Rise & Dine

CANADA

*Savory Secrets from
Canada's Bed & Breakfast Inns*

MARCY CLAMAN

Callawind
Publications Inc.

MONTREAL, CANADA

Rise & Dine Canada: Savory Secrets from Canada's Bed & Breakfast Inns

Cataloguing in Publication Data

Claman, Marcy, 1963–
    Rise & dine Canada : savory secrets from Canada's
bed & breakfast inns

Includes index.
ISBN 1-896511-06-6

    1. Cookery, Canadian.   2. Bed and breakfast
accommodations—Canada.   I. Title. II. Title: Rise and
dine Canada.

TX715.C53 1996   641.5'3   C96-900516-4

Cover illustration and design by Shari Blaukopf
Book design by Marcy Claman

10 9 8 7 6 5 4 3 2 1

Printed in Canada
All product/brand names are trademarks or registered trademarks of their respective trademark holders

Callawind Publications Inc. (E-mail: callawind@accent.net)
   3383 Sources Boulevard, Suite 205, Dollard-des-Ormeaux, Quebec, Canada H9B 1Z8
   2083 Hempstead Turnpike, Suite 355, East Meadow, New York, USA 11554-1730

This book is dedicated to my parents,
Perry and Lorraine,
who always encouraged me to put as much
syrup on my French toast as I wanted.

Acknowledgments

A heartfelt thank you goes out to all the bed & breakfast inns described in this book for allowing me to publish their recipes, and especially for their encouragement and unfailing interest throughout the project.

Thank you to Tracy Fairchild for her friendship and superb taste in editing.

The Rise & Dine cookbook series wouldn't be as mouth-watering without Shari Blaukopf's beautiful cover illustration and design.

My family and friends have been a constant source of inspiration from the beginning and I thank them for giving me the feedback I needed to make this book the best it could be.

Lenny makes the best French toast (except he never cleans up!) — I married him anyway.

Also from Callawind Publications:

Rise & Dine: Savory Secrets from America's Bed & Breakfast Inns
(recommended by *Food & Wine Magazine,* June 1996)

Contents

Measurement Equivalents

Metric:

¼ teaspoon = 1 milliliters rounded
½ teaspoon = 2 milliliters rounded
1 teaspoon = 5 milliliters
1 tablespoon = 15 milliliters rounded
¼ cup = 65 milliliters
⅓ cup = 82 milliliters
½ cup = 125 milliliters
⅔ cup = 165 milliliters
¾ cup = 185 milliliters
1 cup = 250 milliliters

250°F = 130°C
275°F = 140°C
300°F = 150°C
325°F = 165°C
350°F = 180°C
375°F = 190°C
400°F = 200°C
425°F = 215°C
450°F = 230°C
475°F = 240°C

Margarine/butter:

¼ cup = ½ stick (⅛ pound)
½ cup = 1 stick (¼ pound)
1 cup = 2 sticks (½ pound)
1½ cups = 3 sticks (¾ pound)
2 cups = 4 sticks (1 pound)

Miscellaneous:

3 teaspoons = 1 tablespoon
2 tablespoons = ⅛ cup
4 tablespoons = ¼ cup
5⅓ tablespoons = ⅓ cup
8 tablespoons = ½ cup
12 tablespoons = ¾ cup
16 tablespoons = 1 cup
1 cup = ½ pint
2 cups = 1 pint
4 cups = 1 quart
2 pints = 1 quart
4 quarts = 1 gallon

Introduction

What's a bed & breakfast (or B&B) inn? *It's a charming home-away-from-home that includes a heavenly breakfast, warm ambience, hospitable innkeepers, and the interesting company of other guests. Now, when was the last time you enjoyed such comforts at your average hotel or motel?*

I'm a true breakfast lover and, while driving in the countryside on our honeymoon, my husband Lenny and I came upon an oh-so-quaint and inviting B&B. Too good to pass up, we signed on for a trial stay and the promise of a delectable breakfast. We weren't disappointed (even today I remember those wonderful apricot pancakes!). And so began our initiation to the charm and culinary delights of B&B travel.

Some years later, winding our way home from yet another B&B stay (with an unforgettable *homemade* apple strudel still on my taste buds), I was struck with the idea for a bed & breakfast cookbook. This idea became the original, best-selling *Rise & Dine: Savory Secrets from America's Bed & Breakfast Inns*. I was quite content to be a one-book wonder, however the success of the first book begged the inevitable question: Why not write a Canadian sequel featuring the delights to be found north of the 49° parallel?

Rise & Dine Canada includes 81 B&Bs and more than 250 guest-tested recipes reflecting Canada's diverse culture, history, and geography — ingredients that uniquely flavor the Canadian B&B experience. If this book whets your appetite for exploring Canada's B&Bs, use it to guide you in your travels. Why not try a restored nineteenth-century Victorian mansion, where you're served a three-course gourmet breakfast on antique china by the flicker of candlelight? Or, perhaps a log cabin on the lone prairie is more your style?

Whatever your taste in culinary adventures or your budget, you're bound to find a B&B or two in this book that fits perfectly. For your information, each recipe is accompanied by a description of the contributing B&B, along with a guide to cost for double occupancy (excluding taxes) in Canadian dollars. Please note that rates are current as of this book's printing and are subject to change without notice:

$ = under $50 $$ = $50 – $89 $$$ = $90 – $120 $$$$ = over $120

Here's to many memorable B&B meals and travel adventures — right from your kitchen table!

— Marcy Claman

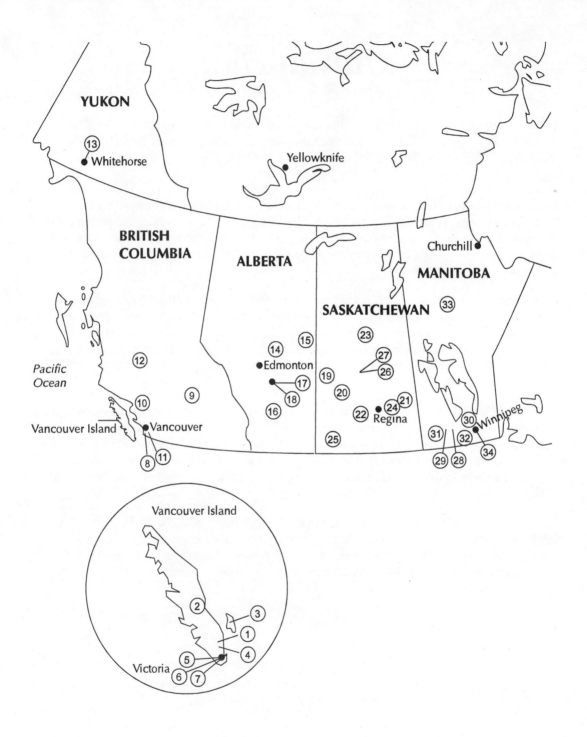

B&B Locator Map
(referenced to Index of B&Bs)

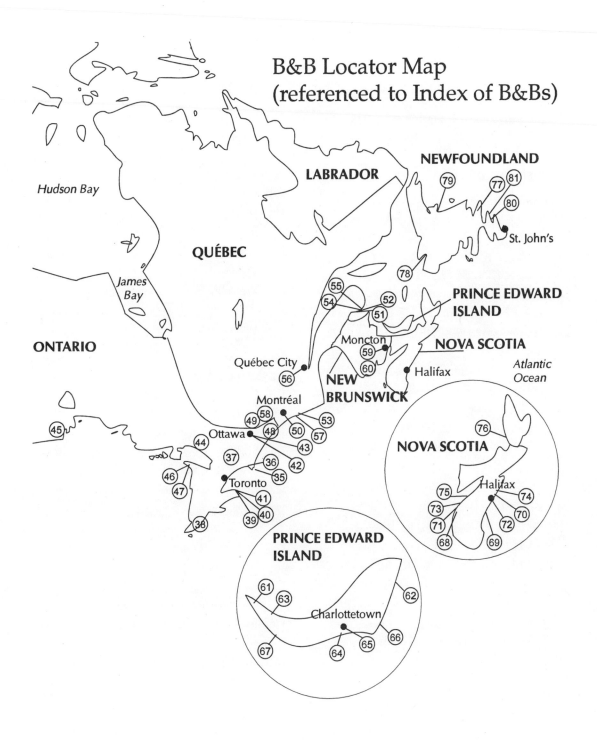

Index of B&Bs

Numbers in square brackets refer to B&B locations on the locator map (pages 8 – 9). Numbers in italics following B&Bs refer to the page number(s) on which they appear in the book.

Nova Scotia

Cape Breton Island:

Newfoundland

Beverages & Cereals

Apple-Cranberry Juice

2 quarts chilled apple juice
2 cups chilled cranberry juice (recipe follows)
2 teaspoons lemon juice

Combine juices and refrigerate. *Variation:* For a refreshing punch, add 4 cups ginger ale before serving. *Makes 10 cups.*

Cranberry juice:
1 quart fresh cranberries
2 quarts boiling water
2 – 3 cinnamon sticks
Juice of 2 lemons
Juice of 2 oranges
Honey to taste

Pour cranberries into boiling water. Add cinnamon sticks and bring to a boil. Simmer 20 – 30 minutes (until berries are very mushy). Mash the berries, then cool to lukewarm. Take out cinnamon sticks. Strain the juice and press the berry pulp to get out all the juice. Add the other fruit juices and honey to taste. Chill. *Makes 3 quarts.*

Bay View Farm / La Ferme Bay View

Helen and Garnett Sawyer
PO Box 21, 337 New Carlisle
West, Route 132
New Carlisle, Québec G0C 1Z0
Tel: (418) 752-2725 / 6718
$

ABOUT THE B & B

Between New Carlisle and Bonaventure, Bay View Farm offers country hospitality in a beautiful seaside environment on the rugged Baie des Chaleurs coastline of Québec's Gaspé Peninsula. Seaside accommodations include five comfortable guest rooms and a fully equipped country house. At breakfast, enjoy Bay View's farm-fresh eggs, meat, homemade muffins, scones, jams, jellies, and beverages, as well as fresh fruits and vegetables in season from the farm's garden and orchards. Additional meals are available on request at reasonable rates. Handicrafts are on display throughout the house. Enjoy the breathtaking panoramic seascapes, participate in the Bay View Folk Festival (second weekend of August) with folk music and dancing, or visit Percé Rock and the archaeological caves of St. Elzéar.

SEASON

May – November

ACCOMMODATIONS

5 rooms with shared baths;
1 private cottage with
private bath

Elgin Manor B&B

Penny and Dave Grimshaw
RR #2
Port Sandfield, Ontario P0B 1J0
Tel: (705) 765-5325
$$ – $$$$

ABOUT THE B&B

Nestled on a quiet bay of picturesque Lake Joseph, you'll find the unique and heartwarming Elgin Manor B&B, a 1920s Tudor home surrounded by English gardens and a water's edge fireplace. In keeping with the timeless, historical traditions for which the Muskoka Lakes are known, you're sure to see several antique wooden boats (called "launches") or even the historic steamship Segwun pass by the dock as you sit in a wooden Muskoka chair. The manor is decorated with antiques throughout and guest rooms are tastefully appointed with handmade quilts. Old-fashioned picnic lunches complete with wicker baskets and antique launch excursions can be arranged. Situated in the heart of Muskoka cottage country (two hours north of Toronto), the area offers year-round activities — from summer nature walks, fishing, swimming, canoeing, and midnight strolls under a million glistening stars, to local artisan tours and winter ice skating, snowshoeing, and cross-country skiing across the panoramic countryside.

SEASON

all year

ACCOMMODATIONS

3 rooms with private baths;
1 honeymoon cabin with
private bath

Bedtime Tea

"When pouring yourself a cup of this soothing tea, be sure to use your favorite antique teapot, cup, and saucer. You're sure to dream pleasant dreams! At Elgin Manor, we pick the herbs fresh from our garden." — Penny Grimshaw

Handful of fresh or ½ handful of dried chamomile leaves
Handful of fresh or ½ handful of dried mint leaves
8 cups hot water

Combine herbs in a teapot full of hot water until tea has been steeped to your desired strength. ***Makes 8 cups.***

Beyond the Pale Oatmeal

3 cups water
1⅔ cups large flake rolled oats
2 eggs, lightly beaten
½ cup maple syrup
¼ cup dark molasses
¼ cup brown sugar
⅔ cup raisins
¼ cup chopped nuts (walnuts, pecans, or almonds)
½ teaspoon ground cinnamon
½ teaspoon ground ginger
¼ teaspoon freshly ground nutmeg

Milk or half-and-half cream (10 – 18%)

Preheat oven to 350°F. Heat water to boiling in a saucepan. Reduce heat to medium-low. Add oats. Cook and stir for 5 minutes. Add all other ingredients, stir, and pour into an oven-proof dish. Bake 1 hour (or microwave on medium-low for 1 hour). Sprinkle edges of open soup bowls with cinnamon, then spoon in oatmeal. Serve with milk or cream. *Tip:* You can omit the raisins and serve brandy- or Grand Marnier-soaked raisins or currants on the side, if desired. *Serves 4 – 6.*

Lakewinds

Jane and Stephen Locke
PO Box 1483, 328 Queen Street
Niagara-on-the-Lake, Ontario
L0S 1J0
Tel: (905) 468-1888
Fax: (905) 468-1061
$$$$

ABOUT THE B&B

A special experience awaits you at Lakewinds, a circa-1881, restored Victorian manor hosted by Jane and Stephen Locke. Situated on an acre of quiet trees and gardens, Lakewinds offers unparalleled views of the Niagara-on-the-Lake Golf Club and Lake Ontario. Elegantly appointed with antiques, guest rooms have been designed for comfort and privacy and all feature private baths. Guests are invited to the games room for billiards or cards and, in summer, can enjoy refreshing dips in the heated pool or simply relax in rocking chairs on the veranda. Sumptuous breakfasts feature fruits, vegetables, and herbs from Jane's garden. Only one-and-a-half hours south of Toronto, Niagara-on-the-Lake is a charming town offering world-class theater, shops, fine restaurants, and beautiful parks — all with a turn-of-the-century ambience. The many estate wineries in the area offer tours and tastings, while golf, tennis, and countless hiking and biking trails await the active visitor.

SEASON

all year

ACCOMMODATIONS

4 rooms with private baths

Chaplin's Country B&B

Kathy and Ron Chaplin
RR #5, PO Box 43
Saskatoon, Saskatchewan
S7K 3J8
Tel: (306) 931-3353
$

ABOUT THE B&B

*E*xperience the wide open spaces and blue sky of Canada's prairies at *Chaplin's Country B&B, a working farm with Jersey cows, pigs, sheep, goats, and chickens. Enjoy a rest on the veranda and view awesome sunsets, or stroll through the barnyard and watch the evening milking. Relax in the gracious country home with handmade spiral staircase, knotty pine paneling, and prairie antiques. For privacy, the guest bedrooms, TV lounge, and bathroom are all on the second floor. Chaplin's country breakfast, including French toast with homemade syrups, sausage, fresh fruit in season, and beverages, is a real eye-opener, while an evening snack of apple cake and hot cider always hits the spot. Only 15 minutes away, Saskatoon offers many fine restaurants, shops, and attractions. Other area diversions include the Western Development Museum, Wanuskewin Heritage Park, University of Saskatchewan, and numerous provincial parks and golf courses. Kathy and Ron pride themselves on their prairie hospitality and comfortable facilities.*

SEASON

all year

ACCOMMODATIONS

3 rooms with shared bath

Breakfast Punch

2 quarts ginger ale (8½ cups)
2 quarts Sprite lemon-lime carbonated drink (8½ cups)
12-ounce can frozen orange juice, thawed
1 teaspoon banana extract
1 teaspoon vanilla

Mix together gently in a large plastic container with a tight fitting screw lid (so as not to lose the fizz). ***Makes about 4½ quarts.***

Fruit Smoothie

½ cup unsweetened frozen raspberries, thawed
½ cup sweetened frozen strawberries, thawed
2 cups orange juice
1 teaspoon honey
1 banana

Combine all ingredients in a blender until smooth. *Makes approximately 4 cups.*

Sproule Heritage Place B&B

Vera and Winston Sproule
PO Box 43, Site 14, RR #1
Strathmore, Alberta T1P 1J6
Tel: (403) 934-3219
$$

ABOUT THE B&B

While Sproule Heritage Place B&B has been featured by both Hallmark USA and Alberta Government Telephone in their television commercials, this farm actually had less high-profile beginnings. In 1909, it was little more than a well-trodden buffalo trail when the Scheer family settled on the open prairie east of Calgary. Years later, the stately house and barn became a landmark to travelers on a road that today is the Trans-Canada Highway. Vera and Winston Sproule purchased the farm in 1985 and began extensive renovations to restore its 1920s elegance. As a result, the site has been declared an Alberta Registered Historic Resource. Artisans and designers of furniture and quilts, Vera and Winston (a country pastor for four years in the Yukon and 24 years in Alberta) assure you a comfortable bed in one of three charming bedrooms and an interesting breakfast.

SEASON

all year

ACCOMMODATIONS

1 room with private bath;
2 rooms with shared bath

Northgate B&B

June and Carl Leschied
106 Main Street
Lewisporte, Newfoundland
A0G 3A0
Tel: (709) 535-2258
$$

ABOUT THE B&B

Experience true Newfoundland hospitality at Northgate B&B, a large and beautifully restored country-style home overlooking Lewisporte harbor. Upon arrival, enjoy afternoon tea in one of the sitting rooms with fireplace and hardwood floors before lounging in one of four charming guest rooms with either private or shared bath. The large dining room is where a wholesome full breakfast of Northgate's own fresh brown eggs, homemade bread, cereals, and wild berry jams is served — all in a smoke-free environment. Northgate is located near craft shops, a museum, laundromat, provincial parks and swimming areas, scenic villages, strawberry "U-picks," and salmon rivers. Explore the beautiful islands of Notre Dame Bay on your hosts' 40-foot tour boat. Experience lunch beside an iceberg or a cookout on a former old-time island settlement. Trips can be arranged to Beothuk Indian haunts or to a remote island cabin for a one- or two-night stay.

SEASON

May 1 – October 31

ACCOMMODATIONS

2 rooms with private baths;
2 rooms with shared bath

Healthy Porridge

"Very healthful, high in fiber, and scrumptious!"
— June Leschied

1 cup large flake rolled oats
2 – 3 prunes, cut-up
2 – 3 dried apricots
½ green apple, peeled, cored, and chopped
2 tablespoons lemon juice
Raisins
Water just to cover ingredients

Fresh milk or half-and-half cream (10 – 18%)

Soak all ingredients in water overnight. In the morning, bring to a gentle boil and stir. Serve with fresh milk or cream (no sugar is needed!). *Serves 3.*

Old-Fashioned Ice Tea

"Best served dockside on summer afternoons while you relax in a Muskoka chair and watch antique wooden boats pass by." — Penny Grimshaw

1-quart antique mason jar filled with cold water
2 flavored tea bags of your choice (lemon recommended)
Sugar to taste
½ cup fresh mint leaves
3 lemon slices, seeds removed

Put tea bags in mason jar with cold water and place in a sunny window for approximately 2 – 3 weeks. Turn the jar upside down periodically to mix the tea and water. Once the mixture looks the color of tea, strain and add sugar to taste. Serve chilled in a tall glass. Top with fresh mint leaves and a slice of lemon. *Makes 4 cups.*

Elgin Manor B&B

Penny and Dave Grimshaw
RR #2
Port Sandfield, Ontario P0B 1J0
Tel: (705) 765-5325
$$ – $$$$

ABOUT THE B&B

Nestled on a quiet bay of picturesque Lake Joseph, you'll find the unique and heartwarming Elgin Manor B&B, a 1920s Tudor home surrounded by English gardens and a water's edge fireplace. In keeping with the timeless, historical traditions for which the Muskoka Lakes are known, you're sure to see several antique wooden boats (called "launches") or even the historic steamship Segwun pass by the dock as you sit in a wooden Muskoka chair. The manor is decorated with antiques throughout and guest rooms are tastefully appointed with handmade quilts. Old-fashioned picnic lunches complete with wicker baskets and antique launch excursions can be arranged. Situated in the heart of Muskoka cottage country (two hours north of Toronto), the area offers year-round activities — from summer nature walks, fishing, swimming, canoeing, and midnight strolls under a million glistening stars, to local artisan tours and winter ice skating, snowshoeing, and cross-country skiing across the panoramic countryside.

SEASON

all year

ACCOMMODATIONS

3 rooms with private baths;
1 honeymoon cabin with
private bath

Cornelius White House
Bed & Breakfast

Bonnie and Frank Evans
8 Wellington Street
Bloomfield, Ontario K0K 1G0
Tel/Fax: (613) 393-2282
$ – $$

ABOUT THE B&B

Located on the historic Loyalist Parkway in the west end of a farming community, the Cornelius White House is named for its original owner, a Dutch settler who built this charming red-brick house in 1862. Today, a sense of history and design combine with European furnishings and accents to create a rather unique bed and breakfast. Three guest rooms on the second floor open onto the cathedral ceiling sitting room, and there's also a suite on the main floor. The B&B is air conditioned and is a non-smoking environment. A full breakfast, consisting of fruit, a hot main course, and freshly baked goods, is served in the adjoining Dutch Treat Tea Room. Outstanding restaurants are nearby, as well as antique and craft shops, galleries, studios, and museums. Cornelius White House is just 10 minutes from the Sandbanks and Outlet Beach provincial parks (boasting the largest freshwater sand dunes in the world). Prince Edward County is a cyclist's dream come true complete with panoramic views and gentle rolling hills.

SEASON

all year

ACCOMMODATIONS

2 rooms with private baths;
2 rooms with shared bath

Orange Juice Spritzer

"Some people can't function in the morning until they've had their coffee. With me, it's orange juice!" — Bonnie Evans

6-ounce can frozen orange juice, thawed
1 cup cold water
1 tablespoon lemon juice
1½ cups lemon-lime flavored carbonated drink
Orange slices

In a large pitcher, combine thawed orange juice, water, and lemon juice. Just before serving, slowly add carbonated drink; stir gently to blend. Serve over ice and garnish with orange slices. ***Makes 4 cups.***

Tom's Oatmeal

2 cups water
¼ cup raisins
¾ cup large flake rolled oats
¼ cup triticale flakes*
1 apple, peeled, cored, and cut into chunks
½ teaspoon ground cinnamon

Half-and-half cream (10 – 18%) and maple syrup, or
    brown sugar

*Note: Similar in appearance to rolled oats, this product is made from the
kernels of a plant that is a cross between wheat and rye.*

In a saucepan, bring water and raisins to a boil. Add oats and
triticale flakes. Cover and reduce heat to simmer until cooked
(about 10 – 12 minutes). Stir only very occasionally (flakes
should appear separated, not mushy). Add apple and cinnamon
approximately 3 minutes before serving (apples should be
cooked but firm). Serve hot with fresh cream and maple syrup
or brown sugar. *Serves 3 – 4.*

Karriage House (1908) Bed & Breakfast

Sue and Tom Chamberlain
5215-47 Street
Wetaskiwin, Alberta T9A 1E1
Tel: (888)/(403) 352-5996
$$

ABOUT THE B&B

Built in 1908 in Alberta's
oldest city, Karriage House
still retains its original
architecture, with arches, alcoves,
curved walls, and fine woodwork.
Surrounded by hedges, big spruce
trees, and tall fences, Karriage House
is a perfect hideaway for that special
weekend. Experience the charm of
the cozy second-floor bedrooms with
shared bath or the intimacy of the
summer guest cottage. Savor an
evening by the fire in the living
room or browse in the Curio Shop,
featuring antiques, collectibles,
dried flowers, and original artwork.
A wholesome breakfast is served in
the dining room or on the deck. Tom
is a great cook and loves skiing
and restoring old cars. Sue enjoys
gardening, decorating, art, and eat-
ing Tom's cooking! In summer,
Tom manages the original Reynolds
Museum, founding place of the
Reynolds-Alberta Museum of Trans-
portation. Forty-five minutes from
Edmonton, Karriage House is within
walking distance of year-round
recreation facilities and the historic
downtown. Your hosts can arrange
biplane and antique aircraft flights.

SEASON

all year

ACCOMMODATIONS

2 rooms with shared bath;
1 summer cottage with
private bath

Weston Lake Inn Bed & Breakfast

Susan Evans and Ted Harrison
813 Beaver Point Road
Salt Spring Island
British Columbia V8K 1X9
Tel: (250) 653-4311
$$$

ABOUT THE B&B

Nestled on a well-tended knoll of flowering trees and shrubs overlooking Weston Lake, the inn is a serene and comfortable adult getaway on the rural south end of Salt Spring Island. The three tastefully decorated guest bedrooms have private baths, down duvets, and fresh flower bouquets. Original Canadian art and beautiful petit-point (crafted by host Ted) grace the interior of the inn. Guests have the exclusive use of a cozy fireside lounge with library, TV, and VCR, and an outdoor hot tub perched above the lake. Creative breakfasts feature fresh eggs from the inn's chickens, and produce from the large, organic garden, such as berries, herbs, and asparagus in season. Near Victoria, Salt Spring Island offers a mild climate, exceptional beauty, a thriving community of artists and craftspeople, and an abundance of outdoor activities. Since opening Weston Lake Inn in 1986, hosts Susan and Ted have been fine-tuning their B&B craft, restoring the house, landscaping, and enjoying their 10-acre paradise with guests. Susan loves gardening, while Ted loves sailing and offers charters aboard their 36-foot sloop.

SEASON

all year

ACCOMMODATIONS

3 rooms with private baths

Weston Lake Granola

"While we have made adaptations to the originals over time, we gratefully acknowledge that many of our best ideas have come from our guests! This granola is great as a cereal with fruit and milk or yogurt, or as a snack." — Susan Evans

5 cups large flake rolled oats
1 cup whole raw hazelnuts, almonds, or pecans
1 cup sunflower seeds
¾ cup sesame seeds
1 cup flaked unsweetened coconut
1 cup soy flour*
1 cup non-instant skim milk powder
1 cup honey
1 cup vegetable oil

*Note: Available at health food stores.

Preheat oven to 300°F. Combine first 7 ingredients; set aside. Combine honey and vegetable oil (heat honey gently in microwave first to ease the combining). Combine both mixtures, and spread on 2 baking sheets. Bake 27 – 30 minutes, stirring at 10-minute intervals, until golden brown. Cool and store in a large airtight sandwich bag in the refrigerator. ***Makes 10 cups.***

Muffins

Boston Muffins

"This recipe, which is at least 75 years old, is from the recipe files of Grandma Avery who lived in the Ottawa valley."
— *Anne MacWhirter*

¾ cup shortening
1 cup brown sugar
1 egg
½ cup molasses
1 teaspoon baking soda
1½ cups milk
½ teaspoon ground cinnamon
½ teaspoon ground cloves
3 cups all-purpose flour
Raisins and/or chopped walnuts (optional)

Preheat oven to 350°F. Mix shortening and sugar. Add egg, molasses, baking soda, and milk. Mix dry ingredients and add to above. Add raisins and/or walnuts, if desired. Place batter into greased muffin cups. Bake 30 minutes. *Makes 2 dozen muffins.*

Buttermilk Saskatoon Berry Muffins

"Saskatoon berries are a favorite to most Saskatchewanites — on a hot July day, families go berry picking in nearby Saskatoon bushes. A breakfast at Company House is not complete without these muffins." — Jill Whiting

1 cup fresh (washed and drained) or frozen (thawed and
    drained) Saskatoon berries or blueberries
2 cups all-purpose flour
½ cup sugar
2½ teaspoons baking powder
½ teaspoon baking soda
½ teaspoon salt
1 teaspoon lemon zest
1 egg
1 cup buttermilk
⅓ cup vegetable oil
Sugar

Preheat oven to 400°F. Grease 12 muffin cups. Combine flour, sugar, baking powder, baking soda, salt, and lemon zest in a large mixing bowl. Stir until well blended. Beat egg, buttermilk, and oil together in a separate bowl until well mixed. Make a well in center of dry ingredients and pour in buttermilk mixture. Stir just until dry ingredients are moistened (mixture should be somewhat lumpy). Fold in berries. Fill prepared muffin cups two-thirds full of batter. Sprinkle tops with sugar. Bake 20 – 25 minutes or until a wooden pick inserted in muffin's center comes out clean. Remove from pan and serve piping hot.
Makes 1 dozen muffins.

Company House Bed & Breakfast

Jill and Jerry Whiting
PO Box 1159
172 Company Avenue
Fort Qu'Appelle, Saskatchewan
S0G 1S0
Tel: (306) 332-6333
$$

ABOUT THE B&B

Company House is located in the beautiful Qu'Appelle Valley, northeast of Regina, Saskatchewan, in the resort town of Fort Qu'Appelle. The house, built in the early 1900s, contributes to a restful atmosphere with its ornately decorated tin ceiling, bright chandeliers, beveled glass windows, maple hardwood floors, and ceramic tile fireplaces with cherrywood mantles. Guests can relax in front of the fireplace or feel at home in their own private lounge complete with television and library. There are two large guest rooms with comfortable double beds. Enjoy a continental or hearty home-cooked breakfast every morning in the quiet dining room. Company House is within walking distance of beaches, fishing, canoeing, birdwatching, hiking, tennis, and shopping (which includes local pottery art and native crafts). Close by are golf courses, ski hills, cross-country and skidoo trails, and many historical sites.

SEASON

all year

ACCOMMODATIONS

2 rooms with shared bath

Wooded Acres
Bed & Breakfast

Elva and Skip Kennedy
4907 Rocky Point Road, RR #2
Victoria, British Columbia
V9B 5B4
Tel: (250) 478-8172 or
(250) 474-8959
$$$

ABOUT THE B&B

Elva and Skip's country house truly is a labor of love, made from scratch with logs from their property. The emptiness that settled in once their children had "grown and flown" inspired Elva and Skip to turn their dream home into an old-fashioned B&B. Secluded in three acres of forest, Wooded Acres invites you to relax in your own sheltered hot tub amidst the pleasures and relics of bygone times. Enjoy a full breakfast of fresh-daily house specialties (including scones and biscuits) served at your convenience. Bedrooms are decorated with antiques, queen beds, and cozy down-filled duvets, while candlelight and lace add a special touch throughout the B&B. As British Columbia's capital, Victoria is known for its breathtaking scenery, beaches, and wilderness parks. The area offers a wealth of walking trails, golf courses, fishing and birdwatching areas, and numerous venues for local artisans. Wooded Acres is located conveniently close to all amenities in Victoria (30 minutes away) and the rural splendor of Sooke (20 minutes away).

SEASON

all year

ACCOMMODATIONS

2 suites with private baths

Chocolate Chip-Banana Muffins

2 cups all-purpose flour
2 teaspoons baking powder
½ teaspoon salt
Pinch of cream of tartar
½ cup butter
¾ cup sugar
2 eggs
½ cup milk
1 teaspoon vanilla
1 banana, mashed
½ cup small chocolate chips
1 teaspoon ground cinnamon
1 teaspoon brown sugar

Preheat oven to 375°F. Mix flour, baking powder, salt, and cream of tartar in a bowl. Make a well in the center and set aside. In a separate bowl, cream butter and sugar and beat in eggs one at a time. Add milk and vanilla, and mix. Add banana and chocolate chips, and mix. Pour banana mixture into the well of dry ingredients. Stir just to moisten. Place batter into greased muffin cups and sprinkle tops with cinnamon-brown sugar mixture. Bake 20 – 25 minutes. *Tip:* Place water in any unused muffin cups to prevent damage. ***Makes 10 large muffins.***

Chocolate-Zucchini Muffins

¾ cup butter
2 cups sugar
3 eggs
2 teaspoons almond extract
½ cup milk
2 cups grated zucchini
2½ cups all-purpose flour
½ cup cocoa powder
2½ teaspoons baking powder
1½ teaspoons baking soda
½ teaspoon salt
2 teaspoons ground cinnamon
Sliced almonds

Preheat oven to 375°F. Cream butter. Add sugar and cream mixture together. Add eggs one at a time, mixing after each one. Add almond extract and milk, and mix. Add grated zucchini and mix. Sift dry ingredients and stir into batter until just moistened. Place batter into greased muffin cups and top with a few sliced almonds. Bake 20 – 25 minutes. *Tip:* These muffins freeze well. *Makes 2 dozen muffins.*

Wooded Acres Bed & Breakfast

Elva and Skip Kennedy
4907 Rocky Point Road, RR #2
Victoria, British Columbia
V9B 5B4
Tel: (250) 478-8172 or
(250) 474-8959
$$$

ABOUT THE B&B

Elva and Skip's country house truly is a labor of love, made from scratch with logs from their property. The emptiness that settled in once their children had "grown and flown" inspired Elva and Skip to turn their dream home into an old-fashioned B&B. Secluded in three acres of forest, Wooded Acres invites you to relax in your own sheltered hot tub amidst the pleasures and relics of bygone times. Enjoy a full breakfast of fresh-daily house specialties (including scones and biscuits) served at your convenience. Bedrooms are decorated with antiques, queen beds, and cozy down-filled duvets, while candlelight and lace add a special touch throughout the B&B. As British Columbia's capital, Victoria is known for its breathtaking scenery, beaches, and wilderness parks. The area offers a wealth of walking trails, golf courses, fishing and birdwatching areas, and numerous venues for local artisans. Wooded Acres is located conveniently close to all amenities in Victoria (30 minutes away) and the rural splendor of Sooke (20 minutes away).

SEASON

all year

ACCOMMODATIONS

2 suites with private baths

The Blossoms
Bed and Breakfast

Berna and Bert Critchlow
RR #1
Westfield, New Brunswick
E0G 3J0
Tel: (506) 757-2962
$$

ABOUT THE B&B

The beautiful vistas of the St. John River are an integral part of The Blossoms's charm. What's more, this lovely modern home is surrounded by herb and flower gardens and shady wooded walks. The landscaped grounds slope down to the water, where you can launch a canoe or simply watch the ospreys dive and the bald eagles glide by. Three guest rooms are distinctively and comfortably furnished, each with double beds, private baths, and balconies that overlook the gardens and water. Breakfast is served on the deck or in the dining room (both of which overlook the river), and offers a choice of fresh fruit, home-baked muffins and breads, or a cooked meal if preferred. The spacious living room offers an extensive and eclectic library and music collection. Hostess Berna gives herbal and wreath-making workshops in the on-site craft store. Area attractions include canoeing, hiking, birdwatching, golfing, tennis, and swimming. St. John — with its theater, antique and craft shops, art galleries, historic walks, and excellent museum — is a short drive away.

SEASON

April – November

ACCOMMODATIONS

3 rooms with private baths

Citrus Blueberry Muffins

"These muffins really add zest to your morning!"
— Berna Critchlow

2 cups all-purpose flour
1 cup sugar
2 teaspoons baking powder
Pinch of salt
1 cup fresh or frozen (thawed and drained) blueberries
Juice and zest of 1 lemon
1 cup melted butter or margarine
1 egg, beaten
1 cup milk

Topping:
2 tablespoons sugar
Remaining juice and lemon zest
2 tablespoons melted butter

Preheat oven to 400°F. Mix first 4 ingredients together. Fold in blueberries and *half* of lemon juice and zest. Add melted butter, beaten egg, and milk, and combine. Bake in greased muffin cups for 20 minutes. Mix topping sugar and remaining lemon juice and zest in a shallow bowl. Brush baked muffins with melted butter and dip each in lemon mixture. Allow to cool. *Makes 1 dozen muffins.*

Cranberry-Orange Muffins

2 cups all-purpose flour
1 cup sugar
1½ teaspoons baking powder
½ teaspoon baking soda
1 teaspoon salt
2 tablespoons vegetable oil
¾ cup orange juice
Zest of 1 orange
1 egg, well beaten
1 cup chopped fresh cranberries

Preheat oven to 400°F. Sift flour, sugar, baking powder, baking soda, and salt together in a large bowl. In a separate bowl, combine oil, orange juice, orange zest, and beaten egg. Add dry ingredients, mixing just enough so flour disappears into mixture. Gently fold in cranberries. Spray muffin cups with non-stick cooking spray and fill them three-quarters full with muffin mixture. Bake 20 minutes. Best served warm. *Tip:* You can also freeze fresh cranberries in season and, when ready to use, let thaw slightly and chop. *Makes 1 dozen muffins.*

Willow House B&B / La Maison des Saules

Pat Le Baron and
Allan Watson
30 Western Avenue
PO Box 906
Sutton, Québec J0E 2K0
Tel: (514) 538-0035
$$

ABOUT THE B&B

A lovely 96-year-old Loyalist-style home with views of a running brook and pond, Willow House is situated in the hub of an artisan community with many local arts and crafts shops nearby. Pat's claim to fame is home-baking, and her specialties include ginger-lemon, blueberry, poppy seed, and carrot-bran muffins, and squash, oatmeal, and granola breads. (Suppers or lunches can be arranged on request.) Other Willow House niceties include a private garden where you can watch an endlessly varied number of bird species come and go, and a cozy lounge where you can while away the hours listening to classical music (with Pat's miniature collie, Chloe, to keep you quiet company). Situated in the Eastern Townships, Sutton is a popular getaway for cycling, hiking, walking, golf, boating, skiing, antique and outlet shopping, and admiring spectacular fall foliage. About one-and-three-quarter hours from Montréal and a half hour from the Vermont border, Willow House welcomes both children and pets.

SEASON

all year

ACCOMMODATIONS

4 rooms with shared baths

Gîte à la ferme
MACDALE
Bed and Breakfast

Anne and Gordon MacWhirter
365 Route 132, Hope
PO Box 803
Paspébiac, Québec G0C 2K0
Tel: (418) 752-5270
$

ABOUT THE B&B

For a relaxing holiday, visit the Gaspé Peninsula and MACDALE Bed and Break-fast. Situated overlooking Chaleur Bay on an active, fifth-generation beef farm, this spacious three-story home offers two family rooms and a variety of guest accommodations. The aroma of fresh coffee and assorted muffins and pastries will awaken you and whet your appetite for an old-fashioned home-baked breakfast using farm-fresh eggs. Thanks to MACDALE's central location, tourist attractions such as world-famous Percé Rock and Forillon Park are well within day-trip driving distance. A seawater therapy resort is just minutes away, as are many museums, points of historical interest, and sports facilities. Anne is a first grade teacher while Gordon has recently retired from teaching junior high school mathematics.

SEASON

all year

ACCOMMODATIONS

1 loft with private bath;
4 rooms with shared baths

Doughnut Muffins

1¾ cups all-purpose flour
1½ teaspoons baking powder
½ teaspoon salt
½ teaspoon ground nutmeg
¼ teaspoon ground cinnamon
¾ cup sugar
1 egg
¾ cup milk
⅓ cup vegetable oil

Coating:
1 teaspoon ground cinnamon
¾ cup sugar
Melted butter

Preheat oven to 350°F. Combine dry ingredients. Mix egg, milk, and oil and add to dry ingredients, stirring just until combined. Place batter into greased muffin cups and bake 20 – 25 minutes. Shake out immediately from muffin pan. Combine cinnamon and sugar for coating. Dip muffin in melted butter, then in sugar-cinnamon mixture. Serve warm or at room temperature. *Makes 1 dozen muffins.*

Fruity Yogurt Muffins

2 cups all-purpose flour
⅓ cup sugar
1 teaspoon baking powder
1 teaspoon baking soda
½ teaspoon salt
1½ cups finely diced fruit of your choice (such as strawberries)
1 tablespoon lemon juice
1¼ cups plain yogurt
¼ cup melted butter

Preheat oven to 350°F. Mix together dry ingredients in a large bowl. Toss fruit into flour mixture just to cover. Mix wet ingredients in a separate bowl, then add to dry mixture. Pour into a greased 12-cup muffin pan and bake 20 minutes. *Tip:* Place water in any unused muffin cups to prevent damage. *Makes 10 muffins.*

Mecklenburgh Inn

Suzi Fraser
78 Queen Street
Chester, Nova Scotia B0J 1J0
Tel/Fax: (902) 275-4638
www.destination-ns.com/
lighthouse/mecklenburgh
$$

ABOUT THE B&B

Constructed by shipwrights at the turn of the century, Mecklenburgh Inn is a historic 1890 bed and breakfast located in the heart of seaside Chester, which has catered to summer visitors and sailing enthusiasts for over 150 years. Sleep in the spacious and comfortably appointed bedrooms filled with period furniture and other interesting objects Suzi has collected over the years, then enjoy a delicious breakfast while you plan the day ahead. You might wander the historic village streets, stopping to watch the yacht races on Mahone Bay, or browse through craft shops and boutiques. Or, maybe a sailboat ride, bicycle ride, or game of golf or tennis would be more your style. Later, relax on the balcony while the sun settles over the western shore and village activity lulls. You might consider an evening meal at one of the excellent restaurants in the area or catch a play at the Chester Playhouse. Before drifting off to sleep, you can wind down in the living room chatting by the fire or perusing travel books and magazines.

SEASON

May 24 – November 7

ACCOMMODATIONS

4 rooms with shared baths

Silver Fox Inn

Julie Simmons
61 Granville Street
Summerside
Prince Edward Island C1N 2Z3
Tel: (800) 565-4033 or
(902) 436-4033
$$

ABOUT THE B&B

The name of this inn recalls the fascinating story of two poor trappers who went from rags to riches developing the silver fox industry in Prince Edward Island from 1880 to 1914. The Silver Fox Inn is a charming reminder of the past and enjoys its own distinctive heritage. Built in 1892 as a private residence, it was designed by the famed architect William Critchlow Harris (1854 – 1913), whose brother Robert Harris gained world recognition as a portrait artist (his painting entitled "The Fathers of Confederation" is known to every Canadian). The Silver Fox has been carefully preserved and retains the original beauty of its spacious rooms with fireplaces and fine woodwork. Six bedrooms, each with private bath, feature period furnishings. Breakfast is available to guests, including freshly baked muffins and biscuits, and home-made preserves. The quiet location is central to Summerside's business and shopping district. Annual area events include the Lobster Carnival, Hydroplane Regatta, Highland Gathering, and reenactments of "Tall Ship" launching parties.

SEASON

all year

ACCOMMODATIONS

6 rooms with private baths

Maple-Bran Muffins

1 cup all-purpose flour
3 teaspoons baking powder
½ teaspoon salt
¼ cup sugar
1 cup bran (use only natural bran)
1 egg, beaten
½ cup milk
½ teaspoon vanilla
5 tablespoons melted butter
3 tablespoons maple syrup

Preheat oven to 400°F. Mix flour, baking powder, salt, and sugar. Mix in bran. Combine egg, milk, vanilla, butter, and maple syrup in a separate bowl. Make a well in dry ingredients and add liquid mixture, combining lightly. Place batter into a prepared 12-cup muffin pan and bake 20 minutes. *Tip:* Place water in any unused muffin cups to prevent damage. *Makes 8 muffins.*

Miracle Date and Pecan Muffins

"If you like your muffins with crunch, don't leave out the pecans!" — Doloris Paquin

1½ cups chopped dates
2 teaspoons baking soda
1 cup boiling water
1 cup Miracle Whip salad dressing or mayonnaise
¾ cup brown sugar
½ cup bran
1½ cups all-purpose flour
½ teaspoon ground cinnamon
½ teaspoon ground nutmeg
¼ cup chopped pecans

Preheat oven to 375°F. In a large bowl, pour boiling water over dates and baking soda. Mix and allow to cool. Add Miracle Whip and brown sugar, mixing well. Add bran, mixing well. Sift in flour and spices, stirring to blend. Fill a greased 12-cup muffin pan and, to add crunch, top with pecans. Bake 20 minutes. *Makes 1 dozen muffins.*

The Green Door Bed & Breakfast

Doloris Paquin
PO Box 335, 376 Berford Street
Wiarton, Ontario N0H 2T0
Tel: (519) 534-4710
$ – $$

ABOUT THE B&B

"Completely comfortable, wonderfully welcoming," is how one recent guest described The Green Door. Built at the turn of the century, this red-brick, stately restored Victorian house is situated on Wiarton's main street and is within a few minutes' walk of shops and restaurants. The main floor has a charming and spacious living room with bay windows and dining room for guests' comfort and pleasure. Up the wooden staircase are three guest bedrooms, two with double beds and one with two single beds, as well as a large guest bathroom. The high ceilings and spacious rooms lend an airy feeling with all the comforts and coziness of home. Outside, enjoy the large garden, maple-shaded deck, and barbecue facilities.

SEASON

all year

ACCOMMODATIONS

1 room with private bath;
2 rooms with shared bath

Twin Pillars
Bed & Breakfast

Bev Suek and Joe Taylor
235 Oakwood Avenue
Winnipeg, Manitoba R3L 1E5
Tel: (204) 284-7590
Fax: (204) 452-4925
E-mail: eht516@freenet.mb.ca
$ – $$

ABOUT THE B&B

Enjoy turn-of-the-century *hospitality and ambience at Twin Pillars, aptly named for the two stately white pillars out front. Inside, you'll find a friendly, homey atmosphere with beautiful antique-filled rooms and lively conversation with congenial hosts Bev and Joe. Twin Pillars welcomes children and dog lovers (there's a resident dog in the host area). Group catering, baby-sitting, free laundry facilities, and designated smoking rooms are also offered. The house specialty is a breakfast of home-baked croissants and home-made jams. Situated in a quiet residential area, Twin Pillars is across from a beautiful park, and down the street from a vintage movie house, restaurants, and a bus route up at the corner. Assiniboine Park and Zoo is 20 minutes by car, while downtown and the Forks National Park and Market are each 10 minutes by car.*

SEASON

all year

ACCOMMODATIONS

4 rooms (including 1 suite)
with shared baths

Oat Bran-Raisin Muffins

¼ cup vegetable oil
¾ cup brown sugar
1 cup all-purpose flour
2 teaspoons baking powder
¼ teaspoon salt
1 cup buttermilk
1 egg
1 teaspoon baking soda
1 cup oat bran
⅔ cup raisins

Preheat oven to 400°F. Whisk together oil, brown sugar, flour, baking powder, and salt. Gently add remaining ingredients. Fill paper-lined muffin cups three-quarters full with batter. Bake approximately 20 minutes. *Tip:* Place water in any unused muffin cups to prevent damage. *Makes 18 muffins.*

Overnight Bran-Raisin Muffins

"A weaving trick of mine is to count out loud, which I suggest you try when adding the separate cups of ingredients for this recipe. This way, if you're interrupted, you're more likely to remember where you were!" — Ann Fleischer

6 eggs
1 cup vegetable oil
Scant 2 cups sugar
1 teaspoon salt
1 teaspoon baking soda
2 teaspoons baking powder
1 tablespoon molasses
3 cups milk
3 cups all-purpose flour
5 cups bran
½ cup raisins

Mix first 7 ingredients. Add milk. Add flour, 1 cup at a time, mixing after each addition. Add bran, 1 cup at a time, mixing after each addition. Add raisins and let mixture sit overnight in the refrigerator — that's the secret. In the morning, remove from refrigerator about ¾ hour before baking. Preheat oven to 400°F. Pour into greased muffin pans and bake 20 minutes. **Makes 4 dozen muffins.**

Cedar Gables

Ann and Don Fleischer
4080 Magog Road
North Hatley, Québec J0B 2C0
Tel: (819) 842-4120
$$ – $$$

ABOUT THE B&B

Established in 1985 as North Hatley's premier B&B, Cedar Gables is a large circa-1890 house located on beautiful Lake Massawippi in the heart of Québec's magnificent Eastern Townships (30 minutes from the US border and one-and-a-half hours from Montréal). The house is exquisitely decorated with many antique Orientals and a few surprises. Bright and colorful guest rooms offer lake or garden views, coordinated bed and bath linens, Yardley soaps, terry robes, and oh-so-comfy beds with spreads by innkeeper Ann herself — an expert weaver and spinner. Breakfasts are hearty and memorable. While enjoying your custom-blend coffee, you'll be able to count no less than 30 fresh fruits in your fruit cup and sample up to 26 different homemade jams (banana daiquiri is a favorite!). In winter, cozy up to one of the three active fireplaces and play games, read, or listen to music. In summer, lounge on the lakeside sun deck, swim, canoe, or fish. The unique village of North Hatley, where some of the finest dining in North America is available — is a five-minute walk away.

SEASON

all year

ACCOMMODATIONS

5 rooms (including 1 suite) with private baths

The Varey House

Lorraine Delisle-Joyner
PO Box 1675, 105 Johnson Street
Niagara-on-the-Lake, Ontario
L0S 1J0
Tel: (905) 468-3252
Fax: (416) 323-9249
$$$

ABOUT THE B&B

*A*round 1837, George Varey, a tailor, built his house on the site of a building destroyed during the War of 1812. Each guest room features its own decor and private bathroom, and guests are served a delicious buffet breakfast. The charm and warmth of the parlor and living room offer a relaxing place to enjoy afternoon refreshments or to meet new friends after a day of sightseeing or before an evening of theater. Bicycles are available for exploring the recreational trails around Niagara-on-the-Lake and along the scenic Niagara River. "One of the best preserved nineteenth-century towns in North America" (Treasury of Canadian Bed and Breakfast), Niagara-on-the-Lake is a haven for artists and artisans, theater lovers, and history buffs. Its antique shops, art galleries, summer theater, historic homes and inns, and recreational activities attract tourists year after year. As Canada's premier wine-growing region, the area also attracts wine aficionados for local winery tours and tasting.

SEASON

April – December

ACCOMMODATIONS

4 rooms with private baths

Peach Muffins

"The Niagara region of Ontario is aptly called 'Fruitland' and, every August, a Peach Festival is held here."
— *Lorraine Delisle-Joyner*

2 cups all-purpose flour
1 tablespoon baking powder
¼ teaspoon salt
1 egg
¾ cup sugar
⅓ cup melted butter
1 cup milk
2 fresh peaches, peeled, pitted, and sliced
1 tablespoon brown sugar
¼ teaspoon ground cinnamon

Topping:
¼ cup brown sugar
1 teaspoon ground cinnamon

Preheat oven to 400°F. Combine flour, baking powder, and salt. Fork-beat the egg with sugar, butter, and milk. With a mixing spoon, combine flour mixture with egg mixture. Toss peaches with brown sugar and cinnamon. Fold peaches into batter. Combine topping ingredients and sprinkle over muffins. Bake in a greased, 12-cup muffin pan for 20 – 25 minutes (can also be baked in a loaf pan at 350°F for 45 – 50 minutes). *Makes 1 dozen muffins.*

Poppy Seed Muffins

1¼ cups sugar
1¼ cups vegetable oil
1 cup evaporated skim milk
3 eggs
2½ cups all-purpose flour
2¼ teaspoons baking powder
⅛ teaspoon salt
¼ cup poppy seeds
1¼ teaspoons vanilla

Preheat oven to 350°F. Combine the sugar, oil, evaporated milk, and eggs with an electric mixer until well blended. Sift the flour, baking powder, and salt together. Add to the egg mixture and beat on low. Add the poppy seeds and vanilla, beating until smooth. Pour batter into a 12-cup, greased muffin pan and bake 20 minutes. *Makes 1 dozen muffins.*

Morrison Manor

Nancy and Jerry Morrison
RR #1
Morpeth, Ontario N0P 1X0
Tel: (519) 674-3431
$$

ABOUT THE B&B

Built in 1989 especially as a B&B, Morrison Manor is just a few minutes from Rondeau Provincial Park — an ideal setting in which to enjoy the warmth and charm of this three-story hand-crafted log home and the natural environment of the park. On the first floor of the manor, guests are invited to use the cozy living room with fireplace if they wish. A full country breakfast is served in the large dining room where fresh herbs hang overhead. Six guest bedrooms and baths are located on the second floor, and two large private suites that overlook fields, a pond, and the full length of Rondeau Bay are located on the third floor. Each room reflects its own country style, and has a door that opens onto a large sitting porch. Besides the park, the area features a winery, buffalo farm, art gallery, cultural center, antique shops, car races, seasonal festivals, and much more. Nancy, a secondary school teacher, and Jerry, a quality-control technician, enjoy cooking, gardening, traveling, theater-going, birdwatching, walking, decorating, and playing shuffleboard.

SEASON

all year

ACCOMMODATIONS

2 suites with private baths;
6 rooms with shared baths

Hilltop Acres
Bed & Breakfast

Janice and Wayne Trowsdale
Route 166
Bideford, Prince Edward Island
(Mailing address: PO Box 3011
Ellerslie, Prince Edward Island
C0B 1J0)
Tel/Fax: (902) 831-2817
$

ABOUT THE B&B

Enjoy the quiet of the country and a "home-away-from-home" atmosphere in this renovated 1930s residence in historic Bideford — where Anne of Green Gables author Lucy Maud Montgomery first taught school from 1894 to 1895. Relax on the second-story balcony overlooking scenic Malpeque Bay or in the large living room. Stroll about the three-acre lawn, play horseshoes, Frisbee, or croquet, or bike or walk around the 75-acre property. Bedrooms have a double bed, two single beds, or a queen waterbed, with the use of a four-piece shared bath (for guests only). Hilltop Acres specializes in homemade muffins and preserves served in the guest breakfast room. Just minutes from the village of Tyne Valley, the Green Provincial Park, and the Shipbuilding Museum, Hill-top Acres is also a half hour from golf courses and shopping centers, and one hour from the Borden car ferry. Your hosts are non-smokers and enjoy meeting and sharing the history and culture of the area. Janice is an office clerk and Wayne is a school bus driver, carpenter, and handyman.

SEASON

June – October
(off-season by reservation)

ACCOMMODATIONS

4 rooms with shared bath

Quick Banana Muffins

"I have had many requests from my guests to share this recipe. The wheat-oat flour gives extra flavor and my guests like the hint of cinnamon on top." — Janice Trowsdale

Scant ½ cup corn oil
1 cup sugar
1 egg
4 teaspoons milk
½ teaspoon vanilla
2 ripe bananas, mashed
1½ cups wheat-oat flour
1 teaspoon baking soda
½ teaspoon salt
Cinnamon sugar

Preheat oven to 350°F. Cream oil and sugar. Add egg, milk, vanilla, and mashed bananas. Mix. Add flour, baking soda, and salt and mix until moistened. Pour into a prepared 12-cup muffin pan. Sprinkle tops of muffins with cinnamon sugar and bake 20 – 25 minutes. ***Makes 1 dozen muffins.***

Rhubarb-Oat Muffins

¼ cup vegetable oil
¾ cup brown sugar
1 cup all-purpose flour
2 teaspoons baking powder
1 teaspoon baking soda
¼ teaspoon salt
1 cup buttermilk
1 egg
⅓ cup oat bran
⅓ cup large flake rolled oats
⅓ cup wheat germ
1¼ cups chopped rhubarb

Preheat oven to 400°F. Combine oil, brown sugar, flour, baking powder, baking soda, and salt. Add buttermilk, egg, oat bran, oatmeal, and wheat germ. Mix gently, then fold in rhubarb. Fill paper-lined muffin cups three-quarters full with batter. Bake approximately 20 minutes. *Tip:* Place water in any unused muffin cups to prevent damage. *Makes about 14 muffins.*

Twin Pillars Bed & Breakfast

Bev Suek and Joe Taylor
235 Oakwood Avenue
Winnipeg, Manitoba R3L 1E5
Tel: (204) 284-7590
Fax: (204) 452-4925
E-mail: eht516@freenet.mb.ca
$ – $$

ABOUT THE B&B

Enjoy turn-of-the-century hospitality and ambience at Twin Pillars, aptly named for the two stately white pillars out front. Inside, you'll find a friendly, homey atmosphere with beautiful antique-filled rooms and lively conversation with congenial hosts Bev and Joe. Twin Pillars welcomes children and dog lovers (there's a resident dog in the host area). Group catering, baby-sitting, free laundry facilities, and designated smoking rooms are also offered. The house specialty is a breakfast of home-baked croissants and home-made jams. Situated in a quiet residential area, Twin Pillars is across from a beautiful park, and down the street from a vintage movie house, restaurants, and a bus route up at the corner. Assiniboine Park and Zoo is 20 minutes by car, while downtown and the Forks National Park and Market are each 10 minutes by car.

SEASON

all year

ACCOMMODATIONS

4 rooms (including 1 suite)
with shared baths

The Lookout at Schooner Cove

Marj and Herb Wilkie
3381 Dolphin Drive
Nanoose Bay, British Columbia
V0R 2R0
Tel/Fax: (604) 468-9796
$$

ABOUT THE B&B

Situated halfway between Victoria and Tofino on unspoiled Vancouver Island, this West Coast contemporary cedar home stands in a woodsy setting of rocks and tall evergreens. The wrap-around deck affords a 180° view of Georgia Strait and the majestic mountains beyond. Relax and savor this "little bit of heaven" or hike, golf, kayak, sail, fish, or sightsee. Take a day trip to the wild western shore of the island and the Pacific Rim National Park or to charming Victoria. The vacation suite will accommodate four people and, with its fully equipped kitchen, makes a popular headquarters for an island stay. Hearty breakfasts are served within full view of the ocean activities. The Wilkies ran a store in New York's Catskill mountains for 15 years before discovering this paradise. They enjoy hiking, golf, crafts, reading, games, puzzles, and especially meeting their guests and helping them plan a memorable stay.

SEASON

May – October
(or by arrangement)

ACCOMMODATIONS

1 vacation suite
with private bath;
1 room with private bath;
1 room with shared bath

Rhubarb-Pecan Muffins

"Voted the best muffins ever by hundreds of enthusiastic guests!" — Marj Wilkie

2 cups all-purpose flour
¾ cup sugar
1½ teaspoons baking powder
½ teaspoon baking soda
1 teaspoon salt
¾ cup chopped pecans
1 large egg, beaten
¼ cup vegetable oil
¾ cup orange juice
2 teaspoons orange zest
1¼ cups chopped rhubarb (fresh works best)
Halved pecans

Preheat oven to 350°F. In a large bowl, mix first 6 dry ingredients. In a smaller bowl, beat together egg, oil, and orange juice. Mix in orange zest and rhubarb. Pour wet ingredients into dry and mix quickly. Spoon batter into a greased 12-cup muffin pan, decorate each muffin with a half pecan, and bake 25 – 30 minutes. *Makes 1 dozen muffins.*

The Lookout at Schooner Cove

Sourdough Blueberry Muffins

4 cups sourdough sponge batter*
1½ cups whole-wheat flour
¼ cup nonfat powdered milk
1 teaspoon salt
½ cup sugar
1 egg
½ cup melted butter
¾ cup blueberries
1 teaspoon baking soda
1 tablespoon water

*Note: In the evening (or at least 12 hours before using), make the sponge batter (see pages 69 – 70).

Preheat oven to 375°F. Reserve 1 cup of sponge batter and return it to your clean starter container. Sift flour, powdered milk, salt, and sugar into a bowl. Make a well in the center. Mix egg and butter thoroughly with the remaining sponge. Add this to the well in the flour. Stir only enough to moisten the flour. Add blueberries. Dissolve baking soda in water, and add to the batter just before filling greased muffin cups three-quarters full. Bake 30 – 35 minutes. *Tip:* Before baking, put water in unused muffin cups to prevent damage. *Makes 20 mini or 1 dozen regular-sized muffins.*

Hawkins House Bed & Breakfast

Carla Pitzel and Garry Umbrich
303 Hawkins Street
Whitehorse, Yukon Territory
Y1A 1X5
Tel: (403) 668-7638
Fax: (403) 668-7632
$$$

ABOUT THE B&B

To stay at the Hawkins House Bed & Breakfast is to share a once-in-a-lifetime Yukon experience with your hosts Carla, Garry, and their two sons. Each guest room in this custom-built, luxury Victorian B&B highlights a different Yukon theme and features private bath and balcony, oak floor, bar sink and refrigerator, cable TV and VCR. Guests can take a Jacuzzi soak in the Fleur de Lys Room, watch Native videos in the First Nations Room, step back into gold rush days in the Victorian Tea Rose Room, or admire the splendid view of the SS Klondike paddlewheeler and Canyon Mountain from the balcony of the Fireweed Room. Especially geared to the business traveler, Hawkins House provides the convenience of private telephone line and answering machine, fax service, and work table with light and computer jack. Breakfast is a homemade feast of northern and international delights — from the home-smoked salmon pâté and moose sausage to jams, syrups, and sourdough pastries.

SEASON

all year

ACCOMMODATIONS

4 rooms with private baths

Brookside Hospitality Home

Pearl and Lloyd Hiscock
PO Box 104
Sunnyside, Newfoundland
A0B 3J0
Tel: (709) 472-4515
$

ABOUT THE B&B

You'll be welcomed like family at Brookside Hospitality Home, a well-maintained ranch-style dwelling in the rural community of Sunnyside. Pearl and Lloyd have lived in Sunnyside practically all their lives and know what Newfoundland hospitality is all about. Get to know them and their miniature collie, Lady, over a cup of tea or coffee, which is provided along with a bed-time snack. In the morning, make your way to the breakfast nook overlooking the water where home-made bread and jam, cereals, and juices await you. Radio, cable TV, laundry facilities, and ample parking are also available. Let your well-informed hosts direct you to the best sights in the province. Lloyd is a boat enthusiast and you may want to look in on his latest boat building project in the shed. Pearl keeps busy with her household responsibilities. Brookside is about one-and-a-half hours' drive from the Argentia Ferry to North Sydney, Nova Scotia, and one hour's drive from St. John's, capital of Newfoundland.

SEASON

all year

ACCOMMODATIONS

2 rooms with shared bath

Spiced Apple Muffins

1½ cups all-purpose flour
1 cup sugar
2 teaspoons baking powder
2 teaspoons ground cinnamon
1 teaspoon baking soda
1 cup peeled, cored, and chopped apple
½ cup raisins or walnuts
2 eggs
½ cup melted butter
½ cup buttermilk or add 1½ teaspoons lemon juice to ½ cup milk

Preheat oven to 400°F. In a large bowl, mix flour, sugar, baking powder, cinnamon, and baking soda. Add apple and raisins or walnuts, tossing to coat. In a small bowl, beat eggs. Add butter and buttermilk and beat with a fork. Add to flour mixture and stir just until blended. Fill greased muffin cups two-thirds full. Bake 15 – 20 minutes. *Makes 1 dozen muffins.*

Strawberry-Oatmeal Muffins

"A great snack anytime!" — Isabel Christie

1½ cups all-purpose flour
1 tablespoon baking powder
½ teaspoon ground cinnamon
½ teaspoon salt
¾ cup quick-cooking rolled oats
¼ cup butter or margarine
½ cup sugar
1 egg, beaten
1 cup milk
½ teaspoon almond extract
1 cup hulled and diced fresh strawberries (or frozen
    strawberries, thawed, well drained, and diced)
Melted butter
Ground nutmeg

Preheat oven to 400°F. Mix together flour, baking powder,
cinnamon, salt, and oats. Cream together butter, sugar, and egg.
Stir dry ingredients into creamed mixture alternately with milk.
Add almond extract. Fold in prepared strawberries. Spoon into
a greased 12-cup muffin pan. Bake 25 minutes or until golden
brown. Brush with melted butter and sprinkle with nutmeg.
Makes 1 dozen muffins.

Riverdell Estate

Clare and Isabel Christie
68 Ross Road
Dartmouth, Nova Scotia
B2Z 1B4
Tel/Fax: (902) 434-7880
$$ – $$$

ABOUT THE B&B

Nestled among the trees
beside a babbling brook,
Riverdell offers modern
luxury with good, old-fashioned
hospitality. Antiques, collectibles,
and handmade quilts adorn this
charming Cape Cod home. Large,
clean rooms with private or shared
baths include two "special occasion" suites — both with double
whirlpool and one with fireplace.
There's lots of space to read, relax,
or birdwatch from the sunny
Florida Room where your homemade breakfast is served. All this
is within minutes of the ocean
beach, golf course, and Dartmouth
and Halifax — two cities full of
adventure. Whatever your leisure
interests may be, your knowledgeable hosts Clare and Isabel will
ensure you get the most out of
your stay.

SEASON

all year

ACCOMMODATIONS

4 rooms with private baths;
2 rooms with shared baths

Au Fil des Saisons

Odile Côté and David Leslie
324, 21E Rue
Québec City, Québec G1L 1Y7
Tel: (418) 648-8168
$$

ABOUT THE B&B

A warm, friendly, and healthy stay awaits you at Au Fil des Saisons. Just a five-minute drive from historic and charming Old Québec, this two-story brick house resides on a quiet, tree-lined residential street with ample parking. An ecologically healthy environment is created with natural products and materials, such as cotton sheets, wool comforters, hardwood floors, and antique furniture, and, needless to say, this B&B is non-smoking. Two inviting bedrooms on the second floor share a common bathroom. In warm weather, take pleasure in rocking on the deck near the garden or contemplating the good life by the pond. When the winds blow cold, warm up in the living room and sip some tea in front of a fire. In the morning, follow your nose down to a feast of organically grown and homemade foods, where you can chat with your hosts to a background of classical music. Odile and David will provide you with tourist guides and maps and take the time to ensure you make the most of your visit to picturesque Québec City and the surrounding region.

SEASON

all year

ACCOMMODATIONS

2 rooms with shared bath

Whole-Wheat Fruit Muffins

"The original recipe came from a friend who made these muffins for us at Christmas. It has evolved over time and this is the way we like them the best. We use organic ingredients for this recipe wherever possible." — David Leslie

2 cups whole-wheat pastry flour (soft, finely milled, low-gluten flour)
1 teaspoon baking powder without alum*
2 eggs
1 teaspoon vanilla
½ cup milk
½ cup maple syrup or honey
¼ cup melted butter
1½ cups berries or chopped fruit of your choice (such as blueberries, raspberries, strawberries, bananas, or apples)

Note: Available at health food stores.

Preheat oven to 350°F. Mix together flour and baking powder. In a second bowl, mix eggs, vanilla, milk, and maple syrup. Pour contents of second bowl into first one. Add butter and fruit, and mix all ingredients. Pour into a greased 12-cup muffin pan. Bake 25 minutes. **Makes 1 dozen muffins.**

Wild Blueberry-Buttermilk Muffins

"These muffins are especially good when the wild blueberries are in season, but are equally good using frozen ones. Simply fold them in quickly and don't overwork the batter."
— Janice Trowsdale

2 cups all-purpose flour
2½ teaspoons baking powder
½ teaspoon salt
6 tablespoons butter
½ cup white sugar
½ cup brown sugar
2 eggs
¾ cup buttermilk
2 cups wild blueberries

Topping (optional):
½ teaspoon ground cinnamon
4 teaspoons sugar
¼ cup ground walnuts

Preheat oven to 400°F. In a bowl, combine flour, baking powder, and salt. In another bowl, cream butter and sugars; beat in eggs and then add the buttermilk until well blended. Pour wet mixture over the dry and stir until just moistened. Fold in blueberries and divide batter equally into a greased 12-cup muffin pan. Mix topping ingredients and sprinkle over muffins. Bake 20 – 25 minutes. *Makes 1 dozen muffins.*

Hilltop Acres Bed & Breakfast

Janice and Wayne Trowsdale
Route 166
Bideford, Prince Edward Island
(Mailing address: PO Box 3011
Ellerslie, Prince Edward Island
C0B 1J0)
Tel/Fax: (902) 831-2817
$

ABOUT THE B&B

Enjoy the quiet of the country and a "home-away-from-home" atmosphere in this renovated 1930s residence in historic Bideford — where Anne of Green Gables author Lucy Maud Montgomery first taught school from 1894 to 1895. Relax on the second-story balcony overlooking scenic Malpeque Bay or in the large living room. Stroll about the three-acre lawn, play horseshoes, Frisbee, or croquet, or bike or walk around the 75-acre property. Bedrooms have a double bed, two single beds, or a queen waterbed, with the use of a four-piece shared bath (for guests only). Hilltop Acres specializes in homemade muffins and preserves served in the guest breakfast room. Just minutes from the village of Tyne Valley, the Green Provincial Park, and the Shipbuilding Museum, Hilltop Acres is also a half hour from golf courses and shopping centers, and one hour from the Borden car ferry. Your hosts are non-smokers and enjoy meeting and sharing the history and culture of the area. Janice is an office clerk and Wayne is a school bus driver, carpenter, and handyman.

SEASON

June – October
(off-season by reservation)

ACCOMMODATIONS

4 rooms with shared bath

Quick & Yeast Breads

Butter Rolls

1 tablespoon salt
Scant ½ cup sugar
2 cups boiling water
1 cup margarine (butter is not better!)
2 packages active dry yeast (2 tablespoons)
2 eggs, beaten
7 cups all-purpose flour

Dissolve salt and sugar in boiling water. Add margarine and dissolve. When cooled to lukewarm, add yeast and wait 5 – 10 minutes until dissolved. Add beaten eggs and 2 cups flour and stir until smooth. Add remaining 5 cups flour and stir until well blended. Cover well and refrigerate overnight or until doubled in size. In the morning, punch down dough, turn it out on a lightly floured surface, and knead for 2 – 3 minutes. Let it rest for 10 minutes covered with the bowl (this will help the dough to warm up). Divide dough into 3 parts. Roll each part into a circle. Cut into equal-sized triangles and roll up each piece beginning at the wide end. Place on a lightly greased cookie sheet and let rise until doubled in size. Preheat oven to 425°F and bake 5 minutes until lightly golden. Turn out on the counter to cool. *Makes 4 dozen rolls.*

Cedar Gables

Ann and Don Fleischer
4080 Magog Road
North Hatley, Québec J0B 2C0
Tel: (819) 842-4120
$$ – $$$

ABOUT THE B&B

Established in 1985 as North Hatley's premier B&B, Cedar Gables is a large circa-1890 house located on beautiful Lake Massawippi in the heart of Québec's magnificent Eastern Townships (30 minutes from the US border and one-and-a-half hours from Montréal). The house is exquisitely decorated with many antique Orientals and a few surprises. Bright and colorful guest rooms offer lake or garden views, coordinated bed and bath linens, Yardley soaps, terry robes, and oh-so-comfy beds with spreads by innkeeper Ann herself — an expert weaver and spinner. Breakfasts are hearty and memorable. While enjoying your custom-blend coffee, you'll be able to count no less than 30 fresh fruits in your fruit cup and sample up to 26 different homemade jams (banana daiquiri is a favorite!). In winter, cozy up to one of the three active fireplaces and play games, read, or listen to music. In summer, lounge on the lakeside sun deck, swim, canoe, or fish. The unique village of North Hatley, where some of the finest dining in North America is available — is a five-minute walk away.

SEASON

all year

ACCOMMODATIONS

5 rooms (including 1 suite)
with private baths

Fresh Start Bed & Breakfast

Innis and Sheila MacDonald
2720 Gottingen Street
Halifax, Nova Scotia B3K 3C7
Tel: (902) 453-6616
$ – $$

ABOUT THE B&B

Fresh Start B&B is an 1895 Victorian mansion, one of the few North End houses to escape destruction by the Halifax Explosion of 1917. It's located in an interesting area populated by families, artists, craftspeople, and students. Citadel Hill, historic properties, and the uniquely designed Hydrostone District are within walking distance. Halifax is a friendly city with many restaurants, live theater, wonderful crafts, and a lively nightlife. In July, visitors come for the International Tattoo Festival and, in August, for the International Buskers Festival. Conveniently located on a bus route, informal Fresh Start lets guests decide when to check in and check out. Laundry service and off-street parking are available, and breakfast tastes great! Guests enjoy relaxing in solitary quiet, visiting with hosts and other guests, reading in the library, or watching TV. The two owners are sisters and nurses. They are also enthusiastic grandmothers and travelers! Innis likes gardening, crafts, and social activism, while Sheila likes cooking and reading.

SEASON

all year

ACCOMMODATIONS

2 rooms with private baths;
6 rooms with shared baths

Cape Breton Breakfast Bread

"Molasses, buttermilk, and oatmeal were staples in many Nova Scotia homes. This bread, which we often serve at Fresh Start, was a childhood treat. It's wonderful with a dish of applesauce." — Innis and Sheila MacDonald

2 cups buttermilk
¾ cup molasses
2 teaspoons baking soda
1 teaspoon salt
1 cup whole-wheat flour
1 cup all-purpose flour
1 cup large flake rolled oats
½ cup raisins

Preheat oven to 400°F. Grease a 9 x 5 x 3" loaf pan. Combine buttermilk, molasses, baking soda, and salt. In a separate bowl, combine flours and oatmeal. Make a well in the center of dry ingredients and blend in buttermilk mixture. Fold in raisins. Bake 1 hour, reducing oven temperature to 350°F when loaf is put in. *Tip:* This bread is great for toasting when it's a couple of days old. *Makes 1 loaf.*

Cinnamon Twist Bread – with a Twist

"Our main goal is to serve a well-prepared, delicious breakfast geared to our guests' preferences."
— *Simon Vermegen*

2 teaspoons active dry yeast
¼ cup honey
13 ounces all-purpose flour
⅔ cup lukewarm milk
1 egg yolk
Pinch of salt

Mix yeast with some honey and 1 ounce of the flour. Add ¼ cup of the lukewarm milk and mix well. Let this stand until the yeast becomes active and bubbly (this is called a sponge). Place the remainder of the honey and flour, and the egg yolk and salt in a mixing bowl. Add the sponge and three-quarters of the remaining milk (don't add all the milk, as different flours in different seasons can react differently — the dough should have a soft and dry feel to it). Mix with a mixer for approximately 5 minutes (this is to develop the gluten in the dough). Cover with a clean tea towel or clean plastic wrap and let it proof in a warm, draft-free place to double its size.

(continued on next page)

Cobble House Bed & Breakfast

Ingrid and Simon Vermegen
3105 Cameron-Taggart Road
RR #1
Cobble Hill, British Columbia
V0R 1L0
Tel/Fax: (250) 743-2672
$$

ABOUT THE B&B

Cobble House B&B is located on southeastern Vancouver Island in beautiful British Columbia, in a rural area with wineries and many recreational opportunities. Victoria and the world-famous Butchart Gardens are about an hour away, as is ferry access from Washington State and mainland British Columbia. The new home, which was designed and built by the hosts, is nestled on its own private 40-acre forest with a creek. Guests are invited to make themselves at home in a warm, welcoming, and relaxing environment. The very spacious and colorful Hummingbird, Jay, and Heron rooms are decorated with wicker and antiques. Your host Simon is a former executive chef and prepares a delicious breakfast, always with guests' preferences in mind. The host family, which includes two beloved dogs, has lots of hobbies and interests — antique car restoration, miniature train collecting, reading, crafts, decorative painting, antique collecting — but never enough time to enjoy them all!

SEASON

all year

ACCOMMODATIONS

3 rooms with private baths

During the proofing, make the following:

Cinnamon mix:
5 ounces butter or margarine (or mix half butter and
    half margarine)
5 ounces brown sugar
1 ounce ground cinnamon
½ ounce ground ginger
2 medium apples, peeled, cored, and diced
4 ounces raisins

Mix butter and spices well. Line a greased 12 x 3½ x 2½" baking pan with half of this butter-spice mixture.

When dough is ready, punch it down. Dust work surface with some flour, and place dough on the table. Mix in the apples and raisins and split dough in 3 equal portions. Roll the portions into rolls the length of the baking pan. Braid these rolls together, place in baking pan, and spread the remaining butter-spice mixture over the top. Cover with a towel or plastic wrap and let it proof in a warm, draft-free place until doubled in size. Preheat oven to 350°F – 375°F and bake approximately 25 – 30 minutes.

Note: Since every oven is different, temperature and placement in the oven may affect baking time. Therefore, keep close watch over the baking process when baking this bread for the first time. ***Makes 1 loaf.***

Country White Bread

1 cup lukewarm water
2 tablespoons sugar
2 packages active dry yeast (2 tablespoons)
4 cups lukewarm water
2 tablespoons salt
4 tablespoons canola oil
14 – 16 cups all-purpose flour

Dissolve sugar in 1 cup lukewarm water. Add yeast and let stand 3 – 5 minutes until dissolved and bubbly; stir. In a separate bowl, stir 4 cups lukewarm water, salt, and oil together. Combine both mixtures together. Gradually add flour (about 11 – 12 cups), and keep adding just until dough can be picked up from the bowl. Cover with a cloth and let rise in a warm place until doubled in size. Punch down. Knead, incorporating more flour, until a soft dough forms. Shape into 4 loaves and place on lightly greased pans. Cover and let loaves rise again until doubled in size. Preheat oven to 350°F and bake 30 minutes or until done. *Makes 4 loaves.*

Sanford House Bed & Breakfast

Elizabeth and Charlie Le Ber
PO Box 1825, 20 Platt Street
Brighton, Ontario K0K lH0
Tel/Fax: (613) 475-3930
$$

ABOUT THE B&B

Sitting majestically on the crest of a hill, Sanford House Bed & Breakfast is a red-brick Victorian home close to Main Street in the friendly town of Brighton. This century-old home with turret and covered veranda has offstreet parking, a separate guest entrance, and three large, bright, and comfortable bedrooms. Guests can choose to relax in the round turret room; in the lounge with television, VCR, videos, board games, and books; in the spacious, bright Victorian parlor; or on the veranda. Delicious home-baked breakfasts, often spotlighting apples grown in nearby orchards, are served in the guest dining room. It's a short drive to beautiful Presqu'ile Provincial Park's sandy beaches, nature trails, fine bird-watching area, and marsh boardwalk. If antique hunting is a passion, there are numerous antique establishments right in Brighton and the surrounding area. Apple-fest, a celebration of the harvest in September, is a particularly lovely time to visit the area. When not entertaining their B&B guests, Elizabeth and Charlie enjoy cycling and birdwatching.

SEASON

all year

ACCOMMODATIONS

3 rooms with shared bath

Orchard Lane
Bed & Breakfast

Yvonne Parker
13324 Middle Bench Road
Oyama, British Columbia
V4V 2B4
Tel: (250) 548-3809
$$

ABOUT THE B&B

Smack dab between Kelowna and Vernon, there awaits Orchard Lane, a newly built Victorian B&B nestled in a private orchard. From the sprawling veranda, this rural setting gives way to a panoramic view of the beautiful Central Okanagan Valley, while nearby Kalamalka and Wood lakes reflect the hills and distant mountains. Inside, a welcoming foyer and spiral staircase lead to romantic and comfortable bedrooms. Visitors lounge in the formal living room with fireplace, stroll through the flower gardens or nearby orchard, admire the terraced landscaping framed by giant trees, or take a refreshing dip in the outdoor hot tub. Your hostess, Yvonne, serves a full gourmet breakfast — made from produce grown in her vegetable garden — in the formal dining room or on the veranda. You'll quickly discover that one of her favorite hobbies is craft collecting, which is evident throughout the house. Alpine skiing, fishing, biking, hiking, and other recreational choices await you and there are golf courses and beaches aplenty to explore. This area is truly a corner of paradise.

SEASON

all year

ACCOMMODATIONS

2 rooms with shared bath

Date Bread

1 teaspoon baking soda
¾ cup boiling water
1 cup chopped dried dates
¾ cup sugar
1 tablespoon butter
1 teaspoon vanilla
1 egg
½ cup chopped walnuts
1¾ cups all-purpose flour

Preheat oven to 350°F. Add soda to boiling water. Pour over chopped dates. Cream sugar and butter. Add vanilla and egg, mixing well. Mix chopped walnuts with flour and add alternately with date mixture to the creamed mixture. Bake in a greased loaf pan about 1 hour. *Makes 1 loaf.*

David's Sweet Sourdough Bread

"My cousin's husband, Ken, is a bread-making expert and he's the one who taught me how to bake bread. I now have a sourdough starter and have since taken his basic recipe and made it my own. We use organic ingredients for this recipe wherever possible."— David Leslie

Starter:

2 cups whole-wheat bread flour (a commercial flour that can be bought from your local bakery)

2 cups lukewarm water

In a ceramic or glass bowl, mix flour with water. Cover and leave at room temperature. Stir with a wooden spoon each morning and evening for 4 days. At that point, the starter should have a fermented smell similar to beer. Put the starter in a glass container in your refrigerator — this is the sourdough "mother," which should be used every week to remain vibrant (if you don't have an abundance of yeast spores in your kitchen, add 1 package active dry yeast and 2 teaspoons honey to the starter).

(continued on next page)

Au Fil des Saisons

Odile Côté and David Leslie
324, 21E Rue
Québec City, Québec G1L 1Y7
Tel: (418) 648-8168
$$

ABOUT THE B&B

A warm, friendly, and healthy stay awaits you at Au Fil des Saisons. Just a five-minute drive from historic and charming Old Québec, this two-story brick house resides on a quiet, tree-lined residential street with ample parking. An ecologically healthy environment is created with natural products and materials, such as cotton sheets, wool comforters, hardwood floors, and antique furniture, and, needless to say, this B&B is non-smoking. Two inviting bedrooms on the second floor share a common bathroom. In warm weather, take pleasure in rocking on the deck near the garden or contemplating the good life by the pond. When the winds blow cold, warm up in the living room and sip some tea in front of a fire. In the morning, follow your nose down to a feast of organically grown and homemade foods, where you can chat with your hosts to a background of classical music. Odile and David will provide you with tourist guides and maps and take the time to ensure you make the most of your visit to picturesque Québec City and the surrounding region.

SEASON

all year

ACCOMMODATIONS

2 rooms with shared bath

1. In the evening, prepare the sourdough sponge batter:
1 cup sourdough starter
2 cups bread flour
1½ cups water

Mix. Cover and let form bubbles overnight at room temperature.

2. Next morning, prepare the dough:
1 cup sourdough sponge batter
1 teaspoon salt
⅓ cup maple syrup or honey
2½ cups bread flour
1 cup raisins (optional)

Take out 1 cup sponge, mixing the rest of the sponge back into the refrigerated sourdough "mother." Add above ingredients to sponge. Mix and then knead for 5 minutes. Place in a lightly greased bowl, cover, and let rise during the day at room temperature.

3. That evening:
Punch down and knead for 5 minutes. Shape into a loaf and butter outside surface. Place in a buttered 8 x 4" glass mold. Cover and let rise in a warm spot overnight.

4. Next morning:
Preheat oven to 325°F. Bake 1 hour. *Makes 1 loaf.*

Dill Bread

1 package fast rising instant yeast (1 tablespoon)
2¼ – 2½ cups all-purpose flour
¼ cup lukewarm water
1 cup creamed cottage cheese, at room temperature
2 tablespoons sugar
1 tablespoon dried onion
1 tablespoon butter
2 teaspoons dill seed
1 teaspoon salt
¼ teaspoon baking soda
1 egg, unbeaten
Melted butter
Sprinkle of salt

Add yeast to flour, and set aside. Preferably in a food processor, combine — one at a time — the water, cottage cheese, sugar, onion, butter, dill seed, salt, soda, egg, and flour-yeast mixture, beating well after each addition. Lightly grease an 8" round casserole and place dough inside. Cover with a towel and keep in a warm place until dough is doubled in size. Preheat oven to 350°F and bake 40 – 50 minutes. After removing from the oven, brush the top of the bread with melted butter and sprinkle with salt. *Makes 1 loaf.*

Gwenmar Guest Home

Joy and Keith Smith
PO Box 59, RR #3
Brandon, Manitoba R7A 5Y3
Tel: (204) 728-7339
Fax: (204) 728-7336
E-mail: smithj@docker.com
$

ABOUT THE B&B

Space, privacy, and quiet is what you'll find at Gwenmar. This 1914 heritage home was the summer retreat of Manitoba's former Lt. Governor (from 1929 to 1934), J.D. McGregor, who named the estate after his daughter Gwen. Since 1980, Joy and Keith Smith have welcomed B&B guests to this relaxing countryside escape. Gwenmar breakfasts are memorable, particularly the home-baked bread and jams and jellies made from Gwenmar's wild berries. Joy, a home economist, is an avid gardener and a major contributor to Canada's heritage seed program, while Keith is a retired agrologist involved in overseas projects. In the summer, you can visit with them on the big, shaded veranda or go for secluded walks on the beautiful grounds or in the valley. In the winter, sit by the fire or go cross-country skiing. Gwenmar is also a short drive from downtown Brandon, with shopping, restaurants, water-slide, air museum, golf courses, and the childhood home of Stone Angel author Margaret Laurence.

SEASON

all year

ACCOMMODATIONS

2 rooms with private baths;
2 rooms with shared bath

Company House
Bed & Breakfast

Jill and Jerry Whiting
PO Box 1159
172 Company Avenue
Fort Qu'Appelle, Saskatchewan
S0G 1S0
Tel: (306) 332-6333
$$

ABOUT THE B&B

Company House is located in the beautiful Qu'Appelle Valley, northeast of Regina, Saskatchewan, in the resort town of Fort Qu'Appelle. The house, built in the early 1900s, contributes to a restful atmosphere with its ornately decorated tin ceiling, bright chandeliers, beveled glass windows, maple hardwood floors, and ceramic tile fireplaces with cherrywood mantles. Guests can relax in front of the fireplace or feel at home in their own private lounge complete with television and library. There are two large guest rooms with comfortable double beds. Enjoy a continental or hearty home-cooked breakfast every morning in the quiet dining room. Company House is within walking distance of beaches, fishing, canoeing, birdwatching, hiking, tennis, and shopping (which includes local pottery art and native crafts). Close by are golf courses, ski hills, cross-country and skidoo trails, and many historical sites.

SEASON

all year

ACCOMMODATIONS

2 rooms with shared bath

Multi-grain Bread

Step 1:
4 cups boiling water
⅓ cup each of wheat flakes, rye flakes, oat flakes, and barley flakes (or any 1⅓ cups combination)
⅓ cup each of cracked wheat, millet seed, flax seed, and sesame seed

Add cereals to boiling water. Let cool (you can also leave overnight).

Step 2:
2 cups warm water
⅓ cup vegetable oil
⅓ cup molasses
⅔ cup evaporated milk

Add to cereal mixture.

Step 3:
1 – 2 teaspoons sugar or honey
2 cups lukewarm water
3 packages active dry yeast (3 tablespoons)

Dissolve sugar or honey in water. Add yeast. Leave for 10 minutes until frothy. Stir well.

(continued on next page)

Step 4:
6 – 8 cups flour (3 – 4 cups each all-purpose and whole-wheat flour)

Put cereal mixture and yeast liquid into a large bowl and beat in flour (using a hand mixer if available). Transfer to a lightly greased bowl, cover, and leave in a warm place for about 1½ hours (or until spongy and the flour on top cracks).

Step 5:
3 tablespoons salt (essential unfortunately)

Punch down. Add salt to dough.

Step 6:
4 cups each (approximately) all-purpose and whole-wheat flour

Work in by hand alternate cups of all-purpose and whole-wheat flour (don't make the dough too hard and dry). Knead well (approximately 5 – 10 minutes).

Step 7:
Let rise covered with a damp cloth until doubled in size.

Step 8:
Sesame seeds

Punch down. Divide into 6 loaves. Put in greased pans. Sprinkle sesame seeds on top. Let rise until doubled in size. (Each loaf weighs about 2 pounds.)

Step 9:
Preheat oven to 450°F, then turn down to 375°F and bake loaves for 40 – 50 minutes or until they sound hollow when tapped underneath. *Makes 6 loaves.*

Anna's
Bed and Breakfast

Anna and Robert Doorenbos
204 Wolf Street
Thompson, Manitoba R8N 1J7
Tel: (204) 677-5075
$ – $$

ABOUT THE B&B

Visit Anna's Bed and Breakfast to experience what Canadian Dutch hospitality is all about. This adult-oriented and non-smoking B&B offers a private guest suite with its own entrance and parking space, two single beds, private bath, kitchenette, and den with TV and telephone. Anna enjoys cooking and will get your day off to a delicious start with a full breakfast served in the main dining room. Oriental meals are another specialty and, along with traditional meals, are available for an additional charge. The greenhouse, which is connected to the cozy and informal living room, opens onto the deck and lends a summer atmosphere to the home — even in the dead of winter! Thompson is the home base of travelers to fly-in fishing lodges and Churchill (Manitoba) and other northern communities. It also boasts the longest alpine ski season in Manitoba. Guest pick-up can be arranged as well as scenic touring by car. Your hosts Anna and Robert moved to Canada from Holland and have lived in Thompson since 1971. Robert, an award winning visual artist, originates from Egypt and Anna from Indonesia.

SEASON

all year

ACCOMMODATIONS

1 suite with private bath

No-Fail Banana Bread

"This recipe, which my daughter-in-law gave me, makes a no-fail, moist loaf."— Anna Doorenbos

½ cup butter or margarine
1 cup sugar
2 eggs
1 cup very ripe bananas (about 3 medium), mashed
1¾ cups all-purpose flour
1 teaspoon baking soda
½ teaspoon baking powder
½ teaspoon salt

Preheat oven to 350°F. Cream butter and sugar together. Beat in eggs one at a time until smooth. Add mashed bananas and blend. In a second bowl, stir flour with baking soda, baking powder, and salt. Add to banana mixture, stirring only to moisten. Bake 1 hour or until done. *Makes 1 loaf.*

Nova Scotia Brown Bread

"Copies of this recipe are always on hand to give to our guests, so now there are variations being made from Alabama to Zimbabwe!" — Monica Cobb

Step 1:
4 cups quick-cooking rolled oats
1 tablespoon salt
½ cup cornmeal
1 cup molasses
¼ cup softened lard or vegetable shortening
8 cups hot water

In a large bowl, combine above ingredients.

Step 2:
3 packages active dry yeast (3 tablespoons)
1 tablespoon sugar
1 cup lukewarm water

Combine in a separate bowl and let rise.

Step 3:
Combine ingredients from step 1 and 2.

(continued on next page)

Bread and Roses Country Inn

Monica and Richard Cobb
PO Box 177, 82 Victoria Street
Annapolis Royal, Nova Scotia
B0S 1A0
Tel: (902) 532-5727
$$

ABOUT THE B&B

Bread and Roses Country Inn is a rare Nova Scotia example of a brick masonry Queen Anne Revival house. Built circa 1882, this non-smoking inn has many fine design details, such as a large entrance hall with sweeping staircase, intricate woodwork, and etched glass windows. The nine guest rooms on three floors are all distinctively decorated with antiques. The owners' eclectic art collection, which includes whimsical Nova Scotia folk art, contemporary Canadian paintings, and Inuit sculpture, is displayed throughout the house. Breakfast includes Monica's brown bread and granola, local preserves, yogurt, juice, and tea or coffee. Guests enjoy gathering in the parlor each evening for tea and sweets to share stories of their Nova Scotian adventures. Nearby are historic sites, museums, artists' studios, golfing, walking trails, and excellent restaurants. Port Royal, Canada's oldest permanent European settlement (1605) is a short drive away. Having traveled extensively throughout the Maritime provinces, Monica and Richard can provide touring tips tailored to your interests.

SEASON

March 1 – October 30

ACCOMMODATIONS

9 rooms with private baths

Step 4:
16 cups (approximately) all-purpose flour

Gradually add flour to combined mixture. Keep adding until the dough is firm enough to knead. Turn out onto a lightly floured board and knead for approximately 10 minutes (this is very hard work!). *Variation:* You can use any type of flour — all-purpose, whole-wheat, wheat, oat, or any combination — however, add more yeast if using heavier flour.

Place dough in a lightly greased bowl covered with a tea towel, which will stop the dough from drying out. Leave dough to rise in a warm place until doubled in size. Punch down. Remove from bowl and cut dough into 6 pieces. Form dough into loaves and put into lightly greased pans. Let rise once more until doubled in size, covered with a tea towel. Preheat oven to 350°F and bake 45 minutes. When ready, the bread should sound hollow when tapped. Let cool on wire racks. *Tip:* This bread freezes well. *Makes 6 loaves.*

Overnight Rolls

"Nothing can beat the smell of bread baking in the morning, especially if you don't have to get up at the crack of dawn to make the necessary preparations!" — Judy Hill

1 package active dry yeast (1 tablespoon)
½ cup lukewarm water
1 teaspoon sugar
2 cups lukewarm water
2½ teaspoons salt
½ cup sugar
½ cup vegetable oil
3 eggs, well beaten
6½ cups all-purpose flour

Rhubarb and apple compote (see recipe on page 175)

At around 5 p.m., combine the first 3 ingredients in a large bowl. Let stand for 10 minutes. Grease 3 12-cup muffin pans. Add the remaining ingredients and knead well (approximately 5 – 10 minutes). Place in a lightly greased bowl, cover, and let rise in a warm spot until doubled in size. Punch down at 1-hour intervals 4 times, then form into clover rolls (3 small rounds placed in each muffin cup). Cover and leave to rise overnight on the kitchen counter. In the morning, bake 15 minutes in a preheated 350°F oven. Serve with rhubarb and apple compote. *Tip:* Freezes well. *Makes 3 dozen rolls.*

The Edwardian Bed & Breakfast

Judy and Jordan Hill
50 Mount Edward Road
Charlottetown
Prince Edward Island C1A 5S3
Tel/Fax: (902) 368-1905
$$$

ABOUT THE B&B

The Edwardian is an elegant 1850s Victorian home, originally the country estate of William Pope, one of the Fathers of Canadian Confederation. Judy and Jordan's interests are obvious as you explore this B&B; period antiques, an extensive art collection, flower arrangements, old books and artifacts, and family quilts are displayed throughout. Jordan's country garden is a focal point for discussion along with the conservatory and parlor fireplace. This B&B has won a number of heritage and beautification awards thanks to loving restoration efforts and attention to overall detail. The four guest rooms feature private baths, double or queen beds, duvets, ceiling fans, and a garden view. As your day begins, Jordan picks a bouquet for the table and Judy prepares one of her memorable breakfasts around an Eastlake walnut dining table set with bone china and sterling silver. It's only a short walk to the center of lovely Charlottetown — birthplace of Canada — where theater, waterfront activities, and year-round dining and shopping await.

SEASON

all year

ACCOMMODATIONS

4 rooms with private baths

River Park Farm

Margaret Whetter
PO Box 310
Hartney, Manitoba R0M 0X0
Tel/Fax: (204) 858-2407
$$

ABOUT THE B&B

River Park Farm is a Victorian guest home built in 1910 on 10 acres of lawn and garden on the banks of the historic Souris River. Recently restored and redecorated, the heritage farmstead has a cozy and casual charm that often sparks memories of childhood visits to a grandma's home in the country. Guests can glimpse deer, raccoons, woodchucks, and many birds while breakfasting on the veranda or in the sun room. Grain elevators in the distance are silhouetted against beautiful prairie sunrises and sunsets. There are walking trails along the river, a nearby golf course and swimming pool, and canoes available either for professional or self-guided trips. Margaret Whetter, the owner and hostess, is a home economist who considers cooking an art form and an act of love. She finds the opportunity to share the stories of her guests' lives a great privilege.

SEASON

all year

ACCOMMODATIONS

4 rooms with shared baths; 7-bed attic room with private bath

Pineapple-Coconut Braid

"This is my basic bread dough recipe — with a tasty variation. It's quick, requires no hands-on kneading, and is foolproof! You do, however, need a fairly heavy-duty mixer with a dough hook." — Margaret Whetter

Dough:
3 cups very hot water
⅓ cup vegetable oil
⅓ cup sugar
2 large eggs
1 teaspoon lemon zest
¼ teaspoon ground mace
7 – 8 cups all-purpose flour
2 packages fast rising instant yeast (2 tablespoons)
1 tablespoon salt

Pineapple mixture:
1½ cups crushed pineapple and juice
1½ tablespoons cornstarch
½ cup sugar
3 teaspoons lemon juice

Flaked toasted coconut

(continued on next page)

In the large mixing bowl with regular beaters, combine water, oil, sugar, eggs, lemon zest, and mace. Beat until frothy. Add 4 cups flour with yeast mixed in and beat well. Remove beaters and replace with dough hook. Add approximately 3 – 4 more cups flour and salt, mixing thoroughly until a soft dough forms. Let stand 15 minutes (still in mixing bowl with dough hook in). Turn on mixer for about 1 minute. Let stand another 15 minutes. Turn mixer on again for about 1 minute to stir down the risen dough. It's now ready to form into braided loaves.

While bread is rising in mixer, cook pineapple and juice, cornstarch, and sugar in a saucepan until thick. Add lemon juice. Cool mixture. When dough is ready, divide it in half. Divide each half into 3 pieces and roll each piece into a 13 x 6" rectangle. Spread pineapple mixture over each (saving some for glaze) and roll up from long side (as for cinnamon buns). Seal edges. On each of 2 greased cookie sheets, place 3 rolls seam side down, 1" apart. Braid, then pinch ends together. Let rise until doubled in size. Preheat oven to 375°F and bake about 20 minutes. While hot, glaze with leftover pineapple mixture and sprinkle with toasted coconut. *Tip:* To make basic bread, simply omit the lemon zest, mace, and pineapple mixture, then braid or shape into loaves or rolls. *Makes 2 braided loaves.*

Australis
Guest House

Carol and Brian Waters
35 Marlborough Avenue
Ottawa, Ontario K1N 8E6
Tel/Fax: (613) 235-8461
$ – $$

ABOUT THE B&B

The oldest established and operating B&B in the Ottawa area, Australis Guest House is a multiple winner of the Ottawa Hospitality Award and has been recommended by Newsweek. Located downtown on a quiet, tree-lined street, one block from the Rideau River (with its ducks and swans) and Strathcona Park, Australis is but a 20-minute walk from the Canadian Parliament buildings. This stately, 60-year-old house boasts leaded windows, fireplaces, oak floors, and eight-foot high stained glass windows overlooking the hall. Three spacious guest rooms, including a suite and private bathroom, display many of the hosts' collectibles gathered while living in different parts of the world. Hearty and delicious breakfasts, featuring award-winning home-baked breads and pastries, ensure you'll start the day just right. Off-street parking and free pick-up and delivery to and from the bus and train stations are available. Your hosts' Australian and English heritages combined with their time in Canada create a truly international and relaxed B&B experience.

SEASON

all year

ACCOMMODATIONS

1 room with private bath;
2 rooms (including 1 suite)
with shared bath

Pumpkin and Plum Loaf

1 cup butter
1 teaspoon orange zest
1 cup sugar
3 eggs
¼ cup orange juice
¾ cup cold mashed pumpkin*, cooked fresh or canned
1 cup chopped orange sections (peeled) and pitted sliced plums (unpeeled), marinated 15 minutes in their own juices
2 cups all-purpose flour
1 teaspoon baking powder
⅓ cup milk

*Note: Use ordinary pumpkin (not butternut) and don't add butter and milk when mashing it.

Preheat oven to 350°F – 375°F. Cream butter, orange zest, and sugar together until light and fluffy. Add eggs one at a time, beating well after each addition. Stir in orange juice, pumpkin, and marinated oranges and plums. Combine flour and baking powder, and sift alternately with enough milk to give batter a soft consistency. Spread into a greased, deep loaf pan and bake 1 – 1¼ hours. Let stand 5 minutes, then turn onto a wire rack to cool. *Makes 1 loaf.*

Rusks

"This recipe was a favorite at the Kilsyth Agricultural Fair of 1917 in Ontario. It comes from a newspaper clipping."
— *Pat and Bill Latimer*

4 tablespoons butter
4 tablespoons sugar
1 teaspoon salt
1 pint scalded milk
1 package active dry yeast (1 tablespoon) dissolved in
    ¼ cup lukewarm water
6 cups (approximately) all-purpose flour
2 eggs, well beaten

Dissolve butter, sugar, and salt in scalded milk. When this mixture has cooled to lukewarm, add the dissolved yeast and 3 cups flour. Cover tightly and set in a warm place to form a sponge (wait at least 2 hours for the sponge to be covered with large air bubbles). Add eggs and enough flour to dough to make a stiff batter. Knead until smooth and elastic (about 10 minutes). Place in a lightly greased bowl, cover, and allow to rise until doubled in size. Punch down. Divide the dough in half and shape each half into a rectangular roll. Place each roll on a lightly greased baking sheet. Cover loosely and let rise until doubled in size. Preheat oven to 375°F. Bake 15 minutes. Reduce temperature to 350°F and bake an additional 10 – 15 minutes or until tops are brown. Let cool. Slice the bread about ½" thick and place slices, flat side down, on a baking sheet. Bake in a preheated 250°F oven for about 1 hour or until the slices are light brown and completely crisp throughout. *Makes about 3 dozen small rusks.*

Latimer on Oxford

Pat and Bill Latimer
37 Oxford Street West
Moose Jaw, Saskatchewan
S6H 2N2
Tel: (306) 692-5481
$ – $$

ABOUT THE B&B

Built in 1911, this faithfully restored foursquare Neo-Greek Revival home greets you with Corinthian columns decorated with cherubs, which support the front balcony. The solid oak front door with acanthus leaf appliqué and beveled oval glass beckons and welcomes you to come inside. Interior oak picture frame floors, leaded glass windows, pocket doors, and plate rails recall an era when quality craftsmanship, natural materials, and functional design ruled the day. Choose from the Oriental, Western, and Victorian guest rooms with shared bath, or the elegant Violet guest room with private bath. Also on the site is a little red coach house with exposed beams and hay loft. Plan your visit to coincide with the Moose Jaw Minuet breakfast and your morning is begun with a cheer. Another specialty produced by the heartland oven are golden brown rusks. Temple Gardens Thermo Mineral Spa, the museum and public library, City Hall, shops, and restaurants are a 10-minute walk downtown. Your hosts' interests include art, literature, and music.

SEASON

all year

ACCOMMODATIONS

1 room with private bath;
3 rooms with shared bath

Cold Comfort Farm

Marilyn and Kennedy Wells
PO Box 105
Alberton, Prince Edward Island
C0B 1B0
Tel: (902) 853-2803
$

ABOUT THE B&B

Cold Comfort Farm takes its name from an English comic novel and is not a description of the hospitality offered! Situated on Matthews Road off route 12 near the town of Alberton, the house was built during Prince Edward Island's silver fox ranching boom early in the century, and is surrounded by gardens and farmland on the coast of an ocean inlet. Rooms are furnished with a mix of traditional Prince Edward Island and European furniture, reflecting the owners' long residence abroad. There is an extensive library, and conversation or solitude are equally available. Breakfast features home baking, fresh fruit, and Cold Comfort's own granola. An excellent golf course, beautiful red and white sand beaches, and a number of good restaurants are nearby.

SEASON

mid-June – mid-September

ACCOMMODATIONS

3 rooms with shared bath

Scottish Baps

"These soft and chewy rolls are the breakfast roll of choice in Scotland." — Marilyn Wells

¾ cup milk
¾ cup water
¼ cup lard
2 teaspoons sugar
1½ teaspoons salt
1 package active dry yeast (1 tablespoon)
5 cups all-purpose flour

Mix milk and water in a saucepan and heat to lukewarm. Add lard, sugar, and ½ teaspoon salt. Stir until dissolved. Dissolve yeast in about ½ cup of this milk mixture. Sift flour and remaining salt into a large, warmed bowl. Make a well in center of dry ingredients and pour in dissolved yeast. Work yeast into flour by hand, adding enough milk mixture to make a soft but manageable dough (depending on the quality of flour, you may need up to 4 tablespoons more or less liquid). Knead dough vigorously until shiny and pliable. Roll into a ball. Cover bowl with a damp cloth and leave in a warm place until dough has doubled in size.

Preheat oven to 475°F. Punch down dough; knead lightly and divide into 12 even-sized balls. Arrange them well-spaced apart on 2 – 3 baking sheets. Flour palms generously and flatten balls into discs, them press a hole in center of each bap with your thumb (this is a characteristic feature of a Scottish bap). Cover and leave baps to rise again until puffy (about 20 minutes). Bake about 10 minutes, so that baps are just golden under their floury coating. Serve very fresh. *Makes 1 dozen baps.*

Sesame Crisp Bread (Norwegian Flat Bread)

Dough:
1½ cups all-purpose flour
1 cup whole-wheat flour
½ teaspoon salt
1 cup warm water

Topping:
1 egg, beaten
Sesame seeds
Garlic powder
Dried dill weed
Other seasonings, such as red pepper flakes, sautéed onion
    and bacon, poppy seeds, grated Parmesan cheese, and
    seasoning salt

Combine flours and salt in a mixing bowl. Stir well to blend.
Add water and stir with a wooden spoon until mixture forms
a soft dough. Turn onto a floured board and knead well for
10 minutes. Place in a lightly greased bowl for 2 hours to relax
the gluten and allow the dough to be rolled very thin. Divide
dough into 4 parts. Roll each piece into a very thin oval (about
12" in diameter). Preheat oven to 425°F. Place on lightly greased
baking sheets and brush with the beaten egg. Sprinkle with
sesame seeds and other toppings and seasonings as wished.
Prick dough well with a fork (or bread will puff badly). Bake
10 – 15 minutes. Serve whole, breaking off pieces as needed.
Makes 4 flat breads.

Gwenmar Guest Home

Joy and Keith Smith
PO Box 59, RR #3
Brandon, Manitoba R7A 5Y3
Tel: (204) 728-7339
Fax: (204) 728-7336
E-mail: smithj@docker.com
$

ABOUT THE B&B

*S*pace, privacy, and quiet is
what you'll find at Gwenmar.
This 1914 heritage home was
the summer retreat of Manitoba's
former Lt. Governor (from 1929 to
1934), J.D. McGregor, who named
the estate after his daughter Gwen.
Since 1980, Joy and Keith Smith
have welcomed B&B guests to this
relaxing countryside escape. Gwenmar breakfasts are memorable,
particularly the home-baked bread
and jams and jellies made from
Gwenmar's wild berries. Joy, a home
economist, is an avid gardener and
a major contributor to Canada's
heritage seed program, while Keith is
a retired agrologist involved in overseas projects. In the summer, you
can visit with them on the big,
shaded veranda or go for secluded
walks on the beautiful grounds or
in the valley. In the winter, sit by
the fire or go cross-country skiing.
Gwenmar is also a short drive
from downtown Brandon, with
shopping, restaurants, water-slide,
air museum, golf courses, and the
childhood home of Stone Angel
author Margaret Laurence.

SEASON

all year

ACCOMMODATIONS

2 rooms with private baths;
2 rooms with shared bath

Hawkins House
Bed & Breakfast

Carla Pitzel and Garry Umbrich
303 Hawkins Street
Whitehorse, Yukon Territory
Y1A 1X5
Tel: (403) 668-7638
Fax: (403) 668-7632
$$$

ABOUT THE B&B

To stay at the Hawkins House Bed & Breakfast is to share a once-in-a-lifetime Yukon experience with your hosts Carla, Garry, and their two sons. Each guest room in this custom-built, luxury Victorian B&B highlights a different Yukon theme and features private bath and balcony, oak floor, bar sink and refrigerator, cable TV and VCR. Guests can take a Jacuzzi soak in the Fleur de Lys Room, watch Native videos in the First Nations Room, step back into gold rush days in the Victorian Tea Rose Room, or admire the splendid view of the SS Klondike paddlewheeler and Canyon Mountain from the balcony of the Fireweed Room. Especially geared to the business traveler, Hawkins House provides the convenience of private telephone line and answering machine, fax service, and work table with light and computer jack. Breakfast is a homemade feast of northern and international delights — from the home-smoked salmon pâté and moose sausage to jams, syrups, and sourdough pastries.

SEASON

all year

ACCOMMODATIONS

4 rooms with private baths

Sourdough Starter

"I'm notorious for forgetting to save my starter. I get talking to guests as I cook and I don't take any out, so I end up making new starter every month! Good thing my starter didn't come over the Chilkoot Pass during the gold rush as some have. Sourdough isn't for a beginner cook, but it's a fun challenge for an experienced one." — Carla Pitzel

2 cups all-purpose flour
3 tablespoons sugar
1 package active dry yeast* (1 tablespoon)
2 cups lukewarm water

Note: Using yeast makes up for the lack of yeast spores in the air of your kitchen. If you want to make a real starter (i.e., you have an abundance of yeast spores in the air from past bread making), omit the yeast and add 4 tablespoons sugar to the starter — it will sour the same, only it will take about 5 days. If you make it this way, you will need fresh ground organic flour and pure water (which hasn't been chlorinated or treated), otherwise it may not work.

In a 1-gallon crock, add all ingredients. Stir mixture until it is a smooth, thin paste. Cover and set in a warm place on the kitchen counter to sour. Stir it several times a day. In 2 or 3 days, your sourdough starter will be ready. It if smells like stinky socks, throw it away! If it has a yeasty-alcohol smell, it's fine.

(continued on next page)

If you want to use this starter, prepare the sponge batter (recipe follows) at least 12 hours before you plan to make your sourdough recipe. If you don't need to use your starter right away, store it accordingly (see next).

Storing your starter

Your starter will keep indefinitely in a clean, covered glass container in the refrigerator. Never use a metal container or leave a metal spoon in the starter or sponge. If your starter hasn't been used for several weeks, it may need to sit out an extra night at warm room temperature before using.

Sponge batter

The sponge batter is what gives sourdough its characteristic flavor. It must be prepared at least 12 hours before adding additional ingredients.

1 cup sourdough starter
2 cups lukewarm water
2 cups all-purpose flour

Measure 1 cup starter from your refrigerated container and place it in a warmed earthenware bowl. Slowly stir in the lukewarm water. Stir in the flour and mix until the batter is smooth. Cover tightly and set the bowl in a warm place, free from drafts, to develop at least 12 hours or overnight. In the morning, the sponge will have gained half again its bulk and will be covered with air bubbles. It will have a pleasant, yeasty odor.

This recipe makes 4 cups sponge batter. Return 1 cup of this batter to your refrigerated starter (this "feeds" your starter by replenishing the amount used to make the sponge batter). You're now left with 3 cups sponge batter for your sourdough recipe. If this will not be enough, increase the sponge batter recipe by one-half or double it.

The Inn
on St. Andrews

Joan Peggs
231 St. Andrews Street
Victoria, British Columbia
V8V 2N1
Tel: (800) 668-5993 or
(604) 384-8613
Fax: (604) 384-6063
E-mail: joan.peggs@vonline.com
$$

ABOUT THE B&B

The Inn on St. Andrews is as lovely today as when it was built in 1913 by Edith Carr, eldest sister of the famous Canadian artist and author, Emily Carr. This Tudor-style heritage property charms with its elegant woodwork, stained and beveled glass, and large bright bedrooms. After a wholesome breakfast in the formal dining room, you can congregate in the sunroom overlooking the east garden or sun deck overlooking the west garden, in the cozy TV room, or in the larger drawing room. The inn is ideally located in James Bay, close to Victoria's inner harbor with ferry and seaplane terminals, the Parliament buildings, the Royal British Columbia Museum, famed Empress Hotel, and downtown shops. A short walk brings you to Beacon Hill Park and the oceanfront. Your host Joan Peggs believes in modern comfort and old-fashioned hospitality, and provides guests with her own map highlighting walking and driving destinations and recommended restaurants.

SEASON

all year

ACCOMMODATIONS

1 room with private bath;
2 rooms with shared bath

Spicy Cheese Corn Bread

(Recipe from Joan Peggs Eggs, written and published by Joan Peggs, 1996)

¾ cup cornmeal
1 cup milk
½ cup whole-wheat flour
½ cup all-purpose flour
4 teaspoons baking powder
¼ cup sugar
½ teaspoon cayenne pepper
½ cup grated medium cheddar cheese
1 egg
⅓ cup vegetable oil

Béchamel sauce (see recipe on page 224)

Preheat oven to 400°F. Lightly grease a 9" square pan. Mix together cornmeal and milk in a medium bowl. Allow to stand 5 minutes. In a large mixing bowl, sift together flours, baking powder, sugar, and cayenne pepper. Stir in cheese. Place egg and oil in a blender jar and blend for 10 seconds. Add to cornmeal mixture. Stir well. Add cornmeal mixture to flour mixture. Combine, using a fork, until dry ingredients are just moistened. Pour into the prepared pan. Bake 25 minutes or until cake tests done. Serve hot. Serve with 1 tablespoon béchamel sauce per serving. *Tip:* To make basic corn bread, omit cheese and cayenne pepper. *Serves 10.*

Sun-dried Tomato Bread

"I adapted this from an olive bread recipe. It can also be adapted to include such ingredients as smoked salmon, black olives, and green olives." — Joy Smith

7 cups all-purpose flour
2 packages fast rising instant yeast (2 tablespoons)
½ tablespoon salt
⅔ cup chopped sun-dried tomatoes
3 generous tablespoons olive oil
Scant 2 cups lukewarm water

Mix all ingredients together to form a soft dough (you may not need to add all the water). Knead for 10 minutes until smooth and elastic. Place dough in a lightly greased bowl, cover with a towel, and let rise in a warm place until doubled in size. Punch down, divide dough in half, shape into round loaves, and place on a greased pan. Cover and let rise again until doubled in size. Preheat oven to 375°F and bake 30 minutes. *Makes 2 large loaves.*

Gwenmar Guest Home

Joy and Keith Smith
PO Box 59, RR #3
Brandon, Manitoba R7A 5Y3
Tel: (204) 728-7339
Fax: (204) 728-7336
E-mail: smithj@docker.com
$

ABOUT THE B&B

Space, privacy, and quiet is what you'll find at Gwenmar. This 1914 heritage home was the summer retreat of Manitoba's former Lt. Governor (from 1929 to 1934), J.D. McGregor, who named the estate after his daughter Gwen. Since 1980, Joy and Keith Smith have welcomed B&B guests to this relaxing countryside escape. Gwenmar breakfasts are memorable, particularly the home-baked bread and jams and jellies made from Gwenmar's wild berries. Joy, a home economist, is an avid gardener and a major contributor to Canada's heritage seed program, while Keith is a retired agrologist involved in overseas projects. In the summer, you can visit with them on the big, shaded veranda or go for secluded walks on the beautiful grounds or in the valley. In the winter, sit by the fire or go cross-country skiing. Gwenmar is also a short drive from downtown Brandon, with shopping, restaurants, water-slide, air museum, golf courses, and the childhood home of Stone Angel author Margaret Laurence.

SEASON

all year

ACCOMMODATIONS

2 rooms with private baths;
2 rooms with shared bath

Bruce Gables B&B

Elsie and Jorn Christensen
PO Box 448, 410 Berford Street
Wiarton, Ontario N0H 2T0
Tel: (519) 534-0429
Fax: (519) 534-0779
$$

ABOUT THE B&B

Whether in French, German, Spanish, Danish, or English, Elsie and Jorn bid you "welcome" to Bruce Gables, their spacious turn-of-the-century Victorian home. Relax in the large living room, which has been restored to its Victorian splendor and furnished with period furniture and antiques. Two of the three large bedrooms have bay windows that overlook the town of Wiarton and the clear blue waters of Colpoy's Bay. A hearty breakfast is served in the elegant dining room where you'll dine on your choice of crêpes, pancakes, waffles, French toast, eggs Benedict/Florentine, omelets, or any style of eggs. Picnic tables and a gas barbecue located in the garden are available for the guests to use. Known as "Gateway to the Bruce," the town of Wiarton makes a perfect headquarters for exploring the Bruce Peninsula. With the Georgian Bay to the east and Lake Huron to the west, the Bruce offers abundant water recreation, not to mention some of the most breathtaking scenery in Ontario from its high limestone bluffs. In addition, the area's provincial parks are natural habitats for many varieties of birds and animals.

SEASON

May – October

ACCOMMODATIONS

3 rooms with shared baths

Traditional Lemon Loaf

½ cup margarine
1 cup sugar
2 eggs
½ cup milk
1½ cups all-purpose flour
1 teaspoon baking powder
1 teaspoon salt
1 teaspoon vanilla
Zest of 1 lemon

Glaze:
Juice of 1 lemon
⅓ cup sugar

Preheat oven to 325°F. Mix margarine and sugar in a food processor. Add eggs one at a time. Add milk and sifted dry ingredients alternately. Add vanilla and lemon zest. Mix until well blended. Pour batter into a greased and floured loaf pan and bake 1 hour. Glaze warm cake with combined ingredients. *Makes 1 loaf.*

Trinity Bay Tea Loaf

2 cups strong tea
1 cup raisins
2½ cups all-purpose flour
1 cup sugar
1 teaspoon salt
2 teaspoons ground nutmeg
2 teaspoons ground cinnamon
2 teaspoons baking soda
¼ teaspoon ground cloves
½ cup shortening

Preheat oven to 350°F. Pour hot tea over raisins and let cool (this can be done anytime). Sift dry ingredients and cut in shortening. Add tea mixture and stir until moistened. Bake 50 – 60 minutes in a greased loaf pan. *Makes 1 loaf.*

Campbell House

Tineke Gow and Family
Trinity, Newfoundland
(Mailing address:
24 Circular Road, St. John's
Newfoundland A1C 2Z1)
Tel/Fax: (709) 753-8945 or
(709) 464-3377 (in season)
E-mail:
heritage@voyager.newcomm.net
www.newcomm.net/campbell
$$

ABOUT THE B&B

This heritage home was built around 1840 for an Irish navigational teacher, James Campbell, considered to be the foremost nautical teacher in Newfoundland at a time when Trinity was a thriving commercial center with a bustling harbor. A 1993 Southcott Award-winner for excellence in restoration, Campbell House is furnished with period antiques and offers a magnificent view of the ocean from every room. Throughout June and July, you might even spot an iceberg or two from your bedroom window! Members of the host family are ardent gardeners and musicians, and may treat you to an impromptu concert of traditional fiddle music. Nearby easy walking trails take you through myriad Atlantic wildflowers and breathtaking land and seascape vistas. Local boat tours leave Trinity several times daily to bring you close to marine wildlife, such as puffins, murres, bald eagles, and whales.

SEASON

May – October

ACCOMMODATIONS

4 rooms with private baths

Norwood
Bed & Breakfast

Pat and Roland Jensen
201 Norwood Court
Wetaskiwin, Alberta T9A 3P2
Tel: (888)/(403) 352-7880
Fax: (403) 352-8850
$$

ABOUT THE B&B

Seventeen-year residents of Wetaskiwin, Pat and Roland Jensen offer old-fashioned B&B hospitality in their new home full of country charm. An old-style double bed and antiques grace one guest room, while Victorian decor illuminates the queen-bedded room. Guests share a full bathroom, Jacuzzi, and a sitting room with white baby grand piano, games, books, and CD stereo system. Served in the formal dining room or on the sunny patio, a typical full breakfast consists of fruit salad, home-baked muffins and breads, homemade jams, a cooked entrée, and beverages. A smoking area is available outside on the deck. Norwood welcomes children but not pets as there's a resident 15-pound cat named Little Guy (who doesn't visit the guest rooms). After a day exploring such museums as Canada's Aviation Hall of Fame and the Alberta Central Railway Museum, shopping at antique, ladieswear, and gift shops, or playing a few rounds of golf, guests can refresh themselves with a soak in the outdoor hot tub. Norwood B&B is only a 45-minute drive from Alberta's capital, Edmonton.

SEASON

all year

ACCOMMODATIONS

2 rooms with shared bath

Two-Hour Bread or Buns

"The original recipe called for shortening or lard, all-purpose flour only, and eggs. I replaced these with healthier ingredients." — Pat Jensen

3 cups lukewarm water
½ cup sugar
6 tablespoons light olive oil
1 teaspoon salt
Scant ½ cup egg substitute, such as Egg Beaters (or 2 eggs)
2 packages fast rising instant yeast (2 tablespoons)
2 cups whole-wheat flour
7 – 8 cups all-purpose flour

Mix all of the above (except all-purpose flour) with a wooden spoon in a large mixing bowl. Still using the wooden spoon, stir in just enough all-purpose flour to get dough past the sticky stage. Roll out onto a floured surface and knead until smooth and elastic (approximately 10 minutes). Place dough in a lightly oiled bowl covered with a tea towel and let rise for approximately 15 minutes. Punch down and repeat rise and punch-down sequence 2 more times.

(continued on next page)

Divide the dough into 4 equal parts and shape into loaves or buns. Place in lightly oiled loaf pans or on sheets. Let rise until doubled in size. Preheat oven to 350°F and bake approximately 25 minutes. *Tips:* Recipe can be doubled or tripled. Bread freezes well. Simply pop a frozen, cooked loaf in the microwave for about 1½ minutes and it tastes like it was just baked. *Makes 4 loaves or 4 dozen buns.*

Montréal Oasis

Lena Blondel
3000 Breslay Road
Montréal, Québec H3Y 2G7
Tel: (514) 935-2312
$$

ABOUT THE B&B

In pilgrim days, the evergreen tree was a sign of shelter, good food, and warm hospitality. It's fitting, then, that two towering evergreens frame the door to Montréal Oasis. This charming B&B with original leaded windows and slanted ceilings is located in downtown Montréal's west end, close to the Fine Arts Museum, chic Crescent Street and Greene Avenue shopping and restaurants, and the "main drag," St. Catherine Street. The beautiful and safe neighborhood with its spacious Elizabethan-style houses and pretty gardens is locally referred to as the Priest Farm district — once a holiday resort for priests. Originally from Sweden, your world-traveled hostess Lena has lived in many countries around the globe, which is evident from the African, Asian, and Swedish art that graces the B&B. The three guest rooms feature Scandinavian and Québecois furniture. Lena loves good food, and serves three-course gourmet breakfasts featuring delicious, fresh ingredients. A friendly Siamese cat resides on the main floor.

SEASON

all year

ACCOMMODATIONS

3 rooms with shared baths

Vortbread

"This is a Swedish bread I only make in winter. It's dark in color, tasty, and goes well with cold weather, strong cheddar, and scrambled eggs seasoned with nutmeg and garnished with fresh parsley." — Lena Blondel

5 teaspoons active dry yeast
1 tablespoon sea salt
3 cups rye flour
1 cup all-purpose flour (plus a little extra, if needed)
3 tablespoons butter or margarine
⅓ cup dark maple syrup
½ tablespoon orange zest
1 teaspoon freshly ground ginger or ½ tablespoon pounded
     anise seeds and ½ tablespoon pounded fennel seeds
2 cups porter ale

Mix yeast with sea salt and flours; set aside. Melt butter and add maple syrup, orange zest, ginger, and porter. Heat until lukewarm. Add to yeast-flour mixture. Knead well, adding more all-purpose flour until dough is smooth and elastic. Place in a lightly greased bowl, cover with a towel, and let rise in a warm place until doubled in size. Punch down. Work the dough on a wheat-floured board until smooth. Shape into 2 loaves and place in a lightly greased baking pan. Let rise again until doubled in size. Bake in a preheated oven at 400°F for 40 minutes. ***Makes 2 loaves.***

Wheat Germ Bread

½ cup butter
½ cup sugar
2 eggs
1 teaspoon vanilla
½ cup all-purpose flour
½ cup whole-wheat flour
¼ teaspoon salt
3½ teaspoons baking powder
1 cup milk
1 cup wheat germ

Preheat oven to 350°F. Cream butter and sugar. Add eggs and vanilla, stirring to blend. Combine dry ingredients and add alternately with milk to egg mixture. Fold in wheat germ. Place batter in a greased 8 x 4 x 3" loaf pan (or double the recipe and place in a greased tube pan). Bake 40 minutes. ***Makes 1 loaf.***

Park View Bed & Breakfast

Gladys and Carson Langille
254 Cameron Street
Moncton, New Brunswick
E1C 5Z3
Tel: (506) 382-4504
$$

ABOUT THE B&B

This Art Deco home was built in 1940 as a residence for Mrs. Inez Robinson, owner of Moncton's first business college. The architectural plans came from the 1939 New York World's Fair and this was the first Art Deco home in Moncton. The curved living room windows look out on beautiful Victoria Park in the city's center. Opened as a B&B in 1989, this charming home provides three guest rooms with cable TV, telephones, and exquisite shared bath, spacious living room with fireplace, elegant dining room, and cozy kitchen. Your hosts provide a warm welcome, a hearty, full home-cooked breakfast of your choice, and a wealth of information about the area. Gladys is a part-time school teacher, while Carson enjoys playing bridge and painting landscapes. A collection of works by local artists graces their walls. Nearby is superb dining, shopping, beaches, parks, museums, galleries, theater, a must-see tidal bore (where the tide goes up and down very quickly), and infamous Magnetic Hill (you'll never believe this is possible unless you experience it yourself!).

SEASON

all year

ACCOMMODATIONS

3 rooms with shared bath

Cakes & Pies

Almond-Banana-Raspberry Breakfast Cake

¾ cup sugar
½ cup margarine
3 eggs
1 banana, mashed
¼ cup milk
¼ cup sour cream
1 teaspoon almond extract
2 cups all-purpose flour
1½ teaspoons baking powder
1½ cups fresh raspberries

Frosting:
1 cup confectioners' sugar
¼ cup softened margarine
1 – 2 teaspoons lemon juice

Preheat oven to 350°F. Lightly butter a 9" square pan. In a large bowl, combine sugar, margarine, eggs, and banana. Beat until light and fluffy. Beat in milk, sour cream, and almond extract. Add flour and baking powder. Stir just until moistened. Pour half of batter in pan and top with berries. Pour remaining batter over berries. Bake 50 – 55 minutes. Remove from oven and let cool. In the meantime, prepare frosting. In a small bowl, beat sugar and margarine. Add enough lemon juice to obtain a spreadable consistency. Spread over warm cake. *Serves 9.*

Fraser House

Sheila and Dennis Derksen
PO Box 211, 33 1st Street East
Letellier, Manitoba R0G 1C0
Tel: (204) 737-2284
$

ABOUT THE B&B

Memories are made at this elegant and romantic 1916 home. Hardwood floors, area rugs, and antique furniture enhance the home's Victorian decor. Spacious rooms combined with great hospitality make your stay most enjoyable. Relax in the parlor or on the veranda or patio with a beverage and home-baked goodies. Breakfast may consist of a puffy egg pancake or freshly baked croissants and muffins, along with the season's fresh fruit, served in the formal dining room. Fraser House is located just a few minutes north of the US border in the heart of Manitoba's bustling agricultural area, and is near golf, fishing, shopping, and skiing. Sheila enjoys crafting projects and holds painting classes during the winter months, while Dennis enjoys carpentry and is employed as a fertilizer dealer.

SEASON

all year

ACCOMMODATIONS

2 rooms with shared bath

Spring Valley Guest Ranch

Jim Saville
PO Box 10
Ravenscrag, Saskatchewan
S0N 0T0
Tel: (306) 295-4124
$$

ABOUT THE B&B

Come relax and enjoy an afternoon visit or an overnight stay at Spring Valley Guest Ranch. This three-story, 1913 character home is nestled in a tall grove of cottonwood poplars, in a pleasant wooded valley with many wild varieties of flora and fauna along a spring-fed stream. Over 1,000 acres of hills and valleys beckon you either on foot or on horseback. You are invited to dine, choosing from a unique menu, in the licensed Country Tea Room, which houses over 200 duck replicas. Live poultry, sheep, horses, and a donkey await your visit in the barnyard. The craft shop in the log cabin is filled with treasures of leather, wood, pottery, and knitted and beaded crafts — all made by local artists. An excellent area for naturalists, photographers, and hikers, Ravenscrag is only 20 minutes from Cypress Hills Provincial Park, on the Alberta border.

SEASON

all year

ACCOMMODATIONS

4 rooms with shared baths;
1 log cabin with shared bath

Angel Food Cake

"If you raise chickens and get lots of extra 'cackleberries,' you can use the egg whites for this recipe and leftover egg yolks for my jelly roll (see recipe on page 140), both great for afternoon or after-dinner treats." — Jim Saville

1 cup cake flour
½ cup sugar
1¼ cups egg whites (approximately 10 egg whites)
1 cup sugar
1¼ teaspoons cream of tartar
¼ teaspoon salt
1 teaspoon vanilla
Fresh berries or fruit of your choice

Preheat oven to 350°F. Sift flour and ½ cup sugar together 4 times; set aside. Beat egg whites until soft peaks form, then gradually add the sugar, cream of tartar, and salt, and beat until stiff (but not dry) peaks form. Add vanilla. Fold flour mixture gently into liquid mixture. Pour into an ungreased angel food cake pan and bake 45 minutes. Top with fresh berries or fruit of your choice. *Serves 12.*

Apple Streusel Coffee Cake

2¼ cups all-purpose flour
¾ cup sugar
¾ cup butter or margarine
½ teaspoon baking powder
½ teaspoon baking soda
1 egg, beaten
¾ cup buttermilk or sour milk
19-ounce can apple pie filling
⅓ cup currants
½ teaspoon ground cinnamon

Island clotted cream topping (see recipe on page 299)

Preheat oven to 375°F. Combine flour and sugar in a large bowl. Cut in butter until mixture is crumbly; set aside ½ cup of mixture. To the remainder, add baking powder and soda. Separately, combine egg and buttermilk. Add to dry ingredients, stirring just until moistened. Spread two-thirds of batter over the bottom and part way up sides of a greased 9" springform pan. Combine pie filling, currants, and cinnamon; spoon over batter. Drop spoonfuls of remaining batter over filling. Sprinkle with reserved crumb mixture. Bake approximately 1 hour. Cool 10 minutes before serving. Serve with island clotted cream topping. *Tip:* Freezes well. *Variation:* Instead of apple pie filling, currants, and cinnamon, try cherry pie filling with ½ teaspoon almond extract mixed in and slivered almonds sprinkled on top with the reserved crumb mixture. *Serves 12.*

The Edwardian Bed & Breakfast

Judy and Jordan Hill
50 Mount Edward Road
Charlottetown
Prince Edward Island C1A 5S3
Tel/Fax: (902) 368-1905
$$$

ABOUT THE B&B

The Edwardian is an elegant 1850s Victorian home, originally the country estate of William Pope, one of the Fathers of Canadian Confederation. Judy and Jordan's interests are obvious as you explore this B&B; period antiques, an extensive art collection, flower arrangements, old books and artifacts, and family quilts are displayed throughout. Jordan's country garden is a focal point for discussion along with the conservatory and parlor fireplace. This B&B has won a number of heritage and beautification awards thanks to loving restoration efforts and attention to overall detail. The four guest rooms feature private baths, double or queen beds, duvets, ceiling fans, and a garden view. As your day begins, Jordan picks a bouquet for the table and Judy prepares one of her memorable breakfasts around an Eastlake walnut dining table set with bone china and sterling silver. It's only a short walk to the center of lovely Charlottetown — birthplace of Canada — where theater, waterfront activities, and year-round dining and shopping await.

SEASON

all year

ACCOMMODATIONS

4 rooms with private baths

Mecklenburgh Inn

Suzi Fraser
78 Queen Street
Chester, Nova Scotia B0J 1J0
Tel/Fax: (902) 275-4638
www.destination-ns.com/
lighthouse/mecklenburgh
$$

ABOUT THE B&B

Constructed by shipwrights at the turn of the century, Mecklenburgh Inn is a historic 1890 bed and breakfast located in the heart of seaside Chester, which has catered to summer visitors and sailing enthusiasts for over 150 years. Sleep in the spacious and comfortably appointed bedrooms filled with period furniture and other interesting objects Suzi has collected over the years, then enjoy a delicious breakfast while you plan the day ahead. You might wander the historic village streets, stopping to watch the yacht races on Mahone Bay, or browse through craft shops and boutiques. Or, maybe a sailboat ride, bicycle ride, or game of golf or tennis would be more your style. Later, relax on the balcony while the sun settles over the western shore and village activity lulls. You might consider an evening meal at one of the excellent restaurants in the area or catch a play at the Chester Playhouse. Before drifting off to sleep, you can wind down in the living room chatting by the fire or perusing travel books and magazines.

SEASON

May 24 – November 7

ACCOMMODATIONS

4 rooms with shared baths

Apple Tart

Crust:
1¼ cups all-purpose flour
⅓ cup sugar
¼ cup ground nutmeg
½ teaspoon baking powder
½ teaspoon salt
½ cup cold unsalted butter
1 whole egg
1 tablespoon milk

Filling:
8-ounce package cream cheese, softened
¼ cup sugar
2 egg yolks
½ teaspoon vanilla

Topping:
3 apples, peeled, cored, and thinly sliced
⅓ cup sugar
½ teaspoon cornstarch
½ teaspoon ground cinnamon

Preheat oven to 350°F. Grease a 10" tart pan. Combine flour, sugar, nutmeg, baking powder, and salt in a food processor. Cut in butter. Beat egg and milk in a separate bowl, then add to flour mixture. Blend until it forms a ball. Pat dough into the prepared pan. Blend cream cheese and sugar in food processor, then add egg yolks and vanilla and blend until smooth. Spread filling evenly over crust. Arrange apples on top. Combine sugar, cornstarch, and cinnamon and sprinkle over apples. Bake 30 minutes. Reduce temperature to 300°F and bake an additional 10 minutes. *Serves 6 – 8.*

Blueberry Coffee Cake

1 cup sugar
¼ cup softened shortening
1 egg
½ cup milk
2 cups all-purpose flour
2 teaspoons baking powder
½ teaspoon salt
1 teaspoon vanilla
2 cups blueberries, washed and well drained

Crumb topping:
½ cup sugar
⅓ cup all-purpose flour
½ teaspoon ground cinnamon
¼ cup softened butter

Preheat oven to 375°F. Mix sugar, shortening, and egg. Stir in milk. Sift next 3 dry ingredients together and stir into batter along with vanilla. Blend in blueberries. Pour batter into a greased 9" square pan. Combine crumb topping ingredients and sprinkle on top of batter. Bake 45 – 50 minutes. *Serves 12.*

Silver Fox Inn

Julie Simmons
61 Granville Street
Summerside
Prince Edward Island C1N 2Z3
Tel: (800) 565-4033 or
(902) 436-4033
$$

ABOUT THE B&B

The name of this inn recalls the fascinating story of two poor trappers who went from rags to riches developing the silver fox industry in Prince Edward Island from 1880 to 1914. The Silver Fox Inn is a charming reminder of the past and enjoys its own distinctive heritage. Built in 1892 as a private residence, it was designed by the famed architect William Critchlow Harris (1854 – 1913), whose brother Robert Harris gained world recognition as a portrait artist (his painting entitled "The Fathers of Confederation" is known to every Canadian). The Silver Fox has been carefully preserved and retains the original beauty of its spacious rooms with fireplaces and fine woodwork. Six bedrooms, each with private bath, feature period furnishings. Breakfast is available to guests, including freshly baked muffins and biscuits, and homemade preserves. The quiet location is central to Summerside's business and shopping district. Annual area events include the Lobster Carnival, Hydroplane Regatta, Highland Gathering, and reenactments of "Tall Ship" launching parties.

SEASON

all year

ACCOMMODATIONS

6 rooms with private baths

Barbara Ann's Bed 'n Breakfast Vacation Farm

Barbara Ann and Ted Witzaney
PO Box 156
Denzil, Saskatchewan S0L 0S0
Tel: (306) 358-4814
$

ABOUT THE B&B

*S*pecially geared for families, Barbara Ann's B&B is located on the Witzaney farm, where they've been raising crops and hogs since 1911. The petting zoo includes traditional farm animals and more exotic ones, including a llama and Muscovy ducks. Barbara Ann's breakfast and other meals served on request feature farm-fresh milk, eggs, cheese, and vegetables; home-baked goods, such as buns, pies, and cookies; homemade jams, jellies, relishes, and pickles; and the farm's home-raised pork, which includes the specialty of the house — homemade sausages. Picnic and barbecue facilities, sandbox and swing set, horseshoe pit, lawn bowling, badminton, and an 18-hole miniature golf course are all on the property. When not tending to guests, Barbara Ann enjoys sewing and craft making, while Ted enjoys woodworking. Both like to spend time with their 10 grandchildren. Denzil is about a half-hour drive west of Unity, Saskatchewan, and a 45-minute drive east of Provost, Alberta.

SEASON

all year

ACCOMMODATIONS

2 rooms with shared bath

Coffee-Walnut Coffee Cake

½ cup soft margarine
½ cup sugar
2 large eggs
⅓ cup chopped walnuts
1 tablespoon coffee extract
1 cup all-purpose flour
Pinch of salt
1 tablespoon baking powder

Filling:
⅓ cup soft margarine
1 cup confectioners' sugar
2 teaspoons milk
2 teaspoons coffee extract
Walnut halves

Preheat oven to 325°F. Butter 2 7"-diameter straight-sided layer cake pans and line the bottom with buttered wax paper. Put the margarine, sugar, eggs, chopped walnuts, and coffee extract in a bowl. Sift in the flour with the salt and baking powder. Beat these ingredients with a wooden spoon for 2 or 3 minutes until well combined. Divide the mixture between the prepared pans, level the surface, and bake 35 – 40 minutes (until cake tops are spongy to the touch). When baked, turn cakes out on a wire rack to cool before removing lining paper.

Make the filling while cakes are baking. Beat the margarine, sugar, milk, and coffee extract in a bowl until smooth. Sandwich the cakes together with two-thirds of the filling between them. Top with remaining filling. Mark the filling with the prongs of a fork in a decorative pattern. Place walnut halves on top of cake. *Serves 12 – 14.*

Cornelius White House Cake

"Our boys don't especially enjoy cake with icing, so we have this sponge-type cake on hand just about all the time. It's very moist and can stay fresh for days (that is, if it's not all gobbled up right away!)." — Bonnie Evans

1 yellow cake mix (Duncan Hines recommended)
1 large vanilla instant pudding mix
¾ cup vegetable oil
4 eggs
¾ cup sweet sherry
1 tablespoon ground nutmeg
Confectioners' sugar
Fresh fruit and whipped cream (optional)

Preheat oven to 350°F. Mix first 6 ingredients together. Beat for about 5 minutes. Pour into a greased angel food pan. Bake approximately 1 hour, checking after 45 minutes. Turn out on a cake rack, cool, and sprinkle with confectioners' sugar. Also delicious topped with fruit and whipped cream. *Serves 10 – 12.*

Cornelius White House
Bed & Breakfast

Bonnie and Frank Evans
8 Wellington Street
Bloomfield, Ontario K0K 1G0
Tel/Fax: (613) 393-2282
$ – $$

ABOUT THE B&B

Located on the historic Loyalist Parkway in the west end of a farming community, the Cornelius White House is named for its original owner, a Dutch settler who built this charming red-brick house in 1862. Today, a sense of history and design combine with European furnishings and accents to create a rather unique bed and breakfast. Three guest rooms on the second floor open onto the cathedral ceiling sitting room, and there's also a suite on the main floor. The B&B is air conditioned and is a non-smoking environment. A full breakfast, consisting of fruit, a hot main course, and freshly baked goods, is served in the adjoining Dutch Treat Tea Room. Outstanding restaurants are nearby, as well as antique and craft shops, galleries, studios, and museums. Cornelius White House is just 10 minutes from the Sandbanks and Outlet Beach provincial parks (boasting the largest freshwater sand dunes in the world). Prince Edward County is a cyclist's dream come true complete with panoramic views and gentle rolling hills.

SEASON

all year

ACCOMMODATIONS

2 rooms with private baths;
2 rooms with shared bath

Chaplin's Country B&B

Kathy and Ron Chaplin
RR #5, PO Box 43
Saskatoon, Saskatchewan
S7K 3J8
Tel: (306) 931-3353
$

ABOUT THE B&B

Experience the wide open spaces and blue sky of Canada's prairies at Chaplin's Country B&B, a working farm with Jersey cows, pigs, sheep, goats, and chickens. Enjoy a rest on the veranda and view awesome sunsets, or stroll through the barnyard and watch the evening milking. Relax in the gracious country home with handmade spiral staircase, knotty pine paneling, and prairie antiques. For privacy, the guest bedrooms, TV lounge, and bathroom are all on the second floor. Chaplin's country breakfast, including French toast with homemade syrups, sausage, fresh fruit in season, and beverages, is a real eye-opener, while an evening snack of apple cake and hot cider always hits the spot. Only 15 minutes away, Saskatoon offers many fine restaurants, shops, and attractions. Other area diversions include the Western Development Museum, Wanuskewin Heritage Park, University of Saskatchewan, and numerous provincial parks and golf courses. Kathy and Ron pride themselves on their prairie hospitality and comfortable facilities.

SEASON

all year

ACCOMMODATIONS

3 rooms with shared bath

Country Apple Cake

4 eggs
2 cups sugar
1 cup vegetable oil

3 cups all-purpose flour
3 teaspoons baking powder
½ teaspoon salt

4 apples, peeled, cored, and sliced (McIntosh recommended)
2 tablespoons sugar
2 tablespoons ground cinnamon

½ cup orange juice
2 teaspoons vanilla
Poppy seeds

Frosting:
1 cup confectioners' sugar
3 – 4 tablespoons lemon juice

Preheat oven to 350°F. In 3 separate bowls: Beat well the eggs, sugar, and oil; mix flour, baking powder, and salt; mix apples, sugar, and cinnamon. Add flour mixture to egg mixture, then add orange juice and vanilla. Pour ½ cup of batter into a greased and floured tube pan, then add half of apple mixture. Add the rest of the batter, then remaining apples. Sprinkle with poppy seeds. Bake 1¼ hours. Mix confectioners' sugar with lemon juice, then drip over warm cake. *Serves 12 – 16.*

Fars Foun (Flan Breton)

"This recipe comes from my Bretonne-Canadian roots. It's called 'Fars Foun' in Breton." — Anne-Marie Bansfield

1 cup pitted prunes, raisins, or fresh pitted cherries in season
¾ cup all-purpose flour
½ cup sugar
3 large eggs or 4 small–medium eggs
2 cups whole milk (homogenized is best), at room temperature
2 tablespoons melted butter
1 tablespoon vanilla
Pinch of salt

Preheat oven to 350°F. Butter a deep pie plate or large Pyrex casserole. Cover the bottom of the dish with either prunes, raisins, or cherries. In a bowl, combine remaining ingredients in order given; add the milk little by little, ending with the addition of butter and vanilla. Pour over fruit in pie plate. Bake 40 – 50 minutes until a knife inserted in the flan's center comes out clean. The top should be golden and firm to the touch. **Serves 6.**

Le Gîte Park Avenue B&B

Anne-Marie and Irving Bansfield
54 Park Avenue
Ottawa, Ontario K2P 1B2
Tel: (613) 230-9131
$$

ABOUT THE B&B

A bright, airy ambience and artistic decor awaits you at Park Avenue B&B, an elegant, brick 1906 home located in a charming residential area of downtown Ottawa, Canada's capital. In addition to high-quality beds done up in classic cotton and linen sheets and duvets, each guest room is furnished with desk and swivel chair, rocking chair, bookshelves, excellent lighting, and attractive works of art. Ideal for families, the third-floor suite has two bedrooms and a private bath. The mood throughout the house is one of relaxation and warmth. Park Avenue B&B is close to the Parliament buildings, art galleries and museums, and is only three minutes away (by foot) from the Rideau Canal, which freezes into the world's longest skating rink. Ottawa has a number of exciting festivals and activities, including Winterlude, a winter carnival held each February. Anne-Marie and Irving make it a point to know what's going on when in Ottawa so they can advise their guests on what to see and do.

SEASON

all year

ACCOMMODATIONS

1 suite with private bath;
2 rooms with shared bath

Hawkins House Bed & Breakfast

Carla Pitzel and Garry Umbrich
303 Hawkins Street
Whitehorse, Yukon Territory
Y1A 1X5
Tel: (403) 668-7638
Fax: (403) 668-7632
$$$

ABOUT THE B&B

To stay at the Hawkins House Bed & Breakfast is to share a once-in-a-lifetime Yukon experience with your hosts Carla, Garry, and their two sons. Each guest room in this custom-built, luxury Victorian B&B highlights a different Yukon theme and features private bath and balcony, oak floor, bar sink and refrigerator, cable TV and VCR. Guests can take a Jacuzzi soak in the Fleur de Lys Room, watch Native videos in the First Nations Room, step back into gold rush days in the Victorian Tea Rose Room, or admire the splendid view of the SS Klondike paddlewheeler and Canyon Mountain from the balcony of the Fireweed Room. Especially geared to the business traveler, Hawkins House provides the convenience of private telephone line and answering machine, fax service, and work table with light and computer jack. Breakfast is a homemade feast of northern and international delights — from the home-smoked salmon pâté and moose sausage to jams, syrups, and sourdough pastries.

SEASON

all year

ACCOMMODATIONS

4 rooms with private baths

Hawkins House Shortcake

"This recipe is my all-time favorite and the only three-ingredient cake I know. It's really quick to prepare for those unexpected guests who just drop in. We serve it with wild Yukon berries and whipped cream." — Carla Pitzel

Dough:
4 eggs, separated
4 tablespoons vanilla sugar*
4 tablespoons all-purpose flour

Topping:
1 banana
Fresh berries

Sweetened whipped cream (beat together):
1 – 3 tablespoons confectioners' sugar
½ teaspoon vanilla
1 cup whipping cream (35%)

Note: Vanilla sugar is found in German specialty stores or delicatessens. If not available, use regular sugar and add ½ teaspoon vanilla to the beaten egg yolks.

(continued on next page)

Preheat oven to 400°F. Butter a shortcake pan. Beat egg whites in a small bowl until stiff. Transfer to a large bowl. Beat egg yolks in a small bowl with vanilla sugar until thick and pale yellow. Pour over egg whites and blend, making sure all the egg whites are mixed in (there should be no lumps of meringue). Fold in flour. Spoon batter into the pan. Cook in the oven for 10 minutes, reduce temperature to 350°F, and leave in another 20 minutes. When cake is cooled, remove from pan. Cut a large banana lengthwise into 4 slices. Curve the banana slices along the inside rim of the cake. Cover the top of the cake with fresh berries. Top the whole works with sweetened whipped cream. *Serves 10.*

Barbara Ann's Bed 'n Breakfast Vacation Farm

Barbara Ann and Ted Witzaney
PO Box 156
Denzil, Saskatchewan S0L 0S0
Tel: (306) 358-4814
$

ABOUT THE B&B

*S*pecially geared for families, Barbara Ann's B&B is located on the Witzaney farm, where they've been raising crops and hogs since 1911. The petting zoo includes traditional farm animals and more exotic ones, including a llama and Muscovy ducks. Barbara Ann's breakfast and other meals served on request feature farm-fresh milk, eggs, cheese, and vegetables; home-baked goods, such as buns, pies, and cookies; homemade jams, jellies, relishes, and pickles; and the farm's home-raised pork, which includes the specialty of the house — homemade sausages. Picnic and barbecue facilities, sandbox and swing set, horseshoe pit, lawn bowling, badminton, and an 18-hole miniature golf course are all on the property. When not tending to guests, Barbara Ann enjoys sewing and craft making, while Ted enjoys woodworking. Both like to spend time with their 10 grandchildren. Denzil is about a half-hour drive west of Unity, Saskatchewan, and a 45-minute drive east of Provost, Alberta.

SEASON

all year

ACCOMMODATIONS

2 rooms with shared bath

*H*azelnut Coffee Cake

¾ cup brown sugar
1 cup all-purpose flour
1 cup whole-wheat flour
1 teaspoon baking soda
1 teaspoon baking powder
1 teaspoon ground cinnamon
1 teaspoon ground nutmeg
½ teaspoon salt
⅔ cup milk
1 egg
¼ cup honey
½ cup ground hazelnuts

Topping:
1 cup sifted confectioners' sugar
1 – 2 tablespoons hot milk
½ cup whole hazelnuts

Preheat oven to 350°F. Mix first 8 dry ingredients together. Combine milk, egg, and honey and add to dry ingredients, blending well. Fold in ground hazelnuts. Pour batter into a greased, 9" square baking pan and bake 1 hour or until cake tests done. Cool slightly then remove from pan. Combine confectioners' sugar and hot milk, and beat until smooth. Drizzle carefully with a spoon over top of cooled cake in a lattice or cross-hatch design. Place whole hazelnuts in boxes formed by lattice design. *Serves 12.*

Heart-Healthy Applesauce Cake

"A favorite with guests, this applesauce cake has no eggs."
— Anna Doorenbos

½ cup margarine or butter
1 cup brown sugar
1 cup unsweetened applesauce
2 cups all-purpose flour
1 teaspoon baking soda
1 teaspoon ground cinnamon
½ teaspoon ground cloves
½ teaspoon salt
½ cup raisins
½ cup slivered almonds

Preheat oven to 350°F. Cream margarine or butter. Beat in sugar. Gradually add applesauce. Sift together remaining ingredients (except nuts and raisins) and add to creamed mixture. Add raisins and nuts. Spread in a greased loaf pan and bake 1 hour or until done. *Serves 12.*

Anna's Bed and Breakfast

Anna and Robert Doorenbos
204 Wolf Street
Thompson, Manitoba R8N 1J7
Tel: (204) 677-5075
$ – $$

ABOUT THE B&B

Visit Anna's Bed and Breakfast to experience what Canadian Dutch hospitality is all about. This adult-oriented and non-smoking B&B offers a private guest suite with its own entrance and parking space, two single beds, private bath, kitchenette, and den with TV and telephone. Anna enjoys cooking and will get your day off to a delicious start with a full breakfast served in the main dining room. Oriental meals are another specialty and, along with traditional meals, are available for an additional charge. The greenhouse, which is connected to the cozy and informal living room, opens onto the deck and lends a summer atmosphere to the home — even in the dead of winter! Thompson is the home base of travelers to fly-in fishing lodges and Churchill (Manitoba) and other northern communities. It also boasts the longest alpine ski season in Manitoba. Guest pick-up can be arranged as well as scenic touring by car. Your hosts Anna and Robert moved to Canada from Holland and have lived in Thompson since 1971. Robert, an award winning visual artist, originates from Egypt and Anna from Indonesia.

SEASON

all year

ACCOMMODATIONS

1 suite with private bath

Elgin Manor B&B

Penny and Dave Grimshaw
RR #2
Port Sandfield, Ontario P0B 1J0
Tel: (705) 765-5325
$$ – $$$$

ABOUT THE B&B

Nestled on a quiet bay of picturesque Lake Joseph, you'll find the unique and heartwarming Elgin Manor B&B, a 1920s Tudor home surrounded by English gardens and a water's edge fireplace. In keeping with the timeless, historical traditions for which the Muskoka Lakes are known, you're sure to see several antique wooden boats (called "launches") or even the historic steamship Segwun pass by the dock as you sit in a wooden Muskoka chair. The manor is decorated with antiques throughout and guest rooms are tastefully appointed with handmade quilts. Old-fashioned picnic lunches complete with wicker baskets and antique launch excursions can be arranged. Situated in the heart of Muskoka cottage country (two hours north of Toronto), the area offers year-round activities — from summer nature walks, fishing, swimming, canoeing, and midnight strolls under a million glistening stars, to local artisan tours and winter ice skating, snowshoeing, and cross-country skiing across the panoramic countryside.

SEASON

all year

ACCOMMODATIONS

3 rooms with private baths;
1 honeymoon cabin
with private bath

Hummingbird Layer Cake

"Hummingbirds are seen throughout Muskoka from May to September. I serve this cake with afternoon tea on the deck near the bright red hummingbird feeders (which may have 8 – 10 visiting birds at one time) so guests can enjoy their beautiful colors and hear the wonderful sound of their wings buzzing." — Penny Grimshaw

2½ cups all-purpose flour
2¼ cups sugar
1 teaspoon fine salt
1 teaspoon baking soda
1 teaspoon ground cinnamon or mixed spice
3 eggs
1½ cups vegetable oil
2 teaspoons vanilla
8-ounce can crushed pineapple, drained
2 cups mashed or chopped bananas

Icing:
½ cup butter
8-ounce package cream cheese
1 teaspoon vanilla
3 – 4 cups confectioners' sugar

Fresh edible flowers
Fresh fruit

(continued on next page)

Preheat oven to 350°F. In a mixing bowl, combine first 5 ingredients. In a small bowl, beat eggs, then add oil and vanilla, mixing again. Add egg mixture to flour mixture. Stir in fruit. Spoon batter into 3 greased 8" layer pans. Bake 25 minutes or until done. Turn pans upside down onto cooling racks so layers can cool. Once cool, frost the top of each layer with icing. Assemble one on top of another and frost sides of cake. Decorate with edible fresh flowers and fruit to resemble a hummingbird (use fruit as the body and flower petals as the wings). Cake can be refrigerated. *Serves 10 – 12.*

Brookside Hospitality Home

Pearl and Lloyd Hiscock
PO Box 104
Sunnyside, Newfoundland
A0B 3J0
Tel: (709) 472-4515
$

ABOUT THE B&B

You'll be welcomed like family at Brookside Hospitality Home, a well-maintained ranch-style dwelling in the rural community of Sunnyside. Pearl and Lloyd have lived in Sunnyside practically all their lives and know what Newfoundland hospitality is all about. Get to know them and their miniature collie, Lady, over a cup of tea or coffee, which is provided along with a bedtime snack. In the morning, make your way to the breakfast nook overlooking the water where home-made bread and jam, cereals, and juices await you. Radio, cable TV, laundry facilities, and ample parking are also available. Let your well-informed hosts direct you to the best sights in the province. Lloyd is a boat enthusiast and you may want to look in on his latest boat building project in the shed. Pearl keeps busy with her household responsibilities. Brookside is about one-and-a-half hours' drive from the Argentia Ferry to North Sydney, Nova Scotia, and one hour's drive from St. John's, capital of Newfoundland.

SEASON

all year

ACCOMMODATIONS

2 rooms with shared bath

Impossible Pie

"After this has baked, you have a definite bottom crust, a lovely custard filling, and a rich butter-coconut topping."
— Pearl Hiscock

4 eggs
¼ cup melted butter
1 cup sugar
½ cup all-purpose flour
½ teaspoon baking powder
¼ teaspoon salt
1 cup flaked unsweetened coconut
2 cups milk
1 teaspoon vanilla

Preheat oven to 350°F. Mix together all ingredients. Pour into a buttered 10" glass pie plate and bake 1 hour. *Serves 6.*

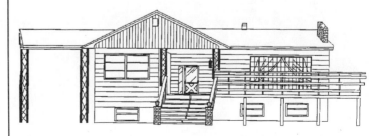

Lazy Dazy Cake

"This cake freezes well and can be made ahead of time. It's an excellent cake to serve with tea or cocoa as a welcoming treat for guests." — Mona Adamson

1 cup all-purpose flour
1 teaspoon baking powder
1 cup sugar
Pinch of salt
2 eggs
1 teaspoon vanilla
½ cup milk
2 tablespoons butter

Topping:
2 tablespoons melted butter
2 tablespoons half-and-half cream (10 – 18%)
5 tablespoons brown sugar
⅓ cup slivered almonds or flaked unsweetened coconut

Preheat oven to 350°F. Mix first 4 ingredients together. Beat eggs with vanilla; add to dry mixture. Bring milk and butter to a boil; let cool to lukewarm. Add to the above mixture and mix until smooth. Pour into a greased 8" square pan and bake about 25 minutes. When done, mix topping ingredients and cover top of cake. Bake an additional 5 – 10 minutes until brown and bubbly. *Tip:* You can reduce the sugar to ¾ cup without any adverse effects. *Serves 12 – 16.*

Lindsay House Bed & Breakfast

Mona and Dixon Adamson
1904-1st Avenue East
Prince Albert, Saskatchewan
S6V 2B5
Tel: (306) 764-4337
$$

ABOUT THE B&B

Lindsay House is named after its original owner, Sir James Hawkins Lindsay, who built the residence in 1906 and lived there until his death in 1958. It is said that he entertained two Canadian prime ministers at Lindsay House, William Lyon Mackenzie King and Sir Wilfred Laurier. Retaining its original structure, this three-story brick house offers four rooms on the second floor with shared bathrooms. Guests have use of the den with wood burning fireplace, parlor or TV room (also with a wood burning fireplace). Served in the formal dining room, breakfast consists of juice, fresh fruit salad, homemade muffins, scones, or croissants, and a different entrée each day (guest preferences or dietary needs can be accommodated). The inn is non smoking; guests can, however, smoke on the wraparound veranda. Prince Albert is situated close to the park land of the north and this B&B is just a five-minute walk from the city center. Mona and Dixon both enjoy gardening and spend many a summer day tending to their flower and vegetable garden.

SEASON

all year

ACCOMMODATIONS

4 rooms with shared baths

Park View
Bed & Breakfast

Gladys and Carson Langille
254 Cameron Street
Moncton, New Brunswick
E1C 5Z3
Tel: (506) 382-4504
$$

ABOUT THE B&B

This Art Deco home was built in 1940 as a residence for Mrs. Inez Robinson, owner of Moncton's first business college. The architectural plans came from the 1939 New York World's Fair and this was the first Art Deco home in Moncton. The curved living room windows look out on beautiful Victoria Park in the city's center. Opened as a B&B in 1989, this charming home provides three guest rooms with cable TV, telephones, and exquisite shared bath, spacious living room with fireplace, elegant dining room, and cozy kitchen. Your hosts provide a warm welcome, a hearty, full home-cooked breakfast of your choice, and a wealth of information about the area. Gladys is a part-time school teacher, while Carson enjoys playing bridge and painting landscapes. A collection of works by local artists graces their walls. Nearby is superb dining, shopping, beaches, parks, museums, galleries, theater, a must-see tidal bore (where the tide goes up and down very quickly), and infamous Magnetic Hill (you'll never believe this is possible unless you experience it yourself!).

SEASON

all year

ACCOMMODATIONS

3 rooms with shared bath

Mandarin Orange Coffee Cake

2 cups all-purpose flour
1 cup sugar
2½ teaspoons baking powder
1 teaspoon salt
½ teaspoon ground nutmeg
½ cup margarine
¾ cup milk
1 egg
1 teaspoon vanilla
11-ounce can drained mandarin oranges

Preheat oven to 350°F. Combine first 5 dry ingredients. Cut in margarine until fine crumbs form. Reserve ½ cup crumbs for topping. To the remainder, add milk, egg, and vanilla. Spread batter in an 8 x 8" greased pan. Spread oranges on top. Cover with crumbs. Bake 40 – 45 minutes. *Serves 9 – 12.*

Open-faced Fruit Cake with Wild Blueberry Filling

"My friend gave me this recipe 30 years ago while she was living in the southern province of Limburg in Holland. I'm still using it today because it uses a minimal amount of fat and eggs. I pick wild muskeg blueberries in the bushes at the back of our house and keep them in the freezer for whenever I make this cake."— Anna Doorenbos

¼ cup margarine or butter
¼ cup sugar
1 egg
1 teaspoon vanilla
1 cup all-purpose flour
½ cup skim milk or 1% milk
Low-fat cooking spray
Wild blueberry filling (recipe follows) or fresh or canned fruit
    of your choice

Vanilla ice cream or whipped cream

(continued on next page)

Anna's Bed and Breakfast

Anna and Robert Doorenbos
204 Wolf Street
Thompson, Manitoba R8N 1J7
Tel: (204) 677-5075
$ – $$

ABOUT THE B&B

Visit Anna's Bed and Breakfast to experience what Canadian Dutch hospitality is all about. This adult-oriented and non-smoking B&B offers a private guest suite with its own entrance and parking space, two single beds, private bath, kitchenette, and den with TV and telephone. Anna enjoys cooking and will get your day off to a delicious start with a full breakfast served in the main dining room. Oriental meals are another specialty and, along with traditional meals, are available for an additional charge. The greenhouse, which is connected to the cozy and informal living room, opens onto the deck and lends a summer atmosphere to the home — even in the dead of winter! Thompson is the home base of travelers to fly-in fishing lodges and Churchill (Manitoba) and other northern communities. It also boasts the longest alpine ski season in Manitoba. Guest pick-up can be arranged as well as scenic touring by car. Your hosts Anna and Robert moved to Canada from Holland and have lived in Thompson since 1971. Robert, an award winning visual artist, originates from Egypt and Anna from Indonesia.

SEASON

all year

ACCOMMODATIONS

1 suite with private bath

Preheat oven to 350°F. Cream butter with sugar. Add egg and vanilla, beating well. Stir in flour and milk alternately until batter is smooth. Spray a 9" flan form with cooking spray and pour batter into it. Bake 25 – 30 minutes. Turn out of form onto a plate, fill with blueberry filling and glaze (recipes follow). Nice served with vanilla ice cream or whipped cream. *Serves 8 – 12.*

Wild blueberry filling:
1½ cups washed wild blueberries
¼ – ½ cup sugar
Juice of ½ lemon
½ cup water
Pinch of ground cinnamon
Cornstarch

Bring ingredients (except cornstarch) to a boil and let simmer for 5 minutes. Thicken with cornstarch and remove from heat. Pour on open-faced cake.

Glaze:
1) **If using fresh fruit**
   Package of powdered fresh fruit glaze

2) **If using canned fruit**
   Juice from canned fruit
   Cornstarch or tapioca

Prepare powdered glaze according to package directions or mix juice from canned fruit with a thickener (such as cornstarch or tapioca). Brush on cake.

Orange Peel-Sherry Cake

2 cups candied orange peels
⅔ cup sweet sherry
1 cup margarine
1½ cups sugar
4 eggs
2½ cups all-purpose flour
1 teaspoon baking powder

Soak the candied peel in ⅓ cup sherry overnight (cover with plastic wrap). Preheat oven to 350°F. Cream margarine and sugar until fluffy. Add eggs one at a time, mixing well after each addition. Combine flour and baking powder, then add to margarine mixture, mixing just until moistened. Fold in sherry-soaked orange peels. Spread mixture into a greased and floured bundt pan. Bake 65 – 75 minutes. Cool for 20 minutes in the pan, then invert. Wrap cake in cheesecloth. Soak the cheesecloth with remaining ⅓ cup sherry. Cover the wrapped cake in aluminum foil and refrigerate for 4 days. *Tips:* When serving, cut small pieces (this cake is quite filling!). Wrap any leftovers back in the cheesecloth and foil and refrigerate. Cake will keep for about 2 weeks. *Serves 24.*

Bread and Roses Country Inn

Monica and Richard Cobb
PO Box 177, 82 Victoria Street
Annapolis Royal, Nova Scotia
B0S 1A0
Tel: (902) 532-5727
$$

ABOUT THE B&B

Bread and Roses Country Inn is a rare Nova Scotia example of a brick masonry Queen Anne Revival house. Built circa 1882, this non-smoking inn has many fine design details, such as a large entrance hall with sweeping staircase, intricate woodwork, and etched glass windows. The nine guest rooms on three floors are all distinctively decorated with antiques. The owners' eclectic art collection, which includes whimsical Nova Scotia folk art, contemporary Canadian paintings, and Inuit sculpture, is displayed throughout the house. Breakfast includes Monica's brown bread and granola, local preserves, yogurt, juice, and tea or coffee. Guests enjoy gathering in the parlor each evening for tea and sweets to share stories of their Nova Scotian adventures. Nearby are historic sites, museums, artists' studios, golfing, walking trails, and excellent restaurants. Port Royal, Canada's oldest permanent European settlement (1605) is a short drive away. Having traveled extensively throughout the Maritime provinces, Monica and Richard can provide touring tips tailored to your interests.

SEASON

March 1 – October 30

ACCOMMODATIONS

9 rooms with private baths

Brio Haus

Diana and Les Habkirk
3005 Brio Entrance
Whistler, British Columbia
V0N 1B3
Tel: (800) 331-BRIO (2746)
or (604) 932-3313
E-mail: briohaus@whistler.net
$$ – $$$

ABOUT THE B&B

Brio Haus is an intimate
bed and breakfast located
in Canada's premier ski
resort area. Enjoy charming rooms,
fitted with cozy goose down duvets,
in a European-style alpine home,
and awake to a full home-baked
breakfast, often featuring one of the
pear specialties of the house. After
wintertime skiing or summertime
hiking, canoeing, and horseback
riding, you can prepare your own
snacks and dinners in the guest
kitchen loaded with amenities. After
that, warm yourself by the evening
fire in the guest lounge and watch
a variety of complimentary movies.
Or, ease sore muscles after an active
day with a soak in the Jacuzzi
moon tub and sauna. Brio Haus is
centrally located, an easy walk to
Whistler Village and ski lifts via the
Valley Trail, and right across the
street from the golf course. Diana
and Les spent many years as a bus
tour guide team in the Canadian
Rockies before opening their lodge
in 1989. Les now runs the local
transit system and Diana works full
time seeing to the needs of her B&B
guests.

SEASON

all year

ACCOMMODATIONS

3 rooms with shared bath

Pear Coffee Cake

"Pears were always a special treat when I was growing up in Kansas, and this recipe originates with my mother. My sister loved the fruit so much that her childhood nickname was (you guessed it) 'Pear.' " — Diana Habkirk

3 tablespoons brown sugar
2 tablespoons all-purpose flour
¼ teaspoon ground nutmeg
1 tablespoon butter

2 cups all-purpose flour
1 teaspoon baking powder
½ teaspoon baking soda
½ teaspoon salt
½ teaspoon ground cinnamon
⅛ teaspoon ground cloves

5 tablespoons butter
¾ cup sugar
1 egg
1½ teaspoons orange zest
⅓ cup orange juice
1 pear, peeled, cored, and chopped
1 cup bran flake cereal
⅔ cup chopped walnuts

(continued on next page)

Preheat oven to 350°F.

Combine in bowl 1: Brown sugar, 2 tablespoons flour, and nutmeg; cut in 1 tablespoon butter.

Combine in bowl 2: 2 cups flour, baking powder and soda, salt, cinnamon, and cloves.

Combine in (large) bowl 3: 5 tablespoons butter and sugar. Beat until fluffy. Add egg and orange zest. Beat well. Add dry ingredients in bowl 2 to this sugar-egg mixture, alternating with orange juice. Stir in pear, cereal, and walnuts. Mix well. Spread batter into a greased 9 x 5 x 2" pan. Sprinkle with brown sugar mixture in bowl 1. Bake 30 minutes. *Serves 12.*

Sanford House Bed & Breakfast

Elizabeth and Charlie Le Ber
PO Box 1825, 20 Platt Street
Brighton, Ontario K0K 1H0
Tel/Fax: (613) 475-3930
$$

ABOUT THE B&B

Sitting majestically on the crest of a hill, Sanford House Bed & Breakfast is a red-brick Victorian home close to Main Street in the friendly town of Brighton. This century-old home with turret and covered veranda has offstreet parking, a separate guest entrance, and three large, bright, and comfortable bedrooms. Guests can choose to relax in the round turret room; in the lounge with television, VCR, videos, board games, and books; in the spacious, bright Victorian parlor; or on the veranda. Delicious home-baked breakfasts, often spotlighting apples grown in nearby orchards, are served in the guest dining room. It's a short drive to beautiful Presqu'ile Provincial Park's sandy beaches, nature trails, fine bird-watching area, and marsh boardwalk. If antique hunting is a passion, there are numerous antique establishments right in Brighton and the surrounding area. Apple-fest, a celebration of the harvest in September, is a particularly lovely time to visit the area. When not entertaining their B&B guests, Elizabeth and Charlie enjoy cycling and birdwatching.

SEASON

all year

ACCOMMODATIONS

3 rooms with shared bath

Pecan-Sour Cream Coffee Cake

Topping:
¾ cup dark brown sugar
1 tablespoon all-purpose flour
1 teaspoon ground cinnamon
¼ cup butter
1 cup chopped pecans

Batter:
1½ cups unbleached or all-purpose flour
1 teaspoon baking powder
½ teaspoon baking soda
2 eggs
¾ cup sour cream
¼ cup maple syrup
1 teaspoon vanilla

Preheat oven to 375°F. Prepare topping by mixing together sugar, flour, and cinnamon. Cut in butter with a fork or pastry blender. Add pecans, tossing to make mixture crumbly, then set aside. To make batter: Sift together flour, baking powder, and baking soda. In a separate bowl, beat eggs until thickened. Add sour cream, maple syrup, and vanilla to eggs, and beat well. Gently combine egg mixture with flour mixture. Add 1 cup topping mixture, stirring gently. Pour batter into a buttered 8" square baking pan. Sprinkle with remaining topping mixture. Bake 35 minutes. Serve warm. **Serves 9.**

Prairie Fresh Fruit Tarts

9 ounces cream cheese, softened
⅓ cup sugar
4 teaspoons lemon juice
1 cup whipping cream (35%) or whipped topping
24 small tart shells, baked
Fresh berries or sliced fruit in season

Sprigs of mint, snips of nasturtium leaves, or orange zest

Beat cream cheese until smooth. Add sugar and lemon juice, blending well. Fold in whipping cream or whipped topping. Spoon into tart shells. Chill. To serve, top with berries or fresh fruit. Garnish with sprigs of mint, snips of nasturtium leaves, or orange zest. *Makes 2 dozen small tarts.*

Peters Place

Joan and Calvin Peters
6430 PR 241 North
Cartier, Manitoba R4K 1B4
Tel: (204) 864-2106
$

ABOUT THE B&B

Experience rural Canada and the people who live there at Peters Place — a 500-acre, family-operated grain farm. Offering peace and quiet along the Assiniboine River, Peters Place is ideal for B&B travelers who want the best of both worlds — country relaxation with close proximity to the urban sights of Winnipeg. It's also a good base from which to tour points of historic interest, such as Lower Fort Garry at Selkirk or the museum at Portage la Prairie. Excellent golf facilities are within a 10-minute drive. For those who enjoy natural parkland, Beaudry Park is open year-round for hikers or cross-country skiers. If time and weather permit, your hosts will take you to watch the beaver on the Assiniboine at dusk, give you a ride in their old Model T or on one of their restored farm tractors, and take you inside their Canadian National Railway caboose. Bountiful breakfasts are served in the family dining area and every effort is made to accommodate special preferences or diets.

SEASON

April – October

ACCOMMODATIONS

2 rooms with shared bath

Longview
Bed & Breakfast

Charlene and Bob Siemens
PO Box 53
Fiske, Saskatchewan S0L 1C0
Tel: (306) 377-4786
$

ABOUT THE B&B

Peaceful surroundings, nature walks, farm-fresh meals, and barnyard animals are what you can expect at Longview, a working prairie farm southwest of Saskatoon. While listening to the howl of the coyote, fall asleep in your private guest cottage with its own bath and deck, then wake up to the crow of the rooster. Join hosts Charlene and Bob in their home for a hearty breakfast (and other meals if requested) — all of which take advantage of the produce, eggs, and meat produced on the farm. For those who want to really get away from it all, Longview offers a rustic cottage surrounded by a grove of trees and a choir of birds. A short drive away, you can find ancient petroglyphs and teepee rings. Your hosts especially welcome families, and enjoy visiting with their guests and sharing their love of the land.

SEASON

May – September

ACCOMMODATIONS

private cottage (3 rooms
with shared bath);
rustic cabin

Prairie Treat Pie

"When we have out-of-province visitors, we make sure to serve them Saskatoon berries, 'the pride of the prairies,' in some form. This pie is our all-time favorite."
— Charlene Siemens

4 cups Saskatoon berries or blueberries
1 tablespoon lemon juice
2 tablespoons water
1 cup sugar
1 tablespoon cornstarch
Pastry for 1 double-crust pie (9")
1 tablespoon butter
Milk (optional)
Sprinkle of sugar (optional)

Preheat oven to 425°F. Simmer berries, lemon juice, and water for 10 minutes, covered. Mix sugar and cornstarch and add to berry mixture. Bring to a boil and cool slightly. Place filling in lower pastry crust and dot with butter. Cover with other crust, seal edges, and cut vents in top crust. If desired, brush pie top lightly with milk and sprinkle with sugar. Bake 15 minutes. Reduce oven to 350°F and bake 30 minutes longer. *Serves 6 – 8.*

Quick Coffee Cake

"My neighbor Joan Tiede shared this delicious recipe with me and I, in turn, have passed it along to many of our guests."
— Vera Sproule

1 cup sour cream
1 teaspoon baking soda
½ cup soft butter
1 cup sugar
2 eggs
1¾ cups all-purpose flour
2 teaspoons baking powder
1 cup brown sugar
1 cup chopped pecans or walnuts

Preheat oven to 350°F. Mix together sour cream and baking soda; set aside. Beat butter and sugar. Add eggs, flour, and baking powder and beat until just moistened. Add sour cream mixture and gently combine. Pour half the batter into a greased 8 x 8 x 2" pan. Sprinkle with ½ cup brown sugar and ½ cup nuts. Pour remaining batter over nuts and top with remaining brown sugar and nuts. Bake 40 – 45 minutes. **Serves 10.**

Sproule Heritage Place B&B

Vera and Winston Sproule
PO Box 43, Site 14, RR #1
Strathmore, Alberta T1P 1J6
Tel: (403) 934-3219
$$

ABOUT THE B&B

While Sproule Heritage Place B&B has been featured by both Hallmark USA and Alberta Government Telephone in their television commercials, this farm actually had less high-profile beginnings. In 1909, it was little more than a well-trodden buffalo trail when the Scheer family settled on the open prairie east of Calgary. Years later, the stately house and barn became a landmark to travelers on a road that today is the Trans-Canada Highway. Vera and Winston Sproule purchased the farm in 1985 and began extensive renovations to restore its 1920s elegance. As a result, the site has been declared an Alberta Registered Historic Resource. Artisans and designers of furniture and quilts, Vera and Winston (a country pastor for four years in the Yukon and 24 years in Alberta) assure you a comfortable bed in one of three charming bedrooms and an interesting breakfast.

SEASON

all year

ACCOMMODATIONS

1 room with private bath;
2 rooms with shared bath

Hawkins House Bed & Breakfast

Carla Pitzel and Garry Umbrich
303 Hawkins Street
Whitehorse, Yukon Territory
Y1A 1X5
Tel: (403) 668-7638
Fax: (403) 668-7632
$$$

ABOUT THE B&B

To stay at the Hawkins House Bed & Breakfast is to share a once-in-a-lifetime Yukon experience with your hosts Carla, Garry, and their two sons. Each guest room in this custom-built, luxury Victorian B&B highlights a different Yukon theme and features private bath and balcony, oak floor, bar sink and refrigerator, cable TV and VCR. Guests can take a Jacuzzi soak in the Fleur de Lys Room, watch Native videos in the First Nations Room, step back into gold rush days in the Victorian Tea Rose Room, or admire the splendid view of the SS Klondike paddlewheeler and Canyon Mountain from the balcony of the Fireweed Room. Especially geared to the business traveler, Hawkins House provides the convenience of private telephone line and answering machine, fax service, and work table with light and computer jack. Breakfast is a homemade feast of northern and international delights — from the home-smoked salmon pâté and moose sausage to jams, syrups, and sourdough pastries.

SEASON

all year

ACCOMMODATIONS

4 rooms with private baths

Rosehip Torte

"This is our signature cake, which I traditionally make with rosehip jelly (but any jelly will do). Be careful slicing this cake — it's light as a feather." — Carla Pitzel

Dough (made 1 day in advance):
⅔ cup butter
⅔ cup sugar
1½ cups all-purpose flour
1 egg
1 cup ground hazelnuts or almonds

Whipped cream filling:
2 cups whipping cream (35%)
2 tablespoons sifted confectioners' sugar
1 teaspoon vanilla

Rosehip jelly (see recipe on page 308)
Rolled marzipan
Marzipan figurines
Fresh flowers

Mix butter, sugar, flour, egg, and nuts together in a bowl. Turn dough onto a floured surface and knead until it forms a nice soft ball. Wrap the dough in a plastic bag and leave in the refrigerator for 1 day.

(continued on next page)

Next day, preheat oven to 350°F. Cut 5 wax paper rounds to neatly fit the greased bottoms of 5 10"-diameter springform pans. Lightly butter one side of the 5 wax paper rounds and put them butter side up in each pan. Divide the dough into 5 equal pieces.

Put a mound of dough in each pan and press it to the edges to make a thin round layer of dough. Bake about 15 minutes (they're overdone if edges become too brown). Cool cakes and don't forget to peel off the wax paper!

Whip cream until stiff. Add sugar and vanilla. Spread rosehip jelly over the tops of all layers. To assemble, put 1 layer on your cake plate. Spread a quarter of the whipped cream over the jelly. Repeat with the other 3 layers. On remaining top layer, cover the jelly with rolled marzipan. Decorate with marzipan figurines and fresh flowers. *Serves 12.*

Norwood
Bed & Breakfast

Pat and Roland Jensen
201 Norwood Court
Wetaskiwin, Alberta T9A 3P2
Tel: (888)/(403) 352-7880
Fax: (403) 352-8850
$$

ABOUT THE B&B

Seventeen-year residents of Wetaskiwin, Pat and Roland Jensen offer old-fashioned B&B hospitality in their new home full of country charm. An old-style double bed and antiques grace one guest room, while Victorian decor illuminates the queen-bedded room. Guests share a full bathroom, Jacuzzi, and a sitting room with white baby grand piano, games, books, and CD stereo system. Served in the formal dining room or on the sunny patio, a typical full breakfast consists of fruit salad, home-baked muffins and breads, homemade jams, a cooked entrée, and beverages. A smoking area is available outside on the deck. Norwood welcomes children but not pets as there's a resident 15-pound cat named Little Guy (who doesn't visit the guest rooms). After a day exploring such museums as Canada's Aviation Hall of Fame and the Alberta Central Railway Museum, shopping at antique, ladieswear, and gift shops, or playing a few rounds of golf, guests can refresh themselves with a soak in the outdoor hot tub. Norwood B&B is only a 45-minute drive from Alberta's capital, Edmonton.

SEASON

all year

ACCOMMODATIONS

2 rooms with shared bath

Sourdough Chocolate Cake

½ cup sourdough starter (see recipe on page 69)
1 cup lukewarm water
¼ cup nonfat dry milk
1½ cups all-purpose flour

1 cup sugar
½ cup shortening
1 teaspoon vanilla
1½ teaspoons baking soda
1 teaspoon ground cinnamon
½ teaspoon salt
2 eggs
3 ounces semisweet chocolate squares, melted

Preheat oven to 350°F. Mix sourdough starter, water, milk, and flour. Cover with plastic wrap and let stand 2 – 3 hours until bubbly. In a separate bowl, cream together next 6 ingredients. Add eggs, one at a time, beating well after each. Add melted chocolate squares. Combine sourdough mixture and chocolate mixture together and mix well. Place batter in a 13 x 9" pan. Bake 25 – 30 minutes. *Serves 15.*

Spanish Cheesecake with Strawberry-Rhubarb Topping

"Absolutely delicious and elegant." — Marlene Scullion

1 pound cream cheese
3 tablespoons butter
1½ cups sugar
2 large eggs
½ teaspoon ground cinnamon
1 teaspoon lemon zest
¼ cup all-purpose flour
½ teaspoon salt
Confectioners' sugar

Preheat oven to 400°F. Cream together cheese, 1 tablespoon butter, and sugar (don't beat). Stir in eggs, blending well after each. Add cinnamon, lemon zest, flour, and salt. Mix well. Butter a round cake, flan, or springform pan with remaining 2 tablespoons butter and pour in batter. Bake 12 minutes. Reduce temperature to 350°F and bake 25 – 30 minutes more. Cool. Sprinkle with confectioners' sugar. When ready to serve, spoon topping (recipe follows) over individual slices. **Serves 8+.**

(continued on next page)

The Open Door / La Porte Ouverte

Marlene and Glenn Scullion
239 Thomas Lefebvre Road
Davidson, Québec J0X 1R0
Tel: (819) 683-2991
Fax: (819) 683-2201
$$

ABOUT THE B&B

The Open Door B&B is nestled on the sandy shores of the Ottawa River, about a one-and-a-quarter-hour drive from the nation's capital. Located in the historic Pontiac region, the area is an inspiring combination of the traditions found in both English and French Canada. Rivers, lakes, and forests surrounding The Open Door provide a backdrop of natural beauty rarely found today. Since January 1993, The Open Door has played host to many international visitors and small conferences. A charming, comfortable atmosphere is created with a tasteful decor of Canadian country antiques. Delicious home cooking is graciously served in the beautiful sunroom overlooking a wide expanse of the river. Numerous seasonal activities are available on the premises or by arrangement. Marlene and Glenn are a recently retired couple from the broadcasting industry. Glenn is also a gifted pianist and Marlene an artist, and they both take great pride in ensuring their guests have a wonderful stay.

SEASON

all year

ACCOMMODATIONS

3 rooms with shared bath;
1 cabin with private bath;
2-bedroom guest house
with private bath

Strawberry-rhubarb topping:
2 cups fresh hulled or frozen (thawed and drained) strawberries
2 cups chopped rhubarb
Sugar to taste
Fresh lemon juice

Simmer ingredients together until rhubarb is tender. Spoon over cheesecake. *Tip:* This sauce can be made ahead and served cold or warm.

Sugarless, Butterless, Eggless Cake

2 cups raisins
1 cup dates
2 teaspoons vanilla
2 teaspoons ground cinnamon
1 teaspoon ground nutmeg
2 cups water
½ cup sunflower or olive oil
1 orange, cut-up (including peel)
Any other fruit you may wish to add

2¼ cups whole-wheat flour
½ cup walnuts
1 teaspoon baking powder
2 teaspoons baking soda

Boil first set of ingredients for 10 minutes. Let cool. Preheat oven to 300°F. Add dry ingredients together, then add to cooled mixture, stirring just to moisten. Place batter in a greased 10" tube pan. Bake 1 hour. *Serves approximately 16.*

Lake Crescent Inn

Evelyn and Bruce Warr
PO Box 69
Robert's Arm, Newfoundland
A0J 1R0
Tel: (709) 652-3067
Fax: (709) 652-3056
$

ABOUT THE B&B

When you think of Newfoundland, think peaceful lifestyle, clean air and rivers, and superb hospitality — all of which you'll find at Lake Crescent Inn. Walk along the quiet roads and beautiful beaches, visit fishermen in the various communities along the route, or go iceberg or whale watching (in season). Boating trips can also be arranged, so why not give cod jigging or salmon fishing a try? Be sure to bring along your camera to capture the moment you reel in your first fish (you might even see "Cressie," the lake monster!). The inn offers four bedrooms and two bathrooms, one with whirlpool and shower. Breakfasts are a homemade feast of muffins, jams, jellies, and breads, and a special health-conscious menu is also available. A Jiggs dinner is served on Sundays from 5:00 p.m., and a Fish Platter dinner is served on Fridays from 5:00 p.m. (other meals can be provided upon request).

SEASON

all year

ACCOMMODATIONS

4 rooms with shared baths

Gaeste-Haus Kroker

Patricia Kroker
PO Box 202
Bruderheim, Alberta T0B 0S0
Tel: (403) 796-3621
$$

ABOUT THE B&B

Only a short drive yet worlds away from the hustle and bustle of Edmonton, Gaeste-Haus Kroker invites you to relax in the charm and comfort of this 1927 brick Victorian guest house. You can choose to enjoy the peaceful ambience of the entire upper level or mingle with other guests in the French Provincial-furnished parlor. Wind down your evening with a snack of homemade dessert. Awaken in the morning to freshly brewed coffee and a hearty breakfast on fine china in the elegantly furnished dining room. Relax on the veranda or in front of the outdoor fireplace, and stroll about the spacious lawn and garden. A former registered nurse, town councilor, and town mayor, hostess Patricia Kroker enjoys gardening, baking, and traveling, and will make your visit an enjoyable and memorable experience. Area attractions include Elk Island National Park, West Edmonton Mall, Ukrainian Cultural Heritage Village, and Beaverhill Lake.

SEASON

all year

ACCOMMODATIONS

3 rooms with shared bath

Swedish Rhubarb Meringue

"I grow rhubarb in my garden and I'm always on the lookout for delicious ways to serve it. This recipe hails from a Swedish B&B I visited, where I helped my hostess (who worked full time) with the cooking. It was a big hit with her guests and is now a big hit with mine." — Patricia Kroker

⅔ cup margarine
2 cups all-purpose flour
2 tablespoons sugar

5 cups diced rhubarb
4 egg yolks (save whites for meringue)
2 cups sugar
4 tablespoons all-purpose flour
¼ teaspoon salt
1 cup evaporated milk or whipping cream (35%)

4 egg whites
5 tablespoons sugar

Preheat oven to 350°F. Mix first 3 ingredients and press into the bottom of a 13 x 9" pan. Prick the bottom with a fork and bake 10 minutes. Mix remaining ingredients and pour over crust. Bake 45 minutes. To make meringue, beat egg whites until foamy in an electric mixer or by hand. While continuing to beat, add sugar 1 tablespoon at a time. Meringue is ready when stiff peaks form. Spoon over rhubarb mixture and bake at 300°F – 350°F 8 – 10 minutes or until meringue is browned. *Serves 12.*

White Pound Cake

1 cup butter
1½ cups sugar
½ cup milk
½ cup warm water
1 teaspoon lemon juice
1 teaspoon vanilla
3 cups all-purpose flour
2 teaspoons baking powder
½ teaspoon salt
3 eggs
Confectioners' sugar
Orange and lemon slices

Preheat oven to 325°F. Cream butter. Add sugar and cream mixture together. Add milk slowly and mix. Gradually add warm water, lemon juice, and vanilla, and mix. Sift dry ingredients together and add alternately with eggs (one at a time) to the butter mixture. Beat well after each addition. Place batter in a greased 9" tube pan and bake 1 hour. Let cool. Sprinkle the top with confectioners' sugar and decorate with fruit slices. *Serves 8 – 10.*

Wooded Acres
Bed & Breakfast

Elva and Skip Kennedy
4907 Rocky Point Road, RR #2
Victoria, British Columbia
V9B 5B4
Tel: (250) 478-8172 or
(250) 474-8959
$$$

ABOUT THE B&B

Elva and Skip's country house truly is a labor of love, made from scratch with logs from their property. The emptiness that settled in once their children had "grown and flown" inspired Elva and Skip to turn their dream home into an old-fashioned B&B. Secluded in three acres of forest, Wooded Acres invites you to relax in your own sheltered hot tub amidst the pleasures and relics of bygone times. Enjoy a full breakfast of fresh-daily house specialties (including scones and biscuits) served at your convenience. Bedrooms are decorated with antiques, queen beds, and cozy down-filled duvets, while candlelight and lace add a special touch throughout the B&B. As British Columbia's capital, Victoria is known for its breathtaking scenery, beaches, and wilderness parks. The area offers a wealth of walking trails, golf courses, fishing and birdwatching areas, and numerous venues for local artisans. Wooded Acres is located conveniently close to all amenities in Victoria (30 minutes away) and the rural splendor of Sooke (20 minutes away).

SEASON

all year

ACCOMMODATIONS

2 suites with private baths

Tranquil Acres B&B / Gîte à la ferme

Myra Roussy
PO Box 103, 252 route Lévesque
Port-Daniel, Québec G0C 2N0
Tel: (418) 396-3491
$

ABOUT THE B&B

Myra Roussy loves to show guests around her south-shore Gaspé working beef/cattle farm and introduce them to all the animals, including cows, pigs, chickens, sheep, and a friendly band of cats (who love to have their pictures taken!). Located on a quiet secondary road just off the main highway (Route 132), the renovated farmhouse captures the true flavor of country style and offers a beautiful view of Bay Chaleur. Fully home-baked breakfasts consist of dishes made with ingredients from the farm's fruit and vegetable garden. You can pitch in and help with the farm chores or simply relax in the spacious yard, soaking in the sights and smells of the countryside. The natural beauty of the Gaspé region is world renowned. Famous Percé Rock (one of the coast's main attractions) is a one-hour drive away, while Paspébiac historic site and a spa specializing in seawater therapy is a 20-minute drive away. Other nearby attractions include the Bonaventure Island Bird Sanctuary, golf courses, and New Richmond historic village.

SEASON

all year

ACCOMMODATIONS

3 rooms with shared bath

Wild Strawberry Tarts with Coconut Topping

"I make the jam for this recipe with wild strawberries that are found growing throughout the countryside during July."
— Myra Roussy

1 pound lard
1 egg mixed with 1 cup warm water
3 tablespoons baking powder
½ teaspoon salt
4 cups all-purpose flour
Wild strawberry jam

Preheat oven to 375°F. Mix together lard and egg with an electric mixer. Combine dry ingredients and gradually add to wet mixture. Roll out dough on a floured board and cut out round circles to fit into regular-sized, greased muffin cups. Place 1 teaspoon of jam in each tart. If desired, cover with coconut topping (recipe follows). *Variation:* Try raspberry jam instead of strawberry. Bake 10 – 15 minutes until tart is golden. ***Makes 3 dozen tarts.***

Coconut topping (optional):
½ cup margarine
½ cup sugar
2 eggs
1 cup flaked unsweetened coconut
1 teaspoon vanilla

Mix all ingredients well. Cover each strawberry tart with 1 tablespoon of this topping before baking.

Other Baked Goods & Desserts

Norwood
Bed & Breakfast

Pat and Roland Jensen
201 Norwood Court
Wetaskiwin, Alberta T9A 3P2
Tel: (888)/(403) 352-7880
Fax: (403) 352-8850
$$

ABOUT THE B&B

Seventeen-year residents of Wetaskiwin, Pat and Roland Jensen offer old-fashioned B&B hospitality in their new home full of country charm. An old-style double bed and antiques grace one guest room, while Victorian decor illuminates the queen-bedded room. Guests share a full bathroom, Jacuzzi, and a sitting room with white baby grand piano, games, books, and CD stereo system. Served in the formal dining room or on the sunny patio, a typical full breakfast consists of fruit salad, home-baked muffins and breads, homemade jams, a cooked entrée, and beverages. A smoking area is available outside on the deck. Norwood welcomes children but not pets as there's a resident 15-pound cat named Little Guy (who doesn't visit the guest rooms). After a day exploring such museums as Canada's Aviation Hall of Fame and the Alberta Central Railway Museum, shopping at antique, ladieswear, and gift shops, or playing a few rounds of golf, guests can refresh themselves with a soak in the outdoor hot tub. Norwood B&B is only a 45-minute drive from Alberta's capital, Edmonton.

SEASON

all year

ACCOMMODATIONS

2 rooms with shared bath

Applesauce Sourdough Doughnuts

2⅔ cups all-purpose flour
1½ teaspoons baking powder
½ teaspoon baking soda
1 teaspoon salt
½ teaspoon ground nutmeg
½ teaspoon ground cinnamon
¼ cup buttermilk
½ cup sourdough starter (see recipe on page 69)
2 tablespoons shortening
½ cup sugar
2 egg yolks
½ teaspoon vanilla
½ cup applesauce
Vegetable oil

Mix together all ingredients except oil. Roll out onto a floured surface and knead well until well mixed and smooth. Roll out dough to about ½" thickness and cut with a well-floured doughnut cutter. Cover and let stand until doubled in size. Deep fry in vegetable oil heated to 390°F until golden brown (these doughnuts take slightly longer to cook). *Variations:* Substitute 1 whole egg instead of 2 egg yolks and ¼ teaspoon ground mace instead of vanilla. *Makes 2 dozen doughnuts.*

Apple Squares

"Because the Annapolis Valley is the apple growing region of Nova Scotia, desserts served at evening tea often feature one of the 10 local varieties. My own preference is for Idared and Gravenstein apples." — Monica Cobb

1½ cups sugar
3 eggs
1 cup canola oil
1 teaspoon vanilla
2 cups all-purpose flour
1 teaspoon baking powder
1 tablespoon ground cinnamon
2 cups peeled, cored, and chopped apples

Preheat oven to 350°F. Beat together sugar and eggs. Add oil and vanilla. In a separate bowl, mix flour, baking powder, and cinnamon. Add to liquid mixture. Fold in apples. Grease a 13 x 9" pan and pour in batter. Bake 40 minutes. Invert when cooled and cut into squares. Store in an airtight container. Keeps moist for about 5 days. ***Makes approximately 18 squares (3 x 2").***

Bread and Roses Country Inn

Monica and Richard Cobb
PO Box 177, 82 Victoria Street
Annapolis Royal, Nova Scotia
B0S 1A0
Tel: (902) 532-5727
$$

ABOUT THE B&B

Bread and Roses Country Inn is a rare Nova Scotia example of a brick masonry Queen Anne Revival house. Built circa 1882, this non-smoking inn has many fine design details, such as a large entrance hall with sweeping staircase, intricate woodwork, and etched glass windows. The nine guest rooms on three floors are all distinctively decorated with antiques. The owners' eclectic art collection, which includes whimsical Nova Scotia folk art, contemporary Canadian paintings, and Inuit sculpture, is displayed throughout the house. Breakfast includes Monica's brown bread and granola, local preserves, yogurt, juice, and tea or coffee. Guests enjoy gathering in the parlor each evening for tea and sweets to share stories of their Nova Scotian adventures. Nearby are historic sites, museums, artists' studios, golfing, walking trails, and excellent restaurants. Port Royal, Canada's oldest permanent European settlement (1605) is a short drive away. Having traveled extensively throughout the Maritime provinces, Monica and Richard can provide touring tips tailored to your interests.

SEASON

March 1 – October 30

ACCOMMODATIONS

9 rooms with private baths

Humber Gallery Hospitality Home

Edna and Eldon Swyer
26 Roberts Drive
Little Rapids, Newfoundland
A2H 6C3
(Mailing address: PO Box 15
Corner Brook, Newfoundland
A2H 6C3)
Tel: (709) 634-2660
$

ABOUT THE B&B

A popular stop for the British royal family, the town of Little Rapids (near Corner Brook) is home to Humber Gallery, an impressive cedar abode with cathedral ceilings, fireplace, wraparound sun deck, two guest rooms with double beds, one guest room with twin beds, and full and half guest bathrooms. Humber serves a nutritious breakfast, while other meals and guests' use of the barbecue and picnic area can be arranged. An excellent spot for an overnight stay when going or coming from Gros Morne National Park, this B&B is in the heart of the Humber Valley Reserve near Marble Mountain Ski Resort, mini-golf facilities, "U-pick" strawberry farms, Bay of Islands tourist attractions, South Brook and Pasadena beaches on Deer Lake, and the Humber River. Edna and Eldon will be happy to provide you with maps, tourist literature, a licensed salmon fishing guide, and insider tips on area attractions.

SEASON

June – September;
February – mid-April

ACCOMMODATIONS

3 rooms with shared baths

Apricot-Fig Pudding

"A Christmas favorite in our home." — Edna Swyer

Sprinkle of sugar
2 cups bread crumbs
1¼ cups all-purpose flour
1¼ teaspoons baking soda
1 teaspoon ground cinnamon
1 teaspoon ground mace
1 teaspoon ground cloves
1 teaspoon salt
1 cup chopped walnuts
1 cup dried figs or dates
1 cup chopped dried apricots
2 cups raisins
1 cup suet (or vegetable oil or margarine)
1 cup brown sugar
2 eggs
1 cup milk
1 teaspoon vanilla
¼ cup prune juice

Grease a pudding mold. Sprinkle sides with sugar. Mix remaining ingredients together and place in mold. Place mold on a trivet in a heavy kettle over 1" boiling water. Partially cover kettle so as to let some steam escape. Set temperature on high heat. As steam begins to escape, use low heat and continue cooking for 1½ – 2 hours (replenish with boiling water as needed). Serve hot. *Serves 6 – 8.*

Aussie Damper

"With its simple, basic ingredients, the damper is easily prepared over an open campfire and often used by drovers during cattle drives in the outback. It's served for breakfast with golden maple syrup or, as Australians call it, 'Cocky's Joy,' since 'Cocky' is slang for someone from the bush."
— Carol Waters

1 cup whole-wheat self-rising flour*
2 cups self-rising flour
¼ teaspoon salt or to taste
2 teaspoons sugar
½ cup milk
¾ cup (approximately) water
Additional milk (or water) and flour for topping

Note: Often used for quick breads and cakes, this is flour to which salt and baking powder have been added.

Preheat oven to 450°F – 475°F. Sift flours, salt, and sugar in a bowl. Make a well in the center and pour in milk and most of the water, all at once. Mix with a knife to a moist, sticky dough. Add more water if necessary. Turn onto a lightly floured surface, knead into 8 round shapes, and place on a greased tray. Pat dough out to a 6" circle. With a sharp knife, cut 2 slits about ½" across dough like a cross (don't cut right to the edge). Brush tops with milk or water, and sift a little extra flour over tops. Bake 10 minutes, reduce oven to 350°F – 375°F, and bake 20 – 30 minutes until golden brown. *Makes 8 dampers.*

Australis Guest House

Carol and Brian Waters
35 Marlborough Avenue
Ottawa, Ontario K1N 8E6
Tel/Fax: (613) 235-8461
$ – $$

ABOUT THE B&B

The oldest established and operating B&B in the Ottawa area, Australis Guest House is a multiple winner of the Ottawa Hospitality Award and has been recommended by Newsweek. Located downtown on a quiet, tree-lined street, one block from the Rideau River (with its ducks and swans) and Strathcona Park, Australis is but a 20-minute walk from the Canadian Parliament buildings. This stately, 60-year-old house boasts leaded windows, fireplaces, oak floors, and eight-foot high stained glass windows overlooking the hall. Three spacious guest rooms, including a suite and private bathroom, display many of the hosts' collectibles gathered while living in different parts of the world. Hearty and delicious breakfasts, featuring award-winning home-baked breads and pastries, ensure you'll start the day just right. Off-street parking and free pick-up and delivery to and from the bus and train stations are available. Your hosts' Australian and English heritages combined with their time in Canada create a truly international and relaxed B&B experience.

SEASON

all year

ACCOMMODATIONS

1 room with private bath;
2 rooms (including 1 suite)
with shared bath

Le Gîte
Park Avenue B&B

Anne-Marie and Irving Bansfield
54 Park Avenue
Ottawa, Ontario K2P 1B2
Tel: (613) 230-9131
$$

ABOUT THE B&B

A bright, airy ambience and artistic decor awaits you at Park Avenue B&B, an elegant, brick 1906 home located in a charming residential area of downtown Ottawa, Canada's capital. In addition to high-quality beds done up in classic cotton and linen sheets and duvets, each guest room is furnished with desk and swivel chair, rocking chair, bookshelves, excellent lighting, and attractive works of art. Ideal for families, the third-floor suite has two bedrooms and a private bath. The mood throughout the house is one of relaxation and warmth. Park Avenue B&B is close to the Parliament buildings, art galleries and museums, and is only three minutes away (by foot) from the Rideau Canal, which freezes into the world's longest skating rink. Ottawa has a number of exciting festivals and activities, including Winterlude, a winter carnival held each February. Anne-Marie and Irving make it a point to know what's going on when in Ottawa so they can advise their guests on what to see and do.

SEASON

all year

ACCOMMODATIONS

1 suite with private bath;
2 rooms with shared bath

"Bake" Biscuits

"Adding the coconut gives these delicious biscuits a wonderfully tropical taste." — Irving Bansfield

3 cups all-purpose flour
½ teaspoon salt
1½ tablespoons baking powder
1 teaspoon sugar
3 tablespoons shortening (or margarine or butter)
¾ cup lukewarm water
2 tablespoons pure creamed coconut (optional)

Salt cod (see recipe on page 269)

Preheat oven to 375°F. Sift flour, salt, baking powder, and sugar together. Cut in shortening until it resembles coarse meal. Add water, tossing the ingredients lightly with your fingertips. Turn dough out onto a floured board and knead 1 – 2 minutes. Form dough into a ball, then roll it into a round shape about 10" across and ¾" thick, either by hand or with a rolling pin (as long as it's handled briefly and lightly). Place it on a greased cookie sheet. Bake 35 – 40 minutes. Let it sit for 10 minutes before cutting into wedges. Serve warm or at room temperature. Serve with brule jol (salt cod). **Serves 6.**

Baked Lemon Pudding

1 cup sugar
¼ cup all-purpose flour
Dash of salt
Zest of 1 lemon
¼ cup lemon juice
2 egg yolks, beaten
1 cup milk
2 egg whites, stiffly beaten

Preheat oven to 350°F. Combine sugar, flour, salt, and lemon zest. Stir in lemon juice, egg yolks, and milk, mixing thoroughly. Fold in beaten egg whites. Pour into an ungreased baking dish. Set in a pan of hot water 1" deep. Bake 40 – 50 minutes until delicately browned. *Serves 6.*

Le Gîte
Park Avenue B&B

Anne-Marie and Irving Bansfield
54 Park Avenue
Ottawa, Ontario K2P 1B2
Tel: (613) 230-9131
$$

ABOUT THE B&B

A bright, airy ambience and artistic decor awaits you at Park Avenue B&B, an elegant, brick 1906 home located in a charming residential area of downtown Ottawa, Canada's capital. In addition to high-quality beds done up in classic cotton and linen sheets and duvets, each guest room is furnished with desk and swivel chair, rocking chair, bookshelves, excellent lighting, and attractive works of art. Ideal for families, the third-floor suite has two bedrooms and a private bath. The mood throughout the house is one of relaxation and warmth. Park Avenue B&B is close to the Parliament buildings, art galleries and museums, and is only three minutes away (by foot) from the Rideau Canal, which freezes into the world's longest skating rink. Ottawa has a number of exciting festivals and activities, including Winterlude, a winter carnival held each February. Anne-Marie and Irving make it a point to know what's going on when in Ottawa so they can advise their guests on what to see and do.

SEASON

all year

ACCOMMODATIONS

1 suite with private bath;
2 rooms with shared bath

Rowat's Waterside Bed and Breakfast

Marg and Jack Rowat
1397 Borland Road
Williams Lake, British Columbia
V2G 1M3
Tel: (604) 392-7395
$$

ABOUT THE B&B

*E*njoy the tranquility of
Rowat's Waterside B&B,
located on Williams Lake right
beside Scout Island Nature Center
and Wildlife Reserve, in the heart of
Cariboo Country. Walk the nature
trails and return home to put your
feet up and enjoy the view of the lake
and marsh from the open deck (this is
a birdwatcher's paradise!). Rowat's
Waterside is also within walking
distance of mini-golf, parasailing,
restaurants, stampede grounds, and a
short drive away from downtown,
golf and tennis facilities, and a sports
arena. For something completely
different, a one-and-a-half-hour drive
will take you to the Ghost Town
Museum of Barkerville, an old gold
rush town. Rowat's accommodations
include tastefully decorated rooms
with private baths, a fireside guest
lounge with TV, air conditioning,
purified water, and ample parking.
Famous Cariboo Cowboy breakfasts
are served in the dining room or
deckside overlooking the marsh bird
sanctuary. Hosts Marg and Jack are
long-time residents of the Cariboo,
and enjoy craft making, gardening,
meeting people, and the great
outdoors.

SEASON

all year

ACCOMMODATIONS

4 rooms with private baths

Cheesy Beaten Biscuits

4 cups all-purpose flour
4 teaspoons baking powder
1 teaspoon salt
½ cup butter
2 eggs, beaten
1 cup milk
½ cup grated cheddar cheese

Preheat oven to 450°F. Sift dry ingredients together. Add butter, beaten eggs, milk, and cheese, mixing briefly. Drop batter by tablespoonfuls onto an ungreased cookie sheet. Bake until golden (approximately 12 minutes). *Makes 2½ dozen biscuits.*

Chocolate Chip-Apple Cookies

"Because the Annapolis Valley is the apple growing region of Nova Scotia, desserts served at evening tea often feature one of the 10 local varieties. My own preference is for Idared and Gravenstein apples." — Monica Cobb

½ cup margarine
1 cup sugar
1 egg
1½ cups all-purpose flour
½ teaspoon baking soda
1 teaspoon ground ginger
1 cup peeled, cored, and grated apple
1 cup semisweet chocolate chips
½ cup quick-cooking rolled oats

Preheat oven to 350°F. In a large bowl, cream together margarine and sugar. Beat in egg. In a separate bowl, mix together flour, baking soda, and ginger. Stir into creamed mixture. Stir in apple, chocolate chips, and oats. Drop mixture by rounded teaspoonfuls onto a well-greased cookie sheet. Bake approximately 15 minutes. Store in an airtight container. *Makes 2½ dozen cookies.*

Bread and Roses Country Inn

Monica and Richard Cobb
PO Box 177, 82 Victoria Street
Annapolis Royal, Nova Scotia
B0S 1A0
Tel: (902) 532-5727
$$

ABOUT THE B&B

Bread and Roses Country Inn *is a rare Nova Scotia example of a brick masonry Queen Anne Revival house. Built circa 1882, this non-smoking inn has many fine design details, such as a large entrance hall with sweeping staircase, intricate woodwork, and etched glass windows. The nine guest rooms on three floors are all distinctively decorated with antiques. The owners' eclectic art collection, which includes whimsical Nova Scotia folk art, contemporary Canadian paintings, and Inuit sculpture, is displayed throughout the house. Breakfast includes Monica's brown bread and granola, local preserves, yogurt, juice, and tea or coffee. Guests enjoy gathering in the parlor each evening for tea and sweets to share stories of their Nova Scotian adventures. Nearby are historic sites, museums, artists' studios, golfing, walking trails, and excellent restaurants. Port Royal, Canada's oldest permanent European settlement (1605) is a short drive away. Having traveled extensively throughout the Maritime provinces, Monica and Richard can provide touring tips tailored to your interests.*

SEASON

March 1 – October 30

ACCOMMODATIONS

9 rooms with private baths

Norwood
Bed & Breakfast

Pat and Roland Jensen
201 Norwood Court
Wetaskiwin, Alberta T9A 3P2
Tel: (888)/(403) 352-7880
Fax: (403) 352-8850
$$

ABOUT THE B&B

Seventeen-year residents of Wetaskiwin, Pat and Roland Jensen offer old-fashioned B&B hospitality in their new home full of country charm. An old-style double bed and antiques grace one guest room, while Victorian decor illuminates the queen-bedded room. Guests share a full bathroom, Jacuzzi, and a sitting room with white baby grand piano, games, books, and CD stereo system. Served in the formal dining room or on the sunny patio, a typical full breakfast consists of fruit salad, home-baked muffins and breads, homemade jams, a cooked entrée, and beverages. A smoking area is available outside on the deck. Norwood welcomes children but not pets as there's a resident 15-pound cat named Little Guy (who doesn't visit the guest rooms). After a day exploring such museums as Canada's Aviation Hall of Fame and the Alberta Central Railway Museum, shopping at antique, ladieswear, and gift shops, or playing a few rounds of golf, guests can refresh themselves with a soak in the outdoor hot tub. Norwood B&B is only a 45-minute drive from Alberta's capital, Edmonton.

SEASON

all year

ACCOMMODATIONS

2 rooms with shared bath

Chocolate-dipped Fruit

1 cup semisweet chocolate chips
1 – 2 tablespoons shortening
6-ounce package dried apricots
1 pint fresh strawberries

In a saucepan over low heat, melt chocolate chips and shortening, stirring constantly until smooth. Spear fruit with toothpicks and dip into chocolate. Place on waxed paper or stick toothpicks into a Styrofoam block until the chocolate hardens. After chocolate sets, arrange on a serving plate and enjoy. *Serves 6.*

Chocolate Pudding

"Before retiring for the evening, I like to offer my guests this pudding as a nightcap along with tea or coffee."
— *Myra Roussy*

½ cup whole milk (don't use skim)
2 cups mini marshmallows
1¼ cups chocolate chips
1 cup whipped cream

Heat milk and marshmallows over medium heat, adding chocolate chips just before marshmallows have melted. Cool, then add whipped cream. Freeze in dessert cups. Serve directly from the freezer, allowing to thaw slightly for 5 minutes.
Makes 6 puddings.

Tranquil Acres B&B / Gîte à la ferme

Myra Roussy
PO Box 103, 252 route Lévesque
Port-Daniel, Québec G0C 2N0
Tel: (418) 396-3491
$

ABOUT THE B&B

Myra Roussy loves to show guests around her south-shore Gaspé working beef/cattle farm and introduce them to all the animals, including cows, pigs, chickens, sheep, and a friendly band of cats (who love to have their pictures taken!). Located on a quiet secondary road just off the main highway (Route 132), the renovated farmhouse captures the true flavor of country style and offers a beautiful view of Bay Chaleur. Fully home-baked breakfasts consist of dishes made with ingredients from the farm's fruit and vegetable garden. You can pitch in and help with the farm chores or simply relax in the spacious yard, soaking in the sights and smells of the countryside. The natural beauty of the Gaspé region is world renowned. Famous Percé Rock (one of the coast's main attractions) is a one-hour drive away, while Paspébiac historic site and a spa specializing in seawater therapy is a 20-minute drive away. Other nearby attractions include the Bonaventure Island Bird Sanctuary, golf courses, and New Richmond historic village.

SEASON

all year

ACCOMMODATIONS

3 rooms with shared bath

Rowat's Waterside Bed and Breakfast

Marg and Jack Rowat
1397 Borland Road
Williams Lake, British Columbia
V2G 1M3
Tel: (604) 392-7395
$$

ABOUT THE B&B

Enjoy the tranquility of Rowat's Waterside B&B, located on Williams Lake right beside Scout Island Nature Center and Wildlife Reserve, in the heart of Cariboo Country. Walk the nature trails and return home to put your feet up and enjoy the view of the lake and marsh from the open deck (this is a birdwatcher's paradise!). Rowat's Waterside is also within walking distance of mini-golf, parasailing, restaurants, stampede grounds, and a short drive away from downtown, golf and tennis facilities, and a sports arena. For something completely different, a one-and-a-half-hour drive will take you to the Ghost Town Museum of Barkerville, an old gold rush town. Rowat's accommodations include tastefully decorated rooms with private baths, a fireside guest lounge with TV, air conditioning, purified water, and ample parking. Famous Cariboo Cowboy breakfasts are served in the dining room or deckside overlooking the marsh bird sanctuary. Hosts Marg and Jack are long-time residents of the Cariboo, and enjoy craft making, gardening, meeting people, and the great outdoors.

SEASON

all year

ACCOMMODATIONS

4 rooms with private baths

Cinnamon Swirls

3 cups all-purpose flour
⅓ cup sugar
5 teaspoons baking powder
½ teaspoon salt
¾ cup margarine
1 cup milk
1 egg, lightly beaten

Filling:
1 egg
4 tablespoons brown sugar
1½ teaspoons ground cinnamon
3 tablespoons bran buds

Preheat oven to 350°F. Combine flour, sugar, baking powder, and salt. Cut in margarine until mixture resembles crumbs. Mix milk with slightly beaten egg. Stir into flour mixture, working it as little as possible. Place on a floured board and knead about 12 times. Roll out dough to an 18 x 9" rectangle. For filling, beat egg and brush over dough. Sprinkle on brown sugar, cinnamon, and bran buds. Roll up like a jelly roll and cut into 18 slices. Put each slice into a paper-lined muffin cup or all on a greased baking sheet. Bake 25 – 30 minutes. *Makes 18 swirls.*

Cornmeal-Apple Wedges

"We like to accompany these wedges with our special yogurt, made with ½ cup toasted walnuts, 5 tablespoons maple syrup, and 2 cups plain yogurt." — Keith Smith

1½ cups all-purpose flour
⅔ cup cornmeal
⅓ cup brown sugar
1 tablespoon baking powder
1 teaspoon baking soda
¼ teaspoon salt
2 large apples, peeled, cored, and cut into chunks
½ cup currants or raisins
1¼ teaspoons ground cinnamon
Pinch of ground nutmeg
½ cup plain yogurt
¼ cup milk
2 whole eggs and 1 egg white
2 tablespoons vegetable oil

Butter, jelly, or jam

Preheat oven to 375°F. Mix together first 6 dry ingredients. Toss together fruit and spices and add to dry mixture. In a separate bowl, mix yogurt and milk together, and whisk in eggs and oil. Pour yogurt mixture into dry ingredients and mix together until moist. Pat into a 9" greased round pan, leaving top lumpy. Bake 40 – 45 minutes or until done. Cut into wedges and serve warm with butter or jelly. These wedges can also be split, toasted, and served with jam. *Serves 6 – 8.*

Gwenmar Guest Home

Joy and Keith Smith
PO Box 59, RR #3
Brandon, Manitoba R7A 5Y3
Tel: (204) 728-7339
Fax: (204) 728-7336
E-mail: smithj@docker.com
$

ABOUT THE B&B

Space, privacy, and quiet is what you'll find at Gwenmar. This 1914 heritage home was the summer retreat of Manitoba's former Lt. Governor (from 1929 to 1934), J.D. McGregor, who named the estate after his daughter Gwen. Since 1980, Joy and Keith Smith have welcomed B&B guests to this relaxing countryside escape. Gwenmar breakfasts are memorable, particularly the home-baked bread and jams and jellies made from Gwenmar's wild berries. Joy, a home economist, is an avid gardener and a major contributor to Canada's heritage seed program, while Keith is a retired agrologist involved in overseas projects. In the summer, you can visit with them on the big, shaded veranda or go for secluded walks on the beautiful grounds or in the valley. In the winter, sit by the fire or go cross-country skiing. Gwenmar is also a short drive from downtown Brandon, with shopping, restaurants, water-slide, air museum, golf courses, and the childhood home of Stone Angel author Margaret Laurence.

SEASON

all year

ACCOMMODATIONS

2 rooms with private baths;
2 rooms with shared bath

Orchard Lane
Bed & Breakfast

Yvonne Parker
13324 Middle Bench Road
Oyama, British Columbia
V4V 2B4
Tel: (250) 548-3809
$$

ABOUT THE B&B

*S*mack dab between Kelowna and Vernon, there awaits Orchard Lane, a newly built Victorian B&B nestled in a private orchard. From the sprawling veranda, this rural setting gives way to a panoramic view of the beautiful Central Okanagan Valley, while nearby Kalamalka and Wood lakes reflect the hills and distant mountains. Inside, a welcoming foyer and spiral staircase lead to romantic and comfortable bedrooms. Visitors lounge in the formal living room with fireplace, stroll through the flower gardens or nearby orchard, admire the terraced landscaping framed by giant trees, or take a refreshing dip in the outdoor hot tub. Your hostess, Yvonne, serves a full gourmet breakfast — made from produce grown in her vegetable garden — in the formal dining room or on the veranda. You'll quickly discover that one of her favorite hobbies is craft collecting, which is evident throughout the house. Alpine skiing, fishing, biking, hiking, and other recreational choices await you and there are golf courses and beaches aplenty to explore. This area is truly a corner of paradise.

SEASON

all year

ACCOMMODATIONS

2 rooms with shared bath

Danish Pastry Apple Bars

2½ cups all-purpose flour
1 teaspoon salt
1 cup shortening
1 egg yolk
Milk
1 cup cornflakes
8 – 10 tart apples such as Granny Smith, peeled, cored, and sliced (to make 8 cups)
¾ – 1 cup sugar
1 teaspoon ground cinnamon
1 egg white

Topping:
1 cup sifted confectioners' sugar
3 – 4 teaspoons milk

Preheat oven to 375°F. Combine flour and salt; cut in shortening to resemble coarse meal. Beat egg yolk in a measuring cup, adding enough milk to make ⅔ cup liquid. Mix well and stir into flour mixture. On a floured surface, roll half the dough in a 17 x 12" rectangle. Fit dough into and up sides of a greased 15 x 10½ x 1" baking pan. Sprinkle with cornflakes. Top with apples. Combine sugar and cinnamon and sprinkle over top. Roll remaining dough and place over apples. Seal edges. Cut slits in top. Beat egg white until frothy and brush on crust. Bake 50 minutes. Let cool for 10 minutes. Cut into bars. Combine confectioners' sugar and milk, and drizzle on while bars are still warm. *Makes 3 dozen bars.*

Easy Cherry Strudel

"Great for breakfast or as a nice way to greet arriving guests, along with a cup of tea." — *Mona Adamson*

3 eggs
1 cup sugar
½ cup evaporated milk
½ cup vegetable oil
Zest and juice of 1 lemon
1½ cups all-purpose flour
2 teaspoons baking powder
Pinch of salt
Cherry pie filling

Topping:
1 cup all-purpose flour
1 cup margarine
¼ cup sugar

Preheat oven to 350°F. Grease a jelly roll pan. *Tip:* Also make a collar of wax paper to extend about 1 – 2" above the pan to avoid spills in the oven. Beat eggs until thick and lemon-colored; gradually add sugar. Beat in the milk, oil, and lemon zest and juice (mixture should be thick and the consistency of mayonnaise). Combine remaining dry ingredients and quickly stir in. Spread in the prepared pan. Cover with cherry pie filling (apple could also be used). For the topping, blend ingredients together to create a chunky crumb mixture. Sprinkle over cake and bake 30 – 45 minutes or until strudel's top is a light golden brown. *Serves 15.*

Lindsay House Bed & Breakfast

Mona and Dixon Adamson
1904-1st Avenue East
Prince Albert, Saskatchewan
S6V 2B5
Tel: (306) 764-4337
$$

ABOUT THE B&B

L indsay House is named after its original owner, Sir James Hawkins Lindsay, who built the residence in 1906 and lived there until his death in 1958. It is said that he entertained two Canadian prime ministers at Lindsay House, William Lyon Mackenzie King and Sir Wilfred Laurier. Retaining its original structure, this three-story brick house offers four rooms on the second floor with shared bathrooms. Guests have use of the den with wood burning fireplace, parlor or TV room (also with a wood burning fireplace). Served in the formal dining room, breakfast consists of juice, fresh fruit salad, homemade muffins, scones, or croissants, and a different entrée each day (guest preferences or dietary needs can be accommodated). The inn is non smoking; guests can, however, smoke on the wraparound veranda. Prince Albert is situated close to the park land of the north and this B&B is just a five-minute walk from the city center. Mona and Dixon both enjoy gardening and spend many a summer day tending to their flower and vegetable garden.

SEASON

all year

ACCOMMODATIONS

4 rooms with shared baths

The Old Rectory Bed & Breakfast

Carol and Ron Buckley
1519 Highway 358, RR #1
Port Williams, Nova Scotia
B0P 1T0
Tel: (902) 542-1815
Fax: (902) 542-2346
E-mail: orectory@fox.nstn.ca
www.bbcanada.com/568.html
$$

ABOUT THE B&B

*S*hare the warmth of this restored former Victorian rectory with its antiques, unique architecture, and three-acre operating apple orchard and gardens. Choose from one of three spacious bedrooms, one with private half-bath, and the others with shared full bath. Access to an additional bath is on the main floor. Your hosts are Ron, a retired geologist with knowledge of local "rock hounding" areas, and physiotherapist, Carol, who enjoys preparing delicious hot breakfasts with homemade breads and preserves. Visit over evening tea or come for a two-day orchard stay in the fall with apple picking and cider making. The Old Rectory is close to historic Prescott House, Grand Pré Park, hiking trails, birdwatching areas, cultural activities, and many fine restaurants.

SEASON

May 1 – October 31

ACCOMMODATIONS

1 room with private half-bath;
2 rooms with shared bath

Fruit Duff

"This recipe can be made with any fruit. I start the season with rhubarb and move through strawberries, raspberries, blueberries, and apples — all available at the local 'U-pick' or from our own garden." — Carol Buckley

2 tablespoons butter
1 cup all-purpose flour
½ cup sugar
1 tablespoon baking powder
½ teaspoon salt
⅔ cup milk
2 cups sliced fruit or berries of your choice

Preheat oven to 350°F. Melt butter in a 7 or 8" oven-proof frying pan. Mix dry ingredients. Mix in milk. Spoon batter over melted butter. Top with fruit of your choice. Bake 30 minutes. Cut into wedges and serve warm to complete your breakfast. *Tip:* If using apple, try sprinkling a little ground cinnamon and sugar on top before baking. *Serves 8.*

Georg's Famous Apple Strudel

"This is an old German recipe that has become a specialty of the inn's restaurant. People come from near and far for it."
— Georg Kargoll

(Author's note: Elvi and Georg requested that this old family recipe not be converted from the original metric version. If necessary, please consult the metric conversion chart on page 6.)

Dough:
250 grams all-purpose flour
3 tablespoons vegetable oil
Salt to taste
Water as needed (approximately 3 tablespoons)

Filling:
2 kilograms apples (McIntosh or Red Delicious recommended)
80 grams bread crumbs
65 grams raisins
65 grams chopped almonds
1 teaspoon ground cinnamon
½ teaspoon vanilla
Whipping cream (35%)
2 tablespoons melted butter
Confectioners' sugar

Vanilla ice cream and whipped cream

(continued on next page)

Haus Treuburg
Elvi and Georg Kargoll
PO Box 92
Port Hood (Cape Breton Island)
Nova Scotia B0E 2W0
Tel: (902) 787-2116
Fax: (902) 787-3216
$$

ABOUT THE B&B

Port Hood is a pretty little fishing port on Cape Breton Island with lovely sandy beaches and the warmest waters in eastern Canada. It's no wonder, then, that Elvi and Georg Kargoll fell in love with this idyllic setting and decided to open a country inn. Decidedly European and with a distinctly German flair, Haus Treuburg offers two bright and attractively decorated rooms and one suite on the inn's second floor, each with private bath, telephone, and cable TV. There are also three cottages overlooking the ocean, each of which have a large sitting room, a kitchen (with microwave), a separate bedroom, a large full bath, telephone and cable TV, and a deck with a gas barbecue. Haus Treuburg's highly rated restaurant (with Georg as chef) serves a romantic candlelight four-course dinner to the soothing sound of classical music, while a "German Sunday Morning Breakfast" is served in the cozy bar. Bicycles and a small boat are available for exploring the charming surroundings. Guided fishing tours are also offered.

SEASON

May 15 – October 31

ACCOMMODATIONS

3 rooms (including 1 suite)
with private baths;
3 cottages with private baths

Knead flour, oil, salt, and enough water to form a non-sticking dough. Set aside. Peel, core, and slice apples and mix them with the other filling ingredients. Preheat oven to 350°F. Roll out the dough into a very thin rectangle— so thin that you could read a love letter through it!

Brush some whipping cream over the dough. Put the filling lengthwise on half of the dough, and start rolling dough, filling side first. Put the strudel on a greased baking sheet and brush the top with melted butter. Bake 40 minutes. Top with some confectioners' sugar. Serve warm with vanilla ice cream and whipped cream. *Serves 10 – 15.*

Ginger Scones

"There are never any leftovers when I make these delicious scones." — Sharon Spraggett

2 cups all-purpose flour
4 teaspoons baking powder
¼ cup sugar
½ teaspoon salt
½ cup cold butter or margarine
⅓ cup chopped preserved ginger
⅔ cup milk
1 egg white
Sprinkle of sugar

Preheat oven to 450°F. In a large bowl, mix flour, baking powder, sugar, and salt. Cut in butter until crumbly. Add ginger and milk just until the dough sticks together. Turn out onto an ungreased cookie sheet and pat into a round. Flatten with your hand to an 8"-diameter circle. Cut just through into 8 or 10 wedges. Brush with egg white and sprinkle with sugar. Bake 10 – 15 minutes. **Makes 8 or 10 scones.**

Hipwood House B&B

Sharon and Malcolm Spraggett
PO Box 211
1763 Hipwood Road
Shawnigan Lake
British Columbia V0R 2W0
Tel: (250) 743-7855
$$

ABOUT THE B&B

*T*hinking of traveling to beautiful Vancouver Island? If so, take the breathtaking 45-minute drive north of Victoria to the quaint village of Shawnigan Lake, and you'll come upon a peaceful country B&B called Hipwood House. Unwind in one of three spacious guest rooms, enjoy a refreshing cup of tea in the garden, or stroll the trails on Hipwood's two acres (which includes a 50-foot suspension bridge). There's also a putting green, horseshoes, and bad-minton — if you need to work off that full country breakfast! You're also a five-minute walk away from the public beach, local artists' gallery, and museum, and close to boat and water sport rentals on the lake, a seaplane for magnificent air tours, fishing, golf, tennis, and restaurants. Many interesting and picturesque areas are within a half-hour drive. Lifelong residents of Vancouver Island, Sharon and Malcolm are knowledgeable about the area and will help make your stay extra special.

SEASON

all year

ACCOMMODATIONS

1 room with private bath;
2 rooms with shared bath

Orchard Lane
Bed & Breakfast

Yvonne Parker
13324 Middle Bench Road
Oyama, British Columbia
V4V 2B4
Tel: (250) 548-3809
$$

ABOUT THE B&B

Smack dab between Kelowna and Vernon, there awaits Orchard Lane, a newly built Victorian B&B nestled in a private orchard. From the sprawling veranda, this rural setting gives way to a panoramic view of the beautiful Central Okanagan Valley, while nearby Kalamalka and Wood lakes reflect the hills and distant mountains. Inside, a welcoming foyer and spiral staircase lead to romantic and comfortable bedrooms. Visitors lounge in the formal living room with fireplace, stroll through the flower gardens or nearby orchard, admire the terraced landscaping framed by giant trees, or take a refreshing dip in the outdoor hot tub. Your hostess, Yvonne, serves a full gourmet breakfast — made from produce grown in her vegetable garden — in the formal dining room or on the veranda. You'll quickly discover that one of her favorite hobbies is craft collecting, which is evident throughout the house. Alpine skiing, fishing, biking, hiking, and other recreational choices await you and there are golf courses and beaches aplenty to explore. This area is truly a corner of paradise.

SEASON

all year

ACCOMMODATIONS

2 rooms with shared bath

Ginger Snaps

"These cookies are terrific with tea." — *Yvonne Parker*

¾ cup shortening
1 cup sugar
¼ cup molasses
1 egg
2 teaspoons baking soda
2 cups all-purpose flour
½ teaspoon ground cloves
½ teaspoon ground ginger
1 teaspoon ground cinnamon
½ teaspoon salt
Sugar for coating

Melt shortening and let cool. Add sugar, molasses, and egg. Beat well. In a bowl, sift baking soda, flour, cloves, ginger, cinnamon, and salt. Mix dry and wet ingredients together until combined. Chill dough.

Preheat oven to 350°F. Remove dough from refrigerator. Form into 1" balls and roll in sugar (do not flatten). Place on a greased cookie sheet and bake 8 – 10 minutes. *Makes 3 dozen cookies.*

Glacé Lace Cookies

"These thin, crisp wafers last a long time."
— *Anne-Marie Bansfield*

½ cup softened butter (not runny or whipped)
2 cups brown sugar
2 eggs
¾ cup all-purpose flour
2 teaspoons baking powder
½ teaspoon salt

Preheat oven to 375°F. Cream butter with sugar using your fingers. Beat in eggs, one at a time. Stir in flour, baking powder, and salt. Spread foil on baking sheets. Butter lightly. Drop dough by scant teaspoonfuls, about 2" apart (don't flatten — cookies will spread while baking). Bake 5 – 6 minutes until cookies are caramel colored. Test for doneness by lifting one off foil with a spatula. If cookie sticks to foil, bake a little longer. Once ready, place baking sheets in the refrigerator to chill for 5 minutes then peel cookies off the foil (don't try to remove them while they're still hot). *Tip:* Store cookies in tin containers. *Makes 12 dozen cookies.*

Le Gîte
Park Avenue B&B

Anne-Marie and Irving Bansfield
54 Park Avenue
Ottawa, Ontario K2P 1B2
Tel: (613) 230-9131
$$

ABOUT THE B&B

A bright, airy ambience and artistic decor awaits you at Park Avenue B&B, an elegant, brick 1906 home located in a charming residential area of downtown Ottawa, Canada's capital. In addition to high-quality beds done up in classic cotton and linen sheets and duvets, each guest room is furnished with desk and swivel chair, rocking chair, bookshelves, excellent lighting, and attractive works of art. Ideal for families, the third-floor suite has two bedrooms and a private bath. The mood throughout the house is one of relaxation and warmth. Park Avenue B&B is close to the Parliament buildings, art galleries and museums, and is only three minutes away (by foot) from the Rideau Canal, which freezes into the world's longest skating rink. Ottawa has a number of exciting festivals and activities, including Winterlude, a winter carnival held each February. Anne-Marie and Irving make it a point to know what's going on when in Ottawa so they can advise their guests on what to see and do.

SEASON

all year

ACCOMMODATIONS

1 suite with private bath;
2 rooms with shared bath

Park View
Bed & Breakfast

Gladys and Carson Langille
254 Cameron Street
Moncton, New Brunswick
E1C 5Z3
Tel: (506) 382-4504
$$

ABOUT THE B&B

This Art Deco home was built in 1940 as a residence for Mrs. Inez Robinson, owner of Moncton's first business college. The architectural plans came from the 1939 New York World's Fair and this was the first Art Deco home in Moncton. The curved living room windows look out on beautiful Victoria Park in the city's center. Opened as a B&B in 1989, this charming home provides three guest rooms with cable TV, telephones, and exquisite shared bath, spacious living room with fireplace, elegant dining room, and cozy kitchen. Your hosts provide a warm welcome, a hearty, full home-cooked breakfast of your choice, and a wealth of information about the area. Gladys is a part-time school teacher, while Carson enjoys playing bridge and painting landscapes. A collection of works by local artists graces their walls. Nearby is superb dining, shopping, beaches, parks, museums, galleries, theater, a must-see tidal bore (where the tide goes up and down very quickly), and infamous Magnetic Hill (you'll never believe this is possible unless you experience it yourself!).

SEASON

all year

ACCOMMODATIONS

3 rooms with shared bath

Heritage Scones

3 cups all-purpose flour
3 teaspoons baking powder
½ teaspoon salt
1 cup brown sugar
1 cup margarine
1 egg yolk
1 cup milk
1 cup raisins or currants
1 egg white, beaten
Sprinkle of sugar

Preheat oven to 400°F. Mix first 4 dry ingredients. Work in margarine with a fork until well blended. Beat egg yolk and milk together and add to margarine mixture. Add raisins and mix well. On a floured surface, roll dough into a 1"-thick circle. Spread with egg white and sprinkle with sugar. Cut into triangles and place on an ungreased baking sheet. Bake 15 minutes. *Makes 2 dozen scones.*

Honey-glazed Pear Turnovers

"Pears were always a special treat when I was growing up in Kansas, and this recipe originates with my mother. My sister loved the fruit so much that her childhood nickname was (you guessed it) 'Pear.' " — Diana Habkirk

3 pears, peeled, cored, and diced
½ cup chopped pecans
2 tablespoons honey
1½ tablespoons lemon juice
1 tablespoon all-purpose flour
1 teaspoon ground cinnamon
Dash of ground ginger
1 egg white
3 tablespoons water, divided
17-ounce package frozen puff pastry
¼ cup honey
1 tablespoon butter

Preheat oven to 350°F. Combine pears, pecans, 2 tablespoons honey, lemon juice, flour, cinnamon, and ginger in a bowl. Combine egg white and 1 tablespoon water, and blend. Thaw pastry sheets. Unfold and cut each sheet into 4 squares. Place 2 tablespoons pear mixture on pastry in the lower right-hand

(continued on next page)

Brio Haus

Diana and Les Habkirk
3005 Brio Entrance
Whistler, British Columbia
V0N 1B3
Tel: (800) 331-BRIO (2746)
or (604) 932-3313
E-mail: briohaus@whistler.net
$$ – $$$

ABOUT THE B&B

Brio Haus is an intimate bed and breakfast located in Canada's premier ski resort area. Enjoy charming rooms, fitted with cozy goose down duvets, in a European-style alpine home, and awake to a full home-baked breakfast, often featuring one of the pear specialties of the house. After wintertime skiing or summertime hiking, canoeing, and horseback riding, you can prepare your own snacks and dinners in the guest kitchen loaded with amenities. After that, warm yourself by the evening fire in the guest lounge and watch a variety of complimentary movies. Or, ease sore muscles after an active day with a soak in the Jacuzzi moon tub and sauna. Brio Haus is centrally located, an easy walk to Whistler Village and ski lifts via the Valley Trail, and right across the street from the golf course. Diana and Les spent many years as a bus tour guide team in the Canadian Rockies before opening their lodge in 1989. Les now runs the local transit system and Diana works full time seeing to the needs of her B&B guests.

SEASON

all year

ACCOMMODATIONS

3 rooms with shared bath

corner of the pastry square. Moisten edges with the egg mixture and fold in half. Press edges firmly with a fork. Brush with the egg mixture. Place turnovers on a greased baking sheet. Bake 20 minutes. Meanwhile, combine remaining 2 tablespoons water, ¼ cup honey, and butter in a saucepan. Bring to a boil without stirring for 2 minutes. Baste turnovers with glaze. Continue cooking for another 10 minutes or until golden. Baste again and serve. *Makes 8 turnovers.*

Jelly Roll

"If you raise chickens and get lots of extra 'cackleberries,' you can use the egg yolks for this recipe and leftover egg whites for my angel food cake (see recipe on page 81), both great for afternoon or after-dinner treats." — Jim Saville

10 egg yolks
2 whole eggs
3 tablespoons water
1 teaspoon lemon juice
1 cup sugar
1 cup all-purpose flour
1 teaspoon baking powder
1 teaspoon cream of tartar
Jam or favorite pie filling of your choice

Preheat oven to 350°F. Add water and lemon juice to eggs and beat well. Add sugar and beat some more. In a separate bowl, combine remaining dry ingredients. Add dry ingredients to liquid mixture and beat until smooth. Pour on well-greased waxed paper that has been placed into a rectangular well-greased cookie sheet. Bake 10 minutes. Flip out onto a clean, wet tea towel (immediately peel off waxed paper). Spread jam or your favorite filling lengthwise across the jelly roll, then roll up (short end to short end). *Serves 12.*

Spring Valley Guest Ranch

Jim Saville
PO Box 10
Ravenscrag, Saskatchewan
S0N 0T0
Tel: (306) 295-4124
$$

ABOUT THE B&B

Come relax and enjoy an afternoon visit or an overnight stay at *Spring Valley Guest Ranch*. This three-story, 1913 character home is nestled in a tall grove of cottonwood poplars, in a pleasant wooded valley with many wild varieties of flora and fauna along a spring-fed stream. Over 1,000 acres of hills and valleys beckon you either on foot or on horseback. You are invited to dine, choosing from a unique menu, in the licensed Country Tea Room, which houses over 200 duck replicas. Live poultry, sheep, horses, and a donkey await your visit in the barnyard. The craft shop in the log cabin is filled with treasures of leather, wood, pottery, and knitted and beaded crafts — all made by local artists. An excellent area for naturalists, photographers, and hikers, Ravenscrag is only 20 minutes from Cypress Hills Provincial Park, on the Alberta border.

SEASON

all year

ACCOMMODATIONS

4 rooms with shared baths;
1 log cabin with shared bath

Gîte à la ferme
MACDALE
Bed and Breakfast

Anne and Gordon MacWhirter
365 Route 132, Hope
PO Box 803
Paspébiac, Québec G0C 2K0
Tel: (418) 752-5270
$

ABOUT THE B&B

For a relaxing holiday, visit the Gaspé Peninsula and MACDALE Bed and Breakfast. Situated overlooking Chaleur Bay on an active, fifth-generation beef farm, this spacious three-story home offers two family rooms and a variety of guest accommodations. The aroma of fresh coffee and assorted muffins and pastries will awaken you and whet your appetite for an old-fashioned home-baked breakfast using farm-fresh eggs. Thanks to MACDALE's central location, tourist attractions such as world-famous Percé Rock and Forillon Park are well within day-trip driving distance. A seawater therapy resort is just minutes away, as are many museums, points of historical interest, and sports facilities. Anne is a first grade teacher while Gordon has recently retired from teaching junior high school mathematics.

SEASON

all year

ACCOMMODATIONS

1 loft with private bath;
4 rooms with shared baths

Jiffy Pudding

"As the name suggests, this pudding can be made in a jiffy. It's so easy and so good!" — Anne MacWhirter

1 cup all-purpose flour
¾ cup brown sugar
⅓ cup raisins
2 teaspoons baking powder
½ cup milk

Topping:
¾ cup brown sugar
2 tablespoons butter
½ teaspoon vanilla
2 cups boiling water

Preheat oven to 350°F. Mix first 5 ingredients together and pour into a buttered 8" square baking dish. Mix topping ingredients and pour over batter. Bake 30 minutes. Serve warm. *Serves 6 – 8.*

Lemon-Buttermilk Sorbet

2 cups buttermilk
¾ cup white corn syrup
¼ cup honey
Juice and zest of 2 lemons
Fresh mint leaves

Beat to combine first 4 ingredients. Chill for at least 30 minutes. Pour into an ice cream maker and follow manufacturer's directions. When ready, scoop out sorbet and freeze in a plastic container. Allow the sorbet to soften for 15 minutes (or 40 seconds on defrost in the microwave) before serving. Serve in a martini glass garnished with a fresh mint leaf. *Makes 8 single scoops.*

Weston Lake Inn Bed & Breakfast

Susan Evans and Ted Harrison
813 Beaver Point Road
Salt Spring Island
British Columbia V8K 1X9
Tel: (250) 653-4311
$$$

ABOUT THE B&B

*N*estled on a well-tended knoll of flowering trees and shrubs overlooking Weston Lake, the inn is a serene and comfortable adult getaway on the rural south end of Salt Spring Island. The three tastefully decorated guest bedrooms have private baths, down duvets, and fresh flower bouquets. Original Canadian art and beautiful petit-point (crafted by host Ted) grace the interior of the inn. Guests have the exclusive use of a cozy fireside lounge with library, TV, and VCR, and an outdoor hot tub perched above the lake. Creative breakfasts feature fresh eggs from the inn's chickens, and produce from the large, organic garden, such as berries, herbs, and asparagus in season. Near Victoria, Salt Spring Island offers a mild climate, exceptional beauty, a thriving community of artists and craftspeople, and an abundance of outdoor activities. Since opening Weston Lake Inn in 1986, hosts Susan and Ted have been fine-tuning their B&B craft, restoring the house, landscaping, and enjoying their 10-acre paradise with guests. Susan loves gardening, while Ted loves sailing and offers charters aboard their 36-foot sloop.

SEASON

all year

ACCOMMODATIONS

3 rooms with private baths

Fraser House

Sheila and Dennis Derksen
PO Box 211, 33 1st Street East
Letellier, Manitoba R0G 1C0
Tel: (204) 737-2284
$

ABOUT THE B&B

Memories are made at this elegant and romantic 1916 home. Hardwood floors, area rugs, and antique furniture enhance the home's Victorian decor. Spacious rooms combined with great hospitality make your stay most enjoyable. Relax in the parlor or on the veranda or patio with a beverage and home-baked goodies. Breakfast may consist of a puffy egg pancake or freshly baked croissants and muffins, along with the season's fresh fruit, served in the formal dining room. Fraser House is located just a few minutes north of the US border in the heart of Manitoba's bustling agricultural area, and is near golf, fishing, shopping, and skiing. Sheila enjoys crafting projects and holds painting classes during the winter months, while Dennis enjoys carpentry and is employed as a fertilizer dealer.

SEASON

all year

ACCOMMODATIONS

2 rooms with shared bath

Maple Twist Rolls

¾ cup milk
¼ cup margarine
2¾ – 3 cups all-purpose flour
3 tablespoons sugar
½ teaspoon salt
1 package active dry yeast (1 tablespoon) dissolved in
    ¼ cup lukewarm water
1 teaspoon maple extract
1 egg

Filling:
½ cup sugar
⅓ cup chopped pecans
1 teaspoon ground cinnamon
¼ cup melted margarine

Icing:
1 cup confectioners' sugar
2 tablespoons melted margarine
1 tablespoon milk or water
½ teaspoon maple extract

In a small saucepan, heat milk and margarine until lukewarm. In a large mixer bowl, blend lukewarm liquid, 1 cup flour, sugar, salt, yeast, maple extract, and the egg at low speed until moistened. Beat 2 minutes. By hand, stir in remaining flour to

(continued on next page)

form a soft dough. Knead on a floured surface until smooth and elastic (about 2 minutes). Place in a lightly buttered bowl, turning to coat with butter. Cover and let rise in a warm place until doubled in size.

To fill: In a small bowl, combine sugar, nuts, and cinnamon. Set aside. Lightly grease a 12" round pizza pan. Punch down dough, divide into 3, and shape into balls. On a floured surface, roll or press 1 ball of dough over bottom of prepared pizza pan. Brush dough with about one-third of the melted margarine, then sprinkle with one-third of the cinnamon-nut mixture. Repeat layers of dough, melted margarine, and cinnamon mixture.

To shape: Place a glass about 2" in diameter in center of dough. With scissors, cut from outside edge to the glass forming 16 pie-shaped wedges. Twist each wedge 4 times. Remove glass. Let rise until doubled in size. Bake in a preheated 350°F oven for 20 minutes. Cool 5 minutes. In a small bowl, blend icing ingredients until smooth. Drizzle over twists. *Makes 16 rolls.*

Fresh Start
Bed & Breakfast

Innis and Sheila MacDonald
2720 Gottingen Street
Halifax, Nova Scotia B3K 3C7
Tel: (902) 453-6616
$ – $$

ABOUT THE B&B

Fresh Start B&B is an 1895 Victorian mansion, one of the few North End houses to escape destruction by the Halifax Explosion of 1917. It's located in an interesting area populated by families, artists, craftspeople, and students. Citadel Hill, historic properties, and the uniquely designed Hydrostone District are within walking distance. Halifax is a friendly city with many restaurants, live theater, wonderful crafts, and a lively nightlife. In July, visitors come for the International Tattoo Festival and, in August, for the International Buskers Festival. Conveniently located on a bus route, informal Fresh Start lets guests decide when to check in and check out. Laundry service and off-street parking are available, and breakfast tastes great! Guests enjoy relaxing in solitary quiet, visiting with hosts and other guests, reading in the library, or watching TV. The two owners are sisters and nurses. They are also enthusiastic grandmothers and travelers! Innis likes gardening, crafts, and social activism, while Sheila likes cooking and reading.

SEASON

all year

ACCOMMODATIONS

2 rooms with private baths;
6 rooms with shared baths

Nana's Tea Biscuits

"In the 1940s, we lived in a Cape Breton coal mining town where money was scarce. Our grandmother made these biscuits and served them with molasses as a snack or dessert. Molasses was the peanut butter of our childhood and it's still a comfort food for expatriate Cape Bretoners."
— *Innis and Sheila MacDonald*

3 cups all-purpose flour
¼ cup sugar
3 teaspoons baking powder
2 teaspoons cream of tartar
1 teaspoon salt
1 teaspoon baking soda
¾ cup shortening
1¼ cups milk

Strong cheddar cheese

Preheat oven to 400°F. Sift together all the dry ingredients. Cut in shortening with a pastry blender or 2 knives until mixture resembles coarse meal. Add milk and stir briefly — only until mixed. Roll out dough 2" thick on a floured board. Cut with a biscuit cutter (2" diameter). Bake on a lightly greased cookie sheet until they spring back when pressed lightly (approximately 12 minutes). Strong cheddar cheese is a great "go-with." ***Makes 16 biscuits.***

Papaya Scones

⅔ cup buttermilk or plain yogurt (have an additional ¼ cup
    on hand)
1 large egg
3 cups all-purpose flour
4 teaspoons baking powder
½ teaspoon baking soda
½ cup sugar
½ teaspoon salt
½ cup butter
½ cup dried cut-up papaya
¼ cup currants
1 teaspoon orange zest
1 tablespoon softened butter

Butter, fresh preserves, and Devonshire cream

Preheat oven to 375°F. Pour buttermilk into a measuring cup
and beat in egg. In a large bowl, blend together flour, baking
powder, baking soda, sugar, and salt. With a pastry blender or
2 knives, cut butter into the dry mixture until it forms fine
granules. Add papaya, currants, and orange zest, stirring to mix.
Add buttermilk mixture all at once, stirring until a soft dough
forms (you may have to add up to ¼ cup additional buttermilk).
Turn out onto a lightly floured surface and knead 5 – 6 times or
just until well mixed. Roll or pat out dough to about 1" thick.
Cut scones the size of a small glass and place on an ungreased
cookie sheet. Bake 15 – 20 minutes. Brush tops with softened
butter. Serve warm with butter, fresh preserves, and Devonshire
cream. *Makes 12 – 15 scones.*

Bruce Gables B&B

Elsie and Jorn Christensen
PO Box 448, 410 Berford Street
Wiarton, Ontario N0H 2T0
Tel: (519) 534-0429
Fax: (519) 534-0779
$$

ABOUT THE B&B

Whether in French, German, Spanish, Danish, or English, Elsie and Jorn bid you "welcome" to Bruce Gables, their spacious turn-of-the-century Victorian home. Relax in the large living room, which has been restored to its Victorian splendor and furnished with period furniture and antiques. Two of the three large bedrooms have bay windows that overlook the town of Wiarton and the clear blue waters of Colpoy's Bay. A hearty breakfast is served in the elegant dining room where you'll dine on your choice of crêpes, pancakes, waffles, French toast, eggs Benedict/Florentine, omelets, or any style of eggs. Picnic tables and a gas barbecue located in the garden are available for the guests to use. Known as "Gateway to the Bruce," the town of Wiarton makes a perfect headquarters for exploring the Bruce Peninsula. With the Georgian Bay to the east and Lake Huron to the west, the Bruce offers abundant water recreation, not to mention some of the most breathtaking scenery in Ontario from its high limestone bluffs. In addition, the area's provincial parks are natural habitats for many varieties of birds and animals.

SEASON

May – October

ACCOMMODATIONS

3 rooms with shared baths

Willow House B&B / La Maison des Saules

Pat Le Baron and
Allan Watson
30 Western Avenue
PO Box 906
Sutton, Québec J0E 2K0
Tel: (514) 538-0035
$$

ABOUT THE B&B

A lovely 96-year-old Loyalist-style home with views of a running brook and pond, Willow House is situated in the hub of an artisan community with many local arts and crafts shops nearby. Pat's claim to fame is home-baking, and her specialties include ginger-lemon, blueberry, poppy seed, and carrot-bran muffins, and squash, oatmeal, and granola breads. (Suppers or lunches can be arranged on request.) Other Willow House niceties include a private garden where you can watch an endlessly varied number of bird species come and go, and a cozy lounge where you can while away the hours listening to classical music (with Pat's miniature collie, Chloe, to keep you quiet company). Situated in the Eastern Townships, Sutton is a popular getaway for cycling, hiking, walking, golf, boating, skiing, antique and outlet shopping, and admiring spectacular fall foliage. About one-and-three-quarter hours from Montréal and a half-hour from the Vermont border, Willow House welcomes both children and pets.

SEASON

all year

ACCOMMODATIONS

4 rooms with shared baths

Pat's Leftover Bread Pudding

"After wondering what to do with a variety of leftover muffins and breads — should I feed them to Chloe (my hungry pup) or to the birds? — I thought of concocting this delicious recipe. It reminds me of the Christmas puddings I used to enjoy when I was a youngster." — Pat Le Baron

2 eggs
Scant ½ cup sugar
2 cups milk
½ teaspoon ground cinnamon
¼ teaspoon ground nutmeg
4 cups stale bread and/or muffin cubes
¼ cup raisins

Whipped cream or vanilla ice cream

Beat eggs. Add sugar, milk, and spices. Oil a 2-quart baking casserole. Arrange bread or muffin cubes in the dish with raisins and cover with egg-milk liquid. Let stand until well soaked (approximately 15 minutes). Bake in a preheated 350°F oven for 25 – 35 minutes until a knife inserted in pudding's center comes out clean. Serve warm with whipped cream or vanilla ice cream. *Tips:* If bread or muffins aren't stale, put them in the oven for 5 – 10 minutes to dry them out. You can bake this pudding in 2 1-quart casseroles. *Serves 8.*

Peach Cobbler

"This peach cobbler always reminds me of the time I served it to five aviators (as they called themselves) from Paris, who didn't have to tell me it was delicious — their loud 'erotic' moaning and groaning made it obvious! I was thrilled that they liked it so much and, at the same time, a bit embarrassed by their reaction." — Nancy Morrison

1 cup melted butter or margarine
2 28-ounce cans peaches
1 yellow cake mix (no substitution)
Ground cinnamon

Preheat oven to 350°F. Place a ½ cup melted butter in the bottom of a 12 x 9" glass dish. Add the peaches and most of the juice. Add the cake mix over the top without mixing, then add the rest of the butter. Sprinkle with cinnamon. Bake until the delicious smell drives you crazy and the top is browned. *Serves 10 – 12.*

Morrison Manor

Nancy and Jerry Morrison
RR #1
Morpeth, Ontario N0P 1X0
Tel: (519) 674-3431
$$

ABOUT THE B&B

Built in 1989 especially as a B&B, Morrison Manor is just a few minutes from Rondeau Provincial Park — an ideal setting in which to enjoy the warmth and charm of this three-story hand-crafted log home and the natural environment of the park. On the first floor of the manor, guests are invited to use the cozy living room with fireplace if they wish. A full country breakfast is served in the large dining room where fresh herbs hang overhead. Six guest bedrooms and baths are located on the second floor, and two large private suites that overlook fields, a pond, and the full length of Rondeau Bay are located on the third floor. Each room reflects its own country style, and has a door that opens onto a large sitting porch. Besides the park, the area features a winery, buffalo farm, art gallery, cultural center, antique shops, car races, seasonal festivals, and much more. Nancy, a secondary school teacher, and Jerry, a quality-control technician, enjoy cooking, gardening, traveling, theater-going, birdwatching, walking, decorating, and playing shuffleboard.

SEASON

all year

ACCOMMODATIONS

2 suites with private baths;
6 rooms with shared baths

ABOUT THE B&B

Y*ou'll be welcomed like family at Brookside Hospitality Home, a well-maintained ranch-style dwelling in the rural community of Sunnyside. Pearl and Lloyd have lived in Sunnyside practically all their lives and know what Newfoundland hospitality is all about. Get to know them and their miniature collie, Lady, over a cup of tea or coffee, which is provided along with a bed-time snack. In the morning, make your way to the breakfast nook overlooking the water where home-made bread and jam, cereals, and juices await you. Radio, cable TV, laundry facilities, and ample parking are also available. Let your well-informed hosts direct you to the best sights in the province. Lloyd is a boat enthusiast and you may want to look in on his latest boat building project in the shed. Pearl keeps busy with her household responsibilities. Brookside is about one-and-a-half hours' drive from the Argentia Ferry to North Sydney, Nova Scotia, and one hour's drive from St. John's, capital of Newfoundland.*

SEASON

all year

ACCOMMODATIONS

2 rooms with shared bath

Raisin Buns

"The perfect buns for tea." — *Pearl Hiscock*

1 cup butter
3 cups all-purpose flour
5 teaspoons baking powder
¼ cup sugar
½ cup raisins
2 eggs
1½ cups water

Preheat oven to 425°F. Cut butter into combined dry ingredients. Add raisins. Beat eggs well; add eggs and water to dry ingredients, making a soft dough. Place on a floured board and roll out flat to ½" thickness. Cut out buns with a 2"-diameter bun cutter or a round glass with its rim dipped in flour. Place them in a greased pan. Bake about 15 minutes. **Makes 3 dozen buns.**

Raspberry Kuchen

1 egg, well beaten
½ cup sugar
½ cup milk
2 tablespoons vegetable oil
1 cup all-purpose flour
2 teaspoons baking powder
1 cup fresh raspberries

Topping:
½ cup all-purpose flour
½ cup sugar
3 tablespoons butter

Preheat oven to 375°F. In a bowl, combine egg, sugar, milk, and oil; mix well. Sift together dry ingredients and stir into egg mixture. Pour batter into a greased 8" square pan. Sprinkle raspberries over batter. Mix topping flour and sugar. Cut in butter to produce coarse crumbs. Sprinkle topping over raspberries. Bake 25 – 30 minutes or until cake tests done (toothpick trick). Cut into squares and serve warm. *Makes 16 squares.*

Norwood Bed & Breakfast

Pat and Roland Jensen
201 Norwood Court
Wetaskiwin, Alberta T9A 3P2
Tel: (888)/(403) 352-7880
Fax: (403) 352-8850
$$

ABOUT THE B&B

Seventeen-year residents of Wetaskiwin, Pat and Roland Jensen offer old-fashioned B&B hospitality in their new home full of country charm. An old-style double bed and antiques grace one guest room, while Victorian decor illuminates the queen-bedded room. Guests share a full bathroom, Jacuzzi, and a sitting room with white baby grand piano, games, books, and CD stereo system. Served in the formal dining room or on the sunny patio, a typical full breakfast consists of fruit salad, home-baked muffins and breads, homemade jams, a cooked entrée, and beverages. A smoking area is available outside on the deck. Norwood welcomes children but not pets as there's a resident 15-pound cat named Little Guy (who doesn't visit the guest rooms). After a day exploring such museums as Canada's Aviation Hall of Fame and the Alberta Central Railway Museum, shopping at antique, ladieswear, and gift shops, or playing a few rounds of golf, guests can refresh themselves with a soak in the outdoor hot tub. Norwood B&B is only a 45-minute drive from Alberta's capital, Edmonton.

SEASON

all year

ACCOMMODATIONS

2 rooms with shared bath

Bay View Manor / Manoir Bay View

Helen Sawyer Hall
PO Box 21
395 Bonaventure East, Route 132
New Carlisle, Québec G0C 1Z0
Tel: (418) 752-2725/6718
$

ABOUT THE B&B

*O*nce a country store and rural post office, Bay View Manor, a spectacular seaside farm on the rugged Gaspé Peninsula, now welcomes guests from all over the world. Reside in the historic, three-story farmhouse with its five guest rooms and oceanfront view, or choose the private cottage. At Bay View Manor's breakfast table, enjoy dishes (including home-baked goods and homemade jams) prepared with fresh eggs, fruit, and produce from the farm — served extra early, if desired, so you can get a real jump on your day! You can visit Bonaventure's Acadian Museum or the archaeological cave (La Grotte) at Saint Elzéar, or take more distant day trips to Miguasha fossil site and park, famous Percé Rock, Bonaventure Island Bird Sanctuary, or Forillon National Park. Right beside the B&B is the 18-hole Fauvel golf course and venues for numerous land and water sports. Of course, you can simply choose to listen to the ocean waves on the patio and enjoy the tranquility. Helen runs the B&B with her sons.

SEASON

May – November

ACCOMMODATIONS

5 rooms with shared baths;
1 private cottage with private bath

Rhubarb Sauce Drop Cookies

½ cup margarine
1 cup sugar
1 egg
1¾ cups all-purpose flour
½ teaspoon baking powder
½ teaspoon baking soda
½ teaspoon salt
1 teaspoon ground cinnamon
¼ teaspoon ground cloves
¼ teaspoon ground nutmeg
½ cup raisins
1 cup quick-cooking rolled oats
1 cup thick rhubarb sauce (recipe follows)

Preheat oven to 350°F – 375°F. Cream margarine and sugar together. Stir in egg. Sift flour, baking powder and soda, salt, and spices together. Mix in raisins and rolled oats. Add to creamed mixture in 3 portions alternately with thick rhubarb sauce in 2 portions, mixing well after each addition. Drop dough by teaspoonfuls onto greased baking sheets. Bake about 12 minutes. *Makes 3 dozen cookies.*

Rhubarb sauce:
3 cups cubed fresh rhubarb
1 cup water
¾ cup sugar

Boil rhubarb in water for 10 minutes. Add sugar. Stir and let cool.

Saskatoon Dumplings

"This recipe was an old standby of my mother-in-law, Lena Mader, who was an excellent cook and mother of eight boys! It's now become a specialty in our Country Tea Room."
— Jo Mader

Dough:
1 cup all-purpose flour
2 teaspoons sugar
1 heaping teaspoon baking powder
Pinch of salt
2 tablespoons canola oil or melted butter
Milk as needed

Fruit sauce:
2 cups Saskatoon berries or blueberries
½ cup sugar
1 cup water

Vanilla ice cream

Mix dough ingredients with enough milk to produce a very thick batter; set aside.

In a heavy saucepan, mix berries, sugar, and water. Bring to a boil. At once, drop the dumpling dough by heaping spoonfuls into the fruit. Cover and simmer for 15 minutes or until the dough is cooked. Serve hot with a scoop of vanilla ice cream.
Serves 5 – 6.

Bluenose Country Vacation Farm

Jo and Kenneth Mader
PO Box 173
Qu'Appelle, Saskatchewan
S0G 4A0
Tel: (306) 699-7192
$$

ABOUT THE B&B

For an old-fashioned welcome where Mother Nature wraps you in her arms, there's no place like Bluenose Country Vacation Farm. Step back in history as you admire the English split field-stone home — a striking silhouette that has been a landmark on the prairie landscape since 1904. Stroll through the gracious farmyard, pet the farm animals, view the large farm machinery new and old, and spend some time in the Agriculture Education Center, with hands-on displays and model farm machinery for children to play with. After a refreshing swim in the indoor heated pool, try your hand at mini-golf, while the children frolic in the playground. In early morning, the call of a meadowlark breaks the stillness and you're eventually coaxed to the breakfast table by the smells of homemade bread and sizzling bacon. Country high tea is served from May to September, and lunch and dinner meals can also be arranged. Bluenose is a short drive from picturesque Qu'Appelle Valley with its sparkling lakes and sandy beaches, and a few minutes from the town's own stores and attractions.

SEASON

all year

ACCOMMODATIONS

6 rooms with private baths

Chaplin's Country B&B

Kathy and Ron Chaplin
RR #5, PO Box 43
Saskatoon, Saskatchewan
S7K 3J8
Tel: (306) 931-3353
$

ABOUT THE B&B

Experience the wide open spaces and blue sky of Canada's prairies at Chaplin's Country B&B, a working farm with Jersey cows, pigs, sheep, goats, and chickens. Enjoy a rest on the veranda and view awesome sunsets, or stroll through the barnyard and watch the evening milking. Relax in the gracious country home with handmade spiral staircase, knotty pine paneling, and prairie antiques. For privacy, the guest bedrooms, TV lounge, and bathroom are all on the second floor. Chaplin's country breakfast, including French toast with homemade syrups, sausage, fresh fruit in season, and beverages, is a real eye-opener, while an evening snack of apple cake and hot cider always hits the spot. Only 15 minutes away, Saskatoon offers many fine restaurants, shops, and attractions. Other area diversions include the Western Development Museum, Wanuskewin Heritage Park, University of Saskatchewan, and numerous provincial parks and golf courses. Kathy and Ron pride themselves on their prairie hospitality and comfortable facilities.

SEASON

all year

ACCOMMODATIONS

3 rooms with shared bath

Scandinavian Kringler

"This is an excellent morning treat for my B&B guests."
— Kathy Chaplin

Crust:
½ cup chilled butter
1 cup all-purpose flour
2 tablespoons ice water

Puff filling:
1 cup water
½ cup butter
1 cup all-purpose flour
3 eggs
½ teaspoon almond extract

Frosting:
1 cup confectioners' sugar
1 tablespoon softened butter
½ teaspoon almond extract or 1½ teaspoons vanilla
2 – 3 tablespoons milk or cream (any type)
Sliced almonds

(continued on next page)

Preheat oven to 350°F. In a small bowl, cut butter into flour using a pastry blender (or 2 knives) until particles are the size of small peas. Sprinkle with water, 1 tablespoon at a time. Stir with a fork just until a soft dough forms. Divide in half. On a greased cookie sheet, roll out each half into a 12 x 3" strip. In a medium saucepan, heat water and butter to boiling. Remove from heat and immediately stir in 1 cup flour until smooth. Add eggs, one at a time, beating until smooth. Stir in almond extract. Divide batter in half and spoon over each crust, spreading to ¾" from edges. Bake 50 – 60 minutes or until golden brown. Immediately remove from pan and cool (puffed top will shrink and fall). In a small bowl, blend frosting ingredients (except nuts) until smooth. Spread on each kringler. Sprinkle with almonds, then slice. *Serves 16 – 20.*

Bayberry Cliff Inn

Nancy and Don Perkins
RR #4, Little Sands
Murray River
Prince Edward Island C0A 1W0
Tel: (800) 668-3395 or
(902) 962-3395
$$ – $$$

ABOUT THE B&B

Bayberry Cliff Inn is named for the fragrant bayberry bushes that cover the rugged 40-foot cliff on which the inn sits. Incorporating two reconstructed post and beam barns, the inn features intriguing architectural details such as individually shaped rooms and multiple-level living spaces. Bedrooms, lofts, and sitting areas are filled with handmade quilts, antique furniture, and paintings, the result of a lifetime of collecting beautiful things. A large library and breakfast area are on the ground level. Don's hash browns and bacon and Nancy's sourdough pancakes and blueberry muffins all consistently get rave reviews. Don is a retired teacher and Nancy is a marine painter (who has made sure the changeable ocean can be seen from every level of the B&B). Bayberry activities include picking up to 35 different wildflowers, sitting in the whimsical tree perch to watch for marine life, inner-tubing, swimming, and beachcombing. You may cook your own meals on the gas grill or choose from many excellent restaurants a scant 15-minute drive away.

SEASON

May 10 – September 30

ACCOMMODATIONS

3 rooms with private baths;
1 room with shared bath

Sourdough Cinnamon Rolls

"A guest gave me this recipe and a cup of starter that was 25 years old at the time. I have since kept it going and have, in turn, given it away to other guests." — Nancy Perkins

1 cup sourdough sponge batter*
¼ cup vegetable oil
4 tablespoons brown sugar
2 cups all-purpose flour
2 teaspoons baking powder
1 teaspoon baking soda
¼ teaspoon salt

Filling:
1 cup brown sugar
3 tablespoons margarine or butter
1 teaspoon ground cinnamon

White frosting

Note: In the evening (or at least 12 hours before using), make the sponge (see pages 69 – 70).

Preheat oven to 350°F. Put sponge, oil, and brown sugar in a bowl and mix together. Add remaining dough ingredients and mix into a soft dough. Place on a floured surface and roll into a rectangle, ½" thick. Combine filling ingredients and spread over dough. Roll up like a jelly roll and cut into 1" slices. Place rolls on greased cookie sheets, spaced about 1" apart, and press them down lightly with your hand. Bake 20 – 25 minutes. Serve warm with dribbled white frosting. *Makes 24 cinnamon rolls.*

Strawberry Squares

Bottom crust:
¼ cup brown sugar
½ cup margarine
½ cup chopped walnuts or pecans
1 cup all-purpose flour

Preheat oven to 375°F. Combine ingredients and press into a 9 x 9" greased pan. Bake 12 minutes. Cool.

Filling:
1 cup frozen strawberries in syrup
½ cup sugar
Small package strawberry Jell-O
2 packages Dream Whip dessert topping mix

Put first 3 filling ingredients in a saucepan and bring just to a boil. Remove from heat and cool. Prepare 1 package of Dream Whip and add to cooled strawberry mixture. Put this mixture over the bottom crust and chill. Before serving, top with another prepared package of Dream Whip. *Tip:* You can double the recipe for a 13 x 9" pan (approximately 24 squares) or even do a triple batch for a nice thick square. *Makes approximately 16 squares.*

Fairfield Farm Inn

Shae and Richard Griffith
10 Main Street West, Route 1
Middleton, Nova Scotia B0S IP0
Tel/Fax: (800) 237-9896
or (902) 825-6989
$$

ABOUT THE B&B

Fairfield Farm Inn is situated on a 110-acre fruit and vegetable farm famous for its luscious melons. Built in 1886, this Annapolis Valley farmhouse has been completely restored and furnished in period antiques to enhance its original charm. Cozy comforters, king- and queen-sized beds, and private baths grace the five guest rooms. The Annapolis River and Slocum Brook are on the property, as are birdwatching and walking trails, pheasants, and other abundant wildlife. Shae and Richard take pride in offering Maritime hospitality and wholesome country breakfasts, featuring fresh fruit picked from their farm and homemade jams and jellies. Shae is a member of the Acadia University Business School Advisory Board; Richard is a retired military officer. Their hobbies include gardening, antique hunting, reading, and traveling. A few minutes from picturesque fishing villages and the world's highest tides on the Bay of Fundy, Middleton boasts museums, restaurants, boutiques, and theater — all a short walking distance from the inn.

SEASON

all year
(winter by reservation only)

ACCOMMODATIONS

5 rooms with private baths

Weston Lake Inn Bed & Breakfast

Susan Evans and Ted Harrison
813 Beaver Point Road
Salt Spring Island
British Columbia V8K IX9
Tel: (250) 653-4311
$$$

ABOUT THE B&B

Nestled on a well-tended knoll of flowering trees and shrubs overlooking Weston Lake, the inn is a serene and comfortable adult getaway on the rural south end of Salt Spring Island. The three tastefully decorated guest bedrooms have private baths, down duvets, and fresh flower bouquets. Original Canadian art and beautiful petit-point (crafted by host Ted) grace the interior of the inn. Guests have the exclusive use of a cozy fireside lounge with library, TV, and VCR, and an outdoor hot tub perched above the lake. Creative breakfasts feature fresh eggs from the inn's chickens, and produce from the large, organic garden, such as berries, herbs, and asparagus in season. Near Victoria, Salt Spring Island offers a mild climate, exceptional beauty, a thriving community of artists and craftspeople, and an abundance of outdoor activities. Since opening Weston Lake Inn in 1986, hosts Susan and Ted have been fine-tuning their B&B craft, restoring the house, landscaping, and enjoying their 10-acre paradise with guests. Susan loves gardening, while Ted loves sailing and offers charters aboard their 36-foot sloop.

SEASON

all year

ACCOMMODATIONS

3 rooms with private baths

Three Cheese Scones

"While we have made adaptations to the originals over time, we gratefully acknowledge that many of our best ideas have come from our guests!" — Susan Evans

½ cup grated strong cheddar cheese
½ cup grated Emmental cheese
½ cup freshly grated Parmesan cheese
1 whole egg
1 egg yolk
½ cup light cream (18 – 30%)
2 cups all-purpose flour
4 teaspoons baking powder
½ teaspoon salt
¼ cup very cold unsalted butter
1 egg white

Preheat oven to 425°F. Mix the cheddar, Emmental, and ¼ cup Parmesan cheese in a large bowl. In a small bowl, fork-beat the whole egg, egg yolk, and cream until blended. In the bowl of a food processor, mix flour, baking powder, and salt, then cut in butter (if you don't have a food processor, use 2 knives). Fluff flour mixture into cheeses. Add egg mixture all at once, stirring with a fork. Press into a ball and knead gently on a floured surface up to 10 times. Roll into a circle ½" thick. Transfer to a lightly greased baking sheet, brush with the egg white, score into 12 wedges, and sprinkle with the remaining Parmesan. Bake 12 – 15 minutes. *Makes 1 dozen scones.*

Yogurt Scones

"Using the lemon zest makes great biscuits for strawberry shortcakes." — Elaine Landray

2 cups all-purpose flour
2 tablespoons sugar
1 tablespoon baking powder
½ teaspoon baking soda
½ teaspoon salt
½ cup butter or margarine
1 cup plain yogurt

Options:
½ cup grated cheddar cheese or a combination of 2 – 3 kinds of
    cheese (Asiago, Parmesan, and mozzarella recommended)
½ cup raisins or dried cranberries
1 teaspoon lemon zest

Preheat oven to 400°F. Mix dry ingredients. Cut in butter with a pastry blender or 2 knives until blended. Add whichever option you are using (cheese, raisins, cranberries, or lemon zest). Mix in the yogurt and form as for pastry (into a loose ball). Roll out on a floured surface to about ½" thickness. Using a 2"-diameter cutter, cut out biscuits. Place on an ungreased cookie sheet and bake 12 minutes. *Makes 18 scones.*

Linden House B&B

Elaine and Phil Landray
PO Box 1586, 389 Simcoe Street
Niagara-on-the-Lake, Ontario
L0S 1J0
Tel/Fax: (905) 468-3923
$$

ABOUT THE B&B

A warm welcome awaits you at Linden House, a new Cape Cod-style, air conditioned home with private guest wing, featuring two queen rooms and one twin/king room, all with private ensuite bathrooms. The queen rooms feature brass beds and cream wicker furniture, while the twin/king room highlights the nautical flavor with Cape Cod wicker. There is a guest lounge on the same level as the bedrooms with television, VCR, games, and books, or you can choose to enjoy the garden or relax in the gazebo. Non-smoking Linden House offers convenient on-site parking and is located in the old town, just four short blocks from Queen Street with its shopping and theaters. In summer, enjoy water recreation on Lake Ontario or top-notch theater at the Shaw Festival. Your hosts, Elaine and Phil, serve such sumptuous breakfasts — featuring seasonal Niagara fruit — that their guests claim they don't need lunch!

SEASON

April – December

ACCOMMODATIONS

3 rooms with private baths

Appetizers & Side Dishes

Baked Beans

2 cups dried Boston beans (also called navy or pea beans)
½ tablespoon dry mustard
½ cup brown sugar
¼ cup molasses
1 teaspoon salt
Pepper to taste
2 cups diced salt pork
1 onion, chopped

Soak beans for a few hours in enough water to cover. Simmer gently for 1½ hours, then drain. Put in an oven-proof dish or bean crock with the rest of the ingredients except the onion. Stir well. Add enough water to cover. Add the onion and bake in a preheated slow oven (300°F) for 6 – 8 hours, covered. Add boiling water when needed to keep the beans moist. May be left uncovered to brown for the last hour, if desired. *Serves 8.*

Bay View Manor / Manoir Bay View

Helen Sawyer Hall
PO Box 21
395 Bonaventure East, Route 132
New Carlisle, Québec G0C 1Z0
Tel: (418) 752-2725/6718
$

ABOUT THE B&B

Once a country store and rural post office, Bay View Manor, a spectacular seaside farm on the rugged Gaspé Peninsula, now welcomes guests from all over the world. Reside in the historic, three-story farmhouse with its five guest rooms and oceanfront view, or choose the private cottage. At Bay View Manor's breakfast table, enjoy dishes (including home-baked goods and homemade jams) prepared with fresh eggs, fruit, and produce from the farm — served extra early, if desired, so you can get a real jump on your day! You can visit Bonaventure's Acadian Museum or the archaeological cave (La Grotte) at Saint Elzéar, or take more distant day trips to Miguasha fossil site and park, famous Percé Rock, Bonaventure Island Bird Sanctuary, or Forillon National Park. Right beside the B&B is the 18-hole Fauvel golf course and venues for numerous land and water sports. Of course, you can simply choose to listen to the ocean waves on the patio and enjoy the tranquility. Helen runs the B&B with her sons.

SEASON

May – November

ACCOMMODATIONS

5 rooms with shared baths;
1 private cottage with private bath

Montréal Oasis

Lena Blondel
3000 Breslay Road
Montréal, Québec H3Y 2G7
Tel: (514) 935-2312
$$

ABOUT THE B&B

I n pilgrim days, the evergreen tree was a sign of shelter, good food, and warm hospitality. It's fitting, then, that two towering evergreens frame the door to Montréal Oasis. This charming B&B with original leaded windows and slanted ceilings is located in downtown Montréal's west end, close to the Fine Arts Museum, chic Crescent Street and Greene Avenue shopping and restaurants, and the "main drag," St. Catherine Street. The beautiful and safe neighborhood with its spacious Elizabethan-style houses and pretty gardens is locally referred to as the Priest Farm district — once a holiday resort for priests. Originally from Sweden, your world-traveled hostess Lena has lived in many countries around the globe, which is evident from the African, Asian, and Swedish art that graces the B&B. The three guest rooms feature Scandinavian and Québecois furniture. Lena loves good food, and serves three-course gourmet breakfasts featuring delicious, fresh ingredients. A friendly Siamese cat resides on the main floor.

SEASON

all year

ACCOMMODATIONS

3 rooms with shared baths

Berry Soup

"A starter course on a hot summer day." — Lena Blondel

3 cups water
¾ cup concentrated raspberry or strawberry juice (not cocktail)
1 tablespoon potato flour
Chopped fresh fruits of your choice, e.g., ½ cup gooseberries
    and 1 cup red currants, or ½ cup raspberries and
    1 cup blueberries (left whole)
Confectioners' sugar
Whole berries
Fresh mint leaves

Bring water, juice, and potato flour to a boil, stirring constantly. Let cool. Add chopped fresh fruits. Sweeten with confectioners' sugar. Serve in chilled fruit cups decorated generously with whole berries and a mint leaf or two. *Serves 5.*

Bloody Mary Soup

1 medium onion, chopped
3 celery stalks, diced
2 tablespoons butter
2 tablespoons tomato purée or paste
1 tablespoon sugar
5 cups tomato juice
1 tablespoon salt
2 teaspoons Worcestershire sauce
¼ teaspoon pepper
1 tablespoon lemon juice
4 ounces vodka
Chopped fresh chives or parsley

In a large pot, sauté onions and celery in butter until light brown. Add tomato purée and sugar. Sauté 1 minute. Add tomato juice and simmer 8 – 10 minutes. Add other ingredients except vodka and chives or parsley. Strain, then add vodka. Serve either hot or chilled, sprinkled with chives or parsley. *Serves 6.*

Humber Gallery Hospitality Home

Edna and Eldon Swyer
26 Roberts Drive
Little Rapids, Newfoundland
A2H 6C3
(Mailing address: PO Box 15
Corner Brook, Newfoundland
A2H 6C3)
Tel: (709) 634-2660
$

ABOUT THE B&B

A popular stop for the British royal family, the town of Little Rapids (near Corner Brook) is home to Humber Gallery, an impressive cedar abode with cathedral ceilings, fireplace, wraparound sun deck, two guest rooms with double beds, one guest room with twin beds, and full and half guest bathrooms. Humber serves a nutritious breakfast, while other meals and guests' use of the barbecue and picnic area can be arranged. An excellent spot for an overnight stay when going or coming from Gros Morne National Park, this B&B is in the heart of the Humber Valley Reserve near Marble Mountain Ski Resort, mini-golf facilities, "U-pick" strawberry farms, Bay of Islands tourist attractions, South Brook and Pasadena beaches on Deer Lake, and the Humber River. Edna and Eldon will be happy to provide you with maps, tourist literature, a licensed salmon fishing guide, and insider tips on area attractions.

SEASON

June – September;
February – mid-April

ACCOMMODATIONS

3 rooms with shared baths

Montréal Oasis

Lena Blondel
3000 Breslay Road
Montréal, Québec H3Y 2G7
Tel: (514) 935-2312
$$

ABOUT THE B&B

I n pilgrim days, the evergreen tree was a sign of shelter, good food, and warm hospitality. It's fitting, then, that two towering evergreens frame the door to Montréal Oasis. This charming B&B with original leaded windows and slanted ceilings is located in downtown Montréal's west end, close to the Fine Arts Museum, chic Crescent Street and Greene Avenue shopping and restaurants, and the "main drag," St. Catherine Street. The beautiful and safe neighborhood with its spacious Elizabethan-style houses and pretty gardens is locally referred to as the Priest Farm district — once a holiday resort for priests. Originally from Sweden, your world-traveled hostess Lena has lived in many countries around the globe, which is evident from the African, Asian, and Swedish art that graces the B&B. The three guest rooms feature Scandinavian and Québecois furniture. Lena loves good food, and serves three-course gourmet breakfasts featuring delicious, fresh ingredients. A friendly Siamese cat resides on the main floor.

SEASON

all year

ACCOMMODATIONS

3 rooms with shared baths

Broiled Grapefruit

"On cold winter days, I like to serve this grapefruit as an appetizer." — Lena Blondel

2 grapefruits, halved
Brown sugar
4 grapes or strawberries

Remove seeds and loosen sections in each half. Sprinkle some brown sugar over each grapefruit half, and broil in the oven until edges just turn brown. Top with a grape or a strawberry. *Serves 4.*

Cinnamon Baked Pears

"Served as a first course on a cold and snowy morning, this fruit dish hits the spot every time with our guests."
— Madeleine Mercier

6 medium pears
¾ cup fresh or frozen (thawed and drained) blueberries
¾ cup water
3 tablespoons packed brown sugar
1½ tablespoons lemon juice
½ teaspoon ground cinnamon

Preheat oven to 350°F. Peel pears and cut in half lengthwise; scoop out core. Place cut side down in a shallow baking dish. Sprinkle blueberries around pears. Combine water, brown sugar, lemon juice, and cinnamon; pour over pears. Bake, covered, for about 45 minutes or until pears are tender. Baste pears occasionally with pan juices. Serve 2 or 3 halves in a plate, pouring some juice and blueberries on top. *Serves 4 – 6.*

Les Trois Érables

Madeleine and Jacques Mercier
PO Box 852, RR #2
Wakefield, Québec J0X 3G0
Tel: (819) 459-1118
$$

ABOUT THE B&B

Nestled among gentle rolling hills on the banks of the Gatineau River, the historic village of Wakefield is a gateway to beautiful Gatineau Park where you can find ample opportunities for hiking, skiing, or less arduous nature walks — especially beautiful in fall foliage season. Less than a half hour's drive takes you to the heart of Canada's national capital, Ottawa. Les Trois Érables was built at the turn of the century and was the home and office of three generations of village doctors until its B&B transformation in 1988. Rooms are tastefully decorated in soft colors and furnished for comfort and convenience. The sumptuous breakfasts attest to the fact that Madeleine loves to cook. Local restaurants, sports outfitters, and boutiques abound.

SEASON

all year

ACCOMMODATIONS

4 rooms with private baths

Peters Place

Joan and Calvin Peters
6430 PR 241 North
Cartier, Manitoba R4K 1B4
Tel: (204) 864-2106

$

ABOUT THE B&B

Experience rural Canada and *the people who live there at Peters Place — a 500-acre, family-operated grain farm. Offering peace and quiet along the Assiniboine River, Peters Place is ideal for B&B travelers who want the best of both worlds — country relaxation with close proximity to the urban sights of Winnipeg. It's also a good base from which to tour points of historic interest, such as Lower Fort Garry at Selkirk or the museum at Portage la Prairie. Excellent golf facilities are within a 10-minute drive. For those who enjoy natural parkland, Beaudry Park is open year-round for hikers or cross-country skiers. If time and weather permit, your hosts will take you to watch the beaver on the Assiniboine at dusk, give you a ride in their old Model T or on one of their restored farm tractors, and take you inside their Canadian National Railway caboose. Bountiful breakfasts are served in the family dining area and every effort is made to accommodate special preferences or diets.*

SEASON

April – October

ACCOMMODATIONS

2 rooms with shared bath

Cool Cucumber Soup

1 large English cucumber
1 green onion, chopped
2 tablespoons chopped fresh dill
1 cup milk
1 cup plain yogurt
Salt and pepper to taste

Grated carrot, chopped green onion, or sliced cucumber

Using a food processor, blend cucumber, onion, and dill. In a large bowl, whisk milk and yogurt until smooth. Mix both mixtures together, then add salt and pepper to taste. Chill until ready to serve. Garnish with grated carrot, chopped green onion, or sliced cucumber. *Makes 3 – 4 cups.*

Dilled Potato Puff

"My mother, Beth Prior, has an art of making a leftover meal taste like a gourmet delight. This is one of her secret recipes."
— Jo Mader

4 cups cooked potatoes (if leftovers, reheat for easy handling)
½ teaspoon salt
¼ teaspoon pepper
¼ teaspoon garlic salt
½ teaspoon dried dill weed
½ cup sour cream
Grated or sliced cheddar cheese

Gravy and hot meats, or cold cuts

Mash potatoes with seasonings. Beat sour cream into potato mixture and place in a casserole dish. Sprinkle top with cheese. Cover. Place in the microwave on medium power or in the oven at 350°F until heated through and cheese melts. Delicious with gravy and hot meats, or with cold cuts. *Serves 4 – 6.*

Bluenose Country Vacation Farm

Jo and Kenneth Mader
PO Box 173
Qu'Appelle, Saskatchewan
S0G 4A0
Tel: (306) 699-7192
$$

ABOUT THE B&B

For an old-fashioned welcome where Mother Nature wraps you in her arms, there's no place like Bluenose Country Vacation Farm. Step back in history as you admire the English split field-stone home — a striking silhouette that has been a landmark on the prairie landscape since 1904. Stroll through the gracious farmyard, pet the farm animals, view the large farm machinery new and old, and spend some time in the Agriculture Education Center, with hands-on displays and model farm machinery for children to play with. After a refreshing swim in the indoor heated pool, try your hand at mini-golf, while the children frolic in the playground. In early morning, the call of a meadowlark breaks the stillness and you're eventually coaxed to the breakfast table by the smells of homemade bread and sizzling bacon. Country high tea is served from May to September, and lunch and dinner meals can also be arranged. Bluenose is a short drive from picturesque Qu'Appelle Valley with its sparkling lakes and sandy beaches, and a few minutes from the town's own stores and attractions.

SEASON

all year

ACCOMMODATIONS

6 rooms with private baths

Fairfield Farm Inn

Shae and Richard Griffith
10 Main Street West, Route 1
Middleton, Nova Scotia B0S IP0
Tel/Fax: (800) 237-9896
or (902) 825-6989
$$

ABOUT THE B&B

Fairfield Farm Inn is situated on a 110-acre fruit and vegetable farm famous for its luscious melons. Built in 1886, this Annapolis Valley farmhouse has been completely restored and furnished in period antiques to enhance its original charm. Cozy comforters, king- and queen-sized beds, and private baths grace the five guest rooms. The Annapolis River and Slocum Brook are on the property, as are birdwatching and walking trails, pheasants, and other abundant wildlife. Shae and Richard take pride in offering Maritime hospitality and wholesome country breakfasts, featuring fresh fruit picked from their farm and homemade jams and jellies. Shae is a member of the Acadia University Business School Advisory Board; Richard is a retired military officer. Their hobbies include gardening, antique hunting, reading, and traveling. A few minutes from picturesque fishing villages and the world's highest tides on the Bay of Fundy, Middleton boasts museums, restaurants, boutiques, and theater — all a short walking distance from the inn.

SEASON

all year
(winter by reservation only)

ACCOMMODATIONS

5 rooms with private baths

Fresh Fruit Cup

Syrup:
2 cups sugar
4 cups water

1 honeydew
1 cantaloupe
1 pineapple
2 oranges
1 grapefruit
Grapes
Kiwi

Heat sugar and water in a pot until boiling and sugar is dissolved. Cool. Prepare fruit (peel, etc.) and chop into bite-sized pieces. Put in a gallon jar in layers. Cover with cooled syrup. Refrigerate and serve as required. *Tip:* You can vary fruit combination depending on what's in season (strawberries lose their color and ferment faster, and should be used only if you're going to use up the batch fairly quickly). *Serves 15 – 20.*

Granola Parfait

"This is a healthy, attractive dish to be made just before serving so the granola won't go soggy from the yogurt."
— *Yvonne Parker*

Granola:
¾ cup vegetable oil
¾ cup honey
1½ tablespoons vanilla
⅓ cup water
½ tablespoon salt
8 cups quick-cooking rolled oats
1 cup wheat germ
1 cup flaked unsweetened coconut
¾ cup brown sugar
1 cup nuts (combination of chopped peanuts, almonds, sunflower seed, sesame seeds, etc.)

Preheat oven to 300°F. Whip together oil, honey, vanilla, water, and salt until well mixed. Pour this over the remaining ingredients and mix well. Spread ½" deep in shallow, ungreased baking pans. Bake 30 minutes, then stir. Continue baking, stirring every 15 minutes, until golden brown — about 1½ hours. Store in an airtight container until ready to use. Freezes well. *Makes approximately 10 cups.*

(continued on next page)

Orchard Lane
Bed & Breakfast
Yvonne Parker
13324 Middle Bench Road
Oyama, British Columbia
V4V 2B4
Tel: (250) 548-3809
$$

ABOUT THE B&B

Smack dab between Kelowna and Vernon, there awaits Orchard Lane, a newly built Victorian B&B nestled in a private orchard. From the sprawling veranda, this rural setting gives way to a panoramic view of the beautiful Central Okanagan Valley, while nearby Kalamalka and Wood lakes reflect the hills and distant mountains. Inside, a welcoming foyer and spiral staircase lead to romantic and comfortable bedrooms. Visitors lounge in the formal living room with fireplace, stroll through the flower gardens or nearby orchard, admire the terraced landscaping framed by giant trees, or take a refreshing dip in the outdoor hot tub. Your hostess, Yvonne, serves a full gourmet breakfast — made from produce grown in her vegetable garden — in the formal dining room or on the veranda. You'll quickly discover that one of her favorite hobbies is craft collecting, which is evident throughout the house. Alpine skiing, fishing, biking, hiking, and other recreational choices await you and there are golf courses and beaches aplenty to explore. This area is truly a corner of paradise.

SEASON
all year

ACCOMMODATIONS
2 rooms with shared bath

Parfait:
Granola
French vanilla yogurt
Strawberry jam
Cashew nut

To make the parfait: Place about 4 tablespoons granola in a small parfait dish. Place a layer of French vanilla yogurt over granola. Place a teaspoon of strawberry jam over yogurt. Sprinkle some granola over jam and top with a cashew nut. *Makes 1 parfait.*

Homestyle Boursin

"For a while, Boursin cheese was unavailable in Canada due to its high bacterial content, which didn't meet Canadian standards. I started making my own version, which uses fresh herbs grown in my kitchen window and tastes very much like the original — delicious!" — Bonnie Evans

16 ounces softened cream cheese
¼ cup mayonnaise
2 teaspoons Dijon mustard
1 tablespoon finely chopped fresh chives
2 tablespoons finely chopped fresh dill
1 tablespoon finely chopped fresh parsley
1 garlic clove, minced

Crackers

Beat ingredients with an electric mixer until thoroughly blended. Spoon into a 2-cup mold lined with aluminum foil (or small crockery serving bowl). Turn out onto a small serving plate and peel off foil. Serve with crackers. Also good on bagels. *Tip:* Best when made 1 or 2 days ahead. *Makes 2 cups.*

Cornelius White House
Bed & Breakfast

Bonnie and Frank Evans
8 Wellington Street
Bloomfield, Ontario K0K 1G0
Tel/Fax: (613) 393-2282
$ – $$

ABOUT THE B&B

Located on the historic Loyalist Parkway in the west end of a farming community, the Cornelius White House is named for its original owner, a Dutch settler who built this charming red-brick house in 1862. Today, a sense of history and design combine with European furnishings and accents to create a rather unique bed and breakfast. Three guest rooms on the second floor open onto the cathedral ceiling sitting room, and there's also a suite on the main floor. The B&B is air conditioned and is a non-smoking environment. A full breakfast, consisting of fruit, a hot main course, and freshly baked goods, is served in the adjoining Dutch Treat Tea Room. Outstanding restaurants are nearby, as well as antique and craft shops, galleries, studios, and museums. Cornelius White House is just 10 minutes from the Sandbanks and Outlet Beach provincial parks (boasting the largest freshwater sand dunes in the world). Prince Edward County is a cyclist's dream come true complete with panoramic views and gentle rolling hills.

SEASON

all year

ACCOMMODATIONS

2 rooms with private baths;
2 rooms with shared bath

Caron House (1837)

Mary and Mike Caron
PO Box 143
Williamstown, Ontario K0C 2J0
Tel: (613) 347-7338
$$

ABOUT THE B&B

Caron House (1837) is a historic, romantic brick home located in the quaint village of Williamstown (established in 1784). Beautifully decorated and furnished with antiques, the house is in its original state, with working fireplaces, inside shutters, tin ceilings, and wide pine floorboards. Two rooms with shared bath are individually decorated with Laura Ashley wallpaper, antique linens, hooked rugs, quilts, and collectibles. Guests can relax in the Keeping Room (a Colonial term for gathering place) or living room, while a full, candlelit gourmet breakfast — accompanied by classical music — is served in the dining room on fine china, silverware, and crystal. Outside, you'll marvel at the herb and Victorian gardens, and relax on the antique wicker furniture on the back veranda, enjoying the lovely yards, complete with trellis, brick patio, and gazebo. Caron House is one hour's drive from either Montréal or Ottawa; nearby attractions include Upper Canada Village, artisan studios, a bird sanctuary, tennis, cycling, and good restaurants. Mary and Mike are retirees from the corporate world, and enjoy traveling, antique hunting, cooking, gardening, and history.

SEASON

all year

ACCOMMODATIONS

2 rooms with shared bath

Mary's Baked Apple

"The Seaway Valley is home of the McIntosh Red Apple, at its peak in the fall when the local 'Apples and Art Studio and Heritage Tour' is held (the last weekend in September). At that time, studios and heritage sites open their doors and invite the public to enjoy arts of the past and arts in the making. It's also when I like to serve my baked apple recipe — art, if I may say so myself, that can be eaten with more than the eye." — Mary Caron

1 McIntosh apple
¼ cup raisins
Pinch of ground nutmeg
Pinch of ground cinnamon
½ teaspoon freshly grated orange zest
1 teaspoon brown sugar
1 teaspoon butter
Reconstituted orange juice
Sour cream or yogurt

The night before serving, core apples and set them upright in an electric crock pot. In the center of each apple, layer raisins, nutmeg, cinnamon, orange zest, brown sugar, and butter. Pour orange juice to fill pot up to the middle of apples. Cook in crock pot on low overnight. In the morning, top with a dollop of sour cream or yogurt. *Makes 1 baked apple (multiply as required).*

Mussel and Sweet Potato Chowder

"Our single most requested recipe since its introduction in 1992! We use fresh Prince Edward Island blue mussels for this recipe." — Michael Smith

5 pounds mussels
¼ cup water
1 pound onion, chopped
¼ cup butter
4 garlic cloves, chopped
2 pounds sweet potatoes, peeled and grated
8 ounces carrot, grated
3 cups milk
3 cups whipping cream (35%)
2 bay leaves

Place mussels and ¼ cup water in a pot with a tight fitting lid. Place on high heat and steam until the shells open wide (discard any that won't open). Remove meat and set aside, reserving steaming liquid and some shells for garnish. "Sweat" onions in butter for 10 minutes (i.e., sauté at low heat). Add garlic cloves and sweat 5 more minutes. Add grated sweet potatoes and carrots with milk and cream to onion mixture. Add bay leaves and simmer for 30 minutes until vegetables are soft. Purée thoroughly in a blender and strain through a fine, mesh strainer. Add mussel juice and thin to desired consistency. Bring back to heat, add mussels, and serve garnished with spicy butter (recipe follows). *Serves 6 – 8.*

(continued on next page)

The Inn at Bay Fortune

David Wilmer (innkeeper)
and Michael Smith (chef)
Bay Fortune
Prince Edward Island C0A 2B0
Tel: (902) 687-3745
Fax: (902) 687-3540
$$$ – $$$$

ABOUT THE B&B

Built in 1910 as the summer home of Broadway playwright Elmer Harris, this inn has enjoyed a place in the Bay Fortune artists' community ever since. In 1989, innkeeper David Wilmer restored the home to its current splendor, reflecting its heritage and taking full advantage of its location overlooking Bay Fortune and the Northumberland Straight beyond. Uniquely decorated with a combination of island antiques and pieces created by local craftsmen, the 11 guest suites all have private baths and a view of the sea, most with a fireplace-graced sitting area. The dining room is the highest rated in Atlantic Canada by Where to Eat in Canada. Chef Michael Smith has earned an international reputation for his focus on fresh island ingredients, and his contemporary cuisine is recognized for its lively combinations and detailed methods. The Inn at Bay Fortune is close to top-flight golf courses and deep-sea fishing, and less than an hour from Charlottetown, with its active nightlife and some of Canada's best theater.

SEASON

May – October

ACCOMMODATIONS

11 suites with private baths

Spicy butter:
2 tablespoons whipping cream (35%)
¼ cup molasses
¼ teaspoon ground cloves
¼ teaspoon ground allspice
1 teaspoon Tabasco sauce
¼ cup butter

Combine all ingredients and bring to a simmer. Whisk together and drizzle over each bowl of soup.

Polenta

"We serve this especially to guests who have allergies to gluten and other wheat products."
— *Anne-Marie and Irving Bansfield*

3 cups water or milk
¼ teaspoon salt
1 cup cornmeal
1 tablespoon butter
¼ cup grated Parmesan or combination of other grated cheeses
¼ teaspoon ground nutmeg (optional)
Butter

Toppings (optional):
Grated mozzarella cheese
Thinly sliced tomatoes
Cooked bacon or ham pieces

Add salt to water or milk and bring to a boil. Just at the boiling point, add cornmeal in a steady stream, beating without stopping until the polenta is thick and separates from the sides of the pot (about 5 minutes). Remove pot from burner and stir in butter, cheese, and nutmeg. Place polenta in a serving dish, pressing it to the sides and smoothing out the top. Butter the surface and serve. The polenta can also be flattened into a greased casserole or pie plate, topped with cheese, tomato, bacon, or ham pieces, and baked in a preheated 375°F oven for 15 – 20 minutes. *Tip:* Polenta makes a tasty reheated leftover. *Serves 6.*

Le Gîte
Park Avenue B&B

Anne-Marie and Irving Bansfield
54 Park Avenue
Ottawa, Ontario K2P 1B2
Tel: (613) 230-9131
$$

ABOUT THE B&B

A bright, airy ambience and artistic decor awaits you at Park Avenue B&B, an elegant, brick 1906 home located in a charming residential area of downtown Ottawa, Canada's capital. In addition to high-quality beds done up in classic cotton and linen sheets and duvets, each guest room is furnished with desk and swivel chair, rocking chair, bookshelves, excellent lighting, and attractive works of art. Ideal for families, the third-floor suite has two bedrooms and a private bath. The mood throughout the house is one of relaxation and warmth. Park Avenue B&B is close to the Parliament buildings, art galleries and museums, and is only three minutes away (by foot) from the Rideau Canal, which freezes into the world's longest skating rink. Ottawa has a number of exciting festivals and activities, including Winterlude, a winter carnival held each February. Anne-Marie and Irving make it a point to know what's going on when in Ottawa so they can advise their guests on what to see and do.

SEASON

all year

ACCOMMODATIONS

1 suite with private bath;
2 rooms with shared bath

Rhubarb and Apple Compote

"Guests from Japan were curious about what rhubarb looked like after they had been served this compote. Because of communication difficulties, we resorted to bringing a stick of rhubarb from the garden to the dining room table for demonstration purposes. It turns out that the type of rhubarb grown in Japan is used as a vegetable dish." — Judy Hill

1 orange
1 pound fresh or frozen (thawed and drained) rhubarb
1 large apple
¼ cup sugar (plus additional quantity to taste)
Plain yogurt or sour cream
Brown sugar

Grate zest and squeeze juice from orange. Cut rhubarb into 1" lengths. Peel, core, and thinly slice apple. In a saucepan, combine orange peel and juice, rhubarb, apple, and ¼ cup sugar. Cover and bring to a boil. Reduce heat and simmer for 10 minutes or until fruit is soft. Add additional sugar to taste, if desired. Top each serving with yogurt or sour cream and sprinkle with brown sugar. *Tip:* Add a handful of raisins or other dried or fresh fruit you may have on hand. *Serves 8 – 10.*

Smoked Mackerel Pâté

½ pound smoked mackerel, skinned and boned
2 tablespoons lemon juice
8 ounces cream cheese, softened
1 tablespoon butter
2 tablespoons minced onion
½ teaspoon fennel seed
¼ teaspoon black pepper
½ cup finely diced green pepper

Blend mackerel, lemon juice, cream cheese, butter, and spices in a food processor. Remove from processor, then mix in green peppers. Press into a bowl and refrigerate, covered, for at least 3 hours. *Tip:* Smoked herring may be substituted for the smoked mackerel, but be careful to take out all small bones before processing. Great spread on pumpernickel bread, whole-wheat crackers, and French bread. *Makes 2½ cups.*

Bay View Farm / La Ferme Bay View

Helen and Garnett Sawyer
PO Box 21, 337 New Carlisle
West, Route 132
New Carlisle, Québec G0C 1Z0
Tel: (418) 752-2725 / 6718
$

ABOUT THE B&B

Between New Carlisle and Bonaventure, Bay View Farm offers country hospitality in a beautiful seaside environment on the rugged Baie des Chaleurs coastline of Québec's Gaspé Peninsula. Seaside accommodations include five comfortable guest rooms and a fully equipped country house. At breakfast, enjoy Bay View's farm-fresh eggs, meat, homemade muffins, scones, jams, jellies, and beverages, as well as fresh fruits and vegetables in season from the farm's garden and orchards. Additional meals are available on request at reasonable rates. Handicrafts are on display throughout the house. Enjoy the breathtaking panoramic seascapes, participate in the Bay View Folk Festival (second weekend of August) with folk music and dancing, or visit Percé Rock and the archaeological caves of St. Elzéar.

SEASON

May – November

ACCOMMODATIONS

5 rooms with shared baths;
1 private cottage with
private bath

The Blossoms
Bed and Breakfast

Berna and Bert Critchlow
RR #1
Westfield, New Brunswick
E0G 3J0
Tel: (506) 757-2962
$$

ABOUT THE B&B

The beautiful vistas of the St. John River are an integral part of The Blossoms's charm. What's more, this lovely modern home is surrounded by herb and flower gardens and shady wooded walks. The landscaped grounds slope down to the water, where you can launch a canoe or simply watch the ospreys dive and the bald eagles glide by. Three guest rooms are distinctively and comfortably furnished, each with double beds, private baths, and balconies that overlook the gardens and water. Breakfast is served on the deck or in the dining room (both of which overlook the river), and offers a choice of fresh fruit, home-baked muffins and breads, or a cooked meal if preferred. The spacious living room offers an extensive and eclectic library and music collection. Hostess Berna gives herbal and wreath-making workshops in the on-site craft store. Area attractions include canoeing, hiking, birdwatching, golfing, tennis, and swimming. St. John — with its theater, antique and craft shops, art galleries, historic walks, and excellent museum — is a short drive away.

SEASON

April – November

ACCOMMODATIONS

3 rooms with private baths

Spring Compote

"A hit for breakfast, lunch, or dinner." — Berna Critchlow

4 navel oranges, peeled and cut into bite-sized pieces
1 cup fresh hulled strawberries or pitted cherries
½ cup fruity wine (optional)
1 tablespoon freshly grated ginger
3 tablespoons chopped fresh cilantro (also known as coriander)
  or 2 tablespoons chopped fresh mint

Mix lightly and serve chilled. *Serves 4 – 6.*

Vegetable Custard

(Recipe from Joan Peggs Eggs, *written and published by Joan Peggs, 1996)*

4 slices onion, chopped
¼ cup chopped vegetables, such as cauliflower (combine with a
    colorful vegetable for appearance), spinach, Swiss chard,
    zucchini, green/red pepper, broccoli
¾ cup milk
3 eggs
½ teaspoon paprika
Grated cheese or seasoned bread crumbs
Chopped fresh parsley

Buttered toast wedges

Preheat oven to 350°F. Lightly grease 4 custard dishes. Place
onion and vegetable in a microwave-safe dish. Heat 1 minute on
medium-high. Place vegetable mixture in the base of prepared
custard dishes. Microwave milk until scalded. Mix together
egg and paprika. Add scalded milk to egg mixture, stirring
constantly. Pour milk-egg mixture over vegetables. Sprinkle
with grated cheese or seasoned bread crumbs. Place custard
cups in a pan of water (1" deep) and bake 15 – 20 minutes, until
a knife inserted into custard's center comes out clean. Garnish
with parsley. Serve on buttered toast wedges. **Serves 4.**

The Inn on St. Andrews

Joan Peggs
231 St. Andrews Street
Victoria, British Columbia
V8V 2N1
Tel: (800) 668-5993 or
(604) 384-8613
Fax: (604) 384-6063
E-mail: joan.peggs@vonline.com
$$

ABOUT THE B&B

The Inn on St. Andrews is as
lovely today as when it was
built in 1913 by Edith Carr,
eldest sister of the famous Canadian
artist and author, Emily Carr. This
Tudor-style heritage property charms
with its elegant woodwork, stained
and beveled glass, and large bright
bedrooms. After a wholesome break-
fast in the formal dining room, you
can congregate in the sunroom over-
looking the east garden or sun deck
overlooking the west garden, in the
cozy TV room, or in the larger draw-
ing room. The inn is ideally located
in James Bay, close to Victoria's
inner harbor with ferry and seaplane
terminals, the Parliament buildings,
the Royal British Columbia Museum,
famed Empress Hotel, and downtown
shops. A short walk brings you to
Beacon Hill Park and the oceanfront.
Your host Joan Peggs believes in
modern comfort and old-fashioned
hospitality, and provides guests
with her own map highlighting walk-
ing and driving destinations and
recommended restaurants.

SEASON

all year

ACCOMMODATIONS

1 room with private bath;
2 rooms with shared bath

French Toast, Pancakes, & Waffles

Apple-Cinnamon Molasses Pancakes

"Molasses has been used locally as a sweetener since the days of trade with the West Indies. It adds a unique flavor to these pancakes." — Carol Buckley

¾ cup all-purpose flour
¾ cup whole-wheat flour
3 teaspoons baking powder
½ teaspoon baking soda
½ teaspoon salt
½ teaspoon ground cinnamon
2 large apples, cored and peeled
¼ cup molasses
1 egg
1¼ cups sweet or sour milk

Hot applesauce and maple syrup

Mix dry ingredients. Grate apples into dry mixture (watch your fingers!). In a separate bowl, combine wet ingredients and beat. Add wet ingredients to dry mixture just until smooth (don't overmix). Cook approximately ¼ cup batter per pancake on a hot griddle. Serve with hot applesauce and maple syrup. *Makes 10 medium pancakes.*

The Old Rectory Bed & Breakfast

Carol and Ron Buckley
1519 Highway 358, RR #1
Port Williams, Nova Scotia
B0P 1T0
Tel: (902) 542-1815
Fax: (902) 542-2346
e-mail: orectory@fox.nstn.ca
www.bbcanada.com/568.html
$$

ABOUT THE B&B

*S*hare the warmth of this restored former Victorian rectory with its antiques, unique architecture, and three-acre operating apple orchard and gardens. Choose from one of three spacious bedrooms, one with private half-bath, and the others with shared full bath. Access to an additional bath is on the main floor. Your hosts are Ron, a retired geologist with knowledge of local "rock hounding" areas, and physiotherapist, Carol, who enjoys preparing delicious hot breakfasts with homemade breads and preserves. Visit over evening tea or come for a two-day orchard stay in the fall with apple picking and cider making. The Old Rectory is close to historic Prescott House, Grand Pré Park, hiking trails, birdwatching areas, cultural activities, and many fine restaurants.

SEASON

May 1 – October 31

ACCOMMODATIONS

1 room with private half-bath;
2 rooms with shared bath

Sanford House Bed & Breakfast

Elizabeth and Charlie Le Ber
PO Box 1825, 20 Platt Street
Brighton, Ontario K0K 1H0
Tel/Fax: (613) 475-3930
$$

ABOUT THE B&B

S itting majestically on the crest of a hill, Sanford House Bed & Breakfast is a red-brick Victorian home close to Main Street in the friendly town of Brighton. This century-old home with turret and covered veranda has offstreet parking, a separate guest entrance, and three large, bright, and comfortable bedrooms. Guests can choose to relax in the round turret room; in the lounge with television, VCR, videos, board games, and books; in the spacious, bright Victorian parlor; or on the veranda. Delicious home-baked breakfasts, often spotlighting apples grown in nearby orchards, are served in the guest dining room. It's a short drive to beautiful Presqu'ile Provincial Park's sandy beaches, nature trails, fine birdwatching area, and marsh boardwalk. If antique hunting is a passion, there are numerous antique establishments right in Brighton and the surrounding area. Apple-fest, a celebration of the harvest in September, is a particularly lovely time to visit the area. When not entertaining their B&B guests, Elizabeth and Charlie enjoy cycling and birdwatching.

SEASON

all year

ACCOMMODATIONS

3 rooms with shared bath

Baked French Toast à l'Orange

6 slices bread, each 1" thick and crusts removed
2 cups milk
8 eggs
2 tablespoons orange juice concentrate

Orange marmalade sauce:
¼ cup butter
½ cup orange marmalade

Cooked sliced bacon

Cut each bread slice in half diagonally. Allow bread to dry out for a few hours by standing up triangles on their edges, on a plate. Place flat in a shallow glass 13 x 9" dish. Combine milk, eggs, and orange juice concentrate until smooth. Pour over bread. Turn bread triangles over once. Cover and refrigerate until liquid is absorbed (or overnight). Preheat oven to 350°F. Butter another 13 x 9" baking dish and place triangles flat inside. Bake 35 minutes. Combine and heat orange sauce ingredients in a saucepan or in the microwave until hot. Stir well to blend. Pour over baked French toast and serve immediately with a side helping of cooked sliced bacon. *Serves 4 – 6.*

Banana-Oatmeal Waffles

1 cup large flake rolled oats
1 cup all-purpose flour
1 tablespoon baking powder
½ teaspoon baking soda
½ teaspoon ground cinnamon
Pinch of freshly grated nutmeg
3 tablespoons brown sugar
1½ cups buttermilk
2 eggs
2 bananas, sliced
¼ cup melted unsalted butter
Sliced bananas
Warm maple syrup
Sour cream (optional)
Confectioners' sugar

Preheat waffle iron. Combine dry ingredients in a large bowl. Combine buttermilk and eggs in a separate bowl; whisk. Stir wet ingredients into dry and combine (don't overmix). Stir in bananas and melted butter. Bake waffles according to manufacturer's directions. Transfer to serving plates and top with sliced bananas, warm maple syrup, and a dollop of sour cream if wished. Dust with confectioners' sugar. *Makes 8 waffles.*

Mecklenburgh Inn

Suzi Fraser
78 Queen Street
Chester, Nova Scotia B0J 1J0
Tel/Fax: (902) 275-4638
www.destination-ns.com/
lighthouse/mecklenburgh
$$

ABOUT THE B&B

Constructed by shipwrights at the turn of the century, Mecklenburgh Inn is a historic 1890 bed and breakfast located in the heart of seaside Chester, which has catered to summer visitors and sailing enthusiasts for over 150 years. Sleep in the spacious and comfortably appointed bedrooms filled with period furniture and other interesting objects Suzi has collected over the years, then enjoy a delicious breakfast while you plan the day ahead. You might wander the historic village streets, stopping to watch the yacht races on Mahone Bay, or browse through craft shops and boutiques. Or, maybe a sailboat ride, bicycle ride, or game of golf or tennis would be more your style. Later, relax on the balcony while the sun settles over the western shore and village activity lulls. You might consider an evening meal at one of the excellent restaurants in the area or catch a play at the Chester Playhouse. Before drifting off to sleep, you can wind down in the living room chatting by the fire or perusing travel books and magazines.

SEASON

May 24 – November 7

ACCOMMODATIONS

4 rooms with shared baths

Les Trois Érables

Madeleine and Jacques Mercier
PO Box 852, RR #2
Wakefield, Québec J0X 3G0
Tel: (819) 459-1118
$$

ABOUT THE B&B

Nestled among gentle rolling hills on the banks of the Gatineau River, the historic village of Wakefield is a gateway to beautiful Gatineau Park where you can find ample opportunities for hiking, skiing, or less arduous nature walks — especially beautiful in fall foliage season. Less than a half hour's drive takes you to the heart of Canada's national capital, Ottawa. Les Trois Érables was built at the turn of the century and was the home and office of three generations of village doctors until its B&B transformation in 1988. Rooms are tastefully decorated in soft colors and furnished for comfort and convenience. The sumptuous breakfasts attest to the fact that Madeleine loves to cook. Local restaurants, sports outfitters, and boutiques abound.

SEASON

all year

ACCOMMODATIONS

4 rooms with private baths

Blueberry-stuffed French Toast

12 slices home-style white bread, crusts removed and cut into 1" cubes
2 8-ounce packages cold cream cheese, cut into 1" cubes
1 cup fresh blueberries
1 dozen large eggs
⅓ cup maple syrup
2 cups milk

Sauce:
1 cup sugar
2 tablespoons cornstarch
1 cup water
1 cup fresh blueberries
1 tablespoon butter

Arrange half the bread cubes in a buttered 13 x 9" glass baking dish. Scatter the cream cheese over the bread and sprinkle the blueberries over the cream cheese. Arrange the remaining bread cubes over the blueberries. In a large bowl, whisk together the eggs, syrup, and milk and pour evenly over the bread mixture. Cover dish with tin foil and refrigerate overnight. In the morning, remove from refrigerator ¾ hour before baking.

(continued on next page)

Preheat oven to 350°F and bake, covered, for 30 minutes. Remove foil and bake 30 minutes more or until French toast is puffed and golden.

To prepare sauce: In a small saucepan, stir together sugar, cornstarch, and water. Cook over moderately high heat, stirring occasionally, for 5 minutes or until mixture has thickened. Stir in the blueberries and simmer, stirring occasionally, for 10 minutes or until berries have burst. Add the butter and stir the sauce until butter has melted. Serve hot over the blueberry-stuffed French toast. *Serves 6 – 8.*

The Green Door
Bed & Breakfast

Doloris Paquin
PO Box 335, 376 Berford Street
Wiarton, Ontario N0H 2T0
Tel: (519) 534-4710
$ – $$

ABOUT THE B&B

"*Completely comfortable, wonderfully welcoming,*" *is how one recent guest described The Green Door. Built at the turn of the century, this red-brick, stately restored Victorian house is situated on Wiarton's main street and is within a few minutes' walk of shops and restaurants. The main floor has a charming and spacious living room with bay windows and dining room for guests' comfort and pleasure. Up the wooden staircase are three guest bedrooms, two with double beds and one with two single beds, as well as a large guest bathroom. The high ceilings and spacious rooms lend an airy feeling with all the comforts and coziness of home. Outside, enjoy the large garden, maple-shaded deck, and barbecue facilities.*

SEASON

all year

ACCOMMODATIONS

1 room with private bath;
2 rooms with shared bath

Bruce Trail Breakfast Pancakes

"These pancakes are named for the celebrated hiking trail on the Bruce Peninsula, just a short distance away."
— Doloris Paquin

½ cup quick-cooking rolled oats
1¾ cups milk
1 cup all-purpose flour
¾ cup whole-wheat flour
2 tablespoons sugar
1 tablespoon baking powder
½ teaspoon salt
½ teaspoon ground cinnamon
2 eggs
2 tablespoons vegetable oil
2 teaspoons vanilla

Combine oats and milk, and let stand 5 minutes. Mix flours, sugar, baking powder, salt, and cinnamon in a large bowl. Beat eggs, oil, and vanilla into oat mixture with a whisk just until blended. Stir liquid mixture into flour mixture just until moistened (don't worry about lumps). Lightly grease a skillet and place on medium heat. Cook, using about ⅓ cup batter for each pancake, until bubbles form on surface. Turn and brown on the other side. *Makes 8 medium-sized pancakes.*

Canadian Alphabet Pancakes

¾ cup yogurt
¾ cup milk
2 eggs, beaten
¼ cup melted butter
1½ cups all-purpose flour
¼ teaspoon each baking powder, baking soda, and salt

Maple butter (whip together ¼ pound softened butter and
    ½ cup maple syrup)

Combine first 4 ingredients. Fold blended dry ingredients into
liquid mixture (don't overmix). Pour batter onto a greased
griddle from a narrow pouring spout or squeeze bottle, forming
large letters from the alphabet. Cook 2 minutes or until bubbles
appear and underside is golden brown. Turn and cook other
side. Serve with maple butter. *Serves 3 – 4 children (or adults!).*

Peters Place

Joan and Calvin Peters
6430 PR 241 North
Cartier, Manitoba R4K 1B4
Tel: (204) 864-2106
$

ABOUT THE B&B

Experience rural Canada and the people who live there at Peters Place — a 500-acre, family-operated grain farm. Offering peace and quiet along the Assiniboine River, Peters Place is ideal for B&B travelers who want the best of both worlds — country relaxation with close proximity to the urban sights of Winnipeg. It's also a good base from which to tour points of historic interest, such as Lower Fort Garry at Selkirk or the museum at Portage la Prairie. Excellent golf facilities are within a 10-minute drive. For those who enjoy natural parkland, Beaudry Park is open year-round for hikers or cross-country skiers. If time and weather permit, your hosts will take you to watch the beaver on the Assiniboine at dusk, give you a ride in their old Model T or on one of their restored farm tractors, and take you inside their Canadian National Railway caboose. Bountiful breakfasts are served in the family dining area and every effort is made to accommodate special preferences or diets.

SEASON

April – October

ACCOMMODATIONS

2 rooms with shared bath

Caron House (1837)

Mary and Mike Caron
PO Box 143
Williamstown, Ontario K0C 2J0
Tel: (613) 347-7338
$$

ABOUT THE B&B

Caron House (1837) is a historic, romantic brick home located in the quaint village of Williamstown (established in 1784). Beautifully decorated and furnished with antiques, the house is in its original state, with working fireplaces, inside shutters, tin ceilings, and wide pine floorboards. Two rooms with shared bath are individually decorated with Laura Ashley wallpaper, antique linens, hooked rugs, quilts, and collectibles. Guests can relax in the Keeping Room (a Colonial term for gathering place) or living room, while a full, candlelit gourmet breakfast — accompanied by classical music — is served in the dining room on fine china, silverware, and crystal. Outside, you'll marvel at the herb and Victorian gardens, and relax on the antique wicker furniture on the back veranda, enjoying the lovely yards, complete with trellis, brick patio, and gazebo. Caron House is one hour's drive from either Montréal or Ottawa; nearby attractions include Upper Canada Village, artisan studios, a bird sanctuary, tennis, cycling, and good restaurants. Mary and Mike are retirees from the corporate world, and enjoy traveling, antique hunting, cooking, gardening, and history.

SEASON

all year

ACCOMMODATIONS

2 rooms with shared bath

Cherry Breakfast Puff Pancakes

Butter
1 egg
⅓ cup all-purpose flour
⅓ cup milk
Sprinkle of ground nutmeg
Heated cherry pie filling
Confectioners' sugar

Warmed maple syrup

Preheat oven to 400°F. Place a pat of butter in each of 2 5½ x 3½" casserole dishes and put dishes in oven until butter is melted. Combine egg, flour, milk, and nutmeg, and mix slightly. Pour equal amounts of batter into each dish and return to the oven for about 15 – 20 minutes, until puffed and golden. Pour heated cherry pie filling (or filling of your choice) into the center of each puff and top with confectioners' sugar. Serve with warmed maple syrup, if desired. *Makes 2 puff pancakes.*

Chicken Crêpes with Avocado

8 crêpes (see recipe on page 221)
5 tablespoons butter or margarine
5 tablespoons all-purpose flour
1 cup milk
¾ cup chicken broth
¼ cup dry white wine
½ cup grated mozzarella cheese
½ teaspoon Worcestershire sauce
1 teaspoon salt
¼ teaspoon pepper
3 tablespoons chopped fresh parsley
1½ cups cooked diced chicken
¼ cup sliced black olives
8 – 12 avocado slices
Grated mozzarella cheese
Paprika

Preheat oven to 350°F. Prepare crêpes. Melt butter or margarine in a saucepan and stir in flour. Add milk, broth, and wine. Cook, stirring constantly, until mixture is thickened and smooth. Add cheese and stir until melted. Add Worcestershire sauce, salt, pepper, and parsley. Add 1 cup of this sauce to combined chicken and olives. Divide mixture evenly amongst crêpes and roll up. Place seam-side down in a single layer in a greased shallow baking dish. Bake, uncovered, for 15 – 20 minutes or until very hot and lightly browned on top. Before serving, top each crêpe with an avocado slice and pour remaining hot sauce over crêpes. Sprinkle with mozzarella cheese and dust with paprika. If you wish, you can add extra slices of avocado on the plate. *Serves 4.*

Caron House (1837)

Mary and Mike Caron
PO Box 143
Williamstown, Ontario K0C 2J0
Tel: (613) 347-7338
$$

ABOUT THE B&B

Caron House (1837) is a historic, romantic brick home located in the quaint village of Williamstown (established in 1784). Beautifully decorated and furnished with antiques, the house is in its original state, with working fireplaces, inside shutters, tin ceilings, and wide pine floorboards. Two rooms with shared bath are individually decorated with Laura Ashley wallpaper, antique linens, hooked rugs, quilts, and collectibles. Guests can relax in the Keeping Room (a Colonial term for gathering place) or living room, while a full, candlelit gourmet breakfast — accompanied by classical music — is served in the dining room on fine china, silverware, and crystal. Outside, you'll marvel at the herb and Victorian gardens, and relax on the antique wicker furniture on the back veranda, enjoying the lovely yards, complete with trellis, brick patio, and gazebo. Caron House is one hour's drive from either Montréal or Ottawa; nearby attractions include Upper Canada Village, artisan studios, a bird sanctuary, tennis, cycling, and good restaurants. Mary and Mike are retirees from the corporate world, and enjoy traveling, antique hunting, cooking, gardening, and history.

SEASON

all year

ACCOMMODATIONS

2 rooms with shared bath

Norwood
Bed & Breakfast

Pat and Roland Jensen
201 Norwood Court
Wetaskiwin, Alberta T9A 3P2
Tel: (888)/(403) 352-7880
Fax: (403) 352-8850
$$

ABOUT THE B&B

Seventeen-year residents of Wetaskiwin, Pat and Roland Jensen offer old-fashioned B&B hospitality in their new home full of country charm. An old-style double bed and antiques grace one guest room, while Victorian decor illuminates the queen-bedded room. Guests share a full bathroom, Jacuzzi, and a sitting room with white baby grand piano, games, books, and CD stereo system. Served in the formal dining room or on the sunny patio, a typical full breakfast consists of fruit salad, home-baked muffins and breads, homemade jams, a cooked entrée, and beverages. A smoking area is available outside on the deck. Norwood welcomes children but not pets as there's a resident 15-pound cat named Little Guy (who doesn't visit the guest rooms). After a day exploring such museums as Canada's Aviation Hall of Fame and the Alberta Central Railway Museum, shopping at antique, ladieswear, and gift shops, or playing a few rounds of golf, guests can refresh themselves with a soak in the outdoor hot tub. Norwood B&B is only a 45-minute drive from Alberta's capital, Edmonton.

SEASON

all year

ACCOMMODATIONS

2 rooms with shared bath

Crumb-topped French Toast

2 eggs, well beaten
½ cup milk
½ teaspoon salt
½ teaspoon vanilla
6 thick bread slices
1 cup cornflake crumbs
¼ cup melted butter

Cinnamon syrup:
1⅓ cups sugar
⅓ cup water
⅔ cup white corn syrup
1 teaspoon ground cinnamon
5 ounces evaporated milk
½ teaspoon almond extract
1 tablespoon butter

Side of cooked bacon or pork breakfast sausage

Preheat oven to 450°F. Combine eggs, milk, salt, and vanilla, and mix well. Dip bread into egg mixture, then coat both sides with crumbs. Place on a well-greased pan. Drizzle melted butter over bread. Bake 10 minutes. Meanwhile, prepare syrup by combining sugar, water, corn syrup, and cinnamon in a saucepan. Bring to a boil and cook 2 minutes. Remove from heat, then add milk, almond extract, and butter. Serve syrup warm with French toast and a side helping of cooked bacon or sausage. *Serves 4.*

Dutch Cinnamon-Apple Pancake

"This spectacular-looking dish puffs up high around the edges to the delight of hungry guests." — Marj Wilkie

¼ cup butter
⅓ cup brown sugar
2 teaspoons ground cinnamon
1 Granny Smith or Golden Delicious apple, peeled, cored, and thinly sliced
4 eggs
¾ cup milk
¾ cup all-purpose flour
Dash of salt
Confectioners' sugar

Maple syrup, orange-ginger sauce (see recipe on page 303), jam, or topping of your choice

Preheat oven to 425°F. Put butter, brown sugar, and cinnamon into a 10" oven-proof skillet and heat in oven about 6 minutes until very hot and bubbly (don't burn). Add apple slices. Return to oven for 3 minutes. Meanwhile, beat together eggs, milk, flour, and salt. Slowly pour over apple-sugar mixture, distributing batter evenly. Return to oven for 25 minutes or until browned and puffed high at sides. Cut into 6 and sprinkle with confectioners' sugar. Serve with maple syrup, orange-ginger sauce, jam, or topping of your choice. *Tip:* This dish is even more impressive when ingredients are divided into 6 individual oval ramekins. *Serves 6.*

The Lookout at Schooner Cove

The Lookout at Schooner Cove

Marj and Herb Wilkie
3381 Dolphin Drive
Nanoose Bay, British Columbia
V0R 2R0
Tel/Fax: (604) 468-9796
$$

ABOUT THE B&B

Situated halfway between Victoria and Tofino on unspoiled Vancouver Island, this West Coast contemporary cedar home stands in a woodsy setting of rocks and tall evergreens. The wrap-around deck affords a 180° view of Georgia Strait and the majestic mountains beyond. Relax and savor this "little bit of heaven" or hike, golf, kayak, sail, fish, or sightsee. Take a day trip to the wild western shore of the island and the Pacific Rim National Park or to charming Victoria. The vacation suite will accommodate four people and, with its fully equipped kitchen, makes a popular headquarters for an island stay. Hearty breakfasts are served within full view of the ocean activities. The Wilkies ran a store in New York's Catskill mountains for 15 years before discovering this paradise. They enjoy hiking, golf, crafts, reading, games, puzzles, and especially meeting their guests and helping them plan a memorable stay.

SEASON

May – October
(or by arrangement)

ACCOMMODATIONS

1 vacation suite with
private bath;
1 room with private bath;
1 room with shared bath

Norwood
Bed & Breakfast

Pat and Roland Jensen
201 Norwood Court
Wetaskiwin, Alberta T9A 3P2
Tel: (888)/(403) 352-7880
Fax: (403) 352-8850
$$

ABOUT THE B&B

*S*eventeen-year residents of Wetaskiwin, Pat and Roland Jensen offer old-fashioned B&B hospitality in their new home full of country charm. An old-style double bed and antiques grace one guest room, while Victorian decor illuminates the queen-bedded room. Guests share a full bathroom, Jacuzzi, and a sitting room with white baby grand piano, games, books, and CD stereo system. Served in the formal dining room or on the sunny patio, a typical full breakfast consists of fruit salad, home-baked muffins and breads, homemade jams, a cooked entrée, and beverages. A smoking area is available outside on the deck. Norwood welcomes children but not pets as there's a resident 15-pound cat named Little Guy (who doesn't visit the guest rooms). After a day exploring such museums as Canada's Aviation Hall of Fame and the Alberta Central Railway Museum, shopping at antique, ladieswear, and gift shops, or playing a few rounds of golf, guests can refresh themselves with a soak in the outdoor hot tub. Norwood B&B is only a 45-minute drive from Alberta's capital, Edmonton.

SEASON

all year

ACCOMMODATIONS

2 rooms with shared bath

Eggnog French Toast

24-ounce bread loaf, cut into 1" slices
6 large eggs
2¼ cups milk
¼ cup sugar
1 teaspoon rum extract
¼ teaspoon ground nutmeg
Confectioners' sugar

Maple syrup

Preheat oven to 500°F. Place bread slices in a large pan. In a large bowl, fork-beat eggs, milk, sugar, rum extract, and nutmeg until blended. Pour mixture over bread in pan. With a fork, prick bread slices and turn to coat both sides of bread until all the egg mixture is absorbed. Place bread on a large, greased cookie sheet and bake 8 – 10 minutes on each side. Arrange French toast on a warm platter, sprinkle with confectioners' sugar, and serve with maple syrup. *Serves 8.*

French Toast Raphael

6 cups white bread cubes (1 x 1") with crusts removed
6 ounces cream cheese, cut into small cubes
6 eggs, well beaten
1 cup milk
½ teaspoon ground cinnamon
⅓ cup dark maple syrup

Cooked bacon or pork breakfast sausage

Place half of bread cubes in a greased 8 x 8" pan. Dot with cream cheese and cover with remaining bread. Combine remaining ingredients and pour over all. Cover with plastic wrap and refrigerate overnight. In the morning, remove dish from refrigerator about ¾ hour before baking. Preheat oven to 375°F and bake 45 minutes until puffy and golden. Serve immediately with cooked bacon or sausage. *Serves 4.*

Dorrington
Bed & Breakfast

Pat and Helen Gray
13851 19A Avenue
White Rock, British Columbia
V4A 9M2
Tel: (604) 535-4408
Fax: (604) 535-4409
www.bbcanada.com/508.html
$$ – $$$

ABOUT THE B&B

A luxurious and restful escape, Dorrington is a wonderful base for exploring the beauty of Vancouver and its surrounding area. Each of Dorrington's three rooms is themed and has a private bath: The Victorian is graced by a double four-poster bed and period decor; the St. Andrews has a unique queen bed hewn from maple branches and contains many original souvenirs of this famous Scottish golf links; The Windsor is 700 square feet of luxury with a brass, canopied queen bed, fireplace, sitting area, and marble bathroom with a double Jacuzzi tub. Full breakfast is served in the Hunt Salon or on the patio overlooking the gardens, tennis court, pond, and outside hot tub. A short drive from downtown Vancouver, White Rock beach with its promenade and many fine restaurants is three minutes away, while ferries to Victoria and the Gulf Islands are 30 minutes away. If you wish, you can use Dorrington's side-by-side tandem bike for a picnic in one of the many nearby heritage forests. Pat is a marketing consultant and Helen works for a nearby supermarket (but her true love is decorating and it shows at Dorrington!).

SEASON

all year

ACCOMMODATIONS

3 rooms (including 1 suite)
with private baths

Barbara Ann's Bed 'n Breakfast Vacation Farm

Barbara Ann and Ted Witzaney
PO Box 156
Denzil, Saskatchewan S0L 0S0
Tel: (306) 358-4814
$

ABOUT THE B&B

Specially geared for families, Barbara Ann's B&B is located on the Witzaney farm, where they've been raising crops and hogs since 1911. The petting zoo includes traditional farm animals and more exotic ones, including a llama and Muscovy ducks. Barbara Ann's breakfast and other meals served on request feature farm-fresh milk, eggs, cheese, and vegetables; home-baked goods, such as buns, pies, and cookies; homemade jams, jellies, relishes, and pickles; and the farm's home-raised pork, which includes the specialty of the house — homemade sausages. Picnic and barbecue facilities, sandbox and swing set, horseshoe pit, lawn bowling, badminton, and an 18-hole miniature golf course are all on the property. When not tending to guests, Barbara Ann enjoys sewing and craft making, while Ted enjoys woodworking. Both like to spend time with their 10 grandchildren. Denzil is about a half-hour drive west of Unity, Saskatchewan, and a 45-minute drive east of Provost, Alberta.

SEASON

all year

ACCOMMODATIONS

2 rooms with shared bath

French Toast with Apricot Sauce

"If we have fresh cow's cream on hand, I like to serve it along with this dish." — Barbara Ann Witzaney

8 slices white bread, each cut in half
½ cup milk
2 eggs
4 tablespoons sugar
¼ teaspoon vanilla
8-ounce can apricots in syrup
Juice of ½ lemon
2 – 4 tablespoons butter or margarine

Whisk the milk and eggs, then stir in sugar and vanilla; set aside. Make a purée from the apricots and their syrup in a blender or food processor. Stir in lemon juice and heat the purée over moderate heat; keep warm. Dip the bread in the egg mixture and fry both sides in butter until golden brown. Arrange bread slices on warmed plates and pour apricot sauce over them. Serve immediately. *Serves 4.*

French Toast with Honey-Yogurt Sauce

Honey-yogurt sauce:
¼ cup low-fat plain yogurt
1 teaspoon honey

1 egg
⅓ cup skim milk
½ teaspoon orange zest
¼ teaspoon vanilla
Pinch of salt
4 slices white or whole-wheat bread
½ teaspoon margarine
Ground nutmeg

In a small bowl, combine yogurt and honey; set aside. In a shallow bowl, beat together egg, milk, orange zest, vanilla, and salt. Dip each bread slice into egg mixture, coating each side well. In a large non-stick skillet, melt margarine over medium heat; cook bread for 2 minutes per side or until golden brown. Sprinkle with nutmeg. Serve with honey-yogurt sauce. *Serves 2.*

Gwenmar Guest Home

Joy and Keith Smith
PO Box 59, RR #3
Brandon, Manitoba R7A 5Y3
Tel: (204) 728-7339
Fax: (204) 728-7336
E-mail: smithj@docker.com
$

ABOUT THE B&B

Space, privacy, and quiet is what you'll find at Gwenmar. This 1914 heritage home was the summer retreat of Manitoba's former Lt. Governor (from 1929 to 1934), J.D. McGregor, who named the estate after his daughter Gwen. Since 1980, Joy and Keith Smith have welcomed B&B guests to this relaxing countryside escape. Gwenmar breakfasts are memorable, particularly the home-baked bread and jams and jellies made from Gwenmar's wild berries. Joy, a home economist, is an avid gardener and a major contributor to Canada's heritage seed program, while Keith is a retired agrologist involved in overseas projects. In the summer, you can visit with them on the big, shaded veranda or go for secluded walks on the beautiful grounds or in the valley. In the winter, sit by the fire or go cross-country skiing. Gwenmar is also a short drive from downtown Brandon, with shopping, restaurants, water-slide, air museum, golf courses, and the childhood home of Stone Angel author Margaret Laurence.

SEASON

all year

ACCOMMODATIONS

2 rooms with private baths;
2 rooms with shared bath

Seaboard
Bed & Breakfast

Sheila and Barrie Jackson
2629 Crowell Road, RR #2
Porter's Lake, Nova Scotia
B0J 2S0
Tel: (800) SEA-6566 or
(902) 827-3747
$ – $$

ABOUT THE B&B

Seaboard Bed & Breakfast at Lawrencetown Beach is a renovated farmhouse built around 1912. Now the home of Sheila and Barrie Jackson, this large white house across the road from Porter's Lake and the Atlantic Ocean has been an area landmark for many years. Local attractions include international caliber surfing from a sand beach; birdwatching from the shore, local marsh, walking trails, and hills; plus fishing, canoeing, windsurfing, and — in season — skating and cross-country skiing. Seaboard is only 35 minutes from Halifax airport and 30 minutes from the cities of Halifax and Dartmouth, where you can enjoy the casino, restaurants, theaters, and special events. Sheila and Barrie are both keen Scottish country dancers and have aptly named their guest rooms after favorite dances. There are two semi-private bathrooms for the exclusive use of guests. A varied and full home-cooked breakfast is served in the sunny dining room overlooking lake and sea, while tea and coffee are offered in the lounge or on the porch.

SEASON

all year

ACCOMMODATIONS

3 rooms with shared baths

Fried Porridge Pancakes

"We always hope for leftovers when these are served. They go very well as a snack with mid-morning coffee."
— *Sheila Jackson*

2¼ cups quick-cooking rolled oats
3 cups milk
⅓ cup butter
3 large eggs
1½ tablespoons brown sugar
1 teaspoon salt
1½ cups whole-wheat flour
1½ tablespoons baking powder
1½ teaspoons ground cinnamon
¼ cup wheat germ

Yogurt and fruit, maple syrup, or jam

Soak oats in milk for 10 – 15 minutes; set aside. Melt butter; set aside. Beat eggs, and add sugar, salt, and melted butter; set aside. Sift flour, baking powder, and cinnamon together, then add wheat germ. Stir oat mixture and flour mixture into egg mixture. Let stand 5 – 10 minutes. Adjust consistency with a little milk, if wished. Ladle batter onto a hot, lightly greased griddle and cook, turning once when bubbles appear and underside is golden. Keep warm in oven, covered with a clean cloth. Serve hot with yogurt and fruit or maple syrup, or cold with jam. *Makes 4 large or 8 small pancakes.*

Fruit Pancakes

"A generous helping of Canadian bacon and any garnish you like will make this one of your favorites." — Isabel Christie

1 tablespoon butter
1 cup sugar
2 eggs, well beaten
2 cups all-purpose flour
2 teaspoons baking powder
Pinch of salt
½ – ¾ cup milk
1 teaspoon vanilla
Fresh fruit in season

Hot topping of applesauce or apple juice thickened with cornstarch, and sprinkled cinnamon

Cream butter and sugar. Add eggs. Add dry ingredients to creamed mixture alternately with milk (to help keep pancakes thin). Add vanilla and mix briefly. Fry on a hot griddle or in a crêpe pan (use about ¼ cup per pancake). Top pancakes or fill crêpes with any fruit in season (strawberries or blueberries work best in summer, while apples work best in winter). Serve with a hot topping of applesauce or apple juice thickened with cornstarch, and sprinkled cinnamon. *Makes 1 dozen pancakes.*

Riverdell Estate

Clare and Isabel Christie
68 Ross Road
Dartmouth, Nova Scotia
B2Z 1B4
Tel/Fax: (902) 434-7880
$$ – $$$

ABOUT THE B&B

Nestled among the trees beside a babbling brook, Riverdell offers modern luxury with good, old-fashioned hospitality. Antiques, collectibles, and handmade quilts adorn this charming Cape Cod home. Large, clean rooms with private or shared baths include two "special occasion" suites — both with double whirlpool and one with fireplace. There's lots of space to read, relax, or birdwatch from the sunny Florida Room where your home-made breakfast is served. All this is within minutes of the ocean beach, golf course, and Dartmouth and Halifax — two cities full of adventure. Whatever your leisure interests may be, your knowledge-able hosts Clare and Isabel will ensure you get the most out of your stay.

SEASON

all year

ACCOMMODATIONS

4 rooms with private baths;
2 rooms with shared baths

Cobble House
Bed & Breakfast

Ingrid and Simon Vermegen
3105 Cameron-Taggart Road
RR #1
Cobble Hill, British Columbia
V0R 1L0
Tel/Fax: (250) 743-2672
$$

ABOUT THE B&B

Cobble House B&B is located on southeastern Vancouver Island in beautiful British Columbia, in a rural area with wineries and many recreational opportunities. Victoria and the world-famous Butchart Gardens are about an hour away, as is ferry access from Washington State and mainland British Columbia. The new home, which was designed and built by the hosts, is nestled on its own private 40-acre forest with a creek. Guests are invited to make themselves at home in a warm, welcoming, and relaxing environment. The very spacious and colorful Hummingbird, Jay, and Heron rooms are decorated with wicker and antiques. Your host Simon is a former executive chef and prepares a delicious breakfast, always with guests' preferences in mind. The host family, which includes two beloved dogs, has lots of hobbies and interests — antique car restoration, miniature train collecting, reading, crafts, decorative painting, antique collecting — but never enough time to enjoy them all!

SEASON

all year

ACCOMMODATIONS

3 rooms with private baths

Grilled Sabayon Fruit Crêpes

"Our main goal is to serve a well-prepared, delicious breakfast geared to our guests' preferences."
— Simon Vermegen

Crêpes:
1 cup milk
1 egg
3½ ounces all-purpose flour
Pinch of salt
Vegetable oil

Mix first 4 ingredients well, making sure no lumps remain. Heat a small, preferably Teflon-coated frying pan on the stove. Put a little vegetable oil in pan and one-quarter of the batter. Bake until golden brown. Repeat with rest of batter. *Makes 4 crêpes.*

Fruit filling:
½ cup orange juice
2 medium apples, peeled, cored, and cubed
2 oranges, peeled and chopped
Zest of 1 lemon
2 teaspoons cornstarch
2 ounces fresh or frozen (thawed and drained) blueberries
20 raspberries for decoration

(continued on next page)

Place orange juice, apple, orange, and lemon zest in a saucepan on the stove. Bring to a quick boil. Thicken with cornstarch, turn heat down to low, and add blueberries. Keep warm. Turn broiler on and set at 375°F. Place rack at the highest level in the oven.

Maple syrup sabayon:
¼ cup maple syrup
3 eggs
2 teaspoons brandy

Put all ingredients in a stainless steel bowl. Place a pan with water on the stove, bring to a boil, then turn heat to low. Place bowl on top and start beating mixture with a whip until it is foamy and firm.

To serve, place 1 crêpe on an oven-proof plate, put some of the fruit mixture in and fold over, then spoon some of the sabayon on top. Finish the other servings. Place plates in the oven to brown the sabayon (this happens quite quickly — watch it!). Take plates out and decorate with the raspberries. *Serves 4.*

Anna's
Bed and Breakfast

Anna and Robert Doorenbos
204 Wolf Street
Thompson, Manitoba R8N 1J7
Tel: (204) 677-5075
$ – $$

ABOUT THE B&B

Visit Anna's Bed and Breakfast to experience what Canadian Dutch hospitality is all about. This adult-oriented and non-smoking B&B offers a private guest suite with its own entrance and parking space, two single beds, private bath, kitchenette, and den with TV and telephone. Anna enjoys cooking and will get your day off to a delicious start with a full breakfast served in the main dining room. Oriental meals are another specialty and, along with traditional meals, are available for an additional charge. The greenhouse, which is connected to the cozy and informal living room, opens onto the deck and lends a summer atmosphere to the home — even in the dead of winter! Thompson is the home base of travelers to fly-in fishing lodges and Churchill (Manitoba) and other northern communities. It also boasts the longest alpine ski season in Manitoba. Guest pick-up can be arranged as well as scenic touring by car. Your hosts Anna and Robert moved to Canada from Holland and have lived in Thompson since 1971. Robert, an award winning visual artist, originates from Egypt and Anna from Indonesia.

SEASON

all year

ACCOMMODATIONS

1 suite with private bath

Heart-Healthy Buttermilk Pancakes

"Both my husband Robert and I are health conscious, so I've become well versed in heart-healthy cooking . . . without compromising taste. I developed this recipe from one I learned in Winnipeg from a cook in a coffee shop."
— Anna Doorenbos

2 cups all-purpose flour
2 cups buttermilk
2 egg whites
2 tablespoons polyunsaturated vegetable oil, such as corn, sunflower, or canola oil
1 teaspoon baking powder
1 teaspoon baking soda
¼ – ½ teaspoon salt
Polyunsaturated vegetable oil or low-fat cooking spray for frying

Maple syrup, fruit syrup, or honey

Mix all ingredients together in a bowl until batter is lumpy. Ladle batter onto a lightly greased grill on medium heat (350°F), turning pancakes once when bubbles appear and underside is golden. Serve with a variety of toppings, such as maple syrup, fruit syrup, or honey. *Tip:* Try adding slivers of apple or blueberries to the batter. **Makes 16 pancakes.**

Henderson Hotcakes with Chokecherry Syrup

"While making chokecherry jelly one year, I made a mistake and the jelly didn't set. However, we tried the concoction on pancakes and it was a hit! I make the syrup from the chokecherries we pick in the surrounding bush."
— *Jeanette Henderson*

2 cups all-purpose flour
½ cup bran, oat bran, or whole-wheat flour
1½ teaspoons salt
2 tablespoons baking powder
¼ cup sugar
2 eggs, beaten
1¾ cups milk
¼ cup vegetable oil

Mix together dry and liquid ingredients separately. Add liquid mixture to dry mixture, mixing until flour is just moistened (don't overmix). Cook ¼ – ⅓ cup batter per pancake on a greased griddle, turning once when bubbles appear and underside is golden. Top with chokecherry syrup (recipe follows). **Makes 12 – 16 pancakes.**

(continued on next page)

Henderson Hollow

Jeanette and Garry Henderson
RR #1
Austin, Manitoba R0H 0C0
Tel: (204) 466-2857
$

ABOUT THE B&B

A *piece of heaven and a heavenly getaway, Henderson Hollow is a cozy country home set in beautiful, rolling, wooded hills. Simply relax on the large deck or in the screened sun porch surrounded by nature's beauty and abundant wildlife, or enjoy many indoor and outdoor activities (depending on the season). Full home-cooked meals include home-baked bread and cinnamon rolls, and dishes featuring garden-fresh fruits and vegetables. The house is filled with antiques and decorated with many homemade crafts for you to enjoy (or purchase, if you desire). Nearby points of interest include the Austin Agricultural Museum (largest in western Canada), Spruce Woods Provincial Park, Margaret Laurence Museum, and the Thomas Seton Centre. Your hosts' interests include golfing in summer at the many beautiful — and challenging! — surrounding golf courses, and cross-country skiing in winter right from the back door.*

SEASON

all year

ACCOMMODATIONS

1 room with private bath;
2 rooms with shared bath;
campground facilities

Chokecherry syrup:
6½ cups chokecherry juice
8 cups sugar
1 cup cornstarch
1 cup water

Prepare juice by adding 2½ – 3 cups water to 4 quarts chokecherries. Simmer 15 minutes, mash, and place in a cheesecloth bag and allow to drip.

Boil chokecherry juice and sugar for 5 minutes. Dissolve cornstarch in water and add to chokecherry mixture. Boil 5 minutes and seal in sterilized jars. *Variation:* You can substitute blueberries or pincherries for the chokecherries. *Makes approximately 9 cups.*

Lemon French Toast with Strawberry Sauce

12 slices Italian or French bread (don't use ends)
16-ounce jar lemon spread
6 eggs, beaten
½ cup milk
2 tablespoons butter or margarine

Strawberry sauce:
1-pound package frozen sliced strawberries in syrup, thawed
2 tablespoons cold water
2 teaspoons cornstarch

Spread 6 bread slices with lemon spread; cover with remaining bread. In a shallow bowl, mix eggs and milk. Dip each sandwich in egg mixture (let it soak in a bit) and fry in melted butter until golden. Meanwhile, heat strawberries and syrup in a small saucepan. Mix cold water and cornstarch in a cup and add to hot strawberries, stirring constantly until sauce is thickened. To serve, slice each French toast sandwich in half diagonally and spoon some sauce over. *Serves 6.*

Harbour House Bed & Breakfast Inn

Gayle Flebotte
615 Lakeshore Drive
Cold Lake, Alberta T0A 0V2
Tel: (403) 639-2337
$$ – $$$

ABOUT THE B&B

Built in 1989 to complement the Cold Lake Marina, Harbour House is patterned after the Old Coast Guard Station in Virginia Beach, Virginia, and retains all the charm of old New England (where your hostess is originally from). Climb the stairs to the viewing tower where you'll admire the panoramic view of Cold Lake, Alberta's seventh largest lake. Settle into one of 11 individually decorated rooms (most facing the lake), and rest assured of a comfortable night's sleep under feather duvets or hand-stitched quilts. Awake to a breathtaking sunrise over the lake and the aroma of the inn's famous sticky buns or other home-baked goods, fresh fruit specialties, and juice. Gayle's passions include quilting, tap dancing, and making sure her guests enjoy their stay. Nearby Cold Lake Provincial Park is home to over 200 bird species. Harbour House is within walking distance of the beach, with opportunities for fishing and boating. In the near vicinity, you can go mini-golfing and regular golfing, bowling, skiing, and browsing in antique and craft shops.

SEASON

all year

ACCOMMODATIONS

5 rooms with private baths;
6 rooms with shared baths

Nightingale's Landing B&B

Sandy and Jim Nightingale
5305 Granville Street
Granville Ferry, Nova Scotia
B0S 1K0
Tel/Fax: (902) 532-7615
$ – $$

ABOUT THE B&B

*O*verlooking the Annapolis River, Nightingale's Landing is a beautifully restored and much photographed Victorian gingerbread cottage built in 1872 by a prominent Loyalist merchant. With three comfortable bedrooms furnished with period antiques, Nightingale's Landing also offers many unique architectural features, including guest parlors with high ceilings, marble fireplaces, antique chandeliers, and original moldings — all in a quiet village setting on four acres. A gourmet breakfast is served daily in the Victorian country dining room. Just three minutes from Annapolis Royal, Granville Ferry is home to artists, potters, and other artisans with studios. The Annapolis Royal tourism area includes the Habitation at Port Royal (Canada's oldest settlement), historic Fort Anne, and the beautiful Annapolis Royal Gardens. Government employees who spent most of their working lives in Europe, Central America, and the Orient, Sandy enjoys gardening, tole painting, and cooking, while Jim enjoys woodworking.

SEASON

May – October

ACCOMMODATIONS

1 suite with private bath;
2 rooms with shared bath

Lemon-Poppy Seed Pancakes

1 cup whole-wheat flour
1 cup all-purpose flour
1 teaspoon baking powder
1 teaspoon baking soda
¼ teaspoon salt
2 tablespoons poppy seeds
1 lemon
2 cups milk
2 eggs
2 tablespoons honey
¼ cup melted unsalted butter
Confectioners' sugar

Butter and warm maple syrup

Mix the first 6 dry ingredients together in a large bowl until well blended. Grate the lemon zest and add it to the dry ingredients. Squeeze the lemon and add the juice to the milk; set aside. Combine the eggs, honey, and butter in a medium bowl. Add the milk and lemon juice mixture. Add this liquid mixture to the dry ingredients and stir gently until well blended. Pour a ¼ cup batter per pancake onto a hot, lightly oiled griddle or frying pan, turning pancakes when bubbles appear, and cook until done. Sprinkle with confectioners' sugar and serve with butter and warm maple syrup. *Makes 16 pancakes.*

Mom's Dandelion Pancakes

4 eggs
½ teaspoon salt
1½ cups all-purpose flour
1 heaping tablespoon sugar
4 teaspoons baking powder
2 cups milk

Beat eggs until light and fluffy. Add all the other ingredients and mix well. Cook ¼ – ½ cup batter per pancake on a greased griddle, turning once when bubbles appear and underside is golden. Top with dandelion syrup (recipe follows). **Makes approximately 1 dozen large pancakes.**

Dandelion syrup:
250 dandelion flower heads*
Juice of 1 lemon
8 cups water
5 cups sugar

Note: If picking dandelions in the wild, ensure that the area hasn't been sprayed with pesticides or fertilizer.

Wash dandelion flower heads well and place them in a large pot. Squeeze in lemon juice. Add water and bring to a boil. Cover and simmer 1 hour. Remove from heat and let stand, covered, overnight. Strain and add sugar. Boil and reduce heat enough to simmer vigorously for 1½ hours or until mixture has the consistency of maple syrup. Pour over pancakes. Store extra in a sealed glass jar in the refrigerator. *Tip:* Make big batches and seal in sterilized jars as you would for preserves. Once opened, keep in the refrigerator. *Makes 4 cups.*

Courtney Leanne Bed and Breakfast

Louise Studer
3428 Dieppe Street
Saskatoon, Saskatchewan
S7M 3S9
Tel: (306) 382-0444
$ – $$

ABOUT THE B&B

Courtney Leanne Bed and Breakfast is located on the west side of Saskatoon in a quiet neighborhood with large lots. Large, comfortable bedrooms are decorated with quilts and afghans, and homemade soaps are provided in the shared baths. Homemade jams, jellies, and muffins complement a full breakfast that, weather permitting, is served out on the deck overlooking the flower beds, pond, and creek. Situated close to golf courses, the city's downtown, a commuter rail station, and the John G. Diefenbaker Airport, Courtney Leanne offers a piano, billiard table, and local craft display on site and cross-country skiing nearby. In addition to running her B&B and meeting new people, hostess Louise Studer takes pleasure in gardening, interior design, and craft making.

SEASON

all year

ACCOMMODATIONS

3 rooms with shared baths

Rowat's Waterside Bed and Breakfast

Marg and Jack Rowat
1397 Borland Road
Williams Lake, British Columbia
V2G 1M3
Tel: (604) 392-7395
$$

ABOUT THE B&B

Enjoy the tranquility of Rowat's Waterside B&B, located on Williams Lake right beside Scout Island Nature Center and Wildlife Reserve, in the heart of Cariboo Country. Walk the nature trails and return home to put your feet up and enjoy the view of the lake and marsh from the open deck (this is a birdwatcher's paradise!). Rowat's Waterside is also within walking distance of mini-golf, parasailing, restaurants, stampede grounds, and a short drive away from downtown, golf and tennis facilities, and a sports arena. For something completely different, a one-and-a-half-hour drive will take you to the Ghost Town Museum of Barkerville, an old gold rush town. Rowat's accommodations include tastefully decorated rooms with private baths, a fireside guest lounge with TV, air conditioning, purified water, and ample parking. Famous Cariboo Cowboy breakfasts are served in the dining room or deckside overlooking the marsh bird sanctuary. Hosts Marg and Jack are long-time residents of the Cariboo, and enjoy craft making, gardening, meeting people, and the great outdoors.

SEASON

all year

ACCOMMODATIONS

4 rooms with private baths

Mushroom Puff Pancake

1 cup sliced mushrooms
1 tablespoon butter
4 green onions, chopped
½ cup butter
6 medium eggs
¼ teaspoon salt
2 cups milk
1 cup all-purpose flour
¾ cup small-curd cottage cheese
¼ cup grated Parmesan cheese
1 teaspoon baking powder
½ cup grated strong cheddar or mozzarella cheese

Salsa (see recipes on page 271 and page 281)

Preheat oven to 450°F. Sauté mushrooms on medium-low heat in 1 tablespoon butter, stirring often until just brown. Add green onions and cook for 1 minute; set aside. Cut ½ cup butter into small pieces and put into a 10" cast-iron skillet or 13 x 9" baking dish. Heat in oven to melt. Combine eggs and salt in a bowl and beat at high speed for 1 minute. Continue mixing while adding milk, flour, cottage cheese, Parmesan, and baking powder. Fold in mushrooms and onions. Pour into the hot skillet and bake 35 minutes until puffed and lightly browned. Let sit for 5 minutes before cutting into 6. Sprinkle with grated cheese. Serve with salsa. *Serves 6.*

Oatmeal Pancakes with Chunky Apple-Maple Sauce

"For this recipe, I use organically grown apples picked right from my garden." — Margaret Whetter

2 cups milk
1½ cups quick-cooking rolled oats
1 cup all-purpose flour
2 tablespoons sugar
1 teaspoon salt
2½ teaspoons baking powder
2 eggs, beaten
½ cup vegetable oil

Pour milk over oats and let stand 5 minutes. Sift dry ingredients and add, with eggs and oil, to the oat mixture. Stir just until dry ingredients are moistened. Ladle a small amount onto a hot, greased skillet. Turn when bubbles appear and underside of pancakes are golden brown. *Tip:* Don't hesitate to add goodies (apples, bananas, almond-flavored Saskatoon berries, or blueberries) to the batter. Serve with chunky apple-maple sauce (recipe follows). *Makes about 1 dozen pancakes.*

(continued on next page)

River Park Farm

Margaret Whetter
PO Box 310
Hartney, Manitoba R0M 0X0
Tel/Fax: (204) 858-2407
$$

ABOUT THE B&B

River Park Farm is a Victorian guest home built in 1910 on 10 acres of lawn and garden on the banks of the historic Souris River. Recently restored and redecorated, the heritage farmstead has a cozy and casual charm that often sparks memories of childhood visits to a grandma's home in the country. Guests can glimpse deer, raccoons, woodchucks, and many birds while breakfasting on the veranda or in the sun room. Grain elevators in the distance are silhouetted against beautiful prairie sunrises and sunsets. There are walking trails along the river, a nearby golf course and swimming pool, and canoes available either for professional or self-guided trips. Margaret Whetter, the owner and hostess, is a home economist who considers cooking an art form and an act of love. She finds the opportunity to share the stories of her guests' lives a great privilege.

SEASON

all year

ACCOMMODATIONS

4 rooms with shared baths; 7-bed attic room with private bath

Chunky apple-maple sauce:
½ cup maple syrup
1 tablespoon butter
1 teaspoon lemon juice
1 teaspoon ground cinnamon
Pinch of ground nutmeg
6 apples, peeled, cored, and cut into chunks

Bring all ingredients to a boil in a saucepan and cook until apples are tender (6 – 8 minutes). Serve over pancakes. For extra pizzazz, flame the sauce with 2 tablespoons rum.
Tip: This topping is also great over vanilla ice cream.

Old-Fashioned Waffles with Sauce

2 eggs, separated
1½ cups milk
2 tablespoons vegetable oil
2 cups all-purpose flour
4 teaspoons baking powder
1 teaspoon salt
1 tablespoon sugar

Preheat a Belgian waffle maker. In a small bowl, beat egg whites until stiff. Set aside. Beat egg yolks until creamy. Add milk to egg yolks and beat. Mix dry ingredients and gradually add to milk mixture, beating until smooth. Gently fold in egg whites. Reserve ½ cup batter for sauce below. Bake waffles according to manufacturer's directions. *Makes 5 – 6 waffles.*

Sauce:
½ cup waffle batter
½ cup sugar
2 cups scalded milk
1 teaspoon vanilla

Fresh fruit

Combine the waffle batter and sugar. Add to the scalded milk (in a 4-cup bowl or measuring cup) and microwave for 2 minutes. Stir, and microwave for 2 more minutes and stir again. Continue cooking, checking at 1-minute intervals, until sauce has a pudding-like consistency. Stir in the vanilla. Serve over waffles and garnish with fresh fruit.

Longview Bed & Breakfast

Charlene and Bob Siemens
PO Box 53
Fiske, Saskatchewan S0L 1C0
Tel: (306) 377-4786
$

ABOUT THE B&B

Peaceful surroundings, nature walks, farm-fresh meals, and barnyard animals are what you can expect at Longview, a working prairie farm southwest of Saskatoon. While listening to the howl of the coyote, fall asleep in your private guest cottage with its own bath and deck, then wake up to the crow of the rooster. Join hosts Charlene and Bob in their home for a hearty breakfast (and other meals if requested) — all of which take advantage of the produce, eggs, and meat produced on the farm. For those who want to really get away from it all, Longview offers a rustic cottage surrounded by a grove of trees and a choir of birds. A short drive away, you can find ancient petroglyphs and teepee rings. Your hosts especially welcome families, and enjoy visiting with their guests and sharing their love of the land.

SEASON

May – September

ACCOMMODATIONS

private cottage (3 rooms with shared bath); rustic cabin

Orchard Lane
Bed & Breakfast

Yvonne Parker
13324 Middle Bench Road
Oyama, British Columbia
V4V 2B4
Tel: (250) 548-3809
$$

ABOUT THE B&B

S mack dab between Kelowna and Vernon, there awaits Orchard Lane, a newly built Victorian B&B nestled in a private orchard. From the sprawling veranda, this rural setting gives way to a panoramic view of the beautiful Central Okanagan Valley, while nearby Kalamalka and Wood lakes reflect the hills and distant mountains. Inside, a welcoming foyer and spiral staircase lead to romantic and comfortable bedrooms. Visitors lounge in the formal living room with fireplace, stroll through the flower gardens or nearby orchard, admire the terraced landscaping framed by giant trees, or take a refreshing dip in the outdoor hot tub. Your hostess, Yvonne, serves a full gourmet breakfast — made from produce grown in her vegetable garden — in the formal dining room or on the veranda. You'll quickly discover that one of her favorite hobbies is craft collecting, which is evident throughout the house. Alpine skiing, fishing, biking, hiking, and other recreational choices await you and there are golf courses and beaches aplenty to explore. This area is truly a corner of paradise.

SEASON

all year

ACCOMMODATIONS

2 rooms with shared bath

Orchard Lane Waffles

"This recipe can either be halved or made ahead and frozen."
— Yvonne Parker

1 pound butter
4½ cups brown sugar
1 dozen eggs
½ cup evaporated skim milk
2 tablespoons vanilla
5 cups all-purpose flour
5 teaspoons baking powder
1 teaspoon salt
Whipped cream

Fresh fruit, strawberry jam, or maple syrup

Cream butter and sugar. Add eggs, milk, and vanilla. Add dry ingredients sifted together. Bake on a waffle iron according to manufacturer's directions. Top with a dab of whipped cream and serve with fresh fruit, strawberry jam, or maple syrup.
Makes approximately 3 dozen waffles.

Partridgeberry and Blueberry Pancakes

1 whole egg or 2 egg whites, well beaten
1 cup milk
3 tablespoons melted butter or margarine
1¼ cups all-purpose flour
2 teaspoons baking powder
2 tablespoons sugar
½ cup blueberries
½ cup partridgeberries* (also known as mountain cranberries or
    creeping cranberries)
Vegetable oil or butter

Maple syrup, heated partridgeberry jam, or berry sauce

Note: If necessary, substitute coarsely chopped plain cranberries for partridgeberries.

Beat egg, milk, and butter. Gradually stir in dry ingredients (don't overmix). Fold in berries last. Pan fry ½ cup batter per pancake in oil or butter, turning once when bubbles appear and underside is golden. Serve with maple syrup, heated partridgeberry jam, or berry sauce. *Makes 10 – 12 pancakes.*

Lake Crescent Inn

Evelyn and Bruce Warr
PO Box 69
Robert's Arm, Newfoundland
A0J 1R0
Tel: (709) 652-3067
Fax: (709) 652-3056
$

ABOUT THE B&B

When you think of Newfoundland, think peaceful lifestyle, clean air and rivers, and superb hospitality — all of which you'll find at Lake Crescent Inn. Walk along the quiet roads and beautiful beaches, visit fishermen in the various communities along the route, or go iceberg or whale watching (in season). Boating trips can also be arranged, so why not give cod jigging or salmon fishing a try? Be sure to bring along your camera to capture the moment you reel in your first fish (you might even see "Cressie," the lake monster!). The inn offers four bedrooms and two bathrooms, one with whirlpool and shower. Breakfasts are a home-made feast of muffins, jams, jellies, and breads, and a special health-conscious menu is also available. A Jiggs dinner is served on Sundays from 5:00 p.m., and a Fish Platter dinner is served on Fridays from 5:00 p.m. (other meals can be provided upon request).

SEASON

all year

ACCOMMODATIONS

4 rooms with shared baths

Linden House B&B

Elaine and Phil Landray
PO Box 1586, 389 Simcoe Street
Niagara-on-the-Lake, Ontario
L0S 1J0
Tel/Fax: (905) 468-3923
$$

ABOUT THE B&B

A warm welcome awaits you at Linden House, a new Cape Cod-style, air conditioned home with private guest wing, featuring two queen rooms and one twin/king room, all with private ensuite bathrooms. The queen rooms feature brass beds and cream wicker furniture, while the twin/king room highlights the nautical flavor with Cape Cod wicker. There is a guest lounge on the same level as the bedrooms with television, VCR, games, and books, or you can choose to enjoy the garden or relax in the gazebo. Non-smoking Linden House offers convenient on-site parking and is located in the old town, just four short blocks from Queen Street with its shopping and theaters. In summer, enjoy water recreation on Lake Ontario or top-notch theater at the Shaw Festival. Your hosts, Elaine and Phil, serve such sumptuous breakfasts — featuring seasonal Niagara fruit — that their guests claim they don't need lunch!

SEASON

April – December

ACCOMMODATIONS

3 rooms with private baths

Peaches and Cream French Toast

"A wonderful use for the world's best peaches, grown right here on the Niagara Peninsula." — Elaine Landray

3 eggs
3 tablespoons peach preserves
¾ cup half-and-half cream (10 – 18%)
6 slices French bread, each ½" thick

Peach butter:
⅓ cup peach preserves
¼ cup softened butter

4 tablespoons butter
Confectioners' sugar
2 fresh peaches, peeled, pitted, and sliced
Toasted almonds

Maple syrup

In a small bowl, whisk eggs and 3 tablespoons peach preserves. Beat in half-and-half. Place a single layer of bread slices in a 13 x 9" baking dish. Pour egg mixture over bread. Cover and refrigerate a few hours or overnight until most of the liquid is absorbed.

(continued on next page)

In a small bowl, beat ⅓ cup peach preserves and ¼ cup softened butter with an electric mixer until fluffy; chill peach butter until ready to serve.

At serving time, melt 2 tablespoons butter in a large skillet. Add 3 bread slices and cook over medium-high heat until browned, turning once. Remove from skillet and keep warm. Repeat with remaining bread slices and butter. Serve French toast sprinkled with confectioners' sugar and topped with peach slices, toasted almonds, and peach butter (use a melon baller to serve). Serve with maple syrup. *Serves 4 – 6.*

Nightingale's Landing B&B

Sandy and Jim Nightingale
5305 Granville Street
Granville Ferry, Nova Scotia
B0S 1K0
Tel/Fax: (902) 532-7615
$ – $$

ABOUT THE B&B

Overlooking the Annapolis River, Nightingale's Landing is a beautifully restored and much photographed Victorian gingerbread cottage built in 1872 by a prominent Loyalist merchant. With three comfortable bedrooms furnished with period antiques, Nightingale's Landing also offers many unique architectural features, including guest parlors with high ceilings, marble fireplaces, antique chandeliers, and original moldings — all in a quiet village setting on four acres. A gourmet breakfast is served daily in the Victorian country dining room. Just three minutes from Annapolis Royal, Granville Ferry is home to artists, potters, and other artisans with studios. The Annapolis Royal tourism area includes the Habitation at Port Royal (Canada's oldest settlement), historic Fort Anne, and the beautiful Annapolis Royal Gardens. Government employees who spent most of their working lives in Europe, Central America, and the Orient, Sandy enjoys gardening, tole painting, and cooking, while Jim enjoys woodworking.

SEASON

May – October

ACCOMMODATIONS

1 suite with private bath;
2 rooms with shared bath

Sandy's Supreme Baked French Toast

"One of our guests was quite taken with this entrée and asked if it had a name. Another guest, who had spent three days with us, piped up from the adjoining table that it's called 'You Might as Well Leave Today Because it Can't Get Any Better Than This!' " — Sandy Nightingale

8 slices cinnamon-raisin bread, each 1" thick
½ cup melted unsalted butter
4 whole eggs
2 egg yolks
¾ cup sugar
3 cups milk
1 cup whipping cream (35%)
1½ tablespoons vanilla
3 cups fresh berries or sliced fruit (strawberries in June, raspberries in July, blueberries in August, and apples in September and October)
Confectioners' sugar

Preheat oven to 350°F. Brush both sides of bread with the melted butter and arrange in an even, single layer in the bottom of a buttered 13 x 9" pan. Beat together in a bowl the whole eggs and egg yolks, then add the sugar, milk, cream, and vanilla and continue to beat until well mixed. Pour this custard mixture evenly over the bread. Bake 25 minutes or until custard is set. Cool in the pan on a wire rack for 15 minutes. Cut into 8 portions, top with fresh fruit, and sprinkle with confectioners' sugar. *Serves 8.*

Saskatoon Breakfast Puff Pancakes

"I use Saskatoon berries because they are a wonderful almond-flavored wild berry found in the prairies. However, any berry may be substituted." — Margaret Whetter

6 teaspoons butter
4 eggs
1 cup all-purpose flour
1 cup milk
Pinch of ground nutmeg
6 tablespoons Saskatoon berry filling (recipe follows) or
    berry filling of your choice
Confectioners' sugar

Saskatoon berry filling:
2 cups Saskatoon berries
¾ cup sugar
½ cup water
2 tablespoons cornstarch

First, prepare berry filling by heating together all ingredients in a saucepan until sauce thickens and is clear. Set aside.

To make puffs: Preheat oven to 425°F. Place a teaspoon of butter in each cup of a 6-cup muffin pan, or in 6 individual ramekins. Place in oven until butter is melted and pan is hot. Mix eggs, flour, milk, and nutmeg until slightly lumpy. Pour into hot muffin cups. Put a tablespoon of fruit filling into each one. Cook 20 minutes until puffed and golden. To serve, spoon some warm fruit filling on individual plates, place puff on filling, and dust with confectioners' sugar. *Makes 6 puff pancakes.*

River Park Farm

Margaret Whetter
PO Box 310
Hartney, Manitoba R0M 0X0
Tel/Fax: (204) 858-2407
$$

ABOUT THE B&B

River Park Farm is a Victorian guest home built in 1910 on 10 acres of lawn and garden on the banks of the historic Souris River. Recently restored and redecorated, the heritage farmstead has a cozy and casual charm that often sparks memories of childhood visits to a grandma's home in the country. Guests can glimpse deer, raccoons, woodchucks, and many birds while breakfasting on the veranda or in the sun room. Grain elevators in the distance are silhouetted against beautiful prairie sunrises and sunsets. There are walking trails along the river, a nearby golf course and swimming pool, and canoes available either for professional or self-guided trips. Margaret Whetter, the owner and hostess, is a home economist who considers cooking an art form and an act of love. She finds the opportunity to share the stories of her guests' lives a great privilege.

SEASON

all year

ACCOMMODATIONS

4 rooms with shared baths;
7-bed attic room with
private bath

Hawkins House
Bed & Breakfast

Carla Pitzel and Garry Umbrich
303 Hawkins Street
Whitehorse, Yukon Territory
Y1A 1X5
Tel: (403) 668-7638
Fax: (403) 668-7632
$$$

ABOUT THE B&B

To stay at the Hawkins House Bed & Breakfast is to share a once-in-a-lifetime Yukon experience with your hosts Carla, Garry, and their two sons. Each guest room in this custom-built, luxury Victorian B&B highlights a different Yukon theme and features private bath and balcony, oak floor, bar sink and refrigerator, cable TV and VCR. Guests can take a Jacuzzi soak in the Fleur de Lys Room, watch Native videos in the First Nations Room, step back into gold rush days in the Victorian Tea Rose Room, or admire the splendid view of the SS Klondike paddlewheeler and Canyon Mountain from the balcony of the Fireweed Room. Especially geared to the business traveler, Hawkins House provides the convenience of private telephone line and answering machine, fax service, and work table with light and computer jack. Breakfast is a homemade feast of northern and international delights — from the home-smoked salmon pâté and moose sausage to jams, syrups, and sourdough pastries.

SEASON

all year

ACCOMMODATIONS

4 rooms with private baths

Sourdough Pancakes

"Sourdough pancakes are traditional Yukon breakfast fare during our February winter carnival (appropriately called Sourdough Rendezvous), New Year's Day, and on special occasions throughout the year." — Carla Pitzel

4 cups sourdough sponge batter*
1 egg
1 tablespoon vegetable oil
1 teaspoon salt
1 tablespoon sugar
1 teaspoon baking soda
1 tablespoon water

Maple syrup, or strawberries and whipped cream

Note: In the evening (or at least 12 hours before using), make the sponge batter (see pages 69 – 70).

Reserve 1 cup of sponge batter and return it to your clean starter container. Add egg, oil, salt, and sugar to the remaining sponge and beat with a fork to blend all ingredients (if the batter seems a little stiff, add another egg). Just before baking, dissolve soda in water, then add to the batter. Cook 3 tablespoons batter per pancake on a hot, greased griddle. Turn once when bubbles appear and underside is golden. Serve with maple syrup, or strawberries and whipped cream. ***Makes 15 medium-sized pancakes.***

Spartan Apple-Cinnamon Crêpes

"In the Brighton area, the beauty of spring apple blossoms in surrounding orchards gives way to colorful autumn baskets filled with the harvested apple crop at fruit stands. Sanford House offers a bowl of this magnificent fruit in season and features them in some of the hot breakfast entrées."
— *Elizabeth and Charlie Le Ber*

3 eggs
1½ cups milk
1 cup all-purpose flour
4 tablespoons melted butter
2 tablespoons sugar
2 tablespoons Calvados (apple brandy from Normandy, France)

Whisk eggs, then add milk and blend well. Stir in remaining ingredients and beat until smooth and free of lumps. Refrigerate batter overnight. Whisk. Pour a thin layer over the bottom of a hot buttered 5½" skillet and cook at medium heat 1½ minutes on first side and about 30 seconds on second side. Transfer to a towel. Repeat with rest of the batter. *Makes about 14 crêpes.*

(continued on next page)

Sanford House Bed & Breakfast

Elizabeth and Charlie Le Ber
PO Box 1825, 20 Platt Street
Brighton, Ontario K0K 1H0
Tel/Fax: (613) 475-3930
$$

ABOUT THE B&B

Sitting majestically on the crest of a hill, Sanford House Bed & Breakfast is a red-brick Victorian home close to Main Street in the friendly town of Brighton. This century-old home with turret and covered veranda has offstreet parking, a separate guest entrance, and three large, bright, and comfortable bedrooms. Guests can choose to relax in the round turret room; in the lounge with television, VCR, videos, board games, and books; in the spacious, bright Victorian parlor; or on the veranda. Delicious home-baked breakfasts, often spotlighting apples grown in nearby orchards, are served in the guest dining room. It's a short drive to beautiful Presqu'ile Provincial Park's sandy beaches, nature trails, fine birdwatching area, and marsh boardwalk. If antique hunting is a passion, there are numerous antique establishments right in Brighton and the surrounding area. Apple-fest, a celebration of the harvest in September, is a particularly lovely time to visit the area. When not entertaining their B&B guests, Elizabeth and Charlie enjoy cycling and birdwatching.

SEASON

all year

ACCOMMODATIONS

3 rooms with shared bath

Apple-cinnamon filling:
6 tablespoons butter
1½ cups brown sugar
1 cup water
1½ teaspoons ground cinnamon
9 Spartan apples, peeled, cored, and sliced
Confectioners' sugar

Place first 5 ingredients in a microwave-safe casserole. Cook uncovered in the microwave on high power for 8 minutes, stirring twice. Place filling in center of crêpes and fold 2 sides over. Turn crêpes with folded sides under and keep warm. To serve, place 2 filled crêpes on a heated plate with a little of the juices and dust with confectioners' sugar.

Strawberry-Almond French Toast

Strawberry-almond sauce:
10-ounce package frozen strawberries, thawed
Water
½ cup sugar
2 tablespoons cornstarch
½ cup toasted sliced almonds

½ cup all-purpose flour
1½ tablespoons sugar
¼ teaspoon salt
2 cups milk
6 eggs
¼ teaspoon ground nutmeg
18 slices French bread, each 1" thick
1 tablespoon butter or margarine

Drain strawberries, reserving liquid. Add enough water to reserved liquid to measure 1 cup. Combine sugar and cornstarch in a saucepan; gradually add liquid. Cook, stirring constantly, until mixture is clear and thickened. Stir in strawberries and almonds. In a separate bowl, beat flour, sugar, salt, milk, eggs, and nutmeg with a rotary beater until smooth. Soak bread in egg batter until saturated. Heat butter in a large skillet and carefully place bread slices in it (if overcrowded, use a second skillet). Cook over medium-low heat on each side until golden brown. Serve with strawberry-almond sauce. *Serves 6.*

Park View Bed & Breakfast

Gladys and Carson Langille
254 Cameron Street
Moncton, New Brunswick
E1C 5Z3
Tel: (506) 382-4504
$$

ABOUT THE B&B

This Art Deco home was built in 1940 as a residence for Mrs. Inez Robinson, owner of Moncton's first business college. The architectural plans came from the 1939 New York World's Fair and this was the first Art Deco home in Moncton. The curved living room windows look out on beautiful Victoria Park in the city's center. Opened as a B&B in 1989, this charming home provides three guest rooms with cable TV, telephones, and exquisite shared bath, spacious living room with fireplace, elegant dining room, and cozy kitchen. Your hosts provide a warm welcome, a hearty, full home-cooked breakfast of your choice, and a wealth of information about the area. Gladys is a part-time school teacher, while Carson enjoys playing bridge and painting landscapes. A collection of works by local artists graces their walls. Nearby is superb dining, shopping, beaches, parks, museums, galleries, theater, a must-see tidal bore (where the tide goes up and down very quickly), and infamous Magnetic Hill (you'll never believe this is possible unless you experience it yourself!).

SEASON

all year

ACCOMMODATIONS

3 rooms with shared bath

Lakewinds

Jane and Stephen Locke
PO Box 1483, 328 Queen Street
Niagara-on-the-Lake, Ontario
L0S 1J0
Tel: (905) 468-1888
Fax: (905) 468-1061
$$$$

ABOUT THE B&B

A special experience awaits you at Lakewinds, a circa-1881, restored Victorian manor hosted by Jane and Stephen Locke. Situated on an acre of quiet trees and gardens, Lakewinds offers unparalleled views of the Niagara-on-the-Lake Golf Club and Lake Ontario. Elegantly appointed with antiques, guest rooms have been designed for comfort and privacy and all feature private baths. Guests are invited to the games room for billiards or cards and, in summer, can enjoy refreshing dips in the heated pool or simply relax in rocking chairs on the veranda. Sumptuous breakfasts feature fruits, vegetables, and herbs from Jane's garden. Only one-and-a-half hours south of Toronto, Niagara-on-the-Lake is a charming town offering world-class theater, shops, fine restaurants, and beautiful parks — all with a turn-of-the-century ambience. The many estate wineries in the area offer tours and tastings, while golf, tennis, and countless hiking and biking trails await the active visitor.

SEASON

all year

ACCOMMODATIONS

4 rooms with private baths

Sweet Potato Pancakes

2 large sweet potatoes, peeled and grated
1 cup chopped green onion
1½ tablespoons minced hot pepper (such as jalapeño)
1 teaspoon orange zest
3 large eggs
⅓ cup all-purpose flour
Salt and pepper to taste
Vegetable oil
Sour cream or crème fraîche
Sprinkle of chopped green onion

Cooked sweet cured ham

In a large bowl, combine sweet potatoes, onions, hot pepper, orange zest, eggs, and flour. Add seasonings. Heat oil in a large skillet over medium heat. For pancakes, shape about ¼ cup of sweet potato mixture into a small round pancake, about 3" in diameter. Turn pancakes after 3 – 5 minutes or when edges are lightly browned, and cook another 3 – 5 minutes. Keep warm while cooking the rest of the pancakes. Serve with a dollop of sour cream or crème fraîche and a sprinkle of chopped green onion. Very nice served with cooked sweet cured ham. *Makes 25 – 30 pancakes.*

Veggie 'n Cheese Puff Pancake

1 tablespoon butter
½ cup all-purpose flour
½ cup milk
2 eggs, beaten
¼ teaspoon salt
2 tablespoons butter
2 cups chopped broccoli
1 cup finely chopped red onion
1 cup chopped tomato
1½ cups grated cheddar cheese

Fresh fruit salad and croissants

Heat oven to 425°F. In a 9" glass pie pan, melt 1 tablespoon butter. In a small bowl, stir together flour, milk, eggs, and salt. Pour into pie pan. Bake 12 – 15 minutes. Meanwhile, melt 2 tablespoons butter in a skillet and cook vegetables at medium heat. Sprinkle ½ cup cheese on cooked pancake, followed by the vegetables, then the rest of the cheese. Return pancake to oven for 2 minutes to melt cheese. Cut into 4. Serve along with fresh fruit salad and croissants. *Serves 4.*

Fraser House

Sheila and Dennis Derksen
PO Box 211, 33 1st Street East
Letellier, Manitoba R0G 1C0
Tel: (204) 737-2284
$

ABOUT THE B&B

Memories are made at this elegant and romantic 1916 home. Hardwood floors, area rugs, and antique furniture enhance the home's Victorian decor. Spacious rooms combined with great hospitality make your stay most enjoyable. Relax in the parlor, veranda, or patio with a beverage and home-baked goodies. Breakfast may consist of a puffy egg pancake or freshly baked croissants and muffins, along with the season's fresh fruit, served in the formal dining room. Fraser House is located just a few minutes north of the US border in the heart of Manitoba's bustling agricultural area, and is near golf, fishing, shopping, and skiing. Sheila enjoys crafting projects and holds painting classes during the winter months, while Dennis enjoys carpentry and is employed as a fertilizer dealer.

SEASON

all year

ACCOMMODATIONS

2 rooms with shared bath

Caron House (1837)

Mary and Mike Caron
PO Box 143
Williamstown, Ontario K0C 2J0
Tel: (613) 347-7338
$$

ABOUT THE B&B

*C*aron House (1837) is a *historic, romantic brick home located in the quaint village of Williamstown (established in 1784). Beautifully decorated and furnished with antiques, the house is in its original state, with working fireplaces, inside shutters, tin ceilings, and wide pine floorboards. Two rooms with shared bath are individually decorated with Laura Ashley wallpaper, antique linens, hooked rugs, quilts, and collectibles. Guests can relax in the Keeping Room (a Colonial term for gathering place) or living room, while a full, candlelit gourmet breakfast — accompanied by classical music — is served in the dining room on fine china, silverware, and crystal. Outside, you'll marvel at the herb and Victorian gardens, and relax on the antique wicker furniture on the back veranda, enjoying the lovely yards, complete with trellis, brick patio, and gazebo. Caron House is one hour's drive from either Montréal or Ottawa; nearby attractions include Upper Canada Village, artisan studios, a bird sanctuary, tennis, cycling, and good restaurants. Mary and Mike are retirees from the corporate world, and enjoy traveling, antique hunting, cooking, gardening, and history.*

SEASON

all year

ACCOMMODATIONS

2 rooms with shared bath

Whole-Wheat Crêpes

"Delicious crêpes with a wholesome texture that I like to use for my chicken crêpes with avocado recipe (on page 188)."
— Mary Caron

1 cup whole-wheat flour
1¼ cups milk
3 eggs
2 tablespoons melted butter or margarine, cooled
¼ teaspoon salt
Butter for frying

Put all ingredients in a blender and whirl for about 1 minute at high speed. Scrape down sides with a spatula and whirl again at high speed for another 15 seconds. Pour into a bowl and cover. Refrigerate for 1 hour or more. In a crêpe pan, place 1 tablespoon butter. When butter bubbles, swirl it around to coat the pan. Pour in enough batter to thinly coat bottom of pan. Flip when underside browns and edges begin to curl. After about 1 minute, crêpe should be almost done. Repeat with rest of batter. Stack crêpes between wax paper or paper towels and set aside or freeze until needed. *Makes 1½ dozen crêpes.*

Wild Wiarton Berry Waffles

"These wonderfully light waffles are a breakfast favorite. We serve them heart shaped." — Elsie Christensen

3 eggs, separated
¾ cup milk
½ cup melted butter or margarine
¾ cup sour cream
1 teaspoon vanilla
2 teaspoons baking powder
½ teaspoon baking soda
1½ cups all-purpose flour
½ teaspoon salt
Berries of your choice
Confectioners' sugar

Using a beater, beat egg whites until stiff. Beat egg yolks in a large bowl. Add milk, butter, sour cream, and vanilla to egg yolks, beating well. Combine dry ingredients and sift into egg yolk mixture, beating well. Fold egg whites into batter carefully. Bake waffles on a hot, greased waffle iron according to manufacturer's directions. Top with berries and sprinkle with confectioners' sugar. *Makes 8 waffles.*

Bruce Gables B&B

Elsie and Jorn Christensen
PO Box 448, 410 Berford Street
Wiarton, Ontario N0H 2T0
Tel: (519) 534-0429
Fax: (519) 534-0779
$$

ABOUT THE B&B

Whether in French, German, Spanish, Danish, or English, Elsie and Jorn bid you "welcome" to Bruce Gables, their spacious turn-of-the-century Victorian home. Relax in the large living room, which has been restored to its Victorian splendor and furnished with period furniture and antiques. Two of the three large bedrooms have bay windows that overlook the town of Wiarton and the clear blue waters of Colpoy's Bay. A hearty breakfast is served in the elegant dining room where you'll dine on your choice of crêpes, pancakes, waffles, French toast, eggs Benedict/Florentine, omelets, or any style of eggs. Picnic tables and a gas barbecue located in the garden are available for the guests to use. Known as "Gateway to the Bruce," the town of Wiarton makes a perfect headquarters for exploring the Bruce Peninsula. With the Georgian Bay to the east and Lake Huron to the west, the Bruce offers abundant water recreation, not to mention some of the most breathtaking scenery in Ontario from its high limestone bluffs. In addition, the area's provincial parks are natural habitats for many varieties of birds and animals.

SEASON

May – October

ACCOMMODATIONS

3 rooms with shared baths

The Inn on St. Andrews

Joan Peggs
231 St. Andrews Street
Victoria, British Columbia
V8V 2N1
Tel: (800) 668-5993 or
(604) 384-8613
Fax: (604) 384-6063
E-mail: joan.peggs@vonline.com
$$

ABOUT THE B&B

The Inn on St. Andrews is as lovely today as when it was built in 1913 by Edith Carr, eldest sister of the famous Canadian artist and author, Emily Carr. This Tudor-style heritage property charms with its elegant woodwork, stained and beveled glass, and large bright bedrooms. After a wholesome breakfast in the formal dining room, you can congregate in the sunroom overlooking the east garden or sun deck overlooking the west garden, in the cozy TV room, or in the larger drawing room. The inn is ideally located in James Bay, close to Victoria's inner harbor with ferry and seaplane terminals, the Parliament buildings, the Royal British Columbia Museum, famed Empress Hotel, and downtown shops. A short walk brings you to Beacon Hill Park and the oceanfront. Your host Joan Peggs believes in modern comfort and old-fashioned hospitality, and provides guests with her own map highlighting walking and driving destinations and recommended restaurants.

SEASON

all year

ACCOMMODATIONS

1 room with private bath;
2 rooms with shared bath

Zucchini Pancakes with Béchamel Sauce

(*Recipe from* Joan Peggs Eggs, *written and published by Joan Peggs, 1996*)

1 cup whole-wheat flour
1 cup all-purpose flour
4 teaspoons baking powder
2 tablespoons sugar
½ medium onion, chopped
½ – 1 teaspoon Italian seasoning or a mixture of dried oregano, marjoram, and basil
1½ cups grated zucchini
1 cup milk
¼ cup vegetable oil
2 eggs

If using an electric frying pan, set to 350°F. Sift together both flours, baking powder, and sugar. In a large mixing bowl, toss together onion, seasonings, and zucchini. Add flour mixture to zucchini mixture. Combine with a fork. Place milk, oil, and eggs in a blender jar, and blend for 15 seconds. Add to the flour-zucchini mixture, stirring gently with a fork until just mixed (extra milk may be required). Cook in a lightly greased frying pan (either at 350°F or over medium heat). Using ¼ cup batter per pancake, drop batter onto heated surface. Cook until surface is covered with bubbles and underside is golden brown.

(continued on next page)

Turn and cook until underside is golden brown. Serve with béchamel sauce (recipe follows) flavored with Parmesan cheese. *Tip:* Leftover pancakes may be frozen. *Makes 16 – 20 pancakes.*

Béchamel sauce:
2 tablespoons margarine
2 tablespoons all-purpose flour
Salt and pepper
1 cup milk

Place margarine in top section of a double boiler. Place over boiling water to melt margarine. Remove top section of double boiler from heat (water) and add flour and seasonings. Stir to mix melted margarine and flour. Add milk and stir into margarine-flour mixture. Return top section of double boiler to heat and stir constantly until mixture thickens to desired consistency. If cheese is to be added (see variation below), add as the sauce begins to thicken. To prevent further thickening, remove from heat. Cover to prevent skin from forming on surface. *Makes 1 cup.*

Variation: For a cheese sauce, add ½ cup grated cheese (strong cheddar, Parmesan, or Swiss). Cayenne pepper and paprika can be added with cheddar cheese; nutmeg can be added with Parmesan and Swiss cheese.

Tips: Extra béchamel sauce can be frozen (6-ounce yogurt containers work best). Place frozen sauce in the refrigerator to thaw overnight. Next day, either use a double boiler or microwave to reheat. If the sauce is too thick, add a small amount of extra milk.

Quiches, Omelets, Frittatas, & Casseroles

Asparagus and Crab Strata

6 slices white bread
¼ cup softened butter
1 cup grated cheddar cheese
1 cup chopped and cooked fresh asparagus
1 cup cooked crab meat, fresh or canned
4 eggs
1¼ cups milk
1½ tablespoons chopped fresh parsley
½ teaspoon salt
Dash of pepper
½ teaspoon paprika

Preheat oven to 350°F. Grease an 8 x 8" baking dish. Spread butter on one side of bread slices. Arrange 3 slices of bread in dish, buttered side down (if necessary, trim bread to fit pan). Layer cheese, asparagus, and crab meat over bread. Place remaining bread slices, buttered side up, over crab meat. Combine eggs, milk, parsley, salt, pepper, and paprika. Pour egg mixture evenly over bread. Let stand for 10 minutes to absorb. Bake 35 – 45 minutes or until a knife inserted in center comes out clean. *Serves 6.*

Fraser House

Sheila and Dennis Derksen
PO Box 211, 33 1st Street East
Letellier, Manitoba R0G 1C0
Tel: (204) 737-2284
$

ABOUT THE B&B

Memories are made at this elegant and romantic 1916 home. Hardwood floors, area rugs, and antique furniture enhance the home's Victorian decor. Spacious rooms combined with great hospitality make your stay most enjoyable. Relax in the parlor or on the veranda or patio with a beverage and home-baked goodies. Breakfast may consist of a puffy egg pancake or freshly baked croissants and muffins, along with the season's fresh fruit, served in the formal dining room. Fraser House is located just a few minutes north of the US border in the heart of Manitoba's bustling agricultural area, and is near golf, fishing, shopping, and skiing. Sheila enjoys crafting projects and holds painting classes during the winter months, while Dennis enjoys carpentry and is employed as a fertilizer dealer.

SEASON

all year

ACCOMMODATIONS

2 rooms with shared bath

Les Trois Érables

Madeleine and Jacques Mercier
PO Box 852, RR #2
Wakefield, Québec J0X 3G0
Tel: (819) 459-1118
$$

ABOUT THE B&B

Nestled among gentle rolling hills on the banks of the Gatineau River, the historic village of Wakefield is a gateway to beautiful Gatineau Park where you can find ample opportunities for hiking, skiing, or less arduous nature walks — especially beautiful in fall foliage season. Less than a half hour's drive takes you to the heart of Canada's national capital, Ottawa. Les Trois Érables was built at the turn of the century and was the home and office of three generations of village doctors until its B&B transformation in 1988. Rooms are tastefully decorated in soft colors and furnished for comfort and convenience. The sumptuous breakfasts attest to the fact that Madeleine loves to cook. Local restaurants, sports outfitters, and boutiques abound.

SEASON

all year

ACCOMMODATIONS

4 rooms with private baths

Asparagus, Gruyère, and Tarragon Souffléd Omelet

½ pound trimmed asparagus
1 medium red onion, thinly sliced
1½ tablespoons unsalted butter
Pinch of sugar
⅔ cup grated Gruyère cheese
1 tablespoon minced fresh tarragon leaves
4 eggs, separated
2 tablespoons all-purpose flour
Salt and pepper to taste

Preheat oven to 375°F. In a 10" non-stick and oven-proof skillet, simmer asparagus in enough water to cover for 3 – 5 minutes or until just tender. Drain asparagus, rinse under cold water, and pat dry with paper towels. Cut the asparagus crosswise into ¼" pieces and transfer them to a bowl. In the skillet, cook the onion with 1 tablespoon butter over moderate heat, stirring frequently for 5 minutes. Add the sugar and cook, stirring, for 3 – 5 minutes or until onion is golden. Transfer mixture to the bowl with asparagus. Add cheese and tarragon, season to taste, and mix thoroughly.

(continued on next page)

Clean skillet and melt remaining ½ tablespoon butter over moderate heat. Tilt skillet to coat entire surface with butter, then remove from heat. Whisk the egg yolks with the flour and salt and pepper to taste until mixture is thick and lemon-colored.

In another bowl, beat egg whites with a pinch of salt until they just hold stiff peaks. Fold them into the yolk mixture gently but thoroughly and pour egg mixture into the skillet, spreading it evenly. Bake the omelet in the middle of the oven for 7 minutes or until it's puffed. Spoon the filling down the middle and, with a spatula, fold omelet in half to enclose filling. Bake the omelet for 1 minute more or until cheese is melted, then cut in half. *Serves 2.*

The Lookout at Schooner Cove

Marj and Herb Wilkie
3381 Dolphin Drive
Nanoose Bay, British Columbia
V0R 2R0
Tel/Fax: (604) 468-9796
$$

ABOUT THE B&B

Situated halfway between Victoria and Tofino on unspoiled Vancouver Island, this West Coast contemporary cedar home stands in a woodsy setting of rocks and tall evergreens. The wrap-around deck affords a 180° view of Georgia Strait and the majestic mountains beyond. Relax and savor this "little bit of heaven" or hike, golf, kayak, sail, fish, or sightsee. Take a day trip to the wild western shore of the island and the Pacific Rim National Park or to charming Victoria. The vacation suite will accommodate four people and, with its fully equipped kitchen, makes a popular headquarters for an island stay. Hearty breakfasts are served within full view of the ocean activities. The Wilkies ran a store in New York's Catskill mountains for 15 years before discovering this paradise. They enjoy hiking, golf, crafts, reading, games, puzzles, and especially meeting their guests and helping them plan a memorable stay.

SEASON

May – October
(or by arrangement)

ACCOMMODATIONS

1 vacation suite
with private bath;
1 room with private bath;
1 room with shared bath

Bacon and Egg Casserole

"Creates a flavorful beginning to the day, not to mention that my cholesterol-conscious guests appreciate the fact that they each get less than an egg per serving." — Marj Wilkie

2 cups grated medium or strong cheddar cheese
2 tablespoons dried onion
1 cup cooked crumbled bacon or ham chunks
6 eggs
3 cups milk
1½ cups powdered biscuit mix
½ teaspoon pepper
½ teaspoon dry mustard
½ cup melted butter

Preheat oven to 400°F. Butter a 13 x 9" casserole. Sprinkle bottom with cheese, onion, and crumbled bacon or ham chunks. Beat remaining ingredients together and slowly pour over top. Bake 25 – 30 minutes. *Serves 8.*

Barbara Ann's Omelet

3 slices bacon, cut into small pieces
2 small potatoes, peeled and sliced into ¼" slices
8 spinach leaves, stems removed and sliced into ¼" strips
6 eggs, lightly beaten
½ cup plain yogurt
Salt and pepper to taste

Heat bacon briefly in a 10" skillet. Add potatoes and fry until bacon is crisp and potatoes are lightly browned. Add spinach, then remove mixture to a small bowl. Combine eggs, yogurt, salt, and pepper, and pour one-third mixture into skillet. Cook over low heat without stirring. As eggs set on bottom, lift edges to let uncooked liquid run underneath. When omelet has set, place one-third spinach filling on one side of omelet, and fold with a fork. Repeat omelet procedure twice more with remaining egg mixture. Serve immediately. *Makes 3 omelets.*

Barbara Ann's Bed 'n Breakfast Vacation Farm

Barbara Ann and Ted Witzaney
PO Box 156
Denzil, Saskatchewan S0L 0S0
Tel: (306) 358-4814
$

ABOUT THE B&B

*S*pecially geared for families, Barbara Ann's B&B is located on the Witzaney farm, where they've been raising crops and hogs since 1911. The petting zoo includes traditional farm animals and more exotic ones, including a llama and Muscovy ducks. Barbara Ann's breakfast and other meals served on request feature farm-fresh milk, eggs, cheese, and vegetables; home-baked goods, such as buns, pies, and cookies; homemade jams, jellies, relishes, and pickles; and the farm's home-raised pork, which includes the specialty of the house — homemade sausages. Picnic and barbecue facilities, sandbox and swing set, horseshoe pit, lawn bowling, badminton, and an 18-hole miniature golf course are all on the property. When not tending to guests, Barbara Ann enjoys sewing and craft making, while Ted enjoys woodworking. Both like to spend time with their 10 grandchildren. Denzil is about a half-hour drive west of Unity, Saskatchewan, and a 45-minute drive east of Provost, Alberta.

SEASON

all year

ACCOMMODATIONS

2 rooms with shared bath

Mecklenburgh Inn

Suzi Fraser
78 Queen Street
Chester, Nova Scotia B0J 1J0
Tel/Fax: (902) 275-4638
www.destination-ns.com/
lighthouse/mecklenburgh
$$

ABOUT THE B&B

Constructed by shipwrights at the turn of the century, Mecklenburgh Inn is a historic 1890 bed and breakfast located in the heart of seaside Chester, which has catered to summer visitors and sailing enthusiasts for over 150 years. Sleep in the spacious and comfortably appointed bedrooms filled with period furniture and other interesting objects Suzi has collected over the years, then enjoy a delicious breakfast while you plan the day ahead. You might wander the historic village streets, stopping to watch the yacht races on Mahone Bay, or browse through craft shops and boutiques. Or, maybe a sailboat ride, bicycle ride, or game of golf or tennis would be more your style. Later, relax on the balcony while the sun settles over the western shore and village activity lulls. You might consider an evening meal at one of the excellent restaurants in the area or catch a play at the Chester Playhouse. Before drifting off to sleep, you can wind down in the living room chatting by the fire or perusing travel books and magazines.

SEASON

May 24 – November 7

ACCOMMODATIONS

4 rooms with shared baths

Breakfast Casserole

2 cups sour cream
3 cups creamed cottage cheese
2 cups grated cheddar cheese
3 scallions, chopped
½ cup chopped mild green chilies
1 cup cooked corn kernels
10 eggs
½ cup melted butter
½ cup all-purpose flour
1 teaspoon baking powder

Preheat oven to 350°F. Mix all ingredients except last two. Mix together flour and baking powder and add to egg mixture. Pour into a greased 13 x 9" pan and bake 45 minutes. *Serves 12.*

Breakfast Pie

"The following recipe comes from the New Sweden Church 100th Anniversary Cookbook (1894 – 1994), *my husband Winston's first country parish. It's simple, easy, and guests find it really tasty." — Vera Sproule*

Crust:
2½ cups frozen hash browns, thawed and grated (or use grated leftover hash browns)

Filling:
5 eggs
½ cup creamed cottage cheese
⅓ cup milk
½ cup chopped mushrooms
1 green onion, sliced
⅛ teaspoon pepper
1 teaspoon salt
4 drops Tabasco sauce or to taste
1½ cups grated cheddar cheese
½ cup cooked crumbled bacon or finely diced cooked ham
½ cup cornflakes

Preheat oven to 325°F. Press hash browns to form a crust in a 9" greased pie plate. Beat eggs until foamy. Stir in following 8 ingredients. Pour into pie plate. Top with bacon or ham and cornflakes. Bake 40 – 50 minutes. Let stand 3 – 4 minutes before cutting. *Serves 4 – 5.*

Sproule Heritage Place B&B

Vera and Winston Sproule
PO Box 43, Site 14, RR #1
Strathmore, Alberta T1P 1J6
Tel: (403) 934-3219
$$

ABOUT THE B&B

While Sproule Heritage Place B&B has been featured by both Hallmark USA and Alberta Government Telephone in their television commercials, this farm actually had less high-profile beginnings. In 1909, it was little more than a well-trodden buffalo trail when the Scheer family settled on the open prairie east of Calgary. Years later, the stately house and barn became a landmark to travelers on a road that today is the Trans-Canada Highway. Vera and Winston Sproule purchased the farm in 1985 and began extensive renovations to restore its 1920s elegance. As a result, the site has been declared an Alberta Registered Historic Resource. Artisans and designers of furniture and quilts, Vera and Winston (a country pastor for four years in the Yukon and 24 years in Alberta) assure you a comfortable bed in one of three charming bedrooms and an interesting breakfast.

SEASON

all year

ACCOMMODATIONS

1 room with private bath;
2 rooms with shared bath

Barbara Ann's Bed 'n Breakfast Vacation Farm

Barbara Ann and Ted Witzaney
PO Box 156
Denzil, Saskatchewan S0L 0S0
Tel: (306) 358-4814
$

ABOUT THE B&B

Specially geared for families, Barbara Ann's B&B is located on the Witzaney farm, where they've been raising crops and hogs since 1911. The petting zoo includes traditional farm animals and more exotic ones, including a llama and Muscovy ducks. Barbara Ann's breakfast and other meals served on request feature farm-fresh milk, eggs, cheese, and vegetables; home-baked goods, such as buns, pies, and cookies; homemade jams, jellies, relishes, and pickles; and the farm's home-raised pork, which includes the specialty of the house — homemade sausages. Picnic and barbecue facilities, sandbox and swing set, horseshoe pit, lawn bowling, badminton, and an 18-hole miniature golf course are all on the property. When not tending to guests, Barbara Ann enjoys sewing and craft making, while Ted enjoys woodworking. Both like to spend time with their 10 grandchildren. Denzil is about a half-hour drive west of Unity, Saskatchewan, and a 45-minute drive east of Provost, Alberta.

SEASON

all year

ACCOMMODATIONS

2 rooms with shared bath

Broccoli and Cheese Quiche

9" unbaked pie shell
¼ cup grated Parmesan cheese
2 cups finely chopped fresh broccoli
1 cup grated Swiss cheese
¼ cup sliced scallions
3 eggs
⅔ cup chicken broth
½ cup whipping cream (35%)
½ teaspoon salt
¼ teaspoon Tabasco sauce

Preheat oven to 450°F. Prick bottom and corners of pie shell with a fork and bake 5 minutes. Remove from oven and sprinkle with 2 tablespoons Parmesan. Layer half the broccoli over the Parmesan cheese. Over that, layer half the Swiss cheese and scallions. Repeat layers with remaining broccoli, Swiss cheese, and scallions. Beat eggs, then add chicken broth, cream, salt, and Tabasco, mixing well. Pour over mixture in pastry shell. Sprinkle with remaining 2 tablespoons Parmesan. Bake 10 minutes, then reduce heat to 325°F and bake 20 – 25 minutes longer (or until a knife inserted in quiche's center comes out clean). Let stand 5 – 10 minutes before cutting. *Serves 10 – 12.*

Cheese and Onion Pie

Crust:
¾ cup all-purpose flour
½ teaspoon salt
¼ teaspoon dry mustard
1 cup grated strong cheddar cheese
¼ cup melted butter

Filling:
2 tablespoons butter
2 cups thinly sliced onion
1 cup cooked and drained egg noodles
2 eggs, beaten
1 cup hot milk
½ teaspoon salt
Pinch of pepper

Preheat oven to 350°F. To make crust: In a medium bowl, combine flour, salt, dry mustard, and cheese. Stir in melted butter until thoroughly mixed. Press evenly into a 9" pie plate.

To make filling: In a frying pan, melt butter over medium heat. Stir in onions and cook until softened but not brown. Add onions to cooked noodles, and spread evenly in crust. Whisk eggs, milk, salt, and pepper until smooth. Pour evenly over noodles and onions.

Bake 35 – 40 minutes or until set and knife inserted in center of pie comes out clean. Let stand 5 minutes before cutting. *Serves 4 – 6.*

The Varey House

Lorraine Delisle-Joyner
PO Box 1675, 105 Johnson Street
Niagara-on-the-Lake, Ontario
L0S 1J0
Tel: (905) 468-3252
Fax: (416) 323-9249
$$$

ABOUT THE B&B

A round 1837, George Varey, a tailor, built his house on the site of a building destroyed during the War of 1812. Each guest room features its own decor and private bathroom, and guests are served a delicious buffet breakfast. The charm and warmth of the parlor and living room offer a relaxing place to enjoy afternoon refreshments or to meet new friends after a day of sightseeing or before an evening of theater. Bicycles are available for exploring the recreational trails around Niagara-on-the-Lake and along the scenic Niagara River. "One of the best preserved nineteenth-century towns in North America" (Treasury of Canadian Bed and Breakfast), Niagara-on-the-Lake is a haven for artists and artisans, theater lovers, and history buffs. Its antique shops, art galleries, summer theater, historic homes and inns, and recreational activities attract tourists year after year. As Canada's premier wine-growing region, the area also attracts wine aficionados for local winery tours and tasting.

SEASON

April – December

ACCOMMODATIONS

4 rooms with private baths

Sanford House Bed & Breakfast

Elizabeth and Charlie Le Ber
PO Box 1825, 20 Platt Street
Brighton, Ontario K0K 1H0
Tel/Fax: (613) 475-3930
$$

ABOUT THE B&B

Sitting majestically on the crest of a hill, Sanford House Bed & Breakfast is a red-brick Victorian home close to Main Street in the friendly town of Brighton. This century-old home with turret and covered veranda has offstreet parking, a separate guest entrance, and three large, bright, and comfortable bedrooms. Guests can choose to relax in the round turret room; in the lounge with television, VCR, videos, board games, and books; in the spacious, bright Victorian parlor; or on the veranda. Delicious home-baked breakfasts, often spotlighting apples grown in nearby orchards, are served in the guest dining room. It's a short drive to beautiful Presqu'ile Provincial Park's sandy beaches, nature trails, fine birdwatching area, and marsh boardwalk. If antique hunting is a passion, there are numerous antique establishments right in Brighton and the surrounding area. Applefest, a celebration of the harvest in September, is a particularly lovely time to visit the area. When not entertaining their B&B guests, Elizabeth and Charlie enjoy cycling and birdwatching.

SEASON

all year

ACCOMMODATIONS

3 rooms with shared bath

Crispin Apple and Sausage Quiche

"In the Brighton area, the beauty of spring apple blossoms in surrounding orchards gives way to colorful autumn baskets filled with the harvested apple crop at fruit stands. Sanford House offers a bowl of this magnificent fruit in season and features them in some of the hot breakfast entrées."
— Elizabeth and Charlie Le Ber

Pastry:
6 tablespoons cold butter
2 tablespoons lard
1¼ cups all-purpose flour
3 tablespoons ice water

Blend butter and lard together well with a pastry blender or 2 knives, then work in flour. Using fingers, blend mixture well. Make a well in mixture and gradually add ice water while stirring quickly. Gather dough in a ball and allow it to rest in the refrigerator for 2 hours in plastic wrap. Roll out on a lightly floured board and place in a fluted 9" or 10" round quiche dish.

(continued on next page)

Filling:
8 pork breakfast sausages
1 tablespoon butter
1 Crispin or Granny Smith apple, peeled, cored, and chopped
½ cup grated medium cheddar cheese
2 egg yolks
1 whole egg
1 cup milk

Preheat oven to 350°F. Remove sausages from casings and sauté until cooked through, stirring until sausage crumbles. Drain in a colander, then drain further on paper towels. Place in pie crust. Sauté chopped apple in melted butter until softened, then distribute over sausage. Grate cheese and distribute over apple. Beat egg yolks, whole egg, and milk and pour over cheese, apple, and sausage. Bake 50 – 60 minutes or until pie is somewhat firm in center and top is golden. Serve warm. *Serves 4.*

West Bay
Bed & Breakfast

Yvette and Ralf Craig
715 Suffolk Street
Victoria, British Columbia
V9A 3J5
Tel: (604) 386-7330
Fax: (604) 389-0280
CompuServe: 74561,3556
$$ – $$$$

ABOUT THE B&B

Feel the ocean breeze and admire the sweeping views of the Straight of Juan de Fuca and snow-capped Olympic Mountains from the deck of this modern, Mediterranean-style B&B. Only minutes from Victoria's many attractions, West Bay offers three bright and whimsical guest rooms, each with private entrance and bath, king or queen bed, bar refrigerator, and French door entrance to a garden patio. Two rooms have TV, and one a fireplace. Breakfast includes a variety of egg dishes or pancakes, fruit salad, granola muesli, yogurt, beverages, and homemade breads and jams. Chat with guests from around the world at the large dining room table or seat yourself in the more intimate sunroom. Leisurely stroll the scenic ocean boardwalk to Chinatown, Market Square, Inner Harbour, famed Empress Hotel, and a wide assortment of museums, restaurants, theaters, and pubs. Catch one of the many harbor ferries or relax on a walkway bench and watch the nonstop comings and goings of seaplanes, cruise ships, yachts, and ferries.

SEASON

all year

ACCOMMODATIONS

3 rooms with private baths

Dilled Smoked Salmon Quiche

1 medium onion, chopped
2 tablespoons butter
2 tablespoons all-purpose flour
4 eggs
¼ teaspoon dry mustard
Dash of ground nutmeg
¼ teaspoon spike seasoning (available at health food stores)
1 teaspoon dried dill weed
Dash of Tabasco sauce
2 cups milk or light cream (18 – 30%)
¾ cup flaked smoked salmon
6 ounces grated cheddar, Swiss, or Monterey Jack cheese, chilled

Preheat oven to 350°F. Microwave onion and butter in a glass, microwave-safe quiche dish on high for 2 minutes. Add flour and stir. In a bowl, beat eggs, seasonings, and milk until combined. Pour mixture into quiche dish. Sprinkle cheese and smoked salmon on top. Bake 35 – 45 minutes. Let stand 5 minutes before cutting. *Serves 6.*

Doloris' Individual Baked Omelet

¼ cup grated Swiss cheese
¼ cup grated strong cheddar cheese
½ teaspoon dried minced onion
2 eggs, beaten
2 tablespoons milk
Dash of salt and pepper
Sprinkle of paprika

Preheat oven to 350°F. Sprinkle grated cheeses evenly in the bottom of a greased, 4"-diameter baking dish. Mix next 4 ingredients together and pour over cheese. Sprinkle with paprika. Bake 20 – 30 minutes. *Serves 1.*

The Green Door Bed & Breakfast

Doloris Paquin
PO Box 335, 376 Berford Street
Wiarton, Ontario N0H 2T0
Tel: (519) 534-4710
$ – $$

ABOUT THE B&B

"*Completely comfortable, wonderfully welcoming,*" *is how one recent guest described The Green Door. Built at the turn of the century, this red-brick, stately restored Victorian house is situated on Wiarton's main street and is within a few minutes' walk of shops and restaurants. The main floor has a charming and spacious living room with bay windows and dining room for guests' comfort and pleasure. Up the wooden staircase are three guest bedrooms, two with double beds and one with two single beds, as well as a large guest bathroom. The high ceilings and spacious rooms lend an airy feeling with all the comforts and coziness of home. Outside, enjoy the large garden, maple-shaded deck, and barbecue facilities.*

SEASON

all year

ACCOMMODATIONS

1 room with private bath;
2 rooms with shared bath

Hipwood House B&B

Sharon and Malcolm Spraggett
PO Box 211
1763 Hipwood Road
Shawnigan Lake
British Columbia V0R 2W0
Tel: (250) 743-7855
$$

ABOUT THE B&B

Thinking of traveling to beautiful Vancouver Island? If so, take the breathtaking 45-minute drive north of Victoria to the quaint village of Shawnigan Lake, and you'll come upon a peaceful country B&B called Hipwood House. Unwind in one of three spacious guest rooms, enjoy a refreshing cup of tea in the garden, or stroll the trails on Hipwood's two acres (which includes a 50-foot suspension bridge). There's also a putting green, horseshoes, and badminton — if you need to work off that full country breakfast! You're also a five-minute walk away from the public beach, local artists' gallery, and museum, and close to boat and water sport rentals on the lake, a seaplane for magnificent air tours, fishing, golf, tennis, and restaurants. Many interesting and picturesque areas are within a half-hour drive. Lifelong residents of Vancouver Island, Sharon and Malcolm are knowledgeable about the area and will help make your stay extra special.

SEASON

all year

ACCOMMODATIONS

1 room with private bath;
2 rooms with shared bath

Eggs Florentine

"No need to call my guests for breakfast when this dish is baking in the oven — its wonderful aromas do the job for me!" — Sharon Spraggett

2 bunches spinach
1 large clove garlic
1 tablespoon vegetable oil
½ teaspoon salt
2 tablespoons half-and-half cream (10 – 18%)
1 tablespoon butter
2 tablespoons grated Swiss cheese
2 tablespoons butter
1½ tablespoons all-purpose flour
¼ teaspoon each salt and pepper
1 cup milk
6 eggs
⅓ cup grated Swiss cheese

Preheat oven to 350°F. Wash and dry spinach well. Finely chop garlic. In a large frying pan, heat oil. Add spinach and garlic and cover. Cook just until wilted. Drain well and chop. Return to pan and add the ½ teaspoon salt, cream, and 1 tablespoon butter. Mix well. Turn into an 8 x 8" baking dish. Sprinkle with 2 tablespoons grated cheese. Melt 2 tablespoons butter in a saucepan, remove from heat, and add flour, salt, and pepper. Stir until smooth. Stir in milk. Bring sauce to a boil, stirring constantly. Carefully break 6 eggs over cheese and spinach in dish. Cover with sauce. Sprinkle with ⅓ cup cheese. Bake uncovered for 15 – 20 minutes or until eggs are set and top is golden. *Serves 6.*

Fiddlehead Quiche

9" unbaked pie shell
8-ounce package cream cheese, cubed
1 cup milk
4 eggs, beaten
¼ cup chopped onion
1 cup chopped fresh mushrooms
2 tablespoons margarine
10-ounce package frozen fiddleheads*
2 cups grated Swiss cheese
Dash of salt, pepper, and paprika
6 bacon slices, crisply cooked and crumbled

Note: Fiddleheads are baby ferns, available fresh in the spring and frozen year-round.

Preheat oven to 400°F. Place pie shell in a 10" pie plate; flute edge. Prick bottom and sides of pastry with a fork. Bake 12 – 15 minutes or until lightly browned. Combine cream cheese and milk in a saucepan; stir over low heat until smooth. Gradually add cream cheese mixture to eggs, mixing until well blended. In a skillet, sauté onion and mushrooms in margarine; remove from skillet. Steam or boil fiddleheads until just cooked al dente, and drain. Add cooked vegetables, Swiss cheese, and seasonings to cream cheese mixture. Mix well. Pour into the pastry shell. Top with crumbled bacon. Reduce oven temperature to 350°F and bake 35 – 40 minutes or until set. *Serves 8.*

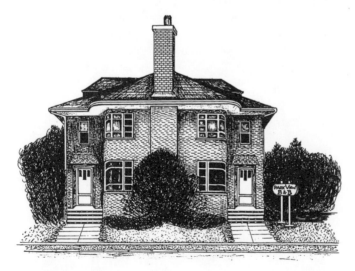

Park View Bed & Breakfast

Gladys and Carson Langille
254 Cameron Street
Moncton, New Brunswick
E1C 5Z3
Tel: (506) 382-4504
$$

ABOUT THE B&B

This Art Deco home was built in 1940 as a residence for Mrs. Inez Robinson, owner of Moncton's first business college. The architectural plans came from the 1939 New York World's Fair and this was the first Art Deco home in Moncton. The curved living room windows look out on beautiful Victoria Park in the city's center. Opened as a B&B in 1989, this charming home provides three guest rooms with cable TV, telephones, and exquisite shared bath, spacious living room with fireplace, elegant dining room, and cozy kitchen. Your hosts provide a warm welcome, a hearty, full home-cooked breakfast of your choice, and a wealth of information about the area. Gladys is a part-time school teacher, while Carson enjoys playing bridge and painting landscapes. A collection of works by local artists graces their walls. Nearby is superb dining, shopping, beaches, parks, museums, galleries, theater, a must-see tidal bore (where the tide goes up and down very quickly), and infamous Magnetic Hill (you'll never believe this is possible unless you experience it yourself!).

SEASON

all year

ACCOMMODATIONS

3 rooms with shared bath

River Run
Cottage & Breakfast

Janice and Bill Harkley
4551 River Road West
Ladner, British Columbia
V4K 1R9
Tel: (604) 946-7778
Fax: (604) 940-1970
$$$$

ABOUT THE B&B

Described in Vancouver Best Places *as "a jewel on the Fraser" and rated "four kisses" in* Best Place to Kiss in the Northwest, *River Run is a romantic, tranquil getaway 30 minutes south of downtown Vancouver. Individual waterfront cottages on the Fraser River with private decks overlooking the river and mountains have wood-burning fireplaces, CD players, telephones, bathrobes, and cozy furnishings. All have private baths, one also equipped with a Jacuzzi tub for two, and one with a soaker tub on the deck. Breakfast is delivered to the cottages at the time specified by guests and includes freshly squeezed juice, home-baked goods, and a variety of entrées. Bicycles, rowboats, and a double kayak are available for guests to explore the delta and the nearby Reifel Migratory Bird Sanctuary. By car, River Run is a 10-minute drive from ferries to Victoria and the Gulf Islands and a 20-minute drive from Vancouver International Airport.*

SEASON

all year

ACCOMMODATIONS

3 cottages with private baths

Fresh Salmon and Leek Quiche

"We're fortunate to have salmon easily available, since the river we live on is one of the most important salmon rivers in British Columbia. Often, after barbecuing, we use some of the leftover fish for this quiche." — Jan Harkley

Crust:
1¼ cups all-purpose flour
¼ teaspoon salt
¼ cup unsalted butter
2 tablespoons lard
1 egg

Filling:
1 – 2 leeks, well rinsed, with white and tender greens cut
    into matchsticks
2 tablespoons butter
1 cup cooked fresh salmon (ensure there are no bones)
1 tablespoon chopped fresh dill or 1 teaspoon dried dill weed
1 cup grated Swiss cheese
4 eggs
1⅓ cups half-and-half cream (10 – 18%)
½ teaspoon salt
½ teaspoon dry mustard

(continued on next page)

Preheat oven to 450°F. Mix together flour and salt. Cut in butter and lard. Beat egg and mix in. Roll out on a floured board and put in a 9" pie pan. In a frying pan, sauté leeks in butter until translucent. Remove from heat and mix in salmon and dill. Spread mixture evenly over pie crust. Sprinkle grated cheese over salmon and leeks. In a separate bowl, beat together eggs, cream, salt, and mustard. Pour over cheese. Bake 10 minutes, then reduce heat to 350°F for another 25 minutes or until center is firm. *Serves 6.*

Le Gîte
Park Avenue B&B

Anne-Marie and Irving Bansfield
54 Park Avenue
Ottawa, Ontario K2P 1B2
Tel: (613) 230-9131
$$

ABOUT THE B&B

A bright, airy ambience and artistic decor awaits you at Park Avenue B&B, an elegant, brick 1906 home located in a charming residential area of downtown Ottawa, Canada's capital. In addition to high-quality beds done up in classic cotton and linen sheets and duvets, each guest room is furnished with desk and swivel chair, rocking chair, bookshelves, excellent lighting, and attractive works of art. Ideal for families, the third-floor suite has two bedrooms and a private bath. The mood throughout the house is one of relaxation and warmth. Park Avenue B&B is close to the Parliament buildings, art galleries and museums, and is only three minutes away (by foot) from the Rideau Canal, which freezes into the world's longest skating rink. Ottawa has a number of exciting festivals and activities, including Winterlude, a winter carnival held each February. Anne-Marie and Irving make it a point to know what's going on when in Ottawa so they can advise their guests on what to see and do.

SEASON

all year

ACCOMMODATIONS

1 suite with private bath;
2 rooms with shared bath

Frittata with Four Cheeses

2 tablespoons butter or margarine
1 onion, finely diced
½ cup diced cooked ham
¼ cup diced cooked potatoes
Freshly chopped basil
Freshly chopped parsley
½ cup vegetables, such as diced red and green pepper,
    mushrooms, and corn kernels
4 eggs
2 tablespoons milk
¾ cup grated cheese combination: Swiss, Gruyère,
    Monterey Jack, and mozzarella
Salt and pepper to taste
Freshly chopped chives or green onion

Preheat oven to 400°F. In a large, oven-proof skillet, heat butter or margarine. Sauté onion. Add ham, potatoes, basil, parsley, and vegetables, and continue to cook. Lightly whisk 4 eggs with milk, then add cheeses, salt, and pepper. Remove skillet from heat and pour in egg mixture. Top with chives or green onion and bake 15 – 20 minutes until the frittata is browned and the center is set. *Serves 6.*

Gouda Baked Eggs with Roasted Red Pepper Coulis

"When serving groups, this baked omelet is easier and faster than making fried omelets one at a time. I like to serve it over a pool of roasted red pepper coulis or a mild salsa."
— Jane Locke

3 garlic cloves, chopped
4 shallots, finely chopped
1 teaspoon dried thyme
1 teaspoon – 1 tablespoon butter
9 eggs, beaten
½ cup grated Gouda cheese

Preheat oven to 350°F. Sauté garlic, shallots, and thyme in butter. Add to beaten eggs. Pour into a greased 9" pie or quiche dish. Bake 15 minutes. Remove, sprinkle with cheese, and cook another 15 minutes. Serve immediately with roasted red pepper coulis (recipe follows). *Serves 4 – 6.*

Roasted red pepper coulis:
1 onion, chopped
2 garlic cloves, chopped

(continued on next page)

Lakewinds

Jane and Stephen Locke
PO Box 1483, 328 Queen Street
Niagara-on-the-Lake, Ontario
L0S 1J0
Tel: (905) 468-1888
Fax: (905) 468-1061
$$$$

ABOUT THE B&B

A special experience awaits you at Lakewinds, a circa-1881, restored Victorian manor hosted by Jane and Stephen Locke. Situated on an acre of quiet trees and gardens, Lakewinds offers unparalleled views of the Niagara-on-the-Lake Golf Club and Lake Ontario. Elegantly appointed with antiques, guest rooms have been designed for comfort and privacy and all feature private baths. Guests are invited to the games room for billiards or cards and, in summer, can enjoy refreshing dips in the heated pool or simply relax in rocking chairs on the veranda. Sumptuous breakfasts feature fruits, vegetables, and herbs from Jane's garden. Only one-and-a-half hours south of Toronto, Niagara-on-the-Lake is a charming town offering world-class theater, shops, fine restaurants, and beautiful parks — all with a turn-of-the-century ambience. The many estate wineries in the area offer tours and tastings, while golf, tennis, and countless hiking and biking trails await the active visitor.

SEASON

all year

ACCOMMODATIONS

4 rooms with private baths

2 tablespoons olive oil
2 cups tomatoes, peeled, seeded, and chopped
1 – 2 fresh hot chilies, seeded and chopped
½ teaspoon dried oregano
Salt and freshly ground pepper to taste
Pinch of sugar
1 tablespoon lime juice
1 sweet red pepper, roasted, peeled, and seeded

In a skillet, sweat onion and garlic in oil until soft. Add tomatoes, chilies, oregano, salt, pepper, sugar, and lime juice; simmer about 2 minutes. Add red pepper. Purée until smooth. *Makes 2 cups.*

Leek and Sage Quiche

1 package cream of leek soup (Knorr recommended)
2 cups milk
5 eggs
2 cups half-and-half cream (10 – 18%)
Scant ¼ cup chopped fresh sage
4 leaves phyllo dough
Melted butter
3 tablespoons bread crumbs
1½ cups grated cheese (mixture of Gruyère, cheddar, and
    Emmental is best)
Fresh sage sprigs

Preheat oven to 375°F. Combine soup mix with milk and heat until boiling and thick. Cool to room temperature (this may be done the night before). Lightly beat eggs and add to soup mixture, then add cream and chopped sage. Brush each leaf of phyllo with melted butter and place in a 9" deep pie dish, folding and fluting overhanging edges for a "frilly" effect. Sprinkle bread crumbs on bottom, then the grated cheese. Pour egg mixture over. Bake 1 hour. Let sit for 10 minutes before cutting. Garnish with sprigs of fresh sage. *Variation:* Try basil or parsley instead of sage. *Serves 8.*

Lakewinds

Jane and Stephen Locke
PO Box 1483, 328 Queen Street
Niagara-on-the-Lake, Ontario
L0S 1J0
Tel: (905) 468-1888
Fax: (905) 468-1061
$$$$

ABOUT THE B&B

A special experience awaits you at Lakewinds, a circa-1881, restored Victorian manor hosted by Jane and Stephen Locke. Situated on an acre of quiet trees and gardens, Lakewinds offers unparalleled views of the Niagara-on-the-Lake Golf Club and Lake Ontario. Elegantly appointed with antiques, guest rooms have been designed for comfort and privacy and all feature private baths. Guests are invited to the games room for billiards or cards and, in summer, can enjoy refreshing dips in the heated pool or simply relax in rocking chairs on the veranda. Sumptuous breakfasts feature fruits, vegetables, and herbs from Jane's garden. Only one-and-a-half hours south of Toronto, Niagara-on-the-Lake is a charming town offering world-class theater, shops, fine restaurants, and beautiful parks — all with a turn-of-the-century ambience. The many estate wineries in the area offer tours and tastings, while golf, tennis, and countless hiking and biking trails await the active visitor.

SEASON

all year

ACCOMMODATIONS

4 rooms with private baths

Latimer on Oxford

Pat and Bill Latimer
37 Oxford Street West
Moose Jaw, Saskatchewan
S6H 2N2
Tel: (306) 692-5481
$ – $$

ABOUT THE B&B

Built in 1911, this faithfully restored foursquare Neo-Greek Revival home greets you with Corinthian columns decorated with cherubs, which support the front balcony. The solid oak front door with acanthus leaf appliqué and beveled oval glass beckons and welcomes you to come inside. Interior oak picture frame floors, leaded glass windows, pocket doors, and plate rails recall an era when quality craftsmanship, natural materials, and functional design ruled the day. Choose from the Oriental, Western, and Victorian guest rooms with shared bath, or the elegant Violet guest room with private bath. Also on the site is a little red coach house with exposed beams and hay loft. Plan your visit to coincide with the Moose Jaw Minuet breakfast and your morning is begun with a cheer. Another specialty produced by the heartland oven are golden brown rusks. Temple Gardens Thermo Mineral Spa, the museum and public library, City Hall, shops, and restaurants are a 10-minute walk downtown. Your hosts' interests include art, literature, and music.

SEASON

all year

ACCOMMODATIONS

1 room with private bath;
3 rooms with shared bath

Moose Jaw Minuet

16 slices brown bread, crusts removed
6 – 8 slices Black Forest ham, edges trimmed
¼ – ½ pound grated strong cheddar cheese
6 large eggs
3 cups homogenized milk
¼ cup finely chopped onion
Salt and pepper to taste
1 teaspoon dry mustard
2 teaspoons Worcestershire sauce
Few drops of Tabasco sauce
¼ cup margarine
1 cup crushed Corn Flakes or Special K cereal

Cover the bottom of a greased 13 x 9" pan with half of the bread slices. Layer the ham, then the grated cheese over the bread slices. Cover the cheese layer with remaining bread slices. Beat eggs, milk, onion, and spices together and pour over the pan contents. Seal the pan with plastic wrap and let stand in the refrigerator overnight. In the morning, remove the dish from refrigerator. Preheat oven to 350°F. Melt margarine and pour over crushed cereal (a rolling pin works well). Sprinkle this mixture over pan contents. Bake uncovered for 1 hour. Remove from oven and let stand 10 minutes before serving. *Serves 8.*

Overnight Sausage Omelet

1 pound pork breakfast sausage
6 slices white bread, crusts removed
1 cup grated cheddar or Emmental cheese
4 eggs
½ teaspoon salt
½ teaspoon dry mustard
2 cups milk

Boil sausage for 20 minutes, then cut into bite-sized pieces. Cube bread. Grease a 12 x 8" casserole. Layer bread, then sausage, and then cheese (1 layer of each for 3 layers in total). Beat eggs until foamy. Add salt, mustard, and milk to eggs, and pour over layered ingredients in casserole. Cover and place in the refrigerator overnight. In the morning, remove dish from refrigerator about ¾ hour before baking. Preheat oven to 350°F and bake 1½ hours uncovered. Serve immediately. *Serves 8 – 10.*

Gîte à la ferme MACDALE Bed and Breakfast

Anne and Gordon MacWhirter
365 Route 132, Hope
PO Box 803
Paspébiac, Québec G0C 2K0
Tel: (418) 752-5270
$

ABOUT THE B&B

For a relaxing holiday, visit the Gaspé Peninsula and MACDALE Bed and Breakfast. Situated overlooking Chaleur Bay on an active, fifth-generation beef farm, this spacious three-story home offers two family rooms and a variety of guest accommodations. The aroma of fresh coffee and assorted muffins and pastries will awaken you and whet your appetite for an old-fashioned home-baked breakfast using farm-fresh eggs. Thanks to MACDALE's central location, tourist attractions such as world-famous Percé Rock and Forillon Park are well within day-trip driving distance. A seawater therapy resort is just minutes away, as are many museums, points of historical interest, and sports facilities. Anne is a first grade teacher while Gordon has recently retired from teaching junior high school mathematics.

SEASON

all year

ACCOMMODATIONS

1 loft with private bath;
4 rooms with shared baths

The Varey House

Lorraine Delisle-Joyner
PO Box 1675, 105 Johnson Street
Niagara-on-the-Lake, Ontario
L0S 1J0
Tel: (905) 468-3252
Fax: (416) 323-9249
$$$

ABOUT THE B&B

*A*round 1837, George Varey, a tailor, built his house on the site of a building destroyed during the War of 1812. Each guest room features its own decor and private bathroom, and guests are served a delicious buffet breakfast. The charm and warmth of the parlor and living room offer a relaxing place to enjoy afternoon refreshments or to meet new friends after a day of sightseeing or before an evening of theater. Bicycles are available for exploring the recreational trails around Niagara-on-the-Lake and along the scenic Niagara River. "One of the best preserved nineteenth-century towns in North America" (Treasury of Canadian Bed and Breakfast), Niagara-on-the-Lake is a haven for artists and artisans, theater lovers, and history buffs. Its antique shops, art galleries, summer theater, historic homes and inns, and recreational activities attract tourists year after year. As Canada's premier wine-growing region, the area also attracts wine aficionados for local winery tours and tasting.

SEASON

April – December

ACCOMMODATIONS

4 rooms with private baths

Quiche Lorraine

9" baked pie shell
6 slices bacon
¾ cup grated Swiss cheese
3 eggs
1¼ cups whipping cream (35%)
½ teaspoon salt
Pinch of pepper and ground nutmeg
1 tablespoon butter

Preheat oven to 350°F. Slice bacon into ¼" pieces and cook until browned. Drain and sprinkle into baked pie shell. Cover with grated cheese. Beat eggs, cream, and seasonings until blended. Gently pour into shell to within ¼" of the top. Dot filling with butter. Bake 25 – 35 minutes or until quiche has slightly puffed and a knife inserted in the center comes out clean. Allow to stand for 10 minutes before cutting. Serve warm or cold.

Tips: The quiche will keep in the refrigerator for about 1 week. To cut calories, replace the heavy whipping cream with light (18 – 30%) or half-and-half (10 – 18%) cream. Homogenized milk also works if you increase the eggs to 4. Don't freeze the quiche as the texture of the filling will be altered. *Serves 4 – 6.*

Reuben Bread Pudding with Maple-Onion Jam

"An interesting, creative brunch dish inspired by our chef's favorite sandwich!" — David Wilmer

2 cups milk
2 tablespoons Dijon mustard
½ teaspoon ground caraway
½ teaspoon salt
½ teaspoon pepper
3 whole eggs
2 egg yolks
8 ounces rye bread (approximately 6 – 8 slices)
6 ounces cooked corned beef
2 ounces sauerkraut
¼ cup chopped fresh chives

Preheat oven to 350°F. Heat milk, Dijon, caraway, salt, and pepper together. Bring to a simmer and remove from heat. Whisk eggs and yolks together in a bowl; slowly add the milk mixture and whisk to combine. Cut the bread into ½" cubes, arrange on a sheet, and bake 15 – 20 minutes until completely toasted and golden brown. Cut the corned beef into ½" cubes and combine with milk mixture, bread cubes, and remaining ingredients. Let rest 20 minutes. Divide the batter into 6 ramekins sprayed with non-stick cooking spray. Place in a water bath half the pudding depth and bake 45 minutes until edges pull away and center sets.

(continued on next page)

The Inn at Bay Fortune

David Wilmer (innkeeper)
and Michael Smith (chef)
Bay Fortune
Prince Edward Island C0A 2B0
Tel: (902) 687-3745
Fax: (902) 687-3540
$$$ – $$$$

ABOUT THE B&B

Built in 1910 as the summer home of Broadway playwright Elmer Harris, this inn has enjoyed a place in the Bay Fortune artists' community ever since. In 1989, innkeeper David Wilmer restored the home to its current splendor, reflecting its heritage and taking full advantage of its location overlooking Bay Fortune and the Northumberland Straight beyond. Uniquely decorated with a combination of island antiques and pieces created by local craftsmen, the 11 guest suites all have private baths and a view of the sea, most with a fireplace-graced sitting area. The dining room is the highest rated in Atlantic Canada by Where to Eat in Canada. Chef Michael Smith has earned an international reputation for his focus on fresh island ingredients, and his contemporary cuisine is recognized for its lively combinations and detailed methods. The Inn at Bay Fortune is close to top-flight golf courses and deep-sea fishing, and less than an hour from Charlottetown, with its active nightlife and some of Canada's best theater.

SEASON

May – October

ACCOMMODATIONS

11 suites with private baths

Tip: The pudding can also be baked in 1 large baking dish and served at the table. Adjust baking time accordingly (approximately 5 – 10 minutes longer). Serve with maple-onion jam (recipe follows). *Serves 6.*

Maple-onion jam:
2 large yellow onions
3 tablespoons olive oil
½ cup maple syrup
¼ teaspoon salt

Peel and slice onions; caramelize them slowly in oil until deep golden brown. *Important:* The key to this recipe is to gradually lower heat as onions cook (this step takes patience!). When onions are brown (not burnt), add maple syrup and simmer 5 minutes. Remove from heat, season with salt, and serve warm.

Sausage and Hash Brown Casserole

"For the hash brown lovers of the world, this is different and delicious." — Marj Wilkie

16-ounce package frozen shredded hash browns
5 eggs
¼ cup milk
2 tablespoons chopped onion
1 tablespoon chopped fresh parsley
1 teaspoon dry mustard
½ teaspoon salt
¼ teaspoon pepper
1 cup grated strong cheddar cheese
8 link sausages
4 tomato slices, cut in halves

Preheat oven to 350°F. Thaw and partially cook hash browns. Combine eggs, milk, onion, parsley, mustard, salt, and pepper. Pour over potatoes in a 13 x 9" baking dish. Sprinkle with ½ cup cheese. Bake 15 – 20 minutes. Meanwhile, cook sausages. Arrange sausages down center of potatoes. Sprinkle with remaining cheese. Place tomato halves along each side of sausages. Return to oven until cheese melts. *Serves 4.*

The Lookout at Schooner Cove

The Lookout at Schooner Cove

Marj and Herb Wilkie
3381 Dolphin Drive
Nanoose Bay, British Columbia
V0R 2R0
Tel/Fax: (604) 468-9796
$$

ABOUT THE B&B

*S*ituated halfway between Victoria and Tofino on unspoiled Vancouver Island, this West Coast contemporary cedar home stands in a woodsy setting of rocks and tall evergreens. The wrap-around deck affords a 180° view of Georgia Strait and the majestic mountains beyond. Relax and savor this "little bit of heaven" or hike, golf, kayak, sail, fish, or sightsee. Take a day trip to the wild western shore of the island and the Pacific Rim National Park or to charming Victoria. The vacation suite will accommodate four people and, with its fully equipped kitchen, makes a popular headquarters for an island stay. Hearty breakfasts are served within full view of the ocean activities. The Wilkies ran a store in New York's Catskill mountains for 15 years before discovering this paradise. They enjoy hiking, golf, crafts, reading, games, puzzles, and especially meeting their guests and helping them plan a memorable stay.

SEASON

May – October
(or by arrangement)

ACCOMMODATIONS

1 vacation suite
with private bath;
1 room with private bath;
1 room with shared bath

Peters Place

Joan and Calvin Peters
6430 PR 241 North
Cartier, Manitoba R4K 1B4
Tel: (204) 864-2106

$

ABOUT THE B&B

Experience rural Canada and the people who live there at Peters Place — a 500-acre, family-operated grain farm. Offering peace and quiet along the Assiniboine River, Peters Place is ideal for B&B travelers who want the best of both worlds — country relaxation with close proximity to the urban sights of Winnipeg. It's also a good base from which to tour points of historic interest, such as Lower Fort Garry at Selkirk or the museum at Portage la Prairie. Excellent golf facilities are within a 10-minute drive. For those who enjoy natural parkland, Beaudry Park is open year-round for hikers or cross-country skiers. If time and weather permit, your hosts will take you to watch the beaver on the Assiniboine at dusk, give you a ride in their old Model T or on one of their restored farm tractors, and take you inside their Canadian National Railway caboose. Bountiful breakfasts are served in the family dining area and every effort is made to accommodate special preferences or diets.

SEASON

April – October

ACCOMMODATIONS

2 rooms with shared bath

Savory Bacon Omelet

4 eggs
¼ cup milk
1 cup cooked crumbled bacon
Freshly ground pepper
½ teaspoon dried sage
1 tablespoon butter
Fresh fruit sections

Toast fingers and apple jelly

Blend all ingredients. In a heavy skillet, melt 1 tablespoon butter, heating until bubbly. Pour omelet mixture gently into bubbling butter. As eggs set, lift edges to let uncooked liquid flood under. Fold once and cut in half. Garnish with fresh fruit sections. Serve with hot thick toast fingers and apple jelly. *Serves 2.*

Seven Layer Casserole

1 – 2" layer sliced potato
1 layer sliced onion
1 layer sliced carrot
¼ cup uncooked rice
14-ounce can peas and liquid
1 pound pork breakfast sausage
10-ounce can vegetable soup
10-ounce can tomato soup diluted with 1 can hot water
Salt and pepper

Preheat oven to 350°F – 375°F. In a large, deep casserole, layer ingredients in order given. Bake covered for 1 hour. Turn sausage and leave casserole uncovered for another hour of baking. *Serves 12 – 14.*

Churchill Farm Bed & Breakfast

Jeanette and Waldron
MacKinnon
RR #3
Bonshaw, Prince Edward Island
C0A 1C0
Tel: (902) 675-2481
$

ABOUT THE B&B

Since 1970, B&B hosts Jeanette and Waldron have welcomed guests to their large, lovingly restored farmhouse. Run as a mixed working farm/B&B until the MacKinnon's retirement from farming in 1982, Churchill Farm offers sweeping views of the surrounding countryside from its large deck. Tea and a full country breakfast are served in the cozy kitchen. Specialties of the house include homemade muffins and jams. Located in the center of Prince Edward Island, Churchill Farm is within driving distance of Charlottetown, Borden Ferry, north and south shore red- and white-sand beaches, fishing, golfing, cross-country skiing, sleigh rides, and restaurants.

SEASON

all year

ACCOMMODATIONS

5 rooms with shared baths

Captain's Quarters B&B

Linda and Arnie Aylward
RR #1
South Gillies, Ontario P0T 2V0
Tel: (807) 475-5630
$$

ABOUT THE B&B

Named in honor of the Aylward sea captains from Nova Scotia, Captain's Quarters is an intimate country bed and breakfast located southwest of the city of Thunder Bay, and a short drive from ski hills, amethyst mines, and fine dining. The modern log home features rustic yet gracious queen-sized bedrooms with private baths. Hiking, cross-country skiing, and golf ranges are available on the property. Expansion plans include a solarium with hot tub. Pancakes with strawberries and whipped cream highlight an extensive and varied breakfast menu created only from fresh, quality products. Another menu favorite, Nova Scotia crab toasties capture the B&B's theme and the East Coast heritage of the host. Golf, gardening, sewing, and crafts are among Linda and Arnie's hobbies.

SEASON

all year

ACCOMMODATIONS

2 rooms with private baths

Shrimp 'n Dill Quiche Tarts

¾ cup grated mozzarella cheese
½ cup coarsely chopped cooked shrimp (canned is fine)
2 tablespoons finely chopped red pepper
1 tablespoon finely chopped green onion
24 small or 18 medium pastry shells (Crisco recommended)
2 eggs
⅔ cup light cream (18 – 30%)
½ teaspoon dried dill weed
Salt and pepper to taste

Preheat oven to 375°F. Sprinkle cheese, shrimp, red pepper, and green onion evenly into prepared pastry shells. Beat eggs, and mix with cream, dill weed, salt, and pepper. Pour into shells over filling. Bake 20 – 25 minutes. Serve warm. *Variation:* Use crab meat instead of shrimp. *Makes 2 dozen small or 18 medium tarts.*

Spinach Omelet

2 10-ounce packages frozen spinach, partially thawed
¼ cup butter
¼ cup all-purpose flour
1 teaspoon salt or to taste
⅛ teaspoon pepper
2 cups half-and-half cream (10 – 18%)
6 – 8 slices thick bacon, cut into ¼" pieces and sautéed
    until partially crisp
3 green onions, chopped
1 cup grated Swiss cheese
6 omelets
¼ cup grated Swiss cheese
Coarsely chopped fresh parsley

In a saucepan, cook partially thawed spinach and drain. In
another saucepan or large cast-iron skillet, melt butter over low
heat and stir in flour, salt, and pepper until blended. Over
medium heat, gradually stir in cream. Cook, stirring constantly,
until thickened. Add cooked spinach, bacon, onions, and 1 cup
Swiss cheese. Cook, stirring, just until cheese melts. Take off
heat. Make omelets (recipe follows). Spoon about ¼ cup spinach
mixture onto omelet and fold. Sprinkle omelet immediately
with Swiss cheese (so it melts) and fresh parsley. Repeat with
rest of omelets. *Tip:* This filling can be used with crêpes too.
Serves 6.

(continued on next page)

Fraser House

Sheila and Dennis Derksen
PO Box 211, 33 1st Street East
Letellier, Manitoba R0G 1C0
Tel: (204) 737-2284
$

ABOUT THE B&B

Memories are made at this
elegant and romantic
1916 home. Hardwood
floors, area rugs, and antique furniture enhance the home's Victorian
decor. Spacious rooms combined
with great hospitality make your
stay most enjoyable. Relax in the
parlor or on the veranda or patio
with a beverage and home-baked
goodies. Breakfast may consist of a
puffy egg pancake or freshly baked
croissants and muffins, along with
the season's fresh fruit, served in the
formal dining room. Fraser House
is located just a few minutes north
of the US border in the heart of
Manitoba's bustling agricultural
area, and is near golf, fishing, shopping, and skiing. Sheila enjoys
crafting projects and holds painting
classes during the winter months,
while Dennis enjoys carpentry and
is employed as a fertilizer dealer.

SEASON

all year

ACCOMMODATIONS

2 rooms with shared bath

Omelet:
2 eggs
2 tablespoons water
Salt and pepper
1 tablespoon butter

Beat together eggs and water. Season to taste with salt and pepper. Melt butter in a pan over medium-high heat (don't let it get brown). When the foaming butter starts to subside, pour in egg mixture. The mixture should set at the edges at once. With a spatula, gently push cooked portions toward the center, tilt, and rotate the pan to allow uncooked egg to flow into the empty spaces. While the top is still moist and creamy, garnish half of omelet with filling. Flip unfilled side over filling and slide onto plate. *Makes 1 omelet (multiply as required).*

Vegetable Casserole Surprise

"This vegetable casserole evolved from necessity. One day, we had unexpected company and an almost empty refrigerator. Our solution was to combine all the bits and pieces we had into a casserole that would serve 10. Everyone loved it and we have since been serving it regularly. You can add and subtract amounts according to your tastes and group size. We have prepared this dish for dinners of up to 100 people."
— *Joan Scott*

2 cups cabbage
4 carrots
1 onion
½ head cauliflower
2 broccoli stalks
1 red pepper
1 green pepper
1 zucchini, 6" long
¼ pound sliced mushrooms
3 garlic cloves, finely chopped
3 tablespoons finely chopped fresh ginger
Salt, pepper, and dried basil to taste

(continued on next page)

Sir William Mackenzie Inn

Joan and Paul Scott
PO Box 255, Highway 48
Kirkfield, Ontario K0M 2B0
Tel/Fax: (705) 438-1278
$$

ABOUT THE B&B

Born in a Kirkfield log cabin in 1849, Canadian railway founder Sir William Mackenzie built his first mansion in Kirkfield in 1888, which became an exciting hub of hospitality for Mackenzie family guests. Today, this carefully restored 40-room home is now a bed and breakfast, offering large bedrooms (many with fireplaces) with private bathrooms. A full hot breakfast awaits your rising, after which you can visit in the popular Games Room. Outside, take the time to explore the estate's 13 acres of tree-shaded lawns and beautiful woods, which create a relaxed atmosphere and form a magnificent backdrop for photographs. A restaurant is also located on the grounds. Innkeeper Paul Scott delights in relating the history of the estate and its original owner, "The Railway King of Canada," to his guests while leading the mansion tour. Sir William Mackenzie Inn is situated a few minutes from the Kirkfield Lift Locks (world's second largest), and is near boating, swimming, golfing, birdwatching, and horseback riding, not to mention cycling trails, mini-golf, go-carting, and a gambling casino.

SEASON

May 1 – October 20

ACCOMMODATIONS

6 rooms with private baths

10-ounce can of cream soup (mushroom, chicken, or broccoli)
4 ounces milk
3 slices mozzarella cheese
Sliced mushrooms or tomato wedges

Breast of chicken and rice

Preheat oven to 350°F. Chop cabbage medium fine. Cut following 7 vegetables into bite-sized pieces. Steam cabbage until just barely cooked (leave crisp). Lay cabbage on bottom of an au gratin pan or rectangular glass casserole dish. Steam other vegetables until crisp (again, don't overcook). Add the zucchini, mushrooms, garlic, ginger, and spices for the last 2 or 3 minutes to avoid overcooking. Spread all these over the cabbage. Pour soup mixed with milk over top. Garnish with cheese slices and either sliced mushrooms or tomato wedges. Bake about 15 minutes. Great for a hot brunch on its own or served alongside breast of chicken and rice. *Serves 8 – 10 generously.*

Vegetable Cheese Omelet

1 green pepper, finely chopped
4 green onions, finely chopped
¼ pound mushrooms, finely chopped
3 tomatoes, finely chopped
Butter
8 eggs, lightly beaten
8 ounces strong cheddar cheese
Chopped fresh chives

Whole-wheat toast and jam

Sauté green pepper, green onions, mushrooms, and tomatoes in butter in a large oven-proof frying pan. Gently pour in beaten eggs. Cook over a low heat until bottom of omelet is set. Preheat oven broiler. Place omelet under the grill for 3 – 4 minutes. As it fluffs (still pale yellow), remove and sprinkle with grated cheese. Return to the broiler until cheese is melted. Omelet will fluff beautifully. Cut in half, then garnish with chives. Serve with whole-wheat toast and jam. *Serves 2.*

Bay View Farm / La Ferme Bay View

Helen and Garnett Sawyer
PO Box 21, 337 New Carlisle
West, Route 132
New Carlisle, Québec G0C 1Z0
Tel: (418) 752-2725/6718
$

ABOUT THE B&B

Between New Carlisle and Bonaventure, Bay View Farm offers country hospitality in a beautiful seaside environment on the rugged Baie des Chaleurs coastline of Québec's Gaspé Peninsula. Seaside accommodations include five comfortable guest rooms and a fully equipped country house. At breakfast, enjoy Bay View's farm-fresh eggs, meat, homemade muffins, scones, jams, jellies, and beverages, as well as fresh fruits and vegetables in season from the farm's garden and orchards. Additional meals are available on request at reasonable rates. Handicrafts are on display throughout the house. Enjoy the breathtaking panoramic seascapes, participate in the Bay View Folk Festival (second weekend of August) with folk music and dancing, or visit Percé Rock and the archaeological caves of St. Elzéar.

SEASON

May – November

ACCOMMODATIONS

5 rooms with shared baths;
1 private cottage with
private bath

Gaeste-Haus Kroker

Patricia Kroker
PO Box 202
Bruderheim, Alberta T0B 0S0
Tel: (403) 796-3621
$$

ABOUT THE B&B

Only a short drive yet worlds away from the hustle and bustle of Edmonton, Gaeste-Haus Kroker invites you to relax in the charm and comfort of this 1927 brick Victorian guest house. You can choose to enjoy the peaceful ambience of the entire upper level or mingle with other guests in the French Provincial-furnished parlor. Wind down your evening with a snack of homemade dessert. Awaken in the morning to freshly brewed coffee and a hearty breakfast on fine china in the elegantly furnished dining room. Relax on the veranda or in front of the outdoor fireplace, and stroll about the spacious lawn and garden. A former registered nurse, town councilor, and town mayor, hostess Patricia Kroker enjoys gardening, baking, and traveling, and will make your visit an enjoyable and memorable experience. Area attractions include Elk Island National Park, West Edmonton Mall, Ukrainian Cultural Heritage Village, and Beaverhill Lake.

SEASON

all year

ACCOMMODATIONS

3 rooms with shared bath

Vegetable Garden Bake

"Since I love to use recipes that call for ingredients I can pick fresh from my garden, this has become one of my favorites. It seems to be a favorite of my guests too since I get lots of compliments every time it's served. I like to dish it up with freshly baked cheese biscuits and pork breakfast sausage."
— Patricia Kroker

5 eggs
⅔ cup vegetable oil
1 tablespoon dried parsley
¾ teaspoon salt
¼ teaspoon pepper
⅔ cup grated Parmesan cheese
1¼ cups chopped onion
3½ cups grated zucchini
¼ cup grated carrot
1¼ cups powdered biscuit mix

Preheat oven to 350°F. Beat eggs in a large mixing bowl until frothy. Mix in oil, parsley, salt, and pepper. Stir in remaining ingredients in order given. Pour into a shallow, greased 9" casserole dish. Bake about 35 minutes. *Serves 8.*

Zucchini Crescent Pie

4 cups unpeeled thinly sliced zucchini
1 cup chopped onion
½ cup margarine
⅓ cup chopped fresh parsley
½ teaspoon salt
½ teaspoon ground pepper
¼ teaspoon garlic powder
¼ teaspoon dried sweet basil
¼ teaspoon dried oregano
2 eggs, well beaten
8 ounces mozzarella cheese, grated
8-ounce package crescent dinner rolls
2 teaspoons prepared mustard

Preheat oven to 375°F. Sauté zucchini and onion in margarine until tender. Stir in parsley and seasonings. In a large bowl, blend eggs and cheese. Stir in vegetable mixture. Separate crescent dough and press over bottom and up sides of an ungreased 9" pie pan to form crust. Spread crust with mustard. Pour vegetable mixture evenly over crust. Bake 18 – 20 minutes. Let stand 10 minutes before cutting. *Serves 6 – 8.*

The Open Door / La Porte Ouverte

Marlene and Glenn Scullion
239 Thomas Lefebvre Road
Davidson, Québec J0X 1R0
Tel: (819) 683-2991
Fax: (819) 683-2201
$$

ABOUT THE B&B

The Open Door B&B is nestled on the sandy shores of the Ottawa River, about a one-and-a-quarter-hour drive from the nation's capital. Located in the historic Pontiac region, the area is an inspiring combination of the traditions found in both English and French Canada. Rivers, lakes, and forests surrounding The Open Door provide a backdrop of natural beauty rarely found today. Since January 1993, The Open Door has played host to many international visitors and small conferences. A charming, comfortable atmosphere is created with a tasteful decor of Canadian country antiques. Delicious home cooking is graciously served in the beautiful sunroom overlooking a wide expanse of the river. Numerous seasonal activities are available on the premises or by arrangement. Marlene and Glenn are a recently retired couple from the broadcasting industry. Glenn is also a gifted pianist and Marlene an artist, and they both take great pride in ensuring their guests have a wonderful stay.

SEASON

all year

ACCOMMODATIONS

3 rooms with shared bath;
1 cabin with private bath;
2-bedroom guest house
with private bath

Egg, Meat, & Fish Main Dishes

Baked Stuffed Salmon in Egg Sauce

1 Atlantic salmon, 5 – 8 pounds, cleaned and scaled
2 teaspoons salt
3 tablespoons lemon juice
⅓ cup butter
1 – 2 medium onions, chopped
½ cup chopped celery
½ cup grated carrot
2 cups white or whole-wheat bread crumbs
1 teaspoon dried savory or sage
1 teaspoon salt
¼ teaspoon pepper
1 egg, beaten
Vegetable oil

Egg sauce:
¼ cup butter
¼ cup all-purpose flour
1½ cups milk
½ – 1 teaspoon salt
Pepper to taste
2 eggs, hard-boiled and chopped
Pinch of chopped fresh parsley

(continued on next page)

Humber Gallery Hospitality Home

Edna and Eldon Swyer
26 Roberts Drive
Little Rapids, Newfoundland
A2H 6C3
(Mailing address: PO Box 15
Corner Brook, Newfoundland
A2H 6C3)
Tel: (709) 634-2660
$

ABOUT THE B&B

A popular stop for the British royal family, the town of Little Rapids (near Corner Brook) is home to Humber Gallery, an impressive cedar abode with cathedral ceilings, fireplace, wraparound sun deck, two guest rooms with double beds, one guest room with twin beds, and full and half guest bathrooms. Humber serves a nutritious breakfast, while other meals and guests' use of the barbecue and picnic area can be arranged. An excellent spot for an overnight stay when going or coming from Gros Morne National Park, this B&B is in the heart of the Humber Valley Reserve near Marble Mountain Ski Resort, mini-golf facilities, "U-pick" strawberry farms, Bay of Islands tourist attractions, South Brook and Pasadena beaches on Deer Lake, and the Humber River. Edna and Eldon will be happy to provide you with maps, tourist literature, a licensed salmon fishing guide, and insider tips on area attractions.

SEASON

June – September;
February – mid-April

ACCOMMODATIONS

3 rooms with shared baths

Preheat oven to 425°F. Combine salt and lemon juice. Rub the salmon inside and out with the mixture. Melt butter in a saucepan. Add onion and celery and cook over medium-low heat until soft (about 10 minutes). Combine in a bowl with carrot, bread crumbs, savory, salt, and pepper. Add beaten egg and mix well. Stuff the salmon with this mixture and skewer closed or sew with a string. Brush surface of the salmon with oil. Place salmon on a lightly greased baking sheet. Bake in the oven, allowing 10 minutes per inch of stuffed thickness of fish. Baste with oil during baking. The salmon is ready when the flesh is no longer translucent and can be pulled away from the backbone with a knife. Let rest 5 – 10 minutes while you cook egg sauce.

In a heavy saucepan, melt butter over medium-low heat. Stir in flour until smooth and remove from heat. Gradually stir in half of the milk. Return to heat and beat until smooth and shiny. Gradually add remaining milk, salt, and pepper. Cook for 2 – 3 minutes until smooth and shiny. Add chopped eggs and stir. Add a pinch of parsley. Serve hot egg sauce in a dish alongside fish. *Serves 8.*

Basilic Tomato and Egg

1 tomato
Olive oil
Chopped fresh basil or fresh pesto
Salt
Freshly grated white pepper
2 eggs
Butter
2 basil leaves

Cut the top of the tomato off. Gently squeeze the tomato to remove juice with the seeds, then chop in small pieces. Sauté tomato for a couple of minutes in olive oil and fresh basil or fresh pesto (dried basil doesn't have enough taste). Add salt and pepper. Add eggs and some butter to the skillet and scramble. Divide egg mixture between 2 plates, garnish with a basil leaf, and serve immediately. Multiply recipe as required. *Serves 2.*

Montréal Oasis

Lena Blondel
3000 Breslay Road
Montréal, Québec H3Y 2G7
Tel: (514) 935-2312
$$

ABOUT THE B&B

In pilgrim days, the evergreen tree was a sign of shelter, good food, and warm hospitality. It's fitting, then, that two towering evergreens frame the door to Montréal Oasis. This charming B&B with original leaded windows and slanted ceilings is located in downtown Montréal's west end, close to the Fine Arts Museum, chic Crescent Street and Greene Avenue shopping and restaurants, and the "main drag," St. Catherine Street. The beautiful and safe neighborhood with its spacious Elizabethan-style houses and pretty gardens is locally referred to as the Priest Farm district — once a holiday resort for priests. Originally from Sweden, your world-traveled hostess Lena has lived in many countries around the globe, which is evident from the African, Asian, and Swedish art that graces the B&B. The three guest rooms feature Scandinavian and Québecois furniture. Lena loves good food, and serves three-course gourmet breakfasts featuring delicious, fresh ingredients. A friendly Siamese cat resides on the main floor.

SEASON

all year

ACCOMMODATIONS

3 rooms with shared baths

Harbour House Bed & Breakfast Inn

Gayle Flebotte
615 Lakeshore Drive
Cold Lake, Alberta T0A 0V2
Tel: (403) 639-2337
$$ – $$$

ABOUT THE B&B

Built in 1989 to complement the Cold Lake Marina, Harbour House is patterned after the Old Coast Guard Station in Virginia Beach, Virginia, and retains all the charm of old New England (where your hostess is originally from). Climb the stairs to the viewing tower where you'll admire the panoramic view of Cold Lake, Alberta's seventh largest lake. Settle into one of 11 individually decorated rooms (most facing the lake), and rest assured of a comfortable night's sleep under feather duvets or hand-stitched quilts. Awake to a breathtaking sunrise over the lake and the aroma of the inn's famous sticky buns or other home-baked goods, fresh fruit specialties, and juice. Gayle's passions include quilting, tap dancing, and making sure her guests enjoy their stay. Nearby Cold Lake Provincial Park is home to over 200 bird species. Harbour House is within walking distance of the beach, with opportunities for fishing and boating. In the near vicinity, you can go mini-golfing and regular golfing, bowling, skiing, and browsing in antique and craft shops.

SEASON

all year

ACCOMMODATIONS

5 rooms with private baths;
6 rooms with shared baths

Breakfast Burritos

"I used to make this in pita bread, but one day the store was out of pita, so I decided to try tortillas. Lo and behold, they became breakfast burritos!" — Gayle Flebotte

4 eggs, beaten
¼ cup milk
Sprinkle of salt and pepper
2 slices cooked ham, chopped
1 green onion, chopped
2 teaspoons butter or margarine
2 large flour tortillas
½ cup grated cheddar cheese

Salsa (see recipes on page 271 and page 281)

Mix eggs, milk, salt, pepper, ham, and onion in a bowl. Scramble egg mixture in melted butter in a skillet. Pile half of scrambled eggs down center of each tortilla, leaving 1" open at each end. Fold one end over eggs then fold sides over eggs. Place seam-side down on a plate. Sprinkle cheese over top. Microwave 60 – 90 seconds or until cheese is melted. Serve with salsa, if desired. *Serves 2.*

Breakfast in One

"For vegetarians, simply omit the bacon or ham."
— *Elaine Landray*

6 slices bread
6 teaspoons butter
1 cup grated Gruyère or Emmental cheese
1 cup cooked chopped ham or crumbled bacon
6 eggs
Salt and pepper
6 teaspoons whipping cream (35%)

Preheat oven to 375°F. Cut the crusts from 6 slices of bread. Roll with a rolling pin. Butter both sides and press each slice into a 6-cup muffin pan (a Texas muffin pan works best). Bake 15 minutes.

Reduce oven to 350°F. Put grated cheeses in the bottoms of toast cups (saving some for topping). Sprinkle ham or bacon over cheese. Break an egg carefully into each cup, add salt and pepper, a dot of butter, and about 1 teaspoon of cream to each, then top with more grated cheese. Bake 18 – 20 minutes. **Serves 6.**

Linden House B&B

Elaine and Phil Landray
PO Box 1586, 389 Simcoe Street
Niagara-on-the-Lake, Ontario
L0S 1J0
Tel/Fax: (905) 468-3923
$$

ABOUT THE B&B

A warm welcome awaits you at Linden House, a new Cape Cod-style, air conditioned home with private guest wing, featuring two queen rooms and one twin/king room, all with private ensuite bathrooms. The queen rooms feature brass beds and cream wicker furniture, while the twin/king room highlights the nautical flavor with Cape Cod wicker. There is a guest lounge on the same level as the bedrooms with television, VCR, games, and books, or you can choose to enjoy the garden or relax in the gazebo. Non-smoking Linden House offers convenient on-site parking and is located in the old town, just four short blocks from Queen Street with its shopping and theaters. In summer, enjoy water recreation on Lake Ontario or top-notch theater at the Shaw Festival. Your hosts, Elaine and Phil, serve such sumptuous breakfasts — featuring seasonal Niagara fruit — that their guests claim they don't need lunch!

SEASON

April – December

ACCOMMODATIONS

3 rooms with private baths

Le Gîte
Park Avenue B&B

Anne-Marie and Irving Bansfield
54 Park Avenue
Ottawa, Ontario K2P 1B2
Tel: (613) 230-9131
$$

ABOUT THE B&B

A bright, airy ambience and artistic decor awaits you at Park Avenue B&B, an elegant, brick 1906 home located in a charming residential area of downtown Ottawa, Canada's capital. In addition to high-quality beds done up in classic cotton and linen sheets and duvets, each guest room is furnished with desk and swivel chair, rocking chair, bookshelves, excellent lighting, and attractive works of art. Ideal for families, the third-floor suite has two bedrooms and a private bath. The mood throughout the house is one of relaxation and warmth. Park Avenue B&B is close to the Parliament buildings, art galleries and museums, and is only three minutes away (by foot) from the Rideau Canal, which freezes into the world's longest skating rink. Ottawa has a number of exciting festivals and activities, including Winterlude, a winter carnival held each February. Anne-Marie and Irving make it a point to know what's going on when in Ottawa so they can advise their guests on what to see and do.

SEASON

all year

ACCOMMODATIONS

1 suite with private bath;
2 rooms with shared bath

Brule Jol (Salt Cod)

"This nutritious salt cod dish originates from my West Indian roots. It's usually accompanied by 'bake' biscuits."
— Irving Bansfield

1 pound (approximately) boneless salt cod
3 – 4 tablespoons finely chopped green onion and/or
    fresh chives
3 – 4 tablespoons finely chopped red and/or yellow pepper
Juice of 1 lemon or lime
3 tablespoons olive oil
Lettuce leaves
2 tomatoes, sliced or wedge-cut
Avocado pear, cut in slender wedges (optional)
Lemon slices

"Bake" biscuits (see recipe on page 121)

Soak the fish in water to cover overnight. Drain. Place fish in a deep skillet and cover again with cold water. Bring to just under a boil — as it starts to simmer, remove from heat, rinse under cold water, and drain. Shred the fish into a bowl. Add chopped onion and peppers. Drizzle with dressing made from lemon or lime juice and olive oil, reserving some to drizzle over entire dish. Arrange cod mixture on some lettuce leaves on a platter. Surround with tomatoes and avocado pear, and drizzle remaining dressing all over the dish. Garnish with lemon slices. Serve with "bake" biscuits. *Tip:* If your taste buds delight in piquant flavor, add a few drops of hot pepper sauce to the dressing. *Serves 6.*

Dutch Toastie

"A Dutch toastie is great at any time of the day. We serve them to our Tea Room patrons for lunch and to our B&B guests for a hearty breakfast." — Bonnie Evans

Slice of bread
Slice of Black Forest ham
Pineapple ring
4 – 6 spears cooked asparagus
Thin cheese slices to cover (Swiss or Gruyère)

Place ingredients on top of bread, in order given, then heat under the broiler until the cheese is melted. ***Serves 1 (multiply as needed).***

Cornelius White House Bed & Breakfast

Bonnie and Frank Evans
8 Wellington Street
Bloomfield, Ontario K0K 1G0
Tel/Fax: (613) 393-2282
$ – $$

ABOUT THE B&B

Located on the historic Loyalist Parkway in the west end of a farming community, the Cornelius White House is named for its original owner, a Dutch settler who built this charming red-brick house in 1862. Today, a sense of history and design combine with European furnishings and accents to create a rather unique bed and breakfast. Three guest rooms on the second floor open onto the cathedral ceiling sitting room, and there's also a suite on the main floor. The B&B is air conditioned and is a non-smoking environment. A full breakfast, consisting of fruit, a hot main course, and freshly baked goods, is served in the adjoining Dutch Treat Tea Room. Outstanding restaurants are nearby, as well as antique and craft shops, galleries, studios, and museums. Cornelius White House is just 10 minutes from the Sandbanks and Outlet Beach provincial parks (boasting the largest freshwater sand dunes in the world). Prince Edward County is a cyclist's dream come true complete with panoramic views and gentle rolling hills.

SEASON

all year

ACCOMMODATIONS

2 rooms with private baths;
2 rooms with shared bath

Henderson Hollow

Jeanette and Garry Henderson
RR #1
Austin, Manitoba R0H 0C0
Tel: (204) 466-2857
$

ABOUT THE B&B

A piece of heaven and a heavenly getaway, Henderson Hollow is a cozy country home set in beautiful, rolling, wooded hills. Simply relax on the large deck or in the screened sun porch surrounded by nature's beauty and abundant wildlife, or enjoy many indoor and outdoor activities (depending on the season). Full home-cooked meals include home-baked bread and cinnamon rolls, and dishes featuring garden-fresh fruits and vegetables. The house is filled with antiques and decorated with many homemade crafts for you to enjoy (or purchase, if you desire). Nearby points of interest include the Austin Agricultural Museum (largest in western Canada), Spruce Woods Provincial Park, Margaret Laurence Museum, and the Thomas Seton Centre. Your hosts' interests include golfing in summer at the many beautiful — and challenging! — surrounding golf courses, and cross-country skiing in winter right from the back door.

SEASON

all year

ACCOMMODATIONS

1 room with private bath;
2 rooms with shared bath;
campground facilities

Eggs Mexicana with Salsa

"We enjoyed this dish so much when visiting Mexico that we decided to adapt it for our Henderson Hollow guests."
— Jeanette Henderson

8 eggs, beaten
2 tablespoons water
½ green pepper, diced
1 hot pepper, diced (such as jalapeño)
1 small onion, diced
1 medium tomato, diced (juice and seeds removed)
1 tablespoon butter or vegetable oil

Beat eggs and water together. Sauté diced vegetables in butter or oil just until tender (don't brown). Stir in beaten eggs and water and continue stirring until cooked. Serve with salsa (recipe follows). *Tip:* If you don't want your eggs too hot, leave the hot pepper whole and remove before serving. *Serves 4.*

Salsa:
6 cups peeled and coarsely diced tomatoes
3 large onions, chopped
¼ cup diced hot pepper (such as jalapeño)

(continued on next page)

1 large green pepper, diced
1 – 2 garlic cloves, minced
2 tablespoons sugar
1½ teaspoons salt
1 teaspoon dried basil
1 teaspoon dried oregano
2 teaspoons dried parsley
½ cup cider vinegar or white vinegar
2 tablespoons cornstarch
¼ cup water
1 cup cooked black beans (optional)
1 cup cooked corn kernels (optional)

Bring diced vegetables, sugar, spices, and vinegar to a boil and simmer 30 minutes or until vegetables are tender. Add black beans and corn, if desired. Dissolve cornstarch in water and stir in. Cook another 10 minutes. Seal in sterilized jars. Refrigerate once opened. *Makes approximately 8 cups.*

Bayberry Cliff Inn

Nancy and Don Perkins
RR #4, Little Sands
Murray River
Prince Edward Island C0A 1W0
Tel: (800) 668-3395 or
(902) 962-3395
$$ – $$$

ABOUT THE B&B

Bayberry Cliff Inn is named for the fragrant bayberry bushes that cover the rugged 40-foot cliff on which the inn sits. Incorporating two reconstructed post and beam barns, the inn features intriguing architectural details such as individually shaped rooms and multiple-level living spaces. Bedrooms, lofts, and sitting areas are filled with handmade quilts, antique furniture, and paintings, the result of a lifetime of collecting beautiful things. A large library and breakfast area are on the ground level. Don's hash browns and bacon and Nancy's sourdough pancakes and blueberry muffins all consistently get rave reviews. Don is a retired teacher and Nancy is a marine painter (who has made sure the changeable ocean can be seen from every level of the B&B). Bayberry activities include picking up to 35 different wildflowers, sitting in the whimsical tree perch to watch for marine life, inner-tubing, swimming, and beachcombing. You may cook your own meals on the gas grill or choose from many excellent restaurants a scant 15-minute drive away.

SEASON

May 10 – September 30

ACCOMMODATIONS

3 rooms with private baths;
1 room with shared bath

Finnish Miners' Pasties

"Given to me by my Finnish father, this recipe was a favorite 'all-in-one' lunch for Finnish miners. The meat is at one end and the dessert at the other! These are great to pack for hikes or picnics." — Nancy Perkins

Dough:
1 cup shortening
1¼ cups boiling water
1 teaspoon salt
4½ – 5 cups all-purpose flour

Meat filling (leave uncooked):
3 small potatoes, diced
1 small onion, diced
Salt and pepper to taste
3 bacon strips, diced
1 carrot, grated

Apple filling:
4 medium apples, peeled, cored, and diced
2 tablespoons sugar
2 teaspoons all-purpose flour
½ teaspoon ground cinnamon
⅛ teaspoon salt

Bacon grease

(continued on next page)

Mix shortening with boiling water and salt. Add just enough flour to make a stiff dough. Chill 1 hour. Turn out onto a floured surface, break off pieces of dough, and roll dough into 4½"-diameter circles; set aside. In separate bowls, mix together ingredients for meat and apple fillings. To assemble pasties, put 1 tablespoon meat filling on right side of circle and 1 tablespoon apple filling on left side of circle. Bring up top and bottom edges and pinch together. Put pastry pinched-side down on a greased baking sheet and pat into the shape of a finger roll. Brush tops with bacon grease. Preheat oven to 350°F and bake 1 hour. *Makes 20 – 24 pasties.*

Fairfield Farm Inn

Shae and Richard Griffith
10 Main Street West, Route 1
Middleton, Nova Scotia B0S IP0
Tel/Fax: (800) 237-9896
or (902) 825-6989
$$

ABOUT THE B&B

Fairfield Farm Inn is situated on a 110-acre fruit and vegetable farm famous for its luscious melons. Built in 1886, this Annapolis Valley farmhouse has been completely restored and furnished in period antiques to enhance its original charm. Cozy comforters, king- and queen-sized beds, and private baths grace the five guest rooms. The Annapolis River and Slocum Brook are on the property, as are birdwatching and walking trails, pheasants, and other abundant wildlife. Shae and Richard take pride in offering Maritime hospitality and wholesome country breakfasts, featuring fresh fruit picked from their farm and homemade jams and jellies. Shae is a member of the Acadia University Business School Advisory Board; Richard is a retired military officer. Their hobbies include gardening, antique hunting, reading, and traveling. A few minutes from picturesque fishing villages and the world's highest tides on the Bay of Fundy, Middleton boasts museums, restaurants, boutiques, and theater — all a short walking distance from the inn.

SEASON

all year
(winter by reservation only)

ACCOMMODATIONS

5 rooms with private baths

Maritime Morning Eggs

2 English muffins
Mayonnaise
Cooked sliced ham
4 eggs, poached
Cheese slices of your choice

Preheat oven to 350°F. Split English muffins with a fork and spread each half generously with mayonnaise. Top with sliced ham. Place in a covered baking dish and warm in oven about 15 minutes. Top with a well-drained poached egg and cheese slice (cut into strips and arranged in a lattice fashion on top of the egg). Return uncovered to oven and bake until cheese just melts. *Quick method:* Warm English muffin with mayonnaise and ham in microwave, uncovered, then broil in oven after placing egg and cheese on top. *Serves 4.*

Nest Eggs

2 – 3 thin slices Black Forest ham
1 egg
1 tablespoon half-and-half cream (10 – 18%)
1 heaping tablespoon grated Swiss cheese
Sprinkle of dried basil
English muffin half

Preheat oven to 350°F. Grease large muffin cups. Line with ham and break egg over top. Add cream and sprinkle with cheese and basil. Bake 20 minutes. Serve on half a toasted English muffin. *Tip:* For baking, place water in any unused muffin cups to prevent damage. *Serves 1 (multiply as required).*

Dorrington Bed & Breakfast

Pat and Helen Gray
13851 19A Avenue
White Rock, British Columbia
V4A 9M2
Tel: (604) 535-4408
Fax: (604) 535-4409
www.bbcanada.com/508.html
$$ – $$$

ABOUT THE B&B

A luxurious and restful escape, Dorrington is a wonderful base for exploring the beauty of Vancouver and its surrounding area. Each of Dorrington's three rooms is themed and has a private bath: The Victorian is graced by a double four-poster bed and period decor; the St. Andrews has a unique queen bed hewn from maple branches and contains many original souvenirs of this famous Scottish golf links; The Windsor is 700 square feet of luxury with a brass, canopied queen bed, fireplace, sitting area, and marble bathroom with a double Jacuzzi tub. Full breakfast is served in the Hunt Salon or on the patio overlooking the gardens, tennis court, pond, and outside hot tub. A short drive from downtown Vancouver, White Rock beach with its promenade and many fine restaurants is three minutes away, while ferries to Victoria and the Gulf Islands are 30 minutes away. If you wish, you can use Dorrington's side-by-side tandem bike for a picnic in one of the many nearby heritage forests. Pat is a marketing consultant and Helen works for a nearby supermarket (but her true love is decorating and it shows at Dorrington!).

SEASON

all year

ACCOMMODATIONS

3 rooms (including 1 suite) with private baths

Captain's Quarters B&B

Linda and Arnie Aylward
RR #1
South Gillies, Ontario P0T 2V0
Tel: (807) 475-5630
$$

ABOUT THE B&B

Named in honor of the Aylward sea captains from Nova Scotia, Captain's Quarters is an intimate country bed and breakfast located southwest of the city of Thunder Bay, and a short drive from ski hills, amethyst mines, and fine dining. The modern log home features rustic yet gracious queen-sized bedrooms with private baths. Hiking, cross-country skiing, and golf ranges are available on the property. Expansion plans include a solarium with hot tub. Pancakes with strawberries and whipped cream highlight an extensive and varied breakfast menu created only from fresh, quality products. Another menu favorite, Nova Scotia crab toasties capture the B&B's theme and the East Coast heritage of the host. Golf, gardening, sewing, and crafts are among Linda and Arnie's hobbies.

SEASON

all year

ACCOMMODATIONS

2 rooms with private baths

Nova Scotia Crab Toasties

"This recipe reflects the East Coast influence of our B&B."
— Arnie Aylward

12 ounces cooked king crab meat, chopped (canned is fine)
¾ cup finely diced celery
¼ – ½ cup mayonnaise (depending on your taste)
½ teaspoon dried dill weed
3 English muffins, halved
6 cheddar cheese slices

Preheat oven to 350°F. Mix the crab, celery, mayonnaise, and dill. Set aside. Lightly toast English muffin halves. Spread crab mixture evenly on muffins. Top with cheddar slices. Place toasties on a baking sheet and bake 10 – 12 minutes.
Makes 6 toasties.

Oasis Poached Eggs

Equal parts chopped fresh parsley, chives, and cilantro
(also known as coriander) or according to taste
1 teaspoon butter
Few drops fresh lemon juice
1 egg, poached
White, black, red, and green crushed peppercorns

Toasted English muffins and dark bread

Add butter to herb mixture and melt in the microwave or in a
pan (don't let it cook). Add a few drops of lemon juice. Place
herb mixture over poached egg and top with peppercorn
mixture. *Tip:* If using unsalted butter, add some sea salt to the
butter. Serve accompanied with a basket of toasted English
muffins and dark bread. Multiply recipe as required. *Serves 1.*

Montréal Oasis

Lena Blondel
3000 Breslay Road
Montréal, Québec H3Y 2G7
Tel: (514) 935-2312
$$

ABOUT THE B&B

*I*n pilgrim days, the evergreen
tree was a sign of shelter, good
food, and warm hospitality. It's
fitting, then, that two towering ever-
greens frame the door to Montréal
Oasis. This charming B&B with
original leaded windows and
slanted ceilings is located in down-
town Montréal's west end, close
to the Fine Arts Museum, chic
Crescent Street and Greene Avenue
shopping and restaurants, and the
"main drag," St. Catherine Street.
The beautiful and safe neighborhood
with its spacious Elizabethan-style
houses and pretty gardens is locally
referred to as the Priest Farm
district — once a holiday resort for
priests. Originally from Sweden,
your world-traveled hostess Lena
has lived in many countries around
the globe, which is evident from the
African, Asian, and Swedish art
that graces the B&B. The three
guest rooms feature Scandinavian
and Québecois furniture. Lena
loves good food, and serves three-
course gourmet breakfasts featuring
delicious, fresh ingredients. A
friendly Siamese cat resides on the
main floor.

SEASON

all year

ACCOMMODATIONS

3 rooms with shared baths

Caron House (1837)

Mary and Mike Caron
PO Box 143
Williamstown, Ontario K0C 2J0
Tel: (613) 347-7338
$$

ABOUT THE B&B

Caron House (1837) is a historic, romantic brick home located in the quaint village of Williamstown (established in 1784). Beautifully decorated and furnished with antiques, the house is in its original state, with working fireplaces, inside shutters, tin ceilings, and wide pine floorboards. Two rooms with shared bath are individually decorated with Laura Ashley wallpaper, antique linens, hooked rugs, quilts, and collectibles. Guests can relax in the Keeping Room (a Colonial term for gathering place) or living room, while a full, candlelit gourmet breakfast — accompanied by classical music — is served in the dining room on fine china, silverware, and crystal. Outside, you'll marvel at the herb and Victorian gardens, and relax on the antique wicker furniture on the back veranda, enjoying the lovely yards, complete with trellis, brick patio, and gazebo. Caron House is one hour's drive from either Montréal or Ottawa; nearby attractions include Upper Canada Village, artisan studios, a bird sanctuary, tennis, cycling, and good restaurants. Mary and Mike are retirees from the corporate world, and enjoy traveling, antique hunting, cooking, gardening, and history.

SEASON

all year

ACCOMMODATIONS

2 rooms with shared bath

Poached Eggs on Black Bean Cakes with Sour Cream

8 eggs, poached (method follows)

Black bean cakes:
3 cups cooked drained black beans (or canned)
2 teaspoons olive oil
½ cup chopped onion
1 clove garlic, minced
2 eggs, well beaten
⅛ teaspoon chili powder
⅛ teaspoon ground cayenne pepper
½ teaspoon salt
¼ teaspoon pepper
1 cup cornmeal
1 tablespoon butter
1 tablespoon olive oil
Sour cream

To poach eggs: Half fill a saucepan with water. Bring water to a boil, then reduce to simmer. Break 1 egg into a small dish, then slide egg into water. Repeat with remaining eggs. Poach up to 4 eggs at a time. Simmer uncovered 3 – 5 minutes. Remove with a slotted spoon.

(continued on next page)

To make bean cakes: Using a blender, finely chop black beans. Remove to a mixing bowl and set aside. In a skillet, heat 2 teaspoons olive oil. Cook onion and garlic a few minutes until tender. Add to beans. Blend in eggs, chili powder, cayenne, salt, and pepper. Stir in ½ cup cornmeal. Form mixture into 8 balls and roll in remaining cornmeal. Flatten balls into ¾"-thick patties (about 3" in diameter). In a skillet, heat butter and 2 tablespoons olive oil. Cook patties over medium-low heat, 4 – 5 minutes on each side.

To serve: Spread a dollop of sour cream over plate, place 2 bean cakes in center of plate and top each with a poached egg. Place a dollop of sour cream over each egg. *Serves 4.*

River Run
Cottage & Breakfast

Janice and Bill Harkley
4551 River Road West
Ladner, British Columbia
V4K 1R9
Tel: (604) 946-7778
Fax: (604) 940-1970
$$$$

ABOUT THE B&B

Described in Vancouver Best Places *as "a jewel on the Fraser" and rated "four kisses" in* Best Place to Kiss in the Northwest, *River Run is a romantic, tranquil getaway 30 minutes south of downtown Vancouver. Individual waterfront cottages on the Fraser River with private decks overlooking the river and mountains have wood-burning fireplaces, CD players, telephones, bathrobes, and cozy furnishings. All have private baths, one also equipped with a Jacuzzi tub for two, and one with a soaker tub on the deck. Breakfast is delivered to the cottages at the time specified by guests and includes freshly squeezed juice, home-baked goods, and a variety of entrées. Bicycles, rowboats, and a double kayak are available for guests to explore the delta and the nearby Reifel Migratory Bird Sanctuary. By car, River Run is a 10-minute drive from ferries to Victoria and the Gulf Islands and a 20-minute drive from Vancouver International Airport.*

SEASON

all year

ACCOMMODATIONS

3 cottages with private baths

River Run Eggs

"One of our all-time favorite breakfasts is this gem created by owner Bill Harkley. It takes about half an hour of preparation but the results are well worth it."
— *Karen Bond, Innkeeper of River Run Cottage & Breakfast*

River Run salsa:
4 Roma (Italian) tomatoes, finely chopped
⅓ cup finely chopped white onion
1 serrano pepper, minced
Juice of ½ lime
1 tablespoon olive oil with chili peppers (or plain)
Salt to taste
¼ cup chopped fresh cilantro (also known as coriander)

2 English muffins
4 eggs, poached
Miracle Whip salad dressing or mayonnaise
Homemade salsa (recipe above)
Grated medium cheddar cheese

Combine salsa ingredients, stirring gently, and place in the refrigerator. Split muffins and warm in toaster. While muffins are warming, poach the eggs (see method on page 279). Spread each muffin half with Miracle Whip and place muffins side by side on a pre-warmed, oven-proof plate. Spread fresh salsa over each muffin half, top with a poached egg, then sprinkle with grated cheddar cheese. Place under broiler until cheese melts and serve immediately. *Serves 2.*

Smoked Salmon Hollandaise

"You can't beat this when the fish are biting!" — *Marj Wilkie*

1 biscuit, freshly baked
4 ounces smoked salmon, warmed
2 eggs, poached
2 tomato slices

Quick hollandaise sauce:
¾ cup butter or margarine
¼ teaspoon salt
Dash of cayenne pepper
1½ tablespoons lemon juice
3 egg yolks

Halve biscuit and pile each half high with warmed smoked salmon. Place poached egg on top of each half. Add a slice of tomato on each egg. Pour hollandaise sauce over all. Multiply recipe as required. *Serves 1.*

To make hollandaise, place butter or margarine in the top of a double boiler. Beat until creamy. Add salt and cayenne. Add lemon juice, a few drops at a time. Beat constantly. Add egg yolks one at a time and beat until mixture is light and fluffy. Place over hot — but not boiling — water for a few minutes, stirring constantly, until sauce is glossy (water shouldn't touch top of double boiler). *Tip:* If you leave the sauce too long, it will separate. *Makes approximately 1 cup.*

The Lookout at Schooner Cove

The Lookout at Schooner Cove

Marj and Herb Wilkie
3381 Dolphin Drive
Nanoose Bay, British Columbia
V0R 2R0
Tel/Fax: (604) 468-9796
$$

ABOUT THE B&B

Situated halfway between Victoria and Tofino on unspoiled Vancouver Island, this West Coast contemporary cedar home stands in a woodsy setting of rocks and tall evergreens. The wrap-around deck affords a 180° view of Georgia Strait and the majestic mountains beyond. Relax and savor this "little bit of heaven" or hike, golf, kayak, sail, fish, or sightsee. Take a day trip to the wild western shore of the island and the Pacific Rim National Park or to charming Victoria. The vacation suite will accommodate four people and, with its fully equipped kitchen, makes a popular headquarters for an island stay. Hearty breakfasts are served within full view of the ocean activities. The Wilkies ran a store in New York's Catskill mountains for 15 years before discovering this paradise. They enjoy hiking, golf, crafts, reading, games, puzzles, and especially meeting their guests and helping them plan a memorable stay.

SEASON

May – October
(or by arrangement)

ACCOMMODATIONS

1 vacation suite with
private bath;
1 room with private bath;
1 room with shared bath

Lake Crescent Inn

Evelyn and Bruce Warr
PO Box 69
Robert's Arm, Newfoundland
A0J 1R0
Tel: (709) 652-3067
Fax: (709) 652-3056
$

ABOUT THE B&B

When you think of Newfoundland, think peaceful lifestyle, clean air and rivers, and superb hospitality — all of which you'll find at Lake Crescent Inn. Walk along the quiet roads and beautiful beaches, visit fishermen in the various communities along the route, or go iceberg or whale watching (in season). Boating trips can also be arranged, so why not give cod jigging or salmon fishing a try? Be sure to bring along your camera to capture the moment you reel in your first fish (you might even see "Cressie," the lake monster!). The inn offers four bedrooms and two bathrooms, one with whirlpool and shower. Breakfasts are a homemade feast of muffins, jams, jellies, and breads, and a special health-conscious menu is also available. A Jiggs dinner is served on Sundays from 5:00 p.m., and a Fish Platter dinner is served on Fridays from 5:00 p.m. (other meals can be provided upon request).

SEASON

all year

ACCOMMODATIONS

4 rooms with shared baths

Sweet and Sour Maritime Catch

1½ pounds cod fillets

Sweet and sour sauce:
½ cup water
2 carrots, cut into small pieces
½ cup brown sugar
⅓ cup white vinegar
2 tablespoons cornstarch
2 tablespoons soy sauce
8-ounce can pineapple chunks
1 green pepper, finely chopped

Batter:
¾ cup water
⅔ cup all-purpose flour
1½ teaspoons salt
½ teaspoon baking powder

Rinse and pat fish dry. In a small saucepan, heat water to boiling and cook carrots 8 – 10 minutes. In another pan, mix brown sugar, vinegar, cornstarch, and soy sauce. Stir in carrots with liquid, pineapple chunks and juice, and green pepper. Heat to boiling, stirring constantly. Boil and stir 1 minute more. Keep warm. Mix together batter ingredients, dip fish in batter, and pan fry. Top with sweet and sour sauce. *Serves 4.*

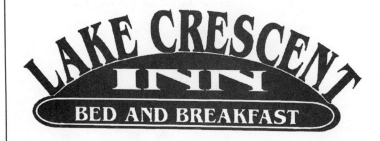

Tarragon Cheesy Eggs

1 teaspoon butter or margarine
3 large eggs
½ cup grated strong cheddar cheese
1 tablespoon finely chopped fresh tarragon

Place butter in a skillet over medium heat. Beat eggs and add along with cheese to skillet, stirring all the time until they are lightly combined. Mix in the tarragon and remove from heat when softly set. *Serves 1 as a main dish or 2 as a side dish.*

The Blossoms Bed and Breakfast

Berna and Bert Critchlow
RR #1
Westfield, New Brunswick
E0G 3J0
Tel: (506) 757-2962
$$

ABOUT THE B&B

The beautiful vistas of the St. John River are an integral part of The Blossoms's charm. What's more, this lovely modern home is surrounded by herb and flower gardens and shady wooded walks. The landscaped grounds slope down to the water, where you can launch a canoe or simply watch the ospreys dive and the bald eagles glide by. Three guest rooms are distinctively and comfortably furnished, each with double beds, private baths, and balconies that overlook the gardens and water. Breakfast is served on the deck or in the dining room (both of which overlook the river), and offers a choice of fresh fruit, home-baked muffins and breads, or a cooked meal if preferred. The spacious living room offers an extensive and eclectic library and music collection. Hostess Berna gives herbal and wreath-making workshops in the on-site craft store. Area attractions include canoeing, hiking, birdwatching, golfing, tennis, and swimming. St. John — with its theater, antique and craft shops, art galleries, historic walks, and excellent museum — is a short drive away.

SEASON

April – November

ACCOMMODATIONS

3 rooms with private baths

The Open Door /
La Porte Ouverte

Marlene and Glenn Scullion
239 Thomas Lefebvre Road
Davidson, Québec J0X 1R0
Tel: (819) 683-2991
Fax: (819) 683-2201
$$

ABOUT THE B&B

The Open Door B&B is nestled on the sandy shores of the Ottawa River, about a one-and-a-quarter-hour drive from the nation's capital. Located in the historic Pontiac region, the area is an inspiring combination of the traditions found in both English and French Canada. Rivers, lakes, and forests surrounding The Open Door provide a backdrop of natural beauty rarely found today. Since January 1993, The Open Door has played host to many international visitors and small conferences. A charming, comfortable atmosphere is created with a tasteful decor of Canadian country antiques. Delicious home cooking is graciously served in the beautiful sunroom overlooking a wide expanse of the river. Numerous seasonal activities are available on the premises or by arrangement. Marlene and Glenn are a recently retired couple from the broadcasting industry. Glenn is also a gifted pianist and Marlene an artist, and they both take great pride in ensuring their guests have a wonderful stay.

SEASON

all year

ACCOMMODATIONS

3 rooms with shared bath;
1 cabin with private bath;
2-bedroom guest house
with private bath

Turkey and Mushroom Croustades

"These are wonderful for happy hour or afternoon tea!"
— Marlene Scullion

Croustade:
20 slices white sandwich bread, crusts removed
Melted butter

Preheat oven to 350°F. Brush both sides of each bread slice with melted butter; press gently into muffin cups. Bake 15 – 20 minutes or until golden. *Tip:* Croustades can be made ahead and frozen.

Filling:
¼ cup butter
1 small onion, finely chopped
1 cup finely chopped mushrooms
6½-ounce can turkey flakes, drained and flaked with a fork
3 tablespoons all-purpose flour

(continued on next page)

1 cup milk
½ teaspoon salt
Pinch of cayenne pepper
Freshly ground black pepper
1 teaspoon lemon juice
Chopped fresh parsley

Preheat oven to 350°F. In a medium saucepan, melt butter. Sauté onion and mushrooms until onion is transparent. Stir in turkey. Sprinkle mixture with flour and blend well. Add milk gradually. Continue heating and stirring until mixture thickens and comes to a boil. Remove from heat and stir in salt, cayenne pepper, black pepper, and lemon juice. Fill each croustade with filling. Place on a cookie sheet and heat for 10 minutes or until bubbly. Sprinkle with chopped parsley and serve hot. *Makes 20 croustades.*

Spreads & Toppings

Angels' Hair Preserves (Carrot Marmalade)

"This nineteenth-century recipe is as heavenly as its name! Guests enjoy it on muffins or fruit bread." — Mary Caron

1 orange
2 – 3 lemons
1¼ cups water
5 cups coarsely grated carrots
7 cups sugar
1 pouch liquid fruit pectin

Cut up orange and 1 lemon; discard seeds. Finely chop fruit and place in a medium saucepan. Squeeze remaining lemons to measure ¼ cup juice; add to fruit. Add water. Bring to a boil, then reduce heat. Cover and simmer 20 minutes, stirring occasionally. Add carrots to fruit mixture. Measure 4½ cups mixture into a 6 – 8 quart pot. Stir in sugar and bring to a full, rolling boil, stirring constantly. Quickly stir in pectin. Boil hard 1 minute, stirring. Remove from heat and skim off foam. Ladle into sterilized, hot jars, leaving ¼" head space, and seal tightly. Store in a cool, dark, dry place. *Makes 8 half-pints.*

Caron House (1837)

Mary and Mike Caron
PO Box 143
Williamstown, Ontario K0C 2J0
Tel: (613) 347-7338
$$

ABOUT THE B&B

Caron House (1837) is a historic, romantic brick home located in the quaint village of Williamstown (established in 1784). Beautifully decorated and furnished with antiques, the house is in its original state, with working fireplaces, inside shutters, tin ceilings, and wide pine floorboards. Two rooms with shared bath are individually decorated with Laura Ashley wallpaper, antique linens, hooked rugs, quilts, and collectibles. Guests can relax in the Keeping Room (a Colonial term for gathering place) or living room, while a full, candlelit gourmet breakfast — accompanied by classical music — is served in the dining room on fine china, silverware, and crystal. Outside, you'll marvel at the herb and Victorian gardens, and relax on the antique wicker furniture on the back veranda, enjoying the lovely yards, complete with trellis, brick patio, and gazebo. Caron House is one hour's drive from either Montréal or Ottawa; nearby attractions include Upper Canada Village, artisan studios, a bird sanctuary, tennis, cycling, and good restaurants. Mary and Mike are retirees from the corporate world, and enjoy traveling, antique hunting, cooking, gardening, and history.

SEASON

all year

ACCOMMODATIONS

2 rooms with shared bath

Lakewinds

Jane and Stephen Locke
PO Box 1483, 328 Queen Street
Niagara-on-the-Lake, Ontario
L0S 1J0
Tel: (905) 468-1888
Fax: (905) 468-1061
$$$$

ABOUT THE B&B

A special experience awaits you at Lakewinds, a circa-1881, restored Victorian manor hosted by Jane and Stephen Locke. Situated on an acre of quiet trees and gardens, Lakewinds offers unparalleled views of the Niagara-on-the-Lake Golf Club and Lake Ontario. Elegantly appointed with antiques, guest rooms have been designed for comfort and privacy and all feature private baths. Guests are invited to the games room for billiards or cards and, in summer, can enjoy refreshing dips in the heated pool or simply relax in rocking chairs on the veranda. Sumptuous breakfasts feature fruits, vegetables, and herbs from Jane's garden. Only one-and-a-half hours south of Toronto, Niagara-on-the-Lake is a charming town offering world-class theater, shops, fine restaurants, and beautiful parks — all with a turn-of-the-century ambience. The many estate wineries in the area offer tours and tastings, while golf, tennis, and countless hiking and biking trails await the active visitor.

SEASON

all year

ACCOMMODATIONS

4 rooms with private baths

Apple Butter

8 cups apple cider
2 quarts apples
2 cups sugar
1 cup corn syrup
1 teaspoon ground cinnamon

Boil the cider until reduced to half its quantity (1 quart). Peel, core, and slice apples. Add apples to the cider and cook slowly until the mixture begins to thicken, stirring most of the time. Add the sugar, corn syrup, and cinnamon. Keep cooking on low heat 2 – 3 hours until a small sample, when cooled on a plate, is of good spreading consistency. *Variation:* Try 1 cup cooked pumpkin instead of corn syrup. *Makes 10 – 12 cups.*

Applesauce Cream

⅔ cup whipping cream (35%)
½ cup applesauce
¼ cup sifted confectioners' sugar
1 tablespoon lemon juice

Beat whipping cream at medium speed with an electric mixer until soft peaks form. Fold in applesauce, confectioners' sugar, and lemon juice. Cover and chill. Serve with waffles or pancakes. *Makes 1½ cups.*

Bay View Manor / Manoir Bay View

Helen Sawyer Hall
PO Box 21
395 Bonaventure East, Route 132
New Carlisle, Québec G0C 1Z0
Tel: (418) 752-2725/6718
$

ABOUT THE B&B

O*nce a country store and rural post office, Bay View Manor, a spectacular seaside farm on the rugged Gaspé Peninsula, now welcomes guests from all over the world. Reside in the historic, three-story farmhouse with its five guest rooms and oceanfront view, or choose the private cottage. At Bay View Manor's breakfast table, enjoy dishes (including home-baked goods and homemade jams) prepared with fresh eggs, fruit, and produce from the farm — served extra early, if desired, so you can get a real jump on your day! You can visit Bona-venture's Acadian Museum or the archaeological cave (La Grotte) at Saint Elzéar, or take more distant day trips to Miguasha fossil site and park, famous Percé Rock, Bona-venture Island Bird Sanctuary, or Forillon National Park. Right beside the B&B is the 18-hole Fauvel golf course and venues for numerous land and water sports. Of course, you can simply choose to listen to the ocean waves on the patio and enjoy the tranquility. Helen runs the B&B with her sons.*

SEASON

May – November

ACCOMMODATIONS

5 rooms with shared baths;
1 private cottage with private bath

Montréal Oasis

Lena Blondel
3000 Breslay Road
Montréal, Québec H3Y 2G7
Tel: (514) 935-2312
$$

ABOUT THE B&B

In pilgrim days, the evergreen tree was a sign of shelter, good food, and warm hospitality. It's fitting, then, that two towering evergreens frame the door to Montréal Oasis. This charming B&B with original leaded windows and slanted ceilings is located in downtown Montréal's west end, close to the Fine Arts Museum, chic Crescent Street and Greene Avenue shopping and restaurants, and the "main drag," St. Catherine Street. The beautiful and safe neighborhood with its spacious Elizabethan-style houses and pretty gardens is locally referred to as the Priest Farm district — once a holiday resort for priests. Originally from Sweden, your world-traveled hostess Lena has lived in many countries around the globe, which is evident from the African, Asian, and Swedish art that graces the B&B. The three guest rooms feature Scandinavian and Québecois furniture. Lena loves good food, and serves three-course gourmet breakfasts featuring delicious, fresh ingredients. A friendly Siamese cat resides on the main floor.

SEASON

all year

ACCOMMODATIONS

3 rooms with shared baths

Beet Sauce

"A guest, chef, and teacher of gourmet cooking in Stratford, Ontario, gave me this unique recipe, which looks stunning on a poached egg. Even if you don't like beets, I guarantee you'll like this sauce!" — Lena Blondel

2¼ pounds cooked beets
Olive oil
Salt and pepper
Dijon mustard
Chopped fresh dill (optional)

Liquefy beets in a juicer. In a saucepan, reduce the juice over low heat until it begins to get thick (at least 15 – 20 minutes). Stir in enough olive oil to get the same consistency as mayonnaise. Add salt, pepper, and Dijon mustard according to taste. The sauce should now be thick, creamy, and dark red. Add some chopped fresh dill, if you desire. Serve over poached eggs. Multiply recipe as required. *Makes about ½ cup.*

Best Ever White Frosting

"This never-fail recipe is great on carrot cake, muffins, and quick breads. Even if you leave it out on the counter, it will not run." — Linda Aylward

⅔ cup milk
3 tablespoons all-purpose flour
½ cup butter
½ cup shortening
¾ cup sugar
1½ teaspoons vanilla
¼ teaspoon salt

In a 1-quart saucepan, mix milk and flour over medium heat. Cook until mixture boils, stirring constantly, and continue to boil for 1 minute. Cool slightly. In a small bowl, with mixer at low speed, beat butter, shortening, and sugar until blended. At high speed, beat until light and fluffy. Reduce speed to low, add milk-flour mixture, vanilla, and salt. At high speed, beat until very fluffy. ***Makes approximately 2½ cups.***

Captain's Quarters B&B

Linda and Arnie Aylward
RR #1
South Gillies, Ontario P0T 2V0
Tel: (807) 475-5630
$$

ABOUT THE B&B

Named in honor of the Aylward sea captains from Nova Scotia, Captain's Quarters is an intimate country bed and breakfast located southwest of the city of Thunder Bay, and a short drive from ski hills, amethyst mines, and fine dining. The modern log home features rustic yet gracious queen-sized bedrooms with private baths. Hiking, cross-country skiing, and golf ranges are available on the property. Expansion plans include a solarium with hot tub. Pancakes with strawberries and whipped cream highlight an extensive and varied breakfast menu created only from fresh, quality products. Another menu favorite, Nova Scotia crab toasties capture the B&B's theme and the East Coast heritage of the host. Golf, gardening, sewing, and crafts are among Linda and Arnie's hobbies.

SEASON

all year

ACCOMMODATIONS

2 rooms with private baths

Weston Lake Inn Bed & Breakfast

Susan Evans and Ted Harrison
813 Beaver Point Road
Salt Spring Island
British Columbia V8K 1X9
Tel: (250) 653-4311
$$$

ABOUT THE B&B

Nestled on a well-tended knoll of flowering trees and shrubs overlooking Weston Lake, the inn is a serene and comfortable adult getaway on the rural south end of Salt Spring Island. The three tastefully decorated guest bedrooms have private baths, down duvets, and fresh flower bouquets. Original Canadian art and beautiful petitpoint (crafted by host Ted) grace the interior of the inn. Guests have the exclusive use of a cozy fireside lounge with library, TV, and VCR, and an outdoor hot tub perched above the lake. Creative breakfasts feature fresh eggs from the inn's chickens, and produce from the large, organic garden, such as berries, herbs, and asparagus in season. Near Victoria, Salt Spring Island offers a mild climate, exceptional beauty, a thriving community of artists and craftspeople, and an abundance of outdoor activities. Since opening Weston Lake Inn in 1986, hosts Susan and Ted have been fine-tuning their B&B craft, restoring the house, landscaping, and enjoying their 10-acre paradise with guests. Susan loves gardening, while Ted loves sailing and offers charters aboard their 36-foot sloop.

SEASON

all year

ACCOMMODATIONS

3 rooms with private baths

Blueberry-Cointreau Jam

4 cups blueberries
3 cups sugar
3 tablespoons fresh lime juice
2 tablespoons Cointreau liqueur

Place washed berries and sugar in a heavy saucepan over low heat until sugar dissolves, stirring constantly. Boil 20 – 25 minutes. Add lime juice and Cointreau, and boil 3 minutes longer. Test consistency. If ready, skim any foam from surface and pour into sterilized jars and seal with paraffin wax. Store in a cool, dark, dry place. *Makes 2 pints.*

Blueberry Hill Sauce

2 cups blueberries
¼ cup maple syrup
1 heaping tablespoon cornstarch mixed with a little cold water
2 tablespoons Cointreau liqueur

Combine blueberries and maple syrup in a small saucepan.
Bring just to a boil on medium heat. Add cornstarch, stirring
until thick, at least 1 minute. Add Cointreau. Serve warm on
pancakes, French toast, or waffles. Store in the refrigerator up to
1 week, or freeze. *Makes 2 cups.*

Weston Lake Inn Bed & Breakfast

Susan Evans and Ted Harrison
813 Beaver Point Road
Salt Spring Island
British Columbia V8K 1X9
Tel: (250) 653-4311
$$$

ABOUT THE B&B

Nestled on a well-tended
knoll of flowering trees and
shrubs overlooking Weston
Lake, the inn is a serene and comfort-
able adult getaway on the rural south
end of Salt Spring Island. The three
tastefully decorated guest bedrooms
have private baths, down duvets,
and fresh flower bouquets. Original
Canadian art and beautiful petit-
point (crafted by host Ted) grace the
interior of the inn. Guests have the
exclusive use of a cozy fireside lounge
with library, TV, and VCR, and an
outdoor hot tub perched above the
lake. Creative breakfasts feature fresh
eggs from the inn's chickens, and pro-
duce from the large, organic garden,
such as berries, herbs, and asparagus
in season. Near Victoria, Salt Spring
Island offers a mild climate, excep-
tional beauty, a thriving community
of artists and craftspeople, and an
abundance of outdoor activities.
Since opening Weston Lake Inn in
1986, hosts Susan and Ted have been
fine-tuning their B&B craft, restor-
ing the house, landscaping, and
enjoying their 10-acre paradise with
guests. Susan loves gardening, while
Ted loves sailing and offers charters
aboard their 36-foot sloop.

SEASON

all year

ACCOMMODATIONS

3 rooms with private baths

Spring Valley Guest Ranch

Jim Saville
PO Box 10
Ravenscrag, Saskatchewan
S0N 0T0
Tel: (306) 295-4124
$$

ABOUT THE B&B

Come relax and enjoy an afternoon visit or an overnight stay at Spring Valley Guest Ranch. This three-story, 1913 character home is nestled in a tall grove of cottonwood poplars, in a pleasant wooded valley with many wild varieties of flora and fauna along a spring-fed stream. Over 1,000 acres of hills and valleys beckon you either on foot or on horseback. You are invited to dine, choosing from a unique menu, in the licensed Country Tea Room, which houses over 200 duck replicas. Live poultry, sheep, horses, and a donkey await your visit in the barnyard. The craft shop in the log cabin is filled with treasures of leather, wood, pottery, and knitted and beaded crafts — all made by local artists. An excellent area for naturalists, photographers, and hikers, Ravenscrag is only 20 minutes from Cypress Hills Provincial Park, on the Alberta border.

SEASON

all year

ACCOMMODATIONS

4 rooms with shared baths;
1 log cabin with shared bath

Dad's Jam

"This favorite of my father was passed down through our family from my fraternal grandmother. When I first opened my B&B in 1988, I offered a variety of jams. This one was always the winner, so now it's the only one I make."
— Jim Saville

1 pound dried apricots (3¼ cups)
4 pounds rhubarb, chopped in ½" pieces
4 pounds sugar (8 cups)
1 unpeeled lemon, chopped
2 unpeeled oranges, chopped

Soak apricots overnight in enough water to cover. Set aside soaking water and cut apricots into quarters. Combine rhubarb, sugar, and apricots and 1 cup soaking water and boil gently for half an hour, stirring to prevent scorching. Add fruit and boil until thick and jelly-like. Pour into hot, sterilized jars and seal tightly. Store in a cool, dark, dry place. *Tips:* Use the heaviest pot you have — it's not so apt to stick and scorch. You can substitute the rhubarb with zucchini, if you desire. **Makes 16 cups.**

Flavored Butters

(Recipes from Joan Peggs Eggs, *written and published by Joan Peggs, 1996)*

1) Whipped Orange Butter

½ cup softened butter
2 tablespoons concentrated orange juice
2 teaspoons confectioners' sugar
1 teaspoon grated fresh ginger

In a small bowl, beat butter until fluffy. Add concentrated orange juice, confectioners' sugar, and ginger and beat until combined. *Tip:* Keeps well in the refrigerator. *Makes ½ cup.*

2) Cinnamon-Honey Butter

¼ cup softened butter
¼ cup honey
1 teaspoon ground cinnamon

Put butter, honey, and cinnamon in a small bowl. Beat until combined. *Variation:* You can use 1 teaspoon ground nutmeg or 1 teaspoon ground ginger in place of the cinnamon. *Tip:* Keeps well in the refrigerator. *Makes ½ cup.*

3) Nut Butter

¼ cup ground nuts (almonds, hazelnuts, or walnuts)
½ cup softened butter
1 teaspoon vanilla (optional)
1 tablespoon confectioners' sugar

In a small bowl, place ground nutmeats and butter. Beat until combined. Flavor with vanilla if desired. *Tip:* Keeps well in the refrigerator. *Makes ½ cup.*

The Inn on St. Andrews

Joan Peggs
231 St. Andrews Street
Victoria, British Columbia
V8V 2N1
Tel: (800) 668-5993 or
(604) 384-8613
Fax: (604) 384-6063
E-mail: joan.peggs@vonline.com
$$

ABOUT THE B&B

The Inn on St. Andrews is as lovely today as when it was built in 1913 by Edith Carr, eldest sister of the famous Canadian artist and author, Emily Carr. This Tudor-style heritage property charms with its elegant woodwork, stained and beveled glass, and large bright bedrooms. After a wholesome breakfast in the formal dining room, you can congregate in the sunroom overlooking the east garden or sun deck overlooking the west garden, in the cozy TV room, or in the larger drawing room. The inn is ideally located in James Bay, close to Victoria's inner harbor with ferry and seaplane terminals, the Parliament buildings, the Royal British Columbia Museum, famed Empress Hotel, and downtown shops. A short walk brings you to Beacon Hill Park and the oceanfront. Your host Joan Peggs believes in modern comfort and old-fashioned hospitality, and provides guests with her own map highlighting walking and driving destinations and recommended restaurants.

SEASON

all year

ACCOMMODATIONS

1 room with private bath;
2 rooms with shared bath

Gwenmar
Guest Home

Joy and Keith Smith
PO Box 59, RR #3
Brandon, Manitoba R7A 5Y3
Tel: (204) 728-7339
Fax: (204) 728-7336
E-mail: smithj@docker.com
$

ABOUT THE B&B

*S*pace, *privacy, and quiet is what you'll find at Gwenmar. This 1914 heritage home was the summer retreat of Manitoba's former Lt. Governor (from 1929 to 1934), J.D. McGregor, who named the estate after his daughter Gwen. Since 1980, Joy and Keith Smith have welcomed B&B guests to this relaxing countryside escape. Gwenmar breakfasts are memorable, particularly the home-baked bread and jams and jellies made from Gwenmar's wild berries. Joy, a home economist, is an avid gardener and a major contributor to Canada's heritage seed program, while Keith is a retired agrologist involved in overseas projects. In the summer, you can visit with them on the big, shaded veranda or go for secluded walks on the beautiful grounds or in the valley. In the winter, sit by the fire or go cross-country skiing. Gwenmar is also a short drive from downtown Brandon, with shopping, restaurants, water-slide, air museum, golf courses, and the childhood home of* Stone Angel *author Margaret Laurence.*

SEASON

all year

ACCOMMODATIONS

2 rooms with private baths;
2 rooms with shared bath

Gooseberry-Orange Marmalade

1 orange, quartered and thinly sliced
¾ cup water
6 cups topped and tailed gooseberries
3 tablespoons lemon juice
4 cups sugar

Simmer orange in water 30 – 45 minutes until tender. Add gooseberries. Boil another 10 minutes. Add lemon juice and sugar. Bring to a full, rolling boil over high heat. Allow to boil 10 – 12 minutes, stirring frequently. Stir another 2 – 5 minutes to suspend fruit (so it doesn't all end up at the bottom). Place in sterilized jars and seal tightly. Store in a cool, dark, dry place.
Makes 6 cups.

Herbed Cookie Cutter Butter

"I cut loon- and heart-shaped butter to serve with my old-fashioned tea biscuits."— Penny Grimshaw

Unsalted butter, cut into ½" slabs
Freshly chopped or dried herbs to taste

Cut slabs of butter into interesting shapes with cookie cutters. Arrange on a plate and sprinkle herbs over top. Garnish as desired. *Tip:* Best if butter is cut immediately after it's removed from refrigerator.

Elgin Manor B&B

Penny and Dave Grimshaw
RR #2
Port Sandfield, Ontario P0B 1J0
Tel: (705) 765-5325
$$ – $$$$

ABOUT THE B&B

Nestled on a quiet bay of picturesque Lake Joseph, you'll find the unique and heartwarming Elgin Manor B&B, a 1920s Tudor home surrounded by English gardens and a water's edge fireplace. In keeping with the timeless, historical traditions for which the Muskoka Lakes are known, you're sure to see several antique wooden boats (called "launches") or even the historic steamship Segwun pass by the dock as you sit in a wooden Muskoka chair. The manor is decorated with antiques throughout and guest rooms are tastefully appointed with handmade quilts. Old-fashioned picnic lunches complete with wicker baskets and antique launch excursions can be arranged. Situated in the heart of Muskoka cottage country (two hours north of Toronto), the area offers year-round activities — from summer nature walks, fishing, swimming, canoeing, and midnight strolls under a million glistening stars, to local artisan tours and winter ice skating, snowshoeing, and cross-country skiing across the panoramic countryside.

SEASON

all year

ACCOMMODATIONS

3 rooms with private baths;
1 honeymoon cabin
with private bath

The Edwardian
Bed & Breakfast

Judy and Jordan Hill
50 Mount Edward Road
Charlottetown
Prince Edward Island C1A 5S3
Tel/Fax: (902) 368-1905
$$$

ABOUT THE B&B

The Edwardian is an elegant 1850s Victorian home, originally the country estate of William Pope, one of the Fathers of Canadian Confederation. Judy and Jordan's interests are obvious as you explore this B&B; period antiques, an extensive art collection, flower arrangements, old books and artifacts, and family quilts are displayed throughout. Jordan's country garden is a focal point for discussion along with the conservatory and parlor fireplace. This B&B has won a number of heritage and beautification awards thanks to loving restoration efforts and attention to overall detail. The four guest rooms feature private baths, double or queen beds, duvets, ceiling fans, and a garden view. As your day begins, Jordan picks a bouquet for the table and Judy prepares one of her memorable breakfasts around an Eastlake walnut dining table set with bone china and sterling silver. It's only a short walk to the center of lovely Charlottetown — birthplace of Canada — where theater, waterfront activities, and year-round dining and shopping await.

SEASON

all year

ACCOMMODATIONS

4 rooms with private baths

Island Clotted Cream Topping

"This is basically a substitute for Devonshire cream enjoyed by the British with tea and scones. Needless to say, our guests from the British Isles consider this a great treat and find our approach of serving it with coffee cake a novel variation on an old theme." — Judy Hill

4-ounce package cream cheese
3 tablespoons brown sugar
Pinch of salt
1 cup whipping cream (35%)

Combine cream cheese, brown sugar, salt, and 3 tablespoons whipping cream. Beat until fluffy. Whip remaining cream until soft peaks form. Fold into first 4 ingredients. Chill and serve with The Edwardian's apple streusel coffee cake (see recipe on page 82) or as a dip with fresh strawberries. *Makes 2 cups.*

Low-calorie Vegetable Dip

2 cups light Miracle Whip salad dressing or light mayonnaise
3 cups plain yogurt
Dried dill weed to taste
Dried minced onion to taste

Fresh raw vegetables

Mix Miracle Whip and yogurt together in a bowl. Add dill weed and minced onion to taste. Serve with fresh raw vegetables.
Tip: This dip will keep in the refrigerator for several days.
Makes 5 cups.

Lake Crescent Inn

Evelyn and Bruce Warr
PO Box 69
Robert's Arm, Newfoundland
A0J 1R0
Tel: (709) 652-3067
Fax: (709) 652-3056
$

ABOUT THE B&B

When you think of Newfoundland, think peaceful lifestyle, clean air and rivers, and superb hospitality — all of which you'll find at Lake Crescent Inn. Walk along the quiet roads and beautiful beaches, visit fishermen in the various communities along the route, or go iceberg or whale watching (in season). Boating trips can also be arranged, so why not give cod jigging or salmon fishing a try? Be sure to bring along your camera to capture the moment you reel in your first fish (you might even see "Cressie," the lake monster!). The inn offers four bedrooms and two bathrooms, one with whirlpool and shower. Breakfasts are a home-made feast of muffins, jams, jellies, and breads, and a special health-conscious menu is also available. A Jiggs dinner is served on Sundays from 5:00 p.m., and a Fish Platter dinner is served on Fridays from 5:00 p.m. (other meals can be provided upon request).

SEASON

all year

ACCOMMODATIONS

4 rooms with shared baths

Hilltop Acres
Bed & Breakfast

Janice and Wayne Trowsdale
Route 166
Bideford, Prince Edward Island
(Mailing address: PO Box 3011
Ellerslie, Prince Edward Island
C0B 1J0)
Tel/Fax: (902) 831-2817
$

ABOUT THE B&B

Enjoy the quiet of the country and a "home-away-from-home" atmosphere in this renovated 1930s residence in historic Bideford — where Anne of Green Gables *author Lucy Maud Montgomery first taught school from 1894 to 1895. Relax on the second-story balcony overlooking scenic Malpeque Bay or in the large living room. Stroll about the three-acre lawn, play horseshoes, Frisbee, or croquet, or bike or walk around the 75-acre property. Bedrooms have a double bed, two single beds, or a queen waterbed, with the use of a four-piece shared bath (for guests only). Hilltop Acres specializes in homemade muffins and preserves served in the guest breakfast room. Just minutes from the village of Tyne Valley, the Green Provincial Park, and the Shipbuilding Museum, Hilltop Acres is also a half hour from golf courses and shopping centers, and one hour from the Borden car ferry. Your hosts are non-smokers and enjoy meeting and sharing the history and culture of the area. Janice is an office clerk and Wayne is a school bus driver, carpenter, and handyman.*

SEASON

June – October
(off-season by reservation)

ACCOMMODATIONS

4 rooms with shared bath

Ma's Rhubarb Marmalade

"My grandmother served me this rhubarb marmalade when I was a little girl."— Janice Trowsdale

12 cups cut-up rhubarb
8 cups sugar
Grated peel and juice of 3 oranges and 2 lemons
19-ounce can crushed pineapple

Put sugar over cut-up rhubarb and let stand overnight. In the morning, add grated peel and juice of oranges and lemons. Add crushed pineapple with its juice. Boil gently for 30 minutes or until thick. Pour into sterilized jars and seal tightly. Store in a cool, dark, dry place. **Makes approximately 7 pints.**

Muskoka Wild Clover-Cranberry Honey

Elgin Manor B&B

Penny and Dave Grimshaw
RR #2
Port Sandfield, Ontario P0B 1J0
Tel: (705) 765-5325
$$ – $$$$

"I purchase fresh cranberries for this recipe from the local cranberry bog, and pick the clover and rose petals right from my garden. Guests enjoy this unusual honey and often like to bring a jar home with them." — Penny Grimshaw

8 cups sugar
½ cup water
80 white wild clover flowers
40 pink wild clover flowers
4 rose petals
1 teaspoon alum (aluminum potassium sulfate)
2 cups cranberries, cooked in hot water until they pop
    (5 minutes on medium temperature)

In a heavy, non-aluminum pot, simmer sugar and water on low heat. Once sugar is dissolved, add clover, rose petals, and alum. Stir and remove from burner. Set aside for 2 – 4 hours. Strain and discard solids. Mix cranberries (left whole) with liquid. Pour into sterilized decorative jars and store in a dry place at room temperature. *Makes 6 cups.*

ABOUT THE B&B

Nestled on a quiet bay of picturesque Lake Joseph, you'll find the unique and heartwarming Elgin Manor B&B, a 1920s Tudor home surrounded by English gardens and a water's edge fireplace. In keeping with the timeless, historical traditions for which the Muskoka Lakes are known, you're sure to see several antique wooden boats (called "launches") or even the historic steamship Segwun pass by the dock as you sit in a wooden Muskoka chair. The manor is decorated with antiques throughout and guest rooms are tastefully appointed with handmade quilts. Old-fashioned picnic lunches complete with wicker baskets and antique launch excursions can be arranged. Situated in the heart of Muskoka cottage country (two hours north of Toronto), the area offers year-round activities — from summer nature walks, fishing, swimming, canoeing, and midnight strolls under a million glistening stars, to local artisan tours and winter ice skating, snowshoeing, and cross-country skiing across the panoramic countryside.

SEASON

all year

ACCOMMODATIONS

3 rooms with private baths;
1 honeymoon cabin
with private bath

Marj and Herb Wilkie
3381 Dolphin Drive
Nanoose Bay, British Columbia
V0R 2R0
Tel/Fax: (604) 468-9796
$$

ABOUT THE B&B

*S*ituated halfway between Victoria and Tofino on unspoiled Vancouver Island, this West Coast contemporary cedar home stands in a woodsy setting of rocks and tall evergreens. The wrap-around deck affords a 180° view of Georgia Strait and the majestic mountains beyond. Relax and savor this "little bit of heaven" or hike, golf, kayak, sail, fish, or sightsee. Take a day trip to the wild western shore of the island and the Pacific Rim National Park or to charming Victoria. The vacation suite will accommodate four people and, with its fully equipped kitchen, makes a popular headquarters for an island stay. Hearty breakfasts are served within full view of the ocean activities. The Wilkies ran a store in New York's Catskill mountains for 15 years before discovering this paradise. They enjoy hiking, golf, crafts, reading, games, puzzles, and especially meeting their guests and helping them plan a memorable stay.

SEASON

May – October
(or by arrangement)

ACCOMMODATIONS

1 vacation suite
with private bath;
1 room with private bath;
1 room with shared bath

Orange-Ginger Sauce

"A taste treat for ginger lovers to serve over pancakes, French toast, or Dutch pancakes." — Marj Wilkie

2 tablespoons peeled and grated fresh ginger
½ teaspoon orange zest
½ cup orange juice
½ cup water
2 tablespoons light corn syrup
1 cup sugar

Combine all ingredients in a small saucepan. Bring to a boil, uncovered, over medium-high heat. Boil 5 minutes. Store in a tightly covered glass jar or plastic container for up to 2 weeks in your refrigerator. *Makes 1½ cups.*

The Lookout at Schooner Cove

Pear and Ginger Jam

"A simple and elegant jam that's very popular with ginger lovers. It's also a good substitute for orange marmalade at breakfast." — Sheila Jackson

3 pounds ripe pears
½ pound crystallized (candied) ginger or ginger in
    syrup (drained)
3 pounds sugar
Juice and grated peel of 1½ lemons

Peel, core, and chop pears. Finely chop ginger. Put pears, ginger, and sugar in a preserving pan with peel and juice of lemons. Heat slowly to a boil, stirring frequently. Boil 10 minutes without stirring. Stir and let cool. Place in sterilized jars and seal tightly. Store in a cool, dark, dry place. **Makes approximately 12 cups.**

Seaboard Bed & Breakfast

Sheila and Barrie Jackson
2629 Crowell Road, RR #2
Porter's Lake, Nova Scotia
B0J 2S0
Tel: (800) SEA-6566 or
(902) 827-3747
$ – $$

ABOUT THE B&B

Seaboard Bed & Breakfast at Lawrencetown Beach is a renovated farmhouse built around 1912. Now the home of Sheila and Barrie Jackson, this large white house across the road from Porter's Lake and the Atlantic Ocean has been an area landmark for many years. Local attractions include international caliber surfing from a sand beach; birdwatching from the shore, local marsh, walking trails, and hills; plus fishing, canoeing, windsurfing, and — in season — skating and cross-country skiing. Seaboard is only 35 minutes from Halifax airport and 30 minutes from the cities of Halifax and Dartmouth, where you can enjoy the casino, restaurants, theaters, and special events. Sheila and Barrie are both keen Scottish country dancers and have aptly named their guest rooms after favorite dances. There are two semi-private bathrooms for the exclusive use of guests. A varied and full home-cooked breakfast is served in the sunny dining room overlooking lake and sea, while tea and coffee are offered in the lounge or on the porch.

SEASON

all year

ACCOMMODATIONS

3 rooms with shared baths

Orchard Lane
Bed & Breakfast

Yvonne Parker
13324 Middle Bench Road
Oyama, British Columbia
V4V 2B4
Tel: (250) 548-3809
$$

ABOUT THE B&B

Smack dab between Kelowna and Vernon, there awaits Orchard Lane, a newly built Victorian B&B nestled in a private orchard. From the sprawling veranda, this rural setting gives way to a panoramic view of the beautiful Central Okanagan Valley, while nearby Kalamalka and Wood lakes reflect the hills and distant mountains. Inside, a welcoming foyer and spiral staircase lead to romantic and comfortable bedrooms. Visitors lounge in the formal living room with fireplace, stroll through the flower gardens or nearby orchard, admire the terraced landscaping framed by giant trees, or take a refreshing dip in the outdoor hot tub. Your hostess, Yvonne, serves a full gourmet breakfast — made from produce grown in her vegetable garden — in the formal dining room or on the veranda. You'll quickly discover that one of her favorite hobbies is craft collecting, which is evident throughout the house. Alpine skiing, fishing, biking, hiking, and other recreational choices await you and there are golf courses and beaches aplenty to explore. This area is truly a corner of paradise.

SEASON

all year

ACCOMMODATIONS

2 rooms with shared bath

Prize Apricot Jam

3 pounds apricots
4½ cups white sugar
¾ cup light-brown sugar
Juice and coarsely grated peel of 1 orange
1 cup crushed pineapple and juice
⅛ teaspoon salt

Wash, pit, and quarter enough apricots to measure 8 cups. Place apricots and other ingredients into a heavy kettle. Bring quickly to a boil, stirring until sugar is dissolved. Cook rapidly, stirring often until 2 thick drops of syrup run together off the side of a cold metal spoon (about 30 – 35 minutes). Ladle into sterilized jars and seal tightly. Store in a cool, dark, dry place. *Makes 8 cups.*

Pumpkin Marmalade

(Recipe from Joan Peggs Eggs, *written and published by Joan Peggs, 1996)*

4 cups fresh pumpkin, chopped into small pieces
3 cups pears or apples, cored and chopped fine
¼ teaspoon salt*
6 cups sugar
3 oranges
3 lemons

Note: The salt heightens the tart flavor of the fruit. If desired, it can be omitted.

Place pumpkin, pears or apples, and salt in a large bowl. Sprinkle with the sugar. Allow to sit overnight. Grate peel of oranges and lemons. Chop pulp, removing seeds. Transfer pumpkin-sugar mixture to a large preserving kettle and add the peel and the pulp. Slowly bring to a boil, stirring frequently. Cook until it tests for jam (2 thick drops of syrup run together off the side of a cold metal spoon) — approximately 40 minutes. Place into sterilized jars and seal tightly. Store in a cool, dark, dry place. *Makes 6 8-ounce jars.*

The Inn on St. Andrews

Joan Peggs
231 St. Andrews Street
Victoria, British Columbia
V8V 2N1
Tel: (800) 668-5993 or
(604) 384-8613
Fax: (604) 384-6063
E-mail: joan.peggs@vonline.com
$$

ABOUT THE B&B

The Inn on St. Andrews is as lovely today as when it was built in 1913 by Edith Carr, eldest sister of the famous Canadian artist and author, Emily Carr. This Tudor-style heritage property charms with its elegant woodwork, stained and beveled glass, and large bright bedrooms. After a wholesome breakfast in the formal dining room, you can congregate in the sunroom overlooking the east garden or sun deck overlooking the west garden, in the cozy TV room, or in the larger drawing room. The inn is ideally located in James Bay, close to Victoria's inner harbor with ferry and seaplane terminals, the Parliament buildings, the Royal British Columbia Museum, famed Empress Hotel, and downtown shops. A short walk brings you to Beacon Hill Park and the oceanfront. Your host Joan Peggs believes in modern comfort and old-fashioned hospitality, and provides guests with her own map highlighting walking and driving destinations and recommended restaurants.

SEASON

all year

ACCOMMODATIONS

1 room with private bath;
2 rooms with shared bath

Fraser House

Sheila and Dennis Derksen
PO Box 211, 33 1st Street East
Letellier, Manitoba R0G 1C0
Tel: (204) 737-2284
$

ABOUT THE B&B

Memories are made at this elegant and romantic 1916 home. Hardwood floors, area rugs, and antique furniture enhance the home's Victorian decor. Spacious rooms combined with great hospitality make your stay most enjoyable. Relax in the parlor or on the veranda or patio with a beverage and home-baked goodies. Breakfast may consist of a puffy egg pancake or freshly baked croissants and muffins, along with the season's fresh fruit, served in the formal dining room. Fraser House is located just a few minutes north of the US border in the heart of Manitoba's bustling agricultural area, and is near golf, fishing, shopping, and skiing. Sheila enjoys crafting projects and holds painting classes during the winter months, while Dennis enjoys carpentry and is employed as a fertilizer dealer.

SEASON

all year

ACCOMMODATIONS

2 rooms with shared bath

Raspberry Syrup

"Great on pancakes, waffles, and fruit-filled omelets and crêpes." — Sheila Derksen

2 cups frozen raspberries, thawed and drained
3 tablespoons sugar
Juice of ½ lemon or 1 tablespoon lemon juice from concentrate
2 ounces orange or peach-flavored liqueur
1 teaspoon cornstarch dissolved in 1 tablespoon cold water

Place first 4 ingredients in a blender and purée at high speed for 10 – 15 seconds. Strain liquid through a fine sieve to remove seeds and pour strained liquid into a saucepan. Bring liquid to a boil and add cornstarch-water mixture. Stir a few minutes until thickened. May be served immediately or refrigerated up to 5 days. ***Makes 1 cup.***

Rosehip Jelly

"I love wild rosehips! Unlike berry picking, rosehip picking is even better after the first frost. Not only do rosehips become sweeter, they also become softer and easier to grind. We pick our rosehips right up to the first snowfall in October."
— Carla Pitzel

Rosehips
Water
Sugar
6-ounce bottle Certo liquid fruit pectin (or 2 packets)

Remove old blooms and stems from the rosehips. For each cup of rosehips, add 1½ cups water and boil until soft. Sieve through a jelly bag. For every 2 cups of extract, add 3 cups of sugar and 1 bottle of Certo. Bring to a boil. Pour carefully into sterilized jars and seal tightly. Store in a cool, dark, dry place. **Tips:** If jelly doesn't set, it becomes rosehip syrup — great on pancakes and waffles! Avoid the temptation to use domestic rosehips, they may be bigger but they may have pesticides and fertilizers. *Makes 4 8-ounce glasses using 2 cups extract.*

Hawkins House Bed & Breakfast

Carla Pitzel and Garry Umbrich
303 Hawkins Street
Whitehorse, Yukon Territory
Y1A 1X5
Tel: (403) 668-7638
Fax: (403) 668-7632
$$$

ABOUT THE B&B

To stay at the Hawkins House Bed & Breakfast is to share a once-in-a-lifetime Yukon experience with your hosts Carla, Garry, and their two sons. Each guest room in this custom-built, luxury Victorian B&B highlights a different Yukon theme and features private bath and balcony, oak floor, bar sink and refrigerator, cable TV and VCR. Guests can take a Jacuzzi soak in the Fleur de Lys Room, watch Native videos in the First Nations Room, step back into gold rush days in the Victorian Tea Rose Room, or admire the splendid view of the SS Klondike paddlewheeler and Canyon Mountain from the balcony of the Fireweed Room. Especially geared to the business traveler, Hawkins House provides the convenience of private telephone line and answering machine, fax service, and work table with light and computer jack. Breakfast is a homemade feast of northern and international delights — from the home-smoked salmon pâté and moose sausage to jams, syrups, and sourdough pastries.

SEASON

all year

ACCOMMODATIONS

4 rooms with private baths

Northgate B&B

June and Carl Leschied
106 Main Street
Lewisporte, Newfoundland
A0G 3A0
Tel: (709) 535-2258
$$

ABOUT THE B&B

Experience true Newfoundland hospitality at Northgate B&B, a large and beautifully restored country-style home overlooking Lewisporte harbor. Upon arrival, enjoy afternoon tea in one of the sitting rooms with fireplace and hardwood floors before lounging in one of four charming guest rooms with either private or shared bath. The large dining room is where a wholesome full breakfast of Northgate's own fresh brown eggs, homemade bread, cereals, and wild berry jams is served — all in a smoke-free environment. Northgate is located near craft shops, a museum, laundromat, provincial parks and swimming areas, scenic villages, strawberry "U-picks," and salmon rivers. Explore the beautiful islands of Notre Dame Bay on your hosts' 40-foot tour boat. Experience lunch beside an iceberg or a cookout on a former old-time island settlement. Trips can be arranged to Beothuk Indian haunts or to a remote island cabin for a one- or two-night stay.

SEASON

May 1 – October 31

ACCOMMODATIONS

2 rooms with private baths;
2 rooms with shared bath

Strawberry-Rhubarb Jam

"My guests' favorite." — June Leschied

5 cups chopped rhubarb
1 cup sugar

1¼ cups sugar
Small package of strawberry Jell-O

Add 1 cup sugar to rhubarb and let stand overnight. In the morning, add another 1¼ cups sugar and bring to a gentle boil until rhubarb is soft. Add Jell-O and stir well. Place in sterilized jars and seal tightly. Store in a cool, dark, dry place. **Makes 5 half-pint jars or 5 cups.**

Vegetable Dip

¾ cup mayonnaise
1½ teaspoons lemon juice
4½ teaspoons honey
4½ teaspoons ketchup
4½ teaspoons dried minced onion
1½ teaspoons curry powder

Fresh raw vegetables

Combine all ingredients and let stand in the refrigerator for a few hours before serving with fresh raw vegetables. *Tip:* This dip will keep in refrigerator for several days. *Makes about 1 cup.*

Lake Crescent Inn

Evelyn and Bruce Warr
PO Box 69
Robert's Arm, Newfoundland
A0J 1R0
Tel: (709) 652-3067
Fax: (709) 652-3056
$

ABOUT THE B&B

When you think of Newfoundland, think peaceful lifestyle, clean air and rivers, and superb hospitality — all of which you'll find at Lake Crescent Inn. Walk along the quiet roads and beautiful beaches, visit fishermen in the various communities along the route, or go iceberg or whale watching (in season). Boating trips can also be arranged, so why not give cod jigging or salmon fishing a try? Be sure to bring along your camera to capture the moment you reel in your first fish (you might even see "Cressie," the lake monster!). The inn offers four bedrooms and two bathrooms, one with whirlpool and shower. Breakfasts are a homemade feast of muffins, jams, jellies, and breads, and a special health-conscious menu is also available. A Jiggs dinner is served on Sundays from 5:00 p.m., and a Fish Platter dinner is served on Fridays from 5:00 p.m. (other meals can be provided upon request).

SEASON

all year

ACCOMMODATIONS

4 rooms with shared baths

The Inn
on St. Andrews

Joan Peggs
231 St. Andrews Street
Victoria, British Columbia
V8V 2N1
Tel: (800) 668-5993 or
(604) 384-8613
Fax: (604) 384-6063
E-mail: joan.peggs@vonline.com
$$

ABOUT THE B&B

The Inn on St. Andrews is as lovely today as when it was built in 1913 by Edith Carr, eldest sister of the famous Canadian artist and author, Emily Carr. This Tudor-style heritage property charms with its elegant woodwork, stained and beveled glass, and large bright bedrooms. After a wholesome breakfast in the formal dining room, you can congregate in the sunroom overlooking the east garden or sun deck overlooking the west garden, in the cozy TV room, or in the larger drawing room. The inn is ideally located in James Bay, close to Victoria's inner harbor with ferry and seaplane terminals, the Parliament buildings, the Royal British Columbia Museum, famed Empress Hotel, and downtown shops. A short walk brings you to Beacon Hill Park and the oceanfront. Your host Joan Peggs believes in modern comfort and old-fashioned hospitality, and provides guests with her own map highlighting walking and driving destinations and recommended restaurants.

SEASON

all year

ACCOMMODATIONS

1 room with private bath;
2 rooms with shared bath

Whipped Cottage Cheese

(Recipe from Joan Peggs Eggs, *written and published by Joan Peggs, 1996)*

"Excellent for pancakes and waffles." — Joan Peggs

1 cup dry or creamed cottage cheese
1 – 2 tablespoons honey
1 – 2 teaspoons lemon juice or vanilla

Place cottage cheese, honey, and flavoring into the small bowl of an electric mixer (a blender or food processor will also work well). Beat on high until well combined and relatively smooth. *Makes 1 cup.*

Zucchini Jam

6 cups peeled, seeded, and grated zucchini
5 cups sugar
¼ cup lemon juice
19-ounce can crushed pineapple, drained
2 small packages peach Jell-O

Prepare zucchini and place in a large saucepan. Add sugar and boil for 6 minutes. Add lemon juice and pineapple. Boil for 6 minutes more. Take off heat and add packages of peach Jell-O. Stir well. Pour into sterilized jars and seal tightly. Store in a cool, dark, dry place. *Makes 5 – 6 cups.*

Gîte à la ferme MACDALE Bed and Breakfast

Anne and Gordon MacWhirter
365 Route 132, Hope
PO Box 803
Paspébiac, Québec G0C 2K0
Tel: (418) 752-5270
$

ABOUT THE B&B

For a relaxing holiday, visit the Gaspé Peninsula and MACDALE Bed and Breakfast. Situated overlooking Chaleur Bay on an active, fifth-generation beef farm, this spacious three-story home offers two family rooms and a variety of guest accommodations. The aroma of fresh coffee and assorted muffins and pastries will awaken you and whet your appetite for an old-fashioned home-baked breakfast using farm-fresh eggs. Thanks to MACDALE's central location, tourist attractions such as world-famous Percé Rock and Forillon Park are well within day-trip driving distance. A seawater therapy resort is just minutes away, as are many museums, points of historical interest, and sports facilities. Anne is a first grade teacher while Gordon has recently retired from teaching junior high school mathematics.

SEASON

all year

ACCOMMODATIONS

1 loft with private bath;
4 rooms with shared baths

Index of Food

Hash brown and sausage casserole, 252

Hawkins House shortcake, 89

Hazelnut coffee cake, 91

Healthy porridge, 19

Heart-healthy
applesauce cake, 92
buttermilk pancakes, 199

Henderson hotcakes with chokecherry syrup, 200

Herbed cookie cutter butter, 298

Heritage scones, 137

Hollandaise sauce, quick, with smoked salmon, 282

Homestyle Boursin, 170

Honey
-cinnamon butter, 296
-glazed pear turnovers, 138
Muskoka wild clover-cranberry, 302
-yogurt sauce, French toast with, 194

Hotcakes, Henderson, with chokecherry syrup, 200

Hummingbird layer cake, 93

Ice tea, old-fashioned, 20

Icing. See Frosting

Impossible pie, 95

Island clotted cream topping, 299

Jam. See Spreads

Jelly roll, 140

Jelly, rosehip, 171

Jiffy pudding, 141

Juice. See also Beverages
apple-cranberry, 14
cranberry, 14

Kringler, Scandinavian, 153

Kuchen, raspberry, 150

Lazy dazy cake, 96

Leek
and sage quiche, 246
and salmon quiche, fresh, 241

Lemon
-buttermilk sorbet, 142
citrus blueberry muffins, 29
French toast with strawberry sauce, 202
loaf, traditional, 73
-poppy seed pancakes, 203
pudding, baked, 122

Loaf. See Bread(s), quick

Low-calorie vegetable dip, 300

Mackerel. See Fish

Mandarin orange coffee cake, 97

Maple
-apple sauce, chunky, oatmeal pancakes with, 207
-bran muffins, 33
butter, with Canadian alphabet pancakes, 186
-onion jam, Reuben bread pudding with, 251
syrup sabayon, with grilled fruit crêpes, 198
twist rolls, 143

Maritime morning eggs, 275

Marmalade. See Spreads

Mary's baked apple, 171

Ma's rhubarb marmalade, 301

Meat. See specific meats

Meringue, Swedish rhubarb, 113

Miracle date and pecan muffins, 34

Molasses apple-cinnamon pancakes, 180

Mom's dandelion pancakes, 204

Moose Jaw minuet, 247

Muffins
apple, spiced, 43
banana, quick, 39
Boston, 25
bran-raisin, overnight, 36
buttermilk Saskatoon berry, 26
chocolate chip-banana, 27
chocolate-zucchini, 28
citrus blueberry, 29
cranberry-orange, 30
date and pecan, miracle, 34
doughnut, 31
fruity yogurt, 32
maple-bran, 33
oat bran-raisin, 35
peach, 37
poppy seed, 38
rhubarb-oat, 40
rhubarb-pecan, 41
sourdough blueberry, 42
strawberry-oatmeal, 44
whole-wheat fruit, 45
wild blueberry-buttermilk, 46

Multi-grain bread, 57

Mushroom
and turkey croustades, 285
puff pancake, 205

Muskoka wild clover-cranberry honey, 302

Mussel and sweet potato chowder, 172

Nana's tea biscuits, 145

Nest eggs, 276

No-fail banana bread, 59

Norwegian flat bread (sesame crisp bread), 68

Nova Scotia brown bread, 60

Nova Scotia crab toasties, 277

Nut butter, 296

Oasis poached eggs, 278

Oat bran-raisin muffins, 35

Oatmeal. See also Cereals
-banana waffles, 182
pancakes with chunky apple-maple sauce, 206
-strawberry muffins, 44

Oat-rhubarb muffins, 40

Old-fashioned ice tea, 20

Old-fashioned waffles with sauce, 208

Omelet(s)
asparagus, Gruyère, and tarragon souffléd, 227
bacon, savory, 253
Barbara Ann's, 230
Doloris' individual baked, 238
Gouda baked eggs with roasted red pepper coulis, 244
method of cooking, 257
plain, 257
sausage, overnight, 248
spinach, 256
vegetable cheese, 260

Onion
and cheese pie, 234
-maple jam, Reuben bread pudding with, 251

Open-faced fruit cake with wild blueberry filling, 98

Orange
butter, whipped, 296
-cranberry muffins, 30
French toast (à l'orange), baked, 181
-ginger sauce, 303
-gooseberry marmalade, 297
juice spritzer, 21
mandarin, coffee cake, 97
marmalade sauce, with French toast, 181
peel-sherry cake, 100

Orchard Lane waffles, 209

Overnight bran-raisin muffins, 36

Overnight rolls, 62

Overnight sausage omelet, 248

Rise & Dine books make unique gifts!

Purchase through your local bookstore or send form along with check or money order to:

Callawind Publications Inc.
3383 Sources Boulevard, Suite 205
Dollard-des-Ormeaux, Quebec, Canada
H9B 1Z8

OR

Callawind Publications Inc.
2083 Hempstead Turnpike, Suite 355
East Meadow, New York 11554-1730
USA

You may return books *in original condition* at any time for a full refund on the purchase price.

Qty	Description	Total
	Rise & Dine: Savory Secrets from America's Bed & Breakfast Inns @ US$14.95 / C$19.95 **each**.	
	Rise & Dine Canada: Savory Secrets from Canada's Bed & Breakfast Inns @ US$14.95 / C$19.95 **each**.	
	Shipping: Surface mail @ US$3.95 / C$4.95 **for 1 book. US$0.80 / C$1.00 for each additional book** (allow 2 – 4 weeks for delivery).	
	7% Goods and Services Tax (GST) for Canadian orders only.	
	Resellers: Please call (514) 685-9109 for more information. *Important: Prices subject to change without notice.*	_____

Name _____   Tel. _____

Address _____

City _____ State/Prov. _____ Zip/Postal code_____

Payment enclosed: ❑ **Check (payable to Callawind Publications)**   ❑ **Money order**

To help us better understand our readers, kindly provide the following information:

Where did you first see this book? _____

Are you buying it for yourself or as a gift? _____

Comments about the book _____

Questions? Call (514) 685-9109 or send e-mail to: **callawind@accent.net**

S0-AJY-690

Fodor's 2009

CARIBBEAN

Where to Stay and Eat
for All Budgets

Must-See Sights
and Local Secrets

Ratings You Can Trust

Fodor's Travel Publications   New York, Toronto, London, Sydney, Auckland
www.fodors.com

FODOR'S CARIBBEAN 2009

Editors: Douglas Stallings, Andrew Collins, Denise Leto, Mark Sullivan, Amanda Theunissen

Editorial Contributors: Carol M. Bareuther, John Bigley, Katherine Dykstra, Lynda Lohr, Elise Meyer, Vernon O'Reilly-Ramesar, Paris Permenter, Elise Rosen, Ramona Settle, Eileen Robinson Smith, Roberta Sotonoff, Jordan Simon, Mark Sullivan, Jane E. Zarem, Michael de Zayas

Editorial Production: Tom Holton

Maps & Illustrations: David Lindroth, Mark Stroud, *cartographers*; Bob Blake, Rebecca Baer, and William Wu *map editors*

Design: Fabrizio LaRocca, *creative director*; Guido Caroti, Siobhan O'Hare, *art directors*; Tina Malaney, Chie Ushio, Ann McBride, *designers*; Melanie Marin, *senior picture editor*; Moon Sun Kim, *cover designer*

Cover Photo: (Montego Bay, Jamaica): Ian Cumming/Axiom

Production/Manufacturing: Angela L. McLean

ISBN 978–1–4000–1942–7

ISSN 1524–9174

SPECIAL SALES

This book is available at special discounts for bulk purchases for sales promotions or premiums. Special editions, including personalized covers, excerpts of existing books, and corporate imprints, can be created in large quantities for special needs. For more information, write to Special Markets/Premium Sales, 1745 Broadway, MD 6-2, New York, New York 10019, or e-mail specialmarkets@randomhouse.com.

AN IMPORTANT TIP & AN INVITATION

Although all prices, opening times, and other details in this book are based on information supplied to us at press time, changes occur all the time in the travel world, and Fodor's cannot accept responsibility for facts that become outdated or for inadvertent errors or omissions. So **always confirm information when it matters,** especially if you're making a detour to visit a specific place. Your experiences—positive and negative— matter to us. If we have missed or misstated something, **please write to us.** We follow up on all suggestions. Contact the Caribbean editor at editors@fodors.com or c/o Fodor's at 1745 Broadway, New York, NY 10019.

PRINTED IN THE UNITED STATES OF AMERICA

10 9 8 7 6 5 4 3 2 1

Your opinion matters. It matters to us. It matters \dent
too. And we'd like to hear it. In fact, we need to hea.

When you share your experiences and opinions, you \
of the Fodor's community. That means we'll not only us
our books better, but we'll publish your names and comme
Throughout our guides, look for "Word of Mouth," excerpts
feedback.

Here's how you can help improve Fodor's for all of us.

Tell us when we're right. We rely on local writers to give you an insid.
tive. But our writers and staff editors—who are the best in the busines.
on you. Your positive feedback is a vote to renew our recommendations
next edition.

Tell us when we're wrong. We're proud that we update most of our guides ever,
year. But we're not perfect. Things change. Hotels cut services. Museums change
hours. Charming cafés lose charm. If our writer didn't quite capture the essence of
a place, tell us how you'd do it differently. If any of our descriptions are inaccurate
or inadequate, we'll incorporate your changes in the next edition and will correct
factual errors at fodors.com immediately.

Tell us what to include. You probably have had fantastic travel experiences that
aren't yet in Fodor's. Why not share them with a community of like-minded travelers? Maybe you chanced upon a beach or bistro or B&B that you don't want to
keep to yourself. Tell us why we should include it. And share your discoveries and
experiences with everyone directly at fodors.com. Your input may lead us to add
a new listing or highlight a place we cover with a "Highly Recommended" star or
with our highest rating, "Fodor's Choice."

Give us your opinion instantly at our feedback center at www.fodors.com/feedback.
You may also e-mail editors@fodors.com with the subject line "Caribbean Editor."
Or send your nominations, comments, and complaints by mail to Caribbean Editor,
Fodor's, 1745 Broadway, New York, NY 10019.

You and travelers like you are the heart of the Fodor's community. Make our community richer by sharing your experiences. Be a Fodor's correspondent.

Happy traveling!

Tim Jarrell, Publisher

MAPS

CONTENTS

ABOUT THIS BOOK

Our Ratings

Sometimes you find terrific travel experiences and sometimes they just find you. But usually the burden is on you to select the right combination of experiences. That's where our ratings come in.

As travelers we've all discovered a place so wonderful that its worthiness is obvious. And sometimes that place is so experiential that superlatives don't do it justice: you just have to be there to know. These sights, properties, and experiences get our highest rating, **Fodor's Choice,** indicated by orange stars throughout this book.

Black stars highlight sights and properties we deem **Highly Recommended,** places that our writers, editors, and readers praise again and again for consistency and excellence.

By default, there's another category: any place we include in this book is by definition worth your time, unless we say otherwise. And we will.

Disagree with any of our choices? Care to nominate a place or suggest that we rate one more highly? Visit our feedback center at www.fodors.com/feedback.

Budget Well

Hotel and restaurant price categories from ¢ to $$$$ are defined in the opening pages of each chapter. For attractions, we always give standard adult admission fees; reductions are usually available for children, students, and senior citizens. Want to pay with plastic? **AE, D, DC, MC, V** following restaurant and hotel listings indicate if American Express, Discover, Diners Club, MasterCard, and Visa are accepted.

Restaurants

Unless we state otherwise, restaurants are open for lunch and dinner daily. We mention dress only when there's a specific requirement and reservations only when they're essential or not accepted—it's always best to book ahead.

Hotels

Hotels have private bath, phone, TV, and air-conditioning and operate on the European Plan (aka EP, meaning without meals), unless we specify that they use the Continental Plan (CP, with a continental breakfast), Breakfast Plan (BP, with a full breakfast), Modified American Plan (MAP, with breakfast and dinner), Full American Plan (FAP, with all meals), or are all-inclusive (AI, including all meals and most activities). We always list facilities but not whether you'll be charged an extra fee to use them, so when pricing

Many Listings
- ★ Fodor's Choice
- ★ Highly recommended
- ⊠ Physical address
- ✢ Directions
- ⌖ Mailing address
- ☎ Telephone
- 🖶 Fax
- ⊕ On the Web
- ✉ E-mail
- ▣ Admission fee
- ☺ Open/closed times
- Ⓜ Metro stations
- ▭ Credit cards

Hotels & Restaurants
- ▣ Hotel
- ↘ Number of rooms
- ᗉ Facilities
- ❶❶ Meal plans
- ✕ Restaurant
- ᗜ Reservations
- ↘ Smoking
- BYOB
- ✕▣ Hotel with restaurant that warrants a visit

Outdoors
- ⊼ Golf
- ⌂ Camping

Other
- ☾ Family-friendly
- ⇨ See also
- ⊠ Branch address
- ☞ Take note

UNITED
STATES

Miami

Key West

Nassau

The Bahamas

Havana

Cuba

Turks and
Caicos Islands

*Little
Cayman*

George
Town

*Cayman
Brac*

*Grand
Cayman*

Puerto Plata

Haiti *Hispaniola*

Port-au-Prince

Santo
Domingo

Montego Bay

Ocho Rios

Jamaica

Kingston

G R E A T E R

Greater Antilles

C a r i b b e a n   *S e a*

0   200 mi
0   200 km

Cartagena   **COLOMBIA**   Maracaibo

ATLANTIC OCEAN

Dominican
Republic

LEEWARD ISLANDS

St. John
Tortola
St.
Thomas
Virgin Gorda
San Juan
Anguilla
St. Barthélemy
St. Maarten/
St. Martin
Saba
Barbuda
Puerto
Rico
St. Eustatius
St. Kitts
Antigua
St.
Croix
Nevis
Montserrat
Marie
Galante
Guadeloupe
Dominica

Leeward Islands

ANTILLES

Martinique
Fort-de-France

WINDWARD ISLANDS

LESSER ANTILLES

St. Lucia
Barbados
St. Vincent
Bridgetown
Bequia
The Grenadines
Carriacou
St. George's
Grenada

Aruba
Curaçao
Bonaire
Willemstad
Islas Los
Roques
Tobago
Port of Spain
Trinidad

La Guaira

Windward Islands
Caracas **VENEZUELA**

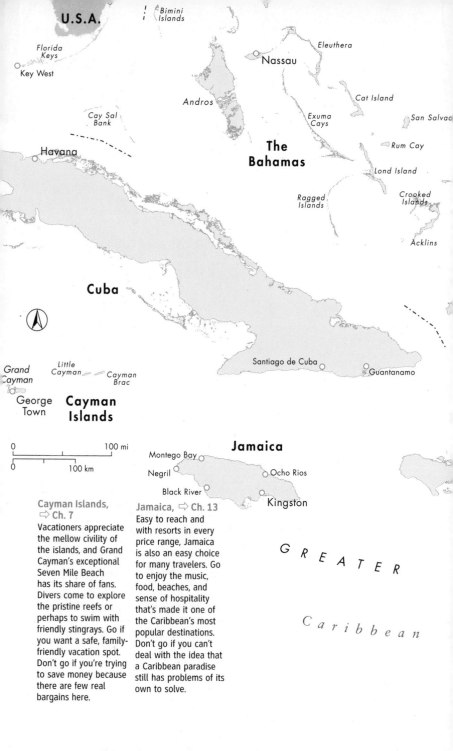

U.S.A.

Bimini
Islands

Florida
Keys

Eleuthera

Key West

Nassau

Cat Island

Andros

San Salvao

Cay Sal
Bank

Exuma
Cays

Rum Cay

Havana

**The
Bahamas**

Lond Island

Ragged
Islands

Crooked
Islands

Acklins

Cuba

Santiago de Cuba

Guantanamo

Grand
Cayman

Little
Cayman

Cayman
Brac

George
Town

**Cayman
Islands**

0   100 mi

0   100 km

Jamaica

Montego Bay

Ocho Rios

Negril

Black River

Kingston

**Cayman Islands,
⇨ Ch. 7**
Vacationers appreciate
the mellow civility of
the islands, and Grand
Cayman's exceptional
Seven Mile Beach
has its share of fans.
Divers come to explore
the pristine reefs or
perhaps to swim with
friendly stingrays. Go if
you want a safe, family-
friendly vacation spot.
Don't go if you're trying
to save money because
there are few real
bargains here.

Jamaica, ⇨ Ch. 13
Easy to reach and
with resorts in every
price range, Jamaica
is also an easy choice
for many travelers. Go
to enjoy the music,
food, beaches, and
sense of hospitality
that's made it one of
the Caribbean's most
popular destinations.
Don't go if you can't
deal with the idea that
a Caribbean paradise
still has problems of its
own to solve.

G R E A T E R

C a r i b b e a n

The Greater Antilles

The islands closest to the United States mainland—composed of Cuba, Jamaica, Haiti, the Dominican Republic, and Puerto Rico—are also the largest in the chain that stretches in an arc from the southern coast of Florida down to Venezuela. Haiti and Cuba aren't covered in this book. The Cayman Islands, just south of Cuba, are usually included in this group.

Turks & Caicos Islands, ⇨ **Ch. 25**
Miles of white sand beaches surround this tiny island chain, only eight of which are inhabited. The smaller islands seem to come from some long-forgotten era of Caribbean life. Go for deserted beaches and excellent diving on one of the world's largest coral reefs. Don't go for nightlife and a fast pace. And don't forget your wallet. This isn't a budget destination.

Dominican Republic, ⇨ **Ch. 10**
Dominicans have beautiful smiles and warm hearts and are proud of their island, which is blessed with pearl-white beaches and a vibrant, Latin culture. Go for the best-priced resorts in the Caribbean and a wide range of activities that will keep you moving day and night. Don't go if you can't go with the flow. Things don't always work here, and not everyone speaks English.

Puerto Rico, ⇨ **Ch. 16**
San Juan is hopping day and night; beyond the city, you'll find a sunny escape and slower pace. So party in San Juan, relax on the beach, hike the rain forest, or play some of the Caribbean's best golf courses. You have the best of both worlds here, with natural and urban thrills alike. So go for both. Just don't expect to do it in utter seclusion.

Puerto Rico

Bayamon

San Juan

Isla de Culebra

Mayaguez

Caguas

Ponce

Isla de Vieques

Anegada

St. Thomas

Tortola

Virgin Gorda

Road Town

Charlotte Amalie

St. John

British Virgin Islands

St. Mac
St. Ma

U.S. Virgin Islands

Christiansted

St. Croix

Lesser Antilles: The Eastern Caribbean

The Lesser Antilles are larger in number but smaller in size than the Greater Antilles, and they make up the bulk of the Caribbean arc. Beginning with the Virgin Islands but going all the way to Grenada, the islands of the Eastern Caribbean form a barrier between the Atlantic Ocean and the Caribbean Sea. The best beaches are usually on the Caribbean side.

Montserrat, ⇨ Ch. 15

Montserrat has staged one of the best comebacks of the new century, returning to the tourism scene after a disastrous volcanic eruption in 1995. Go for exciting volcano eco-tourism and great diving or just to taste what the Caribbean used to be like. Don't go for splashy resorts or nightlife. You'll be happier here if you can appreciate simpler pleasures.

St. Martin, ⇨ Ch. 22

Two nations (Dutch and French), many nationalities, one small island, a lot of development. But there are also more white, sandy beaches than days in a month. Go for the awesome restaurants, excellent shopping, and wide range of activities. Don't go if you're not willing to get out and search for the really good stuff.

U.S. Virgin Islands, ⇨ Ch. 26

A perfect combination of the familiar and the exotic, the U.S. Virgin Islands are a little bit of America set in an azure sea. Go to St. Croix if you like history and interesting restaurants. Go to St. John if you crave a back-to-nature experience. Go to St. Thomas if you want a shop-till-you-drop experience and a big selection of resorts, activities, and nightlife.

British Virgin Islands, ⇨ Ch. 6

The lure of the British Virgins is exclusivity and personal attention, not lavish luxury. Even the most expensive resorts are selling a state of mind rather than state-of-the-art. So go with an open mind, and your stress may very well melt away. Don't go if you expect glitz or stateside efficiency. These islands are about getting away, not getting it all.

Anguilla, ⇨ Ch. 1

With miles of brilliant beaches and a range of luxurious resorts (even a few that mere mortals can afford), Anguilla is where the rich, powerful, and famous go to chill out. Go for the fine cuisine in elegant surroundings, great snorkeling, and funky late-night music scene. Don't go for shopping and sightseeing. This island is all about relaxing and reviving.

St. Barthélemy, ⇨ Ch. 18

If you come to St. Barths for a taste of European village life, not for a conventional full-service resort experience, you will be richly rewarded. Go for excellent dining and wine, great boutiques with the latest hip fashions, and an active, on-the-go vacation. Don't go for big resorts, and make sure your credit card is platinum-plated.

0   100 mi

0   100 km

A T L A N T I C   O C E A N

nguilla

ʰr Valley

Marigot

n

Philipsburg   Gustavia

St. Barthélemy   **Barbuda**

Saba

Oranjestad

St. Eustatius   **St. Kitts**

Basseterre   **Nevis**   St Johns   **Antigua**

Charlestown   English Harbour

Montserrat

Grande-Terre   Le Désirade

Guadeloupe   Abymes

Petite Terre

Pointe-à-Pitre

Basse-Terre

Basse-Terre   Marie
Galante

Les Saintes   Grande-
Bourg

L E E W A R D   I S L A N D S

Portsmouth   Dominica

Roseau

Martinique

St Pierre

Fort-de-France

Antigua, ⇨ **Ch. 2**
Beaches, bone-white and beckoning—one for every day of the year—can be secluded or hopping with activity. History buffs and nautical nuts will appreciate English Harbour, which sheltered Britain's Caribbean fleet in the 18th and 19th centuries. Go for those beaches but also for sailing. Don't go for local culture because all-inclusives predominate. Lovely as it is, the island is more for tourists than travelers.

St. Eustatius, ⇨ **Ch. 19**
St. Eustatius (Statia) is the quintessential low-key island, where the most exciting thing is finding an elusive blue iguana while hiking the Quill. The real thrills are below the surface. Go to dive the wrecks, to hike the island's extinct volcano, and to be among the Caribbean's friendliest people. Don't go if you want to do much else.

Saba, ⇨ **Ch. 17**
With few modern conveniences (no resorts, no fast food, no movie theaters), you can reacquaint yourself with Mother Nature or simply catch your breath. Go to dive in the clear water, to hike to the top of Mount Scenery, and to enjoy the peace. Don't go if you want to lounge on the beach. There is no beach.

St. Kitts & Nevis, ⇨ **Ch. 20**
Things are unhurried on lush, hilly St. Kitts and Nevis. And the locals seem more cordial and courteous—eager to share their paradise with you—than on more touristy Caribbean islands. Go to discover Caribbean history, to stay in a small plantation inn, or just to relax. Don't go for nightlife or shopping. These islands are about laid-back "liming" and maybe buying some local crafts.

Guadeloupe, ⇨ **Ch. 12**
An exotic, tropical paradise, Guadeloupe is covered by a lush rain forest and blessed with a rich, Creole culture that influences everything from its dances to its food. Go if you want to experience another culture—and still have your creature comforts and access to fine beaches. Don't go if you want five-star luxury because it's rare here.

WHAT'S WHERE

The Windward and Southern Islands

The Windward islands—Dominica, Martinique, St. Lucia, St. Vincent, and Grenada— complete the main Caribbean arc. These dramatically scenic southern islands face the tradewinds head on. The Grenadines—a string of small islands between Grenada and St. Vincent—is heaven for sailors. The Southern Caribbean islands—Trinidad, Tobago, Aruba, Bonaire, and Curaçao—are rarely bothered by hurricanes.

Aruba, ⇨ Ch. 3
Some Caribbean travelers seek an undiscovered paradise, some seek the familiar and safe: Aruba is for the latter. On the smallest of the ABC islands, the waters are peacock blue, and the white beaches beautiful and powdery soft. For Americans, Aruba offers all the comforts of home: English is spoken universally, and the U.S. dollar is accepted everywhere.

Bonaire, ⇨ Ch. 5
With only 12,000 year-round citizens and huge numbers of visiting divers, Bonaire still seems largely untouched by tourism. Divers come for the clear water, profusion of marine life, and great dive shops. With a surreal, arid landscape, immense flamingo population, and gorgeous turquoise vistas, you can also have a wonderful land-based holiday.

Curaçao, ⇨ Ch. 8
Rich in heritage and history, Curaçao offers a blend of island life and city savvy, wonderful weather, spectacular diving, and charming beaches. Dutch and Caribbean influences are everywhere, but there's also an infusion of touches from around the world, particularly noteworthy in the great food. Willemstad, the picturesque capital, is a treat for pedestrians, with shopping clustered in areas around the waterfront.

Dominica, ⇨ Ch. 9
Dominica is the island to find your bliss exploring nature's bounty, not in the sun and surf. Go to be active, either diving under the sea or hiking on land. Don't go for great beaches or a big-resort experience. This is one island that's delightfully behind the times.

Martinique, ⇨ Ch. 14
Excellent cuisine, fine service, highly-touted rum, and lilting Franco-Caribbean music are the main draws in Martinique. Go if you're a Francophile drawn to fine food, wine, and sophisticated style. Don't go if you are looking for a bargain and don't have patience. Getting here is a chore, but there are definitely rewards for the persistent.

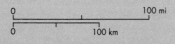

C a r i b b e a n   S e a

Aruba
○ Oranjestad

Bonaire
○ Kralendijk

Curaçao ○ Willemstad

Islas Los Roques

La Guaira

Isla La Tortuga

○ Caracas

0   100 mi
0   100 km

VENEZUELA

Map Labels

St. Kitts

Nevis

L E E W A R D

Antigua

Montserrat

Grande-Terre Guadeloupe

Abymes *Le Désirade*

Basse-Terre Pointe-à-Pitre

I S L A N D S

Basse-Terre *Marie Galante*

Les Saintes Grande-Bourg

Portsmouth

Dominica

Roseau

St Pierre *La Trinité*

Fort-de-France

Martinique

Castries

St. Lucia

W I N D W A R D

Barbados

Bridgetown

Kingstown **St. Vincent**

Bequia

I S L A N D S

The Grenadines

Carriacou

Grenada

St. George's

Tobago

Scarborough

Trinidad

Port of Spain

San Fernando

Text Columns

St. Lucia, ⇨ Ch. 21

One of the most green and beautiful islands in the Caribbean is, arguably, the most romantic. The scenic south and central regions are mountainous and lush, with dense rainforest, endless banana plantations, and fascinating historic sites. Along the west coast, some of the region's most picturesque and interesting resorts are interspersed with dozens of delightful inns, appealing to families as well as lovers and adventurers.

St. Vincent & The Grenadines, ⇨ Ch. 23

Thirty-two perfectly endowed islands and cays have no mass tourism but a lot of old-style Caribbean charm; several have not a small sense of luxury. Tourism isn't even the biggest business in lush, mountainous St. Vincent. Throughout the chain, wildlife trusts protect rare species of flora and fauna, and villa walls ensure privacy for the islands' rich and famous human visitors.

Grenada, ⇨ Ch. 11

The spice business is going strong, but tourism is just as important. On the laid-back island, the only sounds are the occasional abrupt call of a cuckoo in the lush rain forest, the crash of surf in the secluded coves, and the slow beat of a big drum dance. Resorts are mostly small and charming. St. George's, the island's capital, is often called the most beautiful city in the Caribbean.

Trinidad & Tobago, ⇨ Ch. 24

Trinidad and Tobago, the most southerly Caribbean islands, are two different places. Trinidad is an effervescent mix of cultures—mostly descendants of African slaves and East Indian indentured workers—who like to party but also appreciate the island's incredibly diverse ecosystem. Little sister Tobago is laid-back and rustic, with beaches that can match any in the Caribbean.

Barbados, ⇨ Ch. 4

Broad vistas, sweeping seascapes, craggy cliffs, and acre upon acre of sugarcane make up the island's varied landscape. A long, successful history of tourism has been forged from the warm, Bajan hospitality, welcoming hotels and resorts, sophisticated dining, lively nightspots, and, of course, magnificent sunny beaches.

ISLAND FINDER

To help you decide which island is best for you, we've rated each island in several areas that might influence your decision on choosing the perfect Caribbean vacation spot. Each major island covered in this book has been rated in terms of cost from $ (very inexpensive) to $$$$$ (very expensive), and since prices often vary a great deal by season, we've given you a rating for the high season (December through mid-April) and low season (mid-April through November). We've also compared each island's relative strength in several other categories that might influence your decision.

If an island has no marks in a particular column (under "Golf" for example), it means that the activity is not available on the island.

	Cost High Season	Cost Low Season
Anguilla	$$$$	$$$
Antigua	$$$	$$
Aruba	$$$	$$
Barbados	$$$$	$$$$
Bonaire	$$	$$
BVI: Tortola	$$$	$$
BVI: Virgin Gorda	$$$$$	$$$$
BVI: Anegada	$$$$	$$$
BVI: Jost Van Dyke	$$$$	$$$
Cayman Islands: Grand Cayman	$$$$	$$$
Cayman Islands: Little Cayman	$$$	$$$
Cayman Islands: Cayman Brac	$$	$$
Curaçao	$$$$	$$$
Dominica	$$	$
Dominican Republic	$$	$
Grenada	$$$	$$$
Grenada: Carriacou	$$	$
Guadeloupe	$$	$$
Jamaica	$$$	$$
Martinique	$$$	$$
Montserrat	$	$
Puerto Rico	$$$	$$
Saba	$$	$
St. Barthélemy	$$$$$	$$$$
St. Eustatius	$$	$
St. Kitts & Nevis: St. Kitts	$$$	$$
St. Kitts & Nevis: Nevis	$$$$	$$$
St. Lucia	$$$$	$$$
St. Maarten/St. Martin	$$$	$$$
SVG: St. Vincent	$$	$$
SVG: The Grenadines	$$$$	$$$
T&T: Trinidad	$$$	$$
T&T: Tobago	$$$	$$
Turks & Caicos Islands	$$$$*	$$$*
USVI: St. Thomas	$$$$	$$$
USVI: St. Croix	$$	$
USVI: St. John	$$$	$$

* Cost for Provo (Parrot Cay $$$$$, other islands $$)

** Provo Only

Beautiful Beaches	Fine Dining	Shopping	Casinos	Nightlife	Diving	Golf	Eco-tourism	Good for Families
5	4	2		2	1	3	1	2
5	5	4	3	3	2	3	3	3
4	4	4	4	5	3	2	3	4
3	5	3		3	2	5	1	4
3	3	2	1	1	5		4	4
2	3	2		2	3		3	3
5	3	1		1	4		4	3
5	3			1	4		4	4
4	3	1		5	3		4	3
5	4	5		2	4	3	2	4
					4	5	3	3
2					4		3	3
4	4	3	3	4	4	3	4	4
1	3	2		2	5		5	4
5	3	2	3	3	3	5	4	3
4	3	2		1	3	1	4	4
3	1	1			4		3	2
4	2	3	3	3	4	3	5	4
3	3	2	1	2	3	5	5	5
4	4	3	2	3	3	3	3	2
1	1	1		1	4		4	4
3	4	4	4	5	3	4	5	5
	4	2		1	5		4	
4	5	5		2	3			1
1	1	2		1	5		5	3
3	3	3	4	3	3	4	5	5
3	4	2		3	4	5	5	5
3	3	3		3	3	1	5	3
4	5	4	3	4	3	1	2	3
1	2	1	1	1	4		5	3
5	4	1		1	5	5	3	4
3	3	2	3	5	4	4	4	3
4	3	2	3	3	4	3	4	3
5	2**	1	1	1	5	4**	4	3**
3	4	5		2	3	4	2	4
3	3	2	2	2	3	3	3	3
5	3	2		1	3	3	4	5

IF YOU LIKE

Great Beaches

Great beaches aren't all the same. You might dream of sifting your toes in soft white sand with just a hint of warmth. You may love to walk along a virgin beach that is lined with nothing but a 20-foot palm tree. You may be charmed by that cute little crescent that's reachable by a precipitous climb down an almost-sheer rock cliff. You may want to be surrounded by a hundred pairs of beautiful limbs, all smelling slightly of coconut oil. The Caribbean can give you all these. Our favorite beaches aren't always the most famous ones, but part of the fun of taking a tropical vacation is discovering your own favorites, which are sometimes the ones you'd least suspect. Here are a few of the beaches we like:

■ **Baie Orientale, St. Maarten/St. Martin.** There's a good reason why everyone goes here.

■ **The Baths, Virgin Gorda, British Virgin Islands.** Giant boulders form grottoes filled with seawater that you can explore.

■ **Eagle Beach, Aruba.** Once undeveloped, this beach on Aruba's southwestern coast is now hopping and happening.

■ **Half Moon Beach, Providenciales, Turks & Caicos Islands.** A natural ribbon of ivory sand joins two tiny, uninhabited cays.

■ **Macaroni Beach, Mustique, St. Vincent & the Grenadines.** The most famous beach on the most famous Grenadine.

■ **Negril Beach, Jamaica.** Seven miles of sand lined by beach bars, casual restaurants, and hotels in westernmost Jamaica.

■ **Seven Mile Beach, Grand Cayman, Cayman Islands.** Free of litter and peddlers, the best northern sections are a sight to behold.

■ **Shoal Bay, Anguilla.** Sand or talcum powder? You decide.

Boating & Sailing

Whether you charter a crewed boat or captain the vessel yourself, the waters of the Caribbean are excellent for boating and sailing, and the many secluded bays and inlets provide ideal spots to drop anchor and picnic or explore. Once deemed an outward-bound adventure or exclusive domain of the rich and famous, chartering a boat is now considered—and actually is—an affordable and attractive vacation alternative. If you're already a sailor, you may have always wanted to explore beyond your own lake, river, or bay. Well, you can always hire a certified skipper to come along and help you out. If you've never sailed before, you've probably not experienced the delight at dropping anchor at a different beautiful beach every day. There are many great yacht harbors, including these:

■ **Antigua.** Yachtspeople favor the waters here and put in regularly in Nelson's Dockyard, which hosts a colorful annual regatta in late April or early May.

■ **St. Martin.** Marigot's yacht harbor is a jumping-off spot for trips to the nearby islands of Anguilla and St. Barths.

■ **St. Vincent & the Grenadines.** So many islands so close together give you more possibilities than you can possibly enjoy in one vacation.

■ **St. Thomas, U.S. Virgin Islands.** It's easy to charter a yacht in the Virgin Islands, which offer some of the best sailing opportunities in the world.

■ **Tortola, British Virgin Islands.** The best yacht-charter island in the Caribbean, without a doubt.

Diving & Snorkeling

Many people would rather spend their days under the sea rather than on the beach. Generally, the best conditions for diving—clear water and lots of marine life—are also good for snorkelers, though you won't see as much from the surface looking down. If you haven't been certified yet, take a resort course. After learning the basics in a pool, you can often do a short dive from shore. Here are some of the Caribbean's best dive destinations:

■ **Anegada, British Virgin Islands.** The reefs surrounding this flat coral and limestone atoll are a sailor's nightmare but a scuba diver's dream.

■ **Bonaire.** The current is mild, the reefs often begin just offshore, visibility is generally 60 feet to 100 feet, and the marine life is magnificent.

■ **Dominica.** Serious divers know that the pristine, bubbly waters around Dominica's submerged volcanic crater are among the best in the world.

■ **Little Cayman, Cayman Islands.** The drop-off at Bloody Bay Wall goes from 18 feet to more than 1,000 feet—diving doesn't get much better than this.

■ **Saba.** Beside one of the lively Caribbean reefs, the diving on Saba is some of the best in the world.

■ **St. Eustatius.** The waters here are tops for wreck diving.

■ **Tobago Cays, St. Vincent & the Grenadines.** A group of five uninhabited islands surrounds a beautiful lagoon studded with sponges, coral formations, and countless colorful fish.

■ **Turks & Caicos Islands.** The world's third-largest coral reef is visible from the air and packed with exotic marine life, dramatic wall drop-offs, colorful fans, and pristine coral formations.

Golf

What's better than playing the back 9 shaded by swaying palm trees with a view of the crashing surf? Golfers are drawn to excellent Caribbean courses and stunning views, often attached to comfortable and luxurious resorts, where the rest of the family can lounge by the pool while you head off for a morning round before the sun gets too hot. Mild weather year-round means you can be playing golf in the Dominican Republic or Barbados while everyone else is freezing. Here are a few of the best:

■ **Four Seasons Golf Course, Nevis.** The combination of majestic scenery, unbelievably lush landscaping, and Robert Trent Jones Jr.'s wicked layout incorporating ravines and sugar mills, makes this experience well above par even among classic golf resorts.

■ **Hyatt Dorado Courses, Puerto Rico.** Dorado Beach has four world-class, Robert Trent Jones–designed courses that are renowned classics and among Chi Chi Rodríguez's favorites.

■ **Punta Espada Golf Course, Dominican Republic.** The first of three Jack Nicklaus–designed courses at the new Cap Cana development in Punta Cana has already hosted one PGA championship event.

■ **Tobago Plantations Golf & Country Club, Trinidad & Tobago.** The oceanside course—the newest on the island—has amazing views, not to mention challenging greens and fairways.

■ **Trump International Golf Club, Canouan.** This course, the only one in the Grenadines, was designed by Jim Fazio and has astounding views.

IF YOU LIKE

Caribbean History

From the 16th century until the early 19th century, the Dutch, Danes, Swedes, English, French, and Spanish fought bitterly for control of the Caribbean. Some islands have almost as many battle sites as sand flies. Having gained control of the islands and annihilated the Caribs, the Europeans established vast sugar plantations and brought Africans to work the fields. Today the Caribbean population is a rich gumbo of nationalities, and a good deal of the region's history has been preserved. Here are some of the more interesting historical sights:

■ **Christiansted, U.S. Virgin Islands.** Fort Christiansvaern and other historic sights, which are spread out all over town, let you step back into St. Croix's colonial past.

■ **Kurá Hulanda Museum, Curaçao.** This museum and cultural center is at the heart of a rebirth for Curaçao, and its collection documenting African history around the world is worth a special trip.

■ **Nelson's Dockyard, Antigua.** An impeccable restoration of Lord Horatio Nelson's 18th-century headquarters has delightful hotels, restaurants, and crafts shops.

■ **Rose Hall & the Appleton Estate, Jamaica.** Jamaica is home to many former plantation greathouses but none with as rich a history as Rose Hall, which comes complete with haunting legends.

■ **Santo Domingo's Zona Colonial, Dominican Republic.** As you wander the narrow cobbled streets, it's easy to imagine what the city was like in the days of Columbus, Cortés, and Ponce de León, especially now that the zone is well lighted by antique lanterns.

Nightlife

Steel drums, limbo dancers, and jump-ups are ubiquitous in the Caribbean. Jump-ups? Simple. You hear the music, jump up, and dance. Or just indulge the art of "liming" (we call it "hanging out"), which can mean anything from playing pool or dominoes to engaging in heated political debate to dancing.

■ **Aruba.** While it's not everyone's cup of tea, Aruba has a vibrant nighttime scene. You definitely do not have to wait until spring to break free here.

■ **Jamaica.** Reggae Sumfest is the big summer music festival. Both Montego Bay's so-called Hip Strip and Negril's Norman Manley Boulevard are lined with bars and clubs that keep things hopping until late (or early, as the case may be).

■ **Puerto Rico.** With a full range of bars, nightclubs, and every form of entertainment, San Juan is a big, small city that never sleeps. The year-round Le Lai Lo Festival is perhaps the most successful attempt to introduce visitors to local music and dance.

■ **Trinidad.** Port-of-Spain is loaded with lively nightspots, and spontaneity is prized, so you have to keep your ears open for the new parties. The one party you can't miss is Carnival, the Caribbean's biggest and most popular celebration, which draws thousands to the island for days of parades and street parties. Other good Carnival celebrations are on Curaçao and Guadeloupe.

Shopping

Almost as many people go to the Caribbean to shop as to lie on the beach. Whether it's jewelry in St. Maarten, fragrant spices in Grenada, high-end designer fashions in St. Barths, or island crafts almost anywhere, you're likely to come home with a bag full of treasures.

■ **Grenada.** Visit a historic spice plantation, tour a nutmeg-processing plant, and replenish your spice rack with nutmeg, cinnamon sticks, cocoa, and cloves at an outdoor market.

■ **Puerto Rico.** From the boutiques of Old San Juan to ateliers of the young designers elsewhere in metro San Juan to galleries scattered all over the island, there's plenty to see and buy. You may also consider picking up some of the santos created in San Germán.

■ **St. Barthélemy.** Without a doubt, the shopping here for luxury goods and fashion is the best in the Caribbean. The variety and quality are astounding. The unfavorable exchange rates mean fewer bargains for Americans, but the prices here—all duty-free—are still less than what you'd pay in Paris or Saint Tropez.

■ **St. Maarten/St. Martin.** Hundreds of duty-free shops in Phillipsburg make the island the best in the Caribbean for bargain hunters, especially for quality jewelry and perfumes. Marigot has its share of nice boutiques, but unfavorable exchange rates make for fewer good buys on the French side.

■ **St. Thomas, U.S. Virgin Islands.** Main Street in Charlotte Amalie is well known for numerous duty-free shops, selling everything from rum to designer fashions and gems. The Caribbean's biggest cruise port also has several malls.

Staying Active

There's much more to do in the Caribbean than simply lying on the beach, sipping rum punches, or playing a round of golf. Try hiking through rain forests, kayaking through mangroves, or sailing on a board through a windswept bay.

■ **Bird-watching, Trinidad & Tobago.** So the watching part isn't so active, but hiking through the rain forests and savannahs on these sister islands will give you the opportunity to see more bird species than any other place in the Caribbean.

■ **Hiking the Quill, St. Eustatius.** The crater of Statia's extinct volcano is filled with a primeval rain forest and is a top hiking destination.

■ **Horseback Riding at Chukka Cove, Jamaica.** Headquartered at the Ocho Rios polo fields, this company is now Jamaica's top soft-adventure outfitter, having added canopy tours, river rafting, and more to its excellent horseback-riding program.

■ **Kayaking through Bahía Mosquito, Puerto Rico.** Vieques's bioluminiscent bay is best experienced on a kayak tour on a moonless night, when every stroke makes the water light up.

■ **Trekking to Boiling Lake, Dominica.** This bubbly, brackish cauldron is actually a flooded fumarole. A trek here is an unforgettable trip into an otherworldly place.

■ **Windsurfing in Sosúa Bay, Dominican Republic.** Ideal wind conditions have helped to create one of the Caribbean's major windsurfing centers on this north-coast beach.

IF YOU WANT

To Take It Easy on Your Wallet

The Caribbean isn't all about five-star resorts. Often, you may want to save a bit of your vacation cash to eat in elegant restaurants or to shop for the perfect gift. Saving money in the Caribbean doesn't have to mean sacrificing comfort. Sometimes it just means going to a cheaper island, such as the Dominican Republic, Saba, or Dominica. But there are some unique inns and resorts in the Caribbean, where you can sleep for much less and still have a great time.

■ **Bellafonte Chateau de la Mer, Bonaire.** An oceanfront room at this chic, palazzo-style hotel will remind you why you came to the Caribbean.

■ **Carringtons Inn, St. Croix, U.S. Virgin Islands.** A stay at this spacious bed-and-breakfast harks back to a gentler time, when people spent the winter, rather than a week, in the Caribbean.

■ **Horny Toad, St. Maarten/St. Martin.** A marvelous little oceanfront guesthouse with a funky name offers the island's best value for those who want to keep costs down.

■ **Peach & Quiet, Barbados.** This small seaside inn on the southeast coast is the sweetest deal on Barbados.

■ **Rockhouse, Jamaica.** Perched on the cliffs of Negril's West End, unique bungalows blend comfort and rustic style. Regular rooms keep costs down, but if you want to spend a bit more, the dramatic villas are worth every penny.

■ **Rocky Shore Guest House, Grand Cayman, Cayman Islands.** If you really want to connect with Cayman, owners Chris and Trina will treat you right.

To Splurge

The Caribbean's most luxurious resorts are worlds unto themselves. You'll live a privileged existence, if only for the week, and you may be joined by the masters of Wall Street or Hollywood, the jet set or old money. Everyone deserves to splurge at least once, and if that's what you want to do, these are the best places to do it.

■ **Anse Chastanet Hotel, St. Lucia.** Rooms were designed to meld with the mountainside; the new Jade Mountain Club rooms have raised the bar even further.

■ **Bitter End Yacht Club, British Virgin Islands.** Our favorite resort on Virgin Gorda is a haven for yachters, with a top-notch sailing school.

■ **Coral Reef Club, Barbados.** Elegant and stylish without being stuffy, suites are individually designed, beautifully decorated, and wonderfully private.

■ **CuisineArt Resort & Spa, Anguilla.** Upscale but still family-friendly, this resort regains its top ranking after a 2008 room renovation.

■ **Curtain Bluff, Antigua.** This longstanding luxury retreat exudes a timelessness that is hard to match and remains a relative bargain among the top luxury resorts in the Caribbean.

■ **Eden Rock, St. Barthélemy.** St. Barths' original hotel remains one of the island's best.

■ **Paradisus Palma Real Resort, Dominican Republic.** This true luxury all-inclusive is a first for Punta Cana.

To Have the Perfect Honeymoon

Swaying palms, moonlight strolls on the beach, candlelit dinners: no wonder the Caribbean is a favorite honeymoon destination. Whatever you are looking for in a honeymoon—seclusion, privacy, or more active fun—you can certainly find it, and it will usually be on a perfect beach. You can be pampered or just left alone, stay up late or get up with the sun, get out and stay active or simply rest and relax. Our favorites run the gamut, so if you need a place with easy access, or if you want to really get away from it all, we have the perfect spot.

■ **Horned Dorset Primavera, Puerto Rico.** Whisk your beloved to this sunset-kissed hotel and just disappear. You may never leave your elegant oceanfront room. When you do, the restaurant is one of the best in Puerto Rico.

■ **Palm Island, Grenadines.** Enjoy five dazzling beaches for water sports, nature trails for quiet walks, a pool with waterfall, sophisticated dining, impeccable service, exquisite accommodations—and privacy.

■ **Sandals Grande St. Lucian Spa & Beach Resort, St. Lucia.** Big, busy, and all-inclusive, this resort is a favorite of young honeymooners—particularly for its complimentary weddings.

■ **The Somerset, Turks & Caicos Islands.** Provo's most beautiful resort is more focused on your comfort than on attracting a celebrity clientele, so regular folks will still feel at home.

■ **Spice Island Beach Resort, Grenada.** Grenada's best resort has impeccable service, placing it among the Caribbean's finest small resorts.

To Eat Well

Caribbean food is a complex blend of indigenous, African, and colonial influences. Native tubers such as yuca and taro, leafy vegetables like callaloo, and herbs such as cilantro recur in most island cuisines. Africans brought plantains, yams, pigeon peas, and assorted peppers. The Spanish introduced rice, and the British brought breadfruit from the South Pacific. Here are some of our favorite Caribbean restaurants:

■ **Blue by Eric Ripert, Cayman Islands.** Grand Cayman's best restaurant is brought to you by one of New York's finest chefs.

■ **Brandywine Bay, Tortola.** A romantic, candlelit atmosphere coupled with stellar food makes this Tortola's best restaurant.

■ **Iguane Café, Guadeloupe.** Unquestionably original cuisine with influences from around the world is daring and dramatic, not to mention delicious.

■ **KoalKeel, Anguilla.** One of the island's best new restaurants mixes French and West Indian styles to excellent effect.

■ **The Pavilion, Antigua.** Chef Andrew Knoll, a protégé of Emeril Lagasse, has brought a touch of New Orleans verve to this genteel and welcoming restaurant next to Antigua's airport, of all places.

■ **The Verandah, Trinidad.** Phyllis Vieira's free-style Caribbean cuisine is one of the best-kept secrets in Trinidad—well, we can't keep this secret any longer.

WHEN TO GO

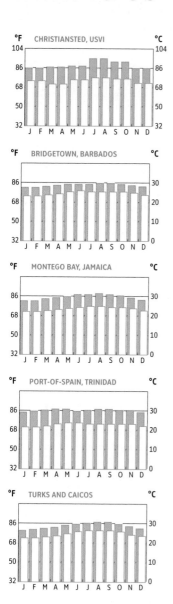

The Caribbean high season is traditionally winter—from December 15 to April 14—when northern weather is at its worst. During this season you're guaranteed the most entertainment at resorts and the most people with whom to enjoy it. It's also the most fashionable, the most expensive, and the most popular time to visit—and most hotels are heavily booked. You must make reservations at least two or three months in advance for the very best places (sometimes a year in advance for the most exclusive spots). Hotel prices drop 20% to 50% after April 15; airfares and cruise prices also fall. Saving money isn't the only reason to visit the Caribbean during the off-season. Temperatures are only a few degrees warmer than at other times of the year, and many islands now schedule their carnivals, music festivals, and other events during the off-season. Late August, September, October, and early November are the least crowded.

Climate

The Caribbean climate is fairly constant. The average year-round temperatures for the region are 78°F to 88°F. The temperature extremes are 65°F low, 95°F high; but, as everyone knows, it's the humidity, not the heat, that makes you suffer, especially when the two go hand in hand.

As part of the late-fall rainy season, hurricanes occasionally sweep through the Caribbean. Check the news daily and keep abreast of brewing tropical storms. The southernmost Caribbean islands (from St. Vincent to Trinidad, along with Aruba, Bonaire, and Curaçao) are generally spared the threat of hurricanes. The rainy season consists mostly of brief showers interspersed with sunshine. You can watch the clouds thicken, feel the rain, then have brilliant sunshine dry you off, all while remaining on your lounge chair. A spell of overcast days or heavy rainfall is unusual, as everyone will tell you.

HURRICANE SEASON

The Atlantic hurricane season lasts from June 1 through November 30, but it's fairly rare to see a large storm in either June or November. Most major hurricanes occur between August and October, with the peak season being in September.

Avoiding the Storms

Keep in mind that hurricanes are more rare the farther south you go. The ABC Islands (Aruba, Bonaire, and Curaçao) as well as Trinidad & Tobago are the least likely to see a direct hit by a hurricane, but all these islands have had their run-ins, so it's not a certainty you'll avoid storms by going south. Similarly, Barbados is less likely to be adversely affected by a strong storm because it lies 100 mi farther east than the rest of the Antilles.

Airlines

Airports are usually closed during hurricanes and many flights cancelled, which results in a disruption of the steady flow of tourists in and out of affected islands. If you are scheduled to fly into an area where a hurricane is expected, check regularly and often with your airline. If flights are disrupted, airlines will usually allow you to rebook at a later date, but you will not get a refund if you have booked a nonrefundable ticket, nor in most cases will you be allowed to change your ticket to a different destination; rather, you will be expected to reschedule your trip for a later date.

Hotels & Resorts

If a hurricane warning is issued and flights disrupted to your destination, virtually every Caribbean resort will waive cancellation and change penalties and will allow you to rebook your trip for a later date; some will allow you to cancel even if a hurricane threatens to strike, even if flights aren't cancelled. Some will give you a refund if you have prepaid for your stay, others will expect you to rebook your trip for a later date. Some large resort companies—including Sandals and SuperClubs—have "Hurricane Guarantees," but these kick in only when flights have been cancelled or when a hurricane is sure to strike.

Travel Insurance:

If you plan to travel to the Caribbean during the hurricane season, it is wise to buy travel insurance that allows you to cancel for any reason. This kind of coverage can be expensive (up to 10% of the value of the trip), but if you have to prepay far in advance for an expensive vacation package, the peace of mind may be worth it. Just be sure to read the fine print; some policies don't kick in unless flights are cancelled and the hurricane strikes, something you may not be assured of until the day you plan to travel. In order to get a complete cancellation policy, you must usually buy your insurance within a week of booking your trip. If you wait until after the hurricane warning is issued to purchase insurance, it will be too late.

Track Those Hurricanes

The obsessive and naturally curious keep a close eye on the Caribbean during Hurricane Season. You can, too. Several Web sites track hurricanes during the season, including ⊕*weather.com,* ⊕*www. hurricanetrack.com,* and ⊕*www.accuweather.com.*

ON THE CALENDAR

The Caribbean's top seasonal events are listed below, and any one of them could provide the stuff of lasting memories. Contact local tourism authorities for exact dates and for further information.

ONGOING January–April	**Carnival** lasts longer on Curaçao than on many other islands: the revelries begin at New Year's and continue until midnight the day before Ash Wednesday. The highlight is the Tumba Festival (dates vary), a four-day musical event featuring fierce competition among local musicians for the honor of having their piece selected as the official road march during parades. Easter Monday's Seú Folklore Parade is made up of groups celebrating the harvest in traditional costumes.
WINTER December	The week before Christmas, the Carriacou **Parang Festival** is a musical and cultural celebration. "Parang" is Spanish for ad-libbing. Costumed singers travel from village to village, creating spontaneous songs based on local gossip and accompanied by guitar, violin, and drums. In odd-numbered years, in early December, Martinique hosts its jazz festival, **Jazz à la Martinique**; in addition to showcasing the best musical talent of the islands, it has attracted such top American performers as Branford Marsalis. So Sabans don't forget what fun is, they hold a **Saba Day** the first weekend in December—three days of band contests, food tastings, and other events. Bicycle racing, arts-and-crafts exhibitions, caroling, and street parties with music and dancing mark **Nine Mornings,** a pre-Christmas tradition in St. Vincent that occurs during the nine days immediately before Christmas.
December–January	St. Croix celebrates Carnival with its **Crucian Christmas Festival,** which starts in late December. After weeks of beauty pageants, food fairs, and concerts, the festival wraps up with a parade in early January.
January	In mid-January, the **Barbados Jazz Festival** is a weeklong event jammed with performances by international artists, jazz legends, and local talent. The **Air Jamaica Jazz & Blues Festival** takes place in Montego Bay, Jamaica, in late January, drawing both music fans and a wide range of talent.
January–February	The **Grenada Sailing Festival,** held at the end of January and early February, includes six days of races and regattas and a

	daylong crafts market and street festival—all organized by the Grenada Yacht Club.
February	Although the pre-Lenten **Carnival** is celebrated all over the Caribbean, the region's biggest and most elaborate celebration is undoubtedly in Trinidad, where it's become a way of life and the most widely anticipated event of the entire year.
	The biggest event of the year is the four-day **Carriacou Carnival,** held in mid-February. Revelers participate in parades, calypso contests, music and dancing, and general frivolity.
SPRING March	Locals and yachties gather at Foxy's bar on Jost Van Dyke in the British Virgin Islands for the annual **St. Patrick's Day** celebration.
	Beginning around March 17 and lasting a week, the **St. Patrick's Day Fiesta** is celebrated in Sauteurs (St. Patrick's Parish), in the north of Grenada, with arts and crafts, agricultural exhibits, food and drink, and a cultural extravaganza with music and dancing.
	On the Dutch side of St. Maarten, early March has the **Heineken Regatta,** with as many as 300 sailboats competing from around the world. (For the experience of a lifetime, some visitors can purchase a working berth aboard a regatta vessel.)
March–April	The **National Music Festival** is held at Kingstown, St. Vincent's Memorial Hall during March and April. The best in Vincentian music and song is presented—folk songs, gospel, calypso, solos and duets, choirs, and group ensembles.
	The Bequia **Easter Regatta** is held during the four-day Easter weekend. Revelers gather to watch boat races and celebrate Bequia's seafaring traditions with food, music, dancing, and competitive games.
	On Union in the Grenadines, the **Easterval Regatta** occurs during the Easter weekend. Festivities include boat races, sports and games, a calypso competition, a beauty pageant, and a cultural show featuring the Big Drum Dance (derived from French and African traditions). Union is one of the few islands (along with Grenada's Carriacou) that perpetuate this festive dance.

ON THE CALENDAR

	During Easter weekend, St. Thomas Yacht Club hosts the **Rolex Cup Regatta,** which is part of the three-race Caribbean Ocean Racing Triangle (CORT), which pulls in yachties and their pals from all over.
Late April–May	**Antigua Sailing Week** draws more than 300 yachts for a series of races in several boat classes. It's like a nautical Kentucky Derby, and the salt air crackles with excitement.
May	Every May, hordes of people head to Tortola for the three-day **BVI Music Festival** to listen to reggae, gospel, blues, and salsa music by musicians from around the Caribbean and the U.S. mainland.
	In early May the weeklong **St. Lucia Jazz Festival,** one of the premier events of its kind in the Caribbean, sees international jazz greats entertain at outdoor venues on Pigeon Island and at various hotels, restaurants, and nightspots throughout the island; free concerts are also held at Derek Walcott Square in downtown Castries.
	On Canouan in the Grenadines, the **Canouan Regatta** is held in mid-May. Besides competitive boat races and sailing events, there are fishing contests, calypso competitions, donkey and crab races, and a beauty pageant.
	The **St. Croix Half Ironman Triathlon** attracts international-class athletes as well as amateurs every May for a 1-mi (2-km) swim, a 7-mi (12-km) run, and a 34-mi (55-km) bike ride; it includes a climb up the Beast on Route 69.
SUMMER June	The weeklong **Bonaire Dive Festival** is filled with educational and fun activities to raise people's awareness of the importance of the world's coral reefs.
	During **Million Dollar Month,** you'll find fishing tournaments on all three of the Cayman Islands (five tournaments in all), each with its own rules, records, and entrance fees; huge cash prizes are awarded, including one for a quarter of a million dollars that's given to the angler who breaks the existing blue marlin record (at this writing 584 pounds).
	The **Creole Blues Festival** is held on Marie-Galante annually, and it's gaining in fame.
	The **St. Kitts Music Festival,** held the last week of June, celebrates everything from R&B to reggae. Among the top inter-

	national acts to perform have been Chaka Khan, Earl Klugh, Kool and the Gang, and Peabo Bryson.
July	Dating from the 19th century, the Barbados **Crop Over Festival**, a monthlong event ending on Kadooment Day (a national holiday), marks the end of the sugarcane harvest.
	The St. Thomas Gamefishing Club hosts its **July Open Tournament** over the July 4 weekend. There are categories for serious marlin anglers, just-for-fun fishermen, and even kids who want to try their luck from docks and rocks.
	St. John dishes up its own version of Carnival with the **July 4** celebration. Weeks of festivities—including beauty pageants and a food fair—culminate in a parade through the streets of Cruz Bay on Independence Day.
Late July–early August	Antigua's **Summer Carnival** is one of the Caribbean's more elaborate, with eye-catching costumes, fiercely competitive bands, and the only Caribbean queen show (aka the Miss Antigua Contest).
	The renowned **Festival del Merengue** is held in late July and early August in Santo Domingo in the Dominican Republic, showcasing name entertainers, bands, and orchestras.
	Music lovers are drawn to Jamaica for the July and August **Reggae Sumfest,** which is getting hotter every year, because the best, brightest, and newest of the reggae stars gather to perform in open-air concerts in MoBay, Jamaica.
	Nevis's version of carnival—**Culturama**—is a summer event, held the end of July and beginning of August, and includes music competitions, art exhibits, and cultural events. It culminates in the daylong last-day jump-up, a colorful parade around the island.
August	Try your hand at sportfishing as anglers compete to land the largest catch at the **BVI Sportfishing Tournament.**
	A month of calypso road shows culminates in the **Grenada Carnival** the second week of August. It's the biggest celebration of the year, with a beauty pageant, a soca monarch competition, continuous steel-pan and calypso music, and a huge Parade of the Bands on the last Tuesday.
	On a Sunday in early August, Point-à-Pitre on Grande-Terre holds the **Fête des Cuisinières,** which celebrates the masters

ON THE CALENDAR

	of creole cuisine with a five-hour banquet that's open to the public. The festival was started in 1916 by a guild of female cooks (the guild still represents a large contingent) who wanted to honor the patron saint of cooks, St. Laurent.
	The **Caribbean Quest Musical Awards**, a festival of regional music from around the islands, is held in early August on the French side of St. Martin.
FALL Late September– early October	The **St. Lucia Billfishing Tournament**, held in late September or early October, attracts anglers from all over the Caribbean, with prizes awarded for the biggest fish and the largest catch; the blue marlin is the most sought-after fish, and everyone hopes to find one that beats the 1,000-pound mark.
October	Grand Cayman sees the carnival-like atmosphere of **Pirates Week** (which really lasts 10 days and includes a mock invasion of Hog Sty Bay by a mock Blackbeard and company). Visitors and locals dress up like pirates and wenches; music, fireworks, and competitions take place island-wide.
	Dominica's **Annual World Creole Music Festival** is held the last weekend in October or first weekend of November. This three-day music and cultural festival draws performers and creole music enthusiasts from around the globe.
	The Dominican Republic **Jazz Festival** is an impressive lineup of international (like Chuck Mangione) and Latino jazz stars (Bobby Sanabria and Carlos Estrada) that runs for three days during the first week of October, with venues in Cabarete, Sosúa, and Puerto Plata. Sea Horse Ranch is a hotbed of activity during the festival, and there's music, dance, and art.
October–November	**Divali,** held in October or November in Trinidad and Tobago and known as the Festival of Lights, is the climax of long spiritual preparation in the Hindu community. Small lamps beautifully illuminate the night, and there are events involving music, dancing, gift exchange, and much hospitality.
November	BET (Black Entertainment Television) sponsors Anguilla's **Tranquility Jazz Festival,** which attracts major musicians such as Hilton Ruiz, James Moody, Bobby Watson, and Vanessa Rubin.

Anguilla

The beach at Little Bay

WORD OF MOUTH

"Anguilla's water looks like you are in a swimming pool, and the sand is so white it hurts your eyes!"

—mustang8

"All [the] beaches are beautiful—long with white sand and crystal clear water—although Shoal Bay East is busier and has day trippers from St. Martin ('busy' in Anguilla is a relative term—the beaches are never really crowded)."

—MaryD

WELCOME TO ANGUILLA

TRANQUIL AND UPSCALE

The island is only 16 mi (26 km) long and 3 mi (5 km) wide at its widest point. A low-lying limestone island, its highest spot is 213 feet above sea level. Since there neither streams nor rivers—only saline ponds used for salt production—water is provided by cisterns that collect rainwater or desalinization plants.

In 1744, Anguillians (as well as privateers from St. Kitts) captured nearby French St-Martin and held it for 4 years; the French retaliated by attacking at Crocus Bay but were repelled.

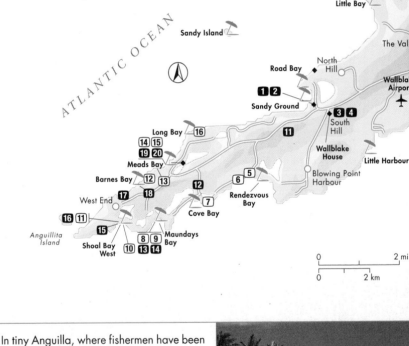

In tiny Anguilla, where fishermen have been heading out to sea for centuries in hand-made boats, the beaches are some of the Caribbean's best and least crowded. Heavy development has not spoiled the island's atmospheric corners, and independent restaurants still thrive. Resorts run the gamut from over-the-top places to quaint inns.

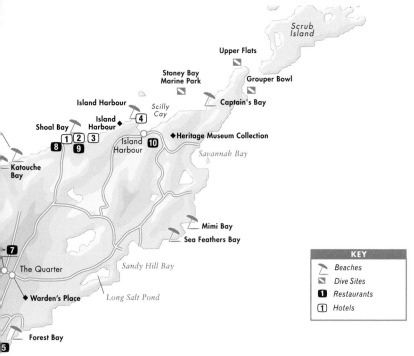

TOP 4 REASONS TO VISIT ANGUILLA

① Miles of brilliant beach ensure you have a quality spot to lounge.

② The dining scene offers fine cuisine in elegant surroundings as well as delicious local food in casual restaurants.

③ A funky late-night local music scene for reggae and string band fans means you don't have to go to bed early.

④ Excellent luxury resorts coddle you in a level of comfort to which you may or may not be accustomed.

ANGUILLA PLANNER

Island Activities

Beach-going and **fine dining** are the two most popular activities on Anguilla. However, if you want to be active, it's not a problem. The **diving** is good, though not excellent. You'll have many options for **day sails** and **snorkeling trips**. And there's even **horseback riding**. For **shopping**, St. Martin is a short ferry ride away. Anguilla's first **golf** course, the Temenos Golf Course, opened in late 2006.

Logistics

Getting to Anguilla: There are no nonstop flights to Anguilla (AXA) from the United States, so you will almost always have to fly through San Juan, St. Maarten, or some other Caribbean island. Most of the airlines flying to Anguilla are Caribbean-based, including Winair and LIAT, so you'll usually be making that short hop in a small plane, but American Eagle makes the trip from San Juan. The other option is a ferry from Marigot in St. Martin or directly from the St. Maarten airport. Many people take this option because it's only a 20-minute trip and relatively inexpensive (about $15 each way). You can also take a private water taxi, but the cost is significantly more.

Hassle Factor: Medium.

Nonstops: None from the U.S.

On the Ground

It's possible to base yourself in Sandy Ground, Rendezvous Bay, Meads Bay, or Upper Shoal Bay and do without a car, but restaurants and resorts are quite spread out, so for the sake of convenience you may wish to rent a car for a few days or for your entire stay. If you do, prepare to drive on the left. Otherwise, the taxi ride from the airport to your hotel will be less than $25 even to the West End (and considerably less if you're going to Sandy Ground). Taxis are fairly expensive on Anguilla, another reason to consider renting a car.

Where to Stay

Anguilla is known for its luxurious resorts and villas, but there are also a few places that mere mortals can afford (and some that are downright bargains).

⇨*For information on hotel meal plans, see Accommodations in Caribbean Essentials.*

WHAT IT COSTS IN U.S. DOLLARS				
$$$$	**$$$**	**$$**	**$**	**¢**
Restaurants				
over $30	$20–$30	$12–$20	$8–$12	under $8
Hotels*				
over $350	$250–$350	$150–$250	$80–$150	under $80
Hotels**				
over $450	$350–$450	$250–$350	$125–$250	under $125

*EP, BP, CP **AI, FAP, MAP Restaurant prices are for a main course and do not include customary 10%–15% service charge. Hotel prices are for two people in a double room in high season and do not include 8% tax, 10%–15% service charge, or meal plans.

Updated by
Elise Meyer

1 PM: **"WHAT DO YOU** mean, you changed the menu? But my snapper," moaned the glamorous mother of three impeccably dressed children, her diamond earrings glittering in the midday sun. The maître d' listened attentively and nodded. "Don't worry, madam, I'm sure the chef will be happy to make it the way you like." "That's all right, Pierre. We'll do that tomorrow. What else would I like?" They consulted the menu together. When lunch materialized, lovely mom took one bite and realized that although she had insisted on eating the same lunch for a dozen years, she might actually like the new dish a teensy bit more.

1 AM: Under the full moon's glow, the beat of the rollicking calypso-tinged reggae had the whole room dancing. First-time visitors mingled with the regulars and the locals, brought together by the magic of the music, the sea air, the rum punch. At last call, they were all the best of friends and agreed to meet again the next night on the other side of the island, where a steel band might or might not appear.

Which is the "real" Anguilla? They both are. And if you want to have an incredibly special Caribbean holiday, make sure that you experience them both.

Peace, pampering, great food, and a wonderful local music scene are among the star attractions on Anguilla (pronounced ang-*gwill*-a). If you're a beach lover, you may become giddy when you first spot the island from the air; its blindingly white sand and lustrous blue-and-aquamarine waters are intoxicating. And, if you like sophisticated cuisine served in casually elegant open-air settings, this may be your culinary Shangri-La. Despite its small size, Anguilla has nearly 70 restaurants ranging from stylish temples of haute cuisine to classic, barefoot beachfront grills.

This dry limestone isle is the most northerly of the Leeward Islands, lying between the Caribbean Sea and the Atlantic Ocean. It stretches, from northeast to southwest, about 16 mi (26 km) and is 3 mi (5 km) across at its widest point. The highest spot is 213 feet above sea level, and there are neither streams nor rivers—only saline ponds once used for salt production. The island's name, a reflection of its shape, is most likely a derivative of *anguille,* which is French for "eel." (French explorer Pierre Laudonnaire is credited with having given the island this name when he sailed past it in 1556.)

In 1631 the Dutch built a fort here, but so far no one has been able to locate its site. English settlers from St. Kitts colonized the island in 1650, with plans to cultivate tobacco and, later, cotton and then sugar. But the thin soil and scarce water doomed these enterprises to fail. Except for a brief period of independence, when it broke from its association with St. Kitts and Nevis in the 1960s, Anguilla has remained a British colony ever since.

From the early 1800s various island federations were formed and disbanded, with Anguilla all the while simmering over its subordinate status and enforced union with St. Kitts. Anguillians twice petitioned for direct rule from Britain and twice were ignored. In 1967, when

St. Kitts, Nevis, and Anguilla became an associated state, the mouse roared; citizens kicked out St. Kitts's policemen, held a self-rule referendum, and for two years conducted their own affairs. To what *Time* magazine called "a cascade of laughter around the world," a British "peacekeeping force" of 100 paratroopers from the Elite Red Devil unit parachuted onto the island, squelching Anguilla's designs for autonomy but helping a team of royal engineers stationed there to improve the port and build roads and schools. Today Anguilla elects a House of Assembly and its own leader to handle internal affairs, while a British governor is responsible for public service, the police, the judiciary, and external affairs.

The territory of Anguilla includes a few islets (or cays, pronounced "keys"), such as Scrub Island, Dog Island, Prickly Pear Cay, Sandy Island, and Sombrero Island. The 10,000 or so residents are predominantly of African descent, but there are also many of Irish background, whose ancestors came over from St. Kitts in the 1600s. Historically, because the limestone land was unfit for agriculture, attempts at enslavement never lasted long; consequently, Anguilla doesn't bear the scars of slavery found on so many other Caribbean islands. Instead, Anguillians became experts at making a living from the sea and are known for their boatbuilding and fishing skills. Tourism is the stable economy's growth industry, but the government carefully regulates expansion to protect the island's natural resources and beauty. New hotels are small, select, and definitely casino-free; Anguilla emphasizes its high-quality service, serene surroundings, and friendly people.

WHERE TO STAY

Tourism on Anguilla is a fairly recent phenomenon—most development didn't begin until the early 1980s, so most hotels and resorts are of relatively recent vintage. The lack of native topography and, indeed, vegetation, and the blindingly white expanses of beach have inspired building designs of some interest; architecture buffs might have fun trying to name some of the most surprising examples. Inspiration largely comes from the Mediterranean: the Greek Islands, Morocco, and Spain, with some Miami-style art deco thrown into the mixture.

Anguilla accommodations basically fall into two categories: grand, sumptuous resorts and luxury resort-villas, or low-key, simple, locally owned inns and small beachfront complexes. The former can be surprisingly expensive, the latter surprisingly reasonable. In the middle are some condo-type options, with full kitchen facilities and multiple bedrooms, which are great for families or for longer stays. At this writing, many properties are in the building, expanding, or planning stages, and by 2009 there may be upward of 1,000 new guest rooms on the island, many in super-deluxe projects. Private villa rentals are becoming more common and are increasing in number and quality every season as development on the island accelerates.

A good phone chat or e-mail exchange with the management of any property is a good idea, as some lodgings don't have in-room TVs, a few have no air-conditioning, and units within the same complex can vary greatly in layout, accessibility, distance to the beach, and view. When calling to reserve a room, ask about special discount packages, especially in spring and summer. Most hotels include continental breakfast in the price, and many have meal-plan options. But keep in mind that Anguilla is home to dozens of excellent restaurants before you lock yourself into an expensive meal plan that you may not be able to change; consider the more flexible voucher offerings. All hotels charge a 10% tax, a $1 per room/per day tourism marketing levy, and—in most cases—an additional 10% service charge.

HOTELS

$$$$ ⬛ **Cap Juluca.** Sybaritic and serene, this 179-acre resort wraps around ☾ breathtaking Maundays Bay, the glittering sand rivaled only by the ★ dramatic domed, white, Moorish-style villas, caring staff, and first-rate sports facilities. Enormous and private, guest rooms are furnished with Moroccan textiles and Brazilian hardwood furniture and have huge marble bathrooms, a few with tubs big enough for two. But the property could stand some maintenance and refurbishing. Private patios, balconies, or sunroofs render sea, sky, and sand part of the decor. The romantic atmosphere makes this resort popular for honeymoons and destination weddings. Ask about special golf packages if you're interested in playing nearby Temenos course. Facilities include a fitness center, an aqua-golf driving range, and an extensive watersports pavilion. There are three room categories, but even the standard ("luxury") accommodations are well laid out, spacious, and comfortable. Flexible multibedroom private villas are beautifully furnished and include a 24-hour-a-day butler. A high point: each morning at the exact moment you specify, continental breakfast appears on your private verandah—the meal includes a basket of fresh-baked pastries, a platter of delicious fresh fruit, and piping-hot coffee. Room TVs are available by request only. At this writing, there was a possibility of the resort changing hands and possibly expanding. **Pros:** Lots of space to stretch out on miles of talcum-soft sand, warm service, romantic atmosphere (no kids). **Cons:** It's sometimes hard to find your room, as the units have strange names or numbers, bathrooms are dated, room TVs only by request. ⬛ *Box 240, Maundays Bay* ☎ *888/858–5822 in U.S., 264/497–6779* ⊕ *www.capjuluca.com* ⬛ *72 rooms, 7 patio suites, 6 pool villas* ⬛ *In-room: refrigerator, no TV, Ethernet. In-hotel: 3 restaurants, room service, bar, tennis courts, pool, gym, spa, beachfront, water sports, no elevator, children's programs (ages 3–14), laundry service* ⬛ *AE, D, MC, V* ⊘ *Closed Sept. and Oct.* ⬛ *CP.*

$$$$ ⬛ **CuisinArt Resort & Spa.** This family-friendly beachfront resort's ☾ design—gleaming white-stucco buildings, blue domes and trim, glass-Fodor'sChoice block walls—blends art deco with a Greek Isle feel. Huge rooms were ★ refurnished and redecorated in 2008, painted in a calming sky-blue and fitted with flat-screen TVs. Guests return in droves to enjoy the casual atmosphere, full-service spa, extensive sports facilities, and the fulfill-every-wish concierge crew, who provide everything from vacation-long nannies to local cell phones to dinner reservations. Continuing facility upgrades include a spacious health club and spa with thalassotherapy tubs. High-season children's programs give parents a chance to enjoy the holiday, too. A hydroponic farm provides ultrafresh organic produce for the two restaurants; tours of the greenhouse, lush tropical gardens, and orchards are fun and engaging. Cooking classes and demonstrations are conducted in the teaching kitchen, and enjoyed at a Chef's Table twice a week. Six private villas are planned for 2009. **Pros:** Family-friendly, great spa and sports, gorgeous beach and gardens. **Cons:** Food service can be slow, pool area is noisy, public areas not inviting. *Box 2000, Rendezvous Bay ☎264/498–2000 or 800/943–3210 ⊕www.cuisinartresort.com ⟋93 rooms, 2 penthouses ⌂In-room: safe, refrigerator, Ethernet. In-hotel: 3 restaurants, bars, tennis courts, pool, gym, spa, beachfront, water sports, bicycles, laundry service ⊟AE, D, MC, V ⊗Closed Sept. and Oct. ⦿EP.*

$$$$ ⚏**Malliouhana Hotel and Spa.** European refinement in a tranquil beach
⟳ setting, attentive service, stellar dining, and a plethora of activities keep
★ the mostly mogul clientele returning year after year, despite nearly universal agreement that a general refurbishment is overdue. An elegant air surrounds the resort's white arches and soaring columns, accented by tile stairways that wrap dramatically around a rocky bluff. With high ceilings, large balconies, marble baths, and sumptuous—if somewhat dated—decor, rooms are so comfortable you might never want to leave. Some suites even have private hot tubs; one has a private swimming pool. Extensive facilities allow you to be as active—or sedentary—as you wish: spend your days snorkeling, waterskiing, or fishing, or just relax at the spa or take a leisurely stroll along mile-long Meads Bay. Those with young ones need not be deterred by the opulence here—Malliouhana is family-friendly. Kids enjoy a beachside pirate-ship playground, playroom, and separate dining facilities. Summertime packages offer two rooms for the price of one. Note the 10% service charge and an additional $20/day electricity surcharge. **Pros:** Huge rooms, elite international clientele, stellar dining on a beautiful terrace over the sea. **Cons:** The beach drops off at the edge, and the water can be rough, guests need to bring lots of cash, shabby outdoor furniture. *Box 173, Meads Bay ☎264/497–6111 or 800/835–0796 ⊕www.malliouhana.com ⟋34 double rooms, 6 junior suites, 7 1-bedroom suites, 2 2-bedroom suites, 2 Jacuzzi suites, 1 honeymoon suite, 1 pool suite ⌂In-room: safe, refrigerator, no TV, Ethernet. In-hotel: 2 restaurants, room service, bar, tennis courts, 3 pools, gym, spa, beachfront, water sports, no elevator, laundry service, public Internet ⊟AE, MC, V ⊗Closed Sept. and Oct. ⦿EP.*

$$$$ ⚏**Sheriva.** This intimate, luxury-villa hotel, opened in 2006, offers a
⟳ glimpse into the future of Anguilla's high-end lodgings. Three cavern-
★ ous private villas containing a total of 20 guest rooms and 7 private swimming pools overlook a broad swath of turquoise sea. The villas can be divided into one- to seven-bedroom residences, completely outfitted with all kinds of amenities: fully equipped offices, exercise rooms,

multiple plasma TVs, video libraries, and poker tables. Besides these perks you have a concierge, a private chef to prepare your meals (meals cost extra), and an attentive housekeeping staff that even does your laundry. Private golf carts shuttle Sheriva guests to nearby Cap Juluca for beach, tennis, spa, and restaurants, with signing privileges. **Pros:** Incredible staff to fulfill every wish, all the comforts of home and more, good value for large family groups. **Cons:** Not on the beach, you risk being spoiled for life by the staff's attentions. ⊠ *Maundays Bay Rd., West End* ☎ *264/498–9898* ⊕ *www.sheriva.com* ↪ *20 rooms* ♿ *In-room: kitchen, DVD, Wi-Fi. In-hotel: pools, laundry service* ⊟ *AE, MC, V* ⏿ *EP.*

$$$–$$$$ ⏿ **Kú.** This all-suites hotel is modeled on the barefoot chic of Miami's ♺ South Beach; the airy white apartments have lime and turquoise deco-★ rative accents, glass and chrome furniture, and balconies overlooking the beach or the pool. It's a great choice for young people because of its chic styling, great facilities, and gentle room rates. Friendly, helpful management and staff keep things running smoothly. The location on the beautiful 1½-mi-long (2½-km-long) sands of Shoal Bay Beach, with its string of lively beach grills and dive shops, is a winner. The open-air restaurant hops at breakfast, lunch, and dinner with omelets, salads, pizza, grilled seafood, and burgers and the famous fish-and-chips of Chef Deon, who also owns the Overlook restaurant. The 70-foot-long beachside bar serves up sophisticated snacks and frosty drinks as well as such entertainments as live music and karaoke, but Shoal Bay regulars know that the spectacular sunsets are reason enough to hang till dark. Top off the whole package with a St. Barths–style beachwear boutique, and a minimarket to provision your unit's kitchen. **Pros:** Beautiful beach with tropical sunsets, the convenience of apartment liv-ing, several walkable dining options. **Cons:** Bathrooms are small, decor is pleasant but not luxurious. ⌂ *Box 51, Shoal Bay East* ☎ *264/497–2011 or 800/869–5827* ⊕ *www.kuanguilla.com* ↪ *27 suites* ♿ *In-room: kitchen, Ethernet. In-hotel: restaurant, bar, pool, gym, spa, beachfront, water sports, no elevator* ⊟ *AE, MC, V* ⏿ *EP.*

$$$ ⏿ **Anguilla Great House Beach Resort.** These traditional West Indian–style bungalows strung along one of Anguilla's longest beaches evoke an old-time Caribbean feel with their cotton-candy colors, and the gen-tle prices and interconnected rooms appeal to families and groups of friends traveling together. Gingerbread trim frames views of the ocean from charming verandahs. Rather basic rooms are decked with local artwork, mahogany and wicker furnishings, tropical-print fabrics, and ceiling fans; some have hand-painted floral borders. Those numbered 111 to 127 offer beach proximity and the best views; newer units aren't as well situated and lack views but have television and Internet access. The restaurant serves a mix of West Indian, Italian, and Continental cuisines; the bartenders proudly ask you to sample their special con-coctions, exemplifying the friendly service. The hotel can arrange in-room massage and other spa treats. **Pros:** Real, old-school Caribbean, young crowd, gentle prices. **Cons:** Rooms are very simple, and bath-rooms are the bare basics. ⊠ *Rendezvous Bay* ⌂ *Box 157, The Valley* ☎ *264/497–6061 or 800/583–9247* ⊕ *www.anguillagreathouse.com*

🛏35 rooms ⚙In-room: refrigerator, dial-up (some). In-hotel: restaurant, pool, gym, beachfront, water sports ▭AE, MC, V ⍢EP.

$$$ 🏨**Sirena.** Young management and a hip, modern look please new and
★ repeat visitors to this low-key resort overlooking Meads Bay. Although small, the attractively redone standard rooms have fresh white paint, flat-screen TVs, comfy beds, and touches of Asian decor. Budget-conscious travelers appreciate the garden suites and larger villas, which have full kitchens. Junior suites have kitchenettes, big granite bathrooms, and whirlpool baths. The restaurant is a gathering spot for guests, many of whom choose a meal plan that includes breakfast and dinner or, for more flexibility, purchase meal vouchers for a part of their stay. Though the five-minute walk to the beach is not the prettiest, you'll find thatched umbrellas and chaises when you get there. **Pros:** Modern, clean, and well-equipped, good value, nice tech amenities. **Cons:** Long walk to the beach with many stairs, ongoing construction next door. ⌂Box 200, Meads Bay ☎264/497–6827 ⊕www.sirena resort.com 🛏20 rooms, 4 suites, 6 villas ⚙In-room: safe, kitchen (some), no TV. In-hotel: restaurant, bar, pools, diving, bicycles, no elevator, public Internet ▭AE, D, MC, V ⍢CP.

$$–$$$ 🏨**Arawak Beach Inn.** These breezy, hexagonal two-story villas are a good choice for a funky, low-key island respite. The pricier units on the top floors are more spacious and a bit quieter and enjoy spectacular views of the rocky shores of boat-dotted Island Harbor and beyond to Scilly Key. Some rooms have large four-poster rattan beds, and some have kitchenettes. Most aren't air-conditioned, and those that are cost more, but the harbor breezes are usually sufficient. The inn's manager, Maria Hawkins, will make you feel like one of the family by the time you leave. Mix your own drinks at the bar—or, if co-owner Maurice Bonham-Carter is around, have him mix you the island's best Bloody Mary. The Arawak Cafe, splashed in psychedelic colors, serves special pizzas and lip-smacking Caribbean comfort food. A small private cove with a sandy beach is a five-minute walk. The common areas have Wi-Fi. **Pros:** Funky, casual crowd, friendly owners, gentle rates. **Cons:** Not on the beach, location makes a car a must, plumbing problems. ⌂Box 1403, Island Harbour ☎264/497–4888, 877/427–2925 reservations only ⊕www.arawakbeach.com 🛏13 rooms, 4 suites ⚙In-room: no a/c (some), safe, kitchen (some), no TV (some). In-hotel: restaurant, bar, pool, beachfront, water sports, no elevator, public Wi-Fi ▭AE, D, MC, V ⍢EP.

VILLAS & CONDOMINIUMS

The tourist office publishes an annual **Anguilla Travel Planner** with informative listings of available vacation apartment rentals. You can contact the **Anguilla Connection** (⌂Box 1369, Island Harbour ☎264/497–9852 or 800/916–3336 ⊕www.luxuryvillas.com) for condo and villa listings.

myCaribbean (☎877/471–2733 ⊕www.mycaribbean.com) is the largest local private villa rental company. Gayle Gurvey and her staff manage and rent more than 100 local villas, and have been in business for almost 10 years.

Ricketts Luxury (☎264/497–6049 ⊕*www.anguillaluxurycollection. com*) is operated by Sue and Robin Ricketts, longtime Anguilla real estate experts who manage a collection of first-rate villas.

$$$$ 🖩 **Altamer.** Architect Myron Goldfinger's geometric symphony of floor-to-ceiling windows, cantilevered walls, and curvaceous floating stair-cases is fit for any king (or CEO)—as is the price tag that goes along with it. Each of the three villas here has a distinct decorative theme and must be rented in its entirety; choose from Russian Amethyst, Brazilian Emerald, or African Sapphire. Striking interiors are filled with custom-made and antique pieces—Murano fixtures, Florentine linens, Turkish kilims, Fabergé ornaments, Tsarist silver candelabras—but still manage to feel airy rather than cluttered. They're also outfitted with the latest gadgetry, from touch-pad stereo systems to wireless Internet. A private butler and eight staff, including a chef, anticipate your every whim. Full conference facilities make this an ideal location for corporate or family retreats of up to 40 people. Planned renovations, slated to begin around 2010, include a luxury yacht marina and additional villas. **Pros:** The last word in luxury and electronic diversions. **Cons:** Construction of proposed marina might be bothersome. ⊠*Shoal Bay West* ☜*Box 3001, The Valley* ☎264/498–4000 ⊕*www.altamer.com* ↪*3 5-bed-room villas* ⚲*In-room: kitchen, VCR (some), Wi-Fi (some). In-hotel: tennis courts, pool, gym, beachfront, water sports, laundry service, public Internet* ⊟*AE, D, DC, MC, V* ☞*1-week minimum* ⧉*AI.*

$$$$ 🖩 **Baccarat Hotel and Residences at Temenos.** "Temenos" is Greek for
★   "sanctuary," and the name is certainly justified. These incomparably glamorous villas were inspired by the pure, spare architecture of Myko-nos and Santorini: sparkling white buildings contrast with the serene blues and greens of the ocean. At this writing, building continues on the 116 new one-, two-, and three-bedroom villas, modeled on the original three super-luxe villas favored by celebrity visitors to Anguilla. The first wave of these is expected to open around 2010. All will have cathedral ceilings, louvered French doors, infinity pools, and enormous marble bathrooms with indoor-outdoor showers. Textural elements are mixed beautifully; marble, granite, wrought iron, mosaic tiles, and woven rugs offset state-of-the-art kitchen and entertainment equipment. The private staff is friendly yet unobtrusive. Of course, sanctuary comes with a high price, but celebrities like Janet Jackson know that you get what you pay for. The beautiful Greg Norman–designed golf course is up and running; soon to come is a state-of-the-art fitness center, three restaurants, four tennis courts, and a 60,000-square-foot clubhouse **Pros:** Luxurious perfection, amazing bathrooms, super service. **Cons:** You'll spend your whole vacation trying to come up with a "con." ☜*Box 1656, Long Bay* ☎264/498–9000 ⊕*www.starwoodhotels. com* ↪*1 5-bedroom villa, 2 4-bedroom villas* ⚲*In-room: kitchen, DVD, Ethernet. In-hotel: tennis courts, pools, gym, beachfront, water sports, laundry service, public Internet* ⊟*AE, D, MC, V* ☞*1-week minimum* ⧉*CP.*

$$$$ 🏠**Caribella.** These spacious Mediterranean-style villas on the broad sands of Barnes Bay are a terrific bargain, especially at the discounted weekly rate. The two-bedroom, two-bathroom villas have full kitchens and daily maid service. The decor is not much to speak of, but the beach is beautiful. **Pros:** Huge amount of space for the cost, beautiful views from huge balconies. **Cons:** Somewhat noisy due to location next to restaurant and construction, very basic decor. *Box 780, Barnes Bay, West End* ☎264/497–6045 ⊕*www.lambertventures.com* ↩6 *villas* &*In-room: kitchen. In-hotel: no elevator* ═MC, V ¶◎¶*EP.*

$$$$ 🏠**Carimar Beach Club.** This horseshoe of bougainvillea-draped Mediterranean-style buildings on beautiful Meads Bay has the look of an upscale Sun Belt condo. Although only two units—No. 1 and No. 6—stand at the water's edge, all have balconies or patios with ocean views. Bright, white, one- and two-bedroom apartments are individually owned and thus reflect their owners' tastes, but most are well-appointed, fully equipped, and carefully maintained. The cordial staff, supreme beachfront location, and several fine restaurants within walking distance make this a popular can be rented for a fee. **Pros:** Tennis courts, easy walk to restaurants and spa, right next door to Malliouihana. **Cons:** No pool or restaurant, no TV, not great a/c. ✉ *Meads Bay* *Box 327, The Valley* ☎264/497–6881 or 800/235–8667 ⊕*www.carimar.com* ↩24 *apartments* &*In-room: kitchen, no TV. In-hotel: tennis courts, beachfront, water sports, no elevator, public Internet* ═AE, D, MC, V ☺*Closed Sept. and Oct.* ¶◎¶*EP.*

$$$$ 🏠**Covecastles Villa Resort.** Though this secluded Myron Goldfinger–designed enclave resembles a series of giant concrete baby carriages from the outside, the sensuous curves and angles of the skylighted interiors bespeak elegance and comfort. Decor in the soaring one- to six-bedroom villas is luxurious but unstuffy: custom-made wicker furniture, raw-silk cushions, and hand-embroidered linens in muted, soothing colors. Louvered Brazilian walnut doors and windows perfectly frame tranquil views of St. Martin, creating living canvases. Units are filled with such high-tech amenities as DVD and CD players. The Point, a super-luxe five-bedroom villa right on the beach, is one of the island's, if perhaps the world's, premier accommodations. The restaurant melds organic to French-Caribbean, the beach beckons, and an unobtrusive staff allows tranquillity to reign. **Pros:** Private beach with reef for snorkeling, great service, classy modern decor. **Cons:** Beach is small and rocky, located at the far end of the island. *Box 248, Shoal Bay West* ☎264/497–6801 or 800/223–1108 ⊕*www.covecastles.com* ↩15 *apartments* &*In-room: DVD (some), Ethernet. In-hotel: restaurant, room service, tennis courts, beachfront, water sports, bicycles, laundry service, no elevator* ═AE, MC, V ¶◎¶*EP.*

$$–$$$$ 🏠**Paradise Cove.** This pretty complex of reasonably priced one- and
⟳   two-bedroom apartments compensates for its location away from the
★   beach with two whirlpools, a large pool, and tranquil tropical gardens where you can pluck fresh guavas for breakfast. The beautiful Cove and Rendezvous bays are just a few minutes' stroll away. Spotless units are attractively appointed with white rattan and natural wicker furniture, gleaming white-tile floors, large kitchens, and soft floral or pas-

tel fabrics from mint to mango. Second-floor units have high-beamed ceilings. Maid service and private cooks are available. Families will appreciate such thoughtful touches as cookies-and-cream pool parties and weekend pizza-making lessons. Very reasonable seven-night packages include a car. **Pros:** Reasonable rates, great pool, lovely gardens. **Cons:** It's a bit far to the beach, decor is bland. ✉ *Box 135, The Cove* ☎ *264/497–6959 or 264/497–6603* ⊕ *www.paradise.ai* ⬎ *12 studio suites, 17 1- and 2-bedroom apartments* ⧉ *In-room: kitchen (some), dial-up. In-hotel: restaurant, bar, pools, gym, laundry facilities, laundry service, public Internet* ⊟ *AE, D, MC, V* ⧉ *EP.*

$$–$$$ ⊞ **Serenity Cottages.** Despite the name of this property, it comprises not cottages but rather large, fully equipped, and relatively affordable studios and one- and two-bedroom apartments in a small complex at the farthest end of glorious Shoal Bay Beach. The restaurant is located on a breezy verandah near the beach. Guests gather on mismatched Adirondack-type chairs for sundowner cocktails. But there isn't much attention from staff. **Pros:** Big apartments, quiet end of beach, snorkeling right outside the door. **Cons:** Generic decor, more condo than hotel in terms of staff, location at the end of Shoal Bay pretty much requires a car, and some extra time to drive to the West End. ✉ *Shoal Bay East, Upper Bay* ☎ *264/497–3328* ⊕ *www.serenity.ai* ⬎ *8 2-bedroom apartments, 2 1-bedroom suites* ⧉ *In-room: kitchen. In-hotel: restaurant, bar, beachfront, public Internet* ⊟ *AE, MC, V* ⊗ *Closed Sept.* ⧉ *EP.*

$$ ⊞ **Allamanda Beach Club.** Youthful, active couples from around the globe happily fill this casual, three-story, white-stucco building hidden in a palm grove just off the beach. Units are neat and simply furnished, with tile floors and pastel matelassé bedspreads; ocean views are best from the top floor. On the ground floor are four large deluxe apartment suites that are great for families. People return year after year, thanks to the management's dedicated hospitality. The creative restaurant, Zara's, is a popular draw, as is the less expensive Gwen's Reggae Grill, a boisterous and colorful beachside joint with an upscale, frat-party atmosphere. Look into special summer packages. **Pros:** Right on Shoal Bay's action, young crowd, good restaurant. **Cons:** Location requires a car; rooms are clean, but not at all fancy, beach and pool lounges are aging poorly. ✉ *Box 662, Upper Shoal Bay Beach* ☎ *264/497–5217* ⊕ *www.allamanda.ai* ⬎ *20 units* ⧉ *In-room: kitchen. In-hotel: 2 restaurants, pool, gym, water sports, public Internet* ⊟ *AE, D, MC, V* ⧉ *EP.*

WHERE TO EAT

Anguilla has an extraordinary number of excellent restaurants, ranging from elegant establishments to down-home seaside shacks. Many have breeze-swept terraces, where you can dine under the stars. Call ahead—in winter to make a reservation and in late summer and fall to confirm if the place you've chosen is open. Anguillian restaurant meals are leisurely events, and service is often at a relaxed pace, so settle in and enjoy. Most restaurant owners are actively and conspicuously present, especially at dinner. It's a special treat to take the time to get to know them a bit when they stop by your table to make sure that you are enjoying your meal.

WHAT TO WEAR

During the day, casual clothes are widely accepted: shorts will be fine, but don't wear bathing suits and cover-ups unless you're at a beach bar. Note that the topless bathing common on some of the French islands is strictly forbidden here. In the evening, shorts are okay at the extremely casual eateries. Elsewhere, women should wear sundresses or nice casual slacks; men will be fine in short-sleeved shirts and casual pants. Some hotel restaurants are more formal and may have a jacket requirement in high season; ask when you make your reservation.

AMERICAN
$$$$
Fodor'sChoice
★

✕**Blanchard's.** This absolutely delightful restaurant, a mecca for foodies, is considered one of the best in the Caribbean. Proprietors Bob and Melinda Blanchard moved to Anguilla from Vermont in 1994 to fulfill their culinary dreams. A festive atmosphere pervades the handsome, airy white room, which is accented with floor-to-ceiling teal-blue shutters to let in the breezes, and colorful artworks by the Blanchards' son Jesse on the walls. A masterful combination of creative cuisine, an upscale atmosphere, attentive service, and an excellent wine cellar (including a selection of aged spirits) pleases the star-studded crowd. The nuanced contemporary menu is ever-changing but always delightful; house classics like corn chowder, lobster cakes, and a Caribbean sampler are crowd pleasers. For dessert, you'll remember concoctions like the key lime "pie-in-a-glass" or the justly famous "cracked coconut" long after your suntan has faded. ⊠ *Meads Bay* ☎*264/497–6100* ⌲*Reservations essential* ▤*AE, MC, V* ☾ *Closed Sun., Aug., and Sept. No lunch.*

$$$-$$$$

✕**Zurra.** The Blanchard's heavenly outpost at the St. Regis Temenos Clubhouse is named for a white, Spanish, tropical-fruit sangria, and the restaurant is as fresh and lovely as its namesake. Sitting on the broad patio, gazing at the glittering sea is a treat for lunch or dinner. Prime aged steaks and chops are char-grilled to perfection, salads sparkle, and the desserts are simply delectable. The afternoon bar menu adds snacks and grilled skewers—it's popular with golfers and their friends. Don't miss a peek at the glass wine cellar, and a tour of Jesse Blanchard's large-scale paintings. ⊠ *Temenos Golf Club* ☎*264/222–8300* ⊕*www. zurrarestaurant.com* ⌲*Reservations essential* ▤*AE, MC, V* ☾*Closed Aug. and Sept.*

ASIAN-FUSION
$$$-$$$$
Fodor'sChoice
★

✕**Hibernia.** Some of the island's most creative dishes are served in this wood-beam cottage restaurant–art gallery overlooking the water at the far eastern end of Anguilla. Unorthodox yet delectable culinary pairings—inspired by chef–owners Raoul Rodriguez and Mary Pat's annual travels to the Far East—include Asian mushroom soup topped with cream of cauliflower, duck breast with Chinese plum and five-spice sauce with black-sesame-crusted gnocchi; a crayfish casserole with steamed rice noodles in basil and coconut milk; and roasted lobster, served with Lao purple rice and artichoke hearts filled with spinach and pine nuts in a vanilla-bean sauce. Every visit here is an opportunity to share in Mary Pat and Raoul's passion for life, expressed through the vibrant combination of setting, art, food, unique tableware, beautiful gardens, and thoughtful hospitality. ⊠*Island Harbour* ☎*264/497–4290* ⊟*MC, V* ⊗*Closed mid-Aug.–mid-Oct. Call for seasonal hrs.*

BARBECUE
$–$$$
★

╳**Smokey's.** There's no sign, so you'll have to ask the way to Cove Bay to find this quintessential Anguillian beach barbecue, part of the Gumbs family mini-empire of authentic and delicious eateries. African-style hot wings, honey-coated ribs, salt-fish cakes, curried chicken roti, and grilled lobsters are paired with local staple side dishes such as spiced-mayonnaise coleslaw, hand-cut sweet-potato strings, and crunchy onion rings. If your idea of the perfect summer lunch is a roadside lobster roll, be sure to try the version here, served on a home-baked roll with a hearty kick of hot sauce. The dinner menu includes crayfish tails and chicken in orange sauce. On Saturday afternoon a popular local band, the Musical Brothers, enlivens the casual, laid-back atmosphere. ⊠*Cove Rd., Cove Bay* ☎*264/497–6582* ⊟*AE, MC, V* ⊗*May–Nov., closed Mon.*

CARIBBEAN
$$$–$$$$

╳**Overlook.** Perched on a cliff high above the bustling harbor of Sandy Ground, chef Deon Thomas's popular and friendly eatery showcases flavorful dishes that combine local and Continental cuisine with a sure hand and a distinct flair. The verandah is pretty, and the orange-and-blue dining room is decorated in island art. The soups stand out: try the carrot-and-apple or pumpkin to start, or perhaps a refreshingly brash gazpacho topped with a basil-Worcestershire granité. At dinner, main courses like roasted grouper curry with coconut-mango chutney as well as braised goat with fragrant rice and peas reflect local flavors, while international touches yield such dishes as oven-crisp duck with Chambord sauce or roasted rack of lamb with rosemary and eggplant tomato ragout. It's closed in summer, when Thomas cooks for lucky fans on Martha's Vineyard. Reservations are recommended. ⊠*Back St., South Hill* ☎*264/497–4488* ⊟*AE, MC, V* ⊗*Closed May–Oct.*

$$–$$$$
★

╳**Tasty's.** Once your eyes adjust to the quirky kiwi, lilac, and coral color scheme, you'll find that breakfast, lunch, or dinner at Tasty's is, well, very tasty. It's open all day long, so if you come off a mid-afternoon plane starving, head right here—it's right near the airport. Chef–owner Dale Carty trained at Malliouhana, and his careful, confident preparation bears the mark of French culinary training, but the menu is classic Caribbean. It's worth leaving the beach at lunch for the lobster salad here. A velvety pumpkin soup garnished with roasted coconut shards is superb, as are the seared jerk tuna and the garlic-infused marinated conch salad. Yummy desserts end meals on a high note. This is one of the few restaurants that do not allow smoking, so take your Cubans elsewhere for an after-dinner puff. Dale also cooks lunch at Bankie Banx's Dune Preserve on the white sands of Rendevous Bay. ⊠*On main road in South Hill* ☎*264/497–2737* ⌲*Reservations essential* ⊟*AE, MC, V* ⊗*Closed Thurs.*

$–$$

╳**English Rose.** Lunch finds this neighborhood hangout packed with locals: cops flirting with sassy waitresses, entrepreneurs brokering deals with politicos, schoolgirls in lime-green outfits doing their homework. The decor is not much to speak of, but this is a great place to eavesdrop or people-watch while enjoying island-tinged specialties like beer-battered shrimp, jerk chicken Caesar salad, snapper creole, and baked chicken. ⊠*Main St., The Valley* ☎264/497–5353 ▤*MC, V* ⊗*Closed Sun.*

ECLECTIC
$$$–$$$$
★
✕**Pimms.** The most coveted tables in this enchanted venue at Cap Juluca are so close to the water that you can actually see fish darting about as you dine. Innovative fare utilizes ultraluxe ingredients from around the world, and the menu includes such creations as organic heirloom tomato sampler with 28-year-old balsamic vinegar, duck confit Greek salad, house-cured duck prosciutto with foie gras, and for a major splurge, Kobe beef rib eye. There are excellent choices for vegetarians, too. A sterling wine list complements the menu (look for regular wine-maker dinners). Your perfect meal could end with chocolate mousse, an aged rum, and a pre-Castro *Cubano.* ⊠*Cap Juluca, Maundays Bay* ☎264/497–6666 ♨*Reservations essential* ▤*AE, MC, V* ⊗*Closed Sept. and Oct. No lunch.*

$$$–$$$$
★
✕**Straw Hat.** Seven picture windows frame seascapes, from floodlighted coral reefs to fishing flotillas, from this covered dock built on pilings directly over the water. By night, the lights of St. Martin and St. Barths twinkle in the distance. But charming owners Peter and Ann Parles, and the sophisticated and original food is the real reason that the restaurant recently celebrated its 10th anniversary. The curried goat here sets the bar for the island. And "fish of the day" here means the fish that was truly caught that day. ⊠*Forest Bay* ☎264/497–8300 ▤*AE, D, MC, V* ⊗*Closed Sun. No lunch.*

$$$–$$$$
Fodor'sChoice
★
✕**Veya.** The stylishly appointed tables glow with flickering candlelight (white-matte sea-urchin votive holders made of porcelain) lining the suavely minimalist, draped, four-sided verandah. A lively lounge where chic patrons mingle and sip mojitos to the purr of soft jazz anchors the room. Inventive, sophisticated, and downright delicious, Carrie Bogar's "Cuisine of the Sun" features thoughtful but ingenious preparations of first-rate provisions. Ample portions are sharable works of art— sample Moroccan-spiced shrimp "cigars" with roast tomato–apricot chutney or Vietnamese-spiced calamari. Jerk-spiced tuna is served with a rum coffee glaze on a juicy slab of grilled pineapple with curls of plantain crisps. Dessert is a must. Sublime warm chocolate cake with chili-roasted banana ice cream and carmelized bananas steals the show. ⊠*Sandy Ground* ☎264/498–8392 ♨*Reservations essential* ▤*AE, MC, V* ⊗*Closed Sun. No lunch.*

$$–$$$$
✕**Zara's.** Chef Shamash Brooks presides at this cozy restaurant with beamed ceilings, terra-cotta floors, colorful artwork, and poolside seating. His kitchen turns out tasty fare that combines Caribbean and Italian flavors with panache. Standouts include a velvety pumpkin soup with coconut milk, crunchy calamari, lemon pasta scented with garlic, herbed rack of lamb served with a roasted apple sauce, and spicy fish fillet steamed in banana leaf. ⊠*Allamanda Beach Club, Upper Shoal Bay* ☎264/497–3229 ▤*AE, D, MC, V* ⊗*No lunch.*

$$
★
✕**Kemia.** Cap Juluca's seaside "hors d'oeuverie" looks like a posh pasha's oasis transported to the Caribbean. Arches, tables, and lamps are embedded with jewel-like mosaic and colored glass; cushy throw

pillows and billowing tent ceilings complete the fantasy. Chef Vernon Hughes prepares a truly global selection of small tapaslike plates that are perfect for sharing in this romantic retreat at the edge of the cerulean waves. Spanish-style shrimp in garlic butter, tiny pots of curries, rare Thai beef salad—it's all delicious. ⊠*Cap Juluca, Maundays Bay* ☎*888/858–5822 in U.S., 264/497–6666* ⚖*Reservations essential* ▭*AE, MC, V* ☉*Closed Sun., Mon., Sept., and Oct. No lunch May–Nov.*

FRENCH ✕**Covecastles.** Elegant, intimate, and—above all—healthy dinners are
$$$$ served here in a garden overlooking beautiful Shoal Bay West. Each season, Dominique Thevenet devises a new menu, innovatively mating French culinary traditions with Caribbean ingredients. The current menu features grilled organic beef tenderloin with lavender oil, spinach and crayfish ravioli in a tomato-garlic sauce, and grilled tuna steak with a juniper berry and port wine cream sauce. Villa guests receive priority for the seven tables, so call ahead for reservations. ⊠*Shoal Bay West* ☎*264/497–6801* ⚖*Reservations essential* ▭*AE, D* ☉*Closed Sept.–Nov. No lunch.*

$$$–$$$$ ✕**KoalKeel.** Originally part of a sugar and cotton plantation, KoalKeel
Fodor's Choice is owned by descendants of the slaves once housed on this very site. A
★ tour is a high point of any meal here, as the buildings are rich in history. A 200-year-old rock oven is used by the on-site bakery upstairs. With a day's notice, you can enjoy a whole chicken that has been slow-roasted from the inside. The menu features a combination of classic French and West Indian specialties. Start with goat cheese baked in puff pastry in a pool of honey vinaigrette; then continue with rack of lamb served with pumpkin gratin or veal chop in a rosemary sauce with caramelized shallots and truffled mashed potato. Be sure to save room for the incredible desserts. Wine lovers take note of the exceptional 15,000-bottle wine cellar, in an underground cistern. Anguilla's savvy early risers show up here for the fresh French bread, croissants, and pain au chocolat that are sold out by 9 AM. ⊠*Coronation Ave., The Valley* ☎*264/497–2930* ⚖*Reservations essential* ▭*AE, MC, V.*

$$$–$$$$ ✕**Michael Rostang at Malliouhana.** Sparkling crystal and fine china, atten-
★ tive service, a wonderful 25,000-bottle wine cellar, and a spectacularly romantic, open-air room complement exceptional haute cuisine rivaling any in the French West Indies. Consulting chef Michael Rostang, renowned for his exceptional Paris bistros, and chef Alain Laurent revamp the menu seasonally, incorporating local ingredients in both classic and contemporary preparations. The ultimate in hedonism is sipping champagne as the setting sun triggers a laser show over the bay, before repairing to your table. ⊠*Meads Bay* ☎*264/497–6111* ⚖*Reservations essential* ▭*AE, D, MC, V* ☉*Closed Sept. and Oct.*

$–$$ ✕**Madeariman Reef Bar & Restaurant.** This casual, feet-in-the-sand bistro right on busy, beautiful Shoal Bay is open for breakfast, lunch, and dinner; the soups, salads, and simple grills here are served with a bit of French flair. Come for lunch and stay to lounge on the beach chaises, or bar-hop between here and Uncle Ernie's barbecue next door. ⊠*Shoal Bay East* ☎*264/497–5750* ▭*AE, MC, V.*

¢–$$ ✕**Geraud's Patisserie.** A stunning array of absolutely delicious French
★   pastries and breads—and universal favorites like cookies, brownies, and muffins—are produced in this tiny shop by Cordon Bleu dynamo Geraud Lavest. Come early morning for cappuccino and croissants, and pick up fixings for a wonderful lunch later (or choose from among the list of tempting daily lunch specials). ✉*South Hill Plaza* ☎*264/497–5559* ▭*AE, MC, V* ⊘*No dinner.*

ITALIAN   ✕**Luna Rosa.** Classic upscale Italian favorites, light and tasty pastas,
$$–$$$$ and luscious vegetables prepared with sensitivity to the importance of
★   authentic ingredients is a winning formula for this 2007 newcomer. The eggplant Parmesan is crisp and light with an intense tomato ragout, and the wild-mushroom risotto is so delicious you may be tempted to lick your plate. The thrilling sea view and charming management are icing on the cake. ✉*Lower South Hill* ☎*264/497–6810* ✍*Reservations essential* ▭*AE, MC, V* ⊘*Closed Sun.*

$$$–$$$$ ✕**Trattoria Tramonto & Oasis Beach Bar.** The island's only Italian restaurant features a dual (or dueling) serenade of Andrea Bocelli on the sound system and gently lapping waves a few feet away. Chef Valter Belli artfully adapts recipes from his home in Emilia-Romagna. Try the delicate lobster ravioli in truffle-cream sauce, or go for a less Italian option: kangaroo steak. For dessert, don't miss the authentic tiramisu. Though you might wander in here for lunch after a swim, when casual dress is accepted, you'll still be treated to the same impressive menu. You can also choose from a luscious selection of champagne fruit drinks, a small but fairly priced Italian wine list, and homemade grappas. Denzel Washington celebrated his 50th birthday here with such close friends as Robert De Niro and Sean "P. Diddy" Combs. ✉*Shoal Bay West* ☎*264/497–8819* ✍*Reservations essential* ▭*MC, V* ⊘*Closed Mon., Sept., and Oct.*

SEAFOOD   ✕**Mango's.** One meal at Mango's and you'll understand why it's a
$$$–$$$$ perennial favorite of repeat visitors to Anguilla. Sparkling-fresh fish
Fodor'sChoice   specialties have starring roles on the menu here. Light and healthy
★   choices like a spicy grilled whole snapper are deliciously perfect. Save room for dessert—the warm apple tart and the coconut cheesecake are worth the splurge. There's an extensive wine list, and the Cuban cigar humidor is a luxurious touch. The proprietor, a former New Jerseyan known islandside as Mango Dave, keeps a watchful eye over his chic domain and over his stylish clientele, a veritable *People* magazine spread in high season. Excellent local live music several nights a week adds to the cheerful party atmosphere. ✉*Barnes Bay* ☎*264/497–6479* ✍*Reservations essential* ▭*AE, MC, V* ⊘*Closed Tues. No lunch.*

SOUTH   ✕**Picante.** This casual, bright-red roadside Caribbean *taqueria*, opened
WESTERN   by a young California couple, serves huge, tasty burritos with a choice
$–$$$ of fillings, fresh warm tortilla chips with first-rate guacamole, and
☺   tequila-lime chicken grilled under a brick. Mexican chocolate pudding
★   makes a great choice for dessert. Seating is at picnic tables; the friendly proprietors cheerfully supply pillows on request. Reservations are recommended. ✉*West End Rd., West End* ☎*264/498–1616* ▭*AE, MC, V* ⊘*Closed Tues. No lunch.*

BEACHES

1

Renowned for their beauty, Anguilla's 30-plus dazzling white-sand beaches are the best reason to visit. You can find long, deserted stretches ideal for walking and beaches lined with bars and restaurants—all accompanied by surf that ranges from wild to glassy-smooth. As anywhere, exercise caution in remote locations, and never swim alone. ⚠ **Do not leave personal property in cars.** Swimming is not recommended at Captain's Bay and Katouche Bay, due to strong westerly currents and potentially dangerous undertows. Do not leave personal items in cars parked at beaches—this can be a problem especially at Little Bay.

NORTHEAST COAST

Captain's Bay. On the north coast just before the eastern tip of the island, this quarter-mile stretch of perfect white sand is bounded on the left by a rocky shoreline where Atlantic waves crash. If you make the grueling four-wheel-drive-only trip along the inhospitable dirt road that leads to the northeastern end of the island toward Junk's Hole, you'll be rewarded with peaceful isolation. The surf here slaps the sands with a vengeance, and the undertow is strong—so wading is the safest water sport.

Island Harbour. These mostly calm waters are surrounded by a slender beach. For centuries Anguillians have ventured from these sands in colorful handmade fishing boats. There are several bars and restaurants (Arawak Cafe, Cote Mer, and Smitty's are best for casual lunches), and this is the departure point for the three-minute boat ride to Scilly Cay, where a thatched beach bar serves seafood. Just hail the restaurant's free boat and plan to spend most of the day (the all-inclusive lunch starts at $40 and is worth the price), Wednesday, Friday, and Sunday only.

NORTHWEST COAST

Barnes Bay. Between Meads Bay and West End Bay, this beach is a superb spot for windsurfing and snorkeling, though in high season it can get a bit crowded with day-trippers from St. Martin. The only public access is on the road to Mango's restaurant and Caribella resort.

Little Bay. Little Bay is on the north coast between Crocus Bay and Shoal Bay, not far from the Valley. Sheer cliffs embroidered with agave and creeping vines rise behind a small gray-sand beach, usually accessible only by water (it's a favored spot for snorkeling and night dives). The easiest way to get here is a five-minute boat ride from Crocus Bay (about $10 round-trip). The hale and hearty can also clamber down the cliffs by rope to explore the caves and surrounding reef; this is the only way to access the beach from the road and is not recommended to the inexperienced climber. Do not leave personal items in cars parked here.

Road Bay. The clear blue waters here are usually dotted with yachts and cargo boats. Several restaurants, including evergreen classic Johnno's, a water-sports center, and lots of windsurfing and waterskiing activity make this area—often called Sandy Ground—a commercial one. The snorkeling isn't very good here, but the sunset vistas are glorious.

Sandy Island. A popular side excursion for Anguilla visitors, Sandy Island is a tiny islet with a lagoon, nestled in coral reefs about 2 mi (3 km) from Road Bay.

SOUTHEAST COAST   **Sandy Hill.** Not far from Sea Feathers Bay, this base for anglers sits between the Valley and Junks Hole at East End. Here you can buy fish and lobster right off the boats and snorkel in the warm waters. Don't plan to sunbathe—the beach is too narrow. But there's very good snorkeling here, and you'll also find great views of St. Martin and St. Barths.

Fodor'sChoice   **Shoal Bay.** Anchored by sea grape and coconut trees and covered in
★   the most exquisite powdery-white coral sand, Shoal Bay—not to be confused with Shoal Bay West at the other end of the island—is one of the Caribbean's prettiest beaches. Restaurants like Gwen's Reggae Grill, Kú, and Madeariman Beach Club offer seafood and tropical drinks; shops sell T-shirts and sunscreen; and the water-sports center arranges diving, sailing, and fishing trips. You can even enjoy a beachside massage.

SOUTHWEST COAST   **Cove Bay.** Lined with coconut palms, this is a quiet spot between Rendezvous Bay and Maundays Bay. You can walk here from Cap Juluca for a change of pace or a beach lunch at Smokey's. There's a fishing boat pier, a dive shop, and a place where you can rent floats, umbrellas, and mats.

Maundays Bay. The dazzling, 1-mi-long (1½-km-long) beach is known for good swimming and snorkeling. You can also rent water-sports gear.

Rendezvous Bay. Here you'll find 1½ mi (2½ km) of pearl-white sand lapped by calm water and with a view of St. Martin. The rockier stretch provides marvelous snorkeling. The expansive crescent houses three resorts, with plenty of open space to go around; stop in for a drink or a meal at one of the hotels. For public access to Rendezous Bay Beach, take the turn off from the main road for Anguilla Great House (between South Hill Plaza and CuisinArt) and follow this road straight to the water.

Shoal Bay West. This glittering bay is a lovely place to spend the day. This mile-long sweep of sand, home to some major restaurants and resorts, is rimmed with mangroves, and there are coral reefs not too far from shore. Punctuate your day with a meal at beachside Trattoria Tramonto. You can reach Shoal Bay West by taking the main road to the West End and turning left at the end of the pavement on a gravel road around the pond. Note that similarly named Shoal Bay is a separate beach on a different part of the island.

SPORTS & THE OUTDOORS

Anguilla's expanding sports options are enhanced by its beautiful first golf course, designed by Greg Norman to accentuate the natural terrain and maximize the stunning ocean views over Rendezvous Bay. Players say the par-72, Troon-managed course is reminiscent of Pebble Beach. Personal experience says: bring a lot of golf balls! The Anguilla Tennis Academy, designed by noted architect Myron Goldfinger, operates in the Blowing Point area. The 1,000-seat stadium, equipped with pro shop and seven lighted courts, was created to attract major international matches and to provide a first-class playing option to tourists and locals.

A Day at the Boat Races

If you want a different kind of trip to Anguilla, try for a visit during Carnival, which starts on the first Monday in August and continues for about 10 days. Colorful parades, beauty pageants, music, delicious food, arts-and-crafts shows, fireworks, and nonstop partying are just the beginning. The music starts at sunrise jam sessions—as early as 4 AM—and continues well into the night. The high point? The boat races. They are the national passion and the official national sport of Anguilla.

Anguillians from around the world return home to race old-fashioned, made-on-the-island wooden boats

that have been in use on the island since the early 1800s. Similar to some of today's fastest sailboats, these are 15 to 28 feet in length and sport only a mainsail and jib on a single 25-foot mast. The sailboats have no deck, so heavy bags of sand, boulders, and sometimes even people are used as ballast. As the boats reach the finish line, the ballast—including some of the sailors—gets thrown into the water in a furious effort to win the race. Spectators line the beaches and follow the boats on foot, by car, and by even more boats. You'll have almost as much fun watching the fans as the races.

BOATING & SAILING

Anguilla is the perfect place to try all kinds of water sports. The major resorts offer complimentary Windsurfers, paddleboats, and water skis to their guests. If your hotel lacks facilities, you can get in gear at **Sandy Island Enterprises** (⊠*Sandy Ground* ☎264/476–6534), which rents Sunfish and Windsurfers and arranges fishing charters. **Island Yacht Charters** (⊠*Sandy Ground* ☎264/497–3743 or 264/235–6555) rents the 35-foot, teak *Pirate* powerboat and the 30-foot Beneteau *Eros* sailboat and organizes snorkeling, sightseeing, and fishing expeditions.

DIVING

Sunken wrecks; a long barrier reef; terrain encompassing walls, canyons, and hulking boulders; varied marine life, including greenback turtles and nurse sharks; and exceptionally clear water—all of these make for excellent diving. Prickly Pear Cay is a favorite spot. **Stoney Bay Marine Park,** off the northeast end of Anguilla, showcases the late-18th-century *El Buen Consejo,* a 960-ton Spanish galleon that sank here in 1772. Other good dive sites include **Grouper Bowl,** with exceptional hard-coral formations; **Ram's Head,** with caves, chutes, and tunnels; and **Upper Flats,** where you are sure to see stingrays.

Anguillian Divers (⊠*Meads Bay* ☎264/497–4750 ⊕*anguilliandivers. com*) is a full-service dive operator with a PADI five-star training center. At Shoal Bay, contact **Shoal Bay Scuba & Watersports** (☎264/497–4371 ⊕*www.shoalbayscuba.ai*). Single-tank dives start at $50, two-tank dives, $80. Daily snorkel trips at 1 PM are $25 per person.

FISHING

Albacore, wahoo, marlin, barracuda, and kingfish are among the fish angled after off Anguilla's shores. You can strike up a conversation with almost any fisherman you see on the beach, and chances are, you'll be a welcome addition on his next excursion. If you'd rather make more formal arrangements, **Johnno's Beach Stop** (☎264/497–2728) in Sandy Ground has a boat and can help you plan a trip.

GOLF

Temenos Golf Club (☎264/498–7000), designed by superstar Greg Norman, is an 18-hole, 7,200-yard championship course, managed by Troon Golf. The course features sweeping sea vistas and an ecologically responsible watering system of ponds and lagoons that snake through the grounds. Greens fees top $400 per person, but include cart, caddie, driving range, and water, but not the service charge of $15.

HORSEBACK RIDING

The scenic Gibbons nature trails, along with any of the island's miles of beaches, are perfect places to ride, even for the novice. Ride English- or western-style or take lessons at **El Rancho Del Blues** (☎264/497–6334). Prices start at $25 to $35 per hour ($50 for two-hour rides).

SEA EXCURSIONS

A number of boating options are available for airport transfers, day trips to offshore cays or neighboring islands, night trips to St. Martin, or just whipping through the waves en route to a picnic spot.

Chocolat (✉*Sandy Ground* ☎*264/497–3394*) is a 35-foot catamaran available for private charter or scheduled excursions to nearby cays. Captain Rollins is a knowledgeable, affable guide. Rates for day sails with lunch are about $80 per person. For an underwater peek without getting wet, catch a ride ($20 per person) on **Junior's Glass Bottom Boat** (✉*Sandy Ground* ☎*264/235–1008* ⊕*www.junior.ai*). Snorkel trips and instruction are available, too. Picnic, swimming, and diving excursions to Prickly Pear Cay, Sandy Island, and Scilly Cay are available through **Sandy Island Enterprises** (☎*264/476–6534*). **No Fear Sea Tours** (✉*The Cove* ☎*264/235–6354*) has three 32-foot speedboats and a 19-foot ski boat. **Funtime Charters** (✉*The Cove* ☎*264/497–6511*) operates five powerboats ranging in size from 32 to 38 feet.

SHOPPING

Anguilla is by no means a shopping destination. In fact, if your suitcase is lost, you will be hard-pressed to secure even the basics on-island. If you're a hard-core shopping enthusiast, a day trip to nearby St. Martin will satisfy. Well-heeled visitors sometimes organize boat or plane charters through their hotel concierge for daylong shopping excursions to

St. Barths. The island's tourist publication, *What We Do in Anguilla,* has shopping tips and is available free at the airport and in shops. Pyrat rums—golden elixirs blending up to nine aged and flavored spirits—are a local specialty available at the Anguilla Rums distillery and several local shops. For upscale designer sportswear, check out the small boutiques in hotels (some are branches of larger stores in Marigot on St. Martin). Outstanding local artists sell their work in galleries, which often arrange studio tours (you can also check with the Antigua Tourist Office).

CLOTHING

Boutique at Malliouhana (✉ *Malliouhana, Meads Bay* ☎264/497–6111) specializes in such upscale designer specialties as jewelry by Oro De Sol, luxurious swim fashion by Manuel Canovas and LaPerla, and Robert LaRoche sunglasses.

★ **Capri Boutique** (✉ *CuisinArt Resort & Spa, Rendezvous Bay* ☎264/498–2000) carries custom designs by the renowned jewelers Alberto & Lina, as well as Helen Kaminski accessories and more brand-name merchandise.

Caribbean Fancy (✉ *George Hill* ☎264/497–3133) sells Ta-Tee's line of crinkle-cotton resort wear, plus books, spices, perfumes, wines, and gift items.

Caribbean Silkscreen (✉ *South Hill* ☎264/497–2272) creates designs and prints them on golf shirts, hats, sweatshirts, and jackets.

Irie Lite (✉ *South Hill* ☎264/497–6526) sells vividly hued beach and resort wear, Reef flip-flops, and French bikinis that appeal to the younger set who also jive to the java and the wireless Internet connection.

Sunshine Shop (✉ *South Hill* ☎264/497–6964) stocks cotton pareus (saronglike beach cover-ups), silkscreen items, cotton resort wear, and hand-painted Haitian wood items.

Why Knot ✉ *West End Rd., right past golf course* ☎264/772–7685) for Fabiana's jewel-color cotton tie-able garments, and the beads and sandals that perfectly accessorize them. If the road sign says "Knot Today" come back later.

Whispers (✉ *Cap Juluca, Maundays Bay* ☎264/497–6666) sells Asian handicrafts and designer resort wear for men and women.

HANDICRAFTS

Anguilla Arts & Crafts Center (✉ *The Valley* ☎264/497–2200) carries island crafts, including textiles and ceramics. Of particular interest are unique ceramics by Otavia Fleming, lovely spotted glaze items with adorable lizards climbing on them. Look for special exhibits and performances—ranging from puppetry to folk dance—sponsored by the Anguilla National Creative Arts Alliance.

Cheddie's Carving Studios (✉ *West End Rd., The Cove* ☎264/497–6027) showcases Cheddie Richardson's fanciful wood carvings and coral and stone sculptures.

Devonish Art Gallery (✉ *West End Rd., George Hill* ☎264/497–2949) purveys the wood, stone, and clay creations of Courtney Devonish, an internationally known potter and sculptor, plus creations by his wife,

Carolle, a bead artist. Also available are works by other Caribbean artists and regional antique maps.

★ **Hibernia Restaurant & Gallery** (⊠ *Island Harbour* ☎ *264/497–4290*) has striking pieces culled from the owners' travels, from contemporary Eastern European artworks to traditional Indo-Chinese crafts.

Loblolly Gallery (⊠ *Coronation St., Lower Valley* ☎ *264/497–6006*), in the historic Rose Cottage, showcases the work of three expats (Marge Morani, Paula Warden, Georgia Young) working in various media and also mounts exhibits from Anguilla's artistic grande dame, Iris Lewis.

★ **Savannah Gallery** (⊠ *Coronation St., Lower Valley* ☎ *264/497–2263*) specializes in works by local Anguillian artists as well as other Caribbean and Central American art, including watercolors, oil paintings from the renowned Haitian St. Soleil group, Guatemalan textiles, Mexican pottery, and brightly painted metal work.

★ The peripatetic proprietors of **World Arts Gallery** (⊠ *Cove Rd., West End* ☎ *264/497–5950 or 264/497–2767*), Nik and Christy Douglas, display a veritable United Nations of antiquities: exquisite Indonesian ikat hangings to Thai teak furnishings, Aboriginal didgeridoos to Dogon tribal masks, Yuan Dynasty jade pottery to Uzbeki rugs. There is also handcrafted jewelry and handbags.

NIGHTLIFE & THE ARTS

In late February or early March, reggae star and impresario Bankie Banx stages Moonsplash, a three-day music festival that showcases local and imported talent around the nights of the full moon. At the end of July is the International Arts Festival, which hosts artists from around the world. BET (Black Entertainment Television) sponsors Tranquility Jazz Festival in November, attracting major musicians such as Hilton Ruiz, James Moody, Bobby Watson, and Vanessa Rubin.

NIGHTLIFE

Most hotels and many restaurants offer live entertainment in high season and on weekends, ranging from pianists and jazz combos to traditional steel and calypso bands. Check the local tourist magazines and newspaper for listings. Friday and Saturday, Sandy Ground is the hot spot; Wednesday and Sunday the action shifts to Shoal Bay East.

The nightlife scene here runs late into the night—the action doesn't really start until after 11 PM. If you do not rent a car, be aware that taxis are not readily available at night. If you plan to take a taxi back to your hotel or villa at the end of the night, be sure to make arrangements in advance with the driver who brings you or with your hotel concierge.

★ The funky **Dune Preserve** (⊠ *Rendezvous Bay* ☎ *264/497–6219*) is the driftwood-fabricated home of Bankie Banx, Anguilla's famous reggae star. He performs here weekends and during the full moon. Kevin Bacon also plays here when he's on the island. There's a dance floor and a beach bar, and sometimes you can find a sunset beach barbecue in progress. In high season there's a $15 cover charge.

Fodor'sChoice Elvis' Beach Bar (⊠*Sandy Ground* ☎*264/772–0637*) is the perfect locale
★ (it's actually a boat) to hear great music and sip the best rum punch on
earth. Check to see if there's a Full-Moon Lunasea party.

★ Things are lively at **Johnno's Beach Stop** (⊠*Sandy Ground* ☎*264/497–
2728*), with live music and alfresco dancing every night and on Sunday afternoon, when just about everybody drops by. This is *the* classic
Caribbean beach bar, attracting a funky eclectic mix, from locals to
movie stars.

★ At the **Pumphouse** (⊠*Sandy Ground* ☎*264/497–5154*), in the old
rock-salt factory, you can find live music most nights—plus surprisingly good pub grub, celebrities like Bruce Willis and Charlie Sheen,
and a minimuseum of artifacts and equipment from 19th-century salt
factories. There's calypso-soca on Thursday; it's open from noon until
3 AM daily, except Sunday.

EXPLORING ANGUILLA

Exploring on Anguilla is mostly about checking out the spectacular
beaches and resorts. The island has only a few roads; some are in bad
condition, but the lack of adequate signage is being addressed. Locals
are happy to provide directions, but having a good map—and using
it—is the best strategy. Get one at the airport, the ferry dock, your
hotel, or the tourist office in the Valley.

WHAT TO SEE

Heritage Museum Collection. Don't miss this remarkable opportunity to
learn about Anguilla. Old photographs and local records and artifacts trace the island's history over 4 millennia, from the days of the
Arawaks. The museum is painstakingly curated by Colville Petty. High
points include the historical documents of the Anguilla Revolution and
the albums of photographs chronicling island life, from devastating
hurricanes to a visit from Queen Elizabeth in 1964. You can see examples of ancient pottery shards and stone tools along with fascinating
photographs of the island in the early 20th century—many depicting
the heaping and exporting of salt and the christening of schooners—
and a complete set of beautiful postage stamps issued by Anguilla since
1967. ⊠*East End at Pond Ground* ☎*264/497-4092* ⌂*$5* ⊘*Mon.–
Sat. 10–5.*

★ **Island Harbour.** Anguillians have been fishing for centuries in the brightly
painted, simple handcrafted fishing boats that line the shore of the harbor. It's hard to believe, but skillful pilots take these little boats out to
sea as far as 50 mi or 60 mi (80 km or 100 km). Late afternoon is the
best time to see the day's catch. Hail the boat to Gorgeous Scilly Cay, a
classic little restaurant offering sublime lobster and Eudoxie Wallace's
knockout rum punches on Wednesday, Friday, and Sunday.

Sandy Ground. Almost everyone who comes to Anguilla stops by its
most developed beach. Little open-air bars and restaurants line the
shore, and there are several boutiques, a dive shop, the Pyrat Rum fac-

tory, and a small commercial pier. This is where you catch the ferry for tiny Sandy Island, just 2 mi (3 km) offshore.

Wallblake House. The only surviving plantation house in Anguilla, Wallblake House was built in 1787 by Will Blake (Wallblake is probably a corruption of his name) and has recently been thoroughly and thoughtfully restored. The place is associated with many a tale involving murder, high living, and the French invasion in 1796. On the grounds are an ancient vaulted stone cistern and an outbuilding called the Bakery (which wasn't used for making bread at all but for baking turkeys and hams). Tours are usually at 10 AM and 2 PM. ✉ *Wallblake Rd., The Valley* ☎ *264/497–6613* ⊕ *www.wallblake.ai* ✉ *Free* ☉ *Mon., Wed., and Fri.*

Warden's Place. This former sugar-plantation greathouse was built in the 1790s and is a fine example of island stonework. It now houses KoalKeel restaurant and a sumptuous bakery upstairs. But for many years it served as the residence of the island's chief administrator, who also doubled as the only medical practitioner. Across the street you can see the oldest dwelling on the island, originally built as slave housing. ✉ *The Valley.*

ANGUILLA ESSENTIALS

To research prices, get advice from other travelers, and book travel arrangements, visit www.fodors.com.

▍ TRANSPORTATION

BY AIR

American Eagle flies several times daily from San Juan. Caribbean Star/TransAnguilla offers daily flights from Antigua, St. Thomas, and St. Kitts and provides air-taxi service on request from neighboring islands. Windward Islands Airways (Winair) wings in daily from St. Thomas and several times a day from St. Maarten. Anguilla Air Services is a reliable charter operation that flies to any Caribbean destination and runs day trips between Anguilla and St. Barths at the reasonable round-trip rate of $175 per person (4 person minimum). LIAT comes in from Antigua, Nevis, St. Kitts, St. Maarten, St. Thomas, and Tortola. Note that LIAT requires all passengers to reconfirm 72 hours in advance, to avoid cancellation of their reservations.

Wallblake Airport is the hub on Anguilla. A taxi ride to the Sandy Ground area runs $7 to $10; to West End resorts it's $16 to $22.

The departure tax is $20, payable in cash at the airport.

Airline Contacts American Eagle (☎264/497–3500). **Anguilla Air Services** (☎264/498–5922). **Caribbean Star/ TransAnguilla** (☎264/497–8690). **LIAT** (☎264/497–5002). **Windward Islands Airways** (☎264/497–2748).

Airport Contacts Wallblake Airport (☎264/497–2719).

BY BOAT & FERRY

Ferries run frequently between Anguilla and St. Martin. Boats leave from Blowing Point on Anguilla approximately every half hour from 7:30 AM to 6:15 PM and from Marigot on St. Martin every half hour from 8 AM to 7 PM. Check for evening ferries, whose schedules are more erratic. You pay a $3 departure tax before boarding, in addition to the $12 one-way fare ($15 in the evening). Don't buy a round-trip ticket, as it restricts you to the boat for which it is purchased. On very windy days the 20-minute trip can be bouncy, so bring medication if you suffer from motion sickness. An information booth outside the customs shed in Blowing Point is usually open daily from 8:30 AM to 5 PM, but sometimes the attendant wanders off. For schedule information, and info on special boat charters, contact Link Ferries. The larger resort hotels usually offer private transfers by speedboat, which meet arrivals at the local boat dock at a cost of about $65 per person. If you need this service, mention it to your reservations representative who will make the arrangements.

Information Link Ferries (☎ 264/497–2231 ⊕ www.link.ai).

BY CAR

Although most of the rental cars on-island have the driver's side on the left as in North America, Anguillian roads are like those in the United Kingdom—driving is on the left side of the road. It's easy to get the hang of, but the roads can be rough, so be cautious, and observe the 30 mph (48 kph) speed limit. Roundabouts are probably the biggest driving obstacle for most. As you approach, give way to the vehicle on your right; once you're in the rotary you have the right of way.

A temporary Anguilla driver's license is required—you can get into real trouble if you're caught driving without one. You get it for $20 (good for three months) at any of the car-rental agencies at the time you pick up your car; you'll also need your valid driver's license from home. Rental rates are about $45 to $55 per day, plus insurance.

Contacts Apex/Avis (✉ Airport Rd. ☎ 264/497–2642). **Triple K Car Rental/Hertz** (✉ Airport Rd. ☎ 264/497–5934).

BY TAXI

Taxis are fairly expensive, so if you plan to explore the island's many beaches and restaurants, it may be more cost-effective to rent a car. Taxi rates are regulated by the government, and there are fixed fares from point to point, which are listed in brochures the drivers should have handy and are also published in the local guide, *What We Do in Anguilla*. It's $24 from the airport or $22 from Blowing Point Ferry to West End hotels. Posted rates are for one or two people; each additional passenger adds $4 to the total and there is sometimes a charge for luggage. You can also hire a taxi by the hourly rate of $25. Surcharges of $2–$5 apply to trips after 6 PM. You'll always find taxis at the Blowing Point Ferry landing and at the airport. You'll need to call them to pick you up from hotels and restaurants, and arrange ahead with the driver who took you if you need a taxi late at night from one of the nightclubs or bars.

Contacts Airport Taxi Stand (☎ 264/235–3828). **Blowing Point Ferry Taxi Stand** (☎ 264/497–6089).

■ CONTACTS & RESOURCES

BANKS & CURRENCY EXCHANGE

Prices quoted throughout this chapter are in U.S. dollars unless otherwise indicated. ATMs dispense American and Eastern Caribbean dollars. Credit cards are not always accepted; some resorts will settle only in cash, but a few accept personal checks. Some restaurants add a charge if you pay with a credit card.

Though the legal tender here is the Eastern Caribbean (EC) dollar, U.S. dollars are widely accepted. (You'll often get change in EC dollars, though.) The exchange rate between U.S. and EC dollars is set at EC$2.68 to the U.S. dollar. Be sure to carry lots of small bills; change for a $20 bill is often difficult to obtain.

ELECTRICITY

The current is 110 volts, the same as in North America; U.S.-standard two-prong plugs will work just fine.

EMERGENCIES

As in the United States, dial 911 in any emergency.

Hospitals Hotel de Health (⊠ Palm Court at Sea Feathers Bay ☎ 264/497–4166) is a well-regarded private medical facility. **Princess Alexandra Hospital** (⊠ Sandy Ground ☎ 264/497–2551). Emergency room and ambulance operate 24 hours a day.

INTERNET, MAIL & SHIPPING

Airmail postcards and letters cost EC$1.50 (for the first ½ ounce) to the United States, Canada, and the United Kingdom and EC$2.50 to Australia and New Zealand. The only post office is in the Valley; it's open weekdays 8 to 4:45. When writing to the island, you don't need a postal code; just include the name of the establishment, address (location or post-office box), and "Anguilla, British West Indies."

The post office, located in the Valley, is open weekdays 8 to 3:30. There's a FedEx office near the airport. It's open weekdays 8 to 5 and Saturday 9 to 1.

Contacts Anguilla Post Office (⊠ Wallblake Rd., The Valley ☎ 264/497–2528). **FedEx** (⊠ Hallmark Bldg., 227 Old Airport Rd., The Valley ☎ 264/497–3575).

SAFETY

Anguilla is a quiet, relatively safe island, but there's no sense in tempting fate by leaving your valuables unattended in your hotel room, on the beach, or in your car. Avoid remote beaches, and lock your car, hotel room, and villa. Most hotel rooms are equipped with a safe to stash your valuables.

TAXES

The departure tax is $20 for adults and $10 for children, payable in cash at the airport, $3 payable in cash at Blowing Point Ferry Terminal. A 10% accommodations tax is added to hotel bills along with a $1 per night marketing tax.

TELEPHONES

To make a local call, dial the seven-digit number. Most hotels will arrange with a local provider for a cell phone to use during your stay. Try to get a prepaid, local one for the best rates. Some GSM international cell phones will work, some not; check with your service before you leave. Hotels usually add a hefty surcharge to all calls.

Cable & Wireless is open weekdays 8–6, Saturday 9–1, and Sunday 10–2. Here, you can rent a cell phone for use during your stay, or purchase Caribbean phone cards for use in specially marked phone booths. Inside the departure lounge at the Blowing Point Ferry dock and at the airport there's an AT&T USADirect access phone for collect or credit-card calls to the United States.

To call Anguilla from the United States, dial 1 plus the area code 264, then the local seven-digit number. From the United Kingdom dial 001 and then the area code and the number. From Australia and New Zealand dial 0011, then 1, then the area code and the number.

To call internationally, dial 1, the area code, and the seven-digit number to reach the United States and Canada; dial 011, 44, and the local number for the United Kingdom; dial 011, 61, and the local number for Australia; and dial 011, 64, and the local number for New Zealand.

Information Cable & Wireless (⊠ Wallblake Rd. ☎ 264/497–3100).

TIPPING

A 10% to 15% service charge is added to all hotel bills, though it doesn't always go to staff.

It's usually expected that you will tip more—$5 per person per day for the housekeeping staff, $20 for a helpful concierge, and $10 per day for the group to beach attendants. It's not uncommon to tip more generously, particularly at higher-end resorts.

Many restaurants include a service charge of 10% to 15% on the bill; it's your choice to tip more if you feel the service is deserving. If there's no surcharge, tip about 15%. If you have taken most meals at your hotel's dining room, approximately $100 per week can be handed to the restaurant manager in an envelope to be divided among the staff.

Taxi drivers should receive 10% of the fare.

TOUR OPTIONS

A round-the-island tour by taxi takes about 2½ hours and costs $40 for one or two people, $5 for each additional passenger. Bennie's Tours is one of the island's more reliable tour operators. Malliouhana Travel & Tours will create personalized package tours of the island. The Old Valley Tour, created by longtime resident Frank Costin, ambles up Crocus Hill, a treasure trove of Anguilla's best-preserved historic edifices, including Ebenezer's Methodist Church (the island's oldest), the Warden's Place, and typical turn-of-the-20th-century cottages (most housing galleries). The tour is by appointment only and offers a fascinating insight into Anguillian architecture, past and present.

Contact the Anguilla Tourist Board or call 264/497–2711 to arrange the tour by Sir Emile Gumbs, the island's former chief minister, of the Sandy Ground area. This tour, which highlights historic and ecological sites, is on Tuesday at 10 AM. The $10 fee benefits the Anguilla Archaeological Historical Society. Gumbs also organizes bird-watching expeditions that show you everything from frigate birds to turtle doves.

Contacts **Anguilla Tourist Office** (✉ Coronation Ave., The Valley ☎ 264/497–2759 or 800/553–4939 ⊕ www.anguilla-vacation. com). **Bennie's Tours** (✉ Blowing Point ☎ 264/497–2788). **Malliouhana Travel &**

Tours (✉ The Quarter ☎ 264/497–2431). **Old Valley Tour** (☎ 264/497–2263).

VISITOR INFORMATION

The Anguilla Tourist Office can provide up-to-the-minute information about attractions, events, and tours.

In Anguilla **Anguilla Tourist Office** (✉ Coronation Ave., The Valley ⊕ www.anguilla-vacation.com ☎ 264/497–2759, 800/553–4939 from U.S. 📠 264/497–2710).

WEDDINGS

Anguilla's beaches and sybaritic resorts, such as Cap Juluca and Malliouhana, provide ideal settings for destination weddings and honeymoons. Several resorts will help plan everything in advance. Some people are discouraged by a fairly lengthy residency period to get an inexpensive marriage license: if one partner lives on Anguilla at least 15 days before the wedding date, the license costs $40; otherwise, you must pay a fee of $284. Allow two working days to process applications, which can be obtained weekdays from 8:30 to 4 at the Judicial Department. Both parties must present proof of identity (valid passport, birth certificate, or driver's license with photo), as well as an original decree of divorce where applicable and death certificate if widowed. Blood tests are not required. There are additional requirements if you wish to marry in the Catholic Church.

Antigua & Barbuda

Heritage Quay, St. John's

WORD OF MOUTH

"Go for sailing week . . . and see why millionaires worldwide flock to Antigua with their multimillion-dollar sailboats; English Harbour turns into a nonstop party."

—antigualover

"Our guide took us through the rain forest and we picked fruit right off the trees. You have to try a piece of black pineapple!"

—Roy_boy

WELCOME TO ANTIGUA & BARBUDA

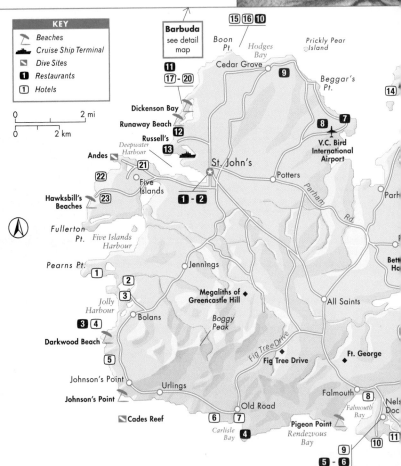

KEY
- Beaches
- Cruise Ship Terminal
- Dive Sites
- **1** Restaurants
- **1** Hotels

0 ——— 2 mi
0 ——— 2 km

Barbuda
see detail
map

15 **16** **10**

Boon Pt.   *Hodges Bay*   Prickly Pear Island

11   Cedar Grove
17 - **20**   **9**   Beggar's Pt.

Dickenson Bay   **8** **7**

Runaway Beach   **12**   V.C. Bird International Airport

Russell's   **13**

Deepwater Harbour

Andes   **21**   St. John's   Potters

22   Five Islands   **1** - **2**

Hawksbill's Beaches   **23**   Parham

Five Islands Harbour

Fullerton Pt.

Pearns Pt.   **1**   Jennings   All Saints

2   Megaliths of Greencastle Hill

3   *Boggy Peak*

Jolly Harbour   Bolans

3 **4**   *Fig Tree Drive*   Ft. George

Darkwood Beach   **5**   Fig Tree Drive

Johnson's Point   Urlings   Falmouth   **8**

Johnson's Point   Old Road   *Falmouth Bay*   Nels Doc

Cades Reef   **6** **7**   Pigeon Point   **10** **11**

Carlisle Bay   **4**   *Rendezvous Bay*

9

5 - **6**

Excellent beaches—365 of them—might make you think that this island has never busied itself with anything more pressing than the pursuit of pleasure. But for much of the 18th and 19th centuries, English Harbour sheltered Britain's Caribbean fleet. These days, pleasure yachts bob where galleons once anchored.

A BEACH FOR EVERY DAY

At 108 square mi (280 square km), Antigua is the largest of the British Leeward Islands. Its much smaller sister island, Barbuda, is 26 mi (42 km) to the north. Together, they are an independent nation and part of the British Commonwealth. The island was under British control from 1667 until it achieved independence in 1981.

ANTIGUA & BARBUDA

2

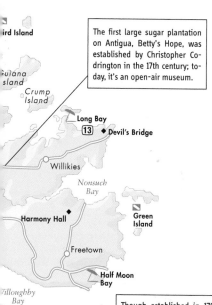

The first large sugar plantation on Antigua, Betty's Hope, was established by Christopher Codrington in the 17th century; today, it's an open-air museum.

Though established in 1704, English Harbour was given much more prominence as a naval station when Horatio Nelson was assigned there in 1784; he expanded the port, which thrived for over 100 years.

TOP 4 REASONS TO VISIT ANTIGUA

1 So many paradisaical beaches of every size provide a tremendous selection for an island its size.

2 Some islands may offer more attractions, but Nelson's Dockyard alone is one of the Caribbean's best examples of historic preservation.

3 With several natural anchorages and tiny islets to explore, Antigua is a major sailing center.

4 Activities galore: land and water sports, sights to see, and nightlife.

ANTIGUA & BARBUDA PLANNER

Island Activities

Because it caters to large numbers of package tourists, Antigua has a fairly wide variety of sports and activity outfitters offering many different kinds of adventure and sightseeing tours that include **hiking, kayaking,** and **snorkeling** trips. Antigua's waters also teem with big-game fish, so **deep-sea fishing** is a popular option. Constant tradewinds also make Antigua an excellent **windsurfing** destination.

The island even has its own "Stingray City" reminiscent of the original in Grand Cayman.

Because of a strong boating culture on the island, **day sails** are also good, and you can rent a **sailboat** for a long or short time. The island is somewhat unsung as a **diving** destination.

Golfers may not be overly impressed by the quality of Antigua's two courses, but they will be pleased with the green fees compared to those on other islands.

A trip to **Barbuda** and its exquisite beach is always welcome. The more adventurous may prefer to get a bit more off the beaten path and make a day trip over to **Montserrat** to see its occasionally spewing, sputtering, active volcano.

Logistics

Getting to Antigua: A fair number of nonstop flights from the U.S. make getting to Antigua (ANU) reasonably easy. Antigua itself is something of a Caribbean hub, as it's a major hub for LIAT. You can continue on a small Carib Aviation plane to Barbuda, or there is ferry service five days a week, though it's geared for day-trippers. Package deals can be a good deal for resorts here.

Hassle Factor: Low for Antigua, Medium for Barbuda.

Nonstops: You can fly nonstop from Atlanta (Delta, twice-weekly in season), Charlotte (USAirways), Miami (American, Caribbean Airlines, Continental), New York–JFK (American, Caribbean Airlines), New York–Newark (Continental).

On the Ground

Antigua's V. C. Bird International Airport, on the northeast coast, is a major hub for traffic between Caribbean islands and for international flights. Montserrat has a small airport with a few daily flights. Taxis meet every flight to Antigua, and drivers will offer to guide you around the island. The taxis are unmetered, but rates are posted at the airport, and drivers must carry a rate card with them. The fixed rate from the airport to St. John's is $10 (although drivers have been known to quote in EC dollars), to Dickenson Bay $13, and to English Harbour $26.

Renting a Car: If you are staying at an isolated resort or wish to sample the island's many fine restaurants, then a car is a necessity, less so if you are staying at an all-inclusive and plan to limit your on-island excursions to a sightseeing tour or two. It's certainly possible to get by without a car, particularly if you are staying near St. John's or English Harbour, but taxi rates mount up quickly (it can cost $50 for the round-trip between St. John's and English Harbour, including a half hour for you to do a bit of exploring). A temporary driving permit is required on the island ($20), and you drive on the left.

Where to Stay

One of the best things about Antigua is that it is lined with many excellent beaches, so you're almost certain to have a good beach regardless of where you stay. Dickenson Bay and Five Islands Peninsula suit beachcombers who want proximity to St. John's, while Jolly Harbour offers affordable options and activities galore. English Harbour and the southwest coast have the best inns and several excellent restaurants—although many close from August well into October; it's also the yachting crowd's hangout. Resorts elsewhere on island are ideal for those seeking seclusion; some are so remote that all-inclusive packages or rental cars are mandatory. Barbuda has three posh resorts.

Luxury Resorts: A fair number of luxury resorts cater to the well-heeled in varying degrees of formality on both Antigua and Barbuda.

All-Inclusive Resorts: Most of the all-inclusives aim for a very mainstream, package-tour kind of crowd—to varying degrees of success—though Sandals Antigua offerings are more upscale.

Small Inns: A few restored small inns can be found around Antigua, but a large concentration is in or near English Harbour.

Hotel & Restaurant Costs

⇨*For information on hotel meal plans, see Accommodations in Caribbean Essentials.*

WHAT IT COSTS IN U.S. DOLLARS

$$$$	$$$	$$	$	¢
Restaurants				
over $30	$20–$30	$12–$20	$8–$12	under $8
Hotels*				
over $350	$250–$350	$150–$250	$80–$150	under $80
Hotels**				
over $450	$350–$450	$250–$350	$125–$250	under $125

*EP, BP, CP **AI, FAP, MAP Restaurant prices are for a main course at dinner and include any taxes or service charges. Hotel prices are per night for a double room in high season, excluding taxes, service charges, and meal plans (except at all-inclusives).

When to Go

The high season runs from mid-December through April; after that time, you can find real bargains, for as much as 40% off the regular rates, particularly if you book an air/hotel package. A fair number of the smaller properties close for at least part of the time between August and October.

The year's big event is **Antigua Sailing Week,** which draws some 300 yachts for a series of races in late April and early May.

Mid-April sees the **Antigua Classic Yacht Regatta,** a five-day event that includes a tall ships race.

Antigua Tennis Week, usually the second week of May, has exhibition games by former greats plus a pro-am tournament.

May also brings the **Antigua & Barbuda Sports Fishing Tournament** in Falmouth.

The **Antigua Music Festival** is in June.

Summer Carnival runs 10 days from the end of July to early August and is one of the Caribbean's more elaborate, with eye-catching costumes and fierce music competitions.

By Jordan
Simon

THE SKIFF SKIMS WATERS RIPPLING from azure to aquamarine, colors so intense they seem almost artificial. An archipelago of islets unfolds before me. We moor off the aptly named Great Bird Island, where brown pelicans dive-bomb for tiny, sun-silvered flying fish inches from my feet as I stroll a stretch of powdered ivory sand. Later, I clamber up the rocks, and my bird's-eye view takes in a flotilla of fishing boats as brightly colored as a child's finger painting. A halo of frigate birds circles overhead, unfurling their wings to a full 8-foot span, resembling a flag proudly flapping in the breeze.

The miracle of Antigua, and especially its astonishingly undeveloped sister island, Barbuda, is that you can still play Robinson Crusoe here. Travel brochures trumpet the 365 sensuous beaches, "one for every day of the year," as locals love saying, though when the island was first developed for tourism, the unofficial count was 52 ("one for every weekend"). Either way, even longtime residents haven't combed every stretch of sand.

The island's extensive archipelago of cays and islets is what attracted the original Amerindian settlers—the Ciboney—at least 4,000 years ago. The natural environment, which is rich in marine life, flora, and fauna, has been likened to a "natural supermarket." Antigua's superior anchorages and strategic location naturally caught the attention of the colonial powers. The Dutch, French, and English waged numerous bloody battles throughout the 17th century (eradicating the remaining Arawaks and Caribs in the process), with England finally prevailing in 1667. Antigua remained under English control until achieving full independence on November 1, 1981, along with Barbuda, 26 mi (42 km) to the north.

Boats and beaches go hand in hand with hotel development, of course, and Antigua's tourist infrastructure has mushroomed since the 1950s. Though many of its grandes dames such as Curtain Bluff remain anchors, today all types of resorts line the sand, and the island offers something for everyone, from gamboling on the sand to gambling in casinos. Environmental activists have become increasingly vocal about preservation and the limiting of development, and not just because green travel rakes in the green. Antigua's allure is precisely that precarious balance and subliminal tension between its unspoiled natural beauty and its something-for-everyone, sun-sand-surf megadevelopment. And, of course, the British heritage persists, from teatime (and tee times) to fiercely contested cricket matches.

WHERE TO STAY

Scattered along Antigua's beaches and hillsides are exclusive, elegant hideaways; romantic restored inns; and all-inclusive hot spots for couples. One trend: top restaurants, including Harmony Hall, have added charming, affordable cottages. Check individual lodgings for restrictions (many have minimum stays during certain high-season periods). Look also for specials on the Web or from tour packagers, since hotels'

Other Hotels to Consider on Antigua

Obviously, we can't include every property deserving mention without creating an encyclopedia. Our favorites receive full reviews, but you might consider the following accommodations, many of which are popular with tour operators.

Antigua Yacht Club Marina & Resort (✉ *Falmouth Harbour* ☎ *268/562–3030* ⊕ *www.aycmarina.com*) is a handsome collection of 19 hotel rooms and 24 studio and 1-bedroom condos (for rent when owners are off-island), climbing a hill with stunning marina views. Accommodations are stylish if spare, with island crafts and the occasional high-tech amenity; the adjacent marina is a center of nautical hubbub with several restaurants, pubs, and shops.

Coconut Beach Club (✉ *Yepton Beach* ☎ *268/462–3239 or 800/361–4621* ⊕ *www.coconutbeachclub.com*) was taken over by CocoBay Resort, which refurbished the neglected rooms in 2004. The beach overlooking the ruins of Ft. James is lovely, the food in the restaurants creative; all units feature smashing sea views, and the price is right—for now.

Hermitage Bay (✉ *Hermitage Bay* ☎ *268/562–5500* ⊕ *www.hermit-agebay.com*) is a deluxe enclave of 30 beachfront and hillside cottages that opened in December 2006 on a secluded, hard-to-reach but pretty stretch of sand. Affecting a look and ambience that borrow from both Carlisle Bay and Curtain Bluff, the minimalist-chic lodgings include a garden shower and private plunge pool. Only time will tell if it can live up to its high ambitions and prices.

Rex Blue Heron (✉ *Johnson's Point* ☎ *268/462–8564 or 800/255–5859* ⊕ *www.rexresorts.com*) is utterly mediocre at best save for three things: a sublime sweep of ecru sand, intimacy (only 64 rooms, most of them overlooking that spectacular beach), and frequent heavily discounted package deals for an international clientele.

Rex Halcyon Cove Beach Resort (✉ *Dickenson Bay* ☎ *268/462–9256 or 800/255–5859* ⊕ *www.rexresorts. com*) is a large, impersonal but admirably outfitted resort (from dive shop to car rental) on one of Antigua's top beaches. It reopened in late 2005 after renovations, though little has been done about the institutional buildings or stampeding tour groups.

---

quoted rack rates are often negotiable. Condo hotels are increasingly popular; although not reviewed in this edition, South Point should open by late 2008 in Falmouth Harbour, and a revamped Hodges Bay Club opened late 2007 on the north shore.

$$$$ ★ **Blue Waters Hotel.** A well-heeled Brit crowd goes barefoot at this swank yet understated retreat. The lobby strikes an immediate note of class, with cast-iron columns, mosaic lamps, towering earthenware urns, fountains, and a central minijungle. The twin beaches are minuscule, but sundecks and gazebos strategically dot the lush hillside for optimum privacy. Rooms are continually refurbished, with such trendy additions as flat-screen TVs and "rainwater" showerheads complementing appealingly old-fashioned vellum prints, intricately

carved furnishings, and classic Italian tile work. Rooms 104 to 116 lack direct beachfront access, but their sizable balconies practically jut over the water. Low-numbered units in the 200 through 600 blocks feature similarly splendid views. The Cove Suites, which are enormous (850 square feet) and elegant, comprise an independent enclave on 5 lavishly landscaped acres with four infinity pools. The three Rock Cottage villas define seclusion. Afternoon tea and nonmotorized water sports are complimentary. The Palm restaurant offers an unmatched setting and fine Caribbean fare and buffets; Vyvien's à la carte restaurant counters with a sophisticated fusion menu and comely neocolonial setting. A breakfast-only plan is available for those who don't want the all-inclusive. **Pros:** Pomp without pretension, exquisite setting, trendy minimalist decor. **Cons:** Small beachfront, trendy minimalist decor. ⊠*Boon Point, Soldiers Bay* ⊡*Box 256, St. John's* ☎*268/462–0290, 800/557–6536 reservations only* ⊕*www.bluewaters.net* ⇗*65 rooms, 32 suites, 3 villas, 4 penthouses* ⬧*In-room: safe, refrigerator, Ethernet. In-hotel: 3 restaurants, room service, bars, tennis court, pools, gym, spa, beachfront, water sports, no elevator, children's programs (ages 5–13), public Internet* ⊟*AE, D, DC, MC, V* ⊘*Closed Sept.* ⦿*AI.*

$$$$
★
Carlisle Bay. This cosmopolitan, boutique sister property of London's trendy One Aldwych hotel daringly eschews everything faux colonial and creole. The monochromatic, magazine-worthy result combines cool, classy minimalism with unsnobbish warmth. Vast, split-level accommodations emulate the Japanese decorative ideal of perfection through simplicity with white walls, black-and-white snapshots, mahogany-and-teak furnishings, mauve and peach fabrics, and chrome-and-glass accents. The bougainvillea garlanding the enormous balcony adds just the right amount of color. Deluxe gadgetry runs the gamut from in-suite plasma TV/DVDs, fiber-optic bed lights, and Gaggia espresso machines to a movie-screening room and library with futuristic Internet stations. The two innovatively trendy restaurants, complimentary nonmotorized water sports, and a soothing spa enhance the luxe ambience. There are kinks—particularly an admirable but inadequate attempt to separate families and romantically inclined couples—but the buff bodies toting cell phones make this a hip, happening see-and-be-scene. **Pros:** Luxury resort, attentive service, family-friendly. **Cons:** Family-friendly, aggressively hip, lovely beach but murky water. ⊠*Carlisle Bay, Old Road, St. Mary's* ⊡*Box 2288, St. John's* ☎*268/484–0000, 800/745–8883, 800/628–8929 reservations only* ⊕*www.carlisle-bay.com* ⇗*88 suites* ⬧*In-room: kitchen (some), DVD, VCR (some), Wi-Fi. In-hotel: 2 restaurants, room service, bars, tennis courts, pool, gym, spa, beachfront, diving, water sports, no elevator, children's programs (ages 3–12), laundry service, public Internet* ⊟*AE, DC, MC, V* ⦿*BP.*

$$$$
Fodor's Choice
★
Curtain Bluff. An incomparable beachfront setting, impeccable service, diligent upgrading by attentive management, superb extras (free scuba diving and deep-sea fishing), effortless elegance: Curtain Bluff is that rare retreat that remains ahead of the times while exuding a magical timelessness. Owner Howard Hulford still patrols the property with cutting shears and wineglass in hand: the lavish gardens and legendary 25,000-bottle wine cellar bespeak his passions, which the loyal mul-

2

tigenerational clientele (yes, families are coddled) shares. Some might find Curtain Bluff stuffy and country-clubby, but guests merely respect one another's privacy. Gorgeous, sunken junior suites—the majority of the rooms—have marble bathrooms, grass mats, Mexican earthenware, deco-funky lamps, and coffered raw-wood ceilings. Stunning duplex suites, in soothing whites and blues, scale the bluff; their hammock-slung terraces alone outclass many hotel rooms. Everyone eventually emerges for exceptional Continental dining and dancing to live bands in the lovely alfresco restaurant, where chef Christophe Blatz also gives cooking and wine-pairing classes. The elegant waterfront spa exemplifies how Curtain Bluff remains a world-class resort that's a bargain in its class. **Pros:** Luxury lodging, sublime food, beautiful beaches, incredible extras. **Cons:** Some find clientele standoffish, lodgings atop bluff not ideal for elderly. ⊠ *Morris Bay* ⏠ *Box 288, St. John's* ☎ *268/462–8400, 888/289–9898 for reservations* ⊕ *www.curtainbluff.com* ⤶ *18 rooms, 54 suites* ⟳ *In-room: safe, no TV, Wi-Fi. In-hotel: 2 restaurants, bar, tennis courts, pool, gym, spa, beachfront, diving, water sports, no elevator, children's programs (ages 4–12), public Internet* ▤ *AE, D* ⊘ *Closed late Aug.–Oct.* ⏐⊚⏐ *AI.*

$$$$
★
Galley Bay. This posh all-inclusive channels the fictional Bali H'ai (with colonial architectural flourishes): there's a man-made lagoon and grotto pool; a bird sanctuary laced with nature trails; a magnificent boardwalk-lined ecru beach; gardens as manicured as the discriminating clientele; thatched-roof public spaces; custom-made bamboo furnishings; art naïf paintings; and African carvings. The soothing, at times crashing surf serenades the creole-style beachfront buildings and romantic Gauguin restaurant (with clever, thatched private-dining alcoves). The handsomely appointed superior and deluxe beachfront units (numbers 47–48 are centrally located; avoid 77–80, which abut potential mosquito breeding grounds) represent the best value, though towering palms slightly obstruct even the second-floor views. Suites are splendid, balancing an old-style plantation look with newfangled necessities (Wi-Fi, flat-screen TV/DVDs). The Gauguin Cottages are charming, especially with the addition of plunge pools, but they're slightly claustrophobic and the walkways separating bedroom from bathroom insufficiently covered. But these are minor quibbles for honeymooning couples and corporate bigwigs escaping the rat race. **Pros:** Luxury lodging, gorgeous beach, impeccable maintenance. **Cons:** Some lodgings are claustrophobic and lack a view, outdoor spa can get hot. ⊠ *Five Islands* ⏠ *Box 305, St. John's* ☎ *268/462–0302, 800/858–4618 reservations only* ⊕ *www.eliteislandresorts.com* ⤶ *98 rooms* ⟳ *In-room: safe, refrigerator, DVD (some), Wi-Fi (some). In-hotel: 3 restaurants, bars, tennis court, pools, gym, spa, beachfront, water sports, bicycles, no elevator, public Internet, no kids under 16* ▤ *AE, D, DC, MC, V* ⊘ *Closed mid-Aug.–early Sept.* ⏐⊚⏐ *AI.*

$$$$
★
Jumby Bay. This refined resort proffers all the makings of a classic Caribbean private island hideaway. The main beach is simply sublime—except when jets whoosh by; fortunately, the butler service offers iPods and DVD players. The air-conditioning, once insufficient because of the majestically high ceilings, has been upgraded. Stan-

dard rooms and junior suites have hand-carved mahogany four-poster beds—though the lighting is poor. Still, the details impress, from the octagonal Rondavel suites' luxuriant indoor-outdoor bathrooms to the luxe villas' hand-painted tile work. The best value for the money are the refurbished Pond Bay Villa ocean-view suites. The cuisine, befitting a Rosewood-managed property, is usually impeccable. Birdsong and sea breeze fill the casual Verandah restaurant. Villa owners, including Robin Leach and Ken Follett, frequent the 18th-century stone-and-mahogany Estate House dining room and its fanciful, pineapple-theme lounge. And privacy is certainly paramount: you can bike along nature trails to the island's many secluded beaches (one lures nesting turtles in season). Guided snorkeling tours are a plus. **Pros:** Luxury lodging, isolated private island location, sterling cuisine. **Cons:** Isolated private island location, jet noise occasionally disturbs the main beach. ⊠ *Long Island* ⬩ *Box 243, St. John's* ☎ *268/462–6000* ⊕ *www.jumbybayresort.com* ⟿ *40 suites, 11 villas* ♿ *In-room: safe, refrigerator, no TV (some), DVD (some), Wi-Fi (some). In-hotel: 2 restaurants, bars, tennis courts, pool, gym, spa, beachfront, water sports, bicycles, no elevator, public Internet* ⊟ *AE, D, MC, V* ⦿ *AI.*

$$$$ 🖼 **St. James's Club.** Forget any prestige the name connotes; this hotel has undergone many incarnations (including one as a Holiday Inn) as the discolored concrete terraces and gaudy plastic accents attest. That said, there's much to recommend it, starting with the peerless location straddling 100 acres on Mamora Bay. Regularly refurbished rooms—flat-screen TVs are the latest upgrade—are commodious and vibrantly decorated (the larger, more-distinctive Premium and Beachfront units are worth the extra cost). Activities galore satisfy the most jaded travelers; in inclement weather you can enjoy movies, trivia contests, and dance classes in the opulent Jacaranda Bar. Though nonmotorized water sports and afternoon tea are complimentary for all guests, most opt for the pricey all-inclusive package, as the remote location discourages dining out. The self-catering two-bedroom villas cascading down the hillside can represent value for large families. Though the restaurants are spectacularly situated over the water, especially Coco's and Piccolo Mondo, food is mostly indifferent. The sometimes unhelpful (or honestly harried) staff and occasional invasion of younger, rowdy Brits on package deals further diminish deluxe pretensions, but this hotel is still a favorite with many travelers who return year after year. **Pros:** Splendid remote location, beautiful beaches. **Cons:** Remote location makes a car a necessity for non-AI guests, tour groups can overrun the resort, uneven food and service. ⊠ *Mamora Bay* ⬩ *Box 63, St. John's* ☎ *268/460–5000 or 800/858–4618* ⊕ *www.eliteislandresorts.com* ⟿ *187 rooms, 72 villas* ♿ *In-room: safe, refrigerator (some). In-hotel: 4 restaurants, room service, bars, tennis courts, pools, gym, spa, beachfront, diving, water sports, no elevator, children's programs (ages 2–12), laundry service, public Internet* ⊟ *AE, D, DC, MC, V* ⦿ *AI.*

$$$$ 🖼 **Sandals Grande Antigua Resort & Spa.** The sumptuous public spaces, lovely beach, glorious gardens, and plethora of facilities almost mask this once-sterling resort's impersonal atmosphere and often apathetic service. Renovations in the original section, now dubbed the Carib-

2

bean Grove, are merely cosmetic and include repainting the buildings in shades of mango, lime, and saffron and adding plunge pools to garden-view rondavels. The few units claiming water vistas (numbers 301–305 are best, while 401–404 lack views but open onto the beach) are cramped, poorly ventilated, and directly in the busiest foot-traffic path. Pluses include a lively atmosphere, activities from cardio training to karaoke, and such extras as complimentary tennis lessons and scuba diving (only spa treatments and weddings incur surcharges). The all-suite Mediterranean Village expansion debuted in November 2007, adding 180 lavish units (starting at 500 square feet and matching marble, mosaic, and mahogany with such contemporary touches as flat-screen TVs); a swim-up bar; private check-in; butler service; two upscale restaurants; a delightful pub; and posh retailers. Architecturally it's a hodgepodge, yet many details impress. **Pros:** Lovely beach, excellent spa, good dining options. **Cons:** Sprawling layout, too bustling, uneven service. ⊠ *Dickenson Bay* ⌕ *Box 147, St. John's* ☎ *268/462–0267, 888/726–3257 reservations only* ⊕ *www.sandals. com* ⤢ *100 rooms, 257 suites, 16 rondavels* ⚷ *In-room: safe, refrigerator, Wi-Fi (some). In-hotel: 7 restaurants, room service, bars, tennis courts, pools, gym, spa, beachfront, diving, water sports, laundry service, public Internet, airport shuttle, no kids* ⊟ *AE, D, DC, MC, V* ⚲ *3-night minimum* ¶⊙ *AI.*

$$$$ ⊞ **Verandah Resort & Spa.** Though local activists disagree, this ecocentric resort on Antigua's wild east coast emphasizes low-impact environmental responsibility without sacrificing upscale contemporary conveniences. The splendid hillside setting overlooks calm, reef-protected Dian Bay; hiking trails snake around the property to Devil's Bridge National Park. Recycling is utilized wherever possible, only nonmotorized water sports are permitted, and the mint-and-apricot creole-style cottages built on stilt-like pylons (which allegedly reduce erosion while enabling greenery to grow under and around) incorporate green materials (solar energy, foam panels, and spray cement to help lower the temperature). There are plentiful activities for kids including ecological edu-tainment and their own pool and restaurant. All 200 sizable, villa-style units offer unobstructed ocean or bay views; vaulted ceilings; stylish touches like granite countertops; liberal use of wood, bamboo, and stone to bring nature indoors; sofa bed and kitchenette (good for families); and such high-tech necessities as flat-screen TVs and Wi-Fi access. Other first-rate facilities include an enormous free-form swimming pool that doubles as a social center, several promising restaurants, a minicinema, and the Tranquility Spa that culls its menu from various global techniques. **Pros:** Gorgeous remote location, sprawling but cleverly centralized, creative spa treatments, good kids' facilities. **Cons:** Remote location makes a car a necessity to explore, smallish beaches, inconsistent food and service. ⊠ *Long Bay* ⌕ *Box 54, St. Philips* ☎ *268/562–6848, 800/858–4618, 866/237–1785 reservations only* ⊕ *www.verandahresortandspa.com* ⤢ *200 suites* ⚷ *In-room: safe, refrigerator, Wi-Fi. In-hotel: 3 restaurants, bars, tennis courts, pools, gym, spa, beachfront, water sports, no elevator, children's programs (ages 4–12), public Internet* ⊟ *AE, D, DC, MC, V* ¶⊙ *AI.*

$$$–$$$$ **Hawksbill by Rex Resorts.** "Location, location, location" is the hospi-
tality industry mantra, and four secluded beaches (including one cloth-
ing-optional strand) compose this resort's main attraction. Verdant
grounds with landscaped walkways, plantation-style cottages trimmed
with gingerbread fretwork and radiant bougainvillea, and a backdrop
of jade mountains maximize Hawksbill's old-time Caribbean feel. Gar-
den-view rooms enjoy restricted water views, making them the best
buy; the original air-conditioned Club units (especially numbers 138–
142) are isolated from the action, but hand-painted tile work, beamed
vaulted ceilings, and superlative vistas make them the choice accommo-
dations—other than the restored, three-bedroom greathouse. Though
a full slate of entertainment is on tap, the mix of honeymooners and
mature couples is generally sedate, thanks to the restful surroundings.
Unfortunately, it has slowly slid downhill since Rex took over, but
book it if you can find an affordable package deal and only seek a
secluded strand—or four. **Pros:** Sublime setting, pretty grounds. **Cons:**
Indifferent food, dated and often worn furnishings, increasingly poor
maintenance. ⊠ *Five Islands* ⊕ *Box 108, St. John's* 🕾 *268/462–0301*
⊕ *www.rexresorts.com* 📞 *111 rooms, 1 three-bedroom villa* ⚷ *In-
room: no a/c (some), safe, refrigerator, no TV. In-hotel: 3 restaurants,
bars, tennis court, pool, spa, beachfront, water sports, no elevator,
public Internet, public Wi-Fi* ⊟ *AE, D, DC, MC, V* ⦿ *AI.*

$$–$$$$ **Jolly Beach Resort.** If you're looking for basic sun-sand-surf fun, this
active resort—Antigua's largest—fits the bill for few bills, luring a gre-
garious blend of honeymooners, families, and singles. Management
diligently gussies up the public areas: there's a faux sugar mill, a free-
form fantasy pool, creole-style vendors' village, attractive gardens, and
a riot of tropical-cocktail colors. Palapas and hammocks dot the long
if crowded beach. The four main restaurants, Italian to Indian, are surprisingly competent, especially the waterfront seafood eatery, Lydia's.
The range of activities and facilities surpasses that of many tonier all-
inclusives. On the downside, service is too often cursory if not curt
and the dilapidated cinder-block structures have peeling paint, chipped
doors, and rusting railings. Most units are cramped and musty with
bizarre, built-in concrete furnishings. "Supersaver" rooms, though the
size of jail cells, represent the top value, especially for singles (only
$10 supplement). Every room has at least a partial sea view. **Pros:**
Inexpensive, great range of activities for the price, good food for a
cheaper AI. **Cons:** Many cramped, ugly rooms, overrun by tour groups;
often impersonal service. ⊠ *Jolly Harbour* ⊕ *Box 2009, Bolans Village* 🕾 *268/462–0061 or 866/905–6559* ⊕ *www.jollybeachresort.com*
📞 *462 units* ⚷ *In-room: safe, refrigerator (some), Wi-Fi (some). In-
hotel: 5 restaurants, bars, tennis courts, pools, gym, beachfront, diving, water sports, no elevator, children's programs (ages 2–12), public
Internet* ⊟ *AE, D, MC, V* ⦿ *AI.*

$$$ **CocoBay.** This healing hillside hideaway aims to "eliminate all poten-
tial worries," by emphasizing simple natural beauty and West Indian
warmth. Pastel-hue, creole-style cottages with gingerbread trim and
distinctive wattle-and-daub terrace dividers have pine floors, sisal rugs,
mosquito netting, and bleached wood louvers. Fresh flowers plucked

from the exquisite gardens add splashes of color. The sparkling bay vistas from every room are restorative in themselves, though a wellness center offers massages, facials, and scrubs, many utilizing indigenous ingredients. Yoga classes and nature hikes further promote de-stressing, though worriers can request complimentary cell phones (you pay for calls). Only the ho-hum food—except at Sheer, which has a surcharge—and pokey beaches somewhat mar the relaxing vibe. **Pros:** Emphasis on local nature and culture, beautiful views. **Cons:** Indifferent food, stifling on breezeless days, difficult climb for elderly. ⊠ *Valley Church* ⌂ *Box 431, St. John's* ☎ *268/562–2400 or 866/692–6094* ⊕ *www. cocobayresort.com* ⟿ *41 rooms, 4 2-bedroom houses* ⌂ *In-room: no a/c, safe, refrigerator, no TV. In-hotel: 2 restaurants, bar, pool, gym, spa, beachfront, water sports, no elevator, public Internet* ▭ *AE, D, MC, V* ⊙ *AI.*

$$–$$$ ▨ **Dickenson Bay Cottages.** If you don't mind a five-minute hike down to
★   the beach, this small hillside complex offers excellent value for families. Lush landscaping snakes around the two-story buildings and pool. The handsomely appointed duplex accommodations feature most of the comforts of home, though the decor is hardly original and the ventilation is poor. Larger units have verandahs with ocean views but aren't worth the higher tariff. Guests enjoy privileges at Rex Halcyon Cove's bustling beach; use of its tennis and water-sports facilities is always discounted. Other dining and recreational options abound along Dickenson Bay. This agreeable enclave is often inexplicably empty, so ask about last-minute reductions and check its Web site for specials. **Pros:** Relatively upscale comfort at down-home prices, walking distance to Dickenson Bay dining and activities. **Cons:** Hike from beach, lacks cross-breeze in many units. ⊠ *Marble Hill* ⌂ *Box 1379, St. John's* ☎ *268/462–4940* ⊕ *www.dickensonbaycottages.com* ⟿ *11 units* ⌂ *In-room: kitchen (some), VCR (some). In-hotel: pool, no elevator* ▭ *AE, DC, MC, V* ⊙ *EP.*

$$–$$$ ▨ **Siboney Beach Club.** This affordable beachfront oasis nestled in a
★   tranquil corner of Dickenson Bay delights with intimacy and warmth, and knowledgeable Aussie owner Tony Johnson gladly acts as a de facto tourist board. Cleverly designed suites have a small bedroom, Pullman-style kitchen, living area, and patio or balcony. Atmospheric touches include island CDs, painted gourds, antique maps, and driftwood wall hangings. A TV can be provided on request, though guests savor the soothing surf counterpointed by crickets, bananaquits, and tree frogs in Tony's extravagant, enchanted garden. Rooms 9 and 10 overlook the sea, and ground-floor units represent fine buys for families—number 3 virtually extends into that lushly landscaped pool area. One drawback: the patios lack screens, forcing a choice between sweltering and swatting pests on rare still days. **Pros:** Friendly service, superb location, great value. **Cons:** No air-conditioning in living room, occasional mosquito problems in ground-floor units. ⊠ *Dickenson Bay* ⌂ *Box 222, St. John's* ☎ *268/462–0806 or 800/533–0234* ⊕ *www. siboneybeachclub.com* ⟿ *12 suites* ⌂ *In-room: safe, kitchen, no TV, Wi-Fi. In-hotel: restaurant, bar, pool, beachfront, no elevator, public Internet* ▭ *AE, D, MC, V* ⊙ *EP.*

$$ ★ **Catamaran Hotel.** The main building at the congenial "Cat Club" evokes a plantation greathouse with verandahs, white columns, and hand-carved doors. The efficiency apartments are ideal for families (the staff dotes on kids), while second-floor deluxe rooms have romantic canopy four-poster beds and scintillating views. Nonmotorized water sports are free at the minuscule, palm- and almond-lined beach, which gazes upon megayachts anchored in the marina. Cell phones and bikes can be rented on-site. Owner-manager Feona Bailey makes improvements yearly (most recently adding the Captain's Quarters restaurant, with lip-smacking barbecue) and personally ensures smooth sailing for travelers seeking true Antiguan flavor. **Pros:** Intimacy, central location, friendly staff. **Cons:** Poky beach (swimming not advised), smallish rooms. ⊠*Falmouth Harbour* ☍*Box 958, St. John's* ☎*268/460–1036 or 800/223–6510* ⊕*www.catamaran-antigua.com* ➟*12 rooms, 2 suites* ⊘*In-room: safe, kitchen. In-hotel: restaurant, bar, pool, beachfront, water sports, no elevator, public Internet* ⊟*D, MC, V* ⊺⊙|*EP.*

$$ **Jolly Harbour Villas.** These duplex, two-bedroom villas ring the marina of a sprawling, 500-acre compound offering every conceivable facility from restaurants and shops to a casino and golf course. The Mediterranean Revival central activity area could put the florid in Florida, with its red-tile roofs, faux stucco, and mustard arcades. The sizable, fully equipped, pastel-hue villas themselves resemble a posh, cookie-cutter retirement village. Opt for those on the south finger, which is closer to the beach, eateries, and most activities, since the free shuttle is erratic and slow. You must pay separately for everything except the pool and kids' club, and the extra $20 per night for air-conditioning is a wise investment: on still days, flies and mosquitoes come out in brute force. Villas represent jolly good value for self-catering families and golfers (unlimited greens fees are $105 per week). Owner, La Perla, is expanding and supposedly upgrading the development—which could mean higher prices. **Pros:** Nice beach, good value, plentiful recreational, dining, and nightlife choices nearby. **Cons:** Mosquito problems, reports of hidden surcharges, inability to charge most restaurants and activities to your villa, some units have 220-volt outlets requiring adaptors. ⊠*Jolly Harbour* ☍*Box 1793, St. John's* ☎*268/462–7771* ⊕*www. jollyharbourantigua.com* ➟*150 villas* ⊘*In-room: no a/c (some), safe, kitchen, no TV (some), DVD (some). In-hotel: 7 restaurants, bars, golf course, tennis courts, pools, beachfront, diving, water sports, no elevator, children's programs (ages 3–11)* ⊟*AE, D, DC, MC, V* ⊺⊙|*EP.*

$$ ☾ **Sunsail Club Colonna.** Those who want to learn to sail or improve their skippering skills should cruise to this instructional facility, justly celebrated worldwide for its affordable sailing and windsurfing schools and family-friendly approach. Sunsail has state-of-the-art equipment, a fine kids' club, and excellent group instruction (all complimentary), but nearly every other aspect of the resort is inferior. However, the expansive free-form pool (though often noisily overrun by kids), handsome public spaces and Mediterranean architecture, sizable rooms (recently brightened with stylish Italian fabrics), and such incentives as discounted greens fees compensate somewhat for the smallish, man-made beaches. The spa could be cleaner, and food veers from inventive to inedible.

Fortunately, management is gradually upgrading every facet of the resort in an effort to make Colonna truly shipshape. Weekly stays are preferred and often discounted. **Pros:** Superlative sailing school, wonderful family programs. **Cons:** Smallish beaches, limited dining options. ⌧*Hodges Bay* ☐*Box 591, St. John's* ☎*268/462–6263 or 800/327–2276* ⊕*www.sunsail.com* ⟲*102 rooms, 12 villas* ⟳*In-room: safe, refrigerator. In-hotel: 2 restaurants, bars, tennis court, pool, gym, spa, beachfront, diving, water sports, no elevator, children's programs (ages 4 months–17), public Internet* ▭*AE, D, MC, V* ⟊*FAP.*

$–$$ 🏨 **Admiral's Inn.** This Georgian brick edifice, originally the shipwright's
★ offices in what is now Nelson's Dockyard, has withstood acts of God and war since the early 18th century. The sturdy walls, occasionally creaking floorboards, even the ancient bar exude history. The finest rooms at "The Ads," as yachties call it, feature the original timbered ceilings—replete with iron braces, whitewashed brick walls, polished hardwood floors, and four-poster beds swaddled in mosquito netting. Those upstairs (numbers 1–3) spy on the yachts in the harbor through Australian pines and stone pillars. Gulls and egrets seem poised to dart into the timbered living room of the two-bedroom Loft (once the dockyard's joinery). Commandeer the complimentary boat and shuttle to nearby beaches when crowds descend on the compound and the inn's captivating terrace restaurant for lunch. **Pros:** Historic ambience, central English Harbour location, fine value. **Cons:** Occasionally noisy when yachties take over the bar, no beach. ⌧*English Harbour* ☐*Box 713, St. John's* ☎*268/460–1027* ⊕*www.admiralsantigua.com* ⟲*14 rooms, 1 2-bedroom apartment* ⟳*In-room: no a/c (some), no TV (some). In-hotel: restaurant, bar, water sports, no elevator* ▭*AE, D, MC, V* ⟊*EP.*

$ 🏨 **Ocean Inn.** Smashing views of English Harbour, affable management, and affordability distinguish this homey inn. The main house has six snug guest rooms (two share a bathroom), but the four hillside cottages are recommended (especially numbers 8 and 9). The owners can provide light dinners with advance notice, though restaurants are only a short hike away. There are several beaches within a 10-minute drive. In season, the small, mural-adorned pool hosts impromptu parties that lure local characters, sea dogs, and eccentric expats for cheap drinks and amusing tall tales. **Pros:** Fabulous views, affable staff, inexpensive. **Cons:** Rickety paths down a steep hill linking cottages, worn rooms need updating, Wi-Fi dodgy. ⌧*English Harbour* ☐*Box 838, St. John's* ☎*268/463–7950 or 888/686–8913* ⊕*www.theoceaninn.com* ⟲*6 rooms, 4 with bath; 4 cottages* ⟳*In-room: refrigerator (some), Wi-Fi. In-hotel: bar, pool, gym, no elevator, public Internet, public Wi-Fi* ▭*AE, V* ⟊*CP.*

WHERE TO EAT

Antigua's restaurants are almost a dying breed since the advent of all-inclusives. But several worthwhile hotel dining rooms and nightspots remain, especially in the English Harbour and Dickenson Bay areas, in addition to many stalwarts. Virtually every chef incorporates local ingredients and elements of West Indian cuisine.

Most menus list prices in both EC and U.S. dollars; if not, ask which currency the menu is using. Always double-check if credit cards are accepted and if service is included. Dinner reservations are needed during high season.

WHAT TO WEAR

Perhaps because of the island's British heritage, Antiguans tend to dress more formally for dinner than dwellers on many other Caribbean islands. Wraps and shorts (no beach attire) are de rigueur for lunch, except at local hangouts.

CARIBBEAN
$$–$$$$

✕**george.** This downtown eatery is a loving evocation of the building owner's original Georgian family home. The contemporary colonial design is stunning: beamed ceilings, teal-and-aqua walls, high-back hardwood chairs, and jalousie shutters that close off to form a second-floor gallery overlooking the busy street scene. The menu updates West Indian classics, from jerk burgers to slow-roasted spareribs with a caramelized passion fruit–pineapple glaze to pepper-seared tuna marinated in sesame-ginger oil. The genial British managers have beefed up the children's and vegetarian menus. If you avoid the priciest items (rack of lamb, lobster) you can dine affordably; indulge in the bartenders' extensive "Naughty List" of cocktails. ⊠ *Market and Redcliffe Sts., St. John's* ☎ *268/562–4866* ▭ *AE, D, MC, V.*

$$–$$$

✕**Papa Zouk.** Who would have thought that a jovial globe-trotting German gent could create a classic Caribbean hangout? But the madras tablecloths, fishnets festooned with Christmas lights, painted bottles of homemade hot sauces, colorful island clientele, and lilting rhythms on the sound system justify the name (zouk is a sultry, musical stew of soul and calypso). Seafood is king, from Guyanese butterfish to Barbudan snapper, usually served either deep-fried or steamed with a choice of such sauces as guava-pepper teriyaki or tomato-basil-coriander. Tangy Caribbean bouillabaisse with garlicky Parmesan mayonnaise and fish 'n' rum (spike it with a vinegar hot sauce) are specialties, as are the knockout rum punches. Finish dinner (and yourself) off with a snifter of aged rum: the tiny bar holds 200 varieties from around the globe. Dine family-style in front or more intimately in back. ⊠ *Hilda Davis Dr., Gambles Terrace, St. John's* ☎ *268/464–7576* ▭ *No credit cards* ⊘ *Closed May–Oct. and Sun. No lunch Mon. and Tues.*

$$–$$$

✕**Russell's.** Convivial owner Russell Hodge had the brilliant idea of restoring a part of Ft. James, with its glorious views of the bay and headlands, and converting it into a semi-alfresco eatery. Potted plants, jazz on the sound system (live musicians Sunday), and red or black hurricane lamps lend a romantic aura to the beamed, stone-and-wood-terrace. The limited menu—local specialties emphasizing seafood—includes fabulous chunky conch fritters and whelks in garlic butter. Russell's sister Faye co-owns Papa Zouk, while sister Valerie runs Shirley Heights Lookout; the Hodges might well be Antigua's first family of food. ⊠ *Fort James* ☎ *268/462–5479* ▭ *No credit cards.*

2

$$–$$$ ✕**Sticky Wicket.** With a dining room framed by flagstone columns and a trendy, open kitchen, this is one of the classiest sports bars imaginable. Cricket is the overriding theme: sit in the posh lounge surrounded by cricket memorabilia or outside on the patio overlooking the equally handsome Stanford Cricket Ground. The menu ranges from snacks, such as the definitive conch fritters, to standouts like fried calamari with lemon-artichoke aioli or anything from the enormous rotisserie. The potent house cocktails and daily specials, not to mention the ambience, remain pure Antillean. This is a splendid respite while waiting for your flight at the airport across the road. ✉*20 Pavilion Dr., Coolidge* ☎*268/481–7000* ▭*AE, D, MC, V.*

CONTINENTAL ✕**The Pavilion.** The airport is a bizarrely incongruous location for a
$$$$ grand restaurant, yet the Pavilion is one of the Caribbean's finest eat-
Fodor'sChoice eries, with tasteful decor, exquisite fare and, yes, jet-set clientele. The
★ building replicates a plantation greathouse; the imposing, ornate main room and silver salver service would be foreboding were it not for the smiling yet ultraprofessional staff. Chef Andrew Knoll, who learned his trade from Emeril Lagasse, proves a worthy BAM-bino. Everything is sourced from top-notch global purveyors (save for fresh local produce such as black pineapple). The chef's New Orleans roots emerge in roasted turkey and gulf shrimp gumbo or "blackened" black grouper with sweet corn–Maine lobster succotash, but he sows his wild "hautes" with such specialties as house-cured foie gras with Royal-Tokaji-ginger braised pears, brioche, and 50-year-old balsamic vinaigrette. Everything is beautifully textured, with a subtle, sophisticated juxtaposition of flavors that slowly detonate on the palate. Go with the decadent degustation wine-pairing menus. The fabulous and fabulously priced list includes some delightfully unusual boutique wines alongside the expected heavy hitters. Ask to tour the 9,000-bottle wine cellar, constructed of antique Wisconsin timber oak, handmade 19th-century Chicago brick, and weathered 17th-century French limestone. A private jet home is optional. ✉*7 Pavilion Dr., Coolidge* ☎*268/480–6800* ⌕*Reservations essential. Jacket required* ▭*AE, D, MC, V* ☉*No dinner Sun., no lunch.*

$$–$$$$ ✕**Coconut Grove.** Coconut palms grow through the roof of this open-
★ air thatched restaurant, flickering candlelight illuminates colorful local murals, waves lap the white sand, and the warm waitstaff provides just the right level of service. Jean-François Bellanger's superbly presented dishes fuse French culinary preparations with island ingredients. Top choices include pan-seared snapper medallions served with roasted sweet potato in a saffron white-wine curry; kingfish tartare accented by tapenade with molasses drizzle and guacamole; and chicken stuffed with creole vegetables in mango-kiwi sauce. The kitchen can be uneven, the wine list is merely serviceable, and the buzzing happy-hour bar crowd lingering well into dinnertime can detract from the otherwise romantic atmosphere. Nonetheless, Coconut Grove straddles the line between casual beachfront boîte and elegant eatery with aplomb. ✉*Siboney Beach Club, Dickenson Bay* ☎*268/462–1538* ▭*AE, D, MC, V.*

ECLECTIC
$$$–$$$$

✕ **The Cove.** Flaming tiki torches flank the entrance of this contemporary architectural take on a plantation greathouse. Inside, a candlelit foyer leads to a handsome polished-wood bar. Scot chef Graham Singer delights in pleasing the eye as well as the palate with exquisite presentations. The upstairs section focuses on what he calls "simpler old-school multicultural food," such as scallop-and-tuna terrine with cucumber and melon emulsion. Downstairs emphasizes more-daring fusion fare (Asian, Mexican, and Italian accents predominate). Sterling starters include braised oxtail terrine with shiitakes, eggdrop soup with shrimp tortellini, and whole quail and lobster over peppered arugula salad with buckwheat-mango vinaigrette. A second downstairs section with an exhibition "courtyard" kitchen lies a few feet above the crashing surf. In fair weather, opt for an upstairs terrace table overlooking the floodlighted ocean. Despite the grandeur, service is warm and welcoming. ✉ *Boon's Point, Soldier's Bay* ☎ *268/562–2683* ⊕ *www.thecove-antigua.com* ⚷ *Reservations essential* ☰ *AE, D, MC, V* ⊘ *No dinner Sun., no lunch Mon.–Sat.*

$$$–$$$$

✕ **Sheer.** This sensuous eatery, a series of tiered wood decks carved into a sheer cliff side, showcases one of the Caribbean's most-ambitious menus. Start with a creative cocktail as you admire the setting sun's pyrotechnics from the staggered, thatched dining nooks, many separated by billowing white-gauze curtains. Chef Nigel Martin revels in daringly unorthodox—even odd—combinations that trigger all sets of taste buds: tuna ceviche and sake-and-wasabi gravlax with Parmesan foam, jellied eggplant relish, and plantain; beef tenderloin tournedos with honey truffled beets, pumpkin rissoles (croquettes), baby leeks, and blue cheese miso; venison carpaccio with andouille-blue potato salad with grapefruit chili; and a dessert of orange-blossom-braised endive (!) with white-chocolate-pistachio *kulfi* (Indian-style ice cream). Sheer closes twice weekly on a rotating schedule, so call ahead. ✉ *CocoBay, Valley Church* ☎ *268/562–2400* ⚷ *Reservations essential* ☰ *AE, D, MC, V* ⊘ *Closed 2 nights per wk. No lunch.*

FRENCH
$$$–$$$$

✕ **Le Bistro.** This Antiguan institution's peach-periwinkle-and-pistachio accents subtly match the tile work, jade chairs, mint china, and painted lighting fixtures. Trellises divide the large space into intimate sections. Chef Patrick Gaducheau delights in blending regional fare with indigenous ingredients, but the kitchen is surprisingly inconsistent, and the service can be stuffy. Opt for daily specials, such as fresh snapper with spinach and grapefruit in thyme-perfumed lime-butter sauce, lobster medallions in basil-accented old-rum sauce with roasted red peppers, and almost anything swaddled in puff pastry. Co-owner Phillippa Esposito doubles as hostess and pastry chef; her passion-fruit mousse and chocolate confections are sublime. ✉ *Hodges Bay* ☎ *268/462–3881* ⚷ *Reservations essential* ☰ *AE, MC, V* ⊘ *Closed Mon. No lunch.*

$$$

✕ **Le Cap Horn.** As Piaf and Aznavour compete with croaking tree frogs in a trellised, plant-filled room lighted by straw lamps, it's easy to imagine yourself in a tropical St. Tropez. From the small but select menu, begin with lobster bisque or escargots in a lovely tomato, onion, and pepper sauce (sop it up with the marvelous home-baked bread); then segue into tiger shrimp swimming in gossamer vanilla-lobster sauce or veal scallop with grapes in cognac sauce. Gustavo Belaunde (he's Peruvian of Catalan extraction) elicits fresh, delicate, almost ethereal flavors from his ingredients; his versatility is displayed in the restaurant's other half, a pizzeria replete with wood-burning oven. Finish with wife Hélène's divine desserts or a cognac and cigar. ✉ *English Harbour* ☎ *268/460–1194* ▭*AE, D, MC, V* ⊘ *Closed Aug., Sept., and Thurs. No lunch.*

ITALIAN
$$–$$$$
★

✕ **La Bussola.** Blend a genuinely *simpatico* welcome with lapping waves, the murmur of jazz, and expert Italian fare and you have Omar Tagliavente and family's recipe for the perfect beachfront bistro. Bleached wood ceilings, billowing white curtains, old island photos of Antigua, and brightly painted plates enhance the relaxed, romantic mood. The presentation is invariably pretty and Omar has a particularly deft hand with seafood; try the salmon grilled in aged balsamic vinegar, lobster thermidor in satiny saffron sauce, or the "fishermen's" spaghetti. Your evening ends with a complimentary grappa, Frangelico, or limoncello (representing northern, central, and southern Italy). La Bussola means "the compass" in Italian, and it certainly takes the right gastronomic direction. ✉ *Runaway Bay* ☎ *268/562–1545* ✍ *Reservations essential* ▭*AE, MC, V* ⊘ *Closed Tues.*

PAN-ASIAN
$$–$$$
★

✕ **East.** Imposing Indonesian carved doors usher you into this bold and sexy Asian fusion spot. Flames flicker in the outdoor lily pond while candles illuminate lacquered dark-wood tables with blood-red napery and oversize fuchsia-color chairs. Exquisite pan-Pacific fare courts perfection through simplicity and precision: prawn spring rolls with hoisin-sweet chili sauce, superlative sashimi, sea scallops with dal and yogurt-cucumber *raita*, and green tea crème brûlée. The small main courses mandate tapas-style dining; the comprehensive wine list is pricey but offers values from intriguing lesser-known regions. ✉ *Carlisle Bay, Old Road, St. Mary's* ☎ *268/484–0000* ✍ *Reservations essential* ▭*AE, D, DC, MC, V.*

$–$$
★

✕ **Kesari.** Adventuresome Aussie chef Darryn Pitman is so enthusiastic about Asian culture and cuisine that he named his son (and this fun, funky, tapas-martini bar) after a popular southern Indian dessert. The just-hip-enough lounge (acid jazz, flickering candles, multihue fountain, low-slung banquettes) is conducive to sampling more than one of the 30-plus cocktails, half of them martinis. Even these display Darryn's brilliant feel for balancing complex tastes. The 20 tapas selections (larger curries and superb sushi are also available) travel the Spice Route from Malaysia (chicken satay) to the Middle East (lamb kebabs with yogurt sauce) in style. His savvy wine selections perfectly complement the flavorful fare. Most nights end in dancing, professional (belly dancers in full regalia) or otherwise (tipsy tabletop), but the vibe remains exuberant without becoming excessive. ✉ *Falmouth Harbour* ☎ *268/460–1361* ▭*MC, V* ⊘ *Closed Mon. and Tues. No lunch.*

BEACHES

Antigua's beaches are public, and many are dotted with resorts that have water-sports outfitters and beach bars. The government does a fairly good job of island-wide maintenance, cleaning up seaweed and garbage, though locals don't always adopt the same prideful attitude. Most restaurant and bars on developed beaches won't charge for beach-chair rentals if you buy lunch or even drinks; otherwise the going rate is usually $3 to $5. Access to some of the finest stretches of sand, such as those at the Five Islands Peninsula resorts (including Galley Bay, Hawksbill by Rex Resorts, and Coconut Beach Club), is somewhat restricted by security gates. Sunbathing topless or in the buff is strictly illegal except on one small beach at Hawksbill by Rex Resorts. Beware that when cruise ships dock in St. John's, buses drop off loads of passengers on most of the west-coast beaches. Choose such a time to tour the island by car, visit one of the more-remote east-end beaches, or take a day trip to Barbuda.

ANTIGUA

Darkwood Beach. This 0.75-mi (1-km) beige ribbon on the southwest coast has stunning views of Montserrat. Although popular with locals on weekends, it's virtually deserted during the week. Waters are generally calm, but there's scant shade, no development other than a basic beach bar, and little to do other than bask in solitude. Its neighbor across the headland (a seven-minute walk along the road), Ffryes Bay, is another fine pristine stretch. ⊕ *2 mi (3 km) south of Jolly Harbour and roughly 0.5 mi (0.75 km) southwest of Valley Church off main coast road.*

Dickenson Bay. Along a lengthy stretch of powder-soft white sand and exceptionally calm water you can find small and large hotels, water sports, concessions, and beachfront restaurants. Be forewarned that many operators such as Big John's Dive can be rather chaotic. Vendors pass by but generally don't hassle sun worshippers. There's decent snorkeling at either point. ⊕ *2 mi (3 km) northeast of St. John's, along main coast road.*

★ **Half Moon Bay.** This 0.75-mi (1-km) ivory crescent is a prime snorkeling and windsurfing area. On the Atlantic side of the island, the water can be quite rough at times, attracting a few intrepid hard-core surfers and wakeboarders. The northeastern end, where a protective reef offers spectacular snorkeling, is much calmer. A tiny bar has restrooms, snacks, and beach chairs. Vendors wander by intermittently; signs of life are few. Half Moon is a real trek (you might end up asking locals directions several times) but one of Antigua's showcase beaches. Follow signs for the villages of St. Philips or Freetown, and pray: all roads are unmarked, and the island's hinterland has no landmarks to guide you. ✉ *On southeast coast, 1.5 mi (2.5 km) from Freetown.*

★ **Johnson's Point/Crab Hill.** This series of connected, deliciously deserted beaches on the southwest coast looks out toward Montserrat, Guadeloupe, St. Kitts, and Nevis. You can explore a ruined fort at one end. Notable beach bar-restaurants include OJ's (try the snapper) and Turner's; both are superb places to applaud the spectacular sunsets, as is the delightful 3 Martini Bar, Restaurant & Apartment across the road. The water is generally placid, though snorkelers will be disappointed. ⊠ *3 mi (5 km) south of Jolly Harbour complex on main west-coast road.*

Pigeon Point. Near Falmouth Harbour lie these two fine white-sand beaches. The leeward side is calmer, the windward side is rockier, and there are sensational views and snorkeling around the point. Several restaurants and bars are nearby, though Bumpkin's satisfies most on-site needs. There are two turnoffs from the main south-coast road; the easiest to identify is just past the turn for the Antigua Yacht Club. ⊠ *Off main south-coast road, southwest of Falmouth.*

Runaway Beach. An often unoccupied stretch of bone-white sand, this beach is still rebuilding after years of hurricane erosion, with just enough palms left for shelter. Both the water and the scene are relatively calm, and beach restaurants such as Sandhaven and La Bussola offer cool shade and cold beer. Hug the lagoon past the entrance to Siboney Beach Club to get here. ⊠ *Approximately 2 mi (3 km) northwest of St. John's, down main north-coast road from Dickenson Bay.*

BARBUDA

Fodor'sChoice
★
Pink Beach. This practically deserted 8-mi (13-km) stretch reaches from Spanish Point to Palmetto Point: you can sometimes walk miles without encountering another footprint. This classic strand is a champagne hue, with sand soft as silk; crushed coral often imparts a rosy glint in the sun, hence its (unofficial) name. There are few signs of life now that Beach House and K Club have closed. The water can be rough with a strongish undertow in spots, though it's mainly protected by the reefs that make the island a diving mecca. If you're coming for the day, hire a taxi to take you here, since none of the roads are well marked. ⊠ *1 mi (1.5 km) from ferry and airstrip along unmarked roads.*

SPORTS & THE OUTDOORS

Several all-inclusives offer day passes that permit use of all sporting facilities from tennis courts to water-sports concessions, as well as free drinks and meals. The cost begins at $40 for singles (but can be as much as $180 for couples at Sandals), and hours generally run from 8 AM to 6 PM, with extensions available until 2 AM. Antigua has long been famed for its cricketers (such as Viv Richards and Richie Richardson); aficionados will find one of the Caribbean's finest cricket grounds right by the airport, with major test matches running January through June.

ADVENTURE TOURS

Antigua is developing its ecotourist opportunities, and several memorable offshore experiences involve more than just snorkeling. The archipelago of islets coupled with a full mangrove swamp off the northeast coast is unique in the Caribbean.

★ **Adventure Antigua** (☎268/727–3261 ⊕*www.adventureantigua.com*) is run by enthusiastic Eli Fuller, who is knowledgeable not only about the ecosystem and geography of Antigua but also about its history and politics (his grandfather was the American consul). His thorough seven-hour excursion (Eli dubs it "re-creating my childhood explorations") includes stops at Guiana Island (for lunch and guided snorkeling; turtles, barracuda, and stingrays are common sightings), Pelican Island (more snorkeling), Bird Island (hiking to vantage points to admire the soaring ospreys and frigate and red-billed tropic birds), and "Hell's Gate" (a striking limestone rock formation where the more intrepid may hike and swim through sunken caves and tide pools painted with pink and maroon algae). The company also offers a fun, shorter "amusement park ride" variation on a racing boat catering to adrenaline junkies who "feel the need for speed."

"Paddles" Kayak Eco Adventure (✉*Seaton's Village* ☎268/463–1944 or 268/560–3782 ⊕*www.antiguapaddles.com*) takes you on a 3½-hour tour of serene mangroves and inlets with informative narrative about the fragile ecosystem of the swamp and reefs and the rich diversity of flora and fauna. The tour ends with a hike to sunken caves and snorkeling in the North Sound Marine Park. Experienced guides double as kayaking and snorkeling instructors, making this an excellent opportunity for novices.

☾ **Stingray City Antigua** (✉*Seaton's Village* ☎268/562–7297) is a carefully reproduced "natural" environment nicknamed by staffers the "retirement home," though the 30-plus stingrays, ranging from infants to seniors, are frisky. You can stroke, feed, even hold the striking gliders, as well as snorkel in deeper, protected waters. The tour guides do a marvelous job of explaining the animals' habits, from feeding to breeding, and their predators (including man).

BICYCLING

Bicycling isn't terribly arduous on Antigua, except in the southernmost region, where the roads soar, dip, and corkscrew. **Bike Plus** (✉*Independence Dr., St. John's* ☎268/462–2453) offers rentals, which run about $15 a day. Everything from racing models to mountain bikes is available.

BOATING

Antigua's circular geographic configuration makes boating easy, while its many lovely harbors and coves provide splendid anchorages. Experienced boaters will particularly enjoy Antigua's east coast, which is far more rugged and has several islets; be sure to get a good nautical map, as there are numerous minireefs that can be treacherous. If you're just looking for a couple of hours of wave hopping, stick to the Dickenson Bay or Jolly Harbour area.

Nicholson Yacht Charters (☎268/460–1530 or 305/433–5533 ⊕*www.nicholson-charters.com*) are real professionals, true pioneers in Caribbean sailing, with three generations of experience. A long-established island family, they can offer you anything from a 20-foot ketch to a giant schooner.

Sunsail (☎268/460–2615 or 800/327–2276 ⊕*www.sunsail.com*) has an extensive modern fleet of dinghies and 32-foot day-sailers available for $25 per half day, $50 for a full day. They also arrange bareboat yachting, often in conjunction with hotel stays.

DIVING

Antigua is an unsung diving destination, with plentiful undersea sights to explore, from coral canyons to sea caves. Barbuda alone features roughly 200 wrecks on its treacherous reefs. The most accessible wreck is the 1890s bark *Andes,* not far out in Deep Bay, off Five Islands Peninsula. Among the favorite sites are **Green Island, Cades Reef,** and **Bird Island** (a national park). Memorable sightings include turtles, stingrays, and barracuda darting amid basalt walls, hulking boulders, and stray 17th-century anchors and cannon. One advantage is accessibility in many spots for shore divers and snorkelers. Double-tank dives run about $90.

Big John's Dive Antigua (⊠*Rex Halcyon Cove Beach Resort, Dickenson Bay* ☎268/462–3483 ⊕*www.diveantigua.com*) offers certification courses and day and night dives. Advantages include the central location, knowledgeable crew, satellite technology sounding the day's best dive sites, free drinks after dives, and exceptionally priced packages. Drawbacks include generally noisy groups and inconsistent maintenance (less safety than hygiene concerns) now that John doesn't personally supervise trips.

Dockyard Divers (⊠*Nelson's Dockyard, English Harbour* ☎268/460–1178), owned by British ex-merchant seaman Captain A. G. "Tony" Fincham, is one of the island's most-established outfits and offers diving and snorkeling trips, PADI courses, and dive packages with accommodations. They're geared to seasoned divers, but staff work patiently with novices.

FISHING

Antigua's waters teem with game fish such as marlin, wahoo, and tuna. Most boat trips include equipment, lunch, and drinks. Figure at least $495 for a half day, $750 for a full day, for up to six people.

The 45-foot Hatteras Sportfisherman **Obsession** (☎268/462–2824) has top-of-the-line equipment, including an international-standard fighting chair, outriggers, and handcrafted rods.

Overdraft (☎268/464–4954 or 268/462–3112 ⊕*www.antiguafishing. com*) is a sleek, spacious fiberglass 40-footer outfitted with the latest techno-gadgetry and operated by Frank Hart, a professional fisherman who knows the waters intimately and regales clients with stories of his trade. He also rents the 26-foot *H2O,* a ProKat versatile enough to accommodate fly-fishing and deeper-water bay bait fishing.

GOLF

Though Antigua hardly qualifies as a duffer's delight, its two 18-hole courses offer varied layouts.

Cedar Valley Golf Club (⊠ *Friar's Hill* ☎ *268/462–0161* ⊕ *www.cedarvalleygolf.ag*), northeast of St. John's, has a par-70, 6,157-yard, 18-hole course. The not terribly well-maintained terrain offers some challenges with tight hilly fairways and numerous doglegs. The 5th hole has exceptional ocean vistas from the top of the tee, while the 9th offers the trickiest design. Greens fees are $35; carts are $30.

Jolly Harbour Golf Course (⊠ *Jolly Harbour* ☎ *268/462–3085 or 268/462–7771* ⊕ *www.jollyharbourantigua.com*) is a par-71, 6,001-yard, 18-hole course designed by Karl Litten. The layout is hilly and lushly tropical, with seven lakes adding to the challenge. Unfortunately, drainage is poor, upkeep spotty, and the pro shop and "19th hole" barely adequate. At least it's reasonable: greens fees are $57.50 ($97.75 including cart).

HORSEBACK RIDING

Comparatively dry Antigua is best for beach rides, though you won't find anything wildly romantic and deserted à la *The Black Stallion*. **Spring Hill Riding Club** (⊠ *Falmouth* ☎ *268/460–7787 or 268/460–1333* ⊕ *www.springhillridingclub.com*) really specializes in equestrian lessons in show jumping and dressage but also offers $40 to $60 trail rides on the beach or through the bush past ruined forts; half-hour private lessons from a British Horse Society instructor are $25.

SAILING & SNORKELING

Not a sailor yourself? Consider signing up for one of the following boat tours. Each tour provides a great opportunity to enjoy the seafaring life while someone else captains the ship.

Miguel's Holiday Adventures (☎ *268/460–9978 or 268/723–7418* ⊕ *www.pricklypearisland.com*) leaves every Tuesday, Thursday, and Saturday morning at 10 AM from the Hodges Bay jetty for snorkeling, rum punches, and lunch at Prickly Pear Island, which offers both shallow- and deepwater snorkeling. In this comfortable family operation, Miguel's wife, Josephine, prepares an authentic, lavish West Indian buffet including lobster, while Miguel and his son Terrence are caring instructors.

Tropical Adventures (☎ *268/462–2064 or 268/480–1225* ⊕ *www.tropicalad.com*) operates Barbuda day trips on the catamaran *Excellence* that overflow with rum and high spirits, as do circumnavigations of Antigua. The company also operates slightly more-sedate, intimate catamaran cruises on the *Tiami*.

Wadadli Cats (☎ *268/462–4792* ⊕ *www.wadadlicats.com*) offers several cruises, including a circumnavigation of the island and snorkeling at Bird Island or Cades Reef, on its five sleek catamarans, including the handsome, fully outfitted *Spirit of Antigua*. Prices are fair, and advance bookers get a free T-shirt.

TENNIS & SQUASH

Most larger resorts have their own tennis courts, but guests have top priority. **BBR Sportive Complex** (⊠ *Jolly Harbour* ☎ *268/462–6260*) offers two clay and two Astroturf courts, instruction, and a squash court. Its lively Steely Bar offers happy hours, theme buffet dinners, and occasional live entertainment or karaoke.

Temo Sports Complex (⊠ *Falmouth Bay* ☎ *268/463–6376 or 268/460–1781*) has four floodlighted, synthetic-grass tennis courts and two glass-backed squash courts.

WINDSURFING & KITEBOARDING

Most major hotels offer windsurfing equipment. The best areas are Nonsuch Bay and the east coast (notably Half Moon and Willoughby bays), which is slightly less protected and has a challenging juxtaposition of sudden calms and gusts.

KiteAntigua (⊠ *Jabberwock Beach* ☎ *268/460–3414 or 268/727–3983* ⊕ *www.kiteantigua.com*) offers lessons in the Caribbean's hot new sport, kite boarding, where a futuristic surfboard with harness is propelled only by an inflated kite; kite-board rentals (for the certified) are also available. The varied lesson packages are expensive but thorough. KiteAntigua closes from September through November, when winds aren't optimal. The center is on a stretch near the airport, but road trips to secret spots are arranged for experienced kite surfers seeking that sometimes harrowing "high."

Patrick Scales of **Windsurfing Antigua** (⊠ *Dickenson Bay* ☎ *268/461–9463 or 268/773–9463*) has long been one of Antigua's, if not the Caribbean's, finest instructors; he now offers a mobile service in high season. He provides top-flight equipment for $25 per hour ($60 per day), all-day lessons for $85, and specialty tours to Half Moon Bay and other favorite spots for experienced surfers.

ZIP-LINING

If you're feeling adventurous, you can play Tarzan and Jane at **Antigua Rainforest Canopy Tours** (⊠ *Fig Dr., Wallings* ☎ *268/562–6363* ⊕ *www.antiguarainforest.com*), which started roping customers at the end of 2006. You should be in fairly good condition for the ropes challenges, which require upper-body strength and stamina, but anyone (vertigo or acrophobia sufferers beware) can navigate the intentionally rickety suspension bridges, then fly (in secure harnesses) over a rain-forest-filled valley from one towering turpentine tree to the next. There will be 23 stations upon completion, as well as a snack bar and interpretive signage. First-timers fear not: the "rangers" are affable, amusing, and accomplished. Admission is $85. It's open daily 8–6.

SHOPPING

Antigua's duty-free shops are at Heritage Quay, one reason so many cruise ships call here. Bargains can be found on perfumes, liqueurs, and liquor (including, of course, Antiguan rum), jewelry, china, and crystal. As for other local items, look for straw hats, baskets, batik, pottery, and hand-printed cotton clothing. Fine artists to look for include Gilly Gobinet, Heather Doram, and Heike Petersen (delightful dolls and quilts).

SHOPPING AREAS

Redcliffe Quay, on the waterfront at the south edge of St. John's, is by far the most appealing shopping area. Several restaurants and more than 30 boutiques, many with one-of-a-kind wares, are set around landscaped courtyards shaded by colorful trees. **Heritage Quay,** in St. John's, has 35 shops—including many that are duty-free—that cater to the cruise-ship crowd, which docks almost at its doorstep. Outlets here include Benetton, the Body Shop, Sunglass Hut, Dolce and Gabbana, and Oshkosh B'Gosh. There are also shops along **St. John's, St. Mary's, High,** and **Long streets.** The tangerine-and-lilac-hue four-story **Vendor's Mall** at the intersection of Redcliffe and Thames streets gathers the pushy, pesky vendors that once clogged the narrow streets. It's jammed with stalls; air-conditioned indoor shops sell some higher-price, if not higher-quality, merchandise. On the west coast the Mediterranean-style, arcaded **Jolly Harbour Marina** holds some interesting galleries and shops.

SPECIALTY STORES

ALCOHOL & TOBACCO

Manuel Dias Liquor Store (✉ *Long and Market Sts., St. John's* ☎ *268/462–0490*) has a wide selection of Caribbean rums and liqueurs.

Quin Farara (✉ *Long St. and Corn Alley, St. John's* ☎ *268/462–3869* ✉ *Heritage Quay, St. John's* ☎ *268/462–1737* ✉ *Jolly Harbour* ☎ *268/462–6245*) has terrific deals on both hard liquor and wines as well as cigars.

ART

Fine Art Framing (✉ *Redcliffe Quay, St. John's* ☎ *268/562–1019*) carries Jennifer Meranto's incomparable hand-colored black-and-white photos of Caribbean scenes; Heather Doram's exquisite, intricately woven "collage" wall hangings; and ever-changing exhibits.

★ **Harmony Hall** (✉ *Brown's Mill Bay, Brown's Mill* ☎ *268/460–4120*) remains Antigua's top exhibition venue. A large exhibit space is used for one-person shows; other rooms display works in various media, from Aussie aboriginal carvings to Antillean pottery. The sublime historic ambience, sweeping vistas, and fine Italian fare compensate for the remote location.

BOOKS & MAGAZINES

The **Best of Books** (⊠ *Lower St. Mary's St., St. John's* ☎ *268/562–3198*) is an excellent, extensive source for everything from local cookbooks and nature guides to international newspapers. Check out the books of Jamaica Kincaid, whose writing about her native Antigua has won international acclaim. You'll also find an intriguing selection of crafts and artworks.

CLOTHING

Exotic Antigua (⊠ *Redcliffe Quay, St. John's* ☎ *268/562–1288*) sells everything from antique Indonesian ikat throws to crepe de chine caftans to Tommy Bahama resort wear.

★ At **Galley Boutique** (⊠ *Nelson's Dockyard, English Harbour* ☎ *268/460–1525*), Janey Easton personally seeks out exclusive creations from both international (Calvin Klein, Adrienne Vittadini) and local Caribbean designers, ranging from swimwear to evening garb. She also sells handicrafts and lovely hammocks.

Jacaranda (⊠ *Redcliffe Quay, St. John's* ☎ *268/462–1888*) sells batik, sarongs, and swimwear as well as Caribbean food, perfumes, soaps, and artwork.

Jingjok (⊠ *Redcliffe Quay* ☎ *268/462–3862*) sells gorgeously hued, handmade batik linen and cotton resort wear.

New Gates (⊠ *Redcliffe Quay, St. John's* ☎ *268/562–1627*) is a duty-free authorized dealer for such name brands as Ralph Lauren, Calvin Klein, and Tommy Hilfiger.

★ **Noreen Phillips** (⊠ *Redcliffe Quay, St. John's* ☎ *268/462–3127*) creates glitzy appliquéd and beaded evening wear—inspired by the colors of the sea and sunset—in sensuous fabrics ranging from chiffon and silk to Italian lace and Indian brocade.

Sunseakers (⊠ *Heritage Quay, St. John's* ☎ *268/462–3618*) racks up every conceivable bathing suit and cover-up—from bikini thongs to sarongs—by top designers.

DUTY-FREE GOODS

Abbott's (⊠ *Heritage Quay, St. John's* ☎ *268/462–3108*) sells luxury items from Breitling watches to Belleek china to Kosta Boda art glass in a luxurious, air-conditioned showroom.

Lipstick (⊠ *Heritage Quay, St. John's* ☎ *268/562–1130*) imports high-priced scents and cosmetics, from Clarins to Clinique and Givenchy to Guerlain.

Passions (⊠ *Heritage Quay, St. John's* ☎ *268/562–5295*) gives Abbott's a run for its (and your) considerable money on luxury brands like Chanel, Hermès, and Lalique.

HANDICRAFTS

★ **Cedars Pottery** (⊠ *St. Claire Estate, Buckleys* ☎ *268/460–5293*) is the airy studio of Michael and Imogen Hunt. Michael produces a vivid line of domestic ware and Zen-simple teapots, vases, and water fountains featuring rich earth hues and sensuous lines. Imogen fashions ethereal paper-clay fish sculptures, and mask-shape, intricately laced light fixtures and candelabras.

Eureka (⊠ *Thames St., St. John's* ☎ *268/560–3654*) spans the globe, from Azerbaijani handblown glass to Zambian weavings and carvings.

Isis (⊠ *Redcliffe Quay, St. John's* ☎ *268/462–4602*) sells island and international bric-a-brac, such as antique jewelry, hand-carved walking sticks, and glazed pottery.

The **Pottery Shop** (⊠ *Redcliffe Quay, St. John's* ☎ *268/562–1264 or 268/462–9503*) sells the work of gifted potter Sarah Fuller, whose hand-painted tiles, wind chimes, and plates and cobalt-blue glazes are striking.

★ **Rhythm of Blue Gallery** (⊠ *Dockyard Dr., English Harbour* ☎ *268/562–2230*) is co-owned by Nancy Nicholson, who's renowned for her exquisite glazed and matte-finish ceramics, featuring Caribbean-pure shades, as well as her black-and-white yachting photos.

Things Local (⊠ *Nelson's Dockyard, English Harbour* ☎ *268/562–5386 or 268/770–5780*) features the wondrous wood carvings of Carl Henry, who fashions local mahogany into boats, fish, and warri boards (warri being an African game brought over to the Caribbean).

JEWELRY

Colombian Emeralds (⊠ *Heritage Quay, St. John's* ☎ *268/462–3462*) is the largest retailer of Colombian emeralds in the world and also carries a wide variety of other gems.

Diamonds International (⊠ *Heritage Quay, St. John's* ☎ *268/481–1880*) has a huge selection of loose diamonds as well as a variety of rings, brooches, bracelets, and pendants. Several resorts have branches.

★ The **Goldsmitty** (⊠ *Redcliffe Quay, St. John's* ☎ *268/462–4601*) is Hans Smit, an expert goldsmith who turns gold, black coral, and precious and semiprecious stones into one-of-a-kind works of art.

NIGHTLIFE

Most of Antigua's evening entertainment takes place at the resorts, which occasionally present calypso singers, steel bands, limbo dancers, and folkloric groups. Check with the tourist office for up-to-date information. In addition, a cluster of clubs and bars pulsate into the night in season around the English/Falmouth Harbour area.

BARS

It's always a party at busy bright trattoria **Abracadabra** (⊠ *Nelson's Dockyard, English Harbour* ☎ *268/460–2701*). Late nights often turn into a disco with live music or DJs spinning reggae and 1980s dance music, while special events run from masquerades to fashion shows.

★ **beach** (⊠ *Dickenson Bay* ☎ *268/480–6940*) is a sophisticated-funky combination of casual beach bar, lounge, and bistro, hung with striking photographs of local scenes.

Castaways (⊠ *Jolly Harbour* ☎ *268/562–4445*) is a boisterous beach bar–bistro with a thatched roof and colorful local murals that serves an inexpensive menu of tapas and pub grub along with occasional entertainment.

The French fare is incidental at **HQ** (⊠*Nelson's Dockyard, English Harbour* ☎*268/562–2563*), where a plush lounge outfitted with cushy sofas and crystal chandeliers hosts slinky jazz combos and pianists. Antony Ricard, the Parisian owner, keeps several instruments on hand for impromptu gigs.

★ **Indigo on the Beach** (⊠*Carlisle Bay, Old Road* ☎*268/480–0000*) is a soigné yet relaxed spot any time of day for creative tapas, salads, grills, and burgers, but the beautiful people turn out in force come evening to pose at the fiber-optically lighted bar, or on white lounges scattered with throw pillows.

The **Inn at English Harbour Bar** (⊠*English Harbour* ☎*268/460–1014*), with its green leather, wood beams, fieldstone walls, 19th-century maps, steering-wheel chandeliers, petit point upholstery, and maritime prints, is uncommonly refined.

The **Mainbrace Pub** (⊠*Copper & Lumber Store Hotel, English Harbour* ☎*268/460–1058*) has a historic ambience and is known as a beer, darts, and fish-and-chips kind of hangout for the boating set.

The **Mad Mongoose** (⊠*Falmouth Harbour* ☎*268/463–7900*) is a wildly popular yachty (and singles) joint, splashed in vivid Rasta colors, with tapas and martini menus, live music Tuesday and Friday, a game room, and satellite TV.

Sandhaven (⊠*Runaway Bay* ☎*268/562–5566*) is a funky place that attracts world-renowned cricketers as well as a jovial crowd for liberal happy hours, an extensive late-night menu running from dirt-cheap burgers and pizza to more-substantial grilled seafood, live mike and karaoke nights, live bands on weekends, and dirty dancing on the sand.

★ **Shirley Heights Lookout** (⊠*Shirley Heights* ☎*268/460–1785*) hosts Sunday-afternoon barbecues that continue into the night with reggae, soca, and steel-band music and dancing that sizzle like the ribs on the grill. Residents and visitors gather for boisterous fun, the latest gossip, and great sunsets. Most tourist groups vanish by 7 PM, when the real partying begins.

★ **Trappa's** (⊠*Main Rd., English Harbour* ☎*268/562–3534*) is a hipster hangout set in a bamboo-walled courtyard hung with huge hibiscus paintings. It serves delectable, sizable tapas (tuna sashimi, deep-fried Brie with black-currant jelly, Thai mango chicken curry, beer-batter shrimp with garlic dip) for reasonable prices (EC$23–EC$46) into the wee hours. Live music is often on the menu.

CASINOS

There are three full casinos on Antigua (at this writing, a fourth was planned to open next to the Sandals Mediterranean Village by 2009), as well as several holes-in-the-wall that have mostly one-arm bandits. Hours depend on the season, so it's best to inquire upon your arrival.

Grand Princess Casino (⊠*Jolly Harbour* ☎*268/562–9900*) occupies slick, three-story digs combining English colonial and Mediterranean Revival elements; Saffron, it's swank Indian restaurant, has surprisingly good food.

You can find abundant slots and gaming tables at the somewhat dilapidated, unintentionally retro (icicle chandeliers, Naugahyde seats, and 1970s soul crooners on the sound system) **King's Casino** (⊠ *Heritage Quay, St. John's* ☎ *268/462–1727*). The best time to go is Friday nights, which jump with energetic karaoke competitions, live bands, and dancing.

Part of the refined Rush complex, **Madison's** (⊠ *Runaway Bay* ☎ *268/ 562–7874* ⊕ *www.rushantigua.com*) offers table games such as Texas Hold 'Em in a handsome space (jazz bands play weekends); Leah's is its sexy waterfront fusion eatery.

DANCE CLUBS

The Coast (⊠ *Heritage Quay, St. John's* ☎ *268/562–2678* ⊕ *www.coast. ag*) attracts a casually swanky, over-21 mix of locals and tourists for fine island food, rollicking live bands, fire-blowing bartenders, and the latest in techno and house in a dockside setting.

Diamond Ice (⊠ *All Saints Rd., St. John's* ☎ *268/562–6828*) is a very local spot, friendly but rowdy, with dance and karaoke competitions throughout the week.

The Gallery (⊠ *Dockyard Dr., English Harbour* ☎ *268/562–5678*) serves up carnivores' delights from the grill, but it's really a prime Grade-A meat market after 10 PM nearly every night, when yachties and locals shimmy to DJ Olivier's soca-house-EuroPop mix.

Rush (⊠ *Runaway Bay* ☎ *268/562–7874*) lures mostly young, lively locals in cool club gear for disco, Latin, and reggae-soca mixes; sea views from the romantic terrace; and the Conors Billiards Lounge (which opens earlier, with happy hours and pub grub).

EXPLORING ANTIGUA

Hotels provide free island maps, but you should get your bearings before heading out on the road. Street names aren't listed (except in St. John's), though *some* easy-to-spot signs lead the way to major restaurants and resorts. Locals generally give directions in terms of landmarks (turn left at the yellow house, or right at the big tree). Wear a swimsuit under your clothes—one of the sights to strike your fancy might be a secluded beach.

WHAT TO SEE

★ **Barbuda.** This flat, 62-square-mi (161-square-km) coral atoll—with 17 mi (27 km) of gleaming white-sand beaches (sand is the island's main export)—is 26 mi (42 km) north of Antigua. Most of the island's 1,200 people live in Codrington. Nesting terns, turtles, and frigate birds outnumber residents at least 10 to 1. Goats, guinea fowl, deer, and wild boar roam the roads, all fair game for local kitchens. A few very basic efficiencies and guesthouses exist, but most visitors stay overnight at the deluxe Coco Point Lodge (two other glam properties have closed). Pink Beach lures beachcombers, a bird sanctuary attracts ornithologists, caves and sinkholes filled with rain forest or underground pools

Barbuda

GOAT ISLAND
RABBIT ISLAND
Goat Pt.
Hog Pt.
Billy Pt.
The Caves
Two Foot Bay
Cedar-Tree Pt.
Codrington Lagoon
Bird Sanctuary
Codrington
Low Bay
Airstrip
Martello Tower
The River Landing
Palmetto Pt.
The Castle
Pink Beach
Airstrip
Spanish Pt.

0   5 miles
0   5 km

(containing rare, even unique crustacean species) attract spelunkers, while reefs and roughly 200 offshore wrecks draw divers and snorkelers. Barbuda's sole historic ruin is the 18th-century, cylindrical, 56-foot-tall **Martello Tower,** which was probably a lighthouse built by the Spaniards prior to English occupation. The **Frigate Bird Sanctuary,** a wide mangrove-filled lagoon, is home to an estimated 400 species of birds, including frigate birds with 8-foot wingspans. Your hotel can make arrangements.

You can fly to Barbuda from Antigua on Carib Aviation, a 15-minute flight, or go by boat on *Barbuda Express,* although despite the catamaran's innovative wave-cutting design and its friendly experienced crew, the 95-minute ride is extremely bumpy ("a chiropractor's nightmare— or fantasy," quipped one passenger). Day trips by air are arranged by D&J Tours (⇨ *Tour Options in Antigua Essentials).*

Betty's Hope. Just outside the village of Pares, a marked dirt road leads to Antigua's first sugar plantation, founded in 1650. You can tour the twin windmills, various ruins, still-functional crushing machinery, and the visitor center's exhibits on the island's sugar era. The private trust overseeing the restoration has yet to realize its ambitious, environmentally aware plans to replant indigenous crops destroyed by the extensive sugarcane plantings. ⊠*Pares* ☎*268/462–1469* ⊕*www.anti-guamuseums.org* ⊡*$2* ⊘*Tues.–Sat. 10–4.*

Devil's Bridge. This limestone arch formation, sculpted by the crashing breakers of the Atlantic at Indian Town, is a national park. Blowholes have been carved by the hissing, spitting surf. The park also encompasses some archaeological excavations of Carib artifacts.

Falmouth. This town sits on a lovely bay backed by former sugar plantations and sugar mills. The most important historic site here is St. Paul's Church, which was rebuilt on the site of a church once used by troops during the Horatio Nelson period.

Fig Tree Drive. This often muddy, rutted, steep road takes you through the rain forest, which is rich in mangoes, pineapples, and banana trees (*fig* is the Antiguan word for "banana"). The rain-forest area is the hilliest part of the island—Boggy Peak, to the west, is the highest point, at 1,319 feet. At its crest, Elaine Francis sells seasonal local fruit juices—ginger, guava, sorrel, passion fruit—and homemade jams at a stall she dubs the Culture Shop. A few houses down (look for the orange windows) is the atelier of noted island artist Sallie Harker (shimmering seascapes and vividly hued fish incorporating gold leaf). You can also pass through several tranquil villages with charming churches, and you'll find Antigua Rainforest Canopy Tours (⇨*Zip-lining under Sports & the Outdoors earlier in this chapter*) here.

Ft. George. East of Liberta—one of the first settlements founded by freed slaves—on Monk's Hill, this fort was built from 1689 to 1720. Among the ruins are the sites for 32 cannons, water cisterns, the base of the old flagstaff, and some of the original buildings.

★ **Harmony Hall.** Northeast of Freetown (follow the signs), this delightful art gallery–cum–restaurant is built on the foundation of a 17th-century sugar-plantation greathouse. Artists Graham Davis and Peter and Annabella Proudlock co-founded the original Jamaican outpost, but the Antigua facility is run by enterprising Italians who operate a superb restaurant and several chic charming cottages. (They also plan to base their "Dragon" Yacht fleet here and run regular regattas.) Its remote location is a headache, but Harmony Hall's seamless blend of historic ambience, panoramic ocean views, stellar food, and sterling service provides a feast for all the senses. Allot the whole afternoon to enjoy lunch, browse through the exhibits, comb the beach, and perhaps even snorkel at nearby Green Island via the property's boat, *Luna.* ⊠*Brown's Mill Bay, Brown's Mill* ☎*268/463–8657 or 268/460–4120* ⊕*www.harmonyhall.com* ⊘*Mid-Nov.–June, daily 10–6.*

Megaliths of Greencastle Hill. It's an arduous climb to these eerie rock slabs in the south-central part of the island. Some say the megaliths were set up by early inhabitants for their worship of the sun and moon or as devices for measuring time astronomically; others believe they're nothing more than unusual geological formations.

Fodor's Choice **Nelson's Dockyard.** Antigua's most famous attraction is the world's only ★ Georgian-era dockyard still in use, a treasure trove for history buffs and nautical nuts alike. In 1671 the governor of the Leeward Islands wrote to the Council for Foreign Plantations in London, pointing out the advantages of this landlocked harbor. By 1704 English Harbour was in regular use as a garrisoned station.

In 1784, 26-year-old Horatio Nelson sailed in on the HMS *Boreas* to serve as captain and second-in-command of the Leeward Island Station. Under him was the captain of the HMS *Pegasus*, Prince William Henry, duke of Clarence, who was later crowned King William IV. The prince acted as best man when Nelson married Fannie Nisbet on Nevis in 1787.

When the Royal Navy abandoned the station at English Harbour in 1889, it fell into a state of decay, though adventuresome yachties still lived there in near-primitive conditions. The Society of the Friends of English Harbour began restoring it in 1951; it reopened with great fanfare as Nelson's Dockyard, November 14, 1961. Within the compound are crafts shops, restaurants, and two splendidly restored 18th-century hotels, the Admiral's Inn and the Copper & Lumber Store Hotel, worth peeking into. (The latter, occupying a supply store for Nelson's Caribbean fleet, is a particularly fine example of Georgian architecture and has an interior courtyard evoking Old England.) The Dockyard is a hub for oceangoing yachts and serves as headquarters for the annual Sailing Week Regatta in late April and early May. Water taxis will ferry you between points for EC$5. The Dockyard National Park also includes serene nature trails accessing beaches, rock pools, and crumbling plantation ruins and hilltop forts.

The **Dockyard Museum,** in the original Naval Officer's House, presents ship models, mock-ups of English Harbour, displays on the people who worked there and typical ships that docked, silver regatta trophies, maps, prints, antique navigational instruments, and Nelson's very own telescope and tea caddy. ⊠ *English Harbour* ☎ *268/481–5022, 268/463–1060, 268/460–1379 for National Parks Authority* ⊕ *www.antiguamuseums.org* ☑ *$2 suggested donation* ☉ *Daily 8–5.*

NEED A BREAK?

The restaurant at the Admiral's Inn (⊠ *Nelson's Dockyard, English Harbour* ☎ *268/460–1027*) is a must for Anglophiles and mariners. Soak up the centuries at the inside bar, where 18th-century sailors reputedly carved their ships' names on the dark timbers. Most diners sit on the flagstone terrace under shady Australian gums to enjoy the views of the harbor complex; yachts seem close enough to eavesdrop. Specialties include pumpkin soup and fresh snapper with equally fresh limes.

Parham. This sleepy village is a splendid example of a traditional colonial settlement. St. Peter's Church, built in 1840 by English architect Thomas Weekes, is an octagonal Italianate building with unusual ribbed wooden ceiling, whose facade is richly decorated with stucco and keystone work, though it suffered considerable damage during an 1843 earthquake.

St. John's. Antigua's capital, with some 45,000 inhabitants (approximately half the island's population), lies at sea level at the inland end of a sheltered northwestern bay. Although it has seen better days, a couple of notable historic sights and some good waterfront shopping areas make it worth a visit.

Signs at the **Museum of Antigua & Barbuda** say PLEASE TOUCH, encouraging you to explore Antigua's past. Try your hand at the educational video games or squeeze a cassava through a *matapi* (grass sieve). Exhibits interpret the nation's history, from its geological birth to its political independence in 1981. There are fossil and coral remains from some 34 million years ago; models of a sugar plantation and a wattle-and-daub house; an Arawak canoe; and a wildly eclectic assortment of objects from cannonballs to 1920s telephone exchanges. The museum occupies the former courthouse, which dates from 1750. The superlative museum gift shop carries such unusual items as calabash purses, seed earrings, warri boards, and lignum vitae pipes, as well as historic maps and local books (including engrossing, detailed monographs on varied subjects by longtime resident, the late Desmond Nicholson). ⊠ *Long and Market Sts.* ☎ *268/462–1469* ⊕ *www.antiguamuseums.org* ☏ *$2 suggested donation* ☉ *Sun.–Thurs. 8:30–4, Fri. 8:30–3, Sat. 10–2.*

At the south gate of the **Anglican Cathedral of St. John the Divine** are figures of St. John the Baptist and St. John the Divine, said to have been taken from one of Napoléon's ships and brought to Antigua. The original church was built in 1681, replaced by a stone building in 1745, and destroyed by an earthquake in 1843. The present neo-baroque building dates from 1845; the parishioners had the interior completely encased in pitch pine, hoping to forestall future earthquake damage. The church attained cathedral status in 1848. Tombstones bear eerily eloquent testament to the colonial days. ⊠ *Between Long and Newgate Sts.* ☎ *268/461–0082.*

Shopaholics head directly for **Heritage Quay,** an ugly multimillion-dollar complex. The two-story buildings contain stores that sell duty-free goods, sportswear, T-shirts, down-island imports (paintings, T-shirts, straw baskets), and local crafts. There are also restaurants, a bandstand, and a casino. Cruise-ship passengers disembark here from the 500-foot-long pier. Expect heavy shilling. ⊠ *High and Thames Sts.*

Redcliffe Quay, at the water's edge just south of Heritage Quay, is the most appealing part of St. John's. Attractively restored (and superbly re-created) buildings in a riot of cotton-candy colors house shops, restaurants, and boutiques and are linked by courtyards and landscaped walkways. At the far south end of town, where Market Street forks into Valley and All Saints roads, haggling goes on every Friday and Saturday, when locals jam the **Public Market** to buy and sell fruits, vegetables, fish, and spices. Ask before you aim a camera; your subject may expect a tip. This is old-time Caribbean shopping, a jambalaya of sights, sounds, and smells.

Shirley Heights. This bluff affords a spectacular view of English Harbour. The heights are named for Sir Thomas Shirley, the governor who fortified the harbor in 1787. At the top is Shirley Heights Lookout, a restaurant built into the remnants of the 18th-century fortifications. Most notable for its boisterous Sunday barbecues that continue into the night with live music and dancing, it serves dependable burgers, pumpkin soup, grilled meats, and rum punches.

Not far from Shirley Heights is the **Dows Hill Interpretation Centre,** where observation platforms provide still more sensational vistas of the English Harbour area. A multimedia sound-and-light presentation on island history and culture, spotlighting lifelike figures and colorful tableaux accompanied by running commentary and music, results in a cheery, if bland, portrait of Antiguan life from Amerindian times to the present. ☎268/460–2777 for National Parks Authority ✆EC$15 ⊘ Daily 9–5.

ANTIGUA & BARBUDA ESSENTIALS

To research prices, get advice from other travelers, and book travel arrangements, visit www.fodors.com.

▮ TRANSPORTATION

BY AIR

In addition to many nonstop flights from the U.S., Carib Aviation flies daily to Barbuda, as well as to neighboring islands. LIAT has daily flights to and from many other Caribbean islands.

Charter flights to Barbuda from Antigua on Carib Aviation cost $60 per person. However, daily seven-seater charter flights are often booked well in advance or canceled without sufficient bookings.

Airline Information American Airlines/ American Eagle (☎268/462–4650). **Carib Aviation** (☎268/462–3147 or 268/481–2900 ⊕www.candoo.com/carib). **Caribbean Airlines** (☎268/480–2900 or 800/723–1111). **Continental Airlines** (☎268/462–5355). **Delta Airlines** (☎800/532–4777). **LIAT** (☎268/480–5600). **US Airways** (☎268/480–5700).

Airport Information V. C. Bird International Airport (VNU ☎268/462–4672 or 268/462–0358).

BY BOAT & FERRY

Barbuda Express runs five days a week (call for the changing schedule), leaving Antigua's Heritage Quay Ferry Dock. The fare is EC$80 one way, EC$140 round-trip (a day tour costs US$120).

Information Barbuda Express (☎268/560–7989, 268/460–0059, or 268/724–7027 ⊕www.antiguaferries.com).

BY CAR

If you are staying on Dickenson Bay, in and around English Harbour, or at an all-inclusive resort, you may not want to rent a car. But if you plan to dine out, then one may be a necessity, since taxi rates can mount up quickly. To rent a car, you need a valid driver's license and a temporary permit ($20), available through the rental agent. Costs start about $50 per day in season, with unlimited mileage, though you may get a better rate if you rent for several days. Most agencies offer automatic, stick-shift, and right- and left-hand drive. Four-wheel-drive vehicles ($55 per day) will get you more places and are refreshingly open; they are also useful because so many roads are full of potholes.

Gasoline in Antigua tends to be more expensive than in the continental United

States. The main roads, by and large, are in good condition, although there are bronco-busting dirt stretches leading to some more-remote locations and a few hilly areas that flood easily and become impassable for a day or two. Driving is on the left, although many locals drive in the middle—or think nothing of stopping at the roadside to chat. Don't be flustered by honking: it's the Caribbean version of hello.

Information Avis (☎268/462–2840). **Budget** (☎268/462–3009). **Dollar** (☎268/462–0362). **Hertz** (☎268/481–4440). **Thrifty** (☎268/462–0976).

BY TAXI

Taxis are unmetered, and although fares mount up quickly, rates are fixed (your driver should have a rate card). Some cabbies may take you from St. John's to English Harbour and wait for a "reasonable" amount of time (about a half hour) while you look around, for about $50. You can always call a cab from the St. John's taxi stand.

Information St. John's taxi stand (☎268/462–5190, 268/460–5353 for 24-hr service).

∎ CONTACTS & RESOURCES

BANKS & EXCHANGE SERVICES

American dollars are readily accepted, although you can usually receive change in EC dollars, so it's really your call as to whether or not you exchange any currency. It's certainly not necessary if you are staying in an all-inclusive resort. The local currency is the Eastern Caribbean dollar (EC$), which is tied to the U.S. dollar and fluctuates only slightly. US$1 is worth approximately EC$2.70; you get a slightly better rate if you exchange money at a bank than at your hotel. Several island banks have ATMs.

Most hotels, restaurants, and duty-free shops take major credit cards; all accept traveler's checks. ATMs (dispensing EC$) are available at the island's banks and at the airport.

Prices quoted throughout this chapter are in U.S. dollars unless otherwise indicated.

ELECTRICITY

Antigua runs on 110 volts, allowing use of most small North American appliances. Outlets are both two- and three-pronged, so bring an adapter.

EMERGENCIES

Ambulance & Fire Ambulance (☎268/462–0251). **Fire** (☎268/462–0044).

Hospitals Holberton Hospital (✉Hospital Rd., St. John's ☎268/462–0251).

Police Police assistance (☎268/462–0125).

INTERNET, MAIL & SHIPPING

Most hotels offer some kind of Internet service; if yours doesn't, the front desk should be able to direct you to one of the small Internet cafés In St. John's, Jolly Harbour, or English Harbour (the operations move around quite a bit). Some restaurants offer free Wi-Fi if you order a meal or even drinks.

Airmail letters to North America cost EC$1.50; postcards, EC75¢. Letters to the United Kingdom cost EC$1.50; postcards EC75¢. Letters to Australia and New Zealand are EC$1.80, postcards EC90¢. The main post office is at the foot of High Street in St. John's. Note that there are no postal codes; when addressing letters to the island, you need only indicate the address and "Antigua, West Indies."

SAFETY

Throughout the Caribbean, incidents of petty theft are increasing. Leave your valuables in the hotel safe-deposit box; don't leave them unattended in your room, on a beach, or in a rental car. Also, the streets of St. John's are fairly deserted at night, so it's not a good idea to wander about alone.

TAXES & SERVICE CHARGES

The departure tax is $20, payable in cash only—either U.S. or EC currency. Hotels collect an 8½% government room tax; some restaurants will add a 7% tax. Hotels and restaurants also usually add a 10% service charge to your bill.

TELEPHONES

GSM tri-band mobile phones from the United States and United Kingdom usually work on Antigua; you can also rent one from Cable & Wireless and APUA (Antigua Public Utilities Authority), though service is occasionally spotty and tariffs can mount up. Basic rental costs range between EC$25 and EC$50 per day (you can buy a SIM card and top it up with regular phone cards), with a EC$300 refundable deposit; typical calls to the United States range between $1.25 and $2 per minute, but you'll certainly save on local calls.

Most hotels have direct-dial phones; other hotels can easily make connections through the switchboard. You can use the Cable & Wireless Phone Card (available in $5, $10, and $20 denominations in most hotels and post offices) for local and long-distance calls. Phone-card phones work much better than the regular coin-operated phones.

To place a local call, simply dial the local seven-digit number. To call Antigua from the United States, dial 1 + 268 + the local seven-digit number.

To call the United States and Canada, dial 1 + the area code + the seven-digit number, or use the phone card or one of the "CALL USA" phones, which are available at several locations, including the airport departure lounge, the cruise terminal at St. John's, and the English Harbour Marina. These take credit cards and, supposedly, calling cards (though Cable & Wireless tacks on a fee).

Information APUA (⊠ Cassada Gardens, St. John's ☎ 268/480–7000 ⊕ www.apuainet. ag). **Cable & Wireless** (⊠ Woods Centre, St.

John's ☎ 268/480–2628 ⊠ Long St., St. John's ☎ 268/480–4236 ⊠ Clare Hall, St. John's ☎ 268/480–4000 ⊕ www.cwantigua.com).

TIPPING

In restaurants it's customary to leave 5% beyond the regular service charge added to your bill if you're pleased with the service. Taxi drivers expect a 10% tip, porters and bellmen about $1 per bag. Maids are rarely tipped, but if you think the service exemplary, figure $2 to $3 per night. Staff at all-inclusives aren't supposed to be tipped unless they've truly gone out of their way.

TOUR OPTIONS

Almost all taxi drivers double as guides, and you can arrange an island tour with one for about $25 an hour. Every major hotel has a cabbie on call and may be able to negotiate a discount, particularly off-season. Several operators specialize in off-road four-wheel-drive adventures that provide a taste of island history and topography. Jolly Harbour–based Caribbean Helicopters offers bird's-eye views both of the island and of Montserrat's ruins and still-simmering volcano. Trips last anywhere from 15 to 45 minutes; prices run $85 to $220. D&J Tours offers day-trippers the chance to experience Barbuda on a round-trip flight with a beach picnic and full tour for $120. Estate Safari Jeep Tours explores the interior, where there are few marked trails and roads are rough. The cost (about $90 per person) includes a visit to Betty's Hope, a hike to the summit of Monk's Hill (affording sensational near-360-degree panoramas of Montserrat, Guadeloupe, and English Harbour and Falmouth Harbour), a botanical walk through the rain forest, and lunch and snorkeling at a secluded beach. Four-wheel off-road adventures by Island Safaris enable you to fully appreciate the island's natural beauty, history, folklore, and cultural heritage as they zoom about the southwest part of Antigua. Hiking is involved, though it's not strenuous. Lunch and snorkeling are also included. Active adventurers will particularly enjoy the combo Land Rover/kayak outback ecotour. Prices start at $85 per person. Mountain to Sea Bike Adventure offers informative, fun, three-hour guided bicycle tours (transfers, equipment, and lunch included) and optional hikes in the Shirley Heights–English Harbour area; they also rent bikes and scooters. Suntours, by far the most professional outfit on Antigua, gives half- and full-day island tours that focus on such highlights as Shirley Heights and English Harbour. Suntours is also the island's American Express representative.

Information **Caribbean Helicopters** (☎268/460–5900 ⊕www.caribbeanhelicopters.com). **D&J Tours** (☎268/773–9766). **Estate Safari Jeep Tours** (☎268/463–4713 or 268/463–2061). **Island Safaris** (☎268/480–1225 ⊕www.tropicalad. com). **Mountain to Sea Bike Adventure** (☎268/721–7350 or 268/770–4837 ⊕www. mountaintoseabikeadventure.com). **Suntours** (⊠Long and Thames Sts., St. John's ☎268/462–4788).

VISITOR INFORMATION

Before You Leave **Antigua & Barbuda Tourist Offices** (☎212/541–4117 in New York City, 305/381–6762in Miami, or 888/268–4227 ⊕www.antigua-barbuda.org). **Barbudaful.net** (⊕www.barbudaful.net).

In Antigua **Antigua & Barbuda Department of Tourism** (⊠Government Complex, Queen Elizabeth Hwy., St. John's ☎268/463–0125 or 268/462–0480). **Antigua Hotels & Tourist Association** (⊠Newgate St., St. John's ☎268/462–0374).

WEDDINGS

Wedding planning is relatively simple in Antigua; most hotels can help with the arrangements, and many offer complete wedding packages (from flowers to catering to videography). No minimum residency or blood test is required for adults 18 and over. Visit the Ministry of Legal Affairs on the outskirts of St. John's any weekday to pay the license application fee of $150. Bring valid passports as proof of citizenship and, in the case of previous marriages, the original divorce or annulment decree; widows or widowers should present the original marriage and death certificates. Then visit the Registrar General's office in downtown St. John's and get a marriage certificate; registration fee is $40. If you marry anywhere but the courthouse in a civil ceremony, you must pay the marriage officer $50. If you prefer a church ceremony, you must receive permission from the clerical authorities. Two or more witnesses must sign the marriage certificate.

Information **Ministry of Legal Affairs** (⊠Queen Elizabeth Hwy., St. John's ☎268/462–0017). **Registrar General** (⊠High St. at Lower Thames St., St. John's ☎268/462–0609).

Aruba

Windsurfing

WORD OF MOUTH

"'[The] most fun thing to do in Aruba [besides chill at the beach] is to rent a jeep and literally drive around the island (the back side is like being on a [different] planet)."

—MG_IslandHopper

"Aruba is a favorite wintertime destination for me, and the high quality of restaurants is one of the reasons. Go and enjoy yourself!!!"

—Lolo12

WELCOME TO ARUBA

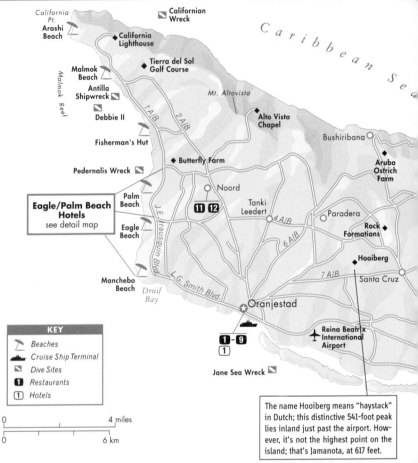

KEY

⌁	Beaches
⏧	Cruise Ship Terminal
◩	Dive Sites
1	Restaurants
①	Hotels

```
0                    4 miles
├────┬────┬────┤
0                    6 km
```

The name Hooiberg means "haystack" in Dutch; this distinctive 541-foot peak lies inland just past the airport. However, it's not the highest point on the island; that's Jamanota, at 617 feet.

The pastel-colored houses of Dutch settlers still grace the waterfront in the capital city of Oranjestad. Winds are fierce, even savage, on the north coast, where you'll find a landscape of cacti, rocky desert, and wind-bent divi-divi trees. On the west coast the steady breezes attract windsurfers to the shallow, richly colored waters.

THE A IN THE ABC ISLANDS

The A in the ABC Islands (the other two being Bonaire and Curaçao), Aruba is small—only 19½ mi (31½ km) long and 6 mi (9½ km) across at its widest point. It became an independent entity within the Netherlands in 1986. The official language is Dutch, but almost every native speaks English and Spanish as well. The island's population is 72,000.

3

ARUBA

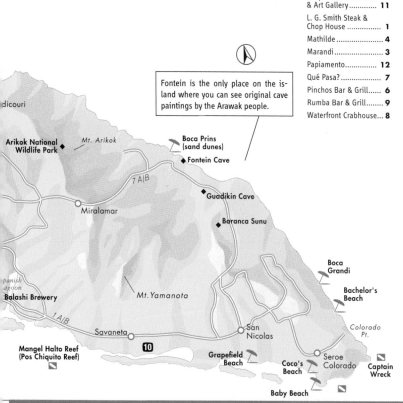

Fontein is the only place on the island where you can see original cave paintings by the Arawak people.

dicouri

Arikok National Wildlife Park ◆   *Mt. Arikok*

Boca Prins (sand dunes)
◆ **Fontein Cave**

7 A|B

◆ **Guadikin Cave**

Miralamar

◆ **Baranca Sunu**

Boca Grandi

panish agoon

Balashi Brewery

Mt. Yamanota

Bachelor's Beach

1 A|B

Colorado Pt.

Savaneta

San Nicolas

10

Mangel Halto Reef (Pos Chiquito Reef)

Grapefield Beach

Coco's Beach

Seroe Colorado

Captain Wreck

Baby Beach

TOP 4 REASONS TO VISIT ARUBA

❶ Nightlife is among the best in the Caribbean. The colorful Kukoo Kunuku party bus picks you up and pours you out at your hotel.

❷ Powder-soft beaches and turquoise waters are legendary.

❸ Great restaurants offer a wide range of cuisine as good as any in the Caribbean.

❹ Aruba's casinos aren't as glitzy as their Las Vegas rivals, but they will please both casual and serious gamblers.

ARUBA PLANNER

Island Activities	Logistics

Island Activities

Soft, sandy **beaches** and turquoise waters are the biggest draws in Aruba. They are often crowded, particularly the best stretches of Eagle Beach, which is the island's—and perhaps one of the Caribbean's—finest. Baby Beach, on the east end of the island, is also good.

But the island also comes alive by night and has become a true **party hot spot**. The **casinos**—though not as elaborate as those in Las Vegas—are among the best of any Caribbean island.

Restaurants are very good, though sometimes expensive.

Diving is good in Aruba, though perhaps not as spectacular as in nearby Bonaire.

Near-constant breezes and tranquil, protected waters have proven to be a boon for **windsurfers,** who have discovered that conditions on the southwestern coast are ideal for their sport.

A largely undeveloped region in Arikok National Wildlife Park is the destination of choice for those wishing to **hike** and explore some wild terrain.

Logistics

Getting to Aruba: Many airlines fly nonstop to Aruba from several cities in North America, and if you need to make connections, it will usually be at a U.S. airport. Aruba is 2½ hours from Miami and 4½ hours from New York. Smaller airlines connect the Dutch islands in the Caribbean, often using Aruba as a hub. The island's state-of-the-art Reina Beatrix International Airport (AUA) is equipped with thorough security, many flight displays, and state-of-the-art baggage handling systems. Travelers to the United States clear U.S. Customs and Immigration before leaving Aruba.

Hassle Factor: Low.

Nonstops: There are nonstop flights from Atlanta (Delta), Boston (American, jetBlue, USAirways), Charlotte (USAirways), Chicago (United—weekly), Fort Lauderdale (Spirit—weekly), Houston (Continental—twice-weekly), Miami (American), Newark (Continental), New York–JFK (American, Delta, jetBlue), New York–LGA (Continental—weekly), Philadelphia (USAirways—twice-weekly), and Washington, DC–Dulles (United), though not all flights are daily.

On the Ground

A taxi from the airport to most hotels takes about 20 minutes. It will cost about $17 to get to the hotels along Eagle Beach, $19 to the high-rise hotels on Palm Beach, and $10 to the hotels downtown. Buses are also an option for traveling around the island and are especially convenient if you are just popping into town from your hotel for a bit of shopping. The hourly bus schedules can be less convenient for getting to the beach, but the price is right, at $1.25 one way ($2.30 round-trip).

Renting a Car: If you want to explore the countryside at your leisure and try different beaches, then you should rent a car, but for just getting to and around town, taxis are preferable, and you can use tour companies to arrange your activities. If you rent a car, try to make reservations before arriving, and rent a four-wheel-drive vehicle if you plan to explore the island's natural sights. Some companies have minimum ages for renting a car.

Where to Stay

Almost all of the resorts are along the island's southwest coast, along L.G. Smith and J.E. Irausquin boulevards, with the larger high-rise properties being farther away from Oranjestad. A few budget places are in Oranjestad itself. Since most hotel beaches are equally fabulous, it's the resort, rather than its location, that's going to be a bigger factor in how you enjoy your vacation.

Large Resorts: These all-encompassing vacation destinations offer myriad dining options, casinos, shops, watersports centers, health clubs, and car-rental desks. The island has only a handful of all-inclusives, though these are gaining in popularity.

Time-shares: Large time-share properties are cropping up in greater numbers, luring visitors who prefer to prepare some of their own meals and have a bit more living space than you might find in the typical resort hotel room.

Boutique Resorts: You'll find a few small resorts that offer more personal service, though not always the same level of luxury as the larger places. But smaller resorts are better suited to the natural sense of Aruban hospitality you'll find all over the island.

Hotel & Restaurant Costs

⇨*For information on hotel meal plans, see Accommodations in Caribbean Essentials.*

WHAT IT COSTS IN U.S. DOLLARS				
$$$$	$$$	$$	$	¢
Restaurants				
over $30	$20–$30	$12–$20	$8–$12	under $8
Hotels*				
over $350	$250–$350	$150–$250	$80–$150	under $80
Hotels**				
over $450	$350–$450	$250–$350	$125–$250	under $125

*EP, BP, CP **AI, FAP, MAP Restaurant prices are for a main course at dinner and include any taxes or service charges. Hotel prices are per night for a double room in high season, excluding taxes, service charges, and meal plans (except at all-inclusives).

When to Go

Aruba's popularity means that hotels are usually booked solid during the high season from mid-December through mid-April or early May, so early booking is essential. During other times of the year, rate reductions can be dramatic.

Aruba doesn't really have a rainy season and rarely sees a hurricane, so you take fewer chances by coming here in late summer and fall. However, if you travel at this time, just remember that hurricanes and tropical storms are not unheard of—just rare.

February or March witnesses a spectacular **Carnival,** a riot of color whirling to the tunes of steel bands and culminating in the Grand Parade, where some of the floats rival the extravagance of those in the Big Easy's Mardi Gras.

By Vernon
O'Reilly-
Ramesar

EVERY EVENING THEY COME TO SIT BY THE SHORE to await the sunset: a family of six visiting from some distant land. During the day the parents may have dined in style, or perhaps laughed a couple of hours away as they gambled in the glitzy casinos downtown. The kids may have gone snorkeling or diving, or perhaps drove an ATV across the arid, moonlike surface of the northern coast. The evening, though, is the time when they all come together as a family to watch the sun dip down below the water. In the tangerine light of another Aruba sunset, they hug and laugh, six happy silhouettes against the Caribbean sky.

Cruise ships gleam in Oranjestad Harbour, while thousands of eager tourists scavenge through souvenir stalls looking for the perfect memento. The mile-long stretch of L. G. Smith Boulevard is lined with cafés, designer stores, and signs for the latest Vegas-style shows. The countryside is dotted with colorful *cunucu* (country-style houses) and small neighborhood shops. Suddenly, the rocky desert landscape is startlingly austere.

Aruba offers an amazingly diverse experience in a small package. Tourists flock here for the sunny climate, perfect waters, and excellent beaches—so much so that the area around beautiful Eagle Beach is an almost unbroken line of hotels, restaurants, and bars. Here on the south coast, the action is nonstop both day and night, while the fiercely rugged north coast is a desolate and rocky landscape that has so far resisted development.

Aruba is the smallest of the ABC islands—only 120 square mi (193 square km) in area—with Bonaire and Curaçao rounding out the trio. In 1986, after much lobbying, Aruba separated from the rest of the Netherlands Antilles to become a separate part of the Kingdom of the Netherlands. Perhaps the separation came so easily because there is so little Dutch presence on the island. The small population of 72,000 is of mainly mixed extraction, and many people show distinct traces of some Amerindian ancestry.

As with Bonaire and Curaçao, the island was originally populated by the Caquetio, an Amerindian people related to the Arawak. After the Spanish conquered the island in 1499, Aruba was basically left alone, since it held little agricultural or mineral appeal. The Dutch took charge of the island in 1636, and things remained relatively quiet until gold was discovered in the 1800s.

Like the trademark *watapana* (divi-divi) trees that have been forced into bonsailike angles by the constant trade winds, Aruba has always adjusted to changes in the economic climate. Mining dominated the economy until the early part of the 20th century, when the mines became unsustainable. Shortly thereafter, Aruba became home to a major oil-refining operation, which was the economic mainstay until the early 1990s, when its contribution to the local economy was eclipsed by tourism. Today, after being so resolutely dedicated to attracting visitors for so many years, Aruba's national culture and tourism industry are inextricably intertwined.

Hotels ▼

Amsterdam
Manor **7**

Aruba
Marriott **1**

Aruban Resort
& Casino **8**

Bucuti Beach .. **10**

Divi Aruba
Beach **11**

Divi Village **13**

Holiday Inn
Sun Spree **2**

Hyatt Regency
Aruba **3**

Mill Resort **6**

MVC Eagle
Beach **9**

Radisson
Aruba **4**

Tamarijn
Aruba **12**

Westin Aruba **5**

Restaurants ▼

Hostaria
Da'Vittorio **1**

Le Dôme **2**

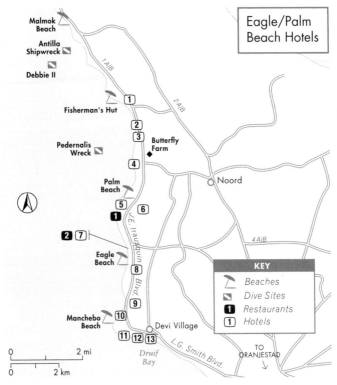

With more than half a million visitors a year, Aruba is not a destination that will appeal to those trying to avoid the beaten path—but you should visit Aruba if you're looking for a nice climate, excellent facilities, lots of nightlife, and no surprises. The U.S. dollar is accepted everywhere, and English is spoken universally, which makes Aruba a popular spot for Americans who want an overseas trip to a place that doesn't feel foreign. In fact, Americans go through U.S. customs right at the airport in Aruba, so there are no formalities upon landing in the United States.

WHERE TO STAY

Hotels on the island are categorized as low-rise or high-rise and are grouped in two distinct areas along L. G. Smith and J. E. Irausquin boulevards north of Oranjestad. The low-rise properties are closer to the capital, the high-rises in a swath a little farther north. Hotel rates, with the exception of those at a few all-inclusives, generally do not include meals or even breakfast. The larger resorts feel like destinations unto themselves, complete with shopping, entertainment, and casinos.

$$$$ 🛏 **Aruba Marriott Resort & Stellaris Casino.** The gentle sound of the surf
★   and splashing waterfalls compete for your attention in this sprawling compound, where everything seems to run smoothly. A spacious

lobby leads either to gardens or to a chic shopping arcade and casino. Recently renovated rooms are spacious (the largest on the island) with massive balconies; most have ocean views, and all have walk-in closets. Suites are even more expansive and have hot tubs. Some of the best dinner shows on the island are held at Wave's Beach Bar and Grill, which is also the perfect place to enjoy the sunset. **Pros:** Large rooms, variety of excellent restaurants, great shopping. **Cons:** Large, impersonal resort, reception can become gridlocked in peak season. ✉ *L. G. Smith Blvd. 101, Palm Beach* ☎ *297/586–9000 or 800/223–6388* ⊕ *www.marriott.com* ⇦ *413 rooms, 20 suites* ♿ *In-room: safe, DVD (some), Ethernet, Wi-Fi. In-hotel: 5 restaurants, bars, tennis courts, pool, gym, spa, beachfront, diving, water sports, concierge, public Wi-Fi* ▬ *AE, D, DC, MC, V* �� *EP.*

$$$$ 🏨 **Divi Aruba Beach Resort Mega All Inclusive.** The main advantage to
☾ staying at this small resort is that it offers a variety of room types, along with the privilege of using the facilities of the adjoining Tamarijn Resort. The beachfront lanais offer the best combination of privacy and views. Because the crowd here can get quite animated—especially with free margaritas so readily available—rooms overlooking the main pool are best avoided. The "Mega" concept allows guests to dine and use the facilities at sister properties. Children under 18 stay free when accompanied by two adults, and the kids' camp even offers Papiamento language lessons. The beach here is gorgeous; nonmotorized water sports are all included in the price, if you can drag yourself off your lounge chair. **Pros:** On wonderful stretch of beach, margarita machines in lobby, common areas feel light and airy. **Cons:** Poolside area can get pretty noisy, the gourmet restaurant isn't that good. ✉ *L. G. Smith Blvd. 93, Manchebo Beach* ☎ *297/582–3300 or 800/554–2008* ⊕ *www.diviaruba.com* ⇦ *203 rooms* ♿ *In-room: refrigerator. In-hotel: 3 restaurants, bars, tennis court, pools, gym, beachfront, diving, water sports, bicycles, children's programs (ages 5–12), laundry service, public Internet* ▬ *AE, D, DC, MC, V* ⌥ *3-night minimum* ⺠ *AI.*

$$$$ 🏨 **Divi Village Golf & Beach Resort.** The newest of the midsize Divi resorts
★ focuses on golf, and although it's just across the road from its sister properties, the atmosphere at this all-suite version is much quieter and more refined. Another difference is the pricing structure; base rates are not all-inclusive, though AI plans that allow you to dine at the Divi Aruba and Tamarijn are available for an additional cost. Happily, the hotel grounds are as lush and well maintained as the 9-hole golf course, and regardless of the meal plan, you get to use the facilities of all Divi resorts on Aruba. Suites are massive and include kitchens; the beach is across the road. Those seeking the ultimate in luxury can book one of the golf villas that overlook the course and have private rooftop Jacuzzis. **Pros:** Excellent golf course, spacious rooms, lushly landscaped grounds. **Cons:** Bit of a hike from some rooms to the lobby, you must cross a busy road to get to the beach. ✉ *J. E. Irausquin Blvd. 93, Oranjestad* ☎ *297/583–5000* ⊕ *www.divivillage.com* ⇦ *250 suites* ♿ *In-room: kitchen, dial-up. In-hotel: 3 restaurants, room service, bars, golf course, tennis courts, pools, no elevator* ▬ *AE, D, DC, MC, V* ⌥ *3-night minimum* ⺠ *EP.*

$$$$ Hyatt Regency Aruba Beach Resort & Casino. This 12-acre resort offers everything from a casino for adults to waterslides for kids, so it's popular with families. Honeymooners head here, too, since the resort is big enough that there are still some quietly romantic corners. The sand-color high-rise building is topped by a distinctive hacienda-style roof, and interconnected pools flow through the compound and end in an ornamental lagoon. Rooms are well equipped, but the balconies are rather small. There's no lack of activities for adults; the resort offers horseback riding, water sports, tennis, and a highly regarded spa. Kids' programs are extensive as well. The restaurants are very good, most notably Ruinas del Mar, which serves fresh seafood with a Continental flair. **Pros:** Beautiful grounds, great for kids, excellent restaurants. **Cons:** Pokey balconies for such a luxury hotel, some rooms are quite a stretch from the beach. ✉ *J. E. Irausquin Blvd. 85, Palm Beach* ☎ *297/586–1234 or 800/554–9288* ⊕ *www.aruba.hyatt.com* ⬧ *342 rooms, 18 suites* ♿ *In-room: safe, Ethernet, Wi-Fi. In-hotel: 6 restaurants, room service, bars, tennis courts, pool, gym, spa, beachfront, diving, water sports, concierge, children's programs (ages 3–12), public Internet* ⊟ *AE, D, DC, MC, V* ⫿◯⫿ *EP.*

$$$$ Radisson Aruba Resort & Casino. Luxury is the key word at this 14-acre resort. Rooms are lavishly equipped and furnished with colonial West Indian–style furniture, including four-poster beds. Large balconies look out onto either ocean views or tropical gardens. The pools are top notch, and even though there's a comprehensive children's program—not to mention a large family contingent—peace and quiet are not hard to find here. The fitness center is dazzling and the spa is the perfect place to unwind from the stresses of everyday life. **Pros:** Rooms have an intimate feel, exercise junkies will love the top-notch facilities, one of the best spas on the island. **Cons:** Restaurants are good but not great, you can never forget you are in a big hotel. ✉ *J. E. Irausquin Blvd. 81, Palm Beach* ☎ *297/586–6555* ⊕ *www.radisson.com* ⬧ *321 rooms, 32 suites* ♿ *In-room: safe, Wi-Fi. In-hotel: 4 restaurants, room service, bars, tennis courts, pools, gym, spa, beachfront, diving, water sports, children's programs (ages 5–12), laundry service, public Internet* ⊟ *AE, D, DC, MC, V* ⫿◯⫿ *EP.*

$$$$ Renaissance Aruba Resort & Casino. This downtown hotel consists of two distinct parts: the Renaissance Marina Hotel and the Renaissance Ocean Suites. Standard rooms are in the marina section, which is on Oranjestad's main drag and overlooks the harbor. The Ocean Suite rooms are larger and have separate living areas and kitchenettes. The main hotel pool actually juts out 25 feet above L. G. Smith Boulevard (swimmers can look down on the street). Rooms here are spacious and well appointed; some overlook the six-floor atrium filled with restaurants and stores. A 40-acre island just offshore has the only private beaches in Aruba and is reserved for hotel guests (the boat to the island leaves from the hotel lobby). Most restaurants in the attached Seaport Mall allow diners to sign for their meals. **Pros:** Right in the heart of the downtown shopping district, lobby and shopping areas are always lively, pool area offers an unmatched view of the port. **Cons:** Rooms overlooking the atrium can be a bit claustrophobic, beach is off-site, hard to find

a quiet spot. ⊠*L. G. Smith Blvd. 82, Oranjestad* ☎*297/583–6000 or 800/421–8188* ⊕*www.renaissancearuba.com* ⤶*291 rooms, 268 suites* ♿*In-room: kitchen (some), Ethernet. In-hotel: 5 restaurants, room service, bars, tennis court, pools, gym, spa, beachfront, diving, water sports, concierge, children's programs (ages 5–12), laundry facilities, public Internet, public Wi-Fi, no-smoking rooms* ⊟*AE, D, DC, MC, V* ⏆*EP.*

$$$$ 🏨**Tamarijn Aruba All Inclusive Beach Resort.** An upscale alternative to its sister property, the Divi Aruba, this resort is pleasantly laid back for an all-inclusive. Guests seeking additional excitement can take a short walk along the beach to the more-rambunctious sister property next door. All rooms are oceanfront and feature blond-wood furnishings and ample balconies. The rate covers food, beverages, entertainment, an array of activities, and even tickets to the weekly Bon Bini Festival. Parents will appreciate the special discount offered on an extra room for the kids. A free shuttle runs to the Alhambra Casino until 3 AM. **Pros:** Stunning beach, access to the Divi Mega All-Inclusive next door, perfect for families. **Cons:** Being right on the beach can mean noise during busy periods, the linear layout means some rooms are quite far from the lobby. ⊠*J. E. Irausquin Blvd. 41, Punta Brabo* ☎*297/525–5200 or 800/554–2008* ⊕*www.tamarijnaruba.com* ⤶*236 rooms* ♿*In-hotel: 3 restaurants, bars, tennis courts, pools, gym, beachfront, water sports, bicycles, public Internet* ⊟*AE, D, DC, MC, V* ⤶*3-night minimum* ⏆*AI.*

$$$$ 🏨**Westin Aruba Resort, Spa & Casino.** Westin added a few extra touches
★   to the already tasteful rooms at the former Wyndham, including flat-screen TVs. The fine restaurants that helped make this hotel a standout choice in the past remain as well (in fact, besides the logo change, it's difficult to tell the difference). Rooms, though not as large as those at some other resorts, are beautifully furnished with plentiful wood accents. The grand public spaces are always decorated with floral displays. Diversions are readily available in the casino and spa; the hotel's Cuban-theme cabaret show at the Cabaret Royale is well worth seeing even if you aren't staying here. Although it isn't cheap, the hotel offers good value for a luxury hotel by Aruba standards. **Pros:** Chic and airy rooms, magnificent beachfront and pool area, comprehensive spa facilities, great restaurants. **Cons:** Immediate area is congested and busy, resort lacks an intimate feel. ⊠*J. E. Irausquin Blvd. 77, Palm Beach* ☎*297/586–4466 or 877/822–2222* ⊕*www.westinaruba.com* ⤶*481 rooms, 81 suites* ♿*In-room: safe, Wi-Fi. In-hotel: 8 restaurants, bars, tennis court, pool, spa, beachfront, diving, water sports, concierge, public Internet* ⊟*AE, D, DC, MC, V* ⏆*EP.*

$$$–$$$$ 🏨**Bucuti Beach Resort.** An extraordinary beach setting, impeccably
Fodor'sChoice understated service, and attention to detail help this elegant Green
★   Globe resort easily outclass anything else on the island. Hacienda-style buildings are surrounded by ecologically sensitive landscaping that suits the island's desertlike environment. Rooms are done in cool creams and feature cherrywood furnishings; there's a distinctly modern and European feel to the entire place. Wireless broadband is available throughout the resort. This hotel is very popular with return visitors,

so book early, as it is frequently sold out in high season. **Pros:** Intimate European feel, impeccable service, ecoconscious hotel means less vacation guilt. **Cons:** Restaurant is not especially good, not close to any shopping and little to buy at hotel. ⊠ *L. G. Smith Blvd. 55B, Eagle Beach* ☎ *297/583–1100* ⊕ *www.bucuti.com* ⏎ *63 rooms, 38 suites, 3 bungalows* ♿ *In-room: safe, refrigerator, Wi-Fi. In-hotel: restaurant, bars, pool, beachfront, bicycles, laundry facilities, public Internet, public Wi-Fi* ⊟ *AE, D, DC, MC, V* ⧫ *CP.*

$$$ 🖾 **Aruban Resort & Casino.** Formerly known as La Cabana this complex of self-contained units sits right across from Eagle Beach. Rooms are all newly renovated and have every imaginable home comfort, including hot tubs. A third of the suites have ocean views. Most common facilities, including the pools, are permanently crowded and usually noisy. There is an excellent children's program that makes this a popular choice for families; those not fond of masses of children should avoid this hotel completely. **Pros:** Self-catering option can be great for families, lots of distractions for the kids. **Cons:** Feels like an apartment complex, public areas are noisy and crowded, beach is across a busy road. ⊠ *J. E. Irausquin Blvd. 250, Eagle Beach* ☎ *297/587–9000 or 800/835–7193* ⊕ *www.thearuban.com* ⏎ *362 suites* ♿ *In-room: safe, kitchen. In-hotel: restaurant, bars, tennis courts, pools, gym, spa, diving, children's programs (ages 5–12), public Internet* ⊟ *AE, D, DC, MC, V* ⧫ *EP.*

$$$ 🖾 **Holiday Inn SunSpree Aruba Beach Resort & Casino.** This popular, family-oriented package-tour hotel has three seven-story buildings filled with spacious rooms lining a sugary, palm-dotted shore. The pool's cascading waterfalls and sundeck, where you can enjoy the Wednesday-evening cocktail party, draws just as large a crowd as the beach. The lobby is usually overflowing with suitcases as the throngs check in and out, so don't expect too much in the way of personalized service from the front desk or the concierge at these busy times. The resort's free program for kids is a boon for families. **Pros:** Affordable and predictable quality, great beachfront location. **Cons:** Hallways have an institutional feel, lines at reception can make you feel you are back at the airport, restaurants are mediocre at best and service can be a problem. ⊠ *J. E. Irausquin Blvd. 230, Palm Beach* ☎ *297/586–3600 or 800/465–4329* ⊕ *www.ichotelsgroup.com* ⏎ *600 rooms, 7 suites* ♿ *In-room: refrigerator, Wi-Fi. In-hotel: 4 restaurants, bars, tennis courts, pools, gym, beachfront, diving, water sports, concierge, children's programs (ages 5–12), public Internet, public Wi-Fi* ⊟ *AE, DC, MC, V* ⧫ *EP.*

$$–$$$ 🖾 **Amsterdam Manor Beach Resort.** An intimate, family-run hotel with a genuinely friendly staff and an authentic Dutch-Caribbean atmosphere, this little place offers excellent value for the money. The gabled mustard-yellow hotel is built around a central courtyard with a waterfall pool and wading pool. Eagle Beach is right across the road (guests can have lunch or dinner served on the beach). The pool bar is buzzing late into the night, and Filo the bartender keeps everyone fully entertained. Tile-floor rooms range from small, elegantly appointed studios (some with ocean-view balconies) to two-bedroom suites with peaked ceilings and whirlpool tubs; all have kitchenettes. The restaurant serves good,

Fodor'sChoice
★

reasonably priced meals. Web junkies can use the free bank of computers near reception. **Pros:** Compound feels like a European village, very good family restaurant, friendly and helpful staff; minigrocery on-site. **Cons:** Across the road from the beach, lacks the boutiques and distractions of a larger hotel. ⊠*J. E. Irausquin Blvd. 252, Eagle Beach* ☎*297/527–1100 or 800/932–6509* ⊕*www.amsterdammanor.com* ⟿*37 studios, 35 suites* ⚲*In-room: safe, kitchen, dial-up. In-hotel: restaurant, bars, pool, water sports, laundry facilities, public Internet, public Wi-Fi, some pets allowed* ⊟*AE, D, MC, V* ⊺⊙⊺*EP.*

$$ ☷ Mill Resort & Suites. ☾ ★ This lovely low-rise resort is deservedly popular with travelers in the know. The staff is genuinely friendly and devoted to the needs of guests. Buildings are laid out around a busy pool and bar area. The open-air Mediterranean-style lobby has free coffee available day and night. The resort's all-inclusive plan, which can be added onto the basic room cost, allows guests the freedom to dine off-property if they wish—although the on-site restaurant is good. Wednesday night draws a crowd from across the island for the all-you-can-eat barbecue, accompanied by live entertainment. The property is a short walk away from the beach. **Pros:** Entire compound has an intimate feel, lively bar area, theme nights are fun. **Cons:** Not on the beach, pool area can be busy and noisy. ⊠*J. E. Irausquin Blvd. 330, Palm Beach* ☎*297/586–7700* ⊕*www.millresort.com* ⟿*64 studios, 128 suites* ⚲*In-room: safe, kitchen (some). In-hotel: restaurant, bar, tennis courts, pools, gym, spa, laundry facilities, public Internet, public Wi-Fi* ⊟*AE, D, DC, MC, V* ⊺⊙⊺*EP.*

$ ☷ MVC Eagle Beach. ☾ ★ For the price and the excellent location across from Eagle Beach, this former vacation facility for the visiting families of Dutch marines is a great bargain. Most guests are still budget-minded Dutch tourists who can live with impeccably clean but basic and simply furnished rooms. Don't come expecting the facilities of a Hilton; however, there's a tennis court, a good restaurant serving hearty fare, and a lively bar. The hotel is also well suited to the needs of families with smaller children, as there are ample play areas and a children's pool. **Pros:** Unbeatable price, popular restaurant with food at affordable prices, since the main language is Dutch you feel that you're someplace other than South Florida here. **Cons:** Spartan accommodations, not for those who want to be away from kids. ⊠*J. E. Irausquin Blvd. 240, Eagle Beach* ☎*297/587–0110* ⊕*www.mvceaglebeach.com* ⟿*16 rooms, 3 suites* ⚲*In-room: no TV. In-hotel: restaurant, bar, tennis court, pool, beachfront, laundry facilities* ⊟*MC, V* ⊺⊙⊺*EP.*

WHERE TO EAT

Aruba has many fine restaurants, so you can expect outstanding meals and international cuisine. Arubans tend to eat their main meal at lunchtime, so feel free to follow suit and save money by trying the lunch menus at the better restaurants. Be sure to try such Aruban specialties as *pan bati* (a mildly sweet bread that resembles a pancake) and *keshi yena* (a baked concoction of Gouda cheese, spices, and meat or seafood in a rich brown sauce). On Sunday you may have a hard time finding a restaurant outside a hotel that's open for lunch, and many restaurants are closed for dinner on Sunday or Monday. Reservations are essential for dinner in high season.

The **Aruba Gastronomic Association** (AGA ⊕*www.arubadining.com*) offers Dine-Around packages that allow visitors to have a three-course dinner at a number of affiliated restaurants. A number of packages, ranging from three dinners ($109) to seven dinners ($245), can be ordered online.

WHAT TO WEAR
Even the finest restaurants require at most a jacket for men and a sundress for women. If you plan to eat in the open air, remember to bring along insect repellent—the mosquitoes sometimes get unruly.

CARIBBEAN
$$–$$$
✕**Brisas del Mar.** Eating at this friendly place overlooking the sea is like dining in a private home. Old family recipes use such indigenous ingredients as the aromatic *yerbiholé* leaf (with a minty basil flavor). Try the steamy fish soup, *keri keri* (shredded fish kissed with annatto, also known as achiote or poor man's saffron), or some of the island's best pan bati. The catch of the day cooked Aruban-style (panfried and covered with creole sauce, or in garlic butter on request) has drawn a crowd for more than 20 years. Reserve early for sunset gazing on the breezy terrace. The restaurant is bus-accessible from hotels. ⊠*Savaneta 222A, Savaneta* ☎297/584–7718 ⊟*AE, MC, V* ⊙*Closed Mon.*

$$–$$$
★
✕**Gasparito Restaurant & Art Gallery.** You can find this enchanting hideaway in a cunucu (country house) in Noord, not far from the hotels. Dine indoors, where works by local artists are showcased on softly lighted walls, or on the outdoor patio. Either way, the service is excellent. The Aruban specialties—pan bati, keshi yena—are feasts for the eye as well as the palate. The standout dish is the Gasparito chicken; the sauce recipe was passed down from the owner's ancestors and features seven special ingredients, including brandy, white wine, and pineapple juice. (The rest, they say, are secret.) Gasparito is an AGA Dine-Around member. ⊠*Gasparito 3, Noord* ☎297/586–7044 ⊟*D, MC, V* ⊙*Closed Sun. No lunch.*

CONTINENTAL
$$$–$$$$
★
✕**Le Dôme.** Eleven thousand bricks were imported from Antwerp to add European flair to this fine-dining spot. Four dining rooms are done in different themes, with the Old World and Galerie rooms being the most atmospheric. The menu changes frequently, but scampi Le Dôme is always listed and worth ordering. The wine list includes more than 250 labels. Savor champagne with the prix-fixe Sunday brunch. Le Dôme is an AGA VIP member. ⊠*J. E. Irausquin Blvd. 224, Eagle Beach* ☎297/587–1517 ⌁*Reservations essential* ⊟*AE, D, MC, V* ⊙*No lunch Sat.*

CUBAN
$$–$$$
★
✕**Cuba's Cookin'.** This funky little establishment is tucked away on an innocuous street downtown. Nightly entertainment, great authentic Cuban food, and a lively crowd are the draws here. The empanadas are excellent, as is the chicken stuffed with plantains. Don't leave without trying the roast pork, which is pretty close to perfection. The signature dish is the *ropa vieja*, a sautéed flank steak served with a rich sauce (the

Cunucu Houses

Pastel houses surrounded by cacti fences adorn Aruba's flat, rugged *cunucu* ("country" in Papiamento). The features of these traditional houses were developed in response to the environment. Early settlers discovered that slanting roofs allowed the heat to rise and that small windows helped to keep in the cool air. Among the earliest building materials was *caliche*, a durable calcium carbonate substance found in the island's southeastern hills. Many houses were also built using interlocking coral rocks that didn't require mortar (this technique is no longer used, thanks to cement and concrete). Contemporary design combines some of the basic principles of the earlier homes with touches of modernization: windows, though still narrow, have been elongated; roofs are constructed of bright tiles; pretty patios have been added; and doorways and balconies present an ornamental face to the world beyond.

name literally translates as "old clothes"). There's always a crowd, as loyal fans and fun-seekers usually crowd the bar area. ⊠ *Wilhelminastraat 27, Oranjestad* ☎297/588–0627 ▤*AE, MC, V* ☉*Closed Sun. mid-Apr.–mid-Dec.*

ECLECTIC

$$$–$$$$

Fodor'sChoice

★

✗ **Marandi.** This seaside restaurant, whose name means "on the water" in Malaysian, is simultaneously cozy and chic. Everything is seductive, from the tables tucked under a giant thatched roof by the water's edge to the dining room, which is unencumbered by a ceiling. The restaurant has moved to a new location on a pier near the airport but seems to have lost none of its charm. The beef cooked in local beer with foie gras, apples, and cabbage is an unusual but tasty option. Reservations are essential at any time, and if you're lucky you can dine at the chef's table, which is right in the kitchen. ⊠*Bucutiweg 50, Oranjestad* ☎297/582–0157 ⚭*Reservations essential* ▤*MC, V* ☉*No lunch.*

$$$–$$$$

★

✗ **Mathilde.** The venerable Chez Mathilde, once the bastion of fine French cuisine on the island, has been transformed into an equally upscale but decidedly more-modern eatery. Billing itself as "island chic," the interior and courtyard have been transformed from the belle epoque decor to a sea of crisp white- and wood-tiled walls. The menu sometimes wanders down memory lane but tends toward Caribbean-influenced offerings such as Brie-crusted grouper served with a fruit salsa. Some have welcomed the changes but others grumble about an unnecessary change to an island institution. If you are not sure about dining here you can still sample the ambience (and watch the posers) at the trendy M lounge. ⊠*Havenstraat 23, Oranjestad* ☎297/583–9200 ⚭*Reservations essential* ▤*AE, D, MC, V* ☉*No lunch Sun.*

$$$–$$$$

★

✗ **Papiamento.** Longtime restaurateurs Lenie and Eduardo Ellis converted their 175-year-old manor into a bistro with an atmosphere that is elegant, intimate, and always romantic. You can feast in the dining room, which is filled with antiques, or outdoors on the terrace by the pool (sitting on plastic patio chairs covered in fabric). The chefs mix Continental and Caribbean cuisines to produce sumptuous seafood and meat dishes. Items cooked "on the stone" are popular as much for the drama of the sizzling stone as for the incredible aromas that envelop you when they are presented. Service can be a bit slow sometimes, so don't come here if you're in a rush. ⊠ *Washington 61, Noord* ☎*297/586–4544* ♨*Reservations essential* ▤*AE, D, MC, V* ⊗*Closed Mon. No lunch.*

$$$–$$$$ ✕**Waterfront Crabhouse.** Amiable, transplanted-American owner Roy Leitch has created a magnet for seafood lovers in the heart of downtown. The waterfront location at the Renaissance Mall lends considerable atmosphere, as do the mural-covered walls and the live music. The Alaskan king crab legs are a sure bet and can easily serve two. Families will appreciate the extensive kids' menu and the huge lobster tank that is bound to provide entertainment for the little ones. ⊠*L. G. Smith Blvd. 82, Oranjestad* ☎*297/583–5858* ▤*AE, D, MC, V.*

$$–$$$$ ✕**Rumba Bar & Grill.** In the heart of Oranjestad, this lively bistro has an open kitchen where you can watch the chef prepare tasty international fare (mostly grilled seafood and beef) over a charcoal grill. The presentations are fanciful, with entrées forming towering shapes over beds of colorful vegetables and sauces. You can dine on the terrace and soak up the local color, or inside amid wicker and warm pink hues; the crowd is always worth watching. It's an AGA Dine-Around member. ⊠*Havenstraat 4, Oranjestad* ☎*297/588–7900* ▤*AE, D, MC, V.*

$$–$$$ ✕**Pinchos Bar & Grill.** Built on a pier, this casual spot—with only 11 tables—has one of the most romantic settings on the island. At night the restaurant glimmers from a distance as hundreds of lights reflect off the water. Guests can watch as chef Robby Peterson prepares delectable meals on the grill in his tiny kitchen. His wife and co-owner, Anabela, keeps diners comfortable and happy. The bar area is great for enjoying ocean breezes over an evening cocktail, and there is live entertainment every weekend. ⊠*L. G. Smith Blvd. 7, Oranjestad* ☎*287/583–2666* ▤*D, MC, V* ⊗*Closed Mon. No lunch.*

Fodor's Choice
★

$$–$$$ ✕**Qué Pasa?** This funky eatery recently moved into new digs down the street from its former address; it now serves as something of an art gallery–restaurant where diners can appreciate the colorful and funky works of local artists while enjoying a meal or savoring a drink. Outdoor spaces are a medley of terra-cotta and deep rusty hues illuminated by strings of lights. Inside, cool white prevails, letting the art stand out. Despite the name, there isn't a Mexican dish on the menu, which includes everything from sashimi to ribs; the fish dishes are especially good. Everything is done with Aruban flair, and the staff is helpful and friendly. The bar area is lively and fun. ⊠ *Wilhelminastraat 18, Oranjestad* ☎*297/583–4888* ▤*MC, V.*

ITALIAN
$$–$$$$ ✕**Hostaria Da' Vittorio.** Part of the fun at this family-oriented spot is watching chef Vittorio Muscariello prepare authentic Italian regional specialties in the open kitchen. The staff helps you choose wines from the extensive list and recommends portions of hot and cold antipasti, risottos, and pastas. Those on a tight budget should stick to the pizza offerings. As you leave, pick up some limoncello (lemon liqueur) or olive oil at the gourmet shop. Be aware that the decibel level of the crowd can be high. A 15% gratuity is automatically added to your

bill. It's an AGA VIP member. ⊠ *L. G. Smith Blvd. 380, Palm Beach* ☎ *297/586–3838* ⊟ *AE, D, MC, V.*

STEAK
$$$–$$$$
★
✕ **L. G. Smith's Steak & Chop House.** A study in teak, cream, and black, this fine steak house offers some of the best beef on the island. Subdued lighting and cascading water create a pleasant atmosphere, and the view over L. G. Smith Boulevard to the harbor makes for an exceptional dining experience. The menu features quality cuts of meat, all superbly prepared. The casino is steps away if you fancy a few pulls at the slots after dinner. ⊠ *Renaissance Aruba Beach Resort & Casino, L. G. Smith Blvd. 82, Oranjestad* ☎ *297/523–6115* ⚑ *Reservations essential* ⊟ *AE, D, DC, MC, V* ⊗ *No lunch.*

$$–$$$$
☺
✕ **El Gaucho Argentine Grill.** Faux-leather-bound books, tulip-top lamps, wooden chairs, and tile floors decorate this Argentina-style steak house, which has been in business since 1977. The key here is meat served in mammoth portions (think 16-ounce steaks). A welcome feature is a children's playroom, which allows adults to dine while the kids are entertained with videos and games. Be warned, though: even with the kids out of sight, the noise level can still be a bit high in this busy restaurant. ⊠ *Wilhelminastraat 80, Oranjestad* ☎ *297/582–3677* ⊟ *MC, V* ⊗ *Closed Sun.*

BEACHES

The beaches on Aruba are legendary: white sand, turquoise waters, and virtually no litter—everyone takes the NO TIRA SUSHI (no littering) signs very seriously, especially considering the island's $280 fine. The major public beaches, which back up to the hotels along the southwestern strip, are usually crowded. You can make the hour-long hike from the Holiday Inn to the Tamarijn without ever leaving sand. Make sure you're well protected from the sun—it scorches fast despite the cooling trade winds. Luckily, there's at least one covered bar (and often an ice-cream stand) at virtually every hotel. On the island's northeastern side, stronger winds make the waters too choppy for swimming, but the vistas are great and the terrain is wonderful for exploring.

Arashi Beach. Just after Malmok Beach, this is a 0.5-mi (1-km) stretch of gleaming white sand. Although it was once rocky, nature—with a little help from humans—has turned it into an excellent place for sunbathing and swimming. Despite calm waters, the rocky reputation has kept most people away, making it relatively uncrowded. ✛ *West of Malmok Beach, on west end.*

☺
★
Baby Beach. On the island's eastern tip (near the refinery), this semicircular beach borders a placid bay that's just about as shallow as a wading pool—perfect for tots, shore divers, and terrible swimmers. Thatched shaded areas are good places to cool off. Down the road is the island's rather unusual pet cemetery. Stop by the nearby snack truck for burgers, hot dogs, beer, and soda. The road to this beach (and several others) is through San Nicolas and along the road toward Seroe Colorado. Just before reaching the beach, keep an eye out for a strange 300-foot natural seawall made of coral and rock that was thrown up

overnight when Hurricane Ivan swept by the island in 2004. ⊠*Near Seroe Colorado, on east end.*

Boca Grandi. This is a great spot for windsurfers, but swimming is not advisable. It's near Seagrape Grove and the Aruba Golf Club toward the island's eastern tip. ⊠*Near Seagrape Grove, on east end.*

Boca Prins. You'll need a four-wheel-drive vehicle to make the trek to this strip of coastline, which is famous for its backdrop of enormous vanilla sand dunes. Near the Fontein Cave and Blue Lagoon, the beach itself is about as large as a Brazilian bikini—but with two rocky cliffs and tumultuously crashing waves, it's as romantic as Aruba gets. This isn't a swimming beach, however. Bring a picnic, a beach blanket, and sturdy sneakers, and descend the rocks that form steps to the water's edge. ⊠*Off 7 A/B, near Fontein Cave.*

Fodor's Choice ★ **Eagle Beach.** On the southwestern coast, across the highway from what is quickly becoming known as Time-Share Lane, is one of the Caribbean's—if not the world's—best beaches. Not long ago it was a nearly deserted stretch of pristine sand dotted with the occasional thatched picnic hut. Now that the resorts have been completed, this mile-plus-long beach is always hopping. When other Caribbean beaches eroded after Hurricane Ivan in 2004, Eagle Beach actually became several feet wider. ⊠*J. E. Irausquin Blvd., north of Manchebo Beach.*

Fisherman's Huts. Next to the Holiday Inn is a windsurfer's haven with good swimming conditions. Take a picnic lunch (tables are available) and watch the elegant purple, aqua, and orange sails struggle in the wind. ⊠*1 A/B, at Holiday Inn SunSpree Aruba.*

Grapefield Beach. To the southeast of San Nicolas, a sweep of blinding-white sand in the shadow of cliffs and boulders is marked by an anchor-shape memorial dedicated to all seamen. Pick sea grapes from January to June. Swim at your own risk; the waves here can be rough. ⊠*Southwest of San Nicolas, on east end.*

Malmok Beach. On the northwestern shore, this small, nondescript beach (where some of Aruba's wealthiest families have built tony residences) borders shallow waters that stretch 300 yards from shore. It's the perfect place to learn to windsurf. Right off the coast here is a favorite haunt for divers and snorkelers—the wreck of the German ship *Antilla,* scuttled in 1940. Take J. E. Irausquin Boulevard to the very end of the road. ⊠*At end of J. E. Irausquin Blvd., Malmokweg.*

Manchebo Beach (*Punta Brabo*). Impressively wide, the shoreline in front of the Manchebo Beach Resort is where officials turn a blind eye to the occasional topless sunbather. This beach merges with Druif Beach, and most locals use the name Manchebo to refer to both. ⊠*J. E. Irausquin Blvd., at Manchebo Beach Resort.*

Palm Beach. This stretch runs from the Westin Aruba Resort, Spa & Casino to the Marriott Aruba Ocean Club. It's the center of Aruban tourism, offering good opportunities for swimming, sailing, and other water sports. In some spots you might find a variety of shells that are great to collect, but not as much fun to step on barefoot—bring sandals just in case. ⊠*J. E. Irausquin Blvd. between Westin Aruba Resort, Spa & Casino and Marriott Aruba Ocean Club.*

🕙 **Rodger's Beach.** Near Baby Beach on the island's eastern tip, this beautiful curving stretch of sand is only slightly marred by its proximity to the oil refinery at the bay's far side. Swimming conditions are excellent here, as demonstrated by the local kids diving off the piers. The snack bar at the water's edge has beach-equipment rentals and a shop. Local bands play Sunday nights from Easter through summer. Drive around the refinery perimeter to get here. ⊠ *Next to Baby Beach, on east end.*

SPORTS & THE OUTDOORS

On Aruba you can participate in every conceivable water sport, as well as play tennis and golf or go on a fine hike through Arikok National Wildlife Park.

BIKING

Pedal pushing is a great way to get around the island; the climate is perfect, and the trade winds help to keep you cool. **Melchor Cycle Rental** (⊠ *Bubali 106B, Noord* ☎ *297/587–1787*) rents ATVs and bikes. **Rancho Notorious** (⊠ *Boroncana, Noord* ☎ *297/586–0508* ⊕ *www. ranchonotorious.com*) organizes mountain-biking tours.

DAY SAILS

If you plan to take a cruise around the island, know that the trade winds can make the waters choppy and that catamaran rides are much smoother than those on single-hull boats. Sucking on a peppermint or ginger candy may soothe your queasy stomach; avoid boating with an empty or overly full stomach. Moonlight cruises cost about $40 per person. There are also a variety of snorkeling, dinner and dancing, and sunset party cruises to choose from, priced from $30 to $60 per person. Many of the smaller operators work out of their homes; they often offer to pick you up (and drop you off) at your hotel or meet you at a particular hotel pier.

★ **Octopus Sailing Charters** (⊠ *Sali-a Cerca 1G, Oranjestad* ☎ *297/586–4281*) operates a trimaran that holds about 20 people. The drinks flow freely during the three-hour afternoon sail, which costs $28. Having a captain named Jethro is almost worth the price of admission in itself. **Red Sail Sports** (⊠ *L. G. Smith Blvd. 17, Oranjestad* ☎ *297/583–1603, 877/733–7245 in U.S.* ⊕ *www.redsailaruba.com*) offers a number of packages aboard its four catamarans, including the 70-foot *Rumba*. The popular sunset sail includes drinks and a lively atmosphere for $45 per person; the dinner cruise package includes a three-course meal and open bar for $95. Red Sail Sports also has locations at the Hyatt and Occidental hotels. **Tranquilo Charters Aruba** (⊠ *Sibelius St. 25, Oranjestad* ☎ *297/586–1418* ⊕ *www.visitaruba.com/tranquilo*), operated by Captain Hagedoorn, offers entertaining cruises, including a six-hour cruise to the south side of the island with lunch for $65. As strange as it sounds, the special "mom's Dutch pea soup" served with lunch is actually very good. Snorkeling equipment and free lessons are included in the package. **Wave Dancer Cruises** (⊠ *Ponton 90, Oranjestad* ☎*297/582–5520* ⊕*www.arubawavedancer.com*), in business since the mid-1970s, offers excellent value for the money. Sunset sails are $37, including drinks and snacks; half-day sails are $45, including snacks, lunch, and drinks. Snorkeling packages are also available.

DIVING & SNORKELING

With visibility of up to 90 feet, the waters around Aruba are excellent for snorkeling and diving. Advanced and novice divers alike will find plenty to occupy their time, as many of the most popular sites—including some interesting shipwrecks—are found in shallow waters ranging from 30 to 60 feet. Coral reefs covered with sensuously waving sea fans and eerie giant sponge tubes attract a colorful menagerie of sea life, including gliding manta rays, curious sea turtles, shy octopuses, and fish from grunts to groupers. Marine preservation is a priority on Aruba, and regulations by the Conference on International Trade in Endangered Species make it unlawful to remove coral, conch, and other marine life from the water.

Expect snorkel gear to rent for about $15 per day and trips to cost around $40. Scuba rates are around $50 for a one-tank reef or wreck dive, $65 for a two-tank dive, and $45 for a night dive. Resort courses, which offer an introduction to scuba diving, average $65 to $70. If you want to go all the way, complete open-water certification costs around $350.

★ **De Palm Watersports** (⊠ *L. G. Smith Blvd. 142, Oranjestad* ☎*297/582–4400 or 800/766–6016* ⊕*www.depalm.com*) is one of the best choices for your undersea experience, and the options go beyond basic diving. You can don a helmet and walk along the ocean floor near De Palm Island, home of huge blue parrot fish. You can even do Snuba—which is like scuba diving but without the heavy air tanks—from either a boat or from an island; it costs $56. **Dive Aruba** (⊠ *Wilhelminastraat 8, Oranjestad* ☎*297/582–7337* ⊕*www.divearuba.com*) offers resort courses, certification courses, and trips to interesting shipwrecks. **Mermaid Sport Divers** (⊠*Bubali 112-J, Sasaki Hwy. between low-rise and high-rise hotels, Oranjestad* ☎*297/587–4103* ⊕*www.scubadivers-aruba.com*) has dive packages with PADI-certified instructors. **Native Divers Aruba** (⊠*Koyari 1, Noord* ☎*297/586–4763* ⊕*www.nativedivers.com*) offers all types of dives; underwater naturalist courses are taught by PADI-certified instructors. **Red Sail Sports** (⊠*J. E. Irausquin Blvd. 83, Oranjestad* ☎*297/586–1603, 877/733–7245 in U.S.* ⊕*www.redsail.com*) has courses for children and others new to scuba diving. An introductory class costs about $79.

FISHING

Deep-sea catches here include barracuda, kingfish, wahoo, bonito, and black-and-yellow tuna. November to April is the catch-and-release season for sailfish and marlin. Many skippered charter boats are available for half- or full-day sails. Packages include tackle, bait, and refreshments. Prices range from $250 to $450 for a half-day charter and from $400 to $600 for a full day.

Pelican Tours & Watersports (⊠ *Pelican Pier, near Holiday Inn and Playa Linda hotels, Palm Beach* ☎ *297/586–3271* ⊕ *www.pelican-aruba. com*) is not just for the surf-and-snorkel crowd; the company will help you catch trophy-size fish. **Red Sail Sports** (⊠ *J. E. Irausquin Blvd. 83, Oranjestad* ☎ *297/586–1603, 877/733–7245 in U.S.* ⊕ *www.redsail. com*) can arrange everything for your fishing trip. Captain Kenny of **Teaser Charters** (⊠ *St. Vincentweg 5, Oranjestad* ☎ *297/582–5088* ⊕ *www.teasercharters.com*) runs a thrilling expedition. The expertise of the crew is matched by a commitment to sensible fishing practices, which include "catch and release" where appropriate and avoiding ecologically sensitive areas. The company's two boats are fully equipped, and the crew seem to have an uncanny ability to locate the best fishing spots.

GOLF

The **Aruba Golf Club** (⊠ *Golfweg 82, San Nicolas* ☎ *297/584–2006*) has a 9-hole course with 20 sand traps, five water traps, roaming goats, and lots of cacti. There are also 11 greens covered with artificial turf, making 18-hole tournaments a possibility. The clubhouse has a bar and locker rooms. Greens fees are $10 for 9 holes, $15 for 18 holes. Golf carts are available.

The **Links at Divi Aruba** (⊠ *J. E. Irausquin Blvd. 93, Oranjestad* ☎ *297/581–4653*), is a 9-hole course designed by Karl Litten and Lorie Viola. The par-36 paspalum grass course (best for seaside courses) takes you past beautiful lagoons. Amenities include a golf school with professional instruction, a swing analysis station, a driving range, and a two-story golf clubhouse with a pro shop. Two restaurants are available: Windows on Aruba for fine dining and Mulligan's for a casual and quick lunch. Greens fees are $75 for 9 holes, $110 for 18 from April to December); guests of the Divi Village Golf & Beach Resort pay a reduced rate.

★ **Tierra del Sol** (⊠ *Malmokweg* ☎ *297/586–0978*), a stunning course, is on the northwest coast near the California Lighthouse. Designed by Robert Trent Jones Jr., this 18-hole championship course combines Aruba's native beauty—cacti and rock formations—with the lush greens of the world's best courses. The $133 greens fee ($88 in summer) includes a golf cart equipped with a communications system that allows you to order drinks for your return to the clubhouse. Half-day golf clinics, a bargain at $45, include lunch in the clubhouse (available Monday, Tuesday, and Thursday). The pro shop is one of the Caribbean's most elegant, with an extremely attentive staff.

HIKING

Despite Aruba's arid landscape, hiking the rugged countryside will give you the best opportunities to see the island's wildlife and flora. Arikok National Wildlife Park is an excellent place to glimpse the real Aruba, free of the trappings of tourism. The heat can be oppressive, so be sure to take it easy, wear a hat, and have a bottle of water handy.

☪ **Aruba Nature Sensitive Hikers** (✉ *Pos Chiquito 13E, Savaneta* ☎ *297/587-*
★ *5017* ⊕ *www.sensitivehikers.com*) is run by Eddy Croes, a former park ranger whose passion for the area is seemingly unbounded. Groups are never larger than eight people, so you'll see as much detail as you can handle. Expect frequent stops when Eddy will ask for silence so that you can hear the sounds of the park. The hikes are done at an easy pace and are suitable for basically anyone. A moonlight walk is available for those looking to avoid the heat.

HORSEBACK RIDING

Ranches offer short jaunts along the beach or longer rides along trails passing through countryside flanked by cacti, divi-divi trees, and aloe vera plants. Ask if you can stop off at Cura di Tortuga, a natural pool that's reputed to have restorative powers. Rides are also possible in Arikok National Wildlife Park. Rates run from $35 for an hour-long trip to $65 for a three-hour tour; private rides cost slightly more.

☪ **Rancho Daimari** (✉ *Tanki Leendert 249, San Nicolas* ☎ *297/587-5674*
⊕ *www.visitaruba.com/ranchodaimari*) will lead your horse to water—either at Natural Bridge or Natural Pool—in the morning or afternoon for $64 per person. The "Junior Dudes" program is tailored to young riders. There are even ATV trips. **Rancho Notorious** (✉ *Boroncana, Noord* ☎ *297/586-0508* ⊕ *www.ranchonotorious.com*) will take you on a tour of the countryside for $45, to the beach to snorkel for $120, or on a three-hour ride up to the California Lighthouse for $70. The company also organizes ATV- and mountain-biking trips.

KAYAKING

Kayaking is a popular sport on Aruba, especially along the south coast, where the waters are calm. It's a great way to explore the coastline. **Aruba Kayak Adventure** (✉ *Ponton 90, Oranjestad* ☎ *297/587-7722* ⊕ *www.arubakayak.com*) has excellent half-day kayak trips, which start with a quick lesson before you paddle through caves and mangroves and along the scenic coast. The tour makes a lunch stop at De Palm Island, where snorkeling is included as part of the $99 package.

SUBMARINE EXCURSIONS

Explore an underwater reef teeming with marine life without getting wet. **Atlantis Submarines** (✉ *Renaissance Marina, L. G. Smith Blvd. 82, Oranjestad* ☎ *297/583-6090* ⊕ *www.atlantisadventures.net*) operates a 65-foot air-conditioned sub, *Atlantis VI*, which takes 48 passengers

95 to 150 feet below the surface along Barcadera Reef ($89 per person). The company also owns the *Seaworld Explorer*, a semisubmersible that allows you to sit and view Aruba's marine habitat from 5 feet below the surface ($37 per person). Make reservations a day in advance.

WINDSURFING

★ The southwestern coast's tranquil waters make windsurfing conditions ideal for both beginners and intermediates, as the winds are steady but sudden gusts rare. Experts will find the Atlantic coast, especially around Grapefield and Boca Grandi beaches, more challenging; winds are fierce and often shift course without warning. Most operators also offer complete windsurfing vacation packages. The up-and-coming sport of kite surfing (sometimes called kite boarding) is also popular in Aruba.

Aruba Boardsailing Productions (⊠*L. G. Smith Blvd. 486, near Fisherman's Huts, Palm Beach* ☎*297/586–3940* 🖶*297/993–1111* ⊕*www. visitaruba.com/arubaboardsailing*) is a major windsurfing center on the island. **Pelican Adventures Tours & Watersports** (⊠*Pelican Pier, near Holiday Inn and Playa Linda hotels, Palm Beach* ☎*297/586–3600* ⊕*www. pelican-aruba.com*) usually has rental boards and sails on hand. **Sailboard Vacations** (⊠*L. G. Smith Blvd. 462, Malmok Beach* ☎*297/586–2527* ⊕*www.sailboardvacations.com*) offers complete windsurf packages, including accommodation. Equipment can be rented for $60 a day. Trade jokes and snap photos with your fellow windsurfers at **Vela Aruba** (⊠*L. G. Smith Blvd. 101, Palm Beach* ☎*297/586–9000 Ext. 6430* ⊕*www.velawindsurf.com*). This is *the* place to make friends. It's a major kite-surfing center as well.

SHOPPING

"Duty-free" *is* a magical term in the Caribbean—but it's not always accurate. The duty-free shopping zone in Aruba closed several years ago, so the only true duty-free shopping is in the departure area of the airport. (Passengers bound for the United States should be sure to shop before proceeding through U.S. customs in Aruba.) Downtown stores often advertise "duty-free prices," with markdowns of up to 25%, but comparison shopping is still advisable. Major credit cards are welcome virtually everywhere; U.S. dollars are accepted almost as readily as the local currency; and traveler's checks can be cashed with proof of identity.

Aruba's souvenir and crafts stores are full of Dutch porcelains and figurines, as befits the island's heritage. Dutch cheese is a good buy (you're allowed to bring up to 10 pounds of hard cheese through U.S. customs), as are hand-embroidered linens and any products made from the native aloe vera plant—sunburn cream, face masks, or skin refreshers. Local arts and crafts run toward wood carvings and earthenware emblazoned with ARUBA: ONE HAPPY ISLAND and the like. Since there's no sales tax, the price you see on the tag is what you pay. (Note that although large stores in town and at hotels include the value-added tax of 3%, tiny shops and studios may add it separately.) Don't try to bargain. Arubans consider it rude to haggle, despite what you may hear to the contrary.

AREAS & MALLS

Oranjestad's **Caya G. F. Betico Croes** is Aruba's chief shopping street, lined with several shops advertising "duty-free prices" (again, these are not truly duty-free), boutiques, and jewelry stores noted for the aggressiveness of their vendors on cruise-ship days.

For late-night shopping, head to the **Alhambra Casino Shopping Arcade** (⊠ *L. G. Smith Blvd. 47, Manchebo Beach*), which is open until midnight. Souvenir shops, boutiques, and fast-food outlets fill the arcade, which is attached to the popular casino. Although small, the **Aquarius Mall** (⊠ *Elleboogstraat 1, Oranjestad*) has some upscale shops. The **Holland Aruba Mall** (⊠ *Havenstraat 6, Oranjestad*) houses a collection of smart shops and eateries. Stores at the **Port of Call Marketplace** (⊠ *L. G. Smith Blvd. 17, Oranjestad*) sell fine jewelry, perfumes, low-priced liquor, batiks, crystal, leather goods, and fashionable clothing. Five minutes from the cruise-ship terminal, the **Renaissance Mall** (⊠ *L. G. Smith Blvd. 82, Oranjestad*), also known as Seaport Mall, has more than 120 stores selling merchandise to meet every taste and budget; the Crystal Casino is also here. The **Royal Plaza Mall** (⊠ *L. G. Smith Blvd. 94, Oranjestad*), across from the cruise-ship terminal, has cafés, a post office (open weekdays 8 to 3:30), and such stores as Nautica, Benetton, Tommy Hilfiger, and Gandelman Jewelers. There's also a Cyber Café for those who want to send e-mail and get their caffeine fix all in one stop.

SPECIALTY STORES

CLOTHING

Confetti (⊠ *Renaissance Mall, L. G. Smith Blvd. 82, Oranjestad* ☎ *297/583–8614*) has the hottest European and American swimsuits, cover-ups, and beach essentials.

★ **Wulfsen & Wulfsen** (⊠ *Caya G. F. Betico Croes 52, Oranjestad* ☎ *297/582–3823*) has been one of the most highly regarded clothing stores in Aruba and the Netherlands Antilles for 30 years. It carries elegant suits for men and linen cocktail dresses for women; it's also a great place to buy Bermuda shorts.

HANDICRAFTS

★ **Art & Tradition Handicrafts** (⊠ *Caya G. F. Betico Croes 30, Oranjestad* ☎ *297/583–6534* ⊠ *Royal Plaza Mall, L. G. Smith Blvd. 94, Oranjestad* ☎ *297/582–7862*) sells intriguing souvenirs. Buds from the *mopa mopa* tree are boiled to form a resin, which is colored using vegetable dyes, then stretched by hand and mouth. Tiny pieces are cut and layered to form intricate designs—these are truly unusual gifts.

The **Artistic Boutique** (⊠*L. G. Smith Blvd. 90–92, Oranjestad* ☎*297/ 588–2468* ⊠*Holiday Inn SunSpree Aruba Beach Resort & Casino, J. E. Irausquin Blvd. 230, Palm Beach* ☎*297/583–3383*) is known for its Giuseppe Armani figurines from Italy, usually sold at a 20% discount; Aruban hand-embroidered linens; gold and silver jewelry; and porcelain and pottery from Spain.

JEWELRY

Filling 6,000 square feet of space, **Boolchand's** (⊠*Renaissance Mall, L. G. Smith Blvd. 82, Oranjestad* ☎*297/583–0147*) sells jewelry and watches. It also stocks leather goods, cameras, and electronics.

If green fire is your passion, **Colombian Emeralds** (⊠*Renaissance Mall, L. G. Smith Blvd. 82, Oranjestad* ☎*297/583–6238*) has a dazzling array. There are also fine European watches.

Kenro Jewelers (⊠*Renaissance Mall, L. G. Smith Blvd. 82, Oranjestad* ☎*297/583–4847 or 297/583–3171*) has two stores in the same mall, attesting to the popularity of its stock of bracelets and necklaces from Ramon Leopard; jewelry by Arando, Micheletto, and Blumei; and various brands of watches. There are also six other locations, including some in major hotels.

PERFUMES

For perfumes, cosmetics, men's and women's clothing, and leather goods (including Bally shoes), stop in at **Aruba Trading Company** (⊠*Caya G. F. Betico Croes 12, Oranjestad* ☎*297/582–2602*), which has been in business since the 1930s.

A venerated name in Aruba, **J. L. Penha & Sons** (⊠*Caya G. F. Betico Croes 11/13, Oranjestad* ☎*297/582–4160 or 297/582–4161*) sells high-end perfumes and cosmetics. It stocks such brands as Boucheron, Cartier, Dior, and Givenchy.

★ **Little Switzerland** (⊠*Caya G. F. Betico Croes 14, Oranjestad* ☎*297/582–1192* ⊠*Royal Plaza Mall, L. G. Smith Blvd. 94, Oranjestad* ☎*297/583–4057*), the Caribbean retail giant, is the place to go for brand-name men's and women's fragrances as well as china, crystal, and fine tableware.

At **Weitnauer** (⊠*Caya G. F. Betico Croes 29, Oranjestad* ☎*297/582– 2790*) you can find specialty Lenox items, as well as a wide range of fragrances.

NIGHTLIFE & THE ARTS

NIGHTLIFE

Unlike many islands, Aruba's nightlife isn't confined to the touristy folkloric shows at hotels. Arubans like to party. They usually start celebrating late, and the action doesn't pick up until around midnight. One uniquely Aruban institution is a psychedelically painted '57 Chevy bus called the **Kukoo Kunuku** (☎*297/586–2010* ⊕*www.kukookunuku. com*). Weeknights you can find as many as 40 passengers traveling among three bars from sundown to around midnight. The $59 fee per passenger includes a so-so dinner, some drinks, and pickup at your hotel. The same company operates the infamous Tatoo party boat, which has a buffet, $1 drinks, live entertainment, and a lot of rowdy behavior for $59. The boat leaves at 7:15 PM from the De Palm pier near the Radisson.

BARS

Bambu (⊠ *Babijn 53, Paradera* ☎*No phone*) is a local joint that offers typical Aruban food, cheap drinks, and a lively crowd on the terrace on weekends.

★ Many visitors, including those on party buses, find their way to **Carlos & Charlie's** (⊠ *Weststraat 3A, Oranjestad* ☎*297/582–0355*)—which may be why most locals shy away from it. You'll find mixed drinks by the yard, Mexican fare, and American music from the 1960s, '70s, and '80s.

Charlie's Bar (⊠*Zeppenfeldstraat 56, San Nicolas* ☎*297/584–5086*) has been an Aruba institution since 1941. It's a bit far from most hotels, but certainly worth the trip. Expect a raucous (and, most likely, very inebriated) crowd. The food here is quite good as well, all the better for padding your stomach before the margaritas.

★ You can watch the crowds from the terrace at **Choose a Name** (⊠*Havenstraat 36, Oranjestad* ☎*297/588–6200*) or climb up on the bar for your karaoke debut; bands also perform several nights a week.

For specialty drinks, try **Iguana Joe's** (⊠*Royal Plaza Mall, L. G. Smith Blvd. 94, Oranjestad* ☎*297/583–9373*). The creative reptilian-theme decor is as colorful as the cocktails.

★ With painted parrots flocking on the ceiling, **Mambo Jambo** (⊠*Royal Plaza Mall, L. G. Smith Blvd. 94, Oranjestad* ☎*297/583–3632*) is daubed in sunset colors. Sip one of several concoctions sold nowhere else on the island, then browse for memorabilia at a shop next door.

With front-row seats to view the green flash—that ray of light that supposedly flicks through the sky as the sun sinks into the ocean—the **Palms Bar** (⊠*Hyatt Regency Aruba Beach Resort & Casino, J. E. Irausquin Blvd. 85, Palm Beach* ☎*297/586–1234*) is the perfect spot to enjoy the sunset.

CASINOS

Aruban casinos offer something for both high and low rollers, as well as live, nightly entertainment in their lounges. Die-hard gamblers might look for the largest or the most active casinos, but many simply visit the casino closest to their hotel.

★ In the casual **Alhambra Casino** (⊠*L. G. Smith Blvd. 47, Oranjestad* ☎*297/583–5000*), a "Moorish slave" named Roger gives every gambler a hearty handshake upon entering.

The smart money is on the **Casablanca Casino** (⊠ *Westin Aruba Resort, Spa & Casino, J. E. Irausquin Blvd. 77, Palm Beach* ☎*297/586–4466*). It's quietly elegant and has a Bogart theme.

Overhead at the **Casino at the Radisson Aruba Resort** (⊠*Radisson Aruba Resort & Casino, J. E. Irausquin Blvd. 81, Palm Beach* ☎*297/586–4045*), thousands of lights simulate shooting stars that seem destined to carry out your wishes for riches. The slots here open at 10 AM, and table action begins at 4 PM.

The ultramodern **Copacabana Casino** (⊠ *Hyatt Regency Aruba Beach Resort & Casino, J. E. Irausquin Blvd. 85, Palm Beach* ☎ *297/586–1234*) is an enormous complex with a Carnival-in-Rio theme and live entertainment.

The **Crystal Casino** (⊠ *Renaissance Aruba Resort & Casino, L. G. Smith Blvd. 82, Oranjestad* ☎ *297/583–6000*) is open 24 hours a day.

The **Excelsior Casino** (⊠ *Holiday Inn SunSpree Aruba Beach Resort & Casino, J. E. Irausquin Blvd. 230, Palm Beach* ☎ *297/586–3600*) has sports betting in addition to the usual slots and table games.

Royal Palm Casino (⊠ *Occidental Grand Aruba, J. E. Irausquin Blvd. 250, Eagle Beach* ☎ *297/587–4665*) is the largest in the Caribbean. It has an expansive, sleek interior; 400 slot machines; a no-smoking slot room and gaming tables; and the Tropicana nightclub.

Low-key gambling can be found at the waterside **Seaport Casino** (⊠ *L. G. Smith Blvd. 9, Oranjestad* ☎ *297/583–6000*).

The **Stellaris Casino** (⊠ *Aruba Marriott Resort, L. G. Smith Blvd. 101, Palm Beach* ☎ *297/586–9000*) is one of the island's most popular.

DANCE & MUSIC CLUBS

★ Popular with locals and tourists, **Café Bahia** (⊠ *Weststraat 7, Oranjestad* ☎ *297/588–9982*) draws a chic crowd every Friday for happy hour. If you come for dinner, stick around for drinking and dancing as the music heats up. On Tuesday night, a band from one of the cruise ships plays local favorites.

★ For jazz and other types of music, try cozy **Garufa Cigar & Cocktail Lounge** (⊠ *Wilhelminastraat 63, Oranjestad* ☎ *297/582–7205*), which serves as a lounge for customers awaiting a table at the nearby Gaucho Argentine Grill (you're issued a beeper so you know when your table is ready). While you wait, have a drink, enjoy some appetizers, and take in the leopard-print carpet and funky bar stools. The ambience may very well draw you back for an after-dinner cognac. There's live entertainment most nights, and the powerful smoke extractor system helps make life bearable for nonsmokers.

THE ARTS

ART GALLERIES

★ **Access** (⊠ *Caya G. F. Betico Croes 16–18, Oranjestad* ☎ *297/588–7837*) showcases new and established artists; it's a major venue for Caribbean art. Located in the downtown shopping district, the gallery is home to a thriving cultural scene that includes poetry readings, chamber music concerts, and screenings of feature films and documentaries. The owner, artist Landa Henriquez, is also a bolero singer.

At **Galeria Eterno** (⊠ *Emanstraat 92, Oranjestad* ☎ *297/583–9607*), you can find local and international artists at work. Be sure to stop by for concerts by classical guitarists, dance performances, visual-arts shows, and plays.

Galeria Harmonia (⊠*Zeppenfeldstraat 10, San Nicolas* ☎*297/584–2969*), the island's largest exhibition space, has a permanent collection of works by local and international artists.

Gasparito Restaurant & Art Gallery (⊠*Gasparito 3, Noord* ☎*297/586–7044*) features a permanent exhibition by Aruban artists.

ISLAND CULTURE

The **Bon Bini Festival,** a year-round folkloric event (the name means "welcome" in Papiamento), is held every Tuesday from 6:30 PM to 8:30 PM at Ft. Zoutman in Oranjestad. In the inner courtyard you can check out the Antillean dancers in resplendent costumes, feel the rhythms of the steel drums, browse among the stands displaying local artwork, and partake of local food and drink. Admission is usually around $3, but can be as high as $10, depending on what is on offer.

EXPLORING ARUBA

Aruba's wildly sculpted landscape is replete with rocky deserts, cactus clusters, secluded coves, blue vistas, and the trademark divi-divi tree. To see the island's wild, untamed beauty, you can rent a car, take a sightseeing tour, or hire a cab for $30 an hour (for up to four people). The main highways are well paved, but on the windward side (the north- and east-facing side) some roads are still a mixture of compacted dirt and stones. Although a car is fine, a four-wheel-drive vehicle will allow you to explore the unpaved interior.

Traffic is sparse, but signs leading to sights are often small and hand-lettered (this is slowly changing as the government puts up official road signs), so watch closely. Route 1A travels southbound along the western coast, and 1B is simply northbound along the same road. If you lose your way, just follow the divi-divi trees, which always lean southwest.

WHAT TO SEE

Alto Vista Chapel. Alone near the island's northwest corner sits the scenic little Alto Vista Chapel. The wind whistles through the simple mustard-color walls, eerie boulders, and looming cacti. Along the side of the road back to civilization are miniature crosses with depictions of the stations of the cross and hand-lettered signs exhorting PRAY FOR US, SINNERS and the like—a simple yet powerful evocation of faith. To get here, follow the rough, winding dirt road that loops around the island's northern tip, or, from the hotel strip, take Palm Beach Road through three intersections and watch for the asphalt road to the left just past the Alto Vista Rum Shop.

Arikok National Wildlife Park. Nearly 20% of Aruba has been designated part of this national park, which sprawls across the eastern interior and the northeast coast. The park is the keystone of the government's long-term ecotourism plan to preserve Aruba's resources and showcases the island's flora and fauna as well as ancient Arawak petroglyphs, the ruins of a gold-mining operation at Miralmar, and the remnants of Dutch peasant settlements at Masiduri. At the park's main entrance,

Arikok Center houses offices, restrooms, and food facilities. All visitors must stop here upon entering so that officials can manage the traffic flow and hand out information on park rules and features. Within the confines of the park are Mt. Arikok and the 620-foot Mt. Yamanota, Aruba's highest peak.

Anyone looking for geological exotica should head for the park's caves, found on the northeastern coast. Baranca Sunu, the so-called Tunnel of Love, has a heart-shape entrance and naturally sculpted rocks farther inside that look like the Madonna, Abraham Lincoln, and even a jaguar. Fontein Cave, which was used by indigenous peoples centuries ago, is marked with ancient drawings (rangers are on hand to offer explanations). Bats are known to make appearances—don't worry, they won't bother you. Although you don't need a flashlight because the paths are well lighted, it's best to wear sneakers.

★ **Aruba Ostrich Farm.** Everything you ever wanted to know about the world's largest living birds can be found at this farm. A large palapa houses a gift shop and restaurant (popular with large bus tours), and tours of the farm are available every half hour. This operation is virtually identical to the facility in Curaçao; it's owned by the same company. ☒ *Makividiri Rd., Paradera* ☎ *297/585–9630* ⊕ *www. arubaostrichfarm.com* ☒ *$12* ☼ *Daily 9–5.*

Balashi Brewery. The factory that manufactures the excellent local beer, Balashi, offers daily tours to the public that will take you through every stage of the brewing process. It makes for a fascinating hour, and the price of the tour includes a free drink at the end. Those more interested in beer drinking than beer making might want to visit the factory any evening from 7 to 10 for happy hour (there is live music on Friday). ☒ *Balashi 75, Balashi* ☎ *297/592–2544* ⊕ *www.balashi.com.*

Butterfly Farm. Hundreds of butterflies from around the world flutter about this spectacular garden. Guided 20- to 30-minute tours (included in the price of admission) provide an entertaining look into the life cycle of these insects, from egg to caterpillar to chrysalis to butterfly. There's a special deal offered here: after your initial visit, you can return as often as you like for free during your vacation. ☒ *J. E. Irausquin Blvd., Palm Beach* ☎ *297/586–3656* ⊕ *www.thebutterflyfarm. com* ☒ *$12* ☼ *Daily 9–4:30; last tour at 4.*

California Lighthouse. The lighthouse, built by a French architect in 1910, stands at the island's far northern end. Although you can't go inside, you can ascend the hill to the lighthouse base for some great views. In this stark landscape, you might feel as though you've just landed on the moon. The lighthouse is surrounded by huge boulders that look like extraterrestrial monsters and sand dunes embroidered with scrub that resemble undulating sea serpents.

Mt. Hooiberg. Named for its shape (*hooiberg* means "haystack" in Dutch), this 541-foot peak lies inland just past the airport. If you have the energy, climb the 562 steps to the top for an impressive view of Oranjestad (and Venezuela on clear days).

Oranjestad. Aruba's charming capital is best explored on foot. L. G. Smith Boulevard, the palm-lined thoroughfare in the center of town, runs between pastel-painted buildings, old and new, of typical Dutch design. You'll find many malls with boutiques and shops here.

The **Archaeological Museum of Aruba** has two rooms chock-full of fascinating artifacts from the indigenous Arawak people, including farm and domestic utensils dating back hundreds of years. ⊠ *J. E. Irausquin Blvd. 2A, Oranjestad* ☎ *297/582–8979* ✉ *Free* ⊙ *Weekdays 8–noon and 1–4.*

★ Learn all about aloe—its cultivation, processing, and production—at **Aruba Aloe,** Aruba's own aloe farm and factory. Guided tours lasting about a half hour will show you how the gel—revered for its skin-soothing properties—is extracted from the aloe vera plant and used in a variety of products, including after-sun creams, soaps, and shampoos. You can purchase the finished goods in the gift shop. ⊠ *Pitastraat 115, Oranjestad* ☎ *297/588–3222* ✉ *$8* ⊙ *Weekdays 8:30–4:30, Sat. 9–1.*

⟳ The **Experience Aruba Panorama** brings the island's history and culture to life in a 22-minute cinematic extravaganza that fills five massive screens and measures 13 feet high and 66 feet wide. The breathtaking shows begin in the Crystal Theater at the Renaissance Aruba Beach Resort & Casino at the top of every hour from 11 to 5. ⊠ *L. G. Smith Blvd. 82, Oranjestad* ☎ *297/583–6000* ✉ *$10* ⊙ *Mon.–Sat. 11–5.*

One of the island's oldest edifices, **Ft. Zoutman** was built in 1796 and played an important role in skirmishes between British and Curaçao troops in 1803. The Willem III Tower, named for the Dutch monarch of that time, was added in 1868 to serve as a lighthouse. Over time, the fort has been a government office building, a police station, and a prison; now its historical museum displays Aruban artifacts in an 18th-century house. ⊠ *Zoutmanstraat, Oranjestad* ☎ *297/582–6099* ✉ *Free* ⊙ *Weekdays 8–noon and 1–4.*

★ The **Numismatic Museum** displays more than 40,000 historic coins and paper money from around the world. A few pieces were salvaged from shipwrecks in the region. Some of the coins circulated during the Roman Empire, the Byzantine Empire, and the ancient Chinese dynasties; the oldest dates to the 3rd century BC. The museum had its start as the private collection of an Aruban who dug up some old coins in his garden. It's now run by his granddaughter. ⊠ *Weststraat, Oranjestad* ☎ *297/582–8831* ✉ *$5* ⊙ *Mon.–Thurs. 9–4, Fri. 9–1, Sat. 9–noon.*

Rock Formations. The massive boulders at Ayo and Casibari are a mystery, as they don't match the island's geological makeup. You can climb to the top for fine views of the arid countryside. On the way you'll doubtless pass Aruba whiptail lizards—the males are cobalt blue, and the females are blue-gray with light-blue dots. The main path to Casibari has steps and handrails the entire way (except on one side), and you must move through tunnels and along narrow steps and ledges to reach the top. At Ayo you can find ancient pictographs in a small cave (the entrance has iron bars to protect the drawings from vandalism).

You may also encounter boulder climbers, who are increasingly drawn to Ayo's smooth surfaces. Access to Casibari is via Tanki Highway 4A; you can reach Ayo via Route 6A. Watch carefully for the turnoff signs near the center of the island on the way to the windward side.

San Nicolas. During the oil refinery heyday, Aruba's oldest village was a bustling port; now its primary purpose is tourism. *The* institution in town is Charlie's Restaurant and Bar. Stop in for a drink and advice on what to see and do in this little town. Aruba's main red light district is located here and will be fairly apparent to even the most casual observer.

ARUBA ESSENTIALS

To research prices, get advice from other travelers, and book travel arrangements, visit www.fodors.com.

■ TRANSPORTATION

BY AIR

Most major U.S. airlines fly to Aruba, and smaller airlines provide connecting flights to and from other Dutch Caribbean islands, making day trips possible, though expensive.

Information American Airlines/American Eagle (☎297/582–2700 ⊕www.aa.com). **Continental** (☎297/588–0044 ⊕www.continental.com). **Delta** (☎297/588–6119 ⊕www.delta.com). **Dutch Antilles Express** (☎297/588–1900 ⊕www.flydae.com). **jet-Blue** (☎801/365–2525 ⊕www.jetblue.com). **Spirit Airlines** (☎ 800/772–7117 ⊕www.spiritair.com). **United Airlines** (☎297/588–6544 ⊕www.united.com). **US Airways** (☎297/588–4162 ⊕www.usairways.com).

Airport Information Reina Beatrix International Airport (AUA ☎297/582–4800 ⊕www.airportaruba.com).

BY BUS

Buses run hourly trips between the beach hotels and Oranjestad. The one-way fare is $1.25 ($2.30 round-trip), and exact change is preferred (so be sure to keep some U.S. change handy if you plan to pay in U.S. currency). There are also minibuses that will pick you up at the same stops for the same price; just be sure to look for the ATA APPROVED SIGN. Buses also run down the coast from Oranjestad to San Nicolas for the same fare.

BY CAR

Aruba has a well-organized public transit system, and taxis and tour companies are readily available, so a rental car is not really necessary for most visitors to the island. Many people come here for the nightlife, so using a taxi will remove any temptation to drink and drive. To rent a car you'll need a driver's license, and you must meet the minimum age requirements of the company (Budget, for example requires drivers to be over 25; Avis, between 23 and 70; and Hertz, over 21). A deposit of $500 (or a signed credit-card slip) is required. Rates are between $44 and $90 a day (local agencies generally have lower rates).

International traffic signs and Dutch-style traffic signals (with an extra light for a turning lane) can be misleading if you're not used to them; use extreme caution, especially at intersections, until you grasp the rules of the road. Speed limits are rarely posted but are usually 50 mph (80 kph) in the countryside. Aside from the major highways, the island's winding roads are poorly marked. Gas prices average about $1.79 a liter (roughly ⅓ gallon), which is reasonable by Caribbean standards.

Information Avis (✉Kolibristraat 14, Oranjestad ☎297/582–8787 ✉Airport ☎297/582–5496 ⊕www.avis.com). **Budget** (✉Kolibristraat 1, Oranjestad ☎297/582–8600 or 800/472–3325 ⊕www.budgetaruba.com). **Dollar** (✉Grendeaweg 15, Oranjestad ☎297/582–2783 ✉Airport ☎297/582–5651 ✉Manchebo Beach Resort, J.E. Irausquin Blvd. 55, Eagle Beach ☎297/582–6696 ⊕www.dollar.com). **Economy** (✉Kolibristraat 5, Oranjestad ☎297/582–5176 ⊕www.economyaruba.com). **Hedwina Car Rental** (✉Bubali 93A, Noord ☎297/587–6442 ✉Airport ☎297/583–0880). **Hertz** (✉Sabana Blanco 35, Oranjestad, near airport ☎297/582–1845 ✉Airport ☎297/582–9112 ⊕www.arubarentcar.com). **National** (✉Tanki Leendert 170, Noord ☎297/587–1967 ✉Airport ☎297/582–5451 ⊕www.nationalcar.com). **Thrifty** (✉Balashi 65, Santa Cruz ☎297/585–5300 ✉Airport ☎297/583–5335 ⊕www.thriftyaruba.com).

TAXIS

There's a dispatch office at the airport; you can also flag down taxis on the street (look for license plates with a "TX" tag). Rates are fixed (i.e., there are no meters; the rates are set by the government and displayed on a chart), though you and the driver should agree on the fare before your ride begins. Add $1 to the fare after midnight, and $2 on Sunday and holidays. An hour-long island tour costs about $60, with up to four people. Rides into town from Eagle Beach run about $17; from Palm Beach, about $15.

Taxi Information Airport Taxi Dispatch (☎297/582–2116).

▮ CONTACTS & RESOURCES

BANKS & EXCHANGE SERVICES

Arubans happily accept U.S. dollars virtually everywhere, so there's no real need to exchange money, except for necessary pocket change (for soda machines or pay phones). The official currency is the Aruban florin (Afl), also called the guilder, which is made up of 100 cents. If you need fast cash, ATMs are easy to find.

ELECTRICITY

Aruba runs on a 110-volt cycle, the same as the United States; outlets are usually the two-prong variety, just as you would find at home.

EMERGENCIES

Hospital Dr. Horacio Oduber Hospital (✉L.G. Smith Blvd. 47, Manchebo Beach ☎297/587–4300).

INTERNET, MAIL & SHIPPING

Aruba is well wired by Caribbean standards. Almost every hotel offers some form of Internet access, ranging from lobby Internet kiosks to high-speed wireless access. SETAR, a local Wi-Fi company, offers wireless access in most of the main hotel areas (and even on the beach if you want to risk bringing your laptop). Prepaid cards must be purchased at one of SETAR's offices). At a cost of only $10 for an entire 24 hours of usage, it is usually cheaper than paying for the service offered by the hotels.

Mailing a letter from Aruba to the United States or Canada costs Afl 2.15 (about $1.20), and a postcard costs Afl 1 (56¢). Expect it to take one to two weeks to arrive at its destination. A letter to Europe is Afl 2.15 ($1.20), and a postcard is Afl 1.25 (60¢). Sending mail to Europe takes two to four weeks, so you'll probably make it home before your letter does. Prices to Australia and New Zealand (three to four weeks) may be slightly higher. When addressing letters to Aruba, don't worry about the lack of formal addresses or postal codes; the island's postal service knows where to go.

LANGUAGE

Everyone on the island speaks English, but the official languages are Dutch and Papiamento. Most locals speak Papiamento—a fascinating, rapid-fire mix of Spanish, Dutch, English, French, and Portuguese—in normal conversation. Here are a few helpful phrases: *bon dia* (good day), *bon nochi* (good night), *masha danki* (thank you very much).

Internet Café Café Internet (✉8 Royal Plaza Mall, Oranjestad ☎297/582–4609).

SETAR Offices Telekiosk Airport (✉Arrival Hall, Reina Beatrix Airport ☎297/583–0525). **Teleshop Irausquinplein** (✉J. E. Irausquinplein, Oranjestad ☎297/582–1871). **Teleshop Palm Beach** (✉Next to Brickell Bay Resort, J. E. Irausquin Boulevard 370, Palm Beach ☎297/586–2042). **Teleshop San Nicholas** (✉Zeppenfeldstraat 33, San Nicholas ☎297/584–8096). **Teleshop Santa Cruz** (✉F. M. Croes Plaza, Santa Cruz 64-C ☎297/585–5400). **Teleshop Seroe Blanco** (✉Administration Bldg., Seroe Blanco z/n ☎297/582–6960).

Post Offices Main Post Office (✉9 J. E. Irausquinplein, Oranjestad ☎297/582–1900). There is also a branch office at Royal Plaza Mall, and others are scattered throughout the island.

SAFETY

Arubans are friendly, so you needn't be afraid to stop and ask anyone for directions. It's a relatively safe island, but common-sense rules still apply. Lock your rental car and leave valuables in your hotel safe. Don't leave bags unattended in the airport, on the beach, or on tour transports. Tap water is okay to drink.

TAXES

The airport departure tax is a hefty $36.75 for departures to the United States and $33.50 to other international destinations (including Bonaire and Curaçao), but the fee is usually included in your ticket price. Hotels collect 8% in government taxes on top of a typical 11% service charge, for a total of 19%. A 3% A. B. B. tax (value-added tax) is included in the price charged in most shops.

TELEPHONES

You can dial international calls directly or call from the SETAR office in the post office building in Oranjestad. Simply dial the seven-digit number in Aruba. AT&T customers can dial 800–8000 from special phones at the cruise dock and in the airport's arrival and departure halls. From other phones, dial 121 to contact the SETAR international operator to place a collect- or calling card call.

Local calls from pay phones, which accept both local currency and phone cards, cost 25¢.

Because hotel phone charges on Aruba can verge on obscene, renting a mobile phone for your stay can save you a ton of money. Chapeau Aruba Business Services offers one-week rental packages for about $69 that include 60 minutes of talk time to the United States; each additional day's rental is only $5, and the phone can be delivered to your hotel for free.

To call Aruba direct from the United States, dial 011–297, followed by the seven-digit number in Aruba.

Information Chapeau Aruba Business Services (☎297/586–4250).

TIPPING

Restaurants generally include a 10% to 15% service charge on the bill; when in doubt, ask. If service isn't included, a 10% tip is standard; if it is included, it's still customary to add something extra, usually small change, at your discretion. Taxi drivers expect a 10% to 15% tip, but it isn't mandatory. Porters and bellhops should receive about $2 per bag; chambermaids, about $2 a day.

TOUR OPTIONS

You can see the main sights in one day, but set aside two days to meander. Romantic horse-drawn carriage rides through the city streets of Oranjestad run $30 for a 30-minute tour; hours of operation are from 7 PM to 11 PM, and carriages depart from the clock tower at the Royal Plaza Mall. Guided tours are your best option if you have only a short time. Aruba's Transfer Tour & Taxi will take you to the main sights on personalized tours that cost $40 per hour. De Palm Tours has a near monopoly on Aruban sightseeing; you can make reservations through its general office or at hotel tour-desk branches. The basic 3½-hour tour hits such highlights of the island. Wear tennis or hiking shoes, and bring a lightweight jacket or wrap, as the air-conditioned bus gets cold.

Information Aruba's Transfer Tour & Taxi (✉Pos Abao 41, Oranjestad ☎297/582–2116). **De Palm Tours** (✉L. G. Smith Blvd. 142, Oranjestad ☎297/582–4400 or 800/766–6016 ⊕www.depalm.com).

VISITOR INFORMATION
Information Aruba Tourism Authority (☎954/767–6477 in Ft. Lauderdale, 201/330–0800 in Weehawken, NJ, or 800/862–7822 ⊕www.aruba.com ✉L. G. Smith Blvd. 172, Eagle Beach, Aruba ☎297/582–3777).

WEDDINGS
Aruba is a popular destination for Caribbean weddings. You must be over the age of 18 and submit the appropriate documents one month in advance. Couples are required to submit birth certificates with raised seals, through the mail or in person, to Aruba's Office of the Civil Registry. They also need an apostille—a document proving they are free to marry—from their country of residence. Most major hotels have wedding coordinators, and there are other independent wedding planners on the island.

With so many beautiful spots to choose from, weddings on Aruba are guaranteed to be romantic. The island's endless beaches are a natural pick, but other choices include the tropical gardens at Arikok National Wildlife Park, the top of one of the natural bridges, or aboard a sunset cruise. And be sure to register for the island's "One Cool Honeymoon" program for special discounts from local businesses.

Wedding Planners Aruba Fairy Tales (✉Box 4151, Noord ☎297/993–0045 ⊕www.arubafairytales.com). **Aruba Weddings for You** (✉Nune 92, Paradera ☎297/583–7638 ⊕www.arubaweddingsforyou.com).

Barbados

Carlisle Bay

WORD OF MOUTH

". . . [B]arbados is good for the first-timer, as it has some of every-thing the Caribbean has to offer . . . except a volcano."

—xkenx

"Nowhere have we found the people more enchanting, the place more inviting, or the culture more interesting."

—Cwalker

WELCOME TO BARBADOS

Broad vistas, sweeping seascapes, craggy cliffs, and acre upon acre of sugarcane… that's Barbados. Beyond that, what draws visitors to the island is the warm Bajan hospitality, the welcoming hotels and resorts, the sophisticated dining, the never-ending things to see and do, the exciting nightspots, and, of course, the sunny beaches.

Hotels .... ▼

Accra Beach
Hotel & Resort **5**

Almond Beach
Village **19**

Almond Casuarina **9**

Bougainvillea
Beach Resort **10**

Cobblers
Cove Hotel **20**

Coconut Court
Beach Resort **3**

The Crane **15**

Divi Southwinds
Beach Resort **8**

Grand Barbados
Beach Resort **1**

Hilton Barbados **2**

Hotel PomMarine **5**

Little Arches Hotel **12**

Little Good Harbour ... **17**

New Edgewater **16**

Peach & Quiet **13**

Port St. Charles **18**

Sandy Bay
Beach Club **7**

The Savannah **4**

Silver Point **14**

South Beach Resort **6**

Turtle Beach
Resort **11**

Restaurants .... ▼

Atlantis Hotel **10**

Bellini's Trattoria **4**

Brown Sugar **2**

Champers **3**

Cliffside Restaurant **9**

The Fish Pot **12**

Josef's Resturant **6**

La Mer **13**

L'Azure at the Crane **8**

Mannie's Suga Suga... **14**

Naniki Restaurant **11**

Pisces **5**

Restaurant at
South Seas **7**

Waterfront Cafe **1**

TOP 4 REASONS TO VISIT BARBADOS

① Great resorts run the gamut—from unpretentious to knock-your-socks-off—in terms of size, intimacy, amenities, and price.

② Golfers can choose from some of the best championship courses in the Caribbean.

③ Great food includes everything from street-party barbecue to international cuisine rivaling the finest dining in the Caribbean.

④ With a wide assortment of land and water sports, sightseeing options, and nightlife, there's always plenty to do.

CHARM AND SOPHISTICATION

Barbados stands apart both geographically and geologically from its Caribbean neighbors; it's a full 100 mi (161 km) east of the Lesser Antilles chain. The top of a single submerged mountain of coral and limestone, the island is 21 mi (34 km) long, 14 mi (22½ km) wide, and relatively flat. The population is about 280,000, and the capital is Bridgetown.

4

BARBADOS

Harrison's Cave, one of the most popular attractions on Barbados, was first mentioned in historical documents in 1795, but it didn't open to the public until 1981.

The surfing is just fine, thanks. Each November, surfers gather at the wild and untamed Bathsheba Soup Bowl for the Independence Classic Surfing Championship.

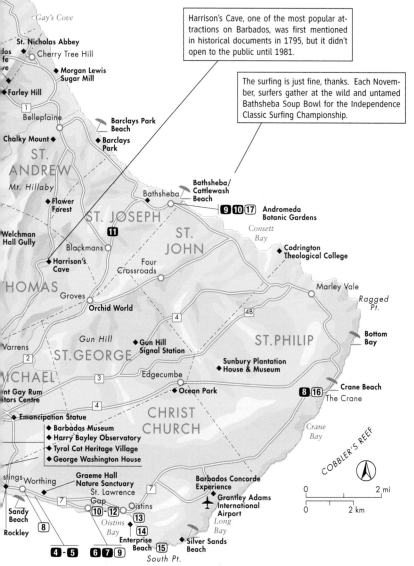

KEY
- Beaches
- Cruise Ship Terminal
- Dive Sites
- **1** Restaurants
- **1** Hotels

Cuckold Pt.

Gay's Cove

St. Nicholas Abbey
Cherry Tree Hill

Morgan Lewis
Sugar Mill

Farley Hill

Belleplaine

Chalky Mount

Barclays Park
Beach

Barclays
Park

ST.
ANDREW

Mt. Hillaby

Bathsheba

Bathsheba/
Cattlewash
Beach

9 10 17 Andromeda
Botanic Gardens

Flower
Forest

ST. JOSEPH

11

ST.
JOHN

Consett
Bay

Welchman
Hall Gully

Blackmans

Codrington
Theological College

Harrison's
Cave

Four
Crossroads

THOMAS

Groves

Orchid World

Marley Vale

Ragged
Pt.

4

4B

Gun Hill

Gun Hill
Signal Station

ST. PHILIP

Bottom
Bay

Varrens

2

ST. GEORGE

Sunbury Plantation
House & Museum

MICHAEL

Edgecumbe

3

nt Gay Rum
itors Centre

4

Ocean Park

Crane Beach

8 16

The Crane

Emancipation Statue

Barbados Museum
Harry Bayley Observatory
Tyrol Cot Heritage Village
George Washington House

CHRIST
CHURCH

Crane
Bay

COBBLER'S REEF

stings
Worthing

Graeme Hall
Nature Sanctuary

St. Lawrence
Gap

7

Barbados Concorde
Experience

Grantley Adams
International
Airport

0   2 mi

Sandy
Beach

8

Rockley

10 12 Oistins

13

Oistins
Bay

14

Enterprise
Beach

15

Silver Sands
Beach

Long
Bay

0   2 km

4 - 5

6 7 9

South Pt.

BARBADOS PLANNER

Island Activities	Logistics
There's always something to do in Barbados, and that's the way most visitors like it. The soft, white **beaches** are good whether you choose to stay in the millionaire's row of resorts on the west coast or the more-affordable south coast.	**Getting to Barbados:** Several airlines fly nonstop to Barbados, but you may have to connect in San Juan or Montego Bay. Barbados is also a regional hub, so sometimes you'll actually make a stopover there en route to a small island, such as Union Island in the Grenadines. Grantley Adams International Airport (BGI) is in Christ Church Parish on the south coast. It's a stunning, modern facility. The airport is about 15 minutes from hotels situated along the south coast, 45 minutes from the west coast, and about 30 minutes from Bridgetown.
Exceptional **golf** courses bring a lot of players to the island, but the private courses—at Royal Westmoreland and Sandy Lane—aren't for the light of wallet.	**Hassle Factor:** Low.
	Nonstops: You can fly nonstop to Barbados from Charlotte (USAirways), Miami (Air Jamaica, American), and New York–JFK (Air Jamaica, American). American Eagle also flies nonstop from San Juan.
The island's **restaurant scene** is excellent; you can choose from street-party barbecue to international cuisine that rivals the finest dining on the planet.	**On the Ground:** Ground transportation is available immediately outside the customs area. Airport taxis aren't metered, but fares are regulated (about $30 to Speightstown, $20 to $22 to west-coast hotels, $10 to $13 to south-coast hotels). Be sure, however, to establish the fare before getting into the cab and confirm whether the price quoted is in U.S. or Barbadian dollars.
Getting out on the water is the favored activity, whether that's on a **snorkeling** day sail, in a **mini-sub**, on a **deep-sea fishing** boat, or from a **dive boat** to explore the island's reefs and wrecks.	**Renting a Car:** If you're staying in a remote location, such as the southeast or east coasts, you may want to rent a car for the duration of your stay. In more-populated areas, where taxis and public transportation are available at the door, you might rent a car or minimoke (a tiny, open-sided convertible similar to a beach buggy, that's popular among tourists in Barbados) for a day or two of exploring on your own. Rates start at about $55 per day during the high season.
In season—from December through April—the conditions around the southern tip of Barbados are ideal for **windsurfing**. All year long, the pounding surf of the east coast draws **surfers** to the Bathsheba Soup Bowl, but the Independence Classic is the highlight every November.	

Where to Stay

Most people stay either in luxurious enclaves on the fashionable west coast—north of Bridgetown—or on the action-packed south coast, within easier reach of small, independent restaurants, bars, and nightclubs. A few inns on the remote southeast and east coasts offer ocean views and tranquillity, but those on the east coast don't have easy access to good swimming beaches. Prices in Barbados are sometimes twice as high in-season as during the quieter months. Most hotels include no meals in their rates, but some offer breakfast or a meal plan; others require you to purchase the meal plan in the high season, and a few offer all-inclusive packages.

Resorts: Great resorts run the gamut—from unpretentious to knock-your-socks-off—in terms of size, intimacy, amenities, and price. Many are well suited for families.

Villas & Condos: Families and longer-term visitors can choose from a wide variety of condos (everything from busy time-share resorts to more-sedate holiday complexes). Villas and villa complexes can be luxurious or simple and everything in between.

Small Inns: A few small, cozy inns can be found in the east and southeast regions of the island.

Hotel & Restaurant Costs

⇨*For information on hotel meal plans, see Accommodations in Caribbean Essentials.*

WHAT IT COSTS IN U.S. DOLLARS

$$$$	$$$	$$	$	¢
Restaurants				
over $30	$20–$30	$12–$20	$8–$12	under $8
Hotels*				
over $350	$250–$350	$150–$250	$80–$150	under $80
Hotels**				
over $450	$350–$450	$250–$350	$125–$250	under $125

*EP, BP, CP **AI, FAP, MAP Restaurant prices are for a main course at dinner and include any taxes or service charges. Hotel prices are per night for a double room in high season, excluding taxes, service charges, and meal plans (except at all-inclusives).

When to Go

Barbados is busiest from December 15 through April 15. Rates in the off-season can be half what they are during this busy period. If you go to Barbados during the high season, be aware that some hotels may require you to buy some kind of meal plan, which is usually not required in the low season.

In mid-January, the **Barbados Jazz Festival** is a weeklong event jammed with performances by international artists, jazz legends, and local talent.

In February the weeklong **Holetown Festival** is held at the fairgrounds to commemorate the date in 1627 when the first European settlers arrived in Barbados.

Gospelfest occurs in May and hosts performances by gospel headliners from around the world.

Dating from the 19th century, the **Crop Over Festival**, a monthlong festival similar to Carnival beginning in July and ending on **Kadooment Day** (a national holiday), marks the end of the sugarcane harvest.

4

By Jane E.
Zarem

THE NUMBER OF TIMES I'VE arrived at Barbados's Grantley Adams International Airport reaches well into the double digits. Recently, something new caught my eye—besides the stunning reconstruction of the airport itself. On the east side of the terminal, a small hangar houses a Concorde—one of seven supersonic airliners retired from British Airway's fleet. That's certainly fitting. After all, a retirement home in Barbados, a British outpost and holiday destination for nearly four centuries, is the dream—and, in fact, the reality—for many Brits. Moreover, Barbados was Concorde's only Caribbean destination during the iconic jetliner's lofty heyday, delivering the well-heeled to their nifty tropical holidays at Mach 2 speed.

Without question, Barbados is the "most British" island in the Caribbean. In contrast to the turbulent colonial past experienced by neighboring islands, which included repeated conflicts between France and Britain for dominance and control, British rule in Barbados carried on uninterrupted for 340 years—from the first established British settlement in 1627 until independence was granted in 1966. That's not to say, of course, that there weren't significant struggles in Barbados, as elsewhere in the Caribbean, between the British landowners and their African-born slaves and other indentured servants.

With that unfortunate period of slavery relegated to the history books, the British influence on Barbados remains strong today in local manners, attitudes, customs, and politics—tempered, of course, by the characteristically warm nature of the Bajan people. ("Bajan," pronounced *bay*-jun, derives phonetically from the British pronunciation of "Barbadian.") In keeping with British-born traditions, many Bajans worship at the Anglican church, afternoon tea is a ritual, cricket is the national pastime (a passion, most admit), dressing for dinner is a firmly entrenched tradition, and patrons at some bars are as likely to order a Pimm's Cup as a rum and Coke. And yet, Barbados is hardly stuffy—this is still the Caribbean, after all.

The long-standing British involvement is only one of the unique attributes that distinguish Barbados from its island neighbors. Geographically, Barbados is a break in the Lesser Antilles archipelago, the chain of islands that stretches in a graceful arc from the Virgin Islands to Trinidad. Barbados is isolated in the Atlantic Ocean, 100 mi (160 km) due east of St. Lucia, its nearest neighbor. And geologically, most of the Lesser Antilles are the peaks of a volcanic mountain range, while Barbados is the top of a single, relatively flat protuberance of coral and limestone—the source of building blocks for many a plantation manor. Many of those historic greathouses, in fact, have been carefully restored. Some are open to visitors.

Bridgetown, both capital city and commercial center, is on the southwest coast of pear-shape Barbados. Most of the 280,000 Bajans live and work in and around Bridgetown, in St. Michael Parish, or along the idyllic west coast or busy south coast. Others reside in tiny villages that dot the interior landscape. Broad sandy beaches, craggy cliffs, and picturesque coves make up the coastline, while the interior is consumed by forested hills and gullies and acre upon acre of sugarcane.

Tourist facilities are concentrated on the west coast in St. James and St. Peter parishes (appropriately dubbed the Platinum Coast) and on the south coast in Christ Church Parish. Traveling along the west coast to historic Holetown, the site of the first British settlement, and continuing to the northern city of Speightstown, you can find posh beachfront resorts, luxurious private villas, and fine restaurants enveloped by lush gardens and tropical foliage. The trendier, more-commercial south coast offers more-competitively priced hotels and beach resorts, and its St. Lawrence Gap area is jam-packed with shops, restaurants, and nightlife. The relatively wide-open spaces along the southeast coast are proving ripe for development, and some wonderful inns and hotels already take advantage of the intoxicatingly beautiful ocean vistas. For their own holidays, though, Bajans escape to the rugged east coast, where the Atlantic surf pounds the dramatic shoreline with unrelenting force.

All in all, Barbados is a sophisticated tropical island with rich history, lodgings to suit every taste and pocketbook, and plenty to pique your interest both day and night—whether you're British or not!

WHERE TO STAY

Most visitors stay on either the fashionable west coast, north of Bridgetown, or on the action-packed south coast. On the west coast, the beachfront resorts in St. Peter and St. James parishes are mostly luxurious, self-contained enclaves. Highway 1, a two-lane road with considerable traffic, runs past these resorts, which can make strolling to a nearby bar or restaurant difficult. Along the south coast, in Christ Church Parish, many hotels are clustered near the busy strip known as St. Lawrence Gap, convenient to dozens of small restaurants, bars, and nightclubs. On the much more remote east coast, a few small inns offer oceanfront views, and get-away-from-it-all tranquillity.

Prices in Barbados can be twice as high in-season (December 15–April 15) compared to the quieter months. Most hotels include no meals in their rates, but some offer breakfast or a meal plan. Others require you to purchase the meal plan in the high season, and a few offer all-inclusive packages.

Resorts run the gamut—from unpretentious to knock-your-socks-off—in terms of size, intimacy, amenities, and price. Families and long-term visitors can choose from a wide variety of villas and condos. A few small, cozy inns are found along the east and southeast coasts, as well as the northwest. They can be ultraluxurious, fairly simple, or something in between.

The lodgings listed below all have air-conditioning, telephones, and TVs in guest rooms unless otherwise noted.

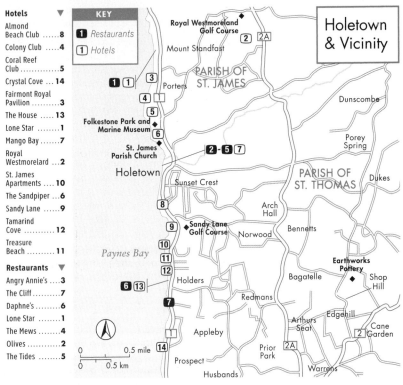

VILLA COMMUNITIES & CONDOMINIUM COMPLEXES

These complexes, which are continually cropping up along the south and west coasts of Barbados, can be an economical option for families, other groups, or couples vacationing together. Nonowner vacationers rent individual units directly from the property managers, the same as reserving hotel accommodations. Units with fully equipped kitchens, two to six bedrooms, and as many baths run $200 to $2,500 per night in the off-season—double that in winter.

SOUTH COAST
$$$–$$$$
★

The Crane. Originally built in 1887 on a seaside bluff on the southeast coast, the Crane is the island's oldest hotel in continuing operation. Today, that original coral-stone hotel building is the centerpiece of a luxurious, 40-acre villa complex. Historic Hotel Apartments are decorated with original antiques, and corner suites have walls of windows and wraparound patios or balconies with panoramic views. The upscale Private Residences—in five modern high-rise buildings—are spacious, individually owned condos with hardwood floors, hand-carved four-poster beds, multiple bathrooms with spa showers, fully equipped kitchens, and private plunge pools. The Crane's original pool is a frequent backdrop for photo shoots, while a huge pool complex nearer the villas includes a spa pool, built in a cliff-top ruin with a 360-degree view, and a half dozen connecting pools and other water features. The adjacent old stable serves as a pool bar. Reef-protected Crane Beach is 98 steps (or an elevator ride) down the cliff. You'll need to rent a car if you expect to spend much time away from the resort grounds. The minimum stay is seven nights in high season; three nights during the rest of the year. **Pros:** Enchanting view, lovely beach, fabulous suites, great restaurants. **Cons:** Remote location, rental car recommended, service tends to be aloof. ⊠ *Crane Bay, St. Philip* ☏*246/423–6220* 🖷*246/423–5343* ⊕*www.thecrane.com* ⇌*4 rooms, 14 suites, 184 villas* ⚒ *In-room: no a/c (some), safe, kitchen (some), refrigerator, DVD (some), VCR (some), Ethernet, Wi-Fi (some). In-hotel: 3 restaurants, room service, bars, tennis courts, pools, gym, spa, beachfront, laundry facilities (some), laundry service, concierge, public Internet, public Wi-Fi* ▤*AE, MC, V* ⦿*EP.*

4

$$-$$$ 🔲**Bougainvillea Beach Resort.** Attractive seaside villas are situated ☻ around the pool or face the beachfront like a private town-house community in this time-share property operated as a hotel, the suites are huge, compared to hotel suites in this price category, and decorated in appealing Caribbean pastels. Each has a sitting area with a pullout sofa—great for families with small kids. All suites have balconies or terraces that overlook either the pool and gardens or the sea. St. Lawrence Gap is a 15-minute westward stroll along the beach or a 20-minute walk along the road. The picturesque fishing village of Oistins is about the same distance in the opposite direction. Guests can have groceries delivered to their room or pre-stocked before arrival. You can even arrange a private cook, who will prepare Bajan specialties. Children under 12 stay free when sharing a room with adults. The minimum stay in high season is seven nights. **Pros:** Big suites, good value, great for families. **Cons:** Bathrooms need updating, sea can be rough for swimming. ⊠ *Maxwell Coast Rd., Maxwell, Christ Church* ☏*246/418–0990* ⊕*www.bougainvillearesort.com* ⇌*138 suites* ⚒ *In-room: dial-up. In-hotel: 2 restaurants, room service, bars, tennis court, pools, gym, spa, beachfront, water sports, no elevator, children's program (ages 3–12), laundry service, public Internet, public Wi-Fi* ▤*MC, V* ⦿*EP.*

$$-$$$ 🔲**Silver Point.** The old Silver Rock Hotel, a haven for windsurfers, has metamorphosed into a trendy boutique villa-hotel. New owners turned the property into a gated community of modern condos that are managed and operated as a hotel. Fifteen one-bedroom, ocean-view suites are decorated in sleek neutral colors and dark mahogany furniture, along with a café-style restaurant, pool, and lounging area. Twenty-two one-bedroom suites were added in 2008 as well as a spa, gym, and two-story open-deck restaurant with a rooftop martini bar. Each unit has coral-stone accents, cedar closets, and iPod dock; suites have granite and marble countertops in both kitchen and bath. Silver Point is perfect for those who like something chic yet fairly remote and secluded—and for those who know that Silver Sands–Silver Rock Beach is the best place for windsurfing and kite surfing. The hotel, which overlooks the beach, offers a special windsurfing package that includes lessons and plenty of time on the water. **Pros:** Classy suites, perfect location for windsurfers, gated community. **Cons:** Not within walking distance of

anything, sea can be rough for swimming, rental car recommended. ✉*Silver Sands, Christ Church* ☎*246/420–4416* ⊕*www.silverpoint hotel.com* ⌨*37 suites* ⌂*In-room: kitchen (some), DVD, VCR, Wi-Fi. In-hotel: 2 restaurants, bar, pools, gym, spa, beachfront, water sports, no elevator, laundry facilities, laundry service, concierge, public Internet, public Wi-Fi, no-smoking rooms* ▤*AE, MC, V* ⎐*EP.*

$$ 🏨**South Beach Resort.** The entrance here is certainly dramatic: guests
☪ take a footbridge from the street across the double-wide lap pool to approach the sleek lobby. This resort is actually a time-share vacation club, but the occasional vacationer wouldn't notice any difference from neighboring resorts. It's run like a hotel, and a very cool hotel at that. Rooms are decorated with quality furniture and fabrics, and the bathrooms are ultramodern. All rooms and suites have an eating area and a pullout sofa in the sitting area, making the accommodations suitable for parents and a couple of kids. Children under 12 stay free in the same room with adults. Accra (Rockley) Beach is just across the street, where beach chairs, water- sports equipment, and other beach toys—as well as drinks and snacks—can be rented or purchased. The restaurant at South Beach serves breakfast only. **Pros:** Beautiful bathrooms, Accra Beach is great for families, Wi-Fi everywhere. **Cons:** More a hotel than a resort, on-site restaurant only serves breakfast, beach is across the street. ✉*Main Rd., Rockley, Christ Church* ☎*246/435–8561* ⊕*www. southbeachbarbados.com* ⌨*22 rooms, 25 suites* ⌂*In-room: kitchen, VCR, Wi-Fi. In-hotel: restaurant, room service, bar, pool, laundry facilities, concierge, public Internet, public Wi-Fi, no-smoking rooms* ▤*AE, MC, V* ⎐*EP.*

WEST COAST 🏨**Port St. Charles.** A luxury residential marina development near his-
$$$$ toric Speightstown on the northwest tip of Barbados, Port St. Charles is a perfect choice for boating enthusiasts who either arrive on their own yacht or plan to charter one during their stay. Each villa is an intimate private home, decorated by the individual owners, and its own mega yacht berth on the property's picturesque lagoon. Port St. Charles also serves as a customs and immigration port of entry for boaters. Villas have one, two, or three bedrooms that surround a man-made lagoon or face the beach. Many have their own private plunge pools. Complimentary water taxis ferry guests around the property during the day—including over to the pool and pool bar at Sunset Island in the middle of the lagoon. **Pros:** A boater's dream, well-appointed units with beautiful views, friendly and safe, great restaurant. **Con:** Not the best spot for little kids. ✉*Hwy. 1B, Heywoods, St. Peter* ☎*246/419–1000* ⊕*www.portstcharles.com* ⌨*31 villas* ⌂*In-room: kitchen, DVD, dialup. In-hotel: 2 restaurants, bars, tennis court, pools, gym, beachfront, water sports, no elevator, laundry facilities, public Internet, no-smoking rooms* ▤*AE, MC, V* ⎐*EP.*

$$$$ 🏨**Royal Westmoreland Villas.** Located on a ridge overlooking the sea,
☪ this villa community was the first of its kind in Barbados, built on a 500-acre estate in the mid-1990s adjoining the Royal Westmoreland Golf Club. Owners and guests value privacy and exclusivity, so access is granted by appointment only. Villas have two, three, or four bedrooms and fully equipped kitchens and dining areas. Cassia Heights

Resort Club villas are modern, two-bedroom town houses located in the center of the estate near the clubhouse; Forest Hills Resort Club villas are two-bedroom houses with a common pool for the exclusive use of Forest Hills guests. Royal villas have vaulted ceilings, three large bedrooms with en-suite bathrooms, and enormous sitting rooms with French doors that open to a terrace and, in some cases, a private swimming pool. When they're not golfing or playing tennis, villa guests can laze around the pool, chill at the spa, or head for the beach at the nearby Colony Club. Only a few are rented to vacationers through Royal Westmoreland; some owners use property management services and outside real estate agencies. **Pros:** Nirvana for golfers, huge accommodations with every possible convenience, lots of activities and amenities for families, private and safe. **Cons:** Very expensive, not on the beach. ⊠*Hwy. 2A, Westmoreland, St. James* ☎*246/422–4653* ⊕*www.royal-westmoreland.com* ⬐*5 villas* ⚑*In-room: kitchen. In-hotel: 3 restaurants, bars, golf course, tennis courts, pools, gym, spa, no elevators, children's program (ages 4–12), laundry facilities, concierge* ▭*AE, MC, V* ⏺*EP.*

4

PRIVATE VILLAS & CONDOS

Local real estate agencies will arrange holiday rentals of privately owned villas and condos along the west coast in St. James and St. Peter. All villas and condos are fully furnished and equipped, including appropriate staff depending on the size of the villa or unit—which can range from one to eight bedrooms. The staff usually works six days a week. Most villas have TVs, DVD and/or VCR and CD players; all properties have telephones, and some have Internet access and/or fax machines. Telephones are usually barred against outgoing overseas calls; plan to use a phone card or calling card. Vehicles are generally not included in the rates, but rental cars can be arranged and delivered to the villa upon request. Linens and basic supplies (e.g., bath soap, toilet tissue, dishwashing detergent) are included.

Units with one to six bedrooms and as many baths run $200 to $2,500 per night in summer—double that in winter. Rates include utilities and government taxes. The only additional cost is for groceries and staff gratuities. A security deposit is required upon booking and refunded seven days after departure.

Rental Agencies Altman Real Estate (⊠*Hwy. 1, Derricks, St. James* ☎*246/432–0840 or 866/360–5292* ⊕*www.aaaltman.com*). **Bajan Services** (⊠*Newton House, Battaleys, St. Peter* ☎*246/422–2618 or 866/978–5239* ⊕*www.bajanservices.com*). **Island Villas** (⊠*Trents Bldg., Holetown, St. James* ☎*246/432–4627* ⊕*www.island-villas.com*).

HOTELS

SOUTH COAST

$$$$

☾

🖼 **Almond Casuarina Beach Resort.** Frequent visitors to the south coast of Barbados have fond memories of the Casuarina Beach Club. Completely renovated, refurbished, and expanded by new owner Almond Resorts, this south coast landmark reopened in early 2008. The lush 8-acre garden of mature bamboo, palm, and fruit trees (and a few resident green monkeys) remains beautifully intact. Blocks of accommodations surround the garden; rooms in a new beachfront building offer mesmerizing sea views; and opportunities for dining, socializing, and water- and land sports abound. A nice touch: everything is included in the room rate—even windsurfing or sailing lessons and an all-day, every-day Kids' Club. Guests also have full access to the dining, recreational, and entertainment facilities at Almond Casuarina's partner hotels on the west coast—Almond Beach Village in Speightstown and Almond Beach Club in St. James. **Pros:** Great beach and beautiful garden, every amenity you could imagine, wonderful for kids. **Con:** Lots of good restaurants to try in nearby St. Lawrence Gap, but you've paid for an all-inclusive. ⊠*St. Lawrence Gap, Dover, Christ Church* ☎*246/428–3600* ⊕*almondresorts.com* ⏦*260 rooms, 7 suites* ⏦*In-room: safe, refrigerator. In-hotel: 3 restaurants, room service, bars, pools, gym, spa, beachfront, water sports, no elevator, children's programs (ages infant–17), concierge, laundry facilities, public Internet* ▤*AE, D, MC, V* ⏦*AI.*

$$$$ 🖼**Divi Southwinds Beach Resort.** The all-suite Divi Southwinds is sit-
⏦ uated on 20 acres of lawn and gardens that are bisected by action-packed St. Lawrence Gap. The bulk of the suites are north of the Gap in a large, unspectacular three-story building offering garden and pool views. The property south of the Gap wraps around a stunning half mile of Dover Beach, where 16 beach villas provide an intimate setting steps from the sand. Whichever location you choose, all suites have separate bedrooms, sofa beds in the sitting room, and full kitchens. It's all within walking distance of lots of shops, restaurants, and nightspots. Kids under 15 stay free in their parents' suite. **Pros:** Beautiful beach, beach villas an excellent value. **Cons:** Few water sports available and none included, some rooms aching for renovations, too pricey for value received. ⊠*St. Lawrence Main Rd., Dover, Christ Church* ☎*246/428–7181* 🖷*246/420–2673* ⊕*www.diviresorts.com* ⏦*121 1-bedroom suites, 12 2-bedroom suites* ⏦*In-room: kitchen. In-hotel: 2 restaurants, bars, tennis courts, pools, gym, beachfront, no elevator, laundry facilities, public Internet* ▤*AE, D, DC, MC, V* ⏦*EP.*

$$$$ 🖼**Hilton Barbados.** Beautifully situated on the sandy Needham's Point
⏦ peninsula, the Hilton Barbados is minutes from Bridgetown. All 350
★ rooms and suites in this high-rise have private balconies overlooking either the ocean or Carlisle Bay; 77 rooms are on executive floors, with a private lounge and concierge services. Meetings are big business here, as the property has the largest hotel meeting space in Barbados. The broad white-sand beach, the sprawling bi-level pool complex, and a host of activities on land and sea make this a hit with vacationing families, as well. Children under 18 stay free in a room with adults, children ages 4 to 12 get a break on meals, and children under 5 eat for free—and parents get one complimentary night of babysitting with a three-night stay. **Pros:** Convenient location, beautiful beach, excellent accommodations, lots of services and amenities. **Cons:** Huge convention hotel, attracts groups. ⊠*Needham's Point, Aquatic Gap, St. Michael* ☎*246/426–0200* 🖷*246/434–5770* ⊕*www.hiltoncaribbean. com/barbados* ⏦*317 rooms, 33 suites* ⏦*In-room: safe, Ethernet, dial-up. In-hotel: 3 restaurants, room service, bars, tennis courts, pools,*

gym, water sports, concierge, children's programs (ages 4–12), public Wi-Fi, no-smoking rooms, some pets allowed ⊟*AE, D, DC, MC, V* ⊚|*EP.*

$$$$ ⊞**Turtle Beach Resort.** Families flock to Turtle Beach because it offers large, bright suites and enough all-included activities for everyone to enjoy. The Tommy Turtle Kids' Club keeps children busy with treasure hunts, supervised swims, games, and other activities from 9 AM to 9 PM each day. That gives parents a chance to play tennis, learn to windsurf or sail, relax at the beach, join the daily shopping excursion to Bridgetown, or enjoy a dinner for two at Asagio's Restaurant. Families also have good times together—cooling off in the three pools, riding the waves on boogie boards, dining buffet style at open-to-the-view Chelonia Restaurant, or having a casual meal at the Waterfront Grill. **Pros:** Perfect for family vacations, nice pools, roomy accommodations, lots of services and amenities. **Cons:** Beach is fairly narrow and congested compared to other south-coast resorts, open vent to hallway can be noisy at night. ⊠*St. Lawrence Gap, Dover, Christ Church* ☎*246/428–7131* 🖷*246/428–6089* ⊕*www.turtlebeachresortbarbados.com* ⬎*161 suites* ⟁*In-room: safe, refrigerator, Ethernet. In-hotel: 3 restaurants, room service, bars, tennis courts, pools, gym, spa, beachfront, diving, water sports, bicycles, children's programs (ages 3–12), laundry service, concierge, public Internet* ⊟*AE, D, DC, MC, V* ⊚|*AI.*

$$$–$$$$ ⊞**Little Arches Hotel.** Off the beaten track just east of the picturesque
★ fishing village of Oistins, this classy boutique hotel has a perfect vantage point overlooking the sea. The small hotel has a distinctly Mediterranean ambience; beautifully appointed rooms are decorated with Italian fabrics, local pottery, and terrazzo flooring. Bathrooms have showers only but feature locally made earthenware sinks. The pool is on the roof, alongside the open-air Café Luna restaurant. The Union Island and Palm Island suites each have a kitchen and a large, ocean-front patio with a private hot tub. Guests who book a 10-day stay are entitled to a choice of a complimentary round of golf at the Barbados Golf Club, an in-room champagne breakfast and massage, or a fully catered day sail. We recommend you leave the kids home if you're staying here, as Little Arches offers pure romance. **Pros:** Stylish accommodations, great restaurant, across from fabulous Miami Beach. **Cons:** Fairly remote, rental car advised. ⊠*Enterprise Coast Rd., Enterprise, Christ Church* ☎*246/420–4689* 🖷*246/418–0207* ⊕*www.littlearches. com* ⬎*8 rooms, 2 suites* ⟁*In-room: safe, kitchen (some), dial-up. In-hotel: restaurant, bar, pool, bicycles, no elevator, laundry service, public Internet* ⊟*MC, V* ⊚|*EP.*

$$$ ⊞**The Savannah.** Convenient, comfortable, and appealing to independent travelers who don't want organized entertainment, the Savannah is a hotel rather than a resort. Nevertheless, it's perfectly situated for walks to the Garrison historic area, the Barbados Museum, the racetrack, and the Graeme Hall Nature Sanctuary—and minutes from Bridgetown by car or taxi. Two modern wings spill down to the beach from the main building, once the historic Sea View Hotel. Definitely opt for a room in one of the modern wings, which overlook a lagoon-style pool that flows between them in graduated steps, from a waterfall at the higher end to a more-traditional pool by the beach; the oceanfront duplex suites at each end are superb. A favorite of local businesspeople, Boucan Restaurant is a buzz of activity at lunchtime. **Pros:** right on the beach, interesting pool, convenient to Bridgetown and sites. **Cons:** not a good choice for kids, rooms are ready for some sprucing up. ⊠ *Garrison Main Rd., Hastings, Christ Church* ☏ *246/435–9473* 🖷 *246/435–8822* ⊕ *www.gemsbarbados.com* ⇱ *90 rooms, 8 suites* △ *In-room: safe, refrigerator, VCR (some), dial-up. In-hotel: 2 restaurants, bars, pools, gym, spa, beachfront, no elevator, laundry service, public Internet, airport shuttle, no-smoking rooms* ⊟ *AE, D, DC, MC, V* ⏃○⏃*CP.*

$$–$$$ 🏨 **Accra Beach Hotel & Resort.** An excellent choice for vacationers preferring a full-service resort in the middle of the busy south coast, Accra is large, it's modern, it faces a great beach, and it's competitively priced. Six duplex penthouse suites—the priciest accommodations—face the sea. Most rooms overlook the large cloverleaf pool or the beach—and some of the oceanfront suites have hot tubs on the balconies. The budget-minded can opt for the less-expensive "island-view" rooms, which face the street. It's not unusual to witness a local couple being married here, and the hotel is a popular meeting venue for businesspeople. That shouldn't interrupt your day lazing on the beach, mingling at the poolside swim-up bar, or dining sumptuously at Wytukai (pronounced Y2K)—the island's only (so far) Polynesian restaurant. **Pros:** Right on a great beach, terrific value, friendly staff. **Con:** Standard rooms are fairly ordinary—opt for a newer one or choose a suite. ⌂ *Hwy. 7, Box 73W, Rockley, Christ Church* ☏ *246/435–8920* 🖷 *246/435–6794* ⊕ *www. accrabeachhotel.com* ⇱ *109 rooms, 37 suites* △ *In-room: safe, refrigerator (some), Ethernet (some), dial-up. In-hotel: 3 restaurants, room service, bars, pool, gym, beachfront, water sports, concierge, laundry service, public Internet, no-smoking rooms* ⊟ *AE, D, MC, V* ⏃○⏃*EP.*

$$ 🏨 **Grand Barbados Beach Resort.** Particularly geared to business travelers, this high-rise hotel is close to Bridgetown and offers executive rooms, abundant business services, and extensive meeting facilities. Leisure travelers also appreciate the comfortable rooms and attentive service—but especially enjoy the hotel's location on beautiful Carlisle Bay. Broad beaches on either side of the building are great for swimming and sunbathing, with powdery white sand and calm water. From guest-room balconies—especially those in the corner rooms—the panoramic view is spectacular. At the far end of a 260-foot-long Victorian pier, five unique suites with over-water patios are a tempting choice for a romantic getaway; the pier is also a perfect spot to watch the sunset. Children under 12 stay free with their parents. **Pros:** Caters to business travelers, beautiful beach, close to Bridgetown, comfortable rooms. **Cons:** Caters to business travelers, hard to compete with newer Hilton Barbados next door. ⌂ *Needham's Point, Box 639, Aquatic Gap, St. Michael* ☏ *246/426–4000* 🖷 *246/429–2400* ⊕ *www.grandbarbados. com* ⇱ *128 rooms, 5 suites* △ *In-room: safe, dial-up, Wi-Fi. In-hotel: 2 restaurants, bars, pool, gym, beachfront, diving, water sports, concierge, laundry service, executive floor, public Internet, public Wi-Fi* ⊟ *AE, DC, MC, V* ⏃○⏃*EP.*

$ ☷**Peach & Quiet.** This small seaside inn on the southeast coast is the
Fodor'sChoice sweetest deal we've found on the entire island. Forego the flashy accou-
★   trements of a resort and, instead, claim one of these stylish suites. With
no in-room noisemakers and no children around, the only sounds you
will hear are the gentle surf and your own conversations. Hands-on
British owners Adrian and Margaret Loveridge have been running
Peach since 1988; they renovated and refurbished the entire property in
2004. Decor in the spacious suites, arranged in whitewashed Mykonos-
inspired buildings, is elegantly spare. Cooled by ceiling fans, each suite
also has a large terrace or balcony; bathrooms have showers only.
Besides lazing in the freshwater pool and windsurfing at nearby beaches
(a five-minute walk), guests enjoy swimming and snorkeling in a natural "rock pool," joining early-morning or late-afternoon walks, and
stargazing at night. You're advised to rent a car. **Pros:** Peace and quiet,
adults-only environment, engaging owners, stargazing and nature
walks are special treats. **Cons:** Inn is closed half of the year, remote
location requires a rental car. ⊠*Inch Marlow Main Rd., Inch Marlow,
Christ Church* ☎*246/428–5682* 🖷*246/428–2467* ⊕*www.peachand
quiet.com* 🛏*22 suites* ⚿*In-room: no a/c, no phone, safe, refrigerator,
no TV. In-hotel: restaurant, bar, pool, water sports, no elevator, no kids
under 16* ⊟*MC, V* ⊗*Closed May–Oct.* ❙⊙❙*EP.*

WEST COAST   ☷**Almond Beach Club & Spa.** Among several similar beachfront resorts
$$$$ south of Holetown, Almond Beach Club distinguishes itself with all-
inclusive rates (only spa and salon services are extra), an adults-only
environment, and reciprocal guest privileges (including shuttle service)
at its enormous sister resort, Almond Beach Village. A horseshoe of
rooms and suites, decorated in a British-colonial theme, faces the sea,
although most units overlook the pools and gardens. Lavish breakfast buffets, four-course lunches, afternoon teas, and intimate dinners
are served in the main dining room—or dine on seafood at Water's
Edge or West Indian cuisine at Enid's, the colorful Bajan restaurant
that also offers free cooking classes. **Pros:** Adults only, intimate atmosphere, short walk to Holetown, next door to Sandy Lane Beach. **Cons:**
Beach erodes to almost nothing at certain times of the year—usually
the result of fall storms. ⊠*Hwy. 1, Vauxhall, St. James* ☎*246/432–
7840* 🖷*246/432–2115* ⊕*www.almondresorts.com* 🛏*133 rooms, 28
suites* ⚿*In-room: safe, refrigerator. In-hotel: 3 restaurants, room service, bars, tennis court, pools, gym, spa, beachfront, water sports, no
elevator, laundry service, public Internet, airport shuttle, no kids under
16* ⊟*AE, D, MC, V* ❙⊙❙*AI.*

$$$$ ☷**Almond Beach Village.** Situated on an 18th-century sugar plantation
♺   north of Speightstown, the Village's 32 acres front a mile-long, pow-
★   dery beach. Rooms and pools at the north end of the property, near a
historic sugar mill, are reserved for adults; at the south end, junior and
one-bedroom suites targeted to families with children are near special
facilities for kids and teens. A plethora of activities—golf, sailing, waterskiing, shopping excursions to Bridgetown, an off-site Bajan picnic, and
more—are all included. Not enough? Hop the shuttle to Almond Beach
Club and enjoy the (adults-only) facilities there. **Pros:** Family resort
with certain areas for adults only, lots to do and all included, compli-

mentary Bajan cooking lessons, sugar mill is a picturesque wedding venue. Cons: It's huge, some liken it to a holiday camp, more emphasis should be placed on room renovations and less on expansion. ⊠*Hwy. 1B, Heywoods, St. Peter* ☎*246/422–4900* 📠*246/422–0617* ⊕*www. almondresorts.com* 🛏*355 rooms, 40 suites* 🚪*In-room: safe. In-hotel: 5 restaurants, room service, bars, golf course, tennis courts, pools, gym, spa, beachfront, water sports, no elevator, children's programs (ages infant–17), public Internet, airport shuttle* ▤*AE, D, MC, V* 🍽*AI.*

$$$$ ★   🏨**Cobblers Cove Hotel.** "English Country" best describes the style of this pretty-in-pink resort, favored by British sophisticates. Flanked by tropical gardens on one side and the sea on the other, each elegant suite has a comfy sitting room with a sofa bed and a wall of louvered shutters that open onto a patio, a trouser press, and a small library of books. For all-out luxury, the sublime (and enormous) Colleton and Camelot penthouse suites each have a richly decorated sitting room, king-size four-poster bed, dressing room, whirlpool bath, private sundeck, and large plunge pool. Socializing occurs in the library, which doubles as a TV lounge, and at the alfresco restaurant, which receives well-deserved raves for superb dining. **Pros:** Very classy establishment, lovely grounds, the penthouse suites are amazing, very quiet. **Cons:** Very quiet, only bedrooms have air-conditioning. ⊠*Road View, Speightstown, St. Peter* ☎*246/422–2291* 📠*246/422–1460* ⊕*www. cobblerscove.com* 🛏*40 suites* 🚪*In-room: safe, refrigerator, no TV, dial-up, Wi-Fi. In-hotel: restaurant, room service, bar, tennis court, pool, gym, spa, beachfront, water sports, no elevator, children's programs (ages 2–12), public Internet, public Wi-Fi, no kids under 12 (Jan.–Mar.)* ▤*AE, D, MC, V* 🍽*BP.*

$$$$ 🏨**Colony Club Hotel.** As the signature hotel of five Elegant Hotel properties on Barbados, the Colony Club is certainly elegant—but with a quiet, friendly, understated style. A lagoon pool meanders through the central gardens, and 20 rooms have private access to the lagoon directly from their patios. Relax on the beach, soak in one of four pools, and enjoy an exquisite meal in the air-conditioned Orchids restaurant or a more-informal repast at the open-air Laguna Restaurant. Nonmotorized water sports, an in-pool scuba-diving lesson, and tennis are all included. A free water taxi provides transportation to two sister hotels located along the west coast. **Pros:** Clubby atmosphere, some rooms open directly onto the lagoon pool. **Cons:** Relatively pricey, beach comes and goes depending on storms. ⊠*Hwy. 1, Porters, St. James* ☎*246/422–2335* 📠*246/422–0667* ⊕*www.colonyclubhotel. com* 🛏*64 rooms, 32 junior suites* 🚪*In-room: safe, refrigerator. In-hotel: 2 restaurants, room service, bars, tennis courts, pools, gym, spa, beachfront, water sports, no elevator, laundry service, public Internet* ▤*AE, DC, MC, V* 🍽*EP.*

$$$$
Fodor's Choice
★   🏨**Coral Reef Club.** Owned and operated by the O'Hara family since the 1950s, the upscale Coral Reef Club offers the elegance and style of Sandy Lane with less formality. Spend your days at the beach or around the pool, taking time out for afternoon tea. Individually designed suites are in pristine coral-stone manses and cottages scattered over 12.5 acres of flower-filled gardens; the public areas ramble along the waterfront.

Garden rooms suit one or two guests and have a small patio or balcony, while junior suites have sitting areas and larger patios or balconies. Luxury cottage suites each have a plunge pool, bedroom, and separate living room with a sofa bed, making them perfect for families. After 7:30 PM, however, kids are not welcome in the dining room. The five pricey Plantation suites and two villas have spacious living rooms, private sundecks and plunge pools, and stereos—and are the only accommodations here that come with TVs (though you can get one for an added charge). Mingle at the bar before dining in the excellent terrace restaurant. **Pros:** Absolutely delightful, elegant yet informal, beautiful suites with huge verandahs, delicious dining, six computers available to guests for free Internet access. **Cons:** No room TVs (if that matters), narrow beach sometimes disappears depending on the weather. ⊠*Hwy. 1, Holetown, St. James* ☎*246/422–2372* 🖷*246/422–1776* ⊕*www.coralreefbarbados.com* ⇲*29 rooms, 57 suites, 2 villas* ⊘*In-room: safe, refrigerator, no TV (some), dial-up, Wi-Fi. In-hotel: restaurant, room service, bar, tennis courts, pools, gym, beachfront, diving, water sports, no elevator, children's programs (ages 2–8), public Internet, no kids under 12 (Jan. 15–Mar. 15)* ⊟*AE, MC, V* ⊘*Closed June* ⑩*BP.*

$$$$ 🏨**Fairmont Royal Pavilion.** Every suite in this adults-oriented resort has ★ a view of the sea from its broad balcony or patio. From ground-floor patios, in fact, you can step directly onto the sand. In the style of a Barbadian plantation house, all rooms have rich mahogany furniture and sisal rugs on ceramic floor tiles; rooms are also equipped with 27-inch flat-screen TVs and DVD/CD players. The resort's traditional, personalized service continues on the beach, where "Beach Butlers" cater to your every seaside whim. Breakfast and lunch are served alfresco near the beach; afternoon tea and dinner, in the exquisite Palm Terrace. **Pros:** Beautiful resort, excellent service—everyone remembers your name, dining is excellent. **Cons:** Dining is expensive ... in fact, everything is expensive. ⊠*Hwy. 1, Porters, St. James BB24051* ☎*246/422–5555* 🖷*246/422–3940* ⊕*www.fairmont.com/royalpavilion* ⇲*72 suite, 1 3-bedroom villa* ⊘*In-room: safe, refrigerator, dial-up. In-hotel: 2 restaurants, room service, bars, tennis courts, pool, gym, beachfront, diving, water sports, no elevator, concierge, laundry service, public Internet, no kids under 12 (Nov.–Apr.), no-smoking rooms* ⊟*AE, D, DC, MC, V* ⑩*EP.*

$$$$ 🏨**Mango Bay.** Mango Bay has a whole new look and attitude. Reopened in 2006 after a $10 million upgrade, returning guests will notice a completely transformed entrance, accommodations elevated to a grander style, the addition of 10 new deluxe rooms and two 1,200-square-foot oceanfront penthouse suites, and a partially enclosed dining room that provides both alfresco and air-conditioned dining options. All-inclusive rates include accommodations, meals, brand-name beverages, and a host of water sports (including waterskiing), as well as off-property sightseeing experiences. Located in the heart of Holetown, this convenient boutique resort is also within walking distance of shops, restaurants, nightspots, historic sites, and the public bus to either Bridgetown or Speightstown. **Pros:** Nice rooms, great food, friendly staff, walk to

Holetown shopping and entertainment. **Cons:** Although heroic measures continue to try to address the problem, a natural drainage stream on the north side of the property can sometimes become odoriferous. ⊠*2nd St., Holetown, St. James* ☎*246/432–1384* 🖷*246/432–5297* ⊕*www.mangobaybarbados.com* ↩*64 rooms, 10 suites, 2 penthouse suites* ⚒*In-room: safe, refrigerator (some), Ethernet. In-hotel: restaurant, bar, pool, beachfront, water sports, public Internet, public Wi-Fi* ▭*AE, D, DC, MC, V* ⦿*AI.*

$$$$
★ 🏨 **The Sandpiper.** This little gem just north of Holetown is every bit as elegant as its sister hotel, Coral Reef Club, yet the atmosphere is more like a private hideaway. Guest rooms and suites are arranged in a loose "S" shape on 7 acres of gardens. One- and two-bedroom suites have a separate living room and full kitchen. Each unit has a CD player; you must rent a TV. The two beachfront Tree Top suites are luxuriously spacious—with bathrooms as big as some Manhattan apartments; each Tree Top Suite has a wraparound terrace with wet bar and plunge pool. Water sports, including waterskiing, are complimentary. Scuba diving, children's programs, massage, and other personal services are available at the Coral Reef Club, which is nearby. **Pros:** Chic and sophisticated, the Tree Top suites are fabulous, the bathrooms are amazing. **Cons:** Beach is small—typical of west-coast beaches, hotel is small and many guests return year after year so reservations can be hard to get. ⊠*Hwy. 1, Holetown, St. James* ☎*246/422–2251* 🖷*246/422–1776* ⊕*www.sandpiperbarbados.com* ↩*22 rooms, 25 suites* ⚒*In-room: safe, kitchen (some), refrigerator, no TV, Ethernet, Wi-Fi. In-hotel: restaurant, room service, bars, tennis courts, pool, gym, beachfront, water sports, public Internet, public Wi-Fi, no kids under 12 (Jan. 15–Mar. 15)* ▭*AE, MC, V* ⊗*Closed Sept.* ⦿*BP.*

$$$$
☾
Fodor'sChoice
★ 🏨 **Sandy Lane Hotel & Golf Club.** Few places on Earth can compare to Sandy Lane's luxurious facilities and ultra-pampering service—or to its astronomical prices. But for the few who can afford to stay here it's an unparalleled experience. The main building of this exquisite resort is a coral-stone, Palladian-style mansion facing a sweeping stretch of beach shaded by mature trees. Guest accommodations, sumptuous in every detail, include three plasma TVs and DVD, full in-room wet bar, a personal butler, and remote-controlled everything—even the draperies! The world-class spa, housed in a magnificent Romanesque building, is a vacation in itself. Add elegant dining, the Caribbean's best golf courses, a tennis center, a full complement of water sports, a special lounge for teenagers, incomparable style ... you get the picture. **Pros:** Top of the line, cream of the crop—no debate about that, the spa is amazing. **Cons:** Over the top for most mortals, you feel like dressing up just to walk through the lobby. ⌖*Hwy. 1, Paynes Bay, St. James BB24024* ☎*246/444–2000* 🖷*246/444–2222* ⊕*www.sandylane.com* ↩*102 rooms, 10 suites, 1 5-bedroom villa* ⚒*In-room: safe, refrigerator, dial-up. In-hotel: 3 restaurants, room service, bars, golf courses, tennis courts, pool, spa, beachfront, water sports, concierge, children's programs (ages 3–12), laundry service, public Internet* ▭*AE, D, DC, MC, V* ⦿*BP.*

$$$$ **Tamarind Cove Hotel.** This Mediterranean-style resort sprawls along 750 feet of prime west-coast beachfront and is large enough to cater to sophisticated couples and active families while at the same time offering cozy privacy to honeymooners. Most rooms provide a panoramic view of the sea. Four-poster beds in 10 luxury oceanfront suites add a touch of romance. Junior suites are great for couples or families with one or two small children; families with older kids might prefer the space and privacy of a one-bedroom suite. Tamarind offers an array of water sports, as well as golf privileges at the Royal Westmoreland Golf Club. Among its three restaurants, Daphne's is a fashionable oasis for wining and dining. A free water taxi shuttles to two sister hotels. **Pros:** Nice location on Paynes Bay beach, lots of free water sports, Daphne's is great. **Cons:** Rooms could use a little loving care, service is a bit slow. ✉*Hwy. 1, Paynes Bay, St. James* ☎*246/432–1332* ⊟*246/432–6317* ⊕*www.tamarindcovehotel.com* ↘*58 rooms, 47 suites* ⌂*In-room: safe, refrigerator. In-hotel: 3 restaurants, room service, bars, tennis courts, pools, gym, beachfront, water sports, no elevator, concierge, laundry service, public Internet* ▭*AE, D, DC, MC, V* ¶⍵*EP.*

$$$$ **Treasure Beach.** Quiet, upscale, and friendly, this boutique all-suites hotel has a residential quality. Many guests—mostly British—are regulars. The rates are relatively expensive when compared to, say, the posh and much larger Coral Reef Club. Nevertheless, the hotel's high number of repeat guests suggests that the ambience here is well worth the price. Two floors of one-bedroom suites form a horseshoe around a small garden and pool. Most have a sea view, but all are just steps from the strip of sandy beach. The superdeluxe Hemmingway Suite blends antiques with modern luxury, an enormous terrace, and a whirlpool tub. All suites have comfortable sitting rooms with ceiling fans, plasma TVs, shelves of books, and open-air fourth walls that can be shuttered at night for privacy. Only the bedrooms are air-conditioned. Suites easily accommodate three adults or two adults and two children. The resort's restaurant enjoys a well-deserved reputation among guests and locals alike for its fine cuisine and pleasant atmosphere. **Pros:** Quiet retreat, congenial crowd, swimming with the turtles just offshore. **Cons:** Narrow beach, only bedrooms are air-conditioned, offshore turtles attract boatloads of tourists. ✉*Hwy. 1, Paynes Bay, St. James BB24009* ☎*246/432–1346* ⊟*246/432–1094* ⊕*www.treasurebeach-hotel.com* ↘*29 suites* ⌂*In-room: safe, refrigerator, dial-up. In-hotel: restaurant, room service, bar, pool, gym, beachfront, water sports, no elevator, laundry service, public Internet, no kids under 2 (Nov.–May 15)* ▭*AE, MC, V* ⊗*Closed Sept.* ¶⍵*EP.*

WHERE TO EAT

First-class restaurants and hotel dining rooms serve quite sophisticated cuisine—often prepared by chefs with international experience—which rivals that served in the world's best restaurants. Most menus include seafood: dorado (also known as dolphinfish—a fish, not the mammal—or mahimahi), kingfish, snapper, and flying fish prepared every way imaginable. Flying fish is so popular that it has officially become

More Barbados Resorts, Hotels & Inns

Because we would like to recommend more places to stay than we have room, here are some additional suggestions:

ON THE EAST COAST

$-$$ **New Edgewater** (✉ *Bathsheba Beach, Bathsheba, St. Joseph* ☎ *246/433-9900* ⊕ *www.newedgewater.com*) has been refurbished but still retains its rustic (some might say funky) beach-house atmosphere.

ON THE SOUTH COAST

$$ **Coconut Court Beach Hotel** (✉ *Main Rd., Hastings Bay, Christ Church BB15156* ☎ *246/427-1655* ⊕ *www.coconut-court.com*) is popular among families, who love the Coco Kids' Club and children's pools. The 82 apartments and efficiencies have kitchenettes; request one with air-conditioning and, if you wish, satellite TV.

$$ **Hotel PomMarine** (✉ *Barbados Community College, Hastings, Christ Church* ☎ *246/228-0900* ⊕ *www.pommarinebarbados.com*) is staffed by Hospitality Institute students at Barbados Community College; the 20 rooms and one self-catering suite here are simple yet comfortable. Hastings Beach is across the street.

$$ **Sandy Bay Beach Club** (✉ *Main Rd., Worthing, Christ Church* ☎ *246/435-8000* ⊕ *www.sandybaybeachclub.com*) is right on broad Sandy Beach; the resort has a water-

fall pool, water sports, and a full-time activities director.

ON THE WEST COAST

$$$$ **Crystal Cove Hotel** (✉ *Hwy. 1, Appleby, St. James* ☎ *246/432-2683* ⊕ *www.crystalcovehotelbarbados.com*) spills down a hillside to the beach where you can swim, sail, snorkel, water-ski, windsurf, or kayak to your heart's content—or play tennis, dip in the pool, or take advantage of the golf privileges.

$$$$ **The House** (✉ *Hwy. 1, Paynes Bay, St. James* ☎ *246/432-5525* ⊕ *www.thehousebarbados.com*) offers privacy, luxury, and service; it's an adult sanctuary next door to sister resort Tamarind Cove.

$$$$ **Little Good Harbour** (✉ *Hwy. 1B, Shermans, St. Peter* ☎ *246/439-3000* ⊕ *www.littlegoodharbourbarbados.com*) is a cluster of classy, spacious one-, two-, and three-bedroom, self-catering cottages overlooking a narrow strip of beach in the far north of Barbados—just beyond the picturesque fishing village of Six Men's Bay.

$$$$ **Lone Star Hotel** (✉ *Hwy. 1, Holetown, St. James* ☎ *246/419-0599* ⊕ *www.thelonestar.com*), a 1940s service station transformed into a chic four-room hotel, is popular among celebs. The restaurant is also extraordinary.

a national symbol. Shellfish also abounds, as do steak, pork, and local black-belly lamb.

Local specialty dishes include *buljol* (a cold salad of pickled codfish, tomatoes, onions, sweet peppers, and celery) and *conkies* (cornmeal, coconut, pumpkin, raisins, sweet potatoes, and spices, mixed together, wrapped in a banana leaf, and steamed). *Cou-cou*, often served with steamed flying fish, is a mixture of cornmeal and okra, usually topped with a spicy creole sauce made from tomatoes, onions, and sweet peppers. Bajan-style pepper pot is a hearty stew of oxtail, beef chunks, and "any other meat" in a rich, spicy gravy and simmered overnight.

For lunch, restaurants often offer a traditional Bajan buffet of fried fish, baked chicken, salads, macaroni pie (macaroni and cheese), and a selection of steamed or stewed local roots and vegetables. Be cautious with the West Indian condiments—like the sun, they're hotter than you think. Typical Bajan drinks, besides Banks Beer and Mount Gay rum, are *falernum* (a liqueur concocted of rum, sugar, lime juice, and almond essence) and *mauby* (a nonalcoholic drink made by boiling bitter bark and spices, straining the mixture, and sweetening it). You're sure to enjoy the fresh fruit or rum punch.

WHAT TO WEAR

The dress code for dinner in Barbados is conservative, casually elegant, and, on occasion, formal—a jacket and tie for gentlemen and a cocktail dress for ladies in the fanciest restaurants and hotel dining rooms, particularly during the winter holiday season. Jeans, shorts, and T-shirts (either sleeveless or with slogans) are always frowned upon at dinner. Beach attire is appropriate only at the beach.

BRIDGETOWN

CARIBBEAN/ SEAFOOD
$$

✕**Waterfront Cafe.** This friendly bistro alongside the Careenage is the perfect place to enjoy a drink, snack, or meal—and to people-watch. Locals and tourists alike gather for all-day alfresco dining on sandwiches, salads, fish, pasta, pepper pot stew, and tasty Bajan snacks such as buljol, fish cakes, or plantation pork (plantains stuffed with spicy minced pork). The panfried flying fish sandwich is especially popular. In the evening you can gaze through the arched windows while savoring nouvelle Caribbean cuisine, enjoying cool trade winds, and listening to live jazz. There's a special Caribbean buffet and steel-pan music on Tuesday night from 7 to 9. ⊠ *The Careenage, Bridgetown, St. Michael* ☎*246/427–0093* ▤*AE, DC, MC, V* ⊘*Closed Sun.*

EAST COAST

CARIBBEAN
$$–$$$$

✕**Cliffside Restaurant.** The outdoor deck of this restaurant in the New Edgewater hotel provides one of the prettiest, breeziest ocean views in all Barbados and, therefore, is a good stop for lunch when touring the east coast. From noon to 3 PM, choose the Bajan buffet or select from the menu. Either way, you might enjoy fried flying fish, roast or stewed chicken, local lamb chops, rice and peas, steamed root vegetables, sautéed plantains, and salad. Afternoon tea with scones, pastries, and sandwiches is served from 3:30 to 6 PM. Dinner is also served but mostly to hotel guests and local residents, who are able to find their way home in the dark on the neighborhood's winding, often unmarked roads. ⊠*Bathsheba Beach, Bathsheba, St. Joseph* ☎*246/433–9900* ⌂*Reservations essential* ▤*AE, MC, V.*

$$–$$$

✕**Atlantis Hotel Restaurant.** People have been stopping by for lunch with a view here since 1945, when Mrs. Enid Maxwell bought this property, a quaint, 19th-century seaside hotel. New owners have kept up Mrs. Maxwell's tradition—all Bajan cuisine that complements the natural environment. Each Wednesday and Sunday the enormous buffet includes pumpkin fritters, rice and peas, breadfruit casserole, steamed fish creole, oven-barbecued chicken, pepper pot, macaroni pie, ratatouille, and more. Homemade coconut pie tops the dessert list. The Atlantis is a lunch stop for organized day tours, so it sometimes get crowded. ⊠ *Atlantis Hotel, Tent Bay, Bathsheba, St. Joseph* ☎ *246/433–9445* ⊟ *AE, MC, V.*

$$–$$$
★
✕**Naniki Restaurant.** Rich wooden beams and stone tiles, clay pottery, straw mats, colorful dinnerware, and fresh flowers from the adjacent anthurium farm set the style here. Huge picture windows and outdoor porch seating allow you to enjoy the exhilarating panoramic view of surrounding hills and, when making the alfresco choice, a refreshing breeze along with your lunch of exquisitely prepared Caribbean standards. Seared flying fish, grilled dorado, stewed lambi (conch), curried chicken, and jerk chicken or pork are accompanied by cou-cou, peas and rice, or salad. On Sunday, lunch is a Caribbean buffet. Vegetarian dishes are always available. ⊠ *Suriname, St. Joseph* ☎ *246/433–1300* ⊟ *AE, DC, MC, V* ⊘ *Closed Mon. No dinner.*

SOUTH COAST

ASIAN/
SEAFOOD
$$$–$$$$
✕**Josef's Restaurant.** The signature restaurant of Austrian restaurateur Josef Schwaiger, in a cliff-side Bajan dwelling surrounded by gardens, is one of the most upscale seaside dining spots on the south coast. Josef's cuisine fuses Asian culinary techniques and Caribbean flavors with fresh seafood. Fruits of the sea—seared yellowfin tuna with mango-cilantro sauce or catch of the day with tomato fondue and creamed potatoes—are prominent, and the wine list is extensive. Try shredded duck with herbed hoisin pancakes as an innovative starter, or let the free-range chicken teriyaki with stir-fry noodles tingle your taste buds. Pasta dishes assuage the vegetarian palate. ⊠ *Waverly House, St. Lawrence Gap, Dover, Christ Church* ☎ *246/435–8245* ⚖ *Reservations essential* ⊟ *AE, MC, V* ⊘ *No lunch.*

CARIBBEAN
$$–$$$
☾
★
✕**Brown Sugar.** Set back from the road in an old traditional home, the lattice-trimmed dining patios here are filled with ferns, flowers, and water features. Brown Sugar is a popular lunch spot for local businesspeople, who come for the nearly 30 delicious local and creole dishes spread out at the all-you-can-eat, four-course Bajan buffet. Here's your chance to try local specialties such as flying fish, cou-cou, buljol, souse, fish cakes, and pepper pot. In the evening, the à la carte menu has dishes such as fried flying fish, coconut shrimp, and plantain-crusted mahimahi; curried lamb, filet mignon, and broiled pepper chicken; and seafood or pesto pasta. Bring the kids—there's a special children's menu with fried chicken, fried flying fish fingers, and pasta dishes. Save room for the warm pawpaw (papaya) pie or Bajan rum pudding with rum sauce. ⊠ *Bay St., Aquatic Gap, St. Michael* ☎ *246/426–7684* ⚖ *Reservations essential* ⊟ *AE, MC, V* ⊘ *No lunch Sat.*

CONTINENTAL
$$$–$$$$
Fodor's Choice
★
✕**Restaurant at South Seas.** Celebrated as one of the best restaurants on Barbados—certainly on the south coast—Chef Barry Taylor creates a tempting menu of dishes in his stylish, waterfront establishment. Raised in both Barbados and Rio and educated in the United States, his cuisine has an international flair. Appetizers might include rose-

mary-scented roasted elk or snow crab and yellowfin tuna cakes. Main courses range from USDA prime beef tenderloin or Peking duckling cooked two ways to Arborio-crusted Vietnamese shrimp or panfried New Bedford scallops. The dining verandah overlooks a quiet cove on one side and beautiful landscaped gardens on the other. The restaurant has one of the most extensive wine, brandy, and vintage rum collections on the island. There's even a cigar menu that lists a dozen Cubans and others from Barbados, Honduras, and the Dominican Republic. Dining here is a very special experience. ⊠ *St. Lawrence Gap, Dover, Christ Church* ☎ *246/420–7423* ⚑ *Reservations essential* ⊟ *AE, MC, V* ⊘ *Closed Sun. No lunch.*

ECLECTIC
$$$–$$$$
★

✕ **Champers.** Chiryl Newman's elegant and popular restaurant and watering hole is an old Bajan home–cum–snazzy seaside restaurant on a quiet lane just off the main south-coast road in Rockley. Luncheon guests—about 75% local businesspeople—enjoy repasts such as char-grilled beef salad, Champers fish pie, grilled barracuda, or chicken and mushroom fettuccine napped in a creamy chardonnay sauce. Dinner guests swoon over dishes such as the roasted rack of lamb with spring vegetables and mint-infused jus, the sautéed sea scallops with stir-fried vegetables and noodles with red Thai curry sauce, and the Parmesan-crusted barracuda with whole-grain mustard sauce. But this isn't nouvelle cuisine. The portions are hearty and the food is well seasoned with Caribbean flavors, "just the way the locals like it," says Newman. The cliff-top setting overlooking Accra Beach offers diners a panoramic view of the sea and a relaxing atmosphere for daytime dining. At night, particularly at the bar, there's a definite buzz in the air. Nearly all the artwork gracing the walls is by Barbadian artists and may be purchased through the on-site gallery. ⊠ *Skeetes Hill, Rockley, Christ Church* ☎ *246/434–3464* ⚑ *Reservations essential* ⊟ *AE, D, DC, MC, V* ⊘ *Closed Sun.*

ITALIAN
$$–$$$

✕ **Bellini's Trattoria.** Classic northern Italian cuisine is the specialty at Bellini's, on the main floor of the Little Bay Hotel. The atmosphere here is smart-casual. Toast the evening with a Bellini cocktail (ice-cold sparkling wine with a splash of fruit nectar) and start your meal with bruschetta, an individual gourmet pizza, or perhaps a homemade pasta dish with fresh herbs and a rich sauce. Move on to the signature garlic shrimp entrée or the popular chicken parmigiana—then top it all off with excellent tiramisu. We recommend making your reservations early; request a table on the Mediterranean-style verandah to enjoy one of the most appealing dining settings on the south coast. ⊠ *Little Bay Hotel, St. Lawrence Gap, Dover, Christ Church* ☎ *246/435–7246* ⚑ *Reservations essential* ⊟ *AE, MC, V* ⊘ *No lunch.*

SEAFOOD
$$$–$$$$
★

✕ **Pisces.** For seafood lovers, this is nirvana. Prepared here in every way—from charbroiled to gently sautéed—seafood specialties may include conch strips in tempura, rich fish chowder, panfried fillets of flying fish with a toasted almond crust and a light mango-citrus sauce, and seared prawns in a fragrant curry sauce. Landlubbers in your party can select from a few chicken, beef, and pasta dishes on the menu. Whatever you choose, the herbs that flavor it and the accompanying vegetables will have come from the chef's own garden. Save room for the bread pudding, yogurt-lime cheesecake, or homemade rum-raisin ice cream. Twinkling white lights reflect on the water as you dine. ⊠ *St. Lawrence Gap, Dover, Christ Church* ☎ *246/435–6564* ✍ *Reservations essential* ⊟ *AE, MC, V* ◷ *No lunch.*

$$$ ✕ **L'Azure at The Crane.** Perched on an oceanfront cliff, L'Azure is an informal luncheon spot by day that becomes elegant after dark. Enjoy seafood chowder or a light salad or sandwich while absorbing the breathtaking view. At dinner, candlelight and a soft guitar enhance a fabulous Caribbean lobster seasoned with herbs, lime juice, and garlic butter and served in its shell; if you're not in the mood for seafood, try the perfectly grilled filet mignon. Sunday is really special, with a Gospel Brunch at 10 AM and a Bajan Buffet at 12:30 PM. ⊠ *The Crane, Crane Bay, St. Philip* ☎ *246/423–6220* ✍ *Reservations essential* ⊟ *AE, MC, V.*

WEST COAST

CARIBBEAN ✕ **Angry Annie's.** You can't miss this place. Outside and inside,
$$–$$$ everything's painted in cheerful Caribbean pinks, blues, greens, and yellows—and it's just steps from the main road. The food is just as lively: great barbecued "jump-up" ribs and chicken, grilled fresh fish or juicy steaks, "Rasta pasta" for vegetarians, and several spicy curries. Eat inside on gaily colored furniture, outside under the stars, or take it away with you. ⊠ *1st St., Holetown, St. James* ☎ *246/432–2119* ⊟ *AE, DC, MC, V* ◷ *No lunch.*

$$–$$$ ✕ **Mannie's Suga Suga.** The beach crowd comes for all-day dining—
◷ breakfast, lunch, and beach-served snacks and drinks—at Barbados's trendiest beach bar on one of its finest strips of sand. Owner-manager Mannie Ward oversees a varied menu of international and Bajan favorites that includes soups, salads, cutters (sandwiches), hot dogs and hamburgers, and barbecued pork, beef, chicken, or fish—and a long list of sides such as fish cakes, rice and peas, fried plantains, potato or breadfruit chips, pumpkin or conch fritters, deep-fried eggplant or zucchini, and garlic bread. Some people change out of their bathing suits and return for the Japanese and Thai cuisine served at dinner, especially on Monday nights when there's a cabaret show. ⊠ *Mullins Beach, Speightstown, St. Peter* ☎ *246/419–4511* ⊟ *MC, V* ◷ *No dinner Thurs. and Sun.*

CONTINENTAL ✕ **The Tides.** Enter into a pretty courtyard and have a cocktail at the
$$$$ cozy bar or the coral-stone lounge in what was once a private man-
★ sion, then proceed to your seaside table. Perhaps the most intriguing feature of this stunning setting—besides the sound of waves crashing onto the shore just feet away—is the row of huge tree trunks growing right through the dining room. The food is equally dramatic. Chef Guy Beasley and his team give a contemporary twist to fresh seafood, fillet of beef, rack of lamb, and other top-of-the-line main courses by adding inspired sauces and delicate vegetables and garnishes. Local residents and repeat visitors agree that the Tides is one of the island's best restaurants. ⊠ *Hwy. 1, Holetown, St. James* ☎ *246/432–8356* ✍ *Reservations essential* ⊟ *MC, V* ◷ *No lunch weekends.*

$$$–$$$$ ✕**The Mews.** Dining at the Mews is like being invited to a very chic
★ friend's home for dinner. This once was, in fact, a private home. The
front room is now an inviting bar, and an interior courtyard is an inti-
mate, open-air dining area. The second floor is a maze of small dining
rooms and dining balconies, but you've come for the food, after all.
The international cuisine is presented with contemporary flair. A plump
chicken breast, for example, will be stuffed with cream cheese, smoked
salmon, and herb pâté and served on a garlic-and-chive sauce. A braised
lamb shank is presented on a bed of cabbage with a port-thyme jus and
creamed potatoes, and fillet of mahimahi is poached in a lemongrass,
ginger, and cilantro broth. The warm molten chocolate cake is a must
for dessert. Some call the atmosphere avant-garde; others call it quaint.
Everyone calls the food delicious. But don't stop at dinner . . . at about
10 PM, the bar begins to bustle. On weekends, the fun spills out into the
street. ⊠*2nd St., Holetown, St. James* ☎*246/432–1122* ⌖*Reserva-
tions essential* ☰*AE, MC, V* ☾*Closed Sun. No lunch.*

ECLECTIC ✕**The Cliff.** Chef Paul Owens' mastery is the foundation of one of the
$$$$ finest dining experiences in the Caribbean, with prices to match. Steep
Fodor'sChoice steps hug the cliff on which the restaurant sits to accommodate those
★ arriving by yacht, and every candlelit table has a sea view. Starters
include smoked salmon ravioli with garlic sauce or grilled portobello
mushroom on greens with truffle vinaigrette; for the main course, try
Caribbean shrimp with a Thai green-curry coconut sauce, veal chop
with a mustard-and-tarragon sauce, or red snapper fillet on a baked
potato cake. Dessert falls into the sinful category, and service is impec-
cable. The prix-fixe menu will set you back $93 per person for a two-
course meal (starter–main course or main course–dessert) or $110 per
person for a three-course meal. Reserve days or even weeks in advance
to snag a table at the front of the terrace for the best view. ⊠*Hwy. 1,
Derricks, St. James* ☎*246/432–1922* ⌖*Reservations essential* ☰*AE,
DC, MC, V* ☾*Closed Sun. Apr. 15–Dec. 15. No lunch.*

$$$–$$$$ ✕**Lone Star.** In the 1940s this was the only commercial garage on the
west coast; today it's the snazzy restaurant in the tiny but chic Lone
Star Hotel, where top chefs in the open-plan kitchen turn the finest
local ingredients into gastronomic delights. The menu is extensive
but pricey, even for lunch. All day, such tasty dishes as fish soup with
rouille, Caesar or Thai chicken salad, tuna tartare, rotisserie chicken,
and linguine with tomato-basil sauce and feta cheese are served in the
oceanfront beach bar. At sunset, the casual daytime atmosphere turns
trendy. You might start with an Oriental tasting plate or a half dozen
oysters, followed by crispy roast duckling, grilled fish of the day, or
lamb cutlets—or choose from one of dozens of other tasty land, sea,
and vegetarian dishes. ⊠*Lone Star Hotel, Hwy. 1, Mount Standfast,
St. James* ☎*246/419–0599* ☰*AE, MC, V.*

$$$ ✕**La Mer.** Enjoy dinner with a view overlooking the pretty, man-made
lagoon at Port St. Charles, the tony villa community that particularly
appeals to boating enthusiasts. Fresh fish from Six Men's Bay, just up
the road, and tender cuts of meat are seared on either of two grills,
wood or lava-rock, while vegetarian dishes might be stirred up at the
wok station. This is a perfect place for a light meal at the Onyx Bar,

just steps from the dock; Sunday brunch; or a romantic dinner. ⊠ *Port St. Charles, Speightstown, St. Peter* 🕾 *246/419–2000* ⌖ *Reservations essential* ⊟ *AE, MC, V* ⊗ *Closed Mon.*

ITALIAN ✕ **Daphne's.** Wedged between the Tamarind Cove Hotel and its sister
$$$–$$$$ hotel, the House, Daphne's is the chic and glamorous Caribbean out-
★ post of the famed London eatery. The chef whips up contemporary ver-
sions of classic Italian dishes. Grilled mahimahi, for example, becomes
"modern Italian" when combined with marsala wine, peperonata, and
zucchini. Perfectly prepared pappardelle with braised duck, red wine,
and oregano is a sublime pasta choice. Light meals, salads, and half
portions of pasta are available at lunch. The extensive wine list fea-
tures both regional Italian and fine French selections. ⊠ *Paynes Bay, St.
James* 🕾 *234/432–2731* ⌖ *Reservations essential* ⊟ *AE, D, MC, V.*

MEDITERRANEAN ✕ **Fish Pot.** Just north of the little fishing village of Six Men's Bay, toward
$$$–$$$$ the far northern west coast of Barbados, this attractive seaside restau-
★ rant serves excellent Mediterranean cuisine and the freshest fish. Gaze
seaward through windows framed with pale green louvered shutters
while lunching on a seafood crepe or perhaps pasta with seafood or
puttanesca sauce; in the evening, the menu may include panfried red
snapper with caper-and-thyme mashed potatoes, seared herb-crusted
tuna on garlic and spinach polenta, sun-dried tomato risotto tossed
with vegetables, and lamb shank braised in red wine. Bright and cheery
by day and relaxed and cozy by night, the Fish Pot offers a tasty din-
ing experience in a setting that's more classy than its name might sug-
gest. ⊠ *Little Good Harbour, Shermans, St. Peter* 🕾 *246/439–3000*
⌖ *Reservations essential* ⊟ *MC, V.*

$$$ ✕ **Olives Bar & Bistro.** This intimate restaurant, a quaint Bajan residence
★ in the center of Holetown, is a favorite west-coast dining spot of local
professionals and visitors alike. Mediterranean and Caribbean flavors
enliven inventive thin-crust pizzas and tasty salads at lunch; the dinner
menu often includes fresh seafood, such as seared yellowfin tuna with
ratatouille or pan-seared sea scallops with basmati rice and steamed
greens. Vegetarian selections are always available. Dine inside, accompanied by the hint of soothing light jazz music, or in the courtyard;
the upstairs bar is a popular spot to mingle over coffee, refreshing
drinks, or snacks (pizza, pastas, salads). ⊠ *2nd St., Holetown, St.
James* 🕾 *246/432–2112* ⊟ *AE, MC, V.*

BEACHES

Bajan beaches have fine white sand, and all are open to the public.
Most have access from the road so nonguest bathers don't have to pass
through hotel properties. When the surf is too high and swimming is
dangerous, a red flag will be hoisted on the beach. A yellow flag—or
a red flag at half-mast—means swim with caution. Topless sunbathing—on the beach or at the pool—is not allowed anywhere in Barbados
by government regulation.

EAST COAST

With long stretches of open beach, crashing ocean surf, rocky cliffs, and verdant hills, the Atlantic (windward) side of Barbados is where Barbadians spend their holidays. But be cautioned: swimming at east-coast beaches is treacherous, even for strong swimmers, and is *not* recommended. Waves are high, the bottom tends to be rocky, the currents are unpredictable, and the undertow is dangerously strong.

Barclays Park. Serious swimming is unwise at this beach, which follows the coastline in St. Andrew, but you can take a dip, wade, and play in the tide pools. A lovely shaded area with picnic tables is directly across the road. ⊠ *Ermy Bourne Hwy., north of Bathsheba, St. Andrews.*

★ **Bathsheba/Cattlewash.** Although it's not safe for swimming, the miles of untouched, windswept sand along the East Coast Road in St. Joseph Parish are great for beachcombing and wading. As you approach Bathsheba Soup Bowl, the southernmost stretch just below Tent Bay, the enormous mushroomlike boulders and rolling surf are uniquely impressive. This is also where expert surfers from around the world converge each November for the Independence Classic Surfing Championship. ⊠ *East Coast Rd., Bathsheba, St. Joseph.*

SOUTH COAST

A young, energetic crowd favors the south-coast beaches, which are broad and breezy, blessed with powdery white sand, and dotted with tall palms. The reef-protected areas with crystal-clear water are safe for swimming and snorkeling. The surf is medium to high, and the waves get bigger and the winds stronger (windsurfers take note) the farther southeast you go.

☾ **Accra Beach.** This popular beach, also known as Rockley Beach, is next to the Accra Beach Hotel. Look forward to gentle surf and a lifeguard, plenty of nearby restaurants for refreshments, a children's playground, and beach stalls for renting chairs and equipment for snorkeling and other water sports. Parking is available at an on-site lot. ⊠ *Hwy. 7, Rockley, Christ Church.*

★ **Bottom Bay.** Popular for fashion and travel industry photo shoots, Bottom Bay is the quintessential Caribbean beach. Surrounded by a coral cliff, studded with a stand of palms, and an endless ocean view, this dreamy enclave is near the southeasternmost tip of the island. Swimming is not recommended, as the waves can be very strong, but it's *the* picture-perfect place for sunbathing, having a picnic lunch, or simply enjoying the view. Park at the top of the cliff and follow the steps down to the beach. ⊠ *Dover, St. Philip.*

Carlisle Bay. Adjacent to the Hilton Barbados and Grand Barbados hotels just south of Bridgetown, this broad half circle of white sand is one of the island's best beaches—but it can become crowded on weekends and holidays. Park at Harbour Lights or the Boatyard, both on Bay Street, where you can also rent umbrellas and beach chairs and buy refreshments. ⊠ *Needham's Point, Aquatic Gap, St. Michael.*

★ **Crane Beach.** An exquisite crescent of pink sand on the southeast coast, Crane Beach is protected by steep cliffs on the land side and a reef on the water side. As attractive as this location is now, it was named not for the elegant long-legged wading birds but for the crane that once hauled and loaded cargo here. Crane Beach usually has a steady breeze and lightly rolling surf that is great for bodysurfing. A lifeguard is on duty. Changing rooms are available at the Crane resort for a small fee (which you can apply toward drinks or a meal at the restaurant). Access is through the hotel and down to the beach via either a cliff-side elevator or 98 steps. ⊠ *Crane Bay, St. Philip.*

Miami Beach. Also called Enterprise Beach, this isolated spot on Enterprise Coast Road, just east of Oistins, is a picturesque slice of pure white sand with cliffs on either side and crystal-clear water. You can find a palm-shaded parking area, snack carts, and chair rentals. Bring a picnic or have lunch across the road at Café Luna in Little Arches Hotel. ⊠ *Enterprise Beach Rd., Enterprise, Christ Church.*

☾ **Sandy Beach.** Next to the Sandy Bay Beach Club resort, this beach has shallow, calm waters and a picturesque lagoon, making it an ideal location for families with small kids. Park right on the main road. You can rent beach chairs and umbrellas, and plenty of places nearby sell food and drink. ⊠ *Hwy. 7, Worthing, Christ Church.*

Silver Sands–Silver Rock Beach. Nestled between South Point, the southernmost tip of the island, and Inch Marlowe Point, Silver Sands–Silver Rock is a beautiful strand of white sand that always has a stiff breeze. That makes this beach the best in Barbados for intermediate and advanced windsurfers and, more recently, kite surfers. ⊠ *Off Hwy. 7, Christ Church.*

WEST COAST

Gentle Caribbean waves lap the west coast, and the stunning coves and sandy beaches are shaded by leafy mahogany trees. The water is perfect for swimming and water sports. An almost unbroken chain of beaches runs between Bridgetown and Speightstown. Elegant homes and luxury hotels face much of the beachfront property in this area, Barbados's Platinum Coast.

West-coast beaches are considerably smaller and narrower than south-coast ones. Also, prolonged stormy weather in September or October may cause sand erosion, temporarily making the beach even narrower. Even so, west-coast beaches are seldom crowded. Vendors stroll by, selling handmade baskets, hats, dolls, and jewelry; owners of private boats offer waterskiing, parasailing, and snorkeling excursions. There are no concession stands, but hotels and beachside restaurants welcome nonguests for terrace lunches (wear a cover-up), and you can buy picnic items at supermarkets in Holetown.

Brighton Beach. Calm as a lake, this is where you can find locals taking a quick dip on hot days. Just north of Bridgetown, Brighton Beach is also the home to the Malibu Beach Club. ⊠ *Spring Garden Hwy., Brighton, St. Michael.*

★ **Mullins Beach.** This lovely beach just south of Speightstown is a perfect place to spend the day. The water is safe for swimming and snorkeling, there's easy parking on the main road, and Mannie's Suga Suga restaurant serves snacks, meals, and drinks—and rents chairs and umbrellas. ⊠ *Hwy. 1, Mullins Bay, St. Peter.*

Paynes Bay. The stretch of beach just south of Sandy Lane is lined with luxury hotels. It's a very pretty area, with plenty of beach to go around and good snorkeling. Public access is available at several locations along Highway 1; parking is limited. Grab a bite to eat and liquid refreshments at Bomba's Beach Bar. ⊠*Hwy. 1, Paynes Bay, St. James.*

SPORTS & THE OUTDOORS

Cricket, football (soccer), polo, and rugby are extremely popular sports in Barbados among participants and spectators alike, with local, regional, and international matches held throughout the year. Contact the Barbados Tourism Authority or check local newspapers for information about schedules and tickets.

DIVING & SNORKELING

More than two dozen dive sites lie along the west coast between Maycocks Bay and Bridgetown and off the south coast as far as the St. Lawrence Gap. Certified divers can explore flat coral reefs and see sea fans, huge barrel sponges, and more than 50 varieties of fish. Nine sunken wrecks are dived regularly, and at least 10 more are accessible to experts. Underwater visibility is generally 80 to 90 feet. The calm waters along the west coast are also ideal for snorkeling. The marine reserve, a stretch of protected reef between Sandy Lane and the Colony Club, contains beautiful coral formations accessible from the beach.

On the west coast, **Bell Buoy** is a large, dome-shape reef where huge brown coral tree forests and schools of fish delight all categories of divers at depths ranging from 20 to 60 feet. At **Dottins Reef,** off Holetown, you can see schooling fish, barracudas, and turtles at depths of 40 to 60 feet. **Maycocks Bay,** on the northwest coast, is a particularly enticing site; large coral reefs are separated by corridors of white sand, and visibility is often 100 feet or more. The 165-foot freighter *Pamir* lies in 60 feet of water off Six Men's Bay; it's still intact, and you can peer through its portholes and view dozens of varieties of tropical fish. **Silver Bank** is a healthy coral reef with beautiful fish and sea fans; you may get a glimpse of the *Atlantis* submarine at 60 to 80 feet. Not to be missed is the *Stavronikita,* a scuttled Greek freighter at about 135 feet; hundreds of butterfly fish hang out around its mast, and the thin rays of sunlight filtering down through the water make fully exploring the huge ship a wonderfully eerie experience.

Farther south, **Carlisle Bay** is a natural harbor and marine park just below Bridgetown. Here you can retrieve empty bottles thrown overboard by generations of sailors and see cannons and cannonballs, anchors, and six unique shipwrecks (*Berwyn, Fox, CTrek, Eilon,* the barge *Cornwallis,* and *Bajan Queen*) lying in 25 to 60 feet of water, all close enough to visit on the same dive. The *Bajan Queen,* a cruise vessel that sank in 2002, is the island's newest wreck.

Dive shops provide a two-hour beginner's "resort" course ($70 to $75) followed by a shallow dive, or a weeklong certification course (about $350). Once you're certified, a one-tank dive runs about $50 to $55;

a two-tank dive is $70 to $80. All equipment is supplied, and you can purchase multidive packages. Gear for snorkeling is available (free or for a small rental fee) from most hotels. Snorkelers can usually accompany dive trips for $20 for a one- or two-hour trip. Most dive shops have relationships with several hotels and offer special dive packages, with transportation, to hotel guests.

On the west coast, **Dive Barbados** (⊠ *Mount Standfast, St. James* ☎ *246/ 422–3133* ⊕ *www.divebarbados.net*), on the beach next to the Lone Star Hotel, offers all levels of PADI instruction, two or three reef and wreck dives daily for up to six divers each time, snorkeling with hawksbill turtles just offshore, as well as underwater camera rental and free transportation.

On the south coast, the **Dive Shop, Ltd** (⊠ *Bay St., Aquatic Gap, St. Michael* ☎ *246/426–9947, 888/898–3483 in U.S., 888/575–3483 in Canada* ⊕ *www.divebds.com*), the island's oldest dive shop, offers daily reef and wreck dives, plus beginner classes, certification courses, and underwater photography instruction. Underwater cameras are available for rent.

Hightide Watersports (⊠ *Coral Reef Club, Holetown, St. James* ☎ *246/432– 0931 or 800/513–5761* ⊕ *www.divehightide.com*) offers three dive trips—one- and two-tank dives and night reef/wreck/drift dives—daily for up to eight divers, along with PADI instruction, equipment rental, and free transportation.

FISHING

Fishing is a year-round activity in Barbados, but its prime time is January through April, when game fish are in season. Whether you're a serious deep-sea fisher looking for marlin, sailfish, tuna, and other billfish or if you prefer angling in calm coastal waters where wahoo, barracuda, and other small fish reside, you can choose from a variety of half- or full-day charter trips departing from the Careenage in Bridgetown. Expect to pay $100 per person for a shared charter; for a private charter, expect to pay $400 per boat for a four-hour half-day or $750 for an eight-hour full-day charter.

Billfisher II (☎ *246/431–0741*), a 40-foot Pacemaker, accommodates up to six guests with three fishing chairs and five rods. Captain Winston ("The Colonel") White has been fishing these waters since 1975. Full-day charters include a full lunch and guaranteed fish (or a 25% refund); all trips include drinks and transportation to and from the boat.

Blue Jay (☎ *246/429–2326* ⊕ *www.bluemarlinbarbados.com*) is a spacious, fully equipped, 45-foot Sport Fisherman with a crew that knows the water's denizens—blue marlin, sailfish, barracuda, and kingfish. Four to six people can be accommodated—it's the only charter boat on the island with four chairs. Most fishing is done by trolling. Drinks, snacks, bait, tackle, and transfers are provided.

Cannon II (☎ *246/424–6107*), a 42-foot Hatteras Sport Fisherman, has three chairs and five rods, and accommodates six passengers; drinks and snacks are complimentary, and lunch is served on full-day charters.

GOLF

Barbadians love golf, and golfers love Barbados. In addition to the courses listed below, Almond Beach Village has a 9-hole, par-3 executive course open only to guests. **Barbados Golf Club** (⊠*Hwy. 7, Durants, Christ Church* ☎*246/428–8463* ⊕*www.barbadosgolfclub.com*), the first public golf course on Barbados, is an 18-hole championship course (6,805 yards, par 72) redesigned in 2000 by golf course architect Ron Kirby. Greens fees are $135 for 18 holes, plus a $20 per-person cart fee. Unlimited three-day and seven-day golf passes are available. Several hotels offer preferential tee-time reservations and reduced rates. Club and shoe rentals are available.

Fodor'sChoice
★ At the prestigious **Country Club at Sandy Lane** (⊠*Hwy. 1, Paynes Bay, St. James* ☎*246/444–2500* ⊕*www.sandylane.com/golf*), golfers can play on the Old Nine or on either of two 18-hole championship courses: the Tom Fazio–designed Country Club Course or the spectacular Green Monkey Course, reserved for hotel guests and club members only. Golfers have complimentary use of the club's driving range. The Country Club Restaurant and Bar, which overlooks the 18th hole, is open to the public. Greens fees in high season are $150 for 9 holes ($130 for hotel guests) or $235 for 18 holes ($200 for hotel guests). Golf carts, caddies, or trolleys are available for hire, as well as clubs and shoes. Carts are equipped with GPS, which alerts you to upcoming traps and hazards, provides tips on how to play the hole, and allows you to order refreshments!

Rockley Golf & Country Club (⊠*Golf Club Rd., Worthing, Christ Church* ☎*246/435–7873* ⊕*www.rockleygolfclub.com*), on the southeast coast, has a challenging 9-hole course (2,800 yards, par 35) that can be played as 18 from varying tee positions. Club and cart rentals are available. Greens fees are $96 for 18 holes and $74 for 9 holes.

★ The **Royal Westmoreland Golf Club** (⊠*Westmoreland, St. James* ☎*246/ 422–4653* ⊕*www.royal-westmoreland.com*) has a world-class Robert Trent Jones Jr.–designed, 18-hole championship course (6,870 yards, par 72) that meanders through the 500-acre property. This challenging course is primarily for villa renters, with a few mid-morning tee times for visitors subject to availability; greens fees for villa renters are $200 for 18 holes, $100 for 9 holes; for visitors, $250 for 18 holes. Greens fees include use of an electric cart (required); club rental is available.

HIKING

Hilly but not mountainous, the northern interior and the east coast are ideal for hiking. The **Arbib Heritage & Nature Trail** (⊠*Speightstown, St. Peter* ☎*246/426–2421*), maintained by the Barbados National Trust, is actually two trails—one offers a rigorous hike through gullies and plantations to old ruins and remote north-country areas; the other is a shorter, easier walk through Speightstown's side streets and past an ancient church and chattel houses. Guided hikes take place on Wednesday, Thursday, and Saturday at 9 AM (book by 3 PM the day before) and cost $7.50.

The **Barbados National Trust** (✉ *Wildey House, Wildey, St. Michael* ☎ *246/ 426–2421* ⊕ *www.hikebarbados.com*) sponsors free walks, called **Hike Barbados,** year-round on Sunday from 6 AM to about 9 AM and from 3:30 PM to 6 PM; once a month, a moonlight hike substitutes for the afternoon hike and begins at 5:30 PM (bring a flashlight). Experienced guides group you with others of similar levels of ability. Stop & Stare hikes go 5 to 6 mi (8 to 10 km); Here & There, 8 to 10 mi (13 to 16 km); and Grin & Bear, 12 to 14 mi (19 to 23 km). Wear loose clothes, sensible shoes, sunscreen, and a hat, and bring your camera and a bottle of water. Routes and locations change, but each hike is a loop, finishing in the same spot where it began. Check local newspapers, call the Trust, or check online for the scheduled meeting place on a particular Sunday.

HORSE RACING

Horse racing is administered by the **Barbados Turf Club** (☎ *246/426– 3980* ⊕ *www.barbadosturfclub.com*) and races take place on alternate Saturdays throughout the year at the Garrison Savannah, a 6-furlong grass oval in Christ Church, about 3 mi (5 km) south of Bridgetown. The important races are the Sandy Lane Barbados Gold Cup, held in late February or early March, and the United Insurance Barbados Derby Day in August. Post time is 1:30 PM. General admission is $5 for grandstand seats and $10 for the clubhouse. (Prices are double on Gold Cup day.)

SEA EXCURSIONS

Minisubmarine voyages are enormously popular with families and those who enjoy watching fish but who don't wish to snorkel or dive. Party boats depart from Bridgetown's Deep Water Harbour for sight-seeing and snorkeling or romantic sunset cruises. Prices are $60 to $80 per person for daytime cruises and $35 to $65 for three-hour sunset cruises, depending on the type of refreshments and entertainment included; transportation to and from the dock is provided. For an excursion that may be less splashy in terms of the party atmosphere but definitely more splashy in terms of the actual experience, turtle tours allow participants to feed and swim with a resident pod of hawksbill and leatherback sea turtles.

Ⓒ The 48-passenger **Atlantis III** (✉ *Shallow Draught, Bridgetown, St. Michael* ☎ *246/436–8929* ⊕ *www.atlantisadventures.com*) turns the Caribbean into a giant aquarium. The 45-minute trip aboard the 50-foot submarine takes you to wrecks and reefs as deep as 150 feet.

Ⓒ Four- and five-hour daytime cruises along the west coast on the 100-foot **MV Harbour Master** (☎ *246/430–0900* ⊕ *www.tallshipscruises.com*) stop in Holetown and land at beaches along the way; evening cruises are shorter but add a buffet dinner and entertainment. Day or night you can view the briny deep from the ship's onboard 34-seat semi-submersible. A daytime cruise on the 57-foot catamaran *Heatwave* (☎ *246/429–9283*) includes stops along the coast for swimming and snorkeling and a barbecue lunch. The sunset cruise includes dinner.

The red-sail **Jolly Roger** (☎*246/228–8142*) "pirate" ship runs four-hour lunch-and-snorkeling sails along the south and west coasts. Be prepared for a rather raucous time, with rope swinging, plank walking, and other games—and plenty of calypso music and complimentary drinks. The sunset cruise, also four hours, includes a buffet dinner, drinks, and entertainment.

The 44-foot CSY sailing yacht **Limbo Lady** (☎*246/420–5418*) sails along the captivating west coast, stopping for a swim, snorkeling, and a Bajan buffet lunch on board. Sunset cruises are another option. The 53-foot catamaran *Tiami* (☎*246/430–0900* ⊕*www.tallshipscruises. com*) offers a luncheon cruise to a secluded bay or a romantic sunset and moonlight cruise with special catering and live music.

Outdoors Barbados (⊕*www.outdoorsbarbados.com*), based in Holetown, has a 32-foot glass-bottom boat from which guests view, snorkel among, and swim with the turtles. Two trips depart daily, at 10 AM and 2 PM. They cover about 6 mi (10 km) of coastline along the west coast, cost $47 per adult, and last two hours each. Hotel transportation, cool drinks, snorkels, and masks are included.

SURFING

The best surfing is on the east coast, at Bathsheba Soup Bowl, but the water on the windward side of the island is safe only for the most-experienced swimmers. Surfers also congregate at Surfer's Point, at the southern tip of Barbados near Inch Marlow, where the Atlantic Ocean meets the Caribbean Sea. **Dread or Dead Surf Shop** (⊠*Hastings Main Rd., Hastings, Christ Church* ☎*246/228–4785* ⊕*www.dreadordead. com*) promises to get beginners from "zero to standing up and surfing" in a single afternoon. The four-hour course—"or until you stand up or give up"—costs $75 per person and includes a board, wax, a rash guard (if necessary), a ride to and from the surf break, and an instructor. Intermediate or experienced surfers can get all the equipment and the instructor for a full day of surfing for $150.

The Independence Classic Surfing Championship (an international competition) is held at Bathsheba Soup Bowl every November—when the surf is at its peak. For information, contact the **Barbados Surfing Association** (☎*246/228–5117* ⊕*www.bsasurf.com*).

WINDSURFING

Barbados is on the World Cup Windsurfing Circuit and is one of the prime locations in the world for windsurfing. Winds are strongest November through April at the island's southern tip, at Silver Sands–Silver Rock Beach, which is where the Barbados Windsurfing Championships are held in mid-January. Use of boards and equipment is often among the amenities included at larger hotels; equipment can usually be rented by nonguests.

More-experienced windsurfers congregate at **Silver Rock Windsurfing Club** (⊠*Silver Sands–Silver Rock Beach, Christ Church* ☎*246/428–2866*), where the surf ranges from 3 to 15 feet and provides an exhilarating windsurfing experience.

SHOPPING

AREAS & MALLS

Bridgetown's **Broad Street** is the primary downtown shopping area. **DaCostas Mall,** in the historic Colonnade Building on Broad Street, has more than 25 shops that sell everything from Piaget to postcards; across the street, **Mall 34** has 22 shops where you can buy duty-free goods, souvenirs, and snacks. At the **cruise-ship terminal** shopping arcade, passengers can buy both duty-free goods and Barbadian-made crafts at more than 30 boutiques and a dozen vendor carts and stalls. **Pelican Craft Centre** is a cluster of workshops halfway between the cruise-ship terminal and downtown Bridgetown, where craftspeople create and sell locally made items.

Holetown and St. Lawrence Gap each have a **Chattel House Village,** a cluster of shops selling local products, fashions, beachwear, and souvenirs. Also in Holetown, **Sunset Crest Mall** has two branches of the Cave Shepherd department store, a bank, a pharmacy, and several small shops; at **West Coast Mall,** you can buy duty-free goods, island wear, and groceries. In Rockley, Christ Church, **Quayside Shopping Center** houses a small group of boutiques, restaurants, and services.

DEPARTMENT STORES

Cave Shepherd (⊠ *Broad St., Bridgetown, St. Michael* ☎ *246/431–2121*) offers a wide selection of clothing and luxury goods; branch stores are in Holetown, at the airport, and at the cruise-ship terminal.

Harrison's (⊠ *Broad St., Bridgetown, St. Michael* ☎ *246/431–5500*) has 11 locations—including its two large stores on Broad Street and one each at the airport and the cruise-ship terminal—offering luxury name-brand goods from the fashion corners of the world.

SPECIALTY ITEMS

ANTIQUES Although many of the private homes, greathouses, and museums in Barbados are filled with priceless antiques, you'll find few for sale—mainly British antiques and some local pieces, particularly mahogany furniture. Look especially for planters' chairs and the classic Barbadian rocking chair, as well as old prints and paintings. **Greenwich House Antiques** (⊠ *Greenwich Village, Trents Hill, St. James* ☎ *246/432–1169*) fills an entire plantation house with vintage Barbadian mahogany furniture, art deco pieces, crystal, silver, china, books, and pictures; it's open daily from 10:30 to 5:30.

ART Perhaps one of the most long-lasting souvenirs to bring home from Barbados is a piece of authentic Caribbean art. The colorful flowers, quaint villages, mesmerizing seascapes, and fascinating cultural experiences and activities that are endemic to the region and familiar to visitors have been translated by local artists onto canvas and into photographs, sculpture, and other media. Gift shops and even some restaurants display local artwork for sale, but the broadest array of artwork will be found in an art gallery. **Gallery of Caribbean Art** (⊠ *Northern Business Centre, Queen St., Speightstown, St. Peter* ☎ *246/419–0585*) is committed to promoting Caribbean art from Cuba to Curaçao, including

Where de Rum Come From

For more than 300 years, a daily "tot" of rum (2 ounces) has been duly administered to each sailor in the British Navy—as a health ration. At times, rum has also played a less-appetizing—but equally important—role. When Admiral Horatio Nelson died in 1805 aboard ship during the Battle of Trafalgar, his body was preserved in a cask of his favorite rum until he could be properly buried.

Hardly a Caribbean island doesn't have its own locally made rum, but Barbados is truly "where de rum come from." Mount Gay, the world's oldest rum distillery, has continuously operated on Barbados since 1703, according to the original deed for the Mount Gay Estate, which itemized two stone windmills, a boiling house, seven copper pots, and a still house. The presence of rum-making equipment on the plantation at the time suggests that the previous owners were actually producing rum in Barbados long before 1703.

Today, much of the island's interior is still planted with sugarcane—where the rum really does come from—and several greathouses, situated on historic sugar plantations, have been restored with period furniture and are open to the public.

To really fathom rum, however, you need to delve a little deeper than the bottom of a glass of rum punch. Mount Gay offers an interesting 45-minute tour of its main plant, followed by a tasting. You can learn about the rum-making process from cane to cocktail, hear more rum-inspired anecdotes, and have an opportunity to buy bottles of its famous Eclipse or Extra Old rum at duty-free prices. Bottoms up!

a number of pieces by Barbadian artists. A branch gallery is located at the Hilton Barbados hotel, Needham's Point.

On the Wall Art Gallery (⊠ #2, *Edgehill Heights, St. Thomas* ☎ *246/425–0223*), next door to Earthworks Pottery, has an array of original paintings by Barbadian artists, along with arts and crafts products. Additional galleries are located in dedicated space at the Tides restaurant on the west coast and Champers restaurant on the south coast.

CLOTHING **Dingolay** (⊠ *Bay St., Bridgetown, St. Michael* ☎ *246/436–2157* ⊠ *Hwy. 1, Holetown, St. James* ☎ *246/432–8709*) sells tropical clothing designed and made in Barbados for ladies and girls as well as shoes, handbags, and accessories from around the world.

Check out the colorful T-shirts from **Irie Blue** (⊠ *Lower Broad St., Bridgetown, St. Michael* ☎ *246/426–8464*), which are designed and made in Barbados. You can also find them in many gift shops.

At **Kosmic Vibes Designs** (⊠ *Spirit Bond Mall 5, Bridgetown, St. Michael* ☎ *246/268–9732*) designer Karen Brathwaite creates linen dresses, pants, and shirts (for women and men) that are made on-site and hand-painted with tropical motifs, tie-dyed in subtle colorations (definitely not your Grateful Dead look), or simply constructed in high style. Hand-beaded jewelry, macramé belts and bags, and other accessories are also designed by Brathwaite and produced in the shop. Custom orders are welcome and will be fulfilled in two weeks or less.

DUTY-FREE GOODS
Duty-free luxury goods—china, crystal, cameras, porcelain, leather items, electronics, jewelry, perfume, and clothing—are found in Bridgetown's Broad Street department stores and their branches, at the cruise-ship terminal shops (for passengers only), and in the departure lounge shops at Grantley Adams International Airport. Prices are often 30% to 40% less than at home. To buy goods at duty-free prices, you must produce your passport, immigration form, or driver's license, along with departure information (e.g., flight number and date) at the time of purchase—or you can have your purchases delivered free to the airport or harbor for pickup. Duty-free alcohol, tobacco products, and some electronic equipment *must* be delivered to you at the airport or harbor.

The anchor shop of **Little Switzerland** (⊠*DaCostas Mall, Broad St., Bridgetown, St. Michael* ☎*246/431–0030*) is at DaCostas Mall, with branches at the cruise-ship terminal and at West Coast Mall, Sunset Crest, in Holetown. Here you can find perfume, jewelry, cameras, audio equipment, Swarovski and Waterford crystal, and Wedgwood china.

The **Royal Shop** (⊠*32 Broad St., Bridgetown, St. Michael* ☎*246/429–7072*) carries fine watches and jewelry fashioned in Italian gold, Caribbean silver, diamonds, and other gems.

HANDICRAFTS
Typical crafts include pottery, shell and glass art, wood carvings, handmade dolls, watercolors, and other artwork (both originals and prints). **Best of Barbados** (⊠*Worthing, Christ Church* ☎*246/421–6900*), was the brainchild of architect Jimmy Walker as a place to showcase the works of his artist wife. Now with seven locations, the shops offer products that range from Jill Walker's frameable prints, housewares, and textiles to arts and crafts in both "native" style and modern designs. Everything is made or designed on Barbados.

Fodor'sChoice
★
Earthworks Pottery (⊠*No. 2, Edgehill Heights, Edgehill Heights, St. Thomas* ☎*246/425–0223*) is a family-owned and -operated pottery shop where you can purchase anything from a dish or knickknack to a complete dinner service or one-of-a-kind art piece. You can find the characteristically blue or green pottery decorating hotel rooms for sale in gift shops throughout the island, but the biggest selection (including some "seconds") is at Earthworks, where you also can watch the potters work.

Pelican Craft Centre (⊠*Princess Alice Hwy., Bridgetown, St. Michael* ☎*246/427–5350*) is a cluster of workshops halfway between the cruise-ship terminal and downtown Bridgetown where craftspeople create and sell locally made leather goods, batik, basketry, carvings, jewelry, glass art, paintings, pottery, and other items. It's open weekdays 9 to 5 and Saturday 9 to 2, with extended hours during holidays or cruise-ship arrivals.

Red Clay Pottery and Fairfield Gallery (⊠*Fairfield House, Fairfield Cross Rd.Fairfield, St. Michael* ☎*246/424–3800*) has been operated by potter Denis Bell all his life, "save a little time spent doing some engineering and raising a family." Visitors are welcome to watch the potters at work in the studio, which is in an old sugar boiling house, and, in the adjacent shop, purchase plates, platters, bowls, place settings, and fine decorative items designed by Bell's daughter, Maggie.

In the chattel houses at **Tyrol Cot Heritage Village** (⊠ *Codrington Hill, St. Michael* ☎ *246/424–2074*) you can watch local artisans make handpainted figurines, straw baskets, clothing, paintings, and pottery—and, of course, buy their wares.

NIGHTLIFE

4

When the sun goes down, the people come out to "lime" (which may be anything from a "chat-up" to a full-blown "jump-up"). Performances by world-renowned stars and regional groups are major events, and tickets can be hard to come by—but give it a try. Most resorts have nightly entertainment in season, and nightclubs often have live bands for listening and dancing. The busiest bars and dance clubs rage until 3 AM. On Saturday nights, some clubs—especially those with live music—charge a cover of about $15.

The **Oistins Fish Fry** is the place to be on weekend evenings, when the south-coast fishing village becomes a convivial outdoor street fair. Barbecued chicken and flying fish are served right from the grill and consumed at roadside picnic tables; servings are huge, and prices are inexpensive—about $5. Drinks, music, and dancing add to the fun.

BARS
Barbados supports the rum industry with more than 1,600 "rum shops," simple bars where men (mostly) congregate to discuss the world (or life in general), drink rum, and eat a "cutter" (sandwich). In more-sophisticated establishments, you can find world-class rum drinks made with the island's renowned Mount Gay and Cockspur brands—and no shortage of Barbados's own Banks Beer.

The **Boatyard** (⊠ *Bay St., Carlisle Bay, Bridgetown, St. Michael* ☎ *246/436–2622*) is a popular pub with both a DJ and live bands; from happy hour until the wee hours, the patrons are mostly local and visiting professionals.

Waterfront Cafe (⊠ *The Careenage, Bridgetown, St. Michael* ☎ *246/427– 0093*) has live jazz in the evening, with a small dance floor for dancing. The picturesque location alongside the wharf is also a draw.

On the south coast, **Bubba's Sports Bar** (⊠ *Main Rd., Rockley, Christ Church* ☎ *246/435–8731*) offers merrymakers and sports lovers live sports on three 10-foot video screens and a dozen TVs, along with a Bajan à la carte menu and, of course, drinks at the bar.

Jumbie's (⊠ *St. Lawrence Gap, Christ Church* ☎ *246/420–7615*) has an open-air party room with either a DJ or live music every night. Happy hours run from 5 PM to 7 PM and again from 10 PM to 1 AM every night and all day Sunday! Obviously, a very happy place to congregate in the evening.

On the west coast, **Coach House** (⊠*Hwy. 1, Paynes Bay, St. James* ☎*246/432–1163*) has live entertainment nightly and international sports via satellite TV.

Lexy's Piano Bar (⊠*2nd St., Holetown, St. James* ☎*246/432–5399*) is a cool, trendy club named for owner Alex Santoriello, a transplanted Broadway singer and actor. A changing roster of singer-pianists play sing-a-long standards, classic rock, R&B, and Broadway tunes. Most any night, you'll find Santoriello there.

Upstairs at Olives (⊠*2nd St., Holetown, St. James* ☎*246/432–2112*) is a sophisticated watering hole. Enjoy cocktails and conversation seated amid potted palms and cooled by ceiling fans—either before or after dinner downstairs.

DANCE CLUBS

After Dark (⊠*St. Lawrence Gap, Dover, Christ Church* ☎*246/435–6547*) attracts mostly young people to live appearances of reggae, calypso, and soca (an upbeat, sexy variation of calypso) headliners such as Krosfyah.

Club Xtreme (⊠*Main Rd., Worthing, Christ Church* ☎*246/228–2582*) attracts a young crowd on Wednesday, Friday, and Saturday nights for the latest DJ-spun alternative, dance, R&B, reggae, and other party music.

The open-air, beachfront **Harbour Lights** (⊠*Upper Bay St., Bridgetown, St. Michael* ☎*246/436–7225*) claims to be the "home of the party animal" and has dancing under the stars most nights to live reggae and soca music.

The **Ship Inn** (⊠*St. Lawrence Gap, Dover, Christ Church* ☎*246/435–6961*) is a large, friendly pub with local band music every night for dancing.

THEME NIGHTS

☾ On Wednesday and Friday evenings at the **Plantation Restaurant and**
★ **Garden Theater** (⊠*St. Lawrence Main Rd., Dover, Christ Church* ☎*246/428–5048*) the Tropical Spectacular calypso cabaret presents "Bajan Roots & Rhythms," a delightful extravaganza that the whole family will enjoy. The show includes steel-band music, fire eating, limbo, and dancing to the reggae, soca, and pop music sounds of popular Barbadian singer John King and the Plantation House Band. The fun begins at 6:30 PM. A Barbadian buffet dinner, unlimited drinks, transportation, and the show cost $75; for the show and drinks only, it's $37.50.

EXPLORING BARBADOS

The terrain changes dramatically from any one of the island's 11 parishes to the next, and so does the pace. Bridgetown, the capital, is a rather sophisticated city. West-coast resorts and private estates ooze luxury, whereas the small villages and vast sugar plantations found throughout central Barbados reflect the island's history. The relentless Atlantic surf shaped the cliffs of the dramatic east coast, and the northeast is called Scotland because of its hilly landscape. Along the lively south coast, the daytime hustle and bustle produce a palpable energy that continues well into the night—at countless restaurants, dance clubs, and nightspots.

BRIDGETOWN

4

This bustling capital city is a major duty-free port with a compact shopping area. The principal thoroughfare is Broad Street, which leads west from National Heroes Square.

Numbers in the margin correspond to points of interest on the Bridgetown map.

WHAT TO SEE **The Careenage.** Bridgetown's natural harbor and gathering place is
2 where, in the early days, schooners were careened (turned on their sides) to be scraped of barnacles and repainted. Today the Careenage serves as a marina for pleasure yachts and excursion boats. A boardwalk skirts the north side of the Careenage; on the south side, a lovely esplanade has pathways and benches for pedestrians and a statue of Errol Barrow, the first prime minister of Barbados. The Chamberlain Bridge and the Charles Duncan O'Neal Bridge cross the Careenage.

3 **National Heroes Square.** Across Broad Street from the Parliament Buildings and bordered by High and Trafalgar streets, this triangular plaza marks the center of town. Its monument to Lord Horatio Nelson (who was in Barbados only briefly in 1777 as a 19-year-old navy lieutenant) predates Nelson's Column in London's Trafalgar Square by 36 years. Also here are a war memorial and a fountain that commemorates the advent of running water on Barbados in 1865.

1 **Nidhe Israel Synagogue.** Providing for the spiritual needs of one of the oldest Jewish congregations in the western hemisphere, this synagogue was formed by Jews who left Brazil in the 1620s and introduced sugarcane to Barbados. The adjoining cemetery has tombstones dating from the 1630s. The original house of worship, built in 1654, was destroyed in an 1831 hurricane, rebuilt in 1833, and restored with the assistance of the Barbados National Trust in 1987. Friday-night services are held during the winter months, but the building is open to the public year-round. Shorts are not acceptable during services but may be worn at other times. ⊠*Synagogue La., St. Michael* ☎246/426–5792 🖾*Donation requested* ☉ *Weekdays 9–4.*

4 **Parliament Buildings.** Overlooking National Heroes Square in the center of town, these Victorian buildings were constructed around 1870 to house the British Commonwealth's third-oldest parliament. A series of stained-glass windows depicts British monarchs from James I to Victo-

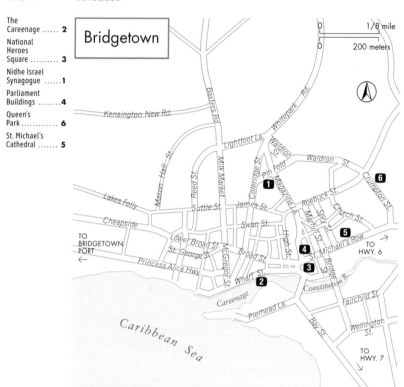

ria. ⊠ *Broad St., St. Michael* ☎ *246/427–2019* ✉ *Donations welcome* ⊙ *Tours weekdays at 11 and 2, when parliament isn't in session.*

❻ Queen's Park. Northeast of Bridgetown, Queen's Park contains one of the island's two immense baobab trees. Brought to Barbados from Guinea, in West Africa, around 1738, this tree has a girth of more than 51 feet. Queen's Park Art Gallery, managed by the National Culture Foundation, is the island's largest gallery; exhibits change monthly. Queen's Park House, the historic home of the British troop commander, has been converted into a theater, with an exhibition room on the lower floor and a restaurant. ⊠ *Constitution Rd., St. Michael* ☎ *246/427–2345 gallery* ✉ *Free* ⊙ *Daily 9–5.*

❺ St. Michael's Cathedral. Although no one has proved it, George Washington, on his only trip outside the United States, is said to have worshipped here in 1751. The original structure was nearly a century old by then. Destroyed twice by hurricanes, it was rebuilt in 1784 and again in 1831. ⊠ *Spry St. east of National Heroes Sq., St. Michael.*

SOUTHERN BARBADOS

Christ Church Parish, which is far busier and more developed than the west coast, is chockablock with condos, high- and low-rise hotels, and beach parks. It is also home to the St. Lawrence Gap and its many places to eat, drink, shop, and party. As you move southeast, the broad, flat terrain comprises acre upon acre of cane fields, interrupted only by an occasional oil rig and a few tiny villages hugging crossroads. Along the byways are colorful chattel houses, the property of tenant farmers. Historically, these typically Barbadian, ever-expandable houses were built to be dismantled and moved as required.

WHAT TO SEE **Barbados Concorde Experience.** Opened to the public in April 2007, the Concorde Experience revolves around the British Airways Concorde G-BOAE (Alpha Echo, for short), that for many years flew between London and Barbados and has now made its permanent home here. Besides boarding the sleek supersonic aircraft itself, you'll learn about how the technology was developed and how this plane differed from other jets. You may or may not have been able to fly the Concorde when it was still plying the Atlantic, but this is your chance to experience some ultramodern history. ⌧*Grantley Adams International Airport, Christ Church* ☎*246/253–6257* ⊕*www.barbadosconcorde.com* ⌧*$17.50* ⊗*Daily 9–5.*

4

Barbados Museum. This intriguing museum, established in 1933 in the former British Military Prison (1815) in the historic Garrison area, has artifacts from Arawak days (around 400 BC) and galleries that depict 19th-century military history and everyday life. You can see cane-harvesting tools, wedding dresses, ancient (and frightening) dentistry instruments, and slave sale accounts kept in a spidery copperplate handwriting. The museum's Harewood Gallery showcases the island's flora and fauna; its Cunard Gallery has a permanent collection of 20th-century Barbadian and Caribbean paintings and engravings; and its Connell Gallery features European decorative arts. Additional galleries include one for children. The Shilstone Memorial Library houses rare West Indian documentation—archival documents, genealogical records, photos, books, and maps—dating back to the 17th century. The museum also has a gift shop and a café. ⌧*Hwy. 7, Garrison Savannah, St. Michael* ☎*246/427–0201 or 246/436–1956* ⊕*www.barbmuse.org.bb* ⌧*$4* ⊗*Mon.–Sat. 9–5, Sun. 2–6.*

Codrington Theological College. An impressive stand of royal palms lines the road leading to the coral-stone buildings and serene grounds of Codrington College, an Anglican seminary opened in 1745 on a cliff overlooking Consett Bay. You're welcome to tour the buildings and walk the nature trails. Keep in mind, though, that beachwear is not appropriate here. ⌧*Sargeant St., Consett Bay, St. John* ☎*246/423–1140* ⊕*www.codrington.org* ⌧*$2.50* ⊗*Daily 10–4.*

Emancipation Statue. This powerful statue of a slave—whose raised hands, with broken chains hanging from each wrist, evoke both contempt and victory—is commonly referred to as the Bussa Statue. Bussa was the man who, in 1816, led the first slave rebellion on Barbados. The work of Barbadian sculptor Karl Brodhagen was erected in 1985 to commemorate the emancipation of the slaves in 1834. ⌧*St. Barnabas Roundabout, intersection of ABC Hwy. and Hwy. 5, Haggatt Hall, St. Michael.*

George Washington House. George Washington slept here! This carefully restored and refurbished 18th-century plantation house in Bush Hill was the only place where the future first president of the United States actually slept outside North America. Teenage George and his older half brother Lawrence, who was suffering from tuberculosis and seeking treatment on the island, rented this house overlooking Carlisle Bay for two months in 1751. Opened to the public in December 2006, the lower floor of the house and the kitchen have period furnishings; the upper floor is a museum with both permanent and temporary exhibits that display artifacts of 18th-century Barbadian life The site includes an original 1719 windmill and bathhouse, along with a stable added to the property in the 1800s—and, of course, a gift shop and small café. Guided tours begin with an informative, 15-minute film appropriately called, "George Washington in Barbados." ⊠ *Bush Hill, The Garrison, St. Michael* ☎ *246/228–5461* ⌖ *$12.50* ⊗ *Mon.–Sat. 9–4:30.*

☼ ★ **Graeme Hall Nature Sanctuary.** This 35-acre oasis, a Barbados National Environmental Heritage Site, sits smack in the middle of the busy commercial area of the south coast. Saved from almost-certain development as a golf course or other commercial use, the sanctuary includes the island's largest inland lake along with ponds and wading pools, swampy marshes and mangroves, observation huts, horticulture exhibits, and two enormous walk-through aviaries filled with brilliantly colored parrots, macaws, flamingos, and ibis. It's interesting, educational, peaceful, and delightful for both adults and kids. ⊠ *Main Rd., Worthing, Christ Church* ☎ *246/435–9727* ⊕ *www.graemehall.com* ⌖ *$12.50* ⊗ *Daily 8–6.*

☼ **Ocean Park.** View stingrays, sharks, moray eels, and other marine life up close and personal at this fun-for-all marine park. Throughout the day, informative talks and feeding demonstrations teach visitors about the underwater creatures on exhibit in the touch pools, mega-tanks, living reef display, mangrove swamp, and freshwater falls. An additional family-fun feature is the adjacent miniature golf course ($2.50 extra). ⊠ *Hwy. 6, Balls Complex, Christ Church* ☎ *246/420–7405* ⊕ *www. oceanparkbarbados.com* ⌖ *$17.50* ⊗ *Daily 9–6.*

★ **Sunbury Plantation House & Museum.** Lovingly rebuilt after a 1995 fire destroyed everything but the thick flint-and-stone walls, Sunbury offers an elegant glimpse of the 18th and 19th centuries on a Barbadian sugar estate. Period furniture, old prints, and a collection of horse-drawn carriages lend an air of authenticity. A buffet luncheon is served daily in the courtyard for $17.50 per person. A five-course candlelight dinner is served ($47.50 per person, reservations required) two nights a week at the 200-year-old mahogany table in the Sunbury dining room. ⊠ *Off Hwy. 5, Six Cross Roads, St. Philip* ☎ *246/423–6270* ⊕ *www. barbadosgreathouse.com* ⌖ *$7.50* ⊗ *Daily 10–5.*

☼ **Tyrol Cot Heritage Village.** This coral-stone cottage just south of Bridgetown was constructed in 1854 and is preserved as an example of period architecture. In 1929 it became the home of Sir Grantley Adams, the first premier of Barbados and the namesake of its international airport. Part of the Barbados National Trust, the cottage is now filled with the late Sir Grantley and Lady Adams' antiques and memorabilia. It's also the centerpiece of an outdoor "living museum," where artisans and craftsmen have their workshops in a cluster of traditional chattel houses. The crafts are for sale, and refreshments are available at the "rum shop." ⊠*Rte. 2, Codrington Hill, St. Michael* ☎*246/424–2074 or 246/436–9033* ⬛*$6* ☉*Weekdays 9–5.*

CENTRAL BARBADOS

On the west coast, in St. James Parish, Holetown marks the center of the Platinum Coast—so called for the vast number of luxurious resorts and mansions that face the sea. Holetown is also where British captain John Powell landed in 1625 to claim the island for King James. On the east coast, the crashing Atlantic surf has eroded the shoreline, forming steep cliffs and prehistoric rocks that look like giant mushrooms. Bathsheba and Cattlewash are favorite seacoast destinations for local folks on weekends and holidays. In the interior, narrow roads weave through tiny villages and along and between the ridges. The landscape is covered with tropical vegetation and is riddled with fascinating caves and gullies.

WHAT TO SEE   **Andromeda Botanic Gardens.** Beautiful and unusual plant specimens from
★   around the world are cultivated in 6 acres of gardens nestled among streams, ponds, and rocky outcroppings overlooking the sea above the Bathsheba coastline. The gardens were created in 1954 with flowering plants collected by the late horticulturist Iris Bannochie. They're now administered by the Barbados National Trust. The Hibiscus Café serves snacks and drinks. ⊠*Bathsheba, St. Joseph* ☎*246/433–9384* ⬛*$8.75* ☉*Daily 9–5.*

★   **Flower Forest.** It's a treat to meander among fragrant flowering bushes, canna and ginger lilies, puffball trees, and more than 100 other species of tropical flora in a cool, tranquil forest of flowers and other plants. A 0.5-mi-long (1-km-long) path winds through the 50-acre grounds, a former sugar plantation; it takes about 30 to 45 minutes to follow the path, or you can wander freely for as long as you wish. Benches located throughout the forest give you a place to pause and reflect. There's also a snack bar, a gift shop, and a beautiful view of Mt. Hillaby. ⊠*Hwy. 2, Richmond Plantation, St. Joseph* ☎*246/433–8152* ⬛*$10* ☉*Daily 9–5.*

☼   **Folkestone Marine Park & Visitor Centre.** On land and offshore, the whole
★   family will enjoy this park just north of Holetown. The museum and aquarium illuminate some of the island's marine life; and for some first-hand viewing, there's an underwater snorkeling trail around Dottins Reef (glass-bottom boats are available for nonswimmers). A barge sunk in shallow water is home to myriad fish, making it a popular dive site. ⊠*Church Point, Holetown, St. James* ☎*246/422–2314* ⬛*Free* ☉*Daily 9–5; museum, weekdays 9–5.*

☼   **Gun Hill Signal Station.** The 360-degree view from Gun Hill, 700 feet
★   above sea level, was what made this location of strategic importance to the 18th-century British army. Using lanterns and semaphore, soldiers

based here could communicate with their counterparts at the Garrison, on the south coast, and at Grenade Hill, in the north. Time moved slowly in 1868, and Captain Henry Wilkinson whiled away his off-duty hours by carving a huge lion from a single rock—which is on the hillside just below the tower. Come for a short history lesson but mainly for the view; it's so gorgeous, military invalids were once sent here to convalesce. ⊠ *Gun Hill, St. George* ☎*246/429–1358* ☜*$4.60* ⊘ *Weekdays 9–5.*

☾ **Harrison's Cave.** This limestone cavern, complete with stalactites, sta-
Fodor's Choice lagmites, subterranean streams, and a 40-foot waterfall, is a rare find
★ in the Caribbean—and one of Barbados's most popular attractions. The cave reopened in 2007, following extensive renovations comprising a new visitor center with interpretative displays, life-size models and sculptures, a souvenir shop, improved restaurant facilities, and access for people with disabilities. The one-hour tours are conducted via electric trams, which fill up fast; reserve ahead of time. ⊠ *Hwy. 2, Welchman Hall, St. Thomas* ☎*246/438–6640* ⊕ *www.harrisonscave. com* ☜*$20* ⊘ *Daily 9–6; last tour at 4.*

Malibu Beach Club & Visitor Centre. Just north of Bridgetown, the fun-loving Malibu Rum people encourage those taking the distillery tour to make a day of it. The beach—which has a variety of water-sports options—is adjacent to the visitor center. Lunch and drinks are served at the beachside grill. ⊠ *Black Rock, Brighton, St. Michael* ☎*246/425– 9393* ⊕ *www.malibu-rum.com* ☜*$7.50, $27.50 with lunch, $37.50 day pass* ⊘ *Weekdays 9–5.*

★ **Mount Gay Rum Visitors Centre.** On this popular 45-minute tour you learn the colorful story behind the world's oldest rum—made in Barbados since the 18th century. Although the distillery is in the far north, in St. Lucy Parish, tour guides explain the rum-making procedure. Both historic and modern equipment is on display, and rows and rows of barrels are stored in this location. The 45-minute tour concludes with a tasting and an opportunity to buy bottles of rum and gift items—and even have lunch. ⊠ *Spring Garden Hwy., Brandons, St. Michael* ☎*246/425–8757* ⊕*www.mountgay.com* ☜*$6, $27.50 with lunch* ⊘ *Weekdays 9–4.*

Orchid World. Follow meandering pathways through tropical gardens filled with thousands of colorful orchids. You'll see Vandaceous orchids attached to fences or wire frames, Schomburgkia and Oncidiums stuck on mahogany trees, Aranda and Spathoglottis orchids growing in a grotto, and Ascocendas suspended from netting in shady enclosures. You'll find seasonal orchids, scented orchids, multicolor Vanda orchids … and more. Benches are well placed to stop for a little rest, admire the flowers, or simply take in the expansive view of the surrounding cane fields and distant hills of Sweet Vale. Snacks, cold beverages, and other refreshments are served in the café. ⊠ *Hwy. 3B, Groves, St, George* ☎*246/433–0306* ☜*$10* ⊘ *Daily 9–5.*

Welchman Hall Gully. This 1.5-mi-long (2-km-long) natural gully is really a collapsed limestone cavern, once part of the same underground network as Harrison's Cave. The Barbados National Trust protects the peace and quiet here, making it a beautiful place to hike past acres of labeled flowers and stands of trees. You can see and hear some interesting birds—and, with luck, a native green monkey. ⊠ *Welchman Hall, St. Thomas* ☎ *246/438–6671* ⌂ *$5.75* ⊙ *Daily 9–5.*

NORTHERN BARBADOS

Speightstown, the north's commercial center and once a thriving port city, now relies on quaint local shops and informal restaurants. Many of Speightstown's 19th-century buildings, with typical overhanging balconies, have been or are being restored. The island's northernmost reaches, St. Peter and St. Lucy parishes, have a varied topography and are lovely to explore. Between the tiny fishing towns along the northwestern coast and the sweeping views out over the Atlantic to the east are forest and farm, moor and mountain. Most guides include a loop through this area on a daylong island tour—it's a beautiful drive.

WHAT TO SEE **Animal Flower Cave.** Small sea anemones, or sea worms (resembling flowers when they open their tiny tentacles) live in small pools in this cave at the island's very northern tip. The view of breaking waves from inside the cave is magnificent. ⊠ *North Point, St. Lucy* ☎ *246/439–8797* ⌂ *$2* ⊙ *Daily 9–4.*

Barbados Wildlife Reserve. The reserve is the habitat of herons, innumerable land turtles, screeching peacocks, shy deer, elusive green monkeys, brilliantly colored parrots (in a large walk-in aviary), a snake, and a caiman. Except for the snake and the caiman, the animals run or fly freely—so step carefully and keep your hands to yourself. Late afternoon is your best chance to catch a glimpse of a green monkey. ⊠ *Farley Hill, St. Peter* ☎ *246/422–8826* ⌂ *$11.50* ⊙ *Daily 10–5.*

Farley Hill. At this national park in northern St. Peter, across the road from the Barbados Wildlife Reserve, the imposing ruins of a plantation greathouse are surrounded by gardens and lawns, along with an avenue of towering royal palms and gigantic mahogany, whitewood, and casuarina trees. Partially rebuilt for the filming of *Island in the Sun,* the classic 1957 film starring Harry Belafonte and Dorothy Dandridge, the structure was later destroyed by fire. Behind the estate, there's a sweeping view of the region called Scotland for its rugged landscape. ⊠ *Farley Hill, St. Peter* ☎ *246/422–3555* ⌂ *$2 per car, pedestrians free* ⊙ *Daily 8:30–6.*

Morgan Lewis Sugar Mill. Built in 1727, the mill was operational until 1945. Today it's the only remaining windmill in Barbados with its wheelhouse and sails intact. No longer used to grind sugarcane, except for occasional demonstrations, it was donated to the Barbados National Trust in 1962 and eventually restored to its original working specifications in 1998 by millwrights from the United Kingdom. The surrounding acres are now used for dairy farming. ⊠ *Cherry Tree Hill, St. Andrew* ☎ *246/422–7429* ⌂ *$5* ⊙ *Weekdays 9–5.*

★ **St. Nicholas Abbey.** There's no religious connection here at all. The island's oldest greathouse (circa 1650) was named after the original

British owner's hometown, St. Nicholas Parish near Bristol, and Bath Abbey nearby. Its stone-and-wood architecture makes it one of only three original Jacobean-style houses still standing in the western hemisphere. It has Dutch gables, finials of coral stone, and beautiful grounds that include an old sugar mill. The first floor, fully furnished with period furniture and portraits of family members, is open to the public. Fascinating home movies, shot by a previous owner's father, record Bajan life in the 1930s. ⊠ *Cherry Tree Hill, St. Peter* ☎ *246/422–5357* 🔊 *$12.50* ⊙ *Weekdays 10–3:30.*

BARBADOS ESSENTIALS

To research prices, get advice from other travelers, and book travel arrangements, visit www.fodors.com.

TRANSPORTATION

AIRPORTS

Grantley Adams International Airport (BGI) is a stunning, modern facility located in Christ Church Parish, on the south coast. The airport is about 15 minutes from hotels situated along the south or east coasts, 45 minutes from the west coast, and about 30 minutes from Bridgetown.

Airport Information Grantley Adams International Airport (BGI ☎ 246/428–7101).

BY AIR

Several international carriers offer frequent nonstop from the U.S. Barbados is also well connected to other Caribbean islands via LIAT. Mustique Airways, SVG Air, and Trans Island Air (TIA) link Barbados with St. Vincent & the Grenadines.

Information Air Jamaica (☎ 246/428–1660 or 800/523–5585). **American Airlines** (☎ 246/428–4170). **Caribbean Airlines** (☎ 246/428–1950 or 800/744–2225). **LIAT** (☎ 246/428–0986 or 888/844–5428). **Mustique Airways** (☎ 246/428–1638). **SVG Air** (☎ 784/457–5124). **Trans Island Air** (☎ 246/418–1654). **US Airways** (☎ 800/622–1015).

BY BOAT

Half the annual visitors to Barbados are cruise passengers. Bridgetown's Deep Water Harbour is on the northwest side of Carlisle Bay, and up to eight cruise ships can dock at the cruise-ship terminal. Downtown Bridgetown is a 0.5-mi (1-km) walk from the pier; a taxi costs about $3 each way.

BY BUS

Bus service is efficient, inexpensive, and plentiful. Blue buses with a yellow stripe are public, yellow buses with a blue stripe are private, and private "Zed-R" vans (so called for their ZR license plate designation) are white with a maroon stripe. All buses travel frequently along Highway 1 (St. James Road) and Highway 7 (South Coast Main Road), as well as inland routes. The fare is Bds$1.50 (75¢) for any one destination; exact change in either local or U.S. currency is appreciated. Buses pass along main roads about every 20 minutes. Stops are marked by small signs on roadside poles that say TO CITY or OUT OF CITY, meaning the direction relative to Bridgetown. Flag down the bus with your hand, even if you're standing at the stop. Bridgetown terminals are at Fairchild Street for buses to the south and east and at Lower Green for buses to Speightstown via the west coast.

BY CAR

Barbados has good roads, but traffic can be busy, particularly around Bridgetown. Small signs tacked to trees and poles at intersections point the way to most attractions, and local people are helpful if you get lost.

Drive on the left, British style. Be mindful of pedestrians and, in the countryside, occasional livestock walking in the road. When someone flashes headlights at you at an intersection, it means "after you." Be especially careful negotiating roundabouts (traffic circles). The speed limit, in keeping with the pace of life and the narrow roads, is 30 mph (50 kph) in the country, 20 mph (30 kph) in town. Bridgetown actually has rush hours: 7 to 9 and 4 to 6. Park only in approved parking areas; downtown parking costs Bds75¢ to Bds$1 per hour.

To rent a car in Barbados, you must have a valid driver's license and major credit card. Most agencies require renters to be between 21 and 75 years of age. Those over 75 may need a certified doctor's note indicating a continuing ability to drive safely. A local driver's permit, which costs $5, is obtained through the rental agency. More than 75 agencies rent cars, jeeps, or minimokes (small, open-sided vehicles), and rates are expensive—about $55 per day for a minimoke to $85 or more per day for a four-wheel-drive vehicle (or $400 to $500 or more per week) in high season, depending on the vehicle and whether it has air-conditioning. Most firms also offer discounted three-day rates. The rental generally includes insurance, pickup and delivery service, maps, 24-hour emergency service, and unlimited mileage.

Information Coconut Car Rentals (⊠Bay St., Bridgetown, St. Michael ☎246/437–0297). **Courtesy Rent-A-Car** (⊠Grantley Adams International Airport, Christ Church ☎246/431–4160). **Drive-a-Matic Car Rental** (⊠Lower Carlton, St. James ☎246/422–3000). **National Car Rentals** (⊠Lower Carlton, St. James ☎246/426–0603). **Sunny Isle Sixt Car Rentals** (⊠Worthing, Christ Church ☎246/435–7979). **Sunset Crest Car Rental** (⊠Sunset Crest, Holetown, St. James ☎246/432–2222).

BY TAXI

Taxis operate 24 hours a day. They aren't metered but charge according to fixed rates set by the government. They carry up to three passengers, and the fare may be shared. For short trips, the rate per mile (or part thereof) should not exceed $1.50. Drivers are courteous and knowledgeable; most will narrate a tour at an hourly rate of about $25 for up to three people. Be sure to settle the price before you start off and agree on whether it's quoted in U.S. or Barbados dollars.

CONTACTS & RESOURCES

BANKS & EXCHANGE SERVICES

The Barbados dollar is pegged to the U.S. dollar at the rate of Bds$1.98 to $1. U.S. paper currency, major credit cards, and traveler's checks are all accepted islandwide. Be sure you know which currency is being quoted when making a purchase. Major credit cards are also readily accepted throughout Barbados.

Barbados National Bank has a branch at Grantley Adams International Airport that's open every day from 8 AM until the last plane lands or departs. ATMs are available 24 hours a day at bank branches, transportation centers, shopping centers, gas stations, and other convenient spots throughout the island.

ELECTRICITY

Electric current on Barbados is 110 volts–50 cycles, U.S. standard. Hotels generally have plug adapters and transformers available for guests who bring appliances from countries that operate on 220-volt current.

EMERGENCIES

Emergency Services Ambulance (☎511). **Fire** (☎311). **Police** (☎211 emergencies, 242/430–7100 nonemergencies).

Hospitals Bayview Hospital (⊠St. Paul's Ave., Bayville, St. Michael ☎246/436–5446). **Queen Elizabeth Hospital** (⊠Martindales Rd., Bridgetown, St. Michael ☎246/436–6450).

4

Pharmacies Grant's (✉ Fairchild St., Bridgetown, St. Michael ☎ 246/436–6120 ✉ Main Rd., Oistins, Christ Church ☎ 246/428–9481). **Knight's** (✉ Lower Broad St., Bridgetown, St. Michael ☎ 246/426–5196 ✉ Super Centre Shopping Center, Main Rd., Oistins, Christ Church ☎ 246/428–6057 ✉ Suncrest Mall, Hwy. 1, Holetown, St. James ☎ 246/432–1290 ✉ Hwy. 1, Speightstown, St. Peter ☎ 246/422–0048).

Scuba-Diving Emergencies Coast Guard Defence Force (24-hour hyperbaric chamber) (✉ St. Ann's Fort, Garrison, St. Michael ☎ 246/427–8819 emergencies, 246/436–6185 nonemergencies). **Divers' Alert Network** (☎ 246/684–8111 or 246/684–2948).

INTERNET, MAIL & SHIPPING

Most hotels and resorts provide Internet access—either free or for a small fee—for their guests. You'll also find Internet cafés in and around Bridgetown, in Holetown and Speightstown on the west coast, and at St. Lawrence Gap on the south coast. Rates range from $2 for 15 minutes to $8 or $9 per hour.

An airmail letter from Barbados to the United States or Canada costs Bds$1.15 per half ounce; an airmail postcard, Bds45¢. Letters to the United Kingdom cost Bds$1.40; postcards, Bds70¢. Letters to Australia and New Zealand cost Bds$2.75; postcards, Bds$1.75. When sending mail to Barbados, be sure to include the parish name in the address.

Information Bean-n-Bagel Internet Cafe (✉ St. Lawrence Gap, Dover, Christ Church ☎ 246/420–4604 ✉ West Coast Mall, Holetown, St. James ☎ 246/432–1103 ✉ The Wharf, Bridgetown, St. Michael ☎ 246/436–7778) . **Clicks-N-Bytes Cafe** (✉ 144 Roebuck St., Bridgetown, St. Michael ☎ 246/427–8939). **Connect Internet Cafe** (✉ Shop 9, 27 Broad St., Bridgetown, St. Michael ☎ 246/228–8648). **ICS Internet Cafe** (✉ St. Lawrence Gap, Dover, Christ Church ☎ 246/428–1513). **Surf 'n' Lime** (✉ Road View, Main Rd., Speightstown, St. Peter ☎ 246/422–5871).

SAFETY

Crime isn't a major problem, but take normal precautions. Lock your room, and don't leave valuables—particularly passports, tickets, and wallets—in plain sight or unattended on the beach. Use your hotel safe. For personal safety, avoid walking on the beach or on unlit streets at night. Lock your rental car, and don't pick up hitchhikers.

Using or trafficking in illegal drugs is strictly prohibited in Barbados. Any offense is punishable by a hefty fine, imprisonment, or both.

TAXES & SERVICE CHARGES

At the airport, each adult passenger leaving Barbados must pay a departure tax of $12.50 (Bds$25), payable in either Barbadian or U.S. currency; children 12 and under are exempt. Although it may be included in cruise packages as a component of port charges, the departure tax is not included in airfare and must be paid in cash by each traveler prior to entering the secure area of the airport.

A 7.5% government tax is added to all hotel bills. A 10% service charge is often added to hotel bills and restaurant checks in lieu of a tip. At your discretion, tip beyond the service charge to recognize extraordinary service.

A 15% V.A.T. is imposed on restaurant meals, admissions to attractions, and merchandise sales (other than duty-free). Prices are often tax inclusive; if not, the V.A.T. will be added to your bill.

TELEPHONES

The area code for Barbados is 246.

Local calls are free from private phones; some hotels charge a small fee. For directory assistance, dial 411. Calls from pay phones cost Bds25¢ for five minutes. Prepaid phone cards, which can be used throughout Barbados and other Caribbean islands, are sold at shops, attractions, transportation centers, and other convenient outlets.

Direct-dialing to the United States, Canada, and other countries is efficient and reasonable, but always check with your hotel to see if a surcharge is added. Some toll-free numbers cannot be accessed in Barbados. To charge your overseas call on a major credit card or U.S. calling card without incurring a surcharge, dial 800/225–5872 (800/CALL–USA) from any phone.

Depending on your carrier, you may find that you can use your cell phone in Barbados to call home, though roaming charges can be expensive. Renting a cell phone if you're planning an extended stay or expect to make a lot of local calls may be a less-expensive alternative. A cell phone can be rented for as little as $5 a day (minimum one-week rental); prepaid cards are available at several locations throughout the island and in varying denominations.

Cell-Phone Rental Global Business Centre (✉ West Coast Mall, Sunset Crest, Holetown, St. James ☎ 246/432–6508 ⊕ www.globalbiz centre.com)

TIPPING
If no service charge is added to your bill, tip waiters 10% to 15% and maids $2 per room per day. Tip bellhops and airport porters $1 per bag. Taxi drivers and tour guides appreciate a 10% tip.

TOUR OPTIONS
A sightseeing tour is a good way to get your bearings and to experience the rich Bajan culture. Taxi drivers will give you a personalized tour of Barbados for about $25 per hour for up to three people. Or you can choose a fascinating helicopter ride, an overland horseback or mountain bike journey, a 4x4 safari expedition, or a full-day bus excursion. The prices vary according to the mode of travel and the number and kind of attractions included. Ask your hotel to help you make arrangements.

Bajan Helicopters offers an eagle's-eye view of the island. The air-conditioned jet helicopters accommodate up to five people for a 30-mi (50-km) "Discover Barbados Tour" or a 50-mi (80-km) "Island Tour." Prices start at $97.50 per person. Highland Adventure Centre offers horseback or mountain bike tours for $50 per person, including transportation, guides, and refreshments. Whether it's your first time on a horse or you're an experienced rider, the chance to view plantation houses, three coastlines, and quaint villages astride a thoroughbred is a thrilling opportunity—don't forget your camera! The mountain bike tour is an exhilarating 7.5-mi (12-km) ride (15% uphill) through the picturesque heart of northern Barbados, ending up at Barclays Park on the east coast. Island Safari will take you to all the popular spots via a 4x4 Land Rover—including some gullies, forests, and remote areas that are inaccessible by conventional cars and buses. The cost for half-day or full-day tours ranges from $45 to $77 per person, including snacks or lunch. L. E. Williams Tour Co. will pick you up at your hotel for a seven-hour narrated bus tour—an 80-mi (130-km) circuit of the best of Barbados. The $62.50 per-person price includes a Bajan buffet lunch and beverages at Atlantis Hotel Restaurant on the rugged east coast.

Information Bajan Helicopters (✉ Bridgetown Heliport, Bridgetown, St. Michael ☎ 246/431–0069 ⊕ www.bajanhe-licopters.com). **Highland Adventure Centre** (✉ Cane Field, St. Thomas ☎ 246/438–8069 or 246/438–8928). **Island Safari** (✉ Main Rd., Bush Hall, St. Michael ☎ 246/429–5337 ⊕ www.barbadostraveler.com). **L. E. Williams Tour Co.** (✉ Hastings, Christ Church ☎ 246/427–1043).

VISITOR INFORMATION
Before You Leave Barbados Tourism Authority (⊕ www.visitbarbados.org ☎ 212/986–6516 in New York City, 305/442–

7471 in Coral Gables, FL, 213/380–2198 in Los Angeles, or 800/221–9831).

In Barbados **Barbados Hotel & Tourism Association** (✉4th Ave., Belleville, St. Michael ☎246/426–5041 📠246/429–2845 🌐www.bhta.org). **Barbados Tourism Authority** (✉Harbour Rd., Bridgetown, St. Michael ☎246/427–2623 📠246/426–4080 🌐www.visitbarbados.org ✉Grantley Adams International Airport, Christ Church ☎246/428–5570 ✉Cruise-ship terminal, Bridgetown, St. Michael ☎246/426–1718).

WEDDINGS

Barbados makes weddings relatively simple for nonresidents, as there are no minimum residency requirements. Most resorts, therefore, offer wedding packages and have on-site wedding coordinators to help you secure a marriage license and plan a personalized ceremony and reception. Alternatively, you may wish to have your wedding at a scenic historic site or botanical garden, on the grounds of a restored greathouse, or at sunset on a quiet beach.

To obtain a marriage license, which often can be completed in less than a half hour, both partners must apply in person to the Ministry of Home Affairs (in the General Post Office building, Cheapside, Bridgetown, open 8:15–4:30 weekdays) by presenting valid passports. If either party was previously married and widowed, you need to present a certified copy of the marriage certificate and a death certificate for the deceased spouse; if either party is divorced, you need a certified copy of the official divorce decree. Nonresidents of Barbados must pay a fee of $75 (Bds$150) plus a stamp fee of $12.50 (Bds$25). Finally, you must make arrangements for an authorized marriage officer (a magistrate or minister) to perform the ceremony.

Bonaire

Flamingos, Washington/Slagbaai National Park

WORD OF MOUTH

"The reason to go is the water. Bonaire is the best shore snorkeling island we have ever visited . . . We often went to several per day, breaking off for lunch and then back out to the reef."

—slk230

"There is an excellent park on the north side of the island, Washington—Slagbaai. We spent most of the day driving around and stopping for views, walks and quick dips . . . [but] it's not paved."

—tully

WELCOME TO BONAIRE

At the market in Kralendijk, hagglers vie for produce brought in by boat from lusher islands. But nature holds sway over human pursuits on this scrubby, cactus-covered landfall. Divers come to explore some of the best sites this side of Australia's Great Barrier Reef. Above the water are more than 15,000 flamingos—the biggest flock in the Western Hemisphere.

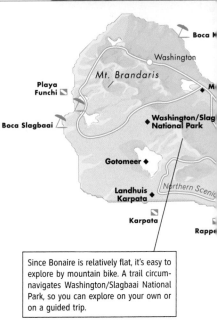

Hotels ▼		Restaurants ▼	
Bellafonte Chateau de la Mer	4	Bistro de Paris	15
Bruce Bowker's	2	Capriccio	9
Buddy Dive Resort	12	City Café	1
Captain Don's Habitat	14	Donna & Giorgio's	13
Coco Palm Garden	6	Kontiki Beach Club	11
Den Laman	1	La Guernica	6
Divi Flamingo	8	Le Flamboyant	8
Golden Reef	10	Mona Lisa	3
Harbour Village	9	Papaya Moon	4
Plaza Resort Bonaire	3	Patagonia Argentina	14
Roomer	5	The Reef	5
Sand Dollar	11	Richard's Waterfront	10
Sorobon Beach	7	Salsa	2
Yachtclub Apartments	13	Wind & Surf	12
		Zeezicht	7

Since Bonaire is relatively flat, it's easy to explore by mountain bike. A trail circum-navigates Washington/Slagbaai National Park, so you can explore on your own or on a guided trip.

TOP 4 REASONS TO VISIT BONAIRE

1 As locals say, you come here to dive, eat, dive, sleep, and dive.

2 You don't have to be a certified diver to appreciate Bonaire's reefs; snorkelers can see a lot of the beauty just below the surface of the water.

3 Tourists came to enjoy the tranquility of the island long before they started exploring offshore.

4 Dining is surprisingly good and varied for such a small island.

DIVER'S PARADISE

With just over 18,000 people, this little island (112 square mi/290 square km) has a real, small-town atmosphere. Kralendijk, the capital, has just 3,000 inhabitants. The entire coastline—from the high-water tidemark to a depth of 200 ft (61 m)—is protected as part of the Bonaire Marine Park, making it one of the best diving destinations in the western hemisphere.

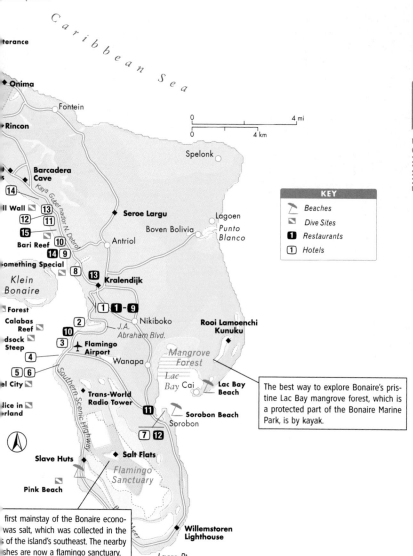

terance

Caribbean Sea

◆ **Onima**

● Fontein

◆ **Rincon**

Spelonk ◆

**Barcadera
Cave**

Kaya Gilberto Nador N. Debrot

⑭

ll Wall ◢ ⑬

⑫ ⑪

⑮

Bari Reef ⑩

⑭ ⑨

omething Special ◢

⑧

*Klein
Bonaire*

◆ **Seroe Largu**

Lagoen
Boven Bolivia *Punto
Blanco*

Antriol

⑧ ⑬ **Kralendijk** ◆

KEY	
◢	*Beaches*
◢	*Dive Sites*
❶	*Restaurants*
①	*Hotels*

① ❶ ❾

Forest

**Calabas
Reef** ◢

dsock ◢
Steep

② ⑩ **Nikiboko**

*J.A.
Abraham Blvd.*

③ ✈ **Flamingo
Airport**

④ **Wanapa**

⑤ ⑥

el City ◢

lice in ◢
rland

◆ **Trans-World
Radio Tower**

⑪

**Rooi Lamoenchi
Kunuku** ◆

*Mangrove
Forest*

*Lac
Bay* Cai **Lac Bay
Beach**

Sorobon Beach
Sorobon

⑦ ⑫

The best way to explore Bonaire's pristine Lac Bay mangrove forest, which is a protected part of the Bonaire Marine Park, is by kayak.

Southern Scenic Highway

Slave Huts ◆ **Salt Flats**

*Flamingo
Sanctuary*

◢

Pink Beach

first mainstay of the Bonaire econo-
was salt, which was collected in the
s of the island's southeast. The nearby
shes are now a flamingo sanctuary.

◆ **Willemstoren
Lighthouse**

Lacre Pt.

0 _____ 4 mi
0 _____ 4 km

BONAIRE PLANNER

Island Activities

Diving—both open-water reef dives and beach dives—is among the best in the world. But there is plenty for nondivers to do as well. **Day sails** are popular for snorkelers who want to see some of the ocean life but who are not certified. **Sportfishing** is also a popular activity, and several captains can take you out to search for big-game fish. Near-constant trade winds make Bonaire a popular **windsurfing** destination. Though things are pretty quiet at night, the island has some very good **restaurants.**

On the Ground

Rental cars and taxis are available, but try to arrange for pickup through your hotel. A taxi will run between $7 and $10 (for up to four people) to most hotels; $18 to the Sorobon Beach Naturist Resort. Fares are 25% extra from 7 PM to midnight and 50% extra from midnight to 6 AM. If you anticipate having to change your flight details while on Bonaire, be mindful of the prospect that some airline counters may close at 5 PM. Many folks just use bicycles to get around, unless they are going more than a few miles.

Logistics

Getting to Bonaire: Most flights from the U.S. connect in San Juan, Montego Bay, or Aruba. If you want to connect through Aruba, you'll more likely than not have to book your flight directly with an island-based airline. Bonaire's Flamingo Airport (BON) is tiny but welcoming (the KLM 747 almost dwarfs the airport when it lands).

Hassle Factor: Medium to High.

Nonstops: The only nonstops are from New York–Newark and Houston (both Continental).

Where to Stay

Alongside the numerous lodges that offer only the basics (mostly catering to divers), you can now find some real resorts. Families can find self-catering accommodations, and many smaller inns will appeal to budget travelers. The best resorts are often on decent beaches, but these are mostly man-made. Almost all the island's resorts are clustered around Kralendijk.

Hotel & Restaurant Costs

⇨*For information on hotel meal plans, see Accommodations in Caribbean Essentials.*

WHAT IT COSTS IN U.S. DOLLARS				
$$$$	$$$	$$	$	¢
Restaurants				
over $30	$20–$30	$12–$20	$8–$12	under $8
Hotels*				
over $350	$250–$350	$150–$250	$80–$150	under $80
Hotels**				
over $450	$350–$450	$250–$350	$125–$250	under $125

By Vernon
O'Reilly
Ramesar

THE WORLD UNDER THE SURFACE is like a blue-tinged dream. Nearby, parrot fish meander through white coral caverns. Ahead, sharp-eyed barracuda move through the water like silver daggers. A manta glides overhead in slow motion like an alien spacecraft. But the enchanting undersea world of Bonaire, like a dream, is an experience done on borrowed time. Breaking the surface is your awakening. Warm air, arid vistas, and the startling gleam of sun on water are your reward.

Bonaire is widely regarded as one of the best destinations in the Caribbean for shore diving, and with good reason. The dry climate and coral composition of the island mean that there's little soil runoff, allowing near perfect visibility in the coastal waters. The islanders have exploited this advantage, and you can find local businesses that cater to virtually every diving need. Even though tourism is the backbone of the economy here, authorities try to ensure that the booming hotel industry does not damage the environment upon which it is based. Thankfully, the fact that most visitors to Bonaire come for the natural beauty has prevented the kind of tourism that has turned neighboring islands like Aruba into commercialized tourist magnets.

Islanders are serious about conserving Bonaire's natural beauty. All the coastal waters of the island were turned into a national park in 1979, and in 1999 Bonaire purchased the 1,500-acre privately owned outlying island of Klein Bonaire to prevent unwanted development. Anyone diving around the island must purchase a one-year permit, and park rangers patrol the waters, handing out hefty fines to people who violate park rules. Spearfishing, removing coral, and even walking on coral are just some of the restricted activities. Rather than restricting legitimate divers, these rules have resulted in a pristine marine environment that makes for a supremely satisfying dive experience. Damage to the reefs caused by rare passing hurricanes is usually quickly repaired by the healthy ecosystem. Small wonder that even the license plates in Bonaire declare it a DIVER'S PARADISE.

Bonaire also offers a variety of experiences above the surface to those willing to explore its 112 square mi (290 square km). The southern salt flats give an interesting glimpse into the island's economic history. Washington–Slagbaai National Park, in the north, has the island's highest peak (784 feet) and is a haven for some of the thousands of flamingos that make Bonaire their home. The near-perfect climate also makes Bonaire the ideal destination for working on a tan or just relaxing.

Although many islanders claim that the name Bonaire comes from the French for "good air," this explanation is unlikely, particularly since the island was never colonized by the French. The island was first inhabited by an Amerindian people (related to the Arawaks) called the Caquetios. Alonso de Ojeda and Amerigo Vespucci landed here in 1499 and claimed it for Spain. It seems likely that they adopted the Amerindian name for the island, which probably sounded very much like Bonaire and which meant "low country." Because the Spanish found little use for the island except as a penal colony, the original inhabitants were shipped off to work on the plantations of Hispaniola, and Bonaire remained largely undeveloped. When the Dutch seized the islands of Aruba, Bonaire, and Curaçao in 1633, they started building the salt industry in Bonaire, which fueled the economy then and which remains an important industry today.

The majority of the 14,000 inhabitants live in and around the capital, Kralendijk. The word almost universally applied to this diminutive city is "cute." It's probably one of the few major downtown areas in the world that can be traversed in under three minutes. Part of the Netherlands Antilles, Bonaire is actually governed from neighboring Curaçao. Legislation has been signed that would see the islands of Bonaire, Saba, and Sint Eustatius becoming directly part of the Netherlands, with Curaçao and Sint Martin becoming autonomous entities within the Kingdom of the Netherlands.

WHERE TO STAY

Although meal plans are available at most hotels, the island has many excellent—and often inexpensive—restaurants. If you're planning a dive holiday, look into the many attractive dive packages.

RENTAL APARTMENTS

If you prefer do-it-yourself home-style comfort over the pampering and other services offered by a hotel, you can rent a fully furnished apartment. **Black Durgon Inn Properties** (☎599/717–5736, 800/526–2370 in U.S. ⊕www.blackdurgon.com) is a small, noncommercial community with its own pier on the water, though no beach. **Bonaire Hotel & Tourism Association** (☎800/388–5951 ⊕www.bonairestays.com) has information on a variety of properties ranging from budget to upscale. **Sun Rentals** (☎599/717–6130 ⊕www.sunrentals.an) offers quite a range of accommodations. You can choose among private ocean-view villas in luxurious areas like Sabadeco, furnished oceanfront apartments (with a pool) in town, or bungalows in Lagoenhill, an inland community. The Sun Oceanfront Apartments are an excellent budget choice for families.

HOTELS

$$$$
☼
Fodor'sChoice
★

☒ **Harbour Village Beach Club.** This snazzy enclave of ocher-color buildings is the benchmark for luxury accommodations on the island. The standard rooms are perfectly fine—though perhaps a bit small; much better are the one-bedroom beachfront villas, which are lavishly appointed and feature outlandishly large marble bathrooms. Room patios open onto either the private beach or the 4-acre tropical garden. Visiting celebrities make this hotel home as much for the beautifully furnished rooms and excellent beach as for the attentive and understated service offered by the well-trained staff. Those seeking a truly romantic experience can order a torch-lighted dinner on the beach. Queen Beatrix of the Netherlands makes this hotel her home when she is on the island. Pros: Great for a secluded getaway, not awash with budget tourists,

The Donkeys of Bonaire

Visitors to Bonaire are often startled by the sight of donkeys lazily roaming about the landscape. In fact, these little equines are considered by islanders an integral part of the modern landscape of Bonaire.

Bonaire has no large indigenous species of mammals. Donkeys were imported to the island in the 1500s to serve the needs of Spanish colonists. They provided an effective means of transport and continued to be used for that purpose for the salt industry that eventually developed. With their minimal water requirements and ability to eat just about any vegetation, the animals proved well adapted to the arid environment. Later, when the salt industry became more mechanized and other forms of transport were introduced, the donkeys were left to wander. With no predators to deal with and little competition for

the scrub and cactus that cover the island, the donkeys have survived, and their numbers have even increased over the years.

Today there are more than 200 wild donkeys roaming the island, and they charm tourists. Islanders often have a more-tarnished view. Roaming about in search of food, donkeys will often push through fences and munch and stomp through ornamental plants. There have also been numerous injuries and a few deadly automobile accidents caused by donkeys wandering on the roads at night.

However, Bonaire's relationship with the ubiquitous quadrupeds seems destined to remain close for the foreseeable future. A donkey sanctuary has been established in the interior to look after ill donkeys and care for orphaned youngsters. The center has more than 80 donkeys in its care.

---

convenient to downtown. Cons: Some rooms are quite far from the beach, grounds can feel a bit deserted. ⊠*Kaya Gobernador N. Debrot 71, Kralendijk* ☎*599/717–7500 or 800/424–0004* 🖷*599/717–7507* ⊕*www.harbourvillage.com* ⇆*16 rooms, 14 1-bedroom suites* ⌂*In-room: safe, refrigerator (some), Wi-Fi. In-hotel: 2 restaurants, room service, bar, tennis courts, pool, gym, beachfront, diving, water sports, laundry service, airport shuttle* ☰*AE, D, DC, MC, V* ⊙*EP.*

$$$ 🏨**Divi Flamingo Resort.** The brightly colored buildings of this resort are a two-minute stroll from downtown, but the main draw is the combination of a top-notch dive program and the only casino on Bonaire. The property features some of the lushest landscaping to be found on this arid island. Rooms are immaculate, and lower-level oceanfront rooms have balconies about 2 feet from the water. Sunbathers will appreciate the beautiful sun pier that affords excellent views of downtown. Chibi Chibi restaurant serves scrumptious seafood dishes and treats guests to a nightly underwater light show. There is live entertainment nightly during high season. Pros: Beautifully landscaped grounds, steps from downtown and restaurants, on-site casino. Cons: Pool can get crowded, beach is quite small. ⊠*J. A. Abraham Blvd. 40, Box 143, Kralendijk* ☎*599/717–8285 or 800/367–3484* 🖷*599/717–8238* ⊕*www.diviflamingo.com* ⇆*129 rooms* ⌂*In-room: safe. In-hotel: 2 restaurants, bar, pools, gym, spa, diving, water sports, no elevator* ☰*AE, D, DC, MC, V* ⊙*EP.*

Fodor's Choice
★

5

$$$ 🏨**Plaza Resort Bonaire.** No other hotel in Bonaire can match the range of activities offered here, with everything from tennis to water sports, not to mention a gorgeous beach. Rooms are exceptionally large and well furnished, with tile floors, but are otherwise unremarkable. This is a sprawling resort, so getting around can be a bit of a hike. Live entertainment on Tuesday nights is a big draw, as is the weekly beach barbecue. The hotel's resident iguanas are docile and friendly and are usually happy to provide guests with a photo opportunity. Pros: Every imaginable recreational activity is available, good shopping in hotel, beautiful grounds. Cons: The size of the compound can make getting around a chore, not an easy walk to downtown. ⊠*J. A. Abraham Blvd. 80, Kralendijk* 🕾*599/717–2500 or 800/766–6016* 🖷*599/717–7133* ⊕*www.plazaresortbonaire.com* 🖙*174 rooms, 48 villas* ♿*In-room: safe, kitchen (some), refrigerator. In-hotel: 3 restaurants, room service, bars, tennis courts, pool, gym, beachfront, diving, water sports, bicycles, children's programs (ages 5–15)* ⊟*AE, D, DC, MC, V* ⏐⚪⏐*EP.*

$$$ 🏨**Sorobon Beach Naturist Resort.** No need to worry about an extensive packing list for Bonaire's only naturist resort, which is on Lac Bay. Clothing is optional everywhere, with nudity enforced on the beach. The rooms are outfitted in an appropriately sparse style but are comfortable and include full kitchens. Rooms are air-conditioned but, inexplicably, only between 7 PM and 7 AM. The property offers Wi-Fi, so it is not unusual to witness the rather bizarre spectacle of guests sitting around getting up close and personal with their laptops. It's worth noting that guests using the beach here are fully visible from the most-popular windsurfing beach on the island, which is right next door. This is definitely a family-oriented property, so those looking for a party center should look elsewhere. Pros: Good deal for families, stunning beachfront; Wi-Fi throughout. Cons: Sunbathing area is visible to windsurfers, miles from shopping and restaurants. ⊠*Sorobon Beach* 🕮*Box 14, Kralendijk* 🕾*599/717–8080 or 800/828–9356* 🖷*599/717–6080* ⊕*www.sorobonbeach.com* 🖙*28 1-bedroom chalets, 1 2-bedroom chalet, 1 3-bedroom house* ♿*In-room: safe, kitchen, no TV. In-hotel: restaurant, bar, beachfront, water sports, laundry service, public Wi-Fi, airport shuttle* ⊟*AE, MC, V* ⏐⚪⏐*EP.*

$$ 🏨**Captain Don's Habitat.** Bonaire's first hotel catering to divers remains
★   a favorite, with a PADI five-star dive center offering more than 20 specialty courses. For a small price difference over the cost of a standard room, studios offer a full kitchen and much more breathing space. Villa suites have spectacular ocean views; downstairs units have massive patios. Rum Runners restaurant serves excellent pizza made in its brick oven. There's little nightlife here other than the usual post-dive chatter before everyone heads off to bed to rest before the next day's activities. The beach is tiny but fine for shore dives or snorkeling, with mesmerizing reef formations 90 feet from shore. Pros: Variety of accommodation types, pizzeria with wood-burning oven, excellent diving facilities. Cons: Little to entertain nondivers, Wi-Fi coverage is spotty. ⊠*Kaya Gobernador N. Debrot 113, Box 88, Kralendijk* 🕾*599/717–8290 or 800/327–6709* 🖷*599/717–8240* ⊕*www.habitatdiveresorts.com* 🖙*24 suites, 9 villas, 20 cottages* ♿*In-room: safe, kitchen (some), refrigerator, Wi-Fi. In-hotel: restaurant, bar, pool, beachfront, diving, water sports, bicycles, no elevator* ⊟*AE, D, DC, MC, V* ⏐⚪⏐*EP.*

$$ **Sand Dollar Condominium Resort.** This condo complex has family-friendly apartments ranging from studios to three-bedrooms, each of which is individually owned and decorated for a comfortable, lived-in feeling. Ocean views from the rooms are great, and the pool is a lovely oasis; the beach, however, is tiny and disappears at high tide. The nearby grocery and ice-cream parlor are handy, and the Chat 'n' Browse cyber-café is a popular place to meet locals and visitors alike. A variety of dive-and-stay packages can be an economical choice for avid divers. Pros: All rooms have great ocean views, well equipped for families, grocery and ATM on property. Cons: Few rooms have phones, no beach bar. ⊠*Kaya Gobernador N. Debrot 79, Box 262, Kralendijk* ☎*599/717–8738 or 800/288–4773* 🖷*599/717–8760* ⊕*www.sanddollarbonaire.com* ⬍*68 condos* ⚙*In-room: no phone (some), kitchen, Wi-Fi. In-hotel: restaurant, bar, tennis courts, pool, beachfront, diving, children's programs (ages 3–17), public Internet* ⊟*AE, D, DC, MC, V* ⊺*EP.*

$–$$ **Bellafonte Chateau de la Mer.** Although it lacks the amenities of a large
Fodor'sChoice resort—including a pool—the intimacy and exclusivity of this elegant
★ palazzo-style hotel near Kralendijk more than compensate. An arched passageway opens out to a breathtaking ocean vista complete with a jetty that seems to have jumped out of the pages of a design magazine. Rooms are chic, with teak and stainless-steel accents that create a clean and breezy feeling. Room balconies are large enough to host a cocktail party for 20 and are perfect for private sunbathing, but to truly experience this hotel, an ocean-view room is essential. The hotel offers a year-round deal whereby guests who pay for six days get a seventh day free. Pros: Elegantly appointed rooms, diving straight from hotel pier, upper rooms have excellent views. Cons: No restaurant or bar, not close to downtown or shopping. ⊠*E. E. G. Blvd. 10, Belnem* ☎*599/717–3333* 🖷*599/717–8581* ⊕*www.bellafontebonaire.com* ⬍*6 studios, 8 1-bedroom suites, 8 2-bedroom suites* ⚙*In-room: kitchen (some), Wi-Fi. In-hotel: diving, laundry service* ⊟*AE, MC, V* ⊺*EP.*

$–$$ **Buddy Dive Resort.** Well-equipped rooms, a nicely landscaped compound, and excellent dive packages keep guests coming back to this large resort. In 2006, the resort joined with the old Lion's Dive resort, next door. The former Lion's Dive rooms are slightly larger, are fully air-conditioned, and offer a greater degree of privacy than the original Buddy Dive rooms. All have the basics you'd expect in a Caribbean resort, including a private balcony or patio. Divers will appreciate the drive-through air-filling station for compressed air or Nitrox in the compound. There's a nice beach and decent restaurants, too. Room packages with a van or pickup are a good idea for those who want to explore the island. Pros: Excellent dive shop, rooms are spacious, open-air restaurant has one of the best ocean views on the island. Cons: Complex can feel like a maze, room amenities vary depending on which side of the property they are located. ⊠*Kaya Gobernador N. Debrot 85, Box 231, Kralendijk* ☎*599/717–5080 or 866/462–8339* 🖷*599/717–8647* ⊕*www.buddydive.com* ⬍*6 rooms, 72 apartments* ⚙*In-room: kitchen (some). In-hotel: 3 restaurants, bar, pools, beachfront, diving, children's programs (ages 5–15), laundry facilities* ⊟*AE, D, MC, V* ⊺*EP.*

5

$–$$ 🏨 **Den Laman Condominiums.** Though the exterior of this property will not win any design awards, the location and beautifully finished interiors are definitely first-class. Rooms are spacious and tastefully done in rattan, teak, and stainless steel. The Ocean View rooms require contortions to see the ocean, so it is best to request an Oceanfront room. For a splurge, rent the huge owner's suite, which features an automatic garage-style door that opens to reveal a private terrace and an incredible ocean vista. One of the island's best seafood restaurants, the Den Laman Restaurant and Bar, is in the building. Pros: Excellent restaurant on-site, rooms are chicly appointed, convenient to downtown. Cons: No elevator means upper rooms can require a climb, common areas feel a little sterile. ⊠*Kaya Gobernador N. Debrot 77, Kralendijk* 🕾*599/717–1700* 🖷*599/717–1710* ⊕*www.denlaman.com* ➪*16 condos* ⟁*In-room: kitchen, safe, Wi-Fi. In-hotel: restaurant, bar, diving, no elevator* ▤*AE, MC, V* �𓏸*EP.*

$ 🏨 **Bruce Bowker's Carib Inn.** The island's first full-time dive instructor,
★ Bruce Bowker, opened this inn in 1980 after moving to Bonaire from the United States. The cozy rooms and Bruce's personal touch have given his resort the highest return-visitor ratio on the island. Most apartment-style units have kitchens, and all bedrooms are air-conditioned. Bruce's background means that the emphasis here is on diving, diving, and more diving. Even though this is a PADI five-star lodge, novice divers can also benefit from the small class sizes. Pros: Intimate and friendly, excellent dive courses, Wi-Fi throughout. Cons: Smaller size means fewer amenities such as shopping, nondivers will find little to entertain them. ⊠*J. A. Abraham Blvd. 46, Box 68, Kralendijk* 🕾*599/717–8819* 🖷*599/717– 5295* ⊕*www.caribinn.com* ➪*10 units* ⟁*In-room: kitchen (some), refrigerator. In-hotel: pool, beachfront, diving, water sports, public Wi-Fi* ▤*D, MC, V* ⟊*EP.*

$ 🏨 **Roomer.** This property, formerly the Great Escape, has changed own-
☾ ership and image to become an excellent, economically priced family hotel. Rooms are on the small side but are each individually decorated with tasteful splashes of color. The hotel restaurant is under a traditional palapa roof and affords a view of the pool and playground. Pros: Very family-oriented, excellent for budget travelers, kid-friendly pool area. Cons: Not on the ocean, miles from downtown. ⊠*E. E. G. Blvd. 97, Belnem* 🕾*599/717–7488* 🖷*599/717–7412* ⊕*www.roomerbonaire. com* ➪*10 rooms* ⟁*In-room: Wi-Fi. In-hotel: restaurant, bar, pool, no elevator* ▤*AE, MC, V* ⟊*EP.*

¢–$ 🏨 **Coco Palm Garden & Casa Oleander.** Three friends and neighbors
☾ operate this series of cozy cottages on adjoining properties, each fully
★ equipped and individually decorated to the point where the hard part is choosing among them. The pool, restaurant, and bar are in the Coco Palm section, all awash with cheerful colors. The property caters primarily to Europeans, so the emphasis is on ambience and efficiency rather than luxurious amenities. This European flavor also means that topless sunbathing is acceptable even around the pool area. Although most rooms have air-conditioning, there is a $10 daily charge for using it. Two larger villas (Nos Kas and BonHome) are down the road and are a good choice for families. This is probably your best value on the island

for ambience, but keep in mind that the beach is a three-minute walk away. Pros: Charming and quirky with no two rooms alike, friendly staff, quiet pool area. Cons: Not close to downtown or shopping, limited on-site dining options. ⊠*Kaya I.R. Randolf Statuuis van Eps 9, Belnem* ☝*Box 216, Kralendijk* ☎*599/717–2108 or 599/790–9080* 🖷*599/717–8193* ⊕*www.cocopalmgarden.org* ⇥*20 rooms, 2 villas* ☝*In-room: kitchen, no TV (some). In-hotel: pool, laundry facilities* ☰*MC, V* ⛝*EP.*

¢–$ ⛝**Golden Reef Inn.** This low-rise lemon-sherbet-hue complex offers comfy rooms and a genuinely intimate feel. Though not directly on a beach, the facilities of nearby Eden Beach are available to guests, and diving expeditions leave directly from the hotel. Cozy rooms are homey and offer a surprising range of amenities, from complimentary breakfast supplies in the fridge to a nice supply of reading materials. Owner Liz Ginocchio takes pains to ensure that guests are comfortable and even takes care of airline arrangements and car rentals on behalf of arriving guests. Her stated policy is "guests first, paperwork after." Pros: Almost unbeatable price and friendly service, virtually any tour or dive can be arranged by the front office, rooms are fully self-contained. Cons: Grounds have little landscaping, basic dining and bar facilities, not on ocean. ⊠*Kaya Den Haag 7, Hato* ☎*599/717–5759* ⊕*www. goldenreefinn.com* ⇥*4 studios, 7 1-bedrooms, 1 2-bedroom villa, 1 1-bedroom villa* ☝*In-room: kitchen, safe. In-hotel: restaurant, bar, pool, diving, public Wi-Fi, laundry facilities* ☰*AE, D, MC, V* ⛝*EP.*

¢ ⛝**Yachtclub Apartments.** Across from Harbour Village, these apartments
★ offer some of the best budget lodging on the island. Large rooms are set in a pristine lemon-yellow compound. Kralendijk is a few minutes' walk away, yet peace and quiet are readily available around the (usually deserted) pool. Room configurations range from studios to a five-bedroom suite. Some of the larger apartments are quite a bit more expensive ($–$$$) than the more-budget-friendly studios and one-bedrooms. Pros: Reasonable price for excellent accommodations, expansive pool area is great for sunbathing, close to several good restaurants. Cons: No ocean view, hotel is on the main road to Kralendijk and can get a bit dusty. ⊠*Kaya Gobernador N. Debrot 52, Kralendijk* ☎*599/717–7424* 🖷*519/717–7372* ⊕*www.yachtclubapartmentsbonaire.com* ⇥*13 apartments* ☝*In-room: safe, kitchen. In-hotel: restaurant, no elevator* ☰*AE, D, MC, V* ⛝*2-night minimum* ⛝*EP.*

WHERE TO EAT

Dining on Bonaire is far less expensive than on Aruba or Curaçao, and you can find everything from Continental to Mexican to Asian fare. Many restaurants serve only dinner—only a few establishments not affiliated with hotels are open for breakfast, so check ahead.

ECLECTIC ✕**City Café/City Restaurant.** This busy waterfront eatery is also one of
$$–$$$ the most reliable nightspots on the island, so it's always hopping day or night. Breakfast, lunch, and dinner are served daily at reasonable prices. Seafood is always featured, as are a variety of sandwiches and salads. The pita sandwich platters are a good lunchtime choice for the

budget challenged. Weekends, there's always live entertainment and dancing. ⊠ *Hotel Rochaline, Kaya Grandi 7, Kralendijk* ☎ *599/717–8286* ⊟ *AE, MC, V.*

$$–$$$ ✕ **Mona Lisa Bar & Restaurant.** Here you can find Continental, Caribbean, and Indonesian fare. Popular bar dishes include Wiener schnitzel and fresh fish with curry sauce. The intimate stucco-and-brick dining room, presided over by a copy of the famous painting of the lady with the mystic smile, is decorated with Dutch artwork, lace curtains, and whirring ceiling fans. The colorful bar adorned with baseball-style caps is a great place for late-night schmoozing and noshing on light snacks or the catch of the day, which is served until 10 PM. There is a four-course fixed-price dinner on offer most evenings for about $46. ⊠ *Kaya Grandi 15, Kralendijk* ☎ *599/717–8718* ⚖ *Reservations essential* ⊟ *AE, MC, V* ⊗ *Closed Sun. No lunch.*

$$–$$$ ✕ **Patagonia Argentinean Steakhouse.** Meat-lovers pack this new, 60-seat, waterfront establishment. Though catering largely to steak-lovers with everything from top sirloin to prime rib, there's a respectable selection of seafood and other meats, too. The quality of some of the lower-priced steaks can be a bit erratic, however, and the use of frozen vegetables is puzzling. The restaurant's popularity can lead to lengthy wait times, but you can mosey over to the cozy bar area to pass some time. ⊠ *Harbour Village Marina, Kralendijk, in lighthouse* ☎ *599/717–7725* ⚖ *Reservations essential* ⊟ *AE, D, MC, V* ⊗ *Closed Mon. No lunch weekends.*

$$–$$$ ✕ **The Reef.** This casual restaurant at the Den Laman Condominiums
★ offers a great variety of family-friendly options. The lunch and dinner menu includes a broad selection, ranging from seafood to pastas. The open-air oceanfront setting is unbeatable and especially great at sunset. ⊠ *Kaya Gobernador N. Debrot 77, Kralendijk* ☎ *599/717–4106* ⊟ *AE, MC, V.*

$$–$$$ ✕ **Salsa.** The chicest eatery in downtown Kralendijk is owned by the same partners who own City Café/City Restaurant. The two-story palapa-covered structure features two totally different dining experiences. The downstairs garden and bar area offers a casual atmosphere with finger foods and tapas. Upstairs is a more-elegant affair with an international menu and is designed for a real evening out. All items on the imaginative world menu are beautifully presented. ⊠ *Kaya Isla Riba, Kralendijk* ☎ *599/717–3558* ⚖ *Reservations essential* ⊟ *AE, MC, V* ⊗ *No lunch.*

$$–$$$ ✕ **Zeezicht Bar & Restaurant.** Zeezicht (pronounced zay-*zeekt* and mean-
★ ing "sea view") serves three meals a day and is a Kralendijk institution. At breakfast and lunch you get basic American fare with an Antillean touch, such as a fish omelet; dinner is more Caribbean and mostly seafood, served either on the terrace overlooking the harbor or in the nautically themed, homey, rough-hewn main room. Locals are dedicated to this hangout, especially for the ceviche, conch sandwiches, and the Zeezicht special soup with conch, fish, and shrimp. The location makes it a popular spot for sunset watchers. ⊠ *Kaya J. N. E. Craane 12, Kralendijk* ☎ *599/717–8434* ⊟ *AE, MC, V.*

$–$$ ✕ **Le Flamboyant.** This intimate restaurant offers good food at affordable
★ prices. The cozy historic house—conveniently downtown—also has a

small gourmet food shop, espresso bar, and lovely cocktail bar. The main attraction is the tree-covered courtyard at the back. Lunch offers a selection of ample sandwiches and salads; dinner is mostly seafood and pastas. There's also a comprehensive vegetarian menu. ⊠*Kaya Grandi 12, Kralendijk* ☎*599/717–3919* ⊟*AE, MC, V* ☉*Closed Sun.*

$–$$ ✕**La Guernica.** This trendy tapas eatery overlooking the boardwalk and
Fodor'sChoice the harbor is great for people-watching; there's outdoor seating as well
★ as a couch- and pillow-filled lounge area. The interior is done in hacienda style with terra-cotta tiles, clay decorations, and comfy lounge chairs. The lunch menu offers a range of sandwiches and salads. This is *the* place to sip a cocktail and be seen. ⊠*Kaya Bonaire 4C, Kralendijk* ☎*599/717–5022* ⊟*AE, MC, V.*

$–$$ ✕**Kontiki Beach Club.** The dining room is a harmonious blend of terracotta tile floors and rattan furnishings around a limestone half-moon bar. There's also a brick terrace for alfresco dining. Chef-owners Miriam and Martin are especially proud of their Dutch *kibbeling* (fish in a beer batter served with chili sauce). There are frequent live jazz performances on the outdoor stage and a constantly changing display of local art on the walls. Although located quite far from downtown, the view of the lagoon and intimate ambience mean it is definitely worth the drive. ⊠*Kaminda Sorobon 64, Lac Bay* ☎*599/717–5369* ⊟*AE, D, MC, V.*

¢–$ ✕**Wind & Surf Beach Bar.** Part of Bonaire Windsurf Place—and located right on the beach—this fun eatery is one of the most casual dining experiences on the island. Tables and chairs are set directly in the sand under a straw-roof structure so that cooling winds sweep through the space. The food is simple but very good; the main offerings are sandwiches, salads, and burgers. The experience of dining with your toes in the sand is sure to leave lingering pleasant memories. The weekly barbecue on Wednesday night with live entertainment is well worth the drive. ⊠*Sorobon Beach* ☎*599/717–2288* ⊟*No credit cards.*

FRENCH ✕**Bistro De Paris.** Any restaurant that welcomes you with a free glass
$$–$$$ of Kir and a personal greeting from the owner should be taken very
Fodor'sChoice seriously. Patrice Rannou has transformed an unassuming house into
★ a lovely bistro serving the best French food on the island. The low-key decor (complete with Perrier-bottle vases) belies the extraordinary food on offer. Lamb-lovers will fall to pieces over the char-grilled chops served with haricots verts and asparagus. The dinner menu is very reasonably priced, but those on an extremely tight budget should at least explore the lunch offerings. Those with kids and a lot of patience may want to try the novelty of the grill stone, which lets diners cook their own meal at the table. Many patrons choose to dine on the outdoor patio. ⊠*Kaya Gobernador N. Debrot 46, Kralendijk* ☎*599/717–7070* ⊟*MC, V* ☉*Closed Sun. No lunch Sat.*

ITALIAN ✕**Capriccio.** This splendid, family-run Italian eatery has plenty to boast
$$–$$$ about. The pastas are handmade daily, and fresh mozzarella is imported
★ from Italy once a week. The wine cellar includes 200 labels and more than 7,000 bottles. You can opt for casual à la carte dining on the terrace or a romantic meal in the tonier, air-conditioned dining room. If

your appetite is hearty, go for the five-course prix-fixe menu. Otherwise, choose one of the 50 regular offerings. ⊠*Kaya Isla Riba 1, Kralendijk* ☎*599/717–7230* ☰*AE, D, MC, V* ⊗*Closed Tues. No lunch Sun.*

$–$$
★
✕**Donna & Giorgio's.** Donna and her Sardinian-born husband, Giorgio, serve delicious home-style meals in this charming restaurant on the main road just outside Kralendijk. With Giorgio in the kitchen, Donna and her daughter greet diners and make them feel at home. Guests may choose to sit in the cozy interior near the bar or outside at one of the tables on the gravel-covered terrace, which is lovely on a cloudless night; however, it's only inches from the road, so there's occasional car noise. You can always find a selection of pizzas and pastas, as well as daily specials displayed on a blackboard outside. Live music on Sunday attracts a large crowd. ⊠*Kaya Grandi 60, near entrance to Divi Flamingo, Kralendijk* ☎*599/717–3799* ☰*MC, V* ⊗*Closed Wed. and Sept.*

MEXICAN
$$–$$$
✕**Papaya Moon Cantina.** Billing itself as Bonaire's first Tex-Mex restaurant, this popular eatery is a newcomer to the Kralendijk dining scene. The menu is comprehensive and offers such traditional favorites as tacos while also including some interesting interpretations of classic Mexican fare. Those seeking a bit of amusement in their dining experience should try the gazpacho, which is served in four shot glasses and topped with avocado cream. ⊠*Kaya Grandi 48, Kralendijk* ☎*599/717–5025* ☰*D, MC, V* ⊗*Closed Tues. No lunch.*

SEAFOOD
$$$–$$$$
★
✕**Richard's Waterfront Dining.** Animated, congenial Richard Beady and his partner, Mario, own this casually romantic waterfront restaurant, which has become one of the island's most recommended—a reputation that's well deserved. The daily menu is listed on large blackboards, and the food is consistently excellent. Fish soup is usually offered and is sure to please, as is the grilled wahoo. ⊠*J. A. Abraham Blvd. 60, Kralendijk* ☎*599/717–5263* ☰*AE, MC, V* ⊗*Closed Mon. No lunch.*

BEACHES

Don't expect long stretches of glorious powdery sand. Bonaire's beaches are small, and though the water is blue (several shades of it, in fact), the sand isn't always white. Bonaire's National Parks Foundation requires all nondivers to pay a $10 annual Nature Fee in order to enter the water anywhere around the island (divers pay $25). The fee can be paid at most dive shops.

Boca Slagbaai. Inside Washington–Slagbaai Park is this beach of coral fossils and rocks with interesting offshore coral gardens that are good for snorkeling. Bring scuba boots or canvas sandals to walk into the water, because the beach is rough on bare feet. The gentle surf makes it an ideal place for swimming and picnicking. Turn left at the "Y" intersection shortly after entering the national park and follow the signs. ✛ *Off main park road, in Washington–Slagbaai National Park.*

Klein Bonaire. Just a water-taxi hop across from Kralendijk, this little island offers picture-perfect white-sand beaches. The area is protected, so absolutely no development has been allowed. Make sure to pack everything before heading to the island, including water and an umbrella to hide under, because there are no refreshment stands, no changing facilities, and almost no shade to be found. Boats leave from the Town Pier, across from the City Café, and the round-trip water-taxi ride costs roughly $14 per person.

Lac Bay Beach. Known for its festive music on Sunday nights, this open bay area with pink-tinted sand is equally dazzling by day. It's a bumpy drive (10 to 15 minutes on a dirt road) to get here, but you'll be glad when you arrive. It's a good spot for diving, snorkeling, and kayaking (as long as you bring your own), and there are public restrooms and a restaurant for your convenience. ⊠ *Off Kaminda Sorobon, Lac Cai.*

Playa Funchi. This Washington–Slagbaai National Park beach is notable for the lagoon on one side, where flamingos nest, and the superb snorkeling on the other, where iridescent green parrot fish swim right up to shore. Turn right at the "Y" intersection after the entrance to the park and follow the signs. ✛ *Off main park road, in Washington–Slagbaai National Park.*

Sorobon Beach. Adjacent to the Sorobon Beach Naturist Resort and its nude beach, this is *the* windsurfing beach on Bonaire. You can find a restaurant-bar next to the resort and windsurfing outfitters on the beach. The public beach area has restrooms and huts for shade, as well as a direct line of sight to the nude section. If driving, take E. E. G. Boulevard (this is the southern route out of Kralendijk) to Kaya I. R. Randolf Statuuis Van Eps then follow this route straight on to Sorobon Beach. ⊠ *Kaya I. R. Randolf Statuuis Van Eps, Sorobon Beach.*

Windsock Beach. Near the airport (just off E. E. G. Boulevard), this pretty little spot, also known as Mangrove Beach, looks out toward the north side of the island and has about 200 yards of white sand along a rocky shoreline. It's a popular dive site, and swimming conditions are also good. ✛ *Off E. E. G. Blvd., near Flamingo Airport.*

SPORTS & THE OUTDOORS

BICYCLING

Bonaire is generally flat, so bicycles are an easy way to get around. Because of the heat it's essential to carry water if you're planning to cycle for any distance and especially if your plans involve exploring the deserted interior. There are more than 180 mi (290 km) of unpaved routes (as well as the many paved roads) on the island.

Cycle Bonaire (⊠ *Kaya Gobernador N. Debrot 77A, Kralendijk* ☎ *599/717–2229*) rents mountain bikes and gear (trail maps, water bottles, helmets, locks, repair and first-aid kits) for $15 a day or $75 for six days; half-day and full-day guided excursions start at $55, not including bike rental.

Tropical Travel (⊠ *J. A. Abraham Blvd. 80, Kralendijk* ☎ *599/717–2500 Ext. 8199*) at the Plaza Resort Bonaire offers bikes for $7 per day or $42 per week.

DAY SAILS & SNORKELING TRIPS

Regularly scheduled sunset sails and snorkel trips are popular (prices range from $25 to $50 per person), as are private or group sails (expect to pay about $425 per day for a party of four).

Bonaire Boating (✉ *Divi Flamingo Resort, J.A. Abraham Blvd. 40, Kralendijk* ☎ *599/790–5353*) offers half- and full-day charters aboard a luxury 56-foot sailing yacht ($395 and $695, respectively), a 57-foot motor yacht ($455 for four hours), or the private charter of a 26-foot Bayliner day cruiser for $295 for three hours. Sunset sailings are also available with drinks for $32 per person.

Kantika di Amor Watertaxi (✉ *Kaya J.N.E. Craane 24, opposite the restaurant It Rains Fishes, Kralendijk* ☎ *599/560–7254 or 599/790–5399*) provides daily rides to Klein Bonaire and drift snorkel and evening cruises with complimentary cocktails.

The **Mushi Mushi** (☎ *599/790–5399*) is a catamaran offering a variety of two- and three-hour cruises starting at $25 per person. It departs from the Bonaire Nautico Marina in downtown Kralendijk (opposite the restaurant It Rains Fishes).

If you want to do some sailing on your own, **Tropical Travel** (✉ *Plaza Resort Bonaire, J.A. Abraham Blvd. 80, Kralendijk* ☎ *599/717–2500 Ext. 8199* ⊕ *www.tropicaltravelbonaire.com*) offers a variety of cruise packages starting at $35 per person.

The **Woodwind** (☎ *599/786–7055* ⊕ *www.woodwindbonaire.com*) is a 37-foot trimaran that offers regular sailing and snorkeling trips as well as charters.

DIVING & SNORKELING

Bonaire has some of the best reef diving this side of Australia's Great Barrier Reef. It takes only 5 to 25 minutes to reach many sites, the current is usually mild, and although some reefs have sudden, steep drops, most begin just offshore and slope gently downward at a 45-degree angle. General visibility runs 60 to 100 feet, except during surges in October and November. You can see several varieties of coral: knobby-brain, giant-brain, elkhorn, staghorn, mountainous star, gorgonian, and black. You can also encounter schools of parrot fish, surgeonfish, angelfish, eel, snapper, and grouper. Beach diving is excellent just about everywhere on the leeward side, so night diving is popular. There are sites here suitable for every skill level; they're clearly marked by yellow stones on the roadside.

Bonaire, in conjunction with *Skin Diver* magazine, has also developed the **Guided Snorkeling Program.** The highly educational and entertaining program begins with a slide show on important topics, from a beginner's look at reef fish, coral, and sponges to advanced fish identification and night snorkeling. Guided snorkeling for all skill levels can be arranged through most resort dive shops. The best snorkeling spots are on the island's leeward side, where you have shore access to the reefs, and along the west side of Klein Bonaire, where the reef is better developed. All snorkelers and swimmers must pay a $10 Nature

Fee, which allows access to the waters around the island and Washington–Slagbaai National Park for one calendar year. The fee can be paid at most dive shops.

Fodor's Choice In the well-policed **Bonaire Marine Park** (⊠ *Karpata* ☎ *599/717–8444* ⊕ *www.bmp.org*), which encompasses the entire coastline around ★ Bonaire and Klein Bonaire, divers take the rules seriously. Don't even *think* about (1) spearfishing; (2) dropping anchor; or (3) touching, stepping on, or collecting coral. In order to dive (as opposed to simply swim and enter the water), you must pay a fee of $25 (used to maintain the park), for which you receive a colored plastic tag (to attach to an item of scuba gear) entitling you to one calendar year of unlimited diving. Checkout dives—dives you do first with a master before going out on your own—are required, and you can arrange them through any dive shop. All dive operations offer classes in free buoyancy control, advanced buoyancy control, and photographic buoyancy control. Tags are available at all scuba facilities and from the Marine Park Headquarters.

DIVE SITES

The *Guide to the Bonaire Marine Park* lists 86 dive sites (including 16 shore-dive-only and 35 boat-dive-only sites). Another fine reference book is the *Diving and Snorkeling Guide to Bonaire,* by Jerry Schnabel and Suzi Swygert. Guides associated with the various dive centers can give you more-complete directions. It's difficult to recommend one site over another; to whet your appetite, here are a few of the popular sites.

★ **Angel City.** Take the trail down to the shore adjacent to the Radio Nederland tower station; dive in and swim south to Angel City, one of the shallowest and most popular sites in a two-reef complex that includes Alice in Wonderland. The boulder-size green-and-tan coral heads are home to black margates, Spanish hogfish, gray snappers, stingrays, and large purple tube sponges.

Bari Reef. Catch a glimpse of the elkhorn and fire coral, queen angelfish, and other wonders of Bari Reef, just off the Sand Dollar Condominium Resort's pier.

★ **Calabas Reef.** Off the coast of the Divi Flamingo Resort, this is the island's busiest dive site. It's replete with Christmas-tree worms, sponges, and fire coral adhering to a ship's hull. Fish life is frenzied, with the occasional octopus putting in an appearance.

Forest. You need to catch a boat to reach Forest, a dive site off the southwest coast of Klein Bonaire. Named for the abundant black-coral forests found in it, the site gets a lot of fish action, including a resident spotted eel that lives in a cave.

Rappel. This spectacular site is near the Karpata Ecological Center. The shore is a sheer cliff, and the lush coral growth is the habitat of some unusual varieties of marine life, including occasional orange sea horses, squid, spiny lobsters, and spotted trunkfish.

Small Wall. One of Bonaire's three complete vertical wall dives (and one of its most popular night-diving spots), Small Wall is in front of the Black Durgon Inn, near Barcadera Beach. Because the access to

Bonaire Marine Park

The Bonaire Marine Park was founded in 1979 in an effort to protect the island's most-precious natural resource. Covering an area of less than 700 acres, the park includes all the waters around the island from the high-water mark to the 60-meter depth. Legislation prevents collecting (or even walking on) coral, using spearguns, or removing marine life. It also means that boats may not drop anchor in most of the island's waters and that divers may not use gloves unless they're needed for ascending or descending a line.

Because the island has so zealously protected its marine environment, Bonaire offers an amazing diversity of underwater life. Turtles, rays, and fish of every imaginable color abound in the pristine waters of the park. The charge ($10 for swimmers and snorkelers, $25 for divers) for a swimming or diving tag allows unlimited use of the park for a year, and every cent goes toward the care and management of the Bonaire Marine Park. And it's money well spent, islanders and most visitors will tell you.

this site is on private property, this is usually a boat-diving site. The 60-foot wall is frequented by squid, turtles, tarpon, and barracuda and has dense hard and soft coral formations; it also allows for excellent snorkeling.

Something Special. South of the marina entrance at Harbour Village Beach Club, this spot is famous for its garden eels. They wave about from the relatively shallow sand terrace looking like long grass in a breeze.

Town Pier. Known for shielding one of Bonaire's best night dives, the pier is right in town, across from the City Café. Divers need permission from the harbormaster and must be accompanied by a local guide.

Windsock Steep. This excellent shore-dive site (from 20 to 80 feet) is in front of the small beach opposite the airport runway. It's a popular place for snorkeling. The current is moderate, the elkhorn coral profuse; you may also see angelfish and rays.

DIVE OPERATORS

Many of the dive shops listed below offer PADI and NAUI certification courses and SSI, as well as underwater photography and videography courses. Some shops are also qualified to certify dive instructors. Full certification courses cost approximately $370; open-water refresher courses run about $185; a one-tank boat dive with unlimited shore diving costs about $37; a two-tank boat dive with unlimited shore diving is about $55. As for equipment, renting a mask, fin, and snorkel costs about $8.50 all together; for a BC and regulator, expect to pay about $16. Check out children's programs like Aquakids and Ocean Classroom—or inquire about their equivalents.

Most dive shops on Bonaire offer a complete range of snorkel gear for rent and will provide beginner training; some dive operations also offer guided snorkeling and night snorkeling. The cost for a guided snorkel session is about $25 and includes slide presentations, transportation to the site, and a tour. Gear rental is approximately $9 per 24-hour period.

Bonaire Dive & Adventure (⊠ *Sand Dollar Condominium Resort, Kaya Gobernador N. Debrot 77A, Kralendijk* ☎ *599/717–2229* ⊕ *www. bonairediveandadventure.com*) is probably the best choice for first-timers who want a stress-free introduction to the sport.

Bonaire Scuba Center (⊠ *Black Durgon Inn, Kaya Gobernador N. Debrot 145, Kralendijk* ☎ *Box 775, Morgan, NJ* ☎ *599/717–5736, 908/566–8866, 800/526–2370 for reservations in U.S.*).

Bruce Bowker's Carib Inn Dive Center (⊠ *J. A. Abraham Blvd. 46, Kralendijk* ☎ *599/717–8819* ⊕ *www.caribinn.com*).

Buddy Dive Resort (⊠ *Kaya Gobernador N. Debrot 85, Kralendijk* ☎ *599/717–5080* ⊕ *www.buddydive.com*).

Captain Don's Habitat Dive Shop (⊠ *Kaya Gobernador N. Debrot 113, Kralendijk* ☎ *599/717–8290* ⊕ *www.habitatdiveresorts.com*).

Dee Scarr's "Touch the Sea" (☎ *Box 369, Kralendijk* ☎ *599/717–8529* ⊕ *www.touchthesea.com*).

Dive Inn (⊠ *Kaya C. E. B. Hellmund, close to South Pier, Kralendijk* ☎ *599/717–8761* ⊕ *www.diveinn-bonaire.com*).

★ **Divi Dive Bonaire** (⊠ *Divi Flamingo Resort & Casino, J. A. Abraham Blvd. 40, Kralendijk* ☎ *599/717–8285* ⊕ *www.diviflamingo.com*).

★ **Larry's Shore & Wild Side Diving** (☎ *599/790–9156* ⊕ *www.larryswild sidediving.com*) is run by a former army combat diver and offers a variety of appealing options ranging from the leisurely to downright scary. This company has become an extremely popular choice, so try to book as early as possible.

Photo Tours Divers (⊠ *Caribbean Court Bonaire, J. A. Abraham Blvd. 82, Kralendijk* ☎ *599/717–3460* ⊕ *www.bonphototours.com*).

Toucan Diving (⊠ *Plaza Resort Bonaire, J. A. Abraham Blvd. 80, Kralendijk* ☎ *599/717–2500* ⊕ *www.toucandiving.com*) offers the Aquakids program for children 5 to 12.

Wanna Dive (⊠ *Hotel Rochaline, Kaya Grandi 7, next to City Café, Kralendijk* ☎ *599/790–8880* ⊕ *www.wannadivebonaire.com*).

FISHING

Captain Cornelis of **Big Game Sportfishing** (⊠ *Kaya Krisolito 6, Santa Barbara* ☎ *599/717–6500* ⊕ *www.bonairefishing.com/biggame*) offers deep-sea charters for those in search of wahoo, marlin, tuna, swordfish, and sailfish. His rates—which cover bait, tackle, and refreshments—average $325 for a half day, $450 for a full day for as many as five people.

Multifish Charters (☎ *599/717–3648* ⊕ *www.bonairefishing.net*) has day or night reef fishing on a 38-foot Bertram twin diesel; the cost for six hours is $420 (six-person maximum). A nine-hour day of deep-sea fishing costs $600 (six-person maximum), including refreshments.

Piscatur Charters (⊠ *Kaya H.J. Pop 3, Kralendijk* ☎ *599/717–8774* ⊕ *www.bonairetours.com/piscatur*) offers light-tackle angler reef fishing for jackfish, barracuda, and snapper from a 15-foot skiff. Rates are $225 for a half day. You can charter the 42-foot Sport Fisherman *Piscatur,* which carries up to six people, for $350 for a half day, $550 for a full day.

HORSEBACK RIDING

☺ You can take hour-long trail rides at the 166-acre **Kunuku Wara-hama Ranch** (⊠*Kaya Guanare 11, east of Kralendijk, off road to Cai* ☎*599/560–7949*) for $20. Guides take you through groves of cacti where iguanas, wild goats, donkeys, and flamingos reside. Reserve one of the gentle pintos or palominos a day in advance, and try to go early in the morning, when it's cool. The ranch, open Tuesday through Sunday from 10 to 6, also has an alfresco restaurant, a golf driving range, and two playgrounds.

KAYAKING

Divers and snorkelers can use kayaks to reach otherwise inaccessible dive sites and simply tow the craft along during their dive. Nondivers can take advantage of the calm waters around the island to explore the coastline and the fascinating stands of mangrove around the Lac Bay area. The mangrove harbors myriad wildlife and acts as a hatchery for marine life. Almost all of the kayaks used are of the sit-on-top variety, which are able to negotiate shallow waters better.

Bonaire Dive & Adventure (⊠*Kaya Gobernador N. Debrot 79, Kralendijk* ☎*599/717–8738 or 800/288–4773* ⊕*www.bonairediveandadventure.com*) rents kayaks and also operates guided trips.

At **Jibe City** (⊠*Sorobon Beach* ☎*599/717–5233, 800/748–8733 in U.S.* ⊕*www.jibecity.com*), which is primarily a windsurfing outfit, kayaks go for $10 (single) and $15 (double) per hour; $25 and $30, respectively, per half day (closed in September).

★ **Mangrove Info & Kayak Center** (⊠*Kaminda Lac 141, on road to Lac Cai, Lac Bay* ☎*599/790–5353* ⊕*www.bonairekayaking.com*) offers guided kayak tours of the mangrove forest at 9 AM and 11 AM daily, for $25 an hour and $43 for two hours. The center houses a unique mangrove aquarium designed to study the Lac Bay mangroves' effect on the global ecosystem as well as a photo gallery showing underwater existence within the forest like never before. The tours are pleasant even for the exercise-challenged and usually provide a great way to work on your tan.

LAND SAILING

☺ This fast-paced activity is basically windsurfing on land using a sail and a three-wheeled apparatus (called a blokart). It can get pretty dusty but is definitely fun and worth a try. **Landsailing Bonaire** (⊠*Kaya Jupiter 4, Belnem* ☎*599/717–8122 or 599/786–8122* ⊕*www.landsailingbonaire.com*) provides training, equipment, and safety clothing for $50 for the first hour.

WINDSURFING

With near constant breezes and calm waters, Bonaire is consistently ranked among the best places in the world for windsurfing. Lac Bay, a protected cove on the east coast, is ideal for windsurfing. Novices will find it especially comforting since there's no way to be blown out to sea. The island's windsurfing companies are headquartered there on Sorobon Beach.

★ The **Bonaire Windsurf Place** (⊠ *Sorobon Beach* ☎ *599/717–2288* ⊕ *www. bonairewindsurfplace.com*), commonly referred to as "the Place," rents the latest Hot Sails Maui, Starboard, and RRD equipment for $40 for two hours or $60 for a full day. A two-hour group lesson costs $45; private lessons are $75 per hour (these rates do not include equipment, which adds at least $35 to the price). A three-day group-lesson package is a bargain at $199, since it includes a one-hour lesson, one hour of practice, and equipment rental; groups are generally limited to four people. Elvis, Roger, and Constantine, who own the place, are all former windsurfing champs.

Jibe City (⊠ *Sorobon Beach* ☎ *599/717–5233, 800/748–8733 in U.S.* ⊕ *www.jibecity.com*) offers lessons for $50 (includes board and sail for beginners only); board rentals start at $20 an hour, $45 for a half day. There are pickups at all the hotels at 9 AM and 1 PM; ask your hotel to make arrangements.

SHOPPING

You can get to know all the shops in Kralendijk in an hour or so, but sometimes there's no better way to enjoy some time out of the sun and sea than to go shopping (particularly if your companion is a dive fanatic and you're not). Almost all the shops are on the Kaya Grandi and adjacent streets and in tiny malls. Harbourside Mall is a pleasant, open-air mall with several fine air-conditioned shops. The most-distinctive local crafts are fanciful painted pieces of driftwood and hand-painted *kunuku,* or little wilderness houses. One word of caution: buy as many flamingo T-shirts as you want, but don't take home items made of goatskin or tortoise shell; they aren't allowed into the United States. Remember, too, that it's forbidden to take sea fans, coral, conch shells, and *all* other forms of marine life off the island.

SPECIALTY STORES

CLOTHING

Benetton (⊠ *Kaya Grandi 29, Kralendijk* ☎ *599/717–5107*) claims that its prices for men's, women's, and children's clothes are 30% lower than in New York.

Best Buddies (⊠ *Kaya Grandi 32, Kralendijk* ☎ *599/717–7570*) stocks a selection of Indonesian batik shirts, pareus, and T-shirts.

At **Island Fashions** (⊠ *Kaya Grandi 5, Kralendijk* ☎ *599/717–7565*) you can buy swimsuits, sunglasses, T-shirts, and costume jewelry.

DUTY-FREE GOODS

Flamingo Airport Duty Free (⊠*Flamingo Airport* ☎*599/717–5563*) sells perfumes and cigarettes.

Perfume Palace (⊠*Harbourside Mall, Kaya Grandi 31, Kralendijk* ☎*599/717–5288*) sells perfumes and makeup from Lancôme, Estée Lauder, Chanel, Ralph Lauren, and Clinique.

HANDICRAFTS

★ **Bon Tiki** (⊠*Kaya C. E. B. Hellmund 3, Kralendijk* ☎*599/717–6877*) sells unique works from Bonaire's finest artists.

Cinnamon Art Gallery (⊠*Kaya A. P. L. Brion 1, Kralendijk* ☎*599/717–7103*), on a side street off Kaya Grandi, offers a selection of fine art from local artists.

JanArt Gallery (⊠*Kaya Gloria 7, Kralendijk* ☎*599/717–5246*), on the outskirts of town, sells unique watercolor paintings, prints, and art supplies; artist Janice Huckaby also hosts art classes.

Whatever you do, make a point of visiting **Jenny's Art** (⊠*Kaya Betico Croes 6, near post office, Kralendijk* ☎*599/717–5004*). Roam around her house, which is a replica of a traditional Bonaire town complete with her handmade life-size dolls and the skeletons of all her dead pets. Lots of fun (and sometimes kitschy) souvenirs made out of driftwood, clay, and shells are all handmade by Jenny.

Maharaj Gifthouse (⊠*Kaya Grandi 11, Kralendijk* ☎*599/717–4402*) has a vast assortment of delft-blue hand-painted china, local artwork, and stainless-steel and crystal items that make great gifts.

JEWELRY

★ **Atlantis** (⊠*Kaya Grandi 32B, Kralendijk* ☎*599/717–7730*) carries a large range of precious and semiprecious gems. The tanzanite collection is especially beautiful. You will also find Sector, Raymond Weil, and Citizen watches, among others, all at great savings. Since gold jewelry is sold by weight here, it's an especially good buy.

Littman's (⊠*Kaya Grandi 33, Kralendijk* ☎*599/717–8160* ⊠*Harbourside Mall, Kaya Grandi 31, Kralendijk* ☎*599/717–2130*) is an upscale jewelry and gift shop where many items are handpicked by owner Steven Littman on his regular trips to Europe. Look for Rolex, Omega, Cartier, and Tag Heuer watches; fine gold jewelry; antique coins; nautical sculptures; resort clothing; and accessories.

NIGHTLIFE

Most divers are exhausted after they finish their third, fourth, or fifth dive of the day, which may explain why there are no full-time discos on Bonaire. Strange as it may sound, the most effective approach to finding the best hot spot is to stand downtown, listen for the loudest music, and then follow your ears. Most of the time nightlife consists of sitting on a quiet beach sipping a local Amstel Bright beer. Top island performers, including the Foyan Boys, migrate from one resort to another throughout the week. You can find information in the free magazines (published once a year) *Bonaire Affair* and *Bonaire Nights*.

The twice-monthly *Bonaire Update Events and Activities* pamphlet is available at most restaurants.

Carnival, generally held in February, is the usual nonstop parade of steel bands, floats, and wild costumes, albeit on a much smaller scale than on some other islands. It culminates in the ceremonial burning in effigy of King Momo, representing the spirit of debauchery.

BARS

Downtown, **City Café** (⊠*Hotel Rochaline, Kaya Grandi 7, Kralendijk* ☎*599/717–8286*) is a wacky hangout splashed in magenta, banana, and electric blue. Here you can find cocktails, snack food, live music on weekends, and karaoke on Wednesday nights.

The Thursday-night happy hour at **Deco Stop Bar** (⊠*Captain Don's Habitat, Kaya Gobernador N. Debrot 113, Kralendijk* ☎*599/717–8286*) is popular.

Karel's (⊠*Kaya J. N. E. Craane 12, Kralendijk* ☎*599/717–8434*) sits on stilts above the sea and is *the* place for mingling—especially Friday and Saturday nights, when there's live island and pop music.

La Guernica (⊠*Kaya Bonaire 4C, Kralendijk* ☎*599/717–5022*), with an ultrachic bar and comfy-couch-lined terrace is the place to be seen on weekend nights.

CASINO

Divi Flamingo Resort (⊠*J. A. Abraham Blvd., Kralendijk* ☎*599/717–8285*) is the only casino on the island and operates until 4 AM.

DANCE CLUBS

★ **City Café** (⊠*Kaya Grandi 7, Kralendijk* ☎*599/717–8286*) is the island's closest thing to a dance club. On weekend nights the restaurant moves the tables aside and it becomes an instant dance floor.

On Sunday afternoon at **Lac Cai** (⊠*Lac Cai*) enjoy the festive Sunday Party, where locals celebrate the day with live music, dancing, and food from 3 to 11. Take a taxi, especially if you plan to imbibe a few rum punches.

EXPLORING BONAIRE

Two routes, north and south from Kralendijk, the island's small capital, are possible on the 24-mi-long (39-km-long) island; either route will take from a few hours to a full day, depending on whether you stop to snorkel, swim, dive, or lounge. Those pressed for time will find that it's easy to explore the entire island in a day if stops are kept to a minimum.

WHAT TO SEE

KRALENDIJK

Bonaire's small, tidy capital city (population 3,000) is five minutes from the airport. The main drag, J. A. Abraham Boulevard, turns into **Kaya Grandi** in the center of town. Along it are most of the island's major stores, boutiques, and restaurants. Across Kaya Grandi, opposite the Littman jewelry store, is Kaya L. D. Gerharts, with several small supermarkets, a handful of snack shops, and some of the better restaurants. Walk down the narrow waterfront avenue called Kaya C. E. B. Hellmund, which leads straight to the **North and South piers.** In the center of town, the Harbourside Mall has chic boutiques. Along this route is **Ft. Oranje,** with its cannons. From December through April, cruise ships dock in the harbor once or twice a week. The diminutive ocher-and-white structure that looks like a tiny Greek temple is the **fish market;** local anglers no longer bring their catches here (they sell out of their homes these days), but you can find plenty of fresh produce brought over from Columbia and Venezuela. Pick up the brochure *Walking and Shopping in Kralendijk* from the tourist office to get a map and full listing of all the monuments and sights in the town.

SOUTH BONAIRE

The trail south from Kralendijk is chock-full of icons—both natural and man-made—that tell Bonaire's mini-saga. Rent a four-wheel-drive vehicle (a car will do, but during the rainy season of October through November the roads can become muddy) and head out along the Southern Scenic Route. The roads wind through dramatic desert terrain, full of organ-pipe cacti and spiny-trunk mangroves—huge stumps of saltwater trees that rise from the marshes like witches. Watch for long-haired goats, wild donkeys, and lizards of all sizes.

☾ ★ **Rooi Lamoenchi Kunuku.** Owner Ellen Herrera restored her family's homestead north of Lac Bay, in the Bonairean *kadushi* (cactus) wilderness, to educate tourists and residents about the history and tradition of authentic kunuku living and show unspoiled terrain in two daily tours. You must make an appointment in advance and expect to spend a couple of hours. ⊠ *Kaya Suiza 23, Playa Baribe* 🕾 *599/717–8490* ⊕ *www. webpagecur.com/rooilamoenchi* 🖃 *$12* ⊗ *By appointment only.*

Salt Flats. You can't miss the salt flats—voluptuous white drifts that look something like mountains of snow. Harvested once a year, the "ponds" are owned by Cargill, Inc., which has reactivated the 19th-century salt industry with great success (one reason for that success is that the ocean on this part of the island is higher than the land—which makes irrigation a snap). Keep a lookout for the three 30-foot obelisks—white, blue, and red—that were used to guide the trade boats coming to pick up the salt. Look also in the distance across the pans to the abandoned solar saltworks that's now a designated **flamingo sanctuary.** With the naked eye you might be able to make out a pink-orange haze just on the horizon; with binoculars you will see a sea of bobbing pink bodies. The sanctuary is completely protected, and no entrance is allowed (flamingos are extremely sensitive to disturbances of any kind).

🕑 **Slave Huts.** The salt industry's gritty history is revealed in Rode Pan, the site of two groups of tiny slave huts. The white grouping is on the right side of the road, opposite the salt flats; the second grouping, called the red slave huts (though they appear yellow), stretches across the road toward the island's southern tip. During the 19th century, slaves working the salt pans by day crawled into these huts to rest. Each Friday afternoon they walked seven hours to Rincon to weekend with their families, returning each Sunday. Only very small people will be able to enter, but walk around and poke your head in for a look.

Willemstoren Lighthouse. Bonaire's first lighthouse was built in 1837 and is now automated (but closed to visitors). Take some time to explore the beach and notice how the waves, driven by the trade winds, play a crashing symphony against the rocks. Locals stop here to collect pieces of driftwood in spectacular shapes and to build fanciful pyramids from objects that have washed ashore.

5

NORTH BONAIRE

The Northern Scenic Route takes you into the heart of Bonaire's natural wonders—desert gardens of towering cacti (kadushi, used to prepare soup, and the thornier *yatu,* used to build cactus fencing), tiny coastal coves, and plenty of fantastic panoramas. The road also weaves between eroded pink-and-black limestone walls and eerie rock formations with fanciful names like the Devil's Mouth and Iguana Head (you'll need a vivid imagination and sharp eye to recognize them). Brazil trees growing along the route were used by Indians to make dye (pressed from a red ring in the trunk). Inscriptions still visible in several island caves were made with this dye.

A snappy excursion with the requisite photo stops will take about 2½ hours, but if you pack your swimsuit and a hefty picnic basket (forget about finding a KFC), you could spend the entire day exploring this northern sector. Head out from Kralendijk on Kaya Gobernador N. Debrot until it turns into the Northern Scenic Route. Once you pass the Radio Nederland towers you cannot turn back to Kralendijk. The narrow road becomes one way until you get to Landhuis Karpata, and you have to follow the cross-island road to Rincon and return via the main road through the center of the island.

Barcadera Cave. Once used to trap goats, this cave is one of the oldest in Bonaire; there's even a tunnel that looks intriguingly spooky. It's the first sight along the northern route; watch closely for a yellow marker on your left before you reach the towering Radio Nederland antennas. Pull off across from the entrance to the Bonaire Caribbean Club, and you can discover some stone steps that lead down into a cave full of stalactites and vegetation.

🕑 **Gotomeer.** This saltwater lagoon near the island's northern end is a popular flamingo hangout. Bonaire is one of the few places in the world where pink flamingos nest. The shy, spindly legged creatures—affectionately called "pink clouds"—are magnificent birds to observe, and there are about 15,000 of them in Bonaire (more than the number of human residents). The best time to catch them at home is January to

June, when they tend to their gray-plumed young. For the best view take the paved access road alongside the lagoon through the jungle of cacti to the parking and observation area on the rise overlooking the lagoon and Washington–Slagbaai National Park beyond.

Landhuis Karpata. This mustard-color building was the manor house of an aloe plantation in the 19th century. The site was named for the *karpata* (castor bean) plants that are abundant in the area—you can see them along the sides of the road as you approach. Notice the rounded outdoor oven where aloe was boiled down before the juice was exported. Although the government has built a shaded rest stop at Karpata, there's still no drink stand.

1,000 Steps. Directly across the road from the Radio Nederland towers on the main road north, you'll see a short yellow marker that points to the location of these limestone stairs carved right out of the cliff. If you trek down the stairs, you can discover a lovely coral beach and protected cove where you can snorkel and scuba dive. Actually, you'll count only 67 steps, but it feels like 1,000 when you walk back up carrying scuba gear.

Onima. Small signposts direct the way to the Indian inscriptions found on a 3-foot limestone ledge that juts out like a partially formed cave entrance. Look up to see the red-stained designs and symbols inscribed on the limestone, said to have been the handiwork of the Arawak Indians when they inhabited the island centuries ago. The pictographs date back at least to the 15th century, and nobody has a clue what they mean. To reach Onima, pass through Rincon on the road that heads back to Kralendijk, but take the left-hand turn before Fontein.

Rincon. The island's original Spanish settlement, Rincon is where slaves brought from Africa to work the plantations and salt fields lived. Superstition and voodoo lore still have a powerful impact here, more so than in Kralendijk, where the townspeople work hard at suppressing old ways. Rincon is now a well-kept cluster of pastel cottages and 19th-century buildings that constitute Bonaire's oldest village. Watch your driving here—goats and dogs often sit right in the middle of the main drag.

Seroe Largu. Just off the main road, this spot, at 394 feet, is one of the highest on the island. A paved but narrow and twisting road leads to a magnificent daytime view of Kralendijk's rooftops and the island of Klein Bonaire. A large cross and figure of Christ stand guard at the peak, with an inscription reading *ayera* (yesterday), *awe* (today), and *semper* (always).

Washington–Slagbaai National Park. Once a plantation producing divi-divi trees (the pods were used for tanning animal skins), aloe (used for medicinal lotions), charcoal, and goats, the park is now a model of conservation. It's easy to tour the 13,500-acre tropical desert terrain on the dirt roads. As befits a wilderness sanctuary, the well-marked, rugged routes force you to drive slowly enough to appreciate the animal life and the terrain. (Think twice about coming here if it has rained recently—the mud you may encounter will be more than inconvenient.) If you're planning to hike, bring a picnic lunch, camera, sunscreen, and plenty of water. There are two routes: the long one (22 mi [35.5 km]) is marked by yellow arrows, the short one (15 mi [24 km]) by green arrows. Goats and donkeys may dart across the road, and if you keep your eyes peeled, you may catch sight of large iguanas camouflaged in the shrubbery.

Bird-watchers are really in their element here. Right inside the park's gate, flamingos roost on the salt pad known as **Salina Mathijs,** and exotic parakeets dot the foot of **Mt. Brandaris,** Bonaire's highest peak, at 784 feet. Some 130 species of birds fly in and out of the shrubbery in the park. Keep your eyes open and your binoculars at hand. Swimming, snorkeling, and scuba diving are permitted, but you're requested not to frighten the animals or remove anything from the grounds. Absolutely no hunting, fishing, or camping is allowed. A useful guide to the park is available at the entrance for about $6. To get here, take the secondary road north from the town of Rincon. The Nature Fee for swimming and snorkeling also grants you free admission to this park. ☎599/717–8444 ⊕ *www.bonairenature.com/washingtonpark* ⌦ *Free but requires payment of Nature Fee ($10)* ⊙ *Daily 8–5; you must enter before 3.*

BONAIRE ESSENTIALS

To research prices, get advice from other travelers, and book travel arrangements, visit www.fodors.com.

▌ TRANSPORTATION

BY AIR

Continental Airlines offers once-weekly direct service to Bonaire (BON) from Houston and Newark. Canadians and Americans will usually have to change planes in San Juan or Aruba. Air Jamaica, American Eagle, and Dutch Antilles Express provide connecting service. KLM offers daily direct flights from Amsterdam.

Information **Air Jamaica** (☎599/717–7747 or 800/523–5585). **American Eagle** (☎599/717–2005 or 800/433–7300). **Continental Airlines** (☎800/231–0856). **Dutch Antilles Express** (☎599/717–0808 ⊕www.flydae.com). **KLM** (☎599/717–7447).

Airport Information **Airport Taxi Stand** (☎599/717–8100). **Flamingo Airport** (BON ☎599/717–3800).

BY BIKE & MOPED

Scooters are a great way to zip around the island. Rates are about $26 per day for a one-seater and up to $32 for a deluxe two-seater. A valid driver's license and cash deposit or credit card are required. Bonaire Motorcycle Shop rents Harley-Davidson motorcycles as well as scooters.

Information **Bonaire Motorcycle Shop** (✉Kaya Grandi 64, Kralendijk ☎599/717–7790). **Macho! Scooter Rentals** (✉J.A. Abraham Blvd. 80, Kralendijk ☎599/717–2500).

BY CAR

You'll need a valid U.S., Canadian, or international driver's license to rent a car, and you must meet the minimum and maximum age requirements (usually 21 and 70) of each rental company. There's a government tax of $3.50 per day per rental; no cash deposit is needed if you pay by credit card.

Gas costs about double what it does in the United States, and you can find stations in Kralendijk, Rincon, and Antriol. Main roads are well paved, but remember that there are also many miles of unpaved roads; the roller-coaster hills at the national park require a strong stomach, and during the rainy season (October through November) mud—called Bonairean snow—can be difficult to navigate. All traffic stays to the right, and there's not a single traffic light. Signs or green arrows are usually posted to leading attractions; if you stick to the paved roads and marked turnoffs, you won't get lost.

Information Avis (⊠ Flamingo Airport, Kralendijk ☎ 599/717–5795). **Budget** (⊠ Flamingo Airport, Kralendijk ☎ 599/717–7424). **Flamingo Car Rental** (⊠ Kaya Grandi 86, Kralendijk ☎ 599/717–8888, 599/717–5588 at airport). **Hertz** (⊠ Flamingo Airport, Kralendijk ☎ 599/717–7221). **Island Rentals** (⊠ Kaya Industria 31, Kralendijk ☎ 599/717–2100). **National** (⊠ Kaya Nikiboko Zuid 114, Kralendijk ☎ 599/717–7940 or 599/717–7907).

BY TAXI

Taxis are unmetered; they have fixed rates controlled by the government. A trip from the airport to your hotel will cost between $7 and $18 for up to four passengers. A taxi from most hotels into town costs between $7 and $10. Fares increase from 7 PM to midnight by 25% and from midnight to 6 AM by 50%. Drivers are usually knowledgeable enough about the island to conduct half-day tours; they charge about $25 per hour for up to four passengers.

Information Taxi Central Dispatch (☎ 599/717–8100).

▌ CONTACTS & RESOURCES

BANKS & EXCHANGE SERVICES

There's no real need to convert your American dollars into the local currency, the NAf guilder. U.S. currency and traveler's checks are accepted everywhere, and the difference in exchange rates is negligible. Banks accept U.S. dollar banknotes at the official rate of NAf 1.78 to the

U.S. dollar, traveler's checks at NAf 1.80. This rate is practically fixed. The rate of exchange at shops and hotels ranges from NAf 1.75 to NAf 1.80. The guilder is divided into 100 cents. You can find ATMs at the airport, in Kralendijk, and at Hato branches of MCB, as well as at the Sand Dollar Condominium Resort and the Plaza Resort; at the Tourism Corporation Bonaire; and at Banco di Caribe on Kaya Grandi.

ELECTRICITY

Bonaire runs on 120 AC/50 cycles. A transformer and occasionally a two-prong adapter are required. Note that some appliances may work slowly (60 cycles are typical in North America), hair dryers may overheat, and sensitive equipment may be damaged.

EMERGENCIES

Emergency Services Ambulance (☎ 599/717–8900). **Fire** (☎ 599/717–8000). **Police emergencies** (☎ 599/717–8000).

Hospital St. Franciscus Hospital (⊠ *Kaya Soeur Bartola 2, Kralendijk ☎ 599/717–8900*).

Pharmacy Botika Bonaire (⊠ Kaya Grandi 27, by Harbourside Mall, Kralendijk ☎ 599/717–8905).

Scuba-Diving Emergencies Scuba-diving emergencies (☎ 599/717–8187).

HOLIDAYS

Public holidays are New Year's Day, Carnival Monday (Monday before Ash Wednesday), Good Friday (Friday before Easter), Rincon Day and Queen's Birthday (April 30), Labor Day (May 1), Bonaire Day (September 6), Antilles Day (October 21), Christmas and the day after (December 25 and 26).

INTERNET, MAIL & SHIPPING

Bonaire is not the ideal place for Internet junkies, as most hotels do not offer even basic dial-up service in rooms, much less Wi-Fi. There are a few cybercafés, the best being Chat 'n' Browse at Sand Dollar Shopping Plaza. Downtown, Cyber City at City Café and Bonaire Access at Harbourside Mall are the most popular. Some hotels offer Wi-Fi, Sand Dollar Condominium Resort being one example.

Airmail postage to North America and Europe is NAf 2.25 for letters and NAf 1.10 for postcards. The main post office is at the southeast corner of Kaya Grandi and Kaya Libertador S. Bolivar in Kralendijk. The post office is open weekdays from 7:30 to noon and 1:30 to 4.

Internet Cafés Bonaire Access (✉Harbourside Mall, Kralendijk ☎No phone). **Chat 'n' Browse** (✉Sand Dollar Shopping Plaza, Kaya Gobernador N. Debrot 79, Kralendijk ☎599/717–2281). **Cyber City** (✉City Café, Kaya Grandi 7, Kralendijk ☎599/717–8286).

LANGUAGE

The official language is Dutch, but the everyday language is Papiamento, a mix of Spanish, Portuguese, Dutch, English, and French, as well as African tongues. You can light up your waiter's eyes if you can say *masha danki* (thank you very much) and *pasa un bon dia* (have a nice day). English is spoken by almost everyone on the island.

SAFETY

Bonaire has a reputation for being friendly and safe, but petty crime exists. Divers who park their cars on the beach while offshore are at high risk of finding broken windows upon their return. The best, though admittedly strange, advice is to leave the vehicle unlocked and windows down when it is parked. The cost of replacing windows on a rental vehicle can be exorbitant, and if there's nothing to steal in the vehicle, the attraction for thieves is gone. Keep your money, credit cards, jewelry, and other valuables in your hotel's safety-deposit box.

TAXES

The departure tax when going to Curaçao is $5.75 (NAf 10.25). For all other destinations it's $20 (NAf 35.60). This tax must be paid in cash at the airport prior to departure. U.S. currency is accepted, but paying in NAf is usually faster. Hotels charge a room tax of $6.50 per person, per night in addition to the V.A.T. (value-added tax). Many hotels add a 10% to 15% service charge to your bill. A V.A.T of 6% is tacked on to dining and lodging costs. V.A.T. may or may not be included in your quoted room rates, so be sure to ask. It's almost always included in restaurant prices.

TELEPHONES

You can make international calls from hotel front desks or from the Telbo central phone company office (next to the tourism office in Kralendijk), which is open 24 hours a day. You can rent a cell phone from CellularOne Bonaire or Chat 'n' Browse at the Sand Dollar Shopping Plaza; the phone will cost you about $3 rental a day (plus a deposit), and you can buy prepaid phone cards—mobile-call costs are about 75% cheaper than hotel calls.

The country code for Bonaire is 599; 717 is the exchange for every four-digit telephone number on the island. When making interisland calls, dial 717 plus the local four-digit number. Local phone calls cost NAf 50¢.

Phone cards from home rarely work on Bonaire. You can try AT&T by dialing 001–800/872–2881 from public phones. To call Bonaire from the United States, dial 011–599/717 plus the local four-digit number.

Information CellularOne Bonaire (✉Kaya Grandi 26, Kralendijk ☎599/717–8787). **Chat 'n' Browse** (✉Sand Dollar Shopping Plaza, Kaya Gobernador N. Debrot 79, Kralendijk ☎599/717–2281).

TIPPING

Most restaurants add a 10% to 12% service charge; if they don't, tip at the same level. Taxi drivers like a 10% tip, but it isn't mandatory. Bellhops should receive $1 per bag.

5

TOUR OPTIONS

Achie Tours has several half- and full-day options. Bonaire Tours & Vacations will chauffeur you around on two-hour tours of either the island's north or south sides or on a half-day city-and-country tour ($28), which visits sights in both regions. Or simply ask any taxi driver for an island tour (be sure to negotiate the price up front). Tropical Travel offers a variety of land- and water-based tours of various lengths starting at $27.

Information **Achie Tours** (✉Kaya Nikiboko Noord 33, Kralendijk ☎599/717–8630). **Bonaire Tours & Vacations** (✉Kaya Gobernador N. Debrot 79, Kralendijk ☎599/717–8738 ⊕www.bonairetours.com). **Tropical Travel** (✉Plaza Resort Bonaire, J.A. Abraham Blvd. 80, Kralendijk ☎599/717–2500).

VISITOR INFORMATION

Before You Leave **Tourism Corporation Bonaire** (✉10 Rockefeller Plaza, Suite 900, New York, NY ☎212/956–5913 or 800/266–2473 ⊕www.infobonaire.com).

In Bonaire **Tourism Corporation Bonaire** (✉Kaya Grandi 2, Kralendijk ☎599/717–8322 or 599/717–8649).

WEDDINGS

With scenic photo opportunities and peaceful surroundings, it's no wonder that couples swoon at the idea of tying the knot on Bonaire. Weddings can be arranged fairly quickly, but it's best to begin planning at least four to six weeks in advance. One member of the couple must apply for temporary residency. Official witnesses must also apply for temporary residency, but most wedding coordinators can arrange for local witnesses. Once temporary residency has been granted, the couple applies for a marriage license and certificate; after the marriage, an apostille (official seal) must be put on the documents. Blood tests are not required.

I Do Bonaire specializes in wedding planning, as does Marvel Tromp of Multro Travel & Tours. The Web site of the Tourism Corporation Bonaire has details if you want to do your own planning. Several resorts on the island have wedding planners, including Harbour Village Beach Club, the Buddy Dive Resort, Captain Don's Habitat, and Plaza Resort Bonaire.

Information **I Do Bonaire** (☎599/717–8778 ⊕www.bonairetours.com). **Multro Travel & Tours** (☎599/717–8334 ⊕www.bonaire weddings.com).

British Virgin Islands

The Baths

WORD OF MOUTH

"Tortola is such a great destination; it is one of my favorite islands. The best was actually chartering a boat out of Tortola and being able to visit a different island every day."

—Sunshine_Lee

"When we arrived at the Top of the Baths we were immediately awe-struck. . . . The immensity of some of the boulders within our limited beginning view is something that just can't be captured on film."

—Maggi

WELCOME TO
BRITISH VIRGIN ISLANDS

NATURE'S LITTLE SECRETS

Most of the 50-some islands, islets, and cays that make up the British Virgin Islands (BVI) are remarkably hilly and volcanic in origin, having exploded from the depths of the sea some 25 million years ago. The exception is Anegada, which is a flat, coral-limestone atoll. Tortola (about 10 square mi/ 26 square km) is the largest member of the chain.

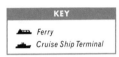

You can still find traces of a primeval rain forest at the top of Sage Mountain, the highest peak in the BVI.

The British Virgin Islands are mostly quiet and casual, so don't expect to party 'til dawn, and definitely leave the tux at home. Luxury here means getting away from it all rather than getting the trendiest state-of-the-art amenities. And the jackpot is the chance to explore the many islets and cays by sailboat.

Flamingo
Pond
Bones
Bight
Red
Pond
Loblolly
Bay
West End
Pt.
Table Bay
Horse
Shoe
Reef
The
Settlement
Pomato
Pt.
Saltheap
Pt.
Lower
Bay
ANEGADA
(15 miles north of Necker Is.)
White
Bay
Budrock
Pond

Sir Richard Branson owns Necker Island, which you can rent for $42,000 per night. Of course you get to share it with 25 of your closest friends.

Prickly Pear
Island
Necker
Island

Mosquito Island
Eustatia Island

Towing
Pt.
North Bay
Cockroach
Island
Virgin
Gorda
Peak
North
Sound
Great
Camanoe
Kitto
Ghut
George
Dog
West
Dog
Long
Bay
Gun Creek
Berchers
Bay
Little
Camanoe
Scrub Island
Great
Dog
Pond
Bay
South Sound
**VIRGIN
GORDA**
Monkey
Pt.
Pusser's Marina
Cay
Handsome
Bay
Anegada Passage
**Beef Island
International Airport**
Spanish Town
**Virgin Gorda
Airport**
Fat Hogs
Bay
Beef Island
Buck
Island
Copper Mine
Pt.
Francis Drake Channel
Fallen Jerusalem
Broken Jerusalem
Round Rock

The giant boulders at The Baths are granite, which isn't usually found in the Caribbean. Scientists theorize that they were carried here by glacial movements during the last Ice Age.

Quart-a-Nancy Pt.
Manchioneel Bay
Salt
Island
Cooper
Island
South
Bay
Ginger Island
Markoe Pt.
Salt
Island Bluff
ig Reef
ay
eter Island
er Island
f

0   4 mi
0   4 km

TOP 4 REASONS TO VISIT THE BRITISH VIRGIN ISLANDS

1 With over 50 islands in the chain, sailors can drop anchor at a different, perfect beach every day.

2 Laid-back luxury resorts offer a full-scale retreat from your everyday life.

3 Diving and snorkeling doesn't get any easier than around Anegada, where vibrant reefs are often just feet from the shore.

4 Your trip isn't complete until you've chilled at the casual beach bars on Jost Van Dyke.

BRITISH VIRGIN ISLANDS PLANNER

Island Activities

The BVI **sailing** scene is one of the best in the world, with Tortola as one of the major charteryacht centers of the Caribbean. It's no wonder that sailing is so popular; most of the best BVI beaches are on deserted islands and are accessible only by boat.

The most famous **beach** in the chain is The Baths on Virgin Gorda, which is lined with giant, round boulders that provide for great off-the-beach snorkeling. Tortola also has its share of beautiful strands, including the beaches at Cane Garden Bay. Jost Van Dyke's White Bay beach is also excellent.

The **nightlife** center of the region is actually a series of simple beach bars on Jost Van Dyke, but yachties in the know are happy to bop over for a drink and to hear Foxy Callwood sing at his eponymous bar and restaurant.

Diving—especially the wreck of the Rhone and the reefs around Anegada—make the BVI a major dive destination. Snorkelers appreciate the many opportunities to snorkel right off the beach, though some better shallow reefs can be reached on a daywail. And **gamefishing** in these waters is also good, as participants in the summer sportfishing tournament will attest.

Logistics

Getting to the BVI: To get to the British Virgin Islands, you must connect in either San Juan or St. Thomas and continue into Tortola on a small plane. You can also take a ferry from Charlotte Amalie or Red Hook on St. Thomas; these ferries also go to Virgin Gorda, but a flight is the only option for Anegada. Separate ferries go from Tortola to Jost Van Dyke and the other island retreats. You can take a tiny island-hopper flight to either Virgin Gorda (VIJ) or Anegada (NGD) from Tortola, but you'll have to book it directly with one of the small island-based airlines.

Hassle Factor: Medium to High.

Nonstops: None from the U.S.

On the Ground

At Tortola's Beef Island airport, taxis hover at the exit from customs. Fares are officially set but are lower per person for more than three passengers. Figure about $15 for up to three people and $5 for each additional passenger for the 20-minute ride to Road Town, and about $20 to $30 for the 45-minute ride to West End. Expect to share your taxi, and be patient if your driver searches for people to fill his cab—only a few flights land each day, and this could be your driver's only run. On Virgin Gorda, if you're staying on North Sound, a taxi will take you from the airport to the dock, where your hotel launch will meet you. If your destination is Leverick Bay, your land taxi will take you there directly. You can also take the North Sound Express directly from the Beef Island airport to Spanish Town or North Sound. On Anegada, your hotel will organize your transportation from the small airstrip.

Renting a Car: Both Tortola and Virgin Gorda have a number of car-rental agencies. Although taxi service is good, you may wish to rent a car to explore farther afield or try many different beaches (you may need to if you are staying at an isolated resort). On Anegada it's possible to rent a car, but most people rely on taxis for transportation. Jost Van Dyke has a single road, and visitors travel on foot or by local taxi.

Where to Stay

Pick your island carefully because each is different, as are the logistics of getting there. **Tortola** gives you a wider choice of restaurants, shopping, and resorts. **Virgin Gorda** has fewer off-resort places to eat and shop, but the resorts themselves are often better, and the beaches are exquisite. **Anegada** is remote and better suited for divers. **Jost Van Dyke** has some classic Caribbean beach bars, along with fairly basic accommodations.

When you want to be pampered and pampered some more, select a remote, **private-island resort** reached only by ferry, or even one of the appealing outer-island resorts that are still somewhat affordable for mere mortals.

If you want to enjoy everything the BVI have to offer, **charter a sailboat** so you can drop anchor where and when you want.

The largest resort in the British Virgin Islands has 120-some rooms, and most have considerably fewer. Luxury here is more about personal service than over-the-top amenities. The best places are certainly comfortable, but they aren't showy. You'll find **villas and condos** in abundance, and they are a good option for families.

Hotel & Restaurant Costs

⇨*For information on hotel meal plans, see Accommodations in Caribbean Essentials.*

WHAT IT COSTS IN U.S. DOLLARS

$$$$	$$$	$$	$	¢
Restaurants				
over $30	$20–$30	$12–$20	$8–$12	under $8
Hotels*				
over $350	$250–$350	$150–$250	$80–$150	under $80
Hotels**				
over $450	$350–$450	$250–$350	$125–$250	under $125

*EP, BP, CP; **AI, FAP, MAP; Restaurant prices are for a main course at dinner, excluding taxes and service charges. Hotel prices are for two people in a double room during high season, excluding taxes, service charges, and meal plans (except for all-inclusives).

When to Go

High season doesn't really get into full swing until Christmas and ends sooner (usually by April 1) than on most Caribbean islands. In the offseason, rates can be a third less.

Locals and yachties gather at Foxy's bar on Jost Van Dyke for the annual **St. Patrick's Day** celebration in March.

Glimpse the colorful spinnakers as sailing enthusiasts gather for the internationally known **BVI Spring Regatta & Sailing Festival,** which begins during the last week in March and continues until the first weekend in April.

Tortola celebrates **Carnival** on and around August 1 to mark the anniversary of the end of slavery in 1834. A slew of activities culminating with a parade through the streets take place in Road Town. Hotels fill up fast, so make sure to reserve your room and rental car rental well in advance.

In August, you can also try your hand at sport fishing, as anglers compete to land the largest catch at the **BVI Sportfishing Tournament**.

6

WITH THE SAILS DOWN AFTER a smooth trip across Sir Francis Drake Channel, our boat glided into White Bay at Jost Van Dyke for an afternoon of snorkeling and sun. A fresh-from-the-sea lobster dinner followed at a shoreside restaurant. The next day we anchored at Cane Garden Bay on Tortola's north shore for a dinghy ride ashore to listen to some hot music, and the day after that at a remote bay where we were the only boat. Traveling by sea is the way to hop around this archipelago of small islands and tiny cays. If a sailing trip isn't on your horizon, take one of the ferries that connect all the islands except Anegada.

The British Virgin Islands (BVI) are in the midst of transition. Once a collection of about 50 sleepy islands and cays, the British Virgin Islands—particularly the main island of Tortola—now sees huge cruise ships crowding its dock outside Road Town. Shoppers clog the downtown area on busy cruise-ship days, and traffic occasionally comes to a standstill. Even the second-largest island, Virgin Gorda, gets its share of smaller ships anchored off the main village of Spanish Town. Despite this explosive growth in the territory's tourism industry, it's still easy to escape the hubbub. Hotels outside Road Town usually provide a quiet oasis, and those on the other islands can be downright serene.

Each island has a different flavor. Want access to lots of restaurants and shopping? Make Tortola your choice. The largest of the BVIs, it covers 10 square mi (26 square km) and sits only a mile from St. John in the United States Virgin Islands (USVI). If you want to kick back at a small hotel or posh resort, try Virgin Gorda. Sitting nearly at the end of the chain, the 8-square-mi (21-square-km) island offers stellar beaches and a laid-back atmosphere. If you really want to get away from it all, the outermost islands, including Anegada and Jost Van Dyke, will fill the bill. Some of the smallest—Norman, Peter, Cooper, and Necker—are home to just one resort or restaurant. Others remain uninhabited specks on the horizon.

Visitors have long visited the BVI, starting with Christopher Columbus in 1493. He called the islands Las Once Mil Virgines—the 11,000 Virgins—in honor of the 11,000 virgin companions of St. Ursula, martyred in the 4th century AD. Pirates and buccaneers followed, and then came the British, who farmed the islands until slavery was abolished in 1834. The BVI are still politically tied to Britain, so the queen appoints a royal governor, but residents elect a local Legislative Council. Offshore banking and tourism share top billing in the territory's economy, but the majority of the islands' jobs are tourism-related. Despite the growth, you can usually find a welcoming smile.

TORTOLA

By Lynda Lohr   Once a sleepy backwater, Tortola is definitely busy these days, particularly when several cruise ships tie up at the Road Town dock. Passengers crowd the streets and shops, and open-air jitneys filled with cruise-ship passengers create bottlenecks on the island's byways. That said, most folks visit Tortola to relax on its deserted sands or linger over lunch at one of its many delightful restaurants. Beaches are never more than a few miles away, and the steep green hills that form Tortola's spine are fanned by gentle trade winds. The neighboring islands glimmer like emeralds in a sea of sapphire. It can be a world far removed from the hustle of modern life, but it simply doesn't compare to Virgin Gorda in terms of beautiful beaches—or even luxury resorts, for that matter.

Initially settled by Taino Indians, Tortola saw a string of visitors over the years. Christopher Columbus sailed by in 1493 on his second voyage to the new world, with Spain, Holland, and France making periodic visits about a century later. Sir Francis Drake arrived in 1595, leaving his name on the passage between Tortola and St. John. Pirates and buccaneers followed, with the British finally laying claim to the island in the late 1600s. In 1741 John Pickering became the first lieutenant governor of Tortola and the seat of the British government moved from Virgin Gorda to Tortola. As the agrarian economy continued to grow, slaves were imported from Africa. The slave trade was abolished in 1807, but slaves in Tortola and the rest of the BVI did not gain their freedom until August 1, 1834, when the Emancipation Proclamation was read at Sunday Morning Well in Road Town. That date is celebrated every year with the island's annual Carnival.

6

Visitors have a choice of accommodations, but most fall into the small and smaller still category. Only Long Bay Resort on Tortola's North Shore qualifies as a resort, but even some of the smaller properties add amenities occasionally add an amenity or two. A couple of new hotel projects are in the works, so look for more growth in the island's hotel industry over the next decade.

WHERE TO STAY

Luxury on Tortola is more about a certain state of mind—serenity, seclusion, gentility, and a bit of Britain in the Caribbean—than about state-of-the-art amenities and fabulous facilities. Some properties, especially the vacation villas, are catching up with current trends, but others seem stuck in the 1980s. But don't let a bit of rust on the screen door or a chip in the paint on the balcony railing mar your appreciation of the ambience. You will likely spend most of your time outside, so the location, size, or price of a hotel should be more of a factor to you than the decor.

Hotels in Road Town don't have beaches, but they do have pools and are within walking distance of restaurants, bars, and shops. Accommodations outside Road Town are relatively isolated, but most face the ocean. Tortola resorts are intimate—only a handful have more than 50 rooms. Guests are treated as more than just room numbers, and many return year after year. This can make booking a room at popular resorts difficult, even off-season, despite the fact that more than half the island's visitors stay aboard their own or chartered boats.

The Chikuzen

Road Town (inset map)

J. R. O'Neal Botanic Gardens

Treasure Isle Rd.

FREE BOTTOM

Waterfront Dr.

Wickhams Cay Rd

PORT PURCELL

Wickhams Cay 2 [1]

Long Bush Rd.

BLYDEN YARD

[1]   Waterfront Dr.   [2]   [3]

[2] Wickhams Cay 1

Peter Island Ferry

[4] [6]

ROAD TOWN

♦ Romasco Place
♦ Sir Olva Georga's Plaza
♦ Ferry Dock
♦ Customs House

Road Bay

Fort Charlotte Rd.

Walling Rd

Cedar Rd

Careening Cove

ROAD REEF

Burnt Point

Old Government House Museum
Fort Burt

0   1/4 mi
0   1/4 km

MacNamara Rd.

Road Town

ATLANTIC OCEAN

Brewers Bay Pinnacle

Shark Bay

Rough Pt.

Hell Hole

Brewers Bay

Brewers Bay

Dubois Pt.

Mt. Healthy National Park
Skyworld

Todman Pk.

Cane Garden Bay Rd

Ridge Rd.

[13]

[12] [9]

Cane Garden Bay

Leonard's

Windy Hill

Joe's Hill Rd.

Road Town see inset

Carrot Bay

Apple Bay

Long Bay West

[9] [6]

Sage Mountain National Park

Ridge Rd.

Dolphin Discovery

[11] [8]

[15]

Sea Cows Bay

Smuggler's Cove

Lower Belmont Bay

[10] [7]

Sage Mtn.

Sea Cows Bay

Great Thatch Island

Steele Pt.

[8]

Zion Hill Rd.

West End

Freshwater Pond

Soper's Hole

[7]

Little Thatch Island

[5]

Soper's Hole

Frenchman's Cay

[4]

Fort Recovery

← TO ST. THOMAS

0   2 mi
0   2 km

The Indians

The Indians

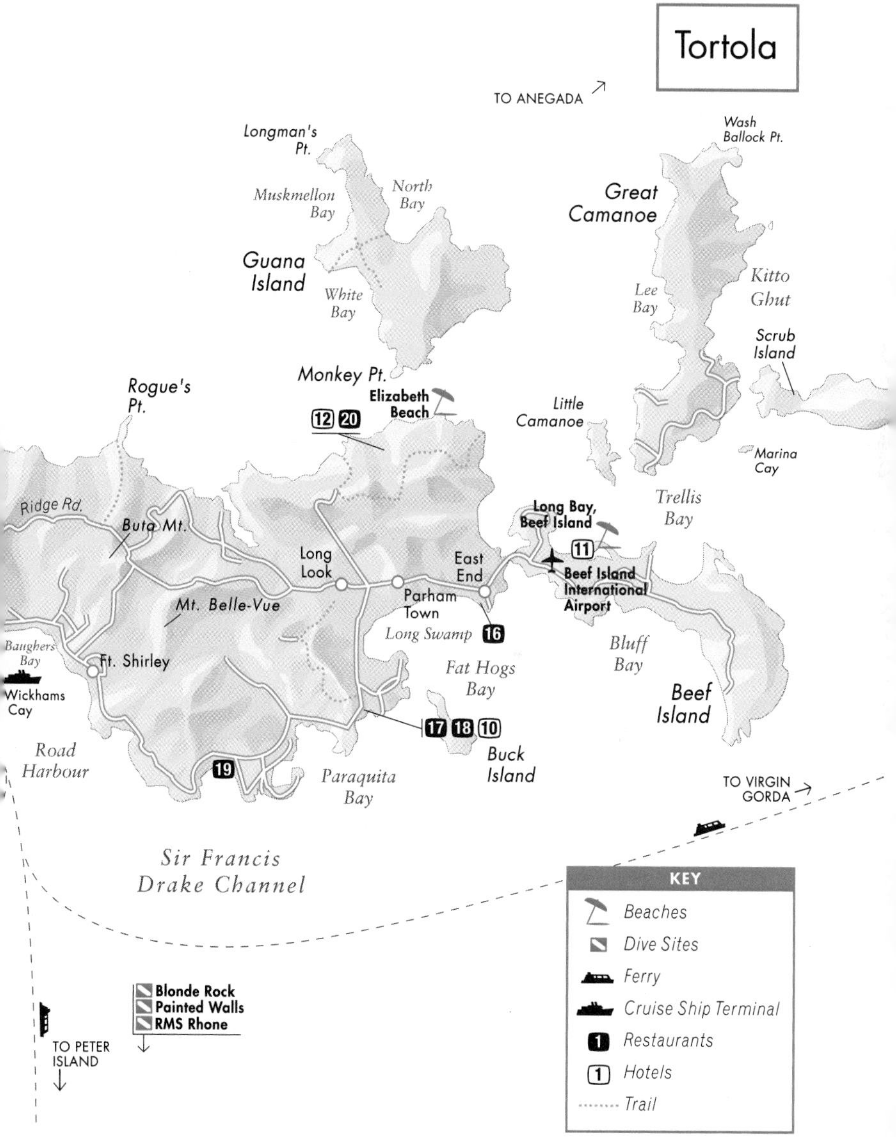

Tortola
TO ANEGADA
Longman's Pt.
Muskmellon Bay
North Bay
Guana Island
White Bay
Great Camanoe
Wash Ballock Pt.
Lee Bay
Kitto Ghut
Scrub Island
Monkey Pt.
Rogue's Pt.
Elizabeth Beach
12 20
Little Camanoe
Marina Cay
Trellis Bay
Ridge Rd.
Buta Mt.
Long Bay, Beef Island
11
Long Look
East End
Beef Island International Airport
Parham Town
Mt. Belle-Vue
Long Swamp
16
Baughers Bay
Ft. Shirley
Wickhams Cay
Fat Hogs Bay
Bluff Bay
Beef Island
17 18 10
Road Harbour
19
Buck Island
Paraquita Bay
TO VIRGIN GORDA
Sir Francis Drake Channel
KEY
Beaches
Dive Sites
Ferry
Cruise Ship Terminal
Restaurants
Hotels
Trail
Blonde Rock
Painted Walls
RMS Rhone
TO PETER ISLAND

Quito's Gazebo **13**
Roti Palace **1**
Sebastian's Beach
Bar & Restaurant **10**
Skywolrd **14**
Spaghetti Junction **3**
Sugar Mill **11**
Turtles **20**

American or British?

Yes, the Union Jack flutters overhead in the tropical breeze, schools operate on the British system, place names have British spellings, Queen Elizabeth II appoints the governor—and the queen's picture hangs on many walls. Indeed, residents celebrate the queen's birthday every June with a public ceremony. You can overhear that charming English accent from a good handful of expats when you're lunching at Road Town restaurants, and you can buy British biscuits—which Americans call cookies—in the supermarkets.

But you can pay for your lunch and the biscuits with American money, because the U.S. dollar is legal tender here. The unusual circumstance is a matter of geography. The practice started in the mid-20th century, when BVI residents went to work in the nearby USVI. On trips home, they brought their U.S. dollars with them.

Soon, they abandoned the barter system, and in 1959, the U.S. dollar became the official form of money. Interestingly, the government sells stamps for use only in the BVI that often carry pictures of Queen Elizabeth II and other royalty with the monetary value in U.S. dollars and cents.

The American influence continued to grow when Americans began to open businesses in the BVI because they preferred its quieter ambience to the hustle and bustle of St. Thomas. Inevitably, cable and satellite TV's U.S.-based programming, along with Hollywood-made movies, further influenced life in the BVI. And most goods are shipped from St. Thomas in the USVI, meaning you can find more American-made Oreos than British-produced Peak Freens on the supermarket shelves.

A few hotels lack air-conditioning, relying instead on ceiling fans to capture the almost constant trade winds. Nights are cool and breezy, even in midsummer, and never reach the temperatures or humidity levels that are common in much of the United States. You may assume that all accommodations listed here have air-conditioning unless we mention otherwise. Remember that some places may be closed during the peak of hurricane season—August through October—to give their owners a much-needed break.

VILLAS

Renting a villa is growing in popularity. Vacationers like the privacy, the space to spread out, and the opportunity to cook meals. As is true everywhere, the most important thing is location. If you want to be close to the beach, opt for a villa on the North Shore. If you want to dine out in Road Town every night, a villa closer to town may be a better bet. Prices per week during the winter season run from around $2,000 for a one- or two-bedroom villa up to $10,000 for a five-room beachfront villa. Rates in summer are substantially less. Most, but not all, villas accept credit cards.

Areana Villas (Box 263, Road Town VG1110 284/494–5864 www. areanavillas.com) represents top-of-the-line properties. Pastel-color villas with one to six bedrooms can accommodate up to 10 guests. Many have pools, whirlpool tubs, and tiled courtyards.

The St. Thomas–based **McLaughlin-Anderson Luxury Villas** (✆*1000 Blackbeard's Hill, Suite 3, St. Thomas USVI00802-6739* ☎*340/776–0635 or 800/537–6246* ⊕*www.mclaughlinanderson.com*) manages nearly three dozen properties around Tortola. Villas range in size from one to six bedrooms and come with full kitchens and stellar views. Most have pools. The company can hire a chef and stock your kitchen with groceries.

Purple Pineapple Villa Rentals (✆*95167 Bermuda Dr., Fernandina Beach, FL 32034* ☎*904/415–1231 or 866/867–8652* ⊕*www.purplepineapple. com*) manages seven luxury homes in locations all over the island. Most have pools, hot tubs, and other amenities. Villas range in size from one to six bedrooms.

Smiths Gore (✆*Box 135, Road Town VG1110* ☎*284/494–2446* ⊕*www. smithsgore.com*) has properties all over the island, but many are in the Smuggler's Cove area. They range in size from two to five to bedrooms. They all have stellar views, lovely furnishings, and lush landscaping.

6

HOTELS & INNS

ROAD TOWN

\$\$ ⌂**Moorings-Mariner Inn.** If you enjoy the camaraderie of a busy marina, this inn on the edge of Road Town may appeal to you. It's a hot spot for charter boaters—usually a lively group—heading out for weeklong sails around the islands. Rooms are spacious and have balconies or porches that are perfect for an afternoon's relaxing. All have pastel accents that complement the peach exteriors. **Pros:** Good dining options, friendly guests, excellent spot to charter boats. **Cons:** Busy location, long walk to Road Town, need car to get around. ⊠ *Waterfront Dr., Box 139,* ☎*284/494–2333 or 800/535–7289* ⇆*36 rooms, 4 suites* ♿*In-room: kitchen (some), refrigerator, dial-up. In-hotel: restaurant, bar, pool, diving, no elevator, public Internet* ▤*MC, V* ⫟*EP.*

\$\$ ⌂**Village Cay Resort & Marina.** If you want to be able to walk to restaurants and shops, you simply can't beat the prime location in the heart of Road Town. It's perfect for charter-yachters who want a night or two in town before heading out to sea, but land-based vacationers like it equally well. Rooms and suites are done in tropical style with tile floors, rattan furniture, and town or marina views. You'll need a car to get to the beach. Otherwise, a tiny pool will have to suffice for your morning swim. **Pros:** Prime location, shops and restaurants nearby, nautical ambience. **Cons:** Little parking, busy street, need car to get around. ⊠ *Wickham's Cay I, Box 145,* ☎*284/494–2771* ⊕*www. igy-villagecay.com* ⇆*21 rooms, 3 suites* ♿*In-room: refrigerator, Ethernet. In-hotel: restaurant, bar, pool, spa, no elevator, public Internet, public Wi-Fi* ▤*AE, MC, V* ⫟*EP.*

OUTSIDE ROAD TOWN

$$$$ **Sugar Mill Hotel.** Though it's not a sprawling resort, this is our favor-
FodorśChoice ite place to stay on Tortola. The rooms are attractively decorated with
★ more than the usual floral spreads and have balconies with good views,
kitchens or kitchenettes, and even some sofa beds. The grounds get
accolades for their lovely gardens, but many say the real reason to
stay here is the easy access to the excellent restaurant, which has both
superb food and a stunning setting in the property's old sugar mill. The
owners, food and travel writers Jeff and Jinx Morgan, have brought
all their expertise to this well-run small resort. The north-shore location puts you across the road from a nice beach, but you need a car to
do anything more than enjoy the sun and sand. **Pros:** Lovely rooms,
excellent restaurant, nice views. **Cons:** On busy road, small beach,
need car to get around. ⊠ *Apple Bay* ⬠ *Box 425, Road Town V1130*
☎ *284/495–4355 or 800/462–8834* ⊕ *www.sugarmillhotel.com* ⟿ *19
rooms, 2 suites, 1 villa, 1 cottage* ⚑ *In-room: safe, kitchen (some), no
TV (some), Wi-Fi. In-hotel: 2 restaurants, bars, pool, beachfront, water
sports, no elevator, public Internet* ⊟ *AE, MC, V* ⦶ *EP.*

$$$$ **Surfsong Villa Resort.** Nested in lush foliage right at the water's edge,
FodorśChoice this small resort on Beef Island provides a pleasant respite for vacation-
★ ers who want a villa atmosphere with some hotel amenities. The hotel
has a chef who whips up meals for an extra charge. A studio villa with
minimal kitchen facilities is tucked up in the trees, but the one- and
two-bedroom villa are right at the water's edge. It takes about a minute
to walk to Sandy Well Bay Beach. Wood furniture and attractive tile
floors provide a comfortable ambience. The public spaces are equally
cozy, with pergolas providing shade. Service such as massage as well
as yoga and Pilates classes are available. **Pros:** Lovely rooms, beautiful beach, chef on call. **Cons:** Need car to get around, no restaurants
nearby. ⊠ *Beef Island* ⬠ *Box 606, Road Town VG1110* ☎ *284/495–
1864* ⊕ *www.surfsong.net* ⟿ *1 suite, 3 villas* ⚑ *In-room: no a/c (some),
safes, gym, kitchen, DVD, Ethernet. In-hotel: beachfront, water sports,
bicycles, no elevator, laundry service, concierge, public Internet, public
Wi-Fi, airport shuttle, no children under 8* ⊟ *MC, V* ⦶ *EP.*

$$$-$$$$ **Fort Recovery Beachfront Villas.** This is one of those small but special
☾ properties, distinguished by friendly service and the chance to get to
★ know your fellow guests rather than the poshness of the rooms and
the upscale amenities. Villas come in several sizes, and all are quaint—
though not fancy—and have good views across the water toward St.
John. A sandy beach stretches seaside, providing calm waters perfect for
kids. The emphasis on wellness is a welcome touch, and beachside yoga
classes are a specialty. The staff is helpful and will arrange day sails
and scuba-diving trips. **Pros:** Beautiful beach, spacious units, historic
site. **Cons:** Need car to get around, isolated location. ⊠ *Waterfront
Dr., Box 239, Pockwood Pond* ☎ *284/495–4354 or 800/367–8455*
⊕ *www.fortrecovery.com* ⟿ *29 suites, 1 villa* ⚑ *In-room: kitchen, dial-
up, Wi-Fi. In-hotel: pool, gym, beachfront, water sports, no elevator,
laundry service, public Internet* ⊟ *AE, MC, V* ⦶ *EP.*

$$$-$$$$ **Long Bay Beach Resort.** Although the service draws an occasional
complaint, the management has been addressing the frosty attitude
of some staff members. Long Bay Beach Resort is still Tortola's only

choice if you want all the resort amenities, including a beach, scads of water sports, tennis courts, and even a pitch-and-putt golf course. Accommodations range from traditional hotel rooms to three-bedroom villas, with lots of choices in between. All have a modern tropical feel with rattan furniture and brightly colored fabrics. Given its relative isolation on the northwest shore, you may not be inclined to make many excursions. Luckily, the Palm Terrace Garden Restaurant serves romantic dinners. **Pros:** Resort atmosphere, good restaurants, many activities. **Cons:** Need car to get around, sometimes curt staff, uphill hike to some rooms. ⊠ *Long Bay* 🖂 *Box 433, Road Town VG1130* ☎ *284/495–4252 or 800/345–0271* ⊕ *www.longbay.com* ↩ *53 rooms, 37 suites, 26 villas* ♿ *In-room: safe, kitchen (some), dial-up. In-hotel: 3 restaurants, bars, tennis courts, pool, gym, spa, beachfront, diving, water sports, no elevator, public Internet, public Wi-Fi* ⊟ *AE, MC, V* ⲓⲟⲓ *EP.*

$$$ ▦ **Sebastian's on the Beach.** Sitting on the island's north coast, Sebastian's definitely has a beachy feel, and that's its primary charm. Rooms vary in amenities and price, with the remodeled beachfront rooms a bit more up-to-date than those that the hotel calls "beach rear." The beachfront rooms have the best views and put you right on the sand. The less expensive rooms are basic, across the street from the ocean, and lack views. Those nearest the intersection of North Coast Road and Zion Hill Road suffer from traffic noise. Although you can eat all your meals at the resort's enjoyable restaurant, the wonderful Sugar Mill Restaurant is just a short drive east. **Pros:** Nice beach, good restaurants, beachfront rooms. **Cons:** On busy road, some rooms nicer than others, need car to get around. ⊠ *Apple Bay* 🖂 *Box 441, Road Town VG1110* ☎ *284/495–4212 or 800/336–4870* ⊕ *www.sebastiansbvi.com* ↩ *26 rooms, 9 villas* ♿ *In-room: refrigerator, no TV (some). In-hotel: restaurant, bar, beachfront, no elevator, public Internet, public Wi-Fi* ⊟ *AE, D, MC, V* ⲓⲟⲓ *EP.*

$$–$$$ ▦ **Lambert Beach Resort.** Although this isolated location on the northeast coast puts you far from Road Town, Lambert Bay is one of the island's loveliest stretches of sand and the main reason to recommend this resort. Rooms are tucked back in the foliage, but you're a few steps away from an afternoon of sunning and swimming. A handful of restaurants in and around nearby Fat Hogs Bay are within easy reach if you have to get off that gorgeous beach. At this writing, construction was set to begin on a complete renovation. Ask about the progress if you fear construction noise will be a problem. **Pros:** Lovely beach, beautiful setting, good restaurant. **Cons:** Bland rooms, isolated location, need car to get around. ⊠ *Lambert Bay, Box 534, East End* ☎ *284/495–2877* ⊕ *www.lambertresort.com* ↩ *38 rooms, 2 villas, 27 condos* ♿ *In-room: kitchen (some), refrigerator, dial-up (some). In-hotel: restaurant, bar, tennis court, pool, spa, beachfront, water sports, no elevator, public Internet* ⊟ *AE, D, MC, V* ⲓⲟⲓ *EP.*

$$ ▦ **Hodge's Creek Marina Hotel.** Sitting marina-side on the island's East End, this hotel puts you in the middle of the nautical action. If you're heading out on a chartered sailboat or if you especially enjoy the marine scene, this is definitely the place for you. Rooms are carpeted and have tiny balconies, but brightly colored spreads and curtains give them a tropical feel. There's a small pool and the CalaMaya Restaurant in the complex. **Pros:** Marina atmosphere, good restaurant, some shopping. **Cons:** Bland rooms, need car to get around. ⊠ *Hodge's Creek* ⌂ *Box 663, Road Town VG1110* ☎ *284/494–5000* ⊕ *www.hodgescreek.com* ⌖ *29 rooms* ⌂ *In-hotel: restaurant, pool, no elevator, public Internet* ⊟ *AE, MC, V* ⦿ *EP.*

$$ 🏨 **Myett's.** Tucked away in a beachfront garden, this tiny hotel puts you right in the middle of Cane Garden Bay's busy nightlife. The restaurant is one of the area's hot spots. Rooms have a typical tropical feel, thanks to the tile floors and rattan furniture. Although you might be content to lounge at the beach and stroll around the bay, you'll need a car to get out and about. **Pros:** Beautiful beach, good restaurant, shops nearby. **Cons:** Busy location, loud music, need car to get around. ⊠ *Cane Garden Bay* ⌂ *Box 556, Cane Garden Bay VG1130* ☎ *284/495–9649* ⊕ *www.myettent.com* ⌖ *6 rooms* ⌂ *In-room: refrigerator. In-hotel: restaurant, spa, beachfront, no elevator, public Internet, public Wi-Fi* ⊟ *AE, MC, V* ⦿ *EP.*

$$ 🏨 **Nanny Cay Hotel.** This quiet oasis is far enough from Road Town to give it a secluded feel but close enough to make shops and restaurants convenient. You're just steps from the hotel's restaurant, boat charters, and the chance to stroll the busy boatyard to gawk at the yachts under repair, but you still have to drive a good 20 minutes to get to the closest beach at Cane Garden Bay. The cheerful rooms, which have tile floors, are enlivened by lots of bright Caribbean colors. **Pros:** Nearby shops and restaurant, pleasant rooms, marina atmosphere. **Cons:** Busy location, need car to get around. ⊠ *Nanny Cay* ⌂ *Box 281, Road Town VG1110* ☎ *284/494–2512* ⊕ *www.nannycay.com* ⌖ *38 rooms* ⌂ *In-room: kitchen (some), refrigerator. In-hotel: 2 restaurants, tennis court, pool, diving, no elevator, public Internet, public Wi-Fi* ⊟ *MC, V* ⦿ *EP.*

WHERE TO EAT

Local seafood is plentiful on Tortola, and although other fresh ingredients are scarce, the island's chefs are a creative lot who apply their skills to whatever the boat delivers. Contemporary American dishes with Caribbean influences are very popular, but you can find French and Italian fare as well. The more expensive restaurants have dress codes: long pants and collared shirts for men and elegant but casual resort wear for women. Prices are often a bit higher than you'd expect to pay back home and the service can sometimes be a tad on the slow side, but enjoy the chance to linger over the view.

ROAD TOWN

CARIBBEAN   ✕ **Roti Palace.** You might be tempted to pass this tiny spot on Road
$–$$ Town's Main Street when you see the plastic tablecloths and fake flow-
★   ers, but owner Jean Leonard's reputation for dishing up fantastic roti is known far and wide. This flatbread is filled with curried potatoes, onions and lobster, chicken, beef, conch, goat, or vegetables. Ask for the bone out if you order the chicken to save yourself the trouble of

fishing them out of your mouth. ⊠ *Main St., Road Town* ☎*284/494–4196* ▭ *No credit cards* ⊙ *Closed Sun.*

ECLECTIC $$–$$$
✕ **CafeSito.** Don't be put off by the pedestrian decor. The chef at this shopping-center spot conjures up delicious dishes that run the gamut from burgers to lobster to chicken alfredo. It's the place to go for pizza smothered with everything from the standard cheese and tomato to the more unusual chicken and bacon. In winter the staff will deliver anything from its menu straight to your hotel. ⊠ *Wickham's Cay I, Waterfront Dr.* ☎*284/494–7412* ▭ *MC, V.*

FRENCH $$$–$$$$
✕ **Le Cabanon.** Birds and bougainvillea brighten the patio of this breezy French restaurant and bar, a popular gathering spot for locals and visitors alike. French onion soup and herring salad are good appetizer choices. From there, move on to the grilled tuna with foie gras, sole in a brown butter sauce, or beef tenderloin with green peppercorn sauce. Save room for such tasty desserts as chocolate cake and crème brûlée, or opt for a platter of French cheeses. ⊠ *Waterfront Dr.* ☎*284/494–8660* ▭ *D, MC, V* ⊙ *Closed Sun.*

ITALIAN $$–$$$$
★
✕ **Spaghetti Junction.** Popular with the boating crowd, this longtime favorite serves up such West Indian dishes as stewed oxtail along with Italian favorites like penne smothered in a spicy tomato sauce, spinach-mushroom lasagna, and angel-hair pasta with shellfish. For something that combines a bit of both, try the spicy jambalaya pasta. You can also find old-fashioned favorites like lobster thermidor on the menu. ⊠*Blackburn Hwy., Baughers Bay* ☎*284/494–4880* ▭ *AE, MC, V* ⊙ *Closed Sun.*

$–$$
★
✕ **Capriccio di Mare.** The owners of the well-known Brandywine Bay restaurant also run this authentic Italian outdoor café. Stop by for an espresso, fresh pastry, a bowl of perfectly cooked penne, or a crispy tomato and mozzarella pizza. Drink specialties include a mango Bellini, an adaptation of the famous cocktail served at Harry's Bar in Venice. ⊠ *Waterfront Dr.* ☎*284/494–5369* ⚞*Reservations not accepted* ▭ *MC, V* ⊙ *Closed Sun.*

SEAFOOD $$$–$$$$
✕ **The Captain's Table.** Select the lobster you want from the pool, but be careful not to fall in—it's in the floor right in the middle of the dining room. The menu also includes traditional conch fritters, steak with mushroom sauce, duckling with a coconut rum glaze, and creative daily specials that usually include freshly caught fish. Ceiling fans keep the dining room cool, but there are also tables on a breezy terrace overlooking the harbor. ⊠ *Wickham's Cay I* ☎*284/494–3885* ▭ *MC, V* ⊙ *No lunch Sat.*

OUTSIDE ROAD TOWN

AMERICAN–
CASUAL
$$$–$$$$
☾
✕ **Pusser's Landing.** Yachters navigate their way to this waterfront restaurant. Downstairs, from late morning to well into the evening, you can belly up to the outdoor mahogany bar or sit downstairs for sandwiches, fish-and-chips, and pizzas. At dinnertime head upstairs for a harbor view and a quiet alfresco meal of grilled steak or local fish. ⊠*Soper's Hole* ☎*284/495–4554* ▭ *AE, MC, V.*

6

$$–$$$$ ✕**Fat Hog Bob's.** With an open-to-the-breeze ambience, this casual eatery dishes up delicious burgers, pastas, and fish dishes for lunch and dinner. That said, folks come here for the ribs simmered to perfection in a spicy sauce. ⊠ *Blackburn Hwy., Hodge's Creek* ☎ *284/494– 1010* ⊟ *MC, V.*

CARIBBEAN   ✕**Quito's Gazebo.** This rustic beachside bar and restaurant is owned and
$$–$$$$ operated by island native Quito Rymer, a multitalented recording star who plays and sings solo on Tuesday and Thursday and performs with his reggae band on Friday and Saturday. The menu is Caribbean, with an emphasis on fresh fish. Try the conch fritters or the chicken roti. ⊠ *Cane Garden Bay* ☎ *284/495–4837* ⊟ *AE, MC, V* ☾ *Closed Mon.*

$$–$$$ ✕**Myett's Garden & Grille.** Right on the beach, this bi-level restaurant and bar is hopping day and night. Chowder made with fresh conch is the specialty here, although the menu includes everything from vegetarian dishes to grilled shrimp, steak, and tuna. There's live entertainment every night in winter. ⊠ *Cane Garden Bay* ☎ *284/495–9649* ⊟ *AE, MC, V.*

CONTINENTAL   ✕**Skyworld.** The top of a mountain is the location for this casually
$$$$ elegant dining room. The menu changes constantly, but look for imagi-
☼   native dishes such as New York strip steak with a brandy and mustard sauce and grilled yellowfin tuna with a pineapple-mango glaze. Other specialties include grilled local fish, roast duck, rack of lamb, and key lime pie. The lunch menu runs to hamburgers and sandwiches with some interesting additions such as a goat cheese tartlet. The restaurant can be crowded at midday when cruise ships dock. ⊠ *Ridge Rd., Joe's Hill* ☎ *284/494–3567* ⊟ *AE, MC, V.*

$$$–$$$$ ✕**Palm Terrace Garden Restaurant.** Relax over dinner in this open-air eatery at Long Bay Beach Resort. Tables are well spaced, offering enough privacy for intimate conversations. The menu changes daily, but several dishes show up regularly. Start your meal with cheese ravioli with wild mushrooms in a garlic cream sauce, Caribbean-style fish and potato chowder, and shrimp cocktail. Entrées include snapper crusted with cornmeal, pan-seared tuna with a mango-caper coulis, and T-bone steak seasoned with peppercorns. There are always at least five desserts to choose from, which might include Belgian chocolate mousse, strawberry cheesecake, or a fluffy lemon and coconut cake. ⊠ *Long Bay Beach Resort, Long Bay* ☎ *284/495–4252* ⊟ *AE, D, MC, V* ☾ *No lunch.*

ECLECTIC   ✕**Eclipse.** This popular waterfront spot isn't much more than a terrace
$$$–$$$$ filled with tables, but you can be caressed by the soft ocean breezes
★   while you're impressed with the cuisine. With dishes from all over the globe, the menu is certainly well traveled. The garden lounge serves lighter fare—try the coconut shrimp, the seafood linguine, or maybe a slice or two of freshly baked pizza. In the main dining room, you can find dishes like bacon and cheese wrapped filet mignon and chicken with a Parmesan cheese and marsala wine sauce, and tuna dusted with seaweed, soy, and ginger. ⊠ *Fat Hog's Bay, East End* ☎ *284/495–1646* ⊟ *MC, V* ☾ *No lunch weekends.*

$$$–$$$$ ✕**Sugar Mill Restaurant.** Candles gleam, and the background music is
Fodor'sChoice peaceful in this romantic restaurant inside a 17th-century sugar mill.
★ Well-prepared selections on the à la carte menu, which changes nightly,
include some pasta and vegetarian entrées. Lobster bisque with basil
croutons and a creamy conch chowder are good starters. Favorite
entrées include fresh fish baked in banana leaves, filet mignon topped
with an herb-cream sauce, pan-roasted quail, and pumpkin and black
bean lasagna. ⊠*Sugar Mill Hotel, Apple Bay* ✆*Box 425, Road Town*
☎*284/495–4355* ⊟*AE, MC, V* ☺*No lunch.*

$$–$$$$ ✕**Sebastian's Beach Bar & Restaurant.** The waves practically lap at your
feet at this beachfront restaurant on Tortola's northern shore. The
menu runs to seafood—especially lobster, conch, and local fish—but
you can also find dishes like ginger chicken and filet mignon. It's a
perfect spot to stop for lunch on your around-the-island tour. Try the
grilled dolphinfish sandwich, served on a soft roll with an oniony tartar
sauce. Finish off with a cup of Sebastian's coffee spiked with home-
brewed rum. ⊠*North Coast Rd., Apple Bay* ☎*284/494–4212* ⊟*AE,
D, MC, V.*

$$$ ✕**CalaMaya.** Casual fare is what you can find at this waterfront res-
taurant. You can always order a burger or lobster salad; the grilled
Kaiser sandwich—shrimp, cheese, and pineapple on a crisp roll—is a
tasty alternative. For dinner, try the snapper with onions, peppers, and
thyme. ⊠*Hodge's Creek Marina, Blackburn Hwy.* ☎*284/495–2126*
⊟*AE, MC, V.*

$$$ ✕**Turtles.** If you're touring the island, Turtles is a good place to stop
for lunch or dinner. Sitting near the ocean at Lambert Beach Resort,
this casual place provides a relaxing respite from the rigors of navigating mountain roads. At dinner you might find tiger shrimp in a curry
sauce or rack of lamb with a raspberry glaze. Lunch favorites include
fried shrimp, fresh tuna on a bun, and pasta dishes. ⊠*Lambert Beach
Resort, Lambert Bay, East End* ☎*284/495–2877* ⊟*AE, D, MC, V.*

$$–$$$ ✕**Jolly Roger Restaurant.** This casual, open-air restaurant near the ferry
terminal is as popular with locals as it is with visitors. The menu ranges
from burgers to rib-eye steak to the island favorite, local lobster. Try
the savory fritters filled with tender local conch and herbs for a good
start to your dinner. End it with a slice of sweet key lime pie. ⊠*West
End* ☎*284/495–4559* ⊟*AE, D, MC, V.*

$$–$$$ ✕**Mountain View.** It's worth the drive up Sage Mountain for lunch or
Fodor'sChoice dinner at this casual restaurant. The view is spectacular—one of the
★ best on Tortola. The small menu includes dishes like veal with a ginger
sauce and grilled mahimahi in a lime-onion sauce. The lobster salad
sandwich is the house lunch specialty. If it's on the menu, don't pass up
the chicken roti. ⊠*Sage Mountain* ✆*Box 4036, Road Town VG1110*
☎*284/495–9536* ⊟*MC, V.*

ITALIAN ✕**Brandywine Bay.** At this restaurant in Brandywine Bay, candlelighted
$$$–$$$$ outdoor tables have sweeping views of nearby islands. Owner Davide
Fodor'sChoice Pugliese prepares foods the Tuscan way: grilled with lots of fresh herbs.
★ The remarkable menu may include duck with a mango sauce, beef
carpaccio, grilled swordfish, and veal chop with ricotta and sun-dried
tomatoes. The homemade mozzarella is another standout. The wine list

is excellent, and the lemon tart and the tiramisu are irresistible. ⊠*Sir Francis Drake Hwy., east of Road Town, Brandywine Bay* ⌂*Box 2914, East End* ☎*284/495–2301* ◬*Reservations essential* ☰*AE, MC, V* ☉*Closed Sun. No lunch.*

BEACHES

Beaches in the BVI are less developed than those on St. Thomas or St. Croix, but they are also less inviting. The best BVI beaches are on deserted islands reachable only by boats, so take a snorkeling or sailing trip at least once. Tortola's north side has several perfect palm-fringed, white-sand beaches that curl around turquoise bays and coves, but none really achieves greatness. Nearly all are accessible by car (preferably a four-wheel-drive vehicle), albeit down bumpy roads that corkscrew precipitously. Some of these beaches are lined with bars and restaurants as well as water-sports equipment stalls; others have absolutely nothing.

Apple Bay. If you want to surf, the area including Little Apple Bay and Capoon's Bay is the spot—although the white, sandy beach itself is narrow. Sebastian's, a casual hotel, caters to those in search of the perfect wave. The legendary Bomba's Surfside Shack—a landmark festooned with all manner of flotsam and jetsam—serves drinks and casual food. Otherwise, there's nothing else in the way of amenities. Good waves are never a sure thing, but you're more apt to find them in January and February. If you're swimming and the waves are up, take care not to get dashed on the rocks. ⊠*North Shore Rd. at Zion Hill Rd.*

Brewers Bay. The water here is good for snorkeling, and you can find a campground with showers and bathrooms and beach bar tucked in the foliage right behind the beach. An old sugar mill and ruins of a rum distillery are off the beach along the road. The beach is easy to find, but the paved roads leading down the hill to it can be a bit daunting. You can get there from either Brewers Bay Road East or Brewers Bay Road West. ⊠*Brewers Bay Rd. E off Cane Garden Bay Rd., or Brewers Bay Rd. W off Ridge Rd.*

Cane Garden Bay. This silky stretch of sand has exceptionally calm, crystalline waters—except when storms at sea turn the water murky. Snorkeling is good along the edges. Casual guesthouses, restaurants, bars, and even shops are steps from the beach in the growing village of the same name. The beach is a laid-back, even somewhat funky place to put down your towel. It's the closest beach to Road Town—one steep uphill and downhill drive—and one of the BVI's best-known anchorages (unfortunately, it can be very crowded). Water-sports shops rent equipment. ⊠*Cane Garden Bay Rd. off Ridge Rd.*

Elizabeth Beach. Home to Lambert Beach Resort, the palm-lined, wide, and sandy beach has parking on its steep downhill access road. Other than at the hotel, which welcomes nonguests, there are no amenities aside from peace and quiet. Turn at the sign for Lambert Beach Resort. If you miss it, you wind up at Her Majesty's Prison. ⊠*Lambert Rd. off Ridge Rd., on eastern end of island.*

Long Bay, Beef Island. The scenery here is superlative: the beach stretches seemingly forever, and you can catch a glimpse of Little Camanoe and Great Camanoe islands. If you walk around the bend to the right, you can see little Marina Cay and Scrub Island. Long Bay is also a good place to search for seashells. Swim out to wherever you see a dark patch for some nice snorkeling. There are no amenities, so come prepared with your own drinks and snacks. Turn left shortly after crossing the bridge to Beef Island. ⊠ *Beef Island Rd., Beef Island.*

Long Bay West. Have your camera ready to snap the breathtaking approach to this stunning, mile-long stretch of white sand. Although Long Bay Resort sprawls along part of it, the entire beach is open to the public. The water isn't as calm here as at Cane Garden or Brewers Bay, but it's still swimable. Rent water-sports equipment and enjoy the beachfront restaurant at the resort. Turn left at Zion Hill Road; then travel about half a mile. ⊠ *Long Bay Rd.*

Smuggler's Cove. After bouncing your way down a pothole-filled dirt road to this beautiful, palm-fringed beach, you'll feel as if you've found a hidden piece of the island. You probably won't be alone on weekends, though, when the beach fills with snorkelers and sunbathers. There's a fine view of Jost Van Dyke from the shore. The beach is popular with Long Bay Resort guests who want a change of scenery, but there are no amenities. Follow Long Bay Road past Long Bay Resort, keeping to the roads nearest the water until you reach the beach. It's about a mile past the resort. ⊠ *Long Bay Rd.*

SPORTS & THE OUTDOORS

DIVING & SNORKELING

Clear waters and numerous reefs afford some wonderful opportunities for underwater exploration. In some spots visibility reaches 100 feet, but colorful reefs teeming with fish are often just a few feet below the sea surface. The BVI's system of marine parks means the underwater life visible through your mask will stay protected.

There are several popular dive spots around the islands. **Alice in Wonderland** is a deep dive south of Ginger Island with a wall that slopes gently from 15 feet to 100 feet. It's an area overrun with huge mushroom-shape coral, hence its name. Crabs, lobsters, and shimmering fan corals make their homes in the tunnels, ledges, and overhangs of **Blonde Rock,** a pinnacle that goes from 15 feet below the surface to 60 feet deep. It's between Dead Chest and Salt Island. When the currents aren't too strong, **Brewers Bay Pinnacle** (20 to 90 feet down) teems with sea life. At the **Indians,** near Pelican Island, colorful corals decorate canyons and grottoes created by four large, jagged pinnacles that rise 50 feet from the ocean floor. The **Painted Walls** is a shallow dive site where corals and sponges create a kaleidoscope of colors on the walls of four long gullies. It's northeast of Dead Chest.

The *Chikuzen,* sunk northwest of Brewers Bay in 1981, is a 246-foot vessel in 75 feet of water; it's home to thousands of fish, colorful corals, and big rays. In 1867 the **RMS** *Rhone,* a 310-foot royal mail steamer, split in two when it sank in a devastating hurricane. It's so well preserved that it was used as an underwater prop in the movie *The Deep*. You can see the crow's nest and bowsprit, the cargo hold in the bow, and the engine and enormous propeller shaft in the stern. Its four parts are at various depths from 30 to 80 feet. Get yourself some snorkeling gear and hop aboard a dive boat to this wreck near Salt Island (across the channel from Road Town). Every dive outfit in the BVI runs scuba and snorkel tours to this part of the BVI National Parks Trust; if you only have time for one trip, make it this one. Rates start at around $60 for a one-tank dive and $90 for a two-tank dive.

Your hotel probably has a dive company right on the premises. If not, the staff can recommend one nearby. Using your hotel's dive company makes a trip to the offshore dive and snorkel sites a breeze. Just stroll down to the dock and hop aboard. All dive companies are certified by PADI, the Professional Association of Diving Instructors, which ensures your instructors are qualified to safely take vacationers diving. The boats are also inspected to make sure they're seaworthy. If you've never dived, try a short introductory dive, often called a resort course, which teaches you enough to get you under water. In the unlikely event you get a case of the bends, a condition that can happen when you rise to the surface too fast, your dive team will whisk you to the decompression chamber at Roy L. Schneider Regional Medical Center Hospital in nearby St. Thomas.

Blue Waters Divers (⊠ *Nanny Cay* ☎ *284/494–2847* ⊠ *Soper's Hole, West End* ☎ *284/495–1200* ⊕ *www.bluewaterdiversbvi.com*) teaches resort, open-water, rescue, and advanced diving courses, and also makes daily dive trips. If you're chartering a sailboat, the company's boat will meet your boat at Peter, Salt, Norman, or Cooper Island for a rendezvous dive. Rates include all equipment as well as instruction. Reserve two days in advance. **Dive Tortola** (⊠ *Prospect Reef* ☎ *284/494–9200* ⊕ *www.divetortola.com*) offers beginner and advanced diving courses and daily dive trips. Trainers teach open-water, rescue, advanced diving, and resort courses. Dive Tortola also offers a rendezvous diving option for folks on charter sailboats.

FISHING

Most of the boats that take you deep-sea fishing for bluefish, wahoo, swordfish, and shark leave from nearby St. Thomas, but local anglers like to fish the shallower water for bonefish. A half day runs about $480, a full day around $850. Call **Caribbean Fly Fishing** (⊠ *Nanny Cay* ☎ *284/494–4797* ⊕ *www.caribflyfishing.com*).

HIKING

☾ Sage Mountain National Park attracts hikers who enjoy the quiet trails that crisscross the island's loftiest peak. There are some lovely views and the chance to see rare species that grow only at higher elevations.

SAILING

Fodor'sChoice
★
☾
The BVI are among the world's most popular sailing destinations. They're clustered together and surrounded by calm waters, so it's fairly easy to sail from one anchorage to the next. Most of the Caribbean's

biggest sailboat charter companies have operations in Tortola. If you know how to sail, you can charter a bareboat (perhaps for your entire vacation); if you're unschooled, you can hire a boat with a captain. Prices vary depending on the type and size of the boat you wish to charter. In season, a weekly charter runs from $1,500 to $35,000. Book early to make sure you get the boat that fits you best. Most of Tortola's marinas have hotels, which give you a convenient place to spend the nights before and after your charter.

If a day-sail to some secluded anchorage is more your spot of tea, the BVI have numerous boats of various sizes and styles that leave from many points around Tortola. Prices start at around $80 per person for a full-day sail, including lunch and snorkeling equipment.

BVI Yacht Charters (✉ *Port Purcell, Road Town* ☎ *284/494–4289 or 888/615–4006* ⊕ *www.bviyachtcharters.com*) offers 31-foot to 71-foot sailboats for charter—with or without a captain and crew, whichever you prefer.

Catamaran Charters (✉ *Nanny Cay Marina, Nanny Cay* ☎ *284/494– 6661 or 800/262–0308* ⊕ *www.catamarans.com*) charters catamarans with or without a captain.

The **Moorings** (✉ *Wickham's Cay II, Road Town* ☎ *284/494–2332 or 800/535–7289* ⊕ *www.moorings.com*), considered one of the world's best bareboat operations, has a large fleet of well-maintained, mostly Beneteau sailing yachts. Hire a captain or sail the boat yourself.

If you prefer a powerboat, call **Regency Yacht Vacations** (✉ *Wickham's Cay I, Road Town* ☎ *284/495–1970 or 800/524–7676* ⊕ *www.regency vacations.com*) for both bareboat and captained sail and powerboat charters.

Sunsail (✉ *Wickham's Cay II, East End* ☎ *284/495–4740 or 800/327– 2276* ⊕ *www.sunsail.com*) offers a full fleet of boats to charter with or without a captain.

Voyages (✉ *Soper's Hole Marina, West End* ☎ *284/494–0740 or 888/869–2436* ⊕ *www.voyagecharters.com*) offers a variety of sailboats for charter with or without a captain and crew.

Aristocat Charters (✉ *West End* ☎ *284/499–1249* ⊕ *www.aristocat charters.com*) sets sail daily to the Indians and Peter Island aboard a 48-foot catamaran.

White Squall II (✉ *Village Cay Marina, Road Town* ☎ *284/494–2564* ⊕ *www.whitesquall2.com*) takes you on regularly scheduled day sails to the Baths at Virgin Gorda, Cooper, the Indians, or the Caves at Norman Island on an 80-foot schooner.

SURFING
Surfing is big on Tortola's north shore, particularly when the winter swells come in to Josiah's and Apple bays. Rent surfboards starting at $25 for a full day.

HIHO (⊠*Trellis Bay, Road Town* ☎*284/494–7694* ⊕*www.go-hiho. com*) has a good surfboard selection for sale or rent. The staff will give you advice on the best spots to put in your board.

WINDSURFING

Steady trade winds make windsurfing a breeze. Three of the best spots for sailboarding are Nanny Cay, Slaney Point, and Trellis Bay on Beef Island. Rates for sailboards start at about $25 an hour or $75 for a two-hour lesson.

Boardsailing BVI (⊠*Trellis Bay, Beef Island* ☎*284/495–2447* ⊕*www. windsurfing.vi*) rents equipment and offers private and group lessons.

SHOPPING

The BVI aren't really a shopper's delight, but there are many shops showcasing original wares—from jams and spices to resort wear to excellent artwork.

SHOPPING AREAS

Many shops and boutiques are clustered along and just off Road Town's **Main Street.** You can shop in Road Town's **Wickham's Cay I** adjacent to the marina. The **Crafts Alive Market** on the Road Town waterfront is a collection of colorful West Indian–style buildings with shops that carry items made in the BVI. You might find pretty baskets or interesting pottery or perhaps a bottle of home-brewed hot sauce. There's an ever-growing number of art and clothing stores at **Soper's Hole** in West End.

SPECIALTY STORES

ART   The **Allamanda Gallery** (⊠*124 Main St., Road Town* ☎*284/494–6680*) carries photography by owner Amanda Baker. **Sunny Caribbee** (⊠*Main St., Road Town* ☎*284/494–2178*) has many paintings, prints, and watercolors by artists from around the Caribbean.

CLOTHES &   **Arawak** (⊠*On dock, Nanny Cay* ☎*284/494–5240* ⊠*Soper's Hole*
TEXTILES   *Marina, West End* ☎*284/495–4262*) carries batik sundresses, sportswear, and resort wear for men and women. There's also a selection of children's clothing. **Hucksters** (⊠*Main St., Road Town* ☎*284/495–7165* ⊠*Soper's Hole Marina, West End* ☎*284/495–3087*) carries nifty souvenirs as well as unusual items for the home. **Latitude 18°** (⊠*Main St., Road Town* ⊠*Soper's Hole Marina, West End* ☎*284/494–7807 for both stores*) sells Maui Jim, Smith, Oakley, and Costa del Mar sunglasses; Freestyle watches; and a fine collection of beach towels, sandals, Crocs, sundresses, and sarongs.

Pusser's Company Store (⊠*Main St. at Waterfront Rd., Road Town* ☎*284/494–2467* ⊠*Soper's Hole Marina, West End* ☎*284/495–4599*) sells nautical memorabilia, ship models, and marine paintings. There's also an entire line of clothing for both men and women, handsome decorator bottles of Pusser's rum, and gift items bearing the Pusser's logo. **Zenaida's of West End** (⊠*Soper's Hole Marina, West End* ☎*284/495–4867*) displays the fabric finds of Argentine Vivian

Jenik Helm, who travels through South America, Africa, and India in search of batiks, hand-painted and hand-blocked fabrics, and interesting weaves that can be made into pareus (women's wraps) or wall hangings. The shop also sells unusual bags, belts, sarongs, scarves, and ethnic jewelry.

FOOD **Ample Hamper** (✉ *Inner Harbour Marina, Road Town* ☎ *284/494–2494* ✉ *Frenchman's Cay Marina, West End* ☎ *284/495–4684* ⊕ *www.amplehamper.com*) has an outstanding collection of cheeses, wines, fresh fruits, and canned goods from the United Kingdom and the United States. The staff will stock your yacht or rental villa. **Best of British** (✉ *Wickham's Cay I, Road Town* ☎ *284/494–3462*) has lots of nifty British food you won't find elsewhere. Shop here for Marmite, Vegemite, shortbread, frozen meat pies, and delightful Christmas crackers filled with surprises. **RiteWay** (✉ *Waterfront Dr., at Pasea Estate, Road Town* ☎ *284/494–2263* ✉ *Fleming St., Road Town* ☎ *284/494–2263* ⊕ *www.rtwbvi.com*) carries a good selection of the usual supplies, but don't expect an inventory like your hometown supermarket. RiteWay will stock villas and yachts.

GIFTS **Bamboushay** (✉ *Nanny Cay Marina, Nanny Cay* ☎ *284/494–0393*) sells handcrafted Tortola-made pottery in shades that reflect the sea. In a brightly painted West Indian house, **Sunny Caribbee** (✉ *Main St., Road Town* ☎ *284/494–2178*) packages its own herbs, teas, coffees, vinegars, hot sauces, soaps, skin and suntan lotions, and exotic concoctions—Arawak Love Potion and Island Hangover Cure, for example.

JEWELRY **Colombian Emeralds International** (✉ *Wickham's Cay I, Road Town* ☎ *284/494–7477*), a Caribbean chain catering to the cruise-ship crowd, is the source for duty-free emeralds and other gems, gold, crystal, and china. **D'Zandra's** (✉ *Wickham's Cay I, Road Town* ☎ *284/494–8330*) carries mostly black coral items set in gold and silver. Many pieces reflect Caribbean and sea themes. **Samarkand** (✉ *Main St., Road Town* ☎ *284/494–6415*) crafts charming gold-and-silver pendants, earrings, bracelets, and pins, many with island themes like seashells, lizards, pelicans, and palm trees. There are also reproduction Spanish pieces of eight (old Spanish coins) that were found on sunken galleons.

PERFUMES & COSMETICS **Flamboyance** (✉ *Palm Grove Shopping Center, Waterfront Dr., Road Town* ☎ *284/494–4099*) carries designer fragrances and upscale cosmetics.

STAMPS The **BVI Post Office** (✉ *Main St., Road Town* ☎ *284/494–3701*) is a philatelist's dream. It has a worldwide reputation for exquisite stamps in all sorts of designs. Although the stamps carry U.S. monetary designations, they can be used for postage only in the BVI.

NIGHTLIFE & THE ARTS

NIGHTLIFE

Like any other good sailing destination, Tortola has watering holes that are popular with salty and not-so-salty dogs. Many offer entertainment; check the weekly *Limin' Times* for schedules and up-to-date information. Bands change like the weather, and what's hot today can be old news tomorrow. The local beverage is the Painkiller, an innocent-tasting mixture of fruit juices and rums. It goes down smoothly but packs quite a punch, so give yourself time to recover before you order another.

By day **Bomba's Surfside Shack** (⊠ *Apple Bay* 🕾 *284/495–4148*), which is covered with everything from crepe-paper leis to ancient license plates to spicy graffiti, looks like a pile of junk; by night it's one of Tortola's liveliest spots. There's a fish fry and a live band every Wednesday and Sunday. People flock here from all over on the full moon, when bands play all night long.At the **Jolly Roger** (⊠ *West End* 🕾 *284/495–4559*) an ever-changing roster of local and down-island bands plays everything from rhythm and blues to reggae and rock every Friday and Saturday—and sometimes Sunday—starting at 8. Local bands play at **Myett's** (⊠ *Cane Garden Bay* 🕾 *284/495–9649*) most nights, and there's usually a lively dance crowd. At the **Pub** (⊠ *Waterfront St., Road Town* 🕾 *284/494–2608*) there's a happy hour from 5 to 7 every day and live blues on Thursday. Courage is what people are seeking at **Pusser's Road Town Pub** (⊠ *Waterfront St., Road Town* 🕾 *284/494–3897*)—John Courage by the pint. Other nights try Pusser's famous mixed drinks, called Painkillers, and snack on the excellent pizza. BVI recording star Quito Rhymer sings island ballads and love songs at **Quito's Gazebo** (⊠ *Cane Garden Bay* 🕾 *284/495–4837*), his rustic beachside bar-restaurant. Solo shows are on Tuesday and Thursday at 8:30; on Friday and Saturday nights at 9:30 Quito performs with his band. There's often live music at **Sebastian's** (⊠ *Apple Bay* 🕾 *284/495–4212*) on Thursday and Sunday evenings, and you can dance under the stars.

THE ARTS

Musicians from around the world take to the stage during the **Performing Art Series** (⊠ *H. Lavity Stoutt Community College, Paraquita Bay* 🕾 *284/494–4994* ⊕ *www.hlscc.edu.vg*), held from October to March each year. Past artists have included Britain's premier a cappella group, Black Voices; the Leipzig String Quartet; and Keith Lockhart and the Serenac Quartet (from the Boston Pops Symphony).

Every May hordes of people head to Tortola for the three-day **BVI Music Festival** (⊠ *Cane Garden Bay* 🕾 *284/495–3378* ⊕ *www.bvimusicfest. net*) to listen to reggae, gospel, blues, and salsa music by musicians from around the Caribbean and the U.S. mainland.

EXPLORING TORTOLA

Tortola doesn't have many historic sights, but it does have lots of beautiful natural scenery. Although you could explore the island's 10 square mi (26 square km) in a few hours, opting for such a whirlwind tour would be a mistake. There's no need to live in the fast lane when you're surrounded by some of the Caribbean's most breathtaking panoramas. Also, the roads are extraordinarily steep and twisting, making driving demanding. The best strategy is to explore a bit of the island at a time. For example, you might try Road Town (the island's tiny metropolis) one morning and a drive to Cane Garden Bay and West End (a little town on, of course, the island's west end) the next afternoon. Or consider a visit to East End, a *very* tiny town located exactly where its name suggests. The north shore is where all the best beaches are found.

ROAD TOWN

The bustling capital of the BVI looks out over Road Harbour. It takes only an hour or so to stroll down Main Street and along the waterfront, checking out the traditional West Indian buildings painted in pastel colors and with corrugated-tin roofs, bright shutters, and delicate fretwork trim. For sightseeing brochures and the latest information on everything from taxi rates to ferry schedules, stop in the BVI Tourist Board office. Or just choose a seat on one of the benches in Sir Olva Georges Square, on Waterfront Drive, and watch the people come and go from the ferry dock and customs office across the street.

> ## ROAD TOWN TRAFFIC TIPS
>
> Road Town's traffic and parking can be horrific. Try to avoid driving along the Waterfront Drive at morning and afternoon rush hours. It's longer, but often quicker, to take a route through the hills above Road Town. (You'll also be treated to some lovely views along the way.) Parking can be very difficult in Road Town, particularly during the busy winter season. There's parking along the waterfront and on the inland side on the eastern end of downtown, but if you're planning a day of shopping, go early to make sure you snag a space.

Fort Burt. The most intact historic ruin on Tortola was built by the Dutch in the early 17th century to safeguard Road Harbour. It sits on a hill on the western edge of Road Town and is now the site of a small hotel and restaurant. The foundations and magazine remain, and the structure offers a commanding view of the harbor. ⊠ *Waterfront Dr., Road Town* 🕾 *No phone* 🖃 *Free* ☉ *Daily dawn–dusk.*

★ **J. R. O'Neal Botanic Gardens.** Take a walk through this 4-acre showcase of lush plant life. There are sections devoted to prickly cacti and succulents, hothouses for ferns and orchids, gardens of medicinal herbs, and plants and trees indigenous to the seashore. From the tourist office in Road Town, cross Waterfront Drive and walk one block over to Main Street and turn right. Keep walking until you see the high school. The gardens are on your left. ⊠ *Botanic Station, Road Town* 🕾 *284/494–3904* 🖃 *$3* ☉ *Mon.–Sat. 9–4:30.*

★ **Old Government House Museum.** The seat of government until 1987, this gracious building now displays a nice collection of items from Tortola's past. The rooms are filled with period furniture, hand-painted china, books signed by Queen Elizabeth II on her 1966 and 1977 visits, and numerous items reflecting Tortola's seafaring legacy. ⊠ *Waterfront Dr., Road Town* 🕾 *284/494–4091* 🖃 *$3* ☉ *Weekdays 9–3, Sat. 9–2.*

AROUND THE ISLAND

Other than spectacular views and some beautiful beaches, Tortola has few must-see attractions. That said, you came to relax, read in the hammock and spend hours at dinner, not to dash madly around the island ticking yet another site off your list. Except for the Dolphin Discovery, where advance booking is recommended, the others are best seen when you stumble upon them on your round-the-island drive.

Cane Garden Bay. Once a sleepy village, Cane Garden Bay is growing into one of Tortola's most important destinations. Stay here at a small hotel or guesthouse or stop by for lunch, dinner, or drinks at a seaside restaurant. You can find a few small stores selling clothing and basics like suntan lotion, and, of course, one of Tortola's most popular beaches is at your feet. The roads in and out of this area are dauntingly steep, so use caution when driving.

Ⓒ **Dolphin Discovery.** Get up close and personal with dolphins as they swim
★ in a spacious seaside pen. There are two different programs that provide a range of experiences. In the Royal Swim, dolphins tow participants around the pen. The less expensive Encounter allows you to touch the dolphins. ⊠*Prospect Reef Resort, Road Town* ☎*284/494–7675* ⊕*www.dolphindiscovery.com* ⊡*Royal Swim $139, Discovery $79* ☉*Encounters daily* 10, noon, 2, and 4; Royal swim daily 11 and 1.

Fort Recovery. The unrestored ruins of a 17th-century Dutch fort sit amid a profusion of tropical greenery on the grounds of Villas of Fort Recovery Estates. There's not much to see here, and there are no guided tours, but you're welcome to stop by and poke around. ⊠*Waterfront Dr., Road Town* ☎*284/485–4467* ⊡*Free.*

Mount Healthy National Park. The remains of an 18th-century sugar plantation can be seen here. The windmill structure has been restored, and you can see the ruins of a mill, a factory with boiling houses, storage areas, stables, a hospital, and many dwellings. It's a nice place to picnic. ⊠*Ridge Rd., Todman Peak* ☎*No phone* ⊕*www.bvinationalparkstrust.org* ⊡*Free* ☉*Daily dawn–dusk.*

★ **Sage Mountain National Park.** At 1,716 feet, Sage Mountain is the highest peak in the BVI. From the parking area, a trail leads you in a loop not only to the peak itself (and extraordinary views) but also to a small rain forest that is sometimes shrouded in mist. Most of the forest was cut down over the centuries to clear land for sugarcane, cotton, and other crops; to create pastureland; or simply to utilize the stands of timber. In 1964 this park was established to preserve what remained. Up here you can see mahogany trees, white cedars, mountain guavas, elephant-ear vines, mamey trees, and giant bullet woods, to say nothing of such birds as mountain doves and thrushes. Take a taxi from Road Town or drive up Joe's Hill Road and make a left onto Ridge Road toward Chalwell and Doty villages. The road dead-ends at the park. ⊠*Ridge Rd., Sage Mountain* ☎*284/494–3904* ⊕*www.bvinationalparkstrust.org* ⊡*$3* ☉*Daily dawn–dusk.*

★ **Skyworld.** Drive up here and climb the observation tower for a stunning 360-degree view of numerous islands and cays. On a clear day you can even see St. Croix (40 mi [64½ km] away) and Anegada (20 mi [32 km] away). ✉*Ridge Rd., Joe's Hill* ☎*No phone* ✉*Free.*

Soper's Hole. On this little island connected by a causeway to Tortola's western end, you can find a marina and a captivating complex of pastel West Indian–style buildings with shady balconies, shuttered windows, and gingerbread trim that house art galleries, boutiques, and restaurants. Pusser's Landing is a lively place to stop for a cold drink (many are made with Pusser's famous rum) and a sandwich and to watch the boats in harbor.

> **FERRY CONFUSION**
>
> The ferry situation is mind-boggling for newcomers to the BVI. Ferries depart from Road Town, West End, and Beef Island, so make sure you get to the right place at the correct time. Sometimes boats bound for Jost Van Dyke, Virgin Gorda, Anegada, St. Thomas, and St. John depart minutes apart, other times the schedule is skimpy. And schedules change at the drop of a hat, particularly in the summer season. To avoid being stranded, call in the morning to make sure the ferry you want is actually going that day.

6

SIDE TRIPS FROM TORTOLA

There are several islands that make great side trips from Tortola, including lovely Marina Cay and tony Peter's Island. Both have great accommodations, so you might want to spend the night.

MARINA CAY

☯ Beautiful little Marina Cay is in Trellis Bay, not far from Beef Island. Sometimes you can see it and its large J-shape coral reefs—a most dramatic sight—from the air soon after takeoff from the airport on Beef Island. Covering 8 acres, this islet is considered small even by BVI standards. On it there's a restaurant, Pusser's Store, and a six-unit hotel. Ferry service is free from the dock on Beef Island.

WHERE TO STAY

$$ ☖ **Pusser's Marina Cay Hotel & Restaurant.** If getting away from it all is your priority, this may be the place for you, because there's nothing to do on this beach-rimmed island other than swim, snorkel, and soak up the sun—there's not even a TV to distract you. Rooms, decorated in simple wicker and wood with floral-print fabrics, are on a hilltop facing the trade winds; two villas look right out to the morning sunrise. The laid-back tempo picks up at 4:30 PM, when charter boaters come ashore to hear local musicians entertain in the bar during happy hour. The restaurant, open for breakfast, lunch, and dinner, offers a menu that ranges from fish and lobster to steak, chicken, and barbecued ribs. Pusser's Painkiller Punch is the house specialty. There's free ferry service from the Beef Island dock for anyone visiting the island, though ferry times and frequency vary with the seasons. **Pros:** Lots of character, beau-

tiful beaches, interesting guests. **Cons:** Older property, ferry needed to get here. ⊠ *West side of Marina Cay* ✆ *Box 76, Road Town, Tortola* ☎*284/494–2174* ⊕*www.pussers.com* ⇆*4 rooms, 2 2-bedroom villas* ⌂*In-room: no a/c, no phone, no TV. In-hotel: restaurant, bar, beachfront, no elevator, public Wi-Fi* ▤*AE, MC, V* ⋈*CP.*

PETER ISLAND

Although Peter Island is home to the resort of the same name, it's also a popular anchorage for charter boaters and a destination for Tortola vacationers. The scheduled ferry trip from Peter Island's shoreside base outside Road Town runs $15 round-trip for nonguests. The island is lush, with forested hillsides sloping seaward to meet white sandy beaches. There are no roads other than those at the resort, and there's nothing to do but relax at the lovely beach set aside for day-trippers. You're welcome to dine at the resort's restaurants.

WHERE TO STAY & EAT

$$$$ ✕⌗**Peter Island Resort.** Total pampering and the prices to match are the ticket at this luxury resort. If you want to while away your days at the beach, enjoy a morning at the spa, stroll the lushly planted grounds, and relax over dinner with other like-minded guests—and have the money to afford the steep rates—this is a good place to do it. For more active types, there are tennis courts and water sports galore. Peter Island is a half-hour ferry ride from Tortola, but once you arrive, you're in another world. The rooms are gorgeous, with thoughtful touches like showers with a view. A couple of villas sit above the hotel rooms. **Pros:** Lovely rooms, nice beach. **Cons:** Need ferry to get here, pricey rates. ⊠*Peter Island* ✆*Box 211, Road Town, Tortola* ☎*284/495–2000 or 800/346–4451* ⊕*www.peterisland.com* ⇆*52 rooms, 3 villas* ⌂*In-room: safe, no TV. In-hotel: 2 restaurants, bar, pool, gym, spa, beachfront, diving, water sports, no elevator, public Internet, public Wi-Fi* ▤*AE, MC, V* ⋈*FAP.*

VIRGIN GORDA

By Lynda Lohr   Virgin Gorda, or "Fat Virgin," received its name from Christopher Columbus. The explorer envisioned the island as a pregnant woman in a languid recline with Gorda Peak being her big belly and the boulders of the Baths her toes. Different in topography from Tortola, with its arid landscape covered with scrub brush and cactus, Virgin Gorda has a slower pace of life, too. Goats and cattle own the right-of-way, and the unpretentious friendliness of the people is winning.

WHERE TO STAY

While villas are scattered all over Virgin Gorda, hotels are centered in and around the Valley, Nail Bay, and in the North Sound area. Except for Leverick Bay Resort, which is around the point from North Sound, all hotels in North Sound are reached only by ferry.

HOTELS & INNS

$$$$ **Biras Creek Resort.** Although Biras Creek is tucked out of the way on
★ the island's North Sound, the get-away-from-it-all feel is actually the
major draw for its well-heeled clientele. Anyway, you're just a five-minute ferry ride from the dock at Gun Creek. There are a handful of other
hotels in the area, but this resort's gourmet meal plan means you won't
want to leave. A member of the exclusive Relais & Châteaux family of
hotels, Biras Creek offers sophisticated suites with separate bedroom
and living areas, though only bedrooms have air-conditioning. Guests
get around on complimentary bicycles. Rates are per couple, per night,
and include everything but beverages. **Pros:** Luxurious rooms, professional staff, good dining options. **Cons:** Expensive rates, isolated location, difficult for people with mobility problems. *Box 54, North
Sound VG1150 284/494–3555 or 800/223–1108 www.biras.com
34 suites In-room: safe, refrigerator, no TV (some), dial-up. In-
hotel: 2 restaurants, bar, tennis courts, pool, spa, beachfront, water
sports, bicycles, no elevator, public Internet, public Wi-Fi AE, MC,
V FAP.*

$$$$ **Bitter End Yacht Club.** Sailing's the thing at this busy hotel and marina
in the nautically inclined North Sound, and since the use of everything
Fodor'sChoice from small sailboats to kayaks to Windsurfers is included in the price,
★ you have no reason not to get out on the water. If you're serious about
taking to the high seas, sign up for lessons at the resort's sailing school.
Of course, if you just want to lounge about on the beachfront chaises
or on your balcony, that's cool. There's a busy social scene, with guests
gathering to swap tales at the hotel's bars. Rooms are bright and cheery,
with the decor leaning toward tropical colors. You can reach the Bitter
End only by a free private ferry. **Pros:** Lots of water sports, good diving opportunities, friendly guests. **Cons:** Expensive rates, isolated location, lots of stairs. *Box 46, North Sound VG1150 284/494–2746
or 800/872–2392 www.beyc.com 87 rooms In-room: no a/c
(some), no TV. In-hotel: 3 restaurants, bar, pool, beachfront, diving,
water sports, no elevator, children's programs (ages 6–18), public Internet, public Wi-Fi AE, MC, V AI.*

$$$$ **Little Dix Bay.** This laid-back luxury resort offers something for everyone, which is why we like it. You can swim, sun, and snorkel on a
★ gorgeous sandy crescent, play tennis or windsurf, or just relax with a
good book. The hotel's restaurants serve stellar food, but you're only a
five-minute drive from Spanish Town's less expensive restaurants and
shopping. Rooms have rattan and wood furniture and a casual feel.
The gardens are gorgeous, with lots of lush plantings kept snipped
to perfection. Depending on when you visit, your fellow guests will
be honeymooners or folks who've spent a week or two in the winter
season for years. **Pros:** Convenient location, lovely grounds, near many
dining options. **Cons:** Expensive rates, very spread out, insular but not
isolated. *Box 70, Little Dix Bay VG1150 284/495–5555 www.
littledixbay.com 98 rooms, 8 suites, 5 villas In-room: safe, refrigerator, no TV, Wi-Fi. In-hotel: 3 restaurants, bars, tennis courts, pool,
gym, spa, beachfront, water sports, no elevator, children's programs
(ages 3–16), public Internet, public Wi-Fi AE, MC, V EP.*

6

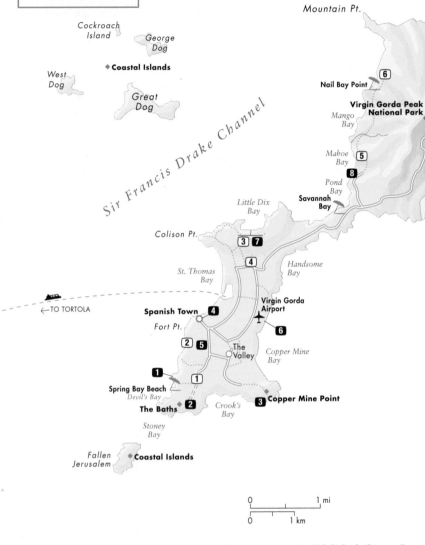

Virgin Gorda

Cockroach Island

George Dog

Coastal Islands

West Dog

Great Dog

Sir Francis Drake Channel

Mountain Pt.

Nail Bay Point ⑥

Virgin Gorda Peak National Park

Mango Bay

Mahoe Bay ⑤

⑧

Pond Bay

Savannah Bay

Little Dix Bay

Colison Pt.

③ ⑦

④

Handsome Bay

St. Thomas Bay

← TO TORTOLA

Spanish Town ④

Virgin Gorda Airport

⑥

Fort Pt.

② ⑤

The Valley

Copper Mine Bay

① 1

① 1

Spring Bay Beach

Devil's Bay

The Baths ② 2

Crook's Bay

③ 3 **Copper Mine Point**

Stoney Bay

Fallen Jerusalem

Coastal Islands

0   1 mi

0   1 km

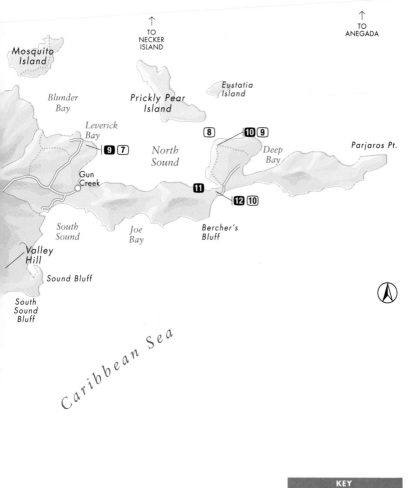

Mosquito
Island

Blunder
Bay

TO
NECKER
ISLAND

Prickly Pear
Island

Eustatia
Island

TO
ANEGADA

Leverick
Bay

9 7

North
Sound

8

10 9

Deep
Bay

Parjaros Pt.

Gun
Creek

11

12 **10**

South
Sound

Joe
Bay

Bercher's
Bluff

Valley
Hill

Sound Bluff

South
Sound
Bluff

Caribbean Sea

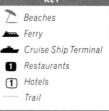

KEY	
⚲	Beaches
⛴	Ferry
🚢	Cruise Ship Terminal
1	Restaurants
1	Hotels
....	Trail

$$–$$$$ 🏨 **Nail Bay Resort.** Rambling up the hill above the coast, this resort
★   offers a wide selection of rooms and suites to fit every need. The beach
is a short walk away from the units at lower elevations, but if you're
staying higher up the hill, you might want to drive to avoid the uphill
trek back to your room. You get cooking facilities (at least microwave,
fridge, toaster oven, and coffeemaker) no matter how small your room.
Part of the road here is in awful condition, but it's being repaved.
There's a restaurant and lots of activities, so you won't need to leave
unless you want to. The rooms and apartments have modern rattan
furniture, tile floors, and nice views. **Pros:** Full kitchens, lovely beach,
close to town. **Cons:** Construction noise, road being repaired, uphill
walk from beach. ✉ *Box 69, Nail Bay VG1150* ☎ *284/494–8000 or
800/871–3551* ⊕ *www.nailbay.com* 🛏 *4 rooms, 4 suites, 8 villas* △ *In-
room: kitchen, VCR. In-hotel: restaurant, bar, tennis court, pool, spa,
beachfront, water sports, no elevator, public Internet, public Wi-Fi*
☰ *AE, MC, V* ⫟ *EP.*

$$$ 🏨 **Olde Yard Village.** All the condos in this upscale complex have at least
partial ocean views. The location, a few minutes' drive from Spanish
Town, is ideal: close enough so that you can easily pop out to dinner
but far enough to make you feel as if you're more isolated than you
really are. You will need a car, though, to make those trips a breeze.
The Olde Yard Village will be building new units over the next several
years, but construction is a bit removed from the existing accommodations. Every condo is decorated to the owner's taste, but you can count
on a comfortable tropical ambience. **Pros:** Close to Spanish Town,
lovely pool, recently built units. **Cons:** No beach, on a busy street, noisy
roosters nearby. ✉ *Box 26, The Valley VG1150* ☎ *284/495–5544 or
800/653–9273* ⊕ *www.oldeyardvillage.com* 🛏 *30 condos* △ *In-room:
kitchen, refrigerator, Wi-Fi. In-hotel: restaurant, 2 tennis courts, bar,
pool, gym, spa, no elevator* ☰ *AE, MC, V* ⫟ *EP.*

$$–$$$ 🏨 **Leverick Bay Resort & Marina.** With its colorful buildings and bustling
marina, Leverick Bay is a good choice. The resort does not have a
great beach, but with easy access to various water-sports activities, a
tasty on-site restaurant, and comfortable and spacious rooms, it's still
appealing. If you prefer an apartment, opt for one of the units stretching up the hillside above the marina. There's a one-week minimum stay
in the apartments. All the accommodations have tile floors and pastel
accents with a tropical feel. **Pros:** Lively location, good restaurant, small
grocery store. **Cons:** Very small beach, no laundry in units, 15-minute
drive to town. ✉ *Box 63, Leverick Bay VG1150* ☎ *284/495–7421 or
800/848–7081* ⊕ *www.leverickbay.com* 🛏 *14 rooms, 4 condos* △ *In-
room: safe, kitchen (some), refrigerator, Wi-Fi. In-hotel: 2 restaurants,
bar, tennis court, pool, spa, beachfront, diving, laundry facilities, public
Internet* ☰ *AE, MC, V* ⫟ *EP.*

$$–$$$ 🏨 **Saba Rock Resort.** Reachable only by a free ferry or by private yacht,
this resort on its own tiny cay isn't for everyone. However, it's good for
folks who want to mix and mingle with the sailors who drop anchor for
the night. The bar and restaurant are busy with yachters gathering for
sundowners, lunch, and dinner. The rooms are spacious, each with a different decor. All have tile floors, rattan or wood furniture, and colorful

spreads and drapes. A resort boat will drop you at nearby North Sound resorts if you need a change of pace. **Pros:** Party atmosphere, convenient transportation, good diving nearby. **Cons:** Tiny beach, isolated location, on a very small island. ⌂*Box 67, North Sound VG1150* ☎*284/495–7711 or 284/495–9966* ⊕*www.sabarock.com* ⌦*7 1-bedroom suites, 2 2-bedroom suites* ♿*In-room: no phone (some), kitchen (some), refrigerator. In-hotel: restaurant, bar, beachfront, water sports, no elevator, public Wi-Fi* ☰*D, MC, V* ⏀*CP.*

$$ ⬛**Fischer's Cove Beach Hotel.** The rooms are modest, the furniture dis-
☾ count-store style, and the walls thin, but you can't beat the location. Budget travelers should consider this hotel if they want a good beach just steps away. If you plan on staying put, you won't even need a car. Spanish Town's handful of restaurants and shopping at Virgin Gorda Yacht Harbor are an easy 15-minute walk away. For better views, opt for the beachfront rooms. **Pros:** Beachfront location, budget price, good restaurant. **Cons:** Very basic units, thin walls, no a/c in some rooms. ⌂*Box 60, The Valley VG1150* ☎*284/495–5252* ⊕*www.fischerscove.com* ⌦*12 rooms, 8 cottages* ♿*In-room: no a/c (some), kitchen (some), refrigerator, no TV (some), dial-up. In-hotel: restaurant, beachfront, no elevator* ☰*AE, MC, V* ⏀*EP.*

VILLAS & VILLA RESORTS

Those craving seclusion would do well at a villa. Most have full kitchens and maid service. Prices per week in winter run from around $2,000 for a one- or two-bedroom villa up to $10,000 for a five-room beachfront villa. Rates in summer are substantially less. On Virgin Gorda a villa in the North Sound area means you can pretty much stay put at night unless you want to make the drive on narrow roads. If you opt for a spot near the Baths, it's an easier drive to town.

The St. Thomas–based **McLaughlin-Anderson Luxury Villas** (✉*1000 Blackbeard's Hill, Suite 3, Charlotte Amalie, USVI* ☎*340/776–0635 or 800/537–6246* ⊕*www.mclaughlinanderson.com*) represents nearly two dozen properties all over Virgin Gorda. Villas range in size from two bedrooms to six bedrooms and come with many amenities, including full kitchens, pools, and stellar views. The company can hire a chef and stock your kitchen with groceries. A seven-night minimum is required during the winter season.

Tropical Care Services (⌂*Box 1039, The Valley VG1150* ☎*284/495–6493* ⊕*www.tropicalcareservices.com*) manages about a dozen properties stretching from the Baths to the Nail Bay area. Several budget properties are included among the more pricey offerings. Most houses have private pools, and a few are right on the beach. A sister company at the same number, Tropical Nannies, provides babysitting services.

Virgin Gorda Villa Rentals (⌂*Box 63, The Valley VG1150* ☎*284/495–7421 or 800/848–7081* ⊕*www.virgingordabvi.com*) manages more than 40 properties near Leverick Bay Resort and Mahoe Bay, so it's perfect for those who want to be close to activities. Many of the accommodations—from studios to six or more bedrooms—have private swimming pools and air-conditioning, at least in the bedrooms. All have full kitchens, are well maintained, and have spectacular views.

6

$$-$$$$ 🏨**Mango Bay Resort.** Sitting seaside on Virgin Gorda's north coast, this collection of contemporary duplex apartments will make you feel right at home. Each apartment is individually owned, so each has a different decor, but you can count on tile floors and tropical accents. The homes come with floats, kayaks, and snorkeling equipment, so you can find plenty to do when you're tired of lounging in the chaise. Giorgio's Table, a popular Italian restaurant, is a short walk away. **Pros:** Nice beach, homey feel, good restaurant nearby. **Cons:** Construction in area, drab decor, some units have lackluster views. ✑ *Box 1062, Mahoe Bay* ☎284/495–5672 ⊕*www.mangobayresort.com* ⬐*14 condos, 5 villas* ♿*In-room: kitchen, dial-up. In-hotel: beachfront, no elevator* ▭*MC, V* ⫶⃝*EP.*

$$-$$$ 🏨**Guavaberry Spring Bay Vacation Homes.** Rambling back from the
★   beach, these hexagonal one- and two-bedroom villas give you all the comforts of home with the striking boulder-fringed beach just minutes away. The villas are best for independent travelers who want to be able to cook or simply head 10 minutes to Spanish Town for a night out. The popular Baths are a short walk away, and snorkeling is excellent. The rooms have dark-wood or white walls, tile floors, and tropical bright spreads and curtains. Not all have sea views. **Pros:** Short walk to the Baths, easy drive to town, great beaches nearby. **Cons:** Sew amenities, older property, basic decor. ✑ *Box 20, The Valley* ☎284/495–5227 ⊕*www.guavaberryspringbay.com* ⬐*12 1-bedroom units, 6 2-bedroom units, 1 3-bedroom unit, 18 villas* ♿*In-room: no a/c (some), no phone, kitchen, no TV (some). In-hotel: beachfront, no elevator, public Internet, public Wi-Fi* ▭*No credit cards* ⫶⃝*EP.*

WHERE TO EAT

Dining out on Virgin Gorda is a mixed bag, with everything from hamburgers to lobster available. Most folks opt to have dinner at or near their hotel to avoid driving on Virgin Gorda's twisting roads at night. The Valley does have a handful of restaurants if you're sleeping close to town.

AMERICAN   ✗**LSL Restaurant.** An unpretentious place along the road to the Baths,
$$$-$$$$ this small restaurant with pedestrian decor still manages to be a local favorite. You can always find fresh fish on the menu, but folks with a taste for other dishes won't be disappointed. Try the veal with mushrooms and herbs in a white wine sauce or the breast of chicken with rum cream and nuts. ⊠*Tower Rd., The Valley* ☎284/495–5151 ▭*MC, V.*

$$-$$$$ ✗**Flying Iguana Restaurant & Bar.** Local art is displayed in this charming
☕   restaurant's comfortable lounge. The open-air dining room looks past the island's tiny airport to the sea. Enjoy classic eggs and bacon for breakfast; for lunch there are sandwiches and juicy hamburgers. The dinner menu includes fresh seafood, grilled chicken, and sizzling steaks. ⊠*Virgin Gorda Airport, The Valley* ☎284/495–5277 ▭*MC, V.*

$$-$$$$ ✗**Mine Shaft Café.** Perched on a hilltop that offers a view of spectacular sunsets, this restaurant near Copper Mine Point serves simple yet well-prepared food, including grilled fish, steaks, and baby back ribs.

Tuesday night features an all-you-can-eat Caribbean-style barbecue. The monthly full-moon parties draw a big local crowd. ⊠ *Copper Mine Point, The Valley* ☎ *284/495–5260* ⊟ *MC, V.*

$$–$$$$ ✕**Restaurant at Leverick Bay.** This bi-level restaurant looks out over North Sound. The fancier upstairs dining room is slightly more expensive, with a menu that includes steaks, lobster, and fresh fish. There's a prime rib special on Saturday night. Below, the bar offers light fare all day—starting with breakfast and moving on to hamburgers, salads, and pizzas until well into the evening. There's a children's menu. ⊠ *Leverick Bay Resort & Marina, Leverick Bay* ☎ *284/495–7154* ⊟ *MC, V.*

$$–$$$ ✕**Bath & Turtle.** You can sit back and relax at this informal tavern with a friendly staff—although the noise from the television can sometimes be a bit much. Well-stuffed sandwiches, homemade pizzas, pasta dishes, and daily specials like conch soup round out the casual menu. Local musicians perform Wednesday and Friday night. ⊠ *Virgin Gorda Yacht Harbour, Spanish Town* ☎ *284/495–5239* ⊟ *AE, MC, V.*

$$ ✕**Fat Virgin's Café.** This casual beachfront eatery offers a straightforward menu of baby back ribs, chicken roti, vegetable pasta, grouper sandwiches, and fresh fish specials for lunch and dinner. You can find a good selection of Caribbean beer. ⊠ *Biras Creek Resort, North Sound* ☎ *284/495–7052* ⊟ *MC, V.*

$$ ✕**Top of the Baths.** At the entrance to the Baths, this popular restaurant starts serving at 8 AM. Tables are on an outdoor terrace or in an open-air pavilion; all have stunning views of the Sir Francis Drake Channel. Hamburgers, coconut chicken sandwiches, and fish-and-chips are among the offerings at lunch. For dessert, the mango raspberry cheesecake is excellent. The Sunday barbecue, served from noon until 3 PM, is an island event. ⊠ *The Valley* ☎ *284/495–5497* ⊟ *AE, MC, V* ⊗ *No dinner.*

CONTINENTAL ✕**Biras Creek Restaurant.** This hilltop restaurant at the Biras Creek Hotel
$$$$ has eye-popping views of North Sound. The four-course prix-fixe menu changes daily and includes several choices per course. For starters, there may be an artichoke, green bean, and wild mushroom salad topped with balsamic vinaigrette, or cream of sweet potato soup accompanied by potato straws. Entrées may include pan-seared snapper over horseradish pearl pasta. The desserts, including a lemon ricotta cheesecake with a spicy passion fruit sauce, are to die for. Dinner ends with Biras Creek's signature offering of cheese and port. ⊠ *Biras Creek Hotel, North Sound* ☎ *284/494–3555 or 800/223–1108* ⚑ *Reservations essential* ⊟ *AE, D, MC, V.*

$$$–$$$$ ✕**Little Dix Bay Pavilion.** For an elegant evening, you can't do better than this—the candlelight in the open-air pavilion is enchanting, the always-changing menu sophisticated, the service attentive. Superbly prepared seafood, meat, and vegetarian entrées draw locals and visitors alike. Favorites include the pan-seared red snapper over homemade linguine, jerk-rubbed rack of lamb with a guava sauce, and a beef tenderloin served with garlic mashed potatoes. The Monday evening buffet shines. ⊠ *Little Dix Bay Resort, Spanish Town* ☎ *284/495–5555* ⚑ *Reservations essential* ⊟ *AE, D, MC, V.*

6

ITALIAN
$$$$

✕ **Giorgio's Table.** Gaze up at the stars and listen to the water lap against the shore while dining on homemade ravioli, beef fillet in a brunello wine sauce, or truffle duck ragout served over pappardelle pasta. House specialties include fresh lobster that you choose yourself from a 5,000-gallon seawater pool. There's also a selection of 120 wines kept in a temperature-controlled cellar. Lunch is more casual and includes pizzas and pasta dishes. ⊠ *Mahoe Bay* ☎ 284/495–5684 ▭ *AE, MC, V.*

> **GROCERY DETOUR**
>
> Virgin Gorda's grocery stores barely equal convenience stores elsewhere. The selection is small and the prices high. Many Virgin Gorda residents head to Tortola or even to St. Thomas to do their shopping. If you're coming here from another island, you might want to bring along one or two items you know you'll need.

$$–$$$

✕ **The Rock Café.** Surprisingly good Italian cuisine is served among the waterfalls and giant boulders that form the famous Baths. For dinner at this open-air eatery, feast on chicken and penne in a tomato-cream sauce, spaghetti with lobster sauce, or fresh red snapper in a butter and caper sauce. For dessert, don't miss the chocolate mousse. ⊠ *The Valley* ☎ 284/495–5482 ▭ *AE, MC, V* ⊘ *No lunch.*

SEAFOOD
$$$$
★

✕ **The Clubhouse.** The Bitter End Yacht Club's open-air waterfront restaurant is a favorite rendezvous for the sailing set, so it's busy day and night. You can find lavish buffets for breakfast, lunch, and dinner, as well as an à la carte menu. Dinner selections include grilled swordfish or tuna, local lobster, chopped sirloin, as well as veggie dishes. ⊠ *Bitter End Yacht Club, North Sound* ☎ 284/494–2745 ⚓ *Reservations essential* ▭ *AE, MC, V.*

BEACHES

Although some of the best beaches are reachable only by boat, don't worry if you're a landlubber, because you can find plenty of places to sun and swim. Anybody going to Virgin Gorda must experience swimming or snorkeling among its unique boulder formations, which can be visited at several sites along Lee Road. The most popular is the Baths, but there are several other similar places nearby that are easily reached.

The Baths. Featuring a stunning maze of huge granite boulders that extend into the sea, this national park is usually crowded midday with day-trippers. The snorkeling is good, and you're likely to see a wide variety of fish, but watch out for dinghies coming ashore from the numerous sailboats anchored offshore. Public bathrooms and a handful of bars and shops are close to the water and at the start of the path that leads to the beach. Lockers are available to keep belongings safe. ⊠ *About 1 mi (1½ km) west of Spanish Town ferry dock on Tower Rd., Spring Bay* ☎ 284/494–3904 ☐ *$3* ⊘ *Daily dawn–dusk.*

Nail Bay. Head to the island's north tip and you can be rewarded with a trio of beaches within the Nail Bay Resort complex that are ideal for snorkeling. Mountain Trunk Bay is perfect for beginners, and Nail Bay and Long Bay beaches have coral caverns just offshore. The resort has a restaurant, which is an uphill walk but perfect for beach breaks. ⊠*Nail Bay Resort, off Plum Tree Bay Rd., Nail Bay* 🕾*No phone* 💷*Free* ☉*Daily dawn–dusk.*

★ **Savannah Bay.** For a wonderfully private beach close to Spanish Town, try Savannah Bay. It may not always be completely deserted, but you can find a spot to yourself on this long stretch of soft, white sand. Bring your own mask, fins, and snorkel, as there are no facilities. The view from above is a photographer's delight. ⊠*Off N. Sound Rd., ¾ mi (1¼ km) east of Spanish Town ferry dock, Savannah Bay* 🕾*No phone* 💷*Free* ☉*Daily dawn–dusk.*

Spring Bay Beach. Just off Tower Road, this national-park beach gets much less traffic than the nearby Baths, and has the similarly large, imposing boulders that create interesting grottoes for swimming. The snorkeling is excellent, and the grounds include swings and picnic tables. ⊠*Off Tower Rd., 1 mi (1½ km) west of Spanish Town ferry dock, Spring Bay* 🕾*284/494–3904* 💷*Free* ☉*Daily dawn–dusk.*

SPORTS & THE OUTDOORS

DIVING & SNORKELING

Where you go snorkeling and what company you pick depends on where you're staying. Many hotels have on-site dive outfitters, but if they don't, one won't be far away. If your hotel does have a dive operation, just stroll down to the dock and hop aboard—no need to drive anywhere. The dive companies are all certified by PADI. Costs vary, but count on paying about $75 for a one-tank dive and $95 for a two-tank dive. All dive operators offer introductory courses as well as certification and advanced courses. Should you get an attack of the bends, which can happen when you ascend too rapidly, the nearest decompression chamber is at Roy L. Schneider Regional Medical Center in St. Thomas.

There are some terrific snorkel and dive sites off Virgin Gorda, including areas around the Baths, the North Sound, and the Dogs. The Chimney at Great Dog Island sports a coral archway and canyon covered with a wide variety of sponges. At Joe's Cave, an underwater cavern on West Dog Island, huge groupers, eagle rays, and other colorful fish accompany divers as they swim. At some sites you can see 100 feet down, but divers who don't want to go that deep and snorkelers will find plenty to look at just below the surface.

☺ The **Bitter End Yacht Club** (⊠*North Sound* 🕾*284/494–2746* ⊕*www.beyc. com*) offers two snorkeling trips a day. **Dive BVI** (⊠*Virgin Gorda Yacht Harbour, Spanish Town* 🕾*284/495–5513 or 800/848–7078* ⊠*Leverick Bay Resort and Marina, Leverick Bay* 🕾*284/495–7328* ⊕*www. divebvi.com*) offers expert instruction, certification, and day trips. **Sunchaser Scuba** (⊠*Bitter End Yacht Club, North Sound* 🕾*284/495–9638 or 800/932–4286* ⊕*www.sunchaserscuba.com*) offers resort, advanced, and rescue courses.

FISHING

The sportfishing here is so good that anglers come from all over the world. **Charter Virgin Gorda**(⊠ *Leverick Bay, North Sound* ☎284/495–7421 ⊕ *www.chartervirgingorda.com)* offers a choice of trips aboard its 46-foot Hatteras, the Mahoe Bay, for full-day marlin hunting. Plan to spend $800 to $1,200.

MINIATURE GOLF

The 9-hole minigolf course **Golf Virgin Gorda** (⊠ *Copper Mine Point, The Valley* ☎284/495–5260) is next to the Mine Shaft Café, delightfully nestled between huge granite boulders.

SAILING & BOATING

The BVI waters are calm, and terrific places to learn to sail. You can also rent sea kayaks, waterskiing equipment, dinghies, and powerboats, or take a parasailing trip.

Ↄ The **Bitter End Sailing & Windsurfing School**(⊠ *Bitter End Yacht Club, North Sound* ☎ 284/494–2746 ⊕ *www.beyc.com)* offers classroom, dockside, and on-the-water lessons for sailors of all levels. Private lessons are $60 per hour.If you just want to sit back, relax, and let the captain take the helm, choose a sailing or power yacht from **Double "D" Charters**(⊠ *Virgin Gorda Yacht Harbour, Spanish Town* ☎ 284/499–2479 ⊕*www.doubledbvi.com).* Rates are $60 for a half-day trip and $95 for a full-day island-hopping excursion. Private full-day cruises or sails for up to eight people run $950. If you'd rather rent a Sunfish or Hobie Wave, check out **Leverick Bay Watersports** ⊠ *Leverick Bay, North Sound* ☎ 284/495–7376 ⊕ *www.watersportsbvi.com.*

WINDSURFING

Ↄ The North Sound is a good place to learn to windsurf: it's protected, so you can't be easily blown out to sea. The **Bitter End Yacht Club** (⊠ *North Sound* ☎284/494–2746 ⊕*www.beyc.com)* gives lessons and rents equipment for $60 per hour for nonguests. A half-day Windsurfer rental runs $80 to $100.

SHOPPING

Most boutiques are within hotel complexes or at Virgin Gorda Yacht Harbour. Two of the best are at Biras Creek and Little Dix Bay. Other properties—the Bitter End and Leverick Bay—have small but equally select boutiques.

CLOTHING

Blue Banana (⊠ *Virgin Gorda Yacht Harbour, Spanish Town* ☎284/495–5957) carries a large selection of gifts, clothing, and accessories.At **Dive BVI** (⊠ *Virgin Gorda Yacht Harbour, Spanish Town* ☎284/495–5513), you can find books about the islands as well as snorkeling equipment, sportswear, sunglasses, and beach bags.**Fat Virgin's Treasure** (⊠ *Biras Creek Hotel, North Sound* ☎284/495–7054) sells cool island-style clothing in tropical prints, a large selection of straw sun hats, and unusual gift items like island-made hot sauces, artistic cards, and locally fired pottery.**Margo's Boutique** (⊠ *Virgin Gorda Yacht Harbour,*

Spanish Town ☎*284/495–5237)* is the place to buy handmade silver, pearl, and shell jewelry. The **Pavilion Gift Shop** (✉*Little Dix Bay Hotel, Little Dix Bay* ☎*284/495–5555)* has the latest in resort wear for men and women, as well as jewelry, books, housewares, and expensive T-shirts. **Pusser's Company Store** (✉*Leverick Bay* ☎*284/495–7369)* has a trademark line of sportswear, rum products, and gift items.

FOOD

The **Bitter End Emporium** (✉*Bitter End Yacht Harbor, North Sound* ☎*284/494–2746)* is the place for such edible treats as local fruits, cheeses, baked goods, and gourmet prepared food to take out. **Buck's Food Market** (✉*Virgin Gorda Yacht Harbour, Spanish Town* ☎*284/495–5423* ✉*Gun Creek, North Sound* ☎*284/495–7368)* is the closest the island offers to a full-service supermarket and has everything from an in-store bakery and deli to fresh fish and produce departments. The **Chef's Pantry** (✉*Leverick Bay* ☎*284/495–7677)* has the fixings for an impromptu party in your villa or boat—fresh seafood, specialty meats, imported cheeses, daily baked breads and pastries, and an impressive wine and spirit selection. The **Wine Cellar & Bakery** (✉*Virgin Gorda Yacht Harbour, Spanish Town* ☎*284/495–5250)* sells bread, rolls, muffins, cookies, sandwiches, and sodas to go.

GIFTS

Flamboyance (✉*Virgin Gorda Yacht Harbour, Spanish Town* ☎*284/495–5946)* has a large line of fragrances, including those inspired by tropical flowers. The **Palm Tree Gallery** (✉*Leverick Bay* ☎*284/495–7479)* sells attractive handcrafted jewelry, paintings, and one-of-a-kind gift items, as well as games and books about the Caribbean. **Reeftique** (✉*Bitter End Yacht Harbor, North Sound* ☎*284/494–2746)* carries island crafts and jewelry, clothing, and nautical odds and ends with the Bitter End logo.

NIGHTLIFE

Pick up a free copy of the *Limin' Times*—available at most resorts and restaurants—for the most current local entertainment schedule.

During high season, **Bath & Turtle** (✉*Virgin Gorda Yacht Harbour, Spanish Town* ☎*284/495–5239)*, one of the liveliest spots on Virgin Gorda, hosts island bands Wednesday and Friday from 8 PM until midnight. Local bands play several nights a week at the **Bitter End Yacht Club** (✉*North Sound* ☎*284/494–2746)* during the winter season. **Chez Bamboo** (✉*Across from Virgin Gorda Yacht Harbour, Spanish Town* ☎*284/495–5752)* is the place for live jazz on Monday night and calypso and reggae on Friday night. The bar at **Little Dix Bay** (✉*Little Dix Bay* ☎*284/495–5555)* presents elegant live entertainment several nights a week in season. The **Mine Shaft Café** (✉*Copper Mine Point, The Valley* ☎*284/495–5260)* has live bands on Wednesday and Friday. The **Restaurant at Leverick Bay** (✉*Leverick Bay Resort & Marina, Leverick Bay* ☎*284/495–7154)* hosts live music on Saturday through Wednesday in season. The **Rock Café** (✉*The Valley* ☎*284/495–5177)* has live bands nearly every night during the winter season.

6

EXPLORING VIRGIN GORDA

One of the most efficient ways to see Virgin Gorda is by sailboat. There are few roads, and most byways don't follow the scalloped shoreline. The main route sticks resolutely to the center of the island, linking the Baths on the southern tip with Gun Creek and Leverick Bay at North Sound. The craggy coast, scissored with grottoes and fringed by palms and boulders, has a primitive beauty. If you drive, you can hit all the sights in one day. The best plan is to explore the area near your hotel (either Spanish Town or North Sound) first, then take a day to drive to the other end. Stop to climb Gorda Peak, which is in the island's center. Signage is erratic, so come prepared with a map.

Fodor's Choice ★ ☻ **The Baths.** At Virgin Gorda's most celebrated sight, giant boulders are scattered about the beach and in the water. Some are almost as large as houses and form remarkable grottoes. Climb between these rocks to swim in the many placid pools. Early morning and late afternoon are the best times to visit if you want to avoid crowds. If it's privacy you crave, follow the shore northward to quieter bays—Spring Bay, the Crawl, Little Trunk, and Valley Trunk—or head south to Devil's Bay. ⊠ *Off Tower Rd., The Baths* 🕾 *284/494–3904* ⊕ *www.bvinational parkstrust.org* 🖼 *$3* ☼ *Daily dawn–dusk.*

Coastal Islands. You can easily reach the quaintly named Fallen Jerusalem Island and the Dog Islands by boat. They're all part of the BVI National Parks Trust, and their seductive beaches and unparalleled snorkeling display the BVI at their beachcombing, hedonistic best. 🕾 *No phone* 🖼 *Free.*

Copper Mine Point. Here stand a tall stone shaft silhouetted against the sky and a small stone structure that overlooks the sea. These are the ruins of a copper mine established 400 years ago and worked first by the Spanish, then by the English, until the early 20th century. The route is not well marked, so turn inland near LSL Restaurant and look for the hard-to-see sign pointing the way. ⊠ *Copper Mine Rd.* 🕾 *No phone* ⊕ *www.bvinationalparkstrust.org* 🖼 *Free.*

Spanish Town. Virgin Gorda's peaceful main settlement, on the island's southern wing, is so tiny that it barely qualifies as a town at all. Also known as the Valley, Spanish Town has a marina, some shops, and a couple of car-rental agencies. Just north of town is the ferry slip. At the Virgin Gorda Yacht Harbour you can stroll along the dock and do a little shopping.

GETTING AROUND

The ferry service from the public dock in Spanish Town can be a tad erratic. Call ahead to confirm the schedule, get there early to be sure it hasn't changed, and ask at the dock whether you're getting on the right boat. The Thursday and Sunday service between Virgin Gorda and St. John is particularly prone to problems.

★ **Virgin Gorda Peak National Park.** There are two trails at this 265-acre park, which contains the island's highest point, at 1,359 feet. Small signs on North Sound Road mark both entrances; sometimes, however, the signs are missing, so keep your eyes open for a set of stairs that disappears into the trees. It's about a 15-minute hike from either entrance up to a small clearing, where you can climb a ladder to the platform of a wooden observation tower and a spectacular 360-degree view. ⊠*North Sound Rd., Gorda Peak* ☎*No phone* ⊕*www.bvi nationalparkstrust.org* ☞*Free.*

JOST VAN DYKE

By Carol M. Bareuther

Named after an early Dutch settler, Jost Van Dyke is a small island northwest of Tortola and is *truly* a place to get away from it all. Mountainous and lush, the 4-mi-long (6½-km-long) island—with fewer than 200 full-time residents—has one tiny resort, some rental houses and villas, a campground, a handful of cars, and a single road. Life definitely rolls along on "island time," especially during the off-season from August to November, when finding a restaurant open for dinner can be a challenge. Water conservation is encouraged, as the source is rainwater collected in basementlike cisterns. Many lodgings will ask you to follow the Caribbean golden rule: "In the land of sun and fun, we never flush for number one." Jost is one of the Caribbean's most popular anchorages, and there's a disproportionately large number of informal bars and restaurants, which have helped earn Jost its reputation as the "party island" of the BVI.

6

WHERE TO STAY

$$-$$$$ ☺ ⊞**White Bay Villas & Seaside Cottages.** There's no missing the beautiful sea views from the verandahs of these hilltop one- to three-bedroom villas and cottages. Accommodations are open-air, with screenless doors and shuttered windows, although there's mosquito netting covering the beds. Almost everything is provided, from linens and beach towels to an occasional bunch of fresh bananas or a ripe papaya from the trees outside. Although there are some small markets on the island, it's a good idea to buy groceries on St. Thomas or Tortola before arriving. White Bay and five beach bars are a short, albeit steep and rocky, walk downhill. A mile away to the east, and also downhill in Great Harbour, there's a small supermarket, half a dozen beach bars and restaurants, a souvenir shop, and water-sports rental. **Pros:** Near Great Harbour and White Bay, incredible views, friendly staff. **Cons:** Steep uphill climbs, delicate septic system. ⊠*White Bay* ⌂*Box 3368, Annapolis, MD21403* ☎*410/571–6692 or 800/778–8066* ⊕*www.jostvandyke. com* ♖*3 villas, 3 cottages* ⌂*In-room: no a/c, kitchen, VCR (some). In-hotel: beachfront, no elevator* ☐*No credit cards* ⦿*EP.*

$$ ⊞**Sandcastle.** This six-cottage hideaway sits on a half-mile stretch of ★ white-sand beach shared by a half dozen beach bars and restaurants. The peach-color cottages are simply furnished. Two-bedroom cottages have outdoor showers and no air-conditioning, but the one-bedroom cottages do have these conveniences. Either way, the Caribbean is no more than 20 feet from your doorstep. There's nothing to do here except relax in a hammock, read, walk the beach, swim, and snorkel.

CLOSE UP

The Laid-Back Lifestyle at its Best

It's the laid-back attitude of Jost Van Dyke, which boasts a beach as its main street and has had electricity only since the 1990s, that makes the famous feel comfortable and everyday folk feel glorious. At no locale is this more so than at Foxy's Tamarind. Foxy Callwood, a seventh-generation Jost Van Dyker and calypsonian extraordinaire, is the star here, strumming and singing rib-tickling ditties full of lewd and laughable lyrics that attract a bevy of boaters and even celebrities like Tom Cruise, Kelsey Grammer, and Steven Spielberg.

What began in the 1970s as a lemonade-stand-size bar, albeit with "modern" fixtures like a galvanized roof and plywood walls, has evolved into a bona fide beach bar with sand floor, wattle walls, and thatched roof that defines the eastern end of the beach

at Great Harbour. Without the glitz of St. Thomas, glamour of St. John, or grace of Tortola, islanders like Foxy knew they needed to carve out their own unique niche—and have done so by appearing to have done nothing at all. Unhurried friendliness and a slice of quintessential Caribbean culture flow freely here.

Foxy, who fished for a living before he started singing for his supper, has traveled the world and had the world come to him for endless parties for Halloween, for Labor Day weekend, and for the New Year. The New York Times named Foxy's one of its three top picks to ring in the millennium. What's the appeal? Foxy sums it up himself: "It's the quantity of people and the quality of the party. You can dance on the tables and sleep on the beach. No one is going to bother you."

Unfortunately, you may find your serenity shattered between 11 AM and 3 PM by the charter-boat day-trippers who arrive on large catamarans for lunch and drinks at the Soggy Dollar Bar. At night, tuck into a casually elegant, four-course candlelight dinner at the Sandcastle Restaurant. For weeklong stays you have the option of a package that includes all breakfasts and most dinners. **Pros:** Beachfront rooms, near restaurants and bars, comfy hammocks. **Cons:** Some rooms lack air-conditioning, beach sometimes clogged with day-trippers. ⊠ *White Bay* ☎ *284/495–9888* ⊕ *www.sandcastle-bvi.com* ⇆ *4 1-bedroom cottages, 2 2-bedroom cottages* ⟲ *In-room: no a/c (some), no TV. In-hotel: restaurant, bar, beachfront, no elevator* ▤ *D, MC, V* ⦿ *EP.*

WHERE TO EAT

Restaurants on Jost Van Dyke are informal (some serve meals family-style at long tables) but charming. The island is a favorite charter-boat stop, and you're bound to hear people exchanging stories about the previous night's anchoring adventures. Most restaurants don't take reservations, and in all cases dress is casual.

$$$$ ✕ **Sandcastle.** Candles illuminate this tiny beachfront dining room during the four-course, prix-fixe affairs. The menu changes frequently, but can include West Indian-style ginger-carrot soup; pan-sautéed fish with a creole sauce; and key lime pie for dessert. Reservations are required by 4 PM for the single dinner seating at 7 PM. There's a BBQ beach buffet on Saturday nights. For lunch you can get flying-fish sandwiches, hamburgers, chicken roti, and conch fritters at the Soggy Dollar Bar, famous as the purported birthplace of the lethal drink called the Painkiller. ⊠*Sandcastle, White Bay* ☏*284/495–9888* ⚑*Reservations essential* ▤*D, MC, V.*

$$–$$$ ✕**Abe's by the Sea.** Specialties at this popular, informal seaside spot include fresh lobster, conch, and spareribs. During the winter season there's a pig roast every Wednesday evening. Wi-Fi access is available for those who want to surf while supping. ⊠*Little Harbour* ☏*284/495–9329* ▤*D, MC, V.*

$$–$$$ ✕**Ali Baba's.** This sandy-floor eatery offers beach-bar dining at its best.
ⓒ Lobster and grilled local fish, including swordfish, kingfish, and wahoo,
★ are specialties. There's a pig roast on Monday night. Beware: Ali Baba's special rum punch is delicious but potent. Dinner reservations are required by 6 PM. ⊠*Great Harbour* ☏*284/495–9280* ⚑*Reservations essential* ▤*AE, MC, V.*

$$–$$$ ✕**Corsairs Beach Bar & Restaurant.** This beach bar is easily recognized
ⓒ by the restored U.S. Army Jeep that adjoins the dining area. Tex-Mex and Caribbean foods star at lunch, with selections ranging from lobster quesadillas to jerk-chicken wings. Northern Italian takes over at night, when you can find seafood pomodoro, which is full of shrimp, fish, squid, and lobster. Live music and a great drink menu keep things moving at night. ⊠*Great Harbour* ☏*284/495–9294* ▤*MC, V.*

$$–$$$ ✕**Foxy's Taboo.** An oasis in the middle of uninhabited marshland at
ⓒ Diamond Cay, this simple, open-air eatery has plastic chairs and tiled wooden tables overlooking a "marina" (really a small dock). But the menu is definitely more upscale here than at Foxy's place in Great Harbour. The Taboo burger at lunch is a hand-formed mound of 100% beef, served with mango chutney and pepper-jack cheese on ciabatta bread. Pizzas have toppings ranging from jalapeño peppers to prosciutto and kalamata olives. Dinner selections include mango-tamarind chicken. There are a dozen or more wines available by the bottle or glass. Don't miss the tiramisu for dessert. Dinner reservations are required by 5 PM. ⊠*Diamond Cay* ☏*284/495–0218* ⚑*Reservations essential* ▤*AE, MC, V* ⊘*Closed Mon. No dinner Sun.*

$$–$$$ ✕**Foxy's Tamarind.** One of the true hot spots in the BVI—and a must-stop
ⓒ for yachties from the world over—Foxy's hosts the madcap Wooden
★ Boat Race every May and throws big parties on New Year's Eve (locals call it "Old Year's Night"), April Fools' Day, and Halloween. This lively place serves local food, has terrific barbecue dinners on Friday and Saturday nights, mixes its own rum punch, and serves its own brand of beer. Famed calypso performer and owner Foxy Callwood plays the guitar and creates calypso ditties about diners. Reservations for dinner are required by 5 PM. ⊠*Great Harbour* ☏*284/495–9258* ⚑*Reservations essential* ▤*AE, MC, V* ⊘*No lunch weekends.*

$$–$$$ ✕**Harris' Place.** Cynthia Harris is famous for her hospitality, along with
ⓒ her family's famous pig-roast buffets and Monday-night lobster spe-
★ cials. This is the hot spot to rub elbows with locals and the charter-boat

crowd for breakfast, lunch, or dinner. ⊠ *Little Harbour* ☎ *284/495–9302* ⊟ *AE, D, MC, V.*

$$–$$$ ✕ **Rudy's Mariner's Rendezvous.** Hamburgers, cheeseburgers, and barbecue ribs are the specialties at this beachfront spot at the extreme western end of Great Harbour. There's a lobster buffet every Thursday night in season. You'll also find a supermarket where you can buy basic groceries. ⊠ *Great Harbour* ☎ *284/495–9282* ⊟ *D, MC, V.*

$$–$$$ ✕ **Sydney's Peace & Love.** Here you can find great lobster, caught aboard owner Sydney Hendrick's own fishing boat, as well as barbecue chicken and ribs. All are served on an open-air terrace or in an air-conditioned dining room at the water's edge. The find here is a sensational (by BVI standards) jukebox. The cognoscenti sail here for dinner, since there's no beach—meaning no irksome sand fleas. ⊠ *Little Harbour* ☎ *284/495–9271* ⊟ *D, MC, V.*

BEACHES & ACTIVITIES

Abe & Eunicy Rentals. Rent one of three types of vehicles—2-door Suzuki ($60 a day), 4-door automatic Jeep ($70 a day), or 4-door automatic Montero ($80 a day)—to explore by land, or a fiberglass dinghy with a 15 horsepower engine ($60 a day) or inflatable dinghy with a 25 horsepower engine, radio, and CD player ($100 a day) for traveling around by sea. There's pick-up and drop-off service from anywhere on the island. ⊠ *Little Harbour* ☎ *284/495–9329* ⊕ *www.abesbythesea. com.*

JVD Scuba and BVI Eco-Tours. See the undersea world around the island with divemaster Colin Aldridge. One of the most impressive dives in the area is off the north coast of Little Jost Van Dyke. Here you can find the Twin Towers: a pair of rock formations rising an impressive 90 feet. A one-tank dive costs $70, two-tank dive $110, and four-hour beginner course $120. ⊠ *Great Harbour* ☎ *284/495–0271* ⊕ *www. bvi-ecotours.com.*

Paradise Jeep Rentals. Even though Jost is a relatively small island, you really need to be in shape to walk from one bay to the next. Renting a jeep is an ideal way to tackle the steep, winding roads. This outfit rents four-door Suzukis for $65 per day and Grand Vitaras for $80. The vehicles are at the gas station in Great Harbour, adjacent to Christine's Bakery. Reservations are a must. ⊠ *Great Harbour* ☎ *284/495–9477.*

Sandy Cay. Just offshore, the little islet known as Sandy Cay is a gleaming scimitar of white sand, with marvelous snorkeling.

♻ **White Bay.** On the south shore, west of Great Harbour, this long stretch
★ of white sand is especially popular with boaters who come ashore for a libation at one of the beach bars.

NIGHTLIFE

★ Jost Van Dyke is the most happening place to go barhopping in the BVI. In fact, yachties will sail over just to have a few drinks. All the spots are easy to find, congregated in two general locations: Great Harbour and White Bay (⇨ *see Where to Eat, above*). On the Great Harbour side you can find Foxy's, Rudy's, and Ali Baba's; on the White Bay side is the One Love Bar and Grill, where Seddy Callwood will entertain you with his sleight of hand, and the Soggy Dollar bar at the Sandcastle restaurant, where legend has it the famous Painkiller was first concocted. If you can't make it to Jost Van Dyke, you can have a Painkiller at almost any bar in the BVI.

ANEGADA

By Carol M.
Bareuther

Fodor's Choice
★

Anegada lies low on the horizon about 14 mi (22½ km) north of Virgin Gorda. Unlike the hilly volcanic islands in the chain, this is a flat coral-and-limestone atoll. Nine miles (14 km) long and 2 mi (3 km) wide, the island rises no more than 28 feet above sea level. In fact, by the time you're able to see it, you may have run your boat onto a reef. (More than 300 captains unfamiliar with the waters have done so since exploration days; note that bareboat charters don't allow their vessels to head here without a trained skipper.) Although the reefs are a sailor's nightmare, they (and the shipwrecks they've caused) are a scuba diver's dream. Snorkeling, especially in the waters around Loblolly Bay on the north shore, is a transcendent experience. You can float in shallow, calm water just a few feet from shore and see one coral formation after another, each shimmering with a rainbow of colorful fish. Such watery pleasures are complemented by ever-so-fine, ever-so-white sand (the northern and western shores have long stretches of the stuff) and the occasional beach bar (stop in for burgers, local lobster, or a frosty beer). The island's population of about 180 lives primarily in a small south-side village called the Settlement, which has two grocery stores, a bakery, and a general store. Many local captains are happy to take visitors out bonefishing.

6

WHERE TO STAY

$$–$$$ **Anegada Reef Hotel.** This may be the busiest place on sleepy Anegada. Although boaters drop anchor in sheltered waters inside the reef and guests from other hotels stop by for lobster salad lunches, the resort itself remains a serene spot. Head here if you want to relax in the shade on a beach that stretches forever, enjoy the company of like-minded folks, and do nothing more strenuous than heading out once or twice to fish or scuba dive in the nearby waters. Rooms are simple but fresh with pastel fabrics. An all-inclusive meal plan is available, however the most exciting 'entertainment' on Anegada is checking out the handful of beach bars and restaurants. **Pros:** Everything you need is nearby, serene setting, gorgeous views. **Cons:** Basic rooms, often a party atmosphere. ⊠ *Setting Point* ☎ *284/495–8002* ⊕ *www.anegadareef.com*

╚20 rooms △In-room: no phone, no TV. In-hotel: restaurant, bar, beachfront, no elevator ⊟MC, V ⊺⊙⫞EP.

$ ⊞ **Neptune's Treasure.** Basic beachside rooms with simple but squeaky-
♺ clean furnishings and air-conditioning that's essential during the summer and fall months are the hallmark of this family-owned guesthouse. If you're happy with a simple place to rest your head while you swim or kayak in crystal-clear waters, sun at the round-the-island beach, enjoy fresh-from-the-sea dinners at the hotel's restaurant, and watch the sun go down, this is the place. If you must move out of the hammock, the hotel will organize an island tour or a fishing expedition. Bonefishing along the flats and deep-sea fishing for blue marlin is some of the best in the world here. **Pros:** Beachfront property, run by a family full of tales of the island. **Cons:** Simple rooms, basic property. ⊠*Between Pomato and Saltheap points* ☎*284/495–9439* ⊕*www.neptunestreasure.com* ╚*9 rooms* △*In-room: no TV. In-hotel: restaurant, beachfront, no elevator* ⊟*MC, V* ⊺⊙⫞*EP.*

WHERE TO EAT

There are between 6 and 10 restaurants open at any one time, depending on the season and on whim. Check when you're on the island.

$$$–$$$$ ✕ **Anegada Reef Hotel Restaurant.** Seasoned yachters gather here nightly to share tales of the high seas. Dinner is by candlelight and always includes famous Anegada lobster, steaks, and succulent baby back ribs—all prepared on the large grill by the little open-air bar. ⊠*Anegada Reef Hotel, Setting Point* ☎*284/495–8002* ⌑*Reservations essential* ⊟*MC, V.*

$$$–$$$$ ✕ **Big Bamboo.** Ice-cold beer, fruity drinks, burgers, fresh fish, barbecued
★ chicken, conch and crab cakes entice a steady stream of barefoot diners to this beach bar for lunch. Dinner is by request only. If your heart is set on lobster, be sure to call in the morning or day before to put in your request. ⊠*Loblolly Bay West* ☎*284/495–2019* ⊟*MC, V.*

$$$–$$$$ ✕ **Pomato Point Restaurant.** This relaxed restaurant and bar sits on a narrow beach a short walk from the Anegada Reef Hotel. Entrées include lobster, stewed conch, and freshly caught seafood. It's open for lunch daily; call by 4 PM for dinner reservations. There's live music each Wednesday evening in season. Be sure to take a look at owner Wilfred Creque's displays of island artifacts, including shards of Arawak pottery and 17th-century coins, cannonballs, and bottles. These are housed in a little one-room museum adjacent to the dining room. ⊠*Pomato Point* ☎*284/495–8038* ⌑*Reservations essential* ⊟*MC, V* ⊙*Closed Sept.*

$$–$$$$ ✕ **Cow Wreck Bar & Grill.** Named for the cow bones that once washed up on shore, this open-air beachside eatery is a fun place to watch the antics of surfers and kite boarders skidding across the bay. Tuck into conch fritters or a lobster salad sandwich for lunch or freshly grilled lobster for dinner. ⊠*Loblolly Bay East* ☎*284/495–8047* ⊟*MC, V.*

$$–$$$$ ✕ **Neptune's Treasure.** The owners catch, cook, and serve the seafood
♺ (lobster is a specialty, as is garlic-studded shark, in season) at this casual

bar and restaurant in the Neptune's Treasure guesthouse. ⊠*Between Pomato and Saltheap points* ☎*284/495–9439* ▭*MC, V.*

BEACHES & ACTIVITIES

Anegada Water Sports. Parasailing, water-skiing, windsurfing, surfing, scuba diving, snorkeling, and bonefishing as well as hiking and bicycling on land can be arranged through this outfit, which also rents a one-bedroom and two-bedroom cottage on Loblolly Beach. ☎*284/495–8359* ⊕*www.loblollycottages.com.*

OTHER BRITISH VIRGIN ISLANDS

COOPER ISLAND

By Lynda Lohr

This small, hilly island on the south side of the Sir Francis Drake Channel, about 8 mi (13 km) from Road Town, Tortola, is popular with the charter-boat crowd. There are no paved roads (which doesn't really matter, as there aren't any cars), but you can find a beach restaurant, a casual hotel, a few houses (some are available for rent), and great snorkeling at the south end of Manchioneel Bay.

\$\$ ✕🖳 **Cooper Island Beach Club.** Cooper Island is one of those Caribbean
Fodor's Choice spots that hark back to an earlier era when frills were few but the
★ peaceful atmosphere was sublime. You usually either love the quiet or hate the isolation. Once you arrive via a complimentary ferry ride from Prospect Reef, Tortola, there's nothing to do but relax, enjoy the sun and the sea, and visit with old and new friends. Rooms are really small suites with basic cooking facilities, but the hotel's restaurant is nearby if you don't want to lug groceries on the ferry. Don't pack your hair dryer or electric shaver, because the wiring can't handle it. Meals run to basics like fish, chicken, and steak. Reservations are essential for the restaurant if you're not a resort guest. **Pros:** Lots of quiet, the Caribbean as it used to be. **Cons:** Small rooms, modest furnishings, need ferry to get here. ⊠*Manchioneel Bay, Road Town* ⌂*Box 512, Turner Falls, MA* ☎*413/863–3162 or 800/542–4624* ⊕*www.cooper-island.com* ⇋*12 rooms* ⌂*In-room: no a/c, no phone, kitchen, no TV. In-hotel: restaurant, bar, beachfront, diving, no elevator, public Wi-Fi* ▭*MC, V* ⅠⓄⅠ*EP.*

GUANA ISLAND

Guana Island sits off Tortola's northeast coast. Sailors often drop anchor at one of the island's bays for a day of snorkeling and sunning. The island is a designated wildlife sanctuary, and scientists often come here to study its flora and fauna. It's home to a back-to-nature resort that offers few activities other than relaxation. Unless you're a hotel guest or a sailor, there's no easy way to get here.

$$$$ ⚜ **Guana Island Resort.** Guana Island is a nature lover's paradise, and it's
★ a good resort if you want to stroll the hillsides, snorkel around the reefs,
and swim at its six beaches, and still enjoy some degree of comfort.
Rooms are simple but charming, with rattan furniture and tile or painted
concrete floors, and are open to the tropical breezes. Once you're here,
you're here. You can spend your time dining and socializing with the
other guests or immersed in that book you never got around to reading.
You can rent the entire 15-room resort if you'd like to vacation with a
group of your friends or family. The hotel's launch picks you up near Terrence B. Lettsome Airport on Beef Island (Tortola's airport) for the short
hop across the water to the resort. **Pros:** Secluded feel, lovely grounds.
Cons: Very expensive, need boat to get here. ⊠ *Guana Island* 🖂 *Box
32, Road Town, Tortola* ☎ *284/494–2354 or 800/544–8262* ⊕ *www.
guana.com* ⇨ *15 rooms, 1 cottage, 1 2-bedroom villa, 1 3-bedroom
villa* ♨ *In-room: no a/c (some), no phone, no TV (some), Wi-Fi. In-hotel:
restaurant, beachfront, water sports, no elevator, public Internet, public
Wi-Fi* ⊟ *AE, MC, V* ◎ *FAP.*

NORMAN ISLAND

This uninhabited island is the supposed setting for Robert Louis Steven-
son's *Treasure Island*. The famed caves at Treasure Point are popular
with day sailors and power boaters. If you land ashore at the island's
main anchorage in the Bight, you can find a small beach bar and behind
it a trail that winds up the hillside and reaches a peak with a fantastic
view of the Sir Francis Drake Channel to the north.

$$ ✕ **Willy T.** The ship, a former Baltic trader and today a floating bar
and restaurant anchored to the north of the Bight, serves lunch and
dinner in a party-hearty atmosphere. Try the jalapeño poppers for
starters. For lunch and dinner, British-style fish-and-chips, West Indian
roti sandwiches, and the barbecued chicken are winners. ⊠ *The Bight*
☎ *284/496–8603* ♨ *Reservations essential* ⊟ *MC, V.*

BRITISH VIRGIN ISLANDS ESSENTIALS

*To research prices, get advice from other
travelers, and book travel arrangements,
visit www.fodors.com.*

∎ TRANSPORTATION

BY AIR

Most travelers to the BVI connect in San
Juan or St. Thomas. You can fly to Tor-
tola, Virgin Gorda, or Anegada but only
on a small plane. Several airlines have
regularly scheduled service to either Tor-
tola or Virgin Gorda. If you have seven or
more people in your party, you can also
charter plane from St. Thomas or San
Juan; Fly BVI is one of the local charter
services.

All three of the BVI's airports—Tortola
(TOC), Virgin Gorda (VIJ), and Ane-
gada (no code)—are classic Caribbean
and almost always sleepy; however, Tor-
tola's Terrence B. Lettsome Airport at
Beef Island can get crowded when several
departures are scheduled close together.

Airline Contacts Air Sunshine (☎284/495–8900 ⊕www.airsunshine.com). **American Eagle** (☎284/495–2559 ⊕www.aa.com). **Cape Air** (☎284/495–1440 ⊕www.flycapeair.com). **Fly BVI** (☎284/495–1747 ⊕www.fly-bvi.com). **LIAT** (☎284/495–2577 ⊕www.liat.com).

Airport Transfers Airport Taxi Association (☎284/495–1982).**Mahogany Rentals & Taxi Service** (⊠Virgin Gorda ☎284/495–5469).

BY BOAT & FERRY

Frequent daily ferries connect Tortola with St. Thomas, where many vacationers use as their main air gateway. Ferries go to and from both Charlotte Amalie and Red Hook. There's huge competition among the Tortola-based ferry companies on the St. Thomas–Tortola runs, with boats leaving close together. As you enter the ferry terminal to buy your ticket, crews may try to convince you to take their ferry.

Ferries also connect St. Thomas with Virgin Gorda, leaving from both Charlotte Amalie and Red Hook, but not daily. Ferries to Virgin Gorda land in Spanish Town.

Leaving both Tortola and Virgin Gorda, all ferries to Red Hook, St. Thomas, stop in St. John first to clear U.S. customs. You can also board in St. John for the trip to the BVI. Since schedules can vary so much, a useful resource is the BVI Tourist Board Web site, which has links to all the ferry companies; these Web sites are the best up-to-date sources of information for specific routes and schedules.

Ferries also link Tortola with Jost Van Dyke, Peter Island, and Virgin Gorda. Tortola has two ferry terminals—one at West End and one in Road Town—so make sure you hop a ferry that disembarks closest to where you want to go.

Contacts Inter-Island Boat Services (☎284/495–4166). **Native Son** (☎284/495–4617 ⊕www.nativesonbvi.com). **New Horizon Ferry Service** (☎284/495–9278 ⊕www.jostvandykeferry.com). **North Sound** **Express** (☎284/495–2138). **Peter Island Ferry** (☎284/495–2000 ⊕www.peterisland.com). **Smith's Ferry** (☎284/495–4495 ⊕www.smithsferry.com). **Speedy's Ferries** (☎284/494–6154 ⊕www.speedysbvi.com). **Tortola Fast Ferry** (☎284/494–2323 ⊕www.tortolafastferry.com).

BY CAR

Driving in the BVI is on the left, British-style, but your car will always have its steering wheel on the left. Speed limits are 20 mph (30 kph) in town and 35 mph (55 kph) outside town but are rarely enforced. Gas is expensive. You need a temporary BVI license, available at the rental-car company for $10 with a valid license from another country. The minimum age to rent a car is 25. Most agencies offer both four-wheel-drive vehicles and cars (often compacts).

Tortola's main roads are well paved, for the most part, but there are exceptionally steep hills and sharp curves; driving demands your complete attention. A main road circles the island, and several roads cross it, almost always through mountainous terrain.

Virgin Gorda has a small road system, and a single, very steep road links the north and south ends of the island. You will probably need a car to get around for at least a few days of your stay unless you plan on staying put at your resort.

Tortola Contacts Avis (⊠Opposite Police Station, Road Town, Tortola ☎284/494–3322). **D&D** (⊠West End Rd., West End, Tortola ☎284/495–4765). **Hertz** (⊠West End, Tortola ☎284/495–4405 ⊠Airport, Tortola ☎284/495–6600 ⊠Road Town, Tortola ☎284/494–6228). **Itgo Car Rental** (⊠Wickham's Cay I, Road Town, Tortola ☎284/494–2639).

Virgin Gorda Contacts L&S Jeep Rental (⊠South Valley, Virgin Gorda ☎284/495–5297 ⊕www.landsjeeprentals.com).**Mahogany Rentals & Taxi Service** (⊠Spanish Town, Virgin Gorda ☎284/495–5469 ⊕mahoganyrentals.puzzlepiece.net).**Speedy's Car Rentals**

6

(⊠The Valley, Virgin Gorda ☏284/495–5240 ⊕www.speedysbvi.com).

BY TAXI

Taxi rates aren't set in the BVI, so you should negotiate the fare with your driver before you start your trip. Fares are per destination, not per person here, so it's cheaper to travel in groups because the fare will be the same whether you have one, two, or three passengers. The taxi number is always on the license plate.

On Tortola, the BVI Taxi Association has stands in Road Town near Wickham's Cay I. The Waterfront Taxi Association picks up passengers from the Road Town ferry dock. The Beef Island Taxi Association operates at the Beef Island–Tortola airport. You can also usually find a West End Taxi Association ferry at the West End ferry dock.

On Virgin Gorda, Andy's Taxi & Jeep Rental offers service from one end of Virgin Gorda to the other. Mahogany Rentals & Taxi Service provides taxi service all over Virgin Gorda.

Tortola Contacts **Airport Taxi Association** (⊠Beef Island Airport, Tortola ☏284/495–1982). **BVI Taxi Association** (⊠Near ferry dock, Road Town, Tortola ☏284/494–3942). **West End Taxi Association** (⊠West End ferry terminal, Tortola ☏284/495–4934). **Waterfront Taxi Association** (⊠Ferry dock, Road Town ☏284/494–6362).

Virgin Gorda Contacts **Andy's Taxi & Jeep Rental** (⊠The Valley, Virgin Gorda ☏284/495–5252). **Mahogany Rentals & Taxi Service** (⊠The Valley, Virgin Gorda ☏284/495–5469).

■ CONTACTS & RESOURCES

BANKS

The currency in the BVI is the U.S. dollar, so there's never a need to change money. ATMs are common in Road Town, Tortola, and around Virgin Gorda Yacht Harbour.

ELECTRICITY

Electricity is 110 volts, the same as in North America, so American appliances work just fine.

EMERGENCIES

Ambulance, Fire & Police **General emergencies** (☏999).

Hospitals & Clinics **Peebles Hospital** (⊠Road Town, Tortola ☏284/494–3497). **Virgin Gorda Government Health Clinic** (⊠The Valley, Virgin Gorda ☏284/495–5337).

Marine Emergencies **VISAR** (☏767 from phone or Marine Radio Channel 16).

INTERNET, MAIL & SHIPPING

There's a post office in Road Town on Tortola. For a small fee, Rush It, in Road Town, offers most U.S. mail and UPS services (via St. Thomas the next day). If you wish to write to an establishment in the BVI, be sure to include the specific island in the address.

There's a post office in Spanish Town on Virgin Gorda. For a small fee, Rush It, in Spanish Town, offers most U.S. mail and UPS services (via St. Thomas the next day). If you wish to write to an establishment in the BVI, be sure to include the specific island in the address.

Many hotels have Internet access for their guests. Internet cafés, however, are harder to find. On Tortola, try Trellis Bay Cybercafé.

Contacts **Rush It** (⊠Road Town, Tortola ☏284/494–4421; ⊠Spanish Town, Virgin Gorda ☏284/495–5821). **Trellis Bay Cybercafé** (⊠Trellis Bay, Tortola ☏284/495–2447).

SAFETY

Although crime is rare, use common sense: don't leave your camera on the beach while you take a dip or your wallet on a hotel dresser when you go for a walk.

TAXES

The departure tax is $5 per person by boat and $20 per person by plane. There's a separate booth at the airport and ferry terminals to collect this tax, which must be paid in cash in U.S. currency. Most hotels add a service charge ranging from 5% to 18% to the bill. A few restaurants and some shops tack on an additional 10% charge if you use a credit card. There's no sales tax in the BVI. However, there's a 7% government tax on hotel rooms.

TELEPHONES

Your mobile phone may or may not work in the BVI. If you're on the south side of Tortola, you may be able to connect to AT&T and Sprint, but other islands are problematic. The BVI have local companies only. Even if your U.S. mainland company assures you that your phone will work, don't count on it.

The area code for the BVI is 284; when you make calls from North America, you need only dial the area code and the number. From the United Kingdom you must dial 001 and then the area code and the number. From Australia and New Zealand you must dial 0011 followed by 1, the area code, and the number.

To call anywhere in the BVI once you've arrived, dial all seven digits. A local call from a pay phone costs 25¢, but such phones are sometimes on the blink. An alternative is a Caribbean phone card, available in $5, $10, and $20 denominations. They're sold at most major hotels and many stores and can be used to call within the BVI, as well as all over the Caribbean, and to access USADirect from special phone-card phones. For credit card or collect long-distance calls to the United States, use a phone-card telephone or look for special USADirect phones, which are linked directly to an AT&T operator. USADirect and pay phones can be found at most hotels and in towns.

Information **USADirect** (☎800/872–2881, 111 from a pay phone).

TIPPING

Tip porters and bellhops $1 per bag. Sometimes a service charge (10%) is included on restaurant bills; it's customary to leave another 5% if you liked the service. If no charge is added, 15% is the norm. Cabbies normally aren't tipped because most own their cabs; add 10% to 15% if they exceed their duties.

TOUR OPTIONS

Romney Associates/Travel Plan Tours can arrange island tours, boat tours, snorkeling and scuba-diving trips, dolphin swims, and yacht charters from its bases on Tortola and Virgin Gorda.

Information **Romney Associates/Travel Plan Tours** (☎284/494–4000).

VISITOR INFORMATION

Contacts **BVI Tourist Board** (✉Ferry Terminal, Road Town, Tortola ☎284/494–3134 ✉Virgin Gorda Yacht Harbour, Spanish Town, Virgin Gorda ☎284/495–5181 ⊕www.bvitourism.com).

WEDDINGS

Getting married in the BVI is a breeze, but you must make advance plans. To make things go smoother, hire a wedding planner to guide you through the ins and outs of the BVI system. Many hotels also have wedding planners on staff to help organize your event. Hotels often offer packages that include the ceremony; accommodations for you, your wedding party and your guests; and extras like massages, sailboat trips, and champagne dinners.

You must apply in person for your license ($110) weekdays at the attorney general's office in Road Town, Tortola, even if you're getting married on Virgin Gorda. You must wait three days to pick it up at the registrar's office in Road Town. If you plan to be married in a church, announcements (called *banns* locally) must be published for three consecutive Sundays in the church bulletin. Only the registrar or clergy can perform ceremonies. The registrar charges $35 at the office and $100 at another location. No blood test is required.

Contacts **BVI Wedding Planners & Consultants** (☎284/494–5306 ⊕www.bviweddings.com).

6

Cayman Islands

Coral reef, Little Cayman Island

WORD OF MOUTH

"We love Eden Rock. We've seen things there we've never seen at any other places we snorkeled. Last year it was the biggest barracuda we'd ever seen . . . the year before it was several turtles."

—SuzieC

"Cayman Brac is VERY laid back. Hardly anyone there. Most tourists are divers . . . The diving at Brac was the best dive vacation we have done."

—Kima

WELCOME TO
CAYMAN ISLANDS

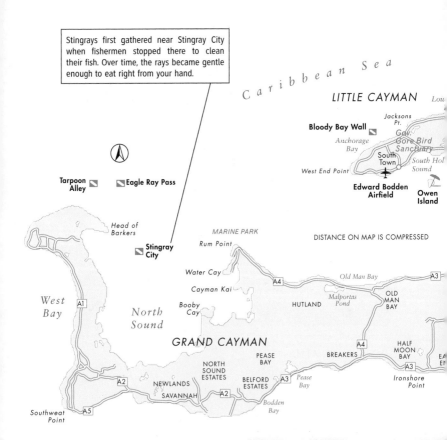

Stingrays first gathered near Stingray City when fishermen stopped there to clean their fish. Over time, the rays became gentle enough to eat right from your hand.

Caribbean Sea

LITTLE CAYMAN   *Lou*

Jacksons Pt.

Bloody Bay Wall

Anchorage Bay   *Gov.*
Gore Bird Sanctuary

South Town   *South Hol Sound*

West End Point

Edward Bodden Airfield   **Owen Island**

Tarpoon Alley   **Eagle Ray Pass**

Head of Barkers

MARINE PARK

DISTANCE ON MAP IS COMPRESSED

Rum Point

Stingray City

Water Cay   *Old Man Bay*   A3

Cayman Kai   A4

West Bay   A1   *North Sound*   *Booby Cay*   *Malportas Pond*   **HUTLAND**   **OLD MAN BAY**

GRAND CAYMAN

A4   **HALF MOON BAY**

PEASE BAY   **BREAKERS**   A3

NORTH SOUND ESTATES   A3   *Pease Bay*

A2   **BELFORD ESTATES**   *Ironshore Point*

NEWLANDS   A2

SAVANNAH   *Bodden Bay*

Southweat Point   A5

Grand Cayman may be the world's largest offshore finance hub, but other offshore activities have put the Caymans on the map. Pristine waters, breathtaking coral formations, and plentiful and exotic marine creatures beckon divers from around the world. Other vacationers are drawn by the islands' mellow civility.

FUN ON AND OFF SHORE

Grand Cayman, which is 22 mi (36 km) long and 8 mi (13 km) wide, is the largest of the three low-lying islands that make up this British colony. Its sister islands (Little Cayman and Cayman Brac) are almost 90 mi (149 km) north and east. The Cayman Trough between the Cayman Islands and Jamaica is the deepest part of the Caribbean.

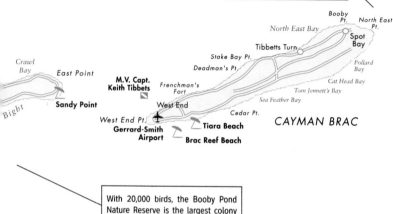

Cayman Brac is named for its 140-foot bluff on the island's eastern end, which is the highest point in the Cayman Islands chain.

With 20,000 birds, the Booby Pond Nature Reserve is the largest colony of the birds in the Caribbean.

7

CAYMAN ISLANDS

OP 4 REASONS TO VISIT THE CAYMAN ISLANDS

Underwater visibility (about 120 feet) is among the best in the Caribbean, and nearby, healthy reefs make this one of the Caribbean's top dive destinations.

With no panhandlers, little crime, and excellent resorts and restaurants, it's an easy place to vacation.

❸ A snorkeling trip to Sting Ray Sandbar is an experience you'll always remember.

❹ Grand Cayman's Seven Mile Beach is one of the Caribbean's best sandy beaches.

CAYMAN ISLANDS PLANNER

Island Activities

Diving is a major draw to all three of the Cayman Islands; the Bloody Bay Wall, off the coast of Little Cayman, is one of the Caribbean's top dive destinations, but there are many sites convenient to Grand Cayman, where shore diving is also good.

One of the most popular activities on Grand Cayman is a dive or snorkeling trip to **Stingray City** or **Stingray Sandbar**; petting and feeding the amazing creatures is a highlight of many Caribbean trips.

On land, Grand Cayman has the most to offer, with plenty of tours and activities, including **semisubmersible tours** of the bay for those who want to see under the waves without getting wet.

Grand Cayman's **Seven Mile Beach** is one of the Caribbean's finest long stretches of sand.

Rock climbers have now discovered the Brac's limestone bluff.

Logistics

Getting to the Cayman Islands: There are plenty of nonstop flights to Grand Cayman (GCM) from the United States. There is also one weekly nonstop from Miami to Cayman Brac (CYB), though most people hop over to the Brac and Little Cayman (LYB) on a small plane from Grand Cayman. Flights land at Owen Roberts Airport (Grand Cayman), Gerrard-Smith Airport (Cayman Brac), or Edward Bodden Airstrip (Little Cayman).

Hassle Factor: Low for Grand Cayman; Medium for Little Cayman and Cayman Brac.

Nonstops: You can fly nonstop to Grand Cayman from Atlanta (Delta), Charlotte (USAirways), Chicago (Cayman Airways), Detroit (Northwest—weekly), Fort Lauderdale (Cayman Airways, Spirit Airlines—twice-weekly), Houston (Cayman Airways), Miami (American, Cayman Airways), New York–JFK (Cayman Airways), New York–Newark (Continental—weekly), and Tampa (Cayman Airways). Cayman Airways also flies weekly from Miami nonstop to Cayman Brac. Air Jamaica offers nonstop flights from both Kingston and Montego Bay.

On the Ground

In Grand Cayman you must take a taxi or rent a car at the airport since most hotels are not permitted to offer airport shuttles. Hotel pickup is more readily available on Cayman Brac and Little Cayman, and taxi service and car rentals are also available on the smaller islands as well.

Renting a Car: It's possible to get by without a car on Grand Cayman if you are staying in the Seven Mile Beach area. You could even walk or ride a bike. If you want to explore the rest of the island—or if you are staying in a condo—you'll need a car. A car is less of a necessity on Cayman Brac or Little Cayman, but cars are available on both islands. To rent a car, bring your valid driver's license, and the car-rental firm will issue you a temporary permit ($7.50). Rates range from $40 to $85 a day. If you're staying in the Seven Mile Beach area of Grand Cayman, most agencies offer free pickup.

Where to Stay

Grand Cayman draws the bulk of Cayman Island visitors. It's expensive during the high season but offers the widest range of resorts, restaurants, and activities both in and out of the water; most resorts are on or near Seven Mile Beach, but a few are north in the West Bay Area, near Rum Point, or on the quiet East End. Both Little Cayman and Cayman Brac are more geared toward serving the needs of divers, who still make up the majority of visitors. Beaches on the Sister Islands, as they are called, don't measure up to Grand Cayman's Seven Mile Beach. The smaller islands are cheaper than Grand Cayman, but with the extra cost of transportation, the overall cost is usually a wash.

Grand Cayman: Grand Cayman has plenty of medium-size resorts as well as the Ritz-Carlton, a large seven-story resort on Seven Mile Beach. The island also has a wide range of condos and villas, many in resortlike compounds on or near Seven Mile Beach and the Cayman-Kai area. There are even a few small guesthouses for budget-minded visitors.

The Sister Islands: Cayman Brac has mostly intimate resorts. Little Cayman has a mix of small resorts and condos, most appealing to divers.

Hotel & Restaurant Costs

⇨*For information on hotel meal plans, see Accommodations in Caribbean Essentials.*

WHAT IT COSTS IN U.S. DOLLARS

$$$$	$$$	$$	$	¢
Restaurants				
over $30	$20–$30	$12–$20	$8–$12	under $8
Hotels*				
over $350	$250–$350	$150–$250	$80–$150	under $80
Hotels**				
over $450	$350–$450	$250–$350	$125–$250	under $125

*EP, BP, CP **AI, FAP, MAP Restaurant prices are for a main course excluding 10% tax and tip. Hotel prices are for two people in a double room in high season, excluding 10% tax, 10%–15% service charge, and meal plans (except at all-inclusives).

When to Go

High season begins in mid-December and continues through early to mid-April. During the low season, you can often get a substantial discount of as much as 40%.

Grand Cayman has two major events: the **Batabano Carnival** in May (or the first week after Easter) is the Cayman Islands' answer to Mardi Gras, though it happens after instead of before Lent.

Pirates Week, Grand Cayman's big fall festival, is in late October. It's a Carnival-like celebration, when visitors and locals dress up as pirates and wenches; music, fireworks, parades, street dances, and competitions take place island-wide.

During the **Cayman Islands International Fishing Tournament** in April, fishermen can enjoy plenty of action and win big prizes.

By Jordan
Simon

A CUSTOMS INSPECTOR TICKS OFF A CHECKLIST OF BANNED ITEMS: "Anything you plan on leaving on Grand Cayman except stress?" After the smiling response, he continues, "You can deposit that anywhere and it will be picked up and disposed of. We looked into stress recycling, but there isn't a call for it."

This British colony, which consists of Grand Cayman, smaller Cayman Brac, and Little Cayman, is one of the Caribbean's most popular destinations. Columbus is said to have sighted the islands in 1503 and dubbed them Las Tortugas after seeing so many turtles in the sea. The name was later changed to Cayman, referring to the caiman crocodiles that once roamed the islands. The Cayman Islands remained largely uninhabited until the late 1600s, when England took them and Jamaica from Spain. Emigrants from England, Holland, Spain, and France arrived, as did refugees from the Spanish Inquisition and deserters from Oliver Cromwell's army in Jamaica; many brought slaves with them as well. The Cayman Islands' caves and coves were also perfect hideouts for the likes of Blackbeard, Sir Henry Morgan, and other pirates out to plunder Spanish galleons. Many ships fell afoul of the reefs surrounding the islands, often with the help of Caymanians, who lured vessels to shore with beacon fires.

Today's Cayman Islands are seasoned with suburban prosperity (particularly Grand Cayman, where residents joke that the national flower is the satellite dish) and stuffed with crowds (the hotels that line the famed Seven Mile Beach are often full, even in the slow summer season). Most of the 52,465 Cayman Islanders live on Grand Cayman, where the cost of living is at least 20% higher than in the United States, but you won't be hassled by panhandlers or feel afraid to walk around on a dark evening (the crime rate is very low). Add political and economic stability to the mix, and you have a fine island recipe indeed.

GRAND CAYMAN

Grand Cayman has long been known for two offshore activities: banking and scuba diving. With 296 banks, the capital, George Town, is relatively modern and usually bustles with activity, but never more so than when two to seven cruise ships are docked in the harbor, an increasingly common occurrence. Accountants in business clothes join thousands of vacationers in their tropical togs, jostling for tables at lunch. When they're not mingling in the myriad shops, vacationers delve into sparkling waters to snorkel and dive, but increasingly, couples are also coming to be married, or at least to enjoy their honeymoon.

In September 2004, Grand Cayman was hit hard by Hurricane Ivan, but the landscape has largely regained its lush greenery, although the effects on the mangroves and large trees are still visible. There is a lot of new construction and plenty of traffic, so check with a local to plan driving time. It can take 45 minutes during rush hours to go 8 mi (13 km).

WHERE TO STAY

Brace yourself for resort prices—there are few accommodations in the lower price ranges. You'll find no big all-inclusive resorts on Grand Cayman (though the Reef Resort does now offer an optional AI plan to its guests), and very few offer a meal plan other than breakfast. Parking is always free at island hotels and resorts.

HOTELS

$$$$ **Grand Cayman Beach Suites.** Hyatt no longer manages this all-suite resort, whose primary recommendation is its beachfront location and trendy eateries, but local ownership has made a seamless transition thus far. The resort lacks landscaping, so the setting is one of concrete and elevators. Nevertheless, the ocean-view suites are plush if a tad worn. The higher the room, the smaller the balcony, but your view becomes increasingly stunning. Suites come with all the latest gadgetry (Wi-Fi, iPod station, flat-screen TV/DVD). Nice touches include canopied beach chairs, and the facilities, led by a Red Sail Sports outpost and ultrahip Bamboo lounge are top notch. **Pros:** Fine beach, superior dining and water-sports facilities, free use of gym (unusual on Grand Cayman), supermarkets and restaurants within walking distance. **Cons:** Most entrances face the street making it noisy weekends, several units need refurbishment, limited parking, music often blaring around the pool. ⊠ *West Bay Rd., Box 1698, Seven Mile Beach* ☎ *345/949–1234* ⊕ *www.grand-cayman-beach-suites.com* ⤶ *53 beach suites* ⌂ *In-room: safe, kitchen, Wi-Fi. In-hotel: 2 restaurants, room service, bars, golf course, pools, gym, spa, beachfront, diving, water sports, concierge, children's programs (ages 3–12)* ⊟ *AE, D, DC, MC, V* ⦿ *EP.*

$$$$ **Ritz-Carlton Grand Cayman.** Posh and pampering without pretension, the Ritz-Carlton offers unparalleled luxury and service infused with a welcome sense of place. The 144-acre resort, as exquisitely manicured as its clientele, is anchored by a seven-story behemoth that faces Seven Mile Beach on the west and the North Sound on the east. Greg Norman designed the golf course; tennis is run by Nick Bollettieri (coach of greats like Andre Agassi); La Prairie operates the sybaritic spa; and the Ambassadors of the Environment children's program was created by none other than Jean-Michel Cousteau. The staff is professional yet discreet, knowing their business not yours. Despite its glam romantic trappings, the resort is family-friendly. Rooms are spacious, hedonistic, and outfitted with high-tech conveniences. **Pros:** Exemplary service, exceptional facilities, extras like naturalist-guided pontoon boat tours of Stingray City. **Cons:** Luxury comes with a high price tag, somewhat sprawling with a confusing layout, long walk to beach (over an interior bridge) from most rooms. ⌕ *Box 32348, KY1-1209, Seven Mile Beach* ☎ *345/943–9000* ⊕ *www.ritzcarlton.com* ⤶ *329 rooms, 12 suites, 24 condominiums* ⌂ *In-room: safe, kitchen (some), refrigerator, DVD, Wi-Fi. In-hotel: 5 restaurants, room service, bar, pools, spa, diving, laundry facilities, children's program (4–12), no-smoking rooms* ⊟ *AE, D, MC, V* ⦿ *BP.*

$$$–$$$$ **Grand Cayman Marriott Beach Resort.** This property received a needed face-lift in 2006; soft, warm colors throughout its public spaces enhance

KEY

- Dive Sites
- 1 Restaurants
- 1 Hotels

Conch Point
Palmetto Point Rd.
Conch Point Rd.
Capt. Reg Parson's Rd.

BARKERS

BIRCH TREE HILL

MOUNT PLEASANT

Head of Barkers

West Bay

BATABANO

CORAL GABLES

NW Point

Town Hall Rd.

North West Point Rd.

West Bay

Orange Canyon

Trinity Caves

Little Salt Creek

Salt Creek

Cemetery Reef

UPPERLAND

Grand Cayman Yacht Club

West Bay Rd.

Governors Creek

Aquarium

GOVERNORS HARBOUR

Seven Mile Beach

The Links at Safehaven Golf Course

Welch Point

Paradise Reef

West Bay

Brittania Golf Course

Galleria Plaza

Galleria Loop

West Shore Center

Marquee Plaza

West Bay Rd.

WHITEHALL ESTATES

North Sound

Eastern Av.

North Sound Rd.

Owen Roberts International Airport

Wreck of the Cali

George Town

Eden Rock

Elgin Av.

Smith Rd.

Crewe Rd.

Black Reef Skate Park

Smith's Cove

S. Church St.

Walkers Rd.

South Sound Rd.

South Sound

Prospect Point

0 ——— 2 mi
0 ——— 2 km

Tarpoon Alley

Boatswain's Beach

Hell

Head Barker

Old Homestead

West Bay

Butterfly Farm

George Town

Southweat Point

Hotels ▼

Christopher Columbus 11

Cobalt Coast 13

Comfort Suites Seven Mile Beach 2

Coral Stone Club 7

Courtyard Marriott 10

Grand Cayman Beach Suites 5

Grand Cayman Marriott 3

Lacovia Condominiums 4

Reef Resort 16

Ritz-Carlton 5

Rocky Shore 12

Shangri-La B&B 14

Sunset House 1

Sunshine Suites 8

Turtle Nest Inn 15

Westin Casuarina 9

Restaurants ▼

Blue by Eric Ripert 14

The Brasserie 1

Breezes by the Bay 4

Calypso Grill 17

Champion House II 5

Chicken Chicken! 10

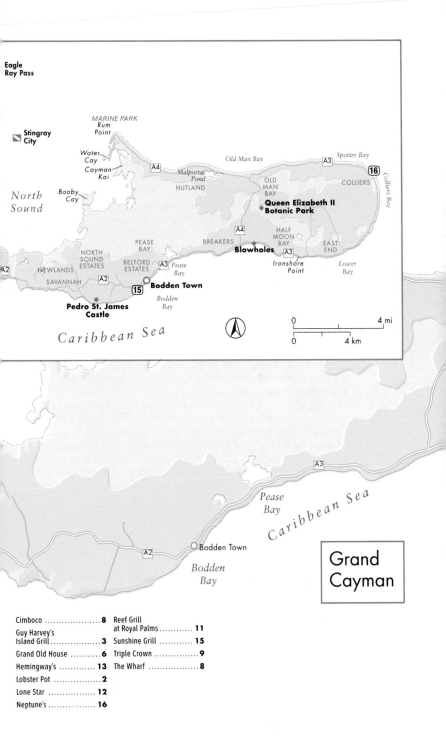

Eagle
Ray Pass

MARINE PARK
*Rum
Point*

**Stingray
City**

*Water
Cay*
*Cayman
Kai*

*Booby
Cay*

*North
Sound*

MARINE PARK
Old Man Bay

[A4]

*Malportas
Pond*

HUTLAND

Spotter Bay

[A3]

[16]

OLD
MAN
BAY

COLLIERS

Colliers Bay

**Queen Elizabeth II
Botanic Park**

PEASE
BAY

BREAKERS

[A4]

HALF
MOON
BAY

EAST
END

NORTH
SOUND
ESTATES

BELFORD
ESTATES

[A3] *Pease
Bay*

Blowholes

[A3]

*Lower
Bay*

NEWLANDS

*Ironshore
Point*

[A2]

SAVANNAH

[A2]

[15] ○ **Bodden Town**

**Pedro St. James
Castle**

*Bodden
Bay*

Caribbean Sea

0   4 mi

0   4 km

[A3]

*Pease
Bay*

[A2]

○ Bodden Town

Caribbean Sea

*Bodden
Bay*

Grand
Cayman

its appeal. The airy, marble lobby has a vaulted ceiling and opens onto a lovely lush, tropical courtyard and turtle lagoon. Large adjoining rooms are ideal for families; all have balconies, hardwood furniture, handsome abstract artworks, and smallish bathrooms. The beach, pool, beach bar, and dive center with water toys fills every waterside need. Add a serene spa, clever man-made reef, and good restaurants, and you never need leave the property. When you do, it's a short walk to more restaurants and stores. **Pros:** Great cocktails and lively bar scene, good snorkeling, surprisingly good food, convenient to both George Town and Seven Mile Beach. **Cons:** Impersonal, often overrun by tour groups and conventioneers, narrowest section of Seven Mile Beach. ⊠ *389 West Bay Rd., Box 30371, Seven Mile Beach* ☎ *345/949–0088 or 800/228–9290* ⊕ *www.marriott.com/gcmgc* ➷ *307 rooms, 4 suites* ⬙ *In-room: safe, refrigerator (some), Wi-Fi. In-hotel: 2 restaurants, room service, bars, pool, spa, beachfront, diving, water sports, laundry facilities, laundry service, public Internet, no-smoking rooms* ▤ *AE, D, DC, MC, V* ⧀⧀ *EP.*

$$$–$$$$ 🖼 **Westin Casuarina Resort & Spa.** The Westin has something to offer
🕐   everyone, from conventioneers to honeymooners to families, not to
★   mention a great location. You can walk a perfect beach, enjoy the sumptuous spa, sweat in the Reebok-powered fitness club, get wet with a Red Sail Sports branch, dine at the marvelous Casa Havana, lounge in the pool with an ocean view, or loll in the suave lounge after dark. The sophisticated room decor includes rich hardwood furnishings and marble-clad bathrooms with pampering showers. Many of the ocean-view rooms have better-than-advertised vistas. The Westin brand signatures have been subtly tailored to the tropics; the kids' club includes trips to the Butterfly and Turtle farms (and piratical skits to scavenger hunts teaching Cayman history). **Pros:** Terrific children's programs, superb beach (the largest resort stretch at 800 feet), sterling dining. **Con:** Occasionally bustling and impersonal when large groups book. ⊠ *West Bay Rd., Box 30620, Seven Mile Beach* ☎ *345/945–3800* ⊕ *www.westincasuarina.net* ➷ *339 rooms, 8 suites* ⬙ *In-room: safe, Ethernet. In-hotel: 3 restaurants, room service, bars, pool, gym, spa, beachfront, diving, water sports, children's programs (ages 4–12), no-smoking rooms* ▤ *AE, MC, V* ⧀⧀ *EP.*

$$$ 🖼 **Cobalt Coast Resort & Suites.** This small hotel is perfect for divers who want a sparkling, spacious room or suite right on the ironshore, far far from the madding crowds. Units have picture windows overlooking the Caribbean, imported Dutch fixtures, and Marimekko fabrics from Finland. The cutting-edge dive operation, Dive Tech, runs smoothly, catering to a wide array of needs, and Duppies restaurant is surprisingly good. As the gracious, gregarious Dutch-born owner, Arie Barendrecht, says "The whole idea is to complement the dive experience." The area also lures anglers so "we'll cook what you bring in." Add great shore diving (especially in the calmer summer season) and this is a no-brainer. **Pros:** Splendid shore diving with a four- or five-minute swim to a 60-foot drop, superb dive outfit, friendly service and clientele. **Cons:** Poky golden sand beach, car necessary especially for nondivers. ⊠ *18-A Sea Fan Dr., West Bay* ☎ *345/946–5656 or*

888/946–5656 ⊕www.cobaltcoast.com ⌦7 rooms, 11 suites ♿In-room: safe, kitchen (some), refrigerator, Wi-Fi. In-hotel: restaurant, bar, pool, diving, laundry facilities, airport shuttle, no elevator ☰AE, D, MC, V ⑪BP.

$$–$$$ **Comfort Suites Seven Mile Beach.** This no-frills all-suites hotel has an ideal location on West Bay Road, next door to the Marriott and near numerous shops, restaurants, and bars. Studios (kitchenette and shower-only bathroom) as well as one- and two-bedroom suites (full kitchens and tubs) are a tad run-down and musty, resembling oversize office cubicles, but have the comforts and conveniences of home, plus complimentary continental breakfast and free Wi-Fi. Regrettably, it looks like a mid-price chain hotel transplanted from the Midwest with little Caribbean flair. The sea is a short walk from the property, but this isn't the nicest part of Seven Mile Beach. Still, this should please families (all units contain sleeper sofas) or groups who want to save a bit on meals. **Pros:** Affordable, nice complimentary extras. **Cons:** Nearly a block from the beach, new condominium blocks sea views, no balconies, bar closes early. ✉ *West Bay Rd., George Town* ☎*345/945–7300 or 877/424–6423* ⊕*www.caymancomfort.com* ⌦*108 suites* ♿*In-room: safe, kitchen, dial-up, Ethernet. In-hotel: restaurant, room service, bar, pool, gym, diving, bicycles, laundry facilities, public Wi-Fi* ☰*AE, D, MC, V* ⑪*CP.*

$$–$$$ **Courtyard by Marriott Grand Cayman.** If you can ignore the unattract-ive parking lot and the busy road between the hotel and the beach, this is a good, well-maintained, even fairly stylish hotel—and a real value. The enormous swimming pool behind the hotel has a relaxing, tropical setting including a splashing fountain. After a hard day of snorkeling (there's another Red Sail Sports outpost) and lounging at the beach, you can visit the seaside beach-bar shack to watch the sunset. Up to two kids under 16 can stay free in their parents' room. The huge, insti-tutional-style but decent Mangrove Grill restaurant serves everything from burgers to a fine salmon with mustard sauce. **Pros:** Good value, congenial staff, great Wednesday BBQ with live music. **Cons:** Pool is delightful but lacks ocean view, attractive but sterile decor throughout. ✉*1590 West Bay Rd., Box 30364, Seven Mile Beach* ☎*345/946–4433* ⊕*www.marriott.com* ⌦*231 rooms, 1 2-bedroom suite* ♿*In-room: refrigerator, Ethernet. In-hotel: 2 restaurants, room service, bars, pool, gym, diving, water sports, laundry facilities, laundry service, public Internet, public Wi-Fi* ☰*AE, D, MC, V* ⑪*EP.*

$$–$$$ **Sunset House.** This amiable seaside resort is on the ironshore south of George Town, close enough for a short trip to stores and restau-rants yet far enough to feel secluded. The rooms are simple and in dire need of sprucing up (decor and condition vary wildly; the 500 block reportedly was scheduled for renovation, while the 400 block offers some of the best views), but good diving and a homey atmosphere are the main attractions. A terrific reef is just steps from the rooms. The thatch-roof My Bar is tremendously popular, and the world-famous Cathy Church's Underwater Photo Centre and Gallery is based here to round out the island's most-comprehensive diving services. **Pros:** Great shore diving and dive shop, lively bar scene, fun international clientele.

7

Cons: Often indifferent service, somewhat run-down, no real swimming beach. ✉ *S. Church St., Box 479GT, George Town* ☎ *345/949–7111 or 800/854–4767* ⊕ *www.sunsethouse.com* ⇌ *58 rooms, 2 suites* ⌂ *In-room: kitchen (some), dial-up, Wi-Fi (some). In-hotel: restaurant, bar, pool, diving, laundry facilities, public Internet, public Wi-Fi, no elevator, no-smoking rooms* ☰ *AE, MC, V* ⦿ *EP.*

$$–$$$ ⛺ **Sunshine Suites Resort.** This friendly, all-suites hotel is an impeccably clean money saver. The slightly musty, faded rooms don't have balconies, patios, or even a view, and both windows and bathrooms are tiny, but each has a complete kitchen, flat-screen TV, and Wi-Fi (laptops can be rented). You can use an outdoor grill for picnics, or enjoy the great cheap food and gossip at the poolside restaurant, a local fave. It's a five-minute walk to Seven Mile Beach, where the resort provides beach chairs and towels near the Westin Casuarina. Breakfast is served poolside. Guests get free access to a nearby local gym, and the resort provides lockers for dive gear. **Pros:** Good value, rocking little restaurant, thoughtful free extras. **Cons:** Poor views, no beach. ✉ *43 Peninsula Ave., off West Bay Rd., Box 30095, George Town* ☎ *345/949–3000 or 877/786–1110* ⊕ *www.sunshinesuites.com* ⇌ *130 suites* ⌂ *In-room: kitchen, Wi-Fi, dial-up. In-hotel: restaurant, bar, pool, laundry facilities* ☰ *AE, D, MC, V* ⦿ *CP.*

$–$$ ⛺ **Turtle Nest Inn.** This affordable, intimate seaside inn has roomy one-
★ bedroom apartments and a pool overlooking a narrow beach with good snorkeling. It's perched at the roadside in Bodden Town. With a new shopping center open in nearby Savannah (west of the hotel) you can find basic supplies some 10 minutes away, but you'll still need to rent a car. The apartments enchant, with arcaded balconies, beamed ceilings, black iron grillwork, vivid throw rugs, and stylish artworks. The meticulous attention to detail is exceptional, from the high-thread-count sheets to the basket of suntan lotions in the lobby for forgetful guests. Other nice touches include World Phones with cheap fixed rates for rent; complimentary use of kayaks, rafts, and snorkeling gear; and fantastic packages including rental car for weeklong stays. **Pros:** Wonderful snorkeling, good value, thoughtful extras, caring staff. **Cons:** Car necessary, occasional rocks and debris on beach, inconsistent Internet and phone service, road noise in back rooms. ✉ *Shamrock Rd., Box 187, Bodden Town* ☎ *345/947–8665* 🖷 *345/947–6379* ⊕ *www. turtlenestinn.com* ⇌ *8 apartments* ⌂ *In-room: kitchen, DVD, Wi-Fi. In-hotel: pool, beachfront, water sports, laundry facilities, Wi-Fi, no elevator* ☰ *AE, D, MC, V* ⦿ *EP.*

GUESTHOUSES

They may be some distance from the beach and short on style and facilities, but these guesthouses offer rock-bottom prices, a friendly atmosphere, and your best shot at getting to know the locals. Rooms are clean and simple, and most have private baths.

$–$$ ⛺ **Rocky Shore Guest House.** Come here if you really want to connect
Fodor'sChoice with Cayman. Owner Chris is a Caymanian artist, a nice young man
★ who will teach you about local crafts. His wife, Trina, runs Cayman Traditional Arts and even offers complete massage services. Both will

help you experience local foods and culture. Since it's in an inland residential area—complete with kids and dogs a half mile (1 km) from Cobalt Coast Resort—you'll need a car (Andy's offers guests a 20% discount). The two cheapest rooms share a bath. The apartments, from studio to three-bedroom, feature all the comforts and functional decor given character by Caymanian crafts such as old bird traps. The rocky beach and ocean are 500 feet away. **Pros:** True Caymanian experience, intriguing demonstrations and workshops, good value especially with weekly packages. **Cons:** Car necessary, no pool. ⊠*30 Grass Piece La., West Bay* ☎*345/926–0119 or 866/845–6943* ≣*345/946–0118* ⊕*www.getaway.ky* ⌫*5 apartments* ⌂*In-room: no phone, kitchen, DVD (some). In-hotel: no elevator* ≡*MC, V* ☉*CP.*

$–$$ ⊞**Shangri-La B&B.** Accomplished pianist George Davidson (he plays
★ regularly at the Westin and offers his jazz CDs for sale) and wife Eileen built this lavish lakeside retreat and truly make guests feel at home. Understated good taste informs every aspect of the house, from the waterfall pool and hot tub to a screened-in patio overlooking the bird-filled lagoon to the carved hardwood furnishings, tatted linens, and ornately embroidered pillows. Not to mention Eileen's scrumptious sumptuous breakfasts (to-die-for bread-and-butter pudding and French toast). Some rooms have romantic touches like four-poster or canopy beds and jetted tubs. Even the sole room sans balcony, Poinciana, has windows overlooking the water. There's an honor bar, and guests have kitchen privileges (with their own shelf in the refrigerator) as well. **Pros:** Use of kitchen, elegant decor. **Cons:** Rental car necessary, not on the beach. ⊠*1 Sticky Toffee La., West Bay* ☎*345/526–1170* ≣*345/946–6491* ⊕*www.shangrilabb.com* ⌫*6 rooms* ⌂*In-room: safe (some), DVD, Wi-Fi. In-hotel: pool, laundry facilities* ≡*AE, MC, V* ☉*BP.*

VILLAS & CONDOMINIUMS

Most condo complexes are very similar, with telephones, satellite TV, air-conditioning, living and dining areas, patios, and parking. Differences are amenities, proximity to town and beach, and the views. As with resorts, rates are higher in winter, and there may be a three- or seven-night minimum. There are dozens of large private villas available on the beach, especially on the North Side near Cayman Kai.

Several of the condo and villa rental companies have Web sites where you can see pictures of the privately owned units and villas they represent. **Cayman Villas** (☎*800/235–5888 or 345/945–4144* ⊕*www. caymanvillas.com*) represents villas and condos on all three Cayman Islands. **Island Dream Villas** (☎*866/978–5908 or 345/940–0318* ⊕*www.islanddreamvillas.com*) represents a few properties on Grand Cayman only. **Island Hideaways** (☎*800/832–2302* ⊕*www.islandhideaways.com*) rents villas all over the Caribbean, including some in the Cayman Islands. **Wimco** (☎*866/850–6140* ⊕*www.wimco.com*), or the West Indies Management Company, is synonymous with quality throughout the world, especially the Caribbean.

$$$$ ⊞**Coral Stone Club.** This exclusive enclave shines in the shadow of the
★ Ritz-Carlton by offering understated barefoot luxury and huge three-bedroom condos. Elegant touches include beveled glass doors, all-new

granite-clad kitchens and bathrooms (with stylish raised basins), deco-inspired art, and arched Palladian windows. Top-floor units have the finest views. Many have four-poster beds and oversize jetted tubs, but all have Wi-Fi, a washer/dryer, screened-in sunbathing patio, and flat-screen TV/DVD. Every guest receives a welcome gift (beach robes and a handcrafted glass platter), and the management can arrange everything from babysitter to chef. **Pros:** Largest ratio of beach and pool space to guests, walking distance to several restaurants and shops, stellar service, excellent off-season deals. **Cons:** Expensive in high season, Ritz-Carlton guests sometimes wander over from their packed section of sand trying to poach beach space. ⊠ *West Bay Rd., Box 30105, Seven Mile Beach* ☎*345/945–5820 or 888/927–2322* 🖷*345/945–5917* ⊕*www.coralstoneclub.com* ⟻*35 3-bedroom condos* ⟠*In-room: kitchen, Wi-Fi. In-hotel: tennis court, pool, gym, beachfront* ▤*AE, MC, V* ⊺❘*EP.*

$$$$ 🏨**Lacovia Condominiums.** The carefully manicured courtyard of this
★ handsome arcaded Mediterranean Revival property could easily be mistaken for a peaceful park. Large shade trees somehow escaped Hurricane Ivan in 2004, and thick, lush gardens overflowing with flowers bloom everywhere; you can feed the iguanas who stake out the frangipani and hibiscus amid the topiary. What's blissfully missing is the usual pressure of traffic, construction, and concrete walls so common in this area of Seven Mile Beach. The condos themselves are nicely kept, their contemporary decor accented by classy tapestries and rugs; all units have a washer/dryer. The beach here is wide and soft, with more wonderful shade trees and thatched gazebos. A shopping center, grocery store, restaurants, dive shops, and nightlife are a short walk away. **Pros:** Central location, exquisite gardens, extensive beach. **Cons:** Rear courtyard rooms can be noisy from traffic and partying from West Bay Road, pool fairly small (though most people prefer the beach). ⊠ *West Bay Rd., Box 32309, Seven Mile Beach* ☎*345/949–7599* ⊕*www.lacovia.com* ⟻*35 1-,2-, and 3-bedroom condos* ⟠*In-room: kitchen, Ethernet. In-hotel: tennis court, pool, gym, beachfront, laundry facilities, no elevator* ▤*AE, D, MC, V* ⊺❘*EP.*

$$$ 🏨**Christopher Columbus.** This enduring favorite is quite a discovery for families, sitting on the peaceful northern end of Seven Mile Beach. Though snorkeling is superb right offshore, the CC's beach is free of rocks; the parrot-green lawn fronting the sand is so perfectly maintained you could play croquet. Thatched cabanas and a gazebo offer shade aplenty. Living rooms and kitchens are enormous; the decor generally favors soft seashell and sunrise colors of pink, mint, and baby blue. Although this is hardly party central, the north building units are quietest. Units 8 and 10 (the latter a particularly good value for families as its "den" has two twin beds) are among the stunners opening onto the beach. **Pros:** Excellent snorkeling, fine beach, great value. **Con:** Car required to access restaurants. ⊠*2013 West Bay Rd., Seven Mile Beach* ☎*345/945–4354 or 866/311–5231* ⊕*www.christophercolumbus condos.com* ⟻*30 2- and 3-bedroom condos* ⟠*In-room: kitchen, Wi-Fi. In-hotel: tennis courts, pool, beachfront, laundry facilities, concierge, no elevator* ▤*AE, D, MC, V* ⊺❘*EP.*

$$–$$$ 🏠**Reef Resort.** This exceedingly well-run time-share property on the less
Fodor's Choice hectic East End offers good value. Each villa has a roomy terrace facing
★ the sea; two-bedroom units can be partitioned, but even the studio has a
microwave and fridge. Every year brings improvements (advance online
check-in, a hurricane-guarantee policy, and a spa and gym since 2007).
You always see a smiling staffer with a paintbrush or hedge clippers.
This cordial, relaxed yet efficient service is a major selling point. Kids
love John Peart (aka Mr. John), the handyman, who conducts regular
fish feedings at the dock. The famous "Barefoot Man" performs at Castaways on Tuesday and Thursday, luring lively locals. The food here (and
killer cocktails at the bar) would tempt anyone an all-inclusive plan is
now an option. **Pros:** Romantically remote, glorious beach, enthusiastic staff (including a crackerjack wedding coordinator). **Cons:** Remote,
few dining options within easy driving distance. ⊠ *Queen's Hwy., Box
20865 SMB, East End* ☎*345/947–3100 or 888/232–0541* ⊕*www.
thereef.com.ky* ⌐*152 suites* ⌂*In-room: safe, kitchen (some), refrigerator. In-hotel: restaurant, bar, tennis court, pools, gym, spa, beachfront,
diving, water sports, bicycles, concierge, laundry facilities, concierge,
no-smoking rooms* ☰*AE, MC, V* ⍒*EP.*

WHERE TO EAT

Grand Cayman dining is casual (even shorts are okay, but *not* beachwear and tank tops, of course). Mosquitoes can be pesky when you are
dining outdoors, especially at sunset, so plan ahead or ask for repellent.
Winter can be chilly enough to warrant a light sweater. You should
make reservations at all but the most-casual places, particularly during the high season.

Prices are about 30% more than those in a major U.S. city. Many restaurants add a 10% to 15% service charge to the bill; be sure to check
before leaving a tip. Alcohol with your meal can send the tab skyrock-
eting. Buy liquor duty-free before you leave the airport and enjoy a
cocktail or nightcap from the comfort of your room or balcony. Cayman customs limits you to two bottles per person.

Don't hesitate to try the local cuisine. Turtle is the traditional specialty
of the Cayman Islands and can be served in soup or stew or as a steak.
Conch, the meat of a large pink mollusk, is ubiquitous in stews and
chowders, fritters and panfried (cracked). Fish—including snapper,
tuna, wahoo, and marlin—is served baked, broiled, steamed, or "Cayman-style" (with peppers, onions, and tomatoes). Caribbean lobster is
available, but there are no other shellfish in local waters. Many of these
dishes would suit any palate, while the unique flavors of salt cod, ackee
(a red tree fruit resembling scrambled eggs in flavor and texture when
cooked), curried goat, or various forms of jerk cuisine may appeal to
the more-adventurous diner.

CARIBBEAN ✗**Breezes by the Bay.** There isn't a bad seat in the house at this nonstop
$–$$$ feel-good fiesta festooned with tiny paper lanterns, Christmas lights,
and Mardi Gras beads (you're "lei'd" upon entering). Wraparound
balconies take in a dazzling panorama from South Sound to Seven

Mile Beach. Rum aficionados will find 34 varieties, and garnishes are impeccably fresh. Equally fresh food at bargain prices, including home-made baked goods and ice creams, isn't an afterthought. Chunky velvety conch chowder served in a bread bowl or near-definitive conch fritters are meals in themselves. Hefty sandwiches are slathered with yummy jerk mayo or garlicky aïoli. Signature standouts include meltingly moist whole fish escoveitch, curry chicken, and jerk-glazed pork chops. ⊠*Harbor Dr., George Town* ☎*345/943–8469* ⊟*AE, MC, V.*

\$–\$\$ ✕ **Champion House II.** Ads trumpet that this restaurant is "where the islanders dine." Indeed they have since the Robinson family started selling takeout from their kitchen in 1965. This favorite overlooks a garden with a cheery tropic motif. The West Indies breakfast and themed lunch buffets are legendary spreads. Local food (curried goat, oxtail with broad beans, turtle soup, and heavy cake) is authentic, hearty, and cheap. Pricier global dishes range from fine Indian vegetarian options like samosas and *masala dal* (lentils simmered with green chilies) to Eisenhower-era standards like bacon-wrapped filet mignon in red wine sauce and scallops braised with sweet peppers in brandy. ⊠*43 Eastern Ave., George Town* ☎*345/949–7882* ⊟*AE, MC, V.*

\$–\$\$ ✕ **Chicken! Chicken!** Devotees would probably award four exclamation
☼ points to the marvelously moist chicken, slow-roasted on a hardwood
★ open-hearth rotisserie. Most customers grab takeout, but the decor is appealing for a fast-food joint; the clever interior replicates an old-time Cayman cottage. Bright smiles and home cooking completely from scratch enhance the authentic vibe. Hearty heaping helpings of sides include scrumptious Cayman-style corn bread, honey-rum beans, jicama coleslaw, and rice and beans. ⊠*West Shore Centre, West Bay Rd., Seven Mile Beach* ☎*345/945–2290* ⊟*AE, MC, V.*

\$–\$\$ ✕ **Sunshine Grill.** This cheerful, cherished locals' secret serves haute
☼ comfort food at bargain-basement prices. Even the poolside building, painted a delectable lemon with lime shutters, whets the appetite. Sunshine ranks high in the island's greatest burger debate, while the jerk chicken egg rolls and fabulous fish tacos elevate pub grub to an art form. Wash it down with one of the many signature libations, like the Painkiller. Take advantage of affordably priced nightly dinner specials (red snapper amandine, Cuban pork loin with *sofrito* (a dip of cilantro, garlic, onions, and oregano). Don't miss Thursday's all-you-can-eat Caribbean BBQ buffet. ⊠*Sunshine Suites, West Bay Rd., Seven Mile Beach* ☎*345/949–3000* ⊟*AE, MC, V.*

CONTINENTAL ✕ **Grand Old House.** This grande dame occupies the Petra Plantation
\$\$\$–\$\$\$\$ House, built in 1908 and transformed into the island's first upscale
Fodor's Choice establishment decades ago. It is that rare restaurant that genuinely
★ transports diners to a gracious era of bygone grandeur sans pretension. The interior rooms recall its plantation house origins. A classical pianist enhances the period ambience, but outside, hundreds of sparkling lights adorn the gazebos to compete with the starry sky. You'll find such expertly executed classics as lobster thermidor and rosemary-garlic-lemon-crusted rack of lamb in merlot reduction, but the increasingly innovative menu has slowly steeped in Asian and even Southwestern influences. Grilled freshwater shrimps float in key lime–garlic sauce

on wakame (seaweed) risotto, while coconut panfried chicken breast is stuffed with mango–pineapple–star anise chutney and covered with a Thai lemongrass sauce. The subtle yet complex flavor interactions, stellar service, and encyclopedic if stratospherically priced wine list ensure legendary landmark status. ⊠*S. Church St., George Town* ☎*345/949–9333* ⚑*Reservations essential* ⊟*DC, MC, V* ☾*Closed Sept. No lunch weekends.*

$$$–$$$$ ✗**Hemingway's.** Willowy palms, hardwood furnishings, a churchlike profusion of candles and torches, whirring paddle fans, wicker, lacquered bamboo, and picture windows opening onto Seven Mile Beach pay tribute to Hemingway's tropic travels. The sushi bar adds a dash of the Far East, while exotic tapas dishes jet from Mumbai to Milan to Madrid (lobster-and-corn lollipops with balsamic-accentuated spicy yogurt dip, slow-cooked guava baby-back spareribs with curried walnuts and organic yogurt). Specialties are described earnestly vis-à-vis their Hemingway significance (lobster because Papa often feasted on it in Key West, paella because bullfighters fascinated him, rum-and-coconut shrimp since Ernest founded "The Royal Order of Shrimp Eaters" in Havana). Entertaining theme nights include Thursday's Taste of Brazil all-you-can-eat *rodizio*. The key lime pie does justice to the restaurant's namesake. ⊠*Grand Cayman Beach Suites, West Bay Rd., Seven Mile Beach* ☎*345/945–5700 or 345/949–1234* ⚑*Reservations essential* ⊟*AE, D, DC, MC, V.*

ECLECTIC ✗**The Brasserie.** Actuaries, bankers, and CEOs frequent this contem-
$$$–$$$$ porary throwback to a colonial country club for lunch and "attitude
★ adjustment" happy hours for cocktails and complimentary canapés. Greg Vassos takes the confusion out of fusion cuisine, whether over terrific bar tapas (like lobster corn dog with red curry aioli and mango salsa) or during Wednesday's Random Acts of Cooking, a multicourse "blind tasting" driven by marketplace cuisine. But any meal encompasses such sterling starters as a trio of local snapper ceviche (coconut, yuzu, and escoveitch marinades) or seared foie gras with smoked maple organic oatmeal and strawberry-lavender foam. Vassos deftly balances flavors and textures without sensory overload: serious food with a sense of playfulness. Save room for desserts, from an artisanal cheese plate to an ice cream and sorbet tasting menu to elaborate architectural confections. ⊠*Cricket Sq., George Town* ☎*345/945–1858* ⚑*Reservations essential* ⊟*AE, MC, V* ☾*No lunch weekends.*

$$$–$$$$ ✗**Calypso Grill.** Shack chic describes this inviting split-level space
★ splashed in Dr. Seuss primary colors contrasting with brick walls, hardwood furnishings, terra-cotta floors, trompe l'oeil shutters, and (real) French doors opening onto sweeping North Sound views. If the interior is like stepping into a Caribbean painting, the outdoor deck serenely surveying frigate birds watchfully circling fishing boats is a Winslow Homer canvas brought to life. George Fowler's menu rightly emphasizes fish hauled in at the adjacent dock, so fresh (and never overcooked) that it almost literally jumps from the plate. You'll never go wrong with the unvarnished catch-of-the-day grilled, blackened, or sautéed. Though this is seafood's turf, landlubbers can savor a veal chop with morel-marsala sauce or a proper rack of lamb. End with

the sticky toffee pudding, which is actually commemorated in a road name. ⊠ *Morgan's Harbour, West Bay* ☎ *345/949–3948* ⚐ *Reservations essential* ⊟ *AE, D, MC, V* ⊙ *Closed Mon.*

$$ ✕ **Cimboco.** This animated celebration of all things fun, funky, and
★ Caribbean is saturated in psychedelic colors. History buffs may be interested to know that the Cimboco was the first motorized sailing ship built in Cayman (in 1927) and for 20 years the main connection/lifeline to the outside world. Everything from breads (superlative bruschetta and jalapeño corn bread) to ice creams is made from scratch. Artisan pizzas betray a (Wolfgang) Puck-ish sensibility with such ingredients as balsamic-roasted eggplant, BBQ jerk chicken, and scallops. Signature items include fire-roasted bacon-wrapped shrimp and caramelized sea scallops with grilled pineapple chutney and ginger mango sauce. Amazingly good desserts start with a moist, intensely rich brownie. The small but well-considered wine list features more than a dozen by the glass. ⊠ *The Marquee, West Bay Rd. at Harquail Bypass, Seven Mile Beach* ☎ *345/947–2782* ⊟ *AE, MC, V.*

ENGLISH ✕ **Triple Crown.** This pub lures lonely lads and lasses with a lengthy list
$$ of draft beers and and a genuine British atmosphere. Popular standbys range from Lancashire hot pot (baked lamb stew topped with sliced potatoes) to a beef-and-ale pie they should freeze for supermarkets, as well the odd fancy effort, such as cider-steamed mussels finished with parsley cream sauce. Smoke-eating machines efficiently minimize haze; big-screen TVs blast major British and occasionally even U.S. sporting events. The bar menu is served until midnight, and prices are generally low for Cayman. ⊠ *Marquee Plaza, Seven Mile Rd., Seven Mile Beach* ☎ *345/943–7821* ⊟ *AE, MC, V.*

ITALIAN ✕ **Neptune's.** Despite pretensions toward decorative dash (faux stone
$$–$$$ arches to mermaid murals), Neptune's thrives precisely because the food eschews fancy frills, stressing tried-and-true preparations that incorporate fresh (and easily obtained) ingredients. The greatest Italian hits menu ranges from *insalata caprese* to carpaccio, lasagna to linguine *fra diavolo.* While seafood reigns supreme, you'll find standout steaks as well. There's a bias toward cream in the sauces, which some find heavenly, others merely heavy. But personable co-owner/chef Raj Kumar gladly accommodates special dietary requirements, including oil- and salt-free options, as well such off-the-menu items as salmon Provençale. Be warned: karaoke takes over on Saturday. ⊠ *Trafalgar Pl., West Bay Rd., Seven Mile Beach* ☎ *345/946–8709* ⊟ *AE, D, MC, V.*

SEAFOOD ✕ **Blue by Eric Ripert.** Chef Eric Ripert consulted on every aspect of the
$$$$ first outpost bearing his name, including the decor and dishware. His
Fodor'sChoice trademark ethereal seafood, flawless not fawning service, soothing
★ sophistication, and refreshing lack of pretension make this one of the Caribbean's finest restaurants. Choose from a regular three-course or the chef's tasting menu. Many dishes are clever improvisational riffs on the mother restaurant, utilizing the island's natural bounty (conch ceviche recalls the famed fluke version). The sensuous counterpoint of flavors, textures, even colors is unimpeachable, as in braised pork belly with gingered pumpkin mousseline and pea shoots in brown butter

jus; sautéed ocean yellowtail in bourbon–lime–guajillo pepper broth with mango-jalapeño salad; or melt-in-mouth almond-honey cake with mandarin orange sorbet and candied kumquats. The vast wine list offers big names but also showcases hot new regions and lesser-known varietals that offer quality and comparative value. ⊠ *Ritz-Carlton Grand Cayman, West Bay Rd., Seven Mile Beach* ☎ *345/943–9000* ⌘ *Reservations essential* ⊟ *AE, D, MC, V* ⊗ *Closed Sun. and Mon. No lunch.*

$$$–$$$$ ✕ **Lobster Pot.** The nondescript building belies the lovely marine-motif decor and luscious seafood at the intimate, second-story restaurant overlooking the harbor. No surprise that fish seem to jump from the plate. Enjoy lobster prepared a dozen ways along with reasonably priced wine, which you can sample by the glass in the cozy bar. The two musts are the Cayman Trio (lobster tail, grilled mahimahi, and garlic shrimp), and the Pot (lobster, giant prawns, and crab), but the kitchen can happily provide reduced-oil and -fat alternatives to most dishes. ⊠ *245 N. Church St., George Town* ☎ *345/949–2736* ⊕ *www. lobsterpot.ky* ⊟ *AE, MC, V* ⊗ *No lunch weekends.*

$$$–$$$$ ✕ **Reef Grill at Royal Palms.** This class act appeals to a casually suave
★ crowd, many of them regulars, who appreciate its consistent quality, attentive yet unobtrusive service, soothing seaside setting, top-notch entertainment, and surprisingly reasonable prices. The space is cannily divided into four areas, each with its own look and feel. Co-owner/ chef George Dahlstrom's gives his perfectly prepared, familiar items just enough twist to satisfy jaded palates: calamari is fried in arborio rice batter with lemon aïoli; the tuna spring roll comes with wasabi and ponzu dipping sauces; melt-in-your-mouth braised short ribs have a caramelized onion demi-glace; and sea scallops are pan-seared with corn, smoked bacon, and lobster mash. Dance the calories off to the estimable reggae, calypso, and soca sounds of Coco Red, then adjourn to the cozy lounge for an aged rum or single malt. ⊠ *West Bay Rd., Seven Mile Beach* ☎ *345/945–6358* ⊟ *AE, MC, V* ⊗ *No dinner Sun.*

$$$–$$$$ ✕ **The Wharf.** The popularity of this large restaurant often leads to impersonal service and mediocre food. But the location, a series of elevated decks and Victorian-style gazebos hugging the sea, is enviable, explaining its enduring appeal. The Ports of Call bar is a splendid place for sunset fanciers, and tarpon feeding off the deck is a nightly (9 PM) spectacle. Stick to simpler fare (creole-style conch fritters, the signature basil-and-pistachio-crusted sea bass) and avoid anything sounding too pretentious. Chef Christian Reiter knows his desserts: Granny Smith apple mille-feuille filled with caramelized apples and cinnamon cream or pistachio–dark chocolate cake with praline Chantilly and mocha ice cream don't disappoint. ⊠ *43 West Bay Rd., Seven Mile Beach* ☎ *345/949–2231* ⌘ *Reservations essential* ⊟ *AE, MC, V* ⊗ *No lunch May–Nov., and weekends in Dec.–Apr.*

$$–$$$$ ✕ **Guy Harvey's Island Grill.** This stylish, sporty upstairs bistro celebrates
★ the sea, from decor to cuisine. You half expect to find Hemingway regaling fellow barflies in the clubby interior with mahogany furnishings, ship's lanterns, porthole windows, whirring ceiling fans, and Harvey's action-packed marine art. The cool blues echo the sea and

7

sky on display from the inviting balcony. Seafood is carefully chosen to exclude overexploited and threatened species. Seasonally changing dishes are peppered with Caribbean influences but pureed through the French chef's formal training. Hence, a silken lobster bisque is served with puff pastry, scallops à la Rockefeller with spinach and béarnaise sauce, and the signature crab cakes with roasted red pepper aioli. You can select your fish baked, pan-sautéed, or grilled. Carnivores needn't despair, with veal medallions in creamy morel sauce or an intensely flavored New York strip with fresh herbs (frites optional). ⊠ *Aquaworld Duty-Free Mall, 55 S. Church St., George Town* ☎ *345/946–9000* ⊟ *AE, D, MC, V.*

TEX-MEX ✕ **Lone Star Bar & Grill.** This temple to sports and the cowboy lifestyle
$–$$ serves a Texas-size welcome and portions. If it can be barbecued, deep-fried, jerked, pulled, or nacho-ized it's probably on the menu. Many locals swear the burgers are Cayman's best. Such Tex-Mex standards as shrimp fajitas are appropriately mouth- and eye-watering, and regulars lick their chops at the reasonable prices. Though the back bar can get rowdy at night, kids are welcome to scamper about (go at lunch when it's less crowded). Monday and Thursday offers all-you-can-eat fajitas, while Tuesday you can gorge on lobster all night. ⊠ *686 West Bay Rd., Seven Mile Beach* ☎ *345/945–5175* ⊟ *AE, MC, V.*

BEACHES

The island is blessed with many fine beaches. These are the very best.

★ **Barkers.** A series of secluded, spectacular beaches are accessed via a dirt road just past Papagallo restaurant. There are no facilities (that's the point!), but some palms offer shade. Unfortunately, the shallow water and rocky bottom discouraging swimming, and it can be cluttered at times with seaweed and debris. ⊠ *Conch Point Rd., Barkers, West Bay.*

★ **Rum Point.** This North Sound beach has hammocks slung in towering casuarina trees, picnic tables, the thatched Wreck Bar & Grill, and Red Sail Sports, which offers various water sports and boats to explore Stingray City. The barrier reef ensures safe snorkeling and soft sand. The bottom remains shallow for a long way from shore, but it's littered with small coral heads, so kids shouldn't wrestle in the water here. The Wreck is ablaze with color—yellow with navy blue trim and orange and green picnic tables—as if trying to upstage the snorkeling just offshore. ⊠ *Rum Point, North Side.*

☾ **Seven Mile Beach.** Grand Cayman's west coast is dominated by the famous
Fodor'sChoice Seven Mile Beach—actually a 6.5-mi-long (10-km-long) expanse of
★ powdery white sand overseeing lapis water stippled with a rainbow of parasails and kayaks. The width of the beach varies with the season; toward the south end it narrows and disappears altogether south of the Marriott, leaving only rock and ironshore. It starts to broaden into its normal silky softness anywhere between Tarquyn Manor and the Reef Grill at Royal Palms. Free of litter and pesky peddlers, it's an unspoiled (though often crowded) environment. Most of the island's resorts, res-

taurants, and shopping centers sit along this strip. At the public beach toward the north end you can find chairs for rent ($10 for the day, including a beverage), a playground, water toys aplenty, two beach bars, restrooms, and showers. The best snorkeling is at either end, by the Marriott and Treasure Island or off the northern section called Cemetery Reef Beach. ⊠ *West Bay Rd., Seven Mile Beach.*

★ **Smith's Cove.** South of the Grand Old House, this tiny but popular, protected swimming and snorkeling spot makes a wonderful beach wedding location. The bottom drops off quickly enough to allow you to swim and play close to shore. Although the beach is slightly rocky, there's little debris or coral heads, plenty of shade, picnic tables, restrooms, and parking. Local scuttlebutt calls it a place for dalliances during work hours; it's also a romantic sunset spot. ⊠ *Off S. Church St., George Town.*

South Sound Cemetery Beach. A narrow, sandy driveway takes you past the small cemetery to a perfect beach. The dock here is primarily used by dive boats during winter storms. You can walk in either direction; the sand is talcum-soft and clean, the water calm and clear (though local surfers take advantage of occasional small reef breaks; if wading, wear reef shoes since the bottom is somewhat rocky and dotted with sea urchins). You'll definitely find no crowds. ⊠ *S. Sound Rd., Prospect.*

Water Cay. If you want an isolated, unspoiled beach, bear left at Rum Point on the North Side and follow the road to the end. When you see a soft, sandy beach, stop your car. Wade out knee deep and look for the large orange starfish. (Don't touch—just look.) ⊠ *North Side.*

SPORTS & THE OUTDOORS

BIRD-WATCHING

Silver Thatch Tours (☎ *345/945–6588 or 345/916–0678* ⊕ *www.earth-foot.org*) is run by Geddes Hislop, who knows his birds and his island (though he's Trinidadian by birth). He specializes in five-hour natural and historic heritage tours that generally culminate at the Queen Elizabeth II Botanic Park's nature trail and lake. The cost is $55 per person for 2 to 10 people, $60 for the early-morning bird-watching–botanic-park tour. Serious birders leave at the crack of dawn, but you can choose the time and leave at the crack of noon instead. The cost includes guide service, pickup & return transport, and refreshments such as local drinks (a great excuse for discourse on herbal medicinal folklore).

DIVING

Pristine clear water, breathtaking coral formations, and plentiful marine life mark the **North Wall**—a world-renowned dive area along the North Side of Grand Cayman. **Trinity Caves**, in West Bay, is a deep dive with numerous canyons starting at about 60 feet and sloping to the wall at 130 feet.

★ Most dive operators offer scuba trips to **Stingray City,** in the North Sound. Widely considered the best 12-foot dive in the world, it's a must-see for adventurous souls. Here dozens of stingrays congregate—tame enough to suction squid from your outstretched palm. You can stand in 3 feet of water at **Stingray Sandbar** as the gentle stingrays glide around your legs looking for a handout. Don't worry—these stingrays are so used to thousands of tourist encounters that they are no danger, and the experience is often a highlight of a Grand Cayman trip.

If someone tells you that the minnows are in at **Eden Rock,** drop everything and dive here (on South Church Street, south of George Town). The schools swarm around you as you glide through the grottoes, and it's an unforgettable experience. The grottoes themselves are safe—not complex caves—and the entries and exits are clearly visible at all times. Snorkelers can enjoy the outside of the grottoes as the reef rises and falls from 10 to 30 feet deep. Avoid carrying fish food unless you know how not to get bitten by eager yellowtail snappers. The waters around Grand Cayman are varied, so if the water looks rough where you are, there's usually a side of the island that's wonderfully calm.

Other good shore-entry snorkeling spots include **West Bay Cemetery,** north of Seven Mile Beach, and the reef-protected shallows of the island's **north and south coasts.** Ask for directions to the shallow wreck of the *Cali* in George Town harbor area; there are several places to enter the water, including a ladder at Rackam's Pub. Among the wreckage you'll recognize the winch and, of course, lots of friendly fish.

As one of the Caribbean's top diving destinations, Grand Cayman is blessed with many top-notch dive operations offering diving, instruction, and equipment for sale and rent. A single-tank boat dive averages $70, a two-tank dive about $100. Snorkel-equipment rental is about $10 to $15 a day. Divers are required to be certified and possess a "C" card. If you're getting certified, to save time during your limited holiday, you can start the book and pool work at home and finish the open-water portion in warm, clear Cayman waters. Certifying agencies offer this referral service all around the world.

Ambassador Divers (⊠ *S. Church St., George Town* ☎ *345/916–1064* ⊕ *www.ambassadordivers.com*) is an on-call guided scuba-diving operation offering dive trips to parties of two to six persons. Co-owner Jason Washington's favorite spots include the excellent dive sites on the West Side and South and North Wall. Ambassador offers two boats, a 28-foot Custom Parker (maximum six divers) and a 45-foot Garcia for private charters. They are available around the clock, and interested divers can be picked up from their hotels or condos. The price for a two-tank boat dive is $95.

Divetech (⊠ *Cobalt Coast Resort & Suites, 18-A Sea Fan Dr., West Bay* ☎ *345/946–5658 or 888/946–5656* ⊕ *www.divetech.com* ⊠ *Turtle Reef, near Boatswain's Beach, West Bay* ☎ *345/949–1700*) has opportunities for shore diving at its lush north-coast location, which provides loads of interesting creatures, a miniwall, and, of course, the North Wall. With quick access to West Bay, the boat is quite comfortable. Technical training (a specialty of owner Nancy Easterbrook) is unparalleled, and the company offers good, personable service as well as the

Learn to Dive

Diving is an exciting experience that does not have to be strenuous or stressful. Almost anyone can enjoy scuba, and it's easy to test the waters via a three-hour resort course costing $100 to $120. After a quick rundown of dos and don'ts, you stand in the shallow end of a pool, learning how to use the mask and fins and breathe underwater with a regulator. The instructor then explains some basic safety skills and before you know it, you're in the drink. The instructor hovers as you float above the reef, watching fish react to you. Don't worry—there are no dangerous fish in Cayman, and they don't bite (as long as you're not "chumming," or handling fish food). You can see corals and sponges, maybe even a turtle or ray. It's an amazing world that you can enter with very little effort.

The resort course only permits shallow, instructor-guided dives in Cayman's calm, clear waters. The next step is full Open Water certification (generally three or four, including several dives, for around $450, less as part of a hotel package). This earns you a C-card, your passport to the underwater world anywhere you travel. From there, addicts will discover dozens of specialty courses. The leading teaching organizations, both with their adherents, are PADI (Professional Association of Dive Instructors) and NAUI (National Association of Underwater Instructors), affectionately nicknamed "Not Another Underwater Idiot" and "Pay and Dive Immediately" (those are the polite versions in scuba's colorful slang). Worry not: Cayman's instructors are among the world's best. And the water conditions just might spoil you.

latest gadgetry; they even mix their own gases and there are multiple dive instructors for different specialties. Snorkel and diving programs are available year-round for children ages eight and up. Excellent prices are a bonus.

Don Foster's Dive Cayman Islands (⊠ *218 S. Church St., George Town* ☎ *345/949–5679 or 800/833–4837* ⊕ *www.donfosters.com*) has a pool with a shower and also snorkeling along the ironshore at Casuarina Point, easily accessed starting at 20 feet, extending to depths of 55 feet. Rates are competitive and there's free shuttle pickup/drop-off along Seven Mile Beach.

Eden Rock Diving Center (⊠ *124 S. Church St., George Town* ☎ *345/949–7243* ⊕ *www.edenrockdive.com*), south of George Town, provides easy access to Eden Rock and Devil's Grotto. It features full equipment rental, lockers, shower facilities, and a full range of PADI courses from a helpful, cheerful staff. Costs for guided shore dives and two-tank dives on its Pro 42 jet boat are cheaper than most outfits, without sacrificing quality or comfort.

★ **Ocean Frontiers** (⊠ *Compass Point, Austin Connelly Dr., East End* ☎ *345/947–7500 or 800/348–6096* ⊕ *www.oceanfrontiers.com*) is an excellent ecocentric operation, offering friendly small-group diving and a technical training facility. Some trips also depart from the Kaibo Yacht Club in Cayman Kai to explore the North Wall; you may even go as far as 12-Mile Bank, where an old 250-foot fuel barge wreck sits in

115-feet depth with strong currents. The company provides valet service, personalized attention, a complimentary courtesy shuttle, and an emphasis on green initiatives and specialized diving, including unguided computer, Touches include hot chocolate and homemade muffins on night dives; the owner Steve is an ordained minister and will conduct weddings in full face masks.

✺ **Red Sail Sports** (☎345/949–8745 or 877/733–7245 ⊕www.redsailcay man.com) offers daily trips from most of the major hotels. Dives are often run as guided tours, a perfect option for beginners. If you're experienced and your air lasts a long time, consult the boat captain to see if he requires that you come up with the group as determined by the first person who runs low on air. There is a full range of kids' dive options for ages 5 to 15. The company also operates Stingray City tours, dinner and sunset sails, and just about every major water sport.

Sunset Divers (✉Sunset House, 390 S. Church St., George Town ☎345/949–7111 or 800/854–4767 ⊕www.sunsethouse.com), a full-service PADI teaching facility located at George Town hostelry catering to the scuba set, has great shore diving and five dive boats to hit all sides of the island. Divers can be independent on their boats as long as they abide by the maximum time and depth standards. Though not directly affiliated with acclaimed underwater shutterbug Cathy Church (whose shop is also at the hotel), she'll often work with them on special courses.

FISHING

If you enjoy action fishing, Cayman waters have plenty to offer. Boats are available for charter, offering fishing options that include deep-sea, reef, bone, tarpon, light-tackle, and fly-fishing. June and July are good all-around months for fishing for blue marlin, yellow- and blackfin tuna, dolphinfish, and bonefish. Bonefish have a second season in the winter months, along with wahoo and skipjack tuna.

Black Princess Charters (☎345/916–6319 or 345/949–0400 ⊕www. fishgrandcayman.com), owned by Captain Chuckie Ebanks, is fully equipped for deep-sea and reef fishing as well as snorkel trips on fully equipped and supplied boats ranging from 17 to 65 feet. His rates are comparatively reasonable and he can arrange clean, inexpensive local accommodations.

Burton's Tourist Information & Activity Services (☎345/949–6598 or 345/ 926–8294) offers a concierge service that can provide information and book virtually any island services.

★ Captain Ronald Ebanks of **R&M Fly Shop & Charters** (☎345/947–3146 or 345/946–0214 ⊕www.flyfishgrandcayman.com) is arguably the island's most knowledgeable fly-fishing guide with more than 10 years' experience in Cayman and Scotland.). He also runs light-tackle trips on a 24-foot Robalo. Everyone from beginners—even children—to experienced casters will enjoy and learn from the trip.

★ **Sea Star Charters** (☎345/949–1016, 345/916–5234 after 8 AM), aka Clinton's Watersports, is run by Clinton Ebanks, a fine and very friendly Caymanian who will do whatever it takes to make sure that you have a wonderful time on his three small, 25- to 31-foot cabin cruisers, enjoying light-tackle, bone-, and bottom-fishing. He's a good choice for beginners and offers a nice cultural experience, as well as sailing charters and snorkeling with complimentary transportation and equipment. Only cash and traveler's checks are accepted.

GOLF

The **Britannia** (⊠ *West Bay Rd., Seven Mile Beach* ☎ *345/949–8020 Ext. 4901 or 345/949–3406* ⊕ *www.britanniavillas.net*) golf course, next to the Grand Cayman Beach Suites, was designed by Jack Nicklaus. The course is really three in one—a 9-hole, par-70 regulation course; an 18-hole, par-57 executive course; and a Cayman course played with a Cayman ball that travels about half the distance of a regulation ball. Green fees are $100 ($110 on Saturday). Amenities include full pro shop and the Britannia Golf Grille.

Formerly the Links at Safehaven, the par-71, 6,605-yard, 18-hole **North Sound Club** (⊠ *Off West Bay Rd., Seven Mile Beach* ☎ *345/945–4155 or 345/947–4653* ⊕ *www.northsoundclub.com*) is infamous among duffers for its strong gusts, giving the ball unexpected loft or backspin. Roy Case factored the wind into his design, which incorporates lots of looming water and sand traps. Wear shorts at least 14 inches long (15 inches for women); no T-shirts are allowed, only collared shirts. Greens fee are $160 ($90 for 9 holes) including cart.

HIKING

★ The National Trust's **Mastic Trail** (⊠ *Frank Sound Rd., entrance by fire station at botanic park, Breakers, East End* ☎ *345/949–0121 for guide reservations* ⊕ *www.nationaltrust.org.ky*), used in the 1800s as the only direct path to and from the North Side, is a rugged 2-mi (3-km) slash through 776 dense acres of woodlands, black mangrove swamps, savannah, agricultural remnants, and ancient rock formations. A comfortable walk depends on weather—winter is better because it's drier, though flowering plants like the banana orchid set the trail ablaze in summer. Call the National Trust to determine suitability and to book a guide for $45; tours are run daily from 9 to 5 by appointment only, regularly on Wednesday at 9 AM. Or walk on the wild side with a $5 guidebook that provides information on the ecosystems you traverse, the endemic wildlife you might encounter, seasonal changes, poisonous plants to avoid, and folkloric uses of various flora. The trip takes about three hours.

HORSEBACK RIDING

Coral Stone Stables (☎ *345/916–4799* ⊕ *www.csstables.com*) offers 90-minute leisurely horseback rides along the white-sand beaches at Bodden Town and inland trails at Savannah; complimentary photos are included. You guide is Nolan Stewart, whose ranch contains 20 horses, chickens, and "randy" roosters. Nolan offers a nonstop narrative on flora, fauna, and history. He's an entertaining, endless font of local information, some of it unprintable.

Ⓒ **Pampered Ponies** (☎ *345/945–2262 or 345/916–2540* ⊕ *www.ponies. ky*) offers what is called "the ultimate tanning machine": horses walking, trotting, and cantering along the beaches and beach trails. You can do either private tours or a variety of guided trips along the uninhabited beach from Conch Point to Morgan's Harbour on the north tip beyond West Bay.

KAYAKING

☙ **Cayman Kayaks** (☎345/746–3249 or 345/926–4467 ⊕www.cayman
★ kayaks.com) explores Grand Cayman's protected mangrove wetlands, providing an absorbing discussion of the indigenous animals (including a mesmerizing stop at a gently pulsing, nonstinging Cassiopeia jellyfish pond) and plants, the effects of hurricanes, and conservation efforts. Even beginners will find the tours easy (the guides dub it low-impact aerobics), and the sit-on-top kayaks are quite stable and comfortable. The Bio Bay tour involves more-strenuous paddling, but the underwater light show is magical. It runs only on moonless nights for full effect and books well in advance. All tours depart from Kaibo Beach Bar in Cayman Kai; the fee is $49 ($25 under 13).

SEA EXCURSIONS

The most-impressive sights in the Cayman Islands are on and underwater, and several submarine-like glass-bottom-boat trips will allow you to see these wonders. Sunset sails, dinner cruises, and other theme (dance, booze, pirate) cruises are available from $20 to $50 per person.

☙ **Atlantis Submarines** (☎345/949–7700 or 866/546–7820 ⊕www.atlan
★ tisadventures.com) takes 48 passengers safely and comfortable along the Cayman Wall down to 100 feet. Try to sit toward the front so you can watch the pilot's nimble maneuverings and the depth gauge. If that literally in-depth tour seems daunting, you can get up-close and personal on the state-of-the-art *Seaworld Explorer* semisubmersible that just cruises the harbor (including glimpses of the *Cali* and *Balboa* shipwrecks). Cost for the submarine is $79 ($89 at night), $39 for the semisubmersible. Children get discounts.

☙ The **Jolly Roger** (☎345/945–7245 ⊕www.jollyrogercayman.com) is a two-thirds replica of Christopher Columbus's 17th-century Spanish galleon *Nina*; the company also owns the *Valhalla,* a wooden Norwegian brig built in 1934 that holds more than 100 passengers. On the afternoon snorkel cruise, play Captain Jack Sparrow while experiencing swashbuckling pirate antics including a trial, sword fight, and walking of the plank; the kids can fire the cannon, help hoist the main sail, and scrub the decks (it's guaranteed that they will love it even if they loathe doing chores at home). The evening options (sunset and dinner sails) are more-standard booze cruises, less appropriate for the kiddies. Prices range from $35 to $60.

On the semisubmersible **Nautilus** (☎345/945–1355 ⊕www.nautilus. ky) you can sit above deck or venture below, where you can view the reefs and marine life through a sturdy glass hull. A one-hour undersea tour is $45. Watch divers feed the fish, or take the Captain's Nemo's Tour that includes snorkeling. As on the Atlantis semisubmersible, you get a close-up look at the Cheeseburger Reef and two of Cayman's mysterious shipwrecks (*Cali* and *Balboa*), with a bit of entertaining educational narrative.

☙ **Sea Trek** (☎345/949–0008 ⊕www.seatrekcayman.com) offers helmet diving, permitting you to walk and breathe 26 feet underwater—without getting your hair wet—for an hour. No training or even swimming ability is required, and you can wear glasses. Guides give a thorough safety briefing, and a sophisticated system of compressors and cylinders provides triple the amount of air necessary for normal breathing, while a safety diver program ensures four distinct levels of backup. The result at near-zero gravity resembles an exhilarating moonwalk. The cost is $75 per person ($70 per person for groups of four or more).

Adrenaline junkies should speed over to **Thriller Cayman** (☎ *345/324–0520 or 345/943–2628* ⊕*www.thrillercayman.ky*), which is often likened to a water roller coaster. The 55-foot, 1,000-hp Thriller 003 speedboat accelerates to 50–60 mph, providing offshore racing thrills without spills. It usually zooms along Seven Mile Beach, but there are also Rum Point Sunday brunch tours. The one-hour joy ride costs $50.

SKATING & SKATEBOARDING

Black Pearl Skate & Surf Park (⊠*Red Bay Rd., Grand Harbour* ☎*345/947–4161* ⊕*www.blackpearl.ky*), a great skating park (skateboards, in-line skates), is the size of a football field and has a flow course, a 60-foot vert ramp, and a standing wave-surf machine. You can rent anything you need.

SNORKELING

Stingray Sandbar is the most popular snorkeling destination by far, and dozens of boats head that way several times a day. It's a not-to-be-missed experience, which you will remember for years to come. The area is always less crowded if you can go on a day when there aren't too many cruise ships in port.

Bayside Watersports (☎*345/949–3200, 866/978–0022 reservations only 10* AM *to 3* PM *weekdays* ⊕*www.baysidewatersports.com*) offers half-day snorkeling trips, North Sound beach lunch excursions, Stingray City and full-day deep-sea fishing, and dinner cruises. The company operates several popular boats out of West Bay's Morgan's Harbour. Full-day trips include lunch and conch diving in season (November–April).

Red Sail Sports (☎*345/949–8745, 345/946–3362, 345/926–2934, or 877/733–7245* ⊕*www.redsailcayman.com*) offers Stingray City, sunset, and evening sails (including dinner in winter) on their luxurious 65-foot catamarans, the *Spirits of Cayman, Poseidon,* and *Ppalu.* They often carry large groups; although the service may not be personal, it will be efficient. In addition to the large cats, a glass-bottom boat takes passengers to Stingray City/Sandbar and nearby coral reefs.

SHOPPING

On Grand Cayman the good news is that there's no sales tax *and* there's plenty of duty-free merchandise. Locally made items to watch for include woven mats, baskets, jewelry made of a marblelike stone called Caymanite (from the cliffs of Cayman Brac), and authentic sunken treasure, though the latter is never cheap. Cigar lovers take note: some shops carry famed Cuban brands, but you must enjoy them on the island; bringing them back to the United States is illegal.

Although you can find black-coral products in Grand Cayman, they're controversial. Most of the coral sold here comes from Belize and Honduras; Cayman Islands marine law prohibits the removal of live coral from its own sea (although most of it has been taken illegally). Black coral grows at a very slow rate (3 inches every 10 years) and is an endangered species. Consider buying other products instead.

AREAS & MALLS

★ The **Anchorage Centre** across from the cruise-ship North Terminal has 10 of the most-affordable stores and boutiques selling duty-free goods from such great brand names as John Hardy, Movado, and Concord, as well as designer ammolite jewelry. Downtown is the **Kirk Freeport Plaza,** known for its boutiques selling fine watches, duty-free china, Gucci goods, perfumes, and cosmetics. Just keep walking—there's plenty of shopping in all directions. Stores in the **Landmark** in George Town sell perfumes, treasure coins, and upscale beachwear; Breezes by the Bay restaurant is upstairs.

SPECIALTY STORES

ART **Artifacts** (⊠ *Cayside Courtyard, Harbour Dr., George Town* ☏ *345/949–2442*) on the George Town waterfront sells Spanish pieces of eight, doubloons, and Halcyon Days enamels (hand-painted collectible pillboxes made in England), as well as antique maps and other collectibles.

★ **Cathy Church's Underwater Photo Centre & Gallery** (⊠ *S. Church St., George Town* ☏ *345/949–7415*) has a collection of the acclaimed underwater shutterbug's spectacular color and limited-edition black-and-white underwater photos. Framed prints are shipped to the United States at no extra charge. Have Cathy autograph her latest coffee-table book and regale you with anecdotes of her latest adventures. She'll schedule private underwater photography instruction as well.

Esteban Gallery (⊠ *3 Dilbert Plaza, Red Bay Rd., George Town* ☏ *345/947–1653*) sells the work of Horacio Esteban, from Cayman Brac, who sculpts mahogany and Caymanite and whose striking striations range in hue from seashell-pink to sienna. His work is beautiful, uniquely Cayman, and worth a look; even such small items as key chains and letter openers make distinctive keepsakes.

★ **Guy Harvey's Gallery & Shoppe** (⊠ *49 S. Church St., George Town* ☏ *345/943–4891*) is where world-renowned marine biologist, conservationist, and artist Guy Harvey showcases his aquatic-inspired art in nearly every conceivable medium, logo tableware, and sportswear (even logo soccer balls and Zippos). Original paintings, sculpture, and drawings are expensive, but there's something (tile art, prints, lithographs, and photos) in most price ranges.

On the shore in George Town, **Island Glassblowing Studio** (⊠ *N. Church St., George Town* ☏ *345/946–1483*) is run by the Zawitowski family of designers, who offer free demonstrations of their incredible skills.

The **Kennedy Gallery** (⊠ *West Shore Centre, West Bay Rd., George Town* ☏ *345/949–8077*) sells paintings, lithographs, and prints by established local artists, notably Joanne Sibley, Lois Brezinski, Charles Long, Miguel Powery, and Leigh Pawling.

★ **Morgan Gallery** (⊠ *Galleria Plaza, West Bay Rd., Seven Mile Beach* ☎ *345/ 943–5566*) offers an eclectic, electric blend of cutting-edge Caymanian work in various media and fine art culled during co-owners Steve Byars and Geraldine Morgan's regular trips through Europe and Asia.

★ **Pure Art** (⊠ *S. Church St., George Town* ☎ *345/949–9133*) purveys wit, warmth, and whimsy right from the wildly colored front steps. About 1.5 mi (2.5 km) south of George Town, its warren of rooms resembles a garage sale run amok or a quirky grandmother's attic spilling over with unexpected finds.

CAMERAS The **Camera Store** (⊠ *Waterfront Centre, N. Church St., George Town*
★ ☎ *345/949–4551*) has friendly and knowledgeable service, lots of duty-free digital cameras, accessories, and fast photo printing from self-service kiosks.

FOODSTUFFS There are seven modern, U.S.-style supermarkets for groceries (three of them have full-service pharmacies) on Grand Cayman. The biggest difference you'll find between these and supermarkets on the mainland is in the prices, which are about 25% to 30% more than at home.

Foster's Food Fair-IGA (⊠ *Airport Centre, 63 Dorcy Dr., George Town* ☎ *345/949–5155* ⊠ *Strand Shopping Center, 46A Canal Point Dr., off West Bay Rd., Seven Mile Beach* ☎ *345/945–4748* ⊠ *Republix Plaza, West Bay Rd., Seven Mile Beach* ☎ *345/949–3214* ⊠ *Morritt's Shopping Centre, 2206 Queens Hwy., East End* ☎ *345/947–2826* ⊠ *Countryside Shopping Center, Savannah* ☎ *345/943–5155*) is the island's biggest chain, with five stores. The Airport Centre and Strand stores have full-service pharmacies. These stores are open from Monday through Saturday, 7 to 11.

★ **Hurley's Marketplace** (⊠ *Grand Harbour Shopping Centre, Red Bay* ☎ *345/947–8488*) is open Monday through Saturday from 7 AM to 10 PM.

Kirk Supermarket & Pharmacy (⊠ *Eastern Ave. near intersection with West Bay Rd., George Town* ☎ *345/949–7022*) is open Monday through Saturday from 7 AM to 10 PM and is a particularly good source for traditional Caymanian fast food (oxtail, curried goat).

The **Tortuga Rum Company** (⊠ *N. Sound Rd., Industrial Park, George Town* ☎ *345/949–7701 or 345/949–7867*) bakes then vacuum-seals more than 10,000 of its world-famous rum cakes daily, adhering to the original "secret" century-old recipe. You can buy a fresh rum cake at the airport on the way home at the same prices as at the factory store.

HANDICRAFTS The **Heritage Crafts Shop** (⊠ *Harbour Dr., George Town* ☎ *345/945–*
& SOUVENIRS *6041*), near the harbor, sells local crafts and gifts. **Pirate's Grotto** (⊠ *Harbour Dr., basement level, below Landmark Shopping Center, George Town* ☎ *345/945–0244*) is a cute store with duty-free liquor and cigars (including Cubans) as well as Cayman Islands souvenirs.

JEWELRY The black-coral creations of **Bernard Passman** (⊠ *Cardinal Ave., George Town* ☎ *345/949–0123*) have won the approval of the British royal family (who chose him to create a wedding present for Prince Charles and Princess Diana).

★ **Mitzi's Fine Jewelry** (⊠ *5 Bay Harbour Centre, West Bay Rd., Seven Mile Beach* ☎ *345/945–5014*) is a treasure trove of salvaged 18th-century coins, silver, Caymanite pieces, and black coral; the store also carries Italian porcelain and the Carrera y Carrera line of jewelry and sculptures. Self-taught, vivacious proprietor Mitzi Callan, who specializes in handmade pieces, is usually on hand to help.

Designer Richard Barile has cultivated a celebrity following for coruscating coral pieces at **Richard's Fine Jewelry** (⊠ *Harbour Dr., George Town* ☎ *345/949–7156*). The large-scale sculptures are extraordinary, including *The Boss,* which took more than a decade to complete.

★ **24K-Mon Jewelers** (⊠ *Buckingham Sq., Seven Mile Beach* ☎ *345/949– 1499*) sells works of art from many jewelers, including Wyland, Merry-Lee Rae, and Stephen Douglas, as well as designs courtesy of owner/goldsmith Gale Tibbetts and her friends, incorporating everything from Swarovski crystals to Spanish doubloons.

NIGHTLIFE

Check the Friday edition of the *Caymanian Compass* for listings of music, movies, theater, and other entertainment. Bars are open during evening hours until 1 AM, and clubs are generally open from 10 PM until 3 AM, but none may serve liquor after midnight on Saturday and none can offer dancing on Sunday.

★ The **Attic** (⊠ *Queen's Court, 2nd fl., West Bay Rd., Seven Mile Beach* ☎ *345/949–7665*) is a chic sports bar with three billiard tables and large-screen TVs; it's on the second floor above "O" Bar. **Bamboo Lounge** (⊠ *Grand Cayman Beach Suites, West Bay Rd., Seven Mile Beach* ☎ *345/947–8744*) is a quiet, refined bar with adjacent sushi restaurant and a good selection of wine by the glass. For a casual drink, visit **Calico Jack's** (⊠ *West Bay Rd., Seven Mile Beach* ☎ *345/945–7850*), a friendly outdoor beach bar at the north end of the public beach with a DJ on Monday and open-mike night on Tuesday, bands every Friday night, and parties during the full moon. You can sit at the bar or swing under a big tree at **Coconut Joe's** (⊠ *Across from Comfort Suites, West Bay Rd., Seven Mile Beach* ☎ *345/943–5637*) and watch the traffic go by. There's a Friday-night DJ. **Margaritaville** (⊠ *Island Village, Cardinal Ave., George Town* ☎ *345/949–6274*) is a huge space that bustles with life; the Friday-evening happy hour is especially popular, and though drinks may be a bit pricier than other waterfront locations, the atmosphere definitely compensates. For a wild and rowdy good time, try the nightclub **Next Level** (⊠ *West Bay Rd. between Grand Cayman Beach Suites and Westin, opposite Marriott, Seven Mile Beach* ☎ *345/946–6398*) or the adjacent Aqua Beach Bar, which has private tiki-hut booths and open mike on Thursday. Check on the live band schedule. The Next Level is a late-night hot spot offering dancing to everything from retro remixes to hip-hop.

★ **"O" Bar** (⊠ *Queen's Court, West Bay Rd., Seven Mile Beach* ☎ *345/943– 6227 or 345/949–7665*) is a trendy dance club with mixed music and flame-throwing, juggling bartenders. An upper-level private loft is available by reservation.

You can watch tarpon feeding at **Rackam's Pub & Restaurant** (⊠ *N. Church St., George Town* ☎*345/945–3860*), a happenin' bar on the water that has complimentary snacks on Friday and a cool misting spray during the hot summer.

★ **Royal Palms** (⊠ *West Bay Rd., George Town* ☎*345/945–6358*) is where local bands play Friday and Saturday nights; it's an outdoor beach bar with plenty of room for dancing under the stars or a great Sunday-afternoon hangout to socialize, sit in the sun, and listen to music. Don't let the location of **Sapphire Lounge** (⊠ *Seven Mile Shops, Seven Mile Beach* ☎*345/946–3496*)—in the back of a plain strip mall—fool you. This is a chic and trendy New York–style martini lounge and sushi bar with more than 30 different drinks—including many martinis—and French-pressed coffee. Choose from bar, tall tables, or sofas; there's new art on the walls every month. You can dance near the water to mellow music at **The Wharf** (⊠ *West Bay Rd., George Town* ☎*345/949–2231*) on Friday and Saturday evenings; there is salsa dancing and lessons on Tuesday.

EXPLORING GRAND CAYMAN

The historic capital of George Town, on the southeast corner of Grand Cayman, is easy to explore on foot. If you're a shopper, you can spend days here; otherwise, an hour will suffice for a tour of the downtown area. To see the rest of the island, rent a car or scooter or take a guided tour. The portion of the island called West Bay is noted for its jumble of neighborhoods and a few attractions. When traffic is heavy, it's about a half hour to West Bay from George Town, but it can be an easier journey now with the opening of a new bypass road that runs parallel to West Bay Road. The less-developed East End has natural attractions from blowholes to botanical gardens, as well as the remains of the island's original settlements. Plan on at least 45 minutes for the drive out from George Town (more than an hour during rush hours). You need a day to explore the entire island—including a stop at a beach for a picnic or swim.

For a wonderful map of the natural attractions, go to the **National Trust** (⊠*S. Church St. north and across street from Sunset House, George Town* ☎*345/949–0121* ⊕*nationaltrust.org.ky*). The Trust sells books and guides to Cayman. The fabulous Web site has more than 50 information sheets on cultural and natural topics from iguanas to schoolhouses. Stop there first before you tour the island.

WHAT TO SEE

☾ **Blowholes.** When the easterly trade winds blow hard, crashing waves force water into caverns and send impressive geysers shooting up as much as 20 feet through the ironshore. The blowholes were partially filled during Hurricane Ivan in 2004, so the water must be rough to recapture the elemental drama that they used to have. ⊠*Frank Sound Rd., roughly 10 mi 16 km) east of Bodden Town, near East End.*

☾ **Boatswain's Beach.** What was Cayman's premier attraction, the Turtle Farm, has been transformed into a marine theme park and rebranded as Boatswain's Beach. The expanded complex now has several shops for souvenirs, jewelry, and cigars as well as restaurants. Still, the turtles remain a central attraction, and you can tour ponds with thousands of them in various stages of growth; some can be picked up from the tanks—a real treat for children and adults as the little creatures flap their fins and splash the water. A nature trail affords a 30-minute guided tour through a butterfly garden, bird-watching spot, and displays of Cayman's native reptiles, including iguanas. A snorkel lagoon provides the adventure of swimming with some of the marine life that are found just offshore from the Cayman coastline. These improvements, along with rest areas and refreshment stands, make Boatswain's Beach worthy of a few hours' visit, but the particularly steep new admission price may keep you away. ⊠*825 Northwest Point Rd., West Bay* ☏*345/949–3894* ⊕*www.boatswainsbeach.ky* ⊠*$55 for comprehensive ticket, $18 for Turtle Farm alone* ☉*Daily 8:30–4:30.*

Bodden Town. In the island's original south-shore capital you can find an old cemetery on the shore side of the road. Graves with A-frame structures are said to contain the remains of pirates. There are also the ruins of a fort and a wall erected by slaves in the 19th century. A curio shop serves as the entrance to what's called the Pirate's Caves ($8), partially underground natural formations that are more hokey (decked out with fake treasure chests and mannequins in pirate garb) than spooky.

☾ **Butterfly Farm.** Your entry fee is good for your entire stay so that you can watch the life-stage changes of the butterflies. It's fun, easy, and interesting and makes a great photo op, particularly early in the morning or on a sunny afternoon. ⊠*Lawrence Rd. across from cinema, Seven Mile Beach* ☏*345/946–3411* ⊕*www.thebutterflyfarm.com* ⊠*$15* ☉*Mon.–Sat. 8:30–4, Sun. 8:30–noon.*

George Town. Begin exploring the capital by strolling along the waterfront Harbour Drive to **Elmslie Memorial United Church,** named after the first Presbyterian missionary to serve in the Caymans. Its vaulted ceiling, wooden arches, and sedate nave reflect the religious nature of island residents. In front of the court building, in the center of town, names of influential Caymanians are inscribed on the **Wall of History,** which commemorates the islands' quincentennial in 2003. Across the street is the Cayman Islands Legislative Assembly Building, next door to the 1919 Peace Memorial Building. In the middle of the financial district is the **General Post Office,** built in 1939. Let the kids pet the big blue iguana statues.

☾ Built in 1833, the home of the **Cayman Islands National Museum** has had several different incarnations over the years, including that of courthouse, jail (now the gift shop), post office, and dance hall. It's small but fascinating, with excellent displays and videos that illustrate local geology, flora, and fauna, and island history. Pick up a walking-tour map of George Town at the museum gift shop before leaving. At this writing, the museum was expected to reopen sometime in late summer 2008, after having been damaged during Hurricane Ivan. ⊠*Harbour Dr., George Town* ☎*345/949–8368* ⊕*www.museum.ky* ⊠*$5* ☽ *Weekdays 9–5, Sat. 10–2.*

Hell. The touristy stopover in West Bay is little more than a patch of incredibly jagged black rock formations. The attractions are the small post office and a gift shop where you can get cards and letters postmarked from Hell. ⊠*Hell Rd., West Bay* ☎*345/949–3358* ⊠*Free* ☽ *Daily 9–6.*

Old Homestead. Formerly known as the West Bay Pink House, this cottage is probably the most-photographed home in Grand Cayman. It was built in 1912 of wattle and daub around an ironwood frame. Cheery Mac Bothwell, who grew up in the house, takes you on tours that present a nostalgic and touching look at life in Grand Cayman before the tourism and banking booms. ⊠*West Bay Rd., West Bay* ☎*345/949–7639* ⊠*$5* ☽ *Mon.–Sat. 8–5.*

⟳ **Pedro St. James Castle.** Built in 1780, the greathouse is Cayman's oldest
★ stone structure and the only remaining late-18th-century residence on the island. The buildings are surrounded by 8 acres of natural parks and woodlands. You can stroll through landscaping of native Caymanian flora and experience one of the most-spectacular views on the island from atop the dramatic Great Pedro Bluff. Don't miss the impressive multimedia theater show complete with smoking pots, misting rains, and two film screens where the story of Pedro's Castle is presented. The show plays on the hour; see it before you tour the site. The poignant outdoor Hurricane Ivan Memorial uses text, images, and symbols to represent important aspects of that horrific 2004 natural disaster. If you want a snack, stop by the relocated—and beloved—Durty Reid's, run by an ex-Marine amputee Vietnam vet who advertises "lousy food, surly help." ⊠*Pedro Castle Rd., Savannah* ☎*345/947–3329* ⊕*www. pedrostjames.ky* ⊠*$10* ☽ *Daily 9–5.*

Fodor's Choice **Queen Elizabeth II Botanic Park.** This 65-acre wilderness preserve show-
★ cases a wide range of indigenous and nonindigenous tropical vegetation. Rare blue iguanas are bred and released in the gardens and are a common sight on the trails. If you're lucky, you'll see the brilliant green Cayman parrot—not just here but virtually anywhere in Cayman. ⊠*Frank Sound Rd., Frank Sound, North Side* ⌂*Box 203, North Side, Grand Cayman* ☎*345/947–9462, 345/947–3558 info line* ⊕*www. botanic-park.ky* ⊠*$10* ☽ *Apr.–Sept., daily 9–6:30; Oct.–Mar., daily 9–5:30 (last admission 1 hr prior to closing).*

CAYMAN BRAC

Cayman Brac is named for its most distinctive feature, a rugged limestone bluff ("brac" in Gaelic) that runs up the center of the 12-mi (19-km) island, culminating in a sheer 140-foot cliff at its eastern end. The Brac, 89 mi (143 km) northeast of Grand Cayman, is accessible via Cayman Airways. With only 1,800 residents—they call themselves Brackers—the island has the feel and easy pace of a small town. Brackers are known for their friendly attitude toward visitors, so it's easy to strike up a conversation.

WHERE TO STAY

Lodgings are small and intimate, and guests are often treated like family. Most resorts offer optional meal plans but there are several restaurants, some of which provide free transport from your hotel. Most restaurants serve island fare (local seafood, chicken, and curries). On Friday and Saturday nights the spicy scent of jerk chicken fills the air; three roadside stands sell takeout dinners. A 1950s-style ice-cream parlor is open on weekends. This is a nature and outdoor island; if the weather is bad, there are no indoor activities, so bring a good book just in case.

$$ **Brac Caribbean and Carib Sands.** These neighboring complexes under the same management offer condos with one to four bedrooms, all individually owned and decorated beyond a "starter" design. The Brac Caribbean balconies overlook the sea; Carib Sands' overlook the water across the extensive pool area. The Captain's Table restaurant and poolside bar at Brac Caribbean is a popular hangout for locals and visitors alike. The Sands grounds are particularly pretty, with buttonwood and ficus "fences" and fragrant oleander bushes buzzing with butterflies. The units here tend to be more vivid though often weirdly configured. Numbers 111 and 114 are particularly stylish digs with splendid views. The Brac Caribbean units feature a more-flowing layout but more-generic decor; ground-floor views are somewhat obscured by foliage. **Pros:** Lively restaurant/bar, pretty beach. **Cons:** Many units could use sprucing up, limited staff. ⬒ *Box 4 SPO, Cayman Brac* ☎*345/948–2265, 345/948–1121, or 866/843–2722* ⊕*www.866thebrac.com* ⬎*42 condos* ⬧*In-room: kitchen, DVD (some), Wi-Fi (some). In-hotel: restaurant, bar, pools, beachfront, diving, bicycles, public Wi-Fi, no elevator* ⊟*AE, MC, V* ⦿*CP.*

$$
★   **Brac Reef Beach Resort.** Popular with divers, this well-run resort features a beautiful sandy beach shaded by sea grape trees. The dock is illuminated nightly, attracting stingrays, tarpon, and other creatures to entertain you on your after-dinner stroll. The motel-style rooms are simple but spotless. The second-floor and end units (118–121, 219–221) offer the best views; the least desirable lack balconies. The buffet-style food is surprisingly good: killer peppery conch chowder, silken lobster bisque, scrumptious garlic bread, live carving station, and plentiful choices like mahimahi with mushroom demi-glace. The crowd tends to be older, with a handful of honeymooners throw in and a few small meetings and vacationing families in summer. **Pros:** Lovely beach, great dive outfit, friendly staff. **Cons:** Uneven stairs, noise from planes, unattractive decor. ⬒ *Box 56, West End, Cayman Brac* ☎*345/948–1323, 727/323–8727 for reservations, in Florida* ⊕*www.bracreef.com* ⬎*40 rooms* ⬧*In-room: dial-up. In-hotel: restaurant, room service, bar, tennis court, pool, gym, spa, beachfront, diving, water sports, bicycles,*

Cayman Brac & Little Cayman

Caribbean Sea

LITTLE CAYMAN

Booby Pt.
North East Pt.
Spot Bay **[11]**
Pollard Bay
North East Bay
Cat Head Bay
Tibbetts Turn
Parrot Preserve
Tom Jennett's Bay
Sea Feather Bay
Stake Bay Pt.
Cayman Brac Museum [10]
Deadman's Pt.
Cedar Pt.
Tiara Beach
Frenchman's Fort
West End
[9]
Brac Reef Beach
West End Pt.
[8]
M.V. Capt. Keith Tibbetts
Gerrard-Smith Airport

CAYMAN BRAC

East Pt.
Sandy Point
Crawl Bay
Charles Bight
Lower Spot Bay
Jacksons Pt.
Little Cayman Research Center
Little Cayman Museum
Owen Island
Gore Bird Sanctuary
Bloody Bay Wall [1]
South Town **[7][5][6][4][3]**
[2]
Edward Bodden Airfield
Anchorage Bay
West End Pt.

KEY
/ Beaches
⬛ Dive Sites
1 Hotels

2 mi
2 km

7

no elevator, laundry service, public Internet, public Wi-Fi, no-smoking rooms ⊟*AE, D, MC, V* ⊙*BP.*

$$ 🏨**Cayman Breakers.** This attractive pink-brick condo development sitting between the bluff and the ironshore on the southeast coast caters to climbers, who come to scale the sheer face of the bluff, as well as divers, who take full advantage of the good shore diving right off the property. Spacious, two-bedroom units favor soft seashell colors and frilly touches (Aubusson-style rugs, shell-embedded mirrors) and have full open kitchens including a dishwasher, as well as a sleeper sofa and washer/dryer. A private shore-dive entrance with a shower and rinse tank is located at the cabana/pool area, slung with hammocks and offering breathtaking views of the bluff and beach. Robert and Nina Banks, the managers who live on-site, are very attentive and helpful. **Pros:** Remote, spectacular views, complimentary bikes. **Cons:** Nearest grocery is a 15-minute drive, gorgeous beach but not ideal for swimming. ✉*Box 202 SPO, Cayman Brac* 🖂*345/948–1463* ⊕*www. caybreakers.com or www.caymancondosonline.com* ⤴*18 2-bedroom condos* ♿*In-room: kitchen, VCR, DVD, Wi-Fi. In-hotel: pool, beachfront, bicycles, no elevator, laundry facilities, no-smoking rooms* ⊟*AE, MC, V* ⊙*EP.*

$ 🏨**Walton's Mango Manor.** This beautifully restored traditional West
★ Indian home has five rooms (all with bath), accented with lovely antique furnishings, model catboats, and bric-a-brac from the Waltons' world travels. Upper-floor units are desirable: their tiny balconies oversee the 500-foot sweep of verdant grounds down to the sea. A spacious, private, seaside cottage called Sea Dreams has a full kitchen, washer/dryer, and Internet access. The tranquil ironshore beach is usually unoccupied; its gazebo has hosted many a wedding ceremony. Walk with owner George, a native Bracker, through the extravagant enchanted landscaping, which include a tiny exquisite synagogue, mosaic gazebo, organic garden in a failed swimming pool, and turtle pond with bridge. Breakfasts feature fresh fruit and luscious jellies from the fruit trees (seven types of mango, key limes, coconuts, plum), wife Lynne's homemade challah bread, and local dishes like salt cod and plantain. **Pros:** True Caymanian hospitality, beautiful grounds, excellent snorkeling. **Cons:** Poky beach across the street, car required. ✉*Box 56 SPO, Stake Bay, Cayman Brac* 🖂*345/948–2551* ⊕*www.waltonsmangomanor.com* ⤴*5 rooms, 1 2-bedroom cottage* ♿*In-room: no TV (some), VCR (some), kitchen (some), Ethernet (some). In hotel: beachfront, no elevator* ⊟*MC, V* ⊙*CP.*

BEACHES

Much of the Brac's coastline is ironshore, though there are several pretty sand beaches, mostly along the southwest coast (where swimmers will also find extensive beds of turtle grass). In addition to the hotel beaches, where everyone is welcome, there is a public beach with good access to the reef; it's well marked on tourist maps. The north-coast beaches, predominantly rocky ironshore, offer excellent snorkeling.

Sculpting Cayman

A sculptor named Foots dreamed since childhood of creating his own version of Plato's lost city of Atlantis. He is seeing his dream fulfilled as he creates huge sculptures of concrete and sinks them in 45 feet of water off the north shore of Cayman Brac. The result is an astounding dive site and artificial reef with more than 100 sculptures covering several acres. The story starts at the Archway of Atlantis (each of the two bases weighs 21,000 pounds). The Elders' Way, lined with 5-foot temple columns, leads to the Inner Circle of Light, where there is a sundial large enough to sit in. Each Elder is modeled after an actual person who has contributed to the Cayman Islands. Foots creates a beautiful story with his creation and is doing this almost entirely on his own; he's made an incredible donation to the divers of the Brac. Foots plans to add a new phase every six months so that the story will go on for a long time before the project is finished.

SPORTS & THE OUTDOORS

DIVING & SNORKELING

Cayman Brac's waters have excellent sea life. The snorkeling off the **north coast** is spectacular, particularly at West End, where coral formations close to shore attract all kinds of critters. Many fish have colonized the Russian frigate—now broken in two—that was scuttled offshore from the site of the former Buccaneer's Inn. An artist named Foots has created an amazing underwater Atlantis. The island's two dive operators offer scuba and snorkel training and PADI certification. Certified divers can purchase à la carte dive packages from the Brac Reef Beach Resort.

★ **Indepth Watersports** (⊠ *Stake Bay* ☎ *345/948–8037, 345/329–6348, or 866/476–2195* ⊕ *www.indepthwatersports.com*). **Reef Divers** (⊠ *Brac Reef Beach Resort, West End* ☎ *345/948–1642* ⊕ *www.bracreef.com*).

HIKING

Free printed guides to the Brac's many heritage and nature trails can be obtained from the **Brac Tourism Office** (⊠ *West End Community Park, west of airport, Cayman Brac* ☎ *345/948–1649*); you can also get the guides at the airport or at your hotel. Traditional routes across the bluff have been cleared and marked; trailheads are identified with signs along the road. It's safe to hike on your own, though some trails are fairly hard going (wear light hiking boots) and others could be better maintained. For those who prefer less-strenuous walking, **Christopher Columbus Gardens** (⊠ *Ashton Reid Dr. [Bluff Rd.], just north of Ashton Rutty Centre*) has easy trails and boardwalks. The park showcases the unique natural flora and features of the bluff, including two cave mouths.

ROCK CLIMBING

If you are experienced and like dangling from ropes 140 feet above a rocky sea, the Brac is the place for you. Ropes and safety gear cannot be rented on the island—you need to bring your own. Through the years,

7

climbers have attached permanent titanium bolts to the **bluff** face, creating some 40 routes. The Cayman Breakers condo community has route maps and descriptions *(⇨ Cayman Breakers in Where to Stay).*

SPELUNKING

If you plan to explore Cayman Brac's caves, wear good sneakers or hiking shoes, as some paths are steep and rocky and some cave entrances reachable only by ladders. **Peter's Cave** offers a stunning aerial view of the picturesque northeastern community of Spot Bay. **Great Cave,** at the island's southeast end, has numerous chambers and photogenic ocean views. In **Bat Cave** you may see bats hanging from the ceiling (try not to disturb them). **Rebecca's Cave** houses the grave site of a 17-month-old child who died during the horrific hurricane of 1932.

EXPLORING CAYMAN BRAC

Cayman Brac Museum. Here you'll find a diverse, well-displayed collection of everyday implements used by previous generations of Brackers. A meticulously crafted scale model of the Caymanian schooner *Alsons* has pride of place. ⊠ *Old Government Administration Bldg., Stake Bay* ☎ *345/948–2622 or 345/244–4446* ⊟ *Free* ⊙ *Weekdays 9–noon and 1–4, Sat. 9–noon.*

Parrot Preserve. The likeliest place to spot the endangered Cayman Brac parrot—and other indigenous birds—is along this National Trust hiking trail off Major Donald Drive, aka Lighthouse Road. The 6-mi (9.5-km) gravel road continues to the lighthouse at the bluff's eastern end, where there's an astonishing view from atop the cliff to the open ocean—the best place to watch the sunrise. ⊠ *Lighthouse Rd., Tibbetts Turn, 0.5 m (1 km) south of town* ☎ *345/948–0319* ⊟ *Free* ⊙ *Daily sunrise–sunset.*

LITTLE CAYMAN

The smallest of the three Cayman Islands, Little Cayman, often referred to as the gem of the Cayman Islands, has a full-time population of only 150, most of whom work in the tourism industry. This 12-square-mi (31-square-km) island is still pristine and has only a sand-sealed airstrip, no official terminal building, and few vehicles. With little commercial development, the island beckons to ecotourists who want to leave the bustle of city life behind. It's probably most well known for its spectacular diving on world-renowned Bloody Bay Wall and adjacent Jackson Marine Park.

WHERE TO STAY

Accommodations are mostly in small lodges, many of which offer meal and dive packages. The meal packages are a good idea; the chefs in most places create wonderful meals.

HOTELS

$$$$ 🏨 **Southern Cross Club.** Little Cayman's first resort was co-founded in
Fodor's Choice the 1950s as a private fishing club by the CEO of Sears-Roebuck and
★ CFO of General Motors, and its focus is still on fishing and diving. The
adventure and barefoot elegance motifs are struck in the semi-open
lobby with African masks, trophy game fish, hand-painted cabinets,
and magnificent indoor-outdoor bar. Psychedelically hued duplex cottages sit on Little Cayman's most-spectacular white-sand beach, with
views of the uninhabited Owen Island and romantic private outdoor
showers. Rooms feature vivid colors and hardwood furniture including
several four-poster beds. Some have separate living rooms; the newest
incorporate ecologically sound aspects like gray-watered gardens and
solar-heated water. Dive services are superb—set your gear up once
and the rest is done for you during your stay. The food is exceptional,
served in various venues, including an air-conditioned split-level dining
room with panoramic views. **Pros:** Barefoot luxury, extras like complimentary use of kayaks and snorkel gear, splendiferous beach. **Cons:**
Not family-friendly. 🏠 *Box 44, South Hole Sound* 📞*345/948–1099
or 800/899–2582* 🌐*www.southerncrossclub.com* 🛏*9 rooms, 3 suites,
1 2-bedroom cottage* ⚒*In-room: no TV, refrigerator (some), Wi-Fi. In-
hotel: restaurant, bar, spa, beachfront, diving, water sports, bicycles,
public Internet, public Wi-Fi, airport shuttle, no kids under 10* ☰*AE,
MC, V* ☉*Closed mid-Sept–mid-Oct.* ⭐*FAP.*

$$$–$$$$ 🏨 **Pirates Point Resort.** Nestled between sea grape and casuarina pines
Fodor's Choice on a sparkling sweep of palapa-dotted sand are 11 bungalow-style
★ rooms, some air-conditioned, others swept by crosswinds through lou-
vers. Walls duplicate the soft colors of a Caribbean dawn; floors and
furnishings are immaculate. In true Caribbean getaway tradition, TV
is banished to the main cottage (where Wi-Fi is available). You'll likely
become fast friends with effervescent owner, Gladys Howard, whose
down-home welcome belies her upscale meals served with fine wines.
Gladys finds time to host weekly champagne parties on the verandah
of her adjacent home and play dominoes after dinner. Somehow Gladys
always wins, slamming tiles down with classic Caribbean vigor. Weekly
stays (preferred) represent huge savings, especially the dive packages.
The large repeat clientele attests that everything from the billeting to
the bill of fare lives up to the billing. **Pros:** Fabulous food, fantas-
tic beach, dynamic dive program, fun-loving staff and owner. **Cons:**
Everyone respects honeymooners' privacy, but this isn't a resort for
antisocial types; tasteful rooms are fairly spare. 🏠 *Box 43, Preston Bay*
📞*345/948–1010* 🌐*www.piratespointresort.com* 🛏*11 rooms* ⚒*In-
room: no a/c (some), no TV. In-hotel: restaurant, bar, gym, beach-
front, diving, water sports, bicycles, airport shuttle, no elevator, public
Internet, public Wi-Fi, no kids under 5* ☰*MC, V* ☉*Closed Sept.–mid
Oct.* ⭐*AI.*

$$$ 🏨 **Little Cayman Beach Resort.** The island's largest resort offers the most
☾ options for fun-seekers. The two-story hotel has modern facilities and
brightly colored rooms, which received a complete refurbishment in
2008 (flat-screen TVs, curved shower rods). They overlook either the
pool area or the ocean (the latter are quieter, especially the 300 block,

farthest from the occasionally raucous Beach Nuts Bar). A full-service spa offers massages utilizing 100% organic marine-based ingredients, as well as hair and nail treatments. The Mermaid Boutique is the island's most upscale shop. Meals are served buffet style. Diving packages are an excellent value. The resort is gradually upgrading various areas and experimenting with ecofriendly practices such as using green-approved organic chemicals. But island warmth remains: it's family-run by Brackers, the children of beloved Linton "Mr. T" Tibbetts, an inspiring self-made millionaire who passionately believes in preserving Caymanian heritage. **Pros:** Extensive facilities, fun crowd. **Cons:** Less-intimate feel than other island resorts, occasionally mediocre food. ⌂ *Box 51, Blossom Village* ☎ *345/948–1033 or 800/327–3835* ⊕ *www.littlecayman.com* ⊃ *40 rooms* ⌂ *In-room: kitchen (some), refrigerator, Wi-Fi. In-hotel: restaurant, bar, tennis court, pool, gym, spa, beachfront, diving, water sports, bicycles, no elevator, public Internet, public Wi-Fi, airport shuttle, parking, no-smoking rooms* ⊟ *AE, MC, V* ⊙ *FAP.*

$$ **Sam McCoy's Diving & Fishing Lodge.** This place is quiet, laid back, and rustic: you can relax in the hammock shed with owner Sam McCoy and listen to his stories. Authentic Caymanian meals are prepared by the family matriarch, Sam's wife Mary, and served family-style in the large dining room overlooking the small pool and the ocean. Eight spartan rooms (aside from walls so vibrantly hued they're headache-inducing) have tiny private baths. McCoy's is a favorite for Saturday-evening barbecues under the stars at the beachside gazebo bar. The immediate area is filigreed with nature trails perfect for bird-watching and meditation. But the real lure is the location, right by Bloody Bay. **Pros:** True Caymanian warmth, ideal location for diving Bloody Bay. **Cons:** Very bare no-frills decor, periodic problems with water pressure, mosquito problem during still summer days. ⌂ *Box 12, North Side* ☎ *345/948–0026 or 800/626–0496* ⊕ *mccoyslodge.com.ky* ⊃ *8 rooms* ⌂ *In-hotel: bar, pool, diving, no elevator* ⊟ *AE, MC, V* ⊙ *AI.*

VILLAS & CONDOS

$$$–$$$$ **Conch Club.** The handsome oceanfront development grafts Caribbean-style gingerbread onto New England maritime architecture with gables and dormers Condos are brilliantly decorated and well equipped, ideal for families or small groups. The town house–style units have vaulted ceilings, full kitchens, private patios, and balconies that look out onto the pool and ocean. Though individually decorated, a fussy grandmotherly-style look out of a Sunbelt retirement community predominates. Diving is offered through Conch Club Divers. Guests can also enjoy the amenities at the Little Cayman Beach Resort (a sister property). Meal plans are available for an additional charge. **Pros:** Splendid views, gorgeous beach. **Cons:** Long walk to Little Cayman Resort's facilities, dated decor. ⌂ *Box 51, Blossom Village* ☎ *345/948–1033 or 888/756–7400* ⊕ *www.conchclub.com* ⊃ *18 2-bedroom condos, 2 3-bedroom condos* ⌂ *In-room: kitchen, DVD, Wi-Fi. In-hotel: pools, spa, diving, bicycles, laundry facilities, public Internet, no elevator* ⊟ *AE, MC, V* ⊙ *EP.*

$$$ **The Club.** These ultramodern, luxurious condos are Little Cayman's newest (from 2002) and nicest units. Each of the three-bedroom residences comes fully equipped, from kitchen to bedroom, with Italian marble, Turkish tiles, elegant accents like arches and crown moldings, state-of-the-art gadgetry from rainfall showerheads to flat-screen TVs, upscale furnishings like four-poster beds, and patios or balconies with scintillating water views. The complex has an outdoor pool with waterfall and Jacuzzi along the beachfront, as well as a dock with inviting hammocks. Guests can use the amenities and sign up for a meal plan at Little Cayman Beach Resort, under the same ownership; it's about a five-minute walk from the Club. Rates do not include housekeeping. **Pros:** Luxurious digs, lovely beach. **Cons:** Housekeeping not included, rear guest bedrooms dark and somewhat cramped. *Box 51, South Hole Sound, Blossom Village* 345/948–1033, 727/323–8727, or 800/327–3835 *www.theclubatlittlecayman.com* 8 condos *In-room: kitchen, DVD, laundry facilities, Wi-Fi. In-hotel: pool, beachfront, bicycles, no elevator, concierge, airport shuttle* AE, MC, V EP.

$$ **Paradise Villas.** The cozy one-bedroom units have beachfront terraces and hammocks. Sunny but spare rooms are simply but immaculately appointed with rattan furnishings, marine artwork and painted driftwood, and muted abstract fabrics. If you get tired of cooking for yourself in the well-equipped kitchen, fine island-style food (not to mention the island's only real bar) is steps away at the Hungry Iguana restaurant. Diving is done with the on-site dive shop; packages that include both room and diving are a sensational value. **Pros:** Good value, friendly staff. **Cons:** Noisy some weekend nights in season, poky beach. *Box 48, South Hole Sound* 345/948–0001 or 877/322–9626 *www.paradisevillas.com* 12 1-bedroom villas *In-room: kitchen. In-hotel: pool, diving, bicycles, no elevator* AE, MC, V Closed mid-Sept.–late Oct. EP.

BEACHES

Fodor'sChoice ★ **Owen Island.** This private island can be reached by rowboat, kayak, or an ambitious 200-yard swim. Anyone is welcome to come across and enjoy the deserted beaches.

Fodor'sChoice ★ **Point o' Sand.** On the easternmost point of the island, this secluded beach is great for wading, shell collecting, and snorkeling. On a clear day you can see 7 mi (11 km) across to Cayman Brac.

SPORTS & THE OUTDOORS

BIRD-WATCHING

★ **Booby Pond Nature Reserve** is home for 20,000 red-footed boobies (the largest colony in the western hemisphere) and Cayman's only breeding colony of magnificent frigate (or man-of-war) birds; other sightings include the near-threatened West Indian whistling duck and vitelline warbler. The RAMSAR Convention, an international treaty for wetland conservation, designated the reserve a wetland of global significance. Near the airport, the sanctuary is open to the public, and has a gift shop and reading library.

DIVING & SNORKELING

Fodor's Choice ★ **Bloody Bay Wall,** on the North Side, begins at a mere 18 feet and plunges to more than 1,000 feet, with visibility often reaching 150 feet—diving doesn't get much better than this. Expect to pay $60 to $75 for a two-tank boat dive. The island is small and susceptible to wind.

Paradise Divers (☎345/948–0001 or 877/322–9626 ⊕www.paradise-divers.com) runs a 46-foot boat from the north coast of Little Cayman to Bloody Bay and Jackson Bay. **Pirate's Point Dive Resort** (☎345/948–1010 ⊕www.piratespointresort.com) has fully outfitted dive boats with dive masters who are great at finding odd and rare creatures. **Reef Divers** (☎345/948–1033), at Little Cayman Beach Resort, also offers a full-service photo and video center. **Sam McCoy's Diving & Fishing Lodge** (☎345/948–0026 or 800/626–0496 ⊕www.mccoyslodge.com.ky) takes small groups on its dive boat. This is the closest dive operation to Bloody Bay (only 10 minutes away) and provides shore diving from Jackson's Point. The **Southern Cross Club** (☎345/948–1099 or 800/899–2582 ⊕www.southerncrossclub.com) limits each of its boats to 12 divers and has its own dock.

FISHING

Bloody Bay, off the north coast, is well known for fishing, and the shallows in South Hole Lagoon are a great spot for tarpon, bonefish, and permit (a large fish related to pompano). Sam McCoy, of **Sam McCoy's Diving & Fishing Resort** (☎345/948–0026 or 800/626–0496 ⊕www.mccoyslodge.com.ky), is among the premier fishermen on the island. The **Southern Cross Club** (☎345/948–1099 or 800/899–2582 ⊕www.southerncrossclub.com) offers light-tackle and deep-sea fishing trips.

EXPLORING LITTLE CAYMAN

Little Cayman Museum. The museum displays relics and artifacts that provide a good overview of this tiny island's history and heritage. ⊠Across from Booby Pond Nature Reserve, Blossom Village ☎No phone at museum, 345/948–1033 for Little Cayman Beach Resort ☑Free ☉Tues. and Thurs. 3–5, by appointment only.

★ **Little Cayman National Trust.** This traditional Caymanian cottage overlooks the Booby Pond Nature Reserve; telescopes on the breezy second-floor deck permit close-up views of their markings and nests, as well as the other feathered friends. Inside you'll find shell collections, panels and dioramas discussing endemic reptiles, and diagrams on the growth and life span of red-footed boobies, frigate birds, egrets, and other island "residents." The shop sells exquisite jewelry made from Caymanite and spider crab shells, extraordinary duck decoys and bird carvings by local artist John Mulak of purple gallinules and black-necked stilts, and great books on history, ornithology, and geology. This is the best place on island for cappuccino, herb tea, cinnamon buns, and scrumptious homemade ice cream (guava, rum raisin, lemongrass, ginger)—a fantastic place to mingle with residents and visitors. ⊠Blossom Village ☎No phone ⊕www.nationaltrust.org.ky ☉Mon.–Sat., 9–noon and 2–6.

CAYMAN ISLANDS ESSENTIALS

To research prices, get advice from other travelers, and book travel arrangements, visit www.fodors.com.

▌ TRANSPORTATION

BY AIR

Almost all nonstop air service is to Grand Cayman, with connecting flights to Cayman Brac and Little Cayman on a small propeller plane. Cayman Airways also flies to both Cayman Brac and Little Cayman; there's also interisland charter service on Island Air.

Airline Contacts **Air Jamaica** (☎345/949-2300 or 800/523-5585 ⊕www.airjamaica.com). **American Airlines/American Eagle** (☎345/949-0666 or 800/744-0006 ⊕www.aa.com). **Cayman Airways** (☎345/949-2311 or 800/422-9626 ⊕www.caymanairways.com). **Continental** (☎345/916-5545 or 800/534-0089 ⊕www.continental.com). **Delta** (☎345/945-8430 or 800/221-1212 ⊕www.delta.com). **Island Air** (☎345/945-0241 ⊕www.islandaircayman.info). **Northwest Airlines** (☎800/225-2525 ⊕www.nwa.com). **Spirit Airlines** (☎800/772-7117 ⊕www.spiritair.com). **US Airways** (☎345/949-7488 or 800/622-1015 ⊕www.usairways.com).

AIRPORTS

Airport Information **Owen Roberts Airport** (GCM ⊠Grand Cayman ☎345/943-7070). **Gerrard-Smith International Airport** (CYB ⊠Cayman Brac ☎345/948-1222). **Edward Bodden Airstrip** (LYB ⊠Little Cayman ☎345/948-0021).

BY BIKE & MOPED

When renting a motor scooter or bicycle, remember to drive on the left and wear sunblock and a helmet. Bicycles ($10 to $15 a day) and scooters ($35 to $40 a day) can be rented in George Town when cruise ships are in port. On Cayman Brac or Little Cayman your hotel can make arrangements for you (most offer complimentary bicycles for local sightseeing).

BY BUS

On Grand Cayman, bus service is efficient, inexpensive, and plentiful, running roughly every 15 minutes. Minivans marked "Omni Bus," most independently operated (there are 38 buses and 24 owners), run from 6 AM to midnight from West Bay to Rum Point. All routes branch from the George Town terminal adjacent to the library on Edward Street and are described in the phone book. The one-way fare from George Town to West Bay via Seven Mile Beach is CI$1.50, to East End destinations CI$2. Some bus stops are well marked; others are flexible. Respond with a wave; then the driver toots his horn.

BY CAR

Driving is easy and usually enjoyable on Grand Cayman. Most visitors, especially if they're staying along Seven Mile Beach, are content taking taxis or a one-day tour to see the sights rather than renting a car. Traffic on the road from Seven Mile Beach to George Town then onto Bodden Town in Grand Cayman is terrible, especially during the 7 to 9 AM and 4:30 to 6:30 PM commuting periods, despite construction of a bypass road. Fortunately, roads are generally well marked and well maintained. One major coastal highway circumnavigates most of the island (remember that no shortcuts divide the extensive East End), though you can get lost in the tangle of side roads in primarily residential West Bay. Exploring Cayman Brac on a scooter is fun and straightforward. You won't really need a car on Little Cayman, though there are a limited number of jeeps for rent; bikes are the preferred mode of transport.

In the Cayman Islands, drive on the left, British style. Be mindful of pedestrians and, in the countryside, occasional livestock walking on the road. When someone flashes headlights at you at an intersection, it means "after you."

7

Be especially careful negotiating round-abouts (traffic circles). Observe the speed limit, which is conservative: 30 mph (50 kph) in the country, 20 mph (30 kph) in town. George Town actually has rush hours: 7 to 9 AM and 4:30 to 6:30 PM. Park only in approved parking areas.

In Grand Cayman, you can find gasoline stations in and around George Town, the airport, and Seven Mile Beach. Although times vary, most open daily with hours that extend into the evening; a few remain open 24 hours a day. There are two gasoline stations on Cayman Brac and one on Little Cayman. Prices are exorbitant, even compared to the Unites States and most of the Caribbean.

Grand Cayman Agencies Ace Hertz (✉ Owen Roberts Airport, Grand Cayman ☎ 345/949-2280 or 800/654-3131 ⊕ www. acerentacarltd.com). **Andy's Rent a Car** (✉ Owen Roberts Airport, Grand Cayman ☎ 345/949-8111 ⊕ www.andys.ky). **Avis** (✉ Owen Roberts Airport, Grand Cayman ☎ 345/949-2468 ⊕ www.aviscayman.com). **Budget** (☎ 345/949-5605 or 800/527-0700 ⊕ www.budgetcayman.com). **Coconut Car Rentals** (✉ Owen Roberts Airport, Grand Cayman ☎ 345/949-4037 or 800/941-4562 ⊕ www.coconutcarrentals.com). **Dollar** (✉ Owen Roberts Airport, Grand Cayman ☎ 345/949-4790 ⊕ www.dollarlac.com). **Economy** (✉ Owen Roberts Airport, Grand Cayman ☎ 345/949-9550 ⊕ www.economy carrental.com.ky). **Marshall's** (✉ Owen Roberts Airport, Grand Cayman ☎ 345/949-2127 ⊕ www.marshalls.ky). **Thrifty** (✉ Owen Roberts Airport, Grand Cayman ☎ 345/949-6640 or 800/367-2277 ⊕ www.thrifty.com).

Cayman Brac & Little Cayman Agencies B&S Motor Ventures (✉ West End, Cayman Brac ☎ 345/948-1646 ⊕ www.bandsmv.com). **CB Rent-a-Car** (✉ Gerrard-Smith Airport, Cayman Brac ☎ 345/948-2424 ⊕ www.cb rentacar.com). **Four D's Car Rental** (✉ Spot Bay, Cayman Brac ☎ 345/948-1599). **McLaughlin Rentals** (✉ Airport Village Square, Little Cayman ☎ 345/948-1000).

BY TAXI

On Grand Cayman, taxis operate 24 hours a day; if you anticipate a late night, however, make pickup arrangements in advance. Call for a cab to be dispatched, as you generally cannot hail one on the street except occasionally in George Town. They carry up to three passengers for the same price. Fares aren't metered; the government sets rates, and they're not cheap, so ask ahead. The tariff increases with the number of riders and bags. To travel in style by limo, you can call A. A. Transportation or Elite Limousine Services. Drivers are courteous and knowledgeable; most will narrate a tour at an hourly rate of about $25 for up to three people. Be sure to settle the price before you start off and agree on whether it's quoted in U.S. or Cayman dollars.

Taxis are scarcer on the Sister Islands; rates are also fixed and fairly prohibitive. Your hotel will provide recommended drivers.

Information A. A. Transportation Services (☎ 345/949-7222 or 345/949-6598). **Charlie's Super Cab** (☎ 345/949-4748). **Elite Limousine Services** (☎ 345/949-5963). **Webster's Taxi Service** (☎ 345/947-1718).

▌ CONTACTS & RESOURCES

BANKS & EXCHANGE SERVICES

You should not need to change money in Grand Cayman, since U.S. dollars are readily accepted, though you may get some change in Cayman dollars, which are worth 25% more than a U.S. dollar. ATMs accepting MasterCard and Visa with Cirrus affiliation are readily available in George Town; you usually have the option of U.S. or Cayman dollars. The Cayman dollar is pegged to the U.S. dollar at the rate of CI$1.25 to $1, and divided into a hundred cents, with coins of 1¢, 5¢, 10¢, and 25¢, and notes of $1, $5, $10, $25, $50, and $100. There's no $20 bill. Traveler's checks and major credit cards are widely accepted. Be sure you know which currency is being quoted when making a purchase.

All prices quoted in this book are in U.S. dollars unless otherwise noted.

ELECTRICITY
Electricity is reliable and is the same as the United States (110 volts/60 cycles).

EMERGENCIES
Although the quality of medical care is adequate on the island, air-ambulance service through Executive Air to Miami is available when necessary within two hours. Double-check the care that you are given and get second opinions when possible.

Diving Emergencies Cayman Hyperbaric (⊠ Hospital Rd., George Town, Grand Cayman ☎ 345/949–2989).

Emergency Services Executive Air (☎ 345/949–7775).

Hospitals Cayman Clinic (⊠ Grand Cayman ☎ 345/949–4234).**George Town Hospital** (⊠ Hospital Rd., George Town, Grand Cayman ☎ 345/949–8600).

INTERNET, MAIL & SHIPPING
In Grand Cayman, most hotels and resorts provide Internet access—either free or for a small fee—for their guests; wireless is increasingly prevalent. You'll also find Internet cafés in George Town and at the easternmost point of the East End. Rates range from $2.50 for 15 minutes to $10 per hour. Several restaurants also advertise free Wi-Fi hot spots. Although there are no cybercafés on the Sister Islands, most of the small hotels have high-speed access in rooms and/or public spaces. Those lacking Wi-Fi or Ethernet usually have a public computer or permit use of the office facilities. A few individual villas get Wi-Fi signals.

Sending a postcard to the United States, Canada, other parts of the Caribbean, or Central America costs CI 25¢. An airmail letter is CI 75¢ per half ounce. To Europe and South America, rates are CI 25¢ for

a postcard and CI 80¢ per half ounce for airmail letters. When addressing letters to the Cayman Islands, be sure to include the new postcodes which have been introduced. You can find postcodes at ⊕ www. caymanpost.gov.ky or on leaflets at any of the islands' post offices. The main post office lies at the intersection of Edward Street and Cardinal Avenue in downtown George Town. There is no home delivery; instead, all mail is delivered to numbered post office boxes. For faster and reliable service to the United States, Federal Express, UPS, and DHL all have locations in the downtown area. Airmail can take two weeks to be delivered to farther-flung areas, including Australia and New Zealand.

Grand Cayman Internet Cafés Café del Sol Internet Cafe (⊠ Marquee Plaza, Seven Mile Beach, Grand Cayman ☎ 345/946–2233 ⊕ www.cafedelsol.ky). **Thirsty Surfer Liquor Store & Internet Cafe** (⊠ Reef Resort, Colliers Bay, East End, Grand Cayman ☎ 345/947–2337).

TAXES
At the airport, each adult passenger leaving Grand Cayman must pay a departure tax of $25 (CI$20), payable in either Caymanian or U.S. currency. It may be included in cruise packages as a component of port charges; it isn't usually added to airfare—check with your carrier, and must be paid in cash by each traveler prior to entering the secure area of the airport.

A 10% government tax is added to all hotel bills. A 10% service charge is often added to hotel bills and restaurant checks in lieu of a tip. There is no V.A.T. or comparable tariff on goods and services.

TELEPHONE
Cable & Wireless (Cayman Islands) Ltd. and Digicel Ltd. are the main providers. The area code for the Cayman Islands is 345. To make local calls (on or between any of the three islands), dial the seven-digit number. Credit cards and calling

cards can be used to call worldwide from any phone and most hotels, though from the latter there's almost always a hefty surcharge, even to access toll-free access numbers for prepaid phone cards.

If you're bringing your own mobile phone and it's compatible with 850/1900 Mhz GSM network or TDMA digital network, you should be able to make and receive calls during your stay, especially from Grand Cayman. Be sure, however, to check with your home provider to be sure that you have roaming service enabled, and note that charges can be astronomical depending on your calling plan. Renting a cell phone if you're planning an extended vacation or expect to make a lot of local calls may be a less-expensive alternative than using your own. Mobile phone rental is available from Cable & Wireless and Digicel; you can stay connected for as little as CI$5 per day plus the cost of a calling card (denominations range from CI$10 to CI$100). International per-minute rates usually range from CI 35¢ to CI 60¢.

Information Cable & Wireless (✉Anderson Square Bldg., Shedden Rd., George Town, Grand Cayman ✉Galleria Plaza, West Bay Rd., George Town, Grand Cayman ☎345/949–7800 ⊕www.cw.ky)

Digicel (✉Cayman Financial Center, 3rd fl., 36A dr Roys Dr., George Town, Grand Cayman ☎345/623–3444 ⊕www.digicelcayman.com).

TIPPING

At large hotels a service charge is generally included and can be anywhere from 6% to 10%; smaller establishments and some villas and condos leave tipping up to you. Although tipping is customary at restaurants, note that some automatically include 15% on the bill—so check the tab carefully. Taxi drivers expect a 10% to 15% tip.

TOUR OPTIONS

A sightseeing tour is a good way to get your bearings and to experience Caymanian culture. Taxi drivers will give you

a personalized tour of Grand Cayman for about $25 per hour for up to three people. Or you can choose a fascinating helicopter ride, a horseback or mountain-bike journey, a 4x4 safari expedition, or a full-day bus excursion. The prices vary according to the mode of travel and the number and kind of attractions included. Ask your hotel to help you make arrangements.

Costs and itineraries for island tours are about the same regardless of the tour operator. Half-day tours average $35 to $50 a person and generally include a visit to Hell and the Turtle Farm at Boatswain Beach aquatic park in West Bay, as well as shopping downtown. Full-day tours ($60 to $75 per person) add lunch, a visit to Bodden Town (the first settlement), and the East End, where you stop at the Queen Elizabeth II Botanic Park, blowholes (if the waves are high) on the ironshore, and the site of the wreck of the *Ten Sails* (not the wreck itself—just the site). The pirate graves in Bodden Town were destroyed during Hurricane Ivan, and the blowholes were partially filled. As you can tell, land tours here are low-key. Children under 12 often receive discounts.

A. A. Transportation Services offers taxis and tour buses. Ask for Burton Ebanks. B. A. McCurley, owner of McCurley Tours, is a free-spirited freewheeling Midwesterner who's lived in Cayman for 24 years and knows everything and everyone on the East End. Not only is she encyclopedic and flexible, she also offers car rentals and transfers for travelers staying on the East End; don't be surprised if she tells you what to order at lunch, especially if it's off the menu. Cayman Island Helicopters offers exhilarating eagle-eye views on three itineraries: $69 for a fly-over of Seven Mile Beach; $105 for a trip adding Stingray City; and $280 for a thrillingly panoramic island-wide aerial tour (discounts are available if you book via the company's Web site). Though the island is flat and mostly arid, the sight of waters rippling from turquoise to tourmaline is exciting enough.

If you prefer another kind of chopper, Cayman Hog Riders delivers on its promise to "go hog wild on the ride of your life," the roar of the engine competing with the roar of the surf as you zoom around the island (the two- and four-hour tours cost $150 to $300 for one, $175 to $325 for two); nothing like a Hell's Angel crowd motoring into Hell! Majestic Tours caters mostly to cruise-ship and incentive groups but also offers similar options to individuals and can customize tours; it's particularly good for West Bay, including Boatswain's Beach and Hell. Native Safari hits the usual sights but emphasize interaction with locals, so you learn about craft traditions, folklore, and herbal medicines. Tropicana Tours offers several excellent Cayman highlights itineraries on its larger buses, including Stingray City stops, as well as reef runner adventures across the North Sound through the mangrove swamps.

Your hotel or villa agent can recommend and organize drivers for tours of the Sister Islands.

Information A. A. Transportation Services (⊠ Grand Cayman ☎ 345/949–7222). **Cayman Hog Riders** (⊠ Grand Cayman ☎ 345/943–8699 or 345/927–8500 ⊕ www. caymanhogriders.com). **Cayman Island Helicopters** (⊠ Grand Cayman ☎ 345/949–4354, 345/929–0116 cell ⊕ www.caymanislandhelicopters.com). **Majestic Tours** (⊠ Grand Cayman ☎ 345/949–7773 ⊕ www.majestic-tours. com). **McCurley Tours** (⊠ Grand Cayman ☎ 345/949–7222). **Native Safari** (⊠ Grand Cayman ☎ 345/324–4778). **Tropicana Tours** (⊠ Grand Cayman ☎ 345/949–0944 ⊕ www. tropicana-tours.com).

VISITOR INFORMATION
The Cayman Islands has tourist offices in the United States, where you can get brochures and maps in advance of your trip. There are also tourism offices on the islands for on-site help.

Before You Leave Cayman Islands Department of Tourism (☎ 305/599–9033 in Miami, 630/705–0650 in Oakbrook Terrace, IL, 212/889–9009 in New York City, 713/461–1317 in Houston, or 877/422–9626 ⊕ www. caymanislands.ky).

In the Cayman Islands Department of Tourism (⊠ Regatta Office Park Leeward 2, West Bay Rd., Box 67GT, George Town, Grand Cayman ☎ 345/949–0623 ⊠ Owen Roberts Airport, Grand Cayman ☎ 345/949–3603 ⊠ West End Rd., North Side, Cayman Brac ☎ 345/948–1649).

WEDDINGS
Getting married in the Cayman Islands is a breeze, and many couples tie the knot here annually. Most choose to say their vows on lovely Seven Mile Beach with the sun setting into the azure sea as their picture-perfect backdrop. Underwater weddings in full scuba gear with schools of fish as impromptu witnesses are also possible (kissing with mask on optional). Cathy Church can photograph your underwater wedding (⇨ *Shopping above*). You can literally leave things up in the air, getting hitched while hovering in a helicopter ("I do; Roger and out," responded one blushing bride over the propeller noise). A traditional church wedding can even be arranged, after which you trot away to your life together in a horse-drawn carriage.

Documentation can be prepared ahead of time or in one day while on the island. There's no on-island waiting period. In addition to the application, you need proof of identity and age (those under 18 must provide parental consent), such as an original or certified birth certificate or passport; a Cayman Islands international embarkation/disembarkation card; and certified or original copies of divorce decrees/death certificates if you have been married before. You must list a marriage officer on the application, and you need at least two witnesses; if you haven't come with friends or family, the marriage officer can help you with that, too. A marriage license costs CI$160 (US$200).

The best way to plan your wedding in the Cayman Islands is to contact a wedding coordinator (resorts such as The Reef, Westin Casuarina, and Ritz-Carlton have one on staff), who will offer a wide variety of packages to suit every taste and budget. All of the logistics and legalities will be properly handled, giving you time to relax and enjoy the wedding of your dreams. The Cayman Islands Department of Tourism keeps a list of wedding coordinators. Or you can order the brochure "Getting Married in the Cayman Islands" from Government Information Services. Vernon Jackson, of Cayman Weddings, is a wonderful marriage officer with a soft accent and a kind heart. You can choose from many different styles of services or rewrite one as you wish.

Information Cayman Weddings (☎ 345/949–8677 ⊕ www.caymanweddings. com.ky). **Deputy Chief Secretary** (✉ Government Administration Bldg., 3rd fl., George Town, Grand Cayman ☎ 345/949–7900 or 345/914–2222). **Government Information Services** (✉ Cricket Sq., George Town, Grand Cayman ☎ 345/949–8092). **Heart of Cayman** (☎ 345/949–1343 ⊕ www.heartofcayman. com).

Curaçao

Playa Lagun

WORD OF MOUTH

"We consider ourselves fortunate to have been to Curaçao. . . . There are many great places to eat—the Blues, Hook's Hut, Jaanchie's, Bistro Le Clochard. . . . We cannot wait to go back again!"

—Knowing

" Before we left everyone told me how expensive it was, and I did not find it to be expensive at all. I thought everything was comparable to what we pay in Philadelphia and reasonable compared to some other islands."

—eileen

WELCOME TO CURAÇAO

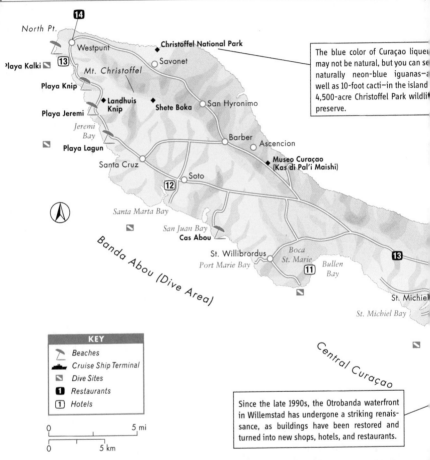

The blue color of Curaçao liqueu may not be natural, but you can se naturally neon-blue iguanas—a well as 10-foot cacti—in the island 4,500-acre Christoffel Park wildli preserve.

KEY

- ⚓ Beaches
- ⚓ Cruise Ship Terminal
- ◿ Dive Sites
- **1** Restaurants
- ① Hotels

Since the late 1990s, the Otrobanda waterfront in Willemstad has undergone a striking renaissance, as buildings have been restored and turned into new shops, hotels, and restaurants.

Willemstad's fancifully hued, strikingly gabled townhouses glimmer across Santa Anna Bay, while vendors at the Floating Market sell tropical fruit from their schooners. Curaçao's diverse population mixes Latin, European, and African ancestries. Religious tolerance is a hallmark here. All people are welcome in Curaçao, and even tourists feel the warmth.

AN ISLAND REBORN
AND REDISCOVERED

The largest and most populous of the Netherlands Antilles is 38 mi (61 km) long and no more than 7½ mi (12 km) wide. Its capital, Willemstad, has been restored and revived over the past few years and is a recognized UNESCO World Heritage Site. The colorful, waterfront townhouses are unique to the island.

Only one maker of the famous orange-flavored Curaçao liqueur is allowed to call itself "authentic": the Senior Curaçao distillery in Saliña Arriba. But the blue color is just an additive.

CURAÇAO

8

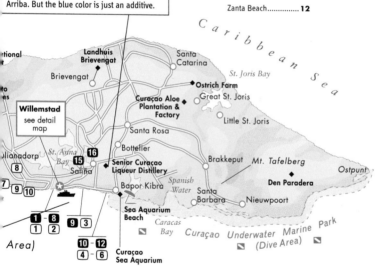

TOP 4 REASONS TO VISIT CURAÇAO

1. Since it sits below the hurricane belt, the weather in Curaçao is almost always alluring, even during the off-season.

2. Carnival is the year's biggest party, drawing an increasing crowd.

3. The island's cultural diversity is reflected in the good food from many different cultures.

4. Striking architecture and fascinating historic sights give you something to see when you're not shopping or lying on the charming beaches.

CURAÇAO PLANNER

Island Activities

The island has many good beaches, not to mention clear, blue water; however, a lot of the beaches on the southeast coast (even the hotel beaches) are a bit rocky. The softer, whiter beaches are on the west coast.

Excellent diving has always been a draw in Curaçao, and a fair percentage of travelers are drawn by the teeming reefs and good shore-diving possibilities.

Day sails are the most popular way to enjoy the water if you don't dive, and all of them offer opportunities for good snorkeling.

Both sides of Willemstad—Punda and the revitalized Otrobanda—offer the shore-bound plenty to occupy their time, making it well worth your while to check out the local sights and do some shopping.

Do stop for a bite to eat at one of the many great restaurants.

By night, you can gamble in a few casinos or check out some of the lively bars and dance clubs.

Logistics

Getting to Curaçao: Most travelers will make a connection in San Juan, Montego Bay, or Aruba. If you want to connect through Aruba, more likely than not you'll have to book your flight on a tiny island-hopper directly with the island-based airline. Hato International Airport (CUR) has car-rental facilities, duty-free shops, and restaurants.

Hassle Factor: Medium–High.

Nonstops: Atlanta (Delta, seasonal), Miami (American), New York–Newark (Continental). American Airlines also offers service from San Juan.

On the Ground

It takes about 20 minutes to get to the hotels in Willemstad by taxi. Taxis have meters, but drivers still use set fares when picking passengers up at the airport. Verify which method your driver will use before setting off; fixed rates apply for up to 4 passengers in a single vehicle. Fares from the airport to Willemstad and the nearby beach hotels run about $15 to $20, and those to hotels at the island's western end about $25 to $40.

Renting a Car: Many of the larger hotels have free shuttles into Willemstad, where you can shop and eat, or you can take a quick, cheap taxi ride; hotels in Willemstad usually provide a free beach shuttle, so it's possible to get by without a car. However, it's still worthwhile to rent a car to explore the island, even if you don't take it for your entire stay. If you're planning to do country driving or rough it through Christoffel Park, a four-wheel-drive vehicle is best. All you need is a valid driver's license. You can rent a car from any of the major car agencies at the airport or have one delivered free to your hotel. Rates range from about $35 to $40 a day for a compact car to about $60–$75 for a four-door sedan or four-wheel-drive vehicle; add 5% tax and optional daily insurance.

Where to Stay

Although Curaçao is the largest of the Dutch Antilles, resort development is concentrated around the capital, Willemstad, so most resorts are within easy reach of town, either by shuttle or even by foot. As the island becomes more developed, visitors have a wider variety of options, and there are a few resorts farther removed as well, but it's the amenities that should drive your decision more than location, so choose the type of lodging that best appeals to your interests and style. Those spending a bit more time—especially Europeans—gravitate to villas and bungalows.

Resorts: Most of Curaçao's larger hotels are midsize resorts of 200 to 300 rooms, and many of them are within easy striking distance of town. There aren't any extravagantly luxurious resorts on the island—and none with mind-boggling nightly rates—but a few of the more-atmospheric properties incorporate restored 18th-century buildings.

Dive Resorts: Most of the resorts catering to divers are smaller operations of fewer than 100 rooms (often much smaller). While some of these are in and around Willemstad, there are also a few on the secluded west end of the island, and that's where shore diving is best.

Villas and Bungalows: Though they are marketed primarily to European travelers who have more time to spend on the island, self-catering accommodations are an option for anyone who has at least a week to spend in Curaçao.

Hotel & Restaurant Costs

⇨*For information on hotel meal plans, see Accommodations in Caribbean Essentials.*

WHAT IT COSTS IN U.S. DOLLARS

$$$$	$$$	$$	$	¢
Restaurants				
over $30	$20–$30	$12–$20	$8–$12	under $8
Hotels*				
over $350	$250–$350	$150–$250	$80–$150	under $80
Hotels**				
over $450	$350–$450	$250–$350	$125–$250	under $125

*EP, BP, CP **AI, FAP, MAP Restaurant prices are for a main course at dinner and include any taxes or service charges. Hotel prices are per night for a double room in high season, excluding taxes, service charges, and meal plans (except at all-inclusives).

When to Go

High season in Curaçao mirrors that in much of the Caribbean, basically from mid-December through mid-April. In the off-season, rates will be reduced at least 25% and often more. Hurricanes and severe tropical storms—though still possible—are rare in Curaçao, which means the island has good weather almost year-round.

The year's big event is **Carnival,** which concludes on Ash Wednesday; it's among the Caribbean's best parties and is beginning to draw visitors in larger numbers.

The **Curaçao International Jazz Festival** is held in May.

The **Curaçao Dive Festival** occurs in late May and features seminars on underwater photography and other dive-related topics.

The **Salsa Festival** is held in June, July, or August.

The **African Diaspora Film Festival** runs for a week in late June and early July, presenting films by black independent filmmakers from around the world.

8

Updated
by Vernon
Ramesar

THE FLOATING PONTOON BRIDGE SWINGS open to let a giant freighter into Willemstad's historic harbor. For a few minutes there will be no crossing by foot from one side of the city to the other, so ferry passengers, chattering gleefully in a multitude of languages, gather at the landing on the Punda side and board for the quick trip across the bay to Otrobanda. Around the bend, a dozen Venezuelan schooners are anchored in the Waaigat Canal, their colorful cargo of fresh fish and produce laid out for sale. On the Handelskade, a man strolls along the harbor with three iguanas draped over his shoulders, luring amused passersby to stop and have a picture taken with the creatures. Nearby, tourists sip frozen margaritas on the patio of an outdoor café under a giant red umbrella. In the background, the splendorous facades of Punda's waterfront town houses glisten in the sunlight.

The sun smiles down on Curaçao, which sits on the outer fringe the so-called hurricane belt, 35 mi (56 km) north of Venezuela and 42 mi (68 km) east of Aruba. The largest of the Dutch Caribbean islands (at approximately 171 square mi [444 square km]), Curaçao is infused not only with European influences, but also with touches of Africa, Latin America, and the rest of the world, reflecting the island's ethnic diversity.

Gentle trade winds help keep the heat in check, and temperatures are generally in the 80s. Water sports—including outstanding reef diving—attract enthusiasts from all over the world. Curaçao claims 38 beaches—some long stretches of silky sand, most smaller coves suitable for picture postcards. In the countryside, the dollhouse look of plantation houses, or *landhuizen* (literally, "land houses"), makes a cheerful contrast to stark cacti and austere shrubbery.

The sprawling city of Willemstad is the island's capital. Its historic downtown and the natural harbor (*Schottegat*) around which it's built are included on UNESCO's World Heritage List, a coveted distinction reserved for the likes of the Palace of Versailles and the Taj Mahal. The "face" of Willemstad delights like a kaleidoscope—rows of sprightly painted town houses with gabled roofs sit perched alongside the steely blue Santa Anna Bay. Local lore has it that in the 1800s, the governor claimed he suffered from migraines and blamed the glare from the sun's reflection off the then-white structures. To alleviate the problem, he ordered the facades painted in colors.

Curaçao was discovered by Alonzo de Ojeda (a lieutenant of Columbus) in 1499. The first Spanish settlers arrived in 1527. In 1634 the Dutch came via the Netherlands West Indies Company. Eight years later Peter Stuyvesant began his rule as governor (in 1647, Stuyvesant became governor of New Amsterdam, which later became New York). Twelve Jewish families arrived in Curaçao from Amsterdam in 1651, and by 1732 a synagogue had been built; the present structure is the oldest synagogue in continuous use in the western hemisphere. Over the years the city built fortresses to defend against French and British invasions—the standing ramparts now house restaurants and hotels. The Dutch claim to Curaçao was recognized in 1815 by the Treaty of

Paris. From 1954 through 2006, Curaçao was the seat of government of the Netherlands Antilles, a group of islands under the umbrella of the Kingdom of the Netherlands. Effective July 2007, Curaçao was granted autonomy (the same status Aruba attained in 1986), and now governs itself independently in all matters aside from defense and foreign policy.

Tourism is on a fast track to surpassing harbor-related activities as the island's primary source of income, with a corresponding surge in hotel development in recent years. The government pumped millions of dollars into the opening of a new airport in 2006, and has committed more funds to an expansion plan to accommodate future growth. The opening of a massive pier has boosted cruise-ship passengers to record numbers. In addition, the government and private sources have invested substantially in the restoration of the island's graceful colonial buildings.

Today, Curaçao's population derives from nearly 60 nationalities—an exuberant mix of Latin, European, and African roots, who speak a Babel of tongues—resulting in superb restaurants and a flourishing cultural scene. Although Dutch is the official language, Papiamento is the vernacular of all the Netherlands Antilles and the preferred choice for communication among the locals. English and Spanish are also widely spoken. The island, like its Dutch settlers, is known for its religious tolerance, and tourists are warmly welcomed.

WHERE TO STAY

You'll generally find hotels at all price levels provide friendly, prompt, detail-oriented service; however, the finer points of service are in some cases still in nascent stages. Many of the large-scale resorts east and west of Willemstad proper have lovely beaches and provide a free shuttle to the city, 5 to 10 minutes away; but you'll find utmost seclusion at hotels on the island's southwestern end, a 30- to 45-minute drive from town. Most hotels in town provide beach shuttles. At this writing, several new resorts were under development, including a 350-room Hyatt Regency resort (expected to open in late 2008 or early 2009); a new Renaissance hotel, entertainment, shopping complex (expected in mid-2008); two other hotel projects (at Caracas Bay and Kontiki Beach) were not expected to open until later in 2009.

VILLAS

♨ Villa and bungalow rentals are especially popular with divers and European visitors and are generally good options for large groups or longer stays. The Curaçao Tourist Board has a complete list of rental apartments, villas, and bungalows on its Web site. The villas at **Livingstone Jan Thiel Resort** (⊠ *Jan Thiel* ☎ *5999/747–0332* ⊕ *www.janthielresort. com*) surround a swimming pool in a low-rise complex that offers a minimarket on-site, free access to the beach across the street, Wi-Fi in the open-air lobby, and a playground and special programs for kids.

Festive decor includes a large painted mural at the entrance and beaded shades on tabletop candleholders at the poolside restaurant.

⟳ The bungalows at **Papagayo Beach Resort** (⊠*Jan Thiel* ☎*5999/747–4333*) give you a unique option: on a whim you can open up a full wall so that your wraparound wooden terrace becomes part of your living space. Suddenly you're as close as it gets to living outdoors. These well-designed and nicely furnished homes include two bedrooms, a full kitchen with dishwasher, and bathroom (showers only). The restaurant menu changes seasonally; the pool bar is a cozy place to meet your neighbors. There's no beachfront, but you get free access to the beach across the street. Special programs and entertainment for kids are offered during school vacation periods.

HOTELS & RESORTS

$$$–$$$$ ⛱ **Avila Hotel.** The right blend of old-world touches, modern amenities, ★ alluring beachfront, attentive staff, and joie de vivre makes this resort the place of choice for the visiting Dutch royalty (well, all guests actually). This well-run hotel on a delightful beach has blossomed around the 18th-century mansion at its center. You'll find every comfort in the modern wings—the Octagon Wing has spacious rooms, sophisticated stone-and-wood decor, flat-screen TVs, and glorious balconies overlooking the ocean; the Blues Wing has waterside wooden decks, whirlpool tubs, and well-stocked kitchenettes. The hotel retains traces of its Dutch heritage in the main lobby, which is dressed like a prim European parlor, with gilt mirrors and gas lamps. Dine under the bulb-lighted boughs of an enormous tree at the Belle Terrace restaurant or at Blues, a gem for its nightlife scene. A unique site for weddings, the Octagon Museum is housed in an 18th-century cupola on hotel grounds. **Pros:** Wide variety of room types and decor, old-world charm, excellent restaurants. **Cons:** No hot water in the older wing of the hotel, staff can be less than helpful with organizing expeditions. ⊠*Penstraat 130, Box 791, Willemstad* ☎*5999/461–4377 or 800/747–8162* ⊕*www.avilahotel.com* ⟷*129 rooms, 11 suites* ⟳*In-room: safe, kitchen (some), refrigerator, Ethernet (some), dial-up. In-hotel: 3 restaurants, bars, tennis court, pool, spa, beachfront, public Internet* ☰*AE, D, DC, MC, V* †⊙†*EP.*

$$$–$$$$ ⛱ **Breezes Curaçao.** You might enjoy the conviviality at the island's ⟳ biggest all-inclusive, but unless you venture off the lushly landscaped grounds, you won't get much taste of the real Curaçao. On the other hand, you won't have much reason to leave: trapeze and trampoline clinics on the beach are among the highlights of the numerous activities included in the room rate. Body-painting contests, beach volleyball, toga parties, karaoke, and much more add to the nonstop merriment. Water massages and pregnancy massages are among the latest additions to the full menu of options at the spa. The casino is one of the island's largest. Don't hesitate to bring the kids, as they'll find plenty of supervised action—like sand-castle building and circus workshops—and get lots of attention. **Pros:** Ample distractions for the whole family, beautiful landscaping.**Cons:** Food is edible but not excellent, some rooms are in need of refurbishing. ⊠*Martin Luther King Blvd. 8, Willems-*

tad ☎*5999/736–7888 or 800/467-8737* ⊕*www.breezes.com* ⇙*285 rooms, 54 suites* ⚑*In-room: safe. In-hotel: 3 restaurants, bars, tennis courts, pools, gym, spa, beachfront, diving, water sports, bicycles, children's programs (ages 2–16), laundry service, public Internet, airport shuttle, no-smoking rooms* ▤*AE, DC, MC, V* ⚐*2-night minimum* ⦾*AI.*

$$$–$$$$ ⌂ **Curaçao Marriott Beach Resort & Emerald Casino.** The cream of the crop

⟳ of Curaçao's resorts beckons you to live it up from the moment you

Fodor's Choice arrive. The grand open-air lobby ushers you into a wonder-world, care-

★ free and unpretentious, embraced by a crescent beach that hugs the resort's edge. Towering palm trees and cheerful bursts of red hibiscus and oleander surround the panoply of laid-back luxury; an attentive staff greets you with pleasantries at every turn. Indulge yourself with a holistic treatment at the spa, frolic at the swim-up bar, try your luck at the alluring—though small—casino, or kick back with a mojito at the Emerald Lounge, which transforms into a disco nightly. Guest rooms, which are attractively outfitted but otherwise standard-issue chain hotel rooms, all have balconies or patios. With myriad options, the breakfast buffet is among the island's best. An all-inclusive option is offered. **Pros:** No need to leave the compound for anything but sightseeing, excellent beach location, first-class spa. **Cons:** Feels big and impersonal, pool area can get very busy. ⊠*Box 6003, Piscadera Bay, Willemstad* ☎*5999/736–8800* ⊕*www.marriott.com* ⇙*237 rooms, 10 suites* ⚑*In-room: safe, Ethernet, dial-up. In-hotel: 4 restaurants, room service, bars, pool, gym, spa, beachfront, diving, water sports, children's programs (ages 5–12), laundry service, public Internet, public Wi-Fi, no-smoking rooms* ▤*AE, D, DC, MC, V* ⦾*EP.*

$$$–$$$$ ⌂ **Hilton Curaçao.** Two beautiful beaches of pillowy white sand beyond

⟳ the open-air lobby make this hotel a jewel in its price range. Don't expect

★ the glamorous life, but you can count on quality and service in both the rooms and the restaurants, which are kept up to high standards. Plenty of creature comforts—like coffeemakers, irons, and hair dryers—are provided in the rooms, which have balconies or patios. Treat yourself to everything from massage to aromatherapy at the spa, play chess on the oversize outdoor game board, or try your luck in the casino. A luminous free-form pool that seems to spill into the ocean invites you to take a dip before lounging with a piña colada. You can also walk over to the lively Hook's Hut for a drink or a meal. Downtown Willemstad is five minutes away by car. **Pros:** Gorgeous beachfront, close to great shopping and off-site restaurants, friendly staff. **Cons:** Hallways are a bit bland, rooms could be in a Hilton anywhere on the planet. ⊠*J. F. Kennedy Blvd., Box 2133, Piscadera Bay* ☎*5999/462–5000* ⊕*www. hiltoncaribbean.com* ⇙*184 rooms, 12 suites* ⚑*In-room: safe, Ethernet. In-hotel: 2 restaurants, room service, bars, tennis courts, pools, gym, spa, beachfront, diving, water sports, concierge, children's programs (ages 4–12), laundry service, executive floor, public Internet, no-smoking rooms* ▤*AE, D, DC, MC, V* ⦾*EP.*

$$$–$$$$ ⌂ **Hotel Kurá Hulanda Spa & Casino.** History comes to life at this quaint

Fodor's Choice hotel. Guest rooms are tucked into restored 18th-century houses built

★ along pebblestone alleyways that diverge from a central courtyard. The

8

pools and gardens are exquisite, especially at night, when lighting casts a romantic glow. Each room is uniquely decorated with Indian and Indonesian fabrics and furnishings; in-room perks include turndown service, robes, Aveda toiletries, and CD players. The opulent Indian-style Bridal Suite is a work of art, with marble floors, hammered sterling silver furniture, and a large plasma TV. The only drawback is a lack of beachfront, but free shuttles will take you to a nearby private beach club or to the more-remote Lodge Kurá Hulanda & Beach Club. The revitalized Otrobanda neighborhood also has great dining within walking distance, and you're a stone's throw from the footbridge to cross over to the Punda side for more shopping and sightseeing. The museum and excellent restaurants are worth a visit even if you don't stay here. **Pros:** Unique historic feel, top-notch restaurants, incredible museum on compound, downtown shopping just steps away. **Cons:** No beach nearby, getting around can be like negotiating a maze. ⊠ *Langestraat 8, Otrobanda, Willemstad* ☎ *5999/434–7700* ⊕ *www.kurahulanda. com* ⇆ *80 rooms, 12 suites* ⋔ *In-room: safe, refrigerator, Ethernet, dial-up. In-hotel: 4 restaurants, room service, bars, pools, gym, spa, no elevator, concierge, laundry service, public Internet, public Wi-Fi, parking (no fee), no-smoking rooms* ▭ *AE, D, MC, V* ⊺⊙⊺*EP.*

$$$–$$$$ 🏨 **Lodge Kurá Hulanda & Beach Club.** On the island's remote western
★ tip, this sprawling resort with tranquil gardens will make you feel far removed from the daily grind. Rooms in two-story villas offer plush comforts, including grand porches (many overlooking the ocean), large televisions, and luxurious bathrooms. The turndown service is a treat before you cuddle up under 300-thread-count Egyptian cotton sheets and comforters. You can explore the nearby caves or hike the trails on the 350-acre property; an activity desk helps coordinate trips anywhere on the island. For a glimpse of underwater magnificence, take a short boat ride to the renowned Mushroom Forest and Watamula dive sites. Or simply get cozy beneath the thatched rotunda of the outdoor lounge, where you'll catch the soothing sounds of a live guitarist some evenings. A free shuttle makes the 45-minute drive to and from town, where you can enjoy all facilities of the Hotel Kurá Hulanda Spa & Casino. An all-inclusive option is available. **Pros:** Perfect for a complete escape, unparalleled ocean views, beautifully appointed rooms. **Cons:** A bit quiet for all tastes, miles away from everything, rental car necessary if you want to leave the resort. ⊠ *Playa Kalki 1, Westpunt* ☎ *5999/839–3600* ⊕ *www. kurahulanda.com* ⇆ *42 rooms, 32 suites* ⋔ *In-room: safe, kitchen (some), refrigerator, Ethernet. In-hotel: 3 restaurants, bar, tennis court, pool, gym, beachfront, diving, water sports, bicycles, no elevator, laundry service, public Wi-Fi* ▭ *AE, D, MC, V* ⊺⊙⊺*EP.*

$$$ 🏨 **Floris Suite Hotel.** Although aesthetically pleasing, the minimalist decor of the spacious suites and the stark open-air lobby of this modernist hotel give it a somewhat aloof feel, perhaps making it better suited for business travel than for a romantic getaway. The friendly staff, however, goes out of its way to make your stay comfortable. Award-winning Dutch interior designer Jan des Bouvrie has used warm mahogany shades offset by cool, sleek stainless-steel adornments in the suites, all of which have a balcony or porch and a full kitchen. A lush tropical garden surrounds the pool, and the beach and dive shop are across the street. **Pros:** Great for a quiet escape, beautifully designed rooms and public spaces. **Cons:** Rather cold feel to the decor, miles from decent shopping and restaurants. ⊠ *J. F. Kennedy Blvd., Box 6246, Piscadera Bay* ☎ *5999/462–6111* ⊕ *www.florissuitehotel.com* ⬅ *71 suites* ⅋ *In-room: kitchen, Ethernet, Wi-Fi. In-hotel: restaurant, room service, bar, tennis court, pool, gym, laundry service, public Internet, no-smoking rooms* ☰ *AE, D, DC, MC, V* ⏣ *EP.*

$$–$$$ 🎖 **Lions Dive & Beach Resort.** Divers are lured by the first-rate program
ⓒ here, but this low-key resort has a lot to offer nondivers as well. The location is great, right on the hip Seaquarium Beach strip that bustles with activity day and night. The open-air beach bar is a popular hangout. Nonmotorized water sports are at your doorstep. Best of all, there's plenty to do nearby, so you don't have to rent a car or take a taxi—at least eight eateries and bars are within walking distance. Admission to the neighboring Sea Aquarium is complimentary for hotel guests. If you do want to go to town, the drive takes about 8 to 10 minutes. All rooms have French doors opening onto a balcony or porch. Rooms with an ocean view—or better yet, the newest rooms right on the beach—are worth the extra cost. **Pros:** Ideal for diving, beautiful private beach and access to Seaquarium Beach, family friendly. **Cons:** Beach can get busy, kids everywhere. ⊠ *Seaquarium Beach, Bapor Kibra z/n* ☎ *5999/434–8888* ⊕ *www.lionsdive.com* ⬅ *102 rooms, 6 suites* ⅋ *In-room: safe, refrigerator, dial-up. In-hotel: 2 restaurants, bar, pools, gym, spa, beachfront, diving, water sports, bicycles, laundry service, public Internet, public Wi-Fi* ☰ *AE, D, DC, MC, V* ⏣ *EP.*

$$–$$$ 🎖 **Sunset Waters Beach Resort.** Serenity seekers are sure to find what
ⓒ they want at this remote resort on a lusciously long stretch of beach. You'll also find scheduled activities, and if you (or the kids) have a special request, the staff will try to accommodate you. The vibe is casual and carefree. Special events like a weekly beach barbecue and Sunday brunch with local food and a steel band engender camaraderie among guests; there's live music most nights. Many guests are drawn by the excellent dive operation and the proximity to the west-end dive sites, including Mushroom Forest. Diving is not included in the rate but is available for a modest charge. Rooms are bright and airy, and many face the ocean, some with dramatic views through floor-to-ceiling windows. (A nude section of the beach can be seen from some rooms.) Complimentary shuttles run to and from town. **Pros:** Beautiful uncrowded beach, bright and airy rooms. **Cons:** North American parents may feel uncomfortable having their kids around topless sunbathers, restaurant food is very basic. ⊠ *Santa Marta Bay* ☎ *5999/864–1233* ⊕ *www.sun setwaters.com* ⬅ *70 rooms* ⅋ *In-room: no phone (some), refrigerator (some). In-hotel: restaurant, bars, tennis court, pool, gym, beachfront, diving, water sports, children's programs (ages 2–16), public Internet* ☰ *AE, D, MC, V* ⏣ *AI.*

$$ 🎖 **Habitat Curaçao.** R, R, and R—rest, relaxation, and round-the-clock shore diving—are what you can look forward to at this resort, which is near a wildlife preserve in a secluded area blanketed by foliage. The dive center is top-notch, and the nearby reef is pristine. The pool

8

affords grand vistas of the serene countryside setting, where nature lovers can explore the nearby hiking trails. Willemstad is a half-hour drive away (a free shuttle runs three times daily). Rooms are brightly outfitted with fabrics designed by local artist Nena Sanchez. Each has a furnished terrace or balcony. There's a shop for essentials, but a full grocery is seven minutes away, so stock your fridge and stay awhile. The larger lanai villas are an excellent value for families or groups. Various meal and dive packages are available. **Pros:** Excellent diving facilities, full-service spa. **Cons:** Far from downtown, a car is essential. ⊠*Coral Estates, Rif St. Marie* ☎*5999/864–8800 or 800/327–6709* ⊕*habitatcuracaoresort.com* ⬭*56 suites, 20 2-bedroom villas* ⬧*In-room: safe, kitchen (some). In-hotel: restaurant, bar, pool, gym, spa, beachfront, diving, no elevator, public Internet, public Wi-Fi* ▭*AE, DC, MC, V* ◎|*EP.*

$$ ⌂**Holiday Beach Hotel & Casino.** Despite the large scale of everything around you, the Holiday Beach manages to offer a cheerful, welcoming ambience that will put you immediately at ease. One tradition is the whimsical main lobby display that changes thematically according to season—like an island version of Macy's windows—just before the entrance to Curaçao's largest, though in no way most glamorous, casino. The crescent beach is dotted with palm trees and palapas for shade. Rooms are airy and bright, and each has a balcony or patio, although the dim interior hallways and reception area exude a motel-like feel. There's a 24-hour Denny's and a video game arcade on-site, and the shops of Willemstad are within walking distance. **Pros:** On the beach and yet close to town, beachfront restaurant and bar, huge casino, Denny's addicts will feel right at home. **Cons:** No Wi–Fi, pool area hosts frequent events and can get noisy. ⊠*Pater Euwensweg 31, Box 2178, Otrobanda, Willemstad* ☎*5999/462–5400 or 800/444–5244* ⊕*www.hol-beach.com* ⬭*200 rooms, 1 suite* ⬧*In-room: safe, refrigerator, Ethernet. In-hotel: 2 restaurants, bars, tennis courts, pool, gym, beachfront, diving, water sports, laundry facilities, laundry service, public Internet, no-smoking rooms* ▭*AE, D, DC, MC, V* ◎|*EP.*

$$ ⌂**Howard Johnson Plaza Hotel & Casino.** Everything the city has to offer is at your doorstep at this colorful hotel on the main square of Otrobanda, an especially coveted location during the holidays and Carnival. At other times, despite the lack of beachfront, it's an acceptable choice for those on a budget, since you can jump in the pool to cool off or jump on a bus to head out for a day at the shore; there's even an on-site casino. Despite uninspiring decor, rooms are light filled and well equipped with hair dryers and irons, and you can request a coffeemaker or refrigerator. For the best view, ask for a room facing the Santa Anna Bay. **Pros:** In the heart of downtown with easy access to Punda, bland but functional rooms. **Cons:** No beach, downtown noise can sometimes be a problem. ⊠*Brionplein, Otrobanda, Willemstad* ☎*5999/462–7800* ⊕*www.hojo-curacao.com* ⬭*50 rooms* ⬧*In-room: safe, refrigerator (some), Ethernet. In-hotel: restaurant, room service, bar, pool, laundry service, executive floor, public Internet, airport shuttle, parking (no fee), no-smoking rooms* ▭*AE, D, DC, MC, V* ◎|*EP.*

$ ☺ **Lagun Blou Dive & Beach Resort.** Travelers on a budget will love this family-owned-and-run hotel that combines a great view with an intimate setting. This small collection of rooms and charming bungalows sits on a cliff overlooking a beautiful cove. Best of all, the beach is just a short walk down. Units are fully equipped with all the comforts of home and include full kitchens. Families will probably find the bungalows to be a great deal as they are priced only slightly higher than an apartment room and can sleep four. **Pros:** Relaxed atmosphere, intimate setting, bargain for families. **Cons:** Far from shopping and restaurants, lacks the amenities of a big resort. ⊠*Seaquarium Beach, Bapor Kibra z/n* ☎*5999/864–0557* ⊕*www.lagunblou.nl* ☞*13 rooms, 8 bungalows* ☖*In-room: safe, kitchen refrigerator, no TV, Wi-Fi. In-hotel: pool, beachfront, diving, laundry facilities* ⊟*MC, V* ☺*EP.*

WHERE TO EAT

Dine beneath the boughs of magnificent old trees, on the terraces of restored mansions and plantation houses, or on the ramparts of 18th-century forts. Curaçaoans partake of generally outstanding fare, with representation from a remarkable smattering of ethnicities. Outdoor or open-air sheltered dining is commonplace; note that most restaurants offer a smoking section or permit smoking throughout. Fine dining tends to be pricey, mostly because of the high cost of importing products to the island. For cheap eats with a local flair, drop by the Old Market for lunch, or stop at one of the snack bars or snack trucks you can find all over the island (have some guilders handy—many of them won't have change for dollars).

8

WHAT TO WEAR

Dress in restaurants is almost always casual (though beachwear isn't acceptable). Some of the resort dining rooms and more-elegant restaurants require that men wear jackets, especially in high season; ask when you make reservations.

CARIBBEAN ✕**Landhuis Daniel.** Many of the tasty meals served here have their roots
$$–$$$ in the restaurant's garden. Fruits, vegetables, and herbs are organically grown at this landmark plantation house—dating from 1711—and used unsparingly in the menu, which changes according to seasonal crop yield. The chef draws on creole, French, and Mediterranean influences for his creations. One option is the prix-fixe "surprise menu"— just tell your waiter your preference for meat, fish, or vegetarian, and any dislikes. There's also a small inn here. ⊠ *Weg Naar, Westpunt* ☎*5999/864–8400* ⊟*AE, MC, V.*

$–$$ ✕**Jaanchi's Restaurant.** You'll be greeted by the owner, Jaanchi himself, a self-described "walking, talking menu," who will recite your choices of delectable dishes for lunch and maybe even a joke or two. The specialty at this sheltered, open-air restaurant is a hefty platter of fresh fish, typically wahoo. Jaanchi's iguana soup, touted in folklore as an aphrodisiac, is famous on the island. It's quite a sight when so-called sugar-thief birds flock to feeders outside the restaurant when the owner periodically fills them with sugar. Although predominantly a lunch spot, the restaurant will accommodate groups of four or more for dinner by prior arrangement. ⊠ *Westpunt 15, Westpunt* ☎*5999/864–0126* ⊟*AE, DC, MC, V.*

CONTINENTAL
$$$–$$$$
★

✕ **Astrolab Observatory.** Although the restaurant's name comes from the collection of astronomical instruments on display, you might leave thinking it comes from the out-of-this-world food. Among the stellar dishes is the roasted reef lobster with a lemon confit. Dine alfresco beneath a massive ficus tree in the gardens of the Kurá Hulanda compound or in the air-conditioned dining room. Depending on how busy it is, the service can range from attentive to downright slow. The extensive wine list is noteworthy. ⊠*Kurá Hulanda, Langestraat 8, Otrobanda, Willemstad* ☎*5999/434–7700* ⌖*Reservations essential* ⊟*AE, DC, MC, V* ☉*Closed Sun. and Mon. No lunch.*

$$$–$$$$
Fodor'sChoice
★

✕ **Bistro Le Clochard.** Built into a 19th-century fort, this romantic gem anchors the entrance to the 21st-century Riffort Village complex, the waterside terrace offering an enchanting view of the floating bridge and harbor. Switzerland and France are the key influences in the sublime preparations. The signature dish is La Potence—a spike-covered metal ball resembling a medieval weapon. It's brought to your table sizzling hot and covered with bits of sizzling tenderloin and sausage, served with various dipping sauces. (A traditional bit of fun is to stake the cost of the meal on not being the first person to drop a morsel.) The cheese fondue definitely keeps diners coming back. Game lovers can have their fill from the seasonal menu. The chicken in curry sauce with exotic fruit is also divine. No matter what, leave room for the sumptuous Toblerone chocolate mousse. ⊠*Harborside Terr., Riffort Village, Otrobanda, Willemstad* ☎*5999/462–5666* ⌖*Reservations essential* ⊟*AE, DC, MC, V.*

$$$–$$$$
★

✕ **Fort Nassau Restaurant.** On a hill above Willemstad, this elegant restaurant is built into an 18th-century fort with a 360-degree view. For the best perspective, sit beside the huge bay windows in the air-conditioned interior; the terrace has a pleasant breeze, but the view is not quite optimal. Among the highlights of the diverse menu is the medley of Caribbean seafood with mahimahi, shrimp, and grilled octopus. Scrumptious desserts will leave you feeling sated. ⊠*Schottegatweg 82, near Juliana Bridge, Otrobanda, Willemstad* ☎*5999/461–3450 or 5999/461–3086* ⌖*Reservations essential* ⊟*AE, D, MC, V* ☉*No lunch weekends.*

ECLECTIC
$$$$

✕ **Gouverneur de Rouville Restaurant & Cafe.** Dine on the verandah of a restored 19th-century Dutch mansion overlooking the Santa Anna Bay and the resplendent Punda skyline. Though not a restaurant for the budget minded, the ambience and food make it worth a visit. Intriguing soup options include Cuban banana soup and Curaçao-style fish soup. *Keshi yena* (stuffed cheese) and spareribs are among the savory entrées. After dinner, you can stick around for live music at the bar, which stays open until 1 AM. ⊠*De Rouvilleweg 9, Otrobanda, Willemstad* ☎*5999/462–5999* ⊟*MC, V.*

$$–$$$
★

✕ **Blues.** Jutting out onto a pier over the ocean, this jazzy spot is an alluring place for dinner. On the menu, designed to look like a vinyl record, are plenty of seafood offerings, including the "Swimming Blues," a harmonious melange of fresh fish, mussels, and more in garlic butter. For meat lovers, the "B.B. King Ribs" holds a spot at the top of the charts. Live music on Thursday and Saturday evening includes seductive vocalists and top-notch musicians. If you'd rather be removed from the scene, you can arrange for a cozy dinner on the beach; whether it's a table for two or for a larger group, you'll be nestled in the sand on colorful oversize pillows. There's also a terrific prix-fixe tapas buffet on Friday. ⊠*Avila Hotel, Penstraat 130, Punda, Willemstad* ☎*5999/461–4377* ⊟*AE, D, DC, MC, V* ⊗*Closed Mon. No lunch.*

$$–$$$ ✕**Kontiki Beach.** Take respite from the sun in what looks like a rain forest burrowed in the sand. Each outdoor table offers shelter from the elements, enveloping you with large, leafy greenery and thatched roofs, and gives you a sense of seclusion from fellow diners. At night, subtle lighting lends a romantic aura. The menu does not offer a huge selection but everything on it is very good. Choices range from pastas and pizza to fish and grilled meats. ⊠*Seaquarium Beach, Bapor Kibra z/n* ☎*5999/465–1589* ⊟*MC, V.*

$$–$$$ ✕**Mambo Beach.** Spread over the sand, this open-air bar and grill serves hearty sandwiches and burgers for lunch; steaks, fresh seafood, and pasta fill the dinner menu. There's an excellent fish buffet on Friday and dinner with a movie on the beach on Tuesday. ⊠*Seaquarium Beach, Bapor Kibra z/n* ☎*5999/461–8999* ⊟*MC, V.*

$–$$$ ✕**La Bahia Seafood & Steakhouse.** As you dine on a sheltered terrace with a remarkable view of the harbor front, you're so close to the passing ships it seems you can almost touch them. "I Had a Lobster at La Bahia" read the T-shirts for sale, but the menu runs the gamut from burgers and pastas to keshi yena and other local specialties. ⊠*Otrobanda Hotel & Casino, Breedestraat, Otrobanda, Willemstad* ☎*5999/462–7400* ⊟*AE, MC, V.*

$$ ✕**Zanta Beach.** Zebra-striped pillows, mood lighting in striking shades of aqua and purple, and periodically changing artwork serve as the perfect accents in this chic lounge. You can opt to dine in a cabana on the seductive outdoor beachfront terrace, where a swimming pool serves as the centerpiece. The menu changes regularly, but tasty staples include the garlic *gambas* (shrimp) with aioli sauce or the penne with smoked salmon. If you're here on Friday, hang around and marvel as the place turns into one of the hottest nightspots on the island. ⊠*Seaquarium Beach, Bapor Kibra z/n* ☎*5999/465–0664 or 5999/521–5379* ♙*Reservations essential* ⊟*MC, V* ⊗*Closed Mon.*

¢–$$ ✕**Time Out Café.** In the shopping heartland of Punda, this outdoor spot serves up light bites like tuna sandwiches and grilled cheese, as well as heartier fare like chicken shwarma. From Breedestraat facing Little Switzerland, take the alley to the left of the store (Kaya A.M. Prince) and walk about 20 yards, or look for the sign in Gomezplein Square and follow the arrow. This is more of a place for lunch but they are open until 7 PM if you're looking for a cheap and cheerful early dinner. ⊠*Keukenplein 8, Punda, Willemstad* ☎*5999/524–5071* ⊟*No credit cards* ⊗*Closed Sun.*

FRENCH $$$–$$$$ ✕ **Larousse.** Diners return time and again for old favorites from a menu of generally traditional French fare, peppered with variants like the chef's so-called Chinese-Russian tomato soup, which blends vodka and garlic in a sweet tomato base. The charming restaurant, with its nine cozy tables (including a tiny no-smoking section), is in a building that dates back to 1742. Original paintings on the walls and white linen tablecloths accentuate the old-fashioned style that the owners lovingly cultivate. Asparagus is used with adoration when it is available on the island and, in season, wild game is prominent among the specials. Insiders come for the stockyard Chicago beef as well as the "salty" lamb (supposedly more tender), imported from Holland. Nothing comes out of a can here: even the ice cream, sauces, and sometimes the chocolate are homemade. ✉ *Penstraat 5, Punda, Willemstad* ☎ *5999/465–5418 or 5999/465–6503* ✍ *Reservations essential* ▭ *AE, MC, V* ⊗ *Closed Mon. No lunch.*

ITALIAN $$–$$$$ ✕ **La Pergola.** Built into the Waterfort Arches, this restaurant and its outdoor terrace are part of an adjoining strip of eateries in a coveted spot perched over the Caribbean. Listen to the rippling waves crash against the rocks as you sip wine and enjoy creative variations on homemade pastas and pizza. The pretty dining room looks like the interior of a Tuscan villa, with its arched, stuccoed ceiling, copper pots adorning the walls, and huge picture windows. The menu changes frequently so there is usually something new to choose should you make multiple visits. ✉ *Waterfort Archesboog 12, Punda, Willemstad* ☎ *5999/461–3482* ▭ *AE, MC, V* ⊗ *No lunch Sun.*

PAN-ASIAN $$–$$$$ ★ ✕ **Jaipur.** The subtle lighting and sound of the nearby waterfall seem to make the food even more sublime at this outdoor Pan-Asian restaurant—with distinct Indian and Thai influences—that's part of the expansive Kurá Hulanda complex. The samosas filled with ground lamb make a great starter, and the tandoori mixed platter—with chicken, shrimp, and lamb kebobs—is a treat. The Thursday-night Asian buffet is a feast for the senses. ✉ *Langestraat 8, Otrobanda, Willemstad* ☎ *5999/461–3482* ▭ *AE, DC, MC, V* ⊗ *Closed Tues. No lunch.*

STEAK $$–$$$ ✕ **Rodeo House of Ribs.** A haven for meat lovers, this family-owned restaurant has been in business since 1980. The staff (dressed in cowboy outfits, of course) keeps the place lively. For kicks, ride the mechanical bull in the backyard: you could win a free meal if you stay up for more than two minutes. There's live music on Saturday nights. ✉ *Fokkerweg 3, Saliña* ☎ *5999/465–9465* ▭ *AE, MC, V.*

BEACHES

Although Curaçao might not be very green, it is surrounded by breathtaking blue. The island has 38 beaches, many of them quite striking, whether small inlets shielded by craggy cliffs or longer expanses of sparkling sand framing picture-perfect waters. Beaches along the southeast coast, even at the hotels, tend to be rocky in the shallow water (wear your reef shoes—some resorts loan them out for free); the west side has more stretches of smooth sand at the shoreline. Exploring the beaches away from the hotels is a perfect way to soak up the island's character. Whether you're seeking a lovers' hideaway, a special snorkeling adventure, or a great spot to wow the kids, you're not likely to be disappointed. There are snack bars and restrooms on many of the larger beaches, but it's at the smaller ones with no facilities where you might find utter tranquillity, especially during the week. Note that most spots with entry fees offer lounge chairs for rent at an additional cost, typically $2 to $3 per chair.

EAST END

☺ **Seaquarium Beach.** This 1,600-foot stretch of sandy beach is divided
★ into separate sections, each uniquely defined by a seaside resort or restaurant as its central draw. By day, no matter where you choose to enter the palm-shaded beach, you can find lounge chairs in the sand, thatched shelters, and restrooms. The sections at Mambo and Kontiki beaches also have showers. The island's largest water-sports center (Ocean Encounters at Lion's Dive) caters to nearby hotel guests and walk-ins. Mambo Beach is always a hot spot and quite a scene on weekends, especially during the much-touted Sunday-night fiesta that's become a fixture of the island's nightlife. The ubiquitous beach mattress is also the preferred method of seating for the Tuesday-night movies at Mambo Beach (check the *K-Pasa* guide for listings—typically B-films or old classics—and reserve your spot with a shirt or a towel). At Kontiki Beach, you can find a spa, a hair braider, and a restaurant that serves refreshing piña colada ice cream. Unless you're a guest of a resort on the beach, the entrance fee to any section is $3 until 5 PM, then free. After 11 PM, you must be 18 or older to access the beach. ✉ *Bapor Kibra z/n, about 1 mi (1.5 km) east of downtown Willemstad.*

8

WEST END

☺ **Cas Abou.** This white-sand gem has the brightest blue water in Curaçao, a treat for swimmers, snorkelers, and sunbathers alike. You can take respite beneath the hut-shaded snack bar. The restrooms and showers are immaculate. The only drawback is the weekend crowds, especially Sunday, when local families descend in droves; come on a weekday for more privacy. You can rent beach chairs, paddleboats, and snorkeling and diving gear. The entry fee is $3. Turn off Westpunt Highway at the junction onto Weg Naar Santa Cruz; follow until the turnoff for Cas Abou, and then drive along the winding country road for about 10 minutes to the beach. ✉ *West of St. Willibrordus, about 3 mi (5 km) off Weg Naar Santa Cruz.*

Playa Jeremi. No snack bar, no dive shop, no facilities, no fee—in fact, there's nothing but sheer natural beauty. It's the kind of beach that's pictured on postcards. Quite a bit of development is planned for this beach, so have a look before it's too late. ✉ *Off Weg Naar Santa Cruz, west of Lagun.*

Playa Kalki. Noted for its spectacular snorkeling, this beach is at the western tip of the island. The Ocean Encounters dive shop is here. ✉ *Westpunt, near Jaanchi's.*

☾ **Playa Knip.** Two protected coves offer crystal-clear turquoise waters. Big (Groot) Knip is an expanse of alluring white sand, perfect for swimming and snorkeling. You can rent beach chairs and hang out under the palapas or cool off with ice cream at the snack bar. There are restrooms here but no showers. It's particularly crowded on Sunday or school holidays. Just up the road, also in a protected cove, Little (Kleine) Knip is a charmer, too, with picnic tables and palapas. Steer clear of the poisonous manchineel trees. There's no fee for these beaches. ✉ *Banda Abou, just east of Westpunt.*

☾ **Playa Lagun.** This northwestern cove is caught between gunmetal-gray cliffs, which dramatically frame the Caribbean blue. Cognoscenti know this as one of the best places to snorkel—even for kids—because of the calm, shallow water. It's also a haven for fishing boats and canoes. There's a small dive shop on the beach, a snack bar (open weekends), and restrooms, but there's no fee. ✉ *Banda Abou, west of Santa Cruz.*

☾ **Playa Porto Mari.** Calm, clear water and a long stretch of white sand are
★ the hallmarks of this beach, which is fine for swimming or just lounging. Without the commercial bustle of Seaquarium Beach, it's one of the best for all-around fun, and therefore draws throngs of local families and tourists on the weekends. A decent bar and restaurant, well-kept showers, changing facilities, and restrooms are all on-site; a nature trail is nearby. The double coral reef—explore one, swim past it, explore another—is a special feature that makes this spot popular with snorkelers and divers (there's a dive shop and a dock). The entrance fee (including one free beverage) is $3 on weekdays, $3.50 on Sunday and holidays. From Willemstad, drive west on Westpunt Highway for 4 mi (7 km); turn left onto Willibrordus Road at the Porto Mari billboard, and then drive 3 mi (5 km) until you see a large church; follow signs on the winding dirt road to the beach. ✉ *Off Willibrordus Rd..*

SPORTS & THE OUTDOORS

☾ For the full gamut of activities in one spot, nature buffs (especially bird-watchers), families, and adventure seekers may want to visit **Caracas Bay island** (☎ *5999/747–0777*). Things to do here include hiking, mountain biking, canoeing, kayaking, windsurfing, jet skiing, and snorkeling. There's a fully equipped dive shop, a restaurant, and a bar on premises. Admission to the scenic area is $3; activities cost extra.

ATVS & SCOOTERS

Hit the road in rugged style behind the wheel of an all-terrain vehicle with **Eric's ATV Adventures** (✉ *Kaya Serafin 63, Willemstad* ☎ *5999/524–7418* ⊕ *www.curacao-atv.com*). All you need for a guided tour of the countryside is a regular driver's license. If you're 10 or older, you can ride as a passenger in the backseat. Helmets and goggles are provided.

Strap on a helmet for an adventurous, guided excursion around the island's most-popular sites with **Scooby's Scooters Curaçao** (⊠ *Breezes Curaçao, Martin Luther King Blvd. 8, Willemstad* ☎ *5999/523–8618* ⊕ *scoobys.curacaoplaza.com*). Visit caves and forts, stop for a swim or snorkel, or even design your own tour if you're a group of four or more people. Three-hour trips are $65 and the fee includes safety equipment, insurance, gas, guide, and pickup at your hotel. There is also a seven-hour buggy tour for $275 per couple which includes lunch. Experience isn't required, but cyclists will have an easier time maneuvering a scooter. You'll get some instruction and the chance to race around a practice course before you go. Children under 16 may ride as passengers. Wear sneakers, sunglasses, and sunscreen; bring a swimsuit and a camera—and you're off!

BIKING

So you wanna bike Curaçao? **Wanna Bike Curaçao** (☎ *5999/527–3720* ⊕ *www.wannabike-curacao.net*) has the fix: kick into gear and head out for a guided mountain-bike tour through the Caracas Bay peninsula and the salt ponds at the Jan Thiel Lagoon. Although you should be fit to take on the challenge, mountain-bike experience is not required. Tour prices vary depending on skill level and duration, and cover the bike, helmet, water, refreshments, park entrance fee, and guide—but don't forget to bring a camera.

DIVING & SNORKELING

8

The **Curaçao Underwater Marine Park** includes almost a third of the island's southern diving waters. Scuba divers and snorkelers can enjoy more than 12.5 mi (20 km) of protected reefs and shores, with normal visibility from 60 to 150 feet. With water temperatures ranging from 75°F to 82°F (24°C to 28°C), wet suits are generally unnecessary. No coral collecting, spearfishing, or littering is allowed. An exciting wreck to explore is the SS *Oranje Nassau*, which ran aground in 1906. The other two main diving areas are Banda Abou, along the southwest coast between Westpunt and St. Marie, and along central Curaçao, which stretches between Bullen Bay to the Breezes Curaçao resort. The north coast—where conditions are dangerously rough—is not recommended for diving.

Introductory scuba resort courses run about $65 for one dive and $130 for two dives. Open-water certification courses run about $350 for the five-dive version. Virtually every operator charges $35 to $45 for a single-tank dive and $65 to $70 for a two-tank dive. One day of unlimited shore diving runs about $22 to $25. Snorkel gear commonly rents for $10 to $15 per day.

Easy Divers at Habitat (⊠ *Habitat Curaçao, Coral Estates, Rif St. Marie* ☎ *5999/864–8305* ⊕ *www.habitatcuracaoresort.com*) offers everything from introductory dives to advanced open-water courses. You are free to dive any time of the night or day, because the abundance of marine life at the house reef makes for easily accessible shore dives right from the resort. In addition, two-tank boat dives are scheduled twice daily.

☾ ★ **Ocean Encounters** (⊠ *Lions Dive & Beach Resort, Seaquarium Beach, Bapor Kibra z/n* ☎ *5999/461–8131* ⊕ *www.oceanencounters.com*) is the largest dive operator on the island. Its operations cover the popular east-coast dive sites including the *Superior Producer* wreck, where barracudas hang out, and the tugboat wreck. West-end hot spots—including the renowned Mushroom Forest and Watamula dive sites—are accessible from the company's outlet at Westpunt. Ocean Encounters offers a vast menu of scheduled shore and boat dives and packages, as well as certified PADI instruction. In July, the dive center sponsors a kids' sea camp in conjunction with the Sea Aquarium.

★ **Sunset Divers** (⊠ *Sunset Waters Beach Resort, Santa Marta Bay* ☎ *5999/864–1708* ⊕ *www.sunsetdiver.com*), the closest full-service PADI operation to the famous Mushroom Forest, offers daily one- and two-tank dives, 24-hour shore diving, and custom dives. The friendly, expert staff takes you to dive sites along the west-side reef system, which has gently sloping walls with lots of coral growth, soft and hard. Lesser known but no less spectacular sites the company often visits include Harry's Hole and Boca Hulu. The house reef is incredible, too, with common sightings of octopus, eel, frogfish, and sea horses—plus there's a submerged small airplane that makes for a great snorkel. The operator has two boats, including a 44-foot yacht for up to 24 divers that's the largest dive boat on the island. Sunset Divers also rents underwater photography gear.

FISHING

Let's Fish (⊠ *Caracasbaaiweg 407N, Caracas Bay* ☎ *5999/561–1812* or *5999/747–4489* ⊕ *www.letsfish.net*), a 50-foot, fully rigged fishing boat, can accommodate groups of up to 11 people on half-day or full-day fishing trips to Klein Curaçao or Banda Abou in search of dolphinfish, marlin, wahoo, and more. With seven fishing vessels among the 14 yachts (and their captains) under his purview, Captain J.R. Van Hutten, nicknamed Captain Jaro, of **Pro Marine Yacht Services** (⊠ *Warawaraweg 7, Van Engelen* ☎ *5999/560–2081* ⊕ *www.curacao boating.com*), is *the* man to see about deep-sea fishing excursions and other fishing trips or parties. Some deals offer free pickup at your hotel. Most boats keep your catch, so check in advance if you want it. You can book the 54-foot yacht *War Eagle*, captained by Jaro himself, and head out in search of marlin, barracuda, mahimahi, and wahoo.

GOLF

In the mood to hit the greens? Try the links at **Blue Bay Curaçao Golf & Beach Resort** (⊠ *Landhuis Blauw, Blue Bay z/n* ☎ *5999/868–1755* ⊕ *www.bluebaygolf.com*). This 18-hole, par-72 course beckons experts and novices alike. Facilities include a golf shop, locker rooms, and a snack bar. Greens fees range from $80 to $100 in high season, and you can rent carts, clubs, and shoes. If you'd like to drive your game to a new level, take a lesson from the house pro ($28 for a half hour).

SEA EXCURSIONS

Many sailboats and motorboats offer sunset cruises and daylong snorkel and picnic trips to Klein Curaçao, the uninhabited island between Curaçao and Bonaire, and other destinations. Prices are around $60 to $75 for a half-day trip (including food and drinks). The half-day "Taste of Curaçao" trip on the *Bounty* (☎5999/560–1887 ⊕*www.bounty adventures.com*), a 90-foot schooner, features sailing, snorkeling, swimming, and rope swinging. It includes an open bar and barbecue lunch. One option aboard the 120-foot Dutch sailing ketch *Insulinde* (☎5999/560–1340 ⊕*www.insulinde.com*) is a snorkeling and scenic tour combo, capped off by a return cruise into the sunset, for $40. The *Mermaid* (☎5999/560–1530 ⊕*www.mermaidboattrips.com*) is a 66-foot motor yacht that carries up to 60 people to Klein Curaçao three times a week. A buffet lunch, beer, and soft drinks are provided at the boat's exclusive beach house, which has picnic tables, shade huts, and facilities. The 76-foot *Miss Ann* (☎5999/767–1579 ⊕*www.missann boattrips.com*) motorboat offers snorkeling or diving, moonlight, and party trips for up to 100 people. For a unique vantage point, soak up the local marine life on a 1½-hour-long tour of the coral reefs aboard the glass-bottom, semisubmersible *Seaworld Explorer* (☎5999/461–0011 ⊕*www.atlantisadventures.net*).

WATER SPORTS

Caribbean Sea Sports (✉*Curaçao Marriott Beach Resort, Piscadera Bay* ☎5999/462–2620 ⊕*www.caribseasports.com*) runs a tight ship when it comes to all sorts of water sports, including kayaking, windsurfing, banana boats, tube rides, diving, and snorkeling. Captain "Good Life" at **Let's Go Watersports** (✉*Santa Cruz Beach 1, Santa Cruz* ☎5999/520–1147 *or 5999/864–0438*) will help you plan kayaking and other boat outings so you can live it up on the water and snorkel in some special spots. He also grills up a tasty lunch at the dock.

SHOPPING

From Dutch classics like embroidered linens, delft earthenware, cheeses, and clogs to local artwork and handicrafts, shopping in Curaçao can turn up some fun finds. But don't expect major bargains on watches, jewelry, or electronics; Willemstad is not a duty-free port (the few establishments that claim to be "duty-free" are simply absorbing the cost of some or all of the tax rather than passing it on to consumers); however, if you come prepared with some comparison prices, you might still dig up some good deals.

SHOPPING AREAS

Willemstad's **Punda** is a treat for pedestrians, with most shops concentrated within a bustling area of about six blocks, giving you plenty of opportunity for people-watching to boot. Closed to traffic, Heerenstraat and Gomezplein are pedestrian malls covered with pink inlaid bricks. Other major shopping streets are Breedestraat and Madurostraat. Here you can find jewelry, cosmetics, perfumes, luggage, and linens—and no shortage of trinkets and souvenirs. Savvy shoppers don't skip town without a stop across the bay to **Otrobanda**, where the Riffort Village Shopping Mall houses a variety of retailers. However, the shops and eateries within are still in flux as development of the adjoining Renaissance hotel and entertainment complex nears completion.

There are also some retail shops in the Kurá Hulanda complex.

SPECIALTY STORES

ART GALLERIES

Gallery Alma Blou (⊠ *Frater Radulphusweg 4, Welgelegen* ☎ *5999/462–8896*) presents works by top local artists; you can find shimmering landscapes, dazzling photographs, ceramics, even African-inspired Carnival masks. **Gallery Eighty-Six** (⊠ *Scharlooweg 76, Punda, Willemstad* ☎ *5999/461–3417*) represents the work of local and international artists. The **Hortence Brouwn Gallery** (⊠ *Kaya Tapa Konchi 12, Brievengat* ☎ *5999/737–2193*) sells sculpted human forms (sometimes abstract) in bronze, cement, marble, and limestone. At the **Nena Sanchez Gallery** (⊠ *Bloempot Shopping Mall, Schottegatweg Oost 17, Bloempot* ☎ *5999/738–2377*), you can find this local artist's cheerful paintings in characteristically bright yellows, reds, greens, pinks, and blues. Her work depicting marine life and island scenes is available in various forms, including posters, mouse pads, and picture frames.

CIGARS

A sweet aroma permeates **Cigar Emporium** (⊠ *Gomezplein, Punda, Willemstad* ☎ *5999/465–3955*), where you can find the largest selection of Cuban cigars on the island, including H. Upmann, Romeo and Julieta, and Montecristo. Visit the climate-controlled cedar cigar room. However, remember that Cuban cigars cannot be taken back to the United States legally.

CLOTHING

Bamali (⊠ *Breedestraat, Punda, Willemstad* ☎ *5999/461–2258*) sells funky, fabulous women's apparel, including Indonesian batik clothing; charming jewelry made of beads, shells, gemstones, and silver; handbags of leather and other fabrics; and lots of other unique accessories. Custom-made clothing is available here, too. Get suited up for the beach at the **Bikini Shop** (⊠ *Seaquarium Beach, Bapor Kibra z/n* ☎ *5999/461–7343*), where you can find women's bathing suits (Vix, Becca, La Goufe) and accessories like cover-ups, flip-flops, and sunglasses. You can find a large selection of Calvin Klein apparel at **Janina** (⊠ *Madurostraat 13, Punda, Willemstad* ☎ *5999/461–1371*), which also carries Levi's jeans. **Mayura** (⊠ *Breedestraat 8, Punda, Willemstad* ☎ *5999/461–7277*) has T-shirts galore, plus souvenirs like Curaçao-themed towels and key chains. **Tommy Hilfiger** (⊠ *Breedestraat 20–21, Punda, Willemstad* ☎ *5999/465–9963*) carries the full designer line for men, women, and children. You can find a large selection of smart men's and women's wear at **Wulfsen & Wulfsen** (⊠ *Wilhelminaplein 1, Punda, Willemstad* ☎ *5999/461–2302*), from European and American designers like Gant, Kenneth Cole, and Passport.

FOODSTUFFS

Centrum Supermarket (⊠ *Weg Naar Bullenbaai z/n, Piscadera* ☎ *5999/869–6222*) is one of the better markets in terms of variety and quality. A bakery is on premises, too. **Toko Zuikertuintje** (⊠ *Zuikertuintjeweg, Santa Rosa* ☎ *5999/737–0188*), a supermarket built on the site of the original 17th-century Zuikertuintje Landhuis, carries all sorts of European and Dutch delicacies.

GIFTS

Boolchand's (⊠ *Heerenstraat 4B, Punda, Willemstad* ☎ *5999/461–6233*) sells electronics, jewelry, Swarovski crystal, Swiss watches, and cameras behind a facade of red-and-white checkered tiles. **Julius L. Penha & Sons** (⊠ *Heerenstraat 1, Punda, Willemstad* ☎ *5999/461–2266*), near the Pontoon Bridge, sells French perfumes and cosmetics, clothing, and accessories in a baroque-style building dating from 1708. At **Little Switzerland** (⊠ *Breedestraat 44, Punda, Willemstad* ☎ *5999/461–2111*) you can find jewelry, watches, crystal, china, and leather goods at significant savings.

HANDICRAFTS

Caribbean Handcraft Inc. (⊠ *Kaya Kakina 8, Jan Thiel* ☎ *5999/767–1171*) offers an elaborate assortment of locally handcrafted souvenirs. It's worth visiting just for the spectacular hilltop view. **Landhuis Groot Santa Martha** (⊠ *Santa Martha Bay* ☎ *5999/864–1323 or 5999/864–2969*) is where artisans with disabilities make ceramic vases, dolls, leather goods, and other products. There's a $3 entrance fee, and it's closed weekends.

JEWELRY

Clarisa (⊠ *Gomezplein 10, Punda, Willemstad* ☎ *5999/461–2006*) specializes in cultured pearls and also carries European gold jewelry and watches. **Different Design** (⊠ *Gomezplein 7, Punda, Willemstad* ☎ *5999/465–2944*) offers gorgeous custom-made pendants and rings of precious gems and gold. **Freeport** (⊠ *Heerenstraat 13, Punda, Willemstad* ☎ *5999/461–9500*) has a fine selection of watches and jewelry (lines include Movado, David Yurman, and Maurice Lacroix). **Gandelman** (⊠ *Breedestraat 35, Punda, Willemstad* ☎ *5999/461–1854*) has watches by Cartier and Rolex, leather goods by Prima Classe, and Baccarat and Daum crystal. **Pieters Jewelers** (⊠ *Gomezplein, Punda, Willemstad* ☎ *5999/465–4774*) carries watches including Seiko, Tissot, and Swatch, as well as gold jewelry, gemstones, and glassware.

LINENS

New Amsterdam (⊠ *Gomezplein 14, Punda, Willemstad* ☎ *5999/461–2437* ⊠ *Breedestraat 29, Punda, Willemstad* ☎ *5999/461–3239*) is the place to price hand-embroidered tablecloths, napkins, and pillowcases, as well as blue delft.

PERFUMES & COSMETICS

The **Yellow House** (⊠ *Breedestraat 23, Punda, Willemstad* ☎ *5999/461–3222*) offers a vast selection of perfumes at low prices.

NIGHTLIFE

Friday is a big night out, with rollicking happy hours and live music at many bars and hotels. And although it might sound surprising, Sunday-night revelry into the wee hours is an island tradition. Pick up a copy of the weekly free entertainment listings, *K-Pasa*, available at most restaurants and hotels. The Web site **Kikotakiko** (⊕ *kikotakiko.com*) lists all the current happenings around the island.

Fodor'sChoice   Outrageous costumes, blowout parades, pulsating Tumba rhythms,
★   miniprocessions known as jump-ups, and frenetic energy character-ize **Carnival.** The season lasts longer here than on many other islands: the revelries begin at New Year's and continue until midnight the day before Ash Wednesday. One highlight is the Tumba Festival (dates vary), a four-day musical event featuring fierce competition between local musicians for the honor of having their piece selected as the offi-cial road march during parades. For the Grand Parade, space is rented along the route and people mark their territory by building wooden stands, some lavishly decorated and furnished.

BARS

Martinis are the specialty at the **Avalon Social Club** (⊠ *Caracasbaaiweg 8, Saliña* ☎ *5999/465–6375*), where a perky crowd pours in for the daily happy hour from 6 to 7. Sushi is a popular choice for lunch or dinner; another standout feature is the Wednesday-night "tapas only" menu. Wednesday-night jam sessions are hot at **De Gouverneur** (⊠ *De Rouvilleweg 9, Otrobanda, Willemstad* ☎ *5999/462–5999*). **Fort Waakzaamheid Tavern** (⊠ *Seru Domi z/n, Willemstad* ☎ *5999/462–3633*)—the name means "Fort Alertness"—is a pleasant place for a cocktail day or night, complete with a panoramic view of the island. **Grand Café de Heeren** (⊠ *Zuikertuintjeweg, Bloempot* ☎ *5999/736–0491*) is a great spot to grab a locally brewed Amstel Bright and meet a happy blend of tourists and transplanted Dutch locals. By day **Hook's Hut** (⊠ *Next to Hilton Curaçao, Piscadera Bay* ☎ *5999/462–6575*) is a beach hangout for locals and tourists stationed at the nearby hotels. The daily happy hour from 5 to 6 kicks off a lively nighttime scene. The outdoor pool table is in terrible shape, but it's one of the few bar tables around.

With giant green leaves and thatched roofs giving each table ultimate seclusion, **Kontiki Beach Club** (⊠ *Seaquarium Beach, Bapor Kibra z/n* ☎ *5999/465–1589*) is a great spot to tuck away and have a drink with your companion if you want to feel alone yet part of the action. If you capture the fun on camera anytime at **Tu Tu Tango** (⊠ *Plaza Mundo Merced, Punda, Willemstad* ☎ *5999/465–4633*), you can send in your photos for posting to its online gallery; there's a lively happy hour on Friday from 6 to 7 PM and silver-screen theme parties once a month, owing to the bar's location behind the cinema. The seaside outdoor deck at the **Waterfort Arches** (⊠ *Waterfortstraat Boog 1, Punda, Willemstad* ☎ *5999/465–0769*) comprises a connecting strip of several bars and restaurants that have live entertainment on various nights of the week. There's never a dull moment at **Wet & Wild Beach Club** (⊠ *Seaquarium Beach, Bapor Kibra z/n* ☎ *5999/561–2477*), where the name speaks for itself every weekend. Friday happy hour features free barbecue; on Saturday a DJ or live band jams until it's too late to care about the time; on Sunday things get charged, starting with happy hour at 6; the fiesta goes on past midnight.

CASINOS

Casino gambling is becoming ever more popular on Curaçao, and hotels are refurbishing their casinos or adding new ones to keep up. Still, the sass and sparkle of the Vegas-style casinos is virtually nonexistent on the island. Although you might hear some hoots and hollers from a craps table, some clanking of coins from the slot machines, and the perpetual din of money changing hands, don't expect bells and whistles, glitzy decor, or cocktail waitresses in thematic costumes. The following hotels have casinos that are open daily: Breezes Curaçao, the Curaçao Marriott Beach Resort & Emerald Casino, the Hilton Curaçao, the Hotel Kurá Hulanda Spa & Casino, the Holiday Beach Hotel & Casino, Howard Johnson Plaza Hotel & casino, and the Otrobanda Hotel & Casino. Even the biggest of these rooms offer only a few card games, and some are limited to slot machines. As for ambience, only the casino at the Marriott—which features pleasant live entertainment some nights—even approaches the class of a Bond-like establishment. A few Texas Hold'em tables are available here, but games only start up when enough players express interest. The Holiday Beach Casino is the largest on the island, and the only one with sports betting—you can watch the live action on TV. Unfortunately, the casino is dreary. Around the island, slot machines open earlier than table games, between 10 AM and 1 PM. Most of the rooms have penny and nickel slots in addition to the higher-priced machines. Tables generally open at 3 PM or 4 PM. Casinos close about 1 AM or 2 AM weekdays; some stay open until 4 AM on weekend nights.

8

DANCE & MUSIC CLUBS

★ Live jazz electrifies the pier at **Blues** (✉ *Avila Hotel, Penstraat 130, Punda, Willemstad* ☎ *5999/461–4377*) on Thursday—*the* night to go—and Saturday. The dance floor at the **Emerald Lounge** (✉ *Curaçao Marriott Beach Resort, Piscadera Bay* ☎ *5999/736–8800*) comes alive on weekends, and is especially steamy on Friday salsa nights. **Mambo Beach** (✉ *Seaquarium Beach, Bapor Kibra z/n* ☎ *5999/461–8999*), an open-air bar and restaurant, draws a hip, young crowd that dances the night away under the stars. On Sunday, come in time for happy hour and warm up for the nightlong party with some beach volleyball. The party heats up on weekends at **Zanta Beach** (✉ *Seaquarium Beach, Bapor Kibra z/n* ☎ *5999/465–0664 or 5999/521–5379*), where the vibe is hip and the live DJ pumps things up.

EXPLORING CURAÇAO

WILLEMSTAD

What does the capital of Curaçao have in common with New York City? Broadway, for one thing. Here it's called Breedestraat, but the origin is the same. Dutch settlers came here in the 1630s, about the same time they sailed through the Verazzano Narrows to Manhattan, bringing with them original red-tile roofs, first used on the trade ships as ballast and later incorporated into the architecture of Willemstad.

The city is cut in two by Santa Anna Bay. On one side is the Punda—crammed with shops, restaurants, monuments, and markets—and on the other is Otrobanda (literally, the "other side"), with lots of narrow, winding streets full of private homes notable for their picturesque gables and Dutch-influenced designs. In recent years the ongoing regeneration of Otrobanda has been apparent, marked by a surge in development of new hotels, restaurants, and shops; the rebirth, concentrated near the waterfront, was spearheaded by the creation of the elaborate Kurá Hulanda complex.

There are three ways to cross the bay: by car over the Juliana Bridge; by foot over the Queen Emma pontoon bridge; or by free ferry, which runs when the pontoon bridge is swung open for passing ships. All the major hotels outside town offer free shuttle service to town once or twice daily. Shuttles coming from the Otrobanda side leave you at Riffort. From here it's a short walk north to the foot of the pontoon bridge. Shuttles coming from the Punda side leave you near the main entrance to Ft. Amsterdam.

Numbers in the margin correspond to points of interest on the Willemstad map.

WHAT TO SEE

⓫ **Curaçao Museum.** Housed in an 1853 plantation house, this small museum is filled with artifacts, paintings, and antiques that trace the island's history. This is also a venue for visiting art exhibitions. ✉ *V.*

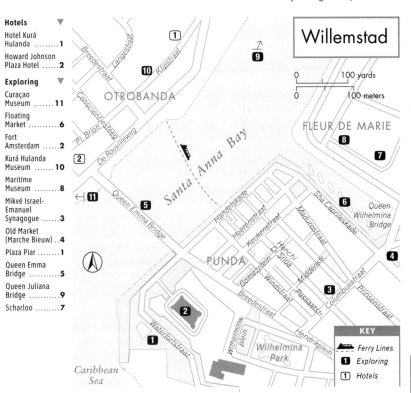

Leeuwenhoekstraat z/n, Otrobanda, Willemstad ☎*5999/462–3873*
Free ☉ Weekdays 9–noon and 2–5, Sun. 10–4.

❻ ★ Floating Market. Each morning dozens of Venezuelan schooners laden with tropical fruits and vegetables arrive at this bustling market on the Punda side of the city. Mangoes, papayas, and exotic vegetables vie for space with freshly caught fish and herbs and spices. The buying is best at 6:30 AM—too early for many people on vacation—but there's plenty of action through the afternoon. Any produce bought here should be thoroughly washed or peeled before being eaten. ⊠*Sha Caprileskade, Punda, Willemstad.*

NEED A BREAK?

For a cooling break from your explorations, Old Vienna Terrace Café (⊠*Handelskade 14, Punda, Willemstad* ☎*5999/461-1502*) serves up scrumptious homemade ice cream. Indulge your sweet tooth with such flavors as green apple, mango, and rum plum. There's also a full menu of light bites and outdoor seating along the harbor.

❷ Ft. Amsterdam. Step through the archway of this fort and enter another century. The entire structure dates from the 1700s, when it was the center of the city and the island's most important fortification. Now it houses the governor's residence, a church (which has a small museum), and government offices. Outside the entrance, a series of majestic gnarled *wayaka* trees are fancifully carved with human forms—the work of local artist Mac Alberto. ⊠*Foot of Queen Emma Bridge, Punda, Willemstad* ☎*5999/461–1139* ☑*Free; $1.75 for church museum* ☉ *Weekdays 9–noon and 2–5, Sun. service at 10.*

🔟 Kurá Hulanda Museum. This fascinating anthropological museum reveals
Fodor'sChoice the island's diverse roots. Housed in a restored 18th-century village,
★ the museum is built around a former mercantile square (Kurá Hulanda means "Holland courtyard"), where the Dutch once sold slaves. An exhibit on the transatlantic slave trade includes a gut-wrenching replica of a slave-ship hold. Other sections feature relics from West African empires, examples of pre-Columbian gold, and Antillean art. The complex is the brainchild of Dutch philanthropist Jacob Gelt Dekker, and the museum grew from his personal collection of artifacts. ⊠*Klipstraat 9, Otrobanda, Willemstad* ☎*5999/462–1400* ⊕*www.kurahulanda. com* ☑*$9* ☉*Daily 10–5.*

❽ Maritime Museum. The museum—designed to resemble the interior of a ship—gives you a sense of Curaçao's maritime history, using model ships, historic maps, nautical charts, navigational equipment, and audiovisual displays. Topics explored in the exhibits include the development of Willemstad as a trading city, Curaçao's role as a contraband hub, the remains of *De Alphen* (a Dutch marine freighter that exploded and sank in St. Anna Bay in 1778 (and excavated in 1984), the slave trade, the development of steam navigation, and the role of the Dutch navy on the island. The museum also offers a two-hour guided tour (Wednesday and Saturday, 2 PM) on its "water bus" through Curaçao's harbor—a route familiar to traders, smugglers, and pirates. The museum is wheelchair accessible. ⊠*Van der Brandhofstraat 7, Scharloo, Willemstad* ☎*5999/465–2327* ⊕*www.curacaomaritime.com* ☑*Museum $10; museum and harbor tour $15* ☉*Tues.–Sat. 10–4.*

❸ Mikvé Israel-Emanuel Synagogue. The temple, the oldest in continuous
★ use in the western hemisphere, is one of Curaçao's most important sights and draws thousands of visitors a year. The synagogue was dedicated in 1732 by the Jewish community, which had already grown from the original 12 families who came from Amsterdam in 1651. They were later joined by Jews from Portugal and Spain fleeing persecution from the Inquisition. White sand covers the synagogue floor for two symbolic reasons: a remembrance of the 40 years Jews spent wandering the desert, and a re-creation of the sand used by secret Jews, or *conversos*, to muffle sounds from their houses of worship during the Inquisition. The **Jewish Cultural Museum** (☎*5999/461–1633*), in back of the synagogue, displays antiques—including a set of circumcision instruments—and artifacts from around the world. Many of the objects are used in the synagogue, making it a "living" museum. English and Hebrew services are held Friday at 6:30 PM and Saturday at 10 AM. Men who attend should wear a jacket and tie. Yarmulkes are provided to men for services and tours. ⊠*Hanchi Snoa 29, Punda, Willemstad* ☎*5999/461–1067* ⊕*www.snoa.com* ☑*$5; donations also accepted* ☉ *Weekdays 9–4:30.*

4 **Old Market** *(Marche Bieuw)*. Local cooks prepare hearty Antillean lunches in coal pots at this covered market behind the post office. Enjoy such Curaçaoan specialties as *funchi* (polenta), goat stew, fried fish, or stewed okra. Prices range from $5 to $7. ⊠ *De Ruyterkade, Punda, Willemstad.*

1 **Plaza Piar.** This plaza is dedicated to Manuel Piar, a native Curaçaoan who fought for the independence of Venezuela under the liberator Simón Bolívar. On one side of the plaza is the Waterfort, built in the late 1820s to help defend the old city. The original cannons are still positioned in the battlements. The foundation, however, now forms the walls of the Howard Johnson Plaza Hotel Curaçao & Casino. ⊠ *Willemstad.*

5 **Queen Emma Bridge.** Affectionately called the Swinging Old Lady by the locals, this bridge connects the two sides of Willemstad—Punda and Otrobanda—across the Santa Anna Bay. The bridge swings open at least 30 times a day to allow passage of ships to and from the sea. The original bridge, built in 1888, was the brainchild of the American consul Leonard Burlington Smith, who made a mint off the tolls he charged for using it: 2¢ per person for those wearing shoes, free to those crossing barefoot. Today it's free to everyone. The bridge was dismantled and completely repaired and restored in 2005. ⊠ *Willemstad.*

9 **Queen Juliana Bridge.** This 1,625-foot-long bridge was completed in 1974 and stands 200 feet above the water. It's the crossing for motor traffic between Punda and Otrobanda and affords breathtaking views (and photo ops) of the city, day and night. ⊠ *Willemstad.*

7 **Scharloo.** The Wilhelmina Drawbridge connects Punda with the once-flourishing district of Scharloo, where the early Jewish merchants built stately homes. The architecture along Scharlooweg (much of it from the 17th century) is magnificent, and, happily, many of the colonial mansions that had become dilapidated have been meticulously renovated. The area closest to Kleine Werf is a red-light district and fairly run-down, but the rest is well worth a visit. ⊠ *Willemstad.*

ELSEWHERE ON CURAÇAO

The Weg Maar Santa Cruz through the village of Soto winds to the island's northwest tip through landscape that Georgia O'Keeffe might have painted: towering cacti, flamboyant dried shrubbery, and aluminum-roof houses. Throughout this *cunucu,* or countryside, you can see fishermen hauling nets, women pounding cornmeal, and an occasional donkey blocking traffic. Land houses—large plantation houses from centuries past—dot the countryside. To explore the island's eastern side from Willemstad, take the coastal road called Martin Luther King Boulevard about 2 mi (3 km) to Bapor Kibra. This is where you can find the Sea Aquarium and the Dolphin Academy. Farther east is a nature park at Caracas Bay and the upscale Spanish Water neighborhood and marina. To the far northeast is Groot St. Joris, home of Curaçao's aloe plantation and one of the largest ostrich-breeding farms outside Africa.

WHAT TO SEE

★ **Christoffel National Park.** The 1,239-foot Mt. Christoffel, Curaçao's highest peak, is at the center of this 4,450-acre garden and wildlife preserve. The exhilarating climb up Mt. Christoffel—a challenge to anyone who hasn't grown up scaling the Alps—takes about two hours for a reasonably fit person. On a clear day, the panoramic view from the peak stretches to the mountain ranges of Venezuela.

Through the park are eight hiking trails and a 20-mi (32-km) network of driving trails (use heavy-treaded tires if you wish to explore the unpaved stretches). All these routes traverse hilly fields full of prickly pear cacti, divi-divi trees, bushy-haired palms, and exotic flowers. Guided nature walks, horseback rides, and jeep tours can be arranged through the main park office. If you're going without a guide, first study the *Excursion Guide to Christoffel Park,* sold at the visitor center. It outlines the various routes and identifies the indigenous flora and fauna. Start out early, as by 10 AM the park starts to feel like a sauna.

Watch for goats and small animals that might cross your path, and consider yourself lucky if you see any of the elusive white-tailed deer. Every day at 4 PM, guides lead 15-minute expeditions to track the protected herd. Birds are abundant, and experts lead the way twice daily. White-tailed hawks may be seen along the green hiking route, white orchids along the yellow hiking route. There are also ancient Indian drawings and caves where you might hear the rustling of bat wings or spot scuttling, nonpoisonous scorpions.

Horseback tours are conducted from Rancho Alfin, which is in the park. Reservations are required. Additionally, most island sports outfitters offer some kind of activity in the park, such as kayaking, specialized hiking tours, and drive-through tours (⇨ *Sports & the Outdoors, above).* ⊠ *Savonet* ☏ *5999/864–0363 for information and tour reservations, 5999/462–6262 for jeep tours, 5999/864–0535 for horseback tours* 🎫*$9* ⊗ *Mon.–Sat. 8–4, Sun. 6–3; last admission 1 hr before closing.*

Curaçao Aloe Plantation & Factory. Drop in for a fascinating tour that takes you through the various stages of production of aloe vera, renowned for its healing powers. You'll get a look at everything from the fields to the final products. At the gift shop, you can buy CurAloe products, including homemade goodies like soap, pure aloe gel, and pure aloe juice, as well as sunscreen and other skin-care products. The plantation is on the way to the Ostrich Farm and run by the same owner. Tours begin throughout the day. ⊠ *Weg Naar Groot St. Joris z/n, Groot St. Joris* ☏ *5999/767–5577* ⊕ *www.aloecuracao.com* 🎫*$4* ⊗ *Mon.–Sat. 9–4; last tour at 3.*

☉ ★ **Curaçao Sea Aquarium.** You don't have to get your feet wet to see the island's underwater treasures. The aquarium has about 40 saltwater tanks filled with more than 400 varieties of marine life. For more up-close interaction, there are several mesmerizing options. You can hand-feed the sharks, stingrays, or sea turtles (or watch a diver do it) at the **Animal Encounters** section, which consists of a 12-foot-deep open-water enclosure. Snorkelers and divers of all skill levels swim freely with tarpon, stingrays, and such. If you prefer to stay dry, there's an underwater observatory in a stationary semi-submarine. It's also possible to swim with the aquarium's six lovable sea lions from Uruguay. Kids as young as three can have their photo taken kissing a sea lion. Reservations for Animal Encounters, including sea lion programs, must be made 24 hours in advance. A restaurant, a snack bar, two photo centers, and souvenir shops are on-site.

At the **Dolphin Academy** (☎5999/465–8900 ⊕*www.dolphin-academy. com*), you can watch a fanciful dolphin show (included with Sea Aquarium admission). For more-up-close interaction, you may choose from several special programs (extra charges apply and reservations are essential) to encounter the dolphins in shallow water, or to swim, snorkel, or dive with them. ⊠*Seaquarium Beach, Bapor Kibra z/n* ☎5999/461–6666 ⊕*www.curacao-sea-aquarium.com* 🖾*$15; animal encounters $54 for divers, $34 for snorkelers; sea lion programs $39– $149; Dolphin Academy $69–$300* ☉*Sea Aquarium daily 8:30–5:30; Dolphin Academy daily 8:30–4:30.*

★ **Den Paradera.** Dazzle your senses at this organic herb garden, where guides will explain the origins of traditional folk medicines used to treat everything from stomach ulcers to diabetes. Owner Dinah Veeris is a renowned expert and author in the field. The kitchen is a factory of sorts where three busy people turn homegrown plants like cactus, aloe vera, and calabash into homemade body- and skin-care products like shampoos, ointments, and oils—all for sale at the gift shop. Reservations are essential for guided tours. ⊠*Seru Grandi Kavel 105A, Banda Riba* ☎5999/767–5608 🖾*$6 with guided tour* ☉*Mon.–Sat. 9–6.*

★ **Hato Caves.** Stalactites and stalagmites form striking shapes in these 200,000-year-old caves. Hidden lighting adds to the dramatic effect. Indians who used the caves for shelter left petroglyphs about 1,500 years ago. More recently, slaves who escaped from nearby plantations used the caves as a hideaway. Hour-long guided tours wind down to the pools in various chambers. Keep in mind that there are 49 steps to climb up to the entrance. To reach the caves, head northwest toward the airport, take a right onto Gosieweg, follow the loop right onto Schottegatweg, take another right onto Jan Norduynweg, a final right onto Rooseveltweg, and follow signs. ⊠*Rooseveltweg z/n, Hato* ☎5999/868–0379 🖾*$7* ☉*Daily 10–5.*

Landhuis Brievengat. This mustard-color plantation house is a fine example of a residence from the island's past. You can see the original kitchen, the 18-inch-thick walls, fine antiques, and the watchtowers once used for lovers' trysts. A Friday-night party is held on the wide wraparound terrace, with bands and plenty to drink ($6 cover charge). On the last Sunday of the month (from 6 PM to 7:30 PM), this estate holds an open house with crafts demonstrations and folkloric shows. It's a 15-minute drive northeast of Willemstad, near Centro Deportivo stadium. ⊠*Brievengat* ☎5999/737–8344 🖾*$1.50* ☉*Mon.–Sat. 9:15–12:15 and 3–6.*

CLOSE UP

Curaçao Liqueur: The Bitter Smell of Success

Some say the famed Curaçao liqueur is what put this spirited island on the map. Oddly, the bitter oranges used to flavor the liqueur weren't recognized for their value until hundreds of years after they were introduced locally. The liqueur is made from the peels of the Laraha orange. In the 16th century, the Spaniards had brought over and planted Valencia oranges, but arid conditions rendered the fruit bitter, and the crops were left to grow in the wild. The plant became known as the Laraha, the so-called Golden Orange of Curaçao.

It was not until the mid-19th century that Edouard Cointreau of France came to appreciate the fragrance of the bitter fruit's dried peels, and he combined them with sweet oranges to make an aperitif. Eventually, the Senior

family created a recipe of its own using the Laraha and began producing Curaçao liqueur commercially in 1896. Today, only Senior's Curaçao is allowed to use the "authentic" label, signifying it is made from the indigenous citrus fruit.

Laraha oranges are harvested twice a year, when the fruit is still green. The peels are sun-dried, then put in a copper still (the original!) with alcohol and water for several days, and finally mixed with Senior's "secret" ingredients and distilled some more. The final product is clear. Colorings (including the famous blue) are added but do not change the flavor. Bartenders, however, use the colorful varieties with great flourish to create fanciful drinks.

Landhuis Kenepa. With the island's largest slave population, this plantation was the site of a revolt in 1795 that spurred the abolition of slavery on the island. The renovated plantation house near the island's western tip is filled with period furnishings and clothing. ⊠ *Weg Naar Santa Cruz, Knip* ☎5999/864–0244 ⊠*$2* ☉ *Weekdays 9–4, weekends 10–4.*

Museo Curaçao *(Kas di Pal'i Maishi).* The thatch-roof cottage is filled with antique furniture, farm implements, and clothing typical of 19th-century colonial life. Out back is a small farm and vegetable garden. Look closely at the fence—it's made of living cacti. There's also a snack bar. A festival featuring live music and local crafts takes place here on the first Sunday of each month. ⊠*Dokterstuin 27, on road to Westpunt from Willemstad, Westpunt* ☎5999/864–2497 ⊠*$2* ☉*Tues.– Fri. 9–4, weekends 9–5.*

☾ **Ostrich Farm.** If you (and the kids) are ready to stick your neck out ★ for an adventure, visit one of the largest ostrich farms outside Africa. Every hour, guided tours show the creatures' complete development from egg to mature bird. Kids enjoy the chance to hold an egg, stroke a day-old chick, and sit atop an ostrich for an unusual photo op. At the **Restaurant Zambezi** you can sample local ostrich specialties and other African dishes (reservations are recommended; closed Monday, no dinner Tuesday). The gift shop sells handicrafts made in southern Africa, including leather goods and wood carvings, as well as products made by local artisans. ⊠*Groot St. Joris* ☎*5999/747-2777* ⊕*www. ostrichfarm.net* ☜*$10* ☉*Tues.–Sun. 9–4.*

Senior Curaçao Liqueur Distillery. The famed Curaçao liqueur, made from the peels of the bitter Laraha orange, is produced at this mansion, which dates to the 1800s. Don't expect a massive factory—it's just a small showroom in an open-air foyer. There are no guides, but delightful old hand-painted posters explain the distillation process, and you can watch workers filling the bottles by hand. Assorted flavors are available to sample for free. If you're interested in buying—the orange-flavor chocolate liqueur is delicious over ice cream—you can choose from a complete selection in enticing packaging, including miniature Dutch ceramic houses. ⊠*Landhuis Chobolobo, Saliña* ☎*5999/461-3526* ⊕*www. curacaoliqueur.com* ☜*Free* ☉*Weekdays 8–noon and 1–5.*

★ **Shete Boka.** The name of this park means "Seven Inlets" in Papiamento. Indeed, the sea has carved out seven magnificent grottoes, the largest of which is Boka Tabla, where you can watch and listen to the waves crashing against the rocks beneath a limestone overhang. Boka Pistol is also spectacular, with thunderous waves smashing into the rocks and jetting up into towering plumes of spray, often leaving rainbows lingering in the mist. Several of the surrounding caverns serve as turtle nesting places; you might also spot flocks of parakeets emerge in formation, hawks soar and dip, and gulls dive-bomb for their lunch. ⊠*Westpunt Hwy., just past village center, Soto* ☜*$2.50* ☉*Daily 8:30–5.*

CURAÇAO ESSENTIALS

8

To research prices, get advice from other travelers, and book travel arrangements, visit www.fodors.com.

■ TRANSPORTATION

BY AIR

In addition to the nonstops on American, Delta, and Continental, you can also connect on American Airlines (via San Juan) or Air Jamaica (via Montego Bay). Aeropostal offers service from Caracas. Dutch Antilles Express offers connecting service from Aruba, Caracas, Santo Domingo, and St. Maarten.

Information Aeropostal (☎5999/839-1166 ⊕www.aeropostal.com). **Air Jamaica** (☎800/523-5585 or 5999/888-2300).. **American Airlines** (☎5999/869-5707). **Continental Airlines** (☎800/231-0856 or 5999/839-1196). **Delta Airlines** (☎800/221-

1212). **Dutch Antilles Express** (☎599/717-0808 ⊕www.flydae.com).

Airport Information Hato International Airport (CUR ☎5999/839-1410).

BY CAR

Most hotels outside Willemstad are just a few minutes away from the city center by taxi, keeping the fares relatively inexpensive for jaunts to go out to dinner or sightseeing in town. So if you don't plan on doing much independent exploring or beach-hopping and are not staying on a remote part of the island, you can get by without renting a car.

Driving in the Netherlands Antilles is the same as in the United States, on the right-hand side of the road, though right turns on red are prohibited. Local laws require drivers and passengers to wear seat belts and motorcyclists to wear helmets. Children under age four must be in child safety seats. There are many gas stations in the Willemstad area as well as in the suburban areas, including two on the main road as you head to the western tip of the island.

Information Avis (☎5999/839–1500 or 800/228–0668). **Budget** (☎5999/868–3466 or 800/472–3325). **Hertz** (☎5999/888–0188). **National Car Rental** (☎5999/869–4433). **Thrifty** (☎5999/461–3089).

BY TAXI

Although meters have been installed in all taxis, technical issues have delayed implementation of their use. Rates are fixed from point to point of your journey. The government-approved rates, which do not include waiting time, can be found in a brochure called "Taxi Tariff Guide," available at the airport, hotels, cruise-ship terminals, and at the tourist board. Rates are for up to four passengers. There's a 25% surcharge after 11 PM. Taxis are readily available at hotels and at taxi stands at the airport, in Punda, and in Otrobanda; in other cases, call Central Dispatch.

Information Central Dispatch (☎5999/869–0752).

▮ CONTACTS & RESOURCES

ADDRESSES

In street addresses that do not specify a house number, the "z/n" is actually a Dutch abbreviation for "zonder nummer" (no number).

BANKS & EXCHANGE SERVICES

U.S. dollars—in cash or traveler's checks—are accepted nearly everywhere, so there's no need to worry about exchanging money. However, you may need small change for pay phones, cigarettes, or soda machines. The currency in the Netherlands Antilles is the florin (also called the guilder) and is indicated by "fl" or "NAf" on price tags. The florin is very stable against the U.S. dollar; the

official rate of exchange at this writing was NAf 1.78 to US$1. There are more than 50 ATM locations on the island that dispense money in the local currency. The airport has an ATM (it dispenses U.S. dollars), as do many bank branches.

Prices quoted throughout this chapter are in U.S. dollars unless otherwise indicated.

ELECTRICITY

The current is 110–130 volts/50 cycles, which is compatible with small North American appliances such as electric razors and hair dryers. Although most hotel rooms have both 110-volt and 220-volt outlets, you might need to borrow an adapter from the front desk if the appropriate outlets aren't situated to your convenience; it's advisable to bring your own.

EMERGENCIES

General Emergencies Ambulance (☎912). **On-call dentists** (☎8888). **On-call doctors** (☎1111). **Police & fire** (☎911).

Hospital St. Elisabeth's Hospital (✉Breedestraat 193, Otrobanda, Willemstad ☎5999/462–5100).

Scuba-Diving Emergencies St. Elisabeth's Hospital (✉Breedestraat 193, Otrobanda, Willemstad ☎5999/462–5100).

Sea Emergencies Coast Guard (☎113).

INTERNET, MAIL & SHIPPING

Internet service is widely available in Curaçao. Most hotels offer access in some form, with data ports, high-speed broadband (ethernet), or Wi-Fi either in your hotel room or in the business center or lobby area of your hotel. There are also several Internet cafés around Willemstad.

There are post offices in Punda, Otrobanda, and Groot Kwartier on Schottegatweg (Ring Road), as well as small branches at the Curaçao World Trade Center and the airport. Some hotels sell stamps and have letter drops; you can also buy stamps at some bookstores. An airmail letter to the United States, Canada, or Europe costs NAf 2.85, a postcard NAf 1.49.

Information **Café Internet** (✉ Handelskade 3B, Punda, Willemstad ☎ 5999/465-5088). **Dot Com** (✉ Saliña Galleries, Saliña ☎ 5999/461-9702). **Suya-Spot Internet C@ fe** (✉ Pietermaaiplein 13, Punda, Willemstad ☎ 5999/461-5388). **Wireless Internet Café** (✉ Hanchi Snoa 4, Punda, Willemstad ☎ 5999/461-0590).

LANGUAGE

Dutch is the official language, but the vernacular is Papiamento—a mixture of Portuguese, Spanish, Dutch, African dialects, and other tongues. One theory holds that the language developed during the 18th century as a mode of communication between landowners and their slaves. Anyone involved with tourism generally speaks English. To guarantee a smile, wish someone *bon dia* (good day) or offer a warm *masha danki* (thank you very much) after someone has performed a service.

SAFETY

Crime is not rampant in Curaçao, but common-sense rules apply. Lock rental cars, and don't leave valuables in the car. Use in-room safes or leave valuables at the front desk of your hotel, and never leave bags unattended at the airport, on tours, or on the beach.

TAXES & SERVICE CHARGES

The airport international departure tax is $32.50 (including flights to Aruba), and the departure tax to other Netherlands Antilles islands is $7. This must be paid in cash, either florins or U.S. dollars. Hotels add a 12% service charge to the bill and collect a 7% government room tax; restaurants typically add 10% to 15%. Most goods and services purchased on the island will also have a 5% OB tax (a goods and services tax) added to the purchase price.

TELEPHONES

Phone service through the hotel operators in Curaçao has improved in recent years. Direct-dial service, both on-island and to elsewhere in the world, is fast and clear.

AT&T Direct service is available from most hotels; your hotel will likely add a surcharge. Dial access is also available at the AT&T calling center at the cruise-ship terminal and at the megapier in Otrobanda. From other public phones, use phones marked LENSO; many more of these have been added around the island in recent years. You can also call direct from the air-conditioned Digicel center using a prepaid phone card (open 8 AM to 5:30 PM, Monday through Saturday, the center also offers Internet access).

To place a local call on the island, dial the seven-digit local number. Pay phones charge NAf 0.50 for a local call—far less than the typical hotel charge. Whether for local or long-distance calling, it's common to use prepaid phone cards, which are widely available around the island, as many pay phones do not accept coins.

To call Curaçao direct from the United States, dial 011–5999 plus the number in Curaçao.

International roaming for most GSM mobile phones is available in Curaçao, so you can make and receive calls on your cell phone as long as you have GSM service and your carrier has a roaming agreement. Local companies are UTS (United Telecommunication Services) and Digicel (formerly Curaçao Telecom). You can also rent a mobile phone or buy a prepaid SIM card for your own phone; if you want to put a local SIM card in your cell phone, be sure to have it unlocked by your company before you travel overseas. Rentals are available at several outlets, including Rent-A-Fone, Yellow Tourism Solutions, and Bright Impex Wireless. Prepaid chips are available at UTS and Digicel.

Information **AT&T Direct** (☎ 800/872-2881). **Bright Impex Wireless** (✉ Gosieweg 75,

8

Willemstad ☎5999/736–6234 or 5999/560–8294). **Digicel** (✉Brionplein H104, Otrobanda, Willemstad ☎5999/699–9518 ✉Schottegatweg Oost 19, Bloempot ☎5999/736–1056). **Rent-A-Fone** (✉Saliña Galleries Unit D-106, Saliña ☎5999/465–8844). **UTS** (✉Rigelweg 2, Groot Davelaar ☎5999/777–0101). **Yellow Tourism Solutions** (✉Curaçao Marriott Beach Resort, Piscadera Bay ☎5999/462–6262).

TIPPING

As service is usually included, tipping at restaurants isn't expected, though if you find the staff exemplary, you can add another 5% to 10% to the bill. A gratuity for taxi drivers is at your discretion, but about 10% is the standard. Tip porters and bellhops about $1 a bag, the hotel housekeeping staff $2 to $3 per day.

TOUR OPTIONS

Most tour operators have pickups at the major hotels, but if your hotel is outside the standard zone, there may be an additional charge of around $3. Tours are available in several languages, including English.

The so-called Trolley Train visits historic sites in Willemstad on a 1½-hour guided tour, one of the most popular run by Atlantis Adventures. This tour begins at Ft. Amsterdam, and there's no hotel pickup. Peter Trips offers full-day island tours departing from the hotels Tuesday, Wednesday, Friday, and Sunday at 9 AM, with visits to many points of interest, including Ft. Amsterdam, Spanish Water, Scharloo, and Ft. Nassau. The cost is $45, and lunch is not included. East- and west-side half-day tours are offered Monday for $22.

Dutch Dream Adventures targets the action seeker with guided canoe and kayak safaris, mountain-bike excursions through Christoffel Park for groups of 10 or more, or custom-designed tours to suit your group's interests. Among the favorites at Taber Tours is the Christoffel National Park/Cas Abou Beach combo: start the day with a guided hike up Mt. Christoffel followed by a tour of the park, and wind up at the beach to relax or snorkel. Yellow Tourism Solutions offers a full range of half- and full-day tours, whether you want to check out town, beaches, or historical sites, or head out with a group for horseback riding, diving, or snorkeling. The company's Yellow Jeep Safari takes you to Christoffel National Park aboard a bright yellow Land Rover, driven by a guide who will take you off the beaten (and paved) path, deep into the park's natural terrain. Although it's aimed primarily at incentive and convention travelers, Explore Curaçao can arrange any activities on the island, from airport transfers to island adventure tours.

Information Atlantis Adventures (✉Hilton Curaçao, J.F. Kennedy Blvd., Box 2133, Piscadera Bay ☎5999/461–0011 ⊕www.atlantisadventures.com). **Dutch Dream Adventures** (☎5999/461–9393 ⊕www.dutchdream-curacao.com). **Explore Curaçao** (✉Cas Coraweg 84, Willemstad ☎5999/747–7714 ⊕www.explore-international.com). **Peter Trips** (☎5999/561–5368 or 5999/465–2703 ⊕www.petertrips.com). **Taber Tours** (✉Dokweg z/n, Willemstad ☎5999/737–6637 ⊕www.tabertours.com). **Yellow Tourism Solutions** (✉Curaçao Marriott Beach Resort, Piscadera Bay ☎5999/462–6262 ⊕www.tourism-curacao.com).

WALKING TOURS

When making reservations for any tour, mention ahead that you speak English. Walking tours of historic Otrobanda, focusing on the unique architecture of this old section of town, are led by architect Anko van der Woude every Thursday (reservations are suggested), leaving from the central clock at Brionplein at 5:15 PM. Jopi Hart offers a walking tour that emphasizes the sociocultural aspects of Otrobanda; it begins at 5:15 PM on Wednesday and departs from the clock at Brionplein. The Talk of the Town tour with Eveline van Arkel will take you through historical Punda to visit sites including Ft. Amsterdam, the restored Ft. Church, the Queen Emma pontoon bridge, and the Mikvé Israel-Emanuel Synagogue (call for reservations; English tours are on Tuesday at 9:30 AM). Gigi leads expert tours of Punda focusing on Jewish heritage, including an insider's look at the synagogue.

Information Anko van der Woude (☎5999/461–3554). **Eveline van Arkel** (☎5999/747–4349 or 5999/562–1861). **Gigi** (☎5999/697–0290). **Jopi Hart** (☎5999/767–3798).

VISITOR INFORMATION

Information Curaçao Tourist Board (⊕www.curacao-tourism.com ✉Pietermaai 19, Punda, Willemstad ☎5999/434–8200 ✉Hato International Airport ☎5999/868–1341).

WEDDINGS

Curaçao's appeal as a destination wedding spot has been rising faster than you can say, "I do." Several resorts and event planners are equipped to help you with the legal requirements and procedures for the marriage itself in addition to arrangements for a reception and/or honeymoon. You and your partner must be living outside the Netherlands Antilles, and you must report to the Register's Office in person at least three days prior to your scheduled marriage. You must notify the Register's Office in writing (from abroad) at least two months ahead of your intended wedding day, stating more than one potential wedding day. You will need to include the following original documents: birth certificate; valid passport (a copy is acceptable at this stage); evidence that you are single; if applicable, evidence that you are divorced or a widow or widower. All of the documents must be current, that is, not more than six months old (with the exception of the passport and birth certificate). The Register's Office may request additional documents, depending on your personal circumstances. Once your documents are received, you will be notified within two weeks of a date and time for your marriage to be performed if every-

thing is in order, of any documents that are lacking or not in order, and/or of any additional documentation you need to supply. A marriage certificate costs NAf 32.50 (about $20). A wedding package costs between NAf 350 (about $200) and NAf 750 (about $425).

Special Events Curaçao–Wedding & Party Planner can help you with the A-to-Zs of wedding logistics, including taking legal steps, booking hotel rooms, and finding the perfect location, caterer, florist, and photographer. Ban Kasa Wedding & Honeymoon Planner Curaçao offers personalized wedding services; a rep will pick you up at the airport and help with every detail from preliminary legal paperwork to your wedding video, and all the options in between (including fireworks, if you want them!).

Several hotels have wedding and honeymoon planners. Among the resorts that specialize in weddings are the Avila Hotel, Breezes Curaçao, Curaçao Marriott Beach Resort & Emerald Casino, Habitat Curaçao, Hotel Kurá Hulanda, the Lodge Kurá Hulanda & Beach Club, and Sunset Waters Beach Resort. The hotels and independent party planners may require more time to assist you with the legal process and other arrangements than what the government requires.

Information Ban Kasa Wedding & Honeymoon Planner Curaçao (✉Kaya Kashimiri 59, Curasol ☎5999/869–5670 ⊕www.bankasa.com). **Office of the Registrar of Curaçao** (✉Burgerlijke Stand Bevolkingsregister en Verkiezengen [BSB&V], A. M. Chumaceiro Blvd. 13, Punda, Willemstad ☎5999/461–1844). **Special Events Curaçao–Wedding & Party Planner** (✉WTC Bldg., Piscadera Bay ☎5999/463–6139 ⊕www.specialevents-curacao.com).

8

Dominica

Scotts Head

WORD OF MOUTH

"I will say it is a wonderful island if you are looking for adventure. Driving around the island was like a scene out of Jurassic Park— dense rain forest and jungle."

—smgapp

"If you are looking for an island that looks just like it did 20 years ago, Dominica is the place for you to return. It's beautiful—very natural and not built up at all."

—MIM04

WELCOME TO DOMINICA

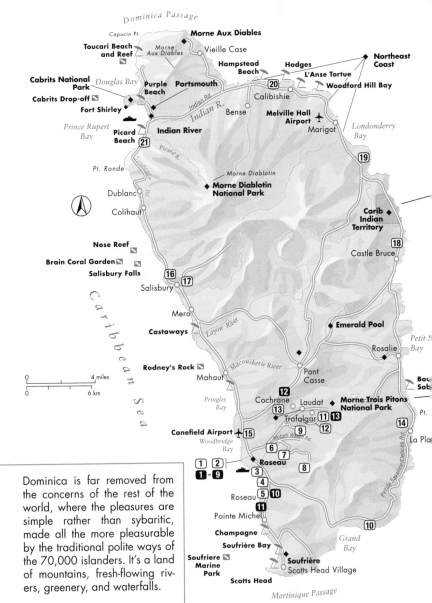

Dominica is far removed from the concerns of the rest of the world, where the pleasures are simple rather than sybaritic, made all the more pleasurable by the traditional polite ways of the 70,000 islanders. It's a land of mountains, fresh-flowing rivers, greenery, and waterfalls.

THE NATURE ISLAND

The island is 29 mi (47 km) long and 16 mi (26 km) wide, with approximately 73,000 citizens. Since it was a British colony (achieving independence in 1978), you may wonder about the prevalence of French names. Although the English first claimed Dominica in 1627, the French controlled it from 1632 until 1759, when it passed back into English hands.

KEY

↗ Beaches
⚓ Cruise Ship Terminal
◩ Dive Sites
❶ Restaurants
① Hotels

The last few remaining Caribs, descendants of the fierce people who were among the earliest Caribbean residents—and for whom the sea is named— live on the northeast coast of Dominica.

Restaurants ▼		Hotels ▼	
Bambuz Restaurant	**11**	Anchorage Hotel	**3**
Cocorico	**8**	Beau Rive	**18**
Cornerhouse Café	**6**	Calibishie	**20**
Crystal Terrace	**10**	Castle Comfort Lodge	**4**
Guiyave	**7**	Cocoa Cottages	**12**
La Robe Creole	**9**	Crescent Moon	**13**
La Maison	**3**	Evergreen Hotel	**5**
Miranda's Corner	**12**	Exotica	**8**
O'Byrnes	**4**	Fort Young Hotel	**1**
Pearl's Cuisine	**2**	Garraway Hotel	**2**
Port of Call	**1**	Hummingbird Inn	**15**
Rainforest Restaurant	**13**	Itassi	**7**
Waterfront Restaurant	**5**	Jungle Bay	**14**
		Papillote	**11**
		Picard Beach Cottages	**21**
		Roseau Valley Hotel	**6**
		Silks Hotel	**19**
		Sunset Bay Club	**16**
		Tamarind Tree	**17**
		Tia's Bamboo Cottages	**9**
		Zandoli	**10**

DOMINICA

9

Morne Trois Pitons National Park was the first UNESCO World Heritage Site in the Lesser Antilles (others are now in St. Kitts and St. Lucia).

TOP 4 REASONS TO VISIT DOMINICA

❶ The island's unspoiled natural environment is the major draw.

❷ The hiking—particularly the hike around Boiling Lake—is exhilarating.

❸ Diving pristine reefs full of colorful sea life or in bubbly, volcanic water is amazing.

❹ For many, an island with no big beach resort is a minus, but if you are the type of person who's going to like Dominica, you know that's a plus.

DOMINICA PLANNER

Island Activities

Although the island has a few brown-sand beaches, they are not a major draw. One of the things you do come for is **diving**, which can be tremendous, particularly in the protected Scotts Head Marine Reserve. **Whale-watching** is also spectacular from November through February, and **hiking** in the island's completely undeveloped rain forest reserves is exciting any time of the year. The island's best **beach** is Champagne, which has steam vents from an underwater volcano just offshore; swimming here is a real experience—you'll feel as if you are adrift in warm, effervescent champagne.

On the Ground

Cab fare from Canefield Airport to Roseau is about $20. The 75-minute drive from Melville Hall Airport to Roseau takes you through the island's Central Forest Reserve and is a tour in itself; the trip costs about $60 by private taxi or $20 per person in a shared taxi. The ferry drops you right in Roseau. If you're staying out on the island, you'll need to rent a car, and you may need a four-wheel-drive to reach some small resorts.

Logistics

Getting to Dominica: There are no nonstops from the U.S., so you'll have to transfer in Antigua, Barbados, Martinique, San Juan, or St. Lucia. There is also a ferry (90 minutes) from Guadeloupe or St. Lucia. Canefield Airport (DCF), about 3 mi (5 km) north of Roseau, is served by only a few small Caribbean-based airlines. Melville Hall Airport (DOM), where most flights arrive, is 75 minutes from Roseau.

Hassle Factor: High, mostly because of the time it takes to travel here.

Nonstops: None.

Where to Stay

There are few upscale options in Dominica and absolutely no large resorts. Most accommodations are in small lodges and guesthouses, though there is one small and one midsize hotel in Roseau.

Hotel & Restaurant Costs

⇨*For information on hotel meal plans, see Accommodations in Caribbean Essentials.*

WHAT IT COSTS IN U.S. DOLLARS				
$$$$	$$$	$$	$	¢
Restaurants				
over $30	$20–$30	$12–$20	$8–$12	under $8
Hotels*				
over $350	$250–$350	$150–$250	$80–$150	under $80
Hotels**				
over $450	$350–$450	$250–$350	$125–$250	under $125

*EP, BP, CP **AI, FAP, MAP Restaurant prices are for a main course at dinner and include any taxes or service charges. Hotel prices are per night for a double room in high season, excluding taxes, service charges, and meal plans (except at all-inclusives).

Updated
by Roberta
Sotonoff

IN DOMINICA, YOU GO TO Mother Nature, or Mother Nature comes to you. Perhaps you will see nature's beauty in underwater silence, swimming in volcanic bubbles while millions of colors dash by; or perhaps you will discover its magnificence hiking steep and narrow stretches of red mud and lush forests on your climb up a mountain volcano. At the end of the day, when you emerge or descend, a rainbow will smile and you can sleep the sleep of the legendary explorer returning from the wild. Any way you choose to experience Dominica, her big and small wonders will awe you.

With all this abundance of nature, there's also a lot of active watching to do—birds flying, turtles hatching, and dolphins and whales jumping. Even when you're not looking, something is sure to capture your gaze. The sensory overload isn't just visual. Your soul may be soothed by the refreshing smell of clean river water and cleaner air; your taste buds will be tantalized by the freshest fruits and vegetables; and your skin will be caressed by the purest natural soaps.

Wedged between the two French islands of Guadeloupe and Martinique, Dominica (pronounced dom-in-*ee*-ka) is as close to the garden of Eden as you're likely to get. Wild orchids, anthurium lilies, ferns, heliconia, and myriad fruit trees sprout profusely. Much of the interior is still covered by luxuriant rain forest and remains inaccessible by road. Here everything grows more intensely: greener, brighter, and bigger. A natural fortress, the island protected the Caribs (the region's original inhabitants) against European colonization. The rugged northeast is still reserved as home to the last survivors of the Caribs, along with their traditions and mythology.

Dominica—29 mi (47 km) long and 16 mi (26 km) wide, with a population of 70,000—did eventually become a British colony; but it attained independence in November 1978 and now has a seat in the United Nations as the central Caribbean's only natural World Heritage Site. Its capital is Roseau (pronounced rose-*oh*); the official language is English, although most locals communicate with each other in Creole; roads are driven on the left; family and place-names are a mélange of English, Carib, and French; and the religion is predominantly Catholic. It's a conservative society. Unlike neighboring Martinique and Guadeloupe, Dominica frowns on topless bathing, and swimsuits should never be worn on the street. The economy is still heavily dependent on agriculture.

With fewer than 100,000 overnight visitors annually, Dominica is a little-known destination with no major hotel chains, but the island's forestry service has preserved more national forests, marine reserves, and parks, per capita, than almost anywhere on Earth.

Dominica is a popular "alternative" Caribbean experience. It's an ideal place to go if you want to really get away—hike, bike, trek, spot birds and butterflies in the rain forest, and explore waterfalls; experience a vibrant culture in Dominica's traditions; kayak, dive, snorkel, or sail in marine reserves; or go out in search of the many resident whale and dolphin species. To experience Dominica, from the elfin woodlands and dense rain forest to the therapeutic geothermal springs and world-class dive sites that mirror the terrestrial terrain, is really to know Earth as it was created.

WHERE TO STAY

Many properties offer packages with dives, hikes, tours, and/or meal plans included, along with all the usual amenities. Some advertise winter rates with a discount for either summer or longer stays.

$$$$ ☐ **Jungle Bay Resort & Spa.** Sweeping views of the untamed Atlantic
★   dominate this resort, which sits on 55 acres of the only developed section of the island's southeast. Hovering over the ocean and surrounded by lush greenery, you may feel as if you are a million miles away from the rest of the world. No matter where you are at this peaceful hideaway, you can always hear the sea. Exercise is a given, as the resort begins at sea level and climbs up to 1,000 feet. Many rooms are perched high on the cliff and have spectacular views. They are rustic with some very nice touches—coffeemaker, refrigerator, fresh fruit, flowers, and a delightful, enclosed outdoor shower. Overlooking the sea and the pool is the resort's restaurant, the Pavilion, which uses local spices and produce in preparing vegetarian, seafood, and chicken dishes as well as tasty cuisine like shrimp curry. The resort's plan that includes meals and activities is a superior value. The Spa du Soleil has cliff-side treatment studios. Jungle Bay Resort is about 2½ hours from the airport and 1 hour from Roseau. **Pros:** Perfect for active vacationers, lovely rooms, outdoor showers. **Cons:** Facility is remote, water is too rough for swimming, a long trek to many of the rooms. ☒*Delices* ⌂*Box 2352, Roseau* ☎*767/446–1789, 866/446–1789 in U.S. and Canada* ⊕*www.junglebaydominica.com* ☞*35 cottages* ⌂*In-room: no phone, no TV. In-hotel: restaurant, bars, pool, spa, no elevator, no kids under 8* ☐*AE, D, MC, V* ☉*CP.*

$$$ ☐ **Silks Hotel.** French taste transformed this 17th-century mansion and
Fodor'sChoice former rum distillery into the poshest resort on the island. The idyllic
★   romantic getaway is surrounded by 1.4 acres of gardens. The common areas and rooms are elegant and plush with a regal blend of African and creole styles. The romantic tower room, which begs for a Juliet to call up a Romeo, is part of a two-level suite that includes a four-poster bed and bathroom with hand-painted French tiles. The only downside to the facility is the lack of bathroom amenities—the only thing supplied is soap. Though the fare at the hotel's restaurant is limited, it is well presented and quite good. The property was renovated in 2007, and a small wine cellar was added. For an additional fee, you can get a car and driver. Pros: Probably the most luxurious lodgings on the islands close to the airport. Cons: More than an hour's drive from Roseau. ☒*Hatton Garden, Marigot* ☎*767/445–8846* ⊕*www.silks-hotel.com* ☞*5 rooms* ⌂*In-hotel: restaurant, pool, no elevator, public Internet, free airport shuttle* ☐*MC, V* ☉*BP.*

$$ ☐ **Beau Rive.** Owner Mark Steele puts Zen-like elegance and creative
★   soul into every detail of this secluded bed-and-breakfast—natural soaps

A Place to Get Soaked

Wotten Waven is no thriving metropolis. In fact, the hamlet at the north end of the Roseau Valley is minuscule. But don't miss it. Hidden in its bush are sulfur-enriched, burping waters, fumaroles, and cascades. A few local entrepreneurs have made it a spa destination. Now, if you are thinking big-time pampering, think again. It is strictly BYOT (bring your own towel). There are three outdoor "spas." Each is unique. **Tia's Bamboo Cottages** are perched on a hill. The springs are at the bottom by the river. Don't want to dip? Well, the owner's preteen daughters at **TiWen Glo Cho** will take you

on a tour down a flowered-bordered path to lush gardens, a small menagerie of native wildlife, and a waterfall. TiWen Glo Cho's state-of-the-art spa is four old-fashioned claw-foot bathtubs. Mineral water is jerry-rigged into them via a series of bamboo poles. **Screw's Sulphur Spa** is the most posh. It offers mud packs and wraps plus three pools, each a different temperature and a different depth. Screw, and that is his name, doesn't let you leave without giving you fresh juice or fruit. Dominica's spas are a far reach from the Golden Door, but then again that is the charm.

in the bath, music gently playing in the lobby, and delicious, freshly prepared food. All rooms are extra spacious and have verandahs with ocean views, but they omit things like TVs, phones, and air-conditioning. It is a place where you can take quiet walks in the citrus and spice gardens or hike along the Richmond River. There's a two-night minimum. **Pros:** Lovely rooms, very good food. **Cons:** Ocean is too rough for swimming, there's only one nightly dinner choice. ⊠ *Between Castle Bruce and Sineku* 🗗 *Box 2424, Roseau* 🕾 *767/445–8992* ⊕ *www.beaurive.com* ⇟ *8 rooms* ⊘ *In-room: no a/c, no phone, no TV. In-hotel: bar, pool, no elevator, public Internet, no kids under 16* ▤ *MC, V* ⧖ *CP.*

9

$$ ⊡ **Crescent Moon Cabins.** In a hidden valley where waterfalls and a ☾ river run rampant, this small, family-run forest resort is so deep in the ★ bush, you might genuinely believe you're camping—except you have the benefit of basic, yet ecofriendly facilities with balconies and hammocks. All cabins have panoramic views; at night, you very well may look up to the stars in awe and wonder how it all began. What makes the property even more unique are hosts Ron and Jean Viveralli, who have pumped agritourism up a notch. Ron, a professionally trained chef, finds inspiration in the greenhouse, goats, chickens, and the fruits that are tenderly cared for by Jean. Ron makes his own coffee, goat cheese, and tofu from scratch. Let Jean or Ron know you want dinner and a gourmet meal will be prepared. This is a great place for active families or for couples looking for romance. But you'll definitely need a 4x4 because the roads leading here are not the best. A stone cottage ($360 per night with three-night minimum) that will accommodate a group or family is the newest addition to the accommodations; there's a two-night minimum on all other rooms. **Pros:** One-of-a-kind property, excellent food. **Cons:** Facilities are about two steps above camping, road here is difficult to navigate. ⊠ *Sylvania* 🗗 *Box 2400, Roseau*

☎767/449–3449 ⊕*www.crescentmooncabins.com* ⇩*4 cabins, 1 cottage* ⏃*In-room: no a/c, no phone, no TV. In-hotel: pool, no elevator, public Internet* ☰*MC, V* ⏉*CP.*

$–$$ ⚏**Calibishie Lodges.** Close to one of Dominica's most picturesque sea-
★   side village, bamboo- and melon-color buildings emerge from behind terraced lemongrass. Six charming one-bedroom, self-contained, balconied units, with comfy furnishings throughout, offer all the comforts of home. The property's interior has been totally renovated to make it even more charming. Bathrooms now have bowl sinks. Add to that the friendliness and care of owners Chris and Linda Vinck. A small swimming pool and sundeck lead off from the Bamboo Bar and Restaurant. Meal plans are available. If the property is full, ask about Dominica Sea View Apartments, which the Vincks also own. **Pros:** Plenty of charm, people-pleasing owners. **Cons:** It's at least an hour's drive from Roseau. ✉*Calibishie Main Rd., Calibishie* ☎767/445–8537 ⊕*www.calibishie-lodges.com* ⇩*6 apartments* ⏃*In-room: no a/c, safe, kitchen, Wi-Fi. In-hotel: restaurant, bar, pool, no elevator, airport shuttle* ☰*D, MC, V* ⏉*BP.*

$–$$ ⚏**Evergreen Hotel.** This family-run, modern oceanfront inn is a nondiv-
☾   er's oasis in diver-friendly Castle Comfort. Located 1 mi (1.5 km) south of Roseau, it has spacious waterfront rooms with large showers and balconies—many with ocean views. A separate honeymoon cottage is in a charming, foliage-filled nook. The Crystal Terrace restaurant, just off the pool, has a creative creole menu. **Pros:** Friendly staff, pleasant surroundings, just 1 mi (1.5 km) from Roseau. **Cons:** One of the few places in the area that doesn't offer diving facilities. ✉*Castle Comfort* ⏏*Box 309, Roseau* ☎767/448–3288 or 767/448–3276 ⊕*www.avirtualdominica.com/evergreen.htm* ⇩*16 rooms, 1 cottage* ⏃*In-room: refrigerator (some). In-hotel: restaurant, bar, pool, no elevator, public Internet* ☰*AE, D, MC, V* ⏉*BP.*

$–$$ ⚏**Fort Young Hotel.** Sitting on the edge of a cliff just to the south of
Fodor's Choice   Roseau, on the site of a former 18th-century-era French fort, this hotel
★   is probably the most urbanlike establishment on the island. The staff is extremely friendly and helpful. Ample-size rooms have balconies with either a limited or full ocean view. Newly remodeled bathrooms have granite vanities. The spacious lobby is quite inviting, and an attached boardwalk has a variety of shops, including a few duty-free ones. The Waterfront Restaurant is one of the island's most upscale and has a romantic atmosphere. **Pros:** Cosmopolitan vibe, friendly staff. **Cons:** Can get crowded during the Friday-night happy hour. ✉*Victoria St., Box 519, Roseau* ☎767/448–5000 ⊕*www.fortyounghotel.com* ⇩*70 rooms, 3 suites* ⏃*In-room: Ethernet (some), Wi-Fi. In-hotel: 3 restaurants, bars, pool, spa* ☰*AE, MC, V* ⏉*EP.*

$–$$ ⚏**Picard Beach Wellness Eco Cottages.** Somewhat pricey by Dominica
☾   standards, these 18 cottages on the grounds of an old, 6-acre coconut plantation and its lovely landscaped gardens are just steps away from Dominica's longest grayish-sand beach. A white picket fence with private gates allows you access to the beach. Each one-bedroom cottage, which is only moderately maintained, accommodates two adults with two children or three adults and has a kitchenette, a living and dining area, and

a verandah. The casual Le Flambeau Restaurant next door serves creole food. **Pros:** One of the few places on the island with spa facilities, nice beach. **Cons:** The property is not well lighted and can be difficult to navigate at night without a flashlight, this part of the island can get pretty buggy. ⊠*Prince Rupert Bay* ⑩*Box 34, Roseau* ☎*767/445–5131* ⊕*www.avirtualdominica.com/picard.htm* ⇖*18 1-bedroom cottages* ⚷*In-room: kitchen, dial-up (some). In-hotel: bar, beachfront, spa, no elevator, public Internet* ▭*AE, D, DC, MC, V* ◯|*EP.*

$ ▥**Castle Comfort Lodge.** The boats anchored just off the pier, the telltale dive log, and the guests in the hot tub with mask imprints on their foreheads give it all away—this is the best dive lodge in Dominica. Located 1 mi (1.5 km) south of Roseau, it offers good all-inclusive packages with top-notch diving and family-style dining. Nondivers who don't want or need fancy amenities will find the rooms adequate and can enjoy the property's pool, plus whale-watching cruises. **Pros:** A favorite retreat for divers, good location. **Cons:** Rooms are very basic. ⊠*Castle Comfort* ⑩*Box 63, Roseau* ☎*767/448–2188 or 888/414–7626* ⊕*www.castlecomfortdivelodge.com* ⇖*15 rooms* ⚷*In-hotel: restaurant, bar, pool, diving, no elevator, public Wi-Fi* ▭*MC, V* ⊘*Closed Sept.* ◯|*EP.*

$ ▥**Cocoa Cottages.** This ecosensitive, hand-constructed wood-and-stone lodge has a cozy tree-house feel, and, though very basic, it's very comfortable. Many of the furnishings are made from recycled materials: bed frames from recycled spools, lamps from coconut shells, and flower pots from bamboo. All beds have colorful madras covers and mosquito nets. Some rooms have balconies and hammock chairs. You can start your day with a cup of hot cocoa or tea made straight from the surrounding trees while you enjoy the melodious sounds of birds, then perhaps have a picnic at a nearby stream or take a nature tour. **Pros:** Rustic and remote. **Cons:** Rustic and remote. ⊠*Trafalgar* ⑩*Box 288, Roseau* ☎*767/448–0412 in Dominica, 954/332–9540 Ext. 1119 in U.S.* ⊕*www.cocoacottages.com* ⇖*6 rooms* ⚷*In-room: no a/c, no phone, no TV. In-hotel: restaurant, bar, no elevator, airport shuttle* ▭*AE, MC, V* ◯|*EP.*

$ ▥**Exotica.** At 1,600 feet, this property is wrapped in mountains and
☾   water—a truly stunning landscape. Solar panels power the red-roof, wooden bungalows and each has a kitchen, bedroom with two extra-long double beds, and a large living room with trundle beds. If you don't want to cook, Fae, a trained nutritionist, serves delicious creole food at the Sugar Apple Café, including produce from her organic garden. Exotica has recently added a new garden restaurant, the Shade House. This is a great place to bird-watch, and the view of the distant ocean from your bungalow is gorgeous. It's so peaceful up here that many guests come for long stays. You may need to rent a jeep to get around. **Pros:** Nice accommodations, friendly staff, good place to take a family. **Cons:** A rental car is needed to get around, it's a drive to the sea. ⊠*Giraudel* ⑩*Box 109, Roseau* ☎*767/448–8839* ⊕*www.exotica-cottages.com* ⇖*6 bungalows* ⚷*In-room: no a/c, kitchen, no TV. In-hotel: 2 restaurants, no elevator* ▭*AE, D, MC, V* ◯|*EP.*

$ 🏨 **Garraway Hotel.** This modern, city-style hotel on the western edge of
⏱ Roseau offers good views from the higher floors. Depending on your
room, you can survey the town's quaint architecture, the ocean, or
the imposing mountains. The second-floor Balizier Restaurant specializes in creole cuisine, with a Wednesday and Friday buffet. You can
have a Sundowner at the Ole Jetty Bar or watch the sunset from the
fifth-floor rooftop terrace. **Pros:** Attractive rooms, well located in the
heart of Roseau. **Cons:** Lower-level rooms do not have good views, a
little impersonal. ⊠*Place Heritage, 1 Dame Eugenia Charles Blvd.,
Box 789, Roseau* ☎*767/449–8800* ⊕*www.garrawayhotel.com* ➥*24
rooms, 7 suites* ⏇*In-hotel: restaurant, bar* ⊟*AE, DC, MC, V* ⏹*EP.*

$ 🏨 **Hummingbird Inn.** The ocean vistas, lushly fragrant garden, and natu-
rally sensuous atmosphere at this hillside retreat provide a romantic
setting for honeymooners and, needless to say, hummingbirds. Beds are
dressed with handmade quilts. Shutters can be left open all night to let
in breezes, soothing honeysuckle scents, and the sounds of the surf. The
Honeymoon Suite has a stately mahogany four-poster bed, a kitchen,
and a patio. The reception area, lounge, and dining terrace are all in
the main house. Phones and TVs are optional. **Pros:** Gorgeous view; if
you are into lizards, this is a sanctuary for the rare iguana delicatissima.
Cons: Very basic rooms, a charge for in-room TV, road to the property
has a very steep turn and is challenging after it rains. ⊠*Morne Daniel
*⏉*Box 1901, Roseau* ☎*767/449–1042* ⊕*www.thehummingbirdinn.
com* ➥*9 rooms, 1 suite* ⏇*In-room: no a/c, kitchen (some). In-hotel:
restaurant, bar, no elevator* ⊟*AE, D, MC, V* ⏹*CP.*

$ 🏨 **Papillote Wilderness Retreat.** Luxuriant vegetation abounds in this
⏱ retreat's 4 acres of botanical gardens—all in the middle of the tropical
forest. This family-friendly, welcoming destination has a mind-boggling
collection of rare and indigenous plants and flowers that are planted
among three secluded mineral pools and stone sculptures; Suite 11 has
its own hot tub. For outdoor activities, the river beckons you to take
a dip, and the 125-foot Trafalgar Falls are a short hike from your
room. The terrace-style Rainforest restaurant, which has spectacular
mountain and valley views, serves excellent local cuisine. A breakfast and dinner plan is available for an additional $40 per day. **Pros:**
Lovely grounds, location inside Morne Trois Pitons National Park,
close to Trafalgar Falls. Cons: A rental car is needed to get most places
from here. ⊠*Trafalgar Falls Rd., Trafalgar* ⏉*Box 2287, Roseau
*☎*767/448–2287* ⊕*www.papillote.dm* ➥*3 rooms, 4 suites* ⏇*In-
room: no a/c, no phone, no TV. In-hotel: restaurant, bar, no elevator
*⊟*AE, D, MC, V* ⊙*Closed Sept.–mid-Oct.* ⏹*EP.*

$ 🏨 **Roseau Valley Hotel.** With tile floors and cheerful decor, this little inn
⏱ is quite inviting. Some rooms have TVs and terraces, while others have
a shared balcony and TV access. Free Internet service is available. The
Waterhole Restaurant specializes in fresh locally grown food. **Pros:**
Reasonable and pleasant. Cons: A 2-mi (3-km) walk to Roseau. ⊠*2 mi
(3 km) east of Roseau, Box 1876, Roseau* ☎*767/449–8176* ⊕*www.
roseauvalleyhotel.com* ➥*10 rooms* ⏇*In-room: kitchen (some), no TV
(some), no a/c. In-hotel: restaurant, bar, pool, no elevator, public Wi-Fi,
airport shuttle* ⊟*AE, MC, V* ⏹*BP.*

$ ⊞ **Sunset Bay Club.** Sunset is a simple but comfortable beachfront resort on a stretch of Dominica's spectacular west coast. Lush gardens filled with scurrying wildlife are crisscrossed by pathways that meander from rooms to garden benches, to the pool, to the sauna hut, and back to the beach and restaurant. The Four Seasons Restaurant is known for its seafood, wide selection of cocktails, and drop-dead gorgeous views. Although most people opt for the all-inclusive plan, a breakfast-only plan is available. In-room TVs are available for a fee. **Pros:** Gardens and views are beautiful, very good food. Cons: Rooms are very basic. ⊠*Batalie Beach, Coulibistrie* ☎*767/446–6522* ⊕*www.sunsetbay club.com* ⇘*12 rooms, 1 suite* ♿*In-room: no a/c, no phone, safe. In-hotel: restaurant, bar, pool, beachfront, diving, no elevator, airport shuttle* ⊟*AE, MC, V* ⍩*BP.*

$ ⊞ **Tamarind Tree Hotel & Restaurant.** The warmth and friendliness of own-
☺ ers Annette and Stefan Loerner-Peyer are this small inn's most valuable asset. Located 100 feet above the Caribbean, the intimate, no-frills hotel has awesome views. A very able Swiss chef produces fine steaks, German bread, and Continental and creole cuisine in its restaurant. The local beer, Kubuli, is on tap—a tap made from plastic plumbing pipes. **Pros:** Extremely friendly owners, good food, only place that you can get Kubuli Beer on tap. Cons: No-frills rooms. ⊠*Salisbury* ⅌*Box 754, Roseau* ☎*888/790–5264* ⊕*www.tamarindtreedominica.com* ⇘*9 rooms* ♿*In-room: refrigerator. In-hotel: restaurant, bar, pool, no elevator* ⊟*MC, V* ⍩*BP.*

$ ⊞ **Zandoli Inn.** Perched on an 80-foot cliff overlooking the southeast
★ Atlantic coast, this small inn has an amazing view—water and then mountains—that is inspiring. Meander through 6 acres of luscious gardens, or have a seat and contemplate the scenery. Upstairs, rooms are elegant and comfortable. Downstairs is the dining room and bar, where hotel guests join owner Linda Hyland for scrumptious organic meals and rum-laced drinks. Farther down the cliff is the plunge pool— under a canopy of orchids; or you can go for a more-adventurous swim from huge boulders in the aqua-blue Atlantic. Pros: Drop-dead vistas. **Cons:** Steep walk to the beach, which is not the best place to take a plunge. ⊠*Roche Cassée, Stowe* ⅌*Box 2099, Roseau* ☎*767/446–3161* ⊕*www.zandoli.com* ⇘*5 rooms* ♿*In-room: no a/c, no phone, no TV. In-hotel: bar, pool, no elevator, laundry service, no kids under 12* ⊟*AE, MC, V* ⍩*EP.*

¢–$ ⊞ **Anchorage Hotel.** Adventure seekers of every age come to this lodge for diving, whale-watching, or other tours led by the in-house tour company. This family-run operation is not unlike Castle Comfort Lodge next door—both offer simple rooms and top-notch activities. The Ocean Terrace Restaurant and Bar is open to dramatic sunsets with visiting yachts in the foreground. Both locals and visitors frequent the weekly buffet dinners with live music. Pros: A fine range of water activities. Cons: No-frill accommodations. ⊠*Castle Comfort* ⅌*Box 34, Roseau* ☎*767/448–2638* ⊕*www.anchoragehotel.dm* ⇘*32 rooms* ♿*In-room: refrigerator (some). In-hotel: restaurant, bar, pool, diving, no elevator, public Internet* ⊟*AE, D, MC, V* ⍩*EP.*

9

¢ 🏠 **Itassi Cottages.** You forget how close these three cottages are to
☾ Roseau as you swing on your hammock overlooking the ocean. On
beautifully landscaped grounds, the two-bedroom cottage can house as
many as six people; the one-bedroom cottage accommodates up to four;
and the studio cottage comfortably sleeps two. Each has a full kitchen
and cable TV, and there's a shared laundry room. They are furnished
with a mix of antiques, straw mats, handmade floral bedspreads, and
calabash lamps. **Pros:** Very friendly atmosphere, great bang for your
buck. Cons: Very simple (but comfortable) accommodations. ⊠*Morne
Bruce* 🕮*Box 2333, Roseau* 📞*767/448–4313* ⊕*www.avirtualdomi-
nica.com/itassi* ⌨*3 cottages* ⟐*In-room: no a/c, kitchen. In-hotel: no
elevator, laundry facilities* ▭*AE, MC, V* ⦿*EP.*

¢ 🏠 **Tia's Bamboo Cottages.** Tia himself built these charming but rustic
cabins, which sit on the side of a hill, amid a picturesque, natural setting. The small wooden guest cottages each have a window, double bed,
mosquito net, sink, toilet, and terrace with a hammock. One cottage
has its own sulfur mineral pool plus a cold shower; others have hot
showers. Below the cottages are two mineral springs, which guests are
free to use. There's a small restaurant, open to the public, serving simple
Caribbean food. **Pros:** Proximity to river and natural springs, extremely
helpful staff. Cons: Cottages are very sparse. ⊠*Wotton Waven, in the
Roseau Valley* 📞*767/448–1998 or 767/440–4352* ⊕*www.avirtual-
dominica.com/tiasbamboocottages* ⌨*3 cottages* ⟐*In-hotel: restaurant, bar, pools* ▭*No credit cards* ☽*Closed June* ⦿*EP.*

WHERE TO EAT

You can expect an abundance of vegetables, fruits, and root crops to
appear on menus around the island. Dominica's economy, after all, is
based on agriculture. Sweet ripe plantains, *kushkush,* yams, breadfruit,
dasheen (also called "taro"), fresh fish, and chicken prepared at least a
dozen different ways are all staples. The local drink is a spiced rum—
steeped with herbs such as anisette (called "nanny") and *pweve* (lemongrass). Dominican cuisine is also famous for its use of local game, such
as the *manicou* (a small opossum) and the *agouti* (a large indigenous
rodent), but you'll have to be an intrepid diner to go that route. At the
time of this writing, the government had banned mountain chicken (a
euphemism for a large frog called *crapaud*) because of problems with
disease. Beware of menus that still include it.

WHAT TO WEAR

Most Dominicans dress nicely but practically when eating out—for
dinner it's shirts and trousers for men and modest dresses for women.
During the day, nice shorts are acceptable at most places; beach attire
is frowned upon, unless of course you're eating on the beach.

CARIBBEAN ✗ **Rainforest Restaurant at Papillote.** Savor a lethal rum punch while loung-
$$$$ ing in a hot mineral bath in the Papillote Wilderness Retreat gardens.
Then try the bracing callaloo soup, dasheen puffs, fish "rain forest"
(marinated with papaya and wrapped in banana leaves), or the succulent freshwater prawns. This handsome Caribbean restaurant has

quite possibly one of the best views in the region. Dine at an altitude cool enough to demand a throw blanket and inspire after-dinner conversation. ⊠*Papillote Wilderness Retreat, Trafalgar Falls Rd., Trafalgar* ☎*767/448–2287* ⊕*www.papillote.dm* ⊴*Reservations essential* ⊟*AE, D, MC, V.*

$$$–$$$$ ✕**La Robe Creole.** A cut-stone building only steps away from the Old
★ Market Plaza houses one of Dominica's best restaurants. In a cozy dining room with wood rafters, ladder-back chairs, and colorful madras tablecloths, you can dine on a meal selected from an eclectic à la carte menu. Local favorites are Titiree (fish balls made from a type of fish called titiree), creole-style wings, and crab backs when in season. The downstairs takeout annex, Mouse Hole, is an inexpensive and tasty place to snack when you're on the run. The restaurant makes its own delicious mango chutney and plantain chips, called *Irie Itals,* which you can buy in local shops. ⊠*3 Victoria St., Roseau* ☎*767/448–2896* ⊕*www.larobecreole.com* ⊟*D, MC, V* ⊗*Closed Sun.*

$$$ ✕**Crystal Terrace Restaurant & Bar.** You can find classic local food with a very elegant twist at this restaurant in the Evergreen Hotel. Dine on a large, airy terrace perched right over the sea, or relax at the bar while sipping a tropical cocktail. Dinners are prix fixe, with a choice of appetizer such as crab back, soup, or salad; entrées of chicken, fish, or other meats served with local produce; and a dessert of fresh fruit or homemade cake and ice cream. Breakfast and lunch are also served here, and reservations are advised. ⊠*Evergreen Hotel, Castle Comfort* ☎*767/448–3288* ☎*767/448–6800* ⊕*www.avirtualdominica. com/evergreen.htm* ⊟*AE, MC, V.*

$$–$$$ ✕**Guiyave.** This popular restaurant in a quaint Caribbean town house also has a shop downstairs serving a scrumptious selection of sweet and savory pastries, tarts, and cakes. These can also be ordered upstairs, along with more-elaborate fare such as garlic shrimp and spicy crab backs, when in season. Choose to dine either in the airy dining room or on the sunny, narrow balcony perched above Roseau's colorful streets—the perfect spot to indulge in one of the fresh-squeezed tropical juices. ⊠*15 Cork St., Roseau* ☎*767/448–2930* ⊟*AE, D, MC, V* ⊗*Closed Tues. and Wed.*

$–$$ ✕**Port of Call Restaurant & Bar.** This haunt of middle-aged barristers and laid-back locals is ideally located, just around the corner from the bay front in downtown Roseau. This breezy restaurant with a soothing gray-and-white color scheme occupies a traditional stone building. The layout is such that you can have your privacy and a relaxing meal. Management here is always ready to meet your needs for home-style local cuisine or a selection of à la carte dishes such as a hamburger and fries, or maybe just an exotic cocktail from the bar. ⊠*3 Kennedy Ave., Roseau* ☎*767/448–2910* ⊟*AE, D, MC, V.*

¢–$ ✕**Miranda's Corner.** Just past Springfield on the way to Pont Casse, you'll begin to see hills full of flowers. At a big bend, a sign on a tree reads MIRANDA'S CORNER, referring to a bar, rum shop, and diner all in one. Here Miranda Alfred is at home, serving everyone from Italian tourists to banana farmers. Many of her ingredients are grown in her adjacent garden. The specialties are numerous, including titiree fish (when it's fresh and in season) and tropical juices. All are prepared with a potion of passion and a fistful of flavor. Miranda's is open for breakfast, lunch, and dinner and is an acceptable pit stop if you are in the area; call ahead to make sure it's open. ⊠ *Mount Joy, Springfield* ☎767/449–2509 ☐MC.

¢–$ ✕Pearl's Cuisine. In a creole town house in central Roseau, chef Pearl, with her robust and infectious character, prepares some of the island's best local cuisine. On her menu that changes daily, she offers such local delicacies as *sousse* (pickled pigs' feet), blood pudding, and rotis. When sitting down to lunch or dinner, ask for a table on the open-air gallery that overlooks Roseau, and prepare for an abundant portion, but make sure you leave space for dessert. If you're on the go, enjoy a quick meal from the daily, varied menu in the ground-floor snack bar. You're spoiled for choice when it comes to the fresh fruit juices. ⊠ *50 King George V St., Roseau* ☎767/448–8707 ☐ *AE, D, MC, V* ⊗ *Closed Sun. No dinner.*

ECLECTIC   **✕La Maison.** The newest restaurant on the island is arguably the island's
$$–$$$ best. Chef Vincent Binet, formerly of Habitacion Chabert (now Silks
Fodor'sChoice   Hotel) has created a modern, minimalist venue with white walls, con-
★   temporary art, Frank Lloyd Wright–styled chairs, and dinnerware that look like warped squares—certainly not what one would expect to find in a Dominican restaurant. Impeccable service and special touches like a timer for brewing tea and chive butter add to the ambience. But the real star is the food. Starters like goat, mozzarella, or blue cheese tartlets with apple-and-raisin salad are lip smacking, while a main course like roast saddle of lamb in garlic sauce is so tender it practically melts in your mouth. ⊠ *4 Fort La., Roseau* ☎767/440–5287 ☐ *AE, D, MC, V* ⊗ *Closed Sun. No lunch Sat.*

$$–$$$ **✕Waterfront Restaurant.** At the southern end of Roseau's bay front, this
☾   elegant and romantic restaurant overlooks the Caribbean coastline.
★   You can dine outdoors on the wraparound verandah while listening to the sound of the sea or indoors in the air-conditioned formal dining room. Executive chef Jermaine Mitchell's menu includes spa-vegetarian choices alongside the traditional international and local dishes. Tropical desserts include cheesecake and guava tart. The menu dips into a wide range of cuisines, from creole specialties like callaloo soup to beef, lamb, duck, and even skewered shrimp with a Thai sauce. No matter what your choice, it will be served by a friendly and efficient waitstaff. The bar's happy-hour steel band adds a nice touch. ⊠ *Fort Young Hotel, Victoria St., Roseau* ☎767/448–5000 ⊕ *www.fortyounghotel. com* ☐ *AE, MC, V.*

$$ **✕Bambuz Restaurant.** Decor is simple—a patio surrounded by a stone-and-bamboo wall, a bar, a garden, and the sea. The menu offers every type of tasty fare, including steaks, shrimp, chicken, and tacos. The house wine is not bad and is reasonably priced. Bambuz's only drawback is that the music is a bit loud. It's located next to Aldive & Watersports. ⊠ *Loubiere Rd., Loubiere* ☎776/448–2899 ☐ *AE, MC, V* ⊗ *Closed Mon.*

¢–$ ✕Cornerhouse Café. Just off the Old Market Plaza, in a historic, three-story stone-and-wood town house, this is Dominica's only true Internet café. An eclectic menu of meals and other treats is on offer to sustain you during your surfing: bagels with an assortment of toppings, delicious soups, fish, sandwiches, salads, cakes, and coffee. Computers are rented by the half hour; relax on soft chairs and flip through books and magazines while you wait. ⊠ *Old and King George V Sts., Roseau* ☎ *767/449–9000* ⊕ *www.avirtualdominica.com/cornerhouse* ⊟ *No credit cards* ⊘ *Closed Sun.*

FRENCH **✕ Cocorico.** It's hard to miss the umbrella-covered chairs and tables at
$–$$ this Parisian-style café on a prominent bay-front corner in Roseau. Breakfast crepes, croissants, baguette sandwiches, and piping-hot café au lait are available beginning at 8:30 AM. Throughout the day you can relax indoors or out and enjoy any of the extensive menu's selections with the perfect glass of wine, and you can even surf the Internet on their computers. In the cellar downstairs, the Cocorico wine store has a reasonably priced selection from more than eight countries. You can also choose from a wide assortment of pâtés and cheeses, crepes, sausages, cigars, French bread, and chocolates. ⊠ *Bay Front at Kennedy Ave., Roseau* ☎ *767/449–8686* ⊟ *MC, V* ⊘ *Closed Sun. No dinner.*

IRISH **✕ O'Byrnes Pub & Grub.** You don't expect to find real Guinness and
¢–$$ shamrocks in Dominica, but this Irish-style pub has both, along with burgers, quesadillas, wings, pizza, and beer. TVs hang from the ceiling of the stone-wall establishment so you can watch all the current sporting events. ⊠ *Castle St., Roseau* ☎ *767/440–4337* ⊟ *MC, V* ⊘ *Closed Sun. and Mon.*

BEACHES

As a volcanic island, Dominica offers many powder-fine black-sand beaches. Found mostly in the north and east, they are windswept, dramatic, and uncrowded, lending themselves more to relaxing than swimming because many have undercurrents. However, slightly farther north there are beautiful secluded white- or brown-sand beaches and coves. Although northeast-coast beaches offer excellent shallow swimming, their wind-tossed beauty can be dangerous; there are sometimes strong currents with the whipped-cream waves. From these beaches you can see the islands of Marie-Galante and Les Saintes and parts of Guadeloupe. On the southwest coast, beaches are fewer and mostly made of black sand and rounded volcanic rocks. Swimming off these rocky shores has its pleasures, too: the water is usually as flat as a lake, deep and blue, and is especially good for snorkeling. In general, the west coast is more for scuba diving and snorkeling than for beach-going.

★ **Champagne.** On the west coast, just south of the village of Pointe Michel, this stony beach is hailed as one of the best spots for swimming, snorkeling, and diving but not for sunning. It gets its name from volcanic vents that constantly puff steam into the sea, which makes you feel as if you are swimming in warm champagne. A new boardwalk leads to the beach from Soufrière/Scotts Head Marine Reserve. ⊠ *1 mi (1.5 km) south of Pointe Michel.*

9

Hampstead Beach. This isolated shoreline on the northeast coast is one of the few really golden-sand beaches on the island. It actually encompasses three bays, of which Batibou Bay is sheltered and calm. Come here to relax, suntan, and swim. You need a 4x4 to get here, but it's worth the long drive and effort. There are no facilities. ⊠ *Off Indian Rd., west of Calibishie.*

L'Anse Tortue. This isolated, golden-sand beach on the northeast coast, which is also known as Turtle Bay, is a favorite for the somewhat adventurous who want to swim and tan and avoid other people without having to drive all the way out to Hampstead Beach. It sits on a cove just past Woodford Hill, and some days the odd surfer finds just the right wave. It's an easy walk down to it from the road. ⊠ *East of Calibishie.*

Mero Beach. The silver-gray stretch of beach is on the west coast, just outside the village of Mero, where the entire community comes to party on Sunday. It's good for sunbathing and swimming. ⊠ *Mero.*

★ **Pointe Baptiste.** Extravagantly shaped, red-sandstone boulders surround this beautiful golden-sand beach. Access is a 15-minute walk, entering through private property, so the beach is quiet and unpopulated. Come here to relax, tan, take dips in the ocean, and climb these incredible rock formations. There are no facilities, but this is one of the nicest beaches on the island. It's near the Pointe Baptiste Guest House. ⊠ *Calibishie.*

Scotts Head. At the southernmost tip of the island, a small landmass is connected to the mainland by a narrow stretch of stony beach separating the Atlantic and the Caribbean. It's a fantastic spot for snorkeling, and you can have lunch at one of the village restaurants. ⊠ *Scotts Head Village.*

SPORTS & THE OUTDOORS

ADVENTURE PARKS

The **Rainforest Aerial Tram** (⊠ *Laudat* ☎ *767/448–8775, 767/440–3266, 866/759–8726 in U.S.* ⊕ *www.rfat.com*) gives you a bird's-eye view of a pristine forest aboard an open, eight-person gondola. For 90 minutes to two hours, you slowly skim the tree-top canopy while a guide provides scientific information about the flora and fauna. At the top, there is an optional walking tour, which is worth the steps. The price is $74. Transportation and lunch are extra. This is a popular attraction for cruise-ship passengers, so try to reserve ahead.

Wacky Rollers (⊠ *Front St., Roseau* ⌂ *Box 900, Roseau* ☎ *767/440– 4386* ⊕ *www.wackyrollers.com*) will make you feel as if you are training for the Marines as you swing on a Tarzan-style rope and grab onto a vertical rope ladder, rappel across zip lines and traverse suspended log bridges, a net bridge, and four monkey bridges (rope loops). It costs $65 for the adult course and should take from 1½ to 3½ hours to conquer the 28 "games." There is also an abbreviated kids' course for $35. Wacky Rollers also organizes adventure tours around the island.

Although the office is in Roseau, the park itself is in Hillsborough Estate, about 20 to 25 minutes north of Roseau.

CYCLING

Cyclists find Dominica's rugged terrain to be an exhilarating challenge, and there are routes suitable for all levels of bikers. **Nature Island Dive** (⊠ *Soufrière* ☎ *767/449–8181* ⊕ *www.natureislanddive.com*) has a fleet of bikes in good condition. You can rent a mountain bike for $25, but if you prefer a knowledgeable guide to lead you through specific areas, the cost ranges up to $65.

DIVING & SNORKELING

Fodor'sChoice
★

Dominica has been voted one of the top 10 dive destinations in the world by *Skin Diver* and *Rodale's Scuba Diving* magazines—and has won many other awards for its underwater sites. They are truly memorable. There are numerous highlights all along the west coast of the island, but the best are those in the southwest—within and around **Soufrière/Scotts Head Marine Reserve.** This bay is the site of a submerged volcanic crater; the Dominica Watersports Association has worked along with the Fisheries Division for years to establish this reserve and has set stringent regulations to prevent the degradation of the ecosystem. Within 0.5 mile (0.75 km) of the shore, there are vertical drops from 800 feet to more than 1,500 feet, with visibility frequently extending to 100 feet. Shoals of boga fish, creole wrasse, and blue cromis are common, and you might even see a spotted moray eel or a honeycomb cowfish. Crinoids (rare elsewhere) are also abundant here, as are giant barrel sponges. There is a $2 fee per person to dive, snorkel, or kayak in the reserve. Other noteworthy dive sites outside this reserve are **Salisbury Falls, Nose Reef, Brain Coral Garden,** and—even farther north— **Cabrits Drop-Off** and **Toucari Reef.** The conditions for underwater photography, particularly macrophotography, are unparalleled. The rates are about $50 for a single tank dive and about $65–$85 for a two-tank dive or from about $95 for a resort course with one open-water dive. All scuba-diving operators also offer snorkeling; equipment rents for $10 to $25 a day; trips with gear range from $15 to $35.

The **Anchorage Dive & Whale Watch Center** (⊠ *Anchorage Hotel, Castle Comfort* ☎ *767/448–2638* ⊕ *www.anchoragehotel.dm*) has two dive boats that can take you out day or night. It also offers PADI instruction (all skill levels), snorkeling and whale-watching trips, and shore diving. One of the island's first dive operations, it has many of the same trips as Dive Dominica.
Cabrits Dive Center (⊠ *Portsmouth* ☎ *767/445–3010, 347/329–4256 from U.S.* ⊕ *www.cabritsdive.com*) is the only PADI five-star dive center in Dominica. Nitrox courses are also available for $250. Since Cabrits is the sole operator on the northwest coast, its dive boats have the pristine reefs almost to themselves, unlike other operations, whose underwater territories may overlap.

Dive Dominica (✉ *Castle Comfort Lodge, Castle Comfort* ☎*954/453–5042 or 888/414–7626* ⊕*www.divedominica.com*), one of the island's dive pioneers, conducts NAUI, PADI, and SSI courses as well as Nitrox certification. With four boats, it offers diving, snorkeling, and whale-watching trips and packages including accommodation at the Castle Comfort Lodge. Its trips are similar to Anchorage's.

Fort Young Dive Centre (✉*Fort Young Hotel, Victoria St., Roseau* ☎*767/448–5000 Ext. 333*) conducts snorkeling, diving, and whale-watching trips departing from the hotel's own dock.

IrieSafari (✉*Soufrière/ScottsHeadMarineReserve, Soufrière* ☎*767/275–7001 or 767/440–7001*) takes snorkelers to Champagne and the nearby tall grasses where turtles like to hang out.

Nature Island Dive (✉*Soufrière* ☎*767/449–8181* ⊕*www.natureisland dive.com*) is run by an enthusiastic crew. Some of the island's best dive sites are right outside its door, and it offers diving, snorkeling, kayaking, and mountain biking as well as resort and full PADI courses.

FISHING

Contact the **Anchorage Hotel** (✉*Castle Comfort* ☎*767/448–2638*) for information about fishing excursions. Fees are $500 for a half-day trip and $800 for a full day.

HIKING

★ Dominica's majestic mountains, clear rivers, and lush vegetation conspire to create adventurous hiking trails. The island is crisscrossed by ancient footpaths of the Arawak and Carib Indians and the Nègres Maroons, escaped slaves who established camps in the mountains. Existing trails range from easygoing to arduous. To make the most of your excursion, you'll need sturdy hiking boots, insect repellent, a change of clothes (kept dry), and a guide. Hikes and tours run $25 to $50 per person, depending on destinations and duration. Some of the natural attractions within the island's national parks require visitors to purchase a site pass. These are sold for varying numbers of visits. A single-entry site pass costs $2, a day pass $5, and a week pass $10.

Local bird and forestry expert **Bertrand Jno Baptiste** (☎*767/446–6358*) leads hikes up Morne Diablotin and along the Syndicate Nature Trail; if he's not available, ask him to recommend another guide.

Hiking guides can be arranged through the **Discover Dominica Authority** (✉*Valley Rd., Roseau* ☎*767/448–2045* ⊕*www.discoverdominica. com*).

The **Forestry Division** (✉*Dominica Botanical Gardens, between Bath Rd. and Valley Rd., Roseau* ☎*767/266–3817*) is responsible for the management of forests and wildlife and has numerous publications on Dominica as well as a wealth of information on reputable guides.

KAYAKING

Dominica has a couple of kayak outfitters that give tours and rent equipment, with rates of about $35 to $70 for guided excursions, and half-day rentals for about $55.

Nature Island Dive (⊠ *Soufrière* ☏ *767/449–8181* ⊕ *www.nature islanddive.com*) gives tours around the Soufrière/Scotts Head Marine Reserve.

Wacky Rollers (⊠ *Front St., Roseau* ☏ *767/440–4386* ⊕ *www.wacky rollers.com*) offers kayaking trips around island waters.

WHALE-WATCHING

Fodor's Choice
★ Dominica records the highest species counts of resident cetaceans in the southern Caribbean region, so it's not surprising that tour companies claim 90% sighting success for their excursions. Humpback whales, false killer whales, minke, and orcas are all occasionally seen, as are several species of dolphin. But the resident sperm whales (they calve in Dominica's 3,000-feet-deep waters) are truly the stars of the show. During your 3½-hour expedition, which costs about $50, you may be asked to assist in recording sightings, data that can be shared with local and international organizations. Although there are resident whales and dolphins and therefore year-round sightings, there are more species to be observed from November through February. Turtle-watching trips are also popular.

The **Anchorage Dive & Whale Watch Center** (⊠ *Anchorage Hotel, Castle Comfort* ☏ *767/448–2638* ⊕ *www.anchoragehotel.dm*) offers whale-watching trips.

Dive Dominica (⊠ *Castle Comfort Lodge, Castle Comfort* ☏ *767/448–2188* ⊕ *www.divedominica.com*) is a major whale-watching operator.

9

SHOPPING

Dominicans produce distinctive handicrafts, with various communities specializing in their specific products. The crafts of the Carib Indians include traditional baskets made of dyed *larouma* reeds and waterproofed with tightly woven *balizier* leaves. These are sold in the Carib Indian Territory and Kalinago Barana Autê as well as in Roseau's shops. Vertivert straw rugs, screw-pine tableware, *fwije* (the trunk of the forest tree fern), and wood carvings are just some examples. Also notable are local herbs, spices, condiments, and herb teas. Café Dominique, the local equivalent of Jamaican Blue Mountain coffee, is an excellent buy, as are the Dominican rums Macoucherie and Soca. Proof that the old ways live on in Dominica can be found in the number of herbal remedies available. One stimulating memento of your visit is rum steeped with *bois bandé* (scientific name *Richeria grandis*), a tree whose bark is reputed to have aphrodisiacal properties. It's sold at shops, vendors' stalls, and supermarkets. The charismatic roadside vendors can be found all over the island bearing trays laden with local and imported souvenirs, T-shirts, and trinkets. Duty-free shopping is also available in specific stores around Roseau.

Dominican farmers island-wide bring their best crops to the Roseau Market, at the end of Dame Eugenia Boulevard and Lainge Lane, every Saturday from 6 AM to 1 PM. It may well be the largest farmers' market in the Caribbean. They start setting up on Friday nights, and often customers begin their shopping then. Vendors are usually out on roadsides when there are cruise ships in port.

MAJOR SHOPPING AREAS

One of the easiest places to pick up a souvenir is the Old Market Plaza, just behind the Dominica Museum, in Roseau. Slaves were once sold here, but today handcrafted jewelry, T-shirts, spices, souvenirs, batik, and lacquered and woven bamboo boxes and trays are available from a group of vendors in open-air booths set up on the cobblestones. These are usually busiest when there's a cruise ship berthed across the street. On these days you can also find a vast number of vendors along the bay front.

SPECIALTY STORES

ART

Most artists work from their home studios, and it often takes the right contact to find them. You can usually see the work of the island's artists at the Old Mill Cultural Center *(⇨ Nightlife & the Arts, below)*. The tree-house studio and café at **Indigo** (⊠ *Bournes* ☎767/445–3486) sells works by in-house artists Clem and Marie Frederick and also serves fresh sugarcane juice or bush teas.

CLOTHING

There's such a wide selection when it comes to clothing stores in Roseau that it really is best to walk around and explore for yourself. However, for classic Caribbean and international designer clothing, there are several reliable boutiques to try. **Ego Boutique** (⊠ *9 Hillsborough St., Roseau* ☎767/448–2336) carries an extensive selection of designer clothing and exquisite crafts and home accessories from around the world.

GIFTS & SOUVENIRS

As cruise-ship visits have increased in frequency, duty-free shops are cropping up, including some name-brand stores, mostly within Roseau's bay front.

Baroon International (⊠ *Kennedy Ave. at Old St., Roseau* ☎767/449–2888) sells unusual jewelry from Asia, the United States, and other Caribbean islands; there are also pieces that are assembled in the store, as well as personal accessories, souvenirs, and special gifts.

Jeweller's International (⊠ *Fort Young Hotel, Victoria St., Roseau* ☎767/440–3319) carries perfumes; crystals; gold-and-silver jewelry alone or with emeralds, diamonds, and other gems; liquor; and other gift items.

For quality leather goods and other personal accessories, try **Land** (⊠*Bay Front, Roseau* ☎767/448–3394) at the Duty-Free Emporium next to the Royal Bank.

In the same Duty Free Emporium, **Smoke & Booze** (⊠*Bay Front, Roseau* ☎767/440–0789) offers a large selection of duty-free cigarettes, cigars, and alcohol.

Whitchurch Duty-Free (⊠*Fort Young Hotel, Victoria St., Roseau* ☎767/448–7177 or 767/448–2181) offers a large assortment of items, including perfumes, leather goods, and designer sunglasses.

HANDICRAFTS

Dominica Pottery (⊠*Bay Front at Kennedy Ave., Roseau* ☎*No phone*) carries products made from various local clays and glazes.

Try**My Tings** (⊠*Cross La. at King George V St., Roseau* ☎776/448–2012 or 776/449–9703) for souvenirs, camera supplies, and phone cards.

Papillote Wilderness Retreat (⊠*Trafalgar* ☎767/448–2287) has an intimate gift shop with local handcrafted goods and particularly outstanding wood carvings by Louis Desire.

For Caribbean arts, crafts, and paintings, visit **Silverline Caribbean Inspiration** (⊠*4 Long La., Roseau* ☎776/440–4171).

Tropicrafts (⊠*Independence St. at Turkey La., Roseau* ☎767/448–2747) has a back room where you can watch local ladies weave grass mats. You can also find arts and crafts from around the Caribbean, local wood carvings, rum, hot sauces, perfumes, and traditional Carib baskets, hats, and woven mats.

NIGHTLIFE & THE ARTS

9

The friendly, intimate atmosphere and colorful patrons at the numerous bars and hangouts will keep you entertained for hours. If you're looking for jazz, calypso, reggae, steel-band, soca (a variation of calypso), cadence-zouk, or jing ping—a type of folk music featuring the accordion, the *quage* (a kind of washboard instrument), drums, and a "boom boom" (a percussion instrument)—you're guaranteed to find it. Wednesday through Saturday nights are really lively, and during Carnival, Independence, and summer celebrations, things can be intense. Indeed, Dominica's Carnival, the pre-Lenten festival, is the most spontaneous in the Caribbean. Other big cultural events include Emancipation celebrations hosted by the National Cultural Council each August.

Fodor's Choice ★ The annual **World Creole Music Festival** (⊕*www.dominica.dm/festivals*) in late October or early November also packs in the action, with three days and nights of pulsating rhythm and music. Creole music enthusiasts come from all over the world to listen to the likes of Kassav, Aswad, and Tabou Combo. Throughout the year, however, most larger hotels have some form of live evening entertainment.

The Original Caribbeans

The Caribbean Sea got its name from the aboriginal inhabitants of the Lesser Antilles known as the Caribs, whose territory ranged as far as the Amazon and the Venezuelan-Columbian Andes. The Island Caribs were a warlike, maritime people who carried out raids on neighboring islands in expertly carved large canoes, thus gradually displacing other inhabitants—such as the Arawaks—from the region.

Linguistically, the name Carib is traced to the Arawak word for "cannibal." However, much of the anthropological data collected by European missionaries regarding actual cannibalism is believed to have been greatly exaggerated, distorting the Caribs' practices. (For that reason, the sequel to *Pirates of the Caribbean*, which was filmed in Dominica, was locally somewhat controversial.) What can't be contested is that the Caribs forcefully resisted European colonization but then dramatically lost power over the Lesser Antilles after two major massacres in the 17th century. One of these incidents occurred in Dominica, where one Carib village is still called Massacre.

By the end of the 18th century, the Caribs, including those from other islands, had mostly retreated into the rugged mountains of northeastern Dominica. Island historian Lennox Honychurch observed: "It is a sad irony that this tribe of seafarers, after whom the waters of the Caribbean have been named, should end up in a corner of the island where access to the sea is almost impossible."

Today, roughly 3,000 Carib descendants live in what is known as the Carib Territory. This area, however, is visually indistinguishable from any other poor, rural community in Dominica. Echoes of their past civilization still glimmer in their baskets made of larouma reed and canoes hollowed out of a single gommier tree.

NIGHTLIFE

Once Friday afternoon rolls around you can sense the mood change. Local bars crank up the music, and each village and community has its own particular nightly entertainment. If by this point in your trip you have made friends with some locals, they will be only too happy to take you to the current hot spot.

Every Friday night from 6 to 8 **Balas Bar & Lounge** (⊠ *Fort Young Hotel, Victoria St., Roseau* ☎ *767/448–5000*) has a very happening rum punch happy hour with a live band and drink specials.

At **Cellars Bar** (⊠ *Sutton Place Hotel, Old St., Roseau* ☎ *767/449–8700*), Wednesday night is Amateur Bartenders Soca Rum Night. Volunteer to be the bartender; taste tests of the featured cocktails are free. Friday is Kubuli Karaoke Night, with patrons competing for prize drinks; it's a real blast and perfect way to totally kick back. Poetry night is Wednesday, and the house trio plays on Friday. It's also open for lunch on Friday.

Symes Zee's (⊠ *34 King George V St., Roseau* ☎ *767/448–2494*) draws a crowd on Thursday night from 10 until the wee hours of the morning, when there's a jazz/blues/reggae band. There's no cover, and the food, drinks, and cigars are reasonably priced.

Warehouse (⊠ *Canefield* ☎ *767/449–1303*), outside Roseau just past the airport, is *the* place to dance on Saturday night. DJs are brought in from other islands to ensure there's variety to all the vibrations. The entrance fee is $5.

THE ARTS

Arawak House of Culture (⊠ *Kennedy Ave. near Government Headquarters, Roseau* ☎ *767/449–1804*), managed by Harry Sealy at the Cultural Division, is Dominica's main performing-arts theater. A number of productions are staged here throughout the year, including plays, recitals, and dance performances.

The **Old Mill Cultural Center** (⊠ *Canefield* ☎ *767/449–1804*) is one of Dominica's historic landmarks. The Old Mill was the island's first sugarcane processing mill and rum distillery. Today, it's a place to learn about Dominica's traditions. Performances and events—including art exhibits—take place here throughout the year.

EXPLORING DOMINICA

Despite the small size of this almond-shape island, it can take a couple of hours to travel between the popular destinations. Many sights are isolated and difficult to find; you may be better off taking an organized excursion. If you do go it alone, drive carefully: roads can be narrow and winding. Plan on eight hours to see the highlights; to fully experience the island, set aside a couple of days and work in some hikes.

WHAT TO SEE

☺ **Cabrits National Park.** Along with Brimstone Hill in St. Kitts, Shirley Heights in Antigua, and Ft. Charlotte in St. Vincent, the Cabrits National Park's Ft. Shirley ruins are among the most significant historic sites in the Caribbean. Just north of the town of Portsmouth, this 1,300-acre park includes a marine park and herbaceous swamps, which are an important environment for several species of rare birds and plants. At the heart of the park is the Ft. Shirley military complex. Built by the British between 1770 and 1815, it once comprised 50 major structures, including storehouses that were also quarters for 700 men. With the help of the Royal Navy (which sends sailors ashore to work on the site each time a ship is in port) and local volunteers, historian Dr. Lennox Honychurch restored the fort and its surroundings, incorporating a small museum that highlights the natural and historic aspects of the park and an open canteen-style restaurant. ⊠ *Portsmouth* ☎ *No phone* 🎫 *$2* 🕐 *Museum daily 8–4.*

☺ **Carib Indian Territory.** In 1903, after centuries of conflict, the Caribbean's
★ first settlers, the Kalinago (more popularly known as the Caribs), were granted a portion of land (approximately 3,700 acres) on the island's northeast coast, on which to establish a reservation with their own chief. Today it's known as Carib Territory, clinging to the northeasterly

9

corner of Dominica, where a group of slightly more than 3,000 Caribs, who resemble native South Americans, live like most other people in rural Caribbean communities. Many are farmers and fishermen; others are entrepreneurs who have opened restaurants, guesthouses, and little shops where you can buy exquisite Carib baskets and other handcrafted items. The craftspeople retain knowledge of basket weaving, wood carving, and canoe building, which has been passed down from one generation to the next.

The Caribs' long, elegant canoes are created from the trunk of a single *gommier* tree. If you're lucky, you may catch canoe builders at work. The reservation's Catholic church in Salybia has a canoe as its unique altar, which was designed by Dr. Lennox Honychurch, a local historian, author, and artist. **L'Escalier Tête Chien** (literally "Snake's Staircase," it's the name of a snake whose head resembles that of a dog) is a hardened lava formation that runs down into the Atlantic. The ocean here is particularly fierce, and the shore is full of countless coves and inlets. According to Carib legend, at night the nearby Londonderry Islets metamorphose into grand canoes to take the spirits of the dead out to sea.

Kalinago Barana Autê (☎767/445–7979 ⊕*www.kalinagobaranaaute. com/about_us*) is Carib Territory's newest addition and the place to learn about Carib customs, history, and culture. A guided, 45-minute tour explores the *village*, stopping along the way to learn about plants, dugout canoes, basket weaving, and *kasava* bread making. The path offers wonderful viewpoints of the Atlantic and a chance to witness Isukati Falls. There are several site packages, but the basic one—which includes admission, tour, and a drink—is about $15.50. It's open daily 9–9.

Ꮯ **Emerald Pool.** Quite possibly the most-visited nature attraction on the island, this emerald-green pool fed by a 50-foot waterfall is an easy trip to make. To reach this spot in the vast Morne Trois Pitons National Park, you follow a trail that starts at the side of the road near the reception center (it's an easy 20-minute walk). Along the way you can pass lookout points with views of the windward (Atlantic) coast and the forested interior. If you don't want a crowd, check whether there are cruise ships in port before going out, as this spot is popular with cruise-ship tour groups.

Ꮯ **Indian River.** The mouth of the Indian River, which flows into the ocean in Portsmouth, was once a Carib Indian settlement. A gentle rowboat ride for wildlife spotting along this river lined with *terra carpus officinalis* trees, whose buttress roots spread up to 20 feet, is not only a relaxing treat but educational and usually entertaining. To arrange such a trip, stop by the visitor center in Portsmouth and ask for one of the "Indian River boys." These young, knowledgeable men are members of the Portsmouth Indian River Tour Guides Association (PIRTGA) and have for years protected and promoted one of Dominica's special areas. Most boat trips take you up as far as Rahjah's Jungle Bar. You can usually do an optional guided walking tour of the swamplands and the remnants of one of Dominica's oldest plantations. Tours last one to three hours, for roughly $10 per person, but the actual price depends on your guide.

Morne Aux Diables. In the far north of Dominica, this peak soars 2,826 feet above sea level and slopes down to Toucari and Douglas bays and long stretches of dark-sand beach. To reach the mountain, take the road along the Caribbean coast. It twists by coconut, cocoa, and banana groves, past fern-festooned embankments, over rivers, and into villages where brightly painted shanties are almost as colorful as all the flora and fauna.

☼ **Morne Diablotin National Park.** The park is named after one of the region's highest mountains, Morne Diablotin—at 4,747 feet, Dominica's highest peak. The peak takes its name, in turn, from a bird, known in English as the black-capped petrel that was prized by hunters in the 18th century. Though the mountain's namesake bird is now extinct on the island, Dominica is still a major birding destination. Of the island's many exotic—and endangered—species, the green-and-purple Sisserou parrot (*Amazona imperialis*) and the Jaco, or red-neck, parrot (*Amazona arausiaca*) are found here in greater numbers than anywhere else in Dominica. Before the national park was established, the Syndicate Nature Trail was protected with the help of some 6,000 schoolchildren, each of whom donated 25¢ to protect the habitat of the flying pride of Dominica, as well as countless other species of birds and other wildlife. The west-coast road (at the bend near Dublanc) runs through three types of forest and leads into the park. The trail offers a casual walk; just bring a sweater and binoculars. The five- to eight-hour hike up Morne Diablotin isn't for everyone. You need a guide, sturdy hiking shoes, warm clothing, and a backpack with refreshments and a change of clothes (including socks) that are wrapped in plastic to keep them dry.

A good guide for Morne Diablotin is local ornithology expert **Bertrand Jno Baptiste** (☎ 767/446–6358).

9

Morne Trois Pitons National Park. A UNESCO World Heritage Site, this 17,000-acre swath of lush, mountainous land in the south-central interior (covering 9% of Dominica) is the island's crown jewel. Named after one of the highest (4,600 feet) mountains on the island, it contains the island's famous "boiling lake," majestic waterfalls, and cool mountain lakes. There are four types of vegetation zones here. Ferns grow 30 feet tall, wild orchids sprout from trees, sunlight leaks through green canopies, and a gentle mist rises over the jungle floor. A system of trails has been developed in the park, and the Division of Forestry and Wildlife works hard to maintain them—with no help from the excessive rainfall and the profusion of vegetation that seems to grow right before your eyes. Access to the park is possible from most points of the compass, though the easiest approaches are via the small mountaintop villages of Laudat (pronounced low-*dah*) and Cochrane.

Fodor'sChoice ★ About 5 mi (8 km) out of Roseau, the Wotten Waven Road branches off toward Sulphur Springs, where you can see the belching, sputtering, and gurgling releases of volcanic hot springs. At the base of Morne Micotrin you can find two crater lakes: the first, at 2,500 feet above sea level, is

Freshwater Lake. According to a local legend, it's haunted by a vindictive mermaid and a monstrous serpent. Farther on is **Boeri Lake,** fringed with greenery and with purple hyacinths floating on its surface.

The undisputed highlight of the park is **Boiling Lake.** Reputedly the world's largest such lake, it's a cauldron of gurgling gray-blue water, 70 yards wide and of unknown depth, with water temperatures from 180°F to 197°F. Although generally believed to be a volcanic crater, the lake is actually a flooded fumarole—a crack through which gases escape from the molten lava below. As many visitors discovered in late 2004, the "lake" can sometimes dry up, though it fills again within a few months and, shortly after that, once more starts to boil. The two- to four-hour (one way) hike up to the lake is challenging (on a very rainy day, be prepared to slip and slide the whole way up and back). You'll need attire appropriate for a strenuous hike, and a guide is a must. Most guided trips start early (no later than 8:30 AM) for this all-day, 7-mi (11-km) round-trip trek.

On your way to Boiling Lake you pass through the **Valley of Desolation,** a sight that definitely lives up to its name. Harsh sulfuric fumes have destroyed virtually all the vegetation in what must once have been a lush forested area. Small hot and cold streams with water of various colors—black, purple, red, orange—web the valley. Stay on the trail to avoid breaking through the crust that covers the hot lava. During this hike you'll pass rivers where you can refresh yourself with a dip (a particular treat is a soak in a hot-water stream on the way back). At the beginning of the Valley of Desolation trail is the **TiTou Gorge,** where you can swim in the pool or relax in the hot-water springs along one side. If you're a strong swimmer, you can head up the gorge to a cave (it's about a five-minute swim) that has a magnificent waterfall; a crack in the cave about 50 feet above permits a stream of sunlight to penetrate the cavern.

Also in the national park are some of the island's most spectacular waterfalls. The 45-minute hike to **Sari Sari Falls,** accessible through the east-coast village of La Plaine, can be hair-raising. But the sight of water cascading some 150 feet into a large pool is awesome. So large are these falls that you feel the spray from hundreds of yards away. Just beyond the village of Trafalgar and up a short hill, is the reception facility, where you can purchase passes to the national park and find guides to take you on a rain-forest trek to the twin **Trafalgar Falls;** the 125-foot high waterfall is called the Father, and the wider, 95-foot high one, the Mother. If you like a little challenge, let your guide take you up the riverbed to the cool pools at the base of the falls (check whether there's a cruise ship in port before setting out; this sight is popular with the tour operators). You need a guide for the arduous 75-minute hike to **Middleham Falls.** It's best if you start at Laudat (the turnoff for the trailhead is just before the village); the trip is much longer from Cochrane Village. The trail takes you to another spectacular waterfall, where water cascades 100 feet over boulders and vegetation and then into an ice-cold pool (a swim here is absolutely exhilarating). Guides for these hikes are available at the trailheads; still, it's best to arrange a tour before even setting out.

Northeast Coast. Steep cliffs, dramatic reefs, and rivers that swirl down through forests of mangroves and fields of coconut define this section of Dominica. The road along the Atlantic, with its red cliffs, whipped-cream waves, and windswept trees, crosses the Hatton Garden River before entering the village of Marigot. In the northeastern region there are numerous estates—old family holdings planted with fruit trees. Beyond Marigot and the Melville Hall Airport is the beautiful Londonderry Estate. The beach here is inspiring, with driftwood strewn about its velvety black sands, which part halfway—where the Londonderry River spills into the Atlantic (swimming isn't advised because of strong currents, but a river bath here is a memorable treat). Farther along the coast, beyond the village of Wesley (which has a gas station and a shop that sells wonderful bread) and past Eden Estate, there are still more beautiful beaches and coves. The swimming is excellent at Woodford Hill Bay, Hodges Beach, Hampstead Estate, Batibou Bay, and L'Anse Tortue. A stop in the charming community of Calibishie is a must; here you'll find bars and restaurants right on the beach, as well as laid-back villas and guesthouses. At Bense, a village in the interior just past Calibishie, you can take a connector road to Chaud Dwe (pronounced show-*dweh*), a beautiful swimming spot in a valley; the only crowd you're likely to encounter is a group of young villagers frolicking in the 15-foot-deep pool and diving off the 25-foot-high rocks.

Portsmouth. In 1782 Portsmouth was the site of the Battle of Les Saintes, a naval engagement between the French and the English. The English won the battle but lost the much-tougher fight against malaria-carrying mosquitoes that bred in the nearby swamps. Once intended to be the capital of Dominica, thanks to its superb harbor on Prince Rupert Bay, it saw as many as 400 ships in port at one time in its heyday, but on account of those swamps, Roseau, not Portsmouth, is the capital today. Maritime traditions are continued here by the yachting set, and a 2-mi (3-km) stretch of sandy beach fringed with coconut trees runs to the Picard Estate area.

Roseau. Although it's one of the smallest capitals in the Caribbean, Roseau has the highest concentration of inhabitants of any town in the eastern Caribbean. Caribbean vernacular architecture and a bustling marketplace transport visitors back in time. Although you can walk the entire town in about an hour, you'll get a much better feel for the place on a leisurely stroll.

For some years now, the Society for Historical Architectural Preservation and Enhancement (SHAPE) has organized programs and projects to preserve the city's architectural heritage. Several interesting buildings have already been restored. **Lilac House,** on Kennedy Avenue, has three types of gingerbread fretwork, latticed verandah railings, and heavy hurricane shutters. The **J. W. Edwards Building,** at the corner of Old and King George V streets, has a stone base and a wooden second-floor gallery. The **Old Market Plaza** is the center of Roseau's historic district, which was laid out by the French on a radial plan rather than a grid, so streets such as Hanover, King George V, and Old radiate from this area. South of the marketplace is the Fort Young Hotel, built as a British fort in the 18th century; the nearby state house, public library, and Anglican cathedral are also worth a visit. New developments at the bay front on Dame M. E. Charles Boulevard have brightened up the waterfront.

The 40-acre **Botanical Gardens,** founded in 1891 as an annex of London's Kew Gardens, is a great place to relax, stroll, or watch a cricket match. In addition to the extensive collection of tropical plants and trees, there's also a parrot aviary. At the Forestry Division office, which is also on the garden grounds, you can find numerous publications on the island's flora, fauna, and national parks. The forestry officers are particularly knowledgeable on these subjects and can also recommend good hiking guides. ⊠ *Between Bath Rd. and Valley Rd.* ☎ *767/448–2401 Ext. 3417* ⊕ *www.da-academy.org/dagardens.html* ⊠ *Free* ⊙ *Mon. 8–1 and 2–5, Tues.–Fri. 8–1 and 2–4.*

The old post office now houses the **Dominica Museum.** This labor of love by local writer and historian Dr. Lennox Honychurch contains furnishings, documents, prints, and maps that date back hundreds of years; you can also find an entire Carib hut as well as Carib canoes, baskets, and other artifacts. ⊠ *Dame M. E. Charles Blvd., opposite cruise-ship berth* ☎ *767/448–8923* ⊠ *$3* ⊙ *Weekdays 9–4:30 and Sat. 9–1; closed Sun except when a cruise ship is in port.*

Soufrière. Tourism is quietly mingling with the laid-back lifestyle of the residents of this gently sunbaked village in the southwest, near one of the island's two marine reserves. Although it was first settled by French lumbermen in the 17th century, it's mainly fishermen you'll find here today. In the village you can find a historic 18th-century Catholic church built of volcanic stone, one of the island's prettiest churches; the ruins of the L. Rose Lime Oil factory; Sulphur Springs, with its hot mineral baths to the east; and the best diving and snorkeling on the island within the **Soufrière/Scotts Head Marine Reserve.** To the west you'll find Bois Cotlette (a historic plantation house) and to the south the Scotts Head Peninsula—at the island's southern tip—which separates the Caribbean from the Atlantic. So if there isn't enough treasure here to satisfy you, there's always the rain forest waiting to be challenged.

DOMINICA ESSENTIALS

To research prices, get advice from other travelers, and book travel arrangements, visit www.fodors.com.

■ TRANSPORTATION

BY AIR

There are no nonstop flights from the United States, but you can connect through San Juan Antigua, Barbados, Martinique, St. Lucia, Trinidad, and Guyana.

Airline Information Air Caraïbes (☎767/448–2181). **American/American Eagle** (☎767/448–0628 or 800/433–7300). **LIAT** (☎767/440–2452, 767/445–7242 for baggage inquiries ⊕www.liatairline.com). **Whitchurch Travel** (☎767/448–2181).

Airport Information Canefield Airport (DCF ☎767/449–2045). **Melville Hall Airport** (DOM ☎767/445–7242).

BY BOAT & FERRY

Express des Isles has regularly scheduled interisland jet catamaran ferry service connecting Dominica to Guadeloupe, Martinique, and St. Lucia; during peak seasons additional arrivals and departures are added. Generally, though, the ferry arrives and departs at the Roseau Ferry Terminal on Monday, Wednesday, Friday, Saturday, and Sunday from Guadeloupe; it continues south to Martinique, as well as St. Lucia, on specific days. The round-trip crossing costs €71 to Martinique, takes approximately 90 minutes, and offers superb views of the other islands.

Information Express des Isles (☎767/448–2181 ⊕www.express-des-iles.com).

BY CAR

Unless you are staying in Roseau or arranging to do extensive guided tours, a car may be a necessity, since cabs can be very expensive. Daily car-rental rates begin at about $40 per day, though you can often pay more if you rent a car for only a day or two (weekly and long-term rates can be negotiated). A refundable $500 to $1,500 deposit is required at the time of pickup. Expect to add approximately $7 to $17 a day for optional collision-damage insurance. You'll need to buy a visitor's driving permit for $12 (EC$30) at one of the airports or at the Traffic Division office on High Street in Roseau.

Roads can be narrow in places, and they meander around the coast and through mountainous terrain. Gasoline stations can be found all over the island. Gasoline is more expensive than in the United States—as of this writing, about $5 per gallon. Driving in Dominica is on the left side, though you can rent vehicles with a steering wheel on either the left or right.

Information Best Deal Car Rental (⊠15 Hanover St., Roseau ☎767/449–9204 or 767/235–3325 ⊕www.bestdealrentacar.com). **Budget Rent-A-Car** (⊠Canefield Industrial Site, Canefield ☎767/449–2080, 800/527–0700 in U.S. ⊕www.budget.com). **Courtesy Car Rentals** (⊠10 Winston La., Goodwill ☎767/445–7763 ⊕www.avirtualdominica.com/courtesycarrental). **Island Car Rentals** (⊠Goodwill Rd., Goodwill ☎767/255–6844 or 767/445–8789 ⊕www.islandcar.dm).

BY TAXI

Taxis and minibuses are available at the airports and in Roseau as well as at most hotels and guesthouses. Rates are fixed by the government (from Melville Hall Airport to Roseau, the fare is $60) but if you opt for a co-op—sharing a taxi (and the fare) with other passengers going in the same direction—you will be able to negotiate a special price (as little as $20 per person from Melville airport to Roseau). Drivers also offer their services for tours anywhere on the island beginning at $25 to $30 an hour for up to four persons; a four- to five-hour island tour will cost

9

approximately $150. It's best to get a recommendation from your hotel. You can recognize a taxi and/or minibus by the H, HA, and HB plates; simply flag them down or make your way to the nearest bus stop. For more information on reputable taxi companies, contact the Dominica Taxi Association or Nature Island Taxi Association.

Information Dominica Taxi Association (☎767/449-9173). Nature Island Taxi Association (☎767/448-1679).

▌CONTACTS & RESOURCES

BANKS & EXCHANGE SERVICES

The official currency is the Eastern Caribbean dollar (EC$). The exchange hovers around EC$2.65 to the US$1. Most Americans will not need to exchange money. U.S. dollars are readily accepted except at the smallest places though, unless you ask, you'll usually get change in EC dollars. Major credit cards are also widely accepted, as are traveler's checks. You can find ATMs in all the banks in Roseau—including Barclays International Bank on Old Street, the Royal Bank of Canada near the cruise-ship berth, Banque Française Commerciale on Queen Mary Street, and the Bank of Nova Scotia on Hillsborough Street—as well as some in larger villages such as Portsmouth. They dispense EC dollars only and accept international bank cards.

Prices throughout this chapter are quoted in U.S. dollars, unless indicated otherwise.

ELECTRICITY

Electric voltage is 220–240 AC, 50 cycles. North American appliances require an adapter and transformer; however, many establishments provide these and often have dual-voltage fittings (110–120 and 220–240 volts).

EMERGENCIES

General Emergencies Ambulance, Police & Fire (☎999).

Hospitals Grand Bay Hospital (✉Grand Bay ☎767/446-3706). Marigot Hospital (✉Marigot ☎767/445-7091). Portsmouth Hospital (✉Portsmouth ☎767/445-5237). Princess Margaret Hospital (✉Federation Dr., Goodwill ☎767/448-2231 or 767/448-2233).

INTERNET, MAIL & SHIPPING

Some hotels and inns have Internet service, but certainly not all. In addition to getting services at the Cornerhouse Café, you can check your e-mail or go online at Cyber Land Internet Café, which has two branches in Roseau and one in Portsmouth. You'll pay about EC$3.50 for 30 minutes of Internet use.

First-class letters to North America cost EC95¢ and those to the United Kingdom cost EC90¢; postcards are EC55¢ to just about anywhere in the world. The general post office is opposite the ferry terminal in Roseau. Dominica is often confused with the Dominican Republic, so when addressing letters to the island, be sure to write: The Commonwealth of Dominica, Eastern Caribbean. Islands in this part of the Caribbean do not use postal codes.

Information Cornerhouse Café (✉Old and King George V Sts., Roseau ☎767/449-9000). Cyber Land Internet Café (✉George St., Roseau ✉Woodstone Shopping Mall, Roseau ✉Grandby St., Portsmouth ☎767/440-2605).

SAFETY

Petty crime can be a problem on Dominica, as with nearly all destinations in the world. It's always wise to secure valuables in the hotel safe and not carry too much money or many valuables around. Remember that if you rent a car to tour the island, you may have to park it in a remote area; don't leave valuables in your vehicle while you're off on a hike or a tour.

TAXES & SERVICE CHARGES

The departure-embarkation tax is EC$55 or about $22, payable in cash only at the airport at the time of departure from the island. Hotels collect a 15% government hotel occupancy tax and restaurants a 15% government V.A.T.

TELEPHONES

Your tri-band GSM mobile phone will work in Dominica, and if your provider will unlock your phone, you can purchase a local SIM card for about EC$27 and use prepaid cell cards. You can also buy a prepaid cell phone for as little as EC$60.

The island has a somewhat adequate telecommunication system and accordingly efficient direct-dial international service. All pay phones are equipped for local and overseas dialing, accepting EC coins, credit cards, or phone cards, which you can buy at many island stores and at the airports. To call Dominica from the United States, dial the area code (767) and the local access code (44), followed by the five-digit local number. On the island, dial only the seven-digit number that follows the area code.

Information AT&T Direct (☎800/872–2881) does not always work. **MCI World Phone** (☎800/888–8000). **Sprint** (☎800/744–2250).

TIPPING

Most hotels and restaurants add a 10% service charge to your bill. A 5% tip for exceptionally good service on top of the service charge is always welcome; otherwise just tip accordingly.

TOUR OPTIONS

Since Dominica is such a nature-centered destination, there's no shortage of certified guides, as well as numerous tour and taxi companies. Ask the staff at your hotel for a recommendation. Generally tours start off in the Roseau area, but most operators will arrange convenient pickups. Prices range between $35 and $75 per person depending on the duration, amenities provided, and number of persons on the excursion. Jonathan Peter of Baggie

Taxi & Tours offers private tours. Dominica Tours is one of the island's largest tour companies, offering a range of hikes and bird-watching trips. Ken's Hinterland Adventure Tours & Taxi Service offers a range of island tours and guided hikes, including some oriented specifically for families with children.

Information Baggie Taxi & Tours (☎767/616–0034 or 767/235–5091). **Dominica Tours** (✉Anchorage Hotel, Castle Comfort ☎767/448–2638 or 767/235–2639 ⊕www.anchoragehotel.dm). **Ken's Hinterland Adventure Tours & Taxi Service** (✉Fort Young Hotel, Victoria St., Roseau ☎767/448–4850 or 866/880–0508 ⊕www.kenshinterlandtours.com).

VISITOR INFORMATION

Before You Leave Discover Dominica Authority (Dominica Tourist Office ⊕www.discoverdominica.com ☎866/522–4057 in the U.S.).

In Dominica Discover Dominica Authority (✉Valley Rd., Roseau ☎767/448–2045 🖷767/448–2045 ✉Old post office, Dame M.E. Charles Blvd., Roseau ☎767/448–2045 Ext. 118 ✉Canefield Airport, Canefield ☎767/449–1242 ✉Melville Hall Airport, Marigot ☎767/445–7051).

Other Web sites A Virtual Dominica (⊕www.avirtualdominica.com). **Visit Dominica** (⊕www.visit-dominica.com).

WEDDINGS

To get married in Dominica, prospective spouses must file an application at least two days prior to the ceremony, and at least one of the parties must have been on the island for a minimum of two days. Non-Dominicans must produce a valid passport and original birth certificate (not a baptismal certificate), and if one of the parties has been married before, a divorce decree or death certificate for the former spouse must be presented as well. The parties to the marriage must sign a statutory declaration on marital status, which must be obtained and sworn in Dominica in the presence of a local lawyer.

9

The parties must also complete and sign an application form "G," which must be witnessed by a magistrate. At least two witnesses must be present at the marriage ceremony. If you marry in Dominica, the tourist office recommends that you deal with a local lawyer. The total cost for the marriage license, marriage ceremony at the Registrar's office, legal fees, and stamps will be approximately $113.

There will be additional costs involved if the marriage takes place in a church or somewhere else on the island.

The Fort Young Hotel offers wedding packages including a bridal bouquet, bottle of champagne, and wedding cake; Papillote Wilderness Retreat and Exotica also have experience organizing weddings for guests.

Dominican Republic

Strumming a merengue

WORD OF MOUTH

"In Punta Cana, walking on the beach with the only goal of 'let's just walk until we get to that point over there' is a daily routine."

—Kep

"The beaches in Cabarete or Sosúa are awesome. Cabarete has one of the longest stretches of beach on the island and it is not the least bit narrow. Cabarete and Sosúa also have great nightlife and restaurants."

—BigBadTea

WELCOME TO THE DOMINICAN REPUBLIC

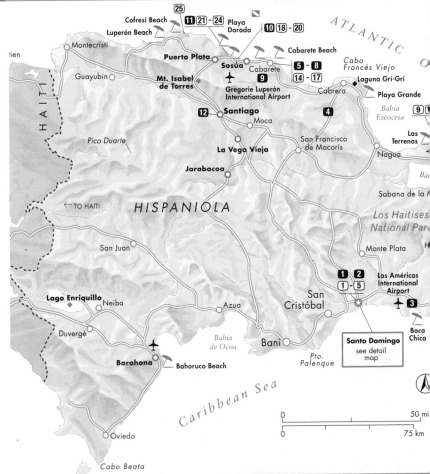

Montecristi
Cofresí Beach
Luperón Beach
25
11 21 - 24 Playa Dorada
10 18 - 20
ATLANTIC
Cabarete Beach
Puerto Plata
Sosúa
Cabarete
Cabo Francés Viejo
5 - 8
14 - 17
Laguna Grí-Grí
Playa Grande
Guayubin
Mt. Isabel de Torres
Gregorie Luperón International Airport
Cabrera
Bahía Escocesa
9
12 Santiago
Moca
San Francisco de Macorís
4
Las Terrenas
Pico Duarte
La Vega Vieja
Nagua
Jarabacoa
Ba
Sabana de la
HISPANIOLA
Los Haitises National Par
TO HAITI
San Juan
Monte Plata
Lago Enriquillo
Neiba
Las Américas International Airport
1 2
1 - 5
San Cristóbal
3
Duvergé
Azua
Boca Chica
Bahía de Ocoa
Bani
Santo Domingo
see detail map
Barahona
Bahoruco Beach
Pto. Palenque
Caribbean Sea
0   50 mi
0   75 km
Oviedo
Cabo Beata

Like the merengue seen on all the dance floors in Santo Domingo, the Dominican Republic is charismatic yet sensuous, energetic yet elegant. The charm of the people adds special warmth: a gracious wave of greeting here, a hand-rolled cigar tapped with a flourish there. Dazzling smiles just about everywhere will quickly beguile you.

LA ISLA ESPAÑOLA

The Dominican Republic covers the eastern two-thirds of the island of Hispaniola (Haiti covers the other third). At 18,765 square mi (48,730 square km), it's the second-largest Caribbean country (only Cuba is larger), and with over 8.8 million people, the second most populous country, too. It was explored by Columbus on his 1492 voyage to the New World.

KEY	
⤢	Beaches
◺	Dive Sites
❶	Restaurants
①	Hotels

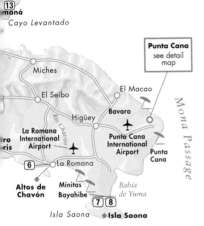

DOMINICAN REPUBLIC

10

TOP 4 REASONS TO VISIT THE DOMINICAN REPUBLIC

❶ There are some 1,000 miles of excellent, pearl-white beaches.

❷ Millions come each year to indulge themselves at the best-value all-inclusive resorts in the Caribbean.

❸ Every imaginable activity—world-class golf, horseback riding, white-water rafting, surfing, diving, wind surfing, and more—is possible here.

❹ The Dominicans love to party, dance, drink, and have a good time at happening bars and clubs.

DOMINICAN REPUBLIC PLANNER

Island Activities

The biggest draw for tourists are powder-soft **beaches**, particularly in Punta Cana, but each of the resort areas has decent beaches.

Windsurfing is best on the north coast, and the top dogs in the sport have found the breezes in Cabarete to be among the most favorable in the Caribbean.

The D.R. also has several of the Caribbean's finest **golf courses.**

Adventure tours are popular in the country's interior, particularly for those travelers who want to get a bit farther off the beaten path and avoid the all-inclusive resorts.

Nightlife is a highlight, particularly in Santo Domingo, where **historical sights** are also a major draw.

However, with so many **all-inclusive resorts,** much of the activity is focused inward, and the majority of tourists never leave their resorts except to go on guided tours and excursions in the immediate vicinity of their hotel.

Logistics

Getting to the Dominican Republic: The D.R. has six major international airports: La Romana (LRM), Puerto Plata (POP), Punta Cana (PUJ), Samaná (AZS), Santiago (STI), and Santo Domingo (SDQ). Plan your air travel carefully so you don't end up flying into Punta Cana when you are staying at Casa de Campo, a two-hour-plus drive. Travel between the island's many developed tourism zones can be arduous and expensive.

Hassle Factor: Low for popular destinations, High for off-the-beaten-path places.

Nonstops: Atlanta (Delta), Charlotte (USAirways), Chicago–O'Hare (United), Ft. Lauderdale (Spirit), Miami (American), New York–JFK (American, JetBlue), New York–Newark (Continental, JetBlue), Philadelphia (USAirways), Washington, DC–Dulles (United). Some American Eagle flights connect in San Juan.

On the Ground

Most package include airport transfers. Otherwise, you'll have to take a local taxi, which can cost as much as $50 if the ride is long (Punta Cana to Uvero Alto, for instance) or as little as $20 (Puerto Plata to Playa Dorada). Very long drives can double the cost (Punta Cana to La Romana, for example) and add 2 hours to your trip.

Renting a Car: If you're staying at an all-inclusive resort, you will probably not need a car. If you're traveling around the D.R., a car can be handy but expensive, averaging $75 per day. Local companies offer substantially better rates; however, you may feel more confident in going with a name brand. To rent a car here, you must have a valid driver's license from your own country, be more than 25 years old, and have a major credit card (or cash deposit). If you do not receive insurance from your credit card (or if it is not included), you'll need to buy insurance, which is also expensive.

Where to Stay

A hotel in **Santo Domingo** allows you to enjoy the capital's great restaurants, nightlife, and historical sights, but most travelers visit the busy, overwhelming city as a day trip.

Boca Chica and **Juan Dolio** offer some of the island's cheapest—but most-mediocre—all-inclusives, along with crowded beaches.

La Romana has Casa de Campo as well as a few resorts on other, better beaches; the region is within reasonable striking distance of Santo Domingo for those needing a taste of history to go with their *plátanos* (plantains).

The isolated, though beautiful, **Barahona** region offers a respite from development and overcrowding but is nearly a four-hour drive from Santo Domingo.

Punta Cana still reigns supreme for its many reasonably priced all-inclusives, but it's better for those looking for a resort-based vacation than for the adventurous.

Samaná is isolated, less developed, and easier to reach now with some flights.

Playa Dorada, the D.R.'s original resort area, is still a land of decent all-inclusives and golf courses, but more-inde-pendent-minded travelers (and all windsurfers) may prefer **Sosúa** and **Cabarete,** where you'll still find a few charming independent inns and small resorts.

Hotel & Restaurant Prices

⇨*For information on hotel meal plans, see Accommodations in Caribbean Essentials.*

WHAT IT COSTS IN U.S. DOLLARS

	$$$$	$$$	$$	$	¢
Restaurants	over $30	$20–$30	$12–$20	$8–$12	under $8
Hotels*	over $350	$250–$350	$150–$250	$80–$150	under $80
Hotels**	over $450	$350–$450	$250–$350	$125–$250	under $125

*EP, BP, CP **AI, FAP, MAP Restaurant prices are for a main course at dinner and include any taxes or service charges. Hotel prices are per night
for a double room in high season, excluding taxes, service charges, and
meal plans (except at all-inclusives).

When to Go

The D.R. is busy year-round. During the somewhat quieter summer season, Europeans flock to the lovely beaches, keeping rates high from mid-June through August, when much of the Caribbean is very quiet indeed. However, in late spring (after Easter until early June) and early fall (September to October) you can get good deals.

Unlike many islands, where rain showers are usually a tempo-rary passing thing, the rains in the D.R. can linger when they do come, especially from June through November.

The largest event in the country is the annual **Jazz Festival** in October, which draws enthusi-asts from all over the world.

Carnival celebrations are held in Santiago and La Vega during the weeks before Lent.

The **Festival del Merengue** is held in Santo Domingo in late July and early August.

10

By Michael
de Zayas,
Elise Rosen,
and Eileen
Robinson
Smith

IT'S *TRANQUILLA* IN THE ZONA COLONIAL at siesta time. Most Dominicans have never given up the habit of taking a siesta after their main midday meal, a vestige of their Spanish heritage. You will be able to hear the distinctive flutter of pigeons' wings as they peck for crumbs among the dramatic ruins of the Bari Hospital. The little old tailor in his ancient shop closes the narrow doors from the inside. The coconut boys and the frying empanada men; the barbers in their gossipy, 1950s-vintage shops; the old women sitting on their white balconies adorned with fuchsia bougainvillea: they'll all be awake soon, but for now you can't help but love the stillness.

The vibrant lifestyle of this sun-drenched, Latin-Caribbean country, where Spanish is the national language and where the people are hospitable and good-natured, makes the Dominican Republic a different cultural experience. If you pick up the rhythm of life here, as freewheeling as the island's trademark merengue, this can be a beguiling tourist destination. And it's still one of the least-expensive Caribbean islands.

Christopher Columbus first claimed the island for Spain on his first New World voyage in 1492 and wrecked his flagship, the *Santa Maria,* on its Atlantic shore on Christmas Eve; later, his brother Bartolomeo founded Santo Domingo de Guzmán (1496), the first city in the New World. With some 300 examples of Spanish-colonial architecture, the Zona Colonial was declared a World Heritage Site by UNESCO in 1990. A throbbing microcosm, there are 100 square blocks of history, very much alive more than five centuries later. Its trendy restaurants, art galleries, boutique hotels, and late-night clubs help make Santo Domingo a superb urban vacation destination.

Dominicans will extend a gracious welcome, saying, "This is your home!" and indeed are happy to share what they have, which is a physically beautiful island bathed by the Atlantic Ocean to the north and the Caribbean Sea to the south. Among its most-precious assets are 1,000 mi (1,600 km) of gorgeous beaches studded with coconut palms and sands ranging from pearl white to golden brown to volcanic black.

The Caribbean sun kisses this exotic land (warm temperatures average 82°F year-round), which occupies two-thirds of the island of Hispaniola, sharing the remainder with the Republic of Haiti. Cuba is due west, and to the east is Puerto Rico. It's a fertile country blessed with resources, particularly cocoa, coffee, rum, tobacco, and sugarcane.

A land of contrasts, the island has alpine landscapes, brown rivers with white-water rapids, rain forests full of wild orchids, and fences of multicolor bougainvillea. Indigenous species from crocodiles to the green cockatoo, symbol of the island, live in these habitats. Bird-watchers, take note: there are 29 endemic species flying around here.

The contrasts don't stop with nature. You can see signs of wealth, for the upper strata of society lives well indeed. In the capital, the movers and shakers ride in chauffeur-driven silver Mercedes. On the country roads you'll be amazed that four people with sacks of groceries and a stalk of bananas can fit on a smoky old *motoconcho* (motorbike-taxi). Similarly, Dominicans can be fair-skinned with light eyes, or black, but mostly they are shades of brown. This is a land of *mestizos,* who are a centuries-old mix of native Indians, Spanish colonists, and African slaves, plus every other nationality that has settled here, from Italian to Arabic.

Accommodations offer a remarkable range—surfers' camps, exclusive boutique hotels, and amazing megaresorts that have brought the all-inclusive hotel to the next level of luxury.

Regrettably, most Dominican towns and cities are neither quaint nor particularly pretty, and poverty still prevails. However, the standard of living has really come up along with the growth of North American tourism. The dollar has weakened against the Dominican peso since 2005, and food prices are higher than they have been, which means prices at all-inclusive resorts are up; however, a vacation in the D.R. can still be a relative bargain.

Islanders have an affinity for all things American: the people, language (more and more speak English), electronic products, fashions, and life-style. A great Dominican dream is to go to the States as a shortstop or pitcher and become the next Sammy Sosa, then return to be a philanthropist in one's own hometown.

WHERE TO STAY

The Dominican Republic has the largest hotel inventory (at this writing approaching 70,000 rooms, with even more under construction) in the Caribbean and draws large numbers of stateside visitors. That is a far cry from the mid-1990s, when most Americans thought it was a country in Latin America if they thought about it at all. Surfers can still find digs for $25 a night in Cabarete, while the new generation of luxurious all-inclusives in Punta Cana and Uvero Alto is simply awesome.

Santo Domingo properties generally base their tariffs on the EP plan—though many include breakfast—and maintain the same room rates year-round. Beach resorts have high winter rates, with prices reduced for the shoulder seasons of late spring and early fall (summer has become another strong season). All-inclusives dominate in Punta Cana. Cabarete was a stronghold of the small inn, but each year it's getting more all-inclusives. Villa rentals are gaining in popularity all over the island.

10

SANTO DOMINGO

The seaside capital of the country is in the middle of the island's south coast. In Santo Domingo, most of the better hotels are on or near the Malecón, with several small, desirable properties in the trendy Colonial Zone, allowing you to feel part of that magical environment. The capital is where you'll find some of the most-sophisticated hotels and restaurants, not to mention nightlife. However, such an urban vacation is best coupled with a beach stay elsewhere on the island.

$$$–$$$$ 🏨**Sofitel Nicolas Ovando.** This luxury hotel, sculpted from the residence
Fodor'sChoice   of the first Governor of the Americas, is the best thing to happen in the
★   Zone since Diego Columbus's palace was finished in 1517. Colonial
rooms have canopied king-size beds, tall ceilings, original stone win-
dow benches, and shutters. Some prefer the sunny (smaller) rooms in
the contemporary annex; with river views, these are smart examples of
French minimalist style. The pool is shaded by trees and tropical plant-
ings, and swimmers leave the sun for a fitness break in the gym. The bar
is a social scene, particularly when the music man plays at cocktail hour,
which includes complimentary hors d'oeuvres. **Pros:** Lavish breakfast
buffet, beautifully restored historic section. **Cons:** Inconsistent service
in the lovely restaurant, hotel could be more lively. ✉ *Calle Las Damas,
Zona Colonial* ☎*809/685–9955 or 800/763–4835* ⊕*www.sofitel.com*
🛏*100 rooms, 4 suites* ⌂*In-room: safe, refrigerator. In-hotel: restau-
rant, room service, bars, pool, gym, concierge, laundry service, public
Internet, public Wi-Fi, parking (no fee), some pets allowed* ⊟*AE, MC,
V* ⍽*BP.*

$–$$ 🏨**Hilton Santo Domingo.** This has become *the* address on the Malecón for
★   businesspeople, convention attendees, and leisure travelers. The six lux-
urious executive floors are wired for business, each with three phones,
Internet ports, actual corner offices with imposing desks and ergonomic
leather chairs, and DSL lines. Suites are geared for longer stays and
have kitchenettes. Creature comforts are satisfied with the plush duvets,
rain showers, and surround sound in the bathrooms, oversize flat-screen
TVs, and gorgeous sea views. Service might just be the best in the country, and rates are surprisingly moderate, particularly with online packages that include a lavish and healthful buffet breakfast. **Pros:** Sunday
Brunch is one of the city's top tickets, great music in the lobby lounge,
best service in Santo Domingo. **Cons:** Little about the hotel is authen-
tically Dominican, hotel can be large and impersonal. ✉*Av. George
Washington 500, Gazcue* ☎*809/685–0000* ⊕*hiltoncaribbean.com/
santodomingo* 🛏*228 rooms, 32 suites* ⌂*In-room: safe, refrigerator,
Ethernet. In-hotel: 2 restaurants, bars, pool, gym, spa, concierge, executive floor, public Internet, public Wi-Fi* ⊟*AE, D, MC, V* ⍽*EP.*

$–$$ 🏨**Renaissance Jaragua Hotel & Casino.** The sprawling, pink oasis is peren-
nially popular, particularly with Americans, for its beautiful grounds
and huge, free-form pool. Fountains splash and hot tubs gurgle. Saunas
bake in what is the capital's largest fitness club—which was undergoing
a needed renovation at this writing. Everything is bigger than life, from
the rooms, where executive-size desks face the satellite TV, to the gigantic suites in the renovated main building to the generous lobby and
huge, lively casino where bands heat up the action. It has the town's
only cabaret theater. Comfy European linens and duvets make sleeping a dream vision. Management and staff are professional and caring.
Check the Web for weekend packages, including even golf, and more.
Pros: Hotel is busy and lively, hotel will match any discount Internet rate, offers an optional all-inclusive plan (rare in Santo Domingo).
Cons: Can be a bit too busy at times, nothing understated about the
decor, some rooms outdated. ✉*Av. George Washington 367, Gazcue*
☎*809/221–2222* ⊕*www.marriott.com* 🛏*292 rooms, 8 suites* ⌂*In-*

room: safe, kitchen, refrigerator (some), dial-up (some). In-hotel: 3 restaurants, bars, tennis courts, pool, gym, spa, concierge, executive floor, public Internet $\equiv$*AE, D, MC, V* ⦿❘*EP.*

$ 📺**Hodelpa Caribe Colonial.** When you leave this little Hernando's Hideaway, the caring staff will say, "Why so soon?" The art deco–style lobby makes clever use of blue objets d'art, as does the high-tech Internet center. Rooms have white-gauze canopies on king-size beds; an allwhite honeymoon suite has a Jacuzzi. Splurge for a suite or a superior room (though even those have tight bathrooms), rather than a subterranean standard. Sit out on your balcony and wave to the neighbors. On Friday nights a Mexican fiesta takes place on the side terrace, with dancers, tequila action, and karaoke. **Pros:** Friendly staff, well managed and efficient. **Cons:** Small bathrooms, standard rooms not on par with others, subsequent renovated colonial buildings have been done better. ⊠*Isabel La Católica 59, Zona Colonial* ☎*809/688–7799 or 888/403–2603* ⊕*www.hodelpa.com* ⬂*52 rooms, 2 suites* ♻*In-room: safe. In-hotel: restaurant, room service, bar, concierge, laundry service, public Internet, parking (no fee)* $\equiv$*AE, MC, V* ⦿❘*BP.*

¢–$ 📺**Hotel La Atarazana.** Ring the bell at this artistically renovated town
★ house, and the white wrought-iron gate opens to a small foyer with a large mirror and long stems of tropical flowers. Left is the kitchen and bar, to the rear is a courtyard furnished with outdoor tables and market umbrellas. A waterfall flows down the coral stone wall; with bamboo and exotic greenery, it's an urban oasis. You may feel as if you are staying with friends—in this case Suzanne and Bernie. She's a Swiss-German economist, he's an architect and designed the hotel and the contemporary lighting fixtures. Rooms, all upstairs, are minimalist and squeaky clean. The courtyard is the setting for the healthful, European-style breakfast and the rum-soaked cocktail hour. **Pros:** Superior service, excellent location near Plaza España but not on a touristy block, rooftop terrace offers views and shaded sitting areas. **Cons:** Front rooms (particularly the one closest to the police station) are noisy in the early morning, no luxurious creature comforts, no restaurant in the hotel. ⊠*La Atarazana 19, next door to police station, Zona Colonial* ☎*809/706–5315* ⊕*www.hotel-atarazana.com* ⬂*7 rooms* ♻*In-room: no a/c (some), no phone, Wi-Fi. In-hotel: bar, no elevator, laundry service, public Internet; public Wi-Fi, no-smoking rooms* $\equiv$*AE, MC, V* ⦿❘*BP.*

10

LA ROMANA

La Romana is on the southeast coast, about a two-hour drive from Santo Domingo and the same distance southwest of Punta Cana. An international airport here has nonstop service from the United States. Casa de Campo's Marina Chavón, with its Mediterranean design and impressive yacht club and villa complex, is as fine a marina facility as can be found anywhere. The shops and restaurants are a big draw for all tourists to the area, as is Altos de Chavón, the re-created 16th-century Mediterranean town on the grounds of Casa de Campo. The resorts in nearby Bayahibe Bay, which has an idyllic, horseshoe-shape beach and a real fishing village, have always been popular with *cap-italeños* and Europeans. North Americans are checking in here and leaving satisfied. Often, when guests want to party down, they buy an inexpensive night-pass to the Viva Wyndham, allowing them entry to the resort's discos along with dinner and drinks. The actual town of La Romana is not pretty or quaint, although it has a lovely central park and is a real slice of Dominican life. The justifiably popular Sunscape Casa del Mar La Romana closes in late 2008 to be transformed into a luxurious Dreams resort and is not reviewed in this edition.

$$$$ ⚃ **Casa de Campo.** At the country's most illustrious resort, golfers vie
☾ for tee-times at the three famed Pete Dye–designed courses. Family
★ reunions in luxury villas are perennially popular. Regular rooms are called casitas and are in two-story, nondescript blocks (ask for one of the six newest) but inside they are soundproof and commodious, with down pillows, walk-in closets, and balconies overlooking the gardens. What's great is that each room (and villa) comes with a golf cart; there's an efficient shuttle, too. Minitas Beach, which although still not expansive, has had many new chic amenities added such as new-Euro furnishings and Balinese sun beds. The restaurant at the beach looks amazing, with contemporary white-sail installations and upgraded cuisine thanks to the new partnership with New York's Le Cirque; high up in Altos de Chavón a second Le Cirque restaurant was expected to open in 2008. Booking just a room (EP) at Casa is possible, but few go this route because the all-inclusive plan is a better value, as are the golf packages. The luxurious Cygalle Healing Spa opened in 2007. **Pros:** Excellent golf and tennis, beach improvements, new spa. **Cons:** Not the greatest beach, expensive food, a bit too sprawling. ⌂ *Box 140, La Romana* ☎*809/523–3333 or 305/856–7083* ⊕*www.casadecampo.com.do* ⇆*267 rooms, 150 villas* ⌂*In-room: safe, refrigerator, kitchen (some), dial-up. In-hotel: 9 restaurants, bars, golf courses, tennis courts, pools, gym, spa, diving, water sports, bicycles, no elevator, children's programs (ages 1–18)* ⊟*AE, MC, V* ⚭*AI.*

$$–$$$ ⚃ **Viva Wyndham Dominicus Palace.** Americans will prefer this classier
☾ sister to that of the nearby Viva Wyndham Dominicus Beach resort, which has a reputation for its excellent animation programs, for its sports, and for its fun atmosphere. An impressive white tent, big enough for a Greek (or Dominican) wedding, is a focal point of the long expanse of beach, which boasts a blue-flag designation for non-polluted waters; by day it's a casual lunch spot, by night it becomes a romantic rendezvous. Guest rooms in the blocks, like the lobby, have a Spanish-colonial style accented with Caribbean colors. The resort has a Green Globe designation for its ecofriendly policies. **Pros:** Absolutely fabulous blue-flag beach, professional dive center, great soothing Metamorphosis Spa. **Cons:** Always busy, no interior transportation even though resort grounds are sprawling, reservations needed for à la carte restaurants. ✉*Playa Bayahibe, Bayahibe* ☎*809/686–5658* ⊕*www.vivaresorts.com* ⇆*330 rooms* ⌂*In-room: safe, refrigerator, Wi-Fi (some). In-hotel: 7 restaurants, bars, tennis courts, pools, gym, spa, beachfront, diving, water sports, no elevator, children's programs (ages 4–16), public Internet, public Wi-Fi* ⊟*AE, MC, V* ⚭*AI.*

$$ ⌂**Iberostar Hacienda Dominicus.**
☾ Iberostar's reputation for excellent
★ cuisine has helped to cement its
popularity with families and incen-
tive groups. The breakfast buffet is
a "Yes!" El Colonial, the gourmet
room, may be one of the best in the
all-inclusive world. Its idyllic beach
with its lighthouse bar doesn't hurt,
either. The crowd here is an inter-
esting mix with some very young
adults, hip families with young
kids, enough French to warrant the
bars' stocking Pernod, and seniors
who are staying as long as three
weeks. A manager's party honoring

> **FOUR SEASONS
> CASA DE CAMPO**
>
> The big news at Casa de Campo
> is that sometime in 2009 a
> brand-new Four Seasons Hotel is
> expected to open on the expan-
> sive resort grounds, offering a
> new level of luxurious accom-
> modations with access to all of
> Casa's great facilities, golf courses,
> and restaurants. The resort will be
> family oriented and have its own
> large spa and beach.

repeat guests can draw a crowd of more than 100 returnees, some who
have decided this is the only place to be. Junior suites are worth the
few dollars more. This resort has familial warmth as well as a definite
fun quotient for singles. **Pros:** Fun resort, gorgeous beach, very family-
friendly. **Cons:** Room decor is a bit outdated, always packed, reserva-
tions at à la carte restaurants not always available and must be made
very early in the morning. ✉*Playa Bayahibe, Bayahibe* ☎*809/688–
3600 or 888/923–2722* ⊕*www.iberostar.com* ⤳*460 rooms, 38 junior
suites* ⌂*In-room: safe, refrigerator. In-hotel: 4 restaurants, bars, tennis
courts, pools, gym, spa, beachfront, diving, water sports, no elevator,
children's programs (ages 4–12), public Internet, public Wi-Fi* ▭*AE,
MC, V* ⍾*AI.*

PUNTA CANA

The easternmost coast of the island has 35 mi (56 km) of incredible
beach punctuated by coco palms; add to that a host of all-inclusive
resorts, an atmospheric thatch-roof airport, and many more direct
flights than any other D.R. resort area, and it's easy to see why this
region—despite having some 24,000 hotel rooms (more than on most
other Caribbean islands) is often sold out. It has become the Cancun
of the D.R., and although you can usually get a room during hurri-
cane season (late August–October), booking far in advance is advis-
able. Look for resorts with spas, which offer a soothing atmosphere
away from the madding crowds, and a litany of both therapeutic and
fun body treatments.

The region commonly referred to as Punta Cana actually encompasses
the beaches and villages of Juanillo, Punta Cana, Bávaro, Cabeza de
Toro, El Cortecito, Arena Gorda, Macao, and Uvero Alto, which hug
an unbroken stretch of the eastern coastline; however, Uvero Alto—
the farthest developed resort area to the north—lies an hour from the
Punta Cana airport.

10

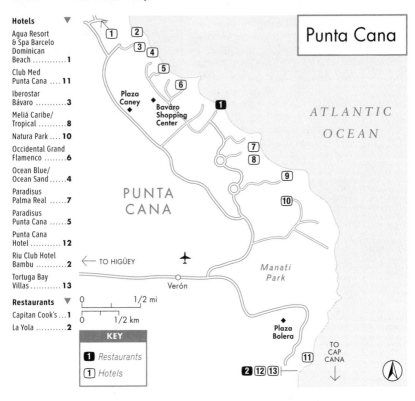

Punta Cana

Plaza
Caney ◆

◆ Bavaro
Shopping
Center

ATLANTIC

OCEAN

PUNTA
CANA

← TO HIGÜEY

Verón

*Manati
Park*

0   1/2 mi

0   1/2 km

◆ Plaza
Bolera

TO
CAP
CANA
↓

KEY

1 *Restaurants*

1 *Hotels*

Cap Cana is a major new development south of the airport. Macao,
which lies between Bávaro and Uvero Alto, is another charmed spot
and is the site of phased luxury residential and resort development
along the beachfront at Rōco Ki. The Westin Rōco Ki Beach & Golf
Resort, the first of several hotels planned here, was slated to open in
September 2008.

$$$$
Fodor'sChoice
★
Agua Resort & Spa. A thatch-roof, open-air lobby welcomes you to
this serene oceanfront resort, where rustic natural beauty and high
architectural style blend seamlessly. The design shows Dominican and
Balinese influences, utilizing materials like *coralina* stone, cane, wicker,
and wood. All rooms have four-post beds with a firm mattress and
Frette linens, a furnished terrace, a large flat-screen TV, and artfully
tiled floor lamps; some have dramatic ocean views. The remarkable
stone bathrooms have porcelain basins and Korres amenities, plus such
thoughtful extras as a toothbrush, toothpaste, and insect repellent. Sec-
ond-level villas are enormous, with soaring thatched-cane roofs. For
a small resort, the pool is quite large, but most guests will be drawn
to the impeccable beach. Beyond the beach is an amazing coral reef
that can turn bright red by night when the light is just so. Service is
superattentive, and the resort can organize horseback riding or helicopter tours, or simply lend you a DVD. This is an adult-oriented

resort, but organized kids' programs serve ages five to nine. Meal plans are available. **Pros:** Serene and remote location, attentive staff, rustic luxury. **Cons:** Mosquitoes, limited nightlife, no clock in room. ⊠*Playa Uvero Alto* ☎*809/468–0000* ⊕*www.aguaresort.com* ⇆*40 rooms, 5 2- or 3-bedroom villas* ⬙*In-room: safe, DVD. In hotel: 2 restaurants, room service, bars, tennis court, pools, gym, spa, beachfront, water sports, no elevator, children's programs (ages 5–9), laundry service, concierge, public Internet, public Wi-Fi, airport shuttle, no-smoking rooms* ⊟*AE, MC, V* ⍟*EP.*

$$$$ 🏨 **Paradisus Palma Real.** The cream of the crop among Punta Cana's lux-
☺ ury all-inclusives, this resort is a showstopper. The average suite, with
Fodor'sChoice flat-screen TV, CD player, balcony or terrace, and semi-open marble
★ bathroom with jet showers and a Jacuzzi for two, is extraordinary. You won't need to upgrade, but if you choose the Royal Service (available for adults only), you'll get a personal butler at your beck and call, private check-in, a private lounge with daytime snacks and evening cocktails, and customized turndown service. Family concierge plans lavish attention on your kids, who get their own check-in, kids' amenities in the rooms, and mini-size robes and slippers. Balinese sun beds—some with thatched roofs—are cozy for lounging beside the glorious pool. The restaurants are situated around a central plaza and are opulently decorated, though admittedly the decor may outshine the food, as is the case in the Mediterranean room. Play at the nearby Cocotal Golf Course is complimentary, but nongolfers will be won over by horseback excursions or the so-called "Scuba Doo," which is basically underwater biking with an oxygen supply. **Pros:** Personalized attention, enticing outdoor spa, complimentary golf. **Cons:** Internet access costs extra, pool chairs and palapas get reserved early. ⊠*Bávaro* ☎*809/688–5000 or 800/688–5000* ⊕*www.paradisuspalmareal.com or www.solmelia. com* ⇆*554 suites* ⬙*In-room: safe, refrigerator, DVD, Ethernet. In-hotel: 7 restaurants, room service, bars, tennis courts, pools, gym, spa, beachfront, diving, water sports, bicycles, children's programs (ages 5– 12), concierge, executive floor, public Wi-Fi, no-smoking rooms* ⊟*AE, D, DC, MC, V* ⍟*AI.*

$$$$ 🏨 **Tortuga Bay Villas.** Shuttered French windows opening to grand vistas
Fodor'sChoice of the sea and a cotton-white private beach are hallmarks of this lux-
★ ury-villa enclave within the grounds of Puntacana Resort & Club. Personal attention is of the essence here; your every desire will be granted, if not anticipated, by your own villa manager, who is accessible by a cell phone provided to you. Although privacy is paramount, there is a simultaneous sense of community. Oscar de la Renta designed the classy colonial-Caribbean rooms, which exude contemporary, understated elegance with a soft palette of colors and plush bed linens. The coralina stone bathrooms are breathtaking and include a Jacuzzi for two; amenities include robes, slippers, and Gilchrist & Soames toiletries. The minibar is stocked with premium liquors, and there's a huge flat-screen TV. A golf cart is included to help you get around, and you can rent a laptop. Villa guests have an exclusive restaurant plus access to all the facilities of the main resort, notably the impeccable Cana Golf Course, designed by P. B. Dye, and the glorious Six Senses

10

Spa. **Pros:** Personal attention, gorgeous sprawling grounds, outstanding golf, VIP check-in at airport. **Cons:** Little nightlife, too isolated for singles. ⊠*Punta Cana* ☎*809/959–8229 or 888/442–2262* ⊕*www. puntacana.com* ⊅*15 one- to four-bedroom villas* ⑂*In-room: safe, kitchen, refrigerator, DVD, Ethernet. In-hotel: 9 restaurants, room service, bars, golf courses, tennis courts, pools, gym, spa, beachfront, diving, water sports, bicycles, no elevator, children's programs (ages 4–12), laundry service, concierge, public Internet, public Wi-Fi, airport shuttle, no-smoking rooms* ▤*AE, D, MC, V* ⏨*BP.*

$$–$$$
☾
★
🖭**Club Med Punta Cana.** Return visitors will surely recognize the playful whimsy and camaraderie that are hallmarks of this family-friendly resort. However, Punta Cana's first all-inclusive has a shiny new face after a $34-million renovation in early 2008 that has infused spark and savvy into this tried-and-true hostelry. Among the upgrades: flat-screen TVs and spiffy new bathrooms in every room, not to mention a brand-new spa with 10 treatment rooms plus special palapas for oceanfront massages. Also set to make a debut were expanded kids' clubs for all age groups, as well as 32 new 750-sqaure-foot oceanfront family suites. Interactive parent and infant learning workshops are among the offerings at the new Baby Club, the only one of its kind in the region. At the teen center, a create-your-own-soda bar is a bubbling hit, and a new skate park gives boarders a venue to show off those ollies and slides. As always, cheery staffers (G.O.s, or "gracious organizers," as they are called) do their best to ensure there's never a dull moment, with yoga, merengue lessons, and circus programs. **Pros:** Inspiring animation staff, something for all ages. **Cons:** Limited dining options, constant bustle. ⊠*Provincia La Altagracia, apartado postal 106, Punta Cana* ☎*809/686–5500 or 800/258–2633* ⊕*www.clubmed.com* ⊅*539 rooms, 32 family suites* ⑂*In-room: safe, refrigerator. In-hotel: 3 restaurants, bars, tennis courts, pools, gym, spa, beachfront, diving, water sports, children's programs (ages infant–17), laundry service, public Internet, public Wi-Fi, airport shuttle* ▤*AE, MC, V* ⏨*AI.*

$$–$$$
☾
★
🖭**Occidental Grand Flamenco Punta Cana.** Plenty of choices for food and fun at this gigantic resort are likely to impress both families and night owls. Most of the tastefully designed, spacious rooms (all of which have a balcony or terrace) got brand-new furnishings in early 2008. A graduated pool—one of the largest in Punta Cana—winds through the handsome grounds, with a swim-up bar that's a hub of activity; a separate quiet pool has no activities nearby, and with so many things going on all day, you may want to escape from time to time. The activity-packed children's program includes a mini-disco every evening, special entertainment for the kids, painting, family games, and theme parties. An ever-popular steak house, a Chinese restaurant, and a sports bar serving American-style fast food are among the dining options. The disco, Mangú, draws crowds until the wee hours. The nightly show rotates on a seven-day cycle. Royal Club guests have an exclusive section of beach, private check-in, a private lounge, free Internet access, and an exclusive à la carte restaurant in a delightful air-conditioned space overlooking the beach. **Pros:** Nightlife is excellent, late-night pizzeria, fun for the whole family. **Cons:** No wheelchair-accessible rooms,

no room-service for standard rooms. ⊠*Bávaro* ☎*809/221–8787* ⊕*www.occidentalhotels.com* ⇆*840 rooms, 25 suites* ♿*In-room: safe, refrigerator. In-hotel: 9 restaurants, room service (some), bars, tennis courts, pools, gym, spa, beachfront, diving, water sports, no elevator, children's programs (ages 4–12), laundry service, concierge (some), executive floor, public Internet, public Wi-Fi, no-smoking rooms* ▤*AE, D, MC, V* ⊠*AI.*

$$–$$$ ⚜**Ocean Blue/Ocean Sand Golf & Beach Resort.** This moderately priced
★ megaresort has a world of charm and exceeds expectations on many fronts. A free trolley traverses the expansive grounds, which are especially pretty at night. All rooms have a balcony or patio, but you pay extra to be near the exquisite beach; some room interiors could use a face-lift. Premium suites, offering oversize marble bathrooms, Jacuzzi tubs, room service, and a VIP lounge, are worth the extra cost. The pool is divided into two sections, with one designated for activities and the other for relaxation. Food at the main buffet is exceptional; house wines are served from bottles, not boxes. The resort's authentic Dominican restaurant is modeled after a traditional home, but if you're craving Americana with a side of fries, try the retro Route 66 diner. Mike's Coffee Shop serves made-to-order frappucinos and other hot and cold java drinks and herbal teas. Guests pay special reduced rates at the White Sands Golf Course; the resort itself has a bowling alley and casino. Service everywhere is prompt and friendly, yet there are some lapses, mainly attributable to linguistic misunderstandings. **Pros:** Free trolley every 10–15 minutes, Mike's Coffee Shop, bowling alley. **Cons:** Limited Internet access even for premium package, some drab interiors. ⊠*Playa Arena Gorda, Bávaro* ☎*809/476–2326* ⊕*www.oceanhotels. net* ⇆*436 junior suites, 272 suites* ♿*In-room: safe, refrigerator. In-hotel: 9 restaurants, bars, golf, tennis courts, pools, gym, spa, beachfront, diving, water sports, bicycles, no elevator, children's programs (ages 4–14), laundry service, public Internet, public Wi-Fi, no-smoking rooms* ▤*AE, MC, V* ⊠*AI.*

$$–$$$ ⚜**Paradisus Punta Cana.** Big-league improvements have been made in recent years at this seasoned tropical getaway, as it has struggled to keep pace with the newer competition. One addition is the Reserve, an ultraexclusive resort within the resort, with 192 suites, separate pools, and first-rate amenities that include an exclusive lounge, as well as concierge and butler service. On the main grounds, the pool complex is like a Hollywood set, with sculptures spouting water and Balinese sun beds; the beach is alluring. An abundance of restaurants—few all-inclusives in Punta Cana offer so many—means you won't go hungry. You can show your more-gregarious side at the karaoke bar—one of the more-convivial spots to mingle—before retreating to your room, where 24-hour room service is available. The venue for the nightly show was being reconstructed as this writing; there's also a casino. A batting cage, a rock-climbing wall, and an archery range make up an action park. Or you can head for the links with unlimited green fees included at the Cocotal Golf Course. **Pros:** Large selection of dining options, 24-hour room service included with standard package, good golf packages. **Cons:** Not recommended for solo travelers, older rooms show

10

signs of wear. ⊠*Bávaro* ☎*809/687–9923 or 800/336–3542* ⊕*www. paradisuspuntacana.solmelia.com* ↩*500 suites, 192 royal suites* ⚏*In-room: safe, refrigerator. In-hotel: 10 restaurants, room service, bars, golf course, tennis courts, pool, gym, spa, beachfront, diving, water sports, bicycles, no elevator, children's programs (ages 5–12), laundry service, public Internet, public Wi-Fi, no-smoking rooms* ⊟*AE, D, DC, MC, V* ⦿*AI.*

$$–$$$ 🏨 **Puntacana Hotel.** The classy granddaddy of all resorts in Punta Cana, ⏱ this charismatic hotel built in the 1970s spearheaded the area's tourism ★ industry and has kept pace with the times. Innovations and renovations consistently delight the well-heeled clientele, who can rely on top-notch service from a polished, attentive staff. A plethora of amenities—not to mention meticulously kept grounds and world-class golf—await guests. All rooms, with dark wood furnishings, stone floors, and floral bedding, have a balcony or terrace. Specialty restaurants are decorated with chic detail, as in Cocoloba, with the incomparable touch of Oscar de la Renta; La Yola charms with its setting overlooking the marina and its sophisticated seafood menu. Housed in the alluring golf club, the Six Senses Spa is a holistic oasis offering marvelous treatments using lemongrass, aloe vera, and tropical fruits grown locally. Zipping along the shore paths in a rented golf cart is an enjoyable way to get where you're going on the grounds, where you can explore hiking trails, swim at a freshwater spring, or visit the petting zoo. Kids' club activities include stretching classes, crafts, minibowling, Nintendo, Spanish lessons, and pony rides. Beachfront family casitas are equipped with baby video monitors. In the nearby Puntacana Village, you'll find a Portuguese restaurant, a much-adored bar, an Oscar de la Renta outlet, an art gallery, and more shops. Meal-plan options are available. **Pros:** Expansive and beautiful grounds, spectacular golf and spa. **Cons:** Limited nightlife on-site, alienating for solo travelers. ⊠*Puntacana Resort & Club, Punta Cana* ☎*809/959–2262 or 888/442–2262* ⊕*www.puntacana.com* ↩*175 rooms, 16 junior suites, 11 suites, 38 casitas* ⚏*In-room: safe, refrigerator (some). In-hotel: 9 restaurants, bars, golf courses, tennis courts, pools, gym, spa, beachfront, diving, water sports, bicycles, no elevator, children's programs (ages 4–12), laundry service, public Internet, public Wi-Fi, airport shuttle, no-smoking rooms* ⊟*AE, MC, V* ⦿*BP.*

$$ 🏨 **Iberostar Bávaro Resort.** Like its two sister resorts, this Spanish doña ⏱ has panache, evidenced in its lobby, an artistic showpiece. It's one of the more-desirable Punta Cana properties, though not one of the newest, and a good value. The dramatic public spaces segue into grounds crisscrossed with lagoons that lead to a broad, beautifully maintained white-sand beach. Although rooms don't compare with the public spaces, the Bávaro's are the sweetest (and most expensive), with a separate sitting area. True to Iberostar's emphasis on quality food and beverages, there are 11 restaurants, including Cajun and gourmet dining rooms. The shows are better than the norm, with house dancers, a band, and vocalists. The Iberostar Punta Cana and Iberostar Dominicana share facilities in the complex, but only guests at the more-expensive Bávaro can dine at that resort's restaurants. **Pros:** Variety of good dining options, fun entertainment, dramatic lobby and grounds. **Cons:** Not singles-oriented, no Internet access in rooms. ✉*Bávaro* ☎*809/221–6500 or 888/923–2722* ⊕*www.iberostar.com* ⛱*590 rooms, 8 apartments* ⚲*In-room: safe, refrigerator. In-hotel: 11 restaurants, room service, bars, tennis courts, pool, gym, spa, beachfront, diving, water sports, no elevator, children's programs (ages 4–12), laundry service, concierge, public Internet, public Wi-Fi* ▤*AE, MC, V* ⏣*AI.*

$$ ⛨ **Riu Clubhotel Bambu.** The most upbeat resort in the giant Riu complex, this bungalow-style, pastel-color caravansary is equally popular among activity-seeking young couples and families. Pumped-up poolside activities and nightly entertainment at the sheltered open-air theater keep guests' spirits and the energy level high. Among the diverse kids' club offerings are water polo, mini golf, badminton, and bowling, as well as a special mini-disco every evening, with face painting once a week. Guests here share access to the facilities of three sister Riu properties (all but the Riu Palace Punta Cana) and the unique Caribbean Street shopping and entertainment village. The Pacha disco and casino within the complex provide some of the best nightlife in the area. Golf packages are available for Riu guests at the nearby Punta Blanca course. Room furnishings are standard and simple (no king-size beds are available here). **Pros:** Lively hub of activity day and night, good kids' club, good golf packages. **Cons:** No king-size beds, no special views, not recommended for solo travelers. ✉*Playa Arena Gorda, Bávaro* ☎*809/221–7575* ⊕*www.riu.com* ⛱*552 rooms, 8 suites* ⚲*In room: safe, refrigerator. In hotel: 5 restaurants, bars, tennis courts, pools, gym, spa, beachfront, diving, water sports, no elevator, children's programs (ages 4–12), laundry service, concierge, public Internet, public Wi-Fi* ▤*AE, D, MC, V* ⏣*AI.*

$–$$ ⛨ **Meliá Caribe Tropical.** At this enormously popular, American-friendly resort, service has been restored and prices have leveled out, making it once again a good value. For an extra $90 per night you can bump up to the VIP Royal Service, which gets you a true apartment suite with butler service, a pillow menu, room service, a stunning pool with a "Grecian ruin," and a private beach area with luxe Indo beds. The restaurant-bar has a delightful breakfast and other repasts. For drinks and appetizers or to get online, swing over to the clubhouse. At least one round of golf is included at the adjacent Cocotal Golf Club, and you get preferred tee times. Know that for most it's a shuttle or train ride to the beach. Flintstone-theme kids' clubs are a hit, with programs for infants to tweens. **Pros:** Proximity to golf course, adjacent to Palma Real Shopping Village. **Cons:** Most rooms far from the beach, many extra charges. ✉*Bávaro* ☎*809/221–1290 or 800/336–3542* ⊕*www.solmelia.com* ⛱*1,144 junior suites* ⚲*In-room: safe, refrigerator, Ethernet. In-hotel: 15 restaurants, room service, bars, golf course, tennis courts, pools, gym, spa, beachfront, water sports, no elevator, children's programs (ages 4 months–13), public Internet, public Wi-Fi* ▤*AE, DC, MC, V* ⏣*AI.*

$–$$ ⛨ **Natura Park Eco-Resort & Spa.** You can feel good about being here as you dine on meals made from wholesome, all-natural ingredients. Carved from a former coconut plantation in 1997, the resort retains a mangrove forest and a natural lake, and exotic birds roam the gardens.

10

The ecosensitive architecture incorporates cut cane, coco palms, local wood, and unearthed stones into the furniture, walkways, and footbridges. Buildings occupy only 10% of the property, and the beach is rather small. This resort appeals to a niche group that prefers low-key, if any, activities. A loft area above the lobby is the designated reading room. Give your body a treat, and take it to the Health Center and Beauty Farm. Comedy and music shows start after dinner, followed by dance music until 1 AM. **Pros:** Healthful food, ecofriendly philosophy and architecture. **Cons:** Limited activities and dining options, small beach, little nightlife. ⊠ *Bávaro* ☎ *809/221–2626* ⊕ *www.blau-hotels. com* ⇱ *490 rooms, 20 suites* ⌂ *In-room: safe, refrigerator. In-hotel: 3 restaurants, bars, tennis courts, pool, spa, beachfront, water sports, no elevator, children's programs (ages 2–12), public Internet, no-smoking rooms* ⊟ *AE, D, MC, V* ⦿ *AI.*

$ **Barceló Dominican Beach.** An exceptional value, this well-managed
★ resort has been infused with upgrades since it was purchased from Ocean Hotels in 2007, and it now exudes appeal rivaling the higher-tier Barceló properties. Many guest rooms have been renovated and all have been outfitted with pillow-top mattresses; all rooms have balconies, satellite TV, and coffeemakers, and the minibar is restocked daily. The gym has all the standard machines—treadmills, stair-steppers, and stationary bikes—and free weights to get (or keep) you in top form. The wonderful Metamorphosis Spa looks out over the ocean, adding another dose of soothing to the mix of treatments. The Spanish restaurant, El Mesón, serves commendable meals in a charming setting, and the Brazilian rodizio grill also gets accolades from guests; a coffee bar will pick you up in the afternoon. Basketball, archery, dance lessons, and Spanish lessons are among the full plate of daytime activities. For nightly fun, two theaters feature a schedule of entertainment on a 14-day rotation; weekly beach parties, a casino, and a disco round out the entertainment options. Wi-Fi is available in all rooms (rare in Punta Cana), although there is an extra cost. **Pros:** Attention to detail, Wi-Fi throughout, great coffee bar. **Cons:** Beach parties can get loud, extra cost for Wi-Fi. ⊠ *Bávaro* ☎ *809/221–0714 Ext. 1801* ⊕ *www. barcelo.com* ⇱ *638 rooms, 94 suites* ⌂ *In-room: safe, refrigerator, Wi-Fi. In-hotel: 9 restaurants, room service (some), bars, tennis courts, pools, gym, spa, beachfront, diving, water sports, bicycles, children's programs (ages 4–12), laundry service, public Internet, public Wi-Fi, no-smoking rooms* ⊟ *AE, DC, MC, V* ⦿ *AI.*

SAMANÁ

Samaná is the name of both the peninsula that curves around the eponymous bay and of the largest town. Las Terrenas is at least a 2½-hour drive from Cabarete. Luckily, El Catey Airport (AZS) now has regular air service from American Eagle from San Juan; otherwise, Takeoff Destination Service offers regular flights from several D.R. airports. The nearest major international airport is Puerto Plata's International Gregorio Luperon, more than a three-hour drive away *(⇨ By Air under Transportation in Dominican Republic Essentials).*

CLOSE UP

Cap Cana

One of the most ambitious new development projects in the Dominican Republic, Cap Cana is a resort and villa complex spread out over 30,000 acres (5 mi [7 km]) of precious beach on bluffs 200 feet above sea level and about 10 minutes south of the Punta Cana airport. In time it will have at least four luxury hotels with 3,000 rooms, 5,000 residential units, six golf courses, a 5,000-seat amphitheater, casinos, a marina with yacht clubs and deep-sea fishing fleet, beach clubs, polo grounds, spas, and tennis and squash courts.

The flagship hotel, the Altabella Sanctuary Cap Cana Golf & Spa, opened in 2008, although some facilities were not complete at this writing. The pioneer of the golf courses, Punta Espada—one of three Jack Nicklaus signature courses planned for the complex—opened in 2006 and is the site of a new PGA Champions Tour event. The second, Las Iguanas, was preparing to open in late 2008. Also already up and running is the exclusive Caletón Beach Club, with

its palapa roof and spectacular pool carved into a coral base. Cap Cana Marina is being built in three phases; it's destined to be the Caribbean's largest, with 500 slips capable of docking yachts of more than 150 feet. Just off the treasured fishing grounds of the Mona Passage between the Dominican Republic and Puerto Rico, the marina will have a port authority and customs, restaurants, shops, and nightclubs. Phase one of the marina was slated to open by May 2008.

Coming soon is the Ritz-Carlton, a billion-dollar mixed-use complex with a 220-room hotel, residences, a spa, a private beach club, five restaurants, and lounges, slated to open in early 2010. Also underway is Donald Trump's $2-billion real estate project, Trump at Cap Cana, which when complete will have a luxury resort, a golf course, golf villas, estate lots, a beach club, a condo hotel, and residences. Kicking off the first phase of development are the Trump Farallon Estates at Cap Cana, which generated record sales of its lot sites.

$$$$
Fodor$Choice
★

ⓘPeninsula House. If you can afford it, a stay here will reset your thinking on what a small luxury property can be; this is one of the best bed-and-breakfasts in the Caribbean, if not the world. The gorgeous Victorian-style plantation house with wraparound verandahs overlooks miles of coconut palms down to the ocean. It's family run and showcases generations' worth of museum-quality sculptures, paintings, and objects d'art, many of which were acquired from the Far East and the Middle East. The art elevates the rooms and common areas to a fascinating visual experience. Dinner, available only to guests, takes place in the central open-air brick courtyard. Dishes, linens, even the stationery you'll find here is refined; to mention that rooms come with flat-screen TVs (the only ones on the Samaná Peninsula at this writing) would be missing the point. No expense has been spared. For heaven's sake, the pool house has a world-class collection of African masks. Is $600 a lot for a room? It's not a full-fledged "resort," but we'd recommend that you consider saving now. In terms of international high-end travel, this is a real steal. The house opened in 2007, doesn't advertise, and the secretive entrance is unmarked from the road. **Pros:** Quiet and

10

remote, luxurious, impeccable guest attention. **Cons:** Expensive, but that's the only drawback we can find. ✉ *Camino Cosón, Las Terrenas* ☎ *809/307–1827 or 809/882–7712* ⊕ *www.thepeninsulahouse.com* ⇥ *6 rooms* ☖ *In room: safe, DVD, Wi-Fi. In-hotel: bar, pool, spa, no elevator, laundry service, public Wi-Fi, no kids under 18* ▤ *AE, D, MC, V* ⦿ *BP.*

$$ ▦ **Bahía Príncipe Cayacoa.** As you might expect of an all-inclusive built in the middle of a setting of immense natural beauty, this place combines the best and worst of everything. Of the four Gran Bahías on the peninsula, only this one doesn't make you feel like a prisoner (although you are still wearing a plastic ID bracelet) since town (and the good food you can find there) is just a five-minute walk away. The best that Cayacoa offers are the mesmerizing views: the ocean, the town, and the rolling green landscape all lie before you from this hilltop perch on the bay. Also, this is the only actual hotel in the town of Samaná. (The next closest, Gran Bahia Samaná, is just 10 minutes away, but feels unpleasantly isolated.) Day visitors can purchase a pass for $70 that includes all food and drinks, and recreation (an excellent choice for cruise passengers). You need to stay a minimum of three nights to dine at the nonbuffet restaurants. Cayacoa has its own spa and disco. Snorkeling and kayaks are included. **Pros:** Beautiful views, fun activities. **Cons:** Bad food, forced to wear ID bracelet. ✉ *Puerto Escondido, Santa Barbara de Samaná* ☎ *809/538–3131* ⊕ *www.bahiaprincipe. com* ⇥ *209 rooms, 86 suites* ☖ *In room: safe, refrigerator. In-hotel: 5 restaurants, room service, bars, pools, gym, spa, beachfront, diving, water sports, laundry service, public Internet, public Wi-Fi* ▤ *AE, D, DC, MC, V* ⦿ *AI.*

$ ▦ **Hotel Las Ballenas Escondidas.** Looking for a truly relaxing and peace-

Fodor's Choice ful setting with a private beach? The French couple who run this place
★ have created a small utopia of gardens and thatch-roof bungalows sloping down to the sea. An infinity-edge pool is in the middle of it all. Ballenas Escondidas is 15 minutes east of Santa Barbara de Samaná, nearly halfway to Las Galeras. This means it's essentially in the middle of nowhere. But where the remoteness and the nice pool and restaurant might seem to imply an all-inclusive experience, there are no forced good times here. At night the ocean is the only music you'll hear. By day, a private terrace with two bamboo chairs overlooks the hibiscus, bougainvillea, coconut trees, and colorful pastels of the other bungalows; a few cats roam the grounds. The hotel offers boating excursions directly from its small beach. Note that rooms have ceiling fans but no air-conditioning. **Pros:** Private, quiet, beautiful.**Cons:** Remote location, thin sheets and older mattresses, no credit cards. ✉ *Los Naranjos* ☎ *809/495–0888* ⊕ *www.ballenas.free.fr* ⇥ *12 bungalows* ☖ *In room: no a/c, no phone, safe, refrigerator, no TV. In-hotel: restaurant, bar, pool, beachfront, laundry service* ▤ *No credit cards* ⦿ *BP.*

$ ▦ **Villa Serena.** The best hotel choice in eastern corner of the peninsula,
★ Villa Serena make a wonderful, relaxed vacation in Samaná a breeze. You'll love the secluded location removed from the hubbub of the main beach; but you'll appreciate being able to walk over to the main street to mix with locals and day-trippers. Included in the price are kayaks,

bicycles, and snorkeling equipment—you can pack a picnic lunch, paddle out to a perfect little island not far offshore, and snorkel around the perimeter. Sensational Room 17 has two balconies and a hammock overlooking the beach. Rooms have bamboo canopy beds with covering scrims. Excursions directly from the premises including the "dream beach" package for a reasonable RD$1,800 per couple—get a tour of all the area's secluded beaches and be dropped off for as long as you like at your favorite. Rooms are available with and without air-conditioning. Prices include a full breakfast. **Pros:** Private beachfront; quiet and secluded property; fine staff. **Cons:** 10-minute walk to town. ⊠*Las Galeras* ☎*809/538–0000* ⊕*www.villaserena.com* ⇔*21 rooms* ♿*In room: no a/c (some), no phone, no TV. In-hotel: restaurants, room service, bar, pool, beachfront, water sports, bicycles, no elevator, laundry service, public Wi-Fi* ⊟*MC, V* ⊺⊙⏐*BP.*

¢ ⊞ **Coyamar.** Coyamar is the most inexpensive of the peninsula's lan-
★ guorous gems. If you don't mind going without air-conditioning, it's hard not to love the hyper-relaxed atmosphere of this family-run small hotel on Playa Bonita. A path wends its way across the yard of orange trees, coconut palms, and bamboo to the beach at the end of the lawn, which has the feel of a small seafront botanic garden. The restaurant, under an enormous thatch roof, serves fresh fish and is a wonderful place to read a book. Coyamar is the creation (the name, in fact, is an invention) of German expat owners Peter and Judith, who designed the environmentally sensitive hotel in the 1990s. Expect to see a shirt-less Peter reading the papers while young son Tao cavorts with his two chow chows, Madox and Balu. Rooms are bright, with peach and light greens. Red floor tiles extend from spacious terraces to the comfortable interiors, which have high ceilings and colorful art. There is no air-conditioning, TV, or phone, but the shutters ensure breezy nights (there are ceiling fans). Don't like the overhead fluorescent lighting at night? Light the candle in your room, and take in the sounds of the surf by flickering light. Life doesn't get simpler. **Pros:** Hands-on owners, green hotel, great value. **Cons:** No a/c, fluorescent lights are dim. ⊠*Playa Bonita1, Las Terrenas* ☎*809/240–5130* ⊕*www.coyamar.com* ⇔*10 rooms* ♿*In room: no a/c, no phone, safe, no TV, Ethernet, Wi-Fi. In-hotel: restaurant, bar, pool, beachfront, no elevator, public Wi-Fi, some pets allowed* ⊟*MC, V* ⊺⊙⏐*CP.*

10

NORTH COAST

The northern coast of the island, with mountains on one side, is also called the Amber Coast because of the large quantities of amber found in the area. The sands on its 75 mi (121 km) of beach are also golden. Major resort areas are Playa Dorada, Cabarete, and Sosúa. Plan to fly into Puerto Plata International Gregorio Luperon Airport.

$$$–$$$$ ⊞ **Casa Colonial Beach & Spa.** Rivals say "over the top" isn't superlative
Fodor$Choice enough to describe this exquisite, all-suites boutique hotel designed
★ by Sara Garcia Cassoni, the first in the D.R. to join the lofty Small Luxury Hotels of the World. White stucco buildings have columns and wrought-iron balustrades and most guests think that it is a restoration

of a colonial mansion. Suites are outfitted with the finest Frette linens. The lobby feels more like a lounge, with a stellar bar; Lucia's, the designer gourmet room, is worthy of this boutique hotel. Upscale spa devotees will savor the Baqua Spa, with its Vichy showers, body wraps, inventory of massages and facials, and refreshing juices. The rooftop sundeck is close to heaven—an infinity pool and four warm Jacuzzis provide several agreeable alternatives to the golden beach. It has also served as a venue for wedding receptions and for private dinners for two. **Pros:** Luxury boutique experience, glorious spa, this is how you would like to live. **Cons:** Can feel empty during the low season, quiet even in the high season, service not as sharp as you would expect for these prices (and few speak good English). ⊠*Playa Dorada, Puerto Plata* ☎*809/320–3232* ⊕*www.casacolonialhotel.com* ⋈*50 suites* ⌂*In-room: dial-up, refrigerator. In-hotel: 2 restaurants, bar, pool, gym, spa, beachfront, concierge, laundry service, public Wi-Fi* ⊟*AE, MC, V* �|O|*EP.*

$$$ 📺**Ocean Point.** Five years in the making, the wait was worth it for the pizzazz of this new five-star, condo complex in the dunes of Kite Beach. This is the good life, as one sits at the pool, shaded by a golden market umbrella and watching the parade of multicolor surf-kites in the big blue ocean. You can take out a kayak or boogie board or just bob around with a pool noodle. The stucco facade of these three-story buildings is attractive; all the condos have expansive terraces and outdoor dining areas. Yet the interiors outshine all, with the fully equipped, Italian designer kitchens being the best attribute, especially for those who want to stay in for dinner. The four-bedroom/four-bath 4,000-square-foot penthouses are tastefully luxurious and worth the extra money if you have a larger family. Mind you, the two-bedroom condos are 1,800 square feet. The two buildings are identical. The reception office and concierge for both projects is in the second phase, in a thatch-roof structure. The concierge can arrange pre-arrival grocery stocking and nanny service, too. **Pros:** Gorgeous views, quality building materials, elevators (!). **Cons:** A 20-minute beach walk to most restaurants, no breakfast or meals available on-site. ⊠*Kite Beach, Carretera Principal, Cabarete* ☎*809/571–0030* ⊕*www.oceanpointdr.com* ⋈*28 2-bedroom condos, 10 4-bedroom penthouses* ⌂*In-room: safe, Ethernet, Wi-Fi. In-hotel: pool, beachfront, laundry facilities, no-smoking rooms (some)* ⊟*AE, D, DC, MC, V* �|O|*EP.*

$$$ 📺**Victorian House.** Roosted on a cliff above breathtaking Sosúa Bay, ★ this boutique hotel is a delightful replica of a Victorian gingerbread house. It's much more low key and not as densely populated as its sister property, the Sosúa Bay Hotel, next door. (You can pipe into its all-inclusive plan.) Check-in is at a white-pillared cottage, originally a settlement house for Jewish refugees in the 1940s. Multilingual concierges pamper independent travelers. Terraces have teak lounge chairs and ottomans, not to mention ever-changing knockout views. **Pros:** Bi-level penthouses are outstanding, consistently good service, small hotel that still offers tie-in meal plan with a nearby sister property. **Cons:** Lack of elevators can be hard if you're on a higher floor, latest renovation not entirely successful. ⊠*Calle Dr. Alejo Martinez 1, El*

Batey, Sosúa ☎809/571–4000 ⬀*32 rooms, 7 junior suites, 8 suites, 3 penthouses* ♿*In-room: safe, kitchen (some), refrigerator. In-hotel: 5 restaurants, room service, bars, pools, gym, beachfront, diving, water sports, bicycles, concierge, no elevator, children's programs (ages 4–12), laundry facilities* ☰*MC, V* ⦿*BP.*

$$ **Natura Cabanas.** This oceanfront ecoparadise offers accommodations
★ in thatch-roof cabanas, such as the Africana, a sophisticated structure made from bamboo, artistic brick, and stonework. The diverse clientele enhances this back-to-nature experience; you might find yourself next to a surfer, a young neurologist, or a yoga aficionado. Lole, the *dueña*, and her caring, bilingual staff promote camaraderie. Healthful breakfasts and lunches are served in one of the two waterfront restaurants where the mellow music is the backdrop for backgammon and conversation. At night the seafood restaurant woos diners. The artistically designed Attabeyra Spa is completely individualistic, and has services like chocolate wraps and massage on the beach. The splendid yoga pavilion is a *palacio*: it is the oceanfront setting for classes, retreats, and weddings. The pool palapa with its colorful Indian sarongs is the setting for romantic dinners for two and VIP parties. There's a special discount if you pay in cash. **Pros:** Good restaurants, caring owners, great spa. **Cons:** Car required, no a/c. ⊠*Playa Perla Marina, Cabarete* ☎☎*809/571–1507* ⊕*www.naturacabana.com* ⬀*11 bungalows* ♿*In-room: no a/c, no phone, kitchen (some), refrigerator, no TV. In-hotel: 2 restaurants, bar, pool, spa, beachfront, no elevator, parking (no fee)* ☰*AE, MC, V* ⦿*CP.*

$$ **Sosúa by the Sea Boutique Beach Resort.** Proudly Canadian owned, this once-dated hotel had a metamorphosis in 2007. Passed from father to son, it has now been completely refurbished with black, queen-size sleigh beds and handsome, minimalist black-and-white decor. The small open-air lobby has comfortable couches and a coffee table in a sitting area. The central pool, dive shop, main restaurant, bar, and "private" beach are still inviting. Joseph's Grape & Grill specialty restaurant, under a white canvas big top, is on a promontory overlooking the crashing surf. The hotel continues to have a mainly returning clientele—older and Canadian—but according to the veteran manager, Americans are starting to discover its charms. **Pros:** All-inclusive plan is optional but an exceptional value, most meals are served à la carte with good house wine, Wi-Fi is available throughout the property. **Cons:** No organized activities or nightlife at hotel, many rooms have no real closets (only a pole with hangers near the bathroom). ⊠*Calle B. Philips, Sosúa* ☎*809/571–3222* ⊕*www.sosuabythesea.com* ⬀*58 rooms, 33 suites* ♿*In room: safe, refrigerator (some), kitchen (some), Wi-Fi. In-hotel: 2 restaurants, bars, pool, beachfront, diving, laundry service, public Internet, public Wi-Fi, no smoking, parking (free)* ☰*AE, MC, V* ⦿*BP.*

$$ **Sun Village Resort & Spa.** Like a sprawling Mediterranean hill town
☯ (be comfortable in your shoes) with an aqua labyrinth of pools, Sun Village keeps climbing higher. It's no longer just a family resort catering to the adjacent Ocean World complex; it's a fun, happening place for sophisticated couples and incentive groups. November's annual film festival attracts an interesting international crowd and is an exciting

10

time to visit. An alluring spa and fitness center features a distinctive pool and Asian garden, plus 205 spa suites with sea views (most regular rooms, alas, have no view). Don't opt for less than a superior room, though all guest rooms will benefit from a modest renovation, which was in the works for 2008 at this writing (ask for a renovated room). The newest offerings, Maxim Bungalows, overlook the property and are exceptional. **Pros:** Great spirit and large fun quotient, the buffet is definitely a notch above, the management and staff go that extra mile to please. **Cons:** Steep hills and stairs here, feels isolated (and is a sizable cab fare if you go somewhere. ⊠*Cofresi Beach, Puerto Plata* ☎*809/970–3364 or 888/446–4695* ⊕*www.sunvillageresorts. com* ⇆*300 rooms, 8 suites, 3 villas* ⟳*In-room: safe. In-hotel: 5 restaurants, bars, tennis courts, pools, gym, spa, beachfront, diving, water sports, bicycles, children's programs (ages 4–12), public Internet, public Wi-Fi* ⊟*AE, MC, V* ⚐*AI.*

$–$$ 🏨 **Gran Ventana Beach Resort.** This resort is characterized by a sophis-
☽ ticated style that sets it apart from the nearby competition. The lobby, with pottery and local drums suspended from the walls, is a contemporary study in Caribbean colors with a fountain. The beach is on a point with unobstructed views to the left. Families are a good share of the market, and this resort is solid as far as the tour operators are concerned, with service and food improving each season. Many couples prefer the larger rooms (sans good ocean views, unfortunately) that surround the quiet pool. A Victorian-style wedding gazebo is popular for nuptials. **Pros:** Consistently good food and service for this price point, plenty of activities for the whole family. **Cons:** Feels busy year-round, the buffet is often better than the free-standing dining rooms. ⊠*Playa Dorada, Puerto Plata* ☎*809/320–2111* ⊕*www.vhhr.com* ⇆*499 rooms, 2 suites, 1 penthouse* ⟳*In-room: safe, refrigerator. In-hotel: 5 restaurants, bars, tennis court, pools, gym, beachfront, water sports, bicycles, no elevator, children's programs (ages 4–12), public Internet* ⊟*AE, MC, V* ⚐*AI.*

$–$$ **Iberostar Costa Dorada.** This resort will dazzle you with its sprawling
★ lobby, its hardwood benches and sculptures, and its curvaceous pool with a central Jacuzzi encircled by Roman pillars. As you swim along you can see the mountains and the beach. Other all-inclusives could learn from Iberostar's excellent buffet; of the à la carte restaurants, the Brazilian is the standout and the Mexican is quite authentic. This resort does a lot right, and yes, there is a spa. Newly repainted, the rooms are somewhat dated but attractive, with their woven wall hangings and bright colors. Many of the staffers speak English here, and the resort itself is close to Puerto Plata, so you can have more contact with real Dominican life. At night, you can watch the entertainment (the music is especially good) from the outdoor seating in the garden. **Pros:** Good management makes for a happy staff and a fun resort, blue-flag beach, top-shelf liquor in the lobby bar. **Cons:** Popularity translates to high-occupancy year-round, no Wi-Fi, pool can be very noisy. ⊠*Playa Costa Dorada, Carretera Luperon, Km 4, Marapica* ☎*809/320–1000 or 888/923–2722* ⊕*www.iberostar.com* ⇆*498 rooms, 18 junior suites* ⟳*In-room: safe, refrigerator. In-hotel: 4 res-*

taurants, bars, tennis courts, pools, gym, spa, beachfront, diving, water sports, no elevator, children's programs (ages 4–12), public Internet ⊟*AE, MC, V* ⊺⊙⎮*AI.*

$ ⬚**Velero Beach Resort.** Laze in the hammock or swing on the palm that
★ bends over the beach while you watch the kite surfers work to become airborne. They're the only thing between you and the horizon at this well-managed hotel and residential enclave with its own beachfront and manicured gardens studded with cacti, orchids, and pottery. Well-heeled Dominicans, hip Americans, and other international guests appreciate that it's removed from the noise of town yet just minutes down the sand from the happening bars. Spacious suites with full kitchens are the best deals; the basic unit has 2 full bedrooms, but lock-outs can divide one larger unit into two smaller units, though the lock-out unit will not have a kitchen. Guests in standard rooms (without kitchens) get a complimentary breakfast at the private beach restaurant. You might ask for the art deco Building 111, which has all been repainted. The views from the penthouses are knockout and an excellent value if three couples share. Ask about the 10% discount for cash. **Pros:** Blenders, microwaves and DVDs in the junior suites and above; new, draped, Balinese sun beds at the pool are wonderfully hedonistic; Velero is blossoming into a wedding and honeymoon venue. **Cons:** No elevators—it's a climb up the spiral staircases, standard rooms are not spacious. ⊠*Calle la Punta 1, Cabarete* ☎*809/571–9727* ⊕*www.velerobeach. com* ⇨*22 2-bedroom suites, 7 penthouses* ᗑ*In-room: safe, kitchen (some), refrigerator, Wi-Fi (some). In-hotel: restaurant, pool, beachfront, no elevator, public Internet, public Wi-Fi* ⊟*MC, V* ⊺⊙⎮*EP.*

¢–$ ⬚**Blue Bay Villa Doradas.** This redo of a 1980s-era resort exceeds your expectations. The stunning, grand entrance (a Sara Garcia design) with its slender, white pillars utilizes white fabric to shelter the lobby from tropical rainfalls. The cushy, woven lounge furniture with bright and floral pillows; the boutique with its tropical whites; the staff in their tropical whites—all make for one attractive island scenario. It provides the backdrop for the weekly manager's party that may be the country's best: a stellar five-piece band, mimosas, and delicious hors d'oeuvres. The exuberant management leads the way to an admirable display of abundance that represents all the à la carte Asian and seafood restaurants as well as the international buffet, from raw oysters to a real turkey dinner. P.S.: This is an adults-only resort—no children allowed; upgrade your room if you can afford it. **Pros:** Great spa, handsome beach club and stellar beachfront, yoga and golf classes included. **Cons:** Mosquitoes are a constant problem, the animated staff and the music are just too loud some days, standard and standard-plus rooms are not luxurious. ⊠*Playa Dorada, Puerto Plata* ☎*809/320–3000, 809/320–1600 for reservations* ⊕*www.bluebayresorts.com* ⇨*245 rooms, 4 suites* ᗑ*In-room: safe, refrigerator. In-hotel: 4 restaurants, bars, tennis courts, pools, gym, spa, beachfront, water sports, bicycles, no elevators, laundry service, concierge, executive floor, public Internet, public Wi-Fi. no smoking rooms, parking (no fee)* ⊟*AE, D, DC, MC, V* ⊺⊙⎮*AI.*

10

¢–$ 🔲 **Villa Taina.** Smack amid the action, steps down from the main drag, this small, German-owned inn encapsulates the original spirit of Cabarete. It caters to the independent traveler and the young and sporty who want more-commodious digs than a surf camp. Enjoy an ample breakfast at Serenada, the beachside restaurant, which is sheltered from the wind by translucent kite boards borrowed from the kite-surfing center; your fellow coffee drinkers may be shielded by German and French newspapers. By night, the revamped restaurant serves international cuisine, with special buffet theme nights, cool sounds, and a fun crowd. The interiors may be a bit dated, but this beach hotel is an excellent value—it even has free in-room DSL lines. Request the quiet rooms (the second floor up to the penthouses) that front the beach. **Pros:** Right in the middle of things, efficient and caring German owner. **Cons:** Small pool, noise of town can be heard in the buildings closest to the street, rooms are on the small side. ✉ *Calle Principal, Cabarete* ☎ *809/571–0722* ⊕ *www.villataina.com* ⇆ *56 rooms, 1 apartment* ⬧ *In-room: refrigerator, Ethernet. In-hotel: restaurant, bar, pool, beachfront, water sports, no elevator* ⊟ *MC, V* ⧄ *BP.*

¢ 🔲 **Hotel Casa Valeria.** In a sweeping, hacienda design—reminiscent of Mexico—this pink adobe, housing both a hotel and a restaurant, is a standout in this quiet neighborhood. Wrought-iron gates open to a courtyard, and most of the simple accommodations face the pool in the rear garden. The proud owners are a Dutch couple. Ärien, in a most efficient manner, has refurbished each of the rooms (some have hand-painted tropical murals), upgraded furnishings, and installed new air-conditioning. Ärien's wife, Diana, adds the feminine touch and softened the courtyard, which is candle-lighted by night. This inn may be cheap, but it's also a great value. Airport transfers are included if you stay a week. **Pros:** Nicely renovated, the owners will transfer you to the airport for half the price of a taxi, rooms have cable TV. **Cons:** These are not deluxe accommodations, service is limited, no views. ✉ *Calle Dr. Rosen, No. 28, El Batey, Sosúa* ☎ *809/571–3536* ⊕ *www.hotelcasavaleria.com* ⇆ *9 rooms* ⬧ *In-room: kitchen (some), no phone. In-hotel: restaurant, pool* ⊟ *MC, V* ⧄ *EP.*

WHERE TO EAT

The island's culinary repertoire includes Spanish, Italian, Middle Eastern, Indian, Japanese, and *nueva cocina Dominicana* (contemporary Dominican cuisine). If seafood is on the menu, it's bound to be fresh. The dining scene in Santo Domingo is the best in the country and probably as fine a selection of restaurants as you will find anywhere in the Caribbean. Keep in mind that the touristy restaurants, such as those in the Colonial Zone, with mediocre fare and just-okay service, are becoming more and more costly, whereas the few fine dining options, like La Residence and Café Bellini, have lowered their prices and are offering a daily special menu with main courses less than $10. Or you can order two generous appetizers for, say, $15. You will have caring service and be sequestered in luxe surroundings away from the tourist hustle. Know that capitaleños dress for dinner and dine late. The crowds pick up after 9:30 PM.

Among the best Dominican specialties are *queso frito* (fried cheese), *sancocho* (a thick stew usually made with five meats and served with rice and avocado slices), *arroz con pollo* (rice with beans and fried chicken parts), *pescado al coco* (fish in coconut sauce), and *plátanos* (plantains) in all their tasty varieties, including *tostones* (fried green plaintains). Shacks and stands that serve cheap eats are an integral part of the culture and landscape, but eat street food at your own risk—more like your own peril. Presidente is the best local beer. Brugal rum is popular with the Dominicans, but Barceló *anejo* (aged) rum is as smooth as cognac, and Barceló Imperial is so special it's sold only at Christmastime.

> **TIP!**
>
> If you are going to the north coast, check out airfares to Santiago, which has numerous direct flights from New York, Newark, and Miami. JetBlue has rates as low as $150 one way. The flight arrives around 4:30 AM, but now that the spiffy Courtyard by Marriott Santiago opened five minutes from the airport, you can bunk there, spend the morning at Centro León, and take a bus or taxi to the north-coast towns of Puerto Plata, Sosúa, and Cabarete. Since JetBlue prices by segments, you could fly out of another destination without penalty.

WHAT TO WEAR

In resort areas, shorts and bathing suits under beach wraps are usually (but not always) acceptable at breakfast and lunch. For dinner, long pants, skirts, and collared shirts are the norm. Restaurants tend to be more formal in Santo Domingo, both at lunch and at dinner, with trousers required for men and dresses suggested for women. Ties aren't required anywhere, but jackets are (even at the midday meal) in some of the finer establishments.

SANTO DOMINGO

10

FRENCH ✕**La Residence.** This fine-dining enclave has always had the setting—
$–$$$ Spanish colonial architecture, with pillars and archways overlooking
★ a courtyard—and an esoteric lunch-dinner menu with high prices that did not always deliver. Now it has a seasoned French chef serving classic yet innovative cuisine with many moderately priced choices. The daily Menu del Chef has a main course for less than $10. It could be brochettes of spit-roasted duck, chicken au poivre, or vegetable risotto. You could start with a salad of panfried young squid for about $5 and go bonkers over the $3 dark- and white-chocolate terrine. Veer from the daily specials menu, and prices can certainly go higher but are still fair; even the grilled fillet and braised oxtail with foie gras sauce and wild mushrooms is reasonable. ⊠*Sofitel Nicolas Ovando, Calle Las Damas, Zona Colonial* ☎809/685–9955 ═AE, MC, V.

ITALIAN ✕ **Café Bellini.** This café has always had a panache far and above its coun-
$–$$$ terparts, for the Italian owners also have the adjacent furniture design
★ center. The moderne, wicker-weave barrel chairs, and the contempo-
rary art and light fixtures are all achingly hip. The menu is the same at
lunch and dinner. The democratic pricing usually offers a main course,
such as the trio of raviolis (spinach, beet, and pumpkin), for about $10,
which works for those on a slim budget. Also, know that an amuse
bouche, perhaps a tomato bruschetta, is usually satisfying. The addition
of grilled portobellos to a classic arugula-and-shaved-Parmesan salad is
brilliant. Main courses are accompanied by pasta or grilled vegetables
and potato. You can enjoy French and Italian liquors here (like pastis
and grappa); dessert might be dark-chocolate mousse and fresh mango
sorbet. Service is laudable, as is the music. ⊠ *Arzobispo Merino, cor-
ner of Padre Bellini, Zona Colonial* ☎ *809/686–3387* ⌕ *Reservations
essential* ▭ *AE, MC, V* ✆ *Closed Sun. No lunch Mon.*

JUAN DOLIO

SEAFOOD ✕ **Restaurante Aura.** This hot beach spot has been the buzz since it opened
$–$$$ in 2005, as it was the first to bring the South Beach experience to Juan
Dolio. The dining area is a large, thatch-roof structure, its trendy white
fabric tied back with a string of conch and seashells. Try relaxing on a
partner chaise, a swinging beach bed, or a hedonistic Balinese sun bed.
On Sunday Aura is slammed, and sports cars and luxury SUVs vie for
parking spots in the lot. And, yes, the seafood is good, from the *lambi*
(conch) to the *langosta* (lobster), not to mention the *parrillada mixta*
(a mix of seafood—mussels, baby lobsters, fresh fish, squid, shrimp),
which gives you all your *mariscos* in one dish. Although the menu can
be pricey, you can keep your tab more moderate by choosing a pizza
or calzone from the wood-burning oven, a few of the excellent sushi
and rolls, or a pasta (such as ravioli with eggplant and prosciutto).
Nutella cheesecake is truly worth its $10 price tag. ■ **TIP** ➔ Wear your
bathing suit and pareo and bring a change of clothes and your sham-
poo. There are now showers in Aura's restrooms, which are a mix of
contemporary fixtures and "rustic" materials. In the ladies' rooms, a
10-foot mirror artistically framed with conch and other shells will tell
you if you're lookin' fine. ⊠ *Calle Principal, Guayacanes, Juan Dolio*
☎ *809/526–2319* ▭ *AE, D, DC, MC, V.*

PUNTA CANA

✕ **La Yola.** As if you were aboard a *yola* (a small fishing boat), you
would feel the gentle breeze blow over the harbor as you dine on a deck
overlooking the Puntacana Marina. Using thatched cane for overhead
shelter, and the ocean as a backdrop, this restaurant's decor blends elements of the region's natural marvels to achieve an utterly gratifying
open-air dining ambience. Delicious cuisine—with both Mediterranean
and Caribbean influences—and attentive service enhance the exceptional experience. Seafood and fish dominate the menu, but you'll also
find beef and chicken selections. The chef will accommodate special

dietary needs. For an appetizer, the spicy tuna tartare with guacamole relish starts you off with a pleasing burst of flavor and satisfying texture. Main plates, including the catch of the day—usually red snapper, grouper, or mahimahi—are artfully prepared and presented. Baked Chilean sea bass with clam-and-cherry-tomato risotto is a savory special. ⊠*Puntacana Resort & Club* ☎*809/959–2262 Ext. 8002* ⌂*Reservations essential* ⊟*AE, MC, V* ⊘*Closed Tues.*

SEAFOOD ✗**Capitan Cook's.** Lobster, king crab legs, and lots of fish are what's
$$–$$$$ cooking at this seafood specialty house on the sand, where the fresh catch is stashed on ice in a fiberglass vault and grilled before your eyes. An à la carte menu is hand-scrawled on a jumbo bulletin board, with prices given in pesos, but U.S. dollars are accepted, too. Despite naysayers who object that the quality of the food has gone downhill, the bazaarlike atmosphere on the waterfront keeps reeling in the tourist crowds. The restaurant offers free round-trip transportation by water taxi from the area hotels (daytime only). Some resorts offer a prix-fixe excursion (around $40) to the restaurant that includes drinks and the parrillada mixta with fries and salad, followed by coffee, fruit, and shots of fiery *mamajuana* (an herbal liqueur). Sit in the sand at the water's edge and watch as the fishermen hang their catch up by the tail. It's wild and crazy as mariachis play *Ai, yai, yai*, vendors hawk Haitian and Dominican art, and waiters sprint to the beach tables delivering sizzling metal cauldrons of the signature parrillada mixta. ⊠*El Cortecito, Bávaro* ☎*809/552–0645* ⌂*Reservations essential* ⊟*MC, V.*

THE NORTH COAST

The Cabarete area in particular—where all-inclusive resorts don't yet totally dominate the scene—has some fun, original restaurants, but these are often small places, so it's important that you make reservations in advance. Expat residents complain that the prices in this town have moved past the good-value-for-money mark; and more and more restaurants are insisting on cash only, be it pesos, dollars, or euros. Sosúa and Playa Dorada each has a lovely fine-dining option, listed below.

10

AMERICAN ✗**Ali's Surf Camp.** You sit at long tables with a disparate group of strang-
CASUAL ers from at least three different countries, surrounded by bullrushes
$ poking up from a lagoon. (Many are kiters who are in residence at the adjacent surf camp, considered Cabarete's best.) You can have a good feed for around 10 bucks. Try grilled, sweet barbecued ribs with fries and a Dominican salad, or the house special, *churrasco* (skirt steak)— and always there's a shooter of mamajuana. The German owner, Ali, changes offerings often, but at this writing German rotisserie chicken is the designated Saturday special. The palapa roof gives the terrace shelter, and the wood-burning oven means flavorful pizza, but best douse yourself with mosquito repellent. You can call to make reservations, and you should if you have a large group. ⊠*Procab Cabarete, Cabarete* ☎*809/571–0733* ⊟*No credit cards* ⊘*No lunch.*

¢–$ ✕ **EZE Bar & Restaurant.** This beach restaurant has a loyal following from breakfast to dinner, from wallet-watchin' windsurfers to wealthy capitaleño families. Menu names reflect the jargon of the surfers who frequent the place, including Bluebird's Salad (chicken tenders over mixed greens with a sweet chili salsa); the EZE Club Dude (curried grilled chicken), and the Rocker (grilled, marinated beef with onions, peppers, tomato, and tzitiki on a soft pita). Frosty, tropical cocktails are excellent, and you can get an energy kick from yogurt and mango smoothies. The blenders also churn out healthful, organic veggie elixirs. Conversely, if you need a bacon cheeseburger fix, this be the place. Dinner is priced similarly to lunch, with more-refined specials, like calamari or even lobster. The manager, Christos, is Bulgarian and so is the mezze platter. ✉ *Cabarete Beach, in front of Carib Wind Center, Cabarete* ☎ *809/880–8779* ▭ *No credit cards.*

CARIBBEAN ✕ **Babanuco Bar & Restaurant.** You want rustic? This is genuine, funked-

$ up Dominican rusticity. Furniture might be a tree stump, decoration a cow horn; tablecloths are raw burlap. The floor is dirt. In the primitive bar hang vintage license plates from French Canada, the United States, and the Netherlands. The food served up by chef-owner Juan Alberto is flavorful and authentic, with seafood a specialty of the *casa*. Try langoustines and lambi, *pulpo* (octopus), land crab, and fillet of fresh, fresh fish. And Juan goes that extra mile, past the ubiquitous creole sauce, like conch in mushroom sauce with fried green bananas and salad. It's cheaper and even more fun if you come with a group. Make a party, and with some notice he can hire musicians for you. ✉ *Off Carretera Río San Juan-Cabrera Entrada de Saltadero, Cabrera* ☎ *809/223–7928* ▭ *No credit cards.*

CONTINENTAL ✕ **Castle Club.** A man's home is his castle. In this one, Doug Beers pre-

$$$ pares creative lunches and dinners for guests who traverse the rocky driveway to enjoy this one-of-a-kind experience. His wife, Marguerite, is the gracious hostess, who shows patrons her home and the artwork strategically positioned between the many open-air arches. Served on antique lace tablecloths strewn with bougainvillea, the well-orchestrated dinner might consist of canapés, carrot-ginger soup, Thai salad, grouper with a ginger–passion fruit sauce, fiesta rice, cold lemon soufflé, and coffee. After dinner, Doug lights a fire in the great room and offers guests a liqueur to warm their interior. You must make reservations in advance since this meal is cooked in the owner's private residence. ✉ *Mocha Rd., between Jamao and Los Brazos, 20 mins from Cabarete* ☎ *809/357–8334 or 809/223–0601* ✉ *castleclub@hotmail.com* ⌂ *Reservations essential* ▭ *No credit cards.*

$–$$$ ✕ **Lucia.** New life has been breathed into Lucia by one of the most well-

★ respected, innovative chefs in the country, Rafael Vasquez. Although it is not as perfect as when he was behind the stove (he is now corporate executive chef for Gran Ventana and Victoria resorts) the menu is comprehensive and contemporary. The setting is as artistic as a gallery, with orchids galore, crisp white linens, and attentive waiters in white guayabera shirts. Guests love the fresh tuna tartare with soy and sweet chili dipping sauces and a smokin' wasabi-lime sorbet. The rich foie gras with apples and a spiced chocolate sauce is as sensual as you find in French territory. Carnivores with more-basic tastes can order an Angus fillet. The molten chocolate volcano with vanilla ice cream is the dessert you want. When the digestif cart is rolled over, be daring with a Brunello grappa or a local Brugal Unico rum. ⊠ *Casa Colonial, Playa Dorada* ☎ *809/320–3232* ⊟ *AE, MC, V.*

$$ ✗ **L'Etoile d'Or.** Behind the French doors, this intimate restaurant is draped with billowing white fabric and displays enough candle power to be ecclesiastical. The menu is now à la carte, and courses are artistically plated, the exception being the vegetables that are served family style. One might begin with a classic like coquilles St. Jacques, followed by king prawns flambéed with Pernod. Service is discreet and professional, the wine list upscale. This is an ideal place for a proposal, and it can follow the traditionally impressive presentation of a Chateaubriand for two with béarnaise sauce, culminated with a "surprise" dessert, something sensually chocolate. ⊠ *Victorian House, Sosúa* ☎ *809/571–4000* ⚱ *Reservations essential* ⊟ *AE, MC, V* ⊘ *Closed Mon. (varies seasonally). No lunch.*

ECLECTIC $–$$ ✗ **Miró Gallery & Restaurant.** Chef-owner Lydia Wazana, a Canadian of Moroccan descent, is a queenpin among the art set, too, and there is always artwork hanging as well as imaginative offerings like Morocco's chicken tagine or Asian seared tuna. Grazers can share tapas such as the Middle Eastern hummus, baba ghanoush, and grilled veggies. Look for items that pair with the incredible curry aioli or spicy pineapple chutney and wasabi potato puree. The menu and master sushi-maker from Lydia's former restaurant, Wabi Sabi, with its classic sashimi and sushi, as well as some fab innovations that include shrimp tempura rolls, are here now. Take a table on the beach (seating out there has been made lounge-y-er) or curl up with your buddies or beaus on the king-size Balinese sun bed, especially on nights when jazz man Roberto tickles the keyboard. ⊠ *Cabarete Beach, Cabarete* ☎ *809/853–6848* ⊟ *No credit cards* ⊘ *Closed Oct. 15–Nov. 15. No lunch.*

SEAFOOD $$–$$$ ★ ✗ **Restaurant at Natura Cabanas.** Seafood is at the heart of the menu here, and appropriately so, for diners listen to the sounds of the waves crashing on coral rock as they fork the catch of the day with a buttery pistachio sauce. Start with the octopus in a mint vinaigrette and then segue to a shellfish pasta in a pink sauce or lobster scampi. It all tastes so fresh. The filet mignon with mixed mushroom sauce is perfection. For dessert enjoy a classic such as a pear poached in red wine à la mode. The wines are French, Spanish, and Chilean (go for the *reservas*). Tables are set with geometric plates, laced linens, and oversize wine glasses. Service is warm, caring, and efficient, the international music atmospheric. ⊠ *Natura Cabanas, Perla Marina, Cabarete* ☎ *809/858–5822 or 809/571–1507* ⚱ *Reservations essential* ⊟ *AE, MC, V.*

10

SANTIAGO

The D.R.'s second city, Santiago, has always been a lovely, provincial place; the draw nowadays is the new, world-class art gallery and museum, Centro León. Most people come from the Puerto Plata area as day-trippers, but a few spend the night, especially if they fly in directly from New York. From Sosúa and Cabarete, it's about a 1½-hour drive on the scenic highway that passes through mountain villages; from Puerto Plata it's about 1 hour, from Santo Domingo 2½ hours. Those who come for the day can at least enjoy lunch in one of Santiago's great restaurants. The long-awaited megahotel, the Gran Cibao, rising like a Maya temple and located between the new Marriott Courtyard and town, was expected to open by late 2008.

ITALIAN
$
★

✕**Il Pasticcio.** Everyone from college students to cigar kings, presidents and politicos, movie producers and stars, packs this eccentrically decorated culinary landmark. Tourists take photos of the bathrooms with their ornate mirrors and Romanesque plaster sinks. Chef-owner Paolo, a true *paisano*, makes this bungalow a personality palace. (He's just added a new yellow Vespa to his collection on display.) His mouthwatering creations are authentic and fresh. Try the great antipasto selections, or commence with the pasticcio salad, which might have smoked salmon, mozzarella, anchovies, capers, and baby arugula. Paolo couples fresh pastas with unexpected sauces, like gnocchi with puttanesca. Even the bread service comes with three sauces, one is like pesto, there's a pomodoro, and the best is a creamy anchovy sauce. They can all be had on pasta, too. Finish with a shot of limoncello and the best tiramisu outside Italy. ⊠ *Calle 3 #5, at Av. Del Llano, Cerros de Gurabo* ☏ *809/582–6061 or 809/276–5466* ☐ *AE, MC, V* ⊘ *Closed Mon.*

BEACHES

The Dominican Republic has more than 1,000 mi (1,600 km) of beaches, including the Caribbean's longest stretch of white sand: Punta Cana–Bávaro. Many beaches are accessible to the public (in theory, all beaches in this country, from the high-water mark down, are open to everyone) and may tempt you to stop for a swim. That's part of the uninhibited joy of this country. Do be careful, though: some have dangerously strong currents, which may be the reason why they are undeveloped.

Fodor'sChoice
★

Playa Bahoruco. This isolated, gorgeous stretch of virgin beach goes on for miles in either direction, with rugged cliffs dropping to golden sand and warm, blue water. It's the ideal wild, undeveloped Caribbean beach, but many sections are pebbly, so you need surf shoes for swimming. Just a little to the south, on the stretch of beach called San Rafael, are beach shacks where you can buy meals of fresh fish, even whole coconut sea bass. ⊠ *Carretera La Costa, Km 17, 8 mi (13 km) south of Barahona.*

Playa Boca Chica. Developed by wealthy industrialist Juan Vicini in the early 1900s, the beach—an immaculate stretch of fine sand—was where entire families moved their households for summer. You can walk far out into the gin-clear waters protected by coral reefs. Unfortunately, some areas are cluttered with plastic furniture, pizza stands, and cottages. The old Hamaca Hotel (now the Coral Hamaca Beach Hotel Casino) was the place to see and be seen; dictator Trujillo kept quarters here; unfortunately, its glory days are long gone. The strip with the rest of the mid-rise resorts is kept busy, particularly on weekends, mainly with Dominican families and some Europeans. If you're staying in the capital, this is the closest good beach, but best to go midweek. Grab lunch at one of the larger beachfront restaurants like El Pelicano or Neptuno's Club and just hang out on a chaise lounge. ⊠*Autopista Las Americas, 21 mi (34 km) east of Santo Domingo, Boca Chica.*

Playa Cabarete. If you follow the coastal road east from Playa Dorada, you can find this beach, which has strong waves and ideal, steady wind (from 15 to 20 knots), making it an integral part of the international windsurfing circuit. Segments of this beach are strips of golden sand punctuated only by palm trees. In the most commercial area, restaurants and bars are back-to-back, spilling onto the sand. The informal scene is young and fun, with expats and tourists from every imaginable country. ⊠*Sosúa–Cabarete road, Cabarete.*

Playa Dorada. On the north's Amber Coast, this is one of the D.R.'s most established resort areas. Each hotel has its own slice of the beach, which is soft beige sand, with lots of reefs for snorkeling. Gran Ventana Beach Resort, which is on a point, marks the end of the major hotel development. The Atlantic waters are great for windsurfing, waterskiing, and fishing. ⊠*Off Autopista Luperon, 10 mins east of Puerto Plata, Playa Dorada.*

Playa Grande. On the north coast, between the towns of Río San Juan and Cabrera, this long stretch of powdery sand is slated for development—so go while you still can. The public entrance to the beach is about a mile after Playa Grande Golf Course, which is at Km 9. Here, the beach is on a lovely cove, with towering cliffs on both sides. In winter there are waves and some tricky currents, but in summer the water is flat. The only facilities are at the golf club and the not-so-wonderful Occidental Playa Grande Hotel atop a cliff, though a few beach shacks fry up fresh fish, garlicky shrimp, and keep the beer on ice. An outcropping separates this beach from Playa Precioso, which is lovely to walk in winter but more swimmable in warm months. During the week you'll have little company, but on Sunday afternoons (or during the entire Easter week), when the locals are here in full force, the scene is busy and inadvisable. ⊠*Carretera Río San Juan–Cabrera, Km 11.*

Playa Las Terrenas. On the north coast of the Samaná Peninsula, tall palms list toward the sea, and the beach is extensive and postcard perfect, with crystalline waters and soft, golden sand. There's plenty of color—vivid blues, greens, and yellows—as well as colorful characters. Two hotels are right on the beach at Punta Bonita. To the west is Playa El Cosón, opposite Cayo Ballena, a great whale-watching spot (from January to April). Samaná has some of the country's best beaches and drop-dead scenery, the rough roads notwithstanding. ⊠*Carretera Las Terrenas, Las Terrenas.*

10

Playa Sosúa. Sosúa Bay is a gorgeous, natural harbor, renowned for its coral reefs and dive sites, about a 20-minute drive from Puerto Plata. Here, calm waters gently lap at a shore of soft golden sand. Swimming is delightful, except after a heavy rain when litter floats in. From the beach you can see mountains in the background, the cliffs that surround the bay, and seemingly miles of coastline. Snorkeling from the beach can be good, but the best spots are offshore, closer to the reefs. (Don't bother going to "Three Rocks"—save your $20 and snorkel off the beach.) Unfortunately, the backdrop is a string of tents where hawkers push souvenirs, snacks, drinks, and water-sports equipment rentals. Lounge chairs can usually be had for RD$50, so bargain. ⊠ *Carretera Puerto Plata–Sosúa, Sosúa.*

★ **Punta Cana.** One of the best and longest Caribbean beaches is 20 mi (32 km) of pearl-white sand shaded by swaying coconut palms; it forms the backdrop for the busiest of the D. R.'s tourist regions. The area encompasses Cabeza de Torres, Playa Bávaro, and continues all the way around the peninsula to Playa de Uvero Alto. Each hotel has its own strip of sand with rows of chaise lounges, and you can often arrange for a day pass if you call in advance. The stretch between Club Med and the Punta Cana Resort and Club is one of the most beautiful. Few isolated stretches exist anymore. Playa El Cortecito, where the restaurant Captain Cook's sits, is more how life used to be, with fishermen bringing in their catch, though even there you can find souvenir shops and strolling vendors. The public beach at Macao is no longer a good option, having been taken over for four-wheeler excursions and a new Westin resort rising from its sands. There are more-deserted stretches in the Uvero Alto area, but that road is rough and, outside of the existing resorts, has few services. ⊠ *Off Autopista Las Americas, east of Higüey, Punta Cana.*

SPORTS & THE OUTDOORS

Although there's hardly a shortage of activities here, the resorts have virtually cornered the market on sports, including every conceivable water sport. In some cases, facilities may be available only to guests of the resorts.

BIKING & HIKING

Pedaling is easy on pancake-flat beaches, but there are also some steep hills in the D. R. Several resorts rent bikes to guests and nonguests alike. **Iguana Mama** (⊠ *Calle Principal 74, Cabarete* ☏ *809/571–0908 or 809/571–0228* ⊕ *www.iguanamama.com*) has traditional and mountain bikes and will take you on guided rides on the flats or test your mettle on the steep grades in the mountains. Downhill rides, which include a taxi up to the foothills, breakfast, and lunch, cost $85 for a full-day trip, $60 for a half-day trip. Advanced rides, on and off roads, are $40 to $50. Guided hikes cost $35 to $65. In addition, this well-established, safety-oriented company offers horseback riding on the beach and countryside for $40 for two hours, canyoning, and a host of other adventure sports.

BOATING

Sailing conditions are ideal, with constant trade winds. Favorite excursions include day trips to Catalina and Saona islands—both in the La Romana area—and sunset cruises on the Caribbean. Prices for crewed sailboats of 26 feet and longer, with a capacity of 4 to 12 people, range from $120 to $700 a day.

Carib Wind Center (⊠ *Cabarete* ☎ *809/571–0640* ⊕ *www.caribwind. com*) is a renowned windsurfing center (known for decades as Carib BIC Center) that also rents Lasers, 17-foot catamarans, boogie boards, and sea kayaks. It has an Olympic Laser training center with a former racing instructor. Experts—even champions—come to train here. **La Marina Chavón** (⊠ *Casa de Campo, Calle Barlovento 3, La Romana* ☎ *809/523–8646*) has much going on, from sailing to motor yachting and socializing at the Casa de Campo Yacht Club.

Ocean World Marina (⊠ *Cofresi, 3 mi (5 km) west of Puerto Plata* ☎ *809/970–3373 or 809/291–1111* ⊕ *www.oceanworldmarina.com*) is a new state-of-the art marina, strategically positioned between the heavily traveled Florida–Bahamas region and the Puerto Rico–eastern Caribbean region. It has filled a large 300-mi (480-km) void on the north coast where no full-service marina previously existed. The new 35-acre complex, when complete, will feature 120 slips that will accommodate sailboats of up to 200 feet. It is a port of entry with its own immigration and customs office, concierge, laundry and shower facilities, a duty-free shop, food-liquor store, car-rental service (even hourly rentals), marina store with fishing supplies, as well as an entertainment clubhouse, nightclub, casino, and first-class dining facilities

DIVING

Ancient sunken galleons, undersea gardens, and offshore reefs are among the lures here. Most divers head to the north shore. In the waters off Sosúa alone you can find a dozen dive sites (for all levels of ability) with such catchy names as Three Rocks (a deep, 163-foot dive), Airport Wall (98 feet), and Pyramids (50 feet). Some 10 dive schools are represented on Sosúa Beach; resorts have dive shops on-site or can arrange trips for you.

In 1979, three atolls disappeared following a seaquake off Las Terrenas, providing an opportunity for truly memorable dives. Also just offshore from Las Terrenas are the Islas Las Ballenas ("The Whale Islands"), a cluster of four little islands with good snorkeling. A coral reef is off Playa Jackson, a beach accessible only by boat. **Las Terrenas Divers** (⊠ *Playa Bonita, Las Terrenas* ☎ *809/889–2422* ⊕ *www.lt-divers.com*) offers diving lessons and trips; diving equipment rentals start at $30, snorkeling equipment at $15 per day. It is closed Sunday.

10

Northern Coast Aquasports (✉ *Sosúa* ☎ *809/571–1028* ⊕ *www.northern coastdiving.com*) is a five-star, Gold Palm PADI dive center; it's also the only National Geographic Center in the D.R. Professionalism is apparent from the initial classroom and pool practice to the legendary dive sites around beautiful Sosúa Bay, where you can explore the reefs, walls, wrecks, and swim-throughs, from 25 to 130 feet. Successful completion of a three-day course and $350 earns you a PADI Open Water Certification card. Classrooms have air-conditioning and DVDs. There is a fine retail shop in the front, selling gear that includes Maui Jim sunglasses. On Friday nights, the British owners host an authentic curry supper and beer party for their clients.

FISHING

Big-game fishing is big in Punta Cana, with blue and white marlin, wahoo, sailfish, dorado, and mahimahi among the most common catches in these waters. Several fishing tournaments are held every summer. The Puntacana Resort & Club has hosted the ESPN Xtreme Billfishing Tournament every year since 2003. Blue marlin tournaments are held at the La Mona Channel in Cabeza de Toro. Several tour operators offer organized deep-sea fishing excursions.

La Marina Chavón (✉ *Casa de Campo, Calle Barlovento 3, La Romana* ☎ *809/523–8646*) is the best charter option in the La Romana area. Yachts are available for charters by day or night for a romantic sunset cruise. Boats for deep-sea and river fishing are available as well. Costs to charter a boat with a crew, refreshments, bait, and tackle generally range from $598 to $2,013 for a half day, from $796 to $3,334 for a full day. At **Puntacana Marina** (✉ *Puntacana Resort & Club, Punta Cana* ☎ *809/959–2262 Ext. 8004* ⊕ *www.puntacana.com*), on the southern end of the resort, half-day, deep-sea fishing excursions are available for $95 per person, with a minimum of two people, $70 for observers. For a Bertram 33-footer to go after tuna, marlin, dorado, and wahoo, it's $575 for four hours. It costs the same to charter a 45-foot Sportfisherman. Also, ask about the yolas, simple fishing boats with outboards.

GOLF

The D.R. has some of the best courses in the Caribbean, designed by top golf architects. Most charge higher rates during the winter high season; some, but not all, reduce their rates between April and October, so be sure to ask. The new **Nick Faldo Legacy Golf Course** will be a part of the new Westin Rōco Ki when it opens in late 2008.

Fodor'sChoice
★   The **Barceló Bávaro Beach Golf & Casino Resort** (✉ *Bávaro* ☎ *809/686– 5797*) has an 18-hole, par 72 course, open to its own guests and those of other hotels. The course, with numerous water obstacles, was designed by Juan Manuel Gordillo, and was the first in the Bávaro area. The rate for those not staying at Bávaro is $120, which includes green fees, golf cart, and a day pass to the resort, which includes food and beverages for the day. The Famed "Teeth of the Dog" course at **Casa de**

Campo (✉ *La Romana* ☎ *809/523–3333* ⊕ *www.casadecampo.com. do*), with 7 holes on the sea, is often ranked as the number-one course in the Caribbean and is among the top courses in the world. Green fees are $150 per round, per person. Pete Dye has designed this and two other globally acclaimed courses here: Dye Fore, with 18 holes close to Altos de Chavón, hugs a cliff that looks over the sea, a river, and the stunning marina ($150); the Links is an 18-hole inland course ($115). Avid golfers should inquire about the resort's three-day and one-week supplements, or the new Simply Golf Packages. Tee times for all courses must be reserved at least one day in advance by resort guests, earlier for nonguests.

Both challenging and affordable, **Catalonia Caribe Golf Club** (✉ *Catalonia Bávaro Resort, Bávaro* ☎ *809/412–0000* ⊕ *www.cataloniabavaro. com*) is an 18-hole, par-72 course spread out on greens surrounded by five lakes and an abundance of shady palms. Alberto Sola was the designer. Green fees are $75.

Named for the coconut plantation on which it was built, **Cocotal Golf Course** (✉ *Bávaro* ☎ *809/687–4653* ⊕ *www.cocotalgolf.com*), designed by Spaniard José "Pepe" Gancedo, has 18 championship holes and 9 regular holes. It's a challenging par-72 course in a residential community dotted with palm trees and lakes. There's also a driving range, club house, pro shop and golf academy. Green fees are $135 for 18 holes, $80 for 9 holes, including cart.

★ **La Cana Golf Course** (✉ *Puntacana Resort & Club, Punta Cana* ☎ *809/959–4653* ⊕ *www.puntacana.com*) is a breathtaking 18-hole championship course designed by P. B. Dye, with spectacular ocean views—4 holes play right along the water. For resort guests, green fees are $71 for 9 holes, $115 for 18 holes, with cart included; for nonguests, fees are $96 for 9 holes, $156 for 18 holes, and $40 for a golf cart. Reserve two weeks in advance from November through April. Lessons and clinics are offered at the resort.

Los Marlins Championshop Golf Course (✉ *Juan Dolio* ☎ *809/526–1359*) is an 18-hole, 6,400-yard, par-72 course designed by Charles Ankrom. Green fees are $70 for 18 holes including a car, $40 for 9 holes. Golfers get 10% off at the Metro Country Club. A Fuentes Cigar Club, one of the few in the country, is on the second floor. Kids and moms can be seen on the 18-hole miniature golf range when the dads are playing the 18-hole course. The tennis courts are lighted at night. A new deluxe spa is coming on line in 2008.

Golf Digest has named **Playa Dorada Golf Club** (✉ *Playa Dorada, Puerto Plata, next door to Victoria Resort* ☎ *809/320–3472* ⊕ *www.playa doradagolf.com*) one of the top 100 courses outside the United States. It's open to guests of all the hotels in the area, though Victoria guests receive a discount. Green fees for 9 holes are $50, 18 holes $75; caddies are mandatory for foursomes and will cost about $12 for 18 holes, $7 for 9; carts are optional, at $20 and $15, for 18 or 9 holes, respectively. The clubhouse was refurbished with contemporary style for the Salvatore Ferragamo Golf Tournament.

10

Fodor'sChoice **Punta Espada Golf Course** (⊠ *Cap Cana, Carretera Juanillo, Juanillo*
★ *☎809/688–5587*) is an 18-hole par-72 Jack Nicklaus signature golf
course characterized by striking bluffs, lush foliage, and winding
waterways. There's a beach view from most of the holes, and half of
them play right along the ocean. It's the first of three Jack Nicklaus
signature courses planned at Cap Cana, and the site of a new PGA
Champions Tour event that debuted in 2008. Green fees are $175,
which includes golf cart, caddy, tees, two bottles of water, and practice
on the driving range.

HORSEBACK RIDING

The 250-acre **Equestrian Center at Casa de Campo** (⊠ *La Romana*
☎809/523–3333 ⊕ *www.casadecampo.com.do*) has something for
both western and English riders—a dude ranch, a rodeo arena (where
Casa's trademark "Donkey Polo" is played), guided trail rides, and
jumping and riding lessons. Guided rides run about $35 an hour;
lessons cost $56 an hour. There are early morning and sunset trail
rides, too. Handsome, old-fashioned carriages are available for hire,
as well.

Guavaberry Equestrian Center (⊠ *Guavaberry Golf & Country Club,*
Autovia del Este, Km 55, Juan Dolio *☎809/333–4653*) has a clean
stable, good stock, and English and western saddles. Delightful hour-
plus trail rides throughout the extensive grounds of the resort cost $25;
complimentary transportation is provided to all Juan Dolio hotels.

Rancho La Isabella (⊠ *Playa Las Terrenas, behind Hotel Las Cayenas,*
Las Terrenas *☎809/804–8960*) offers rides on Playa Bonita for $18
and Playa Cosón or Las Terrenas for $45.

Rancho Puntacana (⊠ *Puntacana Resort & Club, Punta Cana* *☎809/959–*
2262 ⊕ *www.puntacana.com*) is across from the main entrance of the
resort. A one-hour trail ride winds along the beach, the golf course, and
through tropical forests. The two-hour jungle trail ride has a stopover
at a lagoon fed by a natural spring, so wear your swimsuit under your
long pants. You can also do a three-hour full-moon excursion or take
riding lessons. The stock are Paso Fino horses.

The upscale **Sea Horse Ranch Equestrian Center** (⊠ *Cabarete* *☎809/571–*
3880 or 809/571-4462) is a professional, well-staffed operation. The
competition ring is built to international regulations, and there is a
large schooling ring. An annual invitational jumping event is sanc-
tioned by the Dominican Equestrian Federation. Lessons, including
dressage instruction, start at $35 an hour and endurance rides are $30
for 90 minutes, $50 for three hours, including drinks and snacks—but
make reservations. The most-popular ride includes stretches of beach
and a bridle path across a neighboring farm's pasture, replete with
wildflowers and butterflies. Feel free to tie your horse to a palm tree
and jump into the waves.

TENNIS

There must be a million nets around the island, and most of them can be found at the large resorts.

La Terraza Tennis Club (⊠ *Casa de Campo, La Romana* ☎ *809/523–3333*) has been called the Wimbledon of the Caribbean. This 12-acre facility, perched on a hill with sea views, has 13 Har-Tru courts. Nonmembers are welcome (just call in advance); court time costs $28 an hour, and lessons are $55 an hour with an assistant pro, $69 with a pro.

Occidental Tennis Academy (⊠ *Occidental Club on the Green, Playa Dorada, Puerto Plata* ☎ *809/320–1111 for hotel's main switchboard* ⊕ *www.occidentalhotels.com*) was the first tennis academy in the Caribbean. It's equipped with seven Har-Tru clay and hard courts (night-lighted), as well as a gym, pool, social club, and pro shop. Classes are given and supervised by pros. Programs are for adults and children age five and over. You can get private ($13 an hour) or group classes ($8), in English or Spanish, for beginners to professionals. Courts can also be rented by nonguests.

Sea Horse Ranch (⊠ *Cabarete* ☎ *809/571–2902* ⊕ *www.sea-horse-ranch.com*) has a tennis center with five clay courts, illuminated for night play and open to nonguests. Court time costs $20 per person per hour, with an extra fee of $7 for night play; Instructions, available in four languages, cost $20 per hour.

WIND- & KITESURFING

Fodor's Choice ★ Between June and October, Cabarete Beach has what many consider to be optimal windsurfing conditions: wind speeds at 20 to 25 knots (they come from the side shore) and 3- to-10-foot Atlantic waves. The Professional Boardsurfers Association has included Cabarete in its international windsurfing slalom competition. The novice is also welcome to learn and train on wider boards with light sails.

Carib Wind Center (⊠ *Cabarete* ☎ *809/571–0640* ⊕ *www.caribwind. com*), which has been in business since 1988 as the Carib BIC Center, has just changed its name, owner Ari Bashi explains, because BIC was the name of the boards that he bought exclusively. Now he carries a number of brands including many Olympic Laser boards. Equipment and instruction are offered and lessons are generally $30 to $35 an hour; boards rent for $20 an hour. A gem of a windsurfing club, this family-owned business has many repeat clients and is open year-round. In the complex is its beach bar, EZE, as well as a retail shop. It has all the paraphernalia for surfing and a good variety of sunglasses, including Maui Jim's and some of the best bikinis, cute miniskirts, and dresses in town.

Kitexcite (⊠ *Kite Excite Hotel, Kite Beach, Cabarete* ☎ *809/571–9509, 809/913–0827, or 809/914–9745* ⊕ *www.kitexcite.com*) operates a large school for one of the Caribbean's newest popular sports.

SHOPPING

Cigars continue to be the hottest commodity coming out of the D. R. Many exquisite hand-wrapped smokes come from the island's rich Cibao Valley, and Fuente Cigars—handmade in Santiago—are highly prized. Only reputable cigar shops sell the real thing, and many you will see sold on the street are fakes. You can also buy and enjoy Cuban cigars here, but they can't be brought back to the United States legally. Dominican rum and coffee are also good buys. *Mamajuana,* an herbal liqueur, is said to be the Dominican answer to Viagra. The D. R. is the homeland of designer Oscar de la Renta, and you may want to stop at the chic shops that carry his creations. La Vega is famous for its *diablos cajuelos* (devil masks), which are worn during Carnival. Look also for the delicate, faceless ceramic figurines that symbolize Dominican culture.

Though locally crafted products are often of a high caliber (and very affordable), expect to pay hundreds of dollars for designer jewelry made of amber and larimar. Larimar—a semiprecious stone the color of the Caribbean Sea—is found on the D. R.'s south coast. Prices vary according to the stone's hue; the rarest and most-expensive gems have a milky haze, and the less expensive are solid blue. Amber has been mined extensively between Puerto Plata and Santiago. A fossilization of resin from a prehistoric pine tree, it often encases ancient animal and plant life, from leaves to spiders to tiny lizards. Beware of fakes, which are especially prevalent in street stalls. A reputable dealer can show you how to tell the difference between real larimar and amber and imitations.

Bargaining is both a game and a social activity in the D. R., especially with street vendors and at the stalls in El Mercado Modelo. Vendors are disappointed and perplexed if you don't haggle. They're also tenacious, so unless you really plan to buy, don't even stop to look.

AREAS & MALLS

SANTO DOMINGO

One of the main shopping streets in the Zone is **Calle El Conde,** a pedestrian thoroughfare. With the advent of so many restorations, the dull and dusty stores with dated merchandise are giving way to some hip, new shops. However, many of the offerings, including local designer shops, are still of a caliber and cost that the Dominicans can afford. Some of the best shops are on **Calle Duarte,** north of the Colonial Zone, between Calle Mella and Avenida de Las Américas. **Piantini** is a swanky residential neighborhood that has an increasing number of fashionable shops and clothing boutiques. Its borders run from Avenida Winston Churchill to Avenida Lope de Vega and from Calle Jose Amado Soler to Avenida 27 de Febrero.

Acropolis Mall, between AvenidaWinston Churchill and Calle Rafael Augusto Sanchez, has become a favorite shopping arena for the young and/or hip capitaleños. Stores like Zara and Mango (both from Spain), have today's look without breaking budget. **El Mercado Modelo,** a covered market, borders Calle Mella in the Colonial Zone; vendors here sell a dizzying selection of Dominican crafts. The **Malecón Center,** the latest complex, adjacent to the classy Hilton Santo Domingo, will eventually house 170 shops, boutiques, and services plus several movie theaters. In the tower above are luxury apartments and Sammy Sosa, in one of the penthouses. **Plaza Central** (⊠ *Avs. Winston Churchill and 27 de Febrero, Piantini* ☎ *809/541–5929*) is a major shopping center with high-end shops, a Jenny Polanco shop (an upscale Dominican designer who has incredible white linen outfits, artistic jewelry, purses, and more).

LA ROMANA

Altos de Chavón is a re-creation of a 16th-century Mediterranean village on the grounds of the Casa de Campo resort, where you can find art galleries, boutiques, and souvenir shops grouped around a cobbled square. Extra-special is El Club de Cigaro. **La Marina Chavón,** at the Casa de Campo Marina, is home to more than 60 shops and international boutiques, galleries, and jewelers scattered amid restaurants, an ice-cream parlor, Euro-style bars, and a yacht club. It is a great place to spend some hours shopping and sightseeing while you stare at the extravagant yachts. The chic shopping scene at the marina includes Burberry, Bleu Marine, Pucci, Gucci, Cartier, Montblanc, and Versace. Dominican designer Jenny Polanco's boutique here now includes her line of jewelry and handbags. Although upscale is the operative word here, this does not mean that you cannot buy a postcard, a pair of shorts, or a logo T-shirt. Also, the *supermercado* Nacional at the marina has not only groceries but sundries, postcards, and snacks for much less than you would pay at your resort's shop.

PUNTA CANA

Fodor'sChoice ★ The **Galeriás at Puntacana Village** (⊠ *Puntacana Resort & Club, Punta Cana*) lies within a still-blossoming shopping, dining, and residential complex built on the road between the airport and Puntacana Resort, initially to house employees of the resort; the area has now also become a tourist draw. Four banks are planned in the village, which is already home to a church and a school. The commercial square has an Oscar de la Renta shop, a Portuguese restaurant, a beauty parlor, and an art gallery where you can find locally crafted objects on display, including an exquisite wooden chess set with giant pieces carved to resemble classical musicians on one side and Dominican pop stars on the other. Free transportation is provided to guests at Puntacana Resort & Club.

Fodor'sChoice ★ A standout among the region's shopping centers, **Palma Real Shopping Village** (⊠ *Bávaro* ☎ *809/257–6382*) is a swanky, partially enclosed mall designed with an eye toward light and space. Water fountains and tropical plants infuse life into the bright and airy interior areas beneath the blue-tile roof. Music pipes through the stone-floor plaza in the center, where seating is available, and security is tight. Upscale retail shops, which sell beachwear, clothing, skin-care products, jewelry, and more, line the walls. Several restaurants give visitors welcome dining alternatives beyond the gates of their resorts. There are two banks, ATMs, and

10

a money exchange outlet. Store hours are from 10 AM to 10 PM, but the restaurants stay open later. Shuttle buses run to and from many of the hotels with pickups every two hours. A new movie theater, the first in Punta Cana, was being built here at this writing.

You won't find brand-name shops at **Plaza Uvero Alto** (⊠ *Carretera Uvero Alto, Uvero Alto*), but it's a convenient shopping center for the hotels in the remote Uvero Alto area, with a bank and outdoor ATM, money exchange, Internet café, small pharmacy, gift shops, and two minimarkets (one in the front, the other tucked away in the back row of booths) that sell sundries such as suntan lotion and deodorant at prices that are much cheaper than in the hotels. Behind the first row of enclosed stores, peruse the colorful kiosks full of handicrafts, paintings, ceramics, and other gift items; most shopkeepers here, although very friendly, don't speak much English, so knowing even a few words of Spanish will come in handy.

On the outskirts of Higüey, as you head into town along Carretera Higüey–La Otra Banda, you'll find **Plaza Higüeyana**—an artisan market that draws busloads of tourists—on the right-hand side of the road. Here you can browse through racks and shelves full of souvenirs, like mamajuana, rum, T-shirts, jewelry, crafts and ceramics.

Inside the market, you can take a free tour of the **Museo Vivo Del Tabaco** (☎ *809/551–1128*), where you can see how tobacco is planted, harvested, and rolled into cigars. Near the entrance to the museum, you can also purchase hand-rolled cigars. ⊠ *Carretera Higüey–La Otra Banda, at east end of Higüey* ⊗ *Daily 9–noon and 2–5.*

PUERTO PLATA

In Puerto Plata, a popular shopping street for costume jewelry and souvenirs is **Calle Beller.**

Playa Dorada Plaza (⊠ *Calle Duarte at Avenida 30 de Marzo, Puerto Plata*) is a shopping center in the American tradition; stores here sell everything from cigars, rum, coffee, and herbal remedies to ceramics, trinkets, American clothing brands, Oscar de la Renta tops, and Gottex bathing suits. One of the largest stores here is **Discount Plaza,** the Dominican equivalent of Wal-Mart, and the clothes—bathing suits, flip-flops, caps—are of a similar caliber to what you would find in a U.S. discount chain. Similarly, it has a good assortment of toiletries and rum. The souvenirs are Dominican. You can also buy phone cards here, or make long-distance calls in private booths with cash payments.

The seven showrooms of the **Tourist Bazaar,** on Calle Duarte in Puerto Plata, are in an old mansion with a patio bar.

SPECIALTY STORES

ART

Casa Jardin (⊠ *Balacer Gustavo Medjía Ricart 15, Naco, Santo Domingo* ☎ *809/565–7978*) is the garden studio of abstract painter Ada Balacer. Works by other women artists are also shown; look for pieces by

Yolarda Naranjo, known for her modern work that integrates everything from fiberglass, hair, rocks, and wood to baby dresses. **Galería de Arte Mariano Eckert** (⊠ *Av. Winston Churchill and Calle Luis F. Tomen, 3rd fl., Evaristo Morales, Santo Domingo* ☎ *809/541–7109*) focuses on the work of Eckert, an older Dominican artist who's known for his still-lifes. **Galería de Arte Nader** (⊠ *Rafael Augusto Sanchez 22, between Ensanche Piantini and Plaza Andalucia II, Piantini, Santo Domingo* ☎ *809/687–6674 or 809/544–0878*) showcases top Dominican artists in various media. The gallery staff is well known in Miami and New York and works with Sotheby's. Due to their Taíno, African, and European heritage, artisans creating modern Dominican art forms are using seeds, fiber, bones, coconut skin, cow horns, and African motifs. A good selection is found at **Jorge Caridad** (⊠ *Arzobispo Merino, corner of General Cabral, Zona Colonial, Santo Domingo*).

Lyle O. Reitzel Art Contemporaneo (⊠ *Plaza Andalucia II, Piantini, Santo Domingo* ☎ *809/227–8361*) has, since 1995, specialized in contemporary art and showcases mainly Latin artists, from Mexico, South America, and Spain, and some of the most controversial Dominican visionaries. **Plaza Toledo Bettye's Galeria** (⊠ *Isabel la Católica 163, Zona Colonial, Santo Domingo* ☎ *809/688–7649*) sells a fascinating array of artwork, including Haitian voodoo banners, metal sculptures, even souvenirs, chandeliers, and estate jewelry; the American expat owner, Bettye Marshall, has a great eye and can also rent you a room in one of her B&Bs. **Lisa Kirkman Gallery** (⊠ *Ocean One Plaza, next to Banco Santa Cruz, Cabarete* ☎ *809/571–0108*) has a great selection of nationally acclaimed contemporary masters, up-and-coming artists, and works from the winners of the last biennial art festival (held in Santo Domingo) and of the Eduardo León Jimenez national competition for contemporary artists. The gallery rocks when there is an art opening, and the Indo-Caribbean furnishings (also for sale) create a loungelike atmosphere. Many of the artworks and accessories could be carried on a plane, or shipping can be arranged. At **Miró Gallery & Restaurant** (⊠ *Cabarete Beach, Cabarete* ☎ *809/571–0888*) you can find rotating exhibitions of contemporary art with an emphasis on Latino artists and photographers, especially from the Dominican Republic and Cuba. Opening soiees are social events.

CIGARS & TOBACCO

Cigar King (⊠ *Calle Conde 208, Baguero Bldg., Zona Colonial, Santo Domingo* ☎ *809/686–4987*) keeps Dominican and Cuban cigars in a temperature-controlled cedar room. Near the airport, **La Tabaquería Cigar Club** (⊠ *La Plaza Bolera, Suite 10A, Punta Cana* ☎ *809/959–0040*) is a haven for cigar-lovers, who can watch the handmade production process or relax at the bar with a drink. Fine Dominican and Cuban cigars are for sale, as are humidors and related accessories, from 9 AM to 9 PM daily. You can call the store to arrange transportation.

HOME FURNISHINGS

The exquisite **Nuovo Rinascimento** (⊠ *Plazoleta Padre Billini, Zona Colonial, Santo Domingo* ☎ *809/686–3387*), replete with contemporary furniture and antiques, has a treasure trove of Venetian linens and towels. Shipping can be arranged. The wooden hacienda doors open to a wonderful world of white sculptures and an inner courtyard with a lily-pad-dotted pool. Adjacent is Café Bellini, offering authentic Italian cuisine in a striking contemporary setting.

JEWELRY

Harrisons (⊠*Playa Dorada Plaza, Puerto Plata* ☎*809/586–3933* ⊠*Palma Real Shopping Village, Bávaro* ☎*809/552–8721*) doesn't sell trinkets but rather high-end jewelry, most likely at better prices than in your hometown. For quality larimar and amber with well-designed settings, many in platinum, this is it. Branches can be found in many other tourist destinations, including Cabarete and Sosúa. **L'Ile Au Tresor Au Tresor** (⊠*Conde Plaza (lower floor), Calle Conde, across from Mercure Hotel, Zona Colonial, Santo Domingo* ☎*809/685–3983*), owned by Patrick Joyas, has a *Pirates of the Caribbean* theme, but, that aside, it's fun and owned by a talented Frenchman who has some of the most-attractive and creative designer pieces in native larimar, amber, and even conch. If you have never bought any of these lovely stones because the settings are usually cheesy, or if exquisite, too pricey, then this is your chance. His innovative custom work, with sterling or gold, can be done in 48 hours. **Tesoro Caribeño** (⊠*Plaza Uvero Alto, Local 5, Uvero Alto* ☎*809/707–3355*) has a fine selection of amber and larimar jewelry and other stones amid the colorful shelves full of souvenirs and crafts. Unique pieces are crafted by the same designers who create jewelry for the Harrison's chain, but are sold at generally lower prices. The owner speaks fluent English.

NIGHTLIFE

★ Santo Domingo's nightlife is vast and ever changing. Check with the concierges and hip capitaleños. Get a copy of the free newspaper *Touring, Aqui o Guía de Bares Restaurantes*—available free at the tourist office and at hotels—to find out what's happening. At this writing, there is still a curfew for clubs and bars; they must close at midnight during the week, and 2 AM on Friday and Saturday nights. There are some exceptions to the latter, primarily those clubs and casinos located in hotels. Sadly, the curfew has put some clubs out of business, but it has cut down on the crime and late-night noise, particularly in the Zone.

Dancing is as much a part of the culture here as eating and drinking. As in other Latin countries, after dinner it's not a question of *whether* people will go dancing but *where* they'll go. Move with the rhythm of the merengue and the pulsing beat of salsa (adopted from neighboring Puerto Rico). Among the young, the word is that there's no better place to party in the Caribbean than Santo Domingo's Colonial Zone. Almost every resort in Puerto Plata and Punta Cana has live entertainment, dancing, or both. Many clubs stay open until dawn or until the last couple gives it up. Alas, at this time in Santo Domingo, clubs have to close at midnight during the week, 2 AM on Friday and Saturday.

BARS & CLUBS

SANTO DOMINGO

Doubles (✉ *Calle Arzobispo Meriño 54, Zona Colonial* ☎ *809/688–3833*) looks like a friend's place—that is, if you have a French friend who has a hip sense of interior design and would mix rattan furniture, antiques, subdued lighting, and candles in a space that's centuries old. Spanish tiles add interest to this atmospheric piano bar. **Guácara Taína** (✉ *Av. Mirador del Sur 655* ☎ *809/533–0671*) is a landmark, for it is the only *discoteca* in a cave formerly inhabited by Taíno Indians and, well, bats. (Santo Domingo has a network of natural caves within its city limits.) As you descend and see hundreds of heads bobbing and bodies gyrating among the stalactites, it's a unique sight. Banquettes and seating are carved into the limestone walls ornamented with Taíno pictographs. Alas, the fashionable crowd deserted it maybe 15 years ago, leaving it to the *turistas* and, increasingly, groups of cruise-ship passengers. Cover charge is $10 and includes one drink and Latin music you want to dance to. It's open Thursday–Sunday 9 PM–2 AM.

The **LED** (✉ *Hispaniola Hotel & Casino, Av. Abraham Lincoln at Av. Independencia, Gazcue* ☎ *809/476–7733*) disco is in a hotel, so it is able to stay open later than the other clubs, and that in itself is what has made this a favorite of the young and well-to-do party set. Many a graduation is celebrated here until the wee small hours of the *mañana*. **Marrakesh Café & Bar** (✉ *Hotel Santo Domingo, Av. Abraham Lincoln at Av. Independencia, Gazcue* ☎ *809/221–1511*) is where a sophisticated after-work crowd gathers for American and international music (jazz on Monday) and *Casablanca* style. Complimentary tapas come to the table, and you can get top-shelf liquors. **Nowhere Bar** (✉ *Calle Hostos 205, Zona Colonial* ☎ *809/877–6258*) is hot and the crowd mostly young and affluent, but all ages stop by, including the young Americans going to college in Santo Domingo who have adopted this place. They hang on the first level, where the latest music from the States—plus hip-hop and house—is played. A DJ playing Dominican music packs in the locals on the second floor. Thursday night is the infamous Ladies Night. On Friday and Saturday, local bands take the stage. An artistic renovation of a 16th-century, two-story mansion, this is the bar seen in the movie *Miami Vice* (2006). It has just finished another cosmetic redo and is looking clean and refreshed. It's open Wednesday to Saturday. **Praia** (✉ *Calle Gustavo Mejia Ricart 74, Ensanche Naco* ☎ *809/540–8753*) is a bar and wine lounge, popular with rich Dominicans and tourists. The contemporary design utilizes glass and steel for a cool, minimalist decor. Music is modern and electronic; drinks are expensive.

PUNTA CANA

★ **Montecristo** (✉ *Palma Real Shopping Village, Carretera Cortecito-Bávaro, Bávaro* ☎ *809/552–8999*) is a trendy spot that evolves from a bar to a pulsating disco as the night goes on. The head bartender makes great mixed drinks with a flourish, and the manager is generally accessible to guests—tourists and locals alike. A big video screen serves as the backdrop for the dance floor, which mixes up DJ-spun international club music with merengue, bachata, and salsa rhythms—and some-

10

Annual Jazz

It's shades of Havana in the 1950s, of New York's Harlem in the 1920s, with bearded jazz musicians in berets playing among *cubanos* with white Panama hats and guayabera shirts. It's a fusion of African percussion and drums—bongos and congos, backed up by marimbas and maracas, sexy songbirds and their piano men. It's rotund tuba players and sweat-stained black shirts as trumpet and sax players blow it out.

Every October, the towns of Sosúa, Cabarete, Puerto Plata, and Santiago are transformed into music venues when the biggest names in Latin jazz hit the north coast, including such legends as Chuck Mangione, Sade, Carlos Santana, Mongo Santa Maria, Chu Cho Valdés, and Arturo Sandoval.

As hot as salsa, the pulsating tropical sounds draw thousands of aficiona-dos, from poor students to black-tie patrons of the arts, who come for the music, the energy, the art exhibits, the educational workshops, the sun, and the sea. This is one five-star event that is democratic—most tickets cost about $15.

Sizzling hot nights inevitably climax in impromptu jam sessions at such venues as Miró's Restaurant in Caba-rete and Hemingway's Cafe in Playa Dorada Plaza. In short, the D.R. Jazz Fest is one of the best parties of the year.

Resorts book up early, especially those that are hotbeds of jazz activity, like Sosúa Bay Hotel, Victorian House, and Sea Horse Ranch. Check out the festival's Web site for more information: ⊕ *www.drjazzfestival.com*.

times live music. The club has arrangements with several local hotels for transporting groups. There's no cover charge here, and there's special pricing for various sponsored drinks on different nights.

A favorite among many locals, **Pacha** (⊠ *Riu complex, closest to Riu Naiboa entrance, Bávaro* ☎ *809/221–7575*) plays more merengue and bachata than most of the other dance clubs. Drinks here are a lot cheaper, too. For a beer, expect to pay about RD$80 (or about $2.50); the price can be double in some of the other clubs. Cover charges apply when live bands perform; otherwise it's free to enter, and non–resort guests are welcome.

NORTH COAST

Café Cito (⊠ *On main highway, 0.25 mi [0.5 km] west of Playa Dora-da's main gate, 0.25 mi [0.5 km] east of Iberostar, next to Avis, Carret-era Luperon, Playa Dorada* ☎ *809/586–7923*) is a fun, unpretentious place to feed and hang out, a fave of Canadian expats and turistas. It's owned by a cool guy, Tim Hall, who is from Canada. For an amazingly low price you can have a light meal. But it's the good times, the cama-raderie, the sports on a big screen (via satellite), and the music from the jukebox that make this a welcome break from the Costa Dorada or Playa Dorada resort compounds. On sale are Tim's boxes of select cigars, each a different brand.

Crazy Moon (✉ *Paradise Beach Club & Casino, Playa Dorada* ☎ *809/320–3663*) is a mega dance club that's often filled to capacity. Latin music and hip-hop mixed with Euro sounds are popular. Rest up from time to time at the horseshoe bar, so that you can keep the pace until the wee hours of the mañana. The negativo here is that this worn-out resort and its casino are anything but high-brow.

Gravity (✉ *Playa Nacho Resort, Playa Dorada* ☎ *809/320–6226*) doesn't crank up until after midnight, but it keeps rolling until 4 AM. Locals and tourists hip-hop together.

Hemingway's Cafe (✉ *Playa Dorada Plaza, Puerto Plata* ☎ *809/320–2230*) has long been the rockin' spot for the young at heart who love to party. There's rock or reggae by DJs or live bands, but only big-name merengue bands elicit a cover charge. On Saturday night there's a Latin fiesta, and on Thursday the mike is taken over by karaoke singers. The kitchen closes at 2 AM and serves American-style, fun food and good burgers, with fajitas a specialty.

Mangú Disco (✉ *Holiday Village Golden Beach, Playa Dorada* ☎ *809/320–3800*) is a happening, late-night disco in Playa Dorada, that turistas should check out during their stay. What's novel is that choreographed dancers perform, but they are not exactly Vegas quality. On Ladies Nights, geared to women whose husbands are at the casino tables, the MC and on-stage dancers keep the crowds laughing and learning the local dance steps. The muscular disco kings may peel off their shirts, but they don't go much further. *Putas* (not to mention some *putos*) do hang here, but the action is not as bad (or as obvious) as at many places. Signs warning against bringing in weapons or drugs may make some leery, but know that the government mandates those signs, and the policy is for your safety.

Onno's Bar (✉ *Cabarete Beach, Cabarete* ☎ *809/571–0461*), under new ownership since 2007, is promising many innovations and remains a serious party place. It is usually wall-to-wall and back-to-back as the young and fit pack the dance floor and groove to techno sounds while other multinational youth sit at the tables in the sand. It's easier to get served at the beach bar than the main one, and as you chill, people will pass by, introduce themselves, converse, and then move on. It's fun and friendly, although on Friday and Saturday nights, when it stays open until 3 AM, the scene can be too rowdy.

Lax (✉ *Cabarete Beach, Cabarete* ☎ *809/710–0569*) is a perennially popular, open-air bar that really comes alive by night. You can sit in the sand in lounge chairs or jump into the action under the palapa, where a DJ will be spinning madly or a live band will be rockin'. There's good grazing chow, too, and special theme nights like Thai (not bad, either). Drinks come from the blenders and in pitchers, but be patient, getting one can take time when the bar backs up. As it is next to a small hotel, it must close early now—1 AM.

Ruby's Lounge (✉ *Pedro Clisante corner of Calle Arzeno, the last building in Sosúa Bay complex, Sosúa* ☎ *No phone*) was once the Voodoo

10

Lounge and Sosúa's most upscale bar. The new proprietress, who is named Melanie, is a hip, French-Canadian intent on keeping her two-story lounge and dance club at the same good level and decibel as before. Each night has a different theme, be it karaoke or Latin, and often locally well-known blues and jazz players perform. On weekends it might be a mix of live bands and DJ "Vegas Dave," who really knows how to animate a room. Good news: there is no cover charge and if you start drinking early—from 1 PM to 8 PM—you will enjoy discounted prices. No prostitutes are allowed to solicit here, but sometimes come in after "work" just to chill.

CASINOS

The action can heat up, but gambling here is more a sideline than a raison d'être. Most casinos are in the larger hotels of Santo Domingo, with a couple in Playa Dorada, and more in Punta Cana. All offer slot machines, blackjack, craps, and roulette and are generally open daily from 3 PM to 4 AM, the exception being those in Santo Domingo, which, for now, must close at midnight (2 AM on Friday and Saturday). You must be 18 to enter, and jackets are required at the chic casinos in the capital.

In Santo Domingo, several upscale hotels have casinos: Barceló Gran Hotel Lina Spa; Meliá Santo Domingo Hotel & Casino; Hispaniola Hotel & Casino (attracts a younger crowd); Renaissance Jaragua Hotel & Casino; and the Hilton Santo Domingo.

On the north coast, the Holiday Village Golden Beach in Playa Dorada and Occidental Allegro Playa Dorada both have popular American-style casinos. Breezes in Cabarete has its Casino Carnival which had a glamourous redo in late 2007, and leaving Cabarete is Ocean Sands.

SANTO DOMINGO

Atlantis World Casino (✉ *Av. George Washington 218, Gazcue* ☎ *809/688–8080*), adjacent to the Intercontinental Hotel, is one of the newest and American friendly with slots that accept dollars. Although there's no charge to enter the gaming room, the table minimums are higher than most, so the casino attracts a more-upscale crowd until closing time, which doesn't come until 6 AM.

Majestic Casino (✉ *Hilton Santo Domingo, 1st Level, Av. George Washington, Gazcue* ☎ *809/685–0000*) is the newest of the Malecón casinos, and it is on a par with its Las Vegas counterparts. You'll find 20 gaming tables (even baccarat), a VIP salon, 200 video slots, live music (national and international talent), an upscale restaurant, and more.

NORTH COAST

Ocean World Casino (✉ *3 mi [5 km] west of Puerto Plata, Cofresi* ☎ *809/291–1111* ⊕ *www.oceanworld.net*) is an extravagant casino that was constructed within the Ocean World complex in 2006, and it rivals its counterparts in Las Vegas. The whimsical decor and furnishings are from a fantasy world, and windows offer sea views. The Octopus Bar overlooks the spiffy new marina and its flotilla of yachts. A nocturnal tour of the Ocean World complex can include a sunset happy hour at the Lighthouse Lounge, dinner at Poseidón, and then a Las Vegas–style review, *Bravissimo*, which is a flurry of beautiful dancing girls and guys with incredible voices. If you want the night to continue even later, there's the Lighthouse Disco.

EXPLORING THE DOMINICAN REPUBLIC

SANTO DOMINGO

Parque Independencia separates the old city from modern Santo Domingo, a sprawling, noisy city with a population of close to 2 million. In the making is a new ethnic neighborhood, a Chinatown, to resemble San Francisco's. This predominately Asian neighborhood will be just north of the Colonial Zone, on Calles Mella and Duarte. This barrio will have an ornate archway as its entrance, with street signs and phone booths, etc. getting Asian decoration. Chinese businesses, particularly restaurants, already exist, and a museum and a plaza honoring Confucius are planned.

Numbers in the margin correspond to points of interest on the Santo Domingo map. Note: Hours and admission charges to sites are erratic.

Fodor's Choice ★ Spanish civilization in the New World began in Santo Domingo's 12-block **Zona Colonial.** As you stroll its narrow streets, it's easy to imagine this old city as it was when the likes of Columbus, Cortés, and Ponce de León walked the cobblestones, pirates sailed in and out, and colonists were settling. Tourist brochures tout that "history comes alive here"—a surprisingly truthful statement. Every Thursday to Sunday night at 8:30, a typical folkloric show is staged at Parque Colón and Plaza España. During the Christmas holidays there is an artisans fair and live music concerts. Ask about other cultural events.

A fun horse-and-carriage ride throughout the Zone costs $20 for an hour. The steeds are no thoroughbreds, but they clip right along, though any commentary will be in Spanish. You can also negotiate to use them as a taxi, say to go down to the Malecón. The drivers usually hang out in front of the Sofitel Nicolas Ovando. History buffs will want to spend a day exploring the many "firsts" of our continent. You can get a free walking-tour map and brochures in English at the Secretaria de Estado de Turismo office at Parque Colón (Columbus Park), where you may be approached by freelance, English-speaking guides, who will want to make it all come alive for you. They'll work enthusiastically for $20 an hour for four persons. Wear comfortable shoes.

10

❹ **Alcazar de Colón.** The castle of Don Diego Colón, built in 1517, has 40-inch-thick coral-limestone walls. The Renaissance-style structure, with its balustrade and double row of arches, has strong Moorish, Gothic, and Isabelline influences. The 22 rooms are furnished in a style to which the viceroy of the island would have been accustomed—right

Santo
Domingo

down to the dishes and the viceregal shaving mug. ⊠*Plaza de España off Calle Emiliano Tejera at foot of Calle Las Damas, Zona Colonial* ☎*809/687–5361* ⌸*RD$50* ☾*Mon. and Wed.–Fri. 9–5, Sat. 9–4, Sun. 9–1.*

❽ Calle Las Damas. The Street of the Ladies was named after the elegant
★ ladies of the court who, in the Spanish tradition, promenaded in the evening. Here you can see a sundial dating from 1753 and the Casa de los Jesuitas, which houses a fine research library for colonial history as well as the **Institute for Hispanic Culture**; admission is free, and it's open weekdays from 8 to 4:30. If you follow the street going toward the Malecón, you will pass a picturesque alley fronted by a wrought-iron gate that has perfectly maintained colonial structures that are owned by the Catholic Church.

❾ Casa de Bastidas. There's a lovely inner courtyard here with tropical plants and galleries for temporary exhibitions. ⊠*Calle Las Damas off Calle El Conde, Zona Colonial* ☎*No phone* ⌸*Free* ☾*Tues.–Sun. 9–5.*

❸ Casa del Cordón. This structure, built in 1503, is the western hemisphere's oldest surviving stone house. Columbus's son, Diego Colón, viceroy of the colony, and his wife lived here until the alcazar was finished. It was in this house, too, that Sir Francis Drake was paid a ransom to prevent him from totally destroying the city. ⊠ *Calle Emiliano Tejera at Calle Isabel la Católica, within Banco Popular, Zona Colonial* 🕾 *No phone* 🖼 *Free* ⊗ *Weekdays 8:30–4:30.*

⓫ Casa de Tostado. The house was built in the early 16th century and was the residence of writer Don Francisco Tostado. Note its unique twin Gothic windows. It houses the Museo de la Familia Dominicana (Museum of the Dominican Family), which has exhibits on well-heeled 19th-century Dominican society. The house, garden, and antiquities have all been restored. ⊠ *Calle Padre Bellini 22, near Calle Arzobispo Meriño, Zona Colonial* 🕾 *809/689–5000* 🖼 *RD$50* ⊗ *Thurs.–Tues. 9–2.*

❿ Catedral Santa María la Menor. The coral-limestone facade of the first cathedral in the New World towers over the south side of the Parque Colón. Spanish workmen began building the cathedral in 1514, but left to search for gold in Mexico. The church was finally finished in 1540. Its facade is composed of architectural elements from the late Gothic to the lavish Plateresque style. Inside, the high altar is made of hammered silver. At this writing, a museum was being built for the cathedral's treasures. ⊠ *Calle Arzobispo Meriño, Zona Colonial* 🕾 *809/689–1920* 🖼 *Free* ⊗ *Mon.–Sat. 9–4; Sun. masses begin at 6 AM.*

❶ Iglesia Santa Bárbara. This combination church and fortress, the only one of its kind in Santo Domingo, was completed in 1562. ⊠ *Av. Mella between Calle Isabel la Católica and Calle Arzobispo Meriño, Zona Colonial* 🕾 *809/682–3307* 🖼 *Free* ⊗ *Weekdays 8–noon; Sun. masses begin at 6 AM.*

⓭ El Malecón. Avenida George Washington, better known as the Malecón, runs along the Caribbean and has tall palms, cafés, hotels, and sea breezes.

❷ Monasterio de San Francisco. Constructed between 1512 and 1544, the San Francisco Monastery contained the church, convent, and hospital of the Franciscan order. Sir Francis Drake's demolition squad significantly damaged the building in 1586, and in 1673 an earthquake nearly finished the job, but when it's floodlighted at night, the eerie ruins are dramatic indeed. The Spanish government has donated money to turn this into a beautiful cultural center, but we are still waiting. ⊠ *Calle Hostos at Calle Emiliano, Zona Colonial* 🕾 *809/687–4722.*

❺ El Museo de las Casas Reales. This is a remarkable museum that helps ★ you understand the New World that was discovered by Columbus and the ensuing history of exploration and colonization in the 16th century. Exhibits include everything from Taíno archaeological finds to colonial artifacts, coins salvaged from wrecks of Spanish galleons, authentic colonial furnishings, and a collection of weapons. Additionally, the building in which the collection is housed is one of the most handsome colonial edifices remaining in Santo Domingo and has undergone a careful and complete restoration. Built in the Renaissance style, it was the seat of Spanish government and housed the governor's office as well

10

as the Royal Court. It has beautiful windows done in the Plateresque style. An art gallery, with rotating art shows, is also resident. As a popular upscale wedding venue, it is truly magical when candle-lighted by night. ⊠ *Calle Las Damas right before Plaza de Espana, Zona Colonial* ☎ *809/682–4202* ☜ *RD $30* ⊙ *Tues.–Sun. 9–5.*

❻ Pantheon Nacional. The National Pantheon (circa 1714) was once a Jesuit monastery and later a theater. The real curiosity here is the military guard who stays as still as the statues, despite the schoolchildren who try to make him flinch. ⊠ *Calle Las Damas, near Calle de Las Mercedes, Zona Colonial* ☎ *No phone* ☜ *Free* ⊙ *Mon.–Sat. 10–5.*

❼ Parque Colón. The huge statue of Christopher Columbus in the park named after him dates from 1897 and is the work of sculptor Ernesto Gilbert. Like all the parks in the Zona Colonial, this one has been restored. ⊠ *El Conde at Arzobispo Meriño, Zona Colonial.*

⑭ Plaza de la Cultura. Landscaped lawns, modern sculptures, and sleek buildings make up the Plaza de la Cultura. There are several museums and a theater here. The works of 20th-century Dominican and foreign artists are displayed in the **Museo de Arte Moderno** (☎ *809/682–2154*). Native sons include Elvis Aviles, an abstract painter whose works have a lot of texture. His art combines Spanish influences with Taíno Indian and other Dominican symbols. Tony Capellan is one of the best-known artists, representing the D. R. in major international exhibitions. The **Museo del Hombre Dominicano** (☎ *809/687–3623*) traces the migrations of Indians from South America through the Caribbean islands. The **Teatro Nacional** (☎ *809/687–3191*) stages fascinating performances in Spanish only, but don't let that stop you. When in Rome, you would go to an Italian opera, right? . ⊠ *Plaza de la Cultura, Zona Colonial* ☜ *Museo de Arte Moderno RD$20, Museo del Hombre Dominicano RD$20* ⊙ *Tues.–Sun. 10–5.*

THE EAST COAST

Las Américas Highway (built by the dictator Trujillo so his son could race his sports cars) runs east along the coast from Santo Domingo to La Romana—a two-hour drive. Midway are the well-established beach resorts, Juan Dolio and Sammy Sosa's hometown, San Pedro de Macorís. East of La Romana are Punta Cana and Bávaro, glorious beaches on the sunrise side of the island. Along the way is Higüey, an undistinguished city notable only for its giant concrete cathedral and shrine (someone had a vision of the Virgin Mary here), which resembles a pinched McDonald's arch.

★ **Altos de Chavón.** This re-creation of a 16th-century Mediterranean village sits on a bluff overlooking the Río Chavón, about 3 mi (5 km) east of the main facilities of Casa de Campo. There are cobblestone streets lined with lanterns, wrought-iron balconies, wooden shutters, courtyards swathed with bougainvillea, and **Iglesia St. Stanislaus,** the romantic setting for many a Casa de Campo wedding. More than a museum piece, this village is a place where artists live, work, and play.

Dominican and international painters, sculptors, and artisans come here to teach sculpture, pottery, silk-screen printing, weaving, dance, and music at the school, which is affiliated with New York's Parsons School of Design. They work in their studios and crafts shops selling their finished wares. The village also has an archaeological museum and five restaurants. A 5,000-seat **amphitheater** (☎ *809/523–2424 for Kandela tickets ⊕www.kandela.com.do*) features *Kandela,* a spectacular musical extravaganza showcasing the island's sensuous Afro-Caribbean dance moves, music, and culture. Concerts and celebrity performances by such singers as Julio Iglesias, his son Enrique, Sting, and the Pet Shop Boys share the amphitheater's schedule of events.

Isla Saona. Off the east coast of Hispaniola lies this island, now a national park inhabited by sea turtles, pigeons, and other wildlife. Caves here were once used by Indians. The beaches are beautiful, and legend has it that Columbus once strayed here. Getting here, on catamarans and other excursion boats, is half the fun, but know that it can be a crowd scene. Vendors are allowed to bother visitors and there are a number of beach shacks serving lunch and drinks. The largest island in the national park, it is no longer as pristine as a national park should be.

San Pedro de Macorís. The national sport and the national drink are both well represented in this city, an hour or so east of Santo Domingo. Some of the country's best baseball games are played in Tetelo Vargas Stadium. Many Dominican baseball stars have their roots here, including George Bell, Tony Fernandez, Jose Río, and Sammy Sosa. The Macorís Rum distillery is on the eastern edge of the city. From 1913 the 1920s this was a very important town—a cultural center—and mansions from that era are being restored by the Office of Cultural Patrimony, as are some remaining vestiges of 16th-century architecture and the town's cathedral, which has a pretense to Gothic architecture, even gargoyles. There is a Malecón, a nice promenade along the port, and by night the beer and rum kiosks come alive. The Dominicans, Europeans and now North Americans, who take self-catering apartments or condos in Juan Dolio, frequent San Pedro since it has the closest supermercados (Jumbo, Iberia—which also has a big pharmacy, Zaglul) and other small businesses.

10

SAMANÁ

Back in 1824, a sailing vessel called the *Turtle Dove,* carrying several hundred escaped American slaves, was blown ashore in the spot now occupied by **Santa Barbara de Samaná.** The survivors settled and prospered, and today their descendants number several thousand. The churches here are mostly Protestant; the worshippers live in villages called Bethesda, Northeast, and Philadelphia; and the language spoken is an odd 19th-century form of English mixed with Spanish.

Sportfishing in the Samaná area is considered to be among the best in the world. In addition, about 3,000 humpback whales winter off the coast of the Samaná Peninsula from December to March. Major whale-watching expeditions are being organized and should boost the region's economy without scaring away the world's largest mammals. Postcard-perfect **Playa Las Terrenas** is a remote stretch of gorgeous, pristine Atlantic beaches on the north coast, attracting surfers and windsurfers, the young and offbeat. There's a strong French influence here, with modest seafood restaurants, a dusty but burgeoning main street in the town, a small airfield, a couple of all-inclusive resorts, and several congenial smaller hotels right on the beach. If you're happy just hanging out, drinking rum, and soaking up the sun, this is the place. A highway connecting Samaná to Santo Domingo was nearing completion at this writing, and El Catey International Airport, 45 minutes away from the town of Samaná, has regularly scheduled air service from Puerto Rico on American Airlines. Things they are a changing.

THE NORTH COAST

The Autopista Duarte ultimately leads (a three-to four-hour drive) from Santo Domingo to the north coast, sometimes called the Amber Coast because of its large, rich amber deposits. The coastal area around Puerto Plata, notably Playa Dorada, is a region of well-established, all-inclusive resorts and developments; the north coast has more than 70 mi (110 km) of beaches, with condominiums and villas going up fast. The farther east you go from Puerto Plata and Sosúa, the prettier and less spoiled the scenery becomes. The autopista runs past Cabarete, a village that's a popular windsurfing haunt, and Playa Grande, which has a miraculously unspoiled white-sand beach.

Mt. Isabel de Torres. Southwest of Puerto Plata, this mountain soars 2,600 feet above sea level and is notable for its huge statue of Christ. Up there also are botanical gardens that, despite efforts, still are not memorable. You can choose to hire a knowledgeable English-speaking guide for $5 a person. A cable car takes you to the top for a spectacular view. Know that they usually wait until the cars are filled to capacity before going up—which makes them cozy; and should the electricity happen to go off, there is no backup generator. You should visit in the morning, preferably by 9 AM; by afternoon, the cloud cover rolls in, and you can see practically nothing. Also be advised that the vendors are particularly tenacious. ⊠ *Off Autopista Duarte, follow signs* ☎ *No phone* 🚡 *Cable car RD$250* ⏰ *Mon., Tues., and Thurs.–Sun. 9–5.*

Puerto Plata. Although it has been sleeping for decades, this was a dynamic city in its heyday and it is coming back. You can get a feeling for this past in the magnificent Victorian gazebo in the central **Parque Independencia.** On Puerto Plata's own Malecón, the **Fortaleza de San Felipe** protected the city from many a pirate attack and was later used as a political prison. The nearby **lighthouse** has been restored. Big changes are afoot in this town, which is just realizing what it needs to do to become a tourist destination. The Office of Cultural Patrimony, which has done an admirable job of pulling the Zona Colonial from the darkness, is at work on Puerto Plata. Simultaneously, a group of private business owners and investors have developed a long-term plan for beautifying this city, which has hundreds of classic, wooden ginger-bread buildings. Mansions, including Casa Olivores and the Tapounet Family home, are being restored; a Victorian mansion on Calle Jose del Carmen is now a gallery and coffee shop.

☺ The **Museo de Ambar Dominicano** *(Dominican Amber Museum)* is in a lovely old galleried mansion. It both displays and sells the D.R.'s national stone, semiprecious, translucent amber, which is actually fossilized pine resin that dates from about 50 million years ago, give or take a few millennia. Shops on the museum's first floor sell amber, souvenirs, and ceramics. Dominican amber is considered to be the finest in the world. If you buy from street vendors for a low price, you're probably buying plastic. ✉ *Calle Duarte 61* ☎ *809/586–2848* 💲 *RD$15* 🕙 *Mon.–Sat. 9–5.*

Ocean World Adventure Park is a multimillion-dollar aquatic park in Cofresi with marine and wildlife interactive programs, including dolphin and sea lion shows and encounters, a tropical reef aquarium, stingrays, shark tanks, a rain forest, and a Tiger Grotto inhabited by Bengal tigers! Looking out to the sea, the buffet lunch is delightful but not included in the entrance fee. You don't have to come on a tour, but you must make advance reservations if you want to participate in one of the swims or encounters. For example, if you are brave enough for the shark encounter ($70), you will feed them and touch them in the shark lagoon; the stingray encounter is included as well. If you're staying in the Puerto Plata or Cabarete area, ask at your hotel for tour schedules; if you are at nearby Sun Village, transfers are free. Children must be at least age six to do the dolphin swim, and a photo lab and video service can capture the moment. A private beach, locker room, splashy marina, Las Vegas–style casino, and fine-dining restaurant make for a fascinating mix *(⇨ Casinos and Boating.)* ✉ *In front of Sun Village Resort & Spa, on autopista to Santiago, Cofresi* ☎ *809/291–1000 or 809/291–1111* 🌐 *www.oceanworld.net* 💲 *$55; with many supplements for additional activities and encounters* 🕙 *Daily 9–5.*

Sosúa. This small community was settled during World War II by 600 Austrian and German Jews. After the war many of them returned to Europe or went to the United States, and most who remained married Dominicans. Only a few Jewish families reside in the community today, and there's only the original one-room wooden synagogue.

Sosúa is called Puerto Plata's little sister and consists of two communities—El Batey, the modern hotel development, and Los Charamicos, the old quarter—separated by a cove and one of the island's prettiest beaches. The sand is soft and white, the water crystal clear and calm. The walkway above the beach is packed with tents filled with souvenirs, pizzas, and even clothing for sale—a jarring note. The town had developed a reputation for prostitution, but much is being done to eliminate that and to clean up the more-garish elements. Upscale condos and hotels are springing up, and the up-and-coming Dominican families are coming back to the big houses on the bay.

Museo Judío Sosúa chronicles the immigration and settlement of the Jewish refugees in the 1940s. This is a fascinating place, and depending on who is the docent, you may hear that the Jewish settlers experienced a certain amount of prejudice here when they arrived. The adjacent small, wooden synagogue is the wedding spot for many Jewish couples from abroad. ⊠ *Calle Dr. Rosen at David Stern* ☏ *809/571–1386* 🖃*RD$75* ⊙ *Weekdays 9–1 and 2–4.*

THE CIBAO VALLEY

The heavily trafficked four-lane highway north from Santo Domingo, known as the Autopista Duarte, cuts through the lush banana plantations, rice and tobacco fields, and royal poinciana trees of the Cibao Valley. Along the road are stands where for a few pesos you can buy pineapples, mangoes, avocados, *chicharrones* (fried pork rinds), and fresh-fruit drinks.

Jarabacoa. Nature-lovers should consider a trip to Jarabacoa, in the mountainous region known rather wistfully as the Dominican Alps. There's little to do in the town itself but eat and rest up for excursions on foot, horseback, or by motorbike taxi to the surrounding waterfalls and forests—quite incongruous in such a tropical country. Other activities include adventure tours, particularly white-water rafting or canoe trips, jeep safaris, and paragliding. Accommodations in the area are rustic but homey.

La Vega Vieja. Founded in 1495 by Columbus, La Vega is the site of one of the oldest settlements in the New World. You may find the tour of the ruins of the original settlement, Old La Vega, rewarding. About 3 mi (5 km) north of La Vega is Santo Cerro (Holy Mount), site of a miraculous apparition of the Virgin and therefore many local pilgrimages. The Convent of La Merced is here, and the views of the Cibao Valley are breathtaking. The town's remarkable Concepción de la Vega Church was constructed in 1992 to commemorate the 500th anniversary of the discovery of America. The unusual modern Gothic style—all curvaceous concrete columns, arches, and buttresses—is striking.

La Vega is also celebrated for its Carnival, featuring haunting devil masks. These papier-mâché creations are intricate, fanciful gargoyles painted in surreal colors; spiked horns and real cows' teeth lend an eerie authenticity. Several artisans work in dark, cramped studios throughout the area; their skills have been passed down for generations.

Santiago. The second city of the D.R., where many past presidents were born, sits about 90 mi (145 km) northwest of Santo Domingo and is about an hour's drive from Puerto Plata and 90 minutes from Cabarete via the scenic mountain road. An original route from centuries past, the four-lane highway between Santiago and Puerto Plata is dotted with sugar mills. The Office of Cultural Patrimony is overseeing their restoration. This industrial center has a surprisingly charming, provincial feel; the women of Santiago are considered among the country's most beautiful. High on a plateau is an impressive monument honoring the restoration of the republic. Traditional yet progressive, Santiago is still relatively new to the tourist scene but already has several thriving restaurants and new hotels. It's definitely worth setting aside some time to explore the city. Some colonial-style buildings—with wrought-iron details and tiled porticoes—date from as far back as the 1500s. Others are from the Victorian era, with the requisite gingerbread latticework and fanciful colors, while more-recent construction is noveau Victorian. Santiago is the island's cigar-making center; the Fuente factory is here, though the cigars cannot be bought on the island (if you see them for sale on the streets, they are counterfeit).

Fodor's Choice ★ You can gain an appreciation for the art and skill of Dominican cigar making by taking a tour of **E. León Jimenes Tabacalera** (✉ *Av. 27 de Febrero, Villa Progreso* ☎*809/563–1111 or 809/535–5555*). A free tour takes approximately 90 minutes, and the factory is open daily from 9 to 5. Without question, the **Centro León** is a world-class cultural center for the Dominican arts. A postmodern building with an interior space full of light from a crystal dome, the center includes several attractions, including a multimedia biodiversity show, a museum dedicated to the history of the D. R., a simulated local market, a dramatic showcase of Dominican art and sculpture, galleries for special exhibits, a sculpture garden, an aviary, classrooms, and a replica of the León family's first cigar factory, where a dozen cigar rollers are turning out handmade cigars. There's even a first-rate cafeteria. ✉*Av. 27 de Febrero 146, Villa Progreso* ☎*809/582–2315* ⊕*www.centroleon.org. do* ⊠*RD$50, guides in English RD$150* ⊗*Exhibitions Tues.–Sun. 9–6, public areas daily 9–9.*

THE SOUTHWEST

Barahona. The drive from Santo Domingo zigs and zags through small towns, passing coco and banana plantations until you get on Carretera Azua, a fine highway with mountain views and fences of bougainvillea hiding fields of peppers and flowers. You can bathe in the cascades of icy mountain rivers or in hot thermal springs surrounded by dense foliage, *llanai* vines, and fruit trees. Barahona can be a tropical Garden of Eden.

Lago Enriquillo. The largest lake in the Antilles is near the Haitian border. The salt lake is also the lowest point in the Antilles: 114 feet below sea level. It encircles wild, arid, and thorny islands that serve as sanctuaries for such exotic birds and reptiles as flamingos, iguanas, and caimans— the indigenous crocodile. The area is targeted by the government for improvements and infrastructure designed for ecotourists, but progress continues to be slow. ✉*Hwy. 48 west, 2 mi (3 km) east of Descubierta* ☎*No phone* ⊠*$3* ⊗*Daily 8–5.*

10

DOMINICAN REPUBLIC ESSENTIALS

To research prices, get advice from other travelers, and book travel arrangements, visit www.fodors.com.

∎ TRANSPORTATION

BY AIR

INTERNATIONAL

Most major airlines have nonstop flights to a major airport in the Dominican Republic; some flights connect in San Juan. American Airlines and American Eagle have the most flights to the D. R., flying to all of the island's major airports (primarily from New York–JFK, Miami, and San Juan); American Eagle now offers regularly scheduled service to Samaná from San Juan. Continental, Delta, JetBlue (Santiago, Puerto Plata, and Santo Domingo only), Spirit (Santo Domingo only), and US Airways (Santo Domingo and Punta Cana). Air Caraïbes and Air Antilles Express (only in summer) connect to the French West Indies; LIAT has flights to many of the English-speaking islands. Many visitors fly nonstop on charter flights direct from the U.S. East Coast and Midwest, particularly into Punta Cana; these charters are part of a package and can only be booked through a travel agent.

Information Air Antilles Express (☎809/621–8888). **Air Caraïbes** (☎809/621–8888 in the D. R., 0590/82–47–00 in Guadeloupe). **American Airlines/American Eagle** (☎809/200–5151 in Santo Domingo, 809/200–5151 toll-free elsewhere in the D. R.). **Continental** (☎809/262–1060). **Delta** (☎809/200–9191). **JetBlue** (☎809/200–9898). **LIAT** (☎809/621–8888). **Spirit** (☎809/381–4111). **US Airways** (☎809/540–0505).

DOMESTIC

Aerodomca and Air Century fly out of Higuero Airport in Santo Domingo,

offering charters and transfers. Helidosa Helicopters offers charter service as well as aerial sightseeing excursions. In addition to charter flights, Takeoff Destination Service has some scheduled flights.

Information Aerodomca (⊠La Isabella International Dr. Joaquin Balaguer, Higuero ☎809/567–1195). **Air Century** (⊠La Isabella International Dr. Joaquin Balaguer, Higuero ☎809/566–0888 ⊕www.aircentury. com). **Helidosa Helicopters** (⊠Punta Cana ☎809/688–0744, 809/552–6066, or 809/552–6069). **Takeoff Destination Service** (⊠Punta Cana ☎809/552–1333 or 809/567–1195 ⊕www.takeoffweb.com).

AIRPORTS & TRANSFERS

The Dominican Republic has seven major airports, including Las Américas International Airport, about 15 mi (24 km) outside Santo Domingo; El Catey (an impressive international airport), about 25 mi (40 km) west of Santa Barbara de Samaná; Cibao International Airport in Santiago; Gregorio Luperon International Airport (in Puerto Plata), about 7 mi (11 km) east of Playa Dorada; La Isabela International Dr. Joaquin Balaguer Airport, about 10 mi (16 km) north of Santo Domingo (it is often called Higuero or even Isabela Airport); La Romana–Casa de Campo International Airport near the Casa de Campo resort; Punta Cana International Airport (the busiest, handling some 1.5 million passengers a year); Las Américas in Santo Domingo has been renovated and is now much better than it once was. If you book a package through a travel agent, your airport transfers will almost certainly be included in the price you pay. Look for your company's sign as you exit baggage claim. If you book independently, then you may have to take a taxi or rent a car.

If you leave from one of the busier international airports in Santo Domingo,

Puerto Plata, or Punta Cana, anticipate long lines and be sure to give yourself a full two hours for international check-in.

Information Cibao International Airport (STI ⊠Santiago ☏809/582–4894). **El Catey International Airport** (AZS ⊠Catey). **Gregorio Luperon International Airport** (POP ⊠Puerto Plata ☏809/586–0107 or 809/586–0219). **La Isabella International Dr. Joaquin Balaguer** (DHG ⊠Higuero ☏809/826–4003). **La Romana/Casa de Campo International Airport** (LRM ☏809/556–5565). **Las Américas International Airport** (SDQ ⊠Santo Domingo ☏809/549–0450). **Punta Cana International Airport** (PUJ ☏809/686–8790).

BY BUS

Privately owned, air-conditioned buses are the cheapest way to get around the country. They make regular runs to Santiago, Puerto Plata, Punta Cana, and other destinations from Santo Domingo. Fares are cheap; for example, the one-way bus fare from Santo Domingo to Puerto Plata is about $7.50, and the trip takes 3½ hours.

Metro Buses' deluxe buses have more of an upscale clientele; however, there are no movies.

Caribe Tours sometimes shows bilingual movies (although less and less), keeps the air-conditioning frigid, and is favored by locals and families. Buses are often filled to capacity, especially on weekends and holidays, and the bus music will be Dominican-loud.

Linia Gladys is a small bus line that will get you from the capital to Constanza. If you are in the town of Constanza, call them, they might even pick you up at your hotel.

Espreso Baváro buses depart from Plaza Los Girasoles at Avenida Máximo Gómez at Juan Sánchez Ruiz; the buses are not the best, but the price is right and the American movies current. If you're going to one of the Punta Cana resorts, you get off at the stop before the last and take a cab waiting at the taxi stand.

Frequent service from Santo Domingo to the town of La Romana is provided by Express Bus. Buses depart from Ravelo Street, in front of Enriquillo Park, every hour on the hour from 5 AM to 9 PM; the schedule is exactly the same from La Romana, where they leave from Avenida Camino. In Santo Domingo, there's no office and no phone, but a ticket taker will take your $4 just before departure. There's general chaos, but it all comes together, and at about $4 the price is right. Travel time is about 1¾ hours, and if luck is with you, there may be a first-rate American movie. Once in town, you can take a taxi from the bus stop; rates range from $18 for Casa de Campo to $30 for Iberostar Hacienda Dominicus.

Information Caribe Tours (☏809/221–4422). **Espreso Baváro** (☏809/682–9670). **Linea Gladys** (☏809/565-1223 in Santo Domingo, 809/ 539-2134). **Metro Buses** (☏809/566–7126 in Santo Domingo, 809/586–6062 in Puerto Plata, 809/587–4711 in Santiago).

BY CAR

Driving in the D.R. can be a harrowing and expensive experience; we don't recommend that the typical vacationer rent a car. Many Dominicans drive recklessly, and their cars are often in bad shape (missing headlights, taillights). It's best if you don't drive outside the major cities at night. If you must, use extreme caution, especially on narrow, unlighted mountain roads. Watch out for pedestrians, bicycles, motorbikes (some without headlights), and the occasional stray cow, goat, or horse.

Obtain a good road map from your rental agency, and consult the agent there or your hotel concierge about routes. Although some roads are still full of potholes, the route between Santo Domingo and Santiago is a four-lane divided high-

10

way, and the road between Santiago and Puerto Plata is a smooth blacktop. The highway from Casa de Campo to Punta Cana is also a fairly smooth ride. Surprisingly, many of the scenic secondary roads, such as the "high road" between Playa Dorada and Santiago, are in good shape. Driving is on the right, U.S.-style. The 80-kph (50-mph) speed limit is enforced.

Fill up—and watch—the gas tank; stations are few and far between in rural areas. Prices are higher than in the United States, and are fluctuating between $4.50 and $5 a gallon at this writing. Make certain that attendants don't reach for the super pump. You don't need to be putting that expensive a gas in a rental car. Also, watch as the attendant starts the pump to see that it begins at 000; when he is finished, make certain it says the amount you have paid for.

Most major companies have outlets at Las Américas Airport outside Santo Domingo and at Gregorio Luperon International Airport in Puerto Plata, the airports of choice for most independent travelers who are likely to rent cars. At this time, there are no rent-a-car companies in the Barahona area, so if you want to drive yourself there, you have to pick up a car at Las Americas or in Santo Domingo. In Punta Cana, if you just want a car for a day, you can easily rent from a cheaper local company. For longer rentals, it's best to stick with the majors.

The majors and most of the minors will insist on a license, a passport, and a credit card and that drivers are older than 25. In season, you can expect to pay between $45 and $83 (Kia Picanto) for an automatic with insurance from a major outfit like Budget.

Major Agencies Avis (☎800/331–1084 ⊕www.avis.com ✉Las Américas Airport ☎809/549–0468 ✉Gregorio Luperon International Airport, Puerto Plata ☎809/586–0214 ✉Castillo Marquez, corner Duarte, La Romana ☎809/550–0600). **Budget**

(☎800/472–3325 ⊕www.budget.com ✉Las Américas Airport ☎809/549–0351 ✉Gregorio Luperon International Airport, Puerto Plata ☎809/586–0413). **Europcar** (✉Las Américas Airport ☎809/549–0942 ✉Gregorio Luperon International Airport, Puerto Plata ☎809/586–7979 ✉Punta Cana International Airport, Baváro, Punta Cana ☎809/686–2861). **Hertz** (☎800/654–3001 ⊕www.hertz.com ✉Las Américas Airport ☎809/549–0454 ✉Puerto Plata ☎809/586–0200).

Local Agencies MC Auto Rental Car (✉Las Américas Airport ☎809/549–8911 ⊕www.mccarrental.com). **McBeal** (✉Santo Domingo ☎809/688–6518). **Nelly Rent-a-Car** (✉Las Américas Airport ☎809/530–0036, 800/526–6684 in U.S.)

BY PUBLIC TRANSPORTATION

Motoconchos are a popular, inexpensive mode of transportation in such areas as Puerto Plata, Sosúa, Cabarete, and Jarabacoa. You can flag down one of these motorcycle taxis along rural roads and in town; rates vary from RD$20 per person for a short run, to as much as RD$100 to RD$150 between Cabarete and Sosúa (double after 6 PM).

BY TAXI

Taxis, which are government regulated, line up outside hotels and restaurants. They're unmetered, and the minimum fare in most destinations is about $4, but you can bargain for less if you order a taxi away from the major hotels. Though they are more expensive, hotel taxis are the nicest and the safest option. Freelance taxis aren't allowed to pick up from hotels, so they hang out on the street in front of them. They can be half the cost per ride depending on the distance. Carry some small bills, because drivers rarely seem to have change.

Recommendable radio-taxi companies in Santo Domingo are Tecni-Taxi (which also operates in Puerto Plata) and Apolo. Tecni is the cheapest, quoting RD$80 as a minimum per trip, Apolo, RD$90. Hiring a taxi by the hour—with unlimited stops and a minimum of two hours—is often a better option if you're doing a substantial sightseeing trip. Tecni charges RD$240 per hour but will offer hourly rates only before 6 PM; Apolo charges RD$280 per hour, day or night. When booking an hourly rate, be sure to establish clearly the time that you start.

You can use taxis to travel to out-of-town destinations at quoted rates. Check with your hotel or the dispatcher at the airport. For example, from the Colonial Zone in Santo Domingo to Playa Dorada with Tecni-Taxi is $150. If you book through your hotel concierge, it can be more.

Taxi-Queen works with the Santiago hotels. Drivers have passed security checks and wear their ID tags around their necks. Their cars are not wonderful, and the drivers are unlikely to speak English, but their prices are especially reasonable. Also, they will take you the distance to Sosúa for $45 and Cabarete for $10 more. The going rate for a taxi between Sosúa and Cabarete is $12. However, the rate is the same for one or five persons, night or day. Taxi-Tourismo, the company that services the Cibao Airport in Santiago, charges $80 to Sosúa, $90 to Cabarete, but has safer, more-commodious vehicles, mostly SUVs and minivans.

Information Apolo Taxi (☎809/537–0000; 809/537–1245 for a limo, which must be booked far in advance). **Taxi-Cabarete** (☎809/571–0767 in Cabarete). **Taxi-Queen** (☎809/570–0000, 809/233–3333 in Santiago). **Taxi-Sosúa** (☎809/571–3097 in Sosúa). **Taxi-Tourismo** (☎809/829–3007 in Santiago). **Tecni-Taxi** (☎809/567–2010, 809/566–7272 in Santo Domingo, 809/320–7621 in Puerto Plata).

■ CONTACTS & RESOURCES

BANKS & EXCHANGE SERVICES

The coin of the realm is the Dominican peso (written RD$). At this writing, the exchange rate was approximately RD$34 to US$1. If you are staying at an all-inclu-

sive resort, then you will not need to change money; even vendors at markets near AIs take U.S. dollars, though change may be in Dominican pesos. Make sure you know which currency is being used in any transaction.

If you plan to travel independently around the D.R., then you may need to change some money. *Cambios* (currency exchange offices) can be found throughout the island. Some hotels also change money, but, as a rule, hotels will not give you favorable rates—casinos usually offer better rates. A passport is usually required to cash traveler's checks, though they are not always accepted.

Banco Popular has many locations throughout the country, with ATMs that accept international cards—but they dispense pesos. ATMs (ATH in Spanish, also called *cajeros automaticos*) are widely available in Santo Domingo and tourist towns. As you get out into the country, they become scarce. English is almost always an option for transactions, and you will receive pesos.

Major credit cards are accepted at most hotels, large stores, and restaurants (American Express less often).

ELECTRICITY

The current is 110–120 volts/60 cycles just as in North America. Electrical blackouts occur less frequently than in the past and tend to last a few minutes; most hotels and restaurants have generators.

EMERGENCIES

Medical Clinics Centro Médico Punta Cana (⊠Carretera Bávaro, Friusa, Bávaro ☎809/552–1506). **Centro Médico Sosúa** (⊠Av. Martinez, Sosúa ☎809/571–3949). **Centro Médico Universidad Central del Este** (⊠Av. Máximo Gómez 68, La Esperilla, Santo Domingo ☎809/221–0171). **Clínica Abreu** (⊠Av Independencia at Calle Delegado, Gazcue, Santo Domingo ☎809/688–4411 or 809/687-9654). **Clínica Dr. Brugal** (⊠Calle José del Carmen Ariza 15, Puerto Plata ☎809/586–2519). **Clínica Gómez**

10

Patino (✉ Av. Independencia 701, Gazcue, Santo Domingo ☎ 809/685–9131). **Hospiten** (✉ Bávaro ☎ 809/686–1414). **Servi-Med** (✉ Plaza La Criolla, Sosúa ☎ 809/571–0964 ✉ Calle Principal (next to Helados Bon), Cabarete ☎ 809/571–0964).

HEALTH

Never drink tap water in the D.R.; you should even brush your teeth with bottled water. Food safety has been a recurring problem in the country, but each year standards are more strict and problems are less (look for a hotel or restaurant that has earned an "H" for food service hygiene or that has a Crystal America certification). If you are staying at an all-inclusive resort, try to arrive at the start of a buffet meal, before the food has sat out. Salads can be iffy unless you ask if the greens have been washed in bottled or purified water. Don't buy from the street vendors. If you experience intestinal problems, see a doctor at the earliest opportunity; some people bring prescribed antibiotics from home—not a bad idea.

Mosquito-borne illnesses have been increasing in prevalence throughout the Caribbean, particularly dengue fever. It is particularly important to use a mosquito repellant to protect yourself from mosquito bites; long sleeves and long pants also help. After hurricanes and tropical storms, malaria has been reported in many areas of the D.R, but at this writing there are no public notices specifically regarding the Dominican Republic. It is wise to check with the CDC for the latest information before you travel.

Health Warnings National Centers for Disease Control & Prevention (CDC ☎ 877/394–8747 international travelers' health line ⊕ www.cdc.gov/travel).

INTERNET, MAIL & SHIPPING

Internet access of some kind (often for an extra charge) is ubiquitous in D.R. hotels and resorts. Prices at AIs in particular can be high (often as much as $5 for 30 minutes); service may be very slow, and computers may be old (with Spanish-language keyboards).

Wi-Fi is more prevalent in upscale hotels, particularly in Santo Domingo; it is usually free but generally exists only in the lobby and some public areas, rather than in your room. There are dozens of Internet cafés in Santo Domingo, and several more centrally located in Punta Cana (check the shopping plazas), Cabarete, Sosúa, and Playa Dorada.

Airmail postage to North America for a letter or postcard is RD$40; letters may take more than two weeks to reach their destination or never make it. Or you can pay big money, RD$695, for a "fast mail" stamp (which will take three days) through a new service called EMS INPOSDOM, which is also known as EPS, you can send packages and get a tracking number, but the success rate is not so high. If you need to send a package home, it's more reliable to use FedEx or DHL, though they cost a small fortune.

LANGUAGE

Spanish is spoken in the D.R. Staff at major tourist attractions and front-desk personnel in most major hotels speak some English, but you may have difficulty making yourself understood. Outside the popular tourist establishments, you may have difficulty finding and English speaker.

PROSTITUTION

The D.R. has had a reputation for prostitution and sex tourism, but officials are trying to discourage the practice. Sosúa in particular was a hotbed of prostitution in the late 1990s, particularly drawing male European sex tourists. Town fathers have made vigorous efforts to clean things up—and they have—but prostitution still exists in the now-designated *Zona Rojas*. In Cabarete, it has always been the opposite story: young, local surfer boys target European women. The real action goes down in Punta Cana, with the infamous "spanky hanky" boys—staffers, often waiters, bartenders, and animation staff—who prey on single female guests, especially older ones; such a rendezvous often ends up in a seedy, drive-up, by-the-hour motel, where the woman is expected to pay for both the motel and the boy's services. In Santo Domingo, prostitutes (*putas*) are alive and not always well; they ply their trade, roaming casinos and hotels. In many areas, there's substantial gay prostitution as well. Throughout the D.R., sex bars are usually called "gentlemen's clubs."

SAFETY

Violent crime against tourists in the D.R. is rare, and the island is not generally unsafe. It definitely is safer now that President Lionel Fernandez is back in power. Nevertheless, poverty is everywhere in the D.R., and petty theft (particularly of cell phones), pickpocketing, and purse snatching (thieves usually work in pairs) are most frequent in Santo Domingo. Pay attention, especially when leaving a bank, a cambio, or a casino around the Malecón, and alas, even in the Zona Colonial. Crime has even come to Santiago, so be cautious at night, and lock the doors of your car or taxi. Armed private security guards are a common sight at clubs and restaurants.

Security at the all-inclusive resorts is very good, but petty theft still occurs. Punta Cana remains one of the safest regions, Uvero Alto even more so. Should anyone offer you illegal drugs, you should be aware that the penalties are extremely tough—jail (not pretty), fines, and no parole—and don't even think of bringing any from home. Take hotel-recommended taxis at night. When driving, always lock your car and never leave valuables in it, even when doors are locked. If you have a safe in your hotel room, use it.

TAXES & SERVICE CHARGES

Most Americans must still purchase a $10 tourist card upon arrival (payable in U.S. dollars only); the departure tax of $20 is almost always included in the price of your airline ticket. The government tax (IBIS) is a whopping 16%, and is added to almost everything—bills at restaurants, hotels, sports activities, rental cars, and even many items at the *supermercados*.

TELEPHONES

To call the D.R. from the United States, dial 1, then the area code 809 and the local number. From the D.R. you also need only dial 1 plus the area code, then the number. To make a local call, you must dial 809 plus the seven-digit number (dial 1-809 if you are calling a cell phone). Directory assistance is 1411.

Many resorts block calling cards or charge a high connection fee; however, many resorts have reasonable prices for international calls. The savviest travelers now use Skype, the international calling program that you can download to your laptop. If you didn't lug your notebook, many of the better off-resort Internet cafés offer Skype on their computers and have headphones, too.

Orange and CLARO are the two major cell phone companies in the D.R. If you have a tri-band GSM phone, it will probably work on the island. If you are in the D.R. for an extended period, you can also get a local phone and SIM card. You can even rent from CLARO; however, it's more economical to buy a phone for less than $50 and use prepaid phone cards, which are sold a many stores.

TIPPING

A 10% service charge is included in all hotel and restaurant bills. In restaurants, the bill will say *propino incluido* or simply *servis*. Even then it's still expected that you will tip an extra 5% to 10% if the service was to your liking. In resorts (even at all-inclusives), it's customary to leave at least a dollar per day for the hotel maid. Taxi drivers expect a 10% tip, especially if they've had to lift luggage or to wait for you. Skycaps and hotel porters expect at least $1 per bag. At all-inclusives, some staff (waiters, bartenders, bellmen, maids)

10

are starting to expect tips; you can also leave small presents for your maid (but write a note so they can show security).

VISITOR INFORMATION

Information **Dominican Republic Tourist Office** (☎212/588–1012 in New York City, 305/444–4592 in Miami, 888/374–6361 ⊕www.godominicanrepublic.com).

WEDDINGS

The relative ease of getting married in the D.R. has made it a major destination for Caribbean weddings. There are no residency requirements, nor are blood tests mandatory. Original birth certificates and passports are required. Divorce certificates must be stamped by the Dominican Consulate. If a woman has been divorced, it must have been at least 10 months ago. Single certificates that indicate the bride and groom are indeed single must be stamped by that same consulate. If either party is widowed, a death certificate must be produced along with the previous marriage certificate. These documents must be translated into Spanish and legalized. You must usually submit documents at least two weeks in advance of your wedding, and the cost for processing is at least $75 per person.

As elsewhere in the Caribbean, civil ceremonies, performed by a judge, are easier and require less documentation than those performed in churches. They will be in Spanish unless you arrange for an English translator. Similarly, the legalized wedding certificate will be in Spanish and may not be delivered for a week or more. Most couples arrange their wedding ceremonies through the wedding coordinator at their resort.

A number of resorts cater to the wedding market and provide a gorgeous backdrop for the occasion. A wedding coordinator based at the resort will help you with all the paperwork, and this is the best way to go unless you speak fluent Spanish.

Grenada

WITH CARRIACOU

Grand Anse Beach

WORD OF MOUTH

"You can't go to Grenada and not go to Grand Anse Beach . . . and Saturday's Market in St. George's."

—Mymoosies

"One thing I would do differently next time is buy more chocolate. I bought a box for my friends, and didn't keep enough for myself!"

—Greenie

WELCOME TO GRENADA

THE SPICE ISLAND

A relatively small island, Grenada is 21 mi (34 km) long and 12 mi (19 km) wide; much of the interior is lush rain forest. It's a major producer of spices and flavorings. Carriacou—23 mi (37 km) north of Grenada—is just 13 square mi (34 square km). Tiny Petite Martinique is 2 mi farther north.

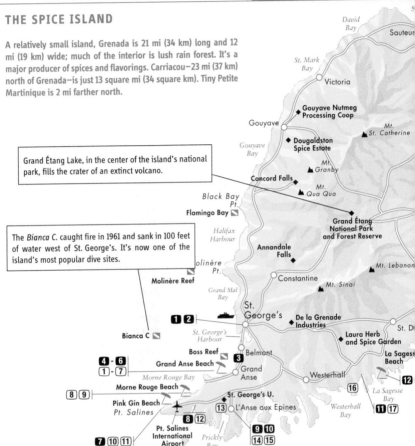

Grand Étang Lake, in the center of the island's national park, fills the crater of an extinct volcano.

The *Bianca C.* caught fire in 1961 and sank in 100 feet of water west of St. George's. It's now one of the island's most popular dive sites.

These days, the people on the Isle of Spice busy themselves cultivating nutmeg, cloves, and other spices. Vestiges of Grenada's once turbulent past have all but disappeared. Renowned for its natural beauty, its fragrant air, and its friendly people, Grenada has lovely beaches and plenty of outdoor and cultural activities.

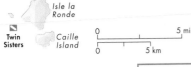

Map labels

Isle la Ronde

Twin Sisters

Caille Island

0   5 mi

0   5 km

n Bridge Island

TO CARRIACOU

Levera Beach

Green Island

Bathway Beach

Leap

Levera National Park and Bird Sanctuary

e Fendue

River Antoine Rum Distillery

li

arl's Airport

Pearl's

Great River Bay

Greenville Cooperative Nutmeg Association

Grenville

Grenville Bay

Telescope Pt.

Marquis

ATLANTIC OCEAN

mme Rose

Grand Bacolet Bay

Gun Pt.

Petite Martinique

Windward

Watering Bay

Hillsborough Bay

Anse le Roche

Sparrow Bay

20 **21** Hillsborough Beach

15 **22**

Belair

Sandy Island

Carriacou Museum

23

14 Hillsborough

Paradise Beach

Lauriston Airport

Grand Bay

Tyrrel Bay Beach

L'Esterre

Kendeace Pt.

16

Tyrrel Bay

Tyrrel Bay

CARRIACOU

White Is.

Saline Island

Frigate Island

Large Island

Kick-em Jenny

KEY

Beaches

Cruise Ship Terminal

Dive Sites

1 Restaurants

1 Hotels

TOP 4 REASONS TO VISIT GRENADA

1 The scent of spices fills the air, perfumes the soap, improves the drinks, and even flavors the ice cream.

2 Nature abounds: Spot monkeys in the mountains, watch birds in the rain forest, join fish in the sea, and build sandcastles on the beach.

3 Friendliness isn't overrated: Grenadians go out of their way to make you feel welcome.

4 With no mega-resorts, you really can get away from it all.

GRENADA PLANNER

Island Activities

Grenada's **beaches** are beautiful, and Grand Anse is among the Caribbean's finest.

It may be hard to pull yourself away from the beach, but be sure to spend a day or two exploring Grenada's lush **scenery.**

The capital city of **St. George's** has a busy harbor, interesting shops, and several historic sites.

A visit to a **spice plantation** and a **nutmeg processing plant** or, if you're adventurous, a guided **hike** in the rain forest, up a mountainside, or to a hidden waterfall is a highlight of most trips.

Little **Carriacou** has a few nice beaches, the best of which is on Sandy Island, which is just offshore from the major town, Hillsborough.

Sailing, particularly to the Grenadines, a small chain of islands north of Carriacou, is exceptional.

Diving, fishing, and **snorkeling** opportunities are also good on both islands.

Logistics

Getting to Grenada & Carriacou: There are no nonstop flights from the U.S., so you have to connect through San Juan or through another nearby island for the short hop on a regional airline. Carriacou is connected by fairly frequent air service from Grenada on small planes and by an inexpensive, 90-minute ferry ride.

Hassle Factor: Medium for Grenada, Medium–High for Carriacou.

Nonstops: None from the U.S.

On the Ground

Point Salines International Airport, at the southwestern tip of Grenada, is a modern facility suitable for the largest jets. Best of all, it's no more than a 10-minute drive from most hotels and resorts. On Carriacou, five minutes south of Hillsborough, Lauriston Airport is a lighted landing strip suitable only for small planes, with a small building for ticket sales and shelter. On Grenada, taxis are always available for transportation between the Point Salines Airport and hotels. Fares to St. George's are $25; to the hotels of Grand Anse and L'Anse aux Épines, $15. Rides taken between 6 PM and 6 AM incur a $4 surcharge. At Carriacou's Lauriston Airport, taxis meet every plane; the fare to Hillsborough is $6.

Renting a Car: On Grenada, having a car or jeep is a convenience if you're staying at a resort in a location other than Grand Anse, which has frequent minibus service. Otherwise, round-trip taxi rides can get expensive if you plan to leave the resort frequently for shopping, meals, or visiting other beaches. Driving is also a reasonable option if you want to explore the island on your own. To rent a car on Grenada, you need a valid driver's license and a local permit (available at the Central Police Station on the Carenage and at some car-rental firms), which costs $12 (EC$30). You can rent a car on Carriacou, but it's easier to take taxis.

Where to Stay

Grenada's tourist accommodations are, for the most part, in the southwest part of the island—primarily on or near Grand Anse Beach or overlooking small bays along the island's southern coast. Nearly all of the island's major beach resorts—including a few that were extensively damaged and then remodeled or even rebuilt—have recovered completely from 2004's Hurricane Ivan. Carriacou is a small island, and its guesthouses are mostly in and around Hillsborough.

Luxury Resorts: Grenada has a handful of luxurious inns and resorts. The best resort on the island (and one of the best in the Caribbean), the Spice Island Beach Resort, re-opened in December 2005 after a major renovation after Hurricane Ivan.

Modest Resorts & Apartment Complexes: Most resorts and hotels on Grenada are small, and many are modest, but that is part of their charm.

Guesthouses: Small guesthouses predominate on Carriacou, where no property has more than 25 rooms.

Hotel & Restaurant Costs

⇨*For information on hotel meal plans, see Accommodations in Caribbean Essentials.*

WHAT IT COSTS IN U.S. DOLLARS				
$$$$	$$$	$$	$	¢
Restaurants				
over $30	$20–$30	$12–$20	$8–$12	under $8
Hotels*				
over $350	$250–$350	$150–$250	$80–$150	under $80
Hotels**				
over $450	$350–$450	$250–$350	$125–$250	under $125

*EP, BP, CP **AI, FAP, MAP Restaurant prices are for a main course at dinner and include any taxes or service charges. Hotel prices are per night for a double room in high season, excluding taxes, service charges, and meal plans (except at all-inclusives).

When to Go

Outside of the high season, which stretches from December 15 to April 15, prices at most Grenada resorts are discounted by up to 40%. There are fewer seasonal changes on Carriacou, where the simple guesthouses are all inexpensive to begin with.

Grenada and Carriacou have some interesting festivals, but you won't find any of the big-scale events as on many islands.

The **Spice Island Billfish Tournament** is held in late January.

The **Grenada Sailing Festival** happens in late January or early February and includes six days of races and regattas.

The Grenada **International Triathlon** is in late April.

Grenada's **Carnival** is a month-long celebration culminating in the second week of August.

The **Carriacou Carnival** in mid-February is the small island's biggest celebration.

The **Carriacou Regatta** in August draws yachts from around the Caribbean.

The Big Drum Dance is the highlight of the **Carriacou Parang Festival**, a musical and cultural celebration held the week before Christmas.

By Jane E.
Zarem

WHILE I WAS WALKING ALONG a narrow street in St. George's during my first visit to Grenada, a young man on the opposite side hollered, "Hey!" He was calling to me. "First time in Grenada?" he asked. Reflexively, though wary, I ever so slightly nodded yes. Then, in a big, friendly voice, he asked, "Are you enjoyin' it?" When I nodded again— affirmatively, of course—his face broadened into a huge smile and, with a big wave, he continued on his way. That, I can affirm based on subsequent visits well into the double digits, is a typical encounter in visitor-friendly Grenada.

Grenada was on a roll. On February 7, 2004, the people on this lush, green, picturesque isle happily celebrated the nation's 30th year of independence. The divisive political events leading to the intervention by U.S. troops in October 1983 had been successfully placed on the back burner of people's minds. And over the following two decades, Grenada had developed a healthy tourism sector and a modern infrastructure, including welcoming hotels and resorts, good roads, up-to-date technology, and reliable utilities. Then, on September 7, 2004, Hurricane Ivan tore through the island, and Grenada was turned upside down.

Grenada lies in the southeastern Caribbean, 12 degrees north of the equator. It is the southernmost of the Windward Islands. Considered outside the hurricane belt, Grenada experiences storm surges from time to time and occasional wind damage when major storms pass by or through its Caribbean neighbors to the north. When Hurricane Ivan's 120-mph winds blew through the island, most Grenadians had never experienced a major hurricane firsthand and, as a result, were taken completely by surprise. Prior to Ivan, the last hurricane to make a direct hit on Grenada was Janet in 1955.

Overnight, countless houses in the countryside were destroyed; roofs were severely damaged or completely torn away; and untold numbers of trees, including those on which the island's lucrative nutmeg crop depends, were toppled. Roads, especially in the less-densely populated north, were impassable for several weeks, while the lifelines of electricity, water, and communications were nonexistent for several months after the storm. One of the most heartbreaking losses was the near total destruction of the recently completed, multimillion-dollar National Stadium, on the north side of St. George's, where Grenadians passionately enjoyed cricket or soccer matches and Carnival festivities.

Although this event forced a sidestep in the island's forward motion, Grenada is once again on a roll. Grenadians stepped up to the plate, and, to all appearances, the island has fully recovered. Mother Nature swiftly brought back the tropical beauty for which Grenada is renowned—although it may be 2010 or so before the nutmeg crop is back to normal. Throughout it all, the people of Grenada retained their friendliness and optimism, the beaches remained beautiful, the sea stayed warm and refreshing. Tourist facilities are either back to normal or bigger and better than before. And the government of China helped Grenada rebuild the National Stadium in time for the World

Cup Cricket series in 2007. All told, horrific Hurricane Ivan and its aftermath couldn't damage the spirit of the Grenadian people.

The nation of Grenada actually consists of three islands: Grenada, the largest, with 120 square mi (311 square km) and a population of 90,000; Carriacou (*car*-ree-a-coo), 23 mi (37 km) north of Grenada, with 13 square mi (34 square km) and a population of about 9,000; and Petite Martinique, 2 mi (3 km) northeast of Carriacou, with just 486 acres and a population of only 900. Carriacou and Petite Martinique are popular for day trips, fishing adventures, or diving and snorkeling excursions, but most of the tourist activity is on Grenada. People interested in a really quiet, get-away-from-it-all vacation will, however, appreciate the simple pleasures of Carriacou during an extended stay.

The island of Grenada itself, just 21 mi (34 km) long and 12 mi (19 km) wide, has 45 beaches and countless secluded coves. Crisscrossed by nature trails and laced with spice plantations, its mountainous interior is mostly consumed by a natural rain forest preserve. St. George's is one of the most picturesque capital cities in the Caribbean, and Grand Anse is one of the region's finest beaches. Nicknamed Isle of Spice, Grenada has long been a major producer of nutmeg, cinnamon, mace, cocoa, and other spices and flavorings. The aroma of spices fills the air in markets, restaurants, and throughout the countryside.

Although he never set foot on the island, Christopher Columbus sighted Grenada in 1498 and named it Concepción. Spanish sailors following in his wake renamed it Granada, after the city in the hills of their homeland. Adapted to Grenade by French colonists, the transformation to Grenada was completed by the British in the 18th century.

Throughout the 17th century, Grenada was the scene of many bloody battles between indigenous Carib Indians and the French. Rather than surrender to the Europeans after losing their last battle in 1651, the Caribs committed mass suicide by leaping off a cliff—now called Carib's Leap or Leapers Hill—in Sauteurs, at the island's northern tip. The French were later overwhelmed by the British in 1762, the beginning of a seesaw of power between the two nations. By the Treaty of Versailles in 1783, Grenada was granted to the British and, almost immediately, thousands of African slaves were brought in to work the sugar plantations. Slavery in Grenada actually began with the French colonization in 1650 and was finally abolished in 1834.

Forts that the French began to protect St. George's Harbour during their colonization of Grenada were later completed and used by the British during theirs. Today, Ft. George and Ft. Frederick are two of the most-visited sites in St. George's. Besides their historical interest, the two locations have magnificent views of the harbor, the capital city itself, and the distant mountains and countryside. Interestingly, not a single shot was fired from either fort for more than two centuries. Then in 1983, Prime Minister Maurice Bishop and several of his supporters were murdered at Ft. George by political foes who had split off from Bishop's party. That event triggered the request from Grenada's governor general and the heads of state of neighboring islands for U.S. troops to intervene, which they did on October 25, 1983.

From that time forward, Grenada's popularity as a vacation destination has increased each year, notwithstanding the temporary effects of Ivan, as travelers continue to seek friendly, exotic islands to visit. Nearly all hotels, resorts, and restaurants in Grenada are family-owned and run by people (mostly Grenadians) whose guests often become their friends. Grenadians, in fact, have a well-deserved reputation for their friendliness, hospitality, and entrepreneurial spirit. You can be sure you'll be "enjoyin' it" when you visit Grenada.

WHERE TO STAY

Lodging options range from simply furnished, inexpensive apartments to elegant suites or villas just steps from the sea. Hotels tend to be small and intimate, with friendly management and attentive staff. All guest rooms are equipped with air-conditioning, an in-room TV, and telephone unless indicated otherwise. During the off-season (April 15 to December 15), prices may be discounted up to 40%.

VILLA COMMUNITIES

As is the case throughout the eastern Caribbean, villa communities are sprouting up like crocuses in spring—everywhere and in profusion. Grenada is one of the last islands to join the party, but properties are opening here quickly. Mount Cinnamon on Grand Anse Beach opened in April 2007. Bacolet Bay Resort & Spa is an extensive villa development underway in St. David's, on the (so far) remote southern coast of Grenada; and Port Louis is a brand-new marina village on the drawing boards—a $500 million project that, when complete in the next few years, will transform the lagoon and St. George's Harbour areas in the capital city. All these developments are investment properties, in which individually owned villas will be made available to nonowner guests through management companies.

$$$$ **Mount Cinnamon.** The first 21 units of what will eventually become a
☾   150-unit villa community opened in April 2007. Beautifully situated on a hillside adjacent to Grand Anse Beach, Mount Cinnamon comprises one-, two-, and three-bedroom villas complete with full kitchens, Bose entertainment systems, cable TV, and such convenient extras as washers and dryers. The rooms themselves are beautifully furnished with contemporary decor and attractive artwork. Each unit has a porch or balcony with a sea view. Most of the bedrooms also have a balcony, and each has its own dressing area and shower. Sitting rooms all have sofa beds, which works well for families. Kids 12 and under stay free. Minimum stay is one week; shorter stays can sometimes be negotiated, based on availability. **Pros:** Excellent location on Grand Anse Beach, good choice for families. **Con:** Ongoing construction over the next few years could be an annoyance. ⊠*Grand Anse, Box 3858, St. George's* ☎*473/439–0000* ⊕*www.mountcinnamongrenada.com*

≤21 units ⚐In-room: safe, kitchen, Wi-Fi. In-hotel: restaurant, bar, tennis court, pool, spa, beachfront, water sports, no elevator, laundry facilities ⊟AE, MC, V ⦿BP.

PRIVATE VILLAS

Villas and private homes are available for rent for a week or longer. The minimum staff includes a maid and a laundress, but a cook, house-keeper, gardener, and others can be arranged.

In Grenada, many rental properties are located in and around L'Anse aux Épines, a beautiful residential peninsula that juts into the sea. In-season rates range from about $1,600 a week for a two-bedroom home with a pool to $8,000 a week for a six-bedroom home on the beach. In Carriacou, in-season rates range from $65 per day for a small cottage or in-town apartment suitable for two people to $185 per day for a villa that accommodates up to six people in the countryside, with panoramic views and a swimming pool.

Information **Down Island Villa Rentals** (✉ *Craigston* ☎ *473/443–8182* ⊕ *www.islandvillas.com*). **Villas of Grenada** (✉ *Box 218, St. George's* ☎ *473/444–1896* ⊕ *www.villasofgrenada.com*).

HOTELS ON GRENADA

$$$$ **Calabash Hotel.** The elegant suites here are in 10 two-story cottages
★ distributed in a horseshoe around 8 acres of gardens that hug a curved beach on Prickly Bay. Each suite has a spacious bedroom and sitting area with rattan and wicker furniture and a verandah, where breakfast is served daily by your maid. Two-thirds of the suites have whirlpool baths; eight have private plunge pools. Complimentary fruit is served on the beach each morning; canapés are delivered to your suite in the evening. Rhodes Restaurant serves memorable cuisine. **Pros:** Pretty location, love those treats, breakfast on the verandah. **Cons:** Pricey, taxi or rental car required to get around. ✉ *L'Anse aux Épines, St. George's* ✉ *Box 382, St. George's* ☎ *473/444–4334* ⊕ *www.calabash hotel.com* ≤*30 suites* ⚐*In-room: kitchen, DVD, dial-up. In-hotel: restaurant, room service, bars, tennis court, pool, gym, spa, beachfront, water sports, no elevator, concierge, laundry service, public Internet* ⊟*AE, MC, V* ⦿*BP.*

$$$$ **Laluna.** You may think you've landed on an island in the South
Fodor'sChoice Pacific, but this upscale enclave is hidden away on a remote, pristine
★ beach near Grenada's Quarantine Point. Laluna's large thatched-roof cottages—each with its own plunge pool—line the beachfront and climb 10 acres of wooded hillside. Owner Bernardo Bertucci, formerly a fashion consultant for Armani and Prada, has infused his elegant style into the breezy, open-plan cottages. Bedrooms open onto large verandahs that serve as indoor-outdoor sitting areas. Bathrooms have showers that partially open to the outdoors. Guests congregate at the comfortable beachfront lounge and bar and have free access to a small CD and video library, a couple of bikes, and a kayak or two. The

resort faces west, assuring beautiful sunset views. **Pros:** Nifty cottages, great restaurant, fabulous beach, attentive staff. **Cons:** The long dirt access road, far from anywhere, fairly confining. ⊠*Morne Rouge, St. George's* ✉*Box 1500, St. George's* ☎*473/439–0001 or 866/452–5862* ⊕*www.laluna.com* ↪*16 cottages* △*In-room: safe, refrigerator, VCR (some), dial-up, Wi-Fi. In-hotel: restaurant, bar, pool, gym, beachfront, water sports, bicycles, no elevator, concierge, laundry facilities, public Internet, public Wi-Fi, no kids under 14 (mid-Dec.–mid-Apr.)* ⊟*AE, MC, V* ♨*EP.*

$$$$

Fodor'sChoice

★

🏨**Maca Bana Villas.** Clustered on a 2-acre hillside overlooking mile-long Magazine Beach, each of Maca Bana's seven villas offers a breathtaking view—of the white sand below, out to sea, up the coastline to pretty St. George's Harbour, and beyond to the cloud-capped mountains. Each villa is named for a tropical fruit, a theme that carries through to the decor. And each has a spacious verandah with a private hot tub. The surrounding gardens are studded with fruit trees, herbal plants, and koi ponds. A small but inviting infinity pool is open to all guests. Villas accommodate two to six persons, but families with young children should be aware of the steep terrain. Roomy kitchens are fully equipped, down to an espresso machine and groceries for your first breakfast. Would-be artists can sign up for lessons with noted artist Rebecca Thompson, the owner's wife. Or perhaps a personal yoga or tai chi lesson on your own deck will do the trick. **Pros:** Roomy villas with amazing views and huge kitchens, excellent restaurant, great beach. **Cons:** Steep hill down to the restaurant and beach, tiny pool. ⊠*Point Salines, St. George's* ☎*473/535–5355* ⊕*www.macabana.com* ↪*2 1-bedroom villas, 5 2-bedroom villas* △*In-room: safe, kitchen, VCR (some), Wi-Fi. In-hotel: restaurant, bar, pool, spa, beachfront, no elevator, laundry facilities, public Wi-Fi* ⊟*AE, MC, V* ♨*EP.*

$$$$

Fodor'sChoice

★

🏨**Spice Island Beach Resort.** Exquisite accommodations in dozens of gleaming white buildings extend along 1,600 feet of Grand Anse Beach. Beachfront "sea grape" suites are steps from the sand, and several luxury pool suites have private gardens and enormous residential-size swimming pools. Two suites are specifically designed for people with mobility problems. Guest rooms are richly decorated with contemporary Asian furniture; bathrooms are enormous, with double-size whirlpool tubs and marble tiles. Throughout the resort, the service is impeccable. Enjoy water sports on the beach, play a game of tennis, or borrow a DVD from the library. Kids enjoy all-day activities at the Nutmeg Pod, which includes a nap room and a four-seat Playstation room with kid-size recliner chairs. **Pros:** Elegant and luxurious yet friendly and casual, perfect beachfront location, excellent staff. **Con:** Haute Caribbean cuisine with limited choices at dinner … occasionally something simpler would be welcome. ⊠*Grand Anse, Box 6, St. George's* ✉*Box 6, St. George's* ☎*473/444–4258* ⊕*www.spiceisland-beachresort.com* ↪*64 suites* △*In-room: safe, DVD, Ethernet, Wi-Fi. In-hotel: 2 restaurants, room service, bar, tennis court, pool, gym, spa, beachfront, diving, water sports, bicycles, no elevator, children's programs (ages 3–12), laundry service, concierge, public Internet* ⊟*AE, D, DC, MC, V* ♨*AI.*

$$$–$$$$ ⬚ **Bel Air Plantation.** On an 18-acre peninsula on Grenada's southeast-
★   ern coast, gaily painted gingerbread cottages dot a verdant hillside.
Beautifully constructed by local craftsmen, the spacious cottages are
luxuriously decorated in a country-casual style, with teak and wicker
furniture, framed botanical prints, and the works of local artisans. Each
one- or two-bedroom cottage has a fully equipped kitchen, Bose enter-
tainment system, CD library, and private verandah. Arrange fishing and
boating charters next door at Grenada Marina. The excellent Water's
Edge restaurant is on-site; rent a car for sightseeing and going to town
(a half-hour drive). **Pros:** Roomy cottages, private, great pool, excel-
lent restaurant. **Cons:** Be prepared to walk up and down the hillside,
far from town … far from anything, in fact. ⊠ *St. David's Point, St.
David's* ✉ *Box 857, LB 125, St. George's* ☎ *473/444–6305* ⊕ *www.
belairplantation.com* 🛏 *11 cottages* △ *In-room: safe, kitchen, DVD,
dial-up. In-hotel: restaurant, room service, bar, pool, spa, no elevator,
concierge, laundry facilities, concierge, public Internet, public Wi-Fi,
airport shuttle, no kids under 15* ⊟ *AE, D, DC, MC, V* ⦾ *EP.*

$$$ ⬚ **Coyaba.** The Cherman family reopened a bigger and better ver-
sion of this popular beachfront resort in 2005. Coyaba, which means
"heaven" in the Arawak language, is situated in a 5.5-acre garden of
palm trees, hibiscus, frangipani, and bougainvillea. It's one of the few
hotels located directly on beautiful Grand Anse Beach. The island's
Amerindian heritage influenced the resort's architecture and interior
design, which includes natural materials, colorful fabrics, and native
artwork. But this is not a rustic environment. The accommodations
are modern, and the decor is beautifully serene; all rooms have a view
of the sea from the private patio or balcony. Three rooms are accessible for guests with disabilities. **Pros:** Excellent beachfront location,
spacious grounds, laid-back atmosphere. **Con:** Rooms are nice but not
extraordinary. ⊠ *Grand Anse, St. George's* ✉ *Box 336, St. George's*
☎ *473/444–4129* ⊕ *www.coyaba.com* 🛏 *80 rooms* △ *In-room: safe,
refrigerator, dial-up. In-hotel: 2 restaurants, bars, tennis court, pool,
gym, spa, beachfront, diving, water sports, no elevator, laundry service*
⊟ *AE, MC, V* ⦾ *EP.*

$$–$$$ ⬚ **Blue Horizons Garden Resort.** A short walk from Grand Anse Beach,
☾   "Blue" is especially popular among divers and nature lovers. All suites
here have separate sitting-dining rooms and one or two beds; studios
have dining alcoves and one bed. All units have kitchenettes and private terraces. Trees and plantings on the 6-acre property are home to
21 species of birds. Popular adventure packages focus on rain-forest
hikes or scuba diving. La Belle Creole restaurant is renowned for its
contemporary West Indian cuisine. **Pros:** Spacious accommodations,
excellent value, good dive and hiking packages. **Cons:** Not directly
on the beach. ⊠ *Grand Anse, St. George's* ✉ *Box 41, St. George's*
☎ *473/444–4316 or 473/444–4592* ⊕ *www.grenadabluehorizons.com*
🛏 *26 suites, 6 studios* △ *In-room: safe, kitchen, dial-up, Wi-Fi. In-
hotel: restaurant, bars, pool, no elevator, laundry service, public Wi-Fi,
no-smoking rooms* ⊟ *AE, D, MC, V* ⦾ *EP.*

$$–$$$ ⬚ **Grenada Grand Beach Resort.** On 20 landscaped acres along a broad
☾   section of beautiful Grand Anse Beach, this resort offers comfort-

able rooms and extensive amenities. Freshwater swimmers enjoy the 300-foot pool with its waterfalls and swim-up bar. Groups sometimes frequent this resort, which has Grenada's largest convention center. Guest rooms all have attractive mahogany furniture, king or twin beds, and a large balcony or patio. Two suites have double-size whirlpool tubs. **Pros:** Huge hotel full of amenities, beautiful beachfront location. **Cons:** Rooms are not extraordinary, popular meeting venue. ⊠ *Grand Anse, St. George's* ✇ *Box 441, St. George's* ☎ *473/444–4371* ⊕ *www. grenadagrand.com* ⬅*238 rooms, 2 suites* ⌂ *In-room: safe, Wi-Fi. In-hotel: 2 restaurants, room service, bars, golf course, tennis courts, pools, gym, beachfront, diving, water sports, no elevator, laundry service, public Wi-Fi* ▱*AE, DC, MC, V* ⏇*BP.*

$$–$$$ ▦**Petit Bacaye Cottage Hotel.** If Robinson Crusoe were to visit Grenada today, he would choose to stay at Petit Bacaye. Hidden along the coast in St. David's, about a half-hour's drive east of Grand Anse and the hustle and bustle of St. George's, Petit Bacaye is a tiny oasis of pure serenity. Just a stone's throw from the palm-fringed beach are five thatched-roof cottages—one double and one with two units, each suitable for two guests; another sleeps four; and the largest sleeps six or seven people. Each cottage has a verandah or sundeck with a view, a kitchen, and large sitting and dining areas—although guests often prefer to take their meals in the restaurant or at a beach barbecue. Each day on the beachfront, fisherman deliver fresh fish that the chef prepares to order. There's a seven-day minimum. **Pros:** Idyllically private and quiet spot, good restaurant, perfect for a wedding or a honeymoon. **Cons:** Remote (you'll need a car), access driveway is steep and scary for drivers. ⊠ *St. David's* ☎ *473/443–2902* ⊕ *www.petitbacaye.com* ⬅*5 cottages* ⌂ *In-room: no a/c, no phone, kitchen, no TV. In-hotel: restaurant, room service, bar, beachfront, no elevator, laundry service, airport shuttle* ▱*MC, V* ⏇ *EP* ⏱ *Closed Aug. and Sept.*

$$–$$$ ▦**True Blue Bay Resort & Marina.** The lawns and gardens at this family-run resort, a former indigo plantation, slope down to True Blue Bay. The Indigo rooms with connecting doors work well for families. Three colorful cottages are near the pool, and four spacious apartments are perched on a cliff overlooking the bay. Each has a living room with a sofa bed, a dining area, and a fully equipped kitchen. Modern villa suites, decorated in Caribbean colors, also have views of the bay. Two beaches are on the bay, and Grand Anse Beach is a five-minute drive away. Arrange yacht charters at the marina or dive excursions at the on-site dive center. **Pros:** Nice accommodations at reasonable prices, busy marina, friendly bar and restaurant. **Cons:** Tiny beach is not great for swimming, rental car is recommended. ⊠ *Old Mill Ave., True Blue Bay, St. George's* ✇ *Box 1414, St. George's* ☎ *473/443– 8783 or 866/325–8322* ⊕ *www.truebluebay.com* ⬅*24 rooms, 4 1-bedroom apartments, 3 2-bedroom cottages, 7 villa suites* ⌂ *In-room: safe, kitchen, dial-up. In-hotel: restaurant, room service, bar, pools, gym, beachfront, diving, water sports, no elevator, laundry service, public Internet* ▱*AE, MC, V* ⏇*CP.*

$$ ▦**Flamboyant Hotel & Villas.** Built on a steep hillside, the rooms at this popular, Grenadian-owned hotel have private verandahs with pan-

oramic views of Grand Anse Bay. One-bedroom suites and two-bed-room, two-bath cottages each have a fully equipped kitchen and sitting room with sofa bed, making this an excellent value for families. Be prepared for lots of stairs (more than 100) to get to Grand Anse Beach. The crab races, after dinner on Monday nights, are legendary. **Pros:** Comparatively inexpensive, great views, nightlife at the Owl bar. **Cons:** Rather ordinary rooms, lots of stairs. ⊠ *Grand Anse, St. George's* 🖰 *Box 214, St. George's* 🖀 *473/444–4247* ⊕ *www.flamboyant. com* 🛏 *38 rooms, 27 suites, 2 cottages* 🖧 *In-room: safe, kitchen (some), refrigerator, DVD (some), VCR (some), dial-up. In-hotel: 2 restaurants, room service, bar, pool, gym, beachfront, diving, water sports, no elevator, laundry service, public Internet* ☰ *AE, D, DC, MC, V* ❢◎❢ *EP.*

$$ ⊡ **Grenadian by Rex Resorts.** This massive beachfront resort on Tam-
Ⅽ arind Bay, favored particularly by Europeans, is minutes from the airport. Guest rooms are in blocks of several two-story, sun-yellow buildings—some along the beach and others on a bluff overlooking the sea. The pool, casual restaurant, and bar are in a beachfront complex but separated from the guest buildings by a large lawn and lake. After dinner, guests gather at the spacious lounge area and enjoy nightly entertainment. **Pros:** Large play area for kids. **Cons:** Rooms are ade-quate but unremarkable, quite a hike from room to beach to lobby, meals are comparatively expensive. ⊠ *Tamarind Bay, Point Salines, St. George's* 🖀 *473/444–3333* ⊕ *www.rexresorts.com* 🛏 *191 rooms, 21 suites* 🖧 *In-room: no a/c (some), safe (some), refrigerator (some), no TV (some), dial-up. In-hotel: 3 restaurants, bars, tennis courts, pool, gym, beachfront, water sports, no elevator, children's programs (ages 4–12), laundry service, no-smoking rooms* ☰ *AE, D, DC, MC, V* ❢◎❢ *EP.*

$$ ⊡ **La Sagesse Nature Centre.** Secluded on La Sagesse Bay—10 mi (16 km) east of the airport (about a 30-minute drive)—the grounds here include a salt-pond bird sanctuary, thick mangroves, nature trails, and 0.5 mi (0.75 km) of tree-shaded beach. Five large guest rooms are in the historic manor house; a nearby beach cottage has two individually rented rooms; and a more-modern beachfront building has two rooms and three suites, two of which are duplex. All accommodations are within 30 feet of the beach, and all except those in the manor house have screened verandahs. Be content to relax here and enjoy the natural surroundings; you'll probably need to rent a car. **Pros:** Rather charm-ing, beautiful beach, excellent restaurant. **Cons:** Remote, you'll need a car to get anywhere else, no Internet access. ⊠ *La Sagesse, St. David's* 🖰 *Box 44, St. George's* 🖀 *473/444–6458* ⊕ *www.lasagesse.com* 🛏 *9 rooms, 3 suites* 🖧 *In-room: no a/c (some), no phone, no TV. In-hotel: restaurant, bar, beachfront, water sports, no elevator, laundry service* ☰ *MC, V* ❢◎❢ *EP.*

$$ ⊡ **Twelve Degrees North.** Named for the latitude at which it sits, this small, secluded inn has one- and two-bedroom suites, all of which face the sea. Accommodations come with a personal housekeeper who cooks breakfast and lunch, cleans, and tends to your laundry. Groceries are stocked for your arrival, along with fresh-cut flowers, rum punch, and a spice basket. Apartments are bright and airy, with modern furniture, a balcony or patio, and woven-grass rugs on the tile floors. **Pros:** Private getaway atmosphere, personalized service, small and quiet. **Cons:** Accommodations are rather unspectacular despite the pretty location, hotel has no Internet of any kind. ✉ *L'Anse aux Épines, St. George's* *Box 241, St. George's* ☎ *473/444–4580* ⊕ *www.twelvedegreesnorth.com* *8 suites* *In-room: no a/c, no phone, no TV. In-hotel: tennis court, pool, beachfront, water sports, no elevator, laundry service, no kids under 15* ▭ *AE, V* *EP.*

$–$$ **Allamanda Beach Resort.** Right on Grand Anse Beach, this small hotel has some rooms with whirlpool baths; many rooms also have connecting doors, making it a good choice for families. All rooms have tile floors and a balcony or patio. At the water-sports center you can find Sunfish and snorkeling equipment. Shopping, restaurants, nightlife, and the minibus to town are right at the doorstep. An all-inclusive option is available, which also includes a massage. **Pros:** Location, location, location, great value. **Cons:** Rooms are fairly basic—don't expect luxury. ✉ *Grand Anse, St. George's* *Box 1025, St. George's* ☎ *473/444–0095* ⊕ *www.allamandaresort.com* *50 suites* *In-room: safe, refrigerator, Wi-Fi. In-hotel: restaurant, tennis court, pool, gym, beachfront, no elevator, public Wi-Fi* ▭ *AE, D, MC, V* *EP.*

$–$$ **Gem Holiday Beach Resort.** Owner Miriam Bedeau and her family operate this no-frills hotel on pretty Morne Rouge Beach. One- and two-bedroom self-catering apartments are small and simple, with kitchenettes, dining-living rooms with mahogany furniture, and private verandahs overlooking the sea. Only the bedrooms are air-conditioned. Fantazia, Grenada's premier (soundproof) dance club, is also on the property. **Pros:** Friendly, family-run hotel on a beautiful beach, excellent restaurant, nightclub on-site. **Cons:** Simple accommodations. ✉ *Morne Rouge, St. George's* *Box 58, St. George's* ☎ *473/444–2288* ⊕ *www.gembeachresort.com* *15 1-bedroom apartments, 4 2-bedroom apartments* *In-room: kitchen, dial-up. In-hotel: restaurant, bar, beachfront, water sports, no elevator, laundry service* ▭ *AE, D, MC, V* *EP.*

HOTELS ON CARRIACOU

$ ★ **Bogles Round House.** Pick your flavor: Lime, Mango, or Plum. Lime cottage is the largest of the three, with room for three or four people; Mango and Plum sleep two comfortably and a third person, if needed. All cottages have double beds with mosquito netting and ceiling fans, along with a galley-style kitchen and shower. The cottages are located in a garden setting about 60 feet from Sparrow Bay, where guests enjoy swimming, snorkeling, and walks on the beach. The centerpiece of the property, however, is the Round House—an art project constructed by the owner's family. **Pros:** The price, the restaurant, the ambience. **Cons:** No a/c, no communication with the outside world (although that may be a "pro" for some). ✉ *Sparrow Bay, Bogles* ☎ *473/443–7841* ⊕ *www.boglesroundhouse.com* *3 cottages* *In-room: no a/c, no phone, kitchen, no TV, Wi-Fi. In-hotel: restaurant, bar, beachfront, no elevator,* *water sports, laundry service, public Internet, public Wi-Fi, some pets allowed, no-smoking rooms* ⊟*MC, V* ⦿|*CP* ⊘*Closed May.*

$ ⬚**Carriacou Grand View Hotel.** The view is lovely, particularly at sunset, from this perch high above Hillsborough Harbour. Though the building is four stories high, its hillside location provides entrances at three levels, making stair-climbing a nonissue, even if you're on the top floor. Guest rooms are pleasant and comfortably furnished; suites have added sitting rooms (large enough for a roll-away bed) and full kitchens. Most bathrooms have showers only. The beach and the town are a 15-minute walk away. **Pros:** Truly a grand view, friendly atmosphere, popular restaurant. **Cons:** Accommodations are basic. ⊠*Beausejour* 🕿🖨*473/443–6348* ⊕*www.carriacougrandview.com* ⬟*7 rooms, 7 suites* ⬙*In-room: no a/c (some), kitchen. In-hotel: restaurant, bar, pool, no elevator, public Internet* ⊟*MC, V* ⦿|*EP.*

$ ⬚**Green Roof Inn.** This small inn operated by a Swedish family has just five rooms—three have private showers, two others share—and a private cottage. All are individually decorated with richly painted walls and pure white fabrics. All rooms have access to a verandah and cooling sea breezes. Beds are draped with mosquito netting. You're guaranteed beautiful views of Hillsborough Bay and the offshore cays—and incredible sunsets night after night. This is a perfect venue for a scuba diving, snorkeling, or beachcombing vacation. **Pros:** Great water view, homey atmosphere, close to town. **Cons:** Rooms are small. ⊠*Hillsborough Bay, Hillsborough* 🕿🖨*473/443–6399* ⊕*www.greenroofinn.com* ⬟*5 rooms, 1 cottage* ⬙*In-room: no a/c, no phone, kitchen (some), refrigerator, no TV, Wi-Fi. In-hotel: restaurant, bar, beachfront, no elevator, public Wi-Fi* ⊟*MC, V* ⦿|*BP.*

¢ ⬚**Ade's Dream Guest House.** By the jetty in Hillsborough, this small guesthouse is a convenient place to rest your weary head after a day snorkeling at Sandy Island or scuba diving at some of Grenada's best dive spots. The accommodations are simple, with queen-size or twin beds and a writing table, but the view of the mountains, sea, neighboring islands, and all the harbor activity is great—and it's certainly priced right. **Pros:** Steps from the jetty, perfect for an overnight on Carriacou. **Cons:** Extremely basic accommodations, don't expect anything special other than the location. ⊠*Main St., Hillsborough* 🕿*473/443–7317* ⊕*www.adesdream.com* ⬟*23 rooms, 16 with bath* ⬙*In-room: no a/c (some), kitchen, no TV. In-hotel: restaurant, beachfront, no elevator, laundry facilities* ⊟*AE, MC, V* ⦿|*BP.*

WHERE TO EAT

Grenada grows everything from lettuce and tomatoes to citrus, mangoes, papaya (called *pawpaw*), callaloo (similar to spinach), dasheen (a root vegetable), christophenes (like squash), breadfruit—the list is endless. And all restaurants prepare dishes with local produce and season them with the many spices grown here. Be sure to try the local flavors of ice cream: soursop, guava, rum raisin, coconut (the best), or nutmeg.

Soups—especially pumpkin and callaloo—are divine and often start a meal. Pepper pot is a savory stew of pork, oxtail, vegetables, and spices. *Oildown,* the national dish, is salted meat, breadfruit, onions, carrots, celery, dasheen, and dumplings all boiled in coconut milk until the liquid is absorbed and the savory mixture becomes "oily." A *roti*—curried chicken, beef, or vegetables wrapped in pastry and baked—is more popular in Grenada than a sandwich.

Fresh seafood of all kinds, including lobster, is plentiful. Conch, known here as *lambi,* often appears curried or in a stew. Crab back, though, is not seafood—it's land crab. Most Grenadian restaurants serve seafood and at least some native dishes.

Rum punches are ubiquitous and always topped with grated nutmeg. Clarke's Court and Westerhall are locally produced and marketed rums. Carib, the local beer, is refreshing, light, and quite good. If you prefer a nonalcoholic drink, opt for fruit punch—a delicious mixture of freshly blended tropical fruit.

WHAT TO WEAR

Dining in Grenada is casual. At dinner, collared shirts and long pants are appropriate for men (even the fanciest restaurants don't require jacket and tie) and sundresses or slacks are fine for women. Beachwear, of course, and other revealing attire should be reserved for the beach.

GRENADA

CARIBBEAN   ✕ **Patrick's Homestyle Cooking.** Patrick Lavine will astound you with both
$$$ his fixed menu of 20 or more local dishes, served family style, and his ebullient and decidedly flamboyant personality. This is Grenadian home-style cooking at its casual best. You'll feast on successive helpings of superb callaloo or pumpkin soup, gingered pork, fried fish, cou-cou (cornmeal cakes), lambi creole, curried goat, oildown, chocolate cake, and more—all for $23 per person. Everything is cooked fresh, so you must call ahead. Then, bring your appetite, your curiosity, and, especially, your sense of humor. ⊠ *Lagoon Rd., St. George's* ☎ *473/440–0364* ⌲ *Reservations essential* ▤ *MC, V.*

$$–$$$ ✕ **The Nutmeg.** West Indian specialties, fresh seafood, great hamburg-
☻   ers, and a waterfront view make this a favorite with locals and visitors alike. It's upstairs on the Carenage (above Sea Change bookstore), with large, open windows from which you can watch the harbor activity as you eat. Try the callaloo soup, curried lambi, fresh seafood, or a steak—or just stop by for a rum punch and a roti. ⊠ *The Carenage, St. George's* ☎ *473/440–2539* ▤ *AE, D, MC, V.*

$–$$$ ✕ **Coconut Beach Restaurant.** Take local seafood, add butter, wine, and Grenadian spices, and you have excellent French creole cuisine. Throw in a beautiful location on Grand Anse Beach, and this West Indian cottage becomes a perfect alfresco spot. Lobster is a specialty, as lobster thermidor or perhaps wrapped in a crepe, dipped in garlic butter, or added to pasta. Homemade coconut pie is a winner for dessert. On Wednesday and Sunday nights in season, dinner is a beach barbecue with live music. ⊠ *Grand Anse, St. George's* ☎ *473/444–4644* ▭ *AE, D, MC, V* ⊗ *Closed Tues.*

$ ✕ **Belmont Estate.** Luncheon is served! If you're visiting the northern reaches of Grenada island, plan to stop for lunch at Belmont Estate, a 400-year-old working nutmeg and cocoa plantation. Settle into the breezy open-air dining room, which overlooks enormous trays of nutmeg, cocoa, and mace drying in the sunshine. A waiter will offer some refreshing local juice and a choice of callaloo or pumpkin soup. Then head to the buffet and help yourself to salad, rice, stewed chicken, beef curry, stewed fish, and vegetables. Dessert may be homemade ice cream, ginger cake, or another delicious confection. Afterward, feel free to take a tour of the museum, cocoa fermentary, sugarcane garden, and old cemetery. Farm animals (and a couple of monkeys) roam the property, and there's often folk music and dancing on the lawn. ⊠ *Belmont, St. Patrick* ☎ *473/442–9524* ⚲ *Reservations essential* ▭ *MC, V* ⊗ *Closed Sat. No dinner.*

CHINESE– ✕ **Tropicana.** The chef-owner here hails from Trinidad and specializes
CARIBBEAN in both Chinese and West Indian cuisine. Local businesspeople seem
$ to be the best customers for the extensive menu of Chinese food, the tantalizing aroma of barbecued chicken notwithstanding. Eat in or take out—it's open from 7:30 AM to midnight. Tropicana is right at the Lagoon Road traffic circle, overlooking the marina. ⊠ *Lagoon Rd., St. George's* ☎ *473/440–1586* ▭ *AE, DC, MC, V.*

ECLECTIC ✕ **Rhodes Restaurant.** The open-air restaurant at the Calabash Hotel,
$$$ named for acclaimed British chef Gary Rhodes, is surrounded by
★ palms, flowering plants, and twinkling lights. Past menus have featured seared yellowfin tuna Benedict as a starter, followed by fillet of red snapper on smoked-salmon potatoes or roast duck breast with leeks and pepper-pot sauce. The passion-fruit panna cotta, light as a soufflé, is nothing short of divine. ⊠ *Calabash Hotel, L'Anse aux Épines, St. George's* ☎ *473/444–4334* ⚲ *Reservations essential* ▭ *AE, MC, V* ⊗ *No lunch.*

$$–$$$ ✕ **Beach House.** At this colorful restaurant a short walk down the beach
★ from Laluna resort, the gleaming white sand and sea views are the perfect backdrop for a salad or pasta luncheon on the deck. At dinner, excellent entrées—rack of lamb, blackened fish, or prime rib—and superb wines give new meaning to the term "beach party." A kids' menu is available, too. ⊠ *Airport Rd., Point Salines, St. George's* ☎ *473/444–4455* ⚲ *Reservations essential* ▭ *AE, MC, V* ⊗ *Closed Sun.*

$$–$$$ ✕ **Water's Edge.** At this Bel Air Plantation restaurant overlooking pris-
★ tine St. David's Harbour, the dining experience is as exquisite as the view is mesmerizing. (The napkins are even folded into the shape of binoculars.) Tables are set on the covered verandah or on the garden patio. The extensive menu includes fish and lobster from the surrounding waters, fresh produce from nearby farms and the resort's own gardens, and imported meats—all delicately flavored with local herbs and spices. ⊠ *Bel Air Plantation, St. David's Point, St. David's* ☎ *473/443–2822* ⚲ *Reservations essential* ▭ *AE, D, MC, V.*

$$ ✕**La Boulangerie.** This combination French bakery and Italian pizzeria, convenient to the hotels at Grand Anse, is a great place for an inexpensive breakfast or light meal—to eat in, take out, or have delivered. You'll find croissants, focaccia and baguette sandwiches, coffee and espresso, and homemade gelato. ⊠*Le Marquis Complex, Grand Anse, St. George's* ☎*473/444–1131* ▭*AE, MC, V.*

ECLECTIC- ✕**La Belle Creole.** The marriage of contemporary and West Indian cuiCARIBBEAN sines and a splendid view of distant St. George's are the delights of this
$$$$ romantic hillside restaurant at the Blue Horizons Garden Resort. The
★ always-changing five-course table d'hôte menu is based on original recipes from the owner's mother, a pioneer in incorporating local products into "foreign" dishes. Try, for instance, Grenadian caviar (roe of the white sea urchin), lobster-egg flan, callaloo quiche, or ginger pork chops. The inspired cuisine, romantic setting, and gracious service are impressive. ⊠*Blue Horizons Garden Resort, Grand Anse, St. George's* ☎*473/444–4316 or 473/444–4592* ⚞*Reservations essential* ▭*AE, D, MC, V.*

SEAFOOD ✕**Red Crab.** Locals and expats love to gather at this pub, especially on
$$–$$$ Saturday night. The curried lambi and garlic shrimp keep the regulars coming back. Seafood, particularly lobster, and steak (imported from the United States) are staples of the menu; hot garlic bread comes with every order. Eat inside or under the stars, and enjoy live music Monday and Friday evenings in season. ⊠*L'Anse aux Épines, near Calabash Hotel, St. George's* ☎*473/444–4424* ⚞*Reservations essential* ▭*AE, MC, V* ☉*Closed Sun.*

$–$$ ✕**Aquarium Restaurant.** As the name suggests, fresh seafood is the speFodor'sChoice cialty here. Many guests spend the day at the adjacent beach (you can
★ rent kayaks or snorkeling gear), then break for a cool drink or satisfying lunch on the deck here. The dining room is surrounded by lush plants and palms, and a waterfall adds romance. The dinner menu always includes fresh fish, grilled lobster, and specialties such as callaloo cannelloni. On Sunday there's a beach barbecue. This place is even convenient to the airport for a preflight meal. ⊠*LaSource Rd., Point Salines, St. George's* ☎*473/444–1410* ⚞*Reservations essential* ▭*AE, D, DC, MC, V* ☉*Closed Mon.*

¢–$$ ✕**La Sagesse Nature Centre.** The perfect spot to soothe a frazzled soul, La Sagesse's open-air seafood restaurant is on a secluded cove in a nature preserve about 30 minutes from Grand Anse. Combine your lunch or dinner with a hike or a day at the beach. Select from sandwiches, salads, or lobster for lunch. Lambi, smoked marlin, tuna steak, and a daily vegetarian entrée may be joined on the dinner menu by specials like chicken française. Transportation is available. ⊠*La Sagesse, St. David's* ☎*473/444–6458* ⚞*Reservations essential* ▭*AE, MC, V.*

CARRIACOU

CARIBBEAN ✕**Bogles Round House.** The Round House restaurant is, in fact, in a small
$$$–$$$$ round structure built with a concrete-filled tree trunk as its central supFodor'sChoice port and a long bench that was once the jawbone of a whale. It's sur★ rounded by gardens and a handful of cottages for rent. Chef Roxanne

Russell is celebrated for her elegant style of Caribbean cuisine. Her three-course, prix-fixe menu, which changes according to market availability, may include such starters as fish cakes and cream of callaloo soup and such entrées rack of lamb au jus and grilled lobster with garlic butter—there's always a vegetarian dish, too. Pasta and pizza are available for kids upon request. Desserts are all homemade, including the ice cream. ⊠ *Sparrow Bay, Bogles* ☎ *473/443–7841* ⌲ *Reservations essential* ⊟ *MC, V* ⊘ *Closed Tues. and Wed.*

$$ ✕ **Callaloo by the Sea Restaurant & Bar.** On the main road, just south of the town jetty, diners enjoy extraordinary views of Sandy Island and Hillsborough Bay. The emphasis is on West Indian dishes and excellent seafood—including lobster, fried fish fingers, and lambi stew—plus sandwiches, salads, and curried chicken. The callaloo soup is outstanding. This is a perfect lunch stop for day-trippers. After you eat, just mosey back to the jetty to catch the ferry back to Grenada. ⊠ *Hillsborough* ☎ *473/443–8004* ⊟ *AE, MC, V* ⊘ *Closed Sept.*

SEAFOOD ✕ **Scraper's.** Scraper's serves up lobster, conch, and the fresh catch of
$$ the day—as well as American-style hamburgers and hot dogs. Dine
⟳ inside or out. It's a simple spot seasoned with occasional calypsonian serenades (by owner Steven "Scraper" Gay, who's a pro). ⊠ *Tyrrel Bay* ☎ *473/443–7403* ⊟ *AE, D, MC, V.*

BEACHES

GRENADA

Grenada has some 80 mi (130 km) of coastline, 65 bays, and 45 white-sand (and a few black-sand) beaches—many in little coves. The best beaches are just south of St. George's, facing the Caribbean, where most resorts are also clustered. Nude or topless bathing, by the way, is against the law if you are in view of others.

Bathway Beach. A broad strip of sand with a natural reef that protects swimmers from the rough Atlantic surf on Grenada's far northern shore, this Levera National Park beach has changing rooms at the park headquarters. ⊠ *Levera, St. Patrick's.*

Fodor'sChoice **Grand Anse Beach.** In the southwest, about 3 mi (5 km) south of St.
★ George's, Grenada's loveliest and most popular beach is a gleaming 2-mi (3-km) semicircle of white sand lapped by clear, gentle surf. Sea grape trees and coconut palms provide shady escapes from the sun. Brilliant rainbows frequently spill into the sea from the high green mountains that frame St. George's Harbour to the north. The Grand Anse Craft & Spice Market is at the midpoint of the beach. ⊠ *Grand Anse, St. George's.*

★ **La Sagesse Beach.** Along the southeast coast, at La Sagesse Nature Center, this is a lovely, quiet refuge with a strip of powdery white sand. Plan a full day of nature walks, with lunch at the small inn adjacent to the beach. ⊠ *La Sagesse, St. David's.*

☾ **Morne Rouge Beach.** One mile (1.5 km) south of Grand Anse Bay, this 0.5-mi-long (0.75-km-long) sheltered crescent has a gentle surf, excellent for swimming. Light meals are available nearby. ✉ *Morne Rouge, St. George's.*

CARRIACOU

Anse La Roche. Like all the beaches on Carriacou, this one—about a 15-minute hike from the village of Prospect, in the north—has pure white sand, sparkling clear water, and abundant marine life for snorkelers. And it's never crowded. ✉ *Windward.*

Hillsborough Beach. Day-trippers can take a dip at this strip of sand adjacent to the jetty. The beach extends for quite a distance in each direction, so there's plenty of room to swim without interference from the boat traffic. ✉ *Hillsborough.*

★ **Paradise Beach.** This long, narrow stretch of sand between Hillsborough and Tyrrel Bay has calm, clear, inviting water, but there are no changing facilities. ✉ *L'Esterre.*

★ **Sandy Island.** This is a truly deserted island off Hillsborough—just a ring of white sand with a few palm trees, surrounded by a reef and crystal-clear waters. Anyone hanging around the jetty with a motorboat will provide transportation for about $10 per person, round-trip. Bring your snorkeling gear and, if you want, a picnic—and leave all your cares behind. ✉ *Hillsborough Bay, Hillsborough.*

Tyrrel Bay Beach. This swath of sand is popular with the sailing set, who use the bay as an anchorage. But beware of the manchineel trees here; they drop poisonous green "apples," and their foliage can burn your skin. ✉ *Harvey Vale.*

SPORTS & THE OUTDOORS

BOATING & SAILING

★ As the "Gateway to the Grenadines," Grenada attracts significant numbers of seasoned sailors to its waters. Large marinas are in the lagoon area of St. George's, at Prickly Bay and True Blue on Grenada's south coast, at St. David's in southeast Grenada, and at Tyrrel Bay in Carriacou. You can charter a yacht, with or without crew, for weeklong sailing vacations through the Grenadines or along the coast of Venezuela. Scenic half- or full-day sails along Grenada's coast cost about $60 per person (with a minimum of four passengers), including lunch or snacks and open bar; a full-day cruise from Grenada to Carriacou may cost $350 to $700, depending on the boat, for up to six people.

Carib Cats (☎ 473/444–3222) departs from the lagoon area of St. George's for a full-day sail along the southwest coast, a half-day snorkel cruise to Molinère Bay, or a two-hour sunset cruise along the west coast. **Footloose Yacht Charters** (☎ 473/440–7949 ⊕ *www.grenadasailing.com*) operates from the lagoon in St. George's and has both sailing and motor yachts available for day trips around Grenada or longer charters to the Grenadines. **Horizon Yacht Charters** (☎*473/439–1000* ⊕*www.horizonyachtcharters.com*), at True Blue Bay Resort, will arrange bareboat or crewed charters, as well as day sails or three-day trips to the Grenadines.

DIVING & SNORKELING

You can see hundreds of varieties of fish and some 40 species of coral at more than a dozen sites off Grenada's southwest coast—only 15 to 20 minutes by boat—and another couple of dozen sites around Carriacou's reefs and neighboring islets. Depths vary from 20 to 120 feet, and visibility varies from 30 to 100 feet.

Off Grenada: A spectacular dive is *Bianca C,* a 600-foot cruise ship that caught fire in 1961, sank to 100 feet, and is now encrusted with coral and serves as a habitat for giant turtles, spotted eagle rays, barracuda, and jacks. **Boss Reef** extends 5 mi (8 km) from St. George's Harbour to Point Salines, with a depth ranging from 20 to 90 feet. **Flamingo Bay** has a wall that drops to 90 feet and is teeming with fish, sponges, sea horses, sea fans, and coral. **Molinère Reef** slopes from about 20 feet below the surface to a wall that drops to 65 feet. It's a good dive for beginners, and advanced divers can continue farther out to view the wreck of the *Buccaneer,* a 42-foot sloop.

Off Carriacou: Kick-em Jenny is an active underwater volcano, with plentiful coral and marine life in the vicinity and, usually, visibility up to 100 feet; though you can't actually dive down 500 feet to reach the actual volcano. **Sandy Island,** in Hillsborough Bay, is especially good for night diving and has fish that feed off its extensive reefs 70 feet deep. For experienced divers, **Twin Sisters of Isle de Rhonde** is one of the most spectacular dives in the Grenadines, with walls and drop-offs of up to 185 feet and an underwater cave.

Most dive operators take snorkelers along on dive trips or have special snorkeling adventures. The best snorkeling in Grenada is at Molinère Point, north of St. George's; in Carriacou, Sandy Island is magnificent and just a few hundred yards offshore. Snorkeling trips cost about $25 per person.

The PADI-certified dive operators listed below offer scuba and snorkeling trips to reefs and wrecks, including night dives and special excursions to the *Bianca C.* They also offer resort courses for beginning divers and certification instruction for more-experienced divers. It costs about $40 to $45 for a one-tank dive, $75 to $80 for a two-tank dive, $50 for trips to the *Bianca C,* $110 to $125 to dive Isle de Rhonde, and $55 to $60 for night dives. Discounted 5- and 10-dive packages are usually offered. Resort courses cost about $80 to $95 and open-water certification runs from $200 to $395.

GRENADA DIVE OPERATORS

Aquanauts Grenada (✉*Grand Anse Beach, Grand Anse, St. George's* ☎*473/444–1126, 888/446–9235 in U.S.* ✉*True Blue Bay Resort, True Blue* ☎*473/439–2500* ⊕*www.aquanautsgrenada.com*) has a multilingual staff, so instruction is available in English, German, Dutch, French, and Spanish. Two-tank dive trips, accommodating no more than eight divers, are offered each morning to both the Caribbean and Atlantic sides of Grenada. **Dive Grenada** (✉ *Flamboyant Hotel, Morne Rouge, St. George* ☎ *473/444–1092* ⊕ *www.divegrenada.net*) offers dive trips twice daily (at 10 AM and 2 PM), specializing in diving the *Bianca C.* **EcoDive** (✉ *Coyaba beach resort, Grand Anse, St. George's* ☎ *473/444–7777* ⊕ *www.ecodiveandtrek.com*) offers two dive trips daily, both drift and wreck dives, as well as weekly trips to dive Isle de Rhonde. The company also runs Grenada's marine conservation and education center, which conducts coral-reef monitoring and turtle projects. **ScubaTech Grenada** (✉ *Calabash Hotel, L'Anse aux Épines, St. George's* ☎ *473/439–4346* ⊕ *www.scubatech-grenada.com*) has two full-time diving instructors and, in addition to daily dive trips, offers the complete range of PADI programs, from discover scuba to dive master.

CARRIACOU DIVE OPERATORS

Arawak Divers (✉ *Tyrrel Bay, Carriacou* ☎ *473/443–6906* ⊕ *www.arawak.de*) has its own jetty at Tyrrel Bay; it takes small groups on daily dive trips and night dives, offers courses in German and English, and provides pickup service from yachts. **Carriacou Silver Diving** (✉ *Main St., Hillsborough, Carriacou* ☎ *473/443–7882* ⊕ *www.scubamax.com*) accommodates up to 12 divers on one of its dive boats and up to 6 on another. The center operates two guided single-tank dives daily as well as individually scheduled excursions.

FISHING

Deep-sea fishing around Grenada is excellent, with marlin, sailfish, yellowfin tuna, and dolphinfish topping the list of good catches. You can arrange sportfishing trips for $375 for a half day to $580 for a full day that accommodate up to five people. **True Blue Sportfishing** (☎ *473/444–2048* ⊕ *www.yesaye.com*) offers big-game charters on its 31-foot *Yes Aye.* It has an enclosed cabin, a fighting chair, and professional tackle. British-born Captain Gary Clifford, who has been fishing since the age of six, has run the company since 1998. Refreshments and courtesy transport are included.

GOLF

Determined golfers might want to try the pleasant, easy 9-hole course at the **Grenada Golf & Country Club** (☎ *473/444–4128*), about halfway between St. George's and Grand Anse. Greens fees are EC$7, and club rental is available; your hotel can make arrangements for you. Popular with local businessmen, this course is convenient to most hotels and is the only public course on the island.

HIKING

Fodor'sChoice

★ Mountain trails wind through **Grand Étang National Park & Forest Reserve** (☎473/440–6160); if you're lucky, you may spot a Mona monkey or some exotic birds on your hike. There are trails for all levels—from a self-guided nature trail around Grand Étang Lake to a demanding one through the bush to the peak of Mt. Qua Qua (2,373 feet) or a real trek up Mt. St. Catherine (2,757 feet). Long pants and hiking shoes are recommended. The cost is $25 per person for a four-hour guided hike up Mt. Qua Qua, $20 each for two or more, or $15 each for three or more; the Mt. St. Catherine hike starts at $35 per person. **EcoTrek** (☎473/444–7777 ⊕*www.ecodiveandtrek.com*) takes small groups on day trips to the heart of the rain forest, where you'll find hidden waterfalls and hot-spring pools. **Henry's Safari Tours** (☎473/444–5313 ⊕*www.spiceisle.com/safari*) offers hiking excursions through rich agricultural land and rain forest to Upper Concord Falls and other fascinating spots. **Telfor Bedeau, Hiking Guide** (☎473/442–6200), affectionately referred to locally as the Indiana Jones of Grenada, is a national treasure. Over the years he has walked up, down, or across nearly every mountain, trail, and pathway on the island. In 2005 he hit the incredible milestone of having hiked 10,000 mi (16,000 km) throughout Grenada over 43 years. His experience and knowledge make him an excellent guide, whether it's an easy walk with novices or the most strenuous hike with experts.

SHOPPING

Grenada is truly a nation of entrepreneurs, from physical businesses with employees and processing operations to self-employed vendors (about one-third of the population) who personally sell their handicrafts in the markets. Some of the unique, locally made goods to look for in gift shops and supermarkets are chocolate candy bars, pain-relief spray, nutmeg jam and syrup, spice-scented soaps and body oils, and fruit- and herb-flavored wine, rum, and liqueur.

Grenada's best souvenirs or gifts for friends back home are spice baskets filled with cinnamon, nutmeg, mace, bay leaves, cloves, turmeric, and ginger. You can buy them for as little as $3 or $5 in practically every shop, at the open-air produce market at **Market Square** in St. George's, at the vendor stalls along the Esplanade near the port, and at the Vendor's Craft & Spice Market on Grand Anse Beach. Vendors also sell handmade fabric dolls, coral jewelry, seashells, and hats and baskets handwoven from green palm fronds.

Here's some local terminology you should know. If someone asks if you'd like a "sweetie," you're being offered a candy. When you buy spices, you may be offered "saffron" and "vanilla." The saffron is really turmeric, a ground yellow root rather than the fragile pistils of crocus flowers; the vanilla is an essence made from locally grown tonka beans, a close substitute but not the real thing. No one is trying to pull the wool over your eyes; these are common local terms. Bargaining is not appropriate in shops and isn't customary with vendors.

AREAS & MALLS

In St. George's, the **Carenage** has several gift shops. On the north side of the harbor, **Young Street** is a main shopping thoroughfare; it rises steeply uphill from the Carenage, then descends just as steeply to the market area. On Melville Street, near the cruise-ship terminal and Market Square, the **Esplanade Mall** has shops that offer duty-free jewelry, electronics, liquor, and gift items, as well as local crafts.

In Grand Anse, a short walk from the resorts, the **Excel Plaza** has shops and services to interest locals and tourists alike, including a full-service health club and a three-screen movie theater. **Grand Anse Shopping Centre** has a supermarket and liquor store, a clothing store, a fast-food restaurant, a pharmacy, an art gallery, and several small gift shops. **Le Marquis Complex** has restaurants, shops, an art gallery, and tourist services. **South City Plaza Mall**, adjacent to the Grand Anse vendor's market, has 35 shops, some that sell duty-free goods, as well as banking facilities and a hotel. **Spiceland Mall** has a modern supermarket with a liquor section, clothing and shoe boutiques for men and women, housewares stores, a wineshop, gift shops, a food court, a bank, and a video-game arcade.

SPECIALTY STORES

ART

Art Grenada (⊠ *Grand Anse Shopping Centre, Suite 7, Grand Anse, St. George's* ☎ *473/444–2317*) sells paintings, drawings, and watercolors exclusively by Grenadian artists, among them Canute Caliste, Lyndon Bedeau, and Susan Mains. Exhibitions change monthly, and you can have your purchases shipped.

BOOKS

A colorful souvenir picture book, a book on island culture and history, a charming local story for kids, a thick novel for the beach, or a paperback for the trip home–all are good reasons to drop into a bookstore. **Sea Change** (⊠ *The Carenage, St. George's* ☎ *473/440–3402*) is nestled underneath the Nutmeg restaurant, right on the waterfront.

DUTY-FREE GOODS

Duty-free shops at the airport sell liquor at impressive discounts of up to 50%, as well as perfumes, crafts, and Grenadian syrups, jams, and hot sauces. You can shop duty-free at some shops in town, but you must show your passport and outbound ticket to benefit from the duty-free prices. **Gitten's** (⊠ *The Carenage, St. George's, St. George* ☎ *473/440–3174* ⊠ *Spiceland Mall, Grand Anse, St. George's* ☎ *473/439–0860* ⊠ *Point Salines International Airport, St. George's* ☎ *473/444–2549*) carries perfume and cosmetics at its three shops.

Mr. Canute Caliste

Self-taught folk artist Canute Caliste, certainly one of Grenada's national treasures, began painting at nine years of age in a colorful, primitive style that hardly changed for nearly 80 years. His charming, childlike paintings depict island life—boatbuilding, bread baking, wedding festivities, courting, farming, dancing, whaling, children's games, even a mermaid.

Born in Carriacou in 1914, Caliste painted in a tiny studio, a simple board building adjacent to his home in the village of L'Esterre. Surrounded by kids, grandkids, and barnyard animals, the artist—with apparently boundless energy—completed up to 16 paintings per day, always labeling, dating, then signing each one: "Mr. Canute Caliste."

A prolific family man, Caliste fathered 23 children and, at his death, had more than 200 grandchildren. Daughter Clemencia Caliste Alexander (his ninth child, with six kids of her own) has worked in the Carriacou Museum, in Hillsborough, since 1978. Her teen-age son, incidentally, inherited his grandfather's skill and style.

Over the years, the price of Caliste's works has skyrocketed. In the early 1990s, visitors to his studio could purchase a barely dry painting for $10 to $25. Today, Caliste paintings are available only from private collectors and fetch hundreds—and often thousands—of dollars. His daughter Clemencia owns a number of early paintings, some of which may be viewed at the Carriacou museum, but they are not for sale. Caliste stopped painting at age 87 but continued to play the fiddle in a local quadrille band. He passed away in 2005, at the age of 91.

Frameable prints of Caliste's amusing paintings are sold at the museum and are certainly delightful mementos of a visit to Grenada and Carriacou. A book called *The Mermaid Wakes*, which is chock-full of prints, is now out of print, but copies may be found by searching used-book sites or Amazon.com.

FOODS

De La Grenade Industries (✉ *St. Paul's* ☎ *473/440–3241*) makes nutmeg and guava jams and jellies, nutmeg syrup, nutmeg liqueur (from a 200-year-old family recipe), and a dozen other kinds of delicious jellies, marmalades, and condiments that are sold at the processing plant and in food stores and gift shops throughout Grenada. **Grenada Chocolate Company** (✉ *Hermitage, St. Patrick's* ☎ *473/442–0050*) makes organic chocolate bars and Smilo cocoa powder from cocoa beans grown at nearby Belmont Estate. Employees at the small factory use antique machinery to roast the beans and mix and temper the chocolate. Then the rich, dark chocolate is molded and wrapped by hand. The candy bars sell in supermarkets and gift shops for about $4 each.

★ The open-air **Market Square** (✉ *Foot of Young St., St. George's*) is a bustling produce market that's open mornings; Saturday is the best—and busiest—time to stock up on fresh fruit to enjoy during your stay. But it's a particularly good place to buy island-grown spices, perhaps the best such market in the entire Caribbean. Crafts, leather goods, and decorative objects are also sold. **Marketing & National Importing Board**

(⊠ *Young St., St. George's, St. George* ☎ *473/440–1791*) stocks fresh fruits and vegetables, spices, hot sauces, and local syrups and jams at lower prices than you can find in most gift shops. At the **Vine Yard** (⊠ *Esplanade Mall, St. George's* ☎ *473/435–5920*) you can buy fruit wines (mango, golden apple, local cherry, sea grape, and pineapple) and flavored rums (nutmeg, vanilla, cocoa, cinnamon, bay leaf, guava, and golden apple) made by Alie Baptiste, who studied chemistry in college and learned about wine making in France. Also an artist, Baptiste individually hand paints the bottles, making them wonderful souvenirs. The wines cost $15; the rums, $18.

GIFTS

Arawak Islands (⊠ *Frequente Industrial Park, St. George's* ☎ *473/444–3577*) produces spice-scented soaps, body oils, perfumes, insect repellents, balms, beeswax candles, and incense made by hand. Shoppers are welcome at the plant, where you can view the manufacturing process, and the company's products and gift baskets are sold in most gift shops. **Figleaf** (⊠ *Le Marquis Complex, Grand Anse, St. George's* ☎ *473/439–1824*) is a small gift shop where you can find an interesting selection of Caribbean arts and crafts, aromatherapy and herbal bath products, and casual clothing. **Imagine** (⊠ *Grand Anse Shopping Centre, Grand Anse, St. George's* ☎ *473/444–4028*) specializes in straw work, ceramics, island fashions, and batik fabrics. **Pssst Boutique** (⊠ *Spiceland Mall, Grand Anse, St. George's* ☎ *473/439–0787*) will catch your eye; it's chock-full of unusual costume jewelry, colorful island clothing, and fascinating gift items for the home.

While it may not seem like much of a gift, a bottle of **Nut-Med Pain Relieving Spray** makes a neat souvenir. The brainchild of agronomist Denis Noel, OBE, whose handful of employees prepare and package the remedy in a facility behind his home in St. Patrick's, Nut-Med spray is made from nutmeg oil, wintergreen or peppermint scent, and "a few other ingredients." It sells like hotcakes in supermarkets and gift shops throughout Grenada for about $12 a bottle.

HANDICRAFTS

★ **Art Fabrik** (⊠ *9 Young St., St. George's* ☎ *473/440–0568*) is a studio where you can watch artisans create batik before turning it into clothing or accessories. In the shop you can find fabric by the yard or fashioned into dresses, shirts, shorts, hats, and scarves. **Tikal** (⊠ *Young St., St. George's* ☎ *473/440–2310*) is known for its exquisite baskets, artwork, jewelry, batik items, and fashions. The **Vendor's Craft & Spice Market at Grand Anse** (⊠ *Grand Anse, St. George's* ☎ *473/444–3780*), managed by the Grenada Board of Tourism, has 82 booths for vendors who sell arts, crafts, spices, music tapes, clothing, produce, and refreshments. It's open daily from 7 to 7.

NIGHTLIFE & THE ARTS

NIGHTLIFE

Grenada's nightlife is centered on the resort hotels and a handful of nightspots—including a huge club, right on the Carenage, that features headliner concerts. During the winter season some hotels have a steel band or other local entertainment several nights a week.

BARS

Banana's Sports Bar (✉ *True Blue, St. George's* ☎ *473/444–4662*) is a casual restaurant and nightspot popular among the students at nearby St. George's University. There's music—Caribbean, salsa, oldies, alternative, pop—and dancing Tuesday through Saturday nights. On weekends, there's a cover charge of EC$10.

DANCE CLUBS

Fantazia (✉ *Morne Rouge, St. George's* ☎ *473/444–2288*) is a popular nightspot; disco, soca, reggae, and international pop music are played from 9:30 PM until the wee hours on weekends. There's a small cover charge of EC$10 to EC$20. **Karma** (✉ *The Carenage, St. George's* ☎ *473/409–2582*) is a spacious (10,000 square feet), first-class entertainment facility with a stage and a dozen plasma TV screens. The club features karaoke on Wednesday nights, "student night" on Thursday, video DJ entertainment on Friday, and special parties and headliner concerts on Saturday nights. The nightclub entrance fee is EC$25; admission for special events runs EC$50 and up. **The Owl** (✉ *Flamboyant Hotel, Grand Anse, St. George's* ☎ *473/444–4247*), open nightly until 3 AM, features karaoke on Thursday night and two happy hours (4–7 and 11–midnight) every night.

THEME NIGHTS

☾ **Gouyave Fish Friday** (✉ *St. Francis and St. Dominic Sts., Gouyave*
★ ☎ *473/444–8430 or 473/444–9490* ⊕ *www.gogouyave.com*) celebrates the deep-sea fishing heritage of the coastal town of Gouyave, about 45 minutes north of St. George's, every Friday night starting at 4 PM and continuing until 1 AM. Street vendors sell freshly caught fish, lobster, and other seafood cooked on open fires, as well as your favorite beverages. Local music and cultural performances make Friday night in Gouyave an entertaining family event.

Rhum Runner (✉ *The Carenage, St. George's* ☎ *473/440–2198*), a 60-foot twin-deck catamaran, leaves from the Carenage at 7:30 PM each Friday and Saturday for a moonlight cruise in the waters around St. George's and Grand Anse, returning about midnight. Tickets are $10, and reservations are recommended. On Wednesday from 6 to 9 there's a sunset dinner cruise for $40 per person; reservations must be made by 4:30 the day before. *Rhum Runner II*, a 72-foot sister ship, operates monthly moonlight cruises the Friday and Saturday nights nearest the full moon for $11 per person—add $2 for a barbecue dinner.

THE ARTS

ISLAND CULTURE

Marryshow Folk Theatre (⊠ *Herbert Blaize St., St. George's* ☎ *473/440–2451*) presents concerts, plays, and special cultural events. Call for a schedule, as productions are sporadic.

EXPLORING GRENADA & CARRIACOU

GRENADA

Grenada is divided into six parishes, including one named St. George, which hold the communities of Grand Anse, Morne Rouge, True Blue, L'Anse aux Épines, and the capital city of St. George's.

WHAT TO SEE

Annandale Falls. A mountain stream cascades 40 feet into a pool surrounded by exotic vines. A paved path leads to the bottom of the falls, and a trail leads to the top. This is a lovely, cool spot for swimming and picnicking. ⊠ *Main interior road, 15 mins northeast of St. George's, St. George's* ☎ *473/440–2452* ⚏ *$1* ⊙ *Daily 9–5.*

Carib's Leap. At Sauteurs (the French word for "leapers"), on the island's northernmost tip, Carib's Leap (or Leapers Hill) is the 100-foot vertical cliff from which the last of the indigenous Carib Indians flung themselves into the sea in 1651. After losing several bloody battles with European colonists, they chose to kill themselves rather than surrender to the French. A visitor center has artifacts and a commemorative display that recounts the event. ⊠ *Sauteurs.*

★ **Concord Falls.** About 8 mi (13 km) north of St. George's, a turnoff from the West Coast Road leads to Concord Falls—actually three separate waterfalls. The first is at the end of the road; when the currents aren't too strong, you can take a dip under the cascade. Reaching the two other waterfalls requires an hour's hike into the forest reserve. The third and most spectacular waterfall, at Fountainbleu, thunders 65 feet over huge boulders and creates a small pool. It's smart to hire a guide. The path is clear, but slippery boulders toward the end can be treacherous without assistance. ⊠ *Off West Coast Rd., St. John's* ⚏ *Changing room $2* ⊙ *Daily 9–5.*

De La Grenade Industries. In the suburb of St. Paul's, five minutes east of St. George's, this company produces syrups, jams, jellies, and a liqueur from nutmeg and other homegrown fruits and spices. The liqueur "recipe" is a 19th-century secret formula. Sybil La Grenade founded the company in 1960 as a cottage industry. Since her tragic death in a car accident in 1991, the company has been overseen by her daughter, Cécile, a U.S.-trained food technologist. You're welcome to watch the manufacturing process and stroll around the adjacent herb and spice gardens. ⊠ *Morne Délice, St. Paul's* ☎ *473/440–3241* ⊕ *www.delagrenade.com* ⚏ *$1* ⊙ *Weekdays 8–5, Sat. 9–12:30.*

🌀 **Dougaldston Spice Estate.** Just south of Gouyave, this historic plantation, now primarily a living museum, still grows and processes spices
the old-fashioned way. You can see cocoa, nutmeg, mace, cloves, and
other spices laid out on giant racks to dry in the sun. A worker will be
glad to explain the process (and will appreciate a small donation). You
can buy spices for about $2 a bag. ⊠ *Gouyave* 🕾 *No phone* 🖹 *Free*
⊙ *Weekdays 9–4.*

🌀 **Gouyave Nutmeg Processing Cooperative.** Touring the nutmeg processing
★ co-op, in the center of the west-coast fishing village of Gouyave (pronounced *gwahve*), is a fragrant, fascinating way to spend half an hour.
You can learn all about nutmeg and its uses, see the nutmegs laid out
in bins, and watch the workers sort them by hand and pack them into
burlap bags for shipping worldwide. The three-story plant turned out
3 million pounds of Grenada's most famous export each year prior to
Hurricane Ivan's devastating effect on the crop in 2004. Locals esti-
mate it will be 2010 before the nutmeg industry returns to that level.
⊠ *Gouyave* 🕾 *473/444–8337* 🖹 *$1* ⊙ *Weekdays 10–1 and 2–4.*

🌀 **Grand Anse.** A residential and commercial area about 5 mi (8 km) south
of downtown St. George's, Grand Anse is named for the world-renowned
beach it surrounds. Grenada's tourist facilities—resorts, restaurants,
some shopping, and most nightlife—are concentrated in this general
area. **Grand Anse Beach** is a 2-mi (3-km) crescent of sand, shaded by
coconut palms and sea grape trees, with gentle turquoise surf. A public
entrance is at Camerhogne Park, just a few steps from the main road.
Water taxis carry passengers between the Esplanade in St. George's and a
jetty on the beach. **St. George's University,** which for years held classes at
its enviable beachfront location in Grand Anse, has a sprawling campus
in True Blue, a nearby residential community. ⊠ *St. George's.*

🌀 **Grand Étang National Park & Forest Reserve.** Deep in the mountainous
★ interior of Grenada is a bird sanctuary and forest reserve with miles
of hiking trails, lookouts, and fishing streams. **Grand Étang Lake** is a
36-acre expanse of cobalt-blue water that fills the crater of an extinct
volcano 1,740 feet above sea level. Although legend has it the lake is
bottomless, maximum soundings are recorded at 18 feet. The informative **Grand Étang Forest Center** has displays on the local wildlife
and vegetation. A forest manager is on hand to answer questions. A
small snack bar and souvenir stands are nearby. ⊠ *Main interior road,
between Grenville and St. George's, St. Andrew's* 🕾 *473/440–6160*
🖹 *$1* ⊙ *Daily 8:30–4.*

🌀 **Grenville Cooperative Nutmeg Association.** Like its counterpart in Gouy-
★ ave, this nutmeg processing plant is open to the public for guided tours.
You can see and learn about the entire process of receiving, drying,
sorting, and packing nutmegs. ⊠ *Grenville, St. Andrew* 🕾 *473/442–
7241* 🖹 *$1* ⊙ *Weekdays 10–1 and 2–4.*

🌀 **Laura Herb & Spice Garden.** The 6.5-acre gardens are part of an old
plantation in the village of Laura, in St. David Parish, just 6 mi (10
km) east of Grand Anse. On the 20-minute tour, you will learn all
about Grenada's indigenous spices and herbs—including cocoa, clove,

nutmeg, pimiento, cinnamon, turmeric, and tonka beans (similar to vanilla)—and how they're used for flavoring and for medicinal purposes. ⊠ *Laura, St. David* ☎ *473/443–2604* ⌑ *$2* ⊙ *Weekdays 8–4.*

Levera National Park & Bird Sanctuary. This portion of Grenada's protected parkland encompasses 450 acres at the northeastern tip of the island, where the Caribbean Sea meets the Atlantic Ocean. A natural reef protects swimmers from the rough Atlantic surf at Bathway Beach. Thick mangroves provide food and protection for nesting seabirds and seldom-seen parrots. The first islets of the Grenadines are visible from the beach. Entrance and use of the beaches and grounds are free. ⊠ *Levera, St. Patrick* ⌑ *Free* ⊙ *Dawn–dusk.*

Pearl's Airport. Just north of Grenville, on the east coast, is the island's original airport, which was replaced in 1984 by Point Salines International Airport. Deteriorating Cuban and Soviet planes sit at the end of the old runway, abandoned after the 1983 intervention, when Cuban "advisers" helping to construct the airport at Point Salines were summarily removed from the island. There's a good view north to the Grenadines and a small beach nearby. ⊠ *Grenville.*

River Antoine Rum Distillery. At this rustic operation, kept open primarily as a museum, a limited quantity of Rivers rum is produced by the same methods used since the distillery opened in 1785. The process begins with the crushing of sugarcane from adjacent fields. The result is a potent overproof rum, sold only in Grenada, that will knock your socks off. ⊠ *River Antoine Estate, St. Patrick's* ☎ *473/442–7109* ⌑ *$2* ⊙ *Guided tours daily 9–4.*

St. George's. Grenada's capital is a bustling West Indian city, most of which remains unchanged from colonial days. Narrow streets lined with shops wind up, down, and across steep hills. Brick warehouses and small shops cling to the waterfront, while pastel-painted homes rise from the waterfront and disappear into steep green hills.

Picturesque **St. George's Harbour,** a submerged volcanic crater, is arguably the prettiest harbor in the Caribbean and the center of town. Schooners, ferries, and tour boats tie up along the seawall or at the small dinghy dock. The **Carenage** (pronounced car-a-*nahzh*), which surrounds horseshoe-shape St. George's Harbour, is the capital's main thoroughfare. Warehouses, shops, and restaurants line the waterfront. The *Christ of the Deep* statue that sits on the pedestrian plaza at the center of the Carenage was presented to Grenada by Costa Cruise Line in remembrance of its ship *Bianca C,* which burned and sank in the harbor in 1961 and is now a favorite dive site.

The **Grenada National Museum** (⊠ *Young and Monckton Sts.* ☎ *473/440–3725* ⌑ *$1* ⊙ *Weekdays 9–4:30, Sat. 10–1*), a block from the Carenage, is built on the foundation of a French army barracks and prison that was originally built in 1704. The small museum has exhibitions of news items, photos, and proclamations relating to the 1983 intervention, along with the childhood bathtub of Empress Joséphine (who was born on Martinique), and other memorabilia from earlier historical periods.

Fodor'sChoice ★

Ft. George (⊠ *Church St.*) is high on the hill at the entrance to St. George's Harbour. It's Grenada's oldest fort—built by the French in 1705 to protect the harbor. No shots were ever fired here until October 1983, when Prime Minister Maurice Bishop and some of his followers were assassinated in the courtyard. The fort now houses police headquarters but is open to the public daily; admission is free. The 360-degree view of the capital city, St. George's Harbour, and the open sea is spectacular.

An engineering feat for its time, the 340-foot-long **Sendall Tunnel** was built in 1895 and named for an early governor. It separates the harbor side of St. George's from the Esplanade on the bay side of town, where you can find the markets (produce, meat, and fish), the cruise-ship terminal, the Esplanade Mall, and the public bus station.

Don't miss St. George's picturesque **Market Square** (⊠ *Granby St.*), a block from the cruise-ship terminal. It's open every weekday morning but really comes alive on Saturday from 8 to noon. Vendors sell baskets, spices, brooms, clothing, knickknacks, coconut water, and heaps of fresh produce. A huge renovation project completed in early 2008 provides permanent cover for the vendors. Historically, Market Square is where parades begin and political rallies take place.

Built in 1825, the beautiful **St. George's Anglican Church** (⊠ *Church St.*) is filled with statues and plaques depicting Grenada in the 18th and 19th centuries.

St. George's Methodist Church (⊠ *Green St. near Herbert Blaize St.*) was built in 1820 and is the oldest original church in the city.

The Gothic tower of **St. George's Roman Catholic Church** (⊠ *Church St.*) dates from 1818, but the current structure was built in 1884; the tower is the city's most visible landmark.

York House (⊠ *Church St.*), dating from 1801, is home to Grenada's Houses of Parliament and Supreme Court. It, the neighboring Registry Building (1780), and Government House (1802) are fine examples of early Georgian architecture.

Overlooking the city of St. George's and the inland side of the harbor, historic **Ft. Frederick** (⊠ *Richmond Hill*) provides a panoramic view of two-thirds of Grenada. The fort was started by the French and completed in 1791 by the British; it was also the headquarters of the People's Revolutionary Government during the 1983 coup. Today you can get a bird's-eye view of much of Grenada from here.

CARRIACOU

Carriacou, the land of many reefs, is a hilly island and has neither lakes nor rivers, so its drinking water comes from rainwater caught in cisterns and purified with bleach. It gets quite arid during the dry season (January through May). Nevertheless, pigeon peas, corn, and fruit are grown here, and the climate seems to suit the mahogany trees used for furniture making and the white cedar critical to the boatbuilding industry that has made Carriacou famous.

Hillsborough is Carriacou's main town. Just offshore, Sandy Island is one of the nicest beaches around (although recent storms and the gradually rising sea have taken their toll on this tiny spit of land). Almost anyone with a boat can give you a ride out to Sandy Island for a small fee (about $10 round-trip), and you can leave your cares on the dock. Rolling hills cut a wide swath through the middle of Carriacou, from Gun Point in the north to Tyrrel Bay in the south.

Interestingly, tiny Carriacou has several distinct cultures. Hillsborough is decidedly English; the southern region, around L'Esterre, reflects French roots; and the northern town of Windward has Scottish ties. African culture, of course, is the overarching influence.

WHAT TO SEE

Belair. For a wonderful bird's-eye view of Hillsborough and Carriacou's entire west coast, drive to Belair, 700 feet above sea level, in the north-central part of the island. On the way, you'll pass by the photogenic ruins of an old sugar mill and the Princess Royal Hospital.

Carriacou Museum. Housed in a building that once held a cotton gin and just one block from the waterfront, the museum has exhibitions of Amerindian, European, and African artifacts, a collection of watercolors by native folk artist Canute Caliste, and a small gift shop with local items. ⊠ *Paterson St., Hillsborough* ☎ *473/443–8288* ⌨ *$2* ⊙ *Weekdays 9:30–4, Sat. 10–4.*

Tyrrel Bay. Picturesque Tyrrel Bay is a large protected harbor in southwest Carriacou. The bay is almost always full of sailboats, powerboats, and working boats—coming, going, or bobbing at their moorings. Edging the bay is a beach with pure white sand; bars, restaurants, a guesthouse, and a few shops face the waterfront.

☻ **Windward.** The small town of Windward, on the northeast coast, is a boatbuilding community. At certain times of year, primarily during school vacations, you may encounter a work in progress along the roadside, where Grenada's Ministry of Culture has set up a training ground for interested youngsters to learn skills from seasoned boatbuilders. Originally constructed for interisland commerce, the boats are now built primarily for fishing and pleasure sailing.

PETITE MARTINIQUE

Petite Martinique (pronounced *pit*-ty mar-ti-*neek*), 10 minutes north of Carriacou by boat, is tiny and residential, with a guesthouse or two but no tourist facilities or attractions—just peace and quiet. Meander along the beachfront and watch the boatbuilders at work. And if by chance there's a boat launching, sailboat race, wedding, holiday, or cultural festival taking place while you're there, you're in for a treat. The music is infectious, the food bountiful, and the spirit lively.

GRENADA ESSENTIALS

To research prices, get advice from other travelers, and book travel arrangements, visit www.fodors.com.

▮ TRANSPORTATION

BY AIR

Air Jamaica's nonstop flight to Barbados continues on to Grenada several times a week. All other flights require travelers to connect in San Juan, Montego Bay, or some other airport in the Caribbean. LIAT offers frequent scheduled service linking Grenada with more than two dozen neighboring islands. SVG Air flies between Grenada and Carriacou, with some flights continuing on to Union Island that connect with flights to St. Vincent or Barbados.

Airline Contacts Air Jamaica (☎473/444–5975 or 800/523–5585). **American Eagle** (☎473/444—2121 or 800/744–0006). **LIAT** (☎888/844–5428). **SVG Air** (☎473/444–3549, 800/744–7285, 473/443–8519 in Carriacou).

Airport Contacts Lauriston Airport (✉Carriacou ☎473/443–6306). **Point Salines International Airport** (✉Grenada ☎473/444–4101).

BY BOAT & FERRY

The high-speed power catamaran *Osprey Express* makes two round-trip voyages daily from Grenada to Carriacou and on to Petite Martinique. The fare for the 90-minute one-way trip between Grenada and Carriacou is $31 per person each way. For the 15-minute trip between Carriacou and Petite Martinique, the fare is $24 round-trip. The boat leaves Grenada from the Carenage in St. George's.

If you're looking for adventure and economy rather than comfort and speed, cargo schooners from Grenada to Carriacou and Petite Martinique also take passengers. Mail boats *Alexia II, Alexia III,* and/or *Adelaide B* depart from the Carenage

in St. George's early Tuesday, Wednesday, Friday, and Saturday mornings for the four-hour voyage to Carriacou; the return trip to Grenada departs Carriacou on Monday, Wednesday, Thursday, and Sunday mornings. The fare between Grenada and Carriacou on these schooners is $10 each way. The *Adelaide B* continues on from Carriacou to Petite Martinique (about a 1½-hour trip); the fare is about $5 each way. Reservations aren't necessary, but get to the wharf at daybreak to be sure you don't miss the boat.

Information Osprey Express (☎473/440–8126 ⊕www.ospreylines.com).

BY CAR

Driving is a constant challenge in the tropics; however, most of Grenada's 650 mi (1,050 km) of paved roads are kept in fairly good condition—albeit steep, curving, and narrow beyond the Grand Anse area. The main road between St. George's and Grand Anse winds along the coast and is heavily traveled. Directions are clearly posted, but having a map on hand is certainly a good idea when you are traveling in the countryside. Driving is on the left, British-style. Gas stations are in St. George's, Grand Anse, Grenville, Gouyave, and Sauteurs.

Some rental agencies impose a minimum age of 21 to rent a car. Rental cars (including four-wheel-drive vehicles) cost $55 to $75 a day or $285 to $375 a week with unlimited mileage. In high season there may be a three-day minimum rental. Rental agencies offer free pickup and drop-off at either the airport or your hotel.

Contacts On Grenada: David's Car Rentals (☎473/444–3399 ⊕www.davidscars.com). **Dollar Rent-A-Car** (☎473/444–4788 ⊕www.dollargrenada.com). **Indigo Car Rentals** (☎473/439–3300 ⊕www.indigocarsgrenada.com). **McIntyre Bros. Ltd.** (☎473/444–3944 ⊕www.caribbeanhorizons.

com). **Y & R Car Rentals** (☎473/444–4448 ⊕www.y-r.com).

On Carriacou: Barba's Auto Rentals (☎473/443–7454 or 473/407–5156).

BY TAXI

Taxis are plentiful, and rates usually adhere to those set by the government. The trip between Point Salines Airport and Grand Anse or L'Anse aux Epines costs $15; between Grand Anse and St. George's, $15; and between Point Salines and St. George's, $25. A $4 surcharge is added for rides taken between 6 PM and 6 AM. Taxis often wait for fares at hotels and at the welcome center at the cruise-ship terminal on the north side of St. George's. Taxis can be hired at an hourly rate of $25, as well.

Water taxis are available along the Esplanade, near the port area. For about $6 (EC$15), depending on the number of passengers, a motorboat will transport you on an exciting cruise between St. George's and the jetty at Grand Anse Beach. Water taxis are privately owned, unregulated, and don't follow any particular schedule—so make arrangements for a pickup time if you expect a return trip.

In Carriacou the taxi fare from Lauriston Airport to Hillsborough is $6; from Hillsborough to Belair, the fare is $4; to Prospect, $6; and to Tyrrel Bay or Windward, $8.

▌ CONTACTS & RESOURCES

BANKS & EXCHANGE SERVICES

Prices quoted in this chapter are in U.S. dollars unless otherwise indicated.

Grenada uses the Eastern Caribbean dollar (EC$). The official exchange rate is fixed at EC$2.67 to US$1; taxis, shops, and hotels sometimes have slightly lower rates (EC$2.50 to EC$2.60). You can exchange money at banks and hotels, but U.S. and Canadian paper currency, traveler's checks, and major credit cards—American Express, Diners Club, Dis-

cover, MasterCard, and Visa—are widely accepted. Except on rare occasions, such as when shopping in the duty-free shops at the international airport, you will receive change in EC dollars.

ELECTRICITY

Electric current on Grenada is 220 volts–50 cycles. Appliances rated at 110 volts (U.S. standard) will work only with a transformer and adapter plug. For dual-voltage computers or appliances, you'll still need an adapter plug; some hotels will loan adapters. Most hotels have 110 outlets for electric razors.

EMERGENCIES

Ambulance Carriacou Ambulance (☎774). **St. Andrew's Ambulance** (☎724). **St. George's, Grand Anse, and L'Anse aux Épines Ambulance** (☎434).

Coast Guard Coast Guard (☎399 emergencies, 473/444–1931 nonemergencies).

Hospitals Princess Alice Hospital (✉Mirabeau ☎473/442–7251). **Princess Royal Hospital** (✉Belair, Carriacou ☎473/443–7400). **St. Augustine's Medical Services, Inc.** (✉St. Paul's ☎473/440–6173). **St. George's General Hospital** (✉St. George's ☎473/440–2051).

INTERNET, MAIL & SHIPPING

Many hotels and resorts in Grenada offer free or inexpensive Internet access to their guests. Java-Kool Internet Cafe, on the Carenage in St. George's, is open Monday through Saturday from 9 AM to 9 PM. On Carriacou, Services Unltd. on Main Street in Hillsborough, above Bullen's Tours and a few steps north of the ferry landing, has an Internet café.

Airmail rates for letters to the United States, Canada, and the United Kingdom are EC$1 for a half-ounce letter or postcard; airmail rates to Australia or New Zealand are EC$1.60 for a half-ounce letter or EC$1 for a postcard. When addressing a letter to Grenada, simply write "Grenada, West Indies" after the local address.

Contacts Java-Kool Internet Cafe (✉The Carenage, St. George's ☎473/435–3506). **Services Unltd. Internet Cafe** (✉Main St., Hillsborough, Carriacou ☎473/443–8451).

SAFETY

Crime against tourists isn't a big problem in Grenada, but it's a good idea to secure your valuables in the hotel safe and not leave articles unattended on the beach. Removing bark from trees, taking wildlife from the forest, and removing coral from the sea are all against the law.

TAXES & SERVICE CHARGES

The departure tax, collected at the airport, is $20 (EC$50) for adults and $10 (EC$25) for children ages 5–11, payable in cash in either currency. A $4 (EC$10) departure tax is collected when you are departing from Carriacou. An 8% government tax is added to all hotel and restaurant bills. A 10% service charge is generally added to hotel and restaurant bills.

TELEPHONES

The area code is 473 (easily remembered, because the numbers correspond on the dial to the first three letters of "Grenada"). Local calls are free from most hotels; for directory assistance, dial 411. Prepaid phone cards, which can be used in special card phones throughout the Caribbean for local or international calls, are sold in denominations of EC$20 ($7.50), EC$30 ($12), EC$50 ($20), and EC$75 ($28) at shops, attractions, transportation centers, and other convenient outlets. You can place direct-dial calls from Grenada to anywhere in the world using pay phones, card phones, most hotel room phones, and some mobile phones. For international calls using a major credit card, dial 111; to place a collect call or use a calling card, dial 800/225–5872 from any telephone. Pay phones are available at the airport, the cruise-ship welcome center, the Cable & Wireless office on the Carenage in St. George's, shopping centers, and other convenient locations. Pay phones accept EC25¢ and EC$1 coins, as well as U.S. quarters.

Your own cell phone may work in Grenada, but roaming charges can be expensive. Local cell phones can be rented from the Cable & Wireless office in St. George's, or you can purchase a local prepaid card for your own cell phone at Cable & Wireless or from Digicel Grenada.

Contacts Cable & Wireless (✉The Carenage, St. George's ☎473/440–1000). **Digicel Grenada** (✉Granby St., St. George's ☎473/439–4505).

TIPPING

If the usual 10% service charge is not added to your hotel or restaurant bill, a tip at that amount is appropriate. Additional tipping is discretionary. Bellhops appreciate a tip of $1 per bag; maids, $1 or $2 per night of your stay; taxi drivers and tour guides, 10% of the fare or fee.

TOUR OPTIONS

Guided tours offer the sights of St. George's, Grand Étang National Park & Forest Reserve, spice plantations and nutmeg processing centers, rain-forest hikes and treks to waterfalls, snorkeling trips to local islands, and day trips to Carriacou. A full-day sightseeing tour costs $55 to $65 per person, including lunch; a half-day tour, $40 to $45; a guided hike to Mt. Qua Qua, $45. Grenada taxi drivers will conduct island sightseeing tours for $150 per day or $25 per hour for up to four people. Carriacou minibus drivers will take up to four people on a 2½-hour island tour for $60, and $20 per hour thereafter.

On Adventure Jeep Tour you ride in the back of a Land Rover, safari fashion, along scenic coastal roads, trek in the rain forest, lunch at a plantation, take a swim, and skirt the capital. Caribbean Horizons offers personalized tours of historic and natural island sites, market and garden tours, and excursions to Carriacou. Dennis Henry of Henry's Safari Tours knows Grenada like the back of his hand. He leads adventurous hikes and four-wheel-drive-vehicle nature safaris, or you can design your own tour. Kennedy Jawahir of Kennedy Tours specializes in comprehensive island tours and hiking excursions. Mandoo Tours offers half- and full-day tours following northern, southern, or eastern routes, as well as hikes to Concord Falls and the mountains. Sunsation Tours offers customized and private island tours to all the usual sites and "as far off the beaten track as you want to go." From garden tours or a challenging hike to a day sail on a catamaran, it's all possible.

Contacts Adventure Jeep Tour (☎473/444–5337 ⊕www.adventuregrenada.com). **Caribbean Horizons** (☎473/444–1555 ⊕www.caribbeanhorizons.com). **Henry's Safari Tours** (☎473/444–5313 ⊕www.spiceisle.com/safari). **Kennedy Tours** (☎473/444–1074 ⊕www.kennedytours.com). **Mandoo Tours** (☎473/440–1428 ⊕www.grenadatours.com). **Sunsation Tours** (☎473/444–1594 ⊕www.grenadasunsation.com).

VISITOR INFORMATION

At the south end of the Carenage in St. George's, the Grenada Board of Tourism has its offices.

Before You Leave Grenada Board of Tourism (☎561/588–8176 in Lake Worth, FL, or 800/927–9554 ⊕www.grenadagrenadines.com). **Grenada Hotel Association** (☎473/444–1353, 800/322–1753 in U.S. and Canada ⊕www.grenadahotelsinfo.com).

In Grenada Grenada Board of Tourism (⊠The Esplanade, St. George's ☎473/440–2001 or 473/440–2279 ⊠Pointe Salines, St.

George's ☎473/444–4140 ⊠Main St., Hillsborough, Carriacou ☎473/443–7948).

WEDDINGS

One appeal of marrying in Grenada is that you've already begun to enjoy a lovely island honeymoon before the wedding ceremony occurs. Nonresidents of Grenada must be on the island for a minimum of three working days prior to applying for a marriage license. Most resorts will organize your wedding for you and handle all the necessary legal arrangements once you've arrived in Grenada. Beachside weddings are popular, whether you choose a location on magnificent Grand Anse Beach or one on a tiny secluded cove. Or you may prefer a setting in a tropical garden with soft steel-pan music playing in the background, or in the rain forest, or even on a sailboat.

Your application for a marriage license is made at the Prime Minister's Office in St. George's, and the necessary stamp duty and license fees must be paid there. The process takes approximately two days—slightly longer if either partner is divorced or there are legal issues. Documents you need to present are valid passports, birth certificates, affidavits of single status (from a clergyperson, lawyer, or registry on official letterhead), a divorce decree or former spouse's death certificate if applicable, and evidence of parental consent if either party is under the age of 21. All paperwork must be written in English (or translated and certified).

Information Prime Minister's Office (⊠Ministerial Complex, 6th fl., Botanical Gardens, St. George's ☎473/440–2255).

Guadeloupe

Running on Plage Caravelle, Grande-Terre

WORD OF MOUTH

"Les Saintes has its own personality and I found it much different from St. Barths. It is simple and quiet, no cars, some nice beaches, one that is well maintained, the others maintained by nature. I loved walking around. You can actually hike from one end of the island to the other. The best restaurant was at the Auberge, which is an interesting place to stay."

—Spainfan

WELCOME TO GUADELOUPE

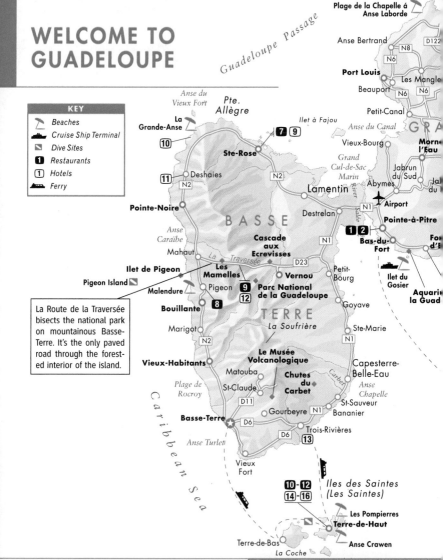

Guadeloupe Passage

KEY

⬎	Beaches
⚓	Cruise Ship Terminal
◣	Dive Sites
1	Restaurants
①	Hotels
⛴	Ferry

La Route de la Traversée bisects the national park on mountainous Basse-Terre. It's the only paved road through the forested interior of the island.

Plage de la Chapelle á Anse Laborde

Anse Bertrand — N8 — D122

Port Louis — Les Mangle

Beauport — N6 — N6

Petit-Canal

Anse du Vieux Fort — Pte. Allègre

Ilet à Fajou — *Anse du Canal* — GRA

La Grande-Anse ⑩

Vieux-Bourg — **Morne l'Eau**

Ste-Rose — 7 9

Grand Cul-de-Sac Marin — Jabrun du Sud — Ja...

⑪ Deshaies — N2 — **Lamentin** — Abymes — du...

N1 ✈ **Airport**

Pointe-Noire — Destrelan — **Pointe-à-Pitre**

Anse Caraïbe — **Cascade aux Ecrevisses** — N1 — **1 2**

Mahaut — *La Traversée* — D23 — **Bas-du-Fort** — Fo... d'...

Ilet de Pigeon — **Les Mamelles** — **Vernou** — Petit-Bourg — ⛴ **Ilet du Gosier**

Pigeon Island ◣ — Pigeon ⑨ — **Parc National de la Guadeloupe** — **Aquari... la Guad**

Malendure — ⑫

Bouillante — 8 — T E R R E — Goyave

Marigot — *La Soufrière* — Ste-Marie

N2 — N1

Vieux-Habitants — **Le Musée Volcanologique** — **Capesterre-Belle-Eau**

Matouba — **Chutes du Carbet** — *Anse Chapelle*

Plage de Rocroy — St-Claude — St-Sauveur

D11 — Bananier

C a r i b b e a n — **Basse-Terre** — Gourbeyre — N1 — St-Sauveur

D6 — Trois-Rivières

Anse Turlet — D6 — ⑬

Vieux Fort — ⑩-⑫ ⑭-⑯ — *Iles des Saintes (Les Saintes)*

Les Pompierres
Terre-de-Haut

Terre-de-Bas — **Anse Crawen**

La Coche

A heady blend of French style and tropical delights, butterfly-shaped Guadeloupe is actually two islands divided by a narrow channel: smaller, flatter, and drier Grand-Terre (Large Land) and wetter and more mountainous Basse-Terre (Low Land). Sheltered by palms, the beaches are beguiling, and the sidewalk cafés are a bit like the Riviera.

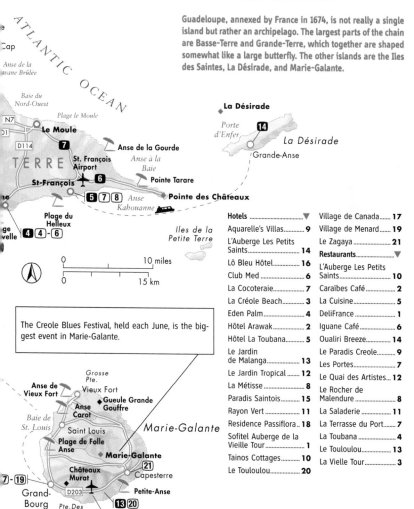

THE BUTTERFLY ISLAND

Guadeloupe, annexed by France in 1674, is not really a single island but rather an archipelago. The largest parts of the chain are Basse-Terre and Grande-Terre, which together are shaped somewhat like a large butterfly. The other islands are the Iles des Saintes, La Désirade, and Marie-Galante.

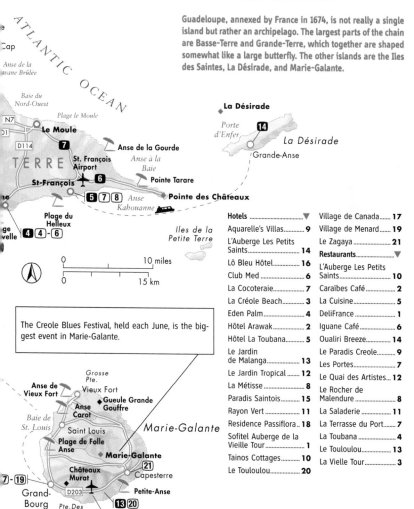

The Creole Blues Festival, held each June, is the biggest event in Marie-Galante.

Hotels ▼	
Aquarelle's Villas	9
L'Auberge Les Petits Saints	14
Lô Bleu Hôtel	16
Club Med	6
La Cocoteraie	7
La Créole Beach	3
Eden Palm	4
Hôtel Arawak	2
Hôtel La Toubana	5
Le Jardin de Malanga	13
Le Jardin Tropical	12
La Métisse	8
Paradis Saintois	15
Rayon Vert	11
Residence Passiflora	18
Sofitel Auberge de la Vieille Tour	1
Tainos Cottages	10
Le Touloulou	20
Village de Canada	17
Village de Menard	19
Le Zagaya	21

Restaurants ▼	
L'Auberge Les Petits Saints	10
Caraïbes Café	2
La Cuisine	5
DeliFrance	1
Iguane Café	6
Oualiri Breeze	14
Le Paradis Creole	9
Les Portes	7
Le Quai des Artistes	12
Le Rocher de Malendure	8
La Saladerie	11
La Terrasse du Port	7
La Toubana	4
Le Touloulou	13
La Vielle Tour	3

TOP 4 REASONS TO VISIT GUADELOUPE

1. Guadeloupe's restaurants highlight the island's fine Creole cuisine.

2. Small, inexpensive inns, called *relais*, give you a genuine island experience and may help you to improve your French.

3. Adventure sports—particularly on the wilder Basse-Terre's Parc National—keep the adrenaline pumping.

4. Remote La Désirade is a truly affordable, friendly island if you want an escape-from-it-all experience.

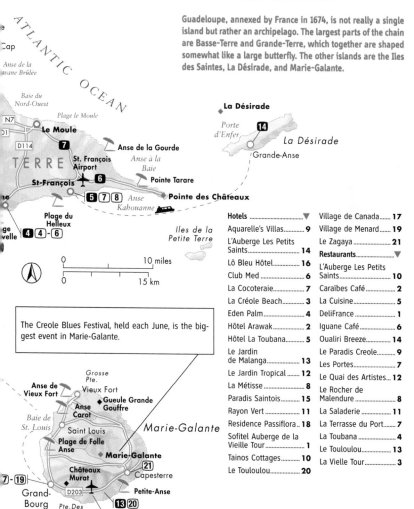

12

GUADELOUPE

GUADELOUPE PLANNER

Island Activities

Guadeloupe's **beaches** can be good, but few resorts are on the island's best, which are mostly along the southern shore of Grand-Terre.

Visitors come instead for good **diving**, the chance to **hike** and explore in Basse-Terre's wild national park.

Good **water sports** make up for sometimes mediocre beaches; windsurfing, sailing, fishing, and jet-skiing are all fun. **Biking** isn't limited to the annual race.

And many travelers enjoy dining at one of Guadeloupe's fine restaurants serving **creole cuisine**.

While **shopping** isn't the best, night owls will find plenty of bars and clubs, as well as a lively music scene.

On the **smaller islands**—Marie-Galante, La Désirade, and Les Saintes—relaxing, sunbathing, and soaking up some old-time Caribbean atmosphere usually rank among the top activities.

Logistics

Getting to Guadeloupe: Although there are a couple of nonstop options, you can also connect through San Juan or another Caribbean island. Some travelers prefer the regularly scheduled ferry service from Dominica, St. Lucia, and Martinique, but the extra travel time certainly increases the hassle factor. The smaller islands—though charming and rewarding destinations—are harder to reach; even with regular ferries and air service, you will almost always need to spend some time on Guadeloupe both coming and going. Aéroport International Pôle Caraïbes, 3 mi (5 km) from Pointe-à-Pitre (PTP), which is a fairly modern airport by Caribbean standards.

Hassle Factor: Medium for Guadeloupe to High for the smaller islands.

Nonstops: You can fly nonstop from Atlanta (Delta) and Miami (Air France, seasonal).

On the Ground

Cabs meet flights at the airport if you decide not to rent a car. The metered fare is about €15 to Pointe-à-Pitre, €15 to Gosier, and €50 to St-François. Fares go up 40% on Sunday and holidays and from 7 PM to 7 AM. You can take a public bus from the airport to downtown Pointe-à-Pitre, but that's not an advisable alternative if you have a lot of luggage.

Renting a Car: If you're based in Gosier or at a large resort, you'll probably only need a car for a day or two of sightseeing. That may be enough, since roundabouts, mountain roads, and fast, aggressive drivers are tiring. Your valid driver's license will suffice for up to 20 days. You can get a rental car from the airport or your hotel. Count on spending between €40 and €60 a day for a small car with standard shift; automatics are considerably more expensive and must be reserved in advance. Some companies, including Europcar, charge a €20 drop-off fee for the airport, even if you pick the car up there. Allow at least 30 minutes to drop off your car at the end of your stay.

Where to Stay

Guadeloupe is actually an archipelago of large and small islands. Grand-Terre has the big package hotels that are concentrated primarily in four or five communities on the south coast, while wilder Basse-Terre has more locally owned hotels. More distant and much quieter are the Iles des Saintes, Marie-Galante, and La Désirade. On each of these smaller islands tourism is but a part of the economy and development is light, and any of them will give you a sense of what the Caribbean used to be.

Resorts: You can certainly opt for a big, splashy resort with all the amenities. Many of the island's large chain hotels cater to French package groups, yet an increasing number of them are being renovated to the degree that they will appeal more to the expectations of Americans.

Relais: These small inns offer a more-personal—and authentic—kind of Caribbean experience.

Villas: Private villas are another option—particularly for families—but the language barrier is often a deterrent to Americans.

Hotel & Restaurant Costs

⇨*For information on hotel meal plans, see Accommodations in Caribbean Essentials.*

WHAT IT COSTS IN U.S. DOLLARS

$$$$	$$$	$$	$	¢
Restaurants				
over $30	$20–$30	$12–$20	$8–$12	under $8
Hotels*				
over $350	$250–$350	$150–$250	$80–$150	under $80
Hotels**				
over $450	$350–$450	$250–$350	$125–$250	under $125

*EP, BP, CP **AI, FAP, MAP Restaurant prices are for a main course at dinner and include V.A.T. and service charge. Hotel prices are per night for a double room in high season and do not include taxes, service charges, and meal plans (except at all-inclusives).

When to Go

The tourism industry thrives during the high season, which lasts from mid-November through May, then the island is quieter the rest of the year. Prices decline 25% to 40% in the off-season.

Carnival is one of the year's highlights, starting in early January and continuing until Ash Wednesday; the celebration finishes with a parade and a huge street party on Mardi Gras.

June's **Creole Blues Festival** on Marie-Galante is gaining in fame and beginning to ensure that the small island's hotels fill up.

In August, the **Tour Cycliste de la Guadeloupe**, which runs over 800 mi (1,290 km) of both Grand-Terre and Basse-Terre, is the Caribbean's answer to the Tour de France.

On one Sunday in mid-August, Pointe-à-Pitre holds a **Fête des Cuisinières** to celebrate creole cuisine. A huge public lunch is followed by a grand ball.

In October, the Union des Arts Culinaires sponsors an upscale **food festival**.

12

By Eileen
Robinson
Smith

URBAN STRESS—BE IT FROM A high-impact life back home or the cacophony of densely populated Pointe-à-Pitre—melts away when you take off in a new Peugeot across the Gabarre Bridge toward Basse-Terre, Guadeloupe's left "wing." Turn the radio dial until you find a good station that will segue from sexy, French love songs to creole soul music and American vocals. Ply the main highway, Route 1, which will take you over velvet green mountains and through variegated rain forests. Detour at any sign that reads CENTRE VILLE. In the center of town, see its life slowly unfold. Back on the road again, you will see makeshift farm stands with a tumble of root vegetables and exotic fruit. Turn off the air-conditioning and let the clean, damp air blow your hair. What could be better? Doing it in a convertible!

It's no wonder that in 1493 Christopher Columbus welcomed the sight of this emerald paradise, where fresh, sweet water flows in cascades. And it's understandable why France annexed it in 1674 and why the British schemed to wrench it from them. In 1749 Guadeloupe mirrored what was happening in the motherland. It, too, was an island divided, between royalists and revolutionaries.

Surprisingly, the resident British sided with the royalists, so Victor Hugues was sent to banish the Brits. While here, he sent to the guillotine more than 300 loyal-to-the-royal planters and freed the slaves, thus all but destroying the plantocracy. An old saying of the French Caribbean refers to *les grands seigneurs de la Martinique et les bonnes gens de la Guadeloupe* (the lords of Martinique and the bourgeoisie of Guadeloupe), and that still rings true. You'll find more aristocratic descendants of the original French planters on Martinique (known as *békés*) and also more "expensive" people, both living and vacationing there. That mass beheading is one of the prime reasons. Ironically, Napoléon—who ultimately ousted the royals—also ousted Hugues and reestablished slavery. It wasn't until 1848 that an Alsatian, Victor Schoelcher, abolished it for good.

Guadeloupe became one of France's *départements d'outremer* in 1946, meaning that it's a dependent of France. It was designated a region in 1983, making it a part of France, albeit a distant part. This brought many benefits to the islanders, from their fine highway systems to the French social services and educational system, as well as a high standard of living. Certain tensions still exist, though the anti-colonial resentment harbored by the older generations is dying out. Guadeloupe's young people realize the importance of tourism to the island's future, and you'll find them welcoming, smiling, and practicing the English and tourism skills they learn in school. Some *français* is indispensable, though you may receive a bewildering response in Creole.

Guadeloupe is a little bit of France, but far from the Metropole. Instead, the culture of this tropical paradise is more Afro-influenced. Savor the earthier pleasures here, exemplified by the wonderful potpourri of whole spices whose heady aromas flood the outdoor markets.

Although Guadeloupe is thought of as one island, it is several, each entity with its own personality. "The mainland" consists of the two largest islands in the Guadeloupe archipelago: Basse-Terre and Grande-Terre, which look something like a butterfly. The outer islands—Les Saintes, Marie-Galante, and La Désirade—are finally being acknowledged as wonderfully unique, unspoiled travel destinations. Tourism officials are now wisely marketing their country as a plural, Les Iles de Guadeloupe. See which one is your place in the sun. *Vive les vacances!*

12

WHERE TO STAY

Most of the island's resort hotels are on Grande-Terre: Gosier, St-François, and Bas-du-Fort are generally considered major resort areas, as is Ste-Anne. With each passing year, the hotels here improve. Often, rates include a buffet breakfast; ask whether this is included in your rate. Many smaller properties do not accept American Express. The renovation of the former Kalenda Hotel in St-François by an American investment group has been stalled. As of January 2008, as dictated by a new French law, all public spaces in hotels are no-smoking, but hotel rooms are considered private, and properties can chose to offer smoking rooms.

VILLAS

French Caribbean International (☎ *800/322–22–23, 805/967–9850 in U.S.* 📠 *805/967–7798* ⊕ *www.frenchcaribbean.com*) handles private villa rentals, from charming cottages in Basse-Terre ($130 to $350 a night) to deluxe sea-view villas in Grande-Terre ($2,600 to $7,000 per week), all with pools. With decades of experience in the French Caribbean, the company has a reputation for honesty and professionalism.

Nouvelles Antilles (☎ *0590/85–00–00* ⊕ *www.nouvellesantilles.com*). This progressive operation, based in St-François, acts as an agent for some 30 villas around the islands, mostly luxurious. In addition, the first online travel agency dedicated to the French West Indies can book your flight, rental car, sports activities, and create a well-priced package. They deal with all the Guadeloupe isles, Martinique, St. Barths, and St. Martin, too, and can customize a multidestination package for groups up to 15.

$$–$$$$ 📷 **Aquarelle's Villas.** At this upscale address on Basse-Terre's north coast, the reception impresses guests with its evolving art shows. In a securely gated community, these 15 homes have private pools on their sundecks, and most have sea views. Furnishings are simple yet fashionable, kitchens are equipped. A stylish, on-site Franco-Creole restaurant serves dinner Wednesday through Sunday and offers room service. Villas have two to five bedrooms and are a good value for families or small groups. There are supplements for breakfast and daily maid service. Some English is spoken. **Pros:** Villas are spacious, the beach has a raw, dramatic beauty. **Cons:** Beach has no chaise lounges, it is a fair walk to the swimmable end. ⊠ *1 Domaine de Nogent, Ste-Rose* ☎ *0590/68–65–23* 📠 *0590/68–38–23* ⊕ *www.aquarelles-villas.com* 🛏 *15 2- to 5-bedroom homes* ⚒ *In-room: no a/c (some), safe, DVD. In-hotel: pool,*

The Life of the Lambi

The *lambi* (lam-bee) by any other name is a Queen Conch or a Stombe Geant. Stingrays consider them a delicacy, as do hermit crabs, lobster, turtles; octopuses wrap their loving arms around them. Yet their main predator is man. He has learned to relish the meat within the copious shell, to the extent that they have been overfished, and harvesting has been limited to four months a year, from October to January.

Ives Tonyon has one of the biggest commercial fishing operations—two 30-foot boats and two mates—on the small, remote island of Désirade. They go out some 2 mi (3 km) for dolphin-fish (mahimahi) and marlin, set traps for lobster, and pull nets for lambi. In two hours they can net about 185 lambi. Three or four make a kilo, which they then sell to La Désirade restaurants for about €20.

At 30, Ives is a nice-looking white man with hazel eyes. When asked his origins, he tells how his was one of the first French families on the island. "Was your father a fisherman?" *"Oui."* "Was your grandfather a fisherman?"

"Oui." "His father and grandfather?" *"Oui, oui."*

FRICASSE OF LAMBI

In these French West Indies, lambi is usually fricasseed. Theodore Compper, owner of La Désirade's Oualiri Beach Hotel & Restaurant, translates while Annie Petronne cooks.

"First you clean the lambi—take out the slimy innards. You can tell by feeling the meat if it is older (six- to eight-years-old) and harder, then you have to pound it out. Otherwise, you just marinade it in fresh lemon juice for 30 minutes, then boil it full tilt for 30 minutes. At the end of the boil, put in a good cup full of *racou*, a seedy, deep-red, creole market spice to which oil has been added. Then cut the lambi in bite-size pieces and put it in the fridge for some hours. Fifteen minutes before serving it, chop onions, garlic, sweet peppers, and parsley and sautée them in oil. Add the red-hue lambi and boil for 15 minutes, adding cold water as you go. Then, *voila!* We serve it with rice, red beans, tomato slices, and shredded carrots."

---

laundry facilities, some pets allowed, no smoking ▭*MC, V* ☉*Closed Sept. 18–Oct. 1* ¶◎¶*EP.*

HOTELS ON GRANDE-TERRE

$$$$ 🏨**La Cocoteraie.** This boutique hotel, with its lobby of dark rattan furnishings and walls of burnt orange and espresso, is a study in refinement. New ownership and management has brought some positive changes: the wall of the restaurant has been opened up to "see the sea" and tables are set on a new deck; another deck looks over the semiprivate beach. Suites have flat-screen TVs and dual, free-form bathroom sinks. Rooms overlooking the glorious pool, which is spanned by a bridge and decorated with magnificent Asian urns, are well-priced. **Pros:** By a calm lagoon, sophisticated clientele, great, international crowd at the Indigo Bar. **Cons:** Spacious suites need more refurbishing for the price, pricey for the quality of construction. ⊠*Av. de l'Europe, St-François*

☎0590/88–79–81 🖷0590/88–78–33 ⊕www.lacocoteraie.com 🛏50 suites 🗘In-room: safe, refrigerator. In-hotel: restaurant, room service, bar, tennis courts, pool, gym, beachfront, no elevator, laundry service, public Internet, parking (no fee), no-smoking rooms ⊟AE, DC, MC, V ⊙Closed Aug. 24–Oct. 21 ⦿BP.

$$$–$$$$
Fodor's Choice
★

Sofitel Auberge de la Vieille Tour. An island classic fashioned around a historic sugar mill, this hotel consistently renews itself. The latest: Désirade, the section of 76 rooms near the pool and beach, has been completely reborn. These rooms now open to private terraces and have fresh white wicker furniture. Everyone loves the hotel's initial welcome: a cool drink and scented towels. After a day at the beach it's back to your bi-level room, with its glass-enclosed bathroom, to watch the lighthouse beam (request Rooms 85 to 90). The lounge is a trip back in time, as guests relax in planter chairs under whirling fans. **Pros:** Most rooms have great views, breakfast (included) is a highlight, the restaurant is one of the island's best. **Cons:** Tremendously expensive, some rooms are in unattractive 1960s-style buildings. ✉Rte. de Montauban, Gosier ☎0590/84–23–23 🖷0590/84–33–43 ⊕www.sofitel.com 🛏143 rooms, 32 deluxe rooms, 1 suite 🗘In-room: safe, refrigerator. In-hotel: 3 restaurants, room service, bars, tennis courts, pool, beachfront, no elevator, public Internet, public Wi-Fi, parking (no fee), no-smoking rooms ⊟AE, MC, V ⦿BP.

$$$
☺
★

Club Med La Caravelle. After a renovation, one of the oldest Caribbean Clubs now has the WOW effect. All the facilities—including the seafront restaurant and its new deck—have a new look and the buffet restaurant now has a separate air-conditioned section. Facing one of the island's best white-sand beaches, the resort is noted for its water sports. The best accommodations are still the oceanfront Marie-Galante wing and the suites in Grande-Terre, all of which are glamorous in the club's latest color scheme: maroons, mauves, and reds. A new villa *residence* is being constructed up on the hill, as is a spa. With four bedrooms, the 20 homes will go into the club's inventory. The children's programs are notably creative, including sports and mini-theater performances. **Pros:** Internet café, exceptional boutique, good service throughout. **Cons:** Club Med experience not to everyone's taste, older standard rooms are small, kid-friendly atmosphere not for everyone. ✉Quartier Caravelle, Ste-Anne ☎0590/85–49–50 or 800/258–2633 🖷0590/85–49–70 ⊕www.clubmed.com 🛏299 rooms, 45 suites 🗘In-room: safe, refrigerator. In-hotel: 2 restaurants, bars, tennis courts, pool, beachfront, water sports, no elevator, children's programs (ages 4–17), laundry service, public Internet, public Wi-Fi, parking (no fee), no-smoking rooms ⊟AE, MC, V ⦿AI.

$$–$$$

Hotel Arawak. A Gosier pioneer since 1973, L'Arawak has emerged from a face-lift with a sleek pastel lobby complete with creole Victorian fretwork and an eye-popping mural of early cane cutting. Nearby, the elliptical bar has a sweeping view of Arawak's long curve of beach. As the mid-rise complex is U-shape, every room has at least a partial sea view. In the renovated wing, refinished furnishings—bamboo with apple-green upholstery—are appealing. Some rooms connect and all have balconies. Sports are a big plus here, and it's fun to watch petanque. **Pros:** Huge new pool and fitness center, low-season rates are about half of high season's, staff and management are welcoming and competent. **Cons:** Aside from beach shack, the mega-dining room is the only option; hallways in unrenovated buildings are dowdy; only double beds or twins throughout property. ⊠*41 Pointe de la Verdure, Gosier* ☎*0590/84–24–24* ⊕*www.hotel-arawak.fr* ⇱*176 rooms, 23 suites* ⬦*In room: safe, refrigerator. In hotel: 2 restaurants, bar, tennis courts, pool, gym, beachfront, diving, water sports, parking (no fee), no smoking rooms* ☰*AE, MC, V* ‖©‖*CP.*

$$–$$$
Fodor'sChoice
★

⌖**Hôtel La Toubana.** Few hotels on Guadeloupe command such a panoramic view of the sea—spanning four islands, no less. The cliff-side suite offers the most dramatic vistas. The bungalows' renovation is complete, including vivid orange outdoor furniture. Swimmers in the infinity pool feel that they can touch the surf, hundreds of feet below. You can also bathe in the small cove, dramatically lighted by night. With its new, luxe spa, La Toubana is now one of the island's *in* places. **Pros:** A special place with sophisticated style; new meeting suite has panoramic views; the orange chairs and table in the pool's shallows add an offbeat touch. **Cons:** The little beach is down the hill by a paved path and has no chaises, bedrooms are small by American standards. ⊠*B. P. 63-Fonds Thezan, Ste-Anne* ☎*0590/88–25–57* 🖷*0590/88–38–90* ⊕*www.toubana.com* ⇱*32 bungalows, 1 suite* ⬦*In-room: kitchen. In-hotel: restaurant, tennis court, pool, spa, no elevator, parking (no fee), no-smoking rooms* ☰*AE, DC, MC, V* ‖©‖*BP.*

$$
★

⌖**La Créole Beach Hotel.** This 10-acre complex is movin' on up thanks to its renovation. Surrounded by mauve market umbrellas and silver patio furniture, the dual pools look enchanting. Families or groups adore the two-bedroom, bi-level Mahogany suite with its minimalist style, kitchen, and enviable sea views. To date, 150 Créole Beach rooms are entirely "new," with crisp, white bedspreads over new mattresses, artwork, LCD TVs, and contemporary bathrooms with hardwood sinks. The oversize rooms and ocean-view suites at Les Palmes resemble those on a teak-appointed yacht. Parisian-trained technicians staff the new Payot spa. The hotel's magic is its fun quotient, which unites everyone, whether you enjoy aqua-aerobics, playing petanque, or moving to a zouk band. **Pros:** Excellent management and long-term staff, good buffets, lovely new gardens. **Cons:** Guest rooms vary wildly in quality (make sure you get a renovated room), beach is small. ⊠*Pointe de la Verdure, Box 61, Gosier* ☎*0590/90–46–46* 🖷*0590/90–46–66* ⊕*www.deshotelsetdesiles.com* ⇱*353 rooms, 15 junior suites, 6 suites, 13 apartments* ⬦*In-room: kitchen (some). In-hotel: 3 restaurants, bar, pool, beachfront, diving, water sports, laundry service, public Internet, public Wi-Fi, parking (no fee), no-smoking rooms* ☰*AE, DC, MC, V* ‖©‖*EP.*

$$

⌖**Eden Palm.** Set away from the tourist zones, this hotel is brimming with sophisticated French style. From the highway, you see a splash of burnt orange amid a pastoral landscape. Impressive wrought-iron gates open to a centuries-old sugar mill bordered by ponds. Each of the duplex bungalows houses two guest rooms with tropical murals and garden terraces. Two new bi-level bungalows have a Jacuzzi on their private deck. Breakfast is a highlight, with French cheeses served

12

on blue-and-gold china. Locals come to Sunday brunch to enjoy the live music. A virgin beach is two minutes away by car. **Pros:** Known for its entertainment, staff is efficient and genuinely caring, Balinese pool beds. **Cons:** You can't see the beach, restaurant has slipped a bit. ⊠*Lieu dit Le Helleux, Ste-Anne* ☎*0590/88–48–48* 🖷*0590/88–48–49* ⊕*www.edenpalm.com* ⤳*57 rooms, 21 suites* ⚒*In-room: safe, refrigerator. In-hotel: restaurant, room service, bar, tennis court, pool, gym, no elevator, parking (no fee), no-smoking rooms, some pets allowed* ☰*AE, MC, V* �"*◯*"*BP.*

$–$$ 🏨**La Métisse.** Pretty as a postcard from a honeymoon couple, this *hôtel de charme* has a new proprietress, Martine Riot. Still the same lovely place where rooms encircle a butterfly-shape pool, it's no longer family- or pet-friendly: quiet is paramount. Sequestered in an upscale residential neighborhood, the property is squeaky clean. Breakfast is particularly lovely; when you draw your drapes, treats appear on your poolside terrace. **Pros:** A safe haven, minibars include French wine. **Cons:** No fun here, rates have escalated, quiet here—shh! ⊠*66 les Hauts de St-François, St-François* ☎*0590/88–70–00* 🖷*0590/88–59–08* ⊕*www.im-caraibes.com/metisse* ⤳*7 rooms* ⚒*In-room: safe, refrigerator, Wi-Fi. In-hotel: pool, no elevator, parking (no fee)* ☰*AE, MC, V* �"*◯*"*CP.*

HOTELS ON BASSE-TERRE

$$–$$$ 🏨**Le Jardin de Malanga.** At this former coffee plantation, the tempting
★ fruit trees may remind you of the Garden of Eden. Two intriguing guest rooms and one suite are in the atmospheric, antiques-filled main house. There is more privacy in the chic, creole-style cottages of courbaril wood; these have patios with hammocks, and monogrammed robes hang in the newly contemporized bathrooms. An infinity pool looks out to the mountains and the sea. **Pros:** A romantic hideaway with history and character, excellent cuisine. **Cons:** Difficult to find and best navigated by day, no TV and not much to do "outside" in the area, the nearest beach is 20 minutes away by car. ⊠*Hermitage, Trois-Rivières* ☎*0590/92–67–57* 🖷*0590/92–67–58* ⊕*www.deshotelsetdesiles.com* ⤳*8 rooms, 1 suite* ⚒*In-room: no TV. In-hotel: restaurant, room service, pool, no elevator, parking (no fee), no-smoking rooms* ☰*AE, MC, V* �"*◯*"*CP.*

$$ 🏨**Rayon Vert.** This romantic hideaway, managed by a bilingual French couple, has the ambience of a private home. Exotic flowers proliferate in the hillside gardens and around the infinity pool, which has an incomparable view of the Bay of Ferry. Opt for one of the larger bungalows (Number 81, 82, 101, or 102), where the sea views are amazing. The modest restaurant's Carib-French fare is both simple and delicious. **Pros:** Interesting, hip (though mostly French) clientele, views from some rooms are amazing. **Cons:** Rooms are spacious but quite simple, decor is dated, steep hill from lower rooms. ⊠*Le Coque Ferry, Deshaies* ☎*0590/28–43–23* 🖷*0590/28–46–27* ⊕*hotel.lerayonvert.free.fr* ⤳*10 rooms, 12 bungalows* ⚒*In-room: refrigerator, VCR (some). In-hotel: restaurant, bar, pool, no elevator, public Internet, parking (no fee)* ☰*MC, V* ⊗*Closed June and Sept.* �"*◯*"*BP.*

$$ ⊞**Tainos Cottages.** Now *this* is a story. A globe-trotting Frenchman designed seven hardwood cottages resembling Guadeloupean *cases* from the 1920s and had them constructed in Indonesia. He imported the cottages and put them on a site overlooking Grande-Anse Beach. The man and his wife (an accomplished chef) filled the raised, open-air bungalows with Persian-style rugs and four-poster beds with mosquito netting. Now you can lounge on elevated Indonesian beds or dip into the pool, which is steps from the sea. **Pros:** Summer rates drop by half, get a discount by booking online, great long beach. **Cons:** Insects, particularly mosquitoes, are a drawback (but they are now using American mosquito magnets that kill them outside the room); most rooms are open-air. ⊠*Plage de Grande-Anse, Deshaies* ☏*0590/28–44–42* 🖷*0590/21–30–20* ⊕*www.tainosvillage.com* ⟲*7 bungalows* ⌂*In-room: no a/c, safe, refrigerator, no TV. In-hotel: restaurant, bar, pool, beachfront, no elevator, public Internet, parking (no fee)* ▤*MC, V* †◎|*CP.*

¢–$ ⊞**Le Jardin Tropical.** Picturesque, immaculate white-and-blue bunga-
☾   lows with gingerbread trim perch on the hillside here. The cluster of terraced buildings and the appealing L-shape pool have an exceptional view of the Caribbean; you're a mile from the closest beach. The largest accommodation can house 10 people (for €150 per night). There's an attractive, open-air common area; you'll also find a breakfast area, billiards room, and a wide-screen satellite TV. **Pros:** The view down the hill is knockout, close to the fun and fine food at Paradis Créole, tasteful room decor. **Cons:** A no-frills place, you will need wheels. ⊠*Rte. de Poirier, Pigeon-Bouillante* ☏*0590/98–77–23* 🖷*0590/98–74–33* ⊕*www.au-jardin-tropical.com* ⟲*6 units* ⌂*In-room: kitchen, no TV. In-hotel: bar, pool, no elevator, public Internet, parking (no fee)* ▤*MC, V* †◎|*EP.*

HOTELS ON ILES DES SAINTES

$$ ⊞**L'Auberge les Petits Saints aux Anarcadiers.** Fashionably eccentric, fun
★   couples, hip families, and serious Caribbeanophiles gravitate to this charismatic inn. After 15 years in business, this landmark was sold to a French couple, Laurence and Jean, who turned things down a notch on the house-party atmosphere, but extend a warm welcome. The pool deck was replaced and furniture upgraded; fitness equipment has been added. With enviable hillside views overlooking the bay, the main building has the charm of decades past, with dormers and gingerbread fretwork. **Pros:** Cool vibe, reminiscent of the island guesthouses of the 1970s, village just down the hill. **Cons:** Do not expect luxury, though improvements continue. ⊠*La Savane, Terre-de-Haut* ☏*0590/99–50–99* 🖷*0590/99–54–51* ⊕*www.petitssaints.com* ⟲*4 bungalows, 4 suites, 2 rooms* ⌂*In-room: dial-up. In-hotel: restaurant, bar, pool, no elevator, public Wi-Fi, airport/ferry shuttle* ▤*AE, MC, V* †◎|*CP.*

$ ⊞**Lô Bleu Hôtel.** The new French owners of what was previously Hotel Cocoplaya tell a familiar story: they came for a cocktail at the beach restaurant and ended up buying the place. The guestroom decor evokes

12

different faraway places like Provence or Africa, but in reality you're just minutes from the main square. Soundproof double windows block out even the annoying drone of the motor scooters. Owner Max Nassah is French/Lebanese, as are the mezes platter and other dishes he serves. **Pros:** Smack on the bay, English is spoken, food is unique on this island. **Cons:** No beautiful grounds, not on a beach, no resort amenities. ⊠*Terre-de-Haut 97137* ☏*0590/92–40–00* 🖷*0590/99–50–41* ⊕*www.lobleuhotel.com* ⊃*10 rooms* ⌂*In-room: refrigerator (some). In-hotel: restaurant, bar, beachfront, no elevator, public Internet* ☰*MC, V* ⌊◎⌉*CP.*

¢–$ 🖬**Paradis Saintois.** You'll feel like the king of the hill as you rock your-
★ self to sleep in your hammock while gazing down on the Caribbean below. The newly renovated apartments (for four to six people) with kitchen terraces are appealing and well maintained by the Swiss managers. Couples should ask for the newest studios, which have hand-crafted stone and tile work. Tricolor boungainvillea surrounds the pool (a second is slated to open in 2008), and the beach is a 10-minute walk away. Guests share the large barbecue grill and the picnic table. The longer you stay, the less you pay. **Pros:** Good fun quotient, super managers. **Cons:** No phones or TVs in rooms, a hike up the hill from town (15 minutes). ⊠*Rte. des Pres Cassin–B. P. I., Terre-de-Haut* ☏*0590/99–56–16* 🖷*0590/99–56–11* ⊕*http://perso.orange.fr/paradis. saintois* ⊃*5 apartments, 2 studios, 1 room* ⌂*In-room: no a/c (some), no phone, kitchen, no TV (some). In-hotel: pools, bicycles, no elevator, laundry service* ☰*MC, V* ⌇*2-night minimum* ⌊◎⌉*EP.*

HOTELS ON MARIE-GALANTE

Accommodations run the gamut from inexpensive, locally owned beach-front bungalows to complexes with foreign owners. **Residence Passi-flora** (⊠*Grand-Bourg* ☏*0590/97–50–48* ⊕*www.residence-passiflora. com*) is composed of two deluxe villas perched on a hillside overlook-ing the sea. The decor is chic French, and there's a Jacuzzi. **Le Toulou-lou** (⊠*Plage de Petite-Anse, Capesterre* ☏*0590/97–32–63* ⊕*www. letouloulou.com*) has four simple stucco bungalows with kitchenettes. You can roll out of your terrace hammock onto the beach. The good creole seafood restaurant is a happening place, with atmospheric music from the beach bar vying with the slapping of the waves. The disco adjacent to the restaurant warms up to hot at night. **Le Village de Canada** (⊠*Section Canada* ☏*0690/50–55–50* ⊕*www.village decanada.com*) has studios, bungalows, and apartments, some with sea views; there's a pool. **Village de Menard** (⊠*Section Canada* ☏*0590/97–09–45* ⊕*www.villagedemenard.com*) consists of squeaky-clean, color-fully decorated bungalows and studios with a pool in a pastoral setting. **Le Zagaya** (⊠*Capesterre* ☏*0590/97–37–84* ⊕*www.le-zagaya.com*), which is decorated in blue and white with marine artifacts and ship doors, offers simple rooms with beds canopied with mosquito netting clustered around a pool. Two bungalows with kitchens are available for longer stays. One of the owners is an Italian chef, so meals are cel-ebratory. The 100-suite **La Cohoba Hôtel** (⊠*Folle Anse, near St-Louis*

☎*0590/97–50–50* 🖷*0590/97–97–96* ⊕*www.cohobahotel.com*), the island's only full-service hotel with a restaurant and beach, is undergoing a badly needed complete renovation.

HOTELS ON LA DÉSIRADE

Even more remote than Marie-Galante, tiny La Désirade has a few simple guesthouses. **Amour D'Oliver** (☎*0590/81–40–52 or 0690/69–66–45*) is small and immaculate, but you'll likely want a car if you stay here. There's no beach, but there's a pool and a barbecue for grilling. **Club Caravelle** (☎*0590/20–04–00* 🖷*0590/20–06–00* ⊕*www.desirade-islands. com*) is inland, but some of the apartments have two floors and sea views. The best views are from the terrace restaurant. **Oualiri Beach Hotel** (☎*0590/20–20–08 or 0690/71–24–76* 🖷*0590/85–51–51* ⊕*www. rendezvouskarukera.com*), a feet-in-the-sand bed-and-breakfast, has sling-back chairs on the beach. Amenities like air-conditioning, cable TV, and in-room Wi-Fi have updated this simple six-room inn. A pioneer from the 1930s, the hotel retains some of its original French windows and doors, patterned tile floors, and fieldstone bar. The beachfront creole restaurant is one of the island's best and the only one with live entertainment.

WHERE TO EAT

Creole cooking is the result of a fusion of influences: African, European, Indian, and Caribbean. It's colorful, spicy, and made up primarily of local seafood and vegetables (including squashlike christophenes), root vegetables, and plantains, always with a healthy dose of pepper sauce. Favorite appetizers include *accras* (salted codfish fritters), *boudin* (highly seasoned blood sausage), and *crabes farcis* (stuffed land crabs). *Langouste* (lobster), *lambi* (conch), *chatrou* (octopus), and *ouassous* (crayfish) are considered delicacies. *Souchy* (like ceviche and Tahitianstyle), raw fish that is "cooked" when marinated in lime juice or similar marinades, is best at seafront restaurants.*Moules et frites* (mussels in broth served with fries) can be found at cafés in Gosier and at the Bas du Fort Marina. As of January 2008, all restaurants and bars are smoke free, as decreed by French law.

Diverse culinary options range from pizza and crepes to Indian cuisine. Look for fine-dining restaurants that belong to the gastronomic association l'Union des Arts Culinaires (UAC). For a quick and inexpensive meal, visit a *boulangerie,* where you can buy luscious French pastries and simple sandwiches. Look for the recommendable chain Délifrance, too. Good news: menu prices seem high but include tax and service (which is split among the entire staff.) If service is to your liking, be generous and leave some extra euros—it's good public relations. In most restaurants in Guadeloupe (as throughout the Caribbean), lobster is the most expensive item on the menu and can easily top €40; price ranges at restaurants listed in this chapter do not include lobster in the price ranges for this reason.

WHAT TO WEAR

Dining is casual at lunch, but beach attire is a no-no except at the more-laid-back marina and beach eateries. Dinner is slightly more formal. Long pants, collared shirts, and skirts or dresses are appreciated, although not required. Guadeloupean ladies like to "dress," particularly on weekends, so don't arrive in flip-flops—they'll be in heels.

GRANDE-TERRE

CAFÉS
$$$
Fodor'sChoice
★

✕**Iguane Café.** Iguanas are indeed the theme here, and you can spy them in unexpected places—juxtaposed with antique cherubs and driftwood mirrors, for example. Unquestionably original cuisine with Asian, Indian, and African influences is Chef Sylvan Serourt's trademark. Begin your sensual *voyage* with foie gras and shallots marinated in balsamic vinegar, then move on to the fishermen's casserole filled with tuna, red snapper, scallops, shrimp, and mussels. Desserts are little marvels, such as the perfect chocolate *moelleux* (molten cake). ⊠*Rte. de La Pointe des Châteaux, 0.5 mi (0.75 km) from airport, St-François* ☎*0590/88–61–37* ☐*AE, MC* ☉*Closed Tues. No lunch Mon. or Wed.–Sat.*

¢–$$
✕**Caraïbes Café.** This sidewalk café straight out of Paris is the in place for lunch and also a spot for a quick breakfast, a fresh juice cocktail (try *corossel/mangue*), a cappuccino, a sundae (*un coupe*), or a pastis while you peoplewatch and listen to French crooners. The *formule* (fixed-price menu) is always the best deal. Service is fast and friendly and can even be in English. ⊠*Pl. de la Victoire, Pointe-à-Pitre* ☎*0590/82–92–23* ☐*MC, V* ☉*Closed Sun. No dinner.*

¢–$
✕**DeliFrance.** For those not in the know, this chain eatery from France is self-service and a safe and sure bet. If you want to take a coffee and fresh croissant for breakfast or a fast and tasty lunch, this be *zee* place. On the colorful awning of this sidewalk café, the words *saladerie* and *sandwicherie* paint the picture. Check out the plat du jour or indulge in a sinful, sweet pastry. ⊠*8 pl. de la Victoire,Pointe-à-Pitre* ☎*0590/83–83–89* ☐*MC, V* ☉*Closed Sun. No dinner.*

FRENCH
$$$–$$$$
★
✕**La Vieille Tour Restaurant.** A historic sugar mill is the backdrop for the artistic creations of Master Chef Denis Schetrit. He is dedicated to preserving great French cuisine, even as he bows to more-recent culinary trends and cleverly utilizes local produce. Foie gras with spicy, exotic fruit chutney is a remarkable appetizer, and the creole bouillabaisse has a depth and

---

> **MORE THAN YOUR BASIC CREOLE COOKING**
>
> The young chefs coming out of the Lycee d'Hotellerie et du Tourisme de Guadeloupe are adding their newfound knowledge to a movement recently afoot, nouvelle creole cuisine. Seasoned French chefs are in place, too, even a master chef (there are only 300 such designated chefs in the world), Denis Schetrit, who reigns at the Sofitel's high-end La Vieille Tour Restaurant. Anchoring the movement are "the ladies," the many female chefs who continue to serve the flavorful creole cuisine that is their heritage.

complexity that will remain in your culinary memory bank. Desserts are dazzling, with lots of towers, sauces, and glacés. ⊠ *Sofitel Auberge de la Vieille Tour hotel, rte. de Montauban, Gosier* ☎ *0590/84–23–23* ⊟ *AE, MC, V* ☉ *Closed Thurs. No lunch.*

$$–$$$$ ✕ **La Cuisine.** It's a bit of Basque country and a lot of Bordeaux, with shades of Morocco in the colorful pillows. If you enjoy raw fish, the red tuna encrusted with sesame seeds is stunningly presented. The chef and proprietor, Frank Le Lan, buys the freshest of food, like the *ouassous* (crawfish) he puts in a salad with a passion-fruit vinaigrette. A terrine made with grapefruit and green tea is a guilt-free dessert. ⊠ *8 Lot Pointes des Pies Saline de l'Est, St-François* ☎ *0590/91–59–06* ⊟ *MC, V* ☉ *Closed Sun.*

$$$ ✕ **La Toubana Restaurant** *(Le Gran Bleu).* Fresh lobsters, a seemingly endless supply of which swim in the canals that beautify the deck, draw many diners. Smoked marlin with green mango is a swell way to begin. The French cuisine gets a delicious Caribbean infusion, as in the tuna with cream of passion-fruit sauce. The inside dining room, although open-air, has deep leather chairs and, in season, a piano player. Lunch patrons dine on the terrace near the infinity pool. With feet dangling in the water and an exotic cocktail in hand, you can watch the sea churn below. ⊠ *Hotel La Toubana, B.P. 63-Fonds Thezan, Ste-Anne* ☎ *0590/88–25–57* ⊟ *AE, MC, V.*

■ **TIP➜** The water thing: Guadeloupe has some of the best-tasting mountain water in the Caribbean isles, but you'll never see anyone drinking it out of the tap. At restaurants, the server will usually ask if you want a bottle of water and if so what kind, *plat?* (plaaa, or flat), meaning "still." Say "Oui, Capes," to request the main island brand. You'll pay €3 to €4 for a big bottle (1.5 liter), half the price of Evian. In your hotel minibar, a small bottle may cost that much. Stop at a gas station, minimart or *supermarche* and buy the big ones for €1.5.

INDIAN   ✕ **Les Portes des Indes.** Dining here is truly a departure: the open-air
$$–$$$ pergola, the blue gates, the pungent aromas, and the bust of Ganesha.
★   Within the paisleycovered menu you can find authentic creole dishes alongside such innovations as boneless chicken with crème fraîche, almonds, and raisins. Keep an eye out for the addictive Indian cheese bread, then cool down with *kulfi,* Indian ice cream topped with ginger confit. The welcome here is always warm and the service dignified. ⊠ *Desvarieux, St-François* ☎ *0590/21–30–87* ⊟ *V* ☉ *Closed early Oct. and Mon. No dinner Sun.*

BASSE-TERRE

CARIBBEAN   ✕ **La Terrasse du Port** *(Chez Mimi).* Pink-striped awnings lead patrons,
$$–$$$ many of whom arrive in BMWs and Citroëns, to this unassuming second-story restaurant. Seafood is the main event, with lobster creole a specialty. And you must love the coquille lambi, the crayfish with reduced lobster bisque, and the shrimp flambéed in *rhum vieux.* Desserts? They're delectable, from the white-chocolate mousse with coconut milk to the fresh mango sorbet. Don't expect chic or trendy, but

the atmosphere is fun. ⊠*Bd. Maritime, Ste-Rose* ☎*0590/28–60–72* ⊟*MC, V* ⊗*Closed Mon. and first 2 wks of Oct. No dinner Sun.*

FRENCH ✕**Le Paradis Créole.** Begin at sunset with one of the *punches maisons* at
$$–$$$ the pool bar so that you can enjoy the remarkable, 360-degree view
★ of the sea. Billed as *gastronomic évolutive*, this is more than just fuel
for the divers who populate this simple hilltop hotel. There is a moderate prix-fixe meal and a changing French menu, often including seafood topped with spicy-fruity sauce. ⊠*Le Paradis Créole Hotel, rte. de Poirier, Pigeon-Bouillante* ☎*0590/98–71–62* ⊟*MC, V* ⊗*Closed Sun. and Mon. No lunch.*

$$–$$$ ✕**Le Rocher de Malendure.** Guests first climb the worn yellow stairs for
★ the panoramic sea views, but return again and again for the food. If
you arrive before noon, when the divers pull in, you might snag one of
the primo tables in a gazebo, which literally hang over the Caribbean.
Begin with a perfectly executed mojito. With fish just off the boat,
don't hesitate to try the sushi *antilliaise* or grilled crayfish and lobster.
⊠*Bord de Mer, Malendure de Pigeon, Bouillante* ☎*0590/98–70–84*
⊟*AE, MC, V* ⊗*Closed Wed. and Sept.–early Oct.*

ILES DES SAINTES

CAFÉS ✕**Le Quai des Artistes.** New arrivals from the ferries are immediately
¢–$ attracted to this second-floor, waterfront café–cum–art gallery, where
they often take breakfast. Under the leather canopy, it's shades of
Greenwich Village with books and newspapers, teas and coffees, wine,
and icy rum cocktails. Contemporary art lines the walls, there for
the buying. International tapas are the main food source and include
sushi and smoked fish plates. Since the kitchen closes at 7 PM, your
only choices after sunset are apéritifs. ⊠*Main dock, Terre-de-Haut*
☎*0590/92–70–98* ⊟*MC, V* ⊗*No dinner.*

ECLECTIC ✕**L'Auberge les Petits Saints aux Anarcadiers Restaurant.** Chef Ives Colas
$$–$$$ has a finger in many cuisines: French, Asian, Italian, and creole. He
insists on top-grade ingredients, like the duck he pairs with mango
and passion-fruit sauce. The lobster here is famous. On the verandah, the night sounds of the tropics vie with sexy French *musique.*
⊠*L'Auberge les Petits Saints aux Anarcadiers, La Savane, Terre-de-Haut* ☎*0590/99–50–99* ⌂*Reservations essential* ⊟*AE, MC, V.*

$–$$ ✕**La Saladerie.** From a sophisticated menu of light plates and the freshest
of fish, you can make a meal of either the fish or beef carpaccio, or the
assorted smoked fish and chilled gazpacho. For dessert, there's a luscious
list of tropical sundaes. Indulge in a snifter of Calvados or Armagnac
and walk the pier to give in to your inner romantic. The French owner
displays his large, mixed-media collages. ⊠*Anse Mire, Terre-de-Haut*
☎*0590/99–53–43* ⊟*MC, V* ⊗*Closed Tues. No dinner Mon.*

MARIE-GALANTE

SEAFOOD ✕**Le Touloulou.** On the curve of Petite-Anse Beach, this ultracasual eat-
$-$$$ ery has tables in the sand. Chef José Viator serves the freshest sea-
food; his standout dish just might be fricassee of conch or octopus
with breadfruit. Set menus start at €20 and often include a shrimp and
fish curry duo. La Pergola's circular bar has the best in rum cocktails
to sip while contemplating the sun's descent. At night the anteroom is
a disco. ⊠*Plage Petite-Anse, Capesterre* ☎*0590/97–32–63* ▬*MC, V*
☺*Closed mid-Sept.–mid-Oct. No dinner Sun.*

LA DÉSIRADE

$-$$ ✕**Oualiri Beach Restaurant.** With tables smack in the sand, on the cov-
☺ ered terrace, and under a conical tent, this beachfront eatery lays out a
bountiful creole buffet on Friday nights and for Sunday brunch. Both
have live entertainment. You can always grab a Continental breakfast,
lunch or dinner, and customize your own €15.50 prix-fixe. Seafood is
the obvious specialty, particularly creole fricassees of lambi and chatrou. Sidle up to the fieldstone bar for a perfect Planters Punch, and
between courses, jump into the sea. Children have their own menus
and love that this is also a *glacier,* with a litany of ice cream flavors;
drizzle your scoops with cajou syrup. P.S. You can check your e-mail
here. Also, owner Theodore Compper will pick you up at the dock or
airport. ⊠*Plage Beau Sejour, Beau Sejour, Le Désirade* ☎*0590/20–
20–08 or 0690/71–24–76* ▬*MC, V.*

BEACHES

Guadeloupe's beaches are generally narrow and tend to be cluttered
with campers-turned-cafés and cars parked in impromptu lots on the
sand. All beaches are free and open to the public; parking fees are rare.
Some hotels allow nonguests to use changing facilities, towels, and
beach chairs for a small fee. On the southern coast of Grande-Terre,
from Ste-Anne to Pointe des Châteaux, you can find stretches of soft
white sand and some sparsely visited stretches. The Atlantic waters on
the northeast coast are too rough for swimming. Along the western
shore of Basse-Terre signposts indicate small beaches. The sand starts
turning gray in Malendure; it becomes volcanic black farther south.
There's one official nude beach, but topless bathing is common.

GRANDE-TERRE BEACHES

L'Autre Bord. The waves on this Atlantic beach give the long expanse of
sand a wild look. The beach, which is protected by an extensive coral
reef, is a magnet for surfers and windsurfers. (Le Toussant Gwanda, a
surfing festival, is generally held here during the first week in November.) You can stroll on the seaside promenade fringed by flamboyant
trees. ⊠*Le Moule.*

★ **Plage Caravelle.** Just southwest of Ste-Anne is one of Grande-Terre's
longest and prettiest stretches of sand, the occasional dilapidated shack

notwithstanding. Protected by reefs, it's also a fine snorkeling spot. Club Med occupies one end of this beach, and nonguests can enjoy its beach and water sports, as well as lunch and drinks, by buying a day pass. You can also have lunch at La Toubana, then descend the stairs to the beach below. ☒*Rte. N4, southwest of Ste-Anne.*

Plage de la Chapelle à Anse-Bertrand. If you want a delightful day trip to the northern tip of Grande-Terre, aim for this spot, one of the loveliest white-sand beaches, whose gentle midafternoon waves are popular with families. When the tide rolls in, it's equally popular with surfers. Several little terrace restaurants at the far end of the beach sate your appetite, but you might want to bring your own shade, because none rent chaise lounges. Before hitting the beach, tour Anse Bertrand. This was where the Caribs made their last stand, and it was a major sugar center. ☒*4 mi (6.5 km) south of La Pointe de la Grand Vigie.*

Plage du Helleux. Except on Sunday, this long stretch of sauvage beach— framed by dramatic cliffs—is often completely deserted in the morning or early afternoon. By 4 PM, you might find 70 or so young surfers, because that's when the waves are right. Many locals take their young children here, but use caution with your own because the current can be strong. The beach has no facilities, but you can get lunch and drinks at the Eden Palm hotel. From Ste-Anne, take the St-François Road about 3 mi (5 km) until you reach the Eden Palm hotel; pass the hotel on your left and take the next right. The beach is about two minutes farther along. ☒*Rte. N4, Lieu-dit le Helleux, Ste-Anne.*

Pointe Tarare. This secluded strip just before the tip of Pointe des Châteaux is the island's only nude beach. If you don't feel comfortable with that, just keep walking and find a private spot. Small bar-cafés are in the parking area, but it's still best to bring some water, snacks, and beach chairs, as there's no place to rent them. What you do have is one of the coast's most dramatic landscapes; looming above are rugged cliffs topped by a huge crucifix. When approaching St-François Marina, go in the direction of Pointe des Châteaux at the roundabout and drive for about 10 minutes. By 2009 the whole area should be dramatically different (all in a good way), for its revitalization will regulate the restaurants, limit traffic to pedestrians—a little train or oxcarts will take you from the parking area—and more. ☒*Rte. N4, southeast of St-François.*

BASSE-TERRE BEACHES

La Grande-Anse. One of Guadeloupe's widest beaches has soft beige sand sheltered by palms. To the west it's a round verdant mountain. There's a large parking area and some food stands, but no other facilities. The beach can be overrun on Sunday, not to mention littered. Right after the parking lot, you can see signage for the creole restaurant Le Karacoli; if you have lunch there (it's not inexpensive), you can *sieste* on the chaise lounges. ☒*Rte. N6, north of Deshaies.*

Malendure. Across from Pigeon Island and the Jacques Cousteau Underwater Park, this long, gray volcanic beach on the Caribbean's calm waters has restrooms, a few beach shacks offering cold drinks and snacks, and a huge parking lot. There might be some litter, but the beach is cleaned regularly. Don't come here for solitude, as the beach is the starting-off point for dive boats, sportfishing boats, glass-bottom boats, and whale-watching vessels. If you're scheduled to do any of the above, you can hang here afterward. Snorkeling from the beach is good. Le Rocher de Malendure, a fine seafood restaurant, is perched on a cliff over the bay. ⊠ *Rte. N6, Bouillante.*

BEACHES ON OTHER ISLANDS

ILES DES SAINTES

Anse Crawen. This 0.5-mi (0.75-km) stretch of white sand is secluded for nude sunbathing, but don't plan on shedding your suit on Sunday, which is family day. To reach it, go past the resort Bois Joli and continue straight until you see the beach. ⊠ *Terre-de-Haut.*

Les Pompierres. This beach is particularly popular with families with small children, as there's a gradual slope, no drop-off, and a long stretch of shallow water. To get here, go to the seamen's church near the main plaza, and then head in the direction of Marigot. Continue until you see Le Salako Snack Bar and some scurrying chickens, and—voilà!—you'll spot a palm-fringed stretch of tawny sand. ⊠ *Terre-de-Haut.*

MARIE-GALANTE

Anse de Vieux Fort. This gorgeous Marie-Galante beach stretches alongside crystal-clear waters that border a large body of freshwater that is ideal for canoeing. It's a surprising contrast from the nearby mangrove swamp you can discover on the hiking trails. The beaches in this area are wide due to the erosion of the sand dunes. It's known as a beach for lovers because of the solitude. Bring your own everything, because this is virgin territory. ⊠ *Rte. D205, just past Pointe Fleur d'Épée, Vieux Fort.*

Petite-Anse. This long, golden beach on Marie-Galante is punctuated with sea grape trees. It's idyllic during the week, but on weekends the crowds of locals and urban refugees from the main island arrive. Le Touloulou's great creole seafood restaurant provides the only facilities. The golden sands are ideal for shelling. ⊠ *6.5 mi (10 km) north of Grand-Bourg via rte. D203, Petite-Anse.*

LA DÉSIRADE

Le Soufleur Plage. To reach one of La Désirade's longest and best beaches from the ferry dock, face town and follow the main road to the right. It's about 15 minutes by car or motor scooter (about €20 a day). White sand, calm waters, and snacks and cold drinks from the beach restaurant await, but there are no chaises, so BYO beach towel. ⊠ *Dpmt. Rd. 207, Le Soufleur.*

SPORTS & THE OUTDOORS

BICYCLING

The French are mad about *le cyclisme*. If you want to be part of this pedal power, take to two wheels. Cycling fever hits the island each August, when hundreds of people converge for the 10-day Tour Cycliste de Guadeloupe, which covers more than 800 mi (1,290 km). If you rent a bicycle, expect to be asked to leave a deposit, but the amount seems to vary; normally you can use a credit card to secure your rental. On Terre-de-Haut, there are a number of shops to the immediate left and right of the ferry dock; the farther from the dock they are, the lower the rates. And you can usually negotiate the price down—a little.

On Grande-Terre, **Eli Sport** (⊠ *Rond Point de Grand-Camp, Grand Camp, Grande-Terre* ☎ *0590/90–37–50*) can set you up with a *vélo tout terrain,* or all-terrain bike. There are no children's bikes, however. The price is right at €10 a day, but reserve as far in advance as possible, or you may find yourself walking instead. **Rent-a-Bike of Ste-Anne** (⊠ *Ste-Anne, Basse-Terre* ☎ *0690/65–05–05*) rents bikes out by the hour (€13). You can opt for a vigorous day (seven hours, with a lunch break, and different degrees of difficulty) of "green" tourism exploring the island with a group (€30). Scooters can be rented as well, and the company organizes hikes and camping trips. **Vert Intense** (⊠ *Basse-Terre, Basse-Terre* ☎ *0590/99–34–73 or 0690/55–40–47* ⊕ *www.vert-intense.com*) is your main Basse-Terre sports connection. The company is known for hiking excursions but also puts together bike excursions. The company prefers that you make a reservation four days in advance.

BOATING & SAILING

If you plan to sail these waters, you should be aware that the winds and currents tend to be strong. There are excellent, well-equipped marinas in Pointe-à-Pitre, Bas-du-Fort, Deshaies, St-François, and Gourbeyre. You can rent a yacht (bareboat or crewed) from several companies. To make a bareboat charter, companies will evaluate your navigational and seamanship skills. If you do not pass, you must hire a skipper or be left on dry land. **Cap Sud** (⊠ *3 pl. Créole, Bas-du-Fort, Grande-Terre* ☎ *0590/90–76–70* ⊕ *www.capsud.net*) has a fleet of eight yachts, including monohulls and catamarans. The sailboats are generally rented as bareboats by the week. The giant yacht-rental company **Sunsail** (⊠ *Bas-du-Fort Marina, Bas-du-Fort, Grande-Terre* ☎ *0590/90–92–02, 410/280–2553, 207/253–5400 in U.S.* ☎ *0590/90–97–99* ⊕ *www.sunsail.com*) has a base on Guadeloupe. Although it's primarily a bareboat operation, you can hire skippers by the week if you have limited experience, or you can get expert instruction in sailing techniques and the local waters. Windsurfers, kayaks, and kite boards can be rented, too, but these must be reserved in advance.

DIVING

The main diving area at the **Cousteau Underwater Park,** just off Basse-Terre near Pigeon Island, offers routine dives to 60 feet. The numerous glass-bottom boats and other crafts make the site feel like a marine parking lot; however, the underwater sights are spectacular. Guides and instructors are certified under the French CMAS (some also have PADI, but none have NAUI). Most operators offer two-hour dives three times per day for about €45 to €50 per dive; three-dive packages are €120 to €145. Hotels and dive operators usually rent snorkeling gear.

Chez Guy et Christian (⊠*Plage de Malendure, Basse-Terre* ☎*0590/98–82–43*) has a good reputation and is well established among those who dive off Pigeon Island. One dive boat departs three times daily and charges €34 a dive. A second dive boat goes to Les Saintes, with two dives, one at a wreck, the other at a reef. The €85 price includes lunch. English-speaking dive masters are PADI certified. Show your Fodor's guide and ask for a discount.

☺ **Les Heures Saines** (⊠*Le Rocher de Malendure, Plage de Malendure, Bouillante, Basse-Terre* ☎*0590/98–86–63, 0690/31–28–42, or 0690/57–30–07* ⊕*www.plongee-guadeloupe.com*) is the premier operator for dives in the Cousteau Underwater Park. Trips to Les Saintes offer one or two dives for average and advanced divers, with plenty of time for lunch and sightseeing. Wreck, night, and Nitrox diving are also available. The instructors, many of them English speakers, are excellent with children. The company also offers sea kayaking and winter whale- and dolphin-watching trips with marine biologists as guides. These tours, aboard a 60-foot catamaran, cost €53.

☺ With more than 10 years of experience, dive master Cedric Phalipon of **Pisquettes Club de Plongée Des Saintes** (⊠*Le Mouillage, Terre-de-Haut, Iles des Saintes* ☎*0590/99–88–80* ⊕*www.pisquettes.com*) knows all the best sites. He gives excellent lessons in English. Equipment is replaced frequently and is of a high caliber. Small tanks are available for kids, who are taken buddy diving.

FISHING

Not far offshore from Pigeon-Bouillante, in Basse-Terre, is a bounty of big-game fish like bonito, dolphinfish, captain fish, barracuda, kingfish, and tuna. You can also thrill to the challenge of the big billfish like marlin and swordfish. Anglers have been known to come back with as many as three blue marlins in a single day. For Ernest Hemingway wannabes, this is it. To reap this harvest, you'll need to charter one of the high-tech sportfishing machines with flying bridges, competent skippers, and mates. The price is $430 to $600 a day, with lunch and drinks included. The boats can accommodate up to six passengers.

With a pair of state-of-the-art boats with covered fly bridges, **Centre de Peche Sportive** (⊠*Malendure de Pigeon, Bouillante, Basse-Terre* ☎*0590/98–70–84* ✐*rocher-malendure@wanadoo.fr*) is known for success in showing anglers where to pull in the big billfish. The per-day rate is €500, and you do get your money's worth; the boat often doesn't come back until sunset, after a fine lunch and cold bevs. You can also go night fishing for swordfish, and the crew will cut the bills and fins off your catch. The company is affiliated with the restaurant Le Rocher de Malendure, which has two simple oceanfront bungalows on the cliffs—a real value for the money. **Michel** (⊠ *Les Galbas, Ste-Anne, Basse-Terre* ☎ *0590/85–42–17 or 0690/55–21–35*) is a reliable big-fishing charter outfit that can usually pick anglers up at their hotel and allow them to charge their €150 to their hotel bill. The mates will be happy to take your picture with your catch of the day.

FOUR-WHEELING

With **Le Haras de Saint-François** (⊠ *Chemin de la Princesse, St-François, Grande-Terre* ☎ *0690/39–90–00*) you can take a four-wheeler quad off road and onto the beach for 2½ hours with a fun guide for €60.

EN ROUTE If you are driving from Ste-Anne to the St-François Marina area, follow signs first to St-François, then look for signs to the marina and Pointe des Châteaux, not St-François centre ville. That is the old town, and a nice detour to see the market, but a circuitous route to the marina.

GOLF

Golf Municipal St-François (⊠ *St-François, Grande-Terre* ☎ *0590/88–41–87* ⊕ *www.saint-francois.golf.com*), across from La Cocoteraie hotel, is an 18-hole, par-71, Robert Trent Jones–designed course (1973); it has an English-speaking pro, a clubhouse, a pro shop, and electric carts for rent. The greens fees are just €25 for 9 holes, €40 for 18; carts rent for €25 for 9 holes and €36 for 18. Chariots (pull carts) rent for just €6 for 18 holes, €4 for 9. There are no caddies. Clubs can be rented for about €25. The course is open daily from 7:30 AM to 6 PM. It's best to reserve tee times a day or two in advance. La Cocoteraie and Golf Marine Hotel guests enjoy a 20% discount. Directly across from the golf course, the simple, inexpensive Golf Marine Hotel is good for golf buddies or sailors wanting a dry berth. ☎ *0590/88–60–60* ⊕ *www.deshotelsetdesiles.com*.

NEED A BREAK? Either before or after your golf game, head to Kolo & Zabriko (⊠ 36 Centre Commercial "Les Arcades,") at roundabout near casino, St-François ☎ 0690/91-06-77) for fresh-squeezed juice, a smoothie, or a very large café au lait in a whimsical, colorful cup with a tiny chocolate chip cookie. Office workers know to come for a salad or take a creative sandwich to go, say, baby shrimp and avocado cream on a fresh-baked roll. Try to choose from among a dozen tropical ice cream flavors.

HIKING

Fodor'sChoice
★

With hundreds of trails and countless rivers and waterfalls, the **Parc National de la Guadeloupe** on Basse-Terre is the main draw for hikers. Some of the trails should be attempted only with an experienced guide. All tend to be muddy, so wear a good pair of boots. Know that even the young and fit can find these outings arduous; the unfit may find them painful. Start off slowly, with a shorter hike, and then go for the gusto. All water sports—even canoeing and kayaking—are forbidden in the center of the park. Scientists are studying the impact of these activities on the park's ecosystem.

> ### A PARK IS RECOGNIZED
>
> In 2007 The Parc National de la Guadeloupe was awarded the prestigious European Charter for Sustainable Tourism in Protected Areas, by the EUROPARC Federation, for an initial period of five years. The award recognizes an ongoing process of sustainable tourism development in cooperation with a wide range of local partners.

Les Heures Saines (⊠ *Le Rocher de Malendure, Plage de Malendure, Bouillante, Basse-Terre* ☎ *0590/98–86–63* ⊕ *www.ecotourisme-guadeloupe.net*), a professional operation that has distinguished itself at sea, has now come ashore to offer freshwater canyoning in a river outside the national park as well as hikes to La Randonnée. There are three different canyoning circuits, including one called the Trail of the Three Waterfalls that lasts six to seven hours. On The Bivouac you spend 24 reality-show-like hours in the forest. For many of these excursions, you have to wait for a group to be assembled. Book as far in advance as you can. Rates range from €45 to €115, for ages 8–14, €28 to €50.

Vert Intense (⊠ *Basse-Terre, Basse-Terre* ☎ *0590/99–34–73 or 0690/55–40–47* ⊕ *www.vert-intense.com*) organizes fascinating hikes in the national park and to the volcano. You move from steaming hot springs to an icy waterfall in the same hike. Guide Eric Barret is patient and safe, and he can bring you to heights that you never thought you could reach, including the top of Le Soufrière. The volcano hike costs only €25 but must be booked four days in advance. A mixed-adventure package spanning three days costs €210. The French-speaking guides, who also know some English and Spanish, can take you to other tropical forests and rivers, where the sport of canyoning can still be practiced. If you are just one or two people, the company can team you up with a group.

HORSEBACK RIDING

A 44-horse stable owned by a female veterinarian, **Le Haras de Saint-François** (⊠ *Chemin de la Princesse, St-François, Grande-Terre* ☎ *0690/39–90–00*) has English lessons and Western trail rides for two hours (€45) or three hours (€60). The latter will take you to the beach, where you can go bareback into the sea.

JET SKIING

The young and sporty French are wild for their *scooters de mer*, but you can't rent a Jet Ski in Guadeloupe unless you have a special license. Instead, **Atmospheres** (⊠*Pointe de la Verdure, Gosier* ☎0690/49–47–28) organizes group excursions for two to five hours that cost €180 to €260. It's a pricey but exhilarating way to enjoy the sea, and you can experience a number of different sites speedily; the full day includes lunch at a remote islet. If you have knee or back problems or are afraid of speed, stay on your chaise lounge: even the twentysomethings are sore afterward.

SEA EXCURSIONS

🔆 **Evasion Tropicale** (⊠*Le Rocher de Malendure, Pigeon-Bouillante, Basse-Terre* ☎0590/98–86–63 ⊕*www.evasiontropicale.org*) operates daylong whale-watching cruises. With the help of the onboard sonar, humpback whales are easy to find from December through March. Trips cost €55 per person, but every passenger must also buy an annual membership to the Association for Study and Census of Turtles, Marine and Mammals of the Caribbean for €25. New on the scene, **Nina** (⊠*St-François Marina, St-François, Grande-Terre* ☎0690/39–90–00) is an 80-foot maxi-catamaran recently relocated from St. Barths. At a swift 12 knots, it plys the waters to the outlying islands, playing French music and serving a French buffet. Attracting an upscale clientele, **Para-doxe** (⊠*St-François Marina, St-François, Grande-Terre* ☎0690/83–62–35) is a top-of-the-line catamaran that sails to Marie-Galante and Les Saintes for €75. It's not your typical booze cruise. Bottles of rum aboard? Sure, but passengers are more likely to be in it for the marine experience and the stopover on nature preserve Petit Terre. The music is soothing and the lunch tasty, with cheesy bread, fresh fish, barbe-cue chicken, ribs, and vegetarian dishes. **Tip Top Cruises** (⊠*35 Rési-dence de la Presqu'île, Bas-du-Fort, Grande-Terre* ☎0590/84–66–36 ✍*tiptopcruise@wanadoo.fr* ⊠*Av. de l'Europe, St-François, Grande-Terre* ☎*No phone*) operates two large catamarans that fly through the water to Les Saintes and other islands, including Marie-Galante and Dominica. It's a full day at sea, with snorkeling, kayaking, and shore excursions, including the little islet of Petit Terre, with its resident population of sea turtles. Lunch is included (there's a supplement for lobster), as well as rum libations. Tip Top has been in the business for years because it runs a clean and tight ship—fun but professional.

WIND- & KITE SURFING

🔆 Most beachfront hotels can help you arrange lessons and rentals. **Centre Nautique** (⊠*Creole Beach Hotel, Pointe de la Verdure, Gosier, Grand-Terre* ☎0590/90–46–59) is run by former windsurfing champions who are instructors of the first degree; the company rents Windsurfers for €20 an hour, Hobie Cats for €32 an hour, and can arrange fishing, cata-maran, and motorboat excursions. **LCS** (⊠*Ste-Anne Lagoon, Ste-Anne, Grande-Terre* ☎0590/88–15–17 ⊕*www.lookasurf.com*), in business since the early 1980s, specializes in lessons for adults and children six and older. Instructors are certified by the French National Federation of Sailing. The company organizes offshore competitions and also runs a retail surf shop. Windsurfing buffs congregate at the **UCPA Hotel Club** (⊠*St-François, Grande-Terre* ☎*0590/88–64–80* ✉*Terre-de-Haut, Iles des Saintes* ☎*0590/99–54–94* ⊕*www.ucpa.com*), where for moderate weekly rates (beginning at €700) they sleep in hostel-style quarters, eat three meals a day, and do a lot of windsurfing. Lessons and boards (also available to nonguests) are included in the package, as are bikes to pedal to the lagoon. A sister club on Terre-de-Haut has a water-sports center in the middle of town, though the hotel itself is out on isolated Baie de Marigot.

SHOPPING

The island has a lot of desirable French products, from designer fashions for women and men and sensual lingerie to French china and liqueurs. As for local handicrafts, you can find attractive wood carvings, madras table linens, island dolls dressed in madras, woven straw baskets and hats, and *salakos*—fishermen's hats made of split bamboo, some covered in madras—which make great wall decorations. Of course, the favorite Guadeloupean souvenir is rum. Look for *rhum vieux*, the top of the line. For foodies, the market ladies sell aromatic fresh spices, crisscrossed with cinnamon sticks, in little baskets lined with madras.

AREAS & MALLS

Grande-Terre's largest shopping mall, **Destrelland,** has more than 70 stores and is just minutes from the airport, which is a shopping destination in its own right. In **Pointe-à-Pitre** you can enjoy browsing in the street stalls around the harbor quay and at the two markets (the best is the Marché de Frébault). The town's main shopping streets are rue Schoelcher, rue de Nozières, and the lively rue Frébault. At the St-John Perse Cruise Terminal there's an attractive mall with about two dozen shops. **Bas-du-Fort**'s two shopping areas are the Cora Shopping Center and the marina, where there are 20 or so shops and quite a few restaurants. In **St-François** there are more than a dozen shops surrounding the marina, some selling French lingerie, swimsuits, and fashions. A supermarket has incredibly good prices on French wines and cheeses, and if you pick up a fresh baguette, you have a picnic. (Then you can go get lost at a secluded beach.)

SPECIALTY STORES

ART

Brigitte Boesch (⊠*St-François, Grande-Terre* ☎*0590/88–48–94*), a German-born painter who has exhibited all over the world, lives in St-François, and her studio is worth a visit. Call for directions. **Gallerie Alamanda** (⊠*La Marina–La Coursive, St-François, Grande-Terre*

☎*0590/88–63–32*) deals exclusively in Haitian art, and while they sell "the same old, same old" (starting at €230), they also have some exquisite work by artists whose work hangs in New York's Museum of Modern Art and others who command prices of nearly €4,000. **Pascal Foy** (✉*Rte. à Pompierres, Terre-de-Haut, Iles des Saintes* ☎*0590/99–52–29*) produces stunning homages to traditional creole architecture: paintings of houses that incorporate collage make marvelous wall hangings. As his fame has grown, his media attention has expanded, so prices have risen.

CLOTHING

Côté Plage (✉*Pl. du Marché, Pointe-à-Pitre, Grande-Terre* ☎*No phone*) sells bikinis, sundresses, and straw beach totes in addition to T-shirts and other ideal island necessities. There's also a line of simple jewelry—turtles, geckos, and sea horses—made of sand and resin. Across from the market, **Dody** (✉*31 rue Frébault, Pointe-à-Pitre, Grande-Terre* ☎*0590/82–18–59*) is the place to go if you want white eyelet (blouses, skirts, dresses, even bustiers). The shop has a high-quality designer line, but you will pay €100 to €300 for a single piece. There's lots of madras, too, which is especially cute in children's clothing. **Le Gall** (✉*La Marina–La Coursive, St-François, Grande-Terre* ☎*No phone*) handles a line of fashionable resort wear for women and children designed by a French painter, Jean Claude Le Gall, that has hand-painted figures like turtles and dolphins on quality cotton knits. There are several other branches of this French favorite across the island.

COSMETICS & PERFUME

L'Artisan Parfumeur (✉*Centre St-John Perse, Pointe-à-Pitre, Grande-Terre* ☎*0590/83–80–25*) sells top French and American brands as well as tropical scents. **L'Atelier du Savon** (✉*Terre-de-Haut, Iles des Saintes* ☎*0590/99–56–44*) makes all of its soaps from vegetable products, with scents including marine spice and mandarin orange. Beautifully packaged gift baskets include bath salts and aromatic oils. **Au Bonheur des Dames** (✉*49 rue Frébault, Pointe-à-Pitre, Grande-Terre* ☎*0590/82–00–30*) sells several different lines of cosmetics and skin-care products in addition to its own perfumes. **Phoenicia** (✉*Bas-du-Fort, Grande-Terre* ☎*0590/90–85–56* ✉*8 rue Frébault, Pointe-à-Pitre, Grande-Terre* ☎*0590/83–50–36* ✉*121 bis rue Frébault, Pointe-à-Pitre, Grande-Terre* ☎*0590/82–25–75*) sells mainly French perfumes. **Vendôme** (✉*8–10 rue Frébault, Pointe-à-Pitre, Grande-Terre* ☎*0590/83–42–84*) is Guadeloupe's exclusive purveyor of Stendhal and Germaine Monteil cosmetics.

HANDICRAFTS

Boutique Alamanda (✉*La Marina–La Coursive, St-François, Grande-Terre* ☎*0590/88–70–13*) carries artistic home furnishings sized to carry home, such as tablecloths, place mats, pillow covers, runners, vases, and decorative accessories. "Out of Africa" bags can be bought to transport your new purchases. The **Centre Artisanat** (✉*Ste-Anne, Grande-Terre* ☎*No phone*) offers a wide selection of local crafts, including art composed of shells, wood, and stone. One of the outlets sells authentic Panama hats. At **Kaz à Lorgé** (✉*25 rue Benoît Cassin, Terre-de-Haut, Iles des Saintes* ☎*0590/99–59–60*) you can find a jumble of handicrafts from around the island and around the world, including prints, mobiles, wall masks, Haitian woodcraft, miniature lobster traps, and cutesy things made from madras. It all fills the two tiny rooms of this gingerbread-covered shop.

★ **Madras Bijoux** (⊠ *115 rue Nozières, Pointe-à-Pitre, Grande-Terre* ☎ *0590/ 82–88–03*) specializes in replicas of authentic creole jewelry; it also creates custom designs and does repairs. At **Maogany Artisanat** (⊠ *Terre-de-Haut, Iles des Saintes* ☎ *0590/99–50–12*), the shop resembles a yacht. Artist and designer Yves Cohen carries batiks and hand-painted T-shirts in luminescent seashell shades. Hand-loomed silk fabrics are embellished with gold thread; others are translucent, like his sensual women's collection. Silk shawls and scarves, hand-embroidered with tropical birds, and his children's collection make great gifts. For men, there are real Panama hats and buccaneer shirts.

LIQUOR & TOBACCO
The airport duty-free stores have a good selection of rum and tobacco. **Délice Shop** (⊠ *45 rue Achille René-Boisneuf, Pointe-à-Pitre, Grande-Terre* ☎ *0590/82–98–24*) is the spot for island rum and edibles from France—from cheese to chocolate.

NIGHTLIFE

Guadeloupeans maintain that the beguine began here, and, for sure, the beguine and mazurkas were heavily influenced by the European quadrille and orchestrated melodies. Their merging together is the origin of West Indian music and it gave birth to zouk (music with an African-influenced Caribbean rhythm) at the beginning of the 1980s. Still the rage here, it has spread not only to France but to other European countries. Many resorts have dinner dancing or offer regularly scheduled entertainment by steel bands and folkloric groups.

The island's performing arts scene is centered on the **Centre des Arts** (⊠ *Pl. des Martyrs de la Liberté, Pointe-à-Pitre, Grande-Terre* ☎ *0590/82–79–78*), where each season is more exciting than the last. Here you'll find exceptional jazz and blues concerts, musical comedies, and even art exhibitions. Hip-hop artists, break-dancers, and classical musicians have all performed here. Prices are democratic. Ask for the special deals.

BARS & NIGHTCLUBS
Club Med (⊠ *Quartier Caravelle, Ste-Anne, Grand-Terre* ☎ *0590/85–49–50*) sells night passes that include all cocktails, dinner with wine, a show in the theater, followed by admission to the disco. Passes cost €90; go on Friday for the gala dinner and the most creative show. It's a super option for single women, who will feel comfortable and safe at the disco, where there are plenty of fun staffers willing to be dance partners.
Something is always happening at the **Creole Beach Hotel** (⊠ *Pointe de la Verdure, Gosier, Grand-Terre* ☎ *0590/90–46–46*). The entertainment is often bands playing beguine and zouk, which are both very dance-

able. The group of primitive dancers and the tom-tom drummers are amazing. Call in advance so that your name will be at the door.

★ The jazzed up **Eden Palm Theater** (⊠ *Eden Palm hotel, Lieu-dit le Hel-leux, Ste-Anne, Grand-Terre* ☎ *0590/88–48–48*) presents a Cuban-influenced Caribbean musical review on Saturday nights. The spec-tacle—like nothing else on the island—has plumage, imaginative cos-tumes, a super sound system and a bevy of dancers. The cost is €60 for dinner and show. On Tuesday nights there is a creole buffet with dancing to a steel band for €40.

Midway (⊠ *Bas-du-Fort Marina, Pointe-à-Pitre, Grand-Terre* ☎ *0590/ 90–03–49*) looks like a hole-in-the-wall, but a lot of good sounds can be heard inside. The piano bar has earned the loyalty of locals, as have the live bands.

Nightly entertainment at **Sofitel Auberge de la Vieille Tour** (⊠ *Rte. de Montauban, Gosier, Grand-Terre* ☎ *0590/84–23–23*) ranges from the talented piano man to jazz combos and, on Thursday, the folklorico ballet. Call first so the security guard has your name.

CASINOS

Both of the island's casinos are on Grande-Terre and have American-style roulette, blackjack, and stud poker. The legal age for gambling is 18, and a new French law dictates that everyone must show their passport. Jacket and tie aren't required, but "proper attire" means no shorts, T-shirts, jeans, flip-flops, or sneakers.

Casino de Gosier (⊠ *Gosier, Grande-Terre* ☎ *0590/84–79–69*) has a bar, restaurant, and cinema. The higher-stakes gambling is behind a closed door. You'll have to pay €10 to be part of that action—or even to watch. It's open daily from 8:30 PM; slot machines open at 10 AM. Townsfolk and tourist alike are waiting to see how the brand new **Casino de St-François** (⊠ *Marina, in front of golf course, nearer to Cen-tre Commercial, St-François, Grande-Terre* ☎ *0590/88–41–31*), under construction at this writing, will turn out. It would have to be a hand-some showplace in comparison to the original, and there will be even more slots and a parking lot.

DISCOS

Night owls should note that carousing here isn't cheap. On the week-end and when there's live music, most discos charge a cover of at least €10, which might go up to as much as €20. Your cover usually includes a drink, and other drinks cost about €12 each, beer as much as €8 in a strip joint. Those you will have to find on your own.

Acapulco (⊠ *1 rue Paul Finette, St-François, Grande-Terre* ☎ *0590/20– 79–18*) is an intimate spot with zouk and other types of music; it has different themes nightly. **Le Cheyenne** (⊠ *Rte. de Montauban, Gosier, Grande-Terre* ☎ *0590/90–01–01*) is a dramatic, Native American–theme disco that continues to draw the crowds. Look for the sculpture of a Cheyenne chief over the grand entrance. On weekends, there's a cover charge when the basement disco is open. (It now has a fine restau-rant, too.) **La Plantation** (⊠ *Gourbeyre, Basse-Terre* ☎ *0590/81–23–37*) is the top spot on Basse-Terre; couples dance to zouk, funk, and house music on the immense mezzanine dance floor. If you like salsa music, **Zenith** (⊠ *Bord de Mer, Bas-du-Fort, Grande-Terre* ☎ *0590/90–72–04*) is one of your best bets. There's a view of the sea and a terrace with a pool.

EXPLORING GUADELOUPE

To see each "wing" of the butterfly, you'll need to budget at least one day. They are connected by a bridge, and Grande-Terre has pretty villages along its south coast and the spectacular Pointe des Châteaux. You can see the main sights in Pointe-à-Pitre in a half day. Touring the rugged, mountainous Basse-Terre is a challenge. If time is a problem, head straight to the west coast; you could easily spend a day traveling its length, stopping for sightseeing, lunch, and a swim. You can make day trips to the islands, but an overnight works best.

GRANDE-TERRE

Ⓒ **Aquarium de la Guadeloupe.** Unique in the Antilles, this aquarium in the marina near Pointe-à-Pitre is a good place to spend an hour. The well-planned facility has an assortment of tropical fish, crabs, lobsters, moray eels, coffer fish, and some live coral. It's also a turtle rescue center. New is the spectacular shark tank. ⊠ *Pl. Créole off rte. N4, Pointe-à-Pitre* ☎ *0590/90–92–38* ⊠ *€8.50* ⊘ *Daily 9–7.*

Ft. Fleur d'Épée. The main attraction in Bas-du-Fort is this 18th-century fortress, which hunkers down on a hillside behind a deep moat. It was the scene of hard-fought battles between the French and the English in 1794. You can explore its well-preserved dungeons and battlements and take in a sweeping view of Iles des Saintes and Marie-Galante. ⊠ *Bas-du-Fort* ☎ *0590/90–94–61* ⊠ *€6* ⊘ *Mon. 10–5, Tues.–Sun. 9–5.*

■ **TIP→** You may find that you adore the tropical ice cream flavors like *mangue* (mango) and *coco* (coconut). You may not realize that *cacahuet* translates to peanut and is addictive!

Gosier. Taking its name from the brown pelicans that nest on the islet of Gosier and along the south coast of Grande-Terre, Gosier was still a tiny village in the 1950s, a simple stopping place between Pointe-à-Pitre and Ste-Anne. However, it grew rapidly in the 1960s, when the beauty of the southern coastline began to bring in tourists in ever-increasing numbers. Today Gosier is Guadeloupe's premier tourist resort while at the same time serving as a chic suburb of Pointe-à-Pitre. People sit at sidewalk cafés reading *Le Monde* as others flip-flop their way to the beach. The town has several hotels, nightclubs, shops, a casino, and a long stretch of sand.

Morne-à-l'Eau. This agricultural town of about 16,000 people has an amphitheater-shape cemetery, with black-and-white-checkerboard tombs, elaborate epitaphs, and multicolor (plastic) flowers. On All Saints' Day (November 1), it's the scene of a moving (and photogenic) candlelight service.

Le Moule. On the Atlantic coast, and once the capital city of Guadeloupe, this port city of 24,000 has had more than its share of troubles: it was bombarded by the British in 1794 and 1809 and by a hurricane in 1928. An important touristic center in past decades, it's experiencing a comeback. A large East Indian population, which originally came to cut cane, lives here. Canopies of flamboyant trees hang over the narrow streets, where colorful vegetable and fish markets do a brisk business. The town hall, with graceful balustrades, and a small 19th-century neoclassical church are on the main square. Le Moule's beach, protected by a reef, is perfect for windsurfing.

Pointe des Châteaux. The island's easternmost point offers a breathtaking view of the Atlantic crashing against huge rocks, carving them into shapes resembling pyramids. There are spectacular views of Guadeloupe's southern and eastern coasts and the island of La Désirade. The dramatic scene is marred by a parking lot filled with tour buses and makeshift bars and snack stands, but if you are spending hours at the beach, you will need the sustenance. On weekends locals come in numbers to walk their dogs, surf, or look for romance. But change is afoot, and the sauvage beach will become gentrified.

Pointe-à-Pitre. Although not the capital, it is the island's largest city, a commercial and industrial hub in the southwest of Grande-Terre. The isles of Guadeloupe have 450,000 inhabitants, 99.6% of whom live in the cities. Pointe-à-Pitre is bustling, noisy, and hot—a place of honking horns and traffic jams and cars on sidewalks for want of a parking place. By day its pulse is fast, but at night, when its streets are almost deserted, you don't want to be there.

The city has suffered severe damage over the years from earthquakes, fires, and hurricanes. In recent years it took heavy hits by Hurricanes Frederick (1979), David (1980), and Hugo (1989). On one side of rue Frébault you can see the remaining French colonial structures; on the other, the modern city. Some of the downtown area has been rejuvenated. The Centre St-John Perse has transformed old warehouses into a cruise-terminal complex that consists of the spartan Hotel St-John, restaurants, shops, and the port authority headquarters. An impressive terminal serves the ferries that depart for Iles des Saintes, Marie-Galante, Dominica, Martinique, and St. Lucia.

The heart of the old city is place de la Victoire; surrounded by wooden buildings with balconies and shutters (including the tourism office) and by sidewalk cafés, it was named in honor of Victor Hugues's 1794 victory over the British. During the French Revolution, Hugues ordered the guillotine set up here so that the public could witness the bloody end of 300 recalcitrant royalists.

Even more colorful is the bustling marketplace, between rues St-John Perse, Frébault, Schoelcher, and Peynier. It's a cacophonous place, where housewives bargain for spices, herbs (and herbal remedies), and a bright assortment of papayas, breadfruits, christophenes, and tomatoes. For fans of French ecclesiastical architecture, there's the imposing **Cathédrale de St-Pierre et St-Paul** (⊠ *Rue Alexandre Isaac at rue de* *l'Eglise*), built in 1807. Although battered by hurricanes, it has fine stained-glass windows and creole-style balconies and is reinforced with pillars and ribs that look like leftovers from the Eiffel Tower. Anyone with an interest in French literature and culture won't want to miss the **Musée St-John Perse,** which is dedicated to Guadeloupe's most famous son and one of the giants of world literature, Alexis Léger, better known as St-John Perse, winner of the Nobel Prize for literature in 1960. Some of his finest poems are inspired by the history and landscape—particularly the sea—of his beloved Guadeloupe. The museum contains a collection of his poetry and some of his personal belongings. Before you go, look for his birthplace at 54 rue Achille René-Boisneuf. ✉*At rues Noizières and Achille René-Boisneuf* ☎*0590/90–01–92* ⌨*€2* ⊙*Thurs.–Tues. 8:30–12:30 and 2:30–5:30.* **Musée Schoelcher** celebrates Victor Schoelcher, a high-minded abolitionist from Alsace who fought against slavery in the French West Indies in the 19th century. The museum contains many of his personal effects, and exhibits trace his life and work. ✉*24 rue Peynier* ☎*0590/82–08–04* ⌨*€3* ⊙*Weekdays 9–5.*

Port Louis. This fishing village of about 7,000 people is best known for Le Soufleur Plage. It was once one of the island's prettiest, but it has become a little shabby. Although the beach is crowded on weekends, it's blissfully quiet during the week. The sand is fringed by flamboyant trees, and there are also spectacular views of Basse-Terre.

Ste-Anne. In the 18th century this town, 8 mi (13 km) east of Gosier, was a sugar-exporting center. Sand has replaced sugar as the town's most valuable asset. La Caravelle (where you can find the Club Med) and the other beaches are among the best in Guadeloupe. On a more spiritual note, Ste-Anne has a lovely cemetery with stark-white tombs.

NEED A BREAK?

Match, a *supermarche* on l'avenue de l'Europe/St-François Marina, has esoteric cheeses and baked goods like pie-size, tropical fruit tarts. Other supermarkets to look for throughout the island that have good deli or bakery departments are those in the Leader Price chain.

★ **St-François.** This was once a simple little village, primarily involved with fishing and harvesting tomatoes. The fish and tomatoes are still here, as are the old creole houses and the lively market with recommendable food stalls in the centre ville, but increasingly, the St-François marina district is overtaking Gosier as Guadeloupe's most fashionable tourist resort area. La Cocoteraie, one of the island's ritziest hotels, is just off l'avenue de l'Europe, which runs between the marina and the rolling fairways and water obstacles of the 18-hole Robert Trent Jones–designed municipal golf course. On the marina side, a string of shops, hotels, bars, and restaurants cater to tourists.

NEED A BREAK?

If you don't want to take time for a two-hour French lunch, watch for gas stations like Shell Boutique, Total Boutique, and Esso Tigermart, which sell food. The Shell station on the left going into St-François has good pizza for

€8, roast chicken, and paninis, as well as tables. A Total might have barbecue ribs, chicken, and turkey.

BASSE-TERRE

Basse-Terre (which translates as "Low-Land") is by far the highest and wildest of the two wings of the Guadeloupe butterfly, with the peak of the Soufrière Volcano topping off at nearly 4,811 feet. Basse-Terre, where you can find the island's national park, is an ecotourist's treasure, with lush, equatorial plant life and adventurous opportunities for hikers and mountain bikers on the old *traces,* routes that porters once took across the mountains. You can still find numerous fishing villages and banana plantations, stretching as far as the eye can see. The northwest coast, between Bouillante and Grande-Anse, is magnificent; the road twists and turns up steep hills smothered in vegetation and then drops down and skirts deep-blue bays and colorful seaside towns. Constantly changing light, towering clouds, and frequent rainbows only add to the beauty.

Basse-Terre. Because Pointe-à-Pitre is so much bigger, few people suspect that this little town of 15,000 is the capital and administrative center of Guadeloupe. But if you have any doubts, walk up the hill to the state-of-the-art Théâtre Nationale, where some of France's finest theater and opera companies perform. Paid for by the French government, it's a sign that Basse-Terre is reinventing itself. Founded in 1640, it has endured not only foreign attacks and hurricanes but sputtering threats from La Soufrière as well. The last major eruption was in the 16th century, though the volcano seemed active enough to warrant evacuating more than 70,000 people in 1975.

The **Jardin Botanique,** or Botanical Garden, is an exquisitely tasteful 10-acre park populated with parrots and flamingos. A circuitous walking trail takes you by ponds with floating lily pads, cactus gardens, and every kind of tropical flower and plant, including orchids galore. A restaurant, with surprisingly good meals, and a snack bar are housed in terraced gingerbread buildings, one overlooking a waterfall, the other the mountains. The garden has a children's park and nature-oriented playthings in the shop. ⊠ *Deshaies* 🕾 *0590/28–43–02* 💷 *€10* 🕘 *Daily 9–6.*

Bouillante. The name means "boiling," and so it's no surprise that hot springs were discovered here. However, the biggest attraction is scuba diving on nearby Pigeon Island, which is accessed by boat from Plage de Malendure. There's a small information kiosk on the

THE COLONY & ITS COSTUMES

If the literature of St-John Perse doesn't entice you to visit the museum dedicated to him, perhaps the new costume exhibits will. See designs that copied the latest Parisian fashions for the isles' French women, who preferred the silk from Lyon, alongside the costumes and turbans of madras cotton worn by *les femmes de couleur* in exhibits that re-create the ambience of the late 19th century.

beach at Plage de Malendure that can help you with diving and snorkeling arrangements.

Cascade aux Ecrevisses. Within the Parc National de la Guadeloupe, Crayfish Falls is one of the island's loveliest (and most popular) spots. There's a marked trail (walk carefully—the rocks can be slippery) leading to this splendid waterfall, which dashes down into the Corossol River—a good place for a dip. Come early, though; otherwise you definitely won't have it to yourself.

Chutes du Carbet. You can reach three of the Carbet Falls (one drops from 65 feet, the second from 360 feet, the third from 410 feet) via a long, steep path from the village of Habituée. On the way up you pass the Grand Étang (Great Pond), a volcanic lake surrounded by interesting plant life. For horror fans there's also the curiously named Étang Zombi, a pond believed to house evil spirits. If there have been heavy rains, *don't even think about it.*

Ilet de Pigeon. This tiny, rocky island a few hundred yards off the coast is the site of the Jacques Cousteau Underwater Park, the island's best scuba and snorkeling site. Although the reefs here are good, they don't rank among the top Caribbean dive spots. Several companies conduct diving trips to the reserve, and it's on the itinerary of some sailing and snorkeling trips *(⇨ Diving and Sea Excursions in Sports & the Outdoors).*

Les Mamelles. Two mountains—Mamelle de Petit-Bourg, at 2,350 feet, and Mamelle de Pigeon, at 2,500 feet—rise in the Parc National de la Guadeloupe. *Mamelle* means "breast," and when you see the mountains, you can understand why they are so named. Trails ranging from easy to arduous lace up into the surrounding mountains. There's a glorious view from the lookout point 1,969 feet up Mamelle de Pigeon. If you're a climber, plan to spend several hours exploring this area. Hark! If there have been heavy rainfalls, cancel your plans.

Le Musée Volcanologique. Inland from Basse-Terre, on the road to Matouba, is the village of St-Claude, where you can see this museum and learn everything you need to know about volcanoes. ⊠ *Rue Victor Hugo, St-Claude* ☎ *0590/78–15–16* ☑ *€4* ⊙ *Daily 9–5.*

★ **Parc National de la Guadeloupe.** This 74,100-acre park has been recognized by UNESCO as a Biosphere Reserve. Before going, pick up a *Guide to the National Park* from the tourist office; it rates the hiking trails according to difficulty, and most are quite difficult indeed. Most mountain trails are in the southern half of the park. The park is bisected by the route de la Traversée, a 16-mi (26-km) paved road lined with masses of tree ferns, shrubs, flowers, tall trees, and green plantains. It's the ideal point of entry to the park. Wear rubber-soled shoes and take along a swimsuit, a sweater, and perhaps food for a picnic. Try to get an early start to stay ahead of the hordes of cruise-ship passengers making a day of it. Check on the weather; if Basse-Terre has had a lot of rain, give it up. In the past, after intense rainfall, rock slides have closed the road for months. ⊠ *Administrative Headquarters, rte. de la Traver-*

sée, St-Claude ☎*0590/80–86–00*
⊕*www.guadeloupe-parcnational.*
com ✉*Free* ☉*Weekdays 8–5:30.*

Pointe-Noire. Pointe-Noire is a good jumping-off point from which to explore Basse-Terre's little-visited northwest coast. A road skirts magnificent cliffs and tiny coves, dances in and out of thick stands of mahogany and gommier trees, and

> ## ZEE DRAINAGE DITCHES
>
> Whether you're driving a car or walking on an unlighted street at night, be aware that there are ditches on the side of the road meant to catch the runoff after a rain.

12

weaves through unspoiled fishing villages with boats and ramshackle houses as brightly colored as a child's finger painting. This town has two small museums devoted to local products. **La Maison du Bois** (☎*0590/98–17–09*) offers a glimpse into the traditional use of wood on the island. Superbly crafted musical instruments and furnishings are for sale. It's open Tuesday to Sunday from 9:30 to 5:30 and charges €1 admission. Across the road from La Maison du Bois is **La Maison du Cacao** (☎*0590/98–25–23* ⊕*maisonducacao.com*), which has exhibits on the operation of a cocoa plantation. Some antique implements are on display, and for your euros you get a hot chocolate. Chocolate bars and other goodies are for sale. It's open daily from 9 to 5 (Sunday only in season) for a €6 admission fee.

Ste-Rose. In addition to a sulfur bath, there are two good beaches (Amandiers and Clugny) and several interesting small museums in Ste-Rose. **Domaine de Séverin** (☎*0590/28–91–86*), free and open daily from 8:30 to 5, is a historic rum distillery with a working waterwheel. A simple open-air dining room has a good menu. A *petit* train traverses the plantation from 9:30 to 10:45 and again from 3:30 to 5:30 from Sunday to Friday; this scenic tour costs €6. A gift shop sells rum, spices, and hot sauces.

★ **Vernou.** Many of the old mansions in this area remain in the hands of the original aristocratic families, the *békés* (Creole for "whites"), who trace their lineage to before the French Revolution. Traipsing along a path that leads beyond the village through the forest, you come to an impressive waterfall at Saut de la Lézarde (Lizard's Leap). It is not always open in low season.

★ **Vieux-Habitants.** This was the island's first colony, established in 1635. Beaches, a restored coffee plantation, and the oldest church on the island (1666) make this village worth a stop. From the riverfront **Musée du Café** (☎*0590/98–54–96*), dedicated to the art of coffeemaking, the tantalizing aroma of freshly ground beans reaches the highway. Plaques and photos tell of the island's coffee history. The shop sells excellent coffee and rum punches (liqueurs). Admission is €6. It's open daily 9 to 5.

ILES DES SAINTES

The eight-island archipelago of Iles des Saintes, often referred to as Les Saintes, dots the waters off the southern coast of Guadeloupe. The islands are Terre-de-Haut, Terre-de-Bas, Ilet à Cabrit, Grand Ilet, La Redonde, La Coche, Le Pâté, and Les Augustins. Columbus discovered them on November 4, 1493 and christened them Los Santos (Les Saintes in French) for All Saints' Day.

Only Terre-de-Haut and Terre-de-Bas are inhabited, with a combined population of little more than 3,000. Many of les Saintois are fair-haired, blue-eyed descendants of Breton and Norman sailors. Unless they are in the tourism industry, they tend to be taciturn and standoffish. Fishing still is their main source of income, and they take pride in their work. The shores are lined with their boats and *filets bleus* (blue nets dotted with orange buoys).

DID YOU KNOW?

For generations, the Saintois fishermen wore hats called *salakos*, which look like inverted saucers, patterned after a hat said to have been brought here by a seafarer from China. You're now more likely to see the younger fishermen in visors and French sunglasses.

★ **Terre-de-Haut.** With 5 square mi (13 square km) and a population of about 1,500, Terre-de-Haut is the largest and most developed of Les Saintes. Its "big city" is Bourg, with one main street lined with bistros, cafés, and shops. Clutching the hillside are trim white houses with bright red or blue doors, balconies, and gingerbread frills.

Terre-de-Haut's ragged coastline is scalloped with lovely coves and beaches, including the seminudist beach at Anse Crawen. The beautiful bay, complete with a "sugarloaf" mountain, has been called a mini Rio. There are precious few vehicles or taxis on island, so you'll often find yourself walking, despite the hilly terrain. Or you can add to the din and rent a motorbike. Take your time on these rutted roads, as around any bend there might be a herd of goats chomping on a fallen palm frond. Two traffic lights have brought a small amount of order to the motorbike hordes. A new ordinance has, too! When aggressively soliciting you, the scooter agencies will not tell you that it is now prohibited to scoot in town from 9 to noon and from 2 to 4.

This island makes a great day trip, but you can really get a feel for Les Saintes if you stay over. It's not unlike St. Barths, but for a fraction of the price.

Fort Napoléon. This gallery holds a collection of 250 modern paintings, influenced by cubism and surrealism. However, this museum is noted for its exhaustive exhibit of the greatest sea battles ever fought. You can also visit the well-preserved barracks and prison cells, or admire the botanical gardens, which specialize in cacti of all sizes and descriptions. ✉ *Grand Bourg* ☎ *0590/37–99–59* 💶 *€5* 🕑 *Daily 9–noon.*

OTHER ISLANDS

La Désirade. "Desirable" is the operative word here. This small, somewhat remote island is an absolute find for those who prefer a road less traveled, who want their beaches long and white, and who don't mind that accommodations are simple if the price and quality are right. The Désirade populace (all 1,700 of them) welcome tourism, and these dear hearts have a warm, old-fashioned sense of community.

12

According to legend, the "desired land" was so named by the crew of Christopher Columbus, whose tongues were dry for want of fresh water when they spied the island; alas, it was the season for drought. The 8-square-mi (21-square-km) island, 5 mi (8 km) east of St-François, is a chalky plateau, with an arid climate, perennial sunshine, cacti, and iguanas. You may even see two male iguanas locked in a prehistoric-looking battle. Rent a four-wheel-drive to climb the zigzag road that leads to the Grande Montagne. Make a photo stop at the diminutive white chapel, which offers a panorama of the sea below. Afraid that you might zig instead of zag down the precipice? Then take a fun, informative van tour that you join near the tourism office at the harbor. The ruins of the original settlement—a leper colony—are on the tour.

Only one road runs around the perimeter of the island, and if you're interested in visiting one of the many gorgeous beaches shaded by coco palms and sea grape trees, you can do that on a scooter. Driving is safer here than anywhere.

NEED A BREAK?

La Désirade has a few cute and casual spots to grab a bite to eat. The goats and their kids that you pass on your island tour may end up in a curry at Chez Nounoune (⊠ *La Providence, La Désirade* ☎ *0590/20–03–59*).

If you're on the beach, you might want to stop by La Payotte (⊠ *Plage de Beauséjour, La Désirade* ☎ *0590/20–01–29*) for the fresh catch, conch, or lobster, or the French owner's famous chicken with a sauce of *noix de cajou* (cashews). Mind you, avoid it when there is a tour group on the island.

★ **Marie-Galante.** This island resonates with history. Columbus sighted this 60-square-mi (155-square-km) island on November 3, 1493, named it after his flagship, the *Maria Galanda,* and sailed on. It's dotted with ruined 19th-century sugar mills, and sugar is still its major product. Honey and 59-proof rum are its other favored harvests. With its rolling hills of green cane still worked by oxen and men with broad-brim straw hats, it's like traveling back in time to when all of Guadeloupe was still a giant farm.

Although it's only an hour by high-speed ferry from Pointe-à-Pitre, the country folk here are still sweet and shy. You can see swarms of yellow butterflies, and maybe a marriage carriage festooned with flowers, pulled by two white oxen. A daughter of the sea, Marie-Galante has some of the archipelago's most gorgeous, uncrowded beaches. Take time to explore the dramatic coast. You can find soaring cliffs—such as the Gueule Grand Gouffre (Mouth of the Giant

Chasm) and Les Galeries (where the sea has sculpted a natural arcade)—and enormous sun-dappled grottos, such as Le Trou à Diable, whose underground river can be explored with a guide. Port Louis, the island's "second city," is the new hip spot. The ferry dock is in Port Louis, and it's also on the charts for yachts and regattas.

> ### COMPETITIONS DES BOEUFS TIRANTS
>
> The annual ox-pulling competitions on Marie-Galante go on for two weeks in November. Where else will you see this in your lifetime?

After sunset, the no-see-ums and mosquitoes can be a real irritation, so always be armed with repellent.

The **Château Murat** (⊠ *Grand-Bourg, Marie-Galante* ☎ *0590/97–94–41*) is a restored 17th-century sugar plantation and rum distillery housing exhibits on the history of rum making and sugarcane production and an admirable *ecomusée,* whose displays celebrate local crafts and customs. It's open daily from 9:15 to 5; admission is free. **Le Moulin de Bézard** (⊠ *Chemin de Nesmond, off D202, Marie-Galante*) is the only rebuilt windmill in the Caribbean. There are two gift shops and a café housed in reproductions of slave quarters with wattle walls. Admission is €4; it's open daily from 10 to 2. You should make it a point to see one of the distilleries, especially **Père Labat** (⊠ *Section Poisson, Grand-Bourg, Marie-Galante* ☎ *0590/97–03–79*), whose rum is considered some of the finest in the Caribbean and whose atelier turns out lovely pottery. Admission is free, and it's open daily from 7 to noon.

GUADELOUPE ESSENTIALS

To research prices, get advice from other travelers, and book travel arrangements, visit www.fodors.com.

I TRANSPORTATION

BY AIR

In addition to nonstop service from Atlanta and Miami, you can also connect in San Juan (American Eagle and Air France). Air Caraïbes connects the island to St. Maarten, Martinique, the Dominican Republic, and Havana, Cuba. LIAT flies from several other Caribbean islands. Air Antilles Express has service to Martinique, St. Martin, St. Barths, and in the summer months to the Dominican Republic. (This service may be extended.) Air Tropical is again flying charters from the St-François airport to Marie-Galante,

Les Saintes, La Désirade, St. Barths, St. Martin, and, well, ask.

Information Air Antilles Express (☎ 0890/64–86–48). **Air Canada** (☎ 0590/21–12–77). **Air Caraïbes** (☎ 0820/83–58–35 or 0590/82–47–00). **Air France** (☎ 0590/21–13–03 or 0820–820–820). **Air Tropical** (☎ 0690/57–26–77). **American Airlines** (☎ 0590/21–11–80 or 0811/30–73–00). **Delta** (☎ 0800/22–56–30). **LIAT** (☎ 0590/21–13–93).

AIRPORTS & TRANSFERS

Aéroport International Pôle Caraïbes (PTP), usually called the Pointe-à-Pitre Airport after the closest major city, is one of the largest and most modern in the Caribbean. Excellent signage makes it very manageable. It has shops, restaurants, and car-rental agencies. There is a tourism information booth in the terminal with bilingual staffers, an ATM, and a currency exchange. Ask your resort if airport transfers can be arranged, as they are almost always cheaper than taking a taxi. Taxi fare to Pointe-à-Pitre is about €15; to Gosier resorts you'll pay about €25, and to St-François it's more than €50.

Information Aéroport International Pôle Caraïbes (☎0590/21–14–72 or 0590/21–14–00).

BY BOAT & FERRY

Ferry schedules and fares often change (expect them to go up as gas prices skyrocket), so phone ahead or confirm them at the tourist office or ferry terminal. Children pay a reduced price, and there's usually not a charge for infants.

You usually travel to the outlying islands in the archipelago in the morning, returning in the afternoon. Brudey Frères ferries travel between Pointe-à-Pitre and Terre-de-Haut and Marie-Galante, and between Terre-de-Haut to Trois-Rivières on Basse-Terre. Comatrile ferries travel from St-François on Grande-Terre to both La Désirade and Marie-Galante. These ferries usually leave in the early morning and again in the afternoon. Both Comatrile and Express des Isles operate ferries between Terre-de-Haut and Marie-Galante. Note: in the low season, you may have to take a complimentary bus from the Pointe-à-Pitre terminal to the ferry dock in Basse-Terre, which can take nearly an hour. That crossing is shorter but rougher.

Express des Iles runs ferries Dominica, Martinique, and St. Lucia. Any of these trips costs about €79, and the daily crossings (with extra departures on weekends), take between three and four hours. Ferries can be crowded on weekends and after music festivals and other events; call to confirm schedules and prices, and in peak times reserve with a credit card.

Small, privately owned boats shuttle passengers between the town of Gosier and the islet of Gosier, where the main attraction is the blinking lighthouse, for about €3. They leave hourly from Le Bord de le Mer restaurant. Guests at the Creole Beach Hotel complex can leave from their dock. This is just a spit of sand in the sea, and you can make-believe that you are Robinson Crusoe. BYO towel, for there are no chaises. On the islet, a beach shack called Ti Robinson grills up snapper, dolphin, and lobster as patrons watch from the nearby hammocks.

Information Brudey Frères Transport Maritime (☎0590/90–04–48, 0590/91–60–87 in Pointe-à-Pitre, 0590/92–69–74 in Trois-Rivières, 0590/92–69–74 in St-François, 0590/97–77–82 in Marie-Galante, 0590/97–77–82 ⊕www.brudey-freres.fr). **Comatrile** (☎0690/50–05–09 or 0590/91–02–45). **Express des Isles** (☎0825/35–90–00 or 0590/91–98–53 ⊕www.express-des-iles.com).

BY CAR

Finding your way from and particularly back to the airport in your rent-a-car can be stressful, for sure. *Porquoi?* Because it is not a straight shot off the highway. Conscientiously follow every sign that has a picture of a plane. You will be traversing a lot of neighborhoods and roundabouts and then a rural area with cane fields. You must return the car to the old (*former*) airport and wait for a shuttle to bring you back to the new airport. Allow an extra hour.

If you're a careful driver and you heed the following tips, exploring the island by car can be fun. Guadeloupe has 1,225 mi (1,976 km) of fine highways, marked as in Europe. Driving around Grande-Terre is relatively easy. Basse-Terre requires more skill to navigate the hairpin bends in the mountains and around the eastern shore; at night these scenic roads are unlighted and treacherous.

Guadeloupeans are fast and oftentimes impatient drivers, and they tailgate. When the fearless motorcycle boys—called hornets—come at you, move aside. Avoid morning and evening rush hours, especially around Pointe-à-Pitre. If you're lost, don't stop to ask people standing on the side of the road; they are waiting for a lift and if you stop they'll jump in. Try to find a gas station and have your map ready, but chances are the attendants speak more Créole than French. Inside, the manager or other customers usually speak French and maybe some English.

Return your vehicle with the same amount of gas or you'll be charged an exorbitant rate. If you return your car with a dirty interior, you might have to pay for cleaning it—Hertz threatens to charge €77. With all agencies, take the walk-around for damage assessment seriously, so that you are not charged for existing dents. You might want a vehicle that takes diesel (*gazole*); which is considerably cheaper than gasoline, but you will pay about €5 more per day for the car. Gas is nearly €7 a gallon. Automatics are few, require advance notice, and are expensive, about €75 per day in high season, whereas your cheapest standard will be about €48 per day. You may feel most comfortable with an American franchise, but Europcar "speaks" English, is professional, and has convertibles from €113 per day.

Information **Avis** (☎0590/21–13–54). **Budget** (☎0590/21–13–49). **Europcar** (☎0590/21–13–52). **Hertz** (☎0590/21–13–46). **Jumbo Car** (☎0590/21–13–50). **Rent A Car** (☎0590/21–13–62) **Sixt** (☎0590/21–13–44).

BY MOPED

The only places in Grande-Terre where tourists can drive scooters relatively safely are around Ste-Anne, St-François, and Gosier. You can rent a Vespa scooter at Equator Moto for about €29 per day, including insurance. You'll need to put down nearly €150 for a deposit. There are numerous vendors by the ferry dock in Terre-de-Haut, Les Saintes, where you can rent mopeds, so search for the best price. Moped traffic in town is restricted during the day, so you may find it eas-

ier to simply walk. Marie-Galante and La Désirade are now the best islands for scooting. The motor scooter rental agents meet the ferry.

Information **Equator Moto** (✉Gosier, Grande-Terre ☎0590/90–36–77). **Loca Sol** (✉Rue du Fort, Grand-Bourg, Marie-Galante ☎0590/97–76–58). **Magaloc** (✉Grand-Bourg, Marie-Galante ☎0590/72–91–33).

BY TAXI

Taxis are metered and fairly pricey. Fares jump by 40% between 7 PM and 7 AM and on Sunday and holidays. Tourist offices or your hotel can arrange for an English-speaking taxi driver. Nicho—of Nicho's Reliable Taxi—speaks perfect English and knows every alternative route when the traffic backs up. Call Narcisse Taxi for an English-speaking, professional taxi driver and tour guide with a minivan. If your French is in order, you can call Radio Cabs.

Information **Narcisse Taxi** (☎0590/94–55–95). **Nicho's Reliable Taxi** (☎0590/74–86–85). **Radio Cabs** (☎0590/82–00–00, 0590/83–09–55, or 0590/20–74–74).

■ CONTACTS & RESOURCES

BANKS & EXCHANGE SERVICES

Few places accept U.S. dollars, so plan on exchanging them for euros. You must change cash or traveler's checks at your hotel (not all change money, and the rate will not be favorable) or a *bureau de change*, and not all of them take traveler's checks. One favorite company is Change Caraïbe, and it has branches near the tourist office and market in Pointe-à-Pitre.

It's easier to use your ATM card to get euros. Make sure you have a four-digit pin number. ATMs, particularly those in smaller towns, don't always accept foreign bank cards. Make sure you have enough cash on hand just in case. On Les Saintes, where there's no longer a bank, the post office will cash traveler's checks. Visa and MasterCard are the credit cards most often accepted, followed by American Express.

ELECTRICITY

Electricity is 220 volts, and plugs have two round prongs. If you're visiting from North America, you'll need both an adapter and a converter.

EMERGENCIES

SAMU is a medical service where you can get to see a doctor fast. However, the receptionists generally do not speak English. SOS Taxi Ambulance can transport you to a hospital quickly, but you may need to have a French-speaking person make the call. SMUR is both an ambulance service and an emergency room.

Emergency Services Ambulance (☎15). **Fire** (☎18). **Police emergencies** (☎17). **SAMU** (☎0590/89–11–00). **SMUR Ambulance of Basse-Terre** (☎0590/80–54–01). **SOS Taxi Ambulance** (☎0590/82–89–33).

Hospitals Centre Hôpitalier (✉Av. Gaston Feuillard, Basse-Terre, Basse-Terre ☎0590/80–54–00). **Centre Hôpitalier de Pointe-à-Pitre** (✉222 rte. Chauvel, Pointe-à-Pitre, Grande-Terre ☎0590/93–47–30 or 0590/89–07–12).

INTERNET, MAIL & SHIPPING

Pointe-à-Pitre has several Internet cafés, including Poly Info and Cyber Café, located mainly on backstreets; the tourist office can give you directions. In Gosier, Cyber Tiger sits across from the Sofitel Auberge de la Vieille Tour. At the St-François marina, there's L'Arobas Café. Expect to pay at least €4 an hour.

Postcards cost €0.80 to the United States, €0.95 to Canada; letters up to 20 grams are €0.80 to the United States, €0.95 to Canada. Stamps can be purchased at post offices, newsstands, tobacco shops, and souvenir shops. When writing to someone in Guadeloupe, be sure to include the name of the specific island in the archipelago (e.g., Grande-Terre, Basse-Terre, Iles des Saintes) as well as the postal code, then "Guadeloupe" followed by "French West Indies."

Information Le Caméléon a Gosier (✉Mare-gaillard, Gosier, Grand-Terre ☎0690/58–84–50). **Cyber Café** (✉20 rue Alexandre Isaac, at Place de Victoire, Pointe-à-Pitre, Grand-Terre). **Cyber Tiger** (✉Res. Grand Gosier Montauban, Gosier, Grand-Terre ☎0590/84–20–54). **L'Arobas Café** (✉La Marina, St-François, Grand-Terre ☎0590/97–17–16). **Poly Info** (✉29 rue Barbes, Pointe-à-Pitre, Grand-Terre ☎0590/20–38–95).

LANGUAGE

The official language is French, though most of the islanders also speak Creole, a lyrical patois that you won't be able to understand. Most of the staff in hotels knows some English as do some taxi drivers, but communicating is decidedly more difficult in the countryside. Arm yourself with a phrase book, a dictionary, patience, and a sense of humor.

SAFETY

Put your valuables in the hotel safe. Don't leave them unattended in your room or on the beach. If you rent a car, always lock it, with luggage and valuables—be it designer sunglasses or a laptop—stashed out of sight. It's not safe to walk around Pointe-à-Pitre at night.

TAXES & SERVICE CHARGES

The *taxe de séjour* (room tax), which varies from hotel to hotel, is usually €1 but never exceeds €1.80 per person per day. Most hotel prices include a 10% to 15% service charge in their rates; if not, it'll be added to your bill. A 15% service charge is included in all restaurant prices, as are taxes.

TELEPHONES

If you need to make many calls outside your hotel, purchase a *télécarte* at the post office or other outlet; these can be used in special phone booths to make cheaper local and international calls. Some hotels charge a connection fee if you use a card from your room phone. It's difficult, but not impossible, to place collect or credit-card calls to the United States.

To make on-island calls, dial 0590 (0690 if it is a cellular) and then the six-digit phone number. To call Guadeloupe from the United States, dial 00–590–590, then the local number. For cell phone numbers, dial 00–590–690, then the local number. If you're in one of the other islands in the French West Indies, dial 0590 and then the local number.

It's possible to buy a cell phone in Guadeloupe. The Orange offices at the airport and the one in Pointe-à-Pitre now accept most U.S. credit cards (but not Amex). You will probably not be able to buy a local SIM card to use in your own mobile phone.

Information Boutique Orange Aéroport (✉Aéroport International Pôle Caraïbes, Abymes ☎0590/21–13–36).

TIPPING

Restaurants are legally required to include a 15% service charge in the menu price, and no additional gratuity is necessary (although appreciated if service is particularly good). Tip skycaps and porters about €1 a bag. Many cab drivers own their own taxis and don't expect a tip. You won't have any trouble ascertaining if a 10% tip is expected. It's a look. Leaving the chambermaid a euro a night is always good form.

TOUR OPTIONS

Guadeloupe has a number of fun, professional tour operators. However, many of the tours are only conducted in French. Emeraude Guadeloupe offers everything from hikes up the volcano to visits to creole homes; guides are certified by the state, but you'll probably need some French to understand everything. GMG Voyage tours can usually be booked through your hotel. The company runs buses north of Basse-Terre to Carbet and to the Severine Distillery, traversing the route des Mamelles. The company also schedules trips to Basse-Terre that include a half-day sail.

Marius Voyages offers excursions to the southern and northern coasts of Basse-Terre; the latter includes a visit to the botanical gardens and a glass-bottom boat ride to Pigeon Island. Excursions go throughout Grande-Terre, providing transport to the ferries for Marie-Galante and Les Saintes; they can even get you to Martinique or Dominica for a couple of nights. Best of all, the company offers airport transfers to hotels in Ste-Anne and St-François for a mere €45 for one or two persons (€80 round-trip). This beats taxi prices and can eliminate the need for a rental car.

Information Emeraude Guadeloupe (✉St-Claude, Basse-Terre ☎0590/81–98–28). **GMG Voyage** (✉Gosier, Grand-Terre ☎0590/21–08–08). **Marius Voyages** (✉Main St., Ste-Anne, Grand-Terre ☎0590/88–19–80).

VISITOR INFORMATION

Information Comité du Tourisme des Iles de Guadeloupe (✉5 sq. de la Banque, Pointe-à-Pitre ☎0590/82–09–30 ⊕www.lesilesdeguadeloupe.com). **French Government Tourist Office** (⊕www.franceguide.com ☎514/288–1904 for public information line, 310/276–2835 in Los Angeles, 312/337–6339 in Chicago).

WEDDINGS

Since getting married in Guadeloupe has a long residency requirement, it's not really feasible to plan a wedding on the island, but it is an exotic honeymoon destination.

Jamaica

Kayaks on the beach at Montego Bay

WORD OF MOUTH

"My husband and I basically came out of this trip astounded at the bad reputation Jamaica gets."

—CaribTraveler

"I have been to many Caribbean beaches and have yet to find one that surpasses Negril when you factor in the local vibe, culture, and laid-backness elements."

—CaribbeanSoul

WELCOME TO JAMAICA

Bloody Bay got its name during the days when Negril was a whaling port; it's also where the pirate Calico Jack Rackham and his crew were captured.

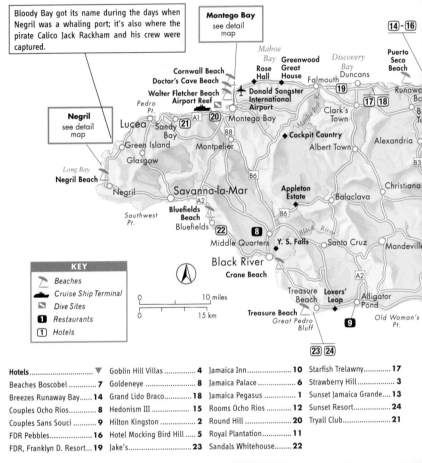

Montego Bay
see detail map

Negril
see detail map

KEY

- Beaches
- Cruise Ship Terminal
- Dive Sites
- **1** Restaurants
- **①** Hotels

0   10 miles

0   15 km

Chances are you will never fully understand Jamaica in all its delightful complexity, but you will probably have a good time trying. You can party in Negril, shop in Montego Bay, or simply relax at one of the island's many all-inclusive resorts, but you'll also discover culture and delicious island cuisine.

OUT OF MANY, ONE

The third-largest island in the Caribbean (after Cuba and Hispaniola), Jamaica is 146 mi (242 km) long and is slightly smaller than the state of Connecticut. It has a population of 2.7 million. With about 800,000 people, the capital, Kingston, is the largest English-speaking city south of Miami (in the Western Hemisphere, at least). The highest point is Blue Mountain Peak at 7,402 feet.

Although you will find spicy, smoky jerk everywhere around Jamaica, its traditional home is in the Boston Bay area, where it's sold in many roadside shacks.

13

JAMAICA

TOP 4 REASONS TO VISIT JAMAICA

① The all-inclusive resort was invented here, and the sprawling beachfront properties are among the best in the Caribbean.

② Golfers will be delighted by the many wonderful courses, primarily in the Montego Bay area.

③ Families will find every conceivable activity, great beaches, and many child-friendly resorts.

④ Jamaica has rich cultural traditions exhibited particularly in local music, art, and cuisine.

JAMAICA PLANNER

Island Activities

Negril has the island's best **beaches**, but there are also good beaches in the southwest and in Montego Bay. Despite the conservative culture of Jamaica, nude sunbathing is common at some resorts.

Tour operators will pick you up from your resort for a wide range of **activities.** Although diving isn't a top activity, dive operators work from all of the island's major resort areas.

Jamaica has some spectacular **golf courses,** the best of which are near Montego Bay.

You can go **rafting** on the slow, lazy Rio Grande, Martha Brae, Black, or White rivers.

Tour operators are coming up with new activities all the time. **Chukka Caribbean Adventures** operates ATV courses, canopy tours, horseback riding, and even a dogsledding adventure.

But as many people seem to be drawn to Jamaica for the music—particularly **reggae,** which originated on the island. **Bob Marley,** one of reggae's most famous stars, is an island legend, and a pilgrimage to the places that were meaningful to him is often on the tourist's agenda.

Logistics

Getting to Jamaica: Donald Sangster International Airport (MBJ), in **Montego Bay**, is the most efficient point of entry for travelers destined for MoBay, Ocho Rios, Runaway Bay, and Negril. Norman Manley International Airport (KIN), in **Kingston,** is the best arrival point for travelers headed to the capital, the south coast, or Port Antonio.

Hassle Factor: Low–High, depending on your distance from MoBay.

Nonstops: Atlanta (Air Jamaica, Delta), Baltimore (Air Jamaica), Charlotte (USAirways), Chicago (Air Jamaica, United), Dallas (American), Detroit (Northwest), Fort Lauderdale (Air Jamaica, Spirit), Houston (Continental), Memphis (Northwest), Miami (Air Jamaica, American), Minneapolis (Northwest), New York–JFK (Air Jamaica, American), New York–Newark (Air Jamaica, Continental), Orlando (Air Jamaica, Spirit), Philadelphia (Air Jamaica, USAirways), Washington, DC–Dulles (United).

On the Ground

If transfers are not included for your trip, you can get shared-van service from the airport in Montego Bay to your final destination. Port Antonio is difficult to reach from MoBay at this writing, so Kingston is a better airport for that destination.

Renting a Car: The average traveler should not rent a car in Jamaica. Rentals are possible but are difficult to arrange on arrival, so make a reservation before your trip. You must be at least 25 years old, have a valid driver's license (from any country), and have a valid credit card. You may be required to post a security of several hundred dollars before taking possession of your car; ask about it when you make the reservation. Rates are also quite expensive, averaging $70 to $120 a day after the addition of the compulsory insurance, which you must usually purchase even if your credit card offers it.

Where to Stay

Montego Bay has the largest concentration of resorts on the island; **Negril** is a more-relaxed haven on the west coast. Both offer a mix of large and small resorts, plus good nightlife. **Runaway Bay** and **Ocho Rios** are more than an hour east of MoBay. **Port Antonio,** a sleepy, laid-back haven, has a few resorts and a quiet atmosphere and is usually accessed by a short flight or long drive from Kingston. The **southwest coast** has a few small resorts, uncrowded beaches, and only one large resort. Few vacationers choose to stay in the capital, **Kingston,** but the immediate area also includes the **Blue Mountains** and the luxe Strawberry Hill resort.

All-inclusive Resorts: Jamaica was the birthplace of the Caribbean all-inclusive resort, which is still the most popular vacation option here. Several of these are open only to couples.

Small Hotels: Particularly in Negril, you'll find smaller, more unique hotels and inns that aren't part of the big chains; however, they aren't always cheap. The Island Outpost company operates several upscale boutique resorts all over Jamaica.

Small Inns: Inexpensive inns, though marketed primarily to European travelers who have more time to spend on the island, are often much less isolated than the big resorts.

Hotel & Restaurant Prices

⇨*For information on hotel meal plans, see Accommodations in Caribbean Essentials.*

WHAT IT COSTS IN U.S. DOLLARS

$$$$	$$$	$$	$	¢
Restaurants				
over $30	$20–$30	$12–$20	$8–$12	under $8
Hotels*				
over $350	$250–$350	$150–$250	$80–$150	under $80
Hotels**				
over $450	$350–$450	$250–$350	$125–$250	under $125

*EP, BP, CP **AI, FAP, MAP Restaurant prices are for a main course at dinner and include any taxes or service charges. Hotel prices are per night for a double room in high season, excluding taxes, service charges, and meal plans (except at all-inclusives).

When to Go

High season in Jamaica runs roughly from mid-December through April. From May through mid-December, you can save from 20% to as much as 40% on rates, more if you use value-oriented travel packagers. There are several annual events in Jamaica that draw huge numbers of visitors.

Air Jamaica's Jazz & Blues Festival is in Montego Bay each January.

In Ocho Rios, the biggest event of the year is the **Ocho Rios Jazz Festival** held each June.

Reggae Sumfest is usually sometime between mid-July and early August.

The **International Marlin Tournament** is held in Port Antonio every October.

The largest islandwide festival is **Carnival,** which is held in Kingston, Ocho Rios, and MoBay every March and April and in Negril every May.

By Paris
Permenter and
John Bigley

"DO YOU SEE THE ACKEE?" We were strolling the banks of the Black River on Jamaica's south coast when we heard the call of a man from a nearby car. He gestured up at an ordinary-looking tree we were near. Between its green leaves peeked small, red fruit, bursting open to reveal large, black seeds like eyes looking out at us. "That's ackee," he said. "We make our national dish from that fruit. You must try some while you are here!"

Jamaicans define enthusiasm. Whether the topic is ackee or dominoes, politics or Carnival, the spirit of this island comes out in every interaction. Although the island is well known for its tropical beauty, reggae music, and cuisine, you may find that your interactions with local residents are what you truly remember.

Although 95% of the population traces its bloodlines to Africa, Jamaica is a stockpot of cultures, including those of other Caribbean islands, Great Britain, the Middle East, India, China, Germany, Portugal, and South America. The third-largest island in the Caribbean (after Cuba and Hispaniola), Jamaica enjoys a considerable self-sufficiency based on tourism, agriculture, and mining.

The island is rich in beauty, but a quick look around reveals widespread poverty and a land where the disparity between the lives of the resort guests and the resort employees is often staggering. High unemployment rates and poor economic opportunities have created a crime problem, one that the tourism board and the government constantly work to resolve. Most safety concerns center on Kingston, with its gang violence. In truth, serious crimes against tourists are rare, but petty theft is sometimes a problem. Property theft is a problem across the island, and there are high rates of burglary and robbery almost everywhere. It's rare to find a middle-class home anywhere without burglar bars.

Where vacationers opt to make their Jamaican home away from home depends on factors ranging from the length of their vacation to personal interests. With its direct air connections to many cities in the United States, Montego Bay (or MoBay) is favored by Americans taking short trips; many properties are just minutes from the airport. Two hours east of the airport lies Ocho Rios (often just "Ochi"), a lush destination that's favored by honeymooners for its tropical beauty and myriad couples-only resorts. Ocho Rios is also a popular cruise port and where you can find one of the island's most recognizable attractions: the stair-step Dunn's River falls, which invites travelers to climb in daisy-chain fashion, hand-in-hand behind a sure-footed guide.

As you continue east from Ocho Rios (although many travelers opt to fly into Kingston and take a short flight), Port Antonio is considered the most beautiful, untouched area of Jamaica, a hideaway for the rich and famous since Errol Flynn first lived there.

More than an hour west of MoBay lies Negril, once a hippie haven and now a growing destination that still hangs on to its laid-back roots despite the addition of several expansive all-inclusive resorts in recent years.

The south coast is more attractive to those travelers looking for funky fun in small, one-of-a-kind resorts and an atmosphere that encourages them to get out and mingle in the community, whether that means a game of dominoes in a local rum shop or a bicycle trip to buy the day's catch from local fisherman. The beaches here don't have the white-sand beauty of their northern cousins, but this area is uncrowded and still largely undiscovered, although it's now home to a large couples-only all-inclusive resort.

Jamaica's capital city, Kingston, is a sharp contrast to the beach destinations. The largest English-speaking city in the western hemisphere south of Miami (with some 800,000 residents), this sprawling metropolis is primarily visited by business travelers or by those who want to learn more about the cultural side of Jamaica, thanks to its numerous galleries, theaters, and cultural programs. But if you really want to understand Jamaica, you can't ignore Kingston.

13

WHERE TO STAY

Jamaica was the birthplace of the Caribbean all-inclusive resort, a concept that started in Ocho Rios and has spread throughout the island, now comprising the lion's share of hotel rooms. Package prices usually include airport transfers, accommodations, three meals a day, snacks, all bar drinks (often including premium liquors) and soft drinks, a full menu of sports options (including scuba diving and golf at high-end establishments), nightly entertainment, and all gratuities and taxes. At most all-inclusive resorts, the only surcharges are for such luxuries as spa and beauty treatments, telephone calls, tours, vow-renewal ceremonies, and weddings (though even weddings are often included at high-end establishments).

The all-inclusive market is especially strong with couples and honeymooners. To maintain a romantic atmosphere (no Marco Polo games by the pool), some resorts have minimum age requirements ranging from 12 to 18. Other properties court families with tempting supervised kids' programs, family-friendly entertainment, and in-room amenities especially for young travelers.

KINGSTON

Visited by few vacationers but a frequent destination for business travelers and visitors with a deep interest in Jamaica heritage and culture, the sprawling city of Kingston is home to some of the island's finest business hotels. Skirting the city are the Blue Mountains, a completely different world from the urban frenzy of the capital city.

$$$$
Fodor'sChoice
★

Strawberry Hill. A 45-minute drive from Kingston—but worlds apart in terms of atmosphere—this exclusive resort was developed by Chris Blackwell, former head of Island Records (the late Bob Marley's label). Perched in the Blue Mountains, it's where the rich and famous go to retreat and relax. The resort has a pool, though this is one Jamaican property not for beach buffs but for those in search of gourmet dining, Aveda spa treatments, and pure relaxation in Georgian-style villas. The villas survey the Blue Mountains from expansive porches, most with an oversize hammock. Every bed has an electric mattress pad to warm things up on chilly evenings; mosquito nets surround you—because there's no air-conditioning, guests usually prefer to keep windows open, which can make it buggy. **Pros:** Stylish accommodations with great mountain views, cool retreat from the heat, best spa in Jamaica. **Cons:** Remote location, limited on-site dining options, too quiet for some guests. ⊠*New Castle Rd., Irishtown* 📞*876/944–8400* ⊕*www. islandoutpost.com* 🛏*12 villas* ⌂*In-room: no a/c, safe, kitchen (some), DVD. In-hotel: restaurant, room service, bar, pool, spa, bicycles, no elevator, laundry service, airport shuttle* ⊟*AE, D, MC, V* �"○"*CP.*

$–$$$ 🏨 **Jamaica Pegasus.** In the heart of the financial district, this 17-story high-rise is popular with business travelers due to its location and business amenities. Popular with locals, the hotel's restaurant offers plenty of Jamaican favorites, such as braised oxtail and grilled snapper. All rooms have balconies and large windows that face the Blue Mountains, the pool, or the Caribbean. There's an excellent business center, duty-free shops, and 24-hour room service. **Pros:** Good business travel facilities, good pool area, easy access to New Kingston business district. **Cons:** Limited leisure activities, no wireless access in guest rooms, 17 floors of guest rooms can mean a wait for an elevator. ⊠*81 Knutsford Blvd., Box 333* 📞*876/926–3690* ⊕*www.jamaicapegasus.com* 🛏*300 rooms, 19 suites* ⌂*In-room: safe, refrigerator (some), Ethernet, dial-up. In-hotel: 3 restaurants, room service, bars, tennis courts, pool, gym, spa, laundry service, concierge, executive floor, public Internet, public Wi-Fi, airport shuttle, parking (no fee), no-smoking rooms* ⊟*AE, D, DC, MC, V* "○"*EP.*

$–$$ 🏨 **Hilton Kingston.** With all the standard amenities travelers expect to see at a high-rise chain hotel, this property ranks as a favorite with business travelers. The expansive marble lobby leads to attractive, well-appointed rooms. The concierge floors offer complimentary cocktails, hors d'oeuvres, and Continental breakfast. Extras include secured-access elevators and in-room coffee and tea setups. **Pros:** Good variety of restaurants, central location, nightly entertainment. **Cons:** Limited leisure activities, limited in-room amenities in most room classes, no balconies. ⊠*77 Knutsford Blvd., Box 112* 📞*876/926–5430* ⊕*www. hiltoncaribbean.com* 🛏*290 rooms, 13 suites* ⌂*In-room: safe, kitchen (some), refrigerator, Ethernet, dial-up. In-hotel: 4 restaurants, room service, bars, pool, gym, spa, laundry service, concierge, executive floor, public Internet, public Wi-Fi, parking (no fee), no-smoking rooms* ⊟*AE, D, DC, MC, V* "○"*CP.*

PORT ANTONIO

There's a sure antidote to the tourist scene in Jamaica's bustling resorts Montego Bay and Ocho Rios: Port Antonio. This quiet community is on Jamaica's east end, 133 mi (220 km) west of Montego Bay, and is favored by those looking to get away from it all. Don't look for mixology classes or limbo dances here; this end of Jamaica is quiet and relaxed. The fun is usually found outdoors, followed by a fine evening meal. The area's must-do activities include rafting Jamaica's own Rio Grande, snorkeling or scuba diving in the Blue Lagoon, exploring the Nonsuch Caves, and having lunch or a drink at the Jamaica Palace.

$$ 🏨 **Jamaica Palace.** The Jamaica Palace might be distinctive for its Jamaica-shape swimming pool and surrounding black-and-white pool terrace—but that's just the beginning of the unusual aspects of this Port Antonio hotel. The white building, marked with palatial columns indoors and out, is designed to resemble a 17th-century Italian palace. Deemed "the art gallery hotel," the facility displays 2,000 pieces of art from paintings to sculptures, some by the hotel's owner. Inside, guest rooms are surprisingly stark, most having beds with curving footboards, flowery spreads, and little other decoration. Pros: Uniquely decorated public areas, large poolside area with plenty of seating, good on-site dining options. Cons: No beach, basic guest rooms, somewhat remote location. ✉ *Box 277, Port Antonio* ☎ *876/993–7720* ⊕ *www.jamaica-palacehotel.com* ♒ *34 rooms, 46 suites* ⚒ *In-room: safe, dialup. In-hotel: 2 restaurants, room service, bars, pool, no elevator, laundry service, public Internet, public Wi-Fi, parking (no fee)* ▭ *MC, V* ⊙ *EP.*

$–$$ 🏨 **Goblin Hill Villas at San San.** This lush 12-acre estate atop a hill overlooking San San Bay is best suited for travelers looking for a home-away-from-home atmosphere, not a bustling resort. Each attractively appointed villa comes with its own dramatic view, plus a staff member to do the grocery shopping, cleaning, and cooking for you. Villas come equipped with cable TV, ceiling fans (with air-conditioning in the bedrooms only), and tropical furnishings; it's sometimes possible to rent the bedroom of one of the two-bedroom villas for a lower per-night cost. The beach is a 10-minute walk away. Excellent car-rental packages are available. Pros: Good for guests who would like a villa experience but the facilities of a hotel, nice bay views from villa terraces and balconies, spacious accommodations. Cons: Long walk to beach, shared lawn and public areas with other villas at complex, somewhat remote location. ✉ *Box 26, San San* ☎ *876/925–8108* ⊕ *www.goblin-hill.com* ♒ *28 villas* ⚒ *In-room: no a/c (some), no phone, kitchen, refrigerator. In-hotel: bar, tennis courts, pool, no elevator* ▭ *AE, D, MC, V* ⊙ *EP.*

$–$$ 🏨 **Hotel Mocking Bird Hill.** With only 10 rooms, some overlooking the sea and all with views of lush hillsides, Mocking Bird Hill is much more like a cozy bed-and-breakfast than a hotel. Owners Barbara Walker and Shireen Aga run an environmentally sensitive operation, with bamboo instead of hardwood furniture, solar-heated water, meals made with local produce in the Mille Fleurs dining terrace, locally produced toiletries and stationery sets, and 7 naturally landscaped acres. There's a free shuttle to Frenchman's Cove beach, about a five-minute drive away. Wedding packages are available. Pros: Numerous ecotourism options, environmentally conscious, excellent dining. Cons: Limited on-site dining, somewhat remote location. ✉ *N. Coast Hwy., Point Ann, Box 254, Port Antonio* ☎ *876/993–7267* ⊕ *www.hotelmocking-*

13

birdhill.com ⟳*10 rooms* ☐*In-room: no a/c, no phone, safe. In-hotel: restaurant, bar, pool, no elevator, laundry service, no-smoking rooms* ▤*AE, MC, V* ▯◯▮*MAP.*

OCHO RIOS

Ocho Rios lies on the north coast, halfway between Port Antonio and MoBay. Rivers, waterfalls, fern-shaded roads, and tropical lushness fill this fertile region. It's a favorite with honeymooners as well as Jamaicans, who like to escape crowded Kingston for the weekend. The area's resorts, hotels, and villas are all a short drive from the frenetic, traffic-clogged downtown, which has a crafts market, boutiques, duty-free shops, restaurants, and several scenic attractions. The community lies 67 mi (111 km) east of Montego Bay, a drive that takes just under two hours thanks to an improved highway.

$$$$ ▦**Beaches Boscobel Resort & Golf Club.** Although this resort is for any-
☼ one—including singles and couples—it's best suited for families, whose
★ children enjoy supervised activities in one of five kids' clubs divided by age, from infants to teens. Some rooms have pull-out sofas, and there are also connecting rooms for large families. Children under age 2 stay free, and special rates cover children under age 16 sharing a room with a parent. The all-inclusive program here is extensive and includes activities for all members of the family as well as nightly activities. Pros: Excellent children's program, numerous dining options, good options for adults including spa and adults restaurants. Cons: Long drive from the airport, beach is a long walk (or an elevator ride) from the rooms, resort is distant from Ocho Rios attractions. ⊠*N. Coast Hwy., Box 2, St. Ann's Bay* ☏*876/975–7777* ⊕*www.beaches.com* ⟳*120 rooms, 110 suites* ☐*In-room: safe, refrigerator. In-hotel: 5 restaurants, bars, tennis courts, pools, gym, spa, beachfront, diving, water sports, children's programs (ages infant–17), laundry service, concierge, public Internet, airport shuttle, parking (no fee), no-smoking rooms* ⟳*2-night minimum* ▤*AE, MC, V* ▯◯▮*AI.*

$$$$ ▦**Couples Ocho Rios.** Renovations in 2004 spiffed up the guest rooms of Jamaica's first all-inclusive resort. Though similar to a Sandals in its creation of a romantic, cozy atmosphere, this Couples resort isn't quite as upscale and tends to draw a somewhat older repeat clientele. Connected by long hallways, rooms are a short walk from the beach; a handful of villa suites are tucked back in the gardens with private plunge pools or hot tubs. The resort is on a nice stretch of beach, and there's also a private island where you can sunbathe in the buff if you want. Weddings are included in the package, as are several off-site excursions. **Pros:** Numerous dining options, free weddings, private island for clothing-optional sunbathing. **Cons:** Long hallways, drab public areas, villas far from the beach. ⊄*Box 330, Tower Isle, St. Mary* ☏*876/975–4271* ⊕*www.couples.com* ⟳*189 rooms, 17 suites* ☐*In-room: safe, refrigerator (some). In-hotel: 5 restaurants, bars, tennis courts, pools, gym, spa, beachfront, diving, water sports, concierge, public Internet, airport shuttle, parking (no fee), no kids under 18* ⟳*3-night minimum* ▤*AE, D, MC, V* ▯◯▮*AI.*

$$$$ 🏨 **Couples Sans Souci Resort & Spa.** This pampering all-inclusive emphasizes relaxation. Rooms—all of which are suites—are soothing, with tile floors, plush linens, large balconies, and a style more Mediterranean than Caribbean. Bathrooms are particularly large and luxurious. Romantic oceanfront suites have oversize whirlpool tubs. Guests have their choice of beaches (one clothing-optional), though both have pebbly sand, and neither is as appealing as the pools. Though the resort is open to couples only, they do not have to be male-female couples. Pros: Excellent spa, upscale accommodations, property is spacious and feels uncrowded. Cons: Some rooms are a long walk from the beach, public areas are a long walk from some rooms, beaches are not as good as others in area. ⊠ *N. Coast Hwy., 2 mi (3 km) east of Ocho Rios, Mammee Bay* ☎ *876/994–1206* ⊕ *www.couples.com* ➟ *148 suites* ⚹ *In-room: safe, refrigerator (some). In-hotel: 4 restaurants, room service, bars, tennis courts, pools, gym, spa, beachfront, no elevator, concierge, laundry service, airport shuttle, no kids under 18* ➣ *3-night minimum* ⊟ *AE, D, DC, MC, V* ⋈ *AI.*

13

$$$$ 🏨 **Goldeneye.** Whether you're a James Bond buff or just a fan of luxury **Fodor's Choice** getaways, this exclusive address 20 minutes east of Ocho Rios holds ★ special appeal. Once the home of Bond author Ian Fleming, the estate is now one of the unique Island Outpost properties. The resort consists of Fleming's home, with three bedrooms and three outdoor baths, as well as a media room, kitchen, and its own private pool and beach. The 15-acre property includes the main house, complete with its own private pool and beach, and three villas tucked into the lush gardens, each with outdoor showers and lots of privacy. Plans call for the addition of more villas as well as a private residential section. Pros: Unique and spacious accommodations, excellent food, plenty of privacy. Cons: Remote location, limited dining options, may be too quiet for some travelers. ⊠ *N. Coast Hwy., Oracabessa* ☎ *876/975–3354* ⊕ *www.islandoutpost.com* ➟ *1 house, 3 villas* ⚹ *In-room: no a/c (some), safe, kitchen, refrigerator, DVD, VCR, Wi-Fi. In-hotel: restaurant, bar, pool (some), beachfront, water sports, no elevator, concierge, parking (no fee)* ⊟ *AE, D, MC, V* ⋈ *AI.*

$$$$ 🏨 **Jamaica Inn.** Start a conversation about elegant Jamaican resorts, and this quietly sophisticated hotel will surely be mentioned. A historic favorite with the rich and famous (one suite is named for guest Winston Churchill), this pricey, genteel resort is known for its attentive staff. Each suite has its own verandah (larger than most hotel rooms) on the private cove's powdery, champagne-color beach. The cliff-top spa is known for its ayurveda and Fijian treatments. Pros: Elegant accommodations, exceptional service, good spa. Cons: Some travelers may feel it's too quiet, too traditional and stiff for some visitors, no in-room television. ⊠ *N. Coast Hwy., east of Ocho Rios, Box 1* ☎ *876/974–2514* ⊕ *www.jamaicainn.com* ➟ *47 suites* ⚹ *In-room: no TV. In-hotel: restaurant, room service, bars, pool, gym, spa, beachfront, water sports, no elevator, laundry service, concierge, no kids under 10 (Apr. 15–Dec. 15), no kids under 12 (Dec. 15–Apr. 15), parking (no fee)* ⊟ *AE, D, MC, V* ⋈ *EP.*

$$$$ 🏨 **Royal Plantation.** Formerly the Royal Plantation at Beaches, this small, adults-only resort now operates independently. More exclusive than any of its sister properties in the Sandals or Beaches chains, the resort puts an emphasis on personal service, fine dining, and a refined atmosphere and does not offer an all-inclusive plan. Built high atop a bluff, it has a feel of exclusivity; all rooms, which are suites, have ocean views, not to mention luxurious bedding, fully stocked in-room bars, CD players, mahogany furniture, and marble baths, many with whirlpool tubs. The most expensive suites have special check-in and luggage services; optional butler service is also available. Steps lead to the beach, where the luxury continues with the services of a beach butler. Pros: Accommodations are expansive and stylish, good dining, room service. Cons: Guest rooms and beach are on different levels, small pool, small beach. ⊠ *N. Coast Hwy., Box 2* ☎ *876/974–5601* ⊕ *www. royalplantation.com* ⇌ *74 suites* ⌂ *In-room: safe, VCR (some), dial-up. In-hotel: 4 restaurants, room service, tennis courts, pool, gym, spa, beachfront, diving, water sports, concierge, no kids under 18* ⟳ *2-night minimum* ⊟ *AE, MC, V* �🍽 *EP.*

$$$ 🏨 **Sunset Jamaica Grande Resort & Spa.** Jamaica's largest conference hotel,
ⓒ   which is right in Ocho Rios, bustles with groups thanks to its expansive conference center. Following an extensive 2005 renovation, it now welcomes a larger percentage of leisure travelers. Rooms, brightened with tropical colors, are divided between two high-rise towers; the best views are found in the north tower. Many guests spend their time at the pool complex, which is built as a replica of Dunn's River falls and includes a meandering river. Kids are kept busy in the complimentary Club Mongoose activity program, and parents can play in an 80-machine slot and video blackjack room. Teens can head to the Jamrock Teen Center. Pros: Nice pool complex, good location for exploring Ocho Rios, good sunset views from some rooms. Cons: Mix of leisure and convention clientele, some restaurants feel crowded, rooms are basic. ⊠ *Main St., Box 100* ☎ *876/974–2200* ⊕ *www.sunsetjamaicagrande.com* ⇌ *730 rooms, 12 suites* ⌂ *In-room: safe, refrigerator (some), dial-up. In-hotel: 6 restaurants, bars, tennis courts, pools, gym, spa, beachfront, water sports, concierge, children's programs (ages 2–12), laundry facilities, laundry service* ⊟ *AE, D, DC, MC, V* �🍽 *AI.*

$ 🏨 **Rooms Ocho Rios.** Adjacent to Sunset Jamaica Grande Resort, this SuperClubs-owned hotel, as its name suggests, has a room-only plan (though with Continental breakfast). Formerly Club Jamaica, the family-friendly hotel offers wireless Internet access. It's favored by business travelers and vacationers who plan to explore the region rather than make a resort their primary destination. Rooms have ocean views and all the basics, decorated in tropical tones. It's an economical choice for independent-minded travelers who would rather sample the town's many restaurants than be tied to an all-inclusive plan. Pros: Good value, good beach, good location from which to explore Ocho Rios. Cons: Small pool area, limited on-site dining options, limited activities. ⊠ *Main St.* ☎ *876/974–6632* ⊕ *www.roomsresorts.com* ⇌ *92 rooms, 5 suites* ⌂ *In-room: safe, kitchen (some), Ethernet, Wi-Fi. In-hotel: restaurant, room service, bar, pool, gym, beachfront, water sports, no*

Other Sandals Resorts on Jamaica

CLOSE UP

The Sandals company has the most hotels of any company on Jamaica. Sandals resorts are open only to couples and are all-inclusive in their pricing. In addition to our favorites, which are reviewed in full in this chapter, the following resorts are also available.

Sandals Dunn's River Villaggio Golf Resort & Spa (⊠ N. Coast Hwy., 2 mi [3 km] east of Ocho Rios, Mammee Bay ☎ 876/972–1610 ⊕ www.sandals.com). Renovated in 2005, this resort lacks extensive facilities, but it has a nice spa and allows guests to shuttle over to other Ocho Rios–area Sandals properties. 243 rooms, 16 suites.

Sandals Grande Ocho Rios Beach & Villa Resort (⊠ N. Coast Hwy., Box 2, Ocho Rios ☎ 876/974–5691 ⊕ www.sandals.com). The largest resort in the Sandals chain includes the "manor" side with greathouse and villas and the "riviera" side with easy beach access. Villas, some fairly far from the public areas, have private pools; some villas have as many as four individual guest suites, each with its own kitchen and living area, that share a single pool. 285 rooms, 244 villas.

Sandals Inn (⊠ Kent Ave., Montego Bay ☎ 876/952–4140 ⊕ www.sandals.com). This small hotel right in MoBay, renovated in 2005, is at the end of Doctor's Cave beach. Guests can catch a shuttle to the other MoBay properties. 52 rooms.

Sandals Montego Bay (⊠ Kent Ave., Montego Bay ☎ 876/952–5510 ⊕ www.sandals.com). Minutes from the airport, this resort is on the largest stretch of beach in MoBay. The almond block of rooms and extensive beach are the resort's best features. 244 rooms.

Sandals Negril Beach Resort & Spa (⊠ Norman Manley Blvd., Negril ☎ 876/957–5216 ⊕ www.sandals.com) is at the top of Seven Mile Beach; in 2007, a block of Negril's first swim-up rooms was added. 137 rooms, 86 suites.

elevator, laundry facilities, laundry service, public Internet, public Wi-Fi, parking (no fee), no-smoking rooms ☰ AE, D, MC, V ⦿ CP.

RUNAWAY BAY

The smallest of the resort areas, Runaway Bay, 50 mi (80 km) east of Montego Bay and about 12 mi (19.5 km) west of Ocho Rios, has a handful of modern hotels, a few all-inclusive resorts, and an 18-hole golf course.

$$$$ **FDR, Franklyn D. Resort.** A favorite for families with very young children, this relaxed resort goes a step beyond the usual supervised kids' programs, assigning you a professional caregiver who will assist you throughout your stay. Kids can take part in a supervised club, but a nanny also assists with in-room help from washing out bathing suits to supervising naps. Guests enjoy spacious one-, two-, and three-bedroom suites. Children under six stay and eat free when staying in a room with their parents. Pros: Good supervised kids' programs, nanny program especially good for young families, spacious accommodations.

Cons: Not appealing to travelers without children, small pool area, rooms need updating. ⊙ *Main St., Runaway Bay* ☎ *876/973–4591* ⊕ *www.fdrholidays.com* ⤝ *76 suites* ⌂ *In-room: safe, kitchen, refrigerator, Ethernet, Wi-Fi. In-hotel: 4 restaurants, bars, tennis court, pool, gym, beachfront, diving, water sports, bicycles, no elevator, children's programs (ages newborn–16), laundry facilities, laundry service, public Wi-Fi, airport shuttle, no-smoking rooms* ☰ *AE, D, MC, V* ⦿ *AI.*

$$$$ 🏨 **Grand Lido Braco.** If you want to experience a Jamaican village almost Disney-style, this resort's for you. Fifteen minutes west of Runaway Bay, the resort is built

TAKING IT OFF

Both Grand Lido Braco and Hedonism III give you an opportunity to go nude. In fact, an entire section of each resort is set aside for nudists. At Grand Lido Braco, the nude rooms are actually all suites that were originally planned as family rooms. In most places in Jamaica, letting it all hang out comes at a premium of up to 20% above the regular rates. You can also take it off at clothing-optional beaches at Hedonism II, Grand Lido Negril, Couples Ocho Rios, Couples Sans Souci, Sunset Beach Resort & Spa, and others.

around a "village" complete with a town square with a fruit lady and peanut man. You can also find the island's largest clothing-optional facilities, which include a pool, hot tub, grill, and tennis courts. The beach—both clothed and clothing-optional sides—is expansive, although not Jamaica's best strip of sand; the large pool complex provides a popular option. Rooms have all the basic amenities but are not very large. Pros: Upscale all-inclusive, 9-hole golf course within walking distance of rooms, separate clothing-optional facilities from beach to tennis courts to grill. Cons: Pebbly beach, some visitors may not like theme park–type creation of Jamaican village, somewhat remote for exploring Ocho Rios attractions. ⊠ *N. Coast Hwy., between Duncans and Rio Bueno, Trelawny* ⊙ *Rio Bueno P.O., Trelawny, Jamaica, WI* ☎ *876/954–0000* ⊕ *www.superclubs.com* ⤝ *226 rooms, 58 suites* ⌂ *In-room: safe. In-hotel: 5 restaurants, room service, bars, golf course, tennis courts, pools, gym, spa, beachfront, diving, water sports, no elevator, concierge, laundry service, public Internet, public Wi-Fi, airport shuttle, no kids under 16* ⥁ *2-night minimum* ☰ *AE, D, DC, MC, V* ⦿ *AI.*

$$$–$$$$ 🏨 **Hedonism III.** Like its more-spartan cousin in Negril, Hedonism III is an adults-only hotel for travelers looking for unsubdued fun that includes a circus clinic and waterslide (through the disco, no less). Unlike its Negril equivalent, however, Hedonism III offers luxurious rooms and Jamaica's first swim-up rooms. The guest rooms, each with mirrored ceilings, have Jacuzzis and CD players. The beach is divided into "nude" and "prude" sides, although a quick look shows that most people leave the suits at home. Scheduled activities include nude body painting and volleyball; the resort even holds Jamaica's only nude weddings. Pros: Swim-up guest rooms, rooms more upscale than Hedonism II, around-the-clock activities. Cons: Spring-break-for-adults–type atmosphere, beach is not as good as others in area, not for travelers looking for a quiet getaway. ⊠ *Main Rd.* ⌂ *Box 250, Ocho Rios, Jamaica, WI* ☎ *876/973–4100* ⊕ *www. superclubs.com* ⇌ *210 rooms, 15 suites* ⌂ *In-room: safe, refrigerator (some). In-hotel: 5 restaurants, bars, tennis courts, pools, gym, spa, beachfront, diving, water sports, no elevator, airport shuttle, no kids under 18* ⊂ *2-night minimum* ⊟ *AE, D, DC, MC, V* ⊙ *AI.*

$$$ ⚏ **Breezes Runaway Bay.** This moderately priced SuperClubs resort, which underwent an extensive renovation and expansion and reopened in 2007, emphasizes an active, sports-oriented vacation—including golf (at the resort's own course), a circus workshop, tennis, and an array of water sports. Expert instruction and top-rate equipment are part of the package. Guests—often Germans, Italians, and Japanese—flock here to dive and snorkel around the reef off the beach, which also makes the bay superbly smooth for swimming. There's also a good golf school. Pros: Extensive sports and water sports options, good food, low-rise room blocks mean easy beach access. Cons: Some public areas can feel crowded, small spa, some restaurants are too small to accommodate demand. ⊠ *N. Coast Hwy., Box 58* ☎ *876/973–6099* ⊕ *www.superclubs.com* ⇌ *220 rooms, 46 suites* ⌂ *In-room: safe, refrigerator, dial-up, Wi-Fi. In-hotel: 5 restaurants, bars, golf course, tennis courts, pools, gym, spa, beachfront, diving, water sports, bicycles, no elevator, laundry service, public Internet, public Wi-Fi, airport shuttle, parking (no fee), no kids under 14, no-smoking rooms* ⊂ *2-night minimum* ⊟ *AE, D, DC, MC, V* ⊙ *AI.*

> **KEEPING IT ON**
>
> If you'd rather enjoy the beach in your swimsuit, remember that most of Jamaica's resorts cater to the traditional beachgoer (and all public beaches require swimsuits by law). Some resorts such as Grand Lido Negril offer "clothing-optional" beaches, which means you're free to keep your swimsuit (or as much of it) on as you like. Only beaches deemed "nude" actually require a birthday-suit dress code.

13

MONTEGO BAY

MoBay has miles of hotels, villas, apartments, and duty-free shops. Although without much cultural stimulus, it presents a comfortable island backdrop for the many conventions it hosts. And it has the added advantage of being the closest resort area to the island's main airport.

$$$$ ⚏ **Half Moon.** With its many room categories, massive villas (with three ☉ to seven bedrooms), shopping village, hospital, school, dolphin swims, ★ golf course, and equestrian center, Half Moon almost seems more like a town than a mere resort. What started out in 1954 as a group of private beach cottages offered for rent during off-season months has blossomed into one of Jamaica's most extensive resorts. Those beach cottages are still available and—just steps away from the sand as well as public areas—remain a great choice. The resort is also home to the island's newest spa, Fern Tree Spa, which opened in 2007 as the island's largest. Pros: Huge beach, many room categories including villas,

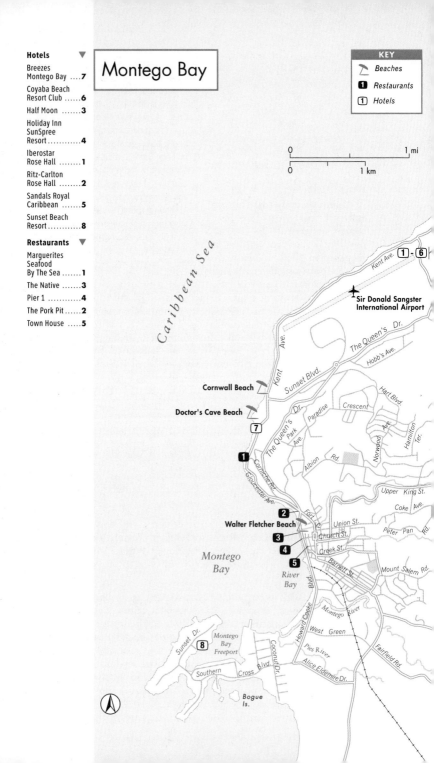

Montego Bay

KEY

⟋ *Beaches*

1 *Restaurants*

[1] *Hotels*

0 ————————— 1 mi

0 ————————— 1 km

Caribbean Sea

Sir Donald Sangster
International Airport

Kent Ave.

The Queen's Dr.

Hobb's Ave.

Hart Blvd.

Sunset Blvd.

Kent Ave.

Cornwall Beach

Doctor's Cave Beach

[7]

The Queen's Dr.

Paradise

Crescent

The Queen's Park Ave.

Norwood Ave.

Hamilton Ter.

1

Albion Rd.

Gloucester Ave.

Corniche Rd.

Upper King St.

Coke Ave.

2

Fort St.

Union St.

Peter Pan Rd.

Walter Fletcher Beach

3

Church St.

4

Creek St.

5

Barnett St.

Mount Salem Rd.

*Montego
Bay*

*River
Bay*

Montego River

Howard Cooke Blvd.

West Green

Sunset Dr.

8

*Montego
Bay
Freeport*

Coconut Dr.

Pies River

Fairfield Rd.

Southern Cross Blvd.

Alice Eldemire Dr.

*Bogue
Is.*

numerous on-site activities. Cons: Some accommodations are a long walk from public areas, some activities are not within walking distance, some accommodations are more recently renovated than others. ⊠ *N. Coast Hwy., 7 mi (11 km) east of Montego Bay* ✆ *Box 80, Montego Bay* ☎ *876/953–2211* ⊕ *www.halfmoon.com* ➳ *34 rooms, 164 suites, 33 villas* ♻ *In-room: safe, kitchen (some), refrigerator, dial-up, Wi-Fi (some). In-hotel: 6 restaurants, room service, bars, golf course, tennis courts, pools, gym, spa, beachfront, diving, water sports, bicycles, no elevator, children's programs (ages infants–17), laundry service, concierge, public Internet, public Wi-Fi, airport shuttle, parking (no fee), no-smoking rooms* ☐ *AE, D, DC, MC, V* ⦿ *EP.*

13

$$$$ 🏨 **Ritz-Carlton Golf & Spa Resort, Rose Hall, Jamaica.** A favorite with conference groups, golfers, and anyone demanding the highbrow service for which the chain is known, this expansive resort lies across the road from the historic Rose Hall estate. Although the luxury hotel is elegant and has solid service, little here sets the mood of a Caribbean resort except its beachfront location and water-sports offerings. If you like high tea, it's offered daily. Along with a full-service spa, there's a fully supervised children's club, making it a popular choice for families. Pros: Excellent meeting and business travel facilities, great golf, good children's program. Cons: Generic atmosphere, small beach, somewhat formal atmosphere for a family-friendly resort. ⊠ *1 Ritz Carlton Dr., St. James* ☎ *876/953–2800* ⊕ *www.ritzcarlton.com* ➳ *427 rooms* ♻ *In-room: safe, refrigerator. In-hotel: 6 restaurants, bars, golf course, tennis courts, pool, gym, spa, beachfront, diving, water sports, concierge, children's programs (ages 5–12), public Internet, public Wi-Fi, airport shuttle* ☐ *AE, D, DC, MC, V* ⦿ *EP.*

$$$$ 🏨 **Round Hill Hotel & Villas.** A favorite of celebrities thanks to its private
★ and elegant villas, this peaceful resort 8 mi (13 km) west of MoBay also offers 36 traditional hotel rooms in the Pineapple House. The hotel rooms are decorated in a refined Ralph Lauren style—done by the designer himself, who owns one of the 27 villas that dot the resort's 98 acres. Each villa includes a personal maid and a cook to make your breakfast, and most have private pools. It's a fairly quiet place, with a small beach and limited dining options, but most guests return again and again because of the personal service and excellent management. Pros: Personal service, stylish accommodations, quiet atmosphere. Cons: Somewhat remote location, costly, some villas do not have pools. ⊠ *N. Coast Hwy., Montego Bay* ☎ *876/956–7050* ⊕ *www.roundhill jamaica.com* ➳ *36 rooms, 27 villas* ♻ *In-room: refrigerator, dial-up. In-hotel: restaurant, room service, bar, tennis courts, pool, gym, spa, beachfront, diving, water sports, concierge, no elevator* ☐ *AE, D, DC, MC, V* ⦿ *EP.*

$$$$ 🏨 **Sandals Royal Caribbean Resort & Private Island.** Four miles (6.5 km) east of the airport, this elegant resort—the most upscale of the three Sandals properties in MoBay—consists of Jamaican-style buildings arranged in a semicircle around attractive gardens. Less boisterous than Sandals Montego Bay, it offers a few more-civilized touches, including afternoon tea. In the evenings, a colorful "dragon boat" transports you to Sandals's private island for meals at an Indonesian restaurant. Pros:

Numerous room categories, offshore dining, complimentary shuttle to other Sandals resorts in Montego Bay. Cons: Some guests might feel the resort is too quiet, smaller beach than Sandals Montego Bay, couples-only policy means some guests can't stay here. ⊠ *N. Coast Hwy.* ⌖ *Box 167, Montego Bay* ☎*876/953–2231* ⊕*www.sandals. com* ⥱*176 rooms, 14 suites* ♿*In-room: safe, refrigerator (some), Ethernet. In-hotel: 4 restaurants, room service (some), bars, tennis courts, pools, gym, spa, beachfront, diving, water sports, no elevator, laundry service, concierge, public Internet, airport shuttle, parking (no fee), no kids under 18, no-smoking rooms* ⌖*2-night minimum* ▱*AE, D, DC, MC, V* ⫴*AI.*

$$$$ ▧ **Tryall Club.** Well known among golfers, Tryall lies 15 mi (24 km)
★   west of MoBay. The sumptuous villas—each of which has a private pool—and pampering staff lend a home-away-from-home atmosphere. The beautiful seaside golf course is considered one of the meanest in the world and hosts big-money tournaments. Golfers are more than willing to accept the relative isolation for easy access to the great course, but this resort is even farther out than Round Hill. Pros: Excellent golf, villa experience with the conveniences of a resort, good family program. Cons: Remote location, shared public facilities, somewhat formal. ⊠ *N. Coast Hwy., Sandy Bay* ☎*876/956–5660* ⊕*www.tryallclub.com* ⥱*56 villas* ♿*In-room: kitchen. In-hotel: restaurant, bars, golf course, tennis courts, pool, gym, spa, beachfront, water sports, children's programs (ages 5–12), no elevator* ▱*AE, D, DC, MC, V* ⫴*EP.*

$$$–$$$$ ▧ **Coyaba Beach Resort & Club.** Owners Joanne and Kevin Robertson live on the grounds of this small resort, interacting with guests and giving the intimate property a relaxing, welcoming ambience. From the plantation-style greathouse to the guest rooms, which are decorated with colonial prints and hand-carved mahogany furniture, you feel the graciousness and comforting atmosphere reminiscent of a country inn. Pros: Quiet atmosphere of an inn, excellent restaurants, good-size private beach. Cons: Located directly on North Coast Highway, fairly small pool, climb to third-floor rooms can be difficult without elevator. ⊠ *Montego Bay, Little River* ☎*876/953–9150* ⊕*www.coyaba-resortjamaica.com* ⥱*50 rooms* ♿*In-room: safe, refrigerator (some). In-hotel: 3 restaurants, room service, bars, tennis court, pool, gym, spa, beachfront, water sports, no elevator, laundry service, concierge, public Internet, parking (no fee), no-smoking rooms* ▱*AE, D, MC, V* ⫴*EP.*

$$$–$$$$ ▧ **FDR, Pebbles.** A slightly more-grown-up version of its sister resort,
☺   FDR, Pebbles bills itself as a soft-adventure experience for families. Although you're still assigned a vacation nanny for personalized babysitting if you have young kids, the family experience is taken a step further here with many more supervised programs for teens, including campouts. Thirty minutes east of Montego Bay, the resort has the feel of a campground, with wooden room blocks, which are not as big or amenity filled as those at FDR, Franklyn D. Resort. Each junior suite is paneled with cedar and pine, highlighted with trim in tropical colors. Up to three children under age 16 can share a room with two parents; kids under 6 stay and eat free when sharing a room with parents. Pros:

Individual nannies for families, good supervised kids program, good selection of activities for older children. Cons: May not pack appeal for travelers without kids, far from local attractions and activities, property can be noisy. ⊠*Main St., Falmouth* ☎*876/954–4821* ⊕*www. fdrholidays.com* ➥*96 junior suites* ♿*In-room: refrigerator, Wi-Fi. In-hotel: 3 restaurants, bar, tennis court, pool, gym, spa, beachfront, water sports, bicycles, no elevator, children's programs (ages newborn– 16), laundry service, public Internet, public Wi-Fi, airport shuttle, no-smoking rooms* ⊟*AE, D, MC, V* ⏐◎⏐*AI.*

$$$–$$$$ ⊞**Holiday Inn SunSpreeResort.** Family fun is tops here, although many couples and singles are also drawn to the moderate prices and good location, 6 mi (9.5 km) east of the airport. You can find seven-room blocks spread along the long beach and large public areas that can, at times, feel a bit overrun with kids and the noise they produce. Adults can find some peace in the quiet pool, which has its own swim-up bar. On the other side of the grounds, a lighted 9-hole miniature golf course offers night play. Shoppers will be happy with the moderately priced shopping mall directly across the street. Children 12 and under stay and eat free. Pros: Good family atmosphere, easy access to shopping area, complimentary self-serve laundry. Cons: Numerous children mean some areas can be noisy, only nonmotorized water sports, hotel located directly beside North Coast Highway. ⊠*N. Coast Hwy.* ✉*Box 480, Montego Bay* ☎*876/953–2485* ⊕*www.montegobayjam. sunspreeresorts.com* ➥*524 rooms, 27 suites* ♿*In-room: safe, dial-up, Wi-Fi. In-hotel: 4 restaurants, room service, bars, tennis courts, pools, beachfront, diving, water sports, children's programs (ages 6 months– 12), laundry facilities, laundry service, concierge, airport shuttle, parking (no fee), no-smoking rooms* ⊟*AE, D, DC, MC, V* ⏐◎⏐*AI.*

$$$–$$$$ ⊞**Iberostar Rose Hall Beach.** Located 20 minutes east of the Montego
☺ Bay airport, this all-inclusive resort, opened in 2007, the first of several planned phases. An extensive array of dining options (including three à la carte restaurants that require reservations) and activities are offered, although motorized water sports and scuba diving incur an additional fee. Operated by a European company, the resort has some of the same feel as the brand's popular Mexico properties, which are noted for the Mexican atmosphere with thatch-roof poolside palapas, Spanish lessons, tropical dance lessons, and around-the-clock action. Pros: Numerous on-site activities, easy access to airport and into Montego Bay, complimentary minibar. Cons: Hotel construction continues on adjacent Iberostar properties, high-rise setup can mean elevator wait, more-limited all-inclusive program than some others. ⊠*N. Coast Hwy. east of Montego Bay* ☎*876/680–0000* ⊕*www.iberostar. com* ➥*334 rooms, 32 suites* ♿*In-room: safe, refrigerator, dial-up. In-hotel: 4 restaurants, room service, bars, pools, gym, spa, beachfront, diving, water sports, children's programs (ages 4–12), laundry service, concierge, public Internet, airport shuttle, parking (no fee)* ⊟*AE, D, MC, V* ⏐◎⏐*AI.*

$$–$$$ ⊞**Sunset Beach Resort & Spa.** Often packed with charter groups, this
☺ expansive resort is a very good value if you don't mind mass tourism. With one of Jamaica's best (and most-used) lobbies, a water park, a

13

teen center, and excellent beaches on a peninsula jutting out into the bay, the facilities here help to redeem the motel-basic rooms. You can choose among three beaches (one clothing optional) or, when it's time to take a break from the sun, hit the spa or slots-only casino. Pros: Excellent beaches, good restaurants, numerous on-site activities. Cons: Can be crowded, high-rise setup means lines for the elevator, somewhat remote location if you want to explore Montego Bay. ⊠ *Freeport ☐ Box 1168, Montego Freeport, Montego Bay ☎876/979–8800 ⊕www.sunsetbeachresort.com ↝430 rooms, 15 suites △In-room: safe, dial-up. In-hotel: 4 restaurants, bars, tennis courts, pools, spa, gym, beachfront, water sports, children's programs (ages 2–12), laundry service, concierge, public Internet, airport shuttle, parking (no fee) ▭AE, MC, V ⚭AI.*

$–$$ ⌂ Breezes Montego Bay. A good choice for those on a budget, this active resort near the airport is especially favored by young travelers. Right on Montego Bay's "Hip Strip," the resort places you steps away from nearby nightclubs and shops. The beach is the great Doctor's Cave, a public strand with a beach-club atmosphere, so you aren't sealed off from the locals (whether that's a plus or a minus is up to you). Rooms have white-tile floors, cozy love seats (leather sofas in the oceanfront suites), carved wooden headboards, and big marble bathrooms. A popular circus workshop and free weddings are also part of the package. Pros: Easy access to Hip Strip restaurants and bars, easy access to airport, good value. Cons: Can be noisy, no private beach, more of a hotel than resort feel. ⊠ *Gloucester Ave. ☎876/940–1150 ⊕www. superclubs.com ↝124 rooms △In-room: safe, VCR (some). In-hotel: 3 restaurants, bars, tennis court, pool, beachfront, diving, water sports, airport shuttle, no kids under 14 ↜2-night minimum ▭AE, D, DC, MC, V ⚭AI.*

$–$$ ⌂ Starfish Trelawny. A real bargain, this all-inclusive resort is operated
ⓒ by SuperClubs but with fewer extras than you find in the company's other resorts. Some motorized water sports, for example, including waterskiing, banana boat rides, snorkeling trips, and scuba diving, are not included in the all-inclusive price. For beach lovers, the best option would be the garden-level cottages (especially popular with larger groups), which are just off the beach, but most guest rooms are found in high-rise towers. The resort is family-friendly from restaurants to nightly entertainment, although the late-night disco is aimed at adults. The resort has a rock-climbing wall, a circus workshop, "ice-skating" on a special plastic surface, and for an additional cost unlimited trapeze sessions. Pros: Good value, excellent children's program, numerous activities. Cons: High-rise balconies can be scary with small children, limited all-inclusive program, doesn't appeal to guests not traveling with children. ⊠ *N. Coast Hwy., Falmouth ☎876/954–2450 ⊕www. starfishresorts.com ↝349 rooms △In-room: safe, Wi-Fi (some). In-hotel: 6 restaurants, room service, bars, tennis courts, pools, gym, spa, beachfront, diving, water sports, children's programs (ages 6 months– 12), public Internet, airport shuttle ↜2-night minimum ▭AE, D, DC, MC, V ⚭AI.*

NEGRIL

Some 50 mi (80 km) west of MoBay, Negril was once a hippie hangout, favored for its inexpensive mom-and-pop hotels and laid-back atmosphere. Today there's still a bohemian flair, but the town's one of the fastest-growing tourism communities in Jamaica, with several large all-inclusives along Bloody Bay, northeast of town. The main strip of Negril Beach and the cliffs are still favored by vacationers who like to get out and explore.

13

$$$$ ⌨ **The Caves.** Although set on 2 tiny acres, this petite resort packs a lot of punch in its cliff-side location, drawing the Hollywood set as well as travelers looking for boutique-style pampering. Thatch-roof cottages are individually designed with vivid colors and hand-carved furniture, every one offering spectacular sunset views. The cottages are built above the natural sea caves that line the cliffs, one of which is used for private romantic dinners. TVs are available, but only if you ask. Pros: Stylish and unique accommodations, personal service, quiet atmosphere. Cons: Limited on-site dining options, may be too quiet for some travelers, no beach (on cliffs). ⊠*Lighthouse Rd.* ☏*876/975–3354* ⊕*www.islandoutpost.com* ⌨*6 suites, 3 cottages* △*In-room: no a/c (some), refrigerator (some), dial-up. In-hotel: restaurant, pool, spa, water sports, bicycles, no elevator, public Wi-Fi, no kids under 16* ⊟*AE, D, MC, V* ⓄⓁ*AI.*

$$$$ ⌨ **Couples Negril.** This resort emphasizes romance and relaxation and is a more-laid-back alternative to the nearby Sandals Negril. The resort has a good beachfront along Bloody Bay, north of the funkier Negril Beach, although Negril's bohemian nature is still reflected throughout the nine low-rise buildings. The property is decorated by a rainbow of colors, and lively art by local craftspeople peppers public spaces. Rooms are similarly bright and roomy but are not luxurious. All land and water activities, selected excursions, and weddings are included in the rates. **Pros:** Plenty of dining options, bartender service on the beach, free weddings. **Cons:** Restaurants can book up early, dated decor, social directors a little too intrusive. ⊠*Norman Manley Blvd.* ☏*Box 35, Hanover, Jamaica, WI* ☏*876/957–5960* ⊕*www.couples.com* ⌨*216 rooms, 18 suites* △*In-room: safe, refrigerator (some). In-hotel: 4 restaurants, bars, tennis courts, pools, gym, spa, beachfront, diving, water sports, no elevator, concierge, airport shuttle, no kids under 18* ☞*3-night minimum* ⊟*AE, D, MC, V* ⓄⓁ*AI.*

$$$$ ⌨ **Couples Swept Away Negril.** Sports-minded couples are welcomed
★ to this all-suites resort known for its expansive menu of sports offerings, top-notch facilities (the best in Jamaica and among the best in the Caribbean), and emphasis on healthful cuisine. If you're looking for an active vacation that is still sprinkled with a hint of romance, it's your best option in Negril. The suites are in 26 two-story tropical villas—each with a private verandah overlooking the sea or a lush garden area—spread out along a 0.5-mi (0.75-km) stretch of gorgeous beach. Across the road lies one of Jamaica's best sports complexes, with classes and high-end equipment and instruction. A 2006 expansion added amenities ranging from new restaurants to an Internet café.

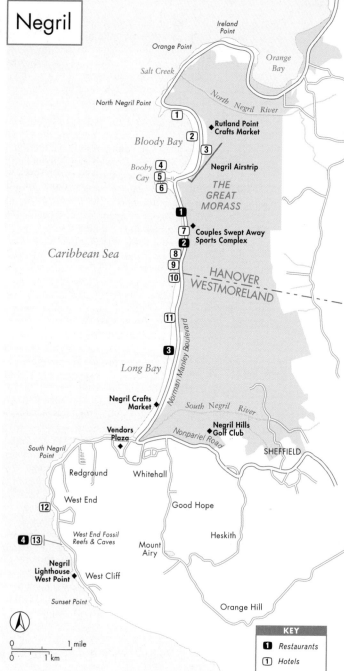

Negril

*Ireland
Point*

Orange Point

*Orange
Bay*

Salt Creek

North Negril River

North Negril Point

◆ Rutland Point
Crafts Market

Bloody Bay

Negril Airstrip

*Booby
Cay*

**THE
GREAT
MORASS**

Caribbean Sea

◆ Couples Swept Away
Sports Complex

HANOVER
WESTMORELAND

Norman Manley Boulevard

Long Bay

Negril Crafts
Market ◆

South Negril River

Vendors
Plaza ◆

Negril Hills ◆
Golf Club

Nonpariel Road

SHEFFIELD

*South Negril
Point*

Redground

Whitehall

Good Hope

West End

Heskith

*West End Fossil
Reefs & Caves*

Mount
Airy

Negril
Lighthouse
West Point ◆

West Cliff

Sunset Point

Orange Hill

0 ——— 1 mile
0 ——— 1 km

KEY

1 *Restaurants*

1 *Hotels*

Pros: Excellent fitness and sports facilities, emphasis on health continues with meal options, free weddings. **Cons:** Healthful emphasis not for everyone, some facilities located across the road from resort, minimum stay restrictive for some. ⊠ *Norman Manley Blvd.* ✆ *Box 3077, Westmoreland, Jamaica, WI* ☎ *876/957–4061* ⊕ *www.couples. com* ⌘ *134 suites* ⊜ *In-room: safe. In-hotel: 6 restaurants, bars, tennis courts, pools, gym, spa, beachfront, diving, water sports, no elevator, concierge, airport shuttle, no kids under 18* ☞ *3-night minimum* ⊟ *AE, D, DC, MC, V* ⊠ *AI.*

13

$$$$
★
⌘ **Grand Lido Negril.** A cursory look around the marble-clad lobby decorated with fine art and elegant columns might give the impression that this upscale all-inclusive is a tad stuffy. But fancy touches are balanced by an expansive clothing-optional beach (including its own hot tub, bar, and grill), giving you one of Jamaica's best resorts, where it's fun to dress for dinner but equally good to strip down for a day of fun in the sun. The clothed beach is one of the best strips of sand in Negril. Appealing to an upscale crowd of all stripes, the mood here is quiet and relaxing—much different than at Hedonism II, which is just next door. Low-rise rooms, both oceanfront and garden suites, are stylish; many offer French doors just steps from the sand. Pros: Excellent beaches, good dining, elegant setting. Cons: Some rooms need updating, central public area lacks view, clothing-optional pool is small. ⊠ *Norman Manley Blvd., Box 88* ☎ *876/957–5010* ⊕ *www.superclubs.com* ⌘ *210 suites* ⊜ *In-room: safe, refrigerator. In-hotel: 6 restaurants, room service, bars, tennis courts, pools, gym, spa, beachfront, diving, water sports, no elevator, laundry service, concierge, public Internet, public Wi-Fi, airport shuttle, no kids under 16, no-smoking rooms* ☞ *2-night minimum* ⊟ *AE, D, DC, MC, V* ⊠ *AI.*

$$$–$$$$
★
⌘ **Hedonism II.** Promising a perpetual spring break for adults, who are drawn to the legendary party atmosphere, this resort gets a lot of repeat business. Although you can find "prude" activities ranging from a rock-climbing wall to an expansive gym, it's the nude side that's perpetually sold out. Guest rooms received a makeover in 2004, and although they don't match the opulence of those at Hedonism III, they include TVs, multihead showers, and (of course) mirrors over the beds. Singles must allow the resort to match them with a same-sex roommate or pay a hefty supplement. Many nude travel groups plan vacations en masse here several times a year; another peak time is Halloween, when guests celebrate the resort's anniversary with wild costumes and decorated guest rooms. Pros: Good beaches, more economical than some adult all-inclusives, numerous activities. Cons: Spring-break atmosphere not for everyone, nude beach and pool frequently overcrowded, rooms remain fairly basic. ⊠ *Norman Manley Blvd., Rutland Point, Box 25* ☎ *876/957–5200* ⊕ *www.superclubs.com* ⌘ *280 rooms, 15 suites* ⊜ *In-room: safe. In-hotel: 6 restaurants, bars, tennis courts, pools, gym, spa, beachfront, diving, water sports, bicycles, concierge, public Internet, no elevator, airport shuttle, no kids under 18* ☞ *2-night minimum* ⊟ *AE, D, DC, MC, V* ⊠ *AI.*

$$$–$$$$
⌘ **Sunset at the Palms Resort & Spa.** Formerly Negril Cabins, this relaxed all-inclusive is a favorite with ecotourists. It was the world's first hotel

to receive Green Globe Certification for environmentally sustainable tourism, and the management works to maintain that status. Rooms here are in tree-house-like cottages amid towering royal palms. Open and airy, rooms have floral bedspreads, gauzy curtains, natural-wood floors, and high ceilings. The beach is across the street, along with activities including nonmotorized water sports. Nature enthusiasts can also take a walk with the resort's resident gardener. Pros: Environmentally conscious hotel, beautiful grounds, unique accommodations. Cons: Beach is across street, eco-emphasis not for everyone, not within walking distance of many Negril Beach attractions and restaurants. ⊠ *Norman Manley Blvd., Box 118* ☎ *876/957–5350* ⊕ *www.sunsetatthepalms.com* ⊷ *65 rooms, 4 suites* △ *In-room: safe. In-hotel: 3 restaurants, bars, tennis court, pool, gym, spa, water sports, public Internet, no elevator, airport shuttle* ⊟ *AE, D, MC, V* ⏃ *AI.*

$$–$$$$ ⌂ **ClubHotel Riu Negril.** Far north of Negril on Bloody Bay, this massive ☺ resort has a decent, sandy beachfront. A lack of personalized service is balanced by good bang for the buck, decent food, and extensive activities and facilities. Rooms are attractive, but those in the second and third blocks are a *very* long walk from everything, with no resort shuttle to help your weary feet. The programs for kids are slightly better here than at the Riu Tropical Bay, which is equally large and next door. Pros: Economical all-inclusive, family travelers find plenty of children on-site, good on-site dining. Cons: Pools and public areas can be overcrowded with families, many rooms a long walk from public areas, long walk from attractions of Negril Beach. ⊠ *Norman Manley Blvd.* ☎ *876/957–5700* ⊕ *www.riu.com* ⊷ *420 rooms, 18 junior suites* △ *In-room: safe, refrigerator. In-hotel: 4 restaurants, bars, tennis courts, pools, gym, spa, beachfront, diving, water sports, no elevator, children's programs (ages 4–12), laundry service, public Internet, airport shuttle* ⊟ *AE, D, MC, V* ⏃ *AI.*

$$–$$$ ⌂ **Point Village Resort.** Feeling more like an apartment complex than a beach resort, Point Village can make you feel as if you're planting some roots in Negril. With both an all-inclusive and room-only plan, you have the option of having it all or not. Kitchens help out those who must keep an eye on their budget. Though it's at the north end of Negril, which is mostly adults-only (Hedonism II and Grand Lido Negril are neighbors), this resort is fairly friendly to families. Rooms have tile floors and basic furnishings, and each is individually decorated. The sprawling complex has two small crescent beaches, rocky grottoes to explore, and fine snorkeling offshore. One child age 13 and under stays free when sharing a room with parents. Pros: Good value for families, large guest rooms, families find many on-site activities. Cons: Travelers without children may find public areas overcrowded with kids, small beaches, room decor outdated. ⊠ *Norman Manley Blvd., Box 105* ☎ *876/957–5170* ⊕ *www.pointvillage.com* ⊷ *99 studios, 66 apartments* △ *In-room: kitchen. In-hotel: 3 restaurants, bars, tennis court, pool, beachfront, water sports, no elevator, children's programs (ages newborn–12)* ⊟ *AE, D, MC, V* ⏃ *AI.*

$$ ⌂ **Charela Inn.** Directly on Negril Beach, this quiet hotel is understated but elegant in a simple way and has a widely praised French-Jamaican restaurant. Each quiet room has a private balcony or a covered patio. You can opt for a room-only plan if you want to explore neighboring restaurants along the beach, but most guests go all-inclusive. Children up to nine years old can stay in their parents' room for no additional charge; there's an $18 per-night charge for kids 10 to 15 years, although no children are permitted in deluxe guest rooms. The Saturday-night folkloric show draws guests from all over Negril. Pros: Great dining, good beach location, good value for families. Cons: Dated room decor, some guest rooms are small, facilities are not luxurious. ⊠*Norman Manley Blvd., Box 3033* ☎*876/957–4277* ⊕*www. charela.com* ⌨*49 rooms* ⌂*In-room: safe. In-hotel: restaurant, bar, pool, beachfront, water sports, no elevator, laundry service* ⌁*5-night minimum mid-Dec.–mid-Apr., 3-night minimum mid-Apr.–mid-Dec.* ▭*D, MC, V* ⧖*EP.*

$$ 🖼 **Country Country.** Owned by Kevin and Joanne Robertson, who also own Montego Bay's Coyaba, this small hotel carries the same home-away-from-home feel of its north-coast cousin but with a distinct Negril charm. Rooms are housed in brightly painted cottages designed by Jamaican architect Ann Hodges (known for her work at Goldeneye and Strawberry Hill); the cottages come alive with country-style touches like gingerbread trim. The oversize rooms all have a private patio. For an additional fee, you can add a meal plan, although most guests find plenty of restaurant choices within the area. Pros: Charming guest rooms, oversize accommodations, good location on Negril Beach. Cons: May be too small for some travelers, some rooms can be noisy at night due to nearby Margaritaville, limited on-site dining options. ⊠*Norman Manley Blvd.* ☎*876/957–4273* ⊕*www.countryjamaica. com* ⌨*20 rooms* ⌂*In-room: safe, refrigerator. In-hotel: restaurant, room service, bar, beachfront, no elevator* ▭*AE, MC, V* ⧖*BP.*

$$ 🖼 **Negril Gardens Beach Resort.** This long-established, brightly colored, low-rise resort epitomizes the relaxed and funky style for which Negril has long been known. Guests are always just a quick walk from Negril's 7-mi-long (11-km-long) beach. Rooms are fairly basic, but those beachside get some noise from nearby clubs until the wee hours. The resort is under Sandals management but operates separately from either the Sandals or Beaches chain, welcoming couples, singles, and families. Children under two stay free, but each room has a maximum occupancy of three persons. Pros: Good value, good beach location, friendly and helpful staff. Cons: Some rooms don't have patios or balconies, some rooms can be noisy at night due to nearby nightclubs, parents with more than one child will have to rent two rooms. ⊠*Norman Manley Blvd., Box 3058* ☎*876/957–4408* ⊕*www.negril gardensresort.com* ⌨*65 rooms* ⌂*In-room: safe. In-hotel: restaurant, bars, pool, beachfront, water sports, no elevator* ⌁*2-night minimum* ▭*AE, D, MC, V* ⧖*AI.*

$$ 🖼 **Rockhouse Hotel.** With a spectacular cliff-side location like that of the
Fodor's Choice Caves—but without the high price tag—the small and trendy Rock-
★ house delivers both resort comforts and funky style. Rooms and villas are built from rough-hewn timber, thatch, and stone and are filled with furniture that echoes the nature theme. Although double the price of

a regular room, villas ($$$), which have outdoor showers and private sundecks above the cliffs, are worth the splurge. Studios have outdoor showers but are otherwise like the regular rooms, which seem pleasantly rustic. You can ask for a TV—but only to watch videos. To be honest, you're far better off enjoying the sunsets, for which Negril is known. There's a thatch-roof Jamaican restaurant, a spa, yoga, kayaking, and a cliff-top infinity pool and bar. Pros: Excellent dining, unique accommodations, beautiful pool area. Cons: No beach, may be too quiet for some visitors, traditional rooms are not nearly as nice as the villas. ⊠ *West End Rd., Box 3024* ☎*876/957–4373* ⊕*www.rockhousehotel.com* ☞*14 rooms, 20 villas* ♿*In-room: safe, no TV. In-hotel: restaurant, bars, pool, water sports, no elevator, no kids under 12* ☰*AE, MC, V* ¶⊙*EP.*

$–$$ ⊞**Coco La Palm.** This quiet, friendly hotel on the beach has oversized rooms (junior suites average 540 square feet) in octagonal buildings around the pool. Some junior suites have private patios or terraces; most of these overlook the gardens (only 11 rooms have ocean views). The resort makes a good home base from which to explore Negril Beach, or you can just relax under one of the tall coconut palms. The beachside restaurant is open-air and casual. Pros: Good beach location, large guest rooms, good on-site dining. Cons: Small pools, dated room decor, few ocean-view rooms. ⊠*Norman Manley Blvd.* ☎*876/957–4227* ⊕*www.cocolapalm.com* ☞*76 rooms* ♿*In-room: safe, refrigerator, DVD, Ethernet. In-hotel: 2 restaurants, room service, bar, pools, beachfront, no elevator, laundry facilities, laundry service, public Internet, parking (no fee)* ☰*AE, DC, MC, V* ¶⊙*EP.*

SOUTH COAST

In the 1970s, Negril was Jamaica's most relaxed place to hang out. Today that distinction is held by the south coast, a long stretch of coastline ranging from Whitehouse to Treasure Beach. Here local residents wave to cars, and travelers spend their days exploring local communities and their nights in local restaurants. The best way to reach the south coast is from Montego Bay, driving overland, a journey of 90 minutes to two hours, depending on the destination.

$$$$ ⊞**Sandals Whitehouse European Village & Spa.** The newest Sandals resort
Fodor'sChoice   in Jamaica and the first major resort on the south coast, this property
★   is one of the most upscale properties in the chain. The resort consists of several "villages" constructed with Italian, Dutch, and French architectural touches. The resort is surrounded by a 500-acre nature preserve and lies on a 2-mi-long (3-km-long) beach. Pros: Great beach with no vendors, numerous dining options, stylish accommodations in all room classes. Cons: Some travelers won't like Disneyish re-creation of European styles, dining at other Sandals is available as part of package but there is no transportation to other properties due to distance, Whitehouse area can be bug-ridden and hot. ⊠*Whitehouse* ☎*876/957–5216* ⊕*www.sandals.com* ☞*304 rooms, 54 suites* ♿*In-room: safe, refrigerator. In-hotel: 7 restaurants, bars, tennis courts,*

pools, gym, spa, beachfront, diving, water sports, concierge, airport shuttle, no kids under 18 ⚓ *2-night minimum* ☰*AE, MC, V* ⓘ*AI.*

$–$$$$ 🏨 **Jake's.** The laid-back, neighborly feel of the south coast is epitomized ★ by Jake's, a relaxed place that's fun, funky, and friendly. Co-owner Jason Henzell, now president of Island Outpost, is active in community development and encourages his guests to get out and mingle in the area, whether that means fishing with the locals or hitting a rum shop. Each villa here (designed by Jason's mother, a theatrical designer) is unique, but some are not especially roomy. Pros: Unique accommodations, infused with south-coast friendliness, personalized service. Cons: Rooms can be cramped when housebound during rainy periods, few amenities, remote location. ✉*Calabash Bay, Treasure Beach* ☎*876/965–3000* ⊕*www.islandoutpost.com* 🛏*15 villas* ⚹*In-room: no a/c (some), no phone, safe, kitchen (some), refrigerator (some), no TV. In-hotel: 2 restaurants, pool, beachfront, water sports, bicycles, no elevator, public Wi-Fi, parking (no fee)* ☰*AE, D, MC, V* ⓘ*EP.*

$–$$$ 🏨 **Sunset Resort & Villas.** Next door to Jake's, this resort lacks the style of its attention-getting neighbor, but it still offers a friendly getaway that's lovingly owner-managed. Rooms are unique and oversize, though some of the decor strikes us as a bit too fussy and frilly. The owners are happy to advise guests about local fun and activities. The open-air restaurant serves beside a large, Astroturf-covered pool area. Pros: Friendly staff, rooms are comfortably large, good location on Calabash Bay. Cons: Decor is dated and fussy, remote location, pool area is dated. ✉*Calabash Bay, Treasure Beach* ☎*876/965–0143* ⊕*www.sunsetresort.com* 🛏*14 rooms* ⚹*In-room: no phone, refrigerator. In-hotel: restaurant, pool, beachfront, no elevator* ☰*AE, D, MC, V* ⓘ*EP.*

WHERE TO EAT

Although many cultures have contributed to Jamaica's cuisine, it has become a true cuisine in its own right. It would be a shame to travel to the heart of this complex culture without having at least one typical island meal. Probably the most famous Jamaican dish is jerk pork—the ultimate island barbecue. The pork (purists cook a whole pig) is covered with a paste of Scotch bonnet peppers, pimento berries (also known as allspice), and other herbs and cooked slowly over a coal fire. Many aficionados believe the best jerk comes from Boston Beach, near Port Antonio. Jerk chicken and fish are also seen on many menus. The ever-so-traditional rice and peas, also known as "coat of arms," is similar to the *moros y cristianos* of Spanish-speaking islands: white rice cooked with red kidney beans, coconut milk, scallions, and seasonings.

The island's most famous soup—the fiery pepper pot—is a spicy mixture of salt pork, salt beef, okra, and the island green known as callaloo. Patties (spicy meat pies) elevate street food to new heights. Although patties actually originated in Haiti, Jamaicans excel at making them. Curried goat is another island standout: young goat is cooked with spices and is more tender and has a gentler flavor than the lamb for which it was substituted by immigrants from India. Salted fish was

Barbecue, Jamaica-Style

Jamaica is well known for its contributions to the world of music, but the island is also the birthplace of a cooking style known as jerk. Modern jerk originated in the 1930s along Boston Beach, east of Port Antonio. Here, the first wayside stands sprang up on the side of the road, offering fiery jerk served in a casual atmosphere. Today, jerk stands are everywhere on the island, but many aficionados still return to Boston Beach for the "real thing."

The historic origins of jerk are unknown (some say the Maroons brought the practice from Africa; others say the cooking style came to the island with the Caribs and the Arawaks). The practice of jerking meat was first recorded in 1698 by a French priest, who wrote of a jerk pit made with four forked sticks with crosspieces covered with a grill made of sticks. On the grill was placed a whole pig, stuffed with lime juice, salt, pimento, and spices that helped preserve the meat in the hot climate.

Today, jerk is still cooked in a pit that contains a fire made from pimento wood. The meat, which is primarily pork but can also be chicken, goat, or fish, is marinated with jerk sauce. Every cook has his own favorite recipe, but most include allspice (pimento) berries, cloves, garlic, onion, ginger, cinnamon, thyme, and peppers. Commercial jerk sauces are also available. Once the jerk is cooked to perfection, it's served up with side dishes such as breadfruit, rice and peas, and a bread called festival.

once the best that islanders could do between catches. Out of necessity, a breakfast staple (and the national dish of Jamaica) was invented. It joins seasonings with salt fish and ackee, a red fruit that grows on trees throughout the island. When cooked in this dish, ackee reminds most people of scrambled eggs.

There are fine restaurants in all the resort areas, many in the resorts themselves, though the Kingston area has the widest selection. Many restaurants outside the hotels in MoBay and Ocho Rios will provide complimentary transportation.

WHAT TO WEAR

Dinner dress is usually casual chic (or just plain casual at many local hangouts, especially in Negril). There are a few exceptions in Kingston and at the top resorts; some require semiformal wear (no shorts; collared shirts for men) in the evening during high season. People tend to dress up for dinner; men might be more comfortable in nice slacks, women in a sundress.

KINGSTON

JAMAICAN ✕ **Strawberry Hill.** A favorite with Kingstonians for its elegant Sunday
$$$–$$$$ brunch, Strawberry Hill is well worth the drive from the city. The open-
★ air terrace has a spectacular view of Kingston and the countryside.
Entrées range from steamed snapper with coconut-scented rice to jerk-

marinated chicken with rice and peas. ⊠*New Castle Rd., Irishtown* ☎*876/944–8400* ⩘*Reservations essential* ▤*AE, D, MC, V.*

$$–$$$ ✕**Norma's on the Terrace.** Jamaican food with a gourmet touch (they call it fusion Jamaican) is the specialty of the day at this often-lauded restaurant, the creation of Jamaica's best-known chef, Norma Shirley. The restaurant is a favorite with Kingstonians, although visitors and locals alike come here for dishes like chicken thighs with guava cream and double-smoked pork chops marinated in Red Stripe beer. ⊠*Devon House, 26 Hope Rd., Kingston* ☎*876/968–5488* ▤*AE, D, MC, V* ⊘*Closed Sun.*

13

PORT ANTONIO

JAMAICAN ✕**Norma's at the Marina.** Another showcase for the culinary talents
$–$$ of Jamaican celebrity chef Norma Shirley (other Norma's locations include Kingston and Negril), this seaside restaurant serves gourmet dishes with a Jamaican twist. Start with an appetizer of smoked marlin or grilled deviled ocean crab back, then move on to entrées such as grilled shrimp in Jamaican herbs and mango salsa or pork riblets with local seasonings. ⊠*Errol Flynn Marina, Ken Wright Dr.* ☎*876/993–9510* ▤*AE, MC, V* ⊘*Closed Mon.*

¢–$ ✕**Boston Jerk Centre.** Actually a collection of about half a dozen open-air stands, this supercasual eatery is a culinary capital in Jamaica thanks to its fiery jerk pits. Stroll up to the open pits, fired by pimento logs and topped with a piece of corrugated roofing metal, locally called zinc, and order meat by the quarter, half, or full pound; chicken, pork, goat, and fish are top options. Side dishes are few but generally include festival (a rolled bread similar to a Southern hush puppy) and rice and peas. ⊠*Boston Beach on Rte. A4 east of Port Antonio* ☎*No phone* ▤*No credit cards.*

OCHO RIOS

ECLECTIC ✕**Evita's Italian Restaurant.** Just about every celebrity who has visited
$$–$$$ Ocho Rios has dined at this hilltop restaurant, and Evita has the pic-
Fodor'sChoice tures to prove it. Guests feel like stars themselves, with attentive wait-
★ staff helping to guide them through a list of about 30 kinds of pasta, ranging from lasagna Rastafari (vegetarian) and fiery jerk spaghetti to *rotelle colombo* (crabmeat with white sauce and noodles). Kids under 12 eat for half price, and light eaters will appreciate half portions. The restaurant offers free transportation from area hotels. ⊠*Mantalent Inn, Eden Bower Rd.* ☎*876/974–2333* ▤*AE, D, MC, V.*

JAMAICAN ✕**Ocho Rios Village Jerk Centre.** This blue-canopied, open-air eatery is
¢–$ a good place to park yourself for frosty Red Stripe beer and fiery jerk pork, chicken, or seafood. Milder barbecued meats, also sold by weight (typically, 0.25 or 0.5 pound makes a good serving), turn up on the fresh daily chalkboard menu posted on the wall. It's lively at lunch, especially when passengers from cruise ships swamp the place. ⊠*Da-Costa Dr.* ☎*876/974–2549* ▤*D, MC, V.*

¢–$ ✕ **Scotchie's Too.** The Ocho Rios branch of the longtime Montego Bay
Fodor'sChoice   favorite has already been lauded by international chefs for its excel-
★   lent jerk. The open-air eatery offers plates of jerk chicken, sausage,
fish, pork, and ribs, all accompanied by *festival* (a rolled bread similar
to a Southern hush puppy), *bammy* (fried cassava bread), and some
fire-breathing hot sauce. Be sure to step over to the kitchen to watch
the preparation of the jerk over the pits. ⊠ *N. Coast Hwy., Drax Hall*
☎ *876/794–9457* ⊟ *AE, D, MC, V.*

MONTEGO BAY

$$–$$$ ✕ **Town House.** Most of the rich and famous who have visited Jamaica
over the decades have eaten here. You find daily specials, delicious variations of standard dishes (red snapper papillote, with lobster, cheese,
and wine sauce, is a specialty), and many Jamaican favorites (like
curried chicken with breadfruit and ackee). The 18th-century Georgian house is adorned with original Jamaican and Haitian art. There's
alfresco dining on the stone patio. ⊠ *16 Church St.* ☎ *876/952–2660*
⌂ *Reservations essential* ⊟ *AE, D, DC, MC, V.*

¢–$$ ✕ **The Native.** Shaded by a large poinciana tree and overlooking Glouces-
★   ter Avenue, this open-air stone terrace serves Jamaican and interna-
tional dishes. To go native, start with smoked marlin, move on to the
boonoonoonoos platter (a sampler of local dishes), and round out with
coconut pie or *duckanoo* (a sweet dumpling of cornmeal, coconut, and
banana wrapped in a banana leaf and steamed). Live entertainment
and candlelit tables make this a romantic choice for dinner on week-
ends. ⊠ *29 Gloucester Ave.* ☎ *876/979–2769* ⌂ *Reservations essential*
⊟ *AE, MC, V.*

JAMAICAN   ✕ **Pork Pit.** A favorite with many MoBay locals, this no-frills eatery
¢–$ serves Jamaican specialties including some fiery jerk—note that it's
spiced to local tastes, not watered down for tourist palates. Many get
their food to go, but you can also find picnic tables just outside. ⊠ *27*
Gloucester Ave. ☎ *876/940–3008* ⊟ *MC, V.*

SEAFOOD   ✕ **Marguerites Seafood By the Sea.** At this romantic pier-side dining
$$–$$$ room and seaside pier, flambé is the operative word. Lobster, shrimp,
fish, and several desserts are prepared in dancing flames as you sip an
exotic cocktail. The Caesar salad, prepared table-side, is also a treat.
⊠ *Gloucester Ave.* ☎ *876/952–4777* ⌂ *Reservations essential* ⊟ *AE,*
D, MC, V ⊘ *No lunch.*

$$–$$$ ✕ **Pier 1.** After tropical drinks at the deck bar, you'll be ready to dig
into the international variations on fresh seafood; the best are the
grilled lobster and any preparation of island snapper. Several party
cruises leave from the marina here, and on Friday night the restaurant
is mobbed by locals who come to dance. ⊠ *Off Howard Cooke Blvd.*
☎ *876/952–2452* ⊟ *AE, MC, V.*

NEGRIL

CARIBBEAN ✕**Rick's Cafe.** It's hard to keep a good café–tourist attraction down,
$$–$$$ even when a force like Hurricane Ivan blows through and sends much
of the establishment into the sea. Rick's has rebuilt and is bigger than
ever, with two floors of dining options along with poolside cabanas for
rent—as well as the cliff diving and sunset views the restaurant has been
known for since 1974. Menu options range from escoveitch shrimp to
jerk chicken skewers to steak. ✉*1 White Hall Rd.* ☎*876/957–4621*
⊕*www.rickscafejamaica.com* ▭*AE, D, MC, V.*

13

$$–$$$ ✕**Norma's on the Beach.** Although it's in the modest boutique hotel Sea
★ Splash, make no mistake: this is Jamaica dining at some of its finest. Norma is Norma Shirley, one of Jamaica's best-known culinary
artists, often called the Julia Child of the Caribbean. Opt for terrace
or candlelit dining. Her dressed-up Jamaican fare is prepared with a
creative flair. Try callaloo-stuffed chicken breast or jerk chicken pasta.
✉*Sea Splash Hotel, Norman Manley Blvd.* ☎*876/957–4041* ▭*AE,
MC, V.*

ECLECTIC ✕**Kuyaba on the Beach.** This charming thatch-roof eatery has an interna-
¢–$$ tional menu—including curried conch, kingfish steak, grilled lamb with
sautéed mushrooms, and several pasta dishes—plus a lively ambience,
especially at the bar. There's a crafts shop on the premises, and chaise
lounges line the beach; come prepared to spend some time, and don't
forget a towel and bathing suit. ✉*Norman Manley Blvd.* ☎*876/957–
4318* ▭*AE, D, MC, V.*

SEAFOOD ✕**Cosmo's Seafood Restaurant & Bar.** Owner Cosmo Brown has made this
$$–$$$ seaside open-air bistro a pleasant place to spend the afternoon—and
maybe stay on for dinner. Fish is the main attraction, and the conch
soup—a house specialty—is a meal in itself. You can also find lobster
(grilled or curried), fish-and-chips, and the catch of the morning. Cus-
tomers often drop cover-ups to take a dip before coffee and dessert and
return to lounge in chairs scattered under almond and sea grape trees
(there's an entrance fee of $1.50 for the beach). ✉*Norman Manley
Blvd.* ☎*876/957–4330* ▭*AE, MC, V.*

SOUTH COAST

ECLECTIC ✕**Jack Sprat Restaurant.** It's no surprise that this restaurant shares its
$$–$$$ home resort's bohemian style (it's the beachside dining spot at Jake's).
From the casual outdoor tables to the late-night dance-hall rhythm, it's
a place to come and hang loose. Jerk crab joins favorites like pizzas
and jerk chicken on the menu, all followed by Kingston's Devon House
ice cream (try the coconut). ✉*Jake's, Calabash Bay, Treasure Beach*
☎*876/965–3583* ▭*AE, MC, V.*

JAMAICAN ✕**Little Ochie.** This casual beachside eatery is a favorite with locals and
¢–$$ travelers, favored for its genuine Jamaican dishes like fish tea, escov-
★ eitch fish, peppered shrimp, jerk chicken, seapuss (octopus), and more.
Most of the seafood is brought in by fishermen just yards away. For
Treasure Beach guests, a favorite way to reach Little Ochie is by boat.

✉ *About 7 mi (11 km) south of A2, Alligator Pond* ☎ *876/965–4449* ⊕ *www.littleochie.com* ☐ *AE, MC, V.*

¢ ✕ **Billy's Place.** A true side-of-the-road stop on the South Coast Highway, Billy's Place serves fiery Jamaican food including scorching peppered shrimp caught just behind the kitchen. Dining's mostly a grab-and-go affair although stands next door provide local desserts like fresh jelly coconut to cool the burn. ✉ *A2 about 30 mins east of Whitehouse, Middlequarters* ☎ *876/366–4182* ☐ *No credit cards.*

BEACHES

With its 200 mi (325 km) of beaches, it's no surprise that Jamaica's stretches of sand range in quality, atmosphere, and crowds. Some of the best beaches are private, owned by the resorts and accessible only to resort guests or travelers who have purchased a day pass to gain access to the facilities. Other beaches are public, although many include a small admission charge.

In general, a few beautiful beaches are found on the north coast, the sand growing lighter and finer as you travel west to Negril, which, with a 7-mi (11-km) stretch of some of the Caribbean's finest coastline, ranks as one of the region's top beaches. As you head south, you find the beaches become smaller and often rockier, but also less crowded with both tourists and resorts. Many resort beaches (especially those at adults-only properties) offer nude or clothing-optional sections. However, nudity (or even toplessness) is not tolerated on public beaches. Jamaica is a very conservative, religious country, and public beaches, where locals visit, do not accept less than a full bathing suit.

PORT ANTONIO

Blue Lagoon. Though the beach is small, the large lagoon has to be seen to be believed. The cool, spring-fed waters cry out to swimmers and are a real contrast to the warmer sea waters. Floating docks encourage you to sun a little, or you can lie out on the small beach. Just how deep is the Blue Lagoon? You might hear it's bottomless (Jacques Cousteau verified that it is not), but the lagoon has been measured at a depth of 180 feet. At present, freelance operators at the gates sometimes offer entry but, for current (and official) conditions, call the Port Antonio office of the Jamaica Tourist Board. ✉ *9 mi (13 km) east of Port Antonio, 1 mi (1.5 km) east of San San Beach.*

Boston Bay. Considered the birthplace of Jamaica's famous jerk-style cooking, it's the beach where some locals make the trek just to buy dinner. You can get peppery jerk pork at any of the shacks spewing scented smoke along the beach. While you're there, you'll also find a small beach perfect for an after-lunch dip, although these waters are occasionally rough and much more popular for surfing. ✉ *11 mi (18 km) east of Port Antonio.*

★ **Frenchman's Cove.** This picturesque, somewhat secluded beach is petite perfection. Protected by two outcroppings that form the cove, the inlet's calm waters are a favorite with families. A small stream trickles into the cove. You'll find a bar and restaurant serving fried chicken right on the beach. If this stretch of sand looks a little familiar, you just might have seen it in the movies; it has starred in *Club Paradise, Treasure Island* (the Charlton Heston version), and *The Mighty Quinn*. If you are not a guest of Frenchman's Cove, admission is $4.50. ⊠*Rte. A4, 5 mi (8 km) east of Port Antonio.*

San San Beach. This small beach has beautiful blue water. Just offshore, Monkey Island is a good place to snorkel (and, sometimes, surf). ⊠*5 mi (8 km) east of Port Antonio.*

13

OCHO RIOS

Dunn's River Falls Beach. You'll find a crowd (especially if there's a cruise ship in town) at the small beach at the foot of the falls. Although tiny—especially considering the crowds that pack the falls—it's got a great view, as well as a beach bar and grill. Look up from the sands for a spectacular view of the cascading water, whose roar drowns out the sea as you approach. ⊠*Rte. A1 between St. Ann's Bay and Ocho Rios.*

James Bond Beach. Another alternative near Ocho Rios—if you don't mind the drive—is in the community of Oracabessa. This beach, on the estate of James Bond's creator, the late Ian Fleming, is owned by former Island Records producer Chris Blackwell, so it's no surprise that it often rocks with live music performances on the bandstand. Guests of Goldeneye enjoy it for free; visitors must pay $5 per person. The beach is open daily except Monday from 9:30 to 6. ⊠*Oracabessa.*

Turtle Beach. One of the busiest beaches in Ocho Rios is not the prettiest, but it's usually lively, and has a mix of both residents and visitors. It's next to the Sunset Jamaica Grande and looks out over the cruise port. ⊠*Main St.*

RUNAWAY BAY

Puerto Seco Beach. This public beach looks out on Discovery Bay, the location where, according to tradition, Christopher Columbus first came ashore on this island. The explorer sailed in search of freshwater but found none, naming the stretch of sand Puerto Seco, or "dry port." Today the beach is anything but dry; concession stands sell Red Stripe beer and local food, including jerk and patties, to a primarily local beach crowd. ⊠*Discovery Bay, 5 mi (8 km) west of Runaway Bay.*

MONTEGO BAY

★ **Doctor's Cave beach.** Montego Bay's tourist scene has its roots right on the Hip Strip, the bustling entertainment district along Gloucester Avenue. Here a sea cave's waters were said to be curative and drew many travelers to bathe in them. Though the cave was destroyed by a hurricane generations ago, the beach is always busy and has a perpetual spring-break feel. It's the best beach in Jamaica outside one of the more-developed resorts, thanks to its plantation-style clubhouse with changing rooms, showers, gift shops, bar, grill, and even a cybercafé. There's a fee for admission; beach chairs and umbrellas are also for rent. Its location within the Montego Bay Marine Park—where there are protected corals and marine life—makes it a good spot for snorkeling. More-active travelers can opt for parasailing, glass-bottom boat rides, or jet skiing. ⊠ *Gloucester Ave., Montego Bay.*

♻ **Walter Fletcher Beach.** Though not as pretty as Doctor's Cave beach, or as tidy, Walter Fletcher Beach is home to Aquasol Theme Park, which offers a large beach (with lifeguards and security), water trampolines, Jet Skis, banana boat rides, Wave Runners, glass-bottom boats, snorkeling, tennis, go-cart racing, a disco at night, a bar, and a grill. Twice a week—on Wednesday and Friday—Aquasol throws a beach bash with a live reggae show and beach party. Near the center of town, the beach has protection from the surf on a windy day. This means you can find unusually fine swimming here; the calm waters make it a good bet for children. ⊠ *Gloucester Ave., Montego Bay.*

NEGRIL

Fodor'sChoice **Negril Beach.** Stretching for 7 mi (11 km), the long, white-sand beach
★ in Negril is arguably Jamaica's finest. It starts with the white sands of Bloody Bay north of town and continues along Long Bay all the way to the cliffs on the southern edge of town. Some stretches remain undeveloped, but there are increasingly few. Along the main stretch of beach, the sand is public to the high-water mark, so a nonstop line of visitors and vendors parade from end to end. The walk is sprinkled with many good beach bars and open-air restaurants, some of which charge a small fee to use their beach facilities. Bloody Bay is lined with large all-inclusive resorts, and these sections are mostly private. Jamaica's best-known nude beach, at Hedonism II, is always among the busiest; only resort guests or day-pass holders may sun here. ⊠ *Norman Manley Blvd.*

THE SOUTH COAST

If you're looking for something off the main tourist routes, head for Jamaica's largely undeveloped southwest coast. Because the population in this region is sparse, these isolated beaches are some of the island's safest, with hasslers practically nonexistent. You should, however, use common sense; never leave valuables unattended on the beach.

★ **Treasure Beach.** The most atmospheric beach in the southwest is in the community of Treasure Beach, which comprises four long stretches of sand as well as many small coves. Though it isn't as pretty as those to the west or north—it has more rocks and darker sand—the idea that you might be discovering a bit of the "real" Jamaica more than makes up for the small negatives. Both locals and visitors use the beaches here, though you're just as likely to find it completely deserted save a friendly beach dog. ⊠ *Treasure Beach township.*

SPORTS & THE OUTDOORS

The tourist board licenses all recreational activity operators and outfitters, which should ensure you of fair business practices as long as you deal with companies that display its decals.

BIRD-WATCHING

Jamaica is a major bird-watching destination, thanks to its varied habitat. The island is home to more than 200 species, some seen only seasonally or in particular parts of the island. Generally the early-morning and late-afternoon hours are the best time for spotting birds. Many bird-watchers flock here for the chance to see the vervian hummingbird (the second-smallest bird in the world, larger only than Cuba's bee hummingbird) or the Jamaican tody (which nests underground).

★ A great place to spot birds is the **Rocklands Bird Sanctuary & Feeding Station** (⊠ *Anchovy* ☎ *876/952–2009*), which is south of Montego Bay. The station was the home of the late Lisa Salmon, one of Jamaica's first amateur ornithologists. Here you can sit quietly and feed birds—including the doctor bird, recognizable by its long tail—from your hand. A visit costs $10. About 10 minutes from Negril, **Royal Palm Reserve** (⊠ *Springfield Rd., Sheffield* ☎ *876/957–3736*) is home to 50 bird species, including the West Indian whistling duck, which comes to feed at the park's Cotton Tree Lake. The park is also home to the Jamaican woodpecker, Jamaican oriole, Jamaican parakeet, and spectacular streamertail hummingbirds, who flit among the thick vegetation. Admission to the reserve is $10.

DIVING & SNORKELING

Jamaica isn't a major dive destination, but you can find a few rich underwater regions, especially off the north coast. MoBay, known for its wall dives, has **Airport Reef** at its southwestern edge. The site is known for its coral caves, tunnels, and canyons. The first marine park in Jamaica, the **Montego Bay Marine Park,** was established to protect the natural resources of the bay; a quick look at the area and it's easy to see the treasures that lie beneath the surface. The north coast is on the edge of the Cayman Trench, so it boasts a wide array of marine life.

Thanks to a marine area protected since 1966, the Ocho Rios region is also a popular diving destination. Through the years, the protected area grew into the **Ocho Rios Marine Park,** stretching from Mammee Bay and Drax Hall to the west to Frankfort Point on the east. Top dive sites in the area include **Jack's Hall,** a 40-foot dive dotted with all types of coral; **Top of the Mountain,** a 60-foot dive near Dunn's River falls with many coral heads and gorgonians; and the **Wreck of the** *Katryn,* a 50-foot dive to a deliberately sunk 140-foot former minesweeper.

With its murkier waters, the southern side of the island isn't as popular for diving, especially near Kingston. **Port Royal,** which is near the airport, is filled with sunken ships that are home to many different varieties of tropical fish. Prices on the island range from $45 to $80 for a one-tank dive. All the large resorts have dive shops, and the all-inclusive places sometimes include scuba diving in their rates. To dive, you need to show a certification card, though it's possible to get a small taste of scuba diving and do a shallow dive—usually from shore—after taking a one-day resort diving course, which almost every resort with a dive shop offers. A couple of places stand out.

Jamaqua Dive Centre (⊠ *Club Ambiance, Runaway Bay* ☎ *876/973-4845* ⊕ *www.jamaqua.com*) is a five-star PADI facility specializing in small dive groups. Along with dives, Jamaqua Dive Centre has a large menu of instructional courses ranging from snorkeling to rescue dive courses. You can also find underwater cameras for rent here. **Scuba Jamaica** (⊠ *Half Moon, N. Coast Hwy., Montego Bay* ☎ *876/381-1113* ⊕ *www.scuba-jamaica.com*) offers serious scuba facilities for dedicated divers. This PADI and NAUI operation also offers Nitrox diving and instruction as well as instruction in underwater photography, night diving, and open-water diving. There's a pickup service for the Montego Bay, Runaway Bay, Discovery Bay, and Ocho Rios areas.

DOLPHIN SWIM PROGRAMS

Dolphin lovers find two well-run options in both Montego Bay and Ocho Rios. **Dolphin Cove at Treasure Reef** (⊠ *N. Coast Hwy., adjacent to Dunn's River falls, Ocho Rios* ☎ *876/974-5335* ⊕ *www.dolphincovejamaica.com*) offers dolphin swims as well as lower-priced dolphin encounters for ages eight and up; dolphin touch programs for ages six and over; or simple admission to the grounds, which also includes a short nature walk. Programs cost between $45 and $195, depending on your depth of involvement with the dolphins. Advance reservations are required. **Dolphin Cove Half Moon** (⊠ *N. Coast Hwy., Montego Bay* ☎ *876/953-2211* ⊕ *www.dolphinswimjamaica.com*) is home to dolphins available for swims and encounters only with guests of Half Moon.

FISHING

Port Antonio makes deep-sea-fishing headlines with its annual Blue Marlin Tournament in October, and MoBay and Ocho Rios have devotees who exchange tales (tall and otherwise) about sailfish, yellowfin tuna, wahoo, dolphinfish, and bonito. Licenses aren't required, and you can arrange to charter a boat at your hotel. A chartered boat (with captain, crew, and equipment) costs about $500 to $900 for a half day or $900 to $1,500 for a full-day excursion, depending on the size of the boat.

The **Glistening Waters Marina** (⊠ *N. Coast Hwy., Falmouth* ☎ *876/954-3229* ⊕ *www.glisteningwaters.com*) offers charter trips from the Falmouth area. Thirty boats moored at the Glistening Waters Marina offer deep-sea fishing charters; the marina also has nighttime pontoon boat trips for a look at the lagoon, whose iridescence is caused by microscopic dinoflagellates that become luminescent when they move. For less-serious anglers, Jamaica has several fishing parks. These offer lake fishing as well as nature walks, picnics, birding, and a family-friendly atmosphere. The easiest to reach is **Royal Palm Reserve** (⊠*Springfield Rd., Sheffield* ☎*876/957–3736*), about 10 minutes from Negril. Visitors can rent gear and try their luck at catching African perch or tarpon in Cotton Tree Lake. There's an admission price of $10 to visit the park and a $5 charge for fishing; you can also purchase any fish you catch to take back to your villa or resort for the night's dinner if you like.

GOLF

Golfers appreciate both the beauty and the challenges offered by Jamaica's courses. Caddies are almost always mandatory throughout the island, and rates are $15 to $45 per round of golf. Cart rentals are available at all courses except Manchester Club; costs are $20 to $40. Some of the best courses in the country are found near MoBay.

The Runaway Bay golf course is found at **Breezes Runaway Bay** (⊠*N. Coast Hwy., Runaway Bay* ☎*876/973–7319*). This 18-hole course has hosted many championship events (greens fees are $80 for nonguests; guests play for free) and is also home to an extensive golf academy.

East of Falmouth, try **Grand Lido Braco Golf Club** (⊠*Trelawny* ☎*876/ 954–0010*), between Duncans and Rio Bueno, a 9-hole course with lush vegetation (nonguests should call for fee information). Caddies are not mandatory on this course.

★ **Half Moon** (⊠*Montego Bay* ☎*876/953–2560*), a Robert Trent Jones–designed 18-hole course 7 mi (11 km) east of town, is the home of the Red Stripe Pro Am (greens fees are $105 for guests, $150 for nonguests). In 2005 the course received an upgrade and once again draws international attention. **Ironshore SuperClubs Golf Club** (⊠*Montego Bay* ☎*876/953–3681*), 3 mi (5 km) east of the airport, is an 18-hole links-style course (greens fees are $50).

In the hills, the 9-hole **Manchester Club** (⊠*Caledonia Rd., Mandeville* ☎*876/962–2403*) is the Caribbean's oldest golf course and charges greens fees of about $17.

Great golf, rolling hills, and a "liquor mobile" go hand in hand at the 18-hole **Negril Hills Golf Club** (⊠*Sheffield Rd., Negril* ☎*876/957–4638*), the only golf course in Negril, which is east of town; the greens fees are $28.75 for 9 holes or $57.50 for 18 holes.

★ The newest course in Jamaica, which opened in January 2001, is the White Witch course at the **Ritz-Carlton Golf & Spa Resort, Rose Hall** (⊠*1 Ritz Carlton Dr., Rose Hall, St. James* ☎*876/518–0174*). The greens fees at this 18-hole championship course are $179 for resort guests, $199 for nonguests, and $99 for a twilight round.

The **Rose Hall Resort & Country Club** (⊠*N. Coast Hwy., Montego Bay* ☎*876/953–2650*), 4 mi (6.5 km) east of the airport, hosts several invitational tournaments (greens fees run $115 for guests, $150 for nonguests) at the 18-hole championship Cinnamon Hill Ocean Course.

The golf course at **Sandals Golf & Country Club** (✉ *Ocho Rios* ☎ *876/975–0119*) is 700 feet above sea level (greens fees for 18 holes are $100, or $70 for 9 holes for nonguests; complimentary greens fees for guests).

Fodor's Choice   **Tryall Club** (✉ *N. Coast Hwy., Sandy Bay* ☎ *876/956–5681*), 15 mi (24
★   km) west of Montego Bay, has an 18-hole championship course on the site of a 19th-century sugar plantation (greens fees are $85 for guests, $125 for nonguests).

HORSEBACK RIDING

Fodor's Choice   Riders with an interest in history can combine both loves on a horse-
★   back tour at **Annandale Plantation** (✉ *Ocho Rios* ☎ *876/974–2323*). The 600-acre plantation is high above Ocho Rios and today serves as a working farm, although in its glory days it hosted dignitaries such as the Queen Mother. Ocho Rios has excellent horseback riding, but the best of the operations is **Chukka Caribbean Adventures** (✉ *Llandovery, St. Ann's Bay* ☎ *876/972–2506* ⊕ *www.chukkacaribbean.com*). Starting out at Chukka Cove, trainers here originally exercised the polo ponies by taking them for therapeutic rides in the sea; soon there were requests from visitors to ride the horses in the water. The company now offers a three-hour beach ride that ends with a bareback swim on the horses in the sea from a private beach. It's a highlight of many trips to Jamaica. **Hooves** (✉ *Windsor Rd., St. Ann's Bay* ☎ *876/972–0905* ⊕ *www. hoovesjamaica.com*) has several guided tours along beach, mountain, and river trails. One of the most interesting offerings is the Bush Doctor Mountain Ride, which takes visitors back into rural Jamaica for a two-hour look at the countryside, whose residents still often depend on the services of bush doctors who utilize local plants for treatments. Rather than be part of a guided group ride, you can opt to rent a horse by the hour at **Prospect Plantation** (✉ *Ocho Rios* ☎ *876/994–1058*), which offers horseback riding for $58 per hour; advance reservations are required. For the adventurous, Prospect Plantation also offers guided camel rides.

In the Braco area near Trelawny (between Montego Bay and Ocho Rios), **Braco Stables** (✉ *Duncans* ☎ *876/954–0185* ⊕ *www.bracostables.com*) offers guided rides including a bareback romp in the sea. Two estate rides are offered a day for $70, and riders are matched to horses based on riding ability. The trip also includes complimentary refreshments served poolside at the Braco greathouse. Experienced riders can also opt for a mountain ride ($84) for a more-rugged two-hour tour.

MOUNTAIN BIKING

Jamaica's hilly terrain creates a challenge for mountain bikers, though there are easier rides, especially near the beaches and on the western end of the island. Heavy, unpredictable traffic on the North Coast Highway makes it off-limits for bikers, but country roads and hilly trails weave a network through the countryside.

★ **Blue Mountain Bicycle Tours** (✉*121 Main St., Ocho Rios* ☎*876/974–7075* ⊕*www.bmtoursja.com*) takes travelers on guided rides in the spectacular Blue Mountains. The excursion, an all-day outing, starts high and glides downhill, so all levels of riders can enjoy the tour. The trip ends with a dip in a waterfall; the package price includes transportation from Ocho Rios or Kingston, brunch, lunch, and all equipment. From its location outside Montego Bay, **Chukka Caribbean Adventures** (✉*Sandy Bay, Hanover* ☎*876/972–2506* ⊕*www.chukkacaribbean. com*) offers both biking and ATV tours. There's a minimum age of 16 on the ATV tours. The noisy ATVs jostle and splash their way along trails on a 10-mi (16-km) ride through the hills before returning so visitors can take a dip in the sea. From its Ocho Rios location, **Chukka Caribbean Adventures** (✉*Llandovery, St. Ann's Bay* ☎*876/972–2506* ⊕*www.chukkacaribbean.com*) offers a 3½-hour bike tour through St. Ann's Bay and the village of Mount Zion with several stops and even snorkeling at the end. There is also an ATV tour. There's a minimum age of 6 for bikes, 16 for ATVs.

RIVER RAFTING

Jamaica's many rivers mean a multitude of freshwater experiences, from mild to wild. Relaxing rafting trips aboard bamboo rafts poled by local boatmen are almost a symbol of Jamaica and the island's first tourist activity outside the beaches. Recently, soft-adventure enthusiasts have also been able to opt for white-water action as well with guided tours through several operators.

Fodor'sChoice Bamboo rafting in Jamaica originated on the **Rio Grande,** a river in
★ the Port Antonio area. Jamaicans had long used the bamboo rafts to transport bananas downriver; decades ago actor and Port Antonio resident Errol Flynn saw the rafts and thought they'd make a good tourist attraction, and local entrepreneurs quickly rose to the occasion. Today the slow rides are a favorite with romantic travelers and anyone looking to get off the beach for a few hours. The popularity of the Rio Grande's trips spawned similar trips down the **Martha Brae River,** about 25 mi (40 km) from MoBay. Near Ocho Rios, the **White River** has lazy river rafting in the daytime, followed by romantic river floats at night with the passage lighted by torches.

★ **Jamaica Tours Limited** (✉*Providence Dr., Montego Bay* ☎*876/953–3700* ⊕*www.jamaicatoursltd.com*) conducts trips down the River Lethe, approximately 12 mi (19 km; a 50-minute trip) southwest of MoBay; the four-hour excursion costs about $54 per person, includes lunch, and takes you through unspoiled hill country. Bookings can also be made through hotel tour desks. **Rio Grande Tours** (✉*St. Margaret's Bay* ☎*876/993–5778*) guides raft trips down the Rio Grande; the cost is $52 per raft (allow an additional $5–$10 for boatman tips). **River Raft Ltd.** (✉*66 Claude Clarke Ave., Montego Bay* ☎*876/952–0889* ⊕*www.jamaicarafting.com*) leads trips down the Martha Brae River, about 25 mi (40 km) from most hotels in MoBay. The cost is $45 per person for the 1½-hour river run. **South Coast Safaris Ltd.** (✉*1 Crane*

13

St., Black River ☎876/965–2513) takes visitors on slow cruises up the river to see the birds and other animals, including crocodiles.

For white-water buffs, several operators offer guided tours of varying levels, ranging from tubing to kayaking. **Chukka Caribbean Adventures** (✉*Ocho Rios and Montego Bay* ☎876/972–2506 ⊕*www.chukka caribbean.com*) offers white-water tubing on the White River, a soft adventure that doesn't require any previous rafting experience. Rafters travel in a convoy along the river and through some gentle rapids.

If you're looking for a more-rugged adventure, then consider a white-water rafting trip with **Caliche Rainforest** (✉*Montego Bay* ☎876/957–5569 ⊕*www.whitewaterraftingmontegobay.com*); you must be at least 14 years old for this trip. The company also offers a less-strenuous rafting trip for all ages.

SHOPPING

Shopping is not really one of Jamaica's high points, though you will certainly be able to find things to buy. Good choices include Jamaican crafts, which range from artwork to batik fabrics to baskets. Wood carvings are one of the top purchases; the finest carvings are made from the Jamaican national tree, lignum vitae, or tree of life, a dense wood that requires a talented carver to transform the hard, blond wood into dolphins, heads, or fish. Bargaining is expected with crafts vendors. Naturally, Jamaican rum is another top souvenir—there's no shortage of opportunities to buy it at gift shops and liquor stores—as is Tia Maria, the Jamaican-made coffee liqueur. Coffee (both Blue Mountain and the less-expensive High Mountain) is sold at every gift shop on the island as well. The cheapest prices are found at the local grocery stores, where you can buy coffee beans or ground coffee.

AREAS & MALLS

In **MoBay** the crafts market on **Market Street** is a compendium of stalls, each selling much the same thing. Come prepared to haggle over prices and to be given the hard sell; if you're in the right mood, though, the whole experience can be a lot of fun and a peek into Jamaican commerce away from the resorts. Montego Bay is also home to some traditional shopping malls where prices are set; you can shop in air-conditioned comfort. **Holiday Inn Shopping Centre** is one of the best. It's directly across the street from the Holiday Inn and has jewelry, clothing, and crafts stores. The most-serious shopping in town is at **Half Moon Village,** east of Half Moon resort. The bright yellow buildings are filled with the finest and most-expensive wares money can buy, but the park benches and outdoor pub here make the mall a fun stop for window-shoppers as well.

With the laid-back atmosphere of **Negril**, it's no surprise that most shopping involves straw hats, baskets, and T-shirts, all plentiful at the **Rutland Point** crafts market on the north edge of town or at the old crafts market in town. For more-serious shopping, head to **Time Square,** known for its luxury goods ranging from jewelry to cigars to watches. The gated shopping area has air-conditioned stores with high-dollar items.

Ocho Rios has several malls, and they are less hectic than the one in MoBay. Shopping centers include **Pineapple Place, Ocean Village, Taj Mahal,** and **Coconut Grove.** A fun mall that also serves as an entertainment center is **Island Village,** near the cruise port. The open-air mall includes Reggae Xplosion, shops selling Jamaican handicrafts, duty-free goods and clothing, a Margaritaville restaurant, and a small beach area with a water trampoline and water sports.

13

A shopping tour of the **Kingston** area should include **Devon House,** the place to find things old and new made in Jamaica. The greathouse is now a museum with antiques and furniture reproductions; boutiques and an ice-cream shop—try one of the tropical flavors (mango, guava, pineapple, and passion fruit)—fill what were once stables.

SPECIALTY STORES

COFFEE
Java lovers will find beans and ground coffee at gift shops throughout the island as well as at the airport. The lowest prices are found in local supermarkets; check the **Hi-Lo Supermarket** (⊠ *West End Rd., Negril* ☎ *876/957–4546*). But if the store is out of Blue Mountain, you may have to settle for High Mountain coffee, the locals' second-favorite brand.

HANDICRAFTS
Gallery of West Indian Art (⊠ *11 Fairfield Rd., Montego Bay* ☎ *876/952–4547*) is the place to find Jamaican and Haitian paintings. A corner of the gallery is devoted to hand-turned pottery (some painted) and beautifully carved and painted birds and animals.

★ **Harmony Hall** (⊠ *Rte. A1, Ocho Rios* ☎ *876/975–4222*), an eight-minute drive east of the main part of town, is a restored greathouse, where Annabella Proudlock sells her unique wooden boxes (their covers are decorated with reproductions of Jamaican paintings). Also on sale—and magnificently displayed—are larger reproductions of paintings, lithographs, and signed prints of Jamaican scenes and hand-carved wooden combs. In addition, Harmony Hall is well known for its shows by local artists.

Things Jamaican (⊠ *Devon House, 26 Hope Rd., Kingston* ☎ *876/926–1961* ⊠ *Sangster International Airport, Montego Bay* ☎ *876/952–4212*) sells some of the best Jamaican crafts—from carved wooden bowls and trays to reproductions of silver and brass period pieces.

Wassi Art Pottery Works (⊠ *Bougainvillea Dr., Great Pond, Ocho Rios* ☎ *876/974–5044*) produces one-of-a-kind works of art in terra-cotta. Visitors can stroll through the studio, watching local artists produce colorful pots in an array of shapes and sizes.

LIQUOR & TOBACCO

As a rule, only rum distilleries, such as Appleton's and Sangster's, have better deals than the airport stores. Best of all, if you buy your rum at the airport stores, you don't have to tote all those heavy, breakable bottles to your hotel and then to the airport. (Note that if you purchase rum—or other liquids, such as duty-free perfumes—outside the airport, you'll need to place them in your checked luggage when returning home. If you purchase liquids inside the secured area of the airport, you may board with your liquids but, after clearing U.S. Customs on landing, you will need to place the liquids in your checked bag if continuing on another flight.)

There are several good cigar shops in Negril. Fine handmade cigars are available at the Montego Bay airport or at one of the island's many cigar stores. You can also buy Cuban cigars almost everywhere, though they can't be brought legally back to the United States. **Cigar King** (⊠ *7 Time Square Mall, Negril* ☎ *876/957-3315*) has a wide selection of cigars, along with a walk-in humidor.

RECORDS & CDS

The **Bob Marley Experience & Theatre** (⊠ *Half Moon Shopping Village, Montego Bay* ☎ *876/953-3449*) has a 68-seat theater where you can watch a documentary on the life and works of the reggae great, but it's mostly a huge shop filled with Marley memorabilia, such as CDs, books, and T-shirts. **Reggae Yard & Island Life** (⊠ *N. Coast Hwy., Island Village, Ocho Rios* ☎ *876/675-8795*), the largest music store in Ocho Rios, is adjacent to Reggae Xplosion. The offerings include an extensive selection of reggae CDs as well as other types of Caribbean music.

NIGHTLIFE

Nightlife includes both on-property shows at the all-inclusive resorts and nightclubs ranging from indoor clubs to beach bashes. For starters, there's reggae, popularized by the late Bob Marley and the Wailers and performed today by son Ziggy Marley, Jimmy Tosh (the late Peter Tosh's son), Gregory Isaacs, Jimmy Cliff, and many others. If your experience of Caribbean music has been limited to steel drums and Harry Belafonte, then the political, racial, and religious messages of reggae may set you on your ear; listen closely and you just might hear the heartbeat of the people. Dance hall is another island favorite, as is soca.

ANNUAL EVENTS

Fodor's Choice ★ In January, Montego Bay is packed with music fans for the **Air Jamaica Jazz & Blues Festival** (☎ *800/568-3247* ⊕ *www.airjamaicajazzandblues. com*) held at the Rose Hall Aqueduct. Those who know and love reggae should visit Montego Bay between mid-July and August for the **Red Stripe Reggae Sumfest** (⊕ *www.reggaesumfest.com*). This weeklong concert—at the Bob Marley Performing Arts Center (a field set up with a temporary stage), in the Freeport area of MoBay—showcases local talent and attracts such big-name performers as Third World and Ziggy Marley and the Melody Makers.

In Ocho Rios, the biggest event of the year is the **Ocho Rios Jazz Festival** (☎876/927–3544 ⊕ *www.ochoriosjazz.com*) held each June. The event, which started in 1991 as a one-day concert, now spans eight days and draws many top names.

DANCE & MUSIC CLUBS

For the most part, the liveliest late-night happenings throughout Jamaica are in the major resort hotels, with the widest variety of spots probably in Montego Bay. Some of the all-inclusives offer a dinner and disco pass from about $50 to $100; to buy a pass, call ahead the afternoon before to check availability and be sure to bring a photo ID with you. Pick up a copy of the *Daily Gleaner,* the *Jamaica Observer,* or the *Star* (available at newsstands throughout the island) for listings on who's playing when and where. In Negril, trucks with loudspeakers travel through the streets in the afternoon announcing the hot spot for the evening.

In Montego Bay, the **Brewery** (⊠ *Shop 4, Miranda Ridge, Gloucester Ave., Montego Bay* ☎876/940–2433) is a popular sports bar. **Hurricanes Disco** (⊠ *Breezes Montego Bay Resort, Gloucester Ave., Montego Bay* ☎876/940–1150) is packed with locals and visitors from surrounding small hotels thanks to a $50 night pass (which includes dinner and drinks).

★ With its location right on what's deemed Montego Bay's Hip Strip, the colorful **Margaritaville Caribbean Bar & Grill** (⊠ *Gloucester Ave., Montego Bay* ☎876/952–4777 ⊠ *Norman Manley Blvd., Negril* ☎876/957–4467 ⊠ *Island Village, Ocho Rios* ☎876/675–8800) boasts a springbreak crowd during the season with a fun-loving atmosphere any night of the year; there is also a location at the Montego Bay airport. **Walter's** (⊠ *39 Gloucester Ave., Montego Bay* ☎876/952–9391) is a downtown favorite.

★ You can find Negril's best live music at **Alfred's Ocean Palace** (⊠ *Norman Manley Blvd., Negril* ☎876/957–4735 ⊕ *www.alfreds.com*), with live performances right on the beach.

★ The sexy, always packed disco at **Hedonism II** (⊠ *Norman Manley Blvd., Negril* ☎876/957–5200) is the wildest dance spot on the island; Tuesday (pajama night) and Thursday (toga night) are tops. For nonguests, night passes are $75 and cover everything from 6 PM to 3 AM; bring a photo ID to obtain a pass, but you should call ahead for a reservation. The **Jungle** (⊠ *Norman Manley Blvd., Negril* ☎876/957–4005) is the hottest nightspot in Negril, with two raised bars and a circular dance floor.

In Ocho Rios, the colorful **Margaritaville Caribbean Bar & Grill** (⊠ *Island Village, Turtle River Rd., Ocho Rios* ☎876/675–8800) boasts a fun-loving atmosphere any night of the year. It's very popular with younger travelers, reflected in a calendar of weekly nightlife activities, which includes plenty of all-night parties.

In Port Antonio, the hottest nightlife in town is not at the hotels, but at local joints such as the **Roof Club** (⊠ *11 West St., Port Antonio* ☎ *No phone*). Open Thursday to Sunday night, the second-floor club plays dance-hall hits.

EXPLORING JAMAICA

Touring Jamaica can be both thrilling and frustrating. Rugged (albeit beautiful) terrain and winding (often potholed) roads make for slow going. Before you set off to explore the island by car, *always* check conditions prior to heading out, but especially in the rainy season from June through October, when roads can easily be washed out. Primary roads that loop around and across the island are two-lane routes but are not particularly well marked. Numbered addresses are seldom used outside major townships, locals drive aggressively, and people and animals seem to have a knack for appearing on the street out of nowhere. That said, Jamaica's scenery shouldn't be missed. To be safe and avoid frustration, stick to guided tours and licensed taxis.

If you're staying in Kingston or Port Antonio, set aside at least one day for the capital's highlights and another for a guided excursion to the Blue Mountains. If you have more time, head for Mandeville. You can find at least three days' worth of activity right along MoBay's boundaries; you should also consider a trip to Cockpit Country or Ocho Rios. If you're based in Ocho Rios, be sure to visit Dunn's River falls; you may also want to stop by Firefly or Port Antonio. If Negril is your hub, take in the south shore, including Y. S. Falls and the Black River.

Numbers in the margin correspond to points of interest on the Jamaica map.

SOUTHEAST

Fodor'sChoice
★
Blue Mountains. Best known as the source of Blue Mountain coffee, these mountains rising out of the lush jungle north of Kingston are a favorite destination with adventure travelers, hikers, and birders as well as anyone looking to see what lies beyond the beach. You can find guided tours to the mountains from the Ocho Rios and Port Antonio areas as well as from Kingston. Unless you're traveling with a local, don't try to go on your own; the roads wind and dip, hand-lettered signs blow away, and you could easily get lost. It's best to hire a taxi (look for red PPV license plates to identify a licensed taxi) or to take a guided tour.

One place worth a visit—especially if you're interested in coffee—is **Mavis Bank** (⊠ *Mavis Bank* ☎ *876/977–8005*) and its Jablum coffee plant. An hour-long guided tour is $8; inquire when you arrive at the main office.

Kingston. Few leisure travelers—particularly Americans—take the time to visit Kingston, because it's not reachable on a day trip from anywhere on the island besides Ocho Rios or the Blue Mountains. It's also a tough city to love. It's big and, all too often, bad, with gang-controlled neighborhoods that are known to erupt into violence, especially near election time.

However, if you've seen other parts of the island and yearn to know more about the heart and soul of Jamaica, Kingston is worth a visit despite big-city security concerns. The government and business center is also a cultural capital, home to numerous dance troupes, theaters, and museums. Indeed, Kingston seems to reflect more of the true Jamaica—a wonderful cultural mix—than do the sunny havens of the north coast. As one Jamaican put it, "You don't really know Jamaica until you know Kingston." It's also home to the University of the West Indies, one of the Caribbean's largest universities. In March 2007 Kingston played host to cricket's World Cup, serving as the site of the opening ceremonies and drawing the attention of the world to the island.

Kingston sprawls in every direction. To the west, coming in from Spanish Town, lie some of the city's worst slums, in the neighborhoods of Six Miles and Riverton City. Farther south, Spanish Town Road skirts through a high-crime district that many Kingstonians avoid. In the heart of the business district, along the water, the pace is more peaceful, with a lovely walk and parks on Ocean Boulevard. Also here is the Jamaica Convention Centre, home of the U.N. body that creates all laws for the world's seas. From the waterfront you can look across Kingston Harbour to the Palisadoes Peninsula. This narrow strip is where you can find Norman Manley International Airport and, farther west, Port Royal, the island's former capital, which was destroyed by an earthquake. Downtown Kingston is considered unsafe, particularly at night, so be careful whenever you go.

Most travelers head to New Kingston, north of downtown. This is the home to hotels and offices as well as several historic sites. New Kingston is bordered by Old Hope Road on the east and Half Way Tree Road (which changes to Constant Spring Road) on the west. The area is sliced by Hope Road, a major thoroughfare that connects this region with the University of the West Indies, about 15 minutes east of New Kingston.

North of New Kingston, the city gives way to steep hills and magnificent homes. East of here, the views are even grander as the road winds into the Blue Mountains. Hope Road, just after the University of the West Indies, becomes Gordon Town Road and starts twisting up through the mountains—it's a route that leaves no room for error.

Devon House, built in 1881 and bought and restored by the government in the 1960s, is filled with period furnishings, such as Venetian crystal chandeliers and period reproductions. You can take a guided tour of the two-story mansion (built with a South American gold miner's fortune) only on a guided tour. On the grounds you can find some of the island's best crafts shops as well as one of the few mahogany trees to have survived Kingston's ambitious but not always careful development. ✉ *26 Hope Rd.* ☎ *876/929–6602* 🎫 *House tour $5* ⊗ *House Mon.–Sat. 9:30–4:30.*

The artists represented at the **National Gallery** may not be household names in other countries, but their paintings are sensitive and moving. You can find works by such Jamaican masters as intuitive painter John Dunkley, and Edna Manley, a sculptor who worked in a cubist style. Among other highlights from the 1920s through 1980s are works by the artist Kapo, a self-taught painter who specialized in religious images. Reggae fans should look for Christopher Gonzalez's controversial statue of Bob Marley (it was slated to be displayed near the National Arena but was placed here because many Jamaicans felt it didn't resemble Marley). ✉ *12 Ocean Blvd., near waterfront* ☎ *876/922–1561* 🎫 *$2* ⊗ *Tues.–Thurs. 10–4:30, Fri. 10–4, Sat. 10–3.*

★ At the height of his career, Bob Marley built a recording studio—painted Rastafarian red, yellow, and green—which now houses the **Bob Marley Museum.** The guided tour takes you through the medicinal herb garden, his bedroom, and other rooms wallpapered with magazine and newspaper articles that chronicle his rise to stardom. The tour includes a 20-minute biographical film on him; there's also a reference library if you want to learn more. Certainly there's much here that will help you to understand Marley, reggae, and Jamaica itself. A striking mural by Jah Bobby, *The Journey of Superstar Bob Marley,* depicts the hero's life from its beginnings, in a womb shaped like a coconut, to enshrinement in the hearts of the Jamaican people. ✉ *56 Hope Rd.* ☎ *876/927–9152* ⊕ *www.bobmarley-foundation.com* 🎫 *$10* ⊗ *Mon.–Sat. 9:30–4.*

Spanish Town. Twelve miles (19 km) west of Kingston on Route A1, Spanish Town was the island's capital when it was ruled by Spain. The town has Georgian Antique Square, the Jamaican People's Museum of Crafts and Technology (in the Old King's House stables), and St. James, the oldest cathedral in the western hemisphere. Spanish Town's original name was Santiago de la Vega, meaning St. James of the Plains.

EAST COAST

Port Antonio. The first Port Antonio tourists arrived in the early 20th century seeking a respite from New York winters. In time, the area became fashionable among a fast-moving crowd that included everyone from Rudyard Kipling to Bette Davis; today, celebs such as Tom Cruise, Eddie Murphy, Brooke Shields, and Denzel Washington dodge the limelight with a getaway in this quiet haven. Although the action has moved elsewhere, the area can still weave a spell. Robin Moore wrote *The French Connection* here, and Broadway's tall and talented Tommy Tune found inspiration for the musical *Nine* while being pampered at Trident.

Port Antonio has also long been a center for some of the Caribbean's finest deep-sea fishing. Dolphin (the delectable fish, not the lovable mammal) is the likely catch here, along with tuna, kingfish, and wahoo. In October the weeklong Blue Marlin Tournament attracts anglers from around the world. By the time they've all had their fill of beer, it's the fish stories—rather than the fish—that carry the day.

A good way to spend a day in Port Antonio is to laze in the deep-azure water of the **Blue Lagoon** (⊠*1 mi [1.5 km] east of San San Beach*). Although there's not much beach to speak of, you can find a water-sports center, changing rooms, and a soothing mineral pool. As this book went to press the lagoon was officially closed, but was occasionally open. Check with tourism officials for an update.

Queen Street, in the residential Titchfield area, a couple of miles north of downtown Port Antonio, has several fine examples of Georgian architecture.

★ **Boston Beach.** A short drive east of Port Antonio is Boston Beach, a don't-miss destination for lovers of jerk pork. The recipe originated with the Arawaks, the island's original inhabitants, but was perfected by the Maroons, the former slaves who refused to surrender to the English when they took over the island. Eating almost nothing but wild hog preserved over smoking coals enabled these former slaves to survive years of fierce guerrilla warfare with the English. Jerk resurfaced in the 1930s, and the spicy barbecue drew diners from around the island. Today a handful of small jerk stands, collectively known as the Boston Jerk Centre, offers fiery flavors cooled by some festival bread and a cold Red Stripe. ⊠*Rte. A4, east of Port Antonio.*

★ **Rio Grande.** The Rio Grande is a granddaddy of river-rafting attractions: an 8-mi-long (13-km-long) swift, green waterway from Berrydale to Rafter's Rest (it flows into the Caribbean at St. Margaret's Bay). The trip of about three hours is made on bamboo rafts pushed along by a raftsman who is likely to be a character. You can pack a picnic lunch and eat it on the raft or on the riverbank; wherever you lunch, a Red Stripe vendor will appear at your elbow. A restaurant, a bar, and souvenir shops are at Rafter's Rest. The trip costs about $52 per two-person raft plus a tip for the boatman. *(For more information on companies that arrange river-rafting excursions, see River Rafting in Sports & the Outdoors, above.)*

Somerset Falls. Located on the Daniels River, these falls are in a veritable botanical garden. A concrete walk to the falls takes you past the ruins of a Spanish aqueduct and Genesis Falls before reaching Hidden Falls. At Hidden Falls, you board a boat and travel beneath the tumbling water; more-daring travelers can swim in a whirlpool or jump off the falls into a pool of water. A bar and restaurant specializing in local seafood is a great place to catch your breath. ⊠*Rte. A4, west of Port Antonio* ☎*876/913–0046* ⊕*www.somersetfallsjamaica.com* 💲*$7.50* ☉*Daily 9–5.*

NORTH COAST

Montego Bay. Today many explorations of MoBay are conducted from a reclining chair—frothy drink in hand—on Doctor's Cave beach. As home of the north-shore airport, Montego Bay is the first taste most visitors have of the island. It's the second-largest city in Jamaica and has a busy cruise pier west of town. Travelers from around the world come and go in this bustling community year-round. The name Montego is derived from *manteca* ("lard" in Spanish). The Spanish first named this Bahía de Manteca, or Lard Bay. Why? The Spanish once shipped hogs from this port city. Jamaican tourism began here in 1924, when the first resort opened at Doctor's Cave beach so that health-seekers could "take the waters." If you can pull yourself away from the water's edge, you'll find some interesting colonial sights in the surrounding area.

★ The **Greenwood Great House** has no spooky legend to titillate, but it's much better than Rose Hall at evoking life on a sugar plantation. The Barrett family, from whom the English poet Elizabeth Barrett Browning descended, once owned all the land from Rose Hall to Falmouth; they built this and several other greathouses on it. (The poet's father, Edward Moulton Barrett, "the Tyrant of Wimpole Street," was born at nearby Cinnamon Hill, the estate of the late country singer Johnny Cash.) Highlights of Greenwood include oil paintings of the Barretts, china made for the family by Wedgwood, a library filled with rare books from as early as 1697, fine antique furniture, and a collection of exotic musical instruments. There's a pub on-site as well. It's 15 mi (24 km) east of Montego Bay. ⊠*Greenwood* ☎*876/953–1077* ⊕*www.greenwoodgreathouse.com* ☜*$12* ⊙*Daily 9–6.*

Fodor's Choice In the 1700s **Rose Hall** may well have been the greatest of greathouses
★ in the West Indies. Today it's popular less for its architecture than for the legend surrounding its second mistress, Annie Palmer. As the story goes, Annie was born in 1802 in England to an English mother and Irish father. When she was 10, her family moved to Haiti, and soon her parents died of yellow fever. Annie was adopted by a Haitian voodoo priestess and soon became skilled in the practice of voodoo. Annie moved to Jamaica, married, and built Rose Hall, an enormous plantation spanning 6,600 acres with more than 2,000 slaves. It's across the highway from the Rose Hall Resort & Country Club. ⊠*N. Coast Hwy.* ☎*876/953–9982* ☜*$15* ⊙*Daily 9–6.*

★ **Bob Marley Centre & Mausoleum.** Travelers with an interest in Bob Marley won't want to miss Nine Mile, the community where the reggae legend was born and is buried. Today his former home is a shrine to his music and values. Tucked behind a tall fence, the site is marked with green and gold flags. Tours are led by Rastafarians, who take visitors through the house and point out the single bed that Marley wrote about in "Is This Love." Visitors also step inside the mausoleum where the singer is buried with his guitar. The site includes a restaurant and gift shop. Visitors from Ocho Rios can arrange transport by taxi, but the round-trip fare is about $175; a less-expensive option is a guided tour. ⊠*Rhoden Hall, Nine Mile* ☎*876/995–1763* ☜*$15* ⊙*Daily 9–4.*

13

Cockpit Country. Fifteen miles (24 km) inland from MoBay is one of the most untouched areas in the West Indies: a terrain of pitfalls and potholes carved by nature in limestone. For nearly a century after 1655 it was known as the Land of Look Behind, because British soldiers nervously rode their horses through here on the lookout for the guerrilla freedom fighters known as Maroons. Former slaves who refused to surrender to the invading English, the Maroons eventually won their independence. Today their descendants live in this area, untaxed and virtually ungoverned by outside authorities. Most visitors to the area stop in Accompong, a small community in St. Elizabeth Parish. You can stroll through town, take in the historic structures, and learn more about the Maroons—considered Jamaica's greatest herbalists.

The **Martha Brae River,** a gentle waterway about 25 mi (40 km) southeast of Montego Bay, takes its name from an Arawak Indian who killed herself because she refused to reveal the whereabouts of a local gold mine to the Spanish. According to legend, she agreed to take them there and, on reaching the river, used magic to change its course, drowning herself and the greedy Spaniards with her. Her *duppy* (ghost) is said to guard the mine's entrance. Rafting on this river is a very popular activity. Martha Brae River Rafting *(⇨ River Rafting in Sports & the Outdoors, above)* arranges trips.

★ **Cranbrook Flower Forest & River Head Adventure Trail.** You can enjoy the north-coast rivers and flowers without the crowds at this botanical reserve filled with blooming orchids, ginger, and ferns. This park is the private creation of Ivan Linton, who has pampered the plants of this former plantation since the early 1980s. Today Linton proudly points out the birds-of-paradise, croton, ginger, heliconia, and begonias as if they were his dear children. The grounds are perfect for a picnic followed by a hike alongside shady Laughlin's Great River. The path climbs high into the hills to a waterfall paradise. Donkey rides, picnicking, croquet, wading, and volleyball are also available here. The complex includes a snack shop and restrooms. ☒ *5 mi (8 km) east of Runaway Bay, 1 mi (1.5 km) off N. Coast Hwy.* ☎ *876/770–8071* 🌐 *www.cranbrookff.com* 🎟 *$10* 🕓 *Daily 9–5.*

Fodor's Choice ★ **Dunn's River Falls.** One of Jamaica's most popular attractions is an eye-catching sight: 600 feet of cold, clear mountain water splashing over a series of stone steps to the warm Caribbean. The best way to enjoy the falls is to climb the slippery steps: don a swimsuit, take the hand of the person ahead of you, and trust that the chain of hands and bodies leads to an experienced guide. The leaders of the climbs are personable fellows who reel off bits of local lore while telling you where to step; you can hire a guide's service for a tip of a few dollars. After the climb, you exit through a crowded market, another reminder that this is one of Jamaica's top tourist attractions. If you can, try to schedule a visit on a day when no cruise ships are in port. ☒ *Off Rte. A1, between St. Ann's Bay and Ocho Rios* ☎ *876/974–2857* 🎟 *$15* 🕓 *Daily 8:30–5.*

Green Grotto Caves. An especially good choice for rainy days, this series of caves offers guided 45-minute tours that include a look at a subterranean lake. The caves have a rich history as a hiding place for everyone from pirates to runaway slaves to the Spanish governor, when he was on the run from the British. It's a good destination if you want to see some of Jamaica's caves without really going off the beaten path. Hard hats are required throughout the tour. ⊠*N. Coast Hwy., 2 mi (3 km) east of Discovery Bay* ☎*876/973–2841* ⊕*www.greengrottocavesja. com* ⊠*$20* ☉*Daily 9–4.*

Ocho Rios. Although Ocho Rios isn't near eight rivers as its name would seem to indicate, it does have a seemingly endless series of cascades that sparkle from limestone rocks along the coast. (The name Ocho Rios came about because the English misunderstood the Spanish *las chorreras*—"the waterfalls.") The town itself isn't very attractive and can be traffic-clogged, but the area has several worthwhile attractions, including the very popular and touristic Dunn's River falls. A few steps from the main road in Ocho Rios are some of the most charming inns and oceanfront restaurants in the Caribbean. Lying on the sand of what seems to be your very own cove or swinging gently in a hammock while sipping a tropical drink, you'll soon forget the traffic that's just a stroll away. The original "defenders" stationed at the Old Fort, built in 1777, spent much of their time sacking and plundering as far afield as St. Augustine, Florida, and sharing their booty with the local plantation owners who financed their missions. Fifteen miles (24 km) west is Discovery Bay, where Columbus landed and where there's a small museum with such artifacts as ships' bells and cannons and iron pots used for boiling sugarcane. Don't miss a drive through Fern Gully, a natural canopy of vegetation filtered by sunlight. (Jamaica has the world's largest number of fern species, more than 570.) To reach the stretch of road called Fern Gully, take the A3 highway south of Ocho Rios.

★ Jamaica's national motto is "Out of Many, One People," and at the **Coyaba River Garden & Museum and Mahoe Waterfalls** you can see exhibits on the many cultural influences that have contributed to the creation of the one. The museum covers the island's history from the time of the Arawak Indians up to the present day. A guided 45-minute tour through the lush 3-acre garden, which is 1.5 mi (2.5 km) south of Ocho Rios, introduces you to the flora and fauna of the island. The complex includes a crafts and gift shop and a snack bar. ⊠*Shaw Park Estate, Shaw Park Ridge Rd.* ☎*876/974–6235* ⊕*www.coyabagardens.com* ⊠*$5* ☉*Daily 8–5.*

In the open-air Island Village shopping and entertainment center, which is owned by Island Records tycoon Chris Blackwell, **Reggae Xplosion** traces the history of Jamaican music. Ska, mento, dance hall, reggae, and more are featured in a series of exhibits spanning two stories. Special sections highlight the careers of some of Jamaica's best-known talents, including Bob Marley, Peter Tosh, and Bunny Wailer. The museum includes a gift shop with recordings and collectibles. ⊠*N. Coast Hwy., Island Village* ☎*876/675–8895* ⊕*www.islandjamaica. com* ⊠*$15* ☉*Mon.–Sat. 9–5.*

★ **Firefly.** About 20 mi (32 km) east of Ocho Rios in Port Maria, Firefly was once Sir Noël Coward's vacation home and is now maintained by the Jamaican National Heritage Trust. Although the setting is Eden-like, the house is surprisingly spartan, considering that he often entertained jet-setters and royalty. He wrote *High Spirits, Quadrille,* and other plays here, and his simple grave is on the grounds next to a small stage where his works are occasionally performed. Recordings of Coward singing about mad dogs and Englishmen echo over the lawns. Tours include a walk through the house and grounds where Coward is buried. The view from the house's hilltop perch is one of the best on the north coast, making Firefly well worth the price of admission. ⊠ *Port Maria* ☎ *876/725–0920* ☞ *$10* ⊙ *Mon.–Thurs. and Sat. 9–5.*

★ **Walkerswood Factory.** To learn more about Jamaican cuisine (as well as the island's bountiful supply of herbs, fruits, and spices), visit the source of many sauces and seasonings. Walkerswood Factory produces everything from jerk sauces to jams and pepper sauces. A one-hour guided tour provides a look at herb gardens, a visit to a re-created hut to learn more about historic countryside life, a jerk marinade demonstration, and sampling Walkerswood products. The site includes a gift shop and snack bar featuring local dishes. ⊠ *About 6 mi (10 km) south of Ocho Rios on A3 in Walkerswood, St. Ann's Bay* ☎ *876/917–2318* ⊕ *www.walkerswood.com* ☞ *$15* ⊙ *Mon.–Sat. 9–4.*

WEST COAST

Negril. In the 18th century, English ships assembled here in convoys for dangerous ocean crossings. The infamous pirate Calico Jack and his crew were captured right here while they guzzled rum. All but two of them were hanged on the spot; Mary Read and Anne Bonney were pregnant at the time, so their executions were delayed.

On the winding coast road 55 mi (89 km) southwest of MoBay, Negril was once Jamaica's best-kept secret, but it has begun to shed some of its bohemian, ramshackle atmosphere for the attractions and activities traditionally associated with MoBay. One thing that hasn't changed around this west-coast center (whose only true claim to fame is a 7-mi [11-km] beach) is a casual approach to life. As you wander from lunch in the sun to shopping in the sun to sports in the sun, you'll find that swimsuits and cover-ups are common attire.

Negril stretches along the coast south from horseshoe-shape Bloody Bay (named when it was a whale-processing center) along the calm waters of Long Bay to the lighthouse. Nearby, divers spiral downward off 50-foot-high cliffs into the deep green depths as the sun turns into a ball of fire and sets the clouds ablaze with color. Sunset is also the time when Norman Manley Boulevard, which intersects West End Road, comes to life with bustling bistros and ear-splitting discos.

♻ Even nonguests can romp at **Hedonism II** (⊠ *Norman Manley Blvd., Rutland Point* ☎ *876/957–5200*). The resort beach is divided into "prude" and "nude" sides; a quick look around reveals where most guests pull their chaise lounges. Nude volleyball, body-painting contests, and shuffleboard keep daytime hours lively; at night most action occurs in the high-tech disco or in the hot tub. Your day pass (which gives you access from 10 to 5 for $65) includes food and drink and participation in water sports, tennis, squash, and other activities. Night passes ($75) cover dinner, drinks, and entrance to the disco. Day or night, reservations are a must; bring a photo ID as well.

For families, **Kool Runnings Waterpark** (⊠ *Norman Manley Blvd.* ☎ *876/ 957–5418* ⊕ *www.koolrunnings.com*) makes a good beach alternative on days when the sea is rough or for travelers not staying at beachfront properties. Admission to the park ($28) includes 10 waterslides and a quarter-mile lazy river float ride; a go-kart track and climbing wall each incur a separate charge. Kids under 48 inches tall can't use some slides so a discounted rate is charged. The park is open Tuesday through Sunday from 10 to 7.

Negril's **lighthouse** (⊠ *West End Rd.*) has guided ships past Jamaica's rocky western coast since 1895. You can stop by the adjacent caretaker's cottage from 11 to 7 (except Tuesday) and, for the price of a tip, climb the spiral steps for the best view in town.

Nature lovers can see more than 100 species of local plants as well as numerous birds and even crocodiles at **Royal Palm Reserve** (⊠ *East of Negril on Sheffield Rd., turn left on Springfield Rd.* ☎ *876/957–3736* ⊕ *www.royalpalmreserve.com*), located on the southern side of the Great Morass. Admission is $10, and the reserve is open daily from 9 to 6.

SOUTH COAST

★ **Appleton Estate.** On a guided tour, you learn about the history of rum making. After a bit of rum history, starting with the days when sugarcane was crushed by donkey power, tours then progress into the modern factory, where one of Jamaica's best-known products is bottled. After the tour, samples flow freely. There's also a good restaurant here serving genuine Jamaican dishes. ⊠ *Hwy. B6, Siloah* ☎ *876/963–9215* ⊕ *www.appletonrum.com* ☑ *$12* ⊗ *Mon.–Sat. 9–4.*

Lovers' Leap. As legend has it, two slaves who were also lovers chose to jump off this 1,700-foot cliff rather than be recaptured by their master. Today it's a favorite stop for its view of the coast (as well as the lover's punch at the bar). Tours of local cacti are available, and a miniature farm demonstrates the dry-farming technique used in this area. ⊠ *Yardley Chase, Treasure Beach* ☎ *876/965–6634* ☑ *Free* ⊗ *Daily.*

Mandeville. At 2,000 feet above sea level, Mandeville is considerably cooler than the coastal areas 25 mi (40 km) to the south. Its vegetation is also lusher, thanks to the mists that drift through the mountains. But climate and flora aren't all that separate it from the steamy coast: Mandeville seems a hilly tribute to all that's genteel in the British character. The people here live in tidy cottages with gardens around a village green; there's even a Georgian courthouse and a parish church.

★ **Y. S. Falls.** A quiet alternative to Dunn's River falls in Ocho Rios, the falls are tucked in a papaya plantation and reached via motorized jitney. If you aren't staying on the south coast, companies in Negril offer half-day excursions. ⊠ *2 Market St., Black River, north of A2, just past town of Middle Quarters* ☎ *876/634–2454* ⊕ *www.ysfalls.com* ⊠ *$12* ☉ *Tues.–Sun. 9:30–4.*

EN ROUTE Although the constant roar of speeding trucks keeps the site from being idyllic, **Bamboo Avenue,** the section of Route A1 between Middle Quarters and Lacovia, is an often-photographed stretch of highway that's completely canopied with tall bamboo. Roadside vendors sell chilled coconuts, cracking them with machetes to reveal the jelly inside.

13

JAMAICA ESSENTIALS

To research prices, get advice from other travelers, and book travel arrangements, visit www.fodors.com.

▌ TRANSPORTATION

BY AIR

AIR TRAVEL TO JAMAICA

Jamaica is well served by major airlines. Cayman Airways connects Jamaica to Grand Cayman and Cayman Brac.

Information Air Canada (☎888/247–2262 in U.S., 888/991–9063 in Jamaica, 876/952–5160 in Montego Bay). **Air Jamaica** (☎800/523–5585 in U.S., 888/359–2475 in Jamaica, 876/952–4300 in Montego Bay). **American Airlines** (☎800/433–7300 in U.S., 800/744–0006 in Jamaica). **British Airways** (☎800/247–9297 in U.S., 800/247–9297 in Jamaica). **Cayman Airways** (☎800/422–9626 in U.S., 876/926–1762 in Kingston, 876/924–8092 in Montego Bay). **Continental Airlines** (☎800/231–0856 in U.S., 800/231–0856 in Jamaica, 876/952–5530 in Montego Bay). **Delta Airlines** (☎800/241–4141 in U.S., 800/221–1212 in Jamaica, 876/940–1834 in Montego Bay). **Northwest Airlines** (☎800/225–2525). **Spirit Airlines** (☎586/791–7300 or 800/772–7117). **United Airlines** (☎800/864–8331 in U.S., 876/979–5845 or 800/538–2929 in Jamaica). **US Airways** (☎800/622–1015).

AIR TRAVEL AROUND JAMAICA

Tim Air and International Airlink offer charter service between Montego Bay's Sangster International Airport and airports in Port Antonio, Ocho Rios, Runaway Bay, Kingston, and Negril. Scheduled service is available on International Airlink between Montego Bay and Kingston. Charter helicopter service is provided by Island Hoppers to Ocho Rios.

Information International Airlink (☎888/247–5465 ⊕www.intlairlink.com). **Island Hoppers** (☎876/974–1285 ⊕www.jamaicahelicoptertours.com). **Tim Air** (☎876/952–2516 in Montego Bay ⊕www.timair.com).

AIRPORTS & TRANSFERS

Many all-inclusive resorts include the cost of airport transfers in their rates. If yours doesn't, you'll have to book a shared-van service at the airport. It's not a cheap transfer to most resort areas from MoBay because of the distances involved. Expect to pay $18 per person one way from Montego Bay to Negril, $25 to Ocho Rios, and $35 to Boscobel (rates are in U.S. dollars).

Major Airports Donald Sangster International Airport (MBJ ⊠Montego Bay ☎876/952–3124 ⊕www.mbjairport.com). **Norman Manley International Airport** (KIN

✉Kingston ☎876/924–8452 ⊕www.manley-airport.com.jm).

Minor Airports Boscobel Aerodrome (✉8 mi [14 km] east of Ocho Rios, Oracabessa ☎876/975–3101). **Negril Aerodrome** (✉Negril ☎876/957–5016).

BY CAR

Driving in Jamaica can be an extremely frustrating chore. You must constantly be on guard—for enormous potholes, people and animals darting out into the street, as well as aggressive drivers. With a one-lane road encircling the island, local drivers are quick to pass other cars—and sometimes two cars will pass simultaneously (inspiring the "undertakers love overtakers" signs seen throughout the island). Gas stations are open daily but accept cash only. Gas costs roughly double the price found in the United States. Driving in Jamaica is on the left, British-style.

Information Budget (☎876/924–8762 in Kingston, 876/979–0438 in Montego Bay ⊕www.budget.com). **Hertz** (☎876/924–8028 in Kingston, 876/952–4250 in Montego Bay ⊕www.hertz.com). **Island Car Rentals** (☎876/924–8075 in Kingston, 876/952–7225 in Montego Bay ⊕www.islandcarrentals.com). **Jamaica Car Rental** (☎876/952–5586 in Montego Bay).

BY TAXI

Some but not all of Jamaica's taxis are metered. If you accept a driver's offer of his services as a tour guide, be sure to agree on a price before the vehicle is put into gear. (Note that a one-day tour should run about $150 to $180, in U.S. dollars, depending on distance traveled.) All licensed taxis display red Public Passenger Vehicle (PPV) plates. Cabs can be called by phone or flagged down on the street. Rates are per car, not per passenger, and 25% is added to the metered rate between midnight and 5 AM. Licensed minivans are also available and bear the red PPV plates. JUTA is the largest taxi franchise with offices in all resort areas.

Information JUTA Kingston (☎876/927–4534 ⊕www.jutakingston.com). **JUTA Montego Bay** (☎876/952–0813 ⊕www.jutatoursjamaica.net). **JUTA Negril** (☎876/957–9197 ⊕www.jutatoursnegrilltd.com). **JUTA Ocho Rios** (☎876/974–2292). **JUTA Port Antonio** (☎876/993–2684).

▌ CONTACTS & RESOURCES

BANKS & EXCHANGE SERVICES

Currency exchange is available at the major airports, in hotels, and in area banks. However, few Americans bother to exchange money, since American dollars are widely accepted. Some ATM machines in Jamaica don't accept American ATM cards, while others will accept American ATM cards and dispense U.S. dollars. Major credit cards are widely accepted throughout the island, although cash is required at gas stations, in markets, and in many small stores. Discover and Diners Club are accepted at many resorts. The official currency is the Jamaican dollar. At this writing the exchange rate was about J$70 to US$1. Prices quoted throughout this chapter are in U.S. dollars, unless otherwise noted.

ELECTRICITY

Like the electrical current in North America, the current in Jamaica is 110 volts but only 50 cycles, with outlets that take two flat prongs. Some hotels provide 220-volt plugs as well as special shaver outlets.

EMERGENCIES

Emergency Services Ambulance and Fire Emergencies (☎110). **Police Emergencies & Air Rescue** (☎119). **Scuba-Diving Emergencies** (✉St. Ann's Bay Hospital, St. Ann's Bay ☎876/972–2272).

Hospitals Cornwall Regional Hospital (✉Mount Salem, Montego Bay ☎876/952–5100). **Mo Bay Hope Medical Center** (✉Half Moon, Montego Bay ☎876/953–3981). **Port Antonio Hospital** (✉Naylor's Hill, Port Antonio ☎876/993–2646). **St. Ann's Bay Hospital** (✉Main St., St. Ann's Bay ☎876/972–2272).

University Hospital of the West Indies
(✉Mona, Kingston ☎876/927–1620).

INTERNET, MAIL & SHIPPING

Internet service is becoming more common, and most hotels offer at least limited service, either at public terminals (often free at the all-inclusive resorts) to Wi-Fi. Postcards may be mailed anywhere in the world for J$50. Letters cost J$60 to the United States and Canada, J$70 to Europe, J$90 to Australia and New Zealand. Due to costly and slow air-shipping service, most travelers carry packages home, even large wood carvings.

SAFETY

Crime in Jamaica is, unfortunately, a persistent problem, so don't let the beauty of the island cause you to abandon the caution you would practice in any unfamiliar place. Many of the headlines are grabbed by murders in Kingston, often gang-related; violent crimes are, for the most part, largely a problem for residents who live in the city. Visitors should be extremely cautious about visiting many of the neighborhoods in Kingston that are outside the business district of New Kingston.

Property crime is an islandwide problem. Utilize your in-room safe and be sure to lock all doors—including balconies—when you leave your room or villa. Traveler's checks are a good idea in Jamaica, being safer than cash (just keep a record of the check numbers in a secure place so they can be replaced if necessary). Never leave your car unlocked, and never leave valuables inside it, even when locked. Ignore efforts, however persistent, to sell you ganja (marijuana), which is illegal across the island.

TAXES

The departure tax is $27 and must be paid in cash if it's not added to the cost of your airline tickets; this policy varies by carrier, although most ticket prices now include the departure tax. Jamaica has replaced the room occupancy tax with a V.A.T. of 15% on most goods and services, which is already incorporated into the prices of taxable goods. Since May 2005, incoming air passengers are charged a $10 tourism enhancement fee; incoming cruise passengers pay a $2 fee; both these fees are almost always included in the price of your airline ticket or cruise passage.

TELEPHONES

Cellular service is expanding throughout Jamaica, especially in Kingston and in the resort areas (service remains sporadic in the mountainous regions). GSM cell phones equipped with tri-band or world-roaming service will find coverage throughout much of the coastal region. Cellular service averages about $1.50 to $2 per minute on the island. Prepaid SIM cards are a more-economical way for travelers who plan to make a large number of local calls.

To dial Jamaica from the United States, just dial 1 + the area code 876. Some U.S. phone companies, such as MCI, provide only limited credit-card calls from Jamaica because they've been victims of fraud. The best option is to purchase Jamaican phone cards, sold in most stores across the island.

TIPPING

Most hotels and restaurants add a 10% service charge to your bill. When a service charge isn't included, a 10% to 20% tip is expected. Tips of 10% to 20% are customary for taxi drivers as well. However, many all-inclusives have a strict no-tipping policy.

TOUR OPTIONS

Because most vacationers don't rent cars for both safety and cost reasons, guided tours are a popular option if you want to take a break from the beach and explore. Check with your hotel concierge for information on half- and full-day tours that offer pickup at your resort. Jamaica's size and slow roads mean that you can't expect to see all the island on any one trip; even a full-day tour will concentrate on just one part of the island. Most of the tours are

13

similar in both content and price. If you're in Montego Bay, tours often include one of the plantation houses in the area. Several Negril-based companies offer tours to Y. S. Falls on the south coast. Tours from Ocho Rios might include any of the area's top attractions, including Dunn's River falls, Kingston, or Mayfield Falls. In almost all cases, you'll arrange your tour through the tour desk of your resort. However, a few of these tours are quite unique, including the following.

Visitors to the south coast, Mandeville, and Kingston areas can experience more of the real Jamaica through Countrystyle, which offers unique, personalized tours of island communities. You're linked with community residents based on your interests; tours can include anything from bird-watching in Mandeville to nightlife in Kingston.

Reggae buffs visiting the Ocho Rios area enjoy the Zion Bus Line, which includes a visit to Bob Marley's boyhood home. Travelers ride a country-style bus painted in bright colors to the island's interior and the village of Nine Mile. The tour includes a look at the simple home where Marley was born and is now buried.

Information **Countrystyle Peace Village** (⊠ 62 Ward Ave., Mandeville ☎ 876/962–7758 or 876/488–7207 🖷 876/962–1461 ⊕ www. countrystylecommunitytourism.com). **Zion Bus Line** (⊠ Chukka Caribbean Adventures, Llandovery, St. Ann's Bay ☎ 876/972–2506 ⊕ www. chukkacaribbean.com).

VISITOR INFORMATION

Before You Leave **Jamaica Tourist Board** (⊕ www.visitjamaica.com ☎ 305/665–0557 in Miami).

In Jamaica **Jamaica Tourist Board** (⊠ 64 Knutsford Blvd., Kingston ☎ 876/929–9200, 888/995–9999 on-island help line ⊠ Cornwall Beach, Montego Bay ☎ 876/952–2445 ⊠ City Centre Plaza, Port Antonio ☎ 876/993–3051).

WEDDINGS

Thanks to its accommodating marriage laws, tropical beauty, and bountiful couples-only resorts, Jamaica is one of the top wedding destinations in the Caribbean. Several all-inclusives, including Super-Clubs and Couples, offer free wedding ceremonies, including the officiant's fee, marriage license, tropical flowers, a small wedding cake, champagne, and more.

Most couples work with their resort's wedding coordinator in advance of their visit to handle the legal paperwork. You can marry after only 24 hours on the island if you've applied for your license and supplied all necessary forms beforehand. You need to supply proof of citizenship (a passport or certified copy of your birth certificate signed by a notary public), written parental consent for couples under age 18, proof of divorce with the original or certified copy of the divorce decree if applicable, and copy of the death certificate if a previous marriage ended in death. Blood tests are not required.

Martinique

The swaying palms of Les Salines

WORD OF MOUTH

"A little bit of French can be important. As in France, people in Martinique will be friendly and helpful if they know you're at least trying in their language."

—xkenx

"Martinique has always been my true love. I prefer the north, with its hikes and wild beaches. There is a very special hotel, Le Domaine Saint Aubin there . . . ."

—Tellurian

WELCOME TO MARTINIQUE

PARIS IN THE TROPICS

The largest of the Windward Islands, Martinique is 425 square mi (1,101 square km). The southern part of the island is all rolling hills and sugarcane fields; it's also where you'll find the best beaches and most development. In the north are craggy cliffs, lush vegetation, and one of the Caribbean's largest volcanoes, Mont Pelée.

At 4,600 feet, Mont Pelée is one of the tallest volcanoes in the Caribbean. It last erupted in 1902, killing some 30,000 people in just two minutes.

Martinique Passa;

Macoub
Grand-Rivière
Anse-
Ceron **Habitation Céron**

Le Prêcheur

Mont Pelée

Le Morne
Rouge
N2

St-Pierre
Rade de St-Pierre
Musée Gauguin
Neisson Distillery **6**

Carbet Morne
Aqualand Vert
N2

Bellefontaine

Case-Pil

*Ca
r
i
b
b
e
a
n

S
e
a*

The impressionist painter Paul Gauguin lived in Carbet after he was dismissed from a job working on the Panama Canal.

0		5 mi
0	5 km	

KEY	
⌁	*Beaches*
1	*Restaurants*
1	*Hotels*

Joie de vivre is the credo in this French enclave, which is often characterized as a Caribbean suburb of Paris. Exotic fruit grows on the volcanoes' forested flanks amid a profusion of wild orchids and hibiscus. The sheer lushness of it all inspired the tropical paintings of one-time resident Paul Gauguin.

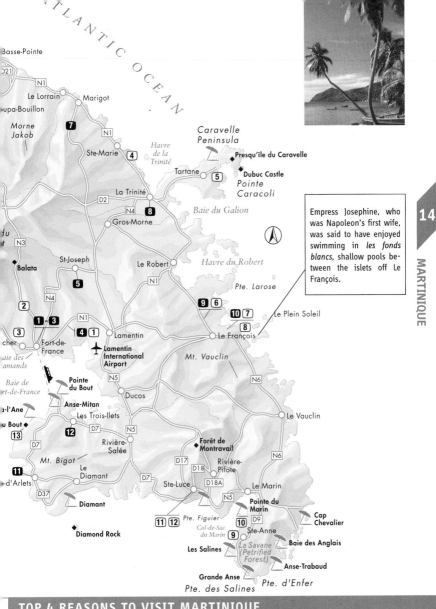

ATLANTIC OCEAN

Basse-Pointe

Le Lorrain · Marigot

oupa-Bouillon

Morne Jakob · **7**

Ste-Marie **4**

Havre de la Trinité

Tartane **5**

Caravelle Peninsula

◆ Presqu'île du Caravelle

◆ Dubuc Castle

Pointe Caracoli

La Trinité D2

N4 **8**
Gros-Morne

Baie du Galion

du N3

◆ **Balata**

St-Joseph **5**

Le Robert N1

Havre du Robert

Pte. Larose

9 6

14

Empress Josephine, who was Napoleon's first wife, was said to have enjoyed swimming in *les fonds blancs*, shallow pools between the islets off Le François.

MARTINIQUE

10 7 Le Plein Soleil

8

2
1 - **3**
3
cher **4 1** Lamentin
Fort-de-France
aie des amands

✈ **Lamentin International Airport**

Le François

Mt. Vauclin

Baie de rt-de-France

a-l'Ane

Pointe du Bout

Ducos N5

N6

Anse-Mitan
Les Trois-Îlets

u Bout ◆
13

12 D7

N5

Rivière-Salée

Forêt de Montravail ◆

Le Vauclin

Mt. Bigot

11
-d'Arlets

Le Diamant D7

D37

Diamant

D17

D18

Rivière-Pitote

Ste-Luce D18A

N6

Le Marin

Pointe du Marin

◆ *Diamond Rock*

11 12 *Pte. Figuier*
Cul-de-Sac du Marin
Les Salines

10 D9

9 Ste-Anne

La Savane (Petrified Forest)

Cap Chevalier

Baie des Anglais

Anse-Trabaud

Grande Anse
Pte. des Salines

Pte. d'Enfer

TOP 4 REASONS TO VISIT MARTINIQUE

1 A magical sensuality infuses everything; it will awaken dormant desires and fuel existing fires.

2 A full roster of beautiful beaches will let you enjoy sun and sand.

3 Excellent French food, not to mention French music and fashion make the island a paradise for Francophiles.

4 Hospitable, stylish, small hotels abound, but there are big resorts, too, if you want that scene.

MARTINIQUE PLANNER

Island Activities

Martinique has plenty of **beaches** for relaxing, including some nice white-sand beaches south of Fort-de-France. Anse Corps de Garde in Ste-Luce and Les Saline in Ste-Anne are among the nicest.

You'll get a better taste of the island if you take part in the myriad outdoor activities. Martinique is a major **sailing** center (the Moorings has a large charter base there); **windsurfing** is also popular, as is **deep-sea fishing**. On land, there are **canopy tours**, **mountain-biking** excursions, and **horseback riding**.

Shoppers will enjoy inexpensive French wines and the fresh-from-France fashions available in Fort-de-France's boutiques. Locally made jewelry and baskets can also be good buys.

Most hotels have entertainment during the high season, but there are also plenty of **nightspots** for dancing, though the crowds tend to be younger (and mostly local).

Enjoying fine **French and creole cuisine** is also at the top of many people's lists; the island has many wonderful restaurants. Travelers looking to save on high euro prices may find relative bargains on the many prix-fixe menus (some of which include wine).

Logistics

Getting to Martinique: Although there are just a few nonstop flights, connections are still available through St. Lucia, St. Maarten, and Guadeloupe on smaller island-hopper planes. It's also possible to get to Martinique by ferry from Dominica, Guadeloupe, or St. Lucia, a less-desirable though affordable trip. The modern Lamentin International Airport (FDF) is about a 15-minute taxi ride from Fort-de-France and some 40 minutes from Les Trois-Ilets Peninsula.

Hassle Factor: Medium to High.

Nonstops: You can fly nonstop from Atlanta (Delta, weekly) or Miami (Air France, seasonal), but most travelers connect in San Juan (American Eagle). There's also a nonstop charter from New York–JFK (by Club Med, weekly in season).

On the Ground

Taxis in Martinique are expensive, so airport transfer costs must become a part of your vacation budget. From the airport to Fort-de-France you'll pay at least €30; from the airport to Pointe du Bout, about €35; and to Tartane, about €40. A 40% surcharge is levied between 7 PM and 6 AM and on Sunday. This means that if you arrive at night, depending on where your hotel is, it may be cheaper (although not safer) to rent a car from the airport and keep it for 24 hours than to take a taxi to your hotel.

Renting a Car: It's worth the hassle to rent a car—if for only a day or two—so that you can explore more of the island. Just be prepared for a manual shift, steep mountainous roads, and heavy traffic. Prices are expensive, about €70 per day or €330 per week (unlimited mileage) for a manual shift, perhaps more for an automatic, which is rare. You may save money by waiting to book your car rental on the island for a reduced weekly rate from a local agency. There's an extra charge if you drop the car off at the airport, having rented it somewhere else on the island. A valid U.S. driver's license and International Driver's Permit are needed to rent a car for up to 20 days.

Where to Stay

Martinique's accommodations range from tiny inns called relais créoles to splashy tourist resorts—some all-inclusive—and restored plantation houses. Several hotels are clustered in Point du Bout on Les Trois-Ilets Peninsula, which is connected to Fort-de-France by ferry. Other clusters are in Ste-Luce and Le François, but other hotels and relais can be found all over the island. Since Martinique is the largest of the Windward Islands, this can mean a substantial drive to your hotel after a long flight or ferry trip. You may want to stay closer to the airport on your first night.

Large Resorts: There are only a few deluxe properties on the island. Those that lack megastar ratings offer an equally appealing mixture of charisma, hospitality, and French style. Larger hotels often have the busy, slightly frenetic feel that the French seem to like.

Relais Créoles: Small, individually owned inns are still available on Martinique, though they may be far removed from the resort clusters.

Villas: Groups and large families can save money by renting a villa, but the language barrier and need for a car can make this a less-desirable option.

Hotel & Restaurant Costs

⇨*For information on hotel meal plans, see Accommodations in Caribbean Essentials.*

WHAT IT COSTS IN U.S. DOLLARS

$$$$	$$$	$$	$	¢
Restaurants				
over $30	$20–$30	$12–$20	$8–$12	under $8
Hotels*				
over $350	$250–$350	$150–$250	$80–$150	under $80
Hotels**				
over $450	$350–$450	$250–$350	$125–$250	under $125

*EP, BP, CP **AI, FAP, MAP Restaurant prices are for a main course at dinner and include any taxes or service charges. Hotel prices are per night for a double room in high season, excluding taxes, service charges, and meal plans (except at all-inclusives).

When to Go

High season runs from mid-November through May, and the island can be quiet the rest of the year, with some hotels closing down for months, particularly in September and October. Those places that remain open offer significant discounts.

Martinique's **Carnival** begins in January and runs until Lent, not unlike Mardi Gras in New Orleans.

About 20 days into Lent there's a mini-Carnival called **Mi-carême**; this one-day hiatus from abstinence includes a rash of parties and dances before sober times return until Easter.

Early August sees the **Tour des Yoles Rondes** point-to-point yawl race.

In odd-numbered years, the early-December **Jazz à la Martinique** festival usually draws a wide range of international talent, including such top performers as Branford Marsalis.

14

By Eileen
Robinson
Smith

AS AMERICAN KIDS ARE PUTTING their costumes together for a Halloween night of black and orange, businesses here are closing their shutters at midday for a four-day weekend: *La Toussaint*. On All Saints' Day, Martinicans make their annual pilgrimage to honor their dead at cemeteries gleaming white from this year's coat of paint on the aboveground tombs and crypts. The women selling plastic flowers are stationed across the street; the peanut lady, nuts wrapped in conical brown paper, sits at the front gate. Taxis and cars pull up as the dark curtain of night comes down. Hundreds of candles illuminate the black-and-white checkerboard tiles and photos of departed loved ones. Tears glisten on the cheeks of a *grandmé re*. But this is also an annual family reunion where relatives kiss each other warmly on both cheeks.

Numerous scattered ruins and other historical monuments reflect the richness of Martinique's sugarcane plantocracy, of *rhum* and the legacy of slavery. The aristocratic planters are gone, but some things haven't changed so much. The island's economy depends on *les bananes* (bananas), *l'ananas* (pineapples), cane sugar, rum, fishing, and even—*voilà*—tourism, though it is not the lifeblood of the island. Martinicans will be glad you came, but there's no gushing welcome. Most islanders just go about their business, with thousands employed in government jobs offering more paid holidays than most Americans can imagine. Martinicans enjoy their time off, celebrating everything from *le fin de la semaine* (the weekend) to Indian feast days, sailboat races, and Carnival.

Christopher Columbus first sighted this gorgeous island in 1502, when it was inhabited by the fierce Caraïbes, who had terrorized the peace-loving Arawaks. The Arawaks called their home Madinina (the Isle of Flowers), and for good reason. Exotic wild orchids, frangipani, anthurium, jade vines, flamingo flowers, and hundreds of vivid varieties of hibiscus still thrive here.

Though the actual number of French residents does not exceed 15% of the total population, Martinique is still a part of France, an overseas *département* to be exact, and French is the official language, though the vast majority of the residents also speak Creole. In colonial days, Martinique was the administrative, social, and cultural center of the French Antilles, a rich, aristocratic island famous for its beautiful women. The island even gave birth to an empress, Napoléon's Joséphine. It saw the full flowering of a plantocracy, with servants and soirees, wine cellars and snobbery. Islanders still enjoy a fairly high standard of living, and the per-capita GNP is the highest of any island in the French Antilles.

Martinique is the largest stronghold of the *békés*—the descendants of the original French planters—and they are still the privileged class on any of the French-Caribbean islands. Many control Martinique's most profitable businesses from banana plantations and rum distilleries to car dealerships. The island's elite dress in designer outfits straight off the Paris runways. In the airport waiting room, you can almost always tell the *Martiniquaises* by the well-tailored cut of their fashionable clothes.

Located between the Caribbean and the Atlantic, Martinique is 425 square mi (1,101 square km) in size and 72 mi (120 km) south of sister island Guadeloupe. English-speaking Dominica is Martinique's nearest neighbor, 15 mi (25 km) to the north. South is St. Lucia, 22 mi (37 km) away.

Of the island's 392,000 inhabitants, 100,000 live in Fort-de-France and its environs. Martinique has 34 separate municipalities; some little fishing villages on the lush north coast seem to be stuck in time.

If you believe in magic, Martinique has it, as well as a sensuality that fosters romance. It has become known as the island of *revenants*, those who always return. *Et pourquoi non?*

14

WHERE TO STAY

Larger hotels usually include a big buffet breakfast of eggs, fresh fruit, cheese, yogurt, croissants, baguettes, jam, and café au lait. Smaller *relais* (inns) often have open-air terrace kitchenettes. At almost all properties, you can request smoking or no-smoking rooms; the new French law banning smoking in public places went into effect January 2008. Alas, hotel rooms are considered private. Most hotels do not have elevators and many are built on hillsides, so if you have issues with stairs- or path-climbing, be sure to ask about that. An American company has earned the bid to take over the former Kalenda in Pointe du Bout and it is slated to be a 200-plus-room facility. Habitation Le Grange, a northern plantation-hotel that had its glory days in decades past, has been sold. It will not reopen as a hotel. The unexpected closure of La Plantation Leyritz made front-page headlines.

VILLAS & CONDOMINIUMS

If you're staying a week or longer, you can often save money by renting a villa or apartment with a kitchen where you can prepare your own meals. The more-upscale rentals come with French-speaking maids and/ or cooks. Don't forget to add in the cost of a car rental to your vacation budget. **French Caribbean International** (☎ 800/322–2223 ⊕ *www.french caribbean.com*), an English-speaking reservation service operated for decades by Gerard Hill, can help you with both villa rentals and hotel rooms. At the **Villa Rental Service** (☎ 0596/71–56–11 🖷 0596/63–11– 64) an English-speaking staffer can help you find a home, a villa, or an apartment to rent for a week or a month. Most properties are in the southern part of the island near good beaches.

$$$　📺**Villa Thalèmont.** Located on the breezy Atlantic coast, on a point facing the ocean, with a wide sweep of lawn, this private villa is 15 minutes from the unspoiled town of Le François. A charming wooden villa embellished with Victorian fretwork, it replicates the colonial homes of the plantation era, with its wooden trey ceilings and floors of green ebony. Authentic African art, fabrics, and hand-hewn wooden furnishings make this villa unique, a study in white with some

CLOSE UP

A How-To for Dining in Martinique

Dining in Martinique is a delightful culinary experience, but as with driving here, it is best to get some directions before you head out. First of all, as in France, *entrées* are appetizers; the main courses will usually be labeled as follows: *poissons* (fish); *viandes* (meat); or *principal plats* (literally, main courses). You will notice that the appetizers are almost as expensive as the mains—and if the appetizer is foie gras you'll pay just as much as for a main course, but it is oh so worth it.

Entrecote is a sirloin steak, usually cut too thin. A filet mignon is a rarity, but you will see *filet mignon du porc,* which is pork tenderloin. *Ouassous* are incredible freshwater crayfish. Don't be alarmed when they are served with their heads on. Similarly, if a fish dish does not specify fillet, you will be looking into its eyes while carving flesh from its bones.

Every respectable restaurant has an admirable wine *carte,* and the offerings will be almost completely French, with few half bottles. Wines by the glass are often swill and are best avoided.

Finally, don't ever embarrass yourself by asking for a doggie bag: you will be considered gauche!

ocher tiled floors. With three bedrooms, two bathrooms, and a well-equipped, French cook's kitchen, a family or double-couples will love this villa. On the back lawn, a grill and a maxi-market umbrella shading a teak table and chairs invite alfresco dining. Guests have pool privileges at a nearby boutique hotel/restaurant. Pictures of the villa are available from the villa manager, Marie Montabord Marc. **Pros:** Gorgeous ocean views, diving float, 10 minutes by small boat to two islets. **Cons:** A car is a must, the road is "rough." ⊠*Point Thalèmont, Le François* ☎*0696/37–16–46 or 0596/71–35–24 for villa manager, Marie Montabord Marc* ⌘ *marie_montabord_marc@hotmail.com* ➦*3 bedrooms* ⌂*no a/c (some), DVD, Ethernet, weekly maid service, beachfront, laundry facilities* ▭*No credit cards (international wire transfer allowed for deposit only)* ⌖*1-week min., 5-person max.*

SOUTH OF FORT-DE-FRANCE

$$$$ **Cap Est Lagoon Resort & Spa.** A member of the Relais and Châteaux
★ group, Martinique's most exclusive resort has brought back the wealthy, international set. The staff strives to make sure that guests leave satisfied. Contemporary villas (some bi-level) have a Franco-Caribbean design, with Southeast Asian influences; most have a view of the crystalline lagoon. The less-expensive garden rooms have water views from their second-floor bedrooms, but no private plunge pools. All suites have CD-DVD players and plasma TVs. Discriminating guests (as well as nonguests) can indulge themselves at the elegant Spa by Guerlain; from the soft music to the minimalist decor, it's a soothing place to enjoy professional treatments. Sports activities include kayaking, kite surfing, yoga, and exploring the neighboring islands by yacht. **Pros:** Sophisticated and elegant, big main pool, island's most contemporary

bar/lounge but with a Martinican feel, and Franco-Caribbean gourmet room. **Cons:** Not a whole lot to do, somewhat isolated, beach is not expansive. ⊠ *Quartier Cap Est, Le François* ☎ *0596/54–80–80 or 800/735–2478* ⊕ *www.capest.com* ↘ *50 suites* ⚒ *In-room: refrigerator, DVD, dial-up. In-hotel: 2 restaurants, room service, bars, tennis court, pool, gym, spa, beachfront, water sports, no elevator, concierge, laundry service, public Internet, public Wi-Fi* ⊟ *AE, MC, V* ⊧⦶ *BP.*

> ### FRENCH PLUMBING
>
> If you aren't familiar with hand-held showers and intricate levers, you can easily flood the bathroom and scald yourself. When the bellman gives you the walk-through, ask him to explain the plumbing. For example, toilets have two depressors; one is for a quick flush, the other a strong and serious flush. Bidets are common. In self-catering villas, if there is a washing machine or a dishwasher, make sure you have a lesson.

$$$$ ⚎ **Sofitel Bakoua Martinique.** Impres-
★ sive wrought-iron gates open to what is, undoubtedly, one of Martinique's best resorts. French guests call it a "human hotel," where one can cocoon. Formerly an estate, the original structure has that East India Company look, with cane-and-teak plantation-style furnishings and terra-cotta tiles. From the circular bar and the adjacent pool, the views of the yachts in the bay are magical. Walk down the pier to the thatched-roof rotunda that shades the Coco Bar. Suites, like the Amanda, are a throwback to gracious estate living. Down pillows and European linens, as well as comfy window seats, give the petite, beach-level rooms a sumptuous feel. The staff, once a bit aloof, is usually efficient and friendly. Nightly entertainment makes this one of the island's social centers. **Pros:** New sailboat for charter, no more birds at breakfast stealing bites, new dock. **Cons:** Constructed in stages so some rooms show age while others are fresh, facades are not all pretty, service can be inconsistent. ⊠ *Pointe du Bout, Les Trois-Ilets* ☎ *0596/66–02–02* ⊕ *www.sofitel.com* ↘ *133 rooms, 6 suites* ⚒ *In-room: safe, refrigerator. In-hotel: 3 restaurants, bars, tennis courts, pool, beachfront, water sports, no elevator, public Internet, public Wi-Fi, parking (no fee), no-smoking rooms* ⊟ *AE, DC, MC, V* ⊧⦶ *BP.*

$$$ ⚎ **Club Med Buccaneer's Creek.** Reborn in 2006 as one of the French
Fodor'sChoice chain's most upscale villages, this flagship is part of Club Med's strategy
★ of meeting the more-refined needs of international travelers. There are several dozen suites, a full-service spa, and a huge seaside pool with sensual Indonesian beds scattered around its periphery. The cuisine at the main buffet is consistently appealing and often amazing, such as when seared foie gras is offered as an appetizer. Situated on one of the island's best beaches, the resort attracts an international mix of singles, couples, and a few families. This branch has always had a fun environment, and that hasn't changed. Everyone parties until the wee hours, heading out the next day to the spa for a rejuvenating massage, so they can do it all over again. **Pros:** hip, still seems new, Club Med spirit is contagious. **Cons:** the one stand-alone restaurant is not memorable, heavy occupancy, some first-timers just don't fancy the Club Med style.

14

⊠ *Pointe Marin, Ste-Anne* ☎ *0596/76–72–72* ⊕ *www.clubmed.com* ⤶ *249 rooms, 44 suites* ⚬ *In-room: safe, refrigerator. In-hotel: 3 restaurants, bar, tennis courts, pool, gym, spa, beachfront, water sports, no elevator, laundry service, public Internet, public Wi-Fi, parking (no fee), no-smoking rooms* ⊟ *AE, MC, V* ⦿ *AI.*

$$–$$$ 🏨 **Le Plein Soleil.** Long one of our favorites, this heavenly hideaway
Fodor's Choice   that underwent a complete transformation in 2006 has been featured
★   so frequently in French, international, and American media that it has become a celebrity hotel. The existing accommodations in creole *cases* (cottages)—painted red, purple, and subtle earth tones—have been enlarged, soundproofed, completely refurnished, and given updated bathrooms and terraces that maximize the glorious sea view. Each now has a flat-screen TV, and the decor throughout is enlivened with the latest designer offerings from Bangkok. Scattered throughout the lush grounds are four bi-level bungalows with private plunge pools. Indian massage is now offered, and the included breakfast has reached a higher, creative level. With a fishpond at its entrance, the terrace restaurant has been expanded, adding a deck with a monumental view. **Pros:** Stimulating client mix, owner is on-site and accessible, sophisticated and artistic ambience is unique in Martinique. **Cons:** Rough road (particularly in rainy season), somewhat remote hilltop location, smallest rooms have small bathrooms. ⊠ *Villa Lagon Sarc, Pointe Thalèmont, Le François* ☎ *0596/38–07–77* ⊕ *www.hotelpleinsoleil.fr/hotel* ⤶ *16 bungalows* ⚬ *In-room: safe, refrigerator, Wi-Fi. In-hotel: restaurant, pool, no elevator, public Internet, public Wi-Fi, parking (no fee)* ⊟ *MC, V* ⦿ *BP.*

$–$$ 🏨 **Karibea Sainte Luce Resort.** This complex of three once-independent
☺   hotels, which share facilities, is on a nice stretch of beach and offers rooms at the right price. The Amyris Hotel—the best of the bunch—is all junior suites; with enviable views of the idyllic cove, superior rooms are just that, and have kitchenettes to boot. Also on the beach is the simpler Amandiers Hotel (if you go this route, you'll be happier with a superior room). However, a standard junior suite at Amyris is just €10 more than a standard room at Amandiers. All-new bathrooms are going into the Amandiers. The comfy Caribia apartments, across the street from the two beachfront hotels, have all-new rattan furniture packages with colorful, tropical flowers, terrace kitchens (some new appliances), garden views, and a small but well-stocked commissary. **Pros:** Larger loggia rooms in Amandiers are best for Americans yet cost 25% more, can walk the beach to town or take shuttle for just €4 round-trip, guests can use amenities at all-three hotels. **Cons:** Best with a rental car, no bellmen, no chaises on beach. ⊠ *Quartier Désert, Ste-Luce* ☎ *0596/62–12–00, 0596/62–11–91 for reservations* ⊕ *www.karibea.com* ⤶ *116 rooms (Amandiers), 108 junior suites (Amyris), 75 apartments (Caribia)* ⚬ *In-room: safe, kitchen (some), refrigerator. In-hotel: 2 restaurants, bars, tennis court, pools, beachfront, water sports, no elevator, children's programs (ages 4–11), public Internet, public Wi-Fi, parking (no fee)* ⊟ *AE, MC, V* ⦿ *EP.*

$–$$ 🏨 **Manoir de Beauregard.** Built in the 18th century, this plantation house has thick stone walls, mullioned windows, and loads of character. The three original rooms upstairs in the manor house are the best. Number 1 is lovely, with toile fabrics, but Number 3 is huge, with wood-beam ceilings, an antique wicker chaise, rockers, and a four-poster bed. The rooms in the modern annex lack charisma. The bungalows, built of rich Brazilian wood, are much more attractive. The restaurant is well regarded. Owned by the St. Cyr family, the hotel hosts many local weddings and art exhibits. **Pros:** Character and history, walking distance to simple, authentic town of Ste-Anne, in greathouse you can visualize yesteryear. **Cons:** Not much going on, no resort amenities, no beach. ⊠ *Chemin des Salines, Ste-Anne* ☎ *0596/76–73–40* ⊕ *www.manoirde beauregard.com* ⇆ *11 rooms, 3 bungalows* ⅃ *In-room: kitchen (some). In-hotel: restaurant, bar, pool, no elevator, parking (no fee)* ▤ *MC, V* ⊙ *Closed Sept. and Oct.* ⏁ *CP.*

14

$ 🏨 **Pierre & Vacances.** This family-oriented lodging is a happening place, ↻ with good music and tropical flowers in the pillared lobby. Energetic (but not annoying) staffers make the sports really enjoyable, whether it's *aqua gym* or scuba diving. If you overexert yourself, recuperate with a reflexology massage with essential oils. The amphitheater is the setting for many *serious* parties and concerts. The apartments, which are soundproof and have kitchenettes, are attractive but not luxurious. The best are those on the higher floors, and they are worth the climb for the knockout views. A small but diverse commissary supplies most simple cooking needs. **Pros:** Strong fun quotient, substantial roster of activities, many staffers speak English. **Cons:** Densely populated, rooms simple and not chic, lots of kids. ⊠ *Pointe Philippeau, Lieu-dit "Pavillon," Ste-Luce* ☎ *0596/62–12–62* ⊕ *www.pierrevacances.com* ⇆ *337 apartments* ⅃ *In-room: safe, kitchen. In-hotel: 3 restaurants, bars, tennis court, pool, beachfront, diving, water sports, no elevator, children's programs (ages 3–12), laundry service* ▤ *AE, MC, V* ⊙ *Closed Sept.–mid-Oct.* ⏁ *EP.*

FORT-DE-FRANCE & POINTS NORTH

$$ 🏨 **Le Domaine Saint Aubin.** This former estate is perched on a hilltop overlooking the sea, so it has a breathtaking view. An interesting Parisian couple returned to the husband's homeland and lovingly restored the 19th-century creole manor house with six simple guest rooms opening onto a verandah. The original rooms on the first floor of the main house have neither the charm nor the island antiques found in the public areas, but the newer rooms have some antiques and more style. Seven rooms (five doubles and two bi-level "quadruples") have been carved out of the original stables, and three four-room lodges, built in the same Louisiana-style architecture, house a fitness room and a conference room. A new media room with a wide-screen plasma TV is a most welcome addition. The restaurant is elegant, and has a fixed-price menu. **Pros:** You can daydream yourself into a more-gracious era, hip owners are scintillating company, wheelchair-accessible rooms. **Cons:** Somewhat remote location requires a car, original rooms are not stylish. ⊠ *Petite Rivière Salée, off rte. 1, La Trinité* ☎ *0596/69–34–77 or 0696/40–99–59* ⊕ *www.ledomainesaintaubin.com* ⇆ *30 rooms* ⅃ *In-*

room: no TV. In-hotel: restaurant, pool, no elevator, public Internet, Wi-Fi, parking (no fee) ▤*MC, V* ⦿*CP.*

$$ 🏨**La Valmenière Hôtel.** This high-rise, perched on a hillside overlooking Fort-de-France, is the closest to the airport (5 mi [8 km]) and is ideal for first- or last-night stays. The style is French *moderne*, and the lobby looks super, with espresso-color furnishings. The place has an efficient and caring staff and is constantly upgrading. The "business corner" as well as the meeting room in the lobby stay busy. The Valmenière stays well occupied with business travelers and in-the-know sojourners. Leisure time can be spent mocking the traffic below from the infinity pool or bubbling in the hot tub on the solarium level. There's a fun bar-brasserie, and Friday night is particularly convivial with a piano man playing. Inquire about the weekend packages. **Pros:** Always alive and active, fine dining restaurant, new suites with balconies. **Cons:** Primarily a business hotel, rooms are large but simplistic, lack panache. ✉*Av. des Arawaks, Fort-de-France* ☎*0596/75–75–75* ⊕*www.karibea.com* ⟿*116 rooms, 4 suites* ⚲*In-room: safe, refrigerator, Wi-Fi. In-hotel: 2 restaurants, room service, bar, pool, gym, laundry service, public Internet, public Wi-Fi, no-smoking rooms* ▤*AE, MC, V* ⦿*EP.*

$–$$ 🏨**Squash Hôtel.** This well-run business hotel is ideally located if you need to sleep close to the airport (15 minutes away) or want to explore Fort-de-France (10 minutes). The lobby is done in blue and white, with attractive wicker furnishings. The front-desk staff is efficient and bilingual. Although the rooms aren't luxurious, they are cheery and bright, with a fresh look and comfortable furnishings. Breakfast is a bountiful buffet at the terrace restaurant by the pool. Afterward you may be tempted to stay put and enjoy the panorama of the sea and the city. If you want to go into town, there's a bus just down the hill for €1. **Pros:** Key staffers speak English, close to city but with suburban quiet, always good Franco-Caribbean cuisine. **Cons:** Not a handsome facade, few resort amenities. ✉*3 bd. de la Marne, Fort-de-France* ☎*0596/72–80–80* ⊕*www.karibea.com* ⟿*102 rooms, 2 suites, 1 business suite* ⚲*In-room: safe, refrigerator, Wi-Fi. In-hotel: restaurant, bar, pool, gym, public Internet, public Wi-Fi* ▤*AE, DC, MC, V* ⦿*BP.*

$ 🏨**Engoulevent.** This small bed-and-breakfast in the suburbs about 10 minutes from Fort-de-France has deluxe suites with contemporary decor, as well as up-to-date amenities like Wi-Fi. Breakfast is lovely, and you can also opt to have dinner, a gastronomic table d'hôte with wine. Personalized service by a "retired" French couple is a hallmark. **Pros:** Rooms are four-star, unique on the island, exceptional food. **Cons:** Madame is sometimes *overly* attentive, not all the benefits of a hotel, best with a car. ✉*22 rte. de l'Union Didier, Fort-de-France* ☎*0596/64–96–00* ⊕*www.engoulevent.com* ⟿*5 suites* ⚲*In-room: safe, refrigerator, dial-up, Wi-Fi. In-hotel: pool, gym, no elevator, public Wi-Fi, airport shuttle, parking (no fee), no-smoking rooms* ▤*MC, V* ⦿*BP.*

¢–$ 🏨**La Caravelle.** The energetic Mahler family has transformed this simple hotel with their artwork from Africa, where patriarch Jean-Paul worked for several decades as a hotel manager. The one-bedroom apartment above the restaurant is handsome. Several of the "family" rooms connect, making them good for groups. The refurbished apartment conveniently has two bathrooms. There is a feel-good breakfast, with fresh local bread and yogurt that is served—as is dinner—at the terrace restaurant, with its awesome view of mountains and ocean. Teak chairs and tables on its verandah look smart, as does the overhanging red tin roof. **Pros:** Caring service, interesting international family, good cuisine. **Cons:** No pool; still a simple, French hotel, breakfast extra. ⊠ *Anse L'Etang, Tartane, La Trinité* ☎ *0596/58–07–32* ⊕ *www.hotel-la-caravelle-martinique.com* ➪ *14 studios, 1 apartment* ♿ *In-room: kitchen. In-hotel: restaurant, no elevator* ⊟ *MC, V* ⊙| *EP.*

WHERE TO EAT

Martinique cuisine is a fusion of African and French and is certainly more international and sophisticated than that of its immediate island neighbors. The influx of young chefs, who favor a contemporary, less-caloric approach, has brought exciting innovations to the table. This *haute nouvelle creole* cuisine emphasizes local products, predominantly starchy tubers like plaintains, white yams, yucca, and island sweet potatoes, as well as vegetables like breadfruit, christophene, and taro leaves. Many creole dishes have been Francofied, transformed into mousselines, terrines, and gratins topped with creamy sauces. And then there's the bountiful harvest of the sea—*lambi* (conch), *langouste* (clawless local lobsters), and dozens of species of fish predominate, but you can also find *ouassous* (freshwater crayfish, which are as luscious as jumbo prawns).

Some local creole specialties are *accras* (cod or vegetable fritters), *crabes farcis* (stuffed land crab), and *feroce* (avocado stuffed with salt fish and farina). You can fire up fish and any other dish with a hit of hot *chien* (dog) sauce. Not to worry—it's made from onions, shallots, hot peppers, oil, and vinegar. To cool your jets, have a 'ti punch—four parts white rum and one part sugarcane syrup.

Supermarkets often have snack bars that serve sandwiches, as do the bakeries and larger gas stations like Esso and Total. *Supermarkets,* such as Champion, have good deli sections and sell French wines for significantly less than at home. DeliFrance, the French chain, has locations in most tourist areas. Travelers on a budget will find creperies and pizzarias, even an African pizza place in Le François. In Fort-de-France's city market, ladies serve up creole prix-fixe meals that can include accras, fricassee of octopus and conch, chicken in coconut milk, or grilled whole fish. (Ask for Chez Carole's).

Menu prices include tax and service. Prix-fixe menus, sometimes with wine, can help keep costs in line.

WHAT TO WEAR

For dinner, casual resort wear is appropriate. Generally, men do not wear jackets and ties, as they did in decades past, but they do wear collared shirts. Women typically wear light cotton sundresses, short or long. At dinnertime, beach attire is too casual for most restaurants.

Nice shorts are okay for lunch, depending on the venue, but jeans and shorts aren't acceptable at dinner. Keep in mind that in Martinique lunch is usually a wonderful three-course, two-hour affair.

SOUTH OF FORT-DE-FRANCE

FRENCH
$$$–$$$$
★

✕ **Le Béleme.** To really experience this place, start with a cocktail in the superchic bar lined with black-and-white photographs; a simple 'ti punch gets an elaborate presentation. Le Béleme is the special-occasion restaurant for well-heeled residents who enjoy innovative cuisine served in a contemporary setting. Alas, it is not inexpensive, but the complimentary *amuse-bouche* may save you an appetizer, although the lobster ravioli is luscious. The *tatin de foie gras* and caramelized green bananas with a shallot-and-lime confit can be had with 24 hours' notice. The menu changes seasonally and features such creations as roast guinea hen with foie gras and morrel mushrooms, dramatically presented by a bevy of servers. Lunch (here or at the beach restaurant), although less glamorous, is still a treat, and provides a more-affordable alternative. ✉*Cap Est Lagoon Resort & Spa, Quartier Cap Est, Le François* ☎*0596/54–80–80* ⌕*Reservations essential* ▭*AE, MC, V.*

$$$
★

✕ **Le Plein Soleil Restaurant.** Perennially popular with the chic set, Le Plein Soleil has a smashing new look. But it's the original, contemporary menu that cements its well-deserved reputation. The young Martinican chef, Nathanael Ducteil, continues to draw applause for his use of the latest techniques from France coupled with remarkable twists on local products. At lunch, the terrace has a hilltop sea view, and by night the mood is romantic, the service fine, the music heady. You might have a lobster medallion flambéed with vintage rum or a thick, tuna steak roasted with lemon confit and stacked on mushroom risotto. Owner Jean-Christophe has brought superb lettuce and herbs plants from Paris for the hotel's garden. The finale might be an inventive basil custard topped with a red berry coulis. ✉*Hôtel Le Plein Soleil, Villa Lagon Sarc, Pointe Thalèmont, Le François* ☎*0596/38–07–77* ⌕*Reservations essential* ▭*MC, V* ⊗*No dinner Sun.*

THAI
$$
★

✕ **La Case Thai.** This restaurant is as soothing as a spa, with a lily pond, tumbled pottery, orchids suspended from the trees, and sophisticated music. Not so the bumpy dirt road. But all is forgotten when you join the animated crowd for a house cocktail of lychee liqueur, passion fruit, and two different kinds of rum. Stagger multiple small courses of all your Thai favorites, making sure that someone orders something served in a pineapple. If a dish doesn't make your mouth go zing, you can ask the Thai chefs to heat it up. Afterward, explore the fascinating boutique with everything from Southeast Asian furnishings to silver jewelry. ✉*Les Trois-Ilets* ☎*0596/48–13–25* ⌕*Reservations essential* ▭*AE, MC, V* ⊗*Closed Sun. and Mon.*

FORT-DE-FRANCE & POINTS NORTH

CAFÉ
$$
★

✕**Mille & Une Brindilles.** At this trendy salon you can order anything from a glass of wine to an aromatic pot of tea in flavors like vanilla or mango. You'll find a litany of tapenades, olive cakes, flans, and cou cou on the prix-fixe menu. Fred, the bubbly Parisian who is both chef and proprietress, is the queen of terrines and she makes a delicious tart (like Roquefort and pear) or pâté out of any vegetable or fish. The Saturday brunch (€22) is a very social occasion. The best-ever desserts, like the Amadéus—as appealing as the classical music that plays—and *moelleux au chocolat* (a rich chocolate-and-coffee pudding), are what you would want served at your last meal on Earth. Look for the sign, for the place is easy to miss. ✉*27 rte. de Didier, Didier, Fort-de-France* ☎*0596/71–75–61* 🚫*No credit cards* ⊗*Closed Sun. and Wed. No dinner.*

14

CARIBBEAN
$$$–$$$$

✕**Le Brédas.** This culinary experience necessitates a trip into the interior, down winding roads where the dense foliage is junglelike. It's best navigated, at least for the first time, by day; come for lunch, but return for a memorable dinner. Martinican chef Jean-Charles Brédas is well known, having worked in some of the better restaurants in Martinique and Manhattan. His lovely wife is a gracious hostess. The tasteful decor includes taupe linen runners on large tables speckled with colored-glass bits; the ceramic plates are the creations of an esteemed local potter. The foie gras is perfectly executed, especially when it's served with green bananas caramelized with rum and pineapple. (This appetizer, his signature dish, is a whopping €33.) One laudable main *plat* is the robust and tender beef marinated in cocoa, orange, and cardamom. The terrace dining room of this century-old house is covered by a peaked white awning. ✉*Entrée Presqu'île, St. Joseph* ☎*0596/57–65–52* 🚫*MC, V* ⊗*No dinner Sun. and Mon.*

$–$$

✕**Le Colibri.** Gregarious Joel Paladino is lovingly continuing a family culinary tradition with this little local spot in the island's northeastern reaches. You'll be impressed by the picturesque ocean views as well as the cuisine that his lovely twin sisters prepare. Begin with deep-green callaloo soup with crab or delicious conch pie, then move on to grilled lobster with a christophene gratin (assuming you don't mind the splurge) or the rabbit baked with prunes (if you do). Some of the traditional creole dishes, like stuffed pigeon with coconut sauce, conch fricassee, and *cochon au lait* (suckling pig), are favorites on Sunday. There's always a lower-price plat du jour. ✉*4 rue des Colibris, Morne-des-Esses, Ste-Marie* ☎*0596/69–91–95* 🚫*AE, MC, V* ⊗*Closed Mon.*

ECLECTIC
$

✕**Soup Bar du Centre Ville.** A sign reading NO OPIUM SMOKING is just one of the details that make this artsy eatery so much fun. This is one place that the island's colorful characters will tell you about if they think you're hip. Wild-looking art decorates one wall; on the other is a surfboard, signed by its American owner, who added: THANKS FOR THE SOUP. The list of soups is extensive, and includes local specialties like *soupe z'habitant,* a flavorful puree of green vegetables with pigs' tails added for flavor. Because a German owns the place, you can also get goulash and cold cream of cucumber soup. No matter what you order, the price is right: a huge bowl with some rolls is about €7. This place is a venue for art exhibits and live music. And yes, there is German beer. ⊠ *120 rue Martine, Fort-de-France* ☎*0596/60–48–96* ⊟*MC, V* ⊙*Closed Sun. No lunch Sat.*

FRENCH
$$–$$$$
Fodor'sChoice
★

✕ **La Belle Epoque.** In a wealthy suburb high above Fort-de-France, this antiques-filled dining room offers a truly fine-dining experience, from the professional service to the sparkling crystal stemware. The food is divine, and the young, talented chef has modernized a menu steeped in classical French tradition. The quality of meat is excellent, particularly the lamb and the hard-to-find cuts such as sweetbreads. The menu has an entire page devoted to foie gras, including an incredibly delicious portion encrusted in blue poppy seeds with red vine-leaf caramel. The prix-fixe meal can help keep costs down; check the daily offering and its price. Owner Martine Diacono, a statuesque blonde, makes this a personality palace. ⊠ *97 rte. de Didier, Didier, Fort-de-France* ☎*0596/64–41–19* ⊟*MC, V* ⊙*Closed Sun. No lunch Mon. or Sat.*

$$$

✕ **Le Dôme.** Sepia-tone lithographs of old St-Pierre adorn the walls of this gourmet restaurant with a panoramic view of Fort-de-France. The prix-fixe meals can be an especially good value, but the most-intriguing dishes are à la carte, which are rather pricey. Foie gras with local pleurotte mushrooms and pineapple chutney is an excellent starter. The cassoulet of scallops or veal medallions in a ginger sauce with Duchesse potatoes and bacon-wrapped asparagus are just a couple of the outstanding main courses. Ask about the specially priced wine of the month. ⊠ *Valmenière Hôtel, av. des Arawaks, Fort-de-France* ☎*0596/75–75–75* ⊟*AE, MC, V.*

$$–$$$

✕ **La Table de Mamy Nounou.** If you looked at this eatery's business card, you'd expect a creole menu served by an elderly island lady. Not! It's owned by a French family. The elegant Madame Mahler will greet you; her husband, Jean-Paul, presides as chef (he's accruing awards) and her son, Bastien, eloquently describes the menu in the King's English. Have an aperitif while you admire the view from the lounge decorated with fascinating African antiques. Savor the pumpkin velouté, and go on to the house-made foie gras with Sauternes jelly. A good main course is the combination of fish, shrimp, and scallops with a cinnamon-cider sauce. Even the sides here are special, like the tatin of pineapples with eggplant caviar. Finish with the *marquise au chocolat,* with rum-soaked chestnuts, and a quality cigar. ⊠ *Anse L'Etang, Tartane, La Trinité* ☎*0596/58–07–32* ⊟*MC, V.*

SEAFOOD
$–$$

✕ **Chez Les Pecheurs.** This is the kind of beach restaurant you search for but seldom find. It began when owner Palmont still made his living by fishing. Now the pink-and-blue boat-of-the-boss is the best one bobbin'. People come for the fisherman's platter (the catch of the day) with a special red sauce, ripe tomatoes, and perfect red beans and rice. Fresh "crayfish on the barbie" can usually be had Thursday through Saturday. Bottles of Neisson rum are plunked in front of a table of, say, French doctors taking a time-out from their medical conference. On Friday night and Sunday, local bands play, and on Saturday a deejay gets everyone up and dancing in the sand. ⊠ *Le Bord de Mer, Carbet* ☎ *0596/76–98–39 or 0696/23–95–59* ▤ *MC, V.*

BEACHES

All of Martinique's beaches are open to the public, but hotels charge a fee for nonguests to use changing rooms and other facilities. There are no official nudist beaches, but topless bathing is prevalent. Unless you're an expert swimmer, steer clear of the Atlantic waters, except in the area of Cap Chevalier (Cape Knight) and the Caravelle Peninsula. The white-sand beaches are south of Fort-de-France; to the north, the beaches are silvery black volcanic sand. Some of the most pleasant strips of sand are around Ste-Anne, Ste-Luce, and Havre du Robert.

Anse Corps de Garde. On the southern Caribbean coast, this is one of the island's best long stretches of white sand. The public beach has picnic tables, restrooms, sea grape trees, and crowds, particularly on weekends, when you can find plenty of wandering food vendors. The water is calm, with just enough wave action to remind you it's the sea. From Fort-de-France, exit to the right before you get to the town of Ste-Luce. You first see signs for the Karibea Hotels and then one for Corps de Garde, which is on the right. At the stop sign take a left. ⊠ *Ste-Luce.*

Anse-Mitan. This is not the French Riviera, though there are often yachts moored offshore. This long stretch of beach can be particularly fun on Sunday. Small, family-owned seaside restaurants are half hidden among palm trees and are footsteps from the lapping waves. Nearly all offer grilled lobster and some form of music, perhaps a zouk band. Inexpensive waterfront hotels line the clean, golden beach, which has excellent snorkeling just offshore. Chaise lounges are available for rent from hotels for about €6. When you get to Pointe du Bout, take a left at the yellow office of Budget Rent-A-Car, then the next left up a hill, and park near the little white church. ⊠ *Pointe du Bout, Les Trois-Ilets.*

Anse Tartane. This patch of sand is on the wild side of the Caravelle Peninsula. It's what the French call a *sauvage* (virgin) beach, and the only people you are likely to see are brave surfers who ride the high waves or some local families. The surf school here has taught many kids the ropes. Résidence Oceane looks down on all of this action but doesn't have a restaurant. Turn right before you get to La Trinité, and follow the route de Château past the Caravelle hotel. Instead of following the signs to Résidence Oceane, veer left and go downhill when you see the ocean. The road runs right beside the beach. There are several bays and *pointes* here, but if you keep heading to the right, you can reach the surf school. ⊠ *Tartane.*

Diamant Beach. The island's longest beach has a splendid view of Diamond Rock, but the waters are rough, with lots of wave action. Often the beach is deserted, especially midweek, which is more reason to swim with prudence. Happily, it's a great place for picnicking and beachcombing; there are shade trees aplenty, and parking is abundant and free. The hospitable, family-run Diamant les Bains hotel is a good lunch spot; if you eat lunch there, the management may let you wash off in the pool overlooking the beach. From Les Trois-Ilets, go in the direction of Rivière Salée, taking the secondary road to the east, toward Le Diamant. A coastal route, it leads to the beach. ⊠ *Le Diamant.*

🕓 **Pointe du Bout.** The beaches here are small, man-made, and lined with resorts, including the Sofitel Bakoua Martinique. Each little strip is associated with its resident hotel, and security guards and closed gates make access difficult. However, if you take a left across from the main pedestrian entrance to the marina—between the taxi stand and the former Kalenda Hotel—then go left again, you will reach Sofitel's beach, which has especially nice facilities and several options for lunch and drinks. If things are quiet—particularly during the week—one of the beach boys may rent you a chaise; otherwise, just plop your beach towel down, face forward, and enjoy the delightful view of the Fort-de-France skyline. The water is dead calm and quite shallow, but it eventually drops off if you swim out a bit. ⊠ *Pointe du Bout, Les Trois-Ilets.*

Pointe du Marin. Stretching north from Ste-Anne, this is a good wind-surfing and waterskiing spot. It's also a popular family beach, with restaurants, campsites, and clean facilities available for a small fee. Club Med is on the northern edge, and you can purchase a day pass. From Le Marin, take the coastal road to Ste-Anne. Make a right before town, toward Domaine de Belfond. You can see signs for Pointe du Marin. ⊠ *Marin.*

★ **Les Salines.** A short drive south of Ste-Anne brings you to a mile-long cove lined with soft white sand and coconut palms. The beach is awash with families and children during holidays and on weekends but quiet during the week. The far end—away from the makeshift souvenir shops—is most appealing. The calm waters are safe for swimming, even for the kids. You can't rent chaise lounges, but there are showers. Food vendors roam the sand. From Le Marin, take the coastal road toward Ste-Anne. You will see signs for Les Salines. If you see the sign for Pointe du Marin, you have gone too far. ⊠ *Ste-Anne.*

SPORTS & THE OUTDOORS

BOATING & SAILING

You can rent Hobie Cats, Sunfish, and Sailfish by the hour from most hotel beach shacks. As for larger crafts, bareboat charters can be had for $1,900 to $7,000 a week, depending on the season and the size of the craft. The Windward Islands are a joy for experienced sailors, but the channels between islands are often windy and have high waves. You must have a sailing license or be able to prove your nautical prowess, though you can always hire a skipper and crew. Prior to setting out, you can get itinerary suggestions; the safe ports in Martinique are many. If you charter for a week, you can go south to St. Lucia or Grenada or north to Dominica, Guadeloupe, and Les Saintes. One-way sailing to St. Martin or Antigua is a popular choice.

■ **TIP**➔ **CAUTION:** Don't even consider striking out on the rough Atlantic side of the island unless you're an experienced sailor. The Caribbean side is much calmer—more like a vast lagoon.

Moorings Antilles Françaises (⊠*Le Marin* ☎*0596/74–75–39, 888/952–8420 in U.S., 727/535–1446 outside U.S.* ⊕*www.moorings.com*), one of the largest bareboat operations in the world, has 10 boats in Martinique, both catamarans and monohulls. Boats can be rented fully crewed and/or fully provisioned.

Punch Croisières (⊠*Bd. Allègre, Le Marin* ☎*0596/74–89–18* ⊕*www. punch-croisieres.com*) is a local, French-owned charter company with a fleet of 15 sailboats, 13 of which are catamarans from 38 to 57 feet; they go out bareboat or crewed.

Sunsail (⊠*Le Marin* ☎*0596/74–77–61, 888/350–3568 in U.S.* ⊕*www. sunsail.com*) is one of the largest yacht-charter companies in the world. Although it's primarily a bareboat operation, those with limited experience can hire skippers by the week. Ocean kayaks can be rented, too, and must be reserved in advance. Check the Web site for discount deals even in winter.

Windward Island Cruising Company (⊠*Le Marin* ☎*0596/74–31–14* ⊕*www.sailing-adventure.com*) has sailboats from 30 to 70 feet.

CANOPY TOURS

Canopy tours—also known as tree-topping tours—are relatively new to Martinique. Even younger kids can join in the fun on some courses. However, if your body parts—particularly knees and elbows—are not as supple as they once were, or if you're afraid of heights, stay back at the hotel pool. The "tour" consists of a series of wooden ladders and bridges suspended from the trees, connected with zip lines. Participants are secured in harnesses and ropes that hitch to them like dog leashes. You connect to a cable and then fly and bellow like Tarzan until you get to the other side. Advance reservations are usually required.

Mangofil (⊠*Domaine de Château Gaillard, Les Trois-Ilets* ☎*0596/68–08–08* ✆*mangofil2@wanadoo.fr*) is a professionally run operation overseen by two young Frenchmen who managed a similar park in France. All of the platforms, ladders, and stations were installed by members of a special union in France that specializes in such work. Safety is key here, but there's also a lot of fun. The boys have a sense of humor, and their full-moon parties are a hoot. The cost is €20 per person.

Mohawk Aventures (⊠*Domaine de Sigy, Le Vauclin* ☎*0696/92–20–19 or 0696/28–07–76*) is next to a banana-packing facility. Although not as professionally run as Mangofil (nor is English spoken as much), it's much more convenient to Le François. There are three adult courses and two appealing courses for children (based on age) and an attractive snack bar. The cost is €20 per person, and the facility is open every day except Monday.

CANYONING

Canyoning, which involves hiking the canyons of the rain forests, usually along and through rivers, sliding over the rocks, then plunging down the cascades into icy pools, is relatively new to Martinique. It's ordinarily a costly sport, but members of **Club d'Escalade et Montagne** (☎0596/52–64–04 *for Pascal Gall, 0596/61–48–41 for Patrick Picard, 0696/26–07–78 for Olivier Motton*), who can be called directly at their homes, will guide those wanting to experience this wet adventure for €25 for a four- to six-hour trek.

CYCLING

Mountain biking is popular in mainland France, and now it has reached Martinique. You can rent a VTT (*Vélo Tout Terrain*), a bike specially designed with 18 speeds to handle all terrains, for €15 with helmet, delivery, and pickup from your hotel, although it requires a €150 credit card deposit. **V. T. Tilt** (✉*Les Trois-Ilets* ☎*0596/66–01–01* ⊕*www.vttilt.com*) has an English-speaking owner who loves to put together groups for fun tours, either half day or full, which includes lunch. They can be beach, river, or mountain rides; tours of plantations or horse ranches; and historic, adventure, or nature experiences.

DAY SAILS

The **Coconasse** (✉*Pointe du Bout Marina, Les Trois-Ilets* ☎*0696/23–83–51* ⊕*www.coconasse.com*) is a classic charter yacht that holds up to 10 passengers. The seasoned skipper is Italian, as are the lunch and Chianti he serves. A full day is €72, a half day €38. Both include drinks. You can also book a two-day passage to St. Lucia for €270.

The catamaran **Kata Mambo** (✉*Pointe du Bout Marina, Les Trois-Ilets* ☎*0696/81–90–08 or 0596/66–10–23* ⊕*www.katamambo.com*) offers a variety of options for half-day (€36) or full-day (€74, €84 for lobster lunch) sails to St-Pierre. For €75, you also get a 4x4 adventure through sugarcane and banana plantations. The full-day trip includes unlimited rum libations; a good, multicourse lunch (half lobsters are €10 extra) with wine; and great CD sounds in four languages. This is a fun day. The fact that they've been in the biz since the early 1990s attests to their professionalism.

DIVING & SNORKELING

Martinique's underwater world is decorated with multicolor coral, crustaceans, turtles, and sea horses. Expect to pay €40 to €45 for a single dive; a package of three dives is around €110.

Okeanos Club (✉*Pierre & Vacances, Ste-Luce* ☎*0596/62–52–36* ⊕*www.okeanos-club.com*) has a morning trip close to shore; in the afternoon, the boats go farther into open water. Lessons (including those for kids 8 to 12) with a PADI-certified instructor can be conducted in English. It's always a fun experience. The dive shop looks out to Diamant Rock, which has wonderful underwater caves and is one of the preferred dives on the island.

Planète Bleue (✉ *Pointe du Bout Marina, Les Trois-Ilets* ☎ *0596/66–08–79*) has a big, up-to-date dive boat, hand-painted with tropical fish and waves, so it's impossible to miss. The English-speaking international crew is proud to have been in business since the early 1990s. The company hits 20 sites, including the Citadel and Salomon's Pool. A boat goes out mornings and afternoons. Thursday is a full day on the north coast, with breakfast, lunch, and all drinks included. Half-day dives include gear and a 'ti punch. Sunday is a day of rest, except for the first one in the month, when it's off to Diamant Rock.

FISHING

14

Deep-sea fishing expeditions in these waters hunt down tuna, barracuda, dolphinfish, kingfish, and bonito, and the big ones—white and blue marlins. You can hire boats from the bigger marinas, particularly in Pointe du Bout, Le Marin, and Le François; most hotels arrange these Hemingwayesque trysts, but will often charge a premium. If you call several days in advance, companies can also put you together with other anglers to keep costs down. The **Centre de Peche** (✉ *Port de Plaisance, bd. Allègre, Le Marin* ☎ *0596/76–24–20 or 0696/28–80–58*), a fully loaded Davis 47-foot fishing boat, is a sportfisherman's dream. It goes out with a minimum of four anglers for €195 per person for a half day, or €390 per person for a full day, including lunch. Nonanglers can come for the ride for €95 and €190, respectively. Captain Yves speaks English fluently and is a fun guy.

GOLF

The 18-hole **Golf Country Club de la Martinique** (✉ *Les Trois-Ilets* ☎ *0596/68–32–81* ⊕ *www.golfmartinique.com*) has a par-71 Robert Trent Jones course with an English-speaking pro, pro shop, bar, and restaurant. The club offers special greens fees to cruise-ship passengers. Normal greens fees are €32 for 9 holes and €46 for 18; an electric cart costs another €30 for 9, €46 for 18. For those who don't mind walking while admiring the Caribbean view between the palm trees, club trolleys are €6. There are no caddies.

HIKING

Two-thirds of Martinique is designated as protected land. Trails, all 31 of them, are well marked and maintained. At the beginning of each, a notice is posted advising on the level of difficulty, the duration of a hike, and any interesting facts. The **Parc Naturel Régional de la Martinique** (✉ *9 bd. Général de Gaulle, Fort-de-France* ☎ *0596/73–19–30*) organizes inexpensive guided excursions year-round. If there have been heavy rains, though, give it up. The tangle of ferns, bamboo trees, and vines is dramatic, but during rainy season, the springs and waterfalls and wet, muddy trails will negate any enthusiasm.

HORSEBACK RIDING

Horseback riding excursions can traverse scenic beaches, palm-shaded forests, sugarcane fields, and a variety of other tropical landscapes. Trained guides often include running commentaries on the history, flora, and fauna of the island.

At **Black Horse Ranch** (⊠ *Les Trois-Ilets* ☎ *0596/68–37–80*), one-hour trail rides (€35) go into the countryside and across waving cane fields; two hours on the trail (€40) bring riders near a river. Only western saddles are used for adults; children can ride English. Semiprivate lessons in French or English are €40 a person, less for kids if they can join a group.

Habitation Cerón (⊠ *Anse Cerón* ☎ *0596/52–94–53 or 0596/52–97–03*), a 600-acre former plantation, has trails that run through the rain forest. A 90-minute ride is just €35. An equestrian center offers private lessons, with either English or western saddles, for €30 an hour. Pony rides range from €6 to €15.

Some guides are English-speaking at **Ranch de Caps** (⊠ *Cap Macré, Le Marin* ☎ *0596/74–70–65 or 0696/23–18–18*), where you can take a half-day ride (western) on the wild southern beaches and across the countryside for €45. Rides go out in the morning (8:30 to noon) and afternoon (1:30 to 5) every day but Monday. If you can manage a full day in the saddle, it costs €75. A real treat is the full-moon ride. Most of the mounts are Anglo-Arabs. Riders are encouraged to help cool and wash their horses at day's end. Reserve in advance. Riders of all levels are welcomed.

Ranch Jack (⊠ *Anse-d'Arlets* ☎ *0596/68–37–69 or 0696/92–26–58* ⊕ *ranch.jack@wanadoo.fr*) has trail rides (English style) across some beautiful country for €35 an hour; half-day excursions for €50 (€58 with transfers from nearby hotels) go through the fields and forests to the beach. The lessons for kids are recommendable.

KAYAKING

Ecofriendly travelers will love skimming the shallow bay while paddling to bird and iguana reserves. Rent colorful fiberglass kayaks to explore the crystalline Havre du Robert, with its shallow pools (called *fonds blanc*), petite beaches, and islets such as Iguana Island. You'll receive one of the island's warmest welcomes at **Les Kayaks du Robert** (⊠ *Pointe Savane, Le Robert* ☎ *0596/65–33–89*). After a memorable half-day paddle through shallow lagoons and mangrove swamps chasing colorful fish, you can enjoy a complimentary planter's punch, all for €20 per person. A guided group trip costs slightly more.

WINDSURFING

At **Bliss** (⊠ *Anse Bonneville Trinité, near Résidence Oceane, Tartane* ☎ *0596/58–00–96* ⊕ *www.surfmartinique.com*), individual (€30) or group (€20) lessons are given to newcomers age five and up. English and Spanish are spoken. Surf- and body boards (with fins) can also be rented for three hours for €14, or €24 for the day.

UPCA Vauclin (⊠ *Le Plage, Le Vauclin* ☎*0596/74–33–68* ⊕*www.ucpa. com*) rents out windsurfing boards at slightly better prices than most other outfitters.

SHOPPING

★ French fragrances, designer scarves and sunglasses, fine china and crystal, leather goods, wine (amazingly inexpensive at supermarkets), and liquor are all good buys in Fort-de-France. Purchases are further sweetened by the 20% discount on luxury items when paid for with certain credit cards. Among the items produced on the island, look for *bijoux creole* (local jewelry, such as hoop earrings and heavy bead necklaces), white and dark rum, and handcrafted straw goods, pottery, and tapestries.

AREAS & MALLS

The area around the cathedral in Fort-de-France has a number of small shops that carry luxury goods. Of particular note are the shops on rue Victor Hugo, rue Moreau de Jones, rue Antoine Siger, and rue Lamartine. The **Galleries Lafayette** department store on rue Schoelcher in downtown Fort-de-France sells everything from perfume to pâté. On the outskirts of Fort-de-France, the **Centre Commercial de Cluny, Centre Commercial de Dillon, Centre Commercial de Bellevue,** and **Centre Commercial la Rond Point** are among the major shopping malls.

You can find more than 100 thriving businesses—from shops and department stores to restaurants, pizzerias, fast-food outlets, a superb supermarket, and the Galleria Hotel—at **La Galleria** in Le Lamentin. In Pointe du Bout there are a number of appealing tourist shops and boutiques, both in and around **Village Créole.**

SPECIALTY STORES

CHINA & CRYSTAL

Cadet Daniel (⊠*72 rue Antoine Siger, Fort-de-France* ☎*0596/71–41–48*) sells Lalique, Limoges, and Baccarat.

Roger Albert (⊠*7 rue Victor Hugo, Fort-de-France* ☎*0596/71–71–71*) carries designer crystal.

■**TIP➔** So you want to look French, *oui?* Yes, buy French designer resort wear, but the secret is a cool, sexy French haircut. Both ladies and men vie for appointments at **Hair du Temps** (⊠*Arcade La Pagerie, Point du Bout, Les Trois-Ilets* ☎*0596/66–02–51*). Note that haircut prices do not include a blow-dry—that's extra, as are hair spray and mousse—€6 extra for whichever you choose!

14

CLOTHING

Bisous Sucrés (✉ *Village Créole, Pointe du Bout, Les Trois-Ilets* ☎ *0596/74–77–04*) offers a unique children's collection, including jewelry, madras dollies, and teeny underwear.

Coté Plage Sarl (✉ *Village Créole, Pointe du Bout, Les Trois-Ilets* ☎ *0596/66–13–00*) stocks French sailor jerseys in creative colors, youthful straw purses in bold hues, fun teenage jewelry, and ladies' bathing suits.

Lynx Optique (✉ *20 rue Lamartine, Fort-de-France* ☎ *0596/71–38–48*) has the latest designer sunglasses from Chanel, Gucci, Dior, Cartier, and Versace. And if you need a pair of prescription lenses, they can take care of that, too.

Mounia (✉ *Rue Perrinon, near old House of Justice, Fort-de-France* ☎ *0596/73–77–27*), owned by a former Yves Saint Laurent model, carries the top French designers for women and men. It will have you opening your wallet wide. Hope for a *solde* (sale).

HANDICRAFTS

The work of **Antan Lontan** (✉ *213 rte. de Balata, Fort-de-France* ☎ *0596/64–52–72*) has to be seen. Sculptures, busts, statuettes, and artistic lamps portray the Creole women and the story of the Martiniquaise culture.

Art et Nature (✉ *Ste-Luce* ☎ *0596/62–59–19*) carries Joel Gilbert's unique wood paintings, daubed with 20 to 30 shades of earth and sand.

Artisanat & Poterie des Trois-Ilets (✉ *Les Trois-Ilets* ☎ *0596/68–18–01*) allows you to watch the creation of Arawak- and Carib-style pots, vases, and jars.

Atelier Céramique (✉ *Le Diamant* ☎ *0596/76–42–65*) displays the ceramics, paintings, and miscellaneous souvenirs of owners and talented artists David and Jeannine England, members of the island's small British expat community.

★ **Bois Nature** (✉ *La Semair, Le Robert* ☎ *0596/65–77–65*) is all about mood and mystique. The gift items begin with scented soap, massage oil, aromatherapy sprays, and perfumes. Then there are wind chimes, mosquito netting, and sun hats made of coconut fiber. The big stuff includes natural wood-frame mirrors and furniture à la Louis XV.

Domaine Château Gaillard (✉ *Rte. des Trois-Ilets, Les Trois-Ilets* ☎ *0596/68–15–68*), a large two-story shopping complex, sells both handicrafts and tropical floral compositions. You can find pottery, jewelry, toys, paintings, and gifts. Coffee and chocolate are also for sale, as are antique creole and French women's costumes—a sexy bustier or Empire-cut vest—for high prices.

At **Galerie Jecy** (✉ *Pointe du Bout Marina, Les Trois-Ilets* ☎ *0596/66–04–98*), owner Stephanie designs fanciful, colorful metalwork that is artistic enough to be called sculpture; her island themes include starfish, octopus, geckos, and impressive billfish. She also sells more-portable souvenirs like colorful wooden napkin rings, fruit plates, and trivets.

Galerie de Sophen (✉ *Pointe du Bout, Les Trois-Ilets* ☎ *0596/66–13–64*), across from the Village Créole, is a combination of Sophie and Henry, both in name and content. This art gallery showcases the work (originals and limited prints) of a French couple who live aboard their sailboat and paint the beauty of the sea and the island, from exotic birds to banana trucks.

JEWELRY

At **Thomas de Rogatis** (⊠*22 rue Antoine Siger, Fort-de-France* ☎*0596/70–29–11*), authentic bijoux creole jewelry, popularized after the abolition of slavery and seen in many museums, is for sale.

PERFUME

Roger Albert (⊠*7 rue Victor Hugo, Fort-de-France* ☎*0596/71–71–71*) stocks such popular scents as those by Dior, Chanel, and Guerlain.

NIGHTLIFE & THE ARTS

14

Martinique is dotted with lively discos and nightclubs, but a good deal of the fun is to be had by befriending Martinicans, French residents, and other expats and hope they will invite you to their private parties. As for casinos, French law now requires everyone to show his passport; the legal gambling age is 18.

CASINOS

On the outskirts of Fort-de-France, the classy **Casino Batelière Plaza** (⊠*Schoelcher* ☎*0596/61–73–23*) is built in a striking nouveau–plantation house style. It has both slot machines and table games. Slots open at 10 AM, but table games don't start until after 7:30 PM. You'll have to fork over a €10 admission (includes a drink) and be properly attired (jacket and tie for men, dresses for women for table games; dressy casual for slots). There's entertainment on weekends. It's open Sunday night, along with its restaurant with live music, when most places are closed up tight.

The interior of this new casino in a major tourist zone, **Casino Trois-Ilets** (⊠*Turn right off rte. de Trois Ilets to rte. de Pointe du Bout and it's on right, Trois-Ilet* ☎*0596/66–00–30*) was designed with a French Quarter ambience and houses 70 slot machines, blackjack, U.S. roulette, and craps (Friday and Saturday). The casino is open daily 10 AM to 3 AM; the moderately priced fine-dining restaurant upstairs is open Sunday night, too. On weekends, jazz is the sound—live Caribbean, creole, and standard.

DANCE CLUBS

Your hotel or the tourist office can put you in touch with the current "in" places. It's also wise to check on opening and closing times and cover charges. For the most part, the discos draw a mixed crowd— Martinicans and tourists, and although a younger crowd is the norm, people of all ages go dancing here.

L'Amphore (⊠*Pointe du Bout, Les Trois-Ilets* ☎*0596/66–03–09 or 0696/80–79–40*) is a hot bar and club where the young and restless dance to funk, soul, tribal, house, techno, and disco, as well as international music from the '70s and '80s. The dress code is strict: no shorts, bandanas, or sandals. Follow the road to Anse-Mitan; the club is on the left before the little church. The VIP room is bottle-service only. The club is open weekends only during the low season and more often during the high season, when there's usually a cover.

The latest buzz, the **Coconuts Club** (⊠*Quartier Laugier, Riviére-Salée* ☎*0596/68–20–49*) houses a restaurant, bar-lounge, and disco. The motto here is "Life is a party!"

Crazy Nights (⊠*Ste-Luce* ☎*0596/68–56–68*) remains popular because it's all about having one crazy time. With upward of 1,000 partying people, your chances are good. Live concerts are frequent, but dancing and hip-swinging are the priorities.

Le Top 50 (⊠*Zone Artisanale, La Trinité* ☎*0596/58–61–43*) is one of the few nightspots in the area where tourists, surfers, and locals all come together to party.

Yucca Bar (⊠*Zac de Rivière Roche, Fort-de-France* ☎*0596/60–48–36*), with a Mexican motif, is known for showcasing innovative bands, usually on Wednesday. Take a taxi, go with local friends, or get good directions, because the area is deserted at night. The club is especially popular on the weekend. If you go early for the Tex-Mex buffet, you can avoid the cover charge.

FOLKLORIC PERFORMANCES

Most leading hotels offer nightly entertainment in season, including the marvelous **Grands Ballets de Martinique,** one of the finest folkloric dance troupes in the Caribbean. Consisting of a bevy of musicians and dancers dressed in traditional costume, the ballet revives the Martinique of yesteryear through dance rhythms such as the beguine and the mazurka. They appear on Friday at the Sofitel Bakoua hotel, in a dinner performance coupled with an authentic creole buffet. On Saturday night they perform at Hotel La Pagerie in Point du Bout, where admission includes a rum drink. **Tche Kreyal,** another folkloric ballet group, which has some 20 performers—many of them children—performs at Les Amandiers in Ste-Luce on Friday. At the Amyris Hotel, the **Kalenda Ballet** dances on Thursday night. In addition, many restaurants offer live entertainment, usually on weekends.

MUSIC CLUBS

Jazz musicians, like their music, tend to be informal and independent. They rarely hold regular gigs. Zouk mixes Caribbean rhythm and an Occidental tempo with creole lyrics. Jacob Devarieux is the leading exponent of this style, and he occasionally performs on the island. Otherwise, you're likely to hear one of his followers.

Calebasse Café (⊠*19 bd. Allègre, Le Marin* ☎*0596/74–69–27*) pleases a diverse—though mostly older—crowd. Jazz is the norm, and there's often a talented local singer. Funky and hip, the interior is a bit rough, but civilized. On Saturday night, if you don't make a reservation you will not have a seat. The food here isn't wonderful, but if you have the conch tart and the grilled lobster, you'll leave satisfied and avoid the cover charge. There's sometimes a beach party. The place is closed Monday.

At **Club Med Buccaneer's Creek** (⊠*Pointe du Marin, Ste-Anne* ☎*0596/76–83–36*), you can buy a night pass that, at €150, might seem expensive, but it includes an impressive buffet dinner, a show in the theater (Friday is the best night), and dancing at the disco until the wee hours. Single women feel comfortable here, and they find willing and very able dance partners.

La Marine (⊠*Marina Pointe du Bout, Les Trois-Ilets* ☎*0596/66–02–32*) is an animated bar and restaurant with live entertainment, mainly on weekends.

The feet-in-the-sand restaurant and bar called **La Méridienne** (⊠*Plage de Anse L'Etang, Tartane* ☎*0596/58–79–91*) is the place for live music, especially acid jazz.

Le Ponton (⊠*On point, behind Sofitel Bakoua, Pointe du Bout, Les Trois-Ilets* ☎*0596/66–05–45*) is a fun waterfront restaurant that attracts a lot of boating types when the DJ cranks it up and particularly when live bands play on the weekends. The music is local: reggae, French, and Latin.

Sofitel Bakoua Martinique (⊠*Pointe du Bout, Les Trois-Ilets* ☎*0596/66–02–02*) has nightly entertainment, from talented piano men to vocalists and jazz combos; the quality of the entertainment is known island wide.

La Villa Créole (⊠*Anse Mitan* ☎*0596/66–05–53*) is a restaurant whose French owner, Guy Bruere-Dawson, has been singing and strumming the guitar since the mid-1980s—everything from François Cabrel to Elton John, some Italian ballads, and original ditties. Other singers perform on Friday and Saturday nights. In order to see the show, you must order dinner, lobster being the best option. There's also a small dance floor.

14

EXPLORING MARTINIQUE

The northern part of the island will appeal to nature lovers, hikers, and mountain climbers. The drive from Fort-de-France to St-Pierre is particularly impressive, as is the one across the island, via Morne Rouge, from the Caribbean to the Atlantic. This is Martinique's wild side—a place of waterfalls, rain forest, and mountains. The highlight is Mont Pelée. The south is the more-developed half of the island, where the resorts and restaurants are located, as well as the beaches.

SOUTH OF FORT-DE-FRANCE

Diamond Rock. This volcanic mound is 1 mi (1.5 km) offshore from the small, friendly village of Le Diamant and is one of the island's best diving spots. In 1804, during the squabbles over possession of the island between the French and the English, the latter commandeered the rock, armed it with cannons, and proceeded to use it as a strategic battery. The British held the rock for nearly a year and a half, attacking any French ships that came along. The French got wind that the British were getting cabin fever on their isolated island and arranged for barrels of rum to float up on the rock. The French easily overpowered the inebriated sailors, ending one of the most curious engagements in naval history.

Forêt de Montravail. A few miles north of Ste-Luce, this tropical rain forest is ideal for a short hike. Look for the interesting group of Carib rock drawings.

Le François. With some 16,000 inhabitants, this is the main city on the Atlantic coast. Many of the old wooden buildings remain and are juxtaposed with concrete structures. The classic West Indian cemetery, with its black-and-white tiles, is still here, and a marina is at the end of town. Two of Martinique's best hotels are in this area, as well as some of the most upscale residences. Le François is also noted for its snorkeling. Offshore are the privately owned Ilets de l'Impératrice. The islands received that name because, according to legend, this is where Empress Joséphine came to bathe in the shallow basins known as *fonds blanc* because of their white-sand bottoms. Group boat tours leave from the harbor and include lunch and drinks. Prices vary *(⇨ Sports & the Outdoors)*. You can also haggle with a fisherman to take you out for a while on his boat. There's a fine bay 6 mi (9.5 km) farther along the coast where you can swim and go kayaking. The town itself is rather lackluster but authentic, and you'll find a number of different shops and supermarkets, owned by truly lovely, helpful residents.

★ The **Habitation Clément** offers a glimpse into Martinique's colonial past, into the elegance and privilege of plantation society, and is complete with Creole ladies in traditional gowns moving about the grounds. The Palm Grove, with an avenue of palms and park benches, is delightful. It was all built with the wealth generated by its rum distillery, and its 18th-century splendor has been lovingly preserved. There's fine art displayed and classical music plays. Framed vintage labels from rum bottles track the changes in the marketing of rum over the centuries. Enjoy the free tastings at the bar and wander into the retail shop. Consider the Canne Bleu, Grappe Blanche, or one of the aged rums, some bottled as early as 1952. ⊠ *Domaine de l'Acajou, Le François* ☎ *0596/54–62–07* ⊕ *www. habitation-clement.fr* ☒ €9 ⊙ *Daily 8:30–5:30.*

Lamentin. There's nothing pretty about Lamentin; the international airport is its most notable landmark. The rest of the town is a sprawling industrial and commercial zone. But many people come here for shopping in the big, fancy shopping mall Euromarché. La Galleria, a second megamall of roughly 100 shops and boutiques, offers everything from pâté de foie gras and Camembert to CDs and sunglasses.

Le Marin. The yachting capital of Martinique is also known for its colorful August carnival and its Jesuit church, circa 1766. From Le Marin a narrow road leads to picturesque Cap Chevalier, about 1 mi (1.5 km) from town. Most of the buildings are white and very European. The marina is lively, and there are waterfront restaurants and clubs.

Pointe du Bout. This tourist area has a marina and several resort hotels, among them the Sofitel Bakoua. The ferry to Fort-de-France leaves from here. A cluster of boutiques, ice-cream parlors, and rental-car agencies forms the hub from which restaurants and hotels of varying caliber radiate, but it's a pretty quiet place in the low season. The beach at Anse-Mitan, which is a little west of Pointe du Bout proper, is one of the best on the island. There are also numerous small restaurants and inexpensive guesthouses here.

NEED A BREAK? Walking down from the Sofitel, at the first cluster of shops on the left is a new gelato shop marked simply: Gelato Artisan Glacier Italian. It's the real deal!

14

Ste-Anne. A lovely white-sand beach and a Catholic church are the highlights of this town on the island's southern tip. There are a bevy of small, inexpensive cafés offering seafood and creole dishes, pizza parlors, produce markets, and barbecue joints—it's fun and lively. To the south of Ste-Anne is Pointe des Salines, the southernmost tip of the island and site of Martinique's best beach.

EN ROUTE Near St. Anne is La Savane des Pétrifications, the Petrified Forest. This desertlike stretch was once swampland and is a veritable geological museum.

Ste-Luce. This quaint fishing village has a sleepy main street with tourist shops and markets, and you can see some cool types taking a Pernod. From the sidewalk cafés there are panoramic sea views of St. Lucia. Nearby are excellent beaches and several resorts. To the east is Pointe Figuier, an excellent spot for scuba diving.

Les Trois-Ilets. Named after the three rocky islands nearby, this lovely little village (population 3,000) has unusual brick-and-wood buildings roofed with antique tiles. It's known for its pottery, straw, and wood-work but above all as the birthplace of Napoléon's empress Joséphine. In the square, where there's also a market and a fine *mairie* (town hall), you can visit the simple church where she was baptized Marie-Joseph Tascher de la Pagerie. The Martinicans have always been enormously proud of Joséphine, even though her husband reintroduced slavery on the island and most historians consider her to have been rather shallow.

★ A stone building that held the kitchen of the estate where Joséphine grew up houses the **Musée de la Pagerie.** It contains an assortment of memorabilia pertaining to her life and rather unfortunate loves, including a marriage certificate and a love letter written straight from the heart by Napoléon in 1796. The main house blew down in the hurricane of 1766, when she was three, and the family lived for years above the sugarcane factory—a hot, odoriferous, and fly-ridden existence. At 16 she was wed (an arranged marriage because her father was a gambling man in need of money) to Alexandre de Beauharnais. After he was assassinated during the Revolution she married Napoléon. ⊠ *Les Trois-Ilets* ☎ *0596/68–33–06* ⊠ *€5* ☼ *Tues.–Fri. 9–5:30, weekends 9:30–12:30 and 3–5.*

Down a dirt road, a Martinican has called up the past with **La Savane des Esclaves** *(the Savannah of the Slaves)*, a re-created slave village. This labor of love was created by Gilbert Larose, who has a fascination with the lives of his ancestors. This is an in-depth look at that major element in Martinique's history and culture, with food tastings and artisan demonstrations. Saturday from 9 AM to noon is Tradition Morning, with elaborate tastings, demonstrations, and traditional dance lessons. ✉*Quartier La Ferme* ☎*0596/68–33–91 or 0696/22–79–05* 🎫€5; *Sat. morning €20* ⊘ *Daily 10–noon and 2–5.*

NEED A BREAK? | Just steps down the hill from the church in Les Trois-Ilets, a simple patissiere, recognized by its awning, brews fresh coffee and bakes wonders like éclairs with chocolate custard interiors. Sit down at a table or take it to go.

Le Vauclin. The return of the fishermen at noon is the big event in this important fishing port on the Atlantic. There's also the 18th-century Chapel of the Holy Virgin. Nearby is the highest point in the south, Mont Vauclin (1,654 feet). A hike to the top rewards you with one of the best views on the island.

FORT-DE-FRANCE

With its historic fort and superb location beneath the towering Pitons du Carbet on the Baie des Flamands, Martinique's capital—home to about one-third of the island's 360,000 inhabitants—should be a grand place. It isn't. But an ambitious redevelopment project, now under way, hopes to make it one of the most attractive cities in the Caribbean. The plan includes the renovation of the Savane Park, the construction of a spectacular waterfront promenade, and the Pointe Simon Business and Tourist Center, which will have a 100-room hotel, luxury apartment building and a massive shopping center. All is slated to be finished in 2010. Alas, the tourist office, formerly on the waterfront, has moved to temporary quarters in the suburb of Schoelcher, so it's not readily accessible to the carless.

The most pleasant districts of Fort-de-France—Didier, Bellevue, and Schoelcher—are up on the hillside, and you need a car (or a taxi) to reach them. But if you try to drive here, you may find yourself trapped in gridlock in the warren of narrow streets downtown. Parking is difficult, and it's best to try for one of the garages or—as a second choice—outdoor public parking areas. A taxi or ferry may be a better alternative.

There are some good shops with Parisian wares (at Parisian prices) and lively street markets that sell, among other things, human hair for wigs. Near the harbor is a marketplace where local crafts, souvenirs, and spices are sold. The town can be fun, and you probably should see it. But the heat, exhaust fumes, and litter tend to make exploring here a chore rather than a pleasure. At night the city feels dark and gloomy, with little street life except for the extravagantly dressed prostitutes who openly parade around after 10 PM. If you plan to go out, it's best to go with a group, and preferably Martinicans.

The **Bibliothèque Schoelcher** is the wildly elaborate Romanesque public library. It was named after Victor Schoelcher, who led the fight to free the slaves in the French West Indies in the 19th century. The eye-popping structure was built for the 1889 Paris Exposition, after which it was dismantled, shipped to Martinique, and reassembled piece by ornate piece. ⊠ *At rue de la Liberté, runs along west side of La Savane, and rue Perrinon* ☎ *0596/70–26–67* 🖙 *Free* ⊘ *Mon. 1–5:30, Tues.– Fri. 8:30–5:30, Sat. 8:30–noon.*

★ **Le Musée Régional d'Histoire et d'Ethnographie** is a learning experience that is best undertaken at the beginning of your vacation, so you can better understand the history, background, and people of the island. Housed in an elaborate former residence (circa 1888) with balconies and fretwork, it has everything from displays of the garish gold jewelry that prostitutes wore after emancipation to reconstructed rooms of a home of proper, middle-class Martinicans. There's even a display of creole headdresses with details of how they were tied to indicate if a woman was single, married, or otherwise occupied. ⊠ *10 bd. Général de Gaulle* ☎ *0596/72–81–87* 🖙 *€3* ⊘ *Mon. and Wed.–Fri. 8:30–5, Tues. 2–5, Sat. 8:30–noon.*

The Galerie de Biologie et de Géologie at the **Parc Floral et Culturel,** in the northeastern corner of the city center, will acquaint you with the island's exotic flora. There's also an aquarium. The park contains the island's official cultural center, where there are sometimes free evening concerts. ⊠ *Pl. José-Marti, Sermac* ☎ *0596/71–66–25* 🖙 *Grounds free, aquarium €5.60, gallery €2* ⊘ *Park daily dawn–10* PM; *aquarium daily 9–7; gallery Tues.–Fri. 9:30–12:30 and 3:30–5:30, Sat. 9–1 and 3–5.*

Rue Victor Schoelcher runs through the center of the capital's primary shopping district, a six-block area bounded by rue de la République, rue de la Liberté, rue Victor Severe, and rue Victor Hugo. Stores sell Paris fashions and French perfume, china, crystal, and liqueurs, as well as local handicrafts.

The Romanesque **St-Louis Cathedral** , with its lovely stained-glass windows, was built in 1878, the sixth church on this site (the others were destroyed by fires, hurricanes, and earthquakes). ⊠ *Rue Victor Schoelcher.*

The heart of Fort-de-France is **La Savane,** a 12.5-acre park filled with trees, fountains, and benches. It's a popular gathering place and the scene of promenades, parades, and impromptu soccer matches. Along the east side are numerous snack wagons. Alas, it's no longer a desirable oasis, what with a lot of litter and other negatives often found in urban parks. A statue of Pierre Belain d'Esnambuc, leader of the island's first settlers, is unintentionally upstaged by Vital Dubray's vandalized—now headless—white Carrara marble statue of the empress Joséphine, Napoléon's first wife. Diagonally across from La Savane, you can catch the ferries for the 20-minute run across the bay to Pointe du Bout and the beaches at Anse-Mitan and Anse-à-l'Ane. It's relatively cheap as well as stress-free—much safer, more pleasant, and faster than by car.

The most imposing historic site in La Savane (and in Fort-de-France) is **Fort St-Louis,** which runs along the east side of La Savane. It's open Monday through Saturday from 9 to 3; admission is €4.

Schoelcher. Pronounced "shell-*share,*" this upscale suburb of Fort-de-France is home to the University of the French West Indies and Guyana, as well as Martinique's largest convention center, Madiana.

NORTH OF FORT-DE-FRANCE

Ajoupa-Bouillon. This flower-filled 17th-century village amid pineapple fields is the jumping-off point for several sights. The Saut Babin, a 40-foot waterfall, is a half-hour walk from Ajoupa-Bouillon. The Gorges de la Falaise is a river gorge where you can swim.

Les Ombrages botanical gardens has marked trails through the rain forest. ⊠ *Ajoupa-Bouillon* ☎ *No phone* ☎ *€4* ⊙ *Daily 9–5:30.*

☾ **Aqualand.** This U.S.-style water park is a great place for families to have a wet, happy day. The large wave pool is well tended; little ones love it, as they do the pirate's galleon in their own watery playground. Older kids may prefer to get their thrill from the slides, including the hairpin turns of the Giant Slalom, the Colorado slide, and the Black Hole, which winds around in total darkness. In the best French tradition, the fast-food options are top notch, including crepes, salads, and even beer. Inquire about catching a weekend Somatour shuttle boat. Nouvelle Frontier organizes tours that include the park. Phone first during the low season. ⊠ *Rte. des Pitons, Carbet* ☎ *0596/78–40–00* ⊕ *www.aqualand-martinique.fr* ☎ *€17.50* ⊙ *Daily 10–6.*

Balata. This quiet little town has two sights worth visiting. Built in 1923 to commemorate those who died in World War I, **Balata Church** is an exact replica of Paris's Sacré-Coeur Basilica.

The **Jardin de Balata** *(Balata Gardens)* has thousands of varieties of tropical flowers and plants. There are shaded benches from which to take in the mountain views. You can order anthurium and other tropical flowers to be delivered to the airport. ⊠ *Rte. de Balata, Balata* ☎ *0596/64–48–73* ☎ *€7* ⊙ *Daily 9–5.*

Basse-Pointe. On the route to this village on the Atlantic coast at the island's northern end you pass many banana and pineapple plantations. Just south of Basse-Pointe is a **Hindu temple** built by descendants of the East Indians who settled in this area in the 19th century. The view of Mont Pelée from the temple is amazing.

Bellefontaine. This colorful fishing village has pastel houses on the hillsides and beautifully painted *gommiers* (fishing boats) bobbing in the water. Look for the restaurant built in the shape of a boat.

Dubuc Castle. At the eastern tip of the Presqu'île du Caravelle are the ruins of this castle, once the home of the Dubuc de Rivery family, who owned the peninsula in the 18th century. According to legend, young Aimée Dubuc de Rivery was captured by Barbary pirates, sold to the

Ottoman Empire, became a favorite of the sultan, and gave birth to Mahmud II. You can park your car right after the turnoff for Résidence Oceane and walk the dirt road to the ruins.

Habitation Céron. This area has had many lives since its first in 1658 as a *habitation,* or sugar plantation. The owners, Louis and Laurence des Grottes, continue to create new options for visitors to their 600-acre property, the latest of which is a fleet of "quads" (four-wheel all-terrain vehicles) to provide a racy alternative to hiking through the rain forest. You can now opt for the same run on horseback from the equestrian center. Self-guided or guided tours through the plantation buildings include a video that describes when the factory was still producing sugar, rum, and *manioc* (yucca). Admission is waived if you have lunch, which you can carry to the nearby beach, though it's nicer to sit on the terrace. ⊠ *Anse Céron* ☎ *0596/52–94–53 or 0596/52–97–03* 🖾 *€6, quad tours €25–€40* ⊘ *Daily 9:30–5.*

14

Macouba. Named after the Carib word for "fish," this village was a prosperous tobacco town in the 17th century. Today its cliff-top location affords magnificent views of the sea, the mountains, and—on clear days—the neighboring island of Dominica.

The **JM Distillery** (☎ *0596/78–92–55*) produces some of the best *vieux rhum* on the island. A tour and samples are free.

Macouba is the starting point for a spectacular drive, the 6-mi (9.5-km) **Route to Grand' Rivière** (☎ *0596/55–72–74 for Syndicat d'Initiative Riverain*) on the northernmost point. This is Martinique at its greenest: groves of giant bamboo, cliffs hung with curtains of vines, and human-size tree ferns that seem to grow as you watch them. Literally at the end of the road is Grand' Rivière, a colorful, sprawling fishing village at the foot of high cliffs. The Syndicat d'Initiative Riverain in Macouba can arrange hiking and boating excursions.

Le Morne Rouge. This town sits on the southern slopes of the volcano that destroyed it in 1902. Today it's a popular resort spot and offers hikers some fantastic mountain scenery. From Le Morne Rouge you can start the climb up the 4,600-foot **Mont Pelée.** But don't try scaling this volcano without a guide unless you want to get buried alive under pumice stones. Instead, drive up to the Refuge de l'Aileron. From the parking lot it's 1 mi (1.5 km) up a well-marked trail to the summit. Bring a sweatshirt, because there's often a mist that makes the air damp and chilly. From the summit follow the route de la Trace (route N3), which winds south of Le Morne Rouge to St-Pierre. It's steep and winding, but that didn't stop the *porteuses* of old: balancing a tray, these women would carry up to 100 pounds of provisions on their heads for the 15-hour trek to the Atlantic coast.

Musée Gauguin. Martinique was a brief stop in Paul Gauguin's wanderings, but a decisive moment in the evolution of his art. He arrived from Panama in 1887 with friend and fellow painter Charles Laval and, having pawned his watch at the docks, rented a wooden shack on a hill above Carbet. Dazzled by the tropical colors and vegetation,

Gauguin developed a style, his Martinique period, that directly anticipated his Tahitian paintings. Disappointingly, this modest museum has only reproductions and some original letters and documents relating to the painter. Also remembered here is the writer Lafcadio Hearn. In his endearing book *Two Years in the West Indies* he provides the most extensive description of the island before St-Pierre was buried in ash and lava. ⊠ *Anse-Turin, Carbet* 🕾 *0596/78–22–66* 🎟 *€6* ⊘ *Daily 9–5:30.*

Neisson Distillery. The "Mercedes" of Martinique rum brewers is a small, family-run operation whose rum is produced from pure sugarcane juice rather than molasses. It's open for tours and tastings, and the shop sells *rhum extra-vieux* (vintage rum) that truly rivals cognac. ⊠ *Carbet* 🕾 *0596/78–07–90* ⊕ *www.neisson.com* 🎟 *Free* ⊘ *Daily 9–4.*

Le Prêcheur. This quaint village, the last on the northern Caribbean coast, is surrounded by volcanic hot springs. It was the childhood home of Françoise d'Aubigné, who later became the Marquise de Maintenon and the second wife of Louis XIV. At her request, the Sun King donated a handsome bronze bell, which still hangs outside the church. The Tomb of the Carib Indians commemorates a sadder event. It's a formation of limestone cliffs, from which the last of the Caraïbes are said to have flung themselves to avoid capture by the marquise's forebears.

Presqu'île du Caravelle. Much of the Caravelle Peninsula, which juts 8 mi (13 km) into the Atlantic Ocean, is under the protection of the Regional Nature Reserve and offers places for trekking, swimming, and sailing. This is also the site of Anse-Spoutourne, an open-air sports and leisure center operated by the reserve. Tartane has a popular surfing beach with brisk Atlantic breezes.

☾ **Ste-Marie.** The winding, hilly route to this town of some 20,000 offers breathtaking views of the rugged Atlantic coastline. Ste-Marie is the commercial capital of the island's north. Look for a picturesque mid-19th-century church here.

The **Musée du Rhum,** operated by the St. James Rum Distillery, is housed in a graceful, galleried creole house. Guided tours take in displays of the tools of the trade and include a visit and tasting at the distillery. It can be a somewhat wild scene when a dozen or more tour buses pull in, though. It's closed during harvest, so call ahead. ⊠ *Ste-Marie* 🕾 *0596/69–30–02* 🎟 *Free* ⊘ *Weekdays 9–5, weekends 9–1.*

After navigating the narrow road, you probably won't find more-cordial hostesses than those here at **Le Musée de la Banane.** Excellent graphics and beautiful prints tell the story of the banana (Martinique's primary export) as it makes its way from the fields to your table. A vintage creole cottage serves as a well-stocked retail shop, and there's a bar and lunch counter with lots of edibles made from bananas. ⊠ *Habitation Limbé* 🕾 *0596/69–45–52* 🎟 *€6* ⊘ *Daily 9–5.*

St-Pierre. The rise and fall of St-Pierre is one of the most remarkable stories in the Caribbean. Martinique's modern history began here in 1635. By the turn of the 20th century St-Pierre was a flourishing city of 30,000, known as the Paris of the West Indies. As many as 30 ships at a time stood at anchor. By 1902 it was the most modern town in the Caribbean, with electricity, phones, and a tram. On May 8, 1902, two thunderous explosions rent the air. As the nearby volcano erupted, Mont Pelée split in half, belching forth a cloud of burning ash, poisonous gas, and lava that raced down the mountain at 250 mph. At 3,600°F, it instantly vaporized everything in its path; 30,000 people were killed in two minutes.

■TIP➡ **Did You Know?** One man survived the volcano's eruption. His name was Cyparis, and he was a prisoner in an underground cell in the town's jail, locked up for public drunkenness. Later, he went on the road with Barnum & Bailey Circus as a sideshow attraction.

14

The **Cyparis Express,** a small tourist train, will take you around to the main sights with running narrative (in French) for a half hour on Saturday, an hour on weekdays for €10.

An Office du Tourisme is on the *moderne* seafront promenade. Stroll the main streets and check the blackboards at the sidewalk cafés before deciding where to lunch. At night some places have live music. Like stage sets for a dramatic opera, there are the ruins of the island's first church (built in 1640), the imposing theater, the toppled statues. This city, situated on its naturally beautiful harbor and with its narrow, winding streets, has the feel of a European seaside hill town. Although many of the historic buildings need work, stark modernism has not invaded this burg. As much potential as it has, this is one town in Martinique where real estate is cheap—for obvious reasons.

For those interested in the eruption of 1902, the **Musée Vulcanologique Frank Perret** is a must. Established in 1932 by Frank Perret, a noted volcanologist, the museum houses photographs of the old town, documents, and a number of relics—some gruesome—excavated from the ruins, including molten glass, melted iron, and contorted clocks stopped at 8 AM. ⊠*Rue Victor Hugo* ☎*0596/78–15–16* 🎫*€5* 🕙*Daily 9–5.*

If you want to know more about volcanoes, earthquakes, and hurricanes, check out **Le Centre de Découverte des Sciences de la Terre.** Housed in a sleek building, this earth-science museum has high-tech exhibits and interesting films. ⊠*Habitation Perinelle* ☎*0596/52–82–42* ⊕*www.cdst.org* 🎫*€5* 🕙*Wed.–Sun. 9–5.*

★ An excursion to **Depaz Distillery** is one of the island's nicest treats. For four centuries it has sat at the foot of the volcano. In 1902 the greathouse was destroyed in the eruption, but soon after it was courageously rebuilt and the fields replanted. A self-guided tour includes the workers' gingerbread cottages and an exhibit of art and sculpture made from wooden casks and parts of distillery machinery. The tasting room sells their rums, including golden and aged rum (notably *rhum doré*) and distinctive liqueurs made from ginger and basil. ⊠*Mont Pelée Plantation* ☎*0596/78–13–14* 🎫*Free* 🕙*Mon.–Sat. 9–5.*

MARTINIQUE ESSENTIALS

To research prices, get advice from other travelers, and book travel arrangements, visit www.fodors.com.

▌TRANSPORTATION

BY AIR

Many travelers connect in San Juan, but there are a handful of nonstop flights from the U.S. to Martinique. Additionally, Air Antilles Express flies from Guadeloupe, St. Maarten, St. Barths, and, in some months, Santo Domingo in the Dominican Republic. Air Caraïbes flies from Guadeloupe, St. Maarten, St. Barths, and Santo Domingo. LIAT connects Martinique with the English-speaking "down islands." It code-shares with Air Caraïbes.

Information Air Antilles Express (☎0890/64–86–48 or 0596/42–16–71 ⊕www.airantilles.com). **Air Caraïbes** (☎0596/42–16–52, 0890/64–47–00, or 0820/83–58–35 ⊕www.aircaraibes.com). **Air France** (☎0820/82–08–20 or 0892/68–29–72). **American Eagle** (☎0590/21–13–66 in Guadeloupe). **Delta** (☎800/22–56–30 ⊕www.delta.com). **LIAT** (☎0596/42–16–11, 0590/21–13–93 in Guadeloupe, 888/844–5428 in U.S. ⊕www.liatairline.com).

AIRPORTS & TRANSFERS

Lamentin International Airport is a clean, contemporary airport, small enough to be managed easily. Short- and long-term parking lots are immediately in front of the terminal. You will need €1 and €2 coins to pay for parking on the way out. The airport is in the commercial area of Lamentin, a 15-minute taxi ride from Fort-de-France, and some 40 minutes from Les Trois-Ilets Peninsula. A public bus stop is diagonally across the highway from the airport. The bus to Fort-de-France costs €1.

Information Lamentin International Airport (FDF ☎0596/42–16–00).

BY BOAT & FERRY

Martinique can be reached by ferry. Express des Îles operates ferries to Dominica, Guadeloupe, and St. Lucia. Any of these trips costs in the neighborhood of €79 one way, and the crossings generally take between three and four hours, or even five on a bad day. Most of these services are daily, with extra departures on weekends, but call ahead to confirm schedules and prices. The services can be crowded on weekends and after music festivals and other popular events.

Weather permitting, *vedettes* (ferries) operate daily between Quai d'Esnambuc in Fort-de-France and the marinas in Pointe du Bout, Anse-Mitan, and Anse-à-l'Ane. Any of these trips takes about 20 minutes, and the ferries operate about every 30 minutes on weekdays, with long waits in the low season. Two companies, Vedettes Madinina and Caribéenne de Transport Maritime, operate the ferries. If you buy a round-trip ticket (about €6) you must use the return ticket for the same ferry company. The ferry is the best way to go into the capital, where traffic and parking are a tropical nightmare.

Information Caribéenne de Transport Maritime (☎0596/42–41–25). **Express des Îles** (☎0825/35–90–00 or 0596/63–12–11 ⊕www.express-des-iles.com). **Vedettes Madinina** (☎0596/63–06–46 ⊕www.vedettesmadinina.com).

BY CAR

The main highways, about 175 mi (280 km) of well-paved and well-marked roads, are excellent, but only in a few areas are they lighted at night. Many hotels are on roads that are barely passable, so get wherever you're going by nightfall or prepare to lose your way. Then tell a stranger: "*Je suis perdu!*" (I am lost). It elicits sympathy. Drive defensively; although Martinicans are polite and lovely people, they drive with aggressive abandon.

Martinique, especially Fort-de-France and environs, is plagued with heavy traffic; if you must drive into Fort-de France, do it on a weekend. Absolutely avoid the Lamentin Airport area and Fort-de-France during weekday rush hours, roughly 7 to 10 AM and 4 to 7:30 PM, and on Sunday night. Even the smaller towns like La Trinité have rush hours. Traffic can also be bad on weekend nights. Watch, too, for *dos d'ânes* (literally, donkey backs), speed bumps that are hard to spot—particularly at night. If you hit one, you'll know it. Gas is costly, nearly $7 per gallon.

Of the many agencies, JumboCar is the most likely to cut a deal, but few of its staffers speak English. Europcar will deliver the car to you and later pick it up, and its rates are usually among the lowest. If you're staying in Ste-Anne, and particularly if you're at Club Med, Euro Soleil Car is a small operation that has exceptionally good prices.

Information Avis (☎0596/42-11-00). **Budget** (☎0596/42-04-04). **Euro Soleil Car** (☎0596/76-93-34). **Europcar** (☎0596/42-42-42). **Hertz** (☎0596/51-01-01). **JumboCar** (☎0596/42-22-22 or 0820/22-02-30).

BY TAXI
Taxis, which are metered, are expensive, though you can try bargaining by offering to pay a flat rate to your destination. Drivers of M. Marital Mercedes Taxis speak English, Spanish, and German as well as French. At Taxi de Place you will find some English-speaking drivers, lots of courtesy, and new SUVs. J. Peloponese provides luxury service in new Mercedes-Benz cars.

Locals take *collectifs* (vans holding up to 10 passengers) that cost just a few euros and depart from the waterfront in Fort-de-France to all parts of the island. Don't be shy, because it can mean the difference between paying €3 and, say, €60 for a taxi to reach the same destination. Drivers don't usually speak English. Buses also are an option and are even cheaper. The tourist offices can help with maps and information.

Information J. Peloponese Taxis (☎0696/25-61-02). **M. Marital Mercedes Taxis** (☎0596/64-20-24, 0696/45-69-07 mobile). **Taxi de Place** (☎0696/31-91-05).

▮ CONTACTS & RESOURCES

BANKS & EXCHANGE SERVICES
The euro is the official currency in Martinique. U.S. dollars are accepted in some hotels but generally at an unfavorable rate. You can usually get the best rate by withdrawing euros from ATMs. Banks no longer exchange currency or traveler's checks; however, *bureaux de change* such as Change Caraïbes—which has offices at the airport and in Fort-de-France (14 rue Victor Hugo and Le Bord de Mer)—still will exchange both and usually offers fair rates.

You can find ATMs at the airport and at branches of the Crédit Agricole bank, which is on the Cirrus and Plus systems and also accepts Visa and MasterCard.

Major credit cards are accepted by most hotels and restaurants, but some establishments accept neither credit cards nor traveler's checks, particularly once you get away from Fort-de-France and Pointe du Bout. Many establishments don't accept American Express in any case.

ELECTRICITY
Most tourist locations are equipped with 220-volt electrical outlets. If you're coming from North America and plan to use your own appliances, bring a converter and an adapter.

EMERGENCIES
Emergency Services Ambulance (☎0596/70-36-48 or 0596/71-59-48). **Fire** (☎18). **Police** (☎17).

Hospitals CHG Louis Domergue (✉R Strade, La Trinité ☎0596/66-46-00). **Hôpital Maison Retraite** (✉Les Trois-Îlets ☎0596/66-30-00).

14

Hôpital du Marin (✉Bd. Allègre, Marin ☎0596/74–92–05). **Hôpital Pierre Zabla Quitman** (✉Lamentin ☎0596/55–20–00). **Hôpital de St-Pierre** (✉Rue Percée, St-Pierre ☎0596/78–14–93).

HEALTH

The water in Martinique is safe, but *no one* drinks from the tap. Always come armed with mosquito repellent; dengue fever has been reported on the island, though it is more prevalent after hurricanes and strong tropical storms.

INTERNET, MAIL & SHIPPING

In Fort-de-France you can check your e-mail at the Cyber Club Caraibe, open weekdays from 8 AM to 8 PM and Saturday 8 AM to 10 PM. Internet Haut Depot is a new Internet café that also has other business services, like document scanning and color copying. You'll have to climb to the second floor, where you will be welcomed by the bilingual French owner.

In Pointe du Bout, you can check your e-mail at Prolavnet (and have your clothes laundered at the same time). In Le Marin, the Calebasse Café, a music venue by night, has an Internet station. It's closed Monday. You can also get Internet service at the island's main post office and in some of the branches in towns like Le François.

Airmail letters to the United States and Canada cost €0.95 for up to 20 grams; postcards cost €0.80. Stamps can be purchased from post offices, tobacco shops, and newsstands. Letters to Martinique should include the name of the business, street (if available), town, and postal code, as well as "Martinique" and "French West Indies." Mail is extremely slow, both ways.

Information Calebasse Café (✉19 bd. Allègre, Le Marin ☎0596/74–84–20). **Cyber Club Caraïbe** (✉16 rue François Arago, Fort-de-France ☎0596/70–31–62 ⊕www.cyber-clubcaraibe.com). **Internet Haut Depot** (✉61 rue Victor Hugo, Fort-de-France ☎0596/63–

12–20). **Prolavnet** (✉Village Créole, Pointe du Bout ☎0596/66–07–79).

LANGUAGE

Although French is the official language, many Martinicans also speak Creole. As in France, you will find a warmer reception if you attempt to speak French first, asking if English is spoken.

SAFETY

Martinique is a reasonably safe island, and generally you will not feel threatened. In Fort-de-France, however, exercise the same safety precautions you would in any large city. It's best not to be downtown at night unless you're with a group, preferably Martinicans. Never leave jewelry, money, or designer sunglasses unattended on the beach or in your car. Keep your laptop under wraps, even in your hotel room, and put valuables in hotel safes.

TAXES & SERVICE CHARGES

A resort tax varies from city to city. Each has its own tax, with most between €0.76 and €1.25 per person per day; the maximum is €2.25. Rates quoted by hotels usually include a 10% service charge; however, some hotels add 10% to your bill.

TELEPHONES

There are no coin-operated phone booths. Public phones use a *télécarte*, which you can buy at post offices, café-tabacs, hotels, and bureaux de change.

To place a local or interisland call you have to dial all 10 numbers, beginning with 0596 and then the six-digit number. To call Martinique from the United States, dial 011–596–596 plus the local six-digit number (yes, you must dial *596 twice*). If calling from Guadeloupe, dial 0596 and then the six digits. Numbers with the 0696 prefix are for cell phones. To call the United States from Martinique, dial 00+1, then the area code, then the local number.

Information AT&T (☎800/99–00–11). **Bell** (☎800/99–00–16). **MCI** (☎800/99–00–19).

TIPPING

All restaurants include a 15% service charge in their menu prices. You can always add to this if you feel that service was particularly good, especially if it's a place you intend to frequent. They will remember the generous Americans.

TOUR OPTIONS

Your hotel front desk can help arrange a personalized island tour with an English-speaking driver. It's also possible to hire a taxi for the day or half day; there are set rates for certain itineraries, and if you share the ride with others the per-person price will be whittled down. La Belle Kréole runs one of the most fun excursion boats to *les fonds blanc*, also known as Empress Joséphine's baths. You can experience the unique Martinican custom of eating accras, drinking planter's punch, and smoking cigarettes in waist-deep water. The price of the trip depends on whether you have lobster, fish, or chicken. Madinina Tours offers half- and full-day jaunts (lunch included) by sea and air. You can go by boat to St-Pierre on the north coast or by air to the Grenadines or St. Lucia. Madinina has tour desks in most of the major hotels.

Information **La Belle Kréole** (⊠Baie du Simon ☎0596/54–96–46 or 0696/29–93–13). **Madinina Tours** (⊠Lamentin Airport, Lamentin ☎0596/42–17–07 ⊕www.madininatours. com).

VISITOR INFORMATION

Before You Leave **Martinique Promotion Bureau** (☎800/391–4909 in U.S., 310/271–6665 in Beverly Hills, 312/751–7800 in Chicago ⊕www.martinique.org.com).

In Martinique **Comité Martiniquais du Tourisme** (⊠BP 7124- Pointe de Jaham, Schoelcher, Fort-de-France ☎0596/61–61–77 ⊕www.martiniquetourisme.com). **Office du Tourisme de Fort-de-France** (⊠76 rue Lazare Carnot, Fort-de-France ☎0596/60–27–73).

WEDDINGS

Since getting married in Martinique requires a long residency requirement, it's not really feasible to plan a wedding on the island, but this sensual island is so suited for a honeymoon.

14

Montserrat

St. Patrick's Day Festival

WORD OF MOUTH

"I read three full books while I was there . . . the pace is wonderfully relaxed. Let me just say this, if your idea of a vacation is an island resort, this is probably not the place for you. If you want to experience a different type of place on this planet of yours, meet some genuinely friendly people, relax, and actually become a little more educated . . . this may be what you are looking for."

—SAnParis

WELCOME TO MONTSERRAT

It's been more than a decade since the Soufrière Hills Volcano erupted, and Montserrat is slowly coming back to life. Though the volcano continues to rumble, the island is otherwise as peaceful as the Caribbean gets, almost a throwback to another time, with the occasional modern convenience (and convenience store) thrown in. Montserrat draws eco-tourists, divers, and those who simply want to experience the Caribbean as it once was.

Hotels	▼	Jumping Jack's	5
Erindell Villa	3	Tina's	1
Gingerbread Hill	2	Ziggy's	3
Tropical Mansion	1		
Restaurants	▼		
Gourmet Gardens	4		

The island's best beach (the sole white-sand beach on the island) is accessible only by boat—or a very steep trail that we don't recommend.

You can visit the Daytime Entry Zone from 6 AM to 6 PM daily, depending on how active the volcano is on any particular day.

Caribbean Sea

Rendezvous B

Little B

Carr's Bay

1

1

Cudjoehe

Bunkum Bay

St.

Woodlands Bay

3
Runaway Ghaut

Montserrat National Trust

Lime Kiln Bay

3 4

Olves
Saler

Old Towne

Montse
Vol
Observa

Old Road Bay

Iles Bay

Cork Hill

DAYTIME ENTRY ZONE

Foxes Bay

Bransby Pt.

Richmond Hill

Plymouth

KEY

1	*Restaurants*
1	*Hotels*

TOP 4 REASONS TO VISIT MONTSERRAT

1 Volcano lovers and other eco-tourists will experience a landscape that's been pretty much left alone for a decade, a rarity in the Caribbean.

2 You'll find tranquillity in abundance; if you want to lay back and relax, this is the place for you.

3 It's a buyer's market. Until the tourists come thundering back, value abounds here.

4 There's virtually no crime, and locals will welcome you with open arms. You won't find a friendlier place in the Caribbean.

THE EMERALD ISLE OF THE CARIBBEAN

Montserrat is a small island about 25 mi (40 km) southwest of Antigua. Named by Columbus after a Catholic abbey near Barcelona—Santa Maria de Montserrate—the island was settled predominantly by Irish Catholics who had once been indentured servants in the West Indies. The numbers of Irish waned, but their influence remained. The island rumbled into the media in 1995, when the Soufrière Hills Volcano suddenly erupted and covered the capital, Plymouth, in ash.

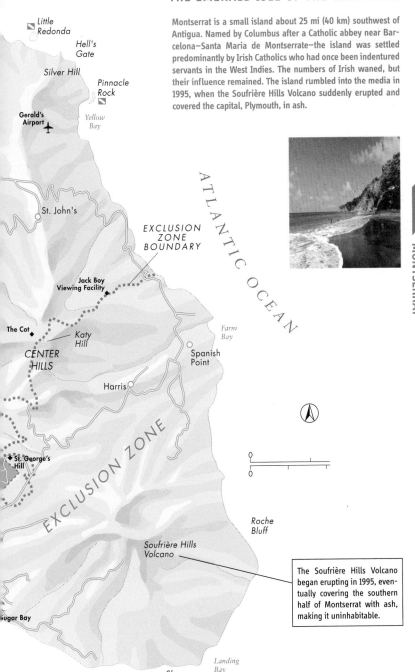

Little Redonda

Hell's Gate

Silver Hill

Pinnacle Rock

Gerald's Airport ✈

Yellow Bay

ATLANTIC OCEAN

○ St. John's

EXCLUSION ZONE BOUNDARY

Jack Boy Viewing Facility ◆

The Cot ◆

Katy Hill

CENTER HILLS

Farm Bay

○ **Spanish Point**

Harris ○

◆ **St. George's Hill**

EXCLUSION ZONE

Roche Bluff

Soufrière Hills Volcano

The Soufrière Hills Volcano began erupting in 1995, eventually covering the southern half of Montserrat with ash, making it uninhabitable.

Sugar Bay

Guadeloupe Passage

Shoe Rock

Landing Bay

0
0

15

MONTSERRAT

MONTSERRAT PLANNER

Island Activities

You come to Montserrat for **ecotourism,** including volcano viewing. There's surprisingly varied **diving** in amazingly pristine waters. **Hiking** through unspoiled rain forest is another attraction. The showcase beach is **Rendezvous Bay,** a cliff shadowed cove accessible only by boat or vigorous hike.

Logistics

Getting to Montserrat: There are no nonstop flights to Montserrat from North America. You can transfer on either Antigua or St. Maarten for a Winair flight (most departures are scheduled to coincide with the international flight schedule into the two islands) into the small but well-designed Gerald's Airport. At one time, there was also ferry service from Antigua, but it no longer operates.

Hassle Factor: Medium to high.

Nonstops: Some to Antigua and St. Maarten, but none to Montserrat.

On the Ground

Though you can take taxis, you'll best appreciate Montserrat's quiet beauty if you rent a car and do some exploring on your own. Rates start at around $35 a day, but gas is expensive. Prepare to drive on your left, break for rambling goats and chickens, and negotiate some steep, winding roads. The fixed taxi fare from the airport ranges from $6 (for Tropical Mansion) to $22 (to the Olveston/Salem area villas).

When to Go

The year's big event is **St. Patrick's Day,** which ushers in a week of festivities, highlighted by musical concerts and masquerades à la Carnival. **Tourism Week,** usually late September or early October, encourages village competitions in music, dance, crafts, and food.

Where to Stay

With a few small guest houses, villas, and one small hotel, Montserrat has no large-scale development. The island's best hotel, Vue Point, is closed at this writing because of the volcano.

Hotel and Restaurant Costs

⇨*For information on hotel meal plans, see Accommodations in Caribbean Essentials.*

WHAT IT COSTS IN U.S. DOLLARS				
$$$$	$$$	$$	$	¢
Restaurants				
over $30	$20–$30	$12–$20	$8–$12	under $8
Hotels*				
over $350	$250–$350	$150–$250	$80–$150	under $80
Hotels**				
over $450	$350–$450	$250–$350	$125–$250	under $125

*EP, BP, CP **AI, FAP, MAP Restaurant prices are for a main course at dinner and include any taxes or service charges. Hotel prices are per night for a double room in high season, excluding taxes, service charges, and meal plans (except at all-inclusives).

By Jordan
Simon

A POLICE ESCORT WAITS PATIENTLY as I stroll the ash-blanketed streets of Montserrat's capital, Plymouth. Behind me, cattle surreally meander through a vast gray expanse—the hardened mudflows that Montserrat's volcano spewed like nature's spittle—flanked by startlingly emerald greensward. Before me, a seemingly endless, pristine beach glistens like black pearls in the sun. The graceful Georgian buildings I fondly recall from my first visit in 1991 poke up like restless sprites: the bell turret of the War Memorial, the gables of Government House. Suddenly I stop short to avoid plunging through a collapsed roof. Spears of sunlight illuminate a droll yet dreamlike store display: untouched rows of sneakers and Swatches in a former shop—a good 15 feet underground.

Aficionados have always regarded Montserrat as an idyllic, fairy-tale island. But in 1995, Grimm turned grim when the Soufrière Hills volcano erupted, literally throwing the island into the fire. The frilly Victorian gingerbreads of the capital, Plymouth, were buried, much of the tourism infrastructure was wiped out, and more than half the original 11,000 residents departed and have not been able to return. Though the volcano still belches (plumes of ash are visible from as far as Antigua), plucky locals joke that new beachfront is being created. The volcano itself is an ecotourism spot drawing travelers curious to see the awesome devastation. Ironically, other fringe benefits exist. Volcanic deposits enriched the already fertile soil; locals claim their fruit and vegetable crops have increased and improved. The slightly warmer waters have attracted even more-varied marine life for divers and snorkelers to appreciate, along with new underwater rock formations.

Although an "Exclusion Zone" covers half the island, the rest is safe; in fact, the zone was slightly retracted after the volcano's lava dome partially collapsed during a pyroclastic flow in July 2003. Seismologists and vulcanologists conduct regular risk analyses and simulation studies; as a result, the Daytime Exclusion Zone shrank after a May 2006 collapse, then expanded again after activity in late 2007 into 2008. Visitors expecting mass devastation are in for a surprise; Montserrat ranks among the region's most pristine, serene destinations, its luxuriant vegetation and jagged green hills justifying the moniker Emerald Isle (most locals are descended from Irish settlers, whose influence lingers in place and family names, folklore, jigs, even a wispy brogue). The combined Carnival and Christmas festivities go on for nearly a month, when the island is awash with color, from calypso competitions to parades and pageants.

Other than the volcano, the steamiest activities are the fiercely contested domino games outside rum shops. That may soon change. The government speaks optimistically of building a new golf course, developing spa facilities to offer volcanic mud baths, even running tours—pending safety assessments—of Plymouth as a haunting Caribbean answer to Pompeii. An airport has been constructed, partly in the hope of recapturing the villa crowd that once frequented the island. But these developments—as well as debates over the new capital and threatened lawsuits against the British government for restricting access and utility service to homesites—will simmer for quite some time. One thing won't change: the people, whether native-born or expat, are among the warmest anywhere. Chat them up, and don't be surprised if you're invited to a family dinner or beach picnic.

WHERE TO STAY

Currently, the island primarily offers villas (housekeepers and cooks can be arranged) or guesthouses, the latter often incorporating meals by request in the rate (ask if the 7% tax and 10% service charge are included); and there is one small hotel. Regrettably, Montserrat's oldest, classiest hostelry, the Osborne family's Vue Pointe Hotel, which bravely kept rising—literally—like a phoenix from the ashes, has shuttered indefinitely, probably permanently; but check their Web site (⊕ *www.vuepointe.com*) for updates.

VILLA RENTALS

In the pre-volcano (and Hurricane Hugo) days, when an international roster of celebrity musicians (Elton to Eric, the Rolling Stones to Sting) recorded at Sir George Martin's Air Studios, Montserrat was a favored spot for many rich and famous Britons (and the occasional American) to vacation. Today you can luxuriate in one of the handsome villas they called home when visiting and do so for comparatively affordable rates.

The leading villa rental company in Montserrat is **Tradewinds Real Estate** (✎ *Box 365, Olveston* ☎ *664/491–2004* ⊕ *www.tradewindsmontserrat.com*). Many of its 20-plus deluxe properties, ranging from one to four bedrooms, have plunge pools, amazing water vistas, and ultramodern conveniences from DVD players and Internet access to gourmet kitchens. Recommended properties with beach access and/or strategic hillside locations include Mango Falls, Casa del Sol, Cythera, and Vest View. Caring owners Susan Edgecombe and her mother, Betty Dix, really try to match guest to villa, remaining available throughout your stay to make any additional arrangements and offer touring and activity suggestions. Rates run from $875 to $2,500 per week in high season.

Another recommended option, in business since 1962, is **Montserrat Enterprises** (✎ *Box 58, Hilltop, St. Peters* ☎ *664/491–2004* ⊕ *www.montserratenterprises.com*). Its inventory is generally smaller, but most of its properties offer splendid views and amenities.

HOTELS & GUESTHOUSES

$ 🖼 **Tropical Mansion Suites.** Despite the grandiose name, this is little more than a motel with neocolonial architectural pretensions. A slight soullessness pervades the space, which lacks the warmth of family-run guesthouses. Nonetheless, it's the most "modern" hotel on the island and quite comfortable. Rooms are clean and fairly spacious, with an upscale motor-lodge look, but balconies (save for Room 202, where Prince Philip stayed) regrettably face the interior courtyard, rather than the verdant sweep of hills undulating down to the sea. Though the institutional basement restaurant has received a face-lift, insist on patio seating. Meals are mostly buffet and adequate, if overpriced. **Pros:** Currently only full-service lodging, centrally located. **Cons:** Far from beaches, mediocre and comparatively pricey food. ⌂ *Box 404, Sweeney's* ☎ *664/491–8767* ⊕ *www.tropicalmansion.com* ↩ *17 rooms, 1 suite* ⌂ *In-room: no a/c (some), kitchen (some), refrigerator, Wi-Fi. In-hotel: restaurant, bar, pool, no elevator, public Internet* ▤ *AE, D, MC, V* ⑩ *CP.*

¢–$ ⊡ **Gingerbread Hill.** This secluded mountainside retreat offers remark-
★ able value, splendid views, utter tranquillity, and exquisite grounds, where you can pluck your breakfast straight from the mango, banana, citrus, papaya, and coconut trees. Owners David and Clover Lea laughingly call themselves "unrepentant but well-done hippies," and they are—in the best sense of respecting nature, supporting local culture, and being self-sufficient. This Renaissance couple built the villas themselves, utilizing recycled or indigenous materials wherever possible. Clover is an artist and trained masseuse (ladies only); David is a documentary videographer, who will give you fascinating perspectives on the volcano. Oldest son Jesse conducts tours and records island music. Two villas have such clever creative touches as trompe-l'oeil window frames and hand-painted tiles, as well as wraparound verandahs with extraordinary views. The cozy Backpacker's Special has a microwave, CD player, and fridge. Reasonably priced meals are available (daughter-in-law Kristina Mae is a mean baker), utilizing fixings from the hydroponic gardens and fresh eggs from the family's chickens. **Pros:** Environmentally conscious, superb value, fascinating owners, delightful menagerie including birds. **Cons:** Car necessary, perhaps too "granola" for some. ⌂ *Box 246, St. Peter's* ☎ *664/491–5812* ⊕ *www. volcano-island.com* ↩ *2 rooms, 2 villas* ⌂ *In-room: no a/c, kitchen (some), refrigerator (some), no TV (some), DVD (some). In-hotel: bicycles, no elevator, laundry facilities, public Internet, airport shuttle* ▤ *No credit cards* ⑩ *EP.*

¢ ⊡ **Erindell Villa Guesthouse.** This tranquil rain-forest retreat is a photo album in the making, overflowing with character and characters. Memorable snapshots run from lush gardens framed by emerald hills and azure sea to colorful cocktail hours brimming with bonhomie and island gossip. Warm and witty Lou and Shirley Spycalla treat you like family, offering such complimentary extras as meet-and-greet airport service, snack baskets, Internet, and a cell phone loaner when hiking or beachcombing. Separate entrances guarantee privacy in the two snug, self-contained units (the poolside room is larger). If you'd rather not cook, you can feast en famille in the kitchen on enticing themed meals, then follow up with hotly contested board games or hilarious karaoke. **Pros:** engaging owners, beautiful landscaping, fun make-shift entertainment including karaoke. **Cons:** hike to beach, karaoke evenings. ⌂ *Gros Michel Dr., Woodlands* ☎ *664/491–3655* ⊕ *www. erindellvilla.com* ↩ *2 rooms* ⌂ *In-room: no a/c, refrigerator. In-hotel:*

15

restaurant, pool, no elevator, laundry service, public Internet, airport shuttle ⊟No *credit cards* ⊠CP.

WHERE TO EAT

Restaurants are casual affairs indeed, ranging from glorified rum shops to hotel dining rooms. Most serve classic Caribbean fare, including such specialties as goat water (a thick stew of goat meat, tubers, and vegetables that seems to have been bubbling for days), the increasingly hard-to-find mountain chicken (giant frogs), saal-fish kiac (codfish fritters), home-brewed ginger beer, and freshly made juices from soursop, mango, blackberry (different from the North American species), guava, tamarind, papaya, and gooseberry.

WHAT TO WEAR

Dress is informal even at dinner, though skimpy attire is frowned upon by the comparatively conservative islanders. Long pants are preferred, albeit not required, for men in the evening.

CARIBBEAN ✗**Tina's.** This pretty, seafoam-green-and-white wooden building is gar-
$–$$$ landed year-round with Christmas lights, a harbinger of the good vibes within. It's the best place to eavesdrop on island gossip, as government functionaries file in for lunch (at least when day-trippers don't take over). Dine either in a trim room or on a breezy verandah (admittedly sans view). Occasionally you'll find old-time dishes like souse, but the menu is generally more upscale: specialties include velvety pumpkin soup, proper escargots, and tender lobster in sultry creole sauce or (even better) tangy garlic sauce; entrées are served with heaping helpings of salads and sides. Fine desserts (moist carrot cake and wonderfully textured coconut pie) end the meal and surprisingly good take-away pizza is available. ⊠*Brades* ☎664/491–3538 ⊟No *credit cards*.

ECLECTIC ✗**Royal Palm Club.** This gem feels
$$$–$$$$ like an update on a colonial
★ Maugham tale, down to the eccentric expats, rumors of royal visits, and wildly eclectic yet elegant decor. Though it technically operates as a "private membership club," anyone can call for reservations. The gingerbread-trim house, swallowed up in extravagant gardens, reputedly hosted Queen Elizabeth II and Princess Margaret during their 1962 trip. The interior features a marvelous mosaic bar (casual wine-and-pasta dinners are served here and at the downstairs poolside bar), stone walls, hardwood floors, stained glass, Turkish throw rugs, Indonesian kites, and

READER LODGING RECOMMENDATION

Montserrat's lodging scene remains in a state of flux. But many small, often charming accommodations crop up as locals and expats try to earn additional income. Fodors.com forum users recommend **Bunkum Beach Guest House** (⊠*Palm Loop* ☎664/491–5348 or 664/491–4562 ⊕*www.bunkumbeachguesthouse.com*). The price ranges from $5 for a "backpacker" special room to $875 per week for a two-bedroom villa. We can certainly recommend the pristine beach setting.

CLOSE UP

Luck of the Irish

Montserrat's first European settlers were persecuted English and Irish Catholics brought from Protestant St. Kitts by Englishman Thomas Warner in 1632. Seventeen years later, Oliver Cromwell sentenced many Irish political prisoners to work in the island's lucrative sugarcane fields. A 1678 census recorded that more than half the islanders were Irish. Their influence lingers today, starting with the shamrock passport stamp. The national flag bears a crest of the legendary Irish figure of Erin with a harp, while the names of both towns (Galway, Bunkum) and inhabitants (Maloney, Frith) hark back to Eire. The national dish, goat water, recalls a traditional Irish stew, while the rollicking *Bam-chick-a-lay* wouldn't be out of place in *River-*

dance. Montserrat is the only country outside Ireland where St. Patrick's Day is a public holiday; March 17 ushers in a week of celebrations across the island, the wearing of the green assuming a distinctly Caribbean beat with live calypso, reggae, and iron band music. Indeed, Montserrat's true African heritage is just as pronounced: many newborns are still given "jumbie" nicknames to fool those evil spirits, and the related jumbie dances, designed to propitiate or ward them off, are lusty and vibrant. The two traditions happily merge in the engaging people, such as Rootsman (aka Murphy), proprietor of the eponymous Carr's Bay bar, fervently discussing his homemade herbal remedies in a lyrical, lilting brogue.

17th-century French sideboards. The enclosed patio, doubling as the main dining room, enchants with sweeping Caribbean views and fluttering butterflies. Doug Simonson works wonders with limited ingredients; four-course set menu choices might include sautéed salmon and tiger shrimp over lime-christophene risotto or slow-roasted pork tenderloin in orange marmalade sauce. Lovely, though pricey, rooms are for rent and villas are in the planning stages. The peripatetic co-owners include the delightful Trevor Stephenson, who will regale you with his "Lifestyles of the poor and infamous" anecdotes. ⊠ *Woodlands* ☎ 664/491–2671 ⊕ *www.montserrat-royalpalmvilla.com* ⚓ *Reservations essential* ⊟ *No credit cards* ⊘ *No lunch Mon.–Sat.*

$$$ ✕**Ziggy's.** Vivacious owners John and Marcia Punter literally hacked Montserrat's most elegant eatery from the rain forest. They poured a concrete floor and dressed it with a white rectangular tent, pergolas, palm fronds, potted plants, hardwood chairs, bronze sculpted candlesticks, and colorful Moroccan-inspired table settings. The menu (posted on a blackboard) changes daily. Generally well-executed dishes lean more toward bistro fare (emphasizing beef entrecôte or grilled marinated lamb over such island staples as chicken and fish); the signature butterfly shrimp usually precede entrées. A decent wine list enhances the meal; save room for the Chocolate Sludge. Though the schedule is erratic (reconfirm reservations), the location hard to find, and the service too relaxed, the ambience is appealingly serene and upscale. ⊠ *Mahogany La., Woodlands* ☎ 664/491–8282 ⊕ *www.ziggysrestaurant.com* ⚓ *Reservations essential* ⊟ *No credit cards* ⊘ *No lunch.*

$$ ✕ **Gourmet Gardens.** This tranquil, secluded spot—a classic gingerbread chattel-house replica echoing the adjacent historic buildings of the former Olveston estate—fulfills more than half the name's promise. There are few more delightful experiences than relaxing on Mariet's verandah amid a virtual botanical garden or beneath the huge, shady tamarind tree. Lunches are excellent value, but Sunday brunch is the winner (scrumptious eggs Benedict). "Gourmet" is a slight exaggeration, but the global menu more than satisfies most palates and wallets. Specialties include stroganoff, chicken cordon bleu, and any dessert (try the chocolate mousse or cheesecake). ⊠ *Olveston* ☎ *664/491–7859* ⚲ *Reservations essential* ⊟ *No credit cards* ⊙ *No dinner Wed.*

$–$$ ✕ **Jumping Jack's.** Danny and Margaret Sweeney moved their beachfront
★ eatery to their home due to safety concerns in Old Road Bay, but it still gives off a nautical vibe and certainly jumps Friday nights when they stay open until 10:30 (they close at 7:30 other nights). The decor—fishnets, Danny's tournament trophies, and photos of him displaying his prize catches—reflects the specialty: tuna, wahoo, and other freshly caught fish. But Margaret utilizes whatever ingredients are available. You might get lucky and have a chance to try her chicken satay, lasagna, or flaky, flavorful pies (chicken-and-mushroom, pork, or steak-and-kidney) that elevate traditional English pub grub to an art form. The sublime sticky toffee pudding, mango-ginger crumble, and pear tart justify Margaret's declaration, "I'd rather make desserts than clean the house!" ⊠ *Hibiscus Dr., Olveston* ☎ *664/491–5645* ⊟ *No credit cards* ⊙ *Closed Mon., Tues., Thurs., and Sat.*

BEACHES

Montserrat's beaches are public and, with one exception, composed of soft, light to dark gray volcanic sand.

Little Bay. Boats chug in and out of the port at the northern end of this otherwise comely crescent with calm waters. Several beach bars—Log-On (get passionate owner Arthur Brokes talking about the environment) and Shizzle ma Nizzle—provide cool shade and cooler drinks. Carlton's Fish Net Bar in the Festival Village specializes in barbecued stuffed trunkfish (a shellfish delicacy); the Good Life also offers fine food. You may see locals casting lines for their own dinner. ⊠ *Approximately 1.5 mi (2.5 km) north of Brades off the main road; look for turnoffs to Little Bay.*

★ **Rendezvous Bay.** The island's sole white-sand beach is a perfect cove tucked under a forested cliff whose calm, unspoiled waters are ideal for swimming and offer remarkable snorkeling. It's accessible only via the sea or a steep trail that runs over the bluff to adjacent Little Bay (you can also negotiate boat rides from the fishermen who congregate there). There are no facilities or shade, but its very remoteness and pristine reef teeming with marine life lend it exceptional charm. ⊠ *Rendezvous Bay.*

Woodlands/Bunkum Bays. The only drawback to this secluded strand is the occasionally rough surf (children should be closely monitored). The breezy but covered picnic area on the cliff is one of the best vantage points to watch migratory humpback whales in spring and nesting green and hawksbill turtles in early fall. (From here, hike north then down across a wooden bridge to even less trammeled Bunkum Bay, which lacks facilities but has a friendly guesthouse.) ⊠ *At turnoff just outside Woodlands village.*

SPORTS & THE OUTDOORS

BIKING

Mountain biking is making a comeback, with a wide network of trails through the lush Centre Hills. Bikes are also a wonderful way to explore the island, and enjoy the lovely coastal vistas along the main road. Ecocentric expat James Naylor runs **Imagine Peace Bicycles** (⊠ *BBC Complex, main road, Brades* ☎ *664/491–8809*), which rents state-of-the-art equipment from Cygnal and Mongoose ($10 to $15 per day) and conducts tours through the countryside.

15

DIVING

More than 30 practically pristine dive sites surround Montserrat. The even more bountiful marine life has had time to recover from the predations of human activities, while the pyroclastic flows formed boulders, pinnacles, ledges, and walls that anchor new coral reefs. **Carr's Bay** is a favorite for shore dives, with arrow crabs, basket stars, turtles, and shimmering blue tang darting about hulking boulders and a small, colorful cave; night dives are particularly memorable as millions of bioluminescent microorganisms glow when disturbed. The shallow reefs surrounding **Woodlands Bay** feature varied underwater topography, including a small, colorful cave and thousands of banded coral shrimp, copper sweepers, sergeant majors, four-eyed butterfly fish, jackknife, attenuated trumpetfish, and turtles. **Rendezvous Bay** may be the finest spot for both snorkeling and diving, thanks to a sheltered reef and lack of ash or silt. You come face-to-face with spotted morays, porcupine fish, snake eels, octopuses, and more. You can even hang out with thousands of (harmless) fruit bats in partly submerged caves. Other top dive sites include **Lime Kiln Bay** and **Bunkum Bay,** as well as the spectacular submarine rock formations around **Little Redonda** and the **Pinnacles** off the rougher, more-challenging northeastern shores.

The **Green Monkey Dive Shop** (⊠ *Little Bay* ☎ *664/491–2628* ⊕ *www. divemontserrat.com*) offers PADI certification, snorkeling trips, and a variety of dives. Scuba Master Troy Depperman customizes trips for clients' interests and skill levels. The most intriguing regular option is Dive Redonda, a tour of the island "Kingdom of Redonda" located just 15 mi (24 km) northwest of Montserrat. The 45-minute boat ride offers scintillating views of the coast and Soufrière Hills volcano. Once there, underwater attractions include leviathan southern stingrays, morays, turtles, nurse sharks, and barracudas cruising around 6-foot barrel sponges and darting in and out of the caves and coral-encrusted barge at the "World's End" on the island's northernmost point. They also run nature hikes and ecotours.

☾ Dive master Bryan Cunningham took over Wolf Krebs's **Seawolf Diving School** (✉ *Main road, Woodlands* ☎ *664/491-7807* ⊕ *www.seawolf divingschool.com*), which offers PADI certification; shore, kayak, and boat dives; snorkeling trips (including a stop at a very cool bat cave); and even underwater photography classes utilizing state-of-the-art SeaLife equipment. Bryan and wife Tish are particularly good with kids: the shop stocks underwater Frisbees and torpedoes, as well as specialized children's gear.

FISHING

Deep-sea fishing (wahoo, bonito, shark, marlin, and yellowfin tuna) is superb, since the waters aren't disturbed by leviathan cruise ships. Affable **Danny Sweeney** (✉ *Olveston* ☎ *664/491–5645*) has won several regional tournaments, including Montserrat's Open Fishing Competition. Half-day charters (up to four people) are $250. Though schools of game fish amazingly cavort just 2 to 3 mi (3 to 5 km) offshore, Danny's depth sounder picks up action in deeper waters. An extra bonus on the open sea are the gripping views of the volcanic devastation.

HIKING

Montserrat's lush, untrammeled rain forest teeming with exotic flora, fauna, and birdlife is best experienced on foot. The tourist office provides lists of hiking trails, from easy to arduous. Nine of the most dramatic routes are gradually being upgraded as part of the Montserrat Tourism Development Project; in addition to improving their definition, the government will also be building viewing platforms and providing interpretative information at strategic points. Still, if you're not experienced or fit, go with a guide; always wear sturdy shoes and bring water. Most marked trails run through the biologically diverse, scenic Centre Hills region, offering stirring lookouts over the volcano's barren flanks, surrounding greenery, and ash-covered villages in the Exclusion Zone. The rain forest is home to many regionally endemic wildlife species (tree frogs, dwarf geckos, anoles, mountain chicken—actually a type of frog, and the half-snake/half-lizard galliwasp), as well as most of the 34 resident birds, from red-billed tropic birds to the rare national bird, the Montserrat oriole, with its distinctive orange-and-black plumage. The Silver Hills in the north are vastly different, with dry and deciduous forests and open plains blanketing a defunct, heavily faulted and eroded volcano; views here might provide a glimpse of how southern Montserrat will look millions of years from now.

Scriber Tours (☎ *664/491–2546, 664/491–3412, or 664/492–2943*) is run by James "Scriber" Daley ("a describer since I was little"), an employee of the Agricultural Department legendary for his uncanny birdcalls. He leads nature hikes through the rain forest for $20 to $40;

he'll hire additional guides if there are more than 10 people per group, ensuring personal attention. Scriber also explains indigenous flora, from 42 fern species (kids love when he "tattoos" them with silver fern leaves) to others prized for medicinal properties (you might collect the makings of bush tea for back pain or menstrual cramps). He also conducts a memorable, if brief, evening mountain-chicken tour, distributing flashlights to find the foot-long frogs.

SHOPPING

Montserrat offers a variety of local crafts and does a brisk trade in vulcanology mementos (many shops sell not only postcards and striking photographs but small bottles of gray ash capped by colorful, homemade cloth).

David Lea (⊠ *Gingerbread Hill, St. Peter's* ☏ *664/491–5812* ⊕ *www. volcano-island.com*) has chronicled Montserrat's volcanic movements in a fascinating eight-part video series, *The Price of Paradise,* each entry a compelling glimpse into the geological and social devastation—and regeneration. These, as well as rollicking local-music CDs by his son and other musicians, are available at his studio. **Jus' Looking** (⊠ *Gerald's Airport, Gerald's* ☏ *664/491–2752 or 664/492–2752*) is a terrific last-minute stop for high-quality local arts and crafts, such as photos, ceramics, painted gourds, and treats like Volcano Rum and homemade gingerbread liqueur (with a slice of gingerbread pickling inside the bottle). They also sell low-priced souvenirs. **Luv's Cotton Store** (⊠ *Salem* ☏ *664/491–3906*) is the best source for sportswear made from sea island cotton, celebrated for its softness and high quality. Also occupying the National Trust building, the **Montserrat Philatelic Bureau** (⊠ *Salem* ☏ *664/491–2042* ⊕ *www.montserratstampbureau. com*) sells a wealth of unusual stamps, including handsome first-day covers. **Oriole Gift Shop** (⊠ *Salem* ☏ *664/491–3086*), run by the Montserrat National Trust, is an excellent source for books on Montserrat (look for the *Montserrat Cookbook* and works by the island's former acting governor, Sir Howard Fergus), as well as handicrafts (wonderful dolls, hand-painted boxes, and calabash purses) and locally made food products. **Woolcock's Craft & Photo Gallery** (⊠ *BBC Bldg., Brades* ☏ *664/491–2025*) promotes the work of local artists like Donaldson Romeo and sells spectacular photos of the volcano as well as of indigenous birds and other wildlife.

NIGHTLIFE

Although Montserrat is better known for another kind of wildlife, Friday-night revelers lime in roadside rum shops scattered around the island, often spilling out on the street as part of the informal evening culture. There's no closing time, and many bars serve yummy, authentic local food. **Garry Moore's Wide Awake Bar** (⊠ *Salem* ☏ *664/491–7156*) is a perennial favorite that doesn't close as long as customers are thirsty. Don't be afraid to wake Garry to pay your tab: he often naps at the bar (when he isn't complaining—mostly humorously—about a plumber's hard life and long hours). Mild-mannered restaurant by day, **Good Life** (⊠*Little Bay* ☎*664/491–4576*) often transforms on weekends into a strobe-lighted disco, blasting the latest Caribbean and Euro-house mixes and attracting every young single ready to mingle. **Howe's Rum Shop** (⊠*St. John's* ☎*664/491–3008*) is the best spot for shooting pool and the breeze over luscious fried and barbecued chicken, liberally daubed with mouth- and eye-watering homemade sauces and seasonings. Lydia, the owner of the **Treasure Spot** (⊠*Cudjoe Head* ☎*664/493–2003*), often books the island's up-and-coming musicians (usually One Man Band but also Pops Morris, Hero, and Basil) to play weekends.

Eight years in development, the impressive, colonnaded **Montserrat Cultural Centre** (⊠*Little Bay* ☎*664/491–4242* ⊕*www.montserrat culturalcentre.com*) and its 500-seat, state-of-the-art Sir George Martin Auditorium presents craft demonstrations, folkloric and fashion shows, pageants, movies (with popcorn and hot dogs), and the occasional dance and theatrical performance. Check with the tourist board or the local newspaper listings for the current schedule.

EXPLORING MONTSERRAT

Though the more-fertile—and historic—southern half of Montserrat was destroyed by the volcano, emerald hills still reward explorers. Hiking and biking are the best ways to experience this island's unspoiled rain forest, glistening black-sand beaches, and lookouts over the devastation.

The Cot. A fairly strenuous Centre Hills trail leads to one of Montserrat's few remaining historic sites—the ruins of the once-influential Sturges family's summer cottage—as well as a banana plantation. Its Duck Pond Hill perch, farther up the trail, dramatically overlooks the coastline, Garibaldi Hill, Old Towne, abandoned villages, and Plymouth.

Jack Boy Viewing Facility. This vantage point—replete with telescope, barbecue grill and tables for picnickers, landscaped grounds, and washrooms—provides bird's-eye views of the old W. H. Bramble airport and eastern villages damaged by pyroclastic flows. ⊠*Jack Boy Hill.*

★ **Montserrat National Trust.** The MNT's Natural History Centre aims to conserve and enhance the island's natural beauty and cultural heritage. The center has exhibits on Arawak canoe building, colonial sugar and lime production (the term "limey" was first applied here to English sailors trying to avoid scurvy), indigenous marine life, West Indian cricket, and the history of Sir George Martin's Air Studios, which once lured top musicians from Dire Straits to Stevie Wonder and Paul McCartney. Eventually one archival exhibit will screen videos of Montserrat's oral history related by its oldest inhabitants. The lovingly tended botanical gardens in back make for a pleasant stroll. ⊠*Main road, Olveston* ☎*664/491–3086* ⊠*$2 suggested donation* ☉*Mon.–Sat. 10–4.*

Fodor'sChoice **Montserrat Volcano Observatory.** The island's must-see sight occupies
★ capacious, strikingly postmodern quarters with stunning vistas of the
Soufrière Hills volcano—a lunarscape encircled by brilliant green—and
Plymouth in the distance. The MVO staff runs half-hour tours that
explain monitoring techniques on sophisticated computerized equipment in riveting detail and describe the various pyroclastic surge deposits and artifacts on display. One room re-creates the sensation of being
there through 3-D interactive volcano cams, a high-impact film with
IMAX footage, working seismometers (kids can jump up and down to
manufacture vibrations), and other real-time monitoring instruments.
⊠*Flemings* ☎*664/491–5647* ⊕*www.mvo.ms* ⊠*Observatory free,*
tours $4 ⊙ *Weekdays 8:30–4:30. Tours Tues. and Thurs. at 2; call*
ahead for other times.

**NEED A
BREAK?**

D&D Bar and Grocery (⊠*Flemings* ☎*664/491–9730*) is an unprepossess-
ing shack, just downhill off the first right turn from the MVO. Owner Dawn
Davis mastered mixology while working at Nisbet Plantation on Nevis, and
she proudly offers more than 100 libations at her Lilliputian bar (and accepts
challenges). She also bakes sublime bread and serves delectable, cheap
local fare (souse, fishwater [fish soup], baked chicken) on weekends.

15

Plymouth. Montserrat's former capital has been off-limits to general
tourists due to volcanic activity since the May 2006 dome collapse.
Prior to that, the adventuresome could stroll its streets, albeit at their
own risk; check with the police department to see if the situation has
changed again. Once one of the Caribbean's loveliest towns, facing
the vividly hued sea, it now resembles a dust-covered lunarscape, with
elegant Georgian buildings buried beneath several feet of ash, mud, and
rubble (though rain is slowly washing layers away). Entry is officially
possible only with a police escort (lest you fall through a rickety roof),
but this can be arranged with the police headquarters in Brades or
through the Montserrat Tourist Board. A hazard allowance of EC$150
is charged per individual or group. ⊠*Plymouth* ☎*664/491–2230 for*
Montserrat Tourist Board ⊠*Police escort EC$150* ⊙ *Daily during*
daylight hrs with police escort.

Richmond Hill. If you're not feeling overly daring (or would rather not
pay the hazard allowance), this formerly affluent suburb of Plymouth,
which is within the Daytime Entry Zone, is just north of the former
capital and also offers a riveting panorama. You can see the 18th-cen-
tury sugar mill that once housed the Montserrat Museum and poke
around the abandoned (for now) Montserrat Springs Hotel, where a
few items remain just as they were left on the front desk during the
mass exodus that began in 1995). You might encounter a goat or cow
nibbling mushrooms growing through the cracks in the pool and tennis court. The hot springs of the hotel are down the hill by the beach,
which has grown substantially and become a favorite liming spot of
locals and expats. ⊠*Richmond Hill* ⊙ *Daylight hrs.*

Runaway Ghaut. Montserrat's *ghauts* (pronounced guts) are deep ravines
that carry rainwater down from the mountains to the sea. This natural

spring, a short, well-marked walk into the hilly bush outside Woodlands, was the site of bloody colonial skirmishes between the British and French. The legend is more interesting than the trail: "Those that drink its water clear they spellbound are, and the Montserrat they must obey." If you don't want to hike or picnic, a drink from the roadside faucet should ensure that you return to Montserrat in your lifetime. ⊠ *Main road, just south of Woodlands.*

St. George's Hill. The only access to this incredible vantage point over the devastation is across the Belham Valley, through a once-beautiful golf course now totally covered by volcanic mudflow. This, too, was removed from the Daytime Entry Zone due to increased volcanic activity, but could be reinstated at any time. If it's accessible on your visit, be aware that routes aren't signposted on the rough road, which is often impassable after heavy rains, so it's best to hire an experienced guide. You'll drive through Cork Hill and Weekes, villages for the most part spookily intact (there's no way to provide utilities, though some enterprising souls are slowly installing solar power and water cisterns). Close to the summit, the equally eerie, abandoned, stark-white wind generator project and the giant satellite dishes of the Gem and Antilles radio stations resemble abstract art installations awaiting completion by Christo. At the top, Ft. St. George contains sparse ruins, including a few cannons, but the overwhelming sight is the panorama of destruction, an unrelenting swath of gray offset by vivid emerald fields and the turquoise Caribbean. ⊠ *St. George's Hill* ☉ *Daylight hrs.*

MONTSERRAT ESSENTIALS

To research prices, get advice from other travelers, and book travel arrangements, visit www.fodors.com.

▪ TRANSPORTATION

BY AIR

The $18.5 million Gerald's Airport (MNI) opened in July 2005. Winair offers several daily 20-minute flights on 19-seat Twin Otters from Antigua and St. Maarten.

Information Winair (☎664/491–6988, 664/491–6030, 888/255–6889 in U.S. ⊕www.fly-winair.com).

BY CAR & TAXI

Temporary driving licenses are available for $20 at the police headquarters in Brades, which is open 24 hours weekdays. You can rent jeeps and cars starting at $40 per day.

One main road—twisting up, down, and around many steep hills—runs from the north, down each side of the island, with little unnamed side roads streaming inland. Most addresses don't have street names or house numbers, but just ask anyone to direct you. You're best off initially with local guides, who will know where the best views are—and which parts of the island are off-limits due to volcanic activity. Respect the signs and closed gates that indicate the Exclusion Zone boundaries; though the Daytime Entry Zone is now open 24/7, you should avoid it at night.

Driving is on the left; the well-paved main road zigs, zags, climbs, and plummets precipitously, while many equally winding side roads are pocked with potholes. There are no traffic lights but a few zebra pedestrian crossings; beware wandering pigs and goats. Gasoline in Montserrat tends to be quite expensive.

Taxis are unmetered and most rates are fixed; sample fares from the airport include $6 to Tropical Mansion and $22 to the Olveston/Salem area villas.

Car Rentals Jefferson Car Rental (✉Palm Loop ☎664/491–2126). **Montserrat Enterprises** (✉St. Peters ☎664/491–2431). **Neville Bradshaw Agencies** (✉Olveston ☎664/491–5270).

❚ CONTACTS & RESOURCES

BANKS & EXCHANGE SERVICES

Local currency is the Eastern Caribbean dollar (EC$), which is tied to the U.S. dollar and fluctuates only slightly. US$1 is worth approximately EC$2.70; you get a slightly better rate if you exchange money at a bank than at your hotel (the exchange is sometimes rounded down to EC$2.50 in simpler transactions). American dollars are readily accepted, although you usually receive change in EC$.

Most hotels, restaurants, and shops take major credit cards; all accept traveler's checks. ATM machines (dispensing EC$) are available at the Royal Bank of Canada and the Bank of Montserrat.

Prices quoted throughout this chapter are in U.S. dollars unless otherwise indicated.

ELECTRICITY

Montserrat runs on 220 volts, but most lodgings also utilize 110 volts, permitting use of small North American appliances. Outlets may be either two- or three-pronged, so bring an adaptor.

EMERGENCIES

Ambulance & Fire Ambulance (☎411 or 664/491–2802). **Fire** (☎911).

Hospital Glendon Hospital (✉St. John's ☎664/491–2552 or 664/491–7404).

Police Police (☎999).

INTERNET, MAIL & SHIPPING

There was one Internet café in Brades, which now operates from the owner's home very erratically; another is expected to open by 2009. Most lodgings have some form of Internet.

Airmail letters to North America and the United Kingdom cost EC$3; postcards, EC$2.25. Letters to Australia and New Zealand cost EC$3; postcards, EC$2.25. The main post office is in the Government House in Brades. Note that there are no postal codes; when addressing letters to the island, you need only indicate the address and "Montserrat, West Indies."

TAXES & SERVICE CHARGES

The departure/airport security tax is $21, payable in cash only—either U.S. or EC currency. Day-trippers from Antigua spending less than 24 hours on Montserrat pay only an EC$10 "security charge" and no departure tax on Antigua. Hotels collect a 10% government room tax, guesthouses and villas 7%. Hotels and restaurants also usually add a 10% service charge to your bill.

TELEPHONES

Most accommodations have direct-dial phones; others can easily make connections through the switchboard. You can use the Cable & Wireless phone card (available in $5, $10, and $20 denominations in most hotels and post offices) for local and long-distance calls. Phone-card phones work much better than the regular coin-operated phones. Currently, mobile phones can't be rented, though one can be purchased for an average cost of EC$300 from Cable & Wireless.

To place a local call, simply dial the local seven-digit number. To call Montserrat from the United States, dial 1 + 664 + the local seven-digit number.

To call the United States and Canada, dial 1 + the area code + the seven-digit number, or use the phone card.

15

Information **Cable & Wireless** (⊠ Sweeney's ☎ 664/491–1000)

TIPPING

In restaurants it's customary to leave 5% beyond the regular service charge added to your bill if you're pleased with the service. Taxi drivers expect a 10% tip, porters and bellmen about $1 per bag. Maids are rarely tipped, but if you think the service exemplary, figure $2 to $3 per night.

TOUR OPTIONS

Jenny's Tours arranges day trips to Montserrat—including transportation from Antigua, an island tour, breakfast, and lunch—starting at $180 per person.

Joe "Fergus" Phillip, who operates Avalon Tours, often e-mails updates on Montserrat to visitors. Jadine Collins-Glitzenhirn (a wild woman in the best sense, who can take you on impromptu adventures)

runs JIG Promotions. Reuben Furlonge is another hardy helpful local (and a "goat water specialist;" you may be stopped along the way by locals inquiring if he's made a batch). All are friendly, knowledgeable, reliable taxi and tour drivers.

Information **Avalon Tours** (⊠ Manjack ☎ 664/491–3432 or 664/492–1565). **Furlonge Taxi & Tours** (⊠ Geralds ☎ 664/491–4376 or 664/492–2790). **Jenny's Tours** (⊠ Woods Centre, Box W471, St. John's ☎ 268/461–9361). **JIG Promotions** (⊠ Davy Hill ☎ 664/491–2752 or 664/492–2752).

VISITOR INFORMATION

The Montserrat Tourist Board lists accommodations, restaurants, activities, car-rental agencies, and tours available on the island.

Information **Montserrat Tourist Board** (⊠ Olveston ☎ 664/491–2230 ⊕ www.visit montserrat.com

Puerto Rico

Fuerte San Cristóbal, San Juan

WORD OF MOUTH

"Old San Juan is clean and beautiful with blue cobblestone streets and an abundance of restaurants, art galleries, and shops. We bought some art and even some handmade teak dominoes. We will definitely stop back here again in our travels."

—CandV

"Most of the islands have pretty shades of blue and green. But I was in Culebra, and the water there sparkled like I never saw water sparkle before. It was like looking at diamonds!!!!!"

—noonema

WELCOME TO PUERTO RICO

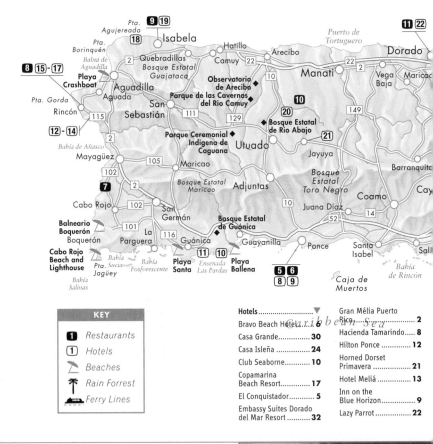

Pta. Agujereada
Pta. Borinquén
Balna de Aguadilla
9 **19**
18
Isabela
Hatillo
Camuy **22**
Arecibo
Puerto de Tortuguero
11 **22**
Dorado
Quebradillas
Bosque Estatal Guajataca
2
22
Manati
Vega Baja
Maric
8 **15** - **17**
Playa Crashboat
Aguadilla
Aguada
Observatorio de Arecibo ◆
10
2
Pta. Gorda
San Sebastián
Parque de las Cavernas del Rio Camuy ◆
10
149
Rincón
115
111
129
20
Bosque Estatal de Rio Abajo ◆
21
12 - **14**
2
Parque Ceremonial Indigena de Caguana ◆
Utuado
Jayuya
Bahía de Añasco
105
Maricao
Bosque Estatal Toro Negro
Barranquit
Mayagüez
102
Bosque Estatal Maricao
Adjuntas
Coamo
Cay
7
2
10
Cabo Rojo
102
San Germán
Juana Díaz
14
Balneario Boquerón
Boquerón
101
La Parguera
116
Bosque Estatal de Guánica ◆
Guánica
Guayanilla
Ponce
52
Santa Isabel
Sal
Cabo Rojo Beach and Lighthouse
Bahía Sucia
Pta. Jagüey
Bahía Fosforescente
11 **10**
Playa Santa
Ensenada Las Pardas
Playa Ballena
5 **6**
8 **9**
Caja de Muertos
Bahía de Rincón
Bahía Salinas

Caribbean Sea

KEY	
1	Restaurants
1	Hotels
⌇	Beaches
🌴	Rain Forrest
⛴	Ferry Lines

Mother Spain is always a presence here—on a sun-dappled cobblestone street, in the shade of a colonial cathedral or fort. Yet multifaceted Puerto Rico pulses with New World energy. The rhythms of the streets are of Afro-Latin salsa and bomba. And the U.S. flag flaps in the salty breezes wherever you go.

SPANISH AMERICAN

Puerto Rico is 110 mi (177 km) long and 35 mi (56 km) wide. With a population of almost 4 million, it's among the biggest Caribbean islands. The first Spanish governor was Juan Ponce de León in 1508; he founded Old San Juan in 1521. The United States won the island in the Spanish-American War in 1917 and made it a commonwealth in 1952.

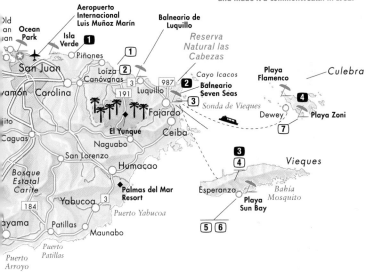

16

PUERTO RICO

TOP 4 REASONS TO VISIT PUERTO RICO

❶ Happening clubs and discos make San Juan one of the Caribbean's nightlife capitals, rivaling even Miami.

❷ Great restaurants run the gamut from elegant places in San Juan to simple spots serving delicious *comida criolla*.

❸ Beaches—both developed and wild—suit the needs of surfers, sunbathers, and families.

❹ Nature abounds, from the underground Río Camuy to El Yunque, the only Caribbean national forest.

PUERTO RICO PLANNER

Island Activities

Because of its size, Puerto Rico supports virtually any activity you might imagine. The west coast is one of the Caribbean's major **surfing** destinations; the north-central region has one of the world's largest underground river systems for **spelunking**; El Yunque is the only Caribbean entry in the national forest system and a mecca for **hikers** and **mountain bikers.**

Large resorts support several excellent **golf courses** and **tennis** facilities; and the surrounding waters are good for **fishing** and **diving.**

Puerto Rico is also lined with several excellent **beaches,** including a few on Vieques that are only now open to the public after many long years. The tiny island of Culebra also has some of Puerto Rico's most beautiful white-sand beaches.

The island is dotted with interesting **historical sights,** and San Juan itself is one of the oldest cities in the western hemisphere. San Juan is also one of the most vibrant cities, with excellent **restaurants,** happening **nightclubs,** and great **shopping.**

Logistics

Getting to Puerto Rico: San Juan (SJU) is the Caribbean hub for American Airlines, but many other nonstop flights make it one of the most convenient Caribbean destinations to reach. The island also has airports in Aguadilla (BQN), Fajardo (FAJ), Ponce (PSE), and Mayagüez (MAZ), and on the islands of Vieques (VQS) and Culebra (CPX). Culebra and Vieques can also be reached by ferry.

Hassle Factor: Low for San Juan, Medium to High for areas outside San Juan

Nonstops: San Juan has nonstop service from Atlanta (Delta), Boston (American, JetBlue), Charlotte (USAirways), Chicago (American, United), Dallas (American), Fort Lauderdale (Spirit), Houston (Continental), Miami (American), New York–Newark (Continental), New York–JFK (American, Delta, JetBlue, United), New York–LaGuardia (Delta), Orlando (Delta, JetBlue, Spirit), Philadelphia (American, United, USAirways), and Washington–Dulles (United). Aguadilla has nonstop service from New York–JFK (JetBlue) and New York–Newark (Continental). Ponce has nonstop service from New York–Newark (Continental, JetBlue).

On the Ground

San Juan taxis have fixed zones; beyond San Juan, you can get fix-rate car or van service to major resort areas east of San Juan (or to Fajardo if you are catching the ferry for Vieques or Culebra). If you are planning to stay outside San Juan.

Renting a Car: It's not really worthwhile to rent a car if you are staying in San Juan; taxis are more cost-effective. However, if you want to explore the island for a day or two, then a car is a necessity. A car is also needed if you are staying somewhere else on the island, with the possible exception of a large resort that you don't plan to leave except on a guided tour (though even some of those charge for parking). A car is almost a necessity if you are staying on Vieques or Culebra and want to explore the island or visit a distant beach.

Where to Stay

If you want easy access to shopping, dining, and nightlife, then you should stay in San Juan, which also has decent—though by no means the island's best—beaches. Most of the other large, deluxe resorts are along the northeast coast. There are also a few resorts along the southern coast. Rincón, in the west, has a concentration of resorts and great surfing. Other small inns and hotels are around the island in the interior, including a few around El Yunque. Look to Vieques and Culebra if you want to find excellent beaches and little development. Many larger resorts in Puerto Rico charge resort fees, which are uncommon elsewhere in the Caribbean.

Big Hotels: San Juan's beaches are lined with large-scale hotels offering all the amenities, including happening restaurants and splashy casinos. The majority are spread out along Condado and Isla Verde beaches.

Upscale Beach Resorts: All over the island—but particularly along the north coast—large tourist resorts offer all the amenities along with a hefty dose of isolation. Just be prepared for expensive food and few nearby off-resort dining opportunities.

Paradores: Small inns (many offering home-style *comida criolla* cooking) are spread out around the island, though they are rarely on the beach.

Hotel & Restaurant Costs

⇨*For information on hotel meal plans, see Accommodations in Caribbean Essentials.*

WHAT IT COSTS IN U.S. DOLLARS

$$$$	$$$	$$	$	¢
Restaurants				
over $30	$20–$30	$12–$20	$8–$12	under $8
Hotels*				
over $350	$250–$350	$150–$250	$80–$150	under $80
Hotels**				
over $450	$350–$450	$250–$350	$125–$250	under $125

*EP, BP, CP **AI, FAP, MAP Restaurant prices are for a main course at dinner and include any taxes or service charges. Hotel prices are per night for a double room in high season, excluding taxes, service charges, and meal plans (except at all-inclusives).

When to Go

San Juan in particular is very expensive—many would say overpriced—during the busy tourist season from mid-December through mid-April; during the off-season, you can get good deals all over the island, with discounts of up to 40% off high-season rates.

Weeklong **patron saint's festivals** happen throughout the year all over the island, so you can almost always find a celebration going on somewhere in Puerto Rico.

Of course, the pre-Lenten **Carnival** is celebrated in Puerto Rico, as it is on so many islands. Ponce's celebration is the most famous, but several towns and regions have parades, music competitions, beauty pageants, and other parties.

Easter week sees spring breakers and Puerto Ricans filling up every beach.

The **Pablo Casals Festival of Classical Music** in early June is a popular event in San Juan itself.

In November the annual **Festival of Puerto Rican Music** takes place in San Juan and other venues.

16

By Mark
Sullivan

SUNRISE AND SUNSET ARE BOTH worth waiting for when you're in Puerto Rico. The pinks and yellows that hang in the early-morning sky are just as compelling as the sinewy reds and purples that blend into the twilight. It's easy to compare them, as Puerto Rico is the smallest of the Greater Antilles. At 110 mi (177 km) long and 35 mi (56 km) wide, you can easily have breakfast in Fajardo, looking eastward over the boats headed to enchanted islands like Vieques and Culebra, then settle down for a lobster dinner in Rincón as the sun is sinking into the inky-blue water. That leaves you plenty of time in between to explore the southern coast, perhaps stopping to see the fanciful firehouse in Ponce or the charming colonial chapel in San Germán.

Known as the Island of Enchantment, Puerto Rico conjures a powerful spell. Here, traffic actually leads you to a "Road to Paradise," whether you're looking for a pleasurable, sunny escape from the confines of urbanity or a rich supply of stimulation to quench your cultural and entertainment thirst. On the island you have the best of both worlds, natural and urban thrills alike; and although city life is frenetic enough to make you forget you're surrounded by azure waters and warm sand, traveling a few miles inland or down the coast can easily make you forget you're surrounded by development.

Puerto Rico was populated primarily by Taíno Indians when Columbus landed in 1493. In 1508 Ponce de León established a settlement and became the first governor; in 1521 he founded what is known as Old San Juan. For centuries, while Africans worked on the coastal sugarcane fields, the French, Dutch, and English tried unsuccessfully to wrest the island from Spain. In 1898, as a result of the Spanish-American War, Spain ceded the island to the United States. In 1917 Puerto Ricans became U.S. citizens, and in 1952 Puerto Rico became a semiautonomous commonwealth.

Since the 1950s, Puerto Rico has developed exponentially, as witnessed in the urban sprawl, burgeoning traffic, and growing population (estimated at nearly 4 million); yet, *en la isla* (on the island) a strong Latin sense of community and family prevails. *Puertorriqueños* are fiercely proud of their unique blend of heritages.

Music is another source of Puerto Rican pride. Like wildflowers, *velloneras* (jukeboxes) pop up almost everywhere, and when one is playing, somebody will be either singing or dancing along—or both. Cars often vibrate with *reggaetón*, a hard, monotonous beat with lyrics that express social malaise. Salsa, a fusion of West African percussion, jazz, and other Latin beats, is the trademark dance. Although it may look difficult to master, it's all achieved by just loosening your hips. You may choose to let your inhibitions go by doing some clubbing *a la vida loca* made famous by pop star Ricky Martin. Nightlife options are on par with any cosmopolitan city—and then some.

By day you can drink in the culture of the Old World; one of the richest visual experiences in Puerto Rico is Old San Juan. Originally built as a fortress by the Spaniards in the early 1500s, the Old City has myriad attractions that include restored 16th-century buildings and

200-year-old houses with balustraded balconies of filigreed wrought iron that overlook narrow cobblestone streets. Spanish traditions are also apparent in the countryside festivals celebrated in honor of small-town patron saints. For quiet relaxation or experiences off the beaten track, visit coffee plantations, colonial towns, or outlying islets where nightlife is virtually nonexistent.

And of course you don't come to a Caribbean island without taking in some of the glorious sunshine and natural wonders. In the coastal areas, the sun mildly toasts your body, and you're immediately healed by soft waves and cool breezes. In the misty mountains, you can wonder at the flickering night flies and the star-studded sky while the *coquís* (tiny local frogs) sing their legendary sweet lullaby. On a moonless night, watch the warm ocean turn into luminescent aqua-blue speckles on your skin. Then there are the island's many acres of golf courses, numerous tennis courts, rain forests, and dozens of beaches that offer every imaginable water sport.

WHERE TO STAY

16

In San Juan, the best beaches are in Isla Verde, though Condado is more centrally located. Old San Juan offers easy access to dining and nightlife. Outside San Juan, particularly on the east coast, you can find self-contained luxury resorts that cover hundreds of acres. Around the island, government-sponsored *paradores* are rural inns, others offer no-frills apartments, and some are large hotels located close to either an attraction or beach.

VILLAS & CONDOS

In the west, southwest, and south—as well as on the islands of Vieques and Culebra—smaller inns, and condominiums for short-term rentals are the norm. Villa rentals are increasingly popular. **Culebra Island Realty** (⊠ *Calle Escudero, Dewey* ☎ *787/742–0052* ⊕ *www.culebraisland realty.com*) has a few dozen properties for rent, ranging from studios to three-bedroom houses. **Island West Properties & Beach Rentals** (⊠ *Rte. 413, Km 1.3, Box 700, Rincón* ☎ *787/823–2323* ⊕ *www.islandwest rentals.com*) can help you rent villas in Rincón by the day, week, or the month For condos or villas on Vieques, contact **Rainbow Realty** (⊠ *Rte. 996, Esperanza, Vieques* ☎ *787/741–4312* ⊕ *www.enchanted-isle. com/rainbow*).

OLD SAN JUAN

$$$$

Fodor'sChoice

★

El Convento. Carmelite nuns once inhabited this 350-year-old convent, but they never had high-tech gadgets like in-room broadband connections or plasma TVs. The accommodations here beautifully combine the old and the new. All guest rooms have hand-hewn wood furniture, shuttered windows, and mahogany-beamed ceilings, but some have a little extra. Room 508 has two views of the bay, while Rooms 216, 217, and 218 have private walled patios. Guests gather for the complimentary wine and hors d'oeuvres that are served before dinner. The second-floor

Picoteo and the courtyard Café del Níspero are good dining choices. **Pros:** Beautiful, historic structure, atmosphere to spare, near plenty of dining options. **Cons:** A bit of a chain-hotel feel, near some noisy bars. ⊠*100 Calle Cristo, Old San Juan* ⊡*Box 1048,* ☎*787/723–9020 or 800/468–2779* ⊕*www.elconvento.com* ⇌*63 rooms, 5 suites* ☖*In-room: safe, DVD, Ethernet, Wi-Fi. In-hotel: 3 restaurants, bars, pool, gym, concierge, laundry service, public Internet, public Wi-Fi, parking (fee), no-smoking rooms* ⊟*AE, D, DC, MC, V* ⸬*EP.*

$$$$ ▦**Sheraton Old San Juan Hotel.** This hotel's triangular shape subtly echoes the cruise ships docked nearby. Rooms facing the water have dazzling views of these behemoths as they sail in and out of the harbor. (Interior rooms, however, face black concrete walls.) The rooms have been plushly renovated and have nice touches like custom-designed beds. On the top floor you'll find a sunny patio with a pool and whirlpool bath. Renovations in 2007 brought two new restaurants—a steak house and a burger joint—and an expansion to what used to be a small casino. **Pros:** Harbor views, near many dining options, good array of room types. **Cons:** Noise from casino overwhelms lobby and restaurants, extra charges for everything from bottled water to Internet access. ⊠*100 Calle Brumbaugh, Old San Juan,* ☎*787/721–5100 or 866/376–7577* ⊕*www.sheratonoldsanjuan.com* ⇌*200 rooms, 40 suites* ☖*In-room: safe, refrigerator, Ethernet. In-hotel: 2 restaurants, room service, bar, pool, gym, laundry service, executive floor, public Internet, parking (fee), no-smoking rooms* ⊟*AE, D, DC, MC, V* ⸬*EP.*

$$$ ▦**Chateau Cervantes.** There's nothing like this hotel anywhere in San
★ Juan—or Puerto Rico, for that matter. The brainchild of local fashion icon Nono Maldonado, this luxury lodging has a look that's completely au courant. Bursts of color from red pillows or gold upholstery on the banquettes add considerable warmth. And the amenities are above and beyond other hotels. Splurge for one of the larger suites and you get a butler who will come to mix cocktails; the two-level presidential suite comes with a car and driver. The rooftop terrace has a bar, a hot tub, and an area for massages. **Pros:** Gorgeous rooms, great international restaurant, quiet side-street location. **Cons:** No views, a bit pricey for what you get. ⊠*329 Calle Recinto Sur, Old San Juan,* ☎*787/724–7722* ⊕*www.cervantespr.com* ⇌*6 rooms, 6 suites* ☖*In-room: safe, Wi-Fi. In-hotel: restaurant, bar, concierge, laundry service* ⊟*AE, D, DC, MC, V* ⸬*EP.*

$$–$$$ ▦**Gallery Inn.** You can shop from your bed at this 200-year-old man-
★ sion, as owner Jan D'Esopo has filled the rooms with her own artworks. And not just the rooms, either; the hallways, the staircases, and even the roof are lined with her fascinating bronze sculptures. Even if you aren't a guest, D'Esopo is pleased to show you around and may even offer you a glass of wine. (Just make sure that Campeche, one of her many birds, doesn't try to sneak a sip.) No two rooms are alike, but all have four-poster beds, hand-woven tapestries, and quirky antiques filling every nook and cranny. There are views of the coastline from several of the rooms, as well as from the spectacular rooftop terrace. **Pros:** One-of-a-kind lodging, ocean views, wonderful concerts. **Cons:** No restaurant, an uphill walk from the rest of Old San Juan. ⊠*204–206*

Calle Norzagaray, Old San Juan, ☎787/722–1808 ⊕*www.thegallery inn.com* ↪*13 rooms, 10 suites* ⌂*In-room: no a/c (some), refrigerator (some), no TV. In-hotel: no elevator, no-smoking rooms* ▭*AE, DC, MC, V* ⴼ◯*CP.*

GREATER SAN JUAN

$$$$　🖽 **La Concha—a Renaissance Resort.** A gem of the architectural movement called Tropical Modernism, La Concha has been treated to a $181 million renovation, and it looks as good as it did when it first opened in 1958. No, it actually looks better. After consulting with original architect Toro Ferrer, the design team has restored many of the original elements, such as the round-roof pool cabanas that give the front facade such a distinctive look. But they also insisted that it appeal to modern tastes, so the glassed-in lobby (centered around a bar serving dozens of kinds of rum) opens out onto a spacious patio with a multilevel swimming pool. The ample rooms have a geometric feel, with all the lines pointing out to sea. They are also marvels of intelligent design—for example, that sleek leather sofa is actually a full-size pullout bed. **Pros:** Amazing architecture, near the city's best shopping, all rooms face the ocean. **Cons:** Ongoing construction at two nearby properties, rooms near the pool area can be noisy. ⊠*1077 Av. Ashford, Condado,* ☎787/721–8500 ⊕*www.laconcharesort.com* ↪*232 rooms, 16 suites* ⌂*In-room: safe, refrigerator, Ethernet, Wi-Fi. In-hotel: 4 restaurants, room service, bars, pool, beachfront, laundry service, public Wi-Fi, no-smoking rooms.* ▭*AE, D, DC, MC, V* ⴼ◯*EP.*

16

$$$$
ↂ
Fodor'sChoice
★
🖽 **Ritz-Carlton San Juan Hotel, Spa & Casino.** The elegance of marble floors and gushing fountains won't undermine the feeling that this is a true beach getaway. The hotel's sandy stretch is lovely, as is the cruciform pool, which is lined by statues of the hotel's signature lion. Works by Latin American artists adorn the lobby lounge and the hallways leading to the well-equipped business center. Rooms have a mix of traditional wooden furnishings and wicker pieces upholstered in soft fabrics. Though most room windows are sealed shut to muffle airport noise, many suites open onto terraces. A full-service spa begs to pamper you with aloe body wraps and *parcha* (passion-fruit juice) massages. Tastefully so, the lavish casino has a separate entrance. In 2007, new balconies on many rooms were unveiled. **Pros:** Top-notch service, excellent restaurant options, pretty pool area. **Cons:** Rather bland facade, very expensive for a San Juan lodging. ⊠*6961 Av. Los Gobernadores, Isla Verde,* ☎787/253–1700 or 800/241–3333 ⊕*www.ritzcarlton. com* ↪*403 rooms, 11 suites* ⌂*In-room: refrigerator, Ethernet. In-hotel: 3 restaurants, room service, bars, tennis courts, pool, gym, spa, concierge, children's programs (ages 4–12), laundry service, executive floor, public Wi-Fi, parking (fee), no-smoking rooms* ▭*AE, D, DC, MC, V* ⴼ◯*EP.*

$$$
Fodor'sChoice
★
🖽 **El San Juan Hotel & Casino.** For decades the don't-miss destination in Isla Verde, this hotel is again on everyone's list after a complete renovation in 2007. First, what hasn't changed: the intricately carved mahogany in the lobby. Now, however, there are three new bars beneath the

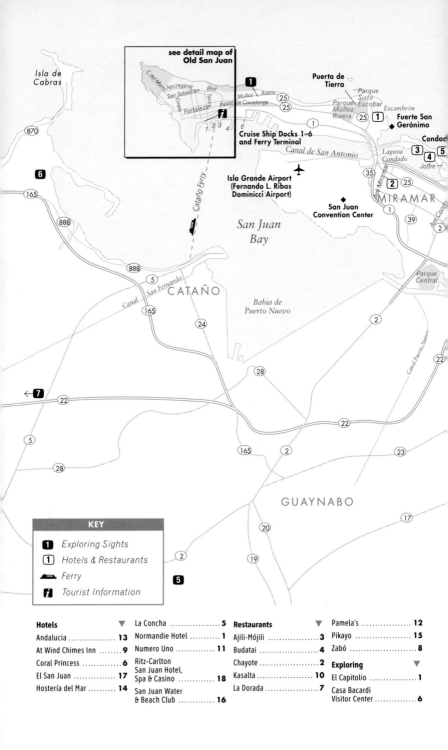

see detail map of
Old San Juan

KEY

1 *Exploring Sights*
1 *Hotels & Restaurants*
Ferry
Tourist Information

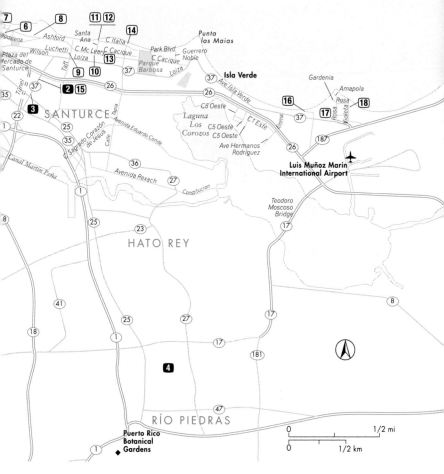

Greater San Juan

ATLANTIC OCEAN

7 6 8 11 12 14

Magdalena Ashford Santa Ana C Italia Punta las Maias
Luchetti C Mc Lean C Cacique Park Blvd Guerrero Noble
Wilson Loiza C Cacique Parque Barbosa Loiza **Isla Verde**
Plaza del Mercado de Santurce Taft 9 10 37 37 Ave Isla Verde Gardenia
35 37 2 15 26 26 Amapola
22 3 **SANTURCE** C5 Oeste C1 Este 16 Rosa 18
1 25 Laguna Los Corozos C5 Oeste 37 Violeta
35 C Sagrado Corazon de Jesus Calle Avenida Eduardo Conde C5 Oeste 17 187
Canal Martin Peña 36 Ave Hermanos Rodriguez 26
1 Avenida Rexach 27 Constitucion **Luis Muñoz Marín International Airport**
25 23 **HATO REY**
41 Teodoro Moscoso Bridge
18 25 27 17
1 17
4 181 8
47
RÍO PIEDRAS
1 **Puerto Rico Botanical Gardens**

0 ____ 1/2 mi
0 ____ 1/2 km

coffered ceiling. In the center is the Blue Bar, down a few steps and set below a massive oval-shape chandelier. To the right is the burnished warmth of Gold Bar, and to the left is the shimmering Silver Bar. Just outside is the completely redone pool area. A trio of poolside cabanas with unbelievable amenities like television and air-conditioning can be reserved, as can any of the four-poster beds hung with gauzy curtains. Rooms are larger than most on the island, and have sleek modern furnishings in white with a few colorful accents. **Pros:** Beautiful pool, superlative dining options in and near hotel, on a great beach. **Cons:** Casino noise in the lobby, self-parking lot is a long walk from the front door of the hotel. ⊠*6063 Av. Isla Verde, Isla Verde,* ☎*787/791–1000* ⊕*www.elsanjuanhotel.com* ⌁*332 rooms, 57 suites* ⌂*In-room: safe, refrigerator, VCR, Ethernet, Wi-Fi. In-hotel: 8 restaurants, room service, bars, tennis courts, pools, gym, beachfront, concierge, children's programs (ages 5–17), laundry service, public Wi-FI, parking (fee), no-smoking rooms* ▤*AE, DC, MC, V* ⏇*EP.*

$$–$$$ ▦**San Juan Water & Beach Club.** There's water everywhere at this bou-
★   tique hotel, from the droplets that decorate the reception desk to the deluge that runs down the glass walls of the elevators. Guest rooms, all of which are decorated in a minimalist style, have an under-the-sea feel because of the soft glow of blue neon. Four rooms are equipped with telescopes for stargazing or people-watching along the beach. No matter which room you choose, you'll have a view of the ocean. The lobby's Liquid lounge is a popular stop along the party trail for hipsters. Wet, the rooftop bar, lets you recline on white leather sofas as you take in the view of the skyline. **Pros:** Fun atmosphere, interesting design, great dining and nightlife options. **Cons:** Lack of closet space in rooms, long walk around block to Condado restaurants. ⊠*2 Calle Tartak, Isla Verde,* ☎*787/728–3666 or 888/265–6699* ⊕*www.water andbeachclubhotel.com* ⌁*84 rooms* ⌂*In-room: safe, VCR, Ethernet. In-hotel: restaurant, room service, bars, pool, gym, beachfront, concierge, laundry service, public Wi-Fi, parking (fee), no-smoking rooms* ▤*AE, D, DC, MC, V* ⏇*EP.*

$–$$ ▦**Coral Princess.** This art deco building—one of the few left in Condado—has personality to spare. The ample guest rooms subtly reflect the hotel's heritage with crisp lines and simple furnishings. The hotel is a block from the neighborhood's main drag, so you don't have to fight the crowds every time you walk out the front door. The beach is five minutes away, but you can always take advantage of the swimming pool on the palm-shaded terrace or the hot tub on the rooftop. **Pros:** Just off the main drag, lots of privacy, pretty garden. **Cons:** Not on the beach, some traffic noise, no restaurant. ⊠*1159 Av. Magdalena, Condado,* ☎*787/977–7700* ⊕*www.coralpr.com* ⌁*25 rooms, 1 apartment* ⌂*In-room: kitchen (some), Ethernet. In-hotel: bar, pool, public Wi-Fi* ▤*AE, D, DC, MC, V* ⏇*CP.*

$–$$ ▦**Hostería del Mar.** This small hotel manages to charm you before you even walk in the door. You'll probably pause, as most people do, to admire the pond filled with iridescent goldfish before continuing into the wood-paneled lobby. The decor might be described as South Seas meets South Beach. The spacious guest rooms continue the tropical theme, aided by colorful fabrics and rattan furnishings. Many rooms have views of the beach, which is only a few feet away. Make sure to enjoy the kitchen's creative cuisine, either in the dining room or at a table on the sand. Most of the staff is courteous and helpful. **Pros:** Lovely building, great on-site dining, good value. **Cons:** A long walk to other restaurants, no pool. ⊠ *1 Calle Tapia, Ocean Park,* ☎*787/727–3302 or 877/727–3302* ⊕*www.hosteriadelmarpr.com* ⤶*8 rooms, 5 suites* ⌂*In-room: kitchen (some). In-hotel: restaurant, bar, beachfront, parking (no fee), no elevator, no-smoking room* ▤*AE, D, DC, MC, V* ¶⊙*EP.*

$–$$ ⛨ **Normandie Hotel.** One of the Caribbean's finest examples of art deco
Fodor's Choice   architecture, this ship-shaped hotel hosted high-society types back in
★   the 1930s. After a stem-to-stern renovation, it's ready to sail again. Egyptian motifs in the grand ballroom and other period details have been meticulously restored. Guest rooms, many of them as big as suites, are decorated in sensuous shades of cream and oatmeal. Business travelers will appreciate the huge desks with ergonomic chairs. Those in search of relaxation need look no further than the sparkling pool or the compact spa with its massage area overlooking the ocean. N Bar, on the second floor, has quickly become a see-and-be-seen place for the city's trendy crowd. As this book went to press, the Normandie was expected to become a W Hotel, but no date had been set for the transition. **Pros:** Gorgeous property, professional staff, chic clientele. **Cons:** No real beach, not walking distance to anything. ⊠ *499 Av. Muñoz Rivera, Puerta de Tierra,* ☎*787/729–2929* ⊕*www.normandiepr.com* ⤶*58 rooms, 117 suites* ⌂*In-room: safe, refrigerator, Ethernet, Wi-Fi. In-hotel: 2 restaurants, bars, pool, gym, spa, beachfront, laundry service, public Internet, public Wi-Fi, parking (fee), no-smoking rooms* ▤*AE, MC, V* ¶⊙*EP.*

$–$$ ⛨ **Numero Uno.** The name refers to the address, but Numero Uno is also
★   how this small hotel rates with its guests. It's not unusual to hear people trading stories about how many times they've returned to this relaxing retreat. Behind a whitewashed wall is a patio where you can catch some rays beside the small pool, enjoy a cocktail at the bar, or dine in the restaurant. (It's so good that it draws locals.) A few steps away, a sandy beach beckons; guests are provided with beach chairs and umbrellas. Instead of the usual tropical colors, the rooms are decorated in shades of cream and gray. The custom-made furnishings, including sleek writing desks, have a lot of flair. **Pros:** Friendly atmosphere, great restaurant, good value. **Cons:** A long walk to other restaurants, small pool. ⊠ *1 Calle Santa Ana, Ocean Park,* ☎*787/726–5010* ⊕*www.numero1guesthouse.com* ⤶*11 rooms, 2 apartments* ⌂*In-room: kitchen (some), refrigerator, Ethernet. In-hotel: restaurant, bar, pool, no elevator, beachfront* ▤*AE, MC, V* ¶⊙*CP.*

$ ⛨ **Andalucia.** In a Spanish-style house, this charming little inn lives up
★   to its name with details like hand-painted tiles and ceramic pots filled with greenery. In the central courtyard there's a kidney-shape hot tub big enough for you and four or five of your closest friends. Bamboo headboards and other nice touches give the rooms a tropical feel. Hosts Estaban Haigler and Emeo Cheung give you the warmest welcome imag-

16

inable, making you feel that their home is yours. When we last visited, they had added three more rooms, a couple of which are great for single travelers. One of the prettiest beaches in the city is a five-minute walk away. **Pros:** Affordable rates, helpful hosts, gorgeous courtyard. **Cons:** Not right on the beach, some rooms are smaller than others. ⊠*2011 Calle McLeary, Ocean Park,* ☎*787/232–5478* ⊕*www.andalucia-puertorico.com* ⇔*11 rooms* ⌂*In-room: kitchen (some), refrigerator, Wi-Fi. In-hotel: no elevator, public Internet, public Wi-Fi* ⌾*EP.*

$ ⌘**At Wind Chimes Inn.** Hidden behind a whitewashed wall covered with bougainvillea, this Spanish-style villa has the feel of an exclusive retreat. So much about the place invites you to relax: the patios shaded by royal palms, the terra-cotta-tiled terraces, and the small pool with a built-in whirlpool spa. And there's the soft, ever-present jingling of wind chimes, reminding you that the beach is just a block away. The spacious guest rooms have a tropical feel. The Boat Bar, open only to guests, serves a light menu from 7 AM to 11 PM. **Pros:** Charming architecture, on the edge of Condado, near shops and restaurants. **Cons:** On a busy street, old-fashioned rooms, distracted staff. ⊠*1750 Av. McLeary, Condado,* ☎*787/727–4153 or 800/946–3244* ⊕*www.atwindchimes-inn.com* ⇔*17 rooms, 5 suites* ⌂*In-room: kitchen (some), Wi-Fi. In-hotel: bar, pool, no elevator, public Wi-Fi, parking (fee), no-smoking rooms* ▤*AE, D, MC, V* ⌾*EP.*

EASTERN PUERTO RICO

$$$$ ⌘**Grand Meliá Puerto Rico.** An enviable stretch of pristine coastline is this massive resort, formerly an all-inclusive resort called Paradisus Puerto Rico. (That experiment didn't go so well.) The open-air lobby, with its elegant floral displays, resembles a Japanese garden, and the swimming pool's columns call to mind ancient Greece. If it sounds like there's an identity crisis here, you're right. It's a mishmash of styles that don't come together in a coherent way. But the hotel does fairly well at being all things to all people. The 500 suites, many with their own hot tubs, are spread among two-story bungalows. **Pros:** Beautiful setting, lovely pool area. **Cons:** Neighborhood is full of noisy construction projects, facade is blank and uninviting, unhelpful staff. ⊠*Rte. 968, Km 5.8, Coco Beach* ☎*787/657–1026 or 800/336–3542* ⊕*www. meliahotels.com* ⇔*500 suites* ⌂*In-room: safe, refrigerator. In-hotel: 6 restaurants, room service, bars, golf courses, tennis courts, pool, gym, spa, beachfront, diving, water sports, concierge, children's programs (ages 4–12), laundry service, public Internet, parking (fee)* ▤*AE, D, MC, V* ⌾*AI.*

$$$$ ⌘**Rio Mar Beach Resort & Spa—a Wyndham Grand Resort.** On more than
★   500 acres, this sprawling resort is geared toward outdoor activities. Many people come to play the championship golf courses or hike in the nearby rain forest. But the biggest draw is the 2-mi-long (3-km-long) stretch of sand just steps from the door. There's a kiosk near the swimming pools that rents sailboats and other equipment; a dive shop organizes excursions to nearby places of interest. Even the extensive programs for children are mostly outdoors. The seven-story hotel,

which wraps around lush gardens, never feels overwhelming. Wyndham took over the property in 2007, and among the improvements was adding their comfy "Be Well" beds. The Mandara Spa transports you to the South Pacific with its hand-carved wood furnishings from Bali. **Pros:** On one of the island's best beaches, great restaurants in and near the hotel, plenty of outdoor activities. **Cons:** Dark and depressing parking lot, long lines at check-in desk. ⊠*6000 Río Mar Bul., Río Grande* ☎*787/888–6000 or 877/636–0636* ⊕*www.wyndhamriomar. com* ☞*528 rooms, 72 suites, 59 villas* ⌂*In-room: safe, VCR, Ethernet. In-hotel: 7 restaurants, bars, golf courses, tennis courts, pools, gym, spa, beachfront, diving, water sports, bicycles, concierge, children's programs (ages 4–12), laundry service, public Internet, public Wi-Fi, airport shuttle, parking (fee), no-smoking rooms* ⊟*AE, D, DC, MC, V* ⽥*EP.*

$$$–$$$$
☼
Fodor'sChoice
★

▦**El Conquistador Resort & Golden Door Spa.** The name means "The Conqueror," and this sprawling complex has claimed the northeastern tip of the island for itself. Perched on a bluff overlooking the ocean, it certainly is one of Puerto Rico's loveliest destination resorts. Arranged in five "villages," The whitewashed buildings have a colonial-era feel. Guest rooms were completely renovated—right down to the floors—in 2007. The ultramodern furnishings are all low to the ground, making sure that nothing obscures the ocean views. The resort's beach is on Palomino Island, just offshore; a shuttle boat gets you there in eight minutes. At the resort there are several different pools, as well as a water park for the kids (and the kids at heart). For grown-ups, a branch of the Japanese-influenced Golden Door Spa is widely considered among the Caribbean's best spas. **Pros:** Some of the island's best rooms, unbeatable views of the nearby islands, good dining options in and near hotel. **Cons:** Must take a boat to the beach, long waits at the funicular taking guests between levels, self-parking lot is a long distance from the front door. ⊠*1000 Av. El Conquistador, Box 70001, Fajardo* ☎*787/863–1000 or 800/468–0389* ⊕*www.elconresort.com* ☞*750 rooms, 17 suites, 155 villas* ⌂*In-room: safe, refrigerator, VCR, Ethernet, Wi-Fi. In-hotel: 17 restaurants, bars, golf course, tennis courts, pools, gym, spa, beachfront, diving, water sports, children's programs (ages 4–12), laundry service, public Wi-Fi, airport shuttle, parking (fee), no-smoking rooms* ⊟*AE, D, DC, MC, V* ⽥*EP.*

16

VIEQUES & CULEBRA

$$–$$$$

▦**Inn on the Blue Horizon.** This inn, consisting of six Mediterranean-style villas, was the tiny island's first taste of luxury. It's still one of the most sought-after accommodations, mostly because of its breathtaking setting on a bluff overlooking the ocean. The entire place is often booked months in advance by weddings and other big groups. Everything is geared toward upping the romance quotient, from the intimate guest rooms to the open-air bar, where the staff will make any cocktail you can name—or create a new one and name it after you. **Pros:** Eye-popping view, elegant accommodations, good dining options. **Cons:** Aloof staff, pricey for what you get. ⊠*Rte. 996, Km 4.2, Esperanza, Vieques*

⌂*Box 1556, Vieques* ☎*787/741–3318* ⊕*www.innthebl...horizon. com* ↻*10 rooms* ⌂*In-room: no phone, no TV. In-hotel: restaurant, bar, pool, beachfront, bicycles, no elevator, no kids under 14* ▤*AE, MC, V* �⓪*BP.*

$$ 🔲**Bravo Beach Hotel.** If this boutique hotel were plopped down into
Fodor'sChoice   the middle of South Beach, no one would raise an eyebrow. What was
★   once a private residence has been expanded to include four different
buildings, all with views of nearby Culebra from their balconies. The
guest rooms have a minimalist flair, brightened by splashes of red and
yellow. High-tech offerings include a Sony Playstation in every room.
One of the pools is the setting for the Palms, a chic lounge; the other
is the backdrop for the not-to-be-missed tapas bar. The hotel is on
a pretty stretch of beach, several blocks north of the ferry dock in
Isabel Segunda. **Pros:** Gorgeous building, beautiful pools, good din-
ing options. **Cons:** In unattractive neighborhood, staff sometimes
seems stretched too thin. ⊠*North Shore Rd., Isabel Segunda, Vieques*
☎*787/741–1128* ⊕*www.bravobeachhotel.com* ↻*9 rooms, 1 villa*
⌂*In-room: no phone, Wi-Fi. In-hotel: restaurant, bar, pools, no kids
under 14* ▤*AE, D, MC, V* ⓪*BP.*

$$ 🔲**Club Seaborne.** The prettiest place to stay in Culebra, this cluster of
plantation-style cottages sits on a hilltop overlooking Fulladoza Bay.
The place feels completely isolated, but it is only a mile or so from the
center of town. Opt for one of the rooms surrounding the pool or one
of the spacious villas. The largest sleeps five, making it a favorite of
families. Specializing in seafood, the terrace restaurant ($$–$$$) is one
of the best on the island. The friendly staff are happy to help you set
up snorkeling and diving trips or arrange transportation to the beach.
Pros: Lovely cottages, well-regarded restaurant, nice view. **Cons:** Staff
can seem overworked, some steps to negotiate. ⊠*Calle Fulladoza, Km
1.5, Culebra* ⌂*Box 357, Culebra* ☎*787/742–3169* ⊕*www.clubsea
bourne.com* ↻*3 rooms, 8 villas, 1 cottage* ⌂*In-room: kitchen (some).
In-hotel: restaurant, bar, pool, no elevator* ▤*AE, MC, V* ⓪*CP.*

$$ 🔲**Hacienda Tamarindo.** The century-old tamarind tree rising through
Fodor'sChoice   the center of the main building gives this place its name. The planta-
★   tion-style house, with its barrel-tile roof and wood-shuttered windows,
is one of the most beautiful on the island. It's easy to find a spot all
to yourself, whether it's on a shady terrace or beside the spectacular
pool. The guest rooms were individually decorated by Linda Vail, who
runs the place along with her husband, Burr. "Caribbean chic" might
be the best way to describe her effortless way of combining well-cho-
sen antiques, elegant wicker furniture, and vintage travel posters. The
nicest room might be Number One, which is in a separate building
and has a private terrace overlooking the ocean. **Pros:** Beautiful views,
nicely designed rooms, best breakfasts on the island. **Cons:** Drive to
beaches, small parking lot. ⊠*Rte. 996, Km 4.5, Esperanza, Vieques*
⌂*Box 1569, Vieques* ☎*787/741–8525* ⊕*www.haciendatamarindo.
com* ↻*16 rooms* ⌂*In-room: no phone, no TV, Wi-Fi. In-hotel: pool,
public Wi-Fi, no elevator, parking (free), no kids under 15* ▤*AE, MC,
V* ⓪*BP.*

SOUTHERN PUERTO RICO

$$-$$$ 🖵 **Copamarina Beach Resort.** Without a doubt the most beautiful resort
Ⓒ   on the southern coast, the Copamarina is set on 16 palm-shaded acres
Fodor'sChoice facing the Caribbean Sea. The fruit trees and other plants are meticu-
★   lously groomed, especially around the pair of swimming pools (one
popular with kids, the other mostly left to the adults). All the guest
rooms are generously proportioned, especially in the older building.
Wood shutters on the windows and other touches lend a tropical feel.
The Asian-influenced design of the small spa blends seamlessly with
the rest of the hotel. Both elegant Alexandra and more-casual, alfresco
Las Palmas Café serve good food. **Pros:** Tropical feel, plenty of activities, great dining options. **Cons:** Sand at the beach has a gummy feel,
noise from the many kids. ⊠ *Rte. 333, Km 6.5, Box 805, Guánica*
☎ *787/821–0505 or 800/468–4553* ⊕ *www.copamarina.com* ➷ *104
rooms, 2 villas* ⚇ *In-room: safe, refrigerator, Wi-Fi. In-hotel: 2 restaurants, room service, bars, tennis courts, pools, gym, spa, beachfront,
diving, water sports, laundry facilities* ⊟ *AE, MC, V* ¶◯*EP.*

$$-$$$ 🖵 **Hilton Ponce Golf & Casino Resort.** The south coast's biggest resort sits
on a black-sand beach about 6 km (4 mi) south of Ponce. Everything
on this 80-acre property is massive, beginning with the open-air lobby.
Constructed of reinforced concrete, like the rest of the hotel, it requires
huge signs to point you in the right direction. All its bright, spacious
rooms are decorated in a lush, tropical motif with balconies overlooking the sea. A large pool is surrounded by palm trees and has a
spectacular view of the Caribbean. **Pros:** Good golf, large casino. **Cons:**
Not on beach, isolated location, bland rooms. ⊠ *1150 Av. Caribe, La
Guancha, Ponce* ⚇ *Box 7419, Ponce* ☎ *787/259–7676 or 800/445–
8667* ⊕ *www.hiltoncaribbean.com* ➷ *253 rooms* ⚇ *In-room: safe,
refrigerator, Ethernet. In-hotel: 4 restaurants, room service, bars, golf
courses, tennis courts, pool, gym, spa, beachfront, bicycles, children's
programs (ages 8–12), parking (fee)* ⊟ *AE, D, DC, MC, V* ¶◯*EP.*

$-$$ 🖵 **Mary Lee's by the Sea.** This meandering cluster of apartments sits on
Fodor'sChoice quiet grounds full of brightly colored flowers. It's home to Mary Lee
★   Alvarez, and she'll make you feel like it's yours as well. Most units have
ocean views; in the others you'll catch a glimpse of the mangroves by
the shore as well as of the cactus growing in the nearby Bosque Estatal
de Guánica. Each of the one-, two-, and three-bedroom units is decorated in bright colors. Each is different, but most have terraces hung
with hammocks and outfitted with barbecue grills. You can rent kayaks to drift along the coast or hop a boat bound for Gilligan's Island.
Pros: Truly feels like a home away from home, warm and friendly
owner, near pristine beaches and forests. **Cons:** Weekly maid service
unless more is requested, no nightlife options. ⊠ *Rte. 333, Km 6.7,
Guánica* ⚇ *Box 394, Guánica* ☎ *787/821–3600* ⊕ *www.maryleesby
thesea.com* ➷ *10 apartments* ⚇ *In-room: no phone, kitchen (some),
no TV. In-hotel: laundry facilities, laundry service, some pets allowed*
⊟ *MC, V* ¶◯*EP.*

$ 🖵 **Hotel Meliá.** In the heart of the city, this family-owned hotel has long
been a local landmark. Its neoclassical facade, with flags from a dozen
countries waving in the breeze, will remind you of the small lodgings

16

in Spain. The lobby, with wood-beamed ceilings and blue-and-beige tile floors, is well worn but extremely charming. The best rooms have French doors leading out to small balconies; the six suites have terrific views of the main square. Breakfast is served on the rooftop terrace, which overlooks the mountains. The restaurant, Mark's at the Meliá, is one of the best on the island. **Pros:** Great location on the main square, walking distance to downtown sites, good dining options in and near hotel. **Cons:** Rooms have a faded feel, front rooms are a bit noisy. ✉ *75 Calle Cristina, Ponce Centro, Ponce* 📫 *Box 1431, Ponce* ☎ *787/842–0260 or 800/448–8355* 🌐 *www.hotelmeliapr.com* *72 rooms, 6 suites* *In-room: Wi-Fi. In-hotel: restaurant, bar, pool, public Internet, parking (fee)* 💳 *AE, MC, V* *CP.*

WESTERN & CENTRAL PUERTO RICO

$$$$ Fodor'sChoice ★ **Horned Dorset Primavera.** This is, without a doubt, the most luxurious hotel in Puerto Rico. The 40 whitewashed villas scattered throughout the tropical gardens are designed so you have complete privacy whether you are relaxing in your private plunge pool or admiring the sunset from one of your balconies. The furnishings in each of the two-story villa suites are impeccable, from the hand-carved mahogany table in the downstairs dining room to the four-poster beds in the upstairs bedroom. The marble bathroom has a footed porcelain tub that's big enough for two. (There's a second bath downstairs that's perfect for showering off after a walk on the beach.) Breakfast is served in your room, and lunch is available on a terrace overlooking the ocean. **Pros:** Unabashed luxury, unmatched meals, lovely setting. **Cons:** On a very slender beach, staff is sometimes haughty. ✉ *Rte. 429, Km 3, Box 1132, Rincón* ☎ *787/823–4030 or 800/633–1857* 🌐 *www.horneddorset.com* *22 villas* *In-room: safe, kitchen, no TV. In-hotel: restaurant, bar, pools, gym, beachfront, no kids under 12* 💳 *AE, MC, V* *MAP.*

$$–$$$ **Embassy Suites Dorado del Mar Beach & Golf Resort.** Kids love the free-form pool that shimmers in the courtyard of this beachfront resort. All the suites have separate bedrooms and living rooms but are otherwise uninteresting. Golfers can take in the mountains and the sea at the same time while playing the course designed by the legendary Chi Chi Rodríguez. The Paradise Café serves Caribbean favorites such as crusted sea bass with mango butter. **Pros:** On a gorgeous beach, family-friendly environment. **Cons:** Chain-hotel feel, noisy common areas, parking lot is crowded and confusingly signed. ✉ *201 Dorado del Mar Bul., Dorado* ☎ *787/796–6125* 🌐 *www.embassysuitesdorado.com* *174 suites, 35 condos* *In-room: kitchen, Wi-Fi. In-hotel: 2 restaurants, room service, bar, golf course, tennis courts, pool, gym, laundry facilities, laundry service, no elevator, parking (fee)* 💳 *AE, D, DC, MC, V* *BP.*

$$–$$$ **Rincón Beach Resort.** Although it's a bit off the beaten path, that's part of the allure of this oceanfront hotel. The South Seas–style decor begins in the high-ceilinged lobby, where hand-carved chaises invite you to enjoy the view through the almond trees. The rooms continue the theme with rich fabrics and dark-wood furnishings. A variety of

activities are available, including whale- and turtle-watching in season. At the end of the infinity pool, a boardwalk leads down to the sand. The resort is tucked away in Añasco, about halfway between Rincón to the north and Mayagüez to the south. **Pros:** Beautiful setting, gorgeous pool area, laid-back vibe. **Cons:** Far from dining options, lacks a Puerto Rican flavor. ⊠*Rte. 115, Km 5.8, Añasco* ☎*787/589–9000* ⊕*www.rinconbeach.com* ⤳*112 rooms* ☐*In-room: safe, kitchen (some), refrigerator, dial-up. In-hotel: restaurant, room service, bars, pool, gym, beachfront, diving, water sports, laundry service, parking (no fee)* ☐*AE, D, DC, MC, V* ⵙ*EP.*

$$–$$$ ☷**Villa Montaña.** This secluded cluster of villas, situated on a deserted stretch of beach between Isabela and Aguadilla, feels like a little town. You can pull your car into your own garage, then head upstairs to your airy hotel room or studio-, one-, two-, or three-bedroom villa suites with hand-carved mahogany furniture and canopy beds. Studios have kitchenettes, while the larger villas have full-size kitchens and laundry rooms. Hotel rooms have a verandah or patio and private bath but no kitchenette (a refrigerator may be requested). Eclipse, the open-air bar and restaurant, serves Caribbean-Asian fusion cuisine. **Pros:** An away-from-it-all feel, on a secluded beach, great food. **Cons:** A bit pricey, far from other dining options. ⊠*Rte. 4466, Km 1.9, Box 530, Isabela* ☎*787/872–9554 or 888/780–9195* ⊕*www.villamontana.com* ⤳*38 rooms, 41 villas* ☐*In-room: kitchen (some), DVD. In-hotel: restaurant, tennis courts, pools, gym, laundry facilities* ☐*AE, D, MC, V* ⵙ*EP.*

$–$$ ☷**Casa Isleña.** With its barrel-tiled roofs, wall-enclosed gardens, and ★ open-air dining room, Casa Isleña might remind well-traveled souls of a villa on the coast of Mexico. The secret of its charm is that this little inn retains a simplicity without compromising the romantic flavor of its setting. Several of the terra-cotta-floored rooms have balconies overlooking the pool and the palm-shaded stretch of beach. Others have terraces that face the courtyard. There's also a hot tub and an indoor patio with a soothing, burbling fountain. If it's booked solid—and this happens frequently during high season—there's a second building a few minutes away. **Pros:** Secluded setting, beautiful beach, eye-catching architecture. **Cons:** A bit hard to find, books up quickly. ⊠*Rte. 413, Km 4.8, Barrio Puntas, Rincón* ☎*787/823–1525 or 888/289–7750* ⊕*www.casa-islena.com* ⤳*9 rooms* ☐*In-room: refrigerator (some). In-hotel: restaurant, bar, pool, beachfront, water sports, parking (no fee)* ☐*AE, MC, V* ⵙ*EP.*

$–$$ ☷**Lazy Parrot.** Painted in eye-popping tropical hues, this mountainside ★ hotel doesn't take itself too seriously. Colorful murals of the eponymous bird brighten the open and airy lobby. The accommodations are a bit more subdued, though they continue the tropical theme. Several have colorful fish swimming across the walls, and the family-themed Dolphin Room has—what else?—a stuffed dolphin. Each has a balcony, but if you want to enjoy the view, ask for an upstairs room. Smilin' Joe's restaurant serves red snapper and other excellent seafood dishes. You can sample a parrot-themed concoction at the bar, or browse through the "parrotphernalia" at the small gift shop. An

16

annex with a dozen brand-new poolside rooms opened at end of 2007. **Pros:** Whimsical design, lush setting, friendly staff. **Cons:** Not on the beach, stairs to climb. ⊠*Rte. 413, Km 4.1, Rincón* ☎*787823–5654 or 800/294–1752* ⊕*www.lazyparrot.com* ⚟*23 rooms* ⚐*In-room: refrigerator, Wi-Fi. In-hotel: 2 restaurants, bars, pool, public W-Fi, no elevator* ⊟*AE, D, MC, V* ⎈|*CP.*

$–$$ ⊞**Villas del Mar Hau.** One-, two-, and three-bedroom cottages—painted
★ in cheery pastels and trimmed with gingerbread—are the heart of this beachfront resort. The accommodations aren't luxurious, but if you're looking for an unpretentious atmosphere, you'll have a hard time doing better. If you are planning on cooking, you should consider one of the studios, all of which have full kitchens. Otherwise, the open-air Olas y Arena is known for its excellent fish and shellfish; the paella is especially good. The hotel also has a stable of horses reserved for guests. **Pros:** Laid-back vibe, calm beach, good restaurant. **Cons:** Very basic rooms, a little too kitschy for some. ⊠*Rte. 466, Km 8.9, Box 510, Isabela* ☎*787/872–2045 or 787/872–2627* ⊕*www.paradorvillasdel marhau.com* ⚟*40 cottages* ⚐*In-room: kitchen (some). In-hotel: restaurant, tennis court, pool, laundry facilities* ⊟*AE, MC, V* ⎈|*EP.*

$ ⊞**Casa Grande Mountain Retreat.** This isn't sleeping in a tree house, but
Fodor's Choice it's close. The guest rooms on this 107-acre ranch are in five wooden
★ buildings that sit on platforms high above the varied vegetation. When you lie in the hammock on your private porch, all you can see is mountains in every direction. The furnishings couldn't be simpler—little more than a bed and a dresser—but that's part of the rustic charm. Leave the windows open at night to hear the chorus of tiny tree frogs sing cantatas. **Pros:** Unspoiled setting, great food. **Cons:** Long drive to other dining options, tin roofs are noisy in the rain. ⊠*Rte. 612, Km 0.3, Box 1499, Utuado* ☎*787/894–3939 or 800/343–2272* ⊕*www. hotelcasagrande.com* ⚟*20 rooms* ⚐*In-room: no a/c, no phone, no TV. In-hotel: restaurant, pool, no-smoking rooms, no elevator* ⊟*AE, MC, V* ⎈|*EP.*

$ ⊞**Lemontree Oceanfront Cottages.** Sitting right on the beach, this pair of lemon-yellow buildings hold six apartments of various sizes. Choose from one three-bedroom unit, one two-bedroom unit, two one-bedroom units, or two studios. No matter which you pick, each of the sleek units has a full kitchen, dining area, and private balcony with views of the coastline. Ted and Jane Davis, who bought the place in 2005, have added amenities not so common in this price range, such as plasma televisions, DVD players, and free Wi-Fi. **Pros:** Far from the crowds, friendly on-site owners. Cons: Beach is very narrow, need to drive to shops and restaurants. ⊠*Rte. 429, Km 4.1, Box 200, Rincón* ☎*787/823–6452* ⊕*www.lemontreepr.com* ⚟*6 apartments* ⚐*In-room: kitchen, DVD, Wi-Fi. In-hotel: beachfront, diving, public Wi-Fi, no elevator* ⊟*MC, V* ⎈|*EP.*

¢–$ ⊞**Rincón Surf & Board.** All the rooms here have surfboard racks, which should give you a clue as to who is drawn to this out-of-the-way guesthouse. Two hostel-type rooms with bunk beds—remains of the original lodging concept—are available at $20 per person. One- to three-bed private rooms are ample size and have a clean and fresh feel; some are like small apartments. **Pros:** Great for outdoorsy types, congenial crowd. Cons: Younger crowd, a bit hard to find. ⊠ *Off Rte. 413, Barrio Puntas, Rincón* ☎ *787/823–0610* ⊕ *www.surfandboard.com* ⤳ *13 rooms, 2 hostel rooms* ⌂ *In-room: refrigerator (some). In-hotel: restaurant, pool, beachfront, water sports, parking (no fee)* ⊟ *AE, MC, V* ❑ *EP.*

¢   **Parador Hacienda Gripiñas.** Built on the grounds of a coffee plan-
Fodor'sChoice tation, this 19th-century inn is surrounded on all sides by mountain
★ peaks. Several of the clapboard-walled rooms in the red-roof manor house have private balconies overlooking lush gardens and the spring-fed pool; the nicest are numbers 4 and 5. There are plenty of small parlors where you can relax with a drink from the bar. Breakfast and dinner are included in the room rates. The dining area, which meanders through three different rooms, serves comida criollo fare such as chicken with rice and beans. **Pros:** Set in the coffee fields, interesting old building, good meals. Cons: Isolated location. ⊠ *Rte. 152, Km 1.7, Box 387, Jayuya* ☎ *787/828–1717* ⊕ *www.haciendagripinas.com* ⤳ *19 rooms* ⌂ *In-hotel: restaurant, bar, pools, no elevator* ⊟ *AE, MC, V* ❑ *MAP.*

16

WHERE TO EAT

Your palate will be pleasantly amused by the range of dining choices available in Puerto Rico. In San Juan you can find restaurants serving everything from Italian to Thai, as well as superb local eateries serving comida criolla (traditional homestyle Puerto Rican food). No matter your price range or taste, San Juan is a great place to eat.

Puerto Rican cooking uses a lot of local vegetables: plantains are cooked a hundred different ways—as *tostones* (fried green), *amarillos* (baked ripe), in *mofongo* (mashed, fried plantains), and as chips. Rice and beans with tostones or amarillos are accompaniments to almost every dish. Locals cook white rice with *habichuelas* (red beans), *achiote* (annatto seeds), or saffron; brown rice with *gandules* (pigeon peas); and *morro* (black rice) with *frijoles negros* (black beans). Yams and other root vegetables, such as yucca and *yautía* (yams), are served baked, fried, stuffed, boiled, and mashed. *Sofrito*—a garlic, onion, sweet pepper, coriander, oregano, and tomato puree—is used as a base for practically everything.

Beef, chicken, pork, and seafood are rubbed with *adobo*, a garlic-oregano marinade, before cooking. *Arroz con pollo* (chicken with rice), *sancocho* (beef or chicken and tuber soup), *asopao* (a soupy rice gumbo with chicken or seafood), and *encebollado* (steak smothered in onions) are all typical plates. Also look for fritters served along highways and beaches. You may find *empanadillas* (stuffed fried turnovers), *sorullitos* (cheese-stuffed corn sticks), *alcapurrias* (stuffed green-banana croquettes), and *bacalaítos* (codfish fritters). Caribbean lobster, available mainly at coastal restaurants, is sweeter and easier to eat than Maine lobster, and there's always plentiful fresh dolphinfish and red snapper.

Conch is prepared in a chilled ceviche salad or stuffed with tomato sauce inside fritters.

Puerto Rican coffee is excellent black or *con leche* (with hot milk). Coffee isn't an on-the-go thing here. In cafés like Kasalta, in the Ocean Park neighborhood of San Juan, people linger over it, chatting with friends as they savor every drop. The origin of the piña colada is attributed to numerous places, from the Caribe Hilton to a Fortaleza Street bar. Puerto Rican rums range from light mixers to dark, aged liqueurs. Look for Bacardí, Don Q, Ron Rico, Palo Viejo, and Barrilito.

WHAT TO WEAR

Dress codes vary greatly, though a restaurant's price category is a good indicator of its formality. For less-expensive places, anything but beachwear is fine. Ritzier eateries will expect collared shirts for men (jacket and tie requirements are rare) and chic attire for women. When in doubt, do as the Puerto Ricans often do and dress up.

OLD SAN JUAN

ASIAN
$$–$$$

✕ **Dragonfly.** It's not hard to find this little restaurant—it's the one with crowds milling about on the sidewalk. If you can stand the wait—as you undoubtedly will, since reservations aren't accepted—then you'll get to sample chef Roberto Trevino's Latin-Asian cuisine. (For the best chance of avoiding a frustrating wait, come when it opens at 6 PM.) The *platos* (plates) are meant to be shared, so order several for your tables. Favorites include pork-and-plantain dumplings with an orange dipping sauce, smoked-salmon pizza with wasabi salsa, and lamb spareribs with a tamarind glaze. The dining room, all done up in Chinese red, resembles an opium den. ⊠*364 Calle Fortaleza, Old San Juan,* ☎*787/977–3886* ⌂*Reservations not accepted* ▤*AE, MC, V* ⊘*No lunch.*

$–$$

✕ **Tantra.** This little gem sits square in the middle of Old San Juan's restaurant row, rather ironically called SoFo (South Fortaleza Street). The menu, which combines Indian and Caribbean flavors, has traditional dishes such as tandoori chicken and inventive surprises like beef tenderloin in a casava puree. The jewel-tone interior invites you to linger, and many patrons do so for an after-dinner puff on an Asian water pipe. ⊠*356 Calle La Fortaleza, Old San Juan,* ☎*787/977–8141* ▤*AE, MC, V.*

CARIBBEAN
$$$–$$$$

✕ **Parrot Club.** Loud and lively, this place is intent on making sure everyone is having a good time. You're likely to strike up a conversation with the bartender as you enjoy a passion-fruit cocktail or with the couple at the next table in the covered courtyard. Something about the atmosphere—ear-splitting salsa music and murals of swaying palm trees—makes connecting easy. The menu has contemporary variations of Caribbean classics. You might start with mouthwatering crab cakes or tamarind-barbecued ribs, followed by blackened tuna in a dark rum sauce or seared sea bass with lobster, leek, and scallop confit. ⊠*363 Calle Fortaleza, Old San Juan,* ☎*787/725–7370* ⌂*Reservations not accepted* ▤*AE, DC, MC, V.*

$$–$$$ ✕**La Ostra Cosa.** This restaurant's succulent prawns, grilled and served
★ with garlic butter, are supposed to be aphrodisiacs. Well, everything on
the menu is rated for its love-inducing qualities. (Look out for those
labeled "Ay, ay, ay!") There are some seats indoors, but opt for a seat
in the walled courtyard. With brilliant purple bougainvillea tumbling
down and moonlight streaming through the trees, it's one of the city's
prettiest alfresco dining spots. The gregarious owner, Alberto Nazario,
genuinely enjoys seeing his guests satisfied. He'll sometimes take out
a guitar and sing old folk songs. Don't be surprised if the locals sing
along. ⊠*154 Calle Cristo, Old San Juan,* ☎*787/722–2672* ▤*AE,
MC, V.*

$–$$ ✕**La Fonda del Jíbarito.** Sanjuaneros have favored this casual, family-
run restaurant for years. The conch ceviche and chicken fricassee are
among the specialties on the menu of comida criollo dishes. The back
porch is filled with plants, and the dining room is filled with fanciful depictions of life on the street outside. The ever-present owner,
Pedro J. Ruiz, is filled with the desire to ensure that everyone is happy.
⊠*280 Calle Sol, Old San Juan,* ☎*787/725–8375* ◻*Reservations not
accepted* ▤*AE, MC, V.*

ECLECTIC ✕**Panza.** Tucked discreetly behind gauzy curtains, this restaurant
$$$–$$$$ doesn't have to shout to be heard—chef Roberto Pagan's creative cook-
ing speaks loud and clear. Although it's rather too quaintly divided into
sections called Preface, Essays, and Contents, the menu is a wonderful
mix of different-size dishes, so you can have your own or share a few
with friends. Our favorites include the bacon-wrapped dates with blue
cheese aioli and the tiny tacos stuffed with slow-cooked duck. The half-
moon banquettes in the front window is the perfect place to try any of
the 550 wines from the extensive cellars. ⊠*Chateau Cervantes, 329
Calle Recinto Sur, Old San Juan,* ☎*787/724–7722* ◻*Reservations
essential* ▤*AE, D, DC, MC, V* ☾*Closed Sun.*

$$–$$$ ✕**Amadeus.** Facing Plaza San José, this bright and airy restaurant often
throws open the doors and lets its tables spill into the square. If you
want a little more privacy, there's also an interior courtyard and an
intimate dining room with whitewashed walls, linen tablecloths, and
lazily turning ceiling fans. Expect nouvelle Caribbean appetizers such
as dumplings with guava-rum sauce or plantain mousse with shrimp,
and entrées such as ravioli with a goat-cheese and pork with mango
and sugarcane. ⊠*106 Calle San Sebastián, Old San Juan,* ☎*787/722–
8635* ▤*AE, MC, V* ☾*No lunch Mon.*

$$–$$$ ✕**Barú.** A well-traveled menu has earned Barú a solid reputation among
sanjuaneros, so it's often crowded. The dishes, all served in medium-size
portions so you can order several and share, range from Middle Eastern
to Asian to Caribbean. Favorites include oysters in a soy-citrus sauce,
risotto with green asparagus, and carpaccio made from beef, tuna, or
salmon. More-substantial fare includes filet mignon with horseradish
mashed potatoes and pork ribs with a ginger-tamarind glaze. The din-
ing room, in a beautifully renovated colonial house, is dark and mys-
terious. ⊠*150 Calle San Sebastián, Old San Juan,* ☎*787/977–7107*
▤*AE, MC, V* ☾*Closed Mon. No lunch.*

16

ITALIAN ✕**Sofia.** Ignore the tongue-in-cheek recordings of "That's Amore."
$$–$$$ Everything else in this red-wall trattoria is the real deal, from the gleaming vegetables on the antipasto table to the interesting vintages on the small but well-chosen wine list. Start with the squid stuffed with sweet sausage, then move onto the linguine with clams and pancetta or the cannelloni filled with roasted duck and topped with marscapone cheese. The plates of pasta are huge, so you might want to consider a half-order (which is more the size of a three-quarter order). Save room for—what else?—a tasty tiramisu. ✉ *355 Calle San Francisco, Old San Juan,* ☎ *787/721–0396* ▭ *AE, MC, V.*

SEAFOOD ✕**Aguaviva.** The name means "jellyfish," which explains why this ultra-
$$$–$$$$ cool, ultramodern place has lighting fixtures shaped like that sea crea-
★ ture. Elegantly groomed oysters and clams float on cracked ice along the raw bar. The extensive menu is alive with inventive ceviches, some with tomato or roasted red peppers and olives, and fresh takes on classics like paella. For something more filling, try dorado served with a shrimp salsa, or tuna accompanied by seafood enchiladas. You could also empty out your wallet for one of the *torres del mar,* or towers of the sea. This gravity-defying dish has comes hot or cold and includes oysters, mussels, shrimp—you name it. Oh, and don't pass up the lobster mashed potatoes. Those alone are worth the trip—and the wait. ✉ *364 Calle La Fortaleza, Old San Juan,* ☎ *787/722–0665* ⬤ *Reservations not accepted* ▭ *AE, D, MC, V.*

SPANISH ✕**El Picoteo.** You could make a meal of the small dishes that dominate
$$$ the menu at this tapas restaurant. You won't go wrong ordering the sweet sausage in brandy or the turnovers stuffed with lobsters and passing them around the table. If you're not into sharing, there are five different kinds of paella that arrive on huge plates. There's a long, lively bar inside; one dining area overlooks a pleasant courtyard, whereas the other takes in the action along Calle Cristo. ✉ *El Convento Hotel, 100 Calle Cristo, Old San Juan,* ☎ *787/723–9621* ▭ *AE, D, DC, MC, V.*

$$–$$$ ✕**El Toro Salao.** The name means "The Salty Bull," and there is something about this restaurant that makes the name seem entirely appropriate. (And we're not just talking about the bullfighting posters that decorate one of the two-story-high walls.) This tapas place was opened by Emilio Figueroa, who helped turn the southern end of Calle Fortaleza into the city's top dining destination. El Toro Salao is not on South Fortaleza, but its brash attitude makes it clearly part of the SoFo bunch. There are plenty of small dishes to share, as well as heartier fare like blackened tuna in sweet paprika and grilled octopus with a sundried tomato vinaigrette. The dining room, where a bar illuminated in red gives it a lusty look, is pleasant enough, but the tables that spill out onto an adjacent cobblestone square are even better. ✉ *367 Calle Tetuán, Old San Juan,* ☎ *787/722–3330* ▭ *AE, MC, V* ☺ *Closed Sun. No lunch.*

GREATER SAN JUAN

ASIAN
$$–$$$$

✕**Budatai.** A trio of lighting fixtures—resembling Chinese lanterns designed by Salvador Dalí—let you know that this is not the kind of place that serves moo goo gai pan. This Pan-Asian eatery has the same clean lines and airy spaces as the string of designer stores that are its downstairs neighbors. And judging from the bags they are carrying, many of the hip young customers are fortifying themselves after an exhausting day in Chanel, Gucci, and Ferragamo. This is designer food, and it fits beautifully. Start with the pork dumplings, made with shaved truffles and topped with flying fish roe that adds just the right amount of saltiness. The entrées include soy-glazed salmon with coconut hash and veal steak with lobster mashed potatoes. ✉ *1056 Av. Ashford, Condado,* ☎ *787/725–6919* ✍ *Reservations essential* ▭ *AE, MC, V.*

CAFÉS
$$–$$$
★

✕**Kasalta.** Those who think coffee can never be too strong should make a beeline to Kasalta, which has an amazing inky black brew that will knock your socks off. Make your selection from the display cases full of luscious pastries and other tempting treats. Walk up to the counter and order a sandwich, such as the savory Cubano, or such items as the meltingly tender octopus salad. For dinner there are fish dishes and other more-substantial fare. ✉ *1966 Calle McLeary, Ocean Park,* ☎ *787/727–7340* ▭ *AE, MC, V.*

CARIBBEAN
$$$–$$$$
★

✕**Pamela's.** If you've always dreamed about a table for two on the beach, just steps away from where the waves are crashing on the shore, then head straight for this restaurant in Ocean Park. A dozen or so umbrella-covered tables are set up just outside the white walls of the Numero Uno Guesthouse, the perfect place to take advantage of the cool breezes. (You can also choose a table in the glassed-in solarium if you need the air-conditioning.) The contemporary menu is as memorable as the setting; look for spicy shrimp sautéed with ginger and jalapenõs, or dorado cooked in a banana leaf. ✉ *Numero Uno Guesthouse, 1 Calle Santa Ana, Ocean Park,* ☎ *787/726–5010* ▭ *AE, D, MC, V.*

$$–$$$$
★

✕**Ajili-Mójili.** Set in a plantation-style house, this restaurant sits on the edge of Condado Bay. Some of the elegant dining rooms have a lovely view of the shimmering water and the city skyline. Traditional Puerto Rican food is prepared with a modern flourish. Sample the fried cheese and *bolitas de yautía y queso* (cheese and yam dumplings), then move on to the *gallinita rellena* (stuffed Cornish game hen). The plantain-crusted shrimp in a white-wine herb sauce is delicious, as is the paella overflowing with shrimp, octopus, mussels, chicken, and spicy sausage. Prices, however, are pretty high despite the quality. ✉ *1006 Av. Ashford, Condado,* ☎ *787/725–9195* ▭ *AE, DC, MC, V.*

ECLECTIC
$$$$

✕**Pikayo.** Chef Wilo Benet is clearly a superstar here, and a plasma television lets diners watch everything that's going on in his kitchen. The Puerto Rico native artfully fuses Caribbean cuisine with influences from around the world. Veal is served in a swirl of sweet-pea coucou, for example, and beef medallions are covered with crumbled blue cheese and a red-wine reduction. The regularly changing menu is a feast for the eye as well as the palate, and might include perfectly shaped

16

tostones stuffed with oven-dried tomatoes, or mofongo topped with saffron shrimp. A changing selection of artworks wraps around the minimalist dining room—the restaurant is, after all, inside a museum. It's in Santurce, just south of Condado. ⊠ *Museo de Arte de Puerto Rico, 299 Av. José de Diego, Santurce,* ☎ *787/721–6194* ⊟ *AE, MC, V* ⊗ *Closed Mon. No lunch weekends. No dinner.*

$$$–$$$$ ✕ **Chayote.** Slightly off the beaten path, this chic eatery is definitely an
★   "in" spot. The chef gives haute international dishes tropical panache. Starters include chayote stuffed with prosciutto and corn tamales with shrimp in a coconut sauce. About half the entrées are seafood dishes, including pan-seared tuna with a ginger sauce and red snapper served over spinach. The ginger flan is a must for dessert. It's in Miramar, a few blocks from Condado. ⊠ *Hotel Olimpo Court, 603 Av. Miramar, Miramar,* ☎ *787/722–9385* ⊟ *AE, MC, V* ⊗ *Closed Sun. and Mon. No lunch Sat.*

$$–$$$ ✕ **Zabó.** In a restored plantation house surrounded by a quiet garden, this restaurant seems as if it's out on the island somewhere. If you'd rather be reminded that you're in Condado, there are several tables outside near bustling Avenida Ashford. Make sure to order several of the tasty appetizers—such as breaded calamari in a tomato-basil sauce—so you can share them your dinner companions. Of the notable main courses, try the veal chops stuffed with provolone and pancetta. ⊠ *14 Calle Candida, Condado,* ☎ *787/725–9494* ⊟ *AE, D, DC, MC, V* ⊗ *Closed Sun. and Mon. No lunch Tues.–Thurs.*

SEAFOOD ✕ **La Dorada.** This seafood establishment in the middle of Condado's
$$–$$$ restaurant row is surprisingly affordable. Don't expect much from the dining room, which is more along the lines of a diner. The focus here is the food. The grilled seafood platter is the specialty, but there are plenty of other excellent dishes, including mahimahi in caper sauce and codfish in green sauce. The friendly staff makes you feel genuinely welcome. ⊠ *1105 Av. Magdalena, Condado,* ☎ *787/722–9583* ⊟ *AE, D, MC, V.*

EASTERN PUERTO RICO

SEAFOOD ✕ **Calizo.** There's a string of seafood shacks on the island's northeastern
$$$ coast, all serving delicious fried fish. This open-air eatery, one of the best in the village of Las Croabas, takes things up a notch or two. Look for dishes like conch salad in a spicy vinaigrette, mahimahi in a honey-and-white-wine sauce, or chunks of lobster sautéed in garlic. Wash it all down with an icy cold beer on tap. It's almost across from the Balneario Seven Seas, making it a great place to find sustenance after a day at the beach. ⊠ *Rte. 987, Las Croabas* ☎ *787/706–7337* ⊟ *MC, V.*

$–$$ ✕ **Pulpo Loco by the Sea.** Talk about truth in packaging—the Crazy Octopus has its palm-shaded tables planted firmly in the sand just a few yards from the ocean. As you might guess, octopus, oysters, mussels, and crab lead the lineup at this colorful seafood shack, though you can always munch on local favorites like fried codfish fritters. If your thirst is greater than your hunger, you can opt for a beer served in a plastic cup. The staff is friendly, and seems to know all the customers on a first-name basis. ⊠*Rte. 187, Km 4.5, Piñones* ☏787/791–8382 ⊟*AE, MC, V.*

VIEQUES & CULEBRA

CARIBBEAN ✕**Blue Macaw.** Polished wood and brushed steel give this newcomer
$$$–$$$$ a sleek, sexy look. It's hard to resist the curvy banquette in the front dining room, but on a cool evening it's even harder to pass up a table in the enclosed rear courtyard. The food here isn't about throwing together a lot of different ingredients. Instead, the kitchen turns out a well-traveled menu of classic dishes like crispy dusk with plum sauce, osso buco with braised vegetables, and lamb tenderloin in a raspberry sauce. Not that hungry? There are plenty of smaller dishes that are perfect for sharing, such as quesadillas with smoked chicken. ⊠*Calle Antonio Mellado at Calle Luis Muñoz Rivera, Isabel Segunda, Vieques* ☏787/741–4000 ⚑*Reservations essential* ⊟*AE, MC, V.*

$$–$$$ ✕**Juanita Bananas.** Trees overflowing with bananas, papayas, and pas-
★ sion fruit line the walkway that leads to one of Culebra's best eateries. Chef Jennifer Daubon, whose parents once ran a restaurant on the island, focuses on the freshest local produce, which is why about an acre of land on the surrounding hillside is used for growing vegetables and herbs. The menu changes with the seasons, but look for dishes like lobster *limonjili,* which is medallions of lobster in a fresh lime and garlic sauce. The dining room, with its low lights, soft music, and expansive view, is without a doubt the most romantic in Culebra. ⊠*Calle Melones, Km 1, Dewey, Culebra* ☏787/742–3855 ⚑*Reservations essential* ⊟*MC, V.*

SOUTHERN PUERTO RICO

ECLECTIC ✕**Mark's at the Meliá.** Hidden behind an etched-glass door, this discreet
$$–$$$$ restaurant is one of the best on the island. Chef Mark French has won
Fodor'sChoice praise for his creative blend of European cooking techniques and local
★ ingredients. That skill results in appetizers like terrine of foie gras with dried cherry compote and smoked salmon topped with caramelized mango. The menu changes often, but you're likely to see such entrées as plantain-crusted dorado and rack of lamb with a goat-cheese crust. The chocolate truffle cake draws fans from as far away as San Juan. This is a family-run business, so Mark's wife, Melody, is likely to greet you at the door. ⊠*Hotel Meliá, 75 Calle Cristina, Ponce Centro, Ponce* ☏787/284–6275 ⚑*Reservations essential* ⊟*AE, MC, V* ⊙*Closed Mon. and Tues.*

SEAFOOD ✕**El Ancla.** Families favor this laid-back restaurant, whose dining room
$–$$$ sits at the edge of the sea. The kitchen serves generous and affordable plates of fish, crab, and other fresh seafood with tostones, french fries, and garlic bread. Try the shrimp in garlic sauce, salmon fillet with capers, or the delectable mofongo. Finish your meal with one of the fantastic flans. The piña coladas—with or without rum—are exceptional. ⊠*9 Av. Hostos Final, Ponce Playa, Ponce* ☏787/840–2450 ⊟*AE, MC, V.*

16

WESTERN & CENTRAL PUERTO RICO

CARIBBEAN ✕ **El Fogón de Abuela.** This rustic restaurant on the edge of Dos Bocas
$–$$$ Lake would make any Puerto Rican grandmother envious. The menu
features stews, red snapper (whole or filleted), and fricassees, including
pork chop, goat, and rabbit. You arrive either by taking the public boat
from El Embarcadero on Route 612, by calling the restaurant from the
dock and requesting a boat be sent to pick you up (free of charge), or
by driving to the south side of the lake. From Utuado, take Route 111
to Route 140 to Route 612 and follow that to its end. The restaurant
is open weekends only. ⊠ *Rte. 485, Camuy* ☎ *787/894–0470* ☐ *MC,
V* ⊙ *Closed Mon.–Thurs.*

$–$$ ✕ **Tamboo.** Here is a bar and grill that doesn't fall too much into either
category. The open-air kitchen prepares any number of unusual items,
from king-crab sandwiches to chicken-and-basil wraps. The bar, also
open to the elements, serves a mean margarita. Happy hour sometimes
starts dangerously early—at 10 AM on Saturday. The deck is a great
place to watch the novice surfers wipe out on the nearby beach. A
renovation in 2007 means the place looks great, and every table has a
million-dollar view of the ocean. ⊠ *Beside the Point, Rte. 413, Km 4.7,
Rincón* ☎ *787/823–3210* ☐ *AE, MC, V.*

ECLECTIC ✕ **Happy Belly's.** If you're in the mood for a hamburger or club sand-
$–$$$ wich, this laid-back restaurant is a good choice. The seating is comfort-
able wooden booths that overlook Playa Jobos—the wind that whips
up the waves may also blow away your napkin. In the evening the
menu changes to more-substantial fare, everything from shrimp scampi
to baby back ribs. But many people just come for the socializing and
the sunsets. ⊠ *Rte. 4466, Km 7.5, Isabela* ☎ *787/872–6566* ☐ *AE,
MC, V.*

SEAFOOD ✕ **El Bohío.** Watch seagulls dive for their dinner while you dine on a
$$ covered deck extending out into the bay. The long list of seafood is
prepared in a variety of ways: shrimp comes breaded, stewed, or skew-
ered; conch is served as a salad or cooked in a butter and garlic sauce.
And the lobster can be prepared in just about any way you can imagine.
⊠ *Rte. 102, Km 9.7, Joyuda* ☎ *787/851–2755* ☐ *AE, DC, MC, V.*

SPANISH ✕ **El Ladrillo.** This cozy spot covers its brick walls (*ladrillo* means
$$$–$$$$ "brick") from floor to ceiling with original paintings. Many of the
dishes on the menu are Spanish, which might account for the many
portraits of Don Quixote. There's a wide selection of seafood—try the
zarzuela, a combination of lobster, squid, octopus, and clams. Lobster
is a specialty, and you can order it *a la criolla* (in a spicy stew), *a la
parrilla* (from the grill), or *ajillo* (with a garlic sauce). The steaks are
also good, especially the filet mignon. The red-jacketed waiters really
know their stuff. ⊠ *334 Calle Méndez Vigo, Dorado* ☎ *787/796–2120*
☐ *AE, MC, V.*

BEACHES

By law, the island's *playas* (beaches) are all open to the public despite what resort hotels may want you to believe. *Balnearios,* which are government-run beaches, are equipped with restrooms, changing areas, water fountains, lifeguards, and parking lots. In many cases there are also picnic tables, playgrounds, and camping facilities. Admission is free, and parking is usually $2 or $3. Hours vary, but most balnearios are open daily from 9 to 5. Because of all these amenities, balnearios are popular and can be both busy and dirty. For quiet relaxation, as a general rule, avoid them on the weekends.

GREATER SAN JUAN AREA

The city's beaches can get crowded, especially on weekends. There's free access to all of them, but parking can be an issue in the peak sun hours—arriving early or in the late afternoon is a safer bet.

★ **Balneario de Carolina.** When people talk of "beautiful Isla Verde beach," this is the one they're talking about. A government-maintained beach, this balneario east of Isla Verde is so close to the airport that the leaves rustle when planes take off. The long stretch of sand, which runs parallel to Avenida Los Gobernadores, is shaded by palms and almond trees. There's plenty of room to spread out and lots of amenities: lifeguards, restrooms, changing facilities, picnic tables, and barbecue grills. ⊠ *Carolina* 🅿 *Parking $2* 🕙 *Daily 8–6.*

Balneario de Escambrón. In Puerta de Tierra, this government-run beach is just off Avenida Muñoz Rivera. The patch of honey-color sand has shade provided by coconut palms and surf that's generally gentle. Favored by families, it has lifeguards, bathhouses, bathrooms, and restaurants. ⊠ *Puerta de Tierra* 🅿 *Parking $3* 🕙 *Daily 7–7.*

Playa de Ocean Park. The residential neighborhood east of Condado and west of Isla Verde is home to this 1-mi-long (1.5-km-long) stretch of golden sand. The waters are often choppy but still swimmable—take care, however, as there aren't any lifeguards on duty. Windsurfers say the conditions here are nearly perfect. The beach is popular with young people, particularly on weekends, as well as gay men. Parking is a bit difficult, as many of the streets are gated and restricted to residents. ⊠ *Ocean Park* 🕙 *Daily dawn–dusk.*

Playa del Condado. East of Old San Juan and west of Ocean Park, this long, wide beach is overshadowed by an unbroken string of hotels and apartment buildings. Beach bars, water-sports outfitters, and chair-rental places abound. You can access the beach from several roads off Avenida Ashford, including Calle Cervantes and Calle Candina. The protected water at the small stretch of beach west of the Condado Plaza hotel is particularly calm and popular with families; surf elsewhere in Condado can be a bit strong. The stretch of sand near Calle Vendig (behind the Atlantic Beach Hotel) is especially popular with the gay community. If you're driving, on-street parking is your only option. ⊠ *Condado* 🕙 *Daily dawn–dusk.*

16

EASTERN PUERTO RICO

Balneario de Luquillo. A magnet for families, this government-maintained beach is well equipped with changing areas and restrooms, lifeguards, food stands and picnic areas, and even stands where you can order a cocktail. Its most distinctive facility, though, is the Mar Sin Barreras (Sea without Barriers), a low-sloped ramp leading into the water that allows wheelchair users to take a dip. The beach is off Route 3 as you head toward Fajardo. ⊠ *Off Rte. 3, Luquillo* 🅿 *Parking $2* ☉ *Tues.–Sun. 9–5.*

Balneario Seven Seas. This long stretch of powdery sand near the Reserva Natural Las Cabezas de San Juan may turn out to be the best surprise of your trip. Facilities include picnic tables, changing areas, restrooms, and showers. On weekends, the beach attracts families keen on its calm, clear waters—perfect for swimming and other water sports. ⊠ *Rte. 987, Fajardo* 🅿 *Parking $3* ☉ *Daily 8–6.*

VIEQUES & CULEBRA

Playa Flamenco. On Culebra's north coast is an amazingly lovely stretch of white sand. This beach, with its almost perfect half-moon shape, is consistently ranked as one of the two or three best in the world. Once you see it, you'll know why. Mountains rise up on all sides, making it feel miles away from civilization. This is the only beach on Culebra with amenities such as restrooms, showers, and kiosks selling simple fare. ⊠ *Off Rte. 251, west of the airport, Culebra* ☉ *Daily dawn–dusk.*

Playa Media Luna. An unpaved road east of Playa Sun Bay leads to a pretty little beach that's ideal for children because the water is calm and shallow. This is a good spot to try your hand at snorkeling. Take note, though, that there are no facilities. ⊠ *Off Rte. 997, east of Playa Sun Bay, Vieques* ☉ *Daily dawn–dusk.*

Playa Sun Bay. East of Esperanza this is easily the most popular of the dozens of beaches that ring Vieques. Its white sands skirt a mile-long, crescent-shape bay. You'll find food kiosks, picnic tables, and changing facilities. On weekdays, when the crowds are thin, you might also find wild horses grazing among the palm trees. ⊠ *Rte. 997, Vieques* 🅿 *Parking $3* ☉ *Daily dawn–dusk.*

SOUTHERN PUERTO RICO

Balneario Boquerón. This broad beach of hard-packed sand is fringed with coconut palms. You can find changing facilities, cabins, showers, restrooms, and picnic tables. Nearby, Playa Santa and Ballena golden sand beaches are often deserted. ⊠ *Boquerón* 🅿 *Parking $3* ☉ *Daily 8 AM–10 PM.*

La Playuela. At the southwesternmost tip of the island, there are breathtaking views of salt mines and the stretches of white sand at the foot of the Cabo Rojo Lighthouse, which are part of a protected reserve. Getting to this beach is a bit of an adventure but bliss upon arrival. Access is via a very bumpy road; a four-wheel drive is recommended. ✉*End of Rte. 301, El Combate* ⊙*Daily dawn–dusk.*

WESTERN & CENTRAL PUERTO RICO

Playa Crashboat. This beach near Aguadilla is famous for the colorful fishing boats docked on its shores; its long, beautiful stretch of golden yellow sand; and its clear water, which is perfect for swimming. Named after rescue boats used when Ramey Air Force Base was in operation, this balneario has picnic huts, showers, parking, and restrooms. ✉*1 mi (1.5 km) west of Rte. 107, Aguadilla* ⊙*Daily dawn–dusk.*

Playa de Jobos. Isabela beaches are mostly rough and suitable for surfers, but some sections of this beach are safe and swimmable. On the same stretch, there are a couple of restaurants with oceanfront decks serving light fare and drinks. ✉*Off Rte. 466, Isabela* ⊙*Daily dawn–dusk.*

SPORTS & THE OUTDOORS

16

BOATING & SAILING

Aqua Frenzy Kayaks (✉*At dock area below Calle Flamboyán, Esperanza, Vieques* ☎787/741–0913) rents kayaks and arranges kayak tours of Bahía Mosquito and other areas. Reservations for the excursion to glowing Bahía Mosquito cost $30. Make reservations at least 24 hours in advance. **Blue Caribe Kayaks** (✉*149 Calle Flamboyán, Esperanza, Vieques* ☎787/741–2522 ⊕*www.enchanted-isle.com/blue caribe*) offers kayak trips to Bahía Mosquito for about $30, as well as trips to deserted parts of the coast and to nearby islets. You can also rent a kayak and set off on your own.

★ **Island Adventures** (✉*Rte. 996, Esperanza, Vieques* ☎787/741–0720 ⊕*www.biobay.com*), owned by former schoolteacher Sharon Grasso, will take you to Bahía Mosquito aboard nonpolluting, electrically powered pontoon boats. The best part is leaping into the water, where the outline of your body will be softly illuminated thanks to bioluminescent organisms. The cost is about $30 per person. Percy Rier and Dalberto Arce of **Kayaking Puerto Rico** (✉*HC 4, Box 12672, Río Grande* ☎787/435–1665 ⊕*www.kayakpuertorico.com*) take you on trips that let you explore the coast by kayak, then dip into the water to see what's under the sea. **Las Tortugas Adventures** (✉*Cond. La Puntilla, 4 Calle La Puntilla, Apt. D1–12, Old San Juan* ☎787/725–5169 or 787/889–7734 ⊕*www.kayak-pr.com*) organizes group-kayaking trips to the Reserva Natural Las Cabezas de San Juan and the Bahía Mosquito in eastern Puerto Rico.

CYCLING

Selected areas lend themselves to bike travel. Avoid main thoroughfares, as the traffic is heavy and the fumes are thick. The Paseo Piñones is an 11-mi (18-km) bike path that skirts the ocean east of San Juan. The entire southwest coast of Cabo Rojo also makes for good biking, particularly the broad beach at Boquerón. Parts of oceanside Route 466 in Isabela that are still development-free make gorgeous rides with breathtaking views.

At **Hot Dog Cycling** (⊠ *5916 Av. Isla Verde, Isla Verde, San Juan* ☎ *787/982–5344* ⊕ *www.hotdogcycling.com*), Raul del Río and his son Omar rent mountain bikes for $30 a day. They also organize group excursions to El Yunque and other places out on the island.

DIVING & SNORKELING

The diving is excellent off Puerto Rico's south, east, and west coasts, as well as its nearby islands. Particularly striking are dramatic walls created by a continental shelf off the south coast near La Parguera and Guánica. There's also some fantastic diving near Fajardo and around Vieques and Culebra, two small islands off the east coast. It's best to choose specific locations with the help of a guide or outfitter. Escorted half-day dives range from $65 to $100 for one or two tanks, including all equipment; in general, double those prices for night dives. Packages that include lunch and other extras are more. Snorkeling excursions, which include transportation, equipment rental, and sometimes lunch, start at $50. Equipment rents for about $5 to $10.

Near Gate 5 of the old Ramey Air Force Base, **Aquatica** (⊠ *Rte. 110, Km 10* ☎ *787/890–6071*) offers scuba-diving certification courses as well as snorkeling and surfing trips. **Culebra Divers** (⊠ *4 Calle Pedro Marquez, Dewey, Culebra* ☎ *787/742–0803* ⊕ *www.culebradivers. com*), run by Monica and Walter Rieder, caters to those who are new to scuba diving. You travel to dive sites on one of the company's pair of 26-foot cabin cruisers. One-tank dives are $65, and two-tank dives are $95. The office is in downtown Dewey, across from the ferry terminal. **Parguera Divers** (⊠ *Posada Porlamar, Rte. 304, Km 3.3, La Parguera* ☎ *787/899–4171* ⊕ *www.pargueradivers.com*) offers scuba and snorkeling expeditions and basic instruction on the southwest coast.

At **Sea Ventures Pro Dive Center** (⊠ *Puerto del Rey Marina, Rte. 3, Km 51.4, Fajardo* ☎ *787/863–3483* ⊕ *www.divepuertorico.com*) you can get PADI certified, arrange dive trips to 20 offshore sites, or organize boating and sailing excursions. A two-tank dive for certified divers, including equipment, is $99. **Taíno Divers** (⊠ *Black Eagle Marina, Black Eagle Rd., off Rte. 413* ☎ *787/823–6429* ⊕ *www.tainodivers.com*) has daily snorkeling and diving trips that cost $75 and $109, including lunch. It also has daily trips to Desecheo Island, charters to Mona Island, and scuba PADI certification courses.

FISHING

Puerto Rico's waters are home to large game fish such as marlin, wahoo, dorado, tuna, and barracuda; as many as 30 world records for catches have been set off the island's shores. You can arrange fishing trips with Capt. Francisco "Pochy" Rosario, who runs **Light Tackle Adventure** (⊠*Boquerón* ☎787/849–1430 ⊕*www.lighttackleadventure.8k.com*). His specialty is tarpon, which are plentiful in these waters. Half-day and full-day excursions can be arranged through **Mike Benítez Sport Fishing** (⊠*Club Náutico de San Juan, Miramar, San Juan* ☎787/723–2292 ⊕*www.mikebenitezfishingpr.com*). From the 45-foot *Sea Born* you can fish for sailfish, white marlin, and blue marlin.

GOLF

Aficionados may know that Puerto Rico is the birthplace of golf legend Chi Chi Rodríguez—and he had to hone his craft somewhere. Currently, you can find nearly 20 courses on the island, including many championship links. Be sure to call ahead for tee times; hours vary, and several hotel courses give preference to guests. Greens fees start at about $20 and go up as high as $150. The **Puerto Rican Golf Association** (⊠*58 Calle Caribe, San Juan* ☎787/721–7742 ⊕*www.prga.org*) is a good source for information on courses and tournaments.

The 18-hole Arthur Hills–designed course at **El Conquistador Resort & Golden Door Spa** (⊠*1000 Av. El Conquistador, Fajardo* ☎787/863–6784) is famous for its 200-foot changes in elevation. The trade winds make every shot challenging.

★ Originally sketched out by Robert Trent Jones Sr., the four 18-hole golf courses at the **Hyatt Hacienda del Mar** (⊠*301 Rte. 693, Dorado* ☎787/796–1234) all got a face-lift in 2005. Six new holes and six redesigned holes mean that the Pineapple and the Sugar Cane courses feel completely different. Jack Nicklaus has said that the 4th hole at the East Course is one of the top 10 holes in the world. The West Course is buffeted by constant breezes off the Atlantic, making it tough to negotiate. **Palmas del Mar Country Club** (⊠*Rte. 906, Humacao* ☎787/285–2256 ⊕*www.palmascountryclub.com*) has two good golf courses: the Rees Jones–designed Flamboyán course, named for the nearly six dozen flamboyant trees that pepper its fairway, winds around a lake, over a river, and to the sea before turning toward sand dunes and wetlands. The older, Gary Player–designed Palm course has a challenging par 5 that scoots around wetlands.

★ The spectacular **Rio Mar Beach Resort & Spa** (⊠*6000 Río Mar Bul., Río Grande* ☎787/888–7060 ⊕*www.wyndhamriomar.com*) has a clubhouse with a pro shop and two restaurants set between two 18-hole courses. The River Course, designed by Greg Norman, has challenging fairways that skirt the Mameyes River. The Ocean Course has slightly wider fairways than its sister; iguanas can usually be spotted sunning themselves near its 4th hole. If you're not a resort guest, be sure to reserve tee times at least 24 hours in advance.

16

HORSEBACK RIDING

Horseback riding is a well-established family pastime in Puerto Rico, with *cabalgatas* (group day rides) frequently organized on weekends through mountain towns.

Gaby's World (⊠*Rte. 127, Km 5.1, Yauco* ☎787/856–2609) is a 204-acre horse ranch that conducts half-hour, one-hour, and two-hour rides through the hills surrounding Yauco. There are also pony rides for children.

★ **Hacienda Carabalí** (⊠*Rte. 992, Km 4, north of entrance to El Yunque* ☎787/690–3781), a family-run operation, is a good place to jump in the saddle and ride one of Puerto Rico's Paso Fino horses. Hour-long rides ($32) take you around the 600-acre ranch, while two-hour treks take you to a river where you and your horse can take a dip.

SURFING

The very best surfing beaches are along the northwestern coast from Isabela south to Rincón, which gained notoriety by hosting the World Surfing Championship in 1968. Today the town draws surfers from around the globe, especially in winter, when the waves are at their best.

East of the city, in Piñones, the Caballo has deep- to shallow-water shelf waves that require a big-wave board known as a gun. Playa La Pared, near Balneario de Luquillo, is a surfer haunt with medium-range waves. Numerous local competitions are held here throughout the year.

★ Not far from Playa La Pared, **La Selva Surf Shop** (⊠*250 Calle Fernández Garcia, Luquillo* ☎787/889–6205 ⊕*www.rainforestsafari.com/ selva.html*) has anything a surfer could need, including news about current conditions. **Rincón Surf School** (⊠*Rincón Surf & Board, Rte. 413* ☎787/823–0610 ⊕*www.surfandboard.com*) offers full-day lessons for $89, which includes board rental and transportation. You can also arrange two-, three-, and five-day surfing seminars for $169 to $369.

WINDSURFING

You can get the best windsurfing advice and equipment from Jaime Torres at **Velauno** (⊠*2430 Calle Loíza, Punta Las Marías, San Juan* ☎787/728–8716 ⊕*www.velauno.com*), one of the largest windsurfing centers in the United States. It has rentals, repair services, and classes. It also sells new and used gear and serves as a clearinghouse for information on windsurfing events throughout the island.

SHOPPING

San Juan has the island's best range of stores, but it isn't a free port, so you won't find bargains on electronics and perfumes. You can, however, find excellent prices on china, crystal, clothing, and jewelry. Shopping for local crafts can also be gratifying: you'll run across a lot that's tacky, but you can also find treasures, and in many cases you can watch the artisans at work. Popular items include *santos* (small carved figures of saints or religious scenes), hand-rolled cigars, handmade *mundillo* lace from Aguadilla, *vejigantes* (colorful masks used during Carnival and local festivals) from Loíza and Ponce, and fancy men's shirts called guayaberas.

In Old San Juan—especially on Calles Fortaleza and Cristo—you can find everything from T-shirt emporiums to selective crafts stores, bookshops, art galleries, jewelry boutiques, and even shops that specialize in made-to-order Panama hats. Calle Cristo is lined with factory-outlet stores, including Coach and Ralph Lauren.

With many stores selling luxury items and designer fashions, the shopping spirit in the San Juan neighborhood of Condado is reminiscent of that in Miami. Avenida Ashford is considered the heart of San Juan's fashion district, and you'll find plenty of high-end clothing stores here.

SPECIALTY STORES

16

ART

★ **Galería Botello** (⊠*208 Calle Cristo, Old San Juan, San Juan* ☎*787/723–9987*), a gorgeous gallery, displays the works of the late Angel Botello, who as far back as 1943 was hailed as the "Caribbean Gauguin." His work, which often uses the bright colors of the tropics, often depicts island scenes. There are pieces on display here by other prominent local artists as well.

★ The ultramodern **Galería Raíces** (⊠*314 Av. José de Diego, Santurce, San Juan* ☎*787/723–8909*), half a block south of the Museo de Arte de Puerto Rico, has works by emerging Puerto Rican artists.

CLOTHES

Clubman (⊠*1351 Av. Ashford, Condado, San Juan* ☎*787/722–1867*), after many years of catering to a primarily local clientele, is still the classic choice for gentlemen's clothing.

Prolific designer **David Antonio** (⊠*69 Av. Condado, Condado, San Juan* ☎*787/725–0600*) runs a small shop that's full of surprises. His joyous creations range from updated version of the men's classic guayabera shirt to fluid chiffon tunics for women.

Lisa Cappalli (⊠*151 Av. José de Diego, Condado, San Juan* ☎*787/724–6575*) sells her lacy designs from a boutique in Condado.

The window displays at **Nativa** (⊠*55 Calle Cervantes, Condado, San Juan* ☎*787/724–1396*) are almost as daring as the clothes its sells.

★ **Nono Maldonado** (⊠*1112 Av. Ashford, Condado* ☎*787/721–0456*) is well-known for his high-end, elegant linen designs. He should know a thing or two about style—he worked for many years as the fashion editor of *Esquire*.

Otto (⊠69 *Av. Condado, Condado, San Juan* ☎787/722–4609), owned by local designer Otto Bauzá, stocks his own line of casual wear for younger men.

JEWELRY

For a wide array of watches and jewelry, visit the two floors of **Bared** (⊠154 *Calle Fortaleza, Old San Juan* ☎787/722–2172), with a charmingly old-fashioned ambience. Look for the massive clock face on the corner. **Club Jibarito** (⊠202 *Calle Cristo, Old San Juan* ☎787/724–7797), has a fantastic collection of high-end watches by Jaeger-LeCoultre and other designers. **Joyería Riviera** (⊠257 *Calle Fortaleza, Old San Juan, San Juan* ☎787/725–4000) sells fine jewelry by David Yurman and Rolex watches.

SOUVENIRS

★ **Magia** (⊠99 *Calle Cristo, Old San Juan* ☎787/386–6164) is the cleverest shop in San Juan. At first the items on display look like traditional crafts, but look again and you notice that everything is a little offbeat. A little wooden shrine, for example, might be sheltering an image of Marilyn Monroe.

★ **Mi Pequeño San Juan** (⊠107 *Calle Cristo, Old San Juan* ☎787/977–1636) specializes in tiny versions of the doorways of San Juan. These ceramics, all done by hand right in the shop, are a wonderful souvenir of your stay. You might even find the hotel where you stayed reproduced in plaster.

You can find a world of unique spices and sauces from around the Caribbean, kitchen items, and cookbooks at **Spicy Caribbee** (⊠154 *Calle Cristo, Old San Juan, San Juan* ☎787/625–4690).

NIGHTLIFE & THE ARTS

Qué Pasa, the official visitor's guide, has listings of events in San Juan and out on the island. For daily listings, pick up a copy of the English-language edition of the *San Juan Star.* The Thursday edition's weekend section is especially useful. For the gay scene, check out the monthly *Puerto Rico Breeze;* the free newspaper is found in many businesses, especially in the Condado area.

NIGHTLIFE

Wherever you go, dress to impress. Puerto Ricans have flair, and both men and women love getting dressed up to go out. Bars are usually casual, but if you have on jeans, sneakers, and a T-shirt, you may be refused entry at swankier nightclubs and discos.

In Old San Juan, Calle San Sebastián is lined with bars and restaurants. Salsa music blaring from jukeboxes in cut-rate pool halls competes with mellow Latin jazz in top-flight nightspots. Evenings begin with dinner and stretch into the late hours (often until 3 or 4 in the morning) at the bars of the more-upscale, so-called SoFo (south of Fortaleza) end of Old San Juan. An eclectic crowd heads to the Plaza del Mercado in Santurce after work to hang out in the plaza or enjoy drinks and food in one of the small establishments skirting the farmers' market. Condado and Ocean Park have their share of nightlife, too. Most are restaurant-and-bar environments.

Just east of San Juan along Route 187, funky Piñones has a collection of open-air seaside eateries that are popular with locals. On weekend evenings, many places have merengue combos, Brazilian jazz trios, or reggae bands. In the southern city of Ponce, people embrace the Spanish tradition of the *paseo,* an evening stroll around the Plaza las Delicias. The boardwalk at La Guancha in Ponce is also a lively scene. Live bands often play on weekends. Elsewhere *en la isla,* nighttime activities center on the hotels and resorts.

BARS & MUSIC CLUBS

The wildly popular **El Batey** (⊠ *101 Calle Cristo, Old San Juan, San Juan* ☎ *787/725–1787*) won't win any prizes for its decor. Grab a marker to add your own message to the graffiti-covered walls, or add your business card to the hundreds that cover the lighting fixtures. The jukebox, packed with vintage 45s, has one of the best music selections on the island. At **Liquid** (⊠ *San Juan Water & Beach Club, 2 Calle Tartak, Isla Verde* ☎ *787/725–4664 or 787/725–4675*), the lobby lounge of San Juan's chicest boutique hotel, glass walls are filled with undulating water, and the fashionable patrons drink wild cocktails to pounding music.

CASINOS

By law, all casinos are in hotels, primarily in San Juan. The government keeps a close eye on them. Dress for the larger casinos is on the formal side, and the atmosphere is refined, particularly in the Isla Verde resorts. Casinos set their own hours but are generally open from noon to 4 AM. In addition to slot machines, typical games include blackjack, roulette, craps, Caribbean stud (a five-card poker game), and *pai gow* poker (a combination of American poker and the Chinese game pai gow). Hotels with casinos have live entertainment most weekends, as well as restaurants and bars. The minimum age to gamble (and to drink) is 18.

You may feel as if you're in Las Vegas when you step into the **Inter-Continental San Juan Resort & Casino** (⊠ *5961 Av. Isla Verde, Isla Verde, San Juan* ☎ *787/791–6100*). A torch singer warms up the crowd at a lounge-bar just outside the gaming room. Inside, a garish chandelier, dripping with strands of orange lights, runs the length of a mirrored ceiling. The casino at the **Ritz-Carlton San Juan Hotel, Spa & Casino** (⊠ *6961 Av. Las Gobernadores, Isla Verde, San Juan* ☎ *787/253–1700*) is refined by day or night. There's lots of activity, yet everything is hushed. The only place to gamble in Old San Juan is at the **Sheraton Old San Juan Hotel & Casino** (⊠ *101 Calle Brumbaugh, Old San Juan, San Juan* ☎ *787/721–5100*). You can see the gaming room—expanded in 2007—from the hotel's main stairway, from the balcony above, and from the lobby. Light bounces off the Bahía de San Juan and pours

16

through its many windows; passengers bound off their cruise ships and pour through its many glass doors.

DANCE CLUBS

A long line of young people can be spotted at the door of the chic club **Brava** (✉ *6063 Av. Isla Verde, Isla Verde* ☎ *787/641–3500*), at the El San Juan Hotel & Casino. The two-level club, each with its own DJ and dance floor, is one of the best places for dancing. There's a different theme party Thursday to Saturday.

★ **Candela** (✉ *110 San Sebastián, Old San Juan, San Juan* ☎ *787/977–4305*), a lounge–art gallery housed in a historic building, hosts some of the most innovative local DJs on the island and often invites star spinners from New York or London. This is the island's best showcase for experimental dance music.

With a large dance and stage area and smokin' Afro-Cuban bands, **Rumba** (✉ *152 Calle San Sebastián, Old San Juan, San Juan* ☎ *787/725–4407*) is one of the best parties in town.

GAY & LESBIAN CLUBS

The oceanfront deck bar of the **Atlantic Beach Hotel** (✉ *1 Calle Vendig, Condado, San Juan* ☎ *787/721–6100*) is famed for its early-evening happy hours, with pulsating tropical music, a wide selection of exotic drinks, and ever-pleasant ocean breezes. **Nuestro Ambiente** (✉ *1412 Av. Ponce de León, Santurce, San Juan* ☎ *787/724–9083*) offers a variety of entertainment for women Wednesday through Sunday. The youth-oriented **Starz** (✉ *365 Av. de Diego, at Av. Ponce de León, Santurce, San Juan* ☎ *787/721–8645*) has dancing on Friday and Saturday nights, as well as a popular after-the-beach party on Sunday evening.

THE ARTS

If you're in Old San Juan on the first Tuesday of the month, take advantage of **Noches de Galerias** (☎ *787/723–6286*). Galleries and select museums open their doors after-hours for viewings that are accompanied by refreshments and music. It certainly makes gallery-hopping more festive.

There's something going on nearly every night at the **Centro de Bellas Artes Luis A. Ferré** (✉ *Av. José de Diego at Av. Ponce de León, Santurce, San Juan* ☎ *787/725–7334*), from pop or jazz concerts to plays, opera, and ballet. It's also the home of the San Juan Symphony Orchestra. The **Museo de Arte de Ponce** (✉ *2325 Av. Las Américas, Sector Santa María, Ponce* ☎ *787/848–0505*) occasionally sponsors chamber music concerts and recitals by members of the Puerto Rico Symphony Orchestra.

Check for theater productions and concerts at the **Teatro La Perla** (✉ *Calle Mayor at Calle Cristina, Ponce Centro, Ponce* ☎ *787/843–4322*).

Named for Puerto Rican playwright Alejandro Tapia, **Teatro Tapia** (✉ *Calle Fortaleza at Plaza Colón, Old San Juan, San Juan* ☎ *787/722–0247*) hosts theatrical and musical productions.

EXPLORING PUERTO RICO

OLD SAN JUAN

Old San Juan, the original city founded in 1521, contains carefully pre-served examples of 16th- and 17th-century Spanish colonial architecture. More than 400 buildings have been beautifully restored. Graceful wrought-iron balconies with lush hanging plants extend over narrow streets paved with *adoquines* (blue-gray stones originally used as ballast on Spanish ships). The Old City is partially enclosed by walls that date from 1633 and once completely surrounded it. Designated a U.S. National Historic Zone in 1950, Old San Juan is chockablock with shops, open-air cafés, homes, tree-shaded squares, monuments, and people. You can get an overview on a morning's stroll (bear in mind that this "stroll" includes some steep climbs). However, if you plan to immerse yourself in history or to shop, you'll need a couple of days.

WHAT TO SEE
Numbers in the margin correspond to points of interest on the Old San Juan Exploring map.

16

⓫ Alcaldía. San Juan's city hall was built between 1604 and 1789. In 1841, extensive alterations were made so that it would resemble the city hall in Madrid, with arcades, towers, balconies, and an inner courtyard. Renovations have refreshed the facade of the building and some interior rooms, but the architecture remains true to its colonial style. A municipal tourist information center and an art gallery with rotating exhibits are on the first floor. ⊠ *153 Calle San Francisco, Plaza de Armas, Old San Juan* ☎ *787/724–7171* 🖅 *Free* ⊙ *Weekdays 8–4.*

❽ Capilla del Cristo. According to legend, in 1753 a young horseman named Baltazar Montañez, carried away during festivities in honor of San Juan Bautista (St. John the Baptist), raced down Calle Cristo and plunged over its steep precipice. A witness to the tragedy promised to build a chapel if the young man's life could be saved. Historical records maintain the man died, but legend contends that he lived. (Another version of the story has it that the horse miraculously stopped before plunging over the cliff.) Regardless, this chapel was built, and inside is a small silver altar dedicated to the Christ of Miracles. You can visit any time, even if the gates are closed. ⊠ *End of Calle Cristo, Old San Juan* ☎ *No phone* 🖅 *Free.*

❺ Casa Blanca. The original structure on this site was a wooden house built in 1521 as a home for Ponce de León; he died in Cuba without ever having lived here. His descendants occupied its sturdier replacement, a lovely colonial mansion with tile floors and beam ceilings, for the next 250 years. From the end of the Spanish-American War in 1898 to 1966 it was the home of the U.S. Army commander in Puerto Rico. Several rooms decorated with colonial-era furnishings are open to the public. A guide will show you around, and then you can explore on your own. Don't miss the stairway leading down from one of the bedrooms; alas, despite local lore, it leads to a small room and not to a

Old San Juan

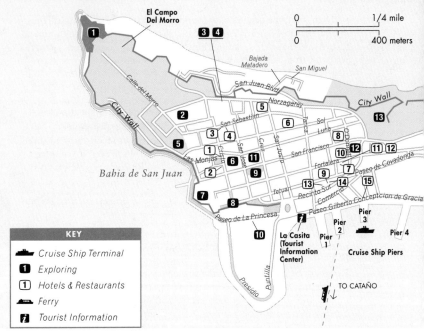

KEY

- 🚢 *Cruise Ship Terminal*
- 1 *Exploring*
- 1 *Hotels & Restaurants*
- ⛴ *Ferry*
- 𝑖 *Tourist Information*

Peaceful Music

Cellist Pablo Casals was one of the 20th century's most influential musicians. Born in Catalonia in 1876, he studied in Spain and Belgium, settled for a time in Paris, then returned to Barcelona. Tours in Europe, the United States, and South America brought him artistic and financial success and opportunities to collaborate with other prominent musicians.

By the advent of the Spanish Civil War, he was an internationally famous musician, teacher, and conductor. He was also an outspoken supporter of a democratic Spain. Forced into exile by Franco's regime, Casals arrived in Puerto Rico, his mother's birthplace, in 1956. There, the 81-year-old maestro continued to work and teach. He established the Casals Festival of Classical Music, making it a home for sublime orchestral and chamber works. For two weeks each June, the Puerto Rico Symphony Orchestra is joined by musicians from all over the world.

In Catalan, Casals first name is "Pau," which appropriately enough means "peace." He and his friend Albert Schweitzer appealed to the world powers to stop the arms race, and he made what many experts say is his greatest work—an oratorio titled "The Manger"—his personal message of peace. Casals died in Puerto Rico in 1973, but his many legacies live on. His favorite instruments, his recordings, and some of his many awards are preserved at the Museo Pablo Casals in Old San Juan.

–Karen English

16

tunnel to nearby El Morro. The lush garden, recently reopened to the public, is a quiet place to unwind. ✉*1 Calle San Sebastián, Old San Juan* ☎*787/725–1454* ⊕*www.icp.gobierno.pr* ✉*$3* ⊘*Tues.–Sat. 9–noon and 1–4.*

❻ Catedral de San Juan Bautista. The Catholic shrine of Puerto Rico had humble beginnings in the early 1520s as a thatch-roof, wooden structure. Hurricane winds tore off the thatch and destroyed the church. It was reconstructed in 1540, when it was given a graceful circular staircase and vaulted Gothic ceilings. Most of the work on the present cathedral, however, was done in the 19th century. The remains of Ponce de León are in a marble tomb near the transept. The trompe l'oeil work on the inside of the dome is breathtaking. Unfortunately, many of the other frescos suffer from water damage. ✉*151 Calle Cristo, Old San Juan* ☎*787/722–0861* ⊕*www.catedralsanjuan.com* ✉*$1 donation suggested* ⊘*Mon.–Sat. 8–5, Sun. 8–2:30.*

❸ Convento de los Dominicos. Built by Dominican friars in 1523, this convent often served as a shelter during Carib Indian attacks and, more recently, as headquarters for the Antilles command of the U.S. Army. Now home to some offices of the Institute of Puerto Rican Culture, the beautifully restored building contains religious manuscripts, artifacts, and art. The institute also maintains a book and music shop on the premises. Classical concerts are held here occasionally. ✉*98 Calle Norzagaray, Old San Juan* ☎*787/721–6866* ✉*Free* ⊘*Mon.–Sat. 9–5.*

⓭ **Fuerte San Cristóbal.** This stone fortress, built between 1634 and 1785, guarded the city from land attacks. Even larger than El Morro, San Cristóbal was known in the 17th and 18th centuries as the Gibraltar of the West Indies. Five freestanding structures are connected by tunnels, and restored units include an 18th-century barracks. You're free to explore the gun turrets, officers' quarters, and passageways. Along with El Morro, San Cristóbal is a National Historic Site administered by the U.S. Park Service; it's a UN World Heritage Site as well. Rangers conduct tours in Spanish and English. ⊠ *Calle Norzagaray at Calle Muñoz Rivera, Old San Juan* ☎ *787/729–6960* ⊕ *www.nps.gov/saju* ➜ *$3; $5 includes admission to El Morro* ☉ *June–Nov., daily 9–5; Dec.–May, daily 9–6.*

❶ **Fuerte San Felipe del Morro.** On a rocky promontory at the northwestern tip of the Old City is El Morro (which translates as "the promontory"), **Fodor'sChoice** a fortress built by the Spaniards between 1540 and 1783. Rising 140 ★ feet above the sea, the massive six-level fortress covers enough territory to accommodate a 9-hole golf course. It is a labyrinth of dungeons, ramps, barracks, turrets, towers, and tunnels. Built to protect the port, El Morro has a commanding view of the harbor. You're free to wander throughout. Tours and a video are available in English. ⊠ *Calle del Morro, Old San Juan* ☎ *787/729–6960* ⊕ *www.nps.gov/saju* ➜ *$3; $5 includes admission to Fuerte San Cristóbal* ☉ *June–Nov., daily 9–5; Dec.–May, daily 9–6.*

❼ **La Fortaleza.** Sitting on a hill overlooking the harbor, La Fortaleza was ★ built as a fortress in 1533. Not a very good fortress, mind you. It was attacked numerous times and taken twice, by the British in 1598 and by the Dutch in 1625. When the city's other fortifications were finished, La Fortaleza was transformed into a palace. Numerous changes to the original primitive structure over the past four centuries have resulted in the present collection of marble and mahogany, medieval towers, and stained-glass galleries. The Western Hemisphere's oldest executive mansion in continuous use, it is still the official residence of the island's governor. Guided tours are conducted several times a day in English and Spanish. Call ahead, as tours are often canceled because of official functions. The tours begin near the main gate in a yellow building called the Real Audiencia. ⊠ *Calle Recinto Oeste, Old San Juan* ☎ *787/721–7000* ⊕ *www.fortaleza.gobierno.pr* ➜ *Free* ☉ *Weekdays 9–5.*

❷ **Museo de las Américas.** On the second floor of the imposing former military barracks, Cuartel de Ballajá, the museum's permanent exhibit, "Las Artes Populares en las Américas," focusing on the popular and folk art of Latin America, contains religious figures, musical instruments, basketwork, costumes, and farming and other implements. ⊠ *Calle Norzagaray at Calle del Morro, Old San Juan* ☎ *787/724–5052* ⊕ *www.museolasamericas.org* ➜ *Free* ☉ *Tues.–Sun. 10–4.*

❹ **Museo de Nuestra Raíz Africana.** The Institute of Puerto Rican Culture created this museum to help Puerto Ricans understand African influences in island culture. On display over two floors are African musical instruments, documents relating to the slave trade, and a list of African words that have made it into popular Puerto Rican culture. ✉*101 Calle San Sebastián, Plaza de San José, Old San Juan* ☎*787/724–4294* ⊕*www.icp.gobierno.pr* ✆*$2* ☉*Tues.–Sat. 8:30–4:30.*

❿ Paseo de la Princesa. This street down at the port is spruced up with flowers, trees, benches, street lamps, and a striking fountain depicting the various ethnic groups of Puerto Rico. At the west end of the paseo, beyond the fountain, is the beginning of a shoreline path that hugs Old San Juan's walls and leads to the city gate at Caleta de San Juan.

❾ Plaza de Armas. The original main square of Old San Juan, this plaza, bordered by calles San Francisco, Fortaleza, San José, and Cruz, has a lovely fountain with 19th-century statues representing the four seasons.

⓬ Plaza de Colón. A statue of Christopher Columbus stands atop a high pedestal in this bustling Old San Juan square. Bronze plaques on the statue's base relate various episodes in the life of the historic explorer.

GREATER SAN JUAN

You'll need to resort to taxis, buses, *públicos* (shared vans), or a rental car to reach the points of interest in "new" San Juan. Avenida Muñoz Rivera, Avenida Ponce de León, and Avenida Fernández Juncos are the main thoroughfares that cross Puerta de Tierra, east of Old San Juan, to the business and tourist districts of Santurce, Condado, Ocean Park, and Isla Verde. Dos Hermanos Bridge connects Puerta de Tierra with Miramar, Condado, and Isla Grande. Isla Grande Airport, from which you can take short hops, is on the bay side of the bridge. On the other side, the Condado Lagoon is bordered by Avenida Ashford, which threads past the high-rise Condado hotels and Avenida Baldorioty de Castro Expreso, which barrels east to the airport and beyond. Due south of the lagoon is Miramar, a residential area with fashionable turn-of-the-20th-century homes and a few hotels and restaurants. Isla Verde, with its glittering beachfront hotels, casinos, discos, and public beach, is to the east, near the airport.

Numbers in the margin correspond to points of interest on the Greater San Juan map.

WHAT TO SEE

❶ El Capitolio. The white-marble capitol, a fine example of Italian Renaissance style, dates from 1929. Its grand rotunda, which can be seen from all over San Juan, was completed in the late 1990s. Fronted by eight Corinthian columns, it provides a very dignified home for the commonwealth's constitution. Guided tours, which take 45 minutes and include visits to the rotunda and other parts of the building, are by appointment only. ✉*Av. Ponce de León, Puerta de Tierra* ☎*787/977–4929* ⊕*www. gotopuertorico.com* ✆*Free* ☉*Weekdays 9–5, weekends 9–2.*

❸ Museo de Arte Contemporáneo de Puerto Rico. This Georgian-style structure, once a public school, displays a dynamic range of works by both established and up-and-coming Puerto Rican artists. Many of the works on display have strong political messages, including pointed commentaries on the island's status as a commonwealth. Only a small part of the permanent collection is on display at any time, but it might be anything from an exhibit of ceramics to a screening of videos. ⊠ *Av. Ponce de León at Av. R. H. Todd, Santurce* ☎ *787/977–4030* ⊕ *www. museocontemporaneopr.org* ✏ *Free* ⊘ *Tues.–Sat. 10–4, Sun. 1–4.*

② **Museo de Arte de Puerto Rico.** One of the biggest museums in the Carib-
☾ bean, this 130,000-square-foot building was once known as San Juan
Fodor'sChoice Municipal Hospital. The beautiful neoclassical building, dating from
★ the 1920s, proved to be too small to house the museum's permanent collection of Puerto Rican art dating from the 17th century to the present. The solution was to build a new east wing, which is dominated by a five-story-tall stained-glass window, the work of local artist Eric Tabales. The collection starts with works from the colonial era, most of them commissioned for churches. Here you'll find works by José Campeche, the island's first great painter. Also well represented is Francisco Oller y Cestero, who was the first to move beyond religious subjects to paint local scenes. There's much more to the museum, including a beautiful garden filled with a variety of native flora and one of the city's best and most expensive restaurants, Pikayo. ⊠ *299 Av. José De Diego, Santurce* ☎ *787/977–6277* ⊕ *www.mapr.org* ✏ *$6* ⊘ *Tues.– Sat. 10–4, Sun. noon–4.*

④ **Museo de Historia, Antropología y Arte.** The Universidad de Puerto Rico's Museum of History, Anthropology and Art has archaeological and historical exhibits that deal with the Native American influence on the island and the Caribbean, the colonial era, and the history of slavery. Art displays are occasionally mounted; the museum's prize exhibit is the painting *El Velorio* (*The Wake*), by the 19th-century artist Francisco Oller. ⊠ *Av. Ponce de León, Río Piedras* ☎ *787/764–0000 Ext. 5852* ⊕ *www.uprrp.edu* ✏ *Free* ⊘ *Mon.–Wed. and Fri. 9–4:30, Thurs. 9–9, weekends 9–3.*

SAN JUAN ENVIRONS

Numbers in the margin correspond to points of interest on the Greater. San Juan map.

WHAT TO SEE

⑥ **Casa Bacardí Visitor Center.** Exiled from Cuba, the Bacardí family built a small distillery here in the 1950s. Today it's one of the world's largest, with the capacity to produce 100,000 gallons of spirits a day and 221 million cases a year. You can hop on a little tram to take a 45-minute tour of the bottling plant, distillery, and museum. Yes, you'll be given a free sample. If you don't want to drive, you can reach the factory by taking the ferry from Pier 2 for 50¢ each way and then a público (shared van) from the ferry pier to the factory for about $2 or $3 per person. ⊠ *Rte. 888, Km 2.6, Cataño* ☎ *787/788–1500 or 787/788– 8400* ⊕ *www.casabacardi.org* ✏ *Free* ⊘ *Mon.–Sat. 8:30–5:30, Sun. 10–5; last tour 1½ hrs before closing.*

⑦ Parque de las Ciencias Luis A. Ferré. The 42-acre Luis A. Ferré Science Park contains a collection of amusing activities and displays. The Transportation Museum has antique cars and the island's oldest bicycle. In the Rocket Plaza, children can experience a flight simulator, and in the planetarium, the solar system is projected on the ceiling. Also on-site are a small zoo and a natural-science exhibit. It's a long drive from central San Juan, though. ⊠ *Rte. 167, Bayamón* ☎ *787/740–6878* ⌧ *$5* ⊙ *Wed.–Fri. 9–4, weekends 10–6.*

❺ Ruinas de Caparra. In 1508 Ponce de León established the island's first settlement here. The Caparra Ruins—a few crumbling walls—are what remains of an ancient fort. The small Museo de la Conquista y Colonización de Puerto Rico (Museum of the Conquest and Colonization of Puerto Rico) contains historical documents, exhibits, and excavated artifacts, though you can breeze through the museum's contents in less time than it takes to say the name. ⊠ *Rte. 2, Km 6.6, Guaynabo* ☎ *787/781–4795* ⊛ *www.icp.gobierno.pr* ⌧ *Free* ⊙ *Tues.– Sat. 8:30–4:20.*

EASTERN PUERTO RICO

16

El Yunque. The 28,000-acre El Yunque National Forest (known as El Yunque after the benevolent spirit Yuquiyú) didn't gain its "rain forest" status for nothing. More than 100 billion gallons of precipitation fall here annually, spawning rushing streams and cascades, 240 tree species, and oversize impatiens and ferns. In the evening, millions of inch-long *coquís* (tree frogs) begin their calls. El Yunque is also home to the *cotorra*, Puerto Rico's endangered green parrot, as well as 67 other types of birds.

Fodor's Choice ★

The forest's 13 hiking trails are well maintained; many of them are easy to walk and less than a mile long. Before you begin exploring, check out the high-tech interactive displays—explaining rain forests in general and El Yunque in particular—at **El Portal** (⊠ *Rte. 191, Km 4.3* ☎ *787/888–1880* ⊛ *www.fs.fed.us/r8/caribbean*), the information center near the northern entrance. This is also a good place to pick up a map of the park and talk to rangers about weather conditions or which trails are open. You can also stock up on water, snacks, film, and souvenirs at the small gift shop. The center is open daily from 9 to 4:30; admission is $3. The park itself, which is free, is open daily 7:30 to 6.

Fajardo. Founded in 1772, Fajardo has historical notoriety as a port where pirates stocked up on supplies. It later developed into a fishing community and an area where sugarcane flourished. (There are still cane fields on the city's fringes.) Today it's a hub for the yachts that use its marinas; the divers who head to its good offshore sites; and for the day-trippers who travel by catamaran, ferry, or plane to the out-islands of Culebra and Vieques. With the most-significant docking facilities on the island's eastern side, Fajardo is often congested and difficult to navigate.

Fajardo is the gateway to the 316-acre **Reserva Natural Las Cabezas de San Juan** (⊠*Rte. 987, Km 6* ☎*787/722–5882 weekdays, 787/860–2560 weekends* ⊕*www.fideicomiso.org/english/index.asp*), a natural preserve where you can wander down boardwalks through seven ecosystems, including lagoons, mangrove swamps, and dry-forest areas. It's a half-hour hike to mangrove-lined Laguna Grande, which at night glows with bioluminescent microorganisms. Call ahead for mandatory guided tours, which are given Wednesday to Sunday at 8:30, 9:30, 10, 10:30, and 2. Admission is $7.

VIEQUES & CULEBRA

Culebra. Culebra is known around the world for its curvaceous coastline. Playa Flamenco, the tiny island's most famous stretch of sand, is considered one of the two or three best beaches in the world. If Playa Flamenco gets too crowded, as it often does around Easter and Christmas, there are many other beaches that will be nearly deserted. There's archaeological evidence that Taíno and Carib peoples lived on Culebra long before the arrival of the Spanish in the late 15th century. The Spanish didn't bother laying claim to it until 1886; its dearth of freshwater made it an unattractive location for a settlement. Although the island now has modern conveniences, its pace seems little changed from a century ago. There's only one town, Dewey, named after U.S. Admiral George Dewey. When the sun goes down, Culebra winds down as well. But during the day it's a delightful place to stake out a spot on Playa Flamenco or Playa Soni and read, swim, or search for shells. So what causes stress on the island? Nada.

Fodor's Choice ★ **Vieques.** This island off Puerto Rico's east coast is famed for its Playa Sun Bay, a gorgeous stretch of sand with picnic facilities and shade trees. In May 2003, the U.S. Navy withdrew from its military operations and turned over two-thirds of Vieques to the local government, which is transforming it into the Vieques National Wildlife Refuge. Vieques has two communities—Isabel Segunda, where the ferries dock, and the smaller Esperanza. Both have restaurants and hotels that will surprise you with their sophistication.

In addition to great beaches, Vieques has one attraction that draws visitors from all over the world. **Bahía Mosquito** *(Mosquito Bay)* is best experienced on moonless nights, when millions of bioluminescent organisms glow when disturbed—it's like swimming in a cloud of fireflies. If you're on the island, this is a not-to-be-missed experience. Several local companies lead trips to the bay, either by kayak or by nonpolluting electric boats.

SOUTHERN PUERTO RICO

Fodor's Choice ★ The 9,900-acre **Bosque Estatal de Guánica**, a United Nations Biosphere Reserve, the Guánica State Forest is a great place for hiking expeditions. It's an outstanding example of a tropical dry coastal forest, with some 700 species of plants ranging from the prickly pear cactus to the gumbo limbo tree. It's also one of the best places on the island for bird-watching, as there are more than 100 types of bird, including the pearly-eyed thrasher, the lizard cuckoo, and the nightjar. One of the most popular hikes is the Ballena Trail, which begins at the ranger station on Route 334. This easy 1.2-mi (2-km) walk, which follows a partially paved road, takes you past a mahogany plantation to a dry plain covered with stunted cactus. A sign reading GUAYACÁN CENTENARIO leads you to an extraordinary guayacán tree with a trunk that measures 6 feet across. ⊠ *Enter along Rte. 334, 333, or 325* ☎ *787/821–5706* 🖾 *Free* ⊙ *Daily 9–5.*

Ponce. The island's second-largest urban area, Ponce shines in 19th-century style with pink-marble-bordered sidewalks, painted trolleys, and horse-drawn carriages. Stroll around the main square, the Plaza las Delicias, with its perfectly pruned India-laurel fig trees, graceful fountains, gardens, and park benches. View the Catedral de Nuestra Señora de la Guadalupe (Our Lady of Guadalupe Cathedral), perhaps even attend the 6 AM mass, and walk down Calles Isabel and Cristina to see turn-of-the-20th-century wooden houses with wrought-iron balconies.

The **Castillo Serrallés** is a splendid Spanish Revival mansion on Vigía Hill. This former residence of the owners of the Don Q rum distillery has been restored with a mix of original furnishings and antiques that recalls the era of the sugar barons. A short film details the history of the sugar and rum industries; tours are given every half hour in English and Spanish. You can also just stroll through the lovely gardens for a reduced admission fee. The 100-foot-tall concrete cross (La Cruceta del Vigía) behind the museum has a windowed elevator, which you can ascend for views of Ponce. ⊠ *17 El Vigía, El Vigía* ☎ *787/259–1774* ⊕ *home.coqui.net/castserr* 🖾 *$6; $9 includes admission to Cruceta del Vigía* ⊙ *Tues.–Thurs. 9:30–5, Fri.–Sun. 9:30–5:30.*

🐾 At the **Centro Ceremonial Indígena de Tibes,** you can find pre-Taíno ruins and burials dating from AD 300 to 700. Some archaeologists, noting the symmetrical arrangement of stone pillars, surmise the cemetery may have been of great religious significance. Be sure to visit the small museum before taking a walking tour of the site. ⊠ *Tibes Indian Ceremonial Center, Rte. 503, Km 2.8, Barrio Tibes* ☎ *787/840–2255 or 787/840–5685* ⊕ *ponce.inter.edu/tibes/tibes.html* 🖾 *$3* ⊙ *Tues.–Sun. 9–noon and 1–4.*

🐾 Just outside Ponce, **Hacienda Buena Vista** is a 19th-century coffee plan-
★ tation. It's a technological marvel—water from the nearby Río Canas was funneled into narrow brick channels that could be diverted to perform any number of tasks, including turning the waterwheel. (Seeing the two-story-tall wheel slowly begin to turn is thrilling, especially for kids.) Nearby is the two-story manor house, filled with furniture that gives a sense of what it was like to live on a coffee plantation nearly 150 years ago. Tours, which are by reservation only, are given at 8:30, 10:30, 1:30, and 3:30. Make sure to call several days ahead to reserve a space on an English-language tour. ⊠ *Rte. 123, Km 16.8, Sector Cor-*

16

ral Viejo ☎787/722–5882 *weekdays, 787/284–7020 weekends* ⚏$5 ⊙ *Fri.–Sun., by reservation only.*

★ The **Museo de Arte de Ponce** is easily identified by the hexagonal galleries on the second floor. The Ponce Museum of Art has one of the best art collections in Latin America, which is why residents of San Juan frequently make the trip down to Ponce. The 3,000-piece collection includes works by famous Puerto Rican artists such as Francisco Oller, represented by a lovely landscape called *Hacienda Aurora.* The highlight of the collection is the mesmerizing *Flaming June,* by Frederick Leighton, which has become the museum's unofficial symbol. ✉*2325 Av. Las Américas, Sector Santa María* ☎787/848–0505 ⊕*www. museoarteponce.org* ⚏$5 ⊙*Daily 10–5.* Two superlative examples of early-20th-century architecture house the **Museo de la Historia de Ponce**, where 10 rooms of exhibits vividly re-create Ponce's golden years, providing fascinating glimpses into the worlds of culture, high finance, and journalism in the 19th century. Hour-long tours in English and Spanish are available, but there's no set time when they start. ✉*51–53 Calle Isabel, Ponce Centro* ☎787/844–7071 *or 787/843–4322* ⚏$3 ⊙*Daily 9–5.*

☼ You haven't seen a firehouse until you've seen the **Parque de Bombas,** a
★ structure built in 1882 for an exposition and converted to a firehouse the following year. Today it's a museum tracing the history—and glorious feats—of Ponce's fire brigade. ✉*Plaza las Delicias, Ponce Centro* ☎787/284–3338 ⚏*Free* ⊙ *Wed.–Mon. 9–5:30.*

San Germán. Around San Germán's (population 39,000) two main squares—Plazuela Santo Domingo and Plaza Francisco Mariano Quiñones (named for an abolitionist)—are buildings done in every conceivable style of architecture found on the island, including Mission, Victorian, creole, and Spanish colonial. The city's tourist office offers a free guided trolley tour. Students and professors from the Inter-American University often fill the center's bars and cafés.

★ One of the oldest Christian religious structures in the Americas, the **Capilla de Porta Coeli** overlooks the long, rectangular Plazuela de Santo Domingo. It's not a grand building, but its position at the top of a stone stairway gives it a noble demeanor. It was Queen Isabel Segunda who decreed that the Dominicans should build a church and monastery in San Germán. A rudimentary structure was built in 1609, replaced in 1692 by the structure that can still be seen today. (Sadly, the monastery was demolished in 1866, leaving only a vestige of its facade.) The Heaven's Gate Chapel now functions as a museum of religious art, displaying painted wooden statuary by Latin American and Spanish artists. ✉*East end of Plazuela Santo Domingo* ☎787/892–5845 ⊕*www. icp.gobierno.pr* ⚏*Free* ⊙ *Wed.–Sun. 8:30–noon and 1–4:15.*

WESTERN & CENTRAL PUERTO RICO
The Puerto Rico Tourism Company calls the western side of the island Porta del Sol and maintains a separate Web site to highlight travel options in the region (⇨ *Visitor Information in Puerto Rico Essentials, below*).

Bosque Estatal de Río Abajo. In the middle of karst country—a region of limestone deposits that is peppered with fissures, caves, and underground streams—the Río Abajo State Forest spans some 5,000 acres and includes huge bamboo stands and silk-cotton trees. Walking trails wind through the forest, which is one of the habitats of the rare Puerto Rican parrot. An information office is near the entrance, and a recreation area with picnic tables is farther down the road. ⊠ *Rte. 621, Km 4.4* ☎ *787/817–0984* ⊠ *Free* ⊘ *Daily dawn–dusk.*

Cabo Rojo. Named for the pinkish cliffs that surround it, Cabo Rojo was founded in 1771 as a port for merchant vessels—and for the smugglers and pirates who inevitably accompanied oceangoing trade. Today the region is known as a family resort destination, and many small, inexpensive hotels line its shores. Seaside settlements such as Puerto Real and Joyuda—the latter has a strip of more than 30 seafood restaurants overlooking the water—are found along the coast. Although you can hike in wildlife refuges at the outskirts of the town of Cabo Rojo, there aren't any area outfitters, so be sure to bring along water, sunscreen, and all other necessary supplies. The neoclassical Cabo Rojo Lighthouse marks the southwesternmost tip of the island.

16

Mayagüez. With a population of slightly more than 100,000, this is the largest city on Puerto Rico's west coast. Although bypassed by the mania for restoration that has spruced up Ponce and Old San Juan, Mayagüez is graced by some lovely turn-of-the-20th-century architecture, such as the landmark art deco Teatro Yagüez and the Plaza de Colón.

☺ Puerto Rico's only zoo, the 35-acre **Zoológico de Puerto Rico,** is just north of downtown. After $13 million in renovations, it's looking pretty spiffy. New on the scene is a 45-foot-tall aviary, which allows you to walk through a rain forest environment as tropical birds fly freely above your head. There's also a new butterfly park where you can let brilliant blue morphos land on your hand, and an arthropodarium where you can get up close and personal with spiders and their kin. There is a $2 charge for parking. ⊠ *Rte. 108, north of Rte. 65* ☎ *787/622–6330* ⊕ *www. parquesnacionalespr.com* ⊠ *$6* ⊘ *Wed.–Sun. 8:30–4.*

★ **Observatorio de Arecibo.** Hidden among pine-covered hills is the world's largest radar-radio telescope. Operated by the National Astronomy and Ionosphere Center of Cornell University, the 20-acre dish lies in a 563-foot-deep sinkhole in the karst landscape. If the 600-ton platform hovering eerily over the dish looks familiar, it may be because it can be glimpsed in scenes from the movie *Contact.* (And, yes, the dish has been used to search for extraterrestrial life.) ⊠ *Rte. 625, Km 3.0* ☎ *787/878–2612* ⊕ *www.naic.edu* ⊠ *$5* ⊘ *June, July, and mid-Dec.–mid-Jan., daily 9–4; mid-Jan.–May and Aug.–mid-Dec., Wed.–Fri. noon–4, weekends 9–4.*

★ **Parque Ceremonial Indígena de Caguana.** The 13 acres of this park were used more than 800 years ago by the Taíno tribes for worship and recreation, including a game—thought to have religious significance—that resembles modern-day soccer. Today you can see 10 *bateyes* (court-yards) of various sizes, large stone monoliths (some with petroglyphs), and re-creations of Taíno gardens. ⊠*Rte. 111, Km 12.3* ☎*787/894–7325* 🖃*$2* ⊙*Daily 8:30–4:30.*

⟳ **Parque de las Cavernas del Río Camuy.** This 268-acre park contains an
Fodor'sChoice enormous cave network and the third-longest underground river in the
★ world. A tram takes you down a trail shaded by bamboo and banana
trees to Cueva Clara, where the stalactites and stalagmites turn the
entrance into a toothy grin. Hour-long guided tours in English and
Spanish lead you on foot through the 180-foot-high cave, which is
teeming with wildlife. You're likely to find blue-eyed river crabs and
long-legged tarantulas. More elusive are the more than 100,000 bats
that make their home in the cave. They don't come out until dark,
but you can feel the heat they generate at the cave's entrance. Tours
are first-come, first-served; plan to arrive early on weekends, when
local families join the crowds. ⊠*Rte. 129, Km 18.9* ☎*787/898–3100*
🖃*$10* ⊙*Wed.–Sun. 8–4; last tour at 3:45.*

Rincón. Jutting out into the ocean along the rugged western coast,
Rincón, meaning "corner" in Spanish, may have gotten its name because
of how it is nestled in a corner of the coastline. The town jumped into
the surfing spotlight after hosting the World Surfing Championship in
1968. Although the beat here picks up from October through April,
when the waves are the best, Rincón, basically laid back and unpretentious, is seeing a lot of development. If you visit between December and
February you might get a glimpse of the humpback whales that winter
off the coast. Because of its unusual setting, Rincón's layout can be a
little disconcerting. The main road, Route 413, loops around the coast,
and many beaches and sights are on dirt roads intersecting it.

PUERTO RICO ESSENTIALS

To research prices, get advice from other travelers, and book travel arrangements, visit www.fodors.com.

▮ TRANSPORTATION

BY AIR

San Juan's busy Aeropuerto Internacional Luis Muñoz Marín has more nonstops than almost any other Caribbean destination. Because it's the Caribbean hub for American Eagle, San Juan is also a good spot from which to hop to other nearby Caribbean islands. Cape Air connects San Juan to St. Thomas and St. Croix. Seaborne Airlines has seaplanes departing from San Juan Piers 6 and 7 to St. Thomas and St. Croix.

Instead of transferring to nearby Aeropuerto Fernando L. Ribas Dominicci (close to Old San Juan and Condado) to take a flight to Vieques or Culebra, most travelers can now fly directly from the internatcional airport. Air Flamenco, Isla Nena Air Service, and Vieques Air Link offer daily flights from both airports in San Juan to Vieques and Culebra. Cape Air flies between the international airport and Vieques.

San Juan is no longer the only gateway into Puerto Rico. If you're headed to the western part of the island, you can fly directly into Aguadilla on either Continental or JetBlue. If the southern coast is your goal, JetBlue and Continental fly to Ponce from Newark.

Major Airlines American Airlines/American Eagle (☎800/433–7300 ⊕www.aa.com). **Continental** (☎800/231–0856 ⊕www.continental.com). **Delta** (☎800/221–1212 ⊕www.delta.com). **JetBlue** (☎800/538–2583 ⊕www.jetblue.com). **Spirit Air** (☎800/772–7117 ⊕www.spiritair.com). **United Airlines** (☎800/864–8331 ⊕www.united.com). **US Airways** (☎800/428–4322 ⊕www.usairways.com).

Regional Airlines Air Flamenco (☎787/724–1818 ⊕www.airflamenco.net). **Cape Air** (☎800/525–0714 ⊕www.flycapeair.com). **Isla Nena Air Service** (☎787/741–6362 or 877/812–5144 ⊕www.islanena.8m.com). **Seaborne Airlines** (☎888/359–8687 ⊕www.seaborneairlines.com). **Vieques Air Link** (☎787/741–8331 or 888/901–9247 ⊕www.vieques-island.com/val).

AIRPORTS & TRANSFERS

Aeropuerto Internacional Luis Muñoz Marín (SJU) is 20 minutes east of Old San Juan in the neighborhood of Isla Verde. San Juan's other airport is the small Fernando L. Ribas Dominicci Airport in Isla Grande (SIG), near the city's Miramar section. From either airport you can catch flights to Culebra, Vieques, and other destinations on Puerto Rico and throughout the Caribbean. (Note that although the Dominicci airport was still operating at this writing, its future was uncertain.) A taxi from the international airport to most parts of San Juan should cost $10 to $19. If you are staying in a hotel outside San Juan, check with your resort to see if it offers transfers; taxi rides outside the San Juan metro area can be very expensive.

Other Puerto Rican airports include Aeropuerto Internacional Rafael Hernández (BQN) in the northwestern town of Aguadilla, Aeropuerto Eugenio María de Hostos (MAZ) in the west-coast community of Mayagüez, Mercedita (PSE) in the south-coast town of Ponce, Aeropuerto Diego Jiménez Torres (FAJ) in the east-coast city of Fajardo, Antonio Rivera Rodríguez (VQS) on Vieques, and Aeropuerto Benjamin Rivera Noriega (CPX) on Culebra.

Information Aeropuerto Antonio Rivera Rodríguez (VQS ⊠Vieques ☎787/741–8358). **Aeropuerto Benjamin Rivera Noriega** (CPX ⊠Culebra ☎787/742–0022). **Aeropuerto Diego Jiménez Torres** (FAJ ⊠Fajardo ☎787/860–3110). **Aeropuerto Eugenio María de Hostos** (MAZ ⊠Mayagüez ☎787/833–0148). **Aeropuerto Fernando L. Ribas Dominicci** (SIG ⊠Isla Grande, San Juan ☎787/729–8711). **Aeropuerto Internacional Luis Muñoz Marín** (SJU ⊠Isla Verde, San Juan ☎787/791–3840). **Aeropuerto Mercedita** (PSE ⊠Ponce ☎787/842–6292). **Aeropuerto Rafael Hernández** (BQN ⊠Aguadilla ☎787/891–2286).

BY BOAT & FERRY

The Autoridad de los Puertos (Port Authority) ferry between Old San Juan (Pier 2) and Cataño costs a mere 50¢ one way. It runs every half hour from 6 AM to 10 PM and every 15 minutes during peak hours.

The Puerto Rico Ports Authority runs passenger ferries from Fajardo to Culebra and Vieques. Service is from the ferry terminal in Fajardo, about a 90-minute drive from San Juan. Advance reservations are not accepted. There are a limited number of seats on the ferries, so get to the terminal in plenty of time, an hour or more ahead of the departure time in Fajardo, somewhat less in Vieques and Culebra.

In Fajardo, the ticket counter is in the small building across the street from the actual terminal. In Vieques and Culebra, the ticket counters are at the entrance to the terminals. There are food kiosks at Fajardo and Vieques that are open even for the early-morning departures. Culebra doesn't have any eateries nearby. The Fajardo–Vieques passenger ferry departs from Vieques weekdays at 9 AM, 1 PM, 3 PM, 4:30 PM, and 8 PM, returning at 6:30 AM, 11 AM, 3 PM, and 6 PM. On weekends ferries depart from Vieques at 9 AM, 3 PM, and 6 PM, returning at 6:30 AM, 1 PM, and

16

4:30 PM. Tickets for the 90-minute journey are $2 each way. The Fajardo-Culebra ferry leaves Culebra daily at 9 AM, 3 PM, and 7 PM, returning at 6:30 AM, 1 PM, and 5 PM. The 90-minute trip is $2.25.

Information **Puerto Rico Ports Authority** (☎787/863-0705).

BY CAR

If you are staying in San Juan, it's more trouble than it's worth to rent a car. However, if you are staying elsewhere on the island, a car is probably a necessity. If you rent a car, a good road map will be helpful in remote areas. A valid driver's license from your country of origin can be used in Puerto Rico for three months. Rates start as low as $39 a day. Several well-marked multilane highways link population centers. Route 26 is the main artery through San Juan, connecting Condado and Old San Juan to Isla Verde and the airport. Route 22, which runs east–west between San Juan and Camuy, and Route 52, which runs north–south between San Juan and Ponce, are toll roads. Route 2, a smaller highway, travels west from San Juan toward Rincón, and Route 3 traverses east toward Fajardo. Route 3 can be mind-numbingly slow, so consider taking Route 66, a toll toad that bypasses the worst of the traffic. Distances are posted in kilometers (1.6 km to 1 mi), whereas speed limits are posted in miles per hour. Some roads in the mountains are very curvy and take longer to cover than the distance on a map might suggest. Most gas stations have both full- and self-service. Hours vary, but stations generally operate daily from early in the morning until 10 or 11 PM; in metro areas many are open 24 hours. Stations are few and far between in the central mountains and other rural areas; plan accordingly.

Major Agencies **Avis** (☎787/721-4499 in San Juan, 787/890-3311 in Aguadilla, 787/863-2735 in Fajardo, 787/833-7070 in Mayagüez). **Budget** (☎787/791-0600 in San Juan). **Hertz** (☎787/791-0840 in San Juan, 787/890-5650 in Aguadilla, 787/832-3314 in Mayagüez, 787/843-1658 in Ponce). **National** (☎787/791-1805 in San Juan). **Thrifty** (☎787/253-2525 in San Juan).

Local Agencies **Carlos Jeep Rental** (☎787/742-3514 in Culebra ⊕www.carlosjeeprental.com). **Charlie Car Rental** (☎787/791-1101 ⊕www.charliecars.com). **Martineau Car Rental** (☎787/741-0087 in Vieques ⊕www.martineaucarrental.com).

BY PUBLIC TRANSIT

The Autoridad Metropolitana de Autobuses (AMA) operates buses that thread through San Juan, running in exclusive lanes on major thoroughfares and stopping at signs marked PARADA. Destinations are indicated above the windshield. Bus B-21 runs through Condado all the way to Plaza Las Américas in Hato Rey. Bus A-5 runs from San Juan through Santurce and the beach area of Isla Verde. Fares are 75¢, and are paid in exact change upon entering the bus. Most buses are air-conditioned and have wheelchair lifts and lock-downs. There is no bus system covering the rest of the island. If you do not have a rental car, your best bet is to travel by públicos (shared vans), which usually hold 17 passengers. They have yellow license plates ending in "P" or "PD," and they scoot to towns throughout the island, stopping in each community's main plaza. They operate primarily during the day; routes and fares are fixed by the Public Service Commission, but schedules aren't set, so you have to call ahead.

Information **AMA** (☎787/767-7979). **Blue Line** (☎787/891-4550). **Choferes Unidos de Ponce** (☎787/764-0540). **Línea Boricua** (☎787/896-6755). **Línea Caborrojeña** (☎787/851-1252). **Línea Sultana** (☎787/765-9377).

BY TAXI

The Puerto Rico Tourism Company has instituted a well-organized taxi program. Taxis painted white and displaying the TAXI TURISTICO logo charge set rates depending on the destination; they run from the airport or the cruise-ship piers to Isla Verde, Condado/Ocean Park, and Old San Juan, with fixed "zone" rates ranging from $9 to $19. If you take a cab going somewhere outside the fixed zones, insist on setting the meter. City tours start at $30 per hour. Metered cabs authorized by the Public Service Commission start at $1 and charge 10¢ for every additional 1/13 mi. In other Puerto Rican towns, you can flag down cabs on the street, but it's easier to have your hotel call one for you. Either way, make sure the driver is clear on whether he or she will charge a flat rate or use a meter to determine the fare. In most places, the cabs are metered.

▮ CONTACTS & RESOURCES

BANKS & MONEY

Puerto Rico, as a commonwealth of the United States, uses the U.S. dollar as its official currency. Credit cards, including Diners Club and Discover, are widely accepted, especially in tourist areas. Automated Teller Machines are readily available and reliable in the cities; many are attached to banks, but you can also find them on the streets and in supermarkets. ATMs are found less frequently in rural areas. Look to local banks such as Banco Popular and First Bank. Citibank also has branches in San Juan, including a convenient Condado branch across from the Radisson Hotel.

ELECTRICITY

Puerto Rico uses the same electrical current as the U.S. mainland, namely 110 volts.

EMERGENCIES

Information Air Ambulance Service (☎787/756–3424 or 800/633–3590). **San Juan Tourist Zone Police** (☎787/726–7020, 787/726–7015 for Condado, 787/728–4770, 787/726–2981 for Isla Verde). **Travelers' Aid** (☎787/791–1034).

INTERNET, MAIL & SHIPPING

In Puerto Rico, Internet cafés are few and far between. If that weren't bad enough, many hotels have yet to install high-speed Internet access in their rooms. Your best bet is to use your hotel business center if you need to send an e-mail. Puerto Rico uses the U.S. postal system, and all addresses on the island carry zip codes. Major post-office branches can be found in most major cities and towns.

Information U.S. Postal Service (✉100 Paseo Colón, Old San Juan, San Juan ✉102 Calle Garrido Morales, Fajardo ✉94 Calle Atocha, Ponce ✉60 Calle McKinley, Mayagüez).

LANGUAGE

Puerto Rico is officially bilingual, but Spanish predominates, particularly outside the tourist areas of San Juan. Although English is widely spoken, you'll probably want to take a Spanish phrase book along on your travels about the island.

SAFETY

San Juan, like any other big city, has its share of petty crime, so guard your wallet or purse on the city streets. Although you certainly can—and should—explore the city and its beaches, use common sense. Don't leave anything unattended on the beach. Leave your valuables in the hotel safe, and stick to the fenced-in beach areas of your hotel. Always lock your car and stash valuables and luggage out of sight. Avoid deserted beaches at night.

TAXES

Accommodations incur a tax: for hotels with casinos it's 11%, for other hotels it's 9%, and for government-approved paradores it's 7%. Ask your hotel before booking. The tax, in addition to the standard 5% to 12% service charge or resort fee applied by most hotels, can add a hefty 20% or more to your bill. There's a 5.5% sales tax in Puerto Rico.

TELEPHONES

Most U.S. mobile phone users will not pay any roaming charges to use their phones in Puerto Rico, though you should confirm that with your company. Puerto Rico's area codes are 787 and 939. Toll-free numbers (prefix 800, 888,

16

or 877) are widely used in Puerto Rico, and many can be accessed from North America (and vice versa). For North Americans, dialing Puerto Rico is the same as dialing another U.S. state or a Canadian province. To make a local call in Puerto Rico you must dial 1, the area code, and the seven-digit number. For international calls, dial 011, the country code, the city code, and the number. Dial 00 for an international long-distance operator. Phone cards are not required but can be useful and are widely available (most drugstores carry them).

TIPPING

Tips are expected, and appreciated, by restaurant waitstaff (15% to 20% if a service charge isn't included), hotel porters ($1 per bag), maids ($1 to $2 a day), and taxi drivers (15% to 18%).

VISITOR INFORMATION

The Puerto Rico Tourism Company has offices at the airports in San Juan and Aguadilla, as well as downtown offices in San Juan, Cabo Rojo, and Ponce.

Before You Leave **Puerto Rico Tourism Company** (☎787/721–2400 or 800/866–7827 ⊕www.gotopuertorico.com).

In Puerto Rico **Culebra Tourism Office** (✉250 Calle Pedro Marquez, Dewey, Culebra ☎787/742–3521). **Fajardo Tourism Office** (✉6 Av. Muñoz Rivera ☎787/863–4013 Ext. 274). **Ponce Municipal Tourist Office** (✉Parque de Bombas, Plaza las Delicias, Ponce ☎787/841–8160). **Puerto Rico Tourism Company** (✉La Casita, Plaza Dársenas, Old San Juan ☎787/722–1709 ✉Aeropuerto Internacional Luis Muñoz Marín ☎787/791–1014 or 787/791–2551 ✉Rte. 100, Km 13.7, Cabo Riojo ☎787/851–7070 ✉9192 Calle Marina, Ponce ☎787/843–0465 ✉Rafael Hernández Airport, Aguadilla ☎787/890–3315). **Vieques Tourism Office** (✉449 Calle Carlos Lebrón, Isabel Segunda, Vieques ☎787/741–5000).

WEDDINGS

If you wish to get married in Puerto Rico, you must get an application from the Demographic Registry Office. There are no special residency requirements, but U.S. citizens must produce a driver's license and non-U.S. citizens must produce a valid passport for identification purposes. If either the bride or groom was previously married, certified copies of a divorce decree or death certificate must be produced as well as a medical certificate. The filing cost is $20. Blood tests are required and must be done within 10 days of the marriage ceremony. The results must be certified and signed by a doctor or hotel physician in Puerto Rico. The cost for the laboratory test in Puerto Rico is about $15 to $25. Both parties must appear at the City Court office to purchase a marriage license. Marriages may then be performed by a judge or any clergyman. The marriage fee is usually between $150 and $350. Most large hotels on the island have marriage coordinators, who can explain the necessary paperwork and help you complete it on time for your marriage ceremony.

Information **Demographic Registry Office** (✉Box 11854, Fernandez Juncos Station, San Juan 00910 ☎787/767–9120).

Saba

Yellow goatfish

WORD OF MOUTH

"Mountainous, lush, quiet, friendly. Great diving, no beaches. Interesting landing and takeoff—very sporting!"

—RoamsAround

"The absolute best [place to dive] that you should not miss is Saba. Just take a small plane, a 10-minute flight from St. Martin to Saba, and dive this sight called Diamond Rock. AMAZING! We saw shark, barracuda, stingray, and tons more. Saba ranks up there with Bonaire in my book."

—MidwestDiver

WELCOME TO SABA

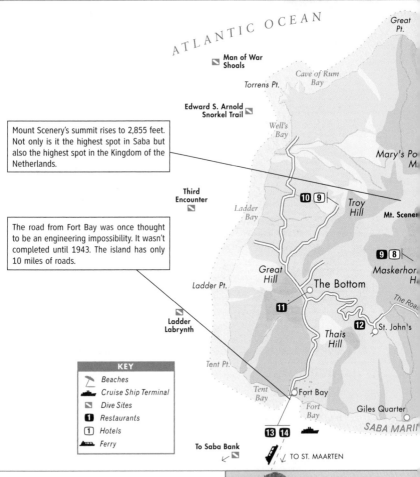

ATLANTIC OCEAN

Great Pt.

Man of War Shoals

Cave of Rum Bay

Torrens Pt.

Edward S. Arnold Snorkel Trail

Well's Bay

Mary's Po M

Mount Scenery's summit rises to 2,855 feet. Not only is it the highest spot in Saba but also the highest spot in the Kingdom of the Netherlands.

Third Encounter

Ladder Bay

10 **9**

Troy Hill

Mt. Scener

The road from Fort Bay was once thought to be an engineering impossibility. It wasn't completed until 1943. The island has only 10 miles of roads.

9 **8**

Maskerhor H

Great Hill

Ladder Pt.

The Bottom

11

The Road

12 St. John's

Ladder Labrynth

Thais Hill

Tent Pt.

KEY

⤢	Beaches
⛴	Cruise Ship Terminal
◪	Dive Sites
1	Restaurants
①	Hotels
⛴	Ferry

Tent Bay

Fort Bay

Fort Bay

Giles Quarter

SABA MARI

13 **14** ⛴

To Saba Bank

TO ST. MAARTEN

Mountainous Saba's precipitous terrain allows visitors to choose between the heights and the depths. The Bottom, the island's capital, was once thought to be the crater of a dormant volcano, from which a trail of 400 rough-hewn steps drops to the sea. Divers can take a different plunge to view the pristine reefs.

THE UNSPOILED QUEEN

Tiny Saba—a dormant volcano that juts out of the ocean to a height of 2,855 feet—is just 5 square mi (13 square km) in size and has a population of about 1,500. One of the Netherlands Antilles, it's 28 mi (45 km) south of St. Maarten and surrounded by some of the richest dive sites in the Caribbean.

Saba's tiny airport, which is built on the only part of the island that's flat enough to accommodate it, has one of the world's shortest runways.

Hotels	▼
Cottage Club	3
Ecolodge Rendez-Vous	8
Gate House	1
Juliana's Hotel	5
El Momo	4
Queen's Garden Resort	9
Mountain Spring Villas	6
Scout's Place	2
Willard's of Saba	7

Restaurants	▼
Brigadoon	4
Family Deli/Bakery	11
Gate House Café	1
In Two Deep	13
King's Crown	12
Lollipop's	11
My Kitchen	6
Pop's Place	14
Rainforest Restaurant	9
Saba's Treasure	2
Scout's Place	3
Swinging Doors	7
Tropics Cafe	5
Willard's of Saba	8

17

SABA

TOP 4 REASONS TO VISIT SABA

① Divers flock to Saba for the clear water and spectacular ocean life.

② Hikers can climb the island's pinnacle, Mount Scenery, but even the less intense trails offer just as many sweeping vistas.

③ Saba reminds you of what the Caribbean used to be: locals are genuine and the tourist traps nonexistent.

④ Several hotels, whose resident nature pros can tell you every thing about local flora and fauna cater to ecotourists.

SABA PLANNER

Island Activities

Forget the beach because there isn't one. Abundant **reefs,** however, are a different story altogether. The island is surrounded by—and zealously preserves—myriad extraordinary **dive sites.** If you don't dive, there are plenty of shallow reefs you can explore by **snorkel.**

If you're not into the briny deep, there's always the **hike** to the top of Mt. Scenery, a breathtaking trip to an even better view, assuming the top isn't shrouded in cloud cover.

Otherwise, it's a very quiet and peaceful place and not a half-bad destination if all you want to do is relax and chat with the ever-friendly locals.

On the Ground

Upon arrival, you can take a taxi from the airport to Hell's Gate for $6, to Windwardside for $8, and to the Bottom for $12.50. While you can rent a car for about ($50 per day, including a full tank of gas and unlimited mileage), few tourists bother; taking the occasional taxi or walking (or even hitch-hiking) is the method of choice. Though if you dare to drive the hairpin turns of the island's road (known as the Road), you won't get lost because there's only one.

Logistics

Getting to Saba: Only one airline (Winair) flies to Saba (SAB), and then only from St. Eustatius and St. Maarten. You can also take *The Edge* or *Dawn II* ferries from St. Maarten; the trip, which takes more than an hour, can be rough and costs $60 round-trip. The ferry schedules are geared to day-trippers, so you must spend a night before and after your Saba stay on St. Maarten.

Hassle Factor: Medium–High.

Nonstops: None.

Where to Stay

Saba's few hotel rooms are primarily in a handful of friendly, tidy inns, or guesthouses perched on ledges or tucked into tropical gardens. Because the island is so small, it doesn't much matter where you stay. Among the choices are one luxury boutique hotel and a couple of splendid, small eco-resorts. There are also more than a dozen apartments, cottages, and villas for rent.

Hotel & Restaurant Costs

⇨*For information on hotel meal plans, see Accommodations in Caribbean Essentials.*

WHAT IT COSTS IN U.S. DOLLARS				
$$$$	**$$$**	**$$**	**$**	**¢**
Restaurants				
over $30	$20–$30	$12–$20	$8–$12	under $8
Hotels*				
over $350	$250–$350	$150–$250	$80–$150	under $80
Hotels**				
over $450	$350–$450	$250–$350	$125–$250	under $125

*EP, BP, CP **AI, FAP, MAP Restaurant prices are for a main course and do not include customary 10%–15% service charge. Hotel prices are for two people in a double room in high season and do not include 8% tax, 10%–15% service charge, or meal plans.

By Katherine
Dykstra

THE SUN IS STILL LOW when I set out to conquer the 1,064 steps that spiral up Mt. Scenery to Saba's summit, with a peak cloaked in a dense, gray haze. The island is so wet that it creates its own clouds, and the crest of Mt. Scenery is almost always overcast. As I climb, the humidity intensifies, and the moss-covered stairs get steeper. It takes me nearly an hour to reach the top, and then something amazing happens. As I look down on the cloud, it miraculously parts, and I find the entire island stretched out before me: sweeping precipices, red roofs huddled together in each of the four villages, the single road that snakes between them, the steeple on the little yellow church. And just as quickly as the cloud parted, it rolls over again. I am left with the feeling that I've seen something very special. It's the very same feeling most people get upon discovering this remote Caribbean island.

One of the Netherlands Antilles, tropical Saba (pronounced *say*-ba) explodes out of the Caribbean Sea just south of St. Maarten (if you've seen the original *King Kong,* you'll recognize its majestic silhouette from the beginning of the film), but the island couldn't be more different. While St. Maarten is all beaches, gambling, and duty-free shopping, Saba is ecotourism, diving, and hiking.

Nearly half of Saba's 5 square mi (13 square km) are covered in verdant tropical rain forest; the other half is sprinkled with petite hamlets composed of white, green-shuttered houses trimmed in gingerbread, roofed in red, and built on grades so steep they seem to defy physics. Flower-draped walls and neat picket fences border narrow paths among the bromeliads, palms, hibiscus, orchids, and Norfolk Island pines. The land dips and climbs à la San Francisco and eventually drops off into sheer cliffs that fall right into the ocean, the fodder for some of the world's most striking dive sites and the primary reason for Saba's cultlike following. Divers seem to relish the fact that they're in on Saba's secret.

17

But word is slowly getting out. Every year more and more tourists are turned on to Saba's charms and make the 11-minute, white-knuckle flight from St. Maarten into the tiny airport (barely the size of an aircraft carrier's, the airstrip is one of the shortest in the world). Indeed, traffic jams along the winding, narrow road (yes, there's really just one) are no longer unheard of. The past few years have seen the opening of a day spa, as well as more restaurants (big advances considering around-the-clock electricity was established only in 1970). But don't fear you will find a booming metropolis; even as it changes, Saba retains an old-world charm.

A major point of local pride is that many Saban families can be traced all the way back to the island's settlement in 1640 (the surnames Hassell, Johnson, and Peterson fill the tiny phone book). And Sabans hold their traditions dear. Saba lace—a genteel art that dates back to the 1870s—is still hand-stitched by local ladies who, on the side, also distill potent, 151-proof Saba Spice, which is for sale in most of the island's mom-and-pop shops. Families follow the generations-old tradition of burying their dead in their neatly tended gardens.

Like the residents of most small towns, the Sabans are a tight-knit group; nothing happens without everyone hearing about it, making crime pretty much a nonissue. But they are eager to welcome newcomers and tend to make travelers feel less like tourists and more like old friends. After all, they're proud to show off their home, which they lovingly call "the unspoiled queen."

WHERE TO STAY

Cable TV is common, but air-conditioning is a rarity.

$$$–$$$$ ⬚ **Willard's of Saba.** Getting to this lavish cliff-side hotel, which literally clings to the mountain 2,000 feet straight up, is no small feat (many a car has had to give up halfway and roll right back down, and most cabs won't even attempt it). However, you may take heart, because once here, you'll have little reason to leave. Among the terraced bungalows you'll find a massage room, hot tub, solar-heated pool, and the only tennis court on the island, not to mention the most stunning views on Saba. We're talking more than 180 degrees. Happily, it's worth almost every penny of the pricey rates. **Pros:** Panoramic views, on-site fitness room, spacious suites. **Cons:** Far from town, expensive rates, scatter-shot lounge. ⌂ *Box 515, Windwardside* ☎ *599/416–2498* ⊕ *www. willardsofsaba.com* ⬚ *9 suites* ⬚ *In-room: no a/c, no TV (some). In-hotel: restaurant, bar, tennis court, pool, gym, no elevator, public Wi-Fi* ⊟ *AE, D, MC, V* ⦿ *EP.*

$$–$$$$ ⬚ **Queen's Garden Resort.** If romance is on the agenda, this is your resort.
★ A quaint stone stairway winds up past the largest pool on the island, all the way to the patio in front of the main building, which houses the King's Crown restaurant. At night, tiki torches flicker and dense foliage gives everything an air of intimacy. That's if you can bear to leave your room: all 12 are decorated dreamily with Dutch colonial and Indonesian furnishings and bestowed with four-poster beds. Be sure to request one of the nine hot-tub suites that open up to panoramic vistas of the village below. **Pros:** Pool bar, private Jacuzzis with sweeping views, rare parking lot. **Cons:** Occasional parties can equal loud and crowded, ever-changing management, ever-changing restaurant staff. ⌂ *1 Troy Hill Dr., Box 4, Troy Hill* ☎ *599/416–3494 or 599/416–3496* ⊕ *www. queenssaba.com* ⬚ *12 suites* ⬚ *In-room: no a/c, safe, kitchen (some). In-hotel: restaurant, bar, pool, no elevator* ⊟ *AE, MC, V* ⦿ *EP.*

$–$$ ⬚ **Juliana's Hotel.** Aesthetics meets affordability here, and this applies to
☺ more than just the reasonable room rates. Everything seems to encom-
★ pass both practicality and pampering. On one side of the hotel, there's the hill that leads to Windwardside's bustling Main Street; on the other, sweeping views of tropical flora end in glimmering blue. Rooms have Wi-Fi service to keep you in touch and balcony hammocks to make you wonder why you want to be. Air-conditioning (Juliana's is one of the few places on the island that has it) and a game room for the kids is the icing on the cake. **Pros:** Across the street from Tropics Café; outdoor, in-rock shower in Orchid Cottage; two on-site computers with free Internet. **Cons:** Close quarters, a hike to get off the property, next door

to ruins of the hurricane-destroyed Captain's Quarters hotel. ⊠ *Wind-wardside* ☎*599/416–2269* ⊕*www.julianas-hotel.com* ⇔*9 rooms, 1 apartment, 2 cottages* ⚬*In-room: a/c (some), refrigerator, Wi-Fi. In-hotel: restaurant, pool, no elevator* ▭*MC, V* ⓞ*BP.*

$ 🏨 **Cottage Club.** Form follows function at these gingerbread bungalows, where the price is right and the proximity to downtown is ideal. Bungalows sprawl down the side of the mountain, affording a bird's-eye view of the surf crashing into the rocks hundreds of feet below. (Nos. 1, 2, and 6 have the most-striking vistas.) The pool is tucked away in the trees, giving it the feel of a true tropical hideaway. Inside, queen-size beds (one room has a king) hang out in scarcely decorated rooms, which come complete with kitchens. **Pros:** Walking distance to Windwardside, lushly landscaped pool, majestic lobby/reception room. **Cons:** Stark suites, no on-site dining. ⊠ *Windwardside* ☎*599/416–2486 or 599/416–2386* ⊕*www.cottage-club.com* ⇔*10 cottages* ⚬*In-room: no a/c, kitchen. In-hotel: pool, no elevator* ▭*AE, D, MC, V* ⓞ*EP.*

$ 🏨 **Ecolodge Rendez-Vous.** If you're serious about getting back to nature, this inn, buried deep in the rain forest, is for you. The lodge is completely solar powered, which means sun showers, no television, and candlelight after dark. A recent renovation added two hot tubs to the property, making a total of four. The 12 cottages contain only the basics (their charm comes from ornate nature-theme wall paintings done by local artist and owner Heleen Cornet). Interspersed among them are herb and vegetable gardens, whose produce is used in the Rainforest Restaurant. A swimming pool—cleaned, of course, with an environmentally sensitive process—and on-site sweat lodge are two more means of relaxation. **Pros:** Candlelit Rainforest Restaurant serves three meals a day, nature-theme cottages, no electricity (good for eco-tourists). **Cons:** Hike to get there, no ocean views, no electricity (not so good for those with electronics). ⊠ *Crispeen Track, Windwardside* ☎*599/416–3348* ⊕*www.ecolodge-saba.com* ⇔*12 cottages* ⚬*In-room: no a/c, no phone, kitchen (some), no TV. In-hotel: restaurant, no elevator* ▭*AE, D, MC, V* ⓞ*EP.*

$ 🏨 **Gate House.** Aptly named, the Gate House rests in Lower Hell's Gate, the Saban equivalent of the suburbs. The rooms are as good an option as any in their price range but are relatively nondescript. The hotel's two high points, however, come in the form of a great French restaurant (the Gate House Café has fare so fine you won't want to eat anywhere else, though the prices might force you to) and the villa, an eight-person enclave nestled among banana trees just down the hill from the main house. The rustic hideaway has a spacious, comfortable living area and its own private pool. Owner Michel is known for taxiing his guests all over the island. **Pros:** Secluded private villa, outdoor terrace perfect for an evening cocktail, attentive on-site owners. **Cons:** Pool area is small, pool furniture scarce, far from everything. ⊠ *Hell's Gate* ☎*599/416–2416* ⊕*www.sabagatehouse.com* ⇔*5 rooms, 1 cottage, 1 villa* ⚬*In-room: no a/c, no TV (some). In-hotel: restaurant, pool, no elevator* ▭*D, MC, V* ⓞ*CP.*

$ 🏨 **Mountain Spring Villas.** In 2005, El Momo's *(⇨below)*owners branched out and up by opening three villas just a short drive up Booby

17

Hill from their original establishment. Though the villas boast the same views as their sibling, with modern amenities like cable TV, ceiling fans, and full kitchens, you won't feel quite as far from home. With three bedrooms, the villas sleep six and are priced both by day and by week for longer sojourns. Visitors have access to El Momo's pool, snack bar, and hammocks. **Pros:** Good for groups, sweeping views, private drive. **Cons:** A strenuous hike to reach, small (900 square feet) for six people, little tropical foliage on the property. ⊠ *Booby Hill* ⌂ *Box 542, Windwardside* ☎ *599/416–2265* ⊕ *www.mountainspringvillas.com* ➳ *3 villas* ⌂ *In-room: no a/c, kitchen, refrigerator. In-hotel: pool, no elevator* ⊟ *AE, D, MC, V* ⊚ *EP.*

$ ⌕ **Scout's Place.** Owned by German dive masters Wolfgang and Barbara Tooten, this all-in-one, no-frills dive resort is especially good for the diver on a tight budget. The finned set will find everything they need: simple accommodations, expert instruction, special packages with Saba Divers, decent grub, and a little late-night fun (people come in droves for Friday-night karaoke)—and all for exactly the right price. In addition to the rooms, for $195 a night in high season you can opt for the two-bedroom cottage with full kitchen and living room. **Pros:** On-site dive shop, multilingual owners, karaoke on Friday. **Cons:** Smallish rooms, some don't get much sunlight, karaoke on Friday. ⊠ *Windwardside* ☎ *599/416–2740* ⊕ *www.scoutsplace.com* ➳ *13 rooms, 1 2-bedroom cottage* ⌂ *In-room: no a/c, kitchen (some), refrigerator (some), Wi-Fi. In-hotel: restaurant, bar, pool, diving, no elevator* ⊟ *MC, V* ⊚ *CP.*

¢–$ ⌕ **El Momo.** If you want to feel as if you're doing your ecological part without giving up every modern convenience, consider these tiny cottages. They're hidden among tropical flora 1,500 feet up Booby Hill. All but two have their own bathrooms, and heated showers are available in addition to solar ones. Take in the view from a hammock in the vegetarian snack bar, or lounge by the pool, which has the only bridge on the island. And be sure to pick up a bottle of the homemade banana rum on your way out; it makes a great gift, or sedative for the flight home. **Pros:** Snack bar/lounge with hammock, cottages buried in the woods, smoke-free property. **Cons:** Tiny accommodations, some shared bathrooms, strenuous hike to get there. ⊠ *Booby Hill* ⌂ *Box 542, Windwardside* ☎ *599/416–2265* ⊕ *www.elmomo.com* ➳ *7 cottages, 5 with bath* ⌂ *In-room: no a/c, kitchen (some), no TV, Wi-Fi. In-hotel: pool, no elevator, no-smoking rooms* ⊟ *AE, D, MC, V* ⊚ *EP.*

WHERE TO EAT

The island might be petite, but there's no shortage of mouthwatering fare from French to fresh seafood to Caribbean specialties. Reservations are necessary, as most of the restaurants are quite small. In addition, some places provide transportation.

WHAT TO WEAR

Restaurants are informal. Shorts are fine during the day, but for dinner you may want to put on slacks or a casual sundress. Just remember that nights in Windwardside can be cool due to the elevation.

CARIBBEAN ✕**Lollipop's.** The expansive view from the wall-to-wall windows more
$–$$$ than makes up for the restaurant's minimal decor. At dinnertime you'll
find a decently priced menu that consists primarily of seafood and vege-
tarian dishes. For Sunday brunch, the best reason to venture here, there
are eggs Benedict, salt fish, johnnycakes, crabmeat, ribs, chicken—the
list goes on and on, and all for $10. The restaurant offers both takeout
and longer weekend hours (9 PM–2 AM) than most other eateries on the
island, but late night is party time, and the place is likely to be packed
to the gills. ⊠*St. John's* ☎*599/416–3330* ▤*MC, V* ⊘*Closed Mon.*

$ ✕**Family Deli/Bakery.** When you get past its rather unimpressive name,
you'll find that this local favorite is beloved for a reason. From the
verandah, which overlooks the bustling main drag, you can get a flavor
for the Bottom at night as you sip Heineken, the island's unofficial beer,
and sup on just-caught seafood. Coconut shrimp and conch stew are
two of the specialties. Or visit during the day for fresh breads, cakes,
and pastries. ⊠*The Bottom* ☎*559/416–3858* ▤*MC, V.*

¢–$ ✕**Pop's Place.** Directly on the water overlooking the pier in Fort Bay is
this itty-bitty come-as-you-are, Caribbean-flavor shack. Inside you'll
find three tables, a tiny bar, and reggae music to really put you in the
mood. Watch the divers come in as you eat lobster sandwiches, the
absolute best on the island. ⊠*Fort Bay* ☎*599/416–3480* ▤*No credit
cards* ⊘*Closed Mon.*

ECLECTIC ✕**Willard's of Saba.** Saba's most expensive restaurant has views of the
$$$–$$$$ sea, a dizzying 2,000 feet below. An enthusiastic, charming cook, Cora-
zon de Johnson fuses international and Asian cuisine. If you miss the
sunset, ask to see her photos of the famous green flash. (She loves to
share when she has time.) Access to the restaurant is up a steep drive;
only a few taxis will make the climb, but you can call the restaurant
to arrange transport. ⊠*Windwardside* ☎*599/416–2498* ▤*AE, D,
MC, V.*

$$–$$$ ✕**King's Crown.** This dimly lighted, highly romantic restaurant is known
for its Saban lobster and tilapia. Come early for cocktails at the out-
door bar, which overlooks the pool—and, below that, the ocean—then
stay late to dance under the stars. Poolside parties, musical events, and
theme nights with international flavors spice things up. At this writing,
the restaurant was due to get a new chef (and a brand-new menu) in
2008. ⊠*1 Troy Hill Dr., Troy Hill* ☎*599/416–3623* ▤*AE, MC, V*
⊘*Closed Tues.*

$$–$$$ ✕**My Kitchen/Mijn Keuken.** Straight from Holland, the owner of this
relaxed restaurant in the heart of town has concocted a seafood-heavy
menu complete with a rotating list of specials determined by the season
and whether the supply boat from St. Maarten was able to dock that
week. The coconut shrimp, crab cakes, and escargots stand out. All
seating is outdoors on the rooftop, allowing you to peer down on the
main drag below or up through latticework to the stars. ⊠*Windward-
side* ☎*599/416–2539* ▤*MC, V* ⊘*Closed Sun.*

$–$$$ ✕**Brigadoon.** Just as many people visit this local favorite for the excep-
★ tional fare as for the entertaining atmosphere, which stars eccentric
co-owner Trish Chammaa, who entertains with jokes and brassy ban-
ter. Trish's husband slaves over supper in the back, and the result is a

17

perfect gastronomic experience. The varied menu includes fresh Saban lobster and a well-priced schwarma plate. The homemade desserts are decadent. ⊠ *Windwardside* ☎ *599/416–2380* ▭ *AE, DC, MC, V* ⊘ *Closed Tues. No lunch.*

$–$$$ ✕ **Scout's Place.** With a new chef at this spacious, oft-hopping restaurant and bar, the food, which runs the gamut from goat stew to spit-roasted chicken, is even better than in years past. And, there's another great reason to come here: the atmosphere. Locals flock to Scout's Place on Friday for karaoke, and there's bound to be a group looking for fun every other night of the week. Sit on the outdoor verandah, which has stunning views of the water, the tiny houses, and the lush forest that make Saba so picturesque. ⊠ *Scout's Place, Windwardside* ☎ *599/416–2740* ▭ *MC, V.*

$$ ✕ **Rainforest Restaurant.** You need a flashlight for the 10-minute hike
★ down the Crispeen Track, by way of the Mt. Scenery Trail, to find this restaurant in the middle of the rain forest. Once you arrive you'll feel you're truly away from it all. Fresh seafood is always available, vegetables are picked fresh from the restaurant's own garden, and the steaks are huge. On Wednesday you can enjoy a guided ecological tour of the island via a slide show while you sup. There's no need for music—the lilting sound of the tree frogs is concert enough. ⊠ *Ecolodge Rendez-Vous, Crispeen Track, Windwardside* ☎ *599/416–3888* ▭ *AE, D, MC, V.*

$–$$ ✕ **Swinging Doors.** A cross between an English pub and an Old West
★ saloon (yes, there are swinging doors), this lively watering hole serves not-to-be-missed barbecue on Tuesday and Friday nights. Pick from ribs, chicken, or ribs and chicken, and don't forget to ask for peanut sauce—you'll be glad you did. Expect plenty of conversation, including some local gossip. ⊠ *Windwardside* ☎ *599/416–2506* ▭ *No credit cards.*

$–$$ ✕ **Tropics Cafe.** Breakfast and lunch are served beside the pool at Juliana's Hotel or in the cabana-style, open-air dining room. The café is owned by the same couple that owns the hotel. Sandwiches, salads, and fresh fish dominate the menu. Two nights a week, Tropics serves dinner. Wednesday is Caribbean night, featuring fresh fish and goat stew. Or go on Friday and for $10 you can bite into a burger and catch a screening of a recently released movie, romantically projected onto a sheet strung up just beyond the pool. ⊠ *Windwardside* ☎ *599/416–2469* ▭ *MC, V* ⊘ *Closed Mon. No dinner Tues., Thurs., or weekends.*

$ ✕ **In Two Deep.** The owners of the Saba Deep dive shop run this lively harborside spot, with its stained-glass window and mahogany bar. The soups and sandwiches (especially the Reuben) are excellent, and the customers are usually high-spirited—most have just come from a dive. Dinner is served on holidays. ⊠ *Fort Bay* ☎ *599/416–3438* ▭ *MC, V* ⊘ *No dinner.*

¢–$ ✕ **Saba's Treasure.** Right in the heart of Windwardside sits this relaxed restaurant whose interior is crafted to look like the interior of a ship. Outside you practically sit on the street (grab one of these chairs for maximum local flavor). Go for a quick meal of stone-oven pizza, the best on the island, or linger over a drink at the tiny bar. ⊠ *Windward-side* ☎ *599/416–2819* ▭ *AE, MC, V* ⊘ *Closed Sun.*

FRENCH   ✕**Gate House Café.** It's well worth the trip to this out-of-the-way loca-
$$–$$$$ tion to sample self-taught chef Michel Job's delicious French cuisine. To
★   complement his entrées, from both land and sea, choose from the extensive wine list, winner of awards from *Wine Spectator* for six years running. Go early for cocktails on the verandah overlooking the ocean and stay late to enjoy Job's flourless Death by Chocolate, which he makes from scratch. Lunch and dinner are served seven days a week, and pickup service is available. ⊠ *Gate House Hotel, Hell's Gate* ☎ *599/416–2416* ▭ *D, MC, V.*

SPORTS & THE OUTDOORS

DIVING & SNORKELING

Fodor'sChoice   Saba is one of the world's premier scuba-diving destinations. Visibil-
★   ity is extraordinary, and dive sites are alive with corals and other sea creatures. Within 0.5 mi (0.75 km) of shore, seawalls drop to depths of more than 1,000 feet. The Saba National Marine Park, which includes shoals, reefs, and seawalls alive with corals and other sea creatures, is dedicated to preserving its marine life.

17

Divers have a pick of 28 sites, including **Third Encounter,** a top-rated pinnacle dive (usually to about 110 feet) for advanced divers, with plentiful fish and spectacular coral; **Man of War Shoals,** another hot pinnacle dive (70 feet), with outstanding fish and coral varieties; and **Ladder Labyrinth,** a formation of ridges and alleys (down to 80 feet), where likely sightings include grouper, sea turtles, and sharks.

Snorkelers need not feel left out: the marine park has several marked spots where reefs or rocks sit in shallow water. Among these sites is **Torrens Point** on the northwest side of the island. Waterproof maps are available from the marine park, the Saba Conservation Foundation, or dive shops.

Expect to pay about $50 for a one-tank dive, around $90 for a two-tank dive. If you're looking for a more-intimate dive experience, try **Saba Deep** (⊠ *Fort Bay* ☎ *599/416–3347* ▭ *599/416–3497* ⊕ *www.sabadeep.com*), which tends to take out smaller groups. The company offers PADI- and/or NAUI-certified instructors. Owned by German divers, **Saba Divers** (⊠ *Windwardside* ☎ *599/416–2740* ⊕ *www.sabadivers.com*) offers multilingual instruction, making this a great option for anyone interested in meeting international divers or in practicing their language skills. It's the only outfit on the island that allows its customers to dive Nitrox for free. **Sea Saba** (⊠ *Windwardside* ☎ *599/416–2246* ⊕ *www.seasaba.com*) will take up to 10 divers out on one of two 40-foot boats; each excursion is accompanied by at least two dive instructors. The staff is both knowledgeable and jovial, making a day on the boat an illuminating and enjoyable experience for any diver.

Every October since 2003, local dive operator Lynn Costenaro, of Sea Saba, orchestrates an event that has become an international attraction. **Sea and Learn** (🕾 *599/416–2246* ⊕*www.seaandlearn.org*) is when pharmacologists, biologists, and other nature experts from all over the world descend on Saba to give presentations, lead field trips, and show off research projects, all of which are designed to increase environmental awareness. Past events have included monitoring undersea octopus checkpoints and studying the medicinal value of indigenous plants. There are even special events for kids. And best of all, it's free. You can sign up online.

HEALTH CLUBS & DAY SPAS

Saba Day Spa (⊠ *Windwardside* 🕾*599/416–3488*) has cozy facilities above Swinging Doors in Windwardside. Owner Sally Myers's expert hands (she was certified in the United States) more than make up for the small size of the establishment. Get a 50-minute massage or minifacial for $60. Appointments are necessary.

HIKING

On Saba you can't avoid hiking, even if you just go to mail a postcard. The big deal, of course, is Mt. Scenery, with 1,064 steps leading to its top. For information about Saba's 18 recommended botanical hikes, check with the **Saba Conservation Foundation** (⊠ *Fort Bay* 🕾*599/416–3295* ⊠*Trail Shop, Windwardside* 🕾*599/416–2630* ⊕*www.sabapark.org*), which maintains trails, or at the foundation's shop in Windwardside. Botanical tours are available on request. Crocodile James (James Johnson) will explain the local flora and fauna. A guided, strenuous, full-day hike through the undeveloped back side of Mt. Scenery costs about $50.

SHOPPING

The history of Saba lace, one of the island's most popular goods, goes back to the late 19th century. Gertrude Johnson learned lace making at a Caracas convent school. She returned to Saba in the 1870s and taught the art that has endured ever since. Saban ladies display and sell their creations at the community center in Hell's Gate and from their houses; just follow the signs. Collars, tea towels, napkins, and other small articles are relatively inexpensive; larger ones, such as tablecloths, can be pricey. The fabric requires some care—it's not drip-dry. Saba Spice is another island buy. Although it *sounds* as delicate as lace and the aroma is as sweet as can be, the base for this liqueur is 151-proof rum. You can find souvenirs, gifts, and *Saban Cottages: A Book of Watercolors*, in almost every shop.

El Momo Folk Art's (⊠ *Windwardside* 🕾*599/416–2518*) shelves overflow with regional crafts, local postcards, handmade jewelry, knickknacks and anything else El Momo can find a spot for.

JoBean Glass (☎599/416–2490) sells intricate handmade glass-bead jewelry as well as sterling silver and gold pieces by artist-owner Jo Bean. She also offers workshops in beadwork.

★ From watercolors of local houses to ocean-inspired sculpture, the **Peanut Gallery** (⊠ *Windwardside* ☎599/416–2509) offers the island's best selection of local and Caribbean art. Take time to browse through the offerings, and you might just walk away with something better than a refrigerator magnet with which to remember your trip.

★ The **Saba Artisan Foundation** (⊠*The Bottom* ☎599/416–3260) turns out hand-screened fabrics that you can buy by the yard or that are already made into resort clothing. It's also a central location where you can buy the famous Saba lace as well as T-shirts and spices.

Sea Saba (⊠ *Windwardside* ☎599/416–2246) carries T-shirts, diving equipment, clothing, and books.

NIGHTLIFE

Check the bulletin board in each village for a list of events, which often include parties. **Scout's Place** (⊠ *Windwardside* ☎599/416–2740) is a popular evening gathering place. The convivial bar can get crowded, and sometimes there's dancing. Go on Friday for karaoke night, when people swarm the spacious dining area. **Lollipops** (⊠*St. John's* ☎599/416–3330) is also busy late night.

17

EXPLORING SABA

Getting around the island means negotiating the narrow, twisting roadway that clings to the mountainside and rises from sea level to almost 2,000 feet. Although driving isn't difficult, just be sure to go slowly and cautiously. If in doubt, leave the driving to a cabbie so you can enjoy the scenery.

The Bottom. Sitting in a bowl-shape valley 820 feet above the sea, this town is the seat of government and the home of the lieutenant governor. The gubernatorial mansion, next to Wilhelmina Park, has fancy fretwork, a steeply pitched roof, and wraparound double galleries. Saba University School of Medicine runs a **medical school** in the Bottom, at which about 320 students are enrolled.

On the other side of town is the Wesleyan Holiness Church, a small stone building with white fretwork. Though it's been renovated and virtually reconstructed over the years, its original four walls date from 1919; go inside and look around. Stroll by the church, beyond a place called the Gap, to a lookout point where you can see the 400 rough-hewn steps leading down to Ladder Bay. This and Fort Bay were the two landing sites from which Saba's first settlers had to haul themselves and their possessions up to the heights. Sabans sometimes walk down to Ladder Bay to picnic. Think long and hard before you do: climbing back requires navigating the same 400 steps.

Engineering Feats

To view Saba from a distance is to be baffled—the island soars out of the Caribbean Sea, cone-shape like the volcano that formed it, with steep, rocky shores providing a seemingly impassable barrier to the outside world. How anyone saw this land as inhabitable is a mystery. But Sabans are a tenacious lot, and they were bound and determined to make this island theirs.

Among the sheer rock walls that surround Saba, at what is now Fort Bay, settlers found a tiny cove where entrance was possible. They navigated rowboats in between the crashing waves, steadied themselves against the swell, and then, waist-deep in water, pulled the boats to shore. Nothing got onto the island without coming this way, not a person, nor a set of dishes, nor a sofa. From there, supplies were hauled up a steep path composed of more than 200 steps (all of different heights and widths) in the hands or on the heads of Sabans. The trail had been carved into the mountain and climbed 820 feet above sea level to the Bottom through a grand crevice. Visitors who were unable to climb were carried to the top at a cost of 30 guilders.

For nearly 300 years after Saba was settled, this was how it was done.

Then, in the early 1900s, the locals decided to build a road. They first approached the Dutch government for help. Legend has it that the Dutch said the grade was too steep, that it could not be done. But the Sabans would not be deterred. They took the matter into their own hands and, with no trained engineers among them, began construction in 1938. The road took five years to complete and now climbs 653 feet out of Fort Bay.

The next feat of engineering came in 1956, when the Technical Economic Counsel of Netherlands Antilles deemed tourism Saba's only market-able resource and decided a pier and an airport had to be built. With only one place flat enough for an airstrip, the airport was built on Flat Point, a solidified lava flow. In 1959, the first conventional single-engine aircraft landed on the 1,300-foot airstrip, one of the shortest in the world. The airport itself opened in 1963. Engineers first tried to build a pier in 1934, but the perpetual waves destroyed it almost immediately. In 1972, the Sabans tried again and were able to build a short, 277-foot-long pier (the sea was simply too deep for anything longer), which was unfortunately too small to accommodate large cruise ships, a major thorn in the tourism industry's side.

Cove Bay. Near the airport on the island's northeastern side, a 20-foot-long strip of rocks and pebbles laced with gray sand is really the only place for sunning. There's also a small tide pool here for swimming.

Flat Point. This is the only place on the island where planes can land. The runway here is one of the world's shortest, with a length of approximately 1,300 feet. Only STOL (short takeoff and landing) prop planes dare land here, as each end of the runway drops off more than 100 feet into the crashing surf below.

Fort Bay. The end of the Road is also the jumping-off place for all of Saba's dive operations and the location of the St. Maarten ferry dock. The island's only gas station is here, as is a 277-foot pier that accommodates the tenders from ships. On the quay are a decompression chamber, one of the few in the Caribbean, and three dive shops. In Two Deep and Pop's Place are two good places to catch your breath while enjoying some refreshments and the view of the water.

Established in 1987 to preserve and manage the island's marine resources, the **Saba National Marine Park** encircles the entire island, dipping down to 200 feet, and is zoned for diving, swimming, fishing, boating, and anchorage. One of the unique aspects of Saba's diving is the submerged pinnacles at about the 70-foot depth mark. Here all forms of sea creatures rendezvous. The information center offers talks and slide shows for divers and snorkelers and provides literature on marine life. (Divers are required to contribute $3 a dive to help maintain the park facilities.) Before you visit, call first to see if anyone is around. ⊠*Saba Conservation Foundation/Marine Park Visitors Center, Fort Bay* ☎*599/416–3295* ⊕*www.sabapark.org* ⊙ *Weekdays 8–4.*

Hell's Gate. The Road makes 14 hairpin turns up nearly 2,000 vertical feet to Hell's Gate. Holy Rosary Church, on Zion's Hill, is a stone structure that looks medieval but was built in 1962. In the community center behind the church, village ladies sell their intricate lace. The same ladies make the potent rum-based Saba Spice, each according to her old family recipe. The intrepid can venture to Lower Hell's Gate, where the Old Sulphur Mine Walk leads to bat caves (with a sulfuric stench) that can—with caution—be explored.

17

Fodor'sChoice **Mt. Scenery.** Stone and concrete steps—1,064 of them—rise to the top of
★ Mt. Scenery. En route to the mahogany grove at the summit, the steps pass giant elephant ears, ferns, begonias, mangoes, palms, and orchids; there are six identifiable ecosystems in all. The staff at the Trail Shop in Windwardside can provide a field guide. Have your hotel pack a picnic lunch, wear sturdy shoes, and take along a jacket and a canteen of water. The round-trip excursion will take about three hours and is best begun in the early morning.

Windwardside. The island's second-largest village, perched at 1,968 feet, commands magnificent views of the Caribbean. Here amid the oleander bushes are rambling lanes and narrow alleyways winding through the hills, and clusters of tiny, neat houses and shops as well as the Saba Tourist Office. At the village's northern end is the Church of St. Paul's Conversion, a colonial building with a red-and-white steeple.

★ Small signs mark the way to the **Saba Museum.** This 150-year-old house, surrounded by lemongrass and clover, was once a sea captain's home. Period pieces on display include a handsome mahogany four-poster bed, an antique organ, and, in the kitchen, a rock oven. You can also look at old documents, such as a letter a Saban wrote after the hurricane of 1772, in which he sadly says, "We have lost our little all." Don't miss the delightful stroll to the museum down the stone-walled Park Lane, one of the prettiest walks in the Caribbean. ⊠ *Windwardside* ☎*No phone* 🖅*$1 suggested donation* ⊙ *Weekdays 10–4.*

SABA ESSENTIALS

To research prices, get advice from other travelers, and book travel arrangements, visit www.fodors.com.

▌ TRANSPORTATION

BY AIR

The approach to Saba's tiny airstrip is as thrilling as a roller-coaster ride. The strip is one of the shortest in the world, but no need to worry, because the de Havilland Twin Otter aircraft are built for it. In fact, the pilot needs only half of the length of the runway to land properly. (If you're nervous, don't sit on the right. The wing seems almost to scrape against the cliff side on the approach.) Once you've touched down on the airstrip, the pilot taxis an inch or two, turns, and deposits you just outside Juancho E. Yrausquin Airport, which first opened in 1963.

Winair is the only airline that flies to Saba—from St. Eustatius and St. Maarten. You must pay a $6 departure tax when leaving Saba by plane for either St. Maarten or St. Eustatius, or $20 if you're continuing on an international flight. (Note: When flying home through St. Maarten from here, list yourself as "in transit" and avoid repaying the tax in St. Maarten, which is $20.)

Airline Contact Winair (☎599/416–2255 or 800/634–4907 ⊕www.fly-winair.com).

Airport Contact Juancho E. Yrausquin Airport (☎599/416–2255).

BY BOAT & FERRY

The Edge, a high-speed ferry, leaves St. Maarten's Pelican Marina in Simpson Bay for Fort Bay on Saba every Wednesday through Sunday at 9 AM and boards for the return trip at about 3:45 PM. The trip, which can be rough, takes just over an hour each way. Round-trip fare is $60, plus 5% extra if you pay by credit card.

Another option for a trip to or from St. Maarten is the *Dawn II,* a 65-foot aluminum vessel that holds 50 people and runs on Tuesday, Thursday, and Saturday between Philipsburg and Fort Bay. *Dawn II* departs Saba at 6:30 AM, arriving at St. Maarten at 8:30 AM, and departs St. Maarten at 5 PM, arriving at Fort Bay at 7 PM. The fare is $35 one-way and $60 for same-day return ticket; a $5 harbor fee is additional. Call ahead to check current schedules.

Contacts Dawn II (☎599/416–3671 ⊕www.sabactransport.com). **The Edge** (☎599/544–2640).

BY CAR

You won't need long to tour the island by car—you can cover the entire circuitous length of the Road in the space of a morning. If you want to shop, have lunch, and do some sightseeing, plan on a full day. If you rent a car, remember that the island's only gas station in Fort Bay closes at 3 PM.

Carless Sabans get around the old-fashioned ways—walking and hitchhiking (very popular and safe). If you choose to thumb rides, you'll need to know the rules of the Road. To get a lift from the Bottom (which actually is near the top of the island), sit on the wall opposite the Anglican church; to catch one in Fort Bay, sit on the wall opposite the Saba Deep dive center, where the Road begins to twist upward. The one and only gas station on the island is in Fort Bay.

Car Rentals Caja's Car Rental (⊠The Bottom ☎599/416–2388).

BY TAXI

Taxis charge a set rate for up to four people per taxi, with an additional cost for each person more than four. The fare from the airport to Hell's Gate is $6, to Windwardside it's $8, and to the Bottom it's $12.50. The fare from the Fort Bay ferry docks to Windwardside is $9.50. A taxi from Windwardside to the Bottom is $6.50.

▌ CONTACTS & RESOURCES

BANKS & EXCHANGE SERVICES

Prices quoted throughout the chapter are in U.S. dollars unless otherwise noted.

U.S. dollars are accepted everywhere, but Saba's official currency is the Netherlands Antilles florin (NAf; also called the guilder). The exchange rate is fixed at NAf 1.80 to US$1. Both First Caribbean International Bank and the Royal Bank of Trinidad and Tobago (RBTT) are in Windwardside and provide foreign-exchange services. RBTT and Windward Island Bank, in the Bottom, both have ATMs.

ELECTRICITY

Saba's current is 110 volts/60 cycles; visitors from North America should have no trouble using their travel appliances.

EMERGENCIES

Hospital A. M. Edwards Medical Center (⊠ The Bottom ☎ 599/416–3289).

Scuba Diving Emergencies Saba Marine Park Hyperbaric Facility (⊠ Fort Bay ☎ 599/416–3295).

INTERNET, MAIL & SHIPPING

An airmail letter to North America or Europe costs NAf 2.25; a postcard, NAf 1.10. Mail can take a week or two to reach the island. The post office is in Windwardside, near Scout's Place, and offers express mail service. When writing to Saba, don't worry about addresses without post-office box numbers or street locations—on an island this size, all mail finds its owner. However, do make sure to include "Netherlands Antilles" and "Caribbean" in the address.

For $5 you can get 30 minutes of Internet access on one of three computers at the Island Communication Services Business Center, which is open weekdays from 10 to 7, Saturday from 10 to 5.

Information Island Communication Services Business Center (⊠ Windwardside ☎ 599/416–2881).

LANGUAGE

Saba's official language is Dutch, but everyone on the island speaks English. Sabans are always willing to help, and they enjoy conversation. If you're open to chatting, you may get some good local advice.

SAFETY

Crime is generally not a problem in Saba. Take along sunscreen and sturdy, no-nonsense shoes that get a good grip on the ground. You may encounter the harmless racer snake while hiking. Don't be alarmed; these snakes lie on rocks to sun themselves but skitter off when people approach.

TAXES & SERVICE CHARGES

You must pay a $6 departure tax when leaving Saba by plane for either St. Maarten or St. Eustatius, or $20 if you're continuing on an international flight. (Note: When flying home through St. Maarten from here, list yourself as "in transit" and avoid repaying the tax in St. Maarten, which is $20.) There's no departure tax when you leave by boat. Several of the larger hotels will tack on a 10% to 15% service charge; others will build it into the rates. Call ahead to inquire about service charges. Hotels add a 5% government tax plus a 3% turnover tax to the cost of a room (sometimes it's tacked on to your bill, and other times it's built into the room rate). Restaurants on Saba usually add a service charge of 10% to 15%.

TELEPHONES

Telephone communications are excellent on the island, and you can dial direct long-distance. There are public phone booths in the Bottom and Windwardside. Phones take prepaid phone cards, which can be bought at stores throughout the island, or local coins. To call Saba from the United States, dial 011 + 599 + 416, followed by the four-digit number.

17

TIPPING

Even if service charges have been added to your bill, it's customary but not necessary to tip hotel personnel and restaurant waitstaff; you should tip taxi drivers, as well. About 10% to 15% should do it.

TOUR OPTIONS

The taxi drivers who meet the planes at the airport or the boats at Fort Bay conduct tours of the island. Tours can also be arranged by dive shops or hotels. A full-day trek costs $40 for one to four passengers and $10 per person for groups larger than four. If you're in from St. Maarten for a day trip, you can do a full morning of sightseeing, stop off for lunch (have your driver make reservations before starting), complete the tour afterward, and return to the airport in time to make the last flight back to St. Maarten. Guides are available for hiking; arrangements may be made through the tourist office or the Trail Shop in Windwardside. Or check out the island in a guided boat tour available for groups of up to 10 on Tuesday and Wednesday. In an hour and a half you will circle the island while learning about its history, its indigenous seabird population, and its coral reefs.

VISITOR INFORMATION

Information Saba Tourist Office (⊕ www. sabatourism.com ☎ 599/416–2231 or 599/416–2322).

WEDDINGS

It isn't difficult to get married on Saba, but it does take a little preparation. A couple of months before you travel, register via e-mail to secure a date and obtain all the necessary information, including the paperwork you need to submit beforehand. Include a letter requesting permission to be married on the island, addressed to the lieutenant governor of Saba. If you choose to be married somewhere other than in the court room at the Government Building, you must submit a written request to the lieutenant governor. Weddings are popular on Saba, and most of the hotels are willing to accommodate and cater provided you plan ahead. (Queen's Garden Resort is a particularly romantic spot.) The actual cost of the wedding ranges from $42 to $62, depending on when and where the ceremony is performed.

Information Lt. Governor of Saba (🖃 Government Offices, The Bottom ⊕ census@ unspoiledqueen.com).

St. Barthélemy

Luxuriating in the surf at Anse á Colombier

WORD OF MOUTH

"The best dinner we had on St. Barths was the pâte, baguettte, brie, and wine that we bought at a French deli and ate at sunset on a totally deserted beach! So romantic!"

—chicgeek

"Don't miss Saline beach! The water is pure turquoise blue and white sand beach—looks like the South Pacific."

—Ashley

WELCOME TO ST. BARTHÉLEMY

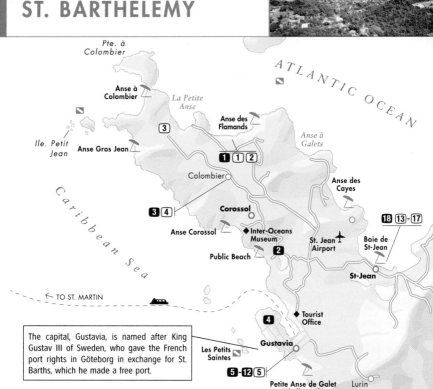

The capital, Gustavia, is named after King Gustav III of Sweden, who gave the French port rights in Göteborg in exchange for St. Barths, which he made a free port.

LA RIVIERA DES CARAÏBES

Just 8 square mi (21 square km), St. Barths is a hilly island with many sheltered bays. New hotels can never have more than 12 rooms, so you will find no high-rise resorts to spoil your views. The French, who had controlled the island since the late 17th century, gave it to Sweden in 1784 but finally reclaimed it in 1877.

Chic travelers put aside their cell phones long enough to enjoy the lovely beaches—long, surf-pounded strands; idyllic crescents crowded by cliffs or forests; glass-smooth lagoons perfect for windsurfing. Nothing on St. Barths comes cheap. But on a hotel's awning-shaded terrace, St. Barths' civilized ways seem worth every penny.

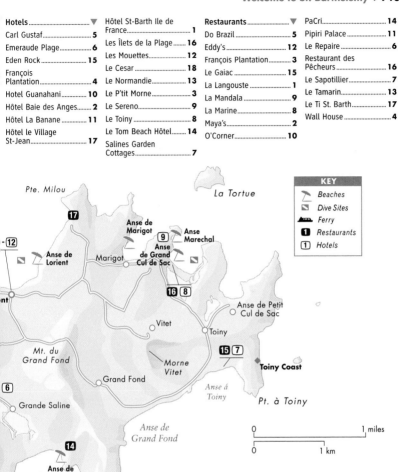

ST. BARTHÉLEMY

18

Gouverneur

TOP 4 REASONS TO VISIT ST. BARTHÉLEMY

1. The island is active, sexy, hedonistic, and hip, with plenty of attractive young people as scenery.

2. If food and wine are your true loves, then you'll find your bliss here.

3. Shopping for stylish clothes and fashion accessories is better nowhere else in the Caribbean.

4. Windsurfing and other water sports make going to the beach more than just a sun-tanning experience.

ST. BARTHÉLEMY PLANNER

Island Activities

St. Barths is about relaxing and reviving in high style. The most popular activity is **fine dining,** and the most popular land-based sport is **shopping.** Most other activities are on the water; the **yachting** scene is strong, as is **windsurfing. Beaches** are numerous and mostly good, though almost never truly great, but you'll definitely want to explore a few of them. The **diving** is good, though not excellent.

On the Ground

Many hotels offer free airport transfers. Otherwise, there's a taxi stand at the airport; unmetered taxis cost about €10 to €25, depending on distance. Settle on a fare before you get in. Taxis virtually disappear at night, so you'll probably need to rent a car during your stay; it's an absolute necessity if you're staying in a villa. You might be able to rent a car directly from your hotel; otherwise, you should reserve one in advance of your trip. Some automatics are available, but you'll most likely get a small, manual four-wheel-drive vehicle. Charges average about $55 a day; automatics usually cost at least a third more.

Logistics

Getting to St. Barths: There are no direct flights to St. Barths (SBH). No, not even on your private Gulfstream. You must fly to another island and then catch a smaller plane for the hop over. Most Americans fly first to St. Maarten, and then take the 10-minute flight to St. Barths, but you can also connect through St. Thomas or San Juan. There are also ferries from St. Martin, but their schedules are really geared for daytrippers.

Hassle Factor: Medium–High.

Nonstops: None.

Where to Stay

Most hotels on St. Barths are small (the largest has just 29 rooms) and stratospherically expensive, but there are a few relative bargains; however, about half of the accommodations on St. Barths are in private villas. Prices drop dramatically in the off-season.

Hotel & Restaurant Costs

⇨*For information on hotel meal plans, see Accommodations in Caribbean Essentials.*

WHAT IT COSTS IN U.S. DOLLARS				
$$$$	$$$	$$	$	¢
Restaurants				
over $30	$20–$30	$12–$20	$8–$12	under $8
Hotels*				
over $350	$250–$350	$150–$250	$80–$150	under $80
Hotels**				
over $450	$350–$450	$250–$350	$125–$250	under $125

By Elise Meyer   **STEPPING ONTO THE VILLA PATIO,** I watch the sun rise over the volcanic mountain, glittering on the cobalt sea, and bathing the hills in a golden light. I stretch lazily, detecting the aroma of freshly brewed coffee. Should breakfast be an almond croissant? Or should we just have the ethereal brioche we discovered yesterday? I decide that a walk to the *boulangerie* is in order, especially in light of that new bikini. Ahhh, another perfect day in paradise. I make a mental note to book another Thai massage for Friday and grab my sunglasses. Is there any way this could be any better?

St. Barthélemy blends the respective essences of the Caribbean and France in perfect proportions. A sophisticated but unstudied approach to relaxation and respite prevails: you can spend the day on a beach, try on the latest French fashions, and watch the sunset while nibbling tapas over Gustavia Harbor, then choose from nearly 100 excellent restaurants for an elegant evening meal. You can putter around the island, scuba dive, windsurf on a quiet cove, or just admire the lovely views.

A mere 8 square mi (21 square km), St. Barths is a hilly island, with many sheltered inlets providing visitors with many opportunities to try out picturesque, quiet beaches. The town of Gustavia wraps itself neatly around a lilliputian harbor lined with impressive yachts and rustic fishing boats. Red-roofed bungalows dot the hillsides. Beaches run the gamut from calm to "surfable," from deserted to packed. The cuisine is tops in the Caribbean, part of the French *savoir vivre* that prevails throughout the island.

Longtime visitors speak wistfully of the old, quiet St. Barths. Development has quickened the pace of life here, that's true, but the island hasn't yet been overbuilt, and a 1982 ordinance limited new tourist lodgings to 12 rooms. The largest hotel—the Guanahani—has fewer than 100 rooms; the island's other rooms are divided among some 40 small hotels and guesthouses. About half the island's visitors stay in private villas. The tiny planes that arrive with regularity still land at the tidy airport only during daylight hours. And although "nightlife" usually means a leisurely dinner and a stargazing walk on the beach, something of a renaissance is under way, and a couple of hot new clubs might give you a reason to pack a pair of dancing shoes.

18

Christopher Columbus discovered the island—called "Ouanalao" by its native Carib Indians—in 1493; he named it for his brother Bartholomé. The first group of French colonists arrived in 1648, drawn by the ideal location on the West Indian Trade Route, but they were wiped out by the Caribs, who dominated the area. Another small group from Normandy and Brittany arrived in 1694. This time the settlers prospered—with the help of French buccaneers, who took advantage of the island's strategic location and protected harbor. In 1784 the French traded the island to King Gustav III of Sweden in exchange for port rights in Göteborg. The king dubbed the capital Gustavia, laid out and paved streets, built three forts, and turned the community into a prosperous free port. The island thrived as a shipping and commercial center until the 19th century, when earthquakes, fires, and hurricanes

Bliss & More

Visitors to St. Barths can enjoy more than the comforts of home by taking advantage of any of the myriad spa and beauty treatments that are now available on the island. Two major hotels, the Isle de France and the Guanahani, have beautiful, comprehensive, on-site spas for their guests. Depending on availability, other visitors to the island can also book services. In addition, scores of independent therapists will come to your hotel room or villa and provide any therapeutic discipline you can think of, including yoga, Thai massage, shiatsu, reflexology, and even manicures, pedicures, and hairdressing. You can find current therapists listed in the local guide, *Ti Gourmet*, or at the Tourist Office in Gustavia.

brought financial ruin. Many residents fled for newer lands of opportunity, and Oscar II of Sweden decided to return the island to France. After briefly considering selling it to America, the French took possession of Saint-Barthélemy again on August 10, 1877.

Today the island is still a free port and is part of an overseas department of France. Arid, hilly, and rocky, St. Barths was unsuited to sugar production and thus never developed an extensive slave base. Most of the 3,000 current residents are descendants of the tough Norman and Breton settlers of three centuries ago. They are feisty, industrious, and friendly—but insular. However, you will find many new, young French arrivals, predominantly from northwestern France and Provence, who speak English well.

WHERE TO STAY

There's no denying that hotel rooms and villas on St. Barths carry high prices, and the current weakness of the dollar makes for a costly respite. You're paying primarily for the privilege of staying on the island, and even at $800 a night the bedrooms tend to be small. Still, if you're flexible—in terms of timing and in your choice of lodgings—you can enjoy a holiday in St. Barths and still afford to send the kids to college.

The most expensive season falls during the holidays (mid-December to early January), when hotels are booked far in advance, usually require a 10- or 14-day stay, and can be double the high-season rates. A 5% government Tourism Tax on room prices (excluding breakfast) went into effect in 2008.

VILLAS & CONDOMINIUMS

On St. Barths, the term "villa" is used to describe anything from a small cottage to a luxurious, modern estate. Today almost half of St. Barths' accommodations are in villas, and we recommend considering this option, especially if you're traveling with friends or family. An advantage to Americans is that villa rates are usually quoted and confirmed in dollars, thus bypassing unfavorable euro fluctuations. Most villas have a small private swimming pool and maid service daily except Sunday. They are well furnished with linens, kitchen utensils, and such electronic playthings as CD and DVD players, satellite TV, and broadband Internet. In-season rates range from $1,400 to $40,000 a week. Most villa-rental companies are based in the United States and have extensive Web sites that allow you to see pictures of the place you're renting; their local offices oversee maintenance and housekeeping and provide concierge services to clients. Just be aware that there are few beachfront villas, so if you have your heart set on "toes in the sand" and a cute waiter delivering your kir royale, stick with the hotels or villas operated by hotel properties.

St. Barth Properties, Inc. (☎508/528–7727 or 800/421–3396 ⊕*www. stbarth.com*), owned by American Peg Walsh—a regular on St. Barths since 1986—represents more than 120 properties here and can guide you to the perfect place to stay. Weekly peak-season rates range from $1,400 to $40,000 depending on the property's size, location, and amenities. The excellent Web site offers virtual tours of most of the villas and even details of availability. An office in Gustavia can take care of any problems you may have and offers some concierge-type services. **Marla** (☎0590/27–62–02 ⊕*www.marlavillas.com*) is a local St. Barth villa-rental company that represents more than 100 villas, many that are not listed with other companies.

Wimco (☎800/932–3222 ⊕*www.wimco.com*), which is based in Rhode Island, oversees bookings for more than 230 properties on St. Barths—they're represented on the island by SiBarth. Rents range from $2,000 to $10,000 for two- and three-bedroom villas; larger villas rent for $7,000 per week and up. Properties can be previewed and reserved on Wimco's Web site (which occasionally lists last-minute specials), or you can obtain a catalog by mail. The company will arrange for babysitters, massages, chefs, and other in-villa services for clients, as well as private air charters.

18

HOTELS

When it comes to booking a hotel on St. Barths, the reservation manager can be your best ally. Rooms within a property can vary greatly. It's well worth the price of a phone call or the time investment of an e-mail correspondence to make a personal connection, which can mean much in arranging a room that meets your needs or preferences. Details of accessibility, views, recent redecorating, meal options, and special package rates are topics open for discussion. Most quoted hotel rates are per room, not per person, and include service charges and airport transfers.

$$$$
★ 　**Carl Gustaf.** This sophisticated hotel right in Gustavia received a welcome overhaul in 2006, and its new incarnation is the last word in luxury. Each apartment-suite is lavishly decorated and equipped with

every modern convenience: iPod-clock radios, multiple flat-screen TVs, and complete minikitchens with a Häagen-Dazs–stocked refrigerator-freezer, and an espresso machine. You even have a computer and printer in the room! The hotel is a good option if you don't want to do much driving—it's within walking distance of everything in town if you don't mind climbing the hill. One- and two-bedroom suites with private decks and black-and-gold tile plunge pools spill down a hill overlooking quaint Gustavia Harbor. Summer rates and special Internet and honeymoon packages are offered. The Carl Gustaf restaurant, known for its classic French cuisine, is spectacular for sunset cocktails and dinner over the twinkle of the harbor lights. **Pros:** Luxurious decor, in-town location, loads of in-room gadgets. **Cons:** It's not very "beachy," outdoor space limited to your private plunge pool. ⊠*Rue des Normands, Box 700, Gustavia* ☎*0590/29–79–00* ⊕*www.hotel carlgustaf.com* ➪*14 suites* ⚲*In-room: kitchen, refrigerator, VCR (some), DVD (some), Ethernet. In-hotel: restaurant, bar, pool, gym, no elevator* ⊟*AE, MC, V* ⊺⊙⊺*CP.*

$$$$
Fodor'sChoice
★
🔲**Eden Rock.** St. Barths' first hotel opened in the 1950s on the craggy bluff that splits Baie de St-Jean. Extensive renovations and an expansion in 2005 raised it into the top category of St. Barth properties. Each of the hotel's 29 unique rooms, suites, and villas is tastefully decorated and luxuriously appointed with plasma satellite TV and high-speed Internet. New, large bathrooms have either deep soaking tubs or walk-in showers; all have loads of fluffy towels and Bulgari suds. The six beachfront villas built on the property are magnificent and sleep up to four, with full kitchens and beautifully appointed modern living areas. Stunning bay views and great service are uniform. In 2008 the resort added three enormous (two- and three-bedroom) super-deluxe villas, each with two private pools, an art gallery, butler service, private cinema, and use of a Mini Cooper. The breakfast buffet, included in the rate, is terrific, and the on-site restaurants are first-rate and deserving of a visit. **Pros:** Chic clientele, beach setting, can walk to shopping and restaurants. **Cons:** Some suites are noisy because of proximity to street. ⊠*Baie de St-Jean 97133* ☎*0590/29–79–99, 877/563–7015 in U.S.* ⊕*www.edenrockhotel.com* ➪*29 rooms, 3 villas* ⚲*In-room: refrigerator, Ethernet. In-hotel: 2 restaurants, bars, pool, water sports, no elevator* ⊟*AE, MC, V* ⊺⊙⊺*BP.*

$$$$
Fodor'sChoice
★
🔲**François Plantation.** A colonial-era graciousness pervades this intimate, exquisite hillside complex of West Indian–style cottages. The rooms have queen-size mahogany four-poster beds and colorful fabrics. Two larger rooms can accommodate an extra bed. The vanishing-edge pool sits atop a very steep hill with magnificent views from its pretty deck. The charming and sophisticated new management are retaining the wonderful, old–St. Barth qualities of the property, including the remarkable gardens, while making necessary improvements. Year-round, the prices are gentle for the island, but the off-season packages, which even include a car, are a real bargain. Villa Plantation, a new one-bedroom house with a private pool, is lovely and quite reasonable, with amazing views. **Pros:** Beautiful gardens, countryside location, wonderful restaurant. **Cons:** Rooms are small, steep hills between cottages, pool, and

main area, need a car to get to beach and town. ⊠*Colombier 97133* ☎*0590/29–80–22* ⊕*www.francois-plantation.com* ⤶*12 rooms, 1 villa* ⚴*In-room: safe, refrigerator, dial-up. In-hotel: restaurant, pool, no elevator* ⊟*AE, MC, V* ⊗*Closed Sept. and Oct.* ⍩*CP.*

$$$$ **Hôtel Baie des Anges.** Everyone is treated like family at this casual
ⓒ   retreat. Ten clean, fresh, and nicely decorated—if somewhat plain—rooms are right on serene Flamands Beach; each has a kitchenette and private terrace. There's also a small pool. The food at La Langouste, the hotel's restaurant, is tasty and reasonably priced. The proprietor also manages a four-bedroom, three-bath villa a bit farther up the hill. **Pros:** On St. Barth's longest beach, family-friendly. **Cons:** Rooms are basic. ⊠*Flamands 97095* ☎*0590/27–63–61* ⊕*www.hotelbaiedesanges. fr* ⤶*10 rooms* ⚴*In-room: safe, kitchen. In-hotel: restaurant, pool, beachfront* ⊟*AE, MC, V* ⍩*EP.*

$$$$ **Hotel La Banane.** Redone in 2006, the nine spacious pavilion-rooms with euro-style contemporary furnishings have yummy names like Watermelon, Pineapple, Grape, and Pomegranate that describe the bright color accents that counterpoint the white interiors. Private baths have every upscale amenity. The hotel's location behind a small shopping center may either be construed as a bother or a convenience, but Lorient Beach is a two-minute walk away. Breakfast is served around the palm-shaded pool. K'fe Massaï, the African-theme restaurant, is very popular. **Pros:** Short walk to beach, friendly and social atmosphere at pool areas, great baths. **Cons:** Rooms are small, location of entrance through parking lot is not attractive. ⊠*Quartier Lorient 97133* ☎*0590/52–03–00* ⊕*www.labanane.com* ⤶*9 rooms* ⚴*In-room: DVD, dial-up. In-hotel: restaurant, bar, pools, no elevator* ⊟*AE, MC, V* ⊗*Closed Sept.–Oct. 15* ⍩*CP.*

$$$$ **Hôtel St-Barth Isle de France.** An obsessively attentive management team
Fodor'sChoice ensures that this intimate, casually refined resort keeps remains among
★   the very best accommodations in St. Barths—if the entire Caribbean. It's not hard to understand why the property boasts a 72% high-season return rate—it just keeps improving each season. A technology upgrade in 2007 added a reception-area computer for guests and broadband to rooms, which are huge and luxuriously outfitted, all with modern four-posters, French fabrics, and fine art, plus superb marble baths (all with a tub or Jacuzzi tub, both rare on the island). The beachside La Case de l'Isle restaurant serves nouvelle cuisine. The spa is by Molton Brown. The beautiful white-sand beach couldn't be more pristine. Good off-season and honeymoon packages help to keep the rates in check. **Pros:** Fabulous beach location, terrific management, great spa. **Cons:** Garden rooms—though large—can be dark, some complaints that the beds are hard. ⊠*Baie des Flamands 97098* ☎*0590/27–61–81* ⊕*www.isle-de-france.com* ⤶*12 rooms, 5 suites, 13 bungalows, 1 2-bedroom villa* ⚴*In-room: refrigerator, DVD, Ethernet. In-hotel: restaurant, room service, bar, tennis court, pools, gym, spa, public Internet* ⊟*MC, V* ⍩*CP* ⊗*Closed Sept.–mid-Oct.*

$$$$ **Hotel Guanahani & Spa.** The only full-service resort on the island has
ⓒ   lovely rooms and suites (14 of which have private pools) and impec-
★   cable personalized service, not to mention one of the only children's

18

programs (though it's more of a nursery). Rooms, all of which have large bathrooms with Clarins toiletries, were redecorated in 2006 in a hip and attractive grape-and-kiwi color scheme; at the same time, a stunningly serene Clarins Spa and Frederic Fekkai hair salon were added. Units vary in price, privacy, view, and distance from activities, so make your preferences known. The Wellness Suite, which is at the top of the property, can serve as your own hedonistic domain after the spa closes at night. Flat-screen TVs, iPod docks, and DVDs are new in all rooms, as is the sometimes dodgy, resort-wide Wi-Fi service; the well-equipped gym is newly expanded, and a renovated tennis court boasts an Astroturf surface. Also here are two well-regarded restaurants, poolside L'Indigo and sophisticated Bartolomeo, which has a lounge with music. **Pros:** Fantastic spa, beachside sports, family-friendly **Cons:** Lots of cats, steep walk to beach. ⊠ *Grand Cul de Sac 97133* ☎ *0590/27–66–60* ⊕ *www.leguanahani.com* ⟳ *34 rooms, 33 suites, 1 3-bedroom villa* ⌂ *In-room: DVD, Wi-Fi. In-hotel: 2 restaurants, room service, bar, tennis courts, pools, water sports, no elevator, children's programs (ages 2–12)* ☰ *AE, MC, V* ⦿ *CP.*

$$$$ 🏠 **Les Îlets de la Plage.** On the far side of the airport, tucked away at the
★   far corner of Baie de St-Jean, these well-priced, comfortably furnished island-style one-, two-, and three-bedroom bungalows (four right on the beach, seven up a small hill) have small kitchens, pleasant open-air sitting areas, and comfortable bathrooms. This is a good choice if you want to be right on the beach with the space and convenience of a villa but the feel of a small resort. Crisp white linens and upholstery, lovely verandahs, and daily deliveries of fresh bread from a nearby bakery add to the pleasantness of the surroundings, though only the bedrooms are air-conditioned. **Pros:** Beach location, apartment conveniences, front porches. **Cons:** No a/c except in guest rooms, right next to the airport. ⊠ *Plage de St-Jean,* ☎ *0590/27–88–57* ⊕ *www.lesilets.com* ⟳ *11 bungalows* ⌂ *In-room: safe, kitchen, dial-up. In-hotel: pool, gym, beachfront, no elevator, concierge* ☰ *AE, MC, V* ⊗ *Closed Sept.–Nov. 1* ⦿ *EP.*

$$$$ 🏠 **Le Sereno.** A St. Barth classic on a beautiful stretch of beach was
Fodor's Choice   reborn as an ultrachic retreat in 2005 (designed by superhot Parisian
★   architect Christian Liaigre). Cutting-edge modern decor and techno amenities create a spare but luxurious, Zen-like serenity. The suites are huge by St. Barth standards and have spacious living areas and private sundecks. Large bathrooms, some with "steeping tubs," have roomy showers and vessel sinks of solid black granite. Other perks include cloud-soft linens and robes from Porthault, Parisian Ex Voto toiletries, high-speed Internet, plasma TVs, and iPod docks (for your own device or their fully loaded ones to borrow). Bedlike poolside lounges for two set the romantic tone for the hip all-day party. **Pros:** Beach location, super chic comfort, fun atmosphere. **Cons:** No a/c in the bathrooms, lots of construction planned for this part of the island over next few years. ⊠ *B.P. 19 Grand-Cul-de-Sac,* ☎ *0590/29–83–00* ⊕ *www.lesereno.com* ⟳ *37 suites and villas* ⌂ *In-room: safe, refrigerator, DVD, Wi-Fi. In-hotel: restaurant, room service, bar, pool, gym, no elevator, laundry service* ☰ *AE, MC, V* ⦿ *EP.*

$$$$ 🏠**Le Toiny.** When perfection is more important than price, choose Le
★ Toiny's romantic villas with mahogany furniture, yards of colored toile,
and heated private pools. Rooms have every convenience of home: lush
bathrooms, fully equipped kitchenettes, and either a stair-stepper or
stationary bike. High-tech amenities include several flat-screen LCD
TVs, stereos, fax machines, and Bang and Olufsen phones. Each suite
has an outdoor shower. Breakfast comes to your terrace each morning,
and in-villa spa services can be provided as well. If ever you want to
leave your villa, Sunday brunch and haute cuisine can be had at the
alfresco Le Gaiac overlooking the Italian-tile pool. New owners are
adding a walking trail to the private beach with a seaside saltwater
pool. Two of the villas are handicap accessible. **Pros:** Extremely private,
luxurious rooms, flawless service. **Cons:** Not on the beach, at least half
an hour drive from town. ⊠*Anse de Toiny 97133* ☎*0590/27–88–88*
⊕*www.letoiny.com* ⛵*14 1-bedroom villas, 1 3-bedroom villa* ⛓*In-
room: safe, refrigerator, DVD, Wi-Fi. In-hotel: restaurant, bar, pool,
no elevator, laundry service* ⊟*AE, DC, MC, V* ⊗*Closed Sept.–late
Oct.* ⦸*CP.*

$$$$ 🏠**Le Tom Beach Hôtel.** This chic but casual boutique hotel right on
busy St. Jean beach is fun for social types. A garden winds around the
brightly painted suites, over the pool via a small footbridge, into the
hopping, open-air restaurant La Plage. The nonstop house party often
spills out onto the terraces and lasts into the wee hours. Big, plantation-
style rooms have high ceilings, cozy draped beds, nice baths, a TV with
DVD player, direct-dial phones, and patios. Oceanfront suites are the
most expensive, but all the rooms are clean and cozy, and were refurbished in 2007 with a romantic white, rose, and lavender color scheme.
Pros: Party central at beach, restaurant, and pool, in-town location.
Cons: Trendy social scene is not for everybody, especially light sleepers.
⊠*Plage St-Jean 97133* ☎*0590/27–53–13* ⊕*www.st-barths.com/tom-
beach-hotel* ⛵*12 rooms* ⛓*In-room: safe, refrigerator, DVD. In-hotel:
restaurant, bar, pool, beachfront, no elevator, public Internet* ⊟*AE,
MC, V* ⦸*CP.*

$$$–$$$$ 🏠**Emeraude Plage.** Right on the beach of Baie de St-Jean, this petite
★ resort consists of small but immaculate bungalows and villas with fully
equipped outdoor kitchenettes on small patios; nice bathrooms add to
the comfort. At this writing, the reception area and units in the D and
F bungalows have been completely renovated in the modern, clean,
white-and-brown color scheme that has become the St. Barth "look";
now there are flat-screen TVs, and, on the patios, new white kitchens.
A new beach pavilion serves breakfast, lunch, and drinks. Check for
ongoing renovations when you inquire about reservations—the higher
priced suites are the renovated ones. The complex is convenient to
nearby restaurants and shops. The beachfront two-bedroom villas are
something of a bargain, especially off-season. **Pros:** Beachfront and in-
town location, good value, cool kitchens on each porch. **Cons:** Smallish
rooms. ⊠*Baie de St-Jean 97133* ☎*0590/27–64–78* ⊕*www.emeraude
plage.com* ⛵*21 bungalows, 4 suites, 2 cottages, 1 villa* ⛓*In-room:
safe, kitchen. In-hotel: bar, beachfront, no elevator, laundry service,
public Internet* ⊟*MC, V* ⊗*Closed Sept.–Oct.* ⦸*EP.*

18

$$–$$$$ 🖼 **Hôtel le Village St-Jean.** For two generations, the Charneau family
★ has offered friendly service and reasonable rates at its small hotel,
making guests feel like a part of the family. Handsome, spacious,
and comfortable, if not particularly trendy-chic, the airy stone-and-
redwood cottages have high ceilings, sturdy furniture, modern baths,
open-air kitchenettes, and lovely terraces with hammocks; one has a
Jacuzzi. You get the advantages of a villa and the services of a hotel
here. The regular rooms have refrigerators, and most have king-size
beds. In addition, there are three lovely villas of various sizes. Regu-
lars are invited to store beach equipment. The location is great—you
can walk to the beach and town from here—and most rooms and cot-
tages have gorgeous views. See if Room 12, 15, or 10, perched on
the edge of the hillside, is available when you book. A lounge with
a plasma TV and Internet access is a popular gathering spot. Rooms
(but not cottages) include continental breakfast in the rates. Cottages
have kitchens; very reasonable summer rates for cottages include a
car. **Pros:** Great value, convenient location, wonderful management.
Cons: Somewhat old-fashioned, can be noisy. ⌂ *Box 623, Baie de St-
Jean 97133* ☎ *0590/27–61–39 or 800/651–8366* ⊕ *www.villagestjean
hotel.com* ⤳ *5 rooms, 20 cottages, 1 3-bedroom villa, 2 2-bedroom
villas* ⌂ *In-room: kitchen (some), no TV. In-hotel: restaurant, bar, pool,
no elevator* ⊟ *AE, MC, V* ⍾ *EP.*

$$ 🖼 **Le P'tit Morne.** Each of the modestly furnished but freshly decorated
and painted mountainside studios has a private balcony with pan-
oramic views of the coastline. The small kitchenettes are adequate for
creating picnic lunches and other light meals. The snack bar serves
breakfast. It's relatively isolated here, however, and the beach is a 10-
minute drive away, but the young and friendly management is eager
to help you enjoy your stay. There are weeklong packages that include
a car, or a dive package. **Pros:** Reasonable rates, great area for hiking.
Cons: Rooms are basic, remote location. ⌂ *Box 14, Colombier 97133*
☎ *0590/52–95–50* ⊕ *www.timorne.com* ⤳ *14 rooms* ⌂ *In-room:
kitchen. In-hotel: pool, no elevator* ⊟ *AE, MC, V* ⍾ *CP.*

$–$$ 🖼 **Les Mouettes.** This guesthouse offers clean, simply furnished, and
economical bungalows that open directly onto the beach. They're also
quite close to the road, which can be either convenient for a quick
shopping excursion or bothersome on account of the noise. Each air-
conditioned bungalow has a bathroom with a shower only, a kitchenette, a patio, one or two double beds making this place a good bet for
families or young visitors on a budget. **Pros:** Right on the beach, family-
friendly. **Cons:** Rooms are basic, right near the road. ⊠ *Lorient Beach
97133* ☎ *0590/27–77–91* ⊕ *www.st-barths.com/hotel-les-mouettes*
⤳ *7 bungalows* ⌂ *In-room: kitchen. In-hotel: beachfront, no elevator*
⊟ *No credit cards* ⍾ *EP.*

$–$$ 🖼 **Salines Garden Cottages.** Budget-conscious beach lovers need look no
further than these small garden cottages, a short stroll from what is
arguably St. Barth's best beach. Each of the five studios is named for
favorite places of the owners: Pavones, Padang, Waikiki, Cap Ferrat, and
Essaouira. There's a small but pleasant pool set in the garden, and each
studio unit has a private terrace. Three have full kitchenettes. You can

choose to join the impromptu house party of the owners and residents, or just stay to yourself. **Pros:** Only property walkable to Salines Beach, quiet, reasonable rates. **Cons:** Far from town, not very private, no phones in rooms. ⊠*Salines,* ☎*0590/51–04–44* ⊕*www.salinesgarden.com* ⤳*5 cottages* ♿*In-room: kitchen (some), Wi-Fi. In-hotel: bar, pool, no elevator, public Wi-Fi* ☉*Closed mid-Aug.–mid-Oct.* ⦿*CP.*

$–$$ ⊡**Le Normandie.** Wendy and Dennis Carlton, longtime St. Barth visitors, have renovated this eight-room inn in a Euro-meets-nautical theme, reflecting the eponymous art deco ocean liner. The rooms are small but stylish and will appeal to young visitors who will appreciate the in-town location, and clubby atmosphere of the tiny pool garden where breakfast and afternoon wine is served. Another thing is sure—there's nothing to compare at this price on the island. And, it's a two-minute walk to the beach. **Pros:** Youthful, house-party atmosphere, friendly. **Cons:** Tiny rooms. ⊠*Quartier Lorient,* ☎*0590/27–61–66* ⊕*www.normandiehotelstbarts.com* ⤳*8 rooms* ♿*In-room: Wi-Fi. In-hotel: bar, pool, no elevator* ⊟*AE, MC, V* ⦿*CP.*

WHERE TO EAT

Dining on St. Barths compares favorably to almost anywhere in the world. Varied and exquisite cuisine, a French flair in the decorations, sensational wine, and attentive service make for a wonderful epicurean experience. St. Barths' style is expressed in more than 80 charming restaurants, from beachfront grills to serious establishments serving five-course meals. On most menus, freshly caught local seafood mingles on the plate with top-quality provisions that arrive regularly from Paris.

Most restaurants offer a chalkboard full of daily specials that are usually a good bet. But even the pickiest eaters will find something on every menu. The weakness of the dollar means that if you're not careful, you could easily spend $150 per person each day on meals. On top of this, restaurant prices have escalated in the last year or two due to fuel surcharges. However, you can dine superbly at a number of the island's better restaurants without breaking the bank, if you watch your wine selections, share appetizers or desserts, and pick up snacks and picnic meals from one of the well-stocked markets. Or, follow the locals to small *crêperies,* cafés, sandwich shops, and pizzerias in the main shopping areas. Lunch is usually less costly than dinner.

Reservations are strongly recommended and, in high season, essential. However, except during Christmas–New Year's it's not usually necessary to book far in advance. A day's—or even a few hours'—notice is usually sufficient. If you enter a restaurant without a reservation, you may not be seated, even if there are empty tables. Restaurant owners on St. Barths take great pride in their service as well as in their food, and they would rather turn you away than slight you on an understaffed evening. At the end of the meal, as in France, you must request the bill. Until you do, you can feel free to linger at the table and enjoy the complimentary vanilla rum that's likely to appear.

18

Check restaurant bills carefully. A service charge (*service compris*) is always added by law, but you should leave the server 5% to 10% extra in cash. You'll usually come out ahead if you charge restaurant meals on a credit card in euros instead of paying with American currency, as your credit card will offer a better exchange rate than the restaurant. Many restaurants serve locally caught lobster (*langouste*); priced by weight, it's usually the most expensive item on a menu and, depending on its size and the restaurant, will range in price from $40 to $60. In menu prices below, it has been left out of the range.

WHAT TO WEAR

A bathing suit and pareu (sarong) are acceptable at beachside lunch spots. Most top it off with a T-shirt or tank top. Jackets are never required and rarely worn, but people dress fashionably for dinner. Casual chic is the idea; women wear whatever is hip, current, and sexy. You can't go wrong in a tank dress or a hippie-chic skirt and top. Nice shorts (not beachy ones) at the dinner table may label a man *américain,* but many locals have adopted the habit, and nobody cares much. Pack a light sweater or shawl for an after-dinner beach stroll.

ASIAN FUSION ✕ **Eddy's.** By local standards, dinner in the pretty, open-air, tropi-
$$–$$$$ cal garden here is reasonably priced. The cooking is French-creole-
★ Asian. Fish specialties, especially the sushi tuna sampler, are fresh and delicious, and there are always plenty of notable daily specials. Just remember some mosquito repellent for your ankles. ⊠ *Rue du Cente-naire* ☎ *0590/27–54–17* ✍ *Reservations not accepted* ▤ *AE, MC, V* ☉ *Closed Sun. No lunch.*

$$–$$$$ ✕ **La Mandala.** Owner Boubou has a couple of popular restaurants on the island, all of which are cute, fun, and have of-the-moment menus and friendly staff. This one offers tasty Thai-influenced food on a sweeping terrace over Gustavia Harbor. The sushi bar is a huge hit with the celebrities that flock here. It's also great for a sunset cocktail. Try the vegetable-curry spring rolls, fish tempura with kimchee sauce, Peking-style duck, or the Thai-scented sea bass steamed in foil. Save room for the apple donuts with Szechwan pepper-and-coriander syrup. ⊠ *Rue de la Sous-Préfecture, Gustavia* ☎ *0590/27–96–96* ▤ *AE, MC, V.*

CARIBBEAN ✕ **Pipiri Palace.** Tucked into a tropical garden, this popular in-town res-
$$$–$$$$ taurant known for its barbecued ribs, beef fillet, and rack of lamb is
★ consistently one of our absolute favorites. Fish-market specialties like red snapper cooked in a banana leaf or grilled tuna are good here, as are grilled duck with mushroom sauce and a skewered surf-and-turf with a green curry sauce. The blackboard lists daily specials that are usually a great choice, like a salad of tomato, mango, and basil. Pierrot, the friendly owner, is sure to take good care of you. ⊠ *Rue Général-de-Gaulle, Gustavia* ☎ *0590/27–53–20* ✍ *Reservations essential* ▤ *MC, V* ☉ *Closed mid-June–July.*

ECLECTIC ✕ **Maya's.** New Englander Randy Gurly and his French–chef wife,
$$$$ Maya, provide a warm welcome and a very pleasant dinner on their
★ cheerful dock decorated with big, round tables and crayon-color canvas chairs, all overlooking Gustavia Harbor. A market-inspired menu

of good, simply prepared and garnished dishes like mahimahi in creole sauce, shrimp scampi, pepper-marinated beef fillet changes daily, assuring the ongoing popularity of a restaurant that seems to be on everyone's list of favorites. ☒*Public, Gustavia* ☎*0590/27–75–73* ⌕*Reservations essential* ▱*AE, MC, V.*

$$$–$$$$ ✕**Do Brazil.** At this cozy restaurant nestled at the cliff side of Gustavia's Shell Beach, you'll be able to sample more of restaurateur Boubou's fusion creations. The menu is more French-Thai than Brazilian, although at dinner there are usually a couple of Brazilian specialties. The decor is vaguely jungle-chic—romantic at night, lively at lunch. The €42 menu is a good deal. Grilled sandwiches at the snack bar on the beachfront level are the perfect lunch. For dinner, choose between varied salads, raw fish, hand-chopped steak tartare, and a variety of fresh-caught grilled fish. The service has been known to be a little relaxed. ☒*Shell Beach, Gustavia* ☎*0590/29–06–66* ⌕*Reservations essential* ▱*AE, MC, V.*

$$$–$$$$ ✕**Le Ti St. Barth Caribbean Tavern.** Chef-owner Carole Gruson captures
★   the funky, sexy spirit of the island in her wildly popular hilltop hot spot. We always come here to dance to great music with the attractive crowd lingering at the bar, lounge at one of the pillow-strewn banquettes, or chat on the torch-lighted terrace. By the time your appetizers arrive, you'll be best friends with the next table. The menu includes Thai beef salad, lobster ceviche, rare grilled tuna with Chinese noodles, and the best beef on the island. Provocatively named desserts, such as Nymph Thighs (airy lemon cake with vanilla custard) and Daddy's Balls (passion fruit sorbet and ice cream) end the meal on a fun note. Around this time someone is sure to be dancing on top of the tables. There's an extensive wine list. The famously raucous full-moon parties are legendary. ☒*Pointe Milou* ☎*0590/27–97–71* ⌕*Reservations essential* ▱*MC, V.*

$$–$$$ ✕**Le Repaire.** This friendly brasserie overlooks Gustavia's harbor and is
★   a popular spot from its early-morning opening at 7 AM to its late-night closing at midnight. Its flexible hours are great if you arrive mid-afternoon and need a good snack before dinner. Grab a cappuccino, pull a captain's chair to the streetside rail, and watch the pretty girls. The menu ranges from cheeseburgers, which are served only at lunch along with the island's best fries, to simply grilled fish and meat. The composed salads always please. Wonderful ice-cream sundaes round out the menu. Try your hand at the billiards table or show up on weekends for live music. ☒*Quai de la République, Gustavia* ☎*0590/27–72–48* ▱*MC, V.*

$$–$$$ ✕**Wall House.** The food can be really good—and the service is always
★   friendly—at this restaurant on the far side of Gustavia harbor. The menu has been changed to emphasize the dishes that Frank, the amiable chef, does best, and the quality of everything continues to rise. Some of the best choices are specialties cooked on the elaborate gas rotisserie, including spit-roasted grouper, stuffed saddle of lamb, or five-spice honey pineapple duck. The pesto gnocchi are out of this world. Local businesspeople crowd the restaurant for the bargain prix-fixe lunch menu. The daily €29 dinner menu is a pretty good deal, too. An old-

18

fashioned dessert trolley showcases some really yummy sweets. ⊠*La Pointe, Gustavia* ☎*0590/27–71–83* ⚗*Reservations essential* ⊟*AE, MC, V* ⊘*Closed Sept. and Oct.*

FRENCH ✕**François Plantation.** This St. Barths favorite has been wonderfully
$$$$ reincarnated with sexy new decor, including pretty white drapery, and
Fodor'sChoice ethnographic black-and-white photos on the walls. Fresh Caribbean
★ produce and seafood combine with European provisions like foie gras, artisanal cheeses, black truffles, and rare spices. First-rate presentation and exceptional service add to (the admittedly costly) delight. Definitely sample the exquisite desserts, such as cucumber-mojito-lemon pound cake. ⊠*François Plantation, Colombier* ☎*0590/29–80–22* ⚗*Reservations essential* ⊟*AE, MC, V* ⊘*Closed Sept. and Oct. No lunch.*

$$$$ ✕**Le Gaïac.** If you're in the mood to dress up, this is the elegant, sophis-
★ ticated restaurant at which to do it. Everything is taken very seriously here. Starched napery and impeccable service complement the blue bay view. Lunch includes chilled, spicy mango soup, salads, and grilled seafood. The dinner menu showcases really serious food: beef fillet with a tamarind glaze and tempura vegetables, coconut-crusted saddle of lamb, lime-infused halibut with banana, and black truffle veal chop cooked in a sea-salt crust: are you salivating? Table-side crêpes suzette are de rigueur, but then again, who could resist lime, orange, or berry soufflé? There's a €43 buffet brunch on Sunday. ⊠*Le Toiny, Anse à Toiny* ☎*0590/29–77–47* ⊟*AE, DC, MC, V* ⊘*Closed Sept.–mid-Oct.*

$$$–$$$$ ✕**La Marine.** This St. Barths harborside classic is run by Carole Gruson, who has created a spiffy decor to match and meld into her hot next-door nightclub, Le Yacht Club. The traditional Thursday- and Friday-night mussels are always a hit, along with lots of other seafood choices. The Caribbean "B.B.Q. night" features all- you-can-eat grilled spiny lobster. It's a good choice for lunch, too. ⊠*Rue Jeanne d'Arc, Gustavia* ☎*0590/27–68–91* ⊟*AE, MC, V.*

$$$–$$$$ ✕**Le Sapotillier.** The romantic brick walls, hand-painted wooden chairs,
★ exquisite white-linen tablecloths, and vivid creole paintings evoke an old-style private island home. The service reminds us of dinner in the "best" homes, but this is not the cooking of your *maman*. Classic French food like rack of lamb, dover sole *meuniere*. and roasted Bresse chicken with potato gratin anchors the menu. Caramelized foie gras with cinnamon spiced pear and *sangria* is not to be missed. The sumptuous chocolate mousse and raspberry soufflé are longtime favorites. ⊠*Rue du Centenaire, Gustavia* ☎*0590/27–60–28* ⚗*Reservations essential* ⊟*MC, V* ⊘*Closed mid-May–late Oct. No lunch.*

$$$–$$$$ ✕**Le Tamarin.** A leisurely lunch here en route to Grand Saline beach is a
★ St. Barths *must*. Delicious French cuisine by Maxime Deschamps, formerly of Le Toiny, is served at this sophisticated open-air restaurant. Artistic salads tempt at lunch, especially the one garnished with with foie gras. Dinner options include a Moroccan-style lamb glazed with mango, along with plenty of daily specials. ⊠*Salines* ☎*0590/27–72–12* ⊟*AE, MC, V* ⊘*Closed Mon.*

$$–$$$ ✕**Le Cesar.** This brand-new restaurant next to Hôtel le Village St-Jean
☺ features excellent, locally caught seafood ably prepared by the former

chef of Le Marine. You can have mussels any day, or good grilled meats with a wide choice of vegetable side dishes. There's a €10 children's menu. The mango *tarte tatin* is a treat. ⊠*Les Hauts de Saint-Jean* ☎0590/27–70–67 ⚠*Reservations essential* ▤*AE, MC, V.*

$$–$$$ ✕**O'Corner.** New on the St. Barths restaurant scene in 2007, O'Corner has received favorable early reports on its cool art deco design, live music, and tasty fresh food offered in small, medium, and large sizes. The music is loud, and the crowd is hip. The real party starts after 11 each evening. It's all under the watchful eye of Hervé Chovet from the former St. Barths Beach Hotel. A mix of salads, stir-fries, grilled meats, and lots of veggie options makes this a great choice for a crowd. There's a plasma TV in the bar. ⊠*Rue du Roi Oscar II, Gustavia* ☎0590/51–00–05 ▤*AE, MC, V.*

ITALIAN ✕**PaCrì.** An adorable, young husband-and-wife team (she is the chef)
$$$–$$$$ serve delicious, huge portions of housemade pasta, wood-oven-fired
★ pizza (at lunch), and authentic Italian main courses, like Pugliese mahimahi, succulent meatballs, and sautéed veal *saltimbocca* on a breezy open terrace right near Saline Beach. The menu changes daily. Don't miss the softball-size hunk of the best artisa nal mozzarella you've ever had, flown in from Italy and garnished with prosciutto or tomato and basil. The eggplant Parmesan appetizer is delicious and more than enough for a meal. Unusual desserts like lemon profiteroles are definitely worth the calories. Gorgeous waitstaff of both sexes add to the general air of voluptuousness. ⊠*Rte. de Saline* ☎0590/29–35–63 ⚠*Reservations essential* ▤*AE, MC, V.*

SEAFOOD ✕**Restaurant des Pêcheurs.** From fresh, morning beachside brioche to
$$–$$$$ a final evening drink in the sexy lounge, you can dine all day in this
★ soaring thatch pavilion that is the epitome of chic. The restaurant at Le Sereno, like the Christian Liaigre–designed resort, is serenity itself. Each menu item is a miniature work of art, beautifully arranged and amiably served. Each day there is a different €44 three-course menu. "Authentic" two-course *Bouillabaisse à l'ancienne,* the famous French seafood stew, is served every Friday, and the chef even gives a class in its preparation, but the menu also lists daily oceanic arrivals from Marseille, and Quiberon on France's Atlantic coast: roasted, salt-crusted, or grilled to perfection. This, and sand between your toes, is heaven. ⊠*Grand Cul-de-Sac* ⚠*Reservations essential* ▤*AE, D, MC, V.*

$$–$$$ ✕**La Langouste.** This tiny beachside restaurant in the pool-courtyard of Hôtel Baie des Anges is run by Anny, the hotel's amiable, ever-present proprietor. It lives up to its name by serving fantastic, fresh-grilled lobster at a price that is somewhat gentler than at most other island venues. Simple, well-prepared fish, pastas, and an assortment of refreshing cold soups are also available. Be sure to try the warm goat cheese in pastry served on a green salad. ⊠*Hôtel Baie des Anges, Flamands Beach* ☎0590/27–63–61 ⚠*Reservations essential* ▤*MC, V* ⊗*Closed May–Oct.*

18

BEACHES

There are many *anses* (coves) and nearly 20 *plages* (beaches) scattered around the island, each with a distinctive personality and each open to the general public. Even in season you can find a nearly empty beach. Topless sunbathing is common, but nudism is forbidden—although both Grande Saline and Gouverneur are de facto nude beaches. Bear in mind that the rocky beaches around Anse à Toiny are not swimmable.

Anse à Colombier. The beach here is the least accessible, thus the most private, on the island; to reach it you must take either a rocky footpath from Petite Anse or brave the 30-minute climb down (and back up) a steep, cactus-bordered—though clearly marked—trail from the top of the mountain behind the beach. Appropriate footgear is a must, and you should know that once you get to the beach, the only shade is a rock cave. Boaters favor this beach and cove for its calm anchorage. ⊠ *Anse à Colombier.*

Anse des Flamands. This is the most beautiful of the hotel beaches—a roomy strip of silken sand. We love to come here for lunch and then spend the afternoon sunning, taking a long beach walk and a swim in the turquoise water. From the beach, you can take a brisk hike to the top of the now-extinct volcano believed to have given birth to St. Barths. ⊠ *Anse des Flamands.*

★ **Anse du Gouverneur.** Because it's so secluded, nude sunbathing is popular here; the beach is truly beautiful, with blissful swimming and views of St. Kitts, Saba, and St. Eustatius. Venture here at the end of the day, and watch the sun set behind the hills. The road here from Gustavia also offers spectacular vistas. Legend has it that pirates' treasure is buried in the vicinity. ⊠ *Anse du Gouverneur.*

Anse de Grand Cul de Sac. The shallow, reef-protected beach is especially nice for small children, fly-fishermen, kayakers, and windsurfers; it has excellent lunch spots, water-sports rentals, and lots of the amusing pelican-like frigate birds that dive-bomb the water fishing for their lunch. ⊠ *Grand Cul de Sac.*

Fodor'sChoice **Anse de Grande Saline.** Secluded, with its sandy ocean bottom, this is just
★ about everyone's favorite beach and great for swimmers, too. Without any major development, it's an ideal Caribbean strand, though it can be a bit windy here, so you can enjoy yourself more if you go on a calm day. In spite of the prohibition, young and old alike go nude. The beach is a 10-minute walk up a rocky dune trail, so be sure to wear sneakers or water shoes. The big salt ponds here are no longer in use, and the place looks a little desolate. ⊠ *Grande Saline.*

Anse de Lorient. This beach is popular with St. Barths families and surfers, who like its rolling waves. Be aware of the level of the tide, which can come in very fast. Hikers and avid surfers like the walk over the hill to Point Milou in the late afternoon sun when the waves roll in. ⊠ *Lorient.*

Baie de St-Jean. Like a mini–Côte d'Azur—beachside bistros, bungalow hotels, bronzed bodies, windsurfing, and lots of day-trippers—the reef-protected strip is divided by Eden Rock promontory, and there's good snorkeling west of the rock. ⊠ *Baie de St-Jean.*

SPORTS & THE OUTDOORS

BOATING & SAILING

St. Barths is a popular yachting and sailing center, thanks to its location midway between Antigua and St. Thomas. Gustavia's harbor, 13 to 16 feet deep, has mooring and docking facilities for 40 yachts. There are also good anchorages available at Public, Corossol, and Colombier. You can charter sailing and motorboats in Gustavia Harbor for as little as a half day. Stop at the Tourist Office in Gustavia for an up-to-the-minute list of recommended charter companies.

Marine Service (⊠*Gustavia* ☎*0590/27–70–34* ⊕*www.st-barths.com/marine.service*) offers full-day outings, either on a 42- or 46-foot catamaran, to the uninhabited Île Fourchue for swimming, snorkeling, cocktails, and lunch. The cost is $100 per person; an unskippered motor rental runs about $260 a day.

Yellow Submarine (⊠*Ferry Dock, Gustavia* ☎*0590/52–40–51* ⊕*www.yellow-submarine.fr*) takes you "six feet under" (the surface of the sea) for a close-up view of St. Barth's coral reefs through large glass portholes. Once a week you can go at night. It costs €40 for adults and €12 for kids under 12. Trips depart hourly starting at 9 AM.

DIVING & SNORKELING

Several dive shops arrange scuba excursions to local sites. Depending on weather conditions, you may dive at **Pain de Sucre, Coco Island**, or toward nearby **Saba**. There's also an underwater shipwreck to explore, plus sharks, rays, sea tortoises, coral, and the usual varieties of colorful fish. The waters on the island's leeward side are the calmest. For the uncertified who still want to see what the island's waters hold, there's an accessible shallow reef right off the beach at Anse de Cayes if you have your own mask and fins. Most of the waters surrounding St. Barths are protected in the island's **Réserve Marine de St-Barth** (⊠*Gustavia* ☎*0590/27–88–18*), which also provides information at its office in Gustavia. The diving here isn't nearly as rich as in the more dive-centered destinations like Saba and St. Eustatius, but the options aren't bad either, and none of the smaller islands offer the ambience of St. Barths.

Plongée Caraïbe (☎*0590/27–55–94*) is recommended for its up-to-the-minute equipment and dive boat. **Splash** (⊠*Gustavia* ☎*0690/56–90–24*) does scuba, snorkeling, and fishing, too. Marine Service operates the only five-star, PADI-certified diving center on the island, called **West Indies Dive** (☎*0590/27–70–34* ⊕*www.westindiesdive.com*). Scuba trips, packages, resort dives, night dives, and certifications start at $90, including gear.

18

FISHING

Most fishing is done in the waters north of Lorient, Flamands, and Corossol. Popular catches are tuna, marlin, wahoo, and barracuda. There's an annual St. Barths Open Fishing Tournament, organized by Ocean Must, in mid-July.

Marine Service (⊠ *Gustavia* ☎ *0590/27–70–34* ⊕ *www.st-barths.com/ marine.service*) arranges ocean-fishing excursions. **Océan Must Marina** (⊠ *Gustavia* ☎ *0590/27–62–25*) arranges deep-sea fishing expeditions as well as bareboat and staffed boat charters.

GOLF

Very well-heeled golf fanatics will be quite pleased with **Fly & Golf** (☎ *0690/30–58–73* ⊕ *www.flygolf.net*), which debuted in 2003. PGA pro and former champion Emmanuel Dussart will arrange tee times and flights from St. Barths to one of the excellent golf courses on Anguilla, St. Thomas, Nevis, or another nearby island. The maximum number of golfers per trip is three. Call about pricing; if you have to think about it, you probably can't afford it.

Golf in Paradise (⊠ *Petit Cul-de-Sac Pond* ☎ *0690/37–46–45*) is a driving range on the water, with a video-golf simulator, and lessons. The company also arranges trips to golf courses on other islands.

HORSEBACK RIDING

Two-hour horseback trail-ride excursions in the morning or the afternoon led by Coralie Fournier are about $40 per person at **St. Barth Equitation** (⊠ *Ranch des Flamands, Anse des Flamands* ☎ *0690/39–87–01*). Instruction is also available.

SHOPPING

Fodor'sChoice
★ St. Barths is a duty-free port, and with its sophisticated crowd of visitors, shopping in the island's 200-plus boutiques is a definite delight, especially for beachwear, accessories, jewelry, and casual wear. It would be no overstatement to say that shopping for fashionable clothing, accessories, and decorative items for the home is better in St. Barths than anywhere else in the Caribbean. New shops open all the time, so there's always something new to discover. Stores often close for lunch from noon to 2, and many on Wednesday afternoon as well, but they are open until about 7 in the evening. A popular afternoon pastime is strolling about the two major shopping areas in Gustavia and St-Jean.

SHOPPING AREAS

In Gustavia, boutiques line the three major shopping streets. Quai de la République, nicknamed rue du Couturier, which is right on the harbor, rivals New York's Madison Avenue or Paris's avenue Montaigne for high-end designer retail, including brand-new shops for **Dior, Louis Vuitton, Tod's, Bulgari, Cartier, Chopard,** and **Hermès.** These shops often carry items that are not available in the United States. The Carré d'Or plaza is great fun to explore. Shops are also clustered in **La Savane Commercial Center** (across from the airport), **La Villa Créole** (in St-Jean), and **Espace Neptune** (on the road to Lorient). It's worth working your way from one end to the other at these shopping complexes—just to see or, perhaps, be seen. Boutiques in all three areas carry the latest in French and Italian sportswear and some haute couture. You probably are not going to find any bargains as long as the euro remains high, but you might be able to snag that *pochette* that is sold out stateside, and in any case, you'll have a lot of fun hunting around.

SPECIALTY STORES

BOOKS

Funny Face Bookstore (✉ *Quai de la République, Gustavia* ☎ *0590/29–60–14*) is a full-service bookstore with hundreds of English titles for adults and kids, plus armchairs, coffee, and Internet access.

CLOTHING

Shopping for up-to-the-minute fashions is as much a part of a visit to St. Barths as going to the beach. Shops change all the time, both in ownership and in the lines that are carried. Current listings are just a general guide. The best advice is simply to go for a long stroll and check out all the shops on the way. The following list is of shops that have an interesting variety of current and fun items, but it's by no means an exhaustive one.

Black Swan (✉ *Le Carré d'Or, Gustavia* ☎ *0590/27–65–16* ✉ *La Villa Créole, St-Jean*) has an unparalleled selection of bathing suits. The wide range of styles and sizes is appreciated. **Boutique Lacoste** (✉ *Rue Du Bord de Mer, Gustavia* ☎ *0590/27–66–90*) has a huge selection of the once-again-chic alligator-logo wear, as well as a shop next door with a complete selection of the Petit Bateau line of T-shirts popular with teens. **Cachemire Crème** (✉ *Rue du Bord du Mer, Gustavia* ☎ *0590/52–48–42*) stocks, as the name suggests, deliciously fine cashmere in unusual styles and a whole tiny line for very lucky children. Right next door to Cachemire Crème, **Cafe Coton** (✉ *Rue du Bord du Mer, Gustavia* ☎ *0590/52–48–42*) is a great shop for men, especially for long-sleeve linen shirts in a rainbow of colors and Egyptian cotton dress shirts. **Calypso** (✉ *Le Carré d'Or, Gustavia* ☎ *0590/27–69–74*) carries resort wear for women by Balenciaga, Lucien Pellat-Finet, and Chloé. **Dovani** (✉ *Rue de la République, Gustavia* ☎ *0590/29–84–77*) has elegant leather goods and Baccarat jewelry. Fans of Longchamp handbags and leather goods will find a good selection at about 20% off

18

stateside prices at **Elysée Caraïbes** (⊠ *Le Carré d'Or, Gustavia* ☎*0590/ 52–00–94*).

Hip Up (⊠ *Rue Général-de-Gaulle, Gustavia* ☎*0590/27–69–33*) stocks a wonderful line of swimwear for all ages; tops and bottoms are sold separately for a practically custom fit, with cute matching accessories like sandals, cargo skirts, and T-shirt tops to complete the look. **Laurent Effel** (⊠ *Rue Général-de-Gaulle, Gustavia*) now has four shops in Gustavia for beautiful leather belts, colorful linen shirts, bags, and shoes. One shop is devoted entirely to exotic leather accessories. Check out **Lili Belle** (⊠ *Pelican Plage, St-Jean* ☎*0590/87–46–14*), for hippie-chic drapey tops, drop-dead bikinis by D nu D, and Stella Forest T-shirts and blouses. Don't miss **Lolita Jaca** (⊠ *Le Carré d'Or, Gustavia* ☎*0590/27–59–98*) for trendy, tailored sportswear. **Mia Zia** (⊠ *Rue du Roi Oscar II, Gustavia* ☎*0590/27–55–48*), which has relocated to big, new, purple quarters in Gustavia, imports wonderful accessories from Morocco, including multicolored, tassled silk and cotton shawls, caftans, and colorful 6-foot-long silk cords to wrap around your wrists, waist, or neck. **Morgan's** (⊠ *La Villa Créole, St-Jean* ☎*0590/27–57– 22*) has a line of popular and wearable casual wear in the trendy vein.

Pati de Saint Barth (⊠ *Passage de la Crémaillière, Gustavia* ☎*0590/29– 78–04*) is the largest of the three shops that stock the chic, locally made T-shirts that have practically become the logo of St. Barths. The newest styles have hand-done graffiti-style lettering. At **Poupette** (⊠ *Rue de la République, Gustavia* ☎*0590/27–94–49*), all the brilliant color-silk and chiffon batik and embroidered peasant skirts and tops are designed by the owner. There also are great belts and beaded bracelets. **Stéphane & Bernard** (⊠ *Rue de la République, Gustavia* ☎*0590/27–69–13*) stocks a well-edited, large selection of superstar French fashion designers, including Rykiel, Tarlazzi, Kenzo, Feraud, and Mugler. Look to **St. Tropez KIWI** (⊠ *St-Jean* ☎*0590/27–57–08* ⊠ *Gustavia* ☎*0590/27– 68–97*) for resort wear. **SUD SUD.ETC.Plage** (⊠ *Galerie du Commerce, St-Jean* ☎*0590/27–98–75*) stocks everything for the beach: inflatables, mats, bags, and beachy shell jewelry. **Saint-Barth Stock Exchange** (⊠ *La Pointe-Gustavia* ☎*0590/27–68–12*), on the far side of Gustavia's harbor, is the island's consignment and discount shop.

COSMETICS

Don't miss the superb skin-care products made on-site from local tropical plants by **Ligne de St. Barths** (⊠ *Rte. de Saline, Lorient* ☎*0590/ 27–82–63*).

FOODSTUFFS

A.M.C (⊠ *Quai de la République, Gustavia*) is a bit older than Match but able to supply anything you might need for housekeeping in a villa, or for a picnic. **JoJo Supermarché** (⊠ *Lorient*) is the well-stocked counterpart to Gustavia's large supermarket and gets daily deliveries of bread and fresh produce. Prices are lower here than at the larger markets. **Match** (⊠ *St-Jean*), a fully stocked supermarket across from the airport, has a wide selection of French cheeses, pâtés, cured meats, produce, fresh bread, wine, and liquor. **Maya's to Go** (⊠ *Galleries du*

Commerce, St-Jean ☎0590/29–83–70) is the place to go for prepared picnics, meals, salads, rotisserie chickens, and more from the kitchens of the popular restaurant. For exotic groceries or picnic fixings, stop by St. Barths' gourmet *traiteur* (takeout) **La Rotisserie** (⊠*Rue du Roi Oscar II, Gustavia* ☎0590/27–63–13 ⊠*Centre Vaval, St-Jean* ☎0590/29–75–69) for salads, prepared meats, groceries from Fauchon, and Iranian caviar.

HANDICRAFTS

The ladies of Corossol produce intricate straw work, wide-brim beach hats, and decorative ornaments by hand. Call the tourist office, which can provide information about the studios of other island artists: Christian Bretoneiche, Robert Danet, Nathalie Daniel, Patricia Guyot, Rose Lemen, Aline de Lurin, and Marion Vinot.

Look for Fabienne Miot's unusual gold jewelry at **L'Atelier de Fabienne** (⊠*Rue de la République, Gustavia* ☎0590/27–63–31). **Chez Pompi** (⊠*On road to Toiny* ☎0590/27–75–67) is a cottage whose first room is a gallery for the naive paintings of Pompi (also known as Louis Ledée). **Couleurs Provence** (⊠*St-Jean* ☎0590/52–48–51) stocks beautiful, handcrafted French-made items like jacquard table linens in brilliant colors; decorative tableware, including trays in which dried flowers and herbs are suspended; and the home fragrance line by L'Occitane. **Kayali** (⊠*Rue de la République, Gustavia* ☎0590/27–64–48) shows varied works by local artists. Local works of art, including paintings, are sold in the bright **Made in St-Barth La Boutique** (⊠*La Villa Créole, St-Jean* ☎0590/27–56–57). Find local stoneware, raku pottery, and other crafts at **St. Barth Pottery** (⊠*Gustavia* ☎0590/27–69–81), next to the post office on the harbor.

JEWELRY

Carat (⊠*Quai de la République, Gustavia*) has Chaumet and a large selection of Breitling watches.

A good selection of watches, including Patek Phillippe and Chanel, can be found at **Diamond Genesis** (⊠*Rue Général-de-Gaulle, Gustavia*). Next door to Cartier, **Oro del Sol** (⊠*Quai de la République, Gustavia*) carries beautiful fine accessories by Bulgari, Ebel, and others. **Sindbad** (⊠*Carré d'Or, Gustavia* ☎0590/27–52–29) is a tiny shop with funky, unique couture fashion jewelry by Gaz Bijou of St. Tropez, crystal collars for your pampered pooch, chunky ebony pendants on silk cord, and other reasonably priced, up-to-the-minute styles.

LIQUOR & TOBACCO

La Cave du Port Franc (⊠*Rue de la République, Gustavia* ☎0590/27–65–27) has a good selection of wine, especially from France. **La Cave de Saint-Barths** (⊠*Marigot* ☎0590/27–63–21) has an excellent collection of French vintages stored in temperature-controlled cellars. **Le Comptoir du Cigare** (⊠*Rue Général-de-Gaulle, Gustavia* ☎0590/27–50–62), run by Jannick and Patrick Gerthofer, is a top purveyor of cigars. The walk-in humidor has an extraordinary selection. Try the Cubans while you are on the island, and take home the Davidoffs. Refills can be shipped stateside. Be sure to try on the genuine Panama hats. **Couleur des Isles**

18

Cuban Cigar (⊠ *Rue Général-de-Gaulle, Gustavia* ☎ *0590/27–79–60*) has many rare varieties of smokeables and good souvenir T-shirts, too. At **M'Bolo** (⊠ *Rue Général-de-Gaulle, Gustavia* ☎ *0590/27–90–54*), be sure to sample the various varieties of infused rums, including lemongrass, ginger, and, of course, the island favorite, vanilla. Bring home some in the beautiful hand-blown bottles.

NIGHTLIFE

"In" clubs change from season to season, so you might ask around for the hot spot of the moment. There's more nightlife than ever in recent memory, and a late (10 PM or later) reservation at one of the club-restaurants will eventually become a front-row seat at a party.

Bar de l'Oubli (⊠ *Rue du Roi Oscar II, Gustavia* ☎ *0590/27–70–06*) is where young locals gather for drinks. **Carl Gustaf** (⊠ *Rue des Normands, Gustavia* ☎ *0590/27–82–83*) lures a more sedate crowd, namely those in search of quiet conversation and sunset watching. **Le Feeling** (⊠ *Lurin* ☎ *0590/52–84–09*) is a cabaret and disco in the Lurin Hills that has special theme nights on Thursday. It opens nightly at midnight for a cabaret show. **Le Nikki Beach** (⊠ *St-Jean* ☎ *0590/27–64–64*) rocks on weekends during lunch, when the scantily clad young and beautiful lounge on the white canvas banquettes. **Le Repaire** (⊠ *Rue de la République, Gustavia* ☎ *0590/27–72–48*) lures a crowd for cocktail hour and its pool table. **Le Santa Fé** (⊠ *Lurin* ☎ *0590/27–61–04*), in the Lurin Hills, features a rowdy crowd, billiards, and satellite TV sports. **Le Sélect** (⊠ *Rue du Centenaire, Gustavia* ☎ *0590/27–86–87*) is St. Barths' original hangout, commemorated by Jimmy Buffett's "Cheeseburger in Paradise." The boisterous garden is where the barefoot boating set gathers for a brew. At this writing the hot spot was **Le Yacht Club** (⊠ *Rue Jeanne d'Arc, Gustavia* ☎ *0690/49–23–33*); although ads call it a private club, you can probably get in anyway.

EXPLORING ST. BARTHÉLEMY

With a little practice, negotiating St. Barths' narrow, steep roads soon becomes fun. Free maps are everywhere, roads are well marked, and painted signs will point you where the tourist office has annotated maps with walking tours that highlight sights of interest. Starting in December 2005, some of the parking congestion on the island was alleviated by the **St-Barth Shuttle**, a fleet of four air-conditioned minibuses with high-season round-trip routes between Gustavia, Flamands, Lorient, and Grand Cul de Sac. The round-trip ticket costs €10.

Numbers in the margin correspond to points of interest on the St. Barthélemy map.

☾ **Corossol.** The island's French-provincial origins are most evident in this two-street fishing village with a little rocky beach. Older local women weave lantana straw into handbags, baskets, hats, and delicate strings of birds. Ingenu Magras's **Inter Oceans Museum** has more than 9,000 seashells and an intriguing collection of sand samples from around the world. You can buy souvenir shells. ✉ *Corossol* ☎ *0590/27–62–97* 🎫 *€3* ⊘ *Tues.–Sun. 9–12:30 and 2–5.*

Gustavia. You can easily explore all of Gustavia during a two-hour stroll. Street signs in both French and Swedish illustrate the island's history. Most shops close from noon to 2, so plan lunch accordingly. A good spot to park your car is rue de la République, where catamarans, yachts, and sailboats are moored. The **tourist office** (☎ *0590/27–87–27* ✉ *odtsb@wanadoo.fr*) on the pier can provide maps and a wealth of information. It's open Monday from 8:30 to 12:30, Tuesday through Friday from 8 to noon and 2 to 5, and Saturday from 9 to noon. On the far side of the harbor known as La Pointe is the charming **Municipal Museum,** where you can find watercolors, portraits, photographs, and historic documents detailing the island's history as well as displays of the island's flowers, plants, and marine life. ☎ *599/29–71–55* 🎫 *€2* ⊘ *Mon., Tues., Thurs., and Fri. 8:30–12:30 and 2:30–6, Sat. 9–12:30.*

St-Jean. The half-mile-long crescent of sand at St-Jean is the island's most popular beach. Windsurfers skim along the water here, catching the strong trade winds. A popular activity is watching and photographing the hair-raising airplane landings. You'll also find some of the best shopping on the island here, as well as several restaurants.

Toiny coast. Over the hills beyond Grand Cul de Sac is this much-photographed coastline. Stone fences crisscross the steep slopes of Morne Vitet, one of many small mountains on St. Barths, along a rocky shore that resembles the rugged coast of Normandy. It's one island beach that's been nicknamed the "washing machine" because of its turbulent surf. Even expert swimmers should beware of the strong undertow here; swimming is generally not recommended.

ST. BARTHÉLEMY ESSENTIALS

To research prices, get advice from other travelers, and book travel arrangements, visit www.fodors.com.

▌ TRANSPORTATION

BY AIR

There are no direct flights to St. Barths. Most North Americans fly first into St. Maarten's Queen Juliana International Airport, from which the island is 10 minutes by air. Flights leave at least once an hour between 7:30 AM and 5:30 PM on Winair. Air Caraïbes, based in Guadeloupe, flies among the French West Indies and to the Dominican Republic. Anguilla Air Services is an excellent charter company that flies to any Caribbean destination and runs day trips between Anguilla and St. Barths, at the very reasonable rate of $175 per person (4-person minimum). St. Barth Commuter is a small, private charter company that can also arrange service. Tradewind Aviation offers charters and regularly scheduled, daily nonstop Premium service from San Juan, Puerto Rico. Flights are timed conveniently to meet early flights from the United States.

18

You must confirm your return interisland flight, even during off-peak seasons, or you may very well lose your reservation. Do not be upset if your luggage has not made the trip with you. It frequently will arrive on a later flight, and your hotel will send a porter to receive it; villa-rental companies may also help you retrieve luggage from the airport, but you may have to beg. It's a good idea to pack a change of clothes, required medicines, and a bathing suit in your carry-on.

Airlines Air Caraïbes (☎0590/27–71–90, 877/772–1005 in U.S. ⊕www.aircaraibes.com). **Anguilla Air Services** (☎264/498–5922 ⊕www.anguillaairservices.com). **St. Barth Commuter** (☎0590/27–54–54 ⊕www. stbarthcommuter.com). **Tradewind Aviation** (☎800/376–7922 ⊕www.tradewindaviation. com). **Winair** (☎0590/27–61–01 or 800/634–4907 ⊕www.fly-winair.com).

Airports Aéroport de St-Jean (☎0590/27–75–81).

BY BIKE & MOPED

Several companies rent motorbikes, scooters, mopeds, and mountain bikes. Motorbikes go for about $30 per day and require a $100 deposit. Helmets are required. Scooter and motorbike rental places are located mostly along rue de France in Gustavia and around the airport in St-Jean. They tend to shift locations slightly.

Information Barthloc Rental (✉Rue de France, Gustavia ☎0590/27–52–81). **Chez Béranger** (✉Rue de France, Gustavia ☎0590/27–89–00). **Ets Denis Dufau** (✉St-Jean ☎0590/27–70–59).

BY BOAT & FERRY

Voyager offers ferry service for day trips between St. Barths, St. Martin (Marigot), and Saba. Round-trips are offered for about $60 per person. There's an additional €12 surcharge for fuel and port fees. All service is from Quai de la République. Private boat charters are also available.

Information Voyager (☎0590/87–10–68 ⊕www.voyager-st-barths.com).

BY CAR

Most travelers to St. Barths rent a car. The new St. Barth Shuttle service can be convenient and much less expensive than a taxi if you're just one or two people, but it still doesn't completely negate the need for a car.

You'll find major rental agencies at the airport. You must have a valid driver's license and be 25 or older to rent, and in high season there may be a three-day minimum. During peak periods, such as Christmas week and February, be sure to arrange for your car rental ahead of time. When you make your hotel reservations, ask if the hotel has its own cars available to rent; some hotels provide 24-hour emergency road service—something most rental companies don't offer. If there are only two of you, think about renting a Smart car. Tiny but powerful on the hills, it's a blast to buzz around in, and also a lot easier to park than larger cars.

Roads are sometimes unmarked, so be sure to get a map. Instead of road signs, look for signs pointing to a destination. These will be nailed to posts at all crossroads. Roads are narrow and sometimes very steep, so check the brakes and gears of your rental car before you drive away, and make a careful inventory of the existing dents and scrapes on the vehicle. Maximum speed on the island is 30 mph (50 kph). Driving is on the right, as in the United States and Europe. St. Barths drivers often seem to be in an unending grand prix and thus tend to keep their cars maxed out, especially and inexplicably when in reverse. Parking is an additional challenge.

There are two gas stations on the island, one near the airport and one in Lorient. They aren't open after 5 PM or on Sunday, but you can use the one near the airport at any time with some credit cards, including Visa, JCB, or Carte Blanche. Considering the short distances, a full tank of gas should last you most of a week.

Information Avis (☎0590/27-71-43). **Budget** (☎0590/27-66-30). **Europcar** (☎0590/27-74-34 ⊕www.st-barths.com/europcar/index.html). **Gumbs** (☎0590/27-75-32). **Gust: Smart of St-Barth** (☎0690/41-66-72). **Hertz** (☎0590/27-71-14). **St. Barth Shuttle** (✉At Mangliers, St. Jean ☎0590/29-44-19). **Turbe** (☎0590/27-71-42 ⊕www.saint-barths.com/turbecarrental/).

BY TAXI

Taxis are expensive and not particularly easy to arrange, especially in the evening. There's a taxi station at the airport and another in Gustavia; from elsewhere you must contact a dispatcher in Gustavia or St-Jean. Technically, there's a flat rate for rides up to five-minutes long. Each additional three minutes is an additional amount. In reality, however, cabbies usually name a fixed rate—and will not budge. Fares are 50% higher from 8 PM to 6 AM and on Sunday and holidays.

Information Gustavia taxi dispatcher (☎0590/27-66-31). **St-Jean taxi dispatcher** (☎0590/27-75-81).

▌CONTACTS & RESOURCES

BANKS & EXCHANGE SERVICES

Banks and ATMs are well located throughout the island, so getting money is rarely a problem. The official currency in St. Barths is the euro; however, dollars are accepted in almost all shops and in many restaurants, though you will probably receive euros in change. Credit cards are accepted at most shops, hotels, and restaurants. In general, American Express charges in dollars; MasterCard charges in euros.

Prices quoted in this chapter are in euros, unless otherwise noted.

ELECTRICITY

Voltage is 220 AC/60 cycles, as in Europe. You can sometimes use American appliances with French plug converters and transformers. Most hotel rooms are conveniently supplied with hair dryers, and most have a shaver plug in the bathroom into which you can plug various rechargeables.

EMERGENCIES

Emergency Services Ambulance & Fire (☎0590/27-62-31). **Police** (☎17 or 0590/27-66-66).

Hospitals Hospital De Bruyn (✉Gustavia ☎0590/27-60-35).

INTERNET, MAIL & SHIPPING

Most hotels provide Internet and e-mail access for guests at the front desk, if not right in the room, but if yours does not, make a visit to the Internet Service at Centre Alizes, which has fax service and 10 computers online. It's open weekdays from 8:30 to 12:30 and 2:30 to 7, as well as on Saturday morning. France Télécom can provide you with temporary Internet access that may let you connect your laptop. If you have a Wi-Fi-equipped laptop, there are hot spots for the area, the Guanahani, and in the parking lot of Oasis Shopping Center in Lorient; service is provided by Antilles Référencement, an excellent computer shop that can set you up with a temporary Internet account or provide other computer support.

Mail is slow. Correspondence between the United States and the island can take up to three weeks to arrive. The main post office is in Gustavia; in season it's open daily 7:30–3, (except for Wed. and Sat., when it closes at noon), but smaller post offices are in St-Jean and Lorient. These are open a few hours each morning. When writing to an establishment on St. Barths, be sure to include "French West Indies" at the end of the address. Because of the slow mail service, faxes are widely used.

Internet Cafés Antilles Référencement (✉Oasis Shopping Centre, Lorient ☎0590/58-97-97). **Centre Alizes** (✉Rue de la République, Gustavia ☎0590/29-89-89).

France Télécom (✉Espace Neptune, St-Jean ☎0590/27–67–00).

Post Offices **Main post office** (✉*Rue Jeanne d'Arc, Gustavia* ☎*0590/27–62–00*). **Lorient post office** (✉Lorient ☎0590/27–61–35). **Saint-Jean post office** (✉Saint-Jean ☎0590/27–64–02).

LANGUAGE

French is the official language, so it can't hurt to pack a phrase book and/or French dictionary. If you speak any French at all, don't be shy. You may also hear Creole, the regional French dialect called patois, and even the Creole of Guadeloupe. Most hotel and restaurant employees speak some English—at least enough to help you find what you need.

SAFETY

There's relatively little crime on St. Barths. Visitors can travel anywhere on the island with confidence. Most hotel rooms have minisafes for your valuables. As anywhere, don't tempt loss by leaving cameras, laptops, or jewelry out in plain sight in your hotel room or villa. Don't walk barefoot at night. There are venomous centipedes that can inflict a remarkably painful sting.

TAXES & SERVICE CHARGES

The island charges a $5 departure tax when your next stop is another French island, $10 if you're off to anywhere else. This is payable in cash only, dollars or euros, at the airport. At this writing, some hotels added an additional 10% to 15% service charge to bills, though most include it in their tariffs. There are no other additional taxes on either hotels or villa rentals.

TELEPHONES

MCI and AT&T services are available. Public telephones do not accept coins; they accept *télécartes,* prepaid calling cards that you can buy at the gas station next to the airport and at post offices in Lorient, St-Jean, and Gustavia. Making an international call using a télécarte

is much less expensive than making it through your hotel.

If you bring a cell phone to the island and wish to activate it for local use, visit St. Barth Eléctronique across from the airport. You can also buy an inexpensive cell phone with prepaid minutes for as little as €20, including some initial air time. Many hotels will rent you a local-service cell phone; ask the manager or concierge.

The country code for St. Barths is 590. Thus, to call St. Barths from the U.S., dial 011 + 590 + 590 and the local six-digit number. Some cell phones use the prefix 690, in which case you would dial 590 + 690. For calls on St. Barths, you must dial 0590 plus the six-digit local number; for St. Martin dial just the six-digit number for the French side, for the Dutch side (Sint Maarten) dial 00–599–54 plus the five-digit number, but remember that this is an international call and will be billed accordingly. To call the United States from St. Barths, dial 001 plus the area code plus the local seven-digit number.

Information **France Télécom** (✉Espace Neptune, St-Jean ☎0590/27–67–00). **St. Barth Eléctronique** (✉St-Jean ☎0590/27–50–50).

TIPPING

Restaurants include a 15% service charge in their published prices, but it's common French practice to leave 5% to 10% *pourboire* (a tip; literally, "for a drink")—in cash, even if you have paid by credit card. When your credit-card receipt is presented to be signed, the tip space should be blank—just draw a line through it—or you could end up paying a 30% service charge. Most taxi drivers don't expect a tip.

TOUR OPTIONS

You can arrange island tours by minibus or car at hotel desks or through any of the island's taxi operators in Gustavia or at the airport. The tourist office runs a variety of tours with varying itineraries that run about €46 for a half day for up to eight people. Mat Nautic can help you arrange to tour the island by water on a Jet Ski or Waverunner. St-Barth Tours and Travel will customize a tour of the island. Wish Agency can arrange customized tours as well as take care of airline ticketing, event planning, maid service, and private party arrangements.

Information **Mat Nautic** (✉Quai du Yacht Club, Gustavia ☎0690/49–54–72). **St-Barth Tours & Travel** (✉Rue Jeanne d'Arc, Gustavia ☎0590/27–52–14). **Wish Agency** (☎0590/29–83–74 ✐wish.agency@wanadoo.fr).

VISITOR INFORMATION

A daily news sheet called *News* lists local happenings like special dinners or music and is available at markets and newsstands. Also, the free weekly *Journal de Saint-Barth*—mostly in French—is useful for current events. The small *Ti Gourmet*

Saint-Barth is a free pocket-size guidebook that's invaluable for addresses and telephone numbers of restaurants and services. Look for the annual *Saint-Barth Tables* for full restaurant menus. Its counterpart, *Saint-Barth Leisures*, contains current information about sports, spas, nightlife, and the arts.

Before You Leave French Government Tourist Office (☎900/990–0040 charges a fee ⊕www.franceguide.com).

In St. Barths Office du Tourisme (✉Quai Général-de-Gaulle ☎0590/27–87–27 ✐odtsb@wanadoo.fr) is an invaluable source for any reliable up-to-the-minute information you may need.

WEDDINGS

Because of the long legal residency requirement, it's not really feasible to get married on St. Barths unless you're a French citizen.

18

St. Eustatius

Fort Oranje, Oranjestad

WORD OF MOUTH

"[C]rime is almost non-existent. . . . Everyone you pass will wave at you, whether they know you or not, and one always enters a shop or place of business with a pleasant . . . greeting."

— Statia

"Although climbing the Quill was a little arduous, it was kind of fun since there was not a soul around except an occasional crab or snake (just one little guy who slithered away as fast as he could)."

— Doug

WELCOME TO ST. EUSTATIUS

Boven Bay

Cocoluch Bay

Fontaan Bay

Venus Bay

Jenkins Bay

Boven

Gilb
Hi

Zeelandia

Little Mountain

Tumble Down Dick Bay

Franklin D **Roosevelt Ai**

Signal Hill

◆ **Ft. Royal**

Interlopers Pt.

Stenara 🟦 **Reef**

Smoke Alley Beach **(Oranje Beach)**

Stenapa Reef, named after the St. Eustatius National Parks Association, was created through the sinking of various ships. It's one of the largest artificial reefs in the Caribbean.

Lower Town

Gallows Bay

Double **Wreck** 🟦

Crooks 🟦 **Castle**

Oranjest see deta map

On November 16, 1776, Fort Oranje fired the first cannon-salute to the new American flag. The first time the Stars and Stripes had been recognized by any country.

KEY

⤢	Beaches
🟦	Dive Sites
🌴	Rain Forest
①	Hotels

Barracuda **Reef** 🟦

Like Saba, tiny Statia is another quiet Caribbean haven for scuba divers and hikers. When the island was called the Emporium of the Western World, warehouses stretched for a mile along the quays, and 200 merchant ships could anchor at its docks. These days it's the day-trippers from St. Martin who walk the quays.

FRIENDLY TRANQUILLITY

A tiny part of the Netherlands Antilles, St. Eustatius (often just called "Statia") is just under 12-square-mi (30-square-km), making it twice as large as Saba. The island, which is 38 mi (63 km) south of St. Maarten, has a population of 2,900. Although there are three beaches, they are better for strolling than swimming.

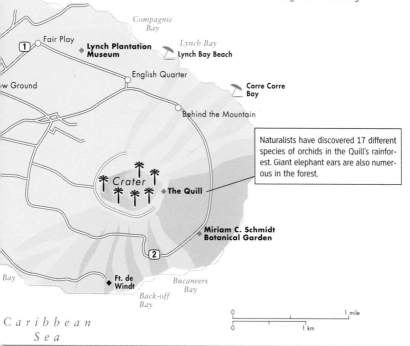

Naturalists have discovered 17 different species of orchids in the Quill's rainforest. Giant elephant ears are also numerous in the forest.

TOP 4 REASONS TO VISIT ST. EUSTATIUS

1. Diving—particularly to its modern and archaeological wrecks—is a highlight in Statia's protected waters.

2. Hiking the Quill, an extinct volcano that holds a primeval rain forest, is the top activity for land lubbers.

3. When you're not diving, you'll be overwhelmed by the genuine friendliness of the people.

4. For anyone interested in 18th-century history, even a day-trip from St. Maarten is a very satisfying experience.

ST. EUSTATIUS PLANNER

Island Activities

St. Eustatius, which is usually referred to as Statia, has **beaches,** but they are fairly rocky, better suited for walking and beachcombing than for swimming and sunning. The more-interesting action is below the waves. Along with Saba, which helps to administer its dive sites as part of the Saba Marine Park, Statia is a major **diving** destination. It has good wreck diving as well as reef diving. If you want to keep your head above water, then the Quill, Statia's extinct volcano, which holds a primeval rain forest, is well worth your time; a guided **hike** here will bring you face to face with all manner of exotic tropical flora and even some fauna.

On the Ground

You could literally walk from the airport runway into town, but if you want to take a taxi, one or two will be waiting for arriving passengers at the airport, and you'll be whisked into Oranjestad for about $5. To explore the island (and there isn't very much of it), car rentals, which cost about $40 to $50 a day, do the job. Statia's roads are generally in good condition (watch out for goats), but there are only 2 gas stations.

Logistics

Getting to St. Eustatius: The only way to get to Statia (EUX) is on one of the regularly scheduled Winair flights from Saba, St. Maarten, or San Juan; you'll have to book this flight yourself, directly with Winair. There is no regularly scheduled ferry service, but flights from St. Maarten and San Juan are fairly frequent and are timed to coincide with the arrival of international flights there.

Hassle Factor: Medium–High.

Nonstops: None.

Where to Stay

Statia has only four hotels, all with 20 rooms or fewer and all within Oranjestad (within walking distance of everything else in town), and a handful bed-and-breakfasts. However, there's nothing on the island that could be described as luxurious. Sometimes the decor, like the redecorated 55-gallon drums–turned–TV stands at King's Well Resort, is quite original.

Hotel & Restaurant Costs

⇨*For information on hotel meal plans, see Accommodations in Caribbean Essentials.*

WHAT IT COSTS IN U.S. DOLLARS				
$$$$	$$$	$$	$	¢
Restaurants				
over $30	$20–$30	$12–$20	$8–$12	under $8
Hotels*				
over $350	$250–$350	$150–$250	$80–$150	under $80
Hotels**				
over $450	$350–$450	$250–$350	$125–$250	under $125

*EP, BP, CP **AI, FAP, MAP Restaurant prices are for a main course at dinner and include any taxes or service charges. Hotel prices are per night for a double room in high season, excluding taxes, service charges, and meal plans (except at all-inclusives).

By Roberta
Sotonoff

THE STARS ARE ABLAZE, BUT it's dark and empty on the road between the Blue Bead Bar & Restaurant and the Gin House Hotel. A chicken running across the road comprises all the traffic, and except for the sound of crickets, there is silence. No need to worry about walking alone. The island of Statia (pronounced *stay-sha*) is safe. How safe? The scuttlebutt is that a St. Maarten police officer sent to serve on the island thinks he is being punished because there is nothing for him to do.

With a population of just fewer than 3,300, it's difficult for someone to commit a crime—or do most anything else—without everyone finding out. Everyone knows everyone, and that's also a blessing. Statians are friendly; they beep their horns and say hello to anyone they see. Even day-trippers are warmly welcomed as friends. There are no strangers here.

Think of the tiny Netherlands Antillean island of St. Eustatius, commonly called Statia, and envision quiet times, strolls through history, and awesome diving and hiking. While many of its neighbors are pursuing the tourist business big-time, Statia just plods along. That's its charm.

The 12-square-mi (31-square-km) island in the Dutch Windward Triangle, 150 mi (241 km) east of Puerto Rico and 38 mi (61 km) south of St. Maarten, was the hub for commerce between Europe and the Americas during the 18th century. When ships carrying slaves, sugar, cotton, ammunition, and other commodities crowded its harbor, it was known as the Emporium of the Western World and the Golden Rock.

With an 11-gun salute to the American "Stars and Stripes" on the brig-of-war *Andrew Doria* on November 16, 1776, Statia's golden age ended. Statia's noteworthy role as the first country to recognize U.S. independence from Great Britain was not a gesture appreciated by the British. In 1781, British Admiral Rodney looted and economically destroyed the island. It has never really recovered.

Indeed, chaos ensued between 1781 and 1816 as the Dutch, English, and French vied for control of the island. It changed hands 22 times. The Netherlands finally won out, and Statia has been a Dutch possession since 1816.

19

Remnants of those bygone days are evident around the island. Hanging off the cliff at the only village, Oranjestad, is the nearly 370-year-old Ft. Oranje, the site from where the famous shots were fired. The original Dutch Reformed Church, built in 1776, sits in its courtyard. Oranjestad itself, on a ridge above the sea, is lush with greenery and bursting with bougainvillea, oleander, and hibiscus. The rest of the island is rather pristine. The eastern side, bordered by the rough waters of the Atlantic, has an untamed quality to it, while extinct volcanoes and dry plains anchor the north end. Statia's crown is the Quill, a 1,968-foot extinct volcano, its verdant crater covered with a primeval rain forest. Hiking to the peak is a popular pastime.

Beaches on the island come and go as the waters see fit, but first-class dive sites lure most visitors to the island. Wrecks and old cannons are plentiful at archaeological dive sites, and modern ships, such as the cable-laying *Charles L. Brown*, have been sunk into underwater craters. Stingrays, eels, turtles, and barracudas live in the undersea Caribbean neighborhood where giant pillar coral, giant yellow sea fans, and reef fingers abound. The sea has reclaimed the walls of Dutch warehouses that have sunk into the sea over the past several hundred years, but these underwater ruins serve as a day-care center for abundant schools of juvenile fish.

On land, beachcombers hunt for blue beads. The 17th-century baubles, found only on Statia, were used to barter for rum, slaves, tobacco, and cotton. The chance of finding one is slim unless you visit the St. Eustatius Historical Foundation Museum. Pre-Columbian artifacts dating back to 500 BC are also on display there.

Besides relying on tourism and the University of St. Eustatius School of Medicine, an accredited, two-year medical school, Statia's economy depends on oil. The northern end of the island is a way station for liquid gold. A 16-million-barrel storage bunker is encased in the Boven, an extinct volcano. It's not unusual to see the hovering tankers loading or unloading oil.

Statia is mostly a short-flight day-trip destination from nearby St. Maarten, where tourists come to explore historical sights and maybe take a quick hike or dive. That might be just enough for some visitors. But those who linger can appreciate the unspoiled island, its history, and its peacefulness. Most of all they will come to enjoy the locals, who make a visit to the island special.

WHERE TO STAY

Renting an apartment is an alternative to staying in a hotel. Although Statia has only a handful of them, several are available for $50 or less per night, but don't expect much beyond a bathroom and kitchenette. Check with the tourist office for options.

$–$$$
★

Old Gin House. Built from 17th- and 18th-century cobblestones, this quaint old cotton warehouse now contains a hotel and restaurant, and offers the island's nicest accommodations. Comfortable, though not lavish, rooms face the gardens and pool of the courtyard. Across the street are four ocean-side units, along with the Seaside Bar and Grill. Free Internet is a nice perk. **Pros:** Conveniently located, good restaurant, attractive setting. **Cons:** Rooms are dark, hotel could use some sprucing up. ⌂Bay Rd., Lower Town, Oranjestad ☎599/318–2319 ⊕www.oldginhouse.com ⥺18 rooms, 2 suites ⌂In-room: refrigerator (some), DVD (some). In-hotel: 2 restaurants, bar, pool, no elevator, public Internet ⊟AE, MC, V ⫶EP.

$–$$
Fodor'sChoice
★

Statia Lodge. Look out from your cottage patio and just beyond the water from the island's nicest digs, and you'll enjoy drop-dead gorgeous views of Nevis on the horizon. Do an about-face and the Quill volcano looms. Each airy yet cozy cottage has attractive teakwood furnishings, tiled floors, ceiling fans, and louver-like walls and French doors, plus a patio with an outdoor kitchenette with tables and chairs. The wood-accented bathrooms each have corner showers. Rates include use of

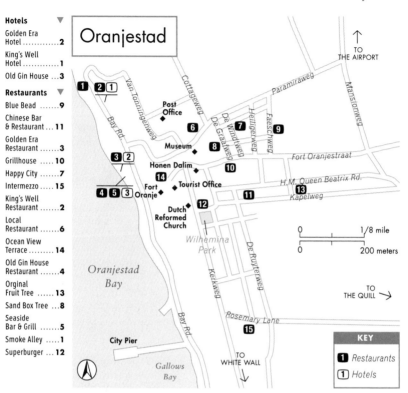

Oranjestad

TO
THE AIRPORT

Post
Office

Museum

Honen Dalim

Fort
Oranje

Tourist Office

Dutch
Reformed
Church

*Wilhemina
Park*

*Oranjestad
Bay*

City Pier

*Gallows
Bay*

TO
WHITE WALL

Fort Oranjestraat

H.M. Queen Beatrix Rd.

Kapelweg

Rosemary Lane

TO
THE QUILL

0   1/8 mile
0   200 meters

KEY

Restaurants

Hotels

either a scooter or, for a bit extra, a car. There's no restaurant, nor TVs or phones—just serenity, as well as a bar that sits alongside the attractive, L-shape swimming pool. Cribs are available for small children. **Pros:** The best views and most modern accommodations on the island. **Cons:** No restaurant, not near the water or town (which is why the car or scooter is necessary), not handicap-accessible. ⊠ *White Wall* ☎*599/318–1900* ⊕*www.statialodge.com* ⬎*8 1-bedroom cottages, 2 2-bedroom cottages* ⚷*In-room: kitchen, no TV. In-hotel: bar, pool, no elevator* ▤*MC, V* ⦵*EP.*

$ **Golden Era Hotel.** This hotel across the street from the Old Gin House has a funky, retro-1960s look. Only half the rooms have a view, but all have tile floors and little terraces. The oceanfront property offers friendly service and a restaurant with great creole food. The staff proudly unveiled a new reception area in 2007, complete with a small gift shop offering up a couple of watches, some perfume, and a some T-shirts. **Pros:** Friendly staff, right on the waterfront, dive shop is next door. **Cons:** Rooms are a bit dark and very basic. ⊠*Bay Rd., Lower Town, Box 109, Oranjestad* ☎*599/318–2345, 800/223–9815 in U.S.* ✉*goldenerahotel@gmail.com* ⬎*19 rooms, 1 suite* ⚷*In-room: refrigerator. In-hotel: restaurant, bar, pool, no elevator* ▤*AE, D, MC, V* ⦵*EP.*

19

$ 🏨 **King's Well Resort.** Win and Laura Piechutzki, along with their macaws, iguanas, cats, and Great Dane, warmly welcome visitors to their little inn. Perched on the wooded cliffs between Upper and Lower Town, the inn has eclectic furnishings, such as TV stands made of decorated oil barrels. All the rooms have balconies, and four have king-size water beds and French doors that face the sea. A cliff-side patio is a pleasant place to watch the sunset. The King's Well Restaurant is probably the only place on the island to get authentic Wiener schnitzel. Weekly rates are available. **Pros:** Eclectic and unusual furnishings, good view of the bay. **Cons:** Not a place for guests not fond of animals, especially iguanas, not on the water or in town. ⊠*On curve of Van Tonningenweg, Smoke Alley, Oranjestad* 🕾*599/318–2538* ⊕*www. kingswellstatia.com* ⟿*12 rooms* ⌂*In-room: refrigerator. In-hotel: restaurant, bar, pool, no elevator* ⊟*D, MC, V* ⍽*BP.*

¢ 🏨 **Country Inn.** Facing Zeelandia Bay and close to the oil terminal and the airport, this folksy little inn is surrounded by a lush, tropical garden. Its six rooms are clean and comfortable but otherwise pretty basic. Owner Iris Pompier prepares lunch and dinner on request. Breakfast costs $5 extra. **Pros:** Very homey, tropical garden is lovely. **Cons:** Not on the water or near town, breakfast isn't complimentary, a vehicle is necessary. ⊠*3 Passionfruit Rd., Concordia* 🕾*599/318–2484* ⟿*6 rooms* ⌂*In-hotel: no elevator* ⊟*No credit cards* ⍽*EP.*

WHERE TO EAT

It's surprising that on such a small island, you can find such a wide range of cuisines: Italian, German, French, Chinese, Indonesian, international, and, of course, Caribbean. What you won't find is anything very fancy. As with most everything on the island, low-key and casual is the name of the game.

ASIAN ✕ **Chinese Bar & Restaurant.** Unless you're into Formica, don't expect
$–$$ to be wowed by the atmosphere at this simple spot. What you will find are large portions of dishes like *bami goreng* (Indonesian-style noodles with bits of beef, pork, or shrimp as well as tomatoes, carrots, bean sprouts, cabbage, soy sauce, and spices); or pork chops with spicy sauce. It's do-it-yourself table hauling if you want to eat outside. ⊠*Queen Beatrix Rd., Upper Town, Oranjestad* 🕾*599/318–2389* ⊟*No credit cards.*

$–$$ ✕ **Grillhouse/San Yen Chinese Bar & Restaurant.** Here is yet another Chinese restaurant that is short on decor—a few tables and a bar—but long on taste. Its special—a dish combining chicken, scallops, shrimp, beef, and sausage with vegetables—is delicious, filling, and well worth the trip. ⊠*Fort Oranjestraat, Upper Town, Oranjestad* 🕾*599/318–2915* ⊟*No credit cards.*

¢–$$ ✕ **Happy City Chinese Bar & Restaurant.** In the island's only strip mall, this tidy restaurant offers more than just Chinese fare. The locals frequent it to sup on Indonesian dishes such as *nasi goreng* (fried rice). ⊠*De Windtweg, Upper Town, Oranjestad* 🕾*599/318–2540* ⊟*No credit cards* ☉*Closed Wed.*

CAFÉS ✕ **Intermezzo.** Statia's newest contribution to the dining scene, a coffeehouse with just a handful of tables, has relocated to a more-festive space. A cheery orange-and-yellow lattice rail decorates the patio seating area. The island's answer to Starbucks is the place to grab an espresso, cappuccino, or latte. Sandwiches and other light fare are also available. Intermezzo closes at 1 PM on Sunday and 3 PM the rest of the week. ✉ *Fort Oranjestraat, Oranjestad* ☎ *599/318–0075* ▤ *No credit cards* ⊗ *No dinner.*

¢ ✕ **Sand Box Tree Bakery.** This is the perfect spot for a quick sandwich; to satisfy your sweet tooth; or to order a wedding, birthday, or other special-occasion cake. It's opposite the Dutch Reformed Church. ✉ *Kerkweg, Upper Town, Oranjestad* ☎ *599/318–2469* ▤ *No credit cards.*

CARIBBEAN ✕ **Golden Era Hotel Restaurant.** Don't pass up this restaurant just because $–$$ it's completely nondescript. Concentrate instead on the tasty seafood and fine creole fare. It has another thing going for it: it's alongside the water, so the sound of the Caribbean is always playing in the background. ✉ *Golden Era Hotel, Bay Rd., Lower Town, Box 109, Oranjestad* ☎ *599/318–2345 or 599/318–2355* ▤ *AE, D, MC, V.*

$–$$ ✕ **Original Fruit Tree Bar and Restaurant.** This traditionally styled Statia eatery—a converted home with simple furnishings—has bougainvillea spilling over its white picket fence. Locals rave about the goat meat, fish, and chicken cutlets as well as the oxtail at this relative newcomer. It is not unusual for patrons to stop by, place an order, and run a few errands while the chef prepares the meal. ✉ *Queen Beatrix Rd., Oranjestad* ☎ *599/318–2584* ▤ *No credit cards.*

$ ✕ **Local Restaurant.** It's hard to miss this place—white lattice towers above the red, yellow, and blue metal fence at the entrance. Its somewhat prosaic name says it all: this is a place for locals to hang out and eat no-frills chicken, fish, oxtail, or goat, served either stewed or fried ✉ *Paramiraweg, Oranjestad* ☎ *599/318–5435* ▤ *No credit cards.*

¢ ✕ **Superburger.** Statia's version of fast food comes from this little hangout, which serves burgers and shakes as well as some West Indian dishes daily from 11:30 to 2. It's a local favorite for lunch. ✉ *Graaffweg, Upper Town, Oranjestad* ☎ *599/318–2412* ▤ *No credit cards* ⊗ *No dinner.*

ECLECTIC ✕ **Blue Bead Bar & Restaurant.** This friendly little restaurant with its $$–$$$ cheerful blue-and-yellow decor is a favorite with locals and the per-★ fect place to watch the sunset. It is one of those places where everyone talks to everyone. There are always daily specials and a menu with an array of choices that include pizza and seafood. ✉ *Bay Rd., Gallows Bay, Lower Town, Oranjestad* ☎ *599/318–2873* ▤ *AE, D, MC, V* ⊗ *Closed Mon.*

$$–$$$ ✕ **King's Well Restaurant.** It's like watching Mom and Dad make dinner to see owners Win and Laura Piechutzki scurry around their open kitchen preparing the night's meal. And don't expect to eat alone, because a meal at this breezy terrace overlooking the sea makes you part of the family. The *rostbraten* (roast beef) and schnitzels are authentic, as Win is German. The fresh lobster is another good choice. ✉ *King's Well Resort, Bay Rd., Lower Town, Oranjestad* ☎ *599/318–2538* ▤ *D, MC, V.*

19

$$–$$$ ✕**Old Gin House Main Dining Room.** In a comfortable dining room that borders a flower-filled courtyard, this bistro serves French cuisine with a West Indian and West African flair. Specialties include Drambuie steak, and a fanciful "floating island" dessert. ⊠ *Old Gin House, Bay Rd., Lower Town, Oranjestad* ☎ *599/318–2319* ▤ *AE, MC, V* ⊘ *Closed Wed. No lunch.*

$$–$$$ ✕**Smoke Alley Bar & Grill.** Owner Michelle Balelo cooks Tex-Mex, Italian, Caribbean, and American food to order at this beachfront hangout. The open-air eatery is the only place on the island where you can get draft beer. There's live music and barbecued meats every Friday night. ⊠ *Gallows Bay, Lower Town, Oranjestad* ☎ *599/318–2002* ▤ *MC, V* ⊘ *Closed Sun.*

$–$$$ ✕**Seaside Bar & Grill.** Set across the street from the Old Gin House, this dapper site is more casual than the hotel's main dining room. The fare is similar, as it's overseen by the same kitchen team. The simple menu includes great scrambled eggs for breakfast, sandwiches and salads for lunch, and dinner specials that always include something from the sea. A snack menu features crab balls and jalapeño poppers. On Wednesday evening there's a barbecue with live music. ⊠ *Old Gin House Hotel, Bay Rd., Lower Town, Oranjestad* ☎ *599/318–2319* ▤ *AE, MC, V.*

$–$$ ✕**Ocean View Terrace.** This spot in the courtyard overlooking the historic Ft. Oranje is a favorite for those who like to watch the sunset. Owner Lauris Redan serves sandwiches and burgers for lunch and local cuisine—baked snapper with shrimp sauce, spicy chicken, tenderloin steak—at dinner. You can get breakfast here, too, and every now and then there's a succulent barbecue. ⊠ *Fort Oranjestraat, Upper Town, Oranjestad* ☎ *599/318–2934* ▤ *No credit cards* ⊘ *No lunch Sun.*

BEACHES

If you lust after a white sandy beach, calm waters, and a place to cool yourself off with a quick dip, you're looking at the wrong island. Statia's beaches are mostly deserted, rocky stretches of pristine shoreline. Many of the beaches on the Caribbean side are here today and reclaimed by the sea tomorrow, while the Atlantic side is untamed with wild swells and a vicious undertow. Walking, shelling, and searching for the elusive blue beads are popular pastimes for beachgoers. It's likely, however, that the only place you will find real blue beads is in the St. Eustatius Historical Foundation.

Lynch Bay Beach. Just two bends north of Corre Corre Bay, light-brown sand covers this small beach on the island's Atlantic side. Opt for walking instead of swimming here. There are turbulent swells and an undertow. ⊠ *Lynch Bay.*

Smoke Alley Beach *(Oranje Beach)*. The color of the sand varies from light beige to black at this rocky beach on the Caribbean side near Gallows Bay. Often, much of the beach is claimed by the sea. The waters are sometimes calm, so snorkeling is possible, but it's usually a better place for a walk than a swim. ⊠ *Oranjestad, north end.*

Diving on Statia

Forget about glitz and nightlife. Statia is the quintessential low-key island. Finding an elusive *iguana delicatissima* on the Quill is probably the most exciting thing you can do on land. Statia's real thrills are underwater.

Long ago, the ocean reclaimed the original seawall built by the Dutch in the 1700s. The sunken walls, remnants of old buildings, cannons, and anchors are now part of an extensive reef system populated by reef fingers, juvenile fish, and other sea creatures.

Statia has more than 30 dive sites protected by the St. Eustatius Marine Park, which has an office on Bay Road in Lower Town. Barracuda swim around colorful coral walls at **Barracuda Reef**, off the island's southwest coast. At **Double Wreck**, just offshore from Lower Town, you can find two tall-masted ships that date from the 1700s. The coral has taken on the shape of these two disintegrated vessels, and the site attracts spiny lobsters, stingrays, moray eels, and large schools of fish. About 100 yards west of Double Wreck is the Japanese ship *Cheng Tong*, which sank in 2004. Off the south end of the island, the sinking of the *Charles L. Brown*, a 1957 cable-laying vessel, which was once owned by AT&T, created another artificial reef when it was sunk in a 135-foot underwater crater. Off the island's western shore, **Stenapa Reef** is an artificial reef created from the wrecks of barges, a harbor boat, and other ship parts. Large grouper and turtles are among the marine life you can spot here. For snorkelers, **Crooks Castle** has several stands of pillar coral, giant yellow sea fans, and sea whips just southwest of Lower Town.

Zeelandia Beach. Walking, shelling, and sunbathing are popular pastimes on this 2-mi (3-km) stretch of black-and-tan sand. Its Atlantic-side location makes it a dangerous place even to put one piggy in the water. ⊠ *Oranjestad.*

19

SPORTS & THE OUTDOORS

DIVING & SNORKELING

Fodor's Choice ★ The island's three dive shops along Bay Road in Lower Town rent all types of gear (including snorkeling gear for about $8 a day), offer certification courses, and organize dive trips. One-tank dives start at $40; two-tank dives are about $75. Both the Saba Marine Park and Quill National Park are under the supervision of **Statia National Parks** (☎599/318–2884 ⊕*www.statiapark.org*). The marine tag fee, which all divers must buy, is used to help offset the costs of preserving the coral and other sea life here; the cost is $3 per day or $15 annually. There are two decompression chambers on the island, and the University of St. Eustatius, a medical school, offers technical training in undersea and hyperbaric medicine.

Dive Statia (⊠ *Bay Rd., Lower Town, Oranjestad* ☎599/318–2435 *or 866/614–3491* ⊕*www.divestatia.com*), a fully equipped and PADI-certified dive shop, has earned PADI's five-star Gold Palm designation. Owners Rudy and Rinda Hees operate the shop out of an old warehouse. In addition to the standard courses, Dive Statia also offers underwater photography courses, Nitrox diving, and DVPs—diver propulsion vehicles—for diving or snorkeling. **Golden Rock Dive Center** (⊠ *Old Gin House, Bay Rd., Lower Town, Oranjestad* ☎ *599/318–2964* ⊕ *www.goldenrockdive.com*), operated by Glenn and Michele Faires, also boasts PADI's Gold Palm designation. In addition to certification courses, the shop offers a National Geographic program that emphasizes conservation. **Scubaqua** (⊠ *Golden Era Hotel, Bay Rd., Lower Town, Oranjestad* ☎ *599/318–2873* ⊕ *www.scubaqua.com*), caters to Europeans as well as Americans. Dive courses are offered in various languages.

HIKING

Trails range from the easy to the "Watch out!" The big thrill here is the Quill, the 1,968-foot extinct volcano with its crater cradling a rain forest. Give yourself two to four hours to complete the hike. The tourist office has a list of 12 marked trails and can put you in touch with a guide. Quill National Park includes a trail into the crater, which is a long, winding, but safe walk. Maps and the necessary $3 permit, which is good for a year, are available at the Statia Marine Park headquarters on Bay Road. Wear layers: it can be cool on the summit and steamy in the interior.

KAYAKING

One excellent way to tour the island is by kayak. Two-person kayaks are available at **Dive Statia** (⊠ *Bay Rd., Lower Town, Oranjestad* ☎ *599/318–2435 or 866/614–3491* ⊕ *www.divestatia.com*) for $20 an hour. Guided tours take paddlers to Black Rock Reef and Jenkins Bay.

SHOPPING

The very limited shopping here is all duty-free. But other than the predictable souvenirs, there's not much to buy. Several shops carry Dutch cheeses and chocolates and an interesting book by Heleen Cornett called *St. Eustatius: Echoes of the Past*. **Mazinga Gift Shop** (⊠ *Fort Oranjestraat, Upper Town, Oranjestad* ☎ *599/318–2245*) is a small department store that sells the basic necessities. The **Paper Corner** (⊠ *Van Tonningenweg, Upper Town, Oranjestad* ☎ *599/318–2208*) sells magazines, a few books, and stationery supplies.

NIGHTLIFE

Statia's nightlife consists of local bands playing weekend gigs and quiet drinks at hotel bars. The island's oldest bar, tiny **Cool Corner** (⊠ *Wilhelminaweg, Upper Town, Oranjestad* ☎ *599/318–2523*), across from the St. Eustatius Historical Foundation Museum, is a lively after-work and weekend hangout. **Smoke Alley Bar & Grill** (⊠ *Lower Town, Gallows Bay* ☎ *599/318–2002*) has live music on Friday night.

EXPLORING ST. EUSTATIUS

Statia is an arid island with a valley between two mountain peaks. Most sights lie in the valley, making touring the island easy. From the airport you can rent a car or take a taxi and be in historic Oranjestad in minutes; to hike the Quill, Statia's highest peak, you can drive to the trailhead in less than 15 minutes from just about anywhere.

Lynch Plantation Museum. Also known as the Berkel Family Plantation, this museum consists of two one-room buildings that show what life was like almost 100 years ago. A remarkable collection preserves this family's history—pictures, eyeglasses, original furnishings, and farming and fishing implements—give a detailed perspective of life on Statia. Call ahead to arrange a private tour. Since it's on the northeast side of the island, you need either a taxi or a car to get there. ⊠ *Lynch Bay* ☎ *599/318–2338* 🖃 *Free* ☾ *By appointment only.*

Miriam C. Schmidt Botanical Garden. As if Statia is not tranquil enough, now comes this new, peaceful 52-acre park. The botanical park is a place of relaxation and quiet. The park has a greenhouse, a palm garden, a kitchen garden, and an observation bird trail. Its location, on the Atlantic side of the Quill *(⇨ below)* on a plot called Upper Company, reveals a superb view of St. Kitts. For a picnic, there's no better place, but the only way to get there is by car or taxi. ⊕ *www.statiapark.org* 🖃 *Suggested donation $5* ☾ *Sunrise–sunset.*

Fodor's Choice ★ **Oranjestad.** Statia's capital and only town sits on the west coast facing the Caribbean. Both Upper Town—with its new cobblestone streets that designate its historic section—and Lower Town are easy to explore on foot.

19

The three bastions of **Ft. Oranje** have clung to these cliffs since 1636. In 1976 Statia participated in the U.S. bicentennial celebration by restoring the fort, and now the black cannons point out over the ramparts. In the parade grounds a plaque, presented in 1939 by Franklin D. Roosevelt, reads, HERE THE SOVEREIGNTY OF THE UNITED STATES OF AMERICA WAS FIRST FORMALLY ACKNOWLEDGED TO A NATIONAL VESSEL BY A FOREIGN OFFICIAL.

Built in 1775, the partially restored **Dutch Reformed Church,** on Kerkweg (Church Way), has lovely stone arches that face the sea. Ancient tales can be read on the gravestones in the adjacent 18th-century cemetery where people were often buried atop one another. On Synagogepad (Synagogue Path), off Kerkweg, is **Honen Dalim** ("She Who Is Charitable to the Poor"), one of the Caribbean's oldest synagogues. Dating from 1738, its exterior is partially restored.

Lower Town sits below Fort Oranjestraat (Fort Orange Street) and some steep cliffs. It is accessible from Upper Town on foot via the zigzagging, cobblestone Fort Road or by car via Van Tonningenweg. Warehouses and shops that were piled high with European imports in the 18th century are either abandoned or simply used to store local fishermen's equipment. Along the waterfront is a lovely park with palms, flowering shrubs, and benches—the work of the historical foundation. Peeking out from the shallow waters are the crumbling ruins of 18th-century buildings, from Statia's days as the merchant hub of the Caribbean. The sea has slowly advanced since then, and it now surrounds many of the stone-and-brick ruins, making for fascinating snorkeling.

In the center of Upper Town is the **St. Eustatius Historical Foundation Museum,** former headquarters of Lord George Rodney, a British admiral during the American Revolution. While here, Rodney confiscated everything from gunpowder to wine in retaliation for Statia's gallant support of the fledgling country. The completely restored house is Statia's most important intact 18th-century dwelling. Exhibits, which were renovated in 2007, trace the island's history from the pre-Columbian 6th century to the present. Statia is the only island thus far where ruins and artifacts of the Saladoid, a newly discovered tribe, have been excavated. ⊠ *Doncker House, 3 Wilhelminaweg, Upper Town, Oranjestad* ☎ *599/318–2288* ⊠ *$3* ⊙ *Weekdays 9–5, weekends 9–noon.*

Fodor'sChoice   **The Quill.** This extinct, perfectly formed, 1,968-foot volcano has a prime-
★   val rain forest in its crater. If you like to hike, you'll want to head here to see giant elephant ears, ferns, flowers, wild orchids, fruit trees, and the endangered *iguana delicatissima* (a large—sometimes several feet long—greenish-gray creature with spines down its back). The volcanic cone rises 3 mi (5 km) south of Oranjestad on the main road. Local boys go up to the Quill by torchlight to catch delectable land crabs. The tourist board or Statia Marine Park will help you make hiking arrangements. Figure on two to four hours to hike the volcano. Make sure to purchase the required $3 permit at the park office before you begin.

ST. EUSTATIUS ESSENTIALS

To research prices, get advice from other travelers, and book travel arrangements, visit www.fodors.com.

▌ TRANSPORTATION

BY AIR

The flight from St. Maarten to Statis's Franklin Delano Roosevelt Airport takes 16 minutes, the flight from Saba 10 minutes, and the flight from St. Kitts 15 minutes. All these short hops are on small planers. Reconfirm your flight, because schedules can change abruptly. The departure fee from the island is $5.65 within the Dutch Caribbean and $12 to all other destinations. If flying out of St.

Maarten, check to see if the international departure fee has already been added into your airline ticket.

Airline Contacts Winair (☎599/545–4237, 599/545–4230, or 599/545–4210)

Airport Contacts Franklin Delano Roosevelt Airport (EUX ☎599/318–2620).

BY CAR

Driving in Statia is not difficult, mostly because there are not that many places to go. Street signs are not plentiful, but anyone you ask for directions will be more than happy to help you. The roads are generally in good condition. Daily rates for a car rental range from $40 to $50.

Contacts **ARC Car Rental** (✉ Oranjestad ☎ 599/318–2595). **Brown's** (✉ White Wall Rd. 8, Oranjestad ☎ 599/318–2266). **Rainbow Car Rental** (✉ Statia Mall, Oranjestad ☎ 599/318–2444). **Walter's** (✉ Chapel Piece, Oranjestad ☎ 599/318–2719).

BY SCOOTER

Zipping around by scooter is another option. Scooter rentals run from $20 to $30 per day and four-wheelers are $30 per day. Insurance is an extra $10 per day.

Contact **L.P.N. Scooter Rentals** (☎ 599/318–4405).

BY TAXI

Taxis meet all flights from Franklin Delano Roosevelt Airport and charge about $5 per person for the drive into town.

■ CONTACTS & RESOURCES

BANKS & CURRENCY EXCHANGE

Prices quoted throughout this chapter are in U.S. dollars, unless noted otherwise.

U.S. dollars are accepted everywhere, but legal tender is the Netherlands Antilles florin (NAf), also referred to as the guilder, and you shouldn't be surprised to receive change in them. The exchange rate was NAf 1.46 to US$1 at this writing. The island's two banks in Upper Town provide foreign-exchange services. There is an ATM at Windward Islands Bank.

EMERGENCIES

Emergency Services **Ambulance** (☎ 912, 599/318–2371, or 599/318–2211). **Fire** (☎ 919 or 699/318–2360). **Police** (☎ 911 or 599/318–2333).

Hospital **Queen Beatrix Medical Center** (✉ 25 H. M. Queen Beatrix Rd., Oranjestad ☎ 599/318–2211 or 599/318–2371).

Scuba Diving Emergencies **St. Eustatius School of Medicine** (✉ Fort Bay ☎ 599/318–2600).

INTERNET, MAIL & SHIPPING

For Web access, drop by the Internet Club on Logeweg near Fort Oranjestraat or the St. Eustatius Jubilee Library in the heart of Oranjestad, across from the Government Administration Building.

The post office is in Upper Town, on Max T. Pandt Boulevard. Airmail letters to North America and Europe are NAf 2.25; postcards, NAf 1.10. When sending letters to the island, be sure to include "Netherlands Antilles" and "Caribbean" in the address.

LANGUAGE

Statia's official language is Dutch (it's used in government documents), but everyone speaks English. Dutch is taught as the primary language in the schools, and street signs are in both Dutch and English.

SAFETY

Statia is relatively crime-free, but common sense should prevail. Lock your rental car when leaving it, store valuables in the hotel safe, and lock your hotel-room door behind you. When driving, particularly at night, be on the lookout for goats, chickens, and other animals that have wandered onto the road. While hiking, you might see the harmless racer snake sunning itself. These snakes are afraid of people and will promptly leave when you arrive.

TAXES & SERVICE CHARGES

The departure tax is $5.65 for flights to other islands of the Netherlands Antilles and $12 to foreign destinations, payable in cash only. Note: when flying home through St. Maarten, list yourself as "in transit" and avoid paying the tax levied in St. Maarten if you are there for less than 24 hours. Hotels collect a 7% government tax and 3% turnover tax. Restaurants charge a 3% government tax and a 10% service charge.

TELEPHONES

Statia has microwave telephone service to all parts of the world. Direct dial is available. There are two pay phones on the

19

island, one near the airport and one in Landsradio. They work with phone cards that you can buy at stores throughout the island. To call Statia from North America, dial 011 + 599 + 318, followed by the four-digit number. To call the United States using an AT&T card, the access number is 001–800/872–2881. To call within the island, dial only the five-digit number that starts with an 8.

TIPPING

Although your hotel or restaurant might add a 10% to 15% service charge, it's customary to tip maids, waitstaff, and other service personnel, including taxi drivers. About 10% for taxi drivers should do it; hotel maids will appreciate about a dollar or two per day, and members of the waitstaff will be grateful for an extra 5% to 10%.

TOUR OPTIONS

Statia's three taxis and two large buses are available for island tours. A 2½-hour outing costs $40 per vehicle for five people (extra persons are $5 each), usually including airport transfer.

The St. Eustatius Historical Foundation Museum sells a booklet detailing a self-guided walking tour of the sights for $3. The tour begins in Lower Town at the marina and ends at the museum. You can do it on your own using the booklet (numbered blue signs on most of the sights correspond to signs in the booklet), but a guide may prove more illuminating.

Contact **St. Eustatius Historical Foundation Museum** (⊠3 Wilhelminaweg, Oranjestad ☎599/318–2288).

VISITOR INFORMATION

At the tourist office, right in the charming courtyard of the government offices, you can pick up maps, brochures, advice, and a listing of 12 marked trails and arrange for guides and tours.

In St. Eustatius **Tourist Office** (⊠Fort Oranjestraat, Oranjestad ☎599/318–2433 or 599/318–2107 ⊟599/318–2433 ⊕www.statiatourism.com ⊗Weekdays 8–noon and 1–5).

WEDDINGS

Marriages in St. Eustatius follow the same rules as on other Netherlands Antilles islands. Couples must be at least 18 years old and submit their documents at least 14 days prior to the wedding date. The application requires notarized original documents to be submitted to the registrar, including birth certificates, passports (for non-Dutch persons), divorce decrees from previous marriages, and death certificates of deceased spouses; six witnesses must be present if the ceremony is to take place outside of the Marriage Hall. The documents must be submitted, in Dutch or English, along with a fee of US$114 to the lieutenant governor of St. Eustatius.

St. Kitts & Nevis

Pinney's Beach, Nevis

WORD OF MOUTH

"When we went to St. Kitts . . . we were looking for a laid back vacation without feeling the pressure of 'we need to do this and this and this' mentally. It was perfect for just that."

—Paulalou

"Nevis is a terrific island if you don't mind dark sand beaches . . . There are . . . scores of old ruins . . ., hiking trails, and small intimate plantation inns where you will be treated like the guest of honor."

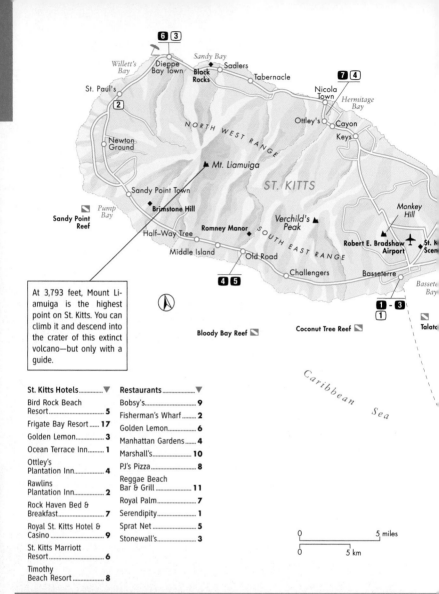

6 **3**

Willett's Bay

Sandy Bay

Dieppe Bay Town
Black Rocks
Sadlers
Tabernacle

St. Paul's

2

7 **4**

Nicola Town
Hermitage Bay

Ottley's
Cayon

Keys

N O R T H   W E S T   R A N G E

Newton Ground

▲ *Mt. Liamuiga*

ST. KITTS

Sandy Point Town

Pump Bay

Brimstone Hill

Monkey Hill

Sandy Point Reef

Romney Manor
Verchild's Peak

Robert E. Bradshaw Airport

St. K Scen

Half-Way Tree

S O U T H   E A S T   R A N G E

Middle Island

Old Road

Challengers
Basseterre

Basset Bay

4 **5**

1 - 3

1

Talat

At 3,793 feet, Mount Liamuiga is the highest point on St. Kitts. You can climb it and descend into the crater of this extinct volcano—but only with a guide.

Bloody Bay Reef

Coconut Tree Reef

C a r i b b e a n   S e a

0   5 miles
0   5 km

TOP 4 REASONS TO VISIT ST. KITTS & NEVIS

1 Both St. Kitts and Nevis are steeped in history; Brimstone Hill Fortress is the Eastern Caribbean's sole man-made UNESCO World Heritage site

2 Luxurious, restored plantation inns can be found on both islands.

3 Both islands have extinct volcanoes and luxuriant rainforests ideal for hikes, as well as fine diving and snorkeling sites.

4 You'll find less development— particularly on Nevis—and more cordial and courteous islanders than on more touristy islands.

WELCOME TO ST. KITTS & NEVIS

THE MOTHER COLONY AND HER SISTER

St. Kitts, a 65-square-mi (168-square-km) island is 2 mi (3 km) from smaller Nevis, about 40 square mi (121 square km). The two former British colonies are joined in a sometimes strained independence. St. Kitts is often called "The Mother Colony," because it was the first permanent English settlement in the Caribbean.

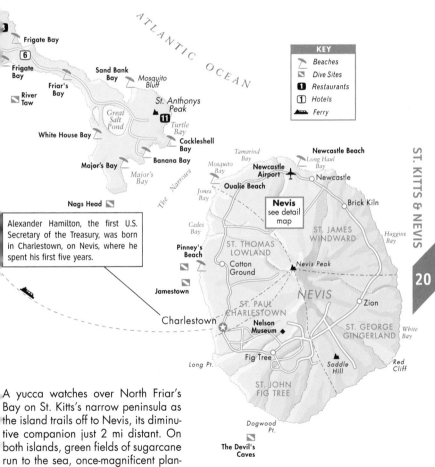

KEY

↗	Beaches
◹	Dive Sites
🔢	Restaurants
①	Hotels
🚢	Ferry

Alexander Hamilton, the first U.S. Secretary of the Treasury, was born in Charlestown, on Nevis, where he spent his first five years.

A yucca watches over North Friar's Bay on St. Kitts's narrow peninsula as the island trails off to Nevis, its diminutive companion just 2 mi distant. On both islands, green fields of sugarcane run to the sea, once-magnificent plantation houses are now luxurious inns, and lovely stretches of uncrowded beach stretch before you.

ST. KITTS & NEVIS PLANNER

Island Activities

Both St. Kitts and Nevis have good but not great **beaches** (Friar's or Frigate Bay are the best choices on St. Kitts, Pinney's or Oualie Beach on Nevis).

St. Kitts offers a wider range of activities, including good **diving, horseback riding, hiking** tours in the rain forest, and **boat rides.**

Nevis has fewer organized activities, but they run the gamut from **wind surfing** to **deep-sea fishing** to **kayaking** to **horseback riding.**

The **Royal St. Kitts Golf Club** was renovated in 2004; other golf courses is being developed at this writing, including one at the Christophe Harbour that is being designed by Tom Fazio.

The Four Seasons Resort Nevis has one of the Caribbean's finest **golf courses** and remains a strong draw for the resort.

Both St. Kitts and Nevis have very good **restaurants.** One of the best dining experiences on either island will be found at one of the fine plantation inn restaurants.

Logistics

Getting to St. Kitts & Nevis: Many travelers connect in Antigua, San Juan, St. Maarten, or St. Thomas. When going to Nevis, it's almost always cheaper to fly into St. Kitts and then take a sea taxi or regularly scheduled ferry to Nevis, but check the schedules or book your sea taxi in advance; a water taxi costs between $20 and $25 one-way per person, and can take as long as 45 minutes. Robert L. Bradshaw International Airport on St. Kitts (SKB) and the smaller, simpler Vance W. Armory International Airport on Nevis (NEV), are still fairly sleepy.

Hassle Factor: Low–Medium for St. Kitts, Medium–High for Nevis.

Nonstops: There are nonstop flights to St. Kitts from Atlanta (Delta–weekly), Charlotte (USAirways–weekly), Miami (American), and New York–JFK (American). There are no nonstop flights from the U.S. to Nevis.

On the Ground

Taxis meet every ferry and flight to St. Kitts or Nevis. The taxis are unmetered, but fixed rates, in EC dollars, are posted at the airport and at the jetty. Note that rates are the same for one to four passengers. On St. Kitts the fares range from EC$32 to Frigate Bay, to EC$72 for the farthest point from the airport. From the airport on Nevis it costs EC$27 to Nisbet Plantation, EC$54 to the Four Seasons, and EC$67 to Montpelier. Before setting off in a cab, be sure to clarify whether the rate quoted is in EC or U.S. dollars. There's a 50% surcharge for trips made between 10 PM and 6 AM.

Renting a Car: If you'd like to dine at the various inns and sightsee for more than one day in St. Kitts, then you should rent a car. If you're staying in the Frigate Bay–Basseterre area, you can get by using taxis and doing a half-day island tour. On Nevis, if you deviate from Main Street in Charlestown, you're likely to have trouble finding your way. You can rent a car for a day or two of exploring if you want, but a tour with a guide is usually easier. On either island, you must get a temporary driving permit (EC$50 on St. Kitts, $24 on Nevis) and drive on the left.

Where to Stay

St. Kitts has a wide variety of places to stay—beautifully restored plantation inns, full-service affordable hotels, simple beachfront cottages, and all-inclusive resorts. One large resort—the Marriott—is more mid-range than upscale and attracts large groups and package tourists. Choose St. Kitts if you want a wider choice of activities and accommodations (you can always do Nevis as a day trip). Nevis is a small island with no large resorts, and most accommodations are upscale—primarily plantation inns and the luxurious Four Seasons. It's much quieter than St. Kitts, so choose it if you want to get away from the hectic island scene and simply relax in low-key comfort and surprisingly high style.

Four Seasons Nevis: Really in a class by itself, the Four Seasons is the only lavish, high-end property on either island. If you can afford it, the resort is certainly one of the Caribbean's finest.

Plantation Inns: Unique to St. Kitts and Nevis are renovated, historic plantation houses that have been turned into upscale inns. On Nevis, the inns are the dominant form of lodging and the main draw. They are usually managed by hands-on owner-operators and offer fine cuisine and convivial hospitality; though not usually on a beach, most of these inns have beach clubs with free private shuttle service.

Hotel & Restaurant Costs

⇨*For information on hotel meal plans, see Accommodations in Caribbean Essentials.*

WHAT IT COSTS IN U.S. DOLLARS

	$$$$	$$$	$$	$	¢
Restaurants					
	over $30	$20–$30	$12–$20	$8–$12	under $8
Hotels*					
	over $350	$250–$350	$150–$250	$80–$150	under $80
Hotels**					
	over $450	$350–$450	$250–$350	$125–$250	under $125

*EP, BP, CP **AI, FAP, MAP Restaurant prices are for a main course at dinner and include any taxes or service charges. Hotel prices are per night for a double room in high season, excluding taxes, service charges, and meal plans (except at all-inclusives).

When to Go

The high season is relatively short, starting in mid-December and stretching into early or mid-April. The shoulder season (roughly April to mid-June and November to mid-December) offers lower rates. Rates are lower still from mid-June through November, but some establishments close.

Carnival on St. Kitts is celebrated during the 10 days right after Christmas.

The **St. Kitts Music Festival** in late June or early July is the biggest event on the island and draws international singing stars.

September on St. Kitts is devoted to **independence festivals**.

Nevis calls its summer carnival **Culturama,** and it's celebrated in late July and early August.

In mid-September, **Heritage Week** celebrates Nevis's history with several celebrations.

The **Nevis Culinary Heritage Exposition** brings in guest chefs for cooking demonstrations and wine tastings the third week of October.

20

By Jordan
Simon

AS I RAMBLE THROUGH THE rain forest, its pristine wildness envelops me like a warm quilt: a banyan tree with roots like the banisters I slid down as a child; bromeliads and orchids strangling mahogany trees in their embrace; green vervet monkeys stealthily clutching fallen, over-ripe mangoes like treasure; iridescent butterflies and hummingbirds competing for prize blooms. But when the trail suddenly disappears into the lush, fragrant undergrowth, I panic momentarily. Then a shifting breeze carries tinkling laughter and clinking cups. Following the sound, I emerge within minutes, sun-blinded, onto a vast, immaculately groomed lawn rolling down to the sea. A quartet of casual yet worldly Brits waves from a table set by a restored 18th-century sugar factory. "You look like you could use a drink," one trills. As I approach, a smiling staffer intercepts me with a tray bearing a cool mint-scented towel and iced bush tea "to calm da nerves."

Variations on that scene are played out on both St. Kitts and Nevis. These idyllic sister islands, just 2 mi (3 km) apart at their closest point, offer visitors a relatively authentic island experience. Both have luxuriant mountain rain forests; uncrowded beaches; historic ruins; towering, long-dormant volcanoes; charming if slightly dilapidated Georgian capitals in Basseterre (St. Kitts) and Charlestown (Nevis); intact cultural heritage; friendly if shy people; and restored, 18th-century sugar plantation inns run by elegant, if sometimes eccentric, expatriate British and American owners.

The islands' history follows the usual Caribbean route: Amerindian settlements, Columbus's voyages, fierce colonial battles between the British and French, a boom in sugar production second only to that of Barbados. St. Kitts became known as the mother colony of the West Indies: English settlers sailed from there to Antigua, Barbuda, Tortola, and Montserrat, while the French dispatched colonists to Martinique, Guadeloupe, St. Martin, and St. Barths.

St. Kitts and Nevis, in addition to Anguilla, achieved self-government as an associated state of Great Britain in 1967. Anguillians soon made their displeasure known, separating immediately, while St. Kitts and Nevis waited until 1983 to become an independent nation. The two islands, despite their superficial similarities, have taken increasingly different routes regarding tourism. Nevis received an economic boost from the Four Seasons, which helped establish it as an upscale destination. St. Kitts, however, has yet to define its identity at a time when most islands have found their tourism niche. A fierce sibling rivalry has ensued.

Though its comparative lack of development is a lure, the Kittitian government is casting its economic net in several directions. Golf, ecotourism, and scuba diving are being aggressively promoted. The St. Kitts Marriott, with 393 hotel rooms and approximately 150 time-share units), is triple the size of any previous hotel, has raised its profile somewhat. This has revived talk of chains like Ritz-Carlton and SuperClubs invading the islandscape (the ultraritzy Auberge Resorts is planning to debut its first Caribbean property in 2009, along with Mandarin Oriental), alongside oft-delayed upmarket villa compounds, a major marine theme park, several golf courses, and the $17-million Beaumont Park horse-racing venue (itself part of a megadevelopment on the island's northwest end). The government hopes the number of available rooms will increase roughly 30% to more than 2,000, according to the "build it and they will come" philosophy. But is St. Kitts ready to absorb all this? The island offers a surprisingly diverse vacation experience while retaining its essential Caribbean flavor. Divers have yet to discover all its underwater attractions, while nature lovers will be pleasantly surprised by the hiking. There's now every kind of accommodation, as well as gourmet dining, golf, and gaming.

Meanwhile, Nevis seems determined to stay even more unspoiled (there are still no traffic lights). Its natural attractions and activities certainly rival those of St. Kitts, from mountain biking and ecohiking to windsurfing and deep-sea fishing, though lying in a hammock and dining on romantic candlelit patios remain cherished pursuits. Pinney's Beach, despite occasional hurricane erosion, remains a classic Caribbean strand. Its historic heritage, from the Caribbean's first hotel to Alexander Hamilton's childhood home, is just as pronounced, including equally sybaritic plantation inns that seem torn from the pages of a romance novel.

Perhaps it's a warning sign that many guests call the catamaran trip to Nevis the high point of their stay on St. Kitts—and many Kittitians build retirement and second homes on Nevis. The sister islands' relationship remains outwardly cordial if slightly contentious. Nevis papers sometimes run blistering editorials advocating independence, though one plebiscite has already failed. St. Kitts and Nevis may separate someday, but for now, their battles are confined to ad campaigns and political debates. Fortunately, well-heeled and barefoot travelers alike can still happily enjoy the many energetic and easygoing enticements of both blissful retreats.

ST. KITTS

20

WHERE TO STAY

St. Kitts has an appealing variety of places to stay—beautifully restored plantation inns (where MAP, including afternoon tea in addition to breakfast and dinner, is encouraged, if not mandatory), full-service affordable hotels, simple beachfront cottages, and all-inclusive resorts. There are also several guesthouses and self-serve condos. Increasing development has been touted (or threatened) for years. The island's first large hotel, the St. Kitts Marriott Resort, is now well established, but any upcoming developments—many quite upscale and primarily residential—are all fewer than 300 units, including the forthcoming sparkling 185-unit Ocean's Edge condo complex on Frigate Bay and the deluxe properties such as Auberge (which opened the affiliated, refined Beach House restaurant on Turtle Beach in 2008) and Mandarin Oriental, which will be part of the grand Christophe Harbour development that will sprawl elegantly across the Southeast Peninsula. On these islands, where breezes generally keep things cool, many, but not all hotels, have air-conditioning.

$$$$ **Golden Lemon.** Perched at the northwest tip of St. Kitts, this serene,
★   scintillating retreat was one of the Caribbean's first true luxury hideaways. Arthur Leaman, a former decorating editor for *House and Garden,* rescued a decaying, 17th-century French plantation house in the early 1960s; his style and panache enliven the entire property. Greathouse rooms (opt for Nos. 1 through 4 and No. 10) feature wrought-iron canopy or four-poster beds and funky touches like leopard-print rugs. One- and two-bedroom soaring, duplex town houses (some with private plunge pools) are equally stylish, with walls painted in luscious colors from pumpkin to blueberry and an eclectic yet harmonious blend of artworks and antiques culled from Arthur and partner Martin Kreiner's travels. Repeat guests cherish the serenity and sterling service; the only caveats are the remote location and rare reports of villagers harassing Americans. EP rates are available, but the location means the all-inclusive packages are the better value. Please note that Arthur and Martin sold the property in 2007, but are expected to remain on property at least through the end of 2008. **Pros:** Pomp without pretension, remote romantic location, impeccably tasteful decor. **Cons:** Small beachfront, car necessary, uncertainty about ownership changes. ⌂ *Box 17, Dieppe Bay* ☎ *869/465–7260 or 800/633–7411* ⊕ *www.goldenlemon.com* ⤵ *9 rooms, 17 villas* △ *In-room: no a/c (some), no TV, dial-up. In-hotel: restaurant, bar, pool, beachfront, no elevator, no kids under 16* ☰ *AE, MC, V* ⊙ *Closed Sept.–mid-Oct.* ⚞*BP.*

$$$–$$$$ **Ottley's Plantation Inn.** You're treated like a beloved relative rather
Fodor's Choice   than a commercial guest at this quintessential Caribbean inn, formerly
★   a sugar plantation, at the foot of Mt. Liamuiga. The 18th-century greathouse (opt for top-floor rooms) and stone cottages hold commodious lodgings with hardwood floors, Laura Ashley–esque trimmings, and wicker and antique furnishings. "Supreme" cottages have plunge pools and whirlpool tubs. You can wander the exquisitely landscaped ornamental gardens, which brilliantly counterpoint the wild adjacent rain forest (filigreed with trails), or visit the rustic-chic spa for one of its exotic treatments. Thoughtful extras include beach and town shuttles, as well as TVs and DVD players for rent. Art and Ruth Keusch and their family set the warm, fun-loving, yet cultured tone. Staff are professional, knowing their business but not yours, providing posh pampering without pomp. **Pros:** Posh yet unpretentious luxury, wonderfully helpful staff and owners, gorgeous gardens. **Cons:** No beach, bumpy access road, long walk from farthest cottages to office. ✉ *Ottley's, southwest of Nicola Town* ☎ *869/465–7234 or 800/772–3039* ⊕ *www.ottleys.com* ⤵ *24 rooms* △ *In-room: safe, no TV (some), Ethernet, Wi-Fi. In-hotel: restaurant, bar, tennis court, pool, spa, no elevator, public Internet, no-smoking rooms* ☰ *AE, D, MC, V* ⚞*EP.*

$$$–$$$$ **Rawlins Plantation Inn.** Civilized serenity awaits at this remote plantation inn between verdant Mt. Liamuiga and the cobalt Caribbean. Twelve acres of lavish, lovingly landscaped grounds are ablaze with

hibiscus, oleander, and plumbago and dotted with the original copper syrup vats. Rooms occupy restored estate buildings (including the sugar mill) and trellised, gingerbread cottages charmingly decorated with local artworks and mahogany furnishings. Days are spent relaxing in one of the many strategically slung hammocks, perhaps contemplating the egrets stalking the palms or the views of St. Maarten and St. Eustatius. Expat artist Kate Spencer's studio is on-site; her husband, Philip, a keen sailor, might be building or restoring classic boats. The refined dining room, given a contemporary edge by a quietly sexy lounge, has always been an island favorite, particularly for its authentic West Indian buffet lunches. Recent upgrades include a new access road that doesn't require chiropractic intervention, and the potentially questionable addition of "Carib Cottages" for sale. **Pros:** Utter tranquillity, exquisite setting, fine kitchen. **Cons:** No beach, uneven service. ⌂ *Box 340, St. Paul's* ☎ *869/465–6221 or 888/790–5264* ⊕ *www.rawlinsplantation.com* ☞ *10 rooms* △ *In-room: no a/c, no phone, no TV. In-hotel: restaurant, bar, tennis court, pool, no elevator, laundry service, public Internet, public Wi-Fi* ⊟ *MC, V* ☺ *Closed Aug. and Sept.* �◎ *BP.*

$$$–$$$$ **St. Kitts Marriott Resort.** There's no question that this flashy, big, bustling beachfront resort offers something for everyone, from families to conventioneers, golfers to gamblers. Unfortunately, it's all monumentally overscaled for tiny, quiet St. Kitts and is almost devoid of real Caribbean charm and flair. Maintenance and staff are diligent, but service is inconsistent and often impersonal. Little things go wrong: phone cards don't work, bills show unwarranted minibar or dining charges, the glorious free-form pools are often surprisingly chilly, breakfast rush hour can mean interminable waits. The property is so vast that only Blocks 600–800 and 1300–1500 can claim true beachfront status; ocean-view rooms often show only a speck of blue. One advantage of its size is that the resort rarely feels crowded (though DJs often blast music to create a party atmosphere). The Marriott scores points for its genuinely soothing Emerald Mist Spa; a splendid kids' area that includes a fully loaded arcade and Club Mongoose (which tries to instill island flavor through nature hikes, limbo lessons, treasure hunts, and crafts classes); cosmopolitan cigar and lobby bars (great sushi); and a fine golf course. Suites are huge and a good value during the off-season, as are the many packages. Some of the huge, gleaming 150-some new time-share units may be occasionally offered in a rental pool, as the guest room inventory has shrunk. **Pros:** Great range of activities, good bars. **Cons:** Impersonal, sometimes inefficient service, surprise extra charges, mediocre food. ⌂ *Box 858, Frigate Bay* ☎ *869/466–1200 or 800/228–9290* ⊕ *www.stkittsmarriott.com* ☞ *393 rooms* △ *In-room: safe, refrigerator, Ethernet. In-hotel: 8 restaurants, room service, bars, golf course, tennis courts, pools, gym, spa, beachfront, water sports, children's programs (ages 5–12), laundry service, public Internet, no-smoking rooms* ⊟ *AE, D, MC, V* ◎ *EP.*

$$–$$$ **Ocean Terrace Inn.** Referred to by locals as OTI, this is a rarity: a smart, intimate business hotel that nonetheless appeals to vacationers. The hillside location, convenient to downtown Basseterre, guarantees

20

marvelous bay views from virtually every room. Luxuriant gardens, room blocks, and a split-level free-form waterfall pool tumble down to the sea. Island touches from masks to murals animate nooks and crannies. Handsomely decorated but tired rooms vary widely in size and style; many deluxe rooms and junior suites (which have a 1960s bachelor-pad look) have kitchenettes or whirlpool tubs. The condos are closer to the water and have great views. The urbane hilltop Waterfalls Restaurant (a local must Friday nights for its West Indian buffet with live music) entices island power brokers. With regular shuttle service to Turtle Beach, courteous helpful staff, and an on-site gym and mini-spa, peaceful OTI promotes rest, not revelries. **Pros:** Excellent service, fine facilities for a small hotel. **Cons:** Must drive to beaches, sprawling layout, some rooms need sprucing up. ⊠ *Wigley Ave, Box 65, Fortlands* ☎*869/465–2754 or 800/524–0512* ⊕*www.oceanterraceinn. com* ➪*71 rooms, 8 condominiums* ⌂*In-room: safe (some), kitchen (some), refrigerator, Wi-Fi. In-hotel: 3 restaurants, bars, pools, gym, water sports, no elevator, public Internet, no-smoking rooms* ⊟*AE, D, MC, V* ⏁*EP.*

$$–$$$ **Rock Haven Bed & Breakfast.** This restful, cozy bed-and-breakfast, a two-minute drive from Frigate Bay beaches (airport transfers are included), provides truly local warmth, courtesy of Judith and Keith Blake. Their gingerbread house and surrounding garden are lovely: the living and dining rooms have carved mahogany doors, crystal chandeliers, English rugs, vividly painted walls hung with equally bold artworks, and hardwood floors. The extensive, breezy verandah seduces with white-wicker chaise lounges, hammocks, and majestic sea views. Two rooms have brass beds draped with mosquito netting. The larger, preferable one has a full kitchen and its own patio and entrance. Judith prepares lavish breakfasts of banana pancakes, pumpkin fritters, and bush teas with ingredients from her herb garden. Islanders also cherish her homemade ice creams, which you can sample on-site. **Pros:** Genuine island hospitality, immaculately maintained, delicious breakfasts. **Cons:** Long walk to beach, no longer value as rates doubled since 2007. ⌂*Box 821, Frigate Bay* ☎*869/465–5503* ⊕*www.rock-haven.com* ➪*2 rooms* ⌂*In-room: no a/c (some), kitchen (some), Wi-Fi. In-hotel: no elevator, laundry service, public Wi-Fi* ⊟*MC, V* ⏁*BP.*

$$ **Royal St. Kitts Hotel & Casino.** This budget-conscious property, the former Allegro Jack Tar, displays a welcome focus on Kittitian culture, evident in everything from the culinary emphasis to the artworks, crafts, and architectural accents (even the curtains were locally designed). Thirty two-story buildings house sizable fresh rooms (80 reopened in the first phase, with another 200 gradually being renovated), some split-level with jetted tubs, all with balconies overlooking the ocean, lagoon, or the golf course. The casino offers table games and more than 100 one-armed bandits; the Lime Beach Bar & Grill promises to become an island hot spot. **Pros:** Terrific value, friendly staff, respect for island tradition. **Cons:** Can be loud when filled with tour groups, needs further renovation in places. ⌂*Box 406, Frigate Bay* ☎*869/465–8651* ⊕*www.royalstkittshotel.com* ➪*282 rooms* ⌂*In-room: safe, kitchenette (some), Wi-Fi. In-hotel: 2 restaurants, bars, tennis court, pools,* *gym, beachfront, children's programs (4–12), no elevator, public Internet, no-smoking rooms □AE, MC, V ⦿AI.*

$–$$ ⚏ **Frigate Bay Resort.** This cheery property's combination of location, value, and polite service compensates for dowdy decor and dire need for minor repairs throughout (current management is gradually freshening the rooms and replacing appliances). Though a shuttle whisks you to nearby Caribbean and Atlantic beaches, you can walk to South Frigate Bay's many restaurants, bars, and water-sports operators. Poolside studios with kitchens are an excellent bargain for self-caterers but tend to be noisier than other rooms. If a water view is paramount, request higher-numbered units in buildings B and C (third-floor units have sweeping vistas over the golf course and Atlantic). The swim-up bar and the thatched, split-level, octagonal restaurant are uncommonly comely drinks spots (though the Continental-Caribbean fare is undistinguished). Best of all are weekly rates that can reduce tariffs by up to 25% per night. **Pros:** Terrific value, easy walk to beaches. **Cons:** No direct beachfront, slightly dilapidated. *⌂Box 137, Frigate Bay* ☎*869/465–8935 or 800/266–2185* ⊕*www.frigatebay.com* ⟻*40 rooms, 24 studios* ⚐*In-room: kitchen (some), refrigerator, Ethernet. In-hotel: restaurant, bar, pool, no elevator, public Internet, public Wi-Fi □AE, D, MC, V ⦿EP.*

$–$$ ⚏ **Timothy Beach Resort.** The only St. Kitts resort sitting directly on a Caribbean beach is incomparably located and restful. Smiling service and simple but sizable apartments make this a great budget find. Comfortable town-house-style units can be blocked off to form standard rooms. The oldest buildings right on the beach are larger and airier, with predictably better views. Third-floor units also have breathtaking vistas, but beware the steep climb. It's an authentic island experience, from the verdant hillside setting to the line-drying sheets flapping in the breeze. Though you get ants on the march during damp weather (don't leave food out!), you also get bananaquits and bullfinches sharing your patio breakfast. Only rattling air-conditioners and rusty chipped fixtures detract from the idyllic atmosphere—and you can always walk to the Marriott if you crave activity. On the beach are the decent Sunset Café, an unaffiliated water-sports concession, and several boisterous beach bars. **Pros:** Unbeatable location, close to the beach action. **Cons:** Worn decor, occasional leaky plumbing, can hear beach bar music weekend nights. *⌂Box 1198, Frigate Bay* ☎*869/465–8597 or 877/942–3224* ⊕*www.timothybeach.com* ⟻*60 apartments* ⚐*In-room: kitchen (some), refrigerator. In-hotel: restaurant, bar, pool, beachfront, no elevator, public Internet □AE, MC, V ⦿EP.*

$ ⚏ **Bird Rock Beach Resort.** This basic, well-maintained hotel crowns a bluff above Basseterre, delivering amazing views of the town, the sea, and the mountains from every vantage point. Two-story buildings in carnival colors wind through small, pretty gardens. The newer rooms are spiffier, with vivid throw rugs and mahogany two-poster beds; studios with kitchenettes and pull-out sofas offer real bargains for families (an additional connecting room costs just $50). Avoid only the 700 block; most other rooms have jaw-dropping panoramas. The tiered sundeck and pool, replete with swim-up bar, and attractive Diana's restaurant rank among the island's top sunset perches. The minuscule man-made beach (a complimentary shuttle drops guests at Frigate Bay), irregular hours, and occasional plumbing problems are a small price to pay and don't seem to bother the laid-back divers and young Europeans who give Bird Rock an appealing international flavor. **Pros:** exuberant friendly clientele, great diving, excellent value, superb views. **Cons:** small man-made beach, insufficient parking. ⊠ *Basseterre Bay, 2 mi [3 km] east of Basseterre* ☏ *Box 227, Basseterre* ☎ *869/465–8914 or 888/358–6870* ⊕ *www.birdrockbeach.com* ⇆ *31 rooms, 19 studios* ⚘ *In-room: kitchen (some), ethernet. In-hotel: 2 restaurants, bars, tennis court, pools, beachfront, diving, water sports, no elevator, public Internet* ⊟ *AE, D, MC, V* ⦿ *EP.*

WHERE TO EAT

St. Kitts restaurants range from funky beachfront bistros to elegant plantation dining rooms (most with prix-fixe menus); most fare is tinged with the flavors of the Caribbean. Many restaurants offer West Indian specialties such as curried mutton, pepper pot (a stew of vegetables, tubers, and meats), and Arawak chicken (seasoned and served with rice and almonds on breadfruit leaf).

WHAT TO WEAR

Throughout the island, dress is casual at lunch (but no bathing suits). Dinner, although not necessarily formal, definitely calls for long pants and sundresses.

CARIBBEAN   ✕ **Golden Lemon.** Evenings at the Golden Lemon hotel's restaurant begin
$$$$ with cocktails and hors d'oeuvres on the bougainvillea-draped flagstone
★   patio. A set three-course dinner is served in a tasteful room with crystal and white wrought-iron chandeliers, high-back cane chairs, delft porcelain, and arched doorways. Tempting dishes range from breadfruit puffs in peanut sauce to lobster cakes with passion-fruit mayonnaise to grilled tilapia with eggplant-and-sweet-pepper relish. Sunday brunch packs the patio for such offerings as banana pancakes and legendary beef stew made with rum. ⊠ *Golden Lemon, Dieppe Bay* ☎ *869/465–7260* ⚑ *Reservations essential* ⊟ *AE, MC, V.*

$$–$$$$ ✕ **Bobsy's.** Locals flock to this semi-alfresco terrace eatery for lively happy hours and, on weekends, for karaoke, sizzling salsa, live bands, and a DJ spinning favorite dance tunes. Vivid colors (scarlet linens, orange walls with mauve and lime trim, turquoise rafters), African masks, and autographed photos of reggae stars attest to the authentic island ambience, as do such fine specialties as pumpkin soup, glazed passion-fruit ribs, and mango-ginger chicken (you can also get hefty burgers and such Continental standbys as lobster thermidor, chicken fettuccine Alfredo, and rack of lamb). ⊠ *Sugar's Complex, Frigate Bay* ☎ *869/466–6133* ⊟ *AE, MC, V* ⦿ *No lunch Sun. or Mon.*

$$–$$$ ✕ **Manhattan Gardens.** Even the tangerine, lemon, and blueberry exterior of this 17th-century gingerbread creole house looks appetizing. Inside, you feel as if you're dining in owner-chef Rosalind Walters's home, with batik hangings, lace tablecloths, and wood carvings. The

rear garden overlooking the sea comes alive for Saturday's Caribbean Food Fest and Sunday's barbecue. The regular menu includes lobster in lemon butter (the one pricey entrée) and mahimahi in lemon-thyme sauce; local specials might consist of goat water (goat stew), souse (pickled pigs' trotters), and curried mutton. It's open for lunch (and some dinners) only when there are reservations. ⊠ *Old Road Town* ☎ *869/465–9121* ⚑ *Reservations essential* ▤ *No credit cards* ⊘ *No dinner Sun.*

CONTINENTAL **✕ Stonewall's.** This lush, tropical courtyard restaurant replete with tin-
$$–$$$ kling fountain was hand-built by the original owners. Banana trees, bougainvillea, and bamboo—filled with a virtual orchestra of chirping tree frogs—grow everywhere. Selections depend on what's fresh and the cook's mood: most popular are the barbecue ribs, and specialties such as herb-crusted rack of lamb or ginger chicken. Lunch items are well priced and include scrumptious coconut-fried shrimp and mango chicken curry crepe. Homemade desserts (such as the six-layer "monster" cake) are not for the calorie- and cholesterol-conscious. Try the house drink, Stone Against the Wall, concocted from Cavalier rum, amaretto, coconut rum, triple sec, pineapple and orange juices, and grenadine. ⊠ *5 Princes St., Basseterre* ☎ *869/465–5248* ▤ *AE, D, MC, V* ⊘ *Closed weekends. No lunch.*

ECLECTIC **✕ Royal Palm.** A 65-foot, spring-fed pool bisects the elegant restaurant
$$$$ at Ottley's Plantation Inn into a semi-enclosed lounge with sea views
★ and a breezy alfresco stone patio. Four-course extravaganzas (dishes are also available à la carte) blend indigenous ingredients with Pacific Rim, Mediterranean, Southwestern, and Latin touches: for example, chili-shrimp corn cakes with chipotle pepper mayonnaise; grilled herb-basted West Indian lobster with tropical sabayon, passion-fruit jus, and lime risotto; or marinated grilled flat iron steak with chipotle drizzle, African cream polenta, and avocado salsa. Finish with simple yet sinful indulgences such as coconut cream cheesecake or mango mousse with raspberry coulis. The combination of superb food, artful presentation, romantic setting, and warm bonhomie is unbeatable. ⊠ *Ottley's Plantation Inn, Ottley's, southwest of Nicola Town* ☎ *869/465–7234* ⚑ *Reservations essential* ▤ *AE, D, MC, V.*

$$–$$$$ **✕ Marshall's.** The pool area of Horizons Villa Resort is transformed into a stylish eatery thanks to smashing ocean views, potted plants, serenading tree frogs, and elegant candlelighted tables. Jamaican chef Verral Marshall fuses ultrafresh local ingredients with global influences. Recommended offerings include pan-seared duck breast with raspberry-ginger sauce or portobello-stuffed tortellini with shrimp in creamy tomato-basil sauce. Most dishes are regrettably more orthodox, and the execution is increasingly uneven. ⊠ *Horizons Villa Resort, Frigate Bay* ☎ *869/466–8245* ⚑ *Reservations essential* ▤ *AE, D, MC, V* ⊘ *No lunch.*

$$–$$$$ **✕ Serendipity.** This stylish restaurant occupies an old creole home whose deck offers lovely views of Basseterre and the bay. As charming as the enclosed patio is, the interior lounge is more conducive to romantic dining, with cushy sofas, patterned hardwood floors, porcelain

20

lamps, and African carvings. The menu reflects co-owner–chef Alexander James's peripatetic postings: you might start with fried Brie with blackberry sauce or beautifully presented spring rolls with plum-soy dipping sauce. Poached salmon with lobster brandy cream sauce and bacon-wrapped beef tenderloin topped with pâté, black truffle slice, and port sauce typify the ambitious main courses. The wine list is well considered; vegetarians will be delighted by the many creative options; and very affordable lunches feature gargantuan tapas-style selections. ⊠*3 Wigley Ave., Fortlands, Basseterre* ☎*869/465–9999* ⊟*AE, D, MC, V* ⊘*Closed Mon. No lunch weekends.*

$$–$$$ ✕**Reggae Beach Bar & Grill.** Treats at this popular daytime watering hole include honey-mustard ribs, coconut shrimp, grilled lobster (a best-buy special Friday nights), decadent bread pudding with rum sauce, and an array of tempting tropical libations. Business cards and pennants from around the world plaster the bar and the open-air space is decorated with a variety of nautical accoutrements, from fishnets and turtle shells to painted wooden crustaceans. You can snorkel here, spot hawksbill turtles, laze in a palm-shaded hammock, or rent a kayak or snorkel gear. Beach chairs are free. Locals come Sunday afternoons for dancing to live bands and for fun but fiercely contested volleyball. ⊠*S.E. Peninsula Rd., Cockleshell Beach* ☎*869/469–9086* ⊟*AE, D, MC, V* ⊘*No dinner Mon.–Thurs.*

ITALIAN   ✕**PJ's Pizza.** "Garbage pizza"—topped with everything but the kitchen
$–$$$ sink—is a favorite, or you can create your own pie. Sandwiches, calzones, simple but lustily flavored pastas (try the goat cheese ravioli in sun-dried tomato sauce or spaghetti with humongous meatballs), and mama-mia classics (eggplant Parmesan to chicken rollatini) are also served. Finish your meal with delicious, moist rum cake. This casual spot, bordering the golf course and open to cooling breezes, is always boisterous (especially during the 9 to 10 happy hour), despite—or perhaps because of—its ironic location beside the Frigate Bay police station. ⊠*Frigate Bay* ☎*869/465–8373* ⊟*AE, D, MC, V* ⊘*Closed Mon. and Sept. No lunch.*

SEAFOOD   ✕**Fisherman's Wharf.** Part of the Ocean Terrace Inn, this extremely
$$–$$$ casual waterfront eatery is decorated in swaggering nautical style, with rusty anchors, casks, buoys, and walls splashed with aqua waves and wild psychedelically hued murals of fishing boats and their catch. Try the excellent conch chowder, followed by fresh grilled lobster or other shipshape seafood, and finish off your meal with a slice of the memorable banana cheesecake. The place is generally hopping, especially on weekend nights when live bands often jam atop the split-level, breeze-swept bar. ⊠*Ocean Terrace Inn, Fortlands, Basseterre* ☎*869/465–2754* ⊟*AE, D, MC, V* ⊘*No lunch.*

$–$$ ✕**Sprat Net.** This simple cluster of picnic tables—sheltered by a bril-
★   liant turquoise corrugated-tin roof and decorated with driftwood, life preservers, photos of coastal scenes, and fishnets—sits on a sliver of sand. Nonetheless, it's an island hot spot. There's nothing fancy on the menu: just grilled fish, lobster, ribs, and chicken served with mountains of coleslaw and peas and rice. But the fish is amazingly fresh:

the fishermen-owners heap their catches on a center table from which you choose your own dinner, then watch it grilled to your specification before dining family-style on paper plates. A new adjacent hut serves up the final food group: pizza. Sprat Net offers old-style Caribbean flavor, with the cheapest drinks and best bands on weekends. No wonder cars line up along the road, creating an impromptu jump-up. ⊠ *Old Road Town* ☎ *869/466–7535* ⊟ *No credit cards* ⊘ *Closed Sept. and Sun. No lunch.*

BEACHES

Beaches on St. Kitts are free and open to the public (even those occupied by hotels). The best beaches, with powdery white sand, are in the Frigate Bay area or on the lower peninsula. The Atlantic waters are rougher, and many black-sand beaches northwest of Frigate Bay double as garbage dumps, though locals bodysurf at Conaree Bay.

Banana/Cockleshell Bays. These twin connected eyebrows of glittering champagne-color sand—stretching nearly 2 mi (3 km) total at the southeastern tip of the island—feature majestic views of Nevis and are backed by lush vegetation and coconut palms. The Rasta-hue Lion Rock Beach Bar (order the knockout Lion Punch) and Reggae Beach Bar & Grill bracket either end of Cockleshell. Locals often come here weekends, throwing bonfire parties at night. The water is generally placid, ideal for swimming. The downside is irregular maintenance, with seaweed (particularly after rough weather) and occasional litter, especially on Banana Bay. Follow Simmonds Highway to the end and bear right, ignoring the turnoff for Turtle Beach. Beach aficionados should check out Majors Bay, the cove just to the west, where you can see locals fishing, at least until Mandarin Oriental debuts in late 2009. ⊠ *Banana Bay.*

★ **Friar's Bay.** Locals consider Friar's Bay, on the Caribbean (southern) side, the island's finest beach. It's a long, tawny scimitar where the water always seems warmer and clearer. Unfortunately, the new Marine World development has coopted nearly half the strand (it's screened by sea grape trees standing sentry). Still, several hopping, happening bars, including Shipwreck, Mongoose, and Sunset Grill, serve terrific, inexpensive local food and cheap, frosty drinks. Chair rentals cost around $3, though if you order lunch you can negotiate a freebie. You can haggle with fishermen here to take you snorkeling off the eastern point, though live coral reefs protect both ends. The waters on the Atlantic (northern) side are rougher, but the beach has a wild, desolate beauty and some good surfing (wind, body, board), though seaweed often washes ashore. Friar's is the first major beach along Southeast Peninsula Drive (aka Simmonds Highway), approximately a mile (1.5 km) southeast of Frigate Bay. ⊠ *Friar's Bay.*

Frigate Bay. The Caribbean side offers talcum-powder-fine beige sand framed by coconut palms and sea grapes, while the Atlantic side (a 15-minute stroll)—the 4-mi-wide (6.5-km-wide) stretch sometimes called North Frigate Bay—is a favorite with horseback riders. South Frigate Bay is bookended by Sunset Café and Oasis. In between are

20

several other lively beach spots, including Cathy's (fabulous jerk ribs), the Monkey Bar, and Mr. X Shiggidy Shack. Most charge $3 to $5 to rent a chair, though they'll often waive the fee if you ask politely and buy lunch. Locals barhop late into Friday and Saturday nights. Waters are generally calm for swimming; the rockier eastern end offers fine snorkeling. The incomparably scenic Atlantic side is—regrettably— dominated by the Marriott (plentiful dining options), attracting occasional pesky vendors. The surf is choppier and the undertow stronger here. On cruise-ship days, groups stampede both sides. Frigate Bay is easy to find, just less than 3 mi (5 km) from downtown Basseterre. ⊠ *Frigate Bay.*

Sand Bank Bay. A dirt road, nearly impassable after heavy rains, leads to a long mocha crescent on the Atlantic. The shallow coves are protected here, making it ideal for families, and it's usually deserted. Brisk breezes lure the occasional windsurfer, but avoid the rocky far left area due to fierce sudden swells and currents. This exceptionally pretty beach lacks facilities and shade, though the ultraluxurious 1,700-acre Auberge Sandy Bank Bay Resort—with spa and golf course—will break ground here in anticipation of a 2009 opening. Enjoy it while you can. As you drive southeast along Simmonds Highway, approximately 10 mi (16 km) from Basseterre, look for an unmarked dirt turnoff to the left of the Great Salt Pond. ⊠ *Sand Bank Bay.*

White House Bay. The beach is rocky, but the snorkeling, taking in several reefs surrounding a sunken tugboat, as well as a recently discovered 18th-century British troop ship, is superb. It's usually deserted, though the calm water (and stunning scenery) makes it a favorite anchorage of yachties. There are no facilities and little shade, but also little seaweed. A dirt road skirts a hill to the right off Simmonds Highway approximately 2 mi (3 km) after Friar's. ⊠ *White House Bay.*

SPORTS & THE OUTDOORS

BOATING & FISHING

Most operators are on the Caribbean side of Frigate Bay, known for its gentle currents. Turtle Bay offers stronger winds and stunning views of Nevis. Though not noted for big-game fishing, several steep offshore drop-offs do lure wahoo, barracuda, shark, tuna, yellowtail snapper, and mackerel. Rates are occasionally negotiable; figure approximately $350 for a four-hour excursion with refreshments. The knowledgeable Todd Leypoldt of **Leeward Island Charters** (⊠ *Basseterre* ☎ *869/465–7474*) takes you out on his charter boat, *Island Lore.* He's also available for snorkeling charters, beach picnics, and sunset-moonlight cruises. **Mr. X Watersports** (⊠ *Frigate Bay* ☎ *869/465–0673*) rents small craft, including motorboats (waterskiing and jet skiing are available). Paddleboats are $15 per hour, sailboats (with one free lesson) $20 to $25 per hour. Mr. X and his cohorts are usually hanging out at the adjacent open-air Monkey Bar. **Reggae Beach Bar & Grill** (⊠ *Cockleshell Beach* ☎ *869/469–9086* ⊕ *www.reggaebeachbar.com*) rents kayaks from the restaurant and can also arrange fishing trips.

DIVING & SNORKELING

Though unheralded as a dive destination, St. Kitts has more than a dozen excellent sites, and the government hopes to increase their visibility by creating several new marine parks. The surrounding waters feature shoals, hot vents, shallows, canyons, steep walls, and caverns at depths from 40 to nearly 200 feet. The St. Kitts Maritime Archaeological Project, which surveys, records, researches, and preserves the island's underwater treasures, has charted several hundred wrecks of galleons, frigates, and freighters dating back to the 17th century. **Bloody Bay Reef** is noted for its network of underwater grottoes daubed with purple anemones, sienna bristle worms, and canary-yellow sea fans that seem to wave you in. **Coconut Tree Reef,** one of the largest in the area, includes sea fans, sponges, and anemones, as well as the Rocks, three enormous boulders with impressive multilevel diving. The only drift dive site, **Nags Head** has strong currents, but experienced divers might spot gliding rays, lobsters, turtles, and reef sharks. Since it sank in 50 feet of water in the early 1980s, the *River Taw* makes a splendid site for less-experienced divers. **Sandy Point Reef** has been designated a National Marine Park and includes Paradise Reef, with swim-through 90-foot sloping canyons, and Anchors Away, where anchors have been encrusted with coral formations. The 1985 wreck of the *Talata* lies in 70 feet of water; barracudas, rays, groupers, and grunts dart through its hull.

Dive St. Kitts (⊠ *2 mi [3 km] east of Basseterre, Frigate Bay* ☎ *869/465–1189* ⊕ *www.divestkitts.com*), a PADI-NAUI facility, offers competitive prices; friendly, laid-back dive masters; and a more-international clientele. The Bird Rock location features superb shore diving: common sightings 20 to 30 feet out include octopuses, nurse sharks, manta and spotted eagle rays, and sea horses. Shore dives are unlimited when you book packages. Kenneth Samuel of **Kenneth's Dive Center** (⊠ *Bay Rd., Newtown* ☎ *869/465–2670* ⊕ *www.kennethsdivecenter.com*), a PADI company, takes small groups of divers with C cards to nearby reefs. Rates average $40 for single-tank dives, $75 for double-tank dives; add $10 to $15 for equipment. Night dives, including lights, are $60, and snorkeling trips (four-person minimum) are $35, drinks included. After 25 years' experience, former fisherman Samuel is considered an old pro (Jean-Michel Cousteau requested his guidance upon his first visit in the 1990s) and strives to keep groups small and prices reasonable. **Pro-Divers** (⊠ *Ocean Terrace Inn, Basseterre* ☎ *869/466–3483* ⊕ *www.prodiversstkitts.com*), is owned by Austin Macleod, a PADI-certified dive master–instructor, and offers resort and certification courses running $115–$390. He offers free introductory scuba courses twice weekly at Ocean Terrace Inn. He also takes groups to snorkeling sites accessible only by boat.

GOLF

St. Kitts hopes to market itself as a golf destination with the remodeling of the Royal St. Kitts Golf Course and the much-delayed opening of the 18-hole La Vallee Golf Course on the island's western side, between Sandy Point and Newton Ground (a stunning layout experiencing financing problems). Two upcoming resort and villa developments include 18-hole courses, one designed by Tom Fazio. The **Royal St. Kitts Golf Club** (⊠ *St. Kitts Marriott Resort, Frigate Bay* ☎ *869/466– 2700* ⊕ *www.royalstkittsgolfclub.com*) is an 18-hole, par-71 links-style championship course that underwent a complete redesign by Thomas McBroom to maximize Caribbean and Atlantic views and increase the challenge (there are now 12 lakes and 83 bunkers). Holes 15 through 17 actually skirt the Atlantic in their entirety, lending new meaning to the term "sand trap." The sudden gusts, wide but twisting fairways, and extremely hilly terrain demand pinpoint accuracy and finesse, yet holes such as 18 require pure power. Greens fees are $140 for Marriott guests in high season, $180 for nonguests. The development includes practice bunkers, a putting green, and a short-game chipping area. The Marriott continues to talk of opening a branch of the Nick Faldo Golf Institute here, perhaps by late 2009.

HIKING

Trails in the central mountains vary from easy to don't-try-it-by-your-self. Monkey Hill and Verchild's Peak aren't difficult, although the Verchild's climb will take the better part of a day. Don't attempt Mt. Liamuiga without a guide. You'll start at Belmont Estate—at the west end of the island—on horseback, then proceed on foot to the lip of the crater, at 2,600 feet. You can go down into the crater—1,000 feet deep and 1 mi (1.5 km) wide, with a small freshwater lake—clinging to vines and roots and scaling rocks, even trees. Expect to get muddy. There are several fine operators (each hotel recommends its favorite); tour rates range from $60 for a rain-forest walk to $90 for a volcano expedition and usually include round-trip transportation from your hotel and picnic lunch.

★ Earl of **Duke of Earl's Adventures** (☎ *869/465–1899*) is as entertaining as his nickname suggests—and his prices are slightly cheaper. He genu-inely loves his island and conveys that enthusiasm, encouraging hikers to swing on vines or sample unusual-looking fruits during his rain-for-est trip. He also conducts a thorough volcano tour to the crater's rim. Greg Pereira of **Greg's Safaris** (☎ *869/465–4121* ⊕ *www.gregsafaris. com*), whose family has lived on St. Kitts since the early 19th century, takes groups on half-day trips into the rain forest and on full-day hikes up the volcano and through the grounds of a private 18th-century greathouse. The rain-forest trips include visits to sacred Carib sites, abandoned sugar mills, and an excursion down a 100-foot coastal can-yon containing a wealth of Amerindian petroglyphs. The Off the Beaten Track Plantation Tour provides a thorough explanation of the role sugar and rum played in the Caribbean economy and colonial wars. He and his staff relate fascinating historical, folkloric, and botanical information. Oliver Spencer of **Off the Beaten Path** (☎ *869/465–6314*) leads rain-forest treks to the ruins of an abandoned coffee plantation taken over by spreading banyan trees, explaining folklore and flora, including herbal remedies, along the way.

HORSEBACK RIDING

Wild North Frigate Bay and desolate Conaree Beach are great for riding, as is the rain forest. Guides from **Trinity Stables** (☎869/465–3226) offer beach rides ($40) and trips into the rain forest ($50). The latter is intriguing as guides discuss plants' medicinal properties along the way (such as sugarcane to stanch bleeding) and pick oranges right off a tree to squeeze fresh juice. Otherwise, the staffers are cordial but shy, but this isn't a place for beginners' instruction.

SEA EXCURSIONS

In addition to the usual snorkeling, sunset, and party cruises (ranging in price from $40 to $80), most companies offer whale-watching excursions during the winter migrating season, January through April. **Blue Water Safaris** (✉Basseterre ☎869/466–4933 ⊕www.bluewatersafaris. com) offers half-day snorkeling trips or beach barbecues on deserted cays, as well as sunset and moonlight cruises on its 65-foot catamaran *Irie Lime*. **Leeward Island Charters** (✉Basseterre ☎869/465–7474) offers day and overnight charters on two 70-foot catamarans—the *Eagle* and *Spirit of St. Kitts*. Day sails are from 9:30 to 4:30 and include a barbecue, an open bar, and use of snorkeling equipment. The Nevis trip stops at Pinney's Beach for a barbecue and at Shooting Bay, a tiny cove in the bullying shadow of a sheer cliff, where petrels and frigate birds inspect your snorkeling skills. The crews are mellow, affable, and knowledgeable about island life.

SHOPPING

St. Kitts has limited shopping, but there are a few small duty-free shops with good deals on jewelry, perfume, china, and crystal. Several galleries sell excellent paintings and sculptures. The batik fabrics, scarves, caftans, and wall hangings of Caribelle Batik are well known. British expat Kate Spencer is an artist who has lived on the island for years, reproducing its vibrant colors on everything from silk pareus (beach wraps) to note cards to place mats. Other good island buys include crafts, jams, and herbal teas. Don't forget to pick up some CSR (Cane Spirit Rothschild), which is distilled from fresh wild sugarcane right on St. Kitts. The Brinley Gold company has made a splash among spirits connoisseurs for its coffee, mango, coconut, lime, and vanilla rums (there is a tasting room at Port Zante).

20

AREAS & MALLS

Most shopping plazas are in downtown Basseterre, on the streets radiating from the Circus. **All Kind of Tings**, a peppermint-pink edifice on Liverpool Row at College Street Ghaut, functions as a de facto vendors' market, where several booths sell local crafts and cheap T-shirts. Its courtyard frequently hosts folkloric dances, fashion shows, poetry readings, and steel-pan concerts. The **Pelican Mall**—a shopping arcade designed to look like a traditional Caribbean street—has 26 stores, a restaurant, tourism offices, and a bandstand near the cruise-ship pier. Directly behind Pelican Mall, on the waterfront, is **Port Zante,** the deep-water cruise-ship pier where a much-delayed upscale shopping-dining complex is becoming a 25-shop area (including the usual large jewelry concerns); the **Amina Market** here is a fine source for cheap local crafts. If you're looking for inexpensive, island-y T-shirts and souvenirs, check out the series of vendors' huts behind Pelican Mall to the right of Port Zante as you face the sea. **Shoreline Plaza** is next to the Treasury Building, right on Basseterre's waterfront. **TDC Mall** is just off the Circus in downtown.

SPECIALTY ITEMS

ART   **Booyork Gallery** (⊠ *College St., Basseterre* ☎ *869/466–9159*) is the atelier of Dennis Richards, who works in a remarkable range of media from pastels to papier-mâché, ceramics to collages: creative Carnival-inspired accessories (incorporating coconut husks, painted ostrich feathers, spangles, and beads), paintings on packed black sand, and wondrous watercolors, both figurative and abstract. Call ahead for appointments. **Spencer Cameron Art Gallery** (⊠ *10 N. Independence Sq., Basseterre* ☎ *869/465–1617*) has historical reproductions of Caribbean island charts and prints, in addition to owner Rosey Cameron's popular Carnevale clown prints and a wide selection of exceptional artwork by Caribbean artists. The gallery will mail anywhere.

HANDICRAFTS   **Caribelle Batik** (⊠ *Romney Manor, Old Road Town* ☎ *869/465–6253*) ★ sells batik wraps, kimonos, caftans, T-shirts, dresses, wall hangings, and the like.

The **Crafthouse** (⊠ *Bay Rd., Southwell Industrial Site, 0.5 mi [1 km] east of Shoreline Plaza, Basseterre* ☎ *869/465–7754*) is one of the best sources for local dolls, wood carvings, and straw work.

★ **Glass Island** (⊠ *The Circus, Basseterre* ☎ *869/466–6771*) sells frames, earrings, and handblown glass vases, bowls, and plates in sinuous shapes and seductive colors.

Island Hopper (⊠ *The Circus, Basseterre* ☎ *869/465–2905*) is a good place for island crafts, especially wood carvings, pottery, textiles, and colorful resort wear, as well as humorous T-shirts and trinkets.

★ **Kate Design** (⊠ *Bank St., Basseterre* ☎ *869/465–5265*) showcases the highly individual style of Kate Spencer, whose original paintings, serigraphs, note cards, and other pieces are also available from her studio outside Rawlins Plantation.

Linen 'n' Things (⊠ *The Circus, Basseterre* ☎ *869/465–5636*) specializes in beautifully textured clothing, accessories, and tableware, as well as local ceramics.

★ The **Potter's House** (⊠ *Camps Estate House, Camps Estate* ☎ *869/465–5947*) is the atelier-home of Carla Astaphan, whose beautifully glazed ceramics and masks celebrate Afro-Caribbean heritage; she also carries marvelous Haitian pieces.

NIGHTLIFE

Most nightlife revolves around the hotels, which host folkloric shows and calypso and steel bands of the usual limbo-rum-and-reggae variety. The growing Frigate Bay "strip" of beach bars, including Monkey Bar, Rainbow, Mr. X Shiggidy Shack, Oasis Sports Bar, and Ziggy's is the place to party hearty weekend nights. A wild wacky evening is promised by **Bob & Elvis The Party Bus** (⊠ *Frigate Bay* ☎ *869/466–8110* ⊕ *www.caribbeanjourneymastrs.com*), as they escort an increasingly raucous crowd via their psychedelically hued bus Tuesday and Thursday to the island's top liming spots. Look for such hard-driving local exponents of soca music as Nu-Vybes, Grand Masters, Small Axe, and up-and-coming Royalton 5; and don't miss the "heavy dance hall" reggae group, House of Judah. The Marriott large, glitzy casino has table games and slots; it was joined in 2007 by a new casino at the Royal St. Kitts Hotel & Casino (formerly the Allegro Jack Tar).

BARS

Caribe Café (⊠ *The Sands Plaza, Suite C14, Bay Rd., Basseterre* ☎ *869/ 465–5282*) gets you wired both ways during the day with free Wi-Fi and high-test espresso. Come evening, it percolates with live music, poetry readings, and special events complementing the cool boho ambience and warm bonhomie. Savor the delectable paninis and biscotti any time as you contemplate the scintillating harbor views.

A favorite happy-hour watering hole is the **Circus Grill** (⊠ *Bay Rd., Basseterre* ☎ *869/465–0143*), a second-floor eatery whose verandah offers views of the harbor and the activity on the Circus.

★ **Keys Cigar Bar** (⊠ *St. Kitts Marriott Resort, Frigate Bay* ☎ *869/466– 1200*) is a surprisingly low-key, classy hangout, with jazz/salsa duos, cushy sofas, high-back straw chairs, chess-set tables, and a superlative selection of aged rums and *Cubanos* (as well as top Dominican and Nicaraguan brands).

★ **Mr. X Shiggidy Shack** (⊠ *Frigate Bay* ☎ *869/762–3983*) is known for its sizzling Thursday-night bonfire parties replete with fire-eaters, raucous karaoke Saturday, and Sunday dinners accompanied by the MRT band; it's also a must-stop on locals' unofficial Friday-night liming circuit of Frigate Bay bars.

Rockies (⊠ *Bird Rock Beach Resort, Basseterre Bay, 2 mi [3 km] east of Basseterre* ☎ *869/465–8914*) is filled with character and characters who scribble humorous words of wisdom—or bar metaphysics—in magic marker on posts ("We're all here because we aren't there," "If you can read this, thank a teacher"). It often rocks weekend evenings when DJ Ronny Rascal spins between live-music sets.

DANCE & MUSIC CLUBS

Popular local DJ Ronnie Rascal entertains at his own nightspot, **Club Atmosphere** (⊠ *Canada Estate* ☎ *869/465–3655*), on most Friday and Saturday nights.

20

SugaR (⊠ *Sugars Complex, Frigate Bay* ☎ 869/465–7777) calls itself the "sweet place to lime," and rocks most evenings with riotous karaoke, "after"-karaoke DJ mixes, Latin Friday, and other theme nights; it also offers slots, pool tables, and a great cheap menu of local specialties.

EXPLORING ST. KITTS

You can explore Basseterre, the capital city, in a half hour or so, and should allow three to four hours for an island tour. Main Road traces the northwestern perimeter of the island through seas of sugarcane and past breadfruit trees and stone walls. Villages with tiny pastel-color houses of stone and weathered wood are scattered across the island, and the drive back to Basseterre around the island's other side passes through several of them. The most spectacular stretch of scenery is on Dr. Kennedy Simmonds Highway, which goes to the tip of the Southeast Peninsula. This ultrasleek modern road twists and turns through the undeveloped grassy hills that rise between the calm Caribbean and the windswept Atlantic, passing the shimmering pink Great Salt Pond, a volcanic crater, and seductive beaches. Major developments are under way, including the Beaumont Park Racetrack near Dieppe Bay, part of an anticipated massive luxury enclave called Kittitian Heights (itself part of the Whitegate Development Project). Construction has resumed on Marine World at South Friar's Bay, a 4-acre theme park with dolphin encounter, stingray lagoon, ecofriendly water-sports center, beach bar and upscale restaurant (Carambola Beach Club, which opened in 2008), nature trail, and aviary.

WHAT TO SEE

Basseterre. On the south coast, St. Kitts's walkable capital is graced with tall palms and flagstone sidewalks; although many of the buildings appear run-down, there are interesting shops, excellent art galleries, and some beautifully maintained houses. Duty-free shops and boutiques line the streets and courtyards radiating from the octagonal **Circus,** built in the style of London's famous Piccadilly Circus.

There are lovely gardens on the site of a former slave market at **Independence Square** (⊠ *Off Bank St., Basseterre*). The square is surrounded on three sides by 18th-century Georgian buildings.

St. George's Anglican Church (⊠ *Cayon St., Basseterre*) is a handsome stone building with a crenellated tower originally built by the French in 1670 and called Nôtre-Dame. The British burned it down in 1706 and rebuilt it four years later, naming it after the patron saint of England. Since then it has suffered a fire, an earthquake, and hurricanes and was once again rebuilt in 1869.

Port Zante (⊠ *Waterfront, behind Circus, Basseterre*) is an ambitious 27-acre cruise-ship pier and marina in an area that has been reclaimed from the sea. The domed welcome center is an imposing neoclassical hodgepodge, with columns and stone arches, shops, walkways, fountains, and West Indian–style buildings housing luxury shops, galleries, and restaurants. A second pier, 1,434 feet long, has a draft that accommodates even leviathan cruise ships. The selection of shops and restaurants (Tiffany Bar and Deli is a find for fantastic local fare) is gradually expanding as well.

In the restored former Treasury Building, the **National Museum** presents an eclectic collection reflecting the history and culture of the island. It's a collaboration of the St. Christopher Heritage Society and the island government. ⊠ *Bay Rd., Basseterre* 🕾 *869/465–5584* 🖃 *EC$1 residents, U.S.$1 nonresidents* ⊘ *Weekdays 9–5, Sat. 9–1.*

NEED A BREAK?

The tropically themed second-floor terrace eatery, Ballahoo (⊠ *Fort St., Basseterre* 🕾 *869/465–4197*) draws a crowd for breakfast, lunch, and dinner. Specialties include chili shrimp, Madras beef curry, and a toasted rum-and-banana sandwich topped with ice cream. At lunchtime, you can watch the bustle of the Circus and enjoy special prices on such dishes as roti bursting with curried chicken or vegetables. Grab fresh local juices (tamarind, guava) if you can. Though the service is lackadaisical bordering on rude, the food is at least plentiful, the daiquiris killer, and the people-watching delightful.

Black Rocks. This series of lava deposits was spat into the sea ages ago when the island's volcano erupted. It has since been molded into fanciful shapes by centuries of pounding surf. ⊠ *Atlantic coast, outside town of Sadlers, Sandy Bay.*

★ **Brimstone Hill.** The well-restored 38-acre fortress, a UNESCO World Heritage Site, is part of a national park dedicated by Queen Elizabeth in 1985. The steep walk up the hill from the parking lot is well worth it if military history and/or spectacular views interest you. After routing the French in 1690, the English erected a battery here, and by 1736 the fortress held 49 guns, earning it the moniker Gibraltar of the West Indies. In 1782, 8,000 French troops laid siege to the stronghold, which was defended by 350 militia and 600 regular troops of the Royal Scots and East Yorkshires. When the English finally surrendered, the French allowed them to march from the fort in full formation out of respect for their bravery (the English afforded the French the same honor when they surrendered the fort a mere year later). A hurricane severely damaged the fortress in 1834, and in 1852 it was evacuated and dismantled. The beautiful stones were carted away to build houses.

20

The citadel has been partially reconstructed and its guns remounted. A seven-minute orientation film recounts the fort's history and restoration. You can see what remains of the officers' quarters, the redoubts, the barracks, the ordnance store, and the cemetery. Its museum collections were depleted by hurricanes, but some pre-Columbian artifacts, objects pertaining to the African heritage of the island's slaves (masks, ceremonial tools, etc.), weaponry, uniforms, photographs, and old newspapers remain. The view from here includes Montserrat and Nevis to the southeast; Saba and St. Eustatius to the northwest; and St. Barths and St. Maarten to the north. Nature trails snake through the tangle of surrounding hardwood forest and savanna (a fine spot to catch the green vervet monkeys—inexplicably brought by the French and now outnumbering the residents—skittering about). ⊠ *Main Rd., Brimstone Hill* ☎ *869/465–2609* ⊕ *www.brimstonehillfortress.org* ⊠ *$8* ⊙ *Daily 9:30–5:30.*

Old Road. This site marks the first permanent English settlement in the West Indies, founded in 1624 by Thomas Warner. Take the side road toward the interior to find some Carib petroglyphs, testimony of even earlier habitation. The largest depicts a female figure on black volcanic rock, presumably a fertility goddess. Less than a mile east of Old Road along Main Road is **Bloody Point,** where French and British soldiers joined forces in 1629 to repel a mass Carib attack; reputedly so many Caribs were massacred that the stream ran red for three days. ⊹ *Main Rd. west of Challengers.*

★ **Romney Manor.** The ruins of this somewhat restored house (reputedly once the property of Thomas Jefferson) and surrounding cottages that duplicate the old chattel-house style are set in 6 acres of glorious gardens, with exotic flowers, an old bell tower, and an enormous, gnarled 350-year-old *saman* tree (sometimes called a rain tree). Inside, at **Caribelle Batik,** you can watch artisans hand-printing fabrics by the 2,500-year-old Indonesian wax-and-dye process known as batik. Look for signs indicating a turnoff for Romney Manor near Old Road.

St. Kitts Scenic Railway. The old narrow-gauge train that had transported sugarcane to the central sugar factory since 1912 is all that remains of the island's once-thriving sugar industry. Two-story cars bedecked in bright Kittitian colors circle the island in just under four hours. Each passenger gets a comfortable, downstairs air-conditioned seat fronting vaulted picture windows and an upstairs open-air observation spot. The conductor's running discourse embraces not only the history of sugar cultivation but the railway's construction, local folklore, island geography, even other agricultural mainstays from papayas to pigs. You can drink in complimentary tropical beverages (including luscious guava daiquiris) along with the sweeping rain-forest and ocean vistas, accompanied by an a cappella choir's renditions of hymns, spirituals, and predictable standards like "I've Been Workin' on the Railroad." There's a break at the halfway point (La Vallee), where cruise-ship passengers disembark. By then, the trip may seem slow as molasses, but it's certainly uniquely Caribbean. ⊠ *Needsmust* ☎ *869/465–7263* ⊕ *www. stkittsscenicrailway.com* ⊠ *$89* ⊙ *June–Sept., departures Mon. at 1 PM and Wed. at 9:30 AM; Oct.–May, departures vary according to cruiseship schedules (call ahead).*

NEVIS

WHERE TO STAY

Most lodgings are in restored manor or plantation houses scattered throughout the island's five parishes (counties). The owners often live at these inns, and it's easy to feel as if you've been personally invited

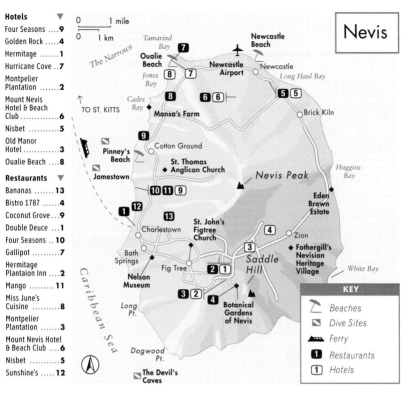

KEY

⤿ Beaches

◺ Dive Sites

⛴ Ferry

❶ Restaurants

[1] Hotels

down for a visit. Before dinner you may find yourself in the drawing room having a cocktail and conversing with the family, other guests, or visitors who have come for a meal. Most inns operate on the MAP plan (including afternoon tea in addition to breakfast and dinner) and offer a free shuttle service to their "private" stretch of beach. If you require TVs and air-conditioning, you're better off staying at hotels and simply dining with the engaging inn owners. Villa Paradiso, a collection of lavish Balinese-inspired three- and four-bedroom villas, formerly run by Abercrombie and Kent's boutique luxury resort division and originally designed by world-renowned decorator Adam Tihany, spill down a verdant hillside to a secluded stretch of Pinney's Beach. The project was in receivership as of this writing, but might reopen.

For approximate costs, see the dining and lodging price chart at the beginning of this chapter.

$$$$ 🏨**Four Seasons Resort Nevis.** This beachfront beauty impeccably com-
⊗ bines world-class elegance with West Indian hospitality, magically
★ appealing to everyone while scrupulously maintaining and upgrad-
ing facilities. Though the public spaces and guest rooms dazzle with mahogany, marble, and crystal, nothing feels overwhelming or over-done. Indeed, consummate taste prevails, redefining the term "under-

20

stated luxury." Service is smiling and solicitous. A beach concierge dispenses everything from books to CDs, circulating regularly with fruit kebabs, Popsicles, and Evian spray. Yes, sometimes it seems overrun by noisy families and conventioneers. And yes, it's pricey. Since all rooms are spacious and elegantly appointed with the latest gadgetry (and the buildings set fairly far back from the water), only those splurging will book the beachfront (or second-floor ocean-view rooms—actually a superior value). Among the amenities here are a state-of-the-art business center, sybaritic spa, and 18-hole Robert Trent Jones Jr. golf course, as well as a model children's club, game room, and turtle program. Good-value packages—and complimentary extras such as nonmotorized water sports and twice-weekly golf clinics—help reduce the sting from the high rates. **Pros:** Luxury without attitude, superlative service, marvelous food, dazzling golf and spa. **Cons:** Pricey, sometimes overrun by conventions, incentive groups (off-season mainly), and families, long walk from farthest rooms to lobby and restaurants. ✉ *Pinney's Beach* ☎ *Box 565, Charlestown* ☎ 869/469–1111, 800/332–3442 in U.S., 800/268–6282 in Canada ⊕ www.fourseasons. com ⟿ 179 rooms, 17 suites, 61 villas ♿ In-room: safe, DVD, Ethernet. In-hotel: 4 restaurants, room service, bars, golf course, tennis courts, pools, gym, spa, beachfront, diving, water sports, bicycles, no elevator, children's programs (ages 2–12), laundry facilities, laundry service, public Internet, no-smoking rooms* ⊟ *AE, D, MC, V* ⊺⊜⫯EP.

$$$$ **Montpelier Plantation.** This Nevisian beauty epitomizes understated
★ elegance and graciously updated plantation living, courtesy of the congenial, cultured Hofmann family. The fieldstone greathouse replicates the 18th-century original; water lilies float serenely in antique copper syrup pots; and the mill now houses an intimate restaurant. Hillside cottages, each with a private verandah and sea views, dot 30 acres of ravishing gardens. The public spaces and guest rooms adopt a chicly minimalist, Asian-inspired aesthetic. Bamboo is brilliantly employed: joined into rustic valances, woven as wall mats, or split for headboards. Each room is distinctive, though all have sisal rugs, Philippine hemp chairs, louvered windows, bowls of fresh flowers, large bathrooms, and a single breathtaking tube filled with orchids and grass hanging above a custom-made canopy platform or mahogany four-poster bed. Attention to detail exemplifies Montpelier: guests register at their leisure once they've settled in; if you pre-ship your bags, they will be unpacked and your clothes pressed before you arrive. Accommodating, longtime staffers (nearly three per room) almost psychically intuit your needs. All you have to do is relax in a hammock contemplating the sea, enjoy complimentary tea by the 60-foot pool bedecked with marvelous local murals, or laze on Montpelier's secluded stretch of Pinney's (a 20-minute complimentary shuttle ride). Guests also have privileges at the new Bistro 1787 in the Botanical Gardens run by executive chef Janice Ryan. **Pros:** Impeccable service, lovely cuisine, exquisite gardens, trendily minimalist decor. **Cons:** Some may find it a little stuffy, no beach on-site. ✉ *Montpelier Estate* ☎ *Box 474, Charlestown* ☎ 869/469–3462 ⊕ www.montpeliernevis.com ⟿ 17 rooms, 1 2-bedroom villa ♿ In-room: no TV. In-hotel: 3 restaurants, bars,

tennis court, pool, beachfront, water sports, no elevator, public Internet, no kids under 8 ⊟*AE, D, MC, V* ☯*Closed late Aug.–early Oct.* ⏃*BP.*

$$$$ ⚏**Nisbet Plantation Beach Club.** At this beachfront plantation inn, pale
★ yellow cottages face a regal, palm-lined grass avenue that sweeps like a dowager's train to the champagne-hue beach. The three categories of faultlessly maintained rooms all have vaulted ceilings, graceful patios, gleaming tile floors, and luscious color schemes (pumpkin to paprika to periwinkle) with such whimsical touches as trompe l'oeil jungle murals. The best buys are the so-called superior units, set back amid the banyan trees. They're nearly as spacious as top-of-the-line rooms and cost about $200 less. Affable service is smoothly unobtrusive (look for special staffers' workshops in traditional Nevisian crafts) and convivial managers welcome guests as if they were coming home. In addition to the soigné greathouse restaurant, you'll find two casual beach eateries and a brilliantly painted deck bar with fantastic sunset views. The small spa specializes in island-infused products created exclusively for the resort. Laundry, afternoon tea, and smiles are complimentary. **Pros:** Glorious setting, the definition of casual elegance, environmentally conscious practices. **Cons:** Long drive to most activities on island, airplanes occasionally whoosh by. ⊠*Newcastle* ☎*869/469–9325 or 800/742–6008* ⊕*www.nisbetplantation.com* ⏃*36 rooms* ⚐*In-room: safe, refrigerator, no TV, dial-up. In-hotel: 3 restaurants, bars, tennis court, pool, gym, spa, beachfront, water sports, no elevator, laundry service, public Internet* ⊟*AE, D, MC, V* ⏃*MAP.*

$$$–$$$$ ⚏**Hermitage Plantation Inn.** A snug 1670 greathouse—reputedly the
★ Caribbean's oldest surviving wooden building—forms the heart of this breeze-swept hillside hideaway. Maureen and Richard "Lupi" Lupinacci and their son Richie are its vivacious soul and will introduce you to everyone who's anyone on Nevis. Lively and laid-back, it attracts a smart (in every sense) set, while remaining down-to-earth and family-friendly—rare for such a refined retreat. The owners' passion for all things Caribbean, from heirloom antiques to vernacular architecture, is apparent. Stone-and-gingerbread cottages are either painstakingly restored originals or meticulous re-creations, with hardwood floors, four-poster canopy beds, and hammock-slung patios or balconies. Families and honeymooners adore the two-story Blue Cottage, but the Loft, Pink House, and Goosepen Cottage are equally sybaritic; the three-bedroom Manor House has its own pool and wraparound porches. The 17th-century stone terraces are embroidered with Maureen's wild, English Romantic–style gardens (pluck your own fruit, or ask the kitchen to prepare a homeopathic bush tea); in genuine plantation fashion, the inn has its own stable, piggery, and livestock. A new "fleet" consisting of a trawler yacht and a sloop will offer sailing and fishing. **Pros:** Wonderful sense of history, delightful owners and clientele, delicious food. **Cons:** Long drive to beach. ⊠*Gingerland* ☎*869/469–3477* ⊕*www.hermitagenevis.com* ⏃*8 rooms, 8 cottages, 1 house* ⚐*In-room: no a/c (some), safe, kitchen (some), refrigerator, no TV (some), Wi-Fi. In-hotel: restaurant, bar, tennis court, pool, no elevator* ⊟*AE, D, MC, V* ⏃*BP.*

20

Off to the Races

CLOSE UP

One of the Caribbean's most festive, endearingly idiosyncratic events is the Nevis Turf and Jockey Club's "Day at the Races," held 10 to 12 times a year on the wild and windswept Indian Castle course. I first experienced the event in the mid-1990s, when I met club president Richard "Lupi" Lupinacci, owner of the Hermitage Plantation Inn. Before even introducing himself, Richard sized me up in the driveway: "You look about the right size for a jockey. How's your seat?" His equally effervescent wife, Maureen, then interceded, "Darling, if you loathe horses, don't worry. In fact, Lupi and I have an agreement about the Jerk and Turkey Club. I get major jewels for every animal he buys."

Since my riding skills were rusty, it was decided that I should be a judge (despite questionable vision, even with glasses). "If it's really by a nose, someone will disagree with you either way," I was reassured. The next day presented a quintessential Caribbean

scene. Although a serious cadre of aficionados (including the German consul) talked turf, the rest of the island seemed more interested in liming and enjoying lively music. Local ladies dished out heavenly barbecued chicken and devilish gossip. Sheep and cattle unconcernedly ambled across the course. But when real horses thundered around the oval, the wooden stands groaned under the weight of cheering crowds, and bookies hand-calculated the payouts.

The irregularly scheduled races continue, albeit now on a properly sodded track, as does the equine hospitality. The **Hermitage Stables** (✉ *Gingerland* ☎ *869/469–3477*) arrange everything from horseback riding to jaunts in hand-carved mahogany carriages. The **Nevis Equestrian Centre** (✉ *Cotton Ground, Pinney's Beach* ☎ *869/469–8118*) offers leisurely beach rides as well as more-demanding canters through the lush hills.

$$$–$$$$
★ 🏨 **Mount Nevis Hotel & Beach Club.** The personable, attentive Meguid family blends the intimacy of the plantation inns, contemporary amenities of the Four Seasons, and typical Nevisian warmth in this hilltop aerie. The former lime plantation (the wild trees' scent wafts on the breeze) affords sterling views from most rooms (request upper floors, which also have marvelous sloped hardwood cathedral ceilings). There's a well-equipped business center, a gym with inspiring water views, Jacuzzis on some outdoor suite decks, and complimentary cell phones (you pay only for calls). Other upscale touches include granite counters, Italian-tile baths, ultramodern kitchens in the superior suites, and CD and DVD players. Standard rooms or junior suites (which have a sitting area and kitchenette) can be combined with the superior suites (whose sofa beds make them good family buys). Some of the 10 new privately owned hillside villas will be in the rental pool. You can luxuriate in a poolside hammock, catch the free shuttle to the beach club and its worthy pizzeria-grill, or take an invigorating hike to the ruins of Thomas Cottle Church, an unusual historic site because both slave owners and slaves worshipped there. **Pros:** Friendly staff, fantastic views, comforts of home at comparatively affordable prices. **Cons:** Lacks beach, long drive to many island activities. ✉ *Shaw's Rd., Mount*

Nevis ✆Box 494, Newcastle ☎869/469–9373 or 800/756–3847 ⊕www.mountnevishotel.com ↩16 suites, 8 junior suites, 8 rooms, 10 villas ⚷In-room: kitchen (some), refrigerator, DVD (some). In-hotel: 2 restaurants, bar, pool, gym, no elevator, public Internet ▭AE, MC, V ⊺⊚|BP.

$$$–$$$$ ⊞**Old Manor Hotel.** Thanks to creative restoration, this inn evokes the physical old-time plantation atmosphere on Nevis (the original cistern is now the pool, and stone outbuildings hold public spaces and guest rooms). The setting is exceptionally pretty, with Mt. Nevis looming in the background, apricot-and-jade buildings enveloped by tropical landscaping, and cannons and rusting sugar-factory equipment forming a virtual abstract sculpture garden. However, despite occasional halfhearted renovations (TVs are still promised), the rooms remain a hodgepodge. The best have exposed wood beams, stone walls, polished hardwood floors, marble double vanities, and four-poster beds. Others are gloomy (reading lights are a chronic problem) or resemble a garage sale, contrasting tatty madras settees with contemporary curved white sofas and soiled rugs. The respected Cooperage restaurant features the "refined Caribbean cuisine" of respected chef Lynn Williams and sensational sea views. **Pros:** Authentic plantation look, excellent under-the-radar restaurant. **Cons:** Lackadaisical service, rooms need refurbishing, no beach or beach club. ⊠*Gingerland ✆Box 70, Charlestown ☎869/469–3445 ⊕www.oldmanornevis.com ↩14 rooms ⚷In-room: no a/c, refrigerator, no TV. In-hotel: 2 restaurants, bars, pool, no elevator, public Internet ▭AE, D, MC, V ⊺⊚|BP.*

$$–$$$$ ⊞**Hurricane Cove Bungalows.** These dramatically set one-, two-, and ★ three-bedroom bungalows cling like glorified tree houses to a cliff overlooking several glittering beaches. Enormous enclosed patios open onto the island's most-glorious vistas; monkeys and pelicans often drop by informally. Every cottage has a full kitchen; many have outdoor gas grills and private swimming pools (those with no pool are especially good buys); it's a short if precipitous walk to Oualie and Lover's beaches. The tiny hotel pool sits in the foundation of a 250-year-old fort, shaded by a magnificent baobab tree. The bungalows are beautifully designed and decorated with beamed ceilings, batik wall hangings, terra-cotta floors, Thai teak furnishings, striking abstract art naïf, and beds swaddled in mosquito netting. Most coveted, especially by honeymooners, are Baobab, Williwaw, Sea Biscuit, and the ultraprivate Monkey cottages. **Pros:** Sensational views, good value for one-bedroom cottages. **Cons:** No air-conditioning for the rare stifling day, minuscule pool, hike back up from beach. ⊠*Hurricane Hill, Oualie Beach ☎869/469–9462 ⊕www.hurricanecove.com ↩13 cottages ⚷In-room: no a/c, kitchen, no TV. In-hotel: pool, no elevator, laundry service ▭AE, D, MC, V ⊙Closed Sept. ⊺⊚|EP.*

$$$ ⊞**Oualie Beach Hotel.** These cozy creole-style gingerbread cottages daubed in cotton-candy colors sit just steps from a hammock-strewn taupe beach overlooking St. Kitts and are carefully staggered to ensure sea views from every room. Deluxe rooms have mahogany canopy four-poster beds and granite vanities, while studios have full kitchen and sofa beds. Unfortunately, many older rooms are slightly musty, with chipped

20

furnishings and faded fabrics. Happily, ecocentric Oualie is noted for its wealth of on-site recreational opportunities from mountain biking to diving, windsurfing to turtle-watching, so you won't spend much time in your room anyway. It's also fairly hopping for a small Nevisian property. The informal restaurant—the domain of talented, enthusiastic chef Jason Bishop—is popular for its West Indian–theme Saturday nights, with live music. Dive packages and numerous Internet specials including early-bird discounts make Oualie excellent value. **Pros:** Fantastic water-sports operations, affordable (especially with recreational packages). **Cons:** Showing some wear. ⊠ *Oualie Beach* 🕾 *869/469– 9735 or 800/682–5431* ⊕ *www.oualiebeach.com* 🛏 *32 rooms* 🕭 *In-room: safe, kitchen (some), refrigerator, VCR (some), Wi-Fi. In-hotel: restaurant, bar, spa, beachfront, diving, water sports, bicycles, no elevator, public Internet, public Wi-Fi* ▤ *AE, D, MC, V* ⧖ *EP.*

$$–$$$ 🏨 **Golden Rock Plantation Inn.** Pam Barry's great-great-great-grandfather built this hillside estate in the early years of the 19th century, and Pam has imbued the inn with her love of Nevisian heritage and nature. The old cistern was converted into a spring-fed swimming pool and the sugar mill into a honeymoon haven with a gorgeous winding bamboo staircase. Cannons placed about the grounds contribute to the historic ambience, as does the extraordinary Eva Wilkin mural in the bar. An avid environmental activist, Pam hacked out nature trails throughout the mountainous, 96-acre property. Green vervet monkeys dash about the premises (they often congregate outside Cottage 1). New ideas and funding, in the form of acclaimed artists Brice Marden and his wife, have infused Golden Rock with a chic, modernist sensibility. They've made what decorators coyly call "a bold statement." Many surfaces— from decks to shutters—have been painted in reds; the pool addition resembles a contemporary-art installation. The aesthetic clashes intriguingly with the historic elements while playing off the richly saturated colors in the landscaping. The gingerbread cottages, which have dazzling ocean views from their patios, likewise received new coats of paint (no more pastels, Pam states) and the island-theme decor may be phased out. The restaurant is being completely overhauled in similar fashion. Some things won't change: free transportation accesses the inn's beach bar (phenomenal rum punches) on Pinney's Beach and a windward strand ideal for seclusion and bodysurfing. And Pam will remain on property as a link to the past and nature advocate. **Pros:** Eco-friendly, arty crowd, glorious grounds. **Cons:** No actual beach though there are two beach clubs, lack of air-conditioning can be a problem on still days. ⊠ *Gingerland* 🖃 *Box 493, Charlestown* 🕾 *869/469–3346* ⊕ *www.golden-rock.com* 🛏 *16 rooms, 1 suite* 🕭 *In-room: no a/c, no TV. In-hotel: 2 restaurants, bar, tennis court, pool, no elevator, public Internet* ▤ *AE, D, MC, V* ⊘ *Closed Sept.–mid-Oct.* ⧖ *EP.*

WHERE TO EAT

Dinner options range from intimate meals at plantation guesthouses (where the menu is often prix fixe) to casual eateries. Seafood is ubiquitous, and many places specialize in West Indian fare. The island is trying to raise its profile as a fine-dining destination by holding NICHE (Nevis International Culinary Heritage Exposition), a gastronomic festival with guest chefs and winemakers offering cooking seminars and tastings during the second half of October.

WHAT TO WEAR

Dress is casual at lunch, although beach attire is unacceptable. Dress pants and sundresses are appropriate for dinner.

For approximate costs, see the dining and lodging price chart at the beginning of this chapter.

CARIBBEAN $$$$ ★ ✕**Miss June's Cuisine.** Dinner with Miss June Mestier, a dynamo originally from Trinidad, could never be called ordinary. The all-inclusive evening begins with cocktails in the ornate living room, followed by dinner in an elegant dining room where tables are set with mismatched china and crystal. Hors d'oeuvres and three courses, including soup and fish, are served. "Now that you've had dinner," Miss June proclaims, "let's have fun," presenting a grand multidish feast highlighting her Trinidadian curries, local vegetable preparations, and meats. "I invite people into my home for dinner and then my manager has the audacity to charge them as they leave!" quips Miss June, who joins guests (who have included Oprah Winfrey, John Grisham, and members of Aerosmith) after dinner for coffee and brandy. Miss June won't kick you out, but she may ask you to turn the lights out as you leave. Her equally vivacious daughter, Simone, plans to add a separate poolside tapas bar, where she would prepare Spanish classics she learned while working in the Canary Islands. ⊠*Jones Bay* ☎*869/469–5330* ⚇*Reservations essential* ▭*MC, V* ⊙*Closed Thurs. and Sat.–Tues. No lunch.*

$$–$$$ ✕**Mango.** This casual beach bar at the Four Seasons has become the latest hot spot for locals and visitors alike, thanks to a gorgeous outdoor deck overlooking the illuminated water, sizzling music, fab drinks, hip decor, and a fairly reasonable menu. You can savor artfully presented Caribbean classics such as ceviche served in coconut shells, a chunky yet velvety conch chowder, lobster and pumpkin fritters with spicy mango dipping sauce, mouth- and eye-watering jerk-spiced swordfish, and barbecued baby back ribs. The kitchen also delights with more-innovative twists, such as blackened wahoo in coconut–Kaffir lime sauce and sugarcane-skewered tiger shrimp with rum-punch glaze and green papaya slaw. ⊠*Four Seasons Resort, Pinney's Beach* ☎*869/469–1111* ▭*AE, D, DC, MC.*

$–$$$ ✕**Sunshine's.** Everything about this beach shack is larger than life, including the Rasta man Llewelyn "Sunshine" Caines himself. Flags and license plates from around the world complement the international patrons (including an occasional movie star), who wander over from the adjacent Four Seasons. Picnic tables are splashed with bright sunrise-to-sunset colors; even the palm trees are painted, though "it gone upscaled," as locals say, with VIP cabanas. Fishermen cruise up with their catch—you might savor lobster rolls or snapper creole. Don't miss the lethal house specialty, Killer Bee rum punch. As Sunshine boasts, "One and you're stung, two you're stunned, three it's a knockout." ⊠*Pinney's Beach* ☎*869/469–1089* ▭*No credit cards.*

20

ECLECTIC   ✕**Hermitage Plantation Inn.** After cocktails in the inn's antiques-filled
$$$$ parlor (the knockout rum punches are legendary), dinner is served on
★   the verandah. Many ingredients are harvested from the inn's herb garden, fruit trees, piggery, and livestock collection; the scrumptious cured
meats, baked goods, preserves, and ice creams are homemade. Sumptuous three- and five-course set menus lovingly prepared by the incomparable (and delightfully named) chef Lovey Boddie might include conch
cakes with lobster sauce; breadfruit-cheddar soufflé; mahimahi with
lemongrass *beurre blanc*, ginger, and tamarind; and white-chocolate-
ginger cheesecake. Bon mots and bonhomie serve as prelude, intermezzo, and coda for a lively evening. ⊠*Gingerland* ☎*869/469–3477*
⌃*Reservations essential* ▭*AE, D, MC, V.*

$$$$ ✕**Montpelier Plantation.** The Hoffman family (Lincoln and Muffin or son
Fodor'sChoice   Tim and daughter-in-law Meredith) presides over a scintillating eve-
★   ning, starting with canapés and cocktails in the civilized Great Room.
Dinner is served on the breezy west verandah, which gazes serenely
upon the lights of Charlestown and St. Kitts. The inventive executive chef, Janice Ryan, utilizes the inn's organic herb gardens and fruit
trees to full advantage. The changing three-course menu might present crispy seafood cake tinged with lemongrass and ginger floating on
coconut-lime sauce, seared swordfish in papaya–black bean salsa, and
a proper herb-crusted rack of lamb in rosemary mustard jus. Meredith
has crafted an exemplary wine list perfectly matched to the cuisine.
The Mill opens on certain nights with sufficient reservations, offering a different set four-course menu accompanied by champagne and
sorbets. Torches light cobblestone steps up to this theatrical faux sugar
mill with crystal sconces, floating candles, and an antique mahogany
gear wheel suspended from the ceiling. Simpler lunches (order the lobster salad) are served on the refreshing patio. ⊠*Montpelier Estate*
☎*869/469–3462* ⌃*Reservations essential* ▭*AE, D, MC, V* ☉*Closed
late Aug.–early Oct.*

$$$$ ✕**Nisbet Plantation Beach Club.** The blissfully air-conditioned greathouse—an oasis of polished hardwood floors, mahogany and cherry-
wood furnishings, equestrian bronzes, antique hurricane lamps, wicker
furnishings, and stone walls—has long been a popular dinner spot.
Tables on the verandah look down the palm-tree-lined fairway to the
sea. The four-course menu combines Continental, Pacific Rim, and
Caribbean cuisines with local ingredients. Sumptuous choices include
chicken and coconut dumpling soup, lobster ravioli in seafood Nantua
sauce, and oven-roasted maple-mustard-glazed duck breast in mandarin orange-cranberry sauce, followed by lemon and vanilla mascarpone
mousse with hazelnut praline. Enjoy an impressively cosmopolitan
selection of cocktails or coffee with silky-soft live music in the civilized
front bar. Witty, dapper maître d' Patterson Fleming (his cravat collection is enviable!) ensures a smooth, swank experience. ⊠*Newcastle*
☎*869/469–9325* ⌃*Reservations essential* ▭*AE, D, MC, V.*

$$$–$$$$ ✕**Coconut Grove.** This thatched-palm roof and rough timber structure
★   sports a sensuous South Seas look, best appreciated on the deck as
the sun fireballs across the Caribbean. Inside, handsome teak furnish-
ings are animated by Buddhas, parrot-hue throw pillows, batik hang-

ings, and gauzy curtains. The service is warm, the champagne properly chilled, and the splendid Pacific Rim–Mediterranean fusion fare seems designed to complement the admirable wine selection—with 4,000 bottles it is second on the sister islands only to that of the Four Seasons—rather than the other way around. Owners Gary and Karin Colt often bring winemaker friends in from Europe for tastings and dinners. Nonetheless, serious foodies won't be disappointed by the likes of plantain rolls with diced tiger shrimp in Colombo (curry) mango coulis, baked baby Camembert with cranberry confiture, house-tea-smoked chicken, or tuna crusted with herbes de Provence and stuffed with tapenade and wild mushrooms. Happy hour, 11 PM–midnight, often ushers in impromptu dancing, continuing the "Bali high" theme. A new downstairs poolside bar and grill is hip-hopping and happening with creative lighter fare during the day and live music many evenings. ⊠*Nelson's Spring, Pinney's Beach* ☎*869/469–1020* ⚖*Reservations essential* ▭*MC, V.*

$$$–$$$$ ✕**Four Seasons Dining Room.** The main restaurant at the Four Seasons
★ is imposing yet romantic: a beamed cathedral ceiling, imported hardwood paneling, parquet floors, flagstone hearth, and china-filled cabinets softened by white linens, towering floral arrangements, and picture windows overlooking the sea. Swiss-born chef Bruno Correa produces a Continental-inspired menu utilizing Caribbean ingredients (he's pioneered working with local farmers to produce micro-vegetables). Presentation is simple yet exquisite: witness the lobster sashimi with caviar on sculpted ice, or diver scallops wrapped in Pata Negra prosciutto in lemongrass sauce. Desserts feature a variety of nightly soufflés, from chocolate to mango. The hotel can arrange a unique interactive dive-and-dine experience, plunging you into the deep to pluck lobster and other marine creatures that Bruno will cook for you later. The wine list is admirably comprehensive with surprisingly fair prices. The adjacent Neve (which counterpoints with aggressively contemporary decor) specializes in Italian grills and bountiful breakfast buffets. The Friday-night beach barbecues are deliciously hedonistic. ⊠*Four Seasons Resort, Pinney's Beach* ☎*869/469–1111* ⚖*Reservations essential* ▭*AE, D, DC, MC, V* ⊗*No lunch.*

$$$ ✕**Mount Nevis Hotel & Beach Club.** The hotel's airy dining room opens onto the terrace and pool with a splendid view of St. Kitts. The elegant yet light menu deftly blends local ingredients with a cornucopia of Caribbean-Continental cuisines, artfully presented by Mexican-born chef Alberto Rodriguez. Sterling starters are sesame tempura shrimp with tamarind oyster sauce or salted fish cake napoleon layered with fresh baby spinach, chorizo, and avocado salsa. Worthy if less-innovative main courses include sautéed black tiger shrimp in scallion-coconut sauce and roast pork loin in apple-merlot sauce. Savor cocktails in the distinctive lounge (accented by sisal rugs, mosaic and painted tiles, towering bamboo stalks, and flowers floating in crystal bowls). Then repair to the sublime open-air dining room, where a pianist holds forth on an illuminated stage by the pool. ⊠*Shaws Rd., Mt. Nevis Estates* ☎*869/469–9373* ⚖*Reservations essential* ▭*AE, MC, V.*

20

$$–$$$ ✗**Bananas.** Peripatetic English owner Gillian Smith's career spans jobs
★ with Disney and Relais & Châteaux, and everything about Bananas
(read lovably nuts) borrows from her wildly diverse experiences. Even
the setting is delightfully deceptive: the classic stone, brick, and wood
plantation greathouse nestled amid extravagant gardens was painstakingly built by Gillian herself in 2006. Her fun, funky, shabby-chic
sensibility informs every aspect of the restaurant. The colonial look
(pith helmets, steamer trunks, beamed ceiling, white wicker, chandeliers dangling from the corrugated tin roof) contrasts with Turkish
kilims, Moroccan lamps, and whimsical touches like a lighted tailor's
dummy and antique tennis rackets. The food is equally eclectic and
globe-trotting, running from bourbon-glazed ribs to lobster tails with
pineapple-ginger salsa. Despite the improvisational ambience, there's
no monkeying around with quality at Bananas. ⊠ *Upper Hamilton
Estate* 🕾 *869/469–1891* ⚠ *Reservations essential* ☰ *MC, V.*

SEAFOOD ✗**Gallipot.** Gallipot attracts locals with ultrafresh seafood at reason-
$$–$$$ able prices, marvelous views of St. Kitts across the road, and sensa-
★ tional sunsets. Large Sunday lunches with ample portions (only one
dish per week, usually classic roast beef and Yorkshire pudding) are a
big draw. The Fosberys built the octagonal bar as an addition to their
small beach house across the street from quiet Tamarind Bay, while
their daughter and son-in-law, Tracy and Julian Rigby, provide fish
through Nevis Water Sports, a charter-fishing company (fishnets and
photos from their sportfishing championships grace the bar). Julian
built a smoker (Tracy dubs it "the eyesore"), where he cures melt-in-
your-mouth wahoo, kingfish, and sailfish carpaccio. Those seeking land
specialties can happily tuck into the smoked duck, steak-and-kidney
pie, or chicken korma curry, seasoned with herbs from Tracy's garden.
⊠ *Tamarind Bay* 🕾 *869/469–8230* ☰ *MC, V* ⊘ *Closed Mon.–Wed.
No dinner Sun.*

$–$$ ✗**Double Deuce.** Mark Roberts, the former chef at Montpelier, decided
★ to chuck the "five-star lifestyle" and now runs this jammed, jamming
beach bar, which lures locals with fine, fairly priced fare, creative
cocktails, and a Hemingway-esque feel (the shack is plastered with
sailing and fishing pictures, as well as Balinese masks, Sabrett's hot
dog umbrellas, and wind chimes). Peer behind the ramshackle bar and
you'll find a gleaming modern kitchen where Mark (and partner Lyndy)
prepare sublime seafood he often catches himself, as well as organic
beef burgers, and lip-smacking ribs. The DD is as cool and mellow as it
gets. Stop by for free Wi-Fi and proper espresso, a game of pool, Thursday-night karaoke, or just to hang out with a Double Deuce Stinger
(Mark's answer to Sunshine's Killer Bee punch). You'll find more than
4,000 songs on the "jukebox"—Akon to ZZ Top, Sarah Vaughan to
Van Morrison; if you can't find your favorite the "DJ" will download it
for you while you take a quick dip. ⊠ *Pinney's Beach* 🕾 *869/469–2222*
⚠ *Reservations essential* ☰ *No credit cards* ⊘ *Closed Mon.*

BEACHES

All beaches are free to the public (the plantation inns cordon off "private" areas on Pinney's Beach for guests), but there are no changing facilities, so wear a swimsuit under your clothes.

Newcastle Beach. This broad swath of soft ecru sand shaded by coconut palms sits at the northernmost tip of the island near Nisbet Plantation, on the channel between St. Kitts and Nevis. It's popular with snorkelers, but beware stony sections and occasional strong currents that kick up seaweed and roil the sandy bottom. You can watch planes take off like seabirds: it's only a three- to four-minute drive east of the airport along Main Road. ⊠ *Newcastle.*

Oualie Beach. South of Mosquito Bay and north of Cades and Jones bays, this beige-sand beach lined with palms and sea grapes is where the folks at Oualie Beach Hotel can mix you a drink and fix you up with water-sports equipment. There's excellent snorkeling amid calm water and fantastic sunset views with St. Kitts silhouetted in the background. Several beach chairs and hammocks ($3 rental if you don't have lunch) line the sand and the grassy "lawn" behind it (this beach expands and erodes constantly). Oualie is at the island's northwest tip, approximately 3 mi (5 km) west of the airport. ⊠ *Oualie Beach.*

★ **Pinney's Beach.** The island's showpiece has almost 4 mi (6.5 km) of soft, golden sand on the calm Caribbean, lined with a magnificent grove of palm trees. The Four Seasons Resort is here, as is the beach pavilion of the Golden Rock Plantation Inn, and casual beach bars such as Sunshine's and the Double Deuce. Regrettably, the waters can be murky and filled with kelp if the weather has been inclement anywhere within a hundred miles, depending on the currents. You can't miss Pinney's: Main Road hugs it, starting just north of Charleston (just take any of the short dirt turnoffs with signage for bars). ⊠ *Pinney's Beach.*

SPORTS & THE OUTDOORS

BIKING

Windsurfing Nevis (⊠ *Oualie Beach* ☎ *869/469–9682* ⊕ *www.bikenevis.com*) offers mountain-bike rentals as well as specially tailored tours on its state-of-the-art Gary Fisher, Trek, and Specialized bikes. The tours ($50–$65), led by Winston Crooke, a master windsurfer and competitive bike racer, encompass lush rain forest, majestic ruins, and spectacular views. Rates vary according to itinerary and ability level but are aimed generally at experienced riders. Winston and his team delight in sharing local knowledge, from history to culture. For those just renting, Winston and Reggie determine your performance level and suggest appropriate routes.

DAY SAILS

Sea Nevis Charters (⊠ *Tamarind Bay* ☎ *869/469–9239*) offers its 44-foot *Sea Dreamer* for snorkeling and island sunset cruises. Captain Les Windley takes you to less-trammeled sites and is a font of information on marine life.

20

DIVING & SNORKELING

The **Devil's Caves** are a series of grottoes where divers can navigate tunnels, canyons, and underwater hot springs while viewing lobsters, sea fans, sponges, squirrel fish, and more. The village of **Jamestown,** which washed into the sea around Ft. Ashby, just south of Cades Bay, makes for superior snorkeling and diving. Reef-protected Pinney's Beach offers especially good snorkeling. Single-tank dives are usually $65, two-tank dives $95.

⟳ **Scuba Safaris** (⊠ *Oualie Beach* ☎*869/469–9518* ⊕*www.scubanevis.*
★ *com*) is a PADI five-star facility, NAUI Dream Resort, and NASDS Examining Station, whose experienced dive masters offer everything from a resort course to full certification. Their equipment is always state-of-the-art, including new underwater scooters. They also provide a snorkeling learning experience that enables you not only to see but to listen to sea life, including whales and dolphins. **Under the Sea** (⊠ *Oualie Beach* ☎*869/469–1291* ⊕*www.undertheseanevis.com*) is the brainchild of Barbara Whitman, a marine biologist from Connecticut. Barbara's mission is to educate snorkelers and divers of all ages about sea life and various ecosystems so they'll appreciate—and respect—what they see. Using hands-on "touch tanks," videos, and self-painted marine murals as familiarization tools, she then offers snorkeling lessons and tours to see the creatures in the wild. Her programs start at $25, and profits go toward educating local schoolchildren about their precious natural environment and increasing ecological awareness.

FISHING

Fishing here focuses on kingfish, wahoo, grouper, tuna, and yellowtail snapper, with marlin occasionally spotted. The best areas are Monkey Shoals and around Redonda. Charters cost approximately $450–$500 per half day, $850–$1,000 per full day, and usually include open bar. *Deep Venture* (⊠ *Oualie Beach* ☎*869/469–5110*), run by fisherman-chef Matt Lloyd, does day-fishing charters, providing a real insight into both commercial fishing and the Caribbean kitchen. **Nevis Water Sports** (⊠ *Oualie Beach* ☎*869/469–9060* ⊕*www.fishnevis.com*) offers sportfishing aboard the 31-foot *Sea Brat* under the supervision of tournament-winning captains Julian Rigby and Ian Gonzaley. Julian, originally from England, and wife Tracy organize the annual Nevis Yacht Club Sports Fishing Tournament, which reels in competitors from all over the Caribbean.

GOLF

Fodor's Choice Duffers doff their hats to the beautiful, impeccably maintained Robert
★ Trent Jones Jr.–designed **Four Seasons Golf Course** (⌕ *18-holes, par-72, 6,766-yards* ⊠ *Four Seasons Resort Nevis, Pinney's Beach* ☎*869/469–1111*): the virtual botanical gardens surrounding the fairways almost qualify as a hazard in themselves. The front 9 holes are fairly flat until the hole 8, which climbs uphill after your tee shot. Most of the truly stunning views are along the back 9. The signature hole is the 15th, a 660-yard monster that encompasses a deep ravine; other holes include bridges, steep drops, rolling pitches, extremely tight and unforgiving fairways, sugar-mill ruins, and fierce doglegs. Attentive attendants can-

vas the course with beverage buggies, handing out chilled, peppermint-scented towels and preordered Cubanos that help test the wind. Greens fees for hotel guests are $125 per person per 9 holes, $190 per 18; nonguests pay $135 and $205 respectively.

HIKING

The center of the island is Nevis Peak—also known as Mt. Nevis—which soars 3,232 feet and is flanked by Hurricane Hill on the north and Saddle Hill on the south. If you plan to scale Nevis Peak, a daylong affair, it's highly recommended that you go with a guide. Your hotel can arrange it (and a picnic lunch) for you. The **Upper Round Road Trail** is a 9-mi (14.5-km) road constructed in the late 1600s that was cleared and restored by the Nevis Historical and Conservation Society. It connects the Golden Rock Plantation Inn, on the east side of the island, with Nisbet Plantation Beach Club, on the northern tip. The trail encompasses numerous vegetation zones, including pristine rain forest, and impressive plantation ruins. The original cobblestones, walls, and ruins are still evident in many places.

★ **Herbert Heights Village Experience** (☎869/469–2856 ⊕*www.herbert heights.com*) is run by the Herbert family, who lead four-hour nature hikes up to panoramic Herbert Heights, where you drink in fresh local juices and the views of Montserrat; the powerful telescope makes you feel as if you're staring right into that island's simmering volcano. The trail formed part of an escape route for runaway slaves. Numerous hummingbirds, doves, and butterflies flit and flutter through the rain forest. The Herberts painstakingly reconstructed thatched cottages that offer a glimpse of village life a century ago at Nelson's Lookout. Hike prices start at $20 (more for donkey transport). The festive activities include crab races, refreshments, rock climbing, and whale-watching in season through a telescope donated by Greenpeace. **Sunrise Tours** (☎869/469–2758 ⊕*www.nevisnaturetours.com*), run by Lynell and Earla Liburd, offers a range of hiking tours, but their most popular is Devil's Copper, a rock configuration full of ghostly legends. Local people gave it its name because at one time the water was hot—a volcanic thermal stream. The area features pristine waterfalls and splendid bird-watching. They also do a Nevis village walk, a Hamilton Estate Walk, an Amerindian walk along the wild southeast Atlantic coast, and trips to the rain forest and Nevis Peak. They love highlighting Nevisian heritage, explaining time-honored cooking techniques, the many uses of dried grasses, and medicinal plants. Hikes range from $20 to $40 per person, and you receive a certificate of achievement. **Top to Bottom** (☎869/469–9080 ⊕*www.walknevis.com*), run by Jim and Nikki Johnston, offers ecorambles (slow tours) and hikes that emphasize Nevis's volcanic and horticultural heritage (including pointing out bat caves and folkloric herbal and "murderous" medicines). The Johnstons are also keen star- and bird-watchers (their Nevis Nights magically explain nocturnal biology, astronomy, even astrology). Kayaks are now available for rent and Jim conducts tours in Long Haul Bay. Three-hour rambles or hikes are $20 per person (snacks and juice included); it's $40 for more-strenuous climbs (two are offered) up Mt. Nevis.

20

HORSEBACK RIDING

Nevis Equestrian Centre (⊠ *Cotton Ground, Pinney's Beach* ☎ *869/469–8118* ⊕ *www.ridenevis.com*) arranges leisurely beach rides, more-demanding trail rides ($60–$90), and lessons from caring, careful owners Erika and John.

KAYAKING

Turtle Tours Nevis (⊠ *Oualie Beach* ☎ *869/465–8503*) offers sea kayaking along the Nevis coast, stopping at an otherwise inaccessible beach underneath a towering cliff for snorkeling and at Pinney's for refreshments and a refreshing view of St. Kitts.

WINDSURFING

★ Waters are generally calm and northeasterly winds steady yet gentle, making Nevis an excellent spot for beginners and intermediates. **Windsurfing Nevis** (⊠ *Oualie Beach* ☎ *869/469–9682*) offers top-notch instructors (Winston Crooke is one of the best in the islands) and equipment for $30 per half hour. Groups are kept small (eight maximum), and the equipment is state-of-the-art from Mistral, North, and Tushingham.

SHOPPING

Nevis is certainly not the place for a shopping spree, but there are some unusual and wonderful surprises, notably the island's stamps, batik, and hand-embroidered clothing. Honey is another buzzing biz. Quentin Henderson, the amiable head of the **Nevis Beekeeping Cooperative,** will even arrange trips by appointment to various hives for demonstrations of beekeeping procedures. Other than a few hotel boutiques and isolated galleries, virtually all shopping is concentrated on or just off Main Street in Charlestown. The lovely old stonework and wood floors of the waterfront Cotton Ginnery Complex make an appropriate setting for stalls of local artisans.

SPECIALTY ITEMS

ART Nevis has produced one artist of some international repute, the late Dame Eva Wilkin, who for more than 50 years painted island people, flowers, and landscapes in an evocative art naïf style. Her originals are now quite valuable, but prints are available in some local shops. The **Eva Wilkin Gallery** (⊠ *Clay Ghaut, Gingerland* ☎ *869/469–2673*) occupies her former atelier (hours are very irregular, so call ahead). If the paintings, drawings, and prints are out of your price range, consider buying the lovely note cards based on her designs; the new owners are also promoting promising regional artists. **Robert Humphreys** (⊠ *Zetlands* ☎ *869/469–3326 or 869/469–6217*) sells his work, flowing bronze sculptures of pirouetting marlins and local birds and animals, at his home, where it's possible to watch the artist at work in his studio.

CLOTHING Most hotels have their own boutiques. **Island Fever** (⊠ *Main St., Charlestown* ☎ *869/469–0867*) has become the island's classiest shop, with an excellent selection of everything from bathing suits and dresses to straw bags and jewelry. **Island Hopper** (⊠ *Main St., Charlestown* ☎ *869/469–*

5430) sells colorful Caribelle Batik clothing and painted coconut bags as well as T-shirts and other Nevis souvenirs.

HANDICRAFTS Cheryl "Cherrianne" Liburd's **Bocane Ceramics** (⊠ *Main St., Stoney Grove* ☎ *869/469–5437*) stocks beautifully designed and glazed local pottery, such as platters painted with marine life, pineapple tea sets, and coffee tables topped with mosaic depictions of chattel houses.

The CraftHouse (⊠ *Pinney's Rd., Charlestown* ☎ *869/469–5505*) is a marvelous source for local specialties from vetiver mats to leather moccasins; there's a smaller branch in the Cotton Ginnery.

Knick Knacks (⊠ *Main St., Neville Bldg. near Ferry Dock, Charlestown* ☎ *869/469–5784*) showcases top local artisans, including Marvin Chapman (stone-and-wood carvings) and Jeannie Rigby (exquisite dolls).

The **Nevis Handicraft Co-op Society** (⊠ *Main St., Charlestown* ☎ *869/469–1746*), next to the tourist office, offers works by local artisans (clothing, ceramic ware, woven goods) and locally produced honey, hot sauces, and jellies (try the guava and soursop).

★ **Newcastle Pottery** (⊠ *Main Rd., Newcastle* ☎ *869/469–1746*), a cooperative, has continued the age-old tradition of hand-built red-clay pottery fired over burning coconut husks. It's possible to watch the potters and purchase wares at their small Newcastle factory.

★ The **Philatelic Bureau** (⊠ *Off Main St., Charlestown* ☎ *869/469–0617*), opposite the tourist office, is the place to go for stamp collectors. St. Kitts and Nevis are famous for their decorative, and sometimes valuable, stamps. Real beauties include the butterfly, hummingbird, and marine-life series.

NIGHTLIFE

★ In season it's usually easy to find a local calypso singer or a steel or string band performing at one of the hotels, notably the Four Seasons and Oualie Beach (which also features string musicians on homemade instruments Tuesday evenings). Scan the posters plastered on doorways announcing informal jump-ups. Though Nevis lacks high-tech discos, many restaurants and bars have live bands or DJs on weekends. **Eddy's Bar & Restaurant** (⊠ *Main St., Memorial Sq., Charlestown* ☎ *869/469–5958*) has traditionally been the place to go on Wednesday nights for a raucous West Indian happy hour. Burgers, shepherd's pie, quesadillas, and a variety of well-prepared food will get you prepared for the long night ahead. The evening will go on and on to the wee hours with karaoke and dancing to a local DJ. **Sunset Beach Club** (⊠ *Clifton Estate* ☎ *869/469–0125*) really goes tropical with flamingo pink walls, lime trim, and rainbow umbrellas shading picnic tables on the beach. Come here for sensational sunsets with St. Kitts as a backdrop; the concoctions will have you seeing stars regardless (watch your step navigating the little wooden bridge over the mangrove "lagoon"). Sunset really buzzes Friday and Saturday nights, when it might be the closest thing

20

to a Nevisian "meet market." The **Water Department Barbecue** (⊠ *Pump Rd., Charlestown* 🕾 *No phone*) is the informal name for a lively Friday-night jump-up that's run by two fellows from the local water department to raise funds for department trips. Friday afternoons the tents go up and the grills are fired. Cars line the streets and the guys dish up fabulous barbecue ribs and chicken—as certain customers lobby to get their water pressure adjusted. It's a classic Caribbean scene.

EXPLORING NEVIS

Nevis's Main Road makes a 21-mi (32-km) circuit through the five parishes; various offshoots of the road wind into the mountains. You can tour Charlestown, the capital, in a half hour or so, but you'll need three to four hours to explore the entire island. Part of the island's charm is its rusticity: there are no traffic lights, goats still amble through the streets of Charlestown, and local grocers announce whatever's in stock on a blackboard (anything from pig snouts to beer).

Numbers in the margin correspond to points of interest on the Nevis map.

Bath Springs. The Caribbean's first hotel, the Bath Hotel, built by businessmann John Huggins in 1778, was so popular in the 19th century that visitors, including such dignitaries as Samuel Taylor Coleridge and Prince William Henry, traveled two months by ship to "take the waters" in the property's hot thermal springs. It suffered extensive hurricane and probably earthquake damage over the years and languished in disrepair until recently. Local volunteers have cleaned up the spring and built a stone pool and steps to enter the waters; now, residents and visitors enjoy the springs, which range from 104°F to 108°F, though signs still caution that you bathe at your own risk, especially if you have heart problems. Upon completion, this promising development will house the Nevis Island Administration offices, massage huts and changing rooms, a restaurant, and a cultural center and historic exhibit on the original hotel property. Follow Main Street south from Charlestown. ⊠ *Charlestown outskirts.*

★ **Botanical Gardens of Nevis.** In addition to terraced gardens and arbors, this remarkable 7.8-acre site in the glowering shadow of Mt. Nevis has natural lagoons, streams, and waterfalls, superlative bronze mermaids, egrets and herons, and extravagant fountains. You can find a proper rose garden, sections devoted to orchids and bromeliads, cacti, and flowering trees and shrubs—even a bamboo garden. The entrance to the Rain Forest Conservatory—which attempts to include every conceivable Caribbean ecosystem and then some—duplicates an imposing Maya temple. A splendid re-creation of a plantation-style greathouse contains the excellent Bistro 1787 (operated by the exemplary Montpelier Plantation), with sweeping sea views, and an upscale shop selling art and Indonesian teak furnishings sourced during the new owner's world travels. ⊠ *Montpelier Estate* 🕾 *869/469–3509* 🖾 *$9* ⊗ *Mon.– Sat. 9–4:30.*

★ **Charlestown.** About 1,200 of Nevis's 10,000 inhabitants live in the capital. The town faces the Caribbean, about 12.5 mi (20 km) south of Basseterre on St. Kitts. If you arrive by ferry, as most people do, you'll walk smack onto Main Street from the pier. It's easy to imagine how tiny Charlestown, founded in 1660, must have looked in its heyday. The weathered buildings still have their fanciful galleries, elaborate gingerbread fretwork, wooden shutters, and hanging plants. The stonework building with the clock tower (1825, but mostly rebuilt after a devastating 1873 fire) houses the courthouse and the second-floor **library** (a cool respite on sultry days). The little park next to the library is Memorial Square, dedicated to the fallen of World Wars I and II. Down the street from the square, archaeologists have discovered the remains of a Jewish cemetery and synagogue (Nevis reputedly had the Caribbean's second-oldest congregation), but there's little to see.

The **Alexander Hamilton Birthplace,** which contains the Museum of Nevis History, is on the waterfront, covered in bougainvillea and hibiscus. This Georgian-style house is a reconstruction of what is believed to have been the American patriot's original home, built in 1680 and thought to have been destroyed during an earthquake in the mid-19th century. Hamilton was born here in 1755 and moved to St. Croix when he was about 12. A few years later, at 17, he moved to the American colonies to continue his education; he became Secretary of the Treasury to George Washington and died in a duel with political rival Aaron Burr. The Nevis House of Assembly occupies the second floor of this building, and the museum downstairs contains Hamilton memorabilia, documents pertaining to the island's history, and displays on island geology, politics, architecture, culture, and cuisine. The gift shop is a wonderful source for historic maps, crafts, and books on Nevis. ⊠ *Low St., Charlestown* ☎ *869/469–5786* ⊕ *www.nevis-nhcs.org* ✉ *$5; $7 includes admission to Nelson Museum* ⊙ *Weekdays 9–4, Sat. 9–noon.*

Eden Brown Estate. This government-owned mansion, built around 1740, is known as Nevis's haunted house, or haunted ruins. In 1822 a Miss Julia Huggins was to marry a fellow named Maynard. However, on the day of the wedding, the groom and his best man had a duel and killed each other. The bride-to-be became a recluse, and the mansion was closed down. Local residents claim they can feel the presence of "someone" whenever they go near the eerie old house with its shroud of weeds and wildflowers. You're welcome to drop by; it's always open, and it's free. ⊠ *East Coast Rd. between Lime Kiln and Mannings, Eden Brown Bay* ☎ *No phone.*

Fothergill's Nevisian Heritage Village. On the grounds of a former sugar plantation–cotton ginnery, this ambitious, ever-expanding project traces the evolution of Nevisian social history, from the Caribs to the present, through vernacular dwellings. Several huts re-create living conditions over the centuries. The Carib chief's thatched hut includes actual relics such as weapons, calabash bowls, clay pots, and cassava squeezers. Wattle-and-daub structures reproduce slave quarters; implements on display include coal pots and sea fans (used as sieves). A post-emancipation chattel house holds patchwork quilts. There's a typical share-

20

cropper's garden, a blacksmithy, and a traditional rum shop (replete with domino players). Management hopes to establish a working still and a small restaurant dispensing authentic Nevisian fare. ⊠*Gingerland* ☎*869/469–5521 or 869/469–7037* 🖃*EC$8* ☉*Mon.–Sat. 9–4.*

Mansa's Farm. Anyone who wants a real sense of island daily life and subsistence should call Mansa. He'll take you past his fruit trees and herb gardens through rows of tomatoes, cucumbers, string beans, eggplant, zucchini, sweet pepper, melons, and more. Discussing the needs for at least partial organic growing practices, he explains how he adapted traditional folk pesticides and describes the medicinal properties of various plants, cultivated and wild. He'll prepare a lunch utilizing his produce, including delectable refreshing fruit drinks. The weekend barbecues are a highlight. All in all, this agri-tourism foray redefines food for thought. ⊠*Cades Bay* ☎*869/469–8520* 🖃*Varies* ☉*Call for appointment.*

Nelson Museum. This collection merits a visit for its memorabilia of Lord Horatio Nelson, including letters, documents, paintings, and even furniture from his flagship. Historical archives of the Nevis Historical and Conservation Society are housed here and are available for public viewing. Nelson was based in Antigua but on military patrol came to Nevis, where he met and eventually married Frances Nisbet, who lived on a 64-acre plantation here. Half the space is devoted to often provocative displays on island life, from leading families to vernacular architecture to the adaptation of traditional African customs, from cuisine to Carnival. ⊠*Bath Rd., outside Charlestown* ☎*869/469–0408* ⊕*www. nevis-nhcs.org* 🖃*$5; $7 includes admission to Museum of Nevis History* ☉*Weekdays 9–4, Sat. 9–noon.*

St. John's Figtree Church. Among the records of this church built in 1680 is a tattered, prominently displayed marriage certificate that reads: HORATIO NELSON, ESQUIRE, TO FRANCES NISBET, WIDOW, ON MARCH 11, 1787. ⊠*Church Ground* ☎*No phone.*

St. Thomas Anglican Church. The island's oldest church was built in 1643 and has been altered many times over the years. The gravestones in the old churchyard have stories to tell, and the church itself contains memorials to Nevis's early settlers. ⊠*Main Rd. just south of Cotton Ground, Jessups* ☎*No phone.*

ST. KITTS & NEVIS ESSENTIALS

To research prices, get advice from other travelers, and book travel arrangements, visit www.fodors.com.

■ TRANSPORTATION

BY AIR

In addition to the nonstop flights, American Eagle has several daily flights into St. Kitts and two daily flights to Nevis from San Juan. Other major domestic airlines fly from their eastern hubs either into Antigua, St. Maarten, San Juan, or St. Thomas, where connections to St. Kitts (and, less frequently, to Nevis) can be made on LIAT, Caribbean Airlines, Carib Aviation, and Winair.

Airline Information American/American Eagle (☎869/465-2273 or 869/469-8995). **Carib Aviation** (☎869/469-9185 in Nevis). **Caribbean Airlines** (☎869/465-2286 or 800/744-2225). **Delta** (☎800/221-1212). **LIAT** (☎869/465-1330). **US Airways** (☎800/428-4322). **Winair** (☎869/465-8010, 869/469-9583 in Nevis).

Airport Information Robert L. Bradshaw International Airport (SKB ✉Golden Rock, St. Kitts ☎465-8013). **Vance W. Amory International Airport** (NEV ✉Newcastle, Nevis ☎869/469-9343).

BY BOAT & FERRY

There are several ferry services between St. Kitts and Nevis, all with byzantine schedules that are subject to abrupt change. Most companies make two or three daily trips. All the ferries take about 30 to 45 minutes and cost $8. You can get up-to-date information about all the options from the central ferry information number or Web site listed below (click on FERRY SCHEDULE).

Sea-taxi service between the two islands is operated by Kenneth Samuel, Nevis Water Sports, Leeward Island Charters, and Austin Macleod of Pro-Divers for $20 one-way in summer, $25 in winter, with a four-person minimum. There's an additional EC$1 tax for port security, paid separately upon departure.

Information Ferry information (☎869/466-4636 ⊕www.leytonms.com). **Kenneth's Dive Centre** (☎869/465-2670). **Leeward Island Charters** (☎869/465-7474). **Nevis Water Sports** (☎869/469-9060). **Pro-Divers** (☎869/465-3223).

BY CAR

You can get by without a car if you are staying in the Frigate Bay–Basseterre area, but if you are staying elsewhere on the island (and if you wish to get out and dine around), you'll need to rent a car. On Nevis, you may wish to rent a car for a day or two of exploring, but roads are so poorly marked that it's often easier to just take taxis and guided tours.

On St. Kitts, present yourself, your valid driver's license, and EC$50 at the police station on Cayon Street in Basseterre to get a temporary driving permit (on Nevis the car-rental agency will help you obtain a local license for $24 at the police station). The license is valid for three months on both islands. On either island, car rentals start at about $40 per day for a compact; expect to pay a few extra bucks for air-conditioning. Most agencies offer substantial discounts when you rent by the week.

Agencies include Avis, which has the best selection of Suzuki and Daihatsu four-wheel-drive vehicles on St. Kitts. Delisle Walwyn also provides an excellent selection and the option of a replacement car for one day on Nevis if you rent for three days or more on St. Kitts. Agencies such as Noel's Courtesy Garage and Striker's Car Rentals offer a wide variety of cars and jeeps for exploring Nevis. TDC/Thrifty Rentals has a wide selection of vehicles and outstanding service; it offers a three-day rental that includes a car on both islands.

20

One well-kept main road circumnavigates St. Kitts and is usually clearly marked, making it difficult to get lost, though the northeast can get a bit bumpy, and the access roads to the plantation inns are notoriously rough. The roads on Nevis are fairly new and generally smooth, at least on the most-traveled north, west, and south sides of the island. The east coast has some potholes, and pigs, goats, and sheep still insist on the right-of-way all around the island. Drivers on both islands tend to travel at a fast clip and pass on curves, so drive defensively. Driving is on the left, British-style, though you will probably be given an American-style car.

Information **Avis** (⊠ S. Independence Sq., Basseterre, St. Kitts ☎ 869/465–6507). **Delisle Walwyn** (⊠ Liverpool Row, Basseterre, St. Kitts ☎ 869/465–8449). **Nevis Car Rentals** (⊠ Newcastle, Nevis ☎ 869/469–9837). **Noel's Courtesy Garage** (⊠ Farms Estate, Nevis ☎ 869/469–5199 ⊕ www.noelcarrental. com). **Striker's Car Rental** (⊠ Hermitage Rd., Gingerland, Nevis ☎ 869/469–2634). **TDC/ Thrifty Rentals** (⊠ Central St., Basseterre, St. Kitts ☎ 869/465–2991 ⊠ Bay Rd., Charlestown, Nevis ☎ 869/469–5690 or 869/469–1005 ⊕ www.tdclimited.com/thriftyrentals).

BY TAXI

Taxi rates are government regulated and are posted at the airport, the dock, and in the free tourist guide. Be sure to clarify whether the quoted fare is in EC or US dollars. There are fixed rates to and from all the hotels and to and from major points of interest. In St. Kitts you can call the St. Kitts Taxi Association. In Nevis, taxi service is available at the airport, by the dock in Charlestown, and through arrangements made at your hotel. On St. Kitts the fares from the airport range from EC$32 to Frigate Bay, to EC$72 for the farthest point from the airport. From the airport on Nevis it costs EC$27 to Nisbet Plantation, EC$54 to the Four Seasons, and EC$67 to Montpelier. There is a 50% surcharge between 10 PM and 6 AM.

Information **Nevis taxi service** (☎ 869/469–5631, 869/469–1483, 869/469–9790 for the airport, 869/469–5515 after dark). **St. Kitts Taxi Association** (☎ 869/465–8487, 869/465–4253, 869/465–7818 after hrs).

▌ CONTACTS & RESOURCES

BANKS & EXCHANGE SERVICES

Legal tender is the Eastern Caribbean (EC) dollar. The rate of exchange at this writing was EC$2.68 to US$1. U.S. dollars are accepted practically everywhere, but you'll usually get change in EC currency. Most large hotels, restaurants, and shops accept major credit cards, but small inns and shops often do not. MasterCard and Visa are the most frequently accepted credit cards. The Royal Bank of St. Kitts has an ATM. There are ATMs on Nevis at the airport, at the Bank of Nova Scotia, at First Caribbean International Bank, and at the St. Kitts-Nevis National Bank. They all accept CIRRUS and PLUS cards but dispense only EC dollars.

Prices quoted throughout this chapter are in U.S. dollars unless otherwise noted.

ELECTRICITY

St. Kitts and Nevis hotels function on 110 volts, 60 cycles, making all North American appliances safe to use.

EMERGENCIES

There are no 24-hour pharmacies on St. Kitts or Nevis, but several pharmacies are open seven days a week, usually until at least 5 PM. Call ahead if it's late in the afternoon.

Ambulance & Fire **Fire emergencies on St. Kitts** (☎ 869/465–2515). **Fire emergencies on Nevis** (☎ 869/469–3444).

Hospitals **Joseph N. France General Hospital** (⊠ Cayon St., Basseterre, St. Kitts ☎ 869/465–2551). **Alexandra Hospital** (⊠ Government Rd., Charlestown, Nevis ☎ 869/469–5473).

INTERNET, MAIL & SHIPPING

Some hotels provide Internet service to their guests (sometimes for a fee, sometimes not), and there is an Internet café in Charlestown, Nevis.

Airmail letters to the United States and Canada cost EC90¢ per half ounce; postcards require EC80¢; to the United Kingdom letters cost EC$1.20, postcards EC$1; to Australia and New Zealand, letters cost EC$1.60, postcards EC$1.20. Mail takes at least 7 to 10 days to reach the United States. St. Kitts and Nevis issue separate stamps, but each honors the other's.

Information Downtown Cybercafe (⊠ Main St., Charlestown, Nevis 🕾 869/469–1999).

SAFETY

On these islands, safety is not a major concern, but take the usual precautions you would at any unfamiliar destination.

TAXES

The departure tax is US$22, payable in cash only. There's no sales tax on either St. Kitts or Nevis. Hotels collect a 9% government tax.

TELEPHONES

Phone cards, which you can buy in denominations of $5, $10, and $20, are handy for making local phone calls, calling other islands, and accessing U.S. direct lines. Many private lines and hotels charge access rates if you use your AT&T, Sprint, or MCI calling card; there's no regularity, so phoning can be frustrating. Pay phones, usually found in major town squares, take EC coins or phone cards. Port Zante has banks of "international" phones that accept credit and, erratically, calling cards. Tri-band GSM phones rentals are available via Cable & Wireless in both St. Kitts and Nevis. Check with the respective tourism offices for alternative providers. Costs are high but not prohibitive, especially if you are going to be on the islands for a week or more.

To make a local call, dial the seven-digit number. To call St. Kitts and Nevis from the United States, dial the area code 869, then access code 465, 466, 468, or 469 and the local four-digit number.

Information Cable & Wireless (⊠ Cayon St., Basseterre, St. Kitts 🕾 869/465–1000 ⊕ www. candw.kn ⊠ Hunkins Plaza, Main St., Charlestown, Nevis 🕾 869/469–5000).

TIPPING

Hotels add up to a 12% service charge to your bill. Restaurants occasionally do the same; ask if it isn't printed on the menu; a 15% tip is appropriate when it isn't included. Taxi drivers typically receive a 10% tip, porters and bellhops $1 per bag; if you feel the service was exemplary, leave $3 to $4 per night for the housekeeping staff.

TOUR OPTIONS

The taxi driver who picks you up will probably offer to act as your guide to the island. Each driver is knowledgeable and does a three-hour tour of Nevis for $75 or a four-hour tour of St. Kitts for $80. He can also make a lunch reservation at one of the plantation restaurants, and you can incorporate this into your tour.

On St. Kitts, Kantours offers comprehensive general island tours, as well as a variety of specialty excursions. The friendly guides at Tropical Tours can run you around St. Kitts ($20 per person), arrange kayaking and snorkeling, and take you to the volcano or rain forest for $52 per person and up.

On Nevis, Fitzroy "Teach" Williams is recommended: he's the former president of the taxi association—even older cabbies call him "the Dean." Kantours arranges half- and full-day tours of the island. TC, a Yorkshire lass who used to drive a double-decker bus in England and has been married to a Nevisian for more than a decade, offers entertaining explorations via TC's Island Tours.

20

Information Fitzroy "Teach" Williams (☎869/469–1140). **Kantours** (☎869/465–2098 in St. Kitts, 869/469–0136 in Nevis ⊕www.kantours.com). **TC's Island Tours** (☎869/469–2911). **Tropical Tours** (☎869/465–4167 ⊕www.tropicalstkitts-nevis.com).

VISITOR INFORMATION
Before You Leave **St. Kitts Tourism Authority** (☎212/535–1234 in New York City, 800/582–6208, 866/556–3847 for Nevis alone ⊕www.stkittstourism.kn).

In St. Kitts & Nevis **Nevis Tourism Authority** (✉Main St., Charlestown, Nevis ☎869/469–7550 or 869/469–1042 ⊕www.nevisisland.com). **St. Kitts Tourism Authority** (✉Pelican Mall, Bay Rd., Box 132, Basseterre, St. Kitts ☎869/465–2620 or 869/465–4040 ⊕www.stkittstourism.kn). **St. Kitts–Nevis Hotel Association** (✉Liverpool Row, Box 438, Basseterre, St. Kitts ☎869/465–5304).

WEDDINGS
St. Kitts and Nevis are both popular wedding locales, and it's relatively easy and fast to obtain a license. Both bride and groom must be in the country for at least 2 full working days (weekdays) before the ceremony, and the cost of a license is $80 (the license fee is reduced to $20 if the parties have been on the island for at least 15 days). You must present a valid passport or birth certificate; if divorced, you must have a divorce decree plus a notarized translation if the document is not in English; if you're widowed, you must have a copy of the death certificate of the deceased spouse. There will be a charge for a civil service from the notary public and the marriage officer, who is the local magistrate. Your hotel will help you make the arrangements; most have wedding coordinators. Couples have often tied the knot on the picturesque 18th-hole lawn overlooking the sea on the Four Seasons golf course, at the various plantation inns, and on the beaches throughout the islands.

St. Lucia

WORD OF MOUTH

"Your choice [of St. Lucia] for a honeymoon is ideal. You won't regret a moment spent. There is so much to do and explore on such a romantic island."

—Progress

"Definitely take some sort of cruise—catamaran or other—along the coast past the Pitons. What a sight they are from the water!"

—Schmerl

WELCOME TO ST. LUCIA

THE CARIBBEAN'S TWIN PEAKS

St. Lucia, 27 mi (43.5 km) by 14 mi (22.5 km), is a volcanic island covered to a large extent by a lush rain forest, which is protected as a national park. The small island has produced two Nobel Prize winners, economist Sir Arthur Lewis and poet Sir Derek Walcott. The most notable geological features are the twin Pitons, each nearly 2,600 feet high.

Soufrière, founded as a French settlement in 1746, was the first colonial capital of St. Lucia. It remains an important cultural and agricultural center of the island.

At 2,619 feet, Petit Piton is actually taller than Gros Piton, which is 2,461 feet. However "Gros" is broader at its base; hence, the name.

KEY	
⊿	Beaches
⚓	Cruise Ship Terminal
◳	Dive Sites
🔟	Restaurants
①	Hotels
⚓	Ferry
🌴	Rain Forest

Explorers, pirates, soldiers, sugar planters, and coal miners have made their mark on this lovely landfall, and the lush tropical peaks known as the Pitons (Gros and Petit) have witnessed them all. Today's visitors come to snorkel and scuba dive in the calm cobalt-blue waters, to sun themselves on the scores of multihued beaches, or to go for a sail off tiny Pigeon Island, which juts off St. Lucia's northwest coast.

TOP 4 REASONS TO VISIT ST. LUCIA

1. Magnificent, lush scenery, particularly in the south and around Soufrière, makes St. Lucia one of the most beautiful Caribbean islands.

2. A popular honeymoon spot, St. Lucia is filled with romantic retreats.

3. Luxurious options include a pampering all-inclusive spa resort, a posh dive resort, and a picturesque resort between the Pitons.

4. The St. Lucia Jazz Festival draws performers—and listeners—from all over the world.

ST. LUCIA PLANNER

Island Activities

The island's **beaches** are decent, but you won't find many long stretches of fine white sand since St. Lucia is a volcanic island; Reduit Beach, in the north, is considered the island's best.

St. Lucia has excellent **diving** along its southwest coast. One upscale resort, Anse Chastanet, specializes in diving from its base near the Pitons.

Deep-sea **fishing** is also good. A **day sail** is one of the best ways to see a good bit of the island and a good way to travel from Castries to Soufrière, or vice versa.

However, St. Lucia's crown jewel is its well-preserved **rain forest,** which can best be explored on a guided hike.

Climbing one of the twin **Pitons** is a rewarding—if arduous—experience and can be done without any special mountain- or rock-climbing experience (though that never hurts). You must hire a guide, however.

Logistics

Getting to St. Lucia: The primary international airport is Hewanorra International Airport (UVF), on the island's southern tip; however, you might have to change planes in San Juan, Barbados, or Montego Bay. American Airlines/American Eagle (via San Juan) and regional airlines fly into George F. L. Charles Airport (SLU) in Castries. Here it could be to your advantage to make a connecting flight (especially if you are staying in the Castries or Rodney Bay area). Those flying into Hewanorra must make the long trip to the north; happily, the trip to Soufrière now takes only 30 minutes.

Hassle Factor: Medium to Medium-High, because of the long drive from Hewanorra International Airport.

Nonstops: There are many nonstop flights from the U.S. to Hewanorra, but none from the U.S. to Castries, which is more convenient to north-coast resorts.

On the Ground

If you land at George F. L. Charles Airport (also referred to as Vigie Airport), in Castries, it's a short drive to resorts in the north, about 20 minutes to Marigot but more than an hour to Soufrière. Everyone landing at Hewanorra faces a long—though scenic—drive north. Taxis are always available at the airports. If you take one, be sure to agree on the fare before you get in. Between Hewanorra and Soufrière expect to pay $55 to $60 each way per taxi (not per person); between Hewanorra and the resorts near Castries, $70 to $75; between George F. L. Charles (Vigie) Airport and nearby resorts, $15 to $25; between Vigie and Soufrière, $70 to $75. A helicopter transfer from Hewanorra is an attractive option, but it costs $120-plus per person.

Renting a Car: Drive yourself if you want to do some exploring and try lots of restaurants; a car is more of a necessity if you are staying at a small inn or hotel away from the beach. If you're staying at an all-inclusive beach resort, taxis would be a better bet. And driving is on the left, British-style; combined with roads that are often in a state of disrepair, the prospect of driving on the island isn't an inviting one for many travelers.

Where to Stay

St. Lucia's lodgings are nearly all concentrated in three locations along the calm Caribbean coast. They're in the greater Castries area between Marigot Bay, a few miles south of the city, and Choc Bay in the north; in and around Rodney Bay and north to Cap Estate; and around Soufrière on the southwest coast near the Pitons. There's only one resort in Vieux Fort, near Hewanorra. Resorts and small inns are tucked into lush surroundings on secluded coves, unspoiled beaches, or forested hillsides. The advantage of being in the north is easier access to a wider range of restaurants; in the south you are limited to your resort's offerings and a few others, mostly in Soufrière.

Big Beach Resorts: Most people choose to stay in one of St. Lucia's many beach resorts, the majority of which are upscale and fairly pricey. Several are all-inclusive, including three Sandals resorts.

Small Inns: If you are looking for something more intimate and often less expensive, a locally owned small inn or hotel is a good option if you don't require being directly on the beach.

Villas: Private apartments and luxury villas are a good choice for families. Many of these are in the north, concentrated in and around Castries, near Cap Estate, and in Marigot Bay.

Hotel & Restaurant Costs

⇨*For information on hotel meal plans, see Accommodations in Caribbean Essentials.*

WHAT IT COSTS IN U.S. DOLLARS

$$$$	$$$	$$	$	¢
Restaurants				
over $30	$20–$30	$12–$20	$8–$12	under $8
Hotels*				
over $350	$250–$350	$150–$250	$80–$150	under $80
Hotels**				
over $450	$350–$450	$250–$350	$125–$250	under $125

*EP, BP, CP **AI, FAP, MAP Restaurant prices are for a main course at dinner and do not include 8% tax or customary 10% service charge. Hotel prices are per night for a double room in high season, excluding 8% tax and meal plans (except at all-inclusives).

When to Go

21

The high season runs from mid-December through mid-April; outside of this period, hotel rates can be significantly cheaper.

In April, the **St. Lucia Golf Open** is an amateur tournament at the St. Lucia Golf Club in Cap Estate.

The **St. Lucia Jazz Festival** in early May is the year's big event; during that week, you may have trouble finding a hotel room at any price.

St. Lucia's summer **Carnival** is held in Castries beginning in late June and continuing into July.

The **St. Lucia Billfishing Tournament** is in late September or early October, attracting anglers from far and wide.

October is Creole Heritage Month, which culminates in **Jounen Kwéyòl Entenasyonnal** (International Creole Day) on the last Sunday of the month.

In late November or early December, the finish of the **Atlantic Rally for Cruisers,** the world's largest ocean-crossing race, is marked by a week of festivities in Rodney Bay.

By Jane E.
Zarem

ALL EYES FOCUS ON ST. Lucia for 10 days each May, when the St. Lucia Jazz Festival welcomes renowned international musicians who perform for enthusiastic fans at Pigeon Island National Park and other island venues. St. Lucians themselves love jazz—and, of course, the beat of Caribbean music resonates through their very souls. The irony is that if you randomly ask 10 St. Lucians to name their favorite kind of music, most would say "country." One possible explanation is that many young St. Lucian men take short-term jobs overseas, cutting sugarcane in Florida and working on farms elsewhere in the South, where they inevitably hear country music. And while the work experience isn't something most remember fondly, the music apparently is.

The pirate François Le Clerc, nicknamed Jambe de Bois (Wooden Leg) for obvious reasons, was the first European "settler" in St. Lucia (pronounced *loo*-sha). In the late 16th century, Le Clerc holed up on Pigeon Island, just off the island's northernmost point, and used it as a staging ground for attacking passing ships. Now Pigeon Island is a national park, a playground for locals and visitors alike, and, as mentioned, the most popular performance venue for the annual St. Lucia Jazz Festival. Several years ago, a man-made causeway attached Pigeon Island to the mainland; today, Sandals Grande St. Lucian Spa & Beach Resort, one of the largest resorts in St. Lucia, and The Landings, a luxury villa community that opened in 2008, are sprawled along that causeway.

St. Lucia has evolved over the years into one of the Caribbean's most popular vacation destinations—particularly for honeymooners and romantics enticed by the island's natural beauty, its many splendid resorts and inns, and its welcoming atmosphere. And the evolution continues. Renewed emphasis from both the public and private sectors is being placed on enhancing the island's tourism product and supporting new and renewed lodgings, activities, and attractions. That's great news for visitors, who already appear delighted with St. Lucia.

Located between Martinique and St. Vincent, and 100 mi (160 km) due west of Barbados, the 27-mi by 14-mi (43.5-km by 22.5-km) island of St. Lucia occupies a prime position in the Caribbean. Its striking natural beauty easily earns it the moniker "Helen of the West Indies." The capital city of Castries and nearby villages in the northwest are home to 40% of the population and, along with Rodney Bay farther north and Marigot Bay just south of the capital, are the general destinations of most vacationers. In the central and southern parts of the island, dense rain forest, jungle-covered mountains, and vast banana plantations dominate the landscape. A torturously winding road follows most of the coastline, bisecting small villages, cutting through mountains, and passing by fertile valleys. On the southwest coast, Petit Piton and Gros Piton, the island's unusual twin peaks that rise out of the sea to more than 2,600 feet, are familiar navigational landmarks for sailors and aviators alike. Divers are attracted to the reefs found just north of Soufrière, the quaint capital city during French colonial times. Most of the natural tourist attractions are in this area. "If you haven't been to Soufrière," St. Lucians will tell you, "you haven't been to St. Lucia."

Like most of its Caribbean neighbors, St. Lucia was first inhabited by the Arawaks and then the Carib Indians. British settlers attempted to colonize the island twice in the early 1600s, but it wasn't until 1651, after the French West India Company secured the island from the Caribs, that Europeans gained a foothold. For 150 years, battles for island possession were frequent between the French and the British, with a dizzying 14 changes in power before the British finally took possession in 1814. The Europeans established sugar plantations, using slaves from West Africa to work the fields. By 1838, when the slaves were emancipated, more than 90% of the population was of African descent—also the approximate proportion of today's 170,000 St. Lucians. Indentured East Indian laborers were brought over in 1882 to help bail out the sugar industry, which collapsed when slavery was abolished and all but died in the 1960s, when bananas became the major crop.

On February 22, 1979, St. Lucia became an independent state within the British Commonwealth of Nations, with a resident governor-general appointed by the queen. Still, the island appears to have retained more relics of French influence—notably the island patois, cuisine, village names, and surnames—than of the British. Most likely, that's because the British contribution primarily involved the English language, the educational and legal systems, and the political structure, while the French culture historically had more impact on the arts—music, dance, and all that jazz!

WHERE TO STAY

Nearly all St. Lucia's villas, hotels, resorts, and inns are concentrated in three locations along the Caribbean coast: the greater Castries area between Marigot Bay, a few miles south of the capital, and Choc Bay in the north; in and around Rodney Bay and north to Cap Estate; and around Soufrière in the southwestern coast near the Pitons. Currently, only one resort is in Vieux Fort, near Hewanorra International Airport, although the area along the southern and southeastern coasts is ripe for development. Resorts and small inns are tucked into lush surroundings on secluded coves, unspoiled beaches, or forested hillsides. The advantage of being in the north is easier access to a wider range of restaurants and nightlife; in the south, you're limited to your own resort's dining options, other resort dining rooms, and a handful of local restaurants in Soufrière. On the other hand, many of the island's natural attractions are in and around Soufrière.

Most people—particularly honeymooners—choose to stay in one of St. Lucia's many beach resorts, most of which are upscale and pricey. Several are all-inclusive, including the three Sandals resorts, two Almond resorts, and three resorts owned and/or managed by Sunswept (the Body Holiday at LeSPORT, Rendezvous, and Jalousie Plantation).

If you're looking for lodgings that are more intimate and less expensive, St. Lucia has dozens of small inns and hotels that are often locally owned, always charming, and often less expensive but that may or may

CLOSE UP

Embracing Kwéyòl

English is St. Lucia's official language, but most St. Lucians speak and often use Kwéyòl—a French-based Creole language—for informal conversations between and among themselves. Primarily a spoken language, Kwéyòl in its written version doesn't look at all like French; pronounce the words phonetically, though—*entenasyonnal* (international), for example, or the word *Kwéyòl* (Creole) itself—and you indeed sound as if you're speaking French.

Pretty much the same version of the Creole language, or patois, is spoken in the nearby island of Dominica. Otherwise, the St. Lucian Kwéyòl is quite different from that spoken in other Caribbean islands with a French and African heritage, such as Haiti, Guadeloupe, and Martinique—or elsewhere, such as Louisiana, Mauritius, and Madagascar. Interestingly, the Kwéyòl

spoken in St. Lucia and Dominica is mostly unintelligible to people from those other locations—and vice versa.

St. Lucia embraces its Creole heritage by devoting the month of October each year to celebrations that preserve and promote Creole culture, language, and traditions. In selected communities throughout the island, events and performances highlight Creole music, food, dance, theater, native costumes, church services, traditional games, folklore, native medicine—a little bit of everything, or *tout bagay*, as you say in Kwéyòl!

Creole Heritage Month culminates at the end of October with all-day events and activities on Jounen Kwéyòl Entenasyonnal, or International Creole Day, which is recognized by all countries that speak a version of the Creole language.

not be directly on the beach. A group of locally owned and operated small hotels, comfortable guesthouses, and self-catering apartments market themselves through the St. Lucia Tourist Board as **INNtimate St. Lucia** (☎ *758/452–4094* ⊕ *www.inntimatestlucia.org*). Accommodations range in size from 3 to 75 rooms.

Luxury villa communities and independent private villas are another alternative in St. Lucia. Virtually all of the villa communities are located in the north near Cap Estate, as well as in south of Castries in Marigot Bay.

VILLAS & CONDOS

Luxury villa communities are an important part of the accommodations mix on St. Lucia, as they can be an economical option for families, other groups, or couples vacationing together. Several villa communities have opened in recent years, and more are on the way. The villa units themselves are privately owned, but nonowners can rent individual units directly from the property managers for a vacation or short-term stay, the same as reserving hotel accommodations. Units with fully equipped kitchens, up to three bedrooms, and as many baths run $200 to $2,500 per night, depending on the size and the season.

21

RODNEY BAY &
CAP ESTATE

$$$$

⊡**Cap Maison.** Opened in July 2008, Cap Maison is a boutique villa community with 22 units that can be configured as up to 50 rooms, junior suites, and oversize one-, two-, or three-bedroom villa suites. The Ocean View Grand Villa suites, for example, measure 3,000 square feet. Built on a seaside bluff, the elegant Spanish Caribbean architecture has wooden jalousie doors and windows, terra-cotta roof tiles, large private balconies, and large roof terraces with a plunge pool. A large infinity pool at the edge of the bluff and a hot tub are available to everyone. Truly luxurious service includes no formal check-in required, an unpacking service upon request, an honor bar, and a personal butler for any little needs and requests that may come up—including arranging a romantic dinner, prepared and served in your suite by one of the resort's chefs. French Caribbean cuisine at the resort's cliff-top Cap Maison restaurant is another option. For extra pampering, there's a full-service spa and a calming Zen garden. The resort is on a seaside cliff, so getting down to Smugglers Cove beach, a secluded crescent of sand, requires walking down (and back up) several steps. The resort also has a 46-foot, 15-passenger powerboat to take guests on day trips to Soufrière or nearby Martinique or on honeymoon cruises. **Pros:** Near the golf course, private and elegant, those rooftop plunge pools. **Cons:** Beach access difficult for those with physical disabilities. ⊠ *Smugglers Cove, Cap Estate, Gros Islet* ⏏ *Box 2188, Gros Islet* ☎ *758/285–1274* ⊕ *www.capmaison.co.uk* ⤶ *11 rooms, 39 suites* ♿ *In-room: kitchen (some), refrigerator, DVD, Wi-Fi. In-hotel: restaurant, room service, bars, pool, gym, spa, beachfront, water sports, no elevator, laundry facilities, public Internet, public Wi-Fi, airport shuttle* ⊟ *AE, MC, V* ⓘ◎ⓘ *EP.*

$$$$

⊡**The Landings.** Managed by RockResorts, the Landings is on 19 acres along the Pigeon Point Causeway, on the northern side of Rodney Bay. Phase I of the condo development—the first 62 units—opened in December 2007. Ultimately, the community will have 231 waterfront residences, ranging in size from 900 to 2,300 square feet (half with plunge pools), constructed in three phases, and completed by 2010. Each unit has a beautifully appointed living; dining room; one, two, or three bedrooms with en suite baths; kitchen; and enormous balcony or terrace. Buildings surround the 80-slip marina, making the atmosphere particularly conducive to yachting and boating. Nevertheless, landlubbers will love the 7,000-square-foot RockResorts Spa™, socializing at the lobby bar in the Grand Pavilion, and soaking up the sun at the beach club or at one of the pools (currently two, with five more to come). Besides preparing your own meals, grab a snack at the gourmet deli, have a light meal on the pier at the Beach Club, or enjoy the latest cuisine concepts in the Trend Room restaurant, where the type of food changes depending on what's "hot" at the time. Guests are also entitled to preferred tee times at the nearby St. Lucia Golf Club. The pampering begins, in fact, with the personalized greeting upon arrival at the airport. **Pros:** Spacious units with modern furnishings, good place for yachties to come ashore, personal chef service. **Con:** Construction through 2010 may create noise and disruption. ⊠ *Pigeon Island causeway, Gros Islet* ☎ *758/458–7300* ⊕ *www.landings.rockresorts.*

com 🖬 *62 units* ᴧ *In-room: kitchen, Ethernet. In-hotel: 3 restaurants, room service, bars, tennis courts, pools, gym, spa, beachfront, water sports, no elevator, concierge, laundry facilities, no-smoking rooms, airport shuttle* ⊟*AE, D, DC, MC, V* ❒*EP.*

$$$–$$$$ 🏨 **Cotton Bay Village.** Opened in 2007, Cotton Bay Village is a villa
☺ community on 9 idyllic acres at the northern tip of the island. Adjacent to the Body Holiday at LeSPORT, a sister operation, it's wedged between a quiet ocean beach and the St. Lucia Golf Club. Luxurious, individually designed and decorated colonial-style town houses and chateau-style villas surround a free-form lagoon pool. Units have spacious sitting rooms, dining terraces, fully equipped kitchens, and one, two, three, or four bedrooms. All are beautifully furnished in eclectic style—painted French furniture, modern metal designs, traditional plantation mahogany. Accommodations also include dedicated service from a personal butler, who carries out special requests and the little chores associated with independent living. Guests may patronize the spa, two bars, a deli, coffee shop, and two restaurants—the Beach Club 14'61" (its latitude and longitude) and a second fine-dining restaurant. Golden-sand Cotton Bay beach is so secluded it's virtually private. Take lessons in windsurfing or kiteboarding, arrange a horseback trek along the beach, or charter a yacht for a day. You're living like royalty here, so you might as well go whole hog. Of course, greens fees at the next-door golf club are free. **Pros:** Truly luxurious accommodations, privacy, family-friendly. **Cons:** Isolated, rental car advised if you plan to leave the property. ✉*Cotton Bay, Cap Estate, Gros Islet* 🕾*758/456–5700* ⊕*www.cottonbayvillage.com* 🖬*74 villas* ᴧ*In-room: kitchen, DVD. In-hotel: 2 restaurants, bars, pool, gym, spa, beachfront, water sports, no elevator, children's programs (ages 3–7)* ⊟*AE, MC, V* ❒*EP.*

$$$–$$$$ 🏨 **Windjammer Landing Villa Beach Resort.** Windjammer's Mediterra-
☺ nean-style villas climb the hillside on one of St. Lucia's prettiest bays. As perfect for families as for a romantic getaway, the resort offers lots to do yet plenty of privacy. Windjammer's stylishly decorated villas can easily be closed off or opened up to become one-, two-, three-, or four-bedroom villa suites. Some have private plunge pools. The resort's reception area opens onto shops, restaurants, and two pools. Eat excellently prepared cuisine in the restaurants, make your own meals, or have dinner prepared and served in your villa. Shuttles whoosh you between villa and activity areas—including two hillside pools connected by a waterfall. **Pros:** Lovely, spacious villas, beautiful sunset views; family friendly. **Cons:** Rent a car if you plan to leave the property, as it's far from the main road. ✉*Labrelotte Bay* 🖂*Box 1504, Castries* 🕾*758/452–0913* ⊕*www.windjammer-landing.com* 🖬*219 rooms* ᴧ*In-room: safe, kitchen (some), refrigerator, DVD. In-hotel: 5 restaurants, room service, bars, tennis courts, pools, gym, spa, beachfront, diving, water sports, no elevator, children's programs (ages 4–12), laundry service, concierge* ⊟*AE, MC, V* ❒*EP.*

MARIGOT BAY   🏨 **Discovery at Marigot Bay.** Five miles (8 km) south of Castries, on the
$$$ mid-west coast of St. Lucia, Discovery at Marigot Bay climbs the hill-
Fodor'sChoice side of what author James Michener called "the most beautiful bay
★ in the Caribbean." Each unit is exquisitely decorated with dark Bali-

nese furniture accented by comfy earth-tone cushions, a four-poster bed with pillow-top mattress, and dark hardwood flooring. Oversize bathrooms have walk-in "drench" showers and double basins set in slate vanities. Each suite has a full kitchen equipped with modern Euro-designer appliances, a spacious living room with a sofa bed and dining area, a balcony or deck, and a washer and dryer; half the suites have private plunge pools. Boats tie up at the resort's dock, and a solar-powered ferry transports guests to the beach or the Rainforest Hideaway restaurant. **Pros:** Pretty bay view, excellent service, oversize accommodations. **Cons:** You'll need a rental car to explore beyond Marigot Bay, beach is picturesque but tiny. ⊠ *Marigot Bay, Box MG7227, Marigot* ☎ *758/458–5300* ⊕ *www.discoverystlucia.com* ⤶ *67 rooms, 57 suites* ⌂ *In-room: safe, kitchen (some), DVD, VCR, ethernet, Wi-Fi. In-hotel: restaurant, room service, bars, pools, gym, spa, water sports, no elevator, laundry facilities, concierge, public Internet, public Wi-Fi* ⊟ *AE, MC, V* ⦶ *EP.*

PRIVATE VILLAS & CONDOS

Local real estate agencies will arrange vacation rentals of privately owned villas and condos that are fully equipped. Most private villas are located in the hills of Cap Estate in the very north of the island, in Rodney Bay or Bois d'Orange, or in Soufrière among St. Lucia's natural treasures. Some are within walking distance of a beach.

All rental villas are staffed with a cook who specializes in local cuisine and a housekeeper; in some cases, a caretaker lives on the property and a gardener and/or night watchman are on staff. All properties have telephones, and some have Internet access and/or fax machines. Telephones may be barred against outgoing overseas calls; plan to use a phone card or calling card. Most villas have TVs, DVDs and/or VCRs, and CD players. All private villas have a swimming pool; condos share a community pool. Vehicles are generally not included in the rates, but rental cars can be arranged and delivered to the villa upon request. Linens and basic supplies (e.g., bath soap, toilet tissue, dish-washing detergent) are included. Pre-arrival grocery stocking can be arranged.

Units with one to nine bedrooms and as many baths run $200 to $2,000 per night, depending on the size of the villa, the amenities, the number of guests, and the season. Rates include utilities and government taxes. Your only additional cost will be for groceries and staff gratuities. A security deposit is required upon booking and refunded after departure less any damages or unpaid miscellaneous charges.

Rental Agencies Island Villas St. Lucia (⊠ *Rodney Bay, Gros Islet* ☎ *758/458–4903* ⊕ *www.island-villas.com/stlucia*). **Tropical Villas** (⊠ *Cap Estate, Gros Islet* ☎ *758/452–8240* ⊕ *www.tropicalvillas.net*).

HOTELS

GREATER CASTRIES

$$$$ ⛤ **Almond Morgan Bay Beach Resort.** Completely refurbished in 2005,
☺   this venerable property is now an all-inclusive resort appropriate for
singles, couples, and families alike offering both quiet seclusion on 22
acres surrounding a stretch of white-sand beach or tons of free sports
and activities. Rooms, each with a private balcony or terrace, are in
several buildings set among tropical gardens or facing the beachfront.
The resort's four restaurants include waterfront Bambou, which serves
a mouthwatering fusion of Caribbean and Asian cuisines; French creole Le Jardin; and seafood restaurant Morgan's Pier, which stretches
dramatically into the bay. Four swimming pools (two designated for
adults only) and all manner of activities are available day and night.
Pros: Family-friendly, lots to do, great atmosphere at Morgan's Pier.
Cons: Resort is huge, beach is small. ⊠*Choc Bay, Gros Islet* ⌐*Box
2167, Castries* ☎*758/450–2511* ⊕*www.almondresorts.com* ⟿*340
rooms* ⌂*In-room: safe. In-hotel: 4 restaurants, bars, tennis courts,
pools, gym, spa, beachfront, water sports, no elevator, concierge, children's programs (ages newborn–16), laundry service, public Internet*
⊟*AE, D, MC, V* ¹⊚¹*AI.*

$$$$ ⛤ **Rendezvous.** Romance is alive and well at this easygoing, all-inclusive resort (for male-female couples only), which stretches along the
dreamy white sand of Malabar Beach opposite the George F. L. Charles
Airport runway. The occasional distraction of prop aircraft taking off
and landing is overshadowed by the beautiful gardens on what was
once a coconut plantation. Accommodations are in cheerful gingerbread cottages, elegant oceanfront rooms with sunset-facing terraces,
or cozy poolside suites. A host of activities and sports are all included.
Buffet-style meals are served at the beachfront terrace restaurant, with
fine dining by reservation at the Trysting Place. **Pros:** Convenient to
Castries and Vigie Airport, great beach, romance in the air. **Cons:** No
room TVs, occasional flyover noise. ⊠*Malabar Beach, Vigie* ⌐*Box
190, Castries* ☎*758/457–7900* ⊕*www.theromanticholiday.com* ⟿*81
rooms, 11 suites, 8 cottages* ⌂*In-room: safe, refrigerator (some), no
TV. In-hotel: 2 restaurants, bars, tennis courts, pools, gym, spa, beachfront, diving, bicycles, no elevator, concierge, laundry service, public
Internet, airport shuttle, no kids under 18* ⊟*AE, D, MC, V* ¹⊚¹*AI.*

$$$$ ⛤ **Sandals Regency St. Lucia Golf Resort & Spa.** One of three Sandals
★   resorts on St. Lucia, this is the second largest and distinguishes itself
with its own 9-hole golf course (for guests only). Like the others, it's for
couples only and is all-inclusive. The resort covers 200 acres on a hillside overlooking the sea on the southern shore of Castries Bay. Guest
rooms are lavishly decorated with rich mahogany furniture and king-
size four-poster beds. Many rooms have private plunge pools. The main
pool, with its waterfall and bridges, and a long crescent beach are focal
points for socializing and enjoying water sports. Massages, scrubs,
and wraps are available at the full-service spa. Six restaurants serve
Asian, Continental, French, Mediterranean, Southwestern, or Caribbean cuisine. An hourly shuttle connects all three Sandals properties.
Pros: Lots to do, picturesque location, on-site golf. **Cons:** Somewhat

isolated location, expert golfers will prefer St. Lucia Golf Club in Cap Estate. ⊠ *La Toc Rd.* ☎ *Box 399, Castries* ☎758/452–3081 ⊕ *www. sandals.com* ☞ *212 rooms, 116 suites* ☐ *In-room: safe. In-hotel: 6 restaurants, room service, bars, golf course, tennis courts, pools, gym, spa, beachfront, diving, water sports, laundry service, executive floor, public Internet, airport shuttle, no kids under 18* ⊟*AE, D, DC, MC, V* ⊙*AI.*

$ ★ 🛏 **Auberge Seraphine.** This is a good choice for independent vacationers who don't require a beachfront location or a breadth of resort activities. Accommodations are spacious, cheerful, and bright. All but six rooms have a water view, and Room 307 has an amazing view from its balcony. A broad, tiled sundeck, the center of activity, surrounds a small pool. Reserve ahead, as business travelers appreciate the Auberge's convenience to downtown Castries, the airport, and great eateries—including the inn's excellent restaurant, which has fine Caribbean, French, and Continental cuisine in addition to a well-stocked wine cellar. **Pros:** Nice pool, good restaurant, Room 307. **Cons:** Somewhat basic accommodations, no beach, no resort activities. ⊠ *Vigie Cove, Castries* ☎ *Box 390, Castries* ☎758/453–2073 ⊕ *www.aubergeseraphine.com* ☞*28 rooms* ☐ *In-room: refrigerator, dial-up. In-hotel: restaurant, bar, pool, no elevator, public Internet* ⊟*AE, MC, V* ⊙*EP.*

RODNEY BAY & CAP ESTATE

$$$$ ☼ 🛏 **Almond Smugglers Cove.** After investing more than $20 million in renovations, this all-inclusive resort opened in 2007 with more food, fun, and features than you'll have time to enjoy in a week. On 60 acres and overlooking a pretty bay at the island's northernmost point, basic but comfortable guest rooms are spread out over a broad hillside; golf cart transportation is available. The resort has five swimming pools, a sandy beach, and a laundry list of water sports to enjoy. The world-class St. Lucia Racquet Club, with seven tennis courts and a squash court, is on-site, and guests get three free 18-hole rounds of golf at the nearby St. Lucia Golf Course. Four dining rooms offer as many cuisines, libations flow freely from four bars, and there's live entertainment nightly. The plethora of planned entertainment lends the resort a holiday camp atmosphere, but families love it. **Pros:** Excellent children's program, superlative tennis facilities, nightly entertainment is family-friendly. **Cons:** Busy, busy, busy . . . not the place for a quiet getaway, guest rooms are spread far and wide on the hillside. ⊠ *Smugglers Cove, Cap Estate, Gros Islet* ☎758/450–0551 ⊕ *www.almondresorts. com* ☞*258 rooms, 100 suites* ☐ *In-room: safe. In-hotel: 4 restaurants, room service, bars, tennis courts, pools, gym, spa, beachfront, water sports, no elevator, children's program (ages newborn–16), laundry service, concierge, public Internet, public Wi-Fi* ⊟*AE, D, MC, V* ⊙*AI.*

$$$$ ★ 🛏 **Body Holiday at LeSPORT.** Even before you leave home, you can customize your own "body holiday" online—from robe size to tee time—at this adults-only resort in luxurious tropical surroundings. Indulge in aromatherapy, a dozen different massages, ayurvedic treatments, wraps, yoga, and personal-trainer services at the splendid Oasis spa; daily treatments are included in the rates. Otherwise, enjoy the beach, scuba diving, golf (greens fees are free at St. Lucia Golf Club, next door),

and other sports. Rooms have marble floors and king-size four-poster or twin beds. The food is excellent at Cariblue (the main dining room), the Club House casual buffet restaurant, the Deli, or the top-of-the-line Tao. Enjoy nightly entertainment at the beachside lounge. Special rates are offered for single guests. **Pros:** Daily spa treatments included, excellent dining, unusual activities such as archery. **Cons:** Unremarkable rooms, small bathrooms with skimpy towels. ⊠ *Cariblue Beach, Cap Estate, Gros Islet* ⌂ *Box 437, Castries* ☎ *758/450–8551* ⊕ *www. thebodyholiday.com* ⇆ *152 rooms, 2 suites* ⌂ *In-room: safe, refrigerator, no TV. In-hotel: 3 restaurants, bars, tennis courts, pools, gym, spa, beachfront, diving, water sports, concierge, public Internet, airport shuttle, no kids under 16* ⊟ *AE, MC, V* ⍓ *AI.*

$$$$ 🏨 **Royal St. Lucian.** This all-suites resort on Reduit (pronounced red-
Ⅽ *wee*) Beach—St. Lucia's best beach—caters to every whim. The reception area has a vaulted atrium, marble walls, a fountain, and a sweeping grand staircase. Just beyond, the free-form pool has Japanese-style bridges, a waterfall, and a swim-up bar. Guest suites are huge, with amenities such as a wide-screen TV, DVD, and stereo equipment. Massages, hydrotherapy, and other treatments can be arranged at the Royal Spa. Dine at the elegant Chic!, the sea-view L'Epicure, or lunch at the casual Beach Tent. Or walk to a dozen or so Rodney Bay restaurants, nightclubs, and shopping areas. Tennis, water-sports facilities, and the children's club are shared with the adjacent Rex St. Lucian hotel. **Pros:** Great beachfront, roomy accommodations, convenient to Rodney Bay Village. **Cons:** Dated guest rooms and baths. ⊠ *Reduit Beach, Rodney Bay, Gros Islet* ⌂ *Box 977, Castries* ☎ *758/452–9999* ⊕ *www. rexcaribbean.com* ⇆ *96 suites* ⌂ *In-room: safe, refrigerator. In-hotel: 3 restaurants, room service, bars, tennis courts, pool, gym, spa, beachfront, diving, water sports, concierge, children's programs (ages 4–12), laundry service, public Internet* ⊟ *AE, DC, MC, V* ⍓ *EP.*

$$$$ 🏨 **Sandals Grande St. Lucian Spa & Beach Resort.** Grand, indeed! And
Fodor'sChoice busy, busy, busy. Couples love this place—particularly young honey-
★ mooners and those getting married here—the biggest and splashiest of the three Sandals resorts on St. Lucia. Several weddings take place each day, in fact. Perched on the narrow Pigeon Island causeway at St. Lucia's northern tip, Sandals Grande offers panoramic views of Rodney Bay on one side and the Atlantic Ocean on the other. All rooms have king-size beds; 24 lagoon-side rooms have swim-up verandahs. With a plethora of land and water sports, a European-style full-service spa, five excellent restaurants, and nightly entertainment, it's never dull. A complimentary shuttle connects all three Sandals properties. **Pros:** Beautiful white-sand beach, lots of water sports, nice spa. **Cons:** The long ride to/from Hewanorra, buffet meals are uninspired. ⊠ *Pigeon Island causeway, Gros Islet* ⌂ *Box 2247, Castries* ☎ *758/455–2000* ⊕ *www.sandals.com* ⇆ *271 rooms, 11 suites* ⌂ *In-room: safe, dial-up. In-hotel: 5 restaurants, room service, bars, tennis courts, pools, gym, spa, beachfront, diving, water sports, laundry service, executive floor, public Internet, airport shuttle, no kids under 18* ⊟ *AE, D, DC, MC, V* ⍓ *AI.*

21

$$ 🏨 **Bay Gardens Beach Resort.** Opened in 2007, this newest of three Bay
☾ Gardens properties in Rodney Bay Village has a prime location directly
on beautiful Reduit Beach. All suites have living and dining areas, full
kitchens, and modern baths; most have views of the sea from the bal-
cony or terrace. The resort's six three-story buildings wrap around a
lagoon-style pool. Water sports and diving are available on the beach,
or arrange a massage in one of the poolside cabanas. Guests may dine
at elegant Mediterranean Pimento's; at Hi Tide, a casual beachside res-
taurant; at the Lo Tide deli; or at any of a dozen or more excellent res-
taurants in the Rodney Bay neighborhood. The Bay Gardens properties
are well known for their friendly hospitality and exceptional service; in
fact, the hotel clientele is 75% repeat guests. Add a beautiful beach to
the equation, and this new addition is sure to be a winner. **Pros:** Idyllic
beachfront location, family friendly, Wi-Fi even on the beach. **Cons:**
While Phase II is underway, construction noise may be an issue; need to
book far in advance. ⊠ *Reduit Beach, Rodney Bay, Gros Islet* ⊕ *Box
1892, Gros Islet* ☎ *758/452–8060* ⊕ *www.baygardensbeachresort.
com* ☞ *72 suites* ↻ *In-room: safe, kitchen, DVD, Ethernet. In-hotel:
3 restaurants, bar, pool, gym, beachfront, diving, water sports, no ele-
vator, children's club (ages 4–12), laundry service, concierge, public
Internet, public Wi-Fi, airport shuttle* ⊟ *AE, D, MC, V* ⦿ *EP.*

$–$$ 🏨 **Coco Palm.** St. Lucia native Allen Chastanet opened this stylish bou-
★ tique hotel in Rodney Bay Village in 2005, adjacent to his Coco Kre-
ole bed-and-breakfast inn. Guests check in and out in the comfort of
their rooms, and personal hosts attend to any requests. Guest rooms—
including six swim-up rooms adjacent to the pool—and a dozen spacious suites are beautifully decorated in French Caribbean plantation
style; yet every modern convenience is also at hand. Cordless phones,
CD and DVD players, free Wi-Fi and Internet access, flat-screen TVs
(in suites), and ultramodern baths with walk-in showers and claw-
foot tubs (in suites) are amenities you'd expect at much pricier resorts.
The excellent Ti Bananne restaurant and bar overlook the pool and
bandstand, and all the action of Rodney Bay Village and beautiful
Reduit Beach are within walking distance. **Pros:** Excellent value, fabulous swim-up rooms, fantastic dining. **Cons:** Not directly on the beach,
noise from nightly entertainment can be annoying. ⊠ *Reduit Beach
Ave., Rodney Bay* ☎ *758/456–2800* ⊕ *www.coco-resorts.com* ☞ *60
rooms, 12 suites* ↻ *In-room: safe, refrigerator, DVD, VCR (some), Wi-
Fi. In-hotel: restaurant, bar, pool, public Internet, public Wi-Fi* ⊟ *AE,
D, MC, V* ⦿ *EP.*

$ 🏨 **Bay Gardens Hotel.** Independent travelers and regional businesspeople
swear by this cheerful, well-run boutique hotel at Rodney Bay Village.
In fact, it's often booked. Never fear: Bay Gardens Inn, a sister property, is next door, and the Bay Gardens Beach Resort, opened in 2007,
is minutes away. Modern, colorful, and surrounded by pretty flower
gardens, the hotel is a short walk to beautiful Reduit Beach (shuttle transportation is also provided), several popular restaurants, and
shops. Some rooms surround the serpentine pool and Jacuzzi and are
close to the restaurant and lobby; more secluded rooms near the back
of the property have easy access to a second pool that's smaller and

quieter. The 16 "Croton" suites added in 2007 have full kitchens and interconnect to become two-bedroom suites. Spices restaurant offers a fairly extensive menu. **Pros:** Excellent service, unusual value, new "Croton" suites are a good bet. **Cons:** Not beachfront, heavy focus on business travelers. ⊠*Rodney Bay* ✉*Box 1892, Castries* ☎*758/452–8060* ⊕*www.baygardenshotel.com* ✈*59 rooms, 28 suites* ♿*In-room: safe, kitchen (some), refrigerator, dial-up. In-hotel: restaurant, room service, bar, pools, no elevator, laundry service, public Internet* ⊟*AE, D, MC, V* ⊙*BP.*

SOUFRIÈRE & MID-COAST

$$$$ ▦**Anse Chastanet Beach Hotel.** Anse Chastanet is magical, if you don't
Fodor's Choice mind the bone-crushing dirt road between the town and the resort and
★ the steep climb to most rooms. But there's the water taxi alternative, or you can soak in the gorgeous isolation; shuttle service is available between the beach and the hillside rooms, 100 steps up. Spectacular rooms, some with stunning Piton vistas, peek through the thick rain forest that cascades down to the sea. Deluxe hillside rooms have a balcony, tile floors, madras fabrics, handmade wooden furniture, and impressive artwork. But you won't find any communication devices, technology, or interruption: it's delightfully peaceful. Diving, jungle biking through the estate's 600 acres, and ocean kayaking are premier activities; rejuvenate afterward at the Kai Belte Spa. **Pros:** Great for divers, Room 14B with the tree growing through the bathroom, the Piton views. **Cons:** Entrance road is difficult to negotiate, steep hillside certainly not conducive to strolling, some may miss in-room TVs and phones. ⊠*Anse Chastanet Rd., Soufrière* ✉*Box 7000, Soufrière* ☎*758/459–7000* ⊕*www.ansechastanet.com* ✈*49 rooms* ♿*In-room: no a/c, no phone, safe, refrigerator, no TV. In-hotel: 2 restaurants, room service, bars, tennis court, spa, beachfront, diving, water sports, bicycles, no elevator, laundry service, public Internet, airport shuttle, no kids under 10* ⊟*AE, MC, V* ⊙*EP.*

$$$$ ▦**Jade Mountain Club.** This premium-level and premium-priced club is a
★ five-level behemoth that looms out of the jungle. The interior is a mass of concrete bridges, each accessing a private suite (called sanctuaries here) that exudes style, luxury, privacy, and comfort. The huge suites share a truly open-space plan—with a missing fourth wall and literally en-suite bathrooms—locally made hardwood furniture, and enormous infinity-edge plunge pools. Guests have a private restaurant, bar, and sky-top terrace at their disposal and can also use sister property Anse Chastanet's facilities. Given the amenities of the sanctuaries, though, it's no wonder that room service is so popular here. Jade Mountain Club sanctuaries are techno-free in terms of communication with the outside world. **Pros:** Amazing rooms, huge in-room pools, incredible Piton views. **Cons:** Sky-high rates, lack of in-room communication, not appropriate for anyone with disabilities. ⊠*Anse Chastanet, Soufrière* ✉*Box 7000, Soufrière* ☎*758/459–4000* ⊕*www.jademountainst lucia.com* ✈*28 suites* ♿*In-room: no a/c, no phone, refrigerator, no TV. In-hotel: restaurant, room service, bar, gym, spa, beachfront, diving, water sports, bicycles, no elevator, laundry service, concierge, public Internet, no children under 15* ⊟*AE, MC, V* ⊙*EP.*

$$$$ 🏨**Jalousie Plantation & Spa.** Located on the most dramatic 192 acres in ☾ St. Lucia, this resort flows down Val des Pitons on the remains of an ★ 18th-century sugar plantation 2 mi (3 km) south of Soufrière. Sugar Mill rooms are large and close to the beach. Clusters of private villas have elegant furnishings, huge bathrooms, and plunge pools; villa suites also have sitting rooms. Shuttles around the property save a climb up and down the hill. Meals range from fine dining to a beach buffet. Dive, windsurf, or sail; play tennis, squash, or pitch-and-putt golf. The spa offers outdoor massage, aromatherapy, and beauty treatments; there are also fitness classes and weight-training sessions. **Pros:** Incomparable scenery, wonderful spa, lots of water sports. **Cons:** Fairly isolated, jungle location means mosquitoes. ⊠ *Anse des Pitons* 🏤 *Box 251, Soufrière* ☎ *800/544–2883 or 758/459–7666* ⊕ *www.jalousie plantation.com* 🛏 *12 rooms, 65 villas, 35 villa suites* 🍴 *In-room: safe, refrigerator, VCR (some), dial-up. In-hotel: 4 restaurants, room service, bars, golf course, tennis courts, pool, gym, spa, beachfront, diving, water sports, no elevator, children's programs (ages 5–12), public Internet, airport shuttle, no-smoking rooms* ▭ *AE, MC, V* 🍽 *EP.*

$$$$ 🏨**Ladera.** One of the most sophisticated small inns in the Caribbean, **Fodor's**Choice the elegantly rustic Ladera is perched 1,100 feet above the sea. An eco- ★ hotel with a local approach to furnishings, food, and staff, each tree house–style suite or villa is uniquely decorated with colonial antiques and local craftsmanship. Each unit has an open fourth wall with a dazzling view of the Pitons as a backdrop for your private plunge pool. The Ti Kai Posé Spa (Creole for "Little House of Rest") offers relaxing and therapeutic massages, beauty services, and restorative bathing pools. Dasheene, the open-air restaurant, has a stunning view of the Pitons. The inn provides shuttle service to Soufrière and its private, fully staffed beach at Anse Jambette, a 20-minute boat ride from the Soufrière dock. **Pros:** Breathtaking Pitons vista, in-room pools, excellent cuisine. **Cons:** Birds have been known to fly into the open-air suites, guests may want a rental car. ⊠ *Val de Pitons, Soufrière* 🏤 *Box 225, Soufrière* ☎ *758/459–7323, 800/223–9868, or 800/738–4752* ⊕ *www. ladera-stlucia.com* 🛏 *21 suites, 6 villas* 🍴 *In-room: no a/c, refrigerator, no TV. In-hotel: restaurant, bars, pool, gym, spa, no elevator, public Internet, airport shuttle, no kids under 14* ▭ *AE, D, MC, V* 🍽 *BP.*

$$$ 🏨**Stonefield Estate Villa Resort.** One 18th-century plantation house and several gingerbread-style cottage villas dot this property. All accommodations have oversize, handcrafted furniture and one or two bathrooms; some villas also have garden showers and plunge pools. Living-dining rooms open onto verandahs with double hammocks and panoramic views, perfectly romantic at sunset. A complimentary shuttle goes to Soufrière or to Jalousie Beach. **Pros:** Very private, lovely pool, great sunset views from villa decks. **Cons:** Meal quality at dinner is inconsistent, you may want a rental car to get around. ⊠ *1 mi (1.5 km) south of Soufrière* 🏤 *Box 228, Soufrière* ☎ *758/459–5648 or 758/459–7037* ⊕ *www.stonefieldvillas.com* 🛏 *16 villas* 🍴 *In-room: no a/c (some), no phone (some), safe, kitchen, refrigerator, VCR (some), no TV (some). In-hotel: restaurant, bar, pool, no elevator, laundry service, public Internet* ▭ *AE, D, MC, V* 🍽 *EP.*

$$–$$$ 🏨 **Ti Kaye Village.** There is a specialness to this aerie overlooking Anse
★ Cochon beach down a mile-long dirt road off the main highway. Gingerbread-style cottages are surrounded by lush greenery and furnished
with handcrafted furniture. Each room has a private garden shower,
a large balcony with double hammock, and wooden louvers in doors
and windows to catch every breeze; some have private plunge pools. Or
you can maneuver the 166-step wooden stairway down the cliff to the
beach—which is one of the best snorkeling sites in St. Lucia. **Pros:** Perfect for a honeymoon or private getaway, garden showers are fabulous,
excellent restaurant. **Cons:** Far from anywhere, all those steps to the
beach. ✉ *Anse Cochon, Castries* 🖂 *Box GM669, Castries* ☎ *758/456-
8101* ⊕ *www.tikaye.com* ⟿ *33 rooms* ♿ *In-room: safe, refrigerator,
no TV. In-hotel: restaurant, bars, pool, gym, beachfront, water sports,
no elevator, laundry service, public Internet, no kids under 12* ☰ *AE,
D, DC, MC, V* ⊚ *BP.*

$–$$ 🏨 **Hummingbird Beach Resort.** Unpretentious and welcoming, this delight-
ful little inn on Soufrière Harbour has rooms in small seaside cabins.
Rooms are simply furnished—a primitive motif emphasized by African
wood sculptures. Most rooms have modern baths; two rooms and a
suite share a bath. A two-bedroom country cottage—with a sitting
room, kitchenette, and spectacular Piton view—is suitable for a family
or two couples vacationing together. The Hummingbird's Lifeline Restaurant is a favorite for locals. **Pros:** Local island atmosphere, small and
quiet, good food. **Cons:** Beach is not great, a "resort" without many
resort amenities. ✉ *Anse Chastanet Rd., Soufrière* 🖂 *Box 280, Soufrière* ☎ *758/459-7232 or 800/223-9815* ⊕ *www.nvo.com/pitonresort*
⟿ *9 rooms, 7 with bath; 1 suite without bath; 1 cottage* ♿ *In-room:
no a/c (some), no TV. In-hotel: restaurant, bar, pool, beachfront, no
elevator, public Internet* ☰ *AE, D, MC, V* ⊚ *BP.*

VIEUX FORT

$$$–$$$$ 🏨 **Coconut Bay.** The only resort in Vieux Fort, Coconut Bay is a sprawl-
♻ ing seaside retreat minutes from St. Lucia's Hewanorra International
Airport. The ocean views are beautiful, and the beach has lovely white
sand; but the resort faces the Atlantic Ocean, so swimming in the sea
is not advised. Instead, you'll find three swimming pools and a water
park with a lazy river, waterslides, and a swim-up bar. The Frégate
Island and Maria Islands are just offshore, and St. Lucia's Pitons and
other natural attractions in Soufrière are 30 minutes by car. Other-
wise, you'll have to be content with the activities in and around the
resort—four restaurants, a full-service spa, and plenty of space to relax
and socialize. **Pros:** Great for families, perfect for windsurfers, friendly
and sociable atmosphere. **Cons:** Rough surf precludes ocean swimming
and water sports, close to the airport but far from everything else.
✉ *Box 246, Vieux Fort* ☎ *758/459-6000* ⊕ *www.coconutbayresort*
andspa.com ⟿ *254 rooms* ♿ *In-room: safe. In-hotel: 4 restaurants,
bars, tennis courts, pools, gym, spa, beachfront, children's programs
(ages 3–12), public Internet* ☰ *AE, MC, V* ⊚ *AI.*

CLOSE UP

Small Hotels & Inns in St. Lucia

Choose one of these seven smaller properties if you're looking for something more intimate than the typical beach resort.

GREATER CASTRIES

$ Villa Beach Cottages (⊠ *Choc Bay, Castries* ☎ *758/450-2884* ⊕ *www. villabeachcottages.com*) line the beach at this family establishment—a favorite of Nobel laureate Sir Derek Walcott. Units are cozy and fairly close together, but each has a balcony facing the water, guaranteeing glorious sunset viewing every evening.

MARIGOT BAY

$-$$ Inn on the Bay (⊠ *Marigot Bay* ☎ *758/451-4260* ⊕ *www.saint-lucia. com*) has just five rooms, and owners Normand Viau and Louise Boucher treat you as a personal guest (adults only). Cool sea breezes obviate the need for a/c, and the stunning views of Marigot Bay are absolutely enchanting from the balcony outside your room and from the pool deck.

RODNEY BAY VILLAGE

$$ Caribbean Jewel Beach Resort (⊠ *Rodney Bay, Gros Islet* ☎ *758/452-9199* ⊕ *www.caribbeanjewelresort.com*) is a true bargain since the 30 units here are huge, modern, and comfortable—and from

every room, the view overlooking Rodney Bay is incredible (request a corner room for the most-expansive view). Suites have full kitchens.

$ Coco Kreole (⊠ *Rodney Bay* ☎ *758/452-0712* ⊕ *www.cocokreole. com*) offers an ambience more reminiscent of the home of a good friend than of a hotel; this 20-room treasure in the center of the action at Rodney Bay Village—and sister to Coco Palm hotel, just behind—is stylish, inexpensive, full of amenities, and close to restaurants, nightspots, and beautiful Reduit Beach.

$$ Ginger Lily (⊠ *Rodney Bay* ☎ *758/458-0300* ⊕ *www.thegingerlilyhotel.com*), a small, modern enclave of 11 rooms, has its own restaurant and a swimming pool and is across the street from Reduit Beach and smack in the middle of Rodney Bay Village.

$-$$ Harmony Suites (⊠ *Rodney Bay* ☎ *758/452-8756* ⊕ *www.harmonysuites.com*) guests (adults only) are scuba divers, boaters, or people who just like being close to Rodney Bay Marina. Of the 30 large suites cloistered around the swimming pool, the 8 waterfront suites are the largest. Reduit Beach is across the road.

WHERE TO EAT

Bananas, mangoes, passion fruit, plantains, breadfruit, okra, avocados, limes, pumpkins, cucumbers, papaya, yams, christophenes (also called chayote), and coconuts are among the fresh local fruits and vegetables that grace St. Lucian menus. The French influence is strong, and most chefs cook with a creole flair. Resort buffets and restaurant fare run the gamut, from steaks and chops to pasta and pizza. Every menu lists fresh fish along with the ever-popular lobster. Caribbean standards include callaloo, stuffed crab back, pepperpot stew, curried chicken or goat, and *lambi* (conch). The national dish of salt fish and green fig—a stew of dried, salted codfish and boiled green banana—is, let's say, an acquired taste. Soups and stews are traditionally prepared in a coal pot, a rustic clay casserole on a matching clay stand that holds the hot coals. Chicken and pork dishes and barbecues are also popular here. Fresh lobster is available in season, which lasts from August through March. As they do throughout the Caribbean, local vendors who set up barbecues along the roadside, at street fairs, and at Friday-night "jump-ups" do a land-office business selling grilled fish or chicken legs, bakes (fried biscuits), and beer—you can get a full meal for about $5. Most other meats are imported—beef from Argentina and Iowa, lamb from New Zealand. Piton is the local brew; Bounty, the local rum.

With so many popular all-inclusive resorts, guests take most meals at hotel restaurants—which are generally quite good and, in some cases, exceptional. It's fun when vacationing, however, to try some of the local restaurants, as well—for lunch when sightseeing or for a special night out.

WHAT TO WEAR

Dress on St. Lucia is casual but conservative. Shorts are usually fine during the day, but bathing suits and immodest clothing are frowned upon anywhere but at the beach. In the evening the mood is casually elegant, but even the fanciest places generally expect only a collared shirt and long pants for men and a sundress or slacks for women.

GREATER CASTRIES

CARIBBEAN ✕ **Restaurant de Palétuvier.** The view from the waterfront restaurant at
$$–$$$ J.J.'s Paradise, a small inn overlooking pretty Marigot Bay, is enchanting, and the seafood prepared by owner-chef Gerard (J.J.) Felix is among the best on the island. Superbly grilled fish with fresh vegetables gets top honors, but you might also enjoy shellfish (lobster, prawns, or lambi), as well as grilled T-bone steak, chicken (roasted, grilled, curried, or creole), pork chops, a vegetarian platter, or something truly exotic such as curried octopus. The welcome is friendly; the atmosphere, casual. Music and entertainment are on the menu most nights, as well. ⊠ *Marigot Bay Rd., Marigot* ☎ *758/451–4076* ⚑ *Reservations essential* ▬ *D, MC, V.*

ECLECTIC ✕ **Rainforest Hideaway.** British chef Jim Verity, whose parents own Dis-
$$$–$$$$ covery at Marigot Bay resort, masters and beautifully presents fusion
Fodor'sChoice fare—in this case, the exotic tastes and flavors influencing classical
★ French cuisine—at this romantic fine-dining hideaway on the north shore of pretty Marigot Bay. It's definitely worth the 20-minute-or-so drive from Castries. A little ferry whisks you to the alfresco restaurant, perched on a dock, where you're greeted with complimentary champagne. You'll be duly impressed by entrées such as balsamic-glazed roast quail, five-spice roast fillet of beef, or citrus-marinated wild salmon, accompanied by rich sauces, exotic vegetables, and excellent wines—not to mention the blanket of stars in the sky overhead and the live jazz several times a week. Sunday brunch is a special treat in this picturesque setting on the bay. ⊠ *Marigot Bay* ☎ *758/286–0511* ⚑ *Reservations essential* ▬ *AE, D, MC, V* ☾ *No lunch.*

FRENCH ✕**Coal Pot.** Popular since the early 1960s, this tiny (only 10 tables)
$$ waterfront restaurant overlooking pretty Vigie Cove is managed by
Fodor'sChoice Michelle Elliott, noted artist and daughter of the original owner, and
★ her French husband, chef Xavier Ribot. For a light lunch, opt for a
Greek or shrimp salad or, perhaps, broiled fresh fish with creole sauce.
Dinner might start with divine lobster bisque, followed by fresh sea-
food accompanied by one (or more) of the chef's fabulous sauces—
ginger, coconut-curry, lemon–garlic butter, or wild mushroom. Hearty
eaters may prefer duck, lamb, beef, or chicken laced with peppercorns,
red wine, and onion or Roquefort sauce. ⊠ *Vigie Marina, Castries*
☎ *758/452–5566* ⌲ *Reservations essential* ⊟ *AE, D, MC, V* ⊙ *Closed
Sun. No lunch Sat.*

$$ ✕**Jacques.** Chef-owner Jacky Rioux creates magical dishes in his open-
★ air garden restaurant (known for years as Froggie Jack's) overlooking
Vigie Cove. The cooking style is decidedly French, as is Rioux, but fresh
produce and local spices create a fusion cuisine that's memorable at
lunch or dinner. You might start with a bowl of creamy tomato-basil or
pumpkin soup, a grilled portobello mushroom, or octopus and conch
in curried coconut sauce. Main courses include fresh seafood, such
as oven-baked kingfish with a white wine and sweet pepper sauce, or
breast of chicken stuffed with smoked salmon in a citrus butter sauce.
The wine list is also impressive. ⊠ *Vigie Marina, Castries* ☎ *758/458–
1900* ⌲ *Reservations essential* ⊟ *AE, MC, V* ⊙ *Closed Sun.*

RODNEY BAY & THE NORTH

ASIAN ✕**Tao.** For exquisite dining, head for Tao at the Body Holiday at LeS-
$$$-$$$$ PORT. Perched on a second-floor balcony at the edge of Cariblue
★ Beach, you're guaranteed a pleasant breeze and a starry sky while
you enjoy fusion cuisine—a marriage of Asian tastes and a Caribbean
touch. Choose from appetizers such as seafood dumplings, sashimi
salad, or miso eggplant timbale, followed by tender slices of pork
loin teriyaki, twice-cooked duck, wok-seared calves' liver, or tandoori
chicken—the results are mouthwatering. Fine wines accompany the
meal, desserts are extravagant, and service is superb. Seating is lim-
ited; hotel guests have priority, so reserve early. ⊠ *The Body Holiday
at LeSPORT, Cap Estate* ☎ *758/450–8551* ⌲ *Reservations essential*
⊟ *AE, MC, V* ⊙ *No lunch.*

ECLECTIC ✕**The Edge.** Innovative Swedish chef Bobo Bergstrom, formerly the
$$$-$$$$ award-winning culinary director at Windjammer Landing and chef de
cuisine at the famed Operakallaren in Stockholm, brought his "Eurob-
bean fusion" cuisine to his own fine-dining establishment, overlooking
the harbor at Harmony Suites hotel. St. Lucian locals and visitors alike
rave about Chef Bobo's culinary feats, the excellent wine list, and the
island's first sushi bar. "Eurobbean" cuisine is a contemporary fusion
style that combines the chef's European heritage, Caribbean traditions
and ingredients, and a touch of Asian influence. Among the dozen start-
ers are a dreamy lobster bisque, scented with saffron and paprika.
Then try snapper braised in fennel bouillon, jerk-marinated and grilled
beef tenderloin, spice-glazed rabbit roulade, or perhaps the five-course

tasting menu. There's sure to be a dish on the extensive menu (or at the sushi bar) that suits everyone in your party, but be sure to leave room for a fabulous dessert. ⊠*Harmony Suites hotel, Rodney Bay* ☎*758/450–3343* ♠*Reservations essential* ☰*AE, MC, V.*

$–$$ ✕**The Lime.** A casual bistro with lime-green gingham curtains, straw
☺ hats decorating the ceiling, and hanging plants, the Lime specializes in local dishes such as spicy jerk chicken or pork and breadfruit salad—as well as char-grilled steak and fresh-caught fish. The meals are well prepared, the portions are plentiful, and the prices are reasonable, which is perhaps why you often see St. Lucians and visitors alike "liming" (an island term that means something akin to hanging around and relaxing) all day and most of the night at this popular restaurant. The Late Lime, a club where the crowd gathers as night turns to morning, is next door. ⊠*Rodney Bay* ☎*758/452–0761* ☰*D, MC, V* ☻*Closed Tues.*

FRENCH ✕**The Great House.** Elegant, gracious, and romantic, the Great House
$$$ was reconstructed on the foundation of an original Cap Estate planta-
★ tion house adjacent to Almond Smugglers Cove Resort. The grandeur of those early days has been revived as well. The waitstaff wears traditional St. Lucian costumes. The chef adds a piquant creole touch to traditional French cuisine—with excellent results. The menu, which changes nightly, might include pumpkin-and-potato soup, local crab back with lime vinaigrette, sautéed Antillean shrimp in a creole sauce, and broiled sirloin with thyme butter and sweet-potato chips. Cocktails at the open-air bar are especially enjoyable at sunset. The Derek Walcott Theatre is next door. ⊠*Cap Estate* ☎*758/450–0450 or 758/450–0211* ♠*Reservations essential* ☰*AE, D, DC, MC, V* ☻*No lunch.*

SOUFRIÈRE

CARIBBEAN ✕**Dasheene Restaurant & Bar.** The terrace restaurant at Ladera resort has
$$$ breathtakingly close-up views of the Pitons and the sea between them,
★ especially beautiful at sunset. Casual by day and magical at night, Executive chef Orlando Satchell describes his creative West Indian menu as "sexy Caribbean." Appetizers may include grilled crab claws with a choice of dips or silky pumpkin soup with ginger. Typical entrées are triggerfish seasoned and soaked in lime and fish stock and cooked in banana leaves, shrimp Dasheene (panfried with local herbs), seared duck breast with passion-fruit jus, or baron fillet of beef with sweet potato and green-banana mash. Light dishes, fresh salads, and sandwiches are served at lunchtime. ✥*Ladera resort, 2 mi (3 km) south of Soufrière* ☎*758/459–7323* ☰*AE, D, DC, MC, V.*

$–$$ ✕**Lifeline Restaurant at the Hummingbird.** The chef at this cheerful restaurant-bar in the Hummingbird Beach Resort specializes in French creole cuisine, starting with fresh seafood or chicken seasoned with local herbs and accompanied by a medley of vegetables just picked from the Hummingbird's garden. Sandwiches and salads are also available. If you stop for lunch, sit outside by the pool for a magnificent view of the Pitons (you can also take a dip), and be sure to visit the batik studio and art gallery of proprietor Joan Alexander and her son, adjacent to the dining room. ⊠*Hummingbird Beach Resort, Anse Chastanet Rd., Soufrière* ☎758/459–7232 ▤*AE, D, MC, V.*

$–$$ ✕**The Still.** If you're visiting Diamond Waterfall, this is a great lunch spot. The two dining rooms seat up to 400 people, so it's a popular stop for tour groups and cruise passengers. The emphasis is on local cuisine using vegetables such as christophenes, breadfruits, yams, and callaloo along with grilled fish or chicken, but there are also pork and beef dishes. All fruits and vegetables used in the restaurant are organically grown on the estate. ⊠*The Still Plantation, Sir Arthur Lewis St., Soufrière* ☎758/459–7261 ▤*MC, V.*

BEACHES

Beaches are all public, but many along the coast, particularly north of Castries, are flanked by hotels. A few secluded stretches of beach on the west coast south of Marigot Bay are accessible primarily by boat and are a popular swimming and snorkeling stop on catamaran or powerboat sightseeing trips. Don't swim along the windward (east) coast, as the Atlantic Ocean is too rough—but the views are spectacular.

Anse Chastanet. In front of the resort of the same name, just north of the city of Soufrière, this palm-studded dark-sand beach has a backdrop of green hills, brightly painted fishing skiffs bobbing at anchor, and the island's best reefs for snorkeling and diving. The resort's gazebos are nestled among the palms; its dive shop, restaurant, and bar are on the beach and open to the public. ⊠*1 mi (1.5 km) north of Soufrière.*

Anse Cochon. This remote dark-sand beach is reached only by boat or via Ti Kaye Village's mile-long access road. The water and adjacent reef are superb for swimming, diving, and snorkeling. Moorings are free, and boaters can enjoy lunch or dinner at Ti Kaye—if you're willing to climb the 166 steps up the hillside. ⊠*3 mi (5 km) south of Marigot Bay.*

Anse des Pitons. Between the Pitons on Jalousie Bay, the white sand on this crescent beach was imported and spread over the natural black sand. Accessible from Jalousie Plantation resort (whose management prefers to call the beach "Forbidden Beach," although it is a public beach like all others on the island) or by boat, the beach offers good snorkeling, diving, and breathtaking scenery. ⊠*Jalousie Bay, 1 mi (1.5 km) south of Soufrière.*

Marigot Beach. Calm waters rippled only by passing yachts lap a sliver of sand studded with palm trees on the north side of Marigot Bay. The beach is accessible by a ferry that operates continually from one side of the bay to the other, and you can find refreshments at adjacent restaurants. ⊠*Marigot Bay.*

Pigeon Point. At this small beach within Pigeon Island National Park, on the northwestern tip of St. Lucia, a restaurant serves snacks and drinks, but this is also a perfect spot for picnicking. ⊠*Pigeon Island.*

★   **Reduit Beach.** This long stretch of golden sand frames Rodney Bay and is within walking distance of many small hotels and restaurants in Rodney Bay Village. The Rex St. Lucian hotel, which faces the beach, has a water-sports center, where you can rent sports equipment and beach chairs and take windsurfing or waterskiing lessons. Many feel that Reduit is the island's finest beach. ⊠ *Rodney Bay.*

Vigie Beach. This 2-mi (3-km) strand runs parallel to the George F.L. Charles Airport runway in Castries, and continues on to become Malabar Beach, the beachfront in front of the Rendezvous resort. ⊠ *Castries, next to the airport.*

SPORTS & THE OUTDOORS

BIKING

Although the terrain is pretty rugged, two tour operators have put together fascinating bicycle and combination bicycle-hiking tours that appeal to novice riders as well as those who enjoy a good workout. Prices range from $60 to $100 per person.

★ **Bike St. Lucia** (⊠ *Anse Chastanet, Soufrière* ☎758/451–2453 ⊕*www. bikestlucia.com*) takes small groups of bikers on Jungle Biking™ tours along trails that meander through the remnants of an 18th-century plantation near Soufrière. Stops are made to explore the French colonial ruins, study the beautiful tropical plants and fruit trees, enjoy a picnic lunch, and take a dip in a river swimming hole or a swim at the beach. If you're staying in the north, you can get a tour that includes transportation to the Soufrière area. **Palm Services Bike Tours** (⊠ *Castries* ☎758/458–0908 ⊕*www.cyclestlucia.com*) is suitable for all fitness levels. Jeep or bus transportation is provided across the central mountains to Dennery, on the east coast. After a 3-mi (5-km) ride through the countryside, bikes are exchanged for shoe leather. The short hike into the rain forest ends with a picnic and a refreshing swim next to a sparkling waterfall—then the return leg to Dennery. All gear is supplied.

BOATING & SAILING

Rodney Bay and Marigot Bay are centers for bareboat and crewed yacht charters. Their marinas offer safe anchorage, shower facilities, restaurants, groceries, and maintenance for yachts sailing the waters of the eastern Caribbean. Charter prices range from $1,750 to $10,000 per week, depending on the season and the type and size of vessel, plus $250 extra per day if you want a skipper and cook. **Bateau Mygo** (⊠ *Marigot Bay* ☎758/451–4772 ⊕*www.bateaumygo.com*) specializes in customized, crewed charters on its 40- to 44-foot yachts for either a couple of days or a week. **Destination St. Lucia (DSL) Ltd.** (⊠ *Rodney Bay Marina, Gros Islet* ☎758/452–8531 ⊕*www.dsl-yachting. com*) offers bareboat yacht charters; vessels range in length from 38 to 51 feet. The **Moorings Yacht Charters** (⊠ *Marigot Bay* ☎758/451–4357 or 800/535–7289 ⊕*www.moorings.com*) rents bareboat and crewed yachts ranging from Beneteau 39s to Morgan 60s.

CRICKET

International and test-series cricket is played at the Beausejour Cricket Ground in Gros Islet and at the impressive National Stadium in Vieux Fort. Contact the tourist board for details on schedules and tickets.

DIVING & SNORKELING

★ **Anse Chastanet,** near the Pitons on the southwest coast, is the best beach-entry dive site. The underwater reef drops from 20 feet to nearly 140 feet in a stunning coral wall. A 165-foot freighter, *Lesleen M,* was deliberately sunk in 60 feet of water near **Anse Cochon** to create an artificial reef; divers can explore the ship in its entirety and view huge gorgonians, black coral trees, gigantic barrel sponges, lace corals, schooling fish, angelfish, sea horses, spotted eels, stingrays, nurse sharks, and sea turtles. **Anse-La-Raye,** midway up the west coast, is one of St. Lucia's finest wall and drift dives and a great place for snorkeling. At the base of **Petit Piton,** a spectacular wall drops to 200 feet. You can view an impressive collection of huge barrel sponges and black coral trees; strong currents ensure good visibility. At the **Pinnacles,** four coral-encrusted stone piers rise to within 10 feet of the surface.

Depending on the season and the particular trip, prices range from about $40 to $60 for a one-tank dive, $175 to $260 for a six-dive package over three days, and $265 to $450 for a 10-dive package over five days. Dive shops provide instruction for all levels (beginner, intermediate, and advanced). For beginners, a resort course (pool training), followed by one open-water dive, runs from $65 to $90. Snorkelers are generally welcome on dive trips and usually pay $25 to $50, which includes equipment and sometimes lunch and transportation.

Buddies (⊠ *Rodney Bay Marina, Rodney Bay* ☎758/452–8406) offers wall, wreck, reef, and deep dives; resort courses and open-water certification with advanced and specialty courses are taught by PADI-certified instructors. **Dive Fair Helen** (⊠ *Vigie Marina, Castries* ☎758/451–7716, *888/855–2206 in U.S. and Canada* ⊕*www.divefairhelen.com*) is a PADI center that offers half- and full-day excursions to wreck, wall, and marine reserve areas, as well as night dives. **Scuba St. Lucia** (⊠ *Anse Chastanet, Soufrière* ☎758/459–7755 ⊕*www.scubastlucia.com*) is a PADI five-star training facility. Daily beach and boat dives and resort and certification courses are offered; underwater photography and snorkeling equipment are available. Day trips from the north of the island include round-trip speedboat transportation.

FISHING

Among the deep-sea creatures you can find in St. Lucia's waters are dolphin (also called dorado or mahimahi), barracuda, mackerel, wahoo, kingfish, sailfish, and white and blue marlin. Sportfishing is generally done on a catch-and-release basis, but the captain may permit you to take a fish back to your hotel to be prepared for your dinner. Neither spearfishing nor collecting live fish in coastal waters is permitted. Half- and full-day deep-sea fishing excursions can be arranged at either Vigie Marina or Rodney Bay Marina. A half day of fishing on a scheduled trip runs about $75–$80 per person. Beginners are welcome. **Captain Mike's** (⊠ *Vigie Marina, Castries* ☎ *758/452-1216 or 758/452-7044* ⊕ *www.captmikes.com*) has a fleet of Bertram powerboats (31 to 38 feet) that accommodate as many as eight passengers; tackle and cold drinks are supplied. **Hackshaw's Boat Charters** (⊠ *Vigie Marina, Castries* ☎ *758/453-0553 or 758/452-3909* ⊕ *www.hackshaws.com*), in business since 1953, runs charters on boats ranging from the 31-foot *Blue Boy* or *Miss T.* to the 50-foot, custom-built *Lady Hack*. **Mako Watersports** (⊠ *Rodney Bay Marina, Rodney Bay* ☎ *758/452-0412*) takes fishing enthusiasts out on the well-equipped six-passenger *Annie Baby*.

GOLF

St. Lucia Golf Club (⊠ *Cap Estate* ☎ *758/452-8523* ⊕ *www.stluciagolf. com*), the only public course, is at the island's northern tip and offers panoramic views of both the Atlantic and Caribbean. It's an 18-hole championship course (6,836 yards, par 71). The clubhouse has a fine-dining restaurant called the Cap Grill that serves breakfast, lunch, and dinner; the Sports Bar is a convivial meeting place any time of day. You can rent clubs and shoes and arrange lessons at the pro shop and perfect your swing at the 350-yard driving range. Depending on the season, greens fees range from $75 for 9 holes to $125 for 18 holes; carts are required and included; club and shoe rentals are available. Reservations are essential. Complimentary transportation from your hotel or cruise ship is provided for parties of three or more people. The St. Lucia Golf Open, a two-day tournament held in March, is open to amateurs; it's a handicap event, and prizes are awarded.

HIKING

The island is laced with trails, but you shouldn't attempt the more-challenging ones on your own. Seasoned hikers may aspire to climb the Pitons, the two volcanic cones rising 2,460 feet and 2,619 feet, respectively, from the ocean floor just south of Soufrière. Hiking is recommended only on Gros Piton, which offers a steep but safe trail to the top. Tourists are permitted to hike Petit Piton, but the second half of the hike requires a good deal of rock climbing, and you'll need to provide your own safety equipment. Hiking the Pitons requires the permission of the St. Lucia Forest & Lands Department and a knowledgeable guide from the **Pitons Tour Guide Association** (☎ *758/459-9748*). The **St. Lucia Forest & Lands Department** (☎ *758/450-2231 or 758/450-2078*) manages trails throughout the rain forest and provides guides who explain the plants and trees you'll encounter and keep you on the right track for a small fee. The **St. Lucia National Trust** (☎ *758/452-5005* ⊕ *www.slunatrust.org*) maintains two trails: one is at Anse La Liberté, near Canaries on the Caribbean coast; the other is on the Atlantic coast, from Mandélé Point to the Frégate Island Nature Reserve. Full-day excursions with lunch cost about $50 to $85 per person and can be arranged through hotels or tour operators.

HORSEBACK RIDING

Creole horses, a breed indigenous to South America and popular on the island, are fairly small, fast, sturdy, and even-tempered animals suitable for beginners. Established stables can accommodate all skill levels and offer countryside trail rides, beach rides with picnic lunches, plantation tours, carriage rides, and lengthy treks. Prices run about $40 for one hour, $50 for two hours, and $70 for a three-hour beach ride and barbecue. Transportation is usually provided between the stables and nearby hotels. Local people sometimes appear on beaches with their steeds and offer 30-minute rides for $10; ride at your own risk.

Atlantic Shores Riding Stable (⊠ *Savannes Bay, Vieux Fort* ☎ *758/454–8668 or 758/484–9769*) is in south St. Lucia; trails take in Honeymoon Beach, mangroves, grassy fields, and the rugged Atlantic coast. **Country Saddles** (⊠ *Marquis Estate, Babonneau* ☎ *758/450–5467 or 758/450–0197*), 45 minutes east of Castries, guides beginners and advanced riders through banana plantations, forest trails, and along the Atlantic coast. **International Riding Stables** (⊠ *Beauséjour Estate, Gros Islet* ☎ *758/452–8139 or 758/450–8665*) offers English- and Western-style riding. The beach-picnic ride includes time for a swim—with or without your horse. **Trim's National Riding Stable** (⊠ *Cas-en-Bas, Gros Islet* ☎ *758/452–8273 or 758/450–9971*), the island's oldest riding stable, offers four sessions per day, plus beach tours, trail rides, and carriage tours to Pigeon Island.

SEA EXCURSIONS

A day sail or sea cruise to Soufrière and the Pitons is a wonderful way to see St. Lucia and, perhaps, the perfect way to get to the island's distinctive natural sites. Prices for a full-day sailing excursion to Soufrière run about $75 to $90 per person and include a land tour to the sulfur springs and the botanical gardens, lunch, a stop for swimming and snorkeling, and a visit to pretty Marigot Bay. Two-hour sunset cruises along the northwest coast cost about $45 per person. Most boats leave from either Vigie Cove in Castries or Rodney Bay.

☽ The 140-foot tall ship **Brig Unicorn** (⊠ *Vigie Cove, Castries* ☎ *758/452–8644*), used in the filming of the TV miniseries *Roots* and more recently the movie *Pirates of the Caribbean*, is a 140-foot replica of a 19th-century sailing ship. Day trips along the coast are fun for the whole family. Several nights each week a sunset cruise, with drinks and a live steel band, sails to Pigeon Point and back. Customized pleasure trips and snorkeling charters can be arranged for small groups (four to six people) through **Captain Mike's** (⊠ *Vigie Cove, Castries* ☎ *758/452–0216 or 758/452–7044* ⊕ *www.captmikes.com*). On *Endless Summer* (⊠ *Rodney Bay Marina, Rodney Bay* ☎ *758/450–8651*), a 56-foot "party" catamaran, you can take a day trip to Soufrière or a half-day swimming and snorkeling trip. For romantics, there's a weekly sunset cruise, with dinner and entertainment. **Mystic Man Tours** (⊠*Bay St., Soufrière* ☎*758/459–7783 or 758/455–9634*) operates whale- and dolphin-watching tours, which are great family excursions. *Surf Queen* (⊠*Vigie Cove, Castries* ☎*758/452–8232*), a trimaran, runs a fast, sleek sail and has a special tour for German-speaking passengers.

L'Express des Iles (⊠*La Place Carenage, Castries* ☎*758/452–2211*) offers an interesting day trip to the French island of Martinique. A hydrofoil departs daily for the 20-mi (32-km) voyage. As you approach Martinique, be sure to be among the first to disembark. There's usually only one immigration-customs agent on duty, and it can take an hour to clear if you're at the end of the line. From Pigeon Island, north of Rodney Bay, you can take a more-intimate cruise to the Pitons aboard the 57-foot luxury cruiser **MV** *Vigie* (⊠*Pigeon Island* ☎*758/452–8232*). For a boat trip to Pigeon Island, the **Rodney Bay Ferry** (⊠*Rodney Bay Marina, Rodney Bay* ☎*758/452–8816*) departs the ferry slip adjacent to the Lime restaurant twice daily for $50 round-trip, which includes the entrance fee to Pigeon Island and lunch; snorkel equipment can be rented for $12.

SIGHTSEEING TOURS

Taxi drivers are well informed and can give you a full tour—and often an excellent one, thanks to government-sponsored training programs. From the Castries area, full-day island tours cost $140 for up to four people; sightseeing trips to Soufrière, $120. If you plan your own day, expect to pay the driver $20 per hour plus tip.

★ **Jungle Tours** (⊠*Cas en Bas, Gros Islet* ☎*758/450–0434*) specializes in rain forest hiking tours for all levels of ability. You're required only to bring hiking shoes or sneakers and have a willingness to get wet and have fun. Prices range from $80 to $90 and include lunch, fees, and transportation via open Land Rover truck. **St. Lucia Helicopters** (⊠*Pointe Seraphine, Castries* ☎*758/453–6950* 🖷*758/452–1553* ⊕*www.stluciahelicopters.com*) offers a bird's-eye view of the island. A 10-minute North Island tour ($55 per person) leaves from Pointe Seraphine, in Castries, continues up the west coast to Pigeon Island, then flies along the rugged Atlantic coastline before returning inland over Castries. The 20-minute South Island tour ($85 per person) starts at Pointe Seraphine and follows the western coastline, circling picturesque Marigot Bay, Soufrière, and the majestic Pitons before returning inland over the volcanic hot springs and tropical rain forest. A complete island tour combines the two and lasts 30 minutes ($130 per person). **St. Lucia Heritage Tours** (⊠*Pointe Seraphine, Castries* ☎*758/451–6058* ⊕*www.heritagetoursstlucia.org*) has put together an "authentic St. Lucia experience," specializing in the local culture and traditions. Groups are small, and some of the off-the-beaten-track sites visited are a 19th-century plantation house surrounded by nature trails, a 20-foot waterfall hidden away on private property, and a living museum presenting Creole practices and traditions. Plan on paying $65 per person for a full-day tour. **Sunlink Tours** (⊠ *Reduit Beach Ave., Rodney Bay* ☎ *758/452–8232 or 800/786–5465* ⊕ *www.sunlinktours.com*) offers dozens of land, sea, and combination sightseeing tours, as well as shopping tours, plantation, and rain forest adventures via jeep safari, deep-sea fishing excursions, and day trips to other islands. Prices range from $20 for a half-day shopping tour to $120 for a full-day land-and-sea jeep safari to Soufrière.

WINDSURFING & KITEBOARDING

Windsurfers and kiteboarders congregate at Anse de Sables Beach, at the southeastern tip of St. Lucia, to take advantage of the blue-water and high-wind conditions that the Atlantic Ocean provides. The **Reef Kite & Surf Centre** (⊠ *Anse de Sables, Vieux Fort* ☎ *758/454–3418*) rents equipment and offers lessons from certified instructors in both windsurfing and kiteboarding. A three-hour beginning windsurfing course costs $90 plus $45 to rent equipment for a half day. For kiteboarding, the three-hour starter course costs $125, including equipment. Kiteboarding is particularly strenuous, so participants must be excellent swimmers and in good physical health.

SHOPPING

The island's best-known products are artwork and wood carvings; clothing and household articles made from both batik and silk-screen fabrics that are designed and produced in island workshops; straw mats and clay pottery. You can also take home straw hats and baskets and locally grown cocoa, coffee, and spices.

AREAS & MALLS

Along the harbor in Castries, you can see rambling structures with bright-orange roofs that house several markets, which are open from 6 AM to 5 PM Monday through Saturday. Saturday morning is the busiest and most colorful time to shop. For more than a century, farmers' wives have gathered at the **Castries Market** to sell produce—which, alas, you can't import to the United States. But you can bring back spices (such as cocoa, turmeric, cloves, bay leaves, ginger, peppercorns, cinnamon sticks, nutmeg, mace, and vanilla essence), as well as bottled hot pepper sauces—all of which cost a fraction of what you'd pay back home. The **Craft Market**, adjacent to the produce market, has aisles and aisles of baskets and other handmade straw work, rustic brooms made from palm fronds, wood carvings, leather work, clay pottery, and souvenirs—all at affordable prices. The **Vendor's Arcade**, across the street from the Craft Market, is a maze of stalls and booths where you can find handicrafts among the T-shirts and costume jewelry.

Gablewoods Mall, on the Gros Islet Highway in Choc Bay, a couple of miles north of downtown Castries, has about 35 shops that sell groceries, wines and spirits, jewelry, clothing, crafts, books, overseas newspapers, music, souvenirs, household goods, and snacks. Along with 54 boutiques, restaurants, and other businesses that sell services and supplies, a large supermarket is the focal point of each **J. Q.'s Shopping Mall**; one is at Rodney Bay and another at Vieux Fort.

The duty-free shopping areas are at **Pointe Seraphine**, an attractive Spanish-motif complex on Castries Harbour with more than 20 shops, and **La Place Carenage**, an inviting, three-story complex on the opposite side of the harbor. You can also find duty-free items in a few small shops at the arcade at the Rex St. Lucian hotel in Rodney Bay and, of course, in the departure lounge at Hewanorra International Airport. You must present your passport and airline ticket to purchase items at the duty-free price.

Marigot Marina Village, on Marigot Bay, has shops and services for boaters and landlubbers alike, including a bank, grocery store, business center, art gallery, an assortment of boutiques, and a French bakery/coffee shop.

Vieux Fort Plaza, near Hewanorra International Airport in Vieux Fort, is the main shopping center in the southern part of St. Lucia. You'll find a bank, supermarket, bookstore, toy shop, and several clothing stores there.

SPECIALTY STORES

ART

Art & Antiques (⊠ *Pointe Seraphine, Castries* ☏ *758/451–4150*) is a museum-type shop opened by artist Llewellyn Xavier and his wife, selling fine art, antique maps and prints, sterling silver and crystal, rich linens, objets d'art, and mere collectibles. **Artsibit Gallery** (⊠ *Brazil and Mongiraud Sts., Castries* ☏ *758/452–7865*) exhibits and sells moderately priced pieces by St. Lucian painters and sculptors. **Caribbean Art Gallery** (⊠ *Rodney Bay Yacht Marina, Rodney Bay* ☏ *758/452–8071*) sells original artwork by local artists, along with antique maps and prints and hand-painted silk. World-renowned St. Lucian artist **Llewellyn Xavier** (⊠ *Cap Estate* ☏ *758/450–9155*) creates modern art, ranging from vigorous oil abstracts that take up half a wall, to small objects made from beaten silver and gold. Much of his work has an environmental theme, created from recycled materials. Xavier's work is on permanent exhibit at major museums in New York and Washington, D.C. Call to arrange a visit to his studio. **Modern Art Gallery** (⊠ *Gros Islet Hwy., Bois d'Orange* ☏ *758/452–9079*) is a home studio, open by appointment only, where you can buy contemporary and avant-garde Caribbean art.

BOOKS & MAGAZINES

Sunshine Bookshop (⊠ *Gablewoods Mall, Castries* ☏ *758/452–3222*) has novels and titles of regional interest, including books by Caribbean authors—among them the works of the St. Lucian Nobel laureate, poet Derek Walcott. You can also find current newspapers and magazines.

Valmont Books (⊠ *Jeremie and Laborie Sts., Castries* ☎ *758/452–3817*) has West Indian literature and picture books, as well as stationery.

CLOTHES & TEXTILES

★ **Bagshaw Studios** (⊠ *La Toc Rd., La Toc Bay, Castries* ☎ *758/452–2139 or 758/451–9249*) sells clothing and table linens in colorful tropical patterns using Stanley Bagshaw's original designs. The fabrics are silk-screened by hand in the adjacent workroom. You can also find Bagshaw boutiques at Pointe Seraphine, La Place Carenage, and Rodney Bay, and a selection of items in gift shops at Hewanorra Airport. Visit the workshop to see how designs are turned into colorful silk-screen fabrics, which are then fashioned into clothing and household articles. It's open weekdays from 8:30 to 5, Saturday 8:30 to 4, and Sunday 10 to 1. Weekend hours may be extended if a cruise ship is in port. **Batik Studio** (⊠ *Hummingbird Beach Resort, on bay front, north of wharf, Soufrière* ☎ *758/459–7232*) has superb batik sarongs, scarves, and wall panels designed and created on-site by Joan Alexander and her son David. At **Caribelle Batik** (⊠ *La Toc Rd., Morne Fortune, Castries* ☎ *758/452–3785*), craftspeople demonstrate the art of batik and silk-screen printing. Meanwhile, seamstresses create clothing and wall hangings, which you can purchase in the shop. The studio is in an old Victorian mansion, high atop Morne Fortune, overlooking Castries. There's a terrace where you can have a cool drink, and there's a garden full of tropical orchids and lilies. Caribelle Batik creations are featured in many gift shops throughout St. Lucia. **Sea Island Cotton Shop** (⊠ *Bridge St., Castries* ☎ *758/452–3674* ⊠ *Gablewoods Mall, Choc Bay* ☎ *758/451–6946* ⊠ *J. Q.'s Shopping Mall, Rodney Bay* ☎ *758/458–4220*) sells quality T-shirts, Caribelle Batik clothing and other resort wear, and colorful souvenirs.

GIFTS & SOUVENIRS

Caribbean Perfumes (⊠ *Jacques restaurant, Vigie Marina, Castries* ☎ *758/453–7249*) blends a half dozen lovely scents for women and two aftershaves for men from exotic flowers, fruits, tropical woods, and spices. Fragrances are all made in St. Lucia, reasonably priced, and available at the perfumery (adjacent to Jacques restaurant) and at many hotel gift shops. **Noah's Arkade** (⊠ *Jeremie St., Castries* ☎ *758/452–2523* ⊠ *Pointe Seraphine, Castries* ☎ *758/452–7488*) has hammocks, wood carvings, straw mats, T-shirts, books, and other regional goods.

HANDICRAFTS

On the southwest coast, halfway between Soufrière and Vieux Fort, you can find locally made clay and straw pieces at the **Choiseul Arts & Crafts Centre** (⊠ *La Fargue* ☎ *758/454–3226*). Many of St. Lucia's artisans come from this area. **Eudovic Art Studio** (⊠ *Morne Fortune, Castries* ☎ *758/452–2747*) is a workshop and studio where you can buy trays, masks, and figures sculpted from local mahogany, red cedar, and eucalyptus wood. At **Zaka** (⊠ *Malgretoute, Soufrière* ☎ *758/457–1504*), you may get a chance to talk with artist and craftsman Simon Gajhadhar, who fashions totems and masks from driftwood and other environmentally friendly sources of wood—taking advantage of all the natural nibs and knots that distinguish each piece. Once the "face" is carved, it is painted in vivid colors to highlight the exaggerated features and provide expression. Each piece is unique.

NIGHTLIFE & THE ARTS

THE ARTS

In early May, the weeklong **St. Lucia Jazz Festival** (⊕ *stluciajazz.org*) is one of the premier events of its kind in the Caribbean. International jazz greats perform at outdoor venues on Pigeon Island and at various hotels, restaurants, and nightspots throughout the island; free concerts are also held at Derek Walcott Square in downtown Castries.

THEATER

The small, open-air **Derek Walcott Center Theatre** (⊠ *Cap Estate, Gros Islet* ☎ *758/450–0551, 758/450–0450 for Great House*), next to the Great House restaurant in Cap Estate, seats 200 people for monthly productions of music, dance, and drama, as well as Sunday brunch programs. The Trinidad Theatre Workshop also presents an annual performance here. For schedule and ticket information, contact the **Great House** restaurant.

NIGHTLIFE

Most resort hotels have entertainment—island music, calypso singers, and steel bands, as well as disco, karaoke, and talent shows—every night in high season and a couple of nights per week in the off-season. Otherwise, Rodney Bay is the best bet for nightlife. The many restaurants and bars there attract a crowd nearly every night.

BARS

The **Captain's Cellar** (⊠ *Pigeon Island, Rodney Bay* ☎ *758/450–0253*) is a cozy Old English–style pub with live jazz on weekends.

DANCE CLUBS

Most dance clubs with live bands have a cover charge of $6 to $8 (EC$15 to EC$20), and the music usually starts at 11 PM. At **Aqua** (⊠ *Rodney Bay* ☎ *758/452–0284*), dance inside or outside on the party deck, starting at 8 PM. **Doolittle's** (⊠ *Marigot Bay* ☎ *758/451–4974*) has live bands and dance music—calypso, soul, salsa, steel band, reggae, and limbo—that changes nightly. At **Indies** (⊠ *Rodney Bay* ☎ *758/452–0727*) you can dance to the hottest rhythms Wednesday, Friday, and Saturday; dress is casual though smart—no hats or sandals, no shorts or sleeveless shirts for men. There's shuttle bus service to and from most major hotels. **Rumours** (⊠ *Rodney Bay* ☎ *758/452–9249*) is a popular nightspot that rocks well into the night. **The Lime and Upper Level at The Lime** (⊠ *Reduit Beach, Rodney Bay* ☎ *758/452–0761*) is a particular favorite of St. Lucians; it's air-conditioned and intimate, with live music, a DJ, or karaoke every night but Tuesday.

THEME NIGHTS

For a taste of St. Lucian village life, head for the **Anse La Raye "Sea-food Friday "** street festival any Friday night. Beginning at 6:30 PM, the main street in this tiny fishing village—about halfway between Castries and Soufrière—is closed to vehicles, and the residents prepare what they know best: fish cakes, grilled or stewed fish, hot bakes (biscuits), roasted corn, boiled crayfish, even grilled-before-your-eyes lobster. Prices range from a few cents for a fish cake or bake to $10 or $15 for a whole lobster. Walk around, eat, chat with the local people, and listen to live music until the wee hours of the morning.

A Friday-night ritual for locals and visitors alike is to head for the **Gros Islet Jump-Up,** the island's largest street party. Huge speakers are set up on the village's main street and blast out Caribbean music all night long. Sometimes there are live bands. When you take a break from dancing, you can buy barbecued fish or chicken, *rotis* (curried chicken, beef, or vegetables wrapped inside a pastry turnover and baked), beer, and soda from villagers who set up cookers right along the roadside. It's the ultimate "lime" experience.

EXPLORING ST. LUCIA

Except for a small area in the extreme northeast, one main route circles all of St. Lucia. The road snakes along the coast, cuts across mountains, makes hairpin turns and sheer drops, and reaches dizzying heights. It takes at least four hours to drive the whole loop. Even at a leisurely pace with frequent sightseeing stops, the curvy roads make it a tiring drive in a single outing.

The West Coast Road between Castries and Soufrière (a 1½- to 2-hour journey) has steep hills and sharp turns, but it's well marked and incredibly scenic. South of Castries, the road tunnels through Morne Fortune, skirts the island's largest banana plantation (more than 127 varieties of bananas, called "figs" in this part of the Caribbean, are grown on the island), and passes through tiny fishing villages. Just north of Soufrière is the island's fruit basket, where most of the mangoes, breadfruit, tomatoes, limes, and oranges are grown. In the mountainous region that forms a backdrop for Soufrière, you will notice 3,118-foot Mt. Gimie (pronounced Jimmy), St. Lucia's highest peak. As you approach Soufrière, you'll also have spectacular views of the Pitons.

The landscape changes dramatically between the Pitons and Vieux Fort on the island's southeastern tip. Along the South Coast Road, the terrain starts as steep mountainside with dense vegetation, progresses to undulating hills, and finally becomes rather flat and comparatively arid. Anyone arriving at Hewanorra International Airport, which is in Vieux Fort, and staying at a resort near Soufrière will travel along this route, a journey of about 30 minutes.

From Vieux Fort north to Castries, a 1¼-hour drive, the East Coast Road twists through Micoud, Dennery, and other coastal villages. It then winds up, down, and around mountains, crosses Barre de l'Isle

Ridge, and slices through the rain forest. The scenery is breathtaking. The Atlantic Ocean pounds against rocky cliffs, and acres and acres of bananas and coconut palms blanket the hillsides. If you arrive at Hewanorra and stay at a resort near Castries, you'll travel along the East Coast Road.

Numbers in the margin correspond to points of interest on the St. Lucia map.

CASTRIES & THE NORTH

Castries, the capital city, and the area north of it are the island's most-developed areas. The roads are straight, mostly flat, and easy to navigate. The beaches are some of the island's best. Rodney Bay Marina and most of the resorts, restaurants, and nightspots are in this area. Pigeon Island, one of the important historical sites, is at the island's northwestern tip.

WHAT TO SEE

Bounty Rum Distillery. St. Lucia Distillers, which produces the island's own Bounty Rum, offers 90-minute "Rhythm and Rum" tours of its distillery, including information on the history of sugar, the background of rum, a detailed description of the distillation process, colorful displays of local architecture, a glimpse at a typical rum shop, Caribbean music, and, of course, a chance to sample the company's rums and liqueurs. The distillery is at the Roseau Sugar Factory in the Roseau Valley, on the island's largest banana plantation, a few miles south of Castries and not far from Marigot. Reservations for the tour are essential. ⊠ *Roseau Sugar Factory, West Coast Rd., Roseau* ☎ *758/451–4258* ⊟ *$5* ☉ *Weekdays 9–3.*

☾ **Castries.** The capital, a busy commercial city of about 65,000 people, wraps around a sheltered bay. Morne Fortune rises sharply to the south of town, creating a dramatic green backdrop. The charm of Castries lies almost entirely in its liveliness, since most of the colonial buildings were destroyed by four fires that occurred between 1796 and 1948. Freighters (exporting bananas, coconut, cocoa, mace, nutmeg, and citrus fruits) and cruise ships come and go daily, making Castries Harbour one of the Caribbean's busiest ports. Pointe Seraphine is a duty-free shopping complex on the north side of the harbor, about a 20-minute walk or 2-minute cab ride from the city center; a launch ferries passengers across the harbor when ships are in port. Pointe Seraphine's attractive Spanish-style architecture houses more than 20 upscale duty-free shops, a tourist information kiosk, a taxi stand, and car-rental agencies. **La Place Carenage,** on the south side of the harbor near the pier and markets, is another duty-free shopping complex with a dozen or shops and a café. **Derek Walcott Square** is a green oasis bordered by Brazil, Laborie, Micoud, and Bourbon streets. Formerly Columbus Square, it was renamed to honor the hometown poet who won the 1992 Nobel prize for literature—one of two Nobel laureates from St. Lucia (the late Sir W. Arthur Lewis won the 1979 Nobel prize in economics). Some of the 19th-century buildings that have survived fire, wind, and rain can be seen on Brazil Street, the square's southern border. On the Laborie Street side, there's a huge, 400-year-old *samaan* tree with leafy branches that shade a good portion of the square. Directly across Laborie Street from Derek Walcott Square is the Roman Catholic **Cathedral of the Immaculate Conception,** which was built in 1897. Though it's rather somber on the outside, its interior walls are decorated with colorful murals reworked by St. Lucian artist Dunstan St. Omer in 1985, just prior to Pope John Paul II's visit. This church has an active parish and is open daily for both public viewing and religious services. At the corner of Jeremie and Peynier streets, spreading beyond its brilliant orange roof, is the **Castries Market.** Full of excitement and bustle, the market is open every day except Sunday. It's liveliest on Saturday morning, when farmers bring their fresh produce and spices to town, as they have for more than a century. Next door to the produce market is the **Craft Market,** where you can buy pottery, wood carvings, and handwoven straw articles. Across Peynier Street from the Craft Market, at the **Vendor's Arcade,** there are still more handicrafts and souvenirs.

Ft. Charlotte. Begun in 1764 by the French as the Citadelle du Morne Fortune, Ft. Charlotte was completed after 20 years of battling and changing hands. Its old barracks and batteries are now government buildings and local educational facilities, but you can drive around and look at the remains, including redoubts, a guardroom, stables, and cells. You can also walk up to the Inniskilling Monument, a tribute to the 1796 battle in which the 27th Foot Royal Inniskilling Fusiliers wrested the Morne from the French. At the military cemetery, which was first used in 1782, faint inscriptions on the tombstones tell the tales of French and English soldiers who died here. Six former governors of the island are buried here as well. From this point atop Morne Fortune you can view Martinique to the north and the twin peaks of the Pitons to the south.

Government House. The official residence of the governor-general of St. Lucia, one of the island's few remaining examples of Victorian architecture, is perched high above Castries, halfway up Morne Fortune—the "Hill of Good Fortune"—which forms a backdrop for the capital city. Morne Fortune has also overlooked more than its share of *bad* luck over the years, including devastating hurricanes and four fires that leveled Castries. Within Government House itself is **Le Pavillon Royal Museum,** which houses important historical photographs and documents, artifacts, crockery, silverware, medals, and awards; original architectural drawings of Government House are displayed on the walls. However, you must make an appointment to visit. ⊠ *Morne Fortune, Castries* ☎ *758/452–2481* 🖼 *Free* 🕘 *Tues. and Thurs. 10–noon and 2–4, by appointment only.*

★ **Marigot Bay.** This is one of the prettiest natural harbors in the Caribbean. In 1778, British admiral Samuel Barrington sailed into this secluded bay-within-a-bay and covered his ships with palm fronds to hide them from the French. Today this picturesque community—where parts of the original movie *Doctor Dolittle* were filmed in the late 1960s—is a favorite anchorage. A 24-hour ferry ($2 round-trip) connects the bay's two shores—a voyage that takes about a minute each way. Marigot Bay has undergone a radical, yet environmentally friendly, transformation. **Discovery at Marigot Bay**—a luxury resort, marina, and marina village with restaurants, bars, grocery store, bakery, boutiques, and other services and activities—has totally revitalized the area and took great pains to protect both the beauty and the ecology of Marigot Bay—including adding *Sunshine Express,* a solar-powered ferry, to transport people across the bay.

Marquis Estate. If you want a close-up view of a working plantation and are willing to get a little wet and muddy in the process, you can tour the island's largest one. The 600-acre Marquis Estate, situated on the northern Atlantic coast, began as a sugar plantation. Now it produces bananas and copra (dried coconut processed for oil) for export, as well as a number of other tropical fruits and vegetables for local consumption. St. Lucia Representative Services Ltd. conducts the tour and will pick you up at your hotel in an air-conditioned bus. You can see the estate by bus or on horseback; a river ride to the coast and lunch at the plantation house are both included. Self-drive tours and private taxi tours aren't permitted. Wear casual clothes. ✉ *Marquis Bay* ☎ *758/452–3762* ۞ *Tours by reservation only.*

☺ ★ **Pigeon Island National Park.** Jutting out from the northwest coast, Pigeon Island is connected to the mainland by a causeway. Tales are told of the pirate Jambe de Bois (Wooden Leg), who once hid out on this 44-acre hilltop islet—a strategic point during the French and British struggles for control of St. Lucia. Now it's a national park and a venue for concerts, festivals, and family gatherings. There are two small beaches with calm waters for swimming and snorkeling, a restaurant, and picnic areas. Scattered around the grounds are ruins of barracks, batteries, and garrisons that date from 18th-century French and English battles. In the Museum and Interpretative Centre, housed in the restored British officers' mess, a multimedia display explains the island's ecological and historical significance. ✉ *Pigeon Island, St. Lucia National Trust, Rodney Bay* ☎ *758/452–5005* ⊕ *www.slunatrust.org* ▣ *$4* ۞ *Daily 9–5.*

☺ ★ **Rain Forest Sky Rides.** Ever wish you could get a bird's-eye view of the rain forest or experience it without hiking up and down miles of mountain trails? Here's your chance. Depending on your athleticism, choose the 75-minute aerial tram ride, the zip-line experience, or both. Either guarantees a magnificent view as you peacefully slip or actively zip through and sometimes above the canopy of the 3,442-acre Castries Waterworks Rain Forest in Babonneau, 30 minutes east of Rodney Bay. On the tram ride, eight-passenger gondolas glide slowly among the giant trees, twisting vines, and dense thickets of vegetation accented by colorful flowers as a tour guide explains and shares anecdotes about the various trees, plants, birds, and other wonders of nature found in the area. The zip line, on the other hand, is a thrilling experience in which you're rigged with a harness, helmet, and clamps that attach to cables strategically strung through the forest. Short trails connect the 10 lines, so riders come down to earth briefly and hike to the next station before speeding through the forest canopy to the next stop. Bring binoculars *and a camera.* ⊠*Chassin, Babonneau* ☎*758/458–5151* ⊕*www.rfat. com* ▣*Tram $72, zip line $60; combo $85* ⊙*Daily 9–4.*

Rodney Bay. About 15 minutes north of Castries, the natural bay and an 80-acre man-made lagoon—surrounded by hotels and many popular restaurants—are named for British admiral George Rodney, who sailed the English Navy out of Gros Islet Bay in 1780 to attack and ultimately decimate the French fleet. Rodney Bay Marina is one of the Caribbean's premier yachting centers and the destination of the Atlantic Rally for Cruisers (transatlantic yacht crossing) each December. Yacht charters and sightseeing day trips can be arranged at the marina. The Rodney Bay Ferry makes hourly crossings between the marina and the shopping complex, as well as daily excursions to Pigeon Island.

SOUFRIÈRE

Soufrière is the destination of most sightseeing trips. This is where you can view the landmark Pitons and explore the French-colonial capital of St. Lucia, with its drive-in volcano, botanical gardens, working plantations, and countless other examples of the natural beauty for which St. Lucia is deservedly famous.

WHAT TO SEE

Diamond Botanical Gardens & Waterfall. These splendid gardens are part of Soufrière Estate, a 2,000-acre land grant made in 1713 by Louis XIV to three Devaux brothers from Normandy in recognition of their services to France. The estate is still owned by their descendants; Joan Du Bouley Devaux maintains the gardens. Bushes and shrubs bursting with brilliant flowers grow beneath towering trees and line pathways that lead to a natural gorge. Water bubbling to the surface from underground sulfur springs streams downhill in rivulets to become Diamond Waterfall, deep within the botanical gardens. Through the centuries, the rocks over which the cascade spills have become encrusted with minerals and tinted yellow, green, and purple. Near the falls, curative mineral baths are fed by the underground springs. For a small fee you can slip into your swimsuit and bathe for 30 minutes in one of the outside pools; a private bath costs slightly more. King Louis XVI of France provided funds in 1784 for the construction of a building with a dozen large stone baths to fortify his troops against the St. Lucian climate. It's claimed that Joséphine Bonaparte bathed here as a young girl while visiting her father's plantation nearby. During the Brigand's War, just after the French Revolution, the bathhouse was destroyed. In 1930 the site was excavated by André Du Boulay, and two of the original stone baths were restored for his use. The outside baths were added later. ⊠*Soufrière Estate, Diamond Rd., Soufrière* ☎*758/452–4759 or 758/454–7565* ▣*$2.75, outside bath $2.50, private bath $3.75* ⊙*Mon.–Sat. 10–5, Sun. 10–3.*

Edmund Forest Reserve. Dense tropical rain forest stretches from one side of the island to the other, sprawling over 19,000 acres of mountains and valleys. It's home to a multitude of exotic flowers and plants, as well as rare birds—including the brightly feathered Jacquot parrot. The Edmund Forest Reserve, on the island's western side, is most easily accessible from just east of Soufrière, on the road to Fond St. Jacques. A trek through the lush landscape, with spectacular views of mountains, valleys, and the sea beyond, can take three or more hours. It takes an hour or so just to reach the reserve by car from the north end of the island. It's a strenuous hike, so you need plenty of stamina and sturdy hiking shoes. Permission from the Forest & Lands Department is required to access reserve trails, and the department requires that a naturalist or forest officer guide you because the vegetation is so dense. ⊠ *East of Fond St. Jacques* ☎ *758/450–2231, 758/450–2078 for Forest & Lands Department* 🎫 *Guide $10, guided tours that include round-trip transportation from your hotel $55–$85* ⊙ *Daily by appointment only.*

Fond Doux Estate. One of the earliest French estates established by land grant (1745 and 1763), 135 hilly acres of this old plantation still produce cocoa, citrus, bananas, coconut, and vegetables; the restored 1864 plantation house is still in use as well. A 30-minute walking tour begins at the cocoa fermentary, where you can see the drying process under way. You then follow a trail through the lush cultivated area, where a guide points out the various fruit- or spice-bearing trees and tropical flowers. Additional trails lead to old military ruins, a religious shrine, and another vantage point for the spectacular Pitons. Cool drinks and a creole buffet lunch are available at the restaurant. Souvenirs, including just-made chocolate balls, are sold at the boutique. ⊠ *Chateaubelair, Soufrière* ☎ *758/459–7545* ⊕ *www.fonddouxestate.com* 🎫 *$6, buffet lunch $14* ⊙ *Daily 9–4.*

Ⓒ **Morne Coubaril.** On the site of an 18th-century estate, a 250-acre land grant by Louis XIV of France in 1713, the original plantation house has been renovated and a farm worker's village has been re-created to show visitors what life was like for both the owners (a single family that owned the landed until 1960) and those who did all the hard labor over the centuries producing cotton, coffee, sugarcane, and cocoa. Cocoa, coconuts, and manioc are still grown on the estate using traditional agricultural methods. Guides show how coconuts are opened and roasted for use as oil and animal feed and how cocoa is fermented, dried, crushed by a man dancing on the beans, and finally formed into chocolate sticks. Manioc roots are grated, squeezed of excess water, dried, and turned into farina and cassava used in baking. The grounds are lovely for walking or hiking, and the view of mountain and sea are spellbinding. The Pitt, a large, open-air restaurant, serves a creole buffet at lunchtime by reservation only. ⊠ *Soufrière* ☎ *758/459–7340* 🎫 *$5.50; $10 including lunch* ⊙ *Daily 9–4:30.*

Fodor'sChoice **The Pitons.** These two unusual mountains, named a UNESCO World ★ Heritage Site in 2004, rise precipitously from the cobalt-blue Caribbean Sea just south of Soufrière. The Pitons are, in fact, the symbol of St. Lucia. Covered with thick tropical vegetation, the massive outcroppings were formed by lava from a volcanic eruption 30 to 40 million years ago. They are not identical twins since—confusingly—2,619-foot Petit Piton is taller than 2,461-foot Gros Piton, though Gros Piton is, as the word translates, broader. Gros Piton is the easier climb, though the trail up even this shorter Piton is one very tough trek and requires the permission of the Forest & Lands Department and a knowledgeable guide. ☎*758/450–2231, 758/450–2078 for St. Lucia Forest & Lands Department, 758/459–9748 for Pitons Tour Guide Association* ✆*Guide services $45* ☉*Daily by appointment only.*

Soufrière. The oldest town in St. Lucia and the former French-colonial capital, Soufrière was founded by the French in 1746 and named for its proximity to the volcano. The wharf is the center of activity in this sleepy town (which currently has a population of about 9,000), particularly when a cruise ship is moored in pretty Soufrière Bay. French-colonial influences can be noticed in the architecture of the wooden buildings, with second-story verandahs and gingerbread trim that surround the market square. The market building itself is decorated with colorful murals. The **Soufrière Tourist Information Centre** (✉*Bay St., Soufrière* ☎*758/459–7200*) provides information about area attractions. Note that outside some of the popular attractions in and around Soufrière, souvenir vendors can be persistent. Be polite but firm if you're not interested in their wares.

☺ **La Soufrière Drive-In Volcano.** As you approach, your nose will pick up
★ the strong scent of the sulfur springs—more than 20 belching pools of muddy water, multicolor sulfur deposits, and other assorted minerals baking and steaming on the surface. Actually, you don't drive in. You drive up within a few hundred feet of the gurgling, steaming mass, then walk behind your guide—whose service is included in the admission price—around a fault in the substratum rock. It's a fascinating, educational half hour, though it can also be pretty stinky on a hot day. ✉*Bay St., Soufrière* ☎*758/459–5500* ✆*$1.25* ☉*Daily 9–5.*

VIEUX FORT & THE EAST COAST

Vieux Fort is on the southeast tip of St, Lucia and the location of Hewanorra International Airport, which serves all jet aircraft arriving and departing St. Lucia. Although less developed for tourism than the island's north and west (although that is expected to change dramatically in coming years), the area around Vieux Fort and along the east coast is home to some of St. Lucia's unique ecosystems and interesting natural attractions.

WHAT TO SEE

Barre de l'Isle Forest Reserve. St. Lucia is divided into eastern and western halves by Barre de l'Isle ridge. A mile-long (1.5-km-long) trail cuts through the reserve, and four lookout points provide panoramic views. Visible in the distance are Mt. Gimie, immense green valleys, both the Caribbean Sea and the Atlantic Ocean, and coastal communities. The reserve is about a half-hour drive from Castries; it takes about an hour to walk the trail—an easy hike—and another hour to climb Mt. La Combe Ridge. Permission from the St. Lucia Forest & Lands Department is required to access the trail in Barre de l'Isle; a naturalist or forest officer guide will accompany you. ✉*Trailhead on East Coast*

Rd., near Ravine Poisson, midway between Castries and Dennery ☏ *758/450–2231 or 758/450–2078* 🖃 *Guide services $10* ⊙ *Daily by appointment only.*

Frégate Island Nature Reserve. A mile-long (1.5-km) trail encircles the nature reserve, which you reach from the East Coast Road near the fishing village of Praslin. In this area, boatbuilders still fashion traditional fishing canoes, called *gommiers* after the trees from which the hulls are made. The ancient design was used by the original Amerindian people who populated the Caribbean. A natural promontory at Praslin provides a lookout from which you can view the two small islets Frégate Major and Frégate Minor and—with luck—the frigate birds that nest here from May to July. The only way to visit is on a guided tour, which includes a ride in a gommier to Frégate Minor for a picnic lunch and a swim; all trips are by reservation only and require a minimum of two people. Arrange visits through your hotel, a tour operator, or the St. Lucia National Trust; many tours include round-trip transportation from your hotel as well as the tour cost. ☒ *Praslin* ☏ *758/452–5005, 758/453–7656, 758/454–5014 for tour reservations* ⊕ *www.sluna trust.org* 🖃 *$18* ⊙ *Daily by appointment only.*

Mamiku Gardens. One of St. Lucia's largest and loveliest botanical gardens surrounds the hilltop ruins of the Micoud Estate. Baron Micoud, an 18th-century colonel in the French Army and governor general of St. Lucia, deeded the land to his wife, Madame de Micoud, to avoid confiscation by the British during one of the many times when St. Lucia changed hands. Locals abbreviated her name to "Ma Micoud," which, over time, became "Mamiku." Nevertheless, the estate did become a British military outpost in 1796 but, shortly thereafter, was burned to the ground by slaves during the Brigand's War. The estate is now primarily a banana plantation, but the gardens themselves—including several secluded or "secret" gardens—are filled with tropical flowers and plants, including delicate orchids and fragrant herbs. Admission includes a guided tour. ☒ *Vieux Fort Hwy., Praslin* ☏ *758/455–3729* 🖃 *$6* ⊙ *Daily 9–5.*

Maria Islands Nature Reserve. Two tiny islands in the Atlantic Ocean, off St. Lucia's southeast coast, compose the reserve, which has its own interpretive center. The 25-acre Maria Major and the 4-acre Maria Minor, its little sister, are inhabited by two rare species of reptiles (the colorful Zandoli Terre ground lizard and the harmless Kouwes grass snake) that share their home with frigate birds, terns, doves, and other wildlife. There's a small beach for swimming and snorkeling, as well as an undisturbed forest, a vertical cliff covered with cacti, and a coral reef for snorkeling or diving. Tours, including the boat trip to the islands, are offered by the St. Lucia National Trust by appointment only; you should bring your own picnic lunch because there are no facilities. ☒ *St. Lucia National Trust Regional Office, Vieux Fort* ☏ *758/452–5005, 758/453–7656, 758/454–5014 for tour reservations* ⊕ *www.slunatrust.org* 🖃 *$35* ⊙ *Aug.–mid-May, Wed.–Sun. 9:30–5, by appointment only.*

Vieux Fort. St. Lucia's second-largest port is where you'll find Hewanorra International Airport. From the Moule à Chique Peninsula, the island's southernmost tip, you can see all of St. Lucia to the north and the island of St. Vincent 21 mi (34 km) south. This is where the waters of the clear Caribbean Sea blend with those of the deeper blue Atlantic Ocean.

ST. LUCIA ESSENTIALS

To research prices, get advice from other travelers, and book travel arrangements, visit www.fodors.com.

▌ TRANSPORTATION

BY AIR

Air Canada has direct weekend service to Hewanorra International Airport in Vieux Fort from Toronto. Air Jamaica flies to Hewanorra from New York via Barbados or Montego Bay. American Airlines flies nonstop daily between Hewanorra and Miami and thrice weekly between Hewanorra and New York (JFK); American also offers connecting service from New York and other major U.S. cities through San Juan via American Eagle to George F. L. Charles Airport in Castries. British Airways flies weekly between London Gatwick and Hewanorra. US Airways flies twice weekly to Hewanorra from Philadelphia and Charlotte. Virgin Atlantic flies nonstop to Hewanorra from London Gatwick.

Air Caraïbes flies between George F. L. Charles Airport and Guadeloupe and Martinique; LIAT flies into George F. L. Charles Airport from several neighboring islands.

Airline Information Air Canada (758/454–6038 www.aircanada.com). **Air Caraïbes** (758/453–0357 www. aircaraibes.com). **Air Jamaica** (758/453–6611 or 800/523–5585 www.airjamaica. com). **American Airlines/American Eagle** (758/452–1820, 758/454–6777, or 800/744–0006 www.aa.com). **British Airways** (758/452–3951 www.britis-hairways.com). **LIAT** (758/452–3056 or

888/844–5428 www.liat.com). **US Airways** (758/454–8186 www.usairways.com). **Virgin Atlantic** (758/454–3610 www. virginatlantic.com).

AIRPORTS & TRANSFERS

St. Lucia has two airports. Hewanorra International Airport accommodates large jet aircraft and is at the southeastern tip of the island in Vieux Fort. George F. L. Charles Airport (also referred to as Vigie Airport) is at Vigie Point in Castries, in the northwestern part of the island, and accommodates only prop aircraft due to its location and runway limitations.

Many large resorts—particularly the all-inclusive ones—and package tour operators provide round-trip airport transfers. That's a significant amenity if you're landing at Hewanorra, as the one-way taxi fare for the 60- to 90-minute ride (depending on whether you're headed to Soufrière or Castries) is expensive—$55 to $75 for up to four passengers. Taxis are always available at the airports.

If you land instead at George F. L. Charles Airport, it's a short drive to resorts in the north, about 20 minutes to Marigot Bay, but more than an hour to Soufrière.

Some people opt for a helicopter transfer between Hewanorra and either Castries or Soufrière, a quick 7- to 10-minute ride with a beautiful view at a one-way cost if $120 to $140 per passenger. Helicopters operate in daylight hours only and carry up to six passengers.

Airport Information George F. L. Charles Airport (SLU 758/452–1156). **Hewanorra International Airport** (UVF 758/454–

6355). **St. Lucia Helicopters** (✉ Pointe Seraphine, Castries ☎758/453–6950 ⊕www. stluciahelicopters.com).

BY BOAT & FERRY

Cruise ships from major lines call at Castries and sometimes off Soufrière. At Port Castries, ships tie up at berths right in town and are convenient to duty-free shops, the market, and transportation for sightseeing excursions. When cruise ships are in port, a water taxi shuttles back and forth between Pointe Seraphine on the north side of the harbor and Place Carenage on the south side of the harbor for $1 per person each way. In Soufrière, ships anchor offshore, and passengers are transferred ashore by tenders.

For visitors arriving at Rodney Bay on their own or chartered yachts, Rodney Bay Marina is an official port of entry for customs and immigration purposes. A ferry travels between the marina and the shopping complex daily on the hour, from 9 to 4, for $4 per person round-trip.

Information Rodney Bay Ferry (☎758/452–8816).

BY BUS

Privately owned and operated minivans constitute St. Lucia's bus system, an inexpensive and efficient means of transportation used primarily by local people. Minivan routes cover the entire island and run from early morning until approximately 10 PM. You may find this method of getting around most useful for short distances, between Castries and the Rodney Bay area, for example; longer hauls can be uncomfortable. The fare between Castries and Gablewoods Mall is EC$1.25; Castries and Rodney Bay, EC$2; Castries and Gros Islet, EC$2.25; Castries and Vieux Fort (a trip that takes more than two hours), EC$7; Castries and Soufrière (a bone-crushing journey that takes even longer), EC$10. Minivans follow designated routes (signs are displayed on the front window); ask at your hotel for the appropriate route

number for your destination. Wait at a marked bus stop or hail a passing minivan from the roadside. In Castries, buses depart from the corner of Micoud and Bridge streets, behind the markets.

In addition to the driver, each minivan usually has a conductor, a young man whose job it is to collect fares, open the door, and generally take charge of the passenger area. If you're sure of where you're going, simply knock twice on the metal window frame to signal that you want to get off at the next stop. Otherwise, just let the conductor or driver know where you're going, and he'll stop at the appropriate place.

BY CAR

To rent a car you must be at least 25 years old and provide a valid driver's license and a credit card. If you don't have an international driver's license, you must buy a temporary St. Lucian driving permit at car-rental firms, the immigration office at either airport, or the Gros Islet police station. The permit costs $20 (EC$54) and is valid for three months. Car-rental rates are usually quoted in U.S. dollars and range from $50 to $80 per day or $300 to $425 per week, depending on the car. Car-rental agencies generally include free pickup at your hotel and unlimited mileage.

St. Lucia has about 500 mi (800 km) of roads, but only about half (281 mi [450 km]) are paved. All towns and villages are connected to major routes. The highways on both coasts are winding and mountainous—particularly on parts of the West Coast Road. Driving in St. Lucia is on the left, British style. Observe speed limits, particularly the 30-mph (50-kph) limit within Castries. Respect no-parking zones; police issue tickets, and penalties start at about $15 (EC$40). And wear your seat belts—it's the law!

Information Avis (✉Vide Bouteille, Castries ☎758/452–2700 ✉Vieux Fort ☎758/454–6325 ✉Vigie ☎758/452–2046 ⊕www.

avisstlucia.com). **Budget** (✉Bois d'Orange, Gros Islet ☎758/452-9887 ✉Vieux Fort ☎758/454-7470 ✉Vigie ☎758/452-3516 ⊕www.budget-stlucia.com). **Cool Breeze Jeep/Car Rental** (✉Soufrière ☎758/459-7729 ⊕www.coolbreezecarrental.com/stlucia). **Courtesy Car Rental** (✉Bois d'Orange, Gros Islet ☎758/452-8140 ⊕www.courtesycarrentals.com). **Hertz** (✉Castries ☎758/452-0679 ✉Vieux Fort ☎758/454-9636 ✉Vigie ☎758/451-7351 ⊕www.sunfuntoursltd.com).

BY TAXI

Taxis are always available at the airports, the harbor, and in front of major hotels. They're unmetered, although nearly all drivers belong to a taxi cooperative and adhere to standard fares. Sample fares for up to four passengers are as follows: Castries to Rodney Bay, $20; Rodney Bay to Cap Estate, $10; Castries to Cap Estate, $25; Castries to Marigot Bay, $25; Castries to Anse La aye, $30; Castries to Soufrière, $70. Always ask the driver to quote the price *before* you get in, and be sure that you both understand whether it's quoted in EC or U.S. dollars. Drivers are careful, knowledgeable, and courteous.

∎ CONTACTS & RESOURCES

BANKS & EXCHANGE SERVICES

The official currency is the Eastern Caribbean dollar (EC$). It's linked to the U.S. dollar at EC$2.67, but, simply for convenience, stores and hotels often exchange at EC$2.50 or EC$2.60. U.S. currency is readily accepted, but you'll receive change in EC dollars—so use your smallest-denomination U.S. bill when making a purchase. Major credit cards and traveler's checks are widely accepted, as well. ATMs are available 24 hours a day at bank branches, transportation centers, and shopping malls, where you can use major credit cards to obtain cash (in local currency only). Major banks on the island include the Bank of Nova Scotia, FirstCaribbean International Bank, and the Royal Bank of Canada.

Prices quoted in this chapter are in U.S. dollars unless otherwise indicated.

ELECTRICITY

The electric current on St. Lucia is 220 volts, 50 cycles, with a square, three-pin plug (U.K. standard). A few large hotels have 110-volt outlets for electric razors only. To use most North American appliances, you'll need a transformer to convert voltage and a plug adapter; dual-voltage computers or appliances will still need a plug adapter. Hotels will sometimes lend you a plug adapter for use during your stay.

EMERGENCIES

Victoria Hospital is St. Lucia's main hospital, on the southwest side of Castries Harbour heading toward La Toc. Regional medical facilities are at Dennery Hospital on the island's east coast, St. Jude's Hospital near Hewanorra International Airport, and Soufrière Hospital in the southwest.

Ambulance & Fire Ambulance and fire emergencies (☎911).

Hospitals Dennery Hospital (✉Main Rd., Dennery ☎758/453-3310). **St. Jude's Hospital** (✉Airport Rd., Vieux Fort ☎758/454-6041). **Soufrière Hospital** (✉W. Quinlan St., Soufrière ☎758/459-7258). **Victoria Hospital** (✉Hospital Rd., Castries ☎758/452-2421).

Police Dial 999. **Marine police** (☎758/453-0770 or 758/452-2595). **Sea-Air Rescue** (☎758/452-2894, 758/452-1182, or 758/453-6664).

HEALTH

Tap water is perfectly safe to drink throughout the island. Be sure to wash fruit thoroughly or, better yet, peel it before eating. Insects can be a real bother during the wet season (July–November), particularly in the rain forest; bring along repellent to ward off mosquitoes and sand flies.

INTERNET, MAIL & SHIPPING

Many hotels and resorts in St. Lucia offer free or inexpensive Internet access to their guests. Internet cafés can be found in and around Rodney Bay Marina. Cable & Wireless maintains a public Internet kiosk at Pointe Seraphine, in Castries, that accepts major credit cards or cash.

The General Post Office is on Bridge Street in Castries and is open weekdays from 8:30 to 4:30; all towns and villages have branches. Postage for airmail letters to the United States, Canada, and the United Kingdom is EC95¢ per ½ ounce; postcards are EC65¢. Airmail letters to Australia and New Zealand cost EC$1.35; postcards, EC70¢. Airmail can take two or three weeks to be delivered—even longer to Australia and New Zealand.

Information CIBS Cafe (⊠ Chisel and St. Louis Sts., Castries ☎ 758/458-2195). **Cyber Connections** (⊠ Rodney Bay Marina, Gros Islet ☎ 758/450-9309). **Destination St. Lucia (DSL) Ltd.** (⊠ Rodney Bay Marina, Gros Islet ☎ 758/452-8531).

LANGUAGE

English is the official language of St. Lucia and is spoken everywhere, but you can often hear local people speaking a French-Creole patois (Kwéyòl) among themselves. If you're interested in learning some patois words and phrases, pick up a copy of *A Visitor's Guide to St. Lucia Patois,* a small paperback book sold in local bookstores for $4.

As in many Caribbean islands, to "lime" is to hang out and a "jump-up" is a big party with lots of dance music (often in the street, as in the village of Gros Islet every Friday night). North American women, especially, will find it charming to be called "milady." And don't be surprised when people in St. Lucia call you "darling" instead of "ma'am" or "sir"—they're being friendly, not forward.

SAFETY

Although crime isn't a significant problem, take the same precautions you would at home—lock your door, secure your valuables, and don't carry too much money or flaunt expensive jewelry on the street.

The Rapid Response Unit is a special police brigade dedicated to visitor security in and around Rodney Bay.

Rapid Response Unit (⊠ Rodney Bay, Gros Islet ☎ 758/452-8155).

TAXES & SERVICE CHARGES

The departure tax is $26 (EC$68), payable in cash only (either EC or U.S. dollars). A government tax of 8% is added to all hotel and restaurant bills. There's no sales tax on goods purchased in shops. Most restaurants add a service charge of 10% to restaurant bills in lieu of tipping.

TELEPHONES

The area code for St. Lucia is 758. You can make direct-dial overseas and inter-island calls from St. Lucia, and the connections are excellent. You can charge an overseas call to a major credit card with no surcharge. From public phones and many hotels, dial 811 and charge the call to your credit card to avoid expensive rates or hotel surcharges. Phone cards can be purchased at many retail outlets and used from any touch-tone telephone (including pay phones) in St. Lucia. You can dial local calls throughout St. Lucia directly from your hotel room by connecting to an outside line and dialing the seven-digit number. Some hotels charge a small fee (usually about EC50¢) for local calls. Pay phones accept EC25¢ and EC$1 coins. Phone cards can be used for local calls, as well as for international calls.

Your cell phone may work, but roaming charges may be prohibitively expensive. Cell phones can be rented from Cable & Wireless offices in Castries, Gablewoods Mall, Rodney Bay Marina, and Vieux Fort; or, if you have an "unlocked" cell phone that uses GSM technology, you can purchase a local SIM card for $20 (which includes an $8 call credit) at Digicel offices in those same areas. The cards can be topped up at hundreds of business locations around the island.

Information **AT&T** (☎800/872–2881). **Cable & Wireless** (☎758/453–9922). **Digicel** (☎758/456–3400 or 758/456–3444).

TIPPING

Most restaurants add a 10% service charge to your bill in lieu of a tip; if one has not been added, a 10% to 15% tip is appropriate for good service. Tip porters and bellhops $1 per bag and hotel maids $1 or $2 per night, although many of the all-inclusive resorts have a no-tipping policy. Taxi drivers and tour guides also appreciate a 10% to 12% tip.

VISITOR INFORMATION

Before You Leave St. Lucia Tourist Board (⊕www.stlucia.org ☎212/867–2950 in New York or 800/456–3984).

In St. Lucia St. Lucia Tourist Board (⊠Sureline Bldg., Vide Bouteille, Box 221, Castries ☎758/452–4094 or 758/452–5968 ⊠Jeremie St., Castries ☎758/452–2479 ⊠Pointe Seraphine, Castries ☎758/452–7577 ⊠Bay St., Soufrière ☎758/459–7419 ⊠George F.L. Charles Airport, Vigie, Castries ☎758/452–2596 ⊠Hewanorra International Airport, Vieux Fort ☎758/454–6644).

WEDDINGS

St. Lucia may be *the* most popular island in all of the Caribbean for weddings and honeymoons. Nearly all of St. Lucia's resort hotels and most of the small inns offer attractive wedding-honeymoon packages, as well as coordinators to handle the legalities and plan a memorable event. Sandals properties offer complimentary weddings to couples booking a minimum-stay honeymoon. Rendezvous, a couples-only resort, is also a popular wedding venue. The most striking setting, though, is probably smack between the Pitons at either Ladera or the Jalousie Plantation.

You can marry on the same day you arrive in St. Lucia if you apply for a "special" marriage license, pay the $200 fee, and have all the necessary documents. You must present valid passports, birth certificates, a divorce decree if either party is divorced, an appropriate death certificate if either party is widowed, and a notarized parental consent if either party is under the age of 18. Most couples opt for the standard marriage license, which costs $125 and requires two days of residence on the island prior to the wedding ceremony. After two days, a local solicitor can apply for a license on your behalf. In either case, special or standard, you can expect additional registrar and certificate fees amounting to about $40. Resort wedding coordinators will help you put together the correct paperwork and, if you wish, will arrange photographer, flowers, musicians, church or other locations for the ceremony, and food and beverage for a reception.

St. Maarten/St. Martin

Beach, Ilet Pinel, Sint Maarten

WORD OF MOUTH

"There are still hidden treasures to be found and special qualities that remain on St. Martin/Maarten."

—Barbara1

"If you want more active night life I would suggest staying on the Dutch side, as that is where most of it is, including casinos. It is better to drive during the day to the French side to explore."

—Snubes

WELCOME TO ST. MAARTEN/ST. MARTIN

If you're on the island during the full moon, head out to Kali's Beach Bar, on lovely Baie de Friar, for the Full Moon Party, an island institution.

KEY

⚑	Beaches
⛴	Cruise Ship Terminal
◼	Dive Sites
⛴	Ferry
❶	Restaurants
⊡	Hotels

TWO NATIONS, ONE ISLAND

St. Maarten/St. Martin is home to approximately 77,000 people from some 70 different countries, but governance of the 37-square-mi (96-square-km) island is split between France and the Netherlands. It's the smallest island in the world divided between two ruling powers. The Dutch capital is Philipsburg; the French capital is Marigot.

Power shoppers will be drawn to Phillipsburg's recently revitalized Front Street, much of which has been turned into a pedestrian mall.

St. Maarten/St. Martin, a half-Dutch, half-French island, is a place where gastronomy flourishes, where most resorts are large rather than small, where casinos draw gamblers, where sporting opportunities are plentiful, and where the sunning, as on the south end of Orient Beach, is *au naturel*.

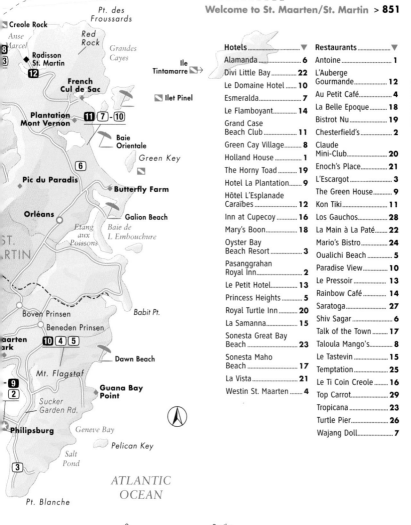

22

ST. MAARTEN & ST. MARTIN

Pt. des Froussards

Creole Rock

Anse Marcel

Radisson St. Martin

Red Rock

Grandes Cayes

Ile Tintamarre →

French Cul de Sac

Ilet Pinel

Plantation Mont Vernon

Baie Orientale

Green Key

Pic du Paradis

Butterfly Farm

Orléans

Galion Beach

Etang aux Poissons

Baie de L.Embouchure

ST. RTIN

Boven Prinsen

Beneden Prinsen

Babit Pt.

aarten ark

Dawn Beach

Mt. Flagstaf

Guana Bay Point

Sucker Garden Rd.

Philipsburg

Geneve Bay

Pelican Key

Salt Pond

ATLANTIC OCEAN

Pt. Blanche

Proselyte Reef

Hotels	▼
Alamanda	6
Divi Little Bay	22
Le Domaine Hotel	10
Esmeralda	7
Le Flamboyant	14
Grand Case Beach Club	11
Green Cay Village	8
Holland House	1
The Horny Toad	19
Hotel La Plantation	9
Hôtel L'Esplanade Caraïbes	12
Inn at Cupecoy	16
Mary's Boon	18
Oyster Bay Beach Resort	3
Pasanggrahan Royal Inn	2
Le Petit Hotel	13
Princess Heights	5
Royal Turtle Inn	20
La Samanna	15
Sonesta Great Bay Beach	23
Sonesta Maho Beach	17
La Vista	21
Westin St. Maarten	4

Restaurants	▼
Antoine	1
L'Auberge Gourmande	12
Au Petit Café	4
La Belle Epoque	18
Bistrot Nu	19
Chesterfield's	2
Claude Mini-Club	20
Enoch's Place	21
L'Escargot	3
The Green House	9
Kon Tiki	11
Los Gauchos	28
La Main à La Paté	22
Mario's Bistro	24
Oualichi Beach	5
Paradise View	10
Le Pressoir	13
Rainbow Café	14
Saratoga	27
Shiv Sagar	6
Talk of the Town	17
Taloula Mango's	8
Le Tastevin	15
Temptation	25
Le Ti Coin Creole	16
Top Carrot	29
Tropicana	23
Turtle Pier	26
Wajang Doll	7

0 — 2 miles
0 — 3 km

TO ST. BARTHÉLEMY

TOP 4 REASONS TO VISIT ST. MAARTEN & ST. MARTIN

1 Grand Case is the island's gastronomic capital, but good food seeps from almost every island pore.

2 Philipsburg is one of the best shopping spots in the Caribbean; with fewer bargains, Marigot is still chock-full of interesting stores.

3 Thirty-seven picture-perfect beaches are spread out all over the island.

4 The wide range of water sports—from sailing to waterskiing, from snorkeling to deep-sea fishing—will meet almost any need.

ST. MAARTEN/ST. MARTIN PLANNER

Island Activities

The island's **beaches** are always a highlight, but few hotels are built on the very best beaches. Baie Orientale, the island's longest and most beautiful stretch of sand, is also the most developed, but even here few of the hotels are directly on the beachfront. You'll likely want to drive around to explore some of the more out-of-the-way spots.

When you're not sunning and swimming, there are many activities to keep you going. **Sailing** and **snorkeling** trips are often the highlight of an island visit.

Fishing is good in the waters around St. Maarten, but the diving is not the best, though there are some good sites.

Baie Orientale is a center for all manner of **water sports**, and you'll see any number of people driving Jet Skis, parasailing, and waterskiing from the shore.

Perhaps one of the best activities on the island is **eating**. St. Martin's restaurants, particularly in Grand Case, are some of the Caribbean's finest.

At night, the **casinos** beckon. But don't expect Las Vegas–style gambling palaces; these casinos are much more modest in scale.

Logistics

Getting to St. Maarten/St. Martin: You'll find many non-stop flights to St. Maarten from U.S., as well as connecting service through San Juan. St. Maarten is a hub for smaller, regional airlines, so it's often easier to make the hop to Anguilla, St. Barths, Saba, or St. Eustatius by making a connection here. The island's main airport is Princess Juliana International Airport (SXM), on the Dutch side. Aeroport de L'Espérance (SFG), on the French side, is small and handles only small planes.

Hassle Factor: Low to Medium.

Nonstops: There are nonstop flights from Atlanta (Delta), Charlotte (USAirways), Chicago (United), Fort Lauderdale (Spirit), Miami (American), New York–JFK (American), New York–Newark (Continental), Philadelphia (USAirways). There are also some nonstop charter flights (including GWV/Apple Vacations from Boston). Many smaller Caribbean-based carriers offer service to St. Maarten.

On the Ground

Most visitors rent a car upon arrival, but taxi service is available at the airport if you don't want to drive yourself, with fixed fares to all hotels on the island, and you'll be able to pay the fare in U.S. dollars. Although the island is small, it's still a long drive to many hotels on the French side, so these taxi fares aren't cheap.

Renting a Car: The best and most economical way to get around St. Maarten is by car, and most people choose to rent a car so they can visit a variety of beaches and restaurants throughout their stay. You can book a car at Juliana International Airport, where all major rental companies have booths, but you still have to take a shuttle to the rental-car lot. There are both major car-rental chains as well as reputable local companies. Rates are among the best in the Caribbean. The only downside is that traffic can be very heavy, particularly around Marigot, where parking is especially difficult during the day.

22

Where to Stay

The island, though small, is well-developed—some say overdeveloped—and offers a wide range of different kinds of lodging. If you want to stay in a larger resort or time-share, concentrate your accommodations search on the Dutch side; the French side has more intimate properties. Just keep in mind that many of the island's best restaurants are in Grand Case, which is a long drive from most Dutch-side hotels. Also remember that at French-side hotels you must pay in euros, so keep that in mind when you budget.

Resorts & Time-Shares: The island's large resorts are often good, but none can be considered truly great. Many have a large time-share component, so beware the hard sell, especially if someone in Philipsburg offers you a "free" booze cruise in return for just a few minutes of your time.

Villas & Condos: Both sides of the island have a wide variety of villas and condos for every conceivable budget. If you look around, it's inevitable that you can find something that meets your needs. Several resort-style condo complexes offer a good alternative to a traditional hotel stay for families and groups.

Small Inns: Small guesthouses and inns can be found on both sides of the island. Some of the best places on the island are actually the smallest and most unassuming. They're also booked solidly year-round, so plan ahead.

Hotel & Restaurant Costs

⇨ *For information on hotel meal plans, see Accommodations in Caribbean Essentials.*

WHAT IT COSTS IN U.S. DOLLARS

$$$$	$$$	$$	$	¢
Restaurants				
over $30	$20–$30	$12–$20	$8–$12	under $8
Hotels*				
over $350	$250–$350	$150–$250	$80–$150	under $80
Hotels**				
over $450	$350–$450	$250–$350	$125–$250	under $125

*EP, BP, CP **AI, FAP, MAP Restaurant prices are for a main course, excluding taxes and service charges. Hotel prices are for two people in a double room in high season, excluding taxes, service charges, and meal plans (except at all-inclusive hotels).

When to Go

The high season begins in December and runs through the middle of April. During the off-season, hotel rooms can be had for as little as half the high-season rates.

The French side's **Carnival** is a pre-Lenten bash of costume parades, music competitions, and feasts. Carnival takes place after Easter on the Dutch side—last two weeks of April—with a parade and music competition.

On the French side, parades, ceremonies and celebration commemorate **Bastille Day** on July 14, and there's more revelry later in the month on **Grand Case Day**.

The Dutch side hosts the **Heineken Regatta** in early March, with as many as 300 sailboats competing from around the world. (For the experience of a lifetime, you can sometimes purchase a working berth aboard a regatta vessel.)

Updated
by Roberta
Sotonoff

THE MAJORITY OF THE YACHT CREW doesn't know the difference between a gaff and a gallow, but that isn't a deterrent for this race. Off they go aboard Dennis Connor's America's Cup winner *Stars and Stripes*. The wind howls through the sails, and Captain Morgan (not the pirate but a sailor from Jamaica) shouts, "Get ready to tack. We can take the lead." The trimmers, grinders, and winchers man their stations. The boat gets within hearing range of its rival, another America's Cup contender, *Canada II*, and friendly barbs are exchanged.

The St. Maarten 12-Metre Challenge is a singular experience. Then again, the island of St. Maarten/St. Martin is also quite unique. Where else can you find a 37-square-mi (96-square-km) island that is governed by two nations—the Netherlands and France—with residents from 70 different countries who speak who knows how many languages? Happily for Americans, who make up the majority of visitors, English works in both nations. Dutch St. Maarten will feel particularly comfortable for Americans, and you're as likely to run into an American expat there as anyone else, on the beach or not. But once you pass the meandering, unmarked border into the French side, you can find more pronounced differences. You'll be hard-pressed to find a washcloth unless your lodgings are very upscale, and it's almost necessary to be an engineer to bypass the safety mechanisms in the electrical outlets. And another thing: though U.S. dollars are happily accepted, be ready for wallet shock. Most things are priced in euros. Almost 4,000 years ago, it was salt and not tourism that drove the little island's economy. Arawak Indians, the island's first known inhabitants, prospered until the warring Caribs invaded, adding the peaceful Arawaks to their list of conquests. Columbus spotted the isle in 1493, but it wasn't populated by Europeans until the 17th century, when it was claimed by the Dutch, French, and Spanish. The Dutch and French finally joined forces to claim the island in 1644, and the Treaty of Concordia partitioned the territory in 1648.

Both sides of the island offer a little European culture along with a lot of laid-back Caribbean ambience. Water sports abound—diving, snorkeling, scuba, sailing, windsurfing, and in late February the Heineken Regatta, with as many as 300 sailboats competing from around the world. (For the experience of a lifetime, some visitors purchase a working berth aboard a regatta vessel.)

With soft trade winds cooling the subtropical climate, it's easy to while away the day relaxing on one of the 37 beaches, strolling Philipsburg's boardwalk, and perusing the shops on Philipsburg's Front Street or the *rues* (streets) of the very French town of Marigot. While luck is an important commodity at St. Maarten's 13 casinos, chance plays no part in finding a good meal at the excellent eateries or after-dark fun in the subtle to sizzling nightlife. Still, the isle's biggest assets are its friendly residents.

Although the island has been heavily developed—especially on the Dutch side—roads could still use work. When cruise ships are in port (and there can be as many as seven at once), shopping areas are

CLOSE UP

Concordia

The smallest island in the world to be shared between two different countries, St. Maarten/St. Martin has existed peacefully in its subdivided state for more than 360 years. The Treaty of Concordia, which subdivided the island, was signed in 1648 and was really inspired by the two resident colonies of French and Dutch settlers (not to mention their respective governments) joining forces to repel a common enemy, the Spanish, in 1644. Although the French were promised the side of the island facing Anguilla and the Dutch the south side of the island, the boundary itself wasn't firmly established until 1817 and then after several disputes (16 of them, to be exact).

Visitors to the island will likely not even notice that they have passed from the Dutch to the French side unless they notice that the roads on the French side feel a little smoother. In 2003, the population of St-Martin (and St-Barthélemy) voted to secede from Guadeloupe, the administrative capital of the French West Indies. That detachment became official in February 2007, and St-Martin is now officially known as the Collectivité de Saint-Martin.

crowded and traffic moves at a snail's pace. Still, these are minor inconveniences compared to the feel of the sand between your toes or the breeze through your hair, gourmet food sating your appetite, or having the ability to crisscross between two nations on one island.

WHERE TO STAY

Scattered up and down the beaches—particularly Simpson Bay and Maho Bay in St. Maarten and Baies Orientale and Nettle in St. Martin—and within the city limits of both Philipsburg and Marigot are a multitude of accommodations. They offer a variety of prices and tastes. Lodgings range from megaresorts like the Sonesta Maho Beach to condos and small inns. On the Dutch side many hotels cater to groups, and although that's also true to some extent on the French side, you can find a larger collection of intimate accommodations there. Timeshares have become extremely popular options, especially since most are available as short-term rentals. Keep in mind that off-season rates (April through the beginning of December) can be as little as half the high-season rates.

HOTELS

DUTCH SIDE

$$$–$$$$ ⬚ **Princess Heights.** Sitting on a hill 900 feet above Oyster Bay, this property's spacious suites offer plenty of privacy. Each tastefully decorated apartment has one or two bedrooms, a kitchen whose side-by-side refrigerator comes stocked with complimentary beverages, marble bathrooms with whirlpool tubs, and a white-balustrade balcony with a smashing view of St. Barths. You also get daily maid service. If you

CLOSE UP

Hot Deals in High Season

The most expensive time to visit St. Maarten/St. Martin is the high season that runs from December to April. But this shouldn't deter bargain hunters. Finding good deals takes perseverance, patience, and flexibility. When you're booking a room, it never hurts to call the hotel directly and ask about special offers. Even the most upscale resorts offer discount rates for certain rooms and certain days of the week during high season. Packages with special themes like water sports or spas can also save you money. Check out deals where kids stay free, you get a free night when you book a certain number of nights, or you're treated to breakfast.

There's a lot of competition at the island's shops and boutiques. Try bargaining, especially in the jewelry stores. Maybe they won't give you a deal, but you won't find out unless you ask. The casinos are always giving something away—chips, drinks, limo service. At restaurants, the prix-fixe lunch or dinner is usually the better deal. On slower nights like Monday and Tuesday, many restaurants offer specials. Look for special offers at the local tourism board and in the local newspaper, the *Daily Herald*.

send a grocery list, your kitchen will be stocked just prior to your arrival. There's a fee for the service, but it saves searching for a grocery store. The property is 4 mi (6 km) from Philipsburg. At this writing, 18 larger suites are scheduled to be completed sometime in 2008. **Pros:** Away from the crowds, friendly staff, every room has a gorgeous view. **Cons:** Numerous steps to climb, not easy to find, need a car to get around. ⊠*156 Oyster Pond Rd., Oyster Pond* ☎*599/543–6906 or 800/441–7227* ⊕*www.princessheights.com* ⇗*15 suites* ⌂*In-room: safe, kitchen, refrigerator, Wi-Fi. In-hotel: pool, gym, beachfront, no elevator, concierge, laundry service* ☰*AE, MC, V* ⎇*EP.*

$$$–$$$$ **Westin St. Maarten, Dawn Beach Resort & Spa.** This glitzy new resort is making a splash—and it isn't because the island's largest freshwater pool is on the property. Two restaurants, four bars, a casino, nightclub, and a slew of activities make it so self-contained that you need never leave the property until you go home. Being a Westin property, it has spacious rooms with the chain's signature beds. Each contemporary-style room is partially carpeted and has a balcony with either an ocean or island view. Large bathrooms have romantic touches like dual showerheads. But what is most heavenly is the hotel's location. Dawn Beach is one of the most scenic spots on the island and *the* place to be at sunrise. The DJ at the trendy Opal nightclub keeps the dance floor hopping until 2 AM. **Pros:** On Dawn Beach, plenty of activities. **Cons:** Chain-hotel decor, lacks charm, a bit off the beaten track. ⊠*144 Oyster Pond Rd., Oyster Pond* ☎*599/543–6700* ⊕*www.westin.com/ stmaarten* ⇗*311 rooms, 6 suites* ⌂*In-room: safe, refrigerator, Ethernet. In-hotel: restaurants, bars, gym, spa, children's program (ages 3–12)* ☰*AE, D, DC, MC, V* ⎇*EP.*

$$–$$$$ **Holland House Beach Hotel.** An ideal location for shop fanatics and sun worshippers, this hotel faces the Front Street pedestrian mall; to the rear is the boardwalk and a lovely stretch of Great Bay Beach.

The open lobby provides easy access from street to beach, and has free Internet access. Rooms are basic but comfortable, with balconies and kitchenettes. Reasonably priced food is served at the open-air seaside restaurant. **Pros:** Excellent location, pleasant property. **Cons:** In a busy location, rooms are nothing fancy. ✉ *43 Front St., Box 393, Philipsburg* ☎ *599/542–2572* ⊕ *www.hhbh.com* ⇌ *48 rooms, 6 suites* △ *In-room: safe, kitchen (some), refrigerator. In-hotel: restaurant, bar, beachfront, public Internet* ▤ *AE, D, DC, MC, V* ○|*EP.*

$$–$$$$ 🏨 **The Inn at Cupecoy.** Overlooking Cupecoy Beach, this cozy little inn oozes comfort and luxury. Rooms are furnished with zebra-skin rugs, antique chaise lounges, and four-poster king-size beds. Large bathrooms have marble vanities and travertine sinks. The complimentary continental breakfast is served poolside. The Market at Cupecoy supplies gourmet foods, baked goods, cheese, and wine, while the Citrus restaurant specializes in French cuisine. The entire inn can be rented out as a five-bedroom villa. **Pros:** Intimate feel, lovely furnishings, near nightlife. **Cons:** Service is hit or miss, atmosphere is too quiet for some. ✉ *130 Lowlands, Cupecoy* ☎ *599/545–4333* ⇌ *5 rooms* △ *In-room: DVD. In-hotel: restaurant, pool, beachfront, no elevator, concierge, airport shuttle* ▤ *AE, D, MC, V* ☉ *Closed Aug. 20–Oct. 20* ○|*CP.*

$$–$$$$ 🏨 **Oyster Bay Beach Resort.** Jutting out into Oyster Bay, this out-of-the-way condo resort sits on the shores of Dawn Beach. Rooms are spacious and tastefully decorated with bright colors. All have balconies that feature a fine view of St. Barths or the marina in Oyster Bay. The open-air lobby is as attractive as the free-form infinity pool. Besides the Jade restaurant, there's Beau Beau's, which features island dishes and dancing waitresses called—of course—the Beaubettes. There's a $5 per day charge for air-conditioning. **Pros:** Lots of activities, nightly entertainment, comfortable accommodations. **Cons:** Isolated location, need a car to get around. ✉ *10 Emerald Merit Rd., Oyster Pond* ⌂ *Box 239, Philipsburg* ☎ *599/543–6040 or 866/978–0212* ⊕ *www.oyster baybeachresort.com* ⇌ *178 condos* △ *In-room: safe, kitchen, VCR (some). In-hotel: 2 restaurants, bar, pool, gym, beachfront, bicycles, no elevator, laundry facilities, public Internet* ▤ *AE, D, MC, V* ○|*EP.*

$$–$$$$ 🏨 **Sonesta Great Bay Beach Resort & Casino.** Location, location, location. Away from the docks that are usually crawling with cruise ships, but only a 10-minute walk to downtown Philipsburg, this resort is especially well positioned. It was closed for well over a year for total renovations. Gorgeous hues of oranges and yellows now accent the comfortable, Caribbean-style guest rooms. All have terraces with fine views. The circular marble lobby faces Great Bay and overlooks the cruise-ship pier on one side and mountains on the other. Its big plus is the white-sand beach, which is rarely crowded. **Pros:** Good location, nice beach, enough activities to keep you busy. **Cons:** Hallways have a hospital-like feel, often filled with groups. ✉ *19 Little Bay Rd., Great Bay* ⌂ *Box 91, Philipsburg* ☎ *599/542–2446 or 800/223–0757* ⊕ *www.sonesta.com/greatbay* ⇌ *210 rooms, 22 studios, 30 suites* △ *In-room: safe, Wi-Fi. In-hotel: 3 restaurants, bars, tennis court, pools, gym, spa, beachfront, water sports, children's programs (ages 4–12)* ▤ *AE, D, DC, MC, V* ○|*EP.*

$$–$$$$ Sonesta Maho Beach Resort & Casino. Las Vegas glitz and glamour rule in the island's largest hotel on beautiful Maho Beach. Whatever your pleasure—sunning or swimming, sailing or shopping, dancing till dawn or pampered yourself in the spa—the island's largest resort also has the widest range of activities. Rooms have balconies with sea or garden views. Not only is its lobby the biggest in the Caribbean, but the resort has a casino, a theater, 5 clubs, 3 restaurants, and 40 shops. Seven other restaurants and an outlet mall surround the resort complex; there's no reason to stray farther. **Pros:** Huge facility, lots of shopping, nonstop nightlife. **Cons:** Internet connection needs upgrading, not the place for a quiet getaway. ⊠*1 Rhine Rd., Box 834, Maho Bay* ☎*599/545–2115, 800/223–0757, or 800/766–3782* ⊕*www.sonesta. com/mahobeach* ⇋*537 rooms* &*In-room: safe, dial-up. In-hotel: 3 restaurants, bars, tennis courts, pools, gym, spa, beachfront, public Wi-Fi* ⊟*AE, D, DC, MC, V* ¦◎¦*EP.*

$$–$$$ Divi Little Bay Beach Resort. Popular with tour groups worrying more about price than posh, this resort offers handsome sea views from the balconies of simple and comfortable rooms. The property borders a lovely, not very crowded beach that juts out into Little Bay. There are more than enough activities to keep you busy, including trips on the bay in the resort's own glass-bottom boat. It's also a quick trip to the heart of Philipsburg. **Pros:** Good location, lovely beach. **Cons:** Packed with package tour groups, hallways are dark. ⊠*Little Bay Rd., Box 961, Philipsburg* ☎*599/542–2333 or 800/367–3484* ⊕*www. diviresorts.com* ⇋*224 rooms* &*In-room: kitchen (some), refrigerator (some), VCR (some). In-hotel: 3 restaurants, bars, tennis court, pools, gym, spa, beachfront, diving, water sports, no elevator, children's programs (ages 3–12), laundry facilities, laundry service* ⊟*AE, D, DC, MC, V* ¦◎¦*EP.*

$$–$$$ La Vista. Hibiscus and bougainvillea line brick walkways that con-
★ nect the 32 wood-frame bungalows and beachfront suites of this intimate and friendly, family-owned resort perched at the foot of Pelican Key. The rooms are somewhat sparsely furnished and have small bathrooms, but have balconies with awesome views. The beach is rocky, but good for snorkeling. **Pros:** Nice views, close to restaurants and bars. **Cons:** No-frills furnishings, not the best beach. ⊠*53 Billy Folly Rd., Pelican Key, Box 2086, Simpson Bay* ☎*599/544–3005 or 888/790– 5264* ⊕*www.lavistaresort.com* ⇋*18 rooms, 32 suites* &*In-room: safe, kitchen (some). In-hotel: restaurant, pools, beachfront, no elevator, laundry facilities* ⊟*AE, D, MC, V* ¦◎¦*EP.*

$–$$$ Mary's Boon Beach Plantation. On a lovely stretch of Simpson Bay,
★ this attractive guesthouse has a shaded courtyard where guests can gather. Pilot Mary Pomeroy chose this site because of its proximity to the airport. (Ask someone to tell you about her life and her mysterious disappearance.) Indonesian-style furniture graces the lobby as well as the rooms. Accommodations have cathedral ceilings, enormous four-poster beds, and verandahs. You'll find an honor bar with free popcorn and a well-known restaurant with a menu that has not changed since the mid-1970s. **Pros:** Small and intimate, interesting history. **Cons:** Rooms are just average, noisy location, mosquitoes abound. ⊠*117*

Simpson Bay Rd., Simpson Bay ☎599/545–7000 ⊕*www.marysboon. com* ⟟37 *rooms* ♿*In-room: kitchen (some), dial-up, Wi-Fi. In-hotel: restaurant, bars, pool, beachfront, no elevator, public Internet* ⊟*AE, D, MC, V* ⦿*EP.*

$–$$

Fodor's Choice ★

🏠**The Horny Toad.** This lovely guesthouse is widely considered the best on this side of the island. Its virtues are many: the stupendous view of Simpson Bay, the clean and comfortable rooms, the creative decor. But the one thing that keeps patrons coming back year after year is the hospitality of owner Betty Vaughn (ask her how the inn got its name). Treating guests like long-lost relatives, she is so welcoming that you simply can't resist her charms. Book early, because the Toad fills up fast. All rooms but one have air-conditioning. **Pros:** Cozy rooms, friendly vibe, beautiful beach is usually deserted. **Cons:** Rooms are very basic, need a car to get around. ⊠*2 Vlaun Dr., Simpson Bay* ☎*599/545–4323 or 800/417–9361* ⊕*www.thehornytoadguesthouse. com* ⟟8 *rooms* ♿*In-room: no a/c (some), kitchen, no TV. In-hotel: beachfront, no elevator, laundry service, public Internet, public Wi-Fi, no kids under 7* ⊟*AE, D, MC, V* ⦿*EP.*

$–$$
★

🏠**Pasanggrahan Royal Inn.** Guests are treated like friends of the family at this cozy inn. The oldest hotel on the island, it once served as the governor's mansion. Walls of the entranceway are lined with pictures of Dutch royalty. Specialty rooms have hand-carved furniture, four-poster beds with mosquito netting, and private balconies. Standard rooms have more of an island flair, with plantation-style furniture. The hotel's restaurant serves excellent meals for a reasonable price; the view looking out over Great Bay isn't bad, either. In case you're wondering, *pasanggrahan* means guesthouse in Indonesian. **Pros:** Well situated, really cozy, friendly staff. **Cons:** On the main drag, crowded beach, small parking lot. ⊠*15 Front St., Box 151, Philipsburg* ☎*599/542–3588 or 599/542–2743* ⊕*www.pasanhotel.com* ⟟31 *rooms* ♿*In-room: safe, refrigerator. In-hotel: restaurant, bar, beachfront, no elevator, public Internet* ⊟*AE, D, MC, V* ⦿*EP.*

$

🏠**Royal Turtle Inn.** This intimate hotel appeals to a wide range of people, from families with children to older travelers to gay couples. It has a great location about three minutes from the main beach. Rooms are nicely furnished, and have romantic touches like four-poster beds. Each has a view of the lagoon. A sundeck is one of the most popular spots on the nicely landscaped grounds. Breakfast at Turtle Pier Restaurant is included. **Pros:** Personalized service, intimate atmosphere. **Cons:** Not on the beach, faces a very busy street. ⊠*114 Airport Rd., Simpson Bay* ☎*599/545–2563* ⊕*www.theroyalturtle.com* ⟟8 *rooms* ♿*In room: refrigerator, Wi-Fi. In hotel: pool* ⊟*MC, V* ⦿*BP.*

FRENCH SIDE

Unless otherwise specified, breakfast is included with the room rate.

$$$$
★

🏠**Green Cay Village.** Surrounded by 5 acres of lush greenery high above Baie Orientale, these villas are a perfect place for families or groups of friends who are looking for privacy and serenity. Each of the West Indian–style villas has its own pretty pool area. The interiors are quite spacious—the largest has three bedrooms, two baths, a living room, a full kitchen, and a dining patio. If you rent just the cheaper studios, you get a kitchenette and a large bedroom with a sitting area. Whichever you choose, the staff can arrange a cook to take care of all your meals. The beach and restaurants are a short walk away. Refrigerators come stocked with essentials like milk and eggs. There are also reserved parking spaces near the villa. **Pros:** Beautiful setting, near Baie Orientale, perfect for families. **Cons:** Need a car to get around, not on the beach. ⊠*Parc de la Baie Orientale, Box 3006, Baie Orientale* ☎*590/87–38–63 or 866/592–4213* ⊕*www.greencayvillage.com* ⇋*16 villas* ⅋*In-room: kitchen, refrigerator, VCR (some). In-hotel: tennis court, pools, no elevator, laundry service, airport shuttle* ▭*AE, MC, V* ⦿*CP.*

$$$$
Fodor'sChoice
★

☷**La Samanna.** A long stretch of white-sand beach borders this dazzling resort. This is the kind of ultrachic retreat where you can arrange for a curtained beach cabana equipped with it own television—for just $200 per day. Rooms are smartly designed with tiled or marble floors, mahogany and teak furnishings, and high-tech toys like DVD players and plasma TVs. A few of the suites have private rooftop sundecks. What separates this hotel from the rest of the island's properties is its high level of service—for example, the management will buy you lunch if you happen to check-in before your room is ready. The hotel offers a wide array of activities, including one-on-one Pilates instruction and yoga at the state-of-the-art workout facility. The Elysées Spa is surrounded by a lush private garden and waterfall. Many treatment rooms include a private outdoor area with a shower. In the main dining room, the menu combines Asian, French, and creole influences. Each course can be paired with a selection of more than 450 different wines from the hotel's award-winning cellar. For cocktails, there's an authentic Moroccan bar. **Pros:** The most luxurious hotel on the island, service is unparalleled, beach is drop dead gorgeous. **Cons:** Very pricey. ⊠*Baie Longue* ⅌*Box 4077, Marigot 97064* ☎*590/87–64–00 or 800/854–2252* ⊕*www.lasamanna.orient-express.com* ⇋*27 rooms, 54 suites* ⅋*In-room: safe, kitchen (some), refrigerator (some), VCR (some). In-hotel: 2 restaurants, bar, tennis courts, pool, gym, spa, beachfront, water sports, no elevator, public Wi-Fi* ▭*AE, MC, V* ⦿*Closed Sept. and Oct.* ⦿*BP.*

$$$–$$$$
☾

☷**Alamanda Resort.** On the white-sand beach of Orient Bay, this hotel has a funky feel. Painted doors decorated with cutout boats, fish, and other oceany things lead to colonial-style suites with terraces that overlook the pool, beach, or the ocean. Two-level rooms also have private decks. Alamanda Café is surrounded by a fragrant tropical garden; the Kakao Beach restaurant looks out toward the ocean. A hotel card gives you access to activities and restaurants at any resort in the area. The staff at the 24-hour activity desk will be happy to arrange island activities. **Pros:** Pleasant property, friendly staff. **Cons:** Need a car to get around, can be difficult to find. ⊠*Baie Orientale* ⅌*BP 5166, Grand Case 97071* ☎*590/52–87–40 or 800/622–7836* ⊕*www.alamanda-resort.com* ⇋*42 rooms* ⅋*In-room: safe, kitchen. In-hotel: 2 restaurants, room service, tennis courts, pool, gym, water sports, no elevator, laundry service, public Internet* ▭*AE, MC, V* ⦿*BP.*

$$$-$$$$ 🛏Le Domaine Hotel. At the end of its charming, open-air lobby, Le Domaine give ways to a tropical garden with a covered path to the sea. All of the spacious, Caribbean-style rooms have lattice-trimmed balconies facing the greenery. Accented in yellow and turquoise, each of the rooms has rounded bathtubs (no showers except for the suites), flat-screen TVs, and in-room safes that can accommodate laptops. A waterfall drops into the attractive pool, and nearby are a gazebo and a hot tub. At La Veranda restaurant, French cuisine is the specialty of chef Philippe Dorange. Therapies from the Caribbean and beyond are on the menu at the Ti Paradis Spa. To reach the hotel, head north at French Cul de Sac. **Pros:** Lovely gardens, beachfront setting. **Cons:** Closed six months a year, very pricey, need a car to get around. ⊠ *Anse Marcel 97150* ☎ *590/52–34–52* ⊕ *www.hotel-le-domaine.com* ⇆ *120 rooms, 18 suites* ⚪ *In-room: safe, kitchen (some). In-hotel: restaurant, room service, bar, pool, gym, spa, beachfront, laundry service, public Internet, airport shuttle* ▤ *AE, DC, MC, V* ☉ *Closed June–Nov.* ⦿ *BP.*

$$$-$$$$ 🛏Esmeralda Resort. The short path from Orient Bay is just long enough to whisk you away from the crowds. Almost all of the upscale villas, which can be configured to meet the needs of different groups, have their own private pool. Caribbean-style rooms all have terraces and fully equipped kitchenettes. A 24-hour activities desk can arrange everything from snorkeling and tennis to car rental and babysitting. The resort has two restaurants—Astrolabe for fine dining and Coco Beach for anything from sushi and burgers. To make your beach life easier, you receive a hotel card for activities at any resort in the area. **Pros:** Beachfront location, pretty pools, plenty of activities. **Cons:** Need a car to get around. ⬡ *Box 5141, Baie Orientale 97071* ☎ *590/87–36–36 or 800/622–7836* ⊕ *www.esmeralda-resort.com* ⇆ *65 rooms* ⚪ *In-room: safe, kitchen (some), refrigerator. In-hotel: 2 restaurants, room service, tennis courts, pools, beachfront, water sports, no elevator, laundry service, public Internet* ▤ *AE, MC, V* ⦿ *EP.*

$$$-$$$$ 🛏Hôtel L'Esplanade Caraïbes. Guests often return to this Mediterranean-style hotel for its quiet elegance and excellent service. When you arrive, you'll find your suite stocked with a welcome basket filled with a baguette, cookies, and other goodies. All the suites at this hilltop abode have beamed ceilings, teak furnishings, and smashing views of the bay and the village of Grand Case from the patios. Two curved stone staircases lead to the gardens and pool. A path down the hillside leads to the fabulous restaurants of Grand Case and the beach. **Pros:** Lovely property, family-friendly feel. **Cons:** Lots of stairs to climb, not on the beach. ⬡ *Box 5007, Grand Case 97150* ☎ *590/87–06–55 or 866/596–8365* ⊕ *www.lesplanade.com* ⇆ *24 units* ⚪ *In-room: safe, kitchen, refrigerator. In-hotel: pools, no elevator, laundry service* ▤ *AE, MC, V* ⦿ *EP.*

$$$-$$$$ 🛏Le Petit Hotel. Surrounded by some of the best restaurants in the Caribbean, this tiny beachfront hotel oozes charm. A Mediterranean staircase leads to its nine spacious rooms and a one-bedroom suite. Each of the rooms has some high-tech touches, such as CD and DVD players and flat-screen TV. Baskets are provided at the self-serve buffet breakfast of croissants, coffee, and freshly squeezed juices; you can then carry these yummies back to your private terrace. Because the hotel has no pool, you're invited to use the pool at nearby Hôtel L'Esplanade Caraïbes. **Pros:** Walking distance to everything in Grand Case, friendly staff. **Cons:** Many stairs to climb, no pool. ⊠ *248 blvd. de Grand Case, Grand Case* ☎ *590/29–09–65* ⊕ *www.lepetithotel.com* ⇗ *9 rooms, 1 suite* ⌂ *In-room: safe, kitchen. In-hotel: beachfront, no elevator* ☰ *AE, MC, V* ⊙ *CP.*

$$-$$$$ ⓒ   🏨 **Le Flamboyant.** The Caribbean-style architecture of this hotel's indoor-outdoor lobby is quite inviting. Rooms are comfortably furnished with carved wood and rattan pieces. Each has a terrace that faces either the garden or the lagoon and is equipped with an outdoor kitchenette. A nightly shuttle to the casinos on the Dutch side is a plus, as are the many recreational activities, including tennis on a lighted tennis court, kayaking and snorkeling in Baie Nettlé, and water aerobics. Meal plans are available. **Pros:** Close to Marigot. **Cons:** Quite pricey for what you get. ⊠ *Rte. des Terres Basses, Baie Nettlé* ☎ *590/87–60–00* ⊕ *www.hmc-hotels.com* ⇗ *200 suites* ⌂ *In-room: safe, kitchen. In-hotel: restaurant, bar, pools, gym, beachfront, no elevator* ☰ *AE, DC, MC, V* ⊙ *Closed early Sept.–mid-Oct.* ⊙ *EP.*

$$-$$$$ ★   🏨 **Grand Case Beach Club.** The bottle of wine at check-in is a nice touch. Then again, there are many nice things about this beachfront property, including a friendly staff and a spectacular view of Anguilla. Fully equipped kitchens have good-size refrigerators and granite counters; CD players are standard in every apartment. Room service is available from the Sunset Café. **Pros:** Comfortable rooms, walking distance to restaurants. **Cons:** Small beach. ⊠ *21 rue de Petit Plage, at north end of blvd. de Grand Case, Box 339, Grand Case* ☎ *590/87–51–87 or 800/344–3016* ⊕ *www.grandcasebeachclub.com* ⇗ *72 apartments* ⌂ *In-room: safe, kitchen, refrigerator, DVD. In-hotel: restaurant, bar, tennis court, beachfront, water sports, no elevator, laundry facilities, laundry service, public Internet* ☰ *AE, MC, V* ⊙ *CP.*

$$-$$$$ ★   🏨 **Hotel La Plantation.** Perched high above Orient Bay, this colonial-style hotel is a charmer. French doors open to a wraparound verandah with an expansive view of Orient Bay. Each spacious villa is composed of a suite and two studios that can be rented together or separately. All are accented with yellow, green, and stenciled wall decorations. Mosquito nets hang over king-size beds, and good-size bathrooms have large showers and two sinks. Alongside the pool is the cozy Café Plantation, where complimentary breakfast is served. Monday's Lobster Night is a deliciously good deal. **Pros:** Relaxing atmosphere, eye-popping views. **Cons:** Small pool, beach is a 10-minute walk away. ⊠ *C5 Parc de La Baie Orientale,* ☎ *590/29–58–00* ⊕ *www.la-plantation.com* ⇗ *17 suites, 34 studios* ⌂ *In-room: safe, kitchen (some), refrigerator. In-hotel: restaurant, tennis courts, pool, gym, no elevator* ⊙ *Closed Sept.–mid-Oct.* ☰ *AE, MC, V* ⊙ *BP.*

PRIVATE VILLAS

Villas are a great lodging option, especially for families who don't need to keep the kids occupied or groups of friends who just like hanging out together. Since these are for the most part freestanding houses, their greatest advantage is privacy. These properties are scattered through the island, often in gated communities or on secluded roads. Some have barebones furnishings, while others are over-the-top luxurious, with gyms, theaters, game rooms, and several different pools. There are private chefs, gardeners, maids, and other staffers to care for both the villa and its occupants.

> ### RADISSON ST. MARTIN RESORT & SPA
>
> The former Le Méridien resort in Anse Marcel has undergone an $80-million facelift and will emerge as the **Radisson St. Martin Resort & Spa** (⌗ BP 581 Marcot Cove, Anse Marsel ☎ 590/ 87–67–09 or 888/201–1718 ⊕ www.radisson.com/stmartin) sometime in late summer 2008. Because the hotel, which will have 189 rooms and 63 suites, was still under construction when this book was being researched, it could not be reviewed.

Villas are secured through rental companies. They offer properties with weekly prices that range from reasonable to more than many people make in a year. Check around, as prices for the same property varies from agent to agent. Rental companies usually provide airport transfers and concierge service, and for an extra fee will even stock your refrigerator.

VILLA RENTAL AGENTS

On the French side of the island, **Caribbean Villas by Blue Escape** (⌗ 2414 *Exposition Blvd., Suite B120, Austin, TX* ☎ 512/472–8832 *or 800/556–4801* ⊕ http://blueescapes.com/) rents villas in Terres Basses, not far from Marigot. **Carimo** (⌗ 23 *rue du Général de Gaulle, Box 220, Marigot* ☎ 590/87–57–58 *or 866/978–5297* ⊕ www.carimo.com) rents villas in the tony Terres Basses area as well as Simpson Bay and Baie Longue. **French Caribbean International** (⌗ 5662 *Calle Real, Suite 333, Santa Barbara, CA* ☎ 805/967–9850 *or 800/322–2223* ⊕ www.french caribbean.com) offers rental properties on the French side of the island. **Island Hideaways** (⌗ 3843 *Highland Oaks Dr., Fairfax, VA* ☎ 800/832– 2302 *or 703/378–7840* ⊕ www.islandhideaways.com), the island's oldest rental company, rents villas on both sides. **Jennifer's Vacation Villas** (⌗ *Plaza Del Lago, Simpson Bay Yacht Club, St. Maarten* ☎ 631/546– 7345 *or 011/599–54–43107* ⊕ www.jennifersvacationvillas.com) rents villas on both sides of the island. **Villas of Distinction** (⌗ 951 *Transport Way, Petaluma, CA* ☎ 800/289–0900 ⊕ www.villasofdistinction.com) is one of the oldest villa-rental companies the French side of the island. **WIMCO** (⌗ *Box 1461, Newport, RI* ☎ 401/849–8012 *or 866/449–1553* ⊕ www.wimco.com) has more hotel, villa, apartment, and condo listings in the Caribbean than just about anyone else.

WHERE TO EAT

Although most people come to St. Maarten/St. Martin for sun and fun, they leave craving the cuisine. That's not surprising as the food is so interesting and varied that the island has come to be known as the gourmet capital of the Caribbean. For an island that covers only 37 square mi, there are more than 400 restaurants from which to choose. During your visit you can sample the best dishes from France, Thailand, Italy, Vietnam, India, Japan, and, of course, the Caribbean.

Many of the best restaurants are in Grand Case, but you should not limit your culinary adventures to that place. There are great dining options throughout the island, from the bistros of Marigot to the romantic restaurants of Cupecoy to the low-key eateries of Simpson Bay. Whether you enjoy dining on fine china in one of the upscale restaurants or off a paper plate at the island's many *lolos* (roadside eateries), St. Maarten/St. Martin's culinary options are sure to appeal to everyone.

During high season, it's essential to **make reservations,** and making them a month in advance is advisable for some of the best places. Often restaurants include a 15% service charge, so go over your bill before tipping. Keep in mind that you can't always leave tips on your credit card, so carry enough cash. A taxi is probably the easiest solution to the parking problems in Grand Case, Marigot, and Philipsburg. Grand Case has two lots—each costs $4—at each end of the main boulevard, but they're always packed.

WHAT TO WEAR

Although appropriate dining attire ranges from swimsuits to sport jackets, casual dress is usually appropriate throughout restaurants on the island. For men, a jacket and khakis or jeans will take you anywhere; for women, dressy pants, a skirt, or even fancy shorts are usually acceptable. Jeans are fine in the less formal eateries. In the listings below dress is casual (and chic) unless otherwise noted, but ask when making reservations if you're unsure.

DUTCH SIDE

ASIAN
$$–$$$

✕ **Wajang Doll.** The *wajang,* a puppet used in traditional plays, lends its name to this popular Indonesian restaurant. Standout dishes include the rijsttafel, an Indonesian specialty that includes 15 to 20 small dishes. Other standouts include *nasi goreng* (fried rice) and such seafood dishes as red snapper. ⊠ *Royal Village Unit 5, Welfare Rd. 58, Cole Bay* ☎ *599/544–2255* ▤ *AE, MC, V* ☉ *Closed Sun. No lunch.*

CAFÉS
¢–$

✕ **Au Petit Café Français.** This tiny bistro is found in the quaint shopping area just off Front Street. It only has a small amount of indoor and outdoor seating, but it's worth the visit for a quick, inexpensive snack or for a freshly ground cup of coffee. Watching employees make crepes is half the fun; eating them is the other half. You can also order hearty salads, pizza, and hot or cold sandwiches on fresh bread. It opens at

11 A.M. ⊠*120 Old St., Philipsburg* ☎*No phone* ▭*No credit cards* ⊘*Closed Sun. No dinner.*

CARIBBEAN
$-$$

✕**Turtle Pier Bar & Restaurant.** The open-air setting, sea breezes, wood-plank floors, and huge lobster tank leave no doubt that you're sitting on a pier in the Caribbean. Unfortunately, the laid-back atmosphere outweighs the average food and slow service. Open seven days a week for breakfast, lunch, and dinner, Turtle Pier has a notable lobster night on Wednesday, buffets on Saturday night, all-you-can-eat rib dinners on Sunday, and live music several nights a week. ⊠*114 Airport Rd., Simpson Bay* ☎*599/545–2562* ▭*AE, D, MC, V.*

CONTINENTAL
$-$$

✕**Chesterfield's.** On the Great Bay waterfront, Chesterfield's is a St. Maarten institution. A five-minute walk from the cruise-ship pier, nautically themed Chesty's is a great place for relaxed meals on the open-air deck. It serves breakfast, lunch, and dinner at reasonable prices. The main fare is steak and seafood, though the menu includes Duck Chesterfield (roast duckling with fresh pineapple-and-banana sauce), peel-and-eat shrimp, and conch fritters. The Mermaid Bar is popular with yachties, locals, and tourists alike. ⊠*Great Bay Marina, Philipsburg* ☎*599/542–3484* ▭*MC, V.*

ECLECTIC
$$$-$$$$
★

✕**Saratoga.** At Simpson Bay Yacht Club, this elegant restaurant lets you choose between the waterfront terrace and the handsome mahogany-paneled dining room. The menu changes daily, but you can never go wrong with one of chef John Jackson's takes on fresh fish, including wahoo, red snapper, and yellowfin tuna. You might start with a spicy ceviche of snapper with mango and tortilla chips, then segue to grilled grouper fillet. The wine list includes 150 different wines, including many by the glass. ⊠*Simpson Bay Yacht Club, Airport Blvd., Simpson Bay* ☎*599/544–2421* ◿*Reservations essential* ▭*AE, D, MC, V* ⊘*Closed Sun. Closed Aug. and Sept. No lunch.*

$$$-$$$$
Fodor'sChoice
★

✕**Temptation.** If you think you know Caribbean cuisine, the constantly changing menu at Temptation just might come as a surprise. Chef Dino Jagtiani, who trained at the Culinary Institute of America, is the mastermind behind dishes like tamarind-glazed mahimahi or caramelized onion-crusted Atlantic salmon. The wine list is extensive and features a number of reasonably priced selections. There are also many inventive cocktails, such as the St. Maartini—a refreshing blend of coconut rum, guava puree, passion fruit juice, and peach schnapps. The dining room is cozy and intimate, with low lighting and live piano music. There's outdoor seating as well. ⊠*Atlantis World Casino, Rhine Rd. 106, Cupecoy* ☎*599/545–2254* ▭*AE, D, MC, V* ⊘*Closed Mon. mid-June–Aug. No lunch.*

$-$$$

✕**The Green House.** The famous happy hour is just one of the reasons people flock to the Green House. This waterfront restaurant balances a relaxed atmosphere, reasonable prices, and quality food with a just-right, flavorful bite. All the beef served is Black Angus, and some people say the burgers and steaks are the best on the island. If you're seeking something spicy, try the deep fried calamari. The daily specials, like the Friday-night "lobster mania," are widely popular. ⊠*Bobby's Marina, Philipsburg* ☎*599/542–2941* ▭*AE, D, MC, V.*

$–$$$ ✕**Oualichi Beach Bar & Restaurant.** Conveniently located on the board-walk, Oualichi has great views of the cruise ships from its nautically themed dining room or outdoor terrace. This is a popular hangout and everyone on the island seems to love the Oualichi pizza. The menu also includes casual fare like sandwiches and wraps. ⊠*Great Bay Beach Boardwalk, Philipsburg* ☎*599/542–4313* ⊟*AE, D, MC, V* ⊗*No lunch Sun.–Wed.*

$$ ✕**Taloula Mango's.** Ribs are the specialty at this casual beachfront res-taurant, but the jerk chicken and thin-crust pizza are not to be ignored. There are also vegetarian options, like the tasty falafel. On weekdays lunch is accompanied by live music; every Friday during happy hour a DJ spins tunes. In case you're wondering, the restaurant got its name from the owner's golden retriever. ⊠*Sint Rose Shopping Mall, off Front St. on beach boardwalk, Philipsburg* ☎*599/542–1645* ⊟*AE, D, MC, V.*

FRENCH   ✕**Antoine.** You'd be hard-pressed to find a more enjoyable evening in
$$$–$$$$ Philipsburg. Owner Jean Pierre Pomarico's warmth shines through as
★   he greets guests and ushers them into the comfy seaside restaurant. Low-key, blue-accented decor, white bamboo chairs, water-colors lin-ing the walls, and candles—along with the sound of the nearby surf—create a relaxing atmosphere. The lobster thermidor (a succulent tail oozing with cream and Swiss cheese) is a favorite, but other special-ties include the seafood linguine and the fillet with shallot butter. At $29, the prix-fixe menu is a great deal. ⊠*119 Front St., Philipsburg* ☎*599/542–2964* ⊕*www.antoinerestaurant.com* ⌂*Reservations essential* ⊟*AE, D, MC, V.*

$$$–$$$$ ✕**L'Escargot.** One of the most venerable restaurants in St. Maarten, L'Escargot is in a 150-year-old creole house. The wraparound veran-dah, the bunches of grapes hanging from the chandeliers, and the Toulouse Lautrec–style murals add to the colorful atmosphere. As the names suggest, snails are the specialty. There are eight different kinds on the menu, but if you can't decide between them just ask owners Jöel and Sonya for the appetizer sampler. You can't go wrong with specialties like rack of lamb and roast duck. There's also a Friday night cabaret show in the tradition of *La Cage aux Folles*. ⊠*96 Front St., Philipsburg* ☎*599/542–2483* ⊕*www.lescargotrestaurant.com* ⊟*AE, MC, V.*

INDIAN   ✕**Shiv Sagar.** The colors of India—notably yellow and green—enliven
$$ this second-floor restaurant in Philipsburg. What it lacks in decor it more than makes up for in flavor. The menu emphasizes northern Indian specialties, including marvelous tandooris and curries, but try one of the less familiar dishes such as *madrasi machi* (red snapper with hot spices) or *saag gosht* (lamb sautéed with spinach). ⊠*20 Front St., opposite First Caribbean International Bank, Philipsburg* ☎*599/542–2299* ⊕*www. shivsagarsxm.com* ⊟*AE, D, DC, MC, V* ⊗*Closed Sun. dinner.*

STEAK   ✕**Los Gauchos Argentine Grill.** You might not expect to find first-quality
$$–$$$$ Argentine meat on an island in the Caribbean, but here it is. The res-
★   taurant, decorated with cow-print chairs, has some of the best beef in town. On Friday, there's an all-you can-eat barbecue ($21.95) accompa-

nied by a steel-pan band. Less carnivorous types will find chicken, fish, and even vegetarian selections on the menu. Selections from Argentina are featured on the wine list. ⊠*Pelican Resort Club Marina, Simpson Bay* ☎*599/544–4084* ▭*D, MC, V.*

VEGETARIAN ✕**Top Carrot.** This vegetarian café and juice bar serves sandwiches, sal-
¢–$ ads, and homemade pastries for breakfast and lunch. Get here early, as the place closed at 6 PM. Favorites include a pastry stuffed with pesto, avocado, red pepper, and feta cheese or a cauliflower, spinach, and tomato quiche. Other health-food specialties include homemade granola and yogurt. Adjacent to the restaurant is a small gift shop with Asian-inspired items plus books on eating healthily. ⊠*Airport Rd., near Simpson Bay Yacht Club, Simpson Bay* ☎*599/544–3381* ▭*MC, V* ⊘*Closed Sun. No dinner.*

FRENCH SIDE

CARIBBEAN ✕**Claude Mini-Club.** An island institution, Claude Mini-Club has
$$–$$$$ delighted patrons with its blend of creole and French food since 1969. The whole place is built tree-house style around the trunks of coconut palms, and the lofty perch mean you have great views of Marigot Harbor. The chairs and tablecloths are a mélange of sunny yellows and oranges. The €40 dinner buffet on Wednesday and Saturday night is legendary. It includes more than 30 dishes, like conch soup, baked ham, blackened goose, and roast pig. Fresh snapper is one of the specialties on the à la carte menu. There's live music nightly. ⊠*Front de Mer, Marigot* ☎*590/87–50–69* ▭*AE, MC, V* ⊘*Closed Sun.*

$–$$$ ✕**Le Ti Coin Creole.** A meal here is like dining with friends. Chef Carl Philips creates the atmosphere and succulent creole cuisine at this cozy spot, like chicken with tamarind sauce and pasta with peppers, onions, and hot sauce. He serves these goodies on the verandah of his mother's house. It's reasonably priced and friendly. What else is do you need? ⊠*Grand Case Blvd., Grand Case* ☎*590/87–92–09* ▭*MC, V.*

$$ ✕**Paradise View.** For some of the best views of Orient Beach, Pinel
★ Island, and St. Barths, head to this place on Baie Orientale. Sit back with cocktails like the ti punch or mango Madness while owner Claudette Davis regales you with stories about the island. Menu choices include everything from sandwiches and salads to ribs and seafood. There's also a good Sunday lunch buffet. ⊠*Hope Hill, Baie Orientale* ☎*590/29–45–37* ▭*AE, MC, V* ⊘*Closed Mon.*

$ ✕**Enoch's Place.** The blue-and-white-stripe awning on a corner of the Marigot Market makes this place hard to miss. But Enoch's cooking is what draws the crowds. Specialties include garlic shrimp, fresh lobster, and rice and beans (like your St. Martin mother used to make). Try the salt fish and fried johnnycake—a great breakfast option. The food more than makes up for the lack of decor, and chances are you'll be counting the days until you can return. ⊠*Marigot Market, Front de Mer, Marigot* ☎*590/29–29–88* ▭*No credit cards* ⊘*Closed Sun. No dinner.*

¢–$ ✕**Talk of the Town.** Although Grand Case is known for its upscale din-
Fodor's Choice ing, you can also find a number of *lolos,* or roadside barbecue stands.
★ One of the most popular is Talk of the Town. With plastic utensils

and paper plates, it couldn't be more informal. The menu includes everything from succulent grilled ribs to stewed conch. Don't miss the johnnycakes and side dishes like plantains, curried rice, beans and coleslaw. The service is friendly, if a bit slow, but sit back with a beer and enjoy the experience. ⊠ *Grand Case Blvd., Grand Case* 🕾 *No phone* ▤ *No credit cards.*

ECLECTIC   ✗ **Le Pressoir.** In a West Indian house painted ravishing shades of yellow
$$$–$$$$ and blue, Le Pressoir has charm to spare. French and creole cuisine
★   dominates the menu, so you'll find dishes like sea scallops in a mango butter sauce and rum-marinated foie gras. Don't miss the seafood special, which includes a first course of shrimp, scallops, and mussels and a second with four types of grilled fish. The name, by the way, comes from the historic salt press that sits opposite the restaurant. ⊠ *30 blvd. de Grand Case, Grand Case* 🕾 *590/87–76–62* ▤ *AE, MC, V* ⊗ *Closed Sun. No lunch.*

$$$–$$$$ ✗ **Rainbow Café.** Refreshing sea breezes mean that these palm-shaded
Fodor'sChoice   tables are always in demand. It has great views of the bay, but the real
★   reason people come to this comfortable bistro is for the food. The menu includes shrimp and scallop with an island-style chutney. The friendly owners and staff make a meal here memorable. Check out the upstairs lounge, which has a cigar and pipe bar. ⊠ *176 blvd. de Grand Case, Grand Case* 🕾 *590/87–55–80* ▤ *AE, MC, V* ⊗ *Closed Sun.*

$$$–$$$$ ✗ **Le Tastevin.** In the heart of Grand Case, Le Tastevin is filled with flowers, plants, and coconut palms. The owners also founded the popular L'Auberge Gourmande across the street. The menu changes frequently, but you might find ambitious offerings like foie gras with figs, crab tartare with tomato, or beef with sauterne sauce. ⊠ *86 blvd. de Grand Case, Grand Case* 🕾 *590/87–55–45* ⩜ *Reservations essential* ▤ *AE, MC, V* ⊗ *Closed mid-Aug.–Sept.*

$$–$$$$ ✗ **Kon Tiki.** Thatched roofs cover the booths at this happening beach bar and restaurant on beautiful Baie Orientale. The food here is great, ranging from casual dishes like burgers and sandwiches to more substantial fare like grilled tuna and mahimahi. There's one potential problem: nude bathers occasionally stroll by, making it somewhat difficult to concentrate on your meal. An added bonus: you can book a variety of water sports right at the restaurant. ⊠ *5 Baie Orientale* 🕾 *590/87–43–27* ▤ *MC, V* ⊗ *No dinner.*

$–$$$ ✗ **La Main à La Pâte.** A great place to people-watch, this restaurant sits
★   on the waterfront at Marina Royale. One of the highlights on the globetrotting menu is the lobster-tail salad, a light concoction full of firm lobster meat and tomato sauce. La Palette Caraïbes, which includes three different fish, includes the tastiest tuna steak on the island. Be sure to try the passion pie with mango ice cream for dessert. The staff is friendly and knowledgeable. ⊠ *Marina Royale, Marigot* 🕾 *590/87–71–19* ▤ *D, MC, V.*

$–$$ ✗ **La Belle Epoque.** A favorite among locals, this sometimes frenzied little
★   bistro is on the marina. Whether you stop for a drink or a meal, you'll soon discover that it's a prime venue for boat- and people-watching. The menu has a bit of everything, from pizza and pasta to lobster

and seafood. There's also a good wine list. ⊠ *Marina Royale, Marigot* ☎ *590/87–87–70* ▤ *AE, MC, V.*

FRENCH
$$$–$$$$
★
✕ Mario's Bistro. This romantic eatery earns raves for its wonderful cuisine and the romantic ambience. Didier Gonnon and Martyne Tardif are out front, while chef Mario Tardif is in the kitchen creating dishes such as sautéed sea scallops with crab mashed potatoes, baked mahimahi with a macadamia nut crust, and rack of lamb with pesto and goat cheese. The open-air, country French–style restaurant is on the canal just after you cross the bridge from Sandy Ground. ⊠ *At Sandy Ground Bridge, Sandy Ground* ☎ *590/87–06–36* ✍ *Reservations essential* ▤ *MC, V* ☾ *Closed Sun. and Aug.–Sept. No lunch.*

$$–$$$$
✕ Bistrot Nu. It's hard to top the simple, unadorned fare and reasonable prices you can find at this intimate restaurant tucked in a Marigot alley. Traditional French and Creole food—coq au vin, fish soup, snails—is served in a friendly, intimate dining room. The prix-fixe menu is a very good value. The place is popular, and the tables are routinely packed until it closes at midnight. It can be difficult to park here, so take your chances at finding a spot on the street—or try a taxi. ⊠ *Rue de Hollande, Marigot* ☎ *590/87–97–09* ▤ *MC, V* ✍ *Reservations essential* ☾ *Closed Sun.*

$$–$$$
✕ L'Auberge Gourmande. One of the best-known restaurants in Grand Case, L'Auberge Gourmande certainly lives up to its reputation. In one of the oldest creole houses in St. Martin, it has elegant arches framing the elegant and charming dining room. Chef Didier Rochat's French cuisine is a delight and includes blue cheese and pecans in phyllo dough, roasted rack of lamb with garlic and herbs, dover sole in lemon butter. The restaurant also has a good selection of wines. ⊠ *89 blvd. de Grand Case, Grand Case* ☎ *590/87–73–37* ▤ *MC, V* ☾ *No lunch.*

$$–$$$
★
✕ Tropicana. This bustling bistro at the Marina Royale has a completely different vibe at lunch and at dinner. Salads are a must for lunch, especially the salad niçoise with medallions of crusted goat cheese. Dinner includes some exceptional steak and seafood dishes. The wine list is quite extensive. Desserts are tasty, and you'll never be disappointed with old standbys like the crème brûlée. You can dine outside or inside along the yacht-filled waterfront. ⊠ *Marina Royale, Marigot* ☎ *590/87–79–07* ▤ *D, MC, V.*

BEACHES

Warm surf and a gentle breeze can be found at the island's 37 beaches, and every one of them is open to the public. What could be better? Each is unique: some bustling and some bare, some refined and some rocky, some good for snorkeling and some good for sunning. Whatever you fancy in the beach landscape department, you can find it here, including a clothing-optional one at the south end of Baie Orientale. If you plan on keeping your valuables, it's a good idea to leave them at the hotel.

St. Maarten vs. St. Martin

If this is your first trip to St. Maarten/ St. Martin, you're probably wondering which side will better suit your needs. That's hard to say, because in some ways the difference between the two can seem as subtle as the hazy boundary line dividing them. But there are some major differences. St. Maarten, the Dutch side, has the casinos, more nightlife and bigger hotels. St. Martin, the French side, has no casinos, less nightlife, and hotels that are smaller and more intimate. Many have kitchenettes, and most include breakfast. Even though there are many very good restaurants on the Dutch side, the French side rules when it comes to gourmet dining. The biggest difference might be currency—the Netherlands Antilles guilder on the Dutch side, the euro on the French side. Of course, many establishments on both sides accept U.S. dollars.

DUTCH SIDE

Cupecoy Beach. This picturesque area of sandstone cliffs, white sand, and shoreline caves is actually a series of beaches that come and go according to the whims of the sea. Though the surf can be rough, it's popular with gay locals and visitors. It's near the Dutch-French border. ⊠ *Cupecoy, between Baie Longue and Mullet Bay.*

★ **Dawn Beach.** True to its name, Dawn Beach is the place to be at sunrise. On the Atlantic side of Oyster Pond, just south of the French border, this is a first-class beach for sunning and snorkeling. It's not usually crowded, and there are several good restaurants nearby. To find it, follow the signs for either Mr. Busby's or Scavenger's restaurant. ⊠ *South of Oyster Pond.*

Great Bay. This is probably the easiest beach to find because it curves around Philipsburg. A bustling, white-sand beach, Great Bay is just behind Front Street. Here you'll find boutiques, eateries, and a pleasant boardwalk. Because of the cruise ships and the salt pond, it's not the best place for swimming. If you must get wet, do it west of Captain Hodge Pier. ⊠ *Philipsburg.*

Little Bay. Although it's popular with snorkelers and divers as well as kayakers and boating enthusiasts, Little Bay isn't as crowded as many other beaches. Maybe it's because the sand is somewhat gravelly. What it does have is panoramic views of St. Eustatius, Philipsburg, the cruise-ship terminal, Saba, and St. Kitts. The beach is west of Fort Amsterdam and accessible via the Divi Little Bay Resort. ⊠ *Little Bay Rd.*

Mullet Bay Beach. Many believe that this mile-long, powdery white-sand beach near the medical school is the island's best. Swimmers like it because the water is usually calm. When the swell is up, the surfers hit the beach. It's also the place to listen for the "whispering pebbles" as the waves wash up. ⊠ *Mullet Bay, south of Cupecoy.*

Simpson Bay Beach. This secluded, half-moon stretch of white-sand beach on the island's Caribbean side is a hidden gem. It's mostly surrounded by private residences. There are no big resorts, no jet skiers, no food concessions, and no crowds. It's just you, the sand, and the water. Southeast of the airport, follow the signs to Mary's Boon and the Horny Toad guesthouses. ⊠ *Simpson Bay.*

FRENCH SIDE

★ **Baie de Friars.** This white stretch of sand has a couple of simple good-food restaurants, calm waters, and a lovely view of Anguilla. The shack with the yellow, red, and green picnic tables belong to Kali's Beach Bar, where every Friday night people come for music, dancing, and a huge bonfire. To get to the beach take National Road 7 from Marigot, go toward Grand Case to the Morne Valois hill, and turn left on the dead-end road. ⊠ *Baie de Friar.*

Baie de Grand Case. A stripe of a beach, this sandy shoreline borders Grand Case, a charming little hamlet with gingerbread-style architecture. The sea is calm, water sports are available, and if the heat becomes too much, you can have a bite to eat at one of the *lolos* (barbecue huts). ⊠ *Grand Case.*

Baie Longue. Though it extends over the French Lowlands, from the cliff at La Samanna to La Pointe des Canniers, the island's longest beach has no facilities or vendors. It's the perfect place for a romantic walk. To get here, take National Road 7 south of Marigot. The entrance marked LA SAMANNA is the first entrance to the beach. ⊠ *Baie Longue.*

Fodor's Choice **Baie Orientale.** Many consider this the island's most beautiful beach, ★ but its satiny white sand, underwater marine reserve, variety of water sports, beach bars, and hotels also make it one of the most crowded. The conservative north end is more family-oriented, while the liberal south end is clothing-optional and eventually becomes full-on nudie territory. To get to Baie Orientale from Marigot, take National Road 7 past Grand Case, past the Aéroport de L'Espérance. ⊠ *Baie Orientale.*

Baie Rouge. Home to a couple of beach bars, Baie Rouge, in the French Lowlands, means Red Bay. It got its name from the lightly tinted, soft sand that borders the shoreline. It's thought to have the best snorkeling beaches on the island. You can swim the crystal waters along the point and explore a swim-through cave. The beach is fairly popular with gay men. Baie Rouge is five minutes from Marigot, off Route 7 at the Nettlé Bay turnoff. ⊠ *Baie Rouge.*

☾ **Ilet Pinel.** A protected nature reserve, this kid-friendly island is a five-minute ferry ride from French Cul de Sac ($6 per person round-trip). The water is clear and shallow, and the shore is sheltered. If you like snorkeling, don your gear and paddle along both sides of the coasts of this pencil-shape speck in the ocean. Off the pier you'll see live lobsters just waiting to become someone's lunch at the isle's two restaurants. A small boutique sells wraps, hats, and T-shirts. Because of its popularity, Ilet Pinel is often crowded. ⊠ *Ilet Pinel.*

SPORTS & THE OUTDOORS

BOATING & SAILING

The island is surrounded by water, so why not get out and enjoy it? The water and winds are perfect for skimming the surf. It'll cost you around $1,000 per day to rent a 28- to 40-foot powerboat, considerably less for smaller boats or small sailboats.

Lagoon Sailboat Rental (⊠ *Airport Rd., near Uncle Harry's, Simpson Bay* ☎ *599/557–0714* ⊕ *www.lagoonsailboatrental.com*) has 20-foot day sailers for rent within Simpson Bay Lagoon for $150 per day, with a half day for $110. Either explore on your own or rent a skipper to navigate the calm, sheltered waters around Simpson Bay Yacht Club and miles of coastline on both the French and Dutch sides of the islands.

The **Moorings** (⊠ *Captain Oliver's Marina, Oyster Pond* ☎ *590/87–32–55 or 888/952–8420* ⊕ *www.moorings.com*) has a fleet of Beneteau yachts as well as bareboat and crewed catamarans for those who opt for a sailing vacation.

Random Wind (☎ *599/544–5148 or 599/557–5742* ⊕ *www.random wind.com*) offers half- and full-day sailing and snorkeling trips on a 54-foot clipper. Charter prices depend on the size of the group and whether lunch is served, but the regularly scheduled Paradise Daysail costs $95 per person. Departures are on the Dutch side, from Ric's Place at Simpson Bay are at 9 AM Tuesday through Friday.

Sailing experience is not necessary for the **St. Maarten 12-Metre Challenge** (⊠ *Bobby's Marina, Philipsburg* ☎ *599/542–0045* ⊕ *www.12metre. com*), one of the island's most popular activities. Participants compete on 68-foot racing yachts, including Dennis Connor's *Stars and Stripes* (the actual boat that won the America's Cup in 1987) and the *Canada II.* Anyone can help the crew grind winches, trim sails, and punch the stopwatch, or you can just sit back and watch everyone else work. The thrill of it is priceless, but book well in advance; this is the most popular shore excursion offered by cruise ships in the Caribbean.

FISHING

You can angle for yellowtail snapper, grouper, marlin, tuna, and wahoo on deep-sea excursions. Costs range from $150 per person for a half day to $250 for a full day. Prices usually include bait and tackle, instruction for novices, and refreshments. Ask about licensing and insurance. **Big Sailfish Too** (⊠ *Anse Marcel* ☎ *690/27–40–90*) is your best bet on the French side of the island. **Lee's Deepsea Fishing** (⊠ *Welfare Rd. 82, Simpson Bay* ☎ *599/544–4233 or 599/544–4234* ⊕ *www.leesfish.com*) organizes excursions, and when you return, Lee's Roadside Grill will cook your tuna, wahoo, or whatever else you catch and keep. **Rudy's Deep Sea Fishing** (⊠ *14 Airport Rd., Simpson Bay* ☎ *599/545–2177 or 599/522–7120* ⊕ *www.rudysdeepseafishing.com*) has been around for years and is one of the more experienced sport-angling outfits.

GOLF

St. Maarten is not a golf destination. Although **Mullet Bay Golf Course** (⊠ *Airport Rd., north of airport* 🕾 *599/545–2801*), on the Dutch side, is an 18-hole course, it's the island's *only* one. Though lately it has been better tended, it's still not in the best of shape and many feel it's not worth the cost.

22

HORSEBACK RIDING

Island stables offer riding packages for everyone from novices to experts. The usual 90-minute ride along the beach costs €50 to $70 for group rides and €70 to $90 for private treks. Reservations are necessary. You can arrange rides directly or through most hotels. **Bayside Riding Club** (⊠ *Galion Beach Rd., Baie Orientale* 🕾 *590/87–36–64 or 599/557–6822* ⊕ *www.baysideridingclub.com*), on the French side, is a long-established outfit that can accommodate all levels of rider riders. On the Dutch side contact **Lucky Stables** (⊠ *Traybay Dr. 2, Cay Bay* 🕾 *599/544–5255 or 599/555–7246*), which offers mountain- and beach-trail rides, including a romantic champagne night ride. Rides start at $45.

KAYAKING

Kayaking is becoming very popular and is almost always offered at the many water-sports operations on both the Dutch and the French sides. Rental starts at about $15 per hour. On the Dutch side, **Blue Bubbles** (⊠ *Westin St. Maarten Dawn Beach Resort & Spa, Oyster Pond* 🕾 *599/542–2333* ⊕ *www.bluebubblesxm.com*) offers lagoon paddles and snorkeling tours by kayak. **TriSport** (⊠ *Airport Rd. 14B, Simpson Bay* 🕾 *599/545–4384* ⊕ *www.trisportsxm.com*) organizes similar kayaking and snorkeling excursions.

On the French side, kayaks are available at **Kayak Tour** (⊠ *French Cul de Sac* 🕾 *599/557–0112 or 690/47–76–72*). Near Le Galion Beach, **Wind Adventures** (⊠ *Orient Bay* 🕾 *590/29–41–57* ⊕ *www.wind-adventures.com*) offers kayaking.

SCUBA DIVING

The water temperature here is rarely below 70°F (21°C). Visibility is often excellent, averaging about 100 feet to 120 feet. The island has more than 40 good dive sites, from wrecks to rocky labyrinths. Beginners and night divers will get a kick out of tugboat *Annie,* which lies in 25 feet to 30 feet of water in Simpson Bay. Right outside of Philipsburg, 55 feet under the water, is the HMS *Proselyte,* once explored by Jacques Cousteau. Although it sank in 1801, the boat's cannons and coral-encrusted anchors are still visible.

Off the north coast, in the protected and mostly current-free Grand Case Bay, is **Creole Rock.** The water here ranges in depth from 10 feet to 25 feet, and visibility is excellent. Other sites off the north coast include

Ilet Pinel, with its good shallow diving; **Green Key,** with its vibrant barrier reef; and **Tintamarre,** with its sheltered coves and geologic faults. On average, one-tank dives start at $51; two-tank dives are about $95. Certification courses start at about $400.

On the Dutch side, the following shops are full-service outfitters and SSI (Scuba Schools International) and/or PADI certified.

Blue Bubbles (⊠*Dawn Beach Resort, Oyster Pond* ☎*599/542–2333* ⊕*www.bluebubblessxm.com*) has several locations, including two in Great Bay. **Dive Safaris** (⊠*Bobby's Marina, Yrausquin Blvd., Philipsburg* ☎*599/544–9001 or 599/545–2401* ⊕*www.divestmaarten.com*) has a shark-awareness dive where participants can watch professional feeders give reef sharks a little nosh. **Ocean Explorers Dive Shop** (⊠*113 Welfare Rd., Simpson Bay* ☎*599/544–5252* ⊕*www.stmaartendiving. com*) is St. Maarten's oldest dive shop, and offers different types of certification courses.

On the French side, **Blue Ocean** (⊠*Sandy Ground Rd., Baie Nettlé* ☎*590/87–89–73* ⊕*www.blueocean.ws*) is a PADI-certified dive center. **Octoplus** (⊠*Blvd. de Grand Case, Grand Case* ☎*590/87–20–62* ⊕*www. octoplus-dive.com*) offers diving certification courses and all-inclusive dive packages. At Grand Case Beach Club, **O2 Limits** (⊠*Blvd. de Grand Case, Grand Case* ☎*690/50–04–00*) offers a variety of dives.

SEA EXCURSIONS

You can take day cruises to Prickly Pear Cay, off Anguilla, aboard the *Lambada,* or sunset and dinner cruises on the 65-foot sail catamaran *Tango* with **Aqua Marina Adventures** (☎*599/544–2640 or 599/544– 2621* ⊕*www.stmaarten-activities.com*). The 50-foot catamaran *Bluebeard II* (⊠*Simpson Bay* ☎*599/577–5935* ⊕*www.bluebeardcharters. com*) sails around Anguilla's south and northwest coasts to Prickly Pear Cay, where there are excellent coral reefs for snorkeling and powdery white sands for sunning. For low-impact sunset and dinner cruises, try the catamaran **Celine** (⊠*Skip Jack's Restaurant, Simpson Bay* ☎*599/545–3961 or 599/552–1535* ⊕*www.sailstmaarten.com*). The sleek 76-foot catamaran **Golden Eagle** (☎*599/542–3323* ⊕*www. sailingsxm.com*) takes day-sailors to outlying islets and reefs for snorkeling and partying.

A cross between a submarine and a glass-bottom boat, the 34-passenger **Seaworld Explorer** (⊠*Blvd. de Grand Case, Grand Case* ☎*599/542– 4078* ⊕*www.atlantisadventures.com*), a semi-submarine, crawls along the water's surface from Grand Case to Creole Rock; while submerged in a lower chamber, passengers view marine life and coral through large windows. Divers jump off the boat and feed the fish and eels.

SNORKELING

Some of the best snorkeling on the Dutch side can be found around the rocks below Fort Amsterdam off Little Bay Beach, in the west end of Maho Bay, off Pelican Key, and around the reefs off Oyster Pond Beach. On the French side, the area around Orient Bay—including Caye Verte, Ilet Pinel, and Tintamarre—is especially lovely and is officially classified and protected as a regional underwater nature reserve. Sea creatures also congregate around Creole Rock at the point of Grand Case Bay. The average cost of an afternoon snorkeling trip is about $45 per person. **Aqua Mania Adventures** (⊠*Pelican Marina, Simpson Bay* ☎*590/544–2640 or 599/544–2621* ⊕*www.stmaarten-activities. com*) offers snorkeling and diving trips, motorized and nonmotorized equipment, and a variety of cruises. The newest activity, called "rock 'n roll safaris," lets participants not only snorkel, but navigate their own motorized rafts. **Blue Bubbles** (⊠*Dawn Beach Resort, Oyster Pond* ☎*599/542–2333* ⊕*www.bluebubblessxm.com*) offers both boat and shore snorkel excursions.

On the French side, **Blue Ocean** (⊠*Sandy Ground Rd., Baie Nettlé* ☎*590/87–89–73* ⊕*www.blueocean.ws*) offers snorkeling trips. **Eagle Tours** (⊠*Bobby's Marina, Philipsburg* ☎*599/542–3323* ⊕*www. sailingsxm.com*) combines sailing, snorkeling, and lunch aboard a 76-foot catamaran. Arrange equipment rentals and snorkeling trips through **Kontiki Watersports** (⊠*Northern beach entrance, Baie Orientale* ☎*590/87–46–89*).

WINDSURFING

The best windsurfing is on Galion Bay on the French side. From November to May, trade winds can average 15 knots. **Club Nathalie Simon** (⊠*Northern beach entrance, Baie Orientale* ☎*590/29–41–57* ⊕*www.wind-adventures.com*) offers rentals and lessons in both windsurfing and kite surfing. One-hour lessons are about €40. **Windy Reef** (⊠*Galion Beach, past Butterfly Farm* ☎*590/87–08–37* ⊕*www. windyreef.fr*) has offered windsurfing lessons and rentals since 1991.

SHOPPING

It's true that the island sparkles with its myriad outdoor activities—diving, snorkeling, sailing, swimming, and sunning—but shopaholics are drawn to the sparkle within the jewelry stores. The huge array of such stores is almost unrivaled in the Caribbean. In addition, duty-free shops offer substantial savings—about 15% to 30% below U.S. and Canadian prices—on cameras, watches, liquor, cigars, and designer clothing. It's no wonder that each year 500 cruise ships make Philipsburg a port of call. On both sides of the island, be alert for idlers. They can snatch unwatched purses.

Prices are in dollars on the Dutch side, in euros on the French side. As for bargains, there are more to be had on the Dutch side.

SHOPPING AREAS

Philipsburg's **Front Street** has reinvented itself. Now it's mall-like, with redbrick walk and streets, palm trees lining the sleek boutiques, jewelry stores, souvenir shops, outdoor restaurants, and the old reliables—including McDonald's and Burger King. Here and there a school or a church appears to remind visitors there's more to the island than shopping. Back Street is where you'll find the **Philipsburg Market Place,** an open-air market where you can haggle for bargains on items such as handicrafts, souvenirs, and cover-ups. **Old Street,** near the end of Front Street, has stores, boutiques, and open-air cafés offering French crepes, rich chocolates, and island mementos. You can find an outlet mall amid the more upscale shops at the **Maho** shopping plaza. The **Plaza del Lago** at the Simpson Bay Yacht Club complex has an excellent choice of restaurants as well as shops.

On the French side, wrought-iron balconies, colorful awnings, and gingerbread trim decorate Marigot's smart shops, tiny boutiques, and bistros in the **Marina Royale** complex and on the main streets, **Rue de la Liberté** and **Rue de la République.** Also in Marigot is the pricey **West Indies Mall** and the **Plaza Caraïbes,** which house designer shops.

SPECIALTY STORES

ART GALLERIES

Maybe it's the vibrant colors, the gorgeous sunlight, or the scenic beauty that stimulates the creative juices of the many artists on the island. It must be something special, because there are a great many artists and and galleries their work.

Céramiques d'art Marie Moine (⊠ *76 rue de la Flibuste, Oyster Pond* ☎ *590/29–53–76)* sells ceramics that are unique and affordable. **Dona Bryhiel Art Gallery** (⊠ *Oyster Pond* ☎ *590/87–43–93)*, before the turn-off to Captain Oliver's Marina, deals mostly in modern figurative paintings by the owner. She will delight you with stories of her life and the paintings, which are steeped in romantic French and Caribbean traditions.

Gingerbread Galerie (⊠ *Marina Royale, Marigot* ☎ *590/87–73–21)* specializes in Haitian art. **Minguet Art Gallery** (⊠ *Rambaud Hill* ☎ *590/87–76–06)*, between Marigot and Grand Case, is managed by the daughter of the late artist Alexandre Minguet. The gallery carries original paintings, lithographs, posters, and postcards depicting island flora and landscapes by Minguet, as well as original works by Robert Dago and Loic BarBotin. **Roland Richardson Gallery** (⊠ *6 rue de la République, Marigot* ☎ *590/87–32–24)* sells oil and watercolor paintings by well-known local artist Roland Richardson. The gallery, with a garden studio in the rear, is worth visiting even if you don't intend to buy a painting, and you may meet the artist himself or his stepmother.

22

CIGARS

The **Cigar Emporium** (⊠ *66 Front St., Philipsburg* ☎ *599/542–2787*) has the island's largest selection of Dominican and Cuban cigars, along with lots of other tobacco items.

DUTY-FREE SHOPS

Carat (⊠ *16 rue de la République, Marigot* ☎ *590/87–73–40* ⊠ *73 Front St., Philipsburg* ☎ *599/542–2180*) sells china and jewelry. **Little Europe** (⊠ *80 Front St., Philipsburg* ☎ *599/542–4371* ⊠ *1 rue du Général de Gaulle, Marigot* ☎ *590/87–92–64*) sells fine jewelry, crystal, and china. **Little Switzerland** (⊠ *52 Front St., Philipsburg* ☎ *599/542–3530* ⊠ *Harbor Point Village, Pointe Blanche* ☎ *599/542–7785* ⊠ *Westin St. Maarten, Dawn Beach* ☎ *599/643–6451*) sells watches, fine crystal, china, perfume, and jewelry. **Manek's** (⊠ *Rue de la République, Marigot* ☎ *590/87–54–91*) sells, on two floors, luggage, perfume, jewelry, Cuban cigars, duty-free liquors, and tobacco products. **Oro Diamante** (⊠ *62-B Front St., Philipsburg* ☎ *599/543–0342*) carries loose diamonds, jewelry, watches, perfume, and cosmetics.

HANDICRAFTS

Visitors to the Dutch side of the island come for free samples at the **Guavaberry Emporium** (⊠ *8–10 Front St., Philipsburg* ☎ *599/542–2965*), the small factory where the Sint Maarten Guavaberry Company makes its guavaberry liqueur. You'll find myriad versions, including one made with jalapeño peppers. Check out the hand-painted bottles. The **Shipwreck Shop** (⊠ *15 and 34 Front St., Philipsburg* ☎ *599/542–5358* ⊕ *www.shipwreckshops.com*) stocks a little of everything: colorful hammocks, handmade jewelry, and lots of the local guavaberry liqueur.

NIGHTLIFE

★ St. Maarten has lots of evening and late-night action. To find out what's doing on the island, pick up *St. Maarten Nights, St. Maarten Quick Pick Guide,* or *St. Maarten Events,* all of which are distributed free in the tourist office and hotels. The glossy *Discover St. Martin/St. Maarten* magazine, also free, has articles on island history and on the newest shops, discos, and restaurants. Or buy a copy of Thursday's *Daily Herald* newspaper, which lists all the week's entertainment.

BARS

On the Dutch side, **Axum Café** (⊠ *7L Front St., Philipsburg* ☎ *599/52–0547*), a 1960s-style coffee shop, offers cultural activities as well as live jazz and reggae. It's open daily, 11:30 AM until the wee hours. **Bamboo Bernies** (⊠ *Caravanserai Resort, 2 Beacon Rd., Simpson Bay* ☎ *599/545–3622*), is an indoor-outdoor tiki bar with a different theme every night. The open-air **Bliss** (⊠ *Caravanserai Resort, Simpson Bay* ☎ *599/545–3996*) plays techno music. **Buccaneer Bar** (⊠ *Behind Atrium Hotel, Simpson Bay* ☎ *599/544–5876*) is the place to enjoy a BBC (Bailey's banana colada) and slice of pizza. **Cheri's Café** (⊠ *Airport Rd., Simpson Bay* ☎ *599/545–3361*), across from Maho Beach Resort &

Casino, features Sweet Chocolate, a lively band that will get your toes tapping and your tush twisting.

The casual **Cliffhanger Beach Bar** (⊠*Cupecoy Beach* ☎*599/552–9440*) is the perfect place to chill out, have a drink, and watch the sunset. The **Ocean Lounge** (⊠*Holland House Hotel, 43 Front St., Philipsburg* ☎*599/542–2572*) is the quintessential people-watching venue. Sip a guavaberry colada and point your chair toward the boardwalk. The **Red Piano** (⊠*Hollywood Casino, Simpson Bay* ☎*599/544–6008*) has live music and tasty cocktails. Starting each night at 8, the pianist at **Soprano's** (⊠*Sonesta Maho Beach Resort, Maho Beach* ☎*599/522–7088*) takes requests for oldies, romantic favorites, or smooth jazz. **Sunset Beach Bar** (⊠*2 Beacon Hill, Beacon Hill* ☎*599/545–3998*) has a relaxed, anything-goes atmosphere. Enjoy live music Wednesday through Sunday as you watch planes from the airport next door fly directly over your head.

On the French side, **Kali's Beach Bar** (⊠*Friars Bay* ☎*690/49–06–81*) is a happening spot with live music until midnight. On Friday night, the big attraction is the huge beach bonfire. **Lady C** (⊠*Simpson Bay* ☎*599/544–4710*), a 70-year-old sailboat, is transformed into a floating party bar. It sits in Simpson Bay Lagoon, making it very convenient for the yachties. At **Pineapple Pete** (⊠*Airport Rd., Simpson Bay* ☎*599/544–6030*) you can groove to live music or visit the game room for a couple of rounds or pool.

CASINOS

The island's casinos—all 14 of them—are found only on the Dutch side. All have craps, blackjack, roulette, and slot machines. You must be 18 years or older to gamble. Dress is casual (but excludes bathing suits or skimpy beachwear). Most casinos are found in hotels, but there are also some independents.

With some of the best restaurants on the island, **Atlantis World Casino** (⊠*106 Rhine Rd., Cupecoy* ☎*599/545–4601*) is a popular destination even for those who don't gamble. It has more than 500 slot machines and gaming tables offering roulette, baccarat, three-card poker, Texas hold-'em poker, and Omaha high poker. **Beach Plaza Casino** (⊠*Front St., Philipsburg* ☎*599/543–2031*), in the heart of the shopping area, has more than 180 slots and multigame machines with the latest in touch-screen technology. Because of its location, it is popular with cruise ship passengers. One of the island's largest gambling joints, **Casino Royale** (⊠*Maho Beach Resort & Casino, Maho Bay* ☎*599/545–2602*) is in bustling Maho, near plenty of restaurants, bars, and clubs. **Coliseum Casino** (⊠*Front St., Philipsburg* ☎*599/543–2101*) is popular with fans of slots, blackjack, poker, or roulette. **Dawn Beach Casino** (⊠*Westin St. Maarten, 144 Oyster Pond Rd., Oyster Pond* ☎*599/543–6700*) is big and glitzy. If you ever get tired of the endless array of slot machines and gaming tables, beautiful Dawn Beach is just outside the door. **Diamond Casino** (⊠*1 Front St., Philipsburg* ☎*599/543–2583*) has 250 slot machines plus the usual tables offering games like blackjack, routlette, and three-card poker. The casino is in the heart of Philipsburg. The **Dolphin Casino** (⊠ *Caravanserai Resort, Simpson Bay* ☎ *599/545–4601*), near the airport, has a giant slot machine at the entrance. In the lobby of the Great Bay Beach Hotel, **Golden Casino** (⊠ *Great Bay Beach Hotel, Little Bay Rd., Great Bay* ☎ *599/542–2446*) is on the small side. But fans say the 84 slots machines and tables with Caribbean poker, blackjack and roulette are more than enough. **Hollywood Casino** (⊠ *Pelican Resort, Pelican Key, Simpson Bay* ☎ *599/544–4463*) has an upbeat theme and a nice late-night buffet. **Jump-Up Casino** (⊠ *1 Emmaplein, Philipsburg* ☎ *599/542–0862*) is near the cruise-ship pier, so it attracts lots of day-trippers. **Paradise Plaza Casino** (⊠ *Airport Rd., Simpson Bay* ☎ *599/543–4721*) has 250 slots and multigame machines. Betting on sporting events is a big thing here, which explains the 20 televisions tuned to whatever game happens to be on at the time. One of the island's largest gaming halls, **Princess Casino** (⊠ *Port de Plaisance, Union Rd., Cole Bay* ☎ *599/544–4311*), has a wide array of restaurants and entertainment options. **Rouge et Noir Casino** (⊠ *Front St., Philipsburg* ☎ *599/542–2952*) is small but busy, catering mostly to cruise-ship passengers. **Tropicana Casino** (⊠ *Welfare Rd., Cole Bay* ☎ *599/544–5654*) offers slot machines and games like poker, blackjack, and roulette, as well as live entertainment and a nightly buffet.

DANCE CLUBS

On the Dutch side, **Greenhouse** (⊠ *Front St., Philipsburg* ☎ *599/542–2941*) plays soca, merengue, zouk, and salsa, and has a two-for-one happy hour that lasts all night Tuesday. **Q-Club** (⊠ *Sonesta Maho Beach Resort, Maho Bay* ☎ *599/545–2632*) is a popular disco at the Casino Royale with music for everyone.

EXPLORING ST. MAARTEN/ST. MARTIN

The best way to explore St. Maarten/St. Martin is by car. Though often congested, especially around Philipsburg and Marigot, the roads are fairly good, though narrow and winding, with some speed bumps, potholes, and an occasional wandering goat herd. Few roads are marked with their names, but destination signs are common. Besides, the island is so small that it's hard to get really lost—at least that is what locals tell you.

A scenic "loop" around the island can take just half a day, including plenty of stops. If you head up the east shoreline from Philipsburg, follow the signs to Dawn Beach and Oyster Pond. The road winds past soaring hills, turquoise waters, quaint West Indian houses, and wonderful views of St. Barths. As you cross over to the French side, the road leads to Grand Case, Marigot, and Sandy Ground. From Marigot, the flat island of Anguilla is visible. Completing the loop brings you past Cupecoy Beach, through Maho and Simpson Bay, where Saba looms in the horizon, and back over the mountain road into Philipsburg.

★ **Butterfly Farm.** A serene, tropical environment envelops visitors in the terrarium-like Butterfly Sphere, where dozens of colorful butterflies flit. At any given time, some 40 species of butterflies, numbering as many as 600, flutter inside the garden under a tented net. Butterfly art and memorabilia are for sale in the gift shop. In case you want to come back, your ticket, which includes a guided tour, is good for your entire stay. ⊠ *Rte. de Le Galion, Quartier d'Orléans* ☎ *590/87–31–21* ⊕ *www. thebutterflyfarm.com* 🖾 *$12* 🕙 *Daily 9–3.*

French Cul de Sac. North of Orient Bay Beach, the French-colonial mansion of St. Martin's mayor is nestled in the hills. Little red-roof houses look like open umbrellas tumbling down the green hillside. The area is peaceful and good for hiking. There's construction, however, as the surroundings are slowly being developed. From the beach here, shuttle boats make the five-minute trip to **Ilet Pinel,** an uninhabited island that's fine for picnicking, sunning, and swimming.

Grand Case. The island's most picturesque town is set in the heart of the French side on a beach at the foot of green hills and pastures. Though it has only a 1-mi-long (1½-km-long) main street, it's known as the restaurant capital of the Caribbean. More than 27 restaurants serve French, Italian, Indonesian, and Vietnamese fare here. The budget-minded love the half-dozen lolos—kiosks at the far end of town that sell savory barbecue and seafood. Grand Case Beach Club is at the end of this road and has two beaches where you can take a dip.

Guana Bay Point. On the rugged, windswept east coast about 10 minutes north of Philipsburg, Guana Bay Point offers isolated, untended beaches and a spectacular view of St. Barths. However, because of the undercurrent, this should be more of a turf than a surf destination.

★ **Le Fort Louis.** Though not much remains of the structure itself, the fort, completed by the French in 1789, commands a sweeping view of Marigot, its harbor, and the English island of Anguilla, which alone makes it worth the climb. There are few signs to show the way, so the best way to find the fort is to go to Marigot and look up. ⊠ *Marigot.*

Marigot. This town has a southern European flavor, especially its beautiful harborfront, with shopping stalls, open-air cafés, and fresh-food vendors. It's well worth a few hours to explore if you're a shopper, a gourmand, or just a Francophile. Marina Royale is the shopping complex at the port, but rue de la République and rue de la Liberté, which border the bay, are also filled with duty-free shops, boutiques, and bistros. The West Indies Mall offers a deluxe shopping experience. There's less bustle here than in Philipsburg, and the open-air cafés are tempting places to sit and people-watch. Marigot doesn't die at night, so you might wish to stay here into the evening—particularly on Wednesday, when the market opens its art, crafts, and souvenir stalls, and on Thursday, when the shops of Marina Royale remain open until 10 and shoppers enjoy live music. From the harborfront you can catch the ferry for Anguilla or St. Barths. Overlooking the town is Le Fort Louis, from which you get a breathtaking, panoramic view of Marigot and the surrounding area. Every Wednesday and Saturday at the foot of Le Fort Louis, there's an open-air food market where fresh fish, produce, fruits, and spices are sold and crowds sample the goods. Parking can be a real challenge during the business day and even at night during the high season.

Orléans. North of Oyster Pond and the Étang aux Poissons (Fish Lake) is the island's oldest settlement, also known as the French Quarter. You can find classic, vibrantly painted West Indian–style homes with elaborate gingerbread fretwork.

22

Philipsburg. The capital of Dutch St. Maarten stretches about a mile (1½ km) along an isthmus between Great Bay and the Salt Pond and has five parallel streets. Most of the village's dozens of shops and restaurants are on Front Street, narrow and cobblestoned, closest to Great Bay. It's generally congested when cruise ships are in port, because of its many duty-free shops and several casinos. Little lanes called *steegjes* connect Front Street with Back Street, which has fewer shops and considerably less congestion. Along the beach is a newly constructed ½-mi-long (1-km-long) boardwalk with restaurants and several Wi-Fi hot spots.

Wathey Square (pronounced watty) is in the heart of the village. Directly across from the square are the town hall and the courthouse, in the striking white building with the cupola. The structure was built in 1793 and has served as the commander's home, a fire station, a jail, and a post office. The streets surrounding the square are lined with hotels, duty-free shops, fine restaurants, and cafés. The **Captain Hodge Pier,** just off the square, is a good spot to view Great Bay and the beach that stretches alongside. The **Sint Maarten Museum** hosts rotating cultural exhibits and a permanent historical display called Forts of St. Maarten–St. Martin. The artifacts range from Arawak pottery shards to objects salvaged from the wreck of the HMS *Proselyte.* ⊠ *7 Front St., Philipsburg* ☎*599/542–4917* ☐*Free* ⊙ *Weekdays 10–4, Sat. 10–2.*

★ **Pic du Paradis.** From Friar's Bay Beach, a bumpy, tree-canopied road leads inland to this peak. At 1,492 feet, it's the island's highest point. There are two observation areas. From them, the tropical forest unfolds below and the vistas are breathtaking. The road is quite isolated, so it's best to travel in groups. It's also quite steep and not in particularly good shape, becoming a single lane as you near the summit; if you don't have a four-wheel-drive vehicle, don't even try it. Parking at the top is iffy, and it's best if you turn around before you park. It may not be so easy later.

Near the bottom of Pic du Paradis is **Loterie Farm,** a peaceful 150-acre private nature preserve opened to the public in 1999 by American expat B. J. Welch. Designed to preserve island habitats, Loterie Farm offers a rare glimpse of Caribbean forest and mountain land. Welch has renovated an old farmhouse and welcomes visitors for hiking, mountain biking, ecotours, or less strenuous activities, such as meditation and yoga. Raves accompany lunch and dinner fare at the Hidden Forest Café since chef Julie Purkis took over the kitchen. The restaurant is open Tuesday through Sunday. The Loterie Farm's newest attraction, the Fly Zone, allows Tarzan wannabes to soar over the forest canopy via a series of ropes, cables, and suspended bridges. The Fly Zone boasts the longest zip lines in the Western Hemisphere. ⊠ *Rte. de Pic du Paradis* ☎ *590/87–86–16 or 590/57–28–55* ⌧ *€5* ☉ *Daily sunrise–sunset.*

Plantation Mont Vernon. Wander past indigenous flora, a renovated 1786 cotton plantation, and an old-fashioned rum distillery at a unique outdoor history and ecomuseum. Along the rambling paths of this former wooded estate, bilingual signs give detailed explanations of the island's agricultural history when its economy was dependent on salt, rum, coffee, sugar, and indigo. There's a complimentary coffee bar along the way and a delightful gift shop at the entrance. ⊠ *Rte. d'Orient-Baie* ☎ *590/29–50–62* ⊕ *www.plantationmontvernon.com* ⌧ *€12* ☉ *Daily 9–5.*

☾ **St. Maarten Park.** This delightful little enclave houses animals and plants indigenous to the Caribbean and South America, including many birds that were inherited from a former aviary. There's also a bat cave filled with fruit bats. The zoo's lone male collared peccary now has a female to keep him company. A family of cotton-topped tamarins also have taken residence at the zoo. All the animals live among more than 100 different plant species. The Monkey Bar is the zoo's charming souvenir shop and sells Caribbean and zoo mementos. This is a perfect place to take the kids when they need a break from the sand and sea. ⊠ *Madame Estate, Arch Rd., Philipsburg* ☎ *599/543–2030* ⌧ *$10* ☉ *Mid-Dec.–mid-Apr., daily 9–5; mid-Apr.–mid-Dec., daily 9:30–6.*

ST. MAARTEN/ST. MARTIN ESSENTIALS

To research prices, get advice from other travelers, and book travel arrangements, visit www.fodors.com.

▮ TRANSPORTATION

AIRPORTS
Aéroport de L'Espérance, on the French side, is small and handles only island-hoppers. Jumbo jets fly into Princess Juliana International Airport, on the Dutch side.

Information Aéroport de L'Espérance (*SFG* ⊠ *Grand Case* ☎ *590/87–53–03).* **Princess Juliana International Airport** (*SXM* ☎ *599/546–7542* ⊕ *www.pjiae.com).*

BY AIR
Many major airlines offer nonstop service from the U.S. Air Caraïbes, Caribbean Airlines, DAE, Insel, LIAT, and Winair (Windward Islands Airways) offer service from other islands in the Caribbean.

Information Air Caraïbes (☎ 590/52-05-10 ⊕ www.aircaraibes.com). **American Airlines** (☎ 599/546-2050 ⊕ www.aa.com). **Caribbean Airlines** (☎ 599/546-7610 ⊕ www.caribbean-airlines.com). **Continental Airlines** (☎ 599/546-7671 ⊕ www.continental.com). **Delta Airlines** (☎ 599/599/546-7615 ⊕ www.delta.com). **Dutch Antilles Express** (☎ 599/546-7842 ⊕ www.flydae.com). **Insel Air** (☎ 599/546-7690 ⊕ www.fly-inselair.com). **jetBlue** (☎ 877/306-4939 ⊕ www.jetblue.com). **KLM** (☎ 546-7695 ⊕ www.klm.com). **LIAT** (☎ 599/546-7677 ⊕ www.

liatairline.com). **Spirit Airlines** (☎599/546–7621 ⊕www.spirit.com). **United** (☎599/546–7681 or 800/864–8331 ⊕www.united.com). **US Airways** (☎599/546–7683 ⊕www.usairways.com). **Winair** (☎599/546–7690 ⊕www.fly-winair.com).

BY BIKE & MOPED

Though traffic can be heavy, speeds are generally slow, so a moped can be a good way to get around. Parking is easy, filling the tank is affordable, and you've got that sea breeze to keep you cool. Scooters rent for as low as €25 per day and motorbikes for €37 a day at Eugene Moto, on the French side. At Go Scoot the bikes are in good repair and the counter clerks are helpful. If you're in the mood for a more substantial bike, contact the Harley-Davidson dealer, on the Dutch side, where you can rent a big hog for $150 a day or $900 per week.

Information Eugene Moto (✉Sandy Ground Rd., Sandy Ground ☎590/87–13–97). **Go Scoot** (✉20 Airport Rd., Simpson Bay ☎599/545–4553 ⊕www.aquaworld-goscoot. com). **Harley-Davidson** (✉71 Union Rd., Cole Bay ☎599/544–2704 ⊕www.h-dstmartin. com).

BY BOAT & FERRY

The *Voyager II* offers daily service from Marigot to St. Barths Tuesday through Saturday. The cost for the 75-minute ride is €88 round-trip. The price includes an open bar, tasty snacks, and port fees; children under 12 travel for about half price. It takes about 30 to 40 minutes to get to St. Barths on the new *Rapid Explorer*, a high-speed catamaran, which departs from the Chesterfield Marina. It's €89 round-trip. Link Ferries make the 20-minute trip between the Marigot waterfront and Blowing Point, on Anguilla, every half hour from 8 AM until 7 PM daily. The fare is $26 round-trip.

The *Dawn II* sails Tuesday, Thursday, and Saturday to Saba. The fare is $80 round-trip. High-speed passenger ferries *Edge I* and *Edge II* motor from Simpson

Bay's Pelican Marina to Saba on Wednesday, Friday, and Sunday in just an hour ($100 round-trip) and to St. Barths on Wednesday, Thursday, and Saturday in 45 minutes ($90 round-trip).

Information Dawn II (☎599/416–3671 ⊕www.sabactransport.com). **Edge I and Edge II** (☎599/544–2640 ⊕www.stmaarten-activities.com). **Link Ferries** (☎264/497–2231 or 264/497–3290 ⊕www.link.ai). **Rapid Explorer** (☎590/27–60–33 ⊕www.sbhonline. com). **Voyager II** (☎590/87–10–68 ⊕www. voyager-st-barths.com).

BY CAR

Most people rent a car so they can more easily reach both sides of the island and interesting beaches. Depending on the time of year, a subcompact car will cost between $25 and $50 a day with unlimited mileage. You can rent a car on the French side, but this rarely makes sense for Americans because of the unfavorable exchange rates.

Most roads are paved and in generally good condition. However, they can be crowded, especially when the cruise ships are in port. Be alert for potholes and speed bumps, as well as the island tradition of stopping in the middle of the road to chat with a friend or yield to someone entering traffic. Few roads are identified by name or number, but most have signs indicating the destination. International symbols are used.

Information Avis (☎599/545–2847 or 590/87–50–60). **Budget** (☎599/545–4030 or 866/978–4447). **Dollar** (☎599/545–3281). **Empress Car Rental** (☎866/978–0849). **Golfe Car Rental** (☎599/545–4541 or 590/51–94–81). **Hertz** (☎599/545–4541 or 590/87–83–71). **Sunshine Car Rental** (☎599/545–2685). **Thrifty** (☎599/545–2393). **Unity Car Rental** (☎599/557–6760).

BY TAXI

The government regulates taxi rates. You can hail cabs on the street or call the taxi dispatch to have one sent for you. On the French side of the island, the minimum rate for a taxi is $4, $2 for each additional passenger. There's a taxi service at the Marigot port near the tourist information bureau. Fixed fares apply from Juliana International Airport and the Marigot ferry to the various hotels around the island. Fares are 25% higher between 10 PM and midnight, 50% higher between midnight and 6 AM.

Information Dutch taxi dispatch (☎147). French taxi dispatch (☎590/87–56–54).

▮ CONTACTS & RESOURCES

BANKS & EXCHANGE SERVICES
It's generally not necessary to change your money in St. Maarten/St. Martin. All banks now have ATMs that accept international cards. Remember, though, that they may issue just dollars or just euros. On the Dutch side, try RBTT or Windward Islands Bank, both of which have several branches on the island. On the French side, try Banque des Antilles Françaises or Banque Française Commerciale. MasterCard, Visa, and American Express are accepted all over the island, Diners Club and Discover on occasion.

Legal tender on the Dutch side is the Netherlands Antilles florin (guilder), written NAf or NLG. At this writing, US$1 was equivalent to NLG 1.43. On the French side, the currency is the euro. The exchange rate at this writing was €1 to US$1.57.

Prices quoted in this chapter are in U.S. dollars unless otherwise noted.

ELECTRICITY
Generally, the Dutch side operates on 110 volts AC (60-cycle) and has outlets that accept flat-prong plugs—the same as in North America. The French side operates on 220 volts AC (60-cycle), with round-prong plugs; you need an adapter and sometimes a converter for North American appliances. The French outlets have a safety mechanism—equal pressure must be applied to both prongs of the plug to connect to the socket.

EMERGENCIES
Emergency Services Dutch-side emergencies (☎911 or 599/542–2222). French-side emergencies (☎17 or 590/52–25–52). **Ambulance or fire emergencies Dutch side** (☎120, 130 for ambulances, 599/542–6001). **Ambulance or fire emergencies French side** (☎18, 590/87–95–01 in Grand Case, 590/87–50–08 in La Savanne). **Police emergencies Dutch side** (☎111 or 599/542–2222). **Police emergencies French side** (☎17 or 590/87–88–35 in Marigot, or 590/87–19–76).

Hospitals Hôpital de Marigot (⊠Rue de l'Hôpital, Concordia ☎590/52–25–25). **St. Maarten Medical Center** (⊠Cay Hill ☎599/543–1111).

INTERNET, MAIL & SHIPPING
Many hotels offer Internet service—some complimentary and some for a fee. There are cybercafés scattered throughout the island and Wi-Fi hot spots on the boardwalk behind Front Street in Philipsburg.

The main Dutch-side post office is on Walter Nisbeth Road in Philipsburg. There's a branch at Simpson Bay on Airport Road. The main post office on the French side is in Marigot, on rue de la Liberté. Letters from the Dutch side to North America and Europe cost ANG2.85; postcards to all destinations are ANG1.45. From the French side, letters up to 20 grams and postcards are €1 to North America. When writing to Dutch St. Maarten, call it "Sint Maarten" and make sure to add "Netherlands Antilles" to the address. When writing to the French side, the proper spelling is "St. Martin," and you add "French West Indies" to the address. Postal codes are used only on the French side.

Information Coconets (⊠29 Hope Estate, Grand Case). **Cyber Link** (⊠53 Front St., Philipsburg). **Internet Corner** (⊠105 rue de Hollande, Marigot).

LANGUAGE

Dutch is the official language of St. Maarten, and French is the official language of St. Martin, but almost everyone speaks English. If you hear a language you can't quite place, it may be Papiamento—a mix of Spanish, Portuguese, Dutch, French, and English—spoken throughout the Netherlands Antilles.

SAFETY

Petty crime can be a problem on both sides of the island. Always lock your valuables and travel documents in your room safe or your hotel's front-desk safe. When sightseeing in a rental car, keep valuables locked in the trunk or car, or better yet, don't leave anything in the car. Never leave your things unattended at the beach. Despite the romantic imagery of the Caribbean, it's not good policy to take long walks along the beach at night.

TAXES

Departure tax from Juliana Airport is $10 to destinations within the Netherlands Antilles and $30 to all other destinations. This tax is included in the cost of many airline tickets, so it's best to check with your airline. If it's not included, the tariff must be paid in cash (dollars, euros, or local currency) at a booth before you get on your plane. If you arrive on the island by plane and depart within 24 hours, you'll be considered "in transit" and will not be required to pay the departure tax. It will cost you €3 (usually included in the ticket price) to depart by plane from L'Espérance Airport and $4 by ferry to Anguilla from Marigot's pier.

Hotels on the Dutch side add a 15% service charge to the bill as well as a 5% government tax, for a total of 20%. Hotels on the French side add 10% to 15% for service and a *taxe de séjour*; the amount of this visitor tax differs from hotel to hotel and can be as high as 5%.

TELEPHONES

Calling from one side of the island to another is an international call. To phone from the Dutch side to the French, you first must dial 00–590–590 for local numbers, or 00–590–690 for cell phones, then the six-digit local number. To call from the French side to the Dutch, dial 00–599, then the seven-digit local number. Because of this, many businesses will have numbers on each side for their customers.

To call a local number on the French side, dial 0590 plus the six-digit number. On the Dutch side, just dial the seven-digit number with no prefix.

For calls to the Dutch side from the United States, dial 011–599/54 plus the local number; for the French side, 011–590–590 plus the six-digit local number. At the Landsradio in Philipsburg, there are facilities for overseas calls and a USADirect phone, where you're directly in touch with an operator who will accept collect or credit-card calls. To call direct with an AT&T credit card or operator, dial 001–800/872–2881. On the French side, AT&T can be accessed by calling 080–099–00–11. If you need to use public phones, go to the special desk at Marigot's post office and buy a *télécarte*. There's a public phone at the tourist office in Marigot where you can make credit-card calls: the operator takes your card number (any major card) and assigns you a PIN (Personal Identification Number), which you then use to charge calls to your card.

TIPPING

Often without consistency, service charges of 10% to 15% may be added to hotel and restaurant bills. Especially in restaurants, be sure to ask if a tip is included; that way, you're not either double tipping or short-changing the staff. Taxi drivers, porters, chambermaids, and restaurant waitstaff depend on tips. The guideline is 10% to 15% for waitstaff and cabbies,

$1 per bag for porters, and $1 to $5 per night for chambermaids.

TOUR OPTIONS

A 2½-hour taxi tour of the island costs $50 for one or two people, $18 for each additional person. Your hotel or the tourist office can arrange it for you. Elle Si Belle offers island tours by van or bus for $15.

Information **Elle Si Belle** (⊠ Airport Blvd., Simpson Bay ☏ 599/545–4954).

VISITOR INFORMATION

Before You Leave **St. Maarten Tourist Office** (Dutch side only ☏ 800/786–2278 or 212/953–2084 in New York City ⊕ www.st-maarten.com). **St. Martin Office of Tourism** (French side only ☏ 877/956–1234 or 212/475–8970 in New York City ⊕ www.st-martin.org).

In St. Maarten/St. Martin **Dutch-side Tourist Information Bureau** (⊠ Cyrus Wathey Sq., Philipsburg ☏ 599/542–2337). **Dutch-side tourist bureau administrative office** (⊠ 33 W. G. Buncamper Rd., in Vineyard Park Bldg., Philipsburg ☏ 599/542–2337). **French-side Office de Tourisme** (⊠ Rte. de Sandy Ground, near Marina Port-Royale, Marigot ☏ 590/87–57–21 or 590/87–57–21).

WEDDINGS

Marriages on St. Maarten follow the same rules as on the other Netherlands Antilles islands; getting married on the French side really isn't feasible because of stringent residency requirements, identical to those in France. Couples must be at least 18 years old and submit their documents at least 14 days prior to the wedding date. The application requires notarized original documents to be submitted to the registrar, including birth certificates, passports (for non-Dutch persons), divorce decrees from previous marriages, death certificates of deceased spouses, and passports for six witnesses if the ceremony is to take place outside of the Marriage Hall. The documents must be submitted in Dutch or English—or else they must be translated into Dutch. The cost for this process is $285.90. Any questions should be directed to the chief registrar.

Information **Chief Registrar** (⊠ Census Office, Soualiga Rd., Philipsburg ☏ 599/542–5647).

St. Vincent & the Grenadines

Tobago Cays, the Grenadines

WORD OF MOUTH

"There is more sightseeing on St. Vincent—absolutely gorgeous, rugged, a step back in time. I would love to go back."

—joan

"If you want to day trip to the various Grenadines, Union Island is your best bet. It's pretty centrally located to Mayreau, Canouan, and the Tobago Cays. And you can fly to Mustique from there on SVG Airways. You can also day trip to Mustique from Bequia on the *Friendship Rose*."

—ejcrowe

www.fodors.com/forums

St. Vincent's La Soufrière volcano last erupted in 1979. The first written description of an eruption here was published in 1718 by Daniel Defoe, author of *Robinson Crusoe*.

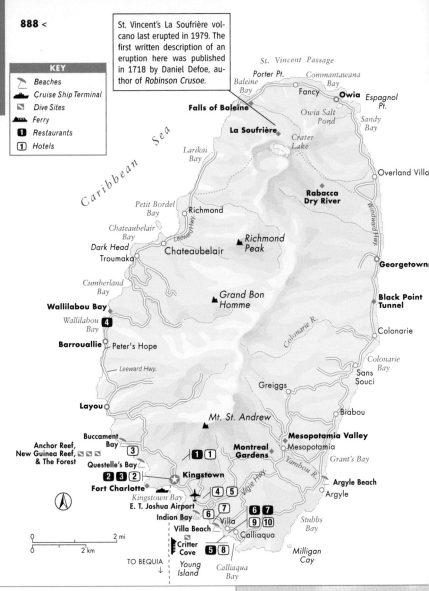

KEY

- Beaches
- Cruise Ship Terminal
- Dive Sites
- Ferry
- **1** Restaurants
- **1** Hotels

St. Vincent Passage

Porter Pt.
Baleine Bay
Commantawana Bay
Fancy
Owia
Espagnol Pt.

Falls of Baleine

Caribbean Sea

La Soufrière
Owia Salt Pond
Sandy Bay

Crater Lake

Larikai Bay

Overland Villa

Petit Bordel Bay
Richmond
Rabacca Dry River

Chateaubelair Bay
Richmond Peak

Dark Head
Troumaka
Chateaubelair

Georgetown

Cumberland Bay

Black Point Tunnel

Wallilabou Bay
Grand Bon Homme
Colonarie

Wallilabou Bay **4**

Barrouallie
Peter's Hope

Colonarie R.

Colonarie Bay

Sans Souci

Leeward Hwy.

Greiggs

Layou
Biabou

Mt. St. Andrew

Buccament Bay **3**

Anchor Reef, New Guinea Reef, & The Forest

Montreal Gardens

Mesopotamia Valley
Mesopotamia

Grant's Bay

Questelle's Bay **2 3 2**

1 1

Fort Charlotte
Kingstown

Yambou R.

Argyle Beach
Argyle

Kingstown Bay
E. T. Joshua Airport
4 5

6 7

7
Indian Bay
6
Villa
9 10

Stubbs Bay

Villa Beach
Calliaqua

Critter Cove
5 8

Young Island

Calliaqua Bay

Milligan Cay

0 —— 2 mi
0 —— 2 km

TO BEQUIA ↓

There are 32 perfectly endowed Grenadine islands and cays in this archipelago that provide some of the Caribbean's best anchorages and prettiest beaches.

WELCOME TO ST. VINCENT & THE GRENADINES

A STRING OF PEARLS

St. Vincent, which is 18 mi (29 km) long and 11 mi (18 km) wide, is the northernmost and largest of the chain of 32 islands that make up St. Vincent & the Grenadines and extend in a string 45 mi southwest toward Grenada. What these islands all have in common is a get-away-from-it-all atmosphere and a virtual lack of large-scale development.

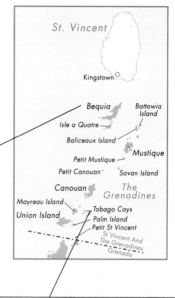

Inhabitants of Bequia, the largest of the Grenadines islands, have long been known for their boat-building skills; now, they are equally recognized for building model boats.

Though they are uninhabited by people, the Tobago Cays and surrounding Horseshoe Reef are rich with underwater marine life, placing this as one of the best snorkeling sites in the world.

Hotels .... ▼	Restaurants .... ▼
Beachcombers 6	Basil's Bar & Restaurant 2
Cobblestone Inn 2	The French Verandah 6
Grand View Beach Hotel 4	Grenadine House 1
Grenadine House 1	Lime Restaurant & Pub 7
The Lagoon Marina Hotel 9	Vee Jay's Rooftop Diner & Pub 3
Mariners Hotel 10	Wallilabou Anchorage 4
Petit Byahaut 3	Young Island Resort 5
Sunset Shores Beach Hotel 7	
Villa Lodge Hotel 5	
Young Island Resort 8	

TOP 4 REASONS TO VISIT ST. VINCENT & THE GRENADINES

1 St. Vincent, with hiking trails, botanical gardens, waterfalls, and dive sites, is a good destination for ecotourism.

2 Since there are few large resorts, you'll find peace and quiet—and no crowds—throughout St. Vincent and the Grenadines.

3 Island-hopping sailing charters are a perfect way to visit the many beautiful Grenadines.

4 Grenadine beaches have brilliant white and powdery soft sand, washed by gentle waves in several shades of blue.

ST. VINCENT & THE GRENADINES PLANNER

Island Activities

Beautiful **beaches** and excellent waters for **sailing** can be found throughout the Grenadines. The beaches on St. Vincent have dark, volcanic sand and, while beautiful, are less than excellent for swimming and sunbathing. You come to these islands to really get away from it all and for **relaxation**, but don't miss the opportunity to do some easy **island-hopping**.

The reef system surrounding the uninhabited Tobago Cays offers some of the best **snorkeling** in the world. Around St. Vincent itself, the waters are rich with marine life, offering **divers** abundant places to explore.

On land, you can **hike** through St. Vincent's verdant forests or **climb** its volcano, La Soufrière. But if you are staying at one of the excellent, luxurious resorts on an isolated Grenadine island, you may be tempted to lie back, immerse yourself in the moment, and do little more than to raise your flag for another rum punch.

Logistics

Getting to St. Vincent and the Grenadines: Until the new international airport becomes a reality (in 2011), you will have to connect in one of six Caribbean islands (Barbados, Grenada, Martinique, St. Lucia, Puerto Rico, or Trinidad) to reach either St. Vincent or any of the Grenadines. Some of the smaller Grenadines require both a flight and a boat ride. Unless you're on a private jet, it's an exhausting, time-consuming trip (it's also fairly expensive), yet people still make the effort to reach some of the most wonderful, unspoiled islands in the Caribbean. Once you've landed on St. Vincent, it's also possible to hop to several different islands for a day or longer by air or by an interisland ferry.

Hassle Factor: High, but worth it.

Nonstops: None from the U.S.

On the Ground

St. Vincent's E.T. Joshua Airport is in ArnoVale, about halfway between Kingstown and Villa Beach. It's a small but busy airport, and it only accommodates turboprop aircraft. In the Grenadines, Bequia and Canouan have small, modern airports. Mustique and Union islands each have an airstrip with frequent regional service. Taxis and buses are readily available at the airport on St. Vincent. The taxi fare to hotels in either Kingstown or the Villa Beach area is $10 (or EC$25). Taxi service is available from the airports on Bequia, Mustique, Canouan, and Union islands.

Renting a Car: You can rent a car on either St. Vincent or Bequia, but rates are fairly expensive, and you must also purchase a temporary driving permit. If you rent a car, though, you'll have more flexibility to go out to dinner and explore the island at your leisure. Many people will be happy to hire a driver for the day or to take a scheduled tour, but the island scenery is dramatically beautiful, so having the freedom to explore at your own pace may be worth the price. A scooter or moped is a less-expensive options.

Where to Stay

Mass tourism hasn't come to St. Vincent and the Grenadines, and the islands' relative isolation means that it probably never will. Most places on St. Vincent are small and simple. If you want luxury and privacy, look to one of the exclusive resorts in the Grenadines, where both can be found in great abundance. If you have the time, it's easy to island-hop by air or by interisland ferry, staying on several islands in simple guesthouses to maximize both your budget and experiences.

Luxury Resorts: Scattered throughout the Grenadines are several fine, luxury resorts, including some that offer a Robinson Crusoe experience without the need to sacrifice the important comforts. Formalities tend to be few, but you will pay handsomely for service, comfort, and privacy.

Simple Resorts and Guesthouses: Most lodgings in St. Vincent are simple, friendly, and relatively inexpensive. There are a lot of guesthouses throughout the islands. Bequia and Union, in particular, have many simple, inexpensive guesthouses.

Villas: Luxurious villas make up the majority of accommodations on Mustique, and they offer every amenity you can imagine. Private villas are also available for rent in Bequia.

Hotel & Restaurant Costs

⇨*For information on hotel meal plans, see Accommodations in Caribbean Essentials.*

WHAT IT COSTS IN U.S. DOLLARS

	$$$$	$$$	$$	$	¢
Restaurants					
	over $30	$20–$30	$12–$20	$8–$12	under $8
Hotels*					
	over $350	$250–$350	$150–$250	$80–$150	under $80
Hotels**					
	over $450	$350–$450	$250–$350	$125–$250	under $125

*EP, BP, CP **AI, FAP, MAP Restaurant prices are for a main course at dinner and include any taxes or service charges. Hotel prices are per night for a double room in high season, excluding taxes, service charges, and meal plans (except at all-inclusives).

When to Go

High season runs roughly from mid-December through mid-April, then rates are usually reduced by at least 40%. Seasonal discounts vary dramatically by resort and by island, with some of the luxury resorts offering better deals periodically throughout the year, though the most-luxurious resorts are always expensive. Inexpensive guesthouses have less seasonal variation in their rates.

The **St. Vincent Blues Fest** is held in mid-March. The **SVG Gospelfest** is held throughout the month of April. Vincy Mas, the St. Vincent **Carnival** celebration, is the island's biggest cultural festival, beginning in June and culminating at the end of July in a huge street party.

Bequia has its own Bequia **Blues Festival** in early February. An **Easter Regatta** brings everyone out to watch boat races. The Bequia **Carnival** is a summer celebration in late June.

The **Canouan Regatta** is held at the end of May. The **Easterval Regatta** on Union Island is on Easter weekend. The two-week Mustique **Blues Festival** begins in early January.

Updated by
Jane E. Zarem

"I KNOW YOU!" AS I walked past the taxi stand on Kingstown's Bay Street, that comment was aimed at me. Sure enough—when I looked back over my shoulder, I noticed one of the drivers smiling at me. He had, in fact, driven me around the island on my visit to St. Vincent the year before. People in St. Vincent and the Grenadines actually have an amusing saying about island living: "You know half the people; the other half knows you!" I think that might be true.

A string of 32 islands and cays composes the single nation of St. Vincent and the Grenadines. SVG, as it's often abbreviated, is in the Windward Islands chain in the southern Caribbean. Mountainous St. Vincent, only 18 mi (29 km) by 11 mi (18 km) and just 13 degrees north of the equator, is the largest and northernmost of the group; the Grenadines extend southwest in a 45-mi (73-km) arc toward Grenada.

St. Vincent is one of the least-"touristy" islands in the Caribbean. That has little to do with it being welcoming or attractive or interesting. In fact, St. Vincent and its people reveal all of those qualities. The Vincentians are friendly, the island is beautiful, and getting around is fairly easy. St. Vincent is simply an unpretentious and relatively quiet island, where fishermen get up at the crack of dawn to drop their nets into the sea, working people go about their day-to-day business in town, and farmers spend backbreaking days working their crops in the countryside.

Most visitors to St. Vincent, it seems, are regional businesspeople, Vincentians who live overseas and travel home to visit family, and vacationers en route to the Grenadines. Hotels and inns are rather small, locally owned and operated, and definitely not glitzy. The only "resort" is on a separate island, 600 feet from the mainland. Restaurants serve mainly local food—grilled fish, stewed or curried chicken, rice, and root vegetables. And the beaches are either tiny crescents of black or brown sand on remote leeward bays or sweeping expanses of the same black sand pounded by Atlantic surf.

St. Vincent's major export is bananas, and banana plants, along with coconut palms and breadfruit trees, crowd more of the island than the 110,000 inhabitants (another 8,800 live on the Grenadines). This has obvious charm for nature lovers. Actually, more and more independent travelers interested in active, ecofriendly vacations are discovering St. Vincent's natural beauty, its active sports opportunities on land and sea, and the richness of its history. They spend their vacation walking or hiking St. Vincent's well-defined jungle trails, catching a glimpse of the rare St. Vincent parrot in the Vermont Valley, exploring exotic flora in the Botanical Garden and in Montreal Gardens, delving into history at Ft. Charlotte, trekking to the spectacular Trinity Falls or the Falls of Baleine, and climbing the active volcano La Soufrière, which last erupted in 1979. Beneath the surface, snorkeling and scuba landscapes are similarly intriguing.

With all that said about down-to-earth, yet still-captivating St. Vincent, the islands of the Grenadines are quite the opposite and will dazzle you with their amazing inns and resorts, fine white-sand beaches, excellent sailing waters, and get-away-from-it-all atmosphere.

Bequia, the largest of the Grenadines, is just south of St. Vincent and a pleasant hour's voyage by ferry—an easy day trip. But Bequia has a large complement of inns, hotels, restaurants, shops, and activities and, therefore, is a popular vacation destination in its own right. Its Admiralty Bay is one of the prettiest anchorages in the Caribbean. With superb views, snorkeling, hiking, and swimming, the island has much to offer the international mix of backpackers and luxury-yacht owners who frequent its shores.

South of Bequia, on the exclusive, private island of Mustique, elaborate villas are tucked into lush hillsides. Mustique does not encourage wholesale tourism, least of all to those hoping for a glimpse of the rich and famous who own or rent villas here. The appeal of Mustique is its seclusion. Nevertheless, Basil's Bar on Brittania Bay and many of the island's lovely beaches are favorite stopovers of the yachting set.

Boot-shape Canouan, just over 5 square mi (11 square km) in area, has been reborn. Still mostly quiet and unspoiled, with only 1,200 or so residents who traditionally earn their living by farming or fishing, Canouan now has paved roads, a clinic, a new fisheries complex, and daily flights from Puerto Rico, St. Lucia, and Barbados bringing well-heeled guests to Raffles Resort Canouan Island. The posh, full-service resort takes up the entire northern third of the island, and boasts one of the Caribbean's most-challenging and most-scenic golf courses and a European-style casino (both of which are Trump enterprises), and has an incredibly inviting spa.

Tiny Mayreau, next in the chain and the smallest inhabited Grenadine, with an area of only 1.5 square mi (4 square km), has fewer than 200 residents—but one of the area's most beautiful beaches. At Saltwhistle Cay, at the narrow northern tip of the island, the Caribbean Sea is often mirror calm; and, just yards away, the rolling Atlantic surf washes the opposite shore. Otherwise, Mayreau has a single unnamed village, one road, rain-caught drinking water, and a couple of inns—but no airport, no bank, and no problems!

Union Island, with its dramatic landscape punctuated by Mt. Parnassus, is the transportation center of the southern Grenadines. Its small but busy airport serves landlubbers, while its yacht harbor and dive operators serve sailors and scuba divers. Clifton, the main town, has shops, restaurants, and a few guesthouses. Ashton, the second significant town, is mainly residential. Union Island is particularly popular among French vacationers who often cruise to the Grenadines on chartered yachts from Martinique or Guadeloupe. Union is a popular spot for yachties to come ashore, restock supplies, and mingle with more-"grounded" folks.

Meanwhile, it took decades to turn the 100-acre, mosquito-infested mangrove swamp called Prune Island into the upscale private resort now known as Palm Island. Today, vacationers who can afford it lounge in luxury on the island's five palm-fringed white-sand beaches.

Petit St. Vincent is another private, single-resort island, reclaimed from the overgrowth by owner-manager Hazen K. Richardson II. The luxury resort's cobblestone cottages are so private that, if you wish, you could spend your entire vacation completely undisturbed.

And finally, the Tobago Cays, five uninhabited islands south of Canouan and east of Mayreau, draw snorkelers and divers who are mesmerized by the marine life here and boaters who are equally impressed with the sheer beauty of the area. Surrounded by a shallow reef, the tiny islands have rustling palm trees, pristine beaches, the clearest water in varying shades of brilliant blue—and plenty of resident fish.

One important thing to keep in mind when considering a vacation trip to St. Vincent and the Grenadines is that the various islands are fairly close together. Whether you travel by boat or by plane, traveling between or among them is not difficult. In fact, St. Vincent and each of the Grenadines are all quite unique. Once there, you'll definitely want to sample more than one.

ST. VINCENT

WHERE TO STAY

With a few exceptions, tourist accommodations and facilities on St. Vincent are in either Kingstown or the Villa Beach area. Most hotel rates are EP, with MAP available as an option; some luxury resorts in the Grenadines offer FAP or all-inclusive plans; and small inns often offer BP or CP. All guest rooms have air-conditioning, TV, and phone, unless stated otherwise.

VILLA COMMUNITIES

Since the island's air service has been limited to small planes operated by regional carriers, huge villa communities and condo complexes are late to arrive in St. Vincent, though an international airport set to open in 2011 likely will change that. The island's first villa community is under construction at Buccament Bay, north of Kingstown. The first phase of Buccament Bay Beach Resort is expected to open in 2009; when complete, the 80-acres beachfront community will have more than 600 one- and two-bedroom town houses, 18 man-made lakes, six restaurants, eight bars, a three-tier swimming pool, a full-service spa, and a golf course.

HOTELS & RESORTS

$$$–$$$$

🛈 **Young Island Resort.** St. Vincent's only true resort is 200 yards offshore (a five-minute ride from Villa Beach by hotel launch) on its own 35-acre island. Airy hillside cottages are decorated in ecru, ocher, and green, with bamboo and rattan furniture. Walls of stone and glass have louvered windows surrounding the sitting areas. Each cottage has a terrace, and bathrooms have garden showers. All cottages have water

Fodor's Choice

★

views despite being hidden in lush tropical vegetation. Two beachfront cottage suites and three on the hillside have separate sitting rooms and private plunge pools; the hillside Duvernette Suite has its own infinity-edge swimming pool and a furnished sundeck. Dine either in the terrace dining room or in a private thatch-roof gazebo. Sailaway packages include two nights touring the Grenadines on a 44-foot sailing yacht. **Pros:** Casually elegant, private white-sand beach, great honeymoon choice or wedding venue, also appropriate for families. **Cons:** No in-room communication devices (unless that appeals to you), noise from nearby nightspots wafts across channel on weekends. ⌂*Box 211, Young Island* ☎*784/458–4826* ⊕*www.youngisland.com* ⇆*23 cottage rooms, 6 cottages suites* � *In-room: no a/c, no phone, safe, refrigerator, no TV. In-hotel: restaurant, room service, bars, tennis court, pool, spa, beachfront, water sports, no elevator, laundry service, public Internet, airport shuttle* ▭*AE, D, MC, V* ⊙*Closed Sept.* �*MAP.*

$$$ 🛏**Petit Byahaut.** Soft-adventure aficionados love this 50-acre ecoretreat, accessible only by a 10-minute boat ride from Buccament Bay (complimentary airport transfers and water taxi for guests). Its picturesque bay front was one of the locations for the *Pirates of the Caribbean* films. Accommodations are in large, open-style cabins, complete with wood floors, private decks, queen-size beds, hammocks, batik artwork, solar-powered lighting, and bathrooms with alfresco, solar-heated rainwater showers. Three meals daily, including candlelight dinners, are served in the open-air dining room, which overlooks the bay. The menu is limited to a couple of choices and always one that's vegetarian. Although well-behaved children are allowed, the rugged terrain and peaceful atmosphere are clearly oriented toward adults. There's a selection of kayaks, endless nature trails, breezy sitting areas, and countless opportunities for bird-watching, along with free use of the scuba and snorkeling equipment and a private black-sand beach. If you tire of the seclusion, excursions are easily arranged. Weekly rates are available. **Pros:** Nature lovers' bliss, good choice for scuba divers. **Cons:** Rustic environment you'll either love or hate. ⌂*Petit Byahaut Bay* ☎*784/457–7008* ⊕*www.petitbyahaut.com* ⇆*4 cabins* ⚪*In-room: no a/c, no phone, no TV. In-hotel: restaurant, bar, beachfront, diving, water sports, no elevator, airport shuttle* ▭*D, MC, V* ⊙*Closed Aug.–Oct.* ⇆*3-night minimum* ⎮*FAP.*

$$–$$$ 🛏**Grenadine House.** Wedged into a residential hillside neighborhood
★ five minutes by taxi from downtown Kingstown and the Botanical Garden, this stylish boutique hotel was rebuilt in the early 1990s on the site of the island's oldest guesthouse (1781) and the home of its first French governor. Completely renovated once again in 2007 by new owners, the inn is favored especially by regional business travelers and perfect for vacationers who want modern comforts in an elegant setting but don't require planned activities or resort features. The hotel does, however, have a pool, a gym, and broad verandahs with sweeping views of the city and the harbor. Rooms are large, with 1930s-style brown-wicker bureaus that contrast against the light-color walls—plain except for a large period travel poster. The European-style service is friendly, efficient, and low-key. Table d'hôte lunch and dinner are available in

the Sapodilla Room, the air-conditioned restaurant on the ground level; breakfast is served on the terrace. Grenadine House and Bequia Beach Hotel on Friendship Bay in Bequia (just renovated and significantly expanded in 2007–08) share the same ownership, so two-island, two-hotel packages are easily arranged. **Pros:** Friendly atmosphere, very attractive rooms, excellent dining. **Cons:** Quiet, residential area far from any beach and a $4 taxi ride to town. ⌂ *Box 2523, Kingstown Park, Kingstown* ☎*784/458–1800, 866/659–8351, or 919/439–4227* ⊕*www.grenadinehouse.com* ↩*20 rooms* ⌂*In-room: safe, Ethernet. In-hotel: restaurant, room service, bar, pool, gym, no elevator, laundry service, public Internet, airport shuttle* ⊟*AE, MC, V* ⍓*CP.*

$$ ⊡ **Grand View Beach Hotel.** In the 1940s, Tony Sardine's family purchased
★ an 8-acre piece of history on a beautiful point of land overlooking Indian Bay and used the greathouse as a private residence until 1965, when it became the Grand View Hotel. But the property has a much longer history: In the 1700s, the area had been Wilkie's Battery, which supported Ft. Duvernette just behind Young Island. And in the 1870s, the main building on the property was converted to a cotton-drying house. Rooms are attractive and comfortable, but not fussy; most offer sweeping vistas of the Grenadines. Luxury rooms have broad terraces with ocean views; two honeymoon suites have king beds and whirlpool tubs. Hallways and walls are filled with the artwork of Caroline Sardine, the owner's daughter, who operates the Little Art Gallery at the hotel's beachside Grand View Grill. Guests and locals enjoy drinks at the Sundowner Bar and West Indian and Continental-style cuisine at Wilkie's restaurant. Sailboats, Windsurfers, and snorkeling equipment are complimentary, but you have to hike down a rather steep hill to the beach. **Pros:** Friendly, family-run boutique vibe, beautiful (grand) sunset views, lots of on-site amenities—including a squash court. **Cons:** That hike down to the beach, a rental car would be handy, a few rooms don't have air-conditioning. ✉ *Villa Point* ☎*784/458–4811* ⊕*www. grandviewhotel.com* ↩*19 rooms, 2 suites* ⌂*In-room: no a/c (some), safe, refrigerator (some), DVD, VCR, Ethernet. In-hotel: 2 restaurants, room service, bars, tennis court, pool, gym, beachfront, water sports, no elevator, laundry service, public Wi-Fi* ⊟*AE, MC, V* ⍓*EP.*

$$ ⊡ **Sunset Shores Beach Hotel.** Down a long, steep driveway off the main road, this lemon-yellow low-rise hotel, in business since 1972, surrounds a small pool and a gigantic and prolific mango tree (help yourself from January through July). It also faces a lovely curve of Indian Bay beachfront. All rooms are large, with patios or balconies. Opt for a room with a water view; otherwise, you'll have to amble over to the poolside bar to get a glimpse of the gorgeous sunsets. The restaurant has a small but varied menu with fresh local fish and lobster (in season); service is friendly and efficient. Local businesspeople frequent the restaurant and conference facilities, yet it primarily caters to vacationers. **Pros:** Excellent location Villa Beach opposite Young Island, pool/bar area lovely at sundown, the price is right. **Cons:** Room decor is rather ordinary, beach is narrow and sometimes next-to-nothing. ⌂ *Box 849, Villa Beach* ☎*784/458–4411* ⊕*www.sunsetshores.com* ↩*32 rooms*

⚲ *In-hotel: restaurant, room service, bars, pool, beachfront, water sports, no elevator, laundry service* ⊟ *AE, D, MC, V* ⦿*EP.*

$–$$ ⊞ **Mariners Hotel.** This friendly, small hotel is on the Villa Beach waterfront, opposite Young Island. Rooms are large, and each has a balcony or terrace facing the water or overlooking the small pool. The French Verandah serves breakfast and lunch with a picturesque view and dinner by candlelight. Other restaurants are nearby, along the waterfront, or you can catch the Young Island ferry to take you to dinner at the resort just across the channel. Although the hotel itself doesn't have a good beach (it's narrow to nonexistent), Mariners guests may use the Young Island beach. The hotel can arrange scuba diving, sportfishing, boat charters, and other activities. **Pros:** Restaurant's French cuisine, guests may use lovely Young Island beach, many water sports available nearby. **Cons:** Rooms large but rather simply decorated, pool small but refreshing. ✉ *Box 859, Villa Beach* ☎*784/457–4000* ⦿*www. marinershotel.com* ⌦*20 rooms* ⚲*In-room: safe, dial-up. In-hotel: restaurant, bars, pool, beachfront, no elevator, public Internet* ⊟*AE, D, MC, V* ⦿*EP.*

$ ⊞ **Beachcombers Hotel.** In 1990, Cheryl Hornsey opened a small (six-room) bed-and-breakfast in her family home overlooking the sea at Villa Beach. Today—through hard work, devotion to details, and much success—the little inn has morphed into a delightful, 31-room, beachfront hotel with a pool, restaurant, and popular bar. Rooms are in the original family home and in a pair of brightly colored (one orange; the other, yellow), three-story buildings. Half the guest rooms overlook the sea; the others face the garden's frenzy of flowers. All are tidy, comfortable, and clean as a whistle. Two enormous penthouse suites each have a full kitchen, elegantly furnished sitting/dining rooms, a modern bath with a whirlpool tub, and a large private balcony with a view of the Grenadines. All rooms, in fact, have patios or balconies with lovely views. Perhaps best of all, Beachcombers offers spa services: aromatherapy, facials, sauna, steam bath, and more. On weekend evenings you can usually find a live band and dancing on the sundeck adjacent to the Beach House restaurant and bar. **Pros:** Great value and location, best beachfront in the area. **Cons:** Popular with small groups so book well ahead, standard rooms are rather "standard" (upgrade to deluxe or penthouse rooms for a relatively insignificant extra fee). ✉ *Box 126, Villa Beach* ☎*784/458–4283* ⦿*www.beachcombershotel.com* ⌦*27 rooms, 4 suites* ⚲*In-room: safe, kitchen (some), refrigerator (some), Ethernet, Wi-Fi. In-hotel: restaurant, room service, bar, pool, spa, beachfront, no elevator, laundry service, public Internet, public Wi-Fi, no-smoking rooms* ⊟*AE, D, MC, V* ⦿*CP.*

$ ⊞ **Lagoon Marina & Hotel.** This hotel overlooking sheltered Blue Lagoon bay may well be the island's busiest. Thanks to its 44-berth marina, there are usually seafaring types liming (hanging out) at the Green Flash restaurant and bar on the second floor overlooking the docks, and plenty of yacht traffic to watch from a couch on your big balcony. Sliding patio doors lead onto these perches. Basic furniture, twin beds, dim lighting, tile bathrooms, and ceiling fans provide an adequate level of comfort, but don't expect luxury. Thick foliage covering a steep hillside

23

on the land side of the property conceal a two-level pool. **Pros:** Busy marina provides great dockside atmosphere, good restaurant, convivial bar. Cons: Simply furnished accommodations ⊠*Blue Lagoon, Box 133, Ratho Mill* ☎*784/458–4308* ⊕*www.lagoonmarina.com* ↩*19 rooms* ☐*In-room: Wi-Fi. In-hotel: restaurant, room service, bar, pools, beachfront, water sports, no elevator, laundry service, public Internet, public Wi-Fi* ☐*MC, V* ⍵*EP.*

$ ⊡**Villa Lodge Hotel.** The venerable Villa Lodge has been welcoming guests since 1961, when a private hillside home was first transformed into a family-operated bed-and-breakfast inn. Additions and renovations over the years turned the inn into a small hotel, but the home-like atmosphere and friendly, personalized service remain. Hotel rooms with king-size beds and small balconies are comfortably yet simply furnished. The eight Breezeville Apartments, which have full kitchens, are better for longer stays. The Patio Restaurant, which attracts local diners as well as hotel guests, offers international cuisine. Indian Bay beach is 100 yards from the hotel. **Pros:** Inexpensive, catch a minibus at the door to go to town or Villa Beach, restaurant is very good. **Cons:** Rooms are large but not fancy; a long stay might become, well, a long stay. ⌂*Box 1191, Indian Bay* ☎*784/458–4641* ⊕*www.villalodge. com* ↩*11 rooms, 8 apartments* ☐*In-room: safe, refrigerator, dial-up. In-hotel: restaurant, bars, pool, no elevator, public Internet* ☐*AE, MC, V* ⍵*EP.*

¢–$ ⊡**Cobblestone Inn.** On the waterfront in "the city," as Vincentians call Kingstown, this small hotel occupies a stone structure formerly used as a warehouse for sugar and arrowroot. Converted to a hotel in 1970, the building has original (1814) Georgian architecture, a sunny interior courtyard, and winding cobblestone walkways and arches. Rooms are tiny, but each has stone walls, rattan furniture, and a private bath. Room No. 5, at the front, is lighter and bigger than most of the others—but noisier, too. A rooftop bar-restaurant serves breakfast and light lunches. The popular Basil's Bar and Restaurant is at ground level. **Pros:** Convenient for an overnight stay if you're taking an early ferry to the Grenadines, neat historical atmosphere, fascinating architecture. **Cons:** Tiny rooms, wandering around the downtown streets at night is not recommended. ⊠*Upper Bay St., Box 867, Kingstown* ☎*784/456–1937* ⊕*www.thecobblestoneinn.com* ↩*19 rooms* ☐*In-hotel: restaurant, bar, no elevator, laundry service, public Internet* ☐*AE, D, MC, V* ⍵*EP.*

WHERE TO EAT

Nearly all restaurants in St. Vincent specialize in local West Indian cuisine, although you can find chefs with broad culinary experience at a few hotel restaurants. Local dishes to try include *callaloo* (similar to spinach) soup, curried goat or chicken, *rotis* (turnovers filled with curried meat or vegetables), fresh-caught seafood (lobster, kingfish, snapper, and mahimahi), local vegetables (avocados, breadfruit, squashlike christophene, and pumpkin) and "provisions" (roots such as yams and dasheen), and tropical fruit (from mangoes and soursop to pineapples and papaya). Fried or baked chicken is available everywhere, often accompanied by "rice 'n' peas" or *pelau* (seasoned rice). The local beer, Hairoun, is brewed according to a German recipe at Campden Park, just north of Kingstown. Sunset is the local rum.

WHAT TO WEAR

Restaurants are casual. You may want to dress up a little—long pants and collared shirts for gents, summer dresses or dress pants for the ladies—for an evening out at a pricey restaurant, but none of the places listed below require gentlemen to wear a jacket or tie. Beachwear, however, is never appropriate in restaurants.

23

CARIBBEAN ✕ **Basil's Bar and Restaurant.** It's not just the air-conditioning that makes
$–$$ this restaurant cool. Downstairs at the Cobblestone Inn, Basil's is owned by Basil Charles, whose Basil's Beach Bar on Mustique is a hangout for the vacationing rich and famous. This is the Kingstown power-lunch venue. Local businesspeople gather for the daily buffet or full menu of salads, sandwiches, barbecued chicken, or fresh seafood platters. Dinner entrées of pasta, local seafood, and chicken are served at candlelit tables. There's a Chinese buffet on Friday, and takeout is available that night only. ⊠ *Cobblestone Inn, Upper Bay St., Kingstown* ☎ *784/457–2713* ▤ *AE, MC, V.*

$–$$ ✕ **Vee Jay's Rooftop Diner & Pub.** Come here for "authentic Vincy cuisine" specials, which are chalked on the blackboard: mutton or fish stew, chicken or vegetable rotis, curried goat, souse, and *buljol* (sautéed codfish, breadfruit, and vegetables). Not-so-Vincy sandwiches, fish-and-chips, and burgers can be authentically washed down with *mauby,* a bittersweet drink made from tree bark; linseed, peanut, passion-fruit, or sorrel punch; local Hairoun beer; or cocktails. Lunch is buffet style. ⊠ *Bay St., Kingstown* ☎ *784/457–2845* ⌂ *Reservations essential* ▤ *AE, MC, V* ☾ *Closed Sun.*

¢–$ ✕ **Wallilabou Anchorage.** Halfway up the Caribbean coast of St. Vincent, this is a favorite luncheon stop for folks sailing the Grenadines, for day-trippers returning from a visit to the Falls of Baleine, and for landlubbers touring the leeward coast. The picturesque view of the bay is enhanced by the period stage sets left behind by the *Pirates of the Caribbean* filmmakers. Open all day (from 8 AM), the bar-and-restaurant serves snacks, sandwiches, tempting West Indian dishes, and lobster in season. Ice, telephones, business services, and shower facilities are available to boaters. ⊠ *Leeward Hwy., Wallilabou Bay* ☎ *784/458–7270* ▤ *AE, MC, V.*

CONTINENTAL ✕ **Young Island Resort Restaurant.** Take the ferry (a two-minute ride from
$$$$ Villa Beach) to Young Island for a delightful lunch or a very special, ★ romantic evening. Stone paths lead to candlelit tables, some in breezy, thatch-roof huts. Tiny waves lap against the shore. Five-course, prix-fixe dinners of grilled seafood, roast pork, beef tenderloin, and sautéed chicken are accompanied by local vegetables; a board of freshly made breads is offered for your selection. Two or three choices are offered for each course. Lunch is à la carte—soups, salads, grilled meats, or fish—and served on the beachfront terrace. ⊠ *Young Island* ☎ *784/458–4826* ⌂ *Reservations essential* ▤ *AE, D, MC, V.*

$$-$$$
Fodor's Choice
★

✕**Grenadine House.** The Sapodilla Room at Grenadine House is a hidden gem—but that shouldn't be the case for long. When new owners renovated the entire hotel in 2007, they installed Chef Winston from Canada via Barbados, and he really knows his stuff. Whet your appetite with a fruity cocktail at the West Indies Bar—the actual bar is from an old English pub, and a gallery of classic black-and-white stills of movie stars graces the walls. Move inside to the dining room and enjoy light and delicious seafood dishes; creamy pasta concoctions; as well as tasty beef, lamb, and chicken entrées that reflect Caribbean flavors. Local people come here for special occasions and business dinners, as this is one of the finest—certainly the most elegant—dining spots on St. Vincent. ⌂*Box 2523, Kingstown Park, Kingstown* ☎*784/456–1800* ⌂*Reservations essential* ▭*AE, MC, V.*

ECLECTIC
$$-$$$
☺

✕**Lime Restaurant & Pub.** Named for the *pursuit* of liming (relaxing), this sprawling waterfront restaurant also has mostly green decor. An extensive all-day menu caters to beachgoers and boaters who drop by for a roti and a bottle of Hairoun—or burgers, curries, sandwiches, gourmet pizzas, pastas, soups, and salads. Dinner choices include fresh seafood, volcano chicken (with a creole sauce that's as spicy as lava is hot), curried goat, and pepper steak. Casual and congenial by day, it's candlelit and romantic at night—enhanced by the twinkling lights of anchored boats and the quiet waves breaking against the seawall. ✉*Young Island Channel, Villa Harbour* ☎*784/458–4227* ▭*AE, D, DC, MC, V.*

FRENCH
$$
Fodor's Choice
★

✕**French Verandah.** Dining by candlelight on the waterfront terrace of Mariners Hotel means exquisite French cuisine with Caribbean flair—and one of the best dining experiences on St. Vincent. Start with a rich soup—traditional French onion, fish with aioli, or callaloo and conch—or escargots, stuffed crab back, or conch salad. Main courses include fresh fish and shellfish grilled with fresh herbs, garlic butter and lime, or creole sauce. Landlubbers may prefer beef bourguignonne, *suprème de poulet* (stuffed chicken breast), or beef tenderloin with béarnaise, Roquefort, or mushroom sauce. For dessert—the *mi-cuit*, a warm chocolate delicacy with vanilla ice cream, is to die for. Lighter, equally delicious fare is served at lunch. Dinner is prix-fixe, at $23 for two courses and $29 for three courses. ⌂*Mariners Hotel, Box 859, Villa Beach* ☎*784/453–1111* ▭*AE, MC, V.*

BEACHES

St. Vincent's origin is volcanic, so the sand on its beaches ranges in color from golden brown to black. Young Island has the only truly white-sand beach, but since the island is private, you must be a guest at the Young Island Resort (or the Mariners Hotel, whose guests have beach privileges) in order to use it. Otherwise, all beaches are public. Villa Beach, on the mainland opposite Young Island, is really more of a waterfront area than a beach. The strip of sand is so narrow it's sometimes nonexistent; nevertheless, boats bob at anchor in the channel, and dive shops, inns, and restaurants line the shore, making this an interesting place to be. On the windward coast, dramatic swaths of broad black sand are strewn with huge black boulders, but the water is rough and unpredictable. Swimming is recommended only in the lagoons, rivers, and bays along the leeward coast.

Argyle. Though this spectacular black-sand beach on St. Vincent's southeast (windward) coast is not safe for swimming, you'll love to watch the surf crashing here.

Buccament Bay. Good for swimming, this tiny black-sand beach is 20 minutes north of Kingstown.

Indian Bay. South of Kingstown and just north of Villa Beach, this beach has golden sand but is slightly rocky; it's good for snorkeling.

Questelle's Bay. This beach (pronounced keet-*ells*), north of Kingstown and next to Campden Park, has a black-sand beach.

SPORTS & THE OUTDOORS

BICYCLING

Bicycles can be rented for about $25 per day, but roads aren't conducive to leisurely cycling. Serious cyclists, however, will enjoy mountain biking in wilderness areas. **Sailor's Wilderness Tours** (⊠ *Middle St., Kingstown* ☎ *784/457–1712, 784/457–9207after hours* ⊕ *www.sailortours.com*) takes individuals or groups on half-day bike tours for $50 per person (which includes 21-speed mountain bike rental).

BOATING & FISHING

Fodor'sChoice ★ From St. Vincent you can charter a monohull or catamaran (bareboat or complete with captain, crew, and cook) to weave you through the Grenadines for a day or a week of sailing—or a full-day fishing trip. One of the most spectacular cruising areas in the world, particularly for sailing, the Grenadines are close enough to allow landfall at a different island nearly every day, yet far enough apart, in some cases, to experience true blue-water sailing. Bequia and Union Island have excellent yacht services and waterfront activity. Mustique is a dream destination, as is Mayreau. Visitors on yachts are welcome to dine at the private Palm Island and Petit St. Vincent resorts. Canouan has come alive in the past few years, and the Tobago Cays are a don't-miss destination for snorkeling and diving. Boats of all sizes and degrees of luxury are available. Charter rates run about $250 per day and up for sailing yachts; fishing trips cost $350 for a half day and $550 for a full day. **Barefoot Yacht Charters** (⊠ *Blue Lagoon, Ratho Mill* ☎ *784/456–9526* ⊕ *www.barefootyachts.com*) has a fleet of catamarans and monohulls in the 32- to 50-foot range. **Crystal Blue Charters** (⊠ *Indian Bay* ☎ *784/457–4532*) offers sportfishing charters on a 34-foot pirogue for both amateur and serious fishermen. **Footloose Charters** (⊠ *Blue Lagoon, Ratho Mill* ☎ *784/458–4308 or 888/952–6013* ⊕ *www.footloosecharters.com*) charters a wide range of 33- to 50-foot monohulls and catamarans, either bareboat or with captain and cook. **Sunsail St. Vincent** (⊠ *Blue Lagoon, Ratho Mill* ☎ *784/458–4308* ⊕ *www.sunsail.com*) charters bareboat and crewed yachts ranging from 30 feet to 50 feet. **TMM Bareboat Vacations** (⊠ *Blue Lagoon, Ratho Mill* ☎ *784/456–9917*

⊕*www.sailtmm.com*) offers fully equipped yachts and catamarans that range from 38 to 51 feet, either bareboat or crewed.

DIVING & SNORKELING

★ Novices and advanced divers alike will be impressed by the marine life in the waters around St. Vincent—brilliant sponges, huge deep-water coral trees, and shallow reefs teeming with colorful fish. Many sites in the Grenadines are still virtually unexplored. Most dive shops offer three-hour beginner "resort" courses, full certification courses, and excursions to reefs, walls, and wrecks throughout the Grenadines. A single-tank dive costs about $65; a two-tank, $115; a 10-dive package, $550. All prices include equipment. It can't be emphasized enough, however, that the coral reef is extremely fragile, and you must only look and never touch.

St. Vincent is ringed by one long, almost continuous reef. The best dive spots are in the small bays along the coast between Kingstown and Layou; many are within 20 yards of shore and only 20 to 30 feet down. **Anchor Reef** has excellent visibility for viewing a deep-black coral garden, schools of squid, sea horses, and maybe a small octopus. **Critter Corner,** just 600 feet off Indian Bay beach, is St. Vincent's hallmark "muck" dive site—a wealth of marine life lurks in and among the sand, silt, sea grass, and boulders. The **Forest,** a shallow dive, is still dramatic, with soft corals in pastel colors and schools of small fish. **New Guinea Reef** slopes to 90 feet and can't be matched for its quantity of corals and sponges. The pristine waters surrounding the **Tobago Cays,** in the southern Grenadines, will give you a world-class diving experience.

Dive Fantasea (⊠ *Villa Beach* ☎*784/457–5560 or 784/457–5577*) offers dive and snorkeling trips to the St. Vincent coast and the Tobago Cays. **Dive St. Vincent** (⊠ *Young Island Dock, Villa Beach* ☎*784/457–4714 or 784/547–4928* ⊕*www.divestvincent.com*) is where NAUI- and PADI-certified instructor Bill Tewes and his staff offer beginner and certification courses and dive trips to the St. Vincent coast and the southern Grenadines. **Indigo Dive** (⊠ *Barefoot Marine Center, Blue Lagoon, Ratho Mill* ☎*784/493–9494* ⊕*www.indigodive.com*) tailors dive experiences for divers of all experience levels.

HIKING

St. Vincent offers hikers and trekkers a choice of experiences: easy, picturesque walks near Kingstown; moderately difficult nature trails in the central valleys; and exhilarating climbs through a rain forest to the rim of an active volcano. Bring a hat, long pants, and insect repellent if you plan to hike in the bush.

Fodor'sChoice **La Soufrière,** the queen of climbs, is St. Vincent's active volcano (which
★ last erupted in April 1979—on Friday the 13th, appropriately enough). Approachable from either the windward or leeward coast, this is *not* a casual excursion for the inexperienced—the massive mountain covers nearly the entire northern third of the island. Climbs are all-day excursions. You'll need stamina and sturdy shoes to reach the top and peek into the mile-wide (1.5-km-wide) crater at just over 4,000 feet. Be sure to check the weather before you leave; hikers have been disappointed

to find a cloud-obscured view at the summit. A guide ($25 to $30) can be arranged through your hotel, the Ministry of Tourism, Youth & Sport, or tour operators. The eastern approach is most popular. In a four-wheel-drive vehicle you pass through Rabacca Dry River, north of Georgetown, and the Bamboo Forest; then it's a two-hour, 3.5-mi (5.5-km) hike to the summit. If you're approaching from the west, near Châteaubelair, the climb is longer—10 to 12 mi (6 to 7 km)—and rougher, but even more scenic. If you hike up one side and down the other, you must arrange in advance to be picked up at the end.

Trinity Falls, in the north, requires a trip by a four-wheel-drive vehicle from Richmond Bay to the interior, then a steep two-hour climb to a crystal-clear river and three waterfalls, one of which forms a whirlpool where you can take a refreshing swim.

Vermont Nature Trails are two hiking trails that start near the top of the Buccament Valley, 5 mi (8 km) north of Kingstown. A network of 1.5-mi (2.5-km) loops passes through bamboo, evergreen forest, and rain forest. In the late afternoon you may be lucky enough to see the rare St. Vincent parrot, *Amazona guildingii*.

SIGHTSEEING TOURS

Several operators on St. Vincent offer sightseeing tours on land or by sea. Per-person prices range from $25 for a two-hour tour to the Botanical Garden to $150 for a day sail to the Grenadines. A full-day tour around Kingstown and either the leeward or windward coast, including lunch, will cost about $65 per person. You can arrange informal land tours through taxi drivers, who double as knowledgeable guides. Expect to pay $25 per hour for up to four people.

Fantasea Tours (⊠ *Villa Beach, St. Vincent* ☎784/457–5555 ⊕*www. fantaseatours.com*) will take you on a 38-foot power cruiser to the Falls of Baleine, Bequia, and Mustique, or to the Tobago Cays for snorkeling. For bird-watchers, hikers, and ecotourists, **HazECO Tours** (⊠*Kingstown, St. Vincent* ☎784/457–8634 ⊕*www.hazecotours.com*) offers wilderness tours, bird-watching expeditions, and hikes to explore the natural beauty and see historic sites throughout St. Vincent. **Sailor's Wilderness Tours** (⊠*Middle St., Kingstown, St. Vincent* ☎784/457–1712 ⊕*www.sailortours.com*) runs the gamut, from a comfortable sightseeing drive (by day or by moonlight) to mountain biking on remote trails to a strenuous hike up La Soufrière volcano. **Sam Taxi Tours** (⊠*Cane Garden, St. Vincent* ☎784/456–4338, 784/458–3686 in Bequia) offers half- and full-day tours of St. Vincent, as well as hiking tours to La Soufrière and scenic walks along the Vermont Nature Trails. Sam's also operates a tour on Bequia that includes snorkeling at Friendship Bay.

SHOPPING

The 12 small blocks that hug the waterfront in **downtown Kingstown** compose St. Vincent's main shopping district. Among the shops that sell goods to fulfill household needs are a few that sell local crafts, gifts, and souvenirs. Bargaining is neither expected nor appreciated. The

cruise-ship complex, on the waterfront in Kingstown, has a collection of a dozen or so boutiques, shops, and restaurants that cater primarily to cruise-ship passengers but welcome all shoppers. The best souvenirs of St. Vincent are intricately woven straw items, such as handbags, hats, slippers, baskets, and grass mats that range in size from place mats to room-size floor mats. If you're inclined to bring home a floor mat, pack a few heavy-duty plastic bags and some twine. The mats aren't heavy and roll or fold rather neatly; wrapped securely, they can be checked as luggage for the flight home. Otherwise, local artwork and carvings are available in galleries, from street vendors, and in shops at the cruise-ship complex.

ANTIQUES & FURNITURE

At Basil's (⊠ *Villa* ☎ *784/456–2602*) is St. Vincent's only antiques and furniture store. Specializing in 200-year-old Asian pieces and the latest creations from Bali, India, and Africa, Basil's collection appeals to fine-furniture collectors as well as those seeking interesting, affordable objets d'art for either home or garden. Even if you're just looking, you might be smitten by the French wines, chocolates, and cheeses.

DUTY-FREE GOODS

At **Gonsalves Duty-Free Liquor** (⊠ *Airport Departure Lounge, Arnos Vale* ☎ *784/456–4781*), spirits and liqueurs are available at discounts of up to 40%. **Voyager** (*R. C. Enterprises Ltd.* ⊠ *Halifax St., Kingstown* ☎ *784/456–1686*), one of the few duty-free shops in St. Vincent, has a small selection of cameras, electronics, watches, china, and jewelry.

FOOD

Whether you're putting together a picnic, stocking your kitchenette, provisioning a yacht, or just want some snacks, **C. K. Greaves Co., Ltd.** (⊠ *Upper Bay St., Kingstown* ☎ *784/457–1074*) is the main supermarket and your best bet. Sunrise Supermarket in Arnos Vale, across the road from the airport, is owned by the same company. Both can be reached by the same phone number, and either store will deliver your order to the dock. **Gourmet Food** (⊠ *Calliaqua* ☎ *784/456–2987*) specializes in delicious breads and imported cheeses and meats, as well as a full range of deli items and other tasty tidbits.

Don't miss visiting **Market Square** (⊠ *Bay and Bedford Sts., Kingstown* ☎ *No phone*). The market is a three-story enclosed building open daily (except Sunday), but really bustles on Friday and Saturday mornings when vendors bring their produce, meats, and fish to market.

LOCAL ART & HANDICRAFTS

★ The **Little Art Gallery** (⊠ *Downstairs, Grand View Grill, Indian Bay* ☎ *784/458–4811*) is owned and operated by Caroline Sardine, an accomplished artist and daughter of the owners of Grand View Beach Hotel. Many of her paintings are on display in the hotel; in the gallery, she offers original art (her own and that of others), along with handcrafted items such as pottery, ceramics, coconut toys, handmade dolls, painted calabashes ("bashees"), goatskin drums, and mahogany carvings. The gallery is in the hotel's beachfront restaurant and is open daily (except Monday) from 2 PM. **Nzimbu Browne** (⊠ *McKie's Hill, Kings-*

town ☎784/457–1677) is a self-taught Vincentian craftsman, artist, musician, and drum maker. He is best known for his original banana art, which he creates from dried banana leaves, carefully selecting and snipping varicolored bits and arranging them on pieces of wood to depict local scenes. Prices range from $15 or $20 for smaller items to several thousands of dollars for larger works sold in galleries. Browne has a kiosk in front of his home but often sets up shop on Bay Street, near the Cobblestone Inn. **St. Vincent Craftsmen's Centre** (⊠ *Frenches St., Kingstown* ☎784/457–2516), three blocks from the wharf, sells locally made grass floor mats, place mats, and other straw articles, as well as batik cloth, handmade West Indian dolls, hand-painted cala-bashes, and framed artwork. No credit cards are accepted. On the leeward coast about a half-hour's drive north of Kingstown, **Wallilabou Craft Centre,** (⊠ *Leeward Highway, Wallilabou* ☎784/456–0078) was established in 1986 as a local cooperative where villagers can learn various techniques for weaving straw and other natural fibers. Workers create baskets, handbags, hats, toys, and other items that are sold in the Kingstown market and make good souvenirs of a visit to St. Vincent.

NIGHTLIFE

Nightlife in St. Vincent consists mostly of once-a-week (in season) hotel barbecue buffets with a steel band or a local string band (usually older gents who play an assortment of string instruments). Jump-ups, so called because the lively calypso music makes listeners jump up and dance, happen around holidays, festivals, and, of course, Vincy Mas—St. Vincent's Carnival, which begins in late June and is the biggest cul-tural event of the year. At nightspots in Kingstown and at Villa Beach, you can join Vincentians for late-night dancing to live or recorded reg-gae, hip-hop, and soca music.

DANCE & MUSIC CLUBS

Dance clubs generally charge a cover of $4 (EC$10), slightly more for headliners. The **Aquatic Bar & Restaurant** (⊠ *Villa Beach* ☎784/458–4205) features live local music on Friday and Saturday nights. The **Attic Sports Bar** (⊠ *1 Melville St., Kingstown* ☎784/457–2558) is above the KFC; you'll hear international jazz and blues on Thursday night; weekend parties begin at 10 PM. **Club Emotions** (⊠ *Grenville St., Kings-town* ☎784/457–2691) has disco music and live bands nightly and attracts a local crowd of mostly young people. **Iguana** (⊠ *Villa Beach* ☎784/457–5557) is a lively scene, with party night on Friday.

THEME NIGHTS

Calliaqua Culture Pot (⊠ *Main Rd., Calliaqua* ☎*No phone*), pronounced cal-uh-*quah*, is a community street party held every Friday evening at 8 PM. Join the crowd for barbecue, beer, dancing to local music, arts and crafts, and cultural performances. On Wednesday and Friday evenings at **Vee Jay's Rooftop Diner & Pub** (⊠ *Bay St., Kingstown* ☎784/457–2845), karaoke accompanies dinner and drinks.

EXPLORING ST. VINCENT

Kingstown's shopping and business district, historic churches and cathedrals, and other points of interest can easily be seen in a half day, with another half day for the Botanical Garden. The coastal roads of St. Vincent offer spectacular panoramas and scenes of island life. The Leeward Highway follows the scenic Caribbean coastline; the Windward Highway follows the more-dramatic Atlantic coast. A drive along the windward coast or a boat trip to the Falls of Baleine requires a full day. Exploring La Soufrière or the Vermont Trails is also a major undertaking, requiring a very early start and a full day's worth of strenuous hiking.

Barrouallie. Once an important whaling village, Barrouallie (*bar*-relly) today is home to anglers earning their livelihoods trawling for blackfish, which are actually small pilot whales. The one-hour drive north from Kingstown, on the Leeward Highway, takes you along ridges that drop to the sea, through small villages and lush valleys, and beside bays with black-sand beaches and safe bathing.

Black Point Tunnel. In 1815, under the supervision of British colonel Thomas Browne, Carib and African slaves drilled this 300-foot tunnel through solid volcanic rock to facilitate the transportation of sugar from estates in the north to the port in Kingstown. The tunnel, an engineering marvel for the times, links Grand Sable with Byrea Bay, just north of Colonarie (pronounced con-a-*ree*).

★ **Falls of Baleine.** The falls are impossible to reach by car, so book an escorted, all-day boat trip from Villa Beach or the Lagoon Marina. The boat ride along the coast offers scenic island views. When you arrive, you have to wade through shallow water to get to the beach. Then local guides help you make the easy five-minute trek to the 60-foot falls and the rock-enclosed freshwater pool the falls create—plan to take a dip.

✪ **Ft. Charlotte.** Started by the French in 1786 and completed by the British
★ in 1806, the fort was named for King George III's wife. It sits on Berkshire Hill, a dramatic promontory 636 feet above sea level, with a stunning view of Kingstown and the Grenadines. Interestingly, cannons face inward—the fear of attack by native peoples was far greater than any threat approaching from the sea, though, truth be told, the fort saw no action. Nowadays the fort serves as a signal station for ships; its ancient cells house historical paintings of the island by Lindsay Prescott.

Georgetown. St. Vincent's second-largest city (and former capital), halfway up the island's east coast, is surrounded by acres and acres of coconut groves. This is also the site of the now defunct Mount Bentinck sugar factory. A tiny, quiet town—with a few streets, small shops, a restaurant or two, and modest homes—it's completely unaffected by tourism. It's also a convenient place to stop for a cool drink or snack or other essential shopping while traveling along the windward coast.

Kingstown. The capital city of St. Vincent and the Grenadines is on the island's southwestern coast. The town of 13,500 residents wraps around Kingstown Bay; a ring of green hills and ridges, studded with

St. Vincent's Complex History

Historians believe that the Ciboney were the first to journey from South America to St. Vincent, which they called Hairoun (Land of the Blessed). The Ciboney ultimately moved on to Cuba and Haiti, leaving St. Vincent to the agrarian Arawak tribes that journeyed north from coastal South America. Not long before Columbus sailed by in 1492, the Arawaks succumbed to the powerful Caribs, who had also paddled north from South America, conquering one island after another en route.

St. Vincent's mountains and forests, however, thwarted European settlement. As colonization advanced elsewhere in the Caribbean, many Caribs fled to St. Vincent. In 1626 the French established a colony, but their success was short-lived; England took over a year later. As "possession" of the island seesawed between France and England, the Caribs continued to make complete European colonization impossible. Ironically, a rift in the Carib community itself enabled the Europeans to gain a foothold.

In 1675 African slaves who had survived a Dutch shipwreck were welcomed into the Carib community. Over time the Carib nation became, for all intents and purposes, two nations—one composed of the original Yellow Caribs, the other of the so-called Black Caribs. Relations between the two groups were often strained. In 1719 tensions rose so high that the Yellow Caribs united with the colonial French against the Black Caribs in what is called the First Carib War. The Black Caribs ultimately retreated to the hills, but they continued to resist the Europeans.

The French established plantations, importing African slaves to work the fertile land. In 1763 the British claimed the island yet again, and a wave of Scottish slave masters arrived with indentured servants from India and Portugal. Communities of direct descendants of the Scots still live near St. Vincent's Dorsetshire Hill and on Bequia.

Meanwhile, the determined French backed the Black Caribs, their previous foe, against the British in 1795's Second Carib War (also known as the Brigands War), during which British plantations were ravaged and burned on the island's windward coast. Black Carib chief Chatoyer managed to push the British troops down the leeward coast to Kingstown. Subsequently, on Dorsetshire Hill high above the town, Chatoyer lost a duel with a British officer. The 5,000 surviving Black Caribs were rounded up and shipped off to Honduras and present-day Belize, where their descendants (the Garifuna people) remain to this day. The few remaining Yellow Caribs retreated to the remote northern tip of St. Vincent, near Sandy Bay, where many of their descendants now live. A monument to Chatoyer has been erected on Dorsetshire Hill, where there's a magnificent westward view over Kingstown and the Caribbean.

The issue of "possession" of St. Vincent has long since been resolved; the nation has been fully independent since 1979 (but still a part of the British Commonwealth). The various ethnic groups have mixed considerably over the years, creating a unique heritage simply described today as "Vincentian."

23

homes, forms a backdrop for the city. This is very much a working city, with a busy harbor and few concessions to tourists. Kingstown Harbour is the only deepwater port on the island.

A few gift shops can be found on and around **Bay Street,** near the harbor. Upper Bay Street, which stretches along the bay front, bustles with daytime activity—workers going about their business and housewives doing their shopping. Many of Kingstown's downtown buildings are built of stone or brick brought to the island in the holds of 18th-century ships as ballast (and replaced with sugar and spices for the return trip to Europe). The Georgian-style stone arches and second-floor overhangs on former warehouses create shelter from midday sun and the brief, cooling showers common to the tropics.

Grenadines Wharf, at the south end of Bay Street, is busy with schooners loading supplies and ferries loading people bound for the Grenadines. The **cruise-ship complex,** south of the commercial wharf, has a mall with a dozen or more shops, plus restaurants, a post office, communications facilities, and a taxi-minibus stand.

An almost infinite selection of produce fills the **Kingstown Produce Market,** a three-story building that takes up a whole city block on Upper Bay, Hillsboro, and Bedford streets in the center of town. It's noisy, colorful, and open Monday through Saturday—but the busiest times (and the best times to go) are Friday and Saturday mornings. In the courtyard, vendors sell local arts and crafts. On the upper floors, merchants sell clothing, household items, gifts, and other products.

Little Tokyo, so called because funding for the project was a gift from Japan, is a waterfront shopping area with a bustling indoor fish market and dozens of stalls where you can buy inexpensive homemade meals, drinks, ice cream, bread and cookies, clothing, and trinkets, and even get a haircut.

St. George's Cathedral, on Grenville Street, is a pristine, creamy yellow Anglican church built in 1820. The dignified Georgian architecture includes simple wooden pews, an ornate chandelier, and beautiful stained-glass windows; one was a gift from Queen Victoria, who actually commissioned it for London's St. Paul's Cathedral in honor of her first grandson. When the artist created an angel with a red robe, she was horrified and sent it abroad. The markers in the cathedral's graveyard recount the history of the island. Across the street is **St. Mary's Cathedral of the Assumption** (Roman Catholic), built in stages beginning in 1823. The strangely appealing design is a blend of Moorish, Georgian, and Romanesque styles applied to black brick. Nearby, freed slaves built the **Kingstown Methodist Church** in 1841. The exterior is brick, simply decorated with quoins (solid blocks that form the corners), and the roof is held together by metal straps, bolts, and wooden pins. **Scots Kirk** (1839–80) was built by and for Scottish settlers but became a Seventh-Day Adventist church in 1952.

Ⓒ A few minutes north of downtown by taxi is St. Vincent's famous **Botan-**
★ **ical Garden.** Founded in 1765, it's the oldest botanical garden in the

western hemisphere. Captain Bligh—of *Bounty* fame—brought the first breadfruit tree to this island for landowners to propagate. The prolific bounty of the breadfruit tree was used to feed the slaves. You can see a direct descendant of this original tree among the specimen mahogany, rubber, teak, and other tropical trees and shrubs in the 20 acres of gardens. Two dozen rare St. Vincent parrots live in the small aviary. Guides explain all the medicinal and ornamental trees and shrubs; they also appreciate a tip at the end of the tour. ⊠ *Off Leeward Hwy., Montrose* ☎ *784/457–1003* ⊠ *$3* ⊗ *Daily 6–6.*

23

La Soufrière. The volcano, which last erupted in 1979, is 4,000 feet high and so huge in area that it covers virtually the entire northern third of the island. The eastern trail to the rim of the crater, a two-hour ascent, begins at Rabacca Dry River.

Layou. Just beyond this small fishing village, about 45 minutes north of Kingstown, are petroglyphs (rock carvings) left by pre-Columbian inhabitants in the 8th century. Arrange a visit through the Ministry of Tourism, Youth & Sport. For $2, Victor Hendrickson, who owns the land, or his wife will escort you to the site.

Mesopotamia Valley. The rugged, ocean-lashed scenery along St. Vincent's windward coast is the perfect counterpoint to the lush, calm west coast. The fertile Mesopotamia Valley (nicknamed Mespo) has a view of dense rain forests, streams, and endless banana and coconut plantations. Breadfruit, sweet corn, peanuts, and arrowroot also grow in the rich soil here. The valley is surrounded by mountain ridges, including 3,181-foot Grand Bonhomme Mountain, and overlooks the Caribbean.

★ **Montreal Gardens.** Welsh-born landscape designer Timothy Vaughn renovated 7.5 acres of neglected commercial flower beds and a falling-down plantation house into a stunning yet informal garden spot. Anthurium, ginger lilies, birds of paradise, and other tropical flowers are planted in raised beds; tree ferns create a canopy of shade along the walkways. The gardens are in the shadow of majestic Grand Bonhomme Mountain, deep in the Mesopotamia Valley, about 12 mi (19 km) from Kingstown. ⊠ *Montreal St., Mesopotamia* ☎ *784/458–1198* ⊠ *$3* ⊗ *Dec.–Aug., weekdays 9–4.*

Owia. The Carib village of Owia, on the island's far northeast coast about two hours from Kingstown, is the home of many descendants of the Carib people of St. Vincent. It's also the home of the **Owia Arrowroot Processing Factory.** Used for generations to thicken sauces and flavor cookies, arrowroot is now used as a finish for computer paper. St. Vincent produces 90% of the world's supply of arrowroot. Close to the village is the **Owia Salt Pond,** created by the pounding surf of the Atlantic Ocean, which flowed over a barrier reef of lava rocks and ridges. Picnic and take a swim before the long return trip to Kingstown.

Rabacca Dry River. This rocky gulch just beyond the village of Georgetown was carved from the earth by the lava flow from the 1902 eruption of nearby **La Soufrière.** When it rains in the mountains, the river goes from dry to a trickle to a gushing river within minutes. Until a bridge was built in 2006 with $2 million in funding provided by the government of Taiwan, drivers would be stranded on one side or the other for an hour or two or, in rare cases, longer.

○ **Wallilabou Bay.** The *Pirates of the Caribbean* left its mark at Wallilabou (pronounced wally-la-*boo*), a location used for filming the recent movies. Many of the buildings and docks built as stage sets remain, giving the pretty bay an intriguingly historic appearance. You can sunbathe, swim, picnic, or buy your lunch at Wallilabou Anchorage. This is a favorite stop for day-trippers returning from the Falls of Baleine and boaters anchoring for the evening. Nearby there's a river with a small waterfall where you can take a freshwater plunge.

THE GRENADINES

The Grenadine Islands are known for great sailing, excellent scuba diving and snorkeling, magnificent beaches, and unlimited chances to relax with a picnic, watch the sailboats, and wait for the sun to set. Each island has a different appeal. Whether you like quiet, nonstop activity, or socializing (as long as you're not looking for wild nightlife), the Grenadines may be your thing.

BEQUIA

Bequia (pronounced *beck*-way) is the Carib word for "island of the cloud." Hilly and green, with several gold-sand beaches, Bequia is 9 mi (14.5 km) south of St. Vincent's southwestern shore; with a population of 5,000, it's the largest of the Grenadines. Although boatbuilding, whaling, and fishing have been the predominant industries here for generations, sailing and Bequia have now become almost synonymous. Bequia's picturesque Admiralty Bay is a favored anchorage for private and chartered yachts. Lodgings range from comfortable resorts and villas to cozy West Indian–style inns. Bequia's airport and frequent ferry service from St. Vincent make this a favorite destination for day-trippers as well. The ferry docks in Port Elizabeth, a tiny town with waterfront bars, restaurants, and shops where you can buy handmade souvenirs, including the exquisitely detailed model sailboats for which Bequia is famous. The Easter Regatta is held during the four-day Easter weekend; revelers gather to watch boat races and celebrate Bequia's seafaring traditions with food, music, dancing, and competitive games.

WHERE TO STAY

VILLAS A number of villas are available for vacation rental in Spring, Friendship Bay, Lower Bay, and other scenic areas of Bequia. They're suitable for from two people to as many as a dozen, and the weekly rentals in high season run from as low as $560 a week for a "sweet and simple" villa to $9,000 or more for an elaborate villa with an Italian-style courtyard, gardens, and pool.

Contact Grenadine Island Villas (⌧ *Port Elizabeth* ☏ *784/529–8046 or 784/455–0969* ⊕ *www.grenadinevillas.com*).

HOTELS *For approximate costs, see the lodging price chart in the St. Vincent & the Grenadines Planner.*

$$$$ 🏨 **Firefly Hotel Bequia.** This small hotel about 2 mi (3 km) north of Port Elizabeth is on a 28-acre sugar plantation that dates back to the late 18th century. In 2007, the owners of Firefly Hotel in Mustique purchased the property from the family that had operated it since 1979 as Spring on Bequia. The hotel's eight original rooms, which the present owners completely renovated, are in three buildings that are made of hand-cut stone and built into the side of a hill overlooking endless coconut palms, the only banana plantation on Bequia, and the beach at Spring Bay. Two additional guest rooms are higher on the hill (Coconut and Sea Cotton), each with a private courtyard with a swimming pool—guests in those accommodations also have free use of a four-wheel-drive vehicle. Meals are served in the Great Restaurant, which also welcomes nonguests. Strolling down to the beach, you'll pass the ruins of the sugar factory, now a potter's studio called Spring Studios. **Pros:** Secluded location, exquisite contemporary rooms with fabulous views, good restaurant and friendly bar. **Cons:** Unless you're in the "high" rooms, you'll want to rent a vehicle; even with a vehicle, negotiating the steep hillside can be daunting. ⊠ *Spring Bay* ☎ *784/458–3414* ⊕ *www.fireflybequia.com* ↪ *10 rooms* ♿ *In-room: refrigerator (some), no TV. In-hotel: restaurant, bar, tennis court, pools, beachfront, water sports, no elevator, airport shuttle, no kids under 12, no-smoking rooms* ☐ *AE, D, MC, V* ⏹ *FAP.*

$$$$ 🏨 **Old Fort Villa.** This stone greathouse of a former sugar estate is now an intimate inn reminiscent of something you might see in Provence or perhaps Burgundy. It's perched high on a cliff and cooled by trade winds, in a spot both remote and stunning. Each guest room has thick stone walls and windows that overlook a panoramic Grenadine vista. Because the nearest beach, aptly called Ravine, is nearly 450 feet down a rather steep path and the water is too rough for swimming, the inn is a good choice for romantics and getaway purists who are content with a pool. Guests have use of a vehicle during their stay. For those who aren't staying here, the Old Fort restaurant is well worth the 10-minute trek from town by car or taxi. **Pros:** Stunning location, attentive hosts, nice honeymoon spot. **Cons:** Rates are by the week, small and quiet. ⊠ *Mount Pleasant* ☎ *784/458–3440* ⊕ *www.oldfortbequia.com* ↪ *4 rooms, 1 suite* ♿ *In-room: no a/c, no TV, Wi-Fi. In-hotel: restaurant, room service, bar, pool, no elevator, laundry service, airport shuttle* ☐ *MC, V* ⏹ *MAP.*

$$$–$$$$ 🏨 **Bequia Beach Hotel & Villas.** Two beachfront properties on Friendship
☼ Bay that were in dire need of some TLC were purchased in 2007 by a
★ Swedish entrepreneur, who also purchased and completely renovated what is now called Grenadine House in St. Vincent. What had been the old Blue Tropic Hotel has been rebuilt as a three-story boutique hotel, with 12 rooms that surround a pool and are furnished in contemporary style, along with a casual café and restaurant with two Swedish chefs who specialize in high-quality Mediterranean cuisine. Family suites accommodate four persons, and a penthouse suite has a Jacuzzi and the ultimate sea view. On the old Bequia Beach Hotel property, six villa

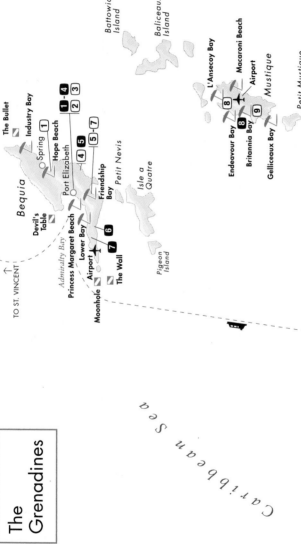

The Grenadines

Bequia

The Bullet
Industry Bay
Spring
Hope Beach
Devil's Table
Port Elizabeth
Admiralty Bay
Princess Margaret Beach
Lower Bay
Moonhole
Airport
The Wall
Friendship Bay
Petit Nevis
Isle a Quatre
Pigeon Island

1 - 4
3
1
2
4
5
5 - 7
6
7

Battowia Island
Baliceaux Island

Mustique

L'Ansecoy Bay
Macaroni Beach
Airport
Endeavour Bay
Britannia Bay
Gelliceaux Bay
Petit Mustique

8
8
9

Savan Island

Petit Canouan

Mahault Bay

TO ST. VINCENT

Caribbean Sea

ATLANTIC OCEAN

Godahl Beach

Canouan

Grand Bay

Glossy Bay

Gibraltar

Airport

Friendship Bay

North Mayreau Channel

Saltwhistle Bay Beach

Saline Bay Beach

Mayreau

Tobago Cays

Sail Rock

Big Sand

Chatham Bay

Union Island

Clifton

Airport

Palm Island

Petit St. Vincent

Martinique Channel

TO
CARRIACOU →

Carriacou

KEY

Beaches
Dive Sites
Ferry
1 Hotels
1 Restaurants

0 —— 4 miles

0 —— 6 km

23

Hotels

Anchorage Yacht Club	15
Bequia Beachfront Villas	6
Bequia Beach Hotel	7
Bigsand Hotel	14
Cotton House	8
Dennis's Hideaway	13
Firefly Bequia	1
Firefly Mustique	9
Frangipani Hotel	2
Friendship Bay Beach Resort	5
Gingerbread Hotel	3
Kings Landing	16
The Old Fort Villa	4
Palm Island Resort	18
Petit St. Vincent Resort	19
Raffles Resort Canouan Island	10
St. Joseph's Apartments	17
Saltwhistle Bay Club	12
Tamarind Beach Hotel & Yacht Club	11

Restaurants

Anchorage Yacht Club	10
L'Auberge des Grenadines	4
Basil's Bar	8
Bigsand Restaurant & Beach Bar	9
Dawn's Creole Garden	6
De Reef	7
Frangipani	1
Gingerbread	2
Lambi's	11
Mac's Pizzeria	3
Old Fort	5

cottages have been newly constructed in Caribbean gingerbread style, with private plunge pools, and either one or two bedrooms. Special packages combine stays at Grenadine House in St. Vincent with a beach vacation at Bequia Beach Hotel & Villas. **Pros:** Beautifully appointed accommodations, everything's brand-new, fabulous beach. **Con:** Ongoing construction of additional suites, restaurant through 2009 could be a nuisance. ⊠*Box 225, Friendship Bay* ☎*784/458–3573* ⊕*www.bequiabeach.com* ↵*12 rooms, 6 cottages, 60 suites* ⌂*In-room: safe, kitchen (some), Ethernet, Wi-Fi. In-hotel: restaurant, bar, pool, beachfront, no elevator, laundry service* ⊟*AE, D, MC, V* ⦿*CP.*

$$-$$$ ⊞ **Bequia Beachfront Villas.** Perfectly located on mile-long (1.5-km-long)
    ℭ   Friendship Bay beach, this is an excellent alternative to a hotel for a couple, a group, or a family. The three villas, which range in size from one to four bedrooms, have enormous living spaces with high ceilings and large porches with panoramic beachfront views, and are luxuriously decorated with attractive, comfortable furniture and extensive artwork. You'll feel like a guest in someone's private and very lovely beach house. Kitchens have full-size, modern appliances as well as every tool, dish, and utensil that you could possibly need. The living rooms have plenty of comfortable seating, large areas for dining, and shelves full of books, games, and magazines. You'll need to rent a car to get around the island and do errands, as the property is fairly isolated. **Pros:** Perfect choice for families or small groups, units are only about 20 feet from the water, huge accommodations with all the comforts of home. **Cons:** Far from town, you'll want a rental jeep to get around, steep hill to road makes it not the best choice for those with disabilities. ⊠*Friendship Bay* ☎*784/457–3423* ⊕*www.bequiabeachfrontvillas.com* ↵*3 villas* ⌂*In-room: kitchen, Wi-Fi. In-hotel: beachfront, no elevator* ⊟*AE, MC, V* ⦿*EP.*

$$-$$$ ⊞ **Gingerbread Hotel.** Easily identified by its decorative fretwork, the
    ℭ   Gingerbread faces the busy Admiralty Bay waterfront. The breezy
    ★   waterfront suites—suitable for three—are large, modern, and stylishly decorated, with bedroom alcoves, adjoining salons, and full kitchens. Downstairs rooms have twin beds and large bay-front porches, while upper rooms have king-size four-poster beds and verandahs; all rooms have a wonderful view of the bay. Decorated and furnished in a sophisticated tropical style, suites have Italian tile floors, blue-and-white geometric-print bed quilts, sheer mosquito netting gathered over beds, and natural wood and rattan furniture throughout. Bathrooms are large and modern. Three economy apartments in a hillside building are comfortable but not luxurious; two of these units are air-conditioned. Gingerbread restaurant serves full meals; for snacks head to the waterfront café. **Pros:** Right in the middle of all the action, lovely waterfront suites suitable for three people, good casual restaurant. **Cons:** You might miss air-conditioning if the breeze isn't cooling enough, no TV. ⊠*Belmont Walkway, Admiralty Bay, Box 191, Port Elizabeth* ☎*784/458–3800* ⊕*www.gingerbreadhotel.com* ↵*7 suites, 3 apartments* ⌂*In-room: no a/c (some), no phone, safe, kitchen, no TV. In-hotel: restaurant, bar, tennis court, beachfront, diving, water sports, no elevator, public Internet, public Wi-Fi* ⊟*MC, V* ⦿*EP.*

23

$$ ☐ **Friendship Bay Beach Resort.** Lars and Magrit Abrahamsson left their busy lives in Sweden back in the mid-1990s and became hoteliers on Bequia. Their sprawling hillside complex hugs the east end of a mile-long (1.5-km-long) arc of white-sand beach on Friendship Bay. Accommodations are in the main building, where rooms are decorated in contemporary style and every room has a sweeping view of the sea. Oceanfront rooms are decorated in island style and have terraces that are steps away from the beach. The open-air Moskito Beach Bar and Restaurant serves seafood and creole cuisine. On Saturday night there's a barbecue and jump-up, and the rope-swing seats at the bar will keep you upright even after a potent rum punch. Breakfast and special dinners are served in the main restaurant, A Touch of Class. **Pros:** Enviable location on Friendship Bay beach, rooms renovated and redecorated in 2007, popular beach bar and grill. **Cons:** No room phone, no room TV, and no room fridge. ☐ *Box 9, Friendship Bay* ☎*784/458–3222* ⊕*www.yachtcharterclub.com/friendshipbay.htm* ⤴*24 rooms, 2 suites* ♿*In-room: no phone, no TV. In-hotel: 2 restaurants, bars, tennis court, beachfront, water sports, no elevator, laundry service* ▭*AE, D, MC, V* ⑩*BP.*

¢–$$ ☐ **Frangipani Hotel.** The venerable Frangipani, owned by former prime minister of St. Vincent and the Grenadines James Mitchell and managed by his daughter, is also known for its friendly waterfront bar and excellent restaurant. Five simple, inexpensive original rooms in the historic shingle-sided sea captain's home have painted-wood walls and floors, grass rugs, and plain furniture and share a bay-front terrace at the front and a cold-water bath at the end of the hall (Room 3 is closest to the bath). Luxurious garden and deluxe hillside units, built of local stone and hardwoods, rise on a gentle slope filled with fragrant frangipani trees; these rooms have tile floors, louvered windows and doors, canopy beds, spacious private baths, and verandahs with spectacular sunset views of the harbor. Two deluxe hillside rooms have air-conditioning. **Pros:** Great waterfront location, beautiful harbor view from hillside rooms, lively bar and restaurant at night. **Cons:** Steep hillside not good for people with disabilities, you might wish for air-conditioning in your room at some times of the year (especially in fall). ⊠*Admiralty Bay, Belmont Walkway, Box 1, Port Elizabeth* ☎*784/458–3255* ⊕*www.frangipanibequia.com* ⤴*15 rooms, 10 with bath* ♿*In-room: no a/c (some), no phone, refrigerator (some), no TV (some). In-hotel: restaurant, room service, bar, tennis court, diving, water sports, no elevator, laundry service* ▭*AE, D, MC, V* ⑩*EP.*

WHERE TO EAT

Dining on Bequia ranges from casual local-style meals to more-elaborate cuisine, and the food and service are both consistently good. Barbecues at Bequia's hotels mean spicy West Indian seafood, chicken, or beef, plus a buffet of side salads, vegetable dishes, and sweet desserts.

CARIBBEAN ✗**Frangipani.** Just before sunset, the yachting crowd comes ashore
$$–$$$ to what is arguably the most popular gathering spot in Bequia—the
★ Frangipani Hotel's waterfront bar. After a drink and a chat, the mood turns romantic, with candlelight and excellent Caribbean cuisine in

the open-air dining room. The à la carte menu emphasizes seafood and local dishes. On Monday nights in high season, a local string band plays catchy tunes; on Friday nights, folksingers entertain. The Thursday Frangi barbecue buffet (about $30) is accompanied by steel-band music and a jump-up. ⊠*Frangipani Hotel, Belmont Walkway, Admiralty Bay, Port Elizabeth* ☎*784/458–3255* ⌖*Reservations essential* ⊟*MC, V.*

$$–$$$ ✕**Old Fort.** The food here is good enough to attract nonguests to the romantic atmosphere of this 1700s-era estate house with one of the best views—and coolest breezes—on the island. At lunch, feast on pumpkin or callaloo soup, crepes, sandwiches, salads, or pasta. At dinner the French creole cuisine focuses on entrées such as spring lamb, tuna steak, lobster, or char-grilled whole snapper, accompanied by homemade bread and curried pigeon peas. ⊠*Old Fort Country Inn, Mount Pleasant* ☎*784/458–3440* ⌖*Reservations essential* ⊟*MC, V.*

$–$$$ ✕**Dawn's Creole Garden.** It's worth the walk uphill to the Creole Garden Hotel for the delicious West Indian food and the view. Lunch options include sandwiches, rotis, fresh mutton, "goat water" (a savory soup with bits of goat meat and root vegetables), fresh fish, and conch. At dinner, the five-course creole seafood, lobster, or vegetarian specials include the christophene (chayote) and breadfruit accompaniments for which Dawn's is known. Barbecue is always available on request. The dinner menu changes daily. There's live guitar music most Saturday nights and a barbecue lunch, with live music, right on the beach on Sunday. ⊠*Creole Garden Hotel, Lower Bay* ☎*784/458–3154* ⌖*Reservations essential* ⊟*AE, MC, V.*

¢–$ ✕**De Reef.** This café-restaurant on Lower Bay is the primary feeding station for long, lazy beach days. When the café closes at dusk, the restaurant takes over—if you've made reservations, that is. For breakfast (from 7) or light lunch, the café bakes its own breads, croissants, coconut cake, and cookies—and blends fresh juices to accompany them. For a full lunch or dinner, conch, lobster, whelk, and shrimp are treated the West Indian way, and the mutton curry is famous. Every other Saturday in season there's a seafood buffet dinner accompanied by live music; on Sunday afternoons there's a music jam. ⊠*Lower Bay* ☎*784/458–3958* ⌖*Reservations essential* ⊟*No credit cards.*

ECLECTIC   ✕**Gingerbread.** The airy dining-room verandah at the Gingerbread
$$–$$$ Hotel offers a panoramic view of Admiralty Bay and the waterfront
☺   activity. The lunch crowd can enjoy barbecued beef kebabs or chicken with fried potatoes or onions, grilled fish, homemade soups, salads, and sandwiches. In the evening, steaks, seafood, and curries are specialties of the house. Save room for warm, fresh gingerbread—served here with lemon sauce. In season, dinner is often accompanied by live music. ⊠*Gingerbread Hotel, Belmont Walkway, Admiralty Bay, Port Elizabeth* ☎*784/458–3800* ⌖*Reservations essential* ⊟*AE, D, MC, V.*

FRENCH   ✕**L'Auberge des Grenadines.** Owned by the French-born Jacques
$$–$$$ Thevenot and his Vincentian wife, Eileen, this quaint restaurant and guesthouse on the waterfront facing Admiralty Bay is convenient for the yachting crowd, day-trippers, and anyone staying a while. The

extensive menu marries French and West Indian cuisines: seafood and local vegetables prepared with a French twist. Lobster is a specialty; select your own from the lobster pool. Light salads and sandwiches are available at lunch. Delicious baguettes and delicate pastries round out any meal. ⊠ *Belmont Walkway, Admiralty Bay, Port Elizabeth* ☎ *784/458–3201* ⌘ *Reservations essential* 🖃 *AE, MC, V.*

PIZZA ✕**Mac's Pizzeria.** Overheard at the dock in Mustique: "We're sailing
$–$$ over to Bequia for pizza." The two-hour sunset sail to Admiralty Bay
℧ is worth the trip to Mac's, which has been serving pizza in Bequia since 1980. Choose from 17 mouthwatering toppings (including lobster), or select homemade quiche, conch fritters, pita sandwiches, lasagna, or soups and salads. Mac's home-baked cookies, muffins, and banana bread (by the slice or the loaf) are great for dessert or a snack. Or top off your meal with a scoop or two of Maranne's homemade ice cream in tropical flavors. The outdoor terrace has water views. ⊠ *Belmont Walkway, Admiralty Bay, Port Elizabeth* ☎ *784/458–3474* ⌘ *Reservations essential* 🖃 *AE, D, MC, V* ⊗ *Closed Mon.*

23

BEACHES

Bequia has clean, uncrowded white-sand beaches. Some are a healthy trek or water-taxi ride from the jetty at Port Elizabeth; others require land transportation.

℧ **Friendship Bay.** This horseshoe-shape, mile-long (1.5-km-long), pro-
★ tected beach on Bequia's mid-south coast can be reached by land taxi. It's a great beach for swimming, snorkeling, and windsurfing; you can rent any equipment you need at Friendship Bay Resort and also grab a bite to eat or a cool drink at the hotel's Moskito Bar and Restaurant.

Hope Bay. Getting to this beach facing Bequia's Atlantic side involves a long taxi ride (about $7.50) and a mile-long (1.5-km-long) walk downhill on a semipaved path. Your reward is a magnificent crescent of white sand, total seclusion, and—if you prefer—nude bathing. Be sure to ask your taxi driver to return at a prearranged time. Bring your own lunch and drinks; there are no facilities. Even though the surf is fairly shallow, swimming may be dangerous because of the undertow.

Industry Bay. This nearly secluded beach is fringed with towering palms on the northeast (windward) side of the island; getting here requires transportation from Port Elizabeth. This beach is good for snorkelers, but there could be a strong undertow. Bring a picnic; the nearest facilities are at Firefly Bequia resort, about a 10- to 15-minute walk.

℧ **Lower Bay.** This broad, palm-fringed beach south of Port Elizabeth and
★ Princess Margaret Beach is reachable by land or water taxi or a healthy hike. It's an excellent beach for swimming and snorkeling. There are restaurants here, as well as facilities to rent water-sports equipment.

℧ **Princess Margaret Beach.** Quiet and wide, with a natural stone arch at
★ one end, the beach is a half-hour hike over rocky bluffs from Port Elizabeth's Belmont Walkway—or you can take a water or land taxi. Though it has no facilities, it's a popular spot for swimming, snorkeling, or snoozing under the palm and sea grape trees.

SPORTS & THE OUTDOORS

BOATING &
SAILING

★

With regular trade winds, visibility for 30 mi (48 km), and generally calm seas, Bequia has some of the best blue-water sailing you can find anywhere in the world, with all kinds of options: day sails or weekly charters, bareboat or fully crewed, monohulls or catamarans—whatever your pleasure. Prices for day trips start at about $125 per person.

Friendship Rose (⊠*Port Elizabeth* 🕾🕾784/458–3373), an 80-foot schooner that spent its first 25 years as a mail boat, was subsequently refitted to take passengers on day trips from Bequia to Mustique and the Tobago Cays. The 65-foot catamaran *Passion* (⊠*Belmont* 🕾784/458–3884), custom-built for day sailing, offers all-inclusive daylong snorkeling and/or sportfishing trips from Bequia to Mustique, the Tobago Cays, and St. Vincent's Falls of Baleine. It's also available for private charter. The Frangipani Hotel owns the *S. Y. Pelangi* (⊠*Port Elizabeth* 🕾784/458–3255 ⊕*www.frangipanibequia.com*), a 44-foot CSY cutter, for day sails or longer charters; four people can be accommodated comfortably, and the cost is $250 per day.

DIVING &
SNORKELING

About 35 dive sites around Bequia and nearby islands are accessible within 15 minutes by boat. The leeward side of the 7-mi (11-km) reef that fringes Bequia has been designated a marine park. The **Bullet**, off Bequia's northeast point, has limited access because of rough seas but is a good spot for spotting rays, barracuda, and the occasional nurse shark. **Devil's Table** is a shallow dive at the northern end of Admiralty Bay that's rich in fish and coral and has a sailboat wreck nearby at 90 feet. **Moonhole** is shallow enough in places for snorkelers to enjoy. The **Wall** is a 90-foot drop, off West Cay. Expect to pay dive operators $50 for a one-tank and $85 for a two-tank dive, including equipment. Dive boats welcome snorkelers for about $10 per person, but for the best snorkeling in Bequia, take a water taxi to the bay at Moonhole and arrange a pickup time.

Bequia Dive Adventures (⊠*Belmont Walkway, Admiralty Bay, Port Elizabeth* 🕾784/458–3826 ⊕*www.bequiadiveadventures.com*) offers PADI instruction courses and takes small groups on three dives daily; harbor pickup and return is included for customers staying on yachts. **Dive Bequia** (⊠*Belmont Walkway, Admiralty Bay, Port Elizabeth* 🕾784/458–3504 ⊕*www.dive-bequia.com*), at the Gingerbread Hotel, offers dive and snorkel tours, night dives, and full equipment rental. Resort and certification courses are available.

SHOPPING

Long renowned for their boatbuilding skills, Bequians have translated that craftsmanship to model-boat building. In their workshops in Port Elizabeth you can watch as hair-thin lines are attached to delicate sails or individual strips of wood are glued together for decking. Other Bequian artisans create scrimshaw, carve wood, crochet, or work with fabric—designing or hand-painting it first, then creating clothing and gift items for sale. Bequia's shops are mostly on Front Street and Belmont Walkway, its waterfront extension, just steps from the jetty where the ferry arrives in Port Elizabeth. North of the jetty there's an open-air market, and farther along the road are the model-boat builders' shops. Opposite the jetty, at Bayshore Mall, shops sell ice cream, baked goods, stationery, gifts, and clothing; there's also a grocery, liquor store, pharmacy, travel agent, and bank. On Belmont Walkway, south of the jetty, shops and studios showcase gifts and handmade articles. Shops are open weekdays from 8 to 5, Saturday 8 to noon.

★ At **Banana Patch Studio** (⊠ *Paget Farm* ☎784/458–3865), you can view and purchase paintings and scrimshaw work by artist Sam McDowell and shell crafts and "sailors' valentines" by his wife, Donna. Sailors' valentines are framed compositions of tiny shells, often with a flower or heart motif and a sentimental message, which 19th-century sailors on long voyages passing through the Caribbean would traditionally commission from local artisans and bring home to their sweethearts. The studio is open by appointment only. **Bequia Bookshop** (⊠ *Belmont Walkway, Port Elizabeth* ☎784/458–3905) has Caribbean literature, plus cruising guides and charts, Caribbean flags, beach novels, souvenir maps, and exquisite scrimshaw and whalebone penknives hand-carved by Bequian scrimshander Sam McDowell. You can visit the studio of French artist **Claude Victorine** (⊠ *Lower Bay* ☎784/458–3150) and admire her delicate hand-painted silk wall hangings and scarves. Large wall hangings cost $100, scarves $50. Her studio is open from noon to 7 PM; it's closed Friday. **Local Color** (⊠ *Belmont Walkway, Port Elizabeth* ☎784/458–3202), above the Porthole restaurant—near the jetty—has an excellent and unusual selection of handmade jewelry, wood carvings, scrimshaw, and resort clothing. **Mauvin's Model Boat Shop** (⊠ *Front St., Port Elizabeth* ☎784/458–3344) is where you can purchase the handmade model boats for which Bequia is known. You can even special-order a replica of your own yacht. They're incredibly detailed and quite expensive—from a few hundred to several thousand dollars. The simplest models take about a week to make.

☼ **Noah's Arkade** (⊠ *Frangipani Hotel, Belmont Walkway, Port Eliza-*
★ *beth* ☎784/458–3424) sells gifts, souvenirs, and contemporary arts and crafts from all over the Caribbean. **Sargeant Brothers Model Boat Shop** (⊠ *Front St., Port Elizabeth* ☎758/458–3344) sells handmade model boats and will build special requests on commission. Housed in the ruins of an old sugar mill, **Spring Pottery & Studios** (⊠ *Spring* ☎784/457–3757) is the working pottery of Mike Goddard and Maggie Overal, with gallery exhibits of ceramics, paintings, and crafts—their own and those of other local artists. All works are for sale. **Withfield Sails** (⊠ *Front St., Port Elizabeth* ☎758/457–3638) repairs and makes sails for real sailboats, but proprietor Withfield M. Laidlow also displays and sells his handmade model boats.

EXPLORING BEQUIA

To see the views, villages, beaches, and boatbuilding sites around Bequia, hire a taxi at the jetty in Port Elizabeth. Several usually line up under the almond trees to meet each ferry from St. Vincent. The driver will show you the sights in a couple of hours, point out a place for lunch, and drop you (if you wish) at a beach for swimming and snorkeling and pick you up later on. Negotiate the fare in advance, but expect to pay about $20 per hour for the tour. Water taxis are available for transportation between the jetty in Port Elizabeth and the beaches. The cost is only a couple of dollars per person each way, but keep in mind that most of these operators are not insured: ride at your own risk.

Admiralty Bay. This huge sheltered bay on the leeward side of Bequia is a favorite anchorage of yachters. Year-round it's filled with boats; in season they're moored cheek by jowl. It's the perfect spot for watching the sun dip over the horizon each evening—either from your boat or from the terrace bar of one of Port Elizabeth's bay-front hotels.

Hamilton Battery. Just north of Port Elizabeth, high above Admiralty Bay, the 18th-century battery was built to protect the harbor from marauders. Today it's a place to enjoy a magnificent view.

★ **Moonhole.** In 1961 American ad executive Tom Johnston and his wife, Gladys, moved to Bequia, purchased this rocky peninsula with a natural moon hole (through which the moon shines during the vernal and autumnal equinoxes), and designed a Flintstone-like stone home overlooking the sea. Over the next 20 years 18 more houses evolved, which are now individually owned as vacation homes. (One of them can be rented for about $1,375 per week.) Moonhole's unique architectural style was determined by the contour of the land, rocks, and trees. Walls and furniture were constructed of local stone, exotic wood, even whalebone, causing the multilevel "houses" to disappear naturally into the hillside. Johnston's son, Jim, and his wife, Sheena, now live at Moonhole and offer tours of their unusual "live-in sculptures" once a week. ⌂ *Box 30, Moonhole* ☎*784/458–3068* ⊕*www.begos.com/ bequiamoonhole* ☞*$22* ⊗ *Tues., by appointment only.*

Mt. Pleasant. Bequia's highest point (an elevation of 881 feet) is a reasonable goal for a hiking trek. Alternatively, it's a pleasant drive. The reward is a stunning view of the island and surrounding Grenadines.

☾ **Oldhegg Turtle Sanctuary.** In the far northeast of the island, Orton
★ "Brother" King, a retired skin-diving fisherman, tends to endangered hawksbill turtles. He'll be glad to show you around and tell you how his project is increasing the turtle population in Bequia. ⊠*Park Beach, Industry* ☎*784/458–3245* ☞*$5 donation requested* ⊗ *By appointment only.*

★ **Port Elizabeth.** Bequia's capital is on the northeast side of Admiralty Bay. The ferry from St. Vincent docks at the jetty, in the center of the tiny town, which is only a few blocks long and a couple of blocks deep. Walk north along Front Street, which faces the water, to the open-air market, where you can buy local fruits and vegetables and some handicrafts; farther along, you can find the model-boat builders' workshops for which Bequia is renowned. Walk south along Belmont Walkway, which meanders along the bay front past shops, cafés, restaurants, bars, and hotels.

CANOUAN

Halfway down the Grenadines chain, this tiny boot-shape island—just 3.5 mi (5.5 km) long and 1.25 mi (2 km) wide—has only about 1,165 residents. But don't let its historically slow pace and quiet ways fool you. Canouan (pronounced *can*-no-wan), which is the Carib word for "turtle," has an airstrip—with night-landing facilities and regularly scheduled flights from St. Vincent, Barbados, and Puerto Rico—and boasts one of the region's largest and most exquisite resorts, a championship golf course, a world-class spa, and a casino! It also claims five of the most pristine white-sand beaches in the Caribbean, and it's a busy port for yacht charters and diving expeditions to the Tobago Cays.

23

WHERE TO STAY

$$$$ 🏨 **Raffles Resort Canouan Island.** The vast bulk of the guest accommoda-
Ⓒ tions at the region's premier resort are in 60 villa-style units sprinkled
Fodor'sChoice around 300 acres of the 1,200-acre resort in an amphitheater setting. A
★ few villas are perched on the 900-foot hillside, next to the golf course. Rooms and suites—designated orchestra or mezzanine level, depending on location—are spectacularly huge (each no less than 600 square feet) and have superb decor, amenities, and views. Each room is assigned its own golf cart for getting around the property. Center stage is an 18th-century Anglican stone church (popular for resort weddings), along with the Galleria Complex—which houses reception, two restaurants and lounges, boutiques, a modern health club (with a boxing ring!), a hair salon, meeting rooms, and a golf pro shop. And as a backdrop, pick the beach, the sea, the mountains, or the Trump International Golf Club, an 18-hole, Jim Fazio–designed, par 72 course touted as one of the best in the Caribbean. Certainly, the view of the Grenadines from the 13th hole is something to write home about—as is the beachfront Amrita Spa. On request, the hotel will "meet and greet" guests in Barbados and arrange flight transfers between Barbados and Canouan. **Pros:** Beautiful accommodations; lots of activities for the entire family; and ahh, the spa! **Cons:** Very expensive, everything is à la carte (except breakfast). ⊠*Carenage Bay, Canouan* 🕾*784/458–8000* ⊕*www. canouan.raffles.com* 🛏*50 rooms, 97 suites, 8 villas* ☖*In-room: safe, kitchen (some), refrigerator, DVD, dial-up, Wi-Fi. In-hotel: 4 restaurants, bars, golf course, tennis courts, pool, gym, spa, beachfront, water sports, bicycles, no elevator, concierge, children's programs (ages 4–14), laundry service, public Internet, public Wi-Fi, airport shuttle* ⊟*AE, D, DC, MC, V* ⊙*BP.*

$$$ 🏨 **Tamarind Beach Hotel & Yacht Club.** Thatched roofs are a trademark of
Ⓒ this beachfront hotel, owned by the same Italian consortium that owns the nearby, superluxe Raffles property. Accommodations are in three buildings facing reef-protected Grand Bay beach. Louvered Brazilian walnut doors in each spacious guest room open onto a spacious veran-dah and a beautiful Caribbean vista. The alfresco Palapa Restaurant serves Italian and Caribbean specialties, grilled meat or fish, pizzas, and pasta prepared by a European chef. Barbecues and themed din-ners rotate throughout the week, and live Caribbean music is featured fairly regularly at the Pirate Cove bar. A 55-foot catamaran is avail-

able for day sails to the Tobago Cays. **Pros:** An excellent, reasonably priced choice on Canouan; excellent setting for diving and boating enthusiasts. Cons: While you can certainly visit Raffles, you might feel envious—until you compare rates. ⊠*Charlestown* ☎784/458–8044 ⊕*www.tamarind.us* ⇄*32 rooms, 8 suites* ⚹*In-room: safe, refrigerator, no TV (some). In-hotel: 2 restaurants, bars, beachfront, diving, water sports, bicycles, no elevator, laundry service, airport shuttle* ▭*AE, MC, V* ⦶*CP.*

BEACHES

⚘ **Godahl Beach.** This lovely stretch of white-sand beach (pronounced *gud-ul*) is at the south end of Carenage Bay and surrounded by the Raffles property, including the resort's beach bar and restaurant and its spa.

Grand Bay. In the center of Canouan on the leeward side is the island's longest beach and the site of Charlestown, the largest town, where ferries dock; it's also called Charlestown Bay.

Mahault Bay. This lovely but remote expanse of beach (pronounced *ma-ho*) is at the northern tip of the island, surrounded by Mt. Royal and accessible through the Raffles property or by sea.

South Glossy Bay. This and other Glossy Bay beaches along the southwest (windward) coast of Canouan are absolutely spectacular. South Glossy Bay is within walking distance of the airport, and the French restaurant at Canouan Beach Hotel is convenient for lunch.

SPORTS & THE OUTDOORS

BOATING The Grenadines has some of the most superb cruising waters in the world. Canouan is at the midpoint of the Grenadines, an easy sail north to St. Vincent, Bequia, and Mustique or south to Mayreau, the Tobago Cays, and beyond. The **Moorings** (⊠*Charlestown* ☎784/482–0653 ☏784/482–0654 ⊕*www.moorings.com*) operates next to Tamarind Beach Hotel & Yacht Club. It has bareboat and crewed yacht charters of monohulls and catamarans ranging in size from 38 to 52 feet.

DIVING & SNORKELING The mile-long (1.5-km-long) reef and waters surrounding Canouan offer excellent snorkeling as well as spectacular sites for both novice and experienced divers. **Gibraltar,** a giant stone almost 30 feet down, is a popular site; plenty of colorful fish and corals are visible. **Windward Bay,** on Canouan's southeast coast, is a large lagoon protected by a barrier reef, making it perfect for snorkeling. The crystalline waters surrounding the nearby **Tobago Cays** offer marvelous diving and snorkeling.

Blue Wave Dive Centre (⊠*Tamarind Beach Hotel, Charlestown* ☎784/458–8044 ☏784/458–8851), a full-service dive facility, offers resort and certification courses and dive and snorkel trips to the Tobago Cays, Mayreau, and Palm Island. **Glossy Dive Club** (⊠*Canouan Beach Hotel, South Glossy Bay* ☎784/458–8888 ☏784/458–8875) is a full-service PADI facility offering dive and snorkel trips to the Tobago Cays and other nearby sites.

GOLF The only 18-hole, championship golf course in St. Vincent and the Grenadines is also one of the best in the Caribbean. Located on the Raffles Resort property, it's operated by Trump Enterprises.

Fodor's Choice **Trump International Golf Club** (⊠ *Raffles Resort, Carenage Bay* ☎ *784/458–*
★ *8000* 🖷 *784/458–8885*) is an 18-hole, par-72 championship course
spread over 60 acres with unparalleled views. The first 9 holes of the
Jim Fazio–designed course, along with holes 10 and 18, are in a pretty
green plain that stretches down to the sea. The rest have been carved
into the mountainside, affording spectacular views of Canouan Island,
the resort itself, and the surrounding Grenadines. The 13th hole offers
a wraparound view; it's also the most challenging, as its unforgiving
green is at the edge of a cliff. Greens fees for 18 holes are $200 for
resort guests, $280 for nonguests; 9 holes, $115 (for resort guests only).
Golf instruction, carts, and rental clubs are available, and a pro shop
and lounge are in the resort.

23

MAYREAU

Mayreau (pronounced *my*-row) is minuscule—just 1.5 square mi
(4 square km). With the exception of 22 acres at its northern tip that
was purchased in 1977 by a German-Canadian family and 21 acres
that comprise the island's single (unnamed) village and were acquired
by St. Vincent and the Grenadines, Mayreau is privately owned by heirs
of the original French plantation owners. Only about 250 residents
live in the hilltop village, and there are no proper roads. Guests at the
resort on Saltwhistle Bay enjoy the natural surroundings in one of the
prettiest locations in the Grenadines—one of the few spots where the
calm Caribbean is separated from the Atlantic surf by only a narrow
strip of beach. It's a favorite stop for boaters, as well, who anchor in
Saltwhistle Bay and come ashore for lunch or dinner. Except for water
sports and hiking, there's not much to do—but everyone prefers it that
way. For a day's excursion, you can hike up Mayreau's only hill (wear
sturdy shoes) to a stunning view of the Tobago Cays. Then stop for
a drink at Dennis' Hideaway and enjoy a swim at Saline Bay beach,
where you may be joined by a few boatloads of cruise-ship passengers.
This pretty little island is a favorite stop for small ships that ply the
waters of the Grenadines and anchor just offshore for the day. The only
access to Mayreau is by boat (ferry, private, or hired), which you can
arrange at Union Island.

WHERE TO STAY
For approximate costs, see the lodging price chart in the St. Vincent &
the Grenadines Planner.

$$$$ 🏠 **Saltwhistle Bay Club.** This little resort is so cleverly hidden among
22 acres of palm and sea grape trees that sailors need binoculars to
be sure it's there at all. Gorgeous Saltwhistle Bay is a half-moon of
crystal-clear water rimmed by almost a mile of sparkling sandy white
beach at the northern tip of Mayreau. Tom and Undine Potter purchased this idyllic spot at the northern tip of Mayreau in 1977, cleared
the land just enough to build four double bungalows out of locally
quarried stone and natural wood, and opened for business in 1979.
Each roomy cottage accommodates two people and is decked out with
wooden shutters, ceiling fans, and a circular stone shower. You can dry

your hair on the breezy second-story verandah atop each bungalow. At the restaurant, individual dining cabanas with stone tables and seats are protected from sun and the occasional raindrop by thatched roofs. You can relish turtle steak, duckling, lobster, and à la carte lunches that may feature lobster salad, a fish sandwich, or even a perfectly prepared BLT. Guests are met at Union Airport and transported to Mayreau by launch. **Pros:** Delightfully natural, great anchorage, excellent all-day dining. Cons: Relatively remote. ⊠*Saltwhistle Bay* ☎*784/458–8444* ⊕*www.saltwhistlebay.com* ⤶*8 units* ⊘*In-room: no a/c, safe, no TV. In-hotel: restaurant, bar, beachfront, diving, water sports, no elevator, public Internet, airport shuttle* ⊟*MC, V* ⊘*Closed Sept. and Oct.* ⓘⓄⓁ*MAP.*

$ ⊡ Dennis' Hideaway. The rooms in this hilltop guesthouse, about a three-minute walk from the beach, are simple: a pair of twin beds, a nightstand, a chair, a private bath, and a place to hang some clothes. Each has a private balcony, with a perfect view of the sun as it sets over Saline Bay. A complete renovation in 2006 added air-conditioning to the guest rooms and a large swimming pool adjacent to the open-air dining terrace. Dennis (who plays guitar two nights a week—and who also happens to be a former shrimp-boat captain and is currently one of the island's three justices of the peace) is a charmer, the seafood (lobster, shrimp, fried squid, sautéed octopus, conch, or kingfish) at the restaurant is great, the drinks are strong, and the view is heavenly. Landlubbers can enjoy rack of lamb, barbecued spareribs or chicken, grilled lamb or pork chops. Dennis will transport inn guests arriving at Union Island Airport on his sailing yacht (a 45-minute voyage) or speedboat (15 minutes). **Pros:** Great value, friendly atmosphere, good restaurant, good base for boaters and divers. Cons: No frills or amenities. ⊠*Saline Bay* ☎*784/458–8594* ⊕*www.dennis-hideaway.com* ⤶*5 rooms* ⊘*In-room: no phone, no TV. In-hotel: restaurant, bar, pool, no elevator* ⊟*No credit cards* ⓘⓄⓁ*BP.*

BEACHES

Saline Bay Beach. This beautiful 1-mi (1.5-km) crescent of sand on the southwest coast has no facilities, but you can walk up the hill to Dennis' Hideaway for lunch or drinks. The dock here is where the ferry that travels between St. Vincent and Union Island ties up, and small cruise ships occasionally anchor offshore to give passengers a beach break.

★ **Saltwhistle Bay Beach.** This beach at the northwestern tip of the island takes top honors—it's an exquisite crescent of powdery white sand, shaded by perfectly spaced palms, sea grapes, and flowering bushes. It's also a popular anchorage for the yachting crowd, who stop for a swim and lunch or dinner at the beachfront Saltwhistle Bay Club.

SPORTS & THE OUTDOORS

BOATING & **Yacht charters, drift-fishing trips, and day sails can be arranged at Den-**
FISHING **nis' Hideaway** (⊠*Saline Bay* ☎*784/458–8594* ⊕*www.dennis-hideaway.com*). Expect to pay $40 per person for drift fishing for 1½ hours and $75–$100 per person (depending on the number of passengers) for a full day of sailing, swimming, and snorkeling—lunch included.

MUSTIQUE

This upscale haven, 18 mi (29 km) southeast of St. Vincent, is only 3 mi (5 km) by 1.25 mi (2 km) at its widest point. The island is hilly and has several green valleys, each with a sparkling white-sand beach facing an aquamarine sea. The permanent population is about 300. Britain's late Princess Margaret put this small, private island on the map after owner Colin Tennant (Lord Glenconner) presented her with a 10-acre plot of land as a wedding gift in 1960 (Tennant had purchased the entire 1,400-acre island in 1958 for $67,500). The Mustique Company—which Tennant formed in 1968 to develop the copra, sea-island cotton, and sugarcane estate into the glamorous hideaway it has become—now manages the privately owned villas, provides housing for all island employees, and operates Mustique Villa Rentals. Arrangements must be made about a year in advance to rent one of the luxury villas that now pepper the northern half of the island. Sooner or later, stargazers see the resident glitterati at Basil's Bar, the island's social center. Proprietor Basil Charles also runs a boutique crammed with clothes and accessories specially commissioned from Bali. A pair of cotton-candy-color, gingerbread-style buildings, the centerpiece of the tiny village, houses a gift shop and clothing boutique. There's a delicatessen-grocery to stock yachts and supply residents with fresh Brie and Moët; an antiques shop is filled with fabulous objets d'art to decorate those extraordinary villas—or to bring home.

The Mustique Blues Festival, held during the first two weeks of February, features artists from North America, Europe, and the Caribbean; shows occur nightly at Basil's Bar. The festival is quite a draw.

WHERE TO STAY

VILLAS Except for the Cotton House and Firefly hotels, Mustique is an island of villas—58 of them, in fact. Villa rentals are arranged solely through Mustique Villa Rentals, even though the villas are privately owned. Villas have two to nine bedrooms, and rentals include a full staff (with a cook), laundry service, and a vehicle or two. Houses range from "rustic" (albeit with en suite bathrooms for every bedroom, phones, pools, and other amenities) to extravagant, expansive, faux-Palladian follies with resident butler. All are elegant and immaculately maintained. Weekly rentals run from $3,000 for a two-bedroom villa in the off-season to $40,000 for a palatial eight-bedroom villa in winter.

Contact **Mustique Villa Rentals** (⌂ *The Mustique Co., Ltd., Box 349, St. Vincent* ☎ *784/458–4621* ⊕ *www.mustique-island.com*).

HOTELS & *For approximate costs, see the lodging price chart in the St. Vincent &*
RESORTS *the Grenadines Planner.*

$$$$ ⊡ **Cotton House.** Mustique's grand hotel, the main building of which
Fodor's Choice was once an 18th-century cotton warehouse, has oceanfront rooms and
★ suites with private walkways leading to the beach, a quartet of elegant ocean-view suites, and three poolside cottages with sunken baths, king-size beds with gauzy netting, and terraces affording stunning views. All have dressing areas, French doors and windows, desks, bathrooms

with marble fittings, your choice of 11 kinds of pillows, and a room TV, VCR, and/or DVD only upon request, ensuring perfect peace. Full unpacking and pressing services upon arrival are included in the rates, as is a weekly sunset cruise. The beachfront spa offers body treatments and has a fitness center on the ground floor. Enjoy breakfast and dinner at the Veranda Restaurant and casual lunches either poolside or at the Beach Terrace. **Pros:** Beautiful rooms, great attention to detail, the pillow menu, excellent dining. **Cons:** Madly expensive, more-sedate atmosphere than, say, Firefly. ⌂ *Box 349, Endeavour Bay* ☎784/456–4777 ⊕*www.cottonhouse.net* ↩*12 rooms, 5 suites, 3 cottages* ⌂*In-room: no phone, safe, no TV, dial-up. In-hotel: 3 restaurants, bars, tennis courts, pool, gym, spa, beachfront, diving, water sports, no elevator, concierge, public Internet, public Wi-Fi, airport shuttle* ▤*AE, D, MC, V* ☉*Closed Sept. and Oct.* ⏺*BP.*

$$$$ ☆ **Firefly.** Tiny and charming, this exclusive, reclusive three-story aerie is wedged into dense tropical foliage on a hillside above Britannia Bay. Originally built as a private villa in the early 1970s, the inn comprises five individually decorated rooms: one has a private deck with hot tub; another, a plunge pool; yet another, an open-air shower. Each is equipped with an iPod (loaded with specially selected music), and speakers. The inn's two pools are connected by a waterfall, and the beach is just down the (rather steep) garden path. The resort is built on a steep hillside, and most rooms are accessible via a spiral staircase, so it is not a suitable choice for guests with young children or folks with disabilities. Guests have free use of a Sunfish sailboat and a "mule," a small motorized buggy commonly used to get around Mustique. All meals are included, as well as picnic lunches, afternoon tea, and sunset snacks. Firefly restaurant serves Caribbean cuisine, gourmet pizza, and pasta dishes. **Pros:** Relaxed and friendly spot, great ocean views from each room, the bar—a hangout for guests and visiting celebrities—features martini and champagne menus. **Cons:** Very expensive, house-party atmosphere may not appeal to all. ⌂ *Box 349, Britannia Bay* ☎784/488–8414 ⊕*www.fireflymustique.com* ↩*5 rooms* ⌂*In-room: refrigerator, no TV, Wi-Fi. In-hotel: restaurant, room service, bar, pools, beachfront, water sports, no elevator, airport shuttle, no kids under 12* ▤*AE, MC, V* ⏺*FAP.*

WHERE TO EAT

For approximate costs, see the dining price chart in the St. Vincent & the Grenadines Planner

$$$–$$$$ ☾ ☆ ✕**Basil's Bar.** Basil's is *the* place to be—and only partly because it's the *only* place to be in Mustique. This rustic eatery is simply a wood deck perched on bamboo stilts over the waves; there's a thatched roof, a congenial bar, and a dance floor that's open to the stars—in every sense. You never know what celebrity may show up at the next table. The food is simple and good—mostly seafood, homemade ice cream, burgers, and salads, great French toast and banana pancakes, the usual cocktails, and unusual wines. Wednesday is "Party Night," with a barbecue; Sunday is "Locals Night," with a buffet of local dishes. ✉*Britannia Bay* ☎784/488–8350 ✍*Reservations essential* ▤*AE, D, MC, V.*

23

BEACHES

Britannia Bay. This beach on the west coast is right next to the Brittania Bay jetty, and Basil's Bar is convenient for lunch.

Endeavour Bay. This is the main beach used by guests of the Cotton House. Swimming and snorkeling are ideal, and a dive shop and water-sports equipment rental are available on-site. The resort's Beach House restaurant and bar are convenient for lunch or snacks.

Geliceaux Bay. One of 10 marine conservation areas designated by St. Vincent and the Grenadines, this beach on the southwest coast is a perfect spot for snorkeling.

L'Ansecoy Bay. At the island's very northern tip, this broad crescent of white sand fringes brilliant turquoise water. Just offshore, the French liner *Antilles* went aground in 1971.

Ⓒ **Macaroni Beach.** Macaroni is Mustique's most famous stretch of fine
Fodor'sChoice white sand—offering swimming (no lifeguards) in moderate surf that's
★ several shades of blue, along with a few palm huts and picnic tables in a shady grove of trees.

SPORTS & THE OUTDOORS

Water-sports facilities are available at the Cotton House, and most villas have sports equipment. Four floodlighted tennis courts are near the airport for those whose villa lacks its own; there's a cricket field for the Brits (matches on Sunday afternoon), and motorbikes or "mules" (beach buggies) to ride around the bumpy roads rent for $65–$85 per day.

DIVING & Mustique is surrounded by coral reefs, and nearly 20 dive sites are
SNORKELING nearby. **Mustique Watersports** (✉ *Cotton House, Endeavour Bay*
Ⓒ ☎784/456–3486 🖷784/456–4565) offers PADI instruction and certi-
fication and has a 28-foot, fully equipped dive boat. Rates are $110 for an introductory course, $85 for a one-tank dive, and $350 for a five-dive package. A special "bubble maker" introduction-to-diving course for children ages 8–11 costs $40. Snorkelers can rent a mask and fins for $10 per hour or $25 per day; snorkeling trips are $40 per person, with a two-person minimum.

HORSEBACK Mustique is the only island in the Grenadines where you can find a fine
RIDING thoroughbred horse or pony to ride. Daily excursions leave from the
Ⓒ **Mustique Equestrian Centre** (☎784/488–8000 ⊕ *www.mustique-island. com*), which is one block from the airport. Rates are $65 per hour for an island trek; private lessons begin at $50. All rides are accompanied, and children over five years are allowed to ride.

PALM ISLAND

A private speck of land (only 135 acres), exquisite Palm Island used to be an uninhabited, mosquito-infested swamp called Prune Island. One intrepid family put heart and soul—as well as muscle and brawn—into taking the wrinkles out of the prune and rechristened it Palm Island. The family cleaned up the five surrounding beaches, built bungalows, planted palm trees, and irrigated the swamp with seawater to kill the mosquitoes. The rustic getaway existed for 25 years before Palm Island's current owners, Elite Island Resorts, dolled up the property, and now it's one of the finest resorts in the Caribbean. Other than the resort, the island is populated only by a handful of privately owned villas. Access is via Union Island, 1 mi (1.5 km) to the west and a 10-minute ride in the resort's launch.

WHERE TO STAY

For approximate costs, see the lodging price chart in the St. Vincent & the Grenadines Planner

$$$$
Fodor'sChoice
★

Palm Island Resort. Perfect for a honeymoon, rendezvous, or luxurious escape, this palm-studded resort offers five dazzling white-sand beaches, a calm aquamarine sea for swimming and enjoying water sports, nature trails for quiet walks, a pool with waterfall, sophisticated dining, impeccable service, and exquisite accommodations. Picture-perfect Casuarina Beach runs the entire length of the western side of the island. Choose a room in a beachfront cottage, a palm-view room in the garden, a plantation suite (ideal for families), or a beachfront island loft that's set on stilts. All have wicker and bamboo furniture, rich fabrics, wooden louvered windows (with screens) on three walls to catch every breeze, and original artwork created by a resident artist, Dr. Patrick Chevalier. A pair of two-bedroom villas—perfect for two couples vacationing together—are spacious, secluded, and modern. They come with their own golf cart and a lightly stocked kitchen, although the all-inclusive meal plan applies to villa guests. The Royal Palm dining room, for guests only, offers a varied table d'hôte menu; the Sunset Grill and Bar near the dock serves seafood, light fare, and drinks and is open to the public for lunch and for dinner by reservation only. An air-conditioned recreation room with comfortable chairs has a TV, Internet access, and a library filled with "take one/leave one" books. **Pros:** Private and romantic, fabulous beach, great snorkeling right outside beachfront cottages 15 and 16. **Cons:** Quiet nights (early to bed and early to rise), fairly isolated. ⊠ *Palm Island* ☎ *784/458–8824* ⊕ *www. eliteislandresorts.com* 🛏 *37 rooms, 9 suites, 2 villas* ♿ *In-room: no phone, safe, kitchen (some), refrigerator, no TV. In-hotel: 2 restaurants, bars, golf course, tennis court, pool, gym, spa, beachfront, water sports, bicycles, no elevator, laundry service, public Internet, public Wi-Fi (some), airport shuttle, no kids under 16 (Dec. 15–Apr. 15)* ▤ *AE, D, DC, MC, V* ❍│*AI.*

PETIT ST. VINCENT

The southernmost of St. Vincent's Grenadines, tiny (113 acres), private Petit St. Vincent, pronounced "Petty" St. Vincent and affectionately called PSV, is ringed with white-sand beaches and covered with tropical foliage. The resort was created in 1968 by Haze Richardson, who remains the current proprietor; several current staff members have worked with him from the beginning. To get here you fly from Barbados to Union Island, where the resort's motor launch meets you for the 30-minute voyage.

WHERE TO STAY

For approximate costs, see the lodging price chart in the St. Vincent & the Grenadines Planner

$$$$ **Petit St. Vincent Resort.** No phones, no TVs, no outside interfer-
★ ences, and no planned activities are particularly appealing when
you can indulge your shipwreck fantasies without foregoing luxury.
Each secluded cobblestone cottage—all of which were renovated and
redecorated in 2007—has a large bedroom, a separate sitting room
with sliding glass walls facing the ocean, a patio, and beach access
(some beaches are rocky, but complimentary reef shoes are provided).
Although the resort does not have air-conditioning, which is rarely a
problem because constant sea breezes and careful design and placement
of cottages ensure that they remain cool even during the heat of midday.
Bathrooms have cobblestone showers. A system of signal flags conveys
your whims to the staff, so you can avoid human encounters entirely if
you wish. Hoist your red flag and nobody *dreams* of approaching; hoist
the yellow and you can promptly receive whatever you desire—or just
a lift to the dining room. Relax, read, swim, and get away from it all
in rustic elegance. Or sail away on a Hobie Cat, Sunfish, Windsurfer,
or kayak. Fishing trips and day sails are available from the dock, as
well. Few families with children stay here, though children who can
amuse themselves are welcome. **Pros:** Beautifully secluded, roomy and
comfortable accommodations, excellent cuisine. Cons: You're pretty
much a captive audience here, some of the beaches are rocky, no pool.
⊠*Petit St. Vincent* ☎784/458–8801 ⊕*www.psvresort.com* ⊡*PSV,
Box 841338, Pembroke Pines, FL 33084* 🖷*784/458–8428* ⬲*22 cottages* ⅑*In-room: no a/c, no phone, no TV. In-hotel: restaurant, room
service, bar, tennis court, beachfront, water sports, no elevator, airport
shuttle* ⊟*AE, MC, V* ⊗*Closed Sept. and Oct.* ⅋*FAP.*

TOBAGO CAYS

Fodor'sChoice A trip to this small group of uninhabited islands, just east of Mayreau
★ in the southern Grenadines and recently declared a wildlife reserve
by the St. Vincent and the Grenadines government, will allow you to
experience some of the best snorkeling in the world. Horseshoe Reef
surrounds five islets, each with tiny palm-lined, white-sand beaches.
The brilliantly colored water (alternating shades of azure and turquoise) is studded with sponges and coral formations and populated
by countless colorful fish. All the major dive operators go here, whether
they're based in St. Vincent or anywhere in the Grenadines. Whether
you're diving, snorkeling, or simply enjoying the boat ride, a visit to
the Tobago Cays is a truly unforgettable experience.

UNION ISLAND

The jagged peak of Mt. Tabol soars 1,000 feet in the air, distinguish-
ing Union Island from its neighbors. Union is a popular anchorage for
French vacationers sailing the Grenadines and a crossroads for others heading to surrounding islands (Palm, Mayreau, and Petit St. Vin-

cent)—just minutes away by speedboat. Clifton, the main town and a port of entry for yachts, is small and commercial, with a bustling harbor, a few simple beachfront inns and restaurants, businesses that cater to yachts, and the regional airstrip—perhaps the busiest in the Grenadines. Hugh Malzac Square, in the center of town, honors the first black man to captain a merchant marine ship. The ship was the *Booker T. Washington*; the time was 1942. Malzac was, of course, from Union Island. Taxis and minibuses are available to get around the island and water taxis go between islands. The Easterval Regatta occurs during the Easter weekend with festivities that include boat races, sports and games, a calypso competition, a beauty pageant, and a cultural show featuring the Big Drum Dance (derived from French and African traditions). Union is one of the few islands (along with Grenada's Carriacou) that perpetuate this festive dance.

Union Island has several small inns and hotels, some directly on the waterfront, others inland, and one directly on Bigsand beach.

WHERE TO STAY

For approximate costs, see the lodging price chart in the St. Vincent & the Grenadines Planner,

$$ **Bigsand Hotel.** Five minutes north of Clifton, Bigsand's small grouping of bright-white, two-story buildings lies just steps from the sea at picturesque Big Sand Beach. Each suite has a large bedroom, an enormous living room furnished with leather couches, and a large bathroom (shower only). Living rooms open to private beachfront porches. Only bedrooms are air-conditioned, but cooling breezes constantly sweep through each suite. Windsurfers, surfboards, kayaks, and snorkeling equipment are complimentary. This is a perfect spot to relax and soak up the Caribbean sun, but you can easily walk to town if you wish. **Pros:** Enviable location on beautiful Bigsand Beach, roomy accommodations, good restaurant. **Cons:** You might want to rent a jeep to get around, hotel charges 4% surcharge for using a credit card. ✉ *Richmond Bay* ☎ *784/485–8447* ⊕ *www.bigsandhotel.com* ➾ *8 rooms, 12 suites* ⚐ *In-room: safe, refrigerator, Wi-Fi. In-hotel: restaurant, room service, bar, beachfront, water sports, bicycles, no elevator, public Internet, airport shuttle* ☰ *AE, MC, V* ⑩ *BP.*

$–$$ **Anchorage Yacht Club.** AYC—a busy marina within walking distance of the airport and for years the "anchor" of Union Island—was purchased in late 2006 by Elite Island Resorts, which also owns Palm Island, the superdeluxe resort just across the channel. As of this writing, AYC was undergoing extensive renovations of its original dozen or so rooms and beachfront cottages, with immediate plans to build a 60-room addition on the north side of the property and renovate the dock area. The owner also plans to reinstall sharks in the seaside shark pool; the original inhabitants escaped in 2004 during Hurricane Ivan. In the meantime, the original rooms are open, the restaurant is busy all day long, and there's even live entertainment some evenings. Dockside amenities include a boutique, a pastry shop, and a soft–ice cream station. AYC is *the* hangout for the yachting crowd. **Pros:** Great location with a beautiful view of the southern Grenadines, busy dock, reasonable rates. **Cons:** Rooms are rather basic (so far), the airport is adjacent to the property. ⊠ *Clifton* ☎ *784/458–8824* ⊕ *www.eliteis-landresorts.com* ↻ *12 rooms* ⌂ *In-room: no phone. In-hotel: restaurant, bar, beachfront, water sports, no elevator, laundry service, public Internet, airport shuttle* ⊟ *AE, MC, V* ‖⊖ *EP.*

$ 🛏 **Kings Landing Hotel.** Owner King Mitchell holds court here, but his grandson recently returned from Canada to operate the hotel for him. Fifteen large, pleasantly furnished rooms face the sea, a small beach is suitable only for wading, and there's a freshwater pool. Each room has a refrigerator; two bungalows have a full kitchen. Breakfast and light meals are served at the poolside bar and grill. The West Indies restaurant is immediately next door for a different dining experience. Divers flock to King's Landing, because Grenadines Dive—the biggest operator in the region—operates from the hotel. For those who want to see some underwater creatures yet stay dry, the hotel has a shark tank. **Pros:** Great for divers, excellent seaside location, good value. **Cons:** Tiny beach, bathrooms have showers only. ⊠ *Clifton* ☎ *784/485–8823* ⊕ *www.kingslandinghotel.com* ↻ *15 rooms, 2 cottages* ⌂ *In-room: no phone, kitchen (some), refrigerator, Ethernet, Wi-Fi. In-hotel: restaurant, bar, pool, beachfront, diving, no elevator, laundry service, public Internet* ⊟ *AE, MC, V* ‖⊖ *BP.*

¢ 🏠 **St. Joseph's Apartments.** Quaint and colorful St. Joseph's Catholic ↻ Church, which the apartments overlook, operates this small hostelry, which began as a community resource center. The meeting room is now used as a lounge—and occasionally for small community meetings or workshops. Each unit has a bedroom and sitting area. Two apartments share a kitchen; the other has its own. A separate West Indian–style cottage, with a full kitchen, is high on the hillside; a dorm room sleeps seven people (linens are provided). The accommodations are small but clean and bright; the view from each verandah is, perhaps, one of the best in the Grenadines. **Pros:** Very inexpensive, dorm room is great for young kids and teenagers, good for brief stays or overnights (although many repeat guests stay longer). **Cons:** Taxi or minibus required to get to town, rooms are very simple. ⊠ *Clifton* ☎ *784/458–8405* ⊕ *www. erikamarine.com/accommodation.html* ↻ *3 apartments, 1 cottage, 1 dorm room* ⌂ *In-room: no a/c (some), kitchen (some), no TV (some), no phone. In-hotel: no elevator, laundry service* ⊟ *MC, V* ‖⊖ *EP.*

WHERE TO EAT

For approximate costs, see the dining price chart in the St. Vincent & the Grenadines Planner.

CARIBBEAN ✕ **Bigsand Restaurant & Beach Bar.** Although the seafood and produce
$$ here are definitely local, diners note a distinctly European finesse in the preparation and presentation at Bigsand, which is owned and operated by Scandinavian expats. Local folks, island visitors, and hotel guests can enjoy breakfast, lunch, or dinner alfresco. Mixed salad, pasta, and sandwiches on homemade bread or panini are great at lunch. You can enjoy a refreshing beer as you watch pelicans dive for their own lunch just offshore. At dinner, the lobster is incredible—or choose the catch

of the day, perfectly sautéed or grilled and served with local vegetables. ⊠*Richmond Bay* ☎784/485–8447 ☲*AE, MC, V.*

$ ✕**Lambi's.** During high season (November to May), Lambi's, which overlooks the waterfront in Clifton, offers a daily buffet for each meal. The dinner buffet includes some 50 dishes, including the specialty, delicious conch creole. In the low season (June to October), dining is à la carte, and you can choose from a menu of fish, chicken, conch, pork, lobster, shrimp, and beef dishes. Lambi is Creole patois for "conch," and the restaurant's walls are even constructed from conch shells. Yachts and dinghies can tie up at the wharf, and there's steel-band music and limbo dancing every night in season. ⊠*Clifton* ☎784/458–8549 ☲*No credit cards.*

SEAFOOD ✕**Anchorage Yacht Club.** You can't get much closer to waterfront dining
$$–$$$ than here at AYC. This is a favorite place for land-side meals—break-
☾ fast, lunch, or dinner—for the yachting crowd. It's also a perfect alternative for guests at Palm Island Resort to get the opposite perspective in terms of the view (and, let's face it, the environment). Freshly baked croissants and other pastries, along with pitchers of fresh-squeezed juice and piping-hot coffee, present the perfect wake up. At lunch, sandwiches, salads, burgers, grilled fish, and more are served with a view. And at dinner, the place comes alive with weekend entertainment (more often in season), as you enjoy fresh seafood cooked to order or, perhaps, a lobster selected from the live lobster pool and prepared to your liking. ⊠*Dockside, Clifton* ☎784/458–8824 ⚐*Reservations essential* ☲*AE, MC, V.*

BEACHES

☾ **Bigsand.** Union has relatively few good beaches, but this one at Richmond Bay on the north shore, a five-minute drive from Clifton, is a pretty crescent of powdery white sand, protected by reefs and with lovely views of Mayreau and the Tobago Cays.

Chatham Bay. The desolate but lovely golden-sand beach at Chatham Bay offers good swimming.

SPORTS & THE OUTDOORS

BOATING & Union is a major base for yacht charters and sailing trips. From a dock
SAILING 500 yards from the Union Island airstrip, you can arrange a day sail throughout the lower Grenadines: Palm Island, Mayreau, the Tobago Cays, Petit St. Vincent, and Carriacou. A full day of snorkeling, fishing, and/or swimming costs about $200 per person for two people or $120 per person for four or more—lunch and drinks included. At **Anchorage Yacht Club** (⊠*Clifton* ☎784/458–8221) you can arrange crewed yacht or sailboat charters for a day sail or longer treks around the Grenadines. The marina is also a good place to stock up on fresh-baked bread and croissants, ice, water, food, and other boat supplies. **Captain Yannis** (⊠*Clifton* ☎784/458–8513) has a charter fleet of three 60-foot catamarans and one 60-foot trimaran. Snorkeling gear, drinks, and a buffet lunch are included in a day sail.

ᴵG & **Grenadines Dive** (⊠*Sunny Grenadines Hotel, Clifton* ☎784/458–8138
 ᴳ ⊕*www.grenadinesdive.com*), run by NAUI-certified instructor Glen-

roy Adams, offers Tobago Cays snorkeling trips and wreck dives at the *Purina*, a sunken World War I English gunboat. A single-tank dive costs $60; multidive packages are discounted. Beginners can take a four-hour resort course, which includes a shallow dive, for $85. Certified divers can rent equipment by the day or week.

ST. VINCENT & THE GRENADINES ESSENTIALS

23

To *research prices, get advice from other travelers, and book travel arrangements, visit www.fodors.com.*

▌TRANSPORTATION

BY AIR

Travelers from North America and Europe arrive at airports in St. Vincent and the Grenadines via regional airlines that connect to major airlines serving six gateways: Barbados, Grenada, Martinique, St. Lucia, Puerto Rico, and Trinidad. Connections are via American Eagle, LIAT, and Grenadines Airways—-an alliance of Mustique Airways and SVG Air. There is a desk at Grantley Adams International Airport in Barbados to assit passengers in transit. American Eagle flies to Canouan via San Juan, St. Lucia, and Barbados. LIAT connects St. Vincent, Bequia, and Union with Barbados, Grenada, and St. Lucia. Grenadines Airways operates shared-charter service linking Barbados with the four airports in the Grenadines, and inter-Grenadine scheduled flights between St. Vincent and the various Grenadines.

Airlines American Eagle (☎784/456–5555 ⊕www.aa.com). **Grenadines Airways** (☎246/418–1654 for shared-charter flights, 784/456–6793 for inter-Grenadine flights ⊕www.grenadineairways. com). **LIAT** (☎784/458–4841 in St. Vincent ⊕www.liatairline.com). **Mustique Airlines** (☎784/458–4380 ⊕www.mustique.com). **SVG Air** (☎784/457–5777 in St. Vincent, 784/458–3713 in Bequia, 784/458–8882 in Canouan, 785/458–8329 in Union ⊕www.svgair.com).

AIRPORTS & TRANSFERS

On St. Vincent, E.T. Joshua Airport is in Arnos Vale, just 10 minutes' drive south of Kingstown. Although it is the nation's largest and busiest airport, its runway configuration limits its use to regional airlines. Work on a new international airport has begun in Argyle, at the southern tip of the island. The new facility, expected to open in 2011, will accommodate long-haul carriers and jet aircraft. In the Grenadines, Bequia and Canouan have airports with lighting for night service; Mustique and Union have small airstrips.

Taxis are always available at the airport in St. Vincent. In Bequia, the taxis—usually pickup trucks, with their beds fitted with seats and an awning—will take you to Port Elizabeth, to the various hotels, or for a day of sightseeing. On Canouan, the resorts generally provide airport transfers, although taxis are available. On Mustique, either transfers are provided or taxis are available. On Union Island, Clifton—the main town—is a short walk from the airport; a jitney from the Anchorage Yacht Club will take you to the dock (a two-minute trip) to meet the launch from Palm Island or Petit St. Vincent; taxis, of course, are also available.

Airports Canouan Airport (CIW ✉Canouan ☎784/458–8049). **E.T. Joshua Airport** (SVD ✉Arnos Vale, St. Vincent ☎784/458–4685). **Grantley Adams International Airport** (BGI ☎246/428–7101). **James F. Mitchell Airport** (BQI ✉Bequia ☎784/458–3948). **Mustique Airport** (MQS ✉Mustique ☎784/458–4380).

Union Airport (UNI ⊠ Clifton, Union
☎ 784/458–8750).

BY BOAT & FERRY

St. Vincent's port accommodates large
passenger ships, and the cruise-ship terminal in Kingstown offers full services
and amenities to passengers. Cruise ships
that call at Port Elizabeth on Bequia, at
Mayreau, and elsewhere in the Grenadines anchor offshore and tender passengers to beaches or waterfront jetties.

Two companies offer frequent ferry services between St. Vincent and Bequia.
Admiralty Transport and Bequia Express
operate two ferries each that make several round-trips daily, Monday through
Saturday, beginning at 6:30 AM in Bequia
and 8 AM in St. Vincent; the latest departure each day is at 5 PM from Bequia and
7 PM from St. Vincent. On Sunday and
public holidays, each company operates
two round-trips, one in the morning and
one in the evening. In St. Vincent, interisland ferries dock at the wharf adjacent
to the cruise-ship terminal in Kingstown;
in Bequia, ferries dock at the jetty in Port
Elizabeth. The one-way trip between St.
Vincent and Bequia takes 60 minutes and
costs $8 each way or $14 round-trip with
the same ferry company.

The interisland ferry, M/V *Barracuda,*
which is also known as "the mail boat,"
operates twice weekly. It leaves St. Vincent on Monday and Thursday mornings, stopping in Canouan, Mayreau,
and Union Island. It makes the return trip
Tuesday and Friday. On Saturday it does
the round-trip from St. Vincent to each
island and returns in a day. M/V *Gem
Star* takes passengers from Kingstown to
Canouan and Union on Tuesday and Friday mornings, returning early Wednesday
and Saturday mornings. Including stopover time, the trip from St. Vincent takes
ours (sometimes via Bequia) to Can-
$12), 4½ hours to Mayreau ($14),
hours to Union Island ($16).

Information Admiralty Transport
(☎☎ 784/458–3348). **M/V Barracuda**
(☎ 784/527–6135). **M/V Bequia Express**
(☎ 784/458–3472). **M/V Gem Star**
(☎ 784/526–1158).

BY BUS

Public buses on St. Vincent are privately
owned, brightly painted minivans with
colorful names like *Confidence, Fully
Loaded, Irie,* and *Who to Blame.* Bus
fares range from EC$1 to EC$6 (40¢
to $2.25) on St. Vincent; the 10-minute
ride from Kingstown to Villa Beach, for
example, costs EC$1.50 (60¢). Buses
operate from early morning until about
midnight. Routes are indicated on a sign
on the windshield, and the bus will stop
on demand. Just wave from the road or
point your finger to the ground as a bus
approaches, and the driver will stop.
When you want to get out, signal by tapping twice above the window by your
seat or ask the conductor, usually a young
boy who rides along to open the door and
collect fares; it's helpful to have the correct change in EC coins. In Kingstown the
central departure point is the bus terminal at the New Kingstown Fish Market.
Buses serve the entire island, although
trips to remote villages are infrequent.

BY CAR

Car rental is available only on St. Vincent
and Bequia. Renting a car on St. Vincent
is a good idea if you would like to explore
the leeward or windward coast on your
own. Either drive is interesting and picturesque, the roads easy to navigate, and the
sights easy to find. If you're planning an
extended stay on St. Vincent and expect
to travel frequently between Kingstown
and, say, the Villa Beach area, a rental car
might be useful—although not necessary,
as both taxis and buses are inexpensive
and readily available. On Bequia, a rental
car will be handy if you're staying for
several days in a remote location—that
is, anywhere beyond Port Elizabeth. For
brief stays, taxis offer prompt service and
will even drop you at the beach and pick
you up later, if you wish.

Rental cars in St. Vincent and Bequia cost about $55 per day or $300 a week, with some free miles. Unless you already have an international driver's license, you'll need to buy a temporary local permit for $30, valid for six months. To get one, present your valid driver's license at the police station on Bay Street or the Licensing Authority on Halifax Street, both in Kingstown, St. Vincent, or the Revenue Office in Port Elizabeth, Bequia.

Avis is the one international agency represented on St. Vincent. Local firms are reliable and offer comparable rates, including some four-wheel-drive vehicles. If you'd prefer to travel in "the slow lane," two-seater scooters or mopeds can be rented for $30 per day or $180 per week from Speedway Bike & Scooter Rental in St. Vincent.

In Bequia, you can rent a four-wheel-drive vehicle from B & G Jeep Rental, a car from Phil's Car Rental, or a Mini-Moke fun car from Parnell's Moke Rental. In Mustique, Mustique Mechanical Services rents cars, Mokes, and motor scooters.

About 360 mi (580 km) of paved roads wind around St. Vincent's perimeter, except for a section in the far north with no road at all, precluding a circle tour of the island. A few roads jut into the interior a few miles, and only one east–west road (through the Mesopotamia Valley) bisects the island. It's virtually impossible to get lost; but if you do make a wrong turn, local folks are friendly and will be happy to point you in the right direction. Roads are narrow in the country, often not wide enough for two cars to pass, and people (including schoolchildren), dogs, goats, and chickens often share the roadway with cars, minibuses, and trucks. Outside populated areas, roads can be bumpy and potholed; be sure your rental car has proper tire-changing equipment and a spare in the trunk. Drive on the left, and toot your horn before you enter blind curves out in the countryside, where you'll encounter plenty of steep hills and hairpin turns.

LOCAL CAR-RENTAL COMPANIES

St. Vincent Avis (✉Airport, Arnos Vale, St. Vincent ☎784/456–6861). **Ben's Auto Rental** (✉Arnos Vale, St. Vincent ☎784/456–2907). **David's Auto Clinic** (✉Sion Hill, St. Vincent ☎784/456–4026). **Speedway Bike & Scooter Rental** (✉Arnos Vale, St. Vincent ☎784/456–4894). **Star Garage** (✉Grenville St., Kingstown, St. Vincent ☎784/456–1743).

Bequia B & G Jeep Rental (✉Port Elizabeth, Bequia ☎784/458–3760). **Parnell's Moke Rental** (✉Port Elizabeth, Bequia ☎784/457–3066). **Phil's Car Rental** (✉Port Elizabeth, Bequia ☎784/458–3304).

Mustique Mustique Mechanical Services (✉Britannia Bay, Mustique ☎784/488–8555).

BY TAXI

Fares are set by the government, but taxis are not metered. Therefore, it's smart to settle on the price before entering the taxi—and be sure you know what currency is being quoted. On St. Vincent, the one-way fare between Kingstown and Villa is about $10 (EC$25).

On some islands, most notably Bequia, water taxis will take you between Port Elizabeth and the beaches for a couple of dollars each way. Keep in mind that these taxi operators aren't regulated or insured, so travel at your own risk.

■ CONTACTS & RESOURCES

BANKS & EXCHANGE SERVICES

Branches of several regional and international banks are in Kingstown, with other branches elsewhere on St. Vincent and in the Grenadines. ATMs are at banks in Kingstown and at their branches.

U.S. dollars are accepted nearly everywhere, although you'll receive change in Eastern Caribbean currency (EC$), which is the official currency and preferred. Large U.S. bills may be difficult to change in small shops. U.S. coins are not accepted anywhere. The exchange rate is fixed at EC$2.67 to US$1. Price quotes in shops are often given in both currencies. Prices quoted in this chapter are in U.S. dollars unless otherwise noted. Major credit cards—including American Express, Diners Club, Discover, Master-Card, and Visa—and traveler's checks are accepted by hotels, car-rental agencies, and some shops and restaurants.

ELECTRICITY

Electricity is generally 220–240 volts, 50 cycles. Some resorts, such as Petit St. Vincent, have 110 volts, 60 cycles (U.S. standard); most have 110-volt shaver outlets. Dual-voltage computers or small appliances will still require a plug adapter (three rectangular pins). Some hotels will lend transformers and/or plug adapters.

EMERGENCIES

ST. VINCENT

Coast Guard **Coast Guard emergencies** (☎911). **Coast Guard nonemergencies** (☎784/457–4578).

Hospital **Milton Cato Memorial Hospital** (⊠Kingstown ☎784/456–1185).

THE GRENADINES

Hospitals **Bequia Casualty Hospital** (⊠Port Elizabeth, Bequia ☎784/458–3294). **Canouan Clinic** (⊠Charlestown, Canouan ☎784/458–8305). **Mustique Company Island Clinic** (⊠Adjacent to Mustique Airport, Mustique ☎784/458–4621 Ext. 353). **Union Island Health Centre** (⊠Clifton, Union ☎784/458–8339).

HEALTH

Water from the tap in your hotel is safe to drink, but bottled water is always available. Fresh fruits and vegetables from the market are safe to eat, but (as at home) you should wash them first. Cooked food ͢ ͢rchased at the market, in small shops, ͢t village snackettes is wholesome and ͢ enjoy.

INTERNET, MAIL & SHIPPING

On St. Vincent, the E@gles Internet Cafe offers high-speed computers and broad-band Internet access for as little as $2 per hour. On Bequia, you'll find a number of Internet cafés in Port Elizabeth. And on Union Island, folks arriving by yacht (or land-based vacationers) will find Internet and all the other business or shipping services they might require at Erika's Marine Services in Clifton.

The General Post Office is on Halifax Street in Kingstown, St. Vincent. Most villages on St. Vincent have branch offices. Bequia's post office is in Port Elizabeth, across from the jetty. Airmail postcards cost EC60¢ to the United States, Canada, and the United Kingdom; airmail letters cost EC90¢ per ounce to the United States and Canada, EC$1.10 to the United Kingdom. When writing to a location in the Grenadines, the address on the envelope should always indicate the specific island name followed by "St. Vincent and the Grenadines, West Indies."

Information **E@gles Internet Cafe** (⊠Halifax St., opposite the General Post Office, Kingstown, St. Vincent). **Erika's Marine Services** (⊠Clifton, Union). **Lenroc Internet Cafe** (⊠Back St., Port Elizabeth, Bequia). **Sunset Internet Cafe** (⊠Front St., Port Elizabeth, Bequia). **Surf 'n' Send Internet Cafe** (⊠Belmont Walkway, Port Elizabeth, Bequia).

LANGUAGE

English is the official language of St. Vincent and the Grenadines. Although there's certainly a Caribbean lilt, you won't hear the Creole patois common on other islands that have a historical French background. One term to listen for is "jump-up," in which case you can expect a party with music and dancing. And if you're going to "lime" at the next "gap," you'll be relaxing—perhaps with a cool drink in hand—down the road. Women travelers find it particularly charming to be referred to as "milady."

SAFETY

There's relatively little crime against tourists here, but don't tempt fate by leaving your valuables lying around or your room or your rental car unlocked. Also, be alert and mindful of your belongings around the wharf areas in Kingstown, which can be congested when passengers are disembarking from ferries or cruise ships.

TAXES & SERVICE CHARGES

The departure tax from St. Vincent and the Grenadines is $15 (EC$40), payable in cash in either U.S. or EC currency; children under 12 are exempt. A government tax of 10% is added to hotel bills; a 15% VAT is added to restaurant checks and other purchases; and a 10% service charge is generally added to hotel bills and often to restaurant checks.

TELEPHONES

The area code for St. Vincent and the Grenadines is 784. Pay phones are readily available and best operated with the prepaid phone cards. Your cell phones should operate in St. Vincent and the Grenadines, but be prepared for hefty roaming charges. Alternatively, mobile phones can be rented on a short-term, pay-as-you-go basisthe two major providers are Digicel and Cable & Wireless. You'll see red Digicel "Top Up Here" signs posted throughout St. Vincent and the Grenadines, indicating places where you can add minutes to your cell phone or phone card.

Local calls are free from private phones and most hotels. Prepaid phone cards, which can be used in special card phones throughout St. Vincent and other Caribbean islands, are sold at shops, transportation centers, and other convenient outlets. (The phone cards can be used for local or international calls.)

Information Cable & Wireless (✉Halifax St.,Kingstown, St. Vincent ☎784/457–1901 ✉Port Elizabeth, Bequia ☎784/458–3999 ✉Charlestown, Canouan ☎784/482–0199 ✉Clifton, Union ☎784/458–8999). **Digicel** (✉Halifax St., Kingstown, St. Vincent ☎784/453–3000).

INTERNATIONAL CALLS

23

When making a collect call to the United States, dial 800/CALLUSA (800/225–5872). For international credit-card calling, dial 800/744–2000.

Information International Operator (☎115). **Operator-Assisted Credit Card Calls** (☎117).

TIPPING

If a 10% service charge has not been added to your restaurant tab, a gratuity at that rate is appropriate. Otherwise, tipping is expected only for special service. For bellmen and porters, $1 per bag is appropriate; for room maids, $2 per day. Taxi drivers and tour guides also appreciate a 10% tip.

VISITOR INFORMATION

Before You Leave St. Vincent & the Grenadines Tourist Office (☎212/687–4981 in New York City, 800/729–1726 ⊕www.svgtourism.com). **St. Vincent & The Grenadines Hotel & Tourism Association** (⊕www.svghotels.com).

In St. Vincent & the Grenadines Bequia Tourism Association (⊕www.bequiatourism.com ✉Main Jetty, Port Elizabeth, Bequia ☎784/458–3286). **St. Vincent & the Grenadines Ministry of Tourism, Youth, and Sport** (✉Upper Bay St., Kingstown, St. Vincent ☎784/457–1502). **Tourist information desks** (✉E. T. Joshua Airport, Arnos Vale, St. Vincent ☎784/458–4685 ✉Union Airport, Clifton, Union ☎784/458–8350).

WEDDINGS

Young Island, Palm Island, Petit St. Vincent, a villa on Mustique, a hilltop on Bequia, a 19th-century church on Canouan, the beach on Mayreau—all are lovely settings for a Caribbean wedding.

Visitors wishing to marry in St. Vincent and the Grenadines must be resident in the country for a minimum of one day before a marriage ceremony can take place. A special marriage license must be obtained from the Ministry of Justice at the Registrar's Office, Granby Street, Kingstown, St. Vincent, on weekdays between 8:30 and 3, excluding the lunch hour. Processing usually takes no more than three hours. You'll need to bring your valid passports, recent birth certificates (issued within the past six months), divorce decrees if you've been divorced, and an appropriate death certificate if either party is widowed. The license fee is $185 (EC$500) plus $7.50 (EC$15 and EC$5) for two required stamps. An official marriage officer, priest, or minister registered in St. Vincent and the Grenadines must officiate at the ceremony, and two witnesses must be present.

Trinidad & Tobago

Carnival in Trinidad

WORD OF MOUTH

"Around January in Trinidad the steel bands will be practicing in their panyards for Panarama. . . . Even if you don't like pan, you can't help but get caught up in the excitement of the music."

—mike

"Of course you know what to expect in birding—it's one of THE places in the world for this. The scarlet ibis flying at dusk are so beautiful."

—l.martin

WELCOME TO TRINIDAD & TOBAGO

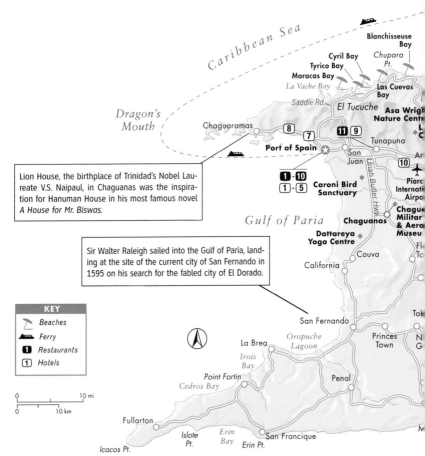

Caribbean Sea

Blanchisseuse Bay

Cyril Bay
Tyrico Bay
Maracas Bay
La Vache Bay
Saddle Rd.

Chupara Pt.

Las Cuevas Bay

El Tucuche

Asa Wrig
Nature Cent

Dragon's Mouth

Chaguaramas

8 **7**

11 **9**

Tunapuna

Port of Spain

San Juan

10

Lion House, the birthplace of Trinidad's Nobel Laureate V.S. Naipaul, in Chaguanas was the inspiration for Hanuman House in his most famous novel *A House for Mr. Biswas.*

1-**10**
1-**5** **Caroni Bird Sanctuary**

Piarc
Internati
Airpo

Chagu
Militar
& Aero
Museu

Gulf of Paria

Chaguanas

Sir Walter Raleigh sailed into the Gulf of Paria, landing at the site of the current city of San Fernando in 1595 on his search for the fabled city of El Dorado.

Dattareya Yoga Centre

Couva

California

Fl
Tc

San Fernando

Tak

KEY
Beaches
Ferry
Restaurants
Hotels

La Brea

Oropuche Lagoon

Princes Town

N
G

Irois Bay

Point Fortin

Penal

Cedros Bay

0   10 mi
0   10 km

Fullarton

Erin Bay

Islote Pt.

San Francique

Erin Pt.

Icacos Pt.

M

The most southerly of the Caribbean islands, Trinidad is also the most colorful. Islanders trace their roots to India, China, and Madeira; and they speak English, Spanish, and French Patois. On much quieter Tobago the most exciting event is often the palm trees swaying high above a gentle arc of a beach.

BUSINESS AND PLEASURE

The two-island republic is the southernmost link in the Antillean island chain, some 9 mi (14½) km off the coast of Venezuela, but Tobago's Main Ridge and Trinidad's Northern Range are believed to represent the farthest reaches of the Andes Mountains. Trinidad is a large petroleum and natural-gas producer. Tiny Tobago is known more for its quiet atmosphere and gorgeous, wild beaches.

24

TRINIDAD & TOBAGO

Tobago

Scarborough

Bacolet Beach was the location where the Disney movie *The Swiss Family Robinson* was filmed. It was also used for many scenes in John Huston's *Heaven Knows, Mr. Allison*.

Hotels ....▼	Monique's......................... **5**
Asa Wright Nature Centre Lodge............. **11**	Pax Guest House **9**
Coblentz Inn **3**	**Restaurants ....▼**
Courtyard by Marriott..................... **7**	A La Bastille............. **10**
	Apsara **7**
Crewes Inn.................... **8**	Il Colosseo **3**
Crowne Plaza................. **4**	Jaffa at the Oval........... **5**
Hilton Trinidad............... **1**	La Boucan **1**
Holiday Inn Express... **10**	Mélange.......................... **9**
Hyatt Regency Trinidad........................ **6**	Tamnak Thai.................. **6**
	Tiki Village..................... **2**
Kapok Hotel..................... **2**	Veni Mangé...................... **4**
Le Grande Almandier..................... **12**	The Verandah **8**
	Wings Restaurant **11**

TOP 4 REASONS TO VISIT TRINIDAD & TOBAGO

1 Trinidad's Carnival is the Caribbean's biggest and best party, but nightlife is hopping the rest of the year, too.

2 Both Trinidad and Tobago are major bird watching destinations; Trinidad itself has more resident species than any other Caribbean island.

3 A melding of many cultures means lively festivals year-round and excellent multicultural cuisine.

4 The steel pan was invented in Trinidad, and excellent bands play all over the island.

TRINIDAD & TOBAGO PLANNER

Island Activities

Trinidad has some good **beaches**—the best being Maracas Bay—but none is as picture-perfect as those on Tobago.

Though they don't have the manicured, country-club elegance you will find on many islands, the **beaches** on **Tobago** feel wilder and hark back to a time when towering hotels didn't line every picturesque Caribbean crescent.

Bird-watching is one of the highlights of a trip to either Trinidad or Tobago; both islands have reserves where you'll see a wide variety of species.

Diving is good off the shores of Tobago, particularly around Arnos Vale Reef, off the island's west coast.

Golfers will do better on Tobago, which has one excellent course and two other good ones.

Nightlife is much better in Port of Spain, with live music being a particular highlight, but Tobago as a whole is much quieter after dark.

Logistics

Getting to Trinidad & Tobago: You can fly nonstop to Trinidad from several U.S. cities, but not directly to Tobago. Most people hop over to Tobago on a small plane from Trinidad. Trinidad's Piarco International Airport (POS), about 30 minutes east of Port of Spain (take Golden Grove Road north to Arouca and then follow Eastern Main Road west for about 10 mi [16 km] to Port of Spain), is a thoroughly modern facility complete with 16 air bridges. Tobago's small Crown Point Airport (TAB) is the gateway to the island.

Hassle Factor: Medium to High.

Nonstops: Nonstops to Trinidad from Atlanta (Delta), Ft. Lauderdale (Spirit), Houston (Continental), Miami (American, Caribbean Airlines), New York–JFK (American, Caribbean Airlines, Delta), New York–Newark (Continental). None to Tobago.

On the Ground

Few hotels provide airport transfers, but you can always ask when you make your reservations. If you've booked a package, sometimes transfers are included. In Trinidad, taxis are readily available at Piarco Airport; the fare to Port of Spain is set at $30 ($45 after 10 PM) and $25 to the Hilton. In Tobago the fare from Crown Point Airport to Scarborough or Grafton Beach is about $50.

Renting a Car: Don't rent a car if you're staying in Port of Spain, but if you're planning to tour Trinidad, you'll need some wheels, as you will if you end up staying out on the island. In Tobago you're better off renting a four-wheel-drive vehicle than relying on expensive taxi service. Be cautious driving on either island, as the country has very lax and seldom enforced drinking and driving laws.

Where to Stay

Trinidad isn't a top tourist destination, so resorts are few and far between, and many are a long drive from Port of Spain and the airport. However, a few ecoconscious options are worth the hassle, particularly if you are a bird-watcher. Tobago has a wide array of lodging options, and it's a much smaller island with better beaches, so your choice of resort is more driven by the amenities you want and your budget—rather than the resort's location.

Hotels: Though they have nice pools and other resort-type amenities, Trinidad's hotels are geared more for business travelers. Options for beachgoers are more limited and farther removed from Port of Spain.

Beach Resorts: Tobago has a nice mix of midsize resorts, including several offering a fair degree of luxury, but there are also many choices for budget-oriented tourists, as is the case in Trinidad, where fewer tourists mean better value at the small beach resorts that cater primarily to locals. Few hotels on either island offer anything but room-only rates, though there are now two all-inclusive resorts on Tobago.

Ecoresorts: Nature lovers, particularly bird-watchers, have an especially good option in Trinidad in the Asa Wright Nature Centre Lodge. Several of Tobago's small resorts are particularly ecoconscious.

Hotel & Restaurant Prices

⇨*For information on hotel meal plans, see Accommodations in Caribbean Essentials.*

WHAT IT COSTS IN U.S. DOLLARS

$$$$	$$$	$$	$	¢
Restaurants				
over $30	$20–$30	$12–$20	$8–$12	under $8
Hotels*				
over $350	$250–$350	$150–$250	$80–$150	under $80
Hotels**				
over $450	$350–$450	$250–$350	$125–$250	under $125

*EP, BP, CP **AI, FAP, MAP Restaurant prices are for a main course at dinner and include any taxes or service charges. Hotel prices are per night for a double room in high season, excluding taxes, service charges, and meal plans (except at all-inclusives).

When to Go

Trinidad is more of a business destination than a magnet for tourists, so hotel rates (particularly in Port of Spain) are much more stable year-round; nevertheless, you can usually get a price break during the traditional Caribbean low season (from May to December). However, Carnival (in January or February) brings the highest rates.

24

Tobago is much more of a tourist destination, but busy periods on Tobago—since it is still more popular with Europeans than Americans—can sometimes differ from the typical vacation periods in the United States.

Trinidad's **Carnival** in January or February is the biggest and best celebration in the Caribbean.

The **Tobago Heritage Festival** is usually held in late July.

Divali, held in October or November and called the festival of lights, is one of the more-popular Hindu festivals in Trinidad.

By Vernon
O'Reilly-
Ramesar

SENSORY OVERLOAD IS INSUFFICIENT TO describe the Queen's Park Savannah on Carnival Tuesday. Thousands of costumed masqueraders in dozens of bands form pulsing sections of color on the dusty path leading to the judging point, the line snaking back as far as the eye can see. The driving sound of steel bands fills the air and barely competes with the throb of massive music trucks blaring soca. The faces in the waiting throng reflect every imaginable ethnic background. Since the wee hours, they have slogged through packed streets to reach this point. Once past the judging area—champions or not—they will continue their musical march until their feet can take no more. On an island built on trade, where the roads are usually packed with honking cars, today the traffic lights are off as Trinis ecstatically celebrate life with a multicultural human traffic jam.

The birthplace of the steel pan (the national instrument), limbo, calypso, and soca (a harder-edged version of calypso), these lush islands can also lay claim to being the economic powerhouse of the Caribbean. Vast oil and gas reserves have led to a high standard of living and a great sense of optimism about the future, where tourism is not the mainstay of the economy. Indeed, the word *tourist* is seldom mentioned here; the preference is for the much friendlier *visitor*. T&T, as the dual-island nation is commonly called, is the southernmost link in the Antillean island chain, lying some 7 mi (11 km) off the coast of Venezuela and safely outside the path of most Caribbean hurricanes. Geologically, though, the islands are actually extensions of the South American mainland. Trinidad's Northern Range is thought to be part of the Andes (and was connected to the mainland as recently as the last Ice Age). This geological history helps explain why the range of flora and fauna is much greater than on other Caribbean Islands. And though connected politically and geologically, Trinidad and Tobago offer dramatically different cultural experiences.

Trinidad's capital city, Port of Spain, is home to some 300,000 of the island's 1.3 million inhabitants. In fact, the capital merges seamlessly with other towns and residential areas to form a dense population belt that runs from Westmoorings in the west to Arima in the east. Downtown Port of Spain is a bustling commercial center complete with high-rise office buildings and seemingly perpetual traffic. Happily, the northern mountain range rises just behind the city and helps to take much of the edge off the urban clamor.

Much of the charm of Trinidad lies in the ethnic mix of the population. The majority of the population is of either African or East Indian background—the descendants of African slaves brought here during the island's relatively short slave history of some 80 years, and indentured East Indian laborers, who came to work the plantations in the 19th century. The island is always buzzing with a variety of celebrations and arts performances that can range from African drumming to classical Indian dance. The national cuisine has also absorbed the best of both cultures. Although these two groups compose more than 80% of the population, other groups such as the French, Spanish, Chinese, and even Lebanese have left their mark.

The Steel Pan

The sound of a steel band playing poolside has become emblematic of the Caribbean. What you may not know is that the fascinating instrument has an interesting and humble history that began in Trinidad.

In 1883 the British government banned the playing of drums on the island, fearful that they were being used to carry secret messages. Enterprising Afro-Trinidadians immediately found other means of creating music. Some turned to cut bamboo poles beaten rhythmically on the ground; these were called Tamboo Bamboo bands, and they soon became a major musical force on the island. With the coming of industry, new materials such as hubcaps and biscuit tins were added as "instruments" in the bands. These metal additions were collectively known as "pan." Later, after the Americans established military bases on the islands during World War II, empty oil drums became available and were quickly put to musical use.

At some point it was discovered that these drums could be cut down, heated in a fire, and beaten into a finely tuned instrument. The steel pan as we know it was thus born. Soon there were entire musical bands playing nothing but steel pans. For years the music gestated in the poorer districts of Port of Spain and was seen as being suitable only for the lower classes of society, a reputation not helped by the fact that the loyal followers of early steel bands sometimes clashed violently with their rivals. Eventually, the magical sound of the "pan" and its amazing ability to adapt to any type of music won it widespread acceptance.

Today the government recognizes the steel pan as the official musical instrument of Trinidad and Tobago. It's played year-round at official functions and social gatherings, but the true time for the steel pan is Carnival. In the annual Panorama festival, dozens of steel bands from around the country compete for the "Band of the Year" title. Some have fewer than a dozen steel pans, while others number in the hundreds. The performance of the larger bands creates a thunderous wall-of-sound effect.

24

Many of the art forms that are considered synonymous with the Caribbean were created on this relatively small island. Calypso was born here, as were soca, limbo, and the steel pan (steel drum). The island can also claim two winners of the Nobel Prize in literature—V.S. Naipaul (2001), who was born in Trinidad and wrote several of his earlier books about the island, and Derek Walcott (1992), a St. Lucian who moved to Trinidad in 1953. Many tourists make a pilgrimage simply to trace the places mentioned in Naipaul's magnum opus, *A House for Mr. Biswas.*

Physically, the island offers an exact parallel to the rain forests of South America, which allows for interesting—and sometimes challenging—ecological adventures. Beach lovers accustomed to the electric blue water and dazzling white sand of coral islands may be disappointed by the beaches on Trinidad. The best beaches are on the north coast, with peach sand, clean blue-green water, and the forest-covered Northern Range as a backdrop. Beaches are almost completely free of hotel development.

Tobago is 23 mi (37 km) northeast of Trinidad. The population here is much less ethnically diverse than that of Trinidad, with the majority being of African descent. Tobagonians have their own dialect and distinct culture. Tourism is much more a part of the island's economy, and you can find excellent resorts and facilities. Tobago also has excellent white-sand beaches.

The two islands have very different histories. Sadly, the Amerindian populations of both islands were virtually wiped out by the arrival of Europeans. After Columbus landed in Trinidad in 1498, the island came under Spanish rule. In an attempt to build the population and provide greater numbers to fend off a potential British conquest, the government at the time encouraged French Catholics from nearby islands to settle in Trinidad. This migration can be seen in the large number of French place-names scattered around the island. Despite this effort, the British conquered the island in 1797.

Tobago had a much more turbulent history. Named after the tobacco that was used by the native Amerindian population, it was settled by the British in 1508. The island was to change hands a total of 22 times before eventually returning to Britain in 1814.

The two islands were merged into one crown colony in 1888, with Tobago being made a ward of Trinidad. Independence was achieved in 1962 under the leadership of Dr. Eric Williams, who became the first prime minister. The islands became an independent republic in 1976 with a bicameral Parliament and an appointed president.

TRINIDAD

WHERE TO STAY

Because Trinidad is primarily a business destination, most accommodations are in or near Port of Spain. Standards are generally good, though not lavish by any means. Port of Spain has a small downtown core—with a main shopping area along Frederick Street—and is surrounded by inner and outer suburbs. The inner areas include Belmont, Woodbrook, Newtown, St. Clair, St. Ann's, St. James, and Cascade. The nearest beach to most hotels is Maracas Bay, which is a half-hour drive over the mountains. Carnival visitors should book many months in advance and be prepared to pay top dollar for even the most modest hotel. The opening in 2008 of the new 428-room Hyatt Regency on the Port of Spain waterfront has added room capacity and means the Hilton Trinidad is now no longer the only big international class hotel on the island.

$$$–$$$$ ▦ **Hilton Trinidad & Conference Centre.** The Hilton was the most upscale
★ hotel on the island before the arrival of the Hyatt Regency, and it still commands a loyal following. On the side of a hill overlooking the

Queen's Park Savannah, it offers beautiful landscaping and breathtaking views of Port of Spain and the Gulf of Paria. Its unique construction means that the lobby is at the top of the hill and guests take an elevator *down* to the rooms. Although rates are high by island standards, you're paying for the comfort of knowing that everything here will be standard Hilton issue. Spa, golf, and wedding packages are available for vacationers. The hotel is undergoing a $32-million upgrade to all rooms and facilities. Work is expected to be completed by the end of 2008. This means that room availability will be lower during the early part of 2008. **Pros:** Great view, full range of hotel services, reliable and consistent service. **Cons:** No longer the best luxury choice on the island, pool area can be very noisy when parties are going on. ✉*Lady Young Rd., Box 442, Port of Spain* ☎*868/624–3211, 800/445–8667 in U.S.* ⊕*www.hiltoncaribbean.com* ➷*386 rooms, 26 suites* ♿*In-room: safe, Ethernet. In-hotel: 2 restaurants, room service, bars, tennis courts, pool, gym, laundry service, executive floor, public Internet* ▭*AE, DC, MC, V* ⎪O⎪*EP.*

$$$–$$$$ ⬚**Hyatt Regency Trinidad.** Trinidad's newest and only full-service hotel on the waterfront is a striking high-rise structure and part of the government's dramatic makeover of the Port of Spain waterfront. It's been designed to provide an insulating environment for business travelers. Rooms are tastefully decorated with bamboo floors and feature fuchsia-accent walls. The lobby has stone walls, a waterfall, palm trees, and generous splashes of bright Caribbean colors. The rooftop pool provides a commanding view of the city. Because of ongoing work along the waterfront, the area around the hotel will be under quite a lot of construction zone until 2010. **Pros:** Spanking new and easily the most upscale hotel on the island, view from the rooftop pool is unbeatable, convenient to downtown and shopping. **Cons:** Right in the middle of a major construction zone, the smell of the wharf can be unpleasant from room balconies ✉*1 Wrightson Rd., Port of Spain* ☎*868/623–2222* ⊕*trinidad.hyatt.com* ➷*428 rooms* ♿*In-room: safe, Wi-Fi. In-hotel: restaurant, room service, bar, gym, spa, laundry service* ▭*AE, DC, MC, V* ⎪O⎪*EP.*

$$$ ⬚**Asa Wright Nature Centre Lodge.** Those seeking to really get away from it all will find this mountain retreat the perfect choice, but the average traveler may find the isolation a bit much. A hotel designed for serious bird-watchers, it's surrounded by 200 acres of wilderness and by streams, waterfalls, and natural pools an hour's drive from the nearest beach or town. From a verandah overlooking the Arima Valley, you can sip a cup of tea (or delicious homegrown coffee) while hummingbirds dart around your head. Rooms in outlying bungalows are simple but adequate; those in the main house are a bit grander and furnished with period furniture but can be noisy. Meals are taken communally in the large dining room, which allows guests to exchange bird stories over good basic food. Well-behaved kids over 12 are welcome, but the lack of TV might prove too much for young minds to bear. **Pros:** Best bird-watching on the island, main house has a wonderful colonial feel, peaceful setting. **Cons:** Miles from anything else on the island, no dining choices, the lack of entertainment options at night can be unnerving. ⬡ *Box 4710, Arima Valley* ☎*868/667–4655 or 800/426–7781* ⊕*www.asawright.org* ⬎*24 rooms, 1 bungalow* ⬧*In-room: no a/c, no TV. In-hotel: restaurant, no elevator, no kids under 12* ☰*MC, V* ⦿*FAP.*

$$ ⬛**Courtyard by Marriott.** This large hotel in the capital offers excellent
★ facilities and a great location. Guests can take advantage of a variety of restaurants, shops, and entertainment possibilities available next door at the ultramodern Movietowne complex. Rooms are spacious and feature lovely high-back wooden headboards on the beds. This hotel caters mainly to business travelers and offers a range of free services, including Wi-Fi, and printing and local faxing at the business center. **Pros:** Excellent location for shopping and dining, large and airy rooms, high service standards. **Cons:** Just off busy highway, the many business travelers can make it feel a bit uncomfortable for leisure guests. ✉*Invader's Bay, Audrey Jeffer's Hwy., Port of Spain* ☎*868/627–5555* ⊕*www.marriott.com* ⬎*116 rooms, 3 suites* ⬧*In-room: safe, refrigerator, Ethernet, Wi-Fi. In-hotel: restaurant, room service, bar, pool, gym, laundry facilities, laundry service, no-smoking rooms* ☰*AE, D, MC, V* ⦿*EP.*

$$ ⬛**Crews Inn Hotel & Yachting Centre.** On Trinidad's western peninsula, this hotel is about 20 minutes from downtown but smack in the middle of the island's most popular nightlife area. The hotel complex caters to the yachting crowd with a huge marina and a wide range of shops. The Lighthouse Restaurant is popular with locals and has a large and lively bar. Rooms are well appointed, with views of the marina and pool. The nearest beach is a 10-minute drive but isn't particularly good. **Pros:** Great view of marina, airy rooms are tastefully decorated, great for yachting enthusiasts. **Cons:** Far from Port of Spain, very limited shopping and dining nearby ✉*Point Gourde, Chaguaramas* ☎*868/634–4384* ⊕*www.crewsinn.com* ⬎*42 rooms, 4 suites* ⬧*In-room: kitchen, VCR (some), Ethernet. In-hotel: restaurant, room service, bars, pool, gym, laundry facilities, laundry service* ☰*AE, MC, V* ⦿*EP.*

$$ ⬛**Crowne Plaza Trinidad.** Proximity to the port and Independence Square is both the draw and the drawback here. From any upper-floor room you have a lovely pastel panorama of the Old Town and of ships idling in the Gulf of Paria, and you're within walking distance of the downtown sights and shops. But with proximity to the action come traffic and noise, especially with major development taking place on the waterfront. Although rooms are adequate, they are not luxurious by any means. A revolving rooftop restaurant called 360 offers a striking view of the city and has a superb Sunday brunch. **Pros:** Close to downtown and the business core, revolving restaurant has wonderful views. **Cons:** There's traffic noise by the pool area, in busy construction zone, port odors can seep into hallways. ✉*Wrightson Rd., Box 1017, Port of Spain* ☎*868/625–3361 or 800/227–6963* ⊕*www.ichotelsgroup. com* ⬎*243 rooms, 5 suites* ⬧*In-room: safe, Ethernet, Wi-Fi. In-hotel: 2 restaurants, room service, bars, pool, gym, laundry service, concierge, public Wi-Fi* ☰*AE, MC, V* ⦿*BP.*

$$ ⬛**Holiday Inn Express & Suites Trincity.** Just five minutes from the airport and with a complimentary shuttle service, this fairly new hotel is popu-

lar with short-stay travelers. Rooms are of the expected standard, and security is tight as befits a hotel that caters primarily to businesspeople. The hotel overlooks a golf course, and the island's largest mall is just a two-minute shuttle ride away. The hotel serves breakfast, but the closest restaurants are at Trincity Mall. Because the hotel is away from the traffic and congestion of Port of Spain, it makes visiting the east-coast and northeast-coast beaches a much less frustrating experience. **Pros:** Convenient to the airport, close to Trincity Mall. **Cons:** Not close to the major urban centers, nearby traffic can be horrendous, has that bland chain-hotel feeling. ⊠*1 Exposition Dr., Trincity* ☎*868/669–6209* ⊕*www.ichotelsgroup.com* ⇄*62 rooms, 20 suites* ⌂*In-room: safe, Ethernet, Wi-Fi. In-hotel: bar, pool, public Wi-Fi, airport shuttle* ▤*AE, D, DC, MC, V* ⊚*BP.*

24

$$ 🔲**Kapok Hotel.** This hotel in a good neighborhood just off Queen's Park Savannah is the best all-around value if you want to stay in the city; it offers a high level of comfort and service. Although it does not have the myriad amenities of the nearby Hilton, many people prefer the more-intimate feel of the Kapok. Rooms vary greatly in size, with the Savannah-facing rooms being generally much larger. Those considering longer stays would be well advised to choose one of the suites with a balcony as the price difference is minimal. The hotel's restaurant, Tiki Village, offers some of the most reliably good food on the island and is popular with locals. Bois Cano, the alfresco bistro and wine bar, is lovely and relaxed and has live jazz on Thursday evenings, not to mention afternoon tea. The Ellerslie Plaza mall is a three-minute walk from the front door. **Pros:** Great location away from downtown noise, more-intimate alternative to Hilton and Hyatt, one of the best restaurants on the island. **Cons:** Lacks some of the services of larger hotels, pool is a bit small. ⊠*16–18 Cotton Hill, St. Clair, Port of Spain* ☎*868/622–5765 or 800/344–1212* ⊕*www.kapokhotel.com* ⇄*73 rooms, 12 suites, 9 studios* ⌂*In-room: safe, kitchen (some), Ethernet. In-hotel: 2 restaurants, room service, pool, gym, laundry facilities, laundry service* ▤*AE, MC, V* ⊚*EP.*

$–$$ 🔲**Coblentz Inn.** This small boutique hotel is bursting at the seams with charm. Just a short drive from downtown in the quiet suburb of Cascade, the hotel offers peace, quiet, and style at a relatively affordable price. Each room is done in a different whimsical theme; the Rumshop Room, for example, comes complete with full bottles of rum and playing cards on the coffee table. Amazingly, for the price, all rooms offer a complimentary, fully stocked minibar. The one so-called "suite" on offer is really just a very large room. **Pros:** rooms have genuine charm, small but attentive staff, common areas are relaxing and great for catching up on reading. **Cons:** restaurant has wildly unreliable food quality, small compound can feel cramped. ⊠*44 Coblentz Ave., Cascade, Port of Spain* ☎*868/621–0541* ⊕*www.coblentzinn.com* ⇄*16 rooms* ⌂*In-room: Wi-Fi. In-hotel: restaurant, room service, no elevator, laundry service, public Wi-Fi* ▤*AE, MC, V* ⊚*BP.*

$ 🔲**Le Grande Almandier.** This low-priced hotel is on Trinidad's remote
★ and beautiful northeast coast. The area is a popular weekend escape for locals who go to experience the lush rain-forest backdrop and expan-

sive beach. Rooms here are cozy, and each is decorated in a different theme. Some rooms are air-conditioned (a rarity for a hotel on this part of the island), but cool ocean breezes are usually quite adequate. The restaurant here serves extraordinary creole dishes featuring seafood caught just off the premises. The nearest shopping or nightlife is a two-hour drive away, so this is strictly a place for those seeking peace, quiet, and good home-style food. **Pros:** right on the beach, great for turtle-watching in season, small with a friendly-family vibe. **Cons:** the north-east coast is at least two hours from the capital, limited shopping and dining options, car is definitely required for any exploring. ⊠ *2 Hosang St., Grande Riviere* ☎ *868/670–1013* ⊕ *www.legrandealmandier.com* ⤳ *10 rooms* ⚐ *In-room: no a/c (some). In-hotel: restaurant, room service, bar, laundry service* ▤ *MC, V* ⧇ *BP.*

¢–$ ▦ **Monique's.** Spacious but simple rooms and proximity to Port of Spain ensure the popularity of this guesthouse, which consists of two separate buildings. Rooms in "Monique's on the Hill" have kitchenettes and sizable balconies, but getting to these rooms is a bit of a trek. The staff are justifiably famous for their friendliness. **Pros:** huge rooms, in a generally quite area, family ownership shows in the concern for the comfort of guests. **Cons:** room decor feels very dated, not within walking distance of shopping or dining. ⊠ *114–116 Saddle Rd., Maraval, Port of Spain* ☎ *868/628–3334 or 868/628–2351* ⊕ *www.moniquestrinidad. com* ⤳ *20 rooms* ⚐ *In-room: kitchen (some), dial-up. In-hotel: bar, no elevator, laundry service, airport shuttle* ▤ *AE, DC, MC, V* ⧇ *CP.*

¢   ▦ **Pax Guest House.** Built in 1932 on the grounds of a hilltop monas-
★   tery, this charming, antiques-furnished guesthouse is ideal for budget travelers seeking a chance to observe nature up close. The 800-foot elevation provides excellent views of the plains to the south as well as the 600-odd acres of monastery grounds to the north. Owners Gerard Ramsawak and Oda van der Haijden are gracious and chatty and over breakfast or dinner, both of which are included, will fill you in on the history of the house and the furniture they have collected from around the world. Afternoon tea in the courtyard is cheap and popular with older locals. **Pros:** magnificent view of northern Trinidad, bird-watching and hiking trails right outside property, tea on the balcony harks back to simpler times. **Cons:** accommodations are Spartan, no access to shopping or nightlife without a car, guests have to be let in at night. ⊠ *Mt. St. Benedict, Tunapuna* ☎ *868/662–4084* ⊕ *www. paxguesthouse.com* ⤳ *18 rooms* ⚐ *In-room: no a/c (some), no phone, no TV (some), Wi-Fi. In-hotel: tennis court, laundry service* ▤ *MC, V* ⧇ *MAP.*

WHERE TO EAT

The food on T&T is a delight to the senses and has a distinctively creole touch, though everyone has a different idea about what creole seasoning is (just ask around, and you'll see). Bountiful herbs and spices include bay leaf, *chadon beni* (similar in taste to cilantro), nutmeg, turmeric, and different varieties of peppers. The cooking also involves a lot of brown sugar, rum, plantain, and local fish and meat. If there's fresh juice on the menu, be sure to try it. You can taste Asian, Indian, African, French, and Spanish influences, among others, often in a single meal. Indian-inspired food is a favorite: rotis (ample sandwiches of soft dough with a filling, similar to a burrito) are served as a fast food; a mélange of curried meat or fish and vegetables frequently makes an appearance, as do vindaloos (spicy meat, vegetable, and seafood dishes). *Pelau* (chicken stewed in coconut milk with peas and rice), a Spanish-influenced dish, is another local favorite. Crab lovers will find large bluebacks curried, peppered, or in callaloo (Trinidad's national dish), a stew made with green dasheen leaves, okra, and coconut milk. Shark-and-bake (lightly seasoned, fried shark meat) is the sandwich of choice at the beach.

24

WHAT TO WEAR

Restaurants are informal: you won't find any jacket-and-tie requirements. Beachwear, however, is too casual for most places. A nice pair of shorts is appropriate for lunch; for dinner you'll probably feel most comfortable in a pair of slacks or a casual sundress.

ASIAN
$$–$$$

✕**Tamnak Thai.** In a beautifully renovated colonial house on Queen's Park Savannah, you can find the best Thai cuisine in Trinidad. On the patio you're surrounded by flowing water and lush foliage; the elegant dining room is a more-intimate (and cooler) experience. Those keeping an eye on their budget may wish to consider sticking to vegetarian dishes, which are tasty and quite economical. Alfresco diners should use insect repellent, as the mosquitoes seem more ravenous than most of the diners. Valet parking is an unusual but welcome touch. ⊠ *13 Queen's Park E, Belmont, Port of Spain* ☎ *868/625–0647* ⊜ *868/623–7510* ⊟ *AE, MC, V* ⊗ *No lunch Sat.–Mon.*

$$–$$$
★

✕**Tiki Village.** Port of Spainers in the know flock to the eighth floor of the Kapok Hotel, where the views of the city day and night are simply spectacular and the food always dependable. The dining room is lined with teak, and the menu includes the best of Polynesian and Asian fare. The Sunday dim sum—with tasting-size portions of dishes such as pepper squid and tofu-stuffed fish—is very popular. ⊠ *Kapok Hotel, 16–18 Cotton Hill, St. Clair, Port of Spain* ☎ *868/622–5765* ⌖ *Reservations essential* ⊟ *AE, MC, V.*

CARIBBEAN
$$–$$$
FodorśChoice
★

✕**The Verandah.** Owner and hostess Phyllis Vieira has been hosting diners since the 1980s and prides herself on her "free-style Caribbean" menu, which is one of the best-kept secrets on the island. But the reasonable prices and consistently excellent cuisine make this a secret we can no longer keep. The open verandah, interior, and courtyard of this beautiful gingerbread-style colonial house provide a suitable setting for the menu, which changes weekly and is brought to you on a blackboard by the attentive, white-garbed staff. ⊠ *10 Rust St., St. Clair, Port of Spain* ☎ *868/622–6287* ⌖ *Reservations essential* ⊟ *No credit cards* ⊗ *Closed Sun. No dinner Mon.–Wed. and Fri.*

$–$$
☾
FodorśChoice
★

✕**Veni Mangé.** The best lunches in town are served in this traditional West Indian house. Credit Allyson Hennessy—a Cordon Bleu–trained chef and local television celebrity—and her friendly, flamboyant sister and partner, Rosemary (Roses) Hezekiah. Despite Allyson's training, home cooking is the order of the day here. The creative creole menu changes regularly, but there's always an unusual and delicious vegetarian entrée. Veni's version of Trinidad's national dish, callaloo, is considered one of the best on the island. The *chip chip* (a small local clam) cocktail is deliciously piquant and is a restaurant rarity. ✉*67A Ariapita Ave., Woodbrook, Port of Spain* ☎*868/624–4597* ♟*Reservations essential* ▭*AE, MC, V* ☾*Closed weekends. No dinner Mon., Tues., or Thurs.*

ECLECTIC ✕**Jaffa at the Oval.** Celebrated chef Joe Brown has taken his culinary
$$$–$$$$ skills to the historic home of West Indies cricket at the Queen's Park Oval. The dining area feels like a colonial gentleman's club with dark woods, coffee-color drapery, and crisp white linens. Cuisine runs the gamut, from sashimi to classic French, so there is likely something to please anyone. If nibbling is more to your taste, choose from the large selection of appetizers. Knowing that you are in the same complex where most of the world's greatest cricketers have played adds to the dining pleasure. ✉*Queens Park Oval, Level 2, 3 Tragarete Rd., St. Clair, Port of Spain* ☎*868/622–6825* ▭*AE, MC, V* ☾*Closed Sun. No lunch Sat.*

$$$–$$$$ ✕**La Boucan.** Trinidadian Geoffrey Holder painted the large mural of a social idyll in Queen's Park Savannah that dominates one wall of the Hilton's main restaurant. A more-leisurely Trinidad is also reflected in the old-fashioned charm of silver service, uniformed waiters, soft lighting, and pink tablecloths. The menu is international, including steaks, seafood grills, and other simple preparations, but you can also find such local specialties as callaloo soup, shrimp creole, and West Indian chicken curry. ✉*Hilton Trinidad & Conference Centre, Lady Young Rd., Port of Spain* ☎*868/624–3211* ▭*AE, DC, MC, V.*

$$–$$$ ✕**Mélange.** Some of the finest and most imaginative food on the island is to be found at this elegant establishment on restaurant row. Chef and owner Moses Ruben uses his years of experience as head chef at the Hilton to create delightfully balanced meals. His imaginative curried crab and dumplings appetizer, which consists of delicately curried crabmeat served on a shell full of miniature dumplings, is an exceptional treat. ✉*40 Ariapita Ave., Woodbrook, Port of Spain* ☎*868/628–8687* ▭*AE, MC, V* ☾*Closed Sun. No lunch Sat., no dinner Mon.*

FRENCH ✕**A La Bastille.** This authentic French brasserie in the heart of Port of
$$–$$$$ Spain makes homemade bread daily, and the menu features many items
★ that are imported straight from Brittany. Tribute is also paid to island ingredients, so you can start your meal with local escargots and end it with delicious mango ice cream. Add a selection of hundreds of wines and you have a memorable dining option. The crepe special on Saturday from 10 to 3 draws an appreciative crowd. ✉*84A Ariapita Ave., Woodbrook, Port of Spain* ☎*868/622–1789* ▭*AE, MC, V* ☾*Closed Sun. No lunch Mon.*

INDIAN ✕**Apsara.** This upscale Indian eatery is one of the few in Trinidad
$$–$$$$ that feature genuine Indian cuisine and not the local (though equally tasty) version. The name means "celestial dancer," and the food here is indeed heavenly. The inviting terra-cotta interior is decorated with

hand-painted interpretations of Moghul art. Choosing dishes from the comprehensive menu is a bit daunting, so don't be afraid to ask for help. The *Husseini boti kebab* (lamb marinated in poppy seeds and masala) is an excellent choice. The restaurant is in the same building as the equally popular Tamnak Thai. ✉*13 Queen's Park E, Belmont, Port of Spain* ☎*868/627–7364 or 868/623–7659* ▭*AE, MC, V* ☉*Closed Sun.*

¢–$ ✗**Wings Restaurant & Bar.** Rum shops and good food are an intrinsic part of Trinidad life, and both are combined in this colorful eatery, which is open only from 10 to 6. Regulars from the nearby university and industrial park flock here at lunchtime to enjoy a wide selection of local Indian food. It can get a bit loud, but at least fans keep the heat in control—just barely. To get here, turn off the Churchill Roosevelt Highway at the FedEx building (north side of the highway) in Tunapuna, and take the first left. ✉*16 Mohammed Terr., Tunapuna* ☎*868/645–6607* ▭*No credit cards* ☉*Closed Sun. No dinner.*

ITALIAN ✗**Il Colosseo.** Calabrian chef Angelo Cofone married a Trinidadian
$$–$$$$ and soon found himself co-owning the island's best Italian restaurant, popular with locals and visiting businesspeople alike. The innovative Italian menu changes regularly, and there is always a daily special. If it's offered, try the calamari done Mediterranean style. The prix-fixe lunch for $19 is a steal and a good way to test the menu. ✉*16 Rust St., St. Clair, Port of Spain* ☎*868/622–8418* ▭*AE, MC, V* ☉*Closed Sun. No lunch Sat.*

BEACHES

Trinidad has some good beaches for swimming and sunning, though none as picture-perfect as those in Tobago. North-coast beaches are the closest to Port of Spain and have peach-color sand, palm trees galore, and excellent water for swimming. The northeast involves a longer drive but offers rugged scenery en route, as well as rougher water and coarser sand. The entire east coast of the island is basically one unbroken beach. Miles of coconut trees line this coast, where finding a secluded spot is never a problem. Unfortunately, the water here tends to be muddy and the undertows dangerous. Although popular with some locals, the beaches of the western peninsula (such as Maqueripe) are not particularly attractive, and the water in this area is often polluted by sewage.

Balandra Bay. On the northeast coast, the beach—popular with locals on weekends—is sheltered by a rocky outcropping and is a favorite of bodysurfers. Much of this beach is suitable for swimming. The noise level on weekends can be a problem for those seeking solace. Take the Toco Main Road from the Valencia Road, and turn off at the signs indicating Balandra (just after Salybia). ✉*Off Valencia Rd. near Salybia.*
Blanchisseuse Bay. On North Coast Road you can find this narrow, palm-fringed beach. Facilities are nonexistent, but it's an ideal spot for a romantic picnic. A lagoon and river at the east end of the beach allow you to swim in freshwater, but beware of floating logs in the river,

as they sometimes contain mites that can cause a body rash (called *bete rouge* locally). You can haggle with local fishermen to take you out in their boats to explore the coast. This beach is about 14 mi (23 km) after Maracas; just keep driving along the road until you pass the Arima turnoff. The coastal and rain-forest views here are spectacular. ⊠ *North Coast Rd. just beyond Arima turnoff.*

Grande Riviere. On Trinidad's rugged northeast coast, Grande Riviere is well worth the drive. Swimming is good, and there are several guesthouses nearby for refreshments, but the main attractions here are turtles. Every year up to 500 giant leatherback turtles come onto the beach to lay their eggs. If you're here at night, run your hand through the black sand to make it glow—a phenomenon caused by plankton. ⊠ *Toco Main Rd. at end of road.*

Las Cuevas Bay. This narrow, picturesque strip on North Coast Road is named for the series of partially submerged and explorable caves that ring the beach. A food stand offers tasty snacks, and vendors hawk fresh fruit across the road. You can also buy fresh fish and lobster from the fishing depot near the beach. You have to park your car in the small car park and walk down a few steps to get to the beach, so be sure to take everything from the car (which is out of sight once you are on the beach). There are basic changing and toilet facilities. It's less crowded here than at nearby Maracas Bay and seemingly serene, although, as at Maracas, the current can be treacherous. ⊠ *North Coast Rd., 7 mi (11 km) east of Maracas Bay.*

Manzanilla Beach. You can find picnic facilities and a pretty view of the Atlantic here, though the water is occasionally muddied by Venezuela's Orinoco River. The Cocal Road running the length of this beautiful beach is lined with stately palms, whose fronds vault like the arches at Chartres. This is where many well-heeled Trinis have vacation homes. The Nariva River, which enters the sea just south of this beach and the surrounding Nariva Swamp, is home to the protected manatee and many other rare species, including the much-maligned anaconda. To get to this beach take the Mayaro turnoff at the town of Sangre Grande. Manzanilla is where this road first meets the coast. ⊠ *Southeast of Sangre Grande.*

★ **Maracas Bay.** This long stretch of sand has a cove and a fishing village at one end. It's *the* local favorite, so it can get crowded on weekends. Lifeguards will guide you away from strong currents. Parking sites are ample, and there are snack bars and restrooms. Try a shark-and-bake ($3, to which you can add any of dozens of toppings, such as tamarind sauce and coleslaw) at one of the beach huts or in the nearby car park (Richard's is by far the most popular). Take the North Coast Road from Maraval (it intersects with Long Circular Road right next to KFC Maraval) over the Northern Range; the beach is about 7 mi (11 km) from Maraval. ⊠ *North Coast Rd..*

Salibea Bay *(Salybia Bay)*. This gentle beach has shallows and plenty of shade—perfect for swimming. Snack vendors abound in the vicinity. Like many of the beaches on the northeast coast, this one is packed with people and music trucks blaring soca and reggae on weekends. It's off the Toco Main Road, just after the town of Matura. ⊠ *Off Toco Main Rd., south of Toco.*

SPORTS & THE OUTDOORS

BIRD-WATCHING

★ Trinidad and Tobago are among the top 10 spots in the world in terms of the number of species of birds per square mile—more than 430, many living within pristine rain forests, lowlands and savannahs, and fresh- and saltwater swamps. If you're lucky, you might spot the collared trogon, Trinidad piping guan (known locally as the common pawi), or rare white-tailed Sabrewing hummingbird. Restaurants often hang feeders outside on their porches, as much to keep the birds away from your food as to provide a chance to see them. Both the Asa Wright Nature Centre and Caroni Bird Sanctuary are major bird-watching destinations (⇨ *Exploring Trinidad, below).*

Winston Nanan (☎ *868/645–1305* ✐ *nantour@tstt.net.tt*) is a self-taught ornithologist who knows the local fauna as well as his own children. He will arrange personal tours in his own car anywhere on the island. His business is based at the Caroni Bird Sanctuary, but his expertise makes a trip with him to the Northern Range or the northeast a must for any true bird-watcher. It won't be cheap, but the personal attention and his willingness to try to find rare species are well worth the expense.

FISHING

The islands off the northwest coast of Trinidad have excellent waters for deep-sea fishing; you may find wahoo, kingfish, and marlin, to name a few. The ocean here was a favorite angling spot of Franklin D. Roosevelt. Through **Bayshore Charters** (⊠ *29 Sunset Dr., Bayshore, Westmoorings* ☎ *868/637–8711)* you can fish for an afternoon or hire a boat for a weekend; the *Melissa Ann* is fully equipped for comfortable cruising, sleeps six, and has an air-conditioned cabin, refrigerator, cooking facilities, and, of course, fishing equipment. Captain Sa Gomes is one of the most experienced charter captains on the islands. Members of the **Trinidad & Tobago Yacht Club** (⊠ *Western Main Rd., Bayshore, Westmoorings* ☎ *868/637–4260)* may be willing to arrange a fishing trip for you.

GOLF

The best course in Trinidad is the 18-hole course at **St. Andrew's Golf Club** (⊠ *Moka, Saddle Rd., Maraval, Port of Spain* ☎ *868/629–2314)*, just outside Port of Spain. Green fees are approximately $45 for 9 holes. The most convenient tee times are available on weekdays.

SHOPPING

Good buys in Trinidad include Angostura bitters, Old Oak or Vat 19 rum, and leather goods, all widely available throughout the country. Thanks in large part to Carnival costumery, there's no shortage of fabric shops. The best bargains for Asian and East Indian silks and cottons can be found in downtown Port of Spain, on Frederick Street and around Independence Square. Recordings of local calypsonians and steel-pan performances as well as *chutney* (a local East Indian music) are available throughout the islands and make great gifts.

AREAS & MALLS

Downtown Port of Spain, specifically **Frederick, Queen,** and **Henry streets,** is full of fabrics and shoes. **Ellerslie Plaza** is an attractive outdoor mall well worth a browse. **Excellent City Centre** is set in an old-style oasis under the lantern roofs of three of downtown's oldest commercial buildings. Look for cleverly designed keepsakes, trendy cotton garments, and original artwork. The upstairs food court overlooks bustling Frederick Street. The **Falls at West Mall,** just west of Port of Spain, is a dazzling temple to upscale shopping that could easily hold its own anywhere in the world. **Long Circular Mall** has upscale boutiques that are great for window-shopping. The **Market at the Normandie Hotel** is a small collection of shops that specialize in indigenous fashions, crafts, jewelry, basketwork, and ceramics. You can also have afternoon tea in the elegant little café.

SPECIALTY ITEMS

CLOTHING A fine designer shop, **Meiling** (⊠ *Kapok Hotel, Maraval, Port of Spain* ☎ 868/627–6975), sells classically detailed Caribbean resort clothing. **Radical** (⊠ *The Falls at West Mall, Western Main Rd., Westmoorings* ☎ 868/632–5800 ⊠ *Long Circular Mall, Long Circular Rd., St. James, Port of Spain* ☎ 868/628–5693 ⊠ *Excellent City Centre, Independence Square, Port of Spain* ☎ 868/627–6110), which carries T-shirts and original men's and women's casual clothing.

DUTY-FREE GOODS Duty-free goods are available only at the airport upon departure or arrival. **De Lima's** (⊠ *Piarco International Airport, Piarco* ☎ 868/669–4738) sells traditional duty-free luxury goods. **Stecher's** (⊠ *Piarco International Airport, Piarco* ☎ 868/669–4793) is a familiar name for those seeking to avoid taxes on fine perfumes, china, crystal, handcrafted pieces, and jewelry. **T-Wee Liquor Store** (⊠ *Piarco International Airport, Piarco* ☎ 868/669–4748) offers deals on alcohol that you probably won't find in many other places around the world.

HANDICRAFTS ★ The tourism office can provide a list of local artisans who specialize in everything from straw and cane work to miniature steel pans. For painted plates, ceramics, aromatic candles, wind chimes, and carved wood pieces and instruments, check out **Cockey** (⊠ *Long Circular Mall, Long Circular Rd., St. James, Port of Spain* ☎ 868/628–6546). The **101 Art Gallery** (*Art Society of Trinidad and Tobago Bldg., At Jamaica Blvd. and St. Vincent Ave., Federation Park, Port of Spain* ☎ 868/628–4081) is Trinidad's foremost gallery, showcasing local artists such as Jackie Hinkson (figurative watercolors); Peter Sheppard (stylized realist local landscapes in acrylic); and Sundiata (semiabstract watercolors). Openings are usually held Tuesday evenings; the gallery is closed Sunday and Monday. **Poui Boutique** (⊠ *Ellerslie Plaza, Long Circular Rd., Maraval, Port of Spain* ☎ 868/622–5597) has stylish handmade batik articles, Ajoupa ware (an attractive, local terra-cotta pottery), and many other gift items. The miniature ceramic houses and local scenes are astoundingly realistic, and are all handcrafted by owners Rory and Bunty O'Connor.

JEWELRY   The design duo of Barbara Jardine and Rachel Ross creates the Alchemy jewelry line. Their handmade works of art with sterling silver, 18K gold, and precious and semiprecious stones are for sale at **Precious Little** (⊠ *5 Pole Carew St., Woodbrook* ☎ *868/622–7655*).

NIGHTLIFE & THE ARTS

NIGHTLIFE

There's no lack of nightlife in Port of Spain, and spontaneity plays a big role—around Carnival time look for the handwritten signs announcing the PANYARD, where the next informal gathering of steel-drum bands is going to be. Gay and lesbian travelers can take advantage of an increasingly lively gay scene in Trinidad, with parties drawing upwards of 200 people on most weekends.

24

★ Two of the island's top nightspots are on a former American army base in Chaguaramas. The **Anchorage/Tsunami Beach Club** (⊠ *Point Gourde Rd., Chaguaramas* ☎ *868/634–4334*) is a good spot for early-evening cocktails and snacks. **Coco Lounge** (⊠ *35 Carlos St.Woodbrook, Port of Spain* ☎ *868/622–6137*) The newest hangout on the popular Ariapita Avenue strip caters to a upscale set who enjoy sipping cocktails in the elegant modern plantation style interior or watching the world go by from the huge verandah. **51° Lounge** (⊠ *51 Cipriani Blvd., Woodbrook, Port of Spain* ☎ *868/627–0051*) is where the smart set hangs out. There's entertainment on most nights, and though admission is often free, it's advisable to call to confirm. Thursday nights are always packed to the rafters, but go after 11 if you want to avoid the karaoke crowd. Don't even think about showing up in shorts, as there's a strict "elegant casual" dress code and an age limit of 25 years and older. **Mas Camp Pub** (⊠ *Ariapita Ave. and French St., Woodbrook, Port of Spain* ☎ *868/627–4042*) is Port of Spain's most dependable nightspot. Along with a bar and a large stage where a DJ or live band reigns, the kitchen dishes up hearty, reasonably priced creole lunches, and if one of the live bands strikes your fancy, chances are you can also buy a tape here.

★ **More Vino** (⊠ *23 O'Connor St., Woodbrook, Port of Spain* ☎ *868/622–8466*) attracts a crowd of young professionals who come to network while sipping one of the more than 100 varieties of wine. Although most people choose to sit outside during the evening, there is also seating available in the air-conditioned interior. Inside, you will also find an astonishing number of bottles on display for consumption on the premises or to take away. Cheeses and other items for nibbling are available, but no proper meals. **Pier 1** (⊠ *Western Main Rd., Chaguaramas* ☎ *868/634–4426*) is *the* place for lively late-night action. You can dance through the night on a large wooden deck jutting into the ocean with gentle sea breezes to cool you down. It's about 20 minutes west of Port of Spain, so get a party together from your hotel and hire a cab. It opens at 9 PM Wednesday through Sunday. For the serious partyers,

Pier 1 offers a "party boat" that leaves on Friday, Saturday, and Sunday night for a floating party for $10. **Sky Bar & Lounge** (⊠ *46 Ariapita Ave., Woodbrook, Port of Spain*) is the new kid on the scene and pulls a lively crowd on Friday and Saturday. The rooftop setting is free of walls and offers dazzling views of Port of Spain harbor. There are occasional live performances and always a large crowd on weekends. There is a nominal admission price of $4 on Friday, when the bar is packed with a mostly gay crowd after 10 PM. **Trotters** (⊠ *Maraval and Sweet Briar Rd., St. Clair, Port of Spain* ☎ *868/627–8768*) is a sports bar in a two-story atrium. You can find an abundance of TV monitors as well as more than 30 varieties of beer from around the globe. It's incredibly popular on weekends despite the pricey drinks.

CARNIVAL

Fodor's Choice ★ Trinidad's version of the pre-Lenten bacchanal is reputedly the oldest in the western hemisphere; there are festivities all over the country, but the most lavish are in Port of Spain. Trinidad's Carnival has the warmth and character of a massive family reunion and is billed by locals (not unreasonably) as "The Greatest Show on Earth."

The season begins right after Christmas, and the parties, called *fêtes*, don't stop until Ash Wednesday. Listen to a radio station for five minutes, and you can find out where the action is. The Carnival event itself officially lasts only two days, from *J'ouvert* (2 AM) on Monday to midnight the following day, Carnival Tuesday. It's best to arrive in Trinidad a week or two early to enjoy the preliminary events. (Hotels fill up quickly, so be sure to make reservations months in advance, and be prepared to pay premium prices for a minimum five-night stay. Even private homes have been known to rent bedrooms for as much as $225 per night.) If you visit during Carnival, try to get tickets to one of the all-inclusive parties where thousands of people eat and drink to the sound of soca music all night long. The biggest Carnival party in Trinidad is **UWI Fête**, which raises money for the university and attracts several thousand people. A ticket will cost you about $80 but includes all drinks and food.

Carnival is about extravagant costumes. Colorfully attired *mas* (troupes), whose membership sometimes numbers in the thousands, march to the beat set by massive music trucks and steel bands. You can visit the various mas "camps" around Port of Spain, where these elaborate getups are put together—the addresses are listed in the newspapers—and perhaps join one that strikes your fancy. Fees run anywhere from $50 to $1,000; you get to keep the costume. As a rule you will find that different bands attract different sorts of participants. **Harts** tends to attract a younger crowd, **Tribe** a more-raucous bunch, and **Brian MacFarlane's The Art Factory** a more-artistic assortment of people. You can also buy your costume online at the tourist board's Web site, which has links to all the major camps. Children can parade in a kiddie carnival that takes place on the Saturday morning the week before the official events.

For several nights before Carnival, costume makers display their work, and the steel bands and calypso singers perform in competitions. The Queen's Park Savannah has been the home for these activities for decades, but the government has announced a plan to replace the existing facilities with a new carnival village and cultural center. Work has begun on the new facilities, but as of this writing, a completion date had not yet been announced. For now, events will continue to be held around the Queen's Park Savannah. There is no doubt whatsoever that they will take place, however, including the crowning of the Calypso Monarch on the Sunday night before Carnival (Dimanche Gras), when the city starts to fill with metal-frame carts carrying steel bands, trucks hauling sound systems, and revelers squeezing into the narrow streets. At midnight on Carnival Tuesday, Port of Spain's exhausted merrymakers go to bed. The next day, feet are sore, but spirits have been refreshed. Lent (and theoretical sobriety) takes over for a while.

24

EXPLORING TRINIDAD

The intensely urban atmosphere of Port of Spain belies the tropical beauty of the countryside surrounding it. You'll need a car and three to eight hours to see all there is to see. Begin by circling the Queen's Park Savannah to Saddle Road, in the residential district of Maraval. After a few miles the road begins to narrow and curve sharply as it climbs into the Northern Range and its undulating hills of dense foliage. Stop at the lookout on North Coast Road; a camera is a must-have here. You pass a series of lovely beaches, starting with Maracas. From the town of Blanchisseuse there's a winding route to the Asa Wright Nature Centre that takes you through canyons of towering palms, mossy grottoes, and imposing bamboo. In this rain forest keep an eye out for vultures, parakeets, hummingbirds, toucans, and, if you're lucky, maybe red-bellied, yellow-and-blue macaws. Trinidad also has more than 600 native species of butterflies and far more than 1,000 varieties of orchids.

Fodor's Choice ★ **Asa Wright Nature Centre.** Nearly 200 acres here are covered with plants, trees, and multihued flowers, and the surrounding acreage is atwitter with more than 200 species of birds, from the gorgeous blue-crowned motmot to the rare (and protected) nocturnal oilbird. If you stay at the center's inn for two nights or more, take one of the guided hikes (included in your room price if you are staying here) to the oilbirds' breeding grounds in Dunston Cave (reservations for hikes are essential). Those who don't want to hike can relax on the inn's verandah and watch birds swoop about the porch feeders—an armchair bird-watcher's delight. You are also more than likely to see a variety of other animal species, including agoutis and alarmingly large golden tegu lizards. This stunning plantation house looks out onto the lush, untouched Arima Valley. Even if you're not staying over, book ahead for lunch (TT$75), offered Monday through Saturday, or for the noontime Sunday buffet (TT$100). The center is an hour outside Blanchisseuse; take a right at the fork in the road (signposted to Arima) and drive another hour (the sign for the center is at milepost 7.75) on Blanchisseuse Road;

East Indians in Trinidad

CLOSE UP

With the abolition of slavery in the British colonies in 1838, many plantation economies like Trinidad were left looking for alternative sources of cheap labor. Trinidad tried to draw Europeans, but the heat made them ineffective. Attention finally turned to the Indian subcontinent, and in 1845 the first ship of Indian laborers arrived in Trinidad. These workers were hired indentured and came mainly from the poorer parts of Uttar Pradesh. They undertook the three-month journey to the New World with the understanding that after their five-year work stint was over, they could reindenture themselves or return to India. The system stayed in place until 1917.

The Indians proved effective on the sugarcane and cocoa plantations, helping them return to prosperity. In an effort to discourage the Indians from returning home, the colony eventually offered a land grant as an incentive for those who chose to stay. Many took up the offer and stayed to make new lives in their adopted homeland. Their descendants still maintain many traditions and, to some extent, language. East Indian culture is a vibrant component of T&T's national culture, and you can find Indian festivals and music sharing center stage at all national events. East Indians actually compose about half the islands' population and are an integral part of Trinidad and Tobago society.

turn right there. *Box 4710, Arima Valley* ☎*868/667–4655* ⊕*www. asawright.org* *$10* ⊗*Daily 9–5. Guided tours at 10:30 and 1:30.*

☺ **Caroni Bird Sanctuary.** This large swamp with mazelike waterways is bordered by mangrove trees, some plumed with huge termite nests. If you're lucky, you may see lazy caimans idling in the water and large snakes hanging from branches on the banks taking in the sun. In the middle of the sanctuary are several islets that are home to Trinidad's national bird, the scarlet ibis. Just before sunset the ibis arrive by the thousands, their richly colored feathers brilliant in the gathering dusk, and as more flocks alight they turn the mangrove foliage a brilliant scarlet. Bring a sweater and insect repellent. The sanctuary's only official tour operator is Winston Nanan (⇨*Bird-watching in Sports & the Outdoors*). ✉½ *hr from Port of Spain; take Churchill Roosevelt Hwy. east to Uriah Butler south; turn right and in about 2 mins, after passing Caroni River Bridge, follow sign for sanctuary* *Free* ⊗*Daily dawn–dusk.*

Chaguaramas Military History & Aerospace Museum. On the former U.S. military base, this is a must-see for history buffs. The exhibits are in a large hangarlike shed without air-conditioning, so dress appropriately. Exhibits cover everything from Amerindian history to the Cold War, but the emphasis is on the two World Wars. There's a decidedly charming and homemade feel to the place; in fact, most exhibits were made by the curator and founder, Commander Gaylord Kelshall of the T&T Coast Guard. The museum is set a bit off the main road but is easily spotted by the turquoise BWIA L1011 jet parked out front (Trinidad and Tobago's former national airline). ⊠ *Western Main Rd., Chaguaramas* ☎*868/634–4391* ⊠*TT$20* ⊗*Mon.–Sat. 9–5.*

🌣 **Dattatreya Yoga Centre.** This impressive temple site was constructed by artisans brought in from India. It is well worth a visit to admire the intricate architectural details of the main temple, learn about Trinidad Hinduism, and marvel at the towering 85-foot statue of the god Hanuman. Krishna Ramsaran, the compound manager, is extremely helpful and proud to explain the history of the center and the significance of the various *murtis* (sacred statues). Kids are welcome, so this makes for a pleasant and educational family outing (kids seem especially interested in the giant elephant statues that guard the temple doors). This is a religious site, so appropriate clothing is required (no shorts), and shoes must be left outside the temple door. It's fine to take pictures of the statue and the temple exterior and grounds, but permission is required to take pictures inside, as it's an active place of worship. The temple is half an hour from Port of Spain; take Churchill Roosevelt Highway east to Uriah Butler south; turn right until the Chase Village flyover; follow the signs south to Waterloo; then follow signs to the temple. ⊠*Datta Dr. at Orangefield Rd., Carapichaima* ☎*868/673–5328* ⊠*Free* ⊗*Daily dawn–dusk, services daily.*

Lopinot Complex. It's said that the ghost of the French count Charles Joseph de Lopinot prowls his former home on stormy nights. Lopinot came to Trinidad in 1800 and chose this magnificent site to plant cocoa. His restored estate house has been turned into a museum—a guide is available from 10 to 6—and a center for parang, the Venezuelan-derived folk music. Although worthwhile for those interested in the finer points of Trinidad history, this may not be worth the long drive for most visitors. ⊠*Take Eastern Main Rd. from Port of Spain to Arouca; look for sign that points north* ☎*No phone* ⊠*Free* ⊗*Daily 6–6.*

🌣 **Point Galera Lighthouse.** An essential stop when touring the northeast, this lighthouse was constructed in 1897 on a stunning cliff and is still actively used to warn ships about the rough waters below, the point where the Atlantic Ocean and Caribbean Sea meet. You can walk out onto a nearby rocky outcropping that marks Trinidad's easternmost point. On most days Tobago is clearly visible from here. A local legend (unprovable) tells that a group of Arawaks jumped off this point to their deaths rather than be captured by the Spanish. You'll pass several beautiful beaches on the drive from Toco to the lighthouse. The journey from Port of Spain takes about two hours; take Churchill Roosevelt Highway east to Valencia Road; follow the road east to Toco Main Road sign; take this road all the way to Toco; from the Toco intersection, follow the sign to Point Galera. ⊠*Galera Rd., 3 mi (5 km) from triangular Toco intersection* ⊠*Free* ⊗*Daily dawn–dusk.*

NEED A BREAK? On the long drive to Point Galera, be sure to stop at Kay's Pot (⊠*Toco Main Rd., Rampanalgas* ☎*No phone*) for a great meal en route. Many consider it worth the drive all by itself. In a corner of the front parking lot of Arthur's Grocery and Bar, Kay serves an incredible array of local food such as *souse*

24

(pickled pigs' feet in a lime-and-cucumber sauce), curried crab, and her signature dish, curried crayfish freshly caught in the pristine mountain streams nearby. The informal atmosphere, low prices, and music pouring out of the bar make for a fun and unusual dining experience.

Port of Spain. Most organized tours begin at the port. If you're planning to explore on foot, which will take two to four hours, start early in the day; by midday the port area can be as hot and packed as Calcutta. It's best to end your tour on a bench in the Queen's Park Savannah, sipping a cool coconut water bought from one of the vendors operating out of flatbed trucks. For about 50¢ he'll lop the top off a green coconut with a deft swing of the machete and, when you've finished drinking, lop again, making a bowl and spoon of coconut shell for you to eat the young pulp. As in most cities, take extra care at night; women should not walk alone. Local police advise tourists and locals to avoid the neighborhoods just east of Port of Spain.

The town's main dock, **King's Wharf,** entertains a steady parade of cruise and cargo ships, a reminder that the city started from this strategic harbor. When hurricanes threaten other islands, it's not unusual to see as many as five large cruise ships taking advantage of the safety of the harbor. It's on Wrightson Road, the main street along the water on the southwest side of town. The national government has embarked on a massive development plan, which means that most of the wharf area is an active construction zone. The plan is to turn the area into a vibrant and attractive commercial and tourism zone. Many spanking-new high-rises have already been built, but the area is likely to be a work in progress for several years.

Across Wrightson Road and a few minutes' walk from the south side of King's Wharf, the busy **Independence Square** has been the focus of the downtown area's major gentrification. Flanked by government buildings and the familiar twin towers of the Financial Complex (they adorn all T&T dollar bills), the square (really a long rectangle) is a lovely park with trees, flagstone walkways, chess tables, and the Brian Lara Promenade (named after Trinidad's world-famous cricketer). On its south side the cruise-ship complex, full of duty-free shops, forms an enclave of international anonymity with the Crowne Plaza Trinidad. On the eastern end of the square is the Cathedral of the Immaculate Conception; it was by the sea when it was built in 1832, but subsequent landfill around the port gave it an inland location. The imposing Roman Catholic structure is made of blue limestone from nearby Laventille.

Frederick Street, Port of Spain's main shopping drag, starting north from the midpoint of Independence Square, is a market street of scents and sounds—perfumed oils sold by sidewalk vendors and music tapes being played from vending carts—and crowded shops. Although it may be tempting to purchase CDs from these street vendors, they are selling pirated material and doing so robs local artists of their livelihood.

At Prince and Frederick streets, **Woodford Square** has served as the site of political meetings, speeches, public protests, and occasional violence. It's dominated by the magnificent Red House, a Renaissance-style building that takes up an entire city block. Trinidad's House of Parliament takes its name from a paint job done in anticipation of Queen Victoria's Diamond Jubilee in 1897. The original Red House was burned to the ground in a 1903 riot, and the present structure was built four years later. The chambers are open to the public.

The view of the south side of the square is framed by the Gothic spires of Trinity, the city's Anglican cathedral, consecrated in 1823; its mahogany-beam roof is modeled after that of Westminster Hall in London. On the north are the impressive Public Library, the Hall of Justice, and City Hall.

If the downtown port area is the pulse of Port of Spain, the great green expanse of **Queen's Park Savannah,** roughly bounded by Maraval Road, Queen's Park West, Charlotte Street, and Saddle Road, is the city's soul. You can walk straight north on Frederick Street and get there within 20 minutes. Its 2-mi (3-km) circumference is a popular jogger's track. The northern end of the Savannah is devoted to plants. A rock garden, known as the Hollows, and a fishpond add to the rusticity. In the middle of the Savannah you will find a small graveyard where members of the Peschier family—who originally owned the land—are buried. Although the perimeter of the Savannah is busy and safe, you shouldn't walk across the park, as there have been occasional reports of muggings. The sheer size of the Savannah makes it difficult for local authorities to patrol, so it is best avoided altogether at night.

A series of astonishing buildings constructed in several 19th-century styles—known collectively as the **Magnificent Seven**—flanks the western side of the Savannah. Notable are Killarney, patterned (loosely) after Balmoral Castle in Scotland, with an Italian-marble gallery surrounding the ground floor; Whitehall, constructed in the style of a Venetian palace by a cacao-plantation magnate and currently the office of the prime minister; Roomor (named for the Roodal and Morgan families—it's still occupied by the Morgans), a flamboyantly baroque colonial house with a preponderance of towers, pinnacles, and wrought-iron trim that suggests an elaborate French pastry; and the Queen's Royal College, in German Renaissance style, with a prominent tower clock that chimes on the hour. Sadly, several of these fine buildings have fallen into advanced decay.

Head over to the southeast corner of the Savannah to see the **National Museum & Art Gallery,** especially its Carnival exhibitions, the Amerindian collection and historical re-creations, and the fine 19th-century paintings of Trinidadian artist Cazabon. ⊠ *117 Upper Frederick St., Port of Spain* ☎ *868/623–5941* ✉ *Free* ☉ *Tues.–Sat. 10–6.* The cultivated expanse of parkland north of the Savannah is the site of the president's and prime minister's official residences and also the **Emperor Valley Zoo & Botanical Gardens.** A meticulous lattice of walkways and local flora, the parkland was first laid out in 1820 for Governor Ralph Woodford. In the midst of the serene wonderland is the 8-acre zoo, which exhibits mostly birds and animals of the region—from the brilliantly plumed scarlet ibis to slithering anacondas and pythons; you can also see (and hear) the wild parrots that breed in the surrounding foliage. The zoo draws a quarter of a million visitors a year. The admission price is a steal, and tours are free. ⊠ *Botanical Gardens, Port of Spain* ☎ *868/622–3530 or 868/622–5343* ▣ *Zoo TT$4, gardens free* ◷ *Daily 9:30–5:30.*

TOBAGO

WHERE TO STAY

Tobago is much more of a tourist destination than Trinidad, and this is reflected in the range of accommodations. Those seeking luxury can find a number of upscale resorts and villas, while the budget-minded can take advantage of several smaller and more-intimate establishments.

For approximate costs, see the dining and lodging price chart in the Trinidad and Tobago Planner at the beginning of this chapter.

$$$$ 🏨 **Coco Reef Resort.** This expansive enclave is just a short distance from
ⓒ the airport but somehow seems miles away. Pink buildings sprawl
★ along a perfect stretch of coast. Just in front of the hotel is the only private (though man-made) beach on the island. The resort has all the usual amenities, including a highly regarded spa. The hotel restaurants are among the best in Tobago, and there's always an animated crowd around the pool bar. Store Bay is, quite literally, next door and Pigeon Point a short walk away. You can't beat the ocean-view villa for its glitz factor, including gold-plated bathroom fittings, a TV the size of a small car, and a private sundeck. Arrive in style by booking the hotel's Rolls (originally owned by Errol Flynn) for the two-minute trip from the airport ($10 per person). **Pros:** Beautifully appointed rooms, the only private beach on the island, impeccable and understated service. **Cons:** Pool area can get a bit too animated, some rooms are quite far from the beach and reception. ⊠ *Coconut Bay, Box 434, Crown Point* ☎ *868/639–8571 or 800/221–1294* ⊕ *www.cocoreef.com* ⇆ *135 rooms, 35 suites, 11 villas* ⌂ *In-room: refrigerator. In-hotel: 2 restaurants, room service, bars, tennis courts, pool, gym, spa, beachfront, diving, water sports* ☰ *AE, D, DC, MC, V* ⦿ *BP.*

$$$$ 🏨 **Plantation Beach Villas.** If you're looking for luxury living in a well-appointed Caribbean villa, you should be blissfully happy here. Each of the six pink, three-bedroom villas is prettily done in colonial style, complete with fretwork; an enormous front porch could easily hold up to six people comfortably. Daily maid service is included in the price. The grounds feature lush landscaping, and the communal pool and bar area is a lively meeting place for villa guests. This property makes an excellent alternative to a regular hotel for larger families. **Pros:** An engaging alternative to a hotel room, on the beach, all the comforts of home and maid service. **Cons:** No restaurants, lacks the diversions of a large hotel. ⊠ *Stone Haven Bay Rd., Black Rock* ⌂ *Box 434, Scarborough* ☎ *868/639–9377* ⊕ *www.plantationbeachvillas.com* ⇆ *6 3-bedroom* *villas* ⚴*In-room: safe, kitchen. In-hotel: bar, pool, beachfront, laundry facilities, laundry service* ☰*AE, MC, V* ¶⊚|*EP.*

$$$$ ⛾ **Villas at Stonehaven.** Perched on a hillside overlooking the ocean, this villa complex sets the standard for luxury self-catering accommodations on Tobago. There are 14 French colonial–style villas in the complex, spaced well enough to allow for maximum privacy. Each 3,700-square-foot, three-bedroom villa has an infinity pool and spectacular views. Individually owned units are all different. A 200-acre bird sanctuary is next door for those who might want a little nature jaunt. Housekeeping is provided, and cooks are available for those who don't wish to make use of the impressive kitchens. The only minor disadvantage here is that the beach is a trek down the hill. Villas are priced for four or six people sharing. **Pros:** As luxurious as Tobago gets, beautiful ocean views from every villa, an infinity pool all to yourself. **Cons:** Restaurant food is barely edible, not on the beach. ⊠*Bon Accord, Grafton Estate, Shirvan Rd., Box 1079, Black Rock* ☎*868/639–9887* ⊕*www.stonehavenvillas.com* ⇆*14 3-bedroom villas* ⚴*In-room: safe, kitchen, dial-up. In-hotel: restaurant, bar, pool, laundry facilities, airport shuttle* ☰*AE, MC, V* ¶⊚|*EP.*

$$–$$$ ⛾ **Blue Haven Hotel.** Justifiably celebrated, this 1940s-era hotel over-
Fodor's Choice looks a spectacular secluded beach on Bacolet Bay just outside Scarbor-
★ ough and has been fully restored and updated to luxury status. Though long neglected, it has been brought back to life by Austrian Karl Pilstl and his wife. The lobby is a study in 1940s perfection and appears now as it must have when Rita Hayworth came through. Rooms have teak floors and glass-partitioned bathrooms (with curtains for private moments); four-poster beds and lavish beddings are standard. Rooms in a new wing have sunken sitting areas. Most activity takes place at the No Problem beach bar, where a barbecue always seems to be in progress. The hotel is surrounded by water on three sides, so every room has a spectacular ocean view. The hotel's restaurant, **Shutters on the Bay,** offers splendid food and an unbeatable atmosphere. Meal plans are available. **Pros:** Historic charm, beautiful beach, more European flair than any other hotel on the island. **Cons:** Lacks the range of services of the larger hotels, beach is a short walk down a hillside. ⊠*Bacolet Bay, Scarborough* ☎*868/660–7400* ⊕*www.bluehavenhotel.com* ⇆*43 rooms, 8 suites, 1 villa* ⚴*In-room: dial-up. In-hotel: restaurant, bars, tennis court, pool, gym, spa, beachfront, no elevator, laundry facilities, laundry service* ☰*AE, DC, MC, V* ¶⊚|*EP.*

$$–$$$ ⛾ **Hilton Tobago Golf & Spa Resort.** The scale and setting of this sprawling plantation-style resort are impressive, but the location is also its biggest drawback. On the windward coast, the beach is minuscule, requiring a complimentary shuttle to the much better Pigeon Point Beach, and the omnipresent sea spray makes all tiled surfaces slippery. The two-story buildings seem to rise magically from the landscape at the end of a gorgeous 18-hole golf course, and the massive atrium lobby, which is filled with local art, has floor-to-ceiling sea views. All rooms are oceanfront (though not all have an ocean view), though the trade-off is a very long walk for guests at each end. All rooms have either a balcony or charming patio. **Pros:** Gorgeous ocean views, excellent restaurants and

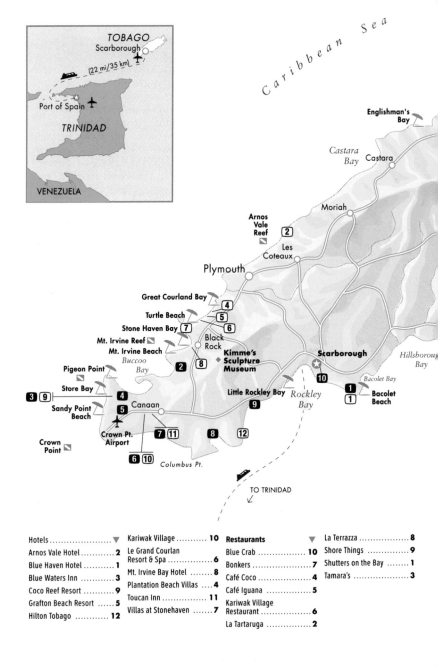

Tobago

Caribbean Sea

TOBAGO
Scarborough
(22 mi/35 km)
Port of Spain
TRINIDAD
VENEZUELA

Englishman's Bay

Castara Bay Castara

Moriah

Arnos Vale Reef [2]
Les Coteaux

Plymouth

Great Courland Bay [4]
Turtle Beach [7] [5]
Stone Haven Bay [7] [6]
Black Rock
Mt. Irvine Reef **Kimme's Sculpture Museum**
Mt. Irvine Beach [2] [8]
Buccoo Bay

Scarborough ★
Hillsborough Bay
[10]
Bacolet Bay

Pigeon Point
Store Bay
[3] [9] [4]
Sandy Point Beach
Little Rockley Bay *Rockley Bay*
[9]
Bacolet Beach [1] [1]

[5] Canaan
[7] [11]
Crown Pt. Airport
[8] [12]

Crown Point

[6] [10]
Columbus Pt.

TO TRINIDAD

St. Giles Island

North Pt.

Lovers Beach

The Sisters

Man O'War Bay

Charlotteville

Bloody Bay

Flagstaff Hill

Parlatuvier

Parlatuvier

Bird of Paradise Island

3

Pigeon Peak

Speyside

Little Tobago

Delaford

King's Bay

Roxborough

Carapuse Bay

t. King George

ATLANTIC OCEAN

KEY	
↗	Beaches
◪	Dive Sites
⛴	Ferry
❶	Restaurants
①	Hotels
......	Trail

0		4 mi
0		4 km

restaurants and entertainment options. **Cons:** No longer managed by Hilton, and hotel's fate still in question at this writing. ⌂*Box 633, Scarborough* ☎*868/660–8500* ⊕*www.hiltoncaribbean.com* ⤵*178 rooms, 22 suites* ⌂*In-room: safe, Wi-Fi. In-hotel: 2 restaurants, bars, golf course, tennis courts, pools, gym, diving, water sports, laundry service* ⊟*AE, MC, V* ⦿*EP.*

$$–$$$ ⌂ **Le Grand Courlan Resort & Spa.** This hotel is more upscale than its sister property, the Grafton Beach Resort, located next door. Rooms have large balconies, and the beach is one of the best on the island. The all-inclusive price includes basic water sports; one spa treatment per day is included, but because of the volume of requests, they sometimes feel rushed. Food is occasionally not great, and service can be a bit slow and impersonal; in truth, both the Coco Reef Resort and the Hilton Tobago offer nicer rooms and better spa treatments and meals for roughly the same price, albeit with à la carte pricing. **Pros:** Beautiful beach, perfect for those who want to get away from screaming children. **Cons:** Other hotels offer better rooms and services for the same price or less, restaurants are mediocre. ⊠*Shirvan Rd., Black Rock* ☎*868/639–9667, 800/468–3750, 800/424–5500 in Canada* ⤵*80 rooms, 3 suites* ⌂*In-room: safe. In-hotel: 3 restaurants, bars, tennis courts, pool, gym, spa, beachfront, diving, water sports, laundry service, no kids under 16* ⊟*AE, MC, V* ⦿*AI.*

$$–$$$ ⌂ **Mt. Irvine Bay Hotel.** Before the Hilton Tobago, the Mt. Irvine was the premier golf hotel on the island, though it's now been eclipsed. Rooms are spacious and perfectly adequate, though not as fancy as those in some other similarly priced hotels on the island. Although the hotel lacks some of the fancier amenities, there's still something magical about its air of 1970s grandeur, which cannot be found at any of the flashy new resorts. A lovely beach, where drinks are served and towels dispensed, sits right across the road. The hotel's restaurants are best avoided, though, since the service is generally slow and the food insipid. **Pros:** Beautiful grounds, perfect for the golf lover, access to one of the prettiest beaches. **Cons:** Public spaces feel dated, poor restaurant service. ⊠*Shirvan Rd., Box 222, Mt. Irvine* ☎*868/639–8871* ⊕*www. mtirvine.com* ⤵*53 rooms, 6 suites, 46 cottages* ⌂*In-room: safe. In-hotel: 3 restaurants, bars, golf course, tennis courts, pool, beachfront, water sports* ⊟*AE, MC, V* ⦿*EP.*

$$ ⌂ **Arnos Vale Hotel.** On 450 hillside acres, this hillside hotel is the perfect retreat for nature lovers and lovers in general. Princess Margaret spent her honeymoon here, and it's easy to see why—the world seems very far away. Rooms are little white cottages set into the hillside, so privacy isn't hard to find. A winding path takes guests down to a picture-perfect beach, pool, and bar. Some of the best snorkeling on the island can be done off the hotel's beach. The hilltop restaurant—furnished with antiques, iron-lattice tables, and a chandelier—has a magnificent patio with sweeping sea views. **Pros:** Complete peaceful setting, beautifully landscaped grounds, large and immaculate rooms. **Cons:** Miles away from dining or shopping, some rooms are quite a hike away from the beach. ⊠*Arnos Vale and Franklin Rds., Box 208, Scarborough* ☎*868/639–2881* ⊕*www.arnosvalehotel.com* ⤵*29 rooms,*

3 suites ⚘*In-room: refrigerator (some), no TV. In-hotel: restaurant, bars, tennis court, pool, beachfront, diving, water sports, no elevator* ▭*AE, DC, MC, V* |◎|*EP.*

$$ 🏨**Blue Waters Inn.** A tropical rain forest creeps up behind this sprawling ★ ecofriendly hotel, which sits on sheltered, turquoise Batteaux Bay with a white-sand beach just east of Speyside. A 90-minute drive from Scarborough, the hotel makes every effort to make guests feel at home. One- and two-bedroom apartments are directly on the beach, and kitchens can be stocked with food for your arrival. The resort caters primarily to divers and bird-watchers, but it's also a fine place from which to explore Tobago's north coast. The restaurant serves the freshest of fish, and barbecue dinners are cooked up on the beach patio. **Pros:** Rooms open onto the beach and are near water, enthusiastic and friendly staff, simple but delicious food. Cons: Long drive from the nearest town. ✉*Batteaux Bay, Speyside* ☎*868/660–4077 or 800/742–4276* ⊕*www. bluewatersinn.com* ⟿*31 rooms, 3 suites, 4 bungalows* ⚘*In-room: kitchen (some), no TV. In-hotel: restaurant, bar, tennis court, beachfront, diving, water sports, public Internet* ▭*AE, MC, V* |◎|*EP.*

$–$$ 🏨**Grafton Beach Resort.** The first all-inclusive hotel in Tobago remains ☼ a very popular choice for young couples. This is not a luxury hotel, and the restaurants are mediocre; however, it is not a bad value for those looking for the basics. Although the hotel is on one of the nicer beaches in Tobago, it is a public beach, and peddlers may sometimes be a problem. Guests here can also use the spa facilities at the tonier Le Grand Courlan for a fee. **Pros:** Large rooms, lively pool area. **Cons:** Mediocre food offerings, free drinks can sometime make for a rowdy crowd. ✉*Shirvan Rd., Black Rock* ☎*868/639–0191* ⟿*102 rooms, 4 suites* ⚘*In-room: safe, refrigerator. In-hotel: 3 restaurants, bars, pool, beachfront, diving, water sports* ▭*AE, MC, V* |◎|*AI.*

$ 🏨**Kariwak Village.** Alan and Cynthia Cloves have created an intimate, ★ tranquil oasis for their loyal guests who return year after year to this holistic retreat. Even the cabanas have been designed with pitched roofs to help "maximize your energy potential." Hearty souls who wish to atone for an excess of nightly rum punches can indulge in daily morning yoga. The bar and restaurant are in a bamboo pavilion and welcome local entertainers on weekends. Choose a garden room for a more-peaceful stay; those near the pool can be noisy. The complex is near the airport, Store Bay, and Pigeon Point but is not on the beach. **Pros:** Cozy and intimate throughout, excellent restaurant, beautiful grounds. **Cons:** The New Age concept may not be to all tastes, no beach. ✉*Box 27, Crown Point* ☎*868/639–8442* ⊕*www.kariwak. com* ⟿*24 rooms* ⚘*In-room: no TV. In-hotel: restaurant, bar, pool* ▭*AE, MC, V* |◎|*EP.*

$ 🏨**Toucan Inn.** This budget hotel near the airport offers simple, clean rooms and a lively social scene. The hotel's restaurant, Bonkers, is a popular hangout for locals and visitors, so entertainment is never far away. Rooms are furnished with locally made teak furniture and comfy beds. Guests staying for a week or more get breakfast included in the rate. The hotel has a small pool, but the beach is a fairly long trek down the road. **Pros:** Great value, good restaurant. **Cons:** Pool and bar area can be a bit raucous on weekends, rooms are serviceable but Spartan, no beach. ✉*Store Bay Local Rd., Crown Point* ☎*868/639–7173* ⊕*www.toucan-inn.com* ➘*20 rooms* ⌂*In-hotel: restaurant, bar, pool* ▤*AE, MC, V* ⦿*EP.*

WHERE TO EAT

Curried crab and dumplings is Tobago's Sunday-dinner favorite. Oil-down—a local dish—tastes better than it sounds: it's a gently seasoned mixture of boiled breadfruit and salt beef or pork flavored with coconut milk. Mango ice cream or a sweet-and-sour tamarind ball makes a tasty finish. You may want to take home some hot-pepper sauce or chutney to a spice-loving friend or relative.

For approximate costs, see the dining and lodging price chart in the Trinidad and Tobago Planner at the beginning of this chapter.

CAFÉ
¢
✕**Shore Things Café & Craft.** With a dramatic setting over the ocean on the Milford Road between Crown Point and Scarborough, this is a good spot to stop for a lunch or coffee break. Survey the view from the deck tables while enjoying a variety of freshly prepared juices (the tamarind is particularly refreshing) and nibbling on excellent sandwiches. The whole-wheat pizza here may well be the best on the island. While waiting for your meal, you can shop for local crafts in the lovely and comprehensive gift shop. ✉*25 Old Milford Rd., Lambeau* ☎*868/635–1072* ▤*MC, V* ⊘*Closed Sun. No dinner.*

CARIBBEAN
$$–$$$
★
✕**Kariwak Village Restaurant.** Recorded steel-band music plays gently in the background at this romantic, candlelit spot in the Kariwak Village complex. In a bamboo pavilion that resembles an Amerindian round hut, Cynthia Clovis orchestrates a very original menu. Whatever the dish, it will be full of herbs and vegetables picked from her organic garden. Be sure to try the delicious homemade ice cream. Friday and Saturday buffets, with live jazz or calypso, are a Tobagonian highlight. ✉*Crown Point* ☎*868/639–8442* ▤*AE, MC, V.*

$$–$$$
★
✕**Shutters on the Bay.** In the stylish Blue Haven Hotel, this restaurant is sure to please even the most-discerning diners. The warm-yellow dining area is on the second floor of a colonial-style building and is surrounded by white push-out shutters that afford a magical view of Bacolet Bay. The menu features a variety of dishes all with a contemporary Caribbean twist. If crayfish is on the menu, get it, as it's a sure pleaser. ✉*Blue Haven Hotel, Bacolet Bay, Scarborough* ☎*868/660–7500* ⌂*Reservations essential* ▤*AE, MC, V.*

¢–$
Fodor'sChoice
★
✕**Blue Crab Restaurant.** The Sardinha family have been serving the best local lunches at their home since the 1980s. The ebullient Alison entertains and hugs diners while her husband, Ken, does the cooking. The food is hearty and usually well seasoned in the creole style. The only bad news here is that the restaurant is rarely open for dinner; the good news is that you may not have room for dinner after lunch. ✉*Robinson and Main Sts., Scarborough* ☎*868/639–2737* ▤*AE, MC, V* ⊘*Closed weekends. No dinner.*

ECLECTIC ✕**Tamara's.** At the elegant Coco Reef Resort you can dine on contem-
$$$$ porary cuisine with an island twist. The peach walls and whitewashed
wooden ceiling make the resort's restaurant feel airy and light, and
island breezes waft through the palm-lined terrace. The prix-fixe menu
changes seasonally, but the fish dishes are sure to please. A full tropical
buffet breakfast is served daily; dinner is served nightly. ⊠ *Coco Reef
Resort, Crown Point, Scarborough* ☎ *868/639–8571* ▱ *AE, MC, V*
☺ *No lunch.*

$$–$$$ ✕**Café Coco.** This smart eatery seats 200, but it's divided into multiple
levels, so there's still a sense of intimacy. Statuary is strewn about with
carefree abandon, and the sound of flowing water permeates the room.
Reasonably priced by Tobago standards, the main courses range from
Cuban stewed beef to shrimp tempura. The zingy *pimento Mexicano,*
mozzarella-stuffed jalapeños and shrimp on a bed of greens, is a great
appetizer. The restaurant is seldom full, so getting a table is usually not
a problem. ⊠ *TTEC Substation Rd. off Crown Point Rd., Crown Point*
☎ *868/639–0996* ▱ *AE, MC, V.*

24

$$–$$$ ✕**Café Iguana.** This funky little restaurant and art gallery is a popular
gathering place evenings as it serves some of the best cocktails on the
island. The menu is eclectic, but there is a distinct Tobago touch to
everything and an emphasis on local ingredients. The crayfish, though
messy to eat, is not to be missed. The art on the walls is available for
sale—you might want to exercise restraint with the cocktails before
deciding to become an art investor. ⊠ *Store Bay Local Rd. at Milford
Rd.Crown Point* ☎ *868/631–8205* ▱ *AE, MC, V.*

$–$$$ ✕**Bonkers.** Despite the rather odd name, this restaurant at the Toucan
Inn is atmospheric and excellent. Designed by expat British co-owner
Chris James, the architecture is a blend of Kenyan and Caribbean
styles, executed entirely in local teak and open on all sides. The menu
is huge; Chris claims it pains him to remove any items, so he just keeps
adding more. You can savor your lobster Rockefeller while enjoying
the nightly entertainment. Open for breakfast and lunch seven days a
week, this is the busiest eatery on the island. ⊠ *Toucan Inn, Store Bay
Local Rd., Crown Point* ☎ *868/639–7173* ▱ *AE, MC, V.*

ITALIAN ✕**La Tartaruga.** Milanese owner Gabriele de Gaetano has created one
$$–$$$ of the island's most delightful dining experiences. Sitting on the large
patio surrounded by lush foliage with Gabriele rushing from table to
table chatting in Italian-laced English is all the entertainment you'll
need. An impressive cellar is stocked solely with Italian wines. ⊠ *Buc-
coo Rd., Buccoo* ☎ *868/639–0940* ⌕ *Reservations essential* ▱ *AE,
MC, V* ☺ *Closed Sun.*

$–$$ ✕**La Terrazza.** This romantic Italian restaurant has lost some of its rustic
Fodor'sChoice charm since moving from its previous location, but great food is still
★ the order of the day. Keisha and Stefano Monti, the husband-and-wife
owners, handle every aspect of the restaurant from the cooking to the
serving. The menu is light, imaginative, and eminently affordable. The
salmon tartare appetizer is heavenly. Stefano, an avid wine collector,
stocks the excellent cellar; Keisha insists that anything he collects be
offered for sale—good news for diners. ⊠ *Tobago Plantations Golf*

Club, Lowlands ☎868/639–8242 ♨*Reservations essential* ▤*MC, V* ☉*Closed Sun. and Mon.*

BEACHES

You won't find manicured country-club sand here. But those who enjoy feeling as though they've landed on a desert island will relish the untouched quality of these shores.

Bacolet Beach. This dark-sand beach was the setting for the films *Swiss Family Robinson* and *Heaven Knows, Mr. Allison*. Though used by the Blue Haven Hotel, like all local beaches it's open to the public. If you are not a guest at the hotel, access to the beach is down a track next door to the hotel. The bathroom and changing facilities on the beach are for hotel guests only. ⊠*Windward Rd. east of Scarborough.*

★ **Englishman's Bay.** This charming, mile-long, somewhat wild beach is usually completely deserted. Keep in mind that the price paid for solitude is a lack of facilities. ⊠*North Side Rd. east of Castara Bay.*

Great Courland Bay. Near Ft. Bennett, the bay has clear, tranquil waters. Along the sandy beach—one of Tobago's longest—you can find several glitzy hotels. A marina attracts the yachting crowd. ⊠*Leeward Rd. northeast of Black Rock, Courland.*

King's Bay. Surrounded by steep green hills, this is the most visually satisfying of the swimming sites off the road from Scarborough to Speyside—the bay hooks around so severely you can feel like you're in a lake. The crescent-shape beach is easy to find because it's marked by a sign about halfway between the two towns. Just before you reach the bay, there's a bridge with an unmarked turnoff that leads to a gravel parking lot; beyond that, a landscaped path leads to a waterfall with a rocky pool. You'll likely meet locals who can offer to guide you to the top of the falls; however, you may find the climb not worth the effort. ⊠*Delaford.*

Lovers Beach. So called because of its pink sand and its seclusion—you have to hire a local to bring you here by boat—it's an isolated and quiet retreat. Ask one of the fishermen in Charlotteville to arrange a ride for you, but be sure to haggle. It should cost you no more than $20 a person for a return ride (considerably less sometimes). ⊠*North coast, reachable only by boat from Charlotteville.*

Mt. Irvine Beach. Across the street from the Mt. Irvine Bay Hotel is this unremarkable beach, but it has great surfing in July and August; the snorkeling is excellent, too. It's also ideal for windsurfing in January and April. There are picnic tables surrounded by painted concrete pagodas and a snack bar. ⊠*Shirvan Rd., Mt. Irvine.*

Parlatuvier. On the north side of the island, the beach is best approached via the road from Roxborough. It's a classic Caribbean crescent, a scene peopled by villagers and fishermen. ⊠*Parlatuvier.*

Pigeon Point Beach. This stunning locale is often displayed on Tobago travel brochures. Although the beach is public, it abuts part of what was once a large coconut estate, and you must pay a token admission (about TT$18) to enter the grounds and use the facilities. ⊠*Pigeon Point.*

Sandy Point Beach. Situated at the end of the Crown Point Airport runway, this beach is abutted by several hotels, so you won't lack for amenities around here. The beach is accessible by walking around the airport fence to the hotel area. ✉ *At Crown Point Airport.*

Stone Haven Bay. A gorgeous stretch of sand is across the street from the Grafton Beach Resort. ✉ *Shirvan Rd., Black Rock.*

Store Bay. The beach, where boats depart for Buccoo Reef, is little more than a small sandy cove between two rocky breakwaters, but the food stands here are divine: several huts licensed by the tourist board to local ladies who sell roti, pelau, and the world's messiest dish—crab and dumplings. Near the airport, just walk around the Crown Point Hotel to the beach entrance. ✉ *Crown Point.*

Turtle Beach. Named for the leatherback turtles that lay their eggs here at night between February and June, it's on Great Courland Bay. (If you're very quiet, you can watch; the turtles don't seem to mind.) It's 8 mi (13 km) from the airport between Black Rock and Plymouth. ✉ *Southern end of Great Courland Bay, between Black Rock and Plymouth.*

24

SPORTS & THE OUTDOORS

BIRD-WATCHING

★ Some 200 varieties of birds have been documented on Tobago: look for the yellow oriole, scarlet ibis, and the comical motmot—the male of the species clears sticks and stones from an area and then does a dance complete with snapping sounds to attract a mate. The flora is as vivid as the birds. Purple-and-yellow *poui* trees and spectacular orange immortelles splash color over the countryside, and something is blooming virtually every season. Pat Turpin and Renson Jack at **Pioneer Journeys** (☎ *868/660–4327 or 868/660–5175* ✉ *pturpin@tstt.net.tt*) can give you information about their bird-watching tours of Bloody Bay rain forest and Louis d'Or River valley wetlands. Naturalist and ornithologist David Rooks operates **Rooks Nature Tours** (✉ *462 Moses Hill, Lambeau* ☎ *868/756–8594* ⊕ *www.rookstobago.com*), offering bird-watching walks inland and trips to offshore bird colonies. He's generally considered to be the best guide on the island.

BOAT TOURS

Tobago offers many wonderful spots for snorkeling. Although the reefs around Speyside in the northeast are becoming better known, **Buccoo Reef,** off the island's southwest coast, is still the most popular—perhaps too popular. Over the years the reef has been damaged by the ceaseless boat traffic and by the thoughtless visiting divers who take pieces of coral as souvenirs. Still, it's worth experiencing, particularly if you have children. Daily 2½-hour tours by glass-bottom boats let you snorkel at the reef, swim in a lagoon, and gaze at Coral Gardens—where fish and coral are as yet untouched. Most dive companies in the Black Rock area also arrange snorkeling tours. There's also good snorkeling near the **Arnos Vale Hotel** and the **Mt. Irvine Bay Hotel.**

Hew's Glass Bottom Boat Tours (✉ *Pigeon Point* ☎ *868/639–9058*) are perfect excursions for those who neither snorkel nor dive. Boats leave daily at 11:30 AM. **Kalina Kats** (✉ *Scarborough* ☎ *868/639–6306*) has a 50-foot catamaran on which you can sail around the Tobago coastline with stops for snorkeling and exploring the rain forest. The romantic sunset cruise with cocktails is a great way to end the day.

DIVING

An abundance of fish and coral thrives on the nutrients of Venezuela's Orinoco River, which are brought to Tobago by the Guyana current. Off the west coast is **Arnos Vale Reef,** with a depth of 40 feet and several reefs that run parallel to the shore. Here you can spot French and queen angelfish, moray eels, southern stingrays, and even the Atlantic torpedo ray. Much of the diving is drift diving in the mostly gentle current. **Crown Point**, on the island's southwest tip, is a good place for exploring the Shallows—a plateau at 50 to 100 feet that's favored by turtles, dolphins, angelfish, and nurse sharks. Just north of Crown Point on the southwest coast, **Pigeon Point** is a good spot to submerge. North of Pigeon Point, long, sandy beaches line the calm western coast; it has a gradual offshore slope and the popular **Mt. Irvine Wall,** which goes down to about 60 feet.

A short trip from Charlotteville, off the northeast tip of the island, is **St. Giles Island.** Here are natural rock bridges—London Bridge, Marble Island, and Fishbowl—and underwater cliffs. The **waters off Speyside** on the east coast draw scuba-diving aficionados for the many manta rays in the area. Exciting sites in this area include Batteaux Reef, Angel Reef, Bookends, Blackjack Hole, and Japanese Gardens—one of the loveliest reefs, with depths of 20 to 85 feet and lots of sponges.

Tobago is considered a prime diving destination, as the clear waters provide maximum visibility. Every species of hard coral and most soft corals can be found in the waters around the island. Tobago is also home to the largest-known brain coral. Generally, the best diving is around the Speyside area. Many hotels and guesthouses in this area cater to the diving crowd with minimalist accommodations and easy access to the water. You can usually get the best deals with these "dive-and-stay" packages. **AquaMarine Dive Ltd.** (✉ *Blue Waters Inn, Batteaux Bay, Speyside* ☎ *868/639–4416* ⊕ *www.aquamarinedive.com*) is on the northeast coast at the Blue Waters Inn and offers a friendly and laid-back approach, which makes it popular with casual divers. **Tobago Dive Experience** (✉ *Manta Lodge, Speyside* ☎ *868/639–7034* ⊕ *www. tobagodiveexperience.com*) offers the most-comprehensive range of courses, including PADI, NAUI, and BSAC. Prices are very competitive, and class sizes are kept small to ensure that all divers get the attention they need. This is also the only dive operation to have locations in both the north and south areas of the island.

FISHING

Dillon's Deep Sea Charters (✉ *Crown Point* ☎ *868/639–9386*) is excellent for full- and half-day trips for kingfish, barracuda, wahoo, mahimahi, blue marlin, and others. Trips start at $165 for four hours, including equipment. With **Hard Play Fishing Charters** (✉ *13 The Evergreen, Old Grange, Mt. Irvine Bay* ☎ *868/639–7108*), colorful skipper Gerard

"Frothy" De Silva helps you bag your own marlin. The cost is $400 for four hours on the 42-foot *Hard Play* or the *Hard Play II*; fly-fishing is also available for $80 per person.

GOLF

★ The 18-hole, par-72 course at the **Mt. Irvine Golf Club** (⊠ *Mt. Irvine Bay Hotel, Shirvan Rd., Mt. Irvine* ☎868/639–8871) was once ranked among the top courses in the Caribbean and among the top 100 in the world, but course maintenance has suffered over the years. Greens fees are $30 for 9 holes, $48 for 18 holes. The 18-hole, PGA-designed championship par-72 course at **Tobago Plantations Golf & Country Club** (⊠ *Lowlands* ☎868/631–0875) is set amid rolling greens and mangroves. It offers some amazing views of the ocean as a bonus. Greens fees are $85 for one round, $150 for two rounds (these rates include a golf cart and taxes). This is the newer of the two main courses on the island and is by far the most popular. The course is well maintained and contains areas of mangrove and forest that are home to many bird species.

Fodor'sChoice

24

HIKING

Ecoconsciousness is strong on Tobago, where the rain forests of the Main Ridge were set aside for protection in 1764, creating the first such preserve in the western hemisphere. Natural areas include Little Tobago and St. Giles islands, both major seabird sanctuaries. In addition, the endangered leatherback turtles maintain breeding grounds on some of Tobago's leeward beaches.

Harris Jungle Tours (⊠ *Golden Grove Rd., Canaan* ☎868/639–0513 ⊕ *www.harris-jungle-tours.com*) is run by the knowledgeable Harris McDonald and offers a variety of tours ranging from strenuous to laid-back. The more adventurous might want to try the rain-forest-at-night tour, which promises the possibility of encounters with some of Tobago's folklore characters, including La Diablesse (a beautifully dressed she-devil with a cloven hoof). **Yes Tourism** (⊠ *Pigeon Point Rd., Crown Point* ☎868/631–0287 ⊕ *www.yes-tourism.com*) offers a comprehensive range of tours for individuals and groups. The Rain Forest tour is an excellent guided hike. Sightseeing tours around Tobago as well as to Trinidad and the Grenadines are also possible.

SHOPPING

The souvenir-bound will do better in Trinidad than in Tobago, but determined shoppers should manage to find a few things to take home. Scarborough has the largest collection of shops, and Burnett Street, which climbs sharply from the port to St. James Park, is a good place to browse.

FOODSTUFFS

Forro's Homemade Delicacies (⊠ *The Andrew's Rectory, Bacolet St., opposite fire station, Scarborough* ☎868/639–2485) sells its own fine line of homemade tamarind chutney, lemon and lime marmalade, hot sauce, and guava and golden-apple jelly. Eileen Forrester, wife of the

Anglican archdeacon of Trinidad and Tobago, supervises a kitchen full of good cooks who boil and bottle the condiments and pack them in little straw baskets—or even in bamboo. Most jars are small, easy to carry, and inexpensive.

HANDICRAFTS

Cotton House (⊠ *Bacolet St., Scarborough* ☎ *868/639–2727*) is a good bet for jewelry and imaginative batik work. Paula Young runs her shop like an art school. You can visit the upstairs studio; if it's not too busy, you can even make a batik square at no charge. **Shore Things Café & Crafts** (⊠ *25 Old Milford Rd., Lambeau* ☎ *868/635–1072*) has a wide variety of souvenir items ranging from masks to music (and everything in between). **Souvenir and Gift Shop** (⊠ *Port Mall, Wrightson Rd., Scarborough* ☎ *868/639–5632*) stocks straw baskets and other crafts.

NIGHTLIFE

Tobago is not the liveliest island after dark, but there's usually some form of nightlife to be found. Whatever you do the rest of the week, don't miss the huge impromptu party, affectionately dubbed Sunday School, that gears up after midnight on all the street corners of Buccoo and breaks up around dawn. Pick your band, hang out for a while, then move on. In downtown Scarborough on weekend nights you can also find competing sound systems blaring at informal parties that welcome extra guests. In addition, "blockos" (spontaneous block parties) spring up all over the island; look for the hand-painted signs. Tobago also has harvest parties on Sunday throughout the year, when a particular village extends its hospitality and opens its doors to visitors.

★ **Bonkers** (⊠ *Toucan Inn, Store Bay Local Rd., Crown Point* ☎ *868/639–7173*) is lively on most evenings, with live entertainment every night except Sunday. **Grafton Beach Resort** (⊠ *Shirvan Rd., Black Rock* ☎ *868/639–0191*) has some kind of organized cabaret-style event every night. Even if you hate that touristy stuff, check out Les Couteaux Cultural Group, which does a high-octane dance version of Tobagonian history. **Kariwak Village** (⊠ *Crown Point* ☎ *868/639–8442*) has hip hotel entertainment and is frequented as much by locals as visitors on Friday and Saturday nights—when one of the better local jazz-calypso bands almost always plays. **The Shade** (⊠ *Milford Rd. and Robert St., Crown Point* ☎ *868/639–9651*), near the gas station, is a sure bet for raucous late-night fun from 7 PM to 4 AM Wednesday through Saturday.

EXPLORING TOBAGO

A driving tour of Tobago, from Scarborough to Charlotteville and back, can be done in about four hours, but you'd never want to undertake this spectacular, and very hilly, ride in that time. The switchbacks can make you wish you had motion-sickness pills (take some along if you're prone). Plan to spend at least one night at the Speyside end of the island, and give yourself a chance to enjoy this largely untouched country and seaside at leisure.

Charlotteville. This delightful fishing village in the northeast is enfolded in a series of steep hills. Fishermen here announce the day's catch by sounding their conch shells. A view of Man O' War Bay with Pigeon Peak (Tobago's highest mountain) behind it at sunset is an exquisite treat.

NEED A BREAK? If you're exploring the windward coast, the funky, inexpensive First Historical Café/Bar (⊠ *Mile Marker 8, Windward Main Rd.* ☎ *868/660–2233*), which is owned by the Washington family, is near Studley Park en route to Charlotte. It's got a thatch roof and a crushed-rock-and-coral floor, and you can eat overlooking the sea on the back porch. The food is simple, featuring such island delights as fruit plates, coconut bread, and fish sandwiches.

Flagstaff Hill. One of the highest points on the island sits at the northern tip of Tobago. Surrounded by ocean on three sides and with a view of other hills, Charlotteville, and St. Giles Island, this was the site of an American military lookout and radio tower during World War II. It's an ideal spot for a sunset picnic. The turnoff to the hill is at the major bend in the road from Speyside to Charlotteville. It's largely unpaved, so the going may be a bit rough.

24

Ft. King George. On Mt. St. George, a short drive up the hill from Scarborough, Tobago's best-preserved historic monument clings to a cliff high above the ocean. Ft. King George was built in the 1770s and operated until 1854. It's hard to imagine that this lovely, tranquil spot commanding sweeping views of the bay and landscaped with lush tropical foliage was ever the site of any military action, but the prison, officers' mess, and several stabilized cannons attest otherwise. Just to the left of the tall wooden figures dancing a traditional Tobagonian jig is the former barrack guardhouse, now housing the small **Tobago Museum.** Exhibits include weapons and other pre-Columbian artifacts found in the area; the fertility figures are especially interesting. Upstairs are maps and photographs of Tobago's past. Be sure to check out the gift display cases for the perversely fascinating jewelry made from embalmed and painted lizards and sea creatures; you might find it hard to resist a pair of bright-yellow shrimp earrings. The **Fine Arts Centre** at the foot of the Ft. King George complex shows the work of local artists. ⊠ *84 Fort St., Scarborough* ☎ *868/639–3970* ⊠ *Fort free, museum TT$2* ☉ *Weekdays 9–5.*

★ **Kimme's Sculpture Museum.** The diminutive and eccentric German-born sculptress Luise Kimme fell in love with the form of Tobagonians and has devoted her life to capturing them in her sculptures. Her pieces can exceed 12 feet in height and are often wonderfully whimsical. Much of her work is done in wood (none of it local), but there are many bronze pieces as well. The museum itself is a turreted structure with a commanding view of the countryside. Most locals refer to it as "The Castle." There are numerous signs in Mt. Irvine directing visitors to the museum. ⊠ *Mt. Irvine* ☎ *868/639–0257* ⊕ *www.luisekimme.com* ⊠ *TT$3.50* ☉ *Sun. 10 AM–2 PM or by appointment.*

St. Giles Island. The underwater cliffs and canyons here off the northeastern tip of Tobago draw divers to this spot where the Atlantic meets the Caribbean. ⊠ *Take Windward Rd. inland across mountains from Speyside.*

Scarborough. Around Rockley Bay on the island's leeward hilly side, this town is both the capital of Tobago and a popular cruise-ship port, but it conveys the feeling that not much has changed since the area was settled two centuries ago. It may not be one of the delightful pastel-color cities of the Caribbean, but Scarborough does have its charms, including several interesting little shops. Whatever you do, be sure to check out the busy Scarborough Market, an indoor and outdoor affair featuring everything from fresh vegetables to live chickens and clothing. Note the red-and-yellow Methodist church on the hill, one of Tobago's oldest churches.

NEED A BREAK?

Ciao Café (✉ *20 Burnett St., Scarborough* ☎ *868/639–3001*) is an essential stop on any visit to the capital and offers a selection of more than 20 flavors of gelato, as well as the usual complement of coffees. You can also get pizza slices and sandwiches if you're looking for a quick snack. There's seating in the air-conditioned interior and a lovely outdoor perch from which to absorb the downtown action sheltered from the blazing sun. Stronger cocktails are also available.

Speyside. At the far reach of Tobago's windward coast, this small fishing village has a few lodgings and restaurants. Divers are drawn to the unspoiled reefs in the area and to the strong possibility of spotting giant manta rays. The approach to Speyside from the south affords one of the most spectacular vistas of the island. Glass-bottom boats operate between Speyside and **Little Tobago Island,** one of the most important seabird sanctuaries in the Caribbean.

TRINIDAD & TOBAGO ESSENTIALS

To research prices, get advice from other travelers, and book travel arrangements, visit www.fodors.com.

▌TRANSPORTATION

BY AIR

Caribbean Airlines, formerly BWIA, is the Trinidad-based national carrier, but many other major airlines offer flights to Trinindad and then onto Tobago from the U.S. To get to Tobago, you will have to hop over from Trinidad on Liat or Caribbean Airlines.

Airline Information **American Airlines** (☎ 868/664–4661). **Caribbean Airlines** (☎ 868/625–1010 or 868/669–3000).

Continental Airlines (☎ 800/461–2744). **Delta Airlines** (☎ 800/221–1212). **LIAT** (☎ 868/627–2942 or 868/623–1838). **Spirit Airlines** (☎ 800/772–7117).

AIRPORTS & TRANSFERS

Authorized airport taxis can be arranged just outside the baggage-claim areas of the airports on both Trinidad and Tobago. (You will certainly be assailed by shouts of "Taxi?" by the nonauthorized drivers as you exit the baggage area.) The trip from the airport into Port of Spain costs about $30 during the day and $45 at night using the authorized taxis. In Tobago, the cost will vary greatly depending on the location of your hotel; a board in the baggage claim area claims to give accurate rates to all the major hotels. Generally, hotels in the Crown Point area should cost about $25 (a bit of a rip-off, as most hotels in that area are within walking distance) while hotels in Scarborough and Grafton Beach will cost approximately $50.

A service available in Trinidad, called 628–8294, will take you from the airport to any point on the island. The cost to get to hotels in Port of Spain is about $16 each way, but you will have to call from the airport or your hotel to arrange the pickup.

Airport Information Crown Point Airport (TAB ☎868/639–0509). **Piarco International Airport** (POS ☎868/669–4101).

BY BOAT & FERRY

The Port Authority maintains ferry service every day between Trinidad and Tobago, although flying is preferable because the seas can be very rough. The trip can be made by either a conventional or high-speed CAT ferry. The ferries leave once a day (from St. Vincent Street Jetty in Port of Spain and from the cruise-ship complex in Scarborough); the trip on the conventional ferry takes about 5 hours and the high-speed CAT takes 2½ hours. The conventional ferry runs TT$75 (round-trip); the round-trip fare for the CAT is TT$100.

Information Port Authority of Trinidad & Tobago (☎868/625–2901 in Port of Spain, 868/639–2181 in Scarborough ⊕www.patnt.com).

BY CAR

Trinidad has excellent roads throughout the island. Be careful when driving during the rainy season, as roads often flood. Never drive into downtown Port of Spain during afternoon rush hour (generally from 3 to 6:30), when traffic is at its heaviest. In Tobago, many roads, particularly in the interior or on the coast near Speyside and Charlotteville, are bumpy, pitted, winding, and/or steep (though the main highways are smooth and fast). On

either island, driving is on the left, in the British style, so remember to look to your right when pulling out into traffic. Also be aware that Tobago has very few gas stations—the main ones are in Crown Point and Scarborough.

Trinidad Car Rentals Auto Rentals (⊠Piarco International Airport, Piarco, Trinidad ☎868/669–2277). **Kalloo's Auto Rentals** (⊠Piarco International Airport, Piarco, Trinidad ☎868/669–5673 ⊕www.kalloos.com). **Southern Sales Car Rentals** (⊠Piarco International Airport, Piarco, Trinidad ☎868/669–2424, 269 from courtesy phone in airport baggage area). **Thrifty** (⊠Piarco International Airport, Piarco, Trinidad ☎868/669–0602).

Tobago Car Rentals Baird's Rentals (⊠Crown Point Airport, Crown Point, Tobago ☎868/639–7054). **Rattan's Car Rentals** (⊠Crown Point Airport, Crown Point, Tobago ☎868/639–8271). **Rollock's Car Rentals** (⊠Crown Point Airport, Crown Point, Tobago ☎868/639–0328). **Singh's Auto Rentals** (⊠Grafton Beach Resort, Shirvan Rd., Black Rock, Tobago ☎868/639–0191 Ext. 53). **Thrifty** (⊠Rex Turtle Beach Hotel, Great Courland Bay, Black Rock, Tobago ☎868/639–8507).

BY TAXI

Taxis in Trinidad and Tobago are easily identified by their license plates, which begin with the letter *H*. Passenger vans, called Maxi Taxis, pick up and drop off passengers as they travel (rather like a bus) and are color-coded according to which of the six areas they cover. Rates are generally less than $1 per trip. (Yellow is for Port of Spain, red for eastern Trinidad, green for south Trinidad, and black for Princes Town. Brown operates from San Fernando to the southeast— Erin, Penal, Point Fortin. The only color for Tobago is blue.) They're easy to hail day or night along most of the main roads near Port of Spain. For longer trips you need to hire a private taxi. Cabs aren't metered, and hotel taxis can be expensive. A taxi service available in Trinidad, called

24

628–TAXI, will take you to the beach for $20 and around town for $10.

Information **628–TAXI** (☎868/628–8294).

❙ CONTACTS & RESOURCES

BANKS & EXCHANGE SERVICES

At this writing, the exchange rate for the Trinidadian dollar (TT$) was about TT$6.34 to US$1. Most businesses on the islands will accept U.S. currency if you're in a pinch. Credit cards and ATM cards are almost universally accepted for payment by businesses, hotels, and restaurants. Cash is necessary only in the smallest neighborhood convenience shops and roadside stalls. Trinidad has ATMs in all but the most remote areas. In Tobago there are only a few in Scarborough and at the airport in Crown Point. Be aware that there are far fewer bank branches in Tobago than in Trinidad.

ELECTRICITY

Electric current is usually 110 volts/60 cycles, but some establishments provide 220-volt outlets.

EMERGENCIES

Emergency Services **Ambulance and fire** (☎990). **Police** (☎999).

Hospitals **Port of Spain General Hospital** (✉169 Charlotte St., Port of Spain, Trinidad ☎868/623–2951). **St. Clair Medical Centre** (✉18 Elizabeth St., St. Clair, Port of Spain, Trinidad ☎868/628–1451) is a private healthcare provider in Port of Spain that is highly recommended. **Scarborough Hospital** (✉Fort St., Scarborough, Tobago ☎868/639–2551).

INTERNET, MAIL & SHIPPING

The local phone company offers a handy dial-up service on both islands called 619–EASY. Simply connect your laptop to the phone line and dial 619–3279 using the word EASY as your username. The charge is 12¢ a minute. Because of crime concerns in Trinidad, it is inadvisable to use Internet cafés in downtown Port of Spain or in areas along the east–west corridor. Almost every hotel offers Internet

service, and newer ones (such as the Marriott) offer wireless high-speed access. In Trinidad, most hotels allow nonguests to use their Internet services for a fee.

In Tobago, the best Internet café in the Scarborough area is J-Puter Tech, which offers access for about $4 an hour. In Crown Point, the most fun choice is the Original House of Pancakes Ltd., which happily combines Internet access and pancakes. The Internet is $5 an hour, but the pancakes are an additional cost.

Postage to the United States and Canada is TT$3.45 for first-class letters and TT$2.25 for postcards; prices are slightly higher for other destinations. The main post offices are on Wrightson Road (opposite the Crowne Plaza) in Port of Spain and in the N.I.B. Mall on Wilson Street (near the docks) in Scarborough. There are no zip codes on the islands. To write to an establishment here, you simply need its address, town, and "Trinidad and Tobago, West Indies."

Internet Cafés **Computer Planet Ltd.** (✉Ariapita Ave. and Luis St., Port of Spain, Trinidad ☎868/622–6888). **J-Puter Tech** (✉20 Burnett St., Scarborough, Tobago ☎868/639–3393). **Jus Click** (✉Royal Palm Plaza, 7 Saddle Rd., Maraval, Trinidad ☎868/628–2316). **Original House of Pancakes Ltd.** (✉Milford Rd. and John Gorman Trace, Crown Point, Tobago ☎868/39–9866).

SAFETY

Travelers should exercise caution in Trinidad, especially in the highly populated east–west corridor and downtown Port of Spain, where walking on the streets at night is not recommended unless you're with a group. A surge in crime on Charlotte Street in Port of Spain suggests that it's best to avoid this street altogether. As a general rule, Tobago is safer than its larger sister island, though this should not lure you into a false sense of security. Petty theft occurs on both islands, so don't leave cash in bags that you check at the airport, and use hotel safes for valuables.

TAXES

Departure tax, payable in cash at the airport, is TT$100. All hotels add a 10% government tax. Prices for almost all goods and services include a 15% V.A.T.

TELEPHONES

The area code for both islands is 868 ("TNT" if you forget). This is also the country code if you're calling to Trinidad and Tobago from another country. From the United States, just dial "1" plus the area code and number.

To make a local call to any point in the country simply dial the seven-digit local number. Most hotels and guesthouses will allow you to dial a direct international call. To dial a number in North America or the Caribbean simply dial "1" and the U.S. or Canadian area code before the number you're calling, but be warned that most hotels add a hefty surcharge for overseas calls. Calls to Europe and elsewhere can be made by checking for the appropriate direct-dial codes in the telephone directory. To make an international call from a pay phone you must first purchase a "companion" card, which is readily available from most convenience shops—then simply follow the instructions on the card. Cards are available in various denominations.

Cell phones here are GSM , but your cell-phone company must have a roaming agreement with Telecommunications Services of Trinidad and Tobago (TSTT) or Digicel in order for your phone to work here. You can also purchase an SIM card to make local calling cheaper in Trinidad, but you'll be assigned a new phone number.

Information Digicel (⊕www.digiceltt.com). **TSTT** (⊕www.tstt.net.tt).

TIPPING

Almost all hotels will add a 10% to 15% service charge to your bill. Most restaurants include a 10% service charge, which is considered standard on these islands. If it isn't on the bill, tip according to service: 10% to 15% is fine. Cabbies expect a token tip of around 10%. At drinking establishments tipping is optional, and the staff at smaller bars may tell you on your way out that you forgot your change.

TOUR OPTIONS

Although any taxi driver in Trinidad or Tobago can take visitors to the major attractions, using a tour company allows for a more-leisurely and educational adventure. Tour operators are also more mindful of the sensitivities of tourists and are much less likely to subject passengers to breakneck speeds and "creative" driving.

In Trinidad, Caribbean Discovery Tours is operated by Stephen Broadbridge. His tours are completely personalized and can include both on- and offshore activities. Tours can range from the strenuous to the leisurely, with prices based on the duration of the expedition and the number of participants. Kalloo's offers tours ranging from a fascinating three-hour tour of Port of Spain to an overnight turtle-watching tour. Sensational Tours & Transport comes highly recommended and is your best choice for island tours. Owner Gerald Nicholas worked for the tourist board for many years and knows the island intimately. He is a complete delight to be with, and his tour prices are the lowest on the island by far.

In Tobago, Frank's Glass Bottom Boat & Birdwatching Tours offers glass-bottom-boat and snorkeling tours of the shores of Speyside; Frank also conducts guided tours of the rain forest and Little Tobago. As a native of Speyside, he's extremely knowledgeable about the island's flora, fauna, and folklore. Tobago Travel is the island's most expe-

24

rienced tour operator, offering a wide variety of services and tours.

In Trinidad **Caribbean Discovery Tours Ltd.** (✉9B Fondes Amandes, St. Ann's, Port of Spain ☎868/624–7281 or 868/620–1989 🖷868/624–8596 ⊕www.caribbeandiscovery tours.com). **Kalloo's** (✉Piarco International Airport, Piarco ☎868/669–5673 or 868/622–9073 ⊕www.kalloos.com). **Sensational Tours & Transport** (✉47 Reservoir Rd., La Pastora, Santa Cruz ☎868/676–2937 or 868/687–7832).

In Tobago **Frank's Glass Bottom Boat & Birdwatching Tours** (✉Speyside ☎🖷868/660–5438). **Tobago Travel** (✉Scarborough ☎868/639–8778).

VISITOR INFORMATION

Before You Leave **Tourism Hotline** (☎888/595–4868). **Trinidad and Tobago Tourism Office** (☎800/748–4224 ⊕www. visittnt.com).

In Trinidad **TDC** (✉Maritime Centre, Level 1, 9 10th Ave., Barataria ☎868/638–7962 🖷868/638–3560 ✉Piarco International Airport, Piarco ☎868/669–5196).

In Tobago **Tobago Division of Tourism** (✉N.I.B. Mall, Wilson St., Level 3, Scarborough ☎868/639–2125 ✉Crown Point Airport, Crown Point ☎868/639–0509).

WEDDINGS

Getting married in Trinidad and Tobago is still not as easy as on some other islands, but idyllic Tobago is still fairly popular as a wedding spot. Both parties must prove that they have been in the country for three days (calculated from the day after arrival). A passport, airline ticket, and proof of divorce (if you've been married before) are all required, as is a $55 license fee. Further information can be obtained from the Registrar General's office. The Coco Reef Resort in Tobago specializes in beach weddings.

Information **Coco Reef Resort** (✉Coconut Bay, Box 434, Crown Point, Tobago ☎868/639–8571 or 800/221–1294 ⊕www. cocoreef.com). **Registrar General** (✉Jerningham St., Scarborough, Tobago ☎868/639–3210 ✉72–74 South Quay, Port of Spain, Trinidad ☎868/624–1660).

Turks & Caicos Islands

Leeward Marina, Providenciales

WORD OF MOUTH

"Grace Bay beach in Turks & Caicos was by far the most beautiful beach that I have seen. We stayed close to the middle of the beach and took a long walk down each side of the beach from our hotel. It was gorgeous. The different colors of blue in the water was an amazing site."

—travelenthusiast

WELCOME TO TURKS & CAICOS ISLANDS

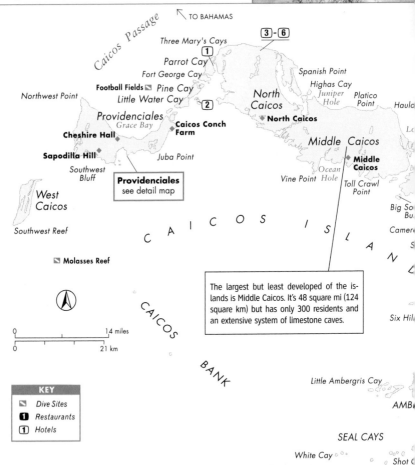

↖ TO BAHAMAS

Caicos Passage

Three Mary's Cays

Parrot Cay

Fort George Cay

Football Fields ◪ Pine Cay

Northwest Point

Little Water Cay

Providenciales

Grace Bay

Cheshire Hall

Sapodilla Hill

Southwest Bluff

Juba Point

Caicos Conch Farm

West Caicos

Southwest Reef

◪ **Molasses Reef**

Providenciales
see detail map

3-**6**

Spanish Point

Highas Cay

North Caicos

Juniper Hole

Platico Point

◆ **North Caicos**

Middle Caicos

◆ **Middle Caicos**

Ocean Hole

Vine Point

Toll Crawl Point

C A I C O S   I S L A

CAICOS

BANK

The largest but least developed of the islands is Middle Caicos. It's 48 square mi (124 square km) but has only 300 residents and an extensive system of limestone caves.

0 |———————| 14 miles
0 |———————| 21 km

Little Ambergris Cay

Six Hil

Big So Bu

Camer

KEY

◪	*Dive Sites*
1	*Restaurants*
1	*Hotels*

SEAL CAYS

White Cay

Shot C

AMB

Only 10 of these 40 islands between the Bahamas and Haiti are inhabited. Divers and snorkelers can explore one of the world's longest coral reefs. Land-based pursuits don't get much more taxing than teeing off at Provo's Provo Golf Club, or sunset-watching from the seaside terrace of a laid-back resort.

GEOGRAPHICAL INFO

Though Providenciales is a major offshore banking center, sea creatures far outnumber humans in this archipelago of 40 islands, where the total population is a mere 25,000. From developed Provo to sleepy Grand Turk to sleepier South Caicos, the islands offer miles of undeveloped beaches, crystal-clear water, and laid-back luxury resorts.

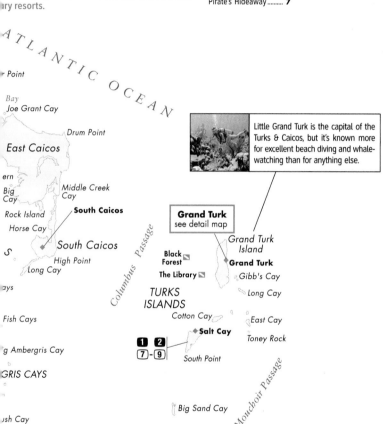

Little Grand Turk is the capital of the Turks & Caicos, but it's known more for excellent beach diving and whale-watching than for anything else.

25

TURKS & CAICOS ISLANDS

TOP 4 REASONS TO VISIT THE TURKS & CAICOS ISLANDS

1 Even on well-developed Provo, there are still miles of deserted beaches without any footprints or beach umbrellas in sight.

2 The third-largest coral reef system in the world is among the world's top dive sites.

3 Island-hopping beyond the beaten path will give you a feel of the past in the present.

4 Destination spas, penthouse suites, and exclusive villas and resorts make celebrity spotting a popular sport.

TURKS & CAICOS ISLANDS PLANNER

Island Activities

The vast majority of people come to the Turks & Caicos to relax and enjoy the clear, **turquoise water**.

The Turks & Caicos Islands are known for **luxurious hotels**, whether on a private island or on Provo itself.

The smaller islands provide a more-**relaxed environment** and substantially less development.

Provo has excellent **beaches**, particularly the long, soft beach along Grace Bay, where most of the island's hotel development has taken place. If you can believe it, some of the smaller, more-isolated islands in the chain have even better beaches.

Reefs are plentiful and are often close to shore, making **snorkeling** excellent. The **reef and wall diving** are among the best in the Caribbean.

The same reefs that draw colorful tropical fish draw big-game fish, so **deep-sea fishing** is also very good.

If you play **golf**, Provo has one of the Caribbean's finest courses.

Logistics

Getting to the Turks & Caicos: Several major airlines fly nonstop to Providenciales from the U.S.; you can also get connecting service via San Juan. If you are going to one of the smaller islands, you'll usually need to make a connection in Provo. All international flights arrive at Providenciales International Airport (PLS). There are smaller airports on Grand Turk (GDT), North Caicos (NCS), Middle Caicos (MDS), South Caicos (XSC), and Salt Cay (SLX). All have paved runways in good condition. Providenciales International Airport has modern, secure arrival and check-in services.

Hassle Factor: Low–High, depending on the island and your home airport.

Nonstops: Atlanta (Delta), Boston (American), Charlotte (USAirways), Dallas (American), Ft. Lauderdale (Spirit), Miami (American), New York–JFK (American), Philadelphia (USAirways).

On the Ground

You can find taxis at the airports, and most resorts provide pickup service as well. A trip between Provo's airport and most major hotels runs about $10 per person. On Grand Turk a trip from the airport to Cockburn Town is about $8; it's $8 to $15 to hotels outside town on Grand Turk. Transfers can cost more on the smaller islands, where gas is much more expensive.

Renting a Car: If you are staying on Provo, you may find it useful to have a car since the island is so large and the resorts so far-flung, if only for a few days of exploring or to get away from your hotel for dinner. On Grand Turk, you can rent a car, but you probably won't need to. Car- and jeep-rental rates average $35 to $80 per day on Provo, plus a $15 surcharge per rental as a government tax. Reserve well ahead of time during the peak winter season. Most agencies offer free mileage and airport pickup service. Several agencies—both locally owned and larger chains—operate on Provo.

Where to Stay

The Turks & Caicos can be a fairly expensive destination. Most hotels on Providenciales are fairly expensive, but there are some moderately priced options; most accommodations are condo-style, but not all resorts are family-friendly. You'll find several upscale properties on the outer islands—including the famous Parrot Cay—but the majority of places are smaller inns. What you give up in luxury, however, you gain back tenfold in island charm. Though the smaller islands are fairly isolated, that's arguably what makes them so attractive in the first place.

Resorts: Most of the resorts on Provo are upscale; many are condo-style, so at least you will have a well-furnished kitchen for breakfast and a few quick lunches. There are two all-inclusive resorts on Provo. A handful of other luxury resorts are on the smaller islands.

Small Inns: Aside from the exclusive, luxury resorts, most of the places on the outlying islands are smaller, modest inns with relatively few amenities. Some are devoted to diving.

Villas & Condos: Villas and condos are plentiful, particularly on Provo and usually represent a good value for families. However, you need to plan a few months in advance to get one of the better choices, less if you want to stay in a more-developed condo complex.

Hotel & Restaurant Prices

⇨*For information on hotel meal plans, see Accommodations in Caribbean Essentials.*

When to Go

High season in Turks & Caicos runs roughly from January through March, with the usual extra-high rates during the Christmas and New Year's holiday period. Several hotels on Provo offer shoulder season rates in April and May. During the off-season, rates are reduced substantially, as much as 40%.

There are three major festivals in the Turks & Caicos. In summer, big names play at the annual **Turks & Caicos Music and Cultural Festival** usually held in August.

In October, Provo is overrun with celebrities for the **Turks & Caicos International Film Festival**, with the movies shown on giant projection screens by the beach.

At the end of November, the **Turks & Caicos Conch Festival** offers native boat races, live music, and conch recipe competitions.

25

WHAT IT COSTS IN U.S. DOLLARS				
$$$$	**$$$**	**$$**	**$**	**¢**
Restaurants				
over $30	$20–$30	$12–$20	$8–$12	under $8
Hotels*				
over $350	$250–$350	$150–$250	$80–$150	under $80
Hotels**				
over $450	$350–$450	$250–$350	$125–$250	under $125

*EP, BP, CP **AI, FAP, MAP Restaurant prices are for a main course at dinner and include any taxes or service charges. Hotel prices are per night for a double room in high season, excluding taxes, service charges, and meal plans (except at all-inclusives).

By Ramona
Settle

WITH WATER SO TURQUOISE THAT it glows, you may find it difficult to stray far from the beach. You may find no need for museums, no desire to see ruins, or even read books. You may find yourself hypnotized by the many neon hues of blues. The Turks & Caicos have some of the most beautiful water in the world, so you can expect almost all of your activities here to be water-based. And the beaches are among the most incredible you will ever see. Don't be surprised if you wake up on your last morning and realize that you have never strayed far from the beach or those mesmerizing views.

A much-disputed legend has it that Columbus first discovered these islands in 1492. Despite being on the map for longer than most other island groups, the Turks & Caicos Islands (pronounced *kay*-kos) still remain part of the less-discovered Caribbean. More than 40 islands—only 8 inhabited—make up this self-governing British overseas territory that lies just 575 mi (862 km) southeast of Miami on the third-largest coral reef system in the world.

Although ivory-white, soft sandy beaches and breathtaking turquoise waters are shared among all the islands, the landscapes are a series of contrasts; from the dry, arid bush and scrub on the flat, coral islands of Grand Turk, Salt Cay, South Caicos, and Providenciales to the greener, foliage-rich undulating landscapes of Middle Caicos, North Caicos, Parrot Cay, and Pine Cay.

The political and historical capital island of the country is Grand Turk, but most of the tourism development, which consists primarily of boutique hotels and condo resorts, has occurred in Providenciales, thanks to the 12-mi (18-km) stretch of ivory sand that is Grace Bay. Once home to a population of around 500 people plus a few donkey carts, Provo has become a hub of activity, resorts, spas, restaurants, and water sports with a population of around 15,000. It's the temporary home for the majority of visitors who come to the Turks & Caicos.

Despite the fact that most visitors land and stay in Provo, the Turks & Caicos National Museum—predictably a stickler for tradition—is in Grand Turk. The museum tells the history of the islands that have all, at one time or another, been claimed by the French, Spanish, and British as well as many pirates, long before the predominately North American visitors discovered its shores.

Marks of the country's colonial past can be found in the wooden and stone, Bermudian-style clapboard houses—often wrapped in deep-red bougainvillea—that line the streets on the quiet islands of Grand Turk, Salt Cay, and South Caicos. Donkeys roam free in and around the salt ponds, which are a legacy from a time when residents of these island communities worked hard as both slaves and then laborers to rake salt (then known as "white gold") bound for the United States and Canada. In Salt Cay the remains of wooden windmills are now home to large osprey nests. In Grand Turk and South Caicos, the crystal-edge tidal ponds are regularly visited by flocks of rose-pink flamingos hungry for the shrimp to be found in the shallow, briny waters.

Sea Island cotton, believed to be the highest quality, was produced on the Loyalist .plantations in the Caicos Islands from the 1700s. The native cotton plants can still be seen dotted among the stone remains of former plantation houses in the more-fertile soils of Middle Caicos and North Caicos. Here communities in tiny settlements have retained age-old skills using fanner grasses, silver palms, and sisal to create exceptional straw baskets, bags, mats, and hats.

> ### WHERE WHEN HOW
>
> Check out ⊕ *www.wherewhen-how.com*, a terrific source with links to every place to stay, all the restaurants, excursions, and transportation. You can pick up the printed version of the magazine all around the island, or subscribe before you go so you know what do while in the Turks & Caicos.

In all, only 25,000 people live in the Turks & Caicos Islands; more than half are "Belongers," the term for the native population, mainly descended from African and Bermudian slaves who settled here beginning in the 1600s. The majority of residents work in tourism, fishing, and offshore finance, as the country is a haven for the overtaxed. Indeed, for residents and visitors, life in "TCI" is anything but taxing. But while most visitors come to do nothing—a specialty in the islands—this does not mean there's nothing to do.

25

THE CAICOS

PROVIDENCIALES

Passengers typically become oddly silent when their plane starts its descent, mesmerized by the shallow, crystal-clear turquoise waters of Chalk Sound National Park. This island, nicknamed Provo, was once called Blue Hills after the name of its first settlement. Just south of the airport and downtown area, Blue Hills still remains the closest thing you can get to a more-typical Caicos Island settlement on this, the most developed of the island chain. Most of the modern resorts, exquisite spas, water-sports operators, shops, business plazas, restaurants, bars, cafés, and the championship golf course are on or close by the 12-mi (18-km) stretch of Grace Bay beach. In spite of the ever-increasing number of taller and grander condominium resorts—either completed or under construction—it's still possible to find deserted stretches on this priceless, ivory-white shoreline. For guaranteed seclusion, rent a car and go explore the southern shores and western tip of the island, or set sail for a private island getaway on one of the many deserted cays nearby.

Progress and beauty come at a price: there is considerable construction on the island. No worry—it does not take away from the gorgeous beaches and wonderful dinners. Although you may start to believe that every road leads to a construction site (or is under construction itself), there are, happily, plenty of sections of beach where you can escape the din.

While you may be kept quite content enjoying the beachscape and top-notch amenities of Provo itself, it's also a great starting point for island-hopping tours by sea or by air as well as fishing and diving trips. Resurfaced roads should help you get around and make the most of the main tourism and sightseeing spots.

WHERE TO STAY

For approximate costs, see the dining and lodging price chart in the Turks & Caicos Planner, at the beginning of this chapter.

VILLA RENTALS   A popular option on Provo is renting a self-catering villa or private home. For the best villa selection, plan to make your reservations three to six months in advance.

Prestigious Properties (*Prestige Pl., Grace Bay* ☎*649/946–5355* ⊕*www. prestigiousproperties.com*) offers a wide selection of modest to magnificent villas in the Leeward, Grace Bay, and Turtle Cove areas of Providenciales. **T. C. Safari** (☎*649/941–5043* ⊕*www.tcsafari.tc*) has exclusive oceanfront properties in the beautiful and tranquil Sapodilla Bay–Chalk Sound neighborhood on Provo's southwest shores.

HOTELS &   🏨 **Amanyara.** If you need seclusion, peace, and tranquillity with a
RESORTS   zenlike atmosphere, this is your place. All accommodations are in pavil-
$$$$ ions, which are simply furnished with an Asian minimalist flair yet have such luxuries as TVs, DVD players, and surround-sound systems. A movie room and well-stocked library are among the few entertainment options, but small touches, such as a shoe rack at the beach and huggies to keep your bottled water cool, are welcome. No need to sign for anything here—the staff will always remember you by name. When it comes to dining, expect an Asian-influenced menu and very high prices; reports on the quality of food have been mixed. One thing is for certain; it's a long, pricey ride to other restaurants, not to mention excursions. This is a place to come if you are looking for peace and quiet in a remote location on a stunning beach. There is construction on-site, but you can't see it from the beach. A unique feature is that rates include the minibar (except spirits) and all long-distance phone calls. **Pros:** On one of the best beaches on Provo, resort is quiet and secluded. **Cons:** Isolated; far from restaurants, excursions, and other beaches. ✉*Northwest Point* ☎*649/941–8133* ⊕*www.amanresorts.com* ⇱*40 pavilions* ⌂*In-room: safe, refrigerator, DVD. In-hotel: 2 restaurants, room service, bar, tennis courts, pool, gym, spa, beachfront, diving, water sports, no elevator, airport shuttle* ☲*AE, MC, V* ⏐☉*EP.*

$$$$ 🏨 **Beaches Turks & Caicos Resort & Spa.** The largest resort in the Turks
☾   & Caicos Islands can satisfy families as eager to spend time apart as
★   together. Younger children and teenagers will appreciate a children's park, complete with video-game center, waterslides, a swim-up soda bar, and even a teen disco. Parents may prefer the extensive spa, pretty beach, and complimentary scuba diving. Rooms, suites, and cottage villas are decorated in standard tropical themes, but the resort's major draw is found outside the rooms, where there are numerous activities and a choice of dining options, from a 1950s-style diner to a Japanese restaurant. This is one of the company's top resorts, with a generally

helpful staff and excellent amenities. Butler service is included for the presidential and penthouse suites. In early 2009, look for the new Italian Village and one of the biggest water parks in the Caribbean to open. **Pros:** Great place for families, all-inclusive. **Cons:** With an all-inclusive plan you miss out on great restaurants, construction on the east side of the property. ⊠*Lower Bight Rd., Grace Bay* 🖷*649/946–8000 or 800/726–3257* ⊕*www.beaches.com* ⟿*359 rooms, 103 suites* ⌂*In-room: safe, dial-up. In-hotel: 9 restaurants, bars, tennis courts, pools, gym, spa, beachfront, diving, water sports, bicycles, no elevator (some buildings), concierge, children's programs (ages newborn–12), public Internet* ⊟*AE, MC, V* ⏱*AI.*

$$$$ 🖫**Grace Bay Club & Villas at Grace Bay Club.** This small and stylish resort
☪ retains a loyal following because of its helpful, attentive staff and aura
★ of unpretentious elegance. The architecture is reminiscent of Florence, with terra-cotta rooftops and a shaded courtyard, complete with fountain. Suites, all with sweeping sea views, have earthy tiles, luxurious white Egyptian cotton–covered beds, and Elemis toiletries. The ground-floor suites, fronted by large arched patios and lush azaleas, have a palatial feel and turquoise water views. New, ultraluxurious villas offer families a Grace Bay experience with a large pool, a bar and grill, and an impressive range of children's activities, including a bouncy castle in Kids Town, as well as kayaking trips and all sorts of "edutainment" to keep even teenagers well occupied. There are also cookies, of course. There is construction ongoing at Grace Bay Club Estates, so ask for a room on the Villas side of the property. **Pros:** Gorgeous pool and restaurant lounge areas with outdoor couches, daybeds, and fire pits. **Cons:** No children allowed at Anacaona restaurant, construction on two sides. ⏍*Box 128, Grace Bay* 🖷*649/946–5050 or 800/946–5757* ⊕*www.gracebayclub.com* ⟿*59 suites* ⌂*In-room: safe, kitchen, VCR (some), Ethernet, Wi-Fi. In-hotel: 2 restaurants, room service, bar, tennis courts, pools, spa, beachfront, water sports, bicycles, concierge, laundry facilities, laundry service, public Internet, public Wi-Fi, no children under 12 in some rooms* ⊟*AE, D, MC, V* ⏱*CP.*

$$$$ 🖫**Point Grace.** Provo's answer to Parrot Cay has attracted celebrity guests, including Donatella Versace. Asian-influenced rooftop domes blend with Romanesque stone pillars and wide stairways in this plush resort, which offers spacious beachfront suites and romantic cottages surrounding the centerpiece: a turquoise infinity pool with perfect views of the beach. Antique furnishings, four-poster beds, and art reproductions give a classic style to the rooms. The second-story cottage suites are especially romantic. Bleached-wood cottages, on the sand dune, house a thalassotherapy spa presided over by elegant French spa manager Edmonde Sidibé. Other highlights include the restaurants, particularly the beautiful Grace's Cottage. Honeymooners can arrange a transfer in an authentic London taxi. **Pros:** Relaxing environment, beautiful pool. **Cons:** Can be stuffy (signs around the pool remind you to be quiet). ⏍*Box 700, Grace Bay* 🖷*649/946–5096 or 888/924–7223* ⊕*www.pointgrace.com* ⟿*23 suites, 9 cottage suites, 2 villas* ⌂*In-room: safe, kitchen, VCR (some). In-hotel: 2 restaurants, room service, bars, pool, spa, beachfront, water sports, bicycles, no elevator (some buildings), concierge, laundry*

Providenciales

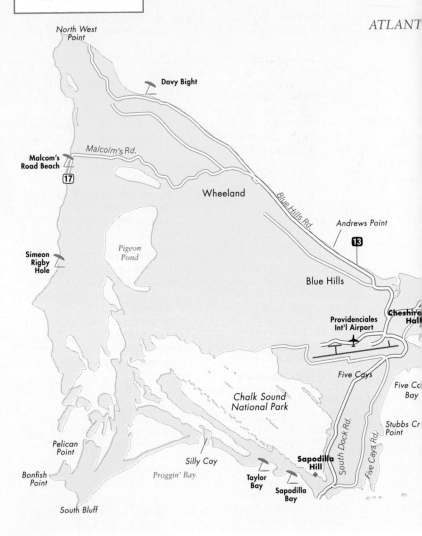

North West Point

Davy Bight

Malcolm's Rd.

Malcom's Road Beach

17

Wheeland

Blue Hills Rd.

Andrews Point

13

Simeon Rigby Hole

Pigeon Pond

Blue Hills

Providenciales Int'l Airport

Cheshire Hall

Five Cays

Five Cays Bay

Chalk Sound National Park

Stubbs Cr Point

Pelican Point

Silly Cay

South Dock Rd.

Five Cays Rd.

Bonfish Point

Proggin' Bay

Taylor Bay

Sapodilla Hill

Sapodilla Bay

South Bluff

ATLANT

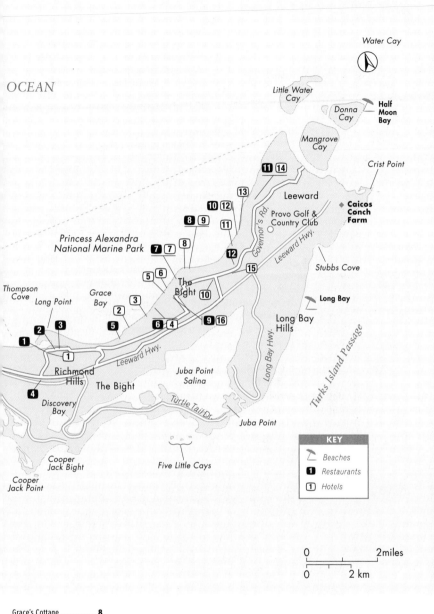

Water Cay

OCEAN

Little Water Cay

Donna Cay

Half Moon Bay

Mangrove Cay

Crist Point

Leeward

Provo Golf & Country Club

Caicos Conch Farm

Stubbs Cove

Princess Alexandra National Marine Park

Governor's Rd.

Leeward Hwy.

Long Bay

Thompson Cove

Long Point

Grace Bay

The Bight

Long Bay Hills

Richmond Hills

Leeward Hwy.

Juba Point Salina

Long Bay Hwy.

Turks Island Passage

Discovery Bay

The Bight

Turtle Tail Dr.

Juba Point

Cooper Jack Bight

Five Little Cays

Cooper Jack Point

KEY	
🔖	Beaches
1	Restaurants
1	Hotels

0		2 miles
0	2 km	

service, public Internet, no-smoking rooms ⊟*AE, D, MC, V* ⊘*Closed Sept.* ⊚*CP.*

$$$$ 🖫**Regent Palms.** High on luxury
☾ and glitz, this is a place to see and be seen. The infinity pool, one of the chicest in the Caribbean, has sun pods (round, white cushioned loungers), a swim-up bar, and iPods to borrow. Suites, which have colonial-style furnishings and luxurious bedding and appointments, have two or three bedrooms but can be subdivided to create one-bedroom suites and regular rooms (which will have only a kitchenette); all bedrooms have a separate terrace. One big plus for families is the washer and dryer in all but regular rooms. The Regent Hotels Group

REQUESTING ROOMS

Most of the resorts on Provo are composed of privately owned condos placed into the resort's rental pool when the owners are not present. Unlike at chain hotels and resorts, you cannot request a particular building, floor, or room unless you are a repeat visitor. If you fall in love with the condo, you can probably purchase it, or one that's similar. There are no taxes in T&C except for a onetime Stamp Duty tax—no property tax and no rental tax—which makes owning your own piece of paradise even more tempting.

has taken over management and has greatly improved the service. The spa is stunningly beautiful, offering every treatment imaginable; it certainly ranks among the best in the Caribbean. A new unique feature in the rooms is access to every radio statio in the world, so you can hear reports from back home while you're in paradise. **Pros:** Great people-watching, lively atmosphere, one of the best spas in the Caribbean. **Cons:** Some would say busy not lively, a little formal and stuffy (cover-ups are required when you go to the pool). ⊠*Grace Bay* ☎*649/946–8666* ⊕*www.regenthotels.com* ⇗*72 suites* ⚘*In-room: safe, kitchen (some), DVD, Wi-Fi. In-hotel: 2 restaurants, room service, bar, tennis court, pool, gym, spa, beachfront, water sports, concierge, children's programs (ages 4–12), laundry facilities, public Wi-Fi, airport shuttle* ⊟*AE, D, MC, V* ⊚*BP.*

$$$$ 🖫**The Somerset.** This luxury resort has the "wow" factor, starting with
Fodor's Choice the architecture, followed by the service, and ending in your luxuri-
★ ously appointed suite. What sets the Somerset apart is that it is also a comfortable place to stay that is more focused on your comfort and enjoyment than in attracting a celebrity clientele. A laid-back unpretentiousness means you don't have to dress up to go to the pool. Unmatched service makes you feel at home. A modern pool deck is equipped with a resistance pool and underwater speakers. The oversize suites are equipped with such extras as a plasma TV, an XBox system, a wine chiller, and Viking appliances, including a washer and dryer, so you don't need to pack heavily. It doesn't get better than this. **Pros:** The most beautiful architecture on Provo. **Cons:** Having to leave! ⊠*Princess Dr., Grace Bay* ☎*649/946–5900* ⊕*www.thesomerset.com* ⇗*53 suites* ⚘*In-room: safe, kitchen, DVD, Wi-Fi. In-hotel: restaurant, room service, bar, pool, gym, beachfront, water sports, bicycles, children's programs (3–16), public Wi-Fi, concierge, laundry facilities* ⊟*AE, MC, V* ⊚*CP.*

From Salt Glows to Thalassotherapy

A Turks Island Salt Glow, where the island's sea salt is mixed with gentle oils to exfoliate, smooth, and moisturize the skin, is just one of the treatments you can enjoy in one of the island spas. Being pampered spa-style has become as much a part of a Turks & Caicos vacation as sunning on the beach. Marine-based ingredients fit well with the Grace Bay backdrop at the Thalasso Spa at **Point Grace,** where massages take place in two simple, bleached-white cottages standing on the dune line, which means you have a spectacular view of the sea-blue hues if you manage to keep your eyes open. The Regent Spa at the **Regent Palms** offers individual treatments with a water feature by day, a fire feature at night. Their signature body scrub uses hand-crushed local conch shells

to smooth the skin. But the widest choice of Asian-inspired treatments (and the most-unforgettable scenery) can be found at the 6,000-square-foot Como Shambhala Spa at the **Parrot Cay Resort,** which has outdoor whirlpools and a central beech-wood lounge overlooking the shallow turquoise waters and mangroves. Provo also has a noteworthy day spa that's not in one of the Grace Bay resorts. Manager Terri Tapper of **Spa Tropique** (⌧ *Ports of Call, Grace Bay Rd., Grace Bay* ☎ *649/941–5720* ⊕ *www. spatropique.com*) blends Swedish, therapeutic, and reflexology massage techniques using oils made from natural plants and products produced locally and within the Caribbean region. The Turks Island Salt Glow has become one of her most popular treatments.

$$$$ 🏨 **Turks & Caicos Club.** On the quieter, western end of Grace Bay, this
★ intimate all-suites hotel is one of a handful with a gated entrance. The buildings are in a colonial style with lovely gingerbread trim. Though the resort aims for an aura of exclusivity, the staff is warm and friendly. Safari-themed suites, complete with raised four-poster beds and spacious balconies, are a definite plus to this quiet retreat. The rates include a full American breakfast. Check the Web site for unique packages, including one with a professional photographer. **Pros:** Incredible lush grounds, on one of the best stretches of Grace Bay beach, great snorkeling from the beach. **Cons:** Small bathrooms. ⌧ *West Grace Bay beach, Box 687, West Grace Bay* ☎ *649/946–5800 or 888/482–2582* ⊕ *www.turksandcaicosclub.com* ➭ *21 suites* ♿ *In-room: safe, DVD, Wi-Fi, kitchen, dial-up. In-hotel: restaurant, room service, bar, pool, gym, beachfront, water sports, bicycles, no elevator, laundry facilities, public Wi-Fi, airport shuttle* ⊟ *AE, MC, V* ⊘ *Closed Sept.* ⦿ *BP.*

$$$$ 🏨 **The Tuscany.** This luxury, gated condo complex at the end of Grace Bay beach is gorgeous. All the condos have three bedrooms with designer furnishings and spacious balconies with oceanfront views; each condo also has three baths and a laundry room, which makes sharing a breeze even if you're not family. Lined by palm trees, the pool has a Tuscan feel and is one of the most beautiful on Provo. One unique feature is guests have use of their own cell phones, along with preset numbers for restaurants and excursions, for use wherever they go during their stay. **Pros:** Luxurious, all condos with ocean views, beautiful pool. **Cons:**

No restaurant and far from the best restaurants, very expensive for self-catering. ⌂ *Box 623, Grace Bay* 🕾 *649/941–4667* ⊕ *www.the tuscanyresort.com* ⇌ *30 condos* ⛄ *In-room: kitchen. In-hotel: tennis court, pool, gym, beachfront, public Wi-Fi* ☰ *AE, MC, V* ⦾ *EP.*

$$$$ 🎟 **Villa Renaissance.** This is luxury for the self-catering tourist. Although it's not a full-service resort, guests do get daily maid service, afternoon tea or coffee at the Pavillion Bar, and a weekly manager's cocktail reception. There is no restaurant on-site, but the location puts you in walking distance to some of the island's best restaurants. The front desk is always willing to help with concierge service. There is a lighted tennis court, a fitness center, and bicycles for the active. The gorgeous suites have stunning balconies or patios facing the ocean. Resembling a small Tuscan village square, it is one of the most beautiful buildings on Provo. **Pros:** Luxury for less, one of the prettiest courtyards in Provo. **Cons:** No restaurant, not full-service resort. ⌂ *Box 592, Grace Bay* 🕾 *649/941– 5300 or 877/285–8764* ⊕ *www.villarenaissance.com* ⇌ *20 suites* ⛄ *In- room: safe, kitchen, DVD, dial-up. In-hotel: bar, pool, spa, beachfront, bicycles, laundry facilities* ☰ *AE, MC, V* ⦾ *EP.*

$$$–$$$$ 🎟 **The Alexandra.** All the comfortable, spacious rooms at this beach-
ⓒ   front condo resort have some type of ocean or pool view—no looking at parking lots here. Amenities and appointments are decidedly upscale: granite countertops, stainless-steel appliances, a washer and dryer, and feather-top pillows on the beds. With the friendliest service on the island, the staff will make you feel like family. At this writing, there is some construction at the back of the property, which has prompted the management to offer specials, and these can be some of the best deals on Provo. **Pros:** Luxury for less, all rooms have ocean views. **Cons:** Lots of construction in the vicinity, temporary reception gives a bad first impression. ⊠ *Princess Dr., Grace Bay* 🕾 *649/946– 5807 or 800/704–9424* ⊕ *www.alexandraresort.com* ⇌ *88 rooms* ⛄ *In-room: safe, kitchen (some), DVD, Wi-Fi. In-hotel: restaurant, bar, tennis courts, pool, gym, beachfront, water sports, laundry facilities.* ☰ *AE, D, MC, V* ⦾ *EP.*

$$$–$$$$ **Ocean Club Resorts.** Enormous locally painted pictures of hibiscus make
ⓒ   a striking first impression as you enter the reception area at one of the
★   island's most well-established condominium resorts. Regular shuttles run along the 0.5-mi (1-km) stretch of Grace Bay beach between two artfully landscaped properties, Ocean Club and Ocean Club West. Both resorts claim some of Provo's best amenities. Ocean Club has the advantage of a quieter location away from most of the development and is just a short walk from Provo Golf & Country Club. Ocean Club West has a larger pool with a swim-up bar. Management and service are superb, as are the special value packages offered throughout most of the year. Plenty of beach and pool toys make Ocean Club a good family option. **Pros:** Family-friendly resort with shuttles between the two shared properties. **Cons:** Both resorts are showing their age. ⌂ *Box 240, Grace Bay* 🕾 *649/946–5880 or 800/457–8787* ⊕ *www.ocean clubresorts.com* ⇌ *174 suites: 86 at Ocean Club, 88 at Ocean Club West* ⛄ *In-room: safe, kitchen (some), VCR (some), dial-up. In-hotel: 2 restaurants, bars, tennis court, pools, gym, spa, beachfront, diving,*

CLOSE UP

What Is a Potcake?

Potcakes are indigenous dogs of the Bahamas and Turks & Caicos Islands. Traditionally, the stray dogs would be fed from the leftover scraps of food that formed at the bottom of the pot; this is how they got their name. Much is being done these days to control the stray dog population. The TCSPCA and Potcake Place are two agencies working to adopt out the puppies. You can "travel with a cause" by adopting one of these gorgeous pups; they come with all the shots and all the papers required to bring them back home to the United States. Even if you don't adopt, you can help by volunteering as a carrier—bringing one back to its adopted family. Customs in the States is actually easier when you are bringing back a potcake! For more information on how you can help, check out the Web site for Potcake Place (⊕ www.potcakeplace.com).

25

water sports, no elevator, concierge, laundry facilities, public Internet, public Wi-Fi ⊟*AE, D, MC, V* ⊙*EP.*

$$$–$$$$ 🏨 **Royal West Indies Resort.** With a contemporary take on colonial archi-
★ tecture and the outdoor feel of a botanical garden, this unpretentious
resort has plenty of garden-view and beachfront studios and suites
for moderate self-catering budgets. Room 135 on the western corner
has the most dramatic ocean views. Right on Grace Bay beach, the
property has a small restaurant and bar for poolside cocktails and
dining. Ask at the reception desk for help and advice on where to
go explore. Special packages and free-night offers are available dur-
ing the low season. **Pros:** The best bang for the buck on Provo, on
one of the widest stretches of Grace Bay beach. **Cons:** Club Med next
door can be noisy, construction on the other side. ⌂*Box 482, Grace
Bay* ☎*649/946–5004 or 800/332–4203* ⊕*www.royalwestindies.com*
➾*99 suites* ⌃*In-room: safe, kitchen, VCR (some), Ethernet, dial-
up. In-hotel: restaurant, bar, pools, beachfront, water sports, bicycles,
no elevator, concierge, laundry facilities, laundry service, no-smoking
rooms* ⊟*AE, MC, V* ⊙*EP.*

$$$–$$$$ 🏨 **Sands at Grace Bay.** Spacious gardens and two pools are surrounded
ⓒ by six rather impersonal three-story buildings at this otherwise well-
appointed resort. Guests can expect friendly and helpful staff and
excellent amenities, including a spa, good-size fitness room, and a
beachside cabana restaurant called Hemingway's. Sparkling ocean
views from huge screened patios and floor-to-ceiling windows are best
in the oceanfront suites in Blocks 3 and 4, which are also closest to
the beach, restaurant, and pool. A complete renovation begun in 2007
has added a beautiful new lobby and made the rooms more luxurious.
Pros: One of the best places for families, central location to shops and
numerous restaurants. **Cons:** Renovation incomplete at this writing,
so not all rooms are updated yet. ⌂*Box 681, Grace Bay* ☎*649/941–
5199 or 877/777–2637* ⊕*www.thesandsresort.com* ➾*118 suites*
⌃*In-room: safe, kitchen (some), dial-up, Wi-Fi. In-hotel: restaurant,
bar, tennis court, pools, gym, spa, beachfront, water sports, bicycles,
no elevator (some buildings), concierge, laundry facilities, laundry ser-*

vice, public Internet, no-smoking rooms, some pets allowed ☰*AE, MC, V* ⦿*EP.*

$$$ ⌨ **Club Med Turkoise.** Guests still fly in from the United States, Europe, and Canada to enjoy the scuba diving, windsurfing, and waterskiing on the turquoise waters at the doorsteps of the area's first major resort. Rooms in the village are basic and set in small, colorful bungalows that were renovated in 2007. In contrast to the otherwise tranquil Grace Bay resorts, this energetic property has a vibrant party atmosphere, nightly entertainment, and even a flying trapeze, catering primarily to fun-loving singles and couples. **Pros:** All-inclusive, active. **Cons:** Although the rooms have been updated, the grounds are showing their age. ⊠*Grace Bay* ☎*649/946–5500 or 888/932–2582* ⊕*www.clubmed.com* ⇩*293 rooms* ♿*In-hotel: 2 restaurants, bars, tennis courts, pool, gym, beachfront, diving, water sports, bicycles, no elevator, laundry service, public Internet, no kids under 18* ☰*AE, D, MC, V* ⦿*AI.*

$$ ⌨ **Caribbean Paradise Inn.** Not far from Grace Bay beach—but tucked away inland about a 10-minute walk from the beach—this two-story bed-and-breakfast has terra-cotta walls and cobalt-blue trimmings. If you get to know manager Jean-Luc Bohic, you can sometimes persuade him to prepare a barbecue. Rooms are smaller than the usual Provo offerings and are simply decorated with balconies overlooking the palm-fringed pool. **Pros:** Pay less by staying a block from the beach. **Cons:** Front desk not always manned. ⌂*Box 673, Grace Bay* ☎*649/946–5020* ⊕*www.paradise.tc* ⇩*16 rooms* ♿*In-room: safe, Wi-Fi, kitchen (some). In-hotel: bar, pool, no elevator, public Internet, no-smoking rooms* ☰*AE, MC, V* ⦿*CP.*

$–$$ ⌨ **Sibonné.** Dwarfed by most of the nearby resorts, the smallest hotel on Grace Bay beach has snug (by Provo's spacious standards) but pleasant rooms with Bermuda-style balconies and a completely circular but tiny pool. Of course, the pool is hardly used because the property is right on the beach. Rooms on the second floor have airy, vaulted ceilings; downstairs rooms have views of and access to the attractively planted courtyard garden, replete with palms, yellow elder, and exotic birdlife. The popular beachfront Bay Bistro serves breakfast, lunch, and dinner. Book early to get one of the two simple value rooms or the beachfront apartment, complete with four-poster bed, which is four steps from the beach; all three are usually reserved months in advance. **Pros:** Closest property to the beach, the island's best bargain on the beach. **Cons:** Pool is small and dated. ⊠*Princess Dr., Box 144, Grace Bay* ☎*649/946–5547 or 800/528–1905* ⊕*www.sibonne.com* ⇩*29 rooms, 1 apartment* ♿*In-room: safe, dial-up. In-hotel: restaurant, bar, pool, beachfront, water sports, bicycles, laundry service* ☰*AE, MC, V* ⦿*CP.*

$–$$ ⌨ **Turtle Cove Inn.** This pleasant two-story inn offers affordable and comfortable lodging in Turtle Cove Marina. All rooms have either a private balcony or patio overlooking the lush tropical gardens and pool or the marina. Besides the dockside Aqua Bar and Terrace, there's also a souvenir shop and liquor store. The inn is ideally situated for divers looking to roll from their beds into the ocean. **Pros:** Very reasonable prices for Provo, nice marina views, popular and inexpensive restaurant. **Cons:** Not on the beach, requires a car to get around. ⊠*Turtle*

Cove Marina, Box 131, Turtle Cove ☎*649/946–4203 or 800/887–0477* ⊕*www.turtlecoveinn.com* ➫*28 rooms, 2 suites* ⚐*In-room: safe, dial-up, refrigerator. In-hotel: restaurant, bar, pool, bicycles, no elevator, no-smoking rooms* ⊟*AE, D, MC, V* Ⓞ|*EP.*

WHERE TO EAT

There are more than 50 restaurants on Provo, from casual to elegant, with cuisine from Asian to European (and everything in between). You can spot the islands' own Caribbean influence no matter where you go, exhibited in fresh seafood specials, colorful presentations, and a tangy dose of spice. Pick up a free copy of *Where When How's Dinning Guide* magazine, which you will find all over the island; it contains menus, Web sites, and pictures of all the restaurants.

For approximate costs, see the dining and lodging price chart in the Turks & Caicos Planner, at the beginning of this chapter.

CARIBBEAN
$$–$$$
Ⓒ

✕ **Simba.** Fishbowl-size glassware is all part of the charm at this larger-than-life, safari-themed poolside restaurant at the quieter end of Grace Bay. For the price, presentation of the Caribbean-inspired dishes with fruity twists like the grouper with curry and mango sauce is above expectations. A plus: this is one of just a few places with indoor, air-conditioned seating, but you need a car to get here (unless staying at theTurks & Caicos Club). ⊠*Turks & Caicos Club, West Grace Bay* ☎*649/946–5888* ⚐*Reservations essential* ⊟*AE, D, MC, V* ⓄNo dinner Wed.

$–$$$
✕ **Da Conch Shack.** An institution in Provo for many years, this brightly colored beach shack is justifiably famous for its conch and seafood. The legendary specialty, conch, is fished freshly out of the shallows and either cooked, spiced, cracked, or fried to absolute perfection. On Friday nights, you can dance in the sand after dinner. This is freshest conch anywhere on the island, as the staff dive for it only after you've placed your order, but if you don't like seafood, there are not many other choices. ⊠*Blue Hills* ⊟*No credit cards* ⓄNo lunch.

DELI
¢–$
✕ **Angela's Top o' the Cove New York Style Delicatessen.** Order deli sandwiches, salads, and enticingly rich desserts and freshly baked pastries at this island institution on Leeward Highway, just south of Turtle Cove. From the deli case you can buy the fixings for a picnic; the shelves are stocked with an eclectic selection of fancy foodstuffs, as well as beer and wine. It's open at 6:30 AM for a busy trade in coffees, cappuccinos, and frappaccinos. This is the best cheesesteak you'll ever have outside Philly, but the location isn't in the heart of where most tourists are staying (it's worth the drive, though). ⊠*Leeward Hwy., Turtle Cove* ☎*649/946–4694* ⊟*AE, MC, V* ⓄNo dinner.

ECLECTIC
$$$$
Fodor's Choice
★
✕ **Coyaba Restaurant.** Located behind Grace Bay Club and next to Caribbean Paradise Inn, this posh eatery serves nostalgic favorites with tempting twists in conversation-piece crockery and in a palm-fringed setting. Chef Paul Newman uses his culinary expertise for the daily-changing main courses, which include exquisitely presented dishes such as crispy whole yellow snapper fried in Thai spices. To minimize any possible pretension, he keeps the resident expat crowd happy with tra-

25

ditional favorites like lemon meringue pie, albeit with his own tropical twist. Don't skip dessert; Paul makes the most incredible chocolate fondant you will ever have. The service is seamless. ⊠ *Off Grace Bay Rd., beside Caribbean Paradise Inn, Grace Bay* ☎ *649/946–5186* ⚖ *Reservations essential* ☰ *AE, MC, V* ☯ *Closed Tues. No lunch.*

$$$$ ✕**Grace's Cottage.** At one of the prettiest dining settings on Provo, tables
★ are artfully set under wrought-iron cottage-style gazebos and around the wraparound verandah, which skirts the gingerbread-covered main building. In addition to such tangy and exciting entrées as panfried red snapper served with roasted pepper sauce or melt-in-your-mouth grilled beef tenderloin served with truffle-scented mashed potatoes, the soufflés are well worth the 15-minute wait and the top-tier price tag. Portions are small, but the quality is amazing. Service is impeccable (ladies are provided a small stool so that their purse is not on the ground. ⊠ *Point Grace, Grace Bay* ☎ *649/946–5096* ⚖ *Reservations essential* ☰ *D, MC, V* ☯ *No lunch.*

$$$–$$$$ ✕**Anacaona.** At the Grace Bay Club, this palapa-shaded restaurant has
★ become a favorite of the country's chief minister. But despite the regular presence of government bigwigs, the restaurant continues to offer a memorable dining experience minus the tie, the air-conditioning, and the attitude. Start with a bottle of fine wine; then enjoy the light and healthy Mediterranean-influenced cuisine. The kitchen utilizes the island's bountiful seafood and fresh produce. Oil lamps on the tables, gently revolving ceiling fans, and the murmur of the trade winds add to the Eden-like environment. The entrancing ocean view and the careful service make it an ideal choice when you want to be pampered. Just added: the world's first Infinity Bar, which seems to spill right into the ocean. Children under 12 are not allowed. Long pants and collared shirts are required. ⊠ *Grace Bay Club, Grace Bay* ☎ *649/946–5050* ⚖ *Reservations essential* ☰ *AE, D, MC, V.*

$$$–$$$$ ✕**Bay Bistro.** You simply can't eat any closer to the beach than here,
☻ the only restaurant in all of Provo that is built directly on the sand. Although service can be slow, the food and setting are excellent. You dine on a covered porch surrounded by palm trees and will be able to hear the waves lapping even after dark. The oven-roasted chicken is the best on the island. Junior, the best bartender on the island, can bring your drink balanced on the top of his head if he's not too busy. Brunch on weekends is very popular. Lines can be long if you don't have a reservation. ⊠ *Sibonné, Princess Dr., Grace Bay* ☎ *649/946–5396* ☰ *AE, MC, V* ☯ *No dinner Mon.*

$$$–$$$$ ✕**O'Soleil.** At the Somerset, this is one of the few indoor restaurants on Provo. White-on-white decor under vaulted ceilings give it a Miami-chic ambience. The executive chef uses mixed international influences, everything from Caribbean to Asian to European in his dishes. Ask for simpler off-the-menu options for the children. Sunday brunch, when they have it, is the best anywhere, but it's not offered every weekend (call to confirm). ⊠ *The Somerset, Princess Dr., Grace Bay* ☎ *649/946–5900* ☰ *AE, D, MC, V.*

$$–$$$$ ✕**Gecko Grille.** You can eat indoors surrounded by giant, painted
☻ banana-leaf murals of camouflaged geckos or out on the garden patio,

where the trees are interwoven with tiny twinkling lights. Creative "Floribbean" fare combines native specialties with exotic fruits and zesty island spices and includes Black Angus steaks grilled to perfection. Pecan-encrusted grouper is a longtime menu favorite. Service is among the friendliest on Provo. Wear bug spray at night if sitting outdoors. ⊠ *Ocean Club, Grace Bay* ☎ *649/946–5885* ⊟ *AE, D, MC, V* ☉ *Closed Mon.*

$$$ ✕ **Caicos Café.** There's a pervasive air of celebration on the tree-shaded terrace of this popular eatery. Choose from grilled seafood, steak, lamb, or chicken served hot off the outdoor barbecue. Owner-chef Pierrik Marziou adds a French accent to his appetizers, salads, and homemade desserts, along with an outstanding collection of fine French wines. Wear bug spray at night. ⊠ *Grace Bay* ☎ *649/946–5278* ⊟ *AE, D, MC, V* ☉ *Closed Sun.*

$$$ ✕ **Magnolia Wine Bar & Restaurant.** Restaurateurs since the early 1990s,
★ hands-on owners Gianni and Tracey Caporuscio make success seem simple. Expect well-prepared, uncomplicated choices that range from European to Asian to Caribbean. The atmosphere is romantic, the presentations attractive, and the service careful. It's easy to see why the Caporuscios have a loyal following. The adjoining wine bar includes a handpicked list of specialty wines, which can be ordered by the glass. The marine setting is a great place to watch the sunset. ⊠ *Miramar Resort, Turtle Cove* ☎ *649/941–5108* ⊟ *AE, D, MC, V* ☉ *Closed Mon. No lunch.*

ITALIAN ✕ **Baci Ristorante.** Aromas redolent of the Mediterranean waft from the
$$–$$$ open kitchen as you enter this intimate eatery east of Turtle Cove. Outdoor seating is on a romantic canal-front patio, one of the lovelier settings on Provo. The menu offers a small but varied selection of Italian dishes. Veal is prominent on the menu, but main courses also include pasta, chicken, fish, and brick-oven pizzas. House wines are personally selected by the owners and complement the tasteful wine list. Try the tiramisu for dessert with a flavored coffee drink. Wear bug spray at night. ⊠ *Harbour Town, Turtle Cove* ☎ *649/941–3044* ⊟ *AE, MC, V.*

SEAFOOD ✕ **Aqua Bar & Terrace.** This popular restaurant on the grounds of the Tur-
$$–$$$$ tle Cove Inn has an inviting waterfront dining deck, and it just keeps
☺ getting better. Leaning heavily in the direction of locally caught seafood and farm-raised conch, the menu includes longtime favorites like wahoo sushi, pecan-encrusted conch fillets, and grilled fish served with flavorful sauces. A selection of more-casual entrées, including salads and burgers, appeals to the budget-conscious. There are plenty of child-friendly menu options. Bring bug spray, as you're close to the water. ⊠ *Turtle Cove Inn, Turtle Cove Marina, Turtle Cove* ☎ *649/946–4763* ⊟ *AE, MC, V.*

BEACHES

★ **Grace Bay** (⊠ *Grace Bay, on north shore*), a 12-mi (18-km) sweeping stretch of ivory-white, powder-soft sand on Provo's north coast is simply breathtaking and home to migrating starfish as well as shallow snorkeling trails. The majority of Provo's beachfront resorts are along

25

★ this shore. **Half Moon Bay** (⊠ *15 mins from Leeward Marina, between Pine Cay and Water Cay, accessible only by boat*) is a natural ribbon of sand linking two uninhabited cays; it's only inches above the sparkling turquoise waters and one of the most gorgeous beaches on the island. It's only a short boat ride away from Provo, and most of the island's tour companies run excursions there or simply offer a beach drop-off, including Silverdeep, J&B Tours, and Caicos Dream Tours (⇨ *Boat-*

Fodors Choice *ing & Sailing, below)*. **Malcolm's Beach** (⊠ *Malcolm's Beach Rd., keep*
★ *straight after passing Amanyara turn-off*) is one of the most stunning beaches you'll ever see, but you'll need a high-clearance vehicle to reach it. Bring your own food and drinks since there are no facilities or food service unless you have made an arrangement with Amanyara to eat at the resort. The best of the many secluded beaches and pristine sands around Provo can be found at **Sapodilla Bay** (⊠ *North of South Dock, at end of South Dock Rd.*), a peaceful 0.25-mi (0.5-km) cove protected by Sapodilla Hill, where calm waves lap against the soft sand, and yachts and small boats move with the gentle tide.

SPORTS & THE OUTDOORS

BICYCLING   Most hotels have bicycles available, or it's possible to rent one from an independent company. You can rent mountain bikes at **Scooter Bob's** (⊠ *Turtle Cove Marina, Turtle Cove* ☎ 649/946–4684 ⊕ *www.provo. net/scooter*) for $15 a day.

BOATING &   Provo's calm, reef-protected seas combine with constant easterly trade winds
SAILING   for excellent sailing conditions. Several multihull vessels offer charters with snorkeling stops, food and beverage service, and sunset vistas. Prices range from $39 for group trips to $600 or more for private charters.

☾ **Caicos Dream Tours** (☎ 649/243–3560 ⊕ *www.caicosdreamtours.com*) offers several different snorkeling trips, including one that has you diving for conch before lunch on a gorgeous beach. The company also offers private charters. For sightseeing below the waves, try the semi-submarine operated by **Caicos Tours** (⊠ *Turtle Cove Marina, Turtle Cove* ☎ 649/231–0006 ⊕ *www.caicostours.com*). You can stay dry within the small, lower observatory as it glides along on a one-hour tour of the reef, with large viewing windows on either side. The trip costs $39. **J&B Tours** (☎ 649/946–5047 ⊕ *www.jbtours.com*) offers half- and full-day excursions to other islands that make for a great day on the beach and in the water. **Sail Provo** (☎ 649/946–4783 ⊕ *www.sailprovo.com*) runs 52-foot and 48-foot catamarans on scheduled half-day, full-day, sunset, and kid-friendly glowworm cruises, where underwater creatures light up the sea's surface for several days after each full moon. **Silverdeep** (☎ 649/946–5612 ⊕ *www.silverdeep.com*) sailing trips include time for snorkeling and beachcombing at a secluded beach. The *Atabeyra,* run by **Sun Charters** (☎ 649/941–5363 ⊕ *www.suncharters.tc*), is a retired rumrunner and the choice of residents for special events.

DIVING   The island's many shallow reefs offer excellent and exciting snorkel-
Fodors Choice   ing relatively close to shore. Try **Smith's Reef,** over Bridge Road east of
★ Turtle Cove.

Scuba diving in the crystalline waters surrounding the islands ranks among the best in the Caribbean. The reef and wall drop-offs thrive with bright, unbroken coral formations and lavish numbers of fish and marine life. Mimicking the idyllic climate, waters are warm all year, averaging 76°F to 78°F in winter and 82°F to 84°F in summer. With minimal rainfall and soil runoff, visibility is usually good and frequently superb, ranging from 60 feet to more than 150 feet. An extensive system of marine national parks and boat moorings, combined with an ecoconscious mind-set among dive operators, contributes to an uncommonly pristine underwater environment.

Dive operators in Provo regularly visit sites at **Grace Bay** and **Pine Cay** for spur-and-groove coral formations and bustling reef diving. They make the longer journey to the dramatic walls at **North West Point** and **West Caicos** depending on weather conditions. Instruction from the major diving agencies is available for all levels and certifications, even technical diving. An average one-tank dive costs $45; a two-tank dive, $90. There are also two live-aboard dive boats available for charter working out of Provo.

☺ With a certified marine biologist on staff, **Big Blue Unlimited** (⊠ *Leeward Marina, Leeward* ☎ *649/946–5034* ⊕ *www.bigblue.tc*) specializes in ecofriendly diving adventures, including special trips for kids involving kayaking through the mangroves or walking along nature trails. It also offers Nitrox and Trimix. **Caicos Adventures** (⊠ *La Petite Pl., Grace Bay* ☎ *649/941–3346* ⊕ *www.tcidiving.com*), run by friendly Frenchman Fifi Kuntz, offers daily trips to West Caicos, French Cay, and Molasses Reef. **Dive Provo** (⊠ *Ports of Call, Grace Bay* ☎ *649/946–5040 or 800/234–7768* ⊕ *www.diveprovo.com*) is a PADI five-star operation that runs daily one- and two-tank dives to popular Grace Bay sites. **Provo Turtle Divers** (⊠ *Turtle Cove Marina, Turtle Cove* ☎ *649/946–4232 or 800/833–1341* ⊕ *www.provoturtledivers.com*), which also operates satellite locations at the Ocean Club and Ocean Club West, has been on Provo since the 1970s. The staff is friendly, knowledgeable, and unpretentious. The *Turks & Caicos Aggressor II* (☎ *800/348–2628* ⊕ *www. turksandcaicosaggressor.com*), a live-aboard dive boat, plies the islands' pristine sites with weekly charters from Turtle Cove Marina.

FISHING   The islands' fertile waters are great for angling—anything from bottom-and reef-fishing (most likely to produce plenty of bites and a large catch) to bonefishing and deep-sea fishing (among the finest in the Caribbean). Each July the Caicos Classic Catch & Release Tournament attracts anglers from across the islands and the United States who compete to catch the biggest Atlantic blue marlin, tuna, or wahoo. For any fishing activity, you are required to purchase a $15 visitor's fishing license; operators generally furnish all equipment, drinks, and snacks. Prices range from $100 to $375, depending on the length of trip and size of boat. For deep-sea fishing trips in search of marlin, sailfish, wahoo, tuna, barracuda, and shark, look up **Gwendolyn Fishing Charters** (⊠ *Turtle Cove Marina, Turtle Cove* ☎ *649/946–5321* ⊕ *www.fishtci.com*). You can rent a boat with a captain for a half- or full-day of bottom- or bonefishing through **J&B Tours** (⊠ *Leeward Marina, Leeward* ☎ *649/946–5047*

Diving the Turks & Caicos Islands

CLOSE UP

Scuba diving was the original water sport to draw visitors to the Turks & Caicos Islands in the 1970s. Aficionados are still drawn by the abundant marine life, including humpback whales in winter, sparkling clean waters, warm and calm seas, and the coral walls and reefs around the islands. Diving in the Turks & Caicos—especially off Grand Turk, South Caicos, and Salt Cay—is still considered among the best in the world.

Off Providenciales, dive sites are along the north shore's barrier reef. Most sites can be reached in anywhere from 10 minutes to 1½ hours. Dive sites feature spur-and-groove coral formations atop a coral-covered slope. Popular stops like **Aquarium, Pinnacles,** and **Grouper Hole** have large schools of fish, turtles, nurse sharks,

and gray reef sharks. From the south side dive boats go to **French Cay, West Caicos, South West Reef,** and **Northwest Point.** Known for typically calm conditions and clear water, the West Caicos Marine National Park is a favorite stop. The area has dramatic walls and marine life, including sharks, eagle rays, and octopus, with large stands of pillar coral and huge barrel sponges.

Off Grand Turk, the 7,000-foot coral wall **drop-off** is actually within swimming distance of the beach. Buoyed sites along the wall have swim-through tunnels, cascading sand chutes, imposing coral pinnacles, dizzying vertical drops, and undercuts where the wall goes beyond the vertical and fades beneath the reef.

⊕*www.jbtours.com*). Capt. Arthur Dean at **Silverdeep** (⊠*Leeward Marina, Leeward* ☎649/946–5612 ⊕*www.silverdeep.com*) is said to be among the Caribbean's finest bonefishing guides.

GOLF   The par-72, 18-hole championship course at **Provo Golf & Country Club**

Fodor'sChoice (⊠*Governor's Rd., Grace Bay* ☎649/946–5991 ⊕*www.provogolf-*

★   *club.com*) is a combination of lush greens and fairways, rugged limestone outcroppings, and freshwater lakes and is ranked among the Caribbean's top courses. Fees are $160 for 18 holes with shared cart. Premium golf clubs are available. **Turks & Caicos Miniature Golf** (⊠*Long Bay Rd., Leeward* ☎649/231–4653) is open every day and even offers a free shuttle service to most Grace Bay hotels. A round costs $15, and there is an on-site bar and grill where you can eat after your golf game.

HORSEBACK   Provo's long beaches and secluded lanes are ideal for trail rides on

RIDING   horseback. **Provo Ponies** (☎649/946–5252 ⊕*www.provo.net/provo ponies*) offers morning and afternoon rides for all levels of experience. A 45-minute ride costs $45; an 80-minute ride is $65. The rates include transportation from all major hotels.

PARASAILING   A 15-minute parasailing flight over Grace Bay is available for $70 (single) or $120 (tandem) from **Captain Marvin's Watersports** (☎649/231–0643), who will pick you up at your hotel for your flight. The views as you soar over the bite-shape Grace Bay area, with spectacular views of the barrier reef, are truly unforgettable.

TENNIS You can rent equipment at **Provo Golf & Country Club** (⊠ *Grace Bay* ☎ *649/946–5991* ⊕ *www.provogolfclub.com*) and play on the two lighted courts, which are among the island's best courts. Nonmembers can play until 5 PM for $10 per hour (reservation required).

WINDSURFING Windsurfers find the calm, turquoise water of Grace Bay ideal. **Windsurfing Provo** (⊠ *Ocean Club, Grace Bay* ☎ *649/946–5649* ⊠ *Ocean Club West, Grace Bay* ☎ *649/231–1687* ⊕ *www.windsurfingprovo. tc*) rents kayaks, motorboats, Windsurfers, and Hobie Cats and offers windsurfing instruction.

SHOPPING

There are several main shopping areas in Provo: Grace Bay has the newer Saltmills complex and La Petite Place retail plaza, the new Regent Village, as well as the original Ports of Call shopping village. Two markets on the beach near the Ocean Club and the Beaches Turks & Caicos Resort & Spa allow for barefooted shopping. Handwoven straw baskets and hats, polished conch-shell crafts, paintings, wood carvings, model sailboats, handmade dolls, and metalwork are crafts native to the islands and nearby Haiti. The natural surroundings have inspired local and international artists to paint, sculpt, print, craft, and photograph; most of their creations are on sale in Providenciales.

★ **Anna's Art Gallery & Studio** (⊠ *The Saltmills, Grace Bay* ☎ *449/231–3293*) sells original artworks, silk-screen paintings, sculptures, and handmade sea-glass jewelry. **ArtProvo** (⊠ *Regent Village, Grace Bay* ☎ *649/941–4545*) is the island's largest gallery of designer wall art; also shown are native crafts, jewelry, handblown glass, candles, and

★ other gift items. **Bamboo Gallery** (⊠ *Leeward Hwy., The Market Place* ☎🖶 *649/946–4748*) sells Caribbean art, from vivid Haitian paintings to wood carvings and local metal sculptures, with the added benefit that artists are usually on hand to describe their works. **Caicos Wear Boutique** (⊠ *La Petite Pl., Grace Bay Rd., Grace Bay* ☎ *649/941–3346*) is filled with casual resort wear, including Caribbean-print shirts, swimsuits from Brazil, sandals, beach jewelry, and gifts. **Greensleeves** (⊠ *Central Sq., Leeward Hwy., Turtle Cove* ☎🖶 *649/946–4147*) offers paintings and pottery by local artists, baskets, jewelry, and sisal mats and bags. **Royal Jewels** (⊠ *Providenciales International Airport* ☎ *649/941–4513* ⊠ *Arch Plaza* ☎ *649/946–4699* ⊠ *Beaches Turks & Caicos Resort & Spa, Grace Bay* ☎ *649/946–8285* ⊠ *Club Med Turkoise, Grace Bay* ☎ *649/946–5602*) sells gold and other jewelry, designer watches, perfumes, fine leather goods, and cameras—all duty-free—at several outlets. If you need to supplement your beach-reading stock or are looking ☪ for island-specific materials, visit the **Unicorn Bookstore** (⊠ *In front of*

★ *Graceway IGA Mall, Leeward Hwy., Grace Bay* ☎ *649/941–5458*) for a wide assortment of books and magazines, lots of information and guides about the Turks & Caicos Islands and the Caribbean, and a large children's section with crafts, games, and art supplies.

For a large selection of duty-free liquor, visit **Discount Liquors** (⊠ *Leeward Hwy., east of Suzie Turn Rd.* ☎ *649/946–4536*). Including a large fresh-produce section, bakery, gourmet deli, and extensive meat counter,

25

Graceway IGA Supermarket (⊠ *Leeward Hwy., Grace Bay* ☎ 649/941–5000), Provo's largest, is likely to have what you're looking for. Be prepared for sticker shock, as prices are much higher than you would expect at home. Besides having a licensed pharmacist on duty, **Lockland Trading Co.** (⊠ *Neptune Plaza, Grace Bay* ☎ 649/946–8242) sells flavored coffees, snacks, ice cream, and a selection of souvenirs.

NIGHTLIFE

While Provo is not known for its nightlife, there's still some fun to be found after dark. On Friday nights you can start off by dancing in the sand at Da Conch Shack *(⇨ Where to Eat, above)* followed by live bands at Calico Jack's. Thursday-night and Saturday-night hot spots include Danny Buoy's. On Saturday nights at Turks & Caicos Miniature Golf you can play a round, sing karaoke, and dance the night away all in one night (⇨ *Golf, above*). Keep abreast of events and specials by checking **TCI eNews** (⊕ *www.tcienews.com*).

Residents and tourists alike flock to the **BET Soundstage & Gaming Lounge** (⊠ *Leeward Hwy., Grace Bay* ☎ 649/941–4318) for video lottery games, live music and other entertainment, a casino, and a late-night disco almost every night. **Bonnie's** (⊠ *Lower Bight Rd., Grace Bay* ☎ 649/941–8452) is a favorite local spot for sports events, movie nights, and endless happy-hour specials. On Friday nights you can find a local band and lively crowd at **Calico Jack's Restaurant & Bar** (⊠ *Ports of Call, Grace Bay* ☎ 649/946–5129). The new **Casablanca Casino** (⊠ *Grace Bay Rd., Grace Bay* ☎ 649/941–3737) has brought slots, blackjack, American roulette, poker, craps, and baccarat back to Provo. Open from 7 PM until 5 AM, this is the last stop for the night. Grace Bay Club has introduced the new Infinity Bar, the only one of its kind in the world, which gives the impression it goes directly into the ocean. A popular gathering spot for locals to shoot pool, play darts, slam dominoes, and catch up on gossip is **Club Sodax Sports Bar** (⊠ *Leeward Hwy., Grace Bay* ☎ 649/941–4540). You won't go hungry with snacks such as conch and fish fingers, jerk pork, and typical native dishes. **Danny Buoy's** (⊠ *Grace Bay Rd., Grace Bay* ✛ *Across from Carpe Diem Residences* ☎ 649/946–5921) is a popular Irish pub.

EXPLORING PROVIDENCIALES

☺ **Caicos Conch Farm.** On the northeast tip of Provo, this is a major mariculture operation, where the mollusks are farmed commercially (more than 3 million conch are here). Guided tours are available; call to confirm times. The small gift shop sells conch-related souvenirs, and the world's only pet conchs, Sally and Jerry, seem more than happy to come out of their shells. ⊠ *Leeward-Going-Through, Leeward* ☎ 649/946–5330 ⊕ *www.caicosconchfarm.com* ☐ *$6* ☉ *Mon.–Sat. 9–4.*

Cheshire Hall. Standing eerily just west of downtown Provo are the remains of a circa-1700 cotton plantation owned by Loyalist Thomas Stubbs. A trail weaves through the ruins, where interpretive signs tell the story of the island's doomed cotton industry. A variety of local plants are also identified. To visit, you must arrange for a tour through the Turks & Caicos National Trust. The lack of context can be disappointing for history buffs; a visit to North Caicos Wades Green Plantation or the Turks & Caicos National Museum could well prove a better fit. ⊠*Near downtown Providenciales* ☎*649/941–5710 for National Trust* ⊕*www.turksandcaicos.tc/nationaltrust* ⊠*$5* ⊙*Daily, by appointment.*

ⓒ **Sapodilla Hill.** On this cliff overlooking the secluded Sapodilla Bay, you can discover rocks carved with the names of shipwrecked sailors and dignitaries from TCI maritime and colonial past. The less adventurous can see molds of the carvings at Provo's International Airport. ⊠*Off South Dock Rd., west of South Dock.*

LITTLE WATER CAY

ⓒ
★ This small, uninhabited cay is a protected area under the Turks & Caicos National Trust. On these 150 acres are two trails, small lakes, red mangroves, and an abundance of native plants. Boardwalks protect the ground, and interpretive signs explain the habitat. The cay is home to about 2,000 rare, endangered rock iguanas. Experts say the iguanas are shy, but these creatures actually seem rather curious. They waddle right up to you, as if posing for a picture. Several water-sports operators from Provo and North Caicos include a stop on the island as a part of their snorkel or sailing excursions (it's usually called "Iguana Island"). There's a $5 fee for a permit to visit the cay, and the proceeds go toward conservation in the islands.

PARROT CAY

Once said to be a hideout for pirate Calico Jack Rackham and his lady cohorts Mary Read and Anne Bonny, the 1,000-acre cay, between Fort George Cay and North Caicos, is now the site of an ultraexclusive hideaway resort.

For approximate costs, see the dining and lodging price chart in the Turks & Caicos Planner, at the beginning of this chapter.

$$$$ 🏨 **Parrot Cay Resort.** This private paradise—a favorite for celebrities and
Fodor's Choice aspiring ones—comes with all the trimmings you'd expect for the sub-
★ stantial price. Elaborate oceanfront villas border the island, and their wooden, Far Eastern feel contrasts with the rather bland hillside terracotta and stucco building that houses the spacious suites. Suite and villa interiors are a minimalist and sumptuous mix of cool-white interiors, Indonesian furnishings, and four-poster beds. The villas are the ultimate indulgence, with heated lap pools, hot tubs, and butler service. The resort's main pool is surrounded by a round, thatched bar and the Asian-inspired Lotus restaurant. The giant Como Shambhala Spa takes destination spas to a whole new level with Indonesian and Balinese therapists. **Pros:** Impeccable service, gorgeous secluded beach, the spa is considered one of the best in the world. **Cons:** Only two restaurants on the entire island, can be difficult to get back to Provo for excursions. ⊠*Parrot Cay* 🏨*Box 164, Providenciales* ☎*649/946–7788* ⊕*www. parrotcay.como.bz* ⚓*42 rooms, 4 suites, 14 villas* 🛎*In-room: safe,*

kitchen (some), refrigerator, VCR (some), dial-up, Wi-Fi. In-hotel: 2 restaurants, room service, bars, tennis courts, pool, gym, spa, beachfront, water sports, no elevator, laundry service, public Internet, public Wi-Fi, airport shuttle ▭AE, MC, V ⍟BP.

PINE CAY

Pine Cay's 2.5-mi-long (4-km-long) beach is among the most beautiful in the archipelago. The 800-acre private island is home to a secluded resort and around 37 private residences.

For approximate costs, see the dining and lodging price chart in the Turks & Caicos Planner, at the beginning of this chapter.

$$$$ **Meridian Club.** You might feel unplugged when you step onto Pine
Fodor'sChoice Cay, since there is no TV, telephone, or traffic to be found on the tiny
★ private island. The charm of this resort, which was built in the 1970s, is that it never changes, it prides itself on simplicity rather than celebrity. The simple beachfront cottages, most of the staff, and what is perhaps the world's smallest airport (in truth, a gazebo) have all stayed pretty much the same for years. On some nights, you can drive your golf cart to the runway for Drive-In Movie night. The 2.5-mi (4-km) stretch of beach is deserted, and instead of roads you can find nature trails and sun-dappled paths that crisscross the island, which can be explored by bike or on foot. Cuisine is excellent, with fresh seafood and delicious cakes and tarts served at lunch, dinner, and afternoon tea. Far from being an ivory-tower experience, the club enables you to become a part of a small community. Guests are mostly overstressed executives, mature couples, and honeymooners; a large percentage of guests are repeats. Children are welcome only in June and July. **Pros:** The finest beach in T&C, rates are inclusive of some of the best food in the T&C as well as snorkel trips. **Cons:** No TVs, no phones. ⊠*Pine Cay* ☎649/946–7758 *or* 866/746–3229 ⊕*www.meridianclub.com* ➾12 *rooms, 1 cottage, 7 private homes* ♿*In-room: no a/c, no phone, no TV, room service. In-hotel: restaurant, bar, tennis court, pool, beachfront, water sports, bicycles, no elevator, laundry service, public Internet, no kids under 12* ▭AE, D, MC, V ⍟*Closed Aug.–Oct.* ⍟AI.

NORTH CAICOS

Thanks to abundant rainfall, this 41-square-mi (106-square-km) island is the lushest of the Turks & Caicos. Bird lovers can see a large flock of flamingos here, anglers can find shallow creeks full of bonefish, and history buffs can visit the ruins of a Loyalist plantation. Although there's no traffic, almost all the roads are paved, so bicycling is an excellent way to sightsee. The island is predicted to become one of the next tourism hot spots, and foundations have been laid for condo resorts on Horse Stable Beach and Sandy Point. Even though it's a quiet place, you can find some small eateries around the airport and in Whitby, giving you a chance to try local and seafood specialties, sometimes served with homegrown okra or corn.

Coming Attractions

The buzz about Turks & Caicos has increased steadily over the last five years, a fact that hasn't missed the ears of developers. Grace Bay, a 12-mi (18-km) stretch of ivory sand on Providenciales, is still a favored location for new properties, including the stunning **Regent Grand**, a grander version of its sister property, Villa Renaissance. **Seven Stars,** a seven-story condominium resort, will be taking the destination to new heights, quite literally; because of its height, Seven Stars will have views like no other resort on Grace Bay. **Windsong** will add some new features to Provo, with a beach bar that appears to be under the water of the pool; it will even have outdoor air conditioner. At this writing, all three of these new resorts are expected to open by summer 2008. Given the volume of construction, it is worth asking your hotel about nearby construction projects to avoid the noise, dust, and obstructed views that can sometimes result.

25

You can now reach North Caicos from Provo with a daily ferry from Walkin Marina in Leeward; the trip takes about 30 minutes (⇨ *By Boat & Ferry in Turks & Caicos Essentials*). If you rent a car on North Caicos, you can even drive on the new causeway to Middle Caicos, a great day trip from Provo.

WHERE TO STAY

For approximate costs, see the dining and lodging price chart in the Turks & Caicos Planner, at the beginning of this chapter.

$$ 🖼️ **Bottle Creek Lodge.** Colorful, self-contained bungalows are scattered close to the water, providing a get-away-from-it-all feeling. Although this small resort is not close to the best beaches of North Caicos, it's the perfect place for fishing and relaxing. Bonefishing is right outside your door; the owners also have motorboats available for deep-sea fishing. You'll be welcomed as if you are coming home, and the restaurant has some of the best food on the island. It's possible to use Paypal if you don't have a credit card for payment. **Pros:** Very colorful and peaceful, great fishing. **Cons:** Not close to the best beaches in North Caicos, requires a car. ⊠ *Belmont* ☎ *649/946–7080* ⊕ *www. bottlecreeklodge.com* ➡ *3 rooms* ⊧ *In-room: kitchen, no phone, no TV, Wi-Fi. In-hotel: restaurant, room service, bar, water sports, bicycles, laundry service, public Internet, some pets allowed, no-smoking rooms* ☰ *MC, V* ⑩ *EP.*

$–$$ 🖼️ **Ocean Beach Hotel & Condominiums.** On Whitby Beach, this horseshoe-shape two-story, solar-paneled resort offers ocean views, comfortable and neatly furnished apartments, and a freshwater pool at quite reasonable rates. The Silver Palm restaurant is a welcome addition to the on-site amenities, which also include a dive and water-sports operation called Beach Cruiser. Unit 5 has the best views over the beach—especially for honeymooners, who automatically receive a 10% discount. You pay extra for air-conditioning, however. **Pros:** On the best beach of North Caicos. **Cons:** You need a car to get anywhere on North Caicos. ⊠ *Whitby* ☎ *649/946–7113, 800/710–5204, 905/690–3817 in Canada*

⊕*www.turksandcaicos.tc/oceanbeach* ⇆*10 suites* ⓧ*In-room: kitchen (some), no TV (some). In-hotel: restaurant, bar, pool, beachfront, diving, water sports, bicycles, no elevator, laundry service, public Internet* ▭*AE, D, MC, V* ⊘*Closed June 15–Oct. 15* ⍾*EP.*

$ 🏨**Pelican Beach Hotel.** North Caicos islanders Susan and Clifford Gardiner built this small palmetto-fringed hotel in the 1980s on the quiet, mostly deserted Whitby Beach. The couple's friendliness and insights into island life, not to mention Susan's home-baked bread and island dishes (Cliff's favorite is her cracked conch and island lobster), are the best features. Over the years upkeep of the property has been somewhat inconsistent, but rooms are nevertheless comfortable. Best is the line of cottage-style rooms (numbered 1 through 6), which is exactly five steps from the windswept beach. **Pros:** The beach is just outside your room. **Cons:** At this writing, rooms are still in the very slow process of being renovated and updated. ✉*Whitby* ☎*649/946–7112* ⊕*www.pelicanbeach.tc* ⇆*14 rooms, 2 suites* ⓧ*In-room: no phone, no TV. In-hotel: restaurant, bar, beachfront, bicycles, water sports, no elevator* ▭*MC, V* ⊘*Closed Aug. 15–Sept. 15* ⍾*MAP.*

BEACHES

The beaches of North Caicos are superb for shallow snorkeling and sunset strolls, and the waters offshore have excellent scuba diving. Horse Stable Beach is the main beach for annual events and beach parties. Whitby Beach usually has a gentle tide, and its thin strip of sand is bordered by palmetto plants and taller trees.

EXPLORING NORTH CAICOS

Flamingo Pond. This is a regular nesting place for the beautiful pink birds. They tend to wander out in the middle of the pond, so bring binoculars.

Kew. This settlement has a small post office, a school, a church, and ruins of old plantations—all set among lush tropical trees bearing limes, papayas, and custard apples. Visiting Kew will give you a better understanding of the daily life of many islanders.

♻ **Wades Green.** Visitors can view well-preserved ruins of the greathouse, overseer's house, and surrounding walls of one of the most successful plantations of the Loyalist era. A lookout tower provides views for miles. Contact the National Trust for tour details. ✉*Kew* ☎*649/941–5710 for National Trust* ⌑*$5* ⊘*Daily, by appointment only.*

MIDDLE CAICOS

At 48 square mi (124 square km) and with fewer than 300 residents, this is the largest and least developed of the inhabited islands in the Turks & Caicos chain. A limestone ridge runs to about 125 feet above sea level, creating dramatic cliffs on the north shore and a cave system farther inland. Middle Caicos has rambling trails along the coast; the Crossing Place Trail, maintained by the National Trust, follows the path used by the early settlers to go between the islands. Inland are quiet settlements with friendly residents. North Caicos and Middle

Caicos are now linked by a new causeway; since they are now linked by a road, it's possible to take a ferry from Provo to North Caicos, rent a car, and explore both North Caicos and Middle Caicos.

WHERE TO STAY

For approximate costs, see the dining and lodging price chart in the Turks & Caicos Planner, at the beginning of this chapter.

$$ ⬚ **Blue Horizon Resort.** At this resort, undulating cliffs skirt one of the most dramatic beaches in the Turks & Caicos. Blue-tin roofs mark the small self-contained open-plan cottages. Screened-in porches and careful positioning ensure that all of the cottages have unobstructed views along the cliffs and out to sea. The lack of amenities and development is actually what makes this spot so special. Tropical Cottage has large, attractive murals; Dragon View cottage has spectacular views of Dragon Cay and is closest to the Crossing Place trail that winds along the cliff tops. **Pros:** Breathtaking views of Mudjin Harbor from the rooms, lack of amenities and development make you feel like you're away from it all. **Cons:** Lack of amenities and development may be too isolated for some. ⊠ *Mudjin Harbor, Conch Bar* ☎ *649/946–6141* ⊕ *www.bhresort.com* ⌑ *5 cottages, 2 villas* ⚑ *In-room: no a/c (some), no phone (some), kitchen (some), no TV (some). In-hotel: beachfront, water sports, bicycles, no elevator, laundry service* ⊟ *AE, MC, V* ⊙ *EP.*

25

EXPLORING MIDDLE CAICOS

↻ **Conch Bar Caves.** These limestone caves have eerie underground lakes and milky-white stalactites and stalagmites. Archaeologists have discovered Lucayan Indian artifacts in the caves and the surrounding area. The caves are inhabited by some harmless bats. If you visit, don't worry—they don't bother visitors. It's best to get a guide. If you tour the caves, be sure to wear sturdy shoes, not sandals.

CAVE TOURS   Taxi driver and fisherman **Cardinal Arthur** (☎ *649/946–6107*) can give you a good cave tour.

Local cave specialist and taxi driver **Ernest Forbes** (☎ *649/946–6140*) is also happy to oblige with a cave tour and may even arrange a fixed-fee lunch at his house afterward if you ask nicely.

SOUTH CAICOS

This 8.5-square-mi (21-square-km) island was once an important salt producer; today it's the heart of the fishing industry. Nature prevails, with long, white beaches, jagged bluffs, quiet backwater bays, and salt flats. Diving and snorkeling on the pristine wall and reefs are a treat enjoyed by only a few.

BEACHES

The beaches at **Belle Sound** on South Caicos will take your breath away, with lagoonlike waters. On the opposite side of the ridge from Belle Sound, **Long Bay** is an endless stretch of beach, but it can be susceptible to rough surf; however, on calmer days this stretch makes you feel you're on a deserted island. Due south of South Caicos is **Big Ambergris Cay,** an uninhabited cay about 14 mi (23 km) beyond the Fish Cays, with a magnificent beach at Long Bay. To the north of South Caicos, uninhabited **East Caicos** has a beautiful 17-mi (27-km) beach on its north coast. The island was once a cattle range and the site of a major sisal-growing industry. Both places are accessible only by boat.

EXPLORING SOUTH CAICOS

At the northern end of the island are fine white-sand beaches; the south coast is great for scuba diving along the drop-off; and there's excellent snorkeling off the windward (east) coast, where large stands of elkhorn and staghorn coral shelter several varieties of small tropical fish. Spiny lobster and queen conch are found in the shallow Caicos Bank to the west and are harvested for export by local processing plants. The bone-fishing here is some of the best in the West Indies.

Beyond the Blue (✉ *Cockburn Town* ☏ *649/231–1703* ⊕ *www.beyond theblue.com*) offers bonefishing charters on a specialized airboat, which can operate in less than a foot of water. Lodging packages are available.

Boiling Hole. Abandoned salinas make up the center of this island—the largest, across from the downtown ballpark, receives its water directly from an underground source connected to the ocean through this boiling hole.

Cockburn Harbour. The best natural harbor in the Caicos chain hosts the South Caicos Regatta, held each year in May.

THE TURKS

GRAND TURK

Just 7 mi (11 km) long and a little over 1 mi (2.5 km) wide, this island, the capital and seat of the Turks & Caicos government, has been a longtime favorite destination for divers eager to explore the 7,000-foot-deep pristine coral walls that drop down only 300 yards out to sea. On shore, the tiny, quiet island is home to white-sand beaches, the National Museum, and a small population of wild horses and donkeys, which leisurely meander past the white-walled courtyards, pretty churches, and bougainvillea-covered colonial inns on their daily commute into town. A cruise-ship complex that opened at the southern end of the island in 2006 brings about 300,000 visitors per year. Despite the dramatic changes this could make to this peaceful tourist spot, the dock is self-contained and is about 3 mi (5 km) from the tranquil, small hotels of Cockburn Town, Pillory Beach, and the Ridge and far from most of the western-shore dive sites. And the influx has also pushed Grand Turk to open up a few new historic sites, including Grand Turk's Old Prison, and the Lighthouse.

All in the Family

Belongers, from the taxi driver meeting you to the chef feeding you, are often connected. "Oh, him?" you will hear. "He my cousin!" As development has been mercifully slow, such family connections, as well as crafts, bush medicine, ripsaw music, storytelling, and even recipes, have remained constant. But where do such traditions come from? Recently, researchers came closer to finding out. Many Belongers had claimed that their great-great-grandparents had told them their forebears had come directly from Africa. For decades their stories were ignored. Indeed, most experts believed that Belongers were descendants of mostly second-generation Bermudian and Caribbean slaves.

In 2005, museum researchers continued their search for a lost slave ship called *Trouvadore*. The ship, which wrecked off East Caicos in 1841, carried a cargo of 193 Africans, captured to be sold into slavery, almost all of whom miraculously survived the wreck. As slavery had been abolished in this British territory at the time, all the Africans were found and freed in the Turks & Caicos Islands. Since there were only a few thousand inhabitants in the islands at the time, these first-generation African survivors were a measurable minority (about 7% of the population then). Researchers have concluded that all the existing Belongers may be linked by blood or marriage to this one incident.

During one expedition, divers found a wrecked ship of the right time period. If these remains are *Trouvadore*, the Belongers may finally have a physical link to their past, to go with their more-intangible cultural traditions. So while you're in the islands, look closely at the intricately woven baskets, listen carefully to the African rhythms in the ripsaw music, and savor the stories you hear. They may very well be the legacy of *Trouvadore* speaking to you from the past. For more information, check out ⊕ *www.slaveshiptrouvadore.com*.

25

WHERE TO STAY

Accommodations include original Bermudian inns, more-modern but small beachfront hotels, and very basic to well-equipped self-catering suites and apartments. Almost all hotels offer dive packages, which are an excellent value.

$$ ☷**Arches of Grand Turk.** Upstairs and downstairs, east- and west-facing balconies from these four ridgetop town houses ensure nicely framed views of both sunrise and sunset. Canadian husband-and-wife team Wally and Cecile Wennick left Florida in the 1990s after more than a decade in the hospitality industry to create this hillside home away from home, less than a five-minute walk from the deserted east beach. The well-equipped town houses are peppered with Cecile's handicrafts, including painted glass bottles, embroidery, and wall hangings that combine to give the airy houses a homespun feel. Weekly housekeeping is included in the rate, but daily maid service costs extra. **Pros:** Quiet getaway, feels like home. **Cons:** Not on the beach, requires a car. ⊠*Lighthouse Rd., Box 226* ☎*649/946–2941* ⊕*www.grandturkarches.com* ⇖*4 town houses* ♿*In-room: kitchen, dial-up, Wi-Fi. In-*

hotel: pool, bicycles, no elevator, laundry service, public Wi-Fi, public Internet ⊟*D, MC, V* ⦿*EP.*

\$\$ 🏨 **Bohio Dive Resort & Spa.** Formerly the Pillory Beach Resort, this resort sits on an otherwise deserted stretch of beach. It's a dream come true for British couple Kelly Shanahan and Nick Gillings, who have created their own retreat on Grand Turk after years of visiting the tiny island. The resort's restaurant is the best on the island. You can relax with yoga sessions or party with the locals at the Sunday sail and kayak races or Thursday-night's "pit party" with roasted meats and music. **Pros:** Has the best restaurant in Grand Turk, on a gorgeous beach, steps away from awesome snorkeling. **Cons:** Rooms are basic and dated, three-night minimum. ⊠*Pillory Beach* ☎*649/946–2135* ⊕*www.bohio resort.com* 🛏*12 rooms, 4 suites* ⚲*In-room: kitchen (some), no phones. In-hotel: restaurant, bars, pool, spa, beachfront, diving, water sports, no elevator, public Internet* ⊟*AE, MC, V* ⦿*3-night minimum* ⦿*EP.*

\$\$ 🏨 **Island House.** Owner Colin Brooker gives his guests a personal intro-
☺ duction to the capital island, thanks to his family's long history here. His years of business travel experience have gone into the comfort-able, peaceful suites that overlook North Creek. Balcony barbecues, shaded hammocks, and flat-screen TVs are among the diversions from the backdrop of splendid island and ocean views. Suites 3 and 7 com-mand the best sunset views. Graduated terraces descend the hillside to a small pool surrounded by pink-and-white climbing bougainvil-lea, creating the feel of a Mediterranean hideaway. An array of inflat-able toys keeps kids happy. The deserted east beach is a 12-minute walk away. If you stay more than three nights, a car is included in the rental price. **Pros:** Full condo units feel like a home away from home. **Cons:** Not on the beach, you need a car to get around. ⊠*Lighthouse Rd., Box 36* ☎*649/946–1519* ⊕*www.islandhouse-tci.com* 🛏*8 suites* ⚲*In-room: kitchen, Wi-Fi. In-hotel: pool, water sports, bicycles, no elevator, laundry facilities, public Wi-Fi, some pets allowed* ⊟*AE, D, MC, V* ⦿*EP.*

\$–\$\$ 🏨 **Osprey Beach Hotel.** Grand Turk veteran hotelier Jenny Smith has trans-
Fodor'sChoice formed this two-story oceanfront hotel with her artistic touches. Palms,
★ frangipani, and deep green azaleas frame it like a painting. Inside, evoca-tive island watercolors, painted by her longtime friend, Nashville artist Tupper Saussay, thread through the property. Vaulted ceilings and Indo-nesian four-poster beds are the highlight of upstairs Suites 51, 52, and 53. Downstairs you can enjoy beach access through your own garden. On the opposite side of Duke Street, the newly built suites have phones, TVs, and Wi-Fi service. **Pros:** Renovated in 2007, best hotel on Grand Turk, walking distance to Front Street, restaurants, and excursions. **Con:** Three-night minimum. ⊠*Duke St., Cockburn Town* ☎*649/946–2666* ⊕*www.ospreybeachhotel.com* 🛏*11 rooms, 16 suites* ⚲*In-room: dial-up (some), Wi-Fi (some), kitchen (some). In-hotel: restaurant, bar, pool, beachfront, water sports, no elevator, laundry service, some pets allowed* ⊟*AE, MC, V* ⦿*3-night minimum* ⦿*EP.*

\$–\$\$ 🏨 **Salt Raker Inn.** A large anchor on the sun-dappled pathway marks the entrance to this 19th-century house, which is now an unpreten-tious inn. The building was built by a shipwright and has a large,

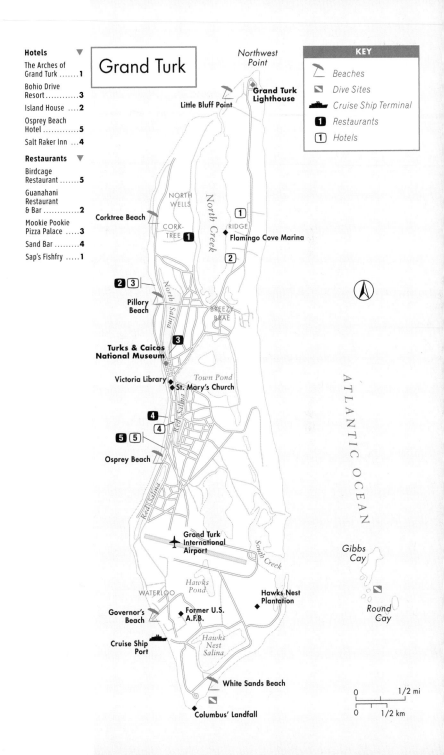

Grand Turk

Hotels ▼

The Arches of
Grand Turk **1**

Bohio Drive
Resort **3**

Island House **2**

Osprey Beach
Hotel **5**

Salt Raker Inn ...**4**

Restaurants ▼

Birdcage
Restaurant **5**

Guanahani
Restaurant
& Bar **2**

Mookie Pookie
Pizza Palace **3**

Sand Bar **4**

Sap's Fishfry **1**

KEY

⚑ Beaches

◩ Dive Sites

🚢 Cruise Ship Terminal

1 Restaurants

1 Hotels

Northwest
Point

**Grand Turk
Lighthouse**

Little Bluff Point

NORTH
WELLS

North Creek

Corktree Beach

CORK-
TREE

1 RIDGE

Flamingo Cove Marina

2

North Salina

Pillory
Beach

BREEZY
BRAE

3

**Turks & Caicos
National Museum**

Town Pond

Victoria Library ◆ St. Mary's Church

Red Salina

4

4

5 5

Osprey Beach

ATLANTIC OCEAN

Red Salina

**Grand Turk
International
Airport**

South Creek

Gibbs
Cay

Hawks
Pond

WATERLOO

**Hawks Nest
Plantation** ◆

Round
Cay

**Governor's
Beach**

◆ Former U.S.
A.F.B.

Hawks
Nest
Salina

**Cruise Ship
Port** 🚢

White Sands Beach

◆ **Columbus' Landfall**

0   1/2 mi

0   1/2 km

breezy balcony with commanding views over the sea, but its best feature is hidden behind the facade: a secret garden of tall tamarind and neme trees, climbing vines, hanging plants, potted hibiscus, climbing bougainvillea, and even a pond. The greenery, as well as providing a quiet spot for natural shade, is home to the inn's Secret Garden Restaurant. Rooms A2, B2, and C2 are nicely shaded havens but have no sea views. Upstairs, Rooms G and H share a balcony with unobstructed views of the ocean and Duke Street. **Pros:** Excellent location that is an easy walk to Front Street, restaurants, and excursions. **Cons:** No no-smoking rooms. ⊠ *Duke St., Box 1, Cockburn Town* ☎ *649/946–2260* ⊕ *www.hotelsaltraker.com* ➪ *10 rooms, 3 suites* ⚙ *In-room: refrigerator, Wi-Fi, dial-up. In-hotel: restaurant, bar, no elevator, laundry service, some pets allowed, public Wi-Fi* ⊟ *D, MC, V* ⊚ *EP.*

WHERE TO EAT

Conch in every shape and form, fresh grouper, and lobster (in season) are the favorite dishes at the laid-back restaurants that line Duke Street. Away from these more-touristy areas, smaller and less-expensive eateries serve chicken and ribs, curried goat, peas and rice, and other native island specialties. Prices are more expensive than in the United States, as most of the produce has to be imported.

AMERICAN
$–$$

✕ **Sand Bar.** Run by two Canadian sisters, this popular beachside bar is a good value, though the menu is limited to fish-and-chips, quesadillas, and similarly basic bar fare. The tented wooden terrace jutting out on to the beach provides shade during the day, making it an ideal lunch spot, but it's also a great place to watch the sunset. The service is friendly, and the local crowd often spills into the street. ⊠ *Duke St., Cockburn Town* ☎ *No phone* ⊟ *MC, V.*

CARIBBEAN
$$–$$$
★

✕ **Birdcage Restaurant.** At the top of Duke Street, this has become the place to be on Sunday and Wednesday nights, when a sizzling barbecue of ribs, chicken, and lobster combines with live "rake-and-scrape" music from a local group called High Tide to draw an appreciative crowd. Arrive before 8 PM to secure beachside tables and an unrestricted view of the band; the location around the Osprey pool is lovely. The rest of the week, enjoy more-elegant and eclectic fare accompanied by an increasingly impressive wine list. ⊠ *Osprey Beach Hotel, Duke St., Cockburn Town* ☎ *649/946–2666* ⊟ *MC, V.*

¢–$

✕ **Mookie Pookie Pizza Palace.** Local husband-and-wife team "Mookie" and "Pookie" have created a wonderful backstreet parlor that has gained well-deserved popularity over the years as much more than a pizza place. At lunchtime, the tiny eatery is packed with locals ordering specials like steamed beef, curried chicken, and curried goat. You can also get burgers and omelets, but stick to the specials if you want fast service, and dine in if you want to get a true taste of island living. By night, the place becomes Grand Turk's one and only pizza take-out and delivery service, so if you're renting a villa or condo, put this spot on speed dial. ⊠ *Hospital Rd., Cockburn Town* ☎ *649/946–1538* ⊟ *No credit cards* ⊙ *Closed Sun.*

ECLECTIC ✕**Guanahani Restaurant & Bar.** Off the town's main drag, this restaurant
$$–$$$ sits on a stunning but quiet stretch of beach. The food goes beyond the
★ usual Grand Turk fare, thanks to the talents of Canadian-born chef
Zev Beck, who takes care of the evening meals. His pecan-encrusted
mahimahi and crispy sushi rolls are to die for. For lunch, Middle Caicos
native Miss Leotha makes juicy jerk chicken to keep the crowd happy.
The menu changes daily. The food is the best in Grand Turk, but it's
also the island's most expensive restaurant. ⊠*Bohio Dive Resort &*
Spa, Pillory Beach ☎*649/946–2135* ▭*MC, V.*

SEAFOOD ✕**Sap's Fishfry.** Down a lesser-known road that runs to the west of
$–$$$ North Creek lies an even lesser-known restaurant. If you survive the
potholed road trip, you will undoubtedly feel you deserve a taste of
the freshly caught grouper, conch, and lobster specialties served at this
small hideaway on the water. This favorite (if slightly scandalous) spot,
is where local married men like to bring their "sweethearts." The prices
and food are certainly good enough to make it the best choice for a
cheap date. Although officially called Sap's, islanders sometimes call it
Chubbies. ⊠*North Creek* ☎*No phone* ▭*No credit cards.*

BEACHES

★ Grand Turk is spoiled for choices when it comes to beach options: sun-
set strolls along miles of deserted beaches, picnics in secluded coves,
beachcombing on the coralline sands, snorkeling around shallow coral
heads close to shore, and admiring the impossibly turquoise-blue waters.
Governor's Beach, a beautiful crescent of powder-soft sand and shallow,
calm turquoise waters that fronts the official British Governor's resi-
dence, called Waterloo, is framed by tall casuarina trees that provide
plenty of natural shade. To have it all to yourself, go on a day when
cruise ships are not in port. On days when ships are in port, the beach
is lined with lounge chairs. For more of a beachcombing experience,
Little Bluff Point Beach, just west of the Grand Turk Lighthouse, is a low,
limestone-cliff-edged, shell-covered beach that looks out onto shallow
waters, mangroves, and often flamingos, especially in spring and sum-
mer. **Pillory Beach,** with sparkling neon turquoise water, is the prettiest
beach on Grand Turk; it also has great off-the-beach-snorkeling.

SPORTS & THE OUTDOORS

CYCLING The island's mostly flat terrain isn't very taxing, and most roads have
hard surfaces. Take water with you: there are few places to stop for
refreshment. Most hotels have bicycles available, but you can also rent
them for $10 to $15 a day from **Oasis Divers** (⊠*Duke St., Cockburn*
Town ☎☎*649/946–1128* ⊕*www.oasisdivers.com*).

DIVING & In these waters you can find undersea cathedrals, coral gardens, and
SNORKELING countless tunnels, but note that you must carry and present a valid
★ certificate card before you'll be allowed to dive. As its name suggests,
the **Black Forest** offers staggering black-coral formations as well as the
occasional black-tip shark. In the **Library** you can study fish galore,
including large numbers of yellowtail snapper. At the Columbus Pas-
sage separating South Caicos from Grand Turk, each side of a 22-mi-
wide (35-km-wide) channel drops more than 7,000 feet. From January

25

through March, thousands of Atlantic humpback whales swim through en route to their winter breeding grounds. **Gibb's Cay,** a small cay a couple of miles off of Grand Turk, makes a great excursion swimming with stingrays.

Dive outfitters can all be found in Cockburn Town. Two-tank boat dives generally cost $60 to $80. **Blue Water Divers** (⊠ *Duke St., Cockburn Town* ☎☎ *649/946–2432* ⊕ *www.grandturkscuba.com*) has been in operation on Grand Turk since 1983 and is the only PADI Gold Palm five-star dive center on the island. Owner Mitch will doubtless put some of your underwater adventures to music in the evenings when he plays at the Osprey Beach Hotel or Salt Raker Inn. **Oasis Divers** (⊠ *Duke St., Cockburn Town* ☎☎ *649/946–1128* ⊕ *www.oasisdivers. com*) specializes in complete gear handling and pampering treatment. It also supplies Nitrox and rebreathers. Besides daily dive trips to the wall, **Sea Eye Diving** (⊠ *Duke St., Cockburn Town* ☎☎ *649/946–1407* ⊕ *www.seaeyediving.com*) offers encounters with friendly stingrays on a popular snorkeling trip to nearby Gibbs Cay.

NIGHTLIFE

On weekends and holidays the younger crowd heads over to the **Nookie Hill Club** (⊠ *Nookie Hill* ☎ *No phone*) for late-night drinking and dancing. Every Wednesday and Sunday, there's lively "rake-and-scrape" music at the **Osprey Beach Hotel** (⊠ *Duke St., Cockburn Town* ☎ *649/946–2666*). On Friday, rake-and-scrape bands play at the **Salt Raker Inn** (⊠ *Duke St., Cockburn Town* ☎ *649/946–2260*).

EXPLORING GRAND TURK

Pristine beaches with vistas of turquoise waters, small local settlements, historic ruins, and native flora and fauna are among the sights on Grand Turk. Fewer than 5,000 people live on this 7.5-square-mi (19-square-km) island, and it's hard to get lost, as there aren't many roads.

Cockburn Town. The buildings in the colony's capital and seat of government reflect a 19th-century Bermudian style. Narrow streets are lined with low stone walls and old street lamps, which are now powered by electricity. The once-vital salinas have been restored, and covered benches along the sluices offer shady spots for observing wading birds, including flamingos that frequent the shallows. Be sure to pick up a copy of the tourist board's Heritage Walk guide to discover Grand Turk's rich architecture.

↻ In one of the oldest stone buildings on the islands, the **Turks & Caicos**
★ **National Museum** houses the Molasses Reef wreck, the earliest shipwreck—dating to the early 1500s—discovered in the Americas. The natural-history exhibits include artifacts left by Taíno, African, North American, Bermudian, French, and Latin American settlers. The museum has a 3-D coral reef exhibit, a walk-in Lucayan cave with wooden artifacts, and a gallery dedicated to Grand Turk's little-known involvement in the Space Race (former Senator John Glenn made his first landfall back on Earth here after his walk on the moon). An interactive children's gallery keeps knee-high visitors even more "edutained." The museum also claims that Grand Turk was Colum-

bus's first landfall in the New World. ⊠*Duke St., Cockburn Town* ☎*649/946–2160* ⊕*www.tcmuseum.org* ✉*$5* ☾*Mon., Tues., Thurs., and Fri. 9–4, Wed. 9–5, Sat. 9–1.*

Grand Turk Lighthouse. More than 150 years old, the lighthouse, built in the United Kingdom and transported piece by piece to the island, used to protect ships in danger of wrecking on the northern reefs. Use this panoramic landmark as a starting point for a breezy cliff-top walk by following the donkey trails to the deserted eastern beach. ⊠*Lighthouse Rd., North Ridge.*

SALT CAY

Fewer than 100 people live on this 2.5-square-mi (6-square-km) dot of land, maintaining an unassuming lifestyle against a backdrop of quaint stucco cottages, stone ruins, and weathered wooden windmills standing sentry in the abandoned salinas. The beautifully preserved island is bordered by picturesque beaches, where weathered green and blue sea glass and pretty shells often wash ashore. Beneath the waves, 10 dive sites are minutes from shore.

25

There are big plans for Salt Cay, which will change the small island forever, though probably not for several years. Gone will be the donkeys and chickens roaming the streets; in their place will be a luxurious resort and new golf course. If you want to see how the Caribbean was when it was laid back, sleepy and colorful, visit the island now before it changes.

WHERE TO STAY

For approximate costs, see the dining and lodging price chart in the Turks & Caicos Planner, at the beginning of this chapter.

$–$$ 🗌**Pirate's Hideaway & Blackbeard's Quarters.** Owner Candy Herwin— true to her self-proclaimed pirate status—has smuggled artistic treasures across the ocean and even created her own masterpieces to deck out this lair. Quirkily decorated rooms show her original style and sense of humor. The African and Crow's Nest suites have private baths; Blackbeard's Quarters is a four-bedroom house with rooms that can be rented separately but share a living room and kitchen (one room has an en-suite bath; the others share a single bath). On a good day, Candy will cook, but only if you entertain her and other guests—whether by reading a sonnet or singing a song. If you love eclectic and artistically inspiring surroundings and want to meet a true pirate queen, this could well be your perfect hideaway. A freshwater pool and gym have been recently added. You can rent golf carts to drive around the island. **Pros:** Artist workshops are offered during peak season. **Cons:** Not directly on the beach. ⊠*Victoria St., South District* ☎*649/946–6909* ⊕*www. saltcay.tc* ⇆*2 suites, 1 house* ⚒*In-room: no a/c (some), no phone, kitchen (some). In-hotel: beachfront, water sports, bicycles, no elevator* ▤*MC, V* ⏀|EP.

$–$$ 🗌**Sunset Reef.** A blue whale on the rooftop denotes this Victoria Street property, which has two very basic villas with excellent ocean views and a whale-watching balcony ideal for communal dining. You must pay extra to use the air-conditioning. **Pros:** Home away from home feel, great balconies for whale-watching. **Cons:** Extra cost for daily maid service. ⊠ *Victoria St., Balfour Town* ☎ *649/941–7753* ⊕ *www. sunsetreef.com* ⇨ *1 1-bedroom villa, 1 2-bedroom villa* ⚐ *In-room: no phone, safe, kitchen, VCR (some). In-hotel: beachfront, water sports, no elevator, laundry facilities, some pets allowed* ☰ *MC, V* ⦿ *EP.*

$–$$ ☷ **Tradewinds Guest Suites.** Yards away from Dean's Dock, a grove of whispering casuarina trees surrounds these five single-story, basic apartments, which offer a moderate-budget option on Salt Cay with the possibility of all-inclusive and dive packages. Screened porches, hammocks overlooking the comings and goings of the small dock, and the friendly staff are the best features. **Pros:** Walking distance to diving, fishing, dining, and dancing. **Cons:** Cost of air-conditioning is not included in basic rates, some may feel isolated with few nighttime activities and no TVs. ⊠ *Victoria St., Balfour Town* ☎ *649/946–6906* ⊕ *www.tradewinds.tc* ⇨ *5 apartments* ⚐ *In-room: no phone, kitchen (some), no TV. In-hotel: beachfront, water sports, bicycles, no elevator* ☰ *MC, V* ⦿ *EP.*

WHERE TO EAT

$–$$ ✕ **Island Thyme Bistro.** Owner Porter Williams serves potent alcoholic creations like the "Wolf" and other creatures, as well as fairly sophisticated local and international cuisine. Look for steamed, freshly caught snapper served in a pepper wine sauce with peas and rice or spicy-hot chicken curry served with a tangy range of chutneys. The airy, trellis-covered spot overlooks the salinas. This is the best place to eat on Salt Cay and the best place to catch up on island gossip. ⊠ *North District* ☎ *649/946–6977* ☰ *MC, V* ⊙ *Closed Wed. mid-May–June and Sept.–late Oct.*

$–$$ ✕ **Pat's Place.** Born and bred on the island, Pat Simmons can give you a lesson in the medicinal qualities of her garden plants and periwinkle flowers as well as excellent native cuisine for a very reasonable price in her typical Salt Cay home. Home cooking doesn't get any closer to home than this. Try conch fritters for lunch and her steamed grouper with okra rice for dinner. Be sure to call ahead, as she cooks only when there's someone to cook for. ⊠ *South District* ☎ *649/946–6919* ⚐ *Reservations essential* ☰ *No credit cards.*

BEACHES

★   The north coast of **Salt Cay** has superb beaches, with tiny, pretty shells and weathered sea glass. Accessible by boat with the on-island tour operators, **Big Sand Cay,** 7 mi (11 km) south of Salt Cay, is tiny and totally uninhabited, but it's also known for its long, unspoiled stretches of open sand.

SPORTS & THE OUTDOORS

DIVING & SNORKELING   Scuba divers can explore the wreck of the *Endymion,* a 140-foot wooden-hull British warship that sank in 1790. It's off the southern point of Salt Cay. **Salt Cay Divers** (⊠ *Balfour Town* ☎ *649/946–6906* ⊕ *www.saltcaydivers.tc*) conducts daily trips and rents all the necessary equipment. It costs around $80 for a two-tank dive.

WHALE-
WATCHING
☙
During the winter months (January through April), Salt Cay is a center for whale-watching, when some 2,500 humpback whales pass close to shore. Whale-watching trips can most easily be organized through your inn or guesthouse.

EXPLORING SALT CAY

Salt sheds and salinas are silent reminders of the days when the island was a leading producer of salt. Now the salt ponds attract abundant birdlife. Island tours are often conducted by motorized golf cart. From January through April, humpback whales pass by on the way to their winter breeding grounds.

Balfour Town. What little development there is on Salt Cay is found here. It's home to several small hotels and a few cozy stores, as well as the main dock and the Green Flash Gazebo, where locals hang out with tourists to watch the sunset and sink a beer.

The grand stone **White House,** which once belonged to a wealthy salt merchant, is testimony to the heyday of Salt Cay's eponymous industry. Still privately owned by the descendants of the original family, it's sometimes opened up for tours. It's worth asking your guesthouse or hotel owner—or any local passerby—if Salt Cay islander "Uncle Lionel" is on-island, as he may give you a personal tour to see the still-intact, original furnishings, books, and medicine cabinet that date back to the early 1800s. ✉ *Victoria St., Balfour Town.*

25

TURKS & CAICOS ISLANDS ESSENTIALS

To research prices, get advice from other travelers, and book travel arrangements, visit www.fodors.com.

■ TRANSPORTATION

BY AIR

The main gateways into the regions are Providenciales International Airport and Grand Turk International Airport. For private planes, Provo Air Center is a full-service FBO (Fixed Base Operator) offering refueling, maintenance, and short-term storage, as well as on-site customs and immigration clearance, a lounge, and concierge services.

Although carriers and schedules can vary according to season, you can find non-stop and connecting flights to Providenciales from several U.S. cities on American, Delta, Spirit Airlines (weekly on Saturday

or Sunday depending on the season), and US Airways. There are also flights from other parts of the Caribbean on Air Turks & Caicos and SkyKing; these airlines also fly to some of the smaller islands in the chain from Provo.

Airline Contacts Air Turks & Caicos (☎649/941–5481 ⊕www.airturksandcaicos.com). **American Airlines** (☎649/946–4948 or 800/433–7300). **Delta** (☎800/241–4141). **SkyKing** (☎649/941–5464 ⊕www.skyking.tc). **Spirit Airlines** (☎800/772–7117 ⊕www.spiritair.com). **US Airways** (☎800/622–1015).

Airport Contacts Grand Turk International Airport (GDT ☎649/946–2233). **Providenciales International Airport** (PLS ☎649/941–5670). **Provo Air Center** (☎649/946–4181 ⊕www.provoaircenter.com).

BY BOAT & FERRY

Begun in 2007, there is now scheduled ferry service on Caribbean Cruisin', which offers daily service with several departures between Provo and North Caicos from Walkin Marina in Leeward. There's a twice-weekly ferry from Salt Cay to Grand Turk (weather permitting).

Information Caribbean Cruisin'
(⊠Walkin Marina, Leeward, Providenciales ☎649/946–5406 or 649/231–4191 ⊕tcimall. tc/northcaicos/images/ferryservice.pdf ✎caribbeancruisin@gmail.com). **Salt Cay Ferry** (☎649/946–6909 ⊕www.turksand caicoswhalewatching.com).

BY CAR

Major reconstruction of Leeward Highway on Providenciales has been completed, and most of the road is now a four-lane divided highway complete with roundabouts. However, the paved two-lane roads through the settlements on Providenciales can be quite rough, although signage is improving. The less-traveled roads in Grand Turk and the family islands are, in general, smooth and paved. Gasoline is expensive, much more so than in the United States.

Driving here is on the left side of the road, British style; when pulling out into traffic, remember to look to your right. Give way to anyone entering a roundabout, as roundabouts are still a relatively new concept in the Turks & Caicos; stop even if you are on what appears to be the primary road. The maximum speed is 40 mph (64 kph), 20 mph (30 kph) through settlements, and limits, as well as the use of seat belts, are enforced.

Avis and Budget have offices on the islands. You might also try local agencies such as Grace Bay Car Rentals, Rent a Buggy, and Tropical Auto Rentals in Provo. Pelican Car Rentals is on North Caicos.

Contacts Avis (⊠Providenciales ☎649/946–4705 ⊕www.avis.tc). **Budget** (⊠Providenciales ☎649/946–4079 ⊕www.

AIRLINE TIP

If you have an afternoon flight, check in your bags early in the morning (keep a change of clothes in a carry-on), then go back to the beach for one last lunch, returning to the airport an hour before your flight departs. It makes for much easier traveling, saves time, and you get your last beach fix.

provo.net/budget). **Grace Bay Car Rentals** (⊠Providenciales ☎649/941–8500 ⊕www. gracebaycarrentals.com). **Pelican Car Rentals** (⊠North Caicos ☎649/241–8275). **Rent a Buggy** (⊠Providenciales ☎649/946–4158 ⊕www.rentabuggy.tc). **Tropical Auto Rentals** (⊠Providenciales ☎649/946–5300 ⊕www. provo.net/tropicalauto).

BY TAXI

Cabs (actually large vans) in Providenciales are metered, and rates are regulated by the government at $2 per person per mile traveled. In Provo call the Provo Taxi & Bus Group for more information. In the family islands, cabs may not be metered, so it's usually best to try to negotiate a cost for your trip when you book your taxi. Many resorts and car-rental agencies offer complimentary airport transfers. Ask ahead of time.

Contact Provo Taxi & Bus Group (☎649/946–5481).

∎ CONTACTS & RESOURCES

BANKS & EXCHANGE SERVICES

Prices quoted in this chapter are in U.S. dollars, which is the official currency in the islands. Major credit cards and traveler's checks are accepted at many establishments. There are ATMs at the branches, at IGA Supermarket, Ports of Call shopping center, and Ocean Club Plaza, all in Provo.

Scotiabank and First Caribbean have offices on Provo, with branches on Grand Turk. Many larger hotels can take care of your money requests. Bring small denominations to the less-populated islands.

ELECTRICITY

Electricity is fairly stable throughout the islands, and the current is suitable for all U.S. appliances (120/240 volts, 60 Hz).

EMERGENCIES

Emergency Services Ambulance & Fire (☎999 or 911). **Police** (☎649/946–2499 in Grand Turk, 649/946–7116 in North Caicos, 649/946–4259 in Provo, 649/946–3299 in South Caicos).

Hospitals Associated Medical Practices (✉Leeward Hwy., Glass Shack, Providenciales ☎649/946–4242). **Grand Turk Hospital** (✉Hospital Rd., Grand Turk ☎649/946–2040).

Scuba Diving Emergencies Associated Medical Practices (✉Leeward Hwy., Glass Shack, Providenciales ☎649/946–4242).

INTERNET, MAIL & SHIPPING

The majority of resorts on the Turks & Caicos offer Wi-Fi service in their public areas, if not in the rooms, so you can keep up with e-mail and the Internet. There are also several Internet cafés, including one in the Ports of Call mall on Provo.

The post office is in downtown Provo at the corner of Airport Road. Collectors will be interested in the wide selection of stamps sold by the Philatelic Bureau. It costs 50¢ to send a postcard to the United States, 60¢ to Canada and the United Kingdom, and $1.25 to Australia and New Zealand; letters, per ½ ounce, cost 60¢ to the United States, 80¢ to Canada and the United Kingdom, and $1.40 to Australia and New Zealand. When writing to the Turks & Caicos Islands, be sure to include the specific island and "Turks & Caicos Islands, BWI" (British West Indies). Delivery service is provided by FedEx, with offices in Provo and Grand Turk.

Contacts FedEx (☎649/946–4682 on Provo). **Philatelic Bureau** (☎649/946–1534).

SAFETY

Although crime is not a major concern in the Turks & Caicos Islands, petty theft does occur here, and you're advised to leave your valuables in the hotel safe-deposit box and lock doors in cars and rooms when unattended.

TAXES & SERVICE CHARGES

The departure tax is $35 and is usually built into the cost of your tickets. If not, it's payable only in cash or traveler's checks. Restaurants and hotels add a 10% government tax. Hotels also add 10% to 15% for service.

TELEPHONES

The area code for the Turks & Caicos is 649. Just dial 1 plus the 10-digit number, including area code, from the United States. To make local calls, dial the seven-digit number. To make calls from the Turks & Caicos, dial 0, then 1, the area code, and the number.

All telephone service is provided by Cable & Wireless and Digicel. Many U.S.–based cell phones work on the islands; use your own or rent one from Cable & Wireless. Internet access is available via hotel-room phone connections or Internet kiosks on Provo and Grand Turk. You can also connect to the World Wide Web from any telephone line by dialing C-O-N-N-E-C-T to call Cable & Wireless and using the user name *easy* and the password *access*. Calls from the islands are expensive, and many hotels add steep surcharges for long distance. Talk fast.

Information Digicel TCI (⊕www.digiceltci.com). **Cable & Wireless** (☎649/946–2200, 800/744–7777 for long distance, 649/266–6328 for Internet access, 811 for mobile service ⊕www.tcimall.tc).

TIPPING

At restaurants, tip 15% if service isn't included in the bill. Taxi drivers also expect a token tip, about 10% of your fare.

25

TOUR OPTIONS

Whether by taxi, boat, or plane, you should try to venture beyond your resort's grounds and beach. The natural environment is one of the main attractions of the Turks & Caicos, yet few people explore beyond the natural wonder of the beach. Big Blue Unlimited has taken ecotouring to a whole new level with educational ecotours, including three-hour kayak trips and more-land-based guided journeys around the family islands. The Coastal Ecology and Wildlife tour is a kayak adventure through red mangroves to bird habitats, rock iguana hideaways, and natural fish nurseries. The North Caicos Mountain Bike Eco Tour gets you on a bike exploring the island, the plantation ruins, the inland lakes, and a flamingo pond with a stop-off at Susan Butterfield's home for lunch. Package costs range from $85 to $225 per person. J&B Tours offers sea and land tours, including trips to Middle Caicos, the largest of the islands, for a visit to the caves, or to North Caicos to see flamingos and plantation ruins. Nell's Taxi offers taxi tours of the islands, priced between $25 and $30 for the first hour and $25 for each additional hour.

Special day excursions are available from local airline Air Turks & Caicos. Trips include whale-watching in Salt Cay, and if you venture to Middle Caicos and North Caicos, in addition to flights, you get a map, water, a lunch voucher, and a mountain bike to explore for the day. Trips start from $99, which includes round-trip air tickets. Day trips to Grand Turk are available with SkyKing. For around $179, you get a round-trip flight to the capital island, a short tour, admission to the Turks & Caicos National Museum, a stop off for lunch, and time to explore on your own.

Contacts Air Turks & Caicos (☎649/946–5481 or 649/946–4181 ⊕www.airturksandcaicos.com). **Big Blue Unlimited** (✉Leeward Marina, Leeward, Providenciales

CELL PHONE TIPS

You can purchase a cheap cell phone at numerous outlets and simply "top-up" (pay as you go). Incoming calls are free, and with the cheap cell, you'll have service even on secluded and isolated beaches. Have your family call you to save on exorbitant island rates and huge roaming charges. Not all cell phones from home will work in the T&C (some do, but you never know which ones until you're actually on-island), even if the phone company tells you it does.

☎649/946–5034 ⊕www.bigblue.tc). **J&B Tours** (☎649/946–5047 ⊕www.jbtours.com). **Nell's Taxi** (☎649/231–0051). **SkyKing** (☎649/941–5464 ⊕www.skyking.tc).

VISITOR INFORMATION

The tourist offices on Grand Turk and Providenciales are open daily from 9 to 5.

Before You Leave Turks & Caicos Islands Tourist Board (954/568–6588 in Ft. Lauderdale or 800/241–0824 ⊕www.turksandcaicostourism.com).

In Turks & Caicos Islands Turks & Caicos Islands Tourist Board (✉Front St., Cockburn Town, Grand Turk ☎649/946–2321 ✉Stubbs Diamond Plaza, The Bight, Providenciales ☎649/946–4970 ⊕www.turksandcaicostourism.com).

WEDDINGS

Beautiful oceanfront backdrops, endless starlight nights, and a bevy of romantic accommodations make the islands an ideal wedding destination. The residency requirement is only 24 hours, after which you can apply for a marriage license to the registrar in Grand Turk; the ceremony can take place at any time after the application has been granted, generally within two to three days. You must present a passport, original birth certificate, and proof of current marital status, as well as a letter stating both parties' occupations, ages, addresses, and fathers' full names. No blood tests are required, and the license fee is $50. The ceremony is conducted by a local minister, justice of the peace, or the registrar. The marriage certificate is filed in the islands, although copies can be sent to your home. There are a number of wedding coordinators on-island, and many resorts offer special wedding packages, which include handling all the details.

Contact Nila Destinations Wedding Planning (☎649/941–4375 ⊕www.nilavacations. com).

25

United States Virgin Islands

Snorkelers, St. Thomas

WORD OF MOUTH

"Much has been written here of the beauty of St. John. All I can say is; its all true! The island is absolutely gorgeous and definitely a place I plan to get back to for a longer visit."

—cmerrell

"Lovely place, lovely people—not a great place for partiers, but for beaches, snorkeling, and quiet fun amid some cool Danish colonial architecture, [St. Croix] was darn near perfect."

—repete

WELCOME TO UNITED STATES VIRGIN ISLANDS

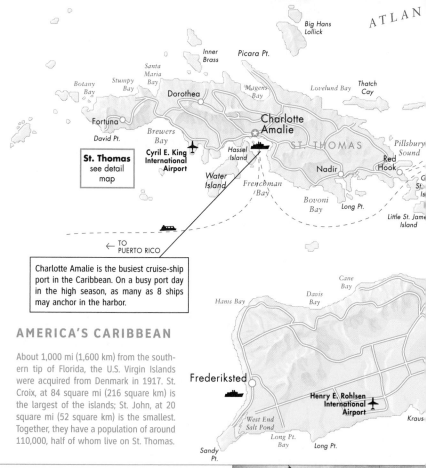

Big Hans Lollick

ATLAN

Picara Pt.

Inner Brass

Santa Maria Bay

Botany Bay

Stumpy Bay

Magens Bay

Lovelund Bay

Thatch Cay

Dorothea

Charlotte Amalie

ST. THOMAS

Fortuna

Brewers Bay

David Pt.

St. Thomas
see detail map

Cyril E. King International Airport

Hassel Island

Pillsbury Sound

Nadir

Red Hook

Water Island

Frenchman Bay

Bovoni Bay

Long Pt.

St. Is

Little St. Jame Island

← TO PUERTO RICO

Charlotte Amalie is the busiest cruise-ship port in the Caribbean. On a busy port day in the high season, as many as 8 ships may anchor in the harbor.

Cane Bay

Davis Bay

Hams Bay

Frederiksted

Henry E. Rohlsen International Airport

West End Salt Pond

Long Pt. Bay

Long Pt.

Kraus

Sandy Pt.

AMERICA'S CARIBBEAN

About 1,000 mi (1,600 km) from the southern tip of Florida, the U.S. Virgin Islands were acquired from Denmark in 1917. St. Croix, at 84 square mi (216 square km) is the largest of the islands; St. John, at 20 square mi (52 square km) is the smallest. Together, they have a population of around 110,000, half of whom live on St. Thomas.

A perfect combination of the familiar and the exotic, the U.S. Virgin Islands are a little bit of home set in an azure sea. With hundreds of idyllic coves and splendid beaches, chances are that on one of the three islands you'll find your ideal Caribbean vacation spot.

TOP 4 REASONS TO VISIT THE UNITED STATES VIRGIN ISLANDS

① St. Thomas is one of the Caribbean's major sailing centers.

② Two-thirds of St. John is a national park, which is criss-crossed by excellent hiking trails.

③ Though Magens Bay on St. Thomas and Trunk Bay on St. John are two of the most perfect beaches you'll ever find, St. Croix's west-end beaches are fetching in their own way.

④ Shopping on both St. Thomas and St. Croix is stellar.

UNITED STATES VIRGIN ISLANDS PLANNER

Island Activities	Logistics

Island Activities

St. Thomas is one of the Caribbean's most important centers for **sailing**.

Beaches are excellent on both St. Thomas and St. John, and good on St. Croix.

Of the three, St. Croix is more known for **diving**, particularly at Cane Bay. St. Croix's Buck Island and its surrounding reefs are also a protected part of the national park system and a great destination for **snorkeling**. The island also has a great **golf** course.

St. Thomas is the most developed of the three islands, but you'll find every imaginable kind of water- and landbased activity, **historic sights**, **golf**, **biking**, and **horseback riding** to mention but a few.

Since most of St. John is a national park, the island is in pristine condition, and its many **hiking** trails are well worth exploring on foot. Off-the beach **snorkeling** is also a popular activity, though some prefer taking a snorkeling and sailing trip to enjoy hard-to-reach beaches in the U.S. and nearby British Virgin Islands.

Logistics

Getting to the U.S. Virgin Islands: It's fairly easy to reach St. Thomas's Cyril E. King Airport (STT) on the west end of the island. St. Croix's Henry Rohlsen Airport (STX) sits outside Frederiksted; the east end is 45 minutes away. If you can't get a nonstop flight to either island, then you can connect in San Juan. You can also take a seaplane between St. Thomas and St. Croix. The only option for St. John is a ferry from either Red Hook or Charlotte Amalie in St. Thomas. Both Caneel Bay and the Westin have private ferries.

Hassle Factor: Low to High, depending on your flight schedule.

Nonstops: You can fly nonstop to St. Thomas from Atlanta (Delta), Charlotte (USAirways), Fort Lauderdale (Spirit), Miami (American), New York–JFK (American) New York–Newark (Continental), Philadelphia (USAirways), Washington, DC–Dulles (United). You can fly nonstop to St. Croix from Atlanta (Delta), Miami (American).

On the Ground

In St. Thomas, shared taxi vans are plentiful at the airport, and fees are per-person. You'll usually be charged a small fee for each piece of luggage. In St. Croix, you'll pay $10 to $20 for a taxi to your hotel. In St. John, safari-style taxi vans meet all the ferries and will drop you at your hotel; as on St. Thomas, the rates are per person.

Renting a Car: If you are renting a villa on any of the three islands, you'll need a car. Otherwise, it's possible to get by with taxis on St. Thomas, but this can be expensive if you need one every day. You'll probably want a car on St. Croix, if only for a few days, to explore the island; if you are staying near Christiansted and your hotel has a shuttle into Christiansted, you might do without one entirely. In St. John, you will probably need a car to get around and to the beach unless you are staying at Caneel Bay or the Westin. To rent a car, you need only a valid driver's license and credit card; the minimum age for drivers is 18, although many agencies won't rent to anyone under the age of 25.

Where to Stay

St. Thomas is the most developed of the Virgin Islands; choose it if you want extensive shopping opportunities and a multitude of activities and restaurants. St. John is the least developed of the three and has a distinct following; it's the best choice if you want a small-island feel and easy access to great hiking. However, most villas there aren't directly on the beach. St. Croix is a sleeper. With accommodations ranging from simple inns to luxury resorts, it's remarkably diverse, but none of the beaches is as breathtaking as those on St. Thomas and St. John.

Resorts: Whether you are looking for a luxury retreat or a moderately priced vacation spot, there's going to be something for you in the USVI. St. Thomas has the most options. St. John has only two large resorts, both upscale; others are small, but it has some unique eco-oriented camping options. St. Croix's resorts are more mid-sized.

Small Inns: Particularly on St. Croix, you'll find a wide range of attractive and accommodating small inns; if you can live without being directly on the beach; these friendly, homey places are a good option. St. Thomas also has a few small inns.

Villas: Villas are plentiful on all three islands, but they are especially popular on St. John, where they represent more than half the available lodging. They're always a good bet for families who can do without a busy resort environment.

⇨For information on hotel meal plans, see Accommodations in Caribbean Essentials.

WHAT IT COSTS IN U.S. DOLLARS

$$$$	$$$	$$	$	¢
Restaurants				
over $30	$20–$30	$12–$20	$8–$12	under $8
Hotels*				
over $350	$250–$350	$150–$250	$80–$150	under $80
Hotels**				
over $450	$350–$450	$250–$350	$125–$250	under $125

*EP, BP, CP; **AI, FAP, MAP. Restaurant prices are for a main course at dinner, excluding tip. Hotel prices are for two people in a double room during high season, excluding 8% tax, service charge and energy surcharges (which can vary significantly), and meal plans (except for all-inclusives).

When to Go

High season coincides with that on most other Caribbean islands, from December through April or May; before and after that time, rates can drop by as much as 25% to 50%, depending on the resort.

St. Thomas's **International Rolex Regatta** in March is a big draw. April is also a great time to visit St. Thomas, as the island comes alive for **Carnival**. The celebrations—steel-drum music, colorful costumes, and dancing in the streets—culminate the last weekend of the month. The big **sport-fishing tournaments** usually begin in May and go through the summer.

The **St. Croix Half Ironman Triathlon** attracts international class athletes as well as amateurs every May. In February and March, the **St. Croix Landmarks Society House Tours** give you a chance to peek inside many historic homes that aren't usually open to the public.

There aren't too many big events on St. John, but **Carnival** tends to bring many people to St. John, as well as the other two U.S. Virgin Islands islands.

26

By Carol M.
Bareuther &
Lynda Lohr

WE PILED INTO THE TAXI van, bags in the back, and set off for our hotel on the opposite end of the island. Minutes later, cars slowed as we crept through the heart of town. But this traffic jam came with a view. Ballast-brick-walled 19th-century buildings touted contemporary buys on gold, diamonds, and emeralds, while turquoise seas glittered on the other side. Then our world turned topsy-turvy. Up we drove at a 45-degree angle or steeper, along former donkey trails to the mountain-ridge road that ran down the spine of the island. From this vantage point, the red-roof buildings and harbor below looked like miniatures on a postcard. Back on level ground, we pulled up to a green-painted van parked alongside stands brimming with tropical produce. "Sorry, I didn't have lunch," our driver apologized as he hopped back into his seat while holding a large paper bag. He pulled out a fried-bread oval, took a bite and passed the rest of the bag back to us. "Here, try a johnnycake," he offered. We were still happily munching as we finally pulled into our hotel. In 40 minutes, we had not merely reached where we were going but had a good idea of where we'd come. True, the U.S. flag blows here, but "America's Paradise" is in reality a delightful mix of the foreign and familiar that offers something for everyone to enjoy.

The U.S. Virgin Islands—St. Thomas, St. John, and St. Croix—float in the Greater Antilles between the Atlantic and Caribbean seas and some 1,000 mi (1,600 km) from the southern tip of Florida. History books give credit to Christopher Columbus for "discovering" the New World. In reality, the Virgin Islands, like the rest of the isles in the Caribbean chain, were populated as long ago as 2000 BC by nomadic waves of seagoing settlers as they migrated north from South America and eastward from Central America and the Yucatán Peninsula.

Columbus met the descendants of these original inhabitants during his second voyage to the New World, in 1493. He anchored in Salt River, a natural bay west of what is now Christiansted, St. Croix, and sent his men ashore in search of fresh water. Hostile arrows rather than welcoming embraces made for a quick retreat. In haste, Columbus named the island Santa Cruz (Holy Cross) and sailed north. He eventually claimed St. John, St. Thomas, and what are now the British Virgin Islands for Spain and at the same time named this shapely silhouette of 60-some islands Las Once Mil Virgenes, for the 11,000 legendary virgin followers of St. Ursula. Columbus believed the islands barren of priceless spices, so he sailed off leaving more than a century's gap in time before the next Europeans arrived.

Pioneers, planters, and pirates from throughout Europe ushered in the era of colonization. Great Britain and the Netherlands claimed St. Croix in 1625. This peaceful coexistence ended abruptly when the Dutch governor killed his English counterpart, thus launching years of battles for possession that would see seven flags fly over this southernmost Virgin isle. Meanwhile, St. Thomas's sheltered harbor proved a magnet for pirates like Blackbeard and Bluebeard. The Danes first colonized the island in 1666, naming their main settlement Taphus for its many beer halls. In 1691 the town received the more respectable name of Charlotte Amalie in honor of Danish king Christian V's wife. It wasn't until 1718 that a small group of Dutch planters raised their country's flag on St. John. As on its sibling Virgins, a plantation economy soon developed.

Plantations depended on slave labor, and the Virgin Islands played a key role in the triangular route that connected the Caribbean, Africa, and Europe in the trade of sugar, rum, and human cargo. By the early 1800s a sharp decline in cane prices due to competing beet sugar and an increasing number of slave revolts motivated Governor General Peter von Scholten to abolish slavery in the Danish colonies on July 3, 1848. This holiday is now celebrated as Emancipation Day.

After emancipation, the island's economy slumped. Islanders owed their existence to subsistence farming and fishing. Meanwhile, during the American Civil War, the Union began negotiations with Denmark for the purchase of the Virgin Islands in order to establish a naval base. However, the sale didn't happen until World War I, when President Theodore Roosevelt paid the Danes $25 million for the three largest islands; an elaborate Transfer Day ceremony was held on the grounds of St. Thomas's Legislature Building on March 31, 1917. A decade later, Virgin Islanders were granted U.S. citizenship. Today the U.S. Virgin Islands is an unincorporated territory, meaning that citizens govern themselves, vote for their own governors, but cannot vote for president or congressional representation.

Nowadays, Virgin Islanders hail from more than 60 nations. Descendants of African slaves are the largest segment of the population, so it's not surprising that they also provide the largest percentage of workers and owners of restaurants, resorts, and shops. The Danish influence is still strong in architecture and street names. Americana is everywhere, too, most notably in recognizable fast-food chains, familiar shows on cable TV, and name-brand hotels. Between this diversity and the wealth that tourism brings, Virgin Islanders struggle to preserve their culture. Their rich, spicy West Indian–African heritage comes to full bloom at Carnival time, when celebrating and playing mas (with abandon) take precedence over everything else.

About 60,000 people live on 32-square-mi (83-square-km) St. Thomas (about the size of Manhattan); 51,000 on the 84 square mi (216 square km) of pastoral St. Croix; and about 5,000 on 20-square-mi (52-square-km) St. John, two-thirds of which is a national park. The backbone of the islands' economy is tourism, but at their heart is an independent, separate being: a rollicking hodgepodge of West Indian culture with a sense of humor that puts sex and politics in almost every conversation. Lacking a major-league sports team, Virgin Islanders follow the activities and antics of their 15 elected senators with the rabidity of Washingtonians following the Redskins. Loyalty to country and faith in God are the rules in the USVI, not the exceptions. Prayer is a way of life, and ROTC is one of the most popular high-school extra-curricular activities.

Although the idyllic images of a tropical isle are definitely here, there's evidence, too, of growing pains. Traffic jams are common, a clandestine drug trade fuels crime, and—particularly on St. Thomas—there are few beaches left that aren't fronted by a high-rise hotel. Virgin Islanders are friendly folks, yet they can be prone to ungracious moments. Saying "Good morning" to the woman behind the jewelry counter, "Good afternoon" to the man who drives your cab, or "Good evening" as you arrive at a restaurant for dinner will definitely pave the way for more pleasantries. Despite fairly heavy development, wildlife has found refuge here. The brown pelican is on the endangered list worldwide but is a common sight in the USVI. The endangered native boa tree is protected, as is the hawksbill turtle, whose females lumber onto the beaches to lay eggs.

With three islands to choose from, you're likely to find your piece of paradise. Check into a beachfront condo on the east end of St. Thomas; then eat burgers and watch football at a beachfront bar and grill. Or stay at an 18th-century plantation greathouse on St. Croix, dine on everything from local food to Continental cuisine, and go horseback riding at sunrise. Rent a tent or a cottage in the pristine national park on St. John; then take a hike, kayak off the coast, read a book, or just listen to the sounds of the forest. Or dive deep into "island time" and learn the art of limin' (hanging out, Caribbean-style) on all three islands.

ST. THOMAS

By Carol M. Bareuther

If you fly to the 32-square-mi (83-square-km) island of St. Thomas, you land at its western end; if you arrive by cruise ship, you come into one of the world's most beautiful harbors. Either way, one of your first sights is the town of Charlotte Amalie. From the harbor you see an idyllic-looking village that spreads into the lower hills. If you were expecting a quiet hamlet with its inhabitants hanging out under palm trees, you've missed that era by about 300 years. Although other islands in the USVI developed plantation economies, St. Thomas cultivated its harbor, and it became a thriving seaport soon after it was settled by the Danish in the 1600s.

The success of the naturally perfect harbor was enhanced by the fact that the Danes—who ruled St. Thomas with only a couple of short interruptions from 1666 to 1917—avoided involvement in some 100 years' worth of European wars. Denmark was the only European country with colonies in the Caribbean to stay neutral during the War of the Spanish Succession in the early 1700s. Thus, products of the Dutch, English, and French islands—sugar, cotton, and indigo—were traded through Charlotte Amalie, along with the regular shipments of slaves. When the Spanish wars ended, trade fell off, but by the end of the 1700s Europe was at war again, Denmark again remained neutral, and St. Thomas continued to prosper. Even into the 1800s, while the economies of St. Croix and St. John foundered with the market for sugarcane, St. Thomas's economy remained vigorous. This prosperity led to the development of shipyards, a well-organized banking system, and a large merchant class. In 1845 Charlotte Amalie had 101 large importing houses owned by the English, French, Germans, Haitians, Spaniards, Americans, Sephardim, and Danes.

Charlotte Amalie is still one of the world's most active cruise-ship ports. On almost any day at least one and sometimes as many as eight cruise ships are tied to the dock or anchored outside the harbor. Gently rocking in the shadows of these giant floating hotels are just about every other kind of vessel imaginable: sleek sailing mono- and multihulls that will take you on a sunset cruise complete with rum punch and a Jimmy Buffett soundtrack, private megayachts that spirit busy executives away, and barnacle-bottom sloops—with laundry draped over the lifelines—that are home to world-cruising gypsies. Huge container ships pull up in Sub Base, west of the harbor, bringing in everything from breakfast cereals to tires. Anchored right along the waterfront are down-island barges that ply the waters between the Greater Antilles and the Leeward Islands, transporting goods like refrigerators, VCRs, and disposable diapers.

The waterfront road through Charlotte Amalie was once part of the harbor. Before it was filled in to build the highway, the beach came right up to the back door of the warehouses that now line the thoroughfare. Two hundred years ago those warehouses were filled with indigo, tobacco, and cotton. Today the stone buildings house silk, crystal, linens, and leather. Exotic fragrances are still traded, but by island beauty queens in air-conditioned perfume palaces instead of through open market stalls. The pirates of old used St. Thomas as a base from which to raid merchant ships of every nation, though they were particularly fond of the gold- and silver-laden treasure ships heading to Spain. Pirates are still around, but today's versions use St. Thomas as a drop-off for their contraband: illegal immigrants and drugs.

WHERE TO STAY

Of the USVI, St. Thomas has the most rooms and the greatest number and variety of resorts. You can let yourself be pampered at a luxurious resort—albeit at a price of $300 to more than $500 per night, not including meals. If your means are more modest, there are fine hotels (often with rooms that have a kitchen and a living area) in lovely settings throughout the island. There are also guesthouses and inns with great views (if not a beach at your door) and great service at about half the cost of what you'll pay at the beachfront pleasure palaces. Many of these are east and north of Charlotte Amalie or overlooking hills—ideal if you plan to get out and mingle with the locals. There are also inexpensive lodgings (most right in town) that are perfect if you just want a clean room to return to after a day of exploring or beach-bumming.

East-end condominium complexes are popular with families. Although condos are pricey (winter rates average $350 per night for a two-bedroom unit, which usually sleeps six), they have full kitchens, and you can definitely save money by cooking for yourself—especially if you bring

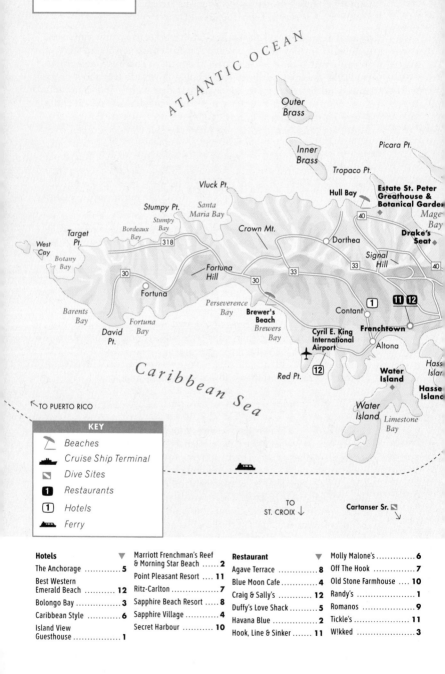

St. Thomas

ATLANTIC OCEAN

Outer Brass

Inner Brass

Picara Pt.

Tropaco Pt.

Hull Bay

Estate St. Peter Greathouse & Botanical Garden

Mage Bay

Vluck Pt.

Santa Maria Bay

Stumpy Pt.

Crown Mt.

Dorthea

Drake's Seat

Signal Hill

Bordeaux Bay

Stumpy Bay

318

Target Pt.

West Cay

Botany Bay

30

Fortuna Hill

30

33

33

40

Barents Bay

Fortuna

Perseverance Bay

Brewer's Beach

Contant

1

11 12

Fortuna Bay

David Pt.

Cyril E. King International Airport

Brewers Bay

Altona

Frenchtown

Hass Islan

Caribbean Sea

Red Pt.

12

Water Island

Hasse Island

TO PUERTO RICO

Water Island

Limestone Bay

KEY

Beaches

Cruise Ship Terminal

Dive Sites

1 Restaurants

1 Hotels

Ferry

TO
ST. CROIX ↓

Cartanser Sr.

Hotels ▼

The Anchorage **5**

Best Western
Emerald Beach **12**

Bolongo Bay **3**

Caribbean Style **6**

Island View
Guesthouse **1**

Marriott Frenchman's Reef
& Morning Star Beach **2**

Point Pleasant Resort **11**

Ritz-Carlton **7**

Sapphire Beach Resort **8**

Sapphire Village **4**

Secret Harbour **10**

Restaurant ▼

Agave Terrace **8**

Blue Moon Cafe **4**

Craig & Sally's **12**

Duffy's Love Shack **5**

Havana Blue **2**

Hook, Line & Sinker **11**

Molly Malone's **6**

Off The Hook **7**

Old Stone Farmhouse **10**

Randy's **1**

Romanos **9**

Tickle's **11**

W!kked **3**

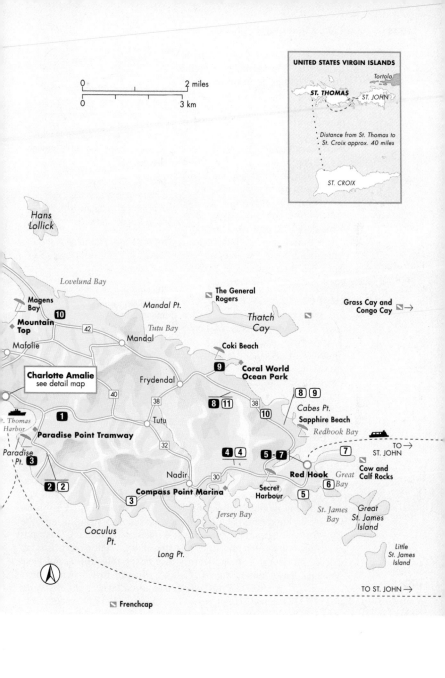

some of your own nonperishable foodstuffs. (Virtually everything on St. Thomas is imported, and restaurants and shops pass shipping costs on to you.) Though you may spend some time laboring in the kitchen, many condos ease your burden with daily maid service and on-site restaurants; a few also have resort amenities, including pools and tennis courts. The east end is convenient to St. John, and it's a hub for the boating crowd, with some good restaurants. The prices below reflect rates in high season, which runs from December 15 to April 15. Rates are 25% to 50% lower the rest of the year.

CHARLOTTE AMALIE

Accommodations in town and near town offer the benefits of being close to the airport, shopping, and a number of casual and fine-dining restaurants. The downside is that this is the most crowded and noisy area of the island. Crime can also be a problem. Don't go for a stroll at night in the heart of town. Use common sense and take the same precautions you would in any major city. Properties along the hillsides are less likely to have crime problems, plus they command a steady breeze from the cool trade winds. This is especially important if you're visiting in summer and early fall.

ST. THOMAS TOP 5

Shop till you drop: Find great deals on jewelry, timepieces, and electronics in Charlotte Amalie.

Tell Fish Stories: Search for trophy-worthy fish from June through October.

Get Your Sea Legs: Cruise between the islands any time of year or join the International Rolex Regatta in March.

Hit the Links: Play through the "Devil's Triangle" at Mahogany Run Golf Course.

Take a Dip: Swim at Magens Bay, considered by many to be one of the most beautiful beaches in the world.

$$–$$$ **Holiday Inn St. Thomas.** Business travelers, those on their way to the British Virgin Islands, or laid-back vacationers who want the convenience of being able to walk to duty-free shopping, sights, and restaurants stay at this harborfront hotel. But if your ideal Caribbean beach vacation means having the beach at your doorstep, this isn't the place for you, despite the presence of a free beach shuttle. Contemporary rooms have such amenities as coffeemakers, hair dryers, ironing boards, and irons. An introductory dive lesson with Admiralty Dive Center is complimentary. Pros: Walking distance to Charlotte Amalie, nice harbor views. Cons: Basic rooms, on a busy street, no water sports. ⊠ *Waterfront Hwy., Box 640,* ☎ *340/774–5200 or 800/524–7389* ⊕ *www.holidayinn.st-thomas.com* ⇨ *140 rooms, 11 suites* ⌂ *In-room: safe, refrigerator, dial-up. In-hotel: restaurant, room service, bar, pool, gym, diving, laundry service, public Internet* ⊟ *AE, D, DC, MC, V* ⎮⊙⎮ *EP.*

$–$$ **The Green Iguana.** Atop Blackbeard's Hill, this B&B offers the perfect mix of gorgeous harbor views, proximity to shopping (five-minute walk), and secluded privacy provided by the surrounding flamboyant trees and bushy hibiscus. Accommodations range from a roomy, top-floor junior suite with two queen beds to a balcony room with queen bed and full kitchen. All rooms have refrigerators, microwave ovens, and coffeemakers. There's also a picnic area with a gas barbecue grill. The managing couple lives on the property and is very helpful in giving restaurant, sightseeing, or beach suggestions. Pros: Personalized service, near the center of town, laundry on premises. Cons: Need a car to get around, neighborhood is sketchy at night. ⊠ *37B Blackbeard's Hill,* ☎ *340/776–7654 or 800/484–8825* ⊕ *www.thegreeniguana.com* ⊅ *6 rooms* ⌂ *In-room: kitchen (some), refrigerator. In-hotel: pool, laundry facilities, no-smoking rooms, no elevator* ⊟ *AE, D, MC, V* ⏊ *EP.*

$–$$ ⊞ **Hotel 1829.** Antique charm is readily apparent in this rambling 19th-century merchant's house, from the hand-painted Moroccan tiles to a Tiffany window. Rooms on several levels range from stylish and spacious suites with vaulted ceilings to small and cozy rooms. The bar is open nightly and attracts locals as well as hotel guests. The second-floor botanical gardens and open-air champagne bar are romantic spots for sunset viewing. Main Street, with its duty-free shops, is a block away. Pros: Close to attractions, old-world charm, breakfast served on the veranda. Cons: Small rooms, tour groups during the day, neighborhood dicey at night. ⊠ *Government Hill, Box 1567,* ☎ *340/776–1829 or 800/524–2002* ⊕ *www.hotel1829.com* ⊅ *15 rooms* ⌂ *In-room: no phone, refrigerator. In-hotel: bar, pool, no kids under 11, no elevator* ⊟ *AE, D, MC, V* ⏊ *CP.*

$–$$ ⊞ **Villa Santana.** Built by exiled General Antonio López Santa Anna of
Fodor's Choice Mexico, this 1857 landmark provides a panoramic view of the har-
★ bor and plenty of West Indian charm, which will make you feel as if you're living in a charming slice of Virgin Islands history. Each of the rooms is unique and lovely. Our two favorites are La Mansion, a former library that is now an elegant villa with a large living area crowned by cathedral ceilings, full kitchen, two baths, and four-poster bed; and El Establo, a three-bedroom house with a full kitchen and laundry facilities that is rented by the week. Modern amenities aren't lacking; you can even sit by the pool with your laptop and indulge in wireless Internet access. Pros: Historic charm, plenty of privacy. Cons: Not on a beach, no restaurant, need a car to get around. ⊠ *2D Denmark Hill,* ☎ *340/776–1311* ⊕ *www.villasantana.com* ⊅ *6 rooms* ⌂ *In-room: no a/c (some), no phone, kitchen (some), no TV (some), Wi-Fi. In-hotel: pool, no elevator* ⊟ *AE, MC, V* ⏊ *EP.*

WEST END

A few properties are in the hills overlooking Charlotte Amalie to the west or near French Town, which is otherwise primarily residential.

$$$ ⊞ **Best Western Emerald Beach Resort.** You get beachfront ambience at this reasonably priced miniresort tucked beneath the palm trees, but the tradeoff is that it's directly across from a noisy airport runway. You'll definitely want to spend time on the white-sand beach, which can be seen from nearly every room in the four three-story, peach-color buildings. Rooms are acceptable, but the tropical-print bedspreads and rattan furnishings look worn. Stay here if you need the beach on a budget or if you have an early-morning flight. Pros: Beachfront location, good value, great Sunday brunch. Cons: Airport noise until 10 PM, on a busy road, limited water sports. ⊠*8070 Lindberg Bay,* ☎*340/777–8800 or 800/780–7234* ⊕*www.emeraldbeach.com* ⚡*90 rooms* ♿*In-room: refrigerator, dial-up. In-hotel: restaurant, bar, tennis courts, pool, gym, beachfront, no elevator* ☰*AE, D, MC, V* ⦿⎮*CP.*

$ 🏨 **Island View Guesthouse.** Perched 545 feet up the face of Crown Mountain, this small inn has a homey feel; the hands-on owners can book tours or offer tips about the best sightseeing spots. Rooms range from a suite with a kitchenette that's perfect for families to two simply furnished verandah rooms that share a bath. The two verandah rooms and six poolside rooms have no air-conditioning, but at this altitude there's always a breeze. Six of the rooms have kitchenettes, so you wouldn't have to eat out for every meal. There's an honor bar for drinks and snacks and a communal verandah where guests congregate for continental breakfasts and home-cooked dinners. Pros: Spectacular views, friendly atmosphere, good value. Cons: Small pool, need a car to get around. ⊠*Rte. 332, Box 1903, Estate Contant* ☎*340/774–4270 or 800/524–2023* ⊕*www.islandviewstthomas.com* ⚡*16 rooms, 14 with private bath* ♿*In-room: no a/c (some), kitchen (some). In-hotel: pool, no elevator, laundry facilities* ☰*AE, MC, V* ⦿⎮*CP.*

EAST END

You can find most of the large, luxurious beachfront resorts on St. Thomas's east end. The downside is that these properties are about a 30-minute drive from town and 45-minute drive from the airport (substantially longer during peak hours). On the upside, these properties tend to be self-contained, plus there are a number of good restaurants, shops, and water-sports operators in the area. Once you've settled in, you don't need a car to get around.

$$$$ 🏨 **Ritz-Carlton, St. Thomas.** Everything sparkles at the island's most luxu-
Fodor's Choice   rious resort, especially after a $40 million renovation that upgraded
★   everything from in-room furnishings to tiling for the walkways. Spa-
☺   cious guest rooms, with high-speed Internet access, private balconies, and marble bathrooms with deep soaking tubs, are in buildings fanning out from the main building. Six somewhat institutional-looking buildings, with two- and three-bedroom condos, sit on their own adjacent beach. The spa, salon, and fitness center serve adults, both body and soul; the Ritz Kids program packs in a full day of activities for kids, including collecting seashells and feeding iguanas. A 54-foot catamaran is a must-do for a day or sunset sail. Pros: Gorgeous views, great water-sports facilities, beautiful beach. Cons: Service is spotty, food can lack flair, isolated location. ⊠*Rte. 317, Box 6900, Estate Great Bay* ☎*340/775–3333 or 800/241–3333* ⊕*www.ritzcarlton. com* ⚡*255 rooms, 20 suites, 2 villas, 81 condos* ♿*In-room: safe, refrigerator, Wi-Fi. In-hotel: 4 restaurants, room service, bars, tennis courts, pools, gym, spa, beachfront, water sports, concierge, children's programs (ages 4–12), laundry service, public Internet, airport shuttle, no-smoking rooms* ☰*AE, D, DC, MC, V* ⦿⎮*EP.*

$$$$ **Wyndham Sugar Bay Resort & Spa.** Though this terra-cotta high-rise
Fodor'sChoice is surrounded by palm trees and lush greenery, rooms and the walk-
★ ways between them have a bit of a generic feel. However, the sixth and
♺ seventh levels of building D have spectacular ocean views. A complete
renovation added plantation-style guest room furnishings, plush car-
peting, and marble-tile bathrooms. The beach is small, although the
nearby pool is replete with waterfalls and colorful cabanas housing hair
braiders and henna tattoo artists that make a day of lounging here idyllic. It's a 99-step hike from guest rooms, however. Health buffs enjoy
the full-service spa and health club, as well as the outdoor fitness trail.
If you're feeling lucky, head to the Ocean Club Gaming Center, where
there are 95 video slot machines. Pros: Gorgeous pool area, full-service
spa, on-site casino. Cons: Some steps to climb, small beach, limited dining options. ⊠ *Rte. 38, Box 6500, Estate Smith Bay* ☎*340/777–7100
or 800/927–7100* ⊕*www.wyndham.com* ↩*300 rooms, 9 suites* ♿*In-
room: safe, refrigerator, dial-up. In-hotel: 2 restaurants, room service,
bar, tennis courts, pool, gym, spa, beachfront, water sports, concierge,
children's programs (ages 4–12), laundry service* ⊟*AE, D, DC, MC,
V* ◯|*AI.*

$$$–$$$$ **Point Pleasant Resort.** Hilltop suites give you an eagle's-eye view of the
east end and beyond, while those in a building adjacent to the reception
area offer incredible sea views. Sea-level junior suites, where the sounds
of lapping waves will lull you to sleep, are smaller. There's a resort
shuttle, but some walking up steep hills is necessary. The beach is tiny,
though some may call it wonderfully private, but three pools give you
more swimming and sunning options. The property also has a labyrinth
of well-marked nature trails to explore. If you like seafood, don't miss
dinner at the Agave Terrace restaurant; Fungi's on the Beach is a casual
alternative. Pros: Lush setting, convenient kitchens, pleasant pools.
Cons: Steep climb from beach, need a car to get around, some rooms
need refurbishing. ⊠*6600 Rte. 38, Estate Smith Bay* ☎*340/775–7200
or 800/524–2300* ⊕*www.pointpleasantresort.com* ↩*128 suites* ♿*In-
room: safe, kitchen, dial-up. In-hotel: 2 restaurants, bar, tennis court,
pools, gym, beachfront, concierge, laundry facilities, public Internet,
no elevator* ⊟*AE, D, DC, MC, V* ◯|*EP.*

26

$$$–$$$$ **Secret Harbour Beach Resort & Villas.** There's not a bad view from
these low-rise studio, one-, and two-bedroom condos, which are either
beachfront or perched on a hill overlooking an inviting cove. All units,
which have white-tile floors and tropical-print wood and wicker fur-
nishings, are spacious; even the studios are more than 600 square feet
and certainly big enough for a family with two children. The pool is
small, but the beach is the real focal point here. Calm seas make for
excellent swimming, and snorkeling is especially good near the small
dock to the east of the cove, where coral outcroppings attract a bevy
of marine life. Watch spectacular sunsets from your balcony or the
beachfront bar. Kids under 13 stay free, making this a good value for
families. Pros: Beautiful beach, good restaurant, secluded location.
Cons: Some rooms are small, car needed to get around, condo owners
are territorial about beach chairs. ⊠*Rte. 317, Box 6280, Estate Naza-
reth* ☎*340/775–6550 or 800/524–2250* ⊕*www.secretharbourvi.com*

🔁*49 suites, 15 studios* ♿*In-room: kitchen. In-hotel: restaurant, bar, tennis courts, pool, gym, beachfront, diving, water sports, no elevator* ▭*AE, MC, V* ⊙*CP.*

$$–$$$ 🔳 **Sapphire Beach Resort & Marina.** A beautiful half-mile-long white-sand beach is the real ace here. After a long succession of owners, Antilles Resorts took control of the property in 2006 and began much-needed refurbishments to the rooms. Changes include new curtains and bedspreads. The property is nicely landscaped on the ocean side, but away from the beach are a long-awaited convention center, marina office, and shopping complex that is still just a big grassy spot occupied by the odd car and piece of construction equipment. Only the pool bar and restaurant are open, but the resort runs a nightly shuttle to the Wyndham Sugar Bay Beach Club & Resort to give guests two more dinner options. Snorkeling equipment, floating mats, one windsurfing lesson and one sail on a Sunfish are complimentary, as is a two-day car rental. Pros: Beachfront location, water sports abound, near ferries. Cons: Some rooms need refurbishing, restaurant fare limited, some construction noise. ✉*6720 Estate Smith Bay 00802* ☎*800/524–2090, 340/773–9150, or 800/874–7897* ⊕*www.sapphirebeachstthomas.com* 🔁*171 suites* ♿*In-room: kitchen (some). In-hotel: restaurant, bar, tennis courts, pool, gym, beachfront, water sports, no elevator, concierge, laundry facilities* ▭*AE, MC, V* ⊙*EP.*

SOUTH SHORE

The south shore of St. Thomas connects town to the east end of the island via a beautiful road that rambles along the hillside with frequent peeks between the hills for a view of the ocean and, on a clear day, of St. Croix some 40 mi (60 km) to the south. The resorts here are on their own beaches. They offer several opportunities for water sports, as well as land-based activities, fine dining, and evening entertainment.

$$$$ 🔳 **Marriott Frenchman's Reef & Morning Star Beach Resorts.** Set majestically
ⓒ   on a promontory overlooking the east side of Charlotte Amalie's harbor, Frenchman's Reef is the high-rise full-service superhotel, while Morning Star is the even more upscale boutique property nestled along the fine white-sand beach. A $25 million refurbishment, complete in 2007, added mahogany furniture, flat-screen televisions, and wireless connections in all the rooms. Meals here include lavish buffets for breakfast and dinner. A rum bar features bottles from around the Caribbean and around the world. Live entertainment and dancing, scheduled activities for all ages, and an hourly boat that shuttles guests to town make having fun easy. Pros: Beachfront location, good dining options, plenty of activities. Cons: Musty smell on lower levels, long walk between resorts. ✉*Rte. 315, Box 7100, Estate Bakkeroe* ☎*340/776–8500 or 800/233–6388* ⊕*www.marriott.com/property/propertypage/sttfr* 🔁*479 rooms, 27 suites* ♿*In-room: safe, refrigerator, dial-up, Wi-Fi. In-hotel: 4 restaurants, room service, bar, tennis courts, pools, gym, spa, beachfront, concierge, children's programs (ages 4–12)* ▭*AE, D, DC, MC, V* ⊙*EP.*

$$$ 🔳 **Bolongo Bay Beach Club.** All the rooms at this family-run resort tucked along a 1,000-foot-long palm-lined beach have balconies with ocean

views; down the beach are 12 studio and two-bedroom condos with full kitchens. This place is more homey than fancy, but the friendliness of the longtime staff keeps visitors coming back. The beach is a bit rocky for swimming, but sails aboard the resort's 53-foot catamaran and excursions arranged by the on-site dive shop are popular. You can opt out of the all-inclusive plan and pay less, but then you'd have to rent a car because the resort is a bit isolated. The creative cuisine at the Beach House, especially the seven-course tasting menu, shouldn't be missed. Pros: Family-run property, on the beach, water sports abound. Cons: A bit run-down, on a busy road, need a car to get around. ⊠ *Rte. 30, Box 7150, Estate Bolongo* ☎*340/775–1800 or 800/524–4746* ⊕*www.bolongobay.com* ⬚*65 rooms, 12 studio and 2-bedroom condos* ⬚*In-room: safe, kitchen (some), refrigerator. In-hotel: 2 restaurants, bar, tennis courts, pool, beachfront, diving, water sports, no elevator* ⊟*AE, D, DC, MC, V* ⦿*EP.*

VILLAS & CONDOMINIUMS

You can arrange private villa rentals through various agents that represent luxury residences and usually have both Web sites and brochures that show photos of the properties they represent. Some are suitable for travelers with disabilities, but be sure to ask specific questions regarding your own needs. **Calypso Realty** (⬚*Box 12178, 00801* ☎*340/774– 1620 or 800/747–4858* ⊕*www.calypsorealty.com*) specializes in rental properties around St. Thomas. **McLaughlin-Anderson Villas** (⊠*100 Blackbeard's Hill, Suite 3,* ☎*340/776–0635 or 800/537–6246* ⊕*www. mclaughlinanderson.com*) handles rental villas throughout the U.S. Virgin Islands, British Virgin Islands, and Grenada. Many villas and condominiums are in complexes on the East End of St. Thomas.

$$$–$$$$ ⬚**The Anchorage.** A beachfront setting and homey conveniences that include full kitchens and washer-dryer units are what you can find in these two- and three-bedroom suites on Cowpet Bay next to the St. Thomas Yacht Club. The complex has two lighted tennis courts, a freshwater pool, and an informal restaurant. Pros: On the beach, good amenities, tasty dining options. Cons: Small pool, noisy neighbors, need car to get around. ⊠*Rte. 317, Estate Nazareth* ⬚*Antilles Resorts, Box 24786, Christiansted, St. Croix* ☎*800/874–7897* ⊕*www.antilles resorts.com* ⬚*11 suites* ⬚*In-room: kitchen. In-hotel: restaurant, bar, gym, tennis courts, pool, beachfront, laundry facilities, no elevator* ⊟*AE, D, MC, V* ⦿*EP.*

$$ ⬚**Sapphire Village.** These high-rise towers feel more like apartment buildings than luxury resorts, so if you're looking for a home away from home, this might be the place. There are full kitchens, so you can avoid pricey restaurant meals. The view from your balcony is the marina and the ocean. The beach, a spectacular half mile of white sand, is a five-minute walk down the hill. There's a restaurant on property and two more down the hill at the Sapphire Beach Resort & Marina. Additional restaurants, a shopping complex, and ferries to St. John are in nearby Red Hook. Pros: Walking distance to Red Hook, nice views, secluded feel. Cons: Small rooms, limited dining options, noisy neighbors. ⊠*Rte. 38, Sapphire Bay* ⬚*Antilles Resorts, Box 24786,*

26

Christiansted, St. Croix ☎340/779–1540 or 800/874–7897 ⊕www.
antillesresorts.com ⟳15 condos ⬧In-room: kitchen. In-hotel: restau-
rant, bar, tennis courts, pools, beachfront, water sports, laundry facili-
ties, no elevator ⊟AE, D, MC, V ⊺⊙⎮EP.

$ ⚏**Caribbean Style.** Couples will enjoy the romantic feel of these private,
★   individually decorated condos. Each has a king-size bed, a reading and
video library, and a kitchen stocked with breakfast foods and special
requests, such as your favorite ice cream or preferred brand of rum.
You can literally toss an ice cube into the sea from the hammock or
lounge chairs on the private porches of the two smaller condos, while
the two larger condos are only about 20 feet away from the rocky
waterfront. Vessup Beach and water sports are a 10-minute walk away.
Couples who would like to tie the knot will find that wedding arrangements, including professional photography, are the owner's specialty.
Pros: Beachfront location, homey rooms, romantic atmosphere. Cons:
No water sports, need a car to get around, bugs are a problem. ⊠*Rte.*
317, at Cabrita Point, Estate Vessup Bay ⬧6501 Red Hook Plaza,
Suite 201, ☎340/715–1117 or 800/593–1390 ⊕www.cstylevi.com/
cstyle_new/html ⟳4 1-bedroom condos ⬧In-room: kitchen. In-hotel:
pool, water sports, no kids under 15, no-smoking rooms, no elevator
⊟AE, MC, V ⊺⊙⎮CP.

WHERE TO EAT

The beauty of St. Thomas and its sister islands has attracted a cadre of
professionally trained chefs who know their way around fresh fish and
local fruits. You can dine on everything from terrific cheap local dishes
such as goat water (a spicy stew) and fungi (a cornmeal polentalike
side dish) to imports such as hot pastrami sandwiches and raspberries
in crème fraîche.

Restaurants are spread all over the island, although fewer are found
on the west and northwest parts of the island. Most restaurants out
of town are easily accessible by taxi and have ample parking. If you
dine in Charlotte Amalie, take a taxi. Parking close to restaurants can
be difficult to find, and walking around after dark isn't advisable for
safety reasons.

If your accommodations have a kitchen and you plan to cook, there's
good variety in St. Thomas's mainland-style supermarkets. Just be prepared for grocery prices that are about 20% higher than those in the
United States. As for drinking, outside the hotels a beer in a bar will
cost between $2 and $3 and a piña colada $5 or more.

WHAT TO WEAR
Dining on St. Thomas is informal. Few restaurants require a jacket and
tie. Still, at dinner in the snazzier places shorts and T-shirts are inap-
propriate; men would do well to wear slacks and a shirt with buttons.
Dress codes on St. Thomas rarely require women to wear skirts, but
you can never go wrong with something flowing.

Prices You Can't Swallow

High food prices in Virgin Islands supermarkets are enough to dull anyone's appetite. Although you'll never match the prices back home, you can shop around for the best deals. If you're staying in a condo or villa (or if you just have a refrigerator in your room), it pays to stock up on the basics at warehouse-type stores like Pricesmart and Cost-U-Less, especially if you are traveling in a group. Even the foods not sold in bulk have lower prices than at supermarkets or convenience stores. Good buys include beverages, meats, produce, and spirits.

After this, head to supermarkets like Plaza Extra, Pueblo, and Food Center. Although the prices aren't as good as at the big-box stores, the selection is better. Finally, if you want to splurge on top-quality meats, exotic produce, imported cheeses, exotic spices, and imported spirits, then finish off your shopping at high-end shops like Marina Market or Gourmet Gallery.

CHARLOTTE AMALIE

AMERICAN
$$–$$$
☾

✕**Greenhouse Bar & Restaurant.** The eight-page menu at this bustling waterfront restaurant offers burgers, salads, and pizza served all day long, along with more upscale entrées like peel-and-eat shrimp, Maine lobster, Alaskan king crab, and Black Angus prime rib for dinner. This is generally a family-friendly place, though the Two-for-Tuesdays happy hour and Friday-night live reggae music that starts thumping at 10 PM draw a lively young-adult crowd. ⊠ *Waterfront Hwy. at Storetvaer Gade* ☎*340/774–7998* ▬*AE, D, MC, V.*

¢–$
Fodor'sChoice
★

✕**Jen's Gourmet Cafe & Deli.** This hole-in-the-wall eatery is the closest thing you can find to a New York–style Jewish deli. Choose the smoked salmon platter for breakfast or hot pastrami on rye at lunch. Homemade desserts like chocolate layer cake, apple strudel, and peaches-and-cream-cheese strudel are yummy. ⊠ *Grand Galleria, 43–46 Norre Gade, Charlotte Amalie* ☎*340/777–4611* ▬*AE, MC, V* ☾*Closed Sun. No dinner.*

CARIBBEAN
$$

✕**Cuzzin's Caribbean Restaurant & Bar.** The top picks in this restaurant in a 19th-century livery stage are the Virgin Islands staples. For lunch, order tender slivers of conch stewed in a rich onion butter sauce, savory braised oxtail, or curried chicken. At dinner the island-style mutton, served in thick gravy and seasoned with locally grown herbs, offers a tasty treat that's deliciously different. Side dishes include peas and rice, boiled green bananas, fried plantains, and potato stuffing. ⊠ *7 Wimmelskafts Gade, also called Back St.* ☎*340/777–4711* ▬*AE, MC, V.*

$–$$
Fodor'sChoice
★

✕**Gladys' Cafe.** Even if the local specialties—conch in butter sauce, salt fish and dumplings, hearty red bean soup—didn't make this a recommended café, it would be worth coming for Gladys's smile. While you're here, pick up a $5 or $10 bottle of her special hot sauce. There are mustard-, oil and vinegar–, and tomato-based versions; the last is the hottest. ⊠ *Waterfront, at Royal Dane Mall* ⌂*28 Dronningens Gade, Charlotte Amelie, St. Thomas* ☎*340/774–6604* ▬*AE* ☾*No dinner.*

26

ECLECTIC
$$$–$$$$
Fodor'sChoice
★

✕**Banana Tree Grille.** The eagle's-eye view of the Charlotte Amalie harbor from this open-air restaurant is as fantastic as the food. Arrive before 6 PM and watch the cruise ships depart from the harbor while you enjoy a drink at the bar. Liz Buckalew, in the restaurant business since the early 1980s, always gives you a warm welcome. For starters try the combination of lobster, shrimp, scallops, and squid marinated in savory herb vinaigrette. The dark rum, honey, and brown sugar-glazed salmon is an excellent entrée. ✉*Bluebeard's Castle, Bluebeard's Hill*✆*Box 302913, Charlotte Amalie, St. Thomas* ☎*340/776–4050* ⌖*Reservations essential* ▭*AE, D, MC, V* ☺*Closed Mon. No lunch.*

FRENCH
$$$–$$$$
★

✕**Hervé Restaurant & Wine Bar.** In the glow of candlelight—at tables impeccably dressed with fine linens, silver settings, and sparkling crystal—you can start off with French-trained Hervé Chassin's crispy conch fritters served with a spicy-sweet mango chutney, then choose from such entrées as black-sesame-crusted tuna with a ginger-raspberry sauce or succulent roast duck with a ginger-tamarind sauce. The passion-fruit cheesecake is to die for. For lunch, quiches, salads, and grilled sandwiches are served in the open-air bistro on the first floor. ✉*Government Hill* ☎*340/777–9703* ⌖*Reservations essential* ▭*AE, MC, V.*

ITALIAN
$$$–$$$$
★

✕**Virgilio's.** For the island's best northern Italian cuisine, don't miss this intimate, elegant hideaway tucked on a quiet side street. Eclectic art covers the two-story brick walls, and the sound of opera sets the stage for a memorable meal. Come here for more than 40 homemade pastas topped with superb sauces—cappellini with fresh tomatoes and garlic or peasant-style spaghetti in a rich tomato sauce with mushrooms and prosciutto. House specialties include osso buco and tiramisu—expertly crafted by chef Ernesto Garrigos, who has prepared these two dishes on the Discovery Channel's Great Chefs of the World series. ✉*18 Main St.* ☎*340/776–4920* ⌖*Reservations essential* ▭*AE, MC, V* ☺*Closed Sun.*

$$

✕**Café Amici.** Set within the historic stonework and cascading tropical blossoms of A. H. Riise Alley, this charming open-air eatery has an Italian name but boasts a menu with Caribbean flair. Choose anything from brick-oven pizzas to fresh salads, open-faced sandwiches, and unique pasta dishes that are cooked to order. House specialties include tamarind barbecued shrimp salad and pizza topped with house-made sausage and apples. ✉*37 Main St.* ☎*340/776–0444* ▭*AE, MC, V* ☺*Closed Sun. No dinner.*

SPANISH
$$$–$$$$
★

✕**Meson Amalia.** Tucked into the alleyway of Palm Passage, this open-air café owned by Antiguan-born Randolph Maynard and his German wife, Helga, serves authentic Spanish cuisine. Try tapas such as mussels in brandy sauce, escargots with mushrooms and herb butter, or Galician-style octopus and baby eels served in a sizzling garlic sauce. Paella is a house specialty, as is the caramel flan. ✉*Palm Passage, 24 Dronnigens Gade* ☎*340/714–7373* ▭*AE, MC, V.*

WEST END

AMERICAN
$$–$$$

✕**Tickle's Dockside Pub.** Nautical types as well as the local working crowd come here for casual fare with homey appeal: chicken-fried steak, meat loaf with mashed potatoes, and baby back ribs. Hearty breakfasts feature eggs and pancakes, while lunch is a full array of burgers, salads, sandwiches, and soups. From November through April, the adjacent marina is full of megayachts that make for some great eye candy while you dine. ⊠ *Crown Bay Marina, Rte. 304, Estate Contant* ☎ *340/776– 1595* ▤ *AE, D, MC, V.*

ECLECTIC
$$$–$$$$
Fodor's Choice
★

✕**Craig & Sally's.** In the heart of Frenchtown, culinary wizard Sally Darash creates menus with a passionate international flavor using fresh ingredients and a novel approach that makes for a delightful dining experience. Sally's constantly changing menu is never the same, which means your favorite dish may not appear again. But there's always something new to tantalize your taste buds, such as yellowtail tuna swimming in a mango, key lime, and habanero sauce. Husband Craig maintains a 300-bottle wine list that's won accolades. ⊕ *22 Honduras St., Frenchtown 00802* ☎ *340/777–9949* ▤ *AE, MC, V* ⊘ *Closed Mon. and Tues. No lunch weekends.*

SEAFOOD
$$

✕**Hook, Line & Sinker.** Anchored right on the breezy Frenchtown waterfront, adjacent to the pastel-painted boats of the local fishing fleet, this harbor-view eatery serves quality fish dishes. The almond-crust yellowtail snapper is a house specialty. Spicy jerk-seasoned swordfish and grilled tuna topped with a yummy mango-rum sauce are also good bets. This is one of the few independent restaurants serving Sunday brunch. ⊠ *2 Honduras, Frenchtown* ☎ *340/776–9708* ▤ *AE, MC, V.*

EAST END

AMERICAN
$$$–$$$$

✕**Blue Moon Café.** Watch the serene scene of sailboats floating at anchor while supping; sunsets are especially spectacular here. Enjoy French toast topped with toasted coconut for breakfast, a grilled mahimahi sandwich with black olive–caper mayonnaise at lunch, or red snapper with pecans, bananas, and a coconut rum sauce for dinner. ⊠ *Secret Harbour Beach Resort, Rte. 32, Red Hook* ☎ *340/779–2080* ▤ *AE, D, MC, V.*

ECLECTIC
$$$–$$$$
Fodor's Choice
★

✕**Old Stone Farmhouse.** Dine in the splendor of a beautifully restored plantation house. For a real treat try executive chef Ric Ade's special tasting menu (a pricey $90 per person). The four-course menu, complete with paired wines, starts off with appetizer selections such as a different sort of surf-and-turf: pan-seared scallops and oxtail stew. A sauerbraten of North American elk served with chestnut spaetzle, sweet-and-sour red cabbage, and gingersnap gravy shows off Ade's creativity with entrées. Desserts include the to-die-for hot chocolate cake served with coffee gelato. Personalized attention makes dining here a delight. ⊠ *Rte. 42, 1 mi (1½ km) west of entrance to Mahogany Run Golf Course, Estate Lovenlund* ☎ *340/777–6277* ⊛ *Reservations essential* ▤ *AE, MC, V* ⊘ *Closed Mon.*

$

✕**Duffy's Love Shack.** If the floating bubbles don't attract you to this zany eatery, the lime-green shutters, loud rock music, and fun-loving waitstaff just might. It's billed as the "ultimate tropical drink shack," and the bartenders shake up such exotic concoctions as the Love Shack Volcano—a 50-ounce flaming extravaganza. The menu has a selection of burgers, tacos, burritos, and salads. Try the grilled mahimahi taco salad or jerk Caesar wrap. Wednesday night is usually a theme party complete with giveaways. ⊠*Rte. 32, Red Hook* ☎*340/779–2080* ⊟*No credit cards.*

IRISH   ✗**Molly Molone's.** This open-air eatery has a devout following among
$$–$$$ locals who live and work on the boats docked nearby. Traditional Irish
☼   dishes include bangers and mash (sausage and mashed potatoes), as well as fresh fish and rich soups and stews. Beware: the resident iguanas will beg for table scraps—bring your camera. Upstairs the same owners run A Whale of a Tale, a pricier seafood eatery that also serves freshly made pasta dishes and fine wines. ⊠*Rte. 32, at American Yacht Harbor, Bldg. D, Red Hook* ☎*340/775–1270* ⊟*MC, V.*

ITALIAN   ✗**Romanos.** Inside this huge old stucco house is a delightful surprise:
$$$–$$$$ a spare yet elegant restaurant serving superb northern Italian cuisine.
★   Try the pastas, either with a classic ragout or a more unique creation such as cream sauce with mushrooms, prosciutto, pine nuts, and Parmesan. ⊠*Rte. 388, at Coki Point, Estate Frydendal* ☎*340/775–0045* ⌐*Reservations essential* ⊟*MC, V* ◷*Closed Sun. No lunch.*

SEAFOOD   ✗**Agave Terrace.** At this open-air restaurant in the Point Pleasant Resort,
$$$–$$$$ the catch of the day—fresh fish served as a steak or a fillet—is listed on the blackboard. More than a dozen sauces, including teriyaki-mango and lime-ginger, liven up your entrée. If you get lucky on a sportfishing day charter, the chef will cook your fish if you bring it in by 3 PM. Come early and have a drink at the Lookout Lounge, which has breathtaking views of the British Virgins. ⊠*Point Pleasant Resort, Rte. 38, Estate Smith Bay* ☎*340/775–4142* ⊟*AE, MC, V* ◷*No lunch.*

$$–$$$ ✗**Off the Hook.** The fish is so fresh here that you may see it coming in from one of the boats tied up at the dock just steps away. For starters try the crispy conch fritters with sweet-hot banana-chili chutney. Entrées include a rib-sticking fish stew with scallops, shrimp, mahimahi, mussels, conch, and calamari swimming in a coconut curry broth. Steak, poultry, and pasta lovers will also find something to please at this open-air eatery. There's also a children's menu. ⊠*Rte. 32, Red Hook* ☎*340/775–6350* ⊟*AE, MC, V* ◷*No lunch.*

SOUTH SHORE

AMERICAN   ✗**W!kked.** Gaze at the boats bobbing in the waves at Yacht Haven
$$–$$$ Grande while forking into casual fare prepared by executive chef
Fodor'sChoice   Brian Katz. Hip cheeseburgers are topped with roasted onions, pep-
★   pers, mushrooms, and smoked Gouda, cheddar, or gorgonzola cheese. Pasta dishes, sizzling steaks, and chicken wings with a choice of five sauces, including ginger-coconut, round out the menu. ⊠*Yacht Haven Grande, 5403 Yacht Haven Grande, Charlotte Amalie* ☎*340/775–8953* ⊟*AE, MC, V.*

ECLECTIC ✕**Havana Blue.** The cuisine here is described as Cuban–Asian, but the
$$–$$$ dining experience is out of this world. A glowing wall of water meets
Fodor'sChoice you as you enter, then you're seated at a table laid with linen and
★ silver that's illuminated in a soft blue light radiating from above. Be
sure to sample the mango mojito, made with fresh mango, crushed
mint, and limes. Entrées include coconut-chipotle ceviche, sugarcane-
glazed pork tenderloin medallions, and the signature dish, miso sea
bass. Hand-rolled cigars and aged rums finish the night off in true
Cuban style. For something really special, request an exclusive table
for two set on Morning Star Beach—you get a seven-course tasting
menu, champagne, and your own personal waiter, all for $375 for two.
⊠*Morningstar Beach Resort, Rte. 315, Box 7100,* ☎*340/715–2583*
⌂*Reservations essential* ⊗*No lunch.*

$$–$$$ ✕**Randy's Bar & Bistro.** There's no view here—even though you're at the
★ top of a hill—but the somewhat hidden location has helped to keep
this one of the island's best dining secrets. This wine shop and deli
caters to a local lunch crowd. At night you forget you're tucked into a
nearly windowless building. The tableside bread for starters is a thick,
crusty focaccia flavored with nearly 10 different vegetables. Try the
Brie-stuffed filet mignon or rack of lamb. After-dinner cigars and wine
complete the experience. ⊠*Al Cohen's Plaza, atop Raphune Hill, ½ mi
(¾ km) east of Charlotte Amalie* ☎*340/777–3199* ▤*AE, D, MC, V.*

26

BEACHES

All 44 St. Thomas beaches are open to the public, although you can
reach some of them only by walking through a resort. Hotel guests
frequently have access to lounge chairs and floats that are off-limits
to nonguests; for this reason you may feel more comfortable at one of
the beaches not associated with a resort, such as Magens Bay (which
charges an entrance fee to cover beach maintenance) or Coki Beach.
Whichever one you choose, remember to remove your valuables from
the car and keep them out of sight when you go swimming.

Brewer's Beach. Watch jets land at the Cyril E. King Airport as you dip
into the usually calm seas. Rocks at either end of the shoreline, patches
of grass poking randomly through the sand, and shady tamarind trees
30 feet from the water give this beach a wild, natural feel. Civilization has arrived, as one or two mobile food vans park on the nearby
road. Buy a fried-chicken leg and johnnycake or burgers and chips to
munch on at the picnic tables. ⊠*Rte. 30, west of University of the
Virgin Islands.*

Fodor'sChoice **Coki Beach.** Funky beach huts selling local foods like meat pates (fried
★ turnovers with a spicy ground-beef filling), picnic tables topped with
☾ umbrellas sporting beverage logos, and a brigade of hair braiders and
taxi men give this beach overlooking picturesque Thatch Cay a Coney
Island feel. But this is the best place on the island to snorkel and scuba
dive. Fish, including grunts, snappers, and wrasses, are like an effervescent cloud you can wave your hand through. Ashore you can find conveniences like restrooms, changing facilities, mask and fin rentals, and
even fish food. ⊠*Rte. 388, next to Coral World Ocean Park.*

Hull Bay. Watch surfers ride the waves here from December to March, when huge swells roll in from north Atlantic storms. The rest of the year, tranquillity prevails. Homer's Snorkel & Scuba Tours is based here, and Homer himself will happily lead you on a day or night snorkel trip to the nearby reefs and out to the uninhabited island of Hans Lollick. Enjoy hot pizza, barbecue ribs, and a game of darts the Hull Bay Hideaway bar and restaurant. ⊠ *Rte. 37, at end of road on north side.*

Fodor's Choice

★

☻

Magens Bay. Deeded to the island as a public park, this heart-shape stretch of white sand is considered one of the most beautiful in the world. The bottom of the bay is flat and sandy, so this is a place for sunning and swimming rather than snorkeling. On weekends and holidays the sounds of music from groups partying under the sheds fill the air. There's a bar, snack shack, and beachwear boutique; bathhouses with restrooms, changing rooms, and saltwater showers are close by. Sunfish and paddleboats are the most popular rentals at the watersports kiosk. East of the beach is Udder Delight, a one-room shop at St. Thomas Dairies that serves a Virgin Islands tradition—a milk shake with a splash of Cruzan rum. Kids can enjoy virgin versions, which have a touch of soursop, mango, or banana flavoring. If you arrive between 8 AM and 5 PM, you pay an entrance fee of $3 per person, $1 per vehicle, and 25¢ per child under age 12. ⊠ *Rte. 35, at end of road on north side of island.*

★ **Morningstar Beach.** Nature and nurture combine at this ¼-mi-long (½-km-long) beach between Marriott Frenchman's Reef and Morning Star Beach Resorts, where amenities range from water-sports rentals to beachside bar service. A concession rents floating mats, snorkeling equipment, sailboards, and Jet Skis. Swimming is excellent; there are good-size rolling waves year-round, but do watch the undertow. If you're feeling lazy, rent a lounge chair with umbrella and order a libation from one of two full-service beach bars. At 7 AM and again at 5 PM, watch the cruise ships glide majestically out to sea from the Charlotte Amalie harbor. ⊠ *Rte. 315, 2 mi (3 km) southeast of Charlotte Amalie, past Havensight Mall and cruise-ship dock.*

★ **Sapphire Beach.** A steady breeze makes this beach a boardsailor's paradise. The swimming is great, as is the snorkeling, especially at the reef near Pettyklip Point. Beach volleyball is big on the weekends. There's also a restaurant, bar, and water-sports rentals at Sapphire Beach Resort & Marina. ⊠ *Rte. 38, Sapphire Bay.*

Secret Harbour. Placid waters make it an easy job to stroke your way out to a swim platform offshore from the Secret Harbour Beach Resort & Villas. Nearby reefs give snorkelers a natural show. There's a bar and restaurant, as well as a dive shop. ⊠ *Rte. 32, Red Hook.*

Vessup Beach. This wild, undeveloped beach is lined with sea-grape trees and century plants. It's close to Red Hook harbor, so you can watch the ferries depart. Calm waters are excellent for swimming. West Indies Windsurfing is here, so you can rent Windsurfers, kayaks, and other water toys. There are no restrooms or changing facilities. It's popular with locals on weekends. ⊠ *Off Rte. 322, Vessup Bay.*

SPORTS & THE OUTDOORS

AIR TOURS

On the Charlotte Amalie waterfront next to Tortola Wharf, **Air Center Helicopters** (✉ *Waterfront, Charlotte Amalie* ☎ *340/775–7335 or 800/619–0013* ⊕ *www.aircenterhelicopters.com*) offers two tours, both pretty pricey: a 17-minute tour of St. Thomas and St. John for $385, and a 25-minute tour that includes St. Thomas, St. John, and Jost Van Dyke priced at $565. Prices are for the entire helicopter, which can accommodate five passengers and a pilot. If you can afford the splurge, it's a nice ride, but in truth, you can see most of the aerial sights from Mountain Top or Paradise Point, and there's no place you can't reach easily by car or boat.

BOATING & SAILING

Calm seas, crystal waters, and nearby islands (perfect for picnicking, snorkeling, and exploring) make St. Thomas a favorite jumping-off spot for day- or weeklong sails or powerboat adventures. With more than 100 vessels from which to choose, St. Thomas is the charter-boat center of the U.S. Virgin Islands. You can go through a broker to book a sailing vessel with a crew or contact a charter company directly. Crewed charters start at $2,000 per person per week, while bareboat charters can start at $1,500 per person for a 50- to 55-foot sailboat (not including provisioning), which can comfortably accommodate up to six people. If you want to rent your own boat, hire a captain. Most local captains are excellent tour guides.

26

Single-day charters are also a possibility. You can hire smaller boats for the day, including the services of a captain if you wish to have someone take you on a guided snorkel trip around the islands.

Island Yachts (✉ *6100 Red Hook Quarter, 18B, Red Hook* ☎ *340/775–6666 or 800/524–2019* ⊕ *www.iyc.vi*)offers sail- or powerboats with or without crews.Luxury is the word at **Magic Moments** (✉ *American Yacht Harbor, Red Hook* ☎ *340/775–5066* ⊕ *www.yachtmagicmoments. com*), where the crew of a 45-foot Sea Ray offers a pampered island-hopping snorkeling cruise. Nice touches include icy-cold eucalyptus-infused washcloths to freshen up and a gourmet wine and lobster lunch. **Stewart Yacht Charters** (✉ *6501 Red Hook Plaza, Suite 20, Red Hook* ☎ *340/775–1358 or 800/432–6118* ⊕ *www.stewartyachtcharters. com*)is run by longtime sailor Ellen Stewart, who is an expert at matching clients with yachts for weeklong crewed charter holidays. Bareboat sail and powerboats, including a selection of stable trawlers, are available at **VIP Yacht Charters** (✉ *South off Rte. 32, Estate Fryden-hoj* ☎ *340/774–9224 or 866/847–9224* ⊕ *www.vipyachts.com*), at Compass Point Marina.

○ **Awesome Powerboat Rentals** (✉ *6100 Red Hook Quarter, Red Hook* ☎ *340/775–0860* ⊕ *www.powerboatrentalsvi.com*), at "P" dock next to the Off the Hook restaurant, offers 22- to 26-foot twin-engine catamarans for day charters. Rates range from $345 to $385 for half- or full-day. A captain can be hired for $115 for a day.If you want to explore the east end of St. Thomas, **Mangrove Adventures** (✉ *Rte. 32,*

Estate Nadir ☎*340/779–2155* ⊕*www.viecotours.com*) offers inflatable boat rentals for $100 per day. **Nauti Nymph** (⊠*6501 Red Hook Plaza, Suite 201, Red Hook* ☎☎*340/775–5066* ☎*800/734–7345* ⊕*www.st-thomas.com/nautinymph*) has a large selection of 25- to 29-foot powerboats. Rates vary from $345 to $540 a day, including snorkel gear, water skis, and outriggers, but not including fuel. You can hire a captain for $115 more.

CYCLING

Water Island Adventures (⊠ *Water Island* ☎*340/714–2186 or 340/775–5770* ⊕*www.waterislandadventures.com*) offers a cycling adventure to the USVI's "newest" Virgin. You take a ferry ride from the West Indian Company dock near Havensight Mall to Water Island before jumping on a Cannondale mountain bike for a 90-minute tour over rolling hills on dirt and paved roads. Explore the remains of the Sea Cliff Hotel, the inspiration for Herman Wouk's book *Don't Stop the Carnival,* then take a cooling swim at beautiful Honeymoon Beach. Helmets, water, a guide, juices, and ferry fare are included in the $75 cost.

DIVING & SNORKELING

Popular dive sites include such wrecks as the *Cartanser Sr.,* a beautifully encrusted World War II cargo ship sitting in 35 feet of water, and the *General Rogers,* a Coast Guard cutter resting at 65 feet. Here you can find a gigantic resident barracuda. Reef dives offer hidden caves and archways at **Cow and Calf Rocks,** coral-covered pinnacles at **Frenchcap,** and tunnels where you can explore undersea from the Caribbean to the Atlantic at **Thatch Cay, Grass Cay,** and **Congo Cay.** Many resorts and charter yachts offer dive packages. A one-tank dive starts at $80; two-tank dives are $99 and up. Call the USVI Department of Tourism to obtain a free eight-page guide to Virgin Islands dive sites. There are plenty of snorkeling possibilities, too.

Admiralty Dive Center (⊠*Holiday Inn St. Thomas, Waterfront Hwy., Charlotte Amalie* ☎*340/777–9802 or 888/900–3483* ⊕*www.admiraltydive.com*)provides boat dives, rental equipment, and a retail store. Four-tank to 12-tank packages are available if you want to dive over several days.

BOB Underwater Adventure (⊠*Crown Bay Marina, Rte. 304, Charlotte Amalie* ☎*340/715–0348* ⊕*www.bobusvi.com*)offers an alternative to traditional diving in the form of an underwater motor scooter called BOB, or Breathing Observation Bubble. A half-day tour, including snorkel equipment, rum punch, and towels, is $99 per person.

Blue Island Divers (⊠*Crown Bay Marina, Rte. 304,Estate Contant* ☎*340/774–2001* ⊕*www.blueislanddivers.com*)is a full-service dive shop that offers both day and night dives to wrecks and reefs.

☾ **Chris Sawyer Diving Center** (☎*340/775–7320 or 877/929–3483* ⊕*www.sawyerdive.vi*) is a PADI five-star outfit that specializes in dives to the 310-foot-long *Rhone,* in the British Virgin Islands. Hotel-dive packages are offered through the Wyndham Sugar Bay Beach Club & Resort.

☾ **Coki Beach Dive Club** (⊠*Rte. 388, at Coki Point, Estate Frydendal* ☎*340/775–4220* ⊕*www.cokidive.com*) is a PADI Gold Palm outfit run by avid diver Peter Jackson. Snorkel and dive tours in the fish-filled reefs off Coki Beach are available, as are classes from beginner to underwater photography.

Snuba of St. Thomas (✉ *Rte. 388, at Coki Point, Estate Smith Bay* ☎ *340/693–8063* ⊕ *www.visnuba.com*) offers something for nondivers, a cross between snorkeling and scuba diving: a 20-foot air hose connects you to the surface. The cost is $68. Children must be eight or older to participate.

Underwater Safaris (✉ *Havensight Mall, Bldg. VI, Rte. 30, Charlotte Amalie* ☎ *340/774–1350* ⊕ *www.scubadivevi.com*) is another PADI five-star center that offers boat dives to the reefs around Buck Island and nearby offshore wrecks.

FISHING

★ Fishing here is synonymous with blue marlin angling—especially from June through October. Four 1,000-pound-plus blues, including three world records, have been caught on the famous North Drop, about 20 mi (32 km) north of St. Thomas. A day charter for marlin with up to six anglers costs $1,500 for the day. If you're not into marlin fishing, try hooking sailfish in winter, dolphin (the fish, not the mammal) in spring, and wahoo in fall. Inshore trips for two to four hours range from $275 to $550, respectively. To find the trip that will best suit you, walk down the docks at either American Yacht Harbor or Sapphire Beach Marina in the late afternoon and chat with the captains and crews.

For marlin, Captain Red Bailey's **Abigail III** (✉ *Rte. 38, Sapphire Bay* ☎ *340/775–6024* ⊕ *www.sportfishvi.com*) operates out of the Sapphire Beach Resort & Marina.

The **Charter Boat Center** (✉ *6300 Red Hook Plaza, Red Hook* ☎ *340/775–7990* ⊕ *www.charterboat.vi*) is a major source for sportfishing charters, both marlin and inshore.

Captain Eddie Morrison, aboard the 45-foot Viking **Marlin Prince** (✉ *American Yacht Harbor, Red Hook* ☎ *340/693–5929* ⊕ *www.marlin prince.com*), is one of the most experienced charter operators in St. Thomas and specializes in fly-fishing for blue marlin.

For inshore trips, **Peanut Gallery Charters** (✉ *Crown Bay Marina, Rte. 304, Estate Contant* ☎ *340/775–5274* ⊕ *www.fishingstthomas.com*) offers trips on its 18-foot *Dauntless* or 28-foot custom sportfishing catamaran.

GOLF

★ The **Mahogany Run Golf Course** (✉ *Rte. 42, Estate Lovenlund* ☎ *340/777–6006 or 800/253–7103* ⊕ *www.mahoganyrungolf.com*) attracts golfers for its spectacular view of the British Virgin Islands and the challenging 3-hole Devil's Triangle. At this Tom and George Fazio–designed par-70, 18-hole course, there's a fully stocked pro shop, snack bar, and open-air clubhouse. Greens and half-cart fees for 18 holes are $150. The course is open daily, and there are frequently informal weekend tournaments. It's the only course on St. Thomas.

26

PARASAILING

The waters are so clear around St. Thomas that the outlines of coral reefs are visible from the air. Parasailers sit in a harness attached to a parachute that lifts them off a boat deck until they're sailing through the sky. Parasailing trips average a 10-minute ride in the sky that costs $75 per person. Friends who want to ride along pay $15 for the boat trip. **Caribbean Watersports & Tours** (⊠*6501 Red Hook Plaza, Red Hook* ☎*340/775–9360* ⊕*www.viwatersports.com*)makes parasailing pickups from 10 locations around the island, including many major beachfront resorts. It also rents Jet Skis, kayaks, and floating battery-power chairs.

SEA EXCURSIONS

Landlubbers and seafarers alike will enjoy the wind in their hair and salt spray in the air while exploring the waters surrounding St. Thomas. Several businesses can book you on a snorkel-and-sail to a deserted cay for a half day that starts at $65 per person or a full day that begins at $110 per person. An excursion over to the British Virgin Islands starts at $115 per person, not including customs fees. A luxury day-long motor-yacht cruise complete with gourmet lunch is $375 or more per person.

For a soup-to-nuts choice of sea tours, contact the **Adventure Center** (⊠*Marriott's Frenchman's Reef Hotel, Rte. 315, Estate Bakkeroe* ☎*340/ 774–2992 or 866/868–7784* ⊕*www.adventurecenters.net*).

The **Charter Boat Center** (⊠*6300 Red Hook Plaza, Red Hook* ☎*340/ 775–7990* ⊕*www.charterboat.vi*)specializes in day trips to the British Virgin Islands and day- or weeklong sailing charters.
Limnos Charters (⊠*Compass Point Marina, Rte. 32, Estate Frydenhoj* ☎*340/775–3203* ⊕*www.limnoscharters.com*)offers one of the most popular British Virgin Islands day trips, complete with lunch, open bar, and snorkel gear. Destinations include the Baths in Virgin Gorda and the sparsely inhabited island of Jost Van Dyke.
Enjoy sailboat racing with **OnDeck Ocean Racing** (⊠*9100 Havensight, Suite 10, Port of Sale Mall, Charlotte Amalie* ☎*340/777–4944* ⊕*www. ondeckoceanracing.com*). During two-hour excursions you participate as a member of the crew. Work the winches, take a turn at the wheel, and maneuver straight to the finish line.
Jimmy Loveland at **Treasure Isle Cruises** (⊠*Rte. 32, Box 6616, Estate Nadir* ☎*340/775–9500* ⊕*www.treasureislecruises.com*) can set you up with everything from a half-day sail to a seven-day U.S. and British Virgin Islands trip that combines sailing with accommodations and sightseeing trips onshore.

SEA KAYAKING

Fish dart, birds sing, and iguanas lounge on the limbs of dense mangrove trees deep within a marine sanctuary on St. Thomas's southeast shore. Learn about the natural history here in a guided kayak-snorkel tour to Patricia Cay or via an inflatable boat tour to Cas Cay for snorkeling and hiking. Both are 2½ hours long. The cost is $65 per person. **Mangrove Adventures** (⊠*Rte. 32, Estate Nadir* ☎*340/779–2155* ⊕*www.viecotours.com*) rents its two-person sit-atop ocean kayaks and inflatable boats for self-guided exploring. In addition, many resorts on St. Thomas's eastern end also rent kayaks.

SUBMARINE TRIPS

Dive 90 feet under the sea to one of St. Thomas's most beautiful reefs without getting wet. **Atlantis Adventures** (⊠*Havensight Mall, Bldg. VI, Charlotte Amalie* ☎*340/776–5650* ⊕*www.atlantisadventures.com*) has a 46-passenger submarine that takes you to a watery world teeming with brightly colored fish, vibrant sea fans, and the occasional shark. A guide narrates the one-hour underwater journey, while a diver makes a mid-tour appearance for a fish-feeding show. The cost is $89. No children shorter than 36 inches are allowed.

WINDSURFING

♺ Expect some spills, anticipate the thrills, and try your luck clipping through the seas. Most beachfront resorts rent Windsurfers and offer one-hour lessons for about $80. If you want to learn, try Pual Stoken's **Island Sol** (☎*340/775–6530* ⊕*www.islandsol.com*). The two-time Olympic athlete charges $125 per hour for private lessons, $75 per hour for group lessons.

One of the island's best-known independent windsurfing companies is **West Indies Windsurfing** (⊠*Vessup Beach, No. 9, Estate Nazareth* ☎*340/775–6530*). Owner John Phillips is the board buff who introduced the sport of kite boarding to the USVI; it entails using a kite to lift a boardsailor off the water for an airborne ride. A private kite-boarding lesson costs $125 per hour, while a semiprivate lesson starts at $85 per hour.

26

SHOPPING

Fodor'sChoice
★ St. Thomas lives up to its billing as a duty-free shopping destination. Even if shopping isn't your idea of how to spend a vacation, you still may want to slip in on a quiet day (check the cruise-ship listings—Monday and Sunday are usually the least crowded) to browse. Among the best buys are liquor, linens, china, crystal (most stores will ship), and jewelry. The amount of jewelry available makes this one of the few items for which comparison shopping is worth the effort. Local crafts include shell jewelry, carved calabash bowls, straw brooms, woven baskets, and dolls. Creations by local doll maker Gwendolyn Harley—like her costumed West Indian market woman—have been little goodwill ambassadors, bought by visitors from as far away as Asia. Spice mixes, hot sauces, and tropical jams and jellies are other native products.

On St. Thomas, stores on Main Street in Charlotte Amalie are open weekdays and Saturday 9 to 5. The hours of the shops in the Havensight Mall (next to the cruise-ship dock) and the Crown Bay Commercial Center (next to the Crown Bay cruise-ship dock) are the same, though occasionally some stay open until 9 on Friday, depending on how many cruise ships are anchored nearby. You may also find some shops open on Sunday if cruise ships are in port. Hotel shops are usually open evenings, as well.

There's no sales tax in the USVI, and you can take advantage of the $1,200 duty-free allowance per family member (remember to save your receipts). Although you can find the occasional salesclerk who will make a deal, bartering isn't the norm.

AREAS & MALLS

The prime shopping area in **Charlotte Amalie** is between Post Office and Market squares; it consists of two parallel streets that run east–west (Waterfront Highway and Main Street) and the alleyways that connect them. Particularly attractive are the historic **A.H. Riise Alley, Royal Dane Mall, Palm Passage,** and pastel-painted **International Plaza.**

Vendors Plaza, on the waterfront side of Emancipation Gardens in Charlotte Amalie, is a central location for vendors selling handmade earrings, necklaces, and bracelets; straw baskets and handbags; T-shirts; fabrics; African artifacts; and local fruits. Look for the many brightly colored umbrellas.

West of Charlotte Amalie, the pink-stucco **Nisky Center,** on Harwood Highway about ½ mi (¾ km) east of the airport, is more of a home-town shopping center than a tourist area, but there's a bank, clothing store, record shop, and Radio Shack.

At the Crown Bay cruise-ship pier, the **Crown Bay Center,** off the Harwood Highway in Sub Base about ½ mi (¾ km) has quite a few shops.

Havensight Mall, next to the cruise-ship dock, may not be as charming as downtown Charlotte Amalie, but it does have more than 60 shops. It also has an excellent bookstore, a bank, a pharmacy, a gourmet grocery, and smaller branches of many downtown stores. The shops at **Port of $ale,** adjoining Havensight Mall (its buildings are pink instead of brown), sell discount goods. Next door to Port of $ale is the **Yacht Haven Grande** complex, with many upscale shops.

East of Charlotte Amalie on Route 38 **Tillett Gardens** is an oasis of artistic endeavor across from the Tutu Park Shopping Mall. The late Jim and Rhoda Tillett converted this Danish farm into an artists' retreat in 1959. Today you can watch artisans produce silk-screen fabrics, candles, watercolors, jewelry, and other handicrafts. Something special is often happening in the gardens as well: the Classics in the Gardens program is a classical music series presented under the stars, Arts Alive is an annual arts-and-crafts fair held in November, and the Pistarckle Theater holds its performances here. **Tutu Park Shopping Mall,** across from Tillett Gardens, is the island's one and only enclosed mall. More than 50 stores and a food court are anchored by Kmart and Plaza Extra grocery store. Archaeologists have discovered evidence that Arawak Indians once lived near the grounds.

Red Hook has **American Yacht Harbor,** a waterfront shopping area with a dive shop, a tackle store, clothing and jewelry boutiques, a bar, and a few restaurants.

Made in St. Thomas

Date palm brooms, frangipani-scented perfume, historically clad dolls, sun-scorched hot sauces, aromatic mango candles: these are just a few of the handicrafts made in St. Thomas.

Justin Todman, aka the Broom Man, keeps the dying art of broom-making alive. It's a skill he learned at the age of six from his father. From the fronds of the date palm, Todman delicately cuts, strips, and dries the leaves, a process that can take up to a week. Then he creatively weaves the leaves into distinctively shaped brooms with birch-berry wood for handles. There are feather brooms, cane brooms, multicolor yarn brooms, tiny brooms to fit into a child's hand, and tall long-handled brooms to reach cobwebs on the ceiling. Some customers buy Todman's brooms—sold at the Native Arts & Crafts Cooperative—not for cleaning but rather for celebrating their nuptials. It's an old African custom for the bride and groom to jump over a horizontally laid broom to start their new life.

Gail Garrison puts the essence of local flowers, fruits, and leaves into perfumes, powders, and body splashes. Her Island Fragrances line includes frangipani-, white ginger-, and jasmine-scented perfumes; aromatic mango, lime, and coconut body splashes; and bay rum aftershave for men. Garrison compounds, mixes, and bottles the products herself in second-floor offices on Charlotte Amalie's Main Street. You can buy the products in the Tropicana Perfume Shop.

Gwendolyn Harley preserves Virgin Islands culture in the personalities of her hand-sewn, softly sculptured historic dolls for sale at the Native Arts & Crafts Cooperative. There are quadrille dancers clad in long, colorful skirts; French women with their neat peaked bonnets; and farmers sporting hand-woven straw hats. Each one-of-kind design is named using the last three letters of Harley's first name; the dolls have names like Joycelyn, Vitalyn, and Iselyn.

Cheryl Miller cooks up ingredients like sun-sweetened papayas, fiery Scotch bonnet peppers, and aromatic basil leaves into the jams, jellies, and hot sauces she sells under her Cheryl's Taste of Paradise line. Five of Miller's products—Caribbean Mustango Sauce, Caribbean Sunburn, Mango Momma Jam, Mango Chutney, and Hot Green Pepper Jelly—have won awards at the National Fiery Foods Show in Albuquerque, New Mexico. You can buy her products at Compass Point Marina as well as Cost-U-Less and the Native Arts & Crafts Cooperative.

Jason Budsan traps the enticing aromas of the islands into sumptuous candles he sells at his Tillett Gardens workshop. Among the scents are Ripe Mango, Night Jasmine, Lime in de Coconut, Frenchie Connection (with vanilla and lavender), and Ripe Pineapple.

26

SPECIALTY ITEMS

ART   **Camille Pissarro Art Gallery.** This second-floor gallery, in the birthplace of St. Thomas's famous artist, offers a fine collection of original paintings and prints by local and regional artists. ⊠*14 Main St., Charlotte Amalie* ☎*340/774–4621.*

The Color of Joy. Find locally made arts and crafts here, including pottery, batik, hand-painted linen and cotton clothing, glass plates and ornaments, and watercolors by owner Corinne Van Rensselaer. There are also original prints by many local artists. ⊠*Rte. 317, about 100 yards west of Ritz-Carlton, Red Hook* ☎*340/775–4020.*

Gallery St. Thomas. Fine art and collectibles are found in this charming gallery, including paintings, wood sculpture, glass, and jewelry that are from or inspired by the Virgin Islands. ⊠*1 Main St., 2nd fl., Charlotte Amalie* ☎*340/777–6363.*

Kilnworks Pottery & Caribbean Art Gallery. A 12-foot statue of a green iguana marks the entrance to this pottery paradise. Owner Peggy Seiwert is best known for her lizard-theme ceramic cups, bowls, and platters. There are also pottery pieces by other local artists, as well as paintings and gift items. ⊠*Rte. 38, across from Toad & Tart English Pub, Estate Smith Bay* ☎*340/775–3979.*

Mango Tango. Works by popular local artists—originals, prints, and note cards—are displayed (there's a one-person show at least one weekend a month) and sold here. There's also the island's largest humidor and a brand-name cigar gallery. ⊠*Al Cohen's Plaza, ½ mi (¾ km) east of Charlotte Amalie* ☎*340/777–3060.*

BOOKS   **Dockside Bookshop.** This place is packed with books for children, travelers, cooks, and historians, as well as a good selection of paperback mysteries, best sellers, art books, calendars, and prints. It also carries a selection of books written in and about the Caribbean and the Virgin Islands. ⊠*Havensight Mall, Bldg. VI, Rte. 30, Charlotte Amalie* ☎*340/774–4937.*

CAMERAS &   **Boolchand's.** Brand-name cameras, audio and video equipment, and binoculars are sold here. ⊠*31 Main St., Charlotte Amalie* ☎*340/776–0794* ⊠*Havensight Mall, Bldg. II, Rte. 30, Charlotte Amalie* ☎*340/776–0302.*

ELECTRONICS

Royal Caribbean. Shop here for cameras, camcorders, stereos, watches, and clocks. ⊠*23 Main St., Charlotte Amalie* ☎*340/776–5449* ⊠*33 Main St., Charlotte Amalie* ☎*340/776–4110* ⊠*Havensight Mall, Bldg. I, Rte. 30, Charlotte Amalie* ☎*340/776–8890.*

CHINA &   **Little Switzerland.** All of this establishment's shops carry crystal from Baccarat, Waterford, and Orrefors; and china from Kosta Boda, Rosenthal, and Wedgwood, among others. There's also an assortment of Swarovski cut-crystal animals, gemstone globes, and many other affordable collectibles. It also does a booming mail-order business; ask for a catalog. ⊠*5 Dronningens Gade, across from Emancipation Garden,Charlotte Amalie* ☎*340/776–2010* ⊠*3B Main St., Charlotte*

CRYSTAL

Amalie ☎*340/776–2010* ✉*Havensight Mall, Bldg. II, Rte. 30, Charlotte Amalie* ☎*340/776–2198.*

Scandinavian Center. The best of Scandinavia is here, including Royal Copenhagen, Georg Jensen, Kosta Boda, and Orrefors. Owners Soøren and Grace Blak make regular buying trips to northern Europe and are a great source of information on crystal. Online ordering is available if you want to add to your collection once home. ✉*Havensight Mall, Bldg. III, Rte. 30, Charlotte Amalie* ☎*340/776–5030 or 800/524–2063.*

CLOTHING **Fresh Produce.** You won't find lime-green mangoes, peachy-pink guavas, or sunny-yellow bananas in this store. But you will find these fun, casual colors in the Fresh Produce clothing line. This is one of only 16 stores to stock 100% of this California-created, tropical-feel line of apparel for women. Find dresses, shirts, slacks, and skirts in small to plus sizes as well as accessories such as bags and hats. ✉*Riise's Alley, Charlotte Amalie* ☎*340/774–0807.*

Local Color. Men, women, and children will find something to choose from among brand-name wear like Jams World, Fresh Produce, and Urban Safari. There's also St. John artist Sloop Jones's colorful, hand-painted island designs on cool dresses, T-shirts, and sweaters. Find tropically oriented accessories like big-brim straw hats, bold-color bags, and casual jewelry. ✉*Royal Dane Mall, at Waterfront, Charlotte Amalie* ☎*340/774–2280.*

Nicole Miller. The New York designer has created an exclusive motif for the USVI: a map of the islands, a cruise ship, and a tropical sunset. Find this print, and Miller's full line of other designs, on ties, scarves, boxer shorts, sarongs, and dresses. ✉*24 Main St., at Palm Passage, Charlotte Amalie* ☎*340/774–8286.*

Tommy Hilfiger. Stop by this shop for classic American jeans and sportswear, as well as trendy bags, belts, ties, socks, caps, and wallets. ✉*Waterfront Hwy. at Trompeter Gade, Charlotte Amalie* ☎*340/777–1189.*

FOODSTUFFS **Belgian Chocolate Company.** Everything at this confectionery shop tastes as good as it smells. Watch chocolates made before your eyes. Specialties include triple-chocolate rum truffles. You can also find imported chocolates here as well. Both the homemade and imported come in decorative boxes, so they make great gifts. ✉*Royal Dane Alley, Charlotte Amalie* ☎*340/774–6675.*

Cost-U-Less. The Caribbean equivalent of Costco and Sam's Club sells everything from soup to nuts, but in giant sizes and case lots. The meat-and-seafood department, however, has family-size portions. A well-stocked fresh produce section and a case filled with rotisserie chicken were added in 2006. ✉*Rte. 38, ¼ mi (½ km) west of Rte. 39 intersection, Estate Donoe* ☎*340/777–3588.*

Food Center. Fresh produce, meats, and seafood, plus an on-site bakery and deli with hot-and-cold prepared foods, are the draw here, espe-

26

cially for those renting villas, condos, or charter boats in the East End area. ✉ *Rte. 32, Estate Frydenhoj* ☎ *340/777–8806.*

Fruit Bowl. For fresh fruits and vegetables, this is the best place on the island to go. ✉ *Wheatley Center, Rtes. 38 and 313 intersection, Charlotte Amalie* ☎ *340/774–8565.*

Gourmet Gallery. Visiting millionaires buy their caviar here. There's also an excellent and reasonably priced wine selection, as well as specialty ingredients for everything from tacos to curries to chow mein. A full-service deli offers imported meats, cheeses, and in-store prepared foods that are perfect for a gourmet picnic. ✉ *Crown Bay Marina, Rte. 304, Estate Contant* ☎ *340/776–8555* ✉ *Havensight Mall, Bldg. VI, Rte. 30, Charlotte Amalie* ☎ *340/774–4948.*

Marina Market. You won't find better fresh meat or seafood anywhere on the island. ✉ *Rte. 32, across from Red Hook ferry, Red Hook* ☎ *340/779–2411.*

Plaza Extra. This large U.S.-style supermarket has everything you need from produce to meat, including fresh seafood, an excellent deli, and a bakery. There's a liquor department, too. ✉ *Tutu Park Shopping Mall, Rte. 38, Estate Tutu* ☎ *340/775–5646.*

PriceSmart. Everything from electronics to housewares is found in this warehouse-size store. The meat, poultry, and seafood departments are especially popular. A small café in front sells pizzas, hot dogs, and the cheapest bottled water on the island—just 75¢ a pop. ✉ *Rte. 38, west of Fort Mylner, Estate Tutu* ☎ *340/777–3430.*

Pueblo Supermarket. This Caribbean chain carries stateside brands of most products—but at higher prices because of shipping costs to the islands. ✉ *Sub Base, ½ mi (¾ km) east of Crown Bay Marina, Estate Contant* ☎ *340/774–4200* ✉ *Rte. 30, 1 mi (1½ km) north of Havensight Mall, Estate Thomas* ☎ *340/774–2695.*

HANDICRAFTS **Caribbean Marketplace.** This is a great place to buy handicrafts from the Caribbean and elsewhere. Also look for Sunny Caribee spices, teas from Tortola, and coffee from Trinidad. ✉ *Havensight Mall, Rte. 30, Charlotte Amalie* ☎ *340/776–5400.*

Down Island Traders. These traders deal in hand-painted calabash bowls; finely printed Caribbean note cards; jams, jellies, spices, hot sauces, and herbs; teas made of lemongrass, passion fruit, and mango; coffee from Jamaica; and handicrafts from throughout the Caribbean. ✉ *Waterfront Hwy. at Post Office Alley, Charlotte Amalie* ☎ *340/776–4641.*

Native Arts & Crafts Cooperative. More than 40 local artists—including schoolchildren, senior citizens, and people with disabilities—create the handcrafted items for sale here: African-style jewelry, quilts, calabash bowls, dolls, carved-wood figures, woven baskets, straw brooms, note cards, and cookbooks. ✉ *Tolbod Gade, across from Emancipation Garden, Charlotte Amalie* ☎ *340/777–1153.*

JEWELRY **Amsterdam Sauer.** Many fine one-of-a-kind designs are displayed at this jeweler's three locations. The Imperial Topaz Collection at the Main Street store is a stunner. ⊠ *1 Main St., Charlotte Amalie* ☎*340/774–2222* ⊠*Havensight Mall, Rte. 30, Charlotte Amalie* ☎*340/776–3828* ⊠*Ritz-Carlton, Rte. 317,Estate Great Bay* ☎*340/779–2308.*

Cardow Jewelry. A chain bar—with gold in several lengths, widths, sizes, and styles—awaits you here, along with diamonds, emeralds, and other precious gems. You're guaranteed 40% to 60% savings off U.S. retail prices or your money will be refunded within 30 days of purchase. ⊠ *33 Main St., Charlotte Amalie* ☎*340/776–1140* ⊠*Havensight Mall, Bldg. I, Rte. 30, Charlotte Amalie* ☎*340/774–0530 or 340/774–5905* ⊠*Marriott Frenchman's Reef Resort, Rte. 315, Estate Bakkeroe* ☎*340/774–0434.*

Colombian Emeralds. Well known in the Caribbean, this store offers set and unset emeralds as well as gems of every description. The watch boutique carries upscale brands like Ebel, Tissot, and Jaeger LeCoultre. ⊠*30 Main St., Charlotte Amalie* ☎*340/777–5400* ⊠*Waterfront at A. H. Riise Mall, Charlotte Amalie* ☎*340/774–1033* ⊠*Havensight Mall, Bldg. V, Rte. 30, Charlotte Amalie* ☎*340/774–2442.*

Diamonds International. Choose a diamond, emerald, or tanzanite gem and a mounting, and you can have your dream ring set in an hour. Famous for having the largest inventory of diamonds on the island, this shop welcomes trade-ins, has a U.S. service center, and offers free diamond earrings with every purchase. ⊠*31 Main St., Charlotte Amalie* ☎*340/774–3707* ⊠*3 Drakes Passage, Charlotte Amalie* ☎*340/775–2010* ⊠*7AB Drakes Passage, Charlotte Amalie* ☎*340/774–1516* ⊠*Havensight Mall, Bldg. II, Rte. 30, Charlotte Amalie* ☎*340/776–0040* ⊠*Wyndham Sugar Bay Beach Club & Resort, Rte. 38, Estate Smith Bay* ☎*340/714–3248.*

H. Stern Jewelers. The World Collection of jewels set in modern, fashionable designs and an exclusive sapphire watch have earned this Brazilian jeweler a stellar name. ⊠*8 Main St., Charlotte Amalie* ☎*340/776–1939* ⊠*Havensight Mall, Bldg. II, Rte. 30, Charlotte Amalie* ☎*340/776–1223* ⊠*Marriott Frenchman's Reef Resort, Rte. 315, Estate Bakkeroe* ☎*340/776–3550.*

Jewels. Name-brand jewelry and watches are in abundance here. Designer jewelry lines include David Yurman, Bulgari, Chopard, and Penny Preville. The selection of watches is extensive, with brand names including Jaeger le Coultre, Tag Heuer, Breitling, Movado, and Gucci. ⊠*Main St., at Riise's Alley, Charlotte Amalie* ☎*340/777–4222* ⊠*Waterfront at Hibiscus Alley, Charlotte Amalie* ☎*340/777–4222* ⊠*Havensight Mall, Bldg. II, Rte. 30, Charlotte Amalie* ☎*340/776–8590.*

Rolex Watches at A. H. Riise. As the Virgin Islands' official Rolex retailer, this shop offers one of the largest selections of these fine timepieces in the Caribbean. An After Sales Service Center assures that your Rolex keeps on ticking for a lifetime. ⊠ *37 Main St., at Riise's Alley, Char-*

26

lotte Amalie ☎*340/776–2303* ✉*Havensight Mall, Bldg. II, Rte. 30, Charlotte Amalie* ☎*340/776–4002.*

LEATHER GOODS   **Coach Boutique at Little Switzerland.** Find a full line of fine leather hand-bags, belts, gloves, and more for women, plus briefcases and wallets for men. Accessories for both sexes include organizers, travel bags, and cell-phone cases. ✉*5 Main St., Charlotte Amalie* ☎*340/776–2010.*

☾ **Zora's.** Fine made-to-order leather sandals are the specialty here. There's also a selection of locally made backpacks, purses, and briefcases in durable, brightly colored canvas. ✉*Norre Gade, across from Roosevelt Park, Charlotte Amalie* ☎*340/774–2559.*

LINENS   **Fabric in Motion.** Fine Italian linens share space with Liberty's of London silky cottons, colorful batiks, cotton prints, ribbons, and accessories at this small shop. ✉*Storetvaer Gade, Charlotte Amalie* ☎*340/774–2006.*

Mr. Tablecloth. The friendly staff here will help you choose from the floor-to-ceiling selection of linens, from Tuscany lace tablecloths to Irish linen pillowcases. The prices will please. ✉*6–7 Main St., Charlotte Amalie* ☎*340/774–4343.*

LIQUOR & TOBACCO   **A. H. Riise Liquors & Tobacco.** This Riise venture offers a large selection of tobacco (including imported cigars), as well as cordials, wines, and rare vintage Armagnacs, cognacs, ports, and Madeiras. It also stocks fruits in brandy and barware from England. Enjoy rum samples at the tasting bar. ✉*37 Main St., at Riise's Alley, Charlotte Amalie* ☎*340/776–2303* ✉*Havensight Mall, Bldg. I, Rte. 30, Charlotte Amalie* ☎*340/776–7713.*

Al Cohen's Discount Liquor. The wine selection at this warehouse-style store is extremely large. ✉*Rte. 30 across from Havensight Mall, Charlotte Amalie* ☎*340/774–3690.*

Tobacco Discounters. Find here a full line of discounted brand-name cigarettes, cigars, and tobacco accessories. ✉*Port of $ale Mall, Rte. 30, next to Havensight Mall, Charlotte Amalie* ☎*340/774–2256.*

MUSIC   **Modern Music.** Shop for the latest stateside and Caribbean CD releases, ☾ plus oldies, classical, and New Age music. ✉*Rte. 30, across from Havensight Mall, Charlotte Amalie* ☎*340/774–3100.*

☾ **Parrot Fish Music.** A stock of standard stateside CDs, plus a good selection of Caribbean artists, including local groups, can be found here. You can browse through the collection of calypso, soca, steel band, and reggae music online. ✉*Back St., Charlotte Amalie* ☎*340/776–4514.*

PERFUME   **Tropicana Perfume Shoppe.** Displayed in an 18th-century Danish building is a large selection of fragrances for men and women, including those locally made by Gail Garrison from the essential oils of tropical fruits and flowers like mango and jasmine. ✉*2 Main St., Charlotte Amalie* ☎*340/774–0010.*

TOYS   **Quick Pics.** Birds sing, dogs bark, and fish swim in this animated toy ☾ land, which is part of a larger electronics and souvenir store. Adults have as much fun trying out the wares as do kids. ⊠*Havensight Mall, Bldg. IV, Rte. 30, Charlotte Amalie* ☎*340/774–3500.*

NIGHTLIFE & THE ARTS

On any given night, especially in season, you can find steel-pan orchestras, rock and roll, piano music, jazz, broken-bottle dancing (actual dancing atop broken glass), disco, and karaoke. Pick up a free copy of the bright yellow *St. Thomas–St. John This Week* magazine when you arrive (it can be found at the airport, in stores, and in hotel lobbies). The back pages list who's playing where. The Friday edition of the *Daily News* carries complete listings for the upcoming weekend.

NIGHTLIFE

BARS **Agave Terrace.** Island-style steel-pan bands are a treat that should not be missed. Steel-pan music resonates after dinner here on Tuesday and Thursday. ⊠*Point Pleasant Resort, Rte. 38, Estate Smith Bay* ☎*340/775–4142.*

Duffy's Love Shack. A live band and dancing under the stars are the big draws for locals and visitors alike. ⊠*Red Hook Plaza, Red Hook* ☎*340/779–2080.*

Epernay Bistro. This intimate nightspot has small tables for easy chatting, wine and champagne by the glass, and a spacious dance floor. Mix and mingle with island celebrities. The action runs from 4 PM until the wee hours Monday through Saturday. ⊠*Frenchtown Mall, 24-A Honduras, Frenchtown* ☎*340/774–5348.*

Greenhouse Bar & Restaurant. Once this favorite eatery puts away the salt and pepper shakers at 10 PM, it becomes a rock-and-roll club with a DJ or live reggae bands raising the weary to their feet six nights a week. ⊠*Waterfront Hwy. at Storetvaer Gade, Charlotte Amalie* ☎*340/774–7998.*

Iggies Beach Bar. Sing along karaoke-style to the sounds of the surf or the latest hits at this beachside lounge. There are live bands on the weekends, and you can dance inside or kick up your heels under the stars. At the adjacent Beach House restaurant, there's Carnival Night, complete with steel-pan music on Wednesday. ⊠*Bolongo Bay Beach Club & Villas, Rte. 30, Estate Bolongo* ☎*340/775–1800.*

Ritz-Carlton, St. Thomas. On Monday nights, catch steel-pan music at this resort's bar. ⊠*Rte. 317, Estate Great Bay* ☎*340/775–3333.*

THE ARTS

THEATER **Pistarkle Theater.** In the Tillett Gardens complex, this air-conditioned theater with more than 100 seats is host to a dozen or more productions annually, plus a children's summer drama camp. ⊠*Tillett Gardens, Rte. 38, across from Tutu Park Shopping Mall, Estate Tutu* ☎*340/775–7877.*

Reichhold Center for the Arts. This amphitheater has its more expensive seats covered by a roof. Schedules vary, so check the paper to see what's

26

on when you're in town. Throughout the year there's an entertaining mix of local plays, dance exhibitions, and music of all types. ⊠ *Rte. 30, across from Brewers Beach, Estate Lindberg Bay* ☎ *340/693–1559.*

EXPLORING ST. THOMAS

St. Thomas is 13 mi (21 km) long and less than 4 mi (6½ km) wide, but it's extremely hilly, and even an 8- or 10-mi (13- or 16-km) trip could take well over an hour. Don't let that discourage you, though; the mountain ridge that runs east to west through the middle and separates the island's Caribbean and Atlantic sides has spectacular vistas.

CHARLOTTE AMALIE

Look beyond the pricey shops, T-shirt vendors, and bustling crowds for a glimpse of the island's history. The city served as the capital of Denmark's outpost in the Caribbean until 1917, an aspect of the island often lost in the glitz of the shopping district.

Emancipation Gardens, right next to the fort, is a good place to start a walking tour. Tackle the hilly part of town first: head north up Government Hill to the historic buildings that house government offices and have incredible views. Several regal churches line the route that runs west back to the town proper and the old-time market. Virtually all the alleyways that intersect Main Street lead to eateries that serve frosty drinks, sandwiches, and West Indian fare. There are public restrooms in this area, too. Allow an hour for a quick view of the sights.

A note about the street names: In deference to the island's heritage, the streets downtown are labeled by their Danish names. Locals will use both the Danish name and the English name (such as Dronningens Gade and Norre Gade for Main Street), but most people refer to things by their location ("a block toward the Waterfront off Main Street" or "next to the Little Switzerland Shop"). You may find it more useful if you ask for directions by shop names or landmarks.

Numbers in the margin correspond to points of interest on the Charlotte Amalie map.

㉒ All Saints Anglican Church. Built in 1848 from stone quarried on the island, the church has thick, arched window frames lined with the yellow brick that came to the islands as ballast aboard ships. Merchants left the brick on the waterfront when they filled their boats with molasses, sugar, mahogany, and rum for the return voyage. The church was built in celebration of the end of slavery in the USVI. ⊠ *Domini Gade* ☎ *340/774–0217* ⊗ *Mon.–Sat. 9–3.*

㉒ Cathedral of St. Peter & St. Paul. This building was consecrated as a parish church in 1848 and serves as the seat of the territory's Roman Catholic diocese. The ceiling and walls are covered with murals painted in 1899 by two Belgian artists, Father Leo Servais and Brother Ildephonsus. The San Juan–marble altar and walls were added in the 1960s. ⊠ *Lower Main St.* ☎ *340/774–0201* ⊗ *Mon.–Sat. 8–5.*

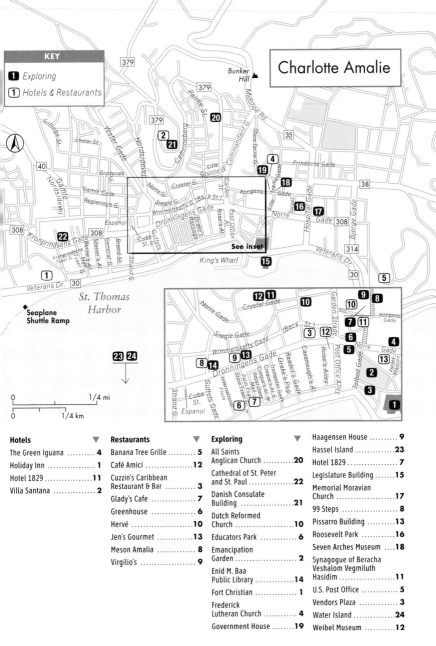

Charlotte Amalie

KEY
- 🔳 Exploring
- 🔲 Hotels & Restaurants

St. Thomas Harbor

Seaplane Shuttle Ramp

0   1/4 mi
0   1/4 km

See inset

King's Wharf

㉑ Danish Consulate Building. Built in 1830 this structure once housed the Danish Consulate. Although the Danish Consul General, Søøren Blak, has an office in Charlotte Amalie, the Danish Consulate is now in the Scandinavian Center in Havensight Mall. This building is not open to the public. ⊠ *Take stairs north at corner of Bjerge Gade and Crystal Gade to Denmark Hill.*

⑩ Dutch Reformed Church. This church has an austere loveliness that's amazing considering all it's been through. Founded in 1744 it's been rebuilt twice following fires and hurricanes. The unembellished cream-color hall gives you a sense of peace—albeit monochromatically. The only other color is the forest green of the shutters and the carpet. Call ahead if you wish to visit at a particular time, as the doors are sometimes locked. ⊠*Nye Gade and Crystal Gade* ☎340/776–8255 ☉ *Weekdays 9–5.*

❻ Educators Park. A peaceful place amid the town's hustle and bustle, the park has memorials to three famous Virgin Islanders: educator Edith Williams, J. Antonio Jarvis (a founder of the *Daily News*), and educator and author Rothschild Francis. The last gave many speeches here. ⊠ *Main St., across from post office.*

❷ Emancipation Garden. Built to commemorate the freeing of slaves in 1848, the garden was the site of a 150th anniversary celebration of emancipation. A bronze bust of a freed slave blowing a symbolic conch shell commemorates this anniversary. The gazebo here is used for official ceremonies. Two other monuments show the island's Danish-American connection—a bust of Denmark's King Christian and a scaled-down model of the U.S. Liberty Bell. ⊠*Between Tolbod Gade and Fort Christian.*

⑭ Enid M. Baa Public Library. Like so many other structures on the north side of Main Street, this large pink building is a typical 18th-century town house. The library was once the home of merchant and landowner Baron von Bretton. He and other merchants built their houses (stores downstairs, living quarters above) across from the brick warehouses on the south side of the street. This is the island's first recorded fireproof building, meaning it was built of ballast brick instead of wood. Its interior of high ceilings and cool stone floors is the perfect refuge from the afternoon sun. You can browse through historic papers or just sit in the breeze by an open window reading the paper. ⊠*Main St.* ☎340/774–0630 ☉ *Weekdays 9–5, Sat. 10–3.*

❶ Fort Christian. St. Thomas's oldest standing structure, this monument was built between 1672 and 1680 and now has U.S. National Landmark status. The clock tower was added in the 19th century. This remarkable building has, over time, been used as a jail, governor's residence, town hall, courthouse, and church. A multimillion dollar renovation project completed in the spring of 2008 stabilized the structure and halted centuries worth deterioration. Check out the **Virgin Islands Museum,** where you can see exhibits on the fascinating history of the region. The gift shop sells local crafts, books, and other souvenirs. ⊠ *Waterfront Hwy., east of shopping district* ☎340/776–4566.

④ Frederick Lutheran Church. This historic church has a massive mahogany altar, and its pews—each with its own door—were once rented to families of the congregation. Lutheranism is the state religion of Denmark, and when the territory was without a minister, the governor—who had his own elevated pew—filled in. ⊠ *Norre Gade* ☎ *340/776–1315* ⊘ *Mon.–Sat. 9–4.*

⑲ Government House. Built in 1867 this neoclassical white brick-and-wood structure houses the offices of the governor of the Virgin Islands. Inside, the staircases are of native mahogany, as are the plaques hand-lettered in gold with the names of the governors appointed and, since 1970, elected. Brochures detailing the history of the building are available, but you may have to ask for them. ⊠ *Government Hill* ☎ *340/774– 0294* ☜ *Free* ⊘ *Weekdays 8–5.*

⑨ Haagensen House. Behind Hotel 1829, this lovingly restored home was built in the early 1800s by Danish entrepreneur Hans Haagensen and is surrounded by an equally impressive cookhouse, outbuildings, and terraced gardens. A lower-level banquet hall now showcases antique prints and photographs. Guided tours begin at the lookout tower at Blackbeard's Castle and continue to the circa-1860s Villa Notman, Haagensen House, and Hotel 1829. The first tour starts at 9:30 AM. ⊠ *Government Hill* ☎ *340/776–1234 or 340/776–1829* ☜ *Tours $35* ⊘ *Oct.–May, daily 9–4; June–Sept., by appointment only.*

㉓ Hassel Island. East of Water Island in Charlotte Amalie harbor, Hassel Island is part of the Virgin Islands National Park, as it has the ruins of a British military garrison (built during a brief British occupation of the USVI during the 1800s) and the remains of a marine railway (where ships were hoisted into dry dock for repairs). You can opt for a three-hour guided tour, which departs from the dock at Marriott's Frenchman's Reef Resort. For $49 per person you can see the ruins as well as the island's flora and fauna.

⑦ Hotel 1829. As its name implies, the hotel was built in 1829, albeit as the private residence of a prominent merchant named Alaxander Lavalette. The building's coral-color facade is accented with fancy wrought-iron railings, and the interior is paneled in dark wood, which makes it feel delightfully cool. From the terrace there's an exquisite view of the harbor framed by brilliant orange bougainvillea. You can combine a visit to this hotel with a walking tour of Haagensen House, Villa Notman, and the lookout tower at Blackbeard's Castle just behind the hotel. ⊠ *Government Hill* ☎ *340/776–1829 or 340/776–1234* ⊕ *www. hotel1829.com* ☜ *Tour $20* ⊘ *Oct.–May, daily 9–4; June–Sept., by appointment only.*

⑮ Legislature Building. Its pastoral-looking lime-green exterior conceals the vociferous political wrangling of the Virgin Islands Senate. Constructed originally by the Danish as a police barracks, the building was later used to billet U.S. Marines, and much later it housed a public school. You're welcome to sit in on sessions in the upstairs chambers. ⊠ *Waterfront Hwy., across from Fort Christian* ☎ *340/774–0880* ⊘ *Daily 8–5.*

26

16 Memorial Moravian Church. Built in 1884 this church was named to commemorate the 150th anniversary of the Moravian Church in the Virgin Islands. ✉ *17 Norre Gade* ☎ *340/776–0066* ✆ *Weekdays 8–5.*

8 99 Steps. This staircase "street," built by the Danes in the 1700s, leads ♺ to the residential area above Charlotte Amalie and Blackbeard's Castle. The castle's tower, built in 1679, was once used by the notorious pirate Edward Teach. If you count the stairs as you go up, you'll discover, as have thousands before you, that there are more than the name implies. ✉ *Look for steps heading north from Government Hill.*

13 Pissarro Building. Housing several shops and an art gallery, this was the birthplace and childhood home of Camille Pissarro, who later moved to France and became an acclaimed impressionist painter. The art gallery contains three original pages from Pissarro's sketchbook and two pastels by Pissarro's grandson, Claude. ✉ *Main St., between Raadets Gade and Trompeter Gade.*

17 Roosevelt Park. First called Coconut Park, this park was renamed in ♺ honor of Franklin D. Roosevelt in 1945. It's a great place to put your feet up and people-watch. A renovation, complete in 2007, added five granite pedestals representing the five branches of the military, bronze urns that can be lighted to commemorate special events, and bronze plaques inscribed with the names of the territory's veterans who died defending the United States. There's also a new children's playground. ✉ *Norre Gade.*

18 Seven Arches Museum. This restored 18th-century home is a striking ★ example of classic Danish–West Indian architecture. There seem to be arches everywhere—seven to be exact—all supporting a "welcoming arms" staircase that leads to the second floor and the flower-framed front doorway. The Danish kitchen is a highlight: it's housed in a separate building away from the main house, as were all cooking facilities in the early days (for fire prevention). Inside the house you can see mahogany furnishings and gas lamps. ✉ *Government Hill, 3 bldgs. east of Government House* ☎ *340/774–9295* ⊕ *www.sevenarches museum.com* ✆ *$5 donation* ✆ *Oct.–July, Mon.–Sat. 10–4; Aug. and Sept., by appointment only.*

11 Synagogue of Beracha Veshalom Vegmiluth Hasidim. The synagogue's Hebrew name translates as the Congregation of Blessing, Peace, and Loving Deeds. The small building's white pillars contrast with rough stone walls, as does the rich mahogany of the pews and altar. The sand on the floor symbolizes the exodus from Egypt. Since the synagogue first opened its doors in 1833 it has held a weekly service, making it the oldest synagogue building in continuous use under the American flag and the second-oldest (after the one on Curaçao) in the western hemisphere. Guided tours can be arranged. Brochures detailing the key structures and history are also available. Next door the Weibel Museum showcases Jewish history on St. Thomas. ✉ *15 Crystal Gade* ☎ *340/774–4312* ⊕ *new.onepaper.com/synagogue* ✆ *Weekdays 9–4.*

5 **U.S. Post Office.** While you buy stamps, contemplate the murals of waterfront scenes by *Saturday Evening Post* artist Stephen Dohanos. His art was commissioned as part of the Works Project Administration (WPA) in the 1930s. ✉ *Tolbod Gade and Main St.*

3 **Vendors Plaza.** Here merchants sell everything from T-shirts to African attire to leather goods. Look for local art among the ever-changing selections at this busy market. ✉ *Waterfront, west of Fort Christian* ☉ *Weekdays 8–6, weekends 9–1.*

24 **Water Island.** This island, the fourth largest of the U.S. Virgin Islands, floats about ¼ mi (½ km) out in Charlotte Amalie Harbor. A ferry goes between Crown Bay Marina and the island several times daily from 6 AM to 6 PM, at a cost of $9 round-trip. The hike from the ferry dock is less than half a mile to Honeymoon Beach, where Brad Pitt and Cate Blanchett filmed a scene of the movie *The Curious Case of Benjamin Button*. Get picnic supplies at Pirate's Ridge Deli, above the beach; or from Heidi's Honeymoon Grill, a mobile food van that pulls up on the weekends; or from the boat that often delivers hot pizza around noon.

12 **Weibel Museum.** In this museum next to the synagogue, 300 years of Jewish history on St. Thomas are showcased. The small gift shop sells a commemorative silver coin celebrating the anniversary of the Hebrew congregation's establishment on the island in 1796. There are also tropically inspired items, like menorahs painted to resemble palm trees. ✉ *15 Crystal Gade* ☎ *340/774–4312* 🎟 *Free* ☉ *Weekdays 9–4.*

AROUND THE ISLAND

To explore outside Charlotte Amalie, rent a car or hire a taxi. Your rental car should come with a good map; if not, pick up the pocket-size "St. Thomas–St. John Road Map" at a tourist information center. Roads are marked with route numbers, but they're confusing and seem to switch numbers suddenly. Roads are also identified by signs bearing the St. Thomas–St. John Hotel and Tourism Association's mascot, Tommy the Starfish. More than 100 of these color-coded signs line the island's main routes. Orange signs trace the route from the airport to Red Hook, green signs identify the road from town to Magens Bay, Tommy's face on a yellow background points from Mafolie to Crown Bay through the north side, red signs lead from Smith Bay to Four Corners via Skyline Drive, and blue signs mark the route from the cruise-ship dock at Havensight to Red Hook. These color-coded routes are not marked on most visitor maps, however. Allow yourself a day to explore, especially if you want to stop to take pictures or to enjoy a light bite or refreshing swim. Most gas stations are on the island's more populated eastern end, so fill up before heading to the north side. And remember to drive on the left!

Although the eastern end has many major resorts and spectacular beaches, don't be surprised if a cow or a herd of goats crosses your path as you drive through the relatively flat, dry terrain. The north side of the island is more lush and hush—fewer houses and less traffic. Here there are roller-coaster routes (made all the more scary because the roads have no shoulders) and incredible vistas. Leave time in the afternoon for a swim. Pick up some sandwiches from delis in the Red Hook area for a picnic lunch, or enjoy a slice of pizza at Magens Bay. A day in the country will reveal the tropical pleasures that have enticed more than one visitor to become a resident.

Butterfly Farm. Step into this 10,000-square-foot mesh enclosure and watch more than 1,000 butterflies from around the world flutter all around you. A 25-minute tour takes you through the life cycle of these beautiful insects. Most people visit in the morning, when there's the most activity. If you're a photographer, you'll probably prefer the afternoon when the butterflies move slower and are easier to capture in a picture. ⊠*Havensight Mall* ☎*340/715–3366* ⊕ *www.thebutterflyfarm. com* ⊡*$15* ⊙*Daily 8:30–5.*

Compass Point Marina. It's fun to park your car and walk around this marina. The boaters—many of whom have sailed here from points around the globe—are easy to engage in conversation. Turn south off Route 32 at the well-marked entrance road just east of Independent Boat Yard. ⊠*Estate Frydenhoj.*

Ⓒ   **Coral World Ocean Park.** This interactive aquarium and water-sports
Fodor's Choice center lets you experience a variety of sea life and other animals. The
★   park has several outdoor pools where you can pet baby sharks, feed stingrays, touch starfish, and view endangered sea turtles. There's also a walk-through aviary where colorful rainbow lorikeets might drink nectar from your hands. Other activities include the Sea Trek Helmet Dive that lets you walk along an underwater trail with a high-tech helmet that provides a continuous supply of air. A Shark Encounter program lets you observe juvenile sharks as they swim around you. A sea lion pool, which opened in 2007, is where you can get a big, wet, whiskered kiss. Also in 2007 the Lorikeet exhibit opened. Buy a cup of nectar for $2 and let these parrot-look-alikes perch on your hand and drink. Coral World also has an offshore underwater observatory, an 80,000-gallon coral reef exhibit (one of the largest in the world), and a nature trail full of lush tropical flowers, ducks, and tortoises. Daily feedings take place at most exhibits. ⊠*Coki Point, north of Rte. 38, Estate Frydendal* ☎*340/775–1555* ⊕*www.coralworldvi.com* ⊡*$18, Sea Lion Splash $99, Sea Trek $68, Shark Encounter $43* ⊙*Daily 9–5.*

Ⓒ   **Drake's Seat.** Sir Francis Drake was supposed to have kept watch over his fleet and looked for enemy ships from this vantage point. The panorama is especially breathtaking (and romantic) at dusk, and if you arrive late in the day you can miss the hordes of day-trippers on taxi tours who stop here to take a picture and buy a T-shirt from one of the many vendors. ⊠*Rte. 40, Estate Zufriedenheit.*

Estate St. Peter Greathouse & Botanical Gardens. This unusual spot is perched on a mountainside 1,000 feet above sea level, with views of more than 20 islands and islets. You can wander through a gallery displaying local art, sip a complimentary rum punch while looking out at the view, or follow a nature trail that leads you past nearly 70 varieties of tropical plants, including 17 varieties of orchids. ⊠*Rte.*

40, Estate St. Peter ☎*340/774–4999* ⊕*www.greathouse-mountaintop. com* ⊠*$12* ⊙*Mon.–Sat. 9–4:30.*

Frenchtown. Popular for its bars and restaurants, Frenchtown is also the home of descendants of immigrants from St. Barthélemy (St. Barths). You can watch them pull up their brightly painted boats and display their equally colorful catch of the day along the waterfront. If you chat with them, you can hear speech patterns slightly different from those of other St. Thomians. Get a feel for the residential district of Frenchtown by walking west to some of the town's winding streets, where tiny wooden houses have been passed down from generation to generation. Next to Joseph Aubain Ballpark, the **French Heritage Museum** (⊠*Intersection of rue de St. Anne and rue de St. Barthélemy* ☎*340/774–2320*)houses artifacts such as fishing nets, accordions, tambourines, mahogany furniture, and historic photographs that illustrate the lives of the French descendants during the 18th through 20th centuries. The museum is open Monday through Saturday from 9 AM to 6 PM. Admission is free. ⊠*Turn south off Waterfront Hwy. at post office.*

☾ **Mountain Top.** Stop here for a banana daiquiri and spectacular views
★ from the observation deck more than 1,500 feet above sea level. There are also shops that sell everything from Caribbean art to nautical antiques, ship models, and T-shirts. Kids will like talking to the parrots—and hearing them answer back. ⊠*Head north off Rte. 33, look for signs* ⊕*www.greathouse-mountaintop.com.*

26

☾ **Paradise Point Tramway.** Fly skyward in a gondola to Paradise Point, an
★ overlook with breathtaking views of Charlotte Amalie and the harbor. There are several shops, a bar, restaurant, and a wedding gazebo; kids enjoy the tropical bird show held daily at 10:30 AM, 1:30 PM, and 3:30 PM. A ¼-mi (½-km) hiking trail leads to spectacular views of St. Croix. Wear sturdy shoes, as the trail is steep and rocky. ⊠*Rte. 30, across from Havensight Mall, Charlotte Amalie* ☎*340/774–9809* ⊕*www. paradisepointtramway.com* ⊠*$18* ⊙*Thurs.–Tues. 9–5, Wed. 9–9.*

Red Hook. In this nautical center there are fishing and sailing charter boats, dive shops, and powerboat-rental agencies at the American Yacht Harbor marina. There are also several bars and restaurants, including Molly Molone's, Duffy's Love Shack, and Off the Hook. One grocery store and two delis offer picnic fixings—from sliced meats and cheeses to rotisserie-roasted chickens, prepared salads, and freshly baked breads. Ferries depart from Red Hook en route to St. John and the British Virgin Islands.

ST. JOHN

By Lynda Lohr The sun slipped up over the horizon like a great orange ball, streaking the sky with wisps of gold. Watching from my porch overlooking Coral Bay, I thanked Mother Nature, as I do almost every day, for providing glorious sunrises, colorful rainbows and green hillsides, and the opportunity to enjoy them all. It was a magnificent start to another gorgeous

St. John day, an island where nature is the engine that fuels the island's economy and brings more than 800,000 visitors a year.

St. John's heart is Virgin Islands National Park, a treasure that takes up a full two-thirds of St. John's 20 square mi (53 square km). The park helps keep the island's interior in its pristine and undisturbed state, but if you go at midday, you'll probably have to share your stretch of beach with others, particularly at Trunk Bay.

The island is booming, and it can get a tad crowded at the ever-popular Trunk Bay Beach during the busy winter season; parking woes plague the island's main town of Cruz Bay, but you won't find traffic jams or pollution. It's easy to escape from the fray, however: just head off on a hike or go early or late to the beach. The sun won't be as strong, and you may have that perfect crescent of white sand all to yourself.

St. John doesn't have a grand agrarian past like her sister island, St. Croix, but if you're hiking in the dry season, you can probably stumble upon the stone ruins of old plantations. The less adventuresome can visit the repaired ruins at the park's Annaberg Plantation and Caneel Bay resort.

In 1675 Jorgen Iverson claimed the unsettled island for Denmark. By 1733 there were more than 1,000 slaves working more than 100 plantations. In that year the island was hit by a drought, hurricanes, and a plague of insects that destroyed the summer crops. With famine a real threat and the planters keeping them under tight reign, the slaves revolted on November 23, 1733. They captured the fort at Coral Bay, took control of the island, and held on to it for six months. During this period, about 20% of the island's total population was killed, the tragedy affecting both black and white residents in equal percentages. The rebellion was eventually put down with the help of French troops from Martinique. Slavery continued until 1848, when slaves in St. Croix marched on Frederiksted to demand their freedom from the Danish government. This time it was granted. After emancipation, St. John fell into decline, with its inhabitants eking out a living on small farms. Life continued in much the same way until the national park opened in 1956 and tourism became an industry.

Of the three U.S. Virgin Islands, St. John, which has 5,000 residents, has the strongest sense of community, which is primarily rooted in a desire to protect the island's natural beauty. Despite the growth, there are still many pockets of tranquillity. Here you can truly escape the pressures of modern life for a day, a week—perhaps, forever.

WHERE TO STAY

St. John doesn't have many beachfront hotels, but that's a small price to pay for all the pristine sand. However, the island's two excellent resorts—Caneel Bay Resort and the Westin St. John Resort & Villas— *are* on the beach. Sandy, white beaches string out along the north coast, which is popular with sunbathers and snorkelers and is where you can find the Caneel Bay Resort and Cinnamon and Maho Bay campgrounds. Most villas are in the residential south-shore area, a 15-minute drive from the north-shore beaches. If you head east you come to the laid-back community of Coral Bay, where there are growing numbers of villas and cottages. A stay outside of Coral Bay will be peaceful and quiet.

If you're looking for West Indian village charm, there are a few inns in Cruz Bay. Just know that when bands play at any of the town's bars (some of which stay open until the wee hours), the noise can be a problem. Your choice of accommodations also includes condominiums and cottages near town; two campgrounds, both at the edges of beautiful beaches (bring bug repellent); ecoresorts; and luxurious villas, often with a pool or a hot tub (sometimes both) and a stunning view.

If your lodging comes with a fully equipped kitchen, you'll be happy to know that St. John's handful of grocery stores sell everything from the basics to sun-dried tomatoes and green chilies—though the prices will take your breath away. If you're on a budget, consider bringing some staples (pasta, canned goods, paper products) from home. Hotel rates throughout the island, though considered expensive by some, do include endless privacy and access to most water sports.

For approximate costs, see the dining and lodging price chart at the beginning of this chapter.

26

HOTELS & INNS

$$$$ ☐ **Caneel Bay Resort.** Well-heeled honeymooners, couples celebrating
Fodor'sChoice anniversaries, and extended families all enjoy Caneel Bay Resort's laid-
★ back luxury. If you want to spend your days sunning on any one of its seven gorgeous beaches, taking a kayak out for a paddle, or enjoy lingering dinners at its fine restaurants, you can find no finer resort on St. John. Your room, which has air-conditioning or can be opened to catch the breezes, won't come with a TV or even a phone (though management will loan you a cellular)—all the better to get away from it all. Rooms look as if they're right out of a magazine; if you opt for one of the beachfront rooms, you can get out of bed and stumble a few steps across the sand to the Caribbean. Otherwise, you can look out on the gardens or the tennis courts. Nightlife runs to steel-pan music or an easy-listening combo; if you want lots of action, go elsewhere. **Pros:** Lovely beaches, gorgeous rooms, lots of amenities. **Cons:** Staff can be chilly, isolated location, rates are pricey. ☒ *Rte. 20, Caneel Bay* ☐ *Box 720, Cruz Bay* ☎ *340/776–6111 or 888/767–3966* ⊕ *www. caneelbay.com* ☐ *166 rooms* ☐ *In-room: no phone, no TV. In-hotel: 4 restaurants, tennis courts, pool, spa, beachfront, diving, water sports, no elevator, children's programs (ages 4–12), public Internet, public Wi-Fi, no-smoking rooms* ☐ *AE, DC, MC, V* ☑ *CP.*

$$$$ ☐ **Westin St. John Resort & Villas.** Other than Caneel Bay, this is the island's only big resort. Although it doesn't provide the same casual luxury, it does have a nice beachfront location and enough activities to keep you busy. That said, most guests rent a car for at least a couple of days to explore the area's many lovely beaches. The hotel is spread over 47 beachfront acres adjacent to Great Cruz Bay, with lushly planted

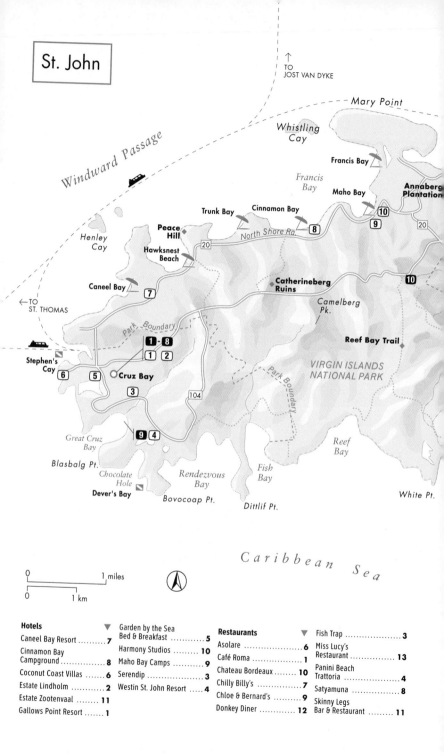

St. John

↑
TO
JOST VAN DYKE

Mary Point

Whistling
Cay

Windward Passage

Francis
Bay

Francis Bay

Maho Bay

Annaberg
Plantation

10

Trunk Bay   Cinnamon Bay

9

Peace
Hill

North Shore Rd.   **8**

20

20

Henley
Cay

Hawksnest
Beach

Catherineberg
Ruins

10

Caneel Bay

Camelberg
Pk.

7

Reef Bay Trail

Park   Boundary

VIRGIN ISLANDS
NATIONAL PARK

←TO
ST. THOMAS

1 - **8**

Stephen's
Cay

1 **2**

Park   Boundary

6   **5**

○Cruz Bay

104

3

Great Cruz
Bay

9 **4**

Reef
Bay

Blasbalg Pt.

Chocolate
Hole

Rendezvous
Bay

Fish
Bay

Dever's Bay   Bovocoap Pt.

Dittlif Pt.

White Pt.

C a r i b b e a n   S e a

0 _____ 1 miles
0 _____ 1 km

Hotels ▼
Caneel Bay Resort **7**
Cinnamon Bay
Campground **8**
Coconut Coast Villas **6**
Estate Lindholm **2**
Estate Zootenvaal **11**
Gallows Point Resort **1**

Garden by the Sea
Bed & Breakfast **5**
Harmony Studios **10**
Maho Bay Camps **9**
Serendip **3**
Westin St. John Resort **4**

Restaurants ▼
Asolare **6**
Café Roma **1**
Chateau Bordeaux **10**
Chilly Billy's **7**
Chloe & Bernard's **9**
Donkey Diner **12**

Fish Trap **3**
Miss Lucy's
Restaurant **13**
Panini Beach
Trattoria **4**
Satyamuna **8**
Skinny Legs
Bar & Restaurant **11**

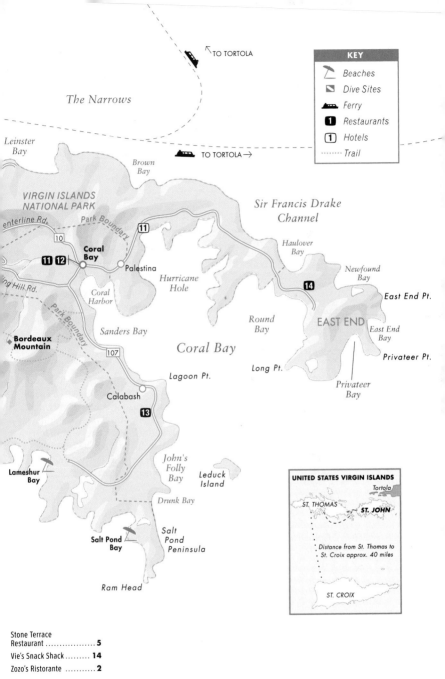

KEY

- Beaches
- Dive Sites
- Ferry
- **1** Restaurants
- **1** Hotels
- Trail

The Narrows

← TO TORTOLA

TO TORTOLA →

Leinster Bay

Brown Bay

VIRGIN ISLANDS NATIONAL PARK

Centerline Rd.

Park Boundary

11

Sir Francis Drake Channel

10

Coral Bay

11 **12**

Palestina

Haulover Bay

Newfound Bay

King Hill Rd.

Coral Harbor

Hurricane Hole

14

East End Pt.

Park Boundary

Sanders Bay

Round Bay

EAST END

East End Bay

Bordeaux Mountain

107

Coral Bay

Lagoon Pt.

Long Pt.

Privateer Pt.

Calabash

Privateer Bay

13

John's Folly Bay

Leduck Island

Lameshur Bay

Drunk Bay

UNITED STATES VIRGIN ISLANDS

Tortola

ST. THOMAS

ST. JOHN

Salt Pond Bay

Salt Pond Peninsula

Distance from St. Thomas to St. Croix approx. 40 miles

Ram Head

ST. CROIX

gardens, a white sandy beach that beckons sunbathers, and nice—but not luxurious—rooms with tropical touches. Those strung out behind the beach put you closest to the water, but even the hillside villas are only a seven-minute stroll to the sand. **Pros:** Entertaining children's programs, pretty pool area, many activities. **Cons:** Mediocre beach, long walk to some parts of the resort, need car to get around. ✉ *Rte. 104, Great Cruz Bay* 🏠 *Box 8310, Cruz Bay* ☎ *340/693–8000 or 800/808–5020* ⊕ *www.westin resortstjohn.com* 🛏 *174 rooms, 134 villas* 🔑 *In-room: safe, refrigerator, Ethernet, Wi-Fi. In-hotel: 4 restaurants, tennis courts, pool, gym, beachfront, diving, water sports, no elevator, children's programs (ages 3–12), public Wi-Fi, no-smoking rooms* ☰ *AE, D, DC, MC, V* ❐*EP.*

> ## ST. JOHN TOP 5
>
> **Beach Hopping:** Hop in your car and make stops at several of the beaches along St. John's North Shore Road.
>
> **Hiking Reef Bay:** Take a ranger-guided hike in Virgin Islands National Park
>
> **Snorkeling at Trunk Bay:** Picture-perfect Trunk Bay is St. John's most popular snorkeling spot.
>
> **Relaxing in a Villa:** There are about 500 vacation villas on St. John.
>
> **Exploring Cruz Bay:** Spend a half day poking around Cruz Bay's varied stores, shopping for that perfect gift for the folks back home.

$$$–$$$$ 🏨 **Estate Lindholm Bed & Breakfast.** Built among old stone ruins on a lushly planted hill overlooking Cruz Bay, Estate Lindholm has a charming setting. The location puts you close to Cruz Bay's restaurants, shopping, and nightlife. You'll feel as if you're out of the fray, but still near enough to run into town when you want. Rooms are sophisticated, with crisp white spreads accented by teak furniture. The sunset views from Asolare restaurant, on the property, provide a stunning end to your day. **Pros:** Lush landscaping, gracious host, pleasant decor. **Cons:** Can be noisy, some uphill walks, on a busy road. 🏠 *Box 1360, Cruz Bay 00831* ☎ *340/776–6121* ⊕ *www.estatelindholm.com* 🛏 *14 rooms* 🔑 *In-room: refrigerator. In-hotel: restaurant, pool, gym, no elevator, no kids under 18, no-smoking rooms* ☰ *AE, D, MC, V* ❐*CP.*

$$$ 🏨 **Garden by the Sea Bed & Breakfast.** A stay here will allow you to live like a local in a middle-class residential neighborhood near a bird-filled salt pond. This cozy B&B is also an easy walk from Cruz Bay. White spreads and curtains provide pristine counterpoints to the blue and green hues in your room. Your hosts serve a delightful breakfast—piña colada French toast is a specialty—on the front deck. It's perfect for folks who enjoy peace and quiet: there are no phones or TVs in the rooms. **Pros:** Homey atmosphere, great breakfasts, breathtaking view from deck. **Cons:** Noise from nearby power substation, some uphill walks, basic amenities. ✉ *Enighed* 🏠 *Box 37, Cruz Bay 00830* ☎ *340/779–4731* ⊕ *www.gardenbythesea.com* 🛏 *3 rooms* 🔑 *In-room: no phone, no TV. In-hotel: no elevator, no-smoking rooms* ☰ *No credit cards* ❐*BP.*

CAMPGROUNDS

St. John has a handful of camping spots ranging from the basic Cinnamon Bay Campground to the relatively comfortable Concordia Studios & Eco-tents. They appeal to those who don't mind bringing their own beach towels from home or busing their own tables at dinner. If you want your piña colada delivered beachside by a smiling waiter, you'd be better off elsewhere.

Cinnamon Bay Campground. Cinnamon Bay Campground sits in the heart of Virgin Islands National Park, a stellar location right at the beach. Tents and rustic cottages are nestled in the trees that stretch behind the shore, and you have easy access to hiking, water sports, and ranger-led evening programs. The amenities are basic, but include propane stoves, cooking equipment, and bed linens; reserve early if you'd like a cottage right behind the beach. Only the screened cottages have electric lights; tenters depend on propane lanterns. Showers and flush toilets, as well as a restaurant and a small store, are a short walk away from the camping area. **Pros:** Beachfront site, hiking trails nearby, lots of activities. **Cons:** Cold showers, can be buggy, some traffic noise. *Flush toilets, drinking water, showers (cold), picnic tables, food service, electricity (some), public telephone, general store, swimming (ocean) ⌿55 tents, 40 cottages, 31 tent sites ⊠Rte. 20, Cinnamon Bay ☏Box 720, Cruz Bay ☎340/776–6330 or 800/539–9998 ⊕www.cinnamonbay.com ⌿Reservations essential ▭AE, MC, V ⊘Closed Sept.*

Maho Bay Camps. Tucked into the greenery along the island's north shore, ecoconscious Maho Bay Camps attracts a sociable crowd that likes to explore the undersea world off the campground's beach or attend on-site seminars. The "tents" (wooden platforms protected from the elements by canvas and screening) are linked by wooden stairs, ramps, and walkways—all of them elevated—so that you can trek around camp, down to the beach, and to the coolish public showers without disturbing the terrain. Although the tents have amenities like real beds and electricity, there are no refrigerators; ice-filled coolers keep your food from spoiling. **Pros:** Friendly atmosphere, tasty food, ecofriendly facility. **Cons:** Many stairs to climb, can be buggy, need a car to get around. *Flush toilets, drinking water, showers (cold), picnic tables, food service, electricity, public telephone, general store, swimming (beach) ⌿114 tent cottages ⊠Maho Bay ☏Box 310, Cruz Bay 00830 ☎340/776–6240 or 800/392–9004 ⊕www.maho.org ⌿Reservations essential ▭AE, MC, V.*

CONDOMINIUM RESORTS & COTTAGES

Many of the island's condos are just minutes from the hustle and bustle of Cruz Bay, but you can find more scattered around the island.

$$$$ Gallows Point Resort. Gallows Point Resort has an excellent waterfront location just outside Cruz Bay's center. You're a short walk to restaurants and shops, but once you step into your condo, the hustle and bustle are left behind. The upper-level apartments have loft bedrooms and the best views. The harborside villas get better trade winds, but they're a tad noisier. Tropical rooms have wicker furniture,

26

tile floors, and brightly colored spreads in colors that reflect the sea and sky. Zozo's Ristorante, a popular spot for sunset watching, serves northern Italian cuisine above the lobby. **Pros:** Walk to shopping, excellent restaurant, comfortably furnished rooms. **Cons:** Some rooms can be noisy, mediocre beach, insufficient parking. ⊠ *Gallows Point, Bay St., Box 58, Cruz Bay* ☎ *340/776–6434 or 800/323–7229* ⊕ *www.gallowspointresort.com* ↩ *60 units* ⚐ *In-room: kitchen, in-room Wi-Fi. In-hotel: restaurant, pool, beachfront, water sports, no elevator, public Internet, public Wi-Fi* ▭ *AE, MC, V* †◎†*EP.*

$$$–$$$$ ⊞ **Coconut Coast Villas.** This small condominium complex with studio, two-, and three-bedroom apartments is a 10-minute walk from Cruz Bay, but is insulated from the town's noise in a sleepy suburban neighborhood. You can swim and snorkel at the small beach or relax poolside and catch some rays. Rooms have a fresh feel; each is a little bit different in decor, with whites, blues, and greens predominating in the color scheme. Colorful artwork by St. John artist Elaine Estern graces the walls. **Pros:** Good snorkeling, full kitchens, walk to Cruz Bay. **Cons:** Small beach, some uphill walks, nearby utility plant can be noisy. ⊠ *Turner Bay* ⏍ *Box 618, Cruz Bay 00831* ☎ *340/693–9100 or 800/858–7989* ⊕ *www.coconutcoast.com* ↩ *9 units* ⚐ *In-room: kitchen, Ethernet. In-hotel: pool, beachfront, no elevator, public Internet* ▭ *MC, V* †◎†*EP.*

$$$–$$$$ ⊞ **Estate Zootenvaal.** Comfortable and casual, this small cottage colony gives you the perfect place to relax. It's certainly out of the way, along the island's East End Road. Although you'll feel that you're getting away from it all, a five-minute drive will bring you to Coral Bay's restaurants, a handful of shops, and tiny grocery store. The small but very private beach across the road is a major plus. **Pros:** Lovely beach, private, near restaurants. **Cons:** Some traffic noise, no air-conditioning. ⊠ *Rte. 10, Hurricane Hole, Zootenvaal* ☎ *340/776–6321* ⊕ *www.estatezootenvaal.com* ↩ *4 units* ⚐ *In-room: no a/c, no phone (some), kitchen, no TV. In-hotel: beachfront, no elevator* ▭ *No credit cards* †◎†*EP.*

$$–$$$ ⊞ **Serendip.** We'd pick Serendip for a budget vacation in a residential locale. This complex offers modern apartments on lush grounds with lovely views. Although this is a property from the 1960s, the units don't feel dated. There are colorful spreads, fully equipped kitchens, and bookshelves filled with good vacation reads. You definitely need a car if you stay here, though; it's about 1 mi (1½ km) up a steep hill from Cruz Bay. **Pros:** Comfortable accommodations, good views, nice neighborhood. **Cons:** No beach, need car to get around, nearby construction. ⊠ *Enighed* ⏍ *Box 273, Cruz Bay 00831* ☎ *340/776–6646 or 888/800–6445* ⊕ *www.serendipstjohn.com* ↩ *10 apartments* ⚐ *In-room: kitchen, Wi-Fi. In-hotel: pool, no elevator* ▭ *MC, V* †◎†*EP.*

$$ ⊞ **Harmony Studios.** These condominium-style units sit hillside at Maho Bay, giving you more of the comforts of home than the tents at the nearby Maho Bay Camp. An ecologically correct environment is one of the draws here. Entryway mats are made of recycled tires, the pristine walls of recycled newspapers, and the electricity comes from the wind and the sun. Best of all, you share access to interesting evening programs and a nice beach at Maho. Be prepared to hike up and down long flights of steep, wooden stairs. **Pros:** Convivial atmosphere, near beach, comfortable units. **Cons:** Lots of stairs, no air-conditioning, need car to get around. ⊠ *Maho Bay* ⊕ *Box 310, Cruz Bay 00830* ☎ *340/776–6240 or 800/392–9004* ⊕ *www.maho.org* ☜ *12 units* ⚭ *In-room: no a/c, no phone, kitchen, no TV. In-hotel: restaurant, beachfront, water sports, no elevator, children's programs (ages 8–16), public Internet, no-smoking rooms* ═ *AE, MC, V* ⫶⃝|*EP.*

PRIVATE CONDOS & VILLAS

Tucked here and there between Cruz Bay and Coral Bay are about 350 private villas and condos (prices range from $ to $$$$). With pools or hot tubs, full kitchens, and living areas, these lodgings provide a fully functional home away from home. They're perfect for couples and extended groups of family or friends. You need a car, since most lodgings are in the hills and very few are at the beach. Villa managers usually pick you up at the dock, arrange for your rental car, and answer questions upon arrival as well as during your stay. Prices drop in the summer season, which is generally after April 15. Some companies begin off-season pricing a week or two later, so be sure to ask.

If you want to be close to Cruz Bay's restaurants and boutiques, a villa in the Chocolate Hole and Great Cruz Bay areas will put you a few minutes away. The Coral Bay area has a growing number of villas, but you'll be about 20 minutes from Cruz Bay. Beaches string out along the North Shore, so you won't be more than 15 minutes from the water no matter where you stay.

26

RENTAL AGENTS

Book-It VI (⊕ *5000 Estate Enighed, PMB 15, Cruz Bay 00830* ☎ *340/693–8555 or 800/416–1205* ☒ *340/693–8480* ⊕ *www.bookitvi. com*) handles villas all across St. John. **Carefree Get-Aways** (⊕ *Box 1626, Cruz Bay 00831* ☎ *340/779–4070 or 888/643–6002* ☒ *340/774–6000* ⊕ *www.carefreegetaways.com*) manages vacation villas on the island's southern and western edges. **Caribbean Villas & Resorts** (⊕ *Box 458, Cruz Bay 00831* ☎ *340/776–6152 or 800/338–0987* ☒ *340/779–4044* ⊕ *www.caribbeanvilla.com*) handles condo rentals for Cruz Views and Gallow's Point Resort, as well as for many private villas. **Caribe Havens** (⊠ *Box 455, Cruz Bay* ☎ *340/776–6518* ☒ *340/776–6518* ⊕ *www.caribehavens.com*) has mainly budget properties scattered around the island. **Catered to Vacation Homes** (⊠ *Marketplace Suite 206, 5206 Enighed, Cruz Bay* ☎ *340/776–6641 or 800/424–6641* ☒ *340/693–8191* ⊕ *www.cateredto.com*) has luxury homes, mainly in the middle of the island and on the western edge. **Cloud 9 Villas** (⊠ *Box 102, Cruz Bay* ☎ *340/693–8495 or 866/693–8496* ☒ *340/693–8191* ⊕ *www.cloud9villas.com*) has several homes, with most in the Gifft Hill and Chocolate Hole area. **Destination St. John** (⊕ *Box 8306, Cruz Bay* ☎ *340/779–4647 or 800/562–1901* ☒ *340/715–0073* ⊕ *www. destinationstjohn.com*) manages villas across the island. **Great Caribbean Getaways** (⊕ *Box 8317, Cruz Bay* ☎ *340/693–8692 or 800/341–2532* ☒ *309/437–9243* ⊕ *www.greatcaribbeangetaways.com*) handles private villas from Cruz Bay to Coral Bay.

Island Getaways (⌂ *Box 1504, Cruz Bay 00831* ☎ *340/693–7676 or 888/693–7676* 📠 *340/693–8923* ⊕ *www.island-getaways.net*) has villas in the Great Cruz Bay–Chocolate Hole area, with a few others scattered around the island. **On-Line Vacations** (⌂ *Box 9901, Emmaus 00830* ☎ *340/776–6036 or 888/842–6632* 📠 *340/693–5357* ⊕ *www.onlinevacations.com*) books vacation villas around St. John. **Private Homes for Private Vacations** (✉ *7605 Mamey Peak, Coral Bay* ☎📠 *340/776–6876* ⊕ *www.privatehomesvi.com*) has homes across the island. **Seaview Vacation Homes** (⌂ *Box 644, Cruz Bay* ☎ *340/776–6805 or 888/625–2963* 📠 *340/779–4349* ⊕ *www.seaviewhomes.com*) handles homes with views of the ocean in the Chocolate Hole, Great Cruz Bay, and Fish Bay areas.

Star Villas (⌂ *1202 Gallows Point, Cruz Bay 00830* ☎ *340/776–6704 or 888/897–9759* 📠 *340/776–6183* ⊕ *www.starvillas.org*) has cozy villas just outside Cruz Bay. **Vacation Vistas** (⌂ *Box 476, Cruz Bay 00831* ☎ *340/776–6462* ⊕ *www.vacationvistas.com*) manages villas mainly in the Chocolate Hole, Great Cruz Bay, and Rendezvous areas. **Windspree** (✉ *7924 Emmaus, Cruz Bay* ☎ *340/693–5423 or 888/742–0357* 📠 *340/693–5623* ⊕ *www.windspree.com*) handles villas mainly in the Coral Bay area.

WHERE TO EAT

The cuisine on St. John seems to get better every year, with culinary-school-trained chefs vying to see who can come up with the most imaginative dishes. There are restaurants to suit every taste and budget—from the elegant establishments at Caneel Bay Resort (where men may be required to wear a jacket at dinner) to the casual in-town eateries of Cruz Bay. For quick lunches, try the West Indian food stands in Cruz Bay Park and across from the post office. The cooks prepare fried chicken legs, pates (meat- and fish-filled pastries), and callaloo.

Some restaurants close for vacation in September and even October. If you have your heart set on a special place, call ahead to make sure it's open during these months.

For approximate costs, see the dining and lodging price chart at the beginning of this chapter.

BORDEAUX

CONTINENTAL   ✕ **Chateau Bordeaux.** This rustic restaurant with a to-die-for view of
$$$$ Coral Bay is a bit out of the way, but worth the trip. Its interior is
★   made elegant with lace tablecloths, glowing candles, and stylish dinner presentations. Start with flaky mahimahi drizzled with a sorrel butter and accompanied by a polenta cake, then segue to lobster fettucine with grilled green beans or rack of lamb topped with roasted corn and tomato couscous. Save room for dessert—the warm flourless chocolate cake is served with a sweet goat cheese mousse and pineapple relish. ✉ *Rte. 10, Bordeaux* ☎ *340/776–6611* ▭ *AE, MC, V* ⊗ *No lunch.*

CORAL BAY & ENVIRONS

AMERICAN ✕**Skinny Legs Bar & Restaurant.** Sailors who live aboard boats anchored
$ just offshore and an eclectic coterie of residents gather for lunch and
★ dinner at this funky spot in the middle of a boatyard-cum-shopping
complex. If owner Moe Chabuz is around, take a gander at his gams;
you'll see where the restaurant got its name. It's a great place for burgers, fish sandwiches, and whatever sports event is on the satellite TV.
⊠*Rte. 10, Coral Bay* ☎*340/779–4982* ⊟*AE, D, MC, V.*

CARIBBEAN ✕**Miss Lucy's Restaurant.** Sitting seaside at remote Friis Bay, Miss Lucy's
$$–$$$ dishes up Caribbean food with a contemporary flair. Dishes like tender
★ conch fritters, a spicy West Indian stew called callaloo, and fried fish
make up most of the menu, but you also find a generous paella filled
with seafood, sausage, and chicken on the menu. Sunday brunches are
legendary, and if you're around when the moon is full, stop by for the
monthly full-moon party. The handful of small tables near the water
are the nicest, but if they're taken or the mosquitoes are swarming, the
indoor tables do nicely. ⊠*Rte. 107, Friis Bay* ☎*340/693–5244* ⊟*AE,
D, MC, V* ⊙*Closed Mon. No dinner Sun.*

$ ✕**Vie's Snack Shack.** Stop by Vie's when you're out exploring the island.
★ Although it's just a shack by the side of the road, Vie's serves up some
great cooking. The garlic chicken legs are crisp and tasty, and the conch
fritters are really something to write home about. Plump and filled with
fresh herbs, a plateful will keep you going for the rest of the afternoon.
Save room for a wedge of coconut pie—called a tart in this neck of
the woods. When you're done eating, a spectacular white-sand beach
across the road beckons. ⊠*Rte. 10, Hansen Bay* ☎*340/693–5033*
⊟*No credit cards* ⊙*Closed Sun. and Mon. No dinner.*

ECLECTIC ✕**Donkey Diner.** In an odd combination that works well for Coral Bay
$–$$$ visitors and residents, this tiny spot along the main road through Coral
Bay sells yummy breakfasts and pizza. Breakfasts can be as ordinary or
as innovative as you like, with the menu running from fried eggs with
bacon to blueberry pancakes to scrambled tofu served with home fries.
Pizzas are equally eclectic, with toppings that include everything from
the usual pepperoni and mushrooms to more exotic corn, raisins, and
kalamata olives. ⊠*Rte. 10, Coral Bay* ☎*340/693–5240* ⊟*No credit
cards* ⊙*Closed Mon. and Tues.*

CRUZ BAY & ENVIRONS

CONTINENTAL ✕**Chloe & Bernard's.** With a menu that focuses on steak and seafood,
$$$$ Chloe & Bernard's is always delightful. The dishes change regularly,
but you might start with a salad of wild field greens, plump grapes, and
candied walnuts drizzled with a roasted apple vinaigrette. Main courses
include red snapper over garlicky mashed potatoes served with sautéed
spinach. ⊠*Westin St. John Resort & Villas, Rte. 104* ☎*340/693–8000*
⊟*AE, MC, V* ⊙*No lunch.*

$$$–$$$$ ✕**Stone Terrace Restaurant.** A delightful harbor view, soft lantern light,
★ and white-linen tablecloths provide the backdrop for this restaurant's
imaginative cuisine. To standards like rack of lamb, the chef adds a
savory dried fruit crust and a cauliflower flan with a mint and sweet
pea sauce. The organic greens salad is drizzled with a Chianti wine vin-

26

aigrette. The desserts change daily, but are always as intriguing as the other courses. ⊠ *Bay St.* ☎ *340/693–9370* ⊟ *MC, V* ⊘ *Closed Mon. No lunch.*

$$$ ✗ **Lime Inn.** Vacationers and mainland transplants who call St. John home flock to this alfresco spot for the congenial hospitality and good food, including all-you-can-eat shrimp on Wednesday nights. Fresh lobster is the specialty, and the menu also includes shrimp-and-steak dishes and such specials as coconut-encrusted chicken breast with plantains and a Thai curry–cream sauce. ⊠ *Lemon Tree Mall, King St.* ☎ *340/776–6425* ⊟ *AE, MC, V* ⊘ *Closed weekends.*

ECLECTIC ✗ **Fish Trap Restaurant and Seafood Market.** The rooms here all open to the
$$$–$$$$ breezes and buzz with a mix of locals and visitors. Start with a tasty
⊙ appetizer like conch fritters or fish chowder (a creamy combination of snapper, white wine, paprika, and secret spices). You can always find steak and chicken dishes, as well as the interesting pasta of the day. ⊠ *Bay and Strand Sts., next to Our Lady of Mount Carmel Church* ☎ *340/693–9994* ⊟ *MC, V* ⊘ *Closed Mon. No lunch.*

$–$$ ✗ **Chilly Billy's.** Although you might stop by this restaurant at lunchtime for a heartburn-inducing St. John Reuben (with turkey, cheese, sauerkraut, and mustard on rye), this restaurant's claim to fame is breakfast. The French toast is one step this side of heaven: before it's fried, the bread is soaked in a mixture of eggs and Bailey's. If you're not one for morning sweets, try a savory breakfast burrito filled with eggs and jalepeño jack cheese. ⊠ *Lumberyard Shopping Center, Boulon Center Rd.* ☎ *340/693–8708* ⊟ *MC, V* ⊘ *No dinner.*

ITALIAN ✗ **Zozo's Ristorante.** Creative takes on old standards coupled with lovely
$$$$ presentations draw the crowds to this restaurant at Gallows Point
Fodor'sChoice Resort. Start with crispy fried calamari served with a pesto mayon-
★ naise. The chef dresses up roasted mahimahi with a pistachio crust and serves it with a warm goat cheese and arugula salad. The slow-simmered osso buco comes with prosciutto-wrapped asparagus and saffron risotto. The sunset views will take your breath away. ⊠ *Gallows Point Resort, Bay St.* ☎ *340/693–9200* ⊟ *AE, MC, V* ⊘ *No lunch.*

$$–$$$ ✗ **Café Roma.** This second-floor restaurant in the heart of Cruz Bay is
⊙ *the* place for traditional Italian cuisine: lasagna, spaghetti and meatballs, and seafood puttanesca. Small pizzas are available at the table, but larger ones are for takeout only. Rum-caramel bread pudding is a dessert specialty. This casual eatery can get crowded in winter, so show up early. ⊠ *Vesta Gade* ☎ *340/776–6524* ⊟ *MC, V* ⊘ *No lunch.*

PAN-ASIAN ✗ **Asolare.** Contemporary Asian cuisine dominates the menu at this
$$$–$$$$ elegant open-air eatery in an old St. John house. Come early and relax
★ over drinks while you enjoy the sunset lighting up the harbor. Start with an appetizer such as pork dumplings served with a glass noodle salad, then move on to entrées such as beef fillet served with pan-roasted potatoes and napa cabbage, or seared tuna served with an apple-and-greens salad. If you still have room for dessert, try the spring roll drizzled with a mango puree and chocolate sauce. ⊠ *Estate Lindholm, Rte. 20 on Caneel Hill* ☎ *340/779–4747* ⊟ *AE, MC, V* ⊘ *No lunch.*

VEGETARIAN
$$ ✗**Satyamuna.** Short on ambience but long on taste, this shopping center restaurant serves delightful vegetarian cuisine with a Mediterranean slant. Order your falafel sandwich, eggplant panini or beanburger at the counter for delivery to your table in the shopping center's arcade. Good people-watching, too. ⊠ *Rte. 108, Cruz Bay* ☎*340/774–3663* ▭*MC, V* ⊗*Closed Sun.*

BEACHES

St. John is blessed with many beaches, and all of them fall into the good, great, and don't-tell-anyone-else-about-this-place categories. Those along the north shore are all within the national park. Some are more developed than others—and many are crowded on weekends, holidays, and in high season—but by and large they're still pristine. Beaches along the south and eastern shores are quiet and isolated.

Cinnamon Bay Beach. This long, sandy beach faces beautiful cays and abuts the national park campground. The facilities are open to the public and include cool showers, toilets, a commissary, and a restaurant. You can rent water-sports equipment here—a good thing, because there's excellent snorkeling off the point to the right; look for the big angelfish and large schools of purple triggerfish. Afternoons on Cinnamon Bay can be windy—a boon for windsurfers but an annoyance for sunbathers—so arrive early to beat the gusts. The Cinnamon Bay hiking trail begins across the road from the beach parking lot; ruins mark the trailhead. There are actually two paths here: a level nature trail (signs along it identify the flora) that loops through the woods and passes an old Danish cemetery, and a steep trail that starts where the road bends past the ruins and heads straight up to Route 10. Restrooms are on the main path from the commissary to the beach and scattered around the campground. ⊠*North Shore Rd., Rte. 20, about 4 mi (6 km) east of Cruz Bay.*

Francis Bay Beach. Because there's little shade, this beach gets toasty warm in the afternoon when the sun comes around to the west, but the rest of the day, it's a delightful stretch of white sand. The only facilities are a few picnic tables tucked among the trees and a portable restroom, but folks come here to watch the birds that live in the swampy area behind the beach. The park offers bird-watching hikes here on Sunday morning; sign up at the visitor center in Cruz Bay. To get here, turn left at the Annaberg intersection. ⊠*North Shore Rd., Rte. 20, ¼ mi (½ km) from Annaberg intersection.*

Hawksnest Beach. Sea grape and waving palm trees line this narrow beach, and there are restrooms, cooking grills, and a covered shed for picnicking. A patchy reef just offshore means snorkeling is an easy swim away, but the best underwater views are reserved for ambitious snorkelers who head farther to the east along the bay's fringes. Watch out for boat traffic—a channel guides dinghies to the beach, but the occasional boater strays into the swim area. It's the closest drivable beach to Cruz Bay, so it's often crowded with locals and visitors. ⊠*North Shore Rd., Rte. 20, about 2 mi (3 km) east of Cruz Bay.*

26

Lameshur Bay Beach. This sea grape–fringed beach is toward the end of a partially paved road on the southeast coast. The reward for your long drive is solitude, good snorkeling, and a chance to spy on some pelicans. The beach has a couple of picnic tables, rusting barbecue grills, and a portable restroom. The ruins of the old plantation are a five-minute walk down the road past the beach. The area has good hiking trails, including a trek (more than a mile) up Bordeaux Mountain before an easy walk to Yawzi Point. ⊠ *Off Rte. 107, about 1½ mi (2½ km) from Salt Pond.*

Maho Bay Beach. This popular beach is below Maho Bay Camps, a wonderful hillside enclave of tent cabins. The campground offers breakfast and dinner at its Pavillion Restaurant, water-sports equipment rentals at the beach, and restrooms. After a five-minute hike down a long flight of stairs to the beach, snorkelers head off along rocky outcroppings for a look at all manner of colorful fish. Watch for a sea turtle or two to cross your path. Another lovely strip of sand with the same name sits right along the North Shore Road. Turn left at the Annaberg intersection and follow the signs about 1 mi (1½ km) for Maho Bay Camps. ⊠ *Off North Shore Rd., Rte. 20, Maho Bay.*

Salt Pond Bay Beach. If you're adventurous, this rocky beach on the scenic southeastern coast—next to Coral Bay and rugged Drunk Bay—is worth exploring. It's a short hike down a hill from the parking lot, and the only facilities are an outhouse and a few picnic tables scattered about. Tide pools are filled with all sorts of marine creatures, and the snorkeling is good, particularly along the bay's edges. A short walk takes you to a pond where salt crystals collect around the edges. Hike farther uphill past cactus gardens to Ram Head for see-forever views. Leave nothing valuable in your car, as reports of thefts are common. ⊠ *Rte. 107, about 3 mi (5 km) south of Coral Bay.*

Fodor'sChoice   **Trunk Bay Beach.** St. John's most-photographed beach is also the pre-
★   ferred spot for beginning snorkelers because of its underwater trail. (Cruise-ship passengers interested in snorkeling for a day flock here, so if you're looking for seclusion, arrive early or later in the day.) Crowded or not, this stunning beach is one of the island's most beautiful. There are changing rooms with showers, bathrooms, a snack bar, picnic tables, a gift shop, phones, lockers, and snorkeling-equipment rentals. The parking lot often overflows, but you can park along the road. ⊠ *North Shore Rd., Rte. 20, about 2½ mi (4 km) east of Cruz Bay.*

SPORTS & THE OUTDOORS

BOATING & SAILING

If you're staying at a hotel or campground, your activities desk will usually be able to help you arrange a sailing excursion aboard a nearby boat. Most day sails leaving Cruz Bay head out along St. John's north coast. Those that depart Coral Bay might drop anchor at some remote cay off the island's east end or even in the nearby British Virgin Islands. Your trip usually includes lunch, beverages, and at least one snorkeling stop. Keep in mind that inclement weather could interfere with your plans, though most boats will still go out if rain

isn't too heavy. If you're staying in a villa, or if your hotel or camp-
★ ground doesn't have an affiliated charter sailboat, contact **St. John Concierge Service**(⊠ *Across from post office, Cruz Bay* ☎*340/777–2665 or
800/808–6025* ⊕*www.stjohnconciergeservice.com*). The capable staff
can find a boat that fits your style and pocketbook. The company also
books fishing and scuba trips.

For a speedier trip to the cays and remote beaches off St. John, you
can rent a power boat from **Ocean Runner** (⊠ *On waterfront, Cruz Bay*
☎*340/693–8809* ⊕ www.oceanrunnerusvi.com). The company rents
one- and two-engine boats for $295 to $695 per day. Gas and oil will
run you $100 to $300 a day extra, depending on how far you're going.
It's a good idea to have some skill with power boats for this self-drive
adventure, but if you don't, you can hire a captain for $110 a day.

Even novice sailors can take off in a small sailboat from Cruz Bay
Beach with **Sail Safaris** (☎*340/626–8181 or 866/820–6906* ⊕*www.
sailsafaris.net*) to one of the small islands off St. John. Guided half-day
tours, rentals, and lessons start at $70 per person.

DIVING & SNORKELING

Although just about every beach has nice snorkeling—Trunk Bay, Cinnamon Bay, and Waterlemon Cay at Leinster Bay get the most praise—
you need a boat to head out to the more remote snorkeling locations
and the best scuba spots. Sign on with any of the island's water-sports
operators to get to spots farther from St. John. If you use the one at
your hotel, just stroll down to the dock to hop aboard. Their boats
will take you to hot spots between St. John and St. Thomas, including
the tunnels at **Thatch Cay,** the ledges at **Congo Cay**, and the wreck of the
General Rogers. Dive off St. John at **Stephens Cay,** a short boat ride out
of Cruz Bay, where fish swim around the reefs as you float downward.
At **Devers Bay,** on St. John's south shore, fish dart about in colorful
schools. **Carval Rock,** shaped like an old-time ship, has gorgeous rock
formations, coral gardens, and lots of fish. It can be too rough here in
winter, though. Count on paying $75 for a one-tank dive and $90 for
a two-tank dive. Rates include equipment and a tour. If you've never
dived before, try an introductory course, called a resort course. Or if
certification is in your vacation plans, the island's dive shops can help
you get your card.

Cruz Bay Watersports (☎*340/776–6234* ⊕*www.divestjohn.com*) has
two locations: in Cruz Bay at the Lumberyard Shopping Complex and
at the Westin St. John Resort. Owners Marcus and Patty Johnston offer
regular reef, wreck, and night dives and USVI and BVI snorkel tours.
The company holds both PADI five-star facility and NAUI Dream
Resort status.**Low Key Watersports** (☎*340/693–8999 or 800/835–7718*
⊕*www.divelowkey.com*), at Wharfside Village, offers one- and two-
tank dives and specialty courses. It's certified as a PADI five-star training facility.

FISHING

Well-kept charter boats—approved by the U.S. Coast Guard—head out to the north and south drops or troll along the inshore reefs, depending on the season and what's biting. The captains usually provide bait, drinks, and lunch, but you need to bring your own hat and sunscreen. Fishing charters run between $550 and $700 per half day for the boat. **Capt. Byron Oliver** (☎*340/693–8339*) takes you out to the north and south drops or closer in to St. John. **Gone Ketchin'** (☎*340/714–1175* ⊕*www.goneketchin.com*), in St. John, arranges trips with old salt Captain Grizz.

HIKING

Although it's fun to go hiking with a Virgin Islands National Park guide, don't be afraid to head out on your own. To find a hike that suits your ability, stop by the park's visitor center in Cruz Bay and pick up the free trail guide; it details points of interest, trail lengths, and estimated hiking times, as well as any dangers you might encounter. Although the park staff recommends long pants to protect against thorns and insects, most people hike in shorts because it can get very hot. Wear sturdy shoes or hiking boots even if you're hiking to the beach. Don't forget to bring water and insect repellent.

Fodor'sChoice
★
The **Virgin Islands National Park** (✉*1300 Cruz Bay Creek, St. John* ☎*340/776–6201* ⊕*www.nps.gov/viis*) maintains more than 20 trails on the north and south shores and offers guided hikes along popular routes. A full-day trip to Reef Bay is a must; it's an easy hike through lush and dry forest, past the ruins of an old plantation, and to a sugar factory adjacent to the beach. It can be a bit arduous for young kids, however. Take the $6 safari bus from the park's visitor center to the trailhead, where you can meet a ranger who'll serve as your guide. The park provides a boat ride back to Cruz Bay for $15 to save you the walk back up the mountain. The schedule changes from season to season; call for times and reservations, which are essential.

HORSEBACK RIDING

Clip-clop along the island's byways for a slower-pace tour of St. John. **Carolina Corral** (☎*340/693–5778*) offers horseback trips and wagon rides down scenic roads with owner Dana Barlett. She has a way with horses and calms even the most novice riders. Rates start at $75 for a 1½-hour horseback ride and $20 for a one-hour wagon ride.

SEA KAYAKING

Poke around crystal bays and explore undersea life from a sea kayak. Rates run about $90 for a full day in a double kayak. Tours start at $50 for a half day. On the Cruz Bay side of the island, **Arawak Expeditions** (☎*340/693–8312 or 800/238–8687* ⊕*www.arawakexp.com*), which operates out of Low Key Watersports in Cruz Bay's Wharfside Village, has professional guides who use traditional and sit-on-top kayaks to ply coastal waters. The company also rents single and double kayaks, so you can head independently to nearby islands like Stephen's Cay. Explore Coral Bay Harbor and Hurricane Hole on the eastern end of the island in a sea kayak from **Crabby's Watersports** (✉*Rte. 107, out-*

side Coral Bay ☎*340/714–2415* ⊕*www.crabbyswatersports.com*). If you don't want to paddle into the wind to get out of Coral Bay Harbor, the staff will drop you off in Hurricane Hole so you can paddle downwind back to Coral Bay. Crabby's also rents snorkel gear, beach chairs, and floats.

WINDSURFING

Steady breezes and expert instruction make learning to windsurf a snap. Try **Cinnamon Bay Campground** (✉*Rte. 20, Cinnamon Bay* ☎*340/693–5902*), where rentals are $40 to $80 per hour. Lessons are available right at the waterfront; just look for the Windsurfers stacked up on the beach. The cost for a one-hour lesson starts at $60, plus the cost of the board rental. You can also rent kayaks, boogie boards, small sailboats, and surfboards.

FREE PARKING

Cruz Bay's parking problem is maddening. Your best bet is to rent a car from a company that allows you to park in their lot. Make sure you ask before you sign on the dotted line if you plan to spend time in Cruz Bay.

SHOPPING

26

AREAS & MALLS

Luxury goods and handicrafts can be found on St. John. Most shops carry a little of this and a bit of that, so it pays to poke around. The Cruz Bay shopping district runs from **Wharfside Village,** just around the corner from the ferry dock, to **Mongoose Junction,** an inviting shopping center on North Shore Road. (The name of this upscale shopping mall, by the way, is a holdover from a time when those furry island creatures gathered at a nearby garbage bin.) Out on Route 104 stop in at the **Marketplace** to explore its gift and crafts shops. At the island's other end, there are a few stores—selling clothes, jewelry, and artwork—here and there from the village of **Coral Bay** to the small complex at **Shipwreck Landing.**

On St. John, store hours run from 9 or 10 to 5 or 6. Wharfside Village and Mongoose Junction shops in Cruz Bay are often open into the evening.

SPECIALTY ITEMS

ART **Bajo el Sol.** This gallery sells works by owner Livy Hitchcock, plus those from a roster of the island's best artists. Shop for oil and acrylics, sculptures, and ceramics. ✉*Mongoose Junction, North Shore Rd., Cruz Bay* ☎*340/693–7070.*

Coconut Coast Studios. This waterside shop, a five-minute walk from Cruz Bay, showcases the work of Elaine Estern. She specializes in undersea scenes. ✉*Frank Bay, Cruz Bay* ☎*340/776–6944.*

BOOKS **National Park Headquarters.** The shop sells several good histories of St. John, including *St. John Back Time,* by Ruth Hull Low and Rafael Lito Valls, and, for linguists, Valls's *What a Pistarckle!*—an explanation of the colloquialisms that make up the local version of English (*pistarckle* is a Dutch Creole word that means "noise" or "din," which pretty much sums up the language here). ✉*Cruz Bay* ☎*340/776–6201.*

CLOTHING **Big Planet Adventure Outfitters.** You knew when you arrived that some place on St. John would cater to the outdoor enthusiasts who hike up and down the island's trails. Well, this outdoor-clothing store is where you can find the popular Naot sandals and Reef footware, along with colorful and durable cotton clothing and accessories by Billabong. The store also sells children's clothes. ⊠ *Mongoose Junction, North Shore Rd., Cruz Bay* ☎ *340/776–6638.*

Bougainvillea Boutique. If you want to look as if you stepped out of the pages of the resort-wear spread in an upscale travel magazine, try this store. Owner Susan Stair carries *very* chic men's and women's resort wear, straw hats, leather handbags, and fine gifts. ⊠ *Mongoose Junction, North Shore Rd., Cruz Bay* ☎ *340/693–7190* ⊠ *Westin Resort and Villas, Rte. 104, Great Cruz Bay* ☎ *340/693–8000 Ext. 1784.*

Jolly Dog. Stock up on the stuff you forgot to pack at this store. Sarongs in cotton and rayon, beach towels with tropical motifs, and hats and T-shirts sporting the Jolly Dog logo fill the shelves. ⊠ *Shipwreck Landing, Rte. 107, Sanders Bay* ☎ *340/693–5333* ⊠ *Skinny Legs Shopping Complex, Rte. 10, Coral Bay* ☎ *340/693–5900.*

Sloop Jones. It's worth the trip all the way out to the island's east end to shop for made-on-the-premises clothing, pillows, and fabrics by the yard splashed with tropical colors. Fabrics are in cotton, linen, and rayon and are supremely comfortable. ⊠ *Off Rte. 10, East End* ☎ *340/779–4001.*

St. John Editions. Shop here for swimsuits and nifty cotton dresses that go from beach to dinner with a change of shoes and accessories. Owner Molly Soper also carries attractive straw hats and inexpensive jewelry. ⊠ *North Shore Rd., Cruz Bay* ☎ *340/693–8444.*

FOOD If you're renting a villa, condo, or cottage and doing your own cooking, there are several good places to shop for food; just be aware that prices are much higher than those at home.

Lily's Gourmet Market. This small store in Coral Bay carries the basics plus meat, fish, and produce. ⊠ *Cocoloba Shopping Center, Rte. 107, Coral Bay* ☎ *340/777–3335.*

Starfish Market. The island's largest store usually has the best selection of meat, fish, and produce. ⊠ *The Marketplace, Rte. 104, Cruz Bay* ☎ *340/779–4949.*

GIFTS **Awl Made Here.** Shop here for locally made leather goods. Owner Tracey Keating creates lovely journal covers, wallets, and belts, but she also does special orders. The store carries other locally made items like imaginative jewelry and hand-painted wine glasses. ⊠ *Skinny Legs Shopping Complex, Rte. 10, Coral Bay* ☎ *340/777–5757.*

Bamboula. Owner Jo Sterling travels the world to find unusual housewares, rugs, bedspreads, accessories, and men's and women's clothes and shoes for this multicultural boutique. ⊠ *Mongoose Junction, North Shore Rd., Cruz Bay* ☎ *340/693–8699.*

Best of Both Worlds. Pricy metal sculptures and attractive artworks hang from this shop's walls; the nicest are small glass decorations shaped like shells and seahorses. ⊠*Mongoose Junction, North Shore Rd., Cruz Bay* ☎*340/693–7005.*

Donald Schnell Studio. In addition to pottery, this place sells unusual hand-blown glass, wind chimes, kaleidoscopes, fanciful fountains, and more. Your purchases can be shipped worldwide. ⊠*Amore Center, Rte. 108, Cruz Bay* ☎*340/776–6420.*

Every Ting. As its name implies, this store has a bit of this and a bit of that. Shop for Caribbean books and CDs, picture frames decorated with shells, and T-shirts with tropical motifs. Residents and visitors also drop by to have a cup of espresso. ⊠*Gallows Point Resort, Bay St., Cruz Bay* ☎*340/693–5820.*

Fabric Mill. Shop here for women's clothing in tropical brights, as well as lingerie, sandals, and batik wraps. Or take home a brilliant-hued bolt from the upholstery-fabric selection. ⊠*Mongoose Junction, North Shore Rd., Cruz Bay* ☎*340/776–6194.*

Mumbo Jumbo. With what may be the best prices in St. John, this cozy shop carries everything from tropical clothing to stuffed sea creatures. ⊠*Skinny Legs Shopping Complex, Rte. 10, Coral Bay* ☎*340/779–4277.*

Nest and Company. In colors that reflect the sea, this cozy store carries perfect take-home gifts. Shop here for soaps in tropical scents, dinnerware, and much more. ⊠*Marketplace Shopping Center, Rte. 108, Cruz Bay* ☎*340/715–2552.*

★ **Pink Papaya.** This store is where you can find the well-known work of longtime Virgin Islands resident M. L. Etre, plus a huge collection of one-of-a-kind gifts, including bright tablecloths, unusual trays, and unique tropical jewelry. ⊠*Lemon Tree Mall, King St., Cruz Bay* ☎*340/693–8535.*

JEWELRY **Caravan Gallery.** Owner Radha Speer travels the world to find much of the unusual jewelry she sells here. And the more you look, the more you see—folk art, tribal art, and masks for sale cover the walls and tables, making this a great place to browse. ⊠*Mongoose Junction, North Shore Rd., Cruz Bay* ☎*340/779–4566.*

Free Bird Creations. Head here for special handcrafted jewelry—earrings, bracelets, pendants, chains—as well as the good selection of water-resistant watches for your beach excursions. ⊠*Wharfside Village, Strand St., Cruz Bay* ☎*340/693–8625.*

Jewels. This branch of a St. Thomas store carries emeralds, diamonds, and other jewels in attractive yellow- and white-gold settings, as well as strings of creamy pearls, watches, and other designer jewelry. ⊠*Mongoose Junction, North Shore Rd., Cruz Bay* ☎*340/776–6007.*

R&I Patton Goldsmiths. Rudy and Irene Patton design most of the lovely silver and gold jewelry displayed in this shop. The rest comes from various designer friends. Sea fans (those large, lacy plants that sway with the ocean's currents) in filigreed silver, starfish and hibiscus pendants in silver or gold, and gold sand-dollar-shape charms and earrings are choice selections. ⊠ *Mongoose Junction, North Shore Rd., Cruz Bay* ☎ *340/776–6548.*

Verace. Jewelry from such well-known designers as Toby Pomeroy and Patrick Murphy fill the shelves. Murphy's stunning gold sailboats with gems for hulls will catch your attention. ⊠ *Wharfside Village, Strand St., Cruz Bay* ☎ *340/693–7599.*

PHOTO   **Cruz Bay Photo.** Pick up disposable cameras, film, and other photo needs,
DEVELOPING   or when your memory card fills up, download your digital photos to a disk or print them out. Shop here also for good-quality sunglasses, a must for your tropical vacation. ⊠ *Wharfside Village, Strand St., Cruz Bay* ☎ *340/779–4313.*

NIGHTLIFE

St. John isn't the place to go for glitter and all-night partying. Still, after-hours Cruz Bay can be a lively little town in which to dine, drink, dance, chat, or flirt. Notices posted on the bulletin board outside the Connections telephone center—up the street from the ferry dock in Cruz Bay—or listings in the island's two small newspapers (the *St. John Sun Times* and *Tradewinds*) will keep you apprised of special events, comedy nights, movies, and the like.

There's calypso and reggae on Friday night at **Fred's** (⊠ *King St., Cruz Bay* ☎ *340/776–6363*). Young folks like to gather at **Woody's** (⊠ *Near ferry dock, across from Subway restaurant, Cruz Bay* ☎ *340/779–4625*), where sidewalk tables provide a close-up view of Cruz Bay's action. After a sunset drink at **Zozo's Ristorante** (⊠ *Gallows Point Resort, Bay St., Cruz Bay* ☎ *340/693–9200*), up the hill from Cruz Bay, you can stroll around town (much is clustered around the small waterfront park). Many of the young people from the U.S. mainland who live and work on St. John will be out sipping and socializing, too.

As its name implies, **Island Blues** (⊠ *Rte. 107, Coral Bay* ☎ *340/776–6800*) is the hot place to go for music at the eastern end of the island. On the far side of the island, landlubbers and old salts listen to music and swap stories at **Skinny Legs Bar & Restaurant** (⊠ *Rte. 10, Coral Bay* ☎ *340/779–4982*).

EXPLORING ST. JOHN

St. John is an easy place to explore. One road runs along the northern shore, another across the center of the mountains. There are a few roads that branch off here and there, but it's hard to get lost. Pick up a map at the visitor center before you start out and you'll have no problems. Few residents remember the route numbers, so have your map in hand if you stop to ask for directions. Bring along a swimsuit for stops at some of the most beautiful beaches in the world. You can spend all day or just a couple of hours exploring, but be advised that the roads are narrow and wind up and down steep hills, so don't expect to get anywhere in a hurry. There are lunch spots at Cinnamon Bay and in Coral Bay, or you can do what the locals do—find a secluded spot for a picnic. The grocery stores in Cruz Bay sell Styrofoam coolers just for this purpose.

If you plan to do a lot of touring, renting a car will be cheaper and will give you much more freedom than relying on taxis; on St. John, taxis are shared safari vans, and drivers are reluctant to go anywhere until they have a full load of passengers. Although you may be tempted by an open-air Suzuki or Jeep, a conventional car can get you just about everywhere on the paved roads, and you'll be able to lock up your valuables. You may be able to share a van or open-air vehicle (called a safari bus) with other passengers on a tour of scenic mountain trails, secret coves, and eerie bush-covered ruins.

WHAT TO SEE

★ **Annaberg Plantation.** In the 18th century, sugar plantations dotted the steep hills of this island. Slaves and free Danes and Dutchmen toiled to harvest the cane that was used to create sugar, molasses, and rum for export. Built in the 1780s, the partially restored plantation at Leinster Bay was once an important sugar mill. Although there are no official visiting hours, the National Park Service has regular tours, and some well-informed taxi drivers will show you around. Occasionally you may see a living-history demonstration—someone making johnnycake or weaving baskets. For information on tours and cultural events, contact the St. John National Park Service Visitors Center. ⊠ *Leinster Bay Rd., Annaberg* ☏ *340/776–6201* ⊕ *www.nps.gov/viis* ⌑ *Free* ☉ *Daily dawn–dusk.*

★ **Bordeaux Mountain.** St. John's highest peak rises to 1,277 feet. Route 10 passes near enough to the top to offer breathtaking vistas. Don't stray into the road here—cars whiz by at a good clip along this section. Instead, drive nearly to the end of the dirt road that heads off next to the restaurant and gift shop for spectacular views at Picture Point and the trailhead of the hike downhill to Lameshur. Get a trail map from the park service before you start. ⊠ *Rte. 10.*

Catherineberg Ruins. At this fine example of an 18th-century sugar and rum factory, there's a storage vault beneath the windmill. Across the road, look for the round mill, which was later used to hold water. In the 1733 slave revolt Catherineberg served as headquarters for the Amina warriors, a tribe of Africans captured into slavery. ⊠ *Rte. 10, Catherineberg.*

Coral Bay. This laid-back community at the island's dry, eastern end is named for its shape rather than for its underwater life—the word *coral* comes from *krawl,* Dutch for "corral." It's a small, quiet, neighborhoody settlement—a place to get away from it all. You'll probably need a four-wheel-drive vehicle if you plan to stay at this end of the island, as some of the rental houses are up unpaved roads that wind around the mountain. If you come just for lunch, a regular car will be fine.

St. John Archaeology

Archaeologists continue to unravel St. John's past through excavations at Trunk Bay and Cinnamon Bay, both prime tourist destinations within Virgin Islands National Park.

Work began back in the early 1990s, when the park wanted to build new bathhouses at the popular Trunk Bay. In preparation for that project, the archaeologists began to dig, turning up artifacts and the remains of structures that date to AD 900. The site was once a village occupied by the Taino, a peaceful group that lived in the area for many centuries. A similar but not quite as ancient village was discovered at Cinnamon Bay.

By the time the Tainos got to Cinnamon Bay—they lived in the area from about AD 1000 to 1500—their society had developed to include chiefs, commoners, workers, and slaves. The location of the national park's busy Cinnamon Bay campground was once a Taino temple that belonged to a king or chief. When archaeologists began digging in 1998, they uncovered several dozen *zemis*, which are small clay gods used in ceremonial activities, as well as beads, pots, and many other artifacts.

Near the end of the Cinnamon Bay dig, archaeologists turned up another less ancient but still surprising discovery. A burned layer indicated that a plantation slave village had also stood near Cinnamon Bay campground; it was torched during the 1733 revolt because its slave inhabitants had been loyal to the planters. Since the 1970s, bones from slaves buried in the area have been uncovered at the water's edge by beach erosion.

Cruz Bay. St. John's main town may be compact (it consists of only several blocks), but it's definitely a hub: the ferries from St. Thomas and the British Virgin Islands pull in here, and it's where you can get a taxi or rent a car to travel around the island. There are plenty of shops in which to browse, a number of watering holes where you can stop for a breather, many restaurants, and a grassy square with benches where you can sit back and take everything in. Look for the current edition of the handy, amusing "St. John Map" featuring Max the Mongoose. To pick up a useful guide to St. John's hiking trails, see various large maps of the island, and find out about current park service programs, including guided walks and cultural demonstrations, stop by the **V.I. National Park Visitors Center** (⊠ *Near baseball field, Cruz Bay* ☎ *340/776–6201* ⊕ *www.nps.gov/viis*). It's open daily from 8 to 4:30.

Elaine Ione Sprauve Library. On the hill just above Cruz Bay is the Enighed Estate greathouse, built in 1757. *Enighed* is the Danish word for "concord" (unity or peace). The greathouse and its outbuildings (a sugar factory and horse-driven mill) were destroyed by fire and hurricanes, and the house sat in ruins until 1982. The library offers Internet access for $2 an hour. ⊠ *Rte. 104, make a right past Texaco station, Cruz Bay* ☎ *340/776–6359* ☎ *Free* ⊙ *Weekdays 9–5.*

Peace Hill. It's worth stopping at this spot just past the Hawksnest Bay overlook for great views of St. John, St. Thomas, and the BVI. On the flat promontory is an old sugar mill. ⊠ *Off Rte. 20, Denis Bay.*

★ **Reef Bay Trail.** Although this is one of the most interesting hikes on St. John, unless you're a rugged individualist who wants a physical challenge (and that describes a lot of people who stay on St. John), you can probably get the most out of the trip if you join a hike led by a park service ranger who can identify the trees and plants on the hike down, fill you in on the history of the Reef Bay Plantation, and tell you about the petroglyphs on the rocks at the bottom of the trail. A side trail takes you to the plantation's greathouse, a gutted but mostly intact structure that maintains vestiges of its former beauty. Take the safari bus from the park's visitor center. A boat takes you from the beach at Reef Bay back to the visitor center, saving you the uphill climb. ⊠*Rte. 10, Reef Bay* ☎*340/776–6201 Ext. 238 reservations* ⊕*www.nps.gov/viis* ✉*Free, safari bus $6, return boat trip to Cruz Bay $15* ☉*Tours at 9:30* AM*, days change seasonally.*

ST. CROIX

By Lynda Lohr

As my seaplane skimmed St. Croix's north coast on the flight from St. Thomas, the island's agrarian past played out below. Stone windmills left over from the days when sugar ruled stood like sentinels in the fields. As we closed in on Christiansted, the big yellow Fort Christianvaern loomed on the waterfront, and the city's red roofs created a colorful counterpoint to the turquoise harbor. A visit to St. Croix, once a Danish colony, always puts me in touch with my Danish roots (my grandmother was a Poulsen). Indeed, history is so popular in St. Croix that planes are filled with Danish visitors who, like other vacationers, come to sun at the island's powdery beaches, enjoy pampering at the hotels, and dine at interesting restaurants, but mainly wish to explore the island's colonial history.

Until 1917 Denmark owned St. Croix and her sister Virgin Islands, an aspect of the island's past that is reflected in street names in the main towns of Christiansted and Frederiksted as well as surnames of many island residents. Those early Danish settlers, as well as those from other European nations, left behind slews of 18th- and 19th-century ruins, all of them worked by slaves brought over on ships from Africa, their descendants, and white indentured servants lured to St. Croix to pay off their debt to society. Some—such as the Christiansted National Historic site, Whim Plantation, the ruins at St. George Village Botanical Garden, the Nature Conservancy's property at Estate Princess, and the ruins at Estate Mount Washington and Judith's Fancy—are open for easy exploration. Others are on private land, but a drive around the island reveals the ruins of 100 plantations here and there on St. Croix's 84 square mi. Their windmills, greathouses, and factories are all that's left of the 224 plantations that once grew sugarcane, tobacco, and other agricultural products at the height of the island's plantation glory.

The downturn began in 1801 when the British occupied the island. The demise of the slave trade in 1803, another British occupation from 1807 to 1815, droughts, the development of the sugar beet industry in Europe, political upheaval, and a depression sent the island on a downward spiral.

St. Croix never recovered from these blows. The end of slavery in 1848, followed by labor riots, fires, hurricanes, and an earthquake during the last half of the 19th century, brought what was left of the island's economy to its knees. The start of prohibition in 1922 called a halt to the island's rum industry, further crippling the economy. The situation remained dire—so bad that President Herbert Hoover called the territory an "effective poorhouse" during a 1931 visit—until the rise of tourism in the late 1950s and 1960s. With tourism came economic improvements coupled with an influx of residents from other Caribbean islands and the mainland, but St. Croix depends partly on industries like the huge oil refinery outside Frederiksted to provide employment.

Today suburban subdivisions fill the fields where sugarcane once waved in the tropical breeze. Condominium complexes line the beaches along the north coast outside Christiansted. Homes that are more elaborate dot the rolling hillsides. Modern strip malls and shopping centers sit along major roads, and it's as easy to find a McDonald's as it is Caribbean fare.

Although St. Croix sits definitely in the 21st century, with only a little effort you can easily step back into the island's past.

WHERE TO STAY

You can find everything from plush resorts to simple beachfront digs in St. Croix. If you sleep in either the Christiansted or Frederiksted area, you'll be closest to shopping, restaurants, and nightlife. Most of the island's other hotels will put you just steps from the beach. St. Croix has several small but special properties that offer personalized service. If you like all the comforts of home, you may prefer to stay in a condominium or villa. Room rates on St. Croix are competitive with those on other islands, and if you travel off-season, you can find substantially reduced prices. Many properties offer money-saving honeymoon and dive packages. Whether you stay in a hotel, a condominium, or a villa, you'll enjoy up-to-date amenities. Most properties have room TVs, but at some bed-and-breakfasts there might be only one in the common room.

Although a stay right in historic Christiansted may mean putting up with a little urban noise, you probably won't have trouble sleeping. Christiansted rolls up the sidewalks fairly early, and humming air-conditioners drown out any noise. Solitude is guaranteed at hotels and inns outside Christiansted and those on the outskirts of sleepy Frederiksted.

For approximate costs, see the dining and lodging price chart at the beginning of this chapter.

HOTELS

CHRISTIANSTED
$$

▦**Hotel Caravelle.** Near the harbor, at the waterfront end of a pleasant shopping arcade, the Caravelle's in-town location puts you steps away from shops and restaurants. Rooms are tasteful and tropical, with white walls and floral-print bedspreads and curtains; most have ocean views. A small pool provides swimming and sunning opportunities. The ever-popular Rum Runners restaurant sits just off the lobby. Pros: Good restaurant, convenient location, convenient parking. Cons: No beach, rundown neighborhood. ⊠*44A Queen Cross St.,* ☎*340/773–0687 or 800/524–0410* ⊕*www.hotelcaravelle.com* ⇘*43 rooms, 1 suite* ⍭*In-room: refrigerator, Ethernet, Wi-Fi. In-hotel: restaurant, bar, pool, public Internet, no elevator* ▭*AE, D, DC, MC, V* ⑭*EP.*

$$

▦**Pink Fancy Hotel.** Offering a connection to the island's elegant past, the venerable hotel is listed on the National Register of Historic Places. Dating from 1780, it became a hotel in 1948. Rooms are filled with antiques, mahogany furnishings, and colorful Oriental rugs. Lush gardens meander around the fenced-in compound, creating a comfortable base for folks who like to get out and about. Guests gather poolside for breakfast and conversation. **Pros:** Homey accommodations, lovely gardens, friendly atmosphere. **Cons:** Rundown neighborhood, no parking lot. ⊠*27 Prince St.,* ☎*340/773–8460 or 800/524–2045* ⊕*www.pinkfancy.com* ⇘*11 rooms* ⍭*In-room: kitchen, Wi-Fi. In-hotel: pool, no elevator, public Wi-Fi, no-smoking rooms* ▭*AE, MC, V* ⑭*CP (some rooms).*

$

▦**Hotel on the Cay.** Hop on the free ferry to reach this lodging in the middle of Christiansted Harbor. Although the island location sounds a bit inconvenient, the ferry ride takes no time at all. The captain zips over to the waterfront whenever he sees someone waiting. Rooms are pleasantly furnished and have harbor views, balconies or patios, and kitchenettes for times when you don't want to eat at the hotel's restaurant. In addition to sunning at the small beach, chatting with fellow travelers, and strolling the lushly planted grounds, you can try snorkeling and other water sports. Keep an eye out for one of the endangered St. Croix ground lizards that call the island home. **Pros:** Quiet atmosphere, convenient location, lovely beach. **Cons:** Accessible only by ferry, no parking available. ⊠*Protestant Cay,* ☎*340/773–2035 or 800/524–2035* ⊕*www.hotelonthecay.com* ⇘*53 rooms* ⍭*In-room: kitchen. In-hotel: restaurant, pool, beachfront, water sports, no elevator, public Internet, public Wi-Fi* ▭*AE, D, MC, V* ⑭*EP.*

$

▦**King Christian Hotel.** A stay at the King Christian puts you right in the heart of Christiansted's historic district. Parts of the building date back to the mid-1700s, but numerous renovations have brought it up to modern standards. Rooms are a bit on the pedestrian side, but floral spreads and pastel walls brighten things up considerably. Unless you're on a rock-bottom budget, don't opt for the depressing rooms in the back. You can hop a ferry to nearby Protestant Cay for an afternoon at the beach when you tire of the pool. You're a quick walk to restaurants, shops, and water-sports excursions. **Pros:** Rooms have ocean views, car rental in lobby, convenient location. **Cons:** No beach, need to take a taxi at night, no parking lot. ⊠*57 King St., Box 24467,* ☎*340/773–*

26

St. Croix

↑
TO
ST. THOMAS

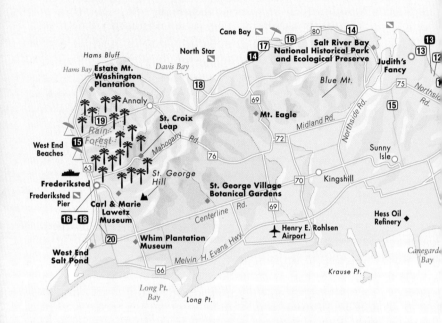

Cane Bay 〰

North Star

Salt River Bay National Historical Park and Ecological Preserve

Hams Bluff

Hams Bay

Davis Bay

Estate Mt. Washington Plantation

Judith's Fancy

Blue Mt.

Annaly

Northside Rd.

St. Croix Leap

Rain Forest

Mt. Eagle

Midland Rd.

Northside Rd.

West End Beaches

Mahogany Rd.

Sunny Isle

Frederiksted

St. George Hill

St. George Village Botanical Gardens

Kingshill

Frederiksted Pier

Carl & Marie Lawetz Museum

Centerline Rd.

Hess Oil Refinery

Canegarde Bay

Whim Plantation Museum

Henry E. Rohlsen Airport

West End Salt Pond

Melvin H. Evans Hwy.

Krause Pt.

Long Pt. Bay

Long Pt.

KEY	
〰	Beaches
〰	Dive Sites
🚢	Cruise Ship Terminal
🌴	Rain Forest
1	Restaurants
1	Hotels

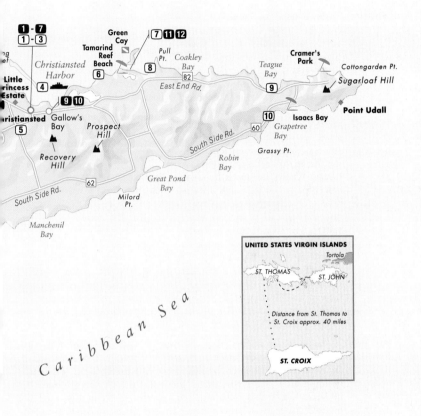

Buck
Island

**Buck Island Reef
National Monument**

1-**7**
①-③

**Green
Cay**
**Tamarind
Reef
Beach**
⑥

7 11 12

Pull
Pt.
8

Coakley
Bay

**Cramer's
Park**

Cottongarden Pt.

*Christiansted
Harbor*

Teague
Bay

Sugarloaf Hill

**Little
Princess
Estate**
④

9 10

East End Rd.
82

9

Point Udall

5

Christiansted Gallow's
Bay

*Prospect
Hill*

10

Isaacs Bay

*Grapetree
Bay*

60

Grassy Pt.

*Recovery
Hill*

*Robin
Bay*

62

*Great Pond
Bay*

South Side Rd.

Milord
Pt.

*Manchenil
Bay*

Caribbean Sea

UNITED STATES VIRGIN ISLANDS

Tortola

ST. THOMAS

ST. JOHN

Distance from St. Thomas to
St. Croix approx. 40 miles

ST. CROIX

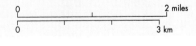

0   2 miles

0   3 km

6330 or 800/524–2012 ⊕www. kingchristian.com ⟿39 rooms ⌂In-room: safe (some), refrigerator. In-hotel: pool, diving, public Internet, public Wi-Fi ▤AE, MC, V �🍴CP.

OUTSIDE   🏨**Carringtons Inn.** Hands-on owners Claudia and Roger Carrington are the real reason to stay here, and they conjure up delicious breakfasts—rum-soaked French toast is a house specialty—dole out advice, and make you feel right at home. Formerly a private home, the comfy bed-and-breakfast is a 10-minute drive from Christiansted. Each room is different, with a decorating theme that reflects a namesake flower. Wicker furniture, handwoven carpets, and balconies in some rooms, colorful spreads, and sea or pool views create an inviting atmosphere. The hillside suburban location means you need a rental car if you stay. **Pros:** Welcoming hosts, tasteful rooms, great breakfasts. **Cons:** No beach, need car to get around. ⊠*4001 Estate Hermon Hill, Christiansted* ☎*340/713–0508 or 877/658–0508* ⊕*www.carringtonsinn.com* ⟿*5 rooms* ⌂*In-room: kitchen (some), refrigerator, no TV. In-hotel: pool, no elevator, public Internet, public Wi-Fi, no-smoking rooms* ▤*AE, MC, V* 🍴*BP.*

EAST END   🏨**The Buccaneer.** For travelers who want everything at their fingertips,
$$$–$$$$ this resort has sandy beaches, swimming pools, and extensive sports
🕐   facilities. A palm-tree-lined main drive leads to the large, pink main building atop a hill; the rest of the resort sits on the grounds of a 300-acre former sugar plantation, where shops, restaurants, and guest quarters are scattered about the manicured lawns. Spacious rooms are tropical in style, with tile floors, four-poster beds, massive wardrobes of pale wood, marble baths, and local art. Beachside doubloon rooms are the largest and are steps from the sand, but you can be perfectly comfortable no matter where you stay. **Pros:** Beachfront location, numerous activities, nice golf course. **Cons:** Pricey rates, insular environment, need car to get around. ⊠*Rte. 82, Box 25200, Shoys* ☎*340/712–2100 or 800/255–3881* ⊕*www.thebuccaneer.com* ⟿*138 rooms* ⌂*In-room: safe, refrigerator, Wi-Fi. In-hotel: 3 restaurants, bar, golf course, tennis courts, pools, gym, spa, beachfront, water sports, children's programs (ages 4–12), no elevator, public Internet, no-smoking rooms* ▤*AE, D, MC, V* 🍴*BP.*

$$$–$$$$ 🏨**Tamarind Reef Hotel.** Spread out along a sandy beach, these low-slung buildings offer casual comfort. Independent travelers who want the

---

ST. CROIX TOP 5

Sailing to Buck Island: Take a boat to the island's best snorkeling spot, or a hike up the hill to take in the stunning view.

Diving the Wall: The Wall is one of the Caribbean's best diving experiences.

Exploring Fort Christiansvaern: This historic fort will let you ponder how life was for early settlers.

Experiencing plantation life: Whim Plantation is a well-preserved example of how the colonial planters lived.

Strolling around Christiansted: You can easily while away the better part of a day in Christiansted, shopping and strolling.

option to eat in or out will enjoy the rooms with basic kitchenettes. The spacious modern rooms have rattan furniture, tropical-print fabrics, and either a terrace or a deck with views of St. Croix's sister islands. Snorkelers can explore a nearby reef, but shallow water makes serious swimming difficult. There's a snack bar just off the beach, and the Galleon Restaurant is next door at Green Cay Marina. **Pros:** Good snorkeling, tasty restaurant, rooms have kitchenettes. **Cons:** Need car to get around, motel-style rooms. ⊠ *5001 Tamarind Reef, off Rte. 82, Annas Hope* ☎ *340/773–4455 or 800/619–0014* ⊕ *www.tamarindreefhotel. com* ⇨ *39 rooms* ♿ *In-room: refrigerator, Wi-Fi. In-hotel: restaurant, pool, water sports, no elevator, no-smoking rooms* ▭ *AE, DC, MC, V* ⎮⊙⎮ *EP.*

$$–$$$ 🏨**Chenay Bay Beach Resort.** The seaside setting and complimentary tennis and water-sports equipment make this resort a real find, particularly for families with active kids. Rooms have ceramic-tile floors, tropical color schemes, rattan furnishings, and front porches. Gravel paths meander among terraced wood or stucco cottages. Other facilities include a large L-shape pool, a protected beach, a picnic area, and a casual restaurant. There's also a reasonably priced shuttle to grocery stores and shopping areas. **Pros:** Beachfront location, good children's program, wide array of water sports. **Cons:** Need car to get around, lacks pizzazz. ⊠ *Rte. 82, Green Cay* ✉ *Box 24600, Christiansted* ☎ *340/773–2918 or 800/548–4457* ⊕ *www.chenaybay.com* ⇨ *50 rooms* ♿ *In-room: kitchen, Wi-Fi. In-hotel: restaurant, bar, tennis courts, pool, beachfront, water sports, no elevator, children's programs (ages 4–12), public Wi-Fi* ▭ *AE, D, MC, V* ⎮⊙⎮ *EP.*

$$–$$$ 🏨**Divi Carina Bay Resort.** An oceanfront location puts most rooms at the Divi Carina Bay Resort close to the beach, but the villas are across the road, behind the main building. Because it has the island's only casino and regular evening entertainment, this resort is your best choice if you enjoy nonstop nightlife. The rooms have rattan and wicker furniture, white-tile floors, and sapphire and teal colors. Although its location on the island's East End puts you a long way from anywhere, the hotel provides a fair amount of activities to keep you busy. **Pros:** Spacious beach, good restaurant, on-site casino. **Cons:** Need car to get around, many stairs to climb, staff seems disinterested. ⊠ *25 Rte. 60, Estate Turner Hole* ☎ *340/773–9700 or 877/773–9700* ⊕ *www.divicarina. com* ⇨ *146 rooms, 2 suites, 20 villas* ♿ *In-room: safe, refrigerator, dial-up, Wi-Fi (some). In-hotel: 2 restaurants, bars, tennis courts, pool, gym, beachfront, water sports, public Internet, public Wi-Fi* ▭ *AE, D, MC, V* ⎮⊙⎮ *EP.*

FREDERIKSTED   🏨**Sandcastle on the Beach.** Right on a gorgeous stretch of white beach,
$$–$$$ this hotel caters primarily to gay men and lesbians, but everyone is welcome. The hotel has a tropical charm that harkens back to a simpler time in the Caribbean; proximity to Frederiksted's interesting dining scene is also a plus. Rooms, which have contemporary decor, tile floors, and bright fabrics, come in several sizes and locations. All have kitchens or kitchenettes, and most have sea views. Packages that include a car and bar privileges are a good value. Although some people bring their kids, the hotel caters more to singles and couples, especially dur-

26

ing the winter season. **Pros:** Lovely beach, close to restaurants, gay-friendly vibe. **Cons:** Neighborhood sketchy at night, need car to get around, no children's activities. ⊠ *127 Smithfield, Rte. 71, Frederiksted* ☎ *340/772–1205 or 800/524–2018* ⊕ *www.sandcastleonthebeach. com* ➷ *8 rooms, 8 suites, 6 villas* ⓬ *In-room: no phone, safe, kitchen (some), VCRs (some). In-hotel: restaurant, pools, gym, beachfront, water sports, no elevator, laundry facilities, public Internet, public Wi-Fi* ⊟ *AE, D, MC, V* ⓄⒾ *CP.*

NORTH SHORE
$$$$
Fodor's Choice
★

▦ **Villa Greenleaf.** This spacious B&B is all about the details—four-poster beds with elegant duvets, towels folded just so, hand-stenciled trim on the walls, and gardens tastefully planted. Staying here is like visiting a well-heeled relative who happens to have home in the Caribbean. The house was built in the 1950s but was totally renovated in 2004. You'll want to spend your days gazing at the lovely view of St. Croix's north shore or relaxing beside the sparkling pool. A car is included in the rates for trips around the island. **Pros:** Tasteful decor, convivial atmosphere, car included in rate. **Cons:** No beach, no restaurants nearby, need car to get around. ⊠ *Island Center Rd., Montpelier* ⓓ *Box 675, Christiansted* ☎ *340/719–1958 or 888/282–1001* ⊕ *www. villagreenleaf.com* ➷ *5 rooms* ⓬ *In-room: safe, refrigerator, Wi-Fi. In-hotel: pool, no elevator, public Wi-Fi* ⊟ *AE, D, MC, V* ⓄⒾ *BP.*

$$–$$$
▦ **Renaissance Carambola Beach Resort.** We like this resort's stellar beachfront setting and peaceful ambience. As of this writing the hotel was in the midst of a massive renovation. The refurbished rooms are lovely, with attractive palm-theme accessories that match the resort's atmosphere. All have terra-cotta floors, ceramic lamps, mahogany ceilings and furnishings, and rocking chairs. Each has a patio and a huge bathroom (shower only). Lushly planted walkways connect the rooms and the hotel's restaurants and pool. **Pros:** Lovely beach, relaxing atmosphere, close to golf. **Cons:** Some dated rooms, need car to get around. ⊠ *Rte. 80, Davis Bay* ⓓ *Box 3031, Kingshill* ☎ *340/778–3800 or 888/503–8760* ⊕ *www.carambolabeach.com* ➷ *151 rooms* ⓬ *In-room: safe, kitchen (some), dial-up. In-hotel: 3 restaurants, tennis courts, pool, gym, spa, beachfront, diving, water sports, no elevator, public Internet, public Wi-Fi* ⊟ *AE, D, DC, MC, V* ⓄⒾ *EP.*

$$
▦ **Cane Bay Reef Club.** These modestly sized lodgings sit seaside in the peaceful community of Cane Bay. They're perfect for folks who don't need every amenity but want to be right at the water's edge. All the rooms in the two-story buildings have no-frills kitchenettes, the usual rattan furniture with tropical accents, and balconies or porches that put you almost on the beach. You can rent dive gear nearby to explore St. Croix's famous Cane Bay Wall. **Pros:** Close to Cane Bay Beach, restaurants nearby, nice views. **Cons:** Need car to get around, decor dated, on busy road. ⊠ *Rte. 80, Cane Bay* ⓓ *Box 1407, Kingshill* ☎ *340/778–2966 or 800/253–8534* ⊕ *www.canebay.com* ➷ *9 units* ⓬ *In-room: kitchen. In-hotel: restaurant, pool, no elevator, public Internet, public Wi-Fi* ⊟ *AE, D, DC, MC, V* ⓄⒾ *EP.*

$$
▦ **Hibiscus Beach Hotel.** This hotel is on a lovely beach—the best reason to stay here. Rooms, each named for a tropical flower, show obvious wear and tear, but all have spacious balconies and are decorated with

brightly colored fabrics. Bathrooms are clean but nondescript—both the shower stalls and the vanity mirrors are on the small side. You'll need a car to get around, as the surrounding neighborhood isn't a great place for walking. **Pros:** Nice beach, good restaurant, close to Christiansted. **Cons:** Dated decor, sketchy neighborhood, need car to get around. ⊠*4131 Estate La Grande Princesse, off Rte. 752, La Grande Princesse* ☎*340/718–4042 or 800/442–0121* ⊕*www.hibiscus beachresort.com* ⇔*38 rooms* ⚭*In-room: safe, refrigerator, dial-up. In-hotel: restaurant, pool, beachfront, water sports, no elevator, public Internet, public Wi-Fi* ☰*AE, D, MC, V* ⑩*CP.*

$$ ⌂**Waves at Cane Bay.** St. Croix's famed Cane Bay Wall is just offshore from this resort, giving it an enviable location. It's a good bet for divers, as there's a dive shop just down the road. Although the hotel's stretch of beach is rocky, you can sunbathe at a small patch of sand beside the pool. Two blue-and-white buildings are where you can find large, balconied rooms decorated in soft pastels. **Pros:** Great diving, restaurants nearby, beaches nearby. **Cons:** Need car to get around, on main road, bland decor. ⊠*Rte. 80, Cane Bay* ⎙*Box 1749, Kingshill* ☎*340/778–1805 or 800/545–0603* ⊕*www.canebaystcroix.com* ⇔*12 rooms* ⚭*In-room: safe, kitchen, Wi-Fi. In-hotel: restaurant, bar, pool, water sports, no elevator* ☰*AE, MC, V* ⑩*EP.*

$-$$ ⌂**Villa Margarita.** This quiet retreat is along a tranquil north-shore beach, about 20 minutes from Christiansted's shops and restaurants. It provides a particularly good base if you want to admire the dramatic views of the windswept coast. Units vary in size, but all come with kitchenettes, tropical furnishings, private balconies, and those spectacular views. Swimming in front of the hotel is difficult because of the shallow water, but other sandy beaches are steps away. The snorkeling nearby is excellent. **Pros:** Friendly host, great views, snorkeling nearby. **Cons:** Isolated location, need car to get around, limited amenities. ⊠*Off Rte. 80, Salt River* ⎙*9024 Salt River, Christiansted* ☎*340/713–1930 or 866/274–8811* ⎙*340/719–3389* ⊕*www.villamargarita.com* ⇔*3 units* ⚭*In-room: no phone, kitchen, refrigerator. In-hotel: pool, no elevator, no kids under 18* ☰*AE, D, MC, V* ⑩*EP.*

CONDOMINIUMS & VILLAS

St. Croix has villas scattered all over the island, but most are in the center or on the East End. Renting a villa gives you all the convenience of home as well as top-notch amenities. Many have pools, hot tubs, and deluxe furnishings. Most companies meet you at the airport, arrange for a rental car, and provide helpful information about the island.

If you want to be close to the island's restaurants and shopping, look for a condominium or villa in the hills above Christiansted or on either side of the town. An East End location gets you out of Christiansted's hustle and bustle, but you're still only 15 minutes from town. North Shore locations are lovely, with gorgeous sea views and lots of peace and quiet.

Island Villas (☎*340/772–0420 or 800/626–4512* ⊕*www.stcroixisland villas.com*) has a supply of villas across the island. **Teague Bay Properties** (☎*800/237–1959* ⊕*www.rentonstcroix.com*) specializes in villas and condominiums across the island, with many on the eastern end. **Vacation St. Croix** (☎*340/778–0361 or 877/788–0361* ⊕*www.vacationst-croix.com*) has villas all around the island.

$$$$ 🏠**Villa Madeleine.** If you like privacy, we think you'll like Villa Madeleine. The two-story villas flow downhill from this condominium resort's centerpiece, a West Indian plantation greathouse. Each villa has a full kitchen and its own pool. The decor evokes the property's natural surroundings: rattan furniture with plush cushions, rocking chairs, and, in some, bamboo four-poster beds. Special touches include pink-marble showers and hand-painted floral wall borders. You definitely need a car for sightseeing. **Pros:** Pleasant decor, full kitchens, private pools. **Cons:** Lower units sometimes lack views, need car to get around. ✉*Off Rte. 82, Teague Bay* 🕎*5014 Villa Madeleine, Christiansted* ☎*340/713–0923 or 800/237–1959* ⊕*www.rentonstcroix.com* 📟*43 villas* △*In-room: kitchen. In-hotel: tennis court, pools, no elevator, public Wi-Fi* ⊟*AE, MC, V* ⦿*EP.*

$$–$$$ 🏠**Club St. Croix.** Sitting beachfront just outside Christiansted, this modern condominium complex faces a lovely sandy beach. You have easy access to shopping and restaurants in nearby Christiansted, but you need a car to get there. Breezes restaurant provides full meal service if you tire of cooking in your fully equipped kitchen. Spacious condos come in different sizes: studios, one-, and two-bedrooms; all have balconies or patios. Rooms have rattan furniture and bright accents. The location near public housing doesn't encourage strolls through the neighborhood. **Pros:** Beachfront location, good restaurant, full kitchens. **Cons:** Need car to get around, sketchy neighborhood. ✉*Rte. 752, Estate Golden Rock* ☎*340/718–9150 or 800/524–2025* ⊕*www.antilles resorts.com* 📟*53 apartments* △*In-room: kitchen, Wi-Fi. In-hotel: restaurant, tennis courts, pool, beachfront, no elevator, public Internet, public Wi-Fi* ⊟*AE, D, MC, V* ⦿*EP.*

$$ 🏠**Colony Cove.** In a string of condominium complexes, Colony Cove lets you experience comfortable beachfront living. Units all have two bedrooms, two bathrooms, and washer–dryer combos, making it a good choice for families. They have typical tropical furnishings with most furniture made of rattan and wicker. Floors are tile. The neighborhood isn't the best, so don't plan on strolling too far at night. **Pros:** Beachfront location, comfortable units, good views. **Cons:** Sketchy neighborhood, need car to get around. ✉*Rte. 752, Estate Golden Rock* ☎*340/718–1965 or 800/524–2025* ⊕*www.antillesresorts.com* 📟*62 apartments* △*In-room: kitchen, dial-up, Wi-Fi. In-hotel: pool, beachfront, no elevator, public Wi-Fi* ⊟*AE, D, MC, V* ⦿*EP.*

$$ 🏠**Sugar Beach.** With all the conveniences of home, Sugar Beach has apartments that are immaculate and breezy. Each unit has a full kitchen and a large patio or balcony with an ocean view; larger ones also have washers and dryers. Although the exteriors are drab stucco, the interiors are enlivened by tropical furnishings. The pool occupies the ruins of a 250-year-old sugar mill. A lovely beach is just steps away, and Christiansted's conveniences are an easy 10-minute drive. It's one of a string of condominium complexes near a public-housing project, so don't walk in the neighborhood at night. **Pros:** Pleasant beach, full kitchens, space to spread out. **Cons:** Sketchy neighborhood, need car to get around. ⊠*Rte. 752, Estate Golden Rock* ☏*340/718–5345 or 800/524–2049* ⊕*www.sugarbeachstcroix.com* ⌑*46 apartments* ♿*In-room: kitchen, Wi-Fi (some). In-hotel: tennis courts, pool, beachfront, no elevator, public Internet, public Wi-Fi* ⊟*AE, D, MC, V* ⍾*EP.*

CAMPGROUNDS

☾ ⚠**Mount Victory Camp.** A remarkable quietude distinguishes this out-of-the-way spread on 8 acres in the island's rain forest. If you really want to commune with nature, you'll be hard-pressed to find a better way to do it on St. Croix. Hosts Bruce and Mathilde Wilson are on hand to explain the environment. You sleep in screened-in tent-cottages perched on a raised platform and covered by a roof. Each has electricity and a rudimentary outdoor kitchen. The shared, spotlessly clean bathhouse is an easy stroll away. The location feels remote, but a lovely sand beach and the Sunset Grill restaurant are a 2-mi (3-km) drive down the hill. In another 10 minutes you're in Frederiksted. **Pros:** Quiet location, friendly hosts, clean bathrooms. **Cons:** Need car to get around, basic facilities. ♿*Flush toilets, drinking water, showers, picnic tables, public Wi-Fi* ⌑*5 tents* ⊠*Creque Dam Rd., Frederiksted* ☏*340/772–1651 or 866/772–1651* ⊕*www.mtvictorycamp.com* ⌑*Reservations essential* ⊟*No credit cards.*

26

WHERE TO EAT

Seven flags have flown over St. Croix, and each has left its legacy in the island's cuisine. You can feast on Italian, French, and American dishes; there are even Chinese and Mexican restaurants in Christiansted. Fresh local seafood is plentiful and always good; wahoo, mahimahi, and conch are most popular. Island chefs often add Caribbean twists to familiar dishes. For a true island experience, stop at a local restaurant for goat stew, curried chicken, or fried pork chops. Regardless of where you eat, your meal will be an informal affair. As is the case everywhere in the Caribbean, prices are higher than you'd pay on the mainland. Some restaurants may close for a week or two in September or October, so if you're traveling during these months it's best to call ahead.

CHRISTIANSTED

CARIBBEAN ✕**Harvey's.** The dining room is plain, even dowdy, and plastic lace
$–$$$ tablecloths constitute the sole attempt at decor—but who cares? The food is delicious. Daily specials, such as mouthwatering goat stew and tender whelks in butter, served with big helpings of rice and vegetables, are listed on the blackboard. Genial owner Sarah Harvey takes great pride in her kitchen, bustling out from behind the stove to chat and urge you to eat up. ⊠*11B Company St.* ☏*340/773–3433* ⊟*No credit cards* ⊘*Closed Sun. No dinner.*

CONTINENTAL ✕**Kendricks.** The chef at this open-air restaurant—a longtime favorite
$$$–$$$$ among locals—conjures up creative contemporary cuisine. To start,
★ try the Alaskan king crab cakes with lemon–black pepper aioli or the warm chipotle pepper with garlic and onion soup. Move on to the house specialty: pecan-crusted roast pork loin with ginger mayon-

naise. ⊠*Company St. and King Cross St.* ☎*340/773–9199* ⊟*MC, V* ⊙*Closed Sun. No lunch.*

$$$–$$$$ ✕**Restaurant Bacchus.** On the chic side, this restaurant is as notable for
★ its extensive wine list as it is for its food. The menu changes regularly but often includes favorites like chopped tuna in a soy-sesame dressing served over crispy wontons. Such entrées as local lobster and fresh fish, steak swimming in mushroom sauce, and baked linguine with shrimp are always popular. For dessert, try the rum-drenched sourdough-bread pudding. ⊠*Queen Cross St., off King St.* ☎*340/692–9922* ⊟*AE, D, MC, V* ⊙*Closed Mon. No lunch.*

$$–$$$$ ✕**Savant.** Savant is one of those small but special spots that locals love.
★ The cuisine is a fusion of Mexican, Thai, and Caribbean—an unusual combination that works surprisingly well. You can find anything from fresh fish to Thai curry with chicken to maple-teriyaki pork tenderloin coming out of the kitchen. With 20 tables crammed into the indoor dining room and small courtyard, this little place can get crowded. Call early for reservations. ⊠*4C Hospital St.* ☎*340/713–8666* ⊟*AE, MC, V* ⊙*Closed Sun. No lunch.*

$$–$$$ ✕**Rum Runners.** The view is as stellar as the food at this highly popular
☾ local standby. Sitting right on Christiansted Boardwalk, Rum Runners
★ serves everything, including a to-die-for salad of crispy romaine lettuce and tender grilled lobster drizzled with lemongrass vinaigrette. More hearty fare includes baby back ribs cooked with the restaurant's special spice blend and Guinness stout. ⊠*Hotel Caravelle, 44A Queen Cross St.* ☎*340/773–6585* ⊟*AE, MC, V.*

ECLECTIC ✕**Avocado Pitt.** Locals gather at this Christiansted waterfront spot for
$ the breakfast and lunch specials as well as for a bit of gossip. Breakfast runs to stick-to-the-ribs dishes like oatmeal and pancakes. Lunches include such dressed-up basics as the Yard Bird on a Bun, a chicken breast sandwich tarted up with a liberal dose of hot sauce. The yellow-fin tuna sandwich is made from fresh fish and gives a new taste to a standard lunchtime favorite. ⊠*King Christian Hotel, 59 Kings Wharf* ☎*340/773–9843* ⊟*AE, MC, V* ⊙*No dinner.*

FRENCH ✕**Café Christine.** A favorite with the professionals who work in down-
$–$$ town Christiansted, Café Christine's presentation is as dazzling as the
★ food. The small menu changes daily, but look for dishes like shrimp salad drizzled with a lovely vinaigrette or a vegetarian plate with quiche, salad, and lentils. Desserts are perfection. If the pear pie topped with chocolate is on the menu, don't hesitate. This tiny restaurant has tables in both the air-conditioned dining room and the outside porch that overlooks historic buildings. ⊠*Apothecary Hall Courtyard, 4 Company St.* ☎*340/713–1500* ⊟*No credit cards* ⊙*Closed weekends and July–mid Nov. No dinner.*

MEDITERRANEAN ✕**Salud Bistro.** This eatery's imaginative menu takes its cue from the
$$–$$$ fresh flavors of the Mediterranean. Start with the savory cheese plate served with homemade bread and crostini before moving on to roasted pumpkin and portobello mushroom pasta tossed with browned butter, sage, toasted pinenuts, and a sprinkle of shaved parmesan. ⊠*Prin-*

cess Shopping Center, Rte. 75, La Grande Princess ☎*340/718–7900* ☐*AE, MC, V* ⊗*Closed Sun.*

OUTSIDE CHRISTIANSTED

ECLECTIC
$$–$$$
☺

✕**Breezez.** This aptly named restaurant is poolside at Club St. Croix condominiums. Visitors and locals are drawn by its reasonable prices and good food. This is *the* place on the island to be for Sunday brunch. Locals gather for lunch, when the menu includes everything from burgers to blackened prime rib with a horseradish sauce. For dessert, try the flourless chocolate torte—a wedge of rich chocolate served with a river of chocolate sauce. ⊠*Club St. Croix, 3220 Golden Rock, off Rte. 752, Golden Rock* ☎*340/718–7077* ☐*AE, D, MC, V.*

$$–$$$
Fodor's Choice
★

✕**Elizabeth's at H2O.** With a lovely beachfront location and stellar food, this restaurant has developed quite a following. Lunch brings out lots of locals for the generous helping of curried chicken salad and a crab cake wrapped in a flavorful tortilla. The piquant horseradish sauce adds a tasty touch. Dinner entrées include a tasty rack of lamb with rosemary demi-glace and roasted red potatoes. ⊠*Hibiscus Beach Resort, off Rte. 752, Estate Princess* ✆*4131 La Grand Princess, Christiansted* ☎*340/718–0735* ☐*AE, D, MC, V.*

ITALIAN
$$$–$$$$

✕**Tutto Bene.** Its muraled walls, brightly striped cushions, and painted trompe-l'oeil tables make Tutto Bene look more like a sophisticated Mexican cantina than an Italian cucina. One bite of the food, however, will clear up any confusion. Written on hanging mirrors is the daily menu, which includes such specialties as veal saltimbocca and scallopine of veal with prosciutto and sage. Desserts, including a decadent tiramisu, are on the menu as well. ⊠*Hospital St., in Boardwalk shopping center* ☎*340/773–5229* ☐*AE, MC, V* ⊗*No lunch.*

EAST END

ECLECTIC
$$$–$$$$

✕**The Galleon.** This popular dockside restaurant is always busy. Start with the Caesar salad or perhaps a flaky layered duck napoleon. The chef's signature dish is a tender filet mignon topped with fresh local lobster. Pasta lovers should sample the linguine with shrimp, mussels, and fish tossed with fresh tomatoes, spinach, and olive oil. Take Route 82 out of Christiansted; then turn left at the sign for Green Cay Marina. ⊠*Annas Hope* ☎*340/773–9949* ☐*MC, V* ⊗*No lunch.*

$$–$$$

✕**The Deep End.** A favorite with locals and vacationers, this poolside restaurant serves up terrific crab-cake sandwiches, London broil with onions and mushrooms, and delicious pasta in various styles. To get here from Christiansted, take Route 82 and turn left at the sign for Green Cay Marina. ⊠*Tamarind Reef Hotel, Annas Hope* ☎*340/713–7071* ☐*MC, V.*

FREDERIKSTED

ECLECTIC
$$$–$$$$
Fodor's Choice
★

✕**Blue Moon.** This terrific little bistro, which has a loyal local following, offers a changing menu that draws on Cajun and Caribbean flavors. Try the spicy gumbo with andouille sausage or crab cakes with a spicy aioli for your appetizer. Chicken, shrimp, sausage, and peppers served over pasta makes a good entrée. The Almond Joy sundae should be

26

your choice for dessert. There's live jazz on Wednesday and Friday. ⊠7 *Strand St.* ☏*340/772–2222* ⊟*AE, MC, V* ☉*Closed Mon.*

$ ✕**Turtles Deli.** Eat outside at this tiny spot just as you enter downtown
☾ Frederiksted. Lunches are as basic as a corned beef on rye or as imaginative as "The Raven" (turkey breast with bacon, tomato, and melted cheddar cheese on French bread). Also good is "The Beast," named after the grueling hill that challenges bikers in the annual triathlon. It's piled high with hot roast beef, raw onion, and melted Swiss cheese with horseradish and mayonnaise. Early risers stop by for cinnamon buns and espresso. ⊠*625 Strand St., at Prince Passage* ☏*340/772–3676* ⊟*No credit cards* ☉*Closed Sun. No dinner.*

FRENCH ✕**Le St. Tropez.** A ceramic-tile bar and soft lighting set the mood at this
$$$–$$$$ Mediterranean-style bistro tucked into a courtyard one block from the waterfront. Seated either inside or on the adjoining patio, you can enjoy grilled meats in delicate sauces. The menu changes daily, often taking advantage of local seafood. The fresh basil, tomato, and mozzarella salad is heavenly. ⊠*227 King St.* ☏*340/772–3000* ⊟*AE, MC, V* ☉*Closed Sun. No lunch Sat.*

OUTSIDE FREDERIKSTED

$$$–$$$$ ✕**Sunset Grill.** As you would expect, this alfresco restaurant is a hot spot
☾ for sunset watchers, as well as a social hub for locals. The ever-changing menu features fish, fish, and more fish. Try the almond-crusted grouper in a soy-butter sauce or whatever else the chef whipped up that day. Those who aren't fond of seafood can pick from dishes like a rib-eye steak for dinner. Desserts might include fresh blueberries and strawberries in a rum sauce. It's about 2 km (1 mi) north of Frederiksted. ⊠*Rte. 63* ☏*340/772–5855* ⊟*MC, V* ☉*Closed Mon.*

NORTH SHORE

ECLECTIC ✕**Off the Wall.** Divers fresh from a plunge at the north shore's popular
$ Cane Bay Wall gather at this breezy spot on the beach. If you want to sit a spell before you order, a hammock beckons. Deli sandwiches, served with delicious chips, make up most of the menu. Pizza and salads are also available. ⊠*Rte. 80, Cane Bay* ☏*340/778–4771* ⊟*AE, MC, V.*

BEACHES

★ **Buck Island.** A visit to this island beach, part of Buck Island Reef National Monument, is a must. The beach is beautiful, but its finest treasures are those you can see when you plop off the boat and adjust your mask, snorkel, and fins to swim over colorful coral and darting fish. Don't know how to snorkel? No problem—the boat crew will have you outfitted and in the water in no time. Take care not to step on those black-pointed spiny sea urchins or touch the mustard-color fire coral, which can cause a nasty burn. Most charter boat trips start with a snorkel over the lovely reef before a stop at the island's beach. An easy 20-minute hike leads uphill to an overlook for a bird's-eye view of the reef below. Find restrooms at the beach. Buck Island is 5 mi (8 km) north of St. Croix.

Cane Bay. The waters aren't always gentle at this breezy north-shore beach, but there are seldom many people around, and the scuba diving and snorkeling are wondrous. You can see elkhorn and brain corals, and less than 200 yards out is the drop-off called Cane Bay Wall. Cane Bay can be an all-day destination. You can rent kayaks and snorkeling and scuba gear at water-sports shops across the road, and a couple of casual restaurants beckon when the sun gets too hot. The beach has no public restrooms. ⊠*Rte. 80, about 4 mi (6 km) west of Salt River.*

West End Beaches. There are several unnamed beaches along the coast road north of Frederiksted, but it's best if you don't stray too far from civilization. For safety's sake, most vacationers plop down their towel near one of the casual restaurants spread out along Route 63. The beachfront Sunset Grill makes a nice spot for lunch. The beach at the Rainbow Beach Club, a five-minute drive outside Frederiksted, has a bar, a casual restaurant, water sports, and volleyball. If you want to be close to the cruise-ship pier, just stroll on over to the adjacent sandy beach in front of Fort Frederik. On the way south out of Frederiksted, the stretch near Sandcastle on the Beach hotel is also lovely. ⊠*Rte. 63, north and south of Frederiksted.*

26

SPORTS & THE OUTDOORS

BOAT TOURS

Almost everyone takes a day trip to Buck Island aboard a charter boat. Most leave from the Christiansted waterfront or from Green Cay Marina and stop for a snorkel at the island's eastern end before dropping anchor off a gorgeous sandy beach for a swim, a hike, and lunch. Sailboats can often stop right at the beach; a larger boat might have to anchor a bit farther offshore. A full-day sail runs about $90, with lunch included on most trips. A half-day sail costs about $60. **Big Beard's Adventure Tours** (☎340/773–4482 ⊕*www.bigbeards.com*) takes you on catamarans, either the *Renegade* or the *Flyer,* from the Christiansted waterfront to Buck Island for snorkeling before dropping anchor at a private beach for a barbecue lunch. **Caribbean Sea Adventures** (☎340/773–2628 ⊕*www.caribbeanseaadventures.com*) departs from the Christiansted waterfront for half- and full-day trips. The **Teroro Charters** (☎340/773–3161 ⊕*www.visitstcroix.com/captainheinz. html*) trimaran *Teroro II* leaves Green Cay Marina for full- or half-day sails. Bring your own lunch.

DIVING & SNORKELING

At **Buck Island,** a short boat ride from Christiansted or Green Cay Marina, the reef is so nice that it's been named a national monument. You can dive right off the beach at **Cane Bay,** which has a spectacular drop-off called the Cane Bay Wall. Dive operators also do boat trips along the Wall, usually leaving from Salt River or Christiansted. **Frederiksted Pier** is home to a colony of sea horses, creatures seldom seen in the waters of the Virgin Islands. At **Green Cay,** just outside Green Cay Marina in the east end, you can see colorful fish swimming around the reefs and rocks. Two exceptional north-shore sites are **North Star** and

Salt River, which you can reach only by boat. At Salt River you can float downward through a canyon filled with colorful fish and coral.

The island's dive shops take you out for one- or two-tank dives. Plan to pay about $65 for a one-tank dive and $90 for a two-tank dive, including equipment and an underwater tour. All companies offer certification and introductory courses called resort dives for novices.

Which dive outfit you pick usually depends on where you're staying. Your hotel may have one on-site. If so, you're just a short stroll away from the dock. If not, other companies are close by. Where the dive boat goes on a particular day depends on the weather, but in any case, all St. Croix's dive sites are special. All shops are affiliated with PADI, the Professional Association of Diving Instructors.

If you're staying in Christiansted, **Dive Experience** (⊠ *1111 Strand St., Christiansted* ☎ *340/773–3307 or 800/235–9047* ⊕ *www.divexp.com*) has PADI five-star status and runs trips to the north-shore walls and reefs in addition to offering the usual certification and introductory classes. **St. Croix Ultimate Bluewater Adventures** (⊠ *Queen Cross St., Christiansted* ☎ *340/773–5994 or 877/567–1367* ⊕ *www.stcroixscuba. com*) can take you to your choice of more than 75 sites; it also offers a variety of packages that include hotel stays.Folks staying in the Judith's Fancy area are closest to **Anchor Dive Center** (⊠ *Salt River Marina, Rte. 801, Salt River* ☎ *340/778–1522 or 800/532–3483* ⊕ *www.anchordivestcroix.com*). The company also has facilities at the Buccaneer hotel. Anchor takes divers to more than 35 sites, including the wall at Salt River Canyon.

Cane Bay Dive Shop (⊠ *Rte. 80, Cane Bay* ☎ *340/773–9913 or 800/338–3843* ⊕ *www.canebayscuba.com*) is the place to go if you want to do a beach dive or boat dive along the north shore. The famed Cane Bay Wall is 150 yards from the five-star PADI facility. This company also has shops at Pan Am Pavilion in Christiansted, on Strand Street in Frederiksted, at the Carambola Beach Resort, and at the Divi Carina Bay hotel.

In Frederiksted, **N2 the Blue** (⊠ *Frederiksted Beach, Rte. 631, Frederiksted* ☎ *340/772–3483 or 888/789–3483* ⊕ *www.n2blue.com*) takes divers right off the beach near Coconuts restaurant, on night dives off the Frederiksted Pier, or on boat trips to wrecks and reefs. **Scuba West** (⊠ *330 Strand St., Frederiksted* ☎ *340/772–3701 or 800/352–0107* ⊕ *www.divescubawest.com*) runs trips to reefs and wrecks from its base in Frederiksted but specializes in showing divers the sea horses that live around the Frederiksted Pier.

FISHING

Since the early 1980s, some 20 world records—many for blue marlin—have been set in these waters. Sailfish, skipjack, bonito, tuna (allison, blackfin, and yellowfin), and wahoo are abundant. A charter runs about $100 an hour per person, with most boats going out for four-, six- or eight-hour trips. **Caribbean Sea Adventures** (⊠ *59 Kings Wharf,*

Christiansted ☎*340/773–2628* ⊕*www.caribbeanseaadventures.com*) will take you out on a 38-foot powerboat called the *Fantasy*.

GOLF

St. Croix's courses welcome you with spectacular vistas and well-kept greens. Check with your hotel or the tourist board to determine when major celebrity tournaments will be held. There's often an opportunity to play with the pros. The **Buccaneer** (⊠*Rte. 82, Shoys* ☎*340/712–2144* ⊕*www.thebuccaneer.com*) has an 18-hole course. It's close to Christiansted, so it's convenient for those staying in or near town. Greens fees are $85 with an additional $20 for cart rental.

★ The spectacular 18-hole course at **Carambola Golf Club** (⊠*Rte. 80, Davis Bay* ☎*340/778–5638* ⊕*www.golfcarambola.com*), in the northwest valley, was designed by Robert Trent Jones Sr. It sits near Carambola Beach Resort. Greens fees are $120 for 18 holes, which includes the use of a golf cart.

The **Reef Golf Course** (⊠*Teague Bay* ☎*340/773–8844*), a public course on the island's east end, has 9 holes. Greens fees are $20, and cart rental is $14.

26

HIKING

Although you can set off by yourself on a hike through a rain forest or along a shore, a guide will point out what's important and tell you why. **Ay-Ay Eco Hike & Tours Association** (⌂*Box 2435, Kingshill 00851* ☎*340/772–4079*), run by Ras Lumumba Corriette, takes hikers up hill and down dale in some of St. Croix's most remote places, including the rain forest and Mount Victory. Some hikes include stops at places like the Carl and Marie Lawaetz Museum and old ruins. The cost is $50 per person for a three- or four-hour hike. There's a three-person minimum. A full-day jeep tour through the rain forest runs $120 per person.

HORSEBACK RIDING

Well-kept roads and expert guides make horseback riding on St. Croix pleasurable. At Sprat Hall, just north of Frederiksted, Jill Hurd runs **Paul & Jill's Equestrian Stables** (⊠*Rte. 58, Frederiksted* ☎*340/772–2880 or 340/772–2627* ⊕*www.paulandjills.com*). She will take you clip-clopping through the rain forest, across the pastures, along the beaches, and over the hilltops—explaining the flora, fauna, and ruins on the way. A 1½-hour ride costs $75.

KAYAKING

Caribbean Adventure Tours (⊠*Salt River Marina, Rte. 80, Salt River* ☎*340/778–1522* ⊕*www.stcroixkayak.com*) takes you on trips through Salt River Bay National Historical Park and Ecological Preserve, one of the island's most pristine areas. All tours run $45. **Virgin Kayak Tours** (⊠*Rte. 80, Cane Bay* ☎*340/778–0071* ⊕*www.virgin kayakco.com*) runs guided kayak trips through the Salt River and rents kayaks so you can tour around the Cane Bay area by yourself. All tours run $45. Kayak rentals are $30 for the entire day.

SHOPPING

AREAS & MALLS

Although the shopping on St. Croix isn't as varied or extensive as that on St. Thomas, the island does have several small stores with unusual merchandise. In Christiansted the best shopping areas are the **Pan Am Pavilion** and **Caravelle Arcade,** off Strand Street, and along **King** and **Company streets.** These streets give way to arcades filled with boutiques. **Gallows Bay** has a blossoming shopping area in a quiet neighborhood. St. Croix shop hours are usually Monday through Saturday 9 to 5, but there are some shops in Christiansted open in the evening. Stores are often closed on Sunday.

The best shopping in Frederiksted is along **Strand Street** and in the side streets and alleyways that connect it with **King Street.** Most stores close Sunday except when a cruise ship is in port. One caveat: Frederiksted has a reputation for muggings, so for safety's sake stick to populated areas of Strand and King streets, where there are few—if any—problems.

SPECIALTY ITEMS

ART **Danica Art Gallery.** Modern paintings by owner Danica David, as well as jewelry, pottery, and other works by various artists, fill this gallery. ⊠ *54 Kings St., Christiansted* ☎ *340/719–6000.*

BOOKS **Undercover Books.** For Caribbean books or the latest good read, try this bookstore across from the post office in the Gallows Bay shopping area. ⊠ *5030 Anchor Way, Gallows Bay* ☎ *340/719–1567.*

CLOTHING **Coconut Vine.** Pop into this store at the start of your vacation, and you'll
Fodor'sChoice leave with enough comfy cotton or rayon batik men's and women's
★ clothes to make you look like a local. Although the tropical designs and colors originated in Indonesia, they're perfect for the Caribbean. ⊠ *1111 Strand St., Christiansted* ☎ *340/773–1991.*

From the Gecko. Come here for the hippest clothes on St. Croix, including superb hand-painted sarongs and other items. ⊠ *1233 Queen Cross St., Christiansted* ☎ *340/778–9433.*

Hot Heads. Hats, hats, and more hats perch on top of cotton shifts, comfortable shirts, and other tropical wear at this small store. If you forgot your bathing suit, this store has a good selection. ⊠ *Kings Alley Walk, Christiansted* ☎ *340/773–7888.*

Pacificotton. Round out your tropical wardrobe with something from this store. Shifts, tops, and pants in Caribbean colors as well as bags and hats fill the racks. ⊠ *1110 Strand St., Christiansted* ☎ *340/773–2125.*

Quiet Storm. With brands that include Fresh Produce, Tommy Bahama, Tori Richard, Roxy, and Quick Silver, shop here for upmarket resort wear and beach accessories. ⊠ *1108 King St., Christiansted* ☎ *340/773–7703.*

FOOD If you've rented a condominium or a villa, you'll appreciate St. Croix's excellent stateside-style supermarkets. Fresh vegetables, fruits, and meats arrive frequently. Try the open-air stands strung out along Route 70 for island produce.

Cost-U-Less. This warehouse-type store is great for visitors because it doesn't charge a membership fee. It's east of Sunny Isle Shopping Center. ⊠*Rte. 70, Sunny Isle* ☎*340/719–4442.*

Plaza Extra. Shop here for Middle Eastern foods in addition to the usual grocery-store items. ⊠*United Shopping Plaza, Rte. 70, Sion Farm* ☎*340/778–6240* ⊠*Rte. 70, Mount Pleasant* ☎*340/719–1870.*

Pueblo. This stateside-style market has two branches. ⊠*Orange Grove Shopping Center, Rte. 75, Christiansted* ☎*340/773–0118* ⊠*Villa La Reine Shopping Center, Rte. 75, La Reine* ☎*340/778–1272.*

Schooner Bay Market. Although it's on the smallish side, Schooner Bay has good-quality deli items. ⊠*Rte. 82, Mount Welcome* ☎*340/773–3232.*

GIFTS **Gone Tropical.** Whether you're looking for inexpensive souvenirs or a special gift, you can probably find it here. On her travels about the world, Margo Meacham keeps her eye out for special delights for her shop—from tablecloths and napkins in bright Caribbean colors to carefully crafted wooden birds. ⊠*5 Company St., Christiansted* ☎*340/773–4696.*

Many Hands. Pottery in bright colors, paintings of St. Croix and the Caribbean, prints, and maps—all made by local artists—make perfect take-home gifts. If your purchase is too cumbersome to carry, the owners ship all over the world. ⊠*21 Pan Am Pavilion, Strand St., Christiansted* ☎*340/773–1990.*

Mitchell-Larsen Studio. Carefully crafted glass plates, sun-catchers, and more grace the shelves of this interesting store. All made on-site by a St. Croix glassmaker, the pieces are often whimsically adorned with tropical fish, flora, and fauna. ⊠*58 Company St., Christiansted* ☎*340/719–1000.*

Fodor'sChoice **Royal Poinciana.** This attractive shop is filled with island seasonings and ★ hot sauces, West Indian crafts, bath gels, and herbal teas. Shop here for tablecloths and paper goods in tropical brights. ⊠*1111 Strand St., Christiansted* ☎*340/773–9892.*

Tesoro. The colors are bold and the merchandise eclectic at this crowded store. Shop for metal sculptures made from retired steel pans, mahogany bowls, and hand-painted place mats in bright tropical colors. ⊠*36C Strand St., Christiansted* ☎*340/773–1212.*

Tradewinds Shop. Whatever the wind blew in seems to land here. Glass sailboats glide across the shelves while metal fish sculptures swim nearby. Candles with tropical motifs, note cards, and costume jewelry jostle for space with Naot sandals. ⊠*53 King St., Christiansted* ☎*340/719–3918.*

HOUSEWARES **Designworks.** If a mahogany armoire or cane-back rocker catches your fancy, the staff will arrange to have it shipped to your home at no charge from its mainland warehouse. Furniture aside, this store has one of the largest selections of local art, along with Caribbean-inspired bric-a-brac in all price ranges. ⊠*6 Company St., Christiansted* ☎*340/713–8102.*

JEWELRY **Crucian Gold.** This store carries the unique gold creations of St. Croix native Brian Bishop. His trademark piece is the Turk's Head ring (a knot of interwoven gold strands), but the chess sets with Caribbean motifs as the playing pieces are just lovely. ⊠*1112 Strand St., Christiansted* ☎*340/773–5241.*

Gold Worker. In silver and gold, the handcrafted jewelry at this tiny store will remind you of the Caribbean. Hummingbirds dangle from silver chains, and sand dollars adorn gold necklaces. The sugar mills in silver and gold speak of St. Croix's past. ⊠*3 Company St., Christiansted* ☎*340/773–5167.*

ib Designs. This small shop showcases the handcrafted jewelry of local craftsman Whealan Massicott. In silver and gold, the designs are simply elegant. ⊠*Company St. at Queen Cross St., Christiansted* ☎*340/773–4322.*

Nelthropp and Low. Specializing in gold jewelry, this store also carries diamonds, emeralds, rubies, and sapphires. Jewelers will create one-of-a-kind pieces to your design. ⊠*1102 Strand St., Christiansted* ☎*340/773–0365 or 800/416–9078.*

Sonya's. Sonya Hough invented the hook bracelet, popular among locals as well as visitors. With hurricanes hitting the island so frequently, she has added an interesting decoration to these bracelets: the swirling symbol used in weather forecasts to indicate these storms. ⊠*1 Company St., Christiansted* ☎*340/778–8605.*

LIQUOR & **Baci Duty Free Liquor and Tobacco.** A walk-in humidor with a good selection of Arturo Fuente, Partagas, and Macanudo cigars is the centerpiece
TOBACCO of this store, which also carries sleek Danish-made watches and Lladró figurines. ⊠*1235 Queen Cross St., Christiansted* ☎*340/773–5040.*

Kmart. The two branches of this discount department store—a large one in the Sunshine Mall and a smaller one mid-island at Sunny Isle Shopping Center—carry a huge line of discounted, duty-free liquor. ⊠*Sunshine Mall, Rte. 70, Frederiksted* ☎*340/692–5848* ⊠*Sunny Isle Shopping Center, Rte. 70, Sunny Isle* ☎*340/719–9190.*

PERFUMES **Violette Boutique.** Perfumes, cosmetics, and skin-care products are the draws here. ⊠*Caravelle Arcade, 38 Strand St., Christiansted* ☎*340/773–2148.*

NIGHTLIFE & THE ARTS

The island's nightlife is ever-changing, and its arts scene is eclectic—ranging from Christmastime performances of *The Nutcracker* to any locally organized shows. Folk-art traditions, such as quadrille dancers, are making a comeback. To find out what's happening, pick up the local newspapers—*V. I. Daily News* and *St. Croix Avis*—available at newsstands. Christiansted has a lively and eminently casual club scene near the waterfront. Frederiksted has a couple of restaurants and clubs offering weekend entertainment.

NIGHTLIFE

Blue Moon (⊠7 *Strand St., Frederiksted* ☎340/772–2222), a waterfront restaurant, is the place to be for live jazz on Wednesday and Friday.Although you can gamble at the island's only casino, it's the nightly music that draws big crowds to **Divi Carina Bay Casino** (⊠*Rte. 60, Estate Turner Hole* ☎340/773–9700). **Fort Christian Brew Pub** (⊠*Boardwalk at end of Kings Alley, Christiansted* ☎340/713–9820 ⊕*www.fortchristianbrewpub.com*) is where locals and visitors listen to live music Wednesday to Saturday. **Hotel on the Cay** (⊠*Protestant Cay, Christiansted* ☎340/773–2035) has a West Indian buffet on Tuesday nights in the winter season, when you can watch a broken-bottle dancer (a dancer who braves a carpet of shattered glass) and mocko jumbie characters.

THE ARTS

Sunset Jazz (⊠*Waterfront, Frederiksted* ☎340/277–0692), has become the hot event in Frederiksted, drawing crowds of both visitors and locals at 6 PM on the third Friday of every month to watch the sun go down and hear good music.

The **Whim Plantation Museum** (⊠*Rte. 70, Estate Whim* ☎340/772–0598), outside of Frederiksted, hosts classical music concerts in winter.

26

EXPLORING ST. CROIX

Although there are things to see and do in St. Croix's two towns, Christiansted and Frederiksted (both named after Danish kings), there are lots of interesting spots in between them and to the east of Christiansted. Just be sure you have a map in hand (pick one up at rental-car agencies, or stop by the tourist office for an excellent one that's free). Many secondary roads remain unmarked; if you get confused, ask for help. Locals are always ready to point you in the right direction.

Numbers in the margin correspond to points of interest on the St. Croix map.

CHRISTIANSTED

Christiansted is a historic Danish-style town that always served as St. Croix's commercial center. Your best bet is to see the historic sights in the morning, when it's still cool. Break for lunch at an open-air restaurant before spending as much time as you like shopping.

In the 1700s and 1800s Christiansted was a trading center for sugar, rum, and molasses. Today there are law offices, tourist shops, and restaurants, but many of the buildings, which start at the harbor and go up the gently sloped hillsides, still date from the 18th century. You can't get lost. All streets lead back downhill to the water.

If you want some friendly advice, stop by the **Visitor Center** (⊠ *Government House, King St.* ☎ *340/773–0495* ⊕ *www.usvitourism.vi*) weekdays between 8 and 5 for maps and brochures.

D. Hamilton Jackson Park. When you're tired of sightseeing, stop at this shady park on the street side of Fort Christiansvaern for a rest. It's named for a famed labor leader, judge, and journalist who started the first newspaper not under the thumb of the Danish crown (his birthday, November 1, is a territorial holiday celebrated with much fanfare in St. Croix). ⊠ *Between Fort Christiansvaern and Danish Customs House.*

Danish Customs House. Built in 1830 on foundations that date from a century earlier, the historic building, which is near Fort Christiansvaern, originally served as both a customs house and a post office. In 1926 it became the Christiansted Library, and it's been a national park facility since 1972. It's closed to the public, but the sweeping front steps make a nice place to take a break. ⊠ *King St.* ☎ *340/773–1460* ⊕ *www.nps.gov/chri.*

Fort Christiansvaern. The large, yellow fortress dominates the waterfront. Because it's so easy to spot, it makes a good place to begin a walking tour. In 1749 the Danish built the fort to protect the harbor, but the structure was repeatedly damaged by hurricane-force winds and had to be partially rebuilt in 1771. It's now a national historic site, the best preserved of the few remaining Danish-built forts in the Virgin Islands. The park's visitor center is here. Rangers are on hand to answer questions. ⊠ *Hospital St.* ☎ *340/773–1460* ⊕ *www.nps.gov/chri* ☎ *$3, includes Steeple Building* ☉ *Weekdays 8–4:30, weekends 9–4:30.*

Government House. One of the town's most elegant structures was built as a home for a Danish merchant in 1747. Today it houses offices. If you're here weekdays from 8 to 4:30, slip into the peaceful inner courtyard to admire the still pools and gardens. A sweeping staircase leads you to a second-story ballroom, still used for official government functions. ⊠ *King St.* ☎ *340/773–1404*

Post Office Building. Built in 1749, Christiansted's former post office was once the Danish West India & Guinea Company warehouse. It now serves as the park's administrative building. ⊠ *Church St.*

Scale House. Constructed in 1856, this was once the spot where goods passing through the port were weighed and inspected. Park staffers now sell a good selection of books about St. Croix history and its flora and fauna. ⊠ *King St.* ☎ *340/773–1460* ⊕ *www.nps.gov/chri* ☉ *Weekdays 8–4:30, weekends 9–4:30.*

Steeple Building. Built by the Danes in 1753, the former church was the first Danish Lutheran church on St. Croix. It's now a museum containing exhibits on the island's Indian inhabitants. It's worth the short walk to see the building's collection of archaeological artifacts, displays on plantation life, and exhibits on the architectural development of Christiansted, the early history of the church, and Alexander Hamilton, the first secretary of the U.S. Treasury, who grew up in St. Croix. Hours are irregular, so ask at the visitor center. ⊠*Church St.* ☎*340/773–1460* ✆ *$3, includes Fort Christiansvaern.*

EAST END

An easy drive (roads are flat and well marked) to St. Croix's eastern end takes you through some choice real estate. Ruins of old sugar estates dot the landscape. You can make the entire loop on the road that circles the island in about an hour, a good way to end the day. If you want to spend a full day exploring, you can find some nice beaches and easy walks with places to stop for lunch.

Buck Island Reef National Monument. Buck Island has pristine beaches that are just right for sunbathing, but there's also some shade for those who don't want to fry. The snorkeling trail set in the reef allows close-up study of coral formations and tropical fish. Overly warm seawater temperatures have led to a condition called coral bleaching that has killed some of the coral. The reefs are starting to recover, but how long it will take is anyone's guess. There's an easy hiking trail to the island's highest point, where you can be rewarded for your efforts by spectacular views of St. John. Charter-boat trips leave daily from the Christiansted waterfront or from Green Cay Marina, about 2 mi (3 km) east of Christiansted. Check with your hotel for recommendations. ⊠*Off north shore of St. Croix* ☎*340/773–1460* ⊕*www.nps.gov/buis*

Point Udall. This rocky promontory, the easternmost point in the United States, is about a half-hour drive from Christiansted. A paved road takes you to an overlook with glorious views. More adventurous folks can hike down to the pristine beach below. On the way back, look for the castle, an enormous mansion that can only be described as a cross between a Moorish mosque and the Taj Mahal. It was built by an extravagant recluse known only as the Contessa. Point Udall is sometimes a popular spot for thieves. Residents advise taking your valuables with you and leaving your car unlocked so they won't break into your car to look inside. ⊠*Rte. 82, Et Stykkeland.*

BETWEEN CHRISTIANSTED & FREDERIKSTED

A drive through the countryside between these two towns will take you past ruins of old plantations, many bearing whimsical names (Morningstar, Solitude, Upper Love) bestowed by early owners. The traffic moves quickly—by island standards—on the main roads, but you can pause and poke around if you head down some side lanes. It's easy to find your way west, but driving from north to south requires good navigation. Don't leave your hotel without a map. Allow an entire day for this trip, so you'll have enough time for a swim at a north-shore beach. Although you can find lots of casual eateries on the main roads, pick up a picnic lunch if you plan to head off the beaten path.

Cruzan Rum Distillery. A tour of the company's factory, established in 1760, culminates in a tasting of its products, all sold here at bargain prices. It's worth a stop to look at the distillery's charming old buildings even if you're not a rum connoisseur. ⊠*West Airport Rd., Estate Diamond* ☎*340/692–2280* ⊕*www.cruzanrum.com* ✆*$4* ☉*Weekdays 9–11:30 and 1–4:15.*

26

CLOSE UP

Turtles on St. Croix

Like creatures from the earth's prehistoric past, green, leatherback, and hawksbill turtles crawl ashore during the annual April-to-November turtle nesting season to lay their eggs. They return from their life at sea every two to seven years to the beach where they were born. Since turtles can live for up to 100 years, they may return many times to nest in St. Croix.

The leatherbacks like Sandy Point National Wildlife Refuge and other spots on St. Croix's western end, but the hawksbills prefer Buck Island and the East End. Green turtles are also found primarily on the East End.

All are endangered species that face numerous natural and man-made predators. Particularly in the Frederiksted area, dogs and cats prey on the nests and eat the hatchlings.

Occasionally a dog will attack a turtle about to lay its eggs, and cats train their kittens to hunt at turtle nests, creating successive generations of turtle-egg hunters. In addition, turtles have often been hit by fast-moving boats that leave large slices in their shells if they don't kill them outright.

The leatherbacks are the subject of a project by the international group Earthwatch. Each summer teams arrive at Sandy Point National Wildlife Refuge to ensure that poachers, both natural and human, don't attack the turtles as they crawl up the beach. The teams also relocate nests that are laid in areas prone to erosion. When the eggs hatch, teams stand by to make sure the turtles make it safely to the sea, and scientists tag them so they can monitor their return to St. Croix.

Judith's Fancy. In this upscale neighborhood are the ruins of an old greathouse and tower of the same name, both remnants of a circa-1750 Danish sugar plantation. The "Judith" comes from the first name of a woman buried on the property. From the guardhouse at the neighborhood entrance, follow Hamilton Drive past some of St. Croix's loveliest homes. At the end of Hamilton Drive the road overlooks Salt River Bay, where Christopher Columbus anchored in 1493. On the way back, make a detour left off Hamilton Drive onto Caribe Road for a close look at the ruins. The million-dollar villas are something to behold, too. ⊠ *Turn north onto Rte. 751, off Rte. 75.*

Little Princess Estate. If the old plantation ruins scattered around St. Croix intrigue you, a visit to this Nature Conservancy project will give you even more of a glimpse into the past. The staff has carved walking paths out of the bush that surrounds what's left of a 19th-century plantation. It's easy to stroll among well-labeled fruit trees and see the ruins of the windmill, the sugar and rum factory, and the laborers' village. This is the perfect place to reflect on St. Croix's agrarian past fueled with labor from African slaves. ⊠ *Off Rte. 75; turn north at Five Corners traffic light* ☎ *340/718–5575* ☺ *Thurs. 3–5.*

Mt. Eagle. At 1,165 feet, this is St. Croix's highest peak. Leaving Cane Bay and passing North Star Beach, follow the coastal road that dips briefly into a forest; then turn left on Route 69. Just after you make the turn, the pavement is marked with the words THE BEAST and a set of giant paw prints. The hill you're about to climb is the famous Beast of the St. Croix Half Ironman Triathlon, an annual event during which participants must cycle up this intimidating slope. ⊠ *Rte. 69.*

Salt River Bay National Historical Park & Ecological Preserve. This joint national and local park commemorates the area where Christopher Columbus's men skirmished with the Carib Indians in 1493 on his second visit to the New World. The peninsula on the bay's east side is named for the event: Cabo de las Flechas (Cape of the Arrows). Although the park is just in the developing stages, it has several sights with cultural significance. A ball court, used by the Caribs in religious ceremonies, was discovered at the spot where the taxis park. Take a short hike up the dirt road to the ruins of an old earthen fort for great views of Salt River Bay. The area also encompasses a coastal estuary with the region's largest remaining mangrove forest, a submarine canyon, and several endangered species, including the hawksbill turtle and the roseate tern. A visitor center sits just uphill to the west. The water at the beach can be on the rough side, but it's a nice place for sunning. ⊠ *Rte. 75 to Rte. 80, Salt River* ☏ *340/773–1460* ⊕ *www.nps.gov/sari* ⊙ *Tues.–Thurs 9–4.*

26

St. George Village Botanical Gardens. At this 17-acre estate, fragrant flora grows amid the ruins of a 19th-century sugarcane plantation village. There are miniature versions of each ecosystem on St. Croix, from a semiarid cactus grove to a verdant rain forest. ⊠ *Rte. 70, turn north at sign, St. George* ☏ *340/692–2874* ⊕ *www.sgvbg.org* ⊡ *$8* ⊙ *Daily 9–5.*

FREDERIKSTED & ENVIRONS

St. Croix's second-largest town, Frederiksted, was founded in 1751. While Christiansted is noted for its Danish buildings, Frederiksted is better known for its Victorian architecture. One long cruise-ship pier juts into the sparkling sea. It's the perfect place to start a tour of this quaint city. A stroll around its historic sights will take you no more than an hour. Allow a little more time if you want to duck into the few small shops. The area just outside town has old plantations, some of which have been preserved as homes or historic structures that are open to the public.

Carl & Marie Lawaetz Museum. For a trip back in time, tour this circa-1750 farm. Owned by the prominent Lawaetz family since 1896, just after Carl Lawaetz arrived from Denmark, the lovely two-story house is in a valley at La Grange. A Lawaetz family member shows you the four-poster mahogany bed Carl and Marie shared, the china Marie painted, the family portraits, and the fruit trees that fed the family for several generations. Initially a sugar plantation, it was subsequently used to raise cattle and grow produce. ⊠ *Rte. 76, Mahogany Rd., Estate Little La Grange* ☏ *340/772–1539* ⊕ *www.stcroixlandmarks. com* ⊡ *$10* ⊙ *Tues., Thurs., and Sat. 10–4.*

Estate Mount Washington Plantation. Several years ago, while surveying the property, the owners discovered the ruins of a sugar plantation beneath the rain-forest brush. The grounds have since been cleared and opened to the public. You can take a self-guided walking tour of the mill, the rum factory, and other ruins. ✉ *Rte. 63, Mount Washington* ☉ *Ruins open daily dawn–dusk.*

Frederiksted. This town is noted less for its danish than for its Victorian architecture, which dates from after the slave rebellion and great fire of July 1848. Across from the pier, Federiksted's **visitor center** (✉ *200 Strand St.* ☎ *340/772–0357* has brochures from numerous St. Croix businesses, as well as a few exhibits about the island. You can stop in weekdays from 8 to 5.

Sitting across from the waterfront in a historic building, the small **Caribbean Museum Center for the Arts** (✉ *10 Strand St.* ☎ *340/772– 2622* ⊕ *www.cmcarts.org*)hosts an always-changing roster of exhibits. Many are cutting-edge multimedia efforts that you might be surprised to find in such an out-of-the way location. The openings are popular events. It's open Wednesday through Friday from noon to 6, Saturday from 10 to 4; admission is free.

Fort Frederiksted (✉ *Waterfront* ☎ *340/772–2021*), completed in 1760, houses a number of interesting historical exhibits and an art gallery. Admission is $3, and it's open weekdays from 8:30 to 4. It's within earshot of the visitor center.

St. Croix Leap. This workshop sits in the heart of the rain forest, about a 15-minute drive from Frederiksted. It sells mirrors, tables, bread boards, and mahogany jewelry boxes crafted by local artisans. ✉ *Rte. 76, Brooks Hill* ☎ *340/772–0421* ☉ *Weekdays 9–5, Sat. 10–5.*

West End Salt Pond. A bird-watcher's delight, this salt pond attracts a large number of winged creatures, including flamingos. ✉ *Veteran's Shore Dr., Hesselberg.*

☾ ★ **Whim Plantation Museum.** The lovingly restored estate, with a windmill, cook house, and other buildings, will give you a sense of what life was like on St. Croix's sugar plantations in the 1800s. The oval-shape greathouse has high ceilings and antique furniture and utensils. Notice its fresh, airy atmosphere—the waterless stone moat around the greathouse was used not for defense but for gathering cooling air. If you have kids, the grounds are the perfect place for them to run around, perhaps while you browse in the museum gift shop. It's just outside of Frederiksted. ✉ *Rte. 70, Estate Whim* ☎ *340/772–0598* ⊕ *www. stcroixlandmarks.com* ☚ *$10* ☉ *Mon.–Sat. 10–4.*

UNITED STATES VIRGIN ISLANDS ESSENTIALS

To research prices, get advice from other travelers, and book travel arrangements, visit www.fodors.com.

∎ TRANSPORTATION

BY AIR

Of all the Virgin Islands, St. Thomas is the most accessible by air, with an abundance of nonstop and connecting flights that can have you at the beach in three to four hours from several East Coast airports. St. Croix also has some nonstop flights You can also get connecting service through San Juan or St. Thomas. Cape Air flies from San Juan and St. Thomas and offers code-share arrangements with all major airlines, so your luggage can transfer seamlessly. Seaborne Airlines flies between St. Thomas, St. Croix, and San Juan. St. John has no air service of any kind.

Airlines American/American Eagle (☎340/776–2560 in St. Thomas, 340/778–2000 in St. Croix). **Cape Air** (☎800/352–0714 ⊕www.flycapeair.com). **Continental** (☎800/231–0856). **Delta** (☎340/777–4177 in St. Thomas, 340/779–3183 in St. Croix). **Seaborne** (☎340/773–6442 ⊕www.seaborneairlines.com). **Spirit** (☎800/772–7117 ⊕www.spiritairlines.com). **United** (☎340/774–9190 in St. Thomas). **US Airways** (☎800/622–1015).

Airports Cyril E. King Airport (STT ✉St. Thomas ☎340/774–5100 ⊕www.viport.com). **Henry Rohlsen Airport** (STX ✉St. Croix ☎340/778–1012 ⊕www.viport.com).

BY BOAT & FERRY

Ferries are a great way to travel around the islands. There's frequent service between St. Thomas and St. John and their neighbors, the BVI. At this writing, proof of citizenship (passport or birth certificate plus government-issued photo ID) is required to travel between the USVI

and BVI by ferry, but on June 1, 2009, a passport will be required.

Actual schedules change regularly, so you should check with the ferry companies to determine the current schedules. The Virgin Islands Vacation Guide & Community (⊕ www.vinow.com) publishes current ferry schedules on its Web site.

Ferries to St. John leave daily from both Charlotte Amalie and Red Hook. From Charlotte Amalie the trip takes 45 minutes and costs $10. The first ferry to St. John leaves at 9, the last at 5:30; from St. John to Charlotte Amalie, the first ferry leaves at 7:15 AM, the last at 3:45.

More frequent ferries to St. John leave from Red Hook, take 15 to 20 minutes, and cost $5; there's an additional charge of $2 for each piece of luggage. The first ferry from Red Hook to St. John leaves at 6:30 AM, the last at midnight; from St. John back to Red Hook, the first ferry leaves at 6 AM, the last at 11 PM. About every hour, there's a car ferry, which costs $52 round-trip; you should arrive at least 25 minutes before departure.

Reefer is the name given to both of the brightly colored 26-passenger skiffs that run between the Charlotte Amalie waterfront and Marriott Frenchman's Reef hotel every day on the half hour from 8 to 5. It's a good way to beat the traffic (and is about the same price as a taxi) to Morning Star Beach. The one-way fare is $6 per person, and the trip takes about 15 minutes.

There's daily service between Charlotte Amalie or Red Hook, on St. Thomas, and West End or Road Town, Tortola, BVI, by either Smith's Ferry or Native Son, and to Virgin Gorda, BVI, by Smith's Ferry. The fare is $22 one-way or $40 round-trip, and the trip from Charlotte Amalie takes 45 minutes to an hour to West End,

26

up to 90 minutes to Road Town; from Red Hook the trip is only a half hour.

The 2¼-hour trip from Charlotte Amalie to Virgin Gorda costs $35 one-way and $60 round-trip. From Red Hook and Cruz Bay, Inter-Island offers service on Thursday and Sunday; Speedy's offers service on Tuesday, Thursday, and Saturday.

On Friday, Saturday, and Sunday a ferry operates among Red Hook, Cruz Bay, and Jost Van Dyke; the trip takes 45 minutes and costs $50 per person round-trip.

A ferry run by V.I. Sea Trans connects St. Thomas and St. Croix Friday through Monday. It leaves St. Thomas from the Charlotte Amalie Waterfront at 9:30 AM and 6:45 PM. Trips leave Gallows Bay, St. Croix, at 7:30 AM and 4:30 PM.

Information Inter-Island Boat Service (☎340/776–6597). **Native Son** (☎340/774–8685 ⊕www.nativesonbvi.com). **Reefer** (☎340/776–8500 Ext. 6814 ⊕www. marriottfrenchmansreef.com).**V.I. SeaTrans** (☎340/776–5494 ⊕www.goviseatrans.com).

BY BUS

On St. Thomas, the island's large buses make public transportation a very comfortable—though slow—way to get from east and west to Charlotte Amalie and back (service to the north is limited). Buses run about every 30 minutes from stops that are clearly marked with VITRAN signs. Fares are $1 between outlying areas and town and 75¢ in town.

Modern Vitran buses on St. John run from the Cruz Bay ferry dock through Coral Bay to the far eastern end of the island at Salt Pond, making numerous stops in between. The fare is $1 to any point.

Privately owned taxi vans crisscross St. Croix regularly, providing reliable service between Frederiksted and Christiansted along Route 70. This inexpensive ($1.50 one-way) mode of transportation is favored by locals, and though the many stops on the 20-mi (32-km) drive between the two main towns make the ride slow, it's never dull. Vitran public buses aren't the quickest way to get around the island, but they're comfortable and affordable. The fare is $1 between Christiansted and Frederiksted or to places in between.

BY CAR

Throughout the U.S. Virgin Islands, driving is on the left, British-style, but cars have steering wheels on the left. All major roads are paved, but on both St. Thomas and St. John you will find many curving roads and hills; St. Croix is much more flat. The law requires that everyone in a car wear a seat belt.

On St. Thomas traffic can get pretty bad, especially in Charlotte Amalie at rush hour (7 to 9 and 4:30 to 6). Cars often line up bumper to bumper along the waterfront. If you need to get from an East End resort to the airport during these times, find the alternate route (starting from the East End, Route 38 to 42 to 40 to 33) that goes up the mountain and then drops you back onto Veterans Highway. If you plan to explore by car, be sure to pick up the latest edition of "Road Map St. Thomas–St. John," which includes the route numbers *and* the names of the roads that are used by locals. It's available anywhere you find maps and guidebooks.

The terrain in St. John is very hilly, the roads winding, and the blind curves numerous. You may suddenly come upon a huge safari bus careening around a corner or a couple of hikers strolling along the side of the road. Major roads are well paved, but once you get off a specific route, dirt roads filled with potholes are common. For such driving, a four-wheel-drive vehicle is your best bet. Be aware that you can't bring all rental cars over to St. John from St. Thomas. Even more important, the barge service is very busy, so you can't always get a space.

Unlike St. Thomas and St. John, where narrow roads wind through hillsides, St. Croix is relatively flat, and it even has a four-lane highway. The speed limit on the Melvin H. Evans Highway is 55 mph (88 kph) and between 35 to 40 mph (55 to 65 kph) elsewhere. Roads are often unmarked, so be patient—sometimes getting lost is half the fun. On St. Croix, where the big HOVENSA refinery is located, gas prices are much closer to what you might expect to pay stateside.

CAR RENTALS IN ST. THOMAS

Avis, Budget, and Hertz all have counters at Cyril E. King Airport. Dependable Car Rental offers pickups and drop-offs at the airport and to and from major hotels. Cowpet Rent-a-Car is on the east end of the island. Discount has a location at Bluebeard's Castle hotel. Avis is at the Marriott Frenchman's Reef, Havensight Mall (adjacent to the cruise-ship dock), and Seaborn Airlines terminal on the Charlotte Amalie waterfront; Budget has branches at the Sapphire Beach Resort & Marina and at the Havensight Mall, adjacent to the main cruise-ship dock.

Information Avis (☎340/774–1468). **Budget** (☎340/776–5774). **Cowpet Rent-a-Car** (☎340/775–7376). **Dependable Car Rental** (☎340/774–2253 or 800/522–3076). **Discount** (☎340/776–4858). **Hertz** (☎340/774–1879).

CAR RENTALS IN ST. JOHN

Best is just outside Cruz Bay near the public library, off Route 10. Cool Breeze is in Cruz Bay across from the Creek. Courtesy is in Cruz Bay next to the police station. Delbert Hill Taxi & Jeep Rental Service is in Cruz Bay across from Lemon Tree Mall, just around the corner from the ferry dock. Denzil Clyne is across from the Creek. O'Connor Jeep is in Cruz Bay across from the Islandia building. St. John Car Rental is across from Wharfside Village shopping center on Bay Street in Cruz Bay. Spencer's Jeep is across from the Creek in Cruz Bay.

Information Best (☎340/693–8177). **Cool Breeze** (☎340/776–6588 ⊕www.coolbreezecarrental.com). **Courtesy** (☎340/776–6650 ⊕www.courtesycarrental.com). **Delbert Hill Taxi & Jeep Rental Service** (☎340/776–6637). **Denzil Clyne** (☎340/776–6715). **O'Connor Car Rental** (☎340/776–6343 ⊕www.oconnorcarrental.com). **St. John Car Rental** (☎340/776–6103 ⊕www.stjohncarrental.com). **Spencer's Jeep** (☎340/693–8784 or 888/776–6628 ⊕www.spencersjeeprental.com).

CAR RENTALS IN ST. CROIX

Atlas is outside Christiansted but provides pickups at hotels. Avis is at Henry Rohlsen Airport and at the seaplane ramp in Christiansted. Budget has branches at the airport, in the King Christian Hotel in Christiansted, and at the Renaissance Carambola Beach Resort. Judi of Croix delivers vehicles to your hotel. Midwest is outside Frederiksted but arranges pick-up at hotels. Olympic and Thrifty are outside Christiansted but will pick up at hotels.

Information Atlas (☎340/718–2886 or 800/426–6009). **Avis** (☎340/778–9355 ⊕www.avis.com). **Budget** (☎340/778–9636 ⊕www.budgetstcroix.com). **Judi of Croix** (☎340/773–2123 or 877/903–2123 ⊕www.judiofcroix.com). **Midwest** (☎340/772–0438 or 877/772–0438 ⊕www.midwestautorental.com). **Olympic** (☎340/773–8000 or 888/878–4227 ⊕www.stcroixcarrentals.com). **Thrifty** (☎340/773–7200 ⊕www.thrifty.com).

BY TAXI

USVI taxis don't have meters because fare rates are standard. Fares are per person, not per destination, and drivers usually take multiple fares, especially from the airport, ferry docks, and the cruise-ship terminals (on St. Thomas and St. Croix). Many taxis are open safari vans, but some are air-conditioned vans. Taxis of all shapes and sizes are available at various ferry, shopping, resort, and airport areas, and they also respond to phone calls.

26

ST. THOMAS

There are taxi stands in Charlotte Amalie across from Emancipation Garden (in front of Little Switzerland, behind the post office) and along the waterfront. But you probably won't have to look for a stand, as taxis are plentiful and routinely cruise the streets.

Information **East End Taxi** (☎340/775–6974). **Islander Taxi** (☎340/774–4077). **VI Taxi Association** (☎340/774–4550).

ST. JOHN

Taxis meet ferries arriving in Cruz Bay. Most drivers use vans or open-air safari buses. You can find them congregated at the dock and at hotel parking lots. You can also hail them anywhere on the road. Almost all trips will be shared, and prices are per person. Paradise Taxi will pick you up if you call, but most of the drivers don't provide that service. If you need one to pick you up at your rental villa, ask the villa manager for suggestions on whom to call or arrange a ride in advance. Some small cruise ships stop at St. John to let passengers disembark for a day. The main town of Cruz Bay is near the area where the ships drop off passengers. If you want to swim, the famous Trunk Bay is a $6 taxi ride per person from town.

Information **Paradise Taxi** (☎340/714–7913).

ST. CROIX

Taxis, generally station wagons or minivans, are a phone call away from most hotels and are available in downtown Christiansted, at the Henry E. Rohlsen Airport, and at the Frederiksted pier during cruise-ship arrivals. In Frederiksted all the shops are a short walk away, and you can swim off the beach. Most ship passengers visit Christiansted on a tour; a taxi will cost $24 for one or two people.

Information **Antilles Taxi Service** (☎340/773–5020). **St. Croix Taxi Association** (☎340/778–1088).

▌CONTACTS & RESOURCES

BANKS

The U.S. dollar is used throughout the U.S. Virgin Islands, so Americans will have no need to change money. All major credit cards are accepted by most hotels, restaurants, and shops.

On St. Thomas, conveniently located ATMs can be found in Charlotte Amalie, Red Hook, and Havensight Mall.

St. John has two banks, both of which are in Cruz Bay.

St. Croix has branches of Banco Popular in Orange Grove and Sunny Isle shopping centers. V.I. Community Bank is in Orange Grove Shopping Center and in downtown Christiansted. Scotia Bank has branches in Sunny Isle, Frederiksted, Christiansted, and Sunshine Mall.

EMERGENCIES

Coast Guard **Marine Safety Detachment** (☎340/776–3497 in St. Thomas and St. John, 340/772–5557 in St. Croix). **Rescue Coordination Center** (☎787/289–2041 in San Juan, PR).

Emergency Services **Air Ambulance Network** (☎800/327–1966). **Medical Air Services** (☎340/777–8580 or 800/643–9023).

Hospitals in St. Thomas **Roy L. Schneider Hospital & Community Health Center** (✉Sugar Estate ✛1 mi [1½ km] east of Charlotte Amalie ☎340/776–8311).

Hospital in St. John **Myrah Keating Smith Community Health Center** (✉Rte. 10, east of Cruz Bay, Susannaberg ☎340/693–8900).

Hospitals in St. Croix **Gov. Juan F. Luis Hospital and Health Center** (✉6 Diamond Ruby, north of Sunny Isle Shopping Center on Rte. 79, Christiansted ☎340/778–6311). **Ingeborg Nesbitt Clinic** (✉516 Strand St., Frederiksted ☎340/772–0260).

Scuba-Diving Emergencies **Roy L. Schneider Hospital & Community Health Center** (✉Sugar Estate, St. Thomas ✛1

mi [1½ km] east of Charlotte Amalie
☎340/776–2686).

INTERNET, MAIL & SHIPPING

ST. THOMAS

The main U.S. Post Office on St. Thomas is near the hospital, with branches in Charlotte Amalie, Frenchtown, Havensight, and Tutu Mall. Postal rates are the same as if you were in the mainland United States, but Express Mail and Priority Mail aren't as quick.

FedEx offers overnight service if you get your package to the office before 5 PM. Shipping services on St. Thomas are also available at Fast Shipping & Communications Nisky Mail Center and at Red Hook Mail Services.

On St. Thomas, Beans, Bytes & Websites is an Internet café in Charlotte Amalie. East End Secretarial Services offers long-distance dialing, copying, and fax services. At Little Switzerland, there's free Internet access along with an ATM, big-screen TV, telephones, and a bar with cold drinks. Near Havensight Mall, go to Soapy's Station or the Cyber Zone at Port of $ale, where there are 16 computers. Rates for Internet access range from $4 to $6 for 30 minutes to $8 to $12 per hour.

Internet Cafés Beans, Bytes & Websites(⊠Royal Dane Mall, behind Tavern on Waterfront, Charlotte Amalie ☎340/775–5262 ⊕www.usvi.net/cybercafe). **Cyber Zone** (⊠Port of $ale, Charlotte Amalie ☎340/714–7743). **East End Secretarial Services** (⊠Upstairs at Red Hook Plaza, Red Hook ☎340/775–5262). **Little Switzerland** (⊠5 Dronnigens Gade, across from Emancipation Garden,Charlotte Amalie ☎340/776–2010). **The Crew Hub** (⊠Havensight Mall, above Budget, Charlotte Amalie ☎340/715–2233).

Shipping Fast Shipping & Communications (⊠Rte. 30, across from Havensight Mall, Charlotte Amalie ☎340/714–7634). **FedEx** (⊠Cyril E. King Airport ☎340/777–4140 ⊕www.fedex.com). **Red Hook Mail Services**

(⊠Red Hook Plaza, Rte. 32, 2nd fl., Red Hook ☎340/779–1890).

ST. JOHN

There's a post office in Cruz Bay, but the lines are often long. The place to go to check your e-mail is Surf da Web in Cruz Bay and Keep Me Posted in Coral Bay. You'll pay $6 a half hour for Internet service.

Internet Cafés ADM Wireless (⊠St. John Marketplace, 2nd fl., Cruz Bay ☎340/715–1469 .**Keep Me Posted** (⊠Cocoloba Shopping Center, Coral Bay ☎340/775–1727 ⊕www.keepmepostedstjohn.com).

Shipping FedEx (⊠St. John ☎800/463–3339).

ST. CROIX

There are post offices at Christiansted, Frederiksted, Gallows Bay, and Sunny Isle on St. Croix. Postal rates are the same as if you were in the mainland United States, but Express Mail and Priority Mail aren't as quick. The FedEx office on St. Croix is in Peter's Rest Commercial Center; try to drop off your packages before 5:30 PM. On St. Croix, check your e-mail and send faxes at A Better Copy in Christiansted. Rates run $5 for a half hour of Internet time.

Shipping FedEx (⊠Peter's Rest Commercial Center, Rte. 708, Peter's Rest, St. Croix ☎800/463–3339).

SAFETY

To be safe, keep your hotel or vacation villa door locked at all times, stick to well-lighted streets at night, and use the same kind of street sense that you would in any unfamiliar territory. If you plan to carry things around, rent a car—not an open-air vehicle—and lock possessions in the trunk. Keep your rental car locked wherever you park. Don't leave cameras, purses, and other valuables lying on the beach while you snorkel for an hour (or even for a minute), no matter how many people are nearby.

26

Regardless of which island you are on, don't wander the streets of the main towns alone at night, whether you are in Charlotte Amalie, Cruz bay, Christiansted, or Frederiksted.

Although crime is not as prevalent in St. John as it is on St. Thomas and St. Croix, it does exist. There are occasional burglaries at villas, even during daylight hours. Lock doors even when you're lounging by the pool. It's not a good idea to walk around Cruz Bay late at night. If you don't have a car, plan on taking a taxi. Since it can be hard to find a taxi in the wee hours of the morning, arrange in advance for a driver to pick you up.

TOUR OPTIONS

ST. THOMAS

Accessible Adventures provides a 2- to 2½-hour island tour aboard a special trolley that's especially suitable for those in wheelchairs. Tours go to major sights like Magens Bay and Mountain Top and include a stop for shopping and refreshments. The cost is $34 per person. The V.I. Taxi Association gives a two-hour tour for two people in an open-air safari bus or enclosed van; aimed at cruise-ship passengers, this $29 tour includes stops at Drake's Seat and Mountain Top. Other tours include a three-hour trip to Coki Beach with a shopping stop in downtown Charlotte Amalie for $35 per person, a three-hour tour that includes a trip up the St. Thomas Skyride for $38 per person, a three-hour trip to the Coral World Ocean Park for $45 per person, and a five-hour beach tour to St. John for $75 per person. For $35 to $40 for two, you can hire a taxi for a customized three-hour drive around the island. Make sure to see Mountain Top, as the view is wonderful.

The *St. Thomas–St. John Vacation Handbook,* available free at hotels and tourist centers, has an excellent self-guided walking tour of Charlotte Amalie on St. Thomas. Blackbeard's Castle conducts a 45-minute to one-hour historic walking tour that starts at Blackbeard's Castle,

then heads downhill to Villa Notman, Haagensen House, and the 99 steps. The cost is $35 per person and includes a tour of Haagensen House and a rum punch. The St. Thomas Historical Trust has published a self-guided tour of the historic district; it's available in book and souvenir shops for $2. Trust members also conduct a two-hour guided historic walking tour by reservation only. Call for more information and to make a reservation.

Information Accessible Adventures (☎340/775–2346 ⊕www.accessvi.com). **Blackbeard's Castle** (☎340/776–1234 or 340/776–1829 ⊕www.blackbeards castle.com). The **St. Thomas Historical Trust** (☎340/774–5541 ⊕www.stthomashistorical trust.org).**V. I. Taxi Association St. Thomas City-Island Tour** (☎340/774–4550 ⊕www. vitaxi.com).

ST. JOHN

In St. John, taxi drivers provide tours of the island, making stops at various sites, including Trunk Bay and Annaberg Plantation. Prices run around $15 a person. The taxi drivers congregate near the ferry in Cruz Bay. The dispatcher will find you a driver for your tour. Along with providing trail maps and brochures about Virgin Islands National Park, the park service also gives several guided tours on- and offshore. Some are only offered during particular times of the year, and some require reservations. For more information, contact the Virgin Islands National Park Visitors Center.

Information V. I. National Park Visitors Center (✉Cruz Bay ☎340/776–6201 ⊕www. nps.gov/viis).

ST. CROIX

St. Croix Safari Tours offers van tours of St. Croix. Excursions depart from Christiansted and last about five hours. Costs run from $45 per person, including admission fees to attractions. St. Croix Transit offers van tours of St. Croix. Tours depart from Carambola Beach Resort, last about three hours, and cost from $5 per person, includes admission fees to some attractions.

Information **St. Croix Safari Tours** (☎340/773-6700 ⊕www.gotostcroix. com/safaritours).**St. Croix Transit** (☎340/772-3333).

VISITOR INFORMATION

Information **USVI Division of Tourism** (✉78-123 Estate Contant, Charlotte Amalie, St. Thomas ☎340/774-8784 or 800/372-8784 ⊕www.usvitourism.vi). **Virgin Islands Hotel & Tourism Association** (☎340/774-6835 ⊕www.virgin-islands-hotels.com).

WEDDINGS

The Virgin Islands provide a lovely backdrop for a wedding. Many couples opt to exchange vows on a white sandy beach or in a tropical garden. The process is easy but does require advance planning. The U.S. Virgin Islands Department of Tourism publishes a brochure with all the details and relevant contact information; you can also download marriage license applications from the Web site.

You must first apply for a marriage license at the Superior Court. The fee is $50 for the application and $50 for the license. You have to wait eight days after the clerk receives the application to get married, and licenses must be picked up in person weekdays, though you can apply by mail.

To make the process easier, most couples hire a wedding planner. If you plan to get married at a large hotel, most have planners on staff, but if you're staying in a villa, at a small hotel or inn, or are arriving on a cruise ship, you'll have to hire your own.

The wedding planner will help you organize your marriage license application as well as arrange for a location, flowers, music, refreshments, and whatever else you want to make your day special. The wedding planner will also hire a clergyman if you'd like a religious service or a nondenominational officiant if you prefer. Indeed, many wedding planners are licensed by the territory as nondenominational officiants and will preside at your wedding.

Superior Court Offices **In St. Croix** (✉Box 929, Christiansted 00820 ☎340/778-9750). **St. Thomas Superior Court** (✉Box 70, St. Thomas00804 ☎340/774-6680).

Wedding Planners **Anne Marie Weddings** (✉5000 Enighed PMB 7, St. John ☎340/693-5153 or 888/676-5701 ⊕www.stjohn weddings.com).**Weddings the Island Way** (✉Box 11694,St. Thomas ☎340/777-6505 or 800/582-4784 ⊕www.weddingstheislandway. com).

26

Caribbean Essentials

PLANNING TOOLS, EXPERT INSIGHT, GREAT CONTACTS

There are planners and there are those who, excuse the pun, fly by the seat of their pants. We happily place ourselves among the planners. Our writers and editors try to anticipate all the issues you may face before and during any journey, and then they do their research. This section is the product of their efforts. Use it to get excited about your trip to Caribbean, to inform your travel planning, or to guide you on the road should the seat of your pants start to feel threadbare.

GETTING STARTED

We're really proud of our Web site: Fodors.com is a great place to begin any journey. Scan Travel Wire for suggested itineraries, travel deals, restaurant and hotel openings, and other up-to-the-minute info. Check out Booking to research prices and book plane tickets, hotel rooms, rental cars, and vacation packages. Head to Talk for on-the-ground pointers from travelers who frequent our message boards. You can also link to loads of other travel-related resources.

▌RESOURCES

ONLINE TRAVEL TOOLS
When either organizing or anticipating a vacation to the Caribbean, you may want to check region-wide online sources for special promotions and local news about a particular island (or islands) before fine-tuning your plans. *For island-specific Web sites, see Visitor Information in the Essentials section at the end of each chapter.*

ALL ABOUT THE CARIBBEAN
CanaNews, an online news network owned by Caribbean Media Corporation, covers important social, political, and economic issues affecting the Caribbean region in both free and members-only sections of its Web site. The Caribbean Newspapers Web site is an online portal for nearly 50 newspaper Web sites that cover the various islands in the Caribbean. The Caribbean Tourism Organization (CTO) is a regional tourism industry association that disseminates research and data on the Caribbean to its members online, as well as destination promotions and other tourism-related news and information on a separate Web site for the general public.

Caribbean Information on the Web CanaNews (⊕www.cananews.net). **Caribbean Newspapers** (⊕www.caribbeannewspapers. com). **Caribbean Tourism Organization (CTO)** (⊕www.caribbeantravel.com).

Currency Conversion Google (⊕www.google.com) does currency conversion. Just type in the amount you want to convert and an explanation of how you want it converted (e.g., "14 Swiss francs in dollars"), and then voilà. **Oanda.com** (⊕www.oanda.com) also allows you to print out a handy table with the current day's conversion rates. **XE.com** (⊕www.xe.com) is a good currency conversion Web site.

Time Zones Timeanddate.com (⊕www.timeanddate.com/worldclock) can help you figure out the correct time anywhere.

Weather Accuweather.com (⊕www.accuweather.com) is an independent weather-forecasting service with good coverage of hurricanes. **Weather.com** (⊕www.weather.com) is the Web site for the Weather Channel.

▌THINGS TO CONSIDER

GOVERNMENT ADVISORIES
As different countries have different world views, look at travel advisories from a range of governments to get more of a sense of what's going on out there. And be sure to parse the language carefully. For example, a warning to "avoid all travel" carries more weight than one urging you to "avoid nonessential travel," and both are much stronger than a plea to "exercise caution." A U.S. government travel warning is more permanent (though not necessarily more serious) than a so-called public announcement, which carries an expiration date.

WORD OF MOUTH

After your trip, be sure to rate the places you visited and share your experiences and travel tips with us and other Fodorites in Travel Ratings and Talk on www.fodors.com.

■ TIP→ Consider registering online with the State Department (https://travelregistration.state.gov/ibrs/), so the government will know to look for you should a crisis occur in the country you're visiting.

The U.S. Department of State's Web site has more than just travel warnings and advisories. The consular information sheets issued for every country have general safety tips, entry requirements (though be sure to verify these with the country's embassy), and other useful details.

General Information & Warnings U.S. Department of State (⊕ www.travel.state.gov).

PASSPORTS & VISAS

With two notable exceptions, all destinations in the Caribbean require U.S. citizens to carry a valid passport when arriving by air. These exception are Puerto Rico, a U.S. commonwealth, and the U.S. Virgin Islands, a U.S. territory. A flight to Puerto Rico is considered a domestic flight, so you need bring only your valid government-issued photo ID. However, travelers to the U.S. Virgin Islands must still provide proof of citizenship, which requires a birth certificate with a raised seal as well as a government-issued photo ID (a passport will always suffice, if you have one).

At this writing, travelers by sea are still allowed to use a photo ID plus a birth certificate with a raised seal to prove citizenship until June 1, 2009. This applies to interisland ferries between the U.S. and British Virgin Islands. However, if you want to pop over to Tortola from either Puerto Rico or St. Thomas by air, you still have to carry a valid passport.

When flying to the Caribbean, children must have passports, as well. And if your child has a different last name, you're advised to carry proof of your relationship—such as a birth certificate with a raised seal.

SHOTS & MEDICATIONS

No special shots or vaccinations are required for Caribbean destinations, but health warnings are sometimes issued, particularly after hurricanes or other natural disasters.

Visitors planning to hike in or explore remote areas or who are undertaking extreme activities and adventures should be sure their tetanus shots are up to date and that they carry along a basic first-aid kit with bandages, hydrogen peroxide, antibiotic cream, and similar items to take care of minor scrapes and injuries.

If you take prescription medicine, make sure you bring enough with you to last through your vacation plus a few extra days, in case your departure is delayed for any reason. Carry your prescribed medications in their original containers. In a real emergency, a local pharmacy could contact your home pharmacy to refill the prescription.

For more information see Health under On the Ground in the Caribbean, below.

■ TIP→ If you travel a lot internationally—particularly to developing nations—refer to the CDC's *Health Information for International Travel* (aka Traveler's Health Yellow Book). Info from it is posted on the CDC Web site (www.cdc.gov/travel/yb), or you can buy a copy from your local bookstore for $24.95.

Health Warnings National Centers for Disease Control & Prevention (CDC ☎877/394–8747 international travelers' health line ⊕ www.cdc.gov/travel). **World Health Organization** (WHO ⊕ www.who.int).

TRIP INSURANCE

What kind of coverage do you honestly need? Do you even need trip insurance at all? Take a deep breath and read on.

We believe that comprehensive trip insurance is especially valuable if you're booking a very expensive or complicated trip (particularly to an isolated region) or if you're booking far in advance. Who knows what could happen six months down the road? But whether or not you get insurance has more to do with how comfortable you are assuming all that risk yourself.

Comprehensive travel policies typically cover trip-cancellation and interruption, letting you cancel or cut your trip short because of a personal emergency, illness, or, in some cases, acts of terrorism in your destination. Such policies also cover evacuation and medical care. Some also cover you for trip delays because of bad weather or mechanical problems as well as for lost or delayed baggage. Another type of coverage to look for is financial default—that is, when your trip is disrupted because a tour operator, airline, or cruise line goes out of business. Generally you must buy this when you book your trip or shortly thereafter, and it's only available to you if your operator isn't on a list of excluded companies.

If you're going abroad, consider buying medical-only coverage at the very least. Neither Medicare nor some private insurers cover medical expenses anywhere outside of the United States (including time aboard a cruise ship, even if it leaves from a U.S. port). Medical-only policies typically reimburse you for medical care (excluding that related to preexisting conditions) and hospitalization abroad, and provide for evacuation. You still have to pay the bills and await reimbursement from the insurer, though.

Expect comprehensive travel insurance policies to cost about 4% to 7% or 8% of the total price of your trip (it's more like 8%–12% if you're over age 70). A medical-only policy may or may not be cheaper than a comprehensive policy. Always read the fine print of your policy to make sure that you are covered for the risks that are of most concern to you. Compare several policies to make sure you're getting the best price and range of coverage available.

Insurance Comparison Sites Insure My Trip. com (☎800/487-4722 ⊕www.insuremytrip. com). **Square Mouth.com** (☎800/240-0369 or 727/490-5803 ⊕www.squaremouth.com).

Medical Assistance Companies AirMed International Medical Group (⊕www. airmed.com) **International SOS** (⊕www. internationalsos.com). **MedjetAssist** (⊕www. medjetassist.com).

Medical-Only Insurers International Medical Group (☎800/628-4664 ⊕www. imglobal.com). **Wallach & Company** (☎800/237-6615 or 540/687-3166 ⊕www. wallach.com).

Comprehensive Travel Insurers Access America (☎866/729-6021 ⊕www. accessamerica.com). **AIG Travel Guard** (☎800/826-4919 ⊕www.travelguard.com). **CSA Travel Protection** (☎800/873-9855 ⊕www.csatravelprotection.com). **HTH Worldwide** (☎610/254-8700 ⊕www.hthworldwide. com). **Travelex Insurance** (☎888/228-9792 ⊕www.travelex-insurance.com). **Travel Insured International** (☎800/243-3174 ⊕www.travelinsured.com).

■**TIP**➔ OK. You know you can save a bundle on trips to warm-weather destinations by traveling in the off-season. But there's also a chance that a severe storm will disrupt your plans. The solution? Look for hotels and resorts that offer storm/hurricane guarantees. Although they rarely allow refunds, most guarantees do let you rebook later if a storm strikes.

BOOKING YOUR TRIP

Unless your cousin is a travel agent, you're probably among the millions of people who make most of their travel arrangements online.

But have you ever wondered just what the differences are between an online travel agent (a Web site through which you make reservations instead of going directly to the airline, hotel, or car-rental company), a discounter (a firm that does a high volume of business with a hotel chain or airline and accordingly gets good prices), a wholesaler (one that makes cheap reservations in bulk and then resells them to people like you), and an aggregator (one that compares all the offerings so you don't have to)?

■ ONLINE

You really have to shop around. A travel wholesaler such as Hotels.com or Hotel Club can be a source of good rates, as can discounters such as Hotwire or Priceline, particularly if you can bid for your hotel room or airfare. Indeed, such sites sometimes have deals that are unavailable elsewhere. They do, however, tend to work only with hotel chains (which makes them just plain useless for getting hotel reservations outside major cities) or big airlines (so that often leaves out upstarts like jetBlue and some foreign or regional carriers).

Also, with discounters and wholesalers you must generally prepay, and everything is nonrefundable. So before you fork over the dough, be sure to check the terms and conditions. Know what a given company will do for you if there's a problem and what you'll have to deal with on your own.

■ **TIP→** To be absolutely sure everything was processed correctly, confirm reservations made through online travel agents,

discounters, and wholesalers directly with your hotel before leaving home.

Booking engines like Expedia, Travelocity, and Orbitz are actually travel agents, albeit high-volume, online ones. And airline travel packagers like American Airlines Vacations and Virgin Vacations—well, they're travel agents, too. But they may still not work with all the world's hotels.

An aggregator site will search many sites and pull the best prices for airfares, hotels, and rental cars from them. Most aggregators compare the major travel-booking sites such as Expedia, Travelocity, and Orbitz; some also look at airline Web sites, though rarely the sites of smaller budget airlines. Some aggregators also compare other travel products, including complex packages—a good thing, as you can sometimes get the best overall deal by booking an air-and-hotel package.

■ WITH A TRAVEL AGENT

If you use an agent—brick-and-mortar or virtual—you'll usually pay a fee for the service. And the service you get from some online agents isn't comprehensive. For example, Expedia and Travelocity don't search for prices on budget airlines like jetBlue, Southwest, or small foreign carriers. That said, some agents (online or not) *do* have access to fares that are difficult to find otherwise, and the savings can more than make up for any surcharge.

A knowledgeable brick-and-mortar travel agent can be a godsend if you're booking a cruise, a package trip that's not available to you directly, an air pass, or a complicated itinerary including several overseas flights. What's more, travel agents that specialize in a destination may have exclusive access to certain deals and insider information or firsthand experience with certain destinations or resorts.

Agents who specialize in specific types of travelers (senior citizens, gays and lesbians, naturists) or types of trips (cruises, luxury travel) can also be invaluable.

■**TIP**➡ Remember that Expedia, Travelocity, and Orbitz are travel agents, not just booking engines. To resolve any problems with a reservation made through these companies, contact them first.

A top-notch agent booking your cruise may get you a cabin upgrade or arrange to have a bottle of champagne chilling in your cabin when you embark. And complain about the surcharges all you like, but when things don't work out the way you'd hoped, it's nice to have an agent to put things right.

Travel agents can still find you good deals for Caribbean travel—sometimes deals you can't book on your own—and agents who specialize in the Caribbean may know about offers that you won't easily uncover by yourself. A few resort companies—Iberostar, for example, which has a big presence in the Dominican Republic—do not allow individuals to book their rooms, so you must book through a travel agent. Some big packagers like Apple Vacations now allow customers to book directly through their Web sites, but they still sell the majority of their trips through affiliated travel agents. Other companies, including Sandals, offer lowest-price guarantees only when you book rooms through travel agents. If you're traveling to the Caribbean from Europe, where air charters are common in high season, you will almost certainly get a better deal on your travel package if you book through a travel agent.

Agent Resources American Society of Travel Agents (☎703/739–2782 ⊕www. travelsense.org).

■ ACCOMMODATIONS

Most hotels and resorts are on the leeward (i.e., Caribbean) side of each island, where the beaches are warmer and sunnier and the calm water is good for snorkeling and swimming. You'll find a few hotels on the windward (i.e., Atlantic) side, where the surf is rough—and most often quite scenic but treacherous for swimming. The most important decision you'll need to make is whether you want to pay the extra price for an oceanfront room. At less-expensive properties, location may mean a difference in price of only $10 to $20 per night, but at luxury resorts on pricey islands, it could amount to as much as $100 or more per night. Always ask how close the property is to a beach. At some hotels you can walk barefoot from your room onto the sand; others may be across a road, a couple of blocks, or a 10-minute drive (or more) away.

If you go to sleep early or are a light sleeper, request a room away from the entertainment area or pool. Air-conditioning isn't a necessity on all islands, many of which are cooled by trade winds, but it can be a plus if you enjoy an afternoon snooze or are bothered by humidity—which is most prevalent from September through November. Breezes are best in second-floor rooms, particularly corner rooms; many hotel rooms have ceiling fans. If you like to sleep without air-conditioning, make sure that the location of your room makes it safe to keep your windows open at night and that the windows have screens. You'll likely notice a candle and box of matches in your room. In even the most-luxurious resorts, the electricity may inexplicably shut off for a while; it's just a fact of Caribbean life. And no matter how diligent the upkeep, humidity and salt air take their toll on metal fixtures.

Most hotels and other lodgings require you to give your credit-card details before they will confirm your reservation. If you don't feel comfortable e-mailing this information, ask if you can fax it (some places even prefer faxes). However you book, get confirmation in writing and have a copy of it handy when you check in.

Be sure you understand the hotel's cancellation policy. Some places allow you to cancel without any kind of penalty—even if you prepaid to secure a discounted rate—if you cancel at least 24 hours in advance. Others require you to cancel a week or more in advance or penalize you the cost of one night. Small inns and bed-and-breakfasts are most likely to require you to cancel far in advance. Most hotels allow children under a certain age to stay in their parents' room at no extra charge, but others charge for them as extra adults; find out the cutoff age for discounts.

■TIP➔ Assume that hotels operate on the European Plan (**EP**, no meals) unless we specify that they use the Breakfast Plan (**BP**, with full breakfast), Continental Plan (**CP**, continental breakfast), Full American Plan (**FAP**, all meals), Modified American Plan (**MAP**, breakfast and dinner) or are **all-inclusive** (**AI**, all meals and most activities).

All the hotels we recommend have private baths unless indicated otherwise.

■ AIRLINE TICKETS

Most domestic airline tickets are electronic; international tickets may be either electronic or paper. With an e-ticket the only thing you receive is an e-mailed receipt citing your itinerary and reservation and ticket numbers.

The greatest advantage of an e-ticket is that if you lose your receipt, you can simply print out another copy or ask the airline to do it for you at check-in. You usually pay a surcharge (up to $50) to get a paper ticket, if you can get one at all.

The sole advantage of a paper ticket is that it may be easier to endorse over to another

> ### WORD OF MOUTH
>
> Did the resort look as good in real life as it did in the photos? Did you sleep like a baby, or were the walls paper thin? Did you get your money's worth? Rate hotels and write your own reviews in Travel Ratings or start a discussion about your favorite places in Travel Talk on www.fodors.com. Your comments might even appear in our books. Yes, you, too, can be a correspondent!

airline if your flight is canceled and the airline with which you booked can't accommodate you on another flight.

■TIP➔ Discount air passes that let you travel economically in a country or region must often be purchased before you leave home. In some cases you can only get them through a travel agent.

CHARTER FLIGHTS

Charter companies rent aircraft and offer regularly scheduled flights (usually nonstops). Charter flights are generally cheaper than flights on regular airlines, and they often leave from and travel to a wider variety of airports. For example, you could have a nonstop flight from Columbus, Ohio, to Punta Cana, Dominican Republic, or from Boston to Antigua.

You don't, however, have the same protections as with regular airlines. If a charter can't take off for mechanical or other reasons, there usually isn't another plane to take its place. If not enough seats are sold, the flight may be canceled. And if a company goes out of business, you're out of luck (unless, of course, you have insurance with financial default coverage; ⇨*Trip Insurance under Things to Consider in Getting Started, above*).

■ RENTAL CARS

When you reserve a car, ask about cancellation penalties, taxes, fees, and any surcharges. All these things can add substantially to your costs. Request car seats if you are traveling with small children when you book.

Rates are sometimes—but not always—better if you book in advance or reserve through a rental agency's Web site. There are other reasons to book ahead, though: for popular destinations, during busy times of the year, or to ensure that you get a certain type of car (four-wheel drive or automatic transmission, for example).

■**TIP**➡ Make sure that a confirmed reservation guarantees you a car. Agencies sometimes overbook, particularly for busy weekends and holiday periods.

Major firms such as Avis, Hertz, and Budget have agencies or affiliates on some Caribbean islands. But don't overlook local firms, whose cars are just as mechanically sound and are priced competitively. On some islands you will have to pay extra to get an automatic transmission, and on a few islands, only manuals will be available; it is always a good idea to verify that you will be able to get an automatic transmission if that is a necessity for you. For exciting treks into remote areas where roads are hilly or unpaved, rent a four-wheel-drive vehicle. On most islands, it's not crucial to reserve a rental car prior to your arrival. Deciding on the spur of the moment to rent a car for a day or two of on-your-own sightseeing is easily accomplished. Many Caribbean islands require you to purchase a temporary driving permit for a small cost (usually less than $20). The rental agency can sometimes provide that for you.

Your driver's license may not be recognized outside your home country, although that is not usually an issue in the Caribbean. You may be able to rent a car with an International Driving Permit (IDP), which can be used only in conjunction with a valid driver's license and which translates your license into 10 languages. Check the American Automobile Association (AAA) Web site for more info as well as for IDPs ($10) themselves.

Major Agencies Alamo (☎800/522–9696 ⊕www.alamo.com).**Avis** (☎800/331–1084 ⊕www.avis.com).**Budget** (☎800/472–3325 ⊕www.budget.com).**Hertz** (☎800/654–3001 ⊕www.hertz.com).**National Car Rental** (☎800/227–7368 ⊕www.nationalcar.com).

CAR-RENTAL INSURANCE

Everyone who rents a car wonders whether the insurance that the rental companies offer is worth the expense. No one—including us—has a simple answer. It all depends on how much regular insurance you have, how comfortable you are with risk, and whether or not money is an issue.

If you own a car, your personal auto insurance may cover a rental to some degree, though not all policies protect you abroad; always read your policy's fine print. If you don't have auto insurance, then seriously consider buying the collision- or loss-damage waiver (CDW or LDW) from the car-rental company, which eliminates your liability for damage to the car. Some credit cards offer CDW coverage, but it's usually supplemental to your own insurance and rarely covers SUVs, minivans, luxury models, and the like. If your coverage is secondary, you may still be liable for loss-of-use costs from the car-rental company. But no credit-card insurance is valid unless you use that card for *all* transactions, from reserving to paying the final bill. All companies exclude car rental in some countries, so be sure to find out about the destination to which you are traveling.

■**TIP**➡ Diners Club offers primary CDW coverage on all rentals reserved and paid for with the card. This means that Diners Club's company—not your own car insurance—pays in case of an accident. It *doesn't* mean your car-insurance company won't raise your rates once it discovers you had an accident.

Some countries require you to purchase CDW coverage or require car-rental companies to include it in quoted rates. Ask your rental company about issues like these in your destination. In most cases it's cheaper to add a supplemental CDW plan to your comprehensive travel-insurance policy *(⇨ Trip Insurance under Things to Consider in Getting Started, above)* than to purchase it from a rental company. That said, you don't want to pay for a supplement if you're required to buy insurance from the rental company.

Some credit-card companies exclude Jamaica in their secondary CDW plans, requiring you to buy full insurance there.

■**TIP**➜ You can decline the insurance from the rental company and purchase it through a third-party provider such as Travel Guard (www.travelguard. com)—$9 per day for $35,000 of coverage. That's sometimes just under half the price of the CDW offered by some car-rental companies.

■ VACATION PACKAGES

Packages *are not* guided excursions. Packages combine airfare, accommodations, and perhaps a rental car or other extras (theater tickets, guided excursions, boat trips, reserved entry to popular museums, transit passes), but they let you do your own thing. During busy periods packages may be your only option, as flights and rooms may be sold out otherwise.

Packages will definitely save you time. They can also save you money, particularly in peak seasons, but—and this is a really big "but"—you should price each part of the package separately to be sure. And be aware that prices advertised on Web sites and in newspapers rarely include service charges or taxes, which can up your costs by hundreds of dollars.

■**TIP**➜ Some packages and cruises are sold only through travel agents. Don't always assume that you can get the best deal by booking everything yourself.

Each year consumers are stranded or lose their money when packagers—even large ones with excellent reputations—go out of business. How can you protect yourself?

First, always pay with a credit card; if you have a problem, your credit-card company may help you resolve it. Second, buy trip insurance that covers default. Third, choose a company that belongs to the United States Tour Operators Association, whose members must set aside funds to cover defaults. Finally, choose a company that also participates in the Tour Operator Program of the American Society of Travel Agents (ASTA), which will act as mediator in any disputes.

You can also check on the tour operator's reputation among travelers by posting an inquiry on one of the Fodors.com forums.

Most major air carriers that fly to the Caribbean offer vacation packages that combine round-trip airfare and lodgings for four, seven, or more nights. Vacation packages can be less expensive than booking your flights and hotel separately if your vacation plans can fit the parameters of the package for the specific time period at the selected resort. Package pricing for vacations to the more-developed islands (St. Thomas, St. Maarten/ St. Martin, Aruba, Puerto Rico, Jamaica, and Grand Cayman, for example) tends to be more competitive and creative.

Airline Vacation Packagers Air Jamaica Vacations (☎800/568–3247 ⊕www.air-jamaicavacations.com). **American Airlines Vacations** (☎800/321–2121 ⊕www.aa vacations.com). **Continental Airlines Vacations** (☎800/301–3800 ⊕www.covacations. com). **Delta Vacations** (☎800/654–6559 ⊕www.deltavacations.com). **US Airways Vacations** (☎800/455–0123 ⊕www.usair waysvacations.com).

Large Agency Packagers American Express Vacations (☎800/335-3342 ⊕www.americanexpressvacations.com). **Apple Vacations** (⊕www.applevacations.com) are mostly sold through travel agents. **Funjet Vacations** (☎888/558-6654 ⊕www.funjet.com). **GoGo Worldwide Vacations** (☎800/541-3788 ⊕www.gogowwv.com) are sold through travel agents. **Liberty Travel** (☎888/271-1584 ⊕www.libertytravel.com).

Online Agency Packagers Cheap Tickets (⊕www.cheaptickets.com). **Expedia** (⊕www.expedia.com). **Orbitz** (⊕www.orbitz.com). **Priceline** (⊕www.priceline.com). **Travelocity** (⊕www.travelocity.com).

Organizations American Society of Travel Agents (ASTA ☎703/739-2782 or 800/965-2782 ⊕www.astanet.com). **United States Tour Operators Association** (USTOA ☎212/599-6599 ⊕www.ustoa.com).

■TIP→ Local tourism boards can provide information about lesser-known and small-niche operators that sell packages to only a few destinations.

TRANSPORTATION

People primarily travel to the Caribbean by air or on a cruise ship that visits several islands. Those who travel by air—especially on nonstop flights—often don't realize how easy it is to combine a visit to one or more nearby islands either via short, reasonably priced hops on a regional airline or by a scenic and inexpensive voyage by ferry.

Anyone visiting San Juan, for example, can fly to the Virgin Islands—either the USVI or the British Virgin Islands—in less than a half hour. Once there, they can travel between and among any or all of the Virgins by ferry or, in the case of St. Croix, seaplane. People visiting Nevis may want to spend a few days next door on St. Kitts; while those visiting St. Martin/St. Maarten can easily take a day trip (or longer trip) by ferry to Anguilla (just 15 minutes away), St. Barths, or Saba, or the quick trip by air to St. Eustatius.

Barbados is a popular destination in and of itself, but it is also the hub of the Eastern Caribbean. Regional carriers make several flights daily between Barbados and Antigua, St. Lucia, Dominica, St. Vincent, the Grenadines (Bequia, Mustique, Canouan, and Union), and Grenada. Flights take no more than 30 minutes—often less. From St. Vincent, of course, frequent and inexpensive ferry service or a 10-minute flight on a tiny plane makes visiting several (or all) of the Grenadines a must. The same is true for Grenada, which is connected by daily ferry service to sister islands Carriacou and Petite Martinique. Similarly, Antigua is a hub for LIAT, from which you can make short, quick hops to St. Kitts, St. Maarten, Guadeloupe, Dominica, or Martinique.

■**TIP➜** Ask the local tourist board about hotel and local transportation packages that include tickets to major museum exhibits or other special events.

■ BY AIR

The flight from New York to San Juan, Puerto Rico, takes 3½ hours; from Miami to San Juan, 2½ hours. Flights from New York to Kingston or Montego Bay, Jamaica, take about 4 hours; from Miami, about an hour. Nonstop flights from New York to Barbados or St. Lucia take about 5 hours. Once you've arrived in the Caribbean, flights between islands are short hops ranging from 10 minutes to 2 hours.

Be sure to confirm your flights on interisland carriers and make sure the carrier has a local contact telephone number for you, as you may be subject to a small carrier's whims: if no other passengers are booked on your flight, particularly if the carrier operates "scheduled charters," you'll be rescheduled onto another flight or at a different departure time (earlier or later than your original reservation) that is more convenient for the airline. Your plane may also make unscheduled stops to pick up more passengers or cargo, which can affect actual departure and arrival times. Don't be concerned; it's all part of the adventure of interisland travel. If you're connecting from an interisland flight to a scheduled overseas departure, be sure to include a substantial buffer of time for these kinds of delays.

If your trip terminates in Puerto Rico, that is considered a domestic destination. Although a U.S. territory, the USVI are treated as an international flight on most carriers, requiring you to check in for your flight with your picture ID and birth certificate with a raised seal. All other Caribbean locations are considered international destinations, and you must appear in person, with your passport, to check in for your flight. Air Jamaica allows passengers to the Caribbean to check in online and then present their passports and luggage at a special Web check-in desk. Some American Airlines flights allow international passengers to check in online and swipe their passports at the airport. It probably won't be long before that is the universal procedure. When you are returning from a Caribbean destination, you may also need to pay departure taxes (which are usually not included in your airfare); if required, departure taxes must be paid in cash.

If a flight is oversold, particularly during busy travel seasons and around holiday periods, the gate agent will usually ask for volunteers to take a later flight and will offer some sort of compensation. On Caribbean routes, this happens most frequently on departures heading north out of San Juan or Miami.

Airlines & Airports Airline and Airport Links.com (⊕ www.airlineandairportlinks.com) has links to many of the world's airlines and airports.

Airline Security Issues Transportation Security Administration (TKA ⊕ www.tsa.gov) has answers for almost every question that might come up.

AIRPORTS

Airports in the Caribbean range from huge, modern, and sometimes stunning international facilities (San Juan, St. Thomas, Trinidad, Montego Bay, Barbados) to tiny but busy airstrips (Tortola, Saba, Canouan, Carriacou) and many airports that fall somewhere in between. San Juan, Montego Bay, St. Maarten, Antigua, and Barbados are regional hubs that link international jet service from North America and Europe with interisland service to airports that cannot accommodate jets. Regardless of the airport's size, be sure to arrive in plenty of time to check in, pay your departure tax, pass through immigration and security, and do any last-minute duty-free shopping. Keep in mind that international flights often close an hour before flight time; if you're not checked in by then, you may not be allowed to check in or

your seat may be given away—and you may have to wait a whole day for the next flight out. U.S.-bound passengers returning from or through Aruba, St. Thomas, or San Juan clear immigration and customs at those respective airports, so allow plenty of time for that, as well, in terms of getting to the airport in time or planning connecting flights. Contact information for respective Caribbean airports is included in the Essentials section of each island chapter.

FLIGHTS

Many carriers fly nonstop or direct routes to the Caribbean from major airports in the United States, including Atlanta, Boston, Charlotte, Chicago, Dallas, Fort Lauderdale, Houston, Miami, New York (JFK), Newark, Philadelphia, and Washington (Dulles). If you live somewhere else in the United States, you'll probably have to make a connection to get to your Caribbean destination. You may also have to make a connection in the Caribbean, most often in San Juan, Montego Bay, Barbados, or St. Maarten.

Most major U.S. airlines fly to some destinations in the Caribbean. The most frequent service, by far, is offered by American Airlines, which has a major hub in San Juan, and Air Jamaica, which has its hub in Montego Bay. American Eagle, an American Airlines subsidiary, operates interisland service from San Juan. Other airlines, such as jetBlue and Spirit, have only a few flights to the Caribbean, but they are all nonstop.

Some destinations are accessible only by small planes operated by local or regional carriers. International carriers will sometimes book those flights for you as part of your overall travel arrangements, or you can confidently book directly with the local carrier, using a major credit card, sometimes online but more often by phone. Unlike the custom among major carriers, schedule changes on most Caribbean airlines normally don't carry a prohibitive penalty, and your credit card may not be charged until after you've taken the flight.

Airline Contacts **Air Jamaica** (☎800/523-5585 ⊕www.airjamaica.com). **American Airlines** (☎800/433-7300 ⊕www.aa.com). **Caribbean Airlines** (☎800/920-4225 ⊕www.caribbean-airlines.com). **Continental Airlines** (☎800/231-0856 ⊕www.continental.com). **Delta Airlines** (☎800/241-4141 ⊕www.delta.com). **jetBlue** (☎800/538-2583 ⊕www.jetblue.com). **Northwest Airlines** (☎800/225-2525 ⊕www.nwa.com). **Spirit Airlines** (☎800/772-7117 or 586/791-7300 ⊕www.spiritair.com). **United Airlines** (☎800/538-2929 ⊕www.united.com). **USAirways** (☎800/622-1015 ⊕www.usairways.com).

Within the Caribbean **Air Caraïbes** (☎877/772-1005 ⊕www.aircaraibes.com). **Air Jamaica Express** (☎800/523-5585 ⊕www.airjamaica.com). **American Eagle** (☎800/433-7300 ⊕www.aa.com). **Cape Air** (☎800/352-0714 or 284/495-2100 ⊕www.flycapeair.com). **Cayman Airways** (☎345/949-8200 or 800/422-9626 ⊕www.caymanairways.com). **Dutch Antilles Express** (☎599/717-0808 ⊕www.flydae.com). **Grenadines Airways (Mustique Air, SVG Air, TIA)** (☎246/418-1654 for shared-charter flights, 784/456-6793 for intra-Grenadines flights ⊕www.grenadineairways.com). **LIAT** (☎866/549-5428, 888/844-5429 within the Caribbean ⊕www.liatairline.com). **Seabourne Airlines** (☎340/773-6442 or 888/359-8687 ⊕www.seaborneairlines.com). **SkyKing** (☎649/941-3136 ⊕www.skyking.tc). **SVG Air** (☎784/457-5124, 800/744-5777 within the Caribbean ⊕www.svgair.com). **Tobago Express** (☎868/627-5160 ⊕www.tobagoexpress.com).

▌ BY BOAT

Interisland ferries are an efficient, interesting, and often inexpensive way to travel around certain areas of the Caribbean. For example, ferries connect Puerto Rico with the outlying islands of Vieques and Culebra; St. Thomas with St. John

and the British Virgin Islands; the various islands of the British Virgin Islands; St. Martin with Anguilla and St. Barths; St. Kitts with Nevis; St. Maarten with Saba and St. Barths; Antigua with Barbados; St. Lucia with Guadeloupe, Martinique, and Dominica; St. Vincent with Bequia and the other islands of the Grenadines; Grenada with Carriacou; and Trinidad with Tobago. In most cases, service is frequent—either daily or several times daily.

▌ BY CAR

Your valid local driver's license or an International Driving Permit (IDP) is recognized in some Caribbean countries. IDPs—available through the AAA—are universally recognized but valid only in conjunction with your regular driver's license. On Guadeloupe, Martinique, and St. Barths, a valid U.S. or EU license is accepted for 20 days; after that, you need an IDP.

Temporary local driving permits are required in several other countries (Anguilla, Antigua, Barbados, the British Virgin Islands, Cayman Islands, Dominica, Grenada, Nevis, St. Kitts, St. Lucia, and St. Vincent and the Grenadines), which you can get at rental agencies or local police offices upon presentation of a valid license and a small fee. St. Lucia and St. Vincent and the Grenadines require a temporary permit only if you don't have an IDP.

Although exploring on your own can give your sightseeing excursions a sense of adventure, tentative drivers should instead consider hiring a taxi for the day. On many islands, driving is on the left (British style). Locals, who are familiar with the roads, often drive fast and take chances. You don't want to get in their way. And you don't want to get lost on dark, winding roads at night.

GASOLINE

Modern gasoline stations (with restrooms and snack shops) are widely available in and around cities and towns but are harder to find in the remote countryside. Gasoline is priced by the liter and, on most islands, is more expensive than in the United States. The equivalent to a gallon of gasoline may cost $6 or more. Most cars, however, are four-cylinder vehicles and get good gas mileage.

ROAD CONDITIONS

Road conditions vary from island to island. Puerto Rico and the Dominican Republic have four-lane highways, as well as tiny, narrow back roads. Jamaica has mostly two-lane roads, but some local drivers seem to think they're on a turnpike. On smaller islands, roads are narrow, often busy, and may be long and straight on islands such as Anguilla or parts of Barbados or steep and winding on mountainous islands such as St. Lucia or Grenada. Although many islands put a great effort into keeping their main roads in good condition, the rainy season takes its toll, leaving new potholes to repair each year.

ROADSIDE EMERGENCIES

If your rental car breaks down, call the rental agency to give you assistance. If you don't have a cell phone that works locally, ask a passerby to make the call for you. Cell phones are becoming ubiquitous in the Caribbean, so that should not be a problem. Be sure, however, that the rental agent provides you with an after-hours telephone number for just such emergencies.

RULES OF THE ROAD

On many islands (Anguilla, Antigua, Barbados, the British Virgin Islands, Cayman Islands, Dominica, Grenada, Jamaica, Nevis, St. Kitts, St. Lucia, St. Vincent and the Grenadines, Trinidad and Tobago, Turks and Caicos, and the U. S. Virgin Islands), be prepared to drive on the left. Speed limits are low, because it's often hard to find a road long and straight enough to *safely* get up much speed. And always wear your seat belt, which is required by law. Drivers are generally courteous; for example, if someone flashes car headlights at you at an intersection, it means "after you." On narrow mountain or country roads, it's a smart idea to tap your horn as you enter a blind curve to let oncoming traffic know you're there.

ON THE GROUND

ADDRESSES

"Whimsical" might best describe some Caribbean addresses. Street names are sometimes as simple as "Main Road" or "Leeward Highway." Street names may be nonexistent in the countryside or the name can change for no apparent reason. And most buildings have no numbers. Addresses throughout this guide may include cross streets, landmarks, and other directionals. But to find your destination you might have to ask a local—and be prepared for directions such as "Go down so, turn at the next gap [road], keep goin' past the church, and you'll see it right there down the hill."

■ COMMUNICATIONS

INTERNET

Nearly all resorts and hotels in the Caribbean have data ports and/or high-speed Internet access in guest rooms. Most offer Internet access—either free or for a small charge—on a designated computer either in a business center or guest lounge. Increasingly, Wi-Fi is available throughout the properties or at least in the public areas for people who bring their own laptops. Internet cafés can be found in downtown areas of the larger cities on most islands. Rates are reasonable and are generally sold in increments of 15 minutes.

Contact Cybercafes (⊕ www.cybercafes.com) lists more than 4,000 Internet cafés worldwide.

PHONES

The good news is that you can now make a direct-dial telephone call from virtually any point on Earth. The better news is that it's getting less expensive to make international calls. Calling from a hotel is usually the most expensive option, although the huge surcharges are pretty much a thing of the past—at least in the Caribbean. Prepaid phone cards usually keep costs to a minimum; they're readily available locally. And then there are mobile phones (⇨ below), which are becoming more prevalent than land lines.

Phone and fax service to and from the Caribbean is modern and efficient. Most hotel rooms have direct-dial telephones with data ports. Prepaid phone cards are used throughout the islands; you can buy them (in various denominations) at many retail shops and convenience stores and use them in special card-only pay phones.

For island area and country codes, see the Essentials sections in individual island chapters. When you are calling home, the country code is 1 for the United States.

CALLING WITHIN THE CARIBBEAN

To make a local call simply dial 9 for an outside line, then the seven-digit local number. Hotel rooms usually have a card or guest directory, which gives dialing instructions. Local calls are often free; some hotels charge $1 per call. Pay phones use either local coins (25¢ or 50¢ in local currency) or prepaid phone cards.

CALLING OUTSIDE THE CARIBBEAN

To make a direct-dial international call from your hotel room, simply dial 9 for an outside line, then dial the overseas country code, the area code, and the phone number. A call to the United States may cost $4 or so for three minutes. Check the customer-information pages of the local phone book (usually one is placed in your hotel room) for sample rates to various international locations.

Calling cards make calling long distance relatively convenient, but you may find the local access number blocked by individual hotels. On some islands, you can dial a toll-free number and use a major credit card to call overseas. And on some islands, toll-free 800 numbers may be altogether inaccessible.

Access Numbers AT&T (☎ 800/225–5288).

MOBILE PHONES

If you have a quad-band phone and your service provider uses the world-standard GSM network, you can probably use your phone abroad. Roaming fees can be steep, however: 99¢ a minute is considered reasonable, and prices on some Caribbean islands can be considerably more expensive. And overseas you normally pay the toll charges for incoming calls. It's almost always cheaper to send a text message than to make a call, since text messages have a very low set fee (often less than 5¢).

If you just want to make local calls, consider buying a new SIM card (note that your provider may have to unlock your phone for you to use a different SIM card) and a prepaid service plan in the destination. You'll then have a local number and can make local calls at local rates. If your trip is extensive, you could also simply buy a new cell phone in your destination, as the initial cost will be offset over time; or buy a prepaid cell phone where you can simply top up the available time in increments of $20, $50, $100 or more.

■ TIP➔ If you travel internationally frequently, save one of your old mobile phones or buy a cheap one on the Internet; ask your cell phone company to unlock it for you, and take it with you as a travel phone, buying a new SIM card with pay-as-you-go service in each destination.

Remember, too, that the electrical current on some islands is 220 volts (as opposed to the 110-volt current found in the United States). You'll need to make sure your cell phone charger is compatible with 220-volt current and bring an appropriate electrical plug adapter if you expect to charge your cell phone battery while you're away.

Contacts Cellular Abroad (☎ 800/287–5072 ⊕ www.cellularabroad.com) rents and sells GMS phones and sells SIM cards that work in many countries. **Mobal** (☎ 888/888–9162 ⊕ www.mobalrental.com) rents mobiles

and sells GSM phones (starting at $49) that will operate in 140 countries. Per-call rates vary throughout the world. **Planet Fone** (☎ 888/988–4777 ⊕ www.planetfone.com) rents cell phones, but the per-minute rates are expensive.

▋ CUSTOMS & DUTIES

Although customs inspectors in some countries inspect all incoming baggage to allay their concerns about smuggling, drug running, or other nefarious activities, many islands wave those tourists who have no goods to declare through customs inspections with only a cursory question or two. Exceptions include major hubs within the Caribbean, such as Jamaica, Puerto Rico, and Antigua. If you're yachting through the islands, note that harbor customs are often thorough, as well.

Nevertheless, customs departments throughout the Caribbean have stepped up their record keeping; most now require incoming passengers to complete and sign a routine customs declaration, listing any gifts you may be bringing for local people or items (other than personal belongings) that may be subject to duty. At this writing, while airlines routinely distribute immigration forms to passengers, they are not distributing the customs forms. Upon arrival at your destination, pick up a customs form in the immigration hall and fill it out while you're waiting in the immigration line.

You're always allowed to bring goods of a certain value back home without having to pay any duty or import tax. But there's a limit on the amount of tobacco and liquor you can bring back duty-free, and some countries have separate limits for perfumes; for exact figures, check with your customs department. The values of so-called "duty-free" goods are included in these amounts. When you shop abroad, save all your receipts, as customs inspectors may ask to see them as well as the items you purchased. If the total value of your goods is more than the duty-free limit, you'll have to pay a tax (most often a flat percentage) on the value of everything beyond that limit.

Individuals entering the United States from the Caribbean are allowed to bring in $800 worth of duty-free goods for your personal use ($1,600 from the U.S. Virgin Islands), including 1 liter of alcohol (2 liters if one was produced in the Caribbean and 5 liters from the USVI), two cartons of cigarettes, and 100 non-Cuban cigars. Antiques and original artwork are also duty-free.

U.S. Information **U.S. Customs and Border Protection** (⊕www.cbp.gov).

▌ DIVING

The Caribbean offers some of the best scuba diving in the world. The reef and waters around Bonaire's entire coast, for instance, incorporate a protected marine park, with scores of dive sites accessible from shore. The Cayman Islands, Turks and Caicos, the British Virgin Islands, St. Lucia, Dominica, and St. Vincent and the Grenadines also offer world-class diving experiences. The water throughout the Caribbean is crystal-clear, often with visibility up to 200 feet, and the quantity and variety of marine life are astounding.

Resorts often offer guests introductory scuba instruction in a pool, followed by a shallow dive; some hotels have on-site dive shops. All dive shops listed in the island chapters of this book offer instruction and certification according to the standards set by either the National Association of Underwater Instructors (NAUI) or the Professional Association of Diving Instructors (PADI). Dive operators offer day and night dives to wrecks, reefs, and underwater walls.

DIVERS ALERT
Don't fly within 24 hours of scuba diving.

Contacts **NAUI Worldwide** (☎813/628–6284 or 800/553–6284 ⊕www.naui.org). **PADI** (☎800/729–7234 or 949/858–7234 ⊕www.padi.com).

▌ EATING OUT

The Caribbean islands offer dining experiences that will delight any palate. You'll find French cuisine with exquisite service, lavish buffets featuring local dishes, fresh seafood served by the waterfront, Italian pasta with a modern twist, Chinese cuisine to eat in or take out, and vegetarian dishes of just-picked produce. Fastfood restaurants usually feature fried or baked chicken, not burgers, but pizza is everywhere.

Local cuisine (which is usually cheaper than what you'll find in upscale international restaurants) could be Spanish-style in Puerto Rico and the Dominican Republic, French creole in St. Lucia and Martinique, Indian in Trinidad, Indonesian in Aruba, jerk (spicy barbecue) in Jamaica, and fresh seafood everywhere. Vegetarians can expect a treat, as the fresh fruit, vegetables, herbs, and spices—both usual and unusual—are plentiful.

For information on food-related health issues, see Health, below.

MEALS & MEALTIMES
Resort breakfasts are frequently lavish buffets that offer tropical fruits and fruit juices, cereal, fresh rolls and pastries, hot dishes (such as codfish, corned-beef hash, and potatoes), and prepared-to-order eggs, pancakes, and French toast. Lunch could be a sit-down meal at a beachfront café or a picnic at a secluded cove. But dinner is the highlight, often combining the expertise of internationally trained chefs with local know-how and ingredients.

Expect breakfast to be served from 7:30 AM to 10 AM; lunch from noon to 2 PM or so; and dinner from 7 PM to about 10 PM—perhaps later on Spanish- or French-heritage islands. Some restaurants have specific mealtimes; others serve continuously all day long.

Unless otherwise noted, the restaurants listed in this guide are open daily for lunch and dinner.

PAYING

Major credit cards (Access, American Express, Barclaycard, Carte Blanche, Diners Club, Discover, EnRoute, Eurocard, MasterCard, Visa) are accepted in most Caribbean restaurants. We note in reviews when credit cards are not accepted.

For guidelines on tipping see Tipping, below.

Price charts for restaurants are included in each destination chapter's Planner.

RESERVATIONS & DRESS

Regardless of where you are, it's a good idea to make a reservation if you can. In some places (St. Barths, for example), it's expected. We mention specifically only when reservations are essential (there's no other way you'll ever get a table) or when they are not accepted. For popular restaurants, book as far ahead as you can (often 30 days), and reconfirm as soon as you arrive. (Large parties should always call ahead to check the reservations policy.) We mention dress only for the very few restaurants where men are required to wear a jacket or a jacket and tie. Shorts and T-shirts at dinner and beach attire anytime are universally frowned upon in restaurants throughout the Caribbean.

WINES, BEER & SPIRITS

The Caribbean is where "de rum come from," so rum is the base of most cocktails—often fruity, festive ones that really pack a punch. Mount Gay and Malibu in Barbados, Bacardí in Puerto Rico, and Cruzan in St. Croix are the big-name Caribbean rum brands whose distilleries are open to the public for tours, tastings, and duty-free shopping. Most islands produce their own artisanal rums, as well.

Many islands also have their own breweries, and the local beers (Red Stripe in Jamaica, Piton in St. Lucia, Banks in Barbados, Carib in Grenada and Trinidad, Hairoun in St. Vincent, Kabuli in Dominica, Medalla in Puerto Rico, Presidente Pilsner in the Dominican Republic, Balashi in Aruba, Wadali from Antigua, Stingray from the Cayman Islands, and so on) are light and refreshing—perfect for hot summer afternoons at the beach.

Wine was not always the best choice in the Caribbean, especially compared to the local beers and festive rum drinks, but good wines are increasingly showing up in Caribbean restaurants, bars, nightclubs, and on supermarket shelves.

Those who prefer a nonalcoholic drink will love the fresh fruit punch, lime squash, or Ting—a carbonated grapefruit drink from Jamaica but also available elsewhere. For something unusual and purely local, try *mauby*, a strong, dark, rather bitter beverage made from the bark of a tree; ginger beer; sea moss, a reputed aphrodisiac made from a combination of of seaweed, sweetener, milk, and spices; and coconut water, the liquid inside a green "jelly coconut" often sold on the street by a "jellyman" who, for 25¢ or 50¢, will nip off the top of the coconut with his sharp machete.

▌ELECTRICITY

You'll often notice a candle and matches on the bedside table in your hotel room. That's because it's not unusual for temporary electrical outages—either storm-related or for unexplained reasons—to occur from time to time throughout the Caribbean. Sometimes it is island-wide, limited to a specific area, or the result of overload on a resort's own generator. Most large resorts do have their own generators and the engineers to tend to them, so power is generally restored within minutes. Be sure to unplug your computer or any other appliances before the power is restored to prevent damage from a power surge.

On most islands the electric current is 110 to 120 volts alternating current (AC), and wall outlets take the same two-prong plugs found in the United States. Exceptions include Dominica, Grenada, St. Lucia, St. Vincent and the Grenadines (other than Petit St. Vincent), and the French islands of Guadeloupe, Martinique, St. Barths, and St. Martin, all of which deliver electric current at 220 volts and require varying kinds of three-prong or large two-prong plugs. When making reservations on any of the islands utilizing 220 volts, check with your specific hotel about current, as some also have 110-volt current available. Many hotels will have plug adapters available at the front desk, which guests can borrow during their stay.

Consider making a small investment in a universal adapter, which has several types of plugs in one lightweight, compact unit. Most laptops and mobile phone chargers are dual voltage (i.e., they operate equally well on 110 and 220 volts), so require only an adapter. These days the same is true of small appliances such as hair dryers. Always check labels and manufacturer instructions to be sure. Don't use 110-volt outlets marked FOR SHAVERS ONLY for high-wattage appliances such as hair dryers.

Contacts Steve Kropla's Help for World Travelers (⊕ www.kropla.com) has information on electrical and telephone plugs around the world. **Walkabout Travel Gear** (⊕ www.walkabouttravelgear.com) has a good coverage of electricity under "adapters."

▌ EMERGENCIES

In case of emergency, make sure you carry some sort of identification with you at all times. If you are taking medication or have allergies, carry that information with you as well in case you are uncon-

scious or otherwise unable to communicate with emergency personnel.

Most islands have direct telephone lines (911 or something similar) that connect with emergency services—police, fire, and ambulance. These emergency numbers, along with contact information for hospitals, clinics, and pharmacies, are listed in the Essentials section of each island chapter.

Be aware that your medical insurance may not cover you when traveling abroad, and hospital and doctor fees for nonresidents can be very expensive. Hospitals, doctors, clinics, and pharmacies generally accept credit cards for payment of medical services and/or prescription drugs.

The United States maintains embassies in Barbados, the Dominican Republic, Grenada, Jamaica, and Trinidad and Tobago. In addition, U. S. consular agents are located in Antigua, Cayman Islands, and Martinique. If you lose your passport or have any other passport-related issues, call or visit the nearest embassy. Local embassies and consular officers can help you in a medical emergency and provide a list of local doctors, dentists, and other medical specialists. American citizens who plan to extend their stay in the Caribbean for longer than three months must register with the appropriate embassy.

United States Embassies & Consulates

United States Embassy, Barbados and Eastern Caribbean (✉ Wildey Business Park, Wildey, St. Michael, Barbados ☎ 246/436–4950 🌐 http://barbados.usembassy.gov). **United States Embassy, Dominican Republic** (✉ César Nicolás Penson St. at Máximo Gómez Av., Santo Domingo, Dominican Republic ☎ 268/726–6531, 809/221–2171 after hours 🌐 www.usemb.gov.do). **United States Embassy, Grenada** (✉ Lance aux Epines, St. George, Grenada ☎ 483/444–1173 ✉ usemb. gd@caribsurf.com). **United States Embassy, Jamaica** (✉ 142 Old Hope Rd., Kingston, Jamaica ☎ 876/702–6000 ✉ St. James Pl., 2nd fl., Gloucester Ave., Montego Bay, Jamaica ☎ 876/952–0160 🌐 http://kingston.usembassy.gov). **United States Embassy, Trinidad and Tobago** (✉ 15 Queen's Park W, Port of Spain, Trinidad and Tobago ☎ 868/622–6371 🌐 http://trinidad.usembassy.gov). **United States Consular Agent, Antigua and Barbuda** (✉ Jasmine Court, Suite 2, Friars Hill Rd., St. John's, Antigua ☎ 268/726–6531 🌐 http:// barbados.usembassy.gov). **United States Consular Agent, Cayman Islands** (✉ Mirco Center, Unit 222, N. Sound Rd., George Town, Grand Cayman ☎ 345/945–8173, 876/702–6055 after hours). **United States Consular Agent, Martinique** (✉ Hotel Valmeniere, Suite 615, Av. des Arawaks, Fort-de-FranceMartinique ☎ 596/596–746–970 ✉ hritchie@outremer. com).

FURTHER READING

Caribbean Style (Crown Publishers) is a coffee-table book with magnificent photographs of the interiors and exteriors of homes and buildings in the Caribbean. Short stories—some dark, some full of laughs—about life in the southern Caribbean made *Easy in the Islands,* by Bob Schacochis, a National Book Award winner. Schacochis has an ear for local patois and an eye for the absurd. In *Coming About: A Family Passage at Sea,* author Susan Tyler Hitchcock details her family's adventures sailing for nine months in the Bahamas and the Caribbean; it's an intimate look at the islands and a wonderful meditation on marriage and family.

Thinking of running away and starting a business on a sun-drenched island? *A Trip to the Beach* by Robert and Melinda Blanchard is the ultimate inspiration. This funny, adventurous tale of how the Blanchards moved to Anguilla, started a restaurant, and learned innumerable lessons (including how to liberate fresh ingredients from the customs warehouse) will have you fantasizing about your own escape. To familiarize yourself with the sights, smells, and sounds of the West Indies, pick up Jamaica Kincaid's *Annie John,* a richly textured coming-of-age novel about a girl growing up on Antigua. The short stories in *At the Bottom of the River,* also by Kincaid, depict island mysteries and manners.

Omeros is Nobel Prize–winning St. Lucian poet Derek Walcott's imaginative Caribbean retelling of the *Odyssey.* Anthony C. Winkler's novels, *The Great Yacht Race, The Lunatic,* and *The Painted Canoe,* provide scathingly witty glimpses into Jamaica's class structure. Meanwhile, if you're heading for Jamaica, be sure to read *The White Witch of Rosehall,* by Herbert G. De Lisser, which relates the fascinating legend of the Rose Hall Plantation—which you can visit. *Wide Sargasso Sea,* by Dominica's Jean Rhys, is a provocative novel set in Jamaica and Dominica that recounts the early life of the first wife of Edward Rochester (pre–*Jane Eyre*). James Michener depicted the islands' diversity in his novel *Caribbean.* To probe island cultures more deeply, read Trinidad's V. S. Naipaul, particularly his *Guerrillas, The Loss of El Dorado, The Enigma of Arrival,* and *A House for Mr. Bizwas*; Eric Williams's *From Columbus to Castro*; and Michael Paiewonsky's *Conquest of Eden. An Embarrassment of Mangoes: A Caribbean Interlude,* by Ann Vanderhoof, is the more-contemporary story of her and her husband's two-year journey around the Caribbean in a 42-foot sailboat, which proves to be both enlightening and entertaining.

Though it was written decades ago, Herman Wouk's hilarious *Don't Stop the Carnival* remains as fresh as ever in its depiction of the trials and tribulations of running a small Caribbean hotel; however, it is somewhat less fresh in its attitudes toward other matters. Mystery lovers should pick up a copy of Agatha Christie's *A Caribbean Mystery*. And kids might enjoy reading the Hardy Boys mystery *The Caribbean Cruise Caper*. If you're keen on specific subjects, such as history, cuisine, folklore, bird-watching, or diving, you'll find wonderful books by local authors on each island.

GAY & LESBIAN TRAVEL

Most of the Caribbean isn't particularly gay- and lesbian-friendly, though some Caribbean islands are more welcoming than others. Puerto Rico is the only one with extensive gay-oriented nightlife, though it is focused almost exclusively in San Juan. In the USVI, St. Thomas has a few gay bars and discos, and the West End of St. Croix has quietly become gay- and lesbian-friendly. Curaçao now reaches out to gay and lesbian travelers. Saba is generally friendly to everyone regardless of sexual orientation. Aruba, St. Maarten, and Trinidad all have some gay nightlife. In general, the French and Dutch islands are the most tolerant islands; the historically British islands are the least tolerant, with Jamaica leading the pack. It is difficult to underestimate how virulent and violent homophobia can be in Jamaica, but the truth is that most of the violence is directed toward Jamaicans, not tourists.

It's important to remember that most Caribbean islands are both religious and conservative, so all travelers need to respect social mores. Nearly every island frowns upon same-sex couples strolling hand in hand down a beach or street, and most public displays of affection (either straight or gay) are also frowned upon.

Upscale resorts for adults, where privacy and discretion are the norm, are often the most welcoming to gay and lesbian travelers, but individually rented villas, many of which have private pools, are another good option. Some couples-only resorts in the Caribbean now allow same-sex couples—and this includes the Sandals and Couples chains, which have changed their policies to welcome all couples—though none of these resorts exactly roll out the red carpet; so you have to ask yourself if you'll be comfortable in such an environment.

▌HEALTH

The most common types of illnesses are caused by contaminated food and water. Especially in developing countries, drink only bottled, boiled, or purified water and drinks; don't drink from public fountains or use ice. You should even consider using bottled water to brush your teeth. Make sure food has been thoroughly cooked and is served to you fresh and hot; avoid vegetables and fruits that you haven't washed (in bottled or purified water) or peeled yourself. If you have problems, mild cases of traveler's diarrhea may respond to Imodium (known generically as loperamide) or Pepto-Bismol. Be sure to drink plenty of fluids; if you can't keep fluids down, seek medical help immediately.

Infectious diseases can be airborne or passed via mosquitoes and ticks and through direct or indirect physical contact with animals or people. Some, including Norwalk-like viruses that affect your digestive tract, can be passed along through contaminated food. If you are traveling in an area where malaria is prevalent, use a repellent containing DEET and take malaria-prevention medication before, during, and after your trip as directed by your physician. Condoms can help prevent most sexually transmitted diseases, but they aren't absolutely reliable and their quality varies from country to country. Speak with your physician and/or check the CDC or

World Health Organization Web sites for health alerts, particularly if you're pregnant, traveling with children, or have a chronic illness.

For information on travel insurance, shots and medications, and medical-assistance companies see Shots & Medications under Things to Consider in Before You Go, above.

SPECIFIC ISSUES IN THE CARIBBEAN

The drinking water supply in resort areas throughout the Caribbean is generally safe, although bottled water is readily available. When touring in remote areas and local villages, always opt for bottled water or alternative bottled beverages.

The major health risk in the Caribbean is sunburn or sunstroke. Having a long-sleeve shirt, a hat, and long pants or a beach wrap available is essential on a boat, for midday at the beach, and whenever you go out sightseeing. Use sunscreen with an SPF of at least 15 (preferably 30) and apply it liberally on your nose, ears, and other sensitive and exposed areas.

Swimmers—even experienced ones—should exercise caution in waters on the windward (Atlantic Ocean) side of the islands. The unseen currents, powerful waves, strong undertows, and rocky bottoms can be extremely dangerous—and lifeguards are rare.

Scuba divers must not fly within 24 hours of scuba diving.

Watch out for black, spiny sea urchins that live on the rocky sea floor in both shallow and deep waters. Stepping on one is guaranteed to be painful for quite some time, as the urchin releases its spikes into the offending body. To remove a spike simply pull it out and apply an antiseptic. To remove an embedded spike, first apply some warm oil (preferably olive oil) to soften and dilate the skin, then remove the spike with a sterile needle.

Poisonous snakes are not endemic to most of the Caribbean, although you should exercise caution while bird-watching in Trinidad. The small lizards native to the islands are harmless and actually keep down the insect population.

The worst insect problem may well be the tiny "no-see-ums" (sand flies) that appear after a rain, near swampy ground, and at the beach around sunset. Mosquitoes can also be annoying and, more importantly, may be carriers of dengue fever, a viral disease that is a growing concern in the Caribbean. Although rarely fatal, the fever, headache, and rash related to dengue fever can last 10 days or more. Malaria has been reported in some parts of the Dominican Republic, particularly rural areas near the Haitian border, and in the city of Kingston, Jamaica; but there have been somewhat wider outbreaks, particularly after hurricanes. Bring along a good insect repellent and use it, particularly at daybreak and sundown, when mosquitoes are most active.

Beware of the manchineel tree that grows near the beach and has fruit that looks like little green apples; it is poisonous and its bark and leaves can burn your skin if you touch them. Even the droplets of water that might reach your skin if you seek protection under the tree during a shower can burn you.

OVER-THE-COUNTER REMEDIES

Island drugstores and supermarkets are well stocked with familiar over-the-counter medicines and other health products that you might need. If you don't see precisely what you want, ask the pharmacist to recommend an appropriate substitute. If you can only use a specific or an uncommon medicine, be sure to bring a sufficient supply with you. Most resorts will sell common, over-the-counter remedies in their gift shops, but prices will be extremely high. It's usually a good idea to put together a small first-aid kit before you go with Benadryl cream, antiseptic wipes, antibiotic cream, adhesive bandages, pain relievers, decongestants, a small bottle of aloe vera gel, and Pepto-Bismol.

■ HOURS OF OPERATION

Though business hours vary from island to island, shops are generally closed Saturday afternoon and all day Sunday. Some shops close for an hour at lunchtime during the week, as well, although this practice is becoming increasingly rare. Farmers' markets are often open daily (except Sunday), but Saturday morning is always the most colorful and exciting time to go.

■ MAIL

Airmail between Caribbean islands and the United States generally takes at least 7 to 14 days.

SHIPPING PACKAGES

Courier services (such as DHL, FedEx, UPS, and others) operate throughout the Caribbean, although not every company serves each island. "Overnight" service is more likely to take two or more days, because of the limited number of flights on which packages can be shipped.

■ MONEY

For island-specific information on banks, currency, service charges, taxes, and tipping in the Caribbean, see the Essentials sections in individual island chapters.

Prices throughout this guide are given for adults. Substantially reduced fees are almost always available for children, students, and senior citizens.

It isn't necessary to exchange funds before leaving home or even at the airport upon arrival. Businesses and individuals on nearly every Caribbean island will accept U.S. paper currency and, to a lesser degree, Canadian dollars and British pounds. You'll always get change in the local currency, however, so use as small a bill as possible. If you would like some local currency for bus fare or small purchases, you can exchange money at your hotel; however, if you are going to an island that uses the euro (particularly Guadeloupe or Martinique), you will have to exchange money or take euros out of a local ATM, and having a few euros on arrival isn't a bad idea.

ATMS & BANKS

Your own bank will probably charge a fee for using ATMs abroad; the foreign bank you use may also charge a fee. Nevertheless, you'll usually get a better rate of exchange at an ATM than you will at a currency-exchange office or even when changing money in a bank. And extracting funds as you need them is a safer option than carrying around a large amount of cash.

■TIP➔ PIN numbers with more than four digits are not recognized at ATMs in many countries. If yours has five or more, remember to change it before you leave.

Debit cards still aren't widely used in the islands, although you can use bank cards and major credit cards to withdraw cash (in local currency) at automatic teller machines (ATMs). ATMs can be found on most islands at airports, cruise-ship terminals, bank branches, shopping centers, gas stations, and other convenient locations.

CREDIT CARDS

Throughout this guide, the following abbreviations are used: **AE**, American Express; **D**, Discover; **DC**, Diners Club; **MC**, MasterCard; and **V**, Visa.

It's a good idea to inform your credit-card company before you travel, especially if you're going abroad and don't travel internationally very often. Otherwise, the credit-card company might put a hold on your card owing to unusual activity—not a good thing halfway through your trip. Record all your credit-card numbers—as well as the phone numbers to call if your cards are lost or stolen—in a safe place, so you're prepared should something go wrong. Both MasterCard and Visa have general numbers you can call (collect if you're abroad) if your card is lost, but you're better off calling the number of your issuing bank, since MasterCard and Visa usually just transfer you to your bank; your bank's number is usually printed on your card.

If you plan to use your credit card for cash advances, you'll need to apply for a PIN at least two weeks before your trip. Although it's usually cheaper (and safer) to use a credit card abroad for large purchases (so you can cancel payments or be reimbursed if there's a problem), note that some credit-card companies *and* the banks that issue them add substantial percentages to all foreign transactions, whether they're in a foreign currency or not. Check on these fees before leaving home, so there won't be any surprises when you get the bill.

Major credit cards are widely accepted at hotels, restaurants, shops, car-rental agencies, other service providers, and ATM machines throughout the Caribbean. The only places that might not accept them are open-air markets or tiny shops in out-of-the-way villages.

Reporting Lost Cards American Express (☎800/992–3404 in the U.S., 336/393–1111 collect from abroad ⊕www.americanexpress.com). **Diners Club** (☎800/234–6377 in the U.S., 303/799–1504 collect from abroad ⊕www.dinersclub.com). **Discover** (☎800/347–2683 in the U.S., 801/902–3100 collect from abroad ⊕www.discovercard.com). **MasterCard** (☎800/622–7747 in the U.S., 636/722–7111 collect from abroad ⊕www.mastercard.com). **Visa** (☎800/847–2911 in the U.S., 410/581–9994 collect from abroad ⊕www.visa.com).

CURRENCY & EXCHANGE

The U.S. dollar is the official currency in Puerto Rico, the U.S. Virgin Islands, and the British Virgin Islands. On Grand Cayman you'll usually have a choice of Cayman or U.S. dollars when you take money out of an ATM and may even be able to get change in U.S. dollars. On most other islands, U.S. paper currency (not coins) is

WORST-CASE SCENARIO

All your money and credit cards have just been stolen. In these days of real-time transactions, this isn't a predicament that should destroy your vacation. First, report the theft of the credit cards to the issuing company. Then get any traveler's checks you were carrying replaced. This can usually be done almost immediately, provided that you kept a record of the serial numbers separate from the checks themselves. If you bank at a large international bank like Citibank or Barclay that operates on the island, go to the closest branch; if you know your account number, chances are you can get a new ATM card and withdraw money right away. **Western Union** (☎*800/325–6000* ⊕*www.westernunion.com*) sends money almost anywhere. Have someone back home order a transfer of money to you to be picked up at an island agency. The order can be made online, over the phone, or at one of the company's offices, which is the cheapest option. The U.S. State Department's **Overseas Citizens Services** (☎*202/647–5225*) can wire money to any U.S. consulate or embassy abroad for a fee of $30. Just have someone back home wire money or send a money order or cashier's check to the state department, which will then disburse the funds as soon as the next working day after it receives them.

usually accepted. When you pay in dollars, however, you'll almost always get change in local currency, so it's best to carry bills in small denominations. The exceptions are at airports—departure-tax payment locations and duty-free shops in the departure lounges—which will generally make every attempt to give you change in U.S. dollars, if you wish. Canadian dollars and British pounds are occasionally accepted, but don't count on this as the norm. The exception to these general rules are the French islands (except for St. Martin), which use the euro; other currency is usually not accepted. If you do need local currency (say, for a trip to one of the French islands), change money at a local bank for the best rate.

With regard to the EC dollar and Barbadian dollar, the exchange rate is fixed, so it makes little difference if you exchange your money in your hotel or at a bank. The exchange rates for the Dominican peso and Jamaican dollar can change.

■TIP➔ Even if a currency-exchange booth has a sign promising no commission, rest assured that there's some kind of huge, hidden fee. (Oh ... that's right. The sign didn't say no *fee*.) And as for rates, you're almost always better off getting foreign currency at an ATM or exchanging money at a bank.

TRAVELER'S CHECKS

Some consider this the currency of the caveman, and it's true that fewer establishments accept traveler's checks these days. Nevertheless, they're a cheap and secure way to carry large sums of money. Both Citibank (under the Visa brand) and American Express issue traveler's checks in the United States, but American Express is better known and more widely accepted. Whatever you do, keep track of all the serial numbers in case the checks are lost or stolen. Keep in mind, too, that small shops may only be able to cash traveler's checks that are in small denominations ($20 vs. $50 or $100).

Contacts **American Express** (☎888/412–6945 in the U.S., 801/945–9450 collect outside the U.S. to speak to customer service ⊕www.americanexpress.com).

▌SAFETY

Most Caribbean destinations are safer than major U.S. cities, but street crime is always a possibility in locations where relatively affluent tourists mingle with significantly poorer locals. As at home, petty crime can be a problem in large urban areas, but violent crimes against tourists—even on islands with higher crime rates such as Jamaica and St. Thomas—are rare. You will avoid most problems by using common sense and simply being as cautious as you would be at home, which means not walking alone in unfamiliar places (especially at night); not going alone to deserted beaches; locking away valuables; not leaving cameras, wallets, or anything else of value unattended or exposed on the beach while swimming; and not flaunting expensive jewelry in public places. Additionally, don't swim alone in unfamiliar waters, and don't swim too far offshore; most beaches have no lifeguards.

If you carry a purse, choose one with a zipper and a thick strap that you can drape across your body; adjust the length so that the purse sits in front of you at or above hip level. If you use a waist pack, attach it so the purse is in the front, not at your back. In a restaurant, stow your purse where you can see it rather than slung over the back of your chair. Carry only enough money in the purse to cover casual spending and utilize your hotel's in-room safe or its front-desk safe deposit box for your remaining valuables.

Be sure to make a photocopy of your passport and a list of all your credit cards and the toll-free customer service number for each issuing company. Keep these items in a separate location from the cards—with your other valuables in the in-room safe in your hotel room, for example—in case your passport or wallet is lost or stolen.

Watch for traffic when crossing the road. Although that may sound like a parent's instruction to a child, visitors from North America, in particular, are not used to cars that travel on the left side of the road—which is the case in many Caribbean islands—and usually fail to look to their left when stepping out into the street. Cars whizz by at quite a clip with little room for error on the narrow, winding, two-lane roads that are common to the islands. So don't forget to look left!

■TIP➔ Distribute your cash, credit cards, IDs, and other valuables between a deep front pocket, an inside jacket or vest pocket, and a hidden money pouch. Don't reach for the money pouch once you're in public.

▌ TAXES

Most Caribbean countries require travelers to pay departure taxes in cash at the time you check in for your flight home. In most cases, you can pay in either local or U.S. currency. Having the exact amount is a wise move to avoid ending up with too much change in the local currency. *For specific departure taxes, see Taxes in the Essentials section of each chapter.*

▌ TIME

The Caribbean islands fall into two time zones. The Cayman Islands, Cuba, Haiti, Jamaica, and the Turks and Caicos Islands are all in the Eastern Standard Time zone, which is five hours earlier than Greenwich Mean Time (GMT). All other Caribbean islands are in the Atlantic Standard Time zone, which is one hour later than Eastern Standard and four hours earlier than GMT. Caribbean islands don't observe daylight saving time, so during that period (March through October) Eastern Standard is one hour behind, and Atlantic Standard is the same time as Eastern Daylight Time.

▌ TIPPING

Just as anywhere else in the world, people in the Caribbean who provide personalized services appreciate a tip. Employees in all-inclusive hotels (e.g., bellhops, maids, waiters, bartenders) are the exception, however, because gratuities are often included in the hotel rates; in some cases, the employees at all-inclusives are specifically prohibited from accepting tips, as at Sandals resorts. At other resorts, tipping may be discouraged but may, in fact, be common, as in the Dominican Republic. Tip as you would in the U.S.: approximately 15%–20% for restaurant bills (unless a service charge is added already), 10% to taxi drivers who act as guides, and $1 to $3 per day for maids in hotels and resorts (leave the tip each morning since different people may clean your room). A few resorts have more formal tipping procedures, and if that is the case, they will be explained to you upon check-in.

INDEX

ABOUT OUR WRITERS

St. Thomas–based writer and dietitian **Carol M. Bareuther** writes about food for the *Virgin Islands Daily News* and serves as the USVI stringer for Reuters. She's the author of two books, including *Sports Fishing in the Virgin Islands*.

Katherine Dykstra is a freelance writer based in New York, but her father lives in Saba, and she visits often. She contributes to a number of newspapers and magazines and wrote the travel column for *Redbook*.

Long-time St. John resident **Lynda Lohr** lives above Coral Bay and writes for numerous publications as well as travel Web sites. She prefers swimming at Great Maho Bay and hiking the island's numerous trails.

Friends of **Elise Meyer** often joke that her middle name is "Let's Go." She has contributed articles to myriad newspapers, magazines, and Web sites. She lives in Connecticut with her husband and children.

Vernon O'Reilly-Ramesar is a broadcaster and writer who divides his life between Trinidad and Canada. He spends much of his time exploring the miracles of the rain forest.

Husband-wife team **Paris Permenter** and **John Bigley** have authored numerous guides to the Caribbean. When they're not in the islands, they edit Lovetripper.com Romantic Travel magazine and ParisandJohn.com from their home base in Texas.

Elise Rosen is a writer and editor in New York. She covered Punta Cana for the Dominican Republic in this year's guide. She's also contributed to *Fodor's Israel*.

On a quest to find the best beaches in the world, **Ramona Settle** chose Providenciales in the Turks & Caicos Islands—where each beach has more beautiful turquoise water than the last—to be her second home. She photographs its beauty in her spare time.

Jordan Simon began his West Indies love affair as a child when his artist mother took him to Haiti. He has since visited and written about nearly every Caribbean island. He writes regularly for national magazines and newspapers. He has authored several books, including *Fodor's Colorado,* and the *Gousha/USA Today Ski Atlas*.

Eileen Robinson Smith moved from the Caribbean to Charleston, South Carolina. She's lived all over the Virgin Islands and has written about about food and travel for *Sky, Caribbean Travel & Life,* and *Condé Nast Traveler.*

Chicago native **Roberta Sotonoff** is a confessed travel junkie who writes to support her habit. Her work has appeared in dozens of domestic and international publications, Web sites, and guidebooks. She writes frequently about the Caribbean.

Mark Sullivan, formerly an editor at Fodor's, is now a freelance writer. In addition to updating our Puerto Rico coverage, he has contributed to several other Fodor's guides and many other publications.

Jane E. Zarem travels frequently to the Caribbean from her Connecticut home. She has contributed to numerous Fodor's guides, among them *New England, USA, Cape Cod, Bahamas, Healthy Escapes,* and *Great American Sports & Adventure Vacations.*

Michael de Zayas has contributed to many Fodor's guides; this time he covered the Samaná peninsula in the Dominican Republic.

Photo Credits